adidas

Blue Ribbon

COLLEGE BASKETBALL YEARBOOK

America's Most Comprehensive Basketball Publication

38 E. Main Street Suite 2A, Buckhannon, W.Va. 26201 ▼ 304-472-0329 ▼ FAX 304-472-7750

Chris Dortch
Editor
Publisher

Dave Link
Associate Editor

Joe Lunardi
Contributing Editor
Tournament Guide Editor

Chris Wallace
Founder
Contributing Editor

Diane Swiger
Executive Assistant

Sara Patterson
Assistant Editor

Stan Crawley
Assistant Editor

Sonny Vaccaro
Consultant

1998-99

CONFERENCES

AMERICA EAST—Charlie Creme (C.C.)
ATLANTIC COAST—Al Featherston (A.F.), Tim Peeler (T.P.)
ATLANTIC 10—Joe Lunardi (J.L.)
BIG EAST—Michael Bradley (M.B.)
BIG SKY—Stephen Dodge (S.D.)
BIG SOUTH—Chris Low (C.L.)
BIG TEN—Dave Jones (D.J.)
BIG 12—Blair Kerkhoff (B.K.)
BIG WEST—Andy Katz (A.K.)
COLONIAL—Dale Bukowski (D.B.)
CONFERENCE USA—Mike DeCourcy (M.D.)
INDEPENDENTS—Greg Pogue (G.P.)
IVY LEAGUE—Bill Avington (B.A.)
MAAC—Bill Doherty (B.D.)
MID-AMERICAN—Rick McCann (R.M.)
MID-CONTINENT—Bill Doherty (B.D.)
MID-EASTERN ATHLETIC—Mike Gore (M.G.)
MIDWESTERN COLLEGIATE—Tom Durso (T.D.)
MISSOURI VALLEY—Kirk Seminoff (K.S.)
NORTHEAST—Bill Doherty (B.D.)
OHIO VALLEY—Chris Low (C.L.)
PACIFIC 10—Jeff Faurado (J.F.)
PATRIOT—Tom Durso (T.D.)
SOUTHEASTERN—Chris Dortch (C.D.), Lee Feinswog (L.F.)
SOUTHERN—Dave Link (D.L.)
SOUTHLAND—Lee Feinswog (L.F.)
SOUTHWESTERN ATHLETIC—Scott Gremillion (S.G.), Lee Feinswog (L.F.)
SUN BELT—Greg Pogue (G.P.)
TRANS-AMERICA—Geoff Cabe (G.C.)
WEST COAST—Paul Buker (P.B.)
WESTERN ATHLETIC—Andy Katz (A.K.)

SPECIAL SECTIONS

BEN WILSON TOP 44 & PROFILES—Brick Oettinger & *Recruiter's Handbook*
HIGH SCHOOLS—Dave Benezra, Mark Mayemura & *Recruiting USA*
JUNIOR COLLEGES—Rick Ball
DIVISION II, III & NAIA—Tony Pettis, Greg Pogue
WOMEN'S DIVISION I—Dan Flesser

DESIGN & PRODUCTION—Dom Roberti, Haverford, PA
PRINTING—CMI Printers, Malvern, PA
COVER ART—Chris Pearl, Pearl and Associates, Boca Raton, FL
OPERATIONS ASSISTANT—Mary Lou Brady
EDITORIAL ASSISTANTS—Chris Dortch II, Lucretia Lawrence

RPI data is supplied by *Collegiate Basketball News*, P.O. Box 3032, Carmel, IN 46032. For additional information, contact Jim Sukup, publisher and editor, at (317) 848-7942. On the internet, go to www.a1.com/rpiratings or write to rpi@indy.net.

PHOTO CREDITS
adidas America, Buffington Studios (J.D. Hinkle, Jr.), Kevin W. Reese (Ben Wilson), MediaWright, Dan Sears, Joe Weiss, Durham Herald-Sun (Elton Brand); Steve Bittner (Steve Francis).

WEB SITES

www.collegebaskets.com
www.ncaatourney.com

adidas Blue Ribbon College Basketball Yearbook is published annually by Blue Ribbon Basketball, Inc. Postage paid at Buckhannon, WV and Malvern, PA. The purpose of *Blue Ribbon* is to promote America's greatest indoor sport, college basketball. The publication does not contain any gambling-related information or advertisements.

Try our other fine publications....

1999 TOURNAMENT PREVIEW

The most ambitious BLUE RIBBON project ever is the 1999 **Tournament Preview**. It will include 80 pages of complete analysis and records for all 64 teams in the NCAA bracket—strengths, weaknesses and potential matchups—plus tournament history and site information. Assembled on Selection Sunday and rushed to you in time for Thursday's tournament opener, the Preview is bound to help with those NCAA picks! Price of $12.95 is a real steal (includes priority shipping).

EARLY SEASON UPDATE/TV GUIDE

The 1998–99 **Early Season Update/TV Guide** will be available in late December/early January.

It will contain more than 70 pages of late-breaking news and team information, *plus*...rosters for all 310 Division I teams, all Division I early signees for 1999-2000, complete television schedules for all networks and the exclusive European report.

Also included will be an early guide to the 1999 NBA draft. All for just $8.45 (includes priority shipping).

adidas Blue Ribbon College Basketball Yearbook

38 E. Main Street Suite 2A
Buckhannon, W.Va. 26201

OR Call 304-472-0329 or 1-800-828-4667
***OR* FAX** 304-472-7750

Back issues of the *Blue Ribbon Yearbook* are available for 1982-83, 1986-87, 1989-90, 1993-94, 1994-95, 1995-96, 1996-97 and 1997-98.
Price of $14.50 includes shipping and handling.

Indicate year(s) and number of copies ______________________

Please send copies of the Early Season Update & Television Guide ($8.45 each) to:

Please send copies of the 1998 Tournament Preview ($12.95 each—add $8.50 for priority shipping) to:

Name ______________________

Street or box ______________________

City ______________________ State ______ Zip code ______________

Telephone ______________________

❑ check or money order enclosed

❑ charge to credit card: ❑ VISA ❑ MasterCard

Name of cardholder ______________________

Number on card ____ — ____ — ____ — ____ Expiration Date ______________

TEAM INDEX

CONTENTS

CONFERENCE INDEX

1998 NCAA TOURNAMENT AND NIT RESULTS

NOTE: The number in parenthesis beside a team is its seed.

NCAA TOURNAMENT RESULTS

FIRST ROUND

EAST REGIONAL
(Hartford, CT)
(1) North Carolina 88, (16) Navy 52
(4) Michigan State 83, (13) Eastern Michigan 71
(8) UNC Charlotte 77, (9) Illinois-Chicago 62
(5) Princeton 69, (12) UNLV 57

(Washington DC)
(7) Indiana 94, (10) Oklahoma 87, OT
(11) Washington 69, (6) Xavier 68
(2) Connecticut 93, (15) Fairleigh Dickinson 85
(14) Richmond 62, (3) South Carolina 61

SOUTH REGIONAL
(Atlanta, GA)
(2) Kentucky 82, (15) South Carolina State 67
(3) Michigan 80, (14) Davidson 61
(10) Saint Louis 51, (7) Massachusetts 46
(6) UCLA 65, (11) Miami 62

(Lexington, KY)
(5) Syracuse 63, (12) Iona 61
(8) Oklahoma State 74, (9) George Washington 59
(1) Duke 99, (16) Radford 63
(4) New Mexico 79, (13) Butler 62

MIDWEST REGIONAL
(Oklahoma City, OK)
(13) Valparaiso 70, (4) Mississippi 69
(8) Rhode Island 97, (9) Murray State 74
(12) Florida State 96, (5) TCU 87
(1) Kansas 110, (16) Prairie View 52

(Chicago, IL)
(11) Western Michigan 75, (6) Clemson 72
(3) Stanford 67, (14) College Of Charleston 57
(2) Purdue 95, (15) Delaware 56
(10) Detroit 66, (7) St. Johns 64

WEST REGIONAL
(Boise, ID)
(10) West Virginia 82, (7) Temple 52
(2) Cincinnati 65, (15) Northern Arizona 62
(3) Utah 85, (14) San Francisco 68
(6) Arkansas 74, (11) Nebraska 65

(Sacramento, CA)
(5) Illinois 64, (12) South Alabama 51
(4) Maryland 82, (13) Utah State 68
(9) Illinois State 82, (8) Tennessee 81, OT
(1) Arizona 99, (16) Nicholls State 60

SECOND ROUND

EAST REGIONAL
(Hartford, CT)
(1) North Carolina 93, (8) UNC Charlotte 83, OT
(4) Michigan State 63, (5) Princeton 56

(Washington, D.C.)
(11) Washington 81, (14) Richmond 66
(2) Connecticut 78, (7) Indiana 68

SOUTH REGIONAL
(Atlanta, GA)
(2) Kentucky 88, (10) Saint Louis 61
(6) UCLA 85, (3) Michigan 82

(Lexington, KY)
(5) Syracuse 56, (4) New Mexico 46
(1) Duke 79, (8) Oklahoma State 73

MIDWEST REGIONAL
(Oklahoma City, OK)
(8) Rhode Island 80, (1) Kansas 75
(13) Valparaiso 83, (12) Florida State 77

(Chicago, IL)
(3) Stanford 83, (11) Western Michigan 65
(2) Purdue 80, (10) Detroit 65

WEST REGIONAL
(Boise, ID)
(10) West Virginia 75, (2) Cincinnati 74
(3) Utah 75, (6) Arkansas 69

(Sacramento, CA)
(1) Arizona 82, (9) Illinois State 49
(4) Maryland 67, (5) Illinois 61

REGIONAL SEMIFINALS

EAST REGIONAL
(Greensboro, NC)
(2) Connecticut 75, (11) Washington 74
(1) North Carolina 73, (4) Michigan State 58

SOUTH REGIONAL
(St. Petersburg, FL)
(2) Kentucky 94, (6) UCLA 68
(1) Duke 80, (5) Syracuse 67

MIDWEST REGIONAL
(St. Louis, MO)
(3) Stanford 67, (2) Purdue 59
(8) Rhode Island 74, (13) Valparaiso 68

WEST REGIONAL
(Anaheim, CA)
(3) Utah 65, (10) West Virginia 62
(1) Arizona 87, (4) Maryland 79

REGIONAL FINALS

EAST REGIONAL
(Greensboro, NC)
(1) North Carolina 75, (2) Connecticut 64

SOUTHEAST REGIONAL
(St. Petersburg, FL)
(2) Kentucky 86, (1) Duke 84

MIDWEST REGIONAL
(St. Louis, MO)
(3) Stanford 79, (8) Rhode Island 77

WEST REGIONAL
(Anaheim, CA)
(2) Utah 87, (1) Arizona 79

FINAL FOUR

(San Antonio, TX)
(S) Kentucky 86, (MW) Stanford 85, OT
(W) Utah 65, (E) North Carolina 59

CHAMPIONSHIP

(S) Kentucky 78, (W) Utah 69

NIT RESULTS

FIRST ROUND
Wednesday, March 11
Georgia Tech 88, Seton Hall 78
North Carolina State 58, Kansas State 39
Penn State 82, Rider 68
Auburn 77, Southern Mississippi 62
Dayton 95, Long Island 92
Georgetown 71, Florida 69
Marquette 80, Creighton 68
Memphis 90, Ball State 67
Minnesota 77, Colorado State 65
UAB 93, Missouri 86
Vanderbilt 73, St. Bonaventure 61
Gonzaga 69, Wyoming 55
Georgia 100, Iowa 93
Fresno State 73, Pacific 70
Hawaii 90, Arizona State 73

Thursday, March 12
Wake Forest 56, UNC-Wilmington 52

SECOND ROUND
Monday, March 16
Penn State 77, Dayton 74
Georgia Tech 80, Georgetown 79
Hawaii 78, Gonzaga 70
Fresno State 83, Memphis 80
Marquette 75, Auburn 60
Minnesota 79, UAB 66

Tuesday, March 17
Vanderbilt 72, Wake Forest 68
Georgia 61, N.C. State 55

THIRD ROUND
Wednesday, March 18
Penn State 75, Georgia Tech 70
Minnesota 73, Marquette 71

Thursday, March 19
Georgia 79, Vanderbilt 65
Fresno State 85, Hawaii 83

SEMIFINALS
New York, NY
Tuesday, March 24
Penn State 66, Georgia 60
Minnesota 91, Fresno State 89 (OT)

THIRD PLACE
New York, NY
Thursday, March 26
Georgia 95, Fresno State 79

CHAMPIONSHIP

New York, NY
Thursday, March 26
Minnesota 79, Penn State 72

ON THE INTERNET

adidas Blue Ribbon may be found on the Internet at:

www.collegebaskets.com
www.ncaatourney.com

e-mail addresses:
Blue Ribbon ....bribbon@msys.net
Joe Lunardi ....jlunardi@sju.edu
Chris Dortch..........dortch@mindspring.com

FROM THE EDITOR

Welcome to the 18th edition of *adidas Blue Ribbon College Basketball Yearbook*. We're pleased with the book, and I know you will be, too.

Before I tell you about some of the positive changes going on at *Blue Ribbon*, I'd like to pay a small tribute to the man who helped make the book what it is today.

Ten years ago, former editor Joe Lunardi brought *Blue Ribbon* into the computer age, leading a team that eventually took over from founder Chris Wallace and positioned the book to succeed in the '90s and beyond. Far too busy with his NBA obligations, Wallace, now Rick Pitino's right-hand man with the Boston Celtics, entrusted the leadership of his beloved *Blue Ribbon* to Lunardi, who introduced computer technology to the editing and production process and recruited a team of high-quality writers and editors.

Somehow, I was included in that group, and for the last seven years, Joe and I have worked side-by-side in making *Blue Ribbon* the premier college basketball publication on the market.

Satisfied with the job he had done, and looking for other challenges, Lunardi stepped down as editor last spring, leaving the controls to me.

Lunardi hasn't left Blue Ribbon completely. He was still a trusted ally in the editing process for the 18th edition—our Top 40 section, complete with several improvements we know you'll love, was edited by Lunardi. And he plans on helping his own brainchild, our popular Tournament Guide, grow. Just as he helped *Blue Ribbon* grow.

With Joe assuming a lesser role in the yearbook's production, I have been free to add my own little touches to the publication. My first move was to recruit several colleagues from my days in the newspaper business. Dave Link, who has covered college basketball for the last 18 years, comes on board as associate editor. Like Joe, Dave is a worthy comrade-in-arms in the arduous task of producing *Blue Ribbon*. There isn't a task too great or small for Dave to tackle.

After Dave joined our group, I was fortunate to add two trusted assistant editors, Stan Crawley and Sara Patterson, present and former newspaper veterans, respectively. Their work in helping edit the millions of words you will soon be reading in *Blue Ribbon* was invaluable.

After our editing team was in place, it was time to recruit more writers to our already-impressive group. I was lucky enough to hire some of the best in the business. Take Dave Jones. He's covered the Big Ten for the *Harrisburg (Pa.) Patriot-News* for the last seven years. In another life, Jones was radio-TV critic for the *Columbus (Ohio) Dispatch*. His excellent writing style reflects the analytical eye with which he covered the broadcast media. And he knows his league inside and out.

The same could be said for Kirk Seminoff, who covers the Missouri Valley Conference for the *Wichita Eagle*. When I was searching for a new MVC writer, I called my friend Blair Kerkhoff at the *Kansas City Star*. Blair writes the Big 12 for *Blue Ribbon*, and I trust his judgement. "Get Kirk," was Blair's quick recommendation. "He's a hoss." In this business, a hoss is one who can write well and meet deadlines. Blair was right about Kirk.

Our effort to bring you the best and most knowledgeable writers in the business extends to our high school coverage. When I made a change in that section this year, I knew immediately who I wanted to hire to write the Top 44 profiles. Brick Oettinger is the dean of recruiting gurus, and as a former college professor at Duke and North Carolina State, he can turn a mean phrase. Our profiles have never been better.

Also new to our high school team are my friends at Recruiting USA, David "The Rockfish" Benezra and Mark Mayemura. Both have backgrounds in coaching, and I trust their judgement when it comes to evaluating talent. The hard-working duo provided our exhaustive, state-by-state, honorable-mention All-America list.

Before I close, I'd be remiss not to mention two more people who work so hard to bring you *adidas Blue Ribbon College Basketball Yearbook*. Diane Swiger runs our office with hard-working efficiency. And Dom Roberti, our production chief, is a tireless computer genius who has taught me how to make my trusty Macintosh Powerbook do incredible things. Thanks to Diane and Dom.

It all adds up to a great book that our long-time *Blue Ribbon* readers can put to good use all season. And for all you first-time readers, dig in. You're about to enjoy a feast.

THE TOP 40

1 Duke
2 Connecticut
3 Stanford
4 Kentucky
5 Maryland
6 Temple
7 Tennessee
8 Michigan State
9 New Mexico
10 Cincinnati
11 Utah
12 Purdue
13 Washington
14 Arizona
15 Oklahoma State
16 North Carolina
17 UCLA
18 Syracuse
19 Xavier
20 Arkansas
21 Indiana
22 Massachusetts
23 Kansas
24 Wake Forest
25 Miami (Fla.)
26 Minnesota
27 Georgia
28 UNLV
29 Oklahoma
30 Texas Christian
31 George Washington
32 Miami (Ohio)
33 Memphis
34 California
35 Rhode Island
36 Clemson
37 St. John's
38 Texas
39 South Carolina
40 UAB

THE REST OF THE FIELD

AMERICA EAST—Delaware
BIG SKY—Northern Arizona
BIG SOUTH—Radford
BIG WEST—Idaho
COLONIAL—Old Dominion
IVY—Pennsylvania
MAAC—Iona
MEAC—South Carolina State
MCC—Detroit
MID-CONTINENT—Oral Roberts
MVC—Creighton
NORTHEAST—St. Francis (N.Y.)
OVC—Murray State
PATRIOT—Navy
SOUTHERN—Davidson
SOUTHLAND—Texas-San Antonio
SUN BELT—Florida International
SWAC—Texas Southern
TAAC—Georgia State
WCC—Pepperdine
AT-LARGE—Georgetown
AT-LARGE—Nebraska
AT-LARGE—North Carolina State
AT-LARGE—Tulsa

1998-99 adidas Blue Ribbon
PLAYER OF THE YEAR

Elton Brand—Duke

Class: Sophomore

Height: 6-8

Weight: 260 lbs.

Position: Forward

Hometown: Peekskill, N.Y.

1996-97 Statistics:

13.4 points per game
7.3 rebounds per game
1.2 blocked shots per game
1.5 steals per game

A question asked of Duke sophomore Elton Brand during the Goodwill Games in New York last summer took him by surprise.

"The reporter asked me what I thought about my chances of being the player of the year in college basketball next season," Brand told the *Greensboro News and Record*. "All I could say was, 'Oh, yeah, really?' I just hadn't thought about it. I guess I'd better get ready for that type of question."

If Brand hadn't thought much about being the player of the year this season, plenty of others had, including *Blue Ribbon*. When all the candidates for our preseason Player of the Year were considered, Brand was a clear-cut choice. It's a tribute to his talent that Brand has already generated that kind of respect despite missing nearly half of Duke's games in his freshman season after suffering a stress fracture in his left foot.

Brand's handiwork at the Goodwill Games proved how far he has come back since his injury.

Before he went down, Brand was leading Duke in scoring and rebounding and was playing as well as any freshman in the country. Though it didn't seem possible Brand could return in time for late-season conference games and the NCAA Tournament, he did just that, but was inconsistent. Not so in the Goodwill Games, won by the United States despite a first-round loss to Puerto Rico.

"I was proud of my consistency in New York," Brand told the *News and Record*. "In every area except free-throw shooting. I'm back at 100 percent now. I've spent time in the weight room this summer for the first time in my life, and I've even quit icing my foot. Besides my low-post game, I feel I've improved at rebounding, blocking shots and running the court."

1998-99 adidas Blue Ribbon
NEWCOMER OF THE YEAR

Steve Francis—Maryland

Class: Junior

Height: 6-3

Weight: 194 lbs.

Position: Guard

Hometown: Takoma Park, Md.

1997-98 Statistics:

25.3 points per game
7.1 rebounds per game
8.7 assists per game
5.3 steals per game

OTHER NEWCOMERS OF IMPACT

Player	Ht	Cl	From	New Team
Courtney Alexander	6-5	JR	Virginia	Fresno State
Tony Akins	6-0	FR	Lilburn, GA	Georgia Tech
Eric Barkley	6-1	FR	Pittsfield, ME	St. John's
Kevin Braswell	6-1	FR	Pittsfield, ME	Georgetown
Rasual Butler	6-7	FR	Philadelphia, PA	LaSalle
Jason Capel	6-7	FR	Norfolk, VA	North Carolina
Jason Collier	7-0	JR	Indiana	Georgia Tech
Ron Curry	6-3	FR	Hampton, VA	North Carolina
Ted Dupay	5-10	FR	Cape Coral, FL	Florida
Keyon Dooling	6-2	FR	Ft. Lauderdale, FL	Missouri
Dan Gadzuric	6-11	FR	Byfield, MA	UCLA
Damon Hancock	6-4	FR	Landcaster, TX	SMU
Kevin Houston	6-4	JR	Seward County (KS) JC	Miami
Dane Fife	6-4	FR	Clarkston, MI	Indiana
Evaldas Jocys	6-9	JR	Western (NE) JC	East Carolina
Freddie Jones	6-4	FR	Gresham, OR	Oregon
Michael LeBlanc	6-6	SO	Connecticut	Vanderbilt
Shawn Marion	6-7	JR	Vincennes (IN) JC	UNLV
Pete Mickeal	6-7	JR	Indian Hills (IA) JC	Cincinnati
Mike Miller	6-8	FR	Mitchell, SD	Florida
Troy Murphy	6-10	FR	Morristown, NJ	Notre Dame
Joel Pryzbilla	7-0	FR	Monticello, MN	Minnesota
Quentin Richardson	6-6	FR	Chicago, IL	DePaul
Chris Porter	6-7	JR	Chipola (FL) JC	Auburn
Silester Rivers	6-6	JR	Utah Valley State JC	BYU
Jaron Rush	6-7	FR	Kansas City, MO	UCLA
Bobby Simmons	6-7	FR	Chicago, IL	DePaul
Gordon Scott	6-5	JR	Barton County (KS) JC	Idaho
Vincent Yarbrough	6-8	FR	Cleveland, TN	Tennessee
B.B. Waldon	6-7	FR	Lakeland, FL	South Florida

Picking the *adidas Blue Ribbon College Basketball Yearbook* Newcomer of the Year is never easy. So many great players enter the Division I ranks each year. How do we pick one from among dozens?

There are two ways, actually, two criteria by which to predict the nation's best newcomer. One school of thought is to choose a player who figures to compile the best statistics. Usually, this is a great player who joins a team down on its luck or in need of talent at a certain position.

The other theory in choosing the top newcomer is to identify a player who could potentially have the greatest impact, a guy who can help his team rise to another level.

With that in mind, our pick for Newcomer of the Year is Maryland point guard Steve Francis. Coaches, recruiting analysts and sports writers we consulted all agreed that Francis is capable of lifting the Terrapins to top 10 status. No less an expert than Maryland coach Gary Williams, a man not given to overstatement, says Francis reminds him of former Terrapin star John Lucas.

We could probably stop right there, but here's more on Francis:

"He's 6-3, which is excellent size for a point guard," said Lou Wilson, Francis' former AAU coach. "He's also an explosive leaper and an excellent defender. He is the prototype all-around, big-time point guard. There's nothing average about him."

Francis started his junior college career at San Jacinto (Texas). San Jac was undefeated when Francis led it to the NJCAA national championship tournament, and the Ravens finished 36-1. Francis averaged 13.5 points, 7.1 assists and 6.6 rebounds as a freshman.

Last year, Francis became the first player to ever lead two undefeated teams to the national championships when his Allegany (Md.) CC team advanced. Francis scored 66 points in Allegany's two games, the fourth-highest two-game total in history.

Francis was chosen a first-team NJCAA All-American, and junior college basketball experts Rick Ball and Phil Henzel picked him as the No. 2-ranked player in the JC ranks a year ago. Look for big things from Steve Francis—and Maryland—this season.

1998-99 adidas Blue Ribbon
ALL-AMERICA TEAM

Brand

Szczerbiak

Hamilton

Miller

McKie

Eschmeyer

MacCulloch

FIRST TEAM

Elton Brand, *Sophomore*	Duke
Wally Szczerbiak, *Senior*	Miami (Ohio)
Richard Hamilton, *Junior*	Connecticut
Andre Miller, *Senior*	Utah
B.J. McKie, *Senior*	South Carolina

Young

Ketner

Padgett

James

SECOND TEAM

Evan Eschmeyer, *Senior*	Northwestern
Scott Padgett, *Senior*	Kentucky
Kenny Thomas, *Senior*	New Mexico
Mateen Cleaves, *Junior*	Michigan State
Trajan Langdon, *Senior*	Duke

Nailon

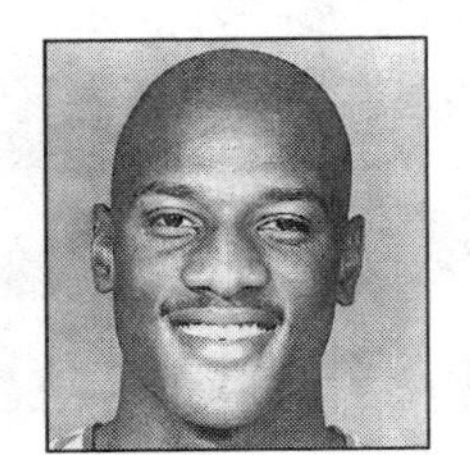
Cummings

Thomas

Jones

THIRD TEAM

Todd MacCulloch, *Senior*	Washington
Tim James, *Senior*	Miami
Jumaine Jones, *Sophomore*	Georgia
Khalid El-Amin, *Sophomore*	Connecticut
Arthur Lee, *Senior*	Stanford

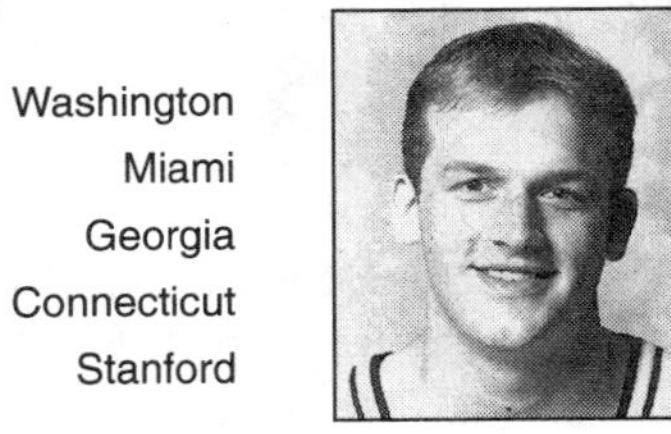
Cardinal

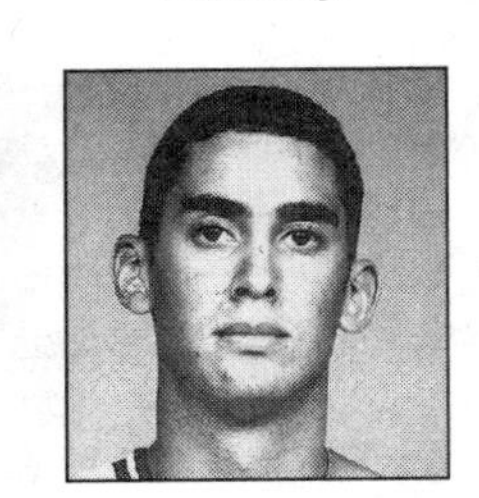
Bramlett

Cleaves

El-Amin

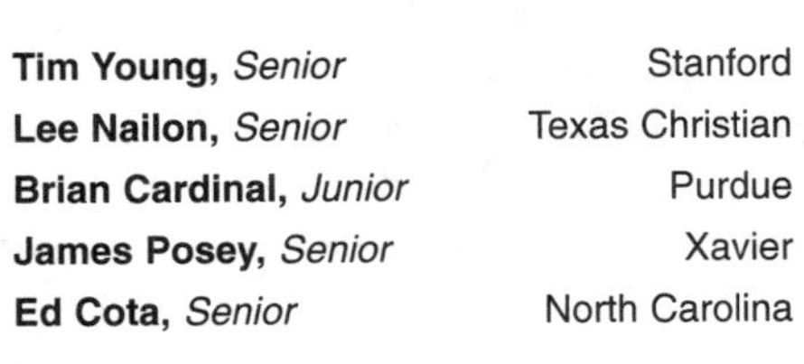

FOURTH TEAM

Tim Young, *Senior*	Stanford
Lee Nailon, *Senior*	Texas Christian
Brian Cardinal, *Junior*	Purdue
James Posey, *Senior*	Xavier
Ed Cota, *Senior*	North Carolina

Posey

Harris

Langdon

Lee

FIFTH TEAM

Lari Ketner, *Senior*	Massachusetts
Vonteego Cummings, *Senior*	Pittsburgh
A.J. Bramlett, *Senior*	Arizona
Tony Harris, *Sophomore*	Tennessee
Dion Glover, *Sophomore*	Georgia Tech

Note—All-America teams do not include newcomers.

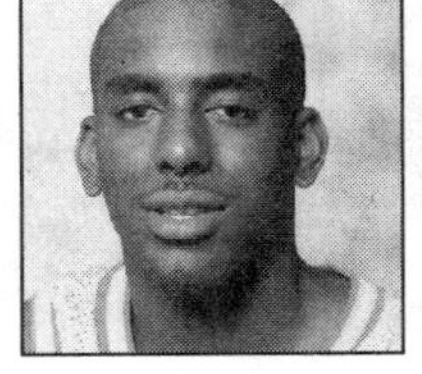
Cota

Glover

1998-99 adidas Blue Ribbon
HONORABLE MENTION ALL-AMERICA TEAM

Damon Arnette, *Senior* Florida Atlantic
Ron Artest, *Sophomore* St. John's
William Avery, *Sophomore* Duke
Matt Baniak, *Sophomore* Saint Louis
Lamont Barnes, *Junior* Temple
Damien Baskerville, *Senior* Weber State
Raja Bell, *Senior* Florida International
Andy Bedard, *Junior* Maine
Jason Bell, *Senior* Virginia Military Institute
Roberto Bergersen, *Senior* Boise State
Ryan Blackwell, *Junior* Syracuse
Pat Bradley, *Senior* Arkansas
Keion Brooks, *Senior* Wright State
Rasheed Brokenborough, *Senior* Temple
Lenny Brown, *Senior* Xavier
Walter Brown, *Senior* Boston University
Jami Bosley, *Junior* Akron
Rodney Buford, *Senior* Creighton
Greg Burston, *Senior* Rider
Geno Carlisle, *Senior* California
Jerry Carstensen, *Junior* Wisconsin-Green Bay
Keith Carter, *Senior* Mississippi
Kris Clack, *Senior* Texas
Charlton Clarke, *Senior* Massachusetts
Craig Claxton, *Junior* Hofstra
Kenyatta Clyde, *Senior* Southern Utah
Lonnie Cooper, *Senior* Louisiana Tech
Ed Cota, *Junior* North Carolina
Avery Curry, *Senior* Idaho
Caswell Cyrus, *Junior* St. Bonaventure
Will Daniel, *Junior* Samford
Baron Davis, *Sophomore* UCLA
Ryan DeMichael, *Senior* Tennessee-Martin
Richy Dominquez, *Sophomore* St. Francis (NY)
Brian Earl, *Senior* Princeton
Lester Earl, *Junior* Kansas
Brian Ehlers, *Junior* Lafayette
Obinna Ekezie, *Senior* Maryland
Bud Eley, *Senior* Southeast Missouri State
Brett Eppenhimer, *Senior* Lehigh
Maurice Evans, *Sophomore* Wichita State
Heshimu Evans, *Senior* Kentucky
Marcus Faison, *Junior* Siena
Marcus Fizer, *Sophomore* Iowa State
Chico Fletcher, *Junior* Arkansas State
Damon Frierson, *Senior* Miami (Ohio)
Jeff Foster, *Senior* Southwest Texas State
Prince Fowler, *Senior* Texas Christian
Jelani Gardner, *Senior* Pepperdine
Quincy Gause, *Senior* Georgia State
Martin Gilliard, *Senior* Bucknell
Javan Goodman, *Senior* Loyola

A.J. Guyton, *Junior* Indiana
Kashif Hameed, *Senior* Iona
Venson Hamilton, *Senior* Nebraska
Ike Harmon, *Junior* Fullerton State
Gregory Harris, *Junior* Mount St. Mary's
Jason Hart, *Junior* Syracuse
Jason Hartman, *Senior* Portland State
Dionte Harvey, *Senior* Southern
Trent Hassell, *Sophomore* Austin Peay
Chris Herren, *Senior* Fresno State
Jermaine Hicks, *Junior* Chicago State
Tim Hill, *Senior* Harvard
Nate Holmstadt, *Senior* Montana State
Chatney Howard, *Senior* James Madison
Jermaine Jackson, *Senior* Detroit
Donnie Johnson, *Senior* Utah State
Michael Jordan, *Junior* Pennsylvania
Kaspars Kambala, *Sophomore* UNLV
Tariq Kirksay, *Junior* Iona
Adam Larrick, *Senior* Charleston Southern
Gabe Lewullis, *Senior* Princeton
Joe Linderman, *Junior* Drexel
Lamont Long, *Junior* New Mexico
Quincy Lewis, *Senior* Minnesota
T.J. Lux, *Senior* Northern Illinois
James Madison, *Junkor* Cleveland State
Mark Madsen, *Junior* Stanford
Demond Mallet, *Junior* McNeese State
Kenyon Martin, *Senior* Cincinnati
Kevin Martin, *Senior* North Carolina-Asheville
Donte Mathis, *Senior* Southwest Texas State
Jason McCutcheon, *Senior* Nicholls State
Hanno Mottola, *Junior* Utah
Ronnie McCollumn, *Sophomore* Centenary
Terrell McIntyre, *Senior* Clemson
Yegor Mescheriakov, *Senior* George Washington
Rick Mickens, *Junior* Central Connecticut State
Brad Millard, *Junior* Saint Mary's
Danny Moore, *Senior* Southwest Missouri State
Ryan Moss, *Senior* Arkansas-Little Rock
Eduardo Najera, *Junior* Oklahoma
Robert O'Kelley, *Sophomore* Wake Forest
Mike Pegues, *Junior* Delaware
Adrian Peterson, *Senior* Oklahoma State
David Phillips, *Junior* Tennessee-Chattanooga
Marshall Phillips, *Senior* Appalachian State
Frantz Pierre-Louis, *Senior* Wagner
Roderick Platt, *Senior* Loyola College
Mark Poag, *Senior* Old Dominion
Reginald Poole, *Senior* Southwestern Louisiana
Laron Profit, *Senior* Maryland
Michael Redd, *Sophomore* Ohio State

Neil Reed, *Senior-* Southern Mississippi
Kareem Reid, *Senior* Arkansas
Antonio Reynolds-Dean, *Senior* Rhode Island
Quentin Richardson, *Freshman* DePaul
Jamie Roberts, *Sophomore* Tennessee State
Rolan Roberts, *Sophomore* Virginia Tech
Ryan Robertson, *Senior* Kansas
Bevon Robin, *Sophomore* Fordham
Shawnta Rogers, *Senior* George Washington
Pepe Sanchez, *Junior* Temple
Matt Santangelo, *Junior* Gonzaga
Eric Schraeder, *Senior* Saint Mary's
Stan Simmons, *Senior* North Carolina-Wilmington
Antonio Smith, *Senior* Michigan State
G.G. Smith, *Senior* Georgia
Omar Sneed, *Senior* Memphis
Rasheed Sparks, *Senior* Morgan State
Isaac Spencer, *Junior* Murray State
Danny Sprinkle, *Senior* Montana State
G.G. Smith, *Senior* Georgia
Anthony Stacy, *Senior* Bowling Green
Greg Stephens, *Senior* East Tennessee State
Greg Stolt, *Senior* Florida
Jason Terry, *Senior* Arizona
Etan Thomas, *Junior* Syracuse
Chris Thunell, *Junior* Southern Illinois
Brian Towne, *Senior* Portland State
Coby Turner, *Senior* Dayton
Brad Traina, *Senior* Central Florida
Wayne Turner, *Senior* Kentucky
Skip Victor, *Senior* Navy
Damiam Walker, *Junior* New Mexico
Raheem Waller, *Senior* South Carolina State
Ben Wandtke, *Senior* Colgate
Fred Warrick, *Senior* Coppin State
Tyrone Washington, *Senior* Mississippi State
Leon Watson, *Senior* Texas-San Antonio
Donald Watts, *Senior* Washington
Sedric Webber, *Senior* College of Charleston
Kris Weems, *Senior* Stanford
Brandon Wharton, *Senior* Tennessee
Brian Williams, *Senior* Alabama
Fred Williams, *Senior* UAB
Tarvis Williams, *Junior* Hampton
Marcus Wilson, *Senior* Evansville
Tim Winn, *Junior* St. Bonaventure
Damian Woolfolk, *Junior* Norfolk State
Mike Wozniak, *Junior* Cal Poly
Rayford Young, *Senior* Texas Tech
Gerald Zimmerman, *Senior* San Francisco

1998-99 adidas Blue Ribbon
WOMEN'S COLLEGE ALL-AMERICA TEAMS & TOP 25

By Dan Fleser, the Knoxville (Tenn.) News-Sentinel

	HT	POS	CL	SCHOOL
FIRST TEAM				
Chamique Holdsclaw	6-2	F	Sr.	Tennessee
Tamika Catchings	6-1	F	So.	Tennessee
Maylana Martin	6-3	F	Jr.	UCLA
Dominique Canty	5-10	G	Sr.	Alabama
Stephanie White-McCarty	5-11	G	Sr.	Purdue
SECOND TEAM				
Amanda Wilson	6-0	F	Sr.	Louisiana Tech
DeMya Walker	6-2	F	Sr.	Virginia
Tamika Whitmore	6-2	C	Sr.	Memphis
Chanel Wright	6-0	G	Sr.	North Carolina
Tamicha Jackson	5-5	G	Jr.	Louisiana Tech
THIRD TEAM				
Svetlana Abrosimova	6-1	F	So.	Connecticut
Lynn Pride	6-2	F	Jr.	Kansas
Noelia Gomez	6-3	C	Sr.	George Washington
Semeka Randall	5-10	G	So.	Tennessee
Nikki Teasley	6-1	G	So.	North Carolina
FOURTH TEAM				
Erin Buescher	6-3	F	So.	Cal-Santa Barbara
Mery Andrade	6-1	F	Sr.	Old Dominion
Angie Braziel	6-3	F	Sr.	Texas Tech
Dalma Ivanyi	5-10	G	Sr.	Florida International
Becky Hammons	5-8	G	Sr.	Colorado State
FIFTH TEAM				
Amy O'Brien	6-1	F	Sr.	Holy Cross
Edwina Brown	5-10	F	Jr.	Texas
Tammi Blackstone	6-4	C	Jr.	Drake
Jackie Stiles	5-8	G	So.	Southwest Missouri State
Erica Gomez	5-9	G	Jr.	UCLA

TOP 25 CAPSULES

1 Tennessee

NICKNAME .... **Lady Volunteers**
COLORS .... **Orange and White**
CONFERENCE .... **Southeastern**
COACH .... **Pat Summitt**
RECORD AT SCHOOL **664-143**
CAREER RECORD **664-143**
LAST SEASON **39-0**
CONFERENCE RECORD .... **14-0 (1st)**
1997-98 FINISH .... **Won National Championship**

STARTERS RETURNING—F Chamique Holdsclaw (6-2 Sr., 23.5 ppg, 8.4 rpg); F Tamika Catchings (6-1, So., 18.2 ppg, 8.0 rpg); C Teresa Geter (6-1, So., 6.3 ppg, 4.8 rpg); G Kellie Jolly (5-10, Jr., 7.6 ppg, 2.3 rpg) G Semeka Randall (5-10 So., 15.9 ppg, 5.3 rpg).

OUTLOOK—Complacency and key injuries might be the biggest potential problems for a team on a 45-game winning streak spanning two seasons. Last season's team returns virtually intact and has added much-needed inside depth with freshmen post players Michelle Snow and Shalon Pillow. The presence of the 6-foot-5 Snow might allow the Lady Vols to increase the pressure of their full-court defense even further.

2 Louisiana Tech

NICKNAME .... **Lady Techsters**
COLORS .... **Red and Columbia Blue**
CONFERENCE .... **Sun Belt**
COACH .... **Leon Barmore**
RECORD AT SCHOOL .... **459-71 (.866)**
CAREER RECORD .... **459-71 (.866)**
LAST SEASON **31-4**
CONFERENCE RECORD .... **13-1 (1st)**
1997-98 FINISH ... **Lost to Tennessee in national final.**

STARTERS RETURNING—F Amanda Wilson (6-0, Sr., 18.5 ppg, 8.8 rpg); F Monica Maxwell (5-9, Sr., 11.9 ppg, 6.4 ppg); G LaQuan Stallworth (5-6, Sr., 11.4 ppg, 3.9 rpg); G Tamicha Jackson (5-5 Jr., 14.6 ppg. 3.3 rpg).

OUTLOOK—Tech has lost only center Alisa Burras, and her play last season was not up to the standards she set the previous season. The new Lady Techsters, including a recruiting class that rivals Connecticut's, is loaded with centers. If the recruits can provide quality depth, Tech could return to the national title game and win.

3 Duke

NICKNAME .... **Blue Devils**
COLORS .... **Royal Blue and White**
CONFERENCE .... **Atlantic Coast**
COACH .... **Gail Goestenkors**
RECORD AT SCHOOL **119-61**
CAREER RECORD **119-61**
LAST SEASON **24-8**
CONFERENCE RECORD .... **13-3 (1st)**
1997-98 RECORD .... **Lost in NCAA West Regional final.**

STARTERS RETURNING—F Peppi Browne (5-11, Jr., 10.7 ppg, 6.2 rpg); C Payton Black (6-4, Sr., 10.5 ppg, 3.6 rpg), C Michele VanGorp (6-6 Sr., 10.4 ppg. 4.1 rpg), G Hilary Howard (5-7 Sr., 9.8 ppg, 3.4 rpg) Nicole Erickson (5-6, Sr., 12.8 ppg , 2 rpg).

OUTLOOK—With five starters back, a Final Four berth would seem to be a reasonable goal. With their height, it would behoove the Blue Devils to have more than a plus-five rebounding margin on the opposition. A tough non-conference schedule that includes Tennessee, Connecticut and Florida could harden this team for the postseason, which is the best measuring stick for a top-five team.

4 Connecticut

NICKNAME .... **Huskies**
COLORS .... **National Flag Blue and White**
CONFERENCE .... **Big East**
COACH .... **Geno Auriemma**
RECORD AT SCHOOL .... **(328-89)**
CAREER RECORD .... **(328-89)**
LAST SEASON **34-3**
CONFERENCE RECORD .... **17-1 (1st)**
1997-98 FINISH ..... **Lost in NCAA East Regional final.**

STARTERS RETURNING—F Svetlana Abrosimova (6-1 So., 14.5 ppg, 5.4 rpg) C Paige Sauer (6-5 Jr., 11.9 ppg, 6.0 rpg) G Amy Duran (5-11 Sr., 9.6 ppg , 3.0 rpg).

OUTLOOK—The Huskies have reloaded with the season's most celebrated recruiting classes, highlighted by national player of the year Tamika Williams and *Parade* All-American Swin Cash, who averaged 30.4 points, 16.9 rebounds and 5.8 blocked shots during her senior high school season. Veteran leadership will be crucial, though, in assimilating the newcomers into a team in transition.

5 Purdue

NICKNAME .... **Boilermakers**
COLORS .... **Old Gold and Black**
CONFERENCE .... **Big Ten**
COACH .... **Carolyn Peck**
RECORD AT SCHOOL **23-10**
CAREER RECORD **23-10**
LAST SEASON **23-10**
CONFERENCE RECORD .... **10-6 (t-3rd)**
1997-98 FINISH .... **Lost in final of NCAA Midwest Regional.**

STARTERS RETURNING—G Stephanie White-McCarty (5-11 Sr., 20.6 ppg, 6.1 rpg); G Ukari Figgs (5-9 Sr., 15.5 ppg, 5.1 rpg); F Tiffany Young (5-11 Jr., 5.1 ppg, 2.0 rpg) F Mackenzie Curless (6-1 Jr., 7.8 ppg, 4.0 rpg); F Michelle Duhart (5.2 ppg, 5.4 rpg).

OUTLOOK—The return of five starters, including one of the nation's best backcourts, speaks for itself in terms of optimism. The departure of Peck, who will be leaving after this season for the WNBA's expansion franchise in Orlando, could create problems. But the team used a competitive trip to Europe this summer to address that issue. The Boilermakers seem poised for a great season.

6 North Carolina

NICKNAME....Tar Heels
COLORS....White and Carolina Blue
CONFERENCE....Atlantic Coast
COACH....Sylvia Hatchell
RECORD AT SCHOOL....241-125
CAREER RECORD....513-205
LAST SEASON....27-7
CONFERENCE RECORD....11-5 (4th)
1997-98....Lost in NCAA Mideast Regional final.

STARTERS RETURNING—F Chanel Wright (6-0 Sr., 13.9 ppg, 3.7 rpg; G Nikki Teasley (6-1, So., 12.9 ppg, 3.5 rpg) G Juana Brown (5-10 So., 8.8 ppg, 4.5 rpg).

OUTLOOK—Despite losing All-American Tracy Reid, this team still is loaded with talent and quickness. The Tar Heels are not big on height, but that shouldn't matter if Wright and Teasley are improved. Teasley presents a height problem for the opposition as a 6-1 point guard.

7 UCLA

NICKNAME....Bruins
COLORS....Blue and Gold
CONFERENCE....Pac-10
COACH....Kathy Oliver
RECORD AT SCHOOL....71-66
CAREER RECORD....71-66
LAST SEASON....20-9
CONFERENCE RECORD....14-4 (2nd)
1997-98 FINISH....Lost in second round of NCAA Tournament.

STARTERS RETURNING—F Maylana Martin (6-3 Jr., 18.8 ppg, 7.4 rpg), F Marie Philman (6-0, Fr., 10.1 ppg, 3.8 ppg), C Janae Hubbard (6-4 Jr., 11.0 ppg, 6.1 rpg), G Erica Gomez, (5-9 Jr., 7.5 ppg, 3.0 rpg).

OUTLOOK—Were it not for a time keeper's error at Alabama, the Bruins might have beaten the Crimson Tide and advanced deep into last season's NCAA Tournament. The key players, notably Martin and Gomez, are back for another go. Hubbard's continued development also is important. The Bruins also need to hope for no injuries. Both Gomez and top reserve Takiyah Jackson have missed past seasons with knee injuries.

8 Kansas

NICKNAME....Jayhawks
COLORS....Crimson and Blue
CONFERENCE....Big 12
COACH....Marian Washington
RECORD AT SCHOOL....480-267
CAREER RECORD....480-267
LAST SEASON....23-9
CONFERENCE RECORD....11-5 (3rd)
1997-98 FINISH....Lost in NCAA West semifinal.

STARTERS RETURNING—F Lynn Pride (6-2 Jr., 14.9 ppg, 6.7 rpg); F Jaclyn Johnson (9.3 ppg, 5.6 rpg), G Suzi Raymant (5-11, Sr., 14.1 ppg, 6.1 rpg), G Jennifer Jackson (5-10, So., 9.0 ppg, 3.2 rpg).

OUTLOOK—The Jayhawks find themselves in a situation similar to two seasons ago, namely plenty of returning talent and a lofty preseason ranking. They took a No. 3 seeding into the 1997 NCAA Tournament but lost a second-round game on their home court to Vanderbilt. If they have enough Pride, the Jayhawks might do more with their potential this season.

9 Virginia

NICKNAME....Cavaliers
COLORS....Blue and Orange
CONFERENCE....Atlantic Coast
COACH....Debbie Ryan
RECORD AT SCHOOL....481-165
CAREER RECORD....481-165
LAST SEASON....19-10
CONFERENCE RECORD....9-7 (5th)
1997-98 FINISH....Lost in second round of NCAA Tournament.

STARTERS RETURNING—F DeMya Walker (6-2, Sr., 16.3 ppg, 8.4 rpg); F Lisa Hosac (6-2, Jr., 7.9 ppg, 6.7 rpg), G Erin Stovall (5-9 So., 9.4 ppg, 2.8 rpg)

OUTLOOK—The Cavaliers receive a big boost from the return of 6-foot Monick Foote, who missed last season with a stress fracture. She had averaged 14 points the previous season and her defense will complement Walker's and the team's overall effort. Elena Kravchenko, a 6-10 sophomore center from Russia, needs to provide more than one rebound per game on average for a team that's rebounding deficient. Virginia's quickness and defense will have to offset suspect shooting.

10 Old Dominion

NICKNAME....Lady Monarchs
COLORS....Slate Blue and Silver
CONFERENCE....Colonial Athletic AssociatioN
COACH....Wendy Larry
RECORD AT SCHOOL....252-91
CAREER RECORD....301-122
LAST SEASON....29-3
CONFERENCE RECORD....16-0 (1st)
1997-98....Lost in semifinal of NCAA East Regional.

STARTERS RETURNING—F Mery Andrade (6-1 Sr., 14.2 ppg, 6.8 rpg); G Aubrey Eblin (5-7 Sr., 11.8 ppg, 2.2 rpg); G Natalie Diaz (5-11 Jr., 6.8 ppg, 2.8 rpg).

OUTLOOK—Despite the loss of point guard Ticha Penicheiro and center Nyree Roberts, there is still talent on this team, as Andrade returns. Her play reflects the hard-nosed competitiveness that has characterized the Lady Monarchs' play during the last two seasons. Diaz might take over at point guard. Old Dominion has recruited/imported several post players to try to fill the void inside.

11 Rutgers

NICKNAME....Scarlet Knights
COLORS....Scarlet and White
CONFERENCE....Big East
COACH....C. Vivian Stringer
RECORD AT SCHOOL....46-42
CAREER RECORD....566-177
LAST SEASON....22-10
CONFERENCE RECORD....14-4 (1st Big East 7)
1997-98 FINISH....Lost in NCAA Mideast semifinal.

STARTERS RETURNING—F Linda Miles (6-0 So., 8.3 ppg, 6.9 rpg); C Jennifer Clemente (6-2 Sr., 3.0, 3.2); G Tomora Young (5-10 Sr., 13.7 ppg, 3.3 rpg); G Natasha Pointer (5-6 So., 14.0 ppg, 4.2 rpg)

OUTLOOK—The Scarlet Knight emerged last season, benefiting from youthful exuberance and a lack of expectations. This season will place a greater premium upon the team's confidence and its competitiveness. Pointer and Young comprise a solid backcourt that should lead Rutgers wherever its headed this season.

12 George Washington

NICKNAME....Colonials
COLORS....Buff and Blue
CONFERENCE....Atlantic 10
COACH....Joe McKeown
RECORD AT SCHOOL....205-76 (.730)
CAREER RECORD....273-96 (.740)
LAST SEASON....20-10
CONFERENCE RECORD ..12-4 (1st in West Division)
1997-98 FINISH....Lost in second round of NCAA Tournament.

STARTERS RETURNING—F Noelia Gomez (6-3 Sr., 17.2 ppg, 6.0 rpg); F Mandisa Turner (6-2 Sr., 6.3 ppg, 5.9 rpg) G Elisa Aguilar (5-8 Jr., 17.2 ppg, 4.9 rpg) G Chasity Myers (5-9 Jr., 8.9 ppg, 4.7 rpg) G Marlo Egleston (5-7 Jr., 7.4 ppg, 2.9 rpg).

OUTLOOK—The return of Spanish imports Gomez and Aguilar maintains George Washington's foundation. More important to the Colonials' success, however, is better overall depth. A key player could be 6-3 sophomore forward Petra Dubovcova, who was averaging 10 points and six rebounds last season before going down after nine games with a torn anterior cruciate knee ligament.

13 North Carolina State

NICKNAME....Wolfpack women
COLORS....Red and White
CONFERENCE....Atlantic Coast
COACH....Kay Yow
RECORD AT SCHOOL....495-202
CAREER RECORD....552-221
LAST SEASON....25-7
CONFERENCE RECORD....12-4 (t-2nd)
1997-98....Lost in national semifinal to Louisiana Tech.

STARTERS RETURNING—F Lyschale Jones (5-10 Sr., 10.8 ppg, 3.0 rpg); F Tynesha Lewis (5-10, So., 11.8 ppg, 4.0 rpg); G Kristen Gillespie (5-11 Sr., 2.8 ppg, 2.4 rpg).

OUTLOOK—Center Chasity Melvin finished her career last season with 37 points against Louisiana Tech. Obviously she will be missed, but 6-foot-6 Summer Erb has considerable experience. The progress of Lewis, an honorable mention All-America as a freshman, will be vital to the Wolfpack's progress.

14 Notre Dame

NICKNAME....Fighting Irish
COLORS....Gold and Blue
CONFERENCE....Big East
COACH....Muffet McGraw
RECORD AT SCHOOL....235-105 (.691)
CAREER RECORD....323-146 (.689)
LAST SEASON....22-10
CONFERENCE RECORD....12-6 (t-2nd, Big East 6)
1997-98 ...Lost in NCAA Midwest Regional semifinal.

STARTERS RETURNING—F Kelley Siemon (6-2 So., 8.0 ppg, 5.2 rpg); C Ruth Riley (6-5 So., 11.5 ppg, 7.3 rpg); G Shelia McMillen (5-10 Sr., 13.6 ppg, 2.7 rpg); G Niele Ivey (5-8 Jr., 8.2 ppg, 3.4 rpg).

OUTLOOK—After a Final Four appearance two seasons ago, a Fighting Irish team that supposedly was rebuilding topped 20 victories last season and scored a second-round NCAA victory over Texas Tech on its home floor. This team figures to be improved on many fronts and ought to be striving for its first victory over conference-rival Connecticut.

15 Arkansas

NICKNAME....Lady Razorbacks
COLORS....Red and White
CONFERENCE....Southeastern
COACH....Gary Blair
RECORD AT SCHOOL....99-95 (.643)
CAREER RECORD....309-98 (.759)
LAST SEASON....22-11
CONFERENCE RECORD....7-7 (t-6th)
1997-98....Lost in national semifinal to Tennessee.

STARTERS RETURNING—F Karyn Karlin (6-1 Jr., 15.2 ppg, 5.5 rpg); G Sytia Messer (5-8 Sr., 12.6 ppg, 4.3 ppg) G Treva Christensen (6-0 Sr., 7.5 ppg, 2.3 rpg).

OUTLOOK—Despite the loss of point guard Christy Smith, Arkansas returns a productive scorer in Karlin and a strong defender in Messer. The Lady Razorbacks are not overly big, but then they weren't last year either. If they can shore up the point-guard position, they will have a chance to build on last season's finish.

16 Texas Tech

NICKNAME....Lady Raiders
COLORS....Scarlet and Black
CONFERENCE....Big 12
COACH....Marsha Sharp
RECORD AT SCHOOL....376-125
CAREER RECORD....376-125
LAST SEASON....26-5
CONFERENCE RECORD....15-1 (1st)
1997-98 FINISH....Lost in second round of NCAA Tournament.

STARTERS RETURNING—F Angie Braziel (6-3 Sr., 14.2 ppg, 6.5 rpg); G Rene Hanebutt (5-8 Sr., 10.2 ppg , 5.5 rpg); G Julie Lake (5-8 Sr., 10.1 ppg, 3.4 rpg) G Melinda Schmucker (5-9 Jr., 3.5 ppg, 2.5 rpg).

OUTLOOK—This ranking probably hinges on Braziel being able to take up more space inside. With forward Alicia Thompson having departed, the state of the Red

Raiders inside game is crucial, not only for points and rebounds, but for creating some space for three-point shooters Hanebutt and Lake.

17 Georgia

NICKNAME...Lady Bulldogs
COLORS...Red and Black
CONFERENCE...Southeastern
COACH...Andy Landers
RECORD AT SCHOOL...459-141 (.765)
CAREER RECORD...541-162 (.770)
LAST SEASON...17-11
CONFERENCE RECORD...8-6 (5th)
1997-98 FINISH...Lost in first round of NCAA Tournament.

STARTERS RETURNING—F Elena Vishniakova (6-3 So., 7.9 ppg, 6.9 rpg); F Angie Ball (6-3 Jr., 4.7 ppg, 4.9 ppg); G Kelly Miller (5-10 So., 17.5 ppg, 5.7 rpg); G Coco Miller (5-10 So., 16.0 ppg, 4.6 rpg); G Pam Irwin (5-10 Sr., 13.6 ppg, 3.1 rpg).

OUTLOOK—The return of five starters should draw the most attention. But the newcomers and the almost-new-comers are really intriguing. Sophomore guard Kiesha Brown missed all but eight games of her freshman season with various injuries. Transfer Deana Nolan adds to a deep perimeter. The freshman class brings much-needed height.

18 California-Santa Barbara

NICKNAME...Gauchos
COLORS...Blue and Gold
CONFERENCE...Big West
COACH...Mark French
RECORD AT SCHOOL...201-121 (.624)
CAREER RECORD...308-221 (.582)
LAST SEASON...27-6
CONFERENCE RECORD...14-1 (1st)
1997-98 FINISH...Lost in second round of the NCAA Tournament.

STARTERS RETURNING—F Kristi Rohr (6-1 Jr., 15.7 ppg, 6.6 rpg); C Nicole Greathouse (6-2 So., 9.9 ppg., 8.3 rpg.); G Erin Buescher (6-3 So., 17.1 ppg, 8.7 rpg); G Stacy Clinesmith (5-5 Jr., 14.0 ppg, 3.4 rpg); Tawnee Cooper (5-9 Jr., 10.8 ppg, 4.3 rpg).

OUTLOOK—UCSB's Thunderdome ought to be rocking this season as the fans cheer a young, talented team that is blossoming. Buescher is one of the most versatile talents in the nation, capable of playing either of the two guard or two forward positions. She led the team in scoring, rebounding, steals and blocked shots last season. A little more help for Buescher would really help the Gauchos.

19 Washington

NICKNAME...Huskies
COLORS...Purple and Gold
CONFERENCE...Pac-10
COACH...June Daugherty
RECORD AT SCHOOL...35-21
CAREER RECORD...159-95
LAST SEASON...18-10
CONFERENCE RECORD...9-9 (t-5th)
1997-98 FINISH...Lost in first round of the NCAA Tournament.

STARTERS RETURNING—F Amber Hall (6-1 Sr., 17.3 ppg, 11.2 rpg); G Jamie Redd (5-10 Sr., 19.3 ppg, 6.6 rpg); G Megan Franza (5-10 So., 7.5 ppg, 1.9 rpg) G Molly Hills (5-9 Sr., 5.6 ppg, 3.2 rpg).

OUTLOOK—Washington's three returning senior starters have played together for three years. Experience is not a problem. But shooting problems linger as the Huskies slipped to .385 percent from the field last season, including .281 percent on three-pointers. If those numbers improve, Washington could rise through the rankings. If not, the Huskies might sink out of Top 25 sight.

20 Stanford

NICKNAME...Cardinal
COLORS...Cardinal and White
CONFERENCE...Pac-10
COACH...Tara VanDerveer
RECORD AT SCHOOL...306-70
CAREER RECORD...458-121
LAST SEASON...21-6
CONFERENCE RECORD...17-1 (1st)
1997-98 FINISH...Lost in first round of NCAA Tournament.

STARTERS RETURNING—F Regan Freuen (6-0 Sr., 5.6 ppg, 1.2 rpg); G Milena Flores (5-6 Jr., 9.7 ppg, 2.9 rpg).

OUTLOOK—Not since the beginning years of VanDerveer's 13-season tenure have the ranks been this thin at Stanford. The season will turn on the contributions of the Cardinal's freshman class, a group headed by prep All-America Lindsey Yamasaki. The 6-foot-1 forward from Oregon City, Ore., about the only top prospect that either UConn or Louisiana Tech didn't sign, might be the best of the bunch. For Stanford's sake, she had better be.

21 Florida

NICKNAME...Lady Gators
COLORS...Orange and Blue
CONFERENCE...Southeastern
COACH...Carol Ross
RECORD AT SCHOOL...165-77 (.682)
CAREER RECORD...165-77 (.682)
LAST SEASON...23-9
CONFERENCE RECORD...10-4 (t-2nd)
1997-98 FINISH...Lost in semifinal of NCAA West Regional.

STARTERS RETURNING—F Talatha Bingham (5-8 Sr., 8.5 ppg, 3.1 rpg), C Tamara Stocks (6-3, So., 10.6 ppg, 4.7 rpg).

OUTLOOK—Despite losing three starters, the Lady Gators return a pair of reserves, forward Tonya Washington and wing player Tiffany Travis, who averaged double-figure scoring last season. As a freshman, Stocks showed the potential to follow DeLisha Milton and Murriel Page and become Florida's next great post player.

22 Southwest Missouri State

NICKNAME...Lady Bears
COLORS...Maroon and White
CONFERENCE...Missouri Valley
COACH...Cheryl Burnett
RECORD AT SCHOOL...226-101
CAREER RECORD...226-101
LAST SEASON...24-6
CONFERENCE RECORD...14-4 (2nd)
1997-98 FINISH...Lost in first round of NCAA Tournament.

STARTERS RETURNING—F Roshonda Reed (6-0 Sr., 13.6 ppg, 6.8 rpg); G Jackie Stiles (5-8 So., 20.6 ppg, 3.8 rpg), G Yen Quach (5-2 Sr., 8.3 ppg, 3.4 rpg) G Sarah Singer (5-9 Jr., 6.1 ppg, 2.5 rpg).

OUTLOOK—Stiles was the Missouri Valley Freshman of the Year, showing why such national powers as Tennessee and Connecticut had recruited her. Stiles' talents offer a considerable upside for the Lady Bears, but they still need to replace departed forward Lisa Davies, the MVC defensive player of the year who averaged 15 points per game.

23 Alabama

NICKNAME...Crimson Tide
COLORS...Crimson and White
CONFERENCE...Southeastern
COACH...Ricky Moody
RECORD AT SCHOOL...199-81 (.711)
CAREER RECORD...199-81 (.711)
LAST SEASON...24-10
CONFERENCE RECORD...10-5 (t-2nd)
1997-98.....Lost in semifinal of NCAA West Regional.

STARTERS RETURNING—G/F Dominique Canty (5-10 Sr., 21.5 ppg, 7.1 rpg); F/C LaToya Caudle (6-3 Sr., 3.3 ppg, 3.9 rpg).

OUTLOOK—This ranking is based primarily on the talents of Canty. Next to Holdsclaw, Canty is the nation's best women's player. She possesses a dazzling combination of power and athleticism. But for this ranking to hold, the Crimson Tide must get something out of a recruiting class that includes a pair of prolific scorers in guards Shondra Johnson and Kaunda Williams.

24 Baylor

NICKNAME...Lady Bears
COLORS...Green and Gold
CONFERENCE...Big 12
COACH...Sonja Hogg
RECORD AT SCHOOL...366-112
CAREER RECORD...59-57
LAST SEASON...20-11
CONFERENCE RECORD...10-6 (t-5th)
1997-98...Lost to Penn State in WNIT final.

STARTERS RETURNING—G Lara Webb (5-10 Sr., 18.8 ppg, 4.3 rpg), G Toya Ellis (5-5 Sr., 13.3 ppg, 3.8 rpg); Kacy Moffitt (6-4 Sr., 15.7 ppg, 6.6 rpg).

OUTLOOK—The return of the Lady Bears' senior trio offers hope to build off last season, which produced the most victories in 16 years. But Baylor is tackling an ambitious schedule. Nine of the Lady Bears' opponents played in the NCAA Tournament. That number could rise to 14, depending on how far they advance in the preseason WNIT. The schedule could make or break this ranking.

25 Colorado State

NICKNAME...Rams
COLORS...Green and Gold
CONFERENCE...Western Athletic
COACH...Tom Collen
RECORD AT SCHOOL...24-6
CAREER RECORD...24-6
LAST SEASON...24-6
CONFERENCE RECORD...11-3 (t-1st)
1997-98 FINISH...Lost in the second round of the NCAA Tournament.

STARTERS RETURNING—G Becky Hammon (5-8 Sr., 23.5 ppg, 3.5 rpg); F Katie Cronin (6-0 Sr., 18.2 ppg, 8.2 rpg); F/C Shannon Randles (6-2 Sr., 7.1 ppg, 5.2 rpg).

OUTLOOK—Hammon is entering the final year of a stellar career at Colorado State. The honorable mention Kodak All-American shot 50 percent from the field last season and 40 percent on three pointers (80 for 199). Cronin provides capable scoring assistance. She's also a three-point sharpshooter (56 of146, .384 percent).

FOR THE RECORD

1997-98 DIVISION I INDIVIDUAL LEADERS

SCORING

SCORING	CL	HT	G	TFG	3FG	FT	PTS	AVG
1. Charles Jones, LIU-Brooklyn	JR	6-3	30	326	116	101	869	29.0
2. Earl Boykins, Eastern Mich.	JR	5-5	29	266	85	129	746	25.7
3. Lee Nailon, Texas Christian	JR	6-9	32	329	1	137	796	24.9
4. Brett Eppehimer, Lehigh	JR	6-0	27	195	92	185	667	24.7
5. Cory Carr, Texas Tech	JR	6-4	27	209	67	143	628	23.3
6. Pat Garrity, Notre Dame	JR	6-9	27	214	40	159	627	23.2
7. Mike Powell, Loyola (Md.)	JR	6-3	28	197	46	207	647	23.1
8. Bonzi Wells, Ball St.	JR	6-5	29	238	53	133	662	22.8
9. Xavier Singletary, Howard	SO	6-6	23	158	71	127	514	22.3
10. Michael Olowokandi, Pacific	JR	7-1	33	310	0	114	734	22.2
11. Antawn Jamison, North Caro.	JR	6-9	37	316	6	184	822	22.2
12. Michael Redd, Ohio St.	FR	6-6	30	241	46	130	658	21.9
13. Evan Eschmeyer, Northwester	JR	6-11	27	200	0	185	585	21.7
14. Matt Harpring, Georgia Tech	JR	6-8	32	230	52	179	691	21.6
15. Saddi Washington, Western M	JR	6-2	29	208	57	153	626	21.6
16. De'Teri Mayes, Murray St.	JR	6-3	33	246	103	116	711	21.5
17. Richard Hamilton, Connectic	SO	6-6	37	270	99	156	795	21.5
18. Mike Jones, Texas Christian	JR	6-3	33	263	62	114	702	21.3
19. Tyronn Lue, Nebraska	JR	6-0	32	240	78	120	678	21.2
20. Rick Kaye, Eastern Ill.	JR	6-5	27	196	44	134	570	21.1
21. DeMarco Johnson, N.C.-Charl	JR	6-9	31	238	18	159	653	21.1
22. Norman Nolan, Virginia	JR	6-8	30	257	0	116	630	21.0
23. Larry Hughes, St. Louis	FR	6-5	32	224	42	180	670	20.9
24. Derrick Dial, Eastern Mich.	JR	6-5	29	222	79	84	607	20.9
25. Tywan Meadows, Idaho St.	JR	6-5	22	156	30	117	459	20.9
26. Omar Sneed, Memphis	JR	6-6	29	231	5	138	605	20.9
27. Jeremy Veal, Arizona St.	JR	6-3	32	244	56	122	666	20.8
28. Corey Brewer, Oklahoma	JR	6-2	33	214	72	186	686	20.8
29. Mark Jones, Central Fla.	JR	6-6	28	220	30	111	581	20.8
30. Roderick Blakney, South Car	JR	5-10	30	197	56	171	621	20.7
31. Paul Pierce, Kansas	JR	6-7	38	287	40	163	777	20.4
32. Antoine Brockington, Coppin	JR	6-2	29	190	78	132	590	20.3
33. Mike Wozniak, Cal Poly SLO	SO	6-2	27	168	83	129	548	20.3
34. Justin Bailey, Hartford	JR	6-2	27	183	36	140	542	20.1
35. Bakari Hendrix, Gonzaga	JR	6-8	33	241	9	165	656	19.9
36. Randy Bolden, Texas Souther	JR	6-2	31	178	94	166	616	19.9
37. Jerome James, Florida A&M	JR	7-1	27	208	0	120	536	19.9
38. Corey Benjamin, Oregon St.	SO	6-6	25	185	29	97	496	19.8
39. Rasaun Young, Buffalo	JR	6-3	28	183	11	177	554	19.8
40. Bryce Drew, Valparaiso	JR	6-3	31	208	94	103	613	19.8
41. Rick Mickens, Central Conn.	SO	6-4	26	179	76	80	514	19.8
42. Raef LaFrentz, Kansas	JR	6-11	30	232	8	121	593	19.8
43. Avery Curry, Idaho	JR	6-0	27	182	48	121	533	19.7
44. Mark Miller, Ill.-Chicago	JR	6-2	27	196	48	91	531	19.7
45. Mike Campbell, LIU-Brooklyn	JR	6-6	32	225	67	112	629	19.7
46. Vonteego Cummings, Pittsbur	JR	6-5	26	173	41	120	507	19.5
47. Fred Meeks, Maine	JR	6-1	24	168	65	66	467	19.5
48. Roberto Bergersen, Boise St	JR	6-6	30	217	60	88	582	19.4
49. David Sivulich, St. Mary's	JR	5-10	26	147	85	125	504	19.4
50. Dan Seigle, Wagner	JR	6-6	29	189	53	130	561	19.3
51. Jarod Stevenson, Richmond	JR	6-7	31	207	82	96	592	19.1
52. Rashod Johnson, Western Mic	JR	6-1	29	189	84	91	553	19.1
53. Jeron Roberts, Wyoming	JR	6-3	28	150	32	200	532	19.0
54. J.R. Henderson, UCLA	JR	6-9	33	228	4	166	626	19.0
55. Rodney Buford, Creighton	JR	6-5	28	189	53	99	530	18.9
56. Raymond Tutt, UC Santa Barb	JR	6-4	26	178	34	102	492	18.9
56. Demond Mallet, McNeese St.	SO	6-1	26	167	94	64	492	18.9
58. B.J. McKie, South Caro.	JR	6-2	31	160	59	205	584	18.8
59. Jarmica Reese, Air Force	JR	6-3	26	166	71	85	488	18.8
60. Damon Frierson, Miami (Ohio	JR	6-4	29	172	40	160	544	18.8
61. Dionte' Harvey, Southern U.	JR	6-4	27	174	80	78	506	18.7
62. Malcolm Johnson, Texas Chri	JR	6-4	33	223	87	83	616	18.7
63. Donte Mathis, Southwest Tex	JR	6-4	28	193	22	114	522	18.6
64. Ansu Sesay, Mississippi	JR	6-9	29	181	21	157	540	18.6
65. T.J. Lux, Northern Ill.	JR	6-9	26	169	5	141	484	18.6
66. Todd MacCulloch, Washington	JR	7-0	30	225	0	107	557	18.6
67. Jamel Thomas, Providence	JR	6-6	29	163	54	156	536	18.5
68. Joe Linderman, Drexel	SO	6-9	28	200	0	116	516	18.4
68. Josh Pittman, N.C.-Ashevill	JR	6-6	28	191	44	90	516	18.4
68. Ralph Biggs, Towson	JR	6-6	28	171	34	140	516	18.4

REBOUNDING

REBOUNDING	CL	HT	G	NO	AVG
1. Ryan Perryman, Dayton	JR	6-7	33	412	12.5
2. Eric Taylor, St. Francis (Pa.)	JR	6-7	27	321	11.9
3. Raef LaFrentz, Kansas	JR	6-11	30	342	11.4
4. Tremaine Fowlkes, Fresno St.	JR	6-8	32	359	11.2
5. Michael Olowokandi, Pacific (Cal.)	JR	7-1	33	369	11.2
6. T.J. Lux, Northern Ill.	JR	6-9	26	289	11.1
7. Thad Burton, Wright St.	JR	6-8	28	305	10.9
8. Allen Ledbetter, Maine	JR	6-7	27	294	10.9
9. Rahshon Turner, Fairleigh Dickins	JR	6-7	29	313	10.8
10. Kenyon Ross, Mississippi Val.	JR	6-6	27	291	10.8
11. K'Zell Wesson, La Salle	JR	6-7	27	290	10.7
11. Evan Eschmeyer, Northwestern	JR	6-11	27	290	10.7
13. Antawn Jamison, North Caro.	JR	6-9	37	389	10.5
14. Rocky Walls, Oral Roberts	JR	6-7	31	325	10.5
15. Jerome James, Florida A&M	JR	7-1	27	282	10.4
16. Jeff Foster, Southwest Tex. St.	JR	6-11	28	285	10.2
17. Robert Traylor, Michigan	JR	6-8	34	344	10.1
18. Carlos Daniel, Washington St.	JR	6-7	28	282	10.1
19. Casey Shaw, Toledo	JR	6-11	27	270	10.0
20. Venson Hamilton, Nebraska	JR	6-10	32	315	9.8
21. Ryan DeMichael, Tenn.-Martin	JR	6-9	26	255	9.8
22. Dennis Davis, Texas Christian	JR	6-9	33	323	9.8
23. Nick Davis, Arkansas	JR	6-9	33	322	9.8
24. Leon Watson, Texas-San Antonio	SO	6-8	27	263	9.7
25. Todd MacCulloch, Washington	JR	7-0	30	292	9.7
26. Ryan Moss, Ark.-Little Rock	JR	6-7	28	272	9.7
27. Michael Ruffin, Tulsa	JR	6-8	31	296	9.5
28. Mark Adamson, Mercer	SO	6-6	25	238	9.5
29. Brian Skinner, Baylor	JR	6-10	28	265	9.5
30. Matt Harpring, Georgia Tech	JR	6-8	32	302	9.4

FIELD GOAL PCT

Min 5 made per game

FIELD GOAL PCT	CL	HT	G	FG	FGA	PCT
1. Todd MacCulloch, Washington	JR	7-0	30	225	346	65.0
2. Ryan Moss, Ark.-Little Rock	JR	6-7	28	167	257	65.0
3. Jarrett Stephens, Penn St.	JR	6-7	31	165	258	64.0
4. Isaac Spencer, Murray St.	SO	6-6	33	171	270	63.3
5. Brad Miller, Purdue	JR	6-11	34	191	302	63.2
6. Zoran Viskovic, Valparaiso	JR	6-11	33	176	280	62.9
7. Kareem Livingston, Appalachian	JR	6-7	29	145	231	62.8
8. David Montgomery, Southeast Mo.	JR	6-8	27	141	227	62.1
9. Travis Lyons, Manhattan	JR	6-5	29	172	277	62.1
10. Leon Watson, Texas-San Antonio	SO	6-8	27	151	245	61.6
11. Evan Eschmeyer, Northwestern	JR	6-11	27	200	328	61.0
12. Michael Olowokandi, Pacific (Ca	JR	7-1	33	310	509	60.9
13. Jermaine Young, Niagara	JR	6-8	27	137	226	60.6
14. Nate Holmstadt, Montana St.	JR	6-8	30	190	315	60.3
15. Ryan Bowen, Iowa	JR	6-7	31	164	272	60.3
16. Chris Thomas, Grambling	SO	6-7	28	140	234	59.8
17. Steve Goodrich, Princeton	JR	6-10	29	152	256	59.4
18. Vince Carter, North Caro.	JR	6-7	38	224	379	59.1
19. Allen Ledbetter, Maine	JR	6-7	27	179	303	59.1
20. Kostas Maglos, Boston College	JR	6-10	31	176	298	59.1
21. Omar Sneed, Memphis	JR	6-6	29	231	395	58.5
22. Stefan Ciosics, Lafayette	JR	6-10	27	160	274	58.4
23. Brian Miles, San Diego	JR	6-8	28	159	273	58.2
24. Hassan Booker, Navy	JR	6-3	30	152	262	58.0
25. Robert Traylor, Michigan	JR	6-8	34	224	387	57.9
26. Antawn Jamison, North Caro.	JR	6-9	37	316	546	57.9
27. Chuck Vincent, Furman	JR	6-7	29	176	306	57.5
28. Erik Nelson, Vermont	JR	6-7	27	164	286	57.3
29. Jerome Jackson, Austin Peay	JR	6-5	28	166	292	56.8
30. Eric Taylor, St. Francis (Pa.)	JR	6-7	27	153	270	56.7

FREE THROW PCT

Min 2.5 made per game

FREE THROW PCT	CL	HT	G	FT	FTA	PCT
1. Matt Sundblad, Lamar	JR	6-2	27	96	104	92.3
2. Louis Bullock, Michigan	JR	6-3	34	123	135	91.1
3. Shammond Williams, North Caro.	JR	6-3	38	133	146	91.1
4. Kevin Ault, Southwest Mo. St.	SO	6-2	32	99	110	90.0
4. Clifton Ellis, Southwest Tex.	JR	6-0	28	72	80	90.0
6. Pete Lisicky, Penn St.	JR	6-4	32	106	119	89.1
7. Danny Sprinkle, Montana St.	JR	6-2	29	73	82	89.0
8. Mike Wozniak, Cal Poly SLO	SO	6-2	27	129	145	89.0
9. Garrett Davis, Stetson	JR	6-3	26	87	98	88.8
10. Arthur Lee, Stanford	JR	6-0	35	164	185	88.6
11. Trajan Langdon, Duke	JR	6-4	36	101	114	88.6
12. Larry Jackson, Liberty	JR	6-1	28	98	111	88.3
13. Sean Colson, N.C.-Charlotte	JR	6-0	29	105	119	88.2
14. Bo Larragan, Marist	JR	6-2	28	112	127	88.2
15. Matt Ricketts, Yale	JR	6-2	26	88	100	88.0
16. Jim Cantamessa, Siena	SO	6-8	29	86	98	87.8
17. Brett Eppehimer, Lehigh	JR	6-0	27	185	211	87.7
18. Jimmie Floyd, Southern Miss.	JR	6-4	33	83	95	87.4

	CL	HT	G	FG	FGA	PCT
19. Rodney Hamilton, Georgia St.	JR	5-9	28	96	110	87.3
20. Andrew Graves, Butler	SO	6-3	30	92	106	86.8
20. Eric Schraeder, St. Mary's (Ca)	JR	6-9	26	92	106	86.8
22. Marcus Wilson, Evansville	JR	6-3	30	124	143	86.7
23. Michael Heary, Navy	JR	6-5	30	125	145	86.2
24. Cory Carr, Texas Tech	JR	6-4	27	143	166	86.1
25. Nathan Smith, American	JR	6-1	26	74	86	86.0
26. Anthony Coomes, Ill.-Chicago	JR	6-1	28	80	93	86.0
27. Matt Heldman, Illinois	JR	6-0	33	98	114	86.0
28. Jason Richey, San Diego St.	JR	6-1	25	96	112	85.7
29. Cuttino Mobley, Rhode Island	JR	6-4	34	131	153	85.6
30. Chris Hollender, Evansville	JR	6-6	30	133	156	85.3

ASSISTS

	CL	HT	G	NO	AVG
1. Ahlon Lewis, Arizona St.	JR	6-0	32	294	9.2
2. Chico Fletcher, Arkansas St.	SO	5-6	29	240	8.3
3. Sean Colson, N.C.-Charlotte	JR	6-0	29	231	8.0
4. Ed Cota, North Caro.	SO	6-1	37	274	7.4
5. Charles Jones, LIU-Brooklyn	JR	6-3	30	221	7.4
6. Anthony Carter, Hawaii	JR	6-1	29	212	7.3
7. Rafer Alston, Fresno St.	JR	6-3	33	240	7.3
8. Mateen Cleaves, Michigan St.	SO	6-2	30	217	7.2
9. Craig Claxton, Hofstra	SO	5-10	31	224	7.2
10. Michael Wheeler, Wagner	JR	5-9	28	197	7.0
11. Doug Gottlieb, Oklahoma St.	SO	6-1	29	201	6.9
12. Shaheen Holloway, Seton Hall	SO	5-10	29	188	6.5
13. Ali Ton, Davidson	JR	6-0	30	193	6.4
14. Robin Kennedy, Nevada	JR	5-11	28	180	6.4
15. Jamar Smiley, Illinois St.	JR	5-11	29	186	6.4
16. Javier Smith, Robert Morris	JR	5-10	27	173	6.4
17. Ryan Robertson, Kansas	JR	6-5	39	248	6.4
18. Rodney Hamilton, Georgia St.	JR	5-9	28	171	6.1
19. Deon Williams, Eastern Wash.	SO	6-2	27	164	6.1
20. Prince Fowler, Texas Christian	JR	5-10	33	200	6.1
21. Leland Redmond, Texas Southern	JR	5-11	28	169	6.0
22. Tyson Wheeler, Rhode Island	JR	5-10	34	205	6.0
23. Joel Fleming, Western Caro.	JR	6-0	27	161	6.0
24. Vonteego Cummings, Pittsburgh	JR	6-5	26	154	5.9
24. Ryan Bundy, Northwestern St.	JR	6-0	26	154	5.9
26. Boney Watson, Sam Houston St.	SO	5-11	24	142	5.9
27. J.R. Camel, Montana	JR	6-2	29	170	5.9
28. Ryan Peterson, Buffalo	FR	5-10	26	152	5.8
29. Jason Kimbrough, Western Mich.	JR	5-11	29	166	5.7
30. Mike Bibby, Arizona	SO	6-2	35	199	5.7

BLOCKED SHOTS

	CL	HT	G	NO	AVG
1. Jerome James, Florida A&M	JR	7-1	27	125	4.6
2. Calvin Booth, Penn St.	JR	6-11	32	140	4.4
3. Alvin Jones, Georgia Tech	FR	6-11	33	141	4.3
4. Etan Thomas, Syracuse	SO	6-9	35	138	3.9
5. Brian Skinner, Baylor	JR	6-10	28	98	3.5
6. Tarvis Williams, Hampton	SO	6-8	26	83	3.2
7. Caswell Cyrus, St. Bonaventure	SO	6-9	32	99	3.1
8. Chris Mihm, Texas	FR	7-0	31	90	2.9
9. Michael Olowokandi, Pacific (Cal.	JR	7-1	33	95	2.9
10. Erik Nelson, Vermont	JR	6-7	27	76	2.8
11. Kenyon Martin, Cincinnati	SO	6-8	30	83	2.8
12. Kashif Hameed, Iona	JR	6-8	33	84	2.5
13. C.J. Black, Tennessee	SO	6-8	29	73	2.5
14. Michael Ruffin, Tulsa	JR	6-8	31	78	2.5
15. Antonio Reynolds-Dean, R.I.	JR	6-7	34	85	2.5
15. Gerben Van Dorpe, Mt. St. Mary's	JR	6-11	28	70	2.5
17. Ryan Chilton, Colorado St.	JR	7-0	29	72	2.5
18. Kirill Misyuchenko, Citadel	JR	7-0	27	67	2.5
19. Kenny Thomas, New Mexico	JR	6-8	32	79	2.5
20. Lamont Barnes, Temple	SO	6-10	30	74	2.5
21. Robert Stevenson, N.C.-Asheville	JR	6-9	28	69	2.5
22. Mamadou N'diaye, Auburn	SO	7-0	30	73	2.4
23. Cal Bowdler, Old Dominion	JR	6-10	28	68	2.4
24. Nick Davis, Arkansas	JR	6-9	33	80	2.4
25. Leon Watson, Texas-San Antonio	SO	6-8	27	65	2.4
25. Freddy Hicks, Arkansas St.	JR	6-7	27	65	2.4
27. Rolan Roberts, Virginia Tech	FR	6-6	27	60	2.2
28. Jeffrion Aubry, Cornell	JR	6-11	24	53	2.2
29. Jonas Sinding, Fairleigh Dickinso	FR	6-9	29	64	2.2
30. Rahshon Turner, Fairleigh Dickins	JR	6-7	29	63	2.2

STEALS

	CL	HT	G	NO	AVG
1. Bonzi Wells, Ball St.	JR	6-5	29	103	3.6
2. Pepe Sanchez, Temple	SO	6-4	27	93	3.4
3. Willie Coleman, DePaul	JR	6-1	30	100	3.3
4. J.R. Camel, Montana	JR	6-2	29	90	3.1
5. Jason Rowe, Loyola (Md.)	SO	5-10	28	86	3.1
6. Damian Owens, West Va.	JR	6-6	32	97	3.0
7. Jason Bell, VMI	JR	6-0	27	79	2.9
8. Mike Jones, Texas Christian	JR	6-3	33	96	2.9
9. Charles Jones, LIU-Brooklyn	JR	6-3	30	87	2.9
10. Mike Campbell, LIU-Brooklyn	JR	6-6	32	89	2.8
11. Joel Hoover, Md.-East. Shore	SO	6-0	27	74	2.7
11. John Thomas, St. Francis (N.Y.)	JR	5-9	27	74	2.7
13. Roderick Blakney, South Caro. St.	JR	5-10	30	82	2.7
14. LaRon Profit, Maryland	JR	6-5	32	87	2.7
15. Jami Bosley, Akron	SO	6-0	21	57	2.7
16. Lenny Brown, Xavier	JR	6-2	30	81	2.7
17. Tim Winn, St. Bonaventure	SO	5-10	26	70	2.7
18. Kenneth Haynes, Grambling	JR	6-0	28	75	2.7
19. Jarion Childs, American	SO	6-0	28	73	2.6
20. Danny Singletary, Coppin St.	JR	6-0	29	75	2.6
21. Issiah Francis, LIU-Brooklyn	JR	6-3	32	82	2.6
22. Ryan Bowen, Iowa	JR	5-7	31	79	2.5
23. Vonteego Cummings, Pittsburgh	JR	6-5	26	66	2.5
24. Lorenzo Hutchinson, Morgan St.	JR	5-11	28	71	2.5
25. Paul Culbertson, Nevada	JR	6-6	27	68	2.5
26. Steve Houston, Texas A&M	SO	6-1	27	67	2.5
27. James Banks, Nicholls St.	SO	6-3	28	69	2.5
28. Franklin Paul, McNeese St.	JR	6-4	20	49	2.5
29. Alex Franco, Tennessee Tech	JR	6-7	29	71	2.4
29. Eric Roberson, Bradley	SO	6-4	29	71	2.4

3-PT FIELD GOAL PCT

Min 2.5 per game and 40%

	CL	HT	G	FG	FGA	PCT
1. Jim Cantamessa, Siena	SO	6-8	29	66	117	56.4
2. Coby Turner, Dayton	JR	6-7	33	61	118	51.7
3. Royce Olney, New Mexico	JR	6-2	25	80	156	51.3
4. Mike Beam, Harvard	JR	6-2	25	41	80	51.3
5. Kenyan Weaks, Florida	SO	6-4	26	61	120	50.8
6. Jaraan Cornell, Purdue	SO	6-3	28	61	122	50.0
6. Matt Langel, Pennsylvania	SO	6-5	26	45	90	50.0
8. Justin Jones, Utah St.	JR	6-3	33	60	121	49.6
9. Mike Warhank, Montana	SO	6-3	30	52	105	49.5
10. Rico Hill, Illinois St.	JR	6-6	30	45	91	49.5
11. Tim Gill, Oral Roberts	JR	6-1	31	95	196	48.5
12. Toby Madison, South Ala.	JR	6-4	28	67	140	47.9
13. Mark Poag, Old Dominion	JR	6-6	28	90	190	47.4
14. Lynn Greer, Temple	FR	6-2	30	50	106	47.2
15. Jarod Stevenson, Richmond	JR	6-7	31	82	174	47.1
16. Andrew Mavis, Northern Ariz.	JR	6-6	29	72	153	47.1
17. Jed Ryan, Pennsylvania	JR	6-7	24	43	93	46.2
18. Kent McCausland, Iowa	JR	6-2	31	74	161	46.0
19. Greg Stolt, Florida	JR	6-8	29	60	131	45.8
20. Sean Wink, Northwestern	FR	6-4	27	86	188	45.7
21. Andy Cavo, New Hampshire	FR	6-6	25	64	142	45.1
22. Louis Bullock, Michigan	JR	6-3	34	93	207	44.9
23. Mike Reno, Monmouth	SO	5-11	27	64	143	44.8
24. Jonathan Baker, Richmond	JR	6-1	31	71	159	44.7
25. Richie Frahm, Gonzaga	SO	6-5	33	77	173	44.5
26. Derrick Hayes, Detroit	JR	6-5	31	51	115	44.3
27. Arthur Lee, Stanford	JR	6-0	35	62	140	44.3
28. Mike Tolman, Boise St.	JR	6-6	30	77	174	44.3
29. Shellord Pinkett, Georgia St.	JR	6-1	28	91	206	44.2
30. B.J. LaRue, Wis.-Green Bay	SO	6-3	29	45	102	44.1

3-PT FIELD GOALS MADE PER GAME

	CL	HT	G	NO	AVG
1. Curtis Staples, Virginia	JR	6-3	30	130	4.3
2. Cedric Foster, Mississippi Val.	JR	5-8	22	86	3.9
3. Charles Jones, LIU-Brooklyn	JR	6-3	30	116	3.9
4. Demond Mallet, McNeese St.	SO	6-1	26	94	3.6
5. Cory Johnson, Southeast Mo. St.	JR	6-0	27	95	3.5
6. Denmark Reid, New Mexico St.	JR	5-11	30	104	3.5
7. Brett Eppehimer, Lehigh	JR	6-0	27	92	3.4
8. Ronnie McCollum, Centenary (La.)	FR	6-3	30	101	3.4
9. Kenny Price, Colorado	JR	6-4	27	90	3.3
10. Seth Schaeffer, Colgate	JR	6-3	28	93	3.3
11. David Sivulich, St. Mary's (Cal.)	JR	5-10	26	85	3.3
12. Corey Reed, Radford	JR	6-6	30	98	3.3
13. Shellord Pinkett, Georgia St.	JR	6-1	28	91	3.3
13. Jermaine Slider, Fairleigh Dickin	JR	6-1	24	78	3.3
15. Nathan Smith, American	JR	6-1	26	84	3.2
16. Mark Poag, Old Dominion	JR	6-6	28	90	3.2
17. Royce Olney, New Mexico	JR	6-2	25	80	3.2
18. Sean Wink, Northwestern	FR	6-4	27	86	3.2
19. De'Teri Mayes, Murray St.	JR	6-3	33	103	3.1
20. Stan Bonewitz, Texas Tech	JR	6-3	27	84	3.1
21. Xavier Singletary, Howard	SO	6-6	23	71	3.1
22. Mike Wozniak, Cal Poly SLO	SO	6-2	27	83	3.1
23. Tim Gill, Oral Roberts	JR	6-1	31	95	3.1
24. Antonio Harvey, Arkansas St.	JR	6-4	29	88	3.0
25. Bryce Drew, Valparaiso	JR	6-3	31	94	3.0
25. Randy Bolden, Texas Southern	JR	6-2	31	94	3.0
27. Shane Hawkins, Southern Ill.	JR	6-2	32	96	3.0
27. Brian Earl, Princeton	JR	6-2	29	87	3.0
29. Casey Green, Southwestern La.	JR	6-3	31	92	3.0
30. Jamie Roberts, Tennessee St.	FR	6-3	29	86	3.0

1997-98 DIVISION I TEAM STATISTICS

SCORING OFFENSE

	G	(W-L)	PTS	AVG
1. Texas Christian	33	(27-6)	3209	97.2
2. LIU-Brooklyn	32	(27-5)	3102	96.9
3. Arizona	35	(30-5)	3177	90.8
4. Florida Int'l	29	(21-8)	2533	87.3
5. Murray St.	33	(29-4)	2862	86.7
6. Southern U.	27	(14-13)	2333	86.4
7. Duke	36	(32-4)	3082	85.6
8. Kansas	39	(35-4)	3300	84.6
9. Cal Poly SLO	28	(14-14)	2367	84.5
10. Arizona St.	32	(18-14)	2703	84.5
11. Cal St. Northridge	28	(12-16)	2356	84.1
12. Purdue	36	(28-8)	3014	83.7
13. Fairleigh Dickinson	30	(23-7)	2511	83.7
14. Xavier	30	(22-8)	2506	83.5
15. Fresno St.	34	(21-13)	2835	83.4
16. Siena	29	(17-12)	2417	83.3
17. UCLA	33	(24-9)	2743	83.1
18. Arkansas	33	(24-9)	2716	82.3
19. North Caro.	38	(34-4)	3113	81.9
20. Mississippi	29	(22-7)	2334	80.5
21. Iona	33	(27-6)	2652	80.4
22. Gonzaga	34	(24-10)	2729	80.3
23. West Va.	33	(24-9)	2647	80.2
24. Northern Ariz.	29	(21-8)	2326	80.2
25. Stanford	35	(30-5)	2807	80.2
26. Iowa	31	(20-11)	2486	80.2
27. Oral Roberts	31	(19-12)	2485	80.2
28. Kentucky	39	(35-4)	3123	80.1
29. Montana St.	30	(19-11)	2398	79.9
30. Eastern Mich.	30	(20-10)	2394	79.8

SCORING DEFENSE

	G	(W-L)	PTS	AVG
1. Princeton	29	(27-2)	1491	51.4
2. South Ala.	28	(21-7)	1526	54.5
3. Col. of Charleston	30	(24-6)	1662	55.4
4. Utah	34	(30-4)	1959	57.6
5. Wyoming	28	(19-9)	1656	59.1
6. Wis.-Green Bay	29	(17-12)	1737	59.9
7. Marquette	31	(20-11)	1860	60.0
8. Temple	30	(21-9)	1820	60.7
9. Bradley	29	(15-14)	1772	61.1
10. N.C.-Wilmington	31	(20-11)	1905	61.5
11. William & Mary	27	(20-7)	1668	61.8
12. Richmond	31	(23-8)	1920	61.9
13. North Caro. St.	32	(17-15)	1988	62.1
14. Colorado St.	29	(20-9)	1802	62.1
15. Columbia	26	(11-15)	1616	62.2
16. Citadel	28	(15-13)	1741	62.2
17. Butler	33	(22-11)	2052	62.2
18. Southern Miss.	33	(22-11)	2057	62.3
19. Wisconsin	31	(12-19)	1940	62.6
20. Detroit	31	(25-6)	1957	63.1
21. Cincinnati	33	(27-6)	2085	63.2
22. Pacific (Cal.)	33	(23-10)	2086	63.2
23. St. Louis	33	(22-11)	2090	63.3
24. Illinois	33	(23-10)	2095	63.5
25. Middle Tenn. St.	28	(19-9)	1781	63.6
26. Northwestern	27	(10-17)	1724	63.9
27. Connecticut	37	(32-5)	2363	63.9
28. Michigan St.	30	(22-8)	1920	64.0
29. Old Dominion	28	(12-16)	1795	64.1
30. Duke	36	(32-4)	2308	64.1

SCORING MARGIN

	OFF	DEF	MAR
1. Duke	85.6	64.1	21.5
2. Texas Christian	97.2	77.9	19.4
3. Kansas	84.6	67.4	17.2
4. North Caro.	81.9	65.6	16.3
5. Arizona	90.8	74.6	16.2
6. Murray St.	86.7	70.7	16.0
7. Princeton	66.5	51.4	15.1
8. Xavier	83.5	68.8	14.7
9. Col. of Charleston	70.1	55.4	14.7
10. Kentucky	80.1	67.0	13.1
11. Cincinnati	76.1	63.2	12.9
12. Northern Ariz.	80.2	67.4	12.8
13. Connecticut	76.6	63.9	12.8
14. Iowa	80.2	67.5	12.7
15. Mississippi	80.5	68.1	12.4
16. Utah	70.0	57.6	12.4
17. Stanford	80.2	68.3	11.9
18. Detroit	74.6	63.1	11.5
19. Purdue	83.7	72.3	11.4
20. West Va.	80.2	69.2	11.1
21. Gonzaga	80.3	69.3	10.9
22. Iona	80.4	69.5	10.8
23. South Ala.	65.0	54.5	10.5
24. LIU-Brooklyn	96.9	86.8	10.2
25. Michigan	77.4	67.2	10.2
26. Montana St.	79.9	69.9	10.1
27. Arkansas	82.3	72.4	9.9
28. Pacific (Cal.)	73.1	63.2	9.8
29. New Mexico	75.7	65.9	9.8
30. Oklahoma St.	78.9	69.2	9.7

WON-LOST PERCENTAGE

	W-L		PCT.
1. Princeton	27	2	.931
2. Kansas	35	4	.897
2. Kentucky	35	4	.897
4. North Caro.	34	4	.895
5. Duke	32	4	.889
6. Utah	30	4	.882
7. Murray St.	29	4	.879
8. Connecticut	32	5	.865
9. Arizona	30	5	.857
9. Stanford	30	5	.857
11. Cincinnati	27	6	.818
11. Iona	27	6	.818
11. Texas Christian	27	6	.818
14. Detroit	25	6	.806
14. Illinois St.	25	6	.806
16. Col. of Charleston	24	6	.800
17. Ill.-Chicago	22	6	.786
18. Purdue	28	8	.778
19. Fairleigh Dickinson	23	7	.767
20. Mississippi	22	7	.759
20. Oklahoma St.	22	7	.759
22. Utah St.	25	8	.758
23. New Mexico	24	8	.750
23. South Ala.	21	7	.750
25. Syracuse	26	9	.743
26. Richmond	23	8	.742
26. South Caro.	23	8	.742
28. William & Mary	20	7	.741
29. Michigan	25	9	.735
29. Rhode Island	25	9	.735

FIELD GOAL PERCENTAGE

	FG	FGA	PCT
1. North Caro.	1131	2184	51.8
2. Northern Ariz.	806	1577	51.1
3. Murray St.	1037	2070	50.1
4. Princeton	684	1374	49.8
5. Pacific (Cal.)	841	1692	49.7
6. Texas Christian	1220	2463	49.5
7. Kansas	1249	2536	49.3
8. Indiana	879	1792	49.1
9. UCLA	985	2011	49.0
10. Michigan	932	1907	48.9
11. Arizona	1146	2350	48.8
12. Washington	843	1729	48.8
13. South Ala.	665	1371	48.5
14. Xavier	848	1752	48.4
15. Purdue	1057	2185	48.4
16. Utah St.	856	1771	48.3
17. Kentucky	1161	2409	48.2
18. Oral Roberts	890	1848	48.2
19. Arizona St.	1019	2118	48.1
20. Niagara	683	1422	48.0
21. Iowa	878	1828	48.0
22. Utah	809	1685	48.0
23. Illinois St.	865	1804	47.9
24. Montana St.	859	1800	47.7
25. Nevada	748	1569	47.7
26. Evansville	726	1526	47.6
27. Duke	1081	2278	47.5
28. Northwestern	570	1203	47.4
29. San Diego	681	1438	47.4
30. Gonzaga	965	2038	47.4

FIELD GOAL PERCENTAGE DEFENSE

	FG	FGA	PCT
1. Miami (Fla.)	634	1672	37.9
2. Bradley	617	1614	38.2
3. Kentucky	892	2324	38.4
4. North Caro.	923	2403	38.4
5. Wyoming	541	1405	38.5
6. Utah	668	1729	38.6
7. Col. of Charleston	616	1591	38.7
8. Temple	620	1599	38.8
9. Marquette	672	1729	38.9
10. Colorado St.	612	1570	39.0
11. Citadel	615	1571	39.1
12. Tulsa	693	1766	39.2
13. Pacific (Cal.)	747	1902	39.3
14. Connecticut	854	2173	39.3
15. Cincinnati	732	1862	39.3
16. Florida A&M	707	1798	39.3
17. Southern Miss.	736	1860	39.6
18. Old Dominion	639	1613	39.6
19. Jackson St.	629	1585	39.7
20. Kansas St.	678	1703	39.8
21. Nebraska	774	1935	40.0
22. UAB	807	2017	40.0
23. Michigan	815	2032	40.1
24. Detroit	670	1668	40.2
25. Kansas	989	2462	40.2
26. Geo. Washington	748	1862	40.2
27. William & Mary	611	1520	40.2
28. Auburn	698	1735	40.2
29. Alabama	775	1923	40.3
30. Cornell	571	1415	40.4

FREE THROW PERCENTAGE

	FT	FTA	PCT
1. Siena	574	715	80.3
2. Montana St.	437	570	76.7
3. Purdue	657	864	76.0
4. Montana	472	621	76.0
5. New Mexico	430	568	75.7
6. Evansville	454	600	75.7
7. Wis.-Green Bay	470	625	75.2
8. Western Mich.	477	639	74.6
9. Arizona St.	493	661	74.6
10. Hartford	541	730	74.1
11. Sam Houston St.	382	516	74.0
12. Penn St.	470	635	74.0
13. Detroit	472	639	73.9
14. Xavier	640	867	73.8
15. Stanford	651	882	73.8
16. UC Irvine	381	517	73.7
17. Southwest Mo. St.	582	791	73.6
18. Yale	435	592	73.5
19. Georgia St.	382	520	73.5
20. Northern Ariz.	460	627	73.4
21. Nevada	481	656	73.3
22. Connecticut	610	832	73.3
23. Texas Christian	559	763	73.3
24. Ill.-Chicago	468	639	73.2
25. Indiana	513	702	73.1
25. St. Mary's (Cal.)	456	624	73.1
27. Utah	588	805	73.0
28. Southwest Tex. St.	486	666	73.0
29. Coppin St.	535	734	72.9
30. Buffalo	510	701	72.8

REBOUND MARGIN

	OFF	DEF	MAR
1. Utah	37.0	27.1	10.0
2. Stanford	41.3	31.9	9.3
3. Fairleigh Dickinson	45.7	36.5	9.1
4. Kansas	43.1	34.2	8.9
5. Michigan St.	39.9	31.0	8.9
6. Southern Ill.	39.9	31.3	8.6
7. Cincinnati	40.1	31.8	8.3
8. Kentucky	42.1	33.9	8.2
9. South Ala.	34.0	26.4	7.6
10. North Caro.	39.8	32.3	7.5
11. St. John's (N.Y.)	42.3	35.1	7.2
12. Michigan	38.6	31.9	6.7
13. Mississippi	41.5	34.9	6.6
14. St. Francis (Pa)	38.5	32.1	6.4
15. Northwestern	33.4	27.3	6.2
16. Southwest Tex. St.	39.6	33.6	6.0
17. Massachusetts	38.5	32.6	5.9
18. Georgetown	40.9	35.0	5.8
19.Pacific (Cal.)	36.9	31.2	5.8
20. Utah St.	35.6	29.8	5.8
21. Iowa	38.3	32.6	5.7
22. San Francisco	35.8	30.3	5.5
23. Murray St.	42.9	37.5	5.4
24. Eastern Ky.	40.6	35.2	5.4
25. Louisiana Tech	35.3	30.0	5.3
26. Navy	40.2	34.9	5.2
27. Texas Christian	44.4	39.2	5.2
28. Oklahoma	38.2	33.0	5.2
29. Toledo	39.5	34.4	5.1
30. Youngstown St.	39.3	34.2	5.1

3 PT FIELD GOAL PERCENTAGE

Min 3.0 p/g and 40%	G	FG	FGA	PCT
1. Northern Ariz.	29	254	591	43.0
2. Utah St.	33	139	324	42.9
3. Pennsylvania	29	223	526	42.4
4. Harvard	26	188	448	42.0
5. Michigan	34	260	621	41.9
6. Ill.-Chicago	28	192	460	41.7
7. Western Mich.	29	209	511	40.9
8. Stanford	35	262	642	40.8
9. Gonzaga	34	274	678	40.4
10. New Mexico	32	301	748	40.2
11. Oral Roberts	31	268	667	40.2
12. Iowa	31	218	543	40.1
13. Florida	29	285	712	40.0
14. South Caro. St.	30	174	436	39.9
15. Richmond	31	241	605	39.8
16. South Ala.	28	129	324	39.8
17. Murray St.	33	205	516	39.7
18. Arkansas St.	29	210	529	39.7
19. Boise St.	30	221	561	39.4
20. Princeton	29	265	681	38.9
21. Evansville	30	193	498	38.8
22. Pacific (Cal.)	33	236	610	38.7
23. Monmouth	27	195	506	38.5
24. Western Ill.	27	174	452	38.5
25. Radford	30	244	636	38.4
26. Air Force	26	196	512	38.3
27. Indiana	32	186	489	38.0
28. Wake Forest	30	235	619	38.0
29. Siena	29	241	636	37.9
30. Towson	28	169	446	37.9

3 PT FIELD GOALS MADE PER GAME

	G	NO	AVG
1. Florida	29	285	9.8
2. LIU-Brooklyn	32	310	9.7
3. North Texas	26	250	9.6
4. New Mexico	32	301	9.4
5. Princeton	29	265	9.1
6. Cal Poly SLO	28	246	8.8
7. Northern Ariz.	29	254	8.8
8. Southeastern La.	26	227	8.7
9. Jacksonville St.	26	225	8.7
10. Oral Roberts	31	268	8.6
11. Cal St. Northridge	28	241	8.6
12. Loyola Marymount	27	231	8.6
13. Tennessee St.	29	248	8.6
14. St. Mary's (Cal.)	27	229	8.5
15. Mississippi Val.	27	227	8.4
16. Fresno St.	34	284	8.4
17. Siena	29	241	8.3
18. La Salle	27	223	8.3
19. Florida Int'l	29	237	8.2
20. Southern Cal	28	228	8.1
21. Radford	30	244	8.1
22. Georgia	35	284	8.1
23. Montana St.	30	243	8.1
24. Gonzaga	34	274	8.1
25. Wake Forest	30	235	7.8
26. Seton Hall	30	234	7.8
27. Richmond	31	241	7.8
28. Fairleigh Dickinson	30	233	7.8
29. Baylor	28	217	7.8
30. Southeast Mo. St.	27	208	7.7
30. Texas Tech	27	208	7.7

DIVISION I COACHING CHANGES FOR 1998-99

School	Former Coach	New Coach
Alabama	David Hobbs	Mark Gottfried
Arizona State	Don Newman	Rob Evans
Chicago State	Phil Gary	Bo Ellis
Clemson	Rick Barnes	Larry Shyatt
Coastal Carolina	Michael Hopkins	Pete Strickland
Colgate	Paul Aiello	Emmett Davis
Colorado State	Stew Morrill	Ritchie McKay
Duquesne	Scott Edgar	Darelle Porter
Fairfield	Paul Cormier	Tim O'Toole
George Washington	Mike Jarvis	Tom Penders
Houston	Alvin Brooks	Clyde Drexler
Howard	Mike McLeese	Kirk Saulny
Idaho State	Herb Williams	Doug Oliver
Iona	Tim Welsh	Jeff Ruland
Iowa State	Tim Floyd	Larry Eustachy
Jacksonville State	Bill Jones	Mark Turgeon
Liberty	Randy Dunton	Mel Hankinson
Long Island	Ray Haskins	Ray Martin
Louisiana Tech	Jim Woolridge	Keith Richard
Loyola of Chicago	Ken Burmeister	Larry Farmer
Mississippi	Rob Evans	Rod Barnes
Mississippi State	Richard Williams	Rick Stansbury
Monmouth	Wayne Szoke	Dave Calloway
Montana	Blaine Taylor	Don Holst
Murray State	Mark Gottfried	Tevester Anderson
New Mexico State	Neil McCarthy	Lou Henson
Niagara	Jack Armstrong	Joe Mihalich
Norfolk State	Michael Bernard	Mel Coleman
Northern Iowa	Eldon Miller	Sam Weaver
Portland State	Ritchie McKay	Joel Sobotka
Providence	Pete Gillen	Tim Welsh
Sam Houston State	Jerry Hopkins	Bob Marlin
San Jose State	Stan Morrison	Phil Johnson
UC-Santa Barbara	Jerry Pimm	Bob Williams
Southern Illinois	Rich Herrin	Bruce Weber
St. John's	Fran Fraschilla	Mike Jarvis
Tennessee Tech	Frank Harrell	Jeff Lebo
Texas	Tom Penders	Rick Barnes
Texas A&M	Tony Barone	Melvin Watkins
UNC Charlotte	Melvin Watkins	Bobby Lutz
Utah State	Larry Eustachy	Stew Morrill
Virginia	Jeff Jones	Pete Gillen
Virginia Commonwealth	Sonny Smith	Mack McCarthy
Western Kentucky	Matt Kilcullen	Dennis Felton
Winthrop	Dan Kenney	Gregg Marshall
Wyoming	Larry Shyatt	Steve McClain

1997-98 CONFERENCE STANDINGS

AMERICA EAST CONFERENCE

Team	Conf W	Conf L	Conf Pct	Full W	Full L	Full Pct
Delaware #	12	6	.667	20	10	.667
Boston U.	12	6	.667	19	11	.633
Hofstra	11	7	.611	19	12	.613
Vermont	11	7	.611	16	11	.593
Hartford	11	7	.611	15	12	.556
Drexel	10	8	.556	13	15	.464
Northeastern	9	9	.500	14	14	.500
New Hampshire	6	12	.333	10	17	.370
Towson	4	14	.222	8	20	.286
Maine	4	14	.222	7	20	.259

ATLANTIC COAST CONFERENCE

Team	Conf W	Conf L	Conf Pct	Full W	Full L	Full Pct
Duke	15	1	.938	32	4	.889
North Caro. #	13	3	.813	34	4	.895
Maryland	10	6	.625	21	11	.656
Clemson	7	9	.438	18	14	.563
Wake Forest	7	9	.438	16	14	.533
Georgia Tech	6	10	.375	19	14	.576
Florida St.	6	10	.375	18	14	.563
North Caro. St.	5	11	.313	17	15	.531
Virginia	3	13	.188	11	19	.367

ATLANTIC10 CONFERENCE

Team	Conf W	Conf L	Conf Pct	Full W	Full L	Full Pct
EAST DIVISION						
Temple	13	3	.813	21	9	.700
Rhode Island	12	4	.750	25	9	.735
Massachusetts	12	4	.750	21	11	.656
St. Bonaventure	6	10	.375	17	15	.531
St. Joseph's	3	13	.188	11	17	.393
Fordham	2	14	.125	6	21	.222
WEST DIVISION						
Xavier #	11	5	.688	22	8	.733
Geo. Washington	11	5	.688	24	9	.727
Dayton	11	5	.688	21	12	.636
Virginia Tech	5	11	.313	10	17	.370
Duquesne	5	11	.313	11	19	.367
La Salle	5	11	.313	9	18	.333

BIG EAST CONFERENCE

Team	Conf W	Conf L	Conf Pct	Full W	Full L	Full Pct
BIG EAST 7						
Syracuse	12	6	.667	26	9	.743
Miami (Fla.)	11	7	.611	18	10	.643
Seton Hall	9	9	.500	15	15	.500
Providence	7	11	.389	13	16	.448
Georgetown	6	12	.333	16	15	.516
Rutgers	6	12	.333	14	15	.483
Pittsburgh	6	12	.333	11	16	.407
BIG EAST 6						
Connecticut #	15	3	.833	32	5	.865
St. John's (N.Y.)	13	5	.722	22	10	.688
West Va.	11	7	.611	24	9	.727
Villanova	8	10	.444	12	17	.414
Notre Dame	7	11	.389	13	14	.481
Boston College	6	12	.333	15	16	.484

#Won conference tournament

BIG SKY CONFERENCE

Team	Conf W	Conf L	Conf Pct	Full W	Full L	Full Pct
Northern Ariz. #	13	3	.813	21	8	.724
Weber St.	12	4	.750	14	13	.519
Eastern Wash.	10	6	.625	16	11	.593
Portland St.*	10	6	.625	15	12	.556
Montana St.	9	7	.563	19	11	.633
Montana	9	7	.563	16	14	.533
Cal St. Northridge	7	9	.438	12	16	.429
Idaho St.	2	14	.125	6	20	.231
Cal St. Sacramento	0	16	.000	1	25	.038

*not Division I

BIG SOUTH CONFERENCE

Team	Conf W	Conf L	Conf Pct	Full W	Full L	Full Pct
N.C.-Asheville	11	1	.917	19	9	.679
Radford #	10	2	.833	20	10	.667
UMBC	6	6	.500	14	14	.500
Liberty	5	7	.417	11	17	.393
Coastal Caro.	4	8	.333	8	19	.296
Winthrop	4	8	.333	7	20	.259
Charleston So.	2	10	.167	5	22	.185

BIG TEN CONFERENCE

Team	Conf W	Conf L	Conf Pct	Full W	Full L	Full Pct
Michigan St.	13	3	.813	22	8	.733
Illinois	13	3	.813	23	10	.697
Purdue	12	4	.750	28	8	.778
Michigan #	11	5	.688	25	9	.735
Iowa	9	7	.563	20	11	.645
Indiana	9	7	.563	20	12	.625
Penn St.	8	8	.500	19	13	.594
Minnesota	6	10	.375	20	15	.571
Wisconsin	3	13	.188	12	19	.387
Northwestern	3	13	.188	10	17	.370
Ohio St.	1	15	.063	8	22	.267

BIG 12 CONFERENCE

Team	Conf W	Conf L	Conf Pct	Full W	Full L	Full Pct
Kansas #	15	1	.938	35	4	.897
Oklahoma St.	11	5	.688	22	7	.759
Oklahoma	11	5	.688	22	11	.667
Nebraska	10	6	.625	20	12	.625
Missouri	8	8	.500	17	15	.531
Baylor	8	8	.500	14	14	.500
Kansas St.	7	9	.438	17	12	.586
Colorado	7	9	.438	13	14	.481
Texas Tech	7	9	.438	13	14	.481
Texas	6	10	.375	14	17	.452
Iowa St.	5	11	.313	12	18	.400
Texas A&M	1	15	.063	7	20	.259

BIG WEST CONFERENCE

Team	Conf W	Conf L	Conf Pct	Full W	Full L	Full Pct
EASTERN DIVISION						
Utah St. #	13	3	.813	25	8	.758
Nevada	11	5	.688	16	12	.571
Boise St.	9	7	.563	17	13	.567
Idaho	9	7	.563	15	12	.556
New Mexico St.	8	8	.500	18	12	.600
North Texas	4	12	.250	5	21	.192
WESTERN DIVISION						
Pacific (Cal.)	14	2	.875	23	10	.697
Cal Poly SLO	7	9	.438	14	14	.500
Cal St. Fullerton	6	10	.375	12	16	.429
UC Irvine	6	10	.375	9	18	.333
Long Beach St.	5	11	.313	10	19	.345
UC Santa Barbara	4	12	.250	7	19	.269

COLONIAL ATHLETIC ASSOCIATION

Team	Conf W	Conf L	Conf Pct	Full W	Full L	Full Pct
William & Mary	13	3	.813	20	7	.741
N.C.-Wilmington	13	3	.813	20	11	.645
Richmond #	12	4	.750	23	8	.742
Old Dominion	8	8	.500	12	16	.429
James Madison	6	10	.375	11	16	.407
George Mason	6	10	.375	9	18	.333
East Caro.	5	11	.313	10	17	.370
American	5	11	.313	9	19	.321
Va. Commonwealth	4	12	.250	9	19	.321

CONFERENCE USA

Team	Conf W	Conf L	Conf Pct	Full W	Full L	Full Pct
AMERICAN DIVISION						
Cincinnati #	14	2	.875	27	6	.818
N.C.-Charlotte	13	3	.813	20	11	.645
St. Louis	11	5	.688	22	11	.667
Marquette	8	8	.500	20	11	.645
Louisville	5	11	.313	12	20	.375
DePaul	3	13	.188	7	23	.233
NATIONAL DIVISION						
Memphis	12	4	.750	17	12	.586
UAB	10	6	.625	21	12	.636
Southern Miss.	9	7	.563	22	11	.667
South Fla.	7	9	.438	17	13	.567
Houston	2	14	.125	9	20	.310
Tulane	2	14	.125	7	22	.241

IVY GROUP

Team	Conf W	Conf L	Conf Pct	Full W	Full L	Full Pct
Princeton	13	0	1.000	27	2	.931
Pennsylvania	10	3	.769	17	12	.586
Yale	7	7	.500	12	14	.462
Harvard	6	8	.429	13	13	.500
Columbia	6	8	.429	11	15	.423
Cornell	6	8	.429	9	17	.346
Dartmouth	4	10	.286	7	19	.269
Brown	3	11	.214	6	20	.231

METRO ATLANTIC ATHLETIC CONFERENCE

Team	Conf W	Conf L	Conf Pct	Full W	Full L	Full Pct
Iona #	15	3	.833	27	6	.818
Rider	12	6	.667	18	10	.643
Siena	10	8	.556	17	12	.586
Niagara	10	8	.556	14	13	.519
Canisius	9	9	.500	13	14	.481
Loyola (Md.)	9	9	.500	12	16	.429
Fairfield	7	11	.389	12	15	.444
Manhattan	7	11	.389	12	17	.414
Marist	7	11	.389	11	17	.393
St. Peter's	4	14	.222	8	19	.296

MID-AMERICAN CONFERENCE

Team	Conf W	Conf L	Conf Pct	Full W	Full L	Full Pct
EAST DIVISION						
Akron	13	5	.722	17	10	.630
Miami (Ohio)	9	9	.500	17	12	.586
Kent	9	9	.500	13	17	.433
Marshall	7	11	.389	11	16	.407
Bowling Green	7	11	.389	10	16	.385
Ohio	3	15	.167	5	21	.192
WEST DIVISION						
Ball St.	14	4	.778	21	8	.724
Western Mich.	14	4	.778	21	8	.724
Eastern Mich. #	13	5	.722	20	10	.667
Toledo	10	8	.556	15	12	.556
Northern Ill.	6	12	.333	10	16	.385
Central Mich.	3	15	.167	5	21	.192

MID-CONTINENT CONFERENCE

Team	Conference W	L	Pct	Full Season W	L	Pct
Valparaiso #	13	3	.813	23	10	.697
Oral Roberts	12	4	.750	19	12	.613
Youngstown St.	11	5	.688	20	9	.690
Western Ill.	11	5	.688	16	11	.593
Buffalo	9	7	.563	15	13	.536
Mo.-Kansas City	7	9	.438	9	18	.333
Southern Utah	4	12	.250	7	20	.259
Northeastern Ill.	3	13	.188	6	19	.240
Chicago St.	2	14	.125	2	25	.074

MID-EASTERN ATHLETIC CONFERENCE

Team	Conference W	L	Pct	Full Season W	L	Pct
Coppin St.	17	1	.944	21	8	.724
South Caro. St. #	16	2	.889	22	8	.733
Hampton	11	7	.611	14	12	.538
Morgan St.	11	7	.611	12	16	.429
Florida A&M	8	10	.444	11	17	.393
Delaware St.	7	11	.389	9	18	.333
Md.-East. Shore	7	11	.389	9	18	.333
North Caro. A&T	7	11	.389	8	19	.296
Howard	5	13	.278	8	20	.286
Bethune-Cookman	1	17	.056	1	26	.037
Norfolk St.	—	—		6	21	.222

MIDWESTERN COLLEGIATE CONFERENCE

Team	Conference W	L	Pct	Full Season W	L	Pct
Detroit	12	2	.857	25	6	.806
Ill.-Chicago	12	2	.857	22	6	.786
Butler #	8	6	.571	22	11	.667
Wis.-Green Bay	7	7	.500	17	12	.586
Loyola (Ill.)	6	8	.429	15	15	.500
Cleveland St.	6	8	.429	12	15	.444
Wright St.	3	11	.214	10	18	.357
Wis.-Milwaukee	2	12	.143	3	24	.111

MISSOURI VALLEY CONFERENCE

Team	Conference W	L	Pct	Full Season W	L	Pct
Illinois St. #	16	2	.889	25	6	.806
Creighton	12	6	.667	18	10	.643
Wichita St.	11	7	.611	16	15	.516
Southwest Mo. St.	11	7	.611	16	16	.500
Indiana St.	10	8	.556	16	11	.593
Bradley	9	9	.500	15	14	.517
Evansville	9	9	.500	15	15	.500
Southern Ill.	8	10	.444	14	18	.438
Northern Iowa	4	14	.222	10	17	.370
Drake	0	18	.000	3	24	.111

NORTHEAST CONFERENCE

Team	Conference W	L	Pct	Full Season W	L	Pct
LIU-Brooklyn	14	2	.875	21	11	.656
Fairleigh Dickinson #	13	3	.813	23	7	.767
St. Francis (Pa.)	10	6	.625	17	10	.630
St. Francis (N.Y.)	10	6	.625	15	12	.556
Mt. St. Mary's	8	8	.500	13	15	.464
Wagner	7	9	.438	13	16	.448
Robert Morris	4	12	.250	8	19	.296
Central Conn. St.	3	13	.188	4	22	.154
Monmouth	3	13	.188	4	23	.148

OHIO VALLEY CONFERENCE

Team	Conference W	L	Pct	Full Season W	L	Pct
Murray St. #	16	2	.889	29	4	.879
Eastern Ill.	13	5	.722	16	11	.593
Middle Tenn. St.	12	6	.667	19	9	.679
Austin Peay	11	7	.611	17	11	.607
Southeast Mo. St.	10	8	.556	14	13	.519
Tennessee St.	8	10	.444	13	16	.448
Eastern Ky.	8	10	.444	10	17	.370
Tennessee Tech	5	13	.278	9	21	.300
Tenn.-Martin	5	13	.278	7	20	.259
Morehead St.	2	16	.111	3	23	.115

#Won conference tournament

PACIFIC-10 CONFERENCE

Team	Conference W	L	Pct	Full Season W	L	Pct
Arizona	17	1	.944	30	5	.857
Stanford	15	3	.833	30	5	.857
UCLA	12	6	.667	24	9	.727
Washington	11	7	.611	20	10	.667
Arizona St.	8	10	.444	18	14	.563
Oregon	8	10	.444	13	14	.481
California	8	10	.444	12	15	.444
Southern Cal	5	13	.278	9	19	.321
Oregon St.	3	15	.167	13	17	.433
Washington St.	3	15	.167	10	19	.345

PATRIOT LEAGUE

Team	Conference W	L	Pct	Full Season W	L	Pct
Lafayette	10	2	.833	19	9	.679
Navy #	10	2	.833	19	11	.633
Bucknell	8	4	.667	13	15	.464
Colgate	5	7	.417	10	18	.357
Lehigh	4	8	.333	10	17	.370
Holy Cross	3	9	.250	7	20	.259
Army	2	10	.167	8	19	.296

SOUTHEASTERN CONFERENCE

Team	Conference W	L	Pct	Full Season W	L	Pct
EASTERN DIVISION						
Kentucky #	14	2	.875	35	4	.897
South Caro.	11	5	.688	23	8	.742
Tennessee	9	7	.563	20	9	.690
Vanderbilt	7	9	.438	20	13	.606
Georgia	7	9	.438	20	15	.571
Florida	6	10	.375	14	15	.483
WESTERN DIVISION						
Mississippi	12	4	.750	22	7	.759
Arkansas	11	5	.688	24	9	.727
Auburn	7	9	.438	16	14	.533
Alabama	6	10	.375	15	16	.484
Mississippi St.	4	12	.250	15	15	.500
LSU	2	14	.125	9	18	.333

SOUTHERN CONFERENCE

Team	Conference W	L	Pct	Full Season W	L	Pct
NORTH DIVISION						
Appalachian St.	13	2	.867	21	8	.724
Davidson #	13	2	.867	20	10	.667
VMI	8	7	.533	14	13	.519
Western Caro.	6	9	.400	12	15	.444
East Tenn. St.	6	9	.400	11	16	.407
N.C.-Greensboro	6	9	.400	9	19	.321
SOUTH DIVISION						
Chattanooga	7	7	.500	13	15	.464
Citadel	6	8	.429	15	13	.536
Wofford	6	8	.429	9	18	.333
Furman	5	9	.357	9	20	.310
Ga. Southern	4	10	.286	10	18	.357

SOUTHLAND CONFERENCE

Team	Conference W	L	Pct	Full Season W	L	Pct
Nicholls St. #	15	1	.938	19	10	.655
Southwest Tex. St.	10	6	.625	17	11	.607
Texas-San Antonio	10	6	.625	16	11	.593
Northwestern St.	10	6	.625	13	14	.481
Northeast La.	8	8	.500	13	16	.448
Texas-Arlington	8	8	.500	13	16	.448
Sam Houston St.	7	9	.438	9	17	.346
Stephen F. Austin	6	10	.375	10	16	.385
McNeese St.	4	12	.250	7	19	.269
Southeastern La.	2	14	.125	6	20	.231

SOUTHWESTERN ATHLETIC CONFERENCE

Team	Conference W	L	Pct	Full Season W	L	Pct
Texas Southern	12	4	.750	15	16	.484
Jackson St.	11	5	.688	14	13	.519
Grambling	10	6	.625	16	12	.571
Southern U.	10	6	.625	14	13	.519
Alcorn St.	8	8	.500	12	15	.444
Prairie View #	6	10	.375	13	17	.433
Alabama St.	6	10	.375	11	17	.393
Mississippi Val.	6	10	.375	6	21	.222
Ark.-Pine Bluff*	3	13	.188	4	23	.148

*not Division I

SUN BELT CONFERENCE

Team	Conference W	L	Pct	Full Season W	L	Pct
South Ala. #	14	4	.778	21	7	.750
Arkansas St.	14	4	.778	20	9	.690
Southwestern La.	12	6	.667	18	13	.581
Ark.-Little Rock	10	8	.556	15	13	.536
New Orleans	9	9	.500	15	12	.556
Louisiana Tech	9	9	.500	12	15	.444
Lamar	7	11	.389	15	14	.517
Western Ky.	6	12	.333	10	19	.345
Jacksonville	6	12	.333	8	19	.296
Tex.-Pan American	3	15	.167	3	24	.111

TRANS AMERICA ATHLETIC CONFERENCE

Team	Conference W	L	Pct	Full Season W	L	Pct
EAST DIVISION						
Col. of Charleston #	14	2	.875	24	6	.800
Florida Int'l	13	3	.813	21	8	.724
Central Fla.	11	5	.688	17	11	.607
Stetson	8	8	.500	11	15	.423
Fla. Atlantic	5	11	.313	5	22	.185
Campbell	4	12	.250	10	17	.370
WEST DIVISION						
Georgia St.	11	5	.688	16	12	.571
Samford	9	7	.563	14	13	.519
Centenary	8	8	.500	10	20	.333
Jacksonville St.	6	10	.375	12	14	.462
Troy St.	5	11	.313	7	20	.259
Mercer	2	14	.125	5	21	.192

WEST COAST CONFERENCE

Team	Conference W	L	Pct	Full Season W	L	Pct
Gonzaga	10	4	.714	24	10	.706
Pepperdine	9	5	.643	17	10	.630
Santa Clara	8	6	.571	18	10	.643
San Francisco #	7	7	.500	19	11	.633
Portland	7	7	.500	14	13	.519
St. Mary's (Cal.)	7	7	.500	11	15	.423
San Diego	5	9	.357	14	14	.500
Loyola Marymount	3	11	.214	7	20	.259

WESTERN ATHLETIC CONFERENCE

Team	Conference W	L	Pct	Full Season W	L	Pct
PACIFIC DIVISION						
Texas Christian	14	0	1.000	27	6	.818
Fresno St.	10	4	.714	21	13	.618
Tulsa	9	5	.643	19	12	.613
Hawaii	8	6	.571	21	9	.700
Southern Methodist	6	8	.429	18	10	.643
San Diego St.	5	9	.357	13	15	.464
Rice	3	11	.214	6	22	.214
San Jose St.	1	13	.071	3	23	.115
MOUNTAIN DIV.						
Utah	12	2	.857	30	4	.882
New Mexico	11	3	.786	24	8	.750
Wyoming	9	5	.643	19	9	.679
Colorado St.	8	6	.571	20	9	.690
UNLV #	7	7	.500	20	13	.606
Brigham Young	4	10	.286	9	21	.300
UTEP	3	11	.214	12	14	.462
Air Force	2	12	.143	10	16	.385

1998-99 JUNIOR COLLEGE ALL-AMERICA TEAM

by Rick Ball

PLAYER	HT	YR	JC, STATE
FIRST TEAM			
Jamie Rosser	6-2	SO	Northwest, MS
Antonio Jackson	6-5	SO	Butler Co., KS
James Zimmerman	6-5	SO	Indian Hills, IA
Marcus Griffin	6-9	SO	Lincoln, IL
Aleksander Radojevic	7-3	SO	Barton Co., KS
SECOND TEAM			
D.J. Wootson	5-11	SO	Cecil, MD
Paul McPherson	6-3	SO	Kennedy King, IL
Rob Griffin	6-6	SO	Southeastern, IA
James Williams	6-9	SO	Dixie, UT
Jermaine Small	6-9	SO	L.A. City, CA
HONORABLE MENTION			
Bernard Barrow	5-9	SO	Kilgore, TX
Lawrence Martin	5-9	SO	Gulf Coast, MS
Bobby Moore	5-9	SO	Vincennes, IN
Ed Suber	5-9	SO	Labette, KS
Everett Stubblefield	5-10	SO	Olney, IL
Corey Fox	5-11	SO	Danville, IL
Michael Johnson	5-11	SO	McCook, NE
Anton Jenifer	5-11	SO	Baltimore, MD
Mike Phillips	5-11	SO	Wabash Valley, IL
Larry Allaway	6-0	SO	Howard, TX
Jason Pryor	6-0	FR	Gulf Coast, FL
Roland Williams	6-0	SO	Trinidad State, CO
Virgil Singleton	6-0	SO	Western, AZ
Brandon Pate	6-0	SO	North Pioneer, AZ
Xon Williams	6-0	SO	Palm Beach, FL
Maurice Baker	6-0	FR	Dixie, UT
Rashad Brooks	6-1	SO	Cecil, MD
Ronnie Jenkins	6-1	FR	Mott, MI
Thomas Watkins	6-1	SO	Mesa, AZ
Amory Sanders	6-1	SO	Three Rivers, MO
Marshall Hyler	6-1	SO	Aquinas, TN
Marcus Tyree	6-1	SO	Bevill State, AL
Charles Walker	6-2	SO	Kemper, MO
Brian Bourbon	6-2	SO	Mineral Area, MO
William Mensah	6-2	SO	Delhi, NY
Anthony Norwood	6-2	FR	Collin Co., TX
Terrick Brown	6-2	SO	Shelby State, TN
Raymond Appleberry	6-2	SO	Holmes, MS
Roy Boone	6-2	SO	Coffeyville, KS
Ravonte Dantzler	6-2	SO	Cloud Co., KS
Donta Wade	6-2	SO	Southeastern, IL
Terrell Smith	6-2	SO	Catonsville, MD
Demetrice Sims	6-2	SO	McLennan, TX
Kenny Dye	6-2	SO	Connors State, OK
Arturo Young	6-2	SO	Brevard, FL
Larry Davis	6-3	SO	N.M. Military
James Murphy	6-3	SO	Kankakee, IL
Jesse Lawrence	6-3	SO	Fort Scott, KS
LaMonte Duncan	6-3	FR	Ranger, TX
Erick Greene	6-3	SO	Kaskaskia, IL
Jeff Walker	6-4	SO	Wabash Valley, IL
Nick Coln	6-4	SO	Northeast, MS
Richard Evans	6-4	SO	Kilgore, TX
Robin Sneed	6-4	SO	Angelina, TX
Maurice Jeffers	6-4	SO	Westark, AR
James Fowler	6-4	SO	Hagerstown, MD
K.T. Turner	6-4	SO	Hutchinson, KS
Chris Rogers	6-4	SO	Bossier Parish, LA
Marc Ridout	6-4	SO	Itawamba, MS
Rayon Holness	6-4	SO	Beaver County PA
Anthony Jones	6-4	SO	Garden City, KS
Ricky Bower	6-4	SO	Ricks, ID
Immanuel McElroy	6-4	FR	Tyler, TX
Stephen Dixson	6-4	SO	Vincennes, IN
Michael Hicks	6-4	SO	Bacone, OK
Nilte Watson	6-4	SO	Lansing, MI
David Sanders	6-4	FR	Tallahassee, FL
Jon Powell	6-5	SO	Owens, OH
Sigfried Hodge	6-5	SO	Mott, MI
James Foster	6-5	SO	Southeastern, IL
David Wall	6-5	SO	Carl Albert, OK
Jason Holmes	6-5	SO	Southwest, MS
John Hicks	6-5	SO	Gulf Coast, MS
DeCoursey Jamison	6-5	SO	Trinity Valley, TX
Shannon Forman	6-5	SO	Northwest, MS
DeMarcus Minor	6-5	SO	Barton Co., KS
Kerry Hendrickson	6-5	SO	Desert, CA
Fred House	6-5	SO	Dixie, UT
Dan Barker	6-6	SO	Indian River, FL
Marhall Sanders	6-6	SO	Brevard, FL
Brian Middleton	6-6	SO	Kishwaukee, IL
Renaldo Johnson	6-6	SO	Carl Albert, OK
Greg Lewis	6-6	SO	Howard, TX
Carlton Brown	6-6	SO	Temple, TX
Reggie York	6-6	SO	South Plains, TX
Jerome Brown	6-6	SO	New Mexico J.C.
Glen Newbold	6-6	SO	Yavapai, AZ
Terrance McLeod	6-6	SO	North Pioneer, AZ
Stan Blackmon	6-6	SO	Odessa, TX
Stephon Bradford	6-6	SO	Compton, CA
Terry Black	6-6	SO	Indian Hills, IA
Reggie Alexander	6-6	SO	Moberly, MO
Mike Marion	6-6	SO	Eastern, UT
Deltorio Campbell	6-6	FR	Northeast, MS
Kevin Paige	6-6	FR	Middle, GA
Angelo Flanders	6-7	SO	Highland, IL
Carl Henderson	6-7	SO	Pensacola, FL
Chris Thompson	6-7	SO	Bossier Parish, LA
Johnny Bosket	6-7	SO	Aiken, SC
Ceneka Shaw	6-7	SO	Hiwassee, TN
Shin Kerr	6-7	SO	Central, FL
Richard Stirgus	6-7	SO	McCook, NE
Tyrone Evans	6-7	SO	Garden City, KS
Clyde Ellis	6-7	SO	Chipola, FL
LaShon Coleman	6-7	SO	Indian Hills, IA
Corey Hightower	6-7	FR	Indian Hills, IA
Ladrick Simon	6-7	SO	Southwestern, CA
R'Cell Harris	6-7	SO	West Valley, CA
Isaac Sanders	6-7	SO	Calhoun, AL
Eric Batchelor	6-7	FR	Northeast, MS
Cedric Taylor	6-7	FR	Garden City, KS
Chico Moore	6-7	SO	Southern, ID
Alex Shorts	6-8	SO	San Jacinto, TX
William Butler	6-8	SO	Santa Fe, FL
Aaron White	6-8	SO	New Mexico Military
Stephone DonDon	6-8	SO	Collin Co., TX
Brian Fisher	6-8	SO	Bevill State, AL
Anthony Evans	6-8	SO	Neosho County, KS
Tajudeen Soyoye	6-8	SO	Meridian, MS
Kenkay Jones	6-8	SO	West Plains, MO
Troy Moore	6-8	SO	Connors State, OK
Kelvin Howell	6-8	SO	Westark, AR
DeeAndre Hulett	6-8	FR	Southestern, IA
Malcolm Battles	6-9	FR	Okaloosa Walton, FL
Arturas Javtokas	6-9	SO	Western, NE
Kareem Bartlett	6-9	SO	Angelina, TX
Dan Gottlieb	6-9	SO	Santa Monica, CA
Donald Oatis	6-9	SO	Lansing, MI
Jon Jones	6-9	SO	Lake Land, IL
Rosmel Blanco	6-9	SO	Bossier Parish, LA
Herb Brown	6-9	SO	Penn Valley, MO
Jamar Gaither	6-9	SO	Butler County, KS
Will Perkins	6-9	SO	Western, IA
Lamar Wright	6-9	SO	Porterville, CA
Julius Hicks	6-9	SO	West Valley, CA
Damian Kirkaldy	6-9	SO	Bacone, CA
Armand Etame	6-9	SO	Rose State, OK
David Watson	6-9	SO	Spartanburg, SC
Austin Larkin	6-9	SO	Coastal, GA
Ken Anaebonam	6-9	SO	Three Rivers, MO
Walter Moore	6-9	FR	McLennan, TX
Charles Kage	6-9	FR	Vincennes, IN
Chris Thomas	6-9	SO	Lawson State, AL
Robert Sanders	6-10	SO	Cincinnati State, OH
Nate Knight	6-10	SO	Valley, UT
Matt McDonald	6-10	SO	San Jose, CA
Kevin Robinson	6-10	SO	Butler County, KS
Chris Anderson	6-10	SO	Blinn, TX
Tomeko Dandridge	6-10	FR	Holmes, MS
David Bivins	6-10	SO	Kennedy King, IL
Joe Casper	6-10	SO	Johnson County, KS
George Aygar	6-10	SO	Bunker Hill, MA
Aaron Brockman	6-10	SO	Allegany, MD
Earnest Brown	6-10	FR	Mesa, AZ
David Dixon	6-11	FR	Tyler, TX
Jermaine Williams	6-11	SO	San Jacinto, TX
Lee Scruggs	6-11	SO	Daytona Beach, FL
Kamani Friend	6-11	SO	Gulf Coast, FL
Jeff Rabey	6-11	SO	Kalamazoo, MI
Ivan Gatto	6-11	SO	Midland, TX
Raynell Brewer	6-11	SO	Gulf Coast, MS

1ST & 2ND TEAM JC ALL-AMERICA PROFILES & TOP 40

by Rick Ball

FIRST TEAM

JAMIE ROSSER—*6-2, 180 lbs., SO, Northwest (Miss.) CC.*
Rosser is a cool point guard from Memphis, Tenn. He scored 13.0 ppg and handed out 6.0 apg as his team went to the NJCAA Tournament in Hutchinson, Kansas last spring. He'll have to do even more for his team this winter. Has SEC and Conference-USA interest.

ANTONIO JACKSON—*6-5, 195 lbs., SO, Butler County (Kansas) CC.*
Jackson is a big perimeter player who can go inside or out easily. He's from the South and likes Alabama, Louisville and UNC Charlotte. Last year, Jackson averaged15.0 ppg and shot 45 percent from the three-point line.

JAMES ZIMMERMAN—*6-5,185 lbs., SO, Indian Hills (Iowa) CC.*
Just modest freshman numbers of 10.0 ppg, 4.0 rpg and 3.0 apg, but he played on a talented 38-0 team. Expect this shooting guard/small forward from High Point, N.C. to have a breakout season.

MARCUS GRIFFIN—*6-9, 235 lbs., SO, Lincoln (Ill.) CC.*
All man at 235 lbs. and committed to Illinois out of Peoria Manual HS and still will go there with his 23.0 ppg and 5.0 blocks per game.

ALEKSANDER RADOJEVIC—*7-3, 235 lbs., SO, Barton County (Kansas) CC.*
Yugoslav native has those great hands to go with a developing 235-lb. frame. Is a B+ student with stats (12.0 ppg, 7.0 rpg) that will definitely grow this year, and is likely to see Mr. Griffin in the Big 10 via Ohio State.

SECOND TEAM

D.J. WOOTSON—5-11, 175 lbs., SO, Cecil (Md.) CC.
A point who gets 28 ppg via the jetstream breaks that he leads or from three-point range. He's also an 81 percent free-throw shooter. Wilmington, Del. is home and he is looking at Georgia State, Virginia Tech and Marist.

PAUL McPHERSON—*6-3, 225 lbs., SO, Kennedy King (Ill.) CC.*
Lefty should be a lineback in the NFL with his size and a 45-inch vertical leap. This small forward likes Houston, Loyola, Wyoming and Appalachian State for his future.

ROB GRIFFIN—*6-6, 220 lbs., SO, Southeastern CC, Iowa.*
Had a 19.0 ppg freshman year, plus 9.0 rpg and 3.0 apg as a small forward and big guard. Won the three-point shooting contest and was leading scorer at the BALLSTARS Top 40 JUCO Camp in 1998. Fielding interest from Iowa State, DePaul and Texas Christian.

JAMES WILLIAMS—*6-9, 225 lbs., SO, Dixie (Utah) CC.*
"Rudy" is a rebounding machine from St. Louis, Mo. He had 14.0 ppg and 8.0 rpg last season and is looking at Mississippi State, Fullerton State and Oklahoma State.

JERMAINE SMALL—*6-9, 215 lbs., SO, Los Angeles (Cal.) CC.*
New Jersey sleeper has really come on. His freshman-year stats of 16.0 ppg and 11.0 rpg have gotten notice from the Big East and Atlantic 10.

TOP 40 TEAMS & COACHES

	TEAM	COACH
1.	Indian Hills, IA	Mike Capaccio
2.	Butler County, KS	Steve Eck
3.	Los Angeles City, CA	Mike Miller
4.	Bacone, OK	Jimmy Voight
5.	Meridian, MS	Dennis Helms
6.	West Valley, CA	Bob Burton
7.	Dixie, UT	Jeff Kidder
8.	Connors State, OK	Bill Muse
9.	Gulf Coast, MS	Bob Weathers
10.	Champlain, VT	Bob Tipson
11.	Tallahassee, FL	Mike Gillespie
12.	Howard, TX	Tommy Collins
13.	Utah Valley State, UT	Jeff Reinert
14.	Kennedy King, IL	Willie Little
15.	San Jacinto, TX	Scott Gernander
16.	Gulf Coast, FL	Joe Pons
17.	Hutchinson, KS	Tim Jankovich
18.	Southeastern, IL	Todd Franklin
19.	Hagerstown, MD	Jim Brown
20.	Three Rivers, MO	Gene Bess
21.	Garden City, KS	Jeremy Cox
22.	Vincennes, IN	Dan Sparks
23.	McLennan, TX	Steve Shields
24.	Southeastern, IA	Joe O'Brien
25.	Kilgore, TX	Scott Schumacher
26.	Bossier Parish, LA	Mike McConathy
27.	Mesa, AZ	Joedy Gardner
28.	Santa Fe, FL	Jeff Burkhamer
29.	Northwest, MS	Don Skelton
30.	Wabash Valley, IL	Rick Hughes
31.	West Plains, MO	Tom Barr
32.	Indian River, FL	Mike Leatherwood
33.	Mott, MI	Steve Schmidt
34.	South Plains, TX	Shawn Scanlan
35.	Northland Pioneer, AZ	Richard Zalenski
36.	Southern, ID	Kevin Jones
37.	Owens, OH	Jim Welling
38.	Allegany, MD	Bob Kirk
39.	Shelby St., TN	Verties Sails, Jr.
40.	McCook, NE	Trace Bevell

1998-99 J.D. HINKLE, JR. NAIA OUTLOOK

by Greg Pogue

NAIA PLAYER OF THE YEAR

WILL CARLTON, Georgetown College (Ky.)—Will Carlton credits his recent past as key to his blossoming success. A top prospect out of Lawrenceburg (Ky.) Anderson County High School, Carlton signed with Utah, where he played his freshman season before transferring before last season to Georgetown College. Working in practices against the likes of Utah stars Keith Van Horn and Michael Doleac, Carlton paid his dues. It paid off last season for Georgetown College, which Carlton led to the NAIA national championship by averaging 19.7 points and 11.9 rebounds and shooting .643 percent from the field. En route to being chosen the NAIA national tournament's MVP, the 6-foot-9, 235-pound junior forward averaged 22 points and 11.4 rebounds while shooting .687 percent from the field. With Carlton and the addition of 6-10 Cincinnati transfer Jackson Julson, the Tigers are the team to beat this season.

NAIA NEWCOMER OF THE YEAR—Marko Wright, Life University

NAIA ALL-AMERICA TEAM

FIRST TEAM

Walter Bethea	5-9	Senior	Park College (Mo.)
Eric Campbell	6-5	Senior	Spring Hill College (Ala.)
Will Carlton	6-9	Junior	Georgetown College (Ky.)
Jack Hartman	6-9	Senior	Biola University (Calif.)
T.J. Walker	6-0	Senior	Azusa Pacific University (Calif.)

SECOND TEAM

Brian Gomes	6-5	Senior	Westmont College (Calif.)
Brian Haskins	6-4	Senior	Lambuth University (Tenn.)
Lanny Knight	6-4	Senior	Texas Wesleyan
Jay Mauck	5-8	Junior	Oklahoma Christian
Tryrian Ridges	6-2	Junior	Union University (Tenn.)

THIRD TEAM

Lamont Barnes	6-4	Junior	Lindsey Wilson College (Ky.)
Larry James	6-6	Junior	Emmanuel College (Ga.)
Brian Watson	6-8	Senior	Montana Tech
Robert White	6-7	Senior	Southern Nazarene (Okla.)
Leronzo Williams	6-5	Senior	Morris College (S.C.)

HONORABLE MENTION

Richard Anderson	6-6	Junior	Simon Fraser University (B.C.)
Marc Bishop	6-1	Senior	University of Findlay (Ohio)
Barry Bowman	6-3	Senior	Georgetown College (Ky.)
Billy Cabbil	6-1	Senior	Faulkner University (Ala.)
Chad Elliott	6-7	Senior	Lubbock Christian (Texas)
Jonathon George	6-5	Senior	Lewis-Clark State College (Idaho)
David Harrison	6-4	Senior	Campellsville College (Ky.)
Curtis Haywood	6-6	Senior	Oklahoma City University
Tracy Hector	6-8	Senior	University of Mobile (Ala.)
John Hester	6-6	Senior	Central State University (Ohio)
Joclin Julmist	6-5	Junior	The Master's College (Calif.)
John Krueger	6-4	Senior	Cedarville College (Ohio)
Jay Martin	6-4	Senior	Oklahoma Baptist University
Archie McClendon	6-7	Senior	Harris-Stowe State (Md.)
Jody McGarity	6-8	Senior	Huston-Tillotson College (Texas)
Monty Montgomery	6-4	Junior	Daemen College (N.Y.)
Gaylon Moore	6-7	Junior	Union University (Tenn.)
Kendrick Moore	6-5	Junior	Voorhees College (S.C.)
Dwayne Miles	6-5	Senior	Georgia Southwestern
Tyce Nasinec	6-4	Senior	Central Washington
Fernando Ortiz	6-4	Junior	St. Vincent College (Pa.)
Gabe Rapier	6-6	Senior	Houston Baptist
Mark Reed	6-4	Senior	Schreiner College (Texas)
Josh Renn	6-7	Senior	Brescia University (Ky.)
Ernest Scott	6-6	Senior	Georgia Southwestern
Terrance Scriven	5-10	Senior	Claflin (S.C.)
Corey Syon	6-1	Senior	Texas Lutheran
Ty Thorn	6-8	Senior	Western Montana College
Jarvis Towns	6-6	Junior	Piedmont College (Ga.)
Kevin VanNice	6-2	Senior	Carroll College (Md.)

NOTE: The *adidas Blue Ribbon* NAIA Outlook is dedicated to the memory of our dear friend, J.D. Hinkle, Jr. The longtime Mayor of Buckhannon, W.Va., and former West Virginia State Senator was one of the biggest supporters NAIA basketball and small college athletics have ever known. Hinkle attended 29 straight NAIA national basketball tournaments in Kansas City, Mo. and sat in the same seat location every year. He was proud of his attendance streak in Kansas City and would go to the tournament, even if only for a day due to his legislative commitments, in order to maintain the streak.

NAIA PRESEASON TOP 20

		(1997-98 record)
1.	Georgetown, Ky.	(36-3)
2.	Azusa Pacific, Calif.	(34-5)
3.	Life, Ga.	(32-4)
4.	Oklahoma City	(26-5)
5.	Union, Tenn.	(30-5)
6.	Incarnate Word, Tex.	(26-5)
7.	Biola, Calif.	(30-7)
8.	Southern Nazarene, Okla.	(29-2)
9.	Park, Mo.	(27-8)
10.	Birmingham-Southern, Ala.	(28-5)
11.	St. Mary's, Texas	(20-7)
12.	Mobile, Ala.	(27-9)
13.	Freed-Hardeman, Tenn.	(24-11)
14.	Houston Baptist	(26-6)
15.	Transylvania, Ky.	(24-9)
16.	Montana State-Northern	(26-9)
17.	St. Vincent, Pa.	(28-5)
18.	David Lipscomb, Tenn.	(26-8)
19.	Olivet Nazarene, Ill.	(28-9)
20.	Oklahoma Baptist	(23-8)

1998-99 NCAA DIVISION II AND III OUTLOOK

NCAA DIVISION II PLAYER OF THE YEAR
Titus Warmsley, Montana State Billings

TITUS WARMSLEY—Any player who can average in the mid-teens in scoring over a season is pretty special. Get up into the high teens and you start talking about All-America potential. Break the 20-point barrier and you have Titus Warmsley of Montana State-Billings. Warmsley averaged 23.0 points last season as a junior, one of the highest totals in Division II last season. Warmsley, a 5-11 guard, also chipped in 4.7 assists per game for good measure and was selected a second-team All-American. Through his efforts, Montana State-Billings won its conference tournament and made the NCAA Division II Tournament.

NEWCOMER OF THE YEAR

Scott Koenen, Southwest State (Minn.)

NCAA DIVISION II ALL-AMERICA TEAM

FIRST TEAM

Antonio Garcia	6-8	Senior	Kentucky Wesleyan
Chris Sykes	6-6	Senior	Delta State (Miss.)
Titus Warmsley	5-11	Senior	Montana State-Billings
Eric Strand	6-9	Senior	Nebraska-Kearney
Antwain Smith	6-8	Senior	St. Paul's (Va.)

SECOND TEAM

Roland Miller	6-4	Senior	East Central Oklahoma
Rodney Dean	6-3	Senior	Central Arkansas
Dana Williams	6-7	Senior	Kentucky Wesleyan
Lee Farrior	6-3	Junior	Longwood (Va.)
Garee Bryant	6-2	Senior	LIU-C.W. Post (N.Y.)

HONORABLE MENTION

Jamie Barker	6-0	Senior	Bentley (Mass.)
Hunter Berg	5-10	Senior	North Dakota
Jeff Boinski	6-5	Senior	Michigan Tech
Cory Brathol	6-7	Junior	Northern Michigan
Anthony Byrd	6-3	Senior	Southern Colorado
Robert Conley	6-6	Senior	Clayton State (Ga.)
Drew Cooper	6-5	Senior	Assumption (Mass.)
William Davis	6-1	Senior	Virginia Union
David Donnelly	6-7	Senior	Stonehill (Mass.)
Kevin Evans	6-3	Junior	St. Andrews (N.C.)
Max Gladieux	6-3	Senior	Bellarmine (Ky.)
Oscar Gonzalez	6-0	Senior	Pittsburg State (Kan.)
Richard Johnson	6-3	Senior	Midwestern State (Texas)
Scott Koenen	6-7	Sophomore	Southwest State (Minn.)
Bryan Moore	6-5	Junior	Assumption (Mass.)
Wayne Morris	6-6	Senior	Shippensburg (Pa.)
Jared Mosley	6-8	Senior	Abliene Christian (Texas)
Jamal Palmer	6-9	Senior	Millersville (Pa.)
Cory Parker	6-5	Junior	Truman State (Mo.)
Adrien Pritchard	6-7	Senior	Queens (N.C.)
Milosh Pujo	6-8	Senior	Lewis (Ill.)
Damon Reed	6-10	Junior	St. Rose (N.Y.)
Dante Ross	5-9	Senior	Cal-Davis
Jared Stevenson	6-1	Junior	Western Washington
John Tomsich	6-10	Senior	LeMonye (N.Y.)
Ray Waits	6-6	Senior	Ferris State (Mich.)
Juan Wiley	6-6	Senior	South Carolina-Aiken

NCAA DIVISION II TOP 20 (1997-98 record)

1. Kentucky Wesleyan (30-3)
2. Virginia Union (27-6)
3. Delta State, Miss. (27-4)
4. Fairmont State, WVa. (27-4)
5. Salem Teikyo, WVa. (28-3)
6. South Dakota State (26-3)
7. Cal State Bakersfield (25-3)
8. Cal Davis (31-2)
9. Central Oklahoma (25-7)
10. West Texas A&M (26-5)
11. Southern Indiana (27-6)
12. Florida Southern (23-7)
13. Nebraska Kierney (25-6)
14. Northern State, S.D. (27-5)
15. St. Rose, N.Y. (27-6)
16. Missouri Western (23-7)
17. Pittsburg State, Kan. (23-7)
18. Adelphi, N.Y. (22-6)
19. Lynn, Fla. (22-7)
20. Queens, N.C. (24-6)

NCAA DIVISION III PLAYER OF THE YEAR
Andy Panko, Lebanon Valley College (PA)

ANDY PANKO—Panko returns for his final year after leading the Labanon Valley Flying Dutchmen to a 20-8 record a year ago. As a junior, Panko led Lebanon Valley to the Eastern College Athletic Conference Southern Regional title as he averaged 25.5 points and 8.7 rebounds while shooting 64 percent from the floor. Panko finished eighth in the Division III in scoring and ninth in field-goal percentage. The 6-8 senior will carry a double-figure scoring streak of 40 games into the 1998-99 season. Last year, Panko was chosen the ECAC Southern Region Player of the Year.

NEWCOMER OF THE YEAR

Ryan William Carter, Wisconsin-Platteville

NCAA DIVISION III ALL-AMERICA TEAM

FIRST TEAM

Andy Panko	6-8	Senior	Lebanon Valley (Pa.)
Adam Doll	6-6	Senior	Simpson College (Iowa)
Jeremy Thompson	6-0	Junior	Ohio Northern
Henry Shannon	6-4	Senior	Maryville (Mo.)
Devean George	6-5	Senior	Augsburg (Minn.)

SECOND TEAM

Michael Shantz	6-5	Senior	Hamilton (N.Y.)
Luke Schmidt	6-7	Senior	Gustavus-Adolphus (Minn.)
Dave Januzzi	6-0	Junior	Wilkes (Pa.)
Josh Estelle	6-0	Senior	Wabash (Ind.)
Chad Tabor	6-4	Senior	Wabash (Ind.)

HONORABLE MENTION

Ryan Gorman	6-8	Senior	Wooster (Ohio)
Rich Williamson	6-7	Senior	Thiel (Pa.)
Merril Brunson	6-4	Junior	Wisconsin-Platteville
Aaron Winkle	6-5	Junior	Calvin (Mich.)
Braheen Cotton	6-4	Senior	Hunter (N.Y.)
Tim Czarnecki	6-6	Junior	Albion (Mich.)
Greg Sutton	6-6	Senior	St. Lawrence (N.Y.)
Rob Hamman	6-7	Senior	Wheaton (Ill.)
Verdel Baskin	6-0	Senior	Colorado College
Korey Coon	6-0	Junior	Illinois Wesleyan
Jason Rusnak	6-4	Senior	Denison (Ohio)
Chad Kahle	6-5	Junior	Defiance (Ohio)
Charles Ridley	6-3	Senior	Wheaton (Ill.)
Josh Wilhelm	6-7	Senior	Carleton (Minn.)
Brad Clark	6-5	Junior	Wisconsin-Oshkosh
Jeff Bell	6-4	Senior	Olivet (Mich.)
Jeff Clement	5-10	Senior	Grinnell (Iowa)
Zach Yoder	6-2	Soph.	Messiah (Pa.)
Eric Joldersma	6-6	Senior	Bethel (Minn.)
Chad Ideus	6-6	Senior	Nebraska-Wesleyan

NCAA DIVISION III TOP 20 (1997-98 record)

1. Wisconsin-Platteville (30-0)
2. Gustavus Adolphus, Minn. (26-4)
3. Catholic, D.C. (25-4)
4. Hunter, N.Y. (28-2)
5. Hamilton, N.Y. (17-10)
6. Wabash, Ind.(22-5)
7. St. Lawrence, N.Y. (24-2)
8. Wooster, Ohio (22-6)
9. Connecticut College (22-4)
10. Wilkes, Pa. (26-5)
11. Augsburg, Minn. (22-4)
12. Wisconsin-Oshkosh (21-3)
13. Nebraska Wesleyan (26-3)
14. Rowan, N.J. (21-8)
15. Simpson, Iowa (22-3)
16. Pomona-Pitzer, Calif. (21-5)
17. Chicago (24-2)
18. Illinois Wesleyan (26-3)
19. Williams, Mass. (26-4)
20. Lebanon Valley, Pa. (20-8)

1998 NBA DRAFT

FIRST ROUND

	Team	Name	College	Height
1.	Los Angeles	Michael Olowokandi	Pacific	7-1
2.	Vancouver	Mike Bibby	Arizona	6-2
3.	Denver	Raef LaFrentz	Kansas	6-11
4.	Toronto	Antawn Jamison	North Carolina	6-9
5.	Golden State	Vince Carter	North Carolina	6-7
6.	Dallas	Robert Traylor	Michigan	6-8
7.	Sacramento	Jason Williams	Florida	6-1
8.	Philadelphia	Larry Hughes	Saint Louis	6-5
9.	Milwaukee	Dirk Nowitzki	DJK Wurzburg (Germany)	6-11
10.	Boston	Paul Pierce	Kansas	6-7
11.	Detroit	Bonzi Wells	Ball State	6-5
12.	Orlando	Michael Doleac	Utah	6-11
13.	Orlando (from Washington)	Keon Clark	UNLV	6-11
14.	Houston	Michael Dickerson	Arizona	6-5
15.	Orlando (from New Jersey)	Matt Harpring	Georgia Tech	6-8
16.	Houston (from New York via Toronto)	Bryce Drew	Valparaiso	6-3
17.	Minnesota	Radoslav Nesterovic	Kinder Bologna (Italy)	7-0
18.	Houston (from Portland via Toronto)	Mirsad Turkcan Efes	Pilsen (Turkey)	6-9
19.	Milwaukee (from Cleveland)	Pat Garrity	Notre Dame	6-9
20.	Atlanta	Roshown McLeod	Duke	6-8
21.	Charlotte	Ricky Davis	Iowa	6-5
22.	L.A. Clippers (from Miami)	Brian Skinner	Baylor	6-10
23.	Denver (from Phoenix)	Tyronn Lue	Nebraska	6-0
24.	San Antonio	Felipe Lopez	St. John's	6-6
25.	Indiana	Al Harrington	St. Patrick's (HS)	6-8
26.	Los Angeles Lakers	Sam Jacobson	Minnesota	6-6.
27.	Seattle	Vladimir Stepania	Union Olimpija Llubljana (Slovenia)	6-11
28.	Chicago	Corey Benjamin	Oregon State	6-6
29.	Utah	Nazr Mohammed	Kentucky	6-10

SECOND ROUND

	Team	Name	College	Height
30.	Dallas (from Toronto)	Ansu Sesay	Mississippi	6-9
31.	L.A. Lakers (from Vancouver)	Ruben Patterson	Cincinnati	6-6
32.	Seattle (from Denver)	Rashard Lewis	Alief-Alsik (HS)	6-10
33.	Seattle (from L.A. Clippers)	Jelani McCoy	UCLA	6-10
34.	Chicago (from Golden State)	Shammond Williams	North Carolina	6-2
35.	Dallas	Bruno Sundov	Split (Croatia)	7-2
36.	Sacramento	Jerome James	Florida A&M	7-1
37.	Philadelphia	Casey Shaw	Toledo	6-11
38.	New York	DeMarco Johnson	UNC-Charlotte	6-8
39.	Milwaukee	Rafer Alston	Fresno State	6-2
40.	Detroit	Korleone Young	Hargrave Military (HS)	6-7
41.	Houston	Cuttino Mobley	Rhode Island	6-4
42.	Orlando	Miles Simon	Arizona	6-5
43.	Washington	Jahidi White	Georgetown	6-10
44.	New York	Sean Marks	California	6-11
45.	L.A. Lakers (from New Jersey)	Toby Bailey	UCLA	6-5
46.	Minnesota	Andrae Patterson	Indiana	6-8
47.	Toronto (from Portland)	Tyson Wheeler	Rhode Island	5-10
48.	Cleveland	Ryan Stack	South Carolina	6-11
49.	Atlanta	Cory Carr	Texas Tech	6-4
50.	Charlotte	Andrew Betts	Long Beach State	7-1
51.	Miami	Corey Brewer	Oklahoma	6-1
52.	San Antonio	Derrick Dial	Eastern Michigan	6-4
53.	Dallas (from Phoenix)	Greg Buckner	Clemson	6-4
54.	Denver (from Indiana)	Tremaine Fowlkes	Fresno State	6-8
55.	Denver (from Seattle)	Ryan Bowen	Iowa	6-7
56.	Vancouver (from L.A. Lakers)	J.R. Henderson	UCLA	6-9
57.	Utah	Torraye Braggs	Xavier	6-8
58.	Chicago	Maceo Baston	Michigan	6-9

DRAFT DAY TRADES

Toronto-Golden State: The Toronto Raptors traded the rights to first-round pick Antawn Jamison (No. 4 overall) to the Golden State Warriors for the rights to first-round pick Vince Carter (No. 5 overall).

Dallas-Milwaukee: The Dallas Mavericks traded the rights to first-round pick Robert Traylor (No. 6 overall) to the Milwaukee Bucks for the rights to first-round pick Dirk Nowitzki (No. 9 overall) and first-round pick Pat Garrity (No. 19 overall).

Dallas-Phoenix: The Dallas Mavericks traded forward Martin Muursepp, guard-forward Bubba Wells and the rights to first-round pick Pat Garrity to the Phoenix Suns for a 1999 first-round draft pick and guard Steve Nash.

San Antonio-Vancouver: The San Antonio Spurs traded forward Carl Herrera and the rights to first-round pick Felipe Lopez (No. 24 overall) to the Vancouver Grizzlies for guard Antonio Daniels.

Utah-Philadelphia: The Utah Jazz traded the rights to first-round pick Nazr Mohammed (No. 29 overall) for a future first-round draft pick.

Atlanta-Chicago: The Chicago Bulls traded the rights to second-round draft pick Shammond Williams (No. 34 overall) to the Atlanta Hawks for the rights to second-round draft pick Cory Carr (No. 49 overall).

L.A. Lakers-Phoenix: The Los Angeles Lakers traded the rights to second round draft pick Toby Bailey (No. 45 overall) to the Phoenix Suns.

THE TOP FORTY

1

DUKE

LOCATION .... **Durham, NC**
CONFERENCE .... **Atlantic Coast (ACC)**
LAST SEASON .... **32-4 (.898)**
CONFERENCE RECORD .... **15-1 (1st)**
STARTERS LOST/RETURNING **2/3**
NICKNAME .... **Blue Devils**
COLORS .... **Blue & White**
HOMECOURT .... **Cameron Indoor Stadium (9,314)**
COACH .... **Mike Krzyzewski (Army '69)**
RECORD AT SCHOOL .... **432-153 (18 yrs.)**
CAREER RECORD .... **505-212 (23 yrs.)**
ASSISTANTS .... **Quin Snyder (Duke '89)**
Johnny Dawkins (Duke '86)
David Henderson (Duke '86)
TEAM WINS (last 5 yrs.) **28-13-18-24-32**
RPI (last 5 yrs.) **4-66-33-9-3**
1997-98 FINISH .... **Lost in NCAA Final Eight.**

COACH AND PROGRAM

Duke nearly completed a four-year climb in 1997-98, from a last-place ACC finish in 1995 to the top of the college basketball world.

The Blue Devils won 32 games, led the nation in scoring margin, spent much of the season ranked No. 1, set an ACC record with 15 league wins and earned a top regional seed in the NCAA Tournament.

Good year, right?

Good for almost anybody else, but just a little short of the standard Mike Krzyzewski established for the program in the late '80s and early '90s. That was a dynasty built on postseason success. Seven times in nine years, Krzyzewski led Duke to the Final Four—including five trips to the title game and a pair of national championships.

The 1997-98 Blue Devils couldn't quite reach that level, not for all their regular season success. Duke made the finals of the ACC Tournament, but lost there to archrival North Carolina. The Devils then won three NCAA Tournament games to reach the Southeast Regional final in St. Petersburg, Fla. There, Krzyzewski's squad built a 17-point lead on Kentucky with nine-and-a-half minutes to play.

"I remember thinking we were (10) minutes away from the Final Four," center Elton Brand said. "I was thinking about cutting down the nets."

But the eventual national champion Wildcats, gaining a measure of revenge for Duke's memorable victory in the '92 East Regional final in Philadelphia, earned the ticket to San Antonio with a furious comeback. The result left the Devils frustrated and still a step away from a return to the heights they climbed so regularly in prior years.

"This was just a taste," Brand said after the game. "We're going to use this experience. This is going to help us in the future."

Krzyzewski had warned anybody who would listen that last season's squad lacked the core of experience which his best teams drew so heavily upon. Not a single player in '98 had ever played in the Sweet 16. Six of his nine top players were freshmen and sophomores.

"There's no way I thought these kids would win 15 conference games and 32 games (overall)," Krzyzewski said. "We had a chance to win the national championship having three freshmen and a sophomore on the court a lot of the time. Because of our reputation, those kids were never really given the pat on the back they deserved."

Duke's unusual combination of inexperience and talented depth led Krzyzewski to play a helter-skelter style—one that would both use as many players as possible and, at the same time, minimize the problems of inexperience.

"We had depth. We had talent, but we had a lot of young guys," Krzyzewski said. "So the plan was to extend, play a lot of people, get more guys involved. We played fast and pressed and didn't set it up very often. There were times we took a few bad shots, but they weren't bad shots in the total thinking because they were aggressive."

As a result of that style, Duke played some wild games, building—and occasionally losing—huge leads. Virginia fell by 44 points in December. A solid Maryland team that beat Kansas and North Carolina went down at home by 32 points, then came to Cameron and lost by 27. UCLA showed up in Durham late in the season and was buried on national television, 120-84.

But not everybody wilted in the face of Duke's pressure. The Blue Devils could play at just one speed, and the inability of Krzyzewski's team to slow things down and protect a lead allowed several poised opponents to erase big margins.

Then-defending national champion Arizona gave the first hint of what would be Duke's crucial flaw in Hawaii, cutting a 21-point second half deficit down to five in the final minute. Three weeks later in Ann Arbor, Michigan erased a 17-point second half lead to hand Duke it's first loss. In Durham in January, Clemson cut 23 points off a 24-point Duke lead and had a shot at the buzzer to win what would have been the greatest comeback in ACC history.

That's why Duke's collapse against Kentucky in St. Petersburg has to be regarded as characteristic of the '98 Blue Devil team. It was not some fluke that Krzyzewski can write off.

Instead, the veteran coach will try to teach his team to play a different tempo in 1998-99.

"I still want to play fast, but I think we can be more situational with it than last year," Krzyzewski said. "We won't be a team that necessarily goes out and forces tempo. I think we'll become a better offensive and defensive team in the halfcourt."

Slowing the tempo a bit will allow Krzyzewski to make full use of his powerful young big men, especially the 6-8, 260-pound Brand. The sophomore from New York appears ready to emerge as one of college basketball's dominant players, but he is just one cog in a talented arsenal that includes All-America sharpshooter Trajan Langdon and proven young veterans such as forward Shane Battier, swingman Chris Carrawell and point guard Will Avery.

Krzyzewski doesn't try to downplay his expectations for the coming season.

"We should be really good," he said. "Physically, mentally, emotionally...what was not a strength is now a strength. We still have talent. We still have depth. Now we also have a more experienced group."

The Blue Devils also have, in Krzyzewski, arguably the most successful coach now working in college basketball. He has the best NCAA Tournament winning percentage of any active coach. Last season he passed Denny Crum and former mentor Bob Knight to take the lead in total Tournament wins among active coaches. When Dean Smith stepped down before last season, Krzyzewski also became the dean of ACC coaches.

It's hard to believe he has been at Duke since 1980. At times, the Blue Devils have wondered how much longer they could hold on to the successful coach. He engaged in serious talks with NBA suitors in 1990 and 1994, then almost quit for health reasons when he had serious back problems in 1995. Even last summer, Krzyzewski still talked wistfully about the prospects of one day coaching in the NBA.

But, within the last year, something changed.

"I love basketball and I respect the NBA," he said this past summer. "But I love college basketball more than pro basketball. It's not as talented, but it's purer. "You can do anything you want defensively (in college basketball) and, therefore, you can do anything you want offensively to counteract it. That, to me, is good."

For the first time, Krzyzewski passed the word to his contacts in the NBA not to bother calling with job inquiries. He signed a new long-term contract with Duke and accepted a position as the school's associate athletic director. His family has just moved into a new home and he is deeply involved in the new "K Lab"—a sports medicine research facility at the university.

At a dedication ceremony for the K Lab, Krzyzewski told the audience that he now plans to be at Duke for a long time.

"There are no lures for me," he said. "I hate to say I'm content because I hate the word content. I'm excited...still excited about being at Duke and doing what I do."

Krzyzewski added that his accomplishments in the late '80s and early '90s were part of another era in college basketball.

"I truly believe college basketball has changed, with so many kids going early (to the NBA)," he said. "The world has changed. To be able to show you can succeed in different time periods is, I think, a challenge. With what we did last season and what we hope to do now, I think we've shown that we can succeed in this time period. That's important to me."

It's important to Duke, too. Because as long as the Blue Devils have Krzyzewski running the program, they can count years like last season as less than spectacular.

STARTERS NOT RETURNING

STEVE WOJCIECHOWSKI (5-11, PG, 5.7 ppg, 2.4 rpg, 4.6 apg, 1.8 tpg, 2.1 spg, 28.2 minutes, .387 FG, .388 3PT). A modestly talented point guard who made himself a lightening rod for what was loved (by some) and hated (by many) about Duke basketball over the last two years.

"He's a common man who's a really good player," Krzyzewski said. "He has uncommon leadership and competitive skills—at the highest level of any kid I've ever coached."

Heading into the 1996-97 season, the Duke coach himself expected "Wojo" to be no more than a solid backup point guard. Instead, the fiery little man from Baltimore made himself a vital player—a point guard with few offensive skills, but with a tenacious defensive presence and one of the best assist/turnover ratios in ACC history.

Wojo came in for considerable abuse at times, but answered his critics on the floor. For instance, he won MVP honors at the Maui Classic after outplaying All-America point guard Mike Bibby of Arizona.

His minutes will go to players with more physical ability (especially Will Avery), but Duke will miss his leadership and his intensity. Wojo's all-out style of play set the tone for the Blue Devils last year.

Who will replace him?

"I don't want anybody to think he has to be Steve, because they'll fail," Krzyzewski said. "We became very dependent on Steve for emotion. I think it will be good for this team if all the players try to step up and give a little bit of what Steve gave us.

"I'd like to see Langdon and Carrawell and Battier be more emotional. I think that would make them better players."

KEY TO ABBREVIATIONS

FR	freshman	ppg	points per game
SO	sophomore	apg	assists per game
JR	junior	spg	steals per game
SR	senior	bpg	blocks per game
F	forward	JC	junior college
C	center	CC	community college
G	guard	HS	high school
lbs	pounds	#	jersey number

ROSHOWN MCLEOD (6-8, SF, 15.3 ppg, 5.6 rpg, 1.2 spg, 23.7 minutes, .494 FG, .411 3PT). The first transfer of the Krzyzewski era proved well worth the precedent. The versatile forward, who played at the same Jersey City, N.J., high school (St. Anthony's) which sent Bobby Hurley to Duke, arrived in Durham after two lackluster seasons at St. John's and promptly established himself as one of the nation's finest offensive players. McLeod gave Duke an inside-outside scoring threat that will be hard to replace.

Ironically, it looked for a time as if McLeod's senior season would be a bust. After a solid junior year in which he was often Duke's only big man on the floor, he reacted poorly to the arrival of several freshmen post players. He floundered to fit in with Brand and Shane Battier, reaching rock bottom with a pre-Christmas performance against Mercer that was so bad it left Krzyzewski fuming and McLeod thinking of quitting.

Instead, McLeod went home over the Christmas break and, after considerable soul-searching, decided to rededicate himself. Coincidentally, soon after his return, Brand suffered the broken foot that opened up more of a role for the 6-8 senior.

McLeod took advantage of the opportunity, establishing himself (along with guard Trajan Langdon) as one of the team's two "go-to" guys. He scored in double figures in 23 of 25 games after the Christmas break and finished as the team's top scorer and No. 3 rebounder. He had the ability to score inside and outside and he was the team's second-best three-point shooter.

McLeod played well enough to earn first-team All-ACC honors and was selected in the first round of the NBA draft by the Atlanta Hawks. Duke still has plenty of players close to his size, but none that possesses as many offensive weapons. McLeod will be missed.

OTHERS NOT RETURNING

MIKE CHAPPELL (6-8, G/F, 7.1 ppg, 2.0 rpg, 14.4 minutes, .434 3PT). The tall, slender swing man from Michigan started Duke's first 21 games, scoring in double figures 12 times. But he fell into a horrible slump after the February loss at North Carolina and ended the regular season with four straight scoreless games. Chappell broke out just in time to provide some timely help off the bench during Duke's NCAA Tournament spurt.

However, faced with the prospect of fighting for playing time in his junior season, Chappell elected to transfer to Michigan State, where he'll have two years of eligibility remaining after sitting out the 1998-99 campaign.

Krzyzewski was surprised and disappointed by Chappell's departure. He had always touted Chappell as a future pro, even when frustrated by the youngster's failure to harness his considerable athletic skills. The Southfield, Mich., product had a sweet jump shot, but rarely displayed his ability to slash to the basket. He also shied away at times from contact inside.

Still, his absence could hurt. Although Duke has plenty of talented wing players, Chappell's unexpected departure means Krzyzewski will have to replace four of his top five three-point shooters.

RICKY PRICE (6-5, G, 2.7 ppg, 8.0 minutes). Set against all of the great success stories at Duke are a handful of notable disappointments. This is one of them.

Price came to Duke in the fall of 1994 as one of the nation's premier prep prospects. Kansas coach Roy Williams was quoted as saying he never felt a recruiting loss more than when Price picked Duke.

But the gregarious, likable Price picked a bad time to come to Duke. His freshman year was marred by an ankle injury and by Krzyzewski's famous back troubles, leading to Duke's first losing season since 1983. Price played a major role in Duke's revival a year later, earning third-team All-ACC honors as the Devils won 18 games and returned to the NCAA Tournament.

It looked as if the quick, explosive swingman was about to live up to his prep hype. But a preseason wrist injury set him back a year later and, although he returned to establish himself as one of the nation's best sixth men as Duke won an unexpected ACC regular season title, the year ended on a sour note. Price played poorly during the Devils' quick exits from the ACC and NCAA Tournaments.

Then real disaster struck. Price, always a fine student, was dismissed from school—reportedly for an honor code violation. He was forced to sit out the first semester of his senior year. He got a job in Durham and worked out alone at the local YMCA. When he rejoined the team after first semester, Price found himself way behind his teammates.

He never found a role with the 97-98 Blue Devils. After averaging over 800 minutes per year and 10.7 ppg in his first three seasons, Price played just 167 minutes and averaged just 2.7 ppg as a senior—almost all of it in garbage time.

Price is a talented player, but, in reality, he was lost to Duke after the 1996-97 campaign.

TODD SINGLETON (6-4, G, 0.7 ppg). A walkon who sat on the bench for three years and never saw any significant action. Krzyzewski rated him a valuable practice player.

PROJECTED STARTERS

TRAJAN LANGDON (6-3, 195 lbs., SR, SG, #21, 14.7 ppg, 2.9 rpg, 1.9 apg, 1.6 tpg, 28.8 minutes, .444 FG, .395 3PT, .886 FT, Anchorage East HS/Anchorage, Ak). If it seems like Langdon has been at Duke forever, that's because he has—almost.

The Alaskan sharpshooter started 24 games for Duke in 1994-95 when he was a freshman, while Krzyzewski was battling his back problems. A year later, it was Langdon who was sidelined for health reasons, missing the 1995-96 season with cartilage damage in his left knee. But he returned to win first-team All-ACC honors a year later, when hit averaged 14.3 ppg and hit 86 three-pointers.

Langdon nearly duplicated those numbers last season, hitting 85 three-pointers and averaging 14.7 ppg. His three-point percentage fell off some (dropping from .441 to .395), but he improved his efficiency inside the three-point line and repeated as a first-team All-ACC choice.

"He's the best shooter in college basketball," Wake Forest coach Dave Odom said.

He's more than that, also contributing mightily as a solid defender and good ballhandler. Krzyzewski points out that Langdon will have to play point guard if he hopes to make it in the pros, so look for Duke's gunnery specialist to do more playmaking this season.

Langdon got some experience in that role this summer. He was the only collegian to play with the U.S. bronze medal team at the World Championships in Athens, Greece.

Originally, Langdon planned to take the summer off and rest. The previous three summers he played minor league baseball in the San Diego Padres organization, but his baseball contract lapsed.

So, when the NBA's labor troubles forced the top pros off the World Championship team and opened up a spot for Langdon, he jumped at the chance. He didn't play a lot (scoring just 20 points in seven games), but was impressive to coach Rudy Tomjanovich.

"I became such a big fan of his," the Houston Rockets coach said. "He's a great team player. He really gives it all. Just because of his shooting alone, he's got to be considered (an NBA prospect). Put that with his work ethic and the way he gives his all, and I think he's going to make it."

Langdon will end his career as the top three-point shooter in Duke history. He is going to challenge Wake Forest's Charlie Davis' ACC career free throw mark. He also has a chance to become only the 21st player in ACC history to win first-team All-Conference honors three times.

Yet, so far, he hasn't accomplished what he came to Duke for—namely, to play in a Final Four. In each of the last two years, Langdon has capped a marvelous regular season with a disappointing postseason performance. So, as great as Langdon's career at Duke has been, there is one gaping hole in his resume.

More than any other player on this Blue Devil team, Langdon will be pushing Duke all the way to St. Petersburg.

ELTON BRAND (6-8, 260 lbs., SO, C, #42, 13.4 ppg, 7.3 rpg, 1.6 tpg, 1.3 bpg, 1.5 spg, 23.5 minutes, .592 FG, .604 FT, Peekskill HS/Peekskill, N.Y.). The timing was awful. The powerful big man from New York was just learning how dominant he could be at the college level. He had followed a 19-point, 12-rebound effort against Villanova with a 21-point, 12-rebound performance against Michigan. He was shooting nearly 70 percent from the floor. Krzyzewski was just about to change his offense to take advantage of Brand's growing maturity and confidence.

That's when it happened. Sliding across the lane during a simple defensive drill, Brand snapped the fifth metatarsal bone in his right foot. Duke would play the next 15 games without him.

Actually, it's a medical miracle Brand returned at all. But the guy who returned to play in Duke's final 10 games was only a shadow of the Elton Brand Duke fans had seen in November and December. He was big and strong, and there were times he could still take over a game (as he did in the second half of a victory over North Carolina), but something was lacking—the quickness and explosiveness that had made Brand one of the nation's most unique and dominating big men.

Well, the rest of the ACC—and college basketball—better get ready. Brand proved over the summer that he's back and better than ever.

He helped lead a team of American collegians to the gold medal in the Goodwill Games. Playing against older and bigger foreign centers, Brand averaged 17.0 ppg (just one point less than USA leader Wally Szczerbiak), a team-high 7.6 rpg and a shot a team-high 65 percent from the floor.

During the Goodwill trials, there were actually coaches who weren't sure Brand belonged on the team. He was too short at 6-8 to play center, they said, and he didn't have the jump shot needed to play power forward.

Wrong.

To begin with, there's his size. Brand has a 7-2 wing span that allows him to compete against taller players. And, while he might not be the world's greatest jump shooter, he is nearly automatic close to the basket. More importantly, few players can match his unique combination of strength and quickness.

Is it any wonder Krzyzewski can't wait to get his hands on Brand again?

"He's going to be better," Krzyzewski said. "Nobody saw who Elton was last year. He was getting ready to show what he can do when he got hurt. At the end of the year, that was not Elton. He really helped us, but Elton's a better player than that."

If he's a better player than last year, then Brand has got to be rated a national Player of the Year candidate. He could also be the first Dukie to turn pro early, making a choice that players such as Grant Hill and Christian Laettner rejected.

"If it happens, it happens," Krzyzewski said. "I hope he has the kind of year that gives him a chance to make that

1997-98 RESULTS

@Army	78-45
Davidson	100-65
#Chaminade	106-70
#Missouri	82-59
#Arizona	95-87
South Carolina State	98-40
North Carolina-Greensboro	93-37
Virginia	103-59
Villanova	94-66
@Michigan (L)	73-81
Mercer	126-64
Portland State	89-39
@Maryland	104-72
North Carolina State	64-50
@Florida State	75-63
@Wake Forest	88-52
Clemson	81-80
@North Carolina A&T	101-66
@Virginia	72-65
Maryland	86-59
Georgia Tech	90-69
@North Carolina (L)	73-97
@North Carolina State	65-49
Florida State	86-72
Wake Forest	78-47
@Clemson	70-66
UCLA	120-84
@Georgia Tech	76-53
North Carolina	77-75
##Virginia	63-41
##Clemson	66-64
##North Carolina (L)	68-83
%Radford	99-63
%Oklahoma State	79-73
%%Syracuse	80-67
%%Kentucky (L)	84-86

@ away games
# Maui Invitational, Lahaina, HI
ACC Tournament, Greensboro Colisuem, Greensboro, NC
% NCAA South Sub-Regional, Lexington, KY
%% NCAA South Regional, St. Petersburg, FL

decision. That's the kind of thing I hope a kid has an opportunity to decide about."

Barring another injury, it is a decision Brand will almost certainly have to make after this season.

SHANE BATTIER (6-8, 230 lbs., SO, PF, #31, 7.6 ppg, 6.4 rpg, 1.1 apg, 1.5 bpg, 1.4 spg, 24.6 minutes, .539 FG, .731 FT, Detroit Country Day School/ Birmingham, Mich.). It's hard to say whether the newcomer from Michigan was more impressive on the court or off it as a freshman.

Off the court, Battier proved to be a loquacious and thoughtful player—perhaps the best postgame interview in the league. On the court, he proved to be that rarest of all commodities—a ready-made defensive ace. In a poll of the league's nine head coaches, Battier was the third-leading vote getter as the ACC's best defender.

He was also a solid rebounder (second on the team to Brand) and showed a nice scoring touch close to the basket. But Battier was content to play defense, rebound and handle the ball. He rarely looked for his shot.

"I'm not an offensive giant," Battier said. "I do everything else, though. That's what I've grown up doing and that's what I'll continue to do until I step away from the court."

All of which is OK with Krzyzewski.

"He's a joy to coach," Krzyzewski said. "Coaches are prone to say they've never seen somebody do this or that, but I have never seen a freshman play defense like Shane Battier. He's like perpetual motion on the defensive end of the court."

Coming out of high school, Battier found himself compared to both Chris Webber (who also played at Detroit Country Day School) and Grant Hill (another personable, versatile 6-8 player at Duke). But Battier proved he was his own man and not a carbon copy of either predecessor.

Battier gave an early indication of both his toughness and his offensive potential during a Blue-White scrimmage, when he suffered a cut over his eye that required stitches. Battier left the floor for temporary repairs, then returned to nail back-to-back three-pointers.

During the season, Battier's offensive contribution fluctuated. He hit a season-high 18 points in the win at Maryland and finished the year strong with a 14-point, seven rebound effort against Syracuse along with 11 points and eight rebounds against Kentucky.

His defense was far more consistent, and sometimes more spectacular. During one sequence against Maryland, he had blocked a shot, made a steal and drew a charge on successive trips down the floor.

The latter is not surprising; Battier drew a school record 29 charges (23 more than the next-best total on the team). His finest moment came at Clemson, when, with Duke leading by just one in the final minute, Clemson's 6-8, 250-pound Harold Jamison tried to power up a shot in Battier's face. The Duke forward not only blocked Jamison's shot, he cupped the ball in his hand and brought it down as a rebound.

Battier gives Krzyzewski so much flexibility on the floor. He can play the post against the strongest power forwards and he can play the wing against the quickest wing forwards. And he handles the ball well enough that there will be times when he is used as the team's primary ballhander.

If Battier's offensive game ever becomes as consistent as his defense—and his work in the postgame interview room—he'll be one of the nation's best players.

CHRIS CARRAWELL (6-6, 210 lbs., JR, SF, #23, 10.1 ppg, 3.7 rpg, 1.1 apg, 1.5 tpg, 22.2 minutes, .482 FG, .641 FT, Cardinal Ritter HS/St. Louis, Mo.). A year after ending his freshman season as Duke's starting center, Carrawell made a smooth transition to the wing as a sophomore. What's next? Point guard?

Don't put it past the hard-nosed junior from St. Louis, who ranks as Duke's most versatile player and maybe as the Blue Devils' toughest competitor.

"That's just my playground nature," Carrawell said. "On the playground, everything's tough. You've got guys trash-talking to you. You've got guys elbowing you. So, when you get to big time Division I ball, you always remember, 'Hey, this is how I came up.'"

Carrawell is one of the best examples of Krzyzewski's refusal to force his players into predetermined roles. One night he might be a defensive stopper, as he was when he helped limit Maryland's explosive Laron Profit to 14 points—on 2-for-13 shooting—in two meetings last year. Or he might decide to hit the boards as he did at Georgia Tech, when led Duke with 10 rebounds in 21 minutes. Or he might take up some of the offensive slack as he did against North Carolina State, when he hit a pair of crucial three-pointers to keep the stubborn 'Pack at arms length in Cameron.

"I try to be a spark," he said. "I try to give scoring, defense...whatever the team needs."

Krzyzewski liked using Carrawell off the bench last season. He started just 10 games, but scored in double figures 22 times.

Throughout his career, Carrawell has displayed an amazing knack of being in the right place at the right time. Even when not at his best, he is dangerous. He proved that at Clemson.

The Tigers trailed Duke the entire game, but scored to take the lead for the first time with just over a minute left. But while Clemson was still celebrating the moment, Carrawell took the inbounds pass, dribbled through the Tiger press and laid in the go-ahead basket to give Duke a lead it wouldn't relinquish. And, a little over a week later, he scored just a single field goal against North Carolina—but it just happened to be the basket that tied the game after Duke had trailed by as many as 17 points in the second half.

WILLIAM AVERY (6-2, 180 lbs., SO, PG, #5, 8.5 ppg, 2.0 rpg, 2.5 apg, 1.7 tpg, 1.0 spg, 19.3 minutes, .427 FG, .296 3PT, Oak Hill Academy, Va./Augusta, Ga.). Easily the most physically gifted backcourt player Krzyzewski has had at Duke, Avery established himself as Steve Wojciechowski's heir apparent at point guard after averaging just over 19 minutes per game last season as a freshman.

Avery possesses surprising strength and explosive quickness. He has good range on his jumper and, even though he shot under 30 percent from beyond the three-point arc, he hit at least one three-pointer in 20 games. He is also an exceptional penetrator with the ability to finish in traffic or to drive and dish off.

The Georgia-born guard showed his talent early, scoring a season high 21 points in a November victory over defending NCAA champ Arizona. He had nine assists in a victory over South Carolina State and led the team in steals five times.

Perhaps the most memorable freshman moment for Avery came in the final seconds of a tie game with Clemson in the semifinals of the ACC Tournament. The guard took an inbounds pass under the Duke basket with 7.8 seconds left, raced the ball upcourt and launched an off-balance shot that hit the rim and bounded long. But Avery followed his shot, rebounded it on the other side of the basket and put it back in at the buzzer to give Duke a 66-64 win.

As good as he was as a freshman, there were times when Avery appeared out of control. Obviously, his questionable shot selection had much to do with his poor shooting percentage. Still, Krzyzewski was reluctant to reign in his talented young guard—just as he is reluctant to pigeon-hole him as a strict playmaker.

"I don't want to restrict William to think of himself as just a point guard," the Duke coach said. "We haven't had a guard like him in our program. I think he's unique."

Krzyzewski sees Avery as a combo guard, capable of scoring from the wing (he was in double figures 15 times as a freshman) or running the show from the point as he did in the second half of Duke's NCAA victory over Syracuse. The score was tied in that regional semifinal game when Avery took over. On five consecutive trips down the floor, he fed Brand for three buckets inside, set up Battier for a short jumper and drilled a three-pointer of his own.

Defensively, Avery has shown he is able to use his quickness very effectively as an on-the-ball defender. He just needs to improve his performance off the ball to become an exceptional defensive player.

1998-99 DUKE SCHEDULE

Nov.	14	Fairfield
	17	*Davidson
	21	South Carolina State
	26-28	#Great Alaska Shootout
Dec.	2	**Michigan State
	5	North Carolina State
	9	Florida
	12	Michigan
	20	North Carolina A&T
	22	***Kentucky
	30	North Carolina-Greensboro
Jan.	3	@Maryland
	6	Georgia Tech
	10	Virginia
	13	@Wake Forest
	16	Florida State
	20	@Clemson
	24	@St. John's
	27	North Carolina
	30	@North Carolina State
Feb.	3	Maryland
	6	@Georgia Tech
	11	@Virginia
	13	Wake Forest
	17	@Florida State
	20	Clemson
	24	@DePaul
	27	@North Carolina
Mar.	4-7	##ACC Tournament

@ Road Games
* Charlotte Coliseum, Charlotte, NC
** Great Eight, United Center, Chicago, IL
*** Continental Airlines Arena, East Rutherford, NJ
\# Anchorage, AK (vs. Notre Dame, first round; also Alaska-Anchorage, Cincinnati, Fresno State, Iowa State, Southern Utah and Saint Mary's)
\## Charlotte Coliseum, Charlotte, NC

KEY RESERVES

CHRIS BURGESS (6-11, 255 lbs., SO, C, #34, 4.3 ppg, 3.2 rpg, 12.6 minutes, .508 FG, .338 FT, Woodbridge HS/Irvine, Calif.). Under normal circumstances, Burgess had a fairly successful freshman year. He averaged more than 12 minutes per game for a team that was ranked No. 1 much of the season, and he showed off the athletic ability that at one time made him the top rated prospect in his class.

But, in a year in which three freshmen classmates played major roles on the team, Burgess was reduced to the role of supporting player.

Two factors kept Burgess from playing a larger role. First, he didn't quite have the strength to battle the more experienced big men in the ACC. Even more significantly, his painful-to-watch work at the foul line kept him on the bench in virtually all close games.

Burgess hit just 26 of 77 free throws, a shockingly low 33.8 percent. On most occasions, he wasn't even close—alternating bricks and air balls with dismaying regularity.

The problem is hard to understand, especially since Burgess, a 70 percent free throw shooter in high school, is an agile player with nice shooting form on his jumpers. Burgess, believing the problem was above the shoulders, engaged a sports psychologist over the summer and claims to have beaten the problem. He has also spent considerable time in the weight room, bulking up to a solid 255 pounds—20 pounds over last year's playing weight.

If Burgess has indeed conquered both freshman-year difficulties, then he could be a formidable addition to Krzyzewski's arsenal this season. He is extremely adept around the basket, either at the high or low post. Only Brand rebounded or drew free throws at a higher rate last year and only Battier blocked shots more frequently.

Krzyzewski would like the option of using Burgess and Brand together as a post combination. That would allow him to move Battier to the wing, presenting opponents with a huge problem (both literally and figuratively).

TAYMON DOMZALSKI (6-10, 245 lbs, SR, C/F, #13, 3.1 ppg, 2.8 rpg, 9.9 minutes, .567 FG, .571 FT, New Mexico Military Institute/Lovington, N.M.). It's easy to forget that this big, strong New Mexican started and played a significant role for Duke in 1995-96. Domzalski, a freshman forced into the lineup before he was ready, started 18 times that year, averaging 6.5 ppg and 5.0 rpg—solid numbers marred only by a propensity for fouling.

Domzalski never got a chance to build on that promising beginning. Sore knees limited him to a few token appearances as a sophomore, while the addition of more talented big men to the roster forced him into a backup role last season.

But Domzalski is quite a backup, as he proved at midseason when a broken foot sidelined Elton Brand. The quiet junior started eight games and turned in some solid performances, including a 10-rebound outing against Clemson.

While Domzalski isn't a big offensive threat, he is strong and aggressive. He showed a nice shooting touch when he played regularly. He hit 81 percent from the foul line as a freshman.

Heading into his senior year, Domzalski's chances of

contributing probably depend more on the health and performance of Brand and Burgess than on anything he might do. And, while there are quite a few other places (even in the ACC) where Domzalski could transfer and start, he appears content to stay at Duke and get his degree.

Domzalski, who aspires to the medical profession, is an excellent student.

NATE JAMES (6-6, 220 lbs., SO, G/F, #14, 3.5 ppg, 1.5 rpg, 1.0 tpg, 6.8 minutes, .429 FG, .500 3PT, .778 FT, Prospect Hall/Frederick, Md.). The powerfully built swingman played in just six games for Duke last season before electing to sit out the season with a high ankle sprain. He was granted an extra season of eligibility under the NCAA's medical hardship rules.

It was the second year in a row that an untimely injury spoiled James' season. As a freshman, he had just earned a starting job in preseason when he ruptured tendons in his thumb and missed the first 14 games of that campaign.

"He's had more bad luck, injury-wise, than any kid I've coached," Krzyzewski said. "He's been the unluckiest time-wise because, each time he got hurt, he was in the process of making a big move—a move the public never saw."

James responded to his injury last season by becoming a conduit between the coaches and the players. Despite his limited playing time, he is one of the team's most respected and liked players. He could help fill the leadership gap caused by Wojciechowski's departure.

James could also help soften the gap left by Chappell's transfer if he can provide Krzyzewski with another dependable three-point shooter. The son of a career Marine officer has hit seven of 20 three-pointers in his limited duty at Duke, but, as a prep senior, he did win a three-point shooting contest at the McDonald's All-America game.

COREY MAGGETTE (6-6, 210 lbs., FR, G/F, 24.0 ppg, 11.0 rpg, .530 FG, .720 FT, Fenwick HS/Oak Park, Ill.). Ever since Krzyzewski's 1986 Duke team lost the NCAA title game to a Louisville squad loaded with athletic mid-sized players, the Blue Devil coach has prized prospects in that mold. So, meet Corey Maggette, the only member of Krzyzewski's 1998 recruiting class.

"He's as good an athlete as we'll have on the team," Krzyzewski said. "He brings athletic ability and versatility to the table. He can play any of the perimeter spots. He can also bring the ball up the court."

Going into the summer before his senior year at Fenwick High School, Maggette was a contender for the No. 1 ranking in his class. A poor shooting performance at the summer camps cost him that honor, but he still has to rank as one of the nation's top prospects.

"He had a monster senior season," John Quinn, the coach at Fenwick High, said.

Maggette finished second in the Illinois Mr. Basketball voting after leading Fenwick to a 28-3 record. He was voted the Catholic League Player of the Year for the second straight season. Duke waged a bitter recruiting battle with homestate Illinois to land Maggette, winning despite whispers that he'll have a tough time earning playing time for the Blue Devils.

His high school coach doesn't agree.

"He's going to work and try to be a part of their rotation, that's his goal now," Quinn said. "If he can start, fine. If he doesn't, he's going to keep his mouth shut and do what he needs to do to get better."

adidas Blue Ribbon Analysis

GRADING SYSTEM

- A+ equal to very best in country—Final Four-caliber unit
- A among the best in the land—worthy of deep NCAA run
- B+ talented, versatile and experienced—NCAA-NIT ability
- B solid and productive winners—league and post-season contenders
- C+ average to above-average—may contend in a weaker league
- C average to mediocre—second division in a strong league
- D+ below average, inconsistent—second division in a weaker league
- D well below average—losing season virtually certain
- F non-Division I ability—an underdog every night

OTHER RETURNEES

JAY HEAPS (5-9, 150 lbs., SR, G, #22, 0.3 ppg, 0.3 rpg, 1.8 minutes, Longmeadow HS/Longmeadow, Mass.). Heaps, one of the nation's premier soccer players, gave some thought to graduating after the first semester of his senior year. He was reportedly talked into staying by Krzyzewski, who really needs Heaps on the practice floor.

Heaps is an excellent ballhander with good quickness, and he is the only player on the Duke roster capable of giving Avery a true point guard to work against in practice. The fiery little playmaker—best remembered for bouncing UNC point guard Jeff McInnis into the press table two years ago, an act that made him a big favorite with the Cameron Crazies—could also fill in during game situations if Krzyzewski feels he needs another ballhandler.

J.D. SIMPSON (6-4, 200 lbs., SO, G, #30, 0.3 ppg, 1.9 minutes, Woodbridge HS/Irvine, Calif.). A former high school teammate of Chris Burgess, Simpson turned down several scholarship offers from mid-level schools to walk on at Duke. Even though Krzyzewski rates him a Division I player, Simpson is unlikely to see any significant minutes for the Blue Devils, except in practice.

OTHER NEWCOMERS

MATT CHRISTENSEN (6-10, 255 lbs., SO, C, ?HS?/Belmont, Ma.). Three years ago, Christensen entered Duke as part of a two-man recruiting class with Taymon Domzalski. He saw little action as a freshman, then took two years off for a Mormon mission to West Germany.

Christensen has returned, but there is an excellent chance he will be redshirted this season. That's the plan for now, although Krzyzewski wants to take a look at his long-missing big man before making a final determination.

It's anybody's guess how Christensen looks after two years away from the game. As a freshman, he was big and strong with decent hands, but he was painfully slow and had little agility.

He played in 13 games that year, scoring 18 points and pulling down 13 rebounds in 70 total minutes of action. He did have nine blocked shots in that span, which is an exceptional rate.

At the worse, Christensen will provide another big body for practice. Most likely, he'll redshirt this year and then inherit Domzalski's duties as a backup post man.

QUESTIONS

Depth at point guard? Avery is the team's only real point guard, and even Krzyzewski vows that he won't be stuck in that role full-time. Can Duke win the national title with a variety of guys sharing the playmaking role?

Leadership? Wojciechowski set the tone for last year's unselfish team and provided its emotional spark. Can someone else—or a combination of players—fill his leadership role?

Three-point shooting? Langdon is a great perimeter shooter, but who else can hit the three-pointer? Avery seems to have potential, but he shot 29 percent last year from distance. James and Carrawell have good percentages, but neither has hit as many as 15 three-pointers in a season.

ANSWERS

Defense! Duke's defense was fabulous a year ago, when opponents turned the ball over more than 20 times per game and shot just 41.1 percent from the field. With Avery to apply pressure on the ball while defensive stoppers Battier and Carrawell work their magic—plus the presence of shot-blockers Brand and Burgess inside—it's a question how anybody will score against this team.

Fab Four! Elton Brand might be the most talented player Krzyzewski has had at Duke, and that's saying a lot at a school where Grant Hill, Danny Ferry and Christian Laettner have been recent stars. But Brand's two freshmen classmates, Will Avery and Shane Battier, are also very special players. If Chris Burgess progresses as expected, that quartet could turn out to be the greatest single recruiting haul since Michigan's Fab Five.

Krzyzewski! The record says it all; he is simply the best tournament coach in the business. Krzyzewski won't buckle under the pressure of Duke's high expectations. He has been ranked No. 1 before. He has also proved a master at adapting his coaching style to the talent on hand. Even "Coach K" rarely has this much talent and, when he has it, Duke rarely stops short of the Final Four.

adidas Blue Ribbon Analysis

BACKCOURT	**A**	**BENCH/DEPTH**	**A**
FRONTCOURT	**A+**	**INTANGIBLES**	**A**

Duke's victory total has climbed steadily since hitting rock bottom in 1995. The Blue Devils have improved from 13 wins in '95 to 18 wins to 24 wins to 32 victories last year.

There should be one more season of improvement.

True, the Blue Devils lost a talented scorer in Roshown McLeod as well as the team's emotional heart in Steve Wojciechowski. But the core of this team, even last year, was and is the talented quartet of players Krzyzewski brought in before the 1997-98 campaign.

Duke has never had a player like Elton Brand, a frontcourt performer with the raw talent to physically dominate anyone he matches up against. And classmates Will Avery and Shane Battier are good enough in their own right to be stars. Chris Burgess hasn't proven he's in that class yet, but he had moments as a freshman which demonstrated why he was once rated the top prospect in the country. And the off-season talk is that Burgess is the most improved player on the team.

That's scary.

If Burgess has stepped up his game, it gives Krzyzewski a wealth of options. He can played Brand and Burgess together, sliding the 6-8 Battier to the wing. With Carrawell and Maggette in the backcourt, that would be a *huge* team. Or he can play Battier at power forward, slide Carrawell in at small forward and, with Avery at the point, field one of the nation's quickest squads.

While Brand is clearly going to be the "go-to" guy, the key to the team would seem to be Avery, the team's only real point guard. Krzyzewski refuses to acknowledge that as a problem, suggesting he can use lineups featuring Langdon, Carrawell and/or Maggette as primary ballhandlers. Before dismissing that idea, remember Krzyzewski's '94 team that used forward Grant Hill as the primary ballhandler; or the '88 and '89 Final Four teams that often put the ball in the hands of forwards Billy King and Danny Ferry.

The real area to watch as the season develops is how well this team plays in the halfcourt. That was the fatal flaw last year. The '97-'98 Blue Devils played superb defense and were the nation's best in a quick, up-tempo game. But it was the only way that team knew how to play and, as a result, it occasionally had trouble holding a lead late in the game—a weakness Kentucky was able to exploit in the Southeast Regional championship game.

That defeat marked the first time Krzyzewski's Blue Devils have lost a regional final—after seven straight victories. In another year, it might have been a crushing disappointment to fall short of the Final Four with a team as good as the Blue Devils were last season. But, coming as it was after three frustrating years with no postseason success, the near-miss was taken as a learning experience, another step on Duke's march back to college basketball prominence.

There will be no such understanding this year. Duke has the talent and now the experience to challenge for the national championship. The Blue Devils have, in Krzyzewski, a coach used to maximizing his team's assets in postseason play.

This will not be a year for near misses or good tries. This is a team that will start the season aiming at the 1999 national championship. Anything less would be a disappointment.

(A.F.)

2

CONNECTICUT

LOCATION .... Storrs, CT
CONFERENCE .... Big East
LAST SEASON .... 32-5 (.865)
CONFERENCE RECORD .... 15-3 (1st, Big East 6)
STARTERS LOST/RETURNING 0/5
NICKNAME .... Huskies
COLORS .... Blue & White
HOMECOURTS .... Gampel Pavilion (8,241)
.... Hartford Civic Center (16,294)
COACH ... Jim Calhoun (American International '68)
RECORD AT SCHOOL .... 272-119 (12 yrs.)
CAREER RECORD .... 522-255 (26 yrs.)
ASSISTANTS .... Dave Leitao (Northeastern '83)
Karl Hobbs (Connecticut '85)
Tom Moore (Boston University '87)
TEAM WINS (last 5 yrs.) 29-28-32-18-32
RPI (last 5 yrs.) 13-8-5-65-4
1997-98 FINISH .... Lost in NCAA Final Eight.

COACH AND PROGRAM

It's time, don't you think? After 12 years of building the Big East's best program (don't even try to tell us about Syracuse), Jim Calhoun deserves a Final Four.

Deserves not to have Christian Laettner make a miracle shot in 1990. Deserves better free throw shooting from Donyell Marshall. Deserves not to worry about the draw, like he did in '95 when the Huskies were stuck in the West Region with eventual champion UCLA, the only team capable of running with UConn that year.

Calhoun deserves not to worry about playing North Carolina in Greensboro, as he had to last March. He deserves the opportunity to torture writers from other parts of the country during the endless pre-Final Four press conferences, using his gatling-gun New England delivery and sometimes-unintelligible way of mashing six or eight words into one, giant syllable sandwich.

This, at last, should be the year. The Huskies have the talent, depth, size and experience to be in St. Petersburg in March, playing for all the marbles and giving Big East fans something to cheer about.

Don't mistake this as some sort of sappy plea for justice and good fortune for Calhoun. He doesn't want it, and we don't want to make the case on his behalf. But there are times in sports when destiny seems to take over, and 1998-99 seems like a perfect time for Connecticut to be playing—and even winning—during the last weekend of the season. This may well be Calhoun's best team, top-to-bottom, and that's saying a lot.

It scares us to think what would have happened had Ajou Ajou Deng, the 6-10 freshman frontcourt marvel who did not qualify, made the grade. Connecticut could have had too much talent, if there is such a thing.

Even without Deng, there is more than enough in Storrs to reach the ultimate goal. The question is, can UConn do it? Now that the Huskies have made it to so many regional finals without success, there is a tendency to wonder whether or not Calhoun can get a team over the hump.

Jim Boeheim endured a career's worth of criticism from 1987 to 1996, before taking an overachieving Syracuse team to the national final against Kentucky. Calhoun may have had some bad luck and rough finishes over the years, but the name of the game in college basketball is winning. And winning big.

You can be the only guy ever to win 250 games at two different schools—which Calhoun is—but that doesn't matter to a lot of fans. Everybody wants the rings. And Calhoun doesn't have one.

"I don't know if there is a big difference between getting to the Final Eight and the Final Four," Calhoun says. "But I do know this: We're not going to take any shortcuts to do it.

"I look at things from a long-term view. We've done well for 10 years here, and we're going to continue to do it. If we do that, we'll get to the Final Four, when we're expected to or not expected to."

This year, nearly everybody will expect the Huskies to do so, at least until the playing starts in earnest. In a season where it's tough to find more than a handful of chalk Final Four contenders, the Huskies stand out—along with Duke and Stanford—as full-fledged Florida candidates (try saying that 10 times fast).

Their backcourt, which includes mouthy sophomore point man Khalid El-Amin, smooth senior Ricky Moore and promising role players Rashamel Jones and Albert Mouring, is outstanding. Their frontcourt boasts burly center Jake Voskuhl, one of the country's better interior defenders, strong forward Kevin Freeman, condor-like pivot Souleymane Wane and newcomers Justin Brown and Beau Archibald.

In between is the best of the bunch, 1998 Big East Player of the Year Rip Hamilton, who surrendered an early shot at the pros to gain weight, improve his game, break some school records and maybe win a national championship. But then he went and broke his foot trying out for the USA Basketball World Championship team, and the entire Constitution State panicked.

Not to worry. Although the injury did prohibit Hamilton from working out as hard as he might have during the off-season, it won't prevent him from practicing—or coming off 62 screens every time downcourt and burying yet another feathery jumper.

Calhoun has always liked to play the up-tempo, run-and-gun game. And this year's collection of versatile athletes should give him even better lineup flexibility than he had in 1994-95, which was probably his swiftest, most effective team to date. He has two and even three players at all five positions, something that should foster tremendous practice competition and allow UConn to hit opponents with an array of looks.

The Huskies could go husky, with Wane and Voskuhl down low and Freeman playing small forward. They could go super quick, orbiting Hamilton and a trio of guards around the big men. And there is the popular "everything in-between" option.

"We have Wane and Voskuhl, two 6-11 kids, and Brown, a seven-footer, down low," Calhoun says. "We have Freeman and (soph Edmund) Saunders at the 'four.' Hamilton and Archibald can play the 'three.' Mouring and Jones are (shooting) guards, and Moore and El-Amin play the point. We have some options."

Thanks for clearing that up, coach. Calhoun has options like Bill Clinton has secrets. Like Shawn Kemp has Father's Day cards. Like...well, you get the picture. Now, he has to put it together.

Last year, although Calhoun was none too happy about playing Carolina on the Heels' ersatz homecourt, he had to know it wasn't Connecticut's time. The Huskies were a year removed from an NIT Final Four run and lacked the savvy and experience to win big. Still, even though they were the Big East's youngest team, they posted the best record in league play (15-3) and ran away with the conference tournament.

Now it's time for the next step. Unless Hamilton is unable to go, thereby robbing the Huskies of much-needed star power, Connecticut is loaded and ready. El-Amin has a chance to be one of the best players in the country. Voskuhl and Wane are the perfect big men for the UConn system, and the newcomers give Connecticut exactly what they need—outside shooting (Archibald), inside pop (Saunders) and more depth in the middle (Brown).

If Calhoun does get to the Final Four this year, he won't be doing so as an underdog. The Huskies have so much potential, everybody may forget about all their near-misses, ignore the great story line about how Calhoun finally got to the promised land and just get on with looking at Connecticut as another college basketball giant that doesn't deserve any pity

That wouldn't be so bad, either. Neither would a national championship.

STARTERS NOT RETURNING

None.

OTHERS NOT RETURNING

MONQUENCIO HARDNETT (6-4, G, 5.4 ppg, 2.7 rpg, 1.5 apg, 16.2 minutes, .419 FG, .258 3PT, .675 FT). Hardnett spent just two years at Connecticut after transferring from Middle Georgia JC, and he never fully reached his scoring potential.

Calhoun had hoped the guard would turn into an off-the- bench scoring force last year. Although Hardnett flashed some glimpses of that skill, he never did so consistently. He scored in double figures six times last year, with a pair of 14-point outbursts (vs. Stanford and St. John's). But Hardnett didn't shoot well from the field and was particularly weak from the outside.

By season's end, he was losing minutes and barely played in the NCAA Tournament. Thanks to an arcane NCAA rule, Hardnett did get a chance to showcase his skills as part of the Connecticut team which played a six-game tour of England and Israel during the summer.

His place should be taken this season by Mouring and Archibald.

JEFF CYBART (6-6, F, 0.0 ppg, 0.3 rpg, nine appearances). A walkon who saw action in nine games last year but averaged just a fraction over one minute per game, Cybart pulled down three rebounds and missed all three of his field goal attempts.

SAM FUNCHES (6-9, F, 0.3 ppg, 0.8 rpg, six appearances). Funches played in only six games last year and left the program because of lack of playing time. A willowy forward with a solid shooting touch to 15 feet, Funches will sit out the first term at Southwest Texas State before becoming eligible around holiday time.

PROJECTED STARTERS

RICHARD HAMILTON (6-6, 180 lbs., JR, SF, #32, 21.5 ppg, 4.4 rpg, 2.4 apg, 2.3 tpg, 1.5 spg, 32.5 minutes, .440 FG, .404 3PT, .843 FT, Coatesville HS/Coatesville, Pa.). Last season's Big East Player of the Year was expected to be among the top five players in the nation until he broke the fifth metatarsal bone in his right foot July 8 at the Team USA training camp in Chicago. Although he was expected to be ready for the start of practice, there's no telling when he'll be back to his machine-gunning self.

The fifth metatarsal, which Duke center Elton Brand

1997-98 RESULTS

*Yale	88-57
#Boston University	68-54
#Rhode Island	80-67
*Coppin State	72-50
##Florida State (L)	60-67
##Arizona State	82-61
West Virginia	88-75
@Rutgers	59-44
@Virginia	74-63
*North Carolina-Wilmington	93-55
*Massachusetts	72-55
*Hartford	100-69
*Fairfield	90-63
*Notre Dame	84-58
@Miami (L)	67-76
@Boston College	80-68
*Seton Hall	80-59
*Georgetown	86-72
@St. John's (L)	62-64
@Syracuse	63-54
@Providence	63-56
Rutgers	73-56
*Villanova	80-65
Stanford	76-56
@West Virginia (L)	62-80
*Pittsburgh	92-67
@Notre Dame	88-79
@Villanova	83-76
*Providence	77-68
St. John's	87-58
###Providence	64-55
###Rutgers	64-50
###Syracuse	69-64
%Fairleigh Dickinson	93-85
%Indiana	78-68
%%Washington	75-74
%%North Carolina (L)	64-75

@ away games
* Hartford Civic Center, Hartford, CT
\# Chase NIT, campus sites
\## Chase NIT, Madison Square Garden, NY
\### Big East Tournament, Madison Square Garden, NY
% NCAA East Sub-Regional, Washington, DC
%% NCAA East Regional, Greensboro, NC

also fractured last December, serves as a shock absorber of sorts for the body. Because it sits on the outside of the foot, it receives continued pressure, particularly from somebody who cuts and plants as much as a shooting guard.

In fact, Hamilton believes the Chicago incident wasn't the alpha and omega of the injury. He had been feeling some discomfort in the area before that time, but tried to play through it.

Now, he's rehabbing the injury and hoping to return to the form that made him one of the nation's most dangerous scorers. Although Hamilton went through something of a shooting slump late in 1997-98, he did make the last-second shot that defeated Washington in the Sweet 16 and was a consistently big producer all year.

Hamilton started the year in fine fashion, ripping Boston University for 29 points in game two and he hit Virginia for 33 in early December. His most productive stretch came just after Christmas, when he scored 127 points in four games—including a season-high 38 at Boston College.

Hamilton is perfect for Connecticut's offensive system. He runs the floor well and is adroit at slamming his defender into the never ending series of bone-crunching screens set by Voskuhl, Freeman and company.

The first Huskie to be named conference Player of the Year as a sophomore and only the third in league history to receive the honor (John Bagley and Chris Mullin were the others), Hamilton led the Big East in three-point shooting percentage, free throw percentage and three-point shots made. He became the fastest UConn player to reach 1,000 points and could threaten 2,000 with a big year this season.

Few realize, however, that Hamilton began last year with an injury problem, too. He was kneed in the thigh during preseason drills and took more than two months to recover completely. In fact, Calhoun reports Hamilton lost 12 pounds from his lithe frame during last season. Even that didn't stop him from being a dominant scorer.

"He has an extraordinary basketball IQ," Calhoun says. "He's not just a scorer. He's a player. He can show even more than he has."

RICKY MOORE (6-2, 195 lbs., SR, SG, #21, 7.5 ppg, 3.1 rpg, 3.5 apg, 1.4 tpg, 1.6 spg, 30.3 minutes, .441 FG, .333 3PT, .729 FT, Westside HS/Augusta, Ga.). The arrival of El-Amin pushed Moore out of the spotlight a little, but those who paid attention realized the former point man had a great year nonetheless—distributing the ball, playing his trademark sticky defense and providing a stable counterpart to El-Amin's brashness.

Moore still isn't the most accomplished shooter around, but he can move with the ball, jumps extremely well and plays the kind of predatory defense Calhoun loves. And Moore is still going to have games in which he gets his.

He smoked Notre Dame for 20 points in mid-February, had 18 against St. John's and scored 14 in Connecticut's first-round NCAA win over Fairleigh-Dickinson. If Moore can improve his long-range shooting, he'll be a great collegiate guard.

He protects the ball (only 52 turnovers in 1,122 minutes) and can distribute. He and El-Amin form one of the country's top backcourt tandems.

KHALID EL-AMIN (5-10, 200 lbs., SO, PG, #42, 16.0 ppg, 2.9 rpg, 4.2 apg, 2.7 tpg, 1.8 spg, 29.9 minutes, .424 FG, .365 3PT, .796 FT, North HS/Minneapolis, Minn.). El-Amin sure didn't move quietly into the world of college basketball. He came in firing, both with his hands and his mouth. The cocky freshman told everybody how good he would be and then delivered, finishing second to Hamilton on the team in scoring, leading Connecticut in assists and generally giving the Huskies a much-needed dose of high-octane confidence.

El-Amin showed he could make big shots. He ran the team. He played defense. He created for others. And he did something rare, taking over a top-flight program that had plenty of returning players.

By the time the tourney rolled around, he was the team's spokesman. Of course, it wasn't as if anybody else could get a word in edgewise.

El-Amin may look like a bearded Buddha, what with his burly physique, but Calhoun assures us that this is not some fat kid running his show. And he forecasts big things for El-Amin.

"With a little more time, he'll be able to jump in there and make major contributions at the NBA level," Calhoun says. "At the end of last year, he had only nine percent body fat. He's a very powerful guy. He looks like a fullback, and he is a fireplug. People think he's chunky, but he was playing 37 minutes a game at the end of the year. So it wasn't like he was out of shape.

"He has the air of an older player, but he's just a kid who likes to compete so much. He's a guy who can turn it up when the game's on the line."

El-Amin didn't waste much time establishing himself last year, scoring 23 points in the Huskies' season-opening win over Yale. He scored 30 points against Notre Dame later in the year and hit for 29 on four different occasions. Against North Carolina in the East Regional final, El-Amin led all UConn scorers with 24 points.

He has excellent shooting range, a deceptively quick first step and can play physical defense. He quarterbacked the gold medal-winning Goodwill Games team this summer and should be among the top backcourt performers in the nation this year.

KEVIN FREEMAN (6-7, 226 lbs., JR, PF, #15, 10.3 ppg, 6.6 rpg, 1.5 tpg, 29.5 minutes, .569 FG, .697 FT, Paterson Catholic HS, N.J./Springfield, Ma.). After watching Freeman play during Connecticut's six-game tour of England and Israel this past summer, Calhoun is no doubt thrilled the forward didn't follow through on any ideas—however preliminary they may have been—about transferring to Massachusetts, Virginia or any other school.

Freeman, who wants to become more of a small forward this year, showed he could put the ball on the floor and produce beyond the lane against the British and Israeli pro opposition. He led the Huskies (Hamilton didn't play, due to his injury) with 15.5 ppg, 7.5 rpg and a glittering .667 field goal percentage. He even made 70 percent of his free throws, which is something considering he made just 59.7 percent as a freshman.

Freeman, who goes 6-7, wants to make himself more attractive to the NBA, so he wants to play more on the wing. He was afraid he wouldn't get that opportunity this year. But, with Brown and Saunders joining the front line, there may be some room for him at the small forward spot.

"Kevin is a warrior for us," Calhoun says. "He wants to give us a different look at the 'four' spot and play a little like Donny Marshall did. During the off-season, he just wanted to know where I saw him in the future."

If Calhoun is smart, it's on the court as often as possible. Freeman can rebound, bang inside and, if he continues to improve from the wing, could be a devastating weapon thanks to his strength. He had four double-doubles last year, including a 21-point, 13-rebound performance against Georgetown.

JAKE VOSKUHL (6-11, 235 lbs., JR, C, #43, 6.9 ppg, 7.1 rpg, 1.8 tpg, 1.3 bpg, 23.7 minutes, .565 FG, .675 FT, Strake Jesuit HS/Katy, Tex.). Voskuhl would appear to be right on track along the traditional Huskie pivot timeline. Calhoun is famous for bringing in big men who need a full four years to germinate, and Voskuhl enters the third year of his process making nice progress indeed.

He remains one of the top interior defenders around, but his offensive and rebounding numbers are beginning to swell. Voskuhl tied for eighth among conference board men last year with and was even more impressive (8.4 rpg) during league play. Voskuhl had 11 double-figure rebound games last year and posted five double-doubles, including a 17-point, 15-board performance in a January win over Seton Hall.

But Voskuhl remains reticent with the ball. He took only 177 shots last year and rarely demanded the rock in the pivot. He seems more content to set screens, pass the ball and concentrate on his defense.

He more of the same overseas. Voskuhl took only 22 shots in six games, but he did team with Wane to give the Huskies a solid pivot tandem. Look for him to split time with Wane again this year, since the two may not work all that well together in Calhoun's up-tempo system.

Voskuhl still has two years of growth remaining, just about right for a Connecticut center, and he should be more productive than ever this year, even if that doesn't mean an explosion of shots.

1998-99 CONNECTICUT SCHEDULE

Nov.	15	Quinnipiac
	19	Richmond
	24	*Hartford
	27	*Wagner
Dec.	1	#Washington
	5	Michigan State
	9	@Massachusetts
	12	@Pittsburgh
	23	*Fairfield
	30	*Villanova
Jan.	2	Georgetown
	6	@Boston College
	9	@West Virginia
	12	*Notre Dame
	16	*Pittsburgh
	20	@Miami (Fla.)
	23	Seton Hall
	25	@Georgetown
	30	@St. John's
Feb.	1	*Syracuse
	6	@Stanford
	10	*Boston College
	13	@Seton Hall
	16	Rutgers
	20	Miami (Fla.)
	22	@Providence
	28	@Syracuse
Mar.	3-6	##Big East Tournament

@ Road Games
* Hartford Civic Center, Hartford, CT
# Great Eight, Chicago, IL
Madison Square Garden, NY

KEY RESERVES

RASHAMEL JONES (6-5, 205 lbs., SR, G/F, #3, 4.4 ppg, 2.7 rpg, 1.2 tpg, 14.3 minutes, .424 FG, .233 3PT, .610 FT, 0.8 spg, Trinity Catholic HS, Conn./Port Chester, N.Y.). The arrivals—and subsequent emergence—of Hamilton and El-Amin have pushed Jones further away from the spotlight, but that doesn't mean Calhoun isn't still fond of the swingman.

Anybody who watched Jones on the summer overseas tour knows why. He was third on the team with 12.7 ppg and showed a renewed ability to score from the elbow on in. Jones will never dazzle anybody with his outside shooting acumen, but he can produce off the dribble and, in the Connecticut scheme, that's just fine.

If Jones averages more than 20 minutes per game, that would be surprising. But he'll play a big role. And, as he showed during six double-figure games last year—including a 17-point outburst against Syracuse in the Big East tourney final—he can be quite productive.

ANTRIC KLAIBER (6-10, 215 lbs., SR, F/C, #22, 3.0 ppg, 2.7 rpg, 1.3 tpg, 13.5 minutes, .576 FG, .704 FT, Episcopal HS, Va./Silver Spring, Md.). The arrival of Brown and Saunders' recent eligibility are bad news for Klaiber, a skilled big man without the heft to make significant contributions inside.

Although he has the ability to handle, pass pretty well, shoot with some range and block the occasional shot, Klaiber is something of a positional defensive liability, since he lacks much strength. He didn't see all that much time on the overseas tour (9.7 minutes per game) and will need to make significant strides to get any more than that this year on what could be the nation's deepest team.

Klaiber did have a couple of fine moments last year, like his eight-point, eight-board outburst against Notre Dame, or his eight points and six rebounds against Hartford and Seton Hall. But Klaiber was largely invisible during the Big East season and needs to live with the weights if he wants to become more than a role player in his final year.

SOULEYMANE WANE (6-11, 235 lbs., JR, C/F, #33, 1.9 ppg, 3.8 rpg, 1.1 bpg, 11.8 minutes, .382 FG, .545 FT, Redemption Christian Academy, N.Y./Dakar, Senegal). Don't let last year's stats fool you. Wane is ready to make an impact for the Huskies. A big impact. One need only look at how he handled 21 minutes per game overseas. He was second on Connecticut in rebounding with 6.3 rpg and made 66.7 percent of his field goal attempts.

"Souleymane is coming on like crazy," Calhoun says of Wane, who spent the summer with the Senagalese national team. "He has a 7-7 reach and is going to be a good player."

Wane can move, has the ability to hit the boards (he had 11 rebounds against Notre Dame last year) and can be an imposing defensive presence. He'll team with Voskuhl this year in a solid pivot combination, and it should be interesting to see how well the two play together when they get the chance.

EDMUND SAUNDERS (6-8, 220 lbs., SO, F, #51, 29.9 ppg, 12.0 rpg, Holy Cross HS/Waterbury, Conn.). Finally eligible after spending a year as a partial qualifier, Saunders fortifies the UConn frontcourt with his strength and ability to hit the boards. But Saunders isn't one-dimensional. He scored 2,087 points during his prep career and should provide a strong enough presence at the power forward spot to let Freeman take some turns on the wing.

Although it should take Saunders some time to shake off the rust, he is expected to give the Huskies more depth and versatility up front. A strong interior defender, Saunders is physically mature and should be capable of handling any rough stuff he encounters in the Big East.

BEAU ARCHIBALD (6-6, 210 lbs., JR, F, #5, 10.8 ppg, 4.2 rpg, 4.7 apg, Utah Valley State College, Washington State & Timpview HS/Provo, Ut). The Archibald story is an interesting—and sad—one. Connecticut will be the third stop on a collegiate journey which began at Washington State and continued on to Utah Valley State College.

Archibald's father, Lynn, was a former Brigham Young assistant who died in June, 1997, following a long bout with prostate cancer. While still mourning his father, Archibald was forced to undergo surgery on both knees while at Utah Valley State due to patellar tendonitis. Though he was expected to be fine by the time practice started, the Huskies hope the repair work won't rob Archibald of his lively leaping and prohibit him from getting the necessary spring on his long-range jumper.

If healthy, Archibald will be quite a weapon. He jumps like a kangaroo, passes like, well, a coach's son and can hit the three. At Washington State, he scored 6.1 ppg in 14.3 minutes per game while making 36.4 percent of his treys. He looked strong at Utah Valley State (nine games) before going under the knife.

Archibald will swing between the two wing positions at UConn and will no doubt stretch defenses.

OTHER RETURNEES

ALBERT MOURING (6-3, 175 lbs., SO, G, #23, 1.1 ppg, 0.3 rpg, 15 appearances, Colonel Richardson HS/Preston, Md.). Even though Mouring showed during the England/Israel tour that he can shoot from long range and surprised some with his quick leaping ability on the offensive boards, it's unlikely he'll see an abundance of time in the crowded Connecticut backcourt this year.

Mouring did not become eligible until the second semester of last season and took a while to get acclimated to the Huskie system and the Big East game. He registered his season high with four points against Pittsburgh in mid-February.

Mouring is athletic and plays solid defense, but could use a little more meat on his body.

E.J. HARRISON (6-1, 170 lbs., SR, G, #40, 1.3 ppg, 0.6 rpg, 18 appearances, .421 FG, .333 3PT, .625 FT, Danbury HS/Danbury, Conn.). A valuable practice player, Harrison is a walkon who sees time usually when the game is out of hand. Fortunately for him, that is quite often in Storrs.

Harrison's finest hour last year came against Fairfield, when he scored nine points, good for third on the team stat sheet that night. He also pulled down three boards against the Stags.

OTHER NEWCOMERS

JUSTIN BROWN (7-0, 215 lbs., FR, C, #20, 12.0 ppg, 10.0 rpg, Australian Institute of Sports/Perth, Australia). A member of the Australian junior national team and an alumnus of the same program which produced Chicago Bulls center Luc Longley, Brown is a skilled player with a good shooting touch who should develop into a major contributor at Connecticut—over time.

Brown needs to improve his strength and adapt to the American game, something he should do during practice battles with Voskuhl and Wane. Expect him to show flashes of talent at some moments and struggle at others.

Like other Huskie pivots, he is a project—but one with potential.

QUESTIONS

Health? The Huskies are deep, but injuries to Hamilton and Archibald could hurt them early on. Although Connecticut should be fine in time for Big East play, Calhoun welcomes the opportunity to blend his roster into an efficient rotation.

Frontcourt? Yes, we know Voskuhl is making improvement and Wane has potential. Saunders could be a real enforcer, too, and Brown is a promising newcomer. But, other than Freeman, this team lacks a proven, big-time power guy capable of producing every night.

History? The Huskies have made it to the threshold before, only to be denied entry. This team has the potential to make the Final Four and more, but so have some of its ancestors. Can UConn do it?

ANSWERS

Depth! Few teams in the country have as much talent among their top 10 or 11 players. Connecticut has enough answers at every position and enough mix-and-match performers to give Calhoun limitless lineup options.

Hamilton! If the Ripper's foot heals properly, he'll return to his previous spot as the Big East's most dangerous player and challenge for a pile of national honors. A deadly shooter with a great all-around game, Hamilton is a true star.

El-Amin! Don't believe this one? Well, just ask Khalid. He'll tell you. The soph is a true leader, a pressure performer, a great shooter, tenacious defender and fine distributor. He may be a second-year player, but El-Amin plays like a grizzled vet.

Freeman! He may be the third star on this club, but Freeman could well be poised for a breakout year. He showed increased versatility overseas and will give opponents fits.

adidas Blue Ribbon Analysis

BACKCOURT	A	BENCH/DEPTH	A
FRONTCOURT	B+	INTANGIBLES	A

This is one of the nation's best teams, pure and simple. The Huskies have a dominant player in Hamilton, a deep and explosive backcourt and plenty of promise up front. What else is there?

Well, a Final Four appearance, and that is exactly what UConn is after this year. The Huskies must get improvement from their frontcourt, and the young guys who have played so well the last year or two must grow into veteran producers, capable of beating anybody anywhere. But that should happen.

Hamilton's foot is a concern, particularly if it is slow to heal. He'll need time to get back in game shape and add some muscle to his skinny frame. If he isn't full speed until January (or later), the Huskies may lose a spot in the seeding derby, and that could be a problem. El-Amin shouldn't have any trouble with the sophomore jinx, but one can never tell. If his shot goes south, defenses will spend even more time concentrating on Hamilton.

The newcomers are intriguing. Don't expect too much out of Brown right away, but Archibald will provide some needed bench scoring pop and Saunders should be ferocious inside.

And don't forget about Moore and Jones, the team elders. Each will need to be productive and demonstrate leadership this year if the Huskies are to reach their ultimate goal.

See you in St. Petersburg, Jim.

(M.B.)

3

STANFORD

LOCATION	Stanford, CA
CONFERENCE	Pacific-10
LAST SEASON	30-5 (.857)
CONFERENCE RECORD	15-3 (2nd)
STARTERS LOST/RETURNING	0/5
NICKNAME	Cardinal
COLOR	Cardinal & White
HOMECOURT	Maples Pavilion (7,500)
COACH	Mike Montgomery (Long Beach State '68)
RECORD AT SCHOOL	235-132 (12 yrs.)
CAREER RECORD	389-209 (20 yrs.)
ASSISTANTS	Trent Johnson (Boise State '80)
	Eric Reveno (Stanford '89)
	Blaine Taylor (Montana '82)
TEAM WINS (last 5 yrs.)	27-22-20-22-30
RPI (last 5 yrs.)	68-41-36-19-6
1997-98 FINISH	Lost in NCAA Final Four.

COACH AND PROGRAM

This was not "Mission Impossible," because it had happened once before. Of course, that was in 1942, the college basketball equivalent of the Paleozoic era.

Stanford in the Final Four...

It is a collection of words not assembled in that particular order since before the end of World War II. Heck, since before the Final Four was called the Final Four.

This was a fool's dream, a cruel joke, somebody else's destiny. Arch-rival California was supposed to return to the Final Four before Stanford did. William and Mary (along with three other guys!) had just as good a chance.

But there they were last spring in San Antonio—Art Lee, Mark Madsen, Tim Young and Co.—playing Kentucky in the national semifinals. And giving the Wildcats all they wanted.

"I *love* that team," Kentucky's Heshimu Evans said after the Wildcats escaped with an 86-85 overtime victory on the way to their second crown in three years.

"Oh, they'll definitely be in the top five next year," Kentucky forward Allen Edwards said in that same post-game locker room. "I wouldn't be surprised if they make it back to this next year."

Perhaps, but a larger question is worth addressing: How did Stanford get there in the first place?

Consider the state of the Stanford program before Mike Montgomery arrived as coach for the 1986-87 campaign. In 12 previous seasons, the Cardinal had won 138 games. Montgomery already has 235 victories in his 12-year run at the school.

Stanford had enjoyed just two winning seasons in the past 20 years before Montgomery changed addresses from Montana. The Cardinal has now had winning seasons 11 times in 12 years under Montgomery, including an ongoing run of four straight 20-victory campaigns.

"It was dismal," said Montgomery, recalling the state of the program when he took over. "I thought to myself, 'Wow, this is something.' I mean, it was scary."

"Somebody had to do something," the coach added.

That "somebody" was the Stanford Class of '89, featuring guard Todd Lichti and forward Howard Wright. Those players, recruited by Tom Davis but molded their final three seasons by Montgomery, reached the NCAA Tournament as seniors. It was the school's first return trip to the event in 47 years; in fact, since winning the national crown in '42.

Lichti, who went on to become a first-round NBA draft pick, brought a new attitude to the program.

"He was the most confident freshman I've ever seen come through Stanford," said Eric Reveno, a center in the Class of '89 and now an assistant coach.

"He had so much ability and such a (winning) mentality," said ex-teammate Earl Koberlain, now the director of intercollegiate sports at Stanford. "It was a conscious acknowledgment that, if we were down at crunch time, we were going to Todd."

Lichti, who now plays pro ball in Australia, is proud of his contribution to what Stanford basketball has become.

"You feel like you were sort of the start of it," he said. "A lot of us in that class do feel like we got the ball rolling. We showed other players considering Stanford that it could be done."

In the years since the 26-7 breakthrough of '89, everything has changed. Recruiting has picked up, once docile Maples Pavilion has been transformed into one of the Pac-10's most daunting home arenas—with its loud and obnoxious 750-student "Sixth Man Club"—and expectations have undergone a complete metamorphosis.

Reveno said Montgomery deserves much of the credit.

"Coach Montgomery's style is one that's very well-suited for Stanford: very consistent, very hard-working, very level-headed...a cerebral approach. It's one of sort of maximizing opportunities and minimizing mistakes. It's fit well."

Indeed, better than virtually anyone imagined. And there is no end in sight for projected success on "The Farm." Montgomery, who dug in at Stanford in the early 1990s when he turned down a chance to move to Virginia, isn't going anywhere. He has got virtually his entire team back, too, for what should be an intriguing encore season.

The Cardinal returns players who accounted for 95 percent of the team's scoring and rebounding a year ago. Gone are players who contributed just 12 minutes and one point to the club's five NCAA Tournament games.

Without much question, Stanford should be better than it was a year ago. But what does that mean?

Another 18-0 start? Doubtful. A return trip to the Final Four? Tricky.

"In all likelihood, we will be better than last year," said Montgomery, a man not prone to giving rosy forecasts. "But that doesn't necessarily translate to having a better record."

The key for Stanford will be continuing to compete and improve against a backdrop of altered expectations.

"How the kids deal with it (will be important)," Montgomery said. "The bottom line, other than the fact that we had good players, (is that) last year we were fairly unselfish. Different kids were stepping up in different situations.

"If the mentality changes at all, if guys think, 'I can do this,' if any of that creeps in, it's going to be much more difficult to win because we still don't have a dominant player."

True, but the Cardinal has five solid starters, great size, a deep bench and a coach the equal of any in the country. Stanford also has something it's never enjoyed before: The realization that winning at the highest level is possible.

STARTERS NOT RETURNING

None.

OTHERS NOT RETURNING

PETE VAN ELSWYK (6-9, F, 3.5 ppg, 3.1 rpg, 11.5 minutes, .430 FG). A transfer from South Carolina three years ago, Van Elswyk started 11 games last season but gradually became lost in the shuffle of Stanford's deep frontcourt rotation. The sturdy redhead twice had double-figure rebound games, including 12 early in the Pac-10 season against Southern California. But he never was a big scoring threat.

Van Elswyk played just 11 minutes total in the Cardinal's five postseason games.

KAMBA TSHIONYI (6-2, G, 1.7 ppg, 0.9 rpg, 1.3 apg, 7.7 minutes, .783 FT). A former walkon, Tshionyi was more valuable to the Cardinal as a junior when he gave the team's backcourt some experience off the bench. Last year, as young players developed, Tshionyi's role diminished. He played just one minute in five NCAA Tournament games.

PROJECTED STARTERS

ARTHUR LEE (6-0, 175 lbs., SR, PG, #11, 14.5 ppg, 2.3 rpg, 4.6 apg, 1.1 spg, 28.7 minutes, .428 FG, .443 3PT, .887 FT, North Hollywood HS/Los Angeles, Calif.). Lee spent all of last season trying to answer a most unfair question. Ultimately, his actions spoke much louder than any verbal response he could have given.

The new Brevin Knight? Nope. Simply Art Lee, and that was more than enough.

"They asked him the whole year; it never went away," Montgomery said of the ceaseless comparisons to his All-America predecessor at point guard. "It wasn't fair and there wasn't anything he could do about it. I thought he showed a great deal of patience dealing with the same questions over and over again."

Lee didn't even earn All-Conference honors, but he was the team's most critical player at the end of the season. A year after splitting his time as a backup to both Knight and at the shooting guard spot, Lee became the team's driving force in the NCAA Tournament.

He averaged 20.6 ppg and 5.6 apg in five NCAA games, also hitting all 35 of his free throws to set a tournament record. After scoring 26 points against Kentucky in the national semifinals, including 5-for-5 from three-point distance, Lee was the only player named to the All-Final Four team who did not play in the championship game.

"I think he gained a lot of confidence with his performance at the end of the year," Montgomery said. "It has to make him very confident in his ability to do these kinds of things.

"His job as point guard is to make sure our team is successful by the blending of running our club, making other people effective and taking care of himself. Art has the ability to score and is a great defender. Rather than looking over his shoulder, I think Art can look forward now."

Winner of the Hank Luisetti Award as the team's most valuable player, Lee clearly has established his own identity in the eyes of his teammates.

"Art has a defensive toughness and a scoring threat that Brevin didn't give you," senior forward Pete Sauer told the *San Francisco Chronicle*. "I think Art is stronger defensively than Brevin was. And Art is more of a consistent shooter."

With Lee at the reins, the team relies on a variety of players, rather than simply leaning on Knight's ability to bail them out at crunch time.

"Right now, playing the style we're playing, I think Art's better," added backcourt mate Kris Weems.

Just about the time the comparisons with Knight slowed, Lee brought a different type of controversy on himself by making a "choke" sign while Rhode Island's Tyson Wheeler was in the process of missing three consecutive free throws late in their NCAA Midwest Regional final game.

Lee, who scored 13 of his 26 points in the final 2:05 of that contest to spark a marvelous comeback, apologized for the action afterward. But the NCAA decided three months later to dredge up the matter, issuing Lee a public reprimand for the incident.

"The NCAA was just trying to do their job," Montgomery reasoned. "They're trying to make a real strong stand for sportsmanship, and we certainly understand that. We didn't condone what happened."

Lee scored in double figures in 29 games last season, and had career-high totals of 27 points, 10 assists and four steals against Oregon State. He dished out a career-best 10 assists in three other games, and had two turnovers or fewer in 20 of Stanford's 35 starts.

KRIS WEEMS (6-3, 195 lbs., SR, SG, #3, 12.6 ppg, 3.0 rpg, 2.3 apg, 28.7 minutes, .425 FG, .382 3PT, .826 FT, F.L. Schlage HS/Kansas City, Kan.). A 40-percent career three-point shooter, Weems earned first-team All-Pac-10 honors last season after averaging 14.3 ppg in conference play.

Weems scored a game-winning three-pointer at the buzzer at Washington after dribbling the length of the court, capping a 32-point performance. He scored a career-high 34 points against Oregon, had 29 against Butler, and earned MVP honors in the Cable Car Classic, scoring 32 points in wins over Rhode Island and Santa Clara. He also had 23 points, including 14 in the second half, in an 84-81 victory at UCLA.

But Weems cooled off late in the season, shooting just .246 from the field in the NCAAs, including just 5-for-23 from three-point distance. He averaged only 7.4 ppg in the Tournament.

"Kris needs to be more consistent," Montgomery said. "He needs to be able to attack the basket a little better so he can set up the perimeter stuff. As a senior, he needs to provide us with leadership."

Weems' perimeter shooting skills were developed after his mother, Camille, had a basketball court installed in her huge backyard in Kansas City, ?Mo.?, when Kris was a youngster.

"We made it big enough so that there would be range for three-point shooting, and he would practice and have his friends over," his mother told the *San Francisco Examiner*.

Weems enters his final season ranked No. 2 on Stanford's career list for three-point attempts (350) and No. 3 in three-pointers made (140).

TIM YOUNG (7-1, 245 lbs., SR, C, #55, 11.3 ppg, 8.1 rpg, 1.2 bpg, 27.1 minutes, .514 FG, .763 FT, Harbor HS/Santa Cruz, Calif.). How do you figure Tim Young? Montgomery and Stanford's players regard him as an indispensable, underrated member of the team. They point to his shooting ability in the clutch, his defense, his leadership.

Outsiders often watch him and wonder why his output isn't more prolific. One Bay Area newspaper published an article exploring the question of why Young seemingly misses so many two-foot shots.

The topic irritates Montgomery, who believes most people miss the point with Young.

"So many people just take Tim for granted. He's just so valuable for us in so many ways. Until he goes, you don't realize how much he does for you," the coach said. "Everybody thinks Tim should go up and dunk everything. But he's efficient in the way he plays the game.

"We've got a lot of players capable of doing a lot of things. He fits in very well with what we're doing. I'd like to see Tim's confidence be at the level he deserves."

The fact is, for all his offensive tools, Young is not the primary "go-to" player in the Stanford attack. The Cardinal is so diverse, Young often seems to merely blend. But when it matters, his teammates believe they can rely on him.

"Sometimes he doesn't realize how good he is," Sauer said. "There's not many players in the country who are as big or strong as Tim. And at a given point in every game, we're going to have to count on our center to score."

"There's a lot of pressure on Tim because he's been there for so long," Jarron Collins said. "I don't understand why people criticize him so much. You can learn a lot just by watching Tim Young—the way he attacks practice, his effort.

"He's the leader on the court and we all look to Timmy. That's just the way it is."

In particular, Young's defensive abilities are somewhat overlooked because he is not a flamboyant shot-blocker. But in two games against Washington last year, Young virtually shut down center Todd MacCulloch, prompting Huskies' coach Bob Bender to remove his star during the game in Seattle.

Young, who has used a strict regimen of stretching and yoga to relieve the lower-back problems which plagued him early in his career, tries not to concern himself with the critics.

"It can frustrate me if I want it to, but I just try to ignore that kind of criticism," he said. "I know what I'm capable of and I know my limitations."

An All-Pac-10 pick a year ago, Young registered seven double-doubles, three of them in the NCAA Tournament. In his Stanford career, Young has grabbed 10 rebounds or more 32 times in a game. He holds the school record with 136 career blocked shots.

MARK MADSEN (6-8, 235 lbs, JR, PF, #45, 11.7 ppg, 8.2 rpg, 26.1 minutes, .589 FG, .629 FT, San Ramon Valley HS/Danville, Calif.). There are lots of ways to describe the mayhem Madsen creates on the court with his physical play. Here's how ex-Kentucky center Nazr Mohammed put it after last year's national semifinal: "Nobody compares to Madsen...within the rules."

Two years removed from a Mormon mission to Spain and just one year after hobbling through a freshman season with back and knee injuries, Madsen emerged as a major force for Stanford in 1997-98.

Appropriately nicknamed "Mad Dog," Madsen is a fierce, no-nonsense player, a power forward of just the ilk Dr. Naismith may have had in mind. Occasionally,

1997-98 RESULTS

San Diego	87-57	
#Hawaii-Hilo	98-49	
#Valparaiso	70-65	
#Butler	99-86	
##Georgia	76-74	
@San Diego State	63-42	
Pacific	67-61	
California-Santa Barbara	95-62	
Lehigh	95-42	
###Rhode Island	70-69	
###Santa Clara	69-60	
@Oregon State	68-48	
@Oregon	89-67	
California	84-74	
Southern California	99-62	
UCLA	93-80	
@Washington State	82-72	
@Washington	74-72	
Arizona (L)	75-93	
Arizona State (L)	87-90	ot
@California	74-72	
@Connecticut (L)	56-76	
@UCLA	84-81	
@Southern California	83-59	
Washington	93-70	
Washington State	72-56	
@Arizona State	86-73	
@Arizona (L)	58-90	
Oregon	95-67	
Oregon State	85-77	
%College of Charleston	67-57	
%Western Michigan	83-65	
%%Purdue	67-59	
%%Rhode Island	79-77	
%%%Kentucky (L)	85-86	ot

@ away games
# Big Island Invitational, Hilo, HI
Wooden Classic, Anaheim, CA
Cable Car Classic, San Jose, CA
% NCAA Midwest Sub-Regional, Chicago, IL
%% NCAA Midwest Regional, St. Louis, MO
%%% NCAA Final Four, San Antonio, TX

Madsen's enthusiasm for the game can lead to an elbow that makes contact. As a junior high student, Madsen broke one of his father's ribs while playing in a backyard pickup game.

It's nothing personal.

"You've got to smile when you watch him play," Jarron Collins said. "In the Purdue game, he gave (center Brad) Miller an elbow and split his chin open. That (happens) every day in practice, blood coming out of somebody."

Madsen pleads innocence when asked how this seems to happen.

"Sometimes you walk away and you're bruised up, and sometimes the other guy's bruised up," he said. "I do kind of say, 'Oh, well,' sometimes."

Madsen is the type of paradox that many ferocious athletes are. Away from the game, he is such a gentle soul that he once spent the night sleeping in his backyard to quell the family dog's loneliness. On the floor, he's a wrecking ball in short pants, choosing Dennis Rodman as the topic for a 15-page freshman thesis on role models.

Montgomery appreciates the raw gifts Madsen so relentlessly applies to the game.

"He affects the game by sheer presence," the coach said. "He plays so hard, there are stretches when he goes and gets the ball that nobody can do anything about it.

"I'd like to see him consistent in that and get to the point where he can do 4-5 things and people just throw up their hands."

Along with planting 100 redwood trees on his parent's property last summer, Madsen spent time trying to develop some diversity in his game. He took as many as 600 mid-range jump shots and jump hooks each day.

It's not that Madsen wants to reinvent his game. He just wants to add to it and demonstrate that Cardinal big men are not merely brutes.

"I personally think we have a front line that plays hard, but is not overly bruising," said Madsen, who would be sure to get an argument from almost anyone with first-hand experience. "We have to rely on our skills. We can't rely on a shoving game inside."

But it's always there if Madsen needs it.

PETE SAUER (6-7, 220 lbs., SR, SF, #5, 9.2 ppg, 4.6 rpg, 2.0 apg, 23.8 minutes, .413 FG, .416 3PT, .815 FT, Shady Side Academy/Pittsburgh, Pa.). Perhaps no one on the Stanford team has adjusted to a changing role as much as Sauer, who played power forward two years ago, but stepped out to the small forward slot last season.

He responded by hitting 42 three-point baskets, while still contributing as a solid rebounder. In Pac-10 games, Sauer averaged 10.7 ppg and 5.2 rpg.

"Pete is clearly one of our leaders. All the kids respect him," Montgomery said. "He can shoot it deep, put it on the floor on occasion. We can play him at the 'four' and go small. One of the reasons we've been able to win is we've got several different ways to hurt you, and Pete is one of those."

"Pete's a guy who gets out there and is never afraid to take the big shot," Madsen said.

Sauer, who has started the past 63 games, said he no longer feels like one of the big guys on the team.

"Now when I look up, I've got five or six guys bigger than me," he said. "The way we play, we always play pretty big and strong. So having a big small forward is a way we can play big defensively and rebound well."

Sauer scored 21 points and grabbed 10 rebounds in the team's win over UCLA last season, and he had 23 points and seven rebounds against Arizona. He scored in double figures in 13 games, and led Stanford's frontcourt players with 74 assists.

KEY RESERVES

DAVID MOSELEY (6-4, 198 lbs., JR, G/F, #21, 6.1 ppg, 1.9 rpg, 14.6 minutes, .401 FG, .422 3PT, .769 FT, Mayfield HS/Las Cruces, N.M.). A versatile player who swings between shooting guard and small forward, Moseley is an explosive scorer with the athletic ability to be a disruptive defender. A co-winner of the team's Most Improved Player award, Moseley scored a career-high 20 points against California-Santa Barbara and had 19 points in 15 minutes against Oregon.

He also played well in the NCAA Tournament, contributing 10 points to the win over Purdue and eight, including a pair of timely three-pointers, against Rhode Island. Moseley's 511 minutes were the most among Stanford's reserves, and he should continue to play a significant role off the bench this season.

"He has instant energy," Montgomery said. "He goes in there and he makes things happen. He gets screened a little too easily at times, and he needs to be more consistent. He needs to have a little more confidence in his ability."

JARRON COLLINS (6-9, 240 lbs., SO, F, #31, 3.8 ppg, 3.5 rpg, 13.5 minutes, .530 FG, .609 FT, Harvard-Westlake HS/North Hollywood, CA). Equipped with skills to play power forward or step to the perimeter, Jarron arrived at Stanford a year ago with his twin brother Jason as the biggest-name recruits the school had attracted in years. He did not disappoint.

As a freshman reserve, Jarron scored in double figures four times, including 12 points in a victory over UCLA and again in a key performance against Purdue in the Midwest Regional semifinals. He also had a career-high 11 rebounds in the 67-59 win over the Boilermakers.

"There was no way we were losing that game," Collins said. "I was like that in my high school career. When a big game's there, I'm there. I get intense. I get extremely focused.

"That's something I have to learn as I get older—to keep the intensity and focus against an opponent that you know you can beat."

"I would like to see him be consistent with his play at a level he's capable of," Montgomery echoed. "He's a very capable player. He needs to learn to motivate himself and play at that level all the time. He has a very good feel for the game."

A consensus high school All-America selection who led his team to a 66-4 record and back-to-back California state Division III titles, Collins anticipates a big leap in his performance this season.

"I feel I can do much more as a player," he said. "I've been working on little things—a jump hook, better post moves. A turn-around jump shot isn't going to get it done. You end up with 'Spalding' on your forehead."

Teammate Mark Madsen said fans may be surprised by what they see from Collins this season.

"Jarron's almost 6-10 and he can shoot three-pointers," Madsen said. "You didn't see too much of that from him in games last year. But we saw it in practice. He can get out on the break and handle the ball.

"You look at him and you don't think 'animal,' but he's really tough inside and he plays huge."

Collins likes the fact that he's difficult to pigeon-hole as a player. His words: "I would say I'm in between a 'three' and a 'four.' I'm a three-and-a-half."

RYAN MENDEZ (6-7, 205 lbs., JR, G/F, #32, 5.5 ppg, 2.2 rpg, 12.2 minutes, .462 FG, .474 3PT, .588 FT, Burleson HS/Burleson, Tex.). A phenomenal long-range shooter, Mendez had surgery late last spring to repair a tendon in his knee. As a result, he took most of the summer off, beginning a light workout program in August.

Mendez has come off the bench his first two years at Stanford to score 74 three-point baskets, 45 of them last season. His accuracy behind the arc was the best in the Pac-10 and seventh in school history.

"The fact that he shoots it deep is a tremendous asset," Montgomery said.

Mendez scored in double figures nine times last season, including a career-high 18 points against California-Santa Barbara. He had 13 points, four rebounds and three assists in 20 minutes against Oregon, and 14 points and two steals against Washington. He hit a three-pointer with 44 seconds left in overtime to pull Stanford within a single point against Kentucky.

Now Montgomery wants Mendez to expand his game.

"We want him to get a little stronger defensively and (become) a more physical rebounder," Montgomery said. "If people crowd him, he's got to be able to create off the dribble to set up the other stuff."

MICHAEL MCDONALD (6-0, 170 lbs., SO, G, #4, 1.7 ppg, 0.7 rpg, 1.4 apg, 7.5 minutes, .294 FG, .250 3PT, .688 FT, Long Beach Poly HS/Long Beach, Calif.). The likely heir to Lee's point guard spot a year from now, McDonald played in all 35 games as a freshman, making steady progress as the season unfolded.

He played a key role in Stanford's 84-81 win at UCLA, running the offense for 19 minutes and helping the Cardinal withstand a comeback try by the Bruins. He scored nine points in 13 minutes against Washington and had a season ratio of 49 assists to 27 turnovers.

"Hopefully, he'll be in a spot where people look at him as a potential starter," Montgomery said. "Mike's got to go in with confidence and feel he can do the job. Sometimes last year we were holding our breath.

"He was hurt his senior year in high school, and he's got to get over the fact that he's at Stanford and get up and compete now."

McDonald, whose father Glenn played in the NBA for the Boston Celtics, missed all but two games of his senior year in high school due to a thigh injury. As a junior, he averaged 18.0 ppg, 6.0 apg and 6.0 rpg.

MARK SEATON (6-9, 230 lbs., SR, F, #44, 2.5 ppg, 2.2 rpg, 10.2 ppg, minutes, .674 FG, .455 FT, Servite HS/Cypress, Calif.). Lost a bit in the shuffle of Stanford's deep forward corps, Seaton will have to work hard to emerge from the crowd.

"I'd like for Mark to have a highly successful senior year," Montgomery said. "He's one of the most unselfish kids I've ever had, yet he's highly capable. Over the years he's had some big games for us. I'd like him to have the confidence he needs."

A .621 career shooter, Seaton had 10 points each in wins over Valparaiso and USC last season. He scored a career-high 18 points as a freshman against USC.

JASON COLLINS (6-10, 240 lbs., FR, C, #33, 7.0 ppg, 6.0 rpg, one appearance, Harvard-Westlake HS/North Hollywood, CA). If Stanford fans haven't seen the full scope of Jarron Collins' game, they haven't seen Jason's at all. He frayed the meniscus cartilage in his left knee in preseason workouts last year, played 15 minutes in the season opener against San Diego, then underwent surgery on Dec. 10.

"Jason Collins is a talent," Madsen said. "The media hasn't seen it, the fans haven't seen it. But I've seen it. If he's healthy and his knee is better, it's going to elevate the entire team's game. He changes the dynamics when guards drive to the basket."

"He'll be one more big guy, taking the load off Mark and myself," center Tim Young said. "More than anything, he's an effective rebounder. He's got great hands and a great feel for the game."

Collins, who finished his high school career with 1,500 rebounds to go along with 2,379 points, returns with four years of eligibility.

"I hope he's 100 percent," Montgomery said. "The jury's still out. There'll be a trial and error period for him to try to determine how he's going to accommodate and tolerate the work load. There'll probably be some adjustments on his part, dealing with a little bit of pain and a little bit of swelling. But he could be huge for us."

Montgomery said Collins is all you want in a young post prospect.

"Jason is very physical. He's got long arms, he understands the game, he blocks shots and, defensively, he can be a dominant rebounder. If he can just do those things, the rest is gravy."

1998-99 STANFORD SCHEDULE

Nov.	14	UC-Davis
	18	#Southern Methodist
Dec.	5-6	##BB&T Classic
	17	@Nevada-Reno
	19	@Pacific
	21-22	###Stanford Invitational
	29	*Temple
Jan.	2	Oregon State
	9	California
	14	@Southern California
	16	@UCLA
	21	Washington State
	23	Washington
	28	@Arizona
	30	@Arizona State
Feb.	3	@California
	6	Connecticut
	11	UCLA
	13	Southern California
	18	@Washington
	20	@Washington State
	25	Arizona State
	27	Arizona
Mar.	4	@Oregon
	6	@Oregon State

@ Road Games
* Pete Newell Classic, Oakland, CA
# Chase NIT (If the Cardinal advances, it will face either Southwest Missouri State or Missouri on Nov. 18. Semifinals and finals are Nov. 25 and 27 at Madison Square Garden, NY)
Washington, DC (vs. Maryland, first round; also DePaul, George Washington and Stanford)
Stanford, CA (vs. Elon, first round; also Santa Clara and William & Mary)

OTHER RETURNEES

ALEX GELBARD (6-3, 188 lbs., JR, G, #20, five appearances, Harvard-Westlake HS/Sherman Oaks, CA). A left-handed walkon, Gelbard scored the only basket of his collegiate career against Oregon last season. He was a teammate of Jarron and Jason Collins when they were juniors at Harvard-Westlake HS, averaging 12.0 ppg and 8.0 rpg his senior season.

A third-generation Stanford athlete, Gelbard's father competed on the ski team and his grandfather played soccer.

NEWCOMERS

TONY GIOVACCHINI (6-2, 170 lbs., FR, G, #25, 20.7 ppg, 8.3 rpg, 7.5 apg, Judge Memorial HS/Salt Lake City, Ut.). The third member of his family to play basketball for a Pac-10 school, Giovacchini will fight for playing time off the bench at both guard positions this season.

"He can shoot it, but he's a point guard who can pass it very well," Montgomery said. "The first thing will be how fast he learns what we do and adjusts to this whole Stanford thing. We are not bringing in guys who can't play. I expect him to compete."

Giovacchini's uncle, Paul, played at Stanford (1977-79) and his father, Marty, played at Washington State (1974-77).

Giovacchini was regarded as the most recruited player in the state of Utah last season, and finished his senior season as his team's leader in scoring, rebounding and assists. He was an All-State selection three straight years and

KYLE LOGAN (6-5, 185 lbs., FR, G/F, #12, injured and did not play senior season at Mercersburg Academy/ Mercersburg, Pa.). Logan gives the Cardinal a versatile and athletic player who can swing among three positions—point guard, shooting guard and small forward. He should get some playing time off the bench from the start this season.

"He played at the 'two' and 'three' (positions), but there is a thought he could handle the ball some," Montgomery said. "He's good at the point of attack and he's pretty athletic. He needs to get stronger. We'll see how quickly he adjusts."

As a junior at St. Maria Goretti HS in Hagerstown, Md., Logan averaged 21 points, seven rebounds and three assists. He shot 58 percent from the field and 85 percent from the free-throw line. He scored a season-high 35 points in one game.

QUESTIONS

Expectations? The Cardinal enters a brave new world as a returning Final Four entry and the consensus pick to win the Pac-10. This team has the talent to bring the school its first outright conference crown since 1942, but will have to overcome the sense others may have that it should be automatic.

Complacency? Don't count on it—these are smart fellas—but this trap can sneak up on the best of those who have tasted high-level success for the first time. To stay at the top, the Cardinal will have to be hungrier than ever.

Health? This is the luck factor that all great teams must have on their side. Center Tim Young, hobbled by a back problem two years ago, was largely pain-free last season. But his backup, freshman Jason Collins, missed nearly the entire year after injuring his left knee. Stanford hopes to spend as little time as possible this season in the training room.

ANSWERS

Confidence! Stanford enters this season knowing that it came within a play or two of defeating eventual NCAA champ Kentucky in the Final Four. That creates a reservoir of confidence which cannot be developed otherwise.

Balance! With size, terrific shooting ability, depth and a great floor leader in Art Lee, the Cardinal can beat teams in a variety of ways. No club in the Pac-10 can match Stanford's versatility.

Montgomery! Mike Montgomery proved his mettle at Stanford while coaching under-talented, over-achieving teams. Now he has big-time players, and he is too smart—and too wary—to let them relax.

adidas Blue Ribbon Analysis

BACKCOURT	A	BENCH/DEPTH	A
FRONTCOURT	A+	INTANGIBLES	B+

Stanford is the classic case of, "Be careful what you ask for, you just might get it." The Cardinal long has wanted to become a big-time college basketball program, and they've clearly arrived.

Now they get everything which goes with that status—expectations, pressure and the bulls-eye normally worn by Arizona and UCLA in the Pac-10. Without exception, every conference coach lists the Cardinal as the favorite to win the league championship.

Are Stanford's players overwhelmed at that prospect?

"That's where we want to be," sophomore Jarron Collins said. "We want to be one of the top programs in the nation, so every year our name is mentioned for the Pac-10 title or to make a good NCAA run. We want to be in the elite."

For all its success a year ago, Stanford hardly is invincible. One-sided losses to Arizona (93-75 and 90-58) and Connecticut (76-56) suggested the Cardinal simply wasn't equipped to face ultra-quick foes.

Young said Stanford's ability to overcome those games spoke volumes about the team.

"I can't say I expected to be in the Final Four last year, but I knew we were a resilient team," he said. "We're good at bouncing back from things, like those hard losses against UConn and Arizona. I think we proved we're capable of competing at the highest level in college basketball. That gives us a lot of confidence.

"But, obviously, what kind of team we're going to be is really up to us."

Montgomery agrees, and doesn't sell short the young talent at UCLA and Arizona, or the experience at Washington and Cal.

"If anything, people are going to be more prepared to play us," he said. "We're going to work hard, probably harder than we have in the past. If we don't, we won't be successful."

(J.F.)

4

KENTUCKY

LOCATION	Lexington, KY
CONFERENCE	SEC (Eastern Division)
LAST SEASON	35-4 (.897)
CONFERENCE RECORD	14-2 (1st)
STARTERS LOST/RETURNING	3/2
NICKNAME	Wildcats
COLORS	Blue & White
HOMECOURT	Rupp Arena (23,000)
COACH	Tubby Smith (High Point '73)
RECORD AT SCHOOL	35-4 (1 yr.)
CAREER RECORD	159-66 (7 yrs.)
ASSISTANTS	George Felton (South Carolina '75) Shawn Finney (Fairmont State '85) Mike Sutton (East Carolina '78)
TEAM WINS (last 5 yrs.)	27-28-32-26-34
RPI (last 5 yrs.)	10-4-1-2-2
1997-98 FINISH	Won national championship.

COACH AND PROGRAM

The first signs were evident early last March in the SEC Tournament: Kentucky 99, Arkansas 74; Kentucky 86, South Carolina 56. The Wildcats were playing well, frighteningly well. Well enough, some veteran sportswriters who cover the SEC reasoned, to make a deep run in the NCAA Tournament.

Did those sportswriters have the good sense to back up their gut feelings about Kentucky and pencil the 'Cats in as national champions on their office pools? If they did, their confidence was justified, for winning the title is exactly what the No. 2-seeded Wildcats did.

It was a wild ride through a Big Dance field that was thought to be dominated by its No. 1 seeds—North Carolina, Duke, Kansas and Arizona. Yet, with a 78-69 victory over Utah, Kentucky won its second national championship in three years and its first under rookie head coach Tubby Smith.

Impressive as Kentucky's title run was, it was doubly so considering Smith was in his first season after taking over for the wildly successful and popular Rick Pitino. And the Wildcats had already made back-to-back appearances in the NCAA final.

Most thought Smith, a former Pitino assistant, could do a good job at Kentucky after his old boss bolted for the Boston Celtics. Smith had proven his worth at two former stops, Tulsa and Georgia, taking both teams to the NCAA Tournament's Sweet 16.

But few thought Smith could whip the Wildcats into a championship team so quickly. Isn't there such a thing as an adjustment period when a new coach takes over?

The Wildcats evidently got all their adjustments over with during the regular season. Smith might have worked for Pitino, but he isn't a Pitino clone. The 'Cats didn't press as much as they did the year before, relying more on a rugged, rock-solid halfcourt defense. Neither did Kentucky hoist three-pointers with the abandon it did under Pitino.

At times, Wildcat fans criticized some of Smith's personnel decisions. To his credit, Smith pretended not to hear, and he kept coaching the best way he knew how. We now know that Smith's best is very, very good.

"Tubby Smith did a remarkable job with Kentucky," Arkansas coach Nolan Richardson said. "The team he inherited wasn't the same team that won the national championship, then finished second. His system isn't Rick Pitino's system, so this group of players had to form a trusting relationship with him."

"You have to give Tubby a tremendous amount of credit," Utah coach Rick Majerus said. "To come into a situation like that, I think that speaks to what a great coach he really is. He had to combine new players with existing players, with a new staff and a system that somewhat resembled Rick Pitino's, and yet add his own discernible touches. To me, it's an incredible coaching job."

Typically, Smith downplays his contributions.

"Certainly, Kentucky's a program that had done it before," Smith said. "There's always the possibility you could compete for a national championship. I've always believed that good players make good coaches."

Perhaps. And there is no question Smith had good players. Still, the 1997-98 Wildcats weren't thought to be anywhere near as talented as the national championship team of two years before. At some point, coaching entered into the equation.

Tubby Smith deserves considerable credit for Kentucky's championship season.

STARTERS NOT RETURNING

JEFF SHEPPARD (6-4, SG, 13.7 ppg, 4.0 rpg, 2.7 apg, 1.6 tpg, 1.2 spg, 28.0 minutes, .444 FG, .376 3PT, .703 FT). Sheppard's decision to redshirt two years ago was a good one, though perhaps not for the reason he had intended.

Sheppard sat out in 1996-97 so he wouldn't have to fight for minutes playing behind Derek Anderson and Ron Mercer. That, former coach Rick Pitino thought, would boost his stock with NBA teams, simply because he could play a lot more minutes in 1997-98.

Well, it didn't quite work out that way. Sheppard did his part by having a solid senior season. But he wasn't drafted, though analysts predicted before the draft he would be selected somewhere near the 40th pick.

The good news was that, by staying in Lexington a fifth season, Sheppard earned another NCAA championship ring.

Make no mistake, Sheppard was a big part of the 'Cats title run. He scored nearly half his career points (521) in his senior season. And 211 of those came in the last 14 games, when Sheppard lifted Kentucky on his back and carried the 'Cats as far as he could.

Three times in those 14 games, Sheppard topped his previous career-high in points. He averaged nearly 20 points per game in the NCAA Tournament, including a 27-point effort against Stanford in the Final Four.

Sheppard, a great leaper and jump shooter, will be missed, but, as always at Kentucky, there are talented players waiting to fill in.

ALAN EDWARDS (6-5, SF, 9.2 ppg, 3.2 rpg, 3.3 apg, 25.4 minutes, 1.7 tpg, 1.1 spg, .444 FG, .292 3PT, .639 FT). Edwards showed immeasurable courage last season, when his mother, Laura Mae, was dying of cancer. She lost her battle late in the season, but Edwards missed just two games. He returned as though on a mission, scoring 15 points and passing for five assists in an SEC Tournament victory over South Carolina.

Edwards went on to average 12.8 ppg, 4.0 apg and 3.0 rpg in the NCAA Tournament. His big three-pointer against Duke in the South Region finals helped start Kentucky's amazing rally to win that game.

Edwards was a solid player, but his contributions can be duplicated by senior Heshimu Evans.

NAZR MOHAMMED (6-10, C, 12.0 ppg, 7.2 rpg, 1.5 tpg, 1.9 bpg, 21.0 minutes, .597 FG, .652 FT). Mohammed was one of college basketball's greatest success stories in recent years. Recruited as an overweight project by former coach Rick Pitino, Mohammed slimmed down, improved his game and became a first-round NBA draft pick.

Evidence of how far Mohammed's game progressed came last season, when he was chosen first-team All-SEC. He started the year as a backup to Jamaal Magloire, but quickly supplanted him and became a dominant low-post scorer.

Mohammed also improved his defense. His 75 blocked shots were a career-high. Fifteen of those blocks came in the NCAAs, including five in the opening minutes against UCLA. That set the game's tone as the 'Cats won, 94-68, in the Sweet 16.

Mohammed originally said he wanted to return "and dominate college basketball" as a senior. But he later changed his mind and declared himself eligible for the NBA draft.

On draft day, Mohammed was chosen by the Utah Jazz as the 29th and final pick in the first round, but an hour later his rights were traded to the Philadelphia 76ers.

"Mohammed was in my Top 10," 76ers' coach Larry Brown told *The 'Cats Pause*. "You never understand how these guys drop, but I'm happy."

Mohammed has a positive attitude as he heads to the next level.

"I think, offensively, I can give a lot to the team," Mohammed told *The 'Cats Pause*. "But also defensively I can do a lot. Plus, I feel I have a good work ethic and I'm coachable. I'm going to go in and work hard."

Kentucky fans can attest to that.

OTHERS NOT RETURNING

CAMERON MILLS (6-3, G, 4.4 ppg, 1.5 rpg, 11.2 minutes, .417 FG, .473 3PT, .956 FT). Mills was one of the best shooters in college basketball. Though he didn't play a lot of minutes compared to the starters and key reserves, he came in handy when Smith needed a long-range shooting threat.

Mills shot 38-for-87 from three-point range last season, and also shot 22-for-23 from the free throw line. He wasn't quite as effective in last year's NCAA Tournament as he was the season before, when he shot 63 percent from three-point range and averaged 11.3 ppg in six games; still, Mills had his moments.

His three-pointer against Duke with 2:14 to play gave the 'Cats an 81-80 lead. And Mills hit two huge three-pointers that helped Kentucky rally to beat Utah in the championship game.

Smith hopes newcomers—most notably Todd Tackett—can assume Mills' role as Kentucky's designated long-range bomber.

PROJECTED STARTERS

WAYNE TURNER (6-2, 187 lbs., SR, PG, #5, 9.3 ppg, 3.1 rpg, 4.4 apg, 2.4 tpg, 1.6 spg, 28.2 minutes, .481 FG, .368 3PT, .620 FT, Beaver Country Day School/Boston, Mass.). Coaches tend to be fiercely loyal to their point guards, especially one so capable as Turner.

"He's one of the best point guards in the country," Smith said, "if not the best point guard in the country. I wouldn't take anybody else over him."

It's easy to see why Smith is so fond of Turner. When the circumstances are crucial, Turner plays his best. Turner took over the point guard spot late in his sophomore season and was instrumental in Kentucky's drive to the NCAA title game. Likewise, Turner was a key cog in the Wildcats' championship run last season.

"He was a big key," Smith said. "He's obviously the guy who made our team go. As he went, so did our team."

Turner has the complete package of skills. He wasn't supposed to be a shooter, but he put in a lot of work on his jumper and last season shot better-than-average from three-point range.

Turner shot 56 percent from the free throw line his first two seasons, but improved to 62 percent last year. And he shot 48 percent from the field.

Turner's shooting is just a bonus, for he has all the other numbers befitting a great point guard. Last year, he handed out 173 assists, fifth in the SEC. He also had 62 steals, leading the Wildcats in that department for the third straight year. His assist-to-turnover ratio was just under 2-1, another excellent barometer of a point guard's worth.

Turner doesn't even need these numbers to validate his presence. Winning and great defense are his forte, and the record speaks for itself. In Turner's three seasons at Kentucky, the Wildcats have won two national championships and advanced to the championship game three times.

Just as he did the season before, Turner significantly raised the level of his play in March. At the SEC Tournament, he was chosen the MVP after scoring 33 points, grabbing six rebounds and passing for a tournament-high 19 assists in three games.

In the NCAAs, Turner was steady. His 16 points and eight assists keyed a huge, fourth-round victory over Duke and earned him the South Region MVP award. At the Final Four, Turner directed the Wildcats' offense to perfection and helped engineer a tempo change in the championship game against Utah.

"If there's one player we can't do without, it's Wayne Turner," Smith said.

SCOTT PADGETT (6-9, 229 lbs., SR, PF, #34, 11.5 ppg, 6.5 rpg, 2.1 apg, 2.2 tpg, 1.3 spg, 27.9 minutes, .476 FG, .374 3PT, .853 FT, St. Xavier HS/Louisville, Ky.). *Blue Ribbon* chose Padgett as a second-team pre-season All-America, and only by the narrowest of margins did he not make the first team. That sums up our feelings about Padgett, one of the most versatile players in the game and a future NBA performer.

Any serious analysis of Padgett's game begins with his shooting touch. We won't demean Padgett to merely say he shoots well for a big man. Padgett is a great shooter, period. When a power forward can step past the three-point line and knock down close to 40 percent of his shots, he becomes a dangerous weapon.

Padgett is a weapon, because, in addition to his three-point stroke, he can also take the ball to the basket and score. How does the defense guard him?

Shorter players can't stop him in the paint. Taller players can't beat get out to the arc fast enough to prevent him from tossing in three-pointers.

"Scott is such a threat," Smith said. "He's a multi-faceted player. At 6-9, he can shoot it with range and pass it. He plays defense and rebounds. He's got the whole package.

"He's a guy we're going to rely on heavily on this year, because we've got fewer weapons than we did last year."

Padgett had done his share of stepping up in big games, even when his teammates were Derek Anderson, Ron Mercer, Nazr Mohammed and Jeff Sheppard. Padgett is the Wildcats' designated assassin. When opponents rally, he seems to always be there with a big basket.

Often, that big basket is a three-pointer.

Padgett has beaten back Tennessee the last two years with timely baskets, did the same thing against Iowa in the 1997 NCAA Tournament and made the game-winner against Duke in last year's NCAA title run. In the regular season, his 24 points helped turn back a determined upset bid by Alabama and his 23 points on the road at Mississippi State helped preserve a 77-71 victory.

Padgett, as Smith said, can do much more than shoot. He had five double-doubles last season, including a 12-point, 13-rebound effort against Alabama in the SEC Tournament. Padgett led the tournament with 26 boards in three games. He was eighth in the SEC in rebounding.

There's more. Padgett was fourth among the Wildcats in assists, third in steals and third in blocked shots. A year ago, Padgett was Kentucky's third-leading scorer. This year, he figures to lead the 'Cats in that department.

"Scott is very capable of being a player who can carry a team," Smith said. "He did it for us last year when he was hot. He'll be a guy we go to a lot this season."

HESHIMU EVANS (6-6, 210 lbs., SR, SF, #14, 8.8 ppg, 5.4 rpg, 1.6 apg, 1.4 tpg, 20.5 minutes, .536 FG, .353 3PT, .628 FT, Manhattan College & East Childs HS/Bronx, N.Y.). If anyone wondered whether Evans could handle the rigors of the SEC after transferring from Manhattan, he quickly put that question to rest. The SEC doesn't award a trophy honoring its best sixth man, but, if it did, Evans would have won it handily.

Seldom has a basketball player been so aptly named. In Swahili, Heshimu means "strong warrior." What a perfect description of Evans, who uses his strength to slash to the basket and battle for rebounds, and his competitiveness to inspire his teammates and befuddle opponents.

Coaches use the term "warrior" all the time, to the point where it has become a cliché. Evans really is a warrior.

Evans wasn't supposed to be a jump shooter, but, lo and behold, he had the numbers at Kentucky, shooting 37 percent from three-point range, good by anyone's standards. Evans knocked in two three-pointers in the second half against Duke and two more in the national championship game against Utah, both sparking Kentucky comebacks.

Averaging 28 minutes in the postseason, Evans put together some big games. He had three double-doubles, including a 22-point, 12-rebound effort against South Carolina and 14 points and 11 rebounds against Duke.

"Heshimu's a versatile player who can play (shooting guard or small forward)," Smith said. "'Mu' shoots it really well. He's developed some consistency from the outside. So I could see him playing the 'two' guard if we needed him to."

More likely, Evans will start at small forward. And there is every reason to think he'll be successful.

Evans started four times last year, averaging 14.0 points and 6.5 rebounds in those games. Smith would pencil in those numbers right now.

JAMAAL MAGLOIRE (6-10, 240 lbs., JR, C, #42, 5.2 ppg, 4.2 rpg, 1.2 tpg, 1.7 bpg, 14.9 minutes, .487 FG, .672 FT, Eastern Commerce HS/Toronto, Ont.). If you

1997-98 RESULTS

Morehead State	88-49	
#George Washington	70-55	
#Arizona (L)	74-89	
#Missouri	77-55	
##Clemson	76-61	
###Purdue	89-75	
*Indiana	75-72	
@Canisius	81-54	
Georgia Tech	85-71	
Tulsa	74-53	
American University	75-52	
Louisville (L)	76-79	
@Ohio	95-58	
Vanderbilt	71-62	
@Georgia	90-79	
@Mississippi State	77-71	
South Carolina	91-70	
Arkansas	80-77	ot
**Alabama	70-67	
@Tennessee	85-67	
@Vanderbilt	63-61	
Florida (L)	78-86	
@Louisiana State	63-61	
@Villanova	79-63	
Tennessee	80-74	
Mississippi (L)	64-73	
@Florida	79-54	
Georgia	85-74	
@Auburn	83-58	
@South Carolina	69-57	
####Alabama	82-71	
####Arkansas	99-74	
####South Carolina	86-56	
%South Carolina State	82-67	
%Saint Louis	88-61	
%%UCLA	94-68	
%%Duke	86-84	
%%%Stanford	86-85	ot
%%%Utah	78-69	

@ away games
* Hoosier Dome, Indianapolis, IN
** Freedom Hall, Louisville, KY
\# Maui Invitational, Lahaina, HI
\## Premier Classic, Phoenix, AZ
\### Great Eight, United Center, Chicago, IL
\#### SEC Tournament, Georgia Dome, Atlanta, GA
% NCAA South Sub-Regional, Atlanta, GA
%% NCAA South Regional, St. Petersburg, FL
%%% NCAA Final Four, San Antonio, TX

thought freshmen Myron Anthony and Ryan Hogan messed up with their little off-the-court antics, consider the bizarre case of Magloire. In late spring, Magloire was riding in a vehicle in Louisville that was stopped by police.

Magloire was clean, but his traveling companions were arrested and charged with possession of marijuana and heroin. One of the men arrested was 51-years-old. Strange bedfellows, to be sure.

"He was with some people he shouldn't have been with that had drugs in the car," Smith said. "He didn't have anything in his pockets, but Jamaal knows that we do not allow (our players) to socialize with grown-ups of that nature or people of that kind.

"We don't condone any of that. That's one of the reasons I'm disappointed in his behavior."

Smith is going to have to come down hard on Magloire. How hard, no one knows, but the 'Cats will probably have to do without him in the early part of the season.

That's a shame, because, after Nazr Mohammed was taken in the NBA draft, Magloire was the obvious choice to become the Wildcats' starting center. He held the job early last season, until an improved Mohammed took it. Now, youngsters Michael Bradley and Jules Camara will have to hold down the position until Magloire returns.

It would be safe to say Magloire is a defensive specialist; he has 145 blocked shots in two seasons, the fourth-highest total in Kentucky history. But he has a decent offensive game, too.

Last year, he shot nearly 50 percent from the field (just as he did as a freshman). He also improved his free throw shooting drastically, from 55 percent his first season all the way to 67 percent.

Clearly, Magloire was and should still play a lot. Smith wouldn't say much about Magloire's status, though.

"It's still up in the air," the coach said. "He's on probation. I'm not sure when he'll be playing. He's got to fulfill some obligations and commitments before he does."

Could one of those obligations be choosing better friends?

TAYSHAUN PRINCE (6-8, 206 lbs., FR, SG, #21, 22.0 ppg, 9.8 rpg, 5.2 apg, 4.0 bpg, Dominguez HS/ Compton, Calif.). Prince was Kentucky's most highly-regarded recruit. *Prep Stars Recruiter's Handbook* ranked him No. 16 in his class and he was a McDonald's and *Parade* All-America.

Observers of informal pickup games and the Wildcats' individual workouts agree that he is as good as advertised. Since signing with Kentucky, Prince has worked hard in the weight room and actually added 18 pounds of muscle to what was a spindly frame.

Prince is a smart player who has a well-rounded game. He is known as a shooter, but can also handle, pass and rebound. The Californian reminds some of a cross between two former UCLA stars, Keith Wilkes (because Prince has a funky release on his lefthanded jumper) and Reggie Miller (the same, wiry body and deadly shot). Prince is also a winner. His high school team won 91 percent of its games during his career (96-9), including the 1997 state championship. Dominguez High was 32-3 in Prince's final season.

Prince was also successful in the classroom (3.3 GPA), but caused some anxious moments for the Kentucky staff and Wildcat fans when it took him longer than anticipated to earn the required score on a standardized test. Prince eventually got the score, though, and he comes to Lexington with a real chance of earning quality minutes as a freshman.

Kentucky doesn't have a clear-cut starter at the shooting guard position, so Prince could fit in there right away. Chances are good that Prince and senior Heshimu Evans will rotate between shooting guard and small forward. That would give Smith some scoring punch at those positions.

"Offensively, Tayshaun has the best ability among our freshmen to help us," Smith said. "I look at newcomers according to what they do best and how they can help us.

"Some will play because we need offense. Tayshaun is one of those players."

KEY RESERVES

SAUL SMITH (6-2, 170 lbs., SO, G, #11 2.5 ppg, 1.0 rpg, 1.4 apg, 13.4 minutes, .360 FG, .286 3PT, .600 FT, Clarke Central HS/Athens, Ga.). Imagine the pressure on Saul Smith. When you're the coach's son, everything you do has to be a little bit better than the other guy, or you can expect to hear about it.

Tubby Smith received mild criticism from some fans for playing his son too much, but those critics didn't realize that Smith was Wayne Turner's only backup. As good as he is, Turner can't go full speed for 40 minutes.

That left a few minutes for Smith, who averaged 13.4 in his freshman season. The youngster wasn't great, but he wasn't bad, either, passing for 51 assists and making 35 steals.

Smith didn't shoot the ball well, but he had his moments. In a five-game stretch after Christmas, Smith made 10 of 11 shots, including six straight across three games. In that span, Smith made six of seven three-pointers.

But scoring points isn't Smith's primary role. Quick and smart (aren't most sons of coaches heady?), Smith was able to give Turner rest by filling in at point guard. That should be Smith's role again this season, though he will have a little more competition for the job with the addition of J.P. Blevins.

MICHAEL BRADLEY (6-10, 230 lbs., SO, F/C, 2.4 ppg, 1.7 rpg, 6.9 minutes, .667 FG, Burncoat HS/Worcester, Mass.). Bradley earned some significant minutes as his freshman season progressed. He played 10 or more minutes just three times in Kentucky's first 18 games, but was a useful reserve in postseason play.

Bradley made big contributions in the SEC Tournament. With starting center Nazr Mohammed in foul trouble and backup Jamaal Magloire suspended, Bradley stepped into the void. Against Alabama, Bradley turned in career-bests in points (10), rebounds (six), steals (two), field goals (four), field goal attempts (seven) and minutes (14).

"Michael Bradley is a very capable center," Smith said. "We don't need a lot of scoring from that position, but he can score when we need it."

MYRON ANTHONY (6-7, 220 lbs., SO, F, #25, 2.3 ppg, 1.2 rpg, 6.3 minutes, .397 FG, .462 3PT, .615 FT, Fletcher HS/Neptune Beach, Fla.). Anthony will play somewhere, once he gets out of Tubby Smith's doghouse.

As young, immature freshmen sometimes do, Anthony got into a bit of trouble last season—leaving the scene of a car accident. Smith doesn't like to publicly denounce his players, but that isn't to suggest he doesn't mete out discipline when required. Anthony will almost certainly miss some games this year due to the incident.

Anthony didn't get a lot of PT as a freshman, but he showed signs of ability. His shooting percentage from three-point range, for example, surprised a few people.

Anthony tended to squeeze a lot of production into his limited time on the court. Returning to his home state, Anthony scored a career-high seven points and grabbed a career-high six rebounds in 12 minutes against Florida.

Anthony will have a chance to compete for minutes at both forward positions, but he's going to have to improve his defense and ballhandling if he wants to earn significant time. He might also want to consider taking a taxi when he leaves campus.

SOULEYMANE CAMARA (6-11, 213 lbs., FR, F/C, #40, 15.1 ppg, 9.7 rpg, 3.7 bpg, Oak Hill Academy, Va./ Dakar, Senegal). With the loss of Nazr Mohammed to the NBA and the uncertain status of Jamal Magloire, Souleymane (call him Jules) Camara might be Kentucky's busiest freshman this season.

"Jules is going to have to play the 'five' spot for us," Smith said. "He's going to have to step up, because we don't have much experience at that position."

That could be good and bad news for Camara. Good because it means more playing time, bad because Camara isn't a back-to-the-basket center.

"He's a finesse player, and that's the way he's always played," Oak Hill coach Steve Smith told *The 'Cats Pause*. "Even with 25 or 30 more pounds on him, he's still going to be that type of player."

Perhaps, but Camara can look forward to playing in the post in addition to relieving Scott Padgett at power forward. Smith judges a freshman's worth by whether he can guard people, and Camara, an excellent athlete, can do that.

Like another African-born center you may have heard of, Camara grew up as a soccer player. Hakeem Olajuwon, to whom Camara has sometimes been compared, got too tall for soccer and gravitated toward a sport at which his size would allow him to excel. The same for Camara. His soccer training has served him well.

"He's got quick feet," Steve Smith said. "I think it's from playing soccer all those years."

Camara has a good range of skills. He can run, pass, handle the ball well for his size and even shoot the three-pointer.

"He's a highly skilled player," Tubby Smith said. "What I see is someone who can help us defensively. He's quick enough to guard a 'three' man."

DESMOND ALLISON (6-5, 193 lbs., FR, F, #32, 34.5 ppg, 10.8 rpg, 9.0 apg, Robinson HS/Tampa, Fla.). If there can be such a thing these days, Allison was a sleeper during the recruiting process. Two summers ago, his grades in need of shoring up, Allison chose to stay home and study rather than travel the summer camp circuit. Thus, he escaped the attention of many recruiting analysts.

He didn't escape Kentucky's attention. Smith and his assistants had Allison on their list, and watched with great interest as Allison got his academic act together and earned the required standardized test score. Once he did, Smith snapped him up.

"Desmond's a real sleeper," Smith said. "I've been really impressed with his work ethic, attitude and all-around athletic ability. I look at kids differently than some. When I see freshmen, I try to find the one who will help the quickest defensively

" Desmond has the best body and the best chance of doing that."

Allison had great statistics in high school. In his three-year varsity career, he averaged more than 30 points per game overall. Allison was hard to stop at that level because he has the ability to take his defender off the dribble, in addition to being a good shooter.

Befitting his status as All-State selection in football and basketball, Allison is a great athlete who can run and jump all night. He is capable of acrobatic slam dunks. Allison's combination of skills, he hopes, will remind Kentucky fans of a former star player.

"I like taking people off the dribble, finding the open man, slashing and driving," Allison told *The 'Cats Pause*. "Kind of like Ron Mercer."

In the long run, he might be closer to Rex Chapman.

TODD TACKETT (6-2, 175 lbs., G, #12, 20.6 ppg, 3.1 apg, Paintsville HS/Paintsville, Ky.). Kentucky wasn't initially interested in Tackett, who committed to Clemson last December. Luckily for Smith, who decided after the NCAA Tournament that the Wildcats needed another shooter, it wasn't too late to get involved with Tackett. Credit goes to Tackett's father, Jerry, who had heard rumors that Kentucky was reconsidering its earlier decision not to recruit Todd.

"I knew the ethics of the school, and they wouldn't approach Todd," the elder Tackett told *The 'Cats Pause*.

1998-99 KENTUCKY SCHEDULE

Nov.	17	Eastern Kentucky
	23	*Wright State
	26-28	#Puerto Rico Shootout
Dec.	1	**Kansas
	5	Miami
	8	***Indiana
	12	Maryland
	19	****Georgia Tech
	22	*****Duke
	26	@Louisville
	29	Tennessee State
Jan.	2	Florida
	5	@South Carolina
	9	@Vanderbilt
	12	Tennessee
	16	@Mississippi
	20	Auburn
	23	Mississippi State
	26	@Georgia
	30	LSU
Feb.	4	@Florida
	6	@Alabama
	13	South Carolina
	17	Georgia
	20	@Arkansas
	24	Vanderbilt
	28	@Tennessee
Mar.	4-7	#SEC Tournament

@ Road Games
* The Crown, Cincinnati, OH
** Great Eight, United Center, Chicago, IL
*** Freedom Hall, Louisville, KY
**** Georgia Dome, Atlanta, GA
***** Continental Airlines Arena, East Rutherford, NJ
# Bayamone, PR (vs. Colorado, first round; also American University-Puerto Rico, Maryland, Pittsburgh, San Francisco, UCLA and Xavier.
Georgia Dome, Atlanta, GA

"So I made the first contact."

Jerry Tackett called Kentucky assistant Shawn Finney early last April and set up a meeting. He brought a tape of his son with him. Three days later, Kentucky offered Todd a scholarship. It didn't take him long to ponder the offer. Tackett was the Wildcats' only spring signee.

"Todd adds depth at shooting guard after the losses of Jeff Sheppard and Cameron Mills to graduation," Smith said. "We were looking for help at the position, and Todd will help us fill that void."

Tackett has a sweet stroke and knows how to free himself for open looks at the basket. He needs to gain strength, but can still fill Cameron Mills' role of designated shooter, even as a freshman.

Tackett is a proven scorer. He set Paintsville's single-game scoring record of 56 points and had 2,082 points in his five-year career. And, just to prove he's not one-dimensional, Tackett passed for a school-record 601 assists.

OTHER RETURNEES

RYAN HOGAN (6-3, 193 lbs., SO, G, #22, 1.1 ppg, 3.8 minutes, .269 FG, .417 3PT, Deerfield HS/Deerfield, Ill.). Like fellow sophomore Myron Anthony, Hogan made a freshman mistake off the court last season when he was pulled over for drunk driving. Suffice to say Smith wasn't too pleased, but he has yet to announce what Hogan's punishment will be. Also like Anthony, Hogan will probably miss some games.

Hogan was recruited to be the heir apparent to Jeff Sheppard at the shooting guard position. Although he played sparingly as a rookie, Hogan showed he had a long-distance stroke, making five of 12 three-pointers.

Hogan's season highlight came against UCLA in the NCAA Tournament He made a pair of three-pointers in the South Region semifinal, matching his career-high point total of six set in the 'Cats season-opener against Morehead State.

Hogan will have to improve defensively to get a strong look at shooting guard. He has a little competition for the job though, with the addition of freshman Tayshaun Prince and senior Heshimu Evans also capable of playing in the backcourt.

STEVE MASIELLO (6-2, 180 lbs., JR, G, #4, 0.6 ppg, 0.2 rpg, 23 appearances). Masiello is a former New York Knicks' ballboy who worked when Pitino was coaching in New York. Pitino invited Masiello to walk on at Kentucky, and he has actually played in 41 games in his first two seasons.

But Masiello played in five fewer games last season than he did as a freshman. His time will be reduced even more this year; Kentucky brought in three freshmen guards.

OTHER NEWCOMERS

J.P. BLEVINS (6-1, 182 lbs., FR, G, #3, 23.7 ppg, 6.6 rpg, 3.6 apg, Metcalfe County HS/Edmonton, Ky.). Blevins is one of those typical Kentucky youngsters who grew up wanting to play for the home state Wildcats. He committed to Kentucky midway through his junior season and, although some recruiting analysts question whether he can play at the SEC level, there can be no discounting Blevins' desire.

Something of a legend in Kentucky, Blevins played varsity basketball when he was a seventh grader. He started at the point from eighth grade on and scored 2,994 career points. Blevins was a first-team All-State pick in his final two seasons by the *Lexington Herald-Leader*, the *Louisville Courier-Journal* and the *Associated Press*.

Blevins is a good ballhandler, who, like fellow freshman Todd Tackett, can also shoot. Blevins once scored 51 points in a game.

Blevins' minutes will be sparse for at least his first season. He has the unenviable task of playing behind Wayne Turner and also the coach's son, Saul Smith.

QUESTIONS

Center? Before the NBA draft and a bad decision or two by Magloire, Kentucky was as strong in the post as any team in the country. Can Michael Bradley and Jules Camara fill the void, especially if Magloire is suspended for any length of time?

Shooting guard? Who will play the position vacated by Jeff Sheppard? Smith has plenty of candidates, but can any of them duplicate Sheppard's contributions of a year ago?

ANSWERS

Tubby Smith! We said it here last year, too. Smith is a great motivator and an excellent coach who knows how to get the most out of his talent. Kentucky's 1998 NCAA title proves that.

Senior leadership! In Wayne Turner, Scott Padgett and Heshimu Evans, Kentucky has three experienced and talented seniors to help take charge of what is basically a young team, with five freshmen and four sophomores.

adidas Blue Ribbon Analysis

BACKCOURT	B+	BENCH/DEPTH	B+
FRONTCOURT	B+	INTANGIBLES	A+

Last season, Tubby Smith proved he is more than capable of running one of the country's top two or three programs. He didn't have to win the national championship to do that. But he got no complaints from Kentucky fans for the title, even though some openly questioned the coach several times during the regular season—especially when the Wildcats were suddenly beatable, including at Rupp Arena.

No one was questioning Smith or his coaching moves after Kentucky disposed of a fine Utah team in the NCAA finals. During the Wildcats' impressive run to the championship, Smith showed he knew what buttons to push—and when to push them.

Kentucky wasn't the most talented team in the NCAA field, at least on paper. But, inspired by Smith's motivational skills, the Wildcats rose to great heights.

What does Smith do for an encore? Kentucky has appeared in the last three NCAA championship games and has brought home two titles. Are the Wildcats that good again?

Had center Nazr Mohammed not decided to turn professional, the Wildcats would have been a lock for St. Petersburg. But, then again, no one should count out Smith.

It isn't as though the talent level is down in Lexington. In Scott Padgett, Smith has a legitimate All-America candidate and a power forward capable of beating opponents inside or outside. Point guard Wayne Turner will be given some All-America consideration, too. He has few equals.

A third senior, Heshimu Evans, was impressive last season, his first after transferring from Manhattan. Padgett, Turner and Evans give Smith a solid nucleus around which to build.

If Smith can fill in around his seniors, he should be able to take the 'Cats on another very deep NCAA Tournament run. First the Wildcats must get by vastly improved Tennessee in the SEC's Eastern Division.

Once Kentucky gets into the postseason, as it has proven repeatedly in the '90s, the Wildcats are often the most dangerous team in the land.

(C.D.)

adidas Blue Ribbon Analysis

GRADING SYSTEM

- A+ equal to very best in country—Final Four-caliber unit
- A among the best in the land—worthy of deep NCAA run
- B+ talented, versatile and experienced—NCAA-NIT ability
- B solid and productive winners—league and post-season contenders
- C+ average to above-average—may contend in a weaker league
- C average to mediocre—second division in a strong league
- D+ below average, inconsistent—second division in a weaker league
- D well below average—losing season virtually certain
- F non-Division I ability—an underdog every night

5

MARYLAND

LOCATION	College Park, MD
CONFERENCE	Atlantic Coast (ACC)
LAST SEASON	21-11 (.656)
CONFERENCE RECORD	10-6 (3rd)
STARTERS LOST/RETURNING	2/3
NICKNAME	Terrapins
COLORS	Red & White, Black & Gold
HOMECOURT	Cole Field House (14,500)
COACH	Gary Williams (Maryland '68)
RECORD AT SCHOOL	164-112 (9 yrs.)
CAREER RECORD	371-240 (20 yrs.)
ASSISTANTS	Billy Hahn (Maryland '75)
	Dave Dickerson (Maryland '90)
	Jimmy Patsos (Catholic University '89)
TEAM WINS (last 5 yrs.)	18-26-17-21-22
RPI (last 5 yrs.)	30-10-35-23-9
1997-98 FINISH	Lost in NCAA Sweet 16.

COACH AND PROGRAM

Maryland coach Gary Williams knows his team is on the verge of running with the big boys. That's why he is looking forward to this year, as the Terrapins welcome back three grizzled veterans who hope to expand on Williams' long list of accomplishments as the Terps' head coach.

Of course, Williams thought he was in the same position three years ago—when he also had three accomplished seniors. Instead, that trio experienced a collectively horrible finale and a season that was full of promise faded into disappointment.

Williams thinks this time will be different, that seniors Laron Profit, Terrell Stokes and Obinna Ekezie will acquit themselves much better than the trio of Johnny Rhodes, Exree Hipp and Duane Simpkins. These three were sophomores back then, so they experienced first-hand what it was like to see a team coast at the end of a season.

Williams thinks they will respond better.

"They know this is their turn," the coach said. "If we are going to be a good team, then our seniors have to be our leaders. They have played in a lot of big games, and they should be used to this type of pressure."

It doesn't hurt, of course, to have a trio of talented newcomers and a barn full of other useful players to keep those seniors—two of which have a history of wayward attention—on the straight and narrow. Junior college sensation Steve Francis, a playmaking point guard with a smooth jumper, will come in and immediately push both Profit and Stokes. Williams wants to develop a productive rotation among them, sometimes putting all three on the court at the same time.

"I think the more ballhandlers you get out there, the better off you are," he said.

There is also the possibility that Francis could simply replace Stokes, who is beginning his third year as a starter, at the point. Stokes did lose the job for a six-game stretch last year to Matt Kovaric, a limited but hard-working senior on last year's team, so he could certainly lose it to one of the most gifted newcomers in the country.

Williams also likes the fact that Francis will push Profit, an athletic guard who doesn't shoot that well from the outside, but who has established a reputation as a solid and dangerous scorer.

Ekezie, on the other hand, won't be pushed so much as he will finally get some help. Redshirt sophomore Mike Mardesich, after slowly developing for two years in the program, is finally ready to contribute regularly. Senior Brian Watkins, sophomore LaRon Cephas and freshman Lonny Baxter are also capable of helping Ekezie in the frontcourt.

If they can find someone to provide consistent outside shooting, the Terps will have one of the deepest and most talented teams Williams has ever coached—and take a true place among the nation's "big boys" this season.

"We might be ready for that," Williams said. "Hopefully, that will be a motivator. Hopefully, our guys won't lay back and think that they have arrived. Every year, especially when you get some attention like we are this year, your role changes. You are not going to sneak up on anybody any more.

"You have to be ready, because teams want to knock you off now. That is what you have to guard against."

Last year, there was no Maryland fade, a malady that kept recent Terp teams from getting the national respect they probably deserved. Williams has done a remarkable job in his nine years at the school, but, because of some high-profile postseason failures, few people seem to know about it.

Maryland and North Carolina are the only two ACC teams (and two of only 11 in the country) that have been to the NCAA Tournament in each of the last five years. If the Terps make it back this year—and they will—it will set a school record for consecutive Tournament appearances.

Yet, prior to last season, it was two first-round defeats in a row for the Terrapins. Their only recent NCAA success came in 1995, when Joe Smith led the team within one game of the Final Four.

In 1997-98, the Terps more than survived history. They scored major regular season upsets over No. 2 Kansas and No. 1 North Carolina. They didn't come close in either game against Duke, losing by a combined total of 59 points in a pair of meetings with the top-ranked Blue Devils, but they were competitive with every other team they played.

And, unlike the year before, the Terps didn't give out at the end of the season. They beat Temple in their regular season finale and nearly upset North Carolina again in the second round of the ACC Tournament.

Maryland then cruised into the Sweet 16 with victories over Utah State and Illinois, but fell to defending champion Arizona in the third round. Not bad for a team that didn't have the maturity or depth that this season's squad will have.

For the second year in a row, the Terrapins play one of the toughest schedules in the nation. Last year's was the RPI's top-rated schedule in the country, thanks to the tough ACC schedule and non-conference games against South Carolina, Kansas, Missouri and Temple.

"We had some really big games early," Williams said. "You get that kind of good pressure in early games and you see how your players react to it. It really exposes them. If you have some things that you are not good at, you find out in December instead of January."

This year, the Terps play in the Puerto Rico Shootout, where they could face UCLA, Kentucky or Arizona. They play at Kentucky, host Stanford and meet Princeton in Baltimore.

"If you look at teams that have been at the top for a long time, this is the kind of schedule that they play," Williams said. "If we want to make a commitment to be there with the big boys, then we have to do the same thing."

STARTERS NOT RETURNING

SARUNAS JASIKEVICIUS (6-4, SF, 12.4 ppg, 3.3 rpg, 3.6 apg, 2.5 tpg, 1.2 spg, 29.3 minutes, .456 FG, .397 3PT, .759 FT). In four years, Jasikevicius never stopped doing the things that made Gary Williams take the short drive to insanity. Even last year, the Lithuanian bomber still made dumbfounding passes and took some unbelievably bad shots.

But he also never lost confidence in his ability to make something happen. Jasikevicius did that on many occasions, particularly in a two-game stretch against Clemson and Georgia Tech which helped solidify the Terps as the ACC's No. 3 team.

Over the years, Jasikevicius improved his defense, his decision-making and his ballhandling. He was the Terps most consistent outside scoring threat last year, something Williams may find hard to replace going into this season. Jasikevicius took and made big shots right until the end of his career.

RODNEY ELLIOTT (6-8, PF, 15.0 ppg, 7.4 rpg, 1.6 apg, 2.1 tpg, 28.9 minutes, .485 FG, .378 3PT, .686 FT). No one knew much about what Elliott could do when he inherited Keith Booth's spot in Maryland's starting lineup last year. He had been a career bench player before he suddenly became Maryland's "go-to" guy.

Elliott responded. His smooth shooting touch seemed unusual for a power forward of his size, but it was developed long ago when Elliott was too skinny to play inside. He filled out by his senior year in college and became not only a deadly shooter, but also a capable inside player who could rebound with the best players in the conference.

He still wasn't sure of his role in the first 10 games of last season, but, by the time the ACC schedule rolled around, Elliott was an important weapon both inside and outside. By season's end, Elliott had nearly doubled his scoring average from the year before and he was the Terps' leading rebounder. That combination earned him a spot on the third-team All-ACC squad.

Elliott was also voted to the ACC Tournament's second team, averaging 14.5 ppg and 9.0 rpg in the 1998 event.

OTHERS NOT RETURNING

MATT KOVARIK (6-5, G, 2.4 ppg, 1.7 rpg, 2.0 apg, 1.2 tpg, 15.3 minutes, .484 FG, .222 3PT, .429 FT). Kovarik was a part of five different teams at Maryland, thanks to a medical redshirt he received after breaking his leg in the preseason of his junior year. During that time, the Terps won more than 100 games and finished in the top half of the ACC standings all five years. Not bad for a guy many thought didn't have the talent to be an ACC player.

Logically, Kovaric had very little to do with the Terps' success. But his development from a hardly-recruited high school player to scout team member at Maryland to a competent ACC point guard was a factor.

Kovaric always did the dirty work. He was a defensive specialist who used his big frame to defend some of the ACC's best players. He filled in when needed and gave Williams decent fill-in minutes when there were injuries to players ahead of him.

He was also important in guiding Maryland through its most turbulent period of last season, the six games in which Stokes was held out of the starting lineup. With Kovarik at the point, Maryland went 4-2, including a stunning upset of No. 2 Kansas.

PROJECTED STARTERS

LARON PROFIT (6-5, 202 lbs., SR, SG, #3, 15.8 ppg, 5.2 rpg, 3.3 apg, 2.8 tpg, 2.7 tpg, 1.1 bpg, 31.5 minutes, .447 FG, .291 3PT, .707 FT, Caesar Rodney HS, Del./ Charleston, S.C.). Profit is perhaps the most gifted athlete on the team. He was a third-team All-ACC pick for the second year in a row and is projected to be the team's best all-star candidate again this year.

Profit does a lot of things well; he just doesn't do them all the time. That's been the biggest drawback of his career at Maryland and a source of frustration for Williams and the coaching staff.

"I think with Laron Profit the whole thing is if he shoots the ball consistently, then he is a good player," Williams said. "He has always been a great talent."

Not necessarily a talented shooter, however. Profit made only 29 percent of his three-point attempts last year, including a paltry 20.8 percent against ACC competition.

Defensively, Profit has done well—especially after inheriting Johnny Rhodes' role as a steal machine, recording 87 swipes last year. He is ranked third on the school's all-time steal list and needs only a eight to move into second place.

As was the case the last two years, all Williams is asking from Profit is to continue to improve and be more consistent. If that happens, then the Terps will finish as one of the top two teams in the ACC.

TERRELL STOKES (6-0, 187 lbs., SR, PG, #12, 5.4 ppg, 2.6 rpg, 4.8 apg, 2.1 tpg, 1.3 spg, 28.1 minutes, .415 FG, .343 3PT, .667 FT, Simon Gratz HS/Philadelphia, Pa). It took a six-game benching to get Stokes' attention last year. This season, Williams hopes all it takes for his senior point guard to be a more consistent and productive player is the arrival of junior college point guard Steve Francis.

Stokes' troubles began in the Terps' ACC opener against Clemson, when he had only two assists and committed a team-high six turnovers. The "expel Terrell" movement began there, but Williams vowed that he wasn't about to make a change.

What the coach did, however, was cut back Stokes minutes, which seemed to help against No. 2 Kansas. Stokes wasn't on the floor as much, but he was there in the final two seconds; he hit a pair of free throws to seal Maryland's 86-83 victory.

However, Stokes' indifferent play began again a game later. Williams responded by putting Matt Kovaric in the starting lineup for six consecutive games.

Stokes, who had been in Williams' doghouse earlier in his career, returned as a starter against North Carolina State and did not really see how the benching helped him or the team that much. However, his productivity went up. Stokes didn't score—which isn't a big part of his game—as much. But he did average more than 1.5 additional assists and 0.5 fewer turnovers than before he was taken out of the lineup.

Stokes is still an offensive liability. He is instead a playmaker and penetrator who plays decent defense instead of adding much scoring to the team. The Terps need some guaranteed scoring, however, and that is why Francis may take minutes away from Stokes.

Williams hopes the internal pressure will help the senior. He also hopes that he can find a way to get Stokes, Profit and Francis on the floor at the same time.

OBINNA EKEZIE (6-10, 262 lbs., SR, C, #54, 12.8 ppg, 6.5 rpg, 1.6 apg, 2.2 tpg, 1.2 bpg, 28.0 minutes, .484 FG, .670 FT, Worcester Academy, Ma./Point Harcourt, Nigeria). Look around the ACC, and you won't find any other team with a true center in its lineup. That doesn't mean Ekezie is one of the best players in the conference, but he is effective in helping the Terps run their breakneck offense.

Ekezie, one of the most improved players in the country two years ago, continued his improvement last year, setting career highs in scoring and rebounding. He played well under pressure and tried to rein in some of his aggressive play, though he still committed more than 100 fouls and was disqualified six times.

Still, he is an inside presence that the Terps need in their guard-oriented, up-tempo offense.

"He is really good for us the way we like to press and fastbreak," Williams said. "He's studied the game. I think he brings an intelligence to the court."

Williams thinks Ekezie is a huge success story. A native of Nigeria, Ekezie played little basketball before attending Worcester Academy in Massachusetts for one year. He has since spent his first three seasons at Maryland, which Ekezie chose because of an engineering/business program instead of its basketball tradition, learning the nuances of the game at its highest collegiate level.

1997-98 RESULTS

*South Carolina (L)	72-76	ot
Fairleigh Dickinson	81-70	
Mount St. Mary's	102-74	
Florida International	117-70	
@Clemson (L)	65-78	ot
#Kansas	86-83	
#George Washington (L)	66-70	
Maryland-Baltimore County	104-66	
North Carolina-Asheville	110-52	
North Carolina-Wilmington	73-36	
@Missouri (L)	79-83	
Duke (L)	72-104	
Florida State	81-74	
@North Carolina State	68-65	
North Carolina	89-83	
@Wake Forest (L)	60-72	
@Georgia Tech	70-67	
Clemson	74-69	
@Duke (L)	59-86	
Virginia	77-70	
@Florida State	68-62	
North Carolina State	78-63	
@North Carolina (L)	67-85	
Wake Forest (L)	79-83	
George Tech	81-69	
@Virginia	74-66	
**Temple	83-66	
##Georgia Tech	83-65	
##North Carolina (L)	73-83	ot
%Utah State	82-68	
%Illinois	67-61	
%%Arizona (L)	79-87	

@	away games
*	BCA Classic, Target Center, Minneapolis, MN
**	Baltimore Civic Center, Baltimore, MD
#	Franklin National Bank Classic, Washington, DC
##	ACC Tournament, Greensboro Coliseum, Greensboro, NC
%	NCAA West Sub-Regional, Sacramento, CA
%%	NCAA West Regional, Anaheim, CA

Ekezie still has a ways to go, Williams believes. His best basketball may still be three or four years away.

"He was forced into the starting lineup about halfway through his freshman year, and he has improved quite a bit every year since," Williams said. "Whether he can make the same jump that he has made the first three years, we'll see. He works hard in the off-season. He has gotten stronger and he has gotten to be a better athlete."

TERENCE MORRIS (6-9, 205 lbs., SO, F, #44, 7.4 ppg, 3.5 rpg, 16.0 minutes, .523 FG, .351 3PT, .695 FT, Thomas Johnson HS/Frederick, Md.). Morris was one of the most heralded freshmen in the ACC last year, but he did not make an immediate impact with the Terps. He took some time getting adjusted to the college game.

Morris led a relatively sheltered prep career at Thomas Johnson High and wasn't exactly sure what to expect when he arrived, amid much acclaim, in College Park. He was painfully shy and quiet, carrying so many expectations, that Williams sheltered him from the media for the first two months of the season.

"He was unique in that he never went to the camps, or played on the AAU teams," Williams said. "He just stayed in Frederick and played in the summer league, pretty much with his high school teammates. He didn't have the exposure.

"A lot of the kids today, they walk in and they have been everywhere and played in big tournaments nationwide and done things like that. Terence never did any of those things."

Morris improved gradually during the course of the season, increasing his numbers significantly over the final 16 games, earning more playing time at critical times in some of the Terps' biggest games. None were bigger than the win over No. 1 UNC, when Morris stepped in and scored three big alley oop dunks that sunk the previously unbeaten Tar Heels.

"By the time we got to the NCAA Tournament, he was in our top five—even though he wasn't starting," Williams said. "I think he is going to be very difficult to keep out of the starting lineup."

This summer, Morris joined teammate Mardesich on a U.S. Select team that participated in the Acropolis Cup in Athens, Greece.

STEVE FRANCIS (6-3, 194 lbs., JR, G, #23, 25.3 ppg, 7.1 rpg, 8.7 apg, .530 FG, .820 FT, 187 steals, Alleghany CC, Md./Takoma Park, Md.). There is little doubt that Francis, one of the most gifted junior college players in the country last year, will play immediately for the Terps. What Williams hopes is that he will be able to play both the point and the shooting guard positions, pushing Stokes and Profit to a higher level of consistency.

"He gives us more versatility in the backcourt than we have ever had before," Williams beamed.

Francis is athletic enough to push Maryland's uptempo offense up the floor at break-neck speed. But Williams also thinks he is a good enough shooter to play the off guard position, where there is a definite opening for a productive scorer. Or—and Williams gets really excited when he talks about this—Francis can step into the backcourt with Profit and Stokes, giving the Terps two point men and a slasher on the perimeter.

Just joining the Terps has been a long and rocky journey for the Maryland native. In the last four years, he has suffered through a broken ankle as a high school junior, the death of his mother as a senior and stops at two different junior colleges.

It was all enough to make Francis consider entering the NBA draft after last season, a transition most scouts believe he could have made much more easily than most of the high school players who go straight to the pros. Along the way, Francis helped lead Alleghany CC to an undefeated regular season, and most people figure he can have the same positive impact on the Terps.

"He's 6-3, which is an excellent size for a point guard," Francis' AAU coach Lou Wilson said. "He's also an explosive leaper and an excellent defender. There is nothing average about him."

Williams hopes that Stokes and Profit discover that on the first day of preseason practice, and that Francis will drive them to become even better.

"That competition in practice is what you want," Williams said. "I think Steve will give us that for sure."

And, by the time the end of the season arrives, who knows what else Francis can do for the Terps?

KEY RESERVES

MIKE MARDESICH (7-0, 245 lbs., SO, F, #33, 5.4 ppg, 4.3 rpg, 18.2 minutes, .424 FG, .622 FT, Worcester Academy, Mass./Conroe, Tex.). This is the guy whose picture is beside the phrase "late bloomer" in the dictionary. Cut from his high school basketball team as a junior, Mardesich didn't have much playing experience—and hardly any interest from colleges offering athletic scholarships—by the time he finished high school.

But, having skipped a grade when his parents moved back to the U.S. from Europe, Mardesich believed he would benefit from an extra year of competition. So he spent a year at Worcester (Ma.) Academy.

He still didn't excite many college scouts, although his 1,310 SAT scores kept Harvard interested. He wasn't even ranked among the top 250 players in the country when he signed with Maryland.

But Williams never considered Mardesich a "project." The kid is seven-feet tall, has good hands and can shoot. Was he lacking anything more than, say, Serge Zwikker?

Williams needed Mardesich to play immediately, but Mardesich stubbornly insisted on redshirting as a freshman. He wanted to get adjusted to college life and learn a little more about basketball.

That year of waiting will pay off now. Mardesich played a little over 18 minutes per game last year, contributing some scoring and rebounding. His biggest contribution of the season, however, was when he stepped in after Ekezie fouled out late in regulation against top-ranked North Carolina. Mardesich scored the game-tying points at the end of regulation, grabbing an Elliott air ball and putting it back to send the game into overtime.

In the extra period, Mardesich showed a few reasons why Williams thinks his young player will succeed in the ACC, as he bullied UNC's Antawn Jamison and Makhtar Ndiaye in the Terps' biggest win of the season. He scored a career-high 14 points and added a team-high nine rebounds.

Williams wants Mardesich to keep maturing this season, so he will be fully ready to step in next year when Ekezie is gone.

BRIAN WATKINS (6-9, 229 lbs., SR, F, #45, 2.1 ppg, 1.7 rpg, 5.3 minutes, .500 FG, .600 FT, Overland HS/Nashville, Tenn.). When Watkins first became eligible for Maryland—he sat out a year after transferring from Notre Dame—the redshirt sophomore scored 11 points in his first appearance. He hasn't scored in double figures since then.

Watkins played in only nine games last year, reaching season-highs of eight points and six rebounds against Florida International.

This year, Watkins will again provide depth in the frontcourt, but Williams has a handful of younger players he wants to develop, probably at the expense of playing time for Watkins.

LARON CEPHAS (6-7, 223 lbs., F, SO, #21, 0.3 ppg, 1.4 rpg, 4.5 minutes, .143 FG, .250 FT, Sanford School/Wilmington, Del.). The Terps could use some depth in the post, and Williams hopes Cephas can provide that this year. He played in 21 games last season and was better at rebounding than scoring.

Like teammate Juan Dixon, Cephas struggled to gain entry into Maryland. He enrolled in January, 1997, and spent the rest of that season as a redshirt. Last year, he was used sparingly.

The former AAU teammate of Maryland's Laron Profit, Cephas is still developing as a post player and his best production is still at least a season away.

DANNY MILLER (6-6, 205 lbs., FR., G, #15 20.5 ppg, 7.9 rpg, 3.4 apg, .451 FG, Rancocas Valley HS/Mt. Holly, N.J.). Williams doesn't like to rush his freshmen into the lineup, and Miller probably will be no exception. Last year, Terence Morris didn't work his way into the team's top five until late February and March.

So Miller, despite all-star credentials, will probably be a versatile role player this year, preparing himself to take over for Profit next season as the Terps' shooting guard. Still, Williams considers Miller his most important recruit in this year's class, mainly because Miller is a high-profile signee who will further establish Maryland's reputation.

Williams thinks it is good for the program to bring in one of the ACC's five incoming McDonald's All-Americas, especially one that was also considering Duke. "It was really important to us to get him here," the coach said.

And it will be really important for Miller to develop into a strong player, which he has the obvious talent to do.

"He's just a great all-around player," Rancocas Valley coach Ron Powell said. "We asked him to do everything for our team—score, rebound, dive on the floor. You name it, he did it and he did it with intensity."

LONNY BAXTER (6-8, 250 lbs., FR, F, #35, 21.4 ppg, 10.3 rpg, .480 FG, .850 FT, Hargrave Military Academy, Va./Silver Spring, Md.). Ekezie is Maryland's only proven muscle man in the post. By the end of the season, Williams hopes Baxter will be able to help in that area.

By all accounts, Baxter is Maryland's burly-man of the future. However, he will be allowed to develop behind Ekezie this season, then step in next year in the post.

Last year, Baxter was a prep school teammate of Korleone Young, a 6-7 forward who went straight into the NBA. Baxter had no trouble making his own mark at the school, averaging double figures in points and rebounding.

"With Obinna Ekezie being a senior, we thought it was important to bring in a player like Lonny who could come in and learn and be ready to play when Obinna left," Williams said. "I'm not worried about where he will fit in, at power forward or at center.

"It doesn't matter to me as long as he can play."<

And this year, he will probably be allowed to sit back, watch and learn from Ekezie.

OTHER RETURNEES

NORMAN FIELDS (6-0, 185 lbs., SR, G, #31, 1.9 ppg, 0.9 rpg, 12 appearances, Mt. St. Michael HS/Mt. Vernon, N.Y.). Fields won a tryout with 300 other Maryland students for the right to walk on to the team in 1995. He is entering his fourth season on the squad and is used primarily as a practice player, helping the team prepare for its next opponent.

Last year, Fields did appear in a career-high 12 games, scoring five points in back-to-back contests against UNC-Asheville and UNC-Wilmington.

MATT HAHN (6-0, 162 lbs., JR, G, #20, 0.9 ppg, five appearances, .250 FG, .200 3PT, .750 FT, Atholton HS/Columbia, Md.). Hahn is entering his third season as a member of the Maryland practice squad. The son of Terrapin assistant coach Billy Hahn, he emulates the opposing point guard in helping the team prepare for upcoming games.

Hahn played in 11 games last year, scoring a career high five points against Mount St. Mary's.

OTHER NEWCOMERS

JUAN DIXON (6-3, 152 lbs., G, FR, #5, 23.4 ppg, 4.5 rpg, Calvert Hall HS/Baltimore, Md.). Dixon, who signed with Maryland in the fall of 1996, didn't enroll at the school until last January, after finally making his qualifying scores and gaining his NCAA eligibility. He never

1998-99 MARYLAND SCHEDULE

Nov.	14	Western Carolina
	17	Maryland-Baltimore County
	20	Hofstra
	23	Duquesne
	26-28	#Puerto Rico Shootout
Dec.	3	Wake Forest
	6-7	##BB&T Bank Classic
	12	@Kentucky
	19	*Princeton
	23	North Texas
	27	South Carolina State
Jan.	3	Duke
	7	@Virginia
	10	North Carolina State
	13	@North Carolina
	19	Georgia Tech
	24	@Clemson
	27	Florida State
	31	@Wake Forest
Feb.	3	@Duke
	6	Virginia
	10	@North Carolina State
	13	North Carolina
	21	@Georgia Tech
	24	Clemson
	27	@Florida State
Mar.	4-7	###ACC Tournament

@ Road Games
* Baltimore Civic Center, Baltimore, MD
\# San Juan, PR (vs. American University-PR, first round; also Colorado, Kentucky, Maryland, Pittsburgh, San Francisco, UCLA and Xavier)
\## MCI Center, Washington, DC (vs. Stanford, first round; also DePaul and George Washington)
\### Charlotte Coliseum, Charlotte, NC

played for the Terps, choosing instead to redshirt, which means he will have four full years of eligibility.

Eventually, Williams wants Dixon to help improve his team's outside shooting, which has plenty to replace with the departures of Elliott and Jasikevicius, the team's two best perimeter shooters.

Dixon was a highly decorated high school player at Baltimore's Calvert Hall. He helped lead his team to the Catholic League tournament finals during the three seasons he was a starter.

"He was capable of carrying us offensively, and he is also a good defender," Calvert Hall coach Mark Amatucci said. "He has proven to be one of the top five guards in the country."

QUESTIONS

Consistency? Sure, Profit and Stokes improved their consistency last year...but not as much as Williams would have liked. They still need to make bigger strides if the Terps want to be considered one of the top teams in the nation.

Outside shooting? The Terps lost their top two perimeter scorers. The returning players shot a meager 31.5 percent from three-point range. To stay with the big boys, the Terps need better productivity outside.

Chemistry? Williams is going to try several combinations, including a three-guard lineup with Profit, Stokes and Francis. How long will he have to experiment, especially in getting playing time for his highly regarded recruits, to find the right combination and the right rotation?

ANSWERS

Experience! Ekezie, Profit and Stokes have had ups and down in their first three years in College Park, but they have all improved dramatically since they first arrived. All three are entering at least their third season in the starting lineup. That experience should pay off for them and the rest of the team this year.

Depth! Williams likes to pressure opponents and run an up-tempo game. He should have more than enough horses in the barn to wear down just about anyone.

Speed! The Terps were already one of the more athletic teams in the conference. The addition of Francis, Miller and Baxter only improves their ability to get up and down the floor.

adidas Blue Ribbon Analysis

BACKCOURT	**A**	**BENCH/DEPTH**	**B+**
FRONTCOURT	**B+**	**INTANGIBLES**	**B+**

The Terrapins have been building for this season for three years now. Profit, Stokes and Ekezie have weathered several storms in their careers and should be ready for a breakout senior season.

However, consistency questions have bothered Profit and Stokes. They improved a little last year from their sometimes immature sophomore season, but Williams hoped for more. The biggest boost they could have, of course, is getting pushed by newcomer Steve Francis, the junior college transfer who is considered one of the best incoming players in college basketball this year.

The Terps made great strides last year, knocking off powers like Kansas and North Carolina. They didn't come close either time against Duke, however, and if they want to become one of the "big boys" of college basketball, they will have to be consistent enough to at least challenge the Blue Devils in the ACC.

Regardless, a great opportunity awaits.

(T.P.)

6

TEMPLE

LOCATION	**Philadelphia, PA**
CONFERENCE	**Atlantic 10 (East Division)**
LAST SEASON	**21-9 (.700)**
CONFERENCE RECORD	**13-3 (1st)**
STARTERS LOST/RETURNING	**2/3**
NICKNAME	**Owls**
COLORS	**Cherry & White**
HOMECOURT	**The Apollo of Temple (10,206)**
COACH	**John Chaney (Bethune-Cookman '55)**
RECORD AT SCHOOL	**356-149 (16 yrs.)**
CAREER RECORD	**581-208 (26 yrs.)**
ASSISTANTS	**Dean Demopoulos (West Chester '77)**
	Nate Blackwell (Temple '90)
	Dan Leibovitz (Pennsylvania '96)
TEAM WINS (last 5 yrs.)	**23-19-20-20-21**
RPI (last 5 yrs.)	**8-37-25-37-30**
1997-98 FINISH	**Lost in NCAA first round.**

COACH AND PROGRAM

The last memory is the most misleading. The 1997-98 Owls crashed spectacularly, losing by 30 points to former Atlantic 10 nemesis West Virginia in the first round of the NCAA West Regional.

It was an aberration; trust us. Without doing the research, there are probably less than a handful of times in John Chaney's 16 seasons that Temple has gone down by a margin even approaching this one—much less in a meaningful game.

What happened that day is easy to explain. The Owls fell behind early, and they fell behind big. So the matchup zone and the controlled tempo and the defensive suction were never factors. Temple had to play from behind, and the Chaney system simply has no contingency for creating extra possessions.

Making it worse was that the Owls couldn't find Idaho with their shots, let alone the baskets at Boise State. Like we said, it was an aberration. The reason we never see such a blowout is that Temple never falls so far behind, so early. Chaney's defense simply won't permit it, and the Owls won't turn the ball over to get on the wrong end of a big run.

Linger if you must, but wise Owls will turn the page on the Mountaineers.

"The point differential by no means distinguishes one (loss) from another," Chaney insisted. "It was nothing you could predict was going to happen."

What we can predict is that the Owls will be back, and then some. We are about to witness not a typically good Chaney team, but a *great* Chaney team. One with a mixture of experience and youth, power and perimeter presence, style and substance.

OK, maybe not style. That is, unless you like an offense which frequently shoots less than 40 percent from the field and whose idea of fun is a long rebound from a three-point brick.

Temple makes its mark at the other end of the court. Always has, always will. At least under Chaney, who has seen players come and go, but whose system wins with lesser talent and can win big with top talent.

Which begs two questions: How high is the talent this year? And how long will Chaney continue dominating North Broad Street?

We'll get into the talent below. Suffice to say this is a group to rival Temple's Final Eight teams of '88, '91 and '93.

As for Chaney, well, the whispers are mounting that he is at least thinking about the inevitable sunset. He has fulfilled one pledge, to coach Temple into its long-sought (and beautiful) new Apollo. He hopes to take one last hurdle into the Final Four.

In the meantime, he has already endorsed long-time assistant Dean Demopoulus as his successor. Should Chaney step down after this season, Demopoulus would be loaded with a similarly talented group next year. Should Chaney wait another year or two, the current nucleus should give him more than one good shot at filling the only gap on his resume.

"They're loaded," suggested one Atlantic 10 observer. "This could be the last round-up."

STARTERS NOT RETURNING

LYNARD STEWART (6-8, PF, 6.9 ppg, 5.2 rpg, 1.1 tpg, 1.3 spg, 28.5 minutes, .520 FG, .570 FT). Stewart is the only significant loss from 1997-98. He was a terrific defender, with long arms and desire and as good a sense of the passing lanes as any recent Owl.

Who can forget the night the Apollo opened? There was Stewart at the head of Temple's matchup zone, cutting the floor in half and making Fresno State look foolish. The Owls' first three baskets came when Jerry Tarkanian's overmatched bunch couldn't make a simply entry pass—not to the post, but to the foul line—and Temple got layups.

Stewart was key in giving the Owls that look, just by being there. He really wasn't much more than workman-like, but it says something that Temple played in the NCAA Tournament during each of his four seasons.

JULIAN DUNKLEY (6-10, SF, 4.5 ppg, 2.2 rpg, 15.7 minutes, .329 FG, .333 3PT, .462 FT). It's not an exaggeration to note that Dunkley may have been the least productive starting player during the Chaney era. Given the way the veteran coach extends his starters—Mark Macon, Nate Blackwell and Terence Stansbury each averaged *over* 40 minutes per game in a single season—it says everything that Dunkley was little more than a nominal starter.

Mostly, he couldn't master the Temple defensive sets. That crime is equal to life imprisonment under Chaney.

The coach might have looked the other way had Dunkley been as good a shooter as advertised, or rebounded with some passion, or clogged the lane, or done almost anything, really. Instead, Dunkley tired of not being good enough and wisely transferred.

It didn't hurt that he could see Mark Karcher (not to mention Quincy Wadley) over his shoulder.

OTHERS NOT RETURNING

MALIK MOORE (6-3, G, 1.3 ppg, 0.9 rpg, 5.7 minutes, .186 FG, .231 3PT, .750 FT). Moore, after sitting out as a freshman, got lost in what might be the nation's deepest backcourt rotation. Then he got lost in the classroom.

Chaney will tolerate the former, but never the latter. Moore was dismissed from the school after only one season in uniform.

MICHAEL TABB (6-9, F, 0.9 ppg, 1.2 rpg, 4.1 minutes, .286 FG, .545 FT). It was hoped that Tabb might help offset the year-early departure of former center Marc Jackson. Instead, the much-traveled big man was overmatched by the demands of Temple and the level of play in the Atlantic 10.

It was a decent gamble, taking Tabb as a Clemson transfer after a stopover at hometown Delaware County (Pa.) CC. It just didn't work out. Tabb could never shake the rust of sitting out the equivalent of two full seasons.

The Owls survived without him last year, and they certainly will again.

PROJECTED STARTERS

LAMONT BARNES (6-10, 230 lbs., JR, PF, #32, 13.8 ppg, 8.0 rpg, 1.9 tpg, 1.3 spg, 2.5 bpg, 33.6 minutes, .579 FG, .660 FT, University Heights Academy/Hopkinsville, Ky.). It is an oversimplification to be sure, but the world according to John Chaney contains a number of truisms. One is that guards should be smart enough to listen to the coach at all times; another is that big men are so dumb that they usually listen to the guards.

Does it surprise anyone that Chaney himself was a star guard? Didn't think so.

But it should be a surprise that Chaney calls Barnes "a very intelligent forward. He has maturity and leadership. He is one of the guys at the hub of this ballclub."

You'd have to have been around the Owls for years to know what kind of high praise that is. Chaney loves his big men, but those adjectives never seemed to find their way into conversations about Ramon Rivas or Tim Perry or Donald Hodge or Duane Causwell. The coach had a soft spot, too, for Marc Jackson, but you'd have to go all the way back to the days of Granger Hall to hear this kind of gushing about a frontcourt player.

Barnes is worth it. His evolution from "nice recruit" to major college star is nearly complete.

Barnes played in Jackson's shadow as a freshman, doing the dirty work and getting out of the way offensively. But he still started all 31 games and one could see the upside, especially the defensive instincts.

As a sophomore, Barnes was forced to the center position by default. Instead of being overmatched, his quickness and leaping ability were tremendous assets. His scoring (from 8.1 ppg in 1996-97) jumped into the all-league range, and his shot-blocking (74) made a stingy Temple defense even better.

"Lamont played an area that was somewhat unnatural to him," Chaney admitted," but he did an excellent job. Our newcomers give him a chance to develop his overall talent in the next two years."

Read "newcomers" as Kevin Lyde. Even if the freshman center is only advanced enough to play the pivot half the time, Barnes will profit. The smiling junior is already mighty good.

RASHEED BROKENBOROUGH (6-4, 185 lbs., SR, SG, #21, 11.8 ppg, 3.3 rpg, 2.0 apg, 2.0 rpg, 1.6 spg, 31.9 minutes, .360 FG, .315 3PT, .670 FT, University City HS/ Philadelphia, Pa.). See Brokenborough in an airport, and he looks more like a starving waiter than a major college "two" guard. He seems shorter than 6-4 and way skinnier than 185 pounds.

Until you try to guard him, or dribble by him, or reach in for a steal. Then that lithe body snaps into action and Brokenborough is gone, launching a jump shot or passing smartly to the post. And, like most Temple perimeter players, his arms always seem to be in your way.

Also like most Temple guards, Brokenborough is a shooter who can't really shoot. The release and the tempo look great, but the results are unmistakable. In two seasons as a full-time starter, Brokenborough is a 36.4 percent shooter and converts an invisible 30.8 percent from three-point range. Yet he has fired away 416 times from the arc in 61 games.

At most places, those numbers would get you dirty looks in an intramural game. At Temple, they call you a star.

The truth, as usual, is somewhere in the middle. Brokenborough is never going to be an NBA player, but he fits the Chaney system. And the Owls win with him. All the pre-college accolades mean nothing here (as Mark Karcher will soon discover); all that matters is doing your job at the defensive end and taking open shots when the ball rotates.

Chaney's response to a poor shooter is never a red light, only to get him more shots. Anyone who remembers Mark Macon would never disagree.

JUAN "PEPE" SANCHEZ (6-4, 198 lbs., JR, PG, #4, 9.6 ppg, 4.1 rpg, 4.9 apg, 2.8 tpg, 3.4 apg, 31.4 minutes, .327 FG, .269 3PT, .743 FT, Bahia Blanca, Argentina). Every year they say Pepe Sanchez is going home to play pro ball, and every year he is back at Temple. Maybe that's because Sanchez has one huge advantage over his predecessors as Chaney's point guard, perhaps the hottest spot in college basketball.

He can pretend not to understand the cagey coach.

Oh, Sanchez speaks English just fine. But, every once in a while, you'll see him roll his eyes or put his palms in the air as he looks away from the bench. The next minute, Sanchez has picked your pocket and created another possession for the Owls.

Sanchez turns the ball over too often for Chaney's taste, but his defense in the matchup zone is unparalleled. "Pepe" was second in the nation in steals and became Temple's all-time single-season leader (with 93) last season.

Now it says here that steals can be the most overrated statistic in basketball. Using it as a gauge of defensive ability is like using stolen bases as a gauge of offensive ability in baseball. Steals are often style, not substance.

The really good defensive point guard gambles only when he can or must. He does not expose his teammates or put the guys behind him in a shorthanded position. He reaches when the time is right.

That is Sanchez, and that is Temple. The crafty junior creates so many extra possessions for his team, and his turnover numbers are well within an acceptable range for any other coach in the sport.

"Experience," said Chaney," is the main thing 'Pepe' brings to us."

And timing. Sanchez, quite appropriately, can't shoot. Yet he sticks three-pointers when it really matters. He turned in the first triple-double under Chaney (10 points, 10 rebounds, 10 assists) vs. La Salle. One night, he might add 10 steals—his career-high is eight—and make it a quadruple-double.

Those eight steals came at Michigan State and Mateen Cleaves, including a pivotal one in the closing minute to help seal a very big victory.

In fact, whenever Temple has a big victory, Sanchez has usually exceeded his averages. He badly turned an ankle late in a game at Dayton last year, and the Owls went on to lose that one as well as a subsequent home contest vs. Xavier (in which Sanchez did not dress).

Look for Sanchez to continue supplying plenty of "pep" this season. And, if he returns next year, the Owls will not miss a beat.

MARK KARCHER (6-5, 210 lbs., SO, SF, #25, 27.5 ppg, 5.0 rpg, 6.7 apg in 1996-97, St. Frances Academy/ Baltimore, Md.). The last Temple recruit with this much advance billing was Mark Macon. As a freshman, Macon was the missing piece as the Owls vaulted to a No. 1 ranking in the wire service polls.

Karcher also joins a very established Temple team. And his superlative offensive skills should be equally welcome on a unit which sometimes treats scoring like bad disease.

"He is a scoring machine," said another Atlantic 10 coach. "It's scary how good he is."

Not that it will matter if Karcher doesn't play defense. Chaney would sit Michael Jordan if he didn't slide in the zone or offer weak side help.

Karcher has had a year to watch and learn. Unfortunately, he could not practice as an academic redshirt. Few players recover easily from such a year off, especially at Temple, where the system is so complex. Even Eddie Jones, in a similar situation, was only a part-time starter once he become eligible.

Yet it will be difficult to ignore Karcher. First, the Owls have a glaring need for offense on the wing. Second, well, Karcher is awfully good.

He was a McDonald's, *Parade* and *USA Today* All-America, making the first team of each. He was the state of Maryland and Baltimore city Player of the Year. He scored an amazing 3,100 points in a four-year varsity career, averaging 22.8 ppg, 9.3 rpg and 5.6 apg along the way.

Karcher creates, he shoots and he scores. On one leg, he would triple the production of Julian Dunkley.

"We're really excited about the new players," Chaney understated. "Mark Karcher we look to as a mix-and-match player."

In Chaney-speak, that means Karcher could play anywhere but center or point guard. And he will, but he'd better at least think about playing some defense.

Temple's gain is a huge loss at Villanova and Maryland, which both thought they had Karcher locked up at various points of his final prep season. When the star recruit became a non-qualifier, however, the Owls were waiting with open arms.

KEVIN LYDE (6-10, 240 lbs., FR, C, #42, 18.0 ppg, 8.0 rpg, 3.5 bpg, Oak Hill Academy, Va./Forest Heights, Md.). The real missing piece at Temple is Kevin Lyde, as the Owls were unexpectedly without a center last year following the early-out of 1996-97 Atlantic 10 Player of the Year Marc Jackson. Jackson left with Chaney's blessing, but that did not diminish the hole his absence created in the middle.

No more. The Owls pushed hard for the starting center at Oak Hill, then scored twice when Lyde committed to Temple and again when he achieved freshman eligibility. This second-team *Parade* All-America should be an immediate starter this season.

If Chaney is happy about that, Lamont Barnes should be ecstatic. The latter just gained substantial real estate around the basket in which he can add new offensive heroics. Lyde's presence should also allow Barnes even more freedom for blocking shots, which makes the interior of the Temple zone as good as its perimeter.

Lyde was rated the No. 4 center prospect in his class and the No. 16 player overall by ESPN. Given normal development, he will be the latest in a long line of outstanding centers at Temple.

Said the *A-10 Hoop Report*: "Lyde was the best (pure) post player in the U.S. last season. He is strong, tough and smart around the goal. He possesses a nice jump shot, drop step, power moves and can also face the basket."

We don't know if Lyde also helps little old ladies across the street, but he won't have to do that as a freshman. All he must do for Temple to be great is defend, rebound, score occasionally, be big and get out of Barnes' way.

KEY RESERVES

QUINCY WADLEY (6-4, 190 lbs., JR, G, #33, 8.0 ppg, 3.4 rpg, 1.5 apg, 1.1 tpg, 1.5 spg, 25.4 minutes, .358 FG, .320 3PT, .810 FT, Harrisburg HS/Harrisburg, Pa.). Wadley is arguably the best sixth man Chaney has had at Temple. Then again, someone had to make up for Julian Dunkley's many weaknesses at small forward.

We doubt many Temple reserves have averaged this many minutes under Chaney. And Wadley earned his as

1997-98 RESULTS

Opponent	Score	
#Auburn	68-42	
*Indiana	59-53	
@Mississippi (L)	74-87	
@Michigan State	56-54	
@Wisconsin	59-49	
Fresno State	76-61	
DePaul	74-43	
@Villanova (L)	57-68	
Rutgers (L)	63-72	
Rhode Island (L)	64-74	
Pennsylvania	67-58	
St. Bonaventure	64-43	
@La Salle	80-66	
Duquesne	75-62	
@Fordham	77-62	
@St. Joseph's	68-62	ot
@Dayton (L)	62-67	
Xavier (L)	73-79	
@Massachusetts	61-47	
Virginia Tech	60-53	
Fordham	59-54	
@Rhode Island	68-67	
St. Joseph's	50-42	
@St. Bonaventure	68-45	
@George Washington	56-49	
**Maryland (L)	66-83	
Massachusetts	74-66	
##St. Joseph's	76-62	
##George Washington (L)	64-78	
%West Virginia (L)	52-82	

@ away games
* CoreStates Spectrum, Philadelphia, PA
** Baltimore Civic Center, Baltimore, MD
# NABC Classic, Albuquerque, NM
Atlantic 10 Tournament, Core States Spectrum, Philadelphia, PA
% NCAA West Sub-Regional, Boise, ID

1998-99 TEMPLE SCHEDULE

Month	Date	Opponent
Nov.	10-11	#Coaches vs. Cancer Classic
	18	Mississippi
	20	Michigan State
	23	*Pennsylvania
Dec.	1	@Penn State
	5	@Indiana
	9	Wisconsin
	14	Florida State
	19	@Rutgers
	29	##Stanford
	31	@Fresno State
Jan.	3	La Salle
	6	St. Bonaventure
	9	@Fordham
	14	St. Joseph's
	16	Rhode Island
	19	@Duquesne
	23	Massachusetts
	30	@St. Bonaventure
Feb.	4	Dayton
	6	@Rhode Island
	9	@St. Joseph's
	14	@Xavier
	16	@Virginia Tech
	20	George Washington
	24	Fordham
	28	@Massachusetts
Mar.	3-6	###Atlantic 10 Tournament

@ Road Games
* The Palestra, Philadelphia, PA
# Madison Square Garden, NY (vs. Georgetown, first round; also Illinois and Wake Forest)
Pete Newell Challenge, Oakland, CA
First Union Spectrum, Philadelphia, PA

a defender, opportunistic scorer and versatile wing man. Wadley is also extremely tough, one of many endearing qualities for Chaney.

Wadley was especially impressive given that he sat out as a freshman. The role he played is more often associated with veterans than first-year guys. When Pepe Sanchez missed two starts with a bum ankle, it was Wadley who got the call (as Brokenborough moved to the point).

Wadley should play a similar role this season. One would think he'd lose minutes given the arrival of Mark Karcher, but Wadley is too valuable for that. Instead, Chaney might load up on wing defenders around Barnes when Lyde is not on the floor.

"From his deeds," said Chaney, "Quincy has been somewhat of a great player."

We think that means the coach likes him.

LYNN GREER (6-2, 165 lbs., SO, G, #14, 7.9 ppg, 1.1 rpg, 1.1 apg, 1.3 tpg, 17.4 minutes, .379 FG, .472 3PT, .806 FT, Engineering & Science HS/Philadelphia, Pa.). If this were football, Greer would be the third down running back, the change of pace guy who makes big plays in spot duty. Greer isn't going to supplant either Sanchez or Brokenborough as a starter, but he is talented enough to start at either guard position. Instead, he will watch and wait and play about half the game behind the two veterans.

Greer does something else which makes him a standout among the Owls (present and past). He connected on 47.2 percent of his three-point attempts to rank 14th in the nation. Defensive orientation notwithstanding, it never hurts to have a guy whose shot goes in the basket a reasonable percentage of the time.

And the Owls lose little with Greer at the other end. He is heady, quick and athletic. He is not as rangy defensively as a typical Temple guard, but he is usually in the right place at the right time.

Greer, the former *Associated Press* Pennsylvania Player of the Year, will be a backcourt starter next season. The position he plays is up to Sanchez.

KEATON SANDERS (6-6, 225 lbs., JR, G/F, #15, 2.1 ppg, 2.7 rpg, 12.3 minutes, .500 FG, .500 FT, Peach County HS/Fort Valley, Ga.). Sanders became a valuable reserve as a sophomore. His 82 minutes as a freshman jumped to 356 in 1997-98.

Sanders gives Temple a little bit more of the little things. He is a strong rebounder, willing defender and aggressive forward who can move around the frontcourt. He won't break a game open with his offense, but the Owls don't need that.

They need a dependable eighth man in a rotation never larger than that under Chaney. Sanders is perfect for the role.

OTHER RETURNEES

None.

OTHER NEWCOMERS

RONALD ROLLERSON (6-10, 290 lbs., FR, C, #30, 16.0 ppg, 13.0 rpg, 5.0 bpg, Faith Christian Academy/ Pennsauken, N.J.). Chaney says he has two center prospects this season in Lyde and Rollerson. The truth is that he has only one.

Rollerson did not play as a prep senior due to a shoulder injury. That and his weight put him reluctantly into the "project" category.

When healthy and in shape, Rollerson can be a player. He was ranked among the nation's top 75 prospects as a junior.

If in uniform, Rollerson should see only deep reserve duty this season. But Temple has a way of hanging onto guys like this and bringing them around.

QUESTIONS

Outside shooting? We say this every year, and it never seems to matter. The Owls always get so many more shots than their opponents, they can afford to shoot a low percentage.

Chemistry? This is rarely an issue at Temple, when guys either do what they are told or seek other opportunities. Of course, rarely have the Owls had two signees the level of Karcher and Lyde. Chaney has some work to do in getting the newcomers to embrace his system.

Schedule? The 1998-99 slate is even tougher than usual. It could make for a rocky start with two first-year regulars. The RPI rewards should come later, however.

ANSWERS

Winning! The Owls do it with shocking regularity. Only six schools have won more (Kentucky, North Carolina, Kansas, St. John's and Duke). Only four have been to more NCAA tournaments (North Carolina, Arizona, Kansas and UCLA). Chaney has been to nine in a row himself, and the Owls have visited the postseason 16 straight times overall.

Defense! We write it every year, and every year it comes true. Scoring against Temple is like questioning Bill Clinton. The answers are never easy.

Talent! Giving John Chaney a Mark Karcher is like giving eyesight to Michaelangelo. If the coach can harness the energy, the results will be spectacular. The rest of the cast was already very good.

adidas Blue Ribbon Analysis

BACKCOURT .... A
BENCH/DEPTH .... B+
FRONTCOURT .... B+
INTANGIBLES .... A+

This is as good as it gets at Temple. The Owls are loaded, adding considerable offense to the usual defensive brilliance. John Chaney may never see the inside of the Final Four, but he has every chance with this nucleus over the next year or two or three.

If he sticks around that long...

If not, the Hall of Fame-bound legend will leave the program in extremely fine shape. His legacy at Temple will be talked about long after he goes back to full-time shopping along Philadelphia's famed Italian market.

John Chaney is one-of-a-kind. And so is the potential of this Temple team.

(J.L.)

7

TENNESSEE

LOCATION .... Knoxville, TN
CONFERENCE .... SEC (Eastern Division)
LAST SEASON .... 20-9 (.690)
CONFERENCE RECORD 9-7 (3rd)
STARTERS LOST/RETURNING 0/5
NICKNAME .... Volunteers
COLORS .... Orange & White
HOMECOURT ...... Thompson-Boling Arena (24,535)
COACH .... Jerry Green (Appalachian State '68)
RECORD AT SCHOOL .... 20-9 (1 yr.)
CAREER RECORD .... 242-187 (15 yrs.)
ASSISTANTS ...... Chris Ferguson (Cumberland '81)
Byron Samuels (UNC-Asheville '86)
Eric Pauley (Kansas '90)
TEAM WINS (last 5 yrs.) 5-11-14-11-20
RPI (last 5 yrs.) 230-116-58-139-26
1997-98 FINISH .... Lost in NCAA first round.

COACH AND PROGRAM

There was a point last season when Jerry Green, seemingly the eternal optimist, was worried about his Tennessee basketball team. The first-year coach had inherited a talented group of players from former coach Kevin O'Neill, who had departed for Northwestern, but the program had so little winning tradition that Green wondered if such a problem could be fixed right away.

After the Vols sunk to a 1-5 start in the Southeastern Conference and were blown away in successive games by South Carolina and Kentucky, panic might have set it, even for the usually unflappable Green.

"I wasn't sure we could win another SEC game," Green said. "At the time, we were so individually oriented. We weren't very team oriented. It seemed like we were willing to accept the role of a loser and that we didn't know how to win."

Just when Green was at the brink of genuine despair, the Vols pulled out of their nose dive. Tennessee fans won't soon forget the night of Jan. 28, when the Vols broke a two-year SEC road losing streak with a convincing victory at Alabama. Though freshman point guard Tony Harris had some brilliant moments before that game, his real coming-out party was in Tuscaloosa. Almost overnight, he had gone from a freshman who thought he had to score all the Vols' big baskets to a seasoned veteran who knew how to get his teammates involved.

The Vols took off after that. They added a second straight road victory at LSU and eventually won eight of 10 games to close out the SEC season. After a homecourt victory over Florida on Feb. 25, Green was reasonably sure the Vols had done enough to attract the attention of the NCAA Tournament selection committee. One victory in the SEC Tournament, Green thought, would seal the deal.

The Vols got that victory, and also got their invitation to the Big Dance. Their stay was short-lived—they lost an 82-81 overtime heartbreaker to Illinois State—but one mission had been accomplished. It was the first time since 1989 that a Tennessee team had played in the NCAAs.

Green, his staff, the players and Vol fans everywhere were disappointed with the first-round ouster, but, after a few days, everyone associated with the program recognized the NCAA trip for the genuine accomplishment it was. And Tennessee fans couldn't be blamed for looking toward this season.

After all, Green had proved his worth by coaching the team to great success without injured starters Charles Hathaway, DaShay Jones and Vegas Davis, all of whom had suffered season-ending injuries. And, save Jones, every key Tennessee player is returning. Throw in the arrival of heralded freshman Vincent Yarbrough, and it's easy to see why the Vol faithful is so excited.

"I don't think people will be laughing at us any more," Green said. "I'm not sure many people in our league had to worry about us before last year. Our kids didn't know how to win. Now, in addition to talent, our kids have confidence that they can win.

"I'm not sure how good we can become, but I think we can be pretty good."

STARTERS NOT RETURNING

None.

OTHERS NOT RETURNING

DASHAY JONES (6-2, G, 7.7 ppg, 3.1 rpg, .524 FG in seven appearances). Few college basketball players ever had more hard luck in their careers than Jones, who kept Tennessee team physicians hopping during his short stay.

Recruited from junior college to play point guard while the Vols were waiting on freshman Tony Harris, Jones never got that chance. In the 1996-97 season, his first at Tennessee, Jones suffered a stress fracture in his right foot during practice. Though he played in 19 games—mostly as a shooting guard—and started 14 of them, his effectiveness was severely limited. Toward the end of the year, having incurred the wrath of former coach Kevin O'Neill, Jones sat on the bench, not so much as taking off his warmups.

Jones got a new beginning when Jerry Green took over as coach last season, but he was barely able to take advantage before the injury jinx struck again. Inserted in the starting lineup after Green opted for a three-guard set, Jones was just starting to play well when, while making a move toward the basket in a game against Wofford, he tore the ACL in his left knee.

Because the injury occurred in Tennessee's seventh game of the season, Jones could not redshirt. His career at Tennessee was over after just 26 games, which meant he essentially got cheated out of a full season.

Green couldn't help but wonder what a healthy Jones might have meant to a team that, because of other injuries, was severely lacking in depth most of the year. In the two games before his injury, Jones scored 15 points and grabbed four rebounds against Appalachian State and had 15 points, nine rebounds and four assists against Tennessee Tech.

SCOTT MOORE (6-11, C, 0.7 ppg, 1.2 rpg, 6.1 minutes). Moore was one of the nicest guys on a team full of nice guys, but, unfortunately, his personality didn't help him on the court. Even though Charles Hathaway was redshirted last season, Moore's minutes did not pick up appreciably from the season before. He got into 21 games and played a total of 129 minutes.

Moore had some offensive skills and could block a shot, but he lacked the speed and quickness necessary to play in an athletic league such as the SEC. With Hathaway coming back and sophomore Isiah Victor ready to claim even more minutes in the frontcourt, Moore realized he would probably play even less as a senior than he did in each of his first three seasons.

To his credit, Moore, who earned his undergraduate degree in just three years at Tennessee, decided he should move on if he wanted to play. With an eye toward a possible pro career overseas, Moore transferred to NAIA Cumberland University, which is near his home in Carthage, Tenn. There, Moore hopes to play enough to make himself marketable to an international pro league.

ANTHONY SEWELL (5-10, G, 0.5 rpg, 0.3 rpg, 16 appearances). Because of injuries, Sewell played more than most walkons could ever hope to. He saw action in 16 games, logging a total of 66 minutes.

Though Green likes to keep everybody on his bench happy, even walkons, it is doubtful Sewell would have played as much as he did if guards DaShay Jones, Aaron Green, Vegas Davis and Tony Harris hadn't missed several games among them with various health problems.

Sewell was rewarded with a scholarship in the second semester, so all those years of serving as practice fodder to the starters accounted for something.

PROJECTED STARTERS

BRANDON WHARTON (6-3, 180 lbs., SR, SG, #15, 15.2 ppg, 3.7 rpg, 3.0 apg, 2.1 tpg, 1.5 spg, 34.1 minutes, .392 FG, .429 3PT, .724 FT, Overton HS/Nashville, Tenn.). With newcomers such as Tony Harris and Isiah Victor on the roster and heart-rending stories such as Charles Hathaway deflecting attention, Wharton was something of a forgotten man at times last season.

Harris' arrival pushed Wharton to shooting guard, where he figured to make an easy transition and become a first-team All-SEC pick. In truth, it took Wharton a while to adjust to his new position. Not having to handle the ball so much was a shock to his system. Eventually, Wharton began to get comfortable with having to look for his shot more and, by season's end, he was Tennessee's leading scorer for the second straight year.

Wharton has been criticized by some for not showing more outward signs of aggression and emotion, and he isn't the best finisher in the world, but there is one thing he can do as well as anyone in college basketball—shoot. A year ago, Wharton used his sweet, lefthanded jumper to connect on 43 percent of his three-point shots, fourth in the SEC. He scored in double figures in a team-high 23 games and led the Vols in scoring five times.

When Wharton was on, he could carry the team. He was red-hot in the first half of the Vols' NCAA Tournament loss to Illinois State, scoring 17 points and making two of two from three-point range. Wharton made seven of eight three-pointers, one shy of the school's single-game record set by Allan Houston, against Georgia. He scored 29 points in that game.

Wharton also proved to be handy filling his old job, if only on a backup basis. When Harris suffered a stress fracture in his leg and had to miss two games, Wharton ran the point. He did so flawlessly in a game against Mississippi, when the Vols, despite not having Harris, Hathaway and Jones, upset the Rebels, then ranked 11th. Harris later said he learned a few things while watching Wharton work.

Green doesn't want Wharton to have to bother with the point this season, but chances are good he will play the position from time to time. Even a bundle of energy like Harris needs a rest now and again.

Far more often, though, Wharton will team with Harris and give the Vols one of the quickest—and best—backcourts in the country.

"Playing the (off) guard wasn't as easy as Brandon thought," Green said. ""He had a little trouble after he moved over. But he began to shoot it really well and he learned to counter the pressure people were putting on him by driving the ball to the basket. We think Brandon is really ready for his senior year."

TONY HARRIS (6-0, 160 lbs., SO, PG, #14, 14.2 ppg, 2.7 rpg, 4.2 apg, 2.0 tpg, 1.3 spg, 31.2 minutes, .366 FG, .322 3PT, .720 FT, East HS/Memphis, Tenn.). It isn't often that a freshman can arrive with the hype Tony Harris did and actually live up to it.

It was obvious from the Vols' first few games of last season that Harris was going to be a difference maker, and it had nothing to do with his physical skills. Not that his speed, quickness and jumping ability aren't put to good use. It's just that Harris' best attribute is his will to win.

"Tony Harris," said Green, "is the most competitive player I've been around."

Harris proved as much in the Vols' second game of the season, against Miami (Ohio). Tennessee struggled most of the game and trailed by double figure margins throughout. Then, with 2:20 left and the Vols trailing by nine, Harris sparked a remarkable comeback that ended when Charles Hathaway scored on a putback at the buzzer.

A month later, Harris again showed his competitiveness when, fighting through leg cramps, he led the Vols to an upset of his hometown Memphis Tigers at the Pyramid. Harris' refuse-to-lose attitude began sifting like a plague through the team, infecting everyone in its path.

For all the mileage he got out of sheer desire, Harris later learned that wasn't enough to survive in the SEC. If Harris had a weakness in the early part of his rookie season, it was that he forced the action, trying to take over games by himself and shooting too often and without much thought.

Ironically, it was an injury which helped Harris overcome that weakness. Sidelined for two games with a stress fracture in his upper right leg, Harris couldn't practice; so he did the next best thing, locking himself in a film room and watching great point guards at work. Harris got another lesson by watching from the Vols' bench as Brandon Wharton, the man he had replaced at the point, directed a stunning upset of then 11th-ranked Mississippi.

"I found out how the good ones did it," Harris said. "They get their teammates involved. I had been talking about doing that all year, but didn't really do it until after I came back (from the injury)."

Tennessee fans won't soon forget that comeback. It happened on a cold January night in Tuscaloosa, Ala. Harris didn't start, but he dominated once he got on the floor, scoring 18 points, passing for a then-career-high six assists and making two of three three-pointers.

Harris went on a subsequent tear, as his shooting improved dramatically along with his assist-to-turnover ratio. The Vols won eight of their next nine games, including upsets of South Carolina and Arkansas and routs of Georgia, Mississippi State and Vanderbilt. Harris earned SEC Player-of-the-Week honors during the Vols' winning streak and also earned the admiration of the league's coaches.

"To me, the thing that makes him great is he plays with incredible emotion every night out," said Florida coach Billy Donovan.

"He can deliver passes to people and he can score," said Kentucky's Tubby Smith. "But he creates a lot of problems defensively and he can really pressure the basketball. He's probably just as big a threat defensively as he is offensively."

No coach in the league was more impressed by Harris than Green.

"Tony had a great year," Green said. "It was about what I expected. I knew that Tony could be a great player. The plus points are obvious, (plus) defense and pushing the ball up the floor and dunking. He's electrifying. Tony was a catalyst to our season. There were times when he said to his teammates, "I'm not gonna' let you guys lose.'"

After his debut, Harris was well-decorated. He was chosen co-Freshman of the Year (along with Georgia's Jumaine Jones) in the SEC and was also a second-team All-SEC pick. Harris was a third-team freshman All-America pick by *Basketball Times*.

Obviously, someone thinks Harris will be able to take his game to another level this season. In August, Harris was chosen along with 24 others as a candidate for the prestigious John Wooden Award. Accordingly, Blue Ribbon placed the sophomore on its preseason All-America fifth team. It would be a surprise to us if he didn't live up to that billing.

C.J. BLACK (6-8, 255 lbs., JR, PF, #43, 12.6 ppg, 6.8 rpg, 1.1 spg, 2.5 bpg, 28.6 minutes, .519 FG, .417 3PT, .741 FT, Brainerd HS/Chattanooga, Tenn.). When his good friend Hathaway went down for the season after surgery to remove a blood clot from his shoulder, Black adopted the high socks look in tribute and was determined to make up for Hathaway's contributions.

Black did that and more. Much more.

After a debut season in which he made the SEC All-Freshman team, Black gained a reputation as a deadly low-post scorer. Last year, Black added a little more to his arsenal. Freed by Green to launch three-pointers when he saw fit, Black did just that and made 10 of 24. Thus, Black became a weapon as a trailer on the fast break, and he also opened up the inside by dragging opposing defenders out past the three-point line.

Without Hathaway, Black had to do a little more damage on the boards, and he did. Black was tops on the team and ninth in the SEC in rebounding, grabbing 10 or more in seven games, including a career-high 13 against Mississippi.

Hathaway's absence also hampered Tennessee's interior defense. Hathaway was a fearsome shot-blocker, and Black, who showed the same skill as a freshman, became a monster in the middle when forced to defend it alone. He blocked a school-record 73 shots, often stunning opponents who didn't realize a man so big could get off his feet so quickly. Black's average of 2.5 bpg led the SEC.

After the season, all Black's numbers added up to a second-team All-SEC selection.

"He had a great year," Green said. "The big thing for him was adjusting so he wasn't locked in totally in the low block. He shot the three with confidence and was still tough down low.

"C.J.'s become a well-rounded player. He can score, get a lot of rebounds and block shots for you. And he's very good for team chemistry."

CHARLES HATHAWAY (6-10, 255 lbs., SO, C, #55, 8.4 ppg, 6.4 rpg, 1.2 apg, 2.6 tpg, 1.0 spg, 2.0 bpg, 21.0 minutes, .464 FG, .517 FT in five appearances, Hillwood HS/Nashville, Tenn.). Before practice last Dec. 1, Hathaway noticed a strange tingling in his right arm. The big man wasn't concerned at the time, but the next morning, Hathaway awoke and found his upper arm had swollen to twice its normal size. Trainer Chad Newman immediately sent Hathaway to Tennessee team physicians, who examined him and determined the swelling was caused by a blood clot in his right shoulder.

"It was scary," Hathaway said. ""At one time they were talking that I could lose my arm. To go from being in the best shape in my life to that...I just couldn't believe it."

On Dec. 5, after the Vols' game against Tennessee Tech, coach Green announced Hathaway's condition. "Our thoughts and prayers are with him," Green said.

Two days later, Hathaway was sent to St. Louis, where noted vascular specialist Rob Thompson performed surgery. Ironically, Hathaway, called "one big muscle" by Newman, had gotten too pumped up; the heavily muscled area in his upper body was restricting blood flow. To correct the problem, Thompson had to trim away muscle and remove a rib.

Thompson's surgery was successful and, though Hathaway briefly hoped he could return by February, he was finished for the season. The good news was that, because Hathaway had played in just five games, he was eligible to receive a medical redshirt. He returns this year with three seasons of eligibility.

1997-98 RESULTS

Opponent	Score	
Winthrop	75-62	
Miami-OH	75-74	
North Carolina-Asheville	75-69	
Austin Peay	74-65	
Appalachian State	69-46	
Tennessee Tech	83-69	
Wofford	92-63	
St. Joseph's	74-54	
@Memphis	68-66	
@Southern California	74-70	
@Florida (L)	69-83	
Auburn (L)	69-74	
@Vanderbilt (L)	79-80	
Mississippi	77-67	
@South Carolina (L)	51-81	
Kentucky (L)	67-85	
@Alabama	84-70	
@Louisiana State	72-65	
Georgia	77-48	
South Carolina	70-69	
@Kentucky (L)	74-80	
Arkansas	74-71	
@Mississippi State	87-63	
Vanderbilt	90-76	
Florida	79-75	
@Georgia (L)	72-77	
#Louisiana State	73-62	
#Arkansas (L)	96-102	
%Illinois State (L)	81-82	ot

@ away games
# SEC Tournament, Georgia Dome, Atlanta, GA
% NCAA West Sub-Regional, Sacramento, CA

There's no question the loss of Hathaway hampered the Vols, at least in certain games in which he would have helped out on the boards and with post defense.

"It was frustrating," Hathaway said. "To sit back and not be able to help my teammates was really tough on me."

Hathaway was around long enough to make perhaps the biggest play of the season. Despite trailing Miami (Ohio) by nine points with 2:20 to play in the second half of a mid-November game, the Vols rallied and won on Hathaway's dramatic put-back of a Tony Harris miss as the buzzer sounded. The basket touched off a riot in Thompson-Boling Arena as fans stormed the floor and mobbed Hathaway. The victory set the tone for what would become a very good year.

Hathaway is ready for more magic moments. He worked hard in the offseason to lose the few extra pounds he gained while rehabilitating. He played in a Nashville summer league with several Vanderbilt and Tennessee State players, and also attended former TSU coach Ed Martin's popular big man camp.

"We think Charles is really going to be an exciting player for us," Green said. "Not many people in college basketball his size can do the things he can do. We're looking forward to seeing him back at full strength, just to see how good he is."

VINCENT YARBROUGH (6-8, 215 lbs., FR, SF, #22, 24.2 ppg, 14.0 rpg, 7.0 apg, 5.2 bpg, Cleveland HS/Cleveland, Tenn.). It's a Saturday night in early August, and Vincent Yarbrough is in the middle of the basketball floor at Tennessee-Chattanooga's Roundhouse, surrounded by autograph-seeking fans. He has just scored 32 points in leading his team of Tennessee high school all-stars to a victory over a team from Georgia.

Though the start of football season is just weeks away, Vol fans have come out on this night to watch basketball. More specifically, they've come to watch Yarbrough, and wonder what he will mean to Tennessee's ever-improving basketball fortunes.

Yes, these people have traditionally been rabid Big Orange football fans, but maybe that was because the basketball team hadn't give them any reason to get excited. After Yarbrough's performance in the all-star game, though, these same fans have a reason to get excited.

"They see him as the missing link," said Tennessee all-star coach Lee Smith, waving his hand at the crowd hovering around Yarbrough. Smith had only heard of Yarbrough's skills before he coached him in the annual game. "He's as good as they say he is. He maybe can do more than they say he can."

That sentiment is shared by Green, who doesn't like to put pressure on newcomers. But the Tennessee coach can't resist talking about Yarbrough's potential.

"Vincent Yarbrough will be an impact player," Green said. "I look for him to have as much or more impact than Tony Harris."

That statement carries some weight, considering it was Harris who, as a freshman, helped lift the Vols to a 20-win season and their first NCAA Tournament appearance since 1989.

Is everyone right about Yarbrough? Most recruiting analysts label him as a can't-miss prospect, a player capable of greatness on the collegiate level and a future in the NBA. Yarbrough was generally regarded among the top dozen seniors in the country last season. And one recruiting service, *Recruiting USA*, ranked him the top player in the country.

"Due to his incredible unselfishness and his ability to mesh with his team, his talents have not been appreciated, I think, by many of my colleagues," said *Recruiting USA*'s David Benezra. "*Recruiting USA* is the only service ranking him No. 1, and we are certainly not afraid to do so.

"You do want to see the No. 1 player dominate, but his talent cannot be denied. Nobody in the class, except for Rashard Lewis (who jumped straight to the NBA), has his up side. People have to remember that he will be a 17-year-old freshman."

Yarbrough has all the skills. It starts with athleticism; he can run and jump all night. Yarbrough is a better-than-average shooter, though even he admits his three-point shot needs a little work. As a defender, Yarbrough's timing, leaping ability and long arms make him a tenacious shot-blocker.

Then there are the intangibles. Despite his youth, Yarbrough is a leader. And, like Tony Harris, he can't stand losing. If this package sounds a bit Jordanesque, well, Vol fans can't wait to see if that could be possible.

KEY RESERVES

RASHARD LEE (6-6, 200 lbs., SR, F, #3, 10.3 ppg, 5.3 rpg, 1.6 apg, 1.5 tpg, 22.8 minutes, .412 FG, .418 3PT, .567, Hillside HS/Durham, N.C.). Freed from the burden of living up to the expectations of former coach Kevin O'Neill, Lee blossomed under Green and became one of the most improved players in the SEC.

With O'Neill as his coach, Lee seemed to play tentatively for fear that a mistake would get him a quick seat on the bench. And, even when Lee was on the floor, he was limited as to what he could attempt. Lee was forbidden to so much as think about taking a three-pointer. At the time, O'Neill didn't think Lee was ready to assume a major portion of the Vols' scoring load.

Partly because injuries took a huge toll on his team last season, Green decided to give Lee a chance. Lee began the year as a starter, was benched because of sub-par defense, then found his way back into the lineup after a 23-point effort against Auburn. Along with a second chance to start, Green gave Lee the green light from beyond the arc, which proved to be a smart move. Lee wound up hoisting 79 three-pointers and made 33 of them.

That previously unseen prowess from the perimeter opened up other aspects of Lee's game. Green says Lee is one of the best penetrators he has coached, which made him tough to guard after opponents had to start respecting his jumper. Lee, an excellent offensive rebounder, was also adept at collecting his share of garbage baskets.

If Lee couldn't find a way to score himself, he was able to pass off to open teammates. He was third on the team with 45 assists. Lee was also fourth in scoring and fourth in rebounding.

"Rashard really gave us a lot," Green said. "He went from being a support person to a front line person"

Never was that more apparent than in a late-season homecourt victory over Vanderbilt. Lee put on a display that night, scoring a career-high 26 points, making four of six three-pointers and grabbing a career-high 11 rebounds. Lee reached double figures in 18 games, and scored nine points in three other contests. As the season progressed, the Vols counted on his scoring contributions.

That much was obvious in Tennessee's final game, an 82-81 overtime loss to Illinois State in the first round of the NCAA Tournament. Lee was four for 18 from the field and one for eight from three-point range. If he had even come close to his season average from the field or three-point range, the Vols would have won.

That performance shouldn't detract from Lee's breakout season, though. Can he do more? It's a good question, considering Lee will have to fight to keep his job. Heralded freshman Vincent Yarbrough will have to play.

"I think I'll let those two decide who's going to play at that spot (small forward)," Green said. "To me, it's not who starts, but who finishes that matters."

TORREY HARRIS (6-10, 240 lbs., SR, F, #40, 3.9 ppg, 4.8 rpg, 1.1 tpg, 20.8 minutes, .512 FG, .431 FT, Piney Woods School/Sardis, Miss.). A year ago, Green correctly forecast that Harris, despite seemingly limited ability, would be a big help to the Vols. Little did Green know how useful Harris would become. When Hathaway was lost for the season, Harris stepped into the starting lineup and provided more than anyone could have hoped.

Besides his usual strong defense—Harris is the Vols' best post defender—he also rebounded better than ever and even developed as a scorer. Harris will never be confused with Shaquille O'Neal in that department, but he more than doubled his scoring average from the previous season as he learned to make layups and even the occasional jump hook.

Harris had a knack for making timely baskets. He scored twice down the stretch of an important home victory over South Carolina, once stealing the ball from Gamecock Ryan Stack underneath the Vols' basket and banking it home. Tennessee's assistant coaches and managers were fond of saying, half jokingly and half with genuine pride, that Harris' usual scoring output was the toughest four points in America.

This season, for the first time in his career, Harris probably won't be pressed into duty as a starter. But be certain that Green won't hesitate to call on the big man, regardless of the situation.

"Torrey won some games for us last year, which I think surprised a lot of our fans," Green said. "It didn't surprise us. He's probably the most coachable player I've ever been around. It's amazing to me that, regardless of how much you challenge him, he tries to get better."

ISIAH VICTOR (6-9, 205 lbs., SO, F, #44, 7.7 ppg, 5.5 rpg, 2.1 tpg, 1.0 bpg, 20.7 minutes, .507 FG, .333 3PT, .575 FT, University Heights Academy/Hopkinsville, Ky.). There was no way Victor could have lived up to the advance billing given him by former Tennessee coach Kevin O'Neill, who couldn't stop talking about Victor when the youngster sat out a redshirt season in 1996-97. To hear O'Neill tell it, Victor was the second-coming of Kareem Abdul-Jabbar, a certain future NBA lottery pick.

Suffice to say Victor didn't exactly lure the NBA scouts to Knoxville in his rookie season, but he showed signs of real ability. Who knows? Maybe one day O'Neill's lottery pick prediction might even come true.

Certainly, Victor has the tools the pros look for. Though he needs to gain some size and strength, Victor is mobile, fairly quick for a big man and has countless post moves in his arsenal. He isn't afraid to step out and shoot from three-point range—ask South Carolina about that—and he plays defense.

As a freshman, Victor played in all 29 games and started seven times. He traveled the typical up-and-down path most freshmen take, but his highs far surpassed his lows. Victor scored 16 points in an upset victory over Mississippi, and matched that career high against Vanderbilt. He had a double-double with 13 points and 10 rebounds against LSU. Victor grabbed 11 rebounds against Georgia and 10 against Florida. Defensively, he had three blocked shots against Kentucky and four steals in the NCAA Tournament game against Illinois State.

And then there was Victor's brightest moment, when, without hesitation, he stepped out past the three-point line and buried a clutch shot that gave the Vols a 66-63 lead with less than three minutes to play in a crucial early-February victory over South Carolina. It was the first three-pointer of his career.

Clearly, Victor has the complete range of skills. But will he get to start this season? Hathaway is returning from a redshirt year; C.J. Black is coming off a great season; and freshman Vincent Yarbrough seems poised to take over the small forward job

Victor could make things interesting. He worked hard on the release of his jumper during the offseason and is even more consistent from long range. If Victor continues to play the way he did in the Vols' last five games of 1997-98—"when he was our most aggressive player," Green said—he could push someone out of the lineup.

"When we asked the players who was doing well in the summer pickup games, they all said Isiah Victor," Green said. "I think he has a great up side. One of the best things he does is catch it on the block and score. Now he's got his shot down from the outside. Now he can

1998-99 TENNESSEE SCHEDULE

Nov.	13	*Arizona
	15	Tennessee State
	17	Northridge State
	19	@Miami (Ohio)
	24	Tennessee-Chattanooga
	30	Western Carolina
Dec.	2	Memphis
	6	Pittsburgh
	10	@St. Joseph's
	19	@South Florida
	22	North Carolina-Greensboro
Jan.	2	@Auburn
	6	LSU
	9	South Carolina
	12	@Kentucky
	20	Georgia
	23	@Florida
	27	@Vanderbilt
	30	Alabama
Feb.	2	@Arkansas
	6	Mississippi State
	10	Florida
	13	Vanderbilt
	17	@Mississippi
	20	@South Carolina
	23	@Georgia
	28	Kentucky
March	4-7	#SEC Tournament

@ Road Games
* BCA Classic, Albuquerque, NM
# Georgia Dome, Atlanta, GA

make the three. Isiah could be a really tough guy to guard."

VEGAS DAVIS (6-3, 215 lbs., JR, G, #34, 6.2 ppg, 3.1 rpg, 1.5 apg, 1.2 spg, 19.7 minutes, .426 FG, .455 3PT, .546 FT, Parker HS/Parker, Ariz.). Davis' season was all but ended on the night of Jan. 28, when, while leading a break in a game at Alabama, he slipped and felt something pop in his left knee. Team doctors later discovered Davis had torn his posterior cruciate ligament.

After Davis' injury, Green must have thought there was some bad mojo working against him. Already, the first-year coach had endured season-ending injuries to center Charles Hathaway and guard DaShay Jones, plus nagging injuries to guards Tony Harris and Aaron Green. The loss of Davis, who had developed into a solid guard and part-time starter, further depleted an already thin bench.

Green really hated to see Davis go down, for the sophomore had been playing well. In 17 games, he scored in double figures five times, including a high of 23 points in an important road victory at Southern California. Davis was also the Vols' best on-ball defender and had improved his outside shot to the point that he was leading Tennessee in three-point shooting at the time of his injury.

Davis ended up as the Vols' three-point percentage leader, but had far fewer attempts than several of his teammates. Green knew he could always count on the numbers Davis produced in that fateful Alabama game: eight points on three of four shooting, two of three from three-point range, three assists, two rebounds and two steals.

At first, Tennessee doctors thought Davis' injury would heal without surgery. He sat out for several weeks, then, after returning to practice before the SEC Tournament, he felt pain in the knee. Davis was presumed lost for the year, but he made a surprise appearance in the Vols' first-round NCAA Tournament loss to Illinois State. Davis played nine minutes in that game, and could have been the hero. His desperation, halfcourt heave at the buzzer came close to going in. If it had, Tennessee would have won 84-82 instead of losing 82-81.

On April 2, Davis underwent surgery to repair his damaged knee.

"We're still counting on Vegas coming back to full strength," Green said. "He's got a great attitude and works hard every day. He might also be the best athlete we've got. He had improved a great deal at the time of his injury."

AARON GREEN (6-2, 200 lbs., SR, G, #5, 4.3 ppg, 1.2 rpg, 1.3 apg, 14.1 minutes, .362 FG, .340 3PT, .686 FT, Sweetwater HS/Sweetwater, Tenn.). Like teammates Charles Hathaway, DaShay Jones and Vegas Davis, Green's season was hampered by injury. In mid-December, he suffered a stress fracture in his right foot and missed five games. Green tried to return from the injury too soon and, although he played through obvious pain, he was ineffective.

In a stretch of eight conference games, Green was scoreless in seven of them. His jump shot, which had been good enough for Green to lead the SEC in three-point shooting (league games only) as a freshman, was missing in action. It was just too painful for Green to jump off or land on his injured foot.

Eventually the injury, and Green's shooting touch, came around. He scored 10 points in an important win over Arkansas, then had the best game of his career when he scored a team-high 23 points, including five of nine from three-point range, in a hard-fought, homecourt victory over Florida.

Teammate Tony Harris was tossed from that game after officials determined he had thrown a high elbow at Florida's Dan Williams. That meant someone had to come through and provide some points. Green was the man in a game which secured third place in the SEC East for the Vols.

With so many bodies ahead of him at shooting guard and small forward, Green's best chance for playing time this season might be as a backup point guard when Harris gets in foul trouble or needs a rest.

"I think he can do it," Green said. "He played there some in high school. And Aaron can pull up and shoot the three, especially against zones. That's something we really need, because we'll see a lot of zones."

OTHER RETURNEES

DEL BAKER (6-5, 200 lbs., SO, G, #32, 1.8 ppg, 1.0 rpg, 7.0 minutes, .354 FG, .296 3PT, 1.000 FT, Cleveland HS/Cleveland, Tenn.). Is he a throw-in or a legitimate SEC player? Before the final third of last season, that's the question many asked about Baker, who happens to be the older brother of new Vol recruit Vincent Yarbrough.

Two years ago, though rival recruiters tried to convince Baker otherwise, former Tennessee coach Kevin O'Neill told the player he was a legitimate SEC prospect, and that he was being signed on his own merits, not just to entice Yarbrough.

Was O'Neill telling Baker what he wanted to hear? Maybe, but last season, Baker showed signs that O'Neill was right, that he could hold his own in the rugged SEC.

Baker endured a typical freshman year. For most of the season, his jump shot was off more than it was on, and his defense was suspect. Then one February night in Starkville, Miss., in a game televised by ESPN, Baker broke loose.

It all started with a steal and two-handed stuff. Thusly inspired, Baker proceeded to score four more baskets, two of them three-pointers. He finished with a career-high 12 points, and Green credited him with being the catalyst for a convincing Tennessee victory.

"He really did have a great game against Mississippi State, and we think he can do it again," Green said. "Over the summer, his name came up as someone who was playing well in the pickup games (among) the players. I'm anxious to see how much he improved over the summer. Del's a great athlete, and he's worked hard on his defense. His best days are before him."

Baker could see some action at shooting guard this season, especially if he has improved his defense. And, if he never does another positive thing for Tennessee, Baker did end up attracting his brother to Knoxville.

"I'd always wanted to play with my brother," Yarbrough said after he signed with the Vols.

OTHER NEWCOMERS

None.

QUESTIONS

Backup point guard? On the rare occasions when Tony Harris gets tired or in foul trouble, who will play the point? Brandon Wharton played there his first two years, but coach Jerry Green would rather keep him at shooting guard. Wharton will still probably play the point some, but Green would have felt better if the Vols could have recruited a backup point man.

Tradition? Tennessee has played so poorly for so long, the Vols don't have a tradition of winning. Can they finally enter a season believing they have enough talent to beat anyone on their schedule? The best teams in the country have a certain attitude about them, something to Vols still need to acquire.

Shooting? Though Tennessee finished second in the SEC in three-point shooting, the Vols connected on just 42 percent of their shots from the field overall last year. Green would have loved to sign another shooter, but, without much playing time to offer, couldn't find a really good one. Trying to improve what he has, Green tore down and rebuilt the jump shots of several veteran players during the offseason.

ANSWERS

Depth! Green can go two-deep at every position without any major drop off in talent.

Size! With Charles Hathaway and C.J. Black in the frontcourt, the Vols won't be pushed around by anyone. Both "bruise brothers," as they are known in Knoxville, weigh more than 250 pounds. Torrey Harris and Isiah Victor, both 6-10, provide better-than-average depth in the post.

Guards! Tony Harris and Brandon Wharton form one of the best backcourts in the nation.

Coaching! Green deserved a lot of credit in his first season at Tennessee for keeping the Vols together and winning despite a rash of injuries. Given a full roster of players, Green will be able to showcase his own talents this year by allowing the Vols to run and press.

adidas Blue Ribbon Analysis

BACKCOURT	**A**	**BENCH/DEPTH**	**A**
FRONTCOURT	**A**	**INTANGIBLES**	**B**

Could this be the Year of the Volunteer in the SEC? Many people think so, but rest assured defending national champion Kentucky will have a thing or two to say about that.

It's been a slow rebuilding process, but Tennessee might finally be ready to do battle with the elite teams in college basketball, including long-time SEC rival Kentucky. All the ingredients are there.

It starts at the top—second-year coach Jerry Green is one of the most respected tacticians in the business. He proved his worth a year ago by leading an injury-depleted team to a 20-victory season and a sport in the NCAA Tournament, Tennessee's first appearance in the Big Dance since 1989.

Green has plenty of talent at his disposal. In the frontcourt, besides menacing Bruise Brothers (as they are known in Knoxville) C.J. Black and Charles Hathaway, a blue-chip small forward has been added in freshman Vincent Yarbrough. Thought by at least one scouting service to be the best high school player in the country last year, Yarbrough should bring the same sort of impact to the Vols that Tony Harris did as a freshman. Yarbrough can do it all—run, jump, shoot, rebound, pass and defend. His only problem is that he might be too unselfish.

In the backcourt, Harris returns after a season which saw him earn SEC Freshman of the Year honors along with Georgia's Jumaine Jones. Harris was the catalyst for much of the Vols' success—longtime Tennessee broadcaster John Ward called him the greatest competitor to wear orange since Bernard King.

Joining Harris for the second straight year is Brandon Wharton, who has put in a solid three years at Tennessee. Wharton can always be counted on for his 15 points per game, plus some of the best three-point shooting in the country.

Behind the starters is a deep bench that includes a solid post player in Torrey Harris, potentially one of the best big men in the league in Isiah Victor, and Rashard Lee, the senior forward who had a breakout season a year ago. Green will make liberal use of his bench, which means the Vols will continue to play an up-tempo style, offensively and defensively.

Add all these ingredients together and you get a team capable of dislodging Kentucky at the top of the SEC's Eastern Division. Can the Vols do that? In a close call, *Blue Ribbon* decided to give an edge to Kentucky, which returns a solid nucleus that includes second-team *Blue Ribbon* preseason All-American Scott Padgett and Wayne Turner, the point guard who has helped lead the Wildcats to a 17-1 record in NCAA Tournament games the last three years.

The most important game in the SEC's regular season could be the last, when Kentucky comes to Knoxville on Feb. 28. The winner could take home the SEC Eastern Division championship.

Regardless of what happens in the regular season, expect a second-straight NCAA Tournament appearance from the Vols, and this time, there won't be a first-round ouster. It wouldn't surprise anyone to see Tennessee advance all the way to the Final Eight.

(C.D.)

adidas Blue Ribbon Analysis

GRADING SYSTEM

A+	equal to very best in country—Final Four-caliber unit
A	among the best in the land—worthy of deep NCAA run
B+	talented, versatile and experienced—NCAA-NIT ability
B	solid and productive winners—league and post-season contenders
C+	average to above-average—may contend in a weaker league
C	average to mediocre—second division in a strong league
D+	below average, inconsistent—second division in a weaker league
D	well below average—losing season virtually certain
F	non-Division I ability—an underdog every night

8

MICHIGAN STATE

LOCATION	East Lansing, MI
CONFERENCE	Big Ten
LAST SEASON	22-8 (.733)
CONFERENCE RECORD	13-3 (t-1st)
STARTERS LOST/RETURNING	0/5
NICKNAME	Spartans
COLOR	Green & White
HOMECOURT	Breslin Center (15,138)
COACH	Tom Izzo (Northern Michigan '77)
RECORD AT SCHOOL	55-36 (3 yrs.)
CAREER RECORD	55-36 (3 yrs.)
ASSISTANTS	Tom Crean (Central Michigan '89)
	Stan Heath (Eastern Michigan '88)
	Mike Garland (Northern Michigan '77)
TEAM WINS (last 5 yrs.)	20-22-16-17-22
RPI (last 5 yrs.)	25-15-78-70-11
1997-98 FINISH	Lost in NCAA Sweet 16.

COACH AND PROGRAM

Four years ago, before Jud Heathcote's final season as head coach, Michigan State made a unique move in an attempt to smooth the transition for his successor and the program. Before that season even began, the university announced Heathcote's young and equally personable assistant—Tom Izzo—would be the head coach the following year.

Consider that transition officially sealed. After a pair of middle-of-the-pack seasons with Izzo coaching players Heathcote recruited, Izzo's third team shot up the Big Ten ladder to the top—claiming the school's first league title in eight years.

The Spartans rode the back of the most exciting young backcourt to hit the conference in a long time. Sophomore Mateen Cleaves and freshman Charlie Bell were the stars, and the Spartans got inspired performances almost nightly from a bunch of undersized baseline players.

Only fifth-year combination guard Thomas Kelley remains from the Heathcote era. Izzo has at once continued the good-humored tradition of his mentor while applying his own stamp to a program rich in history.

Make no mistake, it's the Yoopie's team now (Izzo is from Michigan's upper peninsula, also known as the U.P.). He needn't try to do things as Jud would.

It helps that Izzo feels very comfortable—at least for one more year—with Cleaves as his extension. The big-boned 6-2 point guard glided into the role of leader last season. He shook off the back ailment that slowed his freshman year to a crawl and developed into a deserving league MVP as a mere sophomore.

Falling in behind Cleaves was a line of role players, none particularly adept at scoring, but all springy of step and ready to rumble. Most of them were from the home state, four from the same town—the athletic hotbed of Flint, Mich.—and everyone got along like a happy frat house.

Though his team was outsized by many opponents, Izzo was confident enough in their athleticism to take calculated risks. He commonly sent four men to the offensive glass. Kept fresh by a quality rotation of 10 men unmatched in the conference, the Spartans attacked like wild animals. All hustled; all contributed.

Think about this: Despite placing only Cleaves among the league's top 20 in scoring (even he was just 10th), only Antonio Smith among the top 12 in rebounding and *nobody* in the top 10 of either field goal or free throw percentage, the Spartans won 22 contests.

They did so by planting their style on games like a warrior's flag atop a taken hill. The formula was simple: No one rebounded better; no one defended the perimeter better; no one competed with more gusto.

Yes, Illinois made a late rush to grab a share of the conference title. When third-place Purdue entered East Lansing on the final day of the regular season and won a wonderful battle, MSU was left with an anticlimax.

But the Spartans still made a mark in the NCAAs. Ruining what were probably the two most popular upset calls of the opening weekend, they whipped Eastern Michigan and took apart Princeton to reach Greensboro and the East Region semifinals. There, they ran into roughly 15,000 powder blue-clad true believers. Izzo lost his nerve and kept two men back to guard against North Carolina breakouts. The Spartans fell behind and never quite recovered.

But this year, the March run might be deeper.

Though Cleaves separated his right shoulder in late August in a freak stair-step tumble outside his apartment, he was anticipated back in plenty of time for October practice. And it's not like his jumper stroke—hardly among his many assets—is threatened.

The Spartans have every important player back but one. And they regain the services of their third guard, medically redshirted last year.

The toughest non-conference schedule in the league will toughen State early. And a Big Ten scrambling to reload at the top won't wear the Spartans out in the dog days. This may be the most obvious pick to win the league since Magic Johnson's gang prepared to defend its remarkable runaway '78 title exactly two decades ago. That group only tied for the league crown, but won the national championship.

A lot has to fall together for these Spartans to even reach St. Petersburg. But they're one of a handful of teams nationally with a clear shot.

STARTERS NOT RETURNING

None.

OTHERS NOT RETURNING

DUJUAN WILEY (6-9, F, 6.3 ppg, 3.4 rpg, .624 FG, .723 FT, 16.2 minutes). Maybe no one embodied the style of the '98 team more closely than Wiley, the only significant personnel loss. Wiry and strong, Wiley lacked polish and never really developed any sort of post-up game. But he still managed to rebound from a poor junior season to become a dependable garbage man.

Given a stick-back chance, he rarely missed, leading the Spartans in field goal percentage. Other than Andre Hutson, he was the only Spartan who shot better than 45 percent.

Wiley could run the floor and block shots. The Spartans will miss his hustle inside.

PROJECTED STARTERS

MATEEN CLEAVES (6-2, 190 lbs., JR, PG, #12, 16.1 ppg, 2.5 rpg, 7.2 apg, 2.4 spg, 33.5 minutes, Northern HS/Flint, Mich.). Cleaves is a special player. Izzo is lucky to have had him around for three years, especially these days.

Slimmed down to a fighting weight of 190 after fighting bulk during his back malady, Cleaves displayed dual attributes of size and quickness with the ball that made him hard to handle at both ends. Though not a great shooter, he is the most admirable type of competitor—the one who scores in critical situations, even when he hasn't been playing well.

Typical was his play in the decisive junctures of the Spartans' dreary display at Northwestern. After the Wildcats dragged State into overtime and threatened to spring a mid-season upset that could have unplugged the Big Ten title drive, Cleaves said, "Enough." He took over in the OT, either dishing for points or scoring himself, willing the Spartans to victory.

That knack for getting his offensively-limited teammates the ball where they could score was the special of a championship. Cleaves flirted with the NCAA lead in assists much of the season, just behind Arizona State's Ahlon Lewis.

There are guys who mine assists from pure quickness of penetration and there are bigger guys who wear out defenders by getting an angle and cutting the corner, muscling the defender into a vulnerable position. Cleaves can do both. If he ever learns how to consistently knock down a three-pointer, look out.

At the other end, he is a formidable obstacle, large enough to subtly bump a dribbler off course or impede a cut. His strong hands paw away any ball carelessly positioned, bringing to mind a young Quinn Buckner. And his foot speed allows him to venture into passing lanes for still more steals (his 73 takeaways ranked No. 2 in the Big Ten), knowing he can usually recover in time if he misses.

Cleaves was just recovering from a severely sprained ankle suffered in the World Championships in July when he exited his apartment Aug. 27. Spotting friends, he was distracted and slipped on the steps, falling onto his shoulder.

The shoulder injury kept Cleaves out of action four weeks, his arm in a sling. But, knowing Cleaves, it's hard to imagine such an injury will keep him from conditioning for his junior season, likely his last in college. (Cleaves is close with Spartan junior footballers Sedrick Irvin and Robaire Smith, both of whom are probably headed for the NFL draft in April. It won't shock anyone if all leave MSU at once.)

CHARLIE BELL (6-3, 185 lbs., SO, SG, #14, 9.2 ppg, 4.4 rpg, 1.3 apg, 24.2 minutes, Southwestern HS/Flint, Mich.). In the NCAA Tournament, Bell played as well as his backcourt partner. As a freshman, he stepped in and immediately started 30 games—more than Magic did has a rookie.

Bell supplied pop from the off guard position, not as much through outside shooting (he only hit 19 threes) as through a neat and fearless floor game. He took care of the ball, kept his fouls to a minimum while learning college-level defense, made free throws and, at just 6-3, finished as MSU's No. 3 rebounder.

Bell came on late as a scorer, too. He hit for 22 points in the NCAA first-round win over Eastern Michigan and added 13 in the loss to Carolina.

Yet it was his willingness and ability to expand his game from a mere scorer that delighted Izzo. Bell changed his game from a starring role as a high schooler; he destroyed Glen Rice's prep scoring records to accommodate the needs of the team. About the only tweaking Izzo would like to see from him now is a more accurate three-pointer.

Yet Bell turned himself into a defensive stalwart while playing with astounding poise for a rookie. His upside, one might say, is tremendous.

ANTONIO SMITH (6-8, 250 lbs., SR, PF, #13, 7.9 ppg, 8.7 rpg, 0.9 spg, 29.6 minutes, Northern HS/Flint, Mich.). As is the trend with so many college teams, the Spartans don't have a true center and they lack a traditional post-up scoring threat. The frontcourt contributors are all *de facto* forwards. Most of their interior points result from rebounds and follows—in other words, slop.

Izzo would like to see that change in order to round out the squad's halfcourt potential. The coach lays it right on the line: "If we're going to be half as good as everyone

1997-98 RESULTS

East Tennessee State	82-59	
@Illinois-Chicago (L)	58-70	
#Central Michigan	89-61	
#Gonzaga	70-68	
Temple (L)	54-56	
@Cleveland State	85-54	
Detroit (L)	65-68	
Wright State	95-52	
@South Florida	68-53	
Eastern Illinois	81-69	
@Purdue	74-57	
Wisonsin	63-40	
@Michigan (L)	69-79	
@Minnesota	74-60	
Illinois	68-64	
@Iowa	78-57	
Penn State	71-59	
Indiana	84-66	
@Northwestern	72-66	ot
@Ohio State	84-58	
Iowa	75-64	
@Illinois (L)	63-84	
Minnesota	71-59	
Michigan	80-75	
@Wisconsin	56-47	
Purdue (L)	96-99	ot
##Minnesota (L)	73-76	
%Eastern Michigan	83-71	
%Princeton	63-56	
%%North Carolina (L)	58-73	

@ away games
# Spartan Coca-Cola Classic, East Lansing, MI
Big Ten Tournament, United Center, Chicago, IL
% NCAA East Sub-Regional, Hartford, CT
%% NCAA East Regional, Greensboro, NC

thinks we'll be, we've got to get better play from Antonio Smith offensively."

Maybe no one is a better poster boy for this team than Smith. From purely a hoop sense, he is the Spartans' Dennis Rodman—a spiritual leader, a warrior on the glass and a mason around the tin.

The Big Ten's rebounding champ two years ago as a sophomore (10.6 rpg), Smith is one of a trio of athletic brothers from Flint, one playing in the NFL and the other (Robaire) a star on the Spartan football team. Antonio didn't rebound as prolificly last season as the year before, partly because he had more help.

No problem there. Scoring was something else again. When Smith got the ball within five feet of his own rim, you could hear far-off circus music—the kind that plays when the clowns enter. No shot was too short. Rims cringed in his presence. His FG percentage dropped from .564 to .422—abysmal for a power forward.

"He has to improve his scoring," said Izzo. "He's in there missing shots he can make, shots he knows he can make. He's a great kid. He just has to quit being so unselfish and maybe use the backboard a little more."

Backboards will be happy to hear that. In all seriousness, even if Smith didn't improve a notch, 10 other Big Ten teams would be ecstatic to have him. No one plays harder.

Izzo would love to see an interior man like Smith become a scoring constant. You never know when a perimeter forward will have an off shooting night.

JASON KLEIN (6-7, 200 lbs., SR, SF, #44, 11.2 ppg, 3.7 rpg, 1.3 apg, 27.1 minutes, Grosse Ile HS/Grosse Ile, Mich.). Izzo can't hope to get a much better year than he got in '97-'98 from Klein (11.2 ppg, 3.7 rpg). There is no secret to his game. A full 58 percent of his shots a year ago were three-pointers. Because he hit them at such a high clip, he was a major asset, one the Spartans really needed.

But if that percentage falls too much (he never shot better than .358 before last season), Klein will morph into a liability. He is not a good ballhandler and cannot create shots. Cleaves gets him the ball where he likes it on the wing and he simply strokes.

That is one more reason why Izzo is anxious to create a post threat worthy of double-down defense. If he can find one, Klein will get plenty of open looks.

ANDRE HUTSON (6-8, 210 lbs., SO, F, #34, 7.5 ppg, 5.2 rpg, .613 FG, .754 FT, 21.0 minutes, Trotwood-Madison HS/Trotwood, Ohio). Showing the poise of a senior, Hutson really came on in the second half of the year and had his best games when it mattered most. He scored 21 points in the regular season finale against Purdue and went for 13 points and 10 boards in the NCAA win over Eastern Michigan.

The left-handed Hutson also showed a touch around the hoop that none of the returning Spartans can match. His 61.3 percent shooting was second on the team, as was his 5.2 rpg. In Hutson and Bell, Izzo coaxed two remarkable performances out of freshmen.

While Hutson's fine season was a bit of a surprise, though, the MSU staff are counting on him to continue to improve. It will be interesting to see whether last season was a fluke.

"We'll need him to make the same or more strides than he made last year," Izzo stats flatly.

KEY RESERVES

THOMAS KELLEY (6-2, 190 lbs., SR, G, #3, 8.1 ppg, 2.1 apg in 1996-97, Union HS/Grand Rapids, Mich.). The scary part about the Spartans is—even after Cleaves and Bell—the backcourt is just getting started. In a league that may be stronger around the arc than it's ever been, State looks as deep and talented as anyone.

Kelley would have been the starting off guard last season had he not broken a bone in his right foot the day after scoring 18 points in MSU's first exhibition game. He sat out the season and Bell started instead.

Now Izzo can blend in a veteran with young Bell having a year under his belt. Moreover, Kelley's strong suit—defense—is a perfect complement to Cleaves and Bell. Kelley also gives Izzo versatility; he can play either guard spot on offense, though he has excelled neither as a playmaker (62 assists, 57 turnovers as a junior) nor a long-range shooter (.243 career 3PT).

According to Izzo, Kelley still favored the foot a little as late as the first week of September. But, even at 80 percent, Kelley is quicker than most guards in the conference and he is almost impossible to completely contain one-on-one. He is an extremely good defender on the ball and it is tough for even the slickest penetrators to get by him.

Kelley's presence gives Izzo the option of trapping and pressing in more situations. He also might play three guards a lot.

MORRIS PETERSON (6-6, 210 lbs., JR, F, #42, 8.0 ppg, 3.5 rpg, 18.6 minutes, Northwestern HS/Flint, Mich.). Peterson is a real wild card. It's hard to know exactly how good a shooter he can be.

Peterson spent most of last season wearing a cast on his right wrist, the result of a November fracture, and earned the beloved nickname "The Club." Students took to wearing cut out tube socks on their wrists in his honor. Even with such a handicap, Peterson hit 23 treys.

Regardless, Peterson is a superb athlete and might be the best fastbreak finisher on the team. He was the fourth-best scorer, and he has improved in every season. If he steps up his defense to the level of his teammates, he is a potential star. Izzo thinks it could happen.

"Morris probably made the biggest transformation on our team last year," the coach says. "He went from a high-wire act and offensive juggernaut to a guy who, because of the cast, learned how to play defense and really work hard. I was pleased with his work ethic."

A.J. GRANGER (6-9, 230 lbs., JR, F, #43, 2.6 ppg, 1.8 rpg, 12.0 minutes, Liberty-Benton HS/Findlay, Ohio). Izzo likes Granger because he is smart and knows his way around the post. Mononucleosis in the summer of '97 left him behind during preparations last season, but Izzo still ended up starting him nine games.

Now that MSU needs his points inside, it remains to be seen whether Granger can turn his finesse game into more baskets. Experience on the Big Ten touring team that annually travels Europe might help.

The second half of Granger's freshman year has Izzo hopeful that he can put more points on the board. In fact, the coach feels that Granger could be the guy to enjoy the most significant improvement over the previous season.

DOUG DAVIS (6-3, 170 lbs., SO, G, #30, 2.1 ppg, 0.8 rpg 0.7 apg, 7.7 minutes, Westland HS/Columbus, Ohio). Usually a fourth guard is a deep sub who enters only sporadically. But, in Davis, the Spartans have a guy who played 200 minutes as a rookie, started the Wisconsin game and played in all three NCAA contests.

Davis' durability is a question. He blew out an ankle late in the season against Minnesota and Izzo wants him to add bulk to his light frame. But he is another very quick guard who has already shown nerve from the arc (9-for-23). In Izzo's perfect world, Davis would be Cleaves' backup at the point with Kelley playing mostly the "two."

1998-99 MICHIGAN STATE SCHEDULE

Nov.	13	Northeast Louisiana
	17	@Oakland
	20	@Temple
	27-28	#Coca-Cola Spartan Classic
Dec.	2	*Duke
	5	@Connecticut
	10	@East Tennessee State
	13	Illinois-Chicago
	21-23	##Pearl Harbor Classic
	30	North Carolina-Asheville
Jan.	2	Louisville
	6	@Wisconsin
	9	Michigan
	13	Minnesota
	16	@Illinois
	21	Iowa
	24	@Indiana
	27	Ohio State
	30	Northwestern
Feb.	2	@Penn State
	6	@Iowa
	11	Illinois
	13	@Minnesota
	16	Purdue
	18	@Michigan
	20	Wisconsin
	27 or 28	@Purdue
Mar.	4-7	###Big Ten Conference Tournament

@	Road Games
*	Great Eight, United Center, Chicago, IL
#	East Lansing, MI (vs. Western Michigan, first round; also Central Florida and North Carolina-Wilmington)
##	Laie, HI (vs. Pepperdine, first round; also Alabama, BYU-Hawaii, Oregon State, Texas Tech, Tulsa and Weber State)
###	United Center, Chicago, IL

OTHER RETURNEES

DAVID THOMAS (6-7, 195 lbs., JR, F, #11, 3.5 ppg, 3.8 rpg, 0.8 apg, 14.8 minutes, Notre Dame HS/Brampton, Ont.). The upside is somewhat unknown for Thomas. Skinny and full of spring, Thomas suffered sprains to each knee in December (right) and February (left).

Through six games, he'd averaged 9.0 ppg and 7.8 rpg, indicating he could be a major contributor with one healthy season. Where he fits into this lineup is Izzo's problem.

Sitting him a year might be an option, except that with Duke transfer Mike Chappell arriving next season, it's hard to see how Thomas will get any more playing time a year from now.

LORENZO GUESS (6-3, 190 lbs., SO, G, #5, 0.5 ppg, 0.3 apg, 2.5 minutes, Memorial HS/Wayne, Mich.). A football free safety, Guess is not a necessity. Even so, he saw minutes in seven Big Ten games and legitimate action in the conference tournament. Whether he plays basketball again is up in the air.

STEVE CHERRY (6-6, 190 lbs., SO, F, #25, 0.4 ppg, 0.2 rpg, 1.4 minutes Coldwater HS/Coldwater, Mich.). The "airport unit" is headed by Cherry. He won't play outside of routs.

NEWCOMERS

ADAM BALLINGER (6-9, 225 lbs., FR, F, #55, 25.4 ppg, 9.5 rpg, .637 FG, Bluffton HS/Bluffton, Ind.). This team is as close to a pat hand as you'll find. The two rookies can only hope for mop-up time unless the injuries pile up.

Ballinger has the best chance to strip the warm-ups first. He brings major prep credentials as one of seven finalists for Indiana's legendary "Mr. Basketball" award. Twice he topped 40 points as a post-up scorer.

"He's a kid who has all the offensive post moves," said Izzo. "He's kind of like Bill Laimbeer in that he's not very quick, but he knows how to score."

Ballinger will have to add muscle before he plays much. Izzo chuckled when he said he plans to "throw him over to football (weight training) and let them beat the (crap) out of him for a while."

BRANDON SMITH (5-10, 165 lbs., SO, G, #23, 18.0 ppg, 6.0 apg, 5.0 spg, Pittsford Sutherland HS/Rochester, N.Y.). Smith sat out last season after transferring from Coastal Carolina. He played 14 minutes per game for the Chanticleers in 1996-97, including 32 minutes against the Sweet 16 team from Tennessee-Chattanooga. He never scored more than five points in any game.

Smith averaged 18.0 ppg and 6.0 apg in his senior year at Pittsford Sutherland HS. He is a quick player and a good defender, but isn't expected to play a whole lot this year.

QUESTIONS

Inside scoring? Only one man on this team, Hutson, has shown any touch in the paint at all. In fact, other than Hutson, Thomas is the only man on the roster who shot better than .445. Somebody has to show up here if MSU is to be a genuine post-season player.

Hunger? It's so much fun to play underdog when almost nobody picks you for the first division. Will the Spartans be as hungry as the "hunted" as they were when they were ambushing unsuspecting favorites? Are they mature enough to handle their sudden success?

Pass those December exams? Izzo has lined up a competitive non-con schedule that includes four major tests—Temple (in Philadelphia), Duke (in Chicago), Connecticut (in Hartford) and Illinois-Chicago (in East Lansing). There is also a trek to East Tennessee's death pit in Johnson City, not to mention the inaugural Pearl Harbor Classic in Hawaii (where the opening opponent is Pepperdine, with Tulsa and possibly Alabama on deck).

Cleaves' health? None of the above will matter if Cleaves doesn't recover easily from his shoulder injury.

ANSWERS

Camaraderie! This was a very close team a year ago and, because the roster has barely changed, it should be again. Four former starters became subs last season and accepted roles to help the team. There was no backbiting, no resentment. That needs to be the case again for MSU to make a run at St. Pete.

Perimeter defense! Nobody identifies and goes after three-point specialists like the Spartans. In the :35 shot clock age, where the trey has become top-heavy in importance, it is an asset which cannot be overemphasized.

Izzo's guts! Because he believes in playing the best in order to become the best, Tom Izzo is the kind of guy the Big Ten needs. If his players don't die in the process, they'll be tough come tournament time.

adidas Blue Ribbon Analysis

BACKCOURT	A	BENCH/DEPTH	B+
FRONTCOURT	B	INTANGIBLES	B

In the past, Izzo has stuck his toe in water with defensive pressure and the fastbreak. But he has never really dived in. It may now be the time for both.

This team will be small even when it plays its "big" lineup, and will be tiny when it uses three guards. The Spartans may have to run every chance they get. They also have the overall quickness and depth necessary to trap and press often with several different lineups.

Whether they have the goods to match muscle and bulk with a set-piece halfcourt team featuring a Todd MacCulloch-type in the middle is something else again. Michigan's Robert Traylor gave MSU fits last year.

Another big question: Can this team have as much fun with everyone gunning for it and the experts having picked it to breeze to the title? One thing the Spartans won't do is die worrying about some other opponent's game. Izzo has vowed to that.

Concerned about the volatile transition game of North Carolina, particularly the speed of its big men, Izzo reined in his offensive rebounders and only sent three to the glass on hostile turf in Greensboro. The damage was done in the first half of that Sweet 16 game, when State lost its aggressiveness and fell behind by double digits.

In the end, it didn't matter anyway. The Tar Heels killed a State rally in the second half with several lethal breakouts.

"We weren't afraid of playing them," said Izzo. "The problem was me. I overcoached. As I look back, I did what I thought was right. But we'd won games all year with offensive rebounds.

"Next time, I won't overcoach."

One look at this team, and it's easy to believe there will be a next time very soon.

(D.J.)

9

NEW MEXICO

LOCATION	Albuquerque, NM
CONFERENCE	WAC (Pacific Division)
LAST SEASON	24-8 (.750)
CONFERENCE RECORD	11-3 (2nd, Mountain)
STARTERS LOST/RETURNING	3/2
NICKNAME	Lobos
COLORS	Cherry & Silver
HOMECOURT	The Pit (18,018)
COACH	Dave Bliss (Cornell '65)
RECORD AT SCHOOL	221-99 (10 yrs.)
CAREER RECORD	440-262 (23 yrs.)
ASSISTANTS	Doug Ash (Hanover '71)
	Kevin Lewis (Southern Methodist '86)
	Ron Garcia (New Mexico '81)
TEAM WINS (last 5 yrs.)	23-15-28-25-24
RPI (last 5 yrs.)	55-117-23-14-17
1997-98 FINISH	Lost in NCAA second round.

COACH AND PROGRAM

Dave Bliss has done what he came to do. He has made New Mexico basketball a happening and a regular in the NCAA Tournament. That's why Lobos' fans should rejoice that he signed a long-term deal over the summer. The Lobos have never seen this type of run.

Prior to Bliss' arrival in Albuquerque, the Lobos had been to the NCAA Tournament three times in 85 seasons. New Mexico has now been there six times in the past 10 years.

Prior to 1988, the Lobos had won 20 games only eight times. Bliss has done it nine out of 10 seasons.

New Mexico used to be a "bubble" team every March; now the Lobos are a lock by the end of the WAC schedule. Since 1995-96, the Lobos are 77-21, an average of 26 wins per season. Only nine schools, including New Mexico, have won at least one game in each of the last three NCAA Tournaments.

"We've been able to smooth out the transition periods," Bliss says. "We lost some good players, but we've got Damion Walker and Brian Smith who sat out and we've got Kenny Thomas and Lamont Long back."

It is this type of recruitment planning by Bliss and top assistant Doug Ash—who have been together for 24 seasons, the longest tandem in Division I basketball—that has kept the Lobos in the Top 25. Losing David Gibson, Royce Olney and Clayton Shields would have meant a rebuilding period for past New Mexico teams, even with the caliber of starters returning in Thomas and Long. Instead, the Lobos have become the type of elite program that has players ready to step in and contribute immediately, rather than waiting for them to develop.

Walker, who transferred from Texas Christian, and Smith, a transfer from San Diego, are impact players who can not only keep the Lobos at their present level, but maybe push them even further. Snagging one of the top junior college point guards in the nation (Dontay Hicks) along with the top player in Dallas (Tim Lightfoot) gives them even more hope that they will finally get past the second round of the NCAAs.

New Mexico still needs to do more in the NCAA Tournament to be considered a truly elite program. However, the Lobos are following the correct model by cultivating four-year players and always having someone to step in so as not to lose ground.

And the Lobos have been able to change with their personnel. Don't expect the 1998-99 edition to be a typical three-point shooting team without much regard for the frontcourt.

The emphasis will shift to Thomas and Walker inside, as well as Long slashing to the basket. The defense should be better and possess more quickness on the wings. And The Pit should continue to be one of the toughest homecourts in the nation.

It's no surprise that the Lobos and Utah are the favorites again to win the WAC and fight for the conference tournament championship.

"There's a great feeling around our office. The recruiting is getting a little bit better as a result of how well the team continues to do, not only with the won-loss record, but also in the polls," Bliss says. "And, with the players that we have this year, we should be thought of as a pretty good basketball team again."

Translation: WAC champion, Top 15 ranking and potential Final Eight.

STARTERS NOT RETURNING

DAVID GIBSON (6-2, PG, 5.9 ppg, 2.8 rpg, 3.6 apg, 1.9 tpg, 1.3 spg, 35.4 minutes, .472 FG, .265 3PT, .780 FT). The Lobos are going to miss Gibson because he was the most reliable player on a daily basis. His experience was unmatched; he played more games and more minutes (4,509) than any other player in the history of the school.

Even though there may have been more talented point men, he was extremely intelligent on the court. He'll be missed on the defensive end, too, as the Lobos' top on-the-ball guard. His quickness allowed him to defend any point guard or shooting guard. He was even able to stave off the recruitment of other guards, as the Lobos tried to replace him but never could.

Gibson's departure ended an eight-year run of Albuquerque point guards at the school. Gibson was in charge from 1995-98. He was preceded by Greg Brown (1993-94) and Willie Banks (1991-92).

CLAYTON SHIELDS (6-8, PF, 16.7 ppg, 6.8 rpg, 1.7 apg, 1.5 tpg, 34.7 minutes, .457 FG, .407 3PT, .733 FT). Shields might have been the most versatile player at New Mexico. He was one of the best three-point shooters in the history of the WAC.

He would really create problems for opposing teams with his ability to extend the defense. He forced tough matchups for his size. The Lobos will really miss Shields' shooting and his overall athleticism; he is second-leading scorer in school history.

He was an emotional player. Shields had stretches of erratic shooting and could disappear. He also had his limitations as a rebounder, and UNM may be better off on the boards without him. Shields wasn't physical, but made up for it with his three-point range and ability to break up games.

Shields finished No. 2 in scoring (1,837 points), fifth in rebounding (758), fourth in field goals (641) and fourth in career minutes played (3,865) at New Mexico. The three seniors (Olney, Gibson and Shields) won more games than any other players during a four-year span. UNM was 92-36 from 1995-98, an average of 23 wins per season. The Lobos won a WAC Tournament (1996) and earned three NCAA berths.

ROYCE OLNEY (6-2, SG, 14.8 ppg, 2.5 rpg, 4.0 apg, 1.8 tpg, 1.6 spg, 32.0 minutes, .536 FG, .513 3PT, .754 FT). Every team wished they could have an Olney. He overachieved out of a Class AA school in Truth or Consequences, N.M. No one thought he could play at this level and he ended up being one of the top three-point shooters in college basketball. He was UNM's most valuable player and the team's spirited leader.

When he went down with a knee injury late last season, so, too, did the Lobos' chances to make a deep run in the Tournament. He was a fan favorite, diving into the stands for loose balls. He was a clutch player, always making the big shots.

He wasn't the best athlete, but always made up for his deficiencies with intensity. The Lobos were 21-3 with Olney, averaging 80.3 ppg and shooting 49.8 percent (.431 on three-pointers). Without him, they were 3-5, scoring 62.1 ppg and shooting 39.3 percent (.311 3PT).

"We knew Royce was a good player, but it was hard to evaluate what kind of an effect he had on his teammates," Bliss says. "We didn't know how major a part of our chemistry he was until he was out. Losing one player really jarred us."

OTHERS NOT RETURNING

BEN BAUM (6-11, C, 2.4 ppg, 1.4 rpg, 9.4 minutes, .491 FG, .643 3PT, .833 FT). Baum provided great

1997-98 RESULTS

#Southern California	98-76
New Mexico State	80-79
##Texas Southern	90-67
##Arkansas State	61-51
San Jose State	86-57
@UCLA (L)	58-69
@New Mexico State	62-59
Texas Tech	81-62
###Holy Cross	112-61
###Yale	69-44
Air Force	92-59
Texas Christian	98-77
@Wyoming (L)	55-58
@Colorado State	78-64
UNLV	79-61
@Arizona (L)	70-89
@UTEP	76-69
Brigham Young	72-54
Utah	77-74
Wyoming	89-59
Colorado State	77-62
@Air Force	96-72
@UNLV	75-66
UTEP	95-71
@Texas Christian (L)	64-95
Brigham Young (L)	62-83
@Utah (L)	55-65
####Tulsa	60-59
####Texas Christian	80-73
####UNLV (L)	51-56
%Butler	79-62
%Syracuse (L)	46-56

@	away games
#	NABC Classic, Albuquerque, NM
##	Lobo Classic, Albuquerque, NM
###	Jones Intercable Lobo, Albuquerque, NM
####	WAC Tournament, Thomas & Mack Center, Las Vegas, NV
%	NCAA South Sub-Regional, Lexington, KY

leadership. He had been to the Final Four at Oklahoma State and played in four straight NCAA Tournaments. The Lobos will miss his fire on the court.

When Thomas got in foul trouble against bigger teams, having someone 6-11 helped them offset his loss. Baum was also a great UNM system player because of his ability to shoot the ball from the perimeter.

TOM STARKEY (6-6, F, 1.2 ppg, 1.2 rpg, 2.9 tpg, 4.8 minutes, .263 FG, .200 3PT). Starkey was in over his head with the Lobos. He should have gone mid-major out of high school or redshirted last year. He has transferred to the University of Denver and will sit out this season under NCAA rules.

PROJECTED STARTERS

LAMONT LONG (6-4, 190 lbs., JR, SF, #3, 14.1 ppg, 6.1 rpg, 2.7 apg, 2.0 tpg, 1.5 spg, 37.2 minutes, .461 FG, .318 3PT, .767 FT, Corona del Sol HS/Tempe, Ariz.). Long should be one of the best guards in the country, especially in the West. He is a great slasher with good scoring ability. He could be one of the best all-around players, too. He rebounds, scores and defends.

Long will have to be a "go-to: player, especially with Thomas out for the first semester. He is one of the only players on the Lobos who can create his own shot, take his man with a cross-over dribble and get by him to the basket. He has to be more consistent with his three-point shot by improving his range.

Long plays extremely hard on both ends of the floor and could be the difference in the Lobos becoming a truly elite team. If he has a great year, the Lobos will have a chance to win the WAC and have a deep run in the NCAA Tournament.

Long could lead the Lobos in scoring and be second on the team in rebounding. Bliss wants to play him at shooting guard, but UNM's best lineup has him at small forward. He has played three positions at New Mexico.

"Lamont should be able to step it up a bit and have an outstanding year," Bliss says. "He has to get more serious about things. He has deferred to the older guys, but now he's the older guy and has to discipline himself to take the right attitude toward shooting.

"He has to make the threes and the 'stop and pops.' He hasn't had to worry about much with Charles (Smith), Clayton and Royce. He's capable of the big numbers, but, last year, when we lost Royce, we thought he would pick up even more and he didn't do it."

Long became the team's iron man, playing every minute of the Lobos' last eight games and all but 11 minutes of the final 15. He played all 40 minutes in 17 games overall. He is just 380 points and 171 rebounds away from becoming the 11th member of New Mexico's 1,000-point, 500-rebound club.

KENNY THOMAS (6-8, 255 lbs., SR, C, #4, 16.8 ppg, 9.3 rpg, 3.0 apg, 3.0 tpg, 2.5 bpg, 32.7 minutes, .506 FG, .375 3PT, .767 FT, Albuquerque HS/Albuquerque, N.M.). Thomas has had more to deal with as a college player than maybe any other in recent memory. His career started with a lawsuit against the NCAA (including an injunction to play as a freshman), yet he had an impact year.

After his sophomore year, he reached an agreement with the NCAA to sit out the first semester as a senior. His 1998-99 season will start on Dec. 19, when the Lobos host Sacramento State. New Mexico will only play six games, not including two exhibitions, before Thomas is eligible.

None of those games should have the Lobos worried. They purposely stuffed the first semester with softies, scheduling Washington, Arizona and both New Mexico State encounters after Thomas becomes eligible.

There was speculation Thomas would leave after his junior year, but he decided to return. During the summer, he was arrested for DUI and had to serve two days in jail. The DUI prevented him from trying out for any of the U.S. national teams.

"He's got to get serious about his game," Bliss says. "He's not doing what he needs to do. He has to work harder and can't let his weight balloon. He needs to start answering the bell and be as good as he's supposed to be."

Bliss says Thomas' passing has continued to be exceptional, but he still hasn't reached the potential he showed as a freshman. He was a bull in a china closet that season, but hasn't been the same dominating presence since. He still commits foolish fouls and, to Bliss, "Kenny's a constant reminder that unless you really do it, how do you get any credit for being any good?"

Thomas set high standards for himself after his first WAC Tournament as a frosh. He had 30 points and 17 rebounds in the final against Utah, and hasn't been able to live up to that level. He had to defer inside the past two years with Charles Smith and Shields. This year, he'll be the focal point and should put up big-time numbers.

Sitting out the first semester should make him even hungrier to prove he belongs as a first-team All-America. Thomas has improved his perimeter shooting, and now defenders have to honor that part of his game. His mobility has improved and he has kept his weight down.

Thomas is more under control, and he'll run the floor well. He already has a great presence on the defensive end and should be the best interior defensive player in the WAC. His weakness is his focus; Thomas does not concentrate all of the time.

Much of that has to do with his deferring shots. This is his team now, and Thomas shouldn't sleep-walk through any games. He is a great passer and could be the most dominant low-post player in the country. You have to double-team him, but he'll make you pay for that.

Walker's arrival should take some pressure off Thomas, who can float to the perimeter and use his three-point skills. Bliss is already talking about playing some high-low offense with Thomas at the top of the key and Walker underneath.

What Thomas has to avoid are the disappearing acts, like his season-low three-point, five rebound game against Syracuse in the NCAA Tournament. It was the third time out of five that he has fouled out of an NCAA. He came into that contest averaging 17.5 ppg and 9.3 rpg.

KEVIN HENRY (6-3, 185 lbs., SO, SG, #11, 5.9 ppg, 1.3 rpg, 1.5 apg, 17.2 minutes, .400 FG, .386 3PT, .722 FT Ryan HS/Denton, Tex.). Henry had a decent freshman year after coming in as a point guard who was supposedly going to compete with Gibson. He ended up being a better shooting guard.

Henry will play more on the wing this year. He'll be the Lobos best shooter and is probably their strongest player at guard. He is well-conditioned, but needs to improve his defense. Henry hit big shots for the Lobos, will be counted on to start and will have to shoot well for the Lobos to be successful.

His biggest shot came against Tulsa in the WAC Tournament. Henry replaced Olney in the starting lineup, and his three-pointer won the game and snapped a three-of-four UNM losing streak. In the five postseason (including the WAC tourney), Henry averaged nine points and made 10 three-pointers. He was named to the WAC All-Newcomer team by the coaches and media.

DAMION WALKER (6-7, 225 lbs., JR, PF, #33, 12.2 ppg, 6.5 rpg, 2.2 tpg, 1.1 bpg, 27.1 minutes, .417 FG, .500 3PT, .759 FT in 1996-97, Texas Christian & Lincoln HS/Dallas, Tex.). Walker was a freshman All-America along with Cal's Shareef Abdur-Rahim and Georgia Tech's Stephon Marbury after he averaged 20.5 ppg and 8.8 rpg at TCU in 1995-96. However, his sophomore season wasn't as successful. He had to defer much of his offensive production to the guard tandem of Mike Jones and Malcolm Johnson.

Walker has the ability to return to his freshman numbers both in scoring and rebounding. He'll take a lot of pressure off of Thomas and really improved during his redshirt year.

Walker can now shoot three-pointers, and he'll have a chance to extend the defense. He is a very tough player who doesn't let rebounds get away from him. He still needs to improve his individual defense, but he and Thomas should give the Lobos a top 1-2 punch inside.

As Bliss has said, he'll use both either at the high or low post. Teams that had a tough time guarding Thomas will find it nearly impossible to defend both he and Walker.

This isn't the twin towers, or even a Tim Duncan-David Robinson combination. Thomas and Walker are like a pair of power forwards. However, they are distinctly different bookends. Walker is more content closer to the basket. Thomas would love to float toward the perimeter. The options are endless with these two in the lineup and Long at small forward.

"He's never played with someone like Kenny, and Kenny's never played with someone like Damion," says Bliss, anticipating the dominance of the pair.

DONTAY HICKS (6-1, 175 lbs., JR, PG, #32, 20.8 ppg, 4.7 rpg, 6.7 apg, .489 FG, .330 3PT, .734 FT, Allen County CC, Kan. & Riverside HS/Milwaukee, Wisc.). Hicks comes in as one of the top point guard recruits in the country. He is a very explosive player and will give New Mexico a different look than Gibson.

Gibson was steadier, but Hicks will take more chances—something the Lobos could use on a quicker team. Hicks can break down a defense, and big men like Thomas will benefit from his ability to get inside. His athleticism will also help on defense.

Hicks is more of a scoring point guard, akin to Mookie Blaylock, but he has to adjust to Bliss' system and play under control. He should start at the point and is the key to the Lobos' newcomer class and ultimately their season.

Teams won't be able to play off of Hicks, and he'll give the Lobos something Gibson could not—a scoring threat at the point.

"He's got that flair to his game," Bliss says. "He has all the credentials to handle the ball and pass it effectively. He's a capable, not an outstanding shooter."

1998-99 NEW MEXICO SCHEDULE

Nov.	13	*DePaul
	27-28	#Lobo Classic
Dec	2	Arkansas-Pine Bluff
	8	Texas-Pan American
	19	Cal State Sacramento
	21	McNeese State
	24	@Washington
	28-29	##Lobo Invitational
Jan	2	New Mexico State
	4	@Fresno State
	7	San Diego State
	9	Hawaii
	13	@San Jose State
	16	Arizona
	19	@New Mexico State
	23	@UTEP
	30	Brigham Young
Feb	1	Utah
	6	@Hawaii
	8	@San Diego State
	11	San Jose State
	13	Fresno State
	20	UTEP
	25	@Brigham Young
	27	@Utah
Mar	2-6	###WAC Tournament

@ Road Games
* BCA Classic, Albuquerque, NM
# Albuquerque, NM (vs. Cornell, first round; also LaSalle and Northeastern)
Albuquerque, NM (vs. New Hampshire, first round; also Houston and Portland State)
Thomas & Mack Center, Las Vegas, NV

KEY RESERVES

GREG DAVIS (6-9, 205 lbs., SO, F, #5, 2.0 ppg, 1.3 rpg, 7.7 minutes, .439 FG, .294 3PT, .800 FT, Martin HS/Arlington, Tex.). Davis was competing at the beginning of last season for the fifth starting spot, but got sick (anemia) during the year and lost confidence. He also lost weight, strength and never really recovered.

Davis probably should have redshirted, but, due to short numbers in the frontcourt, could not. He then had a virus this past summer which resulted in a tonsillectomy and dropped his weight below 200 pounds.

Davis is stronger now and should be able to contribute off the bench for the Lobos if Walker or Thomas are in foul trouble. But he could also be a redshirt candidate.

Davis is skilled and a typical Bliss player. He can shoot the three and block shots.

ROLAND HANNAH (6-6, 210 lbs., JR, F, #42, 14.7 ppg, 7.3 rpg, McCook CC, Neb. & Hope HS/Providence, R.I.). Hannah redshirted last year and could be one of the toughest players for the Lobos. He is very versatile on the defensive end and he'll guard anybody on the floor.

He is a good rebounder and will bring toughness to the Lobos. Hannah is limited offensively as an average shooter, but he can finish. The Lobos will play more up-tempo, so he can help them with his ability to flush dunks.

Hannah could start at small forward if UNM wants to start Long at shooting guard. He'll more likely back up Long at small forward or Walker at power forward.

"He's very physical, and there's a reason why we wanted him back," says Bliss, who almost never redshirts junior college transfers. "He served his time and we really think he can help us."

BRIAN SMITH (6-8, 245 lbs., SO, F, #21, 3.1 ppg, 2.5 rpg, .400 FG, .250 3PT, .838 FT in 1996-97, University of San Diego & Salpointe Catholic HS/Tucson, Ariz.). Smith is a tough, hard-nosed player who gives the Lobos their best inside rotation in years. He is similar to the kind of forward often found at Utah.

He is a good defensive, low-post player and can score on the block. He can also step out and hit the three-pointer. Smith has strength and is a solid backup to Walker and Thomas. There shouldn't be much of a dropoff when he enters the game.

Smith handled himself well as a redshirt last year, battling Thomas in practice and toughening him up during the season. The Lobos' scout team last year was one of the best in the country with he, Walker and Hannah.

"He's a blue-collar guy," Bliss says. "He understands his ability and is a typical hard-nosed player. He's like our former player, Greg Schornstein."

TIM LIGHTFOOT (6-4, 170 lbs., FR, G, #10, 21.8 ppg, 5.4 rpg, 160 assists, 92 steals, .466 FG, .356 3PT, .852 FT, Everman HS/Dallas, Tex.). He could be the next Charles Smith, and he could be better than Henry. Lightfoot was the Player of the Year in the Dallas Metro-Plex last season, becoming the second Lobo recruit to receive that honor (Smith did out of Fort Worth).

Lightfoot has great one-on-one ability and can create his own shot. He is the total shooting guard, possessing good quickness and a cross-over dribble. He has to improve on the defensive end, but he should see quality minutes. Lightfoot could even sneak into the starting lineup if he can beat out Henry.

The Lobos were limited after Olney went down last season, but they finally have depth at the point and shooting guard. Lightfoot gives Bliss his deepest and most talented set of perimeter players in his 10 years in Albuquerque.

OTHER RETURNEES

MARCOS WHITE (5-7, 153 lbs., SR, G, #12, 0.4 ppg, 0.1 rpg, 11 appearances, Narbonne HS/Carson, Calif.). White is a reliable walkon. He is also a fan favorite since he has lasted three seasons.

He could help in a pinch.

OTHER NEWCOMERS

JOHN ROBINSON II (6-1, 180 lbs., FR, G, #22, 28.2 ppg, 3.9 rpg, 5.9 apg, 129 steals, .471 FG, .360 3PT, .820 FT, Channelview HS/Houston, Tex.). Robinson is a steady point guard like Gibson, but not as quick, though he is a better shooter. He has good knowledge of the game and should be a solid all-around college player.

Robinson could compete with Hicks for the starting position at the point. He led the city of Houston in scoring last year, but is an average defender. He is the son of a coach and should adapt well to Bliss' hands-on approach.

DREW GAULDEN (6-8, 210 lbs, FR, F, #15, 18.3 ppg, 9.8 rpg, .484 FG, .250 3PT, .721 FT, Canyon HS/Anaheim, Calif.). Gaulden is versatile and athletic, but he's a tweener. He is not big enough to play power forward, but not quick enough to be a "three" man. He has to get stronger and could be called a poor-man's Keith Van Horn.

Gaulden is an average shooter, but can finish with anyone. He is extremely skilled for his size and is a typical Bliss player. He could find some time deep in the small forward rotation.

QUESTIONS

Team shooting? Without Olney, New Mexico is lacking a proven shooter. The Lobos lost two of the top shooters in the WAC in Olney and Shields. The outside shooting must now come from Henry, Long or even Thomas. The Lobos may find themselves doubled-down a lot and will get zoned quite often.

Team defense? The Lobos lose Gibson, Shields and Olney. They have more speed, and but will they be able to get out on the perimeter and also maintain their hold on the defensive boards?

High expectations? How do Thomas and the rest of the Lobos handle expectations of being the WAC favorite and a potential Final Eight team? This is why Thomas stayed in school, and now he has to prove that it was worth the wait.

ANSWERS

Thomas and Walker! They could be the best inside scoring tandem in the country. They have both been All-Americas and should be a great rebounding tandem, too.

Athleticism! This should be the most athletic team Bliss has had in 10 years. The Lobos will be tough to defend at every position, and can run the break better than any other team in the league.

Depth! The Lobos are finally two-deep at every position. Bliss has to let his tight reign go on the freshmen, allowing them to get involved and make a few mistakes.

adidas Blue Ribbon Analysis

BACKCOURT	B	BENCH/DEPTH	B+
FRONTCOURT	A	INTANGIBLES	A

New Mexico will be a tougher, more balanced and better rebounding team than it has been under Bliss. However, that means expectations are even higher for the Lobos to advance deeper in the NCAA Tournament.

They should. There are no excuses for this lot. There is not even an Olney factor. Even if Thomas were to go down—and he is out for the first semester—Walker is more than capable of carrying a team inside.

The Lobos are the clear favorite to win the WAC, but they have to do more than that to appease The Pit faithful and the national media. The Lobos have had shooting guards like Charles Smith. They've had centers like Luc Longley. But they've never had the whole package and depth at every position like they do now.

Expect New Mexico to win key non-conference games in December (Washington) and January (Arizona) and be a realistic Top 10 team come March. The Lobos should be no worse than a Sweet 16 team by the end of the season.

If the Lobos can't go that far with this group, they may never have the chance again.

(A.K.)

10

CINCINNATI

LOCATION	Cincinnati, OH
CONFERENCE	C-USA (American Division)
LAST SEASON	27-6 (.818)
CONFERENCE RECORD	14-2 (1st)
STARTERS LOST/RETURNING	3/2
NICKNAME	Bearcats
COLOR	Red & Black
HOMECOURT	Shoemaker Center (13,176)
COACH	Bob Huggins (West Virginia '77)
RECORD AT SCHOOL	219-77 (9 yrs.)
CAREER RECORD	387-149 (17 yrs.)
ASSISTANTS	Rod Baker (Holy Cross '74)
	Mick Cronin (Cincinnati '96)
TEAM WINS (last 5 yrs.)	22-22-28-26-27
RPI (last 5 yrs.)	27-18-3-16-18
1997-98 FINISH	Lost in NCAA second round.

COACH AND PROGRAM

Let's see: 27 wins, a conference title, a conference tournament crown on top of that, a top five recruiting class and another quite possibly on the way. If this is hell, what the devil goes on in heaven?

Cincinnati spent most of the past two seasons being slowly fed through the NCAA grinder (which is the only way anyone is fed through the NCAA grinder, it seems). For all the trouble school and NCAA investigators went through, and all the money spent by Ohio taxpayers, what did we learn about the way the Bearcats operate their program?

Not a lot, really. By the time Cincinnati went before the infractions committee in August, the charges were reduced to almost nothing: that former point guard Charles Williams was given improper academic aid in establishing his eligibility; that the university failed to sufficiently monitor the program in allowing several players to make unauthorized long- distance phone calls; that assistant coach John Loyer acted unethically. Not a lot more.

The university placed itself on a one-year probation that included minimal sanctions, most notably a ban on recruiting junior college players and a reduction in the number of official visits it could offer prospects. Coach Bob Huggins also had the number of days he would spend away from campus recruiting and fundraising reduced.

While all this was transpiring, the basketball part of the operation proceeded rather nicely, even though it technically was shorthanded the entire time.

With Loyer on an administrative leave and former assistant Larry Harrison moving to a job at DePaul, Huggins got the opportunity to retool his staff and wound up, in some ways, better off. Former California-Irvine coach Rod Baker, who replaced Harrison, brought an outsider's perspective to the Bearcats program along with a voice Huggins respected tremendously. Mick Cronin made tremendous use of the relationships he built while attending UC, working major camps (ABCD, Five-Star) and coaching in a Cincinnati high school to help gather a recruiting class with size and skill.

That class provides a good deal of the reason for the optimism regarding the Bearcats' future, both immediate and near-term. Rarely has Cincinnati had such an abundance of size while Huggins has been coach, and it has been collected without a great sacrifice in terms of athletic ability.

Any doubts about what Huggins can accomplish with a basketball team ought to have been dispelled by his work during the 1997-98 season, when the Bearcats went from outside the preseason Top 25 to a final regular season ranking of No. 9. This despite a 14-game suspension to small forward Ruben Patterson; suspensions of three games each for shooting guard D'Juan Baker, center Kenyon Martin and point guard Michael Horton; early-season injuries to reserve center Ryan Fletcher and reserve guard Shawn Myrick; and the broken hand Fletcher had as he ended the year.

In reality, Huggins should have been a consensus pick as national Coach of the Year. No one else went through so much and accomplished what the Bearcats did. Instead, his unpopularity with many media members led them elsewhere (and only *Basketball Times* chose Huggins for its award).

Cincinnati is one of only three programs to finish the past three seasons ranked in the Top 10, joining Kentucky and Kansas. It is one of only seven programs to conclude the past six seasons with 20 or more victories. The Bearcats have also ended each of the past seven seasons with either a regular season conference championship or a conference tournament title.

Under Huggins during the 1990s, the Bearcats have a .740 winning percentage and 219 victories. Those figures rank 12th and 10th, respectively, among NCAA Division I schools.

The Bearcats will not have to scrape as much to match those accomplishments this year. With the size on hand, they will be able to extend their defense on the perimeter without fear of exposing the frontcourt to foul trouble it can't manage.

"I would like to think we're going to play a little faster and extend the floor more defensively," Huggins said.

The Bearcats retreated from that type of defense when Danny Fortson joined the program and they could not afford to expose him to foul trouble. Last season, it was simply a matter of depth on the inside. No one could afford to get in foul trouble.

If this group of players is able to add backcourt pressure to the halfcourt man-to-man last year's Bearcats played so well, it could become a devastating defensive team. Opponents shot .393 last season, but the disparity between UC's turnovers and those it forced was only about one per game.

Throughout Huggins' tenure, Cincinnati's offense came easily only during Fortson's career, and only then when teams could not concoct a plan to keep the ball from his hands. This team faces a lot of those questions. The guys who figure to grab most of the playing time are most prominently defensive players: Kenyon Martin, Jermaine Tate, Michael Horton. Finding a consistent scoring source with this group will be Huggins' greatest challenge, and the one that determines how much this team is capable of accomplishing.

It's rather important that this team at least make a Sweet 16-type run this year. Instead of focusing on what Cincinnati did with such a short roster and talent so many had dismissed, recent attention has been directed toward the second-round NCAA Tournament loss to West Virginia (which came on a nearly impossible, banked three-pointer by Mountaineers guard Jarrod West).

It was the second consecutive year Cincinnati was

bounced from the Tournament in the second round, both by lower-seeded teams and both by a single point. This could be viewed as an accident, and probably should be for now, given that Huggins made two Final Eight trips and one Final Four in five previous tournaments. But one more such result would no doubt be evidence of a trend.

STARTERS NOT RETURNING

BOBBY BRANNEN (6-7, PF, 14.3 ppg, 8.1 rpg, 1.0 apg, 2.1 tpg, 1.0 spg, 33.9 minutes, .454 FG, .842 FT). The debt the Cincinnati program owes to Brannen is difficult to calculate. As much as anyone, including Huggins, Brannen got the Bearcats through their most difficult times. It was the force of his personality, as well as a game many did not know he possessed, which enabled Cincinnati to remain a force in Conference USA.

Brannen was a co-captain of the Bearcats as a senior, but there was no doubt he was in charge. He was the player his younger teammates respected without hesitation. He worked, so they worked. He listened, so they listened. He refused to quit when Patterson, Baker and Martin were out. So they didn't quit, either.

Brannen recorded double-doubles in seven of Cincinnati's first 10 contests. The game that defined Brannen's season, and the Bearcats' as well, came against Massachusetts at the Rock 'n Roll Shootout in Cleveland just after Christmas. Patterson was well into his suspension, Baker and Martin were in the second of their three-game punishments, and Fletcher was ill with the flu. The latter played anyway, and followed Brannen's lead.

They were up against a Massachusetts team with Lari Ketner, Tyrone Weeks and Ajmal Basit on the front line. Brannen wrecked those guys, getting Weeks into foul trouble and obliterating Ketner with his footwork and flying right elbow. Brannen's 32-point game kept Cincinnati competitive and forced overtime, where the Bearcats won.

Brannen became easier to defend after that, a target for most Cincinnati opponents. He was not hard to take out of a game because of his size, but he continued to battle and the attention paid to him allowed others to contribute points more easily.

He'll be less of a chore to replace tactically than emotionally. It wasn't for his statistics that Marquette coach Mike Deane called Brannen the most valuable player in C-USA. He was chosen first-team All-Conference despite ranking just ninth in the league in scoring.

It is leadership that Cincinnati will miss from Brannen.

RUBEN PATTERSON (6-6, SF, 16.5 ppg, 6.3 rpg, 2.2 apg, 3.5 tpg, 1.2 spg, 27.8 minutes, .472 FG, .269 3PT, .611 FT). After arriving at Cincinnati heralded as the nation's No. 1 junior college player and a nearly indefensible wing athlete, Patterson spent two years struggling to get off the bench for a variety of reasons that had nothing to do with those proclamations.

He missed 14 games of his senior season because he was found to have spent time in his summer employer's condominium and accepting that person's co- signature on a car loan. Cincinnati was 12-2 without him; 15-4 against better competition with him.

Yeah, it was really tough to keep Patterson from the basket, perhaps as tough as any player in the past half-dozen years. But too often he created his own problems by bulling his way into the lane with no concern for avoiding offensive fouls.

He never developed as a shooter the way he was supposed to. Patterson tended to shoot with the fingers on his shooting hand too close together, which created a less firm grip and caused his shots occasionally to wobble as they approached the target.

And he often was benched for defensive reasons, not because he wasn't a superior man-to-man defender—he was, in fact, Cincinnati's best—but because he had trouble with team concepts. Ask him to stop one man, as the UC staff did when Larry Hughes was in the opposite uniform, and he could do it as well as anyone. Ask him to deal with the intricate screen-and-curl game played by Northern Arizona, and Patterson was in trouble.

He could be extremely valuable as a scorer; he hit for 27 points in a win against Rhode Island, 25 in the West Virginia game and a career-high 32 in a road demolition of UAB. He learned of his mother's unexpected death earlier in the day, then went out and dominated the game on offense and defense.

Patterson's athletic ability and one-on-one skills could have been an astonishing combination had he been permitted more time to blend into Cincinnati's operation. It didn't quite work out, but he did make second-team All-Conference and was selected in the second round of the NBA draft by the Los Angeles Lakers.

He will play the coming year in Greece.

D'JUAN BAKER (6-3, SG, 13.4 ppg, 2.6 rpg, 1.1 apg, 2.5 tpg, 1.0 spg, 30.0 minutes, .370 3PT, .867 FT). No one took the West Virginia loss harder than Baker, whose three-pointer with seven seconds left appeared to give the Bearcats a ticket to the Sweet 16. He made that shot from the very spot where he had won the first-round game against Northern Arizona just two days before. Those baskets and his overall Tournament performance overwhelmed the one-word whispers that followed Baker throughout his two seasons at Cincinnati: soft.

Baker sure looked like a marshmallow when he went to Marquette and was shut out while Golden Eagles' guard Aaron Hutchins was topping the 30-point mark. He bore great responsibility for the loss at South Carolina that occurred when Antonio Grant threw in a buzzer-beater to complete a comeback from a 21-point deficit. It was Baker who committed a senseless offensive foul with the Bearcats holding a seven-point lead and Bobby Brannen about to score with just more than a minute left.

Baker's excuse for throwing BJ McKie over the end line? His jersey was being held.

Only at the end did Baker become the offensive player and clutch force Cincinnati had hoped when it signed him out of Midland (Tex.) JC. He began the year with an offensive flourish that showed what he was capable of, hitting for 26, 33, 34 and 26 after opening with an 11-point game against Detroit.

Much of that was against weak competition, though, and when he was suspended three games for making unauthorized long-distance phone calls, he returned without the same confidence. Baker went through a terrible stretch in January and early February.

Yet in Cincinnati's final six games, Baker was in double figures every time, and he hit the game-winning basket not only against Northern Arizona, but also against Saint Louis to clinch the undisputed C-USA title. He was a player Cincinnati could count on, at least by then, to create his own shot and to knock down spot-up threes. There is now no one with quite the same offensive ability in the program.

OTHERS NOT RETURNING

BRENT PETRUS (6-4, G, 2.5 ppg, 2.2 rpg, 12.5 minutes, .644 FG, .708 FT). Petrus played 376 minutes for the Bearcats after walking onto the team in late November, when football season and his career as a quarterback/wideout ostensibly ended. If you add up his rebounds and steals and factor in the considerable number of loose balls he collected, it works out that Petrus picked up one extra possession for Cincinnati for every three minutes or so he spent on the court.

Petrus fell in love with playing for the basketball team, so much so that he chose to travel to Cleveland for the UMass game rather than fly first to Boise for a couple days of football practice. He was a key figure in the UMass win, contributing six points and five rebounds.

During the many suspensions, he started four games and scored a career-high 21 points against Eastern Kentucky. Petrus was valuable as a defensive player and "possession receiver," and for the fact that he rarely made a mental mistake.

JOHN CARSON (6-1, G, 3.1 ppg, 0.8 rpg, 6.9 minutes, .356 FG, .359 3PT, .600 FT). There are those in the Bearcats program who like to believe that spending a year removed from the game as an ineligible freshman ruined Carson. It is more likely he was one of the most egregious recruiting mistakes of Huggins' tenure.

He was recruited as a point guard, and some scouts actually slapped him with a Top 100 tag. But, despite physical strength and a sweet shot, he wasn't nearly quick or fluid enough to play the point at a high major. A program at Cincinnati's level should never sign an academic risk with such limited basketball ability.

In his one season with the Bearcats, he did help win a game at Tulane by hitting two three-pointers. He also made a three in the regular season closer against Saint Louis.

Carson's shooting could make him an asset at a low-major program, which is likely where he'll end up after spending a year in junior college. He was expected to transfer from Cincinnati to Barton County (Kan.) CC.

1997-98 RESULTS

Detroit	76-66	
Arizona State (L)	79-87	
Morehead State	87-57	
Alcorn State	90-76	
Wright State	85-60	
@Xavier (L)	68-88	
Minnesota	81-71	
Eastern Kentucky	106-53	
#Massachusetts	74-66	ot
Winthrop	79-36	
@Houston	81-68	
Memphis	61-54	
Marquette	67-51	
Southern Mississippi	77-61	
@Louisville	71-57	
@Tulane	60-50	
@Marquette (L)	63-66	ot
Rhode Island	88-82	
Louisville	67-61	
@South Carolina (L)	65-67	
@DePaul	109-73	
@UNC Charlotte (L)	62-69	
@Saint Louis	70-43	
South Florida	72-55	
@UAB	93-76	
DePaul	75-38	
UNC Charlotte	68-67	
Saint Louis	61-58	
##Louisville	64-50	
##UAB	100-85	
##UNC Charlotte	71-57	
%Northern Arizona	65-62	
%West Virginia (L)	74-75	

@ away games
\# Rock & Roll Shootout, Cleveland, OH
\## Conference USA Tournament, Shoemaker Center, Cincinnati, OH
% NCAA West Sub-Regional, Boise, ID

PROJECTED STARTERS

MELVIN LEVETT (6-3, 215 lbs., SR, SG, #21, 14.1 ppg, 4.7 rpg, 1.4 apg, 1.8 tpg, 1.0 spg, 29.8 minutes, .417 FG, .378 3PT, .750 FT, Euclid HS/Cleveland, Oh.). Those who watched Levett the least his first two seasons were perhaps the least surprised at his impressive development as a Cincinnati junior. He always looked impressive enough, with astonishing athletic ability and nice shooting form. His free throws suggested he ought to be able to connect on jump shots. But many close to the program wondered if he was together enough to be a reliable, full-time player.

When Patterson was out, Levett made certain he was barely missed. Levett became a steady three-point threat (and even set a school record with 10 in a game against Eastern Kentucky). His perimeter shooting was an important element for an offense that always was a find-it-where-you-can operation. As often as not, the Bearcats found it with Levett behind the arc.

He had 42 points in that game against EKU, but also 20 against Minnesota, 34 against Winthrop, 19 against Houston and Southern Mississippi, and 16 against Memphis. If it seemed Patterson's return might limit his minutes or the importance to the offense, that was dispelled by his 22-point game against Rhode Island (part of a string of five consecutive double-figure games in which Patterson played).

Levett defends well because of his athletic ability and intensity. His energy made him the ideal bench player for the Bearcats, but he only took that role for good in the final 11 games, once Patterson was okay to play. He emerged from the bench to score 26 points in the C-USA clincher against UNC Charlotte, and 15 more against the 49ers in the C-USA tournament championship.

Levett has a knack for big plays even in difficult circumstances. After a miserable 0-for-12 start against UMass in his hometown of Cleveland, he stuck a three-pointer to open the overtime and provide a lead that was not relinquished.

As a senior, Levett will be asked to contribute some leadership but, more important, to start at shooting guard and provide perimeter offense. He is a shoot-and-dunk player, with very little in between, which is a shame because his iffy ballhandling keeps him from getting into traffic and getting himself fouled. He shot well from the free throw line but attempted just 80, which Patterson far exceeded in 14 fewer games. That's the difference between being able to penetrate and not.

Levett's play in the NCAA Tournament was the other concern. He showed he could play well under pressure by averaging 20.5 ppg in the two games that determined the league titles, but, in the NCAAs he was 2-for-11 for five points in 40 combined minutes. This team will need more from him.

KENYON MARTIN (6-8, 230 lbs., JR, C, #4, 9.9 ppg, 8.9 rpg, 1.4 apg, 1.7 tpg, 1.0 spg, 2.7 bpg, 28.6 minutes, .626 FG, .476 FT, Bryan Adams HS/Dallas, Tex.). We said here one year ago: "What Martin does as well as anyone in college is go from standing on the ground to flying in the air in a moment's notice." There now are 83 people who can offer proof of that contention.

Martin was named C-USA defensive player of the year and was second-team All-Conference. His shot-block total ranked among the NCAA leaders, and he also recorded Cincinnati's first triple-double since the days of Oscar Robertson (with 24 points, 23 rebounds and 10 rejections against DePaul).

All three numbers were career-highs. He also pulled a rebound over Kelvin Price's head and threw in a buzzer-beating basket in the UNCC game for the regular season league title.

Although Martin is lean, he continues to grow his body with each year in Cincinnati's outstanding weight program. It is even more important that he develop his offensive skills, because Huggins suggests Martin could become the key player—or close—in Cincinnati's attack.

"I think Kenyon ought to be a 14-15 point-a-game guy," Huggins said. "He's going to get 6-8 off the glass, I think, and he shoots it well enough with mid-range jump shots. He consistently made shots last year when he'd flash up high."

Martin has a flat shot which bothers those who watch him, but they underestimate how accurate he can be with that weapon. He is comfortable coming from the low post, accepting a pass near the foul line and firing a quick turnaround. He does occasionally release that shot on a line and catch the back rim, causing him to miss.

Those who wonder about his ability to make that shot may be confusing his efforts at the free throw line with his regular jumpers. He is less fluid on his foul shots, releasing them from eye-level rather than lifting the ball above his head. When he doesn't extend his elbow on free throws, he hears about it from the bench.

Martin has worked hard at other aspects of his game. He figures to come equipped this season with a jump-hook that could be a devastating weapon because of his ability to get off the deck quickly and to hang in the air once there.

His defensive skills are phenomenal, and his ownership of the lane in the Conference USA tournament (16-10-8 against Louisville) led him to be chosen MVP. He may have more freedom to chase down shots now that he is not the only pure center in the program.

Martin got a late start in eliminating every shot opponents tried; he had 35 of his 83 blocks in the final eight games. He'd have had more than 120 if he had gone at that pace for the whole year.

MICHAEL HORTON (6-1, 200 lbs., SR, PG, #24, 6.0 ppg, 6.0 rpg, 4.8 apg, 3.3 tpg, 1.9 spg, 25.4 minutes, .457 FG, .000 3PT, .461 FT, Allegany CC, Md./Alexandria, Va.). The story of Horton's first season at Cincinnati is more twisted and absurd than a Vonnegut novel. Every time it appeared he was ready to become a consistent, dynamic player for the Bearcats, he retreated. Literally retreated, almost as if he were frightened of success.

He came to Cincinnati with a reputation as the top prospect out of junior college, and he does have remarkably flashy skills which make such assessments somewhat understandable. But his shooting touch is so poor and his competitive nature so sporadic that he did not come close to living up to his rating.

Horton is likable enough and talks about wanting to be the sort of player Cincinnati needs at the point. Occasionally, he was. He passed for eight assists in a win over Minnesota and set a school record with seven steals against Louisville, completely undressing the Cardinals' Cameron Murray.

He played 34 minutes against South Carolina and produced eight points, seven assists and four steals. He had eight assists against Rhode Island in only 24 minutes. He was part of the tag-team defense UC employed against Larry Hughes in a nationally televised game at the Kiel Center, and the Bearcats won in a blowout. Horton is physically strong and laterally quick, and can be a phenomenal defender when he's concentrating.

Horton was 0-for-7 from three-point range, making this the second consecutive year the Bearcats' starting point guard failed to hit a three-point shot all season. He finishes fastbreaks well and is adept at penetrating the lane and completing plays, even if the shots required are extraordinary.

He was far too turnover-prone along the way, averaging six per game in the five defeats he played full-time minutes. He did not handle the ball well against pressure, which didn't show up often because many teams feared the Bearcats' finishing ability too much to defend the entire court. But it hurt most against West Virginia, when he threw it away eight times against the Mountaineers' adequate fullcourt defense.

The thing was, Horton's play in that game seemed as much a psychological matter as physical. He had played his best basketball of the season when the Conference USA Tournament was contested at the Shoemaker Center. With his 38 points, 16 rebounds, 19 assists and only seven turnovers in three games, he should have been the tournament MVP ahead of Kenyon Martin.

But when Horton showed up for the NCAA Tournament, he was out of his comfort zone and his play collapsed. Huggins could stand to watch only 19 minutes of Horton against Northern Arizona, during which he produced three assists and four points. Against the WVU press, with D'Juan Baker and Shawn Myrick not up to the job, there was no other choice but to leave Horton in the game for 34 minutes, and the result was 1-for-5 shooting and eight turnovers.

That will not happen this year. If Horton decides not to accept the challenges presented, he will find himself on the bench and one of the point guard recruits will be playing ahead of him.

PETE MICKEAL (6-7, 220 lbs., JR, SF, #32, 21.9 ppg, 9.3 rpg, Indian Hills CC, Ia. & Rock Island HS/Rock Island, Ill.). No player Cincinnati recruited is more important to this team. He is expected to be a starter, a scorer, a leader.

Mickeal is the prototypical winner, doing whatever is necessary to perform at a championship level. His teams have been 130-5 during the past four seasons, including 72 consecutive victories at Indian Hills and two NJCAA titles.

He went from a 14.3 scoring average his freshman year to 21 points per game in the NJCAA Tournament. He was then MVP of the NJCAA Tournament as a sophomore, when he was the only returning starter from the previous season's club and led his new teammates to a 38-0 record.

He made four plays late in the second half to seal the title game win over Shelby (Tenn.) State: two consecutive baskets, a steal from Shelby star Rico Duncan, then an assist to Alvin Mitchell for a three-pointer that gave Indian Hills a 13-point lead.

Although he is a decent shooter, Mickeal will likely be more of a conduit to the offense. He will battle for baskets and execute Cincinnati's system, and that alone should get him into double figures most nights. Cincinnati is not expecting 20 points per from Mickeal, but does want him to transmit his winner's personality in the same way Brannen did a year ago.

JERMAINE TATE (6-8, 220 lbs., JR, PF, #5, 14.1 ppg, 6.4 rpg, Ohio State & Central Catholic HS/Toledo, Oh.). Tate was frequently dominant defensively when he practiced with the Bearcats last spring after transferring from Ohio State. "That's my partner-in-crime next season," Kenyon Martin said one day, pointing to Tate. Their mission will be to steal scoring opportunities from opponents.

Tate is a proficient shot-blocker, athletic and tough, and a proven high-major player. He averaged 11.0 ppg and 6.9 rpg during his freshman year at Ohio State and was playing well again when a heart ailment forced him to the bench. Physicians have cleared him to play, and he went through UC's three-hour practices from January to March without problems.

At OSU, he scored 23 points against a Kentucky team bound for the Final Four. He set a school freshman record for field goal percentage at .563 and recorded 27 double-figure scoring games.

The expectation is that Tate will move in to start at forward or center, depending on where Martin fits best, once he becomes eligible in December.

1998-99 CINCINNATI SCHEDULE

Nov.	19	@Rhode Island
	25-28	#Great Alaska Shootout
Dec.	5	Oakland
	12	Southwestern Louisiana
	14	Nicholls State
	16	@Minnesota
	19	@UNLV
	22	Houston
	27	*Dayton
	30	North Carolina-Wilmington
Jan.	3	Marquette
	6	DePaul
	9	@Southern Mississippi
	14	@UNC Charlotte
	16	Oklahoma
	21	@Louisville
	23	Saint Louis
	28	Xavier
	30	UAB
Feb.	3	Tulane
	6	@DePaul
	10	@Marquette
	14	@Saint Louis
	17	UNC Charlotte
	21	Louisville
	25	@South Florida
	27	@Memphis
Mar.	3-6	##Conference USA Tournament

@ Road Games
* Rock-N-Roll Shootout, Cleveland OH
\# Anchorage, AK (vs. Southern Utah, first round; also Alaska-Anchorage, Duke, Fresno State, Iowa State, Notre Dame and Saint Mary's)
\## Birmingham-Jefferson Civic Center, Birmingham, AL

KEY RESERVES

RYAN FLETCHER (6-10, 245 lbs., JR, F/C, #24, 3.4 ppg, 3.0 rpg, 14.6 minutes, .378 FG, .596 FT, Middletown HS/Franklin, Oh.). Cincinnati had just about no other inside depth as it navigated the '97-'98 season. Fletcher backed up Brannen and he backed up Martin, and he handled both jobs reasonably well despite being injured much of the season.

He began the year with a leg injury, which set him back in terms of conditioning and skill development (but did not cause him to miss a game). At the end of the year, he had a broken hand that was injured when he slammed it into a basket support in frustration late in the season.

Fletcher was a favorite target of Huggins' anger in practice, and he does tend toward making the silly mistake. If he can eliminate those problems and improve his scoring touch around the basket, he should have a productive season. It's likely Fletcher will begin the year as the starting power forward, because Jermaine Tate does not become eligible until the second semester.

Fletcher has a nice shooting touch from intermediate distances, but tends to rush the ball toward the goal when confronted by traffic and also tried too many three-pointers as a sophomore (13 of his 90 shots were from long range). He is an excellent shot-blocker because he is surprisingly agile for such a big person.

He needs to play more intelligently and to follow instructions more closely, but it appears he is headed toward this. His off-season conditioning work reportedly has been among the best in the program.

SHAWN MYRICK (6-1, 200 lbs., SR, G, #3, 4.5 ppg, 2.1 rpg, 15.0 minutes, .365 FG, .340 3PT, .656 FT, North Idaho CC/Maysville, Ky.). Symptomatic of the recruiting decline at Cincinnati which damaged the program in the past couple years—before Mick Cronin keyed the recruitment of so many top prospects—was the signing of Myrick, who is small for a shooting guard but cannot handle the ball well enough to play the point.

He is a supreme competitor, which he showed when he scored 17 points in the UMass game. He added eight late, clutch points after Horton was hurt against Louisville and later managed 13 (along with 12 rebounds) in a loss at Marquette.

Myrick's lack of size and lateral quickness is a handicap when he is called on to defend opposing shooting guards, and his lack of ballhandling ability prevents Huggins from using him at the point. He had to sit for all but three minutes against West Virginia because of an inability to handle the pressure.

Myrick has a nice three-point touch, but has trouble using it because he usually is defended by bigger players. He didn't hit a three in the final eight games, going 0-for-4 in that span. And he hit only four of 18 after Jan. 18.

It's possible Cincinnati will not be as dependent on Myrick this season because of the new talent assembled. Even last year, he got only 31 minutes in the last five games.

EUGENE LAND (6-7, 200 lbs., FR, F, #33, 19.8 ppg, 10.1 rpg, 3.1 bpg, Roger Bacon HS/Cincinnati, Oh.) The

Bearcats were the winners of a fierce in-city recruiting battle for Land, one of the few top players Cincinnati has produced in recent years.

Land is another terrific athlete, a guy who elevates effortlessly and who comes equipped with nice upper-body strength for a freshman. He has a great knack for scoring in tight, not a classic drop-step sort of post game but a tremendous ability to catch the ball close, soar into the air and drop in a turnaround jumper. His shot is so soft it often falls in the goal after catching a hunk of the rim.

Land shot .611 from the field as a senior and was first-team All-State and the Ohio Division II player of the year. Whether he'll be an effective rebounder early on seems questionable. He does chase the ball, but learning how to establish position will be a challenge.

Land's national rating dipped a bit last summer because he chose not to attend the elite camps or AAU tournaments because of an academic commitment. He has more basketball skill and more athletic ability than some players rated more highly, though.

He will have an opportunity to earn playing time in the first several games because of Tate's absence. Land does not mind playing power forward at the start of his career, because he figures he can eventually develop the skills to be a small forward. It's that sort of attitude that could make him a recruiting steal.

STEVE LOGAN (5-10, 190 lbs., FR, G, #22, 24.3 ppg, 5.8 apg, 2.5 spg, St. Edward HS/Euclid, Oh.). Cincinnati was toying with recruiting an athletic-type point guard, and was making progress with Louisiana's Brandon Dean; then the West Virginia game happened. Huggins decided he needed somebody who could run the show, and Logan started looking a whole lot better.

Logan had been waiting for UC to offer him a scholarship for the better part of a month. In the meantime, he led St. Edward to a state championship in Ohio's largest division and made most of the clutch plays on behalf a team that included top prospects Sam Clancy (USC) and Steve Lepore (Northwestern). Cincinnati's concern about Logan regarded whether or not he'd be athletic enough to defend at the high-major level.

Athletic enough? Maybe, maybe not. The weight at which he is listed is more a goal than reality. But what about intelligence? Or strength? Logan has played most of his career a pound or two heavier than he ought to be, and thus learned the shortcuts to success that so many faster players have not.

Logan understands how to use angles to cut off opponents. Although he has short arms, he is powerfully compact. On offense, he knows how and where to deliver a lead pass on the break. It's nice that a quicker point guard can push the ball up in transition, but so many of them don't know how to get the ball to a teammate who can finish.

Logan is an outstanding shooter from the free throw line and three-point arc. He hit 48 percent on long-distance shots and over 90 percent on foul shots. His presence will force Horton to compete.

It's that simple. If Horton plays with confidence and aggression, Logan could be valuable as a backup. If not, Logan will fight Alvin Mitchell for the starting job.

ALVIN MITCHELL (6-1, 164 lbs., JR, G, #14, 10.4 ppg, 5.2 apg, 2.5 spg, Indian Hills CC, Ia./Omaha, Neb.). Off-the-court problems for recruit Cory Powell led the Bearcats to withdraw a scholarship offer to the athletic wing and permitted them to sign Mitchell, who was Pete Mickeal's junior college teammate.

Mitchell transferred to Indian Hills after spending one season at Nebraska establishing eligibility and another serving as a backup to Tyronn Lue. He got very little playing time in that role, averaging 2.7 ppg and 1.2 apg in 29 games. But there was a point when Lue was hurt, during a Christmas tournament in Puerto Rico, and guess what team he burned for a career-high 16 points?

That effort impressed Huggins, as did Mitchell's play alongside Mickeal. Mitchell transferred from Nebraska when it didn't seem he'd ever get out of Lue's shadow; remember, Lue still had another year's eligibility when he entered the 1998 NBA draft.

Mitchell is an outstanding shooter, hitting .486 from three-point range, and he will be asked to make shots for the Bearcats as a periodic backup to Levett. Mitchell also will have the opportunity to contend for playing time at the point.

OTHER RETURNEES

ALEX MEACHAM (6-0, 165 lbs., SR, G, #41, 0.8 ppg , 0.2 rpg, nine appearances, Roger Bacon HS/Cincinnati, Oh.). It is puzzling to many observers that Huggins doesn't run a program more conducive to walkons, but Meacham is one of the few to make it all the way through a season. Some wonder why an effort-based coach like Huggins would fail to find some charm in the hard work walkons expend in order to be part of the team.

He also is impatient, though, wanting to spend every moment of practice time, well. And walkons have a tough time giving Cincinnati's players the looks they need.

Meacham didn't play his senior year in high school. For a guy away from the game so long, he performed adequately when asked and never complained about his role.

OTHER NEWCOMERS

AARON MCGHEE (6-7, 222 lbs., SO, F, #44, 25.0 ppg, 10.0 rpg, 3.9 bpg, East HS/Aurora, Ill.). McGhee paid a pretty hefty price to be part of the Cincinnati program. His family wrote out-of-state tuition checks for a year so that he could become a Bearcat. A Top 100 recruit out of high school who was not eligible as a freshman, all he could last season do was watch an occasional practice and shoot a few jumpers in his street clothes before anyone arrived .

He is a lefty with a nice shooting touch from long range and the athletic ability and to play either forward spot. He, Land and Fletcher are the contenders to hold down the power forward position until Jermaine Tate can play. But McGhee also figures into the mix at small forward, where he should be the primary backup for Pete Mickeal.

"I think Aaron's really skilled," Huggins said. "I don't know how hard he plays, how quickly he picks things up. I don't have any way of knowing."

What ultimately will determine how good McGhee can become is whether he can add that in-between game Levett has struggled to do. Like Levett, McGhee could be a fine college player without it. He could be devastating by putting the ball on the floor to clear some space for an open shot.

McGhee was a sensation in summer league ball, which has many in Cincinnati excited about his debut.

DONALD LITTLE (6-10, 210 lbs., FR, C, #50, 13.2 ppg, 8.7 rpg, Winchendon School, Ma./Augusta, Ga.). Little not only needs to learn much about playing at the college level, but also about the responsibility of being a team member.

He left the team at Winchendon after having some strategic disagreements with the coach, Mike Byrnes, and it's not like this is a guy who doesn't need to play a lot of basketball. Little jumps well and has the raw tools to be an NBA player, but he needs to understand much about offensive basketball. He was uncomfortable at the offensive end when he played in the adidas ABCD Camp, but always was around the basketball when defense was being transacted.

He averaged four blocks per game in his last year at Mt. Zion (N.C.) Christian Academy and knocked down just about everything at ABCD. He is like many young centers in that his defense is ahead of his offense, but a lot of basketball people believe he has more pro potential than several higher-rated peers. He has that same gift for defending the goal that made Kenyon Martin such a sensation last season.

Huggins expects that, of his two prized freshman frontcourt players, Little may be the less likely to make an early impact because of his need for strength. Cincinnati does not begin classes until much closer to the start of the season than most colleges, which means its outstanding weight program is handicapped.

Little played well on a summer trip to Europe and seemed to be getting his attitude in better shape.

QUESTIONS

Ballhandling? The Bearcats' inability to handle defensive pressure was exposed by West Virginia in the NCAA Tournament. They hope they've resolved that by adding Alvin Mitchell and Steve Logan. If Michael Horton doesn't step up to the challenge, he can now be replaced.

Shooting? D'Juan Baker took an important offensive weapon along with him when he left after his senior season. Melvin Levett showed he can shoot the three, but who else? Mitchell or Logan, perhaps, and maybe Mickeal and McGhee. Or maybe no one?

Chemistry? These guys seem to like each other and want to form a team. But leadership has to emerge, perhaps from Levett and Mickeal, and some guys are going to have to avoid pouting when there aren't enough minutes to go around.

ANSWERS

Frontcounrt full house! The Bearcats are three-deep at every position on the front line, with third stringers who could be in the primary rotation at every other school in the conference. What do you do with all these guys? Win, for one.

Kenyon Martin! His total game continues to progress, with shooting and ballhandling skills improved in the offseason, and he's perhaps the best defensive player in the nation.

Bob Huggins! He showed he was one of the best coaches in college basketball when he took last season's team to 27 wins. He will find a way, in his words, to win again with this bunch.

adidas Blue Ribbon Analysis

BACKCOURT	B	BENCH/DEPTH	B+
FRONTCOURT	A	INTANGIBLES	A

This team should be improved defensively, which is saying something, and certainly there is depth that last year's bunch did not enjoy. The questions then involve the backcourt, scoring and leadership.

Having two guys who were starters for most of the year at guard should be a good thing, and it can be, if Levett is comfortable in the role of a principal scoring option and Horton plays like he wants to win. Offense may not come regularly from one direction, but Levett, Tate and Martin have all been double-figure scorers, and Mickeal figures to contribute in that area.

"A lot will depend on how good the guards are we recruited," Huggins said. "It's yet to be determined if we have a guy who we can throw the ball to and get a (basket). Bake, Bob and Ruben were capable of doing that, and before that there was Danny for three years."

The biggest thing may be the seniors' and Martin's acceptance of Mickeal as a leader. Horton and Levett are not naturals in that role. It should be interesting to see what is done with the captaincy; it may be best to simply slap the title on Mickeal and make it official, even though he's new to the program.

Leadership should be an interesting factor in the development of this team, which could be good enough for a fourth straight Top 10 finish or to at least see the inside of the Sweet 16 once again.

(M.D.)

adidas Blue Ribbon Analysis

GRADING SYSTEM

- A+ equal to very best in country—Final Four-caliber unit
- A among the best in the land—worthy of deep NCAA run
- B+ talented, versatile and experienced—NCAA-NIT ability
- B solid and productive winners—league and post-season contenders
- C+ average to above-average—may contend in a weaker league
- C average to mediocre—second division in a strong league
- D+ below average, inconsistent—second division in a weaker league
- D well below average—losing season virtually certain
- F non-Division I ability—an underdog every night

11
UTAH

LOCATION .... Salt Lake City, UT
CONFERENCE .... WAC (Pacific Division)
LAST SEASON .... 30-4 (.882)
CONFERENCE RECORD .... 12-2 (1st, Mountain)
STARTERS LOST/RETURNING 2/3
NICKNAME .... Utes
COLORS .... Crimson & White
HOMECOURT .... Jon Huntsman Center (15,000)
COACH .... Rick Majerus (Marquette '70)
RECORD AT SCHOOL .... 210-59 (9 yrs.)
CAREER RECORD .... 309-111 (14 yrs.)
ASSISTANTS ... Donny Daniels (Fullerton State '77)
Jeff Judkins (Utah '78)
Brock Brunkhorst (Arizona '85)
TEAM WINS (last 5 yrs.) 14-28-27-29-30
RPI (last 5 yrs.) 152-29-18-5-14
1997-98 FINISH Lost national championship game.

COACH AND PROGRAM

Utah will have a hard time living up to its 1997-98 season, reaching the NCAA title game and coming within five minutes of the national championship. How rare was the Utes' appearance? It was the first time since 1944 that they had played for the title.

What's next? Reality. But, for Utah, that is still a WAC title chase and a win or two in the NCAA Tournament.

In nine years under Rick Majerus, the Utes have become one of the nation's most successful programs. Majerus, the winningest coach in Utah history, has averaged 23 victories per season and taken the Utes to seven NCAAs. He is on a streak in which he has never lost a first-round game. He has taken the Utes to four Sweet 16 appearances in a seven-year span and coached Utah to six WAC titles.

Majerus flirted again with other job openings in the offseason, actually interviewing with Arizona State and Texas. Finances became an issue at ASU, and compatibility was the factor at Texas. Neither worked out, but that may be for the best.

Majerus seems to be a perfect in Utah. He has the free reign he needs under athletic director Chris Hill. He has the type of players he wants, and support from the majority in the community and the administration. He makes plenty of money and is on the verge of having another banner season.

The reason? He's got Andre Miller back for one more year, and he has once again filled his roster with his type of players. Majerus makes it painfully clear when recruiting what everyone's role will be at Utah.

"I'm definitely in charge," Majerus says. "I give guys a lot of range, and you need to have someone who has the vision and direction of the team. They know that when they're being recruited.

"I recruit a kid to be a helluva player and I recruit a player to be a complimentary player. I recruit a kid and tell him what he'll be. You can't have five stars. Well, maybe Duke can, but we can't at Utah."

To play for Majerus you have to defend and rebound. If you don't set picks, you sit. Utah never gives up easy baskets or even second shots off the offensive backboard. Offense doesn't come easily, either.

"Everyone has to share the ball," Majerus says. "Keith (Van Horn) couldn't take any bad shots. We average one bad shot a game, if that. Players know when they've taken a bad shot."

Rebounding is critical to accomplish this controlled game, and Majerus has always had size at Utah.

"When I walk into a gym to recruit," Majerus says, "I always say, 'Show me the bigs, not show me the money. Show me the bigs.' I have a lot of confidence in our ability to develop big men."

It doesn't matter who's on defense. Appearances are deceptive with players like Drew Hansen becoming two-year starters and All-Defensive team members, despite looking like he should be in a YMCA league. The difference is that Utah plays team defense with plenty of help, rather than gambling.

It's this type of team game which keeps Utah in the Top 10 and atop the WAC. Few fans may know the recruits who have filtered into Salt Lake City, but they'll know the name Utah when the Utes are still winning lots of games.

STARTERS NOT RETURNING

MICHAEL DOLEAC (6-11, C, 16.1 ppg, 7.1 rpg, 1.6 tpg, 1.0 bpg, 27.4 minutes, .488 FG, .406 3PT, .805 FT). A three-year starter who had a tremendous body and knew how Majerus wanted to play, Doleac brought Utah toughness in the middle. The Utes relied on him after Keith Van Horn left last year. Majerus said he was one of the best captains he has had at Utah.

Throughout his senior year, Doleac got tougher and more mature. A top student who planned on going to medical school, Doleac knew how to manage his life and stayed injury-free. His scoring average increased every year and he became one of the best post defenders in the nation.

As his career went on, his confidence grew in every aspect of his game. He added a three-point shot and became even more of an offensive threat. Doleac was drafted by the Orlando Magic in the first round.

Just being drafted, let alone in the lottery, proves how far Doleac came from being a gangly center as a freshman.

DREW HANSEN (6-5, SG, 5.5 ppg, 3.1 rpg, 2.1 apg, 27.0 minutes, .438 FG, .456 3PT, .630 FT). A two-year starter who was underrated defensively, Hansen was perfect for Utah. He was a great complimentary player who was committed to Majerus' system and understood his role.

Hansen could knock down a three-pointer, but was also a tireless worker and he played hurt. He provided great leadership, especially considering the Utes never expected much out of him.

Hansen's defensive efforts were phenomenal during his last two years on the team. Plenty of players probably looked at him and laughed, believing they would be able to beat him off the dribble or shoot over him. More often than not, they would find themselves handcuffed from getting open or creating their own shot.

OTHERS NOT RETURNING

DAVID JACKSON (6-3, G, 3.3 ppg, 1.5 rpg, 1.4 apg, 1.2 tpg, 14.6 minutes, .415 FG, .400 3PT, .773 FT). Jackson was not content in Majerus' system and transferred to Oregon, where he'll sit out the year before being eligible in 1999-2000. He was a shooting guard with limited ballhandling skills who could hit the three-pointer and was a decent defender.

Jackson gave the Utes depth, but did not add enough production off the bench.

TRACE CATON (6-4, G, 4.0 ppg, 1.1 rpg, 14.3 minutes, .460 FG, .417 3PT, .833 FT). Caton is heading off on a two-year Mormon Church mission. He was the media's choice as Freshman of the Year in the WAC's Mountain Division.

Before he injured his thigh late in the season, Caton was getting better every game. He was solid, dependable and tough. Caton learned quickly and was committed to how Utah wanted to play.

BRITTON JOHNSEN (6-9, F, 3.5 ppg, 1.6 rpg, 11.1 minutes, .456 FG, .308 3PT, .515 FT). Johnsen is also off on a two-year Mormon mission. He was a McDonald's All-America and the highest-rated recruit ever at Utah, including Van Horn and Andre Miller.

However, he had a patella tendon injury and missed the first 13 games of the season. Because of the injury, Johnsen was never 100 percent. However, once he got on the floor, he gave Utah a player who could play two positions (either small forward or power forward).

Johnsen was getting better defensively as the season went on and was being used as much as Hanno Mottola during the NCAA Tournament. He could outlet exceptionally well, as well as rebound and give Utah tremendous size.

The Utes will miss his versatility. His contributions during victories over Arkansas, Arizona and North Carolina in the NCAA Tournament won't be made up easily.

JON CARLISLE (6-9, F, 2.4 ppg, 2.1 rpg, 10.3 minutes, .565 FG, .618 FT). Carlisle probably would have been the starting center had he not decided to go on a Mormon Church mission for two years (to Ecuador). He gave the Utes size on the front line and provided a decent backup to Doleac.

JORDIE MCTAVISH (6-0, G, 2.7 ppg, 1.0 apg, 9.8 minutes, .361 FG, .357 3PT, .724 FT). McTavish was the backup to Miller, which must be like being the understudy to Tom Cruise. You're not going to get on-screen.

McTavish could never live down stepping in for an injured Miller during the Final Eight loss to Kentucky in '97. He was picked clean on a steal, and the game turned on that play with five minutes left.

McTavish wasn't at the same level, and Utah couldn't afford to take a dramatic step backward when Miller was off the court. A disgruntled McTavish transferred to Idaho State, where he'll certainly be more effective.

GREG BARRATT (6-8, F, 1.8 ppg, 1.9 rpg, 7.2 minutes, .306 FG, .500 FT). Barratt returned from a mission, but rarely played (15 appearances) in the frontcourt. He's off to try and find a better situation, and will sit out at Utah Valley State College this season.

PROJECTED STARTERS

ANDRE MILLER (6-2, 200 lbs., SR, PG, #24, 14.2 ppg, 5.4 rpg, 5.2 apg, 2.5 tpg, 2.1 spg, 31.6 minutes, .549 FG, .333 3PT, .722 FT, Verbum Dei HS/Los Angeles, Calif.). His mother wanted him to declare for the NBA draft, wondering what was left to accomplish. Andre wasn't so sure, especially about his jump shot. Majerus also knew he wanted Miller to stay.

Regardless of the decision, Miller wasn't going to lose. He already has his degree, proving Prop 48 casualties can produce in the classroom. Miller may be the highest-profile academic redshirt to earn his fourth year back.

What Miller didn't know he had was the foresight to make the right choice. Less than a week after the NBA draft, the owners exercised a lockout on the players—freezing out rookies from earning any money over the summer and putting their first-year plans on indefinite hold.

Miller would have been on his own, not playing for the U.S. in the Goodwill Games, not planning on claiming yet another WAC title, not reaping the benefits of being five minutes from an NCAA title. He is easily one of the top

1997-98 RESULTS

Opponent	Score
Fullerton State	87-59
@Weber State	87-72
Southern Utah	66-48
@Loyola Marymount	89-50
California-Irvine	83-54
#Providence	64-58
@Wake Forest	62-53
Utah State	71-55
Azusa Pacific	78-58
Oregon State	69-61
@Wisconsin-Milwaukee	66-51
Rice	73-65
@Brigham Young	71-61
Colorado State	65-51
Wyoming	75-58
@Air Force	57-46
@UNLV	67-54
UTEP	62-56
@New Mexico (L)	74-77
Brigham Young	83-68
@Rice	60-49
@Wyoming (L)	56-62
@Colorado State	60-48
Air Force	55-41
UNLV	79-68
@UTEP	71-49
New Mexico	65-55
##UNLV (L)	51-54
%San Francisco	85-68
%Arkansas	75-69
%%West Virginia	65-62
%%Arizona	76-51
%%%North Carolina	65-59
%%%Kentucky (L)	69-78

@ away games
\# Great Eight, United Center, Chicago, IL
\## WAC Tournament, Thomas & Mack Center, Las Vegas, NV
% NCAA West Sub-Regional, Boise, ID
%% NCAA West Regional, Anaheim, CA
%%% NCAA Final Four, San Antonio, TX

two or three point guards in the nation.

"I would have been sitting around waiting for something to happen," Miller says. "I didn't want to mess around and be in the CBA or overseas somewhere."

Miller went on to win the gold medal for the United States, taking over the championship game against Australia. He was dominant, driving to the lane for layups, stepping up for mid-range jumpers and coming up with a key steal. He was everything to the U.S. He'll do the same for Utah, just as he did last March.

Each of the last three seasons, Miller has earned more rights under Majerus' rule. He wasn't sure where to dribble when he made his starting debut mid-season as a sophomore. The direction came eventually, and so did the confidence.

"Coach always told me to make plays, but don't get out of control," Miller says. "We had players like Keith (Van Horn), and it was my job to drive and kick the ball out to him. The next year, I was more aggressive, shot the ball better and drove."

His drive sped the Utes to an 18-0 start, another WAC title, a No. 2 ranking in the final A.P. poll and the national championship game against Kentucky. He averaged 16.7 ppg, 7.5 rpg, 6.8 apg and 2.0 spg in six NCAA Tournament games, playing with more purpose than any other point guard in the tournament, including Arizona's Mike Bibby, who he rose above with the NCAA's first triple-double since Magic Johnson 19 years earlier.

He was the West Region MVP and had the Final Four award locked up had he not run out of gas in the final minutes of the title game. Up 10 points at halftime, Miller and the rest of the Utes wilted under the Wildcats' press.

"I just remember being tired, being pressed all of the time," Miller says. "We played Arizona, North Carolina and Arkansas, and that was a lot of running for me. We didn't have another person who could dribble the ball. I had to break all of the presses. We were confident, but we didn't sub enough and that got us dragging."

Miller was indeed spent, but not enough to leave Utah in the spring. Majerus used his NBA contacts to find out Miller would go high, but was not a finished product. He knew it, sold Miller on it and advised him to follow Van Horn's and Michael Doleac's path. They were both lottery picks a year after each passed on an early exit.

"I've always erred on the side of caution," Majerus says. "He's the best point I've ever coached. What he's done is improved every season. He's always the first one in the gym and the last one out. He has a feel for the game, a dedication and a passion."

And the coach will reward Miller with more looks, clear-outs, 1-4 spreads and plenty of pick-and-roll (and pick-and-pop) plays that will work for Miller as much as they will for Hanno Mottola, Alex Jensen and Nate Althoff. He'll have a shooter on his wing in transfer Jeremy Killion, and he won't be shy about being the focal point for the first time in four years.

HANNO MOTTOLA (6-10, 230 lbs., JR, PF, #13, 12.5 ppg, 5.3 rpg, 2.3 tpg, 28.2 minutes, .489 FG, .291 3PT, .754 FT, Makelanrinne School/Helsinki, Finland). He gives Utah an inside-outside presence. Mottola can shoot the three-pointer, but has to become a better defender and rebounder. He is a good post passer, has soft hands and can run the floor extremely well for his size.

Mottola will need to pick up the scoring slack for Doleac and become one of the top scoring forwards in the nation. He slipped during the NCAA Tournament, but has to assume a leadership role at the outset of the season.

"He needs to be more aggressive and more physical," Majerus says. "He still plays too much like he's in the European league. He needs to be more physical. I'd like to see him recognize situations more and score more points.

"He's got to score inside. He was a disappointment in the Kentucky game. He had three open looks and couldn't put shots down."

His best game in the NCAA Tournament may have been a 14-point (7-for-12 FG), five-rebound game against Arizona in the West Regional final.

ALEX JENSEN (6-9, 225 lbs., JR, SF, #50, 6.8 ppg, 5.8 rpg, 2.3 apg, 1.4 tpg, 27.9 minutes, .457 FG, .311 3PT, .747 FT, Viewmont HS/Centerville, Ut.). Jensen was a bit slow coming back from his Mormon Church mission last year, but developed into a reliable player. He moves Utah's offense perfectly and is always in the right spots defensively.

Jensen's footwork has improved considerably. He can hit the three-pointer, is a good passer to the post and an outstanding defender. He's got good hands and is committed to what Utah and Majerus want to accomplish. But now he has to score more with Doleac leaving.

"He's the best defender and rebounder that a coach could ever want," Majerus says. "He's a total team player. (But) he's too unselfish. He's got to look to score."

If Jensen can't produce more offensively, the Utes won't win the WAC. He has to help Utah match the kinds of forwards at New Mexico and TCU.

Jensen defended all five positions last year and was named to the NCAA West Region All-Tournament team. He had 14 points, two rebounds and two assists in the NCAA championship loss to Kentucky.

If he can score 14-15 points with 6-8 rebounds this year, he'll more than fulfill his role.

NATE ALTHOFF (6-11, 245 lbs., SO, C, #52, 1.8 ppg, 1.8 rpg, 5.4 minutes, .667 FG, .462 FT, Delano HS/Delano, Minn.). A big body and shot-blocker, Althoff has to work on his stamina, conditioning and become a better defender and rebounder. He has to be a factor for the Utes in Doleac's absence, and likely will start the season at center.

Althoff is limited offensively and will have to finish much better to earn his keep.

"(Nate) is stronger than Doleac and runs the floor better, but he's not as smart," Majerus says. "He'll be a good shot-blocker and has a bounce in his step. He's got good hands, but (is) not as good outside as Doleac."

JEREMY KILLION (6-1, 195 lbs., JR, SG, 27.0 ppg, 5.0 apg, .520 FG, .460 3PT, Palomar JC, Calif. & Rancho Bernardo HS/San Diego, Calif.). Killion is a long-distance shooter who can also put the ball on the floor. He is a great athlete who plays hard, and Majerus is already high on him before the first game—which is more than can be said for most Utah newcomers.

If Killion continues to improve, he could be the starting off guard next to Miller. "He's got a quick release and good range," Majerus says."

KEY RESERVES

TONY HARVEY (6-6, 205 lbs., JR, F, 22.8 ppg, 9.7 rpg, 3.9 spg, Cerritos JC, Calif. & Carson HS/Carson, Calif.). One of the top athletes on the team, Harvey is a 17-foot-and-in shooter. He should be a great defender, but toughness is a question. He can play two spots, picking up a lot of the Utah system during fall individual workouts.

"He primarily will be a defender. (Tony) is a good scorer, but the game has to be brought to him," Majerus says. "He's got good foot speed and good lateral movement."

TYSON JOHNSTON (6-11, 227 lbs., FR, C, 17.7 ppg, 13.7 rpg, 8.0 bpg, Steamboat HS/Steamboat Springs, Colo.). He's got size, can run the floor and block shots. Johnston has got to get tougher to earn minutes ahead of Althoff.

Johnston does have a nice jump hook. If he can produce offensively, he'll have a chance to play as a freshman.

BEN HEUSSER (6-0, 195 lbs., FR, G, 18.8 ppg, 4.5 apg, Preston HS/Preston, Id.). Heusser can hit three-pointers and can go left more than right, but he has to convert at the free-throw line. Heusser played in a small town and no one knows how he'll adjust to this level of competition.

The question is: Will he be another McTavish, or will he actually help the Utes and give Miller the needed breather at the point?

"Heusser's an unknown, but he has a court presence about him," Majerus says. "He can take and hit the open shot."

PHIL CULLEN (6-10, 200 lbs., FR, C, 19.1 ppg, 11.0 rpg, 4.0 apg, 2.0 spg, Chelan HS/Chelan, Wash.). Cullen is a three-point shooter who can put the ball on the court and drive. He's an inside-out player who is also good passer. He'll have to work on his strength. Physically, he may not be able to play in the post just yet.

"He'll contribute with scoring and making free throws," Majerus says. "He's a good shooter who can find ways to score. But he's no Britton Johnsen."

1998-99 UTAH SCHEDULE

Nov.	14	Azuza Pacific
	18	@Utah State
	23-25	#Maui Invitational
Dec.	2	*Rhode Island
	5	@Long Beach State
	9	Weber State
	12	@Texas
	19	Loyola Marymount
	22	St. Francis, PA
	28	Wake Forest
	30	High Point
Jan.	2	Ripon College
	9	Brigham Young
	16	@San Diego State
	18	@Hawaii
	23	San Jose State
	25	Fresno State
	30	@UTEP
Feb	1	@New Mexico
	6	@Brigham Young
	11	San Diego State
	13	Hawaii
	18	@San Jose State
	20	@Fresno State
	25	UTEP
	27	New Mexico
Mar	2-6	##WAC Tournament

@ Road Games
* Great Eight, United Center, Chicago, IL
# Lahaina, HI (vs. Arizona State, first round; also Chaminade, Clemson, Indiana, Kansas State, Michigan and Syracuse)
Thomas & Mack Center, Las Vegas, NV

OTHER RETURNEES

None.

OTHER NEWCOMERS

BRAD CROCKETT (6-6, 205 lbs., FR, F, 16.0 ppg, 10.0 rpg, .470 FG, .820 FT, Viewmont HS/Centerville, Ut.). Crockett is a three-point shooter who can set screens and get shots for others, and he has the ability to hit a mid-range jumper. He's a swing player who likely will play behind Jensen and Tony Harvey.

"He's a role player, and I don't know what we'll get out of him," Majerus says.

ADAM SHARP (6-2, 178 lbs., FR, G, Alta HS/Salt Lake City, Ut.). Sharp redshirted last year after serving a two-year Mormon mission. He could be a role player and a three-point specialist. But Sharp needs to commit himself to defense.

QUESTIONS

Bench? All inexperienced. Harvey, Johnston, Heusser and Cullen will have to play in their first year.

Can they pick up he system? Utah's is one of the most complex systems. How will the newcomers handle it? How will they respond to road and neutral court games early?

Role acceptance? Miller, Mottola and Jensen will score. How will the others handle taking only a few shots instead of a slew?

ANSWERS

Leadership! Miller took over the final of the Goodwill Games and sent a message to every Utah opponent. If the game is on the line, Miller can still win it for Utah.

Athleticism! Harvey, Killion and Miller give it to Utah. The Utes haven't had it for a while.

Versatility! Harvey, Mottola and Jensen can play two spots. Utah can play big (with Mottola and Althoff on the front line). Or the Utes can go with Jensen and Mottola up front, using Harvey and Killion on the wings with Miller.

adidas Blue Ribbon Analysis

BACKCOURT	A	BENCH/DEPTH	B
FRONTCOURT	B+	INTANGIBLES	A

Utah gets an "A" for the backcourt because of Miller and an "A" for intangibles because of Majerus. Those two are enough to get Utah to the top of the WAC and into the NCAA Tournament.

But there's more. Utah has a relatively soft schedule that should allow them only a handful of losses, giving them a record worthy of a high NCAA seed.

The key for the Utes will be the production of Mottola and Jensen, and the development of post players like Althoff, Cullen and Johnston. Killion has to shoot well, too.

Majerus complains that his bench is mostly freshmen,

but it was a year ago, too. It wasn't a problem then, and it shouldn't be one this season.

Expect the Utes to contend for the WAC Pacific Division title with New Mexico, reach the Sweet 16 of the NCAA Tournament and for Miller to be a finalist for Player of the Year nationally.

(A.K.)

12

PURDUE

LOCATION	**West Lafayette, IN**
CONFERENCE	**Big Ten**
LAST SEASON	**28-8 (.778)**
CONFERENCE RECORD	**12-4 (3rd)**
STARTERS LOST/RETURNING	**2/3**
NICKNAME	**Boilermakers**
COLOR	**Old Gold & Black**
HOMECOURT	**Mackey Arena (14,123)**
COACH	**Gene Keady (Kansas State '58)**
RECORD AT SCHOOL	**394-168 (18 yrs.)**
CAREER RECORD	**432-187 (20 yrs.)**
ASSISTANTS	**Frank Kendrick (Purdue '74)**
	Jay Price (Kansas '91)
	Jim Thrash (Eastern New Mexico '68)
TEAM WINS (last 5 yrs.)	**29-25-16-18-28**
RPI (last 5 yrs.)	**1-21-13-20-8**
1997-98 FINISH	**Lost in NCAA Sweet 16.**

COACH AND PROGRAM

A six-year-old audio tape found its way onto the Internet in the middle of last season. It was a five-minute recording of Bob Knight throwing a hissy fit in the Indiana locker room, surreptitiously taped by an anonymous equipment man just before a Purdue game.

What a college basketball fan from outside the Midwest takes away from the recording is the remarkable versatility of Knight in using the F-word. What a Big Ten fan notices is Knight's preoccupation with Purdue that borders on obsession.

The Boilermakers were working on five wins in six tries against the Hoosiers at the time. Gene Keady's boys have continued to get the best of Knight's in the last few years—if not in every game, then always in the standings. Purdue has two thirds and three titles in the last five seasons; Indiana hasn't so much as tied with Purdue in any of those five years.

"It's funny, I used to be his buddy (until) Purdue started winning a lot," Keady likes to joke. That's always followed by, "Nah, Bob's a good guy."

Knight does have something which continues to evade Keady. Never have the Boilermakers played in a Final Four in Keady's 18 years at Purdue; their last was under Lee Rose in 1980, a few weeks before Keady arrived from Western Kentucky.

Knight also has coached three national champions at Indiana. And, so, Roy Firestone never arrives at Keady's door for a photo-op, quail-hunting trip.

If treating Purdue basketball in such a provincial context seems odd, it shouldn't. This program has almost owned the Big Ten the last half-decade. It has either won the league or been right in the thick of the race to the end for five seasons in a row.

In just about any other elite conference, such success would translate into at least one trip to the April ball. Purdue has been close just once, with Glenn Robinson in '94. Grant Hill-led Duke took care of the Boilers that year in a regional final.

Now in his sixties, Keady deserves to have his moment under the network kleigs and the glow of a 50,000-strong dome throng. But whether he'll ever get such a reward is now a dicey proposition.

Keady has another team capable of winning the Big Ten, a young unit without much quality size but plenty of athletes capable of making a run in the NCAAs. But the acronym "NCAA" might have a more depressing connotation than it should around West Lafayette come April.

Purdue was submerged in an investigation by the national governing body of college athletics as *Blue Ribbon* was going to press. Whether Keady's program could escape unscathed was in some doubt.

Of three perceived irregularities, the NCAA was most curious about a $5,000 loan arranged in 1995 by Lafayette banker Bill Powers, allegedly at the behest of Purdue assistant coach Frank Kendrick. The recipient of the loan was Luther Clay, then a prospective freshman attempting to enroll at Purdue from Maine Central Institute, a prep school well known as a way-station for academic partial- or non-qualifiers.

That the loan was arranged—supposedly to settle Clay's tuition bill at MCI—was not necessarily an NCAA violation. That it was not paid back by Clay is the point of contention.

Powers, who is not a Purdue alumnus and claims no allegiance to the school, vehemently denies he was a part of any arrangement with Purdue. He says he understood the loan was to be paid back after Clay earned money from a summer job in '96.

It never was, and the bank wrote it off as a bad debt when Clay transferred again—this time to Rhode Island—in the fall of '96. (Clay played for the Rams last season.)

The investigation was mired in delays as Purdue and the NCAA attempted to build their respective cases. The issue possibly could be resolved at a November hearing in Kansas City. More likely, it will drag on through this season.

How publicity and distraction from the case could affect the current Purdue team—or Kendrick and Keady's future recruiting—is, of course, a salient question. And any sanctions, at this point in Keady's career, could be devastating.

Outwardly, Keady is as breezy as ever. "If I was gonna' cheat, I'd get me some players," he cracked on September, suggesting he has survived on crippled farm hands all these years.

Not quite. In fact, this is the most interesting incoming class at Purdue in quite a while. If it melds with a core of upperclassmen—and that's a big "if"—the Boilermakers could make another two-win splash in the NCAAs similar to last year.

STARTERS NOT RETURNING

CHAD AUSTIN (6-2, SG, 17.0 ppg, 3.7 rpg, 3.7 apg, 2.4 tpg, 1.3 spg, 32.7 minutes, .427 FG, .335 3PT, .763 FT). An all-around guard who wasn't quick enough to play the point or a good enough shooter to shine at the "two," Austin often made up for that with a competitive nature. He made big plays when the Boilermakers needed them most. His backcourt defense was the guts of many important Purdue victories.

One of his weaknesses was shot selection. For a so-so marksman, Austin pulled the trigger a lot. His 497 shots last year ranked fourth in the Big Ten. It's probably unfair, but still telling that his last game as a Boiler was a 4-for-18 disaster in the NCAA loss to Stanford.

BRAD MILLER (6-11, C, 17.2 ppg, 8.9 rpg, 2.5 apg, 3.0 tpg, 1.2 spg, 1.6 bpg, 29.2 minutes, .632 FG, .780 FT). It's hard to bitch about a guy who places among the top five in the Big Ten in scoring (5th), rebounding (3rd), field goal percentage (2nd) and blocked shots (4th), and is 10th in free throw shooting on the side. But Purdue fans found ways. And they weren't entirely unfounded.

Miller also led Purdue in turnovers (101) and had the worst assist-turnover ratio among the six Boilers who played most. There were times when Miller simply disappeared for no apparent reason. He was criticized as soft and lacking nerve for not playing a more physical game.

A noted antagonist was Michigan's Robert Traylor. Some shot-blockers also exposed his lack of lift, notably Penn State's Calvin Booth.

But most of Miller's problems really surrounded the Boilermakers' lack of depth on the baseline. Because of the academic loss of freshman forwards Jamaal Davis and Cameron Stephens, Miller had very little help inside.

That liability eventually shot down the Boilers in the NCAA regional semifinals against towering Stanford. Miller battled Stanford's center, Tim Young, effectively. But the Cardinal overwhelmed Purdue with three other big men.

Miller led the Boilermakers in both points and rebounds in that finale, just as he did during the season. The Boilers will play essentially without a center this year, and they may miss it more than they think.

OTHERS NOT RETURNING

MOSI BARNES (6-0, G, 0.9 ppg, 0.6 rpg, 6.0 minutes, .235 FG, .235 3PT). Barnes, at just 150 pounds, never was tough enough for Keady's taste. He transferred to Eastern Michigan with the coach's hearty good wishes.

Unable to become a factor on the defensive end, his game was limited to occasional work at the point (14 assists, 11 turnovers) and scattergun shooting. That wasn't enough.

PROJECTED STARTERS

ALAN ELDRIDGE (6-1, 185 lbs., SR, PG, #15, 7.2 ppg, 2.6 rpg., 3.6 apg, 2.5 tpg, 1.4 spg, 28.0 minutes., .395 FG, .379 3PT, .814 FT, Wayne HS/Fort Wayne, Ind.). Eldridge has never been the kind of point guard who makes your eyes pop. He's very well conditioned. He's steady, smart and sensible. Those are supposed to be fine attributes at the position.

But Keady would like to see more fire out of him: "I want leadership. I want to see him use that athletic ability to the max. He wants to be cool, but I want him to be mentally tough."

Eldridge can turn it up on defense and really bother point guards who aren't ready for the heat. He has a pretty good three-point shot and isn't afraid to fire in tight games. He is also the best free throw shooter on a team that easily led the league a year ago (.760).

Eldridge substantially improved his assist-turnover ratio last year (1.44), but it still wasn't among the league's top ten. All in all, he's a kid you're not embarrassed to put out there, but he's usually not a difference-maker.

Expect him to start the season at the point again. But it should surprise nobody if Oregon State transfer Carson Cunningham unseats him by January.

BRIAN CARDINAL (6-8, 230 lbs., JR, PF, #35, 12.0 ppg, 4.9 rpg, 1.8 apg, 1.4 tpg, 1.8 spg, 25.7 minutes, .509 FG, .429 3PT, .787 FT, Unity HS/Tolono, Ill.). No one is more despised among Big Ten players than this guy. He

1997-98 RESULTS

Long Island	119-95	
@Valparaiso	73-56	
Northeast Louisiana	107-80	
#UAB	92-64	
#Massachusetts	82-69	
#North Carolina (L)	69-73	
*Kentucky (L)	75-89	
@Louisville	87-69	
##Tennessee-Martin	87-56	
##San Francisco	107-82	
**Xavier	86-84	
Florida A&M	118-77	
Providence	81-79	
Michigan State (L)	57-74	
@Minnesota	83-79	
Penn State	77-55	
@Houston	86-53	
@Illinois	68-58	
@Indiana (L)	88-94	
Ohio State	82-71	
Northwestern	80-45	
@Michigan	89-82	
Wisconsin	82-59	
@Ohio State	107-75	
Indiana	94-89	
Illinois	75-72	
@Iowa (L)	69-88	
@Penn State (L)	63-74	
Minnesota	87-83	
@Michigan State	99-96	ot
###Indiana	76-71	
###Illinois	68-47	
###Michigan (L)	67-76	
%Delaware	95-56	
%Detroit	80-65	
%%Stanford (L)	59-67	

@	away games
*	United Center, Chicago, IL
**	Market Square Arena, Indianapolis, IN
#	Carrs Great Alaska Shootout, Anchorage, AK
##	Boilermaker Invitational, West Lafayette, IN
###	Big Ten Tournament, United Center, Chicago, IL
%	NCAA Midwest Sub-Regional, Chicago, IL
%%	NCAA Midwest Regional, St. Louis, MO

is becoming known as the next Bill Laimbeer. That's a title Cardinal would probably embrace.

He draws charges, he elbows his way into traffic, he dives on the floor, he flops and suckers referees. Cardinal isn't very talented. Everything he's gotten, he's earned.

The son of the Illinois athletic trainer was supposed to be a fair-to-middlin' recruit out of high school. Other than schools in his vicinity, Illinois and Purdue, the most serious suitor he had was probably Penn State.

But Cardinal didn't bat an eye upon entering the league. He immediately made an impact as a freshman with hustle and a willingness to acquire floor burns. He'll serve any number of functions for Keady—setting screens, hitting the boards, popping out for the free throw line jumper.

But his cache of shots is basic. Keady would like to see him add to his repetoire on the blocks and be bolder with a surprisingly accurate three-pointer for a power player. Purdue needs points to replace Miller and Austin's combined 34.2 ppg.

Cardinal should help fill the void.

MIKE ROBINSON (6-6, 210 lbs., JR, SF, #23, 11.3 ppg, 5.3 rpg, 1.7 apg, 1.6 tpg, 24.1 minutes., .511 FG, .214 3PT, .768 FT, Richwoods HS/Peoria, Ill.). For a while, Robinson was thought of in the same terms as McQuay—talented but not particularly motivated to learn. When he was caught stealing CDs his freshman year, it didn't look good.

That all seems like a long time ago. Robinson was the bright spot of a tepid final quarter of the season. His work ethic has completely changed. His touch around the 12-foot range really improved. And he realizes he has the physical tools to get at least a shot at the NBA.

That can be a powerful incentive when a kid reaches upperclass status.

"He didn't used to have the work ethic to be great," said Keady. "Now, he's really grown up."

Robinson was a counselor at Michael Jordan's Chicago summer camp, and got a first-hand glimpse of what makes Jordan what he is—a thirst for excellence so intense that he works on the small cracks in his game in the off-season and adjusts to age by developing subtle skills.

That made an impression on Robinson. That he changed his number from 32 to 23 may not be a coincidence.

Robinson was always an exciting open-court player—tough on the press, fluid on the break. These are commodities in short supply at the small forward spot in the Big Ten. If his jumper and halfcourt moves continue to improve—and they've already gotten pretty good—Robinson could become the "wow" player this league desperately needs.

We'll see.

JARAAN CORNELL (6-3, 200 lbs., JR, SG, #22, 12.8 ppg, 2.9 rpg, 2.3 apg, 1.9 tpg, 1.3 spg, 23.4 minutes, .519 FG, .500 3PT, .813 FT, Clay HS/South Bend, Ind.). It's not an exaggeration to say Purdue's season went south when Cornell went down on Feb. 10 against Indiana with a badly sprained ankle. The Boilermakers were 21-4 to that point.

Cornell's league-leading touch from the arc was zeroed in at the time and, according to Keady, Purdue was "playing as well as any team I've ever had."

Already thin in the frontcourt, the Boilers could not withstand the loss of their long gunner. A devastating road sequence, first to Iowa and then 900 miles east to Penn State three days later, ended in back-to-back losses and Purdue's Big Ten title dreams were toast.

Cornell spent the next six weeks trying to get the ankle back to full strength, but never really did. He still wasn't close to 100 percent when the Boilers lost to Stanford on March 20.

Had he been, Keady's first Final Four would've been even money. A healthy Cornell's amazing long-range consistency could've opened that slugfest up. As it was, Purdue got within three in the final two minutes. With Cornell right, the Boilers might well have been protecting a lead.

Keady says Cornell is healthy now, and that's bad news for a Big Ten that was just beginning to feel his heat. Cornell averaged 20.2 ppg over his last six games before the ankle injury.

GARY MCQUAY (6-7, 215 lbs., JR, PF, #5, 6.0 ppg, 4.6 rpg, 1.2 tpg, 19.3 minutes., .465 FG, .267 3PT, .544 FT, West HS/Gary, Ind.). Much was expected of McQuay as a banger and scorer inside when he came to Purdue. Much was needed from him when Stephens and Davis had to take last year off. But, so far, he has yet to deliver on the promise.

There is nothing wrong with him as a rebounder. In three-fourths the playing time, McQuay pulled down virtually the same number of boards as Cardinal. He is also the Boilers' best returning shot-blocker (1.0 bpg).

Keady is simply concerned that McQuay is doing it all with his body and not enough with his head:

"He's gotta' learn the game—discipline, body balance, staying low on defense. He's gotta' realize it's not Midnight Madness every night. See, his head's the problem; he thinks he's as good as Glenn."

That would be fellow Gary native Glenn Robinson and, yes, it's safe to say, McQuay isn't there yet.

KEY RESERVES

TONY MAYFIELD (6-1, 180 lbs., SR, G, #20, 2.5 ppg, 1.7 rpg, 2.1 apg, 1.4 tpg, 16.6 minutes., .412 FG, .395 3PT, .690 FT, Tyler JC, Tex. & Rufus King HS/Milwaukee, Wisc.). The junior college teammate of Indiana's Rob Turner, Mayfield was brought in last year to provide a stable backup at the point. He performed that duty well.

Mayfield is a lot like Eldridge in both build and playmaking style, and his assist-turnover ratio (1.5) and three-point percentage were actually better. But he is not as good a defender. That means he has a big problem with playing time now that Cunningham is eligible.

Keady claims to "have a soft spot for those juco kids," because he coached junior college ball for a decade at Hutchinson (Kan.) JC. He likes Mayfield because "he's hung in there."

But about the only way Mayfield will equal his minutes of last season is if he handles the ball and shoots with even more proficiency.

CARSON CUNNINGHAM (6-1, 170 lbs., SO, G, #43, 14.9 ppg, 4.7 apg, 2.8 rpg in 1996-97, Oregon State & Andrean HS/Ogden Dunes, Ind.). Without question, Cunningham is the most interesting newcomer to hit the Big Ten this season. Cunningham is something out of one of those cheesy adolescent sports novels.

He is a basketball junkie with such a keen understanding of the game and such anticipation of everyone's moves that he placed fourth in the Pac-10 in assists and led Oregon State in scoring as that rarest of species, the starting freshman point guard. But, the story goes, he grew homesick after a year in the Oregon gloom (he yearned for the delightful northern Indiana winters?) and transferred to Purdue—which had recruited him out of high school.

Cunningham practiced with the Boilers last season, but had to sit out the year as a transfer. That didn't stop his teammates from noticing his skills.

"He's like a six-foot Larry Bird, except with quickness," said Robinson. "He knows you're open before you know you're open."

That's not half of it. Cunningham is the son of a wealthy lawyer and hails from the lofty community of Ogden Dunes along the Lake Michigan shore. He is brilliant as both a student and a conversationalist, and devours new books as most 20-year-olds do new Sony PlayStation games.

And, yeah, the kid looks like a model with piercing blue eyes. So, all things considered, he might even get a date or two.

Back to hoops. If you never caught Cunningham on one of those late-night Barry Tompkins games on Fox and are a tad skeptical, consider that he put up 28 points on future Sweet 16 entry Texas in just his fifth college game.

This is Purdue's point guard of the future, probably starting around Christmas.

GREG MCQUAY (6-6, 215 lbs., JR, F, #32, 14.0 ppg, 8.0 rpg, Southern Idaho JC & West HS/Gary, Ind.). Keady says don't compare the personalities of Gary and his older brother, Greg. Not only is Greg a year more mature, he's been burnished by two seasons of junior college ball.

The book is, Greg is fundamentally more sound yet still as athletic. In fact, though Greg is an inch shorter, he's said to be a better leaper. Keady got a coach in the deal, too; he hired McQuay's old boss, Jim Thrash.

JAMAAL DAVIS (6-7, 215 lbs., SO, F, #40, 18.2 ppg, 8.6 rpg, 4.5 bpg in 1996-97, Merrillville HS/Merrillville Ind.). Had Davis been around for the NCAAs with a season under his belt instead of sitting out, once again, the Stanford game may have been a whole different story.

Davis brings wiry hops and shot-blocking to the frontcourt and will see time behind Robinson or Cardinal. That's provided an old detached ligament injury from high school has been rehabbed correctly.

CAMERON STEPHENS (6-8, 220 lbs., SO, F, #21, 21.5 ppg, 12.5 rpg, South HS/Fort Wayne, Ind.). The other redshirt who might've made a difference between Sweet 16 and Final Four last season. Stephens could play right away as long as he continues to carve off about 40 extra pounds laid on when he was sitting out.

"He's what I call a two-booty," cracked Keady about Stephens' ample rear (at 260 pounds early in the summer). Down to 235 by September, Stephens offers what the Boilers lacked last year—a wide-body with skills. He is capable of getting substantial minutes at either the "four" or "five," especially if Gary McQuay doesn't come around.

1998-99 PURDUE SCHEDULE

Nov.	13	North Carolina-Asheville
	16-27	#Illinois-Chicago
	22	Lafayette
	29	Eastern Illinois
Dec.	5	@Xavier
	8	Illinois State
	11-12	##Boilermaker Invitational
	19	*Butler
	22	**South Carolina
	27	@Providence
Jan.	2	Minnesota
	6	@Penn State
	10	@Wisconsin
	13	Illinois
	16	Indiana
	19	@Ohio State
	23	Michigan
	27	@Northwestern
Feb.	4	Iowa
	6	Ohio State
	9	@Indiana
	13	@Illinois
	16	@Michigan State
	20	Penn State
	23	@Minnesota
	27 or 28	@Michigan State
	Mar. 4-7	###Big Ten Tournament

@ Road Games
* Market Square Arena, Indianapolis, IN
** Jimmy V Classic, East Rutherford, NJ
# Chase NIT (If the Boilermakers advance, they will face either Gonzaga or Memphis on Nov. 18. Semfinals and finals are Nov. 25 & 27 at Madison Square Garden, NY)
West Lafayette, IN (vs. Valparaiso, first round; also Eastern Washington and LaSalle)
United Center, Chicago, IL

OTHER RETURNEES

CHAD KERKHOF (6-1, 170 lbs., JR, G, #11, 0.9 ppg, 0.5 rpg, 4.0 minutes., .333 FG, .429 3PT, .833 FT, Central HS/Greenfield, Ind.). A walkon who scored the first points of his college career last season in mop-up time against Long Island, Kerkhof will also be able to show his grandkids his name in the encyclopedia of the NCAA Tournament. He's in it with two points and two assists against Delaware.

Keady calls Kerkhof his best defensive player, but that still won't get him many minutes in this backcourt.

OTHER NEWCOMERS

RODNEY SMITH (6-6, 205 lbs., FR, F, #31, 13.6 ppg, 6.0 rpg, Pike HS/Indianapolis, Ind.). Though he played for the 30-1 Indiana state champions, Smith hasn't shown conclusively he can shoot from where he'll need to in college. But he adds another lithe body to the mix. He'll compete with two others for whatever time Robinson doesn't gobble up at small forward.

If he proves he can shoot from space, there may be a minute or two behind Cornell, especially when Keady goes to a trapping press where long bodies pay dividends.

MAYNARD LEWIS (6-1, 170 lbs., FR, G, #12, 25.3 ppg, 6.7 rpg, South HS/Terre Haute, Ind.). The runner-up in Indiana's famous "Mr. Basketball" voting, Lewis carries a rep for instant offense. But his chance for playing time depends on how much Keady presses on defense. That could be a lot with this group.

If there's a fifth guard in the rotation, Lewis is it.

JOHN ALLISON (6-10, 215 lbs., FR, C, #54, 14.3

ppg, 8.9 rpg, New Palestine HS/New Palestine, Ind.). Keady and his staff had this beanpole penned in as a redshirt from the get-go. Something along the lines of Matt ten Dam as a long-term project, only about 100 pounds lighter.

So, no one was more stunned than the coach to see that Allison had worked so hard at improving in the last six months that he actually might play some this season. Certainly, Keady could use a real center, if only as a change-up look and a defensive presence.

"He's the biggest surprise on the team," said Keady. "He's great 'cause he doesn't think he's anything great."

QUESTIONS

Chemistry? On paper, this looks like a very tough job of diplomacy for Keady. He has a small core of vets who've earned their chops being invaded by seven kids, all of whom think they deserve playing time.

Point guard? See above. Eldridge has been around this program three years, and here comes a sophomore transfer looking to take his job. And everyone is pretty much predicting it. This is a delicate situation where Eldridge's maturity will be tested.

The investigation? If the NCAA and the university drag along and don't come up with a prompt judgment, no news may be bad news. Getting the mess behind them, whatever the ruling, may be the best for a young unit that figures to peak next season.

ANSWERS

Keady! The guy just keeps rolling along. Joking about another league coach, Keady cracked, "He's always talking about 'I'm tired'. Tired? You talk like that and your players pick up on it. Hell, I'm 61 and none of my players will even play me at H-O-R-S-E anymore. They can't beat me."

Run, run, run! The Big Ten hasn't had a team this equipped to run and press like Arkansas in a long time. If Keady wants to, he has the mid-size athletes and youthful depth to shell-shock a stolid league with high-octane hoops.

Cornell! He's back and, if he's right, the best shooter in the league is going to give a lot of coaches headaches.

adidas Blue Ribbon Analysis

BACKCOURT	B+	BENCH/DEPTH	B+
FRONTCOURT	B	INTANGIBLES	C+

It's very hard to control chemistry. Coaches have a hard enough time recruiting talent to their programs. They just trust and hope they can iron out any conflicts later.

But you never know what happens when 12 personalities are thrown together, especially these days when pro salaries are so monstrous and the stakes for the most talented players are so high.

Michigan State clicked last year with an eclectic blend of youth and maturity. But there was no question about the point guard.

This is a more delicate situation. If the team splits over Eldridge and Cunningham, the season could drain away.

"Chemistry and leadership are my two big questions," said Keady. "We get a bunch of jealousies going, and it could be the pits."

That's not to mention the six other newcomers, all of whom believe they should be getting minutes.

Says Keady: "Kids are always saying, 'If I get more playing time, I can do more.' That's when I say, 'If you get five minutes, do something! You get 20 minutes, do a lot.'"

A simple credo. If the Boilermakers follow it, this could be a very rewarding season.

(D.J.)

13 WASHINGTON

LOCATION .... **Seattle, WA**
CONFERENCE **Pacific-10**
LAST SEASON .... **20-10 (.667)**
CONFERENCE RECORD .... **11-7 (4th)**
STARTERS LOST/RETURNING **2/3**
NICKNAME .... **Huskies**
COLORS .... **Purple & Gold**
HOMECOURT .... **Hec Edmundson Pavilion (7,900)**
COACH .... **Bob Bender (Duke '80)**
RECORD AT SCHOOL .... **67-73 (5 yrs.)**
CAREER RECORD .... **127-130 (9 yrs.)**
ASSISTANTS .... **Byron Boudreaux (Tulsa '87)**
Eric Hughes (Hayward State-CA '89)
Jason Hamilton (Washington '97)
TEAM WINS (last 5 yrs.) **5-9-16-17-20**
RPI (last 5 yrs.) **186-142-92-84-35**
1997-98 FINISH .... **Lost in NCAA Sweet 16.**

COACH AND PROGRAM

Bob Bender says he was flattered. Certainly he was impressed. He even admits he was tempted. But, when it came time last spring to decide whether he should leave Washington for Texas, Bender concluded Seattle had everything he wanted—on and off the basketball court.

"Everybody recognizes what that job has been in the past and what Tom (Penders) made it," Bender said of the Longhorns and their former coach. "It's a perennial Top 20 program with the ability to win a national championship.

"What it came down to when I got back to Seattle was I felt like I was home. There's certainly a lot of things we want to accomplish here. There was no reason to change."

Washington athletic director Barbara Hedges, who already had given Bender a raise one month earlier, bumped his salary again. He now stands to make in the neighborhood of $400,000—including incentives—after the coach decided April 9 to make his stand with the Huskies. But money wasn't the reason he stayed; he could have earned much more with the Longhorns. Bender simply liked the direction he had his Huskies pointed after five seasons.

Washington had slipped to the role of perennial second-division finisher in the Pac-10 by the time Bender arrived from Illinois State before the 1993-94 season. There was no quick fix, as the Huskies struggled to records of 5-22 and 10-17 in his first two years.

From the start, however, there has been steady, noticeable improvement. By year three, Washington was 16-12, earning a berth in the NIT and winning Bender the Pac-10 Coach of the Year award from his peers. The 1996-97 campaign brought an early-season upset of Arizona that seemed to promise big things, but the Huskies weakened in the second round of conference play and wound up sixth. A 17-win season netted another NIT bid.

Finally, last year, Washington broke through. The Huskies' fourth-place Pac-10 finish was their best since 1987. Their NCAA invitation was their first since '86.

At 18-9, Washington seemed to squeak into the postseason. Once there, the Huskies demonstrated they belonged, upending Xavier and Richmond before losing, 75-74, to Connecticut in a memorable Sweet 16 contest.

"You always want it to happen sooner, but sometimes you're better when you make steady, gradual improvement," Bender said. "The foundation might be a little stronger. I really feel that is something we have accomplished."

Bender has taken the program to the point where Washington's image as a "football school" no longer is a anchor, but a benefit.

"One of the reasons I was excited about coming to Washington is the respect I've gained over the years, looking at other institutions that had that same label," he said. "Look at Lon Kruger and what he did at Florida, Pat Kennedy at Florida State. We're fortunate that we have a great football program that can be a huge ally for us in recruiting. It's always been something to point to for credibility, that at Washington you can compete nationally."

The hoop Huskies figure to make further inroads on the national hoops this season. Center Todd MacCulloch along with sharpshooters Donald Watts and Deon Luton give the Huskies three key returning starters, and Bender also recruited well again.

MacCulloch is the Pac-10's top returning scorer and its best big man. Watts emerged last season as one of the league's most dangerous perimeter threats. And Luton continues a surprising evolution from high school center to Pac-10 sniper. The biggest personnel issue on the team is point guard, where sophomore Dan Dickau takes over for departed senior Jan Wooten.

"Point guard is the most competitive position on our team," Bender said. "But we feel very confident because of the way Dan Dickau finished the season."

The greater task for the Huskies will be to understand that things get only tougher, not easier, as they climb the ladder of success.

"Overall, the strength of the league has gotten better and, consequently, the competitiveness you have has to get better," Bender said. "For us, the biggest challenge is going to be so much more mental. Expectations obviously are going to be higher. Everything about this season has already been heightened.

"The schedule is tougher, the Pac-10 is tougher, we won't be able to sneak up on anybody. That takes a special type of maturity to handle."

In particular, Bender understands that playing as one of the acknowledged contenders in the conference requires a different mindset than creeping up as an underdog.

"Your motivation becomes a little different," he said. "You can still call upon the fact that some people might say last year was a magic run, that it wasn't real. But that will definitely not be the sole motivation as we prepare for every game."

STARTERS NOT RETURNING

PATRICK FEMERLING (7-1, C, 5.7 ppg, 6.1 rpg, 25.4 minutes, .476 FG, .602 FT). A three-year letterman, Femerling on July 15 announced his departure from Seattle in favor of a contract with a team in Berlin in the German professional league. Femerling started 19 games for the Huskies last year, as Bender tried hard to make the "twin towers" concept work.

Femerling's interior defensive work was a plus, but he never became an accomplished scoring threat at UW. He had trouble matching up on defense with players capable of stepping out to the perimeter.

Femerling finished his career third on the Huskies' all-time blocked shot list with 84.

JAN WOOTEN (5-10, PG, 5.6 ppg, 2.4 rpg, 2.7 apg, 23.3 minutes, .477 FG, .340 3PT, .725 FT). Wooten started all 30 games for the Huskies and generally gave the team solid, if unspectacular play. Washington could have benefited were Wooten better able to penetrate and dish the ball to MacCulloch, but that was not his forte.

Wooten scored in double figures just five times, with a high game of 12 on two occasions. In three NCAA Tournament games, his scoring dipped to 2.0 ppg, although he averaged 5.3 rpg and had a 9-to-5 assist-to-turnover ratio.

OTHERS NOT RETURNING

CHRIS THOMPSON (6-1, G, 1.3 ppg, 1.0 rpg, 9.6 minutes, .410 FG, .615 FT). Thompson shared the point guard spot with Jan Wooten when both players were juniors, but his playing time greatly diminished last season as Bender opted for Wooten's superior quickness. Thompson was scoreless in 19 of Washington's 30 games, hitting for a season-high six points on two occasions.

PROJECTED STARTERS

DEON LUTON (6-4, 200 lbs., JR, SG, #5, 15.4 ppg, 2.3 rpg, 2.5 apg, 33.7 minutes, .400 FG, .369 3PT, .730 FT, Del City HS/Del City, Okla.). A former high school center, Luton made huge progress as a scoring wing last season, managing double figures 26 times in 30 games. Luton scored a school-record 75 three-pointers, including a single-game record seven against Southern California. With two seasons left, he already ranks second on the school's career list with 101 three-pointers made, just 18 shy of Eldridge Recasner's record.

There is no questioning the perimeter-shooting skills of Luton, whose 17-footer with 11 seconds left helped Washington beat Xavier in the first round of the NCAAs. He shot 7-for-12 from beyond the arc in his 31-point spree at USC.

Now the Huskies need more from Luton.

"We don't want him to be simply a shooter," Bender said. "We want him to be a scorer. Last year, as the season went on, we saw a marked improvement in his ability to put the ball on the floor and get to the basket. That is something that has got to continue to improve."

Likewise, Bender expects Luton to continue becoming a better defensive player.

"Because of his athleticism, he's got to be a guy we're able to put on some of the better scorers in the league," Bender said. "You look how far Deon, a young man who was a high school center, has come in just two short years. This third year, maybe we can see an even greater jump in his skill level on the perimeter."

DONALD WATTS (6-4, 200 lbs., SR, SG, #24, 16.9 ppg, 3.9 rpg, 3.6 apg, 1.6 spg, 33.1 minutes, .476 FG, .308 3PT, .714 FT, Lake Washington HS/Kirkland, Wash.). After two hellish seasons, Watts emerged last year to begin meeting the huge expectations he brought with him to college. A disappointment his first two years at UW, he now is a star in the Pac-10.

"In my coaching career, the most satisfying coaching development has been Donald," Bender said. "He has always been scrutinized throughout his career. He has always been committed and remained patient and worked hard. Last year was the turnaround year, sort of a breakout year for him.

"What I would expect is nothing but a continued improvement."

Watts, the son of former Seattle Sonics star guard Slick Watts, was the consensus Washington state Player of the Year as a senior at Lake Washington HS. Then, as a UW freshman, he struggled mightily, shooting just 22 percent from the field, including 5-for-27 from three-point range. Things hardly got better his sophomore season, when Watts averaged 8.9 ppg on 36 percent shooting.

"Donald is a kid who has been through some tough times, but he's never gotten down, never second-guessed himself," Bender said. "He was always willing to accept a role. And when that role heightened, he was willing to step into that.

"Going into his junior year, we told him, 'This is your time.'"

And it was. Watts scored 21 points in the season opener vs. Saint Mary's and never looked back. He scored in double figures in all but four games and reached 20 points on 13 occasions. He had career games of 28 points against Arizona and California, and also led the team in assists with 107.

Throughout even the worst times, his father was his greatest ally—but also his toughest critic. Slick and Donald Watts talked constantly, the father dissecting his son's game, even if the truth was harsh.

"The first year-and-a-half, I didn't see a lot of stuff I liked a lot," the father told the *Seattle Post-Intelligencer*.

But Donald never lost his confidence, or his nerve.

"A lot of people asked, 'What happened to Donald this? What happened to Donald that?' recalled the son. "Through all the low shooting percentages, all the turnovers, whatever, you still couldn't tell me I couldn't shoot the basketball. You still couldn't tell me I'm not a basketball player. I know who I am, what I am and what I'm capable of."

Donald said he understands and appreciates his father's critical eye.

"I'm a dreamer. I have visions of what I want to be," he said. "He has visions for me, too. I don't think his visions are any greater than what I visualize."

"Because of his dad's career and success," Bender said, "Donald has always had to prove himself. Slick has high expectations, and he does put a lot of those expectations on Donald. But Donald has handled it very well. He knows that when things aren't going well, you've got to work harder."

TODD MACCULLOCH (7-0, 280 lbs., SR, C, #50, 18.6 ppg, 9.7 rpg, 1.3 bpg, 28.2 minutes, .650 FG, .704 FT, Shaftesbury HS/Winnipeg, Manitoba). The one-time oversized youth hockey player from Winnipeg has grown into his role as the Pac-10's most consistent big man.

"He's not Shaq," Connecticut coach Jim Calhoun said before the Huskies met the Huskies in last year's NCAA Sweet 16 matchup. "(But) he's so good for his team. I can't think of the last time we came upon a team and a center that is so efficient."

The two-time national field goal percentage leader, MacCulloch has made two shots for every one he's missed in his college career. That's efficiency. He has also improved his body, his stamina, his ability to stay out of foul trouble and, consequently, on the court. Bender said MacCulloch's improvement mirrors that of the Huskies program itself.

"His greatest improvement last year is he became a focus of defenses we face, and now he's used to that," Bender said. "Mentally, he's learned how to deal with that. He became a better passer and he varied his offense better.

"Before, he was mostly a post-up player. Now he's diversified. He's got a little 15-foot jumper."

MacCulloch scored in double figures 25 times last season and had 15 double-doubles. His best games included a 33-point, 11-rebound effort vs. Portland, a 30-point, 21-rebound game vs. Arizona State, and a 26-point, 17-rebound performance in the return date with ASU.

It wasn't always like this. MacCulloch couldn't bench press 65 pounds just five years ago and, after his first scrimmage with his new teammates at Washington, actually apologized to them for his sad performance.

"They said I wasn't that bad," he told the *Seattle Times*, "but later admitted they thought I was the worst player they had ever seen."

But MacCulloch never gave up on himself.

"One of the real keys to why Todd has done what he's done is his personality," Bender said. "He doesn't get caught up in all his success and, when he does struggle, he doesn't get too down. For a big man, that's very important."

MacCulloch had improved his bench press to 250 pounds by last season, and the rest of his game also has become a load. With 1,201 points, MacCulloch ranks 16th on Washington's all-time list. He also is second all-time with 95 blocked shots. This year he can join Ohio State's Jerry Lucas (1960-62) as the only players to lead the nation in field goal percentage for three consecutive seasons.

THALO GREEN (6-6, 215 lbs., SO, F, #42, 5.3 ppg, 2.5 rpg, 16.0 minutes, .536 FG, .167 3PT, .615 FT, South Salem HS/Salem, Ore.). Green stepped into the starting lineup for the final six games a year ago and helped eliminate the clogging that resulted when Todd MacCulloch and Patrick Femerling both set up inside. Green averaged 8.7 ppg and 3.5 rpg over those six games, five of them victories.

"Offensively, he gave us a much better flow in spreading the floor," Bender said. "It helped Todd because we then were able to open up some things for him. We became much more efficient because Thalo is such an effective passer."

Green twice scored 12 points in a game last year, including vs. UCLA late in the season. In contests in which he took at least four shots, Green shot 50 percent or better in 17 of 20 games. Bender is optimistic that Green's role will continue to evolve this season.

"He's uncanny at his size to score inside in our league," Bender said. "He's a lefthander, he keeps people off balance and he's got great toughness. He is now much better at putting the ball on the floor and getting to the basket, which makes matchups a little more difficult for our opponents.

"What he did for us last year will certainly continue because it is a natural part of his game, understanding the motion offense. His scoring in different manners will make us a little less predictable."

DAN DICKAU (6-0, 170 lbs, SO, PG, #12, 3.8 ppg, 0.9 rpg, 1.0 apg, 9.4 minutes, .420 FG, .533 3PT, .795 FT, Prairie HS/Vancouver, Wash.). The heir to the starting point guard job, Dickau is a confident player and aggressive shooter who must demonstrate an ability to run the team from the point, both offensively and defensively.

"His command of the motion offense and what we are trying to do on the offensive end is certainly greater now," Bender said. "His greatest improvement last year was on the defensive end.

"The point guard position is a trigger position in our defense. His ability to guard the basketball and get the ball into areas that we want it to be against our defense will be critical."

Dickau says his basketball role model is the late Pete Maravich, one of the game's great showmen. Introduced to films of Maravich by his father, Dickau now collects cards, photos and even Maravich's old instructional videos. He wore the nickname "Pistol" on the back of his jersey as an eighth-grader and has tried copying Maravich's flamboyance on the floor.

"My dad also told me I have a good imagination," Dickau told the *Tacoma News Tribune*. "I watch the video, and how he dribbled made people look like an idiot."

Dickau played off the bench at both the point and shooting guard positions last season, and led the team in three-point percentage. He hit 16 of 30 attempts from beyond the arc, including 13 of 20 (.650) over the final 13 games.

A better shooter than Wooten, Dickau scored a career-high 12 points at Arizona and twice had four assists in a game. He hit two three-pointers and had two steals in the Huskies' first-round NCAA Tournament win over Xavier.

1997-98 RESULTS

Opponent	Score	
Saint Mary's	68-65	ot
Boise State	78-68	
James Madison	70-61	
@Portland	70-68	
@Oklahoma State (L)	66-81	
@Brigham Young	83-68	
Old Dominion	86-68	
@South Alabama (L)	52-69	
Gonzaga	88-82	
Washington State	82-76	
Arizona State	92-70	
Arizona (L)	91-110	
@Oregon	81-71	
@Oregon State	70-55	
California	86-84	ot
Stanford (L)	72-74	
@Southern California	101-86	
@UCLA (L)	94-105	
@Arizona (L)	81-112	
@Arizona State (L)	85-94	
Oregon State	84-74	
Oregon	62-61	
@Stanford (L)	70-93	
@California (L)	67-84	
Southern California	91-66	
UCLA	95-94	
@Washington State	70-51	
%Xavier	69-68	
%Richmond	81-66	
%%Connecticut (L)	74-75	

@ away games
% NCAA East Sub-Regional, Washington, DC
%% NCAA East Regional, Greensboro, NC

KEY RESERVES

CHRIS WALCOTT (6-7, 210 lbs., JR, F, #33, 3.9 ppg, 2.8 rpg, 13.0 minutes, .528 FG, .694 FT, Sammamish HS/Bellevue, Wash.). Walcott has made gradual, steady progress in two seasons from a walkon to a serviceable scholarship player for the Huskies. He started five games last season, and scored his first career double-double when he logged 10 points and 10 rebounds against Boise State. He also scored a career-high 14 points—all in the first half—in the Huskies' huge late-season upset of UCLA.

A first-team All-State player as a senior in high school in 1995, Walcott should continue to play a important role off the bench for Washington."

Last year, he erased any doubts about how competitive and productive he could be," Bender said. "His skill level is as good as anybody we put on the floor in the different areas of scoring, rebounding and defending. It's just a matter of him continuing to get stronger."

MICHAEL JOHNSON (6-4, 195 lbs., SO, G, #23, 3.0 ppg, 1.7 rpg, 12.3 minutes, .375 FG, .353 3PT, .692 FT, Ballard HS/Seattle, Wash.). Johnson played in all 30 games as a freshman, but Bender wants him to become a more assertive offensive player this year.

"Every year, all of us as coaches kind of have an 'X' factor, a guy who really has to emerge for us to be as good as we can be," Bender said. "I think Michael has to be that guy, like Donald (Watts) was last year.

"He had some moments, but at other times he was a little hesitant. We expect him to come in and aggressively score the ball when he's on the floor."

A two-time Washington state prep player of the year, Johnson made great defensive progress a year ago,

Bender said. He scored a season-high 11 points in his second collegiate game, against Boise State. He grabbed seven rebounds in a Pac-10 matchup against Washington State.

SENQUE CAREY (6-4, 200 lbs., FR, G, #3, 24.9 ppg, 10.0 rpg, 8.0 apg, St. Francis HS/Mountain View, Calif.). A fall signee last year, Carey should provide the Huskies an immediate boost with his athletic ability and understanding of the game. He was a first-team "Best in the West" selection by the *Long Beach Press-Telegram* and was ranked among the nation's Top 100 players by scouting expert Clark Francis.

Bender is excited about Carey's on-court maturity.

"Senque's understanding of the game is way beyond his years," Bender said. "Many times when I spoke to him after games this past season that he watched us play, it was amazing the feel he had. It's (a) maturity level you don't normally see."

Mark Mayemura, managing editor of *Recruiting USA*, said he viewed Carey as potentially a better prospect than Ray Young, a more-heralded shooting guard who signed with UCLA.

"Right now, Senque has a better halfcourt game than Ray. Ray likes to play up-tempo, but Senque can do both," Mayemura told the *Tacoma News Tribune*. "He's very athletic and quick to the ball. He's a really good shooter and can stroke it from downtown."

Carey could also get a chance to play some at the point guard, likely as Dan Dickau's backup.

Twice the MVP of the West Catholic Athletic League in the San Francisco Bay Area, Carey helped St. Francis to the finals of the Northern California CIF Tournament. As a junior, he averaged 26.0 ppg, 12.7 rpg and 7.8 apg for a 26-3 team.

GRANT LEEP (6-7, 215 lbs., FR, F, #31, 17.3 ppg, Mount Vernon HS/Mount Vernon, Wash.). Born with a name that almost required him to play hoops, Leep should see playing time from the start, especially if his three-point stroke is working.

"What we like in Grant is the flexibility that he brings to us," Bender said. "One thing we will want to take advantage of right away is to let him shoot the ball from three. He comes prepared to step in and play right away because of what he's been through in the Mount Vernon program."

A product of the same high school that spawned former Washington State star Mark Hendrickson, Leep was a two-time All-State selection whose team reached the semifinals of the state tournament as a senior and the finals as a junior.

Leep averaged 18.2 ppg and 8.5 rpg as a junior on a 28-1 team, and was MVP of the WesCo Conference as a sophomore, when he averaged 20.1 ppg and 9.0 rpg.

OTHER RETURNEES

BRYAN BROWN (6-3, 225 lbs., SO, G, #32, 0.9 ppg, 0.4 rpg, 14 appearances, .250 FG, .273 3PT, .333 FT, Mercer Island HS/Mercer Island, Wash.). A second-year walkon, Brown managed just 16 field goal attempts last season, but hoisted up 11 of those from beyond the three-point stripe. His father, former NBA sharpshooter "Downtown" Freddie Brown, must be proud his son wears the same uniform No. 32.

Bryan's older brother, Terik, plays for Oregon. As a senior at Mercer Island HS, Bryan was named MVP of the state tournament while leading his team to the championship.

ANDREW MORITZ (6-1, 165 lbs., JR, G, #11, 0.2 ppg, 0.1 rpg, 10 appearances, .200 FG, Franklin HS/Seattle, Wash.). A third-year walkon player, Moritz has seen action in 15 games during his UW career. He has scored just two points for the Huskies, but Bender says his value is evident in practice, where his background with a winning program benefits those around him.

Moritz was an All-Metro selection his senior year at Franklin HS, where he helped his team to back-to-back state "AA" titles.

DAVID VERSCHUEREN (6-4, 220 lbs., SR, F, #20, 0.0 ppg, 0.3 rpg, four appearances, Issaquah HS/Issaquah, Wash.). A second-year walkon, Verschueren was a four-sport athlete in high school and doubles as a pitcher on the Huskies' baseball team. His role, like that of Moritz, is to provide competition in practice.

OTHER NEWCOMERS

GREG CLARK (6-6, 220 lbs., SO, F, #21, injured and did not play in 1996-97 at Long Beach State, Grossmont HS/La Mesa, Calif.). After sitting out last season as a redshirt transfer, Clark is ready to provide the Huskies with an athletic presence on the wing. The younger brother of Detroit Tigers' first baseman Tony Clark, he signed with Long Beach State out of high school, sat out his freshman season after dislocating a shoulder, then transferred north.

Bender believes Clark will be worth the wait.

"Greg is the most fundamentally sound player I have ever coached," Bender said. "Athletically, he's the Pac-10 prototype. He does everything like a textbook. If I had a young kid watching our game, I'd say to watch Greg Clark and the way he passes it with two hands, the way he rebounds it with two hands."

Clark, the No. 5 all-time scorer in San Diego area history at Grossmont HS, was a first-team "Best in the West" pick by the *Long Beach Press-Telegram* in 1996. The skills he brings to Washington include a solid three-point shot.

MARLON SHELTON (6-10, 260 lbs., FR, C, 8.0 ppg, 10.0 rpg, 6.0 bpg, Rochester HS/Rochester, Mich.). The son of former Oregon State and Seattle Sonics star Lonnie Shelton, Marlon comes to the Huskies with a seven-foot, four-inch wingspan and loads of raw potential. Right now, he is considered a project with limited offensive skills. Then again, that's just how his dad once was described.

Certainly, Shelton's arrival was fortuitous, given the departure weeks later of 7-1 center Patrick Femerling to the German professional league. He came to the Huskies late, after Lonnie made a phone call to the coaching office, suggesting they check out videotapes of his son. Among other things, the staff couldn't help but notice his 42-inch sleeve.

"Because of his size, his skill and his potential, it couldn't be a better fit for us," Bender said. "He's a young man who has an unbelievable future. He has not even started to reach that potential, and yet he comes in a little further ahead than some other guys we've had in our program. His defense and rebounding are very good."

"Hopefully, I'll improve my scoring," Shelton said. "I'm a shot-blocker and a defender. My offense isn't all that much. I'm no Toni Kukoc or anything."

MICHAEL WESTPHAL (6-4, FR, G, 14.0 ppg, Chaparral HS/Scottsdale, Ariz.). The son of new Seattle Sonics coach Paul Westphal joins the Huskies as a walkon. Regarded as a good perimeter shooter, he becomes the fourth son of a former Sonics player to make his way onto the current UW roster.

Paul Westphal played much of his career in Phoenix—and later coached the Suns—but spent one season with the Sonics.

QUESTIONS

Point guard? Dickau showed flashes of promise as a freshman backup last year, but now he must be ready to run a club that views itself as a Top 20 squad. How well he fits those big shoes will go a long way toward determining the Huskies' fortunes.

Expectations? The Huskies' time as underdog is over. There will be no more surprise attacks on the league's elite. Washington is now a member of that club, and achievement will come against a backdrop of raised expectations. That's always tougher.

Frontcourt depth? MacCulloch is a load in the middle, finally a consistent and more polished player as a senior. But he lost his seven-foot sidekick when Patrick Femerling opted for a pro career in his native Germany. Is Lonnie Shelton's son, Marlon, ready to shoulder some of the load up front?

ANSWERS

Todd MacCulloch! There was a time opponents could almost count on MacCulloch running into foul trouble or fatigue. No more. The big Canadian has become a rock in the middle for the Huskies, and one of the top big men in the nation.

Bob Bender! Washington's ability to hold onto Bender when Texas was wooing him saved the program from taking a tumble just as it is reaching for the top of the heap. The Huskies are on solid ground because Bender has built the program gradually and has successfully mined an improving home-state recruiting pool.

Experience! There is no substitute for the lessons Washington learned last season, scratching and clawing at the end of the Pac-10 schedule to secure its postseason bid, then winning twice in its first NCAA Tournament trip in a decade. The payoff should be felt this season.

adidas Blue Ribbon Analysis

BACKCOURT	**B+**	**BENCH/DEPTH**	**B**
FRONTCOURT	**B+**	**INTANGIBLES**	**B+**

The Huskies are not without flaws. They have an unproven point guard, perhaps insufficient depth up front and will rely on several freshmen to play key roles off the bench. Any or all of that could spell trouble on occasion.

Generally speaking, though, Washington's program is in better shape than it has been since the days of Detlef Schrempf and Christian Welp in the mid-1980s. Bob Bender has fashioned a team that features the league's most productive big man and has two explosive, experienced wing players.

Sure the rookie talent is green, but Senque Carey and Grant Leep should provide Washington with an immediate boost. Both are athletic and versatile.

Bender jokes about the fact that he arrived at Washington just as the Pac-10 was taking off. The fact is, Washington's ascension is one factor in the league's overall climb, and the Huskies are fairly well prepared to compete at that higher plane.

"It's been five years and we've made steady steps along the way," Bender said. "The challenges are just as big now. Obviously, postseason (success) last year was huge for us. It was a great run.

"Our goal remains simple: We want to get closer to winning a Pac-10 championship."

The Huskies likely won't get all the way there this season, but they are indeed getting closer. There should be much less worry about an NCAA bid this year.

(J.F.)

1998-99 WASHINGTON SCHEDULE

Nov.	16	North Carolina-Wilmington
	27-29	#Big Island Invitational
Dec.	1	*Great Eight
	5	@Boise State
	8	@Gonzaga
	19	New Mexico State
	24	**New Mexico
	30	Portland
Jan.	3	***Washington State
	7	@Arizona State
	9	@Arizona
	14	Oregon State
	16	Oregon
	21	@California
	23	@Stanford
	28	Southern California
	31	UCLA
Feb.	4	Arizona
	6	Arizona State
	11	@Oregon State
	13	@Oregon
	18	Stanford
	20	California
	25	@Southern California
	27	@UCLA
Mar.	6	Washington State

@ Road Games
* Great Eight, United Center, Chicago, IL
** Key Arena, Seattle, WA
*** Spokane Arena, Spokane, WA
# Hilo, HI (vs. Hawaii-Hilo, first round; also Evansville and Saint Louis)

14

ARIZONA

LOCATION	Tucson, AZ
CONFERENCE	Pacific-10
LAST SEASON	30-5 (.857)
CONFERENCE RECORD	17-1 (1st)
STARTERS LOST/RETURNING	4/1
NICKNAME	Wildcats
COLOR	Cardinal & Navy
HOMECOURT	McKale Center (14,489)
COACH	Lute Olson (Augsberg College '56)
RECORD AT SCHOOL	373-113 (15 yrs.)
CAREER RECORD	565-205 (25 yrs.)
ASSISTANTS	Jim Rosborough (Iowa '66)
	Rodney Tention (San Francisco '88)
	Jay John (Arizona '81)
TEAM WINS (last 5 yrs.)	29-24-27-25-30
RPI (last 5 yrs.)	6-20-14-6-5
1997-98 FINISH	Lost in NCAA Final Eight.

COACH AND PROGRAM

A year ago, Arizona was the defending national champion. The Wildcats had five returning starters and a huge bulls-eye on their chest.

Not surprisingly, given how these things go, there was no repeat NCAA title. But the 1997-98 'Cats were probably better than their champion predecessors.

Heck, all Arizona did was win 30 games. The Wildcats came within a whisker of becoming the first team to post an 18-0 conference record in the two decades since the Pac-8 expanded to the Pac-10.

Now the heat is off. Mike Bibby, Miles Simon and Michael Dickerson have taken their considerable talents to the NBA. In the conference, it is returning Final Four entry Stanford—with all its starters intact—which faces the overwhelming expectations.

Lute Olson must love this.

With superb players back at two key positions—center and point guard—and one of the nation's top recruiting classes, the Wildcats still will be good. Perhaps very good. The point is, they won't have to hear about it hourly from the start of practice in October to the end of March Madness.

This is the best of both worlds for Arizona—a talented team, yet one which faces only modest expectations.

"I think this will be one of the biggest challenges we've had," Olson said. "But we've not gone away very many times."

That wasn't intended as a warning, but it certainly could serve as such. No program in the Pac-10 approaches the consistency Arizona has achieved.

Over the past 11 seasons, Olson's teams have compiled a record of 298-67—working out to an average yearly mark of 27-6. By comparison, all other Pac-10 teams have combined for just three seasons with at least 27 victories during that 11-year span.

So it stands to reason that the Wildcats won't go away this season, or anytime soon. With senior center A.J. Bramlett and senior point guard Jason Terry augmented by a versatile incoming group, Arizona will be a handful once more.

But Olson also knows it will be different than a year ago, when his team wasn't afforded the luxury of an off-night.

"They stepped out there (35) times, and with every team they played it was a huge game," Olson said. "I don't think any team can comprehend that kind of pressure until you've been in that situation.

"Through the years, I don't think we ever face anyone who's not ready to play, just because of the success we've had. But it's not even close to the intensity you see when you talk about playing as the defending national champion. I thought they stood up very well."

Now it's someone else's turn to face at least a taste of that type of pressure.

"No question, it's Stanford," Olson said of the favorite for this year's conference crown. "This is one of those years where everyone can say they've almost got their name on the trophy. We'll see how they'll react, but they did a really nice job last year. I'm sure they feel they can handle the pressure."

For Olson, real-life pressure paid a home visit over the summer when his wife of 44 years, Bobbi, was diagnosed with a relatively advanced form of ovarian cancer. Rumors circulated for weeks, and there was thought in some quarters that Olson might take a leave-of-absence or even retire. Finally, in late August, he and his wife went public.

Dr. David Alberts, Mrs. Olson's oncologist at the Arizona Cancer Center, said she responded well to initial intravenous chemotherapy treatments. "She's only one-quarter through the treatment, but there's every reason to think she'll live a long life," Dr. Alberts said at a news conference.

"Bobbi and I want to assure everyone that she is doing great and we have every reason to believe that her prognosis is excellent," Olson said in a statement. Mrs. Olson was scheduled to undergo surgery in early September, and UA officials said Olson had no plans to leave his job.

When Olson turns his attention back to the team, he will be greeted by seniors Bramlett and Terry, who have helped Arizona to a record of 81-21 during their careers. The pair will be instrumental on a squad which lost more than 60 points and nearly 18 rebounds and 13 assists per game from a year ago.

"We do have excellent leadership from Jason Terry and A.J. Bramlett. They've been there and they know what it takes," Olson said. "Both of them are very positive in their approach with their teammates. I really think they'll do a great job with the young guys."

The Cats' young talent may need some guidance and a little seasoning, but not much else. Olson brought in six new players, plus a bonus for the 1999-2000 season—ex-Wake Forest center Loren Woods. The batch of incoming freshmen will be expected to fill several of the lineup vacancies, and Olson is anxious to see how well they respond.

"It's going to be a fun year because the team has a lot of personality," the coach said. "I think the chemistry will be excellent. The new guys will really fit in with the veterans.

"But we've got some holes to fill and we're going to have to rely on some of the newcomers. Anytime you do that, it's pretty hard to predict how you're going to do. So many games in our league will be contested right to the final minutes, and that's the time period you worry the most about when you're real young."

STARTERS NOT RETURNING

MIKE BIBBY (6-2, PG, 17.2 ppg, 3.0 rpg, 5.7 apg, 2.4 spg, 32.1 minutes, .464 FG, .387 3PT, .755 FT). Bibby spent just two seasons with the Wildcats, but didn't leave before establishing himself as one of the program's greatest players. He directed Arizona to a national championship as a freshman starting at point guard, then piloted the team to a 17-1 conference record last year and a spot in the NCAA West Regional final.

The second pick overall in the 1998 NBA draft, Bibby enjoyed a collegiate record of 55-14; and 30 of those wins came last year when the Wildcats were ranked No. 1 during significant portions of the season.

He was good enough during the regular season to earn the Pac-10's Player of the Year award. But, for the second straight year, Bibby was at his best in March. He averaged a team-best 17.8 ppg in four NCAA games last season and, in 10 postseason contests during his two years in Tucson, averaged 17.9 ppg, 4.5 rpg and 3.5 apg. In two seasons, Bibby wound up with 1,061 points and 377 assists.

From the start, Bibby was cool and understated, preferring the simple, efficient pass to the play with more flair, but also a higher degree of difficulty. Arizona won't see another one like this for a while.

MILES SIMON (6-5, SG, 17.2 ppg, 3.5 rpg, 3.0 apg, 1.3 spg, 31.5 minutes, .476 FG, .368 3PT, .778 FT). No one better represented the swagger of recent Arizona teams than Simon, who grew into a real team leader over his final season-and-a-half.

After sitting out the first 11 games of the 1996-97 season, Simon averaged 18.4 ppg as a junior. Then he hiked that to 22.0 in six NCAA Tournament games, collecting Final Four MVP honors after scoring 30 points in the national championship win over Kentucky.

Simon didn't skip a beat last season, scoring in double figures in 32 of the Wildcats' first 34 games. He scored 20 points or more on 16 occasions, including 11 times in 18 Pac-10 games. One of his rare off games was a six-point performance in the West Regional final loss to Utah.

Simon finished his career with 1,664 points to rank seventh on UA's all-time list. He was chosen in the second round of the NBA draft, 42nd overall, by the Orlando Magic.

MICHAEL DICKERSON (6-5, SF, 18.0 ppg, 4.5 rpg, 1.8 apg, 28.4 minutes, .510 FG, .404 3PT, .758 FT). Dickerson often was the overlooked star of the past two Arizona teams, hidden in shadows created by Bibby and Simon. Yet he finished his fifth on the school's all-time scoring list with 1,791 points, and the Houston Rockets liked him enough to draft the 6-5 sharpshooter 14th overall.

It was Dickerson who picked up the offensive scoring slack two years ago when Simon missed the early portion of the season due to academic problems. And it was Dickerson who led the team in scoring 10 times a year ago, including 30-point outbursts against UCLA and Washington.

But just as Dickerson suffered an ill-timed shooting slump during the team's 1997 title run (2-for-18 in the Final Four and 5-for-28 from three-point range in six NCAA games), he could not deliver in the West Regional final last season against Utah. The Utes, reasoning they could not neutralize all three of Arizona's top offensive guns, played a triangle-and-two alignment, often leaving Dickerson with open perimeter shots. He shot just 2-for-12 and failed to convert from beyond the arc as the Utes posted a stunning 25-point rout.

Bibby and Simon struggled, too, but no one felt worse than the soft-spoken Dickerson.

"I had a chance to step up and get the respect I always feel I should get," he said. "And I didn't do it."

BENNETT DAVISON (6-8, PF, 7.6 ppg, 6.7 rpg, 25.0 minutes, .590 FG, .625 FT). Quick and wiry, Davison was an underrated inside force for the Wildcats, starting at the power forward spot for two seasons. The son of a retired San Francisco cable car operator, Davison fit perfectly with Arizona's fast and sleek perimeter stars of

1997-98 RESULTS

Opponent	Score	
Morgan State	115-53	
#Boston College	99-69	
#Kentucky	89-74	
#Duke (L)	87-95	
North Carolina-Asheville	97-69	
##Kansas (L)	87-90	
@Texas	88-81	
@Baylor	83-68	
Coppin State	99-82	
@Florida State (L)	79-84	
James Madison	92-68	
Kansas State	125-87	
UCLA	87-75	
Southern California	91-72	
@Washington State	94-81	
@Washington	110-91	
Arizona State	127-99	
New Mexico	89-70	
Oregon	87-57	
Oregon State	93-80	
@Stanford	93-75	
@California	70-57	
Washington	112-81	
Washington State	83-61	
@Arizona State	83-82	
@Oregon State	71-70	
@Oregon	81-66	
California	76-73	
Stanford	90-58	
@Southern California (L)	90-91	ot
@UCLA	91-87	
%Nicholls State	99-60	
%Illinois State	82-49	
%%Maryland	87-79	
%%Utah (L)	79-87	

@ away games
# Maui Invitational, Lahaina, HI
Great Eight, Chicago, IL
% NCAA West Sub-Regional, Sacramento, CA
%% NCAA West Regional, Anaheim, CA

the past couple years.

He scored in double figures 12 times last year, including a season-high of 16 points vs. Maryland in the West Regional semifinals. He also grabbed seven or more rebounds on 19 occasions, corralling a career-best 18 in a non-conference game at Baylor.

Davison, who came to Arizona from West Valley JC in the San Francisco Bay Area, averaged 9.7 ppg and 6.4 rpg his first season in Tucson.

OTHERS NOT RETURNING

None.

PROJECTED STARTERS

A.J. BRAMLETT (6-11, 217 lbs., SR, C, #42, 10.4 ppg, 7.4 rpg, 1.0 bpg, 26.7 minutes, .514 FG, .570 FT, La Cueva HS/Albuquerque, N.M.). Bramlett's emergence as a key player for the Wildcats began in the 1997 NCAA title run, when he turned in three of his season's 12 double-figure scoring games. He continued to blossom last year, and the Wildcats expect big things from their senior center.

"He's got a lot of self-confidence and a great work ethic, to where there isn't a second on the court when he isn't working at what he needs to work at. He's extremely coachable," Olson said.

That's the key for most big men, Olson added, and it has been pivotal for Bramlett.

"He's shocked a lot of people who saw him in high school and thought he'd just be an average, at best, college player," Olson said. "If you work hard, run the court all the time and do the work in the weight room, the improvements will amaze people. He's a very bright kid and he picks up things really well."

Even with the team focusing on its perimeter game, Bramlett contributed 21 double-figure scoring efforts last season, including a 17-point, 10-rebound performance against Duke. He had 11 points, 19 rebounds and was a huge defensive factor in a late-season home rout of Stanford.

Now, as the only returning starter, Bramlett will be asked to step into an expanded role. Olson is convinced he's ready.

"Both he and Jason (Terry) have been guys that have really made great sacrifices for the team," Olson said. "Now, with so much of the scoring gone, they'll obviously have the chance to do more."

JASON TERRY (6-2, 169 lbs., SR, PG, #31, 10.6 ppg, 2.4 rpg, 4.4 apg, 1.7 spg, 22.8 minutes, .422 FG, .347 3PT, .827 FT, Franklin HS/Seattle, Wash.). Regarded the past two years as one of the nation's most valuable sixth men, Terry emerges from the considerable backcourt shadow of Bibby and Simon to assume the team's leadership reins. Olson is excited to see what Terry can do as the man running the club on a full-time basis.

"Jason is, above everything else, a team guy. He's going to do what needs to be done for the team to be successful," Olson said. "He has the ability to score, but I don't think that's something he will go out looking for. The important thing will be for him to play the way he's played, which is to involve everyone, so the open man gets the ball and everyone understands what their shots are."

While averaging fewer than 23 minutes per game, Terry nonetheless had 21 double-figure scoring games a year ago, including a 20-point effort at Texas, a 21-point game vs. New Mexico and a 17-point, eight-assist performance against Arizona State.

Perhaps the quickest player in the Pac-10, Terry will continue to be given free reign to take chances on defense. In three seasons, he has totaled 165 steals.

"We'll have guys inside who are pretty good shot-blockers, and that allows a player like Jason to gamble," Olson said. "His game is anticipation. There are times he's going to get beat, because that's the nature of that style. But I think our inside people will make it pretty hard to get to the bucket."

MICHAEL WRIGHT (6-8, 220 lbs., FR, PF, #45, 29.5 ppg, Farragut Academy/Chicago, Ill.). A former high school teammate of Minnesota Timberwolves' star Kevin Garnett, Wright should immediately compete for a starting spot at the Wildcats' vacant power forward slot.

Wright is perhaps the gem of a superb Arizona recruiting class, having been rated as the No. 15 prospect in the nation last year by All-Star Sports. A consensus All-State selection in Illinois as a senior, Wright spent last spring playing on the USA Basketball men's junior world qualifying team.

"From what I understand, he was far and away their most consistent player," Olson said. "He's a big-time rebounder. I think he'll probably end up being the best rebounder we've had (at power forward) for a long time.

"He had a tendency to get into foul trouble in high school because of his aggressiveness, but that is also one of the things that made him such an intriguing prospect. In all the times I saw him play, he never let up and played very hard on both ends of the court."

An honorable mention All-America selection by *USA Today*, Wright led Farragut to a 21-7 record last season.

RUBEN DOUGLAS (6-5, 188 lbs., FR, SG, #5, 34.6 ppg, 9.0 rpg, 4.7 apg, 4.1 spg, Bellarmine-Jefferson HS/Altadena, Calif.). Douglas arrives at Arizona after a prep career in which he was the No. 10 all-time scorer in California high school history with 2,578 points. Olson likes the fact that the Wildcats can call upon Douglas for scoring, but has no fear that this is a player who must shoot the ball to be happy and effective.

"The thing with Ruben was he was on a high school team that needed him to score 40 (points) if they were going to have a chance to win," Olson said. "I've observed him in summer situations, with other good players around him, and he adapted to whatever role he was asked to play.

"One of the biggest adjustments for a guy who scores a lot of points is suddenly he's going to get probably half or a third as many shots as he's taken before. Ruben's got a great disposition. He's a guy who wants to win and he's going to do what he needs to for us to be successful."

Douglas is expected to compete immediately for a starting job at the vacant shooting guard spot. He also has experience at the point, and could be used as a backup to Terry at that position.

He was rated the No. 8 prospect in the *Long Beach Press-Telegram* "Best of the West" poll of coaches before his senior year, when he led the state with 1,073 points. He had games of 56 and 51 points and scored 40 points or more five times in his career.

Douglas was a three-time Player of the Year in the Sante Fe League and a first-team All-State selection this past season. He averaged 27.0 ppg as a junior and 20.2 ppg as a sophomore.

RICHARD JEFFERSON (6-8, 215 lbs., FR, SF, #44, 25.0 ppg, 13.0 rpg, 4.0 apg, 3.0 spg, 4.0 bpg, Moon Valley HS/Phoenix, Ariz.). The son of parents who both attended rival Arizona State, Jefferson arrives at UA as the state's top prep prospect from a year ago. He was the Arizona 4A Player of the Year, leading his team to a 27-3 record.

Olson expects Jefferson to battle for a starting spot at either the wing or power forward position from day one.

"He's just an unbelievable athlete," Olson said. "He can take it to the hole, he shoots the ball well. His biggest adjustment will be on defense. Trying to guards the wings in our league is not an easy thing to do."

Jefferson's stock as a college prospect skyrocketed in the summer of 1997 when he performed well at a camp in Las Vegas and became the subject of a *Sports Illustrated* feature story. He averaged 27.0 ppg, 7.0 rpg and 6.0 apg as a junior.

1998-99 ARIZONA SCHEDULE

Nov.	13	*Tennessee
	25	Texas
	28	@Brigham Young
Dec.	5	**Wyoming
	14	California-Irvine
	19	***Iowa State
	28-30	#Fiesta Bowl Classic
Jan.	2	@UCLA
	4	@Southern California
	7	Washington State
	9	Washington
	14	@Arizona State
	16	@New Mexico
	21	@Oregon
	23	@Oregon State
	28	Stanford
	30	California
Feb.	4	@Washington
	6	@Washington State
	10	Arizona State
	13	Louisiana State
	18	Oregon State
	20	Oregon
	25	@California
	27	@Stanford
Mar.	4	Southern California
	6	UCLA

@ Road Games
* BCA Classic, Albuquerque, NM
** America West Arena, Phoeniz, AZ
*** Las Vegas Shootout, Las Vegas, NV
# Tucson, AZ (vs. Holy Cross, first round; also Florida International and Penn State)

KEY RESERVES

EUGENE EDGERSON (6-6, 210 lbs., JR, F, #33, 4.5 ppg, 5.2 rpg, 17.3 minutes, .486 FG, .704 FT, St. Augustine HS/New Orleans, LA). Edgerson will continue to be just what he has been—a hard-working, physical, raw-boned player whose efforts on defense and under the boards more than compensate for limited offensive tools.

"He's a warrior, a guy who comes to play all the time," Olson said. "His forte has been rebounding and he does a good job defensively. His offense has trailed behind that, just because he's so strong and so aggressive."

Edgerson had a 17-point, 12-rebound performance in last year's season opener vs. Morgan State, then scored in double figures just once more all season. His stats may not be appreciably different this year, either, but his experience and his grit will be invaluable.

DONNELL HARRIS (6-11, 203 lbs., SR, C, #13, 3.3 ppg, 2.9 rpg, 11.4 minutes, .553 FG, .667 FT, North Salinas HS/Salinas, Calif.). After gaining notice with an eight-point, seven-rebound effort in the '97 NCAA title game against Kentucky, Harris took a step backward last year.

He missed 12 games early in the year due to a gall bladder problem that ultimately required surgery. Then he missed three games at the mid-point of the Pac-10 schedule, two of them after being suspended for missing a practice.

After averaging 5.9 ppg and 5.8 rpg as a sophomore, his numbers were barely half that last year, and there was some concern Harris might decide to leave the program. Olson insists Harris will be a valuable member of the team, but only if the player makes it happen.

"There's a lot of ability there. Frankly, it's up to him," Olson said. "It's the last go-round. We'll just have to take a wait-and-see attitude.

"Through the years our seniors have always had great years. It will be interesting. We've got some freshman kids coming in who don't think they'll take a back seat to anybody."

Before his health problems set in, Harris averaged 11.0 ppg and 4.5 rpg the first two games of last season. He had only one other double-figure scoring game all year.

QUYNN TEBBS (6-1, 181 lbs., SO, G, #24, 2.3 ppg, 0.8 rpg, 6.0 minutes, .447 FG, .448 3PT, .600 FT, Bingham HS/Salt Lake City, Ut.). A 23-year-old sophomore, Tebbs spent his first two years out of high school on a Mormon mission in Sao Paulo, Brazil, then redshirted in 1996-97 before seeing his first action last season.

"He's got maturity and a great work ethic," Olson said. "This will be an opportunity to show what he can do."

The owner of a 37-inch vertical leap, Tebbs is an excellent perimeter shooter who scored a career-high nine points last season by hitting three three-pointers in the final 30 seconds of a loss to Duke.

Tebbs' role will increase only if he can hold off the challenge of the Wildcats' highly regarded freshman class.

JUSTIN WESSEL (6-8, 211 lbs., SO, F, #30, 1.2 ppg, 1.2 rpg, 5.6 minutes, .632 FG, .625 FT, Prairie HS/Cedar Rapids, Ia.). After redshirting in 1996-97, Wessel developed last season into a capable backup forward. The coaching staff considers him a versatile player able to pass and handle the ball, and the owner of a solid mid-range shot.

A former Mr. Basketball in Iowa, where he averaged 27.5 ppg and 9.8 rpg as a high school senior, Wessel played in 24 games last season. He played critical minutes in a regular-season-ending game vs. UCLA, and scored a season-high six points against Arizona State.

"He's a good passer and a good shooter," Olson said. "If I had to list our biggest concerns (about him), they're probably on defense and the strength end of it."

LUKE WALTON (6-8, 225 lbs., FR, F, #51, 20.0 ppg, 11.0 rpg, 6.0 apg, University HS/San Diego, Calif.). The son of former UCLA All-America center Bill Walton, Luke has many of the same versatile skills as his father. Arizona's coaches are excited about Walton's ability to pass, shoot and handle the ball for a player his size.

Rated the No. 7 player in the *Long Beach Press-Telegram* "Best in the West" poll last season, Walton will be able to play either the wing or power forward spot for Arizona.

"Luke has a fine all-around game," Olson said. "He has great hands, handles the ball extremely well, shoots it well and can take it to the basket. He has a definite feel for the game, like his dad had.

"Luke has perimeter offensive skills, but is very good with his back to the basket, so he could be an inside-outside guy for us."

Walton played for winners in high school, helping his club to records of 26-4, 25-5 and 28-3 his three seasons on the varsity. The club was 42-0 in conference play those three years.

As a senior, Walton was named the state's Division III Player of the Year and to the All-Academic first-team for San Diego County.

OTHER RETURNEES

JOSH PASTNER (5-11, 174 lbs., JR, G, #12, 0.5 ppg, 0.4 rpg, 17 appearances, .231 FG, .167 3PT, .667 FT, Kingwood HS/Kingwood, Tex.). Originally a walkon at Arizona, Pastner showed himself to be such a valuable practice player that he was awarded a scholarship. He gave up the scholarship this past spring, however, so the Wildcats could award it to Wake Forest transfer Loren Woods.

Pastner is the player on the bench who rarely sits down, and he regularly conducts late-night shooting drills for the benefit of teammates. Mike Bibby credited Pastner's assistance for improvements he made in his game.

"He'll be very important to our ball club," Olson said. "He just has a way of getting everybody pulling in the same direction. He's great with the young guys in terms of getting them to develop the kind of work ethic they need."

Hoping to become a coach someday, Pastner enjoys noting that the Wildcats are 25-0 in games in which he has appeared. It is also a fact, however, that Pastner did not appear in the first half of any of those games.

None of which has prevented Pastner—he of the endless film study and near-coaching staff involvement—from becoming a bit of a cult hero and media darling.

ORTEGE JENKINS (6-2, 218 lbs., SO, G, #43, 1.2 ppg, 0.4 rpg, 13 appearances, .364 FG, .286 3PT, .625 FT, D.S. Jordan HS/Long Beach, Calif.). A top quarterback for the Arizona football team, Jenkins won't join the basketball team until his fall season is complete. His scholarship commitment is to football, and the level of his eventual involvement with the basketball team this year remains uncertain.

"He wants to play," Olson said. "It all depends on how their (football) season goes. If they make it to a bowl game, it will make it that much more difficult for him. It's a tough double."

"O.J.," as his friends and teammates call him, scored four points in six minutes vs. Kansas State last season in his debut, but played sparingly the remainder of the year.

JASON STEWART (5-10, 166 lbs., SR, G, #52, 0.5 ppg, 0.2 rpg, 13 appearances, .200 FG, .750 FT, Gateway Christian HS/Gardena, Calif.). Stewart is a walkon who has played in 19 games over his first two seasons. He actually first practiced with the Arizona women's team, then joined the men's squad.

Stewart's goal is to become a minister someday and he is regarded as the team's spiritual leader. He is 3-for-3 lifetime from the three-point arc in his college career.

OTHER NEWCOMERS

TRAVES WILSON (6-3, 205 lbs., FR, G, #25, Moline HS/Moline, Ill.). Arizona coaches are likening Wilson to former Wildcats defensive ace Reggie Geary. Projected as a combo guard, Wilson is a fierce competitor and great leaper.

"Traves had a great senior season in high school and it really prepared him for what he will have to do at this level," Olson said. "He doesn't have quite the quickness of a Reggie Geary, but he has a very strong upper body.

"Since he can guard guys who are four to five inches taller, he could conceivably contribute (at) any of the three perimeter positions. I think he's going to be a real factor defensively."

A native of the same hometown as Arizona associate head coach Jim Rosborough, Wilson set the all-time scoring record at Moline HS, earning All-State honors in Illinois as a junior and a senior. As a junior, he averaged 17.0 ppg and 8.0 rpg during his junior season.

RICK ANDERSON (6-9 1/2, 205 lbs., FR, F, #22, 22.7 ppg, 12.0 rpg, 4.0 bpg, Long Beach Poly HS/Long Beach, Calif.). The last of six fall signees, Anderson could wind up being redshirted this season. Still growing, he needs the strength that time in the weight room will afford him.

"That was one of the options when Ricky was recruited," Olson said. "It might be the best thing for him, but those kinds of decisions we'll make after we're in practice for a few weeks."

Anderson's father, Gary, played for Olson at Long Beach State, making this the first time Olson has coached a former player's son.

His high school team's MVP as a sophomore, junior and senior, Anderson also earned first-team All-League honors each of those years. As a 4-foot-10 second-grader, Anderson played on a team of fifth and sixth-graders. He said then in a newspaper story that his dream was to grow to be 6-9 "and be like Larry Bird."

NOTABLE REDSHIRT

LOREN WOODS (7-1, 250 lbs., JR, C, 8.8 ppg, 7.1 rpg, 2.3 bpg, 25.2 minutes in 22 games, .401 FG, .670 FT Wake Forest & Cardinal Ritter HS/St. Louis, Mo.). Arizona fans will have to wait a year to see Woods, who sits out this season as a transfer from Wake Forest. He will have two years of eligibility remaining, starting with the 1999-2000 season.

For now, Woods should provide center A.J. Bramlett with a terrific practice foe; he is taller and more agile than anyone Bramlett is likely to see in the Pac-10. Woods is familiar with McKale Center, having played two games there as a freshman in the NCAA Tournament.

Before departing Wake Forest, Woods was on his way to developing into one of the nation's top young big men. He averaged 11.6 ppg and 8.5 rpg the first 14 games last season before taking a seven-game leave of absence. He returned to play the final nine games, but his playing time and effectiveness diminished.

As a freshman, playing alongside Tim Duncan, Woods averaged 6.8 ppg and 5.2 rpg in just 17.5 minutes per game. Those numbers earned him a spot on the *Basketball Times* freshman All-America team and the ACC All-Rookie squad.

A McDonald's All-America as a senior at Cardinal Ritter HS in St. Louis, Woods averaged 21.1 ppg, 13.2 rpg and 6.5 bpg. He led his team to back-to-back state 2A titles and a combined record of 55-6.

QUESTIONS

Experience? There is no way to lose four starters, including three NBA draft picks, and not experience some drop-off. What the Wildcats will miss most is the experience that their talented youngsters simply cannot provide yet.

Jason Terry? Terry steps into the starting point guard and primary leadership role on this team. All available evidence suggests he is more than ready for the assignment. But the landscape is different for him now, without the luxury of playing alongside Bibby, Simon and Dickerson. He is wearing the big shoes now, and he must pull a young team together.

Donnell Harris? Olson has won with young teams in the past (including two years ago, when a freshman point guard directed the 'Cats to the national title). But this is a coach who expects seniors to emerge, and no player in the program faces more questions than Harris—who is talented, but comes off a shaky junior season.

ANSWERS

A.J. Bramlett! Bramlett is living proof that even a 6-11, barely 200-pound center can evolve into an All-Conference player given enough patience and hard work. A.J. still isn't likely to belly-bounce, say, Washington's Todd MacCulloch, but his quickness and wiry strength make him the Wildcats' anchor inside.

Young talent! Olson assembled one of the nation's best recruiting classes just in time for the exodus of star talent from his program. Expect Wright, Douglas and Jefferson, in particular, to make a major impact from the start.

The underdog role! Arizona doesn't have the chance to play this part often, but Olson revels in it. Two years ago—one season ahead of schedule—the 'Cats transformed a fifth-place Pac-10 finish into a national title. A repeat of that epic run is unlikely, but the Wildcats will certainly enjoy watching Stanford wear the mantle of Pac-10 favorite.

adidas Blue Ribbon Analysis

BACKCOURT .... **B+** **BENCH/DEPTH** .... **B+**
FRONTCOURT .... **B+** **INTANGIBLES** .... **A**

It should be obvious by now that Arizona will not recede into the shadows of the Pac-10 race. The Wildcats haven't won fewer than 23 games in any season since 1987, and it's a little hard to fathom this team stumbling.

Nonetheless, Arizona joins UCLA as the two youngest clubs in the Pac-10, and quite possibly the most youthful Top 25 caliber teams in the nation. The Wildcats' edge is their two senior starters, Bramlett and Terry.

Those two, having experienced college basketball at the highest levels, will be a solid foundation from which the Cats' newcomers can build. Arizona's non-conference schedule is typically challenging, but perhaps not the death march recent UA teams have sometimes tackled.

This will allow Arizona to test itself against quality competition, while also growing and assembling confidence. Perhaps by January, but certainly by March, this could be a very uncomfortable team to play.

(J.F.)

15
OKLAHOMA STATE

LOCATION .... **Stillwater, OK**
CONFERENCE .... **Big 12**
LAST SEASON .... **22-7 (.759)**
CONFERENCE RECORD .... **11-5 (t-2nd)**
STARTERS LOST/RETURNING **1/4**
NICKNAME .... **Cowboys**
COLORS .... **Orange & Black**
HOMECOURT .... **Gallagher-Iba Arena (6,381)**
COACH .... **Eddie Sutton (Oklahoma State '58)**
RECORD AT SCHOOL .... **179-77 (8 yrs.)**
CAREER RECORD .... **609-241 (28 yrs.)**
ASSISTANTS .... **Paul Graham (North Texas '74)**
Sean Sutton (Oklahoma State '92)
Randall Dickey (Ouachita Baptist '83)
TEAM WINS (last 5 yrs.) **24-27-17-17-22**
RPI (last 5 yrs.) **18-9-45-46-33**
1997-98 FINISH .... **Lost in NCAA second round.**

COACH AND PROGRAM

Eddie Sutton is one of the game's great comeback stories. His credentials rank among the nation's best.

Last season, he surpassed the 600 career victory mark and ranks ninth among active coaches with 609. Only one of his 28 seasons has ended with a losing record. He is the only coach to take four programs (Creighton, Arkansas, Kentucky and Oklahoma State) to the NCAA Tournament.

But, for all his success, Sutton is also remembered for the stained Kentucky tenure which nearly ended his career.

"I don't know if ever thought I'd be coaching this long," Sutton said. "I was prepared to walk away from it."

That was in 1990, Sutton's crossroads year. The dam had burst at Kentucky. Money had spilled out of a delivery package; there were charges of cheating on an entrance exam, then probation. That one losing season? It was his last with the Wildcats, who turned in a horrid 13-19 mark.

Forced out, Sutton was away from coaching during the 1989-90 season. During that time, he was cleared of wrongdoing at Kentucky and his batteries were recharged. But who would take a chance on a fallen coach?

Oklahoma State, Sutton's alma mater, was in the market. Former Sutton assistant Leonard Hamilton had taken the Miami (Fla.) job a few days after the 1990 season had ended. Sutton, who had inquired about an opening at Kansas State, was warmly welcomed back to Stillwater, where he had played for the legendary Henry Iba in the late 1950s.

Sutton revitalized the program Iba made famous when it was called Oklahoma A&M. The Aggies, as they were known then, won two national championships and played for a third in the 1940s. Playing for Iba and against Ralph Miller at Wichita State, Tex Winter at Kansas State and Dick Harp at Kansas—who had just taken over for Phog Allen—Sutton had a close-up view of some of the game's greatest coaches.

"You couldn't grow up around greater coaches," Sutton said.

Oklahoma State struggled after Sutton's playing career ended in 1958. There were only two NCAA appearances between his playing days and the beginning of his coaching tenure. Then, Sutton's first Cowboy team shared the Big Eight title with Kansas and was the first of five straight to make the NCAA Tournament, culminating with the 1995 Final Four appearance.

The 'Pokes didn't make it back to the NCAAs until last year. They scared the heck out of Duke in the second round before losing by six. The season was one of Sutton's most gratifying. Oklahoma State won its first 11, lost four of eight, then swept through February with seven straight victories. After two consecutive unfulfilling seasons, Sutton had the Cowboys back near the top.

Oklahoma State did it mostly with sophomores and junior Adrian Peterson. The critical game was at Texas Christian right after Christmas. The Cowboys had been 1-12 in road games the previous season. This was their first true road test of 1997-98, and the 'Pokes held on to defeated the nationally-ranked Horned Frogs.

And then there was the 600th victory. It came at home against Texas A&M, giving Sutton a moment to reflect on the roller coaster ride that is his career.

"You know, I could have stayed at Arkansas forever," Sutton said. "While I was there, the only place I ever considered leaving for was Oklahoma State, because it's my alma mater. But the timing was never right."

Word around Stillwater is that Sutton, 62, will coach for three or four more seasons and then turn the program over to his son, Sean, a Cowboys' assistant. Whoever succeeds him, Sutton believes he won't be in coaching long enough to develop gray hair.

"In my opinion, you're going to see fewer and fewer of guy like myself, Norm Stewart, Bob Knight or Don Haskins," Sutton said. "I can't see the young guys of today in it until they're 60. The demands have become too great. They'll wonder if it's worth the trouble."

For Sutton, it clearly has been.

STARTERS NOT RETURNING

BRETT ROBISCH (6-11, C, 15.4 ppg, 8.2 rpg, 33.4 minutes, .500 FG, .308 3PT, .782 FT). Robisch didn't make the All-Big 12 team, but he probably was the league's most valuable player during the second half of the season.

"I don't think people understood how improved he was and how important he was to our team in the second half," said Sutton of Robisch's omission from the honor teams.

Robisch was the Cowboys' leading rebounder and second leading scorer. He shot only 50 percent, but don't be deceived. Robisch was more a finesse player than a banger. Many of his shots came from 8-12 feet.

Robisch is the son of former Kansas great Dave Robisch and his brother, Scott, will be fighting for a starting role on this year's team.

OTHERS NOT RETURNING

CHAD ALEXANDER (6-3, G, 5.4 ppg, 1.8 rpg, 1.0 apg, 16.7 minutes, .395 FG, .388 3PT, .721 FT). Alexander got shoved out of the starting picture a year ago, but gave the Cowboys a solid contributor off the bench. He'll forever be remembered at Oklahoma State for his running left-handed, buzzer-beating throw in from the baseline that gave the Cowboys a one-point victory over Missouri during his junior season.

TOMMY WARNER (6-0, G, 0.6 ppg, 0.1 rpg, seven appearances). Warner was a practice player only.

PROJECTED STARTERS

ADRIAN PETERSON (6-4, 197 lbs., SR, G, #20, 17.7 ppg, 6.7 rpg, 1.7 apg, 1.2 spg, 35.2 minutes, .462 FG, .328 3PT, .799 FT, Oak Grove HS/North Little Rock, Ark.). You hate to get on a guy's case, especially when he is the team's scoring leader for the past two years, but Peterson really hasn't come on strong after an outstanding freshman year. Oh, the numbers have steadily improved, but Peterson teased everybody with a sensational freshman season in which he averaged 11.3 ppg and hit nearly 40 percent of his three-pointers.

"I think that's right," Sutton said. "He was so good as a freshman, and maybe he didn't follow that up the way you might have expected. But he was outstanding for us last year, and I expect him to be better this season."

Peterson is one of those rare breeds in college basketball—a talented senior. He made a wise decision not seriously contemplating an early departure. Unless somebody else snatches it away, Peterson should be the league's Player of the Year.

He has that kind of talent. Peterson is a streak shooter and, when he's on, he can't miss. Peterson changed his pace somewhat last year, reducing his three-point attempts and becoming more of a slasher. The results were positive: Besides increasing his scoring (from 14.2 as a sophomore), Peterson went to the line a team-high 164 times. This is a good thing when you're an 80 percent shooter. Part of his success can be attributed to the addition of Doug Gottlieb, who knew how to set Peterson up in the offense.

With a banner season, Peterson (1,265 career points) could wind up among the top scorers in the program's history, joining the likes of Byron Houston, Bryant Reeves and Bob Kurland. At worst, he'll be the Cowboys first All-Conference player since Reeves and guard Randy Rutherford in 1995.

DESMOND MASON (6-6, 207 lbs., JR, PF, #34, 14.6 ppg, 7.7. rpg, 1.6 apg, 32.7 minutes, .525 FG, .319 3PT, .683 FT, Waxahachie HS/Waxahachie, Tex.). As much as teammate Joe Adkins improved last year, Mason was even better and was named to the Big 12's All-improved team. Mason jumped his scoring average by more than 10 points and more than tripled his rebounding. It was Mason, not starting center Bret Robisch, who provided a more intimidating presence.

Mason lived up to his potential after a disappointing freshman season. He had been selected the top newcomer in the preseason and had the fans in Stillwater drooling after shattering a backboard with a reverse dunk in warm-ups before the opening practice.

But the adjustment was difficult, as it is for many freshmen. Mason shot only 37.7 percent from the floor. He started 12 of 32 games, and wondered about his role.

All that changed last year. Mason was one of three Cowboys to start every game, and he had some of his best moments against top-notch competition like Texas (27 points, 14 rebounds), Oklahoma (21 points) and George Washington (13 points and 13 boards in the first round of the NCAA Tournament).

Mason goes outside for points, but, at 31.9 percent from behind the arc, he is much better in the paint. He doesn't get intimidated by larger players and can score on anybody.

DOUG GOTTLIEB (6-1, 180 lbs., JR, PG, #44, 5.4 ppg, 3.0 rpg, 6.9 apg, 31.2 minutes, .411 FG, .293 3PT, .484 FT, Notre Dame & Tustin HS/Tustin, Calif.). Turnovers were big problems for Oklahoma State in 1996 and 1997. The Cowboys solved it by luring Gottlieb from Notre Dame.

Actually, it wasn't much of a lure. Gottlieb needed a place to play. He left Notre Dame on bad terms after he pled guilty to stealing a teammate's credit card and charging $900 worth of merchandise.

There was an Oklahoma State connection. Gottlieb's father, Bob, had been an assistant for Sutton at Creighton. The Cowboys needed a point guard, and Gottlieb had turned in a nice season for the Fighting Irish, averaging 4.6 ppg and 5.7 apg. He started in 23 of 27 games as a freshman.

"Counting high school, I've been recruited twice and took a total of eight visits," Gottlieb said. "I trusted coach Sutton as much as anybody. When he gave me his word about my role, I felt this is where I belonged."

That role was as an immediate starter, and Gottlieb was a big reason for the Cowboys' fast start—an 11-0 record that included victories over NCAA-bound Washington and Texas Christian. He turned in double-digit assists in four of those games and became the first player in school history to rip off three straight double-digit assist performances.

Against quicker point guards, Gottlieb wasn't as effective. And, when his playmaking ability is reduced, he isn't a good enough shooter to compensate. Even worse than his 41.4 percent from the field was an atrocious 48.6 percent from the line. That figure sometimes forced Sutton to bench his top ballhandler late in close games.

Oklahoma State can survive with Gottlieb turning in a similar performance this season. But, according to Sutton, he has been one of the team's hardest workers on the off-season, working on—what else?—his shooting.

JOE ADKINS (6-2, 193 lbs., JR, SG, #35, 12.6 ppg,

1997-98 RESULTS

Texas-Pan American	103-71	
Creighton	86-70	
Southern Utah	79-58	
North Texas	98-60	
Oral Roberts	73-66	
Washington	81-66	
Arizona State	79-68	
Jackson State	60-58	
Arkansas State	78-62	
@Texas Christian	82-81	
@Texas A&M	100-65	
Nebraska (L)	62-67	
Texas Tech	66-63	
@Missouri (L)	64-70	
@Baylor (L)	95-97	2ot
Texas A&M	94-62	
@Oklahoma	88-84	
@Texas (L)	73-88	
Colorado	86-74	ot
Baylor	85-72	
@Iowa State	81-66	
Oklahoma	70-66	
@Texas Tech	83-81	ot
@Kansas State	64-61	
Texas	80-58	
Kansas (L)	67-71	
#Texas (L)	64-65	
%George Washington	74-59	
%Duke (L)	73-79	

@ away games
# Big 12 Tournament, Kemper Arena, Kansas City, MO
% NCAA South Sub-Regional, Lexington, KY

1998-99 OKLAHOMA STATE SCHEDULE

Nov.	16	Northwestern State
	19-20	#Zippy's Invitational
	28	Texas Christiian
Dec.	1	Florida Atlantic
	5	*UCLA
	12	Arkansas-Little Rock
	20	@Creighton
	22	@UNLV
	30	Southeast Missouri State
Jan.	2	Kansas State
	6	@Texas A&M
	9	@Baylor
	12	Oklahoma
	17	@Texas Tech
	20	Baylor
	23	@Texas
	27	Southern Mississippi
	30	Texas A&M
Feb.	2	Iowa State
	6	@Oklahoma
	10	@Colorado
	14	Texas
	17	@Nebraska
	20	Missouri
	22	@Kansas
	27	Texas Tech
Mar.	4-7	##Big 12 Tournament

@ Road Games
* John Wooden Classic, Anaheim Pond, Anaheim, CA
# Honolulu, HI (vs. Marquette, first round; also Hawaii and Nicholls State)
Kemper Arena, Kansas City, MO

3.0 rpg, 3.4 apg, 29.4 minutes, .415 FG, .327 3PT, .787 FT, John Marshall HS/Oklahoma City, Okla.). Adkins made a huge improvement over his freshman season, when he couldn't shoot straight. That tends to happen in Eddie Sutton's system. Players work so hard on defense that some offense is sacrificed. Adkins is one of the Big 12's better defenders and led the Cowboys with 54 steals last season.

Adkins also became one of the team's designated three-point shooters. He made only 30 percent of his 60 treys as a rookie. In 1997-98, he attempted a team-high 153 and made 41.5 percent. Want more to like? Adkins' 88.0 percent free throw shooting in league games led the Big 12.

Oklahoma State breathed a sigh of relief when Adkins came around. He was one of Sutton's more highly prized recruits and was named the state player of the year in 1996, leading John Marshall HS to the 5A championship in an undefeated season.

Adkins is the brother-in-law of Carl Henry, a former All-Big Eight performer for Kansas in the 1980s.

ALEX WEBBER (6-10, 257 lbs., JR, C, #45, 2.6 ppg, 1.8 rpg, 9.9 minutes, .483 FG, .485 FT, Searcy HS/Searcy, Ark.). Another player with medical problems, Webber missed half of his freshman season with back surgery to remove a ruptured disk. He got through all of last year, although he hardly contributed.

Then, in early August, he suffered injuries to his knees and ankles in an automobile accident. Sutton wasn't certain if Webber would be at full strength for the beginning of fall workouts.

Webber came to Oklahoma State highly touted. He was a consensus Top 100 player who led his high school team to the state championship as a junior. The Cowboys liked his competitiveness, but they haven't had a chance to see much of it during his college career.

Assuming his auto wreck injuries heal, Webber is penciled in as the starting center.

"I told him this summer that he should look at the position as his to lose," Sutton said. "He's got the ability and, when you look at the others on our roster who are trying to beat him out, Webber is the best among them. But we need him to step up."

KEY RESERVES

SCOTT ROBISCH (6-10, 210 lbs., SO, F/C, #40, 3.8 ppg, 2.7 rpg, 8.3 minutes, six appearances, Calvary Academy/Springfield, Ill.). His first two seasons in the program don't even make a good half-season. Injuries have crushed Robisch's development.

As a freshman, he got in five games, scored 10 points and probably would have seen much more playing time. But, at a practice at Colorado, he broke a bone in his hand, suffered tendinitis and was granted a medical redshirt.

Primed for his redshirt freshman season, Robisch got in six games, scored 38 points and looked like he was going to make a contribution. Then he developed a stress fracture in his thigh. Again, he was done for the season.

Robisch is healthy now, and the Cowboys need him to become a serviceable player.

"He needs to get stronger, that's the first thing," Sutton said.

But even a few more muscles won't change Robisch's style, which is different than his brother's. Where Brett played mostly with his back to the basket and got many points on soft hooks or turnarounds, Scott plays more facing the basket.

"He's more of wing-type player, a swing-type player," Sutton said. "Scott can shoot the ball. You can teach the other areas—defense, rebounding, other things—but shooting is an art, and he has the ability to score."

BRIAN MONTONATI (6-9, 220 lbs., JR, F, #30, 2.9 ppg, 1.9 rpg, 7.4 minutes, .483 FG, .750 FT, Fullerton JC, Calif. & Orchard View HS/Muskegon, Mich.). Ready or not, Montonati is going to get more playing time this season. The Cowboys need him. He is big and has some experience, and that's a combination Oklahoma State sorely lacks.

"He'll challenge for a lot of playing time this year," Sutton said. "When you look at who we have available on the front line, there aren't many with his experience. That's in his favor."

The Cowboys will be looking for more games like the one Montonati had against Oklahoma at Stillwater. In a four-point victory, Montonati scored six points in the final two minutes.

Montonati was a two-sport star in high school. His basketball jersey was retired after becoming Orchard View's career scoring leader. He also was an All-Conference wide receiver in football. The 'Pokes would like to see more of that athleticism.

JOHN GILMORE (6-7, 240 lbs., JR, F, #32, 9.1 ppg, 6.1 rpg in 1996-97 at Wisconsin-Milwaukee, also Tyler JC, Tex. & Missouri City HS/Missouri City, Tex.). The depth Sutton has added with Alexander and Gilmore is astounding. Gilmore will slide in behind Desmond Mason and the Cowboys shouldn't drop off much. Gilmore made the All-Midwestern Collegiate Conference freshman team in 1997 before transferring to junior college in his native Texas.

It wouldn't be surprising to see a lineup with Gilmore and Mason, a smaller, quicker front line that can also bang with the bigger boys.

GLENDON ALEXANDER (6-5, 215 lbs., G, JR, #4, 7.9 ppg, 2.6 rpg in the first semester of 1997-98, University of Arkansas & Newman Smith HS/Carrollton, Tex.). So, what do to with the offense with Alexander, once he becomes eligible, in December? The Cowboys have their starting backcourt returning and have perhaps the Big 12's best player—Adrian Peterson—playing Alexander's position.

It appears Alexander will have to sit, and time will tell how that effects Oklahoma State's chemistry. Alexander is good enough to start. He was named to the SEC All-Freshman team in 1996-97 after averaging 9.6 ppg. This after an amazing high school career in which Alexander finished as the state's career scoring leader. As a senior, he scored 1,113 points.

Alexander couldn't beat out three-point specialist Pat Bradley for the starting shooting guard role at Arkansas, so who knows how much playing time he'll get this season in Stillwater?

"He'll challenge our veterans for a lot of playing time," Sutton said.

And that's all. Anything Alexander gets, he'll earn.

OTHER RETURNEES

MICHAEL JOHNSON (6-7, 220 lbs., SO, F, #33, 0.6 ppg, 0.8 rpg, 10 appearances, Shawnee Mission East HS/Leawood, Kan.). Johnson is his high school's career scoring leader, but he did not see much action for the Cowboys last season. He should be more than a practice player this year, though.

His father, Bob, played at Missouri in the early 1970s.

OTHER NEWCOMERS

ROY CANDLEY (7-2, 390 lbs., JR, C, #52, 17.0 ppg, 9.0 rpg, Panola JC, Tex. & Baker HS/Baton Rouge, La.). That's not a typo on the weight. Candley checks in at almost one-fifth of a ton. He would have towered over former Oklahoma State center Bryant "Big Country" Reeves.

The fitness and diet experts at Oklahoma State, who helped mold the once doughy Reeves into an All-America, can't wait to get their hands on Candley. First, they'd like to see about 40-50 pounds come off. Then they want to develop muscle.

Sutton, who never saw Candley play in high school or junior college, will do the rest.

"From looking at film, he's got great hands, a nice shooting touch and can be a good scorer," Sutton said. "But he can't play here at that weight. That needs to come way down."

FREDRIK JONZEN (6-10, 230 lbs., FR, F, #12, Shawnee Mission East HS, Kan./Uppsala, Sweden). Jonzen was a high school teammate of Michael Johnson who caught recruiters' eyes at a camp two summers ago. Jonzen played for a club team (Sallens) in Sweden last year.

Sutton likes his game, but it might be difficult finding playing time for Jonzen.

QUESTIONS

Center? Brett Robisch was one of the Big 12's most underrated players. That will be proven this year as the Cowboys struggle to fill the center slot.

Gottlieb's shooting? At some point, Gottlieb has to shoot it (and sometimes from the free throw line). Oklahoma State hopes the countless hours practicing this summer will pay off.

Next step? The Cowboys haven't been conference champions since 1991. It's been all Kansas and Missouri (once) since. The Cowboys travel to Lawrence late in the season for what may be a conference title showdown; Oklahoma State hasn't won in Allen Field House in the 1990s.

ANSWERS

Backcourt! It's the best in the Big 12. Oklahoma State starts three fine guards—Gottlieb, Adkins and Peterson—and now can bring former prep phenom Glendon Alexander off the bench.

Peterson! A shooter and slasher, he could be the best player in the Big 12.

Tournament tough! It's a safe bet Oklahoma State will make the NCAA Tournament. When it does, look out. The Cowboys haven't lost a first-round game and are 10-6 in NCAA contests overall under Sutton.

adidas Blue Ribbon Analysis

BACKCOURT	**A**	**BENCH/DEPTH**	**B**
FRONTCOURT	**B**	**INTANGIBLES**	**B+**

The Cowboys don't have an inside force or a hot-shooting point guard, but, in between, there isn't a better rotation in the Big 12. Oklahoma State's "middle" might put them over the top.

There are plenty of reasons to like this or most Eddie Sutton-coached teams. They do things right. An Oklahoma State player has led the league in field goal percentage five of the past six years; the Cowboys annually rank among the league leaders in all defensive categories; and the veteran coach knows how to identify and fix problem spots.

Poor point guard play probably prevented the 'Pokes from playing in the NCAA Tournament in 1996 and 1997, so Sutton got Gottlieb. Last season, all of his starters played at least 29.4 minutes, so he got talented transfers to back up the frontcourt and backcourt.

You don't reach 600 career victories without making good decisions, and this could be a major payoff year for Sutton, who has about run out of career milestones. A national championship would be a nice cap, and Sutton may be closer to it with this team than any other.

First, Oklahoma State must assert itself in the Big 12. The Cowboys have finished (or have been seeded) second in five of the past seven conference tournaments, but they haven't gotten past Kansas in six of them. The Cowboys and Jayhawks are the Big 12 favorites and, if comes down to their one league meeting, it's in Lawrence. That's bad news for Oklahoma State, which hasn't won at Allen Field House in this decade.

But Oklahoma State has a nice little home floor winning streak of its own. The 'Pokes have won 78 straight non-conference games at Gallagher-Iba Arena. The record ranks fifth all-time. The Cowboys are chasing UCLA, which won 97 between 1966-1977.

That's mostly a December record, of course. March is where Oklahoma State is pointing this season, and playing well into the second round isn't going to satisfy the Cowboys this time.

(B.K.)

adidas Blue Ribbon Analysis

GRADING SYSTEM

- A+ equal to very best in country—Final Four-caliber unit
- A among the best in the land—worthy of deep NCAA run
- B+ talented, versatile and experienced—NCAA-NIT ability
- B solid and productive winners—league and post-season contenders
- C+ average to above-average—may contend in a weaker league
- C average to mediocre—second division in a strong league
- D+ below average, inconsistent—second division in a weaker league
- D well below average—losing season virtually certain
- F non-Division I ability—an underdog every night

16

NORTH CAROLINA

LOCATION .... Chapel Hill, NC
CONFERENCE .... Atlantic Coast (ACC)
LAST SEASON .... 34-4 (.894)
CONFERENCE RECORD 13-3 (2nd)
STARTERS LOST/RETURNING 4/2
NICKNAME .... Tar Heels
COLORS .... Blue & White
HOMECOURT .... Dean E. Smith Center (21,572)
COACH................. Bill Guthridge (Kansas State '60)
RECORD AT SCHOOL .... 34-4 (1 yr.)
CAREER RECORD .... 34-4 (1 yr.)
ASSISTANTS............. Phil Ford (North Carolina '78)
Dave Hanners (North Carolina '76)
Pat Sullivan (North Carolina '95)
TEAM WINS (last 5 yrs.) 28-28-21-28-34
RPI (last 5 yrs.) 7-1-16-4-1
1997-98 FINISH .... Lost in NCAA Final Four.

COACH AND PROGRAM

Bill Guthridge stepped up to the microphone at a spring press conference and sounded awfully optimistic about his second year as North Carolina's head coach.

"Certainly, I think with Antawn Jamison and Vince Carter coming back, we will be one of the best teams in the country," Guthridge said. "We will probably be ranked No. 1."

Uh, coach, we have some bad news for you...

The Tar Heels won't have either of those All-Americas, both of whom opted to forego their final seasons of college basketball to enter the NBA draft. It was exactly what Tar Heel fans feared all season long—that their team would do well enough in 1997-98 for Jamison, the unanimous choice as the college Player of the Year, and Carter, his vastly talented teammate, to pass up their senior finale.

The bad blue news came about a month after UNC's second consecutive trip to the Final Four. First Jamison, then Carter, sat at a head table with Guthridge and former head coach Dean Smith and announced they were leaving the program.

Asked what he planned to do with the loss of such talent, trying to replace the equivalent of four starters off a Final Four team, Guthridge said: "I think we will punt."

Well, coach, the ride was fun while it lasted...

Then again, it was supposed to be. Guthridge inherited one of the most talented and experienced teams in the country last Oct. 9, when Smith kept his promise and stepped down when he no longer believed he had his whole heart into the job. Smith stayed in the shadows all year long, showing up for only three games at the Smith Center last year.

Guthridge, the career understudy, was suddenly handed a national championship contender. He had little to do in his inaugural year except sit back and enjoy the view from the best seat in the house.

The Tar Heels, with a starting six that averaged over 23 years of age, made the coach look brilliant. He never had to set a starting lineup, because the six players—who accounted for 90 percent of the team's minutes, 92 percent of the team's scoring and nearly 80 percent of its rebounding—rotated every game, with the odd man out determined by alphabetical order.

The Tar Heels had everything they needed at every position. The backcourt was deadly with Ed Cota, Shammond Williams and Vince Carter sharing the responsibilities. The frontcourt had the obvious "go-to" guy in Jamison, with solid contributions from Makhtar Ndiaye and Ademola Okulaja along the way.

The Heels, who led the nation in field goal percentage, made Guthridge the winningest rookie coach in the history of the NCAA. He also picked up the ACC Coach of the Year trophy and a couple of national Coach of the Year awards.

All that for just sitting on the bench and letting his inherited herd of horses run loose. Or so it seemed.

There were a few missteps along the way, but nothing out of the ordinary in the ACC. Guthridge didn't lose his first game until an overtime contest at Maryland in mid-January, the Tar Heels' 18th contest.

They shared the No. 1 position in both polls with crosstown rival Duke, re-energizing a series that had grown almost stale with UNC's dominance in recent years. In both 1997-98 meetings, the Tar Heels and Blue Devils were ranked No. 1 and No. 2. The Tar Heels claimed the first matchup in Chapel Hill and were cruising to lopsided win in Durham until the Blue Devils stormed back in the final 10 minutes.

Duke went on to win the regular season championship, but the Tar Heels took Round 3 fairly easily, winning the ACC Tournament title in Greensboro.

Guthridge wasn't comfortable getting credit for the Tar Heels' success. After UNC won that second consecutive tournament title, he said he still considered his squad "Dean's team."

So, does that mean the 1998-99 Tar Heels are more "Bill's team?"

"I don't know," Guthridge said while looking over his inexperienced roster. "I might want to give it back to Dean."

That wouldn't be hard, since the legendary retired coach has an office two doors down the hall and comes to work every single day.

This year's Tar Heels will be very much like Smith's squad in 1995-96, the season after Jerry Stackhouse and Rasheed Wallace bolted for the NBA after their sophomore campaign. The following year, thanks to the emergence of a kid named Jamison, wasn't the disaster everyone predicted. The Tar Heels still won more than 20 games and finished in the ACC's top three, as they have every year since 1967.

The Tar Heels didn't play well in that postseason, losing second-round games in the ACC and NCAA Tournaments, but Smith was able to right the ship without tarnishing the tradition. Guthridge now appears to be facing a similar task. He knows this will be the first real chance to show off his coaching ability, and all eyes are watching to see if the foundation Smith laid for 36 years is cracking.

Guthridge also knows this: The Tar Heels are better prepared to deal with the loss of Jamison and Carter, who were expected to leave after their junior years, than they were the loss of Stackhouse and Wallace, who both surprised their coaches by turning pro after their sophomore seasons. The Tar Heels have three proven commodities for their starting lineup, with junior Ed Cota at the point, senior Ademola Okulaja at the small forward and sophomore Brendan Haywood at center.

The other two slots are up in the air, as are all backup positions.

One of only two faults anyone found with Guthridge's debut last year was that he didn't develop the bench. The other was that his Tar Heels celebrated too much, showed too much emotion and had an overall lack of control—rather ironic considering the criticism UNC took for years for being too "corporate" and robot-like under Smith.

The Tar Heel reserves, like Guthridge himself, had little to do on the sidelines except celebrate Jamison's acrobatics or Carter's dunks. By late December, the new coach wasn't comfortable enough with his other reserves to get anyone beyond Haywood any significant playing time. So he stuck with his rotation, starting some combination of the same six players all season long.

Guthridge says he doesn't regret that decision now, but there would certainly be fewer questions about the Tar Heels' prospects for this year if anyone had actually seen much out of Max Owens, Brian Bersticker or Michael Brooker.

"It would have maybe helped for this coming year because we could have gotten some of these guys prepared, but I don't think you ever want to play a season preparing for the next season," Guthridge said. "You have to do what is best for that team that year.

"It worked out that we didn't need any depth. By playing those other guys more, it might have gotten us off to a little better start this year, but that is not what we were trying to do last year."

So the early part of this season, when the Tar Heels play in the Preseason NIT and against teams such as Appalachian State, Florida International, Hampton and College of Charleston, will be developmental.

"It might be into January before we get settled into a rotation," Guthridge said. "It might not even happen then.

"We will have to work as hard as we can and see what develops."

It might not be No. 1 in the country, as it might have been with Jamison and Carter still around, but it shouldn't be the lower division of the ACC, either.

STARTERS NOT RETURNING

ANTAWN JAMISON (6-9, PF, 22.2 ppg, 10.5 rpg, 1.6 tpg, 33.2 minutes, .579 FG, .400 3PT, .667 FT). For a guy who never really developed a shot other than the fast putback, Jamison made quite a name for himself. The unanimous national Player of the Year last season, Jamison was the first Tar Heel player since Billy Cunningham to average more than 20 points and 10 rebounds in a season and the first since Michael Jordan to lead the ACC in scoring.

Jamison's decision was fairly obvious. It was a surprise to some that he didn't bolt after his sophomore season, when he again would have been one of the Top 10 players taken in the draft.

Jamison had pushed hard academically and graduated from UNC in little over three years. He helped the team make it to the Final Four in back-to-back seasons. He is the first player in ACC history to be named to the first team as a freshman, sophomore and junior.

Last year, he was the ACC Player of the Year, the ACC Tournament Most Outstanding Player and the unanimous national Player of the Year. What reason, then, was there left to return to school, other than the possibility of setting some personal records, such as becoming the ACC's all-time leading scorer?

"There is not left for me to accomplish," Jamison said at his farewell press conference. "If I stayed, it would be for selfish reasons, to break records and stuff like that.

"It would have been nice to win a national championship, but this was the best decision for me."

Jamison's most impressive quality was his speed. Not only could he run up and down the floor with anyone in the league, the hard-working forward had the quickest shot in the country, both off the pass and off an offensive rebound. That's what made him one of the deadliest and hardest players in the league to stop the last three seasons.

"Relentless" is the word Guthridge most often used to describe Jamison, because of his drive to succeed. He showed that at last year's ACC Tournament, in which he helped the team to its second consecutive title and won MVP honors while playing with a painful pulled groin.

Still, Jamison will have to find a new home. After three years of living off putback shots, Jamison is going to be expected to step outside a little more and face the basket.

Jamison played his entire career at power forward, hardly ever stepping beyond 15 feet for jumpers. However, he did attempt 15 three-point shots last year and his free-throw shooting, once his biggest deficiency, steadily improved during his career.

The scouts—and Jamison, too—believe he will do fine playing the small forward in the NBA.

"In practices, I was playing the 'three,'" Jamison said. "But in games, they needed me to run toward the blocks, so I played the 'four.' If you are successful doing that, why change?

"I don't think the challenge is playing the 'three.' The challenge will just be playing in the NBA."

SHAMMOND WILLIAMS (6-2, SG, 16.8 ppg, 3.2 rpg, 4.2 apg, 2.6 tpg, 1.0 spg, 32.9 minutes, .488 FG, .400 3PT, .911 FT). For a guy who wasn't offered a Division I scholarship coming out of high school, Williams had nothing less than a brilliant career at North Carolina. He wasn't a good ballhandler and sometimes his decision-making was a little shaky, but, when the Tar Heels needed an important shot, they turned to either Jamison or Williams.

More often than not, it was Williams, one of the hardest working players ever to play in Chapel Hill. Most any night during the season, you could find Williams after hours in the Smith Center, tirelessly working on his game. Sometimes he would have company. His brother often came up from Greenville, S.C., just to practice against him.

But, most of the time, it was just Williams and the security personnel. He saw the sun come up over the Smith Center back lot more than once.

In his career, Williams went from being a little used bench player to the school's career three-point leader with 233 bombs to his credit. The ACC Tournament MVP as a junior, Williams became a team leader and vocal spokesman on and off the court as a senior.

Yet with all of his accomplishments, Williams' career was sullied by a couple of incidents. He never thought he got enough credit for contributing to a pair of Final Four squads. He couldn't understand why he was left off the All-ACC second team as a junior and the first team as a senior.

Williams could be pouty and babyish, which he proved by storming off the court in tears at Virginia because of a disagreement in the huddle with Guthridge, a situation that was lovingly referred to as "The Crying Game." It was the contest immediately following his career-high 45 points against Georgia Tech, and the Tar Heels were trailing by 10 points when Williams raced to the locker room, having yet to score more than seven minutes into the game.

The Tar Heels came back and won, while Williams spent the rest of the season answering questions about his behavior that night.

Sadly, Williams' final two seasons ended with horrible shooting performances in the Final Four. He was 1-for-13 in the loss two years ago to Arizona, and 2-for-12 last year against Utah.

It was a shame, really. Williams worked hard to gain his respect, sometimes a little too hard. He got motivation from it and turned into a quality college player. He improved his ballhandling over the last two years and became good enough to get drafted by the NBA's Atlanta Hawks in the second round.

In the end, Williams probably deserved more respect than he received in his career, at least from outside the program, and he likely would have gotten it had he not begged for it so often. His importance will be evident soon enough this year, however, if the Tar Heels struggle with their outside shooting, because no one on the current team can match Williams' perimeter shot.

VINCE CARTER (6-7, SF, 15.6 ppg, 5.1 rpg, 1.9 apg, 1.1 tpg, 1.2 spg, 31.2 minutes, .591 FG, .411 3PT, .680 FT). Watching Carter race the sidelines, turn up the baseline and go airborne for an Ed Cota alley-oop pass was one of the most graceful and spectacular sights of the college basketball season. His polished athletic moves, his ability to shoot the outside shot consistently and his improvement on defense had NBA scouts falling all over themselves. They like the fact that Carter filled out his game to include more than just his exciting dunks as well as the fact that he led the ACC in field goal percentage.

The same scouts believe he has a stronger upside in the long run than Jamison. Carter, an excitable sort who was the ringleader in UNC's celebration madness, wasn't sure about his draft prospects until Dean Smith told him he would go somewhere between No. 4 and No. 10 in the NBA lottery.

"It's the chance of a lifetime," Carter said when he made his announcement. "I feel ready. I think I can handle myself well out there. Hopefully, one day I can be a superstar."

For all of his abilities, however, Carter was never the "go-to" player people kept expecting him to be ever since he arrived on campus from Daytona Beach, Fla. Sure, he took over games every now and then. His 21 points in the first half against Wake Forest as a sophomore were amazing, and he seemed to be the only Tar Heel player actually interested in beating Utah in the Final Four last year.

But he was generally the team's third option, behind Jamison and Williams. If the Tar Heels needed a big shot, especially a jumper on the wing, Williams or even Cota got the call more frequently.

Even last year, people still questioned Carter's desire and his toughness. Nevertheless, the scouts loved his upside and Carter became convinced of his future stardom as they watched him improve in pre-draft workouts.

MAKHTAR NDIAYE (6-9, PF, 5.8 ppg, 4.1 rpg, 1.3 tpg, 1.4 bpg, 23.8 minutes, .481 FG, .273 3PT, .642 FT). Has any player ever had a more horrible exit from a mediocre college career? Ndiaye shamed himself and the program, which has been proud of its relatively unblemished image, at the Final Four last year when he accused Utah freshman Britton Johnsen of using a racial slur during the Tar Heels' loss to the Utes in the Final Four at San Antonio.

Under intense scrutiny, Ndiaye admitted he made the whole thing up, that he was upset after the loss and lashed out when he was informed by some members of the media that Johnsen accused Ndiaye of spitting on him. But, given the racial make up of the Utah team, Ndiaye's comments set off a firestorm of controversy.

Eventually, Ndiaye released an apology to Johnsen, but his actions lingered for weeks. The NCAA, in an unusual move, formally reprimanded Ndiaye for violating "the principle of good sporting behavior that is expected of participants in intercollegiate athletics."

That incident only capped a season in which Ndiaye was often criticized for his overly aggressive play and overly ebullient celebrations. He led the ACC in fouls (133), committing 23 more infractions than anyone else in the league.

In last year's first game against Duke, Ndiaye was so upset by his fifth personal foul, he slammed the ball down on the court. The ensuing technical sparked a Duke comeback that nearly cost UNC the game.

After his team won the ACC Tournament, Ndiaye jumped up on a table and celebrated in front of a section of Duke supporters, including Mike Krzyzewski's wife and daughter. After the Final Four incident, Ndiaye asked the school to help him seek anger management counseling.

That apparently didn't work, either, as soon after the Johnsen incident died down, Ndiaye was arrested for threatening and assaulting a friend of a friend. He was convicted of simple assault and communicating threats in July.

Ndiaye was the only major college transfer ever recruited by Dean Smith. He began his career at Wake Forest, then transferred to Michigan because of recruiting improprieties by the Demon Deacons.

After two years in Ann Arbor, Ndiaye decided he wanted to go elsewhere. Roy Williams convinced Dean Smith to take a chance on this "misunderstood" player, and Smith relented.

In the end, Ndiaye wasn't worth the trouble he caused. Out of all the players UNC loses from last year's team, he alone will not be missed.

OTHERS NOT RETURNING

None.

1997-98 RESULTS

Opponent	Score	
Middle Tennessee State	84-56	
@ Richmond	84-65	
California	71-47	
#UCLA	109-68	
#Seton Hall	95-65	
#Purdue	73-69	
*Louisville	81-72	
##Tennessee-Chattanooga	68-38	
##Virginia Tech	78-57	
Princeton	50-42	
Hampton	92-69	
@Florida State	81-73	
@Georgia	82-80	ot
@Bethune-Cookman	97-46	
@Clemson	73-70	
Georgia Tech	96-75	
Virginia	81-73	
@Maryland (L)	83-89	
Appalachian State	96-63	
@North Carolina State	74-60	
Florida State	103-55	
Clemson	88-79	
@Wake Forest	79-73	
Duke	97-73	
@Georgia Tech	107-100	ot
@Virginia	60-45	
Maryland	85-67	
North Carolina State (L)	72-86	
Wake Forest	72-53	
Duke (L)	75-77	
###North Carolina State	73-46	
###Maryland	83-73	ot
###Duke	83-68	
%Navy	88-52	
%UNC Charlotte	93-83	ot
%%Michigan State	73-58	
%%Connecticut	75-64	
%%%Utah (L)	59-65	

@ away games
* Great Eight, United Center, Chicago, IL
# Carrs Great Alaska Shootout, Anchorage, AK
Harris Teeter Pepsi Challenge, Charlotte, NC
ACC Tournament, Greensboro Coliseum, Greensboro, NC
% NCAA East Sub-Regional, Hartford, CT
%% NCAA East Regional, Greensboro, NC
%%% NCAA Final Four, San Antonio, TX

PROJECTED STARTERS

ED COTA (6-1, 185 lbs., JR, PG, #5, 8.1 ppg, 3.6 rpg, 7.2 apg, 3.0 tpg, 1.5 spg, 33.0 minutes, .493 FG, .303 3PT, .824 FT, St. Thomas More, Conn./ Brooklyn, N.Y.). Cota wants to score. He has always wanted to score. He likes passing the ball to his teammates—which he did at a record rate last year—but he has a real gleam in his eyes going into this season.

"I can score," Cota declared on numerous occasions. "I just don't need to. That's not my job."

In his first two years on campus, the Tar Heels didn't need points from Cota, as Jamison, Carter and Williams were around. Cota still managed to win the ACC Rookie of the Year by being the perfect point guard in the Dean Smith system. He ran the team, distributed the ball and played good defense.

Cota continued that last year, when he led the ACC in assists for the second year in a row and shattered Kenny Smith's single-season school record with 274 dishes. He has averaged more than seven assists per game since he arrived on campus.

In the NCAA Tournament, the unflappable Cota faced huge challenges in back-to-back games, guarding Big 10 Player of the Year Mateen Cleaves of Michigan State and national freshman of the year Kalid El-Amin of Connecticut. Cota, whose nickname is "Easy Ed," didn't bend under pressure, holding Cleaves to 7-for-21 shooting and El-Amin to just two assists in the victories that sent the Tar Heels to the Final Four for the second year in a row.

In five NCAA Tournament games, Cota had 35 assists and only 12 turnovers. Now, Cota will get his chance to put some points on the board. Guthridge hopes that won't be at the expense of the rest of the offense.

"Hopefully, that additional scoring will come naturally within the offense," Guthridge said. "Some people question his scoring ability, but he has scored some big baskets for us."

But this year will be different. With the three top scorers gone, Cota will be a greater part of the offense, whether it is taking his set jump shot from the outside or penetrating the lane. He'll still pass it a lot, but, as he said after Jamison and Carter announced their decisions, "I guess those passes will come back around to me."

ADEMOLA OKULAJA (6-9, 235 lbs., SR, SF, #13, 8.0 ppg, 5.6 rpg, 2.1 apg, 1.6 tpg, 1.2 rpg, 31.3 minutes, .414 FG, .258 3PT, .623 FT, John F. Kennedy School/ Berlin, Germany). Okalaja is certainly a rarity at North Carolina these days: a scholarship senior. There have been precious few of those at the school that has lost five underclassmen to the NBA draft in the last three years.

He will definitely go into the season as the team's on-the-court leader, with 105 career games under his belt. But Okulaja won't be counted on to replace the scoring provided by the trio of Jamison, Carter and Williams.

Generously called a "streaky shooter" in the school's preseason prospectus, Okulaja went through one 13-game stretch in which he missed 24 of 25 three-point shots. In the team's last seven regular season games, Okulaja hit just 33 percent of his field goal attempts.

Opposing teams started leaving Okulaja wide open, daring him to take the jumper, which he invariably missed. One newspaper took to calling the Berlin native "The Achilles Heel."

"That doesn't matter," Okulaja said of his shooting woes. "There is more to my game than shooting."

It's true that Okulaja does a lot more for the Tar Heels than making baskets. He even knocked down some key shots when it mattered, hitting two three-point bombs against Maryland in the ACC Tournament semifinals and tallying 12 points against Connecticut in the game that sent the Tar Heels to the Final Four for the second consecutive year.

Okulaja could be moody at times, but he wasn't bothered by his shooting slump. All that mattered to him was that his teammates remained confident in his abilities.

Okulaja has always felt his most important role was to do the dirty work the Tar Heels need to win games, whether it was playing tenacious defense, making good passes and/or rebounding.

"He will be an excellent stabilizing influence on this young team," Guthridge said of his only recruited senior. "He has to be careful to not feel like he has to do too much this year. That's not a burden one player should take on himself."

Especially one who shoots like Okulaja did during significant portions of last season.

BRENDAN HAYWOOD (7-0, 265 lbs., SO, C, #00,

2.9 ppg, 2.4 rpg, 8.1 minutes, .530 FG, .635 FT, Dudley HS/Greensboro, N.C.). People around the program last year used to say that the Tar Heels had six-and-a-half players they counted on. Haywood, the massive seven-footer with the size 18 shoes, was the "half."

Haywood got more playing time than any reserve outside Guthridge's six starters, playing in every one of the Tar Heels' 38 games. He provided nearly half the non-starter scoring and, as the season progressed, showed that he can make shots in the paint and play polished defense. His 33 blocked shots were third on the team behind Ndiaye and Carter.

Haywood entered school as a mere youngster, only 17-years-old with a little roll of baby fat around the middle. A year older now but no lighter, Haywood will be asked to shoulder more of the burden of the Tar Heels' inside game. How he responds to that responsibility will determine what kind of sophomore season Guthridge has as a coach.

VASCO EVTIMOV (6-10, 230 lbs., SO, PF, #54, 1.5 ppg, 1.4 rpg, 3.8 minutes, .387 FG, .769 FT in 1996-97, Long Island Lutheran, N.Y./Sofia, Bulgaria). It would be easy to say that Evtimov returned from his year of military service a lean, mean fighting machine. That would all be true except for the fact that he served in the French Army.

But Evtimov returned to Chapel Hill this summer about 20 pounds lighter and with a different game than when he left last August for his compulsory military duty. A native of Bulgaria but with French citizenship, Evtimov talked his way into a 10-month stint in France instead of a 16-month stint in Bulgaria.

He missed last year's Final Four season, but now has no further obligations; he can get on with his college and professional career. Evtimov's father was a star basketball player in France.

The most difficult thing about last year for Evtimov was keeping up with the Tar Heels' progress as best he could from his outpost near the Spanish border. He had a fairly cushy assignment of doing little more than playing some basketball for the French junior national team, some pickup soccer and volleyball games, and learning how to shoot a rifle.

"I got off easy," Evtimov told the *News and Observer* of Raleigh (N.C.).

The military brass literally didn't know what to do with the oversized enlistee. They didn't have a uniform, boots or a bed big enough to fit him. He was given an apartment off base and an off-the-rack suit, which he had to wear just like a regulation uniform.

Evtimov did spent a good bit of his time playing for the French junior national team, which helped him shed some pounds and refine his game. He helped the French team to a fifth-place finish in the junior world championships in Sicily.

Now, the former McDonald's All-America believes he has the necessary skills to step in and replace Jamison at power forward, using his improved strength and size to muscle in for rebounds and easy shots. Before he left, Evtimov had shooting guard skills in a power forward body. He frustrated the Tar Heels' staff by taking horrible outside shots and trying to make passes that even Larry Bird couldn't complete.

The staff was in the process of rebuilding that game when Evtimov decided to get his military commitment out of the way and take last year off. Last season was considered a redshirt year, and he will have three years of eligibility remaining.

RONALD CURRY (6-3, 180 lbs., FR, G, #22, 21.9 ppg, 5.5 rpg, 5.7 apg, Hampton HS/Hampton, Va.). Even at North Carolina, where superstars arrive and depart the athletic department on a regular basis, few players have generated the interest of this two-sport star from Virginia.

How else do you explain Guthridge showing up for the first day of football practice? He brought his entire staff out to watch the proceedings, as Curry, the *Parade* High School National Football Player of the Year and the McDonald's National High School Basketball Player of the Year, became the school's first player recruited to play both sports.

He is actually attending UNC on a football scholarship, which he signed last March after reneging on the verbal commitment he made to Virginia in September. It was strongly hinted that Curry made that commitment just to keep recruiters off his back during basketball season.

It seemed to work until the heat turned up on Virginia coach Jeff Jones, who was eventually asked to leave as head coach of his alma mater. Then the recruiting fires re-lit for Curry.

The gridiron hero Florida State football coach Bobby Bowden called the "greatest high school player he's ever seen" still considered Virginia in his final choice, but also took a look at North Carolina and FSU, two places at which he wanted to play both sports.

He finally settled on the Tar Heels, where longtime friend Jason Capel had already signed a letter of intent. His mailbox was soon filled with hate mail from Virginia followers, including a death threat or two, but Curry was unfazed.

He arrived on campus to much hoopla, only a week after he and Capel led their team to its second consecutive AAU national championship. That finished off a staggering list of high-school accomplishments: three consecutive Virginia 3A football titles, another state basketball title and two national championships in the summer with MVP performances strung throughout.

Curry has been asked almost every single day since he became a two-sport star in high school, which he likes better, basketball or football. The general consensus is that he is a better football player, but sees a greater future on the hardwood. Florida State's Charlie Ward went down the same path, and he had a Heisman Trophy in his back pocket.

Curry says he will decide one day between the two, but no time soon. "That's why I came to college, to find out what my niche is," he said.

Curry's football debut didn't take long. He was forced into the lineup on UNC's first possession of its season-opener, when senior quarterback Oscar Davenport suffered a knee injury on the fourth play of the game. Curry had elevated himself to second-team quarterback during the summer, moving ahead of two older players. One of those players left the team, while the other fought it out with another true freshman for third-team duties.

Curry showed why he was named the *Parade* High School Football Player of the Year in that first appearance, completing 12 of 14 passes in one stretch and throwing his first career touchdown pass. With Guthridge sweating profusely, Curry also showed he could scramble, eluding unblocked tacklers with his speed and agility.

Will he make the same kind of impact in basketball? Maybe...if he survives the football season behind a very shaky offensive line.

Though he has been nothing but a point guard during his all-star basketball career, Curry is not about to supplant Cota at that position. But there is a huge opening at shooting guard, one Curry could step into immediately when he finishes with football.

Curry has a soft-spoken demeanor, but has been under intense scrutiny almost since he was featured in his first newspaper feature story as a sixth-grader. He hopes he will fade into the background as a freshman at UNC, which is highly unlikely.

The first few weeks, however, he was able to keep to himself.

"Not many students have said much to me," Curry said in his first interview. "I did a lot of stuff before, but right now I am a regular student. I am not a star here."

Not yet, anyway.

1998-99 NORTH CAROLINA SCHEDULE

Month	Date	Opponent
Nov.	13	Appalachian State
	16-27	#Florida International
	23	@Hampton
	30	@Middle Tennessee State
Dec.	4	*Old Dominion
	5	*College of Charleston
	8	Buffalo
	12	UNC Charlotte
	17	Louisville
	19	@Dartmouth
	22	@Georgia Tech
	29	@California
Jan.	2	Clemson
	6	@Florida State
	13	Maryland
	16	@North Carolina State
	21	Virginia
	23	@Wake Forest
	27	@Duke
	31	Georgia Tech
Feb.	4	@Clemson
	7	Florida State
	13	@Maryland
	17	North Carolina State
	20	@Virginia
	23	Wake Forest
	27	Duke
Mar.	4-7	##ACC Tournament

@ Road Games
* Food Lion Classic, Charlotte, NC
# Chase NIT (If the Tar Heels advance, they will face either the College of Charleston or Georgia on Nov. 18. Semifinals and finals are Nov. 26 & 28 at Madison Square Garden, NY)
Charlotte Coliseum, Charlotte, NC

KEY RESERVES

BRIAN BERSTICKER (6-11, 205 lbs., SO, F/C, #50, 2.6 ppg, 1.3 rpg, 4.6 minutes, .556 FG, Kempsville HS/ Virginia Beach, Va.). Bersticker proved he could dunk last year. And he can whoop and holler with the best players in the country. He contributed more than any other freshman besides Brendan Haywood, but that's not saying much.

So, the question this year is simple: Can Bersticker play in the frontcourt of a top-tier ACC team?

No one found that out last season, when Bersticker was a somewhat lightly regarded recruit playing behind the best player in the country. Bersticker saw action in 19 games, but rarely when it counted.

The coaches like the fact that Bersticker can run the floor, block shots and step outside to hit the 15-foot jumper. He has even bulked up a little over the summer.

Some recruiters called him soft and immediately labeled him a project when he arrived in Chapel Hill. It's true he can't do all the things that Jamison did; but, then, who can?

TERRENCE NEWBY (6-2, 210 lbs., JR, G, #21, 1.2 ppg, 0.2 rpg, 3.9 minutes, .444 FG, .750 3PT, .250 FT, Jordan-Matthews HS/Siler City, N.C.). This is the all-star football player who chose basketball, instead of the other way around, *a la* Ronald Curry. Newby, an All-State selection as a defensive back in high school, will likely benefit the most from Curry's success on the gridiron.

That's because the junior point guard will see more playing time behind Cota, at least until Curry is in basketball shape.

So far, Newby has been little more than a practice player for the Tar Heels, despite arriving at the same time as Cota. He was a football player trying to play basketball, and it wasn't very graceful. He saw less time than any other player on the team two years ago and barely saw an increase in that last year.

Newby can score—he hit six of his eight three-point shots last year in mop-up duty—but he has shown little ability to run the offense, either handling the ball or passing it. With Cota as the only guard on the team with any experience at all, Newby will have to contribute some minutes without being a liability on the court, especially until Curry arrives.

MICHAEL BROOKER (6-6, 200 lbs., SO, #11, 0.6 ppg, 0.5 rpg, 3.7 minutes, .211 FG, .200 3PT, .500 FT, Brentwood Academy, Tenn./Sandersville, Ga.). Brooker was recruited to provide some outside shooting for the Tar Heels, which they will sorely need this year with the departure of Williams and Carter. Brooker has seen precious little action in real games, however, mainly because he is not as athletic as the superstars in front of him.

So far, he has been mostly a practice player and another ecstatic member of the Tar Heels' celebration bunch that was so criticized last year. When he has played, Brooker has not shown the ability to knock down the three-pointer the way he does in practice. He is mostly a standstill shooter, someone who has to have his feet set before he can put up a shot. That doesn't fit well into a motion offense.

Brooker really hasn't been the same since he tore the anterior cruciate ligament in his right knee during a pickup game in his senior year in high school. He was forced to redshirt his freshman season because of it.

This year, he will get the chance to supply some of the outside shooting that Williams provided. He'll be more effective if he can create some of those shots for himself.

MAX OWENS (6-4, 190 lbs., SO, G, #24, 1.4 ppg, 0.8 rpg, 3.5 minutes, .387 FG, .273 3PT, .500 FT, Mt. Zion Academy, N.C./Macon, Ga.). By all accounts, Owens is an outstanding outside player with decent shooting skills, capable ballhandling abilities and the potential to be a strong defender. However, few people saw that in his debut season for the Tar Heels, when most of his shots were alarmingly forced.

Owens, like the rest of the highly touted freshman class, was a spectator most of the season, averaging a little more three minutes in his 20 appearances. Like so many other highly touted high school stars who don't make an immediate impact with the Tar Heels, Owens was rumored to be transferring after his freshman year.

Those rumors proved to be groundless, and that's a good thing for the Tar Heels. With Shammond Williams gone and Curry on football duty, the Heels desperately need help on the perimeter, Owens has to convert his potential into productivity.

That might take a while. Owens missed much of his senior season in high school with a broken leg and made few contributions last year. He essentially has two years of rust to scrape off his game before he can be an effective player for UNC. Early reports are that he has, and that Owens could even open the season in the starting lineup.

JASON CAPEL (6-8, 218 lbs., FR, F/G, #25, 20.2 ppg, 12.0 rpg, St. John's Prospect Hall/Chesapeake, Va.). Capel has the chance to be the most heralded freshman in the country this season, thanks to the absence of Jamison and Carter. Just like when Jerry Stackhouse and Rasheed Wallace left school early and the door was opened for Jamison, Capel has the opportunity to step in immediately and show off the talents that made him one of the most highly sought-after high school players in the country last year.

Capel, the younger brother of former Duke star Jeff Capel and youngest son of Old Dominion head coach Jeff Capel, has the proper lineage to be a collegiate superstar. He absorbed the game for years around the family household, then refined his considerable knowledge of the game at St. John's Prospect Hall, where he helped his team to an undefeated regular season and a No. 1 ranking in the final *USA Today* poll. The *Parade* All-America scored 22 points in the McDonald's game.

How much success Capel has in college, however, could depend on his balky back. Ever since he had a growth spurt in the seventh grade—six inches in 14 weeks—Capel has been bothered by a bulging disk. It's a problem that could probably be corrected by surgery, but his father doesn't think that is a good idea for an 18-year-old.

Capel has been inspected by numerous physicians, including the team doctors at UNC, and they all say it is a problem that won't get worse. But it can be painful, especially when he sits for long periods of time. Capel, who had a special desk for his use at Prospect Hall, missed his first couple of individual workouts with the Tar Heel coaches in September because his back was sore from sitting in class all day.

The elder Capel said the back troubles don't affect his son's game. It certainly didn't seem to hinder Jason this summer, when he and Curry teamed up on the same team to win their second consecutive AAU national championship.

Now that Jason is at UNC, Jeff Capel Sr. is less concerned than ever.

"He's in a position now where he is going to get a lot of help and treatment," dad said. "His back is better than it has been in the last two years. He's really starting to work on his flexibility and strengthening his abdomen to take the strain off his back."

Guthridge and his staff will have to take special precautions all year long to make sure Capel can play at 100 percent, even if that means holding him out every now and then. But, when he's able to play, Jason should be a heavy contributor to the program, though his father doesn't want the expectations to be too high.

"He wants to play right away, no question," the elder Capel said. "He still has to fit in first and pay his dues. You can't go in expecting that, you have to earn it."

KRIS LANG (6-10, 225 lbs., FR, F/C, #42, 18.0 ppg, 12.0 rpg, Hunter Huss HS/Gastonia, N.C.). Generally regarded as the best senior in North Carolina last year, Lang is the least known of the three incoming freshmen—a group rated the second-best recruiting class in the conference behind Wake Forest. And he was still a McDonald's All-America.

Lang should be able to help inside, where the Tar Heels will be looking at several people to replace Jamison and Ndiaye. If he adds some more bulk—he did put on 10 pounds of muscle during the summer—Lang figures he will be ready to play at the highest level of competition.

"I am not an idiot," Lang told the *Greensboro News and Record*. "I need to get bigger to bump in the ACC and last the whole season."

He spent the summer working out at a Gastonia YMCA, trying to beef up. He didn't exactly enjoy it, but, when the UNC coaches suggest a summer workout regimen, the tone doesn't sound as if it is optional.

Lang, who played on the same AAU team as current teammate Brendan Haywood and UNC freshman football player Julius Peppers, needs that additional size if he wants to get playing time this season. He is a good defender, but he won't win many battles in the ACC just because he is taller than his opponent.

As a high school senior, Lang was hampered in January with an elbow injury. But he finished strongly, averaging 24 points and 14 rebounds in his team's final 13 games.

OTHER RETURNEES

BRAD FREDERICK (6-5, 190 lbs., SR, G/F, #35, 0.4 ppg, 0.6 rpg, 4.6 minutes, .333 FG, .500 FT, Lawrence HS/Lawrence, Kan.). Like a few others before him, Frederick has come through the Tar Heels archaic junior varsity program to become a solid contributor on the team. He won't get as many minutes as Pearce Landry did a few years ago to help UNC reach the 1995 Final Four, but Guthridge has no fear of calling on Frederick in sticky situations.

This is his third year with the varsity after playing one year on the JV team, coached by Phil Ford.

A former cross-country champion in Kansas, Frederick won the heart of former coach Dean Smith by setting the record in the team's annual mile run. Then again, there always seemed to be a place for Frederick, since he is also the son of long-time Smith friend Bob Frederick, the athletics director at Kansas.

Still, the younger Frederick earned his spot on the team with his own abilities, which include being a good defender, a decent shooter and a calming influence on a sometimes out of control bench.

ORLANDO MELENDEZ (6-8, 190 lbs., FR, F, #32, 1.3 ppg, 0.3 rpg, 3.5 minutes, McDowell County HS, ?state?/Juana Diaz, P.R.). Melendez is almost as gifted as he is raw. The athletic leaper who could challenge Vince Carter in dunking exhibitions at practice had very little experience playing the game when he arrived at McDowell County High School from Puerto Rico.

He was a late addition to the Tar Heel recruiting class two years ago, only the second player in 36 years of coaching Dean Smith recruited without watching in person. Smith relied on Guthridge's scouting report.

Melendez was impressive athletically when he arrived on campus. But he needs to be stronger before be can be a regular contributor.

He saw some duty in his first three games at UNC, but suffered a soft tissue injury in his left foot just before the Tar Heels left for Alaska. That injury was slow to heal, and Melendez decided in January to seek a medical redshirt.

It was probably just as well. He needed the extra seasoning.

SCOTT WILLIAMS (5-11, 156 lbs., SR, G, #4, 0.2 ppg, 0.2 rpg, 1.7 minutes, .333 FG, .250 FT, Lawrence HS/Lawrence, Kan.). As practice players go, Williams does a good impersonation of the opposing point guard when the Tar Heels are preparing for games. He is even able to give a few minutes on the floor, which is about all you can ask of a walkon who spent two years with the junior varsity.

But Williams, who scored three points all of last year, has a very loyal following. Every now and then, his dad comes to watch his son play for the Tar Heels, which always creates a little stir in Chapel Hill since dad is Kansas coach (and former long-time UNC assistant) Roy Williams.

OTHER NEWCOMERS

None.

QUESTIONS

Experience? Six players scored 90 percent of UNC's points and had 90 percent of its rebounds last year. Only two of those players return. The holes will have to be filled by a talented, but inexperienced group of underclassmen.

Outside shooting? Carter, Williams and even Jamison accounted for nearly three-quarters of the team's three-pointers last year. Some unproven shooters are going to have to step forward to replace that production.

Rotations? Everyone knew where they belonged on last year's team. Guthridge will have to find out in the early part of this season who fits best into which roles. Then he will have to change things around when Curry arrives from his stint with the football team. It should make for an interesting November and December.

ANSWERS

Talent! C'mon, do you seriously believe the cupboard is bare? It still takes two hands to count the number of high school All-Americas on the Tar Heels roster. They have more than any other team besides Duke.

Tradition! It's been 32 years since the Tar Heels finished any lower than third place in the ACC; 28 years since they didn't win 20 games; and 22 years since they were out of the NCAA Tournament. Those streaks didn't end after Stackhouse and Wallace went pro, and no one on this year's team wants them to end on their watch.

Depth! After playing the last two years with only six players, the Tar Heels will have as many as 10 guys from which to choose a regular rotation. Establishing who those regulars will be might take some time, but Guthridge isn't worried about it as long as he has a set rotation by the time the ACC schedule rolls around.

adidas Blue Ribbon Analysis

BACKCOURT	B+	BENCH/DEPTH	B+
FRONTCOURT	B	INTANGIBLES	A

Guthridge doesn't regret not getting his reserves more playing time last year. The Tar Heels were one of the best teams in the nation with only six regulars—a collection of experienced, talented players who didn't need to be off the court more than a few minutes at a time.

Now, however, four of those guys, including a pair of lottery-pick All-Americas, are gone. Few people, Guthridge among them, know what to expect out of the guys left behind. There is little returning scoring and significant worries for a worry-wart coach.

"It could be disastrous," Guthridge said. "We hope it won't be. We are going to work hard for it not to be."

That's always been the annoying thing about the Tar Heels. They always find a way to maintain top-tier status. You know the numbers: 32 years in the ACC's top three; 28 consecutive 20-win seasons; 24 straight NCAA Tournament appearances.

Guthridge understands the challenge of maintaining that tradition. He also knows that students once strung Dean Smith's likeness up a tree when they were dissatisfied with what he was doing.

He is not too worried about the same fate. Not much, anyway.

"As long as they do it in effigy," Guthridge said, "and not the real thing."

(T.P.)

adidas Blue Ribbon Analysis

GRADING SYSTEM

A+	equal to very best in country—Final Four-caliber unit
A	among the best in the land—worthy of deep NCAA run
B+	talented, versatile and experienced—NCAA-NIT ability
B	solid and productive winners—league and post-season contenders
C+	average to above-average—may contend in a weaker league
C	average to mediocre—second division in a strong league
D+	below average, inconsistent—second division in a weaker league
D	well below average—losing season virtually certain
F	non-Division I ability—an underdog every night

17
UCLA

LOCATION .... **Los Angeles, CA**
CONFERENCE **Pacific-10**
LAST SEASON .... **24-9 (.727)**
CONFERENCE RECORD .... **12-6 (3rd)**
STARTERS LOST/RETURNING **3/2**
NICKNAME .... **Bruins**
COLOR .... **Blue & Gold**
HOMECOURT .... **Pauley Pavilion (12,819)**
COACH .... **Steve Lavin (Chapman College, '88)**
RECORD AT SCHOOL .... **48-17 (2 yrs.)**
CAREER RECORD .... **48-17 (2 yrs.)**
ASSISTANTS .... **Michael Holton (UCLA '83)**
Jim Saia (Chapman College '87)
Steve Spencer (Sonoma State '85)
TEAM WINS (last 5 yrs.) **21-31-23-24-24**
RPI (last 5 yrs.) **31-2-24-8-13**
1997-98 FINISH .... **.Lost in NCAA Sweet 16.**

COACH AND PROGRAM

Steve Lavin, prone as he is to lyrical overstatement and colorful references to history and its characters, must be afforded a break on this one. When he says he's looking forward to the start of this season—his third as head coach at UCLA—because the spotlight is finally on basketball, he is not guilty of hyperbole.

Consider what Lavin, a former part-time aide, has endured as a novice head coach in college basketball's toastiest hot seat. He took over on the eve of the season two years ago after Jim Harrick—the man who hired him and just 19 months earlier had won an NCAA title—was fired for falsifying expense account reports.

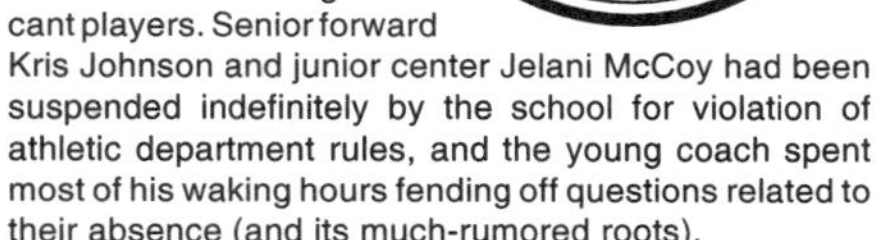

Things were hardly more settled a year ago, when Lavin began the season without two of his most significant players. Senior forward Kris Johnson and junior center Jelani McCoy had been suspended indefinitely by the school for violation of athletic department rules, and the young coach spent most of his waking hours fending off questions related to their absence (and its much-rumored roots).

Now all that controversy is gone, and Lavin is excited. Also gone, of course, are three of the most prolific players in school history. The program will miss graduated seniors Toby Bailey, J.R. Henderson and Johnson, but the coach is still excited. Heck, he is always excited.

"The biggest difference this year is we're not beginning the season in the midst of a crisis," Lavin said. "Our energies are being concentrated on coaching basketball." Lavin, who expects to be more efficient as a teacher on the floor without all the sideshow distractions, said the off-court hassles of the past two years have instilled a toughness in him and his staff.

"It was probably a blessing in disguise that our staff faced that kind of adversity," he said. "In terms of the maturing process, there's no better boot camp that you can go through to earn your stripes.

"We were never under the false pretense that it's going to be easy, because coaching in the '90s is a challenge. I don't think there's a lot I can see down the road that's going to throw me for a loop."

Through it all, Lavin never got the Bruins back to the Final Four, where Bailey, Henderson and Johnson played as freshmen. But he didn't let the ship go astray, either. UCLA won 24 games in each of Lavin's first two seasons, reaching the Final Eight two years ago, the Sweet 16 last March.

"One of the things we're most proud of is the fact that it would have been easy for the team to have an excuse to fail," Lavin said, alluding to Johnson's absence for the first four games along with McCoy's nine-game suspension and ultimate "retirement" from the program.

"The fact that we didn't let any of these hurdles give us an excuse or an 'out' to fail—instead, we win the conference the first year, then this past year go to the Sweet 16, and to not miss a beat in recruiting—that's what we're most proud of as a coaching staff."

This will be a new era of UCLA basketball, with young talent taking over for the three departed seniors. Bailey, Henderson and Johnson combined to average more than 55 points and 18 rebounds last year, and scored a collective 4,941 points in their UCLA careers. They won 102 games in four seasons.

"As basketball players, obviously you lose a great deal of experience and poise," Lavin said. "They played as a group in so many big games over their career. That kind of experience is something that's invaluable to a coach.

"As people, they really carved out some special chapters in the history of UCLA during their four years. They were part of some real highs and real lows here."

Now the Bruins move on, and they hope to do so as soon as possible with sophomore point guard Baron Davis. Davis' ability to come back from a serious knee injury in last year's NCAA Tournament will be central to the Bruins' hopes. He is a phenomenally talented player whose aggressive style on the floor lifts the entire team.

"He has an intensity level you can't teach to a player," Lavin said. "Either you have that competitive drive—that super-human level of intensity that the great athletes have—or you don't.

"Baron's one of those players with that enthusiasm, and there is a contagious effect. He has such an impact on the game."

As Davis rehabs, probably into December, the Bruins will be younger still. But as one talented class exits the university, Lavin welcomes what is considered perhaps the top recruiting group in the nation.

Center Dan Gadzuric, forward JaRon Rush and guard Ray Young all were McDonald's All-America game participants, and French import Jerome Moiso along with forward Matt Barnes are both recruits who would headline the class at most schools. *The Sporting News, Hoop Scoop, PrepStar* and *Basketball News* all proclaimed the UCLA freshman class as the best in the nation.

An ample sample of the gushing:

"This is a phenomenal class, coming on the heels of last year's that was ranked in everybody's top five," said Clark Francis, editor of the *Hoop Scoop* recruiting newsletter. "UCLA is at the top of the mountain right now. No one has recruited better the last couple of years."

"This is a Fab Five recruiting class for UCLA," added Bob Gibbons, who publishes the *All-Star Sports* recruiting newsletter. "This might be UCLA's best recruiting class since the Wooden era."

One prospective newcomer who apparently won't be with the team is 6-8 forward Patrick Ceresa, a member of the Swiss national team, who did not get academic clearance to play. The five remaining newcomers combine to give the Bruins 12 freshmen and sophomores on a 15-man roster. Reserve shooting guard Brandon Loyd is the club's only senior.

"We're probably the youngest team in the country," Lavin suggested.

Few are offering much pity to the Bruins, who have everything except experience. The newcomers all can play at the highest level, and the spring signing of Dutch-born Gadzuric, a physical 6-11, 240-pounder, provides the power in the middle the team otherwise was missing. Certainly there is plenty of speed, plenty of flash and dash.

There is a lot of talent to juggle and a host of egos to keep in line. But Lavin believes the mix will work well.

"A trait I see in all the young guys is competitiveness," Lavin said. "It's obviously a positive thing for the future of our program to have players who have come from great programs."

Lavin knows better than to expect that the season will come and go without a few bumps in the road. Anything short of a complete detour will be OK with him. However, he is optimistic about how this squad will evolve.

"I think it's a team that, as the year goes on, will be fun to watch in terms of their growth and development," he said. "There's no question we're a young basketball team. But it's a team that can make quantum leaps as the season goes on."

STARTERS NOT RETURNING

TOBY BAILEY (6-5, SG, 17.9 ppg, 5.9 rpg, 4.1 apg, 1.2 spg, 35.7 minutes, .443 FG, .423 3PT, .737 FT). One of three Bruins seniors who finished among the Pac-10's top eight scorers a year ago, Bailey was a flashy and versatile player who often rose up at the biggest moments in his career. He gained national notice by scoring 26 points as a freshman in UCLA's NCAA title game victory over Arkansas and, throughout his career, often moved over from his natural shooting guard spot to help at the point.

Bailey wound up No. 4 on the Bruins' career scoring list with 1,846 points, ranking second in three-point field goals (171), first in three-point attempts (501) and sixth in assists (458). He scored in double figures 94 times in his career and started 100 consecutive games. He recorded UCLA's first triple-double by logging 23 points, 10 rebounds and 10 assists as a sophomore against Stephen F. Austin.

Bailey was selected in the second round of the NBA draft, taken 45th overall by the Los Angeles Lakers, who subsequently traded his rights to the Phoenix Suns.

J.R. HENDERSON (6-9, PF, 19.0 ppg, 7.8 rpg, 1.2 spg, 33.1 minutes, .536 FG, .286 3PT, .638 FT). Henderson finished his career ranked in UCLA's top 10 in three major statistical categories—No. 6 in scoring (1,801 points), No. 10 in rebounding (818) and No. 8 in field-goal percentage (.549).

A two-time All-Pac-10 selection, Henderson scored in double figures 31 times in 33 games last season, and was third in the Pac-10 in scoring and sixth in rebounding. He led the team in scoring 13 times last season, including a career-high 32 points vs. Louisville.

Sometimes perceived as lazy because of his smooth, easy-going nature on the floor, Henderson was nonetheless a remarkably consistent performer. He reached double figures 95 times in his career.

Henderson was drafted 56th overall, in the second round, by the NBA's Vancouver Grizzlies.

KRIS JOHNSON (6-4, SF, 18.4 ppg, 5.1 rpg, 32.5 minutes, .519 FG, .409 3PT, .833 FT). Johnson missed the Bruins' first four games due to a suspension that media sources reported was the result of a violation of the school's substance abuse policy. He then returned and had his finest season, including a team-best 21.1 ppg in Pac-10 games.

The son of ex-UCLA great Marques Johnson, Kris developed into a strong inside-outside force for the Bruins. He became a dependable perimeter shooter, but also collected more than 400 rebounds in his college career. An honorable mention All-Pac-10 selection, Johnson was the conference's only player to rank among the top 10 in field goal, three-point and free throw percentages.

He led the team in scoring 15 times, including 14 of UCLA's final 23 games, and topped the 20-point mark 12 times in conference play. In NCAA Tournament play, he led the team with 25 points in a second-round victory over Michigan, then scored 18 points and had eight rebounds in a Sweet 16 loss to Kentucky.

Johnson finished his career with 1,294 points, and his lifetime .807 FT mark ranks sixth on the school's all-time list.

OTHERS NOT RETURNING

JELANI MCCOY (6-9, C, 9.9 ppg, 7.1 rpg, 1.6 bpg, 21.3 minutes in 15 appearances, .600 FG, .522 FT). The team's junior center sat out the start of the season after being suspended—along with Kris Johnson—for a violation of team rules, then played 15 games before quitting the program.

McCoy could have been the interior force the Bruins needed, but he never regained a spot in the starting lineup after his suspension. He often seemed distracted on the floor. Yet McCoy reached double figures in scoring six times and had four double-doubles.

Finally, on Feb. 15, he announced he was leaving the team, citing intense media scrutiny. Nonetheless, McCoy was the first of three UCLA players taken in the NBA draft, going 33rd overall to the Seattle Sonics.

KEVIN DALEY (6-6, F, 1.5 ppg, 0.8 rpg, 3.8 minutes, .444 FG, Artesia HS/Lakewood, Calif.). Daley transferred to Azusa Pacific, a Southern California-based NAIA school, at which he will be immediately eligible. Daley began his career at the University of Nevada-Reno, then transferred to UCLA, where he came off the bench in 11 games. He scored a season-high six points vs. Fullerton State.

VINCE MCGAUTHA (5-11, G, 0.5 ppg, 0.5 rpg, six appearances, .500 FG). A walkon guard, McGautha saw action in just six games last season after playing in 10 the year before. In his two-year UCLA career, he scored 10 total points.

PROJECTED STARTERS

EARL WATSON (6-2, 170 lbs., SO, SG, #25, 5.8 ppg,

3.7 rpg, 3.2 apg, 1.9 spg, 32.0 minutes, .392 FG, .323 3PT, .606 FT, Washington HS/Kansas City, Kan.). Watson was quietly effective as the "other" freshman in the Bruins' starting backcourt. He was the team's only player to start every game, and he played more minutes than any returnee on the roster.

"He may have been our most consistent basketball player last year from start to finish," Lavin suggested. "His contributions are quiet, kind of understated at times. But he's just very steady, especially on defense. He takes charges and has a knack for tracking down loose balls.

"I've never seen anybody his size who rebounds so well. He's got great timing and very strong hands."

Watson had four or more rebounds in 15 games, including efforts of nine vs. New Mexico and eight each against Northern Arizona and Arizona. He scored in double figures five times, including a career-high 15 points vs. rival Southern Cal, in which he hit six of eight shots from the field. Watson had 11 assists against Washington and 10 against Fullerton State, adding five or more steals on three occasions (including seven vs. Fullerton State).

He began his rookie season at the shooting guard spot, but was responsible for handling the ball more as the season progressed, allowing Baron Davis to move about on offense without the ball. Now, with Davis shelved to start the season, Watson's versatility will be critical for the Bruins.

"We can move him around anywhere on the perimeter," Lavin said. "He kind of reminds scouts of Maurice Cheeks."

Lavin has assigned Watson one other duty this season—serving as big brother to UCLA's five incoming freshmen.

"Earl was very homesick early in the year and considered leaving twice. I kid him that I had to sign him three times," Lavin said. "Once he got to the other side on that, that's where the growth took place.

"None of our five freshmen is from L.A., and Earl is in charge of dealing with homesickness. He's been down that path."

BARON DAVIS (6-2 1/2, 190 lbs., SO, PG, #5, 11.7 ppg, 4.0 rpg, 5.0 apg, 2.4 spg, 31.3 minutes, .529 FG, .308 3PT, .676 FT, Crossroads HS/Los Angeles, Calif.). Without much question, Davis was the top freshman guard in the country a year ago. If his rehab goes well and Davis regains his old form, he can make the Bruins special this year.

But when might that happen? UCLA is staying low-key on the topic, but quietly hopes Davis will be ready to go at some point in December.

"The doctors have purposefully not set a target date," Lavin said, "because they're trying to make it clear that until the knee is ready, he won't play. I think Baron would obviously like to be back in early November...but he's making progress with his rehab."

Davis tore the anterior cruciate ligament in his left knee while landing after a spectacular dunk against Michigan in the second round of the NCAAs. Doctors were encouraged by a fairly "clean" situation in surgery, finding no surprises or complications during the procedure.

Before the injury, Davis was playing his best ball of the season. He averaged 12.2 ppg over his final five games, including 16 in the conference-closer against Arizona.

A starter in 31 of the 32 games he played, Davis scored in double figures 19 times, with high games of 22 points vs. Alabama-Birmingham, 21 vs. Washington State and 20 vs. Alaska-Anchorage.

Davis three times had nine assists in a game and combined 13 rebounds with 11 points at UNLV. He had a spectacular game against Northern Arizona, with 17 points, eight steals and six assists.

Davis' biggest drawback as a collegiate rookie was an aggressive nature Lavin believes will work in his favor over the long haul. Last year, however, Davis collected 113 personal fouls, fouling out of nine games, eight of them in Pac-10 play.

"He needs to work on moving his feet more and not gambling and lunging and reaching," Lavin said. "As a coach, you don't ever want to take away their aggressiveness. He just has to learn how to pick his spots.

"He'll probably be more effective at the (NBA) level because they allow the hand-checking, the bumping."

Davis was named Pac-10 Freshman of the Year and was selected to the *Basketball Times* Freshman All-America team.

DAN GADZURIC (6-11, 240 lbs., FR, C, #50, 21.0 ppg, 17.0 rpg, 7.0 bpg, Governor Dummer Academy, Ma./Dem Haag, Holland). The cornerstone of the Bruins' top-ranked recruiting class, Gadzuric is a native Holland, who played the past three seasons at Governor Dummer (Ma.) Academy.

Rated the top player in the nation by *PrepStar*, Gadzuric was a McDonald's All-America selection who scored 15 points in 20 minutes at the prestigious all-star game. He also was a first-team All-America pick by *Parade* and *Slam*, and a third-team choice by *Basketball Weekly*.

"He's kind of a throwback to the old school, traditional low-post player," Lavin said. "He likes to play with his back to the basket. He wants to get the ball on the low block, and he likes to set screens. He wants to take everything hard to the iron, and that's a real positive because we haven't had anyone like that since (George) Zidek."

Most importantly, Gadzuric gives the Bruins a big body to match against the Pac-10's best post players.

"His skill level still has a lot of areas that need work," Lavin said. "But he's a big, strong low-post center, and that's critical in our league—with Stanford and their 49ers' offensive line up front, and Washington with (Todd) MacCulloch."

The recruiting crowd loves Gadzuric's up side.

"Gadzuric is the best big man in the country," said Gibbons of *All-Star Sports*. "He's a tremendous addition (for UCLA). He's the best pure center UCLA has had for a while, maybe going back to the (Bill) Walton days.

"Gadzuric is a strong rebounder and shot blocker and will give the Bruins a physical presence inside, something they've been lacking for the last couple of years," Gibbons added. "Gadzuric has a mature body...he's not your typical incoming college freshman."

JARON RUSH (6-7, 215 lbs., FR, SF, #4, 32.0 ppg, 13.2 rpg, 4.6 apg, 4.0 spg, Pembroke Hill HS/Kansas City, Mo.). A first-team McDonald's and *Parade* All-America selection, Rush is a wing who plays the game with aggression and at a fast pace. "He plays with a kind of reckless abandon," Lavin said. "When he plays, it's just all out."

A former AAU summer league teammate of Earl Watson, Rush figures to compete immediately for a starting job at the wing. Don't be surprised if he instantly becomes the team's top scorer.

"He's like Walter Davis," Lavin said, referring to the ex-NBA star and North Carolina All-America. "It's just so easy for him to score. There are a lot of ways he can get you.

"It's unusual to have that kind of arsenal of offensive weapons. He has the ability to shoot beyond the three-point line. Obviously, he can beat people off the dribble and finish as well as any freshman I've seen. He also can play with his back to the basket and he has a nice mid-range jumper."

Lavin said, as with most freshmen, that Rush's biggest challenge will be adjusting to playing defense.

"All players go through a learning curve," the coach said. "In terms of his ability to play defense, 80 to 90 percent of defense is your heart, being mentally tough."

A finalist for the Naismith Prep Player of the Year award and the nation's top wing prospect, according to *PrepStar* magazine, Rush led his team to the Missouri state 2A title. In the state championship game, he had 26 points, nine rebounds and six blocked shots. He also excelled on the postseason all-star circuit, scoring 18 points at the Hoop Summit and 19 in the McDonald's All-America game.

Rush averaged 27.5 ppg, 12.3 rpg and 4.0 spg as a junior on a 32-0 team that won the state title. He scored 27.3 ppg as a sophomore and 27.2 ppg as a freshman. In four varsity high school seasons, he scored 3,387 points—second in Missouri state history—and led Pembroke HS to a combined record of 112-9. He also had 485 assists and 540 steals.

Rush originally committed to Kansas, then changed his thinking in the spring while opting for UCLA.

TRAVIS REED (6-7, 220 lbs., SO, PF, #13, 4.0 ppg, 2.4 rpg, 12.1 minutes, .523 FG, .333 FT, A.B. Miller HS/Fontana, Calif.). Lavin calls him "the X-factor," and hopes Reed can indeed emerge as a significant factor this season. He has lost weight since last year, added strength and averaged 25 points per game in an L.A. summer league.

"He has a good feel for the game and a knack for scoring," Lavin said. "He played well for us at the end of the season."

Reed scored 11 points in the Bruins' second-round NCAA victory over Michigan, hitting four of five shots from the field. He also delivered an eight-point effort in a mid-conference detour to Duke.

He began the year on a roll, averaging 9.0 ppg over the first five games, including back-to-back 14-point performances against New Mexico and Fullerton State.

1997-98 RESULTS

#North Carolina (L)	68-109	
#Alaska-Anchorage	92-68	
#Alabama-Birmingham	86-72	
##New Mexico	69-58	
Fullerton State	120-91	
Northern Arizona	90-68	
Saint Louis	73-67	
Boise State	81-75	
@UNLV	65-57	
Illinois	74-69	
@Arizona (L)	75-87	
@Arizona State	78-73	
Oregon State	90-72	
Oregon	68-66	
@California	74-73	
@Stanford (L)	80-93	
Southern California	101-84	
Louisville	88-82	
Washington State	88-68	
Washington	105-94	
@Oregon (L)	81-97	
@Oregon State	84-75	
Stanford (L)	81-84	
California	87-84	
@Southern California	82-75	ot
@Duke (L)	84-120	
@Washington State	78-75	
@Washington (L)	94-95	
Arizona State	102-94	
Arizona (L)	87-91	
%Miami	65-62	
%Michigan	85-82	
%%Kentucky (L)	68-94	

@ away games
\# Carrs Great Alaska Shootout, Anchorage, AK
\## John Wooden Classic, Anaheim, CA
% NCAA South Sub-Regional, Atlanta, GA
%% NCAA South Regional, St. Petersburg, FL

KEY RESERVES

RICO HINES (6-4, 210 lbs., SO, G, #22, 1.9 ppg, 1.5 rpg, 10.6 minutes, .341 FG, .308 3PT, .550 FT, Hargrave Military Academy, Va./Greenville, N.C.). Hines developed into a defensive stopper off the bench for the Bruins, and also delivered a key offensive lift in several games.

"Rico played real well for us early and, at the end of the season, made good contributions," Lavin said. "He's a great leader. In every game, he just gives us an unbelievable kind of effort."

Hines played in 23 games, scoring a career-high nine points—including a pair of big three-pointers—in the Bruins' home win over California. "Otherwise, we don't win that game," Lavin said.

Lavin also credits Hines with an excellent defensive performance in the NCAA opener vs. Miami, during which his 20-minute stint included taking a pair of charges. As a sophomore, Hines should compete for a bigger role on the club.

BRANDON LOYD (5-10, 182 lbs., SR, G, #20, 1.3 ppg, 0.3 rpg, 7.5 minutes, .417 FG, .455 3PT, .667 FT, Memorial HS/Tulsa, Okla.). The team's lone senior, Loyd will provide experience and a deep shooting threat, although his skills are somewhat limited.

"He can be invaluable because he's been through the battles," Lavin said. "He's like a hired gun who can come off the bench and shoot the three."

His season high a year ago was nine points against North Carolina, although he scored a career-high 12 vs. Oregon State as a sophomore. Loyd struggled as a true freshman, converting just 27 percent of his three-pointers, but has improved each year, hiking his career accuracy to .363.

BILLY KNIGHT (6-5, 180 lbs., SO, G/F, #3, 2.8 ppg, 0.9 rpg, 6.0 minutes, .444 FG, .387 3PT, .727 FT, Westchester HS/Los Angeles, Calif.). Lavin hopes Knight can evolve into a dependable long-range weapon off the bench.

"Billy Knight's the kind of guy who can come in and

break a game open," said Lavin, who believes Knight and senior Brandon Loyd can both have that effect on things. "He will really help our inside-outside attack. We started him one game and he got 15 points."

That was against Fullerton State, a contest in which he hit six of nine shots—including three of six from beyond the arc—in a 26-minute performance. He also had nine points against Oregon State, converting two of three long-range shots.

Knight's biggest challenge will be to improve his defensive play, and Lavin said he has worked to upgrade his quickness.

RYAN BAILEY (6-3, 200 lbs., SO, G, #21, 8.4 ppg, 4.0 rpg, 113 assists, 34.0 minutes, .408 FG, .270 3PT, .575 FT at Penn State in 1996-97, Loyola HS/Los Angeles, Calif.). Toby's little brother, "Moose," becomes eligible this season after sitting out a year ago as a walkon transfer from Penn State. The starting point guard for the Nittany Lions as a freshman, Bailey could get the chance to play early if Davis is not ready to go.

"I don't think people have an idea of how good a player Ryan Bailey is," Lavin said. "My guess is he and Matt Barnes will be the biggest surprises from a fan's perspective. People have forgotten about him. He's kind of the unknown."

Lavin said Bailey will also get the chance to play shooting guard, but that his greatest contribution likely will come at the point—especially while Davis is on the shelf.

"He's strong, he plays great pressure defense," Lavin said. "He's really improved at penetrating and creating for others. And, for someone his size, he finishes real well around the basket."

Bailey, who scored a season-high 16 points in a win over Bradley two years ago, tied a Penn State freshman record with 113 assists. He started 24 games and averaged 34 minutes after senior Dan Earl was sidelined by a degenerative disk problem in his back and fellow backup Titus Ivory broke his foot.

JEROME MOISO (6-11, 225 lbs., FR, C, #0, Milford Academy, Conn./Guadeloupe, West Indies). First recruited by the Bruins a year-and-a-half ago, Moiso—pronounced Moe-ee-zoe—attended Milford (Conn.) Academy last year to settle his academics. He is a native of Guadeloupe, an island in the West Indies, and a graduate of The INSEP School in Paris.

"He's as skilled a player as anybody in his class—not only in the U.S., but overseas," Lavin said. "He's got very unusual skills for a 6-11 player. He's got instincts and court vision and an ability to pass. He can dribble the ball, he's got an amazing vertical jump and he runs the floor like a wing player."

The Sporting News rated Moiso as the nation's No. 8 center prospect a year ago. The UCLA coaching staff first saw him at the 1997 Hoop Summit international all-star game, where the lefthander had 14 points on 7-for-8 shooting. This past season he played in the Eddie Jones All-Star Classic, where he collected nine points and 11 rebounds.

A forward on the French junior national team, Moiso is regarded as a tremendous shot blocker, but a relatively raw offensive player. Again, though, his potential has basketball people excited.

"Listening to NBA scouts," Lavin said, "some of them feel he can be as strong a post prospect as anyone who's out there."

A year ago, there was some thought—even at *Blue Ribbon*—that Moiso would compete at a Bruin during the latter stages of the 1997-98 season. Instead, he enters 1998-99 with four full season of eligibility.

RAY YOUNG (6-4, 200 lbs., FR, G, #34, 15.0 ppg, 4.0 apg, 4.0 spg at St. Joseph-Notre Dame HS/Alameda, Calif.). The top player to emerge from St. Joseph HS since Jason Kidd, Young is a high-flying shooting guard who played in the McDonald's All-America game with Rush and Gadzuric. Particularly comfortable in an up-tempo game, Young should compete for playing time from the start this season.

"He's someone who, defensively, I think can really help us," Lavin said. "He's a great competitor, plays the game very hard. He wants to work on his jump shot, but he can help us in transition. It's very similar to what Toby (Bailey) had to go through.

"But his strength is defense, and his ability to get into the open court and finish."

As a senior, Young was named the Gatorade Circle of Champions Pacific Region and California Player of the Year, and was a second-team *Parade* magazine All-America pick. Entering the season, he was the No. 2 vote-getter in the *Long Beach Press-Telegram* annual "Best in the West" poll.

Young averaged 17.8 ppg and 7.0 rpg as a junior for a program regarded as the best in Northern California the past half-dozen years. The Pilots compiled a record of 110-17 during Young's four seasons, winning the Northern California title and reaching the state championship game each of the past two seasons.

Young finished his prep career with 1,888 points.

MATT BARNES (6-7, 215 lbs., FR, F, #23, 26.5 ppg, 12.5 rpg, 5.5 apg, 5.8 bpg, Del Campo HS/Fair Oaks, Calif.). An early signee with the Bruins, Barnes was a *Long Beach Press-Telegram* first-team "Best in the West" selection. Also a talented tight end who caught 19 touchdown passes for the Del Campo football team, Barnes is considered a versatile wing player with the ability to post-up, drive the ball to the basket or shoot from the perimeter.

"He's got unbelievable versatility," said Lavin, comparing Barnes to Scottie Pippen and J.R. Henderson. "He's probably most comfortable as a point guard, (as) he sees the floor so well. He loves to pass the ball, which is refreshing."

No doubt, Barnes will be given a great chance to carve out significant playing time right from the start. His ability to play two or three positions adds to his value.

OTHER RETURNEES

SEAN FARNHAM (6-6, 205 lbs., JR, F, #30, 0.1 ppg, 1.1 rpg, nine appearances, De La Salle HS/Clayton, Calif.). A walkon who has helped provide depth in practice, Farnham played in just nine games last year, totaling 25 minutes, 10 rebounds and one point. His role this season is unlikely to change.

MATT HARBOUR (6-1 1/2, 180 lbs., JR, G, #15, 1.2 ppg, 1.0 rpg, eight appearances, .333 FG, Sabino HS/Camarillo, Calif.). A walkon who played in eight games last year and 13 over two seasons, Harbour will continue to be utilized as primarily a practice player. He has played a total of 24 minutes in his UCLA career, scoring 10 points.

TODD RAMASAR (6-5, 200 lbs., SO, G/F, #11, 0.2 ppg, 0.5 rpg, six appearances, Riverside North HS/Corona, Calif.). A walkon guard, Ramasar played in six games last season, scoring just one point. He will continue to make his most meaningful contributions on practice days.

1998-99 UCLA SCHEDULE

Nov.	19	Santa Clara
	26-29	#Puerto Rico Shootout
Dec.	2	Delaware State
	5	*John Wooden Classic
	12	Nevada-Las Vegas
	19	Northridge State
	23	American
	29	Loyola Marymount
Jan.	2	Arizona
	4	Arizona State
	7	@Oregon State
	9	@Oregon
	14	California
	16	Stanford
	20	@Southern California
	23	@Louisville
	28	@Washington State
	31	@Washington
Feb.	4	Oregon
	7	Oregon State
	11	@Stanford
	13	@California
	17	Southern California
	21	Syracuse
	25	Washington State
	27	Washington
Mar.	4	@Arizona State
	6	@Arizona

@ Road Games
* John Wooden Classic, Anaheim Pond, Anaheim, CA
# Bayamone, PR (vs. San Francisco, first round; also American University-PR, Colorado, Kentucky, Maryland, Pittsburgh and Xavier)

OTHER NEWCOMERS

None.

QUESTIONS

Inexperience? The "Baby Bruins" begin the season minus five players who held key roles a year ago—departed seniors Toby Bailey, J.R. Henderson and Kris Johnson, along with junior center Jelani McCoy and recovering point guard Baron Davis. There is just a single senior on the roster, and virtually every key player is in his first or second year of college. The team must grow up fast.

Muscle? The Bruins have been a speed and finesse team for years now, but the 1998-99 squad is especially short on power. It will be left to Dutch freshman center Dan Gadzuric to provide the muscle necessary when teams such as Stanford and Washington visit Pauley Pavilion.

Baron Davis? How soon will the sophomore point guard recover from the knee injury he suffered in last year's NCAA Tournament? Can the Bruins find an adequate replacement in the interim? Will Davis be his old explosive self upon his return? All these questions will help dictate UCLA's fortunes.

ANSWERS

Young talent! UCLA's freshman class—with talent assembled from two states and two foreign countries—may be the best in the country. Add that to a strong corps of sophomores, and there may not be a team in the nation that could beat the Bruins in an under-20 showdown.

Quickness! As usual, the Bruins will be at their best on the run. The sophomore backcourt of Baron Davis and Earl Watson is fleet, but will have to lace on their track shoes to outrun the likes of newcomers JaRon Rush and Ray Young. When the pace quickens, the Bruins should be fun to watch.

Baron Davis! Yeah...him again. When Davis does make it back—and *if* he is whole—he provides the Bruins with a floor leader who will instantly make them better. *Much* better. With its youthful makeup, UCLA figures to come together gradually. That process will be dramatically accelerated when Davis takes the reins again.

adidas Blue Ribbon Analysis

BACKCOURT	**B+**	**BENCH/DEPTH**	**B+**
FRONTCOURT	**B**	**INTANGIBLES**	**B**

UCLA may not look very good at times. The Bruins will make youthful mistakes, will play out of control in stretches and may be overmatched defensively and on the boards on occasion.

And then, look out! When this team gets it together, when the young players dab the moisture behind their ears, Baron Davis returns off the injured list and the rookie talent gains veteran confidence, these guys could be scary.

For years now, UCLA has been a bit unpredictable in this way. The Bruins can be as fluid and graceful as a ballet, or as awkward as a four-year-old on roller skates. There was a bit less of this inconsistency a year ago, with a veteran squad, but there may be a bit more this season with so many newcomers.

But this team will grow throughout the year, aided greatly by better depth than it's had the past two seasons.

"This year, we can simulate game conditions in practice," Lavin said. "Last year, with the disparity (in talent) between the starters and the reserves, that didn't prepare you. Now we're competitive at every position on the floor."

The practice environment is even something Lavin discussed with prospects during his recruiting last year.

"There will be no country club memberships, and that's a real positive thing for us," he said. "We talked with recruits about the fact that if you're worried about the competition, who's behind you, who's next to you, this isn't the place to come."

Juggling that quantity of talent will be a new experience for Lavin. But he sees only the up side.

"It's a team that, by the NCAA Tournament, is going to want to be competitive with the elite programs in the country," Lavin said.

No doubt, the Bruins should be fun to watch. Not always pretty, but always fun.

(J.F.)

18

SYRACUSE

LOCATION	Syracuse, NY
CONFERENCE	Big East
LAST SEASON	26-9 (.743)
CONFERENCE RECORD	12-6 (1st, Big East 7)
STARTERS LOST/RETURNING	2/3
NICKNAME	Orangemen
COLORS	Orange & Blue
HOMECOURT	Carrier Dome (33,000)
COACH	Jim Boeheim (Syracuse '66)
RECORD AT SCHOOL	528-181 (22 yrs.)
CAREER RECORD	528-181 (22 yrs.)
ASSISTANTS	Bernie Fine (Syracuse '67)
	Louis Orr (Syracuse '80)
	Mike Hopkins (Syracuse '93)
TEAM WINS (last 5 yrs.)	23-20-20-19-26
RPI (last 5 yrs.)	16-28-9-60-15
1997-98 FINISH	Lost in NCAA Sweet 16.

COACH AND PROGRAM

Given Jim Boeheim's reputation as a complainer, which has been based—not all that fairly—on sideline histrionics when calls don't go his way, it would seem only right that the prospect of a new season would bring from him predictions of doom, pestilence and NCAA inquiry.

How can a guy who looks absolutely pained if a ref has the temerity to call a foul on one of his players possibly view a Syracuse team objectively? Surely, Boeheim joins guys like Temple's John Chaney in the Lou Holtz School of Team Analysis, which asserts that no coach can possibly praise his players until they have proven themselves over the long haul.

In the Holtz school, Syracuse's season-opener with Colgate is fraught with peril. If the Orange somehow squeeze out a victory over their Patriot League neighbors, Boeheim will no doubt be relieved.

Yet looks deceive. Boeheim might look ready to bitch, but, in recent years, he has seemed more content and confident on the bench. Maybe marriage has mellowed him—although the Syracuse-area press corps may want to dispute that. Perhaps his team's startling advance to the 1996 NCAA title game has brought him a measure of satisfaction, now that his detractors must concede that the smooth-pated coach might actually know what he's doing.

It could be even age. Whatever the cause, Boeheim is forthright about his team's 1998-99 chances. And hopeful.

"I like our team," he says immediately. "I like what we have. We did lose Todd Burgan and Marius Janulis, and they were shooters. If we come close to replacing what they did for us, we might be a better team."

If it seems to you that a summer storm has just cut through a brutally humid day and brought a moment of respite, join the club. Isn't it nice to hear a coach promoting his team, rather than bad-mouthing it?

When Boeheim says he "likes" a club, it must be received in the context of 22 years, 528 wins and a pair of Final Four appearances. With college basketball lacking more than a precious few power teams these days, Syracuse has a chance to make some national waves—especially if it gets some shooters.

If a coach from the Metro Atlantic Athletic Conference says he likes his team, said club could win 16-17 games and challenge for that small conference's title. At Syracuse, it could mean some pretty good things. Boeheim wouldn't like something that won't travel well into the NCAA tourney.

"If we make some shots, we can be a really good team," Boeheim says. "We can even be a Top 10 team." He's right, but Syracuse is going to need some help from the outside. Burgan and Janulis were the team's only perimeter threats last year.

The multi-talented Burgan made 36.6 percent of his three-pointers, while Janulis drilled 39.6 percent. Those numbers may not have put the players among the national leaders, but they did force rivals to respect the Syracuse perimeter game, thereby opening up the lane for forwards Ryan Blackwell and Etan Thomas.

Without Burgan and Janulis, the 'Cuse must rely on a pair of freshmen, Tony Bland and Preston Shumpert, to provide an outside threat. Even if junior point man Jason Hart improves on last year's dreadful (.366 FG, .260 3PT) shooting, the newcomers must produce or the Orangemen will be facing zone after zone.

It seems as if Boeheim is already anticipating such a situation, and is actually talking about using an eight- or nine-man rotation that will press and try to create the ever-popular "easy baskets" which have become such a staple in the brave new world of poor shooters. It's possible that the Syracuse zone, which brought so much success these past few years and even spawned some imitators, might be replaced by an attacking defense designed to force tempo and help take advantage of Orange depth, while also masking its shooting troubles.

It is an interesting development, since Boeheim, after last year's win at Villanova, was adamant in his belief that deep benches and 10-man rotations were not necessary, particularly when the games became important.

"The myth that you have to play eight or nine guys is nonsense—complete, utter nonsense," Boeheim said. "With timeouts every four minutes and two of your own, you don't need it unless you're playing a real pressing, running team. And nobody really presses in college basketball anymore.

"There's no way a guy can't play 40 minutes."

Since Boeheim had only six players who averaged double-figure minutes last year, it is clear he believes in that philosophy. This season, he might have to change his ways a little.

Not only might Syracuse need to press and play more people thanks to its questionable shooting, but the Orangemen have more capable bodies at their disposal this season. For the first time in quite a while, there are 10-11 legitimate candidates on the roster for serious playing time, not just six regulars and a group of hopefuls.

Bland and Shumpert help in that regard, since each freshman is expected to step in and contribute immediately, rather than wait his turn. The same goes for 7-1 sophomore center Billy Celuck, who missed last year, and Kueth Duany, a versatile freshman swingman.

With soph forward Eric Williams expected to make a significant improvement, and classmate Damone Brown no longer the beanpole he was last year, Boeheim has some options. He sure won't be employing a Connecticut-style giddy-up scheme, but it should be interesting to watch the Orangemen during non-conference play, if only to see how many different lineup combinations Boeheim employs.

There will, of course, be certain constants. Hart is back at the point spot, needing only to exercise a little more restraint and good judgment with his shot to become one of the nation's best. Blackwell returns at the small forward position and has the potential to be a star. Now that Burgan is gone, Blackwell won't be deferring to his elders anymore and should use his considerable physical skills to make a season-long statement.

As for Thomas, the nation's most imposing shot-blocker, his developmental curve reaches so far into the clouds that it brings rain. Once he gets comfortable as a primary offensive threat and asserts himself more on the backboards, the Orangemen will have themselves quite a weapon.

No wonder Boeheim "likes" this club so much. There is plenty to favor. And, when play begins and Boeheim goes into his trademark "why me?" act, remember that the guy isn't just a complainer. He does shoot straight, a that's pretty refreshing.

STARTERS NOT RETURNING

TODD BURGAN (6-7, SF, 17.6 ppg, 7.1 rpg, 3.3 apg, 2.9 tpg, 2.0 spg, 36.7 minutes, .404 FG, .366 3PT, .747 FT). Although not appreciated all that much on the national scene, Burgan was a big producer for the Orangemen and one of the Big East's best players. That he didn't make it onto the All-League first-team unit last year is somewhat surprising.

Burgan could do a little of everything. He shot with range. He handled the ball. He was an above-average playmaker. He was second among Orange players in rebounding, assists and steals last year, and finished among the Big East top 10 in four different categories.

Burgan led the Orange in scoring 23 times last year, including the final seven games of the season, when Syracuse advanced to the Big East tourney title game and went to the third round of the NCAA Tournament. He also posted seven double-doubles, including a 20-point, 10-rebound effort against Duke in the NCAA Sweet 16 contest.

Burgan was a playing-time horse, averaging 36.7 minutes per game. Although Syracuse may be able to replace his shooting and his scoring production, it is unlikely to will find a player with enough experience and confidence to take (and make) so many big shots and wear as many hats as Burgan did.

MARIUS JANULIS (6-5, SG, 9.6 ppg, 3.1 rpg, 2.0 apg, 1.7 tpg, 1.3 spg, 32.5 minutes, .410 FG, .396 3PT, .833 FT). Used primarily for his long-range gunning, Janulis was a valuable perimeter player who wasn't going to take all that many defenders off the dribble. But he could saturation bomb defenses if they didn't pay enough attention to him.

A full 67 percent of Janulis' field goal attempts last year were beyond the three-point line, a compelling argument that he was a one-dimensional player. But while Janulis wasn't able to create all that much for himself, he did pass well enough to set up others. And he played some pretty good defense, even if he wasn't the fastest guy on the roster.

Janulis was rarely the first option in the Syracuse offensive scheme, but that didn't prevent him from having several strong performances. He led the Orange in scoring twice last year, against UNC-Greensboro and Connecticut, and hit for 18 points on two occasions, versus Texas Christian and Miami.

Though unheralded, Janulis will be missed, particularly if none of the newcomers can shoot all that well from long range.

OTHERS NOT RETURNING

LASEAN HOWARD (6-6, G/F, 1.9 ppg, 0.8 rpg, 5.8 minutes, .439 FG, .700 FT). The departure of Jason Cipolla was supposed to open up considerable playing time for the physically-gifted Howard, but he was unable

1997-98 RESULTS

North Carolina-Asheville	60-57	
North Carolina-Greensboro	83-53	
Colgate	78-74	
@St. John's	80-73	
@Boston College	70-52	
#Texas Southern	85-73	
#Miami (Ohio)	72-53	
Buffalo	82-70	
##UNLV	71-64	
###Texas Christian	82-78	
###Michigan (L)	61-93	
Rutgers	71-68	
@Providence	77-59	
Louisville	69-65	
Providence (L)	64-76	
Miami	85-67	
@Notre Dame (L)	63-83	
Connecticut (L)	54-63	
@Georgetown	84-66	
@Pittsburgh	84-73	
Seton Hall (L)	61-85	
@Miami	72-63	
West Virginia	73-58	
@Villanova	69-64	
@Rutgers (L)	58-62	
St. John's (L)	65-67	
Pittsburgh	76-61	
Georgetown	77-72	ot
####Villanova	69-66	
####St. John's	69-67	ot
####Connecticut (L)	64-69	
%Iona	63-61	
%New Mexico	56-46	
%%Duke (L)	67-80	

@	away games
#	Carrier Classic, Syracuse, NY
##	Las Vegas Shootout, Las Vegas, NV
###	Puerto Rico Classic, San Juan, PR
####	Big East Tournament, New York, NY
%	NCAA South Sub-Regional, Lexington, KY
%%	NCAA South Regional, St. Petersburg, FL

to capitalize on the opportunity and left Syracuse for Long Beach State, where he will join fellow Orange expatriate Ramel "Rock" Lloyd.

Howard came to Syracuse as a heralded recruit and was expected to be a productive swingman, but he couldn't crack the lineup last year. It became clear as the season went on and the recruiting news trickled in that his future with the program was shaky.

Howard played in 23 games last year, but he averaged only 5.8 minutes and took only 41 shots. Not a great defender, Howard will need to improve his discipline to thrive at his new home.

SAM SPANN (6-6, G/F, 0.5 ppg, 0.3 rpg, eight appearances). It didn't take Spann all that long to realize his future at Syracuse wasn't too bright. Although an outstanding athlete, the man with the name that is equal parts Humphrey Bogart character and Dr. Suess protagonist became disenchanted with his lack of playing time and transferred to Boston University.

He could become a star in the America East Conference.

PROJECTED STARTERS

RYAN BLACKWELL (6-8, 220 lbs., JR, SF, #32, 12.6 ppg, 8.2 rpg, 2.3 apg, 2.6 tpg, 1.4 spg, 35.0 minutes, .478 FG, .344 3PT, .688 FT, Illinois & Pittsford Sutherland HS/Pittsford, N.Y.). There were some who wondered how well Blackwell, who didn't exactly shine—3.9 ppg, 2.9 rpg—during his one year at Illinois, would fare at Syracuse. Boeheim, however, wasn't one of them.

The coach knew what he had the minute Blackwell stepped onto campus, perhaps because he saw the guy play as a prep senior. Although Blackwell graduated from (and was a three-time All-State performer at) nearby Pittsford Sutherland HS, he chose Illinois because of a bond he had formed with then-Illini coach Lou Henson.

Blackwell's family once lived in Champaign, and the youngster had served as a ballboy at Illinois games and had eaten at Henson's house as a kid. (Take it easy. That's not an NCAA violation.)

When Henson left Champaign, so did Blackwell. And Orange fans should be ecstatic.

In his first year with the team, Blackwell was nothing short of spectacular. His no-nonsense game and ability to score from 15 feet and in made him a fine complement to the Syracuse perimeter players. Blackwell also asserted himself immediately on the backboards, leading the team in that category and finishing fifth among Big East players.

Still, Boeheim expects more this year.

"He had a solid year last year, but he didn't want to step in anybody's way," Boeheim says. "He lowered his game and submitted a bit to Burgan."

Don't expect to see that again. In fact, Blackwell may be a bigger (and ultimately better) version of the departed Orange star. Boeheim reports Blackwell has improved his shooting range to three-point quality (he made 11 of 32 treys last year) and is ready to be more than just a second option offensively.

Blackwell showed he could score well last year by hitting for 23 points in the win at Villanova and 21 against Miami (Oh.). He had 11 double-figure rebounding games and could average 10 or more boards this year.

Stardom is waiting for Blackwell. It's up to him whether he wants it or not.

JASON HART (6-3, 177 lbs., JR, PG, #5, 10.2 ppg, 3.6 rpg, 34.2 minutes, .366 FG, .260 3PT, .684 FT, 5.0 apg, 3.5 tpg, 2.3 spg, Inglewood HS/Los Angeles, Calif.). About the only thing preventing Hart from becoming one of the Big East's top players is his shot.

It seemed as if Hart spent part of last season trying to quiet those who said he wasn't good enough from the field during his freshman year. It didn't work. Although Hart had strong numbers in the assist and steal categories, he was an awful shooter from just about anywhere on the court.

"Jason pressed too much last year," Boeheim says. "He was trying to make jump shots. Last year, he didn't have to shoot, because we had Marius and Todd. This year, we need him to make shots."

Hart is quick, creative and difficult to check off the dribble. He can penetrate and sets up his teammates well, particularly those who spread out along the three-point line.

But it's time for him to make the next step and become somebody capable of running the team and making key shots. Hart doesn't have to score 20 per game, even if he thinks he does. He does, however, have to hit open jumpers from the key. And, if he plays with Griffin, he may have to produce from the wing, more uncharted territory for him.

Hart can do it. He had 15 points in the tourney loss to Duke, on 6-for-11 shooting, and he made 7-for-10 against Pittsburgh earlier in the year. Hart scored 22 points against Providence, posted a double-double (19 points, 10 assists) at St. John's and scored 18 against Buffalo.

But those outbursts won't have to be nightly occurrences. If Hart continues to distribute the ball and makes close to half his attempts, the Orangemen will be in great shape.

ETAN THOMAS (6-9, 231 lbs., JR, C, #33, 11.3 ppg, 6.6 rpg, 1.7 tpg, 3.9 bpg, 28.8 minutes, .610 FG, .612 FT, Booker T. Washington HS/Tulsa, Okla.). Last year's Most Improved Player in the Big East, Thomas has enough potential to win it again this year. Known primarily as a shot-blocker, it is time for the big guy to break out in other areas.

Thomas finished fourth in the nation with 3.94 blocks per game last year, and he had some games in which he was positively dominant. He blocked nine shots in the Orangemen's win over Connecticut and had eight swats in the Big East semifinal win over St. John's. When Boeheim says that Thomas is one of the best shot-blockers to come around the league in a long time, he isn't just spouting hyperbole. Thomas is a force.

The question is whether Thomas can become as effective on the offensive end and the backboards as he is patrolling the lane on defense. Thomas has been working on his offensive repertoire and should be a little more potent there, and the departure of Burgan leaves a few more rebounds for him to grab.

"Thomas is not a great offensive player, but he's starting to develop," Boeheim says. "He's done some work on his shot and should make some more free throws. He is a worker."

Thomas hit double figures 21 times last year and was extremely efficient from the field. Against Georgetown, he made 8 of 11 tries en route to 23 points. He was a perfect 6-for-6 against West Virginia two weeks later and finished with 19 points.

ALLEN GRIFFIN (6-1, 175 lbs., SO, SG, #12, 2.4 ppg, 0.9 rpg, 9.2 minutes, .418 FG, .263 3PT, .571 FT, Robeson HS/Brooklyn, N.Y.). Griffin was expected to make an impression during his first year in the program, and he certainly did that. He spelled Hart and showed an ability to play with him, as well. Although Griffin wasn't that much of an offensive force, he certainly proved his worth on defense and proved himself more than capable of taking care of the ball.

"I'm going to play Griffin and Hart together this year, unless somebody else shocks me," Boeheim says. "When you put those guys out there, you can generate some defensive pressure. I'm looking to play some more man-to-man this year."

Griffin was one of the finest players in New York his senior season in high school and, though his contribution to the Syracuse cause last year wasn't all that measurable statistically, he was a steady, versatile reserve. If he is going to start this year, the trick is for him to become more of an offensive force, particularly if he plays the two spot.

Griffin didn't shoot the ball all that well last year, and he took only 67 shots all year. Even his foul shooting was below average.

Still, this is a good, young player. And, unless one or more of the newcomers emerge quickly, Griffin should be in the starting lineup come November.

ERIC WILLIAMS (6-9, 240 lbs., SO, PF, #21, 3.0 ppg, 2.4 rpg, 1.2 tpg, 8.4 minutes, .600 FG, .500 FT, Milford Academy, Conn./Brooklyn, N.Y.). When Williams committed to the Orangemen last summer, many thought Syracuse had gained an immediate star, the kind of frontcourt player who would be dominant. Boeheim cautioned everybody about such optimism, and he was right.

Williams wasn't in great shape a lot of the season and didn't get on the floor all that much, particularly with Blackwell ahead of him. This year, things could change. Williams has hardened his physique and appears ready to make some significant contributions this year—and probably start. Williams won't be a dominant offensive player, since his game is still pretty basic, but he should help on defense and with rebounding.

"He can rebound," Boeheim says. "With him in the lineup (with Blackwell and Thomas), we'll be bigger up front since when we had Derrick Coleman and Rony Seikaly. Williams is really ready. He looks like a beast."

Williams had a couple of promising outings last year, like his seven-point, seven-board game against Texas Southern and an eight-point performance versus Pitt. Although he likes to step away from the basket at times, Williams' primary value to the Orangemen will be as an interior force.

KEY RESERVES

ELVIR OVCINA (6-11, 234 lbs., SR, C/F, #40, 9.6 ppg, 3.1 rpg, 12.1 minutes, .328 FG, .224 3PT, .444 FT, 1.2 apg, 1.0 tpg, Sycamore HS, Ill./Sarajevo, Bosnia). Ovcina, a classic Euro-player with a good outside game and limited inside skills—or desire, for that matter—allows the 'Cuse to go with a high post look at times. He can even be paired with Thomas without much confusion, because the two big men have radically different games.

Ovcina has fine shooting range, but his eye wasn't so sharp last year. That must improve now that Syracuse needs more outside shooting.

Ovcina did have some moments last year, most notably his 12-point outburst against UNC-Greensboro and a six-point, six-block performance in the Big East tourney win over Villanova.

"He gives us a completely different offensive look," Boeheim says of Ovcina. "Other teams have to worry about a big, three-point shooter on the perimeter, but he does have to shoot the ball better this year." Ovcina is a pretty good shot-blocker, but he doesn't show much desire to engage in the rough stuff, as evidenced by his small (2.5 rpg) rebound total. Still, he is a valuable reserve who could average close to 20 minutes per game this year.

DAMONE BROWN (6-8, 205 lbs., SO, F, #25, 1.7 ppg, 0.9 rpg, 3.6 minutes, .417 FG, .500 FT, Seneca Vocational HS/Buffalo, N.Y.). Syracuse fans who watched Brown struggle through his first year on campus had to be wondering why Boeheim made so many favorable comparisons between the skinny forward and former standout (and current assistant coach) Louis Orr.

Although Brown resembled the twiggy Orr in body type, he certainly didn't seem to have Orr's productive game. Brown appeared in only 15 contests last year and virtually disappeared in Big East play, averaging just two minutes in his seven conference appearances.

Well, Boeheim is predicting success for Brown beginning this year. The first reason is bulk. Brown played at a lithe 177 pounds last season. Now, he's up to 205. That will help him considerably, particularly on defense, where Brown has the potential to be pretty good.

Boeheim also thinks Brown will be more versatile with the ball.

"He's going to surprise some people this year,"

1998-99 SYRACUSE SCHEDULE

Nov.	17	Colgate
	19	Coppin State
	23-25	#Maui Classic
Dec.	1	Quinnipiac
	4-5	##Carrier Classic
	9	@West Virginia
	12	Seton Hall
	27	St. Bonaventure
	29	@Notre Dame
Jan.	2	West Virginia
	5	@Villanova
	12	Providence
	16	@Georgetown
	18	@Rutgers
	21	Boston College
	24	South Carolina
	27	St. John's
	30	@Seton Hall
Feb.	1	@Connecticut
	6	Villanova
	8	Miami (Fla.)
	14	@Pittsburgh
	17	Notre Dame
	21	@UCLA
	24	@Boston College
	28	Connecticut
Mar.	3-6	###Big East Tournament

@ Road Games
# Honolulu, HI (vs. Chaminade, first round; also Arizona State, Clemson, Indiana, Kansas State, Michigan and Utah)
Syracuse, NY (vs. Ohio, first round; also Illinois-Chicago and Santa Clara)
Madison Square Garden, NY

Boeheim says. "He can shoot and handle. He needed a year to get stronger."

If Brown is indeed tougher, Boeheim should be correct in his assessment. Brown has tremendous athletic skills—maybe more pure skill than Orr—but he needs to apply it. With Burgan gone, there is an opportunity.

PRESTON SHUMPERT (6-7, 190 lbs., FR, G/F, #3, 28.6 ppg, 10.0 rpg, 4.0 apg, Fort Walton Beach HS/Fort Walton Beach, Fla.). If there is one freshman who could make an immediate impact, it is Shumpert, whom Boeheim praises for his touch and savvy.

"He can shoot it, and he knows how to play the game," Boeheim says. "We'll just have to see how well he can shoot it."

Shumpert was a two-time All-State player at Fort Walton Beach HS and has the ability to score from the inside or outside.

TONY BLAND (6-4, 180 lbs., FR, G, #4, 20.0 ppg, 7.0 rpg, 7.0 apg, Westchester HS/Los Angeles, Calif.). Bland joins Hart as the team's L.A. Connection and brings some needed outside pop to the Syracuse attack.

A two-time first-team All-State performer and a *Parade* All-America, Bland was an early signee with Syracuse and has a good outside shot. He'll most likely begin the season on the bench, but he will certainly get an early look—particularly if he can hit some three-pointers.

KUETH DUANY (6-7, 185 lbs., FR, G/F, #13, 19.5 ppg, 8.0 rpg, 4.0 apg, Bloomington North HS/Bloomington, Ind.). The brother of Wisconsin guard Duany Duany, this swingman was a member of the '97 Indiana state champion and had five 30-point games last year.

Duany falls into the same category as Bland, someone who will get a chance to shine but who will have to make quite an impression to break ahead of Griffin in the starting lineup. Duany is athletic, has pretty good ballhandling skills for a guy his size and can get to the basket.

If Boeheim decides to go with a deeper bench, Duany could be a truly valuable performer, thanks to his versatility.

OTHER RETURNEES

MALIK CAMPBELL (6-3, 178 lbs., SO, G, #10, 1.3 ppg, 0.9 rpg, 5.1 minutes, .350 FG, .571 FT, Turner Carroll HS/Buffalo, N.Y.). Campbell had a relatively undistinguished beginning for the Orange, and it is possible that his contributions to the team could even dwindle this year. It has nothing to do with his talent, rather the facts that Campbell is playing for the Orange football team this fall and won't be available until January, and that fellow soph Allen Griffin looked so good last year that he will probably start alongside Jason Hart.

Campbell saw action in only 15 games last year and, though he flashed the athletic ability and quickness that were expected of him, he struggled with his shot and just didn't have the opportunity to play. Boeheim doesn't shuttle players in and out every two or three minutes.

Campbell could well succeed where Donovan McNabb did not and pull off the football/basketball double, but it will be difficult. Expect him to struggle once he arrives with the team and don't look for any huge contributions, unless there are some injuries.

JASON MALLIN (5-10, 160 lbs., SO, G, #15, 0.0 ppg, 0.0 rpg, four appearances, Clarkstown North HS/New York, N.Y.). A walkon who saw action in just four games last year (and only one Big East game), Mallin has little hope of getting any serious minutes, particularly on a team that has had such a history of short rotations over the past decade.

JOSH WATSON (6-8, 238 lbs., SR, F, #14, Trinity Pawling Prep/Skaneateles, N.Y.). A walkon who didn't play at all last year, Watson has a big body that comes in handy during practices.

adidas Blue Ribbon Analysis

GRADING SYSTEM

- A+ equal to very best in country—Final Four-caliber unit
- A among the best in the land—worthy of deep NCAA run
- B+ talented, versatile and experienced—NCAA-NIT ability
- B solid and productive winners—league and post-season contenders
- C+ average to above-average—may contend in a weaker league
- C average to mediocre—second division in a strong league
- D+ below average, inconsistent—second division in a weaker league
- D well below average—losing season virtually certain
- F non-Division I ability—an underdog every night

OTHER NEWCOMERS

BILLY CELUCK (7-1, 210 lbs., SO, C, #35, 12.5 rpg, Valley View HS/Jessup, Pa.). Celuck sat last year as a partial qualifier and shouldn't expect too much time this year, thanks to his skinny frame and the pivot logjam in front of him.

Celuck came to Syracuse weighing all of 195 pounds. And, though he has "beefed up" to 210, he remains too lean for Big East battle. Unfortunately, his academic situation makes it hard to redshirt him and gives him only three years to develop.

QUESTIONS

Shooting? With Burgan and Janulis gone, the Orangemen are in desperate need of some outside pop. Hart could help. So could Ovcina. But if one of the three freshman perimeter players doesn't emerge offensively, this team is in some trouble.

Rebounding? Burgan's absence means Thomas and Williams must join Blackwell as glass-eaters. Even with Burgan in the lineup, the Orangemen held a relatively slim, plus-1.3 rebounding margin per game last year.

Leadership? Burgan was quite a force in this program during his years there, and it is time for someone to step into his leadership breech. Hart is the natural candidate, but it could be Blackwell. It has to be someone.

ANSWERS

Blackwell! By the time this season is over, the nation will know about Blackwell, a potent forward with inside-outside scoring skills, tremendous rebounding ability and a no-frills approach. He is a budding star.

Hart! Even if he doesn't shoot it better—something he should do—Hart is still a fine point man who plays great defense and can set up teammates well.

Thomas! One of the nation's most imposing defensive forces, Thomas should improve considerably on offense and the backboards this year. He is two strong seasons away from hearing his name called during the NBA draft.

Depth! The Orangemen have their deepest, biggest, most athletic team in years. Boeheim may not use all his resources, but he does have some talent at his disposal.

adidas Blue Ribbon Analysis

BACKCOURT	**B**	**BENCH/DEPTH**	**B+**
FRONTCOURT	**B+**	**INTANGIBLES**	**B+**

Boeheim *should* like this team. All but about two dozen coaches in the nation would trade it for theirs right now. Syracuse has a strong, possibly dominant frontcourt; a good, potentially great, point guard; and some rookie reinforcements with promise.

The key, however, is the outside shooting. If Syracuse doesn't have a viable long-range game, the big guys will go hungry.

That shouldn't be the case. Hart will improve. Blackwell will make one three-pointer per game. Ovcina can hit. And Shumpert or Bland (or both) will emerge.

Syracuse should be an imposing defensive team again, but this year's success won't be just because of the zone. The Orange should be able to press and run a bit more, and that won't require so much heavy lifting in the halfcourt.

In Blackwell and Thomas, Syracuse has a pair of budding stars. Blackwell is fun to watch and incredibly productive, and woe to the person who challenges Thomas when he gets into one of his grooves where every shot is his. If Williams rebounds the way Boeheim thinks he can, this will be one helluva frontcourt.

Hart and Griffin form an interesting backcourt combo, since neither is a true scorer. But their quickness will help on defense, and don't be surprised to see them paired with Bland or Shumpert in a quick lineup.

This should be another good year for Syracuse. If the new guys come along, it could be great.

(M.B.)

19

XAVIER

LOCATION	**Cincinnati, OH**
CONFERENCE	**Atlantic 10 (West Division)**
LAST SEASON	**22-8 (.733)**
CONFERENCE RECORD	**11-5 (t-1st)**
STARTERS LOST/RETURNING	**3/2**
NICKNAME	**Musketeers**
COLORS	**Navy Blue, Gray & White**
HOMECOURT	**Cincinnati Gardens (10,100)**
COACH	**Skip Prosser (Merchant Marine Academy '72)**
RECORD AT SCHOOL	**81-34 (4 yrs.)**
CAREER RECORD	**98-47 (5 yrs.)**
ASSISTANTS	**Jeff Battle (Marshall '85) Mark Gaffney (Bridgewater State '94) Mark Schmidt (Boston College '85)**
TEAM WINS (last 5 yrs.)	**22-23-13-23-22**
RPI (last 5 yrs.)	**60-40-138-30-31**
1997-98 FINISH	**Lost in NCAA first round.**

COACH AND PROGRAM

It took Xavier only three years to accomplish the stated objective, then about three days to throw it all away. Such is life in the NCAA Tournament, when a flat day by a higher seed becomes the legacy of an otherwise fine season.

The Musketeers entered the Atlantic 10 quite boldly prior to the 1995-96 campaign. "In It to Win It" screamed much of the school's literature.

It all seemed a bit too much when Xavier stumbled through its first A-10 season with an 8-8 record. Just a year later, though, the Musketeers were winning the West Division at 13-3. They repeated as division co-champs in 1997-98, but were given little chance of ousting East Division heavyweights Temple or Rhode Island at the conference tourney in Philadelphia.

But the Musketeers waxed the Final Eight-bound Rams in the semifinals, then dodged a bullet when George Washington eliminated Temple. That made for an all-West Division final (somewhat ironic given the eastern domination of the conference). With G.W. out of gas, Xavier cruised to its first Atlantic 10 championship.

Selection Sunday brought a No. 6 seed and a favorable East Region draw. The Musketeers would face Washington (the state) in Washington (the city). Subsequent encounters with South Carolina and/or Connecticut seemed entirely possible.

Except that Xavier, which had averaged 83.5 ppg for the season, shot poorly and was held to 68 points by the Huskies. It was the team's second-lowest offensive output of the year, and the one-point loss left everyone in the program scratching their heads. It didn't help that the Musketeers had the ball, but not a good shot, as time expired.

"As a coach," head man Skip Prosser told the *Cincinnati Enquirer*, "you always question what else you could have done. That's what I've been doing. All you can do is keep working."

And worrying. What should have been a positive summer—with four starting caliber players returning—was soiled, first by the academic woes of two incoming recruits, then by a disastrous injury to swingman Darnell Williams.

Williams, a great scorer and shooter, was arguably the Xavier MVP last season. He was touring with the NIT All-Star team in June when he tore the anterior cruciate ligament in his right knee. Although Williams could conceivably return around mid-season, all indications are that he will redshirt the 1998-99 campaign.

"Any decision," said Prosser, "will be based on what's best for Darnell in the long run."

Other summer losses included power forward Aaron Turner, a 6-7 bruiser from Maine Central Institute, and 6-11 junior college transfer Garvin Davis. Neither made the grade, thinning an already smallish Xavier frontcourt.

The Musketeers will thus attempt an A-10 title defense with a nucleus of three seniors—Lenny Brown, Gary Lumpkin and James Posey—who have been down this road before. Super recruit Lloyd Price will have to be as good as advertised to fill William's void.

If not, Xavier's next memory will be more along the lines of what happened in Washington, D.C., last March than what happened days before in Philadelphia. "Sometimes we played not to lose," Prosser admitted. "I don't have an explanation for it."

This is one case where reading press clippings wouldn't be such a bad idea. When the Musketeers really are "in it to win it," they usually do.

STARTERS NOT RETURNING

DARNELL WILLIAMS (6-5, SF, 17.3 ppg, 3.9 rpg, 2.0 apg, 1.7 tpg, 1.6 spg, 32.9 minutes, .559 FG, .448 3PT, .709 FT). The people who voted Darnell Williams second-team All-Atlantic 10 last season probably meant well; they just weren't paying close enough attention. Williams was the best all-around player on the best all-around team in the league.

He led the high-octane Musketeers in scoring. He shot a marvelous .559 from the field, with 39 three-pointers mixed into a deadly arsenal of slash-and-go maneuvers. He got to the line, he rebounded and he defended like Xavier wing players are supposed to. His stock was rising faster than Wolf Blitzer's ratings.

And then it happened.

Williams, a member of the NIT summer all-star team, was going up for a layup during an exhibition game in Italy. He heard his right knee pop, then shift.

"I'm upset that it happened," Williams told the *Cincinnati Enquirer*. "I've just got to be strong about it. I've got to take it as another step in life."

"It" is the dreaded ACL injury. Some players recover; others do not. And even those on the positive side of the ledger are rarely the same when they first return from surgery.

That's why it seems so likely Williams will not attempt a mid-season return for 1998-99. The best-case scenario following June's reconstructive surgery calls for a January comeback. The real-life scenario is that this explosive swingman has little to gain from a half-hearted senior year.

"You can see why NBA scouts are foaming at the mouth for this kid," said ESPN's Dave Sims.

"You've got to love his game," added St. Joseph's coach Phil Martelli. "He was the one we came in fearing the most."

Translation: If Williams can show that game during a complete senior season in 1999-2000, he's going to make a lot of money playing basketball. A premature return can only put those hopes in jeopardy.

Fortunately for Williams, Xavier coach Skip Prosser agrees. Fortunately for Prosser, he has Lloyd Price waiting in the wings.

TORRAYE BRAGGS (6-8, PF, 13.0 ppg, 8.2 rpg, 2.4 apg, 2.9 tpg, 1.4 spg, 29.7 minutes, .541 FG, .731 FT). Braggs was everything the Musketeers could have wanted during his two years in Cincinnati. He came from junior college as a low-post enforcer, and he performed that role with remarkable consistency.

Braggs numbers were virtually the same as a both junior and a senior. That the Musketeers won two divisional titles and an NCAA game during his tenure in the middle was no coincidence. Braggs took a potential Xavier weakness—the "five" spot—and turned it into a strength.

Braggs, who has signed a contract to play professionally in Spain, will be hard to replace. The Musketeers have no one with his physical presence and may miss their least-known starter most of all.

T.J. JOHNSON (6-7, PF, 5.5 ppg, 3.6 rpg, 1.6 apg, 1.9 tpg, 1.4 spg, 23.3 minutes, .500 FG, .700 FT). The final holdover from Xavier's days in the Midwestern Collegiate Conference, Johnson was a four-year regular and near permanent starter. He wasn't very fast, couldn't jump very high, but was a leader and good soldier even as his role changed.

The one-time MCC Freshman of the Year, Johnson was essentially a role player as the Xavier supporting cast grew around him. Then Braggs began to get many of his shots.

Even so, Johnson accepted his role as a nominal starter. He was usually the first to the bench when super-sub James Posey was inserted. And that was just as well. Limiting Johnson's minutes was the best way to keep him out of foul trouble.

Johnson and Braggs combined to give Xavier a much better halfcourt defense than many expected. Without them, the Musketeers figure to both score and permit more points this winter.

OTHERS NOT RETURNING

NATE TURNER (6-8, F/C, 2.2 ppg, 0.8 rpg, 5.8 minutes in 16 appearances, .565 FG, .500 FT). Injuries slowed the development of this once-promising post man. He opted to leave the program after 16 games a year ago.

Ironically, the Musketeers are hurting for big men as the 1998-99 season begins.

TERRANCE PAYNE (6-6, F, 1.2 ppg, 1.3 rpg, 5.1 minutes, .440 FG, .500 FT). The Musketeers were hoping Payne could produce as a rebounder in spot minutes on the wing. It turned out there weren't many of those minutes available once Darnell Williams went from good to great.

Xavier still has plenty of wing talent, even in Williams' considerable absence. Payne will not be missed.

PAT KELSEY (5-9, G, 1.0 ppg, 5.0 minutes, .294 FG, .400 3PT, .800 FT). The one-time starter at Wyoming made an interesting career choice. He opted to become a deep reserve closer to home rather than continue as a major contributor for a far-away team going nowhere.

Kelsey got in to most games, occasionally spelled Gary Lumpkin at the point and was a leader for the Musketeers. He also saw a lot more wins from the Xavier bench then he would have out west.

PROJECTED STARTERS

GARY LUMPKIN (6-2, 200 lbs., SR, PG, #12, 12.3 ppg, 2.5 rpg, 4.5 apg, 2.3 tpg, 1.4 spg, 33.7 minutes, .385 FG, .295 3PT, .783 FT, William Penn HS/New Castle, Del.). Lumpkin is a very good point guard for the Xavier system. If he returns to form from the three-point line, he could be great.

Lumpkin connected on over 40 percent from distance as both a freshman and sophomore. His slide to 29.5 percent last year was a mystery. If anything, the dominant scoring of Darnell Williams and perimeter presence of Lenny Brown should have made Lumpkin's offense come easier.

Still, the four-year starter did the other parts of his job. He led the team in minutes and assists, and ranked ninth in the conference in free throw shooting. He has started 82 consecutive games, the last 76 alongside Brown, his former high school teammate.

Lumpkin was a first-team All-A10 choice as a sophomore. His shooting was the primary reason he fell to the third team last year. Otherwise, he was and will be the same player again.

LENNY BROWN (6-2, 198 lbs., SR, SG, #4, 14.7 ppg, 3.5 rpg, 3.5 apg, 3.2 tpg, 2.7 spg, 31.9 minutes, .443 FG, .366 3PT, .743 FT, Maine Central Institute/Wilmington, Del.). If Bill and Monica had been together as long as Brown and Lumpkin, they'd be married and divorced by now. The two were teammates and state champions in Delaware, then skipped a year while Brown attended Maine Central Institute. All that did was make them members—and backcourt partners—in the same college class.

"They're one of the most underrated backcourts in America," says Dick Vitale.

They shouldn't be underrated anymore, having won 58 games and counting. Following the upcoming season, they will have played in three straight NCAA Tournaments together. There can't have been too many backcourt pairings over the years which could make that claim.

Brown scores more points, takes more chances defensively and is more outspoken than his partner. He is a lock to break the school's all-time steals record sometime this season. One reason he can take those chances, of course, is the rock-solid presence of Lumpkin.

In the old days, when backcourt players were simply called guards, these two would have thrived. Both can handle, pass, shoot and defend. If you looked only at their statistics, it wouldn't always be clear which is the point man and which is the shooter.

All of which is part of their collective charm.

For his part, Brown joined Lumpkin as a first-team All-Conference choice as a sophomore. He slipped to second team as a junior, but remains highly regarded. He is among 25 finalists for the John Wooden Award.

Last year, Brown was overshadowed a bit by Darnell Williams. This season, it figures to be James Posey in the spotlight.

But Brown will be there just the same, the soul of the Musketeers.

JAMES POSEY (6-8, 210 lbs., SR, PF, #41, 15.3 ppg, 8.4 rpg, 1.3 apg, 2.3 tpg, 2.1 spg, 28.8 minutes, R.B. Chamberlin HS/Twinsburg, Oh.). Posey has got to be the best player in college basketball to never become a full-time starter. In fact, he has started just five times in 59 college games.

1997-98 RESULTS

Toledo	95-76	
Akron	97-73	
Northeast Louisiana	118-61	
Central Michigan	88-54	
@Western Kentucky	93-60	
@Miami-OH (L)	72-80	
Cincinnati	88-68	
*Purdue (L)	84-86	
**DePaul	73-56	
Butler	93-66	
@St. Bonaventure (L)	77-80	
La Salle	104-67	
Fordham	77-43	
@George Washington (L)	73-78	ot
Virginia Tech	77-66	
St. Joseph's	72-62	
@Dayton (L)	82-93	
Duquesne	93-71	
@Temple	79-73	
@La Salle	91-59	
Massachusetts (L)	62-73	
@Virginia Tech	74-63	
George Washington	96-86	
@Duquesne	83-62	
@Rhode Island (L)	68-69	
Dayton	89-84	
#St. Bonaventure	68-44	
#Rhode Island	95-80	
#George Washington	77-63	
%Washington (L)	68-69	

@ away games
* Market Square Arena, Indianapolis, IN
** Rock & Roll Shootout, Cleveland, OH
\# Atlantic 10 Tournament, CoreStates Spectrum, Philadelphia, PA
% NCAA East Sub-Regional, Washington, DC

1998-99 XAVIER SCHEDULE

Nov.	17	@Butler
	21	Chicago State
	23	Morgan State
	26-28	#Puerto Rico Shootout
Dec.	2	Miami (Oh.)
	5	*Purdue
	9	@Toledo
	19	Canisius
	21	Loyola Marymount
	28	@Saint Mary's
Jan.	3	Rhode Island
	6	@Virginia Tech
	9	@Duquesne
	13	St. Bonaventure
	17	George Washington
	20	@Fordham
	23	Virginia Tech
	28	@Cincinnati
	30	@Dayton
Feb.	4	@St. Joseph's
	6	@La Salle
	9	Duquesne
	14	Temple
	16	La Salle
	20	@Massachusetts
	24	Dayton
	27	@George Washington
Mar.	3-6	##Atlantic 10 Tournament

@ Road Games
* The Crowne, Cincinnati, OH
\# San Juan, PR (vs. Pittsburgh, first round; also American University-P.R., Colorado, Kentucky, Maryland, San Francisco and UCLA)
\#\# First Union Spectrum, Philadelphia, PA

All of which means...absolutely nothing. Calling Posey a sixth man is like calling Sammy Sosa a runner-up. Many believe he will become the best-ever Xavier product at the next level.

Posey did nothing to dispel that notion over the summer, starring for the U.S. gold medalists at the 1998 Goodwill Games. His 13 points—off the bench, naturally—were critical in Team USA's title game victory over Australia.

"He's some kind of player," said USA and Minnesota coach Clem Haskins. "I can see why (Xavier) wins. This young man, when he straps it on, gives you everything he's got.

"He plays with reckless abandon, and he comes to play. He doesn't worry about his body. He'll give it all to you."

With great skill, too. Posey is athletic on the perimeter, a tenacious rebounder and the team's leading foul shooter. He also got 63 steals from a non-starting, forward position, which has to be nearly unheard of.

"He's like a praying mantis out there," says Prosser. "He gets his hands on so many passes."

Because of an academic redshirt, this will be only the third season for Posey. Yet he continues to improve dramatically. As a permanent starter this year, the sky is literally the limit for him.

You will hear other names throughout the preseason. Posey will be the best all-around player in the Atlantic 10.

LLOYD PRICE (6-5, 200 lbs., FR, SF, 15.3 ppg, 5.9 rpg, 5.1 apg, 3.1 spg, .562 FG, .407 3PT, .782 FT, Oak Hill Academy, Va./Wilmington, Del.). The plan was to work Price in behind Brown and Darnell Williams, letting this high-flying swingman ease into his hype. Instead, Price will inherit the starting job at small forward due to Williams' summer injury.

Of course, Price would be an instant starter most places. He has been rated as high as 24th in his class (*The Sporting News*) and was the seventh-best shooting guard in the country according to Bob Gibbons. His 25 points and nine rebounds led the Magic Johnson Roundball Classic last April.

When Price got his test score late last spring, there were smiles from here to Cincinnati Gardens. When Williams went down, those smiles turned to sighs of relief that Price was on board.

"At Oak Hill Academy, "he got a chance to play with and against some of the best players in the country," said Prosser. "He has the ability and mental makeup to be a significant contributor to our program."

Price preceded his year at Oak Hill with a fine career at Hodgson Tech in Newark, Delaware. He joins Lumpkin and Lenny Brown as Xavier products from the "Home of Tax Free Shopping." Price averaged 23.0 ppg, 11.8 rpg, 11.5 apg and 6.0 bpg as a junior.

At Oak Hill, Price shot 56.2 percent from the field, 40.7 percent from the arc and 78.2 percent at the line for a 29-2 team which finished seventh in the final *USA Today* poll. He was one of five Oak Hill seniors to accept Division I scholarships.

"Lloyd is very versatile and unselfish," Oak Hill coach Steve Smith said. "He does whatever it takes for the team to win. Lloyd is so athletic, he bounces off the floor."

Indeed, early reports from fall pickups games noted Price dunking over James Posey. This we would pay to see.

DESMOND WALKER (6-8, 225 lbs., JR, PF, 19.8 ppg, 11.2 rpg, 3.5 apg, 3.0 bpg, .520 FG, .600 FT, Florida CC & Greenville HS/Greenville, Ala.). Ideally, Walker would have backed up James Posey this season. Instead, with recruited big men Aaron Turner and Garvin Davis ineligible, Walker may be the starter at the "five" spot. Fellow JC signee Obi Harris is more of a true center, but the Musketeers rarely play with one of those.

"We don't really have a center," Prosser admitted, "and we don't really play with one."

Except that Torraye Braggs and T.J. Johnson, even as power forwards, were at least wide. Neither Posey nor Walker is going to clog the lane.

"Desmond is a well-rounded player," suggested Florida CC coach Rob Flaska. "He's not a great shooter, but he is great scorer."

What the Musketeers really need is defense and rebounding. If Walker can produce half of his junior college numbers at this level, Xavier will be ahead of the game.

KEY RESERVES

MAURICE MCAFEE (6-0, 175 lbs., SO, G, #15, 2.7 ppg, 0.7 rpg, 8.9 minutes, .379 FG, .323 3PT, .556 FT, Buena Vista HS/Saginaw, Mich.). McAfee was often the first guard off the bench by the end of last season. Like most Xavier backcourt performers, he is quick with the ball and a fine defender of same.

"He fits right into our style of play," says Prosser.

Look for McAfee to back up Lumpkin this season. He should no longer have to share that job with Pat Kelsey. And, even though Xavier is looking for point guard help on the recruiting trail, McAfee may have something to say about that next season.

ALVIN BROWN (6-3, 180 lbs., FR, G, #24, 2.8 ppg, seven appearances prior to medical redshirt in 1997-98, Gonzaga HS/Washington, D.C.). Brown's return is the main reason Maurice McAfee should concentrate on a point guard role. Alvin is an ideal backup for namesake Lenny Brown, but a broken bone in his left wrist short-circuited his 1997-98 season.

Brown received a medical redshirt and has four years to recapture the form which made him the *Washington Post* Metro Player of the Year in 1996-97. He led his high school team to a record 30 victories as a senior.

Said Prosser: "Alvin has good shooting range and can score in a variety of ways. He has long arms, which especially help on the defensive end."

Brown is expected to be 100 percent this season. Look for him to move ahead of McAfee in the Xavier backcourt rotation.

OBI HARRIS (6-10, 215 lbs., JR, F/C, 10.0 ppg, 9.0 rpg, 2.5 apg, 4.0 bpg, .610 FG, .630 FT, Tallahassee CC, Fl. & Manatee HS/Bradenton, Fl.). Harris will play immediately as a junior college transfer. He has to. The Musketeers have few other options up front.

"Obi brings size, athleticism and shot-blocking ability," said Prosser. "Right now, his defense is ahead of his offense."

Right now, Harris needs to get stronger. At his size and weight, he may have trouble maintaining the position necessary to become a solid interior defender at this level.

Surely the Musketeers need that quality.

KEVIN FREY (6-7, 230 lbs., FR, F, 17.7 ppg, 9.4 rpg, 2.7 apg, 2.8 bpg, .630 FG, Maine West HS/Chicago, Ill.). The recruiting gurus were split on Frey. He was ranked anywhere from 29th (*Hoop Scoop*) to 86th (Bob Gibbons), though one service called him the sixth-best power forward prospect in the country.

If Frey is anywhere near that level, he will contribute immediately at Xavier. He is the only forward on the roster with a history of bulk and toughness. That's not a knock on the other guys, but more a reflection of their open floor games.

Occasionally, when a game is on the line and the score is tight, it's nice to have someone who will run through a pick or over an opponent for a second shot. If and when Frey becomes that guy, he will be an instant hit for the Musketeers.

Frey played only one season at Maine West HS, but was a first-team All-State selection by every major media outlet in Illinois.

OTHER RETURNEES

REGGIE BUTLER (6-10, 255 lbs., SO, C, #55, 1.1 ppg, 1.6 rpg, 3.5 minutes, .333 FG, .667 FT, Lathrup HS/Southfield, Mich.). Butler has a chance to start for the Musketeers, as does anyone his size who can be productive. However, it is more likely this deep reserve will work his way into a meaningful bench role in the frontcourt.

Butler has never been great scorer, even at his size in high school (7.9 ppg, 11.0 rpg as a senior). He was a redshirt at Xavier in 1996-97, then played only marginally in his collegiate debut (14 appearances) last year.

Can you say "project?"

"Reggie has worked as hard as anyone on the team in the weight room," said Prosser. "The challenge for Reggie is to turn his hard work into productivity."

OTHER NEWCOMERS

None.

QUESTIONS

Post presence? Braggs and T.J. Johnson did their jobs extremely well. There will be nights this season when the Musketeers might be begging for even one of them.

Outside shooting? Neither Lenny Brown or Lumpkin had a particularly good year from the field, although that negative was more than offset by the wonderful season turned in by Darnell Williams. Lloyd Price may be the second coming, but he won't be Williams yet, especially from the outside.

Program? There was offseason turmoil in the front office. Longtime athletic director Jeff Fogelson left somewhat controversially for Seton Hall. Skip Prosser interviewed at Arizona State and was said to have a handshake agreement for that job. Even the new campus arena was delayed. None of this should affect the players, but you never know.

ANSWERS

Seniors! Posey, Lenny Brown and Lumpkin are winners. Posey is a future pro. So few teams have quality seniors anymore that their presence has to help the Musketeers.

Style! Xavier will run you out of the building on offense, capitalize on every mistake with its defense and rotate all kinds of speed on the perimeter. Sometimes the game is over before it starts.

Lloyd Price! The freshman swingman is the real deal, according to all reports. The Musketeers really need him to be in the absence of Darnell Williams.

adidas Blue Ribbon Analysis

BACKCOURT	**B+**	**BENCH/DEPTH**	**B**
FRONTCOURT	**B+**	**INTANGIBLES**	**B+**

With Darnell Williams and at least one of the non-qualifying power players, this was arguably a Top 10 team. Without them, there may not be enough size or depth to match last season.

Then again, Xavier would probably trade an Atlantic 10 championship for an NCAA Tournament victory. And that is a very likely scenario.

The Musketeers are not strong or deep enough to outlast Temple at the top of the conference. However, they are experienced and unique enough to make up for last season's NCAA stumble.

Xavier is no worse than at at-large team and first-round victor. Look for the polls, which always seem to love the Musketeers, to notice them all season long.

(J.L.)

20

ARKANSAS

LOCATION	**Fayetteville, AR**
CONFERENCE	**SEC (Western Division)**
LAST SEASON	**24-9 (.727)**
CONFERENCE RECORD	**11-5 (2nd)**
STARTERS LOST/RETURNING	**2/3**
NICKNAME	**Razorbacks**
COLORS	**Cardinal & White**
HOMECOURT	**Bud Walton Arena (19,200)**
COACH	**Nolan Richardson (UTEP '63)**
RECORD AT SCHOOL	**314-118 (13 yrs.)**
CAREER RECORD	**433-155 (18 yrs.)**
ASSISTANTS	**Mike Anderson (Tulsa '82)**
	Brad Dunn (Western Illinois '81)
	Nolan Richardson III (Langston '91)
TEAM WINS (last 5 yrs.)	**31-32-20-18-24**
RPI (last 5 yrs.)	**2-5-29-58-20**
1997-98 FINISH	**Lost in NCAA second round.**

COACH AND PROGRAM

About an hour after his team's thrilling, 102-96 victory over Tennessee in the second round of the SEC Tournament last March, Arkansas coach Nolan Richardson was still holding court just outside the interview room in the Georgia Dome.

"That was about as good as college basketball gets, wasn't it?" a reporter asked Richardson.

Boss Hog paused for a second, then smiled. "If you didn't like that game," Richardson said, "you don't like basketball."

The SEC and the rest of the country had better get used to more games like it. The Razorbacks are back.

Actually, they never really went away. Arkansas did, after all, advance to the second round of the 1998 NCAA Tournament, where it put a scare into eventual runner-up Utah before falling. But, for the last two years, the proud and perennial champions of the SEC's Western Division had to sit back and watch upstart Mississippi claim the division title.

Arkansas suffered a different setback two years ago after an NCAA investigation ruled former player Sunday Adebayo ineligible. Trying to cooperate with the NCAA, the university slapped itself with sanctions and did not recruit junior college players for two years.

So imagine Richardson's dismay when the NCAA reversed its decision and allowed Adebayo, who was thought to have finished his career at Memphis, to return to Fayetteville for another season. Some observers thought that little brush with the NCAA might drive Richardson to the NBA, but the veteran coach just took it in stride. The man who has junior college, NIT and NCAA championships on his resume went to work and signed one of his best recruiting classes ever, even without JC players.

The guard-heavy class will give the Razorbacks the depth they've been lacking the last couple of years. True, Arkansas might be overly reliant on newcomers this season, but Richardson is particularly dangerous when he has plenty of fresh bodies to plug in and out of his "40 Minutes of Hell" system.

Arkansas will have a solid nucleus of seniors around which to build. Pat Bradley is one of the SEC's feared shooters, Kareem Reid one of its craftier point guards and Derek Hood one of its better rebounders.

It all adds up to another of Richardson's typical teams, one that can wear opponents down with intense defensive pressure. The Hogs' defense, at times, is their best offense.

This season should include a few milestones for Richardson, who will become the winningest coach in school history. He needs just 12 wins to pass Glen Rose, who needed 23 years to produce his 325 wins. Richardson is entering his 14th year.

"I've never taken a job to become the winningest coach," Richardson said. "Games are like report cards. You keep working so you can get the best grades. Becoming the winningest coach will mean a lot more later in my life than it will when it happens.

"After it happens, I'm going to keep working. If I ever get satisfied with something I've accomplished, I don't need to coach any more."

STARTERS NOT RETURNING

NICK DAVIS (6-9, PF, 10.4 ppg, 9.8 rpg, 1.2 apg, 1.3 spg, 2.4 bpg, 26.7 minutes, .510 FG, .472 FT). Toss out the last eight games of the season, when the opposition apparently figured out how to deal with him, and Davis had a great year. He started the season with a 10-point, 15-rebound performance against Northeastern Illinois, then topped that with 22 points and 23 rebounds against Jackson State.

After that, Davis became a rebounding machine, reaching double figures in boards in eight of his next nine games. Davis wound up leading the SEC in rebounding. He was also second in the league in blocked shots. His contributions will be hard to replace.

"He did it all," Richardson said. "He wore down at the end of the season, but we never would have won 24 games without him. We're hoping our forwards will pick up the rebounding slack and that someone else will step forward and take some charges. We should have a little more offensive firepower that will counter the loss of his scoring."

LANDIS WILLIAMS (6-5, SF, 7.4 ppg, 3.3 rpg, 15.8 minutes, .604 FG, .286 3PT, .706 FT). Williams had some solid games last season, but contributed little in the last six contests. He was suspended for the SEC Tournament.

Williams reached double figures nine times a year ago, including a 17-point, four-rebound effort against Alabama State and 17 points and six boards against Auburn.

Williams was a reliable veteran, but his contributions can be replaced.

OTHERS NOT RETURNING

ALI THOMPSON (6-5, SF, 6.3 ppg, 3.4 rpg, 1.1 apg, 17.3 minutes, .430 FG, .333 3PT, .605 FT). Thompson surprised Richardson in late August when he decided to quit the team. As one of four seniors, Thompson would have probably started at small forward and provided leadership for a group of seven freshmen.

"Ali has decided he doesn't want to play basketball anymore," Richardson said. "It is regretful to see a young man get to his senior year and lose interest in playing. However, we wish him luck and happiness in whatever he chooses to do."

Thompson started 15 games in his career and played in 82. He averaged 5.7 ppg and 2.8 rpg in his three seasons. His best year was 1996-97, when he started 11 of 32 games and averaged 7.8 ppg and 3.3 rpg.

Before last season, Thompson had surgery to repair a torn anterior cruciate ligament in his right knee. He was expected to miss the entire season, but was ready for the Southeastern Conference opener against LSU on Jan. 4.

SUNDAY ADEBAYO (6-6, F, 6.2 ppg, 3.6 rpg, 1.3 apg, 15.2 minutes, .511 FG, .677 FT). Adebayo's bizarre career didn't end quite the way he had envisioned. After being ruled ineligible at Arkansas three years ago, he transferred to Memphis, where, most people thought, he played his senior season in 1996-97.

Last fall, the NCAA ruled that it had made a mistake in denying Adebayo eligibility at Arkansas. It allowed him, in an unprecedented move, to return to the Razorbacks for one more season.

Adebayo wasn't eligible until the eighth game and truthfully did not have the impact some thought he would, scoring in double figures just one time in the regular season. But Adebayo earned his keep in the SEC Tournament, when he scored 18 points and grabbed nine rebounds in a wild, second-round victory over Tennessee.

Without the contributions of Adebayo, the Hogs probably would have lost, perhaps putting their NCAA Tournament bid in doubt.

PROJECTED STARTERS

KAREEM REID (5-10, 165 lbs., SR, PG, #12, 11.9 ppg, 2.1 rpg, 5.2 apg, 1.9 tpg, 1.9 spg, 29.5 minutes, .431 FG, .345 3PT, .739 FT, St. Raymond's HS/Bronx, N.Y.). Reid should leave Arkansas as its all-time leader in assists, which says something about the worth of the little guy. Though he was Arkansas' second-leading scorer last year, he is content to run the offense and distribute the ball to his teammates.

Reid is a crafty playmaker. Many times, his seemingly hell-bent drives to the basket thoroughly confuse Arkansas' opponents, because he's so adept at tossing the ball back out to wide-open teammates on the perimeter. With 567 career assists, he needs just 163 this season to pass Lee Mayberry, the school's all-time leader.

Considering Reid has averaged 189 assists per season in his career, he should claim the assist record some time in February. Reid was second in the SEC in assists a year ago.

Reid put in a lot of work on his own offensive game last season, and it showed. A career .412 shooter, Reid shot .431 from the field and .345 from three-point range. In his two previous years, Reid shot just .259 and .233 from behind the arc, so his improved perimeter shooting was a real plus for the Hogs.

Reid also improved his free-throw shooting by nearly four percentage points (to 10th in the SEC). With the game on the line in the late stages, Reid can seal the deal.

Reid is also a cunning defender who excels in Richardson's system, which features, pressure, pressure and more pressure. He had 61 steals last year, fourth in the SEC.

"Kareem Reid is an all-purpose player," Richardson said. "We depend on him for everything."

PAT BRADLEY (6-2, 195 lbs., SR, SG, #22, 14.8 ppg, 2.7 rpg, 1.7 apg, 1.9 tpg, 1.5 spg, 29.3 minutes, .382 FG, .384 3PT, .902 FT, Everett HS/Everett, Ma.). Richardson will never forget his good fortune on a fateful day four years ago when he was watching an AAU game. There to scout Ron Mercer, who ended up at Kentucky, Richardson couldn't help but notice Bradley, who was bombing away from the perimeter.

"We've got to have this guy," Richardson said to himself.

Bradley was surprised to learn of Richardson's interest, but didn't have to have his arm twisted to make the trek from his native New England to Arkansas. Just as Richardson thought, the player has developed into a star.

A year ago, Bradley was a second-team All-SEC pick as he led the Hogs in scoring for the second straight year. He scored in double figures 26 times, reaching his career high of 33 points against the great guards of South Carolina.

"Pat Bradley was fantastic tonight," Gamecock coach Eddie Fogler said after that game.

Bradley is a game-breaking shooter who commands constant defensive attention. Let him slip free, even for an instant, and pay the price. He is a career .407 three-point shooter. Last year, he shot 38 percent from behind the arc (sixth in the SEC) and led the league with his average of 2.8 three-pointers per game. Bradley's 93 three-pointers were the third-highest single-season total in Arkansas history.

Already, Bradley owns the Arkansas record for three-pointers made (273) and attempted (670). He set a school and SEC record for consecutive games with a three-pointer (60). Bradley has at least one trey in 81 of his last 83 games.

As great a shooter as Bradley is, he isn't one-dimensional. Last year, he was third on the team in assists (56) and third in steals (50). He is a career 87 percent free-throw shooter, whose .902 mark last year would have led the SEC if he had enough attempts to qualify.

Bradley might not have to shoot so often this season. A solid recruiting class top-heavy with good guards has improved Arkansas' depth in the backcourt and its overall shooting. Along with backcourt mate Kareem Reid, Bradley will be expected to assume a leadership role.

"We hope the new guys can play with (Bradley and Reid) and get a feel for what we do," Richardson said.

DEREK HOOD (6-8, 220 lbs., SR, PF, #55, 8.4 ppg, 6.1 rpg, 1.7 apg, 2.1 tpg, 1.1 spg, 22.6 minutes, .502 FG, .533 FT, Central HS/Kansas City, Mo.). Hood's numbers were down a bit last year, mainly because Nick Davis was grabbing every rebound in sight, swatting away 80 enemy shots and collecting tons of garbage baskets. But, even though Davis' great year might have overshadowed Hood's performance, the rugged power forward turned in a good season.

Hood, with his funky jumper, has never been known as a scorer. But last season he shot .502 from the field; his career field-goal percentage is .486, so he is doing something right.

Hood excels at the little things. Two years ago, he led

1997-98 RESULTS

Northeastern Illinois	114-56	
Jackson State	97-71	
Oral Roberts	81-75	
*Fresno State	70-69	
Bethune-Cookman	108-42	
Missouri	75-46	
@Louisville	100-83	
Centenary	61-48	
#American-Puerto Rico (L)	59-64	
#Murray State (L)	83-94	
#St. Louis	78-70	
Alabama State	103-48	
Louisiana State	62-59	
Mississippi State	83-70	
@Memphis	75-72	
Florida	89-84	
@Kentucky (L)	77-80	ot
@Auburn	79-65	
Alabama	77-70	
@Louisiana State	85-68	
@Mississippi State	76-73	
Mississippi	100-87	
Vanderbilt	93-83	
@Georgia (L)	70-86	
@Tennessee (L)	71-74	
South Carolina	96-88	
Auburn	107-83	
@Mississippi (L)	65-81	
@Alabama (L)	63-65	
##Tennessee	102-96	
##Kentucky (L)	74-99	
%Nebraska	74-65	
%Utah (L)	69-75	

@ away games
* Premier Classic, Phoenix, AZ
# Puerto Rico Classic, San Juan, PR
SEC Tournament, Georgia Dome, Atlanta, GA
% NCAA West Sub-Regional, Boise, ID

the SEC in rebounding. He is a more than adequate passer, with 143 career assists. His blocked shot total in three years has been consistent: 22, 23 and 27. He defends his position well.

When needed, Hood can also score. He had 16 points against Mississippi and Utah last season. In the Utah game, which happened to be in the second round of the NCAA Tournament, Hood was seven of nine from the field and made both of his free throws.

"Derek Hood has tremendous heart," Richardson has said many times in the past. "He wants to win as much as anyone on our team."

BRANDON DEAN (6-0, 180 lbs., FR, G, #13, 29.0 ppg, 4.0 rpg, 5.0 apg, 3.0 spg, Ouachita Parish HS/ Monroe, La.). The acquisition of Dean can't be understated, for he is as gifted a point guard who could have signed anywhere in the country. He is the heir apparent to Reid at the point, and he won't serve as a mere understudy this season. Dean is going to play—a lot.

"Brandon Dean was ranked by some people as high as anyone we've signed at Arkansas other than Corliss Williamson," Richardson said. "He is capable of becoming one of the best point guards in the country. He needs to be an impact player as a freshman."

Dean would have to be classified as a scoring point guard. He's got all the requisite skills for that—strength, leaping ability and a quick first step to the basket.

"Dean reminds us of (former Arkansas player) Arlyn Bowers because of his build," Richardson told *Hawgs Illustrated*. "He jumps well. He can dunk over Superman. He can create his own shot and he's all over the floor stealing the ball on defense."

Dean's defensive skills caught the attention of several recruiting analysts. "I think he may really help them most defensively because he is so big and strong, really gets after you and is hard to get around," said Ron Briscoe of the *Regional Basketball Report*.

If all this sounds as though Dean is perfect for Richardson's "40 Minutes of Hell" philosophy, well, he is. Dean committed to Clemson in the fall before backing out, and was also recruited heavily by Cincinnati, Kansas, Michigan, UCLA and Kentucky. In the end, he narrowed his choices to LSU, Florida State and Arkansas.

The Hogs won out because Dean realized he was so perfect for what Richardson likes to do. And he wasn't worried in the least that a pair of senior guards will be ahead of him at Arkansas.

"I feel like you just have to go in and compete and play hard," Dean told *Hawgs Illustrated*. "I think the fact that they have so many guards will only help the team. It is an established program with established traditions."

JUSTIN HANKINS (6-9, 220 lbs., FR, F, #44, 25.5 ppg, 14.6 rpg, Elkins HS/Elkins, Ark.). Like new teammate Jason Gilbert, Hankins is an in-state product who grew up wanting to play for Arkansas. Also like Gilbert, Hankins can play more than one position. He has the bulk and skill to play power forward or center.

"He's a banger and a competitor," Richardson told the *Northwest Arkansas Times*. "He'll get after you pretty hard. But he's a big kid who's got some skills. He can handle the ball, shoot, pass. Those are skills that are difficult to teach when they get to this level."

Hankins was ranked No. 89 on the *Prep Stars Recruiter's Handbook* list of the country's top 300 seniors.

KEY RESERVES

JASON JENNINGS (7-0, 275 lbs., SO, C, #52, 4.7 ppg, 2.6 rpg, 9.9 minutes, .510 FG, .689 FT, Bald Knob HS/Bald Knob, Ark.). His status as the only true center on the team should get Jennings into a few games this season, as it did last year. He is the first seven-footer to play for Arkansas since Mike Carpenter in 1985.

You might think a lumbering seven-footer would be lost in the Razorbacks' system, but Jennings saw a fair amount of action as a freshman, playing 288 minutes in 29 games. He shot well and turned back an impressive number of enemy shots (25, third on the team behind Nick Davis and Derek Hood)

Still, there were games in which Jennings' services weren't required. He didn't see a second of playing time, for example, in either of the Hogs' two high-scoring games against Tennessee.

"Jason is a very important part of our team," Richardson said. "We hope, in the November and December games, he will gain some confidence. If he gives us what he's capable of, he can make a difference. His development the day he arrived to now has been very good.

"He doesn't have to start for us, but we'd like to get him up to about 20 minutes per game."

BRANDON DAVIS (6-5, 200 lbs., SO, F, #53, 2.8 ppg, 0.8 rpg, 7.7 minutes, .421 FG, .303 3PT, .632 FT, Fairview HS/Camden, Ark.). As a freshman, Davis found his way into 25 games, during which he showed a willingness to hoist three-pointers. He made 10 of 33, tying him for fourth on the team.

Davis reached double figures three times a year ago. He scored 12 points against Kentucky in the SEC Tournament, and also had 11 points against Northeastern Illinois and 10 against Auburn. Davis is considered to have a huge up side because the former three-sport star (he was All-State in football and also played baseball in high school) is focusing only on basketball.

"Last year was the first time Brandon spent an entire year with just one sport," Richardson said. "Now that he is playing nothing but basketball, he should become a much better player. He has good athletic ability."

JASON GILBERT (5-11, 170 lbs., FR, G, #4, 27.0 ppg, 5.0 apg, Mountain View HS/Mountain View, Ark.). Like all the guards Arkansas signed in its six-man recruiting class, Gilbert is a double-threat. He is a great shooter who can also run the point.

The Arkansas native was actually born in Fayetteville, where his father was an assistant coach at Fayetteville High School, and grew up a Razorback fan.

"Jason cut his teeth on the railings at Barnhill Arena when he was a baby," Gilbert's father, Dwight, told the *Northwest Arkansas Times*. "Now he's going to see what he can do in Walton Arena."

Richardson thinks Gilbert can do a lot.

"Jason Gilbert can have a major impact because of his ability to shoot the ball," Richardson said. "He also understands the game."

Arkansas fans who were thrilled by the super-long-range shooting of former Razorback Al Dillard will appreciate Gilbert. He has Dillard-like range, which means opponents had better check him just inside the midcourt line.

Playing in the Holiday Hoops Tournament at Bud Walton Arena last December, Gilbert swished a 70-footer as the horn sounded to end the first half. The ball rolled under the feet of Arkansas athletic director Frank Broyles and Richardson, both of whom were watching the game from the stands. But the coach didn't need convincing.

""It only took me about a minute and a half to see that Jason could play for us," Richardson told the *Northwest Arkansas Times*. "He's a great shooter, but what I like most is that he makes excellent decisions with the basketball."

1998-99 ARKANSAS SCHEDULE

Nov.	15	Jackson State
	17	Alabama State
	20-22	#Top of the World Classic
	28	Northeast Louisiana
Dec.	5	@Oklahoma
	7	Western Carolina
	16	Southeastern Louisiana
	19	Memphis
	23	@Wake Forest
	30	North Texas State
Jan.	2	@LSU
	6	@Auburn
	9	Mississippi
	13	@Mississippi State
	16	Georgia
	20	Alabama
	23	Providence
	27	LSU
	30	@Mississippi
Feb.	2	Tennessee
	6	@Vanderbilt
	10	@South Carolina
	13	Mississippi State
	16	@Florida
	20	Kentucky
	24	Auburn
	27	@Alabama
Mar.	4-7	SEC Tournament

@ Road Games
\# Fairbanks, AK (vs. Virginia, first round; also Alaska-Fairbanks, Nebraska, New Mexico State, Villanova, Washington State and Wisconsin)
\## Georgia Dome, Atlanta, GA

Richardson shouldn't have to worry about Gilbert concerning matters between the ears. He had a 4.0 grade point average in high school and made a 31 on the ACT.

CHRIS JEFFRIES (6-8, 220 lbs., FR, F, #15, 22.0 ppg, 8.0 rpg, 6.0 apg, Washington Union HS/Fresno, Calif.). He grew up halfway across the country, but, through the magic of TV, Jeffries became an Arkansas fan when he watched some of Richardson's better teams play. His early heroes were Lee Mayberry and Todd Day.

It should come as no surprise, then, that Jeffries' game has been compared to Day's. Like Day, Jeffries is versatile enough to play all three perimeter positions.

"Because of his ability to defend on the perimeter, and his ability to handle the ball, he's dangerous outside," Vonn Webb, Jeffries' high school coach, told the *Arkansas Democrat*. "He has a lot of range and he can knock down the three. It will be difficult for schools, even at the Division I level, to put a guard on him and stop him. With his size, he can also take it inside."

OTHER RETURNEES

CHRIS WALKER (6-5, 195 lbs., JR, G, #41, 2.5 ppg, 1.9 rpg, 11.3 minutes, .377 FG, .267 3PT, .538 FT, Pine Bluff HS/Pine Bluff, Ark.). There isn't much work for a guy who backs up the tireless Reid at point guard, but Walker, who came to Fayetteville as a walkon, did get into 31 games last year and averaged 11.3 minutes.

Walker had 27 assists, but offset them with 32 turnovers. He also had 25 steals, though, so his good plays neutralized his bad ones.

OTHER NEWCOMERS

SERGERIO GIPSON (6-3, 180 lbs., FR, G, #23, 20.6 ppg, 4.3 rpg, 5.3 apg, 3.5 spg, Farmersville HS/ Farmersville, La.). Arkansas raided Louisiana for not just one, but two guards. Before signing point guard Brandon Dean, the Hogs landed Gipson, who is versatile enough to play either backcourt position.

"He can shoot, score points and create shots," Richardson said. "He can play either guard spot, so he's like having two players. Having a swing guard is a plus."

Recruiting analysts also raved about Gipson's versatility.

"I just love him," said Dave Telep of *Prep Stars Recruiter's Handbook*. "He's a crafty lefthander who can player either the point or the 'two' guard. He can really penetrate and get to the goal and also is a legitimate deep shooting threat."

Gipson seriously considered attending Louisiana Tech, which is a 20-minute drive from his home, and also pondered some late interest from Mississippi State before signing with Arkansas. Gipson and Dean are close friends, and might well make up Arkansas' backcourt of the future.

T.J. CLEVELAND (6-1, 180 lbs., FR, G, #20, 19.0 ppg, 6.0 rpg, Minor HS/Birmingham, Ala.). Cleveland, chosen the MVP in the Alabama 6A state tournament after leading Minor High to the championship, obviously had some credentials to earn a scholarship at a Division I school. He was recruited by several, including UAB, UTEP and Murray State.

Family ties influenced his final decision, though. The nephew of Arkansas assistant coach Mike Anderson, Cleveland was convinced to walk on, after which he would be awarded the first available scholarship. Luckily for Cleveland, that scholarship materialized quickly when senior swingman Ali Thompson decided in late August to quit the team.

It was fitting that Cleveland finally end up in Fayetteville.

"He grew up around the program," Anderson said. "He's been coming to the Razorback camp since he was 11 or 12 years old."

Cleveland fits into the mold of the Hogs' other freshman guards, meaning he can play either position.

"He's a combo guard, pretty heady," Anderson said. "And he's a fierce competitor, no doubt about it. We wanted to bring in an abundance of guards this year. Big men stabilize you, but guards take you where you want to go."

JOSH SMITH (6-5, 200 lbs., FR, G, #20, 33.0 ppg, 14.0 rpg, Prairie Grove HS/Prairie Grove, Ark.). Smith joined the program two years ago, but was redshirted last season. He played for a smaller high school, which tempers his gaudy senior-season stats a bit. Still, Smith can shoot. That skill, plus his work ethic, has impressed Richardson.

"Anyone who works as hard as he does has the

possibility of playing," Richardson said.

QUESTIONS

Center? Who will man the middle for the Razorbacks? The massive Jennings played in 29 games a year ago, but does he slow down the Hogs' up-tempo style?

Newcomers? With just six returning veterans, several freshmen will have to play. How many of them will be ready? And how long will it take?

ANSWERS

Guards! In Kareem Reid and Pat Bradley, Arkansas has one of the best backcourts in the SEC. Some talented freshmen guards have been brought in to provide depth.

Style of play! Arkansas is as good at controlling the tempo of a game as any team in the country. The Hogs pressure on defense and attack on offense. It's an exciting brand of basketball to watch.

adidas Blue Ribbon Analysis

BACKCOURT	**A**	**BENCH/DEPTH**	**B**
FRONTCOURT	**B**	**INTANGIBLES**	**A**

After watching upstart Mississippi take over its customary position atop the SEC Western Division standings the last two years, Arkansas is poised to move back into the division's penthouse.

Arkansas' strength is clearly in the backcourt. Kareem Reid is one of the country's best point guards. Pat Bradley is a game-breaking shooter. Several talented freshmen will get a chance to earn minutes behind them.

In the frontcourt, Derek Hood returns for his senior season as one of the SEC's top rebounders. Hood could get some help inside from sophomore center Jason Jennings, or newcomers Justin Hankins and Chris Jeffries. Indeed, at least one other frontcourt player will have to emerge.

Though the Hogs' don't have too much experience behind their three seniors, there is enough depth to allow Richardson to play his favored brand of up-tempo basketball, offensively and defensively.

With so many players of equal ability on his roster, Richardson will be able to use nine or 10 without a drop off in production. That means that Arkansas' "40 minutes of Hell" style will be in full force.

For the rest of the SEC West, that means trouble.

(C.D.)

21

INDIANA

LOCATION	**Bloomington , IN**
CONFERENCE	**Big Ten**
LAST SEASON	**20-12 (.625)**
CONFERENCE RECORD	**9-7 (t-5th)**
STARTERS LOST/RETURNING	**1/4**
NICKNAME	**Hoosiers**
COLORS	**Crimson & Cream**
HOMECOURT	**Assembly Hall (17,357)**
COACH	**Bob Knight (Ohio State '62)**
RECORD AT SCHOOL	**618-220 (27 yrs.)**
CAREER RECORD	**720-270 (33 yrs.)**
ASSISTANTS	**Mike Davis (Thomas Edison '95)** **Pat Knight (Indiana '95)** **John Treloar (Belhaven '78)**
TEAM WINS (last 5 yrs.)	**21-19-19-22-20**
RPI (last 5 yrs.)	**15-30-34-21-21**
1997-98 FINISH	**Lost in NCAA second round.**

COACH AND PROGRAM

The story has been told and retold the last two years around the University of Wisconsin. Everyone really loves the punch line.

Supposedly, current Badger forward Mark Vershaw, then a high school senior of some note, was the target of a hard-sell, conference-call recruiting pitch from Indiana coach Bob Knight and one or more IU assistants. Knight peppered Vershaw with rhetorical questions in his trademark delivery and the teenager dutifully responded.

"You want to attend a respected university, don'tcha Mark?"

"Yes, coach."

"You want to play on a Big Ten champion, don'tcha?"

"Yes, coach."

"And you want to play in the NCAA Tournament, don'tcha?"

"Yes, coach."

Here, Knight tried to close the deal.

"So, why wouldn't you want to come to Indiana University?" Then, Vershaw really closed it.

"You, coach."

Click.

It's not like Knight needed Vershaw. The Hoosier general has ended up with plenty of talent the last few seasons. In fact, an argument could be made that the Hoosiers, who tied for fifth last year in a mediocre Big Ten, started November with the most talented seven-man unit in the league.

But the story is a window to Knight's growing reputation among teenagers as a guy who can be more trouble than he's worth, a guy no Big Ten recruit has to deal with any more to get to the NCAAs or to win a league title.

Discipline? Lon Kruger at Illinois dispenses plenty of it. His players not only love him, but play championship-caliber ball for him.

Defense? Dick Bennett at Wisconsin can teach you how to play serious defense.

Camaraderie? Tom Izzo at Michigan State has built a family atmosphere in East Lansing, one which allows many talented players to accept roles and work happily toward a common goal.

In fact, it can be argued that every asset the IU program has been known for the last quarter century can now be found in greater quantity somewhere else in the Big Ten. What may be most remarkable lately about the Hoosiers is just how hollow they look come March, almost as if some of them want the season to end. With college basketball more competitive than ever, teams that excel aren't just talented and well-coached. The really good ones have some fun, too.

Before the new year, the potential of recent IU teams has been evident. A lively 75-72 loss to eventual national champion Kentucky last season showed the zest of newcomers Rob Turner and William Gladness, as well as the possibilities of a roster that at one point included sophomore center Jason Collier, rookie swingman Luke Recker and holdovers Andrae Patterson, Charlie Miller and A.J. Guyton.

But by the end of recent seasons, that vigor has, without exception, petrified. Indiana is 1-4 over the last four years in the NCAA Tournament. In its last six NCAAs, it has been ousted by a lower-seeded team four times.

Last March, the Hoosiers staggered into the Big Dance with a 2-5 stretch in their last seven games, sweating out a first-round win over last-place Ohio State in the Big Ten Tournament. They very nearly were eliminated again in the NCAA first round (taken to overtime by Oklahoma), before falling to Connecticut two days later.

The Hoosiers almost never look like they're having any fun. More often, they can resemble drones in a sweatshop factory. Gnashing through the day. Fearing the foreman might find some flaw. Stamping out the product. Going home.

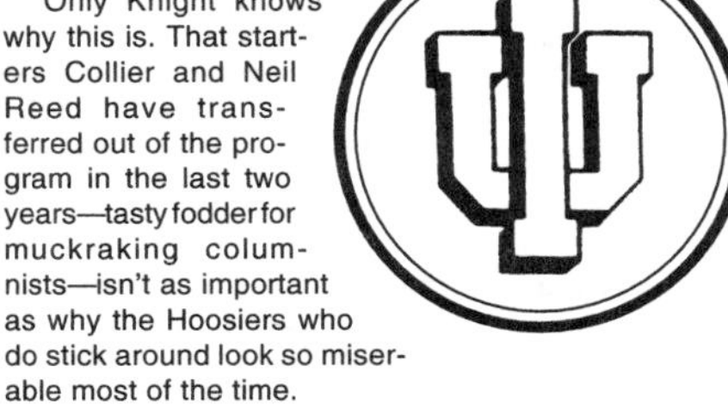

Only Knight knows why this is. That starters Collier and Neil Reed have transferred out of the program in the last two years—tasty fodder for muckraking columnists—isn't as important as why the Hoosiers who do stick around look so miserable most of the time.

One thing is certain: Unless Knight finds a way to cultivate some longer-lasting spirit in his teams, Indiana isn't headed back to the Final Four during the remainder of his tenure and might not even make the NCAA Sweet 16 again. Knight would not be interviewed on the subject, so his take on all of this is hard to know. The Knight comments used below were prepared and faxed by the IU sports information department.

Tactically, many of Knight's problems germinated when the game was dumbed down by the 35-second clock. Before the NCAA decided to whack 10 seconds off the timer in 1994—and especially prior to '86, when no clock existed at all—Indiana was masterful at running defenses through its myriad screens and turning opponents' legs to jelly.

Late in each half, exhausted defenders couldn't move their feet and groped themselves into foul trouble. The Hoosiers won games at the foul line, routinely shooting half-again as many free throws as their opponents. Sore Big Ten losers often whined that Knight intimidated officials, when really the Hoosiers earned their advantage through sheer relentlessness.

That tack doesn't work as well anymore. Last season, Indiana shot virtually the same number of free throws as its Big Ten opponents (339-338).

Carelessness with the ball is often a symptom of fatigue, too. Indiana used to commonly enjoy a substantial edge in turnover margin. But that advantage has dried up, as well. In four of the last five Big Ten seasons, the Hoosiers have committed more turnovers than their opponents—an unprecedented occurrence under Knight.

The 1998-99 team had better have its legs, because it is not big. Other than redshirt freshman Kirk Haston (6-10), no one stands taller than 6-8. In fact, what the Hoosiers need most is the vintage Knight acumen which won three national championships, not a caricature from his coaching past.

STARTERS NOT RETURNING

ANDRAE PATTERSON (6-8, C, 12.6 ppg, 5.8 rpg, 1.8 apg, 25.5 minutes, .495 FG, .278 3PT, .793 FT). The Hoosiers' third-leading scorer and their top rebounder, Patterson provided 240 pounds worth of beef inside. He was also Indiana's leading shot-blocker, with 30 rejections, and his .495 shooting percentage is evidence of an ability to score from the paint. Patterson wasn't a star, just a steady, reliable player who got the job done.

Of course, that was never the expectations when he arrived in Bloomington, so, in the eyes of many, Patterson was an underachiever.

OTHERS NOT RETURNING

CHARLIE MILLER (6-7, F, 3.8 ppg, 2.4 rpg, 13.2 minutes, .365 FG, .227 3PT, .735 FT). Miller provided 10 to 15 minutes per night of mostly ordinary play off the bench. However, he did earn five starts. Given his limited time, Miller rebounded fairly well, leading IU in boards three times.

RICHARD MANDEVILLE (7-0, C, 1.3 ppg, 1.3 rpg, 5.4 minutes, .438 FG, .167 3PT, .714 FT). Seven-footers tend to be very good or very bad; they're seldom just average. Put Mandeville in the "bad" category. He did play in 27 games, starting one, but saw little action during those times.

The most telling stat for Mandeville may be this: 27 games, three blocked shots. That's just not enough for one of the tallest players in Division I.

ROBBIE EGGERS (6-10, F, 0.9 ppg, 1.2 rpg, 4.8 minutes, .368 FG, .429 FT). Eggers saw the fewest minutes of any Hoosier, but still managed a pretty respectable rebounding average, all things considered. There were just too many scorers ahead of him for Knight to justify giving him any more time.

PROJECTED STARTERS

A.J. GUYTON (6-1, 175 lbs., JR, PG, #25, 16.8 ppg, 3.5 rpg, 3.7 apg, 34.0 minutes, .468 FG, .439 3PT, .766 FT, Central HS/Peoria, Ill.). Blessed with the one-on-one skills of a point guard and the three-point accuracy of a "two," Guyton is a true combo guard—a title claimed by many but earned by few. He has the skills to become the single most dangerous offensive force in the league, including a lethal first step and the ability to pull up and fire from almost anywhere on the floor.

Guyton's 987 career points are the seventh best freshman/sophomore scoring total in Hoosier history, and the 79 treys he canned last season were exceeded by only two other IU players. Not only did this guy play in Peoria, he does a pretty fine job of it in Bloomington.

Not that his game couldn't use some fine-tuning. Guyton's assist and steal totals dropped from those of his freshman year, while his turnovers increased.

"The thing we have to do with Guyton is, we have to get him to play without the ball," said Knight. "He's tough with the ball. But he has to learn to play without it at both ends of the floor."

Still, Guyton is clearly the hub of this team. He is the most athletic component and the one most capable of hurting the enemy on all parts of the floor. Witness his feat of collecting 400 points, 100 assists and 100 rebounds in two straight seasons. Only Isiah Thomas has done this at IU.

LUKE RECKER (6-6, 193 lbs., SO, SF, #4, 12.8 ppg, 3.9 rpg, 2.8 apg, 1.5 spg, 29.3 minutes, .491 FG, .321 3PT, .826 FT, DeKalb HS/Waterloo, Ind.). Recker stepped right in as a starter and played well as a freshman. Not terribly quick, he is nonetheless fluid and purposeful in his court movement and plays with a tenacity the Assembly Hall crowd loves. There is nothing superfluous about his game, it's just sturdy as an old farm house. He has the same precocious court awareness that made Damon Bailey such a stunning underclassman.

Displaying considerable enthusiasm, Recker placed second on the team in scoring and minutes played. He's probably not quite good enough to be a 15-plus ppg guy, but with a solid inside-outside game and the ability to hit the open man, not to mention a fine defensive sense, he'll continue to do well.

Expect more of the same out of Recker this season.

WILLIAM GLADNESS (6-8, 220 lbs., SR, PF, #30, 8.6 ppg, 5.1 rpg, 1.3 spg, 24.8 minutes, 5.98 FG, .576 FT, Carl Albert JC, Okla. & West Memphis HS/West Memphis, Ark.). Another talent whose game never quite delivered on the major promise of the late fall was Gladness. The junior college import played hard and well enough down the stretch, just not with the abandon he had earlier.

His agility near the hoop was something IU has lacked lately. Because the Hoosiers are so small this year, he'll have to take care of business around the tin. Knight could really use 15 points and 8-10 rebounds per game from him.

None of the other Hoosiers look capable of that interior production. And, with Patterson gone, there should be considerably more room inside for Gladness to operate.

What should provide Knight with some optimism is that Gladness picked up his game toward the end of the season, averaging in double figures over the last 20 or so games and shooting nearly 60 percent in league contests. He was solid on D, too, snaring 42 steals.

DANE FIFE (6-4, 190 lbs., FR, SG, #11, 25.9 ppg, 4.8 rpg, 5.1 apg, 2.4 spg, Clarkston HS/Clarkston, Mich.). Either immediately or eventually knocking Michael Lewis out of the starting lineup will be Fife, younger brother of former Michigan point guard Dugan Fife. The two aren't very similar.

"Fife is a tough kid," said Knight. "He brings that before anything. We need what this kid can bring to our program. He wants to win. When I think of him, I don't think of his basketball abilities, I think of what he brings to us in terms of wanting to win and knowing how to win and knowing how he's got to play. Obviously, he's going to be a real key."

That Knight got this kid is a testament to his continued clout with certain types of recruits, the Vershaw story be damned. Fife is a primo catch. Then again, so was Patterson and so was Collier. Watching how the rookie develops at IU will be interesting.

What Fife offers is a big guard with pizzazz who can play all types of basketball. In high school and the camps he played a total game—scoring on the catch-and-shoot three-pointer off a screen, slipping passes to wide-open teammates off the drive, playing defense with fangs.

He is quick-footed enough to hang with most shooting guards and can even fill at small forward for a few minutes when Lewis is in the game with Guyton or Turner (7.3 ppg, 2.8 rpg). More mouth-watering is the prospect of Guyton and Fife together, each able to play point or off-guard.

KIRK HASTON (6-10, 230 lbs., FR, C, #35, 20.0 ppg, 12.1 rpg, 5.5 bpg, Perry County HS/Linton, Tenn.). Playing the picking machine will be Haston, the only true center on the team. Knight likes his hands and his increased toughness over the last year in practice. If he can simply rebound consistently in 16-20 minutes per game, Knight would be happy.

Haston picked a good year to join the roster. The Big Ten's returning pivot talent doesn't figure to threaten him much. Redshirting last year allowed him the chance to practice with the Hoosiers for the entire season, and Knight liked the way he seemed to come up with the ball when no one else could.

Indiana needs a rebounder, and if Haston is the guy, it may save some chairs along the bench.

KEY RESERVES

MICHAEL LEWIS (6-1, 180 lbs., JR, G, 6.2 ppg, 4.7 apg, 24.8 minutes, .490 FG, .500 3PT, .832 FT, Jasper HS/Jasper, Ind.). Somewhere in the rotation will be Lewis, who developed into the floor leader last season.

It is easy to underestimate Lewis, but don't let the paper boy appearance fool you. Though not the kind of guy who is going to break anyone down one-on-one, he knows what's going on out there. His assist-to-turnover ratio of 1.9-to-1.0 was among the best in the league last year.

Early-season struggles dampened his scoring average, but Lewis shot the ball much better as the season wore on. And his 83.2 percent from the free throw line is mighty impressive. Still, no one expects Lewis to score. Only eight points in the Big Ten Tournament? So what; he dished 15 assists against just four turnovers in 64 minutes. And how about 15 assists in a game against Iowa? That's called ballhandling.

Lewis and Fife should combine with Guyton to give Knight a very talented backcourt.

ROB TURNER (6-4, 200 lbs., SR, G, #23, 7.3 ppg, 2.8 rpg, 1.8 apg, 18.0 minutes, .436 FG, .250 3PT, .588 FT, Tyler JC, Tex. & Wilmington HS/Wilmington, Del.). Turner made reservations at Knight's doghouse in early February by sometimes playing flimsy defense and violating the coach's sacrosanct four-pass rule. The promise of a .566 field goal percentage (.400 3PT) during the non-conference season dissolved into bad shot selection against league competition.

Turner's numbers dropped to .436 from the field, including .250 from the arc in the Big Ten. And when he mildly criticized IU's structured style to reporters—not exactly the game he played at Tyler (Tex.) JC—Knight took him out of circulation almost completely.

Turner was close to becoming the third one-time starter in two seasons to transfer out in the spring when graduating swingman Charlie Miller persuaded him to stick around for his senior year. It's not an overstatement to say that any chance Indiana has at winning the Big Ten depends on whether Turner and Knight can find common ground.

Turner is a considerable talent who, if happy, could raise the level of this team tremendously. He showed that against Kentucky with 25 points.

It should help that this is his "money year." Turner has the ability to become an NBA draft choice if he regains his outside stroke. And he knows it. But to do that, he needs playing time.

LUKE JIMENEZ (6-3, 195 lbs., JR, G, #12, 3.0 ppg, 1.0 rpg, 12.9 minutes, .526 FG, .488 3PT, .875 FT, Redwood Valley HS/Redwood Valley, Minn.). Jimenez is a useful spare guard who will certainly get spot time at the point. How much will depend largely on how quickly Fife progresses.

For a reserve lead guard, he is dependable with the ball and is a very good shooter when given space. In 665 career minutes, Jimenez has coughed up the ball a startlingly low 31 times. He's also a career .476 three-point shooter. Knight will find him some minutes.

LARRY RICHARDSON (6-8, 220 lbs., JR, C/F, #33, 2.9 ppg, 1.3 rpg, 8.2 minutes, .500 FG, .692 FT, Orange Park HS/Orange Park, Fla.). Richardson, like Gladness, must also progress inside.

"There were times last year when Richardson did some pretty good things," said Knight. "We have to get him playing consistently."

Considering that Gladness and Richardson are the only two guys taller than 6-6 with any experience at all, they'll have to bring their "A" games every night for IU to contend. Richardson has shown flashes of ability, but needs to put together a much more consistent game.

If the past is any indication, though, Knight may need to rely on his newcomers up front.

LYNN WASHINGTON (6-7, 225 lbs., F, #44, 17.5 ppg, 8.0 rpg, San Jose CC, Calif./San Jose, Calif.). Washington is a junior college transfer who should get 8-10 minutes at the "four" spot when Knight elects to play a quick lineup with Gladness at center.

"I really like Washington," said Knight. "Everybody that saw Washington play told us how hard he played and what a tough kid he was. And that's something I don't think we've had in great quantities over the last couple years."

OTHER RETURNEES

None.

OTHER NEWCOMERS

JARROD ODLE (6-8, 205 lbs., FR, F, #43, 26.0 ppg, 11.7 rpg, .460 FG, .800 FT, Oak Hill HS/Converse, Ind.).

1997-98 RESULTS

@Temple (L)	53-59
@Alabama-Brirmingham	80-64
#Hawaii (L)	65-82
#Northeast Louisiana	103-69
Notre Dame	91-80
@Kentucky (L)	72-75
Evansville	85-73
##Wisconsin-Green Bay	72-58
##South Alabama	64-56
###San Francisco	65-52
####Southwest Missouri State	78-66
####Western Michigan	70-63
Iowa (L)	76-89
@Illinois (L)	72-74
Michigan	80-62
Ohio State	83-66
@Northwestern	76-58
Purdue	94-88
@Wisconsin	69-59
@Michigan State (L)	66-84
Minnesota	95-82
Penn State	95-76
@Purdue (L)	89-94
Northwestern	73-55
@Ohio State	74-72
@Michigan (L)	64-112
Illinois (L)	72-82
@Iowa (L)	70-84
#####Ohio State	78-71
#####Purdue (L)	71-76
%Oklahoma	94-87 ot
%Connecticut (L)	68-78

@ away games
# United Airlines Tipoff Classic, Honolulu, HI
Indiana Classic, Bloomington, IN
Pete Newell Challenge, Oakland, CA
Hoosier Classic, Indianapolis, IN
Big Ten Tournament, United Center, Chicago, IL
% NCAA East Sub-Regional, Washington, DC

1998-99 INDIANA SCHEDULE

Nov.	7	*Seton Hall
	8	*South Carolina
	14	Indiana State
	18	UAB
	23-25	#Maui Classic
Dec.	1	@Notre Dame
	5	Temple
	8	**Kentucky
	11-12	##Indiana Classic
	20	San Francisco
	27-28	###Hoosier Classic
	31	@Iowa
Jan.	3	Illinois
	5	@Michigan
	9	@Ohio State
	13	Northwestern
	16	@Purdue
	24	Michigan State
	26	@Minnesota
	31	@Penn State
Feb.	3	Wisconsin
	9	Purdue
	13	@Northwestern
	17	Ohio State
	21	Michigan
	23	@Illinois
	27 or 28	Iowa
Mar.	4-7	####Big Ten Tournament

@ Road Games
* NABC Classic, RCA Dome, Indianapolis, IN
** Freedom Hall, Louisville, KY
# Maui, HI (vs. Kansas State, first round; also Arizona State and Utah)
Bloomington, IN (vs. Boise State, first round; also Bowling Green and Grambling)
Indianapolis, IN (vs. Drake, first round; also Ball State and Bucknell)
United Center, Chicago, IL

Odle is his high school's top career scorer, and he set a school record with 50 points in one game. Still, he seems destined for riding the pines.

On the other hand, the Hoosiers do need help inside. So you never know.

ANTWAAN RANDLE EL (5-11, 180 lbs., FR, #10, Thornton HS/Riverdale, Ill.). This redshirt freshman is the quarterback on the IU football team. Since a bowl game isn't usually in the Hoosiers plans, Randle El should be able to get in basketball shape by mid-December.

His time will probably be limited to short stints, particularly those occasions when Knight wants to turn the defensive screws on the enemy.

KYLE HORNSBY (6-5, 205 lbs., FR, G/F, #32, 23.0 ppg, 9.0 rpg, 6.5 apg, Annacoca HS/Annacoca, La.). Hornsby's floor time depends on how well he can adapt a 60 percent high school three-point shot to college defenses. He leaps well, though—something that can't be coached—and that should help.

TOM GEYER (6-8, 240 lbs., FR, F, #53, Lawrence North HS/Indianapolis, Ind.). Geyer was a walkon last season who redshirted for the year. He was a 1997 McDonald's All-America nominee.

QUESTIONS

Coach Knight? College basketball's favorite novelty act has become a bit tired in seasons past. Bluster doesn't have the same effect when it's being booted out early from the Field of 64.

Rebounding? Only two Hoosiers managed more than four boards per game last year. Good thing IU shot exceptionally well from the floor.

Size? This question related closely to that of rebounding. Indiana just isn't that tall, and was outrebounded last season by more than one per game.

ANSWERS

A.J. Guyton! This guy is the real deal. He began his career with a sparkling freshman campaign and then got even better as a sophomore. If his junior year sees similar improvement, look out.

Experience! Indiana loses some height, but not a lot of stats. Four starters return, along with 77 percent of its points, 71 percent of its rebounds and 87 percent of its assists. And, remember, this team *did* win 20 games a year ago.

adidas Blue Ribbon Analysis

BACKCOURT	B+	BENCH/DEPTH	B
FRONTCOURT	B	INTANGIBLES	C

Given the tools at hand and the Big Ten's overall frontcourt weakness, this team could as well as anyone become the prime challenger to Michigan State. But, then, the Hoosiers should have been in contention to the end last season when they had considerably more experience on the baseline.

If Indiana is ever to recapture its old vigor in this age, Knight has to make it a positive experience to play basketball in Bloomington. Whether he can let that happen is up for debate.

Knight is an incongruent man today: a tactical genius in a time when the game doesn't as much demand his smarts, an absolute ruler in an age when militaristic obedience on the playing fields seems almost passé.

The times won't adapt to him. To succeed again, it looks like he'll have to adapt to them.

(D.J.)

22
MASSACHUSETTS

LOCATION .... Amherst, MA
CONFERENCE .... Atlantic 10 (East Division)
LAST SEASON .... 21-11 (.656)
CONFERENCE RECORD 12-4 (t-2nd)
STARTERS LOST/RETURNING 1/4
NICKNAME .... Minutemen
COLORS .... Maroon & White
HOMECOURT .... Mullins Center (9,493)
COACH ..... James "Bruiser" Flint (St. Joseph's '87)
RECORD AT SCHOOL .... 40-25 (2 yrs.)
CAREER RECORD .... 40-25 (2 yrs.)
ASSISTANTS .... John Robic (Denison '86)
Geoff Arnold (St. Joseph's '86)
Tony Barbee (Massachusetts '93)
TEAM WINS (last 5 yrs.) 28-29-35-19-21
RPI (last 5 yrs.) 11-7-2-47-28
1997-98 FINISH .... Lost in NCAA first round.

COACH AND PROGRAM

Only one UMass regular—senior guard Charlton Clarke—was coached in a game by John Calipari. So, is it safe to call this Bruiser Flint's team yet? More to the point, does it matter?

The Minutemen still play the same way. They are a halfcourt defensive team, a possession-by-possession offensive team and they remain tough as nails. They don't shoot a bunch of three-pointers, don't shuttle a deep rotation onto the floor and their calling card remains a "Refuse to Lose" philosophy.

Massachusetts has lost a few more games under Flint, but that is more a function of the absence of Marcus Camby than it is the upward mobility of Calipari. On balance, Flint is doing just fine, thank you.

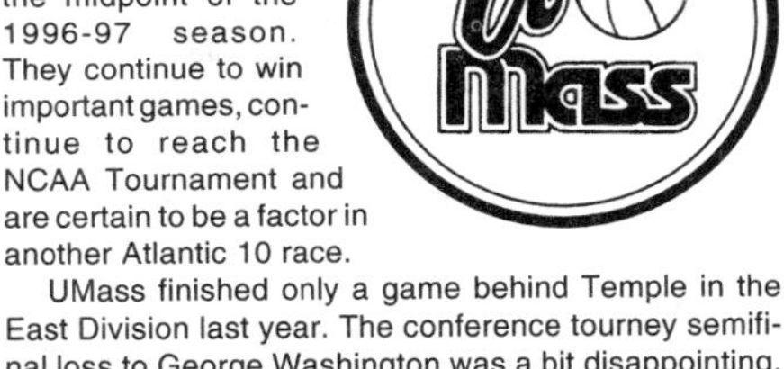

In fact, the Minutemen are 33-14 since the midpoint of the 1996-97 season. They continue to win important games, continue to reach the NCAA Tournament and are certain to be a factor in another Atlantic 10 race.

UMass finished only a game behind Temple in the East Division last year. The conference tourney semifinal loss to George Washington was a bit disappointing. Losing the next week as a No. 7 seed in the NCAA Tournament (to Saint Louis) was harder to swallow. But the Minutemen return all but one key contributor and should be in excellent position to get Flint his first NCAA victory this coming March.

There is some concern that Flint is not as savvy in really big games as his mentor and predecessor. Calipari made a habit of beating No. 1 teams—North Carolina, Arkansas and Kentucky come to mind—and vaulting his program into the headlines. But Flint has come close (UMass took Kansas to the wire in Lawrence last December), and not even Calipari was winning those types of games in his second season.

The real test for Flint is to replenish the talent base. Clarke, Lari Ketner and graduated strongman Tyrone Weeks were holdover players. Emerging guard Monty Mack was already in the Calipari pipeline. "Bruiser" has yet to contribute his own star to the galaxy.

As a program-keeper, judge Flint in a year or two, when the complete Calipari conversion is complete. As a coach, judge him now. No one is UMass history has reached 40 victories faster.

The 1998-99 season will be more of the same in Amherst, only better. Bruiser Flint is about to enjoy his finest hour as a head coach.

STARTERS NOT RETURNING

TYRONE WEEKS (6-7, PF, 10.1 ppg, 8.8 rpg, 1.4 tpg, 1.4 spg, 1.1 bpg, 28.9 minutes, .490 FG, .788 FT). What a success story is Tyrone Weeks.

First he had to sit out as a freshman due to poor academics. Then he gained even more weight on a bigger-than-necessary body. And then he had to find a way to play in a frontcourt dominated by Camby, Donta Bright and Dana Dingle (and Lou Roe before that).

Somewhere along the way, Weeks became an important elder statesman. He kept the players together during the coaching change. He immediately endorsed Flint as the right man for the job. And he got his life together both on and off the court.

Weeks was among the first marquee players to earn back a fourth year of eligibility under the smartly loosened NCAA rules. He graduated on time with his class, then pursued graduate studies while anchoring the frontcourt as a fifth-year senior.

The power forward was admired by everyone in the program. His statistics can be replaced; his presence, maybe not.

OTHERS NOT RETURNING

None.

PROJECTED STARTERS

CHARLTON CLARKE (6-3, 215 lbs., SR, PG, #3, 12.6 ppg, 2.6 rpg, 3.8 apg, 2.4 tpg, 1.3 spg, 35.4 minutes, .408 FG, .346 3PT, .791 FT, St. Raymond's HS/Bronx, N.Y.). Clarke is a typical UMass player: hard-working, overachieving and clutch. He is also the team leader, even though he plays out of position at point guard.

The truth is, Clarke really doesn't have a position. He's a little too slow at the point, not a good enough shooter at off guard and too small for a small forward. Yet all the Minutemen do is win when he is on the floor. When Flint finally figured that out two years ago, Massachusetts went 12-3 down the stretch to secure a near-impossible NCAA bid.

A year ago, Clarke reached double figures in 10 of Massachusetts' last 12 games. He was a back-to-back Player of the Week honoree in February. His three-pointer with two seconds left in regulation forced overtime and ultimately prevented a late-season upset by St. Joseph's.

"He's their MVP," Hawks' coach Phil Martelli learned from first-hand experience. "He is invaluable."

Clarke will likely continue starting as the point guard, but play any other vacancy which occurs during a game. He slides over for Mack and also for Mike Babul in the frontcourt. About the only place he doesn't get is a seat on the bench.

MONTY MACK (6-3, 193 lbs., JR, SG, #5, 13.8 ppg, 3.2 rpg, 3.0 spg, 2.7 tpg, 1.3 tpg, 35.1 minutes, .399 FG, .358 3PT, .788 FT, South Boston HS/Boston, Mass.). So much for redshirt rust. Mack was terrific as a first-year sophomore, and he got better as the season progressed.

Forced to sit his freshman year, Mack worked like crazy to stay ready. It obviously worked. He started all 32 games and played only 10 fewer minutes than Clarke.

Mack wasn't the greatest shooter in the world, but he is an accomplished scorer and defender. The three-pointer should come, as the natural tools are there. Harder to teach are a tough mindset and the necessary defensive intensity. Mack came with those qualities, which make him a perfect fit in Amherst.

A year from now, when Clarke and Lari Ketner are gone, Mack will easily assume the mantle of team leader. By then, he may also be a 20-point scorer.

LARI KETNER (6-10, 268 lbs., SR, C, #4, 15.2 ppg, 7.4 rpg, 1.8 tpg, 2.1 bpg, 30.3 minutes, .523 FG, .644 FT, Roman Catholic HS/Philadelphia, Pa.). OK, Lari, what will it be? Are you the center who plays his best against Raef LaFrentz (Kansas), Brad Miller (Purdue) and Alexander Koul (George Washington)? Or are you the lazy big man who committed 98 fouls and was disqualified three times?

Basically, the Minutemen will go as far as Ketner takes them. And that could be a long way. Ketner has the body and the offensive game to dominate. He can also block shots pretty much whenever he wants to.

It's the "want to" part that often gets in the way, especially on defense. Footwork is a big part of the equation. Ketner has it on offense, so we know he *could* get in better position at the other end. Until then, his overall game is bit of a tease.

One night, that LaFrentz guy was held to 6-for-16 shooting in Lawrence. Miller went 3-for-10 when the Minutemen faced Purdue. Ketner also made Koul disappear on two occasions, including the Atlantic 10 Tournament.

Ketner's offense will always be there. He has a nice touch, can collect offensive rebounds, and uses his body well to seal defenders from the ball and the goal. Clearly,

Ketner will be a first-round NBA draft pick. What he needs next is first-round intensity. It is such a precious commodity, especially with pro salaries spinning out of control.

What do you tell a player like this? "Look, kid, we know you're going to be rich even if you dog it. But, if you play harder, you can make a few million more."

The long-term choice is Ketner's. In the short-term, UMass will push and prod and hope for the best. The guy can really play.

Here is the Ketner quotebook:

• Minnesota coach Clem Haskins, also the U.S. Goodwill Games coach: "I really like Ketner. I like his physical strength and his ability to rebound and defend the goal."

• College of Charleston coach John Kresse: "Ketner has a variety of moves. He is going to be a first-round draft pick."

• Kansas coach Roy Williams: "Ketner is a good rebounder and shot-blocker, and he can score a bit, too. He's not one-dimensional."

• St. Joseph's coach Phil Martelli, an assistant for the Goodwill Games team: "They say he doesn't show up sometimes. Well, you couldn't prove it by me (after Ketner unloaded for a career-high 34 points against the Hawks).

MIKE BABUL (6-6, 204 lbs., JR, SF, #23, 4.1 ppg, 2.8 rpg, 1.6 apg, 1.4 tpg, 23.9 minutes, .435 FG, .600 FT, Attleboro HS/North Attleboro, Mass.). Babul took a huge step forward as a sophomore. Though the numbers above suggest otherwise, he was a significant factor at both ends of the court for the Minutemen.

The defense was obvious. Babul was a member of the Atlantic's 10 All-Defensive team, shutting down the other team's top gun on many occasions. Antonio Granger of Boston College was 2-for-12; Melvin Levett of Cincinnati went 1-for-13; Cuttino Mobley of Rhode Island was 2-for-7; Mark Donnelly of Davidson went 3-for-15; etc.

At the other end, Babul moved the ball and posted more assists than turnovers, quite unusual at his position. He also never takes a bad shot; in fact, he hoisted only six three-pointers all season.

"He fits (the UMass) mold," said one Atlantic 10 coach. "He'll win for you."

1997-98 RESULTS

@Fresno State (L)	64-82	
#Southwestern Louisiana	80-64	
#Purdue (L)	69-82	
#Seton Hall	73-60	
College of Charleston	52-40	
Marshall	61-59	
@Kansas (L)	71-73	
*Boston College	65-57	
##Colorado	79-68	
**Connecticut (L)	55-72	
###Cincinnati (L)	66-74	ot
@St. Joseph's	72-66	
@Fordham	73-55	
George Washington	79-48	
####UNC Charlotte	68-62	ot
Fordham	62-46	
St. Bonaventure	62-50	
@Davidson	82-66	
@Virginia Tech	68-59	
@Rhode Island	74-57	
Dayton	85-69	
Temple (L)	47-61	
@Xavier	73-62	
@Duquesne	74-68	
La Salle	81-71	
Rhode Island (L)	85-87	2ot
St. Joseph's	82-79	ot
@St. Bonaventure (L)	72-70	2ot
@Temple (L)	66-74	
#####Virginia Tech	64-58	
#####George Washington (L)	83-88	
%Saint Louis (L)	46-51	

@ away games
* Fleet Center, Boston, MA
** Hartford Civic Center, Hartford, CT
# Carrs Great Alaska Shootout, Anchorage, AK
Las Vegas Shootout, Las Vegas, NV
Rock & Roll Shootout, Cleveland, OH
Atlantic 10/C-USA Challenge, Providence, RI
Atlantic 10 Tournament, CoreStates Spectrum, Philadelphia, PA
% NCAA South Sub-Regional, Atlanta, GA

AJMAL BASIT (6-9, 248 lbs., JR, PF, #42, 6.8 ppg, 5.4 rpg, 1.6 tpg, 1.5 bpg, 19.4 minutes, .503 FG, .656 FT, St. Anthony's HS/Jersey City, N.J.). Basit broke a bone in his foot and underwent off-season surgery, but is expected to be at full strength as practice gets underway in late October.

A full recovery is Basit's first priority. Right behind that is cementing his position as the team's power forward. Someone has to inherit Tyrone Weeks' minutes (and production), and Basit is the obvious choice.

Not as wide but much more mobile than Weeks, Basit should open up the floor a bit for the Minutemen. UMass won't be Xavier by any means, but the pair of Weeks and Lari Ketner pretty much canceled any fastbreak opportunities.

Basit will also be a different kind of defensive player, but no less effective. Weeks occupied horizontal space; Basit is more vertical. He could reach 2-3 blocked shots per game in more extended minutes.

But he has to be healthy. Without Basit, the Minutemen have a hole they cannot realistically fill. Not even Charlton Clarke can play power forward.

KEY RESERVES

JONATHAN DEPINA (5-9, 175 lbs., SO, G, #10, 3.3 ppg, 1.5 rpg, 2.9 apg, 2.0 tpg, 17.6 minutes, .396 FG, .627 FT, South Boston HS/South Boston, Mass.). DePina would be the starting point guard on most teams. Ironically, he is far and away the best point guard at UMass. It's just that Charlton Clarke has got to play somewhere, and Clarke's presence at the point is the most desirable option with this group.

Even so, DePina saw increasing minutes as his freshman season went along. He is especially effective against teams with smaller point guards, where his size on defense is less of an issue. On the other hand, he can be overmatched against a big point guard such as Temple's Pepe Sanchez.

Trivia: Name the only point guard in America to play regularly and not manage at least a dozen three-point attempts. That would be DePina, who took only three threes all season (making two).

Look for DePina to increase his minutes, his offensive contributions and be ready to assume the job full-time for the 1999-2000 season. He may very well own the school's all-time assist record before he's through.

CHRIS KIRKLAND (6-6, 206 lbs., JR, F, #22, 3.6 ppg, 2.4 rpg, 13.5 minutes, Sto Rox HS/Pittsburgh, Pa.). Kirkland is too small to be a power forward, but that's where he plays best. He may have been Massachusetts' most improved player in 1997-98.

Kirkland stepped up in a big way when Weeks missed the conference tournament opener vs. Virginia Tech. He played a career-high 30 minutes, contributing seven points and six rebounds.

Now that the UMass staff has more confidence in Kirkland, they can turn Basit loose as a free-lance shot-blocker. Kirkland is capable of handling all the bench minutes at the position, and should take another step forward this season.

Kirkland had been miscast as a freshman, as he was used as part of a rotating small forward experiment. He now has his own niche, and both player and team should be better for it.

ANTHONY OATES (6-10, 270 lbs., JR, C, #0, 15.5 ppg, 10.8 rpg, 2.0 bpg, Yavapai JC, Ariz./Tucson, Ariz.). It's a long way from the desert to Amherst, but the Minutemen really wanted depth in the frontcourt. They like to beat on people and win games through attrition; Oates should contribute some to that formula.

Oates will not be a dominant Division I player (he was just a second-team All-Conference selection in junior college). However, numbers are important in a Division I frontcourt. Without Oates, the Minutemen would have only two big bodies to play on the blocks

OTHER RETURNEES

RAFAEL CRUZ (6-2, 185 lbs., SO, G, #13, 1.0 ppg, 0.5 rpg, 13 appearances, Wheeling Park HS/Wheeling, W.Va.). It was hoped that Cruz would push Mack and DePina in an all-rookie backcourt. Instead, he wasn't yet ready to contribute at this level.

Cruz is skilled, however, and should begin to see more time later in his career. That may or may not be this season.

ROSS BURNS (6-3, 180 lbs., SR, G, #12, 0,7 ppg, seven appearances, Cushing Academy/Greenfield, Mass.). Burns was less of a factor as a junior. Injuries pressed this walkon into greater service as a sophomore. Last year, his primary role was again that of a practice player.

ANDREW MACLAY (6-4, 195 lbs., SR, G, #14, four appearances, Stroudsburg HS/Stroudsburg, Pa.). At last look, Maclay was again considering the double duty which makes his college career so interesting. Maclay is the punter for the UMass football team.

In basketball, it has to be an equivalent fourth down situation before the coaches call on Maclay.

OTHER NEWCOMERS

RONELL BLIZZARD (6-8, 215 lbs., FR, F, 16.1 ppg, 9,8 rpg, 6.5 bpg in 1996-97, Sacred Heart HS/Waterbury, Conn.). Blizzard was forced to redshirt as a true freshman due to chronic foot injuries. If healthy, he could challenge for time at either forward position.

His strong suit is a decent perimeter game. Some have likened Blizzard to former UMass small forward Dana Dingle. In the meantime, Blizzard needs to get stronger and gain some experience—even practice—at this level.

KITWANA RHYMER (6-10, 240 lbs., SO, F, #33, 10.0 ppg, 6.0 rpg in 1996-97, St. Raymond's HS/Bronx, N.Y.). Speaking of Dingle, Rhymer follows he and Charlton Clarke to Amherst from St. Raymond's in the Bronx. For now, Rhymer is the least advanced of the three. He is a bit of a late bloomer who posted only modest prep numbers.

But Rhymer picked up the game late after growing up in the Virgin Islands. There is some recent history to suggest that Caribbean big men eventually grow into their bodies.

QUESTIONS

Power? Ketner can be great, which is different from saying he will be great all the time. This year, there is no Tyrone Weeks to police the area.

Depth? The Minutemen typically don't use many players, but the current configuration is one key injury—Ketner, Clarke, Mack—away from disaster.

Timing? UMass should be improved as this cast of characters grows together. However, the Minutemen are doing so at exactly the same time Temple is gearing up for a run at the Final Four. It is the reverse of what Massachusetts did to Temple in the mid-1990s.

1998-99 MASSACHUSETTS SCHEDULE

Nov.	16	#Niagara
Dec.	1	@College of Charleston
	5	@Marshall
	9	Connecticut
	12	*Boston College
	15	@Villanova
	29	Davidson
Jan.	2	Virginia Tech
	5	Iona
	7	@Fordham
	9	@St. Bonaventure
	13	Duquesne
	16	Kansas
	20	@St. Joseph's
	23	@Temple
	26	Fordham
	28	@Dayton
	31	@Texas
Feb.	4	Rhode Island
	7	St. Joseph's
	10	St. Bonaventure
	13	@Rhode Island
	17	@George Washington
	20	Xavier
	23	@La Salle
	28	Temple
Mar.	3-6	##Atlantic 10 Tournament

@ Road Games
* Centrum, Worcester, MA
# Chase NIT (If the Minutemen advance, they face the North Carolina-Asheville/St. John's winner on Nov. 18. Semifinals and finals are Nov. 25 & 27 at Madison Square Garden, NY).
First Union Spectrum, Philadelphia, PA

ANSWERS

Toughness! "Refuse to Lose" lives in Amherst. Give Bruiser Flint credit for maintaining an overachieving spirit instilled by John Calipari (now if only he could inject Ketner with a full-time dose).

Lari Ketner! The big guy has first-team All-America potential. As he goes, so go the Minutemen.

Charlton Clarke! Give him the ball; he'll take (and make) the biggest shots.

adidas Blue Ribbon Analysis

BACKCOURT	**B+**	**BENCH/DEPTH**	**B**
FRONTCOURT	**B**	**INTANGIBLES**	**B**

It's hard to discount a team which can be carried by a player as talented as Ketner. It's hard to overlook a team with contributors as gritty as Clarke and Monty Mack.

Massachusetts should continue its winning ways under Bruiser Flint. "Bruiser" has, in largely unnoticed fashion, won 19 and 21 games in his first two seasons.

Look for similar improvement in 1997-98. Call it 23 wins, second place in the Atlantic 10 East Division and a first-round NCAA Tournament victory.

That would make for another nice season in Amherst, even as expectations remain on the unrealistic side. And Flint may have his first star coming. Shannon Crooks, a 1996 *Boston Globe* "Super Team" member, will be eligible next season after transferring from St. John's.

(J.L.)

23
KANSAS

LOCATION	**Lawrence, KS**
CONFERENCE	**Big 12**
LAST SEASON	**34-9 (.865)**
CONFERENCE RECORD	**15-1 (1st)**
STARTERS LOST/RETURNING	**3/2**
NICKNAME	**Jayhawks**
COLORS	**Crimson & Blue**
HOMECOURT	**Allen Field House (16,300)**
COACH	**Roy Williams (North Carolina '72)**
RECORD AT SCHOOL	**282-62 (10 yrs.)**
CAREER RECORD	**282-62 (10 yrs.)**
ASSISTANTS	**Matt Doherty (North Carolina '84)**
	Neil Dougherty (Cameron '84)
	Joe Holladay (Oklahoma '69)
TEAM WINS (last 5 yrs.)	**27-25-29-34-34**
RPI (last 5 yrs.)	**14-3-4-1-7**
1997-98 FINISH	**Lost in NCAA second round.**

COACH AND PROGRAM

So the Jayhawks move on. Their bitter feelings from yet another failed postseason melt into optimism as a new year approaches. That's how its been for the past four seasons following earlier-than-expected NCAA Tournament punchouts.

In each of the prior years, coach Roy Williams tries to describe the feeling in the days after the upset loss. Four days after the Jayhawks were shocked by Rhode Island in the second round this past March—the earliest dismissal for a Kansas team since 1992—Williams talked about where he is as the head coach of a program which has more victories and the highest winning percentage of any in the 1990s, and also more postseason misfortune.

"I don't mind telling you that this is the first time in my life that I have had any lack of trust or confidence in myself," Williams said. "That bothers me. I want to be able to help those players."

Help them get to a Final Four, that is.

It didn't happen again in 1997-98, and the roll call of great Kansas players who never got out of a regional grew by Raef LaFrentz and Paul Pierce. Yet history is likely to remember the 1996-97 Jayhawks in a more disappointing light. After all, that team possessed four first-round draft picks (Scot Pollard and Jacque Vaughn along with Pierce and LaFrentz). Yes, KU lost to eventual national champion Arizona that year, but it was an Arizona team which, to that point, had barely scraped by South Alabama and College of Charleston.

The '98 Jayhawks weren't ranked No. 1 in the nation all year as they were in '97, but there was a feeling about the team that wasn't there the previous year. Last season's team had more overall weaknesses, but it was a quicker, more athletic team. Kansas wasn't going to be pushed around in the Tournament and, in Pierce and LaFrentz, they had first-team All-Americas who could score at crunch time.

So what happened? The Jayhawks ran into a Rhode Island team with guards so fast the Jayhawks couldn't keep up. Tyson Wheeler and Cuttino Mobley scorched Ryan Robertson and Billy Thomas. Williams said before the game that he was concerned about the matchups, but who takes that seriously? It was a No. 1 seed against a No. 8 seed who many thought would fall to Murray State in the first round.

Yes, the Rams were no fluke; Rhode Island was a Stanford miracle rally away from an improbable Final Four appearance. And, yes, Jim Harrick had done this before to Kansas. In 1990, the second-seeded Jayhawks fell to Harrick's No. 7 UCLA. But those are excuses, and there was no excuse for the way Kansas' season ended.

Onward. Drop the bar for this year's team. There is no All-America talent. Expectations are lower. Maybe that will work better.

Two starters return, although two others started at least nine games apiece. But the Jayhawks have less proven talent than at any time in the past four years. For the first time since 1996, not even an All-Conference player is returning.

So the spin begins.

"Sometimes, when you have such great players, the rest of you sit back and watch them," Robertson said. "You don't play. You rely on their talent. We've done a lot of that. Maybe that's one of the reasons we haven't been successful in the NCAA Tournament. We're not going to have the luxury anymore."

What the Jayhawks really don't have is a proven scorer. Roberton's 8.3 ppg is tops among returning players. The other returning starter, forward T.J. Pugh, averaged 5.7 ppg.

This being Kansas, guys who weren't asked to score will invariably step up. Center Eric Chenowith showed a nice outside touch and forward Lester Earl can be a powerful inside force. Their combined 13.5 ppg will probably double.

Kansas is one of those places which never falls off the map. Not with Williams. The recruiting class wasn't a national Top 10, but it was one of the best two or three in the Big 12. The Jayhawks will be good again, maybe even good enough to win a fifth straight conference title. But this is not a team that will finished 15-1 in the league as it's done for the past two seasons.

One thing is for sure: Williams can't wait to get the season started. Most of the distractions are behind him and, boy, did the Jayhawks make some headlines. First, mega-recruit JaRon Rush backed out of a commitment to Kansas and announced he was going to UCLA. In the process, he called Williams "Roy" on a call-in radio program and was denounced for showing a lack of respect.

The Earl situation never slowed in the off-season. Kansas took public relation hits for continuing to support Earl, even after the player admitted accepting cash, medical treatment and free meals while being recruited by Louisiana State. Earl eventually signed with the Tigers, but transferred to the Jayhawks after one semester.

Former Texas guard Luke Axtell gave Kansas even more of a "Boys Town" feel when he announced he was transferring after a major fallout with former Longhorns coach Tom Penders. Axtell's grades were given to an Austin radio station by an assistant coach, which led to the departure of Penders and his staff.

Player procurement is such a public thing these days. So is the NCAA Tournament. Kansas would like nothing better than to make less news in the former and more in the latter this season.

STARTERS NOT RETURNING

PAUL PIERCE (6-7, SF, 20.4 ppg, 6.3 rpg, 30.4 minutes, .513 FG, .339 3PT, .738 FT). Looking back on it, it's hard to believe Paul Pierce was only third-team All-Conference as a sophomore. You could justify it at the time because at least 10 others were having better seasons. Then Pierce showed up everybody by becoming the Big 12 Tournament MVP and the Jayhawks' leading scorer in every postseason game.

Pierce didn't improve that much as a junior, but he was named first-team All-America, giving the Jayhawks two in the same season for the first time. Pierce became the first Kansas player to average 20 points per game since Danny Manning's senior season.

No doubt, Pierce would be the preseason favorite for national player of the year if he had returned. But, unlike recent KU stars Jacque Vaughn and LaFrentz, Pierce didn't find enough reasons to play his senior year. As the NBA lockout continued through the summer, Pierce wondered if he had done the right thing.

"If somebody were to tell me the NBA would go on hold for a year, then I probably would have stayed in school," Pierce said. "But that's something that's never happened, so I'm happy with my decision."

As a junior, Pierce scored 777 points, the fifth highest total in school history. He went over 50 percent from the floor for the year for the first time, although his three-point percentage dropped more than 10 points.

When he was on, there was no better player in the country. During a game against Oklahoma, Pierce couldn't miss. The performance was so amazing that, during a timeout, as Pierce passed the Oklahoma bench, Sooners coach Kelvin Sampson offered a congratulatory handshake.

With one more year, Pierce would have passed LaFrentz for second on the school's career scoring list, and who knows? Maybe he could have led the Jayhawks

1997-98 RESULTS

Santa Clara	99-73	
Rice	88-61	
#Western Kentucky	75-62	
#UNLV	92-68	
##Arizona State	90-88	ot
##Florida State	73-58	
###Arizona	90-87	
Emporia State, KS	102-50	
####Maryland (L)	83-86	
####Pennsylvania	89-71	
Massachusetts	73-71	
Middle Tennessee State	103-68	
Pepperdine	96-83	
#####Texas Christian	94-78	
@Southern California	74-69	
######Ohio State	69-56	
######Vanderbilt	89-82	
######Hawaii (L)	65-76	
Nebraska	96-76	
Colorado	111-62	
@Texas	102-72	
@Texas A&M	83-65	
Kansas State	69-62	
@Missouri (L)	73-74	
Texas Tech	88-49	
Baylor	94-47	
@Nebraska	82-71	
@Iowa State	83-62	
Missouri	80-70	
@Kansas State	73-58	
@Colorado	81-72	
Iowa State	71-54	
Oklahoma	83-70	
@Oklahoma State	71-67	
#######Kansas State	68-61	
#######Nebraska	91-59	
#######Oklahoma	72-58	
%Prairie View A&M	110-52	
%Rhode Island (L)	75-80	

@	away games
#	Chase NIT, campus sites
##	Chase NIT, Madison Square Garden, NY
###	Great Eight, Chicago, IL
####	Franklin National Bank, Washington, D.C.
#####	Sprint Shootout, Kansas City, MO
######	Outrigger Hotels Rainbow Classic, Honolulu, HI
#######	Big 12 Tournament, Kemper Arena, Kansas City, MO
%	NCAA Midwest Sub-Regional, Oklahoma City, OK

to the Final Four by himself. We'll never know.

RAEF LAFRENTZ (6-11, PF, 19.8 ppg, 11.4 rpg, 1.5 bpg, 30.2 minutes, .548 FG, .712 FT). In some respects, no Kansas player could feel more disappointment about last season than LaFrentz. He passed up a probable top five selection in the NBA draft to return for his senior season with the hope of finally making it to the Final Four.

He started well, scoring 32 points against Arizona in the Great Eight and was averaging over 20 per when his suffered a broken bone in his right (non-shooting) hand that cost him eight games. In his first game back, LaFrentz had 31 points and 15 rebounds against Texas Tech.

Despite the injury and missed time, LaFrentz was named Big 12 Player of the Year and first-team All-America for the second straight season. His chances for national player of the year were dashed by the injury, but LaFrentz had no complaints when the awards were handed out and supported the choice of North Carolina's Antawn Jamison.

LaFrentz became the first Kansas player in 27 years to average double-digits in points and rebounds. He started all 131 games of his career and finished second to Danny Manning in career points (2,066) and rebounds 1,186) at the school. He will be remembered along with Manning, Wilt Chamberlain, Clyde Lovellette and Jo Jo White as among the greatest to ever play for the Jayhawks.

Sadly for LaFrentz, like White, he never made it out of the regionals. LaFrentz never had a dominating performance in 12 career NCAA Tournament games.

LaFrentz surprised some draft experts when he was chosen third by the Denver Nuggets. His stock was rumored to be slipping. Not according to Nuggets GM Dan Issel, who loves LaFrentz's shooting touch and mobility.

BILLY THOMAS (6-4, SG, 13.6 ppg, 3.0 rpg, 26.7 minutes, .468 FG, .401 3PT, .788 FT). Kansas got the improvement it sought from Thomas as a senior, who entered the starting lineup for the first time and responded with a career best scoring average. His three-point shooting remained a constant 40 percent and he finished his career as the program's top long-range bomber. His 269 treys and 691 attempts are school marks.

Yet Thomas would trade all of that for one good, clutch performance in the NCAA Tournament. March could be a nightmare for Thomas.

In 1996, he let a pass for a wide open layup slip through his hands and out of bounds in the final moments of the regional final against Syracuse. In 1997, he rimmed out an open trey that could have sent the Arizona game into overtime. Last season, he missed 13 of 15 three-pointers in the loss to Rhode Island.

At times, he could be a spectacular shooter. He made eight of 11 three-pointers at Texas and five of eight against Arizona State, including one that bounded in to give Kansas a victory in the NIT semifinals.

OTHERS NOT RETURNING

C.B. MCGRATH (5-11, G, 0.7 ppg, 0.9 rpg, 8.7 minutes). Colin Bryant McGrath got more minutes last season than any time since his freshman year, when he was the primary backup at the point.

Kansas is going to miss McGrath, not so much for his hustle but his humor. He was the team prankster, and will forever be remembered around Lawrence for a missed dunk during his junior season that made all the highlight shows.

PROJECTED STARTERS

RYAN ROBERTSON (6-5, 182 lbs., SR, PG, #4, 8.3 ppg, 2.8 rpg, 6.3 apg, 31.3 minutes, .454 FG, .431 3PT, .733 FT, St. Charles West HS/St. Charles, Mo). Here's a statistic any coach would love: When Robertson starts, Kansas is 49-4 over the past two seasons.

Robertson isn't sure about his position. He was a reserve shooting guard for his first two years, except the 11 games he started at the point as a sophomore (when Jacque Vaughn was injured). Last season, Robertson was the starting point guard.

When Kansas signed pure point guard Jeff Boschee, it made Robertson wonder if he was going back to shooting guard.

"I love playing the point, but I've also been blessed with the ability to shoot from outside," Robertson said. "I can play both, and I really don't have a preference."

Robertson can shoot. He led the Jayhawks in three-point percentage for the second time in three seasons and, with a little more accuracy this year, will push Milt Newton (44.6 percent from 1987-89) for the school's career mark. Robertson stands at 43.1.

Robertson's 248 assists were the second-most in school history. Vaughn, who started at the point the previous four years, never had that many in a season. Also, Robertson's 2.66-to-1.00 assist-to-turnover ratio was outstanding.

So why isn't he a slam dunk to return to the starting point guard role? For one thing, at 6-5, he doesn't have the quickness demanded by the position. The Rhode Island backcourt made Kansas painfully aware of the discrepancy in backcourt speed during the NCAA Tournament. Robertson had nine points and five assists in the second-round loss; URI's Tyson Wheeler finished with 20 and eight.

If Boschee starts at the point, Robertson goes to shooting guard and backs up Boschee. If Robertson starts at the point, Kenny Gregory starts at off-guard. Kansas could even go with a smaller, more athletic Boschee-Robertson-Gregory backcourt (with Earl and Pugh up front).

It's always been like this for Robertson. When Vaughn finished, the Jayhawks went hard after a point guard and missed out on Baron Davis (UCLA) and Khalid El-Amin (Connecticut) among others. They were left with Robertson, who did not disappoint.

On a team with many questions on offense, Robertson's shooting is about the only proven commodity. Look for him to fire away even more often this season.

The Robertsons have marked Dec. 23 on the calendar. Kansas plays Saint Louis at the TWA Dome and Ryan's brother, Troy, is a junior for the Billikins.

T.J. PUGH (6-8, 246 lbs., JR, SF, #32, 5.7 ppg, 5.0 rpg, 24.2 minutes, .489 FG, .589 FT, Creighton Prep/ Omaha, Neb.). Thomas Joseph Pugh moved into the starting lineup and became something of the team's blue collar worker. The statistics weren't overwhelming, but his defense was solid enough to earn a spot on the league's All-Defensive team.

"He's the most consistent defensive player I've coached in 10 years," Roy Williams said.

Pugh missed eight games in December and January when he suffered a stress fracture in his foot. His play improved over the second half of the season, and he scored in double figures four times in a 13-game stretch.

A case can be made that he was the team's most underrated player last year. His game is unspectacular, but he doesn't make many mistakes.

"He's not as gifted as some people, but he does what he's supposed to do," Williams said. "He works his tail off."

With the Jayhawks top three scorers gone, Pugh will need to deliver more points. Pugh was a scorer in high school, averaging 25.8 ppg as a senior. He won't do that this season, but half of that production would be huge for the Jayhawks.

LESTER EARL (6-8, 235 lbs., JR, PF, #3, 7.6 ppg, 6.5 rpg, 1.0 bpg, 20.7 minutes, .497 FG, .652 FT, Louisiana State & Glen Oaks HS/Baton Rouge, La.). At press time, LSU did not know if the NCAA had applied additional sanctions for the recruiting violations involving Earl. School officials met with the infractions committee in August, having already reduced scholarships and visits.

The case against LSU was helped by Earl, who was offered immunity for providing his information. He told the NCAA, that among other things, he'd been paid $6,000 by an assistant coach during the recruiting process. All in all, it's been a messy affair. For his part, Kansas coach Roy Williams has maintained that he knew nothing about the violations while LSU was recruiting Earl nor when the player decided to transfer.

Earl was never happy at LSU. He said he felt pressured to attend his hometown school and, upon arriving in Lawrence, said Kansas was where he always wanted to be.

The LSU decision is vital to Earl's future. If the Tigers are found guilty, Earl likely will receive an extra year of eligibility. If that doesn't happen, this will be his final year as a college player.

Kansas has no more athletic performer. Earl earned the nickname "sushi," according to Ryan Robertson, "because he's so raw. Very athletic. There's not a better athlete in the country when it comes to running, jumping, rebounding and going after the ball."

The polish came slowly. Mostly, Earl was good for a game's worth of suffocating defense, sometimes highlighted by a spectacular blocked shot, along with the requisite slam dunks. He can pop a 10-footer and is capable of 20-point games.

But rebounding and defense will continue to be Earl's strengths. Kansas hopes he has two more years to hone his game.

Earl had knee surgery in May and did not play over the summer. He is expected to be at full strength when the season begins.

ERIC CHENOWITH (7-0, 235 lbs., SO, C, #44, 5.9 ppg, 4.9 rpg, 1.6 tpg, 1.6 bpg, 17.0 minutes, .454 FG, .684 FT, Villa Park HS/Villa Park, Calif.). The big guy got thrown into the fire when Raef LaFrentz went down with a broken hand. It was Chenowith, ironically, who broke it, fouling LaFrentz across the hand during a Dec. 26 practice.

Chenowith started 10 games and enjoyed some of his finest moments. He scored 19 points against Nebraska and grabbed 20 rebounds against Texas A&M, the highest single-game board total in the Roy Williams decade.

As you'd expect from a seven-footer who averaged 17 minutes per game, Chenowith blocked a lot of shots. His 62 set a school record for freshmen, and he is already well on his way to the school career record.

As the season got later, Chenowith's playing time decreased. It was a matter of keeping LaFrentz on the floor more often as well as Chenowith's fatigue. But he played well enough to make the league's All-Freshman team and be named second-team freshman All-America by *Basketball Times*.

Chenowith will advance to the starting lineup and, once he gets that field goal percentage in order, he could become one of finest pure centers to play for Williams.

KENNY GREGORY (6-5, 215 lbs., SO, SG, #20, 7.1 ppg, 2.0 rpg, 1.6 apg, 15.8 minutes, .504 FG, .313 3PT, .407 FT, Independence HS/Columbus Oh.). Gregory may start this year, maybe not. It depends on what happens at point guard between Ryan Robertson and Jeff Boschee. If Robertson starts, Gregory should be the off-guard. If it's Boschee, Robertson could move into the second guard spot where he played for most his first two seasons.

But Williams knows he needs to get Gregory more than the minutes he averaged as a freshman. When Kansas lost prized recruit JaRon Rush to UCLA, Rush said the change of heart had to do with the Jayhawks' substitution patterns. Asked to clarify his statement, Rush said he saw where talented players like Gregory weren't getting as much playing time as he believed they should.

But that's what happens at Kansas, which rarely has slots open due to the early departure of underclassmen.

1998-99 KANSAS SCHEDULE

Nov.	13	Gonzaga
	17	@Pennsylvania
	21	Fort Hays State
	27	*UNLV
Dec.	1	**Kentucky
	5	***Pepperdine
	8	Iowa
	12	Southern Cal
	17	DePaul
	19	****Illinois
	23	@St. Louis
Jan.	2	Texas A&M
	6	@Baylor
	9	Iowa State
	11	@Missouri
	16	@Massachusetts
	18	Texas
	24	Missouri
	27	@Nebraska
	30	Colorado
Feb.	1	@Kansas State
	7	@Colorado
	10	Nebraska
	13	@Texas Tech
	17	Kansas State
	20	@Oklahoma
	22	Oklahoma State
	28	@Iowa State
Mar.	4-7	#Big 12 Tournament

@ Road Games
* Tip-Off Classic, Springfield, MA
** Great Eight, Chicago, IL
*** John Wooden Classic, Anaheim, CA
**** Sprint Shootout, Kemper Arena, Kansas City, MO
# Kemper Arena, Kansas City, MO

Yet Gregory never griped about his situation.

"It's not all about talent," Gregory said. "It might be that someone here has more experience." Which was the case last season, when Gregory spelled Billy Thomas.

Gregory is a talented athlete with great hops. He was the Jayhawks' top scorer off the bench and was named to the league's All-Freshman team. Maybe a little more offense was expected, but Gregory must accept some of the blame for poor percentages from behind the arc and at the foul throw line. He was bothered by a sore back most of the season, but did not use it as an excuse.

"I didn't say much about it," Gregory said. "I just tried to play through it, but I wasn't really able to jump like I wanted."

The back problem is now behind Gregory, and a bright future stands before him.

KEY RESERVES

NICK BRADFORD (6-6, 175 lbs., JR, G/F, #21, 4.2 ppg, 2.5 rpg, 1.8 apg, 14.1 minutes, .453 FG, .133 3PT, .604 FT, Fayetteville HS/Fayetteville, Ark.). Things got a little better for Bradford last season, who contributed little during his freshman year. He seemed more comfortable, got his field goal and free throw percentages to acceptable levels, and at times made some terrific passes. His 65 assists ranked fourth on the team, and he was ninth in minutes played.

Now comes a bigger step. Bradford will get more playing time, maybe as much as 20 minutes per game. He needs to become more of an offensive threat, but it is not going to come from trey land. Bradford actually got worse from behind the arc last year, from .136 to .133.

Despite the low numbers, Bradford is one of the team's flashiest performers when in control. When he plays shooting guard, the 6-6 Bradford can smother his opponent on defense.

ASHANTE JOHNSON (6-8, 210 lbs., JR, F, #31, 23.0 ppg, 14.0 rpg, .580 FG, .390 3PT, Canada JC, Calif., University of Utah & Scripps Ranch HS/San Diego, Calif.). Johnson started at Utah and sat out as a redshirt. He appeared in 19 games during the 1996-97 season as a backup to Keith Van Horn. He averaged 7.8 minutes, 1.8 ppg and 1.7 rpg in what was a disappointing campaign.

He came to the Utes highly touted. As a high school senior, he was named the top player in San Diego over UCLA's Jelani McCoy. But it didn't work out at Utah. Yet, at Canada JC, Johnson was the top player for a team that finished 28-4.

The Jayhawks have had great fortune with Division I transfers (Rick Calloway, Rex Walters, Jerod Haase) and mixed results with junior college players. Darrin Hancock helped the 1993 team reach the Final Four. Others didn't pan out. It is often difficult for a junior college player to learn the Jayhawks' system.

Johnson is a gifted athlete who can create offense going to the basket. He is projected as a small forward.

JEFF BOSCHEE (6-1, 185 lbs., FR, PG, #13, 26.0 ppg, 6.0 apg, .520 FG, .380 3PT, .850 FT, Valley City HS/Valley City, N.D.). If Boschee gets the starting nod, he'll be the first KU freshman to start at the point since Jacque Vaughn in 1994. He'll have to earn that position, though.

Since he arrived at Kansas, Roy Williams wanted to establish the program as something of a midwest North Carolina, a place kids growing up in mid-America would want to attend in the same way kids in the East want to be Tar Heels. He found such a player in Boschee, who grew up a Jayhawks fan.

Boschee twice won North Dakota's player of the year award. His high school team finished 20-6 and third in the state. He holds Valley City single-game records for points (46) and assists (12).

JEFF CAREY (6-9, 230 lbs., FR, C, #22, 19.3 ppg, 12.7 rpg in 1996-97 at Camdenton HS/Camdenton, Mo.). Carey elected to sit out as a redshirt last season, a rare measure of patience that undoubtedly will pay off. During summer pickup games at Allen Field House, no less an expert than Paul Pierce praised Carey's improvement.

Carey decided to sit out because the Jayhawks had signed Eric Chenowith to fill out the frontcourt. Now that LaFrentz is gone, Carey will step in and could be the first big man off the bench.

Carey's dad, Ray Bob Carey, played at Missouri in the 1960s, but the Tigers showed little interest in Jeff.

JOHN CRIDER (6-3, 180 lbs., FR, G, #12, 31.3 ppg, 11.1 rpg, 3.5 apg, 3.5 spg, 2.2 bpg, .322 3PT, .796 FT, Horton HS/Horton, Kan.). This is what happens in small-town Kansas when a high school player accepts a scholarship to KU: 500 of the town's 1,800 population show up at the high school to witness Crider's letter of intent. The town proclaims "John Crider Day." Crider gets invited to speak at several schools in the county about the rewards for hard work.

Horton is located about 70 miles northwest of Lawrence, and it had produced at least former Kansas great. A.C. "Dutch" Lonborg, a member of the school's Hall of Fame, played at Kansas and went on to coach and serve as athletic director at Northwestern.

Crider will be a reserve shooting guard. Shooting is what he does best. He spends his summers shooting, six hours a day. He'll assume the role Kenny Gregory had last year when he backed up Billy Thomas.

OTHER RETURNEES

JELANI JANISSE (6-3, 210 lbs., SR, G, #23, 0.7 ppg, 0.8 rpg, 0.3 apg, 3.1 minutes, .625 FG, .600 FT, Los Angeles CC, Calif. & John F. Kennedy HS/Granada Hills, Calif.). Ankle surgery last September limited Janisse's preseason production. His audition as a Division I player came in the first six games, and the results weren't good. Janisse did not seem ready. He played 34 minutes, scored one point, had three assists and 10 turnovers.

After that, Janisse played as many as six minutes in a game only once. Janisse will play more this season, but the Jayhawks made point guard a recruiting priority and landed Boschee.

TERRY NOONER (6-0, 170 lbs., JR, G, #5, 1.0 ppg, 0.2 rpg, 22 appearances, Raytown High/Raytown, Mo.). Nooner was in the same position as Chris Martin a year earlier. He was the only player selected from a walkon tryout.

Nooner scored 22 points in 1997-98, one more than the previous year. His role didn't change in 1998 and it won't change this season. Nooner did come off the bench in the first half against Kansas State in the Big 12 tournament, but that was an exception.

CHRIS MARTIN (6-2, 190 lbs., SR, G, #30, 0.6 ppg, 0.4 rpg, 19 appearances, Cornell College, Ia., Johnson County CC, Kan. & Shawnee Mission South HS/Overland Park, Kan.). Martin emerged from a walkon camp of 61 candidates. "I can't believe they picked me," he said.

But Martin shouldn't sound so insecure. He started 30 games the previous year for Johnson County CC and averaged 11.6 ppg. Martin's season-high as a Jayhawk came in the opener, when he scored three points against Santa Clara.

OTHER NEWCOMERS

MARTIN LONDON (6-3, 180 lbs., FR, G, #24, 17.6 ppg, 6.0 rpg, 4.0 apg, .540 FG, .400 3PT, St. Joseph's HS/Broadview, Ill.). The final player to sign for Kansas, London picked Kansas over primarily Big Ten schools. He will back up at both guard slots and small forward.

Kansas, which usually wows prospects when they visit during the midnight madness practice (a fire marshal looks the other way), did a smart thing with London. Just as impressive is the team's postseason banquet. It always sells out, and some fans who can't buy seats on the basketball floor sit up in the stands. London visited that weekend and signed a few days later.

London grew six inches while in high school, and has added 10 pounds of muscle to his frame since the end of last season. His natural position is off-guard.

QUESTIONS

Offense? The top three scorers are gone. Kansas now needs a player who has never averaged in double figures in college to step up and become a "go-to" guy.

Point guard? It could be Robertson or Boschee. The team needs to know.

Letdown? For four years, this has been the nation's winningest program. The Jayhawks are going to have to cope with more losses in 1998-99.

ANSWERS

Depth! This is always the case at Kansas. No returning All-Conference players, but Robertson and Earl are of that quality. Gregory could be.

Less pressure! No preseason No. 1 ranking, so fans will wonder if this team is good enough to win the Big 12. Kansas has the talent and could develop that underdog mindset, which is a powerful motivator.

Roy Williams! He hasn't caught a break in March lately, but nobody prepares harder than Williams.

adidas Blue Ribbon Analysis

BACKCOURT	**B+**	**BENCH/DEPTH**	**B**
FRONTCOURT	**B+**	**INTANGIBLES**	**B+**

In its 101st season, Kansas finds itself in a different position. None of the Jayhawks have been on a squad ranked lower than eighth in the country. The team has been ranked in the Top 10 for 69 straight wire service polls.

These players have also never lost a home game. The Allen Field House winning streak stands at 60. Yet it wouldn't be a shocking development if Kansas didn't start the season in the Top 10, or if it lost at home this year.

Kansas hasn't had to rebuild since Williams' first season, when he took over the defending national champion. This isn't an overhaul, but it will be a test of his recent recruiting and depth development. Players like Chenowith, Earl, Pugh and Gregory will be expected to pad their stats significantly.

At least one other Big 12 coach believes the fall won't be hard.

"They lose LaFrentz, they lose Pierce, (but) they have Chenowith, they have Robertson and Gregory, and nobody has a player like Lester Earl," Nebraska coach Danny Nee said. "I wouldn't worry much about Kansas."

It's a team that will take Williams back to his earliest days at Kansas. Early practices will be more teaching than coaching. Only Robertson and Pugh have been in the program for more than two years—which is unusual at Kansas, but more typical of college basketball conditions these days.

What kind of team is this? Not even Williams knows. It's about the same size as last season, perhaps a bit quicker and better defensively. LeFrentz and Pierce won no defensive honors. Chenowith, Earl and Pugh all had better credentials in that regard.

But it's pure folly to think Kansas is better off without their two first-round draft picks.

"We'll miss their scoring, of course, but we'll also miss their leadership," Williams said. "They were the players everybody on the team looked up to."

So add leadership to the list of discoveries Williams will need to make in October. It should be fun for him and the Jayhawks, who won't have the burden of expectation as in the past.

The last time Kansas got to the Final Four, in 1993, expectations were low. There were no All-Americas, and the leaders and offensive stars emerged. Hey, it happens.

Look at last year's Final Four. Stanford without Brevin Knight, Utah without Keith Van Horn and Kentucky without Ron Mercer all went farther than most believed they could.

(B.K.)

adidas Blue Ribbon Analysis

GRADING SYSTEM

A+	equal to very best in country—Final Four-caliber unit
A	among the best in the land—worthy of deep NCAA run
B+	talented, versatile and experienced—NCAA-NIT ability
B	solid and productive winners—league and post-season contenders
C+	average to above-average—may contend in a weaker league
C	average to mediocre—second division in a strong league
D+	below average, inconsistent—second division in a weaker league
D	well below average—losing season virtually certain
F	non-Division I ability—an underdog every night

24
WAKE FOREST

LOCATION .... Winston-Salem, NC
CONFERENCE .... Atlantic Coast (ACC)
LAST SEASON .... 16-14 (.533)
CONFERENCE RECORD 7-9 (t-4th)
STARTERS LOST/RETURNING 1/4
NICKNAME .... Demon Deacons
COLORS .... Black & Gold
HOMECOURT ...... Lawrence Joel Coliseum (14,407)
COACH .... Dave Odom (Guilford '65)
RECORD AT SCHOOL .... 182-93 (9 yrs.)
CAREER RECORD .... 220-135 (12 yrs.)
ASSISTANTS Ernie Nestor (Alderson-Broaddus '68)
Frank Haith (Elon College '88)
Russell Turner (Hampden-Sydney '92)
TEAM WINS (last 5 yrs.) 21-26-26-24-16
RPI (last 5 yrs.) 20-6-6-7-37
1997-98 FINISH .... Lost in NIT second round.

COACH AND PROGRAM

Dave Odom knows he shouldn't have, but he couldn't resist. He needed the bodies.

So, for the second year in a row, he went out and signed the ACC's biggest recruiting class—five freshmen and a sophomore transfer. With senior reserve guard Joseph Amonett the only scholarship player on the roster older than a sophomore, Odom knows the Demon Deacons are going to be even younger this year than last.

That's quite a feat. Odom made ACC history last February when he sent out a starting lineup of nothing but freshmen for two consecutive games. There were injuries and other extenuating circumstances which forced that lineup on the court, but it also signaled a total purge of the past—from a team that won back-to-back ACC Tournament titles with Tim Duncan in the lineup to a new generation of players.

By the time the season was over, senior guards Tony Rutland and Jerry Braswell—the starting backcourt for two of the Duncan years—were only role players on a team that ended up winning 16 games and nearly qualified for the NCAA Tournament.

In fact, Odom was rightfully furious his freshman-filled squad didn't get an invitation. Instead, the committee took ACC member Florida State, even though Wake was ranked higher in the RPI, finished a game ahead of the Seminoles in the ACC final standings and completed the regular season far stronger than FSU, whose quality wins all came before January.

"I am absolutely astonished that (the NCAA Selection Committee) would go in the direction they went," said Odom, whose team made it to the second round of the NIT.

So the Deacon's seven-year run of consecutive NCAA appearances—second-longest in ACC behind North Carolina's 22—ended with some sourness. But salving those wounds was the fact that Wake didn't completely fall by the wayside.

So far this decade, the ACC has had two teams, Duke and Georgia Tech, fall from first place to last in only one season. Odom was proud that last year's Deacons, coming off one of the most successful runs in school history with Duncan, didn't let that happen to them.

"To be able to get through that year without the bottom falling out record-wise and still being able to got to a postseason tournament, I think it gives us a good basis from which to build for this year and the years to come," Odom said.

Odom should have plenty to build from with his two huge waves of recruits. A year ago, he signed seven players, including budding star guard Robert O'Kelley, who replaced Rutland at point guard early in the season and went on to become the ACC Freshman of the Year.

Only six of those recruits were admitted to school, but it was enough to stop the bleeding in Wake's decimated frontcourt. This year, Odom brought in five more freshmen and a transfer.

"We will have 11 freshmen and sophomores," Odom said. "That's too many in two classes. It's not something any coach would prefer, but it's a situation that has developed for us.

"We have to make it a positive for us by having lively, competitive workouts and trying to involve more players in the game."

Odom didn't land the powerful frontcourt stud he wanted, but he did add two very important recruits. They are Spanish forward/center Darius Songaila and point guard Broderick Hicks, the latter of whom Odom calls his first true point guard recruit ever.

The Deacons will need the help in the frontcourt, now that Loren Woods—the once heralded successor to Tim Duncan—decided to transfer. Woods, suspended for seven games by Odom because he "was taking the game too seriously," needed some time off. The highly touted seven-footer eventually returned, but never became the star player everyone expected after his All-America prep career. He decided in April to transfer to Arizona.

That leaves very little offensive production inside for the Deacons. Last year's freshman frontcourt of Josh Shoemaker, Raphael Vidauretta and Niki Arinze established themselves as good rebounders and good defenders, but they couldn't score in a brothel.

Arinze, playing out of place in the low post, averaged the most points and rebounds of the three, and he should be even better this year when Odom allows him to return to his natural wing position. He will be challenged there by the offensive skills of freshman recruit Craig Dawson, the nephew of former North Carolina All-America.

Shoemaker and Vidauretta averaged 7.5 ppg between them, but were solid rebounders and defenders. Adding Songaila and forward Antwan Scott should help the offense.

"We didn't have a lot of inside scoring, but we had great defense and rebounding out of Raphael and Josh," Odom said, adding that each had gained more than 15 pounds in the off-season. "They are bigger and stronger and more experienced. They are going to be better inside scorers and they are going to play quite a bit.

"We have enough beef and brawn inside to be good."

The other frontcourt signee was forward Tate Decker, who will sit out this year after transferring from Missouri.

The backcourt needed some help, too, mostly in the way of ballhandling. The Deacons were horrible at times holding onto the ball. They were in the lower half of the ACC standings in turnover margin, last in steals and awful in assist-to-turnover ratio. Not a single returning player on the roster had more assists than turnovers, an astounding statistic for a team that finished in the upper division of its conference.

Odom hopes the arrival of Hicks, plus a couple of slashing wing players, will improve that. Hicks was one of the best high school point guards in the nation last year, averaging 21 points, seven assists and four steals per game.

If Hicks develops the way Odom wants, he should be able to take over at the point and allow O'Kelley to slide over to the shooting guard position, where he belongs. O'Kelley became a star in the league much in the same manner of Randolph Childress, a point guard who looked to shoot more than he looked to pass. It was effective, to be sure, on a team that had such problems getting the post players to score, but Odom admits that O'Kelley would be better off at "two" guard.

"The fact that we have Broderick Hicks here is going to help Robert," Odom said. "It will give Robert the chance to play both positions this year. Last year, he only played one."

Odom wants O'Kelley to be able to shoot more often, even though he attempted 100 shots more than any other player on the team last year.

"We are not going to just throw him the ball and let him have carte blanche," Odom said. "We want him to be within the team concept, but he will have a green light from a shot standpoint. We have got to give him more freedom to take shots."

The other recruits will also help with ballhandling, particularly versatile wing player Ervin Murray, who played both small forward and point guard in leading his team to the North Carolina state 2-A title game for two years in a row.

The thing Odom liked most about the way his freshman class played last year was its fearless style. They didn't know how unusual it was for freshmen to play such a key role in the ACC.

"There are some tremendous advantages to being young, and we found that out last year," Odom said. "They don't tire out as quickly. They are enthusiastic. They have a lot of energy.

"They played a fearless brand of basketball. They weren't afraid to go out and lay it on the line. You've got to believe that's going to continue."

Odom hopes that, as sophomores, that class will instill that same attitude to the new freshmen. He also hopes this year's freshmen will adjust to college life as quickly as last year's team did.

"I think the biggest problem for freshmen, the one I don't think media and fans recognize, is the off-the-court-socialization process," Odom said. "They are still trying to get used to being away from home, learning how to wash their own clothes and making their own schedule each day.

"Those things are really hard. I think the socialization part of being a freshman is harder than the basketball part."

Odom hopes this class will adjust as easily as last year's class. He is not talking about any potential redshirt candidates. He wants to wait until Dec. 1 before making that decision, but, with another class so large, it would certainly be beneficial to spread the talent over three classes instead of two.

"Anything is possible," Odom said. "At this point, I would doubt that any of the five freshmen would be redshirted."

So what's Odom going to do with all his young turks? Run 'em, both up the court on offense and at opponents on defense. At least that's what he's had his assistants working on in the offseason, installing a more up-tempo, pressing attack that is unlike anything Wake Forest has ever tried under Odom, a notorious halfcourt coach in the style of Terry Holland.

He thinks that might change this year.

"I think there will be some subtle changes," Odom said. "But with the number of players were have, we should be able to push it out on the floor and be a little more aggressive and not sit back in the lane as much.

"Fatigue shouldn't be quite as much of a problem. Maybe you'll see some different alignments defensively with some pressure. Our fastbreak would be better, because of more players and more skill than we have had in a while."

1997-98 RESULTS

Virginia Military Institute	88-70	
Navy	67-43	
*Georgetown	56-54	
Liberty	81-47	
Richmond	71-67	
@Davidson	61-56	
Utah (L)	53-62	
@Marshall (L)	66-73	
**Princeton (L)	64-69	
Radford	85-53	
***Virginia (L)	64-73	ot
Clemson	70-66	
@Georgia Tech (L)	63-70	
Duke (L)	52-88	
Maryland	72-60	
@Florida State (L)	59-83	
Missouri	74-65	
Virginia	62-55	
North Carolina (L)	73-79	
@North Carolina State	68-62	
@Clemson (L)	46-71	
Georgia Tech (L)	76-77	
@Duke (L)	47-78	
@Maryland	83-79	
Florida State	69-68	
@North Carolina (L)	53-72	
North Carolina State	71-57	
#Clemson (L)	56-75	
%North Carolina-Wilmington	56-52	
%%Vanderbilt (L)	68-72	

@ away games
* Hall of Fame Classic, Springfield, MA
** Continental Airlines Arena, East Rutherford, NJ
*** Richmond Coliseum, Richmond, VA
# ACC Tournament, Greensboro Coliseum, Greensboro, NC
% NIT first round, Winston-Salem, NC
%% NIT second round, Nashville, TN

Odom admits that it will be hard for him to change his personal coaching style.

"You make changes grudgingly," he said. "You don't just go out and say 'Hey, I'd like to do that.' I know what works for me, and for me to go to an all-out running and pressing game is not likely. That's not the way I think.

"But I do think there will be some subtle changes."

STARTERS NOT RETURNING

TONY RUTLAND (6-2, SG, 12.7 ppg, 2.6 rpg, 3.3 apg, 2.6 tpg, 30.9 minutes, .408 FG, .421 3PT, .805 FT). Rutland never fully recovered, at least in confidence, from the knee surgery he had at the end of his sophomore season, when he helped the team to its second consecutive ACC Tournament title.

Rutland pushed to get back for his junior year, but he had such little success that his confidence was ruined—as was the confidence placed in him by Odom. Rutland and the coach were at odds on several occasions and, by the time Rutland was a senior, nothing seemed to help that relationship.

Rutland opened last year with problems, having to sit out the first two games of the year because of an NCAA suspension, then missing more time after he twisted his injured knee. Eventually, however, O'Kelley became the player many thought Rutland could be, a scoring point guard in the mode of Randolph Childress. It earned him the ACC Rookie of the Year.

Rutland, meanwhile, still saw a lot of time at shooting guard, replacing classmate Braswell at that position He finished fourth in the ACC in three-pointers made and managed to lead the sloppy Deacons in assists.

But his senior year was a far cry from his exploits as a sophomore, when the Deacons were terrific because of his shooting, his defense and his ability to get the ball to Tim Duncan. Those days weren't relived very often last year, because the Deacons had no inside scoring and Rutland's careless ballhandling (72 turnovers were a team high) made him a liability running the offense.

Rutland's career ended with him leading the Deacons in scoring in three of their final four games, including a career-high 28 points in his regular season finale against North Carolina State. Unfortunately, that production was simply too late.

OTHERS NOT RETURNING

LOREN WOODS (7-1, C, 8.8 ppg, 7.1 rpg, 2.3 bpg, 25.2 minutes, .401 FG, .250 3PT, .670 FT). The sad, sad tale of Loren Woods' Wake Forest career ended this spring when the 7-1 center decided he would leave Winston-Salem and find another school. He finally ended up at Arizona.

Woods, a high school superstar known for his shot-blocking abilities, arrived at Wake Forest under the unfortunate shadow of Tim Duncan, a senior during Woods' freshman year. Woods was expected to eventually replace the four-year great.

Odom crow-barred Woods into the Deacon lineup as a freshman at the expense of a less-talented, but better-liked senior named Sean Allen. Woods showed flashes of brilliance and looked at times like he could develop into the ACC's, if not the nation's, best big man. Playing alongside Duncan helped that perception.

But, last year, Woods had to go it alone, and his relationship with the team got decidedly worse. Woods allegedly threatened a teammate in practice one day, causing Odom to suspend the shot-blocking center for seven games. The official explanation was that Woods put too much pressure on himself and was given the time off to reassess the importance of basketball in his life.

When he returned—without much change, it turns out—he saw only limited action in eight of Wake's final nine games.

What went wrong with this "can't-miss" prospect, the first McDonald's All-America ever signed by Odom? Too many expectations, both from himself and from the people around him. While stubbornly trying to prove his manhood, Woods showed that he was a big softie who expected to become the next Duncan, but never worked to achieve that level of success.

STEVEN GOOLSBY (6-4, G/F, 8.2 ppg, 2.6 rpg, 21.3 minutes, .391 FG, .376 3PT, .686 FT). Goolsby was hardly ever much more than a sixth man for the Deacons, even though he ended up starting 11 games last year. He was at his best when he came in to offer some deadly perimeter shooting, as he did in a career-high 19-point performance against top-ranked North Carolina.

In the end, however, Goolsby was a one-dimensional player whose biggest asset was his ability to hit the outside shot. That was nice, but, with O'Kelley and Rutland on the team, it wasn't necessary very often.

JERRY BRASWELL (6-1, G, 4.0 ppg, 2.1 rpg, 16.0 minutes, .420 FG, .378 3PT, .800 FT). After starting all but one game as a junior, Braswell saw his playing time and importance to the team diminish as freshman sensation Robert O'Kelley improved.

Braswell opened the season with a 7-for-7, 20-point performance in place of Tony Rutland, who was serving a two-game suspension by the NCAA. But he lost his starting spot after the Deacons' loss to Utah, when he played like a lost lamb on the court.

As O'Kelley's role increased, Rutland moved to shooting guard and Braswell stayed on the bench. After hitting double figures in his first five games, Braswell scored more than 10 only twice the rest of the season.

PROJECTED STARTERS

ROBERT O'KELLEY (6-1, 185 lbs., SO, SG, #4, 16.6 ppg, 2.1 rpg, 1.8 apg, 2.4 tpg, 29.6 minutes, .417 FG, .421 3PT, .806 FT, White Station HS/Memphis, Tenn.). Finally, Wake Forest got a player who lived up to a similar predecessor. When O'Kelley arrived in Winston-Salem as the highest-ranked member of last year's recruiting class, the obvious comparisons were to former Wake Forest All-America Randolph Childress, a shoot-first point guard who single-handedly led the Deacons to the 1995 ACC Tournament title.

Unlike Woods, who wilted under the constant comparisons to Tim Duncan in his first year on campus, O'Kelley thrived in his rookie year. He made his opening statement three games into the season, stepping in for an injured Rutland and scoring 25 points in a victory over Georgetown. That point total included the game-winning three-pointer with 6.9 seconds left on the clock.

He never shrunk from the pressure of playing in the ACC. He was just as comfortable launching a dozen three-pointers against North Carolina and Duke as he was doing it against Liberty and Radford. In fact, he averaged more than a point more in ACC competition than outside the conference.

He led the Deacons in scoring 18 times and posted the highest scoring average (16.6 ppg) for any Wake freshman sine 1953. At the end of the season, O'Kelley edged Georgia Tech guard Dion Glover for the ACC Freshman of the Year Award, becoming only the second Deacon to ever win it. Rodney Rogers was the first, back in 1991. O'Kelley was also named a first-team freshman All-America by *Basketball Times*.

This season, if Hicks turns out to be the pure point guard Odom expects, O'Kelley will play more at the off-guard position, where he will expected to shoot even more than he did last year. As Odom said earlier, O'Kelley won't have carte blanche, but his green light will be shining brightly all season long.

NIKI ARINZE (6-5, 218 lbs., SO, SF, #20, 7.0 ppg, 6.1 rpg, 24.1 minutes, .426 FG, .167 3PT, .643 FT, Martin Luther King HS/Nashville, Tenn.). Odom has already promised this natural swingman that he won't be forced inside as he was most of last year, when there were few other options in the frontcourt.

Arinze, considered a sleeper in last year's recruiting class, tied Rutland for most starts last season with 24 and was one of only four players to participate in all 30 contests. And the long and lanky player was out of position the whole time.

Still, Arinze is the team's leading returning rebounder and second leading scorer, so he didn't exactly founder on the inside. He even collected a career-high 15 boards against Missouri. Odom thinks Arinze will be better when he gets back to his natural spot on the floor, especially now that he's added nearly 30 pounds since the end of last season (when he was an undersized 180-pounder).

"He will definitely be a full-time perimeter player," Odom promised.

How Arinze reacts to returning to his natural position, flanked by O'Kelley in the backcourt and a more productive frontcourt, will be a key to the Deacons' success.

RAFAEL VIDAURETTA (6-9, 250 lbs., SO, C, #41, 4.5 ppg, 5.8 rpg, 1.9 tpg, 23.5 minutes, .435 FG, .429 3PT, .535 FT, New Hampton School, N.H./Zaragoza, Spain). The only things Vidauretta needs to become a standout player in the ACC are better scoring and fewer fouls. The 6-9 Spanish big man had a strong debut last year and Odom expects bigger things in 1998-99, thanks to more than 20 pounds of muscle he added in the off-season.

Vidauretta was the only player on the roster to start every ACC game for the Deacons last year, and he improved all his numbers over the back half of the season. In the final 12 games, when Woods was absent or limited, Vidauretta averaged 8.3 rpg, leading the Deacons in that category seven times.

Woods' departure might have created even more playing time for Vidauretta this season had not Odom brought in freshmen Darius Songaila and Antwan Scott, who are expected to contribute immediately because of their frontcourt scoring abilities. But neither Vidauretta or fellow sophomore Josh Shoemaker will be pushed completely aside. They did too many things well last year, and Odom will give them both a chance to show they are improved offensively before supplanting them in the lineup.

Vidauretta was considered more of an outside player—a point forward in the mode of former Clemson player Iker Iturbe, who is also from Spain—when he arrived last year. He was still a little overwhelmed playing only inside, but, with soft hands and good rebounding skills, he should continue to improve this year.

JOSH SHOEMAKER (6-9, 235 lbs., SO, PF, #44, 3.0 ppg, 4.2 rpg, 20.0 minutes, .467 FG, .516 FT, Gate City HS/Gate City, Va.). For a guy who was thought to be a redshirt candidate last year, Shoemaker made a pretty big impact for the Deacons. He played in all but one game last year and made 17 starts. He didn't contribute much scoring, but he was a tenacious rebounder.

Shoemaker and McMillan were recruited primarily to take up space, because Odom knew that his entire front line would be decimated the year Duncan, Allen and Ricky Peral graduated. When Vidauretta and former Swedish recruit Joakin Blom had trouble making it through the NCAA clearinghouse, Odom was glad he had that insurance.

Vidauretta, of course, became academically eligible, while Blom, who struck out twice with the clearinghouse, decided to play professionally in Europe. That opened the door for Shoemaker to get more playing time.

That door might close somewhat this year, with the arrival of Songaila and Scott, but Odom liked the way Shoemaker played defense and rebounded last year, so his time on the court won't be completely taken away by more offensively gifted players. Don't expect him, however, to lead the team in minutes played.

BRODERICK HICKS (6-1, 160 lbs., FR, PG, #3, 21.7 ppg, 7.2 apg, 4.1 spg, Stake Jesuit HS/Houston, Tex.). Go through the list of Wake Forest players during Dave Odom's career and try to find a true point guard. You'll be looking until a goat grows wings. There simply aren't any.

Tony Rutland was close. O'Kelley always looks for his shot more than he looks to pass. Randolph Childress

1998-99 WAKE FOREST SCHEDULE

Nov.	10-11	#Coaches vs. Cancer Classic
	18	North Carolina-Greensboro
	21	Mercer
	24	William & Mary
	27	Davidson
	30	@Virginia Military
Dec.	3	@Maryland
	12	@Virginia Tech
	16	Coastal Carolina
	19	East Tennessee State
	23	Arkansas
	28	@Utah
Jan.	2	Virginia
	9	@Clemson
	13	Duke
	16	@Georgia Tech
	20	@Florida State
	23	North Carolina
	28	@North Carolina State
	31	Maryland
Feb.	3	@Virginia
	10	Clemson
	13	@Duke
	16	Georgia Tech
	20	Florida State
	23	@North Carolina
	28	North Carolina State
Mar.	4-7	##ACC Tournament

@ Road Games
\# New York, NY (vs. Illinois, first round; also Georgetown and Temple)
\## Charlotte Coliseum, Charlotte, NC

was a good ballhandler and scorer, but hardly a true point guard.

So Odom is excited about the arrival of Hicks, the smallish playmaker from Houston who led his team to a state championship as a senior. The two-time All-State pick scored 32 points in the title game.

"Broderick Hicks is the first true point guard that we have had here, maybe since Derrick McQueen, and I didn't even recruit him," Odom said. "I think he just needs to get bigger, stronger and more experienced."

Odom plans to use Hicks in some backcourt combination with O'Kelley and Griffin, and to do so right away.

KEY RESERVES

JOSEPH AMONETT (6-5, 195 lbs., SR, G, #11, 2.3 ppg, 11.0 minutes, .316 FG, .211 3PT, .783 FT, Pickett County HS/Byrdstown, Tenn.). Odom likes Amonett a lot. He likes his leadership. He likes the fact that the skinny guard from Tennessee has stuck around to help the team all this time.

He likes him so much that he will give Amonett a chance to win a starting position for the Demon Deacons. It's a nice chance, but one that probably won't result in any increased playing time for Amonett, whose time on the court decreased by five minutes per game last year.

"Joseph has not had as satisfying a three years as we would have liked, but he has still provided us with great leadership," Odom said. "He's probably as intelligent a basketball player as we've had on our roster for a long, long time."

His new teammates are more talented and will be around for a long time after Amonett's final year is over. As the only scholarship player older than a sophomore, he'll be important to offer guidance to his young teammates, but he won't see much more than spot duty in the Deacon lineup.

JAMES GRIFFIN (6-2, 186 lbs., SO, G, #33, 2.3 ppg, 1.1 rpg, 9.6 minutes, .253 FG, .280 3PT, .714 FT, Greenville HS/Greenville, S.C.). One of two freshmen who didn't log more than 20 minutes per game last year, Griffin is still lagging behind his classmates. Odom believes he lacks confidence.

"He has as much ability as anybody on our team," Odom said this fall. "We just have to get his confidence level and his level of mental toughness up, as well.

"I think if he will continue to work in the early practices, that will come around."

Griffin can shoot and score, something he did at a record rate in high school. He was considered by some recruiters as the best player in the Palmetto State in each of his final three years. As a senior, he averaged 32 points per game and had six contests with 40 or more points.

Mostly used as a shooting guard, Griffin can also play a little at the point. Odom hopes to get him into a rotation with O'Kelley and Hicks in the backcourt, giving the Deacons a powerful scoring punch from outside.

Griffin is a shooter, though his .253 field goal percentage doesn't reflect that. He had a rough start to his career, missing 19 of his first 20 shots. He improved with a 10-for-22 after that, but ended the season by making eight of his final 33 shots.

Obviously, Griffin will have to improve those shooting numbers if he wants to be a bigger part of Odom's plans for this season.

DARIUS SONGAILIA (6-9, 239 lbs., FR, F/C, #25, 24.0 ppg, 11.0 rpg, New Hampton School, N.H./ Marijampole, Lithuania). Supposedly, Songailia is everything Woods was not on the inside: an aggressive, bruising frontcourt presence. Woods was dangerous blocking shots, which he did at a faster rate than just about anybody in the league, but was hardly an enforcer.

Songailia averaged in double figures in his only season at New Hampton, the same New England prep school that produced Vidauretta. Songailia and Hicks are definitely the most important players in Wake's recruiting class. Odom didn't get the big-time post scorer that he wanted, but he thinks Songaila is close to that.

"He's an all-court player," Odom told the *Winston-Salem Journal.* "He has a nose for scoring, and we certainly need that."

ANTWAN SCOTT (6-8, 205 lbs., FR, F, #34, 14.4 ppg, 6.2 rpg, 2.4 bpg, .655 FG, Oak Hill Academy, Va./ New Bern, N.C.). With the loss of Loren Woods, the Deacons need scoring production in the low post which they never got from Shoemaker or Vidaureta. Scott can provide some of that, but is still too skinny to give the Deacons the solid combination of scoring, rebounding and defense that Odom wants.

He was a strong complementary player on an Oak Hill team which went 25-2 last year. He played small forward on that team, but Odom will definitely want him with his back to the basket this year.

"He didn't play on the inside, but that was because of the other players on his team," Odom told the *Winston-Salem Journal.* "The year hurt him statistically, but it will help him this year. He will be a better player after playing on the outside."

Odom figures Scott can provide some of the inside scoring the Deacons lacked last year, he just wants to make both sure Scott and Songaila also provide the rebounding and defense which Shoemaker and Vidauretta contributed.

CRAIG DAWSON (6-5, 195 lbs., FR, F, #42, 29.4 ppg, 8.4 rpg, Kinston HS/Kinston, N.C.). Dawson has the blood lines to be a productive scorer in the ACC. The nephew of former UNC All-America Jerry Stackhouse scored nearly 30 points per game as a senior in high school.

Odom thinks Dawson has great scoring skills that still need to be developed. He will use him with Ervin Murray, who is a strong shooter but a suspect ballhandler, on the perimeter. Those two and forward Antwan Scott should be accustomed to playing together. They all participated on the same AAU team for the last two summers.

Dawson was considered a Top 25 prospect heading into his senior year. Some off-the-court problems (he and several other schoolmates were charged with taking clothes out of a Kinston department store without paying for them) and a lackluster senior season dropped him out of the Top 50 at the end of his prep career.

But Odom thinks he has a sleeper with the right background to be successful in the ACC.

ERVIN MURRAY (6-5, 180 lbs., FR, G, #31, 19.5 ppg, 8.2 rpg, 5.5 apg, Wallace-Rose Hill HS/Teachey, N.C.). Versatility is the biggest asset that Murray brings to the Deacon recruiting class. He led his team to the state 2-A championship game as a junior point guard. He moved to small forward as a senior and averaged nearly 20 points per game as Wallace-Rose Hill went undefeated and won the 2-A title.

Odom plans to use him as a wing player of some sort, whether its as a shooting guard or small forward.

OTHER RETURNEES

ARON MCMILLAN (6-9, 245 lbs., SO, F/C, #5, 1.7 ppg, 1.4 rpg, 7.0 minutes, .474 FG, Greensboro Day School/Greensboro, N.C.). The only member of last year's large freshman class who never started a game, McMillan saw action only 14 times all year long and averaged a mere seven minutes in those contests.

He saw most of his action as a reserve when Woods was suspended from the team, playing eight straight games during that time. McMillan showed solid fundamental skills and a decent shooting touch, but he and Griffin were the only members of the freshmen class who didn't seem quite ready to contribute on college basketball's highest level.

The son of nine-year NBA veteran Jim McMillan, Aron has a solid background in the game, but his skills are limited for a big man. He is not very athletic, is glued to the floor, doesn't have good hands and plays a little stiff.

But Odom likes having him around, because he plays hard and he takes up a lot of space in the lane. Those are good attributes, but, with all the frontcourt talent Odom brought in this spring, McMillan needs further development if he wants to contribute this year.

OTHER NEWCOMERS

JIM FITZPATRICK (6-0, 180 lbs., JR, G, #10, 8.3 ppg in 1996-97, Campbell & Flint Hill Academy, Va./Fairfax, Va.). A non-scholarship player, Fitzpatrick sat out last season after transferring to Wake Forest from Campbell. He practiced with the team all of last season and that will essentially be his role again this year.

A starter in 13 of his 15 games as a sophomore at Campbell, Fitzpatrick will give the Deacons depth at the point. He does have some valuable experience. He scored 19 points once against Duke, had 11 assists against East Carolina and had a career-high 24 points against Central Florida in a conference tournament game.

TIM FULLER (6-4, 200 lbs., JR, G, #23, 0.3 ppg, seven appearances, .500 FG, Woodbridge HS/ Woodbridge, Va.). A walkon guard who saw action in seven games last year, Fuller has scored exactly one basket in each of the last two years. He will again be a practice player for Odom's team, helping the Deacons prepare by running an upcoming opponents offense.

QUESTIONS

Experience? The Demon Deacons have one senior and 11 players in the freshman and sophomore classes. Odom must wonder sometimes if he runs a basketball program or a nursery school.

Chemistry? While it's good to have tainted blood purged from the system, some of last year's freshmen might be looking over their shoulder at this year's freshmen for playing time. It's going to be a tough sell for Odom to keep everyone happy.

Ballhandling? The Deacons don't have a single returning player who had more assists than turnovers last year. In fact, no one other than forward Josh Shoemaker is close.

ANSWERS

O'Kelley! The ACC Freshman of the Year will be expected to carry most of the offensive load for the Deacons this year. He showed last season that he can handle it.

Versatility! Odom has so many young legs that he is thinking of running a more up-tempo, pressure style of game. That's not been Odom's style in the past, but he thinks he can take advantage of his deep bench to outrun opponents.

Attitude! Odom loved his fearless freshmen last year. With the departure of Rutland, Braswell and particularly Woods, things should be happier in Winston-Salem this season. If the last year's freshmen can teach this year's class to have the same attitude, the Deacons should be fun to watch and successful in the ACC.

adidas Blue Ribbon Analysis

BACKCOURT	**B+**	**BENCH/DEPTH**	**B+**
FRONTCOURT	**B**	**INTANGIBLES**	**B+**

Last year, Wake Forest could take solace in the fact that the success Odom had built in the previous eight seasons didn't collapse after the Deacons lost the best player in college basketball—Tim Duncan.

The Deacons didn't challenge North Carolina and Duke for the top position in the ACC. Then again, neither did anybody else. But playing with a young team that sometimes had five freshmen starters, the Deacons had an ACC-best 7-5 record against the rest of the league.

"Our team played to a higher level than anybody had a reason to believe that they could," Odom said. "I think what happens is that if you give into, 'Well, we are young and we cannot expect our kids to be successful until they get experience,' then that is what you will get.

"Whatever success we had, we didn't give in mentally at the beginning. We decided that 'we are who we are,' the ACC is what it is and it's up to us to go to them, because they are not going to come back to us. We have to do the same thing this year."

With only one scholarship player above a sophomore, that may sound like a huge challenge. But with so much experience in the sophomore class, Odom doesn't think it will be—especially if those sophomores can instill a similar fearless spirit into this year's freshman class.

"If we can do that," Odom said, "then I think we will have a chance."

(T.P.)

adidas Blue Ribbon Analysis

GRADING SYSTEM

A+	equal to very best in country—Final Four-caliber unit
A	among the best in the land—worthy of deep NCAA run
B+	talented, versatile and experienced—NCAA-NIT ability
B	solid and productive winners—league and post-season contenders
C+	average to above-average—may contend in a weaker league
C	average to mediocre—second division in a strong league
D+	below average, inconsistent—second division in a weaker league
D	well below average—losing season virtually certain
F	non-Division I ability—an underdog every night

25
MIAMI

LOCATION .... **Coral Gables, FL**
CONFERENCE .... **Big East**
LAST SEASON .... **18-10 (.643)**
CONFERENCE RECORD .... **11-7 (2nd, Big East 7)**
STARTERS LOST/RETURNING **1/4**
NICKNAME .... **Hurricanes**
COLORS .... **Orange & Green**
HOMECOURT .... **Miami Arena (15,388)**
COACH.. Leonard Hamilton (Tennessee-Martin '71)
RECORD AT SCHOOL .... **98-129 (8 yrs.)**
CAREER RECORD .... **154-192 (12 yrs.)**
ASSISTANTS .. Dwight Freeman (Western State '82)
Stan Jones (Memphis '84)
Scott Howard (Iowa State '83)
TEAM WINS (last 5 yrs.) **7-15-15-16-18**
RPI (last 5 yrs.) **223-113-103-90-50**
1997-98 FINISH .... **Lost in NCAA first round.**

COACH AND PROGRAM

The temptation was certainly there. Was it ever.

All those seasons Leonard Hamilton would start talking about the injuries and the bad luck, how if only Player A had been healthy or Player B hadn't torn his knee up. Would've. Could've. Should've.

Didn't.

Miami floundered in the Big East, flirting with .500 overall, playing in an NIT or two, teasing us. Each season, we would wonder what might happen if Miami could finally win a game or two on the road.

Everybody knew the story about how the league's northern squads would head south, fleeing brutal February weather, and then get spanked by the 'Canes as visions of the beach danced in their heads.

If only...perhaps...nope. Miami continued to struggle. And some people wondered how Hamilton could keep right on coaching, hoping and moving ahead. At some programs, his losing record would have meant a quick hook.

At others, the 'Canes abysmal attendance figures would have meant the end. College basketball is a business, after all. One look at the awful way television handles the NCAA Tournament (no pay-per-view; too many commercials, etc.) will tell you that. Miami was operating with a poor cash flow, and it wasn't winning games. But Hamilton stayed.

And it looks like Miami A.D. Paul Dee is a genius. Unlike many of his counterparts, who believe that coaches are expendable and the bottom line is everything, Dee stuck with Hamilton.

He saw the evidence that Hamilton was beginning to bring in some top recruits. He saw the line at the school infirmary, where guys who broke ankles jogging or hurt themselves at Midnight Madness went to get fixed up so they could dream some more. He saw how tough it was to draw people to an arena in perhaps the worst part of Miami and, worse yet, miles from campus. And he knew how tough it was for a private institution to raise the necessary funds to build one of those on-campus gems that ring the register and attract recruits.

So Dee stood pat.

Smart move. The payoff came last season, Hamilton's eighth as Miami's coach. The Hurricanes made good on the years of promise by making it to the NCAA Tournament for the first time since 1960. It didn't matter (okay, at the time it did) that the 'Canes went down to UCLA in the first round, thanks to some curious officiating and red-hot performances by J.R. Henderson and Toby Bailey.

The Hurricanes were back, and they looked great.

This year should be greater still. Miami returns 11 letterwinners. It welcomes four pretty good recruits. By winning four times on the road last year in conference play, it proved that northern travel is no longer an insurmountable foe. All hail Hamilton.

Maybe.

"We're going in the right direction, but we need to keep the same type of approach we have always had," Hamilton says. "When people had no confidence in us, we had to feel we had a chance. We haven't arrived yet. We need to maintain our focus."

If you were expecting some sort of in-your-face declaration, sorry. Hamilton doesn't do that. He is serious, bland and rarely good copy. He is also right. Miami made it to an NCAA tourney and lost a first-round game. Delaware did that, too. The trick is to get back and win a couple.

And then keep going. And keep winning. Hamilton is aware the Hurricanes made a dramatic first step, but there is plenty of work left to do.

"We still have not earned the status people are giving us," he says. "People are projecting us to be better, but those are just projections. We haven't established it yet. There are two kinds of progress: projected and actual. We have to do the latter."

Come on, coach, show a little bit of happiness. This is a big thing you have accomplished here. Nobody wants to see the team slip back into the abyss, but enjoy the moment some. Then move on. And move on with confidence.

Miami has four starters back, including first-team All-Big East forward Tim James, a candidate for league Player of the Year honors. The splendid senior, who has been the catalyst in Miami's resurgence and is one of the nation's most underrated players, need only to improve his ballhandling and long-range shooting to be the total package.

But he may not be able to boost his overall numbers, and that's not a bad thing. Because Miami has so much around him, James won't have to score 25 a night—even though he could probably do it.

In fact, this team has an abundance of positives, with point guard the only real question. Miami led the nation in field goal percentage defense last year, holding opponents to a measly .379 from the field, quite an accomplishment. Hamilton is so confident in his team's defense that he used Miami's late-summer trip to Argentina and Uruguay to work on offense, not a bad idea, given the 'Canes' 44 percent shooting success last year.

Miami is an excellent rebounding team, a fact evidenced by their dominance (46-32) of a pretty good UCLA team on the boards in the NCAA tourney. Its frontcourt of James, Mario Bland and swingman Johnny Hemsley is formidable, and junior Vernon Jennings is one of the nation's most versatile players.

If someone (Jennings or newcomers Michael Simmons and Joao Paulo Coelho) can handle the point without serious incident, Miami will be awfully tough to beat. And, in a Big East in which only Connecticut and Syracuse look like sure bets, Miami is poised to cement its recent status as one of the conference's *nouveau riche*. This might be frowned upon in social circles, but is actually encouraged in the world of college basketball; recruits look for the hottest programs, not necessarily the ones with the oldest money.

It's a great time to be a Hurricane basketball fan. Bet you didn't think you would be reading that line any time soon. And, though Hamilton is loathe to pile on the praise, you know he must feel a tremendous sense of accomplishment. So should Dee. Maybe the rest of the college basketball world will watch and see that patience can be a good thing in the long run.

"It doesn't bother me that people aren't paying that much attention," Hamilton says. "The only thing that counts is how we perform when the season starts. Part of developing a basketball team is developing skills. You also need mental maturity.

"We're spending most of the time before the season starts trying to improve our mentality. We have to be able to compete at the highest level."

The 'Canes are just about there.

STARTERS NOT RETURNING

KEVIN NORRIS (5-9, PG, 8.0 ppg, 2.9 rpg, 4.9 apg, 3.0 tpg, 2.4 spg, 30.8 minutes, .342 FG, .341 3PT, .816 FT,). Norris may not have been the best shooter in the world, but he developed into quite a point man for the Hurricanes and he will be missed. A fine passer, aggressive defender and durable floor leader, Norris ran the show for the young Miami club last year and provided plenty of veteran stewardship.

Norris started a record 108 consecutive games for Miami and left the school as its leader in steals and assists. And, though he wasn't exactly an expert marksman, he did lead Miami in three-point accuracy last year, making 34.1 percent of his 135 tries.

Although the Hurricanes return plenty of talent, the loss of Norris could have something of an exponential effect on Miami, since the point guard position is so vital in college basketball today.

OTHERS NOT RETURNING

LUCAS BARNES (6-5, G/F, 9.1 ppg, 4.1 rpg, 1.5 tpg, 24.9 minutes, .508 FG, .111 3PT, .516 FT). Barnes had started all 16 games of his sophomore season when he was suspended for a disciplinary violation and decided to leave school. He was still looking for a home as this publication went to press, but rumor had it that he was considering Southern.

A strong scorer off the wing who could finish well at the basket and showed signs of being a future perimeter star, Barnes was missed by the Hurricanes. If some of the newcomers, most notably Kevin Houston, emerge this year, his absence will not be so critical.

STEVE FRAZIER (6-2, G, 5.6 ppg, 1.8 rpg, 1.8 apg, 1.3 tpg, 21,4 minutes, .355 FG, .288 3PT, .680 FT). Presenting "Exhibit A" in Hamilton's argument that bad luck followed the Hurricanes for several years. Frazier tore his ACL during his first-ever practice at Miami, then suffered another serious knee injury prior to the 1996-97 season.

Those injuries torpedoed what could have been a promising career for Frazier, who finished as a part-time starter last year. He posted five double-figure scoring games and showed an ability to handle the ball.

He didn't, however, shoot it that well, something that troubled him throughout his time in Coral Gables. Once considered a top-flight recruit thanks to a 30.0 ppg average as a prep senior, Frazier was never able to fully recover from all his misfortune.

CHARLES WISEMAN (G, 6-2, 0.9 ppg, 0.8 rpg, 6.2 minutes, .136 FG, .158 3PT, .667 FT). Wiseman played in only 12 games last year, but he did average decent minutes per appearance. One, however, would not classify his play as all that productive.

Wiseman made shot only 3-for-22 from the field last year and, although all three were treys, he missed 16 more from behind the arc.

JAIME WAGGONER (6-2, G, 0.3 ppg, 0.0 rpg, seven appearances). A walkon who saw action in only seven games and made one of five shots last year, Waggoner was more known for his disproportionate totals in fouls (five) and turnovers (three) than his points or rebounds.

1997-98 RESULTS

@Southern Illinois	73-61
Florida Atlantic	69-47
UNC Charlotte	89-72
Eastern Kentucky	86-64
@Jacksonville	74-70
Rutgers	63-55
Georgetown	66-56
Georgia State	80-64
@Memphis	65-57
#Georgia Tech (L)	61-69
@Seton Hall	78-65
@Pittsburgh	73-65
Connecticut	76-67
@West Virginia (L)	84-98
@St. John's (L)	64-73
@Syracuse (L)	67-85
Villanova	78-63
@Boston College	67-57
@Villanova (L)	75-78
Providence	64-54
Syracuse (L)	63-72
Notre Dame	66-57
@Providence (L)	57-59
@Notre Dame	65-59
Seton Hall (L)	71-76
West Virginia	70-66
##Georgetown (L)	56-62
%UCLA (L)	62-65

@ away games
# HIP Health Plan Orange Bowl Classic, Miami, FL
Big East Tournament, Madison Square Garden, NY
% NCAA South Sub-Regional, Atlanta, GA

PROJECTED STARTERS

TIM JAMES (6-7, 221 lbs., SR, PF, #40, 16.8 ppg, 9.4 rpg, 3.1 tpg, 1.5 spg, 1.6 bpg, 31.8 minutes, .485 FG, .235 3PT, .674 FT, Northwestern HS/Miami, Fla.). James is the one who didn't get burned by injury. The one who was able to develop gradually into a star. The one who will be Miami's signature player this year. The senior forward has myriad skills, and Hamilton has been able to nurture James' talent and bring him into the limelight slowly.

James was a deserving first-team All-League choice last year, thanks to a game that sparkled at both ends of the floor. James scored, but he also led the Big East in rebounding and was fourth in blocked shots. He finished second among Hurricanes in steals.

Because of that all-around play, James is one of the league's top players and someone who will be no doubt coveted at the next level. But don't expect a numbers explosion this year. James probably won't have to do it.

"Tim's progress has been somewhat a reflection of the strides the entire team has made," Hamilton says. "He's showing improvement each year. I didn't allow him to feel any pressure to have to carry the team. We're still the type of team that has to win by committee. We need contributions from a lot of guys to win.

"That has allowed him to develop his own niche. There are times when he has had some really big games. There are other games when he didn't attract too much attention, because he's so unselfish that he doesn't disrupt the flow."

When James wants to, however, he can steal the show. He had 13 double-doubles last year and some monstrous individual games. He went for 26 points and 13 rebounds against West Virginia, put up 24 and 12 against Syracuse, and 22 points and 13 boards against Georgetown. James is excellent along the baseline, gets to the basket well off the wing and can finish in the open court.

What he does need is a more accurate shooting eye, both from medium-to-long range and at the free throw line. And it would be good if he cut down on his team-high 88 turnovers and was able to improve on a paltry total of 11 assists.

That said, James is a star, and improving those areas would just make him even more lethal.

JOHNNY HEMSLEY (6-5, 200 lbs., JR, SF, #31, 14.1 ppg, 4.3 rpg, 1.8 apg, 2.5 tpg, 29.9 minutes, .410 FG, .271 3PT, .786 FT, Southern HS/Baltimore, Md.). Hemsley has the potential to be a highly-productive wing scorer, provided he improves his consistency.

"We think Johnny has a knack for scoring and a nose for the basket," Hamilton says. "He's an offensive-minded kid, and we have given him the freedom to be that way. He's improved his overall game."

If that improvement includes outside shooting, the Hurricanes will be in good shape. Hemsley didn't convert all that well from the outside last season, but did make a significant jump in production from his freshman year. Should he replicate that kind of advance this year, look out.

Hemsley hit for 20 or more points five times last year, with a 22-point outburst against Georgia State being the high-water mark. He missed four games toward the end of the season due to a suspension (for a violation of team policy) and took a little while to get his stroke back, but he did score 20 against Georgetown in the first round of the Big East tourney.

MARIO BLAND (6-6, 265 lbs., JR, C, #51, 11.6 ppg, 6.4 rpg, 2.1 tpg, 26.9 minutes, .610 FG, .598 FT, Callaway HS/Jackson, Miss.). A classic space-eater with a quick spring and good foot quickness, Bland is an undersized but productive pivot.

Bland set a Miami single-season record last year by making 61 percent of his field goal attempts, and he was even better in Big East play—sinking 62.1 percent of his tries, the best figure since Patrick Ewing made 64.8 percent in 1983-84. Most of Bland's success came at extremely close range.

No matter. He is a fine inside anchor to the Miami frontcourt and a solid interior defensive presence.

What Bland is not, however, is a shot-blocking terror. Fortunately for him and the Hurricanes, James, who swatted away 45 balls last year, is. So, Bland can concentrate on what he does. That said, he would do well to improve his shaky free throw shooting and grab some more rebounds, particularly on the defensive end. Still, Bland is a good fit for this team, which has enough wing talent to use a basket-bound pivotman.

Bland posted a pair of double-doubles last year and hit the 19-point mark twice, against Rutgers and Syracuse. In the NCAA tourney game against UCLA, he led all Hurricanes with 18 points and added eight rebounds.

VERNON JENNINGS (6-3, 215 lbs., JR, SG, #30, 4.0 ppg, 4.0 rpg, 3.9 apg, 2.1 tpg, 1.7 spg, 23.7 minutes, .295 FG, .167 3PT, .636 FT, Maine Central Institute/College Park, Ga.). Don't look at the stats with Jennings. Look at the facts. The guy can play four positions (all but center). He handles the ball well and creates for his teammates. He plays defense, too.

Jennings may not shoot all that well, but he is indispensable.

He has also been oft-injured. Jennings missed the first eight games of last year while recovering from a broken fifth metatarsal bone in his right foot. He was also injured prior to the 1996-97 season.

"Vernon Jennings hasn't had a pre-season practice during his career here," Hamilton says.

Things look good for this season. Jennings played point during the Hurricanes' South American trip and averaged 5.5 apg in four games. Not bad for a guy who is more suited for a swing position. Jennings will be a fine insurance policy at the point this year if Coelho and Simmons can't handle the full load. And, if his shooting improves, Jennings will be a valuable offensive weapon.

Again, don't judge him game-to-game by his points, rebounds and assists. Look at where he played, whom he guarded and how he facilitated his teammates' success. That's the beauty of Jennings.

JOAO PAULO COELHO (6-2, 185 lbs., SO, PG, Figueira da Foz/Portugal). Coelho comes to Miami with plenty of international experience, including an appearance as the starting point guard on the international team (three points, one assist) which defeated the U.S. All-Stars in '98 Hoop Summit.

Coelho was a member of the Portuguese under-22 national squad. He spent his last two years as a member of FC Porta, the two-time defending national club champion of Portugal. He is a slick playmaker who can hit the outside shot.

He will receive an immediate opportunity to take over the starting point spot at Miami.

KEY RESERVES

ELTON TYLER (6-9, 210 lbs., SO, F, #44, 4.1 ppg, 2.6 rpg, 1.3 tpg, 11.1 minutes, .613 FG, .632 FT, West Roxbury HS/Dorchester, Ma.). Hamilton is hoping Tyler and fellow 6-9 soph Dwayne Wimbley will make the same steps Jennings, Bland and Hemsley did from their first to second years in the program.

The early indications are that Tyler could do that. He led the Hurricanes with 9.3 rpg during the South American trip and showed that he was more aggressive inside. Even though he still isn't all that powerful, Tyler has plenty of potential. He led the team by making 61.3 percent of his field goal attempts last year and, even though he only took 75 shots, Tyler showed an ability to finish close to the basket.

"We gave Tyler and Wimbley a lot of minutes last year, and they understand that," Hamilton says. "We need them to step up this year."

Tyler hit for double figures twice last year, scoring 13 points against Villanova and 11 at West Virginia. His production fell off as the year went on, but that was most likely a function of some weariness. Increased strength and conditioning will mean a lot for him this year.

MIKE BYARS-DAWSON (5-10, 195 lbs., SO, G, #3, 2.5 ppg, 1.0 rpg, 1.0 tpg, 8.9 minutes, .413 FG, .467 3PT, .471 FT, Fort Worth Dunbar HS/Fort Worth, Tex.). Byars-Dawson had a solid debut for the Hurricanes last year and will be expected to help provide some much-needed backcourt depth this season.

The sophomore gave a glimpse of what he can do during a two-game sequence last year, when he scored 14 points on the road against Villanova and 12 versus Providence. A pretty good shooter, Byars-Dawson's size may indicate that he is a point guard, but his game is more suited for the two spot.

Strong at getting to the basket and quick in the open floor, Byars-Dawson brings more speed to the Hurricane lineup.

DWAYNE WIMBLEY (6-9, 240 lbs., SO, F, #34, 1.1 ppg, 2.3 rpg, 8.9 minutes, .355 FG, .474 FT, St. Thomas Aquinas HS/Fort Lauderdale, Fla.). Wimbley made somewhat of a smaller splash than Tyler did last year, but his big body will be in much demand during 1998-99. Like Tyler, he played well during the South American swing and should be ready to make more of an impact this year.

To do that, however, Wimbley needs to improve his shooting and get to the backboards more frequently. A solid offensive rebounder, Wimbley needs to work on converting those boards into points. He didn't have too many offensive highlights last year, scoring six against Florida Atlantic and five against Villanova.

KEVIN HOUSTON (6-4, 215 lbs., JR, G/F, 23.5 ppg, 10.2 rpg, .545 FG, .367 3PT, Seward County CC, Kan./Brooklyn, N.Y.). An NJCAA All-America last year who led his team to a 35-3 record and a trip to the final four, Houston will be expected to provide much-needed offensive firepower from the wing for the Hurricanes.

"We expect him to make more of an immediate impact than the other newcomers," Hamilton says. "He's a scorer."

That's for sure. Houston averaged 33.5 ppg during the NJCAA Tournament and left Seward as the school's second all-time leading scorer. He has the strength to get to the basket and will also light it up from outside. He did, however, take 563 shots last year, a habit he'll have to cut back upon if he wants to see meaningful minutes on Hamilton's team.

MICHAEL SIMMONS (6-0, 185 lbs., FR, G, 12.0 ppg, 5.0 rpg, 7.2 apg, Mercersburg Academy, Pa./Rialto, Calif.). Simmons is a solid point man who will challenge for the starting position this year.

"He has the talent to make a contribution as a freshman," Hamilton says. "He's not your typical freshman, since he is a 19 years-old."

Simmons has excellent ballhandling skills and great shooting range. He has a solid frame that should stand up well to the college game and gained some maturity by spending three years at Mercersburg Academy, some 3,000 miles from his home.

As a junior at Mercersburg, Simmons averaged 16.0 ppg, 4.0 rpg and 9.0 apg.

OTHER RETURNEES

NICK DONOVAN (7-0, 243 lbs., SR, F, #15, 0.7 ppg, 0.8 rpg, 5.1 minutes, .200 FG, .500 FT, King Henry VIII HS/Coventry, England). Donovan gives the Hurricanes height and an international feel on the roster. He does not, however, make much of a contribution during games.

Donovan played in just 11 contests last year, thanks to a torn ACL suffered against Villanova in late January. And, though he did get one start, he was unable to manage more than three points (Villanova, Jacksonville).

The arrivals of Tyler and Wimbley last year made it certain that Donovan would be a valuable practice player but not get onto the court all that often once the real action started. Should he return fully from the knee injury, he may gain some more minutes, but he won't be a regular part of the rotation.

1998-99 MIAMI (FLA.) SCHEDULE

Nov.	13	@Florida Atlantic
	23	@UNC Charlotte
	27	Northern Iowa
Dec.	5	@Kentucky
	8	Boston College
	11	Central Florida
	18	@Georgia State
	22	Memphis
	27	#Ohio State
	30	@Georgetown
Jan.	6	St. John's
	9	Notre Dame
	12	@Rutgers
	16	@West Virginia
	20	Connecticut
	24	@Boston College
	27	Seton Hall
	30	@Pittsburgh
Feb.	3	@St. John's
	6	Georgetown
	8	@Syracuse
	13	@Providence
	16	Villanova
	20	@Connecticut
	23	Pittsburgh
	27	Rutgers
Mar.	3-6	##Big East Tournament

@ Road Games
# HIP Health Plan Orange Bowl Basketball Classic, Miami, FL
Madison Square Garden, NY

JERRY SCHLIE (6-6, 206 lbs., SO, F, #11, 0.4 ppg, 0.0 rpg, seven appearances, Sachem HS/Holbrook, N.Y.). Another little-used reserve, Schlie appeared in seven games last year and logged a total of 12 minutes. Schlie scored a point against Florida Atlantic in the second game of the year and hit a pair of free throws in the loss at West Virginia.

MIKE CURCIO (5-9, 172 lbs., SR, G, #21, 0.3 ppg, 0.3 rpg, three appearances, The Benjamin School/Hobe Sound, Fla.). A walkon who saw action in only three games last year, Curcio scored his lone point of the season in the win over Western Kentucky.

TODD MANUEL (6-2, 182 lbs., SO, G, #14, 1.5 ppg, 1.0 rpg, two appearances, Cardinal Gibbons HS/Lighthouse Point, Fla.). Manuel is a walkon who played only twice last year, but he did hit three of four free throws in the Jan. 10 loss at West Virginia and pulled down a rebound 12 days later against Villanova.

OTHER NEWCOMERS

JOHN SALMONS (6-7, 220 lbs., FR, F, 18.4 ppg, 9.0 rpg, 5.0 apg, Plymouth-Whitemarsh HS/Plymouth Meeting, Pa.). Salmons will most likely be worked into the Miami lineup slowly, thanks to the surfeit of frontcourt players on the roster, but he does have the potential to be a highly productive player some day.

Salmons was rated by Bob Gibbons as one of the nation's Top 100 recruits and was listed 11th among all prep small forwards in another pre-season annual.

"He is an extremely versatile athlete who we think will give us a lot of versatility with his ability to play either the guard or forward position," Hamilton says. "We think he will fit into our system very well." Salmons helped lead Plymouth-Whitemarsh to a 30-3 record and a trip to the Pennsylvania state final four.

QUESTIONS

Point Guard? Norris wasn't the greatest player in the world, but he ran the team, was there every night and played great defense. Replacing him won't be easy. Jennings could be the man, but he's too valuable at other spots to play the point all the time. Miami needs Coelho or Simmons to step up.

Depth? Tyler and Wimbley must emerge as reliable interior players, and Houston has to come off the bench producing or the 'Canes will run out of steam against better opponents.

Scoring? It was a good idea for Miami to work on its offense during the trip to South America. Man does not win by defense alone.

ANSWERS

Tim James! It's time the nation knew more about this guy. A full season scoring 20 per night and grabbing 10 boards should do that. James has an all-around game that could be great if he shoots a little better from outside.

Defense! Even though the Hurricanes lost Norris, they should still be among the nation's leaders in field goal percentage defense, something that contributes to plenty of wins.

Versatility! Jennings can play four positions. Hemsley can line up anywhere on the wing. Bland is whatever you need down low. James can slide to small forward. And so on. Hamilton has plenty of combinations at his disposal.

Newcomers! Even though this class isn't among the top 10-15 in the country, it should fill Miami's needs by providing help at the point and some perimeter pop, two things the Hurricanes need desperately.

adidas Blue Ribbon Analysis

BACKCOURT	B	BENCH/DEPTH	B
FRONTCOURT	B+	INTANGIBLES	B

This a great American success story. Thirteen years after bringing basketball back, Miami made it to the NCAA tourney. That may seem like a long time to some, but you try life as a start-up these days. It ain't easy. Last year was terrific.

And this year should be better. Miami needs only help at the point—and it has some answers at its disposal—to become a team capable of winning a tourney game. James is a star, Bland, Jennings and Hemsley are a solid supporting cast that should improve this year, and there is the chance for a productive bench.

Hamilton was right to preach patience, because it appears as if Miami has been built for the long haul. It wins with defense. It has attracted some pretty solid players the last four years.

And it has carved out a solid niche for itself in the restructured Big East. What the Hurricanes have to do now is finish more strongly than they did last year and become more dangerous on the offensive end. They have the defense and rebounding stuff down pat.

Miami isn't a Final Four contender, but just imagine what it would mean to this program to win an NCAA tourney game—for the first time in school history. Everything is relative and, at Miami, the slow progress which has been made must be judged in the right context.

This is a solid team with one standout that should be tough night after night. Even Hamilton would admit that isn't too bad.

(M.B.)

26

MINNESOTA

LOCATION	Minneapolis, MN
CONFERENCE	Big Ten
LAST SEASON	20-15 (.571)
CONFERENCE RECORD	6-10 (8th)
STARTERS LOST/RETURNING	2/3
NICKNAME	Golden Gophers
COLORS	Maroon & Gold
HOMECOURT	Williams Arena (14,625)
COACH	Clem Haskins (Western Kentucky '67)
RECORD AT SCHOOL	223-154 (12 yrs.)
CAREER RECORD	324-227 (18 yrs.)
ASSISTANTS	Bobby Jones (Western Kentucky '84) Bill Brown (Southwest Missouri State '92) Brent Haskins
TEAM WINS (last 5 yrs.)	21-20-20-31-20
RPI (last 5 yrs.)	21-74-49-3-49
1997-98 FINISH	Won NIT championship.

COACH AND PROGRAM

It's the kind of P.R. person's dream that doesn't come along very often, and the folks at Minnesota aren't letting it pass without a full swing. The Gophers' best players this year are, without question, forward Quincy Lewis and guard Kevin Clark.

You know, the Road to the Final Four is something of a wilderness trail. And, of course, the Gophers will need their two stars to lead the way.

Kind of like...Lewis & Clark.

Oh, my. This is what's called in the sportswritin' trade, "room service." If ever we've seen an entree for a hokey media guide cover, this is it. Wonder if the guys are willing to wear beaver pelts on their heads? Gee, just for a couple hours...

All zaniness aside, Clark and Lewis are two of the 10 best players in the league. The key for Clem Haskins, suddenly a Big Ten coaching veteran entering his 13th season at the school, will be how much help he can get from a couple of newcomers at the point and the pivot. If he gets it, this looks like a team which can give a lot of people trouble.

Certainly, good omens abound. The Gophers finished strong and won the National Invitation Tournament last year, their second such trophy in six seasons. Teams that finish big in the NIT often are too good for it the following year.

And let's not forget, of course, that this team is just two seasons removed from the Final Four. Very quietly, Minnesota put together a season in 1997 that the school's fans will be discussing for ages. Thirty-one wins. A 16-2 conference record. A top seed in the NCAA Tournament. And, perhaps most important, some hard-won respect for the Big Ten.

Then, last season, rocked by the loss of some key, key guys—such as 1997 conference Player of the Year Bobby Jackson—all the Gophers did was go out and blitz the NIT.

As if anyone needed the confirmation, well, yes, Haskins truly earned his place among the coaching elite. And, as always, this season he has plenty of athletes. But, unlike last year, he should have some guys to take care of business around the hoop. It's all a matter of how fast his fresh blood fits in and grows up.

STARTERS NOT RETURNING

ERIC HARRIS (6-3, PG, 13.6 ppg, 4.1 apg, 2.8 rpg, 34.9 minutes, .389 3PT). Harris was one of the best defensive guards the Big Ten has seen, a physical warrior on every possession. He was the kind of guy a point guard didn't need on top of him late in games, harassing and bumping and making every turn of the halfcourt offense a pain.

Harris wasn't a bad shooter, either, especially considering he logged more minutes than anyone on the team.

SAM JACOBSON (6-6, SF, 18.2 ppg, 5.2 rpg, 1.3 spg, 31.1 minutes, .426 FG, .324 3PT, .727 FT). A fearless and high-flying slasher in the mold of Bob Sura, Jacobson will be missed as the main offensive option. He sometimes shot too much and took difficult runners in traffic, but he was never afraid to take the big shot. He also had one-on-one skills to pull it off when isolated late in games.

If anything, last season was the one when Jacobson finally fulfilled the potential that so many people saw in him. He improved his free throw shooting, took much better care of the basketball and controlled his tendency to commit too many fouls. He may not have been the next Kevin McHale—as a lot of Minnesotans had predicted—but that should in no way dull the luster of the season he put together as a senior.

OTHERS NOT RETURNING

None.

PROJECTED STARTERS

QUINCY LEWIS (6-7, 215 lbs, SR, SF, #20, 14.5 ppg, 5.6 rpg, 1.9 apg, 1.9 spg, 29.8 minutes, .457 FG, .678 FT, Parkview HS/Little Rock, Ark.). Moving back to small forward where he belongs should boost Lewis' offensive productivity. Stuck out of position at power forward last season, Lewis didn't fare badly. His spring and timing served him well against bulkier opponents.

But he was a better fit as a wing players two years ago when the Gophers streaked to an undisputed league title and the Big Ten's first Final Four berth in four years. Repeatedly, Lewis made big shots facing the basket in 1996-97, entering as a hired-gun in short spurts.

Lewis' 50 points in two games in last year's inaugural Big Ten Tournament showed he is ready for the challenge Haskins has given him—being the major point-producer on this team. Lewis also looks like a big-game player. He sent the NIT semifinal against Fresno State to overtime with an epic three-pointer, calmly stepping back across the arc after rebounding a Kevin Clark miss in the final seconds. His experience on the gold-medal-winning U.S. Goodwill Games squad, coached by Haskins, can only build his confidence further.

"He's going to be a pro," said Haskins. "He's heady, has good range and he's a deceivingly tough rebounder. He's bulked up from 195 to 215 during his time in the program.

"But we're fortunate to have big people now inside. So Quincy will be facing the bucket the majority of the time."

KEVIN CLARK (6-2, 180 lbs., SR, SG, #10, 11.6 ppg, 4.1 rpg, 2.6 apg, 1.2 spg, 27.9 minutes, .488 FG, .400 3PT, .761 FT, Richmond Hill Academy, Cowley County CC/Savannah, Ga.). The starter at shooting guard, Clark played very well down the stretch a year ago and gained tremendous confidence. He shot .460 from three-point distance in Big Ten games.

Clark was also the Most Valuable Player of the NIT, won by the Gophers in large part because of his big-time performances in New York City. He buried both Penn State and Fresno State at the Garden.

Clark has a great transition game in addition to his long distance prowess. Scoring in the 15-18 point range would be terrific for this former junior college performer. If he and Lewis combine in the 35-point range, the Minnesota offense will be on target.

Clark is explosive along the lines of '97 Final Four star Bobby Jackson, and nearly as productive. He is not as strong as Jackson, but this guy can play.

Clark, who has some injury history, just needs to stay

healthy. God gave him great wheels, and he could be a premier national-level player this season.

KYLE SANDEN (6-11, 260 lbs., SO, PF, #51, 4.4 ppg, 2.3 rpg, 17.0 minutes, .492 FG, .679 FT, Lincoln HS/Thief River Falls, Minn.). Sanden will move away from the pivot this season, where he was eaten alive on defense a year ago. He will play the power forward spot and rotate there with sophomore Antoine Broxsie.

Sanden played last season about as you would expect from a freshman thrust into a starting role in one of the nation's elite conferences. At 6-11 and 260, he was big enough, just not experienced or toned enough to deal with the Eschmeyers, Traylors and Booths. He was abused regularly.

But Sanden did flash surprisingly polished moves as a post-up threat and his nice little bag of shots should develop further from the 'four' spot. He can even drift to the arc or trail on the break for a spot-up three-pointer.

JOEL PRZYBILLA (7-0, 250 lbs., FR, C, #50, 19.5 ppg, 14.2 rpg, Monticello HS/Monticello, Minn.) Przybilla is a heralded post player called the No. 2 entering freshman prospect in nation by Bob Gibbons. Gibbons and other recruiting gurus said the same thing with much certainty when Jerod Ward left Mississippi high school ball for Michigan.

It's unfair and it's a lot of pressure on a teenage kid. But Minnesota's season depends in large part on how much of an immediate impact Przybilla has. He arrives billed as a tremendous shot-blocker. Against Big Ten pivots, many of whom aren't very seasoned, Przybilla could step in and control games if he really is that good.

Though Sanden could start the season at center, Haskins makes no pretense about not wanting to keep him there. He'd much rather move Sanden to power forward and have Przybilla take over as the starting center.

"Joel has the kind of defensive presence of a Bill Walton," said Haskins. "I think right now, today, he's as good as any college player in the country at defending the basket.

"He has a second sense. He can go get the ball and really fire the outlet. I'll tell you, people are gonna' get back off us when we get the rebound. We're gonna come back at you."

1997-98 RESULTS

Villanova	68-55
#Utah State (L)	64-75
Alabama (L)	63-64
Campbell	67-57
Eastern Michigan	65-58
Western Carolina	63-46
Nebraska (L)	66-70
@Cincinnati (L)	71-81
Fresno State	92-72
Sacramento State	100-56
Florida Atlantic	95-45
Purdue (L)	79-83
@Northwestern (L)	59-66
@Penn State (L)	68-75
Michigan State (L)	60-74
Iowa (L)	69-82
@Michigan (L)	57-65
Ohio State	76-53
Wisconsin	58-48
@Indiana (L)	82-95
@Illinois (L)	56-68
Michigan	88-78
@Iowa	73-71
@Michigan State (L)	59-71
Penn State	82-77
@Purdue (L)	83-87
Northwestern	59-54
##Northwestern	64-56
##Michigan State	76-73
##Michigan (L)	69-85
%Colorado State	77-65
%%UAB	79-66
%%%Marquette	73-71
%%%%Fresno State	91-89
%%%%Penn State	79-72

@ away games
# Chase NIT, Minneapolis, MN
% NIT first round, Minneapolis, MN
%% NIT second round, Minneapolis, MN
%%% NIT third round, Minneapolis, MN
%%%% NIT final four, Madison Square Garden, NY

Przybilla is still mechanical on offense, but so what? If he's as good as advertised defensively, Haskins will be able to put a big, paralyzing defense-and-rebounding five on the floor in Przybilla, Broxsie, Lewis, Clark and Simmons. It'll be no picnic playing these guys.

TERRANCE SIMMONS (6-3, 185 lbs., SO, PG, #23, 4.2 ppg, 1.9 rpg, 1.9 apg, 15.2 minutes at Louisiana State University, Haughton HS/Haughton, La.). A transfer from Louisiana State, Simmons is penciled in as the starting point guard. Big and strong at 6-3, he resembles Eric Harris in that he can body guys on defense and get in their face.

Simmons had flashes of very good play at LSU. He played very well as a freshman against Louisville's eventual Final Eight team. But he played mostly shooting guard for the Tigers.

The smoothness of his transition to point guard will determine a great deal about where the Gophers go in '99.

"(Simmons) won't be as far behind as some people anticipate," assured Haskins. "He's worked very hard. He and Kevin Clark give us as good a defensive backcourt as anyone in America. They're two strong guys who can tee it up and get after you."

Haskins is concerned that a structured halfcourt game will initially be tougher for Simmons, who has been more effective in transition in the past.

"When people slow you down, that's the adjustment he's going to have to make," the coach said. "He'll need to learn how to give it up and when to give it up."

KEY RESERVES

KEVIN NATHANIEL (6-5, 210 lbs., G/F, #13, 2.0 ppg, 1.7 rpg, 12.9 minutes, .339 FG, Camarillo HS/Camarillo, Calif.). A ripped-bodied 6-5 swingman with versatility off the bench, Nathaniel can even fill in at the point or play small forward. He is a good enough ballhandler, but can't be out there when the Gophers need points from long distance. He is a lousy shot.

Still, Haskins plans to play Nathaniel 25 minutes or so simply because of his propensity for dirty work—grabbing loose balls, getting the occasional rebound and playing defense. He's a military kid, too, so Haskins is a little partial.

MILES TARVER (6-8, 230 lbs., SR, F, #42, 4.4 ppg, 6.3 rpg, 1.5 apg, 26.6 minutes, St. Joseph's HS, Maine Central Prep/Oakland, Calif.). What a deceptive rebounder. At 215 pounds, Tarver led the Gophers in rebounding. Haskins rightly calls him "one of the toughest guys in the country."

Tarver has busted a gut in the weight room and is buffed up at 230. Combined with his formidable spring, the added muscle should make him a handful at either forward spot. He'll see time at both.

Haskins would like to back Tarver out of the paint more and let him pop the 12-footer from the baseline when available. He bricked his share of gimmies in traffic a year ago, but should boost his scoring by getting out of the crowds and facing up some.

ANTOINE BROXSIE (6-10, 230 lbs., SO, C/F, #40, 1.5 ppg, 2.3 rpg, 10.1 minutes, .526 FG, Tampa Bay Technical/Tampa, Fla.). Broxsie is less subtle and much tougher than Sanden, with whom he will rotate at power forward. A true center who's adept at blocking shots, he excites Haskins with his relentlessness. He won't turn 19 till the New Year and his upside is substantial.

For now, when Haskins needs a banger, Broxsie is his man. He will push for a starting job.

NICK SINVILLE (6-6, 225 lbs., FR, F, #4, 21.1 ppg, 16.2 rpg, 5.3 bpg, Loyola Prep/Shreveport, La.). Sinville and fellow frosh Kevin Burleson, aside from Przybilla, have the best chance of playing right away. Sinville was the Class AA Player of Year in Louisiana. He's a banger, but also has soft hands and can finish around the basket.

"If Miles (Tarver) could finish like Sinville, he'd be Paul Silas," said Haskins.

A two-time all-New Orleans selection, Sinville put up awesome high school numbers at both ends of the floor. He played on an AAU team that placed third in the national AAU Tournament in 1997. Last spring, Sinville was invited to the USA Basketball 22-and-Under National Team Trials in Colorado Springs, Colo.

KEVIN BURLESON (6-3, 190 lbs., FR, G, #12, 15.0 ppg, 8.0 rpg, 8.0 spg, O'Dea HS/Seattle, Wash.). Burleson is from an athletic family. His father Al played in the NFL for the 49ers and Saints. His brother now plays DB for the Washington Huskies. Haskins thinks he might be a sleeper.

Burleson can play either guard slot, and he has a nice sense of where players are. In addition to driving the lane, he showed an ability in high school to pull up and hit from the outside.

OTHER RETURNEES

JASON STANFORD (6-6, 185 lbs., SR, F, #30, 2.0 ppg, 1.6 rpg, 6.3 minutes, Nicolet HS/Milwaukee, Wisc.). Jason is one of the Gophers' twin brothers. He's a bit player who shocked everyone by collecting 11 points and nine rebounds two years ago in a big win over Michigan State.

JERMAINE STANFORD (6-6, 185 lbs., SR, F, #31, 0.4 ppg, 0.7 rpg, 2.6 minutes, Nicolet HS/Milwaukee, Wisc.). Brother Jermaine has played even less. Both he and Jason are all arms and elbows. Haskins loves them so much as practice players that he gave the former walkons each a scholarship last season.

They're back paying their way this year.

OTHER NEWCOMERS

MITCH OHNSTAD (6-2, 175 lbs, SO, G, #34, 10.9 ppg, 2.9 rpg in 1996-97, Cal Poly-San Luis Obispo & Faribault HS/Faribault, Minn.). A transfer from Cal Poly-San Luis Obispo, Ohnstad is a guard who Haskins would like to find spot time for when he needs to push tempo. A point guard at SLO, he is the Gophers' fastest player baseline-to-baseline.

In addition, Ohnstad can also play off-guard. He is a former Minnesota "Mr. Basketball" who shot 37 percent from beyond the arc in his season at Cal Poly.

RYAN KEATING (5-11, 175 lbs., FR, G, #21, Minnetonka HS/Minnetonka, Minn.). If Keating's scholastic career is any indication, Haskins may be forced to give him a long look at the point. Keating was an honorable mention All-America pick who holds his school's record for career assists. His high school assist-to-turnover ratio was 2.3-to-1.0.

DUSTY RYCHART (6-7, 210 lbs., FR, F, #45, 29.0 ppg, 14.8 rpg, Grand Rapids HS/Grand Rapids Minn.). Rychart is athletic and a hard worker, but is too far down on the depth chart to hope for much action.

JOHN AUNE (6-9, 250 lbs., FR, C, #54, 8.0 ppg, 9.0 rpg, Osseo HS/Maple Grove, Minn.). Aune redshirted last season after making the team as a walkon. He's an okay player in the paint, but there is probably too much talent in front of him for him to see any significant time.

GREG HALBERT (6-8, 200 lbs, FR, F, #25, 21.2 ppg, 6.8 rpg, White Bear Lake HS/White Bear Lake, Minn.). Halbert is also a walkon. He plays further out than many big men, and showed himself in high school as something of a ballhandler and defensive stopper.

1998-99 MINNESOTA SCHEDULE

Nov.	21	Appalachian State
	24	Seton Hall
	28	Winthrop
	30	Oregon
Dec.	4	@Fresno State
	12	Eastern Michigan
	16	Cincinnati
	19	@Nebraska
	22	Montana State
	28	Sacramento State
Jan.	2	@Purdue
	6	Northwestern
	9	Penn State
	13	@Michigan State
	16	Iowa
	20	Michigan
	23	@Ohio State
	26	Indiana
	30	@Wisconsin
Feb.	3	Illinois
	7	@Michigan
	10	@Iowa
	13	Michigan State
	17	@Penn State
	23	Purdue
	27	@Northwestern
Mar.	4-7	#Big Ten Tournament

@ Road Games
# United Center, Chicago, IL

QUESTIONS

Are Przybilla and Simmons ready? No one knows that. But Haskins, usually courageous about challenging his teams early, will get his new guys' feet wet right away with some tough non-conference games. There are six legit opponents before the New Year: Seton Hall, Oregon, at Fresno State, Eastern Michigan, Cincinnati, and at Nebraska.

A better start? That's a virtual certainty. Crippled by injuries to Jacobson and Lewis, the Gophers staggered to an 0-6 Big Ten start last season.

Better on the road? Minnesota suffered a relapse of an old plague last year. The Gophers struggled away from Williams Arena in Big Ten play, going 1-7. That makes Haskins 27-78 (.257) in road Big Ten games. To be fair, he was 14-13 in the three seasons preceding 1997-98.

ANSWERS

Haskins! While you don't see him backing down from a confrontation, Haskins seems to have mellowed into a mature leader who less often sends off hyper vibes to his players in tight spots. He'll still toss a sport jacket now and then, but he's calm more often. And his players love him.

Williams Arena! One of the toughest pits in the country, the old brick house is not a pleasant place to be for visitors.

Dee-fense! This has a chance to be one of the nastiest defenses produced by a coach who was a man-eater himself as a pro with the Phoenix Suns and others.

adidas Blue Ribbon Analysis

BACKCOURT	B	BENCH/DEPTH	B
FRONTCOURT	B	INTANGIBLES	B

Since proving critics wrong, this one included, with his defense-based '97 Final Four team, Haskins seems vindicated and comfortable in his role as one of the Big Ten old hands. It takes a confident guy to stay composed in the face of an 0-6 league start.

Haskins was a rock, encouraging his young players, reassuring them that they could improve and learn while their stars mended early-season injuries. Such maturity wears well on the veteran coach. Haskins was at times strident in his younger years, often blaming officiating and taking a Gophers-against-the-world stance that seemed silly.

As for this year, it looks like Haskins' kind of team—young, energetic, ready to attack.

"I just got some kids who need some playing time," Haskins said. "We can make people's life hard the next three or four years."

This unit may be a year away from really making its mark. But it looks good enough for a first-division league finish and an NCAA bid right now. And third place is within reach.

(D.J.)

adidas Blue Ribbon Analysis

GRADING SYSTEM

- A+ equal to very best in country—Final Four-caliber unit
- A among the best in the land—worthy of deep NCAA run
- B+ talented, versatile and experienced—NCAA-NIT ability
- B solid and productive winners—league and post-season contenders
- C+ average to above-average—may contend in a weaker league
- C average to mediocre—second division in a strong league
- D+ below average, inconsistent—second division in a weaker league
- D well below average—losing season virtually certain
- F non-Division I ability—an underdog every night

27

GEORGIA

LOCATION	**Columbia, SC**
CONFERENCE	**SEC (Eastern Division)**
LAST SEASON	**20-15 (.571)**
CONFERENCE RECORD	**7-9 (t-4th)**
STARTERS LOST/RETURNING	**1/4**
NICKNAME	**Bulldogs**
COLORS	**Red & Black**
HOMECOURT	**Stegeman Coliseum (12,401)**
COACH	**Ron Jirsa (Gettysburg '81)**
RECORD AT SCHOOL	**20-15 (1 yr.)**
CAREER RECORD	**20-15 (1 yr.)**
ASSISTANTS	**Michael Hunt (Furman '83)**
	Reggie Rankin (Ohio '89)
	Jerry Waters (Belmont '67)
TEAM WINS (last 5 yrs.)	**14-18—21-24-20**
RPI (last 5 yrs.)	**98-71-26-27-45**
1997-98 FINISH	**Won NIT third-place game.**

COACH AND PROGRAM

Things looked grim for Georgia and rookie head coach Ron Jirsa on the night of Feb. 4, 1998. Catching an emerging Tennessee team that was just about to begin a bombing mission through the SEC, the Bulldogs were crushed, 77-48. The game wasn't as close as that score might indicate.

The 'Dogs looked confused and disorganized and appeared in serious need of a confidence transfusion as the Volunteers tap-danced on their heads, running up the score without really trying. Nothing Georgia tried could even begin to stave off the rout. After the game, the 'Dogs crawled out of Knoxville with a 10-11 record, their hopes for a third-straight NCAA Tournament appearance seemingly dashed.

Clearly, it was gut-check time in Athens. In a players-only meeting, the Bulldogs vowed to never again suffer a tail-kicking the likes of which Tennessee had administered to them. And Jirsa, who had taken over the program from popular Tubby Smith, began to assert himself and put his own stamp on the program as he made some difficult personnel decisions.

The results, though falling short of that coveted NCAA bid, were impressive. After the Tennessee debacle, the Bulldogs won four straight—over Florida, Arkansas, Vanderbilt and Alabama. Losses at Kentucky and South Carolina (by two points) followed, but then came a grudge match against Tennessee. Georgia won, 77-72, and then took out Mississippi State in the first round of the SEC Tournament.

A loss to Mississippi the next day officially doomed any chance of playing in the NCAAs, but the 'Dogs' resume was good enough to land an NIT trip.

Jirsa must have wondered who he had offended among the NIT hierarchy after Georgia was sent in the tournament's first two rounds to Iowa (but won) and then North Carolina State. The 'Dogs won that game, too, then finally got to host against SEC rival Vanderbilt. Georgia won again, thus earning a trip to Madison Square Garden for the semifinals.

There, the Bulldogs' run was finally ended by Penn State, but they regrouped with a consolation game victory over Fresno State. That win was Georgia's 20th of the season and it established a milestone for the program. Never in the school's 93-year history in men's basketball had the 'Dogs won 20 games for three straight years.

Jirsa views his first season as the main man with mixed emotions, but he feels much more pride than disappointment over what his team accomplished.

"To the average fan, it might not have seemed like we had much of an adjustment period at the outset of the season," Jirsa said. "I was the top assistant on Tubby's staff, but there was more there than met the eye. The players had to adjust to a new coach and new staff. And a freshman (Jumaine Jones) had become our leading scorer and shot taker.

"You add to that one of the toughest schedules in the country and, I thought, all things considered, we did a decent job."

Indeed, had the ball bounced the other way a couple of times during Georgia's non-conference schedule, its season might have been drastically different. Two-point losses to North Carolina State, Stanford and North Carolina were particularly disappointing. That late-December loss to the Tar Heels was a real body blow—Georgia had the game, played in Athens, in hand, only to lose in the final minute.

It took the Bulldogs a while to recover, and their early SEC record (five straight losses) proved as much. But once Georgia did right itself, Jirsa had emerged from the long shadows cast by Tubby Smith as his own man. Just as important, the program Smith revitalized was still in good shape.

"I really credit the players and the character they showed in being able to withstand our losing streak at the beginning of the SEC season," Jirsa said. "We should be able to take a little momentum into this season. Traditionally, teams that have done well in the NIT have come back and played well the following year."

STARTERS NOT RETURNING

LORENZO HALL (6-9, C, 4.6 ppg, 3.8 rpg, 15.0 minutes, .539 FG, .411 FT). Hall was used sporadically in his final season. He started 20 games, but, toward the latter half of the year, did not see much action.

Hall's stats weren't all that great, either. He should be more than replaced by the center tandem of Eric DeYoung and Robb Dryden.

Hall, who had been counted on, was virtually a non-factor by the end of last season.

OTHERS NOT RETURNING

LARRY BROWN (6-5, F, 6.3 ppg, 4.2 rpg, 17.9 minutes, .462 FG, .779 FT). For a tight end, Brown made a pretty good power forward. A two-sport contributor who caught touchdown passes on the football field, Brown came in handy as Jirsa's confidence in Lorenzo Hall eroded.

Brown started seven games and turned in several solid performances. He shot respectably from the field and was excellent from the free-throw line.

PHENIZEE RANSOM (6-5, G, 3.9 ppg, 3.1 rpg, 14.3 minutes, .440 FG, .297 3PT, .411 FT). Ransom was off the floor much more than he was on it during his career at Georgia. He had to sit out a redshirt season in 1995-96 after transferring from Winston-Salem State. Then, in his first season in 1996-97, Ransom suffered a knee injury and missed Georgia's first seven games.

Ransom returned that year, but couldn't work his way into former coach Tubby Smith's rotation. He played in just 14 games.

Last season, Ransom played in all 35 games and started five. He shot the ball poorly and had more turnovers (49) than assists (34).

Those numbers would strongly suggest that Ransom won't be missed.

DERRICK DUKES (6-7, F, 7.3 ppg, 1.9 rpg, 12.6 minutes, .376 FG, .353 3PT, .686 FT). Incredibly, though he played just 12.6 minutes per game, Dukes was second on the team in three-pointers made (55) and attempted (156). He was something of a specialist, which was good and bad. Dukes was a better-than-average shooter, but his defense was another matter. That explains why he didn't play more.

PROJECTED STARTERS

G.G. SMITH (5-11, 178 lbs., SR, SG, #12, 13.5 ppg, 2.9 rpg, 4.2 apg, 2.3 tpg, 1.3 spg, 34.3 minutes, .439 FG, .436 3PT, .777 FT, Cascia Hall Prep/Tulsa, Okla.). Talk about loyalty. Smith had every reason to leave Georgia after his father departed in the spring of 1997 for Kentucky. But, rather than follow Tubby, the younger Smith stayed put and did his best to continue the good work started by his father in reviving Georgia's slumbering program.

G.G. didn't talk about it, but one can only imagine how he felt while Kentucky was making its run to the NCAA championship last season. He could have had a good seat on the Kentucky bench—while sitting out a redshirt season—but instead played in the NIT.

If Jumaine Jones is Georgia's most talented player, Smith is its most valuable. Capable of playing either guard spot, Smith eventually proved more helpful as a scorer last season, as backcourt mate Ray Harrison's shooting touch went AWOL. Smith led the 'Dogs and was third in the SEC in three-point shooting last season. He was also fifth in the league in three-pointers per game (2.3).

Smith increased his scoring average by more than two points per game over the year before, and raised his field-goal percentage from 37 percent to 44 percent. He led the 'Dogs in scoring eight times, with a season-high 27 points coming in NIT consolation game against Fresno State

The durable Smith—who led Georgia in minutes played—did not completely forsake his point guard duties. He had his second-straight 100-plus assist season (148) and is ninth on the school's all-time list in that statistic. Smith was eighth in the SEC in assists. He was also 20th in steals (46) and sixth in free-throw percentage (.777).

"G.G. is the epitome of a leader," Jirsa said. "He's done a great job with the ball and without the ball in our motion offense. He shot the ball well last year, and he needs to continue to do that for us. Running the club and being able to score is a tough combination. He can do both."

RAY HARRISON (6-3, 175 lbs., SR, PG, #23, 11.9 ppg, 3.0 rpg, 3.6 apg, 2.8 tpg, 1.5 spg, 33.3 minutes, .385 FG, .290 3PT, .739 FT, Dunwood HS/Lithonia, Ga.). Harrison was having a solid junior season until he suffered a groin injury in January. After that, his offensive production dwindled. The injury caused Harrison to miss two games and also underscored his worth—the Bulldogs lost at home to Vanderbilt and were crushed on the road at Tennessee in Harrison's absence.

More of a slasher than a pure jump shooter, Harrison will probably play more at the point-guard spot this season, allowing backcourt mate G.G. Smith to move over to shooting guard. Harrison shot just 38 percent from the field and 29 percent from three-point range last season. A year earlier, those numbers were 44 and 36.

Despite missing the two games, Harrison's other numbers were consistent with his sophomore production. He had 120 assists (11th in the SEC) and 51 steals (also 11th in the league).

Jirsa can only wonder what sort of season Harrison might have put together had he not been injured. He led Georgia in scoring four times in the first month of the season, notching 24 points against Georgia Southern, 23 against West Virginia, 22 against Texas and 21 against Georgia Tech. He was chosen to the All-Tournament team in the Coaches vs. Cancer Classic and the Delta Air Lines Holiday Classic.

This season, Jirsa is hoping freshman D.A. Layne can give Harrison a little rest.

"Ray and G.G. played so many minutes last year," Jirsa said. "If we can keep their minutes under control, that will make them both better players."

JUMAINE JONES (6-7, 210 lbs., SO, PF, #20, 14.7 ppg, 8.5 rpg, 1.8 tpg, 29.5 minutes, .453 FG, .355 3PT, .785 FT, Mitchell-Baker HS/Camilla, Ga.). Here's a scary thought for the rest of the SEC: Jones, already considered by many experts to be the league's best player, used the summer to get even better. Honing his skills for the gold medal-winning U.S. team at the Goodwill Games, Jones learned a lot about getting physical and maintaining a level of aggression and intensity for extended periods of games.

"It's a lot different than college ball," Jones, who averaged 7.4 ppg and 3.6 rpg, told the *Atlanta Journal-Constitution*. of his Team USA experience "There was a lot more banging than I expected. There's a lot more Dennis Rodmans here. Coach (Clem) Haskins has been on me to get a lot tougher, more aggressive."

Add a healthy dose of toughness and aggression to Jones' game and, well, he just might be ready for the next level. Georgia fans are already worried that this might be Jones' last season in Athens.

Jones, as expected, had a sensational debut. He was the first freshman to lead Georgia in scoring and rebounding in 13 years. He was among the league's leaders in scoring (ninth), rebounding (third), field-goal percentage (sixth) and free-throw percentage (third). Jones also raked in his share of postseason honors, sharing the SEC Freshman of the Year award with Tennessee point guard Tony Harris and also being chosen third-team All-SEC.

As his stats would suggest, Jones possesses a well-rounded game. He can shoot the three-pointer (though at times last season he was overly reliant on it). He can finish on the break with an acrobatic game that reminds some 'Dogs fans of Dominique Wilkins. Late in the year, after his teammates discovered he could post up and score on anybody in the league, Jones became dominant in the paint.

"I think his ability to play inside and outside is what makes him most difficult to guard," Jirsa said. "Our motion offense gives our players a lot of freedom, but you have to read the defense. When a bigger player guards Jumaine, he's able to step out and hit the perimeter shot. When a player not quite as tall or strong is guarding him, he's able to get to the basket."

Jones led Georgia in scoring in 15 games and 21 times was its leading rebounder. His best effort of the season came against Arkansas on his 19th birthday, when he scored 27 points and grabbed 17 boards. Few teams in the country got as much production from or relied as much on a freshman as Georgia did Jones.

"Jumaine had a great year for us," Jirsa said. "When you consider he was just 18 years old playing power forward in the SEC, there's no tougher position. To have the kind of numbers he did was really impressive."

MICHAEL CHADWICK (6-4, 203 lbs., SR, SF, #24, 8.8 ppg, 4.1 rpg, 1.5 apg, 1.7 tpg, 25.3 minutes, .398 FG, .348 3PT, .676 FT, Central HS/Phenix City, Ala.). More than any other player on the roster, Chadwick was affected by the addition of Jumaine Jones, who took more shots—by far—than any Bulldog. Chadwick's scoring averaged plummeted nearly four points per game, and his shooting percentages from the field and the three-point line were down considerably from the prior year.

Suffice to say Chadwick didn't quite look like an All-SEC player, which he was as a sophomore. Jirsa even benched him in mid-December. It was the first time Chadwick hadn't started in more than a year.

Chadwick did have his moments. He scored 20 or more points four times. His two free throws with 28 seconds to play sealed an SEC Tournament victory over Mississippi State. Chadwick had 19 points in that game, the only time all season he led the 'Dogs in scoring.

"Michael plays a role on our team as well as any other player," Jirsa said. "He didn't score as many points last year, but after he adjusted (to Jones), he really came on. Michael's a very good offensive rebounder, and he's proven himself as one of the top defenders in our league."

ERIC DEYOUNG (7-0, 220 lbs., SR, C, #10, 2.3 ppg, 2.7 rpg, 12.3 minutes, .424 FG in 1996-97, Pasco-Hernando CC, Fla. & Frankenmuth HS/Frankenmuth, Mich.). When DeYoung was recruited, the Georgia coaches promised they would redshirt him one season so he could get stronger and work on his game. Jirsa had to swallow hard at times last season as the Bulldogs struggled inside, but he made good on his promise and kept DeYoung on the sidelines.

Jirsa's patience will pay off this season, as DeYoung figures to be the starter at center. He will face competition from 7-1 sophomore Robb Dryden, but DeYoung's experience should allow him to play the bulk of the minutes.

DeYoung's first season at Georgia, in 1996-97, was plagued by a nagging injury to his left leg. At first, doctors diagnosed the problem as a strained calf muscle. Later, it was revealed that DeYoung had suffered a stress fracture. He missed the entire postseason, which hurt the Bulldogs as they fell victim to Tennessee-Chattanooga in the first round of the NCAA Tournament.

DeYoung might have been able to help keep the pesky, undersized Mocs off the boards in that game. He could have meant the difference in a 73-70 decision.

DeYoung hasn't had a lot of time to show what he can do, but he gave a hint in the 1996 Rainbow Classic. He scored the go-ahead basket in a victory over Washington State, then made two big plays in helping the 'Dogs beat Memphis. He saved a loose ball to G.G. Smith, who then passed to Michael Chadwick for the winning basket. Then, DeYoung deflected the Tigers' final shot at the buzzer.

If he can routinely contribute a big play or two per game, Georgia will be OK at center.

"Eric would have helped us last year, but he'll help us more this year," Jirsa said. "Eric is well-rounded; he can do a lot of things. He's can score, he's a good free-throw shooter and a decent passer. He makes other players around him better."

KEY RESERVES

BADI OLIVER (6-8, 212 lbs., JR, F, #13, 2.5 ppg, 1.6 rpg, 10.6 minutes, .443 FG, .538 FT, Cardinal Newman

1997-98 RESULTS

#North Carolina State (L)	45-47	
#Texas	89-87	
Mercer	78-58	
Charleston Southern	116-59	
Georgia Southern	96-74	
Texas	94-76	
*Stanford (L)	74-76	
@Colorado	84-73	
@East Carolina	55-54	
**West Virginia (L)	81-86	
Georgia Tech	77-71	
North Carolina (L)	80-82	ot
@Auburn (L)	62-73	
Kentucky (L)	79-90	
@Florida (L)	77-82	
South Carolina (L)	60-68	
@Mississippi State (L)	64-69	
@Louisiana State	61-52	
Mississippi	70-68	
Vanderbilt (L)	64-68	
@Tennessee (L)	48-77	
Florida	87-77	
Arkansas	86-70	
@Vanderbilt	81-62	
Alabama	78-71	
@Kentucky (L)	74-85	
@South Carolina (L)	76-78	
Tennessee	77-72	
##Mississippi State	79-76	
##Mississippi (L)	67-72	
%Iowa	100-93	
%%North Carolina State	61-55	
%%%Vanderbilt	79-65	
%%%%Penn State (L)	60-66	
%%%%Fresno State	95-79	

@ away games
* John Wooden Classic, Anaheim, CA
** Georgia Dome, Atlanta, GA
# Coaches v. Cancer IKON Classic, East Rutherford, NJ
SEC Tournament, Georgia Dome, Atlanta, GA
% NIT first round, Iowa City, IA
%% NIT second round, Raleigh, NC
%%% NIT third round, Athens, GA
%%%% NIT final four, Madison Square Garden, NY

1998-99 GEORGIA SCHEDULE

Nov.	13	Mercer
	16	#College of Charleston
	23	Marshall
	29	@Texas
Dec.	2	@West Virginia
	4	Furman
	8	@Appalachian State
	13	@Georgia Tech
	19	*Fresno State
	22	East Carolina
	28	Long Island
Jan.	2	@Alabama
	6	Mississippi State
	10	@Florida
	13	Vanderbilt
	16	@Arkansas
	20	@Tennessee
	23	@Mississippi
	26	Kentucky
	30	Auburn
Feb.	3	@Vanderbilt
	6	South Carolina
	13	Florida
	17	@Kentucky
	20	LSU
	23	Tennessee
	27	@South Carolina
March	4-7	##SEC Tournament

@ Road Games
* Georgia Dome, Atlanta, GA
# Chase NIT (If the Bulldogs advance, they will face either Florida International or North Carolina on Nov. 18. Semifinals and finals are Nov. 25 & Nov. 27 at Madison Square Garden, NY.)
Georgia Dome, Atlanta, GA

HS/West Palm Beach, Fla.). Like so many of his teammates, Oliver battled injuries last season. After moving into the starting lineup at center for six of the final seven regular season games, Oliver suffered two concussions in a week and played just four minutes in the Bulldogs' five NIT games.

Oliver's season had its highs and lows. He won a mid-December game against East Carolina with a free throw with no time on the clock. Oliver started twice in December and even led Georgia with eight rebounds against Colorado. Then came the 'Dogs' SEC season, during which Oliver played little, until the end.

He moved into the starting lineup with seven games to play and was making progress until his concussions. Both were suffered in practice.

This year, Oliver probably won't have to play center given the return of Eric DeYoung and the continued development of Robb Dryden. That means Oliver will have to find minutes backing up Jumaine Jones at power forward. Jones played almost 30 minutes per game last year, so Oliver's role could be limited.

JON NORDIN (6-8, 230 lbs., SR, F, #42, 3.2 ppg, 1.5 rpg, 8.5 minutes, .382 FG, .394 3PT, .722 FT, Shiloh HS/Lithonia, Ga.). Two years ago, Nordin started 30 games at power forward. Last season, Nordin didn't even play 30 games, let alone start that many.

With the addition of freshman Jumaine Jones, Nordin didn't start once and played just 8.5 minutes per game. Then an ankle injury suffered late in the season caused him to miss the 'Dogs' last five regular-season games.

Nordin had his moments in his three previous seasons, mainly because he can shoot. He is a career 41 percent three-point shooter, strong by anyone's standards. Even last year, when his numbers were down, Nordin shot well from behind the arc.

Nordin's role probably won't change this year. When Jirsa needs some quick offense, especially from the perimeter, he can turn to Nordin. Last season, he scored 13 points against Kentucky, just the second time in his career he reached double figures against an SEC opponent. Nordin matched that point total in the next game against Florida.

ROBB DRYDEN (7-1, 230 lbs., SO, C, #34, 0.8 ppg, 1.2 rpg, 5.2 minutes, Terry Parker HS/Jacksonville, Fla.). Dryden, who redshirted two years ago, will get a chance to battle for the starting center job with Eric DeYoung.

Dryden played sparingly last season, seeing action in 19 games for an average of 5.2 minutes. An injury was part of the reason he played so little. Dryden was diagnosed with a stress fracture in his fibula in late November, and it was January before he returned. By that time, he had missed nine games.

Dryden logged double figures in minutes just once the rest of the season. He had a season-high five points against Alabama.

Dryden is a good shooter, so Jirsa is hoping he can develop into a productive center and help push DeYoung.

"He's skilled at 7-1," Jirsa said. "I think if he continues to get better and becomes a contributor this year, he can be a good center in this league."

D.A. LAYNE (6-2, 180 lbs., FR, G, #32, 24.3 ppg, 7.2 rpg, 6.0 apg, Wheeler HS/Marietta, Ga.). As anyone who watched the Tennessee-Georgia High School All-Star game in early August knows, Layne can play. He is a strong, athletic scrapper who nearly led his seemingly overmatched Georgia team past the Tennessee All-Stars and their main gun, future SEC foe Vincent Yarbrough, a Tennessee signee.

Layne scored a team-high 20 points in that game, and afterward talked about his future at Georgia.

"I hope I get to play a lot as a freshman," he said. "Coach Jirsa and I have had a long talk about that."

Chances are good Layne will play early and often as the third guard behind starters G.G. Smith and Raymond Harrison. Layne, ranked the No. 61 senior in the country by *Prep Stars Recruiter's Handbook*, is capable of playing either backcourt spot. In the Georgia-Tennessee All-Star game, he displayed a good three-point stroke, making three of six from behind the arc, and also had a couple of great passes for easy baskets.

"D.A. is our third guard," Jirsa said. "He's a tough kid, but his ballhandling and passing are the biggest things he brings to us. Last year, we really didn't have a true ballhandler as our third guard."

OTHER RETURNEES

ADRIAN JONES (6-5, 190 lbs., JR, G, #11, 2.8 ppg, 1.1 rpg, 8.2 minutes, .406 FG, .333 3PT, .556 FT, South Atlanta HS/Atlanta, Ga.). Jones kept team physicians busy all last season as he battled a stress fracture in his foot, a severe ankle sprain and a sprained wrist. The result: He played just 8.2 minutes per game as a sophomore, after playing 14.2 as a freshman.

As if Jones didn't have enough hard luck last year, he suffered some more over the summer, when he re-injured his foot. That latest injury is expected to keep Jones on the sidelines all season, which means he is a logical candidate to be redshirted.

All of which is a blow to the 'Dogs. The way the game is played today, you can't have too many good three-point shooters.

OTHER NEWCOMERS

RYAN LEWIS (6-9, 215 lbs., FR, F, #44, 16.2 ppg, 11.3 rpg, 4.5 bpg, Lakewood HS/St. Petersburg, Fla.). Lewis is the only frontcourt signee in Georgia's class, but he might have a tougher time finding minutes than his fellow freshmen, considering he is projected as a power forward. Lewis starts his career behind Jumaine Jones. and Badi Oliver.

"Ryan Lewis is a candidate to be redshirted," Jirsa said. "We've always redshirted at least one player a year here (dating back to his two years as an assistant under Tubby Smith). It would give Ryan a chance to get stronger and work on his game."

Last season, Lewis led Lakewood High to a 27-10 record and a berth in the Florida Class 5A Final Four.

QUESTIONS

Center? Georgia has good size at the position, but neither 7-0, 225-pound Eric DeYoung nor 7-1, 235-pound Robb Dryden has much experience. DeYoung played 12 minutes per game two years ago and redshirted last season. Dryden saw limited action as a redshirt freshman a year ago.

Backcourt help? Can D.A. Layne provide relief for starters G.G. Smith and Raymond Harrison? If he can, the two seniors will be more effective playing fewer minutes.

ANSWERS

Jumaine Jones! Many thought Jones was the best player in the talent-rich SEC as a freshman. After a summer playing for the gold medal-winning U.S. team in the Goodwill Games, Jones should be even better this year.

Guards! The Bulldogs have a senior backcourt manned by two competitors, Smith and Harrison. Layne could make the guard position a real strength if he can contribute as a freshman.

Scoring! The Bulldogs have plenty of multi-dimensional weapons. Smith, Jones, Harrison, Chadwick and Layne can score from the perimeter or take their defenders to the basket.

adidas Blue Ribbon Analysis

BACKCOURT	B+	**BENCH/DEPTH**	B
FRONTCOURT	B+	**INTANGIBLES**	B

Georgia struggled for a while last season as the Bulldogs settled in under new coach Ron Jirsa, who had taken over for Tubby Smith, his popular and successful former boss. There were some low points in the season, but, after Jirsa decided what he wanted his players to do and they bought into the plan, the Bulldogs started winning.

Georgia's late-season resurgence came too late to earn the Bulldogs their third straight NCAA Tournament bid, but they made the most of their trip to the NIT, advancing all the way to the semifinals in Madison Square Garden. The 'Dogs lost to Penn State, but regrouped for a consolation game victory over Fresno State.

The NIT appearance should give Georgia some positive momentum heading into this season. It's doubtful whether the 'Dogs can challenge for the Eastern Division championship, but they won't roll over and play dead for their division mates. Tennessee, Kentucky and others will have to play their best to keep Georgia in the lower regions of the division standings.

Our call is a third-place finish in the East. That should be good enough to land the Bulldogs an NCAA Tournament bid. Remember, the NCAA took four teams from the East last year.

The division is even stronger now.

(C.D.)

28

UNLV

LOCATION	**Las Vegas, NV**
CONFERENCE	**WAC (Mountain Division)**
LAST SEASON	**20-13 (.606)**
CONFERENCE RECORD	**7-7 (5th, Mountain)**
STARTERS LOST/RETURNING	**1/4**
NICKNAME	**Runnin' Rebels**
COLORS	**Scarlet & Gray**
HOMECOURT	**Thomas & Mack Center (18,500)**
COACH	**Bill Bayno (Sacred Heart '85)**
RECORD AT SCHOOL	**52-39 (3 yrs.)**
CAREER RECORD	**52-39 (3 yrs.)**
ASSISTANTS	**Glynn Cyprien (Texas-San Antonio '90)** **Dave Rice (UNLV '91)** **Greg Vetrone (Long Island '86)**
TEAM WINS (last 5 yrs.)	**15-12-10-22-20**
RPI (last 5 yrs.)	**158-170-22255-47**
1997-98 FINISH	**Lost in NCAA first round.**

COACH AND PROGRAM

It's amazing how much a homecourt winning streak and an NCAA Tournament berth can do to change the perception of a program.

UNLV was looked at as underachieving and a recruiting hotbed gone cold last season. The Runnin' Rebels had one of the top five recruiting classes in the nation last year and had had one of the top junior college classes the previous season.

All the Runnin' Rebels had to show for it was an NIT appearance two years ago and an average finish in the WAC Mountain Division. Then came the streak and the program finally shined as bright as the lights on the strip.

Head coach Bill Bayno scrapped a plan of trying to put the players on the court who should be the best and went with a better combination. With Keon Clark out of the lineup because of a suspension, the Runnin' Rebels rallied to win 10 of its their 13 games—including six straight at home.

The final two regular season victories were over Colorado State and Wyoming. The last four were an unbelievable run through the WAC Tournament, all over teams who were all playing for either a spot or a seed in the NCAA Tournament.

UNLV wasn't favored to win any of them. It beat Hawaii in the first round, Utah in the second, Fresno State in the semifinals and New Mexico in the final. The victory over New Mexico gave UNLV a hard-earned 20-win season and back-to-back 20-win seasons since the final days of the Jerry Tarkanian era.

"It was like a dream," Bayno says. "All those teams, even Colorado State and Wyoming, came at us with an NCAA berth at stake."

Bayno had always been known as a recruiter, but one never able to prove he could coach. He did a decent job of taking UNLV into the NIT the previous year, but was criticized for his handling of the rotation last season.

Finally, he found the right mix—allowing Mark Dickel to take over the team at the point, settling on Brian Keefe at shooting guard, letting Tyrone Nesby take the lead at small forward and using a powerful tandem of Kevin Simmons and Kaspars Kambala inside. The five meshed immediately.

"The obvious goal is to continue the chemistry we had late in the year," Bayno says. "They all worked hard this summer and have gotten better. We only had eight guys in the rotation for the final month."

But that's all they needed. Now he's got more, but shouldn't mess with the overall numbers. All Bayno has to do is plug Shawn Marion into Nesby's place, define the roles off the bench and the Runnin' Rebels should be set.

They've got a schedule laced with games to build their power rating and earn Top 25 consideration. Win some of the high-profile non-conference contests and the Rebels are set to make themselves a Tournament team in December, not on the last day of the season.

"Kevin and Brian have to lead this team and withstand a brutal non-conference schedule," Bayno says. "We've got a chance to be good, but with a tough, tough schedule."

The expectations haven't changed for this squad. Everyone in Las Vegas and the WAC expects them to be a Tournament team and a Top 25 program.

The Rebels were playing like one at the end of last season. They should be one again at the beginning of this season. They must be one at the end, too, or this UNLV staff will be revered only for its recruiting.

STARTERS NOT RETURNING

TYRONE NESBY (6-6, SF, 15.8 ppg, 5.6 rpg, 1.2 apg, 1.6 tpg, 1.3 spg, 32.7 minutes, .385 FG, .333 3PT, .709 FT). Nesby was the team's leading scorer and its emotional leader. His second half was the reason the Runnin' Rebels went on a tear to the NCAA Tournament.

Nesby stepped up and hit big shots when UNLV needed it, especially against New Mexico in the WAC Tournament championship game. He developed deep three-point range and became the Rebels' best three-point shooter. He was the one of the hardest players to defend at small forward in the WAC, mainly because of his ability to take defenses out to the perimeter while also posting up.

With Clark out, Nesby became the team's anchor.

OTHERS NOT RETURNING

KEON CLARK (6-11, C, 14.8 ppg, 8.6 rpg, 32.1 minutes, .548 FG, .667 FT). The team's top shot-blocker and rebounder was in and out of trouble all year. Clark missed the first 11 games due to an NCAA suspension for accepting a free trip from a sports agent. He then played 10 games before leaving the team again for testing positive for marijuana. Even so, he was drafted in the first round by the NBA's Orlando Magic.

Clark was one of the most electric players in the game, bringing an air of excitement with his propensity for blocking shots and his vast array of dunks. He was expected to be one of the most important players in the WAC and should have been an All-America candidate.

But his off-court problems at the end of the season and throughout his senior year canceled any bids for postseason honors. He considered leaving for the NBA after his junior year, but was convinced by Bayno to stay in school. The incident with the agent happened in March after the '97 NIT, but neither player nor coach thought the penalty would be so harsh.

GRANT RICE (6-4, G, JR, 0.6 ppg, 1.3 rpg, 8.5 minutes, .143 FG, .400 FT). Rice was a backup forward and the brother of assistant coach Dave Rice. He did a decent job of filling in early in the season.

Rice did a lot of the dirty work such as setting screens, rebounding and diving on the floor for loose balls. Once the roster became whole in January, he saw very little time.

Rice actually had a year of eligibility remaining, but chose not to take it and to focus instead on graduate school.

TYRELL JAMERSON (6-2, G, 1.4 ppg, 0.5 rpg, 11 appearances, .667 FG, .667 FT). Jamerson was a backup point guard from Las Vegas who walked on and didn't see much time until the end of the season, but he was very popular with his teammates because of his work ethic and ability to get along with everyone. He helped push Mark Dickel in practice, and Dickel credits him for making him a better player.

PROJECTED STARTERS

MARK DICKEL (6-1, 175 lbs., JR, PG, #11, 5.8 ppg, 3.0 rpg, 5.5 apg, 2.4 tpg, 30.3 minutes, .431 FG, .327 3PT, .672 FT, Dunedin, New Zealand). Dickel came on strong during the second half of his sophomore season and established himself as a legitimate Division I point guard. He earned the respect of his teammates and coaches by leading the team and making sure everyone played together.

He is also an underrated shooter. Dickel nailed some key shots during the WAC Tournament, helping the Rebels win the championship on their homecourt. He is no longer afraid to take an open shot.

Dickel has come to realize that he needs to be a part of the offense to be successful. He also has a better understanding of what Bayno wants from him on the floor. He plays with a more natural feel for the game.

Dickel has also grown an inch-and-a-half and gained 10 pounds of muscle by playing with the New Zealand national team. He could be the most improved player in the program. He fought off the challenge of Daniels last year and was on the floor for the important minutes of the second half of the season.

"Greedy and Mark need to accept sharing time and sacrifice their egos a bit," Bayno says. "Playing Greedy at the 'two' last year screwed him up, and Mark went through a midseason slump.

"He was confused and disoriented. Now, Mark's in a groove."

KEVIN SIMMONS (6-8, 230 lbs., SR, PF, #5, 11.5 ppg, 6.4 rpg, 1.9 tpg, 27.1 minutes, .394 FG, .385 3PT, .718 FT, California-Irvine & Tilden HS/Brooklyn, N.Y.). Simmons emerged as the team leader along with Nesby last year, and is now expected to take on that role as the co-captain with Keefe. Simmons is a solid two-way player who has a great natural instinct for the game.

He reads the game exceptionally well and can play either guard, forward or center. He missed 14 games for taking the same illegal trip with Clark. However, Simmons quickly found his stride and, by early February, was making a positive contribution to the team.

He has a chance to play himself into the NBA draft if he can continue to score and rebound and provide the leadership this team needs to get back to the NCAA Tournament. Simmons knows how to get to the basket and finish, and he can work without the ball. He also works hard to get his teammates open, sets good screens and is a decent passer. Simmons has a better grasp on the game than most players on the team.

His defense is underrated and has improved markedly at UNLV. Simmons was only asked to score at Cal-Irvine, but is playing both ends of the court at UNLV.

"Kevin came around a lot quicker," Bayno says. "Kevin busted out against Wyoming (20 points on Jan. 31). Kevin's big thing was the suspension. It got him out of shape. He'll be more effective and more explosive now."

KASPARS KAMBALA (6-9, 250 lbs., SO, C, #34, 11.6 ppg, 7.4 rpg, 2.2 tpg, 24.7 minutes, .521 FG, .721 FT, Homestead HS, Wisc./Riga, Latvia). Kambala was the WAC's Freshman of the Year in the Mountain Division. He had nine double-doubles and got out to a blazing start during Clark's absence.

However, once Clark returned, Kambala struggled in an attempt to mesh his game next to Clark. Ironically, once Clark left the team in February, Kambala's statistics climbed. He is one of the strongest players in the WAC and doesn't back away from a physical challenge.

Kambala lacked some defensive footwork and went to Pete Newell's Big Man Camp in Honolulu this past August. He also spent a week working with NBA assistant Tim Grgurich in Las Vegas. He needed to develop more finesse in his game.

Kambala did that, and has added decent range to his shot. He was thought to be almost too robotic in the post, but he has become agile and can step out to take the 12-15 footer. He is not as much of a low-post player as you would think.

The hope is that Kambala can maintain a consistent mid-range jumper to go with his bruising play underneath the basket. He seems to be at ease knowing the center position is his. He is comfortable, but not satisfied.

"He's got to stay on the floor and be willing to become a better passer," Bayno says. "He struggled versus double-teams. We created such a high standard when he played 40 minutes and nobody was double-teaming him at the beginning of the year.

"His minutes went down and he felt obligated to score 20 and 10. He forced shots and he struggled when they double-teamed him. He has to get five or six shots off of offensive rebounds and continue to defend and rebound."

BRIAN KEEFE (6-4, 190 lbs., SR, SG, #3, 7.7 ppg, 1.8 rpg, 21.9 minutes, .429 FG, .417 3PT, .585 FT, Boston College, California-Irvine & Winchester HS/Winchester, Mass). He is UNLV's top returning perimeter shooter, but it took him most of the year to get his eye back after sitting out half of the season. He had to do that because he had transferred from Boston College.

Keefe previously played at California-Irvine with teammate Kevin Simmons. He needed the benefit of regular minutes. He also needed the minutes to find his groove.

He was a player who Bayno played erratically. Once he settled on Keefe as his shooter, he seemed to relish the role. When Keefe hit his stride, teams couldn't sag on Kambala or anyone else on the low post.

"It took Brian a while to get comfortable with playing," Bayno says. "He was pressing a bit and it was a simple case of not playing competitively for over a year and a half."

SHAWN MARION (6-7, 215 lbs., JR, SF, #31, 23.5 ppg, 13.1 rpg, .600 FG, .750 FT, 2.8 apg, 2.0 spg, 2.9 bpg, Vincennes University, Ind./North Chicago, Ill.). Marion was the top junior college recruit and will be asked to replace another Vincennes product in Nesby.

Marion should have made the U.S. Goodwill Games team; he was the last player cut. He can beat you inside or out. He is a strong finisher and an underrated defender.

1997-98 RESULTS

Loyola Marymount	96-81
#Eastern Michigan	84-66
#@Kansas (L)	68-92
@Southern California	82-72
@Michigan (L)	59-83
@Rhode Island (L)	73-91
Chicago State	86-49
Syracuse (L)	64-71
California-Irvine	77-55
UCLA (L)	57-65
Nevada	62-50
@Tulane	77-61
Air Force	88-77
@New Mexico (L)	61-79
@UTEP (L)	50-62
Brigham Young	76-63
Utah (L)	54-67
Chaminade	77-49
@Colorado State (L)	57-60
@Wyoming (L)	62-73
@Air Force	59-57
Wofford	79-52
UTEP	69-63
New Mexico (L)	66-75
@Brigham Young	84-76
@Utah (L)	68-79
Wyoming	72-66
Colorado State	78-66
##Hawaii	64-59
##Utah	54-51
##Fresno State	76-67
##New Mexico	56-51
%Princeton (L)	57-69

@ away games
# Chase NIT, campus sites
Western Athletic Conference tournament, Las Vegas, NV
% NCAA East Sub-Regional, Hartford, CT

1998-99 UNLV SCHEDULE

Nov.	14	Sacred Heart
	16	Troy State
	21	Southern California
	24	Weber State
	27	*Kansas
Dec.	2	@Nevada
	5	@Arizona State
	12	@UCLA
	19	Cincinnati
	22	Southern Utah
	27	Columbia
	30	Oklahoma State
Jan.	5	Georgetown
	9	Air Force
	14	Rice
	16	Tulsa
	21	@Southern Methodist
	23	@Texas Christian
	28	Wyoming
	30	Colorado State
Feb.	6	@Air Force
	13	@Rice
	15	@Tulsa
	20	Southern Methodist
	22	Texas Christian
	25	@Colorado State
	27	@Wyoming
Mar.	2-6	#WAC Tournament

@ Road Games
* Tip-Off Classic, Springfield, MA
# Thomas & Mack Center, Las Vegas, NV

Several NBA teams were looking at him to come out this past spring. He is arguably the Rebels' best recruit since Larry Johnson. He can also play the "four" or "five" spot if needed.

"Shawn proved in the Goodwill Games tryouts that he could play with anyone in the country," Bayno says. "He's got to improve his physical strength and his ability to shoot the ball.

"In terms of effort and intensity, he may be the fastest kid I've ever coached. He runs the floor as well as anybody. He's obviously got to score and he is great in transition. He's an unbelievable defender and a great rebounder.

"We'll have great balance with him, and he'll fit in."

KEY RESERVES

EDWIN "GREEDY" DANIELS (6-0, 175 lbs., SO, G, #24, 6.7 ppg, 2.9 rpg, 2.8 apg, 2.4 tpg, 1.7 spg, 22.1 minutes, .365 FG, .288 3PT, .551 FT, Cohen HS/New Orleans, La.). Daniels is a talented and very erratic player who never found his niche. He was shuffled back and forth between shooting and point guard. He did lead the team in steals and was a good defender throughout the season. He is probably the Runnin' Rebels best on-the-ball defender.

Bayno plans on playing him exclusively at the point this season. Once UNLV made the decision to use eight players, Daniels became the third member of a three-guard rotation with Dickel and Brian Keefe. He handled it as well as can be expected. He didn't complain and worked harder.

Daniels spent the summer on a traveling All-Star teams coached by Bayno in Tahiti. He has supposedly made good progress and harnessed his erratic behavior with the ball. He sometimes outruns his teammates on the break and needs to learn when to make the pass and when to pull back and put the team in a halfcourt set.

Daniels is still learning how to play the game at this level.

"Greedy has to learn and grow as a point guard," Bayno says. "His intensity and his defense off the bench have to improve. He has to play more controlled and play at different speeds. He needs to give us that defensive spark and get to the loose balls and steals."

DONOVAN STEWART (6-4, 215 lbs., SO, F, #14, 5.4 ppg, 2.9 rpg, 17.8 minutes, .477 FG, .300 3PT, .455 FT, Cheshire Academy, Conn./Rialto, Calif.). He could be the most underrated player in the program. Stewart does all of the little things to win.

He is an excellent screener, rebounder and passer. He can hold his own against bigger players defensively. He needs to develop more range on his shooting.

Right now, Stewart is only effective inside the paint. His best moves are his ability to drive baseline and finish. He can post players up who are smaller than he.

Stewart can play shooting guard and small forward. He was coming off of back surgery a year ago, yet he did not play tentatively. He was even ignored at times by Bayno.

Stewart didn't get regular minutes early, but he, too, was in the eight-man rotation by the end of the season. His rebounding is essential, and he can also get a hot hand.

Stewart is an important player despite the lack of recognition. The coaches think highly of him.

ISSIAH EPPS (6-10, 230 lbs., JR, C, #33, 3.5 ppg, 4.1 rpg, 1.4 bpg, 15.7 minutes, .434 FG, .468 FT, Maine Central Institute/Kingstree, S.C.). Epps was an eligibility casualty who did not join the team until mid-December. It took him a while to get his basketball legs back under him. But, by the end of the season, he was probably UNLV's best defender among its big men.

Epps led the team with 39 blocked shots despite playing in only 27 games. He was coming off of back surgery, which had slowed his development into UNLV's system.

Epps was the part of the successful eight-man rotation by the end of the season, rotating in as Kambala's backup. The goal is for his offense to catch up to his defense so he can become a more regular contributor.

The UNLV staff would like to get eight to 10 points per game out of him as well as seven to eight rebounds and a couple of blocked shots. He'll still play behind Kambala.

DESMOND HEROD (6-5, 190 lbs., FR, G, #0, 30.5 ppg, 13.0 rpg, 4.0 apg, 3.3 spg, Adelphi Academy/Baybridge, N.Y.). One of the top prep scorers in high school history, Herod is coming to UNLV with the idea of being a scorer. He has great range and can hit the three-pointer with regularity. He can get to the basket and can also block shots.

Herod can play himself into the rotation, especially with his shooting. Behind Keefe, there is no consistent three-point threat. Herod is also his logical successor at shooting guard.

OTHER RETURNEES

None.

OTHER NEWCOMERS

CHRIS RICHARDSON (6-7, 170 lbs., FR, F, #20, 18.3 ppg, 10.7 rpg, 3.2 apg, 4.7 spg, Carroll HS/Corpus Christi, Tex.). Richardson was one of the top players in Texas. He has the ability to be a strong rebounder at both ends of the floor. He has decent range offensively, but needs to develop some strength if he is going to defend players at his size or bigger at this level.

Richardson is a long-term weight room project. He could see time, depending on what others do, but is also a possibility for a redshirt.

MATT SIEBRANDT (6-7, 220 lbs., FR, F, #13, 14.9 ppg, 7.5 rpg, 1.7 apg, 1.4 spg, Galena HS/Reno, Nev.). Siebrandt is a physical banger who will find it hard to get playing time unless Epps or Kambala are hurt. He is another possible redshirt candidate.

Siebrandt has good range from the foul line-in and can shoot the three-pointer on occasion. He is also a hard worker, which attracted Bayno to him.

Siebrandt will help push the others in practice, which is important in this program. He'll earn his keep on the scout team this season.

MYRON PIGGIE (6-0, 185 lbs., FR, G, #10, Hargrave Military Academy, Va./Kansas City, Mo.). Piggie could very well redshirt, or he could be used as a deep reserve at the point.

QUESTIONS

Chemistry? UNLV had it at the end of last season. Will it be there again? The Runnin' Rebels have to accept their roles at the outset, or else this season will stop before it starts.

Perimeter shooting? Keefe should provide the necessary three-point shooting, but he needs help from Dickel, Daniels off the bench and Marion at small forward. Simmons could also help spread the defense by taking his man further out to the perimeter.

Post scoring? Kambala has developed much more of a low post game, but it still has a way to go before the Rebels can feel consistently comfortable going inside. Also, Epps has to provide some offense off the bench and Marion will have to get inside plenty. Simmons could be the key to scoring in the post.

ANSWERS

Athleticism! The Runnin' Rebels should get up and down the court as good as any team in the West. Dickel can run the break, and Marion may be the best trailer in the WAC. The Rebels have to use this to their advantage.

Thomas & Mack! UNLV's homecourt during the WAC Tournament was as advantageous as possible in March. The fans were into the chants and made life hell for opposing teams. The Rebels have made basketball a happening again and could go undefeated at home.

Marion! No player entering the WAC has as many expectations as does Marion. He should deliver, and could do for UNLV what Lee Nailon did for TCU last season. Even with Nesby, the Rebels lacked a "go-to" player last season. Marion has the ability to take over games and carry the team.

adidas Blue Ribbon Analysis

BACKCOURT	B	BENCH/DEPTH	B+
FRONTCOURT	B+	INTANGIBLES	B+

UNLV isn't an elite team, but still has all of the pieces to make a run into the second round of the NCAA Tournament. The key for the Runnin' Rebels will be to claim some of the marquee non-conference games.

UNLV needs to get national attention early, and it has the chances. The Rebels have been able to prove it at home, but have to go on the road and pick up a key victory. Meshing Marion into the lineup with Simmons and Kambala will be the most important part of the preseason. That threesome should form one of the most imposing frontcourts in terms of strength and scoring in the West.

UNLV shouldn't be an NCAA bubble team this time. The Rebels should be a lock. If they're not by March, then something has gone terribly wrong.

(A.K.)

29

OKLAHOMA

LOCATION	Norman, OK
CONFERENCE	Big 12
LAST SEASON	22-11 (.667)
CONFERENCE RECORD	11-5 (t-2nd)
STARTERS LOST/RETURNING	2/3
NICKNAME	Sooners
COLORS	Crimson & Cream
HOMECOURT	Lloyd Noble Center (11,100)
COACH	Kelvin Sampson (Pembroke State '78)
RECORD AT SCHOOL	81-44 (4 yrs.)
CAREER RECORD	257-192 (15 yrs.)
ASSISTANTS	Jason Rabedeaux (California-Davis '88)
	Ray Lopes (College of Idaho '87)
	Bennie Seltzer (Washington State '97)
TEAM WINS (last 5 yrs.)	15-23-17-19-22
RPI (last 5 yrs.)	38-13-39-50-54
1997-98 FINISH	Lost in NCAA first round.

COACH AND PROGRAM

We went back and looked at what was written for Oklahoma's preview a year ago.

"Coaches rightfully argue that the NCAA Tournament diminishes the importance of the regular season. A victory or two in March can erase any bad feelings from January, but an underachieving postseason emits all kinds of bad vibes.

"Oklahoma hasn't won an NCAA Tournament game under Kelvin Sampson. The Sooners' NCAA losing streak actually is five, dating back to the Billy Tubbs era. But Oklahoma's postseason problems shouldn't detract from Sampson's achievement.

"For each of the past three years, he's taken a team that's featured one outstanding player and built winning teams around him. For two years it was Ryan Minor. Last season, Nate Erdmann was the centerpiece. Beyond them, the Sooners had average talent but they won enough games to earn an at-large selection into the Tournament."

Ditto that.

Oklahoma's in kind of rut. A nice rut, mind you. The kind of rut nearly every coach in the nation would love. Under Sampson, the Sooners have never not been in the NCAA Tournament or finished in the upper division of the conference.

They took care of business a year ago, overcoming a rash of injuries and beating the teams they were supposed to beat while going 0-4 against the three others that received first round byes in the conference tournament (Kansas, Oklahoma State and Nebraska). That kept Oklahoma's RPI in the 60-70 range most of the season, and that's why the second-place team in the Big 12 was a 10th seed in the NCAAs.

Early-season losses to Butler and Wisconsin in Hawaii, as well as Mississippi State and Memphis before Christmas—only Butler made the NCAA Tournament—raised questions about Oklahoma's strength. There were no impressive non-league victories.

But opening Big 12 play with a 4-0 record, including road triumphs over Colorado and Texas A&M, helped restore some confidence. From there, Oklahoma went on to tie Oklahoma State for second in the conference. It was Sampson's fourth straight winning record in league play.

More consistency under Sampson: Oklahoma has always had one of the league's top players, and they're tough as nails at home. Most of that should be true again in 1998-99.

The only part that's a little different is the absence of a known scoring commodity. Since Sampson arrived for the 1993-94 season, he has always known going into a season who his leading scorer was going to be. Ryan Minor, Nate Erdmann and Corey Brewer all gave Sampson a measure of comfort heading into the year.

"The thing that concerns me about this team is, 'Who's going to be our leader?'" Sampson said. "We've had three great players since I've been here in Ryan, Nate and Corey. Now, we've got go find a way to replace a leader when there's not an obvious one coming up."

But there is a tradeoff. Sampson may not know about his scoring leader, but, for the first time in his OU career, he does know about his starting point guard. Michael Johnson returns.

"He's the reason I'm excited about this year," Sampson said. "He'll allow us to move along faster."

There are plenty of other reasons to like the Sooners. Two other quality starters return, and Sampson believes this is his deepest team in five years at Norman.

Sampson also isn't satisfied with what he has accomplished, which bodes well for him. He wants to go beyond averaging 20 victories per year.

It is time for the Sooners to win an NCAA Tournament game. It almost happened a year ago, when Oklahoma gamely fought back from a 19-point second half deficit to send its first-round game with Indiana into overtime. The Hoosiers prevailed, but it was as close as a Sampson team has come to an NCAA victory.

He also came close to winning his first Big Eight tournament. The underdog Sooners got to the championship game and even led in the second half before falling to third-ranked Kansas. That effort and the game against Indiana gave Sampson and the Sooners a good feeling about this year. It's also nice knowing the team Oklahoma and everybody else has chased throughout most of the 1990s, Kansas, shouldn't be anywhere near as good as it has been recently.

That leaves first-place up for grabs, and the Sooners could be ready to take their shot at the top.

1997-98 RESULTS

Jackson State	75-62	
Texas-Arlington	81-63	
Southwest Texas State	81-68	
#Butler (L)	63-73	
#Wisconsin (L)	64-75	
#Hawaii-Hilo	86-70	
Arkansas-Pine Bluff	82-51	
@Mississippi State (L)	65-67	ot
Memphis (L)	78-80	
Florida-Atlantic	91-65	
North Texas	95-72	
##Coppin State	83-72	
##Alabama	79-61	
@Colorado	69-68	
Kansas State	71-64	
@Texas A&M	76-66	
Texas	91-75	
@Nebraska (L)	43-53	
Iowa State	64-63	
@Baylor	61-60	
Oklahoma State (L)	84-88	
Texas A&M	80-71	
Texas Tech (L)	68-70	
@Texas	81-74	
@Oklahoma State (L)	66-70	
Baylor	75-63	
Missouri	80-76	
@Kansas (L)	70-83	
@Texas Tech	89-56	
###Missouri	58-53	
###Texas	68-55	
###Kansas (L)	58-72	
%Indiana (L)	87-94	ot

@ away games
# Big Island Invitational, Hilo, HI
All-College Tournament, Oklahoma City, OK
Big 12 Tournament, Kemper Arena, Kansas City, MO
% NCAA East Sub-Regional, Washington, DC

STARTERS NOT RETURNING

COREY BREWER (6-1, PG, 20.8 ppg, 5.6 rpg, 3.2 apg, 35.4 minutes, .429 FG, .375 3PT). Sampson isn't ashamed to say Brewer was one of his all-time favorites.

"Corey identified, almost eerily, a sense of who we are with his physicalness, his spirit and intensity," Sampson said. "I'm really not worried about replacing Corey's points. Who is going to establish our work ethic in practice? Who going to get us going in practice when we hit that lull? That's what Corey was about."

He was also about production. Brewer led Oklahoma in scoring in 28 of 33 games in an All-Big 12 season. His 24.4 average in league games led the Big 12, and he was team's top scorer in all 16 conference contests. There wasn't a more valuable player in Big 12 games than Brewer.

He improved his shooting last season and knocked down 72 three-pointers, 55 more than the previous year. His 19.2 ppg career scoring average ranks fourth in school history for players with more than 1,000 points. Only Wayman Tisdale (25.6), Alvin Adams (23.7) and Don Sidle (20.4) have better marks.

Brewer came to Oklahoma the hard way. After high school there were stops at two junior colleges, Navarro in Texas and Carl Albert in Poteau, Okla. He was a big fish in a small pond there, averaging 26.3 ppg and 4.0 apg.

The numbers attracted several top programs, and Oklahoma had an opening at guard. It turned out to be the best recruit of Sampson's in his four seasons.

EVAN "HOOTIE" WILEY (6-11, C, 10.7 ppg, 5.2 rpg, 23.8 minutes, .593 FG). Wiley was the final player recruited by Billy Tubbs. Sampson was the coach when he signed, but it was Tubbs who scouted the talent.

Wiley had a nice season and set a school record for field goal percentage. His career highlight came as a junior, when he made 26 of his first 27 shots from the field. Wiley finished with a career field goal mark of 55.2 percent.

"There are some guys that have a special place in your heart," Sampson said. "Hootie is one of those guys for me. He may not be the best player in the league, but he plays hard and he's gotten better every year."

OTHERS NOT RETURNING

ROBERT ALLISON (6-5, G, 6.3 ppg, 2.2 rpg, 21.1 minutes, .352 FG, .352 3PT). Allison started all 20 of his games, but did not become the big scorer he might have been. He came to Oklahoma with the reputation of a great perimeter shooter and turned out to be in the 35-percent range from behind the arc.

Still, Allison gave the Sooners a steady presence and was better in the second half of the season.

REGGIE BASS (6-2, G, 0.5 ppg, 0.2 rpg, six appearances). Bass joined the team as a walkon practice player two years ago. He played in 11 games in his career, took four shots and made one—a three-pointer.

BOBBY JO EVANS (6-9, F, 1.0 ppg, two appearances). A sad story, as Evans was once seen as the Sooners' next great forward. But chronic knee problems ended his career prematurely. Evans has one year of eligibility remaining and he remains at Oklahoma on scholarship, but he will not play again.

That he remains in school to get his degree is a triumph. Evans became a husband and father as a freshman, and the family remained in his home state of Texas. Evans nearly dropped out of school to get a job and support them, but the family convinced him that college was an opportunity his family could not afford to miss.

PROJECTED STARTERS

MICHAEL JOHNSON (6-0, 170 lbs., SR, PG, #10, 7.1 ppg, 2.8 rpg, 4.3 apg, 1.6 spg, 31.6 minutes, .372 FG, .420 3PT, .753 FT, Highland CC, Ill. & Rancho HS/Las Vegas, Nev.). Sampson's pretty excited about this guy.

"Michael's a great kid, a very coachable kid," he said. "I was pretty hard on him last year, but he weathered the storm, became a better player and was one of our more valuable players down the stretch. I expect him to be one of the better point guards in the Big 12."

Actually, that spot is wide open and Johnson has as much upside as anybody.

Amazingly, this is the first time in five years Sampson knows the identity of his point guard heading into the season. In Johnson, he has a quick, light player who gets by on guile and shooting. Johnson led the Sooners in three-point percentage, which was a much higher mark than his two-point shooting.

Johnson got his OU career off to a great start by matching a school record with 18 assists in a December game. The total was the most by a Division I player last season. Johnson also had nine assists against Texas. He drained all four three-point tries en route to a career-best 19 points against Texas A&M. Johnson played all 45 minutes in the NCAA Tournament loss to Indiana.

Like Humphrey, a hospital trip interrupted Johnson's season. He took a shot to the mouth in Texas and suffered a broken nose and damage to his upper teeth. But Johnson did not miss a game.

EDUARDO NAJERA (6-8, 235 lbs., JR, PF, #21, 10.5 ppg, 5.4 rpg, 28.5 minutes, .425 FG, .265 3PT, .634 FT, Cornerstone Christian/San Antonio, Tex.). Najera's development was slowed by a stress fracture in his left foot. He had started the first 20 games, missed three, then came off the bench for the final 10.

But he was a better player than his freshman year. He was less of a bull in the paint and more of a smooth operator. He cut down on his fouls, shot a little better, scored more. Najera has always been rugged. But he has learned over two season that he possesses some skills that make him a more well-rounded player.

"Not many people saw him at his best last year," Sampson said. "He's the kind of kid who can carry us. He's one of our key, key players. If he's at full speed and having a great year, we will, too."

Najera is an interesting story. Four years ago, he came from his native Chihuahua, Mexico, to San Antonio as an exchange student. Najera spoke no English. The language came along slowly, but the basketball didn't.

At Cornerstone Christian, Najera became a force, averaging 24.8 ppg and 15.4 rpg. He signed with Oklahoma out of high school, but did not have the ACT score to qualify for a scholarship.

Najera enrolled as a part-time student and studied for the test. An ACT score of 11 became a 17, and Najera was enrolled as a 21-year-old freshman. He has become a fan favorite and should be one of the best at his position in the Big 12.

RYAN HUMPHREY (6-8, 225 lbs., SO, SF, #24, 9.2 ppg, 6.5 rpg, 1.8 bpg, 23.3 minutes, .482 FG, .549 FT, Booker T. Washington HS/Tulsa, Okla.). Sampson played

1998-99 OKLAHOMA SCHEDULE

Nov.	14	Northwestern State
	21	Coppin State
	27-28	#Sooner Classic
Dec.	5	Arkansas
	17	Sam Houston State
	21-23	##Puerto Rico Holiday Classic
	29-30	###All College Tournament
Jan.	3	@Iowa State
	6	Texas Tech
	9	Colorado
	12	@Oklahoma State
	16	@Cincinnati
	20	Nebraska
	23	@Kansas State
	25	Texas
	30	@Texas Tech
Feb.	3	@Baylor
	6	Oklahoma State
	10	@Texas
	13	Texas A & M
	15	@Missouri
	20	Kansas
	24	@Texas A & M
	27	Baylor
Mar.	4-7	####Big 12 Tournament

@ Road Games
# Norman, OK (vs. Western Carolina, first round; also Arkansas-Little Rock and Murray State)
San Juan, PR (vs. St. Joseph's, first round; also Alabama-Birmingham, American University-PR, Middle Tennessee State, Mississippi, North Carolina State and Ohio State)
Oklahoma City, OK (vs. Western Kentucky, first round; also Cal Poly SLO and Oral Roberts)
Kemper Arena, Kansas City, MO

it just right with Humphrey. Expectations were getting out of control; the Sooners had won a major recruiting battle; and he was the highest profile recruit in Sampson's tenure. Humphrey was being compared to another player from the same high school, Wayman Tisdale.

Sampson had heard enough, so he started firing off warnings.

"He's going to be a good one, but his offense has a long way to go. It's not there yet," Sampson said. "Don't expect too much."

Perfect. With a few well-chosen words, Sampson diffused a potential problem. Instead of looking at Humphrey's numbers as disappointing—after all, Tisdale was an All-America as a freshman—the prevailing attitude seemed to be that Humphrey had a successful freshman season, earning a spot on the Big 12's All-Freshman team.

Not all went smoothly for Humphrey. On Dec. 17, he was diagnosed with iron-deficiency anemia and missed an early conference game with a precautionary hospital stay.

"The symptoms are the bigger concern," Sampson said. "He has fatigue. He needs to take medicine." It proved not to be a problem. Humphrey played better as the year went on."

His stickback at Baylor beat the buzzer and gave the Sooners a one-point victory. He recorded double-doubles against Alabama (13-13) and Texas Tech (17-11), and matched his season high with 18 points in the NCAA Tournament victory over Indiana.

The season ended on a high note. Humphrey shared the team's top student-athlete award with teammate Renzi Stone.

RENZI STONE (6-10, 255 lbs., JR, C, #33, 4.8 ppg, 4.9 rpg, 22.8 minutes, .509 FG, .705 FT, Jenks HS/Tulsa, Okla.). In a season of bulging disks, busted noses and stress fractures, Stone was a, well, a rock for the Sooners. He didn't get hurt and was one of four players to appear in all 33 games.

There are no surprises with Stone. He gives Oklahoma quality minutes, a basket or two, four or five rebounds, and shoots it better than most. Then he returns to the bench and awaits the next call.

"He gets things done," is how Sampson describes him. "I can think about three games we lose last year if Renzi doesn't produce."

One for sure was a one-point victory at Colorado in the Big 12 opener. Stone scored a career-high 15 points while making six of seven from the floor. At Texas, he had 13 points and a career-best 10 rebounds.

Stone could start at center this year, giving the Sooners an experienced starting front line of Stone, Najera and Humphrey.

KELLEY NEWTON (6-2, 190 lbs., JR, SG, #20, 17.7 ppg, 4.3 apg, 3.9 rpg, .448 3PT, .899 FT, Neosho CC, Kan. & Wyandotte HS/Kansas City, Kan.). Newton will give the Sooners a Robert Allison-type shooter, a three-point gun from the bench. Newton made first-team All-Jayhawk Conference on the strength of his perimeter shooting, while helping Neosho CC to a 27-5 record.

KEY RESERVES

TIM HESKETT (6-1, 180 lbs., SO, G, #14, 9.5 ppg, 2.0 rpg, 2.5 apg, .400 FG, .364 3PT, two appearances, Lexington HS/Lexington S.C.). A year earlier, Heskett averaged 3.9 ppg and shot 32.1 percent on three-pointers. He played a major role for the Sooners off the bench late in the 1997 season, when Oklahoma made its run for NCAA Tournament consideration.

But, after two games last year, Heskett was done. He had suffered a bulging disk and OU was without a promising guard. Heskett scored 15 points in his second game, against Texas-Arlington, before the decision was made to sit out.

In 1997, Heskett had an amazing effect on the Sooners, who collectively seemed to raise their level when he was on the floor. Heskett is a solid, if unspectacular player, but his enthusiasm rubs off on teammates.

"Tim will have an immediate impact on the personality of this team because of his attitude," Sampson said. "That's what leadership is. It's not scoring 20 points. Leadership is winning. Some guys can score three or four points a game and be leaders. Tim is that kind of player."

Heskett is a point guard and, if he stays there, he'll play behind Michael Johnson. But his three-point accuracy should allow him to stay on the floor some at shooting guard.

ERIC MARTIN (6-5, 200 lbs., SR, G, #30, 6.5 ppg, 3.4 rpg, 1.1 apg, .377 FG, .286 3PT, .878 FT, Sullivan JC, Ky. & Fairdale HS/Louisville, Ky.). Martin was another injury problem last season. A bulging disk (see Tim Heskett) kept him out of the final 11 games and from turning in a solid rookie Division I season.

Sullivan will be a valuable reserve, a backup shooting guard, who the Sooners will want on the floor at the end of close games because of free throw shooting. "He can come in and give us instant offense," Sampson said.

Three years ago, Martin started for the national junior college champions. Two years ago, he led Sullivan JC in scoring.

VICTOR AVILA (6-10, 250 lbs., JR, C, #32, 23.7 ppg, 15.3 rpg, 2.1 apg, 2.8 bpg, .628 FG, .371 3PT, .719 FT, Scottsdale CC, Az./Culiacan, Mexico). Avila could have a big impact on the Sooners. He was named second-team junior college All-America and posted some magnificent numbers at Scottsdale CC. He could push Renzi Stone for the starting nod in the middle.

"He has great hands, good instincts and knows how to pass for a big man," Sampson said. "His low post moves are outstanding. We feel fortunate to have him."

Sampson said Avila is better with his back to the basket, which gives him an advantage over Stone. But Avila also shot 37 percent on three-pointers.

He is a native of Mexico, like Najera. They were teammates on the Mexican team during the 1997 World University Games that finished seventh (of 16 entrants) with a 3-3 record.

OTHER RETURNEES

ALEX SPAULDING (6-3, 190 lbs., SO, G, #44, 2.5 ppg, 6.2 minutes, .469 FG, .294 3PT, .920 FT, Williams HS/Burlington, N.C.). Sampson thought about redshirting Spaulding, but, when Heskett went down after two games, there was no choice. He was named Big 12 freshman of the week after scoring a season-high 13 points against Florida Atlantic. His biggest asset is free throw shooting, at 92 percent.

OLEG REZTSOV (7-2, 225 lbs., JR, C, #22, 1997-98 redshirt, Weatherford HS, Tex./Kiev, Ukraine). Reztsov averaged 12 points, nine rebounds and five blocks for Weatherford two years ago, but he played in only a handful of games after suffering a broken foot in December.

Reztsov is from a hoops family. Both parents coach in the Ukraine. His brother and mother have played on Soviet national teams. Reztsov is a project, but should be fun to watch.

He'll be the tallest player to suit up for the Sooners and the first Russian. He also has designed his own web site (www.geocites.com/Coloseum/Loge/8258/).

OTHER NEWCOMERS

J.R. RAYMOND (6-2, 180 lbs., FR, G, #11, 18.1 ppg, 6.1 apg, 3.2 spg, .420 3PT, Mount Zion Christian Academy, N.C./Gastonia, N.C.). Raymond is the Sooners' only freshman recruit and something of an in-between guard.

As Sampson said, "He isn't a true point and not a prototypical 'two' guard.

He's what I call a good guard."

Raymond may redshirt this season.

QUESTIONS

Go-to player? The guy Sampson wants to lead the team, Michael Johnson, isn't a big scorer, or at least he wasn't last year.

NCAA Tournament-itis? At some point, Oklahoma has to win a tournament game. Its only NCAA victory in the decade came in 1990 over Towson State.

Finishing kick? In its 11 losses last season, the Sooners led or were tied in the second half of 10 of them. Oklahoma must learn how to close the deal.

ANSWERS

Free-throw shooting! They just seem to work harder at it at Oklahoma. In 125 games under Sampson, the Sooners are hitting at a 72.2 percent clip.

Michael Johnson! A true point guard who looks pass first, shot second.

Johnson will need to score more, but there may not better a point in the Big 12.

Kelvin Sampson! He finds a way to get things done. Among Big 12 coaches, only Kansas' Roy Williams has been to more consecutive NCAA Tournaments than Sampson's four.

adidas Blue Ribbon Analysis

BACKCOURT	B	BENCH/DEPTH	B
FRONTCOURT	B	INTANGIBLES	B

There's much to like about this Oklahoma team. An experienced player is back at every position except shooting guard. No, there is nobody in the lineup who has averaged more than 10.5 ppg as a college player, but everybody seems to improve in Sampson's system. And players like Johnson, Najera and Humphrey should have their best seasons.

What Oklahoma needs this season is more luck. Too many key players missed too many games, and guys like Johnson played hurt. Sampson wants to develop depth. He thought he had it last year, but yanking redshirts off players isn't his idea of creating a solid playing rotation.

"I think we can go nine deep," Sampson said. "I've never been able to go nine deep since I've been here. When it comes down to crunch time, you have to be down to a seven- or eight-man rotation, but you want the luxury of having that ninth guy."

Another difference this year: Oklahoma should get more points in the paint. Najera, Humphrey, Stone and newcomer Avila (if he lives up to his billing) can all score inside. Going inside more is a goal because the Sooners believe they have good enough perimeter shooting to stretch the defense. Johnson, Heskett, Martin and Newton can all bury the three-pointer at 40 percent.

If it all comes together, this could be Sampson's best year at Oklahoma. The Sooners are capable of finishing first in the Big 12, getting that good seed and winning a game or two in the NCAA Tournament. In other words, it's a team capable of breaking out of the rut.

(B.K.)

30

TEXAS CHRISTIAN

LOCATION	Fort Worth, TX
CONFERENCE	WAC (Mountain Division)
LAST SEASON	27-6 (.818)
CONFERENCE RECORD	14-0 (1st, Pacific)
STARTERS LOST/RETURNING	3/2
NICKNAME	Horned Frogs
COLORS	Purple & White
HOMECOURT	Daniel Meyer Coliseum (7,186)
COACH	Billy Tubbs (Lamar '58)
RECORD AT SCHOOL	80-45 (4 yrs.)
CAREER RECORD	519-245 (24 yrs.)
ASSISTANTS	Brian Fish (Marshall '87)
	Rob Flaska (Michigan Tech '82)
	Conley Phillips (Northwestern State '90)
TEAM WINS (last 5 yrs.)	7-16-15-22-27
RPI (last 5 yrs.)	240-141-94-45-23
1997-98 FINISH	Lost in NCAA first round.

COACH AND PROGRAM

We wouldn't be writing about this team in this section of the yearbook if it weren't for Lee Nailon staying in school. Credit Billy Tubbs.

Tubbs went to Chicago to watch Nailon at the predraft camp in June. He went there to encourage him, but not for the NBA.

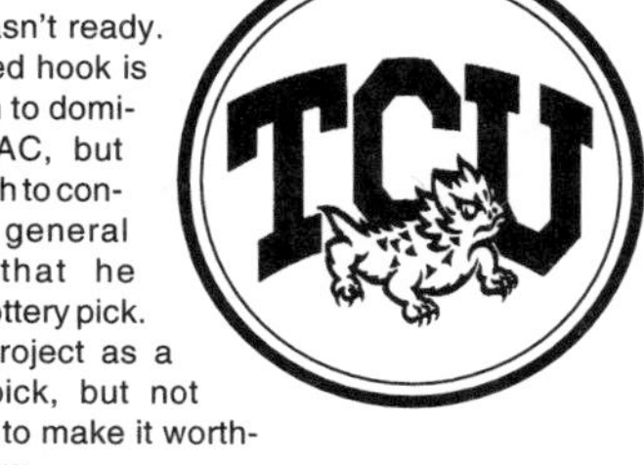

Nailon wasn't ready. His lefthanded hook is good enough to dominate the WAC, but wasn't enough to convince NBA general managers that he should be a lottery pick. Nailon did project as a first-round pick, but not high enough to make it worthwhile—for now.

So, he came back to TCU. And here are the Horned Frogs, a Top 40 team again. Credit Billy Tubbs.

Why? Because Nailon isn't the only reason to put TCU in this elite company. Tubbs has done what he set out to do at Texas Christian. He has made the Horned

Frogs a perennial postseason team by combining transfers and junior college guys that want to play his style. TCU runs, scores and rebounds, and can intimidate any team that doesn't want to keep pace.

And they win.

"We're still (in the Top 40)," Tubbs says. "We planed on being back. I didn't even know Lee was coming back. But I knew we would be good."

With Nailon, they could be even better. Losing to Florida State—which didn't even deserve to be there—in the first round of the NCAA Tournament left the Horned Frogs bitter and hungrier to get back and move beyond the tourney's opening day.

Tubbs may not have the perimeter shooting he did last year with Mike Jones and Malcolm Johnson, but he'll have one of the most productive frontcourts in the nation and one of the best point guards in Prince Fowler.

"Two years ago we were left out (of the NCAAs), and last year we thought we would go further than we did," Tubbs says. "Our lack of success should be a motivating factor to get back and do better. There wasn't a game last year that we couldn't have won. This will be an exciting team and I'll be a better coach."

Tubbs has coached in the Final Four, actually the title game when he was with Oklahoma in 1988. He came to TCU to make the Horned Frogs a program worth watching.

Texas Christian was rarely mentioned in college basketball when Tubbs took over in 1994. Now, the Horned Frogs are a type of team no one wants to play.

In their first year in the WAC, the Horned Frogs made it to the conference tournament final, losing to Utah in the championship game. They were one of the last teams kept out of the NCAAs, eventually losing to Notre Dame in the second round of the NIT. A year later, with Nailon on board, TCU made a mockery of the WAC's Pacific Division, becoming the first team in league history to go undefeated in regular season play.

The Horned Frogs didn't get the appropriate respect nationally, taking almost two months to crack the Top 25. It took a little longer in the coaches' poll, largely because Tubbs' style of scoring—allowing his team to keep going no matter the margin.

He'll tell you they got neglected in the NCAA Tournament, receiving a fifth seed but drawing Florida State in the first round. With Ryan Carroll out and Jones and Johnson unable to hit their shots consistently, the Horned Frogs were bounced early.

Jones, Johnson, Dennis Davis and James Penny are gone, but the Horned Frogs are back where Tubbs always promised they would be—in the Top 40 and a troubling opponent for anyone on their schedule.

"Your only limitation in life is your imagination," Tubbs says. "If you can imagine getting to the Final Four and winning a national championship, you can do it. If you don't have that vision, you can't ever get it done."

STARTERS NOT RETURNING

MIKE JONES (6-3, SG, 21.3 ppg, 5.7 rpg, 5.5 apg, 3.3 tpg, 2.9 spg, 36.8 minutes, .480 FG, .378 3PT, .803 FT). Jones was a scorer, and he scored in every conceivable way.

Jones may have been the best mid-range shooter in the country last year. He was a perfect compliment to Johnson, and vice versa. The two could hit the three together, but only Jones could step around his defender and pull up around the free-throw line. He could also drive inside and get to the basket.

Jones also offered leadership that will be sorely missed. A consensus first-team All-WAC player, he had more professional potential than Johnson, but, like him, was passed over in the NBA draft. His best career performance was a 44-point effort in the '97 WAC Tournament against Fresno State.

"The toughest guy to replace will be Mike Jones," Tubbs says. "He could have been our most valuable player. I don't see us bringing in a guy better than Mike Jones."

MALCOLM JOHNSON (6-4, SG, 18.7 ppg, 4.9 rpg, 2.1 apg, 2.1 tpg, 2.1 spg, 33.1 minutes, .458 FG, .370 3PT, .783 FT). He was a terrific standing shooter, but he was streaky. Johnson would hit eight three-pointers against Fresno State one game and then put up a zero against SMU. In the NCAA Tournament loss to Florida State, Johnson was 1-for-6 on three-pointers.

Johnson was a decent slasher and a good defender who had a long reach. He had 14 20-plus games last season and was a first-team All-WAC member. But he is replaceable in the Horned Frogs' offense.

DENNIS DAVIS (6-9, C, 7.6 ppg, 9.8 rpg, 1.0 apg, 1.9 tpg, 25.2 minutes, .525 FG, .585 FT). Davis was one of the toughest rebounders in the WAC. He was an excellent role player and one of the best defenders in the league. His banging in the post was the perfect compliment to Nailon.

Davis was second in the WAC in rebounding, 22nd nationally. He had 15 double-digit rebounding games last year, but was always limited offensively. There were times when his ineffectiveness drew too much attention to Nailon. However, he was the enforcer to Nailon's productivity. His strength will be missed.

OTHERS NOT RETURNING

JAMES PENNY (6-6, F, 10.5 ppg, 4.9 rpg, 1.3 apg, 1.1 tpg, 1.1 spg, 1.1 bpg, 20.2 minutes, .527 FG, .176 3PT, .735 FT). Penny was one of the best sixth men in the WAC, giving TCU an immediate boost off the bench. He gave the Horned Frogs a different look than Davis.

While Davis would be a banger inside and had limited offensive skills and mobility, Penny would come in and be a shot-blocker, mid-range shooter and a dunker.

However, he was inconsistent. Penny would have some games when he could put up 10-15 points, and others when he would struggle to get four.

PROJECTED STARTERS

PRINCE FOWLER (5-10, 170 lbs., SR, PG, #10, 8.3 ppg, 2.8 rpg, 6.2 apg, 2.2 tpg, 1.3 spg, 34.1 minutes, .392 FG, .385 3PT, .714 FT, Oklahoma & Western HS/Las Vegas, Nev.). Fowler is a very quick point guard who can get into the lane and cause havoc. Now he has to change his game.

TCU needs him to make shots because of the absence of Jones and Johnson. There were times last year when a gimmick defense was used against Fowler and he was lost. Now the pressure will be on him; he had a hard time making shots when he had to last season.

"Prince will be called on more to score," Tubbs says. "I always felt he had the potential to be the best three-point shooter on the team.

"Lee was never the focal point of our offense. Everyone will look to him, which could open up some other things for us. Other players will get shots they normally didn't get.

"I think other players will put up big numbers, and I wouldn't be surprised if it's Prince Fowler."

In the last 10 games of the season, Fowler had 61 assists but committed just 16 turnovers. During the WAC Tournament, which ended with the Horned Frogs losing to New Mexico in the semifinals, Fowler dished out 17 assists with just two turnovers.

Fowler averaged 40 points per game in high school, but immediately took a lesser role at Oklahoma and in his first two years at TCU. However, he never gave up his defense. Fowler was and is the catalyst defensively for the Horned Frogs.

TCU was constantly criticized for being more of an offensive team, but Fowler gave them credibility on the defensive end. He can get after any point guard and harass him into turning the ball over and generating a fastbreak.

LEE NAILON (6-9, 230 lbs., SR, PF, #54, 24.0 ppg, 8.9 rpg, 1.8 apg, 2.9 tpg, 1.1 spg, 1.0 bpg, 33.3 minutes, .554 FG, .737 FT, Butler County CC, Kan. & Clay HS/ South Bend, Ind.). Nailon had one of the most dominant seasons in college basketball, especially by a newcomer. Nailon showcased a soft hook, a low-post spin move and dunk, a mid-range game and aggressive rebounding skills. He finished his remarkable season with a 32-point, eight-rebound performance against Florida State in the NCAA Tournament.

His best game of the season was a five three-pointer effort against Mississippi Valley State, in which he made 23 of 30 field goal attempts. He was the consensus WAC Player of the Year and the MVP in the Pacific Division. He begins this season as a national Player of the Year candidate.

"When you see the people that left this year and the people that are returning, it's amazing that he could win the Player of the Year," Tubbs says. "Everybody who comes into D-I basketball gets better that second year. Mike Jones did and so, too, did Malcolm Johnson.

"I know Lee will be a better player. He'll be the strength of our team."

Tubbs doesn't think he had to twist Nailon's arm on returning. He says the facts were clear that he wouldn't go in the Top 10 of the NBA draft.

"We were ready to go ahead and move forward without him, but, from day one, I thought he really would return," Tubbs says. "It's not that he did poorly in Chicago, but they had him playing small forward and he was out of position. Wayman Tisdale didn't play well there, either. Those things are for the guards."

However, Nailon showed Tubbs that he could play some small forward by stepping out and hitting a few

1997-98 RESULTS

Southwest Missouri State	78-67	
Long Island University	105-95	
@Texas Tech	107-76	
Texas-Pan American	153-78	
Delaware State	138-75	
Morgan State	133-74	
North Texas	113-74	
#Mississippi Valley State	106-83	
#Baylor	99-75	
*Kansas (L)	78-94	
##Iowa State	93-54	
##Syracuse (L)	78-82	
##American-Puerto Rico	105-93	
Oklahoma State (L)	81-82	
@New Mexico (L)	77-98	
Fresno State	91-76	
San Jose State	104-65	
@San Diego State	105-61	
@Hawaii	83-76	
@Southern Methodist	100-82	
Rice	97-67	
Tulsa	102-100	ot
@Fresno State	99-91	
@San Jose State	119-84	
Hawaii	126-84	
San Diego State	91-69	
Southern Methodist	79-70	
New Mexico	95-64	
@Tulsa	57-54	
@Rice	86-73	
###Southern Methodist	71-69	
###New Mexico (L)	73-80	
%Florida State (L)	87-96	

@ away games
* Sprint Shootout, Kansas City, MO
# Texas Christian Tournament, Fort Worth, TX
Puerto Rico Holiday Classic, San Juan, PR
WAC Tournament, Thomas & Mack Center, Las Vegas, NV
% NCAA Midwest Sub-Regional, Oklahoma City, OK

1998-99 TEXAS CHRISTIAN SCHEDULE

Nov.	9	*Rhode Island
	10	*Providence
	14	Oral Roberts
	18	New Orleans
	21	@UTEP
	23	Arkansas State
Dec.	1	North Texas
	5	UTEP
	8	Texas Tech
	19	@Southwest Missouri State
	22	@Oklahoma State
	30	Gonzaga
Jan.	2	North Carolina-Asheville
	11	@Southern Methodist
	14	@Wyoming
	16	@Colorado State
	21	Air Force
	23	UNLV
	28	@Tulsa
	30	@Rice
Feb.	6	Southern Methodist
	11	Wyoming
	13	Colorado State
	20	@Air Force
	22	@UNLV
	25	Rice
	27	Tulsa
Mar.	2-6	##WAC Tournament

@ Road Games
* CoSIDA Classic, Providence, RI
Thomas & Mack Center, Las Vegas, NV

jumpers and handling the ball.

Nailon may be the top returning scorer around, but he is not without flaws. He still tends to get into foul trouble too often and committed four or more fouls in 20 games. He fouled out of only two, but picking up the fourth limited his minutes in a number of games.

He can get frustrated when he feels like he's being picked on by the officials or being double teamed. Nailon will be a No. 1 target all season and will have to deal with the attention. He has handled other negatives well, especially his one off-court problem. Nailon was suspended one game for an alleged assault.

He'll need to be a model citizen on and off the court, maintain his scoring average and lead TCU into the NCAA Tournament to earn any national Player of the Year award.

RYAN CARROLL (6-4, SG, 190 lbs., #25, 3.0 ppg, 2.1 rpg, 1.2 apg, 10.9 minutes, .519 FG, .323 3PT, .900 FT, Longview HS/Longview, Tex.). Carroll showed as a freshman that he could be the next Johnson or Jones. He is a long-armed defender and could become a specialty player. He can also hit the deep three-pointer. He stepped up during the final month of the season, getting a tip-in against Tulsa in TCU's 102-100 overtime win.

Carroll should be the team's starting "two" guard, but a foot injury could delay his spot in the rotation. Carroll had to sit out the Florida State game and then had surgery to repair a tendon tear in his ankle.

"We'd like him to be our starting 'two' or 'three' man," Tubbs says. "He hasn't done anything since last June.

"He makes the critical baskets. He's a good athlete, sees the floor well. It hurt us when we lost him going into the NCAAs. He was the guy who could come in if Malcolm and Mike weren't shooting well."

MARQUISE GAINOUS (6-9, 216 lbs., JR, PF, #33, 24.5 ppg, 9.3 rpg, Jacksonville CC, Fla. & Jones HS/ Orlando, Fla.). Gainous was the key recruit for the Horned Frogs. Tubbs had to get a forward to put next to Nailon or in place of him had he decided to enter the draft.

Tubbs hired Gainous' coach, Rob Flaska, and that package deal is one of the reasons why the Horned Frogs will get back to the NCAA Tournament. Gainous is a low-post scorer who will draw plenty of attention playing next to Nailon. New Mexico has Kenny Thomas and Damion Walker, and the tandem of Nailon and Gainous may only be the second-best in the league, but it's in the top five in the West.

"Gainous is a tremendous offensive player. We lose Dennis Davis' rebounding, (but) Gainous is a better player than Davis and Penny," Tubbs says. "If Lee hadn't come back, we would have still had a player who could get us 20-something a game.

"We had a drop-off offensively at that other forward spot last year, but that won't happen this year."

VLADIMIR JAKSIC (6-8, 233 lbs., JR, SF, #20, 12.7 ppg, 4.1 rpg, Blinn JC, Tex./Zagreb, Croatia). Jaksic was an All-Conference player at Blinn JC and is a typical European forward. He can shoot from the perimeter, making 42 percent of his shots, 39 percent on three-pointers and hitting 73 percent of his free throws.

Tubbs could play Jaksic at small forward next to Nailon and Gainous. It would give the Horned Frogs two bruising forwards inside and a skilled shooting forward alongside them. Tubbs wants scorers at all five positions, and Jaksic shouldn't let him down.

"Vladimir is an extremely good ballhandler and a good shooter at 6-8," Tubbs says. "Where does he fit in? He could play the 'two' or the 'three.'"

KEY RESERVES

SCOTT GRADNEY (6-9, 195 lbs., SR, F, #32, 4.6 ppg, 2.0 rpg, 10.1 minutes, .535 FG, .759 FT, McLennan JC, Tex. & Ballard HS/Louisville, Ky.). Gradney is thin and similar to Penny. He is a high-post forward who can be a good shooter, but he wasn't given the chance last year. He'll have to be more assertive this season if he wants to get on the court.

Tubbs is expecting his newcomers to push Gradney. It's up to him to respond and create his own time by rebounding, knocking down the mid-range jumper and finishing on the fastbreak.

"He's a good scorer, maybe even a better scorer than James Penny," Tubbs says.

His best outing was a 14-point game against Hawaii, in which he hit all six field goal attempts. It was this type of role play by Gradney and the aforementioned effort by Carroll that pushed TCU to an undefeated WAC record.

MICHAEL CAUSEY (6-3, 192 lbs., FR, G, #14, 19.0 ppg, New Hampton Prep, N.H. & Albany HS/Albany, Ga.). Tubbs believes Causey could step in and start at shooting guard if Carroll isn't healthy. Regardless, he will play.

Causey is a scorer who can get points inside and out. He scored more than 2,200 points in high school and was rated as one of the top guards in the nation. He transferred to New Hampton Prep for his senior year after averaging 32 points per game at Albany HS.

"He's a tremendous prospect who can really shoot it," Tubbs says.

SHANNON LONG (6-7, 190 lbs., JR, F, #5, 16.2 ppg, 10.6 rpg, Connors State College, Okla. & Jackson HS/ Jackson, Miss.). Long originally signed with Mississippi State out of high school, but was not get eligible. He spent the past two years at Connors State and was a first-team All-Conference player.

He is a versatile forward who can hit three-pointers and slash to the basket. Long would be wise to duplicate Penny's accomplishments and become instant offense off the bench. He'll get his chances to rotate in with Jaksic at small forward. He could also be a better defender than Jaksic, which would get him more time.

JON DAY (6-10, 233 lbs., JR, C, #31, 6.1 ppg, 5.5 rpg in 1996-97, Lon Morris College, Tex. & McCullough HS/ Houston, Tex.). Day sat out last season, redshirting after arriving from Lon Morris College. His most important role was to bang with Davis and Nailon in practice. Now, he'll have to step in and be a useful reserve for Nailon.

Day doesn't fit into the Horned Frogs' running style, but neither did Davis. Day can rebound and finish, and that's all he'll have to do when he's in the game.

DERALE WILSON (6-5, 195 lbs., JR, G, #22, 10.0 ppg, 5.0 rpg, Seminole JC, Okla. & Carl Albert HS/ Midwest City, Okla.). Wilson was a first-team Oklahoma JC performer, but is more of a role player than a scorer. He could add some defensive pressure and the occasional finish on the fast break.

Tubbs needs guys who can play his up-tempo style, and Wilson can fit in perfectly.

OTHER RETURNEES

THOMAS MCTYER (5-10, 156 lbs., SO, G, #3, 0.8 ppg, 0.6 rpg, 4.3 minutes, .182 FG, .250 3PT, .625 FT, Durango HS/Las Vegas, Nev.). McTyer is similar to his cousin, Prince Fowler, but younger. McTyer will probably get similar time again this season, playing only a few minutes to give Fowler a breather.

His most important role on the team may be pushing Fowler in practice, giving him the type of competition he needs before games. However, McTyer has to improve on his shooting before Fowler leaves.

OTHER NEWCOMERS

REBEL PAULK (6-10, 216 lbs., FR, C, #44, 19.4 ppg, 9.7 rpg, Blanchard HS/Blanchard, Okla.). Paulk is a shot-blocking big man who can score in the low post. His role on this team will be limited by the presence of Nailon and Gainous. However, he could move ahead of Day in the rotation if his defense improves.

Paulk was Oklahoma's small school player of the year, but he'll have to play at a big-time level to earn minutes as a freshman.

LEE MOON, JR. (6-1, 177 lbs., FR, G, #12, New Hampton Prep, N.H.). Moon redshirted last year and probably won't get much time this season. He is the son of Wyoming athletic director Lee Moon, Sr., and his placement on the team directly helped Steve McClain get the Wyoming head job.

McClain recruited Moon for TCU and also helped sign Causey. He went to Texas A&M as an assistant for a month before accepting the Wyoming head coaching job when Larry Shyatt left for Clemson.

QUESTIONS

Perimeter shooting? Who will replace Johnson and Jones? Fowler has to pick up a lot of the offensive slack, a healthy Carroll has to produce and Causey has to shoot well on three-pointers—better than most freshmen who come into a program.

Can Fowler shift responsibilities? No longer is he a set-up man for Jones, Johnson and Nailon. Fowler has to be a scoring point man, but he can't ignore Nailon and Gainous. He has to find balance in his game and continue being a defensive pest.

Frontcourt depth? Nailon and Gainous will get in foul trouble; that's a fact. But who will replace them? Day and Paulk may not be ready to handle the load. Jaksic isn't a low-post scorer, and neither is Wilson or Long. TCU needs Nailon and Gainous on the court for 35 minutes. If they're not, the Horned Frogs are in trouble.

ANSWERS

Nailon! He is a national Player of the Year candidate and has the ability to carry the Horned Frogs to the WAC Mountain title and into the NCAA Tournament. He can score 40 or even 50 points on a given night. Few teams in the country have players who can deliver that kind of production.

Tubbs! The veteran coach is cocky, but he has proven each season that he continues to get better. TCU was an impressive defensive team despite its frenetic offense. He has plugged players into the right spots and continues to make TCU basketball a happening.

Attitude! The Horned Frogs believe they can't lose. They're as confident as any team in the nation.

adidas Blue Ribbon Analysis

BACKCOURT	B	BENCH/DEPTH	B
FRONTCOURT	A	INTANGIBLES	B+

Texas Christian isn't thought of in the same light as most of the Top 40 teams, but that's only because the Horned Frogs were a disappointment in the NCAA Tournament. However, they've got a dominant post player, one of the best point guards and an impact newcomer. They're entertaining and they win.

"We brought in guys who can shoot the ball, so we're not concerned with people dropping off and helping on Lee," Tubbs says. "We've got guys who can stick the shots. With Nailon and Gainous, there aren't too many teams with better players than those two."

Add Fowler, and that's the reason TCU is in the front portion of *Blue Ribbon*. Expect the Horned Frogs to push UNLV for the Mountain Division title, make the NCAA Tournament and perhaps win a game this time.

(A.K.)

31
GEORGE WASHINGTON

LOCATION	**Washington, DC**
CONFERENCE	**Atlantic 10 (West Division)**
LAST SEASON	**24-9 (.727)**
CONFERENCE RECORD	**11-5 (t-1st)**
STARTERS LOST/RETURNING	**1/4**
NICKNAME	**Colonials**
COLORS	**Buff & Blue**
HOMECOURT	**Charles E. Smith Center (5,000)**
COACH	**Tom Penders (Connecticut '67)**
RECORD AT SCHOOL	**first year**
CAREER RECORD	**478-319 (27 yrs.)**
ASSISTANTS	**Rob Wright (Paul Quinn '83)**
	Bonzie Colson (Rhode Island '89)
	Tommy Penders (Texas '95)
TEAM WINS (last 5 yrs.)	**18-18-21-15-24**
RPI (last 5 yrs.)	**47-78-53-86-38**
1997-98 FINISH	**Lost in NCAA first round.**

COACH AND PROGRAM

What does it tell you when the Big East starts hiring underachieving Atlantic 10 coaches?

OK, maybe that's a bit harsh.

But Rhode Island sure looked a whole lot better without Al Skinner, and the second-year Boston College coach still has an awful long way to go in Beantown.

At George Washington, where Mike Jarvis fled suddenly for St. John's, there is a suspicion the Colonials might actually be better without the guy who resurrected their program from the ashes. And there is no denying either statement. G.W. was two years removed from a one-win season when Jarvis arrived, only to become consistent winners through the mid-'90s.

So why is it that no one cried when he left? Maybe it's just that Jarvis was better as an underdog.

As a favorite, he came across as arrogant and defensive. And, though his teams remained good, they never fulfilled the lofty expectations of recent seasons. Jarvis even had the temerity to criticize Atlantic 10 media members a couple of years ago, when the consensus conference favorites staggered in behind Xavier in the weaker West Division.

It was our fault, he implied, that G.W. didn't win big that year. He neglected to mention that the preseason vote was unanimous for the Colonials to grab no worse than a division title, yet they failed to win even an NIT game.

Whatever...

You can bet Jarvis will be charming to the New York media. He is still an underdog in the Big Apple.

Meanwhile, the karma at Foggy Bottom is a whole lot better than on Capitol Hill. G.W. athletic director Jack Kvancz jumped at the chance to hire a childhood friend as his coach. It didn't hurt that the friend was Tom Penders, a free agent of sorts from Texas who has won nearly 500 games in 27 seasons.

Penders had been forced out by the Longhorns after the grades of a player were released to a radio station by an assistant coach. Penders was in the Caribbean at the time, but it didn't seem to matter. The veteran coach claims he was undercut by the Texas administration, for whom he had done nothing but win (and, most recently, survive heart bypass surgery).

Penders was unemployed less than two months when the Colonials called. He inherits an NCAA Tournament team with four returning starters, at least three of whom figure to thrive immediately in his wide-open style.

Was it only 10 years ago that Penders helped put the Atlantic 10 on the map by taking Rhode Island to the Sweet 16? Fellow A-10 member Temple was No. 1 in the nation that year, and the two teams' combined 1988 performance contributed mightily to the conference becoming a regular multiple-bid league.

"That was the furthest any Atlantic 10 teams had ever gone in the Tournament," Penders told the *A-10 Hoop Report*, "and now it's just been very consistent over the last 10 years. The last few years there's either been a team in the Elite Eight or the Final Four. You can't say that about a lot of conferences."

The return of Tom Penders should only help in maintaining that tradition.

1997-98 RESULTS

Howard	101-64	
Delaware	84-79	
American University	74-47	
#Kentucky (L)	55-70	
#Boston College	76-64	
#DePaul	60-46	
@Texas Tech (L)	57-80	
##Pennsylvania	66-62	
##Maryland	70-66	
@Old Dominion	58-56	
UNC Charlotte	93-83	
###Army	91-59	
###George Mason	82-69	
La Salle	78-68	
Duquesne	90-68	
@Massachusetts (L)	48-79	
Xavier	78-73	ot
Dayton	81-61	
@Fordham	71-65	
@Duquesne	94-83	
Virginia Tech	75-61	
@La Salle	82-65	
@St. Joseph's	67-62	
Rhode Island (L)	61-69	
@Dayton (L)	64-78	
@Xavier (L)	86-96	
Temple (L)	49-56	
@Virginia Tech	64-50	
St. Bonaventure	71-67	
####Massachusetts	88-83	
####Temple	78-64	
####Xavier (L)	63-77	
%Oklahoma State (L)	59-74	

@	away games
#	Maui Invitational, Lahaina, HI
##	Franklin National Bank Classic, Washington, DC
###	US Airways Classic, Fairfax, VA
####	Atlantic 10 Tournament, CoreStates Spectrum, Philadelphia, PA
%	NCAA South Sub-Regional, Lexington, KY

STARTERS NOT RETURNING

ALEXANDER KOUL (7-1, C, 12.0 ppg, 6.8 rpg, 2.1 tpg, 1.3 bpg, 26.1 minutes, .567 FG, .561 FT). How does one go from lottery pick to non-factor? Such is the mystery of Koul, who regressed markedly during his final two collegiate seasons.

To be fair, "Sasha" did graduate as the Colonials fifth all-time leading scorer (1,653 points). He also left as the school's all-time leader in blocked shots (187). Yet he and his class never won an NCAA Tournament game; in fact, they once failed to qualify with the best talent in the league.

That would be 1996-97, the season in which Koul stopped progressing. He went from being the only guy in the conference who could make Marcus Camby disappear to being the only seven-foot starter around who could make himself disappear.

Koul stopped running the floor. He had poor defensive positioning. He was too often in foul trouble. And he—not to mention Jarvis—whined about it constantly.

It may seem a ridiculous assertion, but the Colonials should be better this year without him. No, they don't have a center. Then again, Penders doesn't play with one. Can you imagine Koul trying to keep up with a Penders-coached team? The 1998-99 Colonials will probably score 10 more points per game than they did a year ago (73.2 ppg).

"It's addition by subtraction," suggested one Atlantic 10 scout. "And the other (returnees) will thrive in Penders' style."

Very Koul.

But we may not have seen the last of "Sasha." Koul reportedly signed a one-year, $450,000 contract in Turkey, from which he one day hopes to migrate back to the NBA.

OTHERS NOT RETURNING

ANDREI KRIVONOS (6-4, G, 3.3 ppg, 1.9 rpg, 1.2 apg, 14.9 minutes, .394 FG, .269 3PT, .787 FT). You can be sure there won't be many guys like this around under Penders. It's one thing to sign top foreign players; it's another to rely on marginal ones who can't make a jump shot.

Krivonos was a hustler, a hard worker and a willing defender. But he wasn't quick enough to play the point, and his time at shooting guard was severely hampered by his inability to manage the "shooting" part.

The second semester arrival of Mike King rendered Krivonos extinct.

"We have a reputation internationally," Penders told the *A-10 Hoop Report*, "(but) we're going to concentrate more on local talent."

There you have it.

J.J. BRADE (6-5, G, 4.0 ppg, 2.3 rpg, 1.1 apg, 14.4 minutes, .340 FG, .250 3PT, .648 FT). Brade will sit out this season to concentrate on academics, which is bad timing on his part. Brade was a runner and jumper often trapped in G.W.'s halfcourt offensive system. He could have made a nice leap forward under Penders.

Brade started only seven games last year and his time was cut in half from 28 minutes to 14. As with Krivonos, much of that was due to the second semester eligibility of King. Then there is the small matter of a wing player making just two three-pointers in two seasons.

We may not see Brade again in a George Washington uniform.

DARIN GREEN (6-5, F, 2.9 ppg, 0.9 rpg, 8.4 minutes, .396 FG, .111 3PT, 1.000 FT). Green was 18-for-18 from the free throw line as a senior. Problem is, he couldn't take all his shots from there. Elsewhere on the court, particularly with a hand in his face, Green was, well, offensive.

Penders' first priority has to be upgrading the wing positions.

RASHEED HAZZARD (6-0, G, 0.9 ppg, 0.4 rpg, 5.0 minutes, .188 FG, .231 3PT, .350 FT). A non-factor who would have been much better served at a lower-level program. Sadly, no one will remember the contributions of Walk Hazzard's son.

On the court, there simply weren't any, even in 27 appearances.

PROJECTED STARTERS

SHAWNTA ROGERS (5-4, 155 lbs., SR, PG, #54, 14.7 ppg, 4.4 rpg, 4.8 apg, 2.7 tpg, 2.4 spg, 34.1 minutes, .419 FG, .377 3PT, .774 FT, Lake Clifton HS/Baltimore, Md.). Rogers was no longer a gimmick in 1997-98, but a legitimate All-Conference player. He was *so* much better as a junior than a sophomore, it restored everyone's faith in the promise he showed as a second-semester freshman.

As a soph, Rogers was a poor shooter (.340 FG) and a turnover machine. Last season, he significantly boosted his shooting numbers, committed three fewer turnovers in four more appearances and upped his assists total to a career-high 159.

That, ladies and gentleman, is a Division I point guard—regardless of height.

"I think he's the best point guard in the country," gushed his new coach, Tom Penders.

While that may be stretching things a bit, Rogers should be a first-team All-Atlantic 10 performer as a senior. He should also benefit considerably from Penders' high-octane approach.

Rogers can push the ball, make decent decisions on the break and pull up for his own jumpers. He is also an extraordinary rebounder for his height (4.8 career rpg), meaning he can often be his own outlet passer.

Rogers is also learning how and when to take over, especially in big games. He punished Massachusetts for a career-high 28 points in the Atlantic 10 Tournament, and his career-highs in other categories (14 rebounds vs. Dayton; 13 assists vs. Duquesne; eight steals, twice) suggest a player who can be a dominant force from the perimeter. Rogers has also averaged 17.0 ppg in three postseason games.

He was the first marquee player to exploit a loophole in the NCAA eligibility rules, not enrolling at G.W. as a first-semester freshman. Instead he used that term to get his standardized test scores in order, missing only eight games in the process. Second-semester freshman eligibility is now commonplace.

"I like my point guards to be able to score as well as run the ballclub, and I think (Shawnta) can do both," Penders told the *A-10 Hoop Report*. "I think you'll see a significant increase in his numbers, both scoring and assists, because of the tempo of the game."

If so, Rogers will more than live up to his nickname—"Nut."

YEGOR MESCHERIAKOV (6-8, 235 lbs., SR, SF, #55, 12.7 ppg, 4.8 rpg, 2.3 apg, 2.3 tpg, 28.1 minutes, .418 FG, .358 3PT, .752 FT, Republic College of Olympic Reserve/Miksk, Belarus). Mescheriakov dropped from

1998-99 GEORGE WASHINGTON SCHEDULE

Nov.	13	#George Mason
	17	@Illinois
	29	@UNC Charlotte
Dec.	2	@American University
	6-7	##BB&T Classic
	12	Old Dominion
	23	*Siena
	26	Bradley
	30	Ohio
Jan.	2	@Duquesne
	9	La Salle
	14	Dayton
	17	@Xavier
	21	@St. Bonaventure
	23	@Rhode Island
	28	Duquesne
	31	Fordham
Feb.	3	@La Salle
	6	@Virginia Tech
	12	St. Joseph's
	14	@Dayton
	17	Massachusetts
	20	@Temple
	24	Virginia Tech
	27	Xavier
Mar.	3-6	###Atlantic 10 Tournament

@	Road Games
*	Pepsi Arena, Albany, NY
#	Red Auerbach Colonial Classic, Washington, DC
##	Washington, DC (vs. DePaul, first round; also Maryland and Stanford)
###	First Union Spectrum, Philadelphia, PA

second-team All-Atlantic 10 to third team as a junior, but there was no real change in his skill level. It was simply a matter of other players—namely Rogers and rookie guard Mike King—making more shots around him.

Mescheriakov's scoring average dipped from 16.6 ppg to 12.7 ppg, but that will not be an issue under Penders. With fewer defensive responsibilities—and this Belarusian was never a defender, anyway—Merscheriakov could average close to 20 points per game as a senior.

The smooth forward has already caught the eye of pro scouts, who like his range, soft touch and ability to put the ball on the floor. Mescheriakov is adept in traffic and can also get to the glass and finish.

He is capable of monster performances, with career-highs of 31 points (vs. La Salle) and 13 rebounds (twice). It will surprise no one if Mescheriakov hears his name called next June at the NBA draft. Last January, he was named one of the seven best foreign-born college players by *Sports Illustrated.*

"He's a player," said Penders. "I hate to even put a position on him, because he doesn't handle like a guy his size should. He can score inside and out and he's an extremely physical player."

MIKE KING (6-5, 190 lbs., SO, SG, #5, 13.2 ppg, 3.8 rpg, 1.4 apg, 1.8 tpg, 26.5 minutes, .480 FG, .321 3PT, .694 FT, Lake Clifton HS/Baltimore, Md.). King, a one-time prep teammate of Shawnta Rogers, took advantage of the so-called "Rogers Rule" to become eligible last Dec. 29. He became an immediate double-figure performer, giving the Colonials a shooting guard threat they had not replaced since the days of Kwame Evans.

King was hindered by a bum ankle in early February, missing two starts, but recovered to give every indication that would be one of the best in the league at his position. King scores more in traffic than as a standstill shooter, which suggests that he, too, will benefit from the coaching change. He has the body and the athleticism to improve dramatically with a full season of work.

"If there are better backcourts around," said Penders, "I want to see them." King and Rogers should indeed be quite a pair this winter.

"Those are two all-league guys," said a rival A-10 coach. "Throw in Mescheriakov, who I really like, and Tom gets three all-league players right away. He's going to win big at G.W."

PAT NGONGBA (6-8, 224 lbs., SO, PF, #35, 4.3 ppg, 4.4 rpg, 1.4 tpg, 18.3 minutes, .360 FG, .200 3PT, .560 FT, Calvert Hall, Md./Bangui, Central African Republic). There was a debate throughout much of the season among G.W. loyalists. Who should be the power forward, Ngongba or Antxon Iturbe?

Ngongba got more of the hype and most of the starts; Iturbe got more of the minutes. Iturbe was more advanced and more consistent on a team that really needed his dirty work.

So why is Ngongba listed as a starter and Iturbe noted below as a key reserve? Call it the Penders factor. Ngongba is the more athletic of the pair, and his ability to run the floor suggests he will be of great value to the new look Colonials.

Moreover, Ngongba is the more obvious "center" candidate should Penders follow his history and play without a true "five" man.

"We plan to run and press an awful lot," Penders said, to the surprise of no one. "Speed and athleticism are going to be real important."

That huffing and puffing you hear are wind sprints from the returning George Washington frontcourts players. For Ngongba and Itrube, that means "suicides" until the next election.

FRANCISCO DE MIRANDA (6-9, 220 lbs., JR, C, #14, 5.1 ppg, 3.7 rpg, 1.1 tpg, 12.4 minutes, .555 FG, .500 FT, Mencia Lyceum/Breda, The Netherlands). Ngongba and Iturbe are the two best power players in the program. However, it is widely assumed that Penders will rarely use them together. The new coach can probably get by with one slower guy on the floor, but not two.

Hence the opportunity for de Miranda, the Colonials' most improved player in 1997-98. If the sweet-shooting junior can take a similar step forward this season, he could almost double his minutes under the new coach.

de Miranda can run, extend his long arms on defense and make the open jumper. All of which are necessary qualities in an up-tempo attack.

"Ngongba and Francisco de Miranda can both play the center position in my system," Penders told the *A-10 Hoop Report*, "but I have been known to switch lineups and give it a small look."

KEY RESERVES

ANTXON ITURBE (6-8, 252 lbs., SO, PF, #15, 6.4 ppg, 5.5 rpg, 1.1 apg, 1.3 tpg, 23.5 minutes, .646 FG, .433 FT, St. John's Prospect Hall, Md./Vitoria Basque, Spain). Iturbe, if not a starter, will again remain the Colonials' most important reserve. His freshman contributions far exceeded expectations.

The younger brother of former Clemson player Iker Iturbe, Anxton got near-starters' minutes without ever starting a game. He did so by using his big body with abandon, particularly as a defensive enforcer and rebounder. The combination of he and Ngongba also allowed Mescheriakov to play primarily at the small forward position.

Iturbe will score occasionally. He managed 14 points against UNC Charlotte and a double-double (10 points, 10 rebounds) against Kentucky at the Maui Classic.

"He doesn't look like a sophomore," said Penders. "He looks like a 34-year-old NBA veteran. He's one of those guys who, when you talk about your team, may not be mentioned in the first sentence, but he's going to be in your lineup. He's probably going to be the all-purpose guy.

"I've got to get a nickname for him. I think it's going to be 'X-man.' He's very solid. He's the type of guy everybody needs."

We suspect Penders is going to need Iturbe even more than he thinks.

SECO CAMARA (6-5, 202 lbs., SR, F, #44, 4.0 ppg, 1.6 rpg, 11.4 minutes, .323 FG, .274 3PT, .706 FT, Thomas Sumpter Academy, S.C./Lisbon, Portugal). It may be just a hunch, but we think Camara is going to get major minutes as a senior. Like so many recent G.W. wing players, Camara can't shoot a lick. But he can run and jump and finish.

Sound like a Penders type of player?

"He's improved his range," Penders said. "I think we've got some pretty good guards."

On paper, Camara is Mike King's backup. In reality, when the Colonials go "small," he may be the first extra wing man off the bench.

ROEY EYAL (6-2, 160 lbs., SO, G, #12, 1.2 ppg, 0.8 rpg, 1.0 apg, 7.1 minutes, .393 FG, .389 3PT, .600 FT, Boyer HS/Jerusalem, Israel). Penders says Eyal will be Shawnta Rogers' backup, and that may be so. But the fact of the matter is that the Israeli import demonstrated very few Division I skills.

Eyal is not particularly quick or strong, he is not a shooter and even his fine passing skills are muted by an inability to keep up with his teammates. Working is his favor is that Rogers will surely not play 40 minutes, especially at Penders' tempo.

But we doubt the new coach will identify Eyal as his point guard of the future.

OTHER RETURNEES

SAM ANYAN (6-6, 197 lbs., JR, F, #24, 0.6 ppg, 0.4 rpg, 10 appearances, Calvert Hall HS/Baltimore, Md.). Anyan is a walkon who has appeared in 21 games over two seasons. He has now scored 12 points in his college career.

Look for more of the same in 1998-99.

MARK LUND (6-0, 165 lbs., JR, G, #11, 0.1 ppg, 0.3 rpg, seven appearances, Klawock HS/Klawock, Ak.). Team managers everywhere, take heart. Lund advanced from the water bottles as a freshman to walkon status last season. He appeared in seven games and managed a free throw vs. La Salle.

Hey, it may not seem like much, but Division I basketball is a whole lot more fun from an Atlantic 10 bench than it is from Klawock, Alaska.

DANIEL SOARES (6-3, 195 lbs., JR, G, #25, 0.3 ppg, 0.5 rpg, six appearances, Newport Prep, Md./Rio de Janiero, Brazil). The last of three G.W. walkons, Soares at least has good bloodlines. His father, Gabriel, played for the Brazilian national team.

OTHER NEWCOMERS

DORIEN BROWN (6-5, 222 lbs., FR, G, #13, 16.0 ppg, 5.0 rpg, 2.0 apg, St. Thomas More Academy, Conn./Voorhees, NJ). Penders wasted little time in signing his first George Washington player. Ironically, he had been recruiting Brown for Texas before both parties realized G.W. was possibly an even better match.

"I wanted him badly," Penders told the *A-10 Hoop Report*, "and, fortunately, he hadn't signed. That was a big addition for us. He scores, he's strong, he's very physical."

Brown will play when the Colonials go small. It may not take him long to surpass Seco Camara in the rotation.

ANDRY SOLA (6-7, 205 lbs., FR, G/F, #21, 24.o ppg, 11.0 rpg, St. Thomas Aquinas HS/Oakville, Ontario). Sola was called "the best shooter in Canada." What that means in anybody's guess.

If Sola really can shoot, he will play. The Colonials' outside shooting remains a major weakness, though it will be hidden somewhat by Penders' fastbreak intentions.

St. Thomas Aquinas once won 37 straight games with Sola in the lineup. He has been invited to play for the Canadian national team.

ALBERT ROMA (7-0, 225 lbs., C, #3, 11.0 ppg, 7.0 rpg, 2.5 bpg, Winchendon School, Mass./Balenya, Spain). Roma is a fine student and emerging post prospect. His Winchendon teams were a combined 51-12 in two seasons, including 26-7 last year. He shot 57 percent from the field and 83 percent from the line.

Not surprisingly, Roma needs more weight and strength. It is hard to envision him making a major contribution as a freshman. However, he will be groomed for the limited center duty required in the Penders system.

Said the new coach: "He's a very promising rookie."

QUESTIONS

Transition? Some players were glad to see Jarvis go, others were not. We assume most will like the idea once they learn of the green light to fire at will.

Outside shooting? It remains an Achilles' heal for the Colonials and the primary reason they have stumbled in big games the past two seasons. In the days of the three-pointer, it never hurts to make a few. Penders may have to settle for more wide-open two-pointers.

Defense? Jarvis' teams were generally overrated defensively; Penders' group may not even try that hard. There will be nights (Xavier and Rhode Island come to mind) when the Colonials are simply outscored.

ANSWERS

Talent! George Washington has all-league candidates at three positions. Rogers, Mescheriakov and King could start for virtually any team in the Atlantic 10—and beyond.

Fun! The Colonials will be fun to watch. And the sideline arrogance is gone.

Tom Penders! He has won wherever, whenever. And the veteran coach has rarely inherited this kind of returning talent.

adidas Blue Ribbon Analysis

BACKCOURT .... **A** **BENCH/DEPTH** .... **B**
FRONTCOURT .... **B** **INTANGIBLES** .... **B+**

Most look at the collective departure of center Alexander Koul and coach Mike Jarvis and assume the Colonials are about to back-slide. We think the opposite.

Sometimes it is simply time for a change. Give Jarvis credit for recognizing that, and give the Colonials credit for making a prompt hire which will assure that their winning ways continue.

Penders, plain and simple, is a winner. Inheriting Shawta Rogers, Yegor Mescheriakov and Mike King is a bonus. We suspect the new coach will also do a better job of disguising the weaknesses so apparent in G.W.'s prior halfcourt orientation.

But this isn't Texas. Guarding the other team, not just pressing, will be an issue at times. More often that not, though, this George Washington team will have more weapons than the opponent.

All of which spells a return to the NCAA Tournament, a setting in which Tom Penders has always been quite comfortable.

(J.L.)

32

MIAMI (Oh.)

LOCATION .... Oxford, OH
CONFERENCE .... Mid-American (MAC)
LAST SEASON .... 17-12 (.586)
CONFERENCE RECORD .... 9-9 (t-2nd, East)
STARTERS LOST/RETURNING 0/5
NICKNAME .... RedHawks
COLOR .... Red & White
HOMECOURT .... Millett Hall (9,200)
COACH .... Charlie Coles (Miami '65)
RECORD AT SCHOOL .... 38-21 (2 yrs.)
CAREER RECORD .... 130-105 (8 yrs.)
ASSISTANTS .... James Whitford (Wisconsin '94)
Jermaine Henderson (Miami '97)
Don Moormeier (Cincinnati '59)
TEAM WINS (last 5 yrs.) 19-23-21-21-17
RPI (last 5 yrs.) 277-49-76-71-116
1997-98 FINISH .... Lost in conference final.

COACH AND PROGRAM

Charlie Coles expects this to be the best season of his life. And why not? He almost wasn't around to enjoy it.

On Feb. 28, while coaching Miami (Oh.) in a Mid-American Conference Tournament quarterfinal game at Western Michigan, Coles suffered cardiac arrest. The prompt attention of doctors in the crowd and emergency personnel at the game saved his life.

After a television timeout with 11:23 remaining in the first half of a game tied at 14-14, Coles fell flat on his face. Physicians worked on him for 20 minutes before he was taken to a local hospital. The game was delayed nearly two hours.

Coles awoke at Bronson Methodist Hospital in Kalamazoo, Mich., and couldn't talk because of a tube in his mouth. Doctors told him what had happened and gave him a notepad to respond.

He wrote, "Did we win the game?"

Yes, Charlie, they did. After hearing their coach was going to be OK, the RedHawks met and decided to continue playing. Miami went on to upset favored Western Michigan, 67-63.

"This win was definitely dedicated to our leader," forward Wally Szczerbiak said afterward.

The 56-year-old coach, who had heart bypass surgery in 1986 while he was the head coach at Central Michigan, returns to the sidelines this year with the permission of his doctors.

"They're saying I'm ready to go," Coles says. "That's exciting for me. The situation was a poor way for us to get publicity, but it did happen, so I'm trying to put a positive spin on it. It still seems like it only happened yesterday.

"This will be the best season of my life if I can coach, which they tell me I can, so this will be quite a year for me. It's like starting all over again."

The team rallied around their coach and defeated Kent in the MAC Tournament semifinals, before Miami's season ended with a loss to Eastern Michigan in the league finals.

With nearly 100 percent of its scoring and rebounding returning from a 17-12 squad, the RedHawks are picked to win the MAC East title and, possibly, the conference tournament, as well. At least that's what Coles says the other coaches may be thinking.

"The last four or five years, the team that was supposed to do well in the MAC didn't win it," he says. "That's one reason why I wouldn't want to be the favorite. The expectations for us are high, however, and I welcome that. But I'm also telling the team that could be a trap if we believe it.

"The good news is that we have everyone back; the bad news is that we have everyone back. That can be both good and bad. We can turn it into a good situation or, if we don't work hard, it can turn into a bad situation."

It can't possibly be too bad with players such as Szczerbiak and guard Damon Frierson along for the ride.

STARTERS NOT RETURNING

None.

OTHERS NOT RETURNING

JOHN LACKAFF (5-11, G, 1.9 ppg, 8.7 minutes, .308 FG, .275 3PT, .571 FT). Lackaff is a Miami baseball player who joined the basketball squad in a time of need. During the season, injuries and assorted academic and personal problems reduced the RedHawks to only six scholarship players and three walkons.

MARCUS SMITH (6-1, G, 0.7 ppg, nine appearances). Smith is a junior halfback on Miami's football team. He joined the basketball team late and provided backup help.

SHANE ALEXANDER (6-2, G, 0.8 ppg, eight appearances). Alexander suffered a fractured ankle in January and was lost for the season. He did not return to school this year.

PROJECTED STARTERS

DAMON FRIERSON (6-4, 195 lbs., SR, SG, #30, 18.8 ppg, 4.6 rpg, 4.1 apg, 3.4 tpg, 1.5 spg, 38.3 minutes, .398 FG, .339 3PT, .769 FT, Ben Davis HS/Indianapolis, Ind.). Normally a shooting guard, Frierson was forced to play the point last year because of injuries. Despite the switch, he received second-team All-MAC honors. He is regarded as one of the league's better defenders.

Frierson is a durable performer who led the conference in minutes played (1,100) ; he reached 40 minutes or more in 13 games. He is the first basketball-playing member of Miami's "Iron M Strength Club," with a total of 965 lbs. in the bench press (275), hang clean (275) and squat (415). His 33-inch vertical leap is the best on the team.

Frierson was sixth in the league in scoring, fifth in assists, 10th in free throw accuracy and had the ninth-best assist-to-turnover ratio (1.19). He has scored in double figures 65 times in 87 career games and ranks 14th in school history with 1,228 career points. He needs only 50 points to make the top 10.

Frierson went to Italy in June as a member of the NIT college all-star team. His nickname is "Smooth."

WALLY SZCZERBIAK (6-8, 241 lbs., SR, PF, #32, 24.4 ppg, 7.6 rpg, 2.5 apg, 3.4 tpg, 1.1 bpg, 38.2 minutes, .529 FG, .492 3PT, .806 FT, Cold Spring Harbor HS/Cold Spring Harbor, N.Y.). A reasonably well-informed college basketball editor approached St. Joseph's coach Phil Martelli, an assistant this past summer for the U.S. Goodwill Games team, and asked, "Who was the best player at the tryouts?"

"Wally," Martelli answered immediately. "Wally with the funny name, the kid from the 'other' Miami."

Not Elton Brand? Not Khalid-El Amin? Not a handful of other, more high-profile guys?

"Oh, they're all real good," said Martelli. "But Wally might be the best player in the country."

So, welcome to college basketball's version of "Wally World."

Szczerbiak was a first-team All-MAC selection last season. He was definitely a league Player of the Year candidate until breaking a bone in his shooting (right) hand in January, an injury which forced him to miss eight starts.

He played in only 21 of Miami's 29 games (72 percent), which failed to meet the required 75 percent for inclusion in conference and NCAA statistics. Szczerbiak scored 20 or more points 16 times, with seven double-doubles, four 30-point games and a 41-point explosion in a double-overtime victory at Dayton.

Szczerbiak is a viable candidate for All-America honors and NBA draft selection.

"I think he is a carbon copy of Tom Gugliotta from the Minnesota Timberwolves," Northern Illinois coach Brian Hammel says.

This summer, Szczerbiak earned a berth on the U.S. roster for the Goodwill Games and led the Americans to the gold medal by averaging a team-best 17.2 ppg in the five-game tournament. He scored 15 in the gold medal game against Australia and had 20 the night before against Lithuania.

Szczerbiak is a power forward with a shooting guard's game. He has a 30.5-inch vertical leap and bench presses 300-plus pounds.

"He's just one hell of a player," says Minnesota coach Clem Haskins, who had Szczerbiak on the Goodwill Games squad. "He can shoot it outside, take it to the hole. He's a great finisher, a guy who will not only go over you, but through you. There's no nonsense to his game."

Marty Blake, the NBA's director of scouting, says Szczerbiak might be the best shooter in college basketball. He is a first-team *Blue Ribbon* All-America.

Even if you have to buy a satellite dish, find a way to catch Szczerbiak's act this season.

ANTHONY TAYLOR (6-1, 182 lbs., JR, SG, #21, 12.4 ppg, 3.5 rpg, 2.9 apg, 3.1 tpg, 1.2 spg, 36.3 minutes, .440 FG, .375 3PT, .722 FT, Hargrave Military Academy, Va. & North Cambridge Catholic HS/Medford, Mass.). Taylor and Frierson were the only players who started all 29 games last year. He was third on the team in scoring, behind Szczerbiak and Frierson, and had 17 double-figure performances.

His season highlights included 27 points and eight assists in a win over La Salle, and a 22-point, eight-rebound effort in a victory over IUPUI. He also fired in 27 points in a league win over Ohio.

"Anthony had some big games for us, but wasn't as consistent as we'd like him to be," coach Charlie Coles says.

JOHN ESTICK (6-6, 250 lbs., SR, PF, #31, 8.1 ppg, 7.9 rpg, 30.3 minutes, .563 FG, .541 FT, Trinidad State JC, Colo., Iona & Memorial HS/Tulsa, Okla.). You need a road map to follow the career of Estick. He started high school in Brewster, N.Y., and made All-State as a junior. As a senior at Tulsa (Okla.) Memorial HS, he made another All-State team.

His next stop was Iona College, where he averaged 8.0 ppg and 7.8 rpg as a freshman. Estick then enrolled at Trinidad State (Colo.) JC in Colorado, where he was the leading scorer (22.0 ppg) and rebounder (11.0 rpg).

Estick finally arrived at Miami last year and became the RedHawks' bruiser on the inside. He finished fourth in the league in rebounding (7.9 rpg), including 19 in a win over Western Michigan.

In three MAC Tournament games, Estick averaged 11.7 ppg and 10 rpg.

ROB MESTAS (5-10, 185 lbs., JR, PG, #11, 3.3 ppg, 1.8 rpg, four appearances, .333 FG, .250 3PT, .500 FT, Roosevelt HS/Minneapolis, Minn.). Mestas yielded to the pain in his twice-surgically repaired right knee and was finished after four early-season games. He was granted a medical redshirt and has two seasons of eligibility remaining.

He started all 30 games in 1996-97 (4.9 ppg, 138 assists) and ranked third in the MAC in assist-to-turnover ratio (1.94). He shared the team Defensive Player of the Year award with Frierson.

If healthy, Mestas should return to his rightful place as the team's starting point guard. He won't score much, but

1997-98 RESULTS

@Tennessee (L)	74-75
@Dayton	93-86
Wisconsin-Green Bay	64-46
IUPUI	102-75
Virginia Commonweath	85-75
Xavier	80-72
#La Salle	71-66
#Syracuse (L)	53-72
@Bowling Green (L)	59-72
@Central Michigan	86-65
@Western Michigan (L)	47-63
Eastern Michigan	72-64
Toledo (L)	56-76
Akron (L)	51-64
@Kent (L)	65-66
@Marshall	71-54
Ohio	73-58
@Toledo (L)	50-63
@Eastern Michigan (L)	67-71
Ball State	73-67
Northern Illinois	74-71
Kent (L)	52-58
@Akron (L)	63-74
@Ohio	85-53
Marshall	71-60
Bowling Green	61-52
@Western Michigan	67-63
##Kent	64-59
##Eastern Michigan (L)	77-92

@ away games
# Carrier Classic, Syracuse, NY
MAC Tournament, Toledo, OH

will pass and defend. With all the shooters around him, that should be plenty.

KEY RESERVES

MIKE ENSMINGER (6-6, 249 lbs., SO, F, #53, 2.3 ppg, 4.4 rpg, 23.5 minutes, .328 FG, .765 FT, Oak Hills HS/Cincinnati, Oh.). Ensminger started 18 games and averaged 23.5 minutes. He grabbed 10 rebounds in a loss at Eastern Michigan and 12 in a win over Marshall.

If Mestas is healthy, all the RedHawks return to their normal positions. That would mean a sixth-man role for Ensminger, which would make both he and Miami more effective.

REFILOE LETHUNYA (6-8, 222 lbs., JR, F/C, #24, 5.3 ppg, 4.0 rpg, 22.8 minutes, .415 FG, .638 FT, Marshall & Potomac HS/Dumfries, Va.). Lethunya is an interesting story. He was born in London, but grew up in Maseru in the Kingdom of Lesotho in southern Africa before moving to Virginia at age 10. His late grandfather was the king of the village of Mofalani and his grandmother is now queen.

Lethunya has the skills and the size to play both the power forward and center positions.

JAY LOCKLIER (6-11, 227 lbs., SO, C, #40, 3.2 ppg, 1.8 rpg, 11.8 minutes, .550 FG, .833 FT, Christian HS/ Charlotte, N.C.). After playing in the first 13 games of last season, Locklier was declared ineligible in mid-January. His best performance was 11 points and five rebounds in a MAC win at Central Michigan.

JASON STEWART (6-5, 192 lbs., JR, G/F, #5, 16.1 ppg, .275 3PT in 1996-97, Furman University & Norcross HS/Duluth, Ga.). Stewart started 40 of 51 games in two seasons at Furman in the Southern Conference. He scored 30 points against South Carolina State as a sophomore and 20 or more points seven times as a freshman.

He was a member of the Southern Conference All-Freshman team. The Miami starters play a ton of minutes, but Stewart should be no worse than the eight man in the rotation.

JASON GRUNKEMEYER (6-5, 182 lbs., SO, G, #3, 4.4 ppg, 16.5 minutes in 1996-97, Ohio & Moeller HS, Cincinnati, Oh.). Sat out the 1997-98 season as a transfer from across the MAC at Ohio.

Grunkemeyer played in 26 of the Bobcats' 27 games as a freshman, including six as a starter. He led Ohio with a .474 three-point shooting percentage (27-for-57).

The RedHawks will always find room for a shooter.

1998-99 MIAMI (Oh.) SCHEDULE

Nov.	13	@Notre Dame
	19	Tennessee
	22	Dayton
	27	*Boston University
Dec.	2	@Xavier
	3	@Wisconsin-Green Bay
	8	Marshall
	12	@Central Michigan
	22-23	#Fresno State Coors Lite Classic
	30	Northern Illinois
Jan.	2	Western Michigan
	6	@Eastern Michigan
	8	@Buffalo
	13	Toledo
	16	Akron
	20	@Kent
	23	@Marshall
	28	Bowling Green
Feb.	3	Ohio
	6	@Western Michigan
	10	@Ball State
	13	Eastern Michigan
	17	@Toledo
	20	@Bowling Green
	24	Kent
27, Mar. 2-3		##MAC Tournament

@ Road Games
* Halifax, Nova Scotia
# Fresno, CA (vs.San Diego, first round; also Chicago State and Fresno State)
First round Feb. 27 at campus sites. Remainder of tournament March 2-3 at SeaGate Centre, Toledo, OH

OTHER RETURNEES

RICH ALLENDORF (6-10, 248 lbs., SO, F/C, #52, 0.8 ppg, 1.8 rpg, 6.1 minutes, .313 FG, .636 FT, St. Xavier HS/Cincinnati, Oh.). He played sparingly in 22 appearances. Allendorf's season highs were four points and six rebounds.

OTHER NEWCOMERS

BRIAN EDWARDS (6-7, 210 lbs., SO, F, #33, 17.0 ppg, 8.0 rpg, Mackenzie HS/Detroit, Mich.). Edwards was an academic casualty last season who is now eligible. He'll have the opportunity to work off his redshirt rust slowly, as the RedHawks are well stocked at his position.

However, Edwards should be a major contributor next season.

BEN HELMERS (6-1, 172 lbs., FR, G, #11, 19.0 ppg, Badin HS/Hamilton, Oh.). Helmers is a possible candidate for a redshirt year because of the depth in front of him. He made second team All-Ohio in Division II and was the Southwestern District Player of the Year. He was a late signee who originally gave a verbal commitment to Division II St. Michael's College in Vermont.

QUESTIONS

MAC East? Miami is one of five teams in the six-member MAC East Division with five returning starters. The balance of power has definitely shifted eastward. Last year, all three post-season participants—Eastern Michigan and Western Michigan in the NCAAs and Ball State in the NIT—were from the West Division.

Coaching staff? Charlie Coles, the 56-year-old head coach with a history of heart problems, is back on the job, but long-time assistant Ray Martin is the new head coach at Long Island. Martin assumed the head coaching duties last season when Coles suffered cardiac arrest in a MAC Tournament game.

Injuries? Staying healthy is the key. Miami was hit hard by injuries last season, including the loss of superstar forward Wally Szczerbiak for eight games with a broken wrist. The RedHawks were 3-5 in those games. The injuries and other personnel setbacks ruined what might have been a great year.

ANSWERS

Szczerbiak and Frierson! The ultra-talented seniors provide the best one-two punch in the MAC, but don't let it go to their heads. "Very seldom can you say that your best two players are your best two people," Coles says. "I can say that. We have a good group of guys, and they're the best of the best. Wally and Damon make the rest of our team better."

Mestas! The return of a healthy Mestas at point guard is huge. He is a solid playmaker and outstanding defender. More than anything else, he allows Frierson to return to his normal post at shooting guard.

adidas Blue Ribbon Analysis

BACKCOURT	B+	BENCH/DEPTH	B
FRONTCOURT	B+	INTANGIBLES	B

Miami (Oh.) has by far the top talent in the MAC. Szczerbiak is one of the best frontcourt players in the nation, and Frierson isn't far behind at his position. In short, the RedHawks are loaded.

The RedHawks went to postseason play six consecutive times before missing out last year. A rugged non-conference schedule in 1998-99—with games against Notre Dame, Tennessee, Dayton, Xavier and Boston University—was designed with the NCAA Tournament in mind.

"We're playing the good non-conference schedule to get us ready for the MAC season," Coles says. "Our goal is to win the conference tournament, because we know we will get an automatic berth to the NCAA Tournament. That is the ultimate test for our team.

"The non-conference games put us in that arena to be sharp night-in and night-out."

Other MAC schools aren't going to roll over, but Miami doesn't expect them, too. Besides, the RedHawks don't need any help.

"Wally World" is quite a show.

(R.M.)

33
MEMPHIS

LOCATION	Memphis, TN
CONFERENCE	C-USA (National Division)
LAST SEASON	17-12 (.586)
CONFERENCE RECORD	12-4 (1st)
STARTERS LOST/RETURNING	3/2
NICKNAME	Tigers
COLOR	Royal Blue & Gray
HOMECOURT	The Pyramid (20,142)
COACH	Tic Price (Virginia Tech '79)
RECORD AT SCHOOL	17-12 (1 yr.)
CAREER RECORD	80-39 (4 yrs.)
ASSISTANTS	Johnny Jones (LSU '85)
	Fred Rike (West Texas State '89)
	Chip Simms (Georgetown '92)
TEAM WINS (last 5 yrs.)	13-24-22-16-17
RPI (last 5 yrs.)	96-27-19-76-68
1997-98 FINISH	.Lost in NIT second round.

COACH AND PROGRAM

It has not taken long for Tic Price to restore Memphis to a position among the nation's elite programs, which ought to tell you how good this job can be in the proper hands.

Even with the heart of this basketball-rich city's latest harvest performing elsewhere—Tony Harris at Tennessee, Robert O'Kelley at Wake Forest and Cory Bradford at Illinois—Memphis still has assembled sufficient talent to make a serious run at a Top 20 ranking and NCAA Sweet 16 finish.

And one of the best players from last season's NIT team is gone because of academic problems. Yet the Tigers are still good enough to be co-favorites in Conference USA.

When Price took over the Tigers from former coach Larry Finch, he was fortunate former assistant Tom Schuberth had seen to it that power forward Omar Sneed signed a letter of intent. Sneed's arrival placed the program in solid position to complete the recruitment of shooting guard Marcus Moody and point guard Detric Golden.

Price finished the pitch to Moody and Golden, then put the clincher on a nice recruiting salvage job by hiring junior college coach Fred Rike as an assistant. That led to the signing of center Jermaine Ousley. The Tigers now had enough talent to get through a transitional season, allowing Price to begin the process of putting Memphis back into the recruiting game for real.

He chose to take advantage of his strength in Louisiana—as well as attempt to secure the best players in Memphis—and wound up successful in both endeavors.

"We needed bigger people," Price said. "We didn't have size. I really feel my staff did an outstanding job in assembling the talent we did. A lot of games, when we played physically, we just could not match up with most teams."

Recruiting is such an important part of what makes this one of the best jobs in coaching. So many great players grow up in town wanting to be Tigers that Memphis is one of the few city universities which can expect to compete at or near the same level as the major state schools.

If only the city's high schools were educating these players as successfully, there would be even more homegrown riches for Price to enjoy. He signed Terry Rogers, a Top 75 talent and one of the best big men Memphis has produced, but Rogers did not qualify and wound up in junior college. Price did not pursue point guard Brian Kizzie with the vigor he might have, in part because Kizzie was suspect academically. Kizzie signed at Colorado, but did not achieve freshman eligibility.

With the players he had last season—as well as lacking depth and inside strength because of a back injury that bothered Ousley all year—Price did impressive work to bring a division title to the school. He also kept the squad competitive for an NCAA bid until the final week of the season.

Price is strongest as a coach at the defensive end, but the nature of this team meant it was necessary to gamble more to get results. And the Tigers' inability to block shots occasionally made that strategy a disaster. With several capable players on the front line this time, expect the defensive field goal percentage to drop from last season's .446 toward a more impressive number.

"We may be able to force people into pressure areas that we didn't focus on as much last year," Price said. "We'll have enough people that they'll know if they don't play defense, they'll be on the bench."

Offensively, Price tends to rely on his players' individual talents more than perhaps he should. The Tigers were not the toughest team to take out of their system last season. But at least he has guys with a lot of different talents now, and, perhaps, with depth, he'll be more comfortable allowing this team to run. Price says he will, and it would be a good idea because it could ultimately test his popularity with Memphis fans.

Price has two guys who can score in the post with anyone: Sneed, who has proven he can do it at the college level, and freshman Paris London, who still must. He's got fine wing athletes in Moody and sophomore Jimmie Hunter, who may be the biggest surprise in college basketball this season.

There are plenty of points to be had from those players if they're put in the proper positions.

"I think it's certainly going to take some pressure off Omar," Price said. "People will focus on him, but he goes in this year knowing he doesn't have to carry the team like he did a year ago. He knows we'll probably have more weapons.

"There were some times during games when he'd have to pick and choose his spots in terms of when to go all out. But this year, he can blow it out, knowing he'll have somebody to come in for him."

STARTERS NOT RETURNING

DETRIC GOLDEN (5-10, PG, 14.2 ppg, 2.7 rpg, 3.0 apg, 2.7 tpg, 1.5 spg, 35.6 minutes, .430 FG, .439 3PT, .735 FT). A victim of his own academic indifference—and some say his selfishness and stubborn nature—Golden has left the Memphis program and was said to be considering a transfer (virtually impossible from an academic standpoint) or a spot in a European pro league (not extremely likely, given his limited college experience).

It's too bad, because Golden did bring great quickness and a lethal three-point shot to the Memphis offense. "I would love to have Detric, because he was experienced, he'd proven himself," Price said.

Golden led Conference USA in long-distance shooting. He scored 27 points against UAB, 23 against Georgetown, 33 against DePaul and 24 against Fresno State.

Oh, did we mention Memphis lost three of those games? In fact, Memphis was 5-6 when Golden scored 18 points or more, a connection he never really seemed to make.

Let's face it: Golden was not the point guard Memphis needed. He was, instead, a 5-10 shooting guard who did little to keep the Tigers offense flowing. When Southern Mississippi ripped apart the Memphis attack in the Conference USA Tournament quarterfinals, where was Golden? Trying to put it back together? No. He was shooting 6-for-20 from the field.

Golden passed for only 88 assists on the season, which placed him 10th in a league loaded with mediocre point guards. All he would have needed to rack up a half-dozen assists most night was toss 10 entry passes to Omar Sneed.

It remains to be seen whether Memphis will miss Golden when it needs a key three-pointer or when the opposition wants to employ a fullcourt press. When Sneed or Jermaine Ousley or someone else wants the ball, he won't be missed at all.

KELDRICK BRADFORD (6-4, G, 9.8 ppg, 4.8 rpg, 2.4 apg, 2.2 tpg, 1.9 spg, 29.8 minutes, .519 FG, .267 3PT, .720 FT). One of Price's great accomplishments in his first Memphis season was getting Bradford to play like a man most of the time, especially after he played so much of his first season trying hardest to avoid contact.

Bradford threw in a buzzer-beating shot from beyond halfcourt to defeat UNC Charlotte, which was his greatest moment as a Tiger. It may also have been a more decisive moment in the overall Conference USA race than was Kenyon Martin's putback with less than a second left as the 49ers and Cincinnati Bearcats met for the title.

Bradford also put a hammerlock on Larry Hughes in the rookie's first league game, allowing him 18 points on 5-of-15 shooting as the Tigers picked up a six-point win. He led Memphis with 27 points in his final game at The Pyramid, a drilling of Ball State in a head-to-head NIT matchup with first-round draft pick Bonzi Wells.

Bradford was a major contributor to Memphis' division championship, and his steadiness on the wing both offensively and defensively will be the element the Tigers most dearly miss.

HARRY ALLEN (6-2, SG, 6.5 ppg, 2.2 rpg, 2.3 apg, 2.2 tpg, 1.1 spg, 18.8 minutes, .450 FG, .418 3PT, .364 FT). When Allen played in the exhibition games that preceded his first Division I season, he was the most dazzling passer The Pyramid had seen since Penny Hardaway, as well as an impressive three-point shooter. It was a nice two games.

Then reality kicked in. Allen did not play with confidence against high-major competition. It became obvious he was best suited to be a mid- or low-major player. He was versatile and physically rugged, but did not believe he had the ability to compete against the best.

Allen had two decent years with the Tigers, but likely could have done more. He started 22 games at shooting guard, and played really well at season's end—averaging 14 points per game in the NIT.

But Price tended to ride Allen only when he was hot and otherwise set him aside in favor of Marcus Moody. His replacements are dramatically more talented.

OTHERS NOT RETURNING

CODY HOPSON (6-5, F, 1.4 ppg, 1.9 rpg, 9.2 minutes, .234 FG, .167 3PT, .333 FT). A spectacular athlete who had a fair three-point touch, Hopson just didn't understand how to play the game. He did not know how to make the best use of his athletic gifts nor when to play aggressively and when to step back into the system.

Memphis initially had to wait a semester for him to finish his junior college degree, and it hardly seemed worth the trouble when all was said and done. When Hopson missed the 1996-97 season with academic trouble, it seemed unlikely Price would allow him to play last year.

But he was welcomed and given a minor role, including six starts. Hopson rarely shot, but did produce 13 steals—not bad in the time he got.

MICHAEL BRITTIAN (6-9, C, 0.8 ppg, 1.2 rpg, 5.8 minutes, .250 FG). It's hard to think of any player recruited to Memphis in the past half-dozen years who did less during his time on scholarship than Brittian.

He began his career by hitting a few early high-post jumpers in the opening game of the 1996-97 season against Wisconsin, but once the Badgers began guarding him for that shot, it went downhill from there. He could not score in the post, would not pursue available rebounds and all but refused to guard his man.

His gift for making that high-post shot could have been well-utilized by Finch, who didn't want to run a scripted offense. But, then, Brittian's attitude in practice made it reasonable to wonder if setting up shots for him was worth the trouble.

Brittian barely played under Price, who found greater use for the lumbering James Harris.

1997-98 RESULTS

Northeast Louisiana	75-74	ot
@ Vanderbilt (L)	77-86	
Jackson State	73-65	
@Oklahoma	80-78	
Tennessee (L)	66-68	
Miami (L)	57-65	
Tulane	64-59	
Idaho	72-58	
@Saint Louis	68-62	
@Cincinnati (L)	54-61	
Arkansas (L)	72-75	
@North Carolina State (L)	60-71	
South Florida	74-62	
Southern Mississippi	79-67	
UAB	86-70	
@Georgetown (L)	69-73	
@South Florida	70-61	
UNC Charlotte	73-70	
@Houston	76-63	
@UAB (L)	77-88	
DePaul (L)	98-100	2ot
@Southern Mississippi (L)	62-75	
@Tulane	83-77	
Louisville	93-75	
Houston	89-76	
@Marquette	77-65	
#Southern Mississippi (L)	57-85	
%Ball State	90-67	
%%Fresno State (L)	80-83	

@ away games
# Conference USA Tournament, Shoemaker Center, Cincinnati, OH
% NIT first round, Memphis, TN

PROJECTED STARTERS

OMAR SNEED (6-6, 239 lbs., SR, PF, #31, 20.9 ppg, 9.2 rpg, 2.2 apg, 3.1 tpg, 1.7 spg, .585 FG, .238 3PT, .667 FT, San Jacinto JC, Tex./Beaumont, Tex.). Why is it that no one really appreciates what a low- post force can accomplish?

There was no great battle over the services of Sneed when he was entering his sophomore year at San Jacinto (Tex.) JC. Former assistant Tom Schuberth more or less stole him away from the schools in Texas and others that had more to promise—partly because this was an excellent assistant coach who knew how to do his job, but also because other schools did not make a big enough fuss.

The thing about an undersized post player is that, in addition to the scoring he'll provide and the stress he'll put on an opposing defenses in terms of pre-game preparation and foul trouble, they almost always have a great deal of toughness. Sneed surely does.

He led Conference USA in rebounding, finished third in scoring and was chosen first-team All-League. The Memphis people thought he ought to have won the league's player of the year award, and they didn't make a terrible case given that Sneed ranked first in scoring and rebounding in conference games. The voters got it wrong, anyway, in choosing UNCC's DeMarco Johnson. The true winner should have been Larry Hughes.

Sneed got better as the year progressed, averaging 23.8 ppg and 10.3 rpg and topping 60 percent from the field in his final 16 games. He scored 20 or more points 17 times and hit for 30 or better three times. He passes effectively out of double-teams and nearly had as many assists as the Tigers' point guard.

Like any low-post specialist, it is not impossible to take him out of the game. Guard him with a bigger man who blocks shots, and you've got a chance, but it is also possible Sneed will get your bigger man in foul trouble. Put a defender in front of him and one behind him, and he's going to have a tough time getting the ball. Those teams that fronted him often had success because of the Tiger guards' inability to put the ball over top of the defense.

All of this will be more difficult to do now that Memphis has increased its variety of weapons. If the opposing big man commits to Sneed, who guards a healthy Ousley? If you front Sneed, he could move the defender out toward the foul line and leave driving lanes for his quicker teammates.

Sneed has not been extremely adept with the ball away from the basket, but time spent in Memphis' conditioning program might have improved his quickness enough to make a difference in that regard. He did try to extend defenses with three-point shots last season, but was not accurate enough for it to be a factor.

MARCUS MOODY (6-4, 174 lbs., SO, SG, #32, 7.7 ppg, 2.0 rpg, 1.8 apg, 2.0 tpg, 1.4 spg, 23.7 minutes, .364 FG, .254 3PT, .540 FT, Overton HS/Memphis, Tenn.). Our words next to Moody's name in this book got us in trouble last year. We called Moody physically and mentally weak. We said he wasn't ready for the physical nature of Division I ball.

So then he scores 41 points against Oklahoma in his fourth college game. On the road, no less, and suddenly the paper in Memphis is picking out our words to show how Moody was doubted. We look bad, right?

No, actually. We said he was highly skilled, for one thing. And, for much of the season which followed that moment of brilliance, Moody demonstrated precisely the limitations we mentioned. He scored in double figures only six other times.

Take out his Oklahoma numbers, and he connected on just over 33 percent from the field. He shot 126 times from three-point range, even though he made only 32, which backed up the contention that he lacked the mental determination to drive the ball into traffic. Moody tended not to get his feet set beneath him when shooting and occasionally to fade away as he shot, as though he were concerned about being bumped even that far from the goal.

It's easy to stand back and shoot threes. This is what we expected of him last season, and he delivered as forecast but for a one-night aberration.

All of which is not to condemn him. Moody has a tremendous amount of talent and could still have an outstanding college career. It's not out of the question that he could become a pro, if he builds up his body and a taste for contact.

"He really worked hard this summer," Price said. "His upper body strength is much better. He gained 15 pounds and is playing with more confidence.

"He'll stick his nose in there, is getting rebounds. The weight room has really helped his confidence."

This is what you want to hear if you're a Memphis fan, because Moody's ballhandling ability is not going to do him much good if he is merely going to stand behind the line and chuck threes. He's got to get himself into the lane and create plays for himself and his teammates, proving he has the gumption to finish. He's got competition at his position now and, to keep his hold on minutes that might otherwise go to Jimmie Hunter, Moody will have to be productive.

Moody was seen in pickup games during the fall attacking the basket and finishing strong, which could make him a far more impressive player as a sophomore.

JERMAINE OUSLEY (6-9, 238 lbs., SR, C, #4, 9.0 ppg, 6.7 rpg, 1.5 apg, 3.2 tpg, 1.3 spg, 1.0 bpg, 29.7 minutes, .441 FG, .583 FT, Tyler JC, Tex./Milwaukee, Wisc.). You might as well discount all these statistics listed for Ousley. Whether they are a true measure of him as a player will not be seen until the Tigers have played several games this season.

Ousley played all of last year with nagging back pain that resulted from a bulking disk. He rarely practiced. He could not deliver nor absorb the sort of contact necessary to effectively operate in the low post. Imagine what he must have felt when he set himself in the post and felt an opponent's forearm in his back.

The injury should not be a problem this winter. Ousley had surgery in April and enjoyed a healthy summer, displaying his athleticism and creating a great deal of enthusiasm about what he might be for the Tigers in his senior year.

"Jermaine's back is much better. The surgery was successful, and he's been cleared by the doctors to go full speed," Price said. "He went into the weight room and got much stronger.

"His whole game is athleticism. With a bad back, that takes away from his athleticism, so he wasn't as effective. I think you'll see a very exciting layer. He'll have that lateral movement, and can bang inside."

Ousley's offensive skill appeared suspect after last season, but again we're left to wonder how efficient he might be if completely healthy. He is not a shooter; that's for certain. And he doesn't appear to have great post skills.

But that's why he ought to be an ideal complement for Sneed. Ousley doesn't have to be a full-time target to contribute offensively, not if he cleans up Sneed's misses and turns them into baskets.

Where Ousley unquestionably needs work is with free throw shooting. He went to the line enough to demonstrate he isn't very good at it.

KEIRON SHINE (5-10, 165 lbs., JR, PG, #11, 19.2 ppg, 3.4 rpg, 5.7 apg, Okaloosa-Walton JC, Tex. & Craigmont HS/Memphis, Tenn.). When it became apparent that Golden might not be around for another season, Price decided it would be wise to allow Shine to return home to continue his college career. Shine was rated one of the top 20 prospects at the JC level by analyst Rick Ball.

O-W was his second junior college in as many years. He began his career at Hiwassee JC in Tennessee, but left after averaging 11.1 ppg and 5.1 apg and helping Hiwassee to a 30-2 record. Shine is not a great shooter, but may be better at getting his teammates involved than was Golden. He'll likely start at the point and will make it extremely tough to press the Tigers.

"He's a great athlete, has speed, quickness (and) can push the basketball in transition more than we did last year," Price said. "He's got the ability to blow by people, to break people down."

JIMMIE HUNTER (6-4, 200 lbs., SO, SG, 31.0 ppg, Trezevant HS/Memphis, Tenn.). If the Memphis preseason roster listed Hunter, which it doesn't, it likely would not use the name by which most in the city know him. He is "Snap." He is Snap the way Penny is Penny.

Hunter was the overshadowed member of the Memphis high school class of 1997, even though there were those in town who insisted he was the best of the bunch. They failed to understand that however talented Hunter is, he did not compete at the same level as Tony Harris or Robert O'Kelley. But then, these people saw the talent that so many on the national scene did not.

Hunter can shoot, pass, dribble, run, create, defend if he wants and dunk on anyone who comes near. He may be the single most spectacular talent to enter college basketball this season, if indeed he enters college basketball this season and if he is the same player he was before disappearing into NCAA purgatory.

Hunter is on track to join the Tigers at the semester break. He did not qualify for freshman eligibility and was not academically sound enough to be admitted full-time in the fall of 1997. He had to begin as a part-time student and demonstrate the necessary progress to qualify for admission, which is why he can't play until the second term.

Presuming he is okay to play, Hunter can give Memphis the sort of creative force it lacked last season. He does understand the game at a high level, anticipating plays and teammate's actions. He shoots the ball with range and has an amazing ability to finish. The pro scouts have noticed him and like what they see.

"Just put him out there, you've got a chance," Price said. "We could use him at the point if we wanted, but he's more of a wing."

What the coaches want to see now is for Hunter to play with responsibility, with pressure. At Trezevant HS, it was basically a matter of how many points he could score. And when he played club ball with Harris, O'Kelley and Illinois' Cory Bradford, there was very little pressure on Hunter to perform.

He will be an important part of this team, whether he takes over the point guard spot or handles one of the wing positions with the responsibility to generate offense.

KEY RESERVES

SHYRONE CHATMAN (6-3, 200 lbs., SO, G, #15, 3.4 ppg, 1.0 rpg, 10.9 minutes, .365 FG, .682 FT, McKinley HS/Baton Rouge, La.). It will be quite a fight for Chatman to secure some playing time as a Tiger sophomore, but at least he gets to throw the first punch.

While Jimmie Hunter is off completing his eligibility requirements, Chatman will be in practice and in front of Price, trying to prove he is worthy of a role with this club. To do so, he will have to make dramatic improvement as an offensive player.

Price attempted to use him at point guard early last season, an experiment designed to show Golden who was in charge and to find some use for Chatman's toughness. Chatman lasted four minutes and committed four turnovers as the Tigers lost to Vanderbilt.

Chatman is a hard-working player, the sort coaches love up until they see them in a game. Then, they sometimes worry

Chatman did score 21 points in a contest against UAB, including 5-for-11 three-point shooting, and he got 10 in the win against UNC Charlotte in just 15 minutes.

He must have that sort of confidence all the time in order to expand his role. Otherwise, the best Chatman can hope is to get minutes as a defensive specialist once the Tigers have their full complement of wing players.

PARIS LONDON (6-8, 235 lbs., FR, F, #14, 21.9 ppg, 12.4 rpg, Hamilton HS/Memphis, Tenn.) Paris London's stock chart reads like the most volatile issue on Wall Street.

He was among the top five players in his class as a freshman, then a bust as a sophomore. He was back near the top after a brilliant week spent in the company of Shane Battier at camp before his junior season, and followed that with a sizzling performance in the Las Vegas Holiday prep tournament.

Then he went to the ABCD Camp as a senior and undid all the good he'd done. Then came a half-baked senior season which knocked him off the McDonald's All-America list and down to the 30s and 40s in most recruiting rankings.

It seems almost as if London has been a star too long for his own good. So many people have expected so much for such a long time that he may be crumbling under the weight of expectations. He had domestic problems last year that landed him in the headlines on pages which ordinarily discuss matters other than sports. He just doesn't seem to be having a lot of fun.

All of which could change under Price and, if it does, Memphis will be very pleased London signed a letter of intent with the Tigers. Because this is still one of the dozen most talented players in the Class of '98.

He does not shoot the ball well, which is something he needs to be convinced of, but his handle is phenomenal for a player with his size and strength. He can be the sort of scoring machine in the post that Antawn Jamison was at North Carolina.

The difference, of course, is that Jamison wanted to be that kind of player. London ruined his reputation by refusing to go near the lane throughout the summer of 1997. He stood outside and tried to prove he was a small forward instead of getting inside and proving he was a great player.

"We had some individual meetings with our players and that was one thing we touched on with Paris," Price said. "We told him, 'You've made your basketball career by being an outstanding post player. You will, at some point, be able to step out on the wing. Let's work during the year to develop your skills, but focus on your strengths right now.' I think he understands this is what he has to do."

If London listens, he could eventually start at small forward and serve as the last piece of a phenomenal front line. But if put in that position, he must emphasize rebounding, attacking the basket and making use of his ballhandling and passing skills to create offense. If he thinks being a three-man at Memphis means firing three-pointers, he will quickly earn a seat on the bench.

"I think, long-term, Paris is going to be a real special player here," Price said. "I think what's happened is because we've built depth, it'll take pressure off him in terms of having to come right in and be the man. We'll bring him along slowly and, as he progresses, his minutes will progress. I think he knows it's going to take time."

DINNO DANIELS (6-0, 175 lbs., FR, G, #3, 19.1 ppg, 5.7 rpg, 6.5 apg, West Jefferson HS/New Orleans, La.). Price stirred some controversy when he went after Dinno (pronounced Din-O) Daniels rather than hometowner Brian Kizzie, especially since both were considered qualifying risks at the time. Price was right. Daniels will play his freshman season, and Kizzie will not. And Memphis needed one of them to help run this offense.

Kind of like his brother, Greedy Daniels, who plays at UNLV, Daniels is not a pure point guard. He will guard the opposing point as well as one can at his size, but he

1998-99 MEMPHIS SCHEDULE

Nov.	13	North Carolina-Wilmington
	16	#Gonzaga
	21	Northeast Louisiana
	30	Arkansas-Pine Bluff
Dec.	2	@Tennessee
	5	Vanderbilt
	8	Jackson State
	12	Mississippi
	19	@Arkansas
	22	@Miami
	28	Southern Mississippi
Jan.	2	UAB
	7	@South Florida
	10	@UNC Charlotte
	14	Tulane
	17	@Houston
	23	South Florida
	25	Arkansas State
	30	@Southern Mississippi
Feb.	4	@Louisville
	6	Houston
	11	@UAB
	13	@DePaul
	18	Saint Louis
	21	Marquette
	24	@Tulane
	27	Cincinnati
Mar.	3-6	##Conference USA Tournament

@ Road Games
# Chase NIT (If the Tigers advance, they will play either Illinois-Chicago or Purdue on Nov. 18. Semifinals and finals are Nov. 25 and 27 at Madison Square Garden, NY)
Birmingham-Jefferson Civic Center, Birmingham, AL

needs to get stronger. Yet Dinno has exceptionally long arms and uses them well to bother opponents.

Defense will be the primary asset on which he builds his career at Memphis. Remember, Price likes a defense that pressures the ball in the backcourt and makes it difficult to start an offense.

As an offensive player, Daniels is a pretty fair shooter, although it may take a year or so before he's hitting the high 30s in three-point percentage. For now, he'll be at least a threat to score from there.

Daniels will learn in short order what is necessary to run an offense at this level. With Golden gone, Daniels will compete for the starting point job, although it is likely to go to Keiron Shine. Daniels sees the floor well, but has not yet displayed a penchant for the entry passes that will be key as long as Sneed is around.

As a prep player, Daniels was rated No. 84 by the *PrepStars Recruiters Handbook*. His team won a district championship, and he was the *New Orleans Times-Picayune* large school Player of the Year as a senior. In his first two seasons, with his brother as part of the team, Dinno helped win two state titles.

"He brings a certain amount of toughness to the position," Price said. "He'll guard, he's got good ballhandling skills. He'll bring good court savvy. Plus, he's a winner. When he's plays basketball, that's his total focus. He's a very mature player for such a young guy."

SHAMEL JONES (6-9, 220 lbs., SO, F/C, #55, 1.1 ppg, 2.2 rpg in 1996-97, Georgetown & Paul Robeson HS/Brooklyn, N.Y.). After making a very small splash in his first year at Georgetown, Jones left school because the university did not have the necessary programs to deal with his learning disability. He liked The Pyramid when the Hoyas visited in his only season and wondered about transferring there.

It turns out Memphis had the tools to deal with his academic needs. Jones has since flourished in school and should be an important contributor to the Tigers in his debut.

Jones can play any frontcourt position. He shoots well enough to play small forward, even though he was 0-for-6 on threes as a Georgetown freshman.

But his most important role will be as a backup to Ousley. He blocks shots well, with four in a game against Alabama State. And he had 10 rebounds in his most extensive stint at Georgetown, against Delaware State. Memphis will need him for his size and the muscle he can bring to the frontcourt.

"He's very aggressive, plays the game with a lot of intensity," Price said. "He's a kid who might have been our missing link a year ago."

OTHER RETURNEES

JAMES HARRIS (6-9, 242 lbs., SO C, #35, 1.7 ppg, 1.3 rpg, 8.8 minutes, .487 FG, .423 FT, Westbury Christian/Houston, Tex.). A lot of folks wondered how long it would take Price to run Harris out of the program, even though his mother is known to have strong AAU connections in the Houston area. Price instead chose to find some use for Harris, and he did a serviceable job.

Harris cut a lot of weight in order to meet Price's requirements to play. He had arrived at Memphis a year earlier in excess of 270 pounds, but his determination to get in better condition was obvious.

He has few on-court skills. He never passed for an assist in his first year. He struggles to make shots. His season-high for points was only six. But it doesn't hurt to have a big body who can exchange punishment.

It's likely his role will be diminished with the arrival of Shamel Jones and freshman Kelly Wise, but improvement could keep him in the rotation.

OTHER NEWCOMERS

KELLY WISE (6-9, 210 lbs., FR, F, #45, 19.8 ppg, 11.1 rpg, 4.3 bpg, Choctawhatchee HS/Fort Walton Beach, Fla.). With Rogers ineligible, Wise's development as a freshman becomes that much more important for the Tigers. He is athletic, runs well and blocks shots, although he did not have the senior year some had hoped.

"He's got to learn he can't wait, or he'll become the head waiter. The time for him is now. There's an urgency there. Every day, I get the feeling he's falling into that casual mode," Price said. "He's got all the tools in the world to become an excellent player."

Wise was not well-known entering the fall recruiting season because he did not play a lot of summer ball. Those who did see him wondered if he might not need more strength to be an effective player as a freshman. The lack of buzz on Wise did not hurt the Tigers in their pursuit of him.

He was honorable mention All-State, was rated No. 38 in the South by analyst Ron Briscoe and was widely perceived to be a top 150-type of prospect. Wise is likely to be the fourth or fifth big man in Memphis' inside rotation, but he'll have to make a dramatic improvement to get more than a dozen minutes per game.

DANIEL WEAVER (6-9, 220 lbs., FR, F, #41, 13.0 ppg, 8.0 rpg, Bartlett HS/Bartlett, Tenn.). Although he had scholarship offers from such mid-major schools as Missouri-Kansas City, The Citadel and Austin Peay, Weaver decided he wanted to join the Memphis program as a walkon.

He played well in summer ball and preseason pickup games and, given his size, could be more than the average walkon. Weaver is considered to be strong and played in a prep program known for coaching its talent well.

AARON MULVAGH (6-6, 205 lbs., JR, G, #20, 12.7 ppg, 5.0 rpg, .410 3PT in 1996-97, Yavapai CC, Ariz. & South Hadley HS/Springfield, Ma.). Mulvagh's signing was an odd one, especially since he was the second member of last year's fall class. The Tigers committed to him before they knew they'd have success with London, Rogers and some others.

Mulvagh basically was off the charts—meaning he didn't show up at all—when it came to the junior college recruiting analysts. Memphis liked his athletic ability and shooting touch, but he has not played in the most competitive circumstances. Even then did not produce that well.

The stats listed are for his freshman season. He missed much of his sophomore year because of a torn hamstring. It is unlikely he'll be an important player for the Tigers.

QUESTIONS

The point? Losing Golden seems like a plus, but somebody's got to prove he can do the job—whether it's Shine or Daniels or even Jimmie Hunter. Memphis needs greater direction for its offense.

Perimeter shooting? Golden takes the league's best three-point shooter out of the lineup. Moody is inconsistent from long range, but has potential. Hunter also can hit the shot. Somebody's got to. Just don't let London think he's the guy.

Experience? More of Memphis' players are unproven than just about anyone you'll find in this section of *Blue Ribbon*. But that was the case a year ago, as well, and that team won 17 games.

ANSWERS

Omar Sneed! His production was amazing as a junior and, even with more talent on the front line, is likely to improve as he gets the ball more often in scoring position than Golden would allow. Sneed is a producer and a winner.

Size and more size! Instead of limping along with an injured Ousley in the middle, the Tigers get him healthy and—with Jones, Wise and London to help—won't have to overtax him.

"Snap"! If Jimmie Hunter plays, and if he plays like Jimmie Hunter can, the college basketball world will be talking a lot about "Snap" as December turns into January.

adidas Blue Ribbon Analysis

BACKCOURT	B+	BENCH/DEPTH	B
FRONTCOURT	A	INTANGIBLES	B

"We've got a really inexperienced team," Price said. "When you look at our roster, four guys have one year each of Division I basketball. People get excited about the team, but we're still inexperienced."

That still can hurt you in today's college basketball, but it's more a matter of whether those players allow inexperience to become a factor. Because inexperience is common today—with players leaving early for the pros or becoming ineligible—progress rules.

So, yes, success may not be instantaneous for this Tigers team. But it ought to come. Price will be able to extend his defense; he'll be able to cut Shine and Hunter loose to push the ball on the break; he'll be able to guard the opposing point man with Daniels; and he'll be able to get the ball more frequently to Sneed. The guy only averaged 13.6 shots per game last season when the team had almost no other weapons. We ask you again: Do you really think this team will miss Detric Golden?

Not when it's ending the season in the NCAA Tournament, with maybe a win or two along the way.

(M.D.)

34

CALIFORNIA

LOCATION	Berkeley, CA
CONFERENCE	Pacific-10
LAST SEASON	12-15 (.444)
CONFERENCE RECORD	8-10 (t-5th)
STARTERS LOST/RETURNING	1/4
NICKNAME	Golden Bears
COLORS	Blue & Gold
HOMECOURT	New Arena (19,200)
COACH	Ben Braun (Wisconsin '75)
RECORD AT SCHOOL	35-24 (2 yrs.)
CAREER RECORD	368-259 (21 yrs.)
ASSISTANTS	Scott Beeten (Lehigh '71)
	Charles Ramsey (Eastern Michigan '91)
	Louis Reynaud (San Francisco State '82)
TEAM WINS (last 5 yrs.)	22-13-17-23-12
RPI (last 5 yrs.)	29-108-59-15-124
1997-98 FINISH	No conference tournament.

COACH AND PROGRAM

After treading water in basketball no-man's land last year, the Golden Bears are ready to plunge back into the deep end of the pool. California's one-year, NCAA-imposed postseason ban is over, and coach Ben Braun is coaching a team largely of his own choosing.

"We had a lot of things going against us last year, from injuries to probation to whatever, but we managed to overcome all those things to still finish on a strong note," Braun said. "Hopefully, that will carry over to this year."

The Bears definitely view themselves as an NCAA Tournament-caliber team this season, although no one on the current roster has enjoyed the experience. Still, Braun believes simply the chance to compete for the postseason will be a strong lure for his players.

Cal

"You'd like to at least have that carrot out there," he said. "All the players realize the intensity and rewards and excitement of the NCAA (Tournament), and everybody would love that opportunity. It was really tough having that taken away last year."

Braun directed the Bears to 23 victories and a surprise push into the NCAA Sweet 16 in his debut at Cal two years ago. But the Bears lost six seniors from that team, along with power forward/tight end Tony Gonzalez to the NFL. Then the NCAA imposed sanctions for violations committed during ex-coach Todd Bozeman's regime, and a young team entered last season with no experience and no prospect of a tangible reward.

Some fans expected the worst. Braun simply wanted his team to stabilize and continue working for improvement. For the most part, that's what he got.

The Bears were helpless offensively at the outset of the season, reduced to seven scholarship players until transfers Geno Carlisle and Thomas Kilgore became eligible in mid-December. The team came together slowly, but for most of the conference season played the Pac-10 on nearly even terms.

The Bears lost to UCLA by one and three points, to Arizona by three, to Stanford by two and at Washington by two in overtime. Altogether, Cal compiled a record of 0-8 in games decided by three points or less.

"I think we had to go through that to get where we want to be (this) year," Carlisle said. "You grow through those types of losses because nobody wants to go through them again.

"We were always confident. What people have to realize is that was our first year together."

"It was a step to get into those close games," Braun said. "A lot of teams weren't even close with some of those (other) teams. But I don't want our players to settle into losing those games. Hopefully, we draw from last year. Now we've got to get over the hump."

The 1998-99 squad, with no one who ever played a game for Bozeman, is smaller, but also quicker and deeper than a year ago. The Bears also hope to be improved from the perimeter, where their 100 three-point baskets last season were 45 fewer than any other team in the Pac-10. Cal converted a measly .305 from beyond the arc.

The depth and quickness should allow the Bears to play a more aggressive style at both ends. With limited personnel a year ago, Braun was reluctant to pressure too liberally, concerned about fouls and fatigue. Now he can shuttle players on and off the floor and keep a fresh five in the game.

"We have the option of playing guys not as long and playing a little bit more intensely," he said. "We had to kind of walk on eggshells last year, settle into some zones at times. We had to watch guys' minutes, their fouls. It was tough."

Carlisle and Kilgore, the team's two top scorers, and point guard Raymond King give the Bears three experienced backcourt players. They will be joined by Dennis Gates and, hopefully, Donte Smith, standout players last year on high-level high school teams that combined for a record of 54-6.

"You've got to have players who are accustomed to being on winning teams. That's crucial," Braun said. "Without question, they are players of the future for us. We don't want to put pressure on them this year. We just want them to contribute."

Sean Lampley, one of the Pac-10's top freshmen a year ago, and senior Mike Gill return at the forward spots, and JC arrival Carl Boyd should add depth and an athletic presence on the wing. Even without great experience at the post, Braun is confident his team can present matchup problems with its quickness and versatility.

"We've got some guys who are in-between heights, and we've got to turn those guys into a positive for us," he said. "They're good players. But are they guards or forwards? I'm not sure, but I hope the other team's not sure, either. That's what you hope to create."

STARTERS NOT RETURNING

SEAN MARKS (6-11, PF, 9.8 ppg, 7.6 rpg, 26.1 minutes, .478 FG, .182 3PT, .689 FT). The Bears' popular New Zealand-born power forward closed out his career with a largely healthy and productive senior season.

"Kiwi," as his teammates called him, played in 26 of 27 games, a stark contrast to previous seasons when injuries limited his availability and effectiveness. Marks was the Bears' top rebounder, six times reaching double figures. He scored in double figures 15 times, including a season-high 23 points against UCLA.

The club's only senior, Marks was selected 44th in the NBA draft by the New York Knicks, then traded to Toronto.

OTHERS NOT RETURNING

KENYON JONES (6-10, C, 6.0 ppg, 3.7 rpg, 16.7 minutes, .477 FG, .527 FT). After three uneven seasons, Jones announced last spring he was transferring and would play his senior season elsewhere. The Cal coaching staff hardly squawked about his decision.

Jones arrived on campus in the fall of 1995 with fellow Georgia prep star Shareef Abdur-Rahim, but never approached the impact his talented classmate had. Braun and his staff had high hopes for Jones, but were disappointed over two years with his work ethic and lack of consistent productivity.

SEAN JACKSON (6-5, G, 2.1 ppg, 1.1 rpg, 13.9 minutes, .295 FG, .259 3PT, .600 FT). Ex-coach Todd Bozeman's final recruit, Jackson announced last spring he was transferring after two seasons spent largely on the bench.

Jackson arrived at Cal with a reputation as a perimeter shooter, but he converted less than 25 percent of his three-point attempts in two seasons. He started seven games early last season as a sophomore, while Cal awaited the eligibility of Geno Carlisle and Thomas Kilgore. He played just 27 minutes in eight Pac-10 games, however, scoring a total of two points against conference foes.

PROJECTED STARTERS

GENO CARLISLE (6-3, 200 lbs., SR, SG, #25, 17.9 ppg, 3.0 rpg, 2.8 apg, 1.0 spg, 34.7 minutes, .433 FG, .342 3PT, .752 FT, Ottawa Hills HS/Grand Rapids, Mich.). Carlisle enters his senior season as the Pac-10's No. 2 returning scorer, behind only Washington center Todd MacCulloch. Creative and deceptively quick, Carlisle scored in double figures in 19 of the 22 games he played, and accounted for 10 of the team's 14 20-point performances.

Braun was encouraged with Carlisle's gradual improvement on the defensive end, but wants the former Northwestern star to emerge as a team leader this season. Carlisle, who came to Cal to find a winning atmosphere, should be ready to accept an expanded role.

"Geno's a fifth-year senior and he needs to provide more leadership and be a factor for us at both ends of the floor," Braun said. "I think he's capable of being a lot better all-around. He's already proven he can play at the offensive end."

Carlisle scored a season-high 31 points at UCLA, and topped 25 on five other occasions. His three-pointer with nine seconds left forced overtime at Washington, and he became the first Cal player to hit five three-pointers in back-to-back games.

Curiously, Carlisle was dramatically more effective on the road than at home in the New Arena in Oakland. He averaged 21.9 ppg on .493 accuracy in foreign venues, compared to just 14.6 ppg on .370 shooting at home.

An all-state high school star in Michigan, Carlisle averaged 11.7 and 19.7 ppg in two seasons at Northwestern. He enters his senior season having already scored 1,230 points as a collegian.

THOMAS KILGORE (6-2, 185 lbs., SR, SG, #15, 12.9 ppg, 2.2 rpg, 2.6 apg, 2.1 spg, 30.7 minutes, .431 FG, .375 3PT, .713 FT, Union HS/Grand Rapids, Mich.). Kilgore was the most versatile player and best defender in Cal's backcourt last year after transferring from Central Michigan. The one-time All-Freshman selection from the Mid-American Conference missed the first five games of the season before becoming eligible as a transfer, then took his place in the Bears' starting backcourt.

He scored in double figures 15 times and had at least one steal in all but his first game for the club. Ranked third in the Pac-10 with 2.14 steals per game, Kilgore joined Jason Kidd ('93 and '94) and Gene Ransom (1978) as the only Cal players to average at least 2.0 steals per game.

"Thomas gives us some toughness on the floor. He's a pretty hard-nosed player and he's around the ball a lot defensively," Braun said.

Kilgore played at both the shooting guard and point slots last year, but likely will be used primarily at the former position this season. A somewhat unorthodox-looking shooter, Kilgore nonetheless is a good finisher on the break and a surprisingly effective slasher to the hoop.

He had 19 points and seven assists vs. USC, a season-high 21 points and eight assists in a win at Washington State and 18 points in the Bears' late-season victory over Washington. Kilgore sat out the season finale last year after missing a scheduled academic meeting.

"I'm hoping there's a correlation," Braun said. "Those are valuable lessons."

A former Grand Rapids, Mich., high school rival of teammate Geno Carlisle, where both were All-City selections, Kilgore enters his senior year with 847 career points. He averaged 18.9 ppg as a freshman at Central Michigan, including a career-high 35 points in his college debut against Iona.

RAYMOND "CIRCUS" KING (5-10, 155 lbs., JR, PG, #10, 6.5 ppg, 2.8 rpg, 3.3 apg, 1.3 spg, 28.0 minutes, .449 FG, .206 3PT, .667 FT, El Cerrito HS/Richmond, Calif.). No one on the team bent his game so much to satisfy Braun and, by the end of last year, the Bears' starting point guard and head coach seemed comfortable with one another.

"I thought he made great progress, I really did," Braun said. "It was progress that did take some time, but I was pleased with what he was able to do for us at the end of the year."

King provided Cal with by far its quickest player, and its only point guard capable of penetrating and dishing the ball. He also could be a maddeningly erratic player whose game was sprinkled with quick shots and careless passes.

Braun kept him on a yo-yo string early in the season, repeatedly yanking him when King strayed from the plan. But the transfer from San Diego State gradually eliminated some of the excesses from his game and became more the player Braun wanted.

"He was playing like a point guard—distributing the ball, making better decisions," Braun said. "He needs to more consistently knock down the jumper. When he plays at different speeds, he's pretty good. He's getting better at that."

King, who missed most of preseason workouts last year with a bulging disk in his back, enters this season as the starter. But he will face competition from freshman Donte Smith, if eligible—a situation the coaching staff hopes will benefit both players.

King certainly has the edge in experience. Including his one season at San Diego State, he already has started 40 collegiate games. His scored in double figures three times last year, including a 21-point performance against Portland State in which he also had three assists, three steals and just one turnover.

SEAN LAMPLEY (6-7, 210 lbs., SO, PF, #21, 8.4 ppg, 5.2 rpg, 1.7 apg, 24.6 minutes, .449 FG, .263 3PT, .589 FT, St. Francis DeSales HS/Chicago, Ill.). Perhaps the Pac-10's most consistently productive freshman—including UCLA point guard Baron Davis—by the end of last season, Lampley was a pleasant surprise to everyone but the Cal coaching staff.

"Sean really played with a lot of confidence," Braun said. "His intensity level was good, and we're hoping in the coming year we'll see more improvement and he won't be satisfied with where he's been."

His high school profile diminished by an injury-shortened senior season, Lampley started slowly for Cal, but improved steadily. He scored in double figures 11 times, averaging 10.7 ppg over the team's final 15 games. Lampley impressed the right folks, too, saving a couple of his best games for defending national champion Arizona. He had 17 points and 10 rebounds vs. the Wildcats in Oakland, then totaled a career-high 21 points and eight rebounds in the rematch at Tucson. He also played well in Los Angeles, collecting nine points, 12 rebounds, four assists and three blocks against USC.

"He has unlimited potential," Carlisle said of Lampley late last season. "People are just starting to see glimpses of what he can do on a consistent basis."

Comfortable at either forward spot, Lampley most likely will see duty at the power forward position this year, given the team's limited frontcourt experience. His long arms and post-up ability allow him to play effectively against taller defenders, although he also has shown strong ballhandling and perimeter skills.

"Sean Lampley makes plays for you," Braun added. "He's proven we get a pretty good return when we go to him. He's a player who will give us a couple different

1997-98 RESULTS

@North Carolina (L)	47-71
Saint Mary's (L)	61-64
@San Francisco (L)	50-59
@Houston (L)	51-54
Portland State	74-61
#Brigham Young	68-64
##New Hampshire	75-67
##Virginia Commonwelath	66-57
@Oregon (L)	59-66
@Oregon State	84-70
@Stanford (L)	74-84
UCLA (L)	73-74
Southern California	92-82
@Washington (L)	84-86
@Washington State	86-75
Arizona State	82-77
Arizona (L)	57-70
Stanford (L)	72-74
@Rhode Island (L)	63-72
@Southern California	73-43
@UCLA (L)	84-87
Washington State	69-60
Washington	84-67
@Arizona (L)	73-76
@Arizona State (L)	80-99
Oregon State (L)	43-46
Oregon	75-71

@ away games
# Pete Newell Challenge, Oakland, CA
Golden Bear Classic, Berkeley, CA

looks. He can take big guys outside, or post you up on the low block."

Lampley was rated the nation's No. 15 small forward prospect by *Hoop Scoop* in 1997, but missed much of his senior season with a broken foot. He returned to lead his team to a fourth-place finish in the Illinois state tournament, averaging 12.9 ppg, 10.9 rpg and 3.0 bpg. He averaged 21.8 ppg and 10.3 rpg as a junior.

Lampley is the youngest of five brothers, all of whom have played college basketball: Lemone at DePaul, Kevin at Aurora(Ill.) College, Michael at Illinois-Chicago and Lee at Western Kentucky.

FRANCISCO ELSON (7-0, 235 lbs., SR, C, #41, 5.0 ppg, 4.7 rpg, 0.9 bpg, 18.4 minutes, .431 FG, .612 FT, Rotterdam, The Netherlands). Just the second seven-footer in Bears' history and their first in more than 30 years, Elson carries the burden of being the club's only "experienced" big man this season. And that term is relative. A native of The Netherlands, Elson did not begin playing basketball until he was 15, and remains a fairly raw offensive player.

With the departure of senior Sean Marks to the NBA and junior Kenyon Jones via the transfer route, the Bears are looking for Elson to develop into a steady and productive post player.

"He's got to be really dominant in the paint this year," Braun said. "He's got to give us some presence on the floor, not off the floor in foul trouble. I think he can make a lot of improvement. He still hasn't played that many years."

Elson already is a capable rebounder, having snared 17 in a single game against Virginia Commonwealth, an effort that earned him MVP honors in Cal's Golden Bear Classic. Elson had at least two blocked shots in seven games, collecting 25 for the season.

Elson spent his summer playing for the Dutch National Team alongside future UCLA rival Dan Gadzuric. Afterward, he was scheduled to attend the Pete Newell Big Man's Camp.

An honorable mention JC All-America pick at Kilgore College in Texas, Elson scored in double figures four times this past season, including a career-best 12 points vs. Arizona State. The Bears don't need him to be a big scorer, but they need him to show himself as at least a threat at the offensive end.

KEY RESERVES

MIKE GILL (6-6, 210 lbs., SR, F, #33, 10.4 ppg, 3.4 rpg, 1.1 spg, 24.2 minutes, .406 FG, .273 3PT, .780 FT, Dunbar HS/Washington, D.C.). Regarded by Braun as the Bears' most valuable player last season, Gill certainly was the club's most snake-bitten member. He missed four games due to a severe abdominal muscle strain and four more after a badly infected molar landed him in the hospital with a high fever.

"If Mike is healthy, he gives us some scoring punch," Braun said. "He hit some big shots for us last year, and he's a versatile player. He just brings a workmanlike attitude to practice. We expect him to step up and help us in whatever area we need."

When healthy a year ago, Gill was as critical and versatile as any player on the roster. With just seven scholarship players in uniform for the season opener at North Carolina, Gill shifted from his natural small forward spot to point guard. He spent two games at that spot, scoring 13 points against the Tar Heels and 18 in a subsequent game against Saint Mary's.

Between ailments, and back on the wing, he scored 18 points against Southern California and 17 at Washington. Gill closed the season by hitting a 12-foot shot with 7.8 seconds left to break a 71-all tie and lift the Bears to a 75-71 win over Oregon.

Along with sophomore Sean Lampley and JC recruit Carl Boyd, Gill gives the Bears perhaps the best assortment of forwards in the Pac-10. Respected by the coaching staff and his teammates, Gill figures to become a leader in the locker room.

Gill, who lists Dick Vitale as his favorite sports personality, was a Top 40 national prospect out of storied Dunbar HS in Washington in 1995. He spent his freshman season at Pitt, where he averaged 4.1 ppg and 2.0 rpg in 12 games. He then transferred to Compton (Calif.) JC, averaging 21.3 ppg and 9.3 rpg with high games of 40 points and 19 rebounds.

ROBBIE JONES (6-3, 195 lbs., JR, G, #30, 2.1 ppg, 1.7 rpg, 16.7 minutes, .463 FG, .769 FT, Cordova HS/Sacramento, Calif.). Jones came to Cal in 1995-96 and redshirted, then spent one season at Canada JC in nearby Redwood City, averaging 15.1 ppg, 4.0 rpg and 5.0 apg. Then it was back to Cal as a walkon last season, where he developed into an important player on a team strapped for manpower.

Jones played in 23 games last season, 10 of them as a starter. He gave the team a hustling defensive presence in the backcourt, although he was a reluctant and limited offensive contributor.

"With his experience, he'll be a factor," Braun predicted. "He's going to push guys. That's what he did last year. He pushed guys until he got an opportunity to play, and he helped us. He's a role player and I don't think you can ever have enough of those guys."

Jones knew his role and played it competently most of the season. He helped hold Washington State's Chris Crosby to 3-for-13 shooting and scored a career-high 11 points in the season-ender vs. Oregon.

Braun likes him for this reason, too: Jones committed just 11 turnovers in 264 minutes.

CARL BOYD (6-5, 215 lbs., JR, G/F, #23, 17.0 ppg, 4.0 spg, 3.0 apg, Porterville JC/Beloit, Wisc.). The physical and athletic Boyd figures to have the greatest immediate impact of Cal's five newcomers, sliding into either of the wing positions as a starter or early substitute off the bench. A first-team All-State junior college selection, Boyd is considered a larger version of recent Cal star Ed Gray—a scorer more than a shooter, a slasher who also has the ability to post-up near the basket.

"Carl is one of the most versatile players I've ever recruited," Braun said. "He was one of our top recruiting priorities because of the qualities he'll bring to our team.

"He impressed us so much because of his physical and mental toughness and leadership. Our fans will really like watching him play. He definitely plays above the rim."

"He's got the potential to be a highlight-film guy every night," said George Nessman, Boyd's coach at Porterville JC. "He'll challenge every guy in front of him on the break."

Boyd was rated one of the Top 25 junior college recruits nationally by Bob Gibbons of *All-Star Sports*, and earned Player of the Year in the Central Valley Conference. He led Porterville to a 29-6 record and a No. 3 ranking in the state.

He expected to be the top newcomer for Cal in terms of impact this season.

DENNIS GATES (6-4, 190 lbs., FR, P, #5, 11.1 ppg, 3.3 rpg, 3.2 apg, 2.5 spg at Whitney Young HS/Chicago, Ill.). Regarded as a superior defender and a winner, Gates comes to Cal from a Whitney Young program that compiled a record of 60-3 over the past two seasons. A teammate of Top 25 recruit Quentin Richardson, now a freshman at DePaul, Gates helped his club to a 30-1 record and Class AA state title in Illinois last season.

Whitney Young was ranked No. 2 in the country by *USA Today*. Gates was named MVP of the state championship game after scoring 20 points in a 61-56 win over Galesburg.

"He could be the most underrated player in the country," said Clark Francis of *Hoop Scoop*.

"Dennis is a winner in every sense of the word," Braun said. "He is a natural leader and there is no question he is a future leader at Cal. He is an intelligent player who comes from a top-notch academic and athletic school. You like to build programs around players like Dennis Gates."

He may have a future in politics, too. After signing with the Bears, Gates sent an entry into a Cal fans Internet website, assuring them he was excited about coming to Berkeley and that he looked forward to meeting their expectations for him.

A former AAU teammate of fellow Chicagoan Sean Lampley, Gates was a second-team All-City selection and a third-team All-State pick. He was named Chicago's All-Academic Player of the Year.

Braun hopes Gates can have a similar impact at Cal. "I think he's a threat for us," the coach said.

DONTE SMITH (6-2, 185 lbs., FR, G, #3, 28.3 ppg, 6.2 apg, 5.7 rpg, Anacostia HS/Washington, D.C.). The 1998 Washington D.C. Player of the Year, Smith is a scoring point guard who led his team to a 24-5 record and the Interscholastic Athletic Association title in the nation's capital.

"Donte is a natural floor leader," Braun said. "He is a combination player who we project as a point guard. He is not only a very talented player, but he also plays hard. He makes plays and he makes players around him better.

"I think he can contribute. I'm counting on him and Dennis (Gates) to push our older players."

Smith scored a season-high 44 points in one game last year, hitting 11 three-pointers. As a junior, he averaged 20.5 points per game. He was rated among the nation's Top 50 recruits by Bob Gibbons of *All-Star Sports*, and was listed as the No. 21 point guard by *The Sporting News*.

Smith participated in the Capital Classic All-Star Game and was a Top 50 finalist by the McDonald's All-America committee. Anacostia HS coach Tom Hargrove said the Bears landed more than a talented player.

"He's an extremely good guy, one of the better players we've had come through in terms of his character and disposition," Hargrove said. "He's the type of kid you don't mind taking home with you. The basketball will take care of itself and his character will carry him the rest of the way."

The third D.C. player in recent years to wind up at California, Smith has a connection to current Cal senior Mike Gill, whose mother works in the office at Anacostia HS. Smith, a good student, needs two more ACT points to become eligible for the second semester. He carried a 3.65 core GPA in high school.

Smith's projected debut would be Dec. 19 at Brigham Young.

OTHER RETURNEES

JUSTIN LABAGH (6-5, 200, SR, F, 0.4 ppg, 0.4 rpg, five appearances, St. Ignatius HS/San Francisco, Calif.). A fourth-year walkon, Labagh played in five games last year, registering a total of six minutes. But he is considered a valuable enough practice player that he has traveled with the team for road games the past two seasons.

OTHER NEWCOMERS

SHAHAR GORDON (6-10, 240 lbs., FR, C, #40, 8.0 ppg, 10.0 rpg, St. Thomas More Academy, Conn./Tel Aviv, Israel). Cal's final spring signee, Gordon came aboard in June after the Bears lost out to the NBA in pursuit of German teenage prospect Dirk Nowitzki. Even before a scholarship became available, Gordon was so committed to attending Cal he seemed willing to play one year as a walkon.

Cal offered him a scholarship after Nowitzki announced his intentions to turn pro and after Gordon received written confirmation from his native Israel that he had at least a one-year postponement of his military obligation. Quite likely, he will receive a full four-year postponement, enabling him to complete his Cal commitment without interruption.

Gordon is a raw, physical player who comes to Cal from the high-powered St. Thomas More Academy pro-

1998-99 CALIFORNIA SCHEDULE

Nov.	15	@Hawaii
	25	Eastern Washington
	28	@DePaul
Dec.	3	Houston
	5	Rhode Island
	7	Coppin State
	19	@Brigham Young
	21-22	#Golden Bear Classic
	29	*North Carolina
Jan.	2	Oregon
	4	Oregon State
	9	@Stanford
	14	@UCLA
	16	@Southern California
	21	Washington
	23	Washington State
	28	@Arizona State
	30	@Arizona
Feb.	3	Stanford
	11	Southern California
	13	UCLA
	18	@Washington State
	20	@Washington
	25	Arizona
	27	Arizona State
Mar.	4	@Oregon State
	6	@Oregon

@ Road Games
* Pete Newell Challenge, Oakland, CA
# Oakland, CA (vs. Eastern Kentucky first round; also Mississippi State and Southwestern Louisiana)

gram in Oakdale, Conn. Gordon was among seven players on his team that received NCAA scholarship offers.

"Shahar is a player who shows a lot of potential," Braun said. "He is eager to learn and is a very coachable player. He can play strong near the basket, but also possesses good perimeter skills. He'll help us because he plays hard."

Gordon, a member of his country's under-22 national team, is expected to be used in a backup role this year. But he believes the adjustment period to playing American ball was accelerated by his year at St. Thomas More.

"We had a real talented team," Gordon said, "and that's going to give me an edge over other European players who come to the States because they're going to have to make the adjustment once they get here."

SOLOMON HUGHES (6-11, 215 lbs., FR, F/C, #45, 19.0 ppg, 12.0 rpg in 1996-97 at Bishop Montgomery HS/ Torrance, Calif.). Regarded as a Top 40 prospect out of Bishop Montgomery HS two years ago, Hughes originally signed with Tulane as a senior, then changed his mind. Tulane declined to release him from his scholarship commitment, so Hughes spent last year at Fork Union (Va.) Military Academy.

Hughes arrived at California with full eligibility to play four seasons over a five-year span. He picked Cal over a variety of schools, including Florida and Florida State.

Just 6-2 when he entered high school five years ago, Hughes still is adjusting to his recent growth spurt. He has added weight and muscle in the past year, but remains a lean player who utilizes quickness more than power.

"I'm a lot more athletic than I was when I was a (high school) senior," Hughes said. "I can shoot a lot better. Right now I'm stronger facing (the basket), but the post-up part is really coming along."

"I'm excited about Solomon's decision to come to Cal," Braun said. "He's an agile post player who has outstanding potential, and there is tremendous opportunity for him to make an immediate contribution here."

Hughes figures to serve as backup to senior center Francisco Elson and also will see time at the power forward slot.

QUESTIONS

Frontcourt? The Bears lost nearly 14 feet of frontcourt talent when Sean Marks graduated and Kenyon Jones decided to transfer. Francisco Elson showed only glimpses of an offensive game last year, and will need to provide at least a threat from the post while youngsters Solomon Hughes and Shahar Gordon develop.

Inexperience? The Bears return all but two of their top nine players from a year ago, but this team is young in the ways of competing at the top of the conference. None of the Bears has ever played an NCAA Tournament game.

Leadership? With the roster in such flux last year, no one truly emerged as a leader on this team. That must change if the Bears expect to fulfill their expectations and compete for an upper-division spot in the Pac-10. Among the most likely candidates for the leadership mantle: Carlisle, Gill and Lampley.

ANSWERS

Depth! The Bears began last season with just seven eligible scholarship players, and never were afforded the type of manpower needed to play an up-tempo style on a steady basis. This club will bring on reserves like a hockey team, especially in the backcourt and on the wings, where no team in the conference is deeper.

Quickness! Braun likes a balanced approach with an emphasis on muscle, but this team will rely on speed. And that quickness is everywhere, from his backcourt to center Elson, who can run with the best of them.

Opportunity! Last season was a frustrating one for the Bears, who began the year knowing NCAA sanctions would keep them out of the postseason regardless of what they did on the court. With prohibitions now lifted, the Bears are anxious to play with a tangible postseason goal.

adidas Blue Ribbon Analysis

BACKCOURT	**B+**	**BENCH/DEPTH**	**B+**
FRONTCOURT	**B**	**INTANGIBLES**	**B**

After two seasons of transition and the turmoil of an NCAA investigation that resulted from ex-coach Todd Bozeman's transgressions, the Bears are ready to move forward again.

"I like the direction we're going, and I like the pace," Braun said of his program's progress. "Our plan was not to come in and make any quick fixes. We took a big step last year. We weren't doormats; we were competitive. Now we want to be consistently competitive."

Braun has re-energized Cal fans and built a team that can play the style he wants. The Bears will play quick and fierce, using defense to set up offense, attacking whenever possible.

Cal will face matchup difficulties with the league's more physical teams, such as Stanford and Washington. But the Bears hope their lineup provides equally challenging matchups for opponents not equipped with their speed and versatility.

Just how the Bears fit into a hotly contested Pac-10 upper-division will be intriguing to see. Braun believes a key will be the development of leadership that never fully matured last season.

"Sometimes I think our younger guys have shown more leadership than the older players. Someone's got to step up," he said. "We hope the seniors will really carry a hungry attitude, because there's a lot out there for us."

An NCAA Tournament bid is at the top of the Bears' list. And there are more to follow. Braun has already received four verbal commitments from Top 100-caliber high school seniors for the 1999-2000 season.

(J.F.)

35

RHODE ISLAND

LOCATION	**Kingston, RI**
CONFERENCE	**Atlantic 10 (East Division)**
LAST SEASON	**25-9 (.735)**
CONFERENCE RECORD	**12-4 (t-2nd)**
STARTERS LOST/RETURNING	**3/2**
NICKNAME	**Rams**
COLORS	**Light Blue, Dark Blue & White**
HOMECOURT	**Keaney Gymnasium (3,385)**
	Providence Civic Center (12,641)
COACH	**Jim Harrick (Morris Harvey '60)**
RECORD AT SCHOOL	**25-9 (1 yr.)**
CAREER RECORD	**383-169 (18 yrs.)**
ASSISTANTS	**Jerry DeGregorio (St. John's '85)**
	Jim Harrick Jr. (Pepperdine '87)
	Tom Garrick (Rhode Island '89)
TEAM WINS (last 5 yrs.)	**11-7-20-20-25**
RPI (last 5 yrs.)	**123-190-74-35-19**
1997-98 FINISH	**Lost in NCAA Final Eight.**

COACH AND PROGRAM

Mission accomplished.

Rhode Island entered the 1997-98 season hoping to make a significant splash on the national scene. The Rams had hired Jim Harrick to coach a veteran, winning group in the wake of Al Skinner's departure for Boston College. They had taken another chance in admitting renegade recruit Lamar Odom.

They moved a bunch more games to the Providence Civic Center, seeking a bigger slice of the New England college basketball market.

Mostly, the Rams wanted someone to notice their continued winning.

Again, mission accomplished. Harrick's messy exit from UCLA is a distant memory. All that remains is his national championship with the Bruins and the best season in Rhode Island history.

Final Eight good enough for you?

Truth be told, the Rams should have been in the Final Four. The outplayed both of the higher seeds they faced in the NCAA Tournament, speeding by heavily-favored Kansas in the second round and leading Stanford until the bitter end of the Midwest Region championship game.

A turnover here, some missed free throws there, and the Cardinal pulled off a near-miracle comeback. That Stanford was ultimately a better team should in no way diminish what Rhode Island accomplished. The Rams were a testimony to togetherness, veteran leadership and the great power of senior guards.

Even with an arguably more talented cast for 1998-99, URI will have a hard time duplicating all that went right last season.

"It couldn't have been a more magical time," Harrick told the *Providence Journal*. "There is a heavenly father, and he was definitely (with us)."

Even before the NCAA Tournament, they were calling it one of the best seasons in Rhode Island history. No URI team had ever qualified for consecutive NCAA fields; none had played in three straight postseason tournaments.

Some, including this reporter, thought the Rams might be stung in the NCAA opening round by Murray State. URI won by 23 points. No one gave them a prayer against No. 1 seed Kansas in the next round. Well the Rams won again, in Oklahoma City no less, and even more handily than the 80-75 final score would indicate.

The Sweet 16 matchup with Valparaiso was more good fortune (and a great story line, pitting Harrick against son Jim Jr., a Valpo assistant at the time). Finally, in the regional championship game, the Rams coughed up a six-point lead in the last minute to Stanford.

There were tears, but only momentarily. The Rams had captured their state and much of the nation.

Now, three of the starters are gone. But the consensus No. 1 prep player of two years ago is making a pit stop on his way to the NBA. And Harrick remains, as well, despite grumbling a year ago that a big winner would move him up the coaching ladder.

Harrick's career winning percentage is about .700. That he did so again with the Rams last year—and will again this season—is called going with the chalk.

URI fans, enjoy the ride.

STARTERS NOT RETURNING

TYSON WHEELER (5-10, PG, 14.9 ppg, 2.6 rpg, 6.0 apg, 2.9 tpg, 1.3 spg, 34.0 minutes, .402 FG, .363 3PT, .648 FT). Wheeler represents everything good about URI's 1997-98 coming out party. He endured the seven-win disaster that was his freshman season. He suffered through critical losses to St. Joseph's in the NIT quarterfinal ('96) and Atlantic 10 championship game ('97). Wheeler not only endured; he kept smiling throughout.

Some thought Wheeler should have been A-10 Player of the Year as a junior (he lost out to Temple's Mark Jackson). As a senior, he subordinated much of his offense to hard-charging backcourt partner Cut Mobley. Yet he remained the fulcrum of the Rhode Island attack.

It was terribly unfortunate that Wheeler closed his career by missing important free throws at the end of the Stanford game. He had scored 68 points in four NCAA contests up to that point, and was magnificent in the biggest game of his career. Wheeler had danced and dashed through the Stanford trees for a team-high 24 points on 9-for-14 shooting.

Someday, we hope Wheeler looks back and remembers more than that final minute. His entire career was worth smiling about.

CUTTINO MOBLEY (6-4, SG, 17.2 ppg, 4.3 rpg, 2.6 apg, 2.2 tpg, 1.6 spg, 33.3 minutes, .480 FG, .416 3PT, .856 FT). Kansas coach Roy Williams is probably still lying awake at night, seeing visions of Mobley and Wheeler flying by his overmatched guards. Mobley only scored 27 points that day. Together, he and Wheeler outscored a couple of Kansas guys named Pierce and LaFrentz.

And you wonder why the Jayhawks can't get back to the Final Four?

All of which has little to do with Mobley, who rebounded from some injury-stifled campaigns with the best season of his life. He shot judiciously, guarded the perimeter and became a team leader. Let us never forget what a pair of quality senior guards can accomplish in the NCAA Tournament.

Both he and Wheeler were first-team All-Atlantic 10 performers. For one day at least, they outplayed two first-team All-Americas.

JOSHUA KING (6-8, SF, 8.7 ppg, 4.0 rpg, 1.2 apg, 1.2 tpg, 24.8 minutes, .453 FG, .407 3PT, .765 FT). Even Josh King became an all-around player under Harrick. King, who previous forte was to touch opposing players as little as possible, occasionally guarded his man in 1997-98. He shot less as a senior, but was still a dangerous long-distance threat.

The Rams have plenty of new wing players. It remains to be seen if any are the knock-down shooter that King was.

OTHERS NOT RETURNING

JOHN BENNETT (6-7, F, 1.4 ppg, 0.9 rpg, 6.6 minutes, .263 FG, .826 FT). Bennent was even less important to the Rams under Harrick. The arrival of Luther Clay may have had something to do with that. Still, he was always ready when called upon, and he leaves having participated in eight NCAA and NIT games.

MAUREICO GAY (5-10, G, 0.9 ppg, 12 appearances). Gay made the most of his 12 walkon appearances, scoring 11 points.

PROJECTED STARTERS

ANTONIO REYNOLDS-DEAN (6-7, 220 lbs., SR, PF, #34, 11.2 ppg, 7.6 rpg, 1.8 apg, 1.8 tpg, 1.1 spg, 2.5 bpg, 30.6 minutes, .505 FG, .677 FT, Douglass HS/ Atlanta, Ga.). Hype notwithstanding, Reynolds-Dean is now the most accomplished college player in the program. He has started 98 consecutive games in his Rhode Island career, averaging solid scoring and rebounding totals throughout. He began as the A-10 Freshman of the Year, and has kept his game at virtually the same level.

"He may be the most underrated player in the country," said St. Joseph's coach Phil Martelli.

It doesn't seem to matter who surrounds him. Reynolds-Dean plays his 30 minutes, posts about 12 points and eight boards, then goes back to the dorm. Then there are the 194 blocked shots in three seasons.

Reynolds-Dean can score (career-high 27 points vs. Northeastern). He has also collected as many as 19 rebounds in a game. He can play 40 or more minutes if needed, and his quiet demeanor belies a fierce competitive instinct.

1997-98 RESULTS

#North Carolina-Wilmington	78-69	
#@Connecticut (L)	67-80	
@Boston University	86-63	
@Brown	75-57	
*Providence	69-58	
*UNLV	91-73	
*Ohio	85-72	
##Stanford (L)	69-70	
##Pennsylvania	96-89	
@Temple	74-64	
@St. Joseph's	83-68	
Duquesne	83-76	
@La Salle	84-73	
###Tulane	85-61	
@St. Bonaventure (L)	81-86	
Virginia Tech	73-66	
@Cincinnati (L)	82-88	
*Massachusetts (L)	57-74	
@Fordham	75-70	
St. Joseph's	94-76	
*California	72-63	
St. Bonaventure	67-66	
@George Washington	69-61	
*Temple (L)	66-67	
@Massachusetts	87-85	2ot
@Dayton (L)	62-71	
*Xavier	69-68	
Fordham	71-57	
####Dayton	83-70	
###Xavier (L)	80-95	
%Murray State	97-74	
%Kansas	80-75	
%%Valparaiso	74-68	
%%Stanford (L)	77-79	

@ away games
* Providence Civic Center, Providence, RI
\# Chase NIT, campus sites
\## Cable Car Classic, San Jose, CA
\### Bud Light A-10/C-USA Challenge, Providence, RI
\#### Atlantic 10 Tournament, CoreStates Spectrum, Philadelphia, PA
% NCAA Midwest Sub-Regional, Oklahoma City, OK
%% NCAA Midwest Regional, St. Louis, MO

We suspect he has grown up a lot at URI. When he first came north from Atlanta, he did not even bring a winter coat along.

This time next year—at some port of call either in the U.S. or abroad—Reynolds-Dean will be able to buy the coat factory.

LUTHER CLAY (6-9, 225 lbs., JR, C, #35, 9.8 ppg, 6.7 rpg, 1.7 tpg, 28.1 minutes, .492 FG, .604 FT, Purdue & Maine Central Institute/Oberlin, Oh.). In some respects, Clay is the key to the 1998-99 season. He needs to stay healthy and become a consistent force in the middle for the Rams to make a successful transition to an inside-focused team.

Clay has the game. He was once one of the most sought-after prep players in the nation. Coming out of Maine Central Institute, he averaged 17.3 ppg and 11.1 rpg for the national runners-up, becoming a consensus Top 20 prospect.

As a college freshman in 1995-96, Clay appeared in 24 of 32 games for Purdue. He was a marginal performer at best, both on the court and off. His recruitment to Purdue is still being reviewed by the NCAA.

Clay opted to sit out the 1996-97 season and transfer. Guided by his former coach at MCI, Max Good, he chose Rhode Island. The thinking was that the Rams were only a quality center away from making a deep NCAA run.

The irony is that the Rams went much of the season with so-so performances from Clay. He injured an ankle in the preseason, and reportedly was distraught enough to consider quitting the game. He then missed another key contest vs. Massachusetts due to strep throat.

Come tourney time, though, Clay finally became more than a role player. He managed a pair of double-doubles, including a 14-point, 11-rebound effort in the shocking upset of Kansas.

If it is true that Clay needed only to shake off his redshirt year, look for a big season in the middle out of Rhode Island's center.

PRESTON MURPHY (6-1, 180 lbs., SR, PG, #32, 9.1 ppg, 2.7 rpg, 1.5 apg, 1.5 tpg, 1.0 spg, 25.4 minutes, .403 FG, .351 3PT, .659 FT, Nouvel Catholic HS/Saginaw, Mich.). Only one thing is certain about Murphy: No matters how well he plays, he will remain an anonymous contributor to URI's success.

The past two years, he was the third guard behind Wheeler and Mobley. No one seemed to notice his .422 three-point shooting as a sophomore or his 25-plus minutes as a junior. Murphy played almost as much as the starters, so he should have little adjustment to being one as a senior.

Figure on Murphy to play point guard, if only because it is the safest option in this potentially explosive lineup. The Rams surely need someone willing to pass the ball and sacrifice for his teammates.

As Murphy surely remembers the not-so-good times, look for him to be an invaluable—and little-mentioned performer—this season. He understand his role.

LAMAR ODOM (6-9, 220 lbs., SO, SF, 25.1 ppg, 17.2 rpg, 12.0 apg, 5.0 bpg, .607 FG, .475 3PT, .704 FT, Redemption Christian Academy, N.Y./New York, N.Y.). You may have heard of this guy. He has made more all-star teams (and played at more schools) than you have toes on your feet. He has also accomplished something few thought possible.

Lamar Odom is eligible to play Division I college basketball. To do so, he overcame every academic hurdle placed in front of him. He put some unsavory national press about test scores in his rearview mirror. He also turned down separate professional contracts valued at $100,000 (CBA) and $500,000 (Greece).

Why? It seems Odom wants to at least experience college ball before embarking on a certain pay-for-play career. Here is the short-version of his story:

- Odom dominates the New York Catholic League as a 15-year-old sophomore, leading Christ the King HS to the city title. His 36 points in the league final shoot him past Lew Alcindor, Kenny Anderson and Felipe Lopez in the record book.
- Odom finishes his scholastic work at St. Thomas Aquinas HS in Milford, Conn., where he meets current URI assistant Jerry DeGregorio and is recruited by a UCLA coach named Jim Harrick.
- He attends Redemption Christian Academy (Troy, N.Y.) during the 1996-97 season, this after dominating the summer circuit and the signature ABCD camp. Odom finishes at Redemption Christian and is named the *Parade* national Player of the Year.
- Odom signs a letter-of-intent at UNLV, but never enrolls at the school (his SAT scores are questioned in a *Sports Illustrated* article). Odom considers the NBA draft, but opts instead to attend classes at Rhode Island—now with Harrick and DeGregorio on board—as a non-matriculating student.
- After a full year (and summer) of college work, Odom again spurns the NBA draft and becomes eligible as a redshirt sophomore.

"I think Lamar became a man," DeGregorio told the *A-10 Hoop Report*.

Added Odom: "I knew this day would come, and it's finally here so I'm just so happy."

What we have then is the one-time prep player of the year about to begin his collegiate career in a sleepy New England hamlet by the Atlantic Ocean. Odom is by far the top recruit ever signed by Rhode Island, or the Atlantic 10 for that matter.

However long he stays, or whatever the current level of his game, it is hard to imagine that Odom won't be worth the wait.

ZACH MARBURY (6-3, 185 lbs., FR, SG, 25.7 ppg, 3.7 rpg, 3.7 apg, .548 FG, .420 3PT, .716 FT, Milford Academy, Conn./Brooklyn, N.Y.). The younger brother of Minnesota Timberwolves guard and New York City legend Stephon Marbury, the Rams would settle for half of that ability from Zach. Marbury the younger is not a pure point man like his brother. In fact, most think this combo guard is better suited off the ball.

Regardless, Marbury can score from anywhere on the court. And, losing Wheeler and Mobley, the Rams will need some points from the backcourt. CNN/SI calls Marbury one of the nation's Top 10 at the guard position.

How about this for a high school reunion? Marbury, Odom, Tavorris Bell and transfer Ed Brown all toiled for the same Long Island AAU team.

"He's out there, way out there," one A-10 scout said of Marbury, "but he can play."

KEY RESERVES

DAVID ARIGBABU (6-8, 250 lbs., SR, F, #10, 4.5 ppg, 3.3 rpg, 16.2 minutes, .495 FG, .724 FT, Mercer Island HS, Wash./Laatzen, Germany). Ever the good solider, Arigbabu simply does what he is asked in the Rams' frontcourt. That should be more of the same in 1998-99.

He has played in 94 games over three seasons, starting only twice. His minutes have averaged anywhere from 14.9 to 20.4 per game. He provides size, bulk

1998-99 RHODE ISLAND SCHEDULE

Nov.	9	#Texas Christian
	10	#Vanderbilt
	14	@Providence
	19	*Cincinnati
	24	Brown
	28	*Wisconsin
Dec.	2	##Utah
	5	@California
	12	@Ohio
	23	*San Francisco
	27	###Cleveland State
	29	####Sparkletts Invitational
Jan.	3	@Xavier
	10	Dayton
	13	Fordham
	16	@Temple
	21	*La Salle
	23	*George Washington
	27	St. Joseph's
	30	@Duquesne
Feb.	4	@Massachusetts
	6	*Temple
	10	@Virginia Tech
	13	*Massachusetts
	16	@St. Bonaventure
	21	@St. Joseph's
	24	St. Bonaventure
	28	@Fordham
Mar.	3-6	#####Atlantic 10 Tournament

@ Road Games
* Providence Civic Center, Providence, RI
\# CoSIDA Classic, Providence, RI
\## Great Eight, Chicago, IL
\### Gatorade Rock 'n Roll Shootout, Cleveland, OH
\#### Malibu, CA (vs. Pepperdine, first round; also Eastern Michigan and Siena)
\##### First Union Spectrum, Philadelphia, PA

and an experienced presence. Since one never knows which Luther Clay is going to show up, Arigbabu is valuable insurance.

He once scored 16 points (vs. Syracuse) and has pulled down as many as eight rebounds (three times). Arigbabu won't take a bad shot, and he can be used late in close games. His free throw shooting jumped from .535 to .724 last season.

Arigbabu will continue as Rhode Island's first (only?) big man off the bench.

TORY JEFFERSON (6-6, 185 lbs., SO, F, #00, 2.0 ppg, 1.2 rpg, 7.7 minutes, .432 FG, .133 3PT, .800 FT, East HS/Rochester, N.Y.). Jefferson plays the wrong position at the wrong time for Rhode Island. When a Lamar Odom and a Tavorris Bell show up at practice, you'd better not set your heart on a larger role. One guy thinks he should already be in the NBA; the other one jumps over cars (more on that below).

Yet Jefferson could become a key reserve given his ability to shoot the ball. Though his three-point percentage was meager as a freshman, that came in only 15 attempts. His overall shooting and shot selection was not bad for a rookie seeing only spot duty.

Jefferson needs to hang in there at Rhode Island. At least one of the guys ahead of him doesn't figure to be there very long.

TAVORRIS BELL (6-6, 210 lbs., FR, F, 13.1 ppg, 5.2 rpg, 3.1 apg, 2.6 spg, .557 FG, .355 3PT, .682 FT, Winchendon Prep, Mass./Hempstead, N.Y.). Bell played in only 10 games at Winchendon in 1997-98, sidelined by a separated shoulder and ultimately a mid-year transfer to Rhode Island. He did not dress for the Rams at all, and thus retains four full years of eligibility.

During his final season at Hempstead (N.Y.) High, Bell was rated among the nation's Top 50 prospects by Bob Gibbons. He averaged 20.7 ppg, 12.1 rpg, 3.0 apg and 3.0 spg, and was considered by some the best leaper in the country.

AAU coach Gary Charles, who had both Bell and Lamar Odom on the same team, said, "You put a nickel on the moon, and (Bell) will jump and get it." Bell once leaped over a car to dunk at the playground.

We don't suspect there will be many cars in Atlantic 10 arenas this season, but it would make for one helluva halftime promotion.

TIP VINSON (6-4, 190 lbs., FR, G, 23.1 ppg, 7.4 rpg, .566 FG, .412 3PT, .819 FT, St. Thomas Aquinas HS/New Britain, Conn.). Caleb "Tip" Vinson played for URI assistant coach Jerry DeGregorio during his junior season at St. Thomas Aquinas. He then became a Top 100 recruit as a senior in 1997-98.

Vinson was first-team All-State in Connecticut. ESPN called him one of the top 10 prep guards in the country. Bob Gibbons ranked him No. 58 overall.

Vinson is considered a good shooter and quality all-around guard. Prep coaches have referred to him as "intelligent, poised and crafty."

Sounds like a worthy successor to Preston Murphy.

OTHER RETURNEES

None.

OTHER NEWCOMERS

ANDREW WAFULA (6-10, 195 lbs., FR C, #4, 16.1 ppg, 9.8 rpg in 1996-97, Peninsula Christian Academy, Va./Kampala, Uganda). Wafula, who was signed by Harrick just 16 days after he became Rhode Island's coach, has yet to dress for the Rams. He redshirted last year in an effort to gain strength.

Wafula has played only five years of organized basketball. He gained 11 pounds during his final year at Peninsula Christian Academy, but still needs to spend a little more time in the chow line.

Until then, his best shots are likely to come during layup drills.

ED BROWN (6-8, 290 lbs., JR, C, 1.0 ppg, 0.7 rpg in 1996-97, St. John's & Copaigue HS/Amityville, N.Y.). Brown sat out the second semester last year after transferring from St. John's and will be eligible in December. He has worked on his conditioning, but would seem to be too heavy to make a meaningful contribution this season.

Brown played in five of the first seven games last year at St. John's. His career-highs are eight points and four rebounds (vs. West Virginia in 1995-96).

The Rams may need a big body from time to time, and Brown would certainly qualify. For kicks, maybe URI should have him lie down from time to time and let Tavorris Bell jump over him.

MARK TREADWELL (6-5, 220 lbs., FR, F, 6.4 ppg, 4.7 rpg, St. Joseph's HS/Chicago, Ill.). Treadwell was a late and welcome addition for the Rams. He had originally signed a letter-of-intent at Indiana.

Treadwell could be a useful reserve at some point. He has the size and strength to be a good sixth man down the road.

Treadwell played in only seven games as a high school senior at St. Joseph's, suffering a nasty back injury during a dunk attempt. He had been a first-team All-State choice as a junior at Chicago's Westinghouse HS. As a sophomore, he was a second-team All-State selection at Oak Park High.

DAVID SMITH (6-5, 210 lbs., JR, G, William Jewell College, Mo./Columbia, Mo.). Not many walkons go the junior college route. Smith did, however, then sat out last season to improve his chances with the Rams.

Smith's best chance for court time might be before the game. He sang the national anthem prior to a URI contest last year, and could do so this season in uniform (and maybe Bell could jump over him, too!).

QUESTIONS

Backcourt? Tyson Wheeler and Cuttino Mobley were a wonderful combination, playing off one another at both ends of the floor. Neither was afraid to take (and make) clutch shots.

Hangover? After the best season in school history, will the Rams have their feet on the ground when the season gets underway?

Chemistry? On paper, URI looks more like a prep all-star squad than a complete college team. This is not always a good thing. Last time we checked, there is only one ball for every five players.

ANSWERS

Frontcourt! If Clay and Odom are even at 80 percent, they combine with quality senior Antonio Reynolds-Dean to form as good a frontcourt as there is in the country. But it is an awfully volatile mix.

Lamar Odom! Odom could dominate the Atlantic 10, or he could be the centerpiece of a teamwide implosion. We'll probably see both scenarios as the season unfolds.

Jim Harrick! Is he always that calm on the sidelines? It didn't seem that way at UCLA. Yet last season, he was almost fatherly to a veteran URI group. This year, Harrick will need to blend an entirely new set of egos.

adidas Blue Ribbon Analysis

BACKCOURT	B	BENCH/DEPTH	B
FRONTCOURT	B+	INTANGIBLES	B

Make no mistake, the Rams' upside is incredible. They could be right back in the second weekend of the NCAA Tournament.

Just as likely is that Rhode Island suffers tremendously from the lack of an experienced backcourt. The senior guards who carried URI a year ago would be effective policemen for this volatile mixture of players and egos.

Even a perfect frontcourt—which Clay, Reynolds-Dean and Odom could be—is only as good as the guards up top. Preston Murphy is a nice player, but he isn't Wheeler or Mobley. Unless he really takes over, the inmates could be running the asylum.

There is fabulous talent here. What we don't know is whether or not the Rams can come together as a team.

(J.L.)

36
CLEMSON

LOCATION	Clemson, SC
CONFERENCE	Atlantic Coast (ACC)
LAST SEASON	18-14 (.563)
CONFERENCE RECORD	7-9 (t-4th)
STARTERS LOST/RETURNING	2/3
NICKNAME	Tigers
COLORS	Orange & White
HOMECOURT	Littlejohn Coliseum (11,020)
COACH	Larry Shyatt (Wooster '73)
RECORD AT SCHOOL	first year
CAREER RECORD	19-9 (1 yr.)
ASSISTANTS	Scott Duncan (Wooster '78)
	Darren Tillis (Paul Quinn College '96)
	Matt Driscoll (Slippery Rock '92)
TEAM WINS (last 5 yrs.)	18-15-18-23-18
RPI (last 5 yrs.)	80-80-46-11-29
1997-98 FINISH	Lost in NCAA first round.

COACH AND PROGRAM

So, how much would you pay to be a head coach in the ACC?

For first-year Clemson coach Larry Shyatt, that question is easily answered—thanks to the Wyoming judicial system. The figure is somewhere in the neighborhood of $286,000.

Shyatt thought he had hit the coaching jackpot when his old mentor, Rick Barnes, got fed up with living in the shadow of the giants of the ACC and unexpectedly bolted for Texas on Easter Sunday. Shyatt, who had just led Wyoming to a 19-9 record and an appearance in the NIT in his only year as Cowboys' head coach, was the obvious choice to replace his old boss and he was offered a salary somewhere around $400,000 per year.

Shyatt is personable, a good recruiter and the players on the team were already familiar with and fond of his affable nature. One problem: Shyatt had a five-year contract with Wyoming, with a significant buyout clause.

Here's where the story gets fun, a beautiful reflection of our litigious society. Shyatt sued Wyoming, claiming that Wyoming athletic director Lee Moon had made a verbal promise to waive the buyout clause if Clemson came calling. Shyatt filed his lawsuit in South Carolina, hoping to get a favorable ruling in Clemson's home state.

However, that suit was dropped, just in time for Wyoming to file a countersuit demanding payment of the buyout and seeking to keep Shyatt from handling any coaching responsibilities at Clemson until the suit was settled. Eventually, in August, the coach and the school came to a settlement in which he would make five payments between $50,000 and $75,000 to fulfill his contractual obligation.

On court, as opposed to in court, Shyatt is more than familiar with Clemson's roster. As an assistant under Barnes for nine years, Shyatt recruited most of the current players to the South Carolina school before taking the Wyoming job. More importantly, the players know and genuinely like Shyatt, an affable sort who is quick to crack a joke and likely won't run the intense, bone-crunching practices for which Barnes was famous.

Barnes' departure shocked many in this tiny upstate town known more for its football success than basketball prowess. But Barnes embraced his underdog role, both on campus and in the ACC, playing the us-against-them role to the limit with his team. Apparently, it worked.

With a nearly talentless roster that the coach dubbed the "Slab Five," Barnes went to a physical style and won 15 games his first year, including five in the ACC. The next three years, he took the Tigers to the NCAA Tournament, advancing to the Sweet 16 two seasons ago.

But Barnes just about wore out his schtick last season. He continued to play the aggressive, annoying physical style. The Tigers set an ACC record by committing 41 fouls against North Carolina. Six Tiger players fouled out of the game, and the Tigers had to finish with only four players on the court.

There were other criticisms of Barnes' program, too. Tiger players didn't develop while playing for Barnes, it was said. Departed senior Greg Buckner, who followed Barnes from Providence as a high school recruit, was better as a freshman than he was as a senior. Current seniors Harold Jamison and Tom Wideman are no more effectively offensively going into this season as they were when they arrived three years ago.

Last year, when the Tigers returned all five starters from a Sweet 16 team and were ranked No. 5 in one major preseason poll, Clemson stumbled badly out of the gate, losing back-to-back games to Gonzaga and Kentucky in Alaska. Because of injuries to feisty point guard Terrell McIntyre and some other role players, the Tigers saw their record slip to 12-10 by mid-February. Only a late surge at the end of the regular season got them back into NCAA Tournament consideration.

The Tigers bowed out in the second round of the ACC Tournament and in the first round of the NCAAs, and many considered Clemson's season a significant step back from the 23-win effort of a year before. When push came to shove, as it so often did under Barnes, the Tigers had won exactly as many games in Barnes' first four years as they did under predecessors Bill Foster and Cliff Ellis.

There is a simple, four-word explanation of why Barnes left for Texas: North Carolina and Duke. Barnes discovered after four years of fighting it that the ACC mountain was just too hard to climb.

In its best years, Clemson would struggle to get into the top three of the ACC. The rest of the time, well, you do the math.

Barnes is a good enough coach and Texas is a good enough school that he should be able to get into the top two of the Big 12 without having to punch Kansas coach Roy Williams in the nose, as Barnes almost did with Williams' mentor, Dean Smith. Barnes should have a better chance of winning a national championship at Texas than he likely would of winning an ACC championship at Clemson. It's a harsh reality for the North Carolina native, who was fairly comfortable at Clemson—despite his parting shot at the South Carolina school system.

Oh, you heard about that, didn't you? Barnes was waiting to begin a television interview, when he mentioned off-camera that one of the biggest reasons he was leaving Clemson was because his children's schools were "horrible." That didn't play well in the state, and the coach had to do some serious apologizing as the door flung shut on his departure.

Shyatt, who was well-liked in his three years at Clemson, doesn't have to worry about living in Barnes' shadow. A good coach with a bag full of one-liners, he was a welcome replacement for Barnes.

Shyatt went immediately to work with his players, convincing talented forward Tony Christie to stay at the school. Christie and Barnes did not get along, and the junior forward was ready to transfer after last season.

Otherwise, the Tigers had a solid, but not overly impressive, recruiting class. It could have been better, but two players who made verbal commitments to the team, 6-4 Kentucky swingman Todd Tackett and 6-0 Louisiana point guard Brandon Dean, backed out at the last minute. Tackett fulfilled his dream of going to Kentucky, while Dean changed his mind and went to Arkansas.

Of the three players Clemson did sign, two were inked by Barnes—forward Chuckie Gilmore and guard Dustin Braddick. After Shyatt took over, he added guard Will Solomon, a scoring guard Barnes originally recruited and who Shyatt never saw face-to-face.

Gilmore will likely learn his trade in the low post playing behind Jamison and Wideman, while Solomon is projected to be McIntyre's eventual replacement. Braddick is kind of a wild card.

While the Tigers will be in transition during Shyatt's first year at the helm, they still have one of the deepest and most experienced lineups in the ACC. If McIntyre, the team catalyst, stays healthy, Clemson will contend for the upper echelon of the conference and can perhaps get into the top three.

Shyatt hopes that happens for his seniors, who signed with the Tigers after Barnes' first year in town. Those were lean times in the program, but this class came in seven players strong and has a chance to be Clemson's first senior group to reach four consecutive NCAA Tournaments.

"This senior class at Clemson is special to me, because they came here when it was not easy to choose Clemson," Shyatt said. "These guys were not high school All-Americas. Terrell McIntyre was not a top 250 player coming out of high school.

"These guys have already left a mark, because they have prove that Clemson can sustain a run of success, can go to the NCAA Tournament on a consistent basis, not just have a good season every four or five years."

There are some obvious questions to answer, though, such as replacing departed leading scorer Greg Buckner, getting some consistent outside shooting and inside scoring, and making more free throws. The Tigers were one of the worst foul shooting teams in conference history last year, with three regulars under 50 percent. The .614 team wide percentage was the worst since the school began keeping the statistic in 1954.

Shyatt has his work cut out for him, to be sure. But he also has an experienced nucleus of players who have had good success in the ACC. He did an admirable job taking over a Wyoming team that was 12-16 the previous year and leading them to a 19-9 record and a berth in the NIT.

He has more talent and experience to work with this time around.

STARTERS NOT RETURNING

GREG BUCKNER (6-4, 210 lbs., SG, 16.3 ppg, 4.1 rpg, 2.6 apg, 1.5 tpg, 1.6 spg, 31.9 minutes, .537 FG, .328 3PT, .696 FT). For four years, Buckner was the guy Clemson looked to for big plays and critical shots. Most people didn't know that much about him, playing as he did for the tradition-poor Tigers.

But Barnes considered his senior guard one of the biggest impact players on an ACC program in a long, long time. Buckner not only finished his career as the school's third all-time leading scorer, but also in the top 15 in field goals, free throws, assists, rebounds and games played.

Buckner, who signed a letter of intent with Barnes at Providence, backed out of that commitment to follow Barnes to Clemson. The coach was most appreciative. Maybe that's why Buckner started every single game of his career for the Tigers, a school-record 122 of them to be exact.

Buckner spent most of his career playing at the small forward position, but, because of injuries and backcourt troubles, he moved to shooting guard as a senior. That allowed Barnes to insert athletic Tony Christie into the starting lineup.

When the Tigers needed Buckner the most, he came through for them, closing out his final two regular season games with 44 points, 17-for-25 shooting overall and 10-for-12 shooting from the free throw line. He played 61 minutes without a turnover.

Buckner had great all-around skills, from scoring to leadership, from three-point shooting to clutch decision-making. Even though the Tigers have five experienced seniors returning this year, Buckner's presence won't be easily replaced.

"He has been a great leader for us the last four years," Shyatt said. "He had to be a starter and a leader for us from day one his freshman year. That is difficult to replace, but we have some talented players returning who are anxious to contribute in his absence."

Most likely, Shyatt will turn to Terrell McIntyre to take Buckner's place as a scorer and team leader.

IKER ITURBE (6-7, 235 lbs., PF, 5.8 ppg, 2.6 rpg, 1.7 apg, 1.4 tpg, 17.3 minutes, .471 FG, .308 3PT, .653 FT). Iturbe could have returned for his fifth year of eligibility, since he received a medical redshirt two years ago because of a blood clot problem in his shoulder. But he wanted to get on with his professional career in Spain, so he announced in the spring that he would not return.

Iturbe started most of the games in his last three seasons. He didn't have any real flashy skills, being primarily a perimeter player with a post player's body. Sometimes he even would play the unusual point-forward position, running the team's offense with crisp passes and smart plays, but it wasn't often.

The main loss with Iturbe is the leadership he would have provided. But, with a five-member senior class, that experienced leadership is not something the Tigers lack

OTHERS NOT RETURNING

None.

PROJECTED STARTERS

TERRELL MCINTYRE (5-9, 175 lbs., SR, PG, #5, 13.9 ppg, 3.4 rpg, 5.3 apg, 2.3 tpg, 2.0 spg, 32.4 minutes, .427 FG, .361 3PT, .779 FT, Hoke County HS/Raeford, N.C.). The biggest second-guess most ACC observers made of Barnes last year was his decision not to bite the bullet and hold McIntyre out until he was completely recovered from a December foot injury.

McIntyre missed only three games because of the injury, but he persisted in coming back early. Too early, it seemed. McIntyre wasn't practicing with the team, but, beginning in the Jan. 3 game against North Carolina, he tried to play against ACC competition.

The Tigers went 2-7 during a McIntyre-hampered stretch. Could it have been worse without the feisty point guard? Probably not. Had he taken the time to get completely healthy, McIntyre might have been able to better run the team down the stretch.

There is no question McIntyre is the high-octane fuel that makes the Tigers run without knocks and pings. He was still healthy in the Tigers' December ACC opener against Maryland, scoring 21 points with nine rebounds, nine assists and four steals. He tried to help the team just as much while injured, but he was both an offensive and defensive liability.

When he returned to full strength at the very end of the year, McIntyre was his old self. In the regular-season finale, when Clemson was essentially playing Georgia Tech for one of the ACC's NCAA Tournament bids, McIntyre scored 12 points, had seven rebounds, six assists and seven steals.

McIntyre has averaged more than 31 minutes per game his entire career at Clemson. Shyatt hopes to relieve him a little more this year, while still counting on the tiny point guard to provide more scoring and more vocal leadership on the floor.

"Without Greg Buckner, we will ask a little bit of everything from Terrell," Shyatt said. "Last year his injuries showed us the importance of depth. I would like to think we can give him the rest he deserves this year, and that will be important over the long season."

HAROLD JAMISON (6-8, 260 lbs., SR, PF, #32, 9.8 ppg, 7.3 rpg, 24.8 minutes, .592 FG, .481 FT, Holly Hill HS/Vance, S.C.). Everyone keeps waiting for this sculpted specimen to break loose and become a superstar. Time is running out.

1997-98 RESULTS

North Carolina-Wilmington	67-50	
#Iona	79-49	
#Southwest Missouri State	71-67	
#Gonzaga (L)	71-84	
##Kentucky (L)	61-76	
Maryland	78-65	ot
Furman	71-62	
*Illinois (L)	61-71	
South Carolina	62-57	
###Seton Hall	62-59	
Charleston Southern	65-42	
South Carolina State	84-60	
@Western Kentucky	71-52	
North Carolina (L)	70-73	
@Wake Forest (L)	66-70	
Florida State	86-65	
@Duke (L)	80-81	
Virginia	69-52	
@Maryland (L)	69-74	
@North Carolina (L)	79-88	
North Carolina State (L)	80-82	ot
@Georgia Tech (L)	52-70	
Wake Forest	71-46	
Western Carolina	102-67	
@Florida State	78-49	
Duke (L)	66-70	
@Virginia (L)	74-78	ot
@North Carolina State	77-72	
Georgia Tech	76-62	
####Wake Forest	75-56	
####Duke (L)	64-66	
%Western Michigan (L)	72-75	

@ away games
* United Center, Chicago, IL
# Top of the World Shootout, Fairbanks, AK
Premier Classic, Phoenix, AZ
Jimmy V Classic, East Rutherford, NJ
ACC Tournament, Greensboro Coliseum, Greensboro, NC
% NCAA Midwest Sub-Regional, Chicago, IL

Jamison has put up decent numbers for three years as a spot-starting forward, becoming the first Tiger player to ever lead the team in field goal percentage and rebounding for three consecutive seasons. Last year, he averaged more offensive rebounds (3.94) than any player in the ACC.

Jamison was particularly effective down the stretch, when the Tigers needed his scoring and rebounding to get back on the right track for postseason play. He scored 17 points each against Duke and N.C. State, and average more than 8.7 rpg in the team's last seven games.

Shyatt knows Jamison still hasn't consistently lived up to the potential he showed at times in his career, especially in scoring.

"The sand has just about out of the bottle for Harold," Shyatt said. "He has improved every year, but we want him to be the scoring force on the inside like we all know he can."

All you have to do is look at Jamison to know he is a great athlete. He was a highly recruited football player out of high school. Shyatt hopes to take better advantage of those athletic skills.

"He might be the best big man in the country when it comes to running the floor," the coach said. "He's in great shape, and this is a way he can create mismatches."

Jamison has good skills driving to the basket and is particularly adept at getting fouled, which is pretty bad news for Clemson. Jamison's free-throw shooting went from unacceptable as a sophomore to abysmal as a junior. He obviously needs to improve that area, since he was one of nine players in the ACC to get at least 150 free throw attempts last year.

TONY CHRISTIE (6-6, 220, SR, SF, #44, 8.0 ppg, 1.8 rpg, 1.4 apg, 1.3 tpg 22.2 minutes, .444 FG, .415 3PT, .454 FT, St. John's Prospect Hall/Hartford, Conn.). Less than 36 hours after Shyatt was introduced as Barnes' replacement, Christie announced he would stay at the school. "I hope I did some listening to him in the last three days," Shyatt said.

Christie, a talented forward who revealed stunning flashes of brilliance—then often disappeared—had a long list of things to discuss with the new coach. He had been planning to transfer elsewhere for his senior season, because he could no longer get along with the sometimes abusive treatment he felt he received from Barnes.

The coach pushed Christie to get better, especially when it came to his inside penetration, but sometimes that meant kicking him out of practice. Christie wanted to be bigger part of the team's offense. He will likely get his chance this year with Buckner's departure.

"Tony is coming off a tremendous season from three-point range," Shyatt said. "We would like to have him expand his game and score inside, which will help his outside game. He is capable of driving to the hoop and scoring effectively."

Christie, who started 25 games at small forward last year, was the team's best three-point shooter, hitting 54 of his 130 attempts (which ranked No. 4 overall in the ACC). But his offensive game wasn't well-rounded. He scored only 35 baskets inside the arc, contributed less than two rebounds per game and was one of three Tiger players to hit fewer than half his free throws.

Those numbers have to be better for him to be a productive small forward in the ACC.

TOM WIDEMAN (6-10, 250 lbs., SR, C, #33, 4.4 ppg, 4.8 rpg, 19.0 minutes, .533 FG, .433 FT, Walton HS/ Marietta, Ga.). Entering his fourth season as a starter, Wideman still hasn't become the scoring threat Barnes was hoping for three years ago. One of the most aptly named players in ACC history, Wideman takes up a lot of space in the lane and is therefore a great post defender. Some coaches rate him among the best defenders in the league.

But, for three years, Wideman has offered only rebounding and defense, with little or no threat of scoring. For the second year in a row, Wideman finished the season with more rebounds (154) than points (140). That's probably why he's gone from starting 29 games as a freshman to 21 games as a sophomore and 24 as a junior.

Wideman's scoring has never improved since he averaged 5.8 ppg his freshman season. He is an accurate shooter and would be in the top five in field goal percentage in the league if he would take enough shots to qualify.

Wideman was so reluctant to score, he couldn't even make that open 15-footer basketball insiders like to call the "free throw." He, like Jamison, had a higher field goal percentage than free throw mark. His 43 percent shooting from the line was easily the worst of any player in the ACC who started more than 10 games.

Wideman is an intelligent student who has never missed making the dean's list and will likely be an academic All-America. But he commits too many fouls in Clemson's rough-and-tumble style, many of them not of the smartest nature. He fouled out seven times last year, the most of any returning player in the league.

Shyatt loves Wideman's post defense and his offensive rebounding, but it is clear that the senior needs to offer more offensively and improve at the foul line if he is going to help push the Tigers into the ACC's upper division.

VINCENT WHITT (6-6, 185 lbs., JR, SG, #22, 5.5 ppg, 2.8 rpg, 1.2 apg, 1.7 tpg, 18.7 minutes, .400 FG, .077 3PT, .652 FT, Dudley HS/Greensboro, N.C.). Whitt is the most logical successor to Buckner's slashing, scoring role on the perimeter. He is a 6-6 scorer who has averaged barely five points in his first two years on campus and will have to contribute much more than that this year if the Tigers are to be successful.

"Vince is one of our quickest players," Shyatt said. "Because quickness is one of our biggest weaknesses, he is very valuable to us. If there is anyone who can be a team catalyst or the team spark, it can be Vincent Whitt. I say this in the intensity category, without putting any scoring pressure on him."

Whitt was excellent for the first half of his freshman season, filling in for the injured Tony Christie. Those first 19 games seemed to show that the praise he received coming out of high school was justified.

But Whitt unraveled from February to the end of that season, and his playing time was cut nearly in half. His final numbers were disappointing, even though he was named to the league's All-Freshman team.

Last year, Whitt again had his best games in the first half of the season. He had only one double-digit scoring effort in the team's last 15 games, and he played more than 21 minutes only once in that span.

This year, Shyatt needs Whitt to score more often. After all, the Tigers are 11-1 in Whitt's career when he hit double figures in scoring.

KEY RESERVES

JOHNNY MILLER (6-0, 180 lbs., SR, G, #4, 4.3 ppg, 0.9 rpg, 1.7 apg, 1.2 tpg, 15.7 minutes, .298 FG, .284 3PT, .667 FT, Solanco HS/Christiana, Pa.). Fewer players who are described as "shooters" have had a worse season trying to make baskets than Miller did last year, unless it was Vincent Whitt or Andrius Jukunas the year before.

Still, Miller made the biggest shot of the Tigers' season when he drained a three-pointer in the final seconds of the victory at N.C. State, a wide-open jumper that the Wolfpack never bothered to defend because Miller had been in such a horrendous shooting slump.

Miller arrived at Clemson two years ago after transferring from Temple, where he spent two productive seasons as a scorer, but not necessarily a shooter, for the Owls. He set a school and conference record with 73 three-pointers by a freshman.

Even though he was one of the premier high school guards in the country when he initially went to Temple, Miller has never been an accurate shooter. As a freshman he hit only 34 percent of his field goals, 30 percent of his three-pointers and 48 percent of his free throws.

As a sophomore, his field goal percentage and three-point percentage went down by at least five percentage points each. That's about the time shoulder problems and a personality conflict with Temple coach John Chaney sent Miller looking for another school.

However, in his first year of eligibility with the Tigers, lingering knee problems kept Miller from being an impact player. After sitting out an entire season as a transfer, Miller had three knee surgeries in 10 months—including the removal of a cyst the size of a baseball from behind his knee.

"Johnny has had to face a lot of obstacles over the last couple of years," Shyatt said. "It has made him tougher and more mature. If healthy, he can give us a great scoring punch and quickness defensively."

However, Clemson is perpetuating a long myth if it continues to cast Miller as a great shooter who was merely hampered by a knee injury. Miller has never proven he could be an accurate shooter from beyond the arc. A frequent shooter, yes. An accurate shooter, no.

But the Tigers desperately need some outside scoring, and Miller will get plenty of opportunities to establish himself as a deep threat.

MOHAMED WONI (6-9, 235 lbs., JR, C, #34, 3.7 ppg, 2.8 rpg, 15.2 minutes, .523 FG, .658 FT, St. John's Prospect Hall/Ivory Coast, Africa). In his first two years, Woni languished on the Clemson bench for most of the regular season, then stepped in late in the season and shown some flash of potential. He did it as a freshman against Minnesota in the NCAA Tournament, when he had his only career double-double, and again last year against Western Michigan in the Tigers' only NCAA Tournament game.

He ended the 1997-98 season on a good shooting streak, hitting 19 of his last 28 shots. He scored at least eight points in four of his last nine games.

But Woni is a lot like Wideman and Jamison. He is reluctant to shoot and can be too aggressive inside. He has added nearly 20 pounds since he arrived on campus, so he is better able to bang in Clemson's aggressive system. But he hasn't improved his skills enough to make a consistent contribution.

At least Woni can hit free throws at a better rate than Jamison and Wideman, though he seems to have picked up some bad habits from his teammates. Woni made 95 percent of his free throws as a freshman and just 66 percent as a sophomore.

Shyatt expects Woni to play more this season, especially if he can hit the intermediate jump shot.

ANDRIUS JURKUNAS (6-9, 230 lbs., JR, F, #3, 2.4 ppg, 1.7 rpg, 10.7 minutes, .276 FG, .079 3PT, .630 FT in 1996-97, St. John's Prospect Hall/Kaunas, Lithuania). Jurkunas has been hurt so often during his career at Clemson that the school should replace the little swooshes on his sneakers with little red crosses. He sat out all of last year as a medical redshirt because of a knee injury. That came after a foot and knee injury that ruined his sophomore season and deflated his confidence.

Jurkunas started nearly all of the Tigers' games as a freshman, showing versatility that few perimeter players in the ACC had. He not only led the team with 51 three-pointers, a freshman record at Clemson, he also led the team with 34 blocked shots.

He averaged more than eight points per game overall and did all the little things that were expected of him. But, as a sophomore, Jurkunas' confidence was totally shot after he suffered an ankle and knee injury in December. He made only 27 percent of his field goal attempts and was a pitiful 3-for-38 from three-point range.

Taking last season off was probably a good idea for the native Lithuanian. It allowed him to finally heal completely and to regain some of that spent mental energy.

1998-99 CLEMSON SCHEDULE

Nov.	13	Arkansas Pine Bluff
	16	Stetson
	19	Western Carolina
	23-25	#Maui Classic
	30	Radford
Dec.	3	East Tennessee State
	12	North Carolina-Asheville
	16	@South Carolina
	21	South Carolina State
	26	*Furman
	29	**Illinois
Jan.	2	@North Carolina
	5	North Carolina State
	9	Wake Forest
	12	@Florida State
	17	@Virginia
	20	Duke
	24	Maryland
	28	@Georgia Tech
Feb.	4	North Carolina
	6	@North Carolina State
	10	@Wake Forest
	14	Florida State
	17	Virginia
	20	@Duke
	24	@Maryland
	28	Georgia Tech
Mar.	4-7	##ACC Tournament

@ Road Games
* BI-LO Center, Greenville, SC
** BI-LO Center, Greenville, SC
# Maui, HI (vs. Michigan, first round; also Arizona State, Chaminade, Indiana, Kansas State, Syracuse and Utah)
Charlotte Coliseum, Charlotte, NC

If he returns to his freshman shooting form, he will be a big asset. The Tigers need outside shooting.

"Andrius could be a wild card on this team," Shyatt said. "We need to take advantage of his ability to shoot from the outside at 6-9. I am excited to see a healthy Andrius Jurkunas, because he is capable of helping us in so many areas."

But only if he has the confidence to do so.

ADAM ALLENSPACH (7-1, 245 lbs., SO, C, #55, 2.1 ppg, 1.2 rpg, 8.9 minutes, .436 FG, .692 FT, Monroe HS/ Parkland, Fla.). Allenspach is only the second seven-footer to ever play at Clemson. Wayne "Tree" Rollins was the other, and that was nearly a quarter-century ago.

Allenspach played sparingly as the only active freshman on the roster last year, needing more strength and stamina to make himself useful in Clemson's rugged inside game. But he showed some flashed of productivity, starting the final nine games of the regular season and leading the team with 19 blocked shots.

"I was surprised to see that he averaged only about nine minutes (per) game last year," Shyatt said. "He is still maturing physically, but I am excited about his future."

Allenspach wasn't supposed to play at Clemson. He signed a national letter of intent with Boston College after his all-star high school career in Florida. But because of a feud between then-coach Jim O'Brien and the school's administration, that letter was never submitted and Allenspach backed off his commitment.

O'Brien wanted the player to go with him to Ohio State when took the head coaching job there, but, by then, Allenspach had already decided on Clemson, his second choice.

WILL SOLOMON (6-2, 175 lbs., FR, G, #15, 26.4 ppg, 4.0 rpg, 5.0 apg, East Hartford HS/East Hartford, Conn.). Even Shyatt doesn't know what kind of game Solomon really has. The coach has never seen the point guard play, nor did he ever meet with him face-to-face in recruiting.

Solomon was recruited by Barnes, but he had not made up his mind by the time the coach left for Texas. Because of NCAA rules, Shyatt couldn't visit Solomon in Connecticut after he became head coach.

Shyatt talked to Solomon on the phone before he arrived on campus this fall, but he essentially had to take his future point guard sight unseen. This was a first for Shyatt, as far as American-born players were concerned.

"I have signed some international players in the past without a face-to-face meeting, but it is unusual," Shyatt said.

Solomon is an important recruit, since this will be McIntyre's final year of eligibility. He has to learn to run the Clemson offense so he will be ready to inherit that position next year.

OTHER RETURNEES

None.

OTHER NEWCOMERS

DUSTIN BRADDICK (6-5, 200 lbs., FR, G, #24, 15.6 ppg, 7.8 rpg, 3.4 apg, North Charleston HS/Charleston, S.C.). Braddick is the biggest enigma of the Tigers' recruiting class. He is a wing player who was All-State for consecutive seasons at North Charleston High, leading his team to a 25-4 record as a senior.

But Braddick, who signed in the spring with Barnes, was not considered a blue-chip prospect in recruiting circles. Barnes recruited Braddick to add some punch to Clemson's limp outside scoring. Whether the 6-5 wing player can do that is still up for debate and probably won't really be known until Shyatt has a chance to watch him in the fall.

For now, Shyatt sees Braddick as a versatile player in the mold of Buckner and Iturbe. That may change when he gets to know him a little better.

CHUCKIE GILMORE (6-8, 275 lbs., FR, F, #42, 18.9 ppg, 10.8 rpg, 2.5 bpg, 71st HS/Fayetteville, N.C.). Gilmore is a power forward who will be expected to learn from playing with and behind Jamison and Wideman. He is not untalented, but he probably won't contribute much this year.

Gilmore helped his high school team compile a 28-1 record last year, so he knows how to handle success. And he is no stranger to the Tigers' new head coach.

Shyatt actually began recruiting Gilmore two years ago when he was still a Clemson assistant, so he has fairly intimate knowledge of the player's assets and weaknesses. And he doesn't want to pigeon-hole Gilmore as simply a power forward, even though that seems to be the perfect position for him.

"His size is what makes him spectacular," Shyatt told the *Winston-Salem Journal*. "He was always such a strong, dominating, power kind of player when I saw him play.

"I don't think it would be fair right now to make a characterization about his position. Versatility is probably one of the best commodities in basketball, so the more he can play other positions, the greater possibility of him being on the floor."

QUESTIONS

Outside shooting? Between Miller, Jukunas and Whitt—three of the Tigers' primary threats from the perimeter—they made 34 of 165 three-point shots in their last season of play, which was 1996-97 for the redshirted Jurkunas. That's an embarrassing 20.6 percent. Only McIntyre and Christie have shown they can consistently make the long shots. The Tigers need more.

Team speed? Even with the quick-footed McIntyre running the show, the Tigers are woefully lacking the athletic ability to get up and down the floor in fastbreak situations. Shyatt hopes Whitt can inject some speed into the Tigers' plodding halfcourt system.

Free throw shooting? Want to know a big reason why the Tigers were 1-6 in games decided by five points or less. They couldn't buy a free throw. The Tigers were horrible from the line, with three starters making less than half their free throws. The team shot a league-low 61 percent for the season.

ANSWERS

Experience! With four senior starters, all of whom have three years of post-season play, the Tigers know what it takes to win big games and have the leadership to carry it through. They lived through a disappointing junior season and are ready to redeem themselves in their final year.

McIntyre! The plucky little point guard is, when healthy, one of the most exciting players in the conference. He is poised to have a big senior season.

Depth! Along with those four seniors, Shyatt can mix in more than a half-dozen other players into his regular rotation. The Tigers are still going to be a physical team, so those bodies will be needed.

adidas Blue Ribbon Analysis

BACKCOURT .... B **BENCH/DEPTH** .... B+
FRONTCOURT .... B **INTANGIBLES** .... B

Barnes is gone, but he leaves the legacy of re-energizing a school that had never really cared much about basketball. He catered to the football mindset, serving as the roving parking lot reporter for the football tailgate show.

He was a showman who came in and made immediate noise with his confrontations with North Carolina legend Dean Smith. That got Barnes and his team noticed. But, when he finally realized he wasn't going to consistently be among the best programs in the conference, Barnes decided it was time to pack up and leave for a greener chaparral.

He left a solid nucleus for Shyatt to be successful in his first season as the Tigers' head coach. Clemson doesn't have Greg Buckner as its "go-to" guy anymore, but a healthy McIntyre should help offset Buckner's departure.

Don't be surprised if the Tigers are very successful in Shyatt's first year. There were strained relations between Barnes and some of his players last year, particularly because of the coach's strict rules and rugged practices.

Out from under the floodlights, the Tigers' experienced nucleus could shine—maybe enough to get into the ACC's top three. The most important thing to watch for in Shyatt's first year is how the Tigers play at the end of the season. Last year, the Tigers faded in January, February and March.

Will Shyatt's more easy-going style prevent that from happening when it counts?

(T.P.)

37

ST. JOHN'S

LOCATION .... **Jamaica, NY**
CONFERENCE .... **Big East**
LAST SEASON .... **22-10 (.688)**
CONFERENCE RECORD .... **13-5 (2nd, Big East 6)**
STARTERS LOST/RETURNING **2/3**
NICKNAME .... **Red Storm**
COLORS .... **Red & White**
HOMECOURTS .... **Alumni Hall (6,008)**
.... **Madison Square Garden (18,876)**
COACH .... **Mike Jarvis (Northeastern '68)**
RECORD AT SCHOOL .... **first year**
CAREER RECORD .... **253-141 (13 yrs.)**
ASSISTANTS **Mike Jarvis II (Boston University '86)**
Kevin Clark (Clark '81)
TBA
TEAM WINS (last 5 yrs.) **12-14-11-13-22**
RPI (last 5 yrs.) **111-89-107-83-32**
1997-98 FINISH .... **Lost in NCAA first round.**

COACH AND PROGRAM

Nobody expected to be devoting this off-season to figuring out whether Mike Jarvis is a good fit at St. John's.

When a team wins nine more games than it had the previous season and doubles its output from two years prior, most people are generally talking about contract extensions and all that good stuff. Nobody is thinking about forced resignations and soap-opera style happenings.

Add in an NCAA Tournament appearance, albeit a losing one, and most coaches (especially in New York City) would probably spend the summer fighting to pay for a drink.

Well, welcome to St. John's, where Fran Fraschilla is out after turning the program around in two years, and Jarvis is in, after enhancing George Washington's national profile during his eight years in D.C.

Now nobody may ever know whether Fraschilla yelled too loudly (and profanely) at his players. Or whether he actually did moon one of them during a practice. And we can't be sure that he really did want that Arizona State coaching job.

All we know is that St. John's A.D. Ed Manetta wanted Fraschilla out, even if that meant eating the remainder of the coach's contract. This is in addition to paying Jarvis upward of (gulp!) $750,000 per year for seven seasons.

But Manetta seemed enthusiastic about the circumstances, and went so far as to declare himself "ecstatic" at the press conference announcing Jarvis' hiring. And why shouldn't he be? The money isn't coming out of his checkbook.

Jarvis comes to St. John's with something of a difficult mission. He must keep New York's top program moving toward the upper reaches of college basketball, and he may have to do it differently than he has done things before. His United Nations approach, which often led to rosters of players from as many as nine different countries, may not play well in Jamaica (Jamaica, N.Y., that is). Jarvis needs to convince the top New York City kids to stay home and help make new glory days at St. John's.

As one columnist put it while appealing to Jarvis to hire a New Yorker as one of his assistants—something he hadn't done as of late September, although his third staff slot was still open—the new coach needs to find "someone who can tell the difference between the Bronx and Belarus."

Okay, maybe that was a bit of a cheap shot, but the fact remains that Jarvis has become more known lately for assembling rosters which would be best served by calling plays in *Esperanto* than somebody who has participated in mainstream recruiting circles. Jarvis, a man who has never wanted for confidence—at least outwardly—doesn't worry too much about that or the challenge of taking on a program that has a rich basketball tradition.

"It's a chance to have worked in three of the best cities in the country," says Jarvis, who has also worked in Boston and, of course, Washington, D.C. "How many people can say they did that?"

Not many, indeed. But nobody will care whether Jarvis has his hoops passport stamped in three Northeast media centers or a trio of hick towns if the Johnnies don't win. And that's what raises the question of the day: Did St. John's upgrade its coaching position by hiring Jarvis?

There are many who believe it did. Jarvis is a nationally-known coach, a well-respected member and spokesman in the Black Coaches Association, and somebody who has a Sweet 16 appearance along with four other NCAA tourney invitations to his credit. He took a program, George Washington, that was wallowing and made it into a power in one of the nation's rising conferences.

Jarvis compiled a 152-90 record at GW, despite laboring in the considerable shadow of D.C. rival Georgetown—which barely admitted the existence of the Colonial program, despite the BCA ties between Jarvis and Hoya coach John Thompson. Jarvis brings a strong track record to Jamaica. He has a recognizable name and face, thanks in part to a clean dome which is always polished to a high sheen.

There are plenty of reasons why this is a good hire, and also why it was a good move for Jarvis. He comes to a conference with a higher profile than his previous home, even if the Atlantic 10 and Big East are converging every minute. He'll have a bigger budget. He'll play more on TV. He'll even get to toss it up in Madison Square Garden, the world's most famous arena.

"I spent eight of the best years of my life in Washington," Jarvis says. "If you're going to make a change, it's best to be in control of that change, do it for totally positive reasons and do it with the idea of making things better.

"In that vein, I accept the challenge of New York and St. John's. The Atlantic 10 is a great conference with great coaches. And though things were going so well for me at George Washington, that's the time to make a move. When you leave a place, you want to have a going-away party.

"This is my third change. The first was when I went from Cambridge (Rindge and Latin HS) to Boston University. Then, I went from Boston University to George Washington. Now, I'm going from GW to St. John's. I've had three going-away parties."

But do all the St. John's fans want to welcome Jarvis to town with a soiree? The new coach certainly accomplished plenty at GW, but many think he could have done more. His teams always seemed to be stronger early in the year than at the end. His 1993 trip to the Sweet 16 was as much a product of Georgia Tech's first-round belly-flop against Southern as any great performance by the Colonials.

Jarvis is also worthy of criticism about the play of Alexander Koul, who went from sure-fire NBA lottery pick after his sophomore year to an undrafted plodder destined for life in the Euroleagues. And then there is Jarvis' behavior.

Forget about the times he has ducked out after games without talking to media, instances which violated league policy, or refused to shake hands with his opposite number (even after a win). Let's focus on one incident, which, if it had been dealt with properly, would have resulted in a suspension or censure. It happened in the semifinals of the 1997 Atlantic 10 tourney and has been well-chronicled in these pages.

But the tantrum thrown by Jarvis that night was an all-timer which bears repeating. In response to what he considered unfair treatment of Koul by game officials, Jarvis stole and hid the game ball, berated the officials profanely, and ripped off his coat and offered it to the refs while saying, "You've taken everything else, why not take my clothes??"

Charming. If Fraschilla was canned in part because of his behavior behind closed doors, just imagine what that outburst would have forced the St. John's administration to do.

Finally, there are Jarvis' thinly-hidden professional coaching aspirations. Even though he says he is thrilled to be at St. John's, few doubt that the right NBA opportunity would cause him to pack his bags quickly—with or without a going-away party.

So, St. John's definitely gets a coach with a high profile. It gets somebody with a track record. Whether it got the man capable of continuing the work Fraschilla began is anybody's guess.

"What we have to do is win," Jarvis says. "We want to do it in a first-class manner. There are many people in this city who love St. John's, and we want to make sure we do things the right way."

This year, that will mean fielding a team with no true center, most likely a freshman point guard (Erick Barkley), a junior college transfer (Marvis Thornton) replacing one of the school's all-time leading scorers and a sophomore (Ron Artest) who must now become a star, whether he's ready or not. The frontcourt is thin. The collective shooting seems suspect.

Yes, Barkley could join Artest in stardom. Yes, 6-6 freshman Anthony Glover, a Top 30 player, could be declared eligible by the NCAA Clearinghouse (he is enrolled at St. John's this fall) and give St. John's a big boost.

Maybe Fraschilla would have taken a step back with this bunch. Then again, we'll never know. As for Jarvis, he had better get up to speed quickly. They don't want to rebuild again at St. John's.

STARTERS NOT RETURNING

FELIPE LOPEZ (6-6, SF, 17.6 ppg, 4.8 rpg, 2.7 apg, 2.3 tpg, 1.2 spg, 34.6 minutes, .431 FG, .337 3PT, .573 FT). America is a wonderful place. No matter how dark things may seem at times, there is always a shot at redemption. And so it was with Lopez, who began his journey at St. John's expected to be the greatest player in Big East history—if he stayed around that long—and ended it four years later as a first-team All-League choice, a first-round NBA draft selection and a case study in how damaging hype can be.

Lopez was never the savior he was billed as (unfairly) as out of New York City's Rice HS. Instead, he was a gifted player with many rough edges around his game. Lopez didn't shoot the ball well, at first. He didn't work well in halfcourt situations. He didn't pass well. And, though fellow Dominicans loved him nonetheless, many Red Storm fans ridiculed him.

By the time Lopez's senior season dawned, there were those who wondered whether the man once thought to be the Caribbean Michael Jordan would even be an NBA player. But Lopez worked harder than most collegians and concluded his career at St. John's with a flourish.

Lopez finished with 1,927 points, good for third on the school's all-time scoring list—behind Chris Mullin and Malik Sealy—and set school records for three-pointers made in a season and a career. He was drafted 24th overall by San Antonio and shipped to Vancouver on draft day as part of the deal for point man Antonio Daniels.

Although Lopez was no dead-eye marksman, he did improve his outside shooting. And he had some big games last year, including a pair of 27-point performances (against American University of Puerto Rico and Providence). Lopez may never have reached the ridiculous expectations which trailed him when he enrolled at St. John's, but he certainly concluded his career with much to be proud of.

ZENDON HAMILTON (6-11, C, 15.4 ppg, 8.7 rpg, 2.8 tpg, 1.0 bpg, 32.4 minutes, .472 FG, .654 FT). If there was ever a walking, breathing example of how misleading numbers can be, Hamilton is it. He did boast some impressive stats during his career and finished his four years as the school's fifth all-time scorer and fourth rebounder, but the best indication of his "me-first" attitude came on NBA draft day, when the 6-11 pivot went undrafted by a league still dying for big men.

Hamilton scored. He rebounded. But he rarely passed. And he wasn't the most enthusiastic defender, either. Despite posting eight 20-point efforts last year, Hamilton was concerned more with his numbers than the team, a fact evidenced by his 11 assists (total). His blocked shot total did swell, slightly, to 30 for the year, but that is chump change.

An athletic 6-11 player like him should have had triple that. But that's the story of Hamilton's career. He could have been big-time, had he only looked beyond his line on the score sheet.

1997-98 RESULTS

Lafayette	72-49	
St. Francis-NY	83-73	
#American University-Puerto Rico	93-81	
#Georgia Tech (L)	65-77	
#Illinois	83-66	
Syracuse (L)	73-80	
@West Virginia (L)	70-86	
Colgate	69-53	
@Manhattan	84-60	
DePaul	74-70	2ot
##Niagara (L)	63-86	
##Drexel	75-46	
@Notre Dame	79-69	
Seton Hall (L)	59-61	
@Louisville (L)	67-73	
@Georgetown	66-60	
Miami	73-64	
@Providence	63-56	
Connecticut	64-62	
@Pittsburgh	90-83	2ot
Villanova	82-59	
Rutgers	76-58	
Notre Dame (L)	65-73	
@Boston College	91-79	
West Virginia	77-69	
@Seton Hall	64-60	
Boston College	66-61	
@Syracuse	67-65	
@Connecticut (L)	58-87	
###Boston College	91-80	
###Syracuse (L)	67-69	ot
%Detroit (L)	64-66	

@ away games
# Puerto Rico Holiday Classic, San Juan, PR
Chase ECAC Holiday Festival, Madison Square Garden, NY
Big East Tournament, Madison Square Garden, NY
% NCAA Midwest Sub-Regional, Chicago, IL

OTHERS NOT RETURNING

TARIK TURNER (6-5, G, 3.4 ppg, 1.9 rpg, 2.5 apg, 1.7 tpg, 19.1 minutes, .407 FG, .310 3PT, .714 FT). Turner never blossomed into the full-time star point guard that was expected when he joined Lopez and Hamilton on the St. John's campus back in the fall of 94.

That's not to say Turner wasn't an important part of last year's team. He was. He started 17 games, was a solid distributor and a strong defender. But Turner's problem was his outside shot. That and his relative lack of quickness—when compared to other point men—hurt him.

Perhaps lower expectations at the start of his career might have helped Turner, since he never became more than a solid complementary player.

JAMES FELTON (6-9, F, 2.2 ppg, 3.3 rpg, 14.0 minutes, .333 FG, .250 FT). Another member of last year's class, Felton was dismissed after only six games last fall for a violation of team policy. He surfaced for a while at Florida State, but left there. His future is sketchy for now.

Felton could have played a huge role on last year's team, particularly since the Johnnies lacked depth in the frontcourt. But his misbehavior cost him a chance to stand out. An athletic player who can run the floor, it would have taken Felton some time to develop his offensive game, but he could have helped out on the backboards and by blocking shots.

SHANNON CROOKS (6-2, G, 1.9 ppg, 1.3 rpg, 1.0 apg, 1.1 tpg, 8.7 minutes, .327 FG, .458 FT). Crooks was part of the heralded 1997 recruiting class, but a lack of playing time didn't sit too well with him. He transferred to Massachusetts after only one year.

Crooks played in 23 of the Red Storm's 32 games, but he was not given too much extended playing time, perhaps a by-product of his wayward shooting. Tough, physical, yet quick, Crooks was supposed to give the St. John's backcourt some needed depth. That could have happened this year, but the arrivals of Erick Barkley and Marvis Thornton no doubt showed Crooks that more minutes were not guaranteed.

GEOVANNI SOTO (6-6, F, 1.3 ppg, 0.3 rpg, three appearances). A little-used walkon, Soto played a total of three minutes last year but had perfect statistics. He made his only shot from the field and was a perfect 2-for-2 from the free throw line.

PROJECTED STARTERS

LAVOR POSTELL (6-6, 210 lbs., JR, SF, #25, 9.9 ppg, 5.1 rpg, 1.6 apg, 1.6 tpg, 1.0 spg, 29.1 minutes, .452 FG, .333 3PT, .826 FT, Westover HS/Albany, Ga.). Postell may be the Big East's most underrated player.

Even though he will no doubt spend this year in Ron Artest's shadow, after laboring his first two in the shade cast by Lopez and Hamilton, Postell is an extremely valuable contributor who can do a little bit of everything. He will have the chance to show more this season.

Likely to be the Johnnies' starting small forward, unless Jarvis has to play him at guard, Postell is strong off the wing and along the baseline and improved his shooting considerably from his freshman to sophomore seasons. Another jump like that, and he could be scoring 15 per night.

But Postell's true value to the Red Storm won't necessarily be on offense. One of the Big East's hardest-working and most effective perimeter defenders, Postell can lock up the best wing men in the league and make their nights miserable. Jarvis will be able to use him on 6-2 guards, 6-9 forwards and everything in between. Talk about your luxuries.

Postell had a couple of big statistical nights in 1997-98, like his 21-point, eight-rebound showing at Notre Dame and his 17-point game against Miami. With Lopez and Hamilton gone, there will certainly be more points for Postell. And maybe that increased output will get him some more attention.

But, after two years of strong play, the question will be, "What took you so long to notice?"

RON ARTEST (6-6, 233 lbs., SO, PF, #15, 11.6 ppg, 6.3 rpg, 2.0 apg, 2.9 tpg, 1.6 spg, 1.1 bpg, 27.2 minutes, .415 FG, .327 3PT, .526 FT, La Salle Academy/Queensbridge, N.Y.). It may not seem fair to make a sophomore the focal point of a team, but in a sport where freshmen excel and often lead teams to championships, it is possible to argue that Artest is a year late in his ascension. That's a sarcastic comment, of course, since he was right to defer to Lopez and Hamilton last season. But, with no upperclassmen capable of leading the way, Artest must step to the forefront.

He certainly has the talent to do so. A rare physical specimen who goes 233 pounds but can still operate smoothly on the perimeter, Artest is likely to be St. John's starting power forward. On a team with limited height and bulk, that designation is more out of necessity.

He'll play all over the place, a fact evidenced by his 104 three-point attempts last year (second-most on the team). Artest started only 12 games last season, but he demonstrated the ability to score and enough backboard strength to finish third on the team in rebounding.

Artest had 24 points against American University of Puerto Rico in only his third game at St. John's. But his biggest explosion was a 26-point, 13-rebound effort against Boston College. He topped the 20-point mark one other time, against Villanova (21). Artest got better down the stretch, when he showed he had the ability to dominate some day.

Artest does have rare inside-outside skills, but they need polish. His shooting percentage was weak last year, and he was awful (52.6 percent) from the foul line. Artest proved he could create opportunities for others, but his good assist work was often overshadowed by turnovers. He led the team with 92.

It would be wrong to expect Artest to score 20 a night and pull down 10 boards each time out, but there will be nights when he does that—and more. There will also be games in which he struggles. Artest is, after all, a sophomore.

But he is a good one. How much he is able to do will go a long way toward determining whether St. John's is a factor in the Big East, or merely a member of the pack.

TYRONE GRANT (6-7, 245 lbs., SR, PF, #32, 6.8 ppg, 6.9 rpg, 1.3 tpg, 21.3 minutes, .513 FG, .663 FT, Grady HS/Brooklyn, N.Y.). This could be an important year for Grant. With Hamilton gone and the Johnnies in need of some inside fortification, Grant could have a big year. That would be nice, because after a promising debut, this hard-working forward has slipped back somewhat in the past two years.

If Jarvis maintains his halfcourt style, Grant should have ample opportunity to use his solid, lively body down low. He has the ability to come close to a double-double average, even though his rebounds in that situation might outweigh his scoring output. Grant will never dazzle anyone with his offensive game, but he is a bear on the backboards and plays strong positional defense.

Even if Grant does get into double figures on the scoring sheet, his primary work will be in the rebounding department; he'll create most of his offensive opportunities off the backboards. He had 14 rebounds in a big performance against Syracuse in last year's Big East semifinal and had 12 boards in the NCAA loss to Detroit.

Grant may have to play the "five" spot this year, something that could bring foul problems, but he will be a productive, if undersized, pivot.

ERICK BARKLEY (6-1, 185 lbs., FR, PG, 26.0 ppg, 7.3 apg, 4.0 spg, Maine Central Institute/Queens, N.Y.). Part of a great, 35-0 MCI team that sent several players to the Division I ranks, including Villanova's Bobby Smith and Georgetown's Kevin Braswell, Barkley is the plum of this recruiting class and the man expected to step in and grab the starting point guard position.

A McDonald's All-America, Barkley defied the usual all-for-one, one-for-all MCI ethic by erupting for some impressive offensive numbers. But he also set up his teammates well, despite sharing the point responsibilities with Smith.

"He's obviously a great talent who knows how to play," Jarvis says about Barkley, who attracted recruiting attention up and down the Eastern seaboard. "He has won everywhere he has played, and is older and more mature than most freshmen."

Barkley has a good outside shot, works well in the open floor, can create big plays on defense and sets up his teammates well. What else is there? Now all he has to do is put it all together for a Big East contender with title aspirations. No problem, right? Expect Barkley to be given every opportunity to start at the point, but don't expect him to play 35 minutes.

That's the luxury of Charles, who should help make Barkley's initiation a little easier. Still, there is little doubt St. John's needs Barkley to step in and make a big impact his freshman year. Otherwise, it's "Hello, NIT."

MARVIS THORNTON (6-4, 195 lbs., JR, SG, 21.2 ppg, 6.0 apg, Tallahassee JC, Fla./Baltimore, Md.). A stone scorer who should step right into Lopez's shooting guard spot, "Bootsy" was a first-team NJCAA All-America who led Tallahassee JC to a 65-4 record during his two years there and broke former Syracuse starter Jason Cipolla's school scoring record with 1,291 points.

"Thornton is a scorer," Jarvis says. "If we can get him to play a little bit of defense, that will be to our advantage."

Jarvis may be jovial about Thornton's cavalier attitude toward defense now, but he won't tolerate lackadaisical play at that end once the season begins. Yes, St. John's needs his scoring, but Jarvis is unlikely to sacrifice defense for the offensive numbers.

KEY RESERVES

COLLIN CHARLES (5-11, 167 lbs., JR, G, #11, 3.9 ppg, 2.0 rpg, 3.0 apg, 2.0 tpg, 1.0 spg, 21.1 minutes, .389 FG, .341 3PT, .730 FT, Eastern Commerce HS/Toronto, Ont.). One would expect that in the natural scheme of things, Turner's departure would clear the way for Charles, who was a reliable part-time starter last year, to take over the point. That's not necessarily the case. The arrival of the heralded Erick Barkley could force Charles even further to the background.

Last year, he pretty much shared the position with Turner. This season he could be a full-fledged reserve, thanks to Barkley's myriad skills and toughness. That may not be the best thing for Charles, but it would certainly put the Johnnies in a good position.

Charles is a fine distributor whose 3-to-2 assist-to-turnover ratio would make most coaches smile (and was an improvement over his rookie year performance). Jet-quick, Charles is excellent in transition. But he must shoot better from the outside if he wants to mount a serious challenge for the starting job. His 38.9 percent field goal proficiency was not at all acceptable last year.

REGGIE JESSIE (6-7, 213 lbs., SO, G/F, #41, 2.0 ppg, 1.8 rpg, 10.2 minutes, .393 FG, .263 3PT, .444 FT, Bishop Loughlin HS/Queensbridge, N.Y.). Jessie should see increased time this year, but he needs to improve his shooting first. A solid bench player with a strong body who can work well off the wing and inside, Jessie can get to the basket and create some things for himself—and, at times, others.

Jessie struggled with his shot last year, but he did get 10.2 minutes per game. That total isn't likely to sky-rocket, but if he can prove a reliable scorer and ballhandler—traits he showed during his prep career—Jessie could see as many as 15-20 minutes per game.

He is versatile enough to play either wing spot, and his 6-7, 213-pound frame might make him a power forward candidate in the slim St. John's frontcourt.

ALBERT RICHARDSON (6-9, 220 lbs., JR, F,, 20.0 ppg, 11.0 rpg, 2.0 bpg, McCook CC, Neb./New Orleans, La.). Although neither Fraschilla, who recruited Richardson, nor Jarvis is a big fan of junior college players, Richardson fills a significant need for St. John's, bringing size and inside production to the team.

Although it's unlikely Richardson will start immediately, given Grant's experience and talent, he could become a vital cog and the first big man off the bench. A NJCAA honorable mention all-America, Richardson proved he could score and rebound during his two years at McCook CC.

He will be asked to do a little bit of both this season.

DONALD EMANUEL (6-8, FR, F, 12.2 ppg, 10.5 rpg, 2.0 spg, 3.8 bpg, Jones HS/Houston, Tex.). Emanuel will have every opportunity to find a way into the St. John's lineup, since the team does need some size. Rated one of the Top 100 players in the nation and a standout at the '97 summer camps, Emanuel will be asked to back up Artest and even Grant in the Johnnies' frontcourt.

OTHER RETURNEES

CHUDNEY GRAY (6-3, 188 lbs., JR, G, #3, 2.4 ppg, 0.7 rpg, 5.5 minutes, .611 FG, .400 3PT, .286 FT, Rice HS/Bronx, N.Y.). Gray may get a chance at more action now that the Johnnies have a new coach. You know that's what he's hoping, but don't count on it.

Gray spent his first full season (he didn't become eligible until the second semester of his freshman year) as a complementary player and actually saw his minutes per game drop to 5.5 from 7.9. A solid producer close to the basket, Gray will get a chance to find a spot in the regular backcourt rotation.

But, if Anthony Glover becomes eligible, expect Gray's minutes to shrink to their former levels.

MILOS DUMIC (6-10, 220 lbs., SO, C/F, #21, 0.0 ppg, 0.2 rpg, five appearances, St. Joseph's-by-the-Sea HS, N.Y./Bijeljina, Yugoslavia). Jarvis should relate quite well to Dumic, a European import who begins his second year on campus. Dumic played in only five games last year, something that was anticipated given his slight frame and unfamiliarity with the American game. He didn't attempt a shot and grabbed but one rebound.

He could get more action this year, since the Johnnies lack real size. But Dumic must get stronger, tougher and more able to produce on the court if he wants to get any real time.

KAREEM SYED (6-5, 196 lbs., JR, G, #10, 0.0 ppg, 0.0 rpg, two appearances, Hillcrest HS/Kew Gardens, N.Y.). A walkon who appeared in just two games last year and didn't register a single statistic other than his appearances, Syed is expected to remain well out of the rotation once again.

1998-99 ST. JOHN'S SCHEDULE

Nov.	16	#North Carolina-Asheville
	23	Columbia
	30	St. Francis-NY
Dec.	2	Hofstra
	5	@Boston College
	9	Pittsburgh
	12	@Virginia
	19	Fordham
	22	Fairleigh Dickinson
Jan.	2	@Rutgers
	4	Niagara
	6	@Miami (Fla.)
	9	*Seton Hall
	11	*Georgetown
	16	*Rutgers
	20	@Providence
	24	*Duke
	27	@Syracuse
	30	*Connecticut
Feb.	3	*Miami (Fla.)
	6	@Pittsburgh
	9	@West Virginia
	13	*Villanova
	15	Providence
	20	@Georgetown
	24	*Notre Dame
	27	@Villanova
Mar.	3-6	##Big East Tournament

@ Road Games

* Madison Square Garden, NY

Chase NIT (If the Minutemen advance, they face the Massachusetts/Niagara winner on Nov. 18. Semifinals and finals are Nov. 25 & 27 at Madison Square Garden, NY).

Madison Square Garden, NY

OTHER NEWCOMERS

None.

QUESTIONS

Point guard? Charles is not a full-time Big East point man; that has been proven. And, although Barkley brings glittering credentials, he hasn't proven anything on the collegiate level. St. John's needs him to be ready right away or struggle in a league that has plenty of good point men.

Frontcourt depth? Artest and Grant are good starting points, but they play basically the same position. With no center, Grant will be asked to play the pivot, but it is essential that Richardson and Emanuel provide consistent support.

Scoring? Lopez and Hamilton didn't lead the Johnnies to a Final Four, but they filled up the scorebook every night. Artest, Postell and Grant must increase their production, and Thornton must show he is capable of playing at both ends.

Three-point shooting? Lopez only made 33.7 percent of his trey attempts last year, but he was a marksman when compared to his weak-shooting teammates. Artest and Postell could be good situational long-range shooters, but Barkley and Thornton (and perhaps Glover) must emerge as deep threats.

ANSWERS

Artest! It's time for the sophomore to shine. As he showed at the end of last year, this sophomore ready to be a force at both ends of the court.

Postell! This could be his coming-out party, too. Postell is an excellent defender with a rapidly-improving offensive game. He is right on time.

Barkley! He may not be ready to star, but he brings tremendous talent and will benefit from the extra year at MCI. He looks like the classic 1990s lead guard, capable of both scoring and setting up his teammates.

Defense! Last year's team held rivals to 40.7 percent field goal shooting and, with Jarvis aboard, that number could shrink this year. That alone will help the Johnnies challenge in conference.

adidas Blue Ribbon Analysis

BACKCOURT	B	BENCH/DEPTH	B
FRONTCOURT	B	INTANGIBLES	B

It is a little difficult to get a handle on this team, first because of the big graduation losses and then because no one knows the answers to several key questions.

Can Artest step up? How will the team respond to Jarvis' style? Will the frontcourt be deep enough? Can somebody shoot from the outside? Here are the best answers we can come up with:

Yes, Artest will emerge. He has the talent and benefited from a year of developing out of the main spotlight. The Johnnies will play pretty well under Jarvis, at least at the defensive end. The frontcourt will have some trouble, however, unless Richardson turns out to be a stud (junior college players are frequently dicey). And St. John's will indeed struggle from the outside at times.

Sounds like a mixed bag at the start. And it doesn't sound as if the Red Storm is poised to replicate—or improve upon—its 22-win performance last year.

But there is plenty of hope. This is an extremely young team. Artest and Barkley comprise a strong foundation on which to build. If Glover becomes eligible, St. John's will even better set for the future. It will also have a formidable young trio that should be battle-tested by March.

Maybe Fraschilla knew what he was doing when he looked at other job opportunities. Even though St. John's is in New York, there is no guarantee it will get every great player out of the city. It's campus isn't the most picturesque in the world, that's for sure.

But New York is New York, and Jarvis' move to St. John's is definitely a step up on the career ladder. Whether he can help the Red Storm enjoy similar progress remains to be seen.

(M.B.)

38
TEXAS

LOCATION	Austin, TX
CONFERENCE	Big 12
LAST SEASON	14-17 (.452)
CONFERENCE RECORD	6-10 (10th)
STARTERS LOST/RETURNING	1/4
NICKNAME	Longhorns
COLORS	Burnt Orange & White
HOMECOURT	Erwin Special Events Center (16,042)
COACH	Rick Barnes (Lenoir-Rhyne '77)
RECORD AT SCHOOL	first year
CAREER RECORD	202-134 (11 yrs.)
ASSISTANTS	Ricky Stokes (Virginia '74)
	Brain Cousins (Providence '91)
	Ed Kohtala (Maine '81)
TEAM WINS (last 5 yrs.)	26-23-21-18-14
RPI (last 5 yrs.)	37-31-40-32-110
1997-98 FINISH	Lost in conference semifinal.

COACH AND PROGRAM

The setting was as bizarre as you'd want to see. On stage was Texas coach Tom Penders and athletic director DeLoss Dodds. Both were saying Penders wasn't being pushed out, but they couldn't fool anybody.

The previous few weeks, heck, even the whole season had been tumultuous. In some ways, it was ridiculous.

It started sadly, as Penders underwent heart surgery. He had a defibrillator implanted to rectify a condition which surfaced seven years ago. He turned over coaching duties to assistant Tom Oran for two weeks, including two losses in the Coaches vs. Cancer Classic.

TEXAS

Penders watched from his bed.

"That was the worst, the most stressful, frustrating situation I've ever been in," Penders said. "I felt helpless. When you're there, at least you're going down with the ship."

That's exactly where Penders found himself six months later, on a sinking ship. Much more was expected from a team that suffered only one significant loss, Reggie Freeman, from a Sweet 16 team. And the future looked even brighter after signing one of the best recruiting classes in school history.

But little went right for the Longhorns. It started with those two losses in New Jersey (to Princeton and Georgia). Before Big 12 play, there were no satisfying victories.

No real leader was emerging and—worse for the program and for Penders—the team's chemistry was not only bad, it was lethal. The rookies weren't meshing with the veterans, and the veterans weren't stepping up like they should have. The biggest problem was freshman Luke Axtell.

We'll get to him later.

The league schedule started with a home loss to Baylor. In its next three games, Texas lost to Missouri by 22 points, Kansas by 30 and Oklahoma by 16. So the Longhorns, helplessly out of any real postseason ambitions, had to be content with smaller triumphs.

They did sweep nemesis Texas Tech, won a stirring victory at an emotion-charged Texas A&M (playing Texas for the final time in old White Coliseum), picked up a home triumph over NCAA-bound Oklahoma State, then shocked everybody at the conference tournament by upsetting Tech and the Cowboys again to reach the semifinals (before falling to Oklahoma).

A week later, everything started to unravel. While Penders was vacationing in the Caribbean, an assistant coach told an Austin radio station that Axtell was not making satisfactory progress in the classroom. Some of his grades were disclosed. A big mistake; a huge mistake.

Penders hustled back to face the fire and the firing squad. Axtell, it turned out, had been an unhappy camper most of the season. He didn't get along with Penders or most of his teammates.

When the season ended, he and three other players went to Dodds and complained about Penders. But only Axtell transferred (to Kansas). Others who said they were unhappy, including center Chris Mihm and power forward Gabe Muoneke, stuck it out.

Then Penders was gone, an amicable parting we were led to believe at the time. But, after he landed at George Washington, Penders let loose and criticized Dodds. The whole thing was unsightly and the end couldn't come soon enough.

Onward.

After dipping into the Atlantic Coast Conference for a football coach when he hired North Carolina's Mack Brown, Dodds went back there to pluck Rick Barnes from Clemson. Dodds had also talked to, among others, Washington's Bob Bender and Utah's Rick Majerus.

Dodds had been a Barnes fan from his days on the NCAA basketball committee. Committee guys get the best seats, right next to the benches and, during Clemson's tournament games, Dodds was impressed with what he saw.

"He seemed very focused on the game and with his team, and less focused on the officials," Dodds said.

On the surface, it seems like a good hire. Barnes is a winner. It's how he wins that might make Texas fans wonder if Dodds hired the right guy.

In 11 seasons—one at George Mason, six at Providence and four at Clemson—Barnes has had only one losing season. He took teams to the NCAA Tournament five times before winning a game, then he got to the Sweet 16 in 1997. Last year's Tournament run ended prematurely, when Western Michigan upset the Tigers in the first round.

Give Barnes credit for understanding the Texas situation upon arriving in Austin.

"One thing we'll find out here is how committed we are to being a basketball team," he said. "Teams that win are those that believe in each other and work together in tough times."

But Texas fans have a few things to consider before embracing Barnes. First, last year's Clemson team underachieved, which is atypical for Barnes. Last season started with enormous expectations, with the Tigers ranked as high as No. 5 in one poll.

But Clemson lost to Gonzaga in the championship game of the Top of the World Classic and was plagued by inconsistency throughout the season. At one stretch, the Tigers lost four straight in the ACC.

When it got to the NCAAs with an 18-13 record, sixth-seeded Clemson was thought to be a dangerous team. But it couldn't get past Western Michigan.

Then, there is Barnes' style. When it comes attracting basketball fans in the Southwest, style points count. This isn't the ACC, where a defensive-minded approach is encouraged if it can stop North Carolina.

Texans (and most Oklahomans, for that matter) want to be entertained. Penders made an immediate impact by pumping up the volume. Barnes isn't of that ilk. But he is saying the right things.

"As far as style goes, we'll evaluate our talent and make a decision," Barnes said. "The most important thing for a coach is to not ask your players to conform to a style of play.

"But we are going to build a team based on defense. If you want to win championships, you have to defend people."

Texas publicists are quick to point out that Barnes coached four of the 11 highest-scoring teams in Providence history, and the Big East is a defensive-minded conference. This we know about Barnes and his teams: They're aggressive and they don't shy away from challenges.

Barnes' spat with former North Carolina coach Dean Smith is well known. Will he continue the quarrel with Smith's protégé, Roy Williams at Kansas?

Actually, the conference could use some of that fire. And, with Axtell becoming eligible next year, maybe the Longhorns and Jayhawks could get something started.

And why, exactly, did Barnes leave Clemson for Texas? Only his heart knows, but perhaps Barnes feels closer to a conference championship in the Big 12 than he ever did in the ACC.

In 11 years, no Barnes team has finished higher than fourth in the league. But, with plenty of talent returning and the conference looking to be no better than it was a year ago, Texas is in position to challenge Oklahoma State, Kansas, Oklahoma and perhaps Missouri for the Big 12's top spot.

That is, if the chemistry is right. With Barnes, that shouldn't be a problem. He let the players know immediately it was his way or the highway. At his first team meeting, Barnes laid down some laws: No facial hair below the lip; no earrings; no ball caps inside; mandatory team breakfasts at 7:30 a.m.; no headphones as players stroll across campus.

"He scared me at first," said guard Chico Vazquez. "He was straightforward about how he runs things. If you liked it, fine. If you didn't, move on."

Such a style stands in contrast to Penders' looser reins. But, after the disaster of last season, the Longhorns could use a little more structure.

Barnes scored his first recruiting coup in June when he attracted former Texas player of the year Chris Owens, a 6-8 forward who played his freshman season at Tulane.

"Coach Barnes runs a very disciplined system, and I feel like I can be a major player," Owens told the *Lubbock Advance-Journal*. "I wouldn't be going there if he wasn't there."

Owens started 27 games last season, averaging 6.1 ppg and 5.5 rpg for the Green Wave. He is projected as a small forward for the Longhorns, who didn't sign a player taller than 6-3 for this season.

STARTERS NOT RETURNING

LUKE AXTELL (6-8, SF, 13.3 ppg, 4.3 rpg, 28.7 minutes, .428 FG, .393 3PT, .737 FT). Axtell took his game and attitude to Kansas, where he hopes to develop in coach Roy Williams' system. You better believe the wild shots he threw up last season won't be tolerated at Kansas. They wouldn't have been under Rick Barnes, either, and there was some talk that Axtell considered changing his mind once Barnes was hired.

That isn't going to happen. Axtell made a good first impression at Kansas. He showed up with a haircut, after playing with a frizzy, floppy mane for the Longhorns. Proof that Penders had trouble controlling Axtell: He led Texas in three-point attempts with 173 and was second to Kris Clack in all field goal tries.

Axtell had some terrific moments. In his fourth game, he fired in 32 points against Liberty, the most by a Texas freshman since Terrence Rencher in 1992. He had back-to-back games of 6-for-8 three-point shooting against Nebraska and Oklahoma State. He nearly made the Big 12 All-Tournament team by averaging 14.3 ppg in three games as the Longhorns upset their way to the semifinals.

But little did anybody know of Axtell's unhappiness during the season. One of the centerpieces of Penders' heralded recruiting classes—a hometown hero from Austin staying home—did not work out and now seeks peace of mind at Kansas.

"I think the style of play at Kansas is definitely more my style," Axtell said. "Texas was something I had to adapt to. I'm going from one extreme to another. Definitely, I'm looking for more structure."

Because of a Big 12 rule, Axtell has only two years of eligibility at Kansas beginning with the 1999-2000 season.

OTHERS NOT RETURNING

IRA CLARK (6-8, F/C, 6.2 ppg, 3.9 rpg, 17.2 minutes, .517 FG). A role player throughout his career, Clark was banger off the bench. His big game came in a home loss to Baylor in which he had 19 points, 12 rebounds in a career-high 30 minutes.

Maybe Clark should have played more.

BRANDY PERRYMAN (6-2, G, 5.8 ppg, 0.9 rpg, 16.3 minutes, .324 FG, .333 3PT, .917 FT). Perryman didn't have the exclamation point senior season he would have liked. His three-point shooting dipped for a third straight year after a .449 effort as a freshman. Perryman lost playing time to Axtell, who was better at creating his own shot.

There were some high points. Perryman set a school record by playing in 122 consecutive games, every single one of his career. He finished as the school's career leader in free throw percentage at .897 and stands fourth in treys made (210) and attempted (585).

ANTHONY GOODE (6-1, G, 2.2 ppg, 1.9 apg, 9.4 minutes, .355 FG) Goode was a former walkon who once projected as the starting point guard. He started two games early, and played 20 minutes in a December contest against Arizona.

But his playing time fell off and, after logging 10 minutes against Fresno State in late January, Goode played one minute in the final 14. games. Enough of that, he said.

Goode transferred to Texas-Arlington, where he'll have one year of eligibility.

PROJECTED STARTERS

KRIS CLACK (6-5, 215 lbs., JR, SF, #15, 17.3 ppg, 6.6 rpg, 3.2 apg, 1.7 spg, 33.0 minutes, .545 FG, .327 3PT, .729 FT, Anderson HS/Anderson, Tex.). We expected Clack to have a bigger year as a junior, but that's not to say he was a disappointment. Under Penders, Texas had a habit of replacing a "go-to" player with another.

In 1992, Texas lost Joey Wright (21.2 ppg) and replaced him with Dexter Cambridge (12.2 ppg to 21.7 ppg). In 1993, Cambridge was gone and it was Mike Richardson's turn (7.8 ppg to 20.2 ppg). In 1994, Richardson goes and B.J. Tyler raises his average by five points to 22.8 ppg.

Tyler is gone in 1995 and Terrence Rencher goes from 15.9 to 20.8 ppg. Rencher leaves in 1996 and Reggie Freeman jumps from 14.7 to 22.4 ppg.

Clack's average did rise from 12.6 to 17.3 ppg, and he improved in nearly all other areas, but Clack isn't the offensive player others like Freeman were. He is a defensive stud, which Barnes should love. His 181 career steals rank fifth on the Longhorns' career list, and 77 career blocked shots is more than an off-guard's quota. He could become the first player in Texas history to record 200 steals and 100 blocks.

Last season was a difficult year for the Longhorns and Clack. Texas shouldn't have looked to Clack to be its top scoring threat. He is not that kind of player. Oh, his dunks are spectacular. He jumps out of the gym and can slash. But Clack is only an average shooter.

Clack found himself in the uncomfortable position of supporting Penders at the end of the season. While a handful of players complained to A.D. DeLoss Dodds about Penders, captains Clack and Chico Vazquez openly supported their coach.

"I had some disappointment and anger over how the whole thing was handled, but I had to get over it," Clack said. "But looking back on it, was time for a change."

Under Barnes, Clack shouldn't have to adjust his game much. He is a remarkable athlete and can guard anybody in the Big 12 who isn't a center. And Clack has jumped center in each of his three seasons.

Like last year, he'll play shooting guard and small forward. Clack should be Barnes' kind of player. He won't have to score more, and Barnes will give him every opportunity to pad his defensive statistics.

NNADUBEM "GABE" MUONEKE (6-7, 240 lbs., JR, PF, #3, 10.4 ppg, 5.7 rpg, 2.2 apg, 1.0 spg, 25.9 minutes, .431 FG, .262 3PT, .585 FT, Cypress Falls HS/Houston, Tex.). Barnes likes physical basketball, and there is no more physical player in the Big 12 than Muoneke. He loves to mix it up. Sometimes, as it did at Oklahoma, it gets too physical. But, no doubt, Muoneke comes to play.

At times, Muoneke would liked to have been more effective. He shot only 43 percent, hardly acceptable for a power forward who got 27 of his 119 field goals on dunks. He either needs to get more accurate on three-pointers (26.2 percent) or stop shooting them.

Muoneke has terrific hands. He recorded more assists (68) than any power forward in Texas history. His 32 steals ranked second only to Clack's 55.

Muoneke was born in Michigan; his parents are from Nigeria. His full name is Nnadubem Gabriel Enyinaya Muoneke. Texas publicists learned that Nnadubem means "God guide me." Muoneke means "spirit that creates." His brother's name is Chukwudebelum.

Dad is a math professor at Prairie View A&M. Before his freshman season, "Gabe" knocked down legendary Texas running back Earl Campbell during a Midnight Madness scrimmage.

CHRIS MIHM (7-0, 255 lbs., SO, C, #4, 12.4 ppg, 8.0 rpg, 2.0 tpg, 2.9 bpg, 24.8 minutes, .514 FG, .647 FT, Westlake HS/Austin, Tex.). Penders played Mihm immediately, and the big guy lived up to his billing. He turned in the best season for a freshman center at Texas since La Salle Thompson in 1980 and he was named to the Big 12 All-Freshman team. Mihm led Texas in rebounding and his 90 blocked shots set a school record.

Mihm is a Pete Newell Big Man Camp success story. He attended before his senior year in high school and turned into one of the nation's top recruits. Mihm liked it so much, he went back this summer, paying his own way to Hawaii.

He got better as the season went on. In his first 15 games, Mihm averaged 9.3 ppg and shot 45.8 percent from the field. One of those games was a dreadful 3-for-13 shooting performance against Kansas, a game in which the Jayhawks' prized freshman center, Eric Chenowith, seemed to have the upper hand.

From then on, Mihm was terrific, averaging 15.3 ppg, 8.8 rpg and shooting 55.4 percent over his final 16 games. Mihm's biggest shot of the season was an offensive rebound of a Kris Clack jumper in the final moments of a one-point victory at Texas A&M.

"He's going to be a pro," gushed former Aggies coach

1997-98 RESULTS

#Princeton (L)	56-62
#Georgia (L)	87-89
@North Texas	116-94
Liberty	98-70
@Georgia (L)	76-94
American University	78-62
Arizona (L)	81-88
Florida	85-82
Louisiana State	69-63
@Illinois (L)	80-105
Houston	89-71
Baylor (L)	81-87
@Missouri (L)	69-91
Kansas (L)	72-102
@Oklahoma (L)	75-91
Texas Tech	88-79
Nebraska	105-91
@Fresno State (L)	82-90
@Iowa State (L)	82-85
Oklahoma State	88-73
@Texas A&M	81-80
Oklahoma (L)	74-81
@Kansas State (L)	79-83
@Texas Tech	82-80
Texas A&M	87-74
@Baylor (L)	75-80
@Oklahoma State (L)	58-80
Colorado (L)	64-81
##Texas Tech	86-83
##Oklahoma State	65-64
##Oklahoma (L)	55-68

@ away games
# Coaches vs. Cancer IKON Classic, East Rutherford, NJ
Big 12 Tournament, Kansas City, MO

1998-99 TEXAS SCHEDULE

Nov.	17	@Houston
	21	South Florida
	25	@Arizona
	29	Georgia
Dec.	2	@Oral Roberts
	5	*San Diego
	12	Utah
	15	Wisconsin
	19	@Louisiana State
	28-30	#Rainbow Classic
Jan.	2	@Colorado
	6	Iowa State
	10	@Nebraska
	13	Baylor
	16	Kansas State
	18	@Kansas
	23	Oklahoma State
	25	@Oklahoma
	31	Massachusetts
Feb.	3	Texas A&M
	6	@Texas Tech
	10	Oklahoma
	14	@Oklahoma State
	17	Texas Tech
	20	@Texas A & M
	24	@Baylor
	27	Missouri
Mar.	4-7	##Big 12 Tournament

@ Road Games
* San Diego Sports Arena, San Diego, CA
# Honolulu, HI (vs. Mississippi State, first round; also Florida State Hawaii, Murray State, Princeton and Southwestern Louisiana)
Kemper Arena, Kansas City, MO

Tony Barone.

Maybe. There is still plenty of game for Mihm to polish. He should shoot it a little better and cut down on the turnovers. That should happen with experience.

One area in which he needs no tutoring is blocked shots. Credit the Newell camp for that ability. Mihm understands more than most that it is better to redirect a shot in play than swat it 15 rows into the seats.

For a big man, Mihm is nimble, perhaps a result of his tennis career. His father, Gary, played the sport at Marquette. Chris was ranked in Texas as late as 14 years-old.

DEJUAN "CHICO" VAZQUEZ (6-4, 215 lbs., SR, PG, #31, 7.5 ppg, 3.3 rpg, 2.0 apg, 22.6 minutes, .429 FG, .352 3PT, .679 FT, Reagan HS/Austin, Tex.). Vazquez and Kris Clack give Texas two of the best defensive guards in the Big 12. Vazquez had 24 steals and blocked 18 shots. His 52 career blocks rank 10th on the school's career list, a remarkable figure for a point guard. He had some of his better defensive games against the league's top guards, Texas Tech's Cory Carr and Nebraska's Tyronn Lue.

Although Vazquez and Clack played high school ball in Austin, they did not know each other until coming to Texas—or at least get to know each other better. Vazquez's free throw with three seconds left in overtime gave his team a one-point victory over Clack's in a high school game three years ago.

Vazquez has never been asked to be a scorer. He'll be a four-year starter and may not reach 1,000 points (540). But he improved in all major categories. He shouldn't have to add much to those totals to please Barnes, as long he keeps up his end of the bargain on defense.

"Guards have to make good decisions, but you've got to defend first," Barnes said. "You can't run without the ball, so you can create easy baskets with your defense."

BERNARD SMITH (6-3, 190 lbs., SO, SG, #21, 5.9 ppg, 3.2 rpg, 2.2 apg, 1.0 spg, 22.2 minutes, .369 FG, .296 FT, .853 FT, Conroe HS/Conroe, Tex.). Smith played extensively as a freshman, also getting six starting assignments. He didn't shoot it well, but few did for the Longhorns last season. And his shooting did get better Smith hit 35.7 percent on three-pointers over his final 18 games after missing 14 of his first 15 attempts from behind the arc.

Of more concern should be his assist/turnover ratio (66 assists/54 turnovers), and that was the best on a bad ballhandling team last season. In league games, Texas averaged two more turnovers per game than opponents.

Smith was named the Houston-area high school player of the year as a senior and picked Texas over Kansas. Unless Barnes goes with a three guard offense, Smith figures to come off the bench again, but he should get more minutes.

KEY RESERVES

IVAN WAGNER (6-1, 195 lbs., JR, G, #5, 3.1 ppg, 0.8 rpg, 1.2 apg, 10.6 minutes, .239 FG, .107 3PT, .472 FT, North Carolina State & Roosevelt HS/San Antonio, Tex.). Wagner has had some athletic highlights in college. As a freshman at North Carolina State, he scored 29 points in his first game (off the bench against Virginia Military Institute). He followed that with a 17-point effort against Winthrop.

Wagner was playing because of the suspension to two starters. He ended up averaging 3.4 ppg that season.

After sitting out 1996-97 as a transfer, Wagner played in 17 games, starting four, for Texas last year. He had his best outing in a blowout loss to Kansas. Wagner scored 10 points and grabbed five rebounds.

Yet Wagner's major accomplishments have come on the track. He won the 1997 NCAA outdoor high jump with a leap of 7-6 1/2. During an April meet, Barnes took the entire basketball team to watch Wagner compete. It was a togetherness thing that had an impact.

VOHN HUNTER (6-3, 205 lbs., FR, G, 18.6 ppg, 5.0 rpg, St. Raymond's HS/Bronx, N.Y.) Penders made a habit of luring top talent from New York City, and Hunter is the latest. Hunter follows former Longhorns Alex Broadway, Terrence Rencher and Reggie Freeman out of the Big Apple to the Lone Star State.

Hunter is the Longhorn's top recruit and has the best chance to play immediately. He plays both guard spots, but likely will see most of his action backing up Clack at shooting guard. Hunter made a few Top 100 lists, and was ranked as high as No. 62 by ESPN (14th-best shooting guard).

Hunter is the son of former Harlem Globetrotter Bobby Joe Hunter. As a high school player, he was fan of Freeman, who attended Rice before heading to Texas.

NATHANIAL BAILEY (5-10, 175 lbs., JR, G, 14.1 ppg, 4.0 apg, 3.2 spg, North Idaho College, Odessa College, Tex. & Science Hill HS/Johnson City, Tenn.) Bailey committed to Virginia Tech out of high school but he wound up at North Idaho, where he made second team All-Region 18. Texas is his fourth school in four years.

Bailey will backup Vazquez at the point. At Science Hill HS, one of the nation's renowned prep programs, Bailey helped the team to two state championships.

WILLIAM CLAY (6-2, 175 lbs., JR, G, #23, 16.1 ppg, .380 3PT, .800 FT San Jacinto JC, Tex. & Bryan HS/ Bryan, Tex.). Texas didn't shoot three-pointers well, ranking 10th in the Big 12 at 32.9 percent. Clay should help. He set a school record by knocking down 205 in a two-year junior college career, and he had nine in one game as a freshman.

That season, he was a second-team All-Conference choice on a squad that finished 36-1. San Jac went 60-7 in his two years.

In high school, Clay shot 42.1 percent on three-pointers. He made 341 in three years and, as a junior, ranked behind Texas teammate Gabe Muoneke and Texas A&M's Jerald Brown in statewide scoring.

Look for Clay to get Brandy Perryman's minutes.

OTHER RETURNEES

WENDELL CARTER (6-9, 200 lbs., SR, F, 1.7 ppg, 1.3 rpg, 5.2 minutes, .414 FG, .167 FT, North Dakota-Williston & Mirabella Senior Secondary School/San Fernando, Trinidad). Carter played in three of the final 16 games. He got in a season-high 19 minutes in the season's second game, against Georgia, and evidently did not make enough an impression.

If it doesn't work out in basketball, Carter can make it in business. He is a certified welder.

MARLON DRAKES (6-8, 235 lbs., SR, F, #34, 0.8 ppg, 0.9 rpg, 5.1 minutes, .385 FG, .500 FT, North Dakota-Williston & Success Laventille Composite School/ Port of Spain). Drakes didn't see much action a year ago and it's hard to see him playing much more this year. He mostly played behind Chris Mihm.

Drakes played for the 1997 Trinidad and Tobago national team. He was a member of that nation's air force before being granted an honorable discharge in order to attend college.

DREW BROWN (6-6, 200 lbs., SO, F, #30, three appearances, White Station HS/Memphis, Tenn.). Brown, a walkon, appeared in three games. He is the brother of Taryn Brown of the Texas women's team.

His father, also named Drew, played at Southern University and briefly for the Harlem Globetrotters.

FORD ALLEN (6-0, 170 lbs., SO, G, SO, #14, two appearances, Incarnate Word Academy/Corpus Christi, Tex.). A walkon, Allen played a total of two minutes in two games without scoring.

OTHER NEWCOMERS

None.

QUESTIONS

Offense? The departed Axtell was the team's second-leading scorer. Somebody must fill the void and the small forward position.

Chemistry? Nobody outside the team knew about it throughout last season, but the Longhorns may have had the worst chemistry in Division I. Gone are Penders and Axtell, so it should be addition by subtraction.

Philosophy? The players have no choice but to buy into whatever Barnes throws at them, but, if it's a deliberate attack, that's not what most of the players were recruited to do.

ANSWERS

Rick Barnes! A feisty winner everywhere he's been. Texas and Clemson both wear orange, but that's about the only similarity. The Longhorns have more resources and maybe even a deeper desire to be great in basketball.

Defense! If nothing else, the Longhorns will be strong defensively under Barnes—because that's his strong suit. But that shouldn't be a difficult sell with the team.

Kris Clack! Texas' most complete player and one of the Big 12's best.

adidas Blue Ribbon Analysis

BACKCOURT	**B**	**BENCH/DEPTH**	**B**
FRONTCOURT	**B**	**INTANGIBLES**	**B**

Barnes has done his best to smooth over the negative vibes from the end of last season. To most, like Kris Clack, Penders was a popular coach; not all the players wanted him out. There is no problem between Clack and Barnes, but Clack thought Penders was treated unfairly.

Of all college basketball's coaching changes, this one will be the most watched and is the most interesting. Coaches don't usually volunteer to leave the ACC.

Barnes must see something special at Texas. It might not happen this year, but there is enough talent from the Penders' regime to believe Texas will be back in the NCAA Tournament.

The Longhorns are a step behind at least Oklahoma State and Kansas in the Big 12. The schedule contains the usual ruggedness, but that's how Penders—who always thinks RPI—liked it.

Texas seems solid in most areas, but one aspect that must improve is ballhandling. The Longhorns had 42 more turnovers than opponents (31 more in Big 12 games). Part of the problem was the lack of an experienced point guard. Freshman Bernard Smith turned out to be Texas' best at the point, and he had major shooting woes.

The Longhorns are tough and athletic up front, and Barnes should bring out the best in their defensive abilities. In fact, Barnes should bring out the best in all their abilities. That's the kind of coach he is.

Look for Texas to finish third or fourth in the Big 12, grab 18 victories or so, and be is position to be a pest in March.

(B.K.)

39
SOUTH CAROLINA

LOCATION	**Columbia, SC**
CONFERENCE	**SEC (Eastern Division)**
LAST SEASON	**23-8 (.742)**
CONFERENCE RECORD	**11-5 (2nd)**
STARTERS LOST/RETURNING	**2/3**
NICKNAME	**Gamecocks**
COLORS	**Garnet & Black**
HOMECOURT	**Carolina Coliseum (12,401)**
COACH	**Eddie Fogler (North Carolina '70)**
RECORD AT SCHOOL	**85-64 (5 yrs.)**
CAREER RECORD	**227-144 (12 yrs.)**
ASSISTANTS	**Rick Callahan (Salem '80)**
	John Cooper (Wichita State '91)
	Barclay Radebaugh (East Tennessee State '87)
TEAM WINS (last 5 yrs.)	**9-10-19-24-23**
RPI (last 5 yrs.)	**29-48-49-25-12**
1997-98 FINISH	**Lost in NCAA first round.**

COACH AND PROGRAM

If South Carolina could ever get past the first round of the NCAA Tournament, the nation might actually see how far the program has come in five years under coach Eddie Fogler.

Alas, that opening game in the Big Dance has proven to be a king-sized thorn in the Gamecocks' side. Two years ago, Coppin State shocked the college basketball world when, as the 15th-seeded team in the East Regional, it bumped second-seeded South Carolina from the Tournament, 78-65.

The shock of that stunning defeat had barely subsided when the Gamecocks took the floor against their first-round opponent in the 1998 NCAAs. This time the third seed from the East, South Carolina was again ousted, 62-61, by Richmond, a team with a reputation for giant killing.

Disappointed as he was by both losses, Fogler has chosen not to dwell on what he believes is ancient history.

"Getting there (to the NCAA Tournament) is not easy," Fogler said. "You walk such a fine line the last two weeks of the regular season. We're glad to have been able to play in the Tournament the last two years. Of course we would have liked to have done better, but I don't worry about the NCAA Tournament until we get there. This is a new team, with difference circumstances."

The early ousters might have overshadowed how far Fogler has taken the program he inherited—in shambles—five years ago. Rebuilding with homegrown talent mined from South Carolina high schools and the occasional Division I transfer, Fogler took the Gamecocks to the NIT by his third season. Then came the two, ill-fated NCAA berths.

Despite the loss of two key starters, guard Melvin Watson and center Ryan Stack, the Gamecocks are good enough to get their ticket to the Big Dance stamped again. In guard BJ McKie, the Gamecocks have a player many consider the best in the SEC. He will make the big move to point guard this season as Fogler tries to replace Watson.

There are veterans at every other position as well as depth, provided in part by a solid, four-man recruiting class of four freshmen.

Fogler makes no predictions that the Gamecocks are ready to atone for their first-round NCAA Tournament disasters. He is not ready to say his team will even advance to the NCAAs.

"We can have a good team here," Fogler said. "But our league is getting stronger, particularly the East. We're all not going (to the Tournament)."

Perhaps not. But of the five to six NCAA bids the SEC figures to receive this season, chances are still good that South Carolina will claim one of them.

STARTERS NOT RETURNING

MELVIN WATSON (6-1, PG, 11.4 ppg, 3.9 rpg, 4.7 apg, 1.8 spg, 32.1 minutes, .397 FG, .350 3PT, .765 FT). Watson was the heart and soul of South Carolina, a sure-handed, competitive point guard who ran the team and could get his points when needed. Few guards in the country had Watson's combination of quickness and strength.

Watson became a fixture in his freshman season as Fogler began his rebuilding process. He started all but three games during his career, proving as durable as he was talented.

Watson helped lead the Gamecocks to three straight postseason appearances. That South Carolina was upset in the NCAA Tournament's first round the last two years shouldn't be blamed on Watson, who will go down in the school's history as a player who helped re-establish the Gamecocks' proud basketball tradition.

Surprisingly to some, Watson was not drafted by an NBA team. The league's lockout hampered his efforts to land a free-agent deal.

Watson then entertained the idea of signing with a team in Greece, but apparently that deal fell through.

RYAN STACK (6-11, C, 9.6 ppg, 6.0 rpg, 1.8 bpg, 29.8 minutes, .498 FG, .319 3PT, .708 FT). Stack will be missed, and not only because South Carolina doesn't have a big man with his range of skills. Capable of scoring inside or stepping out past the three-point line, Stack was hard to defend.

Smaller, quicker players couldn't stop him in the post. Taller, slower defenders couldn't chase him out to the perimeter in time to prevent Stack from launching three-pointers. He was just good enough from that range to keep the defense honest.

Stack was also a good shot-blocker who made opponents think twice about taking the ball inside. He was South Carolina's blocked shot leader by a wide margin.

Many talent evaluators predicted that Stack, because of his size and versatility, might get a chance to play in the NBA. They were right. He was chosen in the second round (the 48th pick overall) by the Cleveland Cavaliers.

OTHERS NOT RETURNING

ARTHUR CARLISLE (6-6, F, 3.5 ppg, 2.2 rpg in 1996-97). Carlisle left the team in the first semester of last year and transferred to South Carolina State, where he should become an instant starter once he becomes eligible in December. Carlisle did not have the ability to have that sort of impact with the Gamecocks.

PROJECTED STARTERS

BJ MCKIE (6-2, 190 lbs., SR, PG, #3, 18.8 ppg, 3.5 rpg, 3.0 apg, 1.3 spg, 33.0 minutes, .438 FG, .415, .782 FG, Irmo HS/Columbia, S.C.). Whatever BJ McKie ends up accomplishing in his career—and he is on target to accomplish a lot—his greatest contribution to the program came the day he put his signature on scholarship papers.

"When he chose South Carolina, it was a real boost to our program," Fogler said. "What he said by that was, 'I know they haven't been winning at South Carolina, but I'm going to school there and help them win.' That sent a strong message to the kids in our state."

Since McKie's signing, the Gamecocks have mined their home state for most of their top players—at least those who didn't turn pro. Fogler can only imagine how strong his team would have been had he been able to sign Jermaine O'Neal and Kevin Garnett, but both skipped college and went straight to the NBA.

Even without the two big men, South Carolina has cleaned up on local talent. Ten of the 13 players on scholarship are from the Palmetto State. McKie is a big reason for that in-state recruiting success and, for that, Fogler will always remember him.

The coach won't soon forget, either, McKie's decision to forsake the NBA draft after his junior season and stay in school. Had McKie bolted, Fogler would have been faced with replacing his entire starting backcourt, which was generally considered one of the top two or three in college basketball last season. Now, Fogler need only replace former point guard Melvin Watson. He thinks he has a player capable of doing that.

If you guessed that player was McKie, you're right. A shooting guard by trade, McKie nevertheless has playmaking skills (as his 267 career assists would attest). McKie had 93 assists last season, second on the team behind Watson. He also shot 78 percent from the free-throw line, not a bad skill to have for a guy who's going to be handling the ball 90 percent of the time in the closing minutes of games.

"I can tell you that he'll be playing a lot of time at the point," Fogler said. "One of the reasons is he's such a competitor. That's his strongest suit."

McKie can also do a few other things well. His offensive skills jump out at you. Quicker than anyone in the SEC—with the exception of Tennessee's Tony Harris—McKie can blow by defenders for easy layups. And, when he doesn't score, he is usually fouled. We've already mentioned that McKie can cash in from the line.

1997-98 RESULTS

Maryland	76-72 ot
The Citadel	77-58
Belmont University, TN	72-61
#Virginia Tech	74-73
#Tennessee Chattanooga	67-55
@Clemson (L)	57-62
St. Joseph's	77-65
South Carolina State	90-85
Towson State	65-55
@Mississippi (L)	54-73
Vanderbilt	71-70
Louisiana State	70-53
@Kentucky (L)	70-91
@Georgia	68-60
Tennessee	81-51
@Auburn	61-56
@Furman	79-52
Florida	74-72
Cincinnati	67-65
@Vanderbilt	65-61
@Tennessee (L)	69-70
Alabama	74-63
Mississippi State	76-65
@Arkansas (L)	88-96
@Florida	79-74
Georgia	78-76
Kentucky (L)	57-69
##Florida	71-60
##Mississippi	87-77
##Kentucky (L)	56-86
%Richmond (L)	61-62

@ away games
# Harris Teeter Pepsi Challenge, Charlotte, NC
SEC Tournament, Georgia Dome, Atlanta, GA
% NCAA East Sub-Regional, Washington, DC

Adding to McKie's arsenal is his three-point stroke. Never a bad shooter from behind the arc, McKie has turned himself into a great one. Last season he was fifth in the SEC in three-point percentage.

"He's learned to shoot the ball so much better from three," Fogler said. "He was already able to spin and get inside and create contact. Now that his outside shooting has improved, he's become difficult to guard."

It should come as no surprise that McKie led the SEC in scoring last season. He sealed that honor in a head-to-head matchup with his closest pursuer, Ansu Sesay of Mississippi, in the SEC Tournament. McKie scored a career-high 37 points in that game, won by South Carolina, as he made 20 of 22 free throws (all in the second half). McKie wound up averaging 18.8 ppg to Sesay's 18.6 ppg.

McKie has also become a solid defender. He played nothing but zone defense in high school, so his adjustment to playing man-to-man for Fogler was difficult. But each year, he has improved. "He's gotten a lot better defensively," Fogler said, "particularly off the ball."

McKie's package of skills should land him on most All-America teams. He was selected one of 25 players from around the nation to be considered for the John Wooden Award. Most observers of SEC basketball believe McKie will be the SEC's preseason Player of the Year.

Whatever happens, Gamecock fans will always appreciate McKie for his bold decision to sign with a rebuilding program. He has led many others into the fold.

ANTONIO GRANT (6-5, 225 lbs., SO, SF, #35, 6.6 ppg, 4.4 rpg, 1.3 apg, 24.0 minutes, .441 FG, .341 3PT, .635 FT, New Hampton Prep, N.H. & North Augusta HS/North Augusta, S.C.). Grant's debut season of 1996-97 was cut short when he suffered a stress fracture in his foot after just three games. But he was given a medical redshirt year.

Grant clearly used his time on the sidelines wisely. He improved his game to the point that, in his redshirt freshman season, he became a starter.

When Grant was recruited, some considered him an undersized power forward who didn't have a perimeter game. Last season, Grant surprised a lot of people by shooting 34 percent from three-point range. He wasn't afraid to take potential game-winning shots against Florida and Cincinnati in consecutive games in February. He made them both, giving the Gamecocks two-point victories in each game.

At 225 pounds, the chiseled Grant can do more than just score. Defensively, he can guard all three perimeter positions. And he can pass a bit, as his 39 assists would attest. Grant will start at small forward again this season.

"Antonio Grant had a very good year for us," Fogler said. "He developed into an SEC-caliber player."

LERON WILLIAMS (6-7, 225 lbs., SR, PF, #32, 10.3 ppg, 4.3 rpg, 20.0 minutes, .572 FG, .673 FT, University of Florida & Southeast HS/Clearwater, Fla.). Williams is a hulking presence in the paint who makes good use of his time. If his stats were factored out over 40 minutes, he would have averaged 20.7 ppg and 8.7 rpg.

Part of the reason for Williams' production is his efficiency from the field. Leading the Gamecocks in dunks, he shot .572, also tops on the team. His skills were showcased in the SEC Tournament, when he made 11 of 18 shots and averaged 12 points. He scored 19 points and grabbed nine boards against Kentucky.

Of course, some people didn't need to be convinced that Williams, the refugee from Billy Donovan's faster-paced style at Florida, could play. Ask Tennessee, which watched him score 25 points on 12 of 15 shooting. Or Georgia, against which Williams scored 17 points and grabbed eight boards in just 23 minutes. Williams reached double figures in 14 of the 25 games he played after gaining eligibility in December.

Williams isn't perfect. His defense isn't quite up to Fogler's high standards. And he's not adept at passing the ball back out to open teammates when double-teamed in the post. Williams had a whopping two assists.

"Offensively, his numbers per minute played are very, very good," Fogler said. "But we're asking LeRon to get better defensively."

HERBERT LEE DAVIS (6-5, 175 lbs., JR, SG, #14, 4.8 ppg, 1.3 rpg, 16.0 minutes, .379 FG, .238 3PT, .476 FT, Winchendon Prep, Ma. & Georgetown HS,/Georgetown, S.C.). Davis has a legitimate chance of moving into a starting role if he can shake off a nasty sophomore slump. Last season, Davis' jumper went on an extended sabbatical.

"He just lost his confidence," Fogler said. "He's a very skilled athlete who just lost his confidence."

If Davis can rediscover that missing confidence, and his jumper along with it, he could take over the shooting guard job. That spot comes open with the move of BJ McKie to the point.

If Davis were only judged by his freshman statistics, he would seem capable of starting. He shot 37 percent from three-point range two years ago, not bad for a rookie. He also shot a respectable 41 percent from the field.

Last year, Davis couldn't hit the broad side of Carolina Coliseum. He shot 37 percent from the field and a dismal 24 percent from three-point range.

When Davis' jumper isn't falling, he's toast. He hasn't mastered the art of penetrating, as evidenced by his numbers at the free-throw line. Davis has played in 61 games at South Carolina and started four times, but he has only taken 33 free throws. Worse, he has made just 15 of those (.455).

If Davis could learn how to take the ball to the hole and either score or get fouled—something at which McKie excels—he wouldn't put so much pressure on his jumper.

When Davis is on, he can be a game-breaking shooter. Last season against Alabama he scored a career-high 16 points, making six of nine shots, including three for three from three-point range.

"Herbert Lee has good offensive potential," Fogler said. "He's going to be better this year. He's just got to get tougher."

BUD JOHNSON (6-10, 245 lbs., SR, C, #21, 2.2 ppg, 2.5 rpg, 12.0 minutes, .528 FG, .419 FT, Eau Claire HS/ Columbia, S.C.). South Carolina coaches were shaking their heads in joyous disbelief after the Gamecocks' first-round SEC Tournament game against Florida last March. Johnson, something of a disappointment the last two seasons, scored 13 points, making five of six shots, and grabbed 10 rebounds, all in just 17 minutes. South Carolina won, 71-60.

"If Bud could do that for us every night...," a South Carolina assistant said, not finishing his sentence but clearly pondering the possibilities.

Johnson arrived in Columbia in 1995 as one of the highest-ranked prep players in the country. He played accordingly in his freshman season, but his effort was inconsistent at best the last two years.

The numbers tell the story. As a freshman, Johnson shot 54 percent from the field and blocked 38 shots. He started 14 games and averaged 21 minutes.

By his junior season, Johnson's playing time was down to 12 minutes per game and he started just four times. He still shot well (.528), but blocked just five shots. And he made 17 turnovers to only four assists.

Clearly, Johnson struggled.

"It wasn't just any one thing," Fogler said. "It was in all areas. He was error-prone at times. Sometimes he made bad decisions."

This year, the Gamecocks need Johnson to play to his potential.

"He's a key for us," Fogler said. "He's worked hard. He's in the best shape I've ever seen him. I'd be happy for him to rebound, block shots and guard. His rebounding has to be a factor this year."

KEY RESERVES

WILLIAM GALLMAN (6-7, 230 lbs., SR, PF, #20, 5.9 ppg, 5.9 rpg, 21.0 minutes, .431 FG, .571 FT, Chester HS/Chester, S.C.). Gallman is the Gamecocks' resident blue-collar worker, a lunch pail kind of guy who excels at the facets of the game that require effort. Witness his 76 offensive boards in 1997-98, tops on the team.

"Gallman's a real solid player," Fogler said. "He's our best post defender and he is also a good rebounder who likes to bang. He's just a good work ethic kid."

Though Gallman's role kept him, for the most part, out of the limelight last season, he had his moments. He was three for three from the field in an overtime victory over Maryland. He also had 11 points and a career-high 14 rebounds against The Citadel.

Fogler will probably try to find more ways to get the ball in Gallman's hands at crunch time. Last season, he was 14-for-17 from the floor in the final five minutes or overtime of games.

RECUS NIX (6-3, 195 lbs., SR, G, #23, 1.8 ppg, 1.8 rpg, 9.0 minutes, .310 FG, .190 3PT, .714 FT, Allegany CC, Md. & Stall HS/Charleston, S.C.). Nix is academically ineligible for the first semester, but is expected back in December. He averaged just nine minutes last season, but his time steadily increased as Fogler began to use him as a defensive stopper. Nix played 18.3 minutes per game over the last eight games.

Nix might be thrown into the mix of candidates to replace Melvin Watson, but, if he's going to help the Gamecocks, he'll have to improve his shooting and become a little steadier with the ball. His turnovers nearly doubled his assists (29-15) last season.

Nix's shining moment last year came against Cincinnati, when he scored a career-high eight points. Six of those points, including a key three-point play that helped the Gamecocks erase a 23-point deficit, came in the second half.

HAGEN ROUSE (6-3, 165 lbs., JR, G, #13, 1.9 ppg, 0.5 rpg, 8.0 minutes, J.L. Mann HS/Greenville, S.C.). Playing behind Watson and McKie the last two seasons didn't leave a lot of minutes for Rouse, but he did manage to play in 49 games and start three.

This season, Rouse will definitely get on the court more often. If McKie is playing the point, he could get time at shooting guard. In his limited duty over the last two years, Rouse manage to shoot a more-than-respectable .364 from three-point range.

In his best career game, Rouse had back-to-back three-pointers that helped the Gamecocks pull away from Tennessee-Chattanooga last December. He finished with a career-high eight points in that game, to go along with three assists and two steals.

AARON LUCAS (5-11, 170 lbs., FR, G, #5, 22.3 ppg, 5.2 rpg, 2.2 apg, 2.6 spg, Richland Northeast HS/Columbia, S.C.). Fogler intends to use former shooting guard BJ McKie extensively at the point guard position this year, but Lucas might help the coach change his mind. The buzz among the players in South Carolina's off-season pickup games was that Lucas is good enough to force Fogler to play him.

Quick and with a good shooting touch, Lucas was chosen as the South Carolina Player of the Year by the *Columbia State*. He was also chosen the 1998 Coaches Select Player of the Year in South Carolina. That award is based on academics and athletic performance and is voted on by the state's high school basketball coaches.

Lucas led his high school team to a top 10 ranking most of the regular season, and almost single-handedly took Richland Northeast to the third round of the state playoffs. After the season, Lucas shined in the Carolina Classic All-Star game with 13 points and three assists.

"Of our freshman, Tony Kitchings has gotten the most notoriety," Fogler said. "But Aaron Lucas has gotten the second-most notoriety. People who have seen him play know he's darn good."

TONY KITCHINGS (6-10, 260 lbs, FR, C, #50, 16.4 ppg, 13.2 rpg, 2.8 bpg, 2.5 spg, South Aiken HS/Aiken, S.C.). Kitchings, in the vernacular of recruiting analysts, was a good "get" for South Carolina. With the departure of Ryan Stack, South Carolina needed a center. And Kitchings was an in-state product with an excellent resume. The fit seems perfect.

Kitchings was generally regarded among the top 50 high school players in the nation. *Prep Stars Recruiter's Handbook* ranked him No. 50 in its list of the country's top 300 seniors. Kitchings was a three-time South Carolina All-State pick and was one of 12 high school players in the nation chosen to play in the Hoop Summit game during the Final Four last March.

Earlier that month, Kitchings led South Aiken to the AAAA state championship, scoring 15 points and grabbing 21 rebounds in the title game. His rebound and outlet pass led to the winning basket with 0.8 seconds to play.

"Kitchings is a big, strong kid and a very skilled player," Fogler said. "We think all our freshmen are good players. But they are also inexperienced. We've got a lot of players back."

1998-99 SOUTH CAROLINA SCHEDULE

Nov.	8	*Indiana
	23	Wofford
	28	The Citadel
	30	Jacksonville
Dec.	4	**College of Charleston
	5	**Old Dominion
	16	Clemson
	19	East Carolina
	22	***Purdue
	29	South Carolina State
Jan.	2	@Mississippi State
	5	Kentucky
	9	@Tennessee
	13	Florida
	16	@Alabama
	20	@Vanderbilt
	24	@Syracuse
	27	Mississippi
	30	Vanderbilt
Feb.	3	Auburn
	6	@Georgia
	10	Arkansas
	13	@Kentucky
	17	@LSU
	20	Tennessee
	24	@Florida
	27	Georgia
Mar.	4-7	#SEC Tournament

@ Road Games
* NABC Classic, Indianapolis, IN
** Food Lion MVP Classic, Charlotte, NC
*** Jimmy V Classic, East Rutherford, NJ
\# Georgia Dome, Atlanta, GA

OTHER RETURNEES

DAVID ROSS (6-5, 215 lbs., SO, F, #00, 2.2 ppg, 1.2 rpg, 8.0 minutes, Boca Ciega HS/St. Petersburg, Fla.). Ross played in 17 games last season and even started twice, but he has the misfortune of playing behind fellow sophomore Antonio Grant. Ross has a well-rounded game an is an exceptionally good passer.

He made the most of his limited time on the court. He scored 12 points in consecutive games against St. Joseph's and South Carolina State, and he notched four or more points in six games. His playing time should increase marginally this season, but Grant will still get the bulk of the minutes at the small forward spot.

OTHER NEWCOMERS

DAMIEN KINLOCH (6-7, 200 lbs., FR, F, #33, 20.8 ppg, 9.8 rpg, 3.8 bpg, North Charleston HS/Charleston, S.C.). Kinloch is the one South Carolina freshman who wouldn't figure to play a lot, because the Gamecocks are stocked at forward. But who knows? He impressed Fogler during preseason individual drill sessions, and won the admiration of his teammates for his handiwork in pickup games.

Like teammate Jamel Bradley, Kinloch comes from a winning high school program. North Charleston had a 38-game winning streak going until it was broken in the second round of the AAAA state tournament last March.

Kinloch was a first-team All-State pick as a senior, and he also played in the Carolina Classic All-Star game, which matches the best high school players from North and South Carolina. Teamed with future teammate Aaron Lucas, Kinloch paced a 96-93 South Carolina victory with a team-high 16 points, eight rebounds and four blocked shots.

Prep Stars Recruiter's Handbook ranked Kinlock No. 133 on its list of the nation's top 300 seniors.

"I like Kinloch a lot," Fogler said. "He's a very athletic player who can help us."

JAMEL BRADLEY (6-2, 160 lbs., FR, G, #10, 17.7 ppg, 5.3 rpg, 6.1 apg, Woodrow Wilson HS/Beckley, W.V.). Bradley was South Carolina's only recruit in the spring signing period, as Fogler sought to add another body at the point guard position. Without the departed Melvin Watson at the point, Fogler might need help there, especially if he decides to play BJ McKie more at shooting guard.

Bradley, who can play either guard spot, should be able to find work as a freshman, for one important reason—he's a winner.

Last season, he led Woodrow Wilson to a 22-3 record and its second straight West Virginia AAA state championship. He was a first-team All-State pick and an honorable mention All-America by *USA Today*.

A good shooter, Bradley set the West Virginia high school record last season when he shot 95 percent from the free-throw line.

Bradley continued to make his mark even after the season. Playing in the first game of the West Virginia-Ohio All-Star series last June, Bradley scored 32 points (on six three-pointers and eight for eight from the free-throw line) and made two free throws with four seconds left to give his team the win. He was chosen the game's MVP.

Bradley followed that with 17 points in the second game. He also won the three-point shooting contest, making six of 10. If Bradley can shoot anywhere near that well in college, or if he can help run the team, he'll earn significant minutes as a freshman.

QUESTIONS

Point guard? BJ McKie moves from shooting guard to the point. Will he be able to handle the job as well as did his old role? Or, will a freshman eventually take over?

Frontcourt scoring? Will freshman Tony Kitchings be able to step in and provide points? LeRon Williams can't do it all alone.

STRENGTHS

BJ McKie! The choice of most experts as the SEC Player of the Year. With an inside-outside game, McKie is close to unstoppable offensively. Whatever position he plays, McKie should be capable of taking over games.

Coaching! Fogler, with previous stops at Wichita State and Vanderbilt, has proven he is one of the nation's best while enjoying success everywhere he's been.

adidas Blue Ribbon Analysis

BACKCOURT .... B+ BENCH/DEPTH .... B+
FRONTCOURT .... B INTANGIBLES .... B+

One of these years, South Carolina is going to win an NCAA Tournament game. The Gamecocks' recent first-round failures in the Big Dance have overshadowed the rebuilding efforts of coach Eddie Fogler, who has turned the program into a perennial postseason team in just five years.

Fogler appears to have another club that is more than capable of reaching the NCAA Tournament. Even without point guard Melvin Watson, who had led the team so capably for four years, South Carolina is still loaded with veteran talent. And Fogler is very pleased with his four-man recruiting class.

There are several keys to the season. BJ McKie's ability to handle the point guard position is one key. If McKie can replace Watson, then Fogler need only come up with a shooting guard. Candidates abound, so someone should step forward to claim the position fairly quickly.

The frontcourt is in capable hands, too, with LeRon Williams, the Florida transfer, having established himself as a dependable inside scorer. If Bud Johnson, the inconsistent senior center, can live up his high school billing and become more of an offensive threat, South Carolina won't miss the talented Ryan Stack as much.

Without question, Fogler will coach the Gamecocks into a fourth-straight postseason tournament berth. We think South Carolina will finish fourth in the SEC's Eastern Division, which, coupled with a solid performance in the league tournament, will earn the Gamecocks their third straight NCAA bid.

Their first-round opponent had better beware. These guys are getting tired of early spring breaks.

(C.D.)

40
UAB

LOCATION .... Birmingham, AL
CONFERENCE .... C-USA (National)
LAST SEASON .... 21-12 (.636)
CONFERENCE RECORD 10-6 (2nd)
STARTERS LOST/RETURNING 1/4
NICKNAME .... Blazers
COLOR .... Green Gold & White
HOMECOURT .... Bartow Arena (8,500)
COACH .... Murry Bartow (UAB '91)
RECORD AT SCHOOL .... 39-26 (2 yrs.)
CAREER RECORD .... 39-26 (2 yrs.)
ASSISTANTS .... Scott Rigot (Buffalo '86)
Andy Kennedy (UAB '91)
Thomas Johnson (Montevallo '77)
TEAM WINS (last 5 yrs.) 22-14-16-18-21
RPI (last 5 yrs.) 36-127-115-95-64
1997-98 FINISH .... .Lost in NIT second round.

COACH AND PROGRAM

If you wanted to find somebody in Birmingham who figured the only reason Murry Bartow was head coach at UAB was that his father was the boss, it wouldn't have been hard. Walk down the street. Stop into a gas station. Better yet, pick up a paper.

There, on the right day, you'd have read some blistering diatribes authored against Bartow after he'd coached, oh, about a dozen games. The Blazers weren't particularly bad in those games and no one had expected they'd be particularly good, but well, his father was the boss.

If you were watching the team Bartow put on the floor, though, you would have noticed how it was creating points despite being overburdened with non-scorers and how it defended the basket with sound concepts and an acceptable degree of energy. Bartow's first team was not special, it was decent. But it certainly was not a team which should have led anyone to conclude that its coach was out of his league.

Bartow believes in employing as many strong athletes as he can muster in a physical man-to-man defense. It is more difficult to assess what he believes in offensively, because his first couple teams included guard Cedric Dixon, who always seemed to be playing his own game. With Dixon gone, expect the Blazers to play a bit faster, to look for more baskets in transition, to force the ball into the lane and to use their physical strength to its greatest advantage.

There've been so many guys in recent UAB lineups who didn't look like scorers that it was easy to get the idea the Blazers were in-offensive, but Bartow points out they averaged 75 points and scored in the 90s against fine defensive teams such as South Florida and Southern Mississippi. They even topped 100 points against a not-so-fine Houston defense.

"As I look at this team, we have a chance to be one of the higher-scoring teams in the league," Bartow said. "We have four or five different guys who can score in double figures. Maybe not to get you 20, but maybe to get you 12, 13, 14. I think we have a chance to be pretty good offensively."

This is a program that is ready to reach the NCAA Tournament on the basis of solid, consistent improvement. The players in place are as athletic, man-for- man, as most any in Conference USA.

UAB's recruiting has quickly improved in Bartow's two seasons as head coach. He got Willie Mitchell as a transfer from Michigan, Predrag Materic out of junior college and the stars of one of Alabama's best prep teams this decade, LeAndrew Bass and Myron Ransom.

This still is not an easy mission, especially with the lure of the Southeastern Conference so powerful for the players UAB is likely to target. Center Marvin Stone of Huntsville was always a longshot, but Top 25 wing guard Rod Grizzard was right there in town and still chose to head down the highway to Alabama.

This is the most difficult aspect of UAB's program, now that it's no longer a niche school and is competing in a major conference. It must recruit among the elite, and this may be more of a challenge for Bartow than just about any coach in the league—save perhaps for Bobby Lutz at UNC Charlotte, and at least he is in basketball country.

Other schools around the league have special advantages all their own: the homegrown talent base in Memphis, the tradition of Louisville, Cincinnati's Shoemaker Center. UAB is smack in the middle of the most pervasive sports conference in the nation, and doesn't belong to the SEC. This is more of a handicap than some may realize.

You think it doesn't matter? Watch the attendance figures when the Conference USA tournament heads to Birmingham this March.

UAB has managed to maintain an NIT level program as it navigates the transition to major-conference competition. Generally, its teams have had tough kids, but not enough skilled players. Bartow understands that and appears to be trying to attract more players who fit both categories.

It's not as though Bartow merely sat beside his father all those years and did not work to become a coach. No doubt connections helped him get the jobs he had, but he also worked for Bob Knight at Indiana and learned a great deal of basketball there.

Murry Bartow knows what he's doing. Is he his father? Who is? Gene Bartow won more than 600 games, led both Memphis and UCLA to the Final Four and nearly got UAB there just a few years after he started the program from scratch. Murry Bartow's father is one of the great coaches in the game's history. He should not be the measure by which Murry's career is judged.

Rather, he should be examined within the context of Conference USA, a league with more than its share of excellent coaches. In that regard, Murry Bartow is holding his own.

STARTERS NOT RETURNING

CEDRIC DIXON (5-9, PG, 13.3 ppg, 3.1 rpg, 3.2 apg, 2.2 tpg, 1.3 spg, 29.7 minutes, .405 FG, .388 3PT, .743 FT). It's hard to imagine how UAB fans put up with Dixon all these years. Oh, yeah, he led the team in scoring and assists last season, started for most of his career, topped 1,000 points and blah, blah, blah.

For all the things a team sacrifices to put a 5-9 guy on the basketball floor, it just deserves more than Dixon was willing to give in return. He did not provide floor leadership, did not create offense for his team, was not a defensive force. He could score, on occasion, but probably not if the opposing team did its job scouting.

Dixon's 31 points against Houston, that was a typical game. As was his six-point effort in the second-round NIT loss to Minnesota.

"There was a degree of inconsistency with Ced," Bartow said, "but the games he was on, he had some big, big games for us."

The problem with waiting around for Dixon to find his stroke was that he did not add enough to the equation in other areas. Had he learned to be a point guard, a true point guard, using his quickness to push the ball on the break and his shooting touch to keep defenses honest, UAB might have made the NCAA Tournament in one of the past couple years.

Instead, the lack of a full-time, on-court point guard kept all of the Blazers' perimeter players below .450 shooting. They never got easy shots, because there was no one willing to create them.

UAB will be a better basketball team with Dixon gone, no matter the statistics he takes with him.

OTHERS NOT RETURNING

PREDRAG SAVOVIC (6-4, G, 2.4 ppg, 1.0 turnovers, 7.7 minutes, .217 FG, .154 3PT, .724 FT). This is one that will hurt. When Savovic starts showing up in those midnight ESPN games, launching rainbow three-pointers for the Hawaii Rainbows, Bartow might lose a wink of sleep or two over Savovic's decision to transfer.

If it doesn't look like that from the numbers, such is the peril of playing high-major ball as a freshman. But this is a very talented player Riley Wallace will be ever so happy to have next season.

The funny thing is that Savovic began his only season at UAB in extremely promising fashion. He scored 28 points in his first four games, including 13 against Purdue and six against Indiana. He was 1-of-5 from the floor against the Hoosiers and missed two three-point attempts, but the way he played that night in his 17 minutes, you could see there was a player there.

Savovic struggled with his shot and with handling the ball as the season wore on. He was not ready for all of what was required at this level, from the standpoint of playing defense and responding to what defenses presented to him. With that year in the program, he could have been an important player for this club.

"He just didn't want to wait," Bartow said. "He could have helped us this year. He's a good player."

PROJECTED STARTERS

FRED WILLIAMS (6-8, 220 lbs., SR, PF, #22, 11.8 ppg, 7.0 rpg, 1.0 apg, 2.8 tpg, 25.3 minutes, .502 FG, .722 FT, Spartanburg Methodist JC, S.C./Queens, N.Y.). It took a while for Williams to consistently show what he was capable of doing for the Blazers, but by the end of the year he was one of the top players in Conference USA.

Williams did not start, which is something Bartow explains more with his gut than his head. "We got into a situation where we felt comfortable starting the guys we were starting," Bartow said.

That's simple. It also kept Williams down to 25 minutes per game, and he was probably worth more. He'll get them this year.

Williams is a power player, but deceptively athletic. "In the end, he's maybe the fastest guy on our team. He can run by people, is very quick to the ball from a rebounding standpoint," said Bartow.

Williams got only 71 of his 230 rebounds at the offensive end. He's got to be as aggressive going after the ball at that end, especially since it means it would add points to his total.

There is a strong possibility Williams could emerge as a star for the Blazers.

"He's potentially an All-League player," Bartow said. "This year could be a breakout year for him. He's a high-percentage shooter, can really score. He's got a knack for scoring points, and he does it in a very efficient manner."

If there are problems with his game, the first is that he is not a great shooter, although that one is mitigated by the fact he understands he's not a great shooter. The other is that he is inconsistent, perhaps emotional.

Williams closed with six consecutive double-figure games, but preceded that with three games in which he scored a combined 19. He'd catch your eye, though, even in a subpar game.

TORREY WARD (6-3, 210 lbs., JR, SG, #3, 7.3 ppg, 4.4 rpg, 1.3 apg, 1.7 tpg, .539 FG, .726 FT, 20.1 minutes, Phillips HS/Birmingham, Ala.). There are some players you just want to have on your team, and a 6-3 guard who can put up 22 points without ever launching a three-pointer is that type of player.

Ward is the farthest thing from fancy. He tried only two threes all last year, when dozens of players not only his size but a half-foot taller were killing themselves and their teams trying to prove they had that kind of range. Ward is more of an athlete than a shooting guard, but he has understood his limitations as a shooter and ballhandler to this point in his career and could dramatically improve by addressing them.

He had four scoreless games, which was a bad sign, but he got 15 points against Memphis, 17 against Auburn, 20 against Southern Mississippi and recorded a double-double against Missouri in the NIT, with 15 points and 11 boards. Ward closed the season well, averaging 12.3 ppg and hitting 34-for-66 from the field in the final seven games.

He is a garbage player, a guy who cleans up the mess left behind by players considered to be more talented. The only problem with Ward is finding minutes for him, finding where to put him, because he does not shoot and thus makes it difficult to get by when he's playing shooting guard. But his defense is so strong that it can be worth the limitations he imposes.

He started nearly all of the season because Bartow liked to bring Damon Cobb off the bench. UAB's people are very high on him. The school's preseason guide says he is "on the verge of blossoming into a major star for the Blazers." Hard to say where anyone got that notion. Ward is mostly a role player, and role players do not become stars.

"He's very, very athletic," Bartow said. "He's right there. He's got a chance. Last year, he weighed 190, now he's 210. The unknown with Torrey...has his handle improved, and his shot? It's going to be an interesting year for him."

LEANDREW BASS (6-3, 185 lbs., SO, PG, #4, 4.1 ppg, 2.5 rpg, 2.6 apg, 2.2 tpg, 17.1 minutes, .439 FG, .594 FT, West End HS/Birmingham, Ala.). There were probably a lot of times last year when Bartow was relieved he decided to bring Bass along slowly as a freshman point guard. There may be times this year when he wishes he hadn't.

Bass is standing first in line at the point guard spot for UAB. He played nearly half the time for the Blazers there last year, when Dixon was having one of his identity crises, and produced respectable assist numbers in relation to his turnovers for someone not getting the chance to control the flow of the game. He does need to cut down on the number of plays he forces, which will limit his turnover total.

Bass is strong and big for a point guard in an era when small and quick has become the standard. But that need not be a handicap if he can use his size to his advantage.

Bass creates well off the dribble and is more effective than a lot of point guards when he gets in the lane. His vision is not always obscured by the defense.

Shooting is a problem and could cost him the starting job if JC recruit Eric Holmes shows he is a point guard. Bass was 0-for-7 from three-point range last year. For a team that is not loaded with great shooters, it'd be nice to have a guy in the back who can stick a three.

Bass scores other ways, though. He had 17 points in the Conference USA semifinals against Memphis, although that game was not especially competitive. With greater pressure in the NIT, he passed for five assists in 20 minutes against Minnesota.

As a defender, he is especially adept at attacking those less fortunate than himself. He picked up nine steals total in consecutive games against Norfolk State and Houston.

Bass' passing skills are outstanding. In the final six games, he had multiple assists in 14 appearances, even though he only once played more than 25 minutes.

As a high school player, Bass was the driving force behind a West End team that upset several programs with a greater national reputation. He knows how to win and could be the better of Bartow's two choices to run the offense.

"I think he's ready," Bartow said. "Certainly there are some things he has to do to refine his game, but he's very fast with the ball, very competitive. Certainly shooting-wise, he's got to improve over what he did last year. He's a very good penetrator, a guy who understands the game and gets the ball where it needs to go."

DEWAYNE BROWN (6-7, 250 lbs., SR, C, #25, 4.6 ppg, 4.1 rpg, 1.1 tpg, 14.5 minutes, .468 FG, .577 FT, Jones County JC/Bessemer, Ala.). It's almost by default, but not entirely, that Brown holds down the middle of the UAB front line. He is not tall enough, not skilled enough, but he is certainly man enough.

The longer last season went on, the more Bartow relied upon Brown because of the way he clogs up the middle on defense and stands up for himself on the boards. Once his minutes went into the 20s and stayed there, over the final nine games, he averaged 6.8 rpg. He got a career-high 10 against Saint Louis in a key victory that advanced the Blazers to the Conference USA Tournament semifinals.

Brown does tend to get into foul trouble; he had four or more in six of the last eight games, but it's hard for him to play it any differently.

UAB has a few bigger players, but none who've proven they are better for the job. Brown is not going to be a major offensive player for the Blazers. They rarely throw him the ball, expecting him mostly to set screens and collect offensive rebounds. But he could stand to shoot better at the free throw line. He was 41-for-71 last year.

MYRON RANSOM (6-5, 220 lbs., SO, SF, #13, 4.6 ppg, 2.3 rpg, 1.1 tpg, 11.1 minutes, .442 FG, .375 3PT, .652 FT, West End HS/Birmingham, Ala.). The other half of Bartow's recruiting coup two years ago, Ransom is a dynamic athlete whose potential improvement is a key to the Blazers' high hopes.

He had an inconsistent freshman season, flashing brilliance in a 16-minute stint against Indiana, sustaining it with 17 points and eight rebounds against North Texas. When he played with confidence toward the latter part of the season, he hit for eight or more points in six of the final nine games. All of the three- pointers he scored came in that stretch, from Feb. 19 to the end of the season. He did not try one prior to that.

But in between were too many games in which he was not a factor, including several where he barely played.

Ransom works the baseline well, although where a Nate Johnson takes the goal head-on, Ransom tends to slash in sideways and use the backboard. He could be more productive as an offensive rebounder, because, if he went after the ball, he's got the ideal skills to then make a play.

"Certainly Myron is a guy we're waiting very anxiously to see what he's going to do," Bartow said. "He's a guy (who) could break out and have a big year. He's strong, aggressive. He'll tear your head off."

Ransom has the opportunity to become UAB's starting small forward, but he'll have to play consistently and confidently to keep the job with veterans such as Willie Mitchell and Antonio Jackson possibly sitting the bench. Neither of them is a true wing.

Mitchell can play the position; Jackson is a power player who could take a spot in the lineup and force Bartow to juggle other positions. The problem with a Williams-Brown-Ransom front line is that it's awfully small, although Bartow is a coach who uses a lot of combinations and would not be wedded to that group for extended periods if it became a problem.

"In our program, we really can't recruit a better-looking kid than (Ransom). He's a phenomenal athlete," Bartow said. "We're just kind of all waiting to see what he's going to do. We could look up when he's a senior and be looking at an NBA player.

"Last year, he was a freshman, and some games he's not getting minutes and some games he's getting 18. A lot just comes with playing and having a better feel for what we want. I think that will become much clearer to him this year."

1997-98 RESULTS

Arkansas-Pine Bluff	81-51
@Cleveland State	74-58
Indiana (L)	64-80
#Purdue (L)	64-92
#Southwestern Louisiana	76-67
#UCLA (L)	72-86
North Texas	79-73
Vanderbilt (L)	74-85
@Tennessee-Chattanooga	57-55
@Auburn	71-65
##Florida	80-73
Jackson State	84-61
@South Florida	62-48
@Marquette	65-62
Tulane	85-66
Louisville	55-53
@Saint Louis (L)	60-77
@Memphis (L)	70-86
@UNC Charlotte (L)	80-86
Houston	78-61
DePaul (L)	53-54
Memphis	88-77
@Southern Mississippi (L)	56-73
@Tulane	77-69
Cincinnati (L)	76-93
@Houston	104-70
Norfolk State	103-74
South Florida	92-76
Southern Mississippi	93-81
###Saint Louis	76-74
###Cincinnati (L)	85-100
%Missouri	93-86
%%Minnesota (L)	66-69

@ away games
# Carrs Great Alaska Shootout, Anchorage, AK
HIP Orange Bowl Classic, Miami, FL
Conference USA Tournament, Shoemaker Center, Cincinnati, OH
% NIT first round, Columbia, MO
%% NIT second round, Minneapolis, MN

KEY RESERVES

DAMON COBB (6-4, 195 lbs., SR, G, #11, 9.4 ppg, 1.9 rpg, 1.6 apg, 1.6 tpg, 1.3 spg, .411 FG, .421 3PT, .780 FT, 24.0 minutes, Memorial HS/Evansville, Ind.). "As other people scout him, I'm sure they say he's just a shooter," Bartow said. "But, for us, he does a lot of things that help us win."

Cobb is a team captain whom Bartow considers an inspirational leader, the sort of player who will pursue loose balls, throw himself in front of a driving ballhandler to draw a charge and fight for any available possession. He's a bright kid who twice won Conference USA's scholar-athlete award.

He also can shoot like the devil, although athletic teams tend not to have trouble taking him out of the offense. He scored a just 23 points combined in four games against Cincinnati and Memphis.

Cobb was another UAB player who closed the season strong, hitting double figures in all but two of the final 10 games and averaging 14.1 ppg in that stretch. His three-point shooting is the key to nearly all his scoring. Only 19 of his field goals last year came from inside the line, 19 out of 50 attempts, which is quite dreadful when you think about it.

Opponents who pay attention to Cobb should be able to limit him simply by forcing him to take the ball inside the defense. But he can be deadly from long distance when left open. He was 33-for-67 in the last 10 games, a .492 percentage.

"He hits a lot of threes, a lot of big threes late in games,'" Bartow said. Exhibit A in that regard was his 11-point second half against Saint Louis in the Conference USA semifinals.

WILLIE MITCHELL (6-8, 215 lbs., SR, F, #33, 9.5 ppg, 5.0 rpg, 1.3 apg, 1.9 tpg, 21.2 minutes, .421 FG, .286 3PT, .667 FT, Michigan & Pershing HS/Detroit, Mich.). Rare is the McDonald's All-America who winds up at UAB, and rare is the McDonald's All-America who does as little with that designation as Mitchell. He probably should never have had that honor, lacking as the does the athletic explosiveness and offensive polish one would expect from a player regarded as one of the 25 best in all of high school basketball.

Bartow defends Mitchell as someone who got the Blazers "10 and six. Everybody expects so much more, but a lot of guys can't get you 10 and six."

Willie didn't either, not quite. And what he did get would have been fine if he'd put out the same sort of numbers every night. Instead, he was all over the map, mostly putting up the big stats against lesser teams and often taking the night off when it got tough.

Mitchell scored 19 points against UCLA, 13 against Indiana and 12 against Saint Louis, but the Blazers lost all three games by substantial margins. He also had games of four, four and two against Cincinnati, UNC Charlotte and Purdue.

In Conference USA games, he slid to 7.5 ppg. He's not a shooter (6-for-21 on threes) and is one of the Blazers' least impressive defensive players.

Mitchell broke his foot and missed six of the final 10 games, then had offseason surgery to repair damage. He reportedly was dedicated to offseason conditioning and may return an improved player.

"He's kind of an in-between guy," said Bartow, who used him at both small forward and power forward. Bartow does not like to use Williams and Mitchell at the same time because it makes the Blazers a bit sluggish on defense. That fact caused Mitchell's playing time to slide, because Williams emerged as one of the team's best players.

"He's got to get more comfortable, and we've got to get more comfortable with him," Bartow said of Mitchell. "Willie can score. If you get him the ball in the right position, he can get you points. He's a pretty good rebounder."

ANTONIO JACKSON (6-8, 220 lbs., SR, F/C, #34, 7.5 ppg, 4.2 rpg, 1.2 tpg, 19.1 minutes, .508 FG, .589 FT, Wake Forest & Aliceville HS/Aliceville, Ala.). Jackson started all but seven games last season, and he could open this year in the lineup once again. But it's hard to imagine him not playing behind Williams if this team wants to contend for a tournament bid. It also is possible he could play in the middle and fight Brown for a starting spot, which seems the most likely scenario by which Jackson gets extended playing time.

Jackson had nine double-figure scoring games last year—four of them coming in a row against Tulane, Cincinnati, Houston and Norfolk State in early February. He is more skilled than Brown, although he does not rebound as well and does not have the same strength to apply defensively. He is the closest thing this team has to a shot-blocker, but even at that does not average one per game (0.7 bpg).

Although he was a starter, he only occasionally played more than 20 minutes per game. He got 34 minutes against Vanderbilt and had a career game, with 20 points and nine rebounds in early December, and, in 26 minutes against UNC Charlotte, had 19 points and eight rebounds.

So which comes first, the chicken or the egg? Does he produce when given extended minutes, or does he get extended minutes when he produces? His only other 30-minute game was against South Florida, when he had eight points and seven rebounds and would have hit double-figure scoring had he not gone 4-for-8 from the foul line.

PREDRAG MATERIC (6-6, 215 lbs., JR, F/G, #5, 3.4 ppg, 2.3 rpg, 1.2 apg, 1.1 tpg, 16.4 minutes, .333 FG, .373 3PT, .595 FT, Barton County CC, Kan./Sarajevo, Yugoslavia). Materic was not quite the impact player Bartow had hoped upon signing him out of junior college, but at least he has an extra year to try and make something happen. Materic came in as a sophomore, which meant there wasn't as much urgency for him to establish himself.

Materic was heavy in the rotation in the middle of the season, but was only intermittently effective. He was 4-for-6 on threes against Tulane and 2-for-5 against UNC Charlotte, but fell into the trap of only firing long-distance shots. He gradually accomplished less and less as the season progressed and did not hit double-figure minutes in four of the final five games.

Materic is an excellent passer and would be a good complement to Myron Ransom and Willie Mitchell at small forward, bringing an entirely different look to the position.

Bartow intends to play Materic mostly at the small forward because he is well-stocked at shooting guard, and Materic does provide a different look for the Blazers. He is a shooter and scorer, not the kind of defensive athlete that is mostly comprises their frontcourt. However, he's got to find that shooting touch against high-level defense if he's going to get more playing time.

"I would hope we'd get more this year. I don't know how much more," Bartow said. "What he was up against, that takes some getting used to."

ERIC HOLMES (6-3, 185 lbs., JR, G, #21, 19.1 ppg, 2.8 rpg, 3.7 apg, 2.6 spg, Dixie JC, Ut./Pasadena, Calif.). The question right now is whether Holmes will be a shooting guard or point guard for the Blazers, or both. He will compete for starting jobs at both positions, although it appears the first look will be at point guard because there is no one beside Bass at the position.

"He can shoot the ball. He averaged more than three made threes per game," Bartow said. "I like his toughness. He'll actually go to the other end and guard somebody, which helps. He's a tough kid, has a lot of self-confidence."

Holmes played both backcourt positions at Dixie JC and led a 28-5 team in scoring. He was first-team All-Region and ranked No. 44 among JC prospects by analyst Phil Henzel. Henzel listed Holmes as shooting 95-for-244 (.389) on three-pointers at Dixie and .457 from the field overall.

Other programs that recruited Holmes looked at him more as a shooter, but it's hard to figure where he'd fit in that regard with UAB with Ward and Cobb already in place. It's likely he'll get some minutes at each guard spot, and could take over at the point if Bass is a disappointment.

OTHER RETURNEES

IGOR NIKOLIC (7-1, 240 lbs., SO, C, #50, 2.6 ppg, 2.4 rpg, 6.8 minutes, .500 FG, .625 FT, Garden City CC, Kan./Zemun, Serbia). Nikolic redshirted after making five brief appearances and then injuring his knee as a sophomore transfer.

His most extensive action was 14 minutes against Indiana, during which he blocked two shots but did not do much on the boards. He did get four rebounds in each of two seven-minute stints against Arkansas-Pine Bluff and Cleveland State.

Nikolic is more of a European-style player, but, since no one else on this team is an on-the-block offensive player, his basket-facing offense is not necessarily a detriment. If he can rebound and defend the goal at this level, which has not yet been established, he could give UAB an important frontcourt weapon.

FELIX OKAM (6-11, 230 lbs., SR, C, #51, 0.6 ppg, 1.6 rpg, 4.7 minutes, .500 FG, .333 FT, Alabama State/Onitsha, Nigeria). Okam transferred from Alabama State, but has not been able to prove himself at the high-major level. He got walkon style minutes during his second full season at UAB, his appearances dropping from 21 as a sophomore to nine as a junior.

It is unlikely he will be a contributor for the Blazers as a senior.

BILL ARMSTRONG (6-1, G, 0.3 ppg, 0.7 rpg, six appearances, Oneonta HS/Oneonta, Ala.). Armstrong spent his first year in the program as a walkon, seeing action in six games. His only points coming against Norfolk State, which was also his only playing stint longer than a minute.

1998-99 UAB SCHEDULE

Nov.	14	Alcorn State
	18	@Indiana
	22	Tulsa
	24	Cleveland State
	29	@South Alabama
Dec.	1	Texas-Arlington
	5	@Western Kentucky
	8	Jacksonville State
	12	Auburn
	15	Princeton
	21-23	#Puerto Rico Holiday Classic
	30	@Tulane
Jan.	2	@Memphis
	7	Marquette
	9	Houston
	14	@DePaul
	16	@South Florida
	21	Tulane
	24	UNC Charlotte
	30	@Cincinnati
Feb.	4	@Houston
	7	Southern Mississippi
	11	Memphis
	18	South Florida
	20	@Southern Mississippi
	25	@Louisville
	27	Saint Louis
Mar.	3-6	##Conference USA Tournament

@ Road Games
# Bayamone, PR (vs. Ohio State, first round; also America University-PR; Middle Tennessee State, Mississippi, North Carolina State, Oklahoma and St. Joseph's)
Birmingham-Jefferson Civic Center, Birmingham, AL

OTHER NEWCOMERS

None.

QUESTIONS

Interior defense? Because of its size problem, UAB has given up some big numbers to opposing centers. Cincinnati's Kenyon Martin got 19 points, same as Purdue's Brad Miller. Conference USA doesn't have many guys like that, which is a plus.

Point guard? Will it be Bass or Holmes? Will either or a combination of both be consistent enough to direct a tournament-level ballclub?

Consistency? With Bartow's frequent player rotations, it is sometimes hard to get a sense of what this team wants to be. That can be a positive, because the Blazers are hard to scout, but they get lost from time to time themselves.

ANSWERS

Fred Williams! This is a player who perhaps doesn't deserve his own exclamation point, but who will develop into a solid, high-teens scorer and will rebound with most anyone in the league. UAB has needed a "go-to" guy since Carlos Williams left, and Williams should be that guy.

Depth! Bartow can keep reaching into his bench until he finds somebody who's having a good night, plus he's got all the fouls he can use in the post.

Defense! UAB teams most often are no fun to play. Ransom, Ward and Brown will make this group fit that tradition.

adidas Blue Ribbon Analysis

BACKCOURT	**B**	**BENCH/DEPTH**	**A**
FRONTCOURT	**B**	**INTANGIBLES**	**B**

This is not the prettiest team in the *Blue Ribbon* Top 40, but it's a mature group with great athletes who want to play defense and enough gifted shooters to get the ball in the goal.

The Blazers should be more adept at getting the ball where it needs to go, since Dixon will no longer be around to short-circuit the attack. If Williams emerges as a key target and Ward continues his rapid improvement, the Blazers could have two players who are among the most notable in Conference USA.

The key to the season remains the development of the West End HS sophomores, Bass and Ransom. They are the immediate future of UAB basketball and, if they progress from promising freshman years, it will be a bright future. If one or the other is not ready, there are enough players around to take their place in the lineup.

However, if both are on schedule, UAB will be a tough team to keep out of the NCAA field.

(M.D.)

CONFERENCE PREVIEWS

AMERICA EAST CONFERENCE

adidas BLUE RIBBON FORECAST

1. Delaware
2. Drexel
3. Hofstra
4. Maine
5. Boston University
6. Northeastern
7. Vermont
8. Hartford
9. Towson
10. New Hampshire

ALL-CONFERENCE TEAM

G—Andy Bedard, JR, Maine
G—Craig Claxton, JR, Hofstra
F—Walter Brown, SR, Boston University
F—Mike Pegues, JR, Delaware
C—Joe Linderman, JR, Drexel

PLAYER OF THE YEAR

Craig Claxton, JR, Hofstra

NEWCOMER OF THE YEAR

Andy Bedard, JR, Maine

1998-99 CONFERENCE TOURNAMENT

Feb. 27-Mar. 1, 7, Bob Carpenter Center, Newark, DE (Championship game at homecourt of highest remaining seed)

1997-98 CHAMPIONS

Boston University and Delaware (regular season)
Delaware (conference tournament)

1997-98 POSTSEASON PARTICIPANTS

Postseason Record: 0-1 (.000)
NCAA
Delaware (first round)

TOP BACKCOURTS

1. Boston University
2. Hofstra
3. Maine

TOP FRONTCOURTS

1. Delaware
2. Drexel
3. Maine

ON THE WAY UP

Maine

ON THE WAY DOWN

Hartford

INSIDE THE NUMBERS

- 1997-98 conference RPI: 17th (of 30)
- Conference RPI (last 5 years): 19-16-23-13-17

DID YOU KNOW?

Last season, Delaware, Boston University, Hartford and Northeastern each posted victories against every other team in the conference...Maine, which added two transfers from Boston College this season, will welcome Temple transfer Julian Dunkley, a 6-10 forward, next season. Dunkley, one of the nation's top recruits in 1996, will have two seasons remaining at Maine...For the first time since the '93-94 season, America East has no rookie head coaches...The conference championship game will be televised by ESPN for the 12th consecutive year...League commissioner Chris Monach recently signed a three-year contract extension.

(C.C.)

BOSTON UNIVERSITY

LOCATION .... **Boston, MA**
CONFERENCE .... **America East**
LAST SEASON .... **19-11 (.633)**
CONFERENCE RECORD .... **12-6 (t-1st)**
STARTERS LOST/RETURNING **1/4**
NICKNAME .... **Terriers**
COLORS .... **Scarlet & White**
HOMECOURT .... **Case Gym (1,800)**
COACH .... **Dennis Wolff (Connecticut '78)**
RECORD AT SCHOOL .... **77-43 (4 yrs.)**
CAREER RECORD .... **107-61 (6 yrs.)**
ASSISTANTS .... **Don Farquahr (Austin '77)**
Larry Greer (Northeastern '89)
Orlando Vandross (American International '92)
TEAM WINS (last 5 yrs.) **11-15-18-25-19**
RPI (last 5 yrs.) **219-146-119-38-88**
1997-98 FINISH .... **Lost in conference final.**

For much of last season the America East was a topsy-turvy league: Picked to finish seventh, Vermont led the conference until February;. After four straight years in the postseason, Drexel slumped to a losing record. Northeastern beat everyone and lost to everyone. Hartford underachieved, while Delaware, perhaps, overachieved.

At the end, there was Boston University, now a mainstay in America East. The Terriers, picked to win the league, shared the title with Delaware.

"I definitely have the feeling that we have put BU back to where year in and year out we can compete for the top spot," Terriers coach Dennis Wolff said.

Boston University certainly had its moments during the '97-98 season. After a Feb. 3 loss to Northeastern, the Terriers were on a four-game slide and just 5-6 in the league. Then BU won its last seven games and tied Delaware for the conference title

A nine-game winning streak took the Terriers to the America East tournament championship game, where they lost to the Blue Hens, 66-58. It ended a streaky season for the Terriers.

"We had a few injuries and a suspension and it took us into the middle of the year before we all got on the same page," Wolff said. "To be honest, we just played terrifically right up to the end."

That suspension was imposed on **LeVar Folk** and was potentially a wound from which the Terriers might not have healed. But they did.

A December blowup with Wolff over an academic issue resulted in six-game suspension for the 5-10 senior point guard, during which it was unsure if Folk would return. When he finally apologized to his coach, Folk was allowed back. It took another eight games for Folk to get his starting job back and when he did, he made it count.

Folk averaged 15.8 ppg, 6.4 assists and played 37 minutes per game in his first five games back as a starter. He finished the year averaging 11.3 ppg and 5.5 assists (131 total). Folk was second in America East in assists. The suspension is now a distant memory and Folk is again one of the league's top lead guards, a status he has held since his sophomore year.

"Over the last 10 games LeVar was arguably the best player in our league," Wolff said. "I wouldn't trade him for any other point guard in the league."

Folk's assist numbers could continue to climb if he regularly looks to 6-6 senior forward **Walter Brown** (14.7 ppg, 8.9 rpg, .528 FG, 32 blocks). In his first season at Boston University after transferring from Holy Cross, Brown quickly became the Terriers' top player. The wiry, athletic senior led the team in scoring and was fourth in the league in rebounding, earning second-team all-conference honors.

With Joey Beard's dependable work on the boards no longer available, Brown's jumping-jack rebounding style will have to continue to produce results. With those two leading the way, the Terriers topped the conference in rebounding margin last year.

"Joey did a lot of the little things," Wolff said. "Some of these other guys will have to do the same things. Walter is more of a scorer and we are not going to be able to ask Walter to do what Joey was doing. We are going to ask Walter to do the same things, only better."

One of those other guys is 6-6 senior **Matt Curley** (5.3 ppg, 3.2 rpg). BU is going to need more size and Curley could fit the bill.

Curley, the younger brother of former Boston College big men Bill and Mickey Curley, had short streaks of productive minutes a year ago, but nothing sustained. Curley made 13 starts and only Brown and Beard played more minutes among the big men. That time will probably rise. So must the numbers.

"Curley is still a question mark," Wolff said. "I think he is better than the way he played last year."

Otherwise, Wolff will have to rely on a group of young players to increase their output. One such player, 6-7 **Jean Avebe** (3.3 ppg, 3.5 rpg), is back for his junior year, but it's just his fourth year playing in the United States. A native of Yaounde, Cameroon, Avebe is still a little raw in ability and somewhat injury-prone, but he is improving. Despite minor arthroscopic knee surgery in the middle of the season,

1998-99 BOSTON UNIVERSITY SCHEDULE

Nov.	17	UNC Charlotte
	22	@Alabama
	27	*Miami (Ohio)
	30	American
Dec.	5	@Northeastern
	8	@Harvard
	22	Manhattan
	28-29	#Bobcat Holiday Classic
Jan.	3	@Towson
	5	@Delaware
	10	Maine
	12	New Hampshire
	15	@Drexel
	17	@Hofstra
	22	Vermont
	24	@Hartford
	29	Towson
	31	Delaware
Feb.	4	@New Hampshire
	6	@Maine
	10	Northeastern
	13	Hofstra
	15	Drexel
	19	@Vermont
	21	Hartford
26-Mar.	6	##America East Tournament

@ Road Games
* Nova Scotia
# Bozeman, MT (vs. Colorado, first round; also Canisius and Montana State)
Bob Carpenter Center, Newark, DE (Championship game at homecourt of highest seeded team)

Avebe was making significant strides and was a key reserve at the end of the season. By the end of this season he could be much more than that.

"We need Avebe to be more aggressive offensively, but I'm not worried about him defensively or rebounding. He could really blossom," Wolff said.

Wolff has two good-sized freshmen in his four-player recruiting class who will have to be in the mix to give the Terriers some depth. They are 6-7, 220-pound **Jerome Graham** of Washburn HS in North Minneapolis, Minn., and 6-8, 215-pound **Ignacio Rodriguez** of St. Thomas More HS in the Spain's Canary Islands. They are the tallest players on the roster other than 6-10 junior **Ken Michin** (2.5 ppg, 1.6 rpg). Graham earned second-team All-Metro honors as a high school senior, averaging 19.3 ppg. Rodriguez averaged 14 ppg and grabbed 8.1 rpg for a St. Thomas More team that sent seven players to Division I programs.

Michin has been plagued by injuries, most of which can be tied to his weight. He returned to a limited role last year after a redshirt season, but by late-February had ballooned to 280 pounds. He dropped down to 260 before the summer, but Wolff will not let Michin or his decent offensive skills return to the floor until he loses at least 10 more pounds.

The backcourt has no such worries. Folk also has a standout offensive weapon in the backcourt in 6-2 senior **Billy Beal** (13.4 ppg, 2.1 rpg, 60 assists, 67 of 180 three-point shots).

BU came to rely on Beal to step up and he did just that. He earned a starting job in mid-January. His scoring average jumped eight points from his sophomore to junior season and Beal became the Terriers best long-range shooter. Without Beal's heroics, BU's late-season run may never have happened.

The Terriers escaped with a 70-69 victory at Maine in mid-February when Beal made a three-pointer in the final seconds. BU went on to win six more in a row heading into the conference championship game.

Beal finished second on the team in scoring and led in three-pointers, earning third-team all-conference honors.

Even more accurate from long range is 6-4 junior **Mike Costello** (7.8 ppg, 1.6 rpg, 50 assists), who made 39 percent (57 of 146) of his three-point shots. Costello started more games than Beal (25 to 23), but played six fewer minutes per game. Costello and Beal spent plenty of time on the floor together last year and Wolff says they will do so again—even though BU is going with a smaller lineup.

"Mike Costello looks night and day different physically. He's got a great chance to be our most improved player," Wolff said.

Wolff also added two freshmen guards—6-4 **Marshall Crane** of Bishop Brady HS in Concord, N.H., and 6-0 **Dereck Franklin** of Chantilly HS in Chantilly, Va. Crane is a solid outside shooter. He averaged 14.0 ppg for the New Hampshire state runner-up.

Franklin is a combo guard whose 25.0 ppg helped him gain an invitation to play in the Capital Classic all-star game He has the best chance of any of the four freshmen to play immediately.

adidas Blue Ribbon Analysis

BACKCOURT .... **B+** **BENCH/DEPTH** .... **B**
FRONTCOURT .... **C+** **INTANGIBLES** .... **B+**

The Terriers have earned at least a share of the last two regular-season America East titles and have appeared in three straight tournament championship games. Each of those streaks could grow in '99.

Replacing 6-10 forward/center Joey Beard's production and presence is the only significant problem to solve. The Terriers have no player with Beard's combination of size and skills. In fact, no player on the roster seems to be even close.

Matt Curley, Jean Avebe, and perhaps Jerome Graham or Ignacio Rodriguez could end up being keys to whether BU can distance itself from a group of four or five teams vying for the America East title.

"Our season hinges on how we replace Beard," Wolff said.

Everything else seems settled. The distractions created by Folk's suspension won't be there and Walter Brown could be even better as the club's offensive catalyst.

"I think Walter can play better. If he just improves his foul shooting (.638 FT), he'd score 18 points a game," Wolff said.

Billy Beal is a good outside shooter and an even better all-around player. He and Folk can match any guard duo in the conference. Beal and Mike Costello give BU solid long-range weapons on every possession.

Wolff always has a dependable—f not stifling—defense to rely upon. The Terriers were again near the top of the conference in stopping opponents (second in average points allowed, 67.5, and third in field-goal defense, .417).

That kind of defense and three proven and dependable offensive players in Brown, Folk, and Beal will be enough to at least get the Terriers to last season's level. And that, as usual, will have them in the hunt for an NCAA Tournament berth.

(C.C.)

DELAWARE

LOCATION .... **Newark, DE**
CONFERENCE .... **America East**
LAST SEASON .... **20-10 (.666)**
CONFERENCE RECORD .... **12-6 (t-1st)**
STARTERS LOST/RETURNING **4/1**
NICKNAME .... **Fightin' Blue Hens**
COLORS .... **Royal Blue & Gold**
HOMECOURT .... **Acierno Arena/Carpenter Center (5,000)**
COACH .... **Mike Brey (George Washington '82)**
RECORD AT SCHOOL .... **50-38 (3 yrs.)**
CAREER RECORD .... **50-38 (3 yrs.)**
ASSISTANTS .... **Sean Kearney (Scranton '81)**
Kenny Blakeney (Duke '95)
G.R. Myers (Delaware '97)
TEAM WINS (last 5 yrs.) **14-12-15-15-20**
RPI (last 5 yrs.) **166-175-163-154-95**
1997-98 FINISH .... **Lost in NCAA first round.**

Delaware coach Mike Brey loves a good transfer—and for good reason.

In Brey's three years as Delaware's coach, he has signed 17 players. Eight of them were transfers. Most of them have been a big success.

"I think it's because I'm a transfer," said the former Duke assistant. "For the most part our track record has been good. When I got here I said one of our goals should be if we could have a quality transfer sitting out every year."

So far Brey has reached his goal.

In Brey's first year, Keith Davis, a transfer from Virginia Commonwealth, sat out but practiced with the Blue Hens. Davis then started 61 games and was the leader on last year's America East championship team. Two seasons ago, forward **Darryl Presley**, a transfer from Virginia, could only practice with the team, but he became a force at the end of last season.

Last year, the players in waiting were **John Gordon**, a former first-team All-America East guard at Maine, and 7-1 **Ndongo Ndiaye**, a transfer from Providence.

This season, guard Billy Wells, a transfer from Tulane, will practice with the team before assuming the point-guard job in 1999-2000.

"What it does is it keeps you from ever being real young. You always have a man," Brey said. "When Davis became eligible, he was a 21-year-old man who'd been through the battles. And they can't go anywhere else. They can't look over their shoulder. They have to make it work and they are doing it your way."

That experience helped the Blue Hens play their best basketball in February. Delaware won eight of its last 11 conference games and tied preseason favorite Boston University for the regular-season title.

The Blue Hens took advantage of the homecourt in the America East Tournament and earned the school's first NCAA tournament berth since 1992.

Forget that Delaware endured the worst beating in the NCAA Tournament last year with a 39-point loss to Purdue. Last season was still a rousing success.

"Certainly it's gratifying to do in the third year with the group of kids you worked so hard to get in the first two years," said Brey, who went to five Final Fours as an assistant at Duke "It was a tough climb and it feels good, but this year offers a new challenge."

With the most veteran team in America East, the Blue Hens are poised to meet that challenge. Davis (10.6 ppg, 6.4 rpg.) is a key loss, but everyone else is back, led by first-team All-America East forward **Mike Pegues** (16.8 ppg, 6.8 rpg, .511 FG).

Perhaps no player in the league was as consistent as the 6-5, 245-pound Pegues, a junior and former high school teammate of Presley's at DeMatha (Md.) HS, also the alma mater and first coaching stop for Brey.

Pegues scored in double figures in all but one conference game and in all but two games last year. He scored 17 against Purdue and 18 at Boston University in his first game back from a fractured right hand. Pegues could be the most rugged player in America East.

Presley (12.9 ppg, 7.7 rpg, .541 FG percentage, 23 blocked shots), a 6-6 junior, was probably the Blue Hens' best player in March. He scored 41 points and grabbed 37 rebounds in the America East Tournament, including 25 points and 13 rebounds in the championship game against Boston University. Presley was chosen the tournament's most valuable player.

With the problems that doomed him at Virginia and his early inconsistency of last year behind him, Presley seems to be reaching the potential many anticipated when he came out of DeMatha.

"Both Pegues and Presley had great summers and they are very confident young men now," Brey said.

Brey added some frontcourt help for Pegues and Presley with the addition of Ndiaye, who becomes eligible December 21. The 7-1 junior from Senegal will be the tallest player in Blue Hen history. Ndiaye is a raw talent who never was more than a reserve at Providence, averaging 1.6 points and 1.2 rebounds in five games last season.

Ndiaye's size and athleticism should make him an effective shot blocker. With an opportunity for a starting job at Delaware, he may get the chance to prove himself, but he's not a scoring threat like Pegues and Presley. Ndiaye is on the roster, but could sit out this season and have two years left.

Brey didn't use a true center last year, but if he does this season it will either be Ndiaye or 6-10 senior co-captain **John Bennett** (4.0 ppg, 3.1 rpg, 40 blocks).

Bennett doesn't stray too far from the basket, as his career field-goal percentage (.587) would suggest.

Seniors **Fred Gonzalez** (1.5 ppg, 0.5 rpg), a 6-9 forward, and 6-10 center **Mohammed Niang** (0.8 ppg, 0.5 rpg), another Senegal native, will have trouble breaking into the rotation. Each played in 11 games last season. Still, Brey would like to find another post player.

Gordon, a 5-10 junior, returns to his home state after two impressive seasons at Maine. He steps in for Davis at shooting guard, but they are two distinctly different players. As Brey said, Davis "did all the tough stuff" and was the Blue Hens' leader. Gordon's contributions will be many, but far more tangible. Gordon averaged 14.7 points, 2.9 rebounds, 3.3 assists and shot .407 from three-point range at Maine two years ago. An excellent ball-handler, Gordon played point guard at Maine as a sophomore.

"John Gordon is the best shooter I've ever seen," said Northeastern coach Rudy Keeling, who recruited Gordon and coached him during his freshman year at Maine. "I told somebody when he played for me, if he played horse with

1998-99 DELAWARE SCHEDULE

Nov.	14	@American
	18	Delaware State
	23	Rider
	25	@Howard
Dec.	1	@Colgate
	5	@Drexel
	12	*Lafayette
	21-22	#College of Charleston Tournament
	27	@Virginia
Jan.	3	Northeastern
	5	Boston University
	10	Towson
	14	@Vermont
	16	@Hartford
	19	@Hofstra
	22	Maine
	24	New Hampshire
	27	Drexel
	29	@Northeastern
	31	@Boston University
Feb.	7	@Towson
	10	Hofstra
	13	Vermont
	15	Hartford
	18	@Maine
	20	@New Hampshire
26-Mar.	6	##America East Tournament

@ Road Games
* Desmond Conference Challenge, Albany, NY
# Charleston, SC (vs. Charleston Southern, first round; also College of Charleston and Stonybrook)
Bob Carpenter Center, Newark DE (Championship game at homecourt of highest seeded team)

Larry Bird, the game would go on forever."

Gordon could share the point-guard job with 5-11 senior **Tyrone Perry** (9.8 ppg, 3.2 rpg, 90 assists, 54 steals). Perry was Brey's first recruit at Delaware and has been a regular since his arrival. He was the club's leading three-pointer shooter (61 of 149 three-point shots, .409 percent) and free-throw shooter (.786).

Perry's shooting ability will allow Brey to move his guards into the best matchups possible. Often last season, Perry would move to shooting guard late in games while Davis handled the point-guard job.

"We'll worry who handles the ball most of the time later, but they are going to play together. I don't care how small they are. Those two are bulldogs," Brey said.

Perhaps another starter in the three-guard lineup will be 6-4 sophomore **Greg Miller** (6.1 ppg, 1.9 rpg, 49 assists, 36 of 93 three-point shots). He started 22 games as a redshirt freshman.

A similar player is 6-2 junior **Kestutis Marciulionis** (9.7 ppg, 1.6 rpg, 42 assists), who was second on the team behind Perry with 57 three-pointers (.329 from three-point range). The left-handed shooting Lithuanian might be the best backup scoring threat in America East.

Also returning is another Senegal native, 6-5 sophomore forward/guard **Madou Diouf** (2.3 ppg, 1.5 rpg). He played well in spot duty last year until the end of the season. Brey likes his athleticism. Diouf may be a better defensive player than Miller or Marciulionis and he becomes more important with the graduation of Davis.

Tobias Mullen (1.0 ppg, 0.3 rpg) averaged just 2.9 minutes in 10 games last season, but Brey believes the 6-4 senior walkon could also be the defensive specialist. Providing depth will be 6-1 sophomore guard **Dave Arnold** (1.3 ppg, 0.2 rpg).

adidas Blue Ribbon Analysis

BACKCOURT .... B+ BENCH/DEPTH .... B
FRONTCOURT .... B+ INTANGIBLES .... B

The Blue Hens are the favorites in America East and that probably won't change next year. Brey's three most talented players—Darryl Presley, Mike Pegues and John Gordon—are juniors. They want a return trip to the NCAA Tournament in '99.

"I'm not going to sell us short. We think we have a chance to be even more special than last year," Brey said. "But we also know it's fragile."

The only key personnel change is the loss of guard Keith Davis, but that is enough of a loss for Brey.

"Keith Davis was so important to us. The other players listened to him and respected him. He always was the ace in the hole," Brey said.

Brey has plenty of questions about this year's team, but most coaches in the league would love to have players like Pegues, Presley, Gordon, and Tyrone Perry.

Like last year, the league will be very competitive for the top five or six spots. Delaware will be right there near the top.

(C.C.)

DREXEL

LOCATION .... Philadelphia, PA
CONFERENCE .... America East
LAST SEASON .... 13-15 (.464)
CONFERENCE RECORD 10-8 (6th)
STARTERS LOST/RETURNING 5/0
NICKNAME .... Dragons
COLORS .... Blue & Gold
HOMECOURT ... Physical Ed. Athletic Center (2,300)
COACH .... Bill Herrion (Merrimack '81)
RECORD AT SCHOOL .... 147-62 (7 yrs.)
CAREER RECORD .... 147-62 (7 yrs.)
ASSISTANTS Steve Seymour (Bridgewater State '81)
John O'Connor (Penn State '83)
Dino Presley (Kutztown '93)
TEAM WINS (last 5 yrs.) 25-25-27-22-13
RPI (last 5 yrs.) 45-57-50-72-156
1997-98 FINISH .... Lost in conference semifinal.

Last season, Drexel was inconsistent, at times sloppy, and finished with a losing season. All that was unheard of during Bill Herrion's first six years as coach.

Only in his first season, 1991-92, did Herrion fail to reach the 20-victory mark. Now Herrion and the Dragons find themselves trying to bounce back from their first losing season.

"What we went through as a team and a program last season was very difficult," said Herrion of his first losing season in 13 years as a college head coach and assistant.

Oddly, the losing season may help stabilize Drexel basketball, at least for this season.

For the first time in a couple of years, Herrion did not spend the off-season squelching rumors that had him skipping town for other coaching jobs. Herrion could concentrate on his job at Drexel and trying to get the Dragons back to the postseason, where they had finished the four previous years.

Herrion also doesn't have to worry about having a young, inexperienced team. At this time a year ago, Herrion was trying to replace two starters and work four freshmen into the lineup.

Now, it's just about playing and executing. Drexel returns every player from last year's team, including two veterans who could well be the best in America East at their positions: 6-9 junior center **Joe Linderman** and 6-2 senior shooting guard **Mike DeRocckis**.

Linderman was a first-team all-conference player last year after earning the league's rookie-of-the-year award the year before. He led the Dragons in scoring (18.4 ppg), rebounding (8.5 rpg) and field-goal percentage (.524) and had 12 double-doubles.

"Having a 6-9 guy you can throw the ball inside to with positive results is a real luxury at this level," Herrion said. "Linderman is stronger and better, with improved stamina. This year we need him to take ownership of this team and be a leader.

If Linderman gets that much better, the rest of the league is in trouble.

"Linderman is just a hell of a player," Delaware coach Mike Brey said. "He's very difficult to defend in the low post."

DeRocckis (15.4 ppg, 2.9 rpg, 80 assists, 77 of 205 three-point shots) completes perhaps the best inside-outside duo in the conference. For the second straight year, DeRocckis had his field-goal percentage drop (to .384), but he remains among the league's most feared long-range shooters. He was almost as good from three-point range (.376) as he was from everywhere else. Still, it was a far cry from a freshman season when DeRocckis shot .478 from behind the arc.

DeRocckis' shooting woes last season mirrored the team's shooting woes. The Dragons were ninth in the league (.417) in field-goal percentage.

DeRocckis was the Dragons' assist leader nine times and the top rebounder four times. Nobody on the team is more durable. DeRocckis has started all 90 of his collegiate games and last year averaged 37.5 minutes.

"DeRocckis is a man," Brey said. "He's been in the league. He's played in championship games. How do you defend him?"

Just as dependable is 5-7 senior point guard **Greg Gaffney** (4.1 ppg, 2.1 rpg, 119 assists). Gaffney shared the starting job for the first part of the season with 6-1 junior **Bryant Coursey**, but by midseason the job was Gaffney's.

When Coursey was suspended for the last 10 games, Gaffney became the only point guard on the team. Gaffney started 14 games and was the primary reason the Dragons led America East in assist-to-turnover ratio. For every turnover, Gaffney handed out 2.2 assists. He was 21 of 40 from three-point range.

"Greg Gaffney is a rock," Herrion said. "He takes care of the basketball and gets it to the right people."

Coursey gives Drexel the athleticism at the point that Gaffney can't. Coursey (7.4 ppg, 3.7 rpg. 60 assists) started 11 games and scored in double figures seven times. Coursey know how to get his points through penetration. Drexel lost four of five games in one stretch during his suspension.

Tom Dearborn (1.3 ppg, 0.5 rpg), a 6-2 junior, and 6-3 senior **Ross Neisler** (2.0 ppg, 1.2 rpg) will add depth at the wing. Dearborn is a jump shooter—26 of his 30 shots last season came from three-point range (he made 8 of those 26 from). Neisler, who started four games last year, played more than Dearborn, and that probably won't change this season.

Chris Burch from Olney Central JC in St. Louis is the only newcomer. The 6-5 junior is the tallest of the wing players. He averaged 8.9 points and 5.7 rebounds last year.

David Stec (0.2 ppg, 0.2 rpg), 6-4 sophomore walkon, is more of a practice player.

Drexel continued to put players on the league's all-rookie team with last season's selection of 6-6 sophomore forward **Petrick Sanders** (6.6 ppg, 4.5 rpg). The former Philadelphia Public League Player of the Year was a favorite target for his coach's criticism, but by season's end had become the player even Herrion could praise.

"I'm a big fan of Petrick Sanders," Herrion said. "He will be crucial to our success, but I think his strength is that he has played one year already. Now he is really ready to keep playing."

Sanders started 25 games last season.

If Herrion decides to go bigger along the baseline, 6-7 sophomore **Mike Kouser** (5.4 ppg, 4.5 rpg) could get the job as the fifth starter. That may depend on whether Kouser improves his shooting touch (.394 FG percentage). In six starts and 18 minutes per game, Kouser tied Sanders as the Dragons' second-leading rebounder.

Herrion could also decide to go with a smaller, more athletic lineup, which could mean more minutes for 6-5 sophomore **Stephen Starks** (6.8 ppg, 2.7 rpg). Starks has plenty of offensive skills. He was third on the team in double-digit scoring games with nine. Improvements in Starks ball-handling skills could help those numbers improve and if he improves defensively, his mintues will surely increase.

Julius Williams, a 6-4 sophomore guard, started his first eight games, but finished the year playing in just 11 more. Williams (3.1 ppg, 2.0 rpg) shot .305 percent from the field.

Fifth-year senior **Brahin Riley**, a 6-7 forward, will contribute when possible. Riley (1.6 ppg, 2.0 rpg) averaged 9.4 minutes in 27 games.

1998-99 DREXEL SCHEDULE

Nov.	18	*Seton Hall
	24	Monmouth
Dec.	1	Richmond
	5	Delaware
	19	@La Salle
	29-30	#Pepsi-Oneida Classic
Jan.	2	@Maine
	4	@New Hampshire
	8	@Vermont
	10	@Hartford
	15	Boston University
	17	Northeastern
	19	@Towson
	21	@Pennsylvania
	24	Hofstra
	27	@Delaware
	30	Maine
Feb.	1	New Hampshire
	5	Vermont
	7	Hartford
	10	Towson
	13	@Northeastern
	15	@Boston University
	18	**St. Joseph's
	21	@Hofstra
26-Mar.	6	##America East Tournament

@ Road Games
* Continental Airlines Arena, East Rutherford, NJ
** The Palestra, Philadelphia, PA
\# Green Bay, WI (vs. Air Force, first round; also Texas Southern and Wisconsin-Green Bay)
\#\# Bob Carpenter Center, Newark, DE (Championship game at homecourt of highest seeded team)

adidas Blue Ribbon Analysis

BACKCOURT .... B BENCH/DEPTH .... B+
FRONTCOURT .... B INTANGIBLES .... A

Perhaps the biggest reason for Drexel's demise last season was defense. The Dragons' streak of leading the league four straight years ended as they finished fifth in field-goal percentage defense (.428) and third in points allowed (67.6).

"Our youth caught up to us in the end," Herrion said. "We had our moments of brilliance, and equally our moments where we really struggled."

Joe Linderman and Mike DeRocckis may be the two best players in the league at their positions. DeRocckis has worked hard to show he is more than just a stand-still shooter. Linderman is the most skilled big man in the league.

Despite some of the problems of last season, Drexel was still only a tip-in at the buzzer against Boston University from reaching the championship game of the America East Tournament.

"What we went through as a program was very tough, but we showed a lot of improvement down the stretch, and that's what we hope to build on as we start the season," Herrion said.

America East is now more than a two- or three-team race. Drexel is among four or five teams with a shot at the title. That makes for a very interesting February and March.

(C.C.)

HARTFORD

LOCATION .... **West Hartford, CT**
CONFERENCE .... **America East**
LAST SEASON .... **15-12 (.555)**
CONFERENCE RECORD .... **11-7 (t-3rd)**
STARTERS LOST/RETURNING **3/2**
NICKNAME .... **Hawks**
COLORS .... **Scarlet & White**
HOMECOURT .... **The Sports Center (4,475)**
COACH .... **Paul Brazeau (Boston College '81)**
RECORD AT SCHOOL .... **79-87 (6 yrs.)**
CAREER RECORD .... **79-87 (6 yrs.)**
ASSISTANTS . Chris Ostapchuk (Boston College '90)
Stan Nance
TEAM WINS (last 5 yrs.) **16-11-6-17-15**
RPI (last 5 yrs.) **126-176-266-128-153**
1997-98 FINISH .... **Lost in conference quarterfinal.**

Everything seemed to be in place for Hartford's Hawks to make a championship run in 1997-98. They had two senior all-conference forwards in Anthony Bethune and Ryan Howse, an experienced, senior point guard in Keith Bike and a high-scoring swingman in Justin Bailey.

Experience, versatility, proven talent—it was all there.

Yet it didn't work out. Bethune spent the first semester on the bench with academic problems and Hartford got off to a 1-3 start. The inconsistency remained for much of the season—Hartford was good enough to beat contenders Boston University and Hofstra and bad enough to lose to cellar-dwellers Maine and Towson.

Although they rallied with a 7-2 February and finished third in America East, the Hawks fell short of their goal.

"Disappointment probably isn't the right word," Hartford coach Paul Brazeau said. "You want to finish first. You are trying to win the league."

Howse (13.0 ppg, 6.7 rpg), Bethune (17.9 ppg, 5.9 rpg), and Bike (11.4 ppg, 2.9 rpg, 110 assists) are gone, leaving some gaping holes for the Hawks to fill.

"I think other people will pick up the slack. We have three quality seniors and I think we will be better defensively and we should be bigger and more athletic," Brazeau said. "But obviously we have to make up for experience."

Brazeau can feel fortunate that 6-2 senior **Justin Bailey** (20.1 ppg, 5.0 rpg, 87 assists, 59 steals) returns this season. Bailey led the league last year in scoring, steals, and free-throw percentage (.838). Bailey isn't flashy, but does everything well. He beats defenders off the dribble and can hit the open jump shot.

"He's a very motivated basketball player. You can't be unhappy with the season he had," Brazeau said.

With Howse and Bethune drawing attention last season, Bailey was able to roam free. Bailey must now produce as the No. 1 option.

"It's just any other league or situation," Brazeau said. "Teams have guys the other teams want to stop. Now that's Justin and it will force him to raise his game, but he's a senior and four-year starter now. You hope those benefits pay off into a very good senior year."

Junior **Darrick Jackson** (7.6 ppg, 2.8 rpg, 71 assists, 42 steals) split the point-guard job with Bike last season. This year it will be his job to lose. Jackson, 5-10, started 14 games and was the Hawks' third-best three-point shooter (29 of 91). He will need to improve his 71-to-80 assist-to-turnover ratio.

Jackson will be pushed by junior-college transfer **Rylad King** of Western Wyoming CC. King, a 6-0 junior, is quicker and more athletic than Jackson and will at least see plenty of time off the bench.

Sophomore guard **Keyon Smith** (1.6 ppg, 0.6 rpg,) will look for more playing time. Smith, 6-3, averaged 5.6 minutes in 19 games.

It is likely that 6-4 freshman **Manta Storpirstis**, a native of Jonava, Lithuania, will get most of his minutes backing up the two wing spots. Like most of his countrymen who come to play in the United States, Storpirstis is a good shooter.

"He can be a contributor," Brazeau said. "He's a little older and can flat-out stroke it. You always have to find room for scorers."

In the frontcourt, Brazeau will be counting heavily on 6-7 senior center **Chris Eames** (8.0 ppg, 5.3 rpg, 25 blocks, 34 steals), Hartford's only big man with significant playing experience. Eames, a three-year starter, will need to become a more reliable scorer.

Bethune and Howse each played more than 30 minutes a game, leaving little time for any of the younger players last year. Thus, there is next to no experience at the forward spots.

South Alabama transfer **Rob Sawicki** and 6-7 sophomore **Harold Juluke** (0.5 ppg, 1.3 rpg) will likely assume those starting jobs. The 6-10 Syawicky, a sophomore, played very little two years ago for the Jaguars, averaging 1.6 points and 1.4 rebounds, but alongside Eames gives the Hawks some good size. Of the other returnees, Juluke played the most, but averaged only 9.1 minutes in 15 games.

Joe Rose (0.6 ppg, 1.3 rpg), a 6-8 junior, played in 15 games and averaged 4.3 minutes and 6-7 sophomore **Samont Washington** (0.9 ppg, 0.8 rpg) averaged 4.3 minutes in 14 games.

Brazeau has some unknowns in the frontcourt, and three more freshmen post players expand that list: 6-8 **Jay Carter** from Lord Elgin HS in Burlington, Ontario; 6-8 **Rob Doss** from Harding HS in Bridgeport, Conn.; and 6-9 **Todd Jones** from St. Mary's HS in Elizabeth, N.J. They will have every chance to earn minutes immediately.

"It's still too early to tell with these guys," Brazeau said.

Jaron Brown, a 6-4 senior, can play shooting guard or small forward and has been a role player. That could change. Brazeau wants to utilize the size he has recruited in the last two years, but Brown (2.6 ppg, 1.5 rpg) should make a bid for a more significant role. Brown played in all 27 games last year.

adidas Blue Ribbon Analysis

BACKCOURT .... **B** **BENCH/DEPTH** .... **D+**
FRONTCOURT .... **D+** **INTANGIBLES** .... **C+**

It appeared to be a year of underachieving for the Hartford Hawks last season, but that won't be possible this year.

Expectations are much lower in West Hartford. With Justin Bailey and Chris Eames returning, Hartford isn't exactly starting over, but there are too many other questions surrounding the team.

Coach Paul Brazeau must reconstruct a frontcourt around Eames, who will have to be more productive. After Eames, the Hawks are thin in experienced frontcourt players.

Defensively, Hartford needs to improve. Finishing 11-7 in America East was only possible because the Hawks had the league's top scoring offense and one of the worst defenses, allowing 78.4 ppg.

Three of the top four scorers are gone, so the offense will not be as good. If the defense isn't better, it could spell trouble for Hartford.

"We've got to be better defensively," Brazeau said. "That was a big letdown last year."

Brazeau can't ask Justin Bailey to be much better. Bailey became the league's top scorer and perhaps its best all-around player. His biggest problem this season could be pressing, trying to compensate for the lack of proven players around him.

In an ever-improving and more balanced league, the Hawks are a team that will likely take a step backward this season. They look destined for a return to the league's bottom half.

(C.C.)

1998-99 HARTFORD SCHEDULE

Nov.	15	@Georgetown
	18	@Holy Cross
	21	Siena
	24	*Connecticut
Dec.	3-4	#Phoenix Classic
	9	New Hampshire
	12	@Maine
	21	Harvard
	28	@Tulane
Jan.	4	Vermont
	8	@Hofstra
	10	Drexel
	14	Towson
	16	Delaware
	22	@Northeastern
	24	Boston University
	27	@New Hampshire
	31	@Vermont
Feb.	5	Hofstra
	7	@Drexel
	10	Maine
	13	@Towson
	15	@Delaware
	19	Northeastern
	21	@Boston University
26-Mar.	6	##America East Tournament

@ Road Games
* Hartford Civic Center, Hartford, CT
\# Hartford, CT (vs. Yale, first round; also Central Connecticut State and Fordham)
\## Bob Carpenter Center, Newark DE (Championship game at homecourt of highest-seeded team)

HOFSTRA

LOCATION .... **Hempstead, NY**
CONFERENCE .... **America East**
LAST SEASON .... **19-12 (.613)**
CONFERENCE RECORD .... **11-7 (t-3rd)**
STARTERS LOST/RETURNING **1/4**
NICKNAME .... **Flying Dutchmen**
COLORS .... **Gold, White & Blue**
HOMECOURT .... **Physical Fitness Center (2,500)**
COACH .... **Jay Wright (Bucknell '83)**
RECORD AT SCHOOL .... **50-63 (4 yrs.)**
CAREER RECORD .... **50-63 (4 yrs.)**
ASSISTANTS .... **Tom Pecora (Adelphi '83)**
Brett Gunning (UNLV '94)
Eugene Burroughs (Richmond '94)
TEAM WINS (last 5 yrs.) **9-10-9-12-19**
RPI (last 5 yrs.) **285-203-284-195-140**
1997-98 FINISH .... **Lost in conference semifinal.**

When Jay Wright was hired as Hofstra's coach five years ago, he focused on turning the program around by staying close to home and winning recruiting battles. It's been a slow process, but the Flying Dutchmen finally enjoyed the fruits of that labor with a 19-win season and the most conference victories (11) in school history.

This year could be even better. Hofstra should be a contender for the America East championship, thanks in large part to nine native New Yorkers on the 12-man roster.

"When we came to Hofstra, our goal was to make us contenders for the league championship on a year-to-year basis," Wright said.

Wright and his staff have done such a good job recruiting players and keeping them that this year's team has no freshmen. With five starters back and two transfers, they didn't need any freshmen.

The prize catch of the New York recruits was easily 5-11 junior **Craig "Speedy" Claxton**, whom Wright recruited without barely having to leave his office. The Hempstead, N.Y. native became just the second sophomore in the league's history to win player of the year (Northeastern's Reggie Lewis was the other).

Perhaps no player in America East is more dangerous with the ball than Claxton, and he has it in his hands plenty. He's also a dangerous shooter. Claxton (16.3 ppg, 4.6 rpg, 224 assists) led Hofstra in scoring and the league in assists. He was ninth in the nation with his average of 7.2 assists per game.

"He's the one kid in our league who could go a step higher league-wise and still make an impact," Northeastern coach Rudy Keeling said.

Claxton was one of the more improved players in the league as well, and he was good as a freshman. He was able to more than double his assist average and score more last season than his first.

"Claxton is just so explosive, especially off those ball screens. If he comes out and shoots the ball better, then I don't know what the answer is," Delaware coach Mike Brey said.

That may be the only place to exploit Claxton. Of his 375 field-goal attempts (fourth most in the league), only 11 of them were from three-point range. If he can at least become a threat from behind the arc, all of America East becomes his stage.

Claxton is also one of the league's top man-to-man defenders and led America East with 67 steals per game.

"Speedy takes great pride in covering any opponent, no matter what size they are. Every honor that he received was truly deserved," Wright said. "He is the kind of player you want to have the ball at the end of the game because he can make any play necessary to win."

Claxton's improved assist total and Hofstra's subsequent seven-win jump from the '96-97 season may be

1998-99 HOFSTRA SCHEDULE

Nov.	20	@Maryland
	24	Youngstown State
	27-29	#Hawaii-Pacific Thanksgiving Classic
Dec.	2	@St. John's
	8	@Iona
	12	@Towson
	22	@Youngstown State
	26-27	##ECAC Holiday Festival
Jan.	2	@New Hampshire
	4	@Maine
	5	Belmont
	8	Hartford
	10	@Vermont
	15	Northeastern
	17	Boston University
	19	Delaware
	24	@Drexel
	27	Towson
	30	New Hampshire
Feb.	1	Maine
	5	@Hartford
	7	Vermont
	10	@Delaware
	13	@Boston
	15	@Northeastern
	21	Drexel
26-Mar.	6	###America East Tournament

@ Road Games
# Honolulu, HI (vs. Southern Mississippi, first round; also Baylor, Hawaii-Pacific, Illinois State, Iona, Missouri-Kansas City and Virginia Commonwealth)
New York, NY (vs. Georgia Tech, first round; also Iona and Pennsylvania)
Bob Carpenter Center, Newark, DE (Championship game at homecourt of highest seeded team)

most attributed to the arrival of sophomore **Roberto Gittens**. After a bit of a slow start, the 6-6, 230-pound Gittens, who plays in the mold of Larry Johnson, became, at times, a dominating low-post player. He lived up to his billing as an all-New York City high school player.

Gittens (10.7 ppg, 6.7 rpg) was Hofstra's second-leading scorer and rebounder and led the team with a .528 field-goal percentage and 61 blocked shots. Only Vermont's Tony Orciari got more votes for America East Rookie of the Year.

Gittens wasn't the only Dutchman rookie to garner attention. Joining him was 6-5 sophomore guard **Norman Richardson** (8.7 ppg, 3.8 rpg), who twice was chosen America East Rookie of the Week and started 14 games for Wright. That number of starts should increase this season.

Gittens and Richardson flank 6-7 senior center **Duane Posey** (9.6 ppg, 6.8 rpg, 28 steals, 15 blocked shots) in the frontcourt.

Posey became a full-time starter last season and he became a more efficient player, leading the Flying Dutchmen in rebounding. His production improved over his sophomore season, although his minutes only increased by about two a game.

The arrival of Gittens and Richardson took a good bit of playing time and confidence from 6-7 senior **Tim Beckett** (6.8 ppg, 4.4 rpg, 43 of129 three-point shots). Beckett got fewer shots and his scoring average fell five points. It's very unlikely Beckett will regain a starting job and the minutes won't increase unless his three-point shot improves dramatically. He and 6-4 senior guard **Mike Renfro** (7.0 ppg, 2.9 rpg) could find themselves battling for time as reserves at the wing spots.

That's because senior **Anthony Davis** (7.7 ppg, 51 of 153 three-point shots) regained his form last season, and Hofstra welcomes New Hampshire transfer **Jason Hernandez** to the mix this year.

Davis became Hofstra's top man off the bench and led the team in three-pointers. The 6-0 sophomore Hernandez was an all-rookie choice for the Wildcats two seasons ago, averaging 7.8 ppg. He can play both guard positions. Hernandez, along with Davis and Renfro, give Wright plenty of options alongside Claxton in the backcourt.

Renfro, who came to Hofstra from Allegany CC in Maryland, started 24 games at shooting guard, but often gave way to Davis in key situations.

One starter who won't return is 6-7 guard/forward Joe Brown (7.3 ppg, 3.3 rpg), who decided during the summer to transfer to Coppin State. Brown started 18 games last season.

Adding depth to the backcourt will be 6-6 sophomore **Mike Feeley** (0.6 ppg, 17 games), while 5-9 junior walkon **Jeff Fox** will get his chances in practice.

The frontcourt gets deeper at mid-year when 6-8 junior forward and DePaul transfer **Abdou Syllan**, a native of Dakar, Senegal, becomes eligible. Syllan is a good rebounder who grabbed 6.8 rpg in 14 Conference USA games two years ago. His game is not refined, but Syllan has a nose for the ball. He averaged 3.8 ppg in his freshman year for the Blue Demons and once had a 14-point, 14-rebound game against UNC Charlotte.

June surgery to repair the detached retina of 6-7 sophomore **Marc Petit** of New Utrecht HS in Brooklyn, N.Y., has his status in doubt this year. Even a completely healthy Petit will have a difficult time cracking the rotation.

adidas Blue Ribbon Analysis

BACKCOURT .... **A** **BENCH/DEPTH** .... **B**
FRONTCOURT .... **B** **INTANGIBLES** .... **C+**

Hofstra has gone from 10th, to seventh, to a tie for third in the America East race since Jay Wright was hired five seasons ago, and this season should be even better with the former Villanova and UNLV assistant leading the way.

"Hofstra has the most talent in our league," Boston University coach Dennis Wolff said. Most of the other league coaches said the same of the Flying Dutchmen.

The outstanding freshmen years for Roberto Gittens and Norman Richardson have given Wright bookend forwards he didn't know he had at this time last year. With Tim Beckett, Mike Renfro, and Mike Feeley, Wright has options other than his prized sophomores. Anthony Davis, Jason Hernandez, and the versatile Renfro are the perfect complementary players on the wings.

It is Craig Claxton who makes it work for the Flying Dutchmen. He could easily be the best weapon in America East, especially if he finds his outside shooting touch.

Hofstra must now go out and do the job. Several teams can match the Flying Dutchmen's talent and have more experience, especially at winning games.

This is almost the same Hofstra team that won 19 times last season, but was inconsistent enough to lose seven conference games.

Hofstra has not reached the NCAA Tournament since 1977, and getting there in '99 is very possible. The Dutchmen should be in the hunt at a league tournament.

(C.C.)

MAINE

LOCATION .... **Orono, ME**
CONFERENCE .... **America East**
LAST SEASON .... **7-20 (.259)**
CONFERENCE RECORD .... **4-14 (t-9th)**
STARTERS LOST/RETURNING **0/5**
NICKNAME .... **Black Bears**
COLORS .... **Blue & White**
HOMECOURT .... **Alfond Sports Arena (6,000)**
COACH ..... **John Giannini (North Central College '84)**
RECORD AT SCHOOL .... **18-40 (2 yrs.)**
CAREER RECORD .... **186-78 (9 yrs.)**
ASSISTANTS .... **Ted Woodward (Bucknell '86)**
Ed Jones (Maine '94)
Mike Mennenga (Morehead State '93)
TEAM WINS (last 5 yrs.) **12-13-7-11-7**
RPI (last 5 yrs.) **89-189-182-207-259**
1997-98 FINISH .... **Lost in conference first round.**

It looks like better days are ahead for the Maine Black Bears and coach John Giannini.

Giannini went into last season with players who had little experience and even less proven talent. He had just three returning players in the program, and it showed in a seven-win season.

Everybody was saying, "Wait till next year."

Well, next year is here, and Maine appears ready to go from the cellar to title contender.

"This is the first time since our staff arrived that we have a good nucleus of returning players, good incoming players," Giannini said. "We have a full roster and experience. We have not been able to enjoy that over the last two years."

Maine probably won't surprise its opponents.

"I'm going to pick Maine to win the league with their transfers and solid returning players," said Hartford coach

1998-99 MAINE SCHEDULE

Nov.	14	Hampton
	17	@Northwestern
	21	@Fairleigh Dickinson
	23	@Vermont
	28	@Brown
	30	@Providence
Dec.	12	Hartford
	19-20	#UNO Christmas Classic
	30	Sacred Heart
Jan.	2	Drexel
	4	Hofstra
	10	@Boston University
	12	@Northeastern
	16	New Hampshire
	22	@Delaware
	24	@Towson
	27	Vermont
	30	@Drexel
Feb.	1	@Hofstra
	4	Northeastern
	6	Boston University
	10	@Hartford
	14	@New Hampshire
	18	Delaware
	20	Towson
26-Mar.	6	##American East Tournament

@ Road Games
# New Orleans, LA (vs. New Orleans, first round; also Tennessee State and Troy State)
Bob Carpenter Center, Newark, DE (Championship game at homecourt of highest-seeded team)

Paul Brazeau, whose team lost at Maine in one of the Black Bears' most impressive victories last season.

Giannini returns all five starters, but they aren't guaranteed their starting jobs this year. Giannini spent last year watching Boston College transfers **Andy Bedard** and **Nate Fox** in practice, dreaming of the possibilities they could bring to the team.

Bedard already seems to have taken on a leadership role.

"Bedard is like (former Maine guard) John Gordon (now at Delaware)," Delaware coach Mike Brey said. "He's coming back and he wants to win a championship and he's been a hell of a leader."

Bedard, a 6-1 junior, at times was a key guard off the bench, and even a part-time starter, for the Eagles. At other times he was forgotten.

After his sophomore year when he averaged 4.9 points and 2.1 assists, mostly backing up point guard Scoonie Penn, Bedard left BC. When Eagles coach Jim O'Brien left for Ohio State a few months later, Bedard considered a return. Instead, he chose a return to his home state.

Bedard will be expected to run the team. He is the most experienced and big-game-tested player Giannini has had at Maine. He shot .378 from three-point range as a sophomore at Boston College, and that percentage should get better with Bedard coming off the high-post screens of the Bears' second-best player, 6-6 senior forward/center **Allen Ledbetter**.

Ledbetter (16.1 ppg, 10.9 rpg, 42 steals, .591 FG percentage) is a player who goes about his business in a quiet manner. Ledbetter, America East's top rebounder last season, was one of only five players in the nation to average a double-double.

One of the strongest players in America East, Ledbetter is a chiseled 225 pounds and was recently chosen a National Strength Coaches Association All-American. He has created an effective arsenal of pump fakes, drop-step moves, and quick-release jump hooks. He utilizes his broad shoulders to carve out space.

Ledbetter has also worked to develop a jump shot and has good range to 15 feet. Ledbetter, who only fouled out once last season, averaged 35.6 minutes and played all 27 games. Only two players in America East played more: New Hampshire's Matt Acres and Drexel's Mike DeRocckis.

"Allen Ledbetter is a first-team all-conference-type player," said Northeastern coach Rudy Keeling, who coached and recruited Ledbetter while he was still coaching at Maine.

Sophomore **Colin Haynes** gave Ledbetter some surprising help last season. Forced into more minutes (29.6 per game) than Giannini would have liked, the 6-7 Haynes (7.3 ppg., 7.2 rpg) became the top freshman rebounder in the league. It helped that Maine missed more shots than any team in American East.

Haynes, who started more games (26) than any Black Bear except Ledbetter, made 36 of 100 three-point shots.

He may move to the bench if Giannini opts for a stronger offensive lineup that would include Fox at one forward spot.

Fox is from Plainfield, Ill. HS, where he averaged 28 points and 15 rebounds as a senior. He didn't get nearly as much playing time with the Eagles as Bedard and is probably better-suited to the America East than the Big East.

At 245 pounds, Fox , a junior, can mix it up inside, but he's more effective on the perimeter. He's a talented shooter and at 6-8 will have little trouble shooting over defenders. Fox will certainly help a Black Bear team that led the conference in three-pointers made (203 of 598), but was just seventh in percentage (.339).

Thus, Giannini has a dilemma this season: establishing the roles of 6-1 seniors **Marcus Wills** (17.4 ppg, 2.5 rpg, .386 FG, 46 of 135 three-point shots) and **Fred Meeks**, (19.5 ppg, 3.5 rpg, .446 FG, 65 of 152 three-point shots). Wills and Meeks are the two players who took most of the three-point shots a year ago.

With few other options beside Ledbetter and Giannini wanting to establish the up-tempo style, Wills and Meeks were able to run free. They were the only Bears capable of creating their own shot and made a great pair of scorers. That won't change, but their situation will.

Bedard will be running the show, and no longer will Wills be asked to take most of the big shots. Many of those will go to Bedard.

Giannini will try to find help for his two leading scorers in search of a more balanced, team-oriented offense.

Meeks was the second-leading scorer in the conference and does not have the all-around game of Wills.

"Both Fred and Marcus did a very good job last year and showed that they are both explosive scorers," Giannini said. "I expect them to be even better with a better supporting cast around them."

Freshman **Clinton "Huggy" Dye** of Maine Central Institute could be a sleeper. Playing on perhaps the most talented MCI team ever—10 players signed with Division I schools—the 6-2 Dye was lost in the mix. He was a much better player by season's end than he was in November when he committed to Maine.

Dye, from Indianapolis, will learn to play point guard and could also be a scorer. His playing time could increase drastically next season when Wills and Meeks are gone.

Dade Faison (4.4 ppg, 1.9 rpg), a 5-11 junior point guard, was a 25-game starter last season, but will likely lose his job to Bedard. Although he was third in the conference with 139 assists, Faison has limited offensive skills, as evidenced by his .237 three-point percentage and .288 field-goal percentage. His 31.8 minutes per game last season could be cut in half.

Another returnee who may lose some playing time is 6-1 junior guard **Corey Thibodeau** (4.2 ppg, 1.7 rpg). He averaged 19.8 minutes in 26 games, starting four. In the same situation is 6-6 sophomore forward **Todd Tibbetts** (1.5 ppg, 2.0 rpg), who averaged 10.6 minutes in 25 games.

The frontcourt will get help from a healthy **Jamar Croom**, a redshirt freshman from Reading (Penn.) HS. The 6-9, 250-pound Croom sat out last season while a knee injury he suffered in high school healed slowly. Croom is even stronger than Ledbetter, but his offensive skills are limited at this point in his career

Maine hopes to get more production this season from 6-8 senior **Linnell Marshall** (0.6 ppg, 0.6 rpg). He appeared in just five games last season, but has potential to be a solid player.

Giannini signed a very athletic 6-4 guard, Rickey White of Mt. Ararat HS in Maine. He will be academically ineligible this season.

Next season, Giannini will welcome another transfer, 6-10 small forward Julian Dunkley of Temple. He was one of the nation's top recruits in 1996 and will have two years of eligibility.

adidas Blue Ribbon Analysis

BACKCOURT	**B+**	**BENCH/DEPTH**	**C**
FRONTCOURT	**B**	**INTANGIBLES**	**C+**

Women's basketball is big in Maine, which had four straight teams in the NCAA Tournament. Crowds often flock to women's games.

Maine coach John Giannini wants to bring that kind of fanfare to the men's program. Can he match the women's success on the court and in the stands? Wait and see.

It will be his team's talent and his coaching ability that will make Maine a better team and a more attractive drawing card for fans.

How much better may depend on how new point guard Andy Bedard mixes with Marcus Wills and Fred Meeks, two big scorers who like to have the basketball in their hands.

The role of senior forward Andy Ledbetter won't change much, except maybe his ability to make shots in the 15-foot range.

This looks like the season Giannini has been waiting for since he was hired at Maine three years ago. Maine can be a contender in what should be a closely contested race.

(C.C.)

NEW HAMPSHIRE

LOCATION .... **Durham, NH**
CONFERENCE .... **America East**
LAST SEASON .... **10-17 (.370)**
CONFERENCE RECORD .... **6-12 (8th)**
STARTERS LOST/RETURNING **4/1**
NICKNAME .... **Wildcats**
COLORS .... **Blue & White**
HOMECOURT .... **Whittemore Center (7,200)**
COACH .... **Jeff Jackson (Cornell '84)**
RECORD AT SCHOOL .... **17-37 (2 yrs.)**
CAREER RECORD .... **17-37 (2 yrs.)**
ASSISTANTS **Bobby Castagna (Northridge State '75)**
Kevin Mouton (San Francisco '89)
Bob Duffley (Dalhousie '87)
TEAM WINS (last 5 yrs.) **15-19-6-7-10**
RPI (last 5 yrs.) **164-77-277-237-231**
1997-98 FINISH .... **Lost in conference first round.**

What Jeff Jackson is doing at New Hampshire is more than just rebuilding. He's restructuring from the ground floor.

The third-year head coach is changing the ideals, the philosophies and above all changing the personnel at a program without much basketball tradition.

For the second straight offseason, Jackson will have eight new players. The Wildcats' roster looks more like an English 101 attendance list than a basketball team. Seven freshmen, five sophomores, and a junior-college transfer make up the majority of the 15-player team.

"The one thing we are excited about as a coaching staff is that every player in the program is someone we selected or recruited," Jackson said. "It's a much more comfortable situation."

Two returnees to the backcourt are 6-4 junior guard/forward **Carmen Maciariello** (10.4 ppg, 2.3 rpg, 1.9 apg) and 5-10 junior guard **Jelani Phillips** (1.1 ppg, 0.3 rpg). Phillips played in just eight games last year.

With the graduations of big men Matt Acres (13.4 ppg, 6.6 rpg) and Ken Rassi (9.0 ppg, 6.3 rpg), Jackson can now completely install his faster-paced, guard-oriented style. He will do that by building around Maciariello.

The 6-4 shooting guard was the Wildcats' second-leading scorer a year ago and improved late in the season, averaging more than 15.1 points over the last10 games. Most of those points come from behind the three-point arc where Maciariello was 51 for 139 (.367 percent) and ranked in the America East's top 10.

That pales in comparison to teammate **Andy Cavo** (9.9 ppg., 3.0 rpg), who led the league with a .451 three-point percentage (64 for 142). The 6-6 sophomore was the third-best rookie in America East last year, behind only Vermont's Tony Orciari and Hofstra's Roberto Gittens. Cavo is a terrific shooter when left alone. However, 77 percent of his points came from three-pointers. Jackson hopes for, and thinks he can get, more diversity from Cavo this season.

"Those two guys (Maciariello and Cavo) are probably two of the better wing players in the league and they complement each other very well," Jackson said.

Unlike last season, Marciariello and Cavo will be on the court together much of the time and can cause fits for the opposition with their long-range shooting from opposite wings.

Jackson also likes the depth he has behind Maciariello and Cavo. That depth will be provided by 6-2 sophomore **Colin Donahue** (2.0 ppg, 1.5 rpg), 6-7 redshirt freshman **Assane Faye** of Bridgeton (Maine) Academy; and 6-6 freshman **Austin Ganly** of Greely HS in North Yarmouth, Maine.

Donahue, who averaged 14 minutes in 26 games last year, is a good defender and Jackson can use his intensity as a spark off the bench.

Faye, a native of Dakar, Senegal in West Africa, averaged 19 points and 7.5 rebound at Bridgeton, but wasn't ready to play at the Division I level last year. He has added 35 pounds in two years (up to 195) and should be far more prepared. His athleticism will get him playing time, but his game still needs to be refined.

Ganly could step right into some quality minutes. He averaged 16.3 points and 8.0 rebounds, helping Greely to Maine's state Class B championship last season. Ganly won the state's Gatorade Player-of-the-Year award.

"Austin is a terrific athlete and of all the people at that position, he is the most versatile in terms of ball-handling, shooting, and playing defense," Jackson said.

Possibly being pushed out of the rotation are 6-2 sophomore **Brett LeFlem** (0.4 ppg, 0.0 rpg in seven games) and 6-4 redshirt freshman **Chris Brown** of Scituate HS in Boston.

The wing position is New Hampshire's biggest strength, but questions exist at almost every other position.

Who gets Cavo and Maciariello the ball where they can shoot it? Who takes the pressure off when the opponent extends to defend the three-point shot almost exclusively? Therein lies two Wildcat-sized questions.

Jackson went into the Philadelphia area to find two freshmen to replace Carlos Bradberry (9.1 ppg, 3.0 rpg, 109 assists) at the point: **Will Chavis** from Philadelphia's School of Engineering and Science and **Drew Dawson** from Trinity HS in Camp Hill, Pa.

The 5-9, 160-pound Chavis is Jackson's top recruit this year and was tabbed as the probable starter before he arrived at New Hampshire. He will be the quickest point guard New Hampshire has had in a long time.

Chavis, who averaged 27 points, nine assists, and four steals in his senior season, is a talented penetrator and ball handler who honed those skills in the Sonny Hill League in Philadelphia during the summer. Jackson hopes Chavis' size isn't a defensive liability.

"Will is going to make Carmen and Andy and Assane Faye and Austin Ganly and Colin Donahue much more effective from the perimeter," Jackson said. "He gets excited about creating opportunities for other people."

Dawson, the leading scorer in Trinity history, is a little bigger and stronger than Chavis at 5-11, 180 pounds. Jackson calls Dawson "one of the most physically tough players," he's ever been involved with. He was the quarterback on a high school football team that ran the triple option.

Both freshmen point guards will play plenty and imme-

1998-99 NEW HAMPSHIRE SCHEDULE

Nov.	14	Brown
	20-21	#Mohegan Sun Classic
	28	@Yale
Dec.	5	@Virginia
	9	@Hartford
	13	@Dartmouth
	28-29	##Lobo Invitational
Jan	2	Hofstra
	4	Drexel
	9	@Northeastern
	12	@Boston University
	16	@Maine
	19	Vermont
	22	@Towson
	24	@Delaware
	27	Hartford
	30	@Hofstra
Feb.	1	@Drexel
	4	Boston University
	6	Northeastern
	10	@Vermont
	14	Maine
	18	Towson
	20	Delaware
26-Mar.	6	###America East Tournament

@ Road Games
# New Britain, CT (vs. Delaware State, first round; also Brown and Central Connecticut State)
Albuquerque, NM (vs. New Mexico, first round; also Houston and Portland State)
Bob Carpenter Center, Newark, DE (Championship game at homecourt of highest-seeded team)

diately. The 5-10 Phillips (1.1 ppg, 0.3 rpg) played in just eight games last year and will probably see limited playing time again unless the freshmen flop.

Jackson didn't have as much luck recruiting frontcourt talent.

Newcomers **Jeff Senulis** of Mount St. Joseph's HS in Grand Island, N.Y., **Mike Boyd** of Naval Prep and Bexley, Ohio, and **Keil Zepernick** of Nassau CC and Baldwin, N.Y. join sophomores **Ethan Cole** (2.5 ppg, 2.8 rpg) and **Rob Marquardt** (1.3 ppg, 1.1) in the frontcourt. They will collectively try and replace the double-figure point production of Acres and Rassi.

The 6-10 Cole has the most experience to fill that void. Cole played in 25 games a year ago, but only averaged 10.7 minutes. He has good size, strength, and shot-blocking skills (38-inch vertical leap and 11 blocks in his five starts). With a big jump in playing time, the offensive numbers will increase, but Cole will quickly need to become a consistent threat to keep defenses honest.

Marquardt also has good size at 6-11 and 235 pounds, but is still a bit of a mystery. Appendicitis limited him to 19 games last year. He has also had three throat operations, a broken ankle, and a broken nose while at New Hampshire. Marquardt mirrors Cole in his abilities and he should get plenty more time to exhibit them this season. He seems due for some good luck.

Zepernick, a 6-11 junior, has some collegiate experience after two seasons at Nassau, but is still a raw talent. He goes into the center mix with Cole and Marquardt and will challenge them for playing time.

Jackson compares Senulis to Acres and he hopes the 6-8 freshman can be as productive. Senulis scored 1,300 career points at St. Joseph's and was second-team All-Western New York as a senior. He also gives New Hampshire another three-point threat at power forward. Jackson scouted a game in which Senulis made five three-point shots in a three-minute span.

Boyd joined the Wildcats at midseason last year, but never played. Jackson calls the 6-7 freshman "the most athletic player in the program," but he still has limited offensive skills.

adidas Blue Ribbon Analysis

BACKCOURT	**C+**	**BENCH/DEPTH**	**C**
FRONTCOURT	**F**	**INTANGIBLES**	**C**

Jeff Jackson's recruiting class was mentioned by some as being among the top 20 in the East, and that puts in place a solid foundation of players at each position.

However, the roster is still filled with inexperienced players, some in key spots. Jackson will be relying on two freshmen at the point and he has no other options. The frontcourt has no player who has averaged more than Ethan Cole's 10.7 minutes or 2.5 points at this level. That spells trouble.

The nucleus of wing players and shooters is good. If freshman point guard Will Chavis is able learn on the job and can regularly create holes in the defense with penetration, Carmen Maciariello and Andy Cavo will be that much more effective.

Matt Acres and Ken Rassi helped bridge a gap between coaching regimes, but now that they're gone, New Hampshire can become more the type of team Jackson wants.

"We are hoping we can become much more aggressive offensively and improve defensively," Jackson said. "We can also play much more physically. We think we have the most talent we've had here. Granted they are young, but they are also capable."

Without much strength in the frontcourt, New Hampshire could have problems dealing with some of the league's traditionally-strong programs. The Wildcats won't be able to shoot themselves into games and will need more balance. Maybe that comes in a year or two, but not this year. It looks like another second-division finish for the Wildcats.

(C.C.)

adidas Blue Ribbon Analysis

GRADING SYSTEM

A+	equal to very best in country—Final Four-caliber unit
A	among the best in the land—worthy of deep NCAA run
B+	talented, versatile and experienced—NCAA-NIT ability
B	solid and productive winners—league and post-season contenders
C+	average to above-average—may contend in a weaker league
C	average to mediocre—second division in a strong league
D+	below average, inconsistent—second division in a weaker league
D	well below average—losing season virtually certain
F	non-Division I ability—an underdog every night

NORTHEASTERN

LOCATION	**Boston, MA**
CONFERENCE	**Amercia East**
LAST SEASON	**14-14 (.500)**
CONFERENCE RECORD	**9-9 (7th)**
STARTERS LOST/RETURNING	**2/3**
NICKNAME	**Huskies**
COLORS	**Red & Black**
HOMECOURT	**Cabot Gymnasium (2,000)**
COACH	**Rudy Keeling (Quincy '70)**
RECORD AT SCHOOL	**21-34 (2 yrs.)**
CAREER RECORD	**127-156 (10 yrs.)**
ASSISTANTS	**Ken Dempsey (Moravian '83)** **Jay Young (Marist '86)** **Keith Motley (Northeastern '78)**
TEAM WINS (last 5 yrs.)	**5-18-4-7-14**
RPI (last 5 yrs.)	**259-104-288-257-186**
1997-98 FINISH	**Lost in conference quarterfinal.**

Rudy Keeling has shown he can revive a basketball program.

First, he took a Maine team that won nine games in his first season and won 20 games by his sixth.

Now entering his third year at Northeastern, Keeling has transformed the Huskies. They won four games the season before his arrival. Last year they won 14.

Now it's time to prove he can produce and maintain a consistent winner. The .500 record last season was a solid improvement, and so was the nine league victories. Northeastern, which beat every team in the league, seemed to go from bad to mediocre.

"It wasn't so bad coming from where we came from. We had a poor year the year before and we knew it would be a building experience," Keeling said. "But obviously it would have been nice to win a few more games. We win three more, we win the league."

Northeastern will have to make the next leap without leading scorer and rebounder Ty Mack (17.3 ppg, 5.6 rpg), a 6-6 forward. He and 6-7 forward Lamont Clark (4.4 ppg, 4.2 rpg) are gone, so Keeling has two-thirds of his frontcourt to replace.

"Our biggest problem will be replacing Ty Mack. He was such a big part of what we did," Keeling said.

Senior forward **Lin Lattimore** (7.3 ppg, 5.5 rpg) is the one who could play a key role. His minutes and production dropped off from his sophomore season (8.7 ppg, 8.3 rpg), in what amounted to a sub-par year for the third-year starter. Lattimore, 6-7, has mostly played center the last two seasons. This year, Keeling is determined to put Lattimore at his more natural forward spot.

"If we can get him to play like he did two years ago we'll be fine, but he's got to give us some lost-post scoring," Keeling said.

That's because moving Lattimore to power forward creates a question mark at center.

Keeling has tried 6-9 junior **Changa Adams** (0.4 ppg, 1.0 rpg) at times with little success, but with the position so uncertain, Adams could get another opportunity. He couldn't match up physically in his first two seasons, but has gotten stronger during the summer.

Those two years in the program might be the only advantage he has over Keeling's other option, 6-8 freshman **Michael Rainey** from Tulsa (Okla.) Memorial HS. At 220 pounds, Rainey is the biggest player in Keeling's four-man recruiting class and he showed some offensive skills on the high school level. Rainey shot 65 percent and scored nearly 16 points a game as a senior.

Keeling likes to go after players from top high school programs and he got one in **Marquis Wright** from Whitney Young HS in Chicago. Keeling hopes 6-5 junior **Cortez Bond** of Parkland (Ill) CC and 6-6 junior **Tyrone Hammick** of Western Nebraska CC can make significant contributions this season.

Keeling believes Bond can fill Mack's vacated small forward spot. Bond is not the rebounder Mack was, but he is more of an outside threat and could eventually be as productive a scorer. Hammick could back up Bond.

Another player who could help is 6-6 redshirt freshman **Tim West** of Providence-St. Mel HS in Chicago. At 220 pounds, West is one of Keeling's heavier frontcourt players. West averaged 14.1 points as a high school senior.

John Green, a 6-8 senior post player, also returns. Green averaged 1.2 points and 2.9 rebounds last year.

Things are a little more settled in the backcourt. In fact, the Huskies' guards are among the best in America East, especially if 6-0 redshirt freshman **Jean Bain** is fully recovered from the broken wrist that sidelined him last year. Bain, of Bridgton Academy in Medford, Mass., was the most highly-regarded player in last year's recruiting class and is good enough to challenge 6-2 junior **Terry Kringe** and 5-10 senior **Harold Miller** for their starting jobs.

Bain is a slashing scorer who averaged more than 24 points as a high school senior.

"Jean Bain is going to surprise some people. He's going to really help us. He can score and really defend," Keeling said.

Kringe is entering his third season as Northeastern's starting point guard. An America East All-Rookie selection as a freshman, Kringe (7.1 ppg, 2.7 apg, 73 assists) slumped in his sophomore season. With Kringe running the offense, Northeastern was last in America East in assists and he shot just .380 from the field.

Miller (13.5 ppg, 1.7 rpg) had a much better season. He was the Huskies' second-leading scorer and led the team in assists (111). Miller was also Northeastern's leading three-point threat (43 for 107).

Bain's arrival eases a bit the loss of Joe Hicks, who averaged 7.4 points and was selected to the all-rookie team, but has left school.

"Hicks was a very talented player. In many ways losing him is worse than losing Ty because we knew we were losing Ty," Keeling said.

Without Hicks, Keeling will again turn to 6-2 sophomore **Marcus Blossom** (6.6 ppg, 2.9 rpg) for a spark off the bench.

"Any time you can get the production we got out of Marcus as a walkon, it is a very pleasant surprise," Keeling said."He's worked very hard and could even battle for a starting spot."

Blossom took the minutes that might have gone to 6-3 sophomore **Kareen Harris** (2.3 ppg, 0.9 rpg). Harris played in 18 games and will have to show something early to increase his playing time.

adidas Blue Ribbon Analysis

BACKCOURT	**B+**	**BENCH/DEPTH**	**C+**
FRONTCOURT	**D+**	**INTANGIBLES**	**B**

Northeastern should have a very different look this season.

With the graduation of Ty Mack, Huskies coach Rudy

1998-99 NORTHEASTERN SCHEDULE

Nov.	17	@Brown
	20	@Navy
	27-28	#Lobo Classic
Dec.	1	@Marquette
	5	Boston University
	9	@St. Peter's
	19	Harvard
	22	Central Connecticut
Jan.	3	@Delaware
	5	@Towson
	9	New Hampshire
	12	Maine
	15	@Hofstra
	17	@Drexel
	22	Hartford
	24	Vermont
	29	Delaware
	31	Towson
Feb.	4	@Maine
	6	@New Hampshire
	10	@Boston University
	13	Drexel
	15	Hofstra
	19	@Hartford
	21	@Vermont
26-Mar.	6	##America East Tournament

@	Road Games
#	Albuquerque, NM (vs. La Salle, first round; also Cornell and New Mexico)
##	Bob Carpenter Center, Newark, DE (Championship game at homecourt of highest-seeded team)

Keeling will switch to a more guard-oriented attack and probably play a more up-tempo style. In Harold Miller, Keeling has a solid scorer around whom he can build.

Terry Kringe is an experienced point guard who complements Miller. If Jean Bain emerges as the player Keeling thinks he can, then Northeastern has one of the top three guard rotations in the league.

"We're going to play mature guards who have played a while. If you want to build a team you have to start there," Keeling said.

That will have to help make up for a below-average frontcourt that has little proven punch.

The Huskies are still in the transition phase. Keeling has gotten the program back to respectability, but the next step could be more difficult.

"It's a confidence thing," Keeling said."We played a lot of close games last year and when we played the real good teams close, we couldn't find a way to win. That's something we have to do. And we have to beat the teams we are better than."

The improvement of last year may stall with the loss of Mack. Northeastern doesn't seem to have enough talent to make a run at Delaware. The Huskies' goal should be to crack the top four, which seems unlikely. A sixth- or seventh-place finish is more probable.

(C.C.)

TOWSON

LOCATION ..... **Towson, MD**
CONFERENCE ..... **America East**
LAST SEASON ..... **8-20 (.286)**
CONFERENCE RECORD ..... **4-14 (t-9th)**
STARTERS LOST/RETURNING **2/3**
NICKNAME ..... **Tigers**
COLORS ..... **Gold, Black & White**
HOMECOURT ..... **Towson Center (5,000)**
COACH ..... **Mike Jaskulski (St. Norbert '76)**
RECORD AT SCHOOL ..... **8-20 (1 yr.)**
CAREER RECORD ..... **70-68 (5 yrs.)**
ASSISTANTS .... **Tom Sheals (Bethune-Cookman '80)**
Jay Dull (Iowa '80)
Randy Lee (South Carolina '95)
TEAM WINS (last 5 yrs.) **21-12-16-9-8**
RPI (last 5 yrs.) **108-183-137-220-238**
1997-98 FINISH ..... **Lost in conference quarterfinal.**

For Mike Jaskulski, his first season as Towson University's coach can be summed up like this: Mission accomplished. Well, sort of.

Jaskulski vowed to improve the Tiger defense and he did so dramatically. Towson went from America East's worst to first in that category, shaving nearly 13 points off its points-allowed average down to 63.7 ppg last year.

However, defense didn't win a championship in this case. The Tigers' offense went in the other direction, from best to worst in the league. The Tigers' record was a game worse than in 1996-97 and they tied Maine for last in the conference.

This season the defense may have to be even better because Jaskulski must replace his top three scorers in Ralph Biggs (18.4 ppg, 4.8 rpg), Ryan Lexer (10.8 ppg, 4.7 rpg), and Derrick Newton (9.7 ppg, 4.9 rpg). Those graduation losses also consisted of three-fourths of the frontline rotation.

Making matters worse, Towson's top returning scorer, 5-11 junior point guard **Marlin Wise** (6.5 ppg, 2,8 rpg, 81 assists, .456 FG percentage) will be academically ineligible until December. That's not a good way to start the season for a team that had trouble winning close games. Twenty-one of Towson's 28 games were decided by 10 points or less, but the Tigers managed to win just four of those games. They lost to Michigan by three and took America East champion Delaware to overtime twice and lost both times.

Even if Wise is back for the second semester, his return doesn't guarantee him a starting job. He wasn't the best floor leader with just 12 more assists than turnovers. No starting point guard in the league had fewer than his 81 assists. Wise did make 41 percent of his three-point shots (29 for 70), but 5-11 junior **Damon Cason** (4.6 ppg, 2.2 rpg, 74 assists) is also a capable deep shooter (25 of 74 three-point shots), and more importantly Cason is eligible at the start of the season. Jaskulski will give Cason every opportunity to win the job and keep it.

"The Damon Cason of this year and the Damon Cason of last year is a completely different player and person. He's a changed man," Jaskulski said."That would have been a battle even if Marlin was eligible."

Even if Cason's improvement is obvious, Jaskulski will be depending on a pair of transfers to significantly increase the point production from the backcourt. Although 6-4 junior **Torin Ragin**, a transfer from Wyoming, and 6-2 junior **Peter Mauro** from Eastern Utah JC have never played a game for the Tigers, they are two of the more experienced players on a team that returned just five players who played last season.

Ragin practiced with the team last year and Jaskulski already has so much confidence in him that he made the former Cowboy a team captain.

Ragin averaged 3.2 ppg and 2.1 assists in 27 games for Wyoming in '96-'97. Although he made just seven of 23 three-point shots, Ragin will be expected to score from long range.

Mauro can play both guard positions and could battle Cason for the point-guard job. The Brooklyn, N.Y. native has good range on his shot and was a solid offensive threat at Eastern Utah. His adaptation to the defensive scheme could be the determining factor in Mauro's immediate role.

"Inevitably, against good teams the shot clock is going to wind down on you a number of times during a game. I think in Peter and Torin we have two guys who can create opportunities for themselves in those situations," Jaskulski said.

Raul dePablo (5.9 ppg, 1.8 rpg, 47 assists) may not be one of those players, but he is the team's second-leading returning scorer and best shooter. A 6-1 junior, dePablo was second in the conference in three-point accuracy at .431 percent (47 for 109). That was offset a bit by his making just 47, the lowest total for anyone in the league's top five.

Freshman **Danny White** of Jesuit HS in New Orleans was recruited specifically for his defense and thus will be given a look from Jaskulski. However, with a number of veterans ahead of him, the 6-2 White may have to wait to show off those defensive skills.

While Jaskulski can at least feel settled about his personnel in the backcourt, the same can't be said for the frontcourt. **Alphonso Hawes** (3.8 ppg, 4.5 rpg), a center/forward, is the only frontcourt player with significant experience, and the Tigers' only senior was not much help on the offensive end. Despite shooting from inside, Hawes' shooting percentage was .417. The 6-6 Hawes was a 21-game starter who Jaskulski likens to "Dennis Rodman minus the antics" and calls him the Tigers' best defender.

"Alphonso brings a certain toughness to our team and really sets the tone for us," Jaskulski said.

After Hawes it's a guessing game in the frontcourt, although Towson got a big boost two weeks before classes began with the addition of 6-7 **Guy Zenou**, a 22-year-old freshman from Israel. Zenou was considered the best player on Israel's 22-under national team and brings the skills and experience of international competition that many of his teammates don't have.

"Even though he is a little older, Guy has a tremendous upside," Jaskulski said.

Another returnee to the frontcourt is 6-6 **Brian Barber** (2.1 ppg, 1.3 rpg). Barber played 8.1 minutes a game as a freshman and has added 16 pounds—most of it muscle—in the offseason. Expect him to move into the starting lineup at power forward. Jaskulski figures Barber's offseason work made him the leading candidate to be the Tigers' most improved player.

Barber's primary competition comes from three new players: 6-6 sophomore **Josh Davalli**, a transfer from Division II Massachusetts-Lowell; 6-7 freshman **Kerry Augustus**, an all-state player from Georgia; and 6-8 freshman **Shaun Holtz**, an all-state player from Mississippi.

Davalli, from basketball power Cardinal Gibbons HS in Baltimore, may have a jump on the other newcomers because he, like Ragin, spent last season practicing with the Tigers during his transfer year. Jaskulski likes Davalli's defensive versatility, which could get him quality minutes off the bench. He averaged 10.0 ppg and 5.0 rpg at Lowell.

Augustus, from Lassiter HS in Rosewell, Ga., is a late-developing player who may end up more on the perimeter. Holtz, from Crystal Springs, Miss., HS, is a banger who is the only other physical post player beside Hawes.

1998-99 TOWSON SCHEDULE

Nov.	14	@Creighton
	19-21	#Battle for Baltimore
	30	@Michigan
Dec.	7	@Louisville
	12	Hofstra
	19	@Maryland-Baltimore County
	22	Lafayette
	30	American
Jan.	3	Boston University
	5	Northeastern
	10	@Delaware
	14	@Hartford
	16	@Vermont
	19	Drexel
	22	New Hampshire
	24	Maine
	27	@Hofstra
	29	@Boston University
	31	@Northeastern
Feb.	7	Delaware
	10	@Drexel
	13	Hartford
	15	Vermont
	18	@New Hampshire
	20	@Maine
26-Mar.	6	##America East Tournament

@ Road Games
\# Towson, MD (vs. Morgan State, first round; also Loyola College and Maryland-Baltimore County)
\#\# Bob Carpenter Center, Newark, DE (Championship game at homecourt of highest seeded team)

adidas Blue Ribbon Analysis

BACKCOURT	**D**	**BENCH/DEPTH**	**D**
FRONTCOURT	**C+**	**INTANGIBLES**	**C**

Mike Jaskulski may have dramatically improved the defensive mindset at Towson, but his second team of Tigers appears to be starved for offense.

Graduation and defections took two-thirds of the offensive production from a team that was already last in the conference in scoring. No player on the roster has proven he can be anything more than a third or fourth option to score at this point.

"We lost our three top scorers, but in situations like this where you ask where is the offense going to come from, invariably somebody steps up," Jaskulski said.

Those somebodies are likely newcomers Torin Ragin and Pete Mauro. The two transfers may be better at creating offensive chances for themselves and others than Ralph Biggs (18.4 ppg, 4.8 rpg) and Ryan Lexer (10.1 ppg, 4.7 rpg), but those departed players put up some offensive numbers that will be difficult to match.

Marlin Wise's ineligibility until December hurts the depth and versatility of the backcourt, but if Damon Cason has improved as much as Jaskulski says, it may not be a huge factor. Wise may not get a job back.

The proven scoring punch in the frontcourt is even more of an unknown. Just as Ragin and Mauro need to step forward, so too might newcomer Guy Zenou, who has played against tough competition as a member of Israel's 22-under national team. Alphonso Hawes and Brian Barber can be effective rebounders and defenders, but have shown little ability to put the ball in the basket.

With another year in Jaskulski's system, the defense may be even better if the former Miami assistant can overcome the lack of size.

There are too many questions to expect a season like last year's. The Tigers will battle, but will have a difficult time climbing out of America East's bottom three.

(C.C.)

adidas Blue Ribbon Analysis

GRADING SYSTEM

A+	equal to very best in country—Final Four-caliber unit
A	among the best in the land—worthy of deep NCAA run
B+	talented, versatile and experienced—NCAA-NIT ability
B	solid and productive winners—league and post-season contenders
C+	average to above-average—may contend in a weaker league
C	average to mediocre—second division in a strong league
D+	below average, inconsistent—second division in a weaker league
D	well below average—losing season virtually certain
F	non-Division I ability—an underdog every night

VERMONT

LOCATION .... Burlington, VT
CONFERENCE .... America East
LAST SEASON .... 16-11 (.592)
CONFERENCE RECORD 11-7 (t-3rd)
STARTERS LOST/RETURNING 1/4
NICKNAME .... Catamounts
COLORS .... Green & Gold
HOMECOURT .... Patrick Gymnasium (3,228)
COACH .... Tom Brennan (Georgia '71)
RECORD AT SCHOOL .... 136-195 (12 yrs.)
CAREER RECORD .... 188-270 (16 yrs.)
ASSISTANTS .... Jesse Agel (Vermont '84)
Curtis Wilson (Adelphi '91)
TEAM WINS (last 5 yrs.) 12-14-12-14-16
RPI (last 5 yrs.) 209-161-213-197-173
1997-98 FINISH .... Lost in conference quarterfinal.

There was no national championship. There was no America East championship. There wasn't a postseason berth or an All-American, but in many ways last season was a magical one for the Vermont Catamounts.

For the second straight year, Vermont overachieved. The Catamounts appeared to be a lock to finish in the bottom half of the America East standings. They surprised nearly everyone by winning 10 of their first 13 conference games.

When February began, the Catamounts were on target for the league's regular-season title, but a 56-48 loss at Maine started a three-game losing streak and Vermont settled for third place.

Regardless, that was good enough to stand as one of the best seasons in school history. The 11 league wins were a school record and the Catamounts managed to beat each conference opponent at least once.

"Playing on the last day with a chance to tie for the championship was something we've never been close to around here," Vermont coach Tom Brennan said. "I think we got so wrapped up in that, we didn't take care of business in the end."

Vermot lost to Drexel, 51-42, in a conference quarterfinal.

"It was very disappointing, especially when I sat next to (Delaware coach Mike) Brey and saw that big ring on his finger," Brennan joked, referring to Delaware's league championship. "I've been 3-24, I've been 5-22, and we aren't supposed to be successful, so to do it would have been kind of neat. So it was a little disappointing to be that close."

The surprising season was accomplished by one of Brennan's least-experienced teams. Brennan had just one senior. In his 13th season at Vermont, Brennan returns seven of his top eight players.

Unfortunately, the departing senior was Eric Nelson, the Catamounts' top player the last two years and one of the best big men in school history. The 6-7, 230-pound Nelson led Vermont in scoring (16.2 ppg), rebounding (9.1 rpg), field-goal percentage (.573), and blocked shots (76). Where that production comes from in '98-99 will be Vermont's biggest question.

Craig Peper, a 6-8 senior forward, averaged 13 points and 7.7 rebounds in 1996-'97, but dropped to 10.4 ppg and 6.0 rpg last season. The decline was mostly because of a slump the final two months of the season, a slump that coincided with Vermont's losing five of its last seven games.

"He's very quietly had some great numbers here, but he's one of those kids you look at and say, 'He's going to get every rebound, he's going to score every basket,' but that just doesn't happen all the time," Brennan said. "But I think he could have a bust-out senior year."

With Nelson gone, Peper will need to score more, and he has the skills to do it. Peper also has to cut down on his team-leading 83 fouls. The Catamounts don't have the luxury of a player with Peper's offensive skills on the bench.

That's because the other two seniors, **Jared Steele** and **Matt Chotkowski**, are unproven as scorers.

Steele (6.3 ppg, 3.8 rpg) is the most rugged of the three seniors at 6-6, 235 pounds. He was strictly a reserve last season after an injury-plagued sophomore year, but will probably move into Nelson's starting job at center.

Although Steele has struggled to stay in shape throughout his career, Brennan showed faith in his emotional leader by making Steele the Catamounts' captain. In return, Brennan hopes for some on-court toughness and a few more rebounds a game from Steele.

The 6-6 Chotkowski won't bang like Steele or score like Peper, but he is essential to Vermont's success. He will probably come off the bench as Vermont's sixth man. He's a decent rebounder who relies more on his leaping ability, but gets the most of his minutes because of his defense.

"He's a bonus because he can play every position up front, especially defending each position," Brennan said. "If he doesn't start, he could be the best sixth man in the league."

Chotkowski's ability to contribute each night is vital because there is no experience behind him. Freshman **Trevor Gaines** of Farmington (Mich.) HS is a great leaper and has plenty of raw talent, but was only 17 years old when he started college. Brennan likes his ability and thinks the 6-6 Gaines could be a sleeper, but he may need time to mature. Gaines averaged 21 points, 11 rebounds, and 3.5 blocked shots as a high school senior.

Freshman **Corry McLaughlin** of Andover (Mass.) HS began his college career at Fordham, but lasted just a semester and one exhibition game before transferring. When he becomes eligible in January, McLaughlin, at 6-8 and 225 pounds, will bring some much-needed height to the frontcourt. The North Andover, Mass., native averaged 17 points, nine rebounds and four blocks as a high school senior two years ago.

Sophomore **Erik Barrett** of Montpelier (Vt.) HS was redshirted last year. Barrett, 6-8, might help right away and you have to admire his perseverance. Barrett took four years off after high school and grew six inches. That and some hard work made Barrett into a Division I prospect.

Vermont's backcourt is a bit deeper and a little more settled.

Brennan believes he can count on sophomore **Tony Orciari**. As a freshman, Orciari was the Catamounts' second-leading scorer (14.7 ppg) and leader in three-point goals (making 59 of 145), three-point percentage (.407, fifth-best in the league) and free-throw percentage (.778, sixth in the league). The 6-3 Orciari, considered by many to be the best Vermont high school player in the last 20 years, was everything the locals could have wanted. He followed up two Vermont high school Player-of-the-Year awards with the America East Rookie-of-the-Year award.

"They treat him like a rock star around here," Brennan said. "When they announce his name, you think Mick Jagger is coming off the bench."

All of the pressure of being a state hero at age 18 didn't affect Orciari's consistency. He reached double figures 23 times and made a three-pointer in 24 of Vermont's 27 games.

"He's just a joy to coach," Brennan said. "It's like the guy has never watched television in his life. There is just no nonsense. And when Orciari is great, he makes everyone around him better."

Orciari will depend on point guard **David Roach** to get him the basketball. The 5-11 junior led Vermont in assists (109) and minutes. Roach (4.7 ppg, 2.1 rpg) shot just .291 from the field. He played hurt much of last season, which perhaps hurt him offensively and contributed to his low offensive numbers. His scoring average (7.9) and assist totals (127) from his freshman season dropped last year, but he displayed his toughness by not missing a start. His streak is at 54 straight starts.

Another junior, 6-2 **Tobe Carberry** (11.1 ppg, 3.1 rpg, 45 assists) started all 27 games on the other wing. Carberry is not known as a shooter, but was second in three-point attempts (24 for 85). Carberry is a slasher and penetrator, while 6-5 junior guard **Tyler Murphy** (4.3 ppg, 1.7 rpg) is a better shooter. Murphy shot .311 from three-point range, making 19 of 61, but averaged just 14 minutes in 26 games. He started four games.

Sam Meister of Notre Dame Cathedral HS in Chardron, Ohio, is the only freshman guard on the roster. Meister, 6-5, averaged 14 points, 10 rebounds, and six assists and was honorable mention All-Ohio last season. He improves Vermont's backcourt size considerably. He was recruited as a point guard, but has good strength and versatility. Meister could play three positions during his career at Vermont.

Two backups last season were 5-10 junior **Chad Rainey** (0.4 ppg, 0.7 rpg) and 6-4 junior walkon **Brian Nemitz** (1.1 ppg, 0.3 rpg). They combined to make 17 appearances last year and their playing time will be limited again this season.

1998-99 VERMONT SCHEDULE

Nov.	13	@Lehigh
	18	Dartmouth
	21	Holy Cross
	23	Maine
	27-28	#Pepsi-Marist Classic
Dec.	4-5	##Blue And Gold Coca-Cola Classic
	9	Yale
Jan.	4	@Hartford
	8	Drexel
	10	Hofstra
	14	Delaware
	16	Towson
	19	@New Hamphire
	22	@Boston University
	24	@Northeastern
	27	@Maine
	31	Hartford
Feb.	5	@Drexel
	7	@Hofstra
	10	New Hampshire
	13	@Delaware
	15	@Towson
	19	Boston University
	21	Northeastern
	26-28	###America East Tournament

@ Road Games
# Poughkeepsie, NY (vs. Columbia, first round; also Colgate and Marist)
Milwaukee, WI (vs. Tulsa, first round; also Cornell and Marquette)
Bob Carpenter Center, Newark, DE (Championship game at homecourt of highest-seeded team)

adidas Blue Ribbon Analysis

BACKCOURT .... B **BENCH/DEPTH** .... C+
FRONTCOURT .... C+ **INTANGIBLES** .... B

Vermont coach Tom Brennan remembers the day vividly. It was January 2, 1987.

It was his first season as coach, and Vermont was playing host to Niagara. That same night Miami and Penn State were playing for the national football championship in the Fiesta Bowl, and Burlington got hit by a huge snowstorm.

Only about 100 people attended the Vermont-Niagara game, in which Vermont trailed, 58-20, at halftime.

"I walked into the locker room and said to the guys, 'I don't know what you are going to do, but I'm going to go out and thank all these people for coming here tonight,' " Brennan said.

It's considerably different now. Tony Orciari's decision to stay home and play helped boost the attendance to almost 3,000 per game. The Catamounts, meanwhile, have done their best to avoid being blown out of games like that cold night in '87.

In fact, the rest of the America East coaches voted Patrick Gymnasium the toughest place in the conference to play.

Despite the loss of 6-7 forward Erik Nelson, Brennan returns his most experienced team with three seniors in the frontcourt, three juniors guards, and a sophomore starter.

"Among (Jared) Steele, (Craig) Peper, and (Matt) Chotkowski, I have three guys who can fill the bill," Brennan said. "They are all tough kids who have had good careers to this point, and now they are seniors. Now maybe we win some of those games where we're not great, but we're older, more experienced, and have been down the road, especially on the road. ...We think we are going to be good again."

Vermont can be among the upper echelon and should be able to compete with any team in the league on a given night, but don't look for the Catamounts to win the America East title.

(C.C.)

ATLANTIC COAST CONFERENCE

adidas BLUE RIBBON FORECAST

1. Duke
2. Maryland
3. North Carolina
4. Wake Forest
5. Clemson
6. North Carolina State
7. Georgia Tech
8. Florida State
9. Virginia

TOP 40

Clemson, Duke, Maryland, North Carolina, North Carolina State and Wake Forest are ranked among the 1998-99 *adidas Blue Ribbon* Top 40. Extended profiles can be found in the Top 40 section of *Blue Ribbon*.

ALL-CONFERENCE TEAM

G—Ed Cota, SR, North Carolina
G—Trajan Langdon, SR, Duke
G—Terrell McIntyre, SR, Clemson
F—Laron Profit, SR, Maryland
C—Elton Brand, SO, Duke

PLAYER OF THE YEAR

Elton Brand, SO, Duke

NEWCOMER OF THE YEAR

Steve Francis, Jr, Maryland

1998-99 CONFERENCE TOURNAMENT

Mar. 4-7, Charlotte Coliseum, Charlotte, NC

1997-98 CHAMPIONS

Duke (regular season)
North Carolina (conference tournament)

1997-98 POSTSEASON PARTICIPANTS

Postseason Record: 14-8 (.636)

NCAA

North Carolina (Final Four)
Duke (Final Eight)
Maryland (Sweet 16)
Florida State (2nd round)
Clemson

NIT

Georgia Tech (3rd round)
Wake Forest (2nd round)
North Carolina State (2nd round)

TOP BACKCOURTS

1. Maryland
2. Duke
3. Wake Forest

TOP FRONTCOURTS

1. Duke
2. Clemson
3. North Carolina State

ON THE WAY UP

North Carolina State

ON THE WAY DOWN

North Carolina

INSIDE THE NUMBERS

- 1997-98 conference RPI: 1st (of 30)
- Conference RPI (last 5 years): 2-2-1-1-1

DID YOU KNOW?

After years of having some of the longest active coaching streaks in the nation, more than half of the league's coaches are relative newcomers. Five of them—Clemson's Larry Shyatt, Florida State's Steve Robinson, North Carolina's Bill Guthridge, North Carolina State's Herb Sendek and Virginia's Pete Gillen—enter the season with two years experience or less at their current school...Of course, Guthridge, Dean Smith's top assistant for 30 years, fared fairly well as a "newcomer," setting an NCAA record with 34 victories in his rookie year. He also took the Tar Heels to the Final Four...Only one player—Duke's Trajan Langdon—returns from last year's youthful first-team all-conference team. There were three juniors on that team, but UNC's Antawn Jamison and Vince Carter both opted to turn pro. They were the fourth and fifth selections, respectively, by Toronto and Golden State. Then, in an odd twist of draft-day events, Jamison and Carter were immediately swapped for one another...Jamison became the first player in ACC history to be chosen first-team all-ACC as a freshman, sophomore and junior...Three ACC teams have no returning senior players—North Carolina State, Georgia Tech and Virginia. More than 62 percent of the players in the league are either sophomores or freshmen...The ACC Tournament, after a four-year run in Greensboro, returns to the Charlotte Coliseum this spring. The Charlotte Coliseum was home to the event from 1990-94...The ACC had seven teams ranked in both major polls at one point last year.

(T.P.)

FLORIDA STATE

LOCATION .... **Tallahassee, FL**
CONFERENCE .... **Atlantic Coast**
LAST SEASON .... **18-14 (.563)**
CONFERENCE RECORD .... **6-10 (t-6th)**
STARTERS LOST/RETURNING **4/1**
NICKNAME .... **Seminoles**
COLORS .... **Garnet & Gold**
HOMECOURT .... **Tallahassee/Leon County Civic Center (12,500)**
COACH .... **Steve Robinson (Radford '81)**
RECORD AT SCHOOL .... **18-14 (1 yr.)**
CAREER RECORD .... **64-32 (3 yrs.)**
ASSISTANTS **Coleman Crawford (North Alabama '75)**
Jim Platt (Concordia '73)
Tim Juhlin (Northern Iowa '90)
TEAM WINS (last 5 yrs.) **13-12-13-20-18**
RPI (last 5 yrs.) **76-67-90-42-40**
1997-98 FINISH .... **Lost in NCAA second round.**

The strides may not have been huge, but second-year head coach Steve Robinson believes Florida State is better prepared for what will come this year.

If that, indeed, is the case, then Robinson can thank the NCAA Tournament selection committee, which shocked many in the college basketball world by including the long-faded Seminoles in the field of 64 last season.

Florida State began the season with some impressive victories, notably over Elite Eight participant Connecticut at Thanksgiving and defending national champion Arizona at Christmas. The Seminoles even climbed as high as No. 13 in the national polls.

But when ACC season peaked, they went into a steep decline, losing five of their last six regular-season games and falling to North Carolina State in the first round of the ACC Tournament. It hardly looked like a squad that would end the school's five-year NCAA Tournament drought.

Despite finishing behind Wake Forest and Georgia Tech in the ACC standings, the Seminoles were picked over those two ACC teams as the league's fifth team in the field of 64. The committee looked smart when Florida State upset fifth-seeded Texas Christian in the first round, then lost in overtime to upstart Valparaiso in the second round.

"I think we succeeded on a big level," Robinson said of his team's unexpected appearance in the tournament. "We weren't supposed to win against TCU, everybody had pretty much written us off."

To Robinson, that postseason performance showed something about his team. "If you keep trying and keep trying, something good might happen," Robinson said. "If you stop trying, then you have eliminated the possibility that something good might happen. Toward the end of the season we were playing better. We weren't necessarily that successful, but we got a lot of satisfaction out of going to the NCAA Tournament. There were only 64 teams and we were one of the 64."

That may be a difficult feat to repeat in Robinson's second year. He enters this season without four starters from last year. He has six new faces to choose from, including two freshmen, three transfers and a player who sat out for a season.

"That's a lot of new faces," said Robinson. Especially because his recruiting class, though large, is lightly regarded by most analysts.

"We have to give these freshmen the opportunity to grow and mature as basketball players," Robinson said. "We can't expect those freshmen to play at the same level as those seniors we lost."

At the same time, upperclassmen weren't necessarily the best thing about Florida State's team last year. At the end of the season, they appeared to lose focus and positive attitude, playing in a system that was far different from the one they were recruited to play in.

One of those lost starters could have returned this year, but power forward Randell Jackson opted to forego his senior season to enter the NBA draft. That didn't turn out to be such an astute move. Jackson wasn't drafted, and is now playing professionally in Europe.

So, in some regards, the Seminoles aren't as experienced and may not be as talented this year, but what most people expect is a team more willing to follow Robinson's instruction and play Robinson's game, which he developed as a long-time assistant for Roy Williams at Kansas and implemented successfully at Tulsa. In other words, while last year was a step in the right direction, this year's team will go further in building Robinson's program in Tallahassee.

There will certainly be new blood injected into the program, with 6-5 senior shooting guard **Terrell Baker** as the team's lone returning starter. At least two of those new faces will vie for a starting position.

Baker (12.0 ppg, 4.3 rpg) is an offensive threat from the perimeter and a defensive stopper who can shut down the opposition's best perimeter player.

But last year was his first year in the program and the junior college transfer had to search before he found his niche on a squad that returned five starters from an NIT-finalist team the year before.

"We will expect him to do more of those things and add to what he did last year," Robinson said. "For a first-year

1998-99 FLORIDA STATE SCHEDULE

Nov.	13	Sam Houston State
	20	Florida
	24	Idaho
Dec.	1	@Virginia
	6	Auburn
	14	@Temple
	17	@Jacksonville
	20	Georgia Southern
	23	@Butler
	27-30	#Rainbow Classic
Jan.	6	North Carolina
	9	@Georgia Tech
	12	Clemson
	16	@Duke
	20	Wake Forest
	23	North Carolina State
	27	@Maryland
	30	Virginia
Feb.	2	South Florida
	7	@North Carolina
	11	Georgia Tech
	14	@Clemson
	17	Duke
	20	@Wake Forest
	24	@North Carolina State
	27	Maryland
Mar.	4-7	##ACC Tournament

@ Road Games
# Honolulu, HI (vs. Princeton, first round; Hawaii, Mississippi State, Murray State, Southwestern Louisiana, Texas, UNC Charlotte)
Charlotte Coliseum, Charlotte, NC

player, I think he was still just trying to figure it all out at times. He has a better feel for it going into this year."

Not all of the new Seminoles are unfamiliar to Robinson. Two players, both vying to replace Kerry Thompson at point guard, practiced with the Seminoles all of last year.

Adrian Crawford, son of FSU assistant Coleman Crawford, sat out the season after following his father and Robinson from Tulsa, where he played in all 34 games as a freshman. The 6-5 Crawford (4.3 ppg, 2.1 assists at Tulsa in 1996-97) is a sophomore.

"He brings some experience—not only on-the-floor competition, but he knows our system and how we want to play," Robinson said.

Crawford will battle 5-11 sophomore **Delvon Arrington** for time at the point—the team's only experienced player at that position, Devonaire Deas, opted to leave the program in the offseason. Arrington, the first partial qualifier in basketball accepted at an ACC school, sat out all of last season and will have three years of eligibility remaining.

Arrington is athletic and quick and has a stellar prep record. He helped St. Anthony's High of Jersey City, N.J., to three state high school championships, three state Tournament of Champions titles and, as a junior, the *USA Today* national title.

With Crawford, Arrington and Baker, the Seminoles have some options in the backcourt. Freshman **Emanuel Mathis**, a 6-3 shooter from Atlanta's Holy Innocent School, is a scorer who probably needs some time before adjusting to the ACC after playing in Georgia's smallest high school classification. Mathis averaged 28.2 points as a senior and was a first-team Class A all-state pick.

Robinson and his staff are also expecting big things out of 6-8 junior forward **Ron Hale**, who can play at the swing position or at power forward. He flashed some of his potential in the postseason, leading the Seminoles in scoring and rebounding in the two NCAA Tournament games.

"In the offseason, we said 'OK, Ron, this is your opportunity. The window is wide open for you,' " Robinson said. "He had a tremendous summer and worked very hard."

Hale (5.8 ppg, 4.0 rpg) can play inside or outside, making him a good complement to Baker on the wing. Freshman **Antwaun Dixon**, a 6-6 swing player from Atlanta's Wheeler High, will also compete for time on the wing. Dixon averaged 16.0 points and 9.5 rebounds in Georgia's highest classification.

The front court poses some interesting questions for Robinson. He likes 7-2, 218-pound sophomore **Karim Shabazz** now that he has added 20 pounds to his stringbean-like frame.

Shabazz not only put on some weight and added strength, he also got valuable experience this summer at the USA Basketball's National Team Trials for the Goodwill Games team. He was cut, but Robinson thinks the experience will help as he tries to compete against the ACC's best.

Kentucky transfer **Oliver Simmons**, a 6-8, 225-pound junior, was a disappointment in his first year as a Seminole. Simmons (1.9 ppg, 1.3 rpg) will have to be more productive his second time around.

Among the other returning players are 6-7 sophomore swing player **Ronald Thompson** (1.4 ppg, 0.9 rpg), 6-5 walkon point guard Matt Chlebek (1.1 ppg, 0.7 rpg) and walkon forward **Gibson Pierre** (0.4 ppg, 0.6 rpg).

Robinson did most of his recruiting in the front court, with three of his four new signees playing in the post. Forward Damous Anderson, a 6-6, 215-pound junior college transfer, is probably the most ready to contribute early in the season, but he won't get that chance. He did not complete his degree requirements at Metro Atlanta College and was not admitted for the fall semester. He plans to enroll for the spring.

Anderson (21.7 ppg, 11.7 rpg at Metro Atlanta) was a junior college All-American last year. His versatility at small forward and power forward make the coaches optimistic about his future, if he eventually becomes eligible.

Florida State's final signee is 6-10 center **Justin Mott**, who was signed from Barton County Community College in Kansas as a reaction to 6-10 James Felton's decision to leave the program. Felton never played at Florida State. He sat out last year after transferring from St. John's.

Mott was a reserve center in his only year in junior college. He also played one year at Washington State.

Heading into preseason, Robinson expected either Crawford or Arrington to be his starting point guard, with Baker at shooting guard, Hale at small forward and Shabazz at center. Simmons, Anderson and Thompson were expected to battle for the power forward spot.

adidas Blue Ribbon Analysis

BACKCOURT	**C+**	**BENCH/DEPTH**	**C**
FRONTCOURT	**C+**	**INTANGIBLES**	**C**

Robinson has portrayed this year as a season of opportunity for several of his players. Hale has never really been as big a part of the Seminole scheme as the coaches think he should. He'll get plenty of chances to prove himself this year.

No other team in the league has a player with Shabazz's height, but he has to be more durable and more aggressive. Another 20 to 30 pounds would do him good.

The power forward position will be key. Simmons proved little last year. Anderson might help push him along, when (or if) he joins the team. And Thompson is still too inexperienced to know how he will perform.

"We have several guys who have not had the opportunity to play until this year," Robinson said. "Now they are going to have to step into those roles and see if they can make the best of those opportunities."

If not, it will take a lot more than a unexpected invitation from the NCAA Tournament selection committee to get the Seminoles in the field of 64 for the second year in a row.

(T.P.)

GEORGIA TECH

LOCATION	**Atlanta, GA**
CONFERENCE	**Atlantic Coast (ACC)**
LAST SEASON	**19-14 (.576)**
CONFERENCE RECORD	**6-10 (t-6th)**
STARTERS LOST/RETURNING	**3/2**
NICKNAME	**Yellow Jackets**
COLORS	**Crimson & Gray**
HOMECOURT	**Alexander Memorial Auditorium (10,000)**
COACH	**Bobby Cremins (South Carolina '70)**
RECORD AT SCHOOL	**326-204 (17 yrs.)**
CAREER RECORD	**426-274 (23 yrs.)**
ASSISTANTS	**Kent Cantwell (UNC-Asheville '73) Dereck Whittenburg (N.C.State '84) Gary Leiner (Notre Dame '76)**
TEAM WINS (last 5 yrs.)	**16-18-24-9-19**
RPI (last 5 yrs.)	**39-52-11-101-57**
1997-98 FINISH	**Lost in NIT third round.**

Bobby Cremins has his sanity back. At least for now.

About this time last year, the white-haired wonder sounded as though he was ready to jump off the Coca-Cola building in an attempt to wipe out the memories of his worst season as a head coach.

But, thanks to a critical decision by one of the best all-around players in school history to return for his senior season, Cremins was able to turn things around rather quickly.

Thanks for sticking around Matt Harpring, your coach needed it.

Harpring, the second-leading scorer in Tech history and one of the most versatile players to come through the ACC in quite a while, is finally gone, off waiting to make his millions as a first-round draft pick of the Orlando Magic (No. 15 overall).

Because Harpring stayed around for his senior season, though, the Yellow Jackets were able to bounce back from the 9-18 debacle in 1996-97 that left Cremins drained and demoralized.

"After going from first to last the year before, I thought last year was a good kind of comeback year for us," Cremins said. "We got within a hair of making the NCAA Tournament.

"It was a good season, not a great one. But we almost pulled off a great season."

It was certainly better than being at the bottom of the ACC, where the Yellow Jackets finished the year before in Cremins' only losing season as a head coach. That's where they were picked to finish again last year.

While he was enjoying the swan songs of Harpring and forward Michael Maddox, Cremins found some new star candidates who will be expected to help the Yellow Jackets return to the NCAA Tournament this year. Before the 1996-97 season, Tech had been to the Big Dance eight straight years.

Sophomores **Dion Glover** and **Alvin Jones** are the nucleus of Cremins' continued rebuilding. Glover, a 6-4 scoring dynamo, was the runner-up ACC Rookie of the Year to Wake Forest's Robert O'Kelley. Glover (18.0 ppg, 5.0 rpg, 86 assists, 70 steals) showed he will be a future superstar in the ACC, particularly with his postseason performances of 33 points against Seton Hall and 22 against Georgetown in the NIT. Glover was the third-leading freshman scorer in the nation, and was fourth in ACC scoring. He was also second in steals (2.1 spg) and fifth in minutes played (35.2).

"Last year was a great learning year for Dion," Cremins said. "He learned a lot about his game, a lot about himself. Hopefully, he can utilize that experience from last year and really be ready to be a takeover guy this year."

Glover learned even more about his game during the summer as a member of the USA Basketball team in the Goodwill Games. Glover was the gold medal-winning team's fifth leading scorer (8.4 ppg) and shot .485 percent from the field and .571 percent from the three-point line.

What's encouraging to Cremins, of course, is there is plenty of room for improvement. Glover shot only .271 percent from three-point range and was third on the team in total three-pointers. He still makes bad decisions on the court and his defensive efforts never came close to his offensive production.

Jones (6.8 ppg, 6.7 rpg) was one of the biggest surprises in the ACC last year, if not the country. A lightly regarded recruit, the 6-11 Jones earned a starting job in the preseason and set the tone for the entire season by blocking 11 shots in Tech's season-opener against Winthrop. He went on to lead the NCAA with 141 blocked shots, shattering the school record. Jones' average of 4.3 blocks per game was third in the country behind Jerome James of Florida A&M (4.5) and Calvin Booth of Penn State (4.4).

After scaring the socks off Winthrop's players with his barrage of blocks, Jones didn't have another double-figure block effort all year, but he came close. Jones blocked nine Georgetown shots in the NIT, and also had eight-block games against Delaware State, Coastal Carolina and Georgia Southern.

Jones was everything Glover wasn't—a defensive force—but he needs to improve on his offensive production. He still needs work on his strength and endurance and he can help take some scoring pressure off Glover with a little offensive maturity, which Cremins is expecting.

"I think as Alvin matures, he can become a very, very good player," Cremins said.

Jones was slowed this summer with a stress fracture in his foot, but is expected to be at full speed when preseason drills begin.

Jones won't be expected to handle all the inside scoring, at least not after Dec. 11. That's when Indiana transfer **Jason Collier** becomes eligible for the Yellow Jackets. Collier is a sweet-shooting, 7-foot junior who was a *Parade* All-American and Mr. Basketball in Ohio as a high school senior.

Collier (10.7 ppg, 5.2 rpg at Indiana) tired of Bobby

1998-99 GEORGIA TECH SCHEDULE

Nov.	16	Charleston Southern
	20	The Citadel
	27-29	#Big Island Invitational
Dec.	5	Appalachian State
	13	Georgia
	16	Wofford
	19	*Kentucky
	22	North Carolina
	26-27	##ECAC Holiday Classic
	30	Mount St. Mary's
Jan.	2	@North Carolina State
	6	@Duke
	9	Florida State
	16	Wake Forest
	19	@Maryland
	23	@Virginia
	28	Clemson
	31	@North Carolina
Feb.	2	North Carolina State
	6	Duke
	11	@Florida State
	14	@Louisville
	16	@Wake Forest
	21	Maryland
	25	Virginia
	28	@Clemson
Mar.	4-7	###ACC Tournament

@	Road Games
*	Georgia Dome, Atlanta, GA
#	Hilo, HI (vs. New Orleans, first round; also Georgia Tech, Hawaii-Hilo, Saint Louis, Washington, West Virginia and Wisconsin-Green Bay)
##	New York, NY (vs. Hofstra, first round; also Iona and Pennsylvania)
###	Charlotte Coliseum, NC

Knight's relentless pressure last December and called up Cremins, who had recruited Collier out of high school. Tech is probably where Collier belonged anyway—his father Jeff played four years for the Yellow Jackets in the early 1970s.

Collier should be the perfect foil to Jones. He's a smooth-shooting big man who is much better on offense than defense. The combination of the two should give Tech one of the more formidable front lines in the conference, once they get used to being on the floor at the same time.

Unfortunately for Cremins, the rest of his lineup is filled with question marks.

For starters, Cremins is heading into his fifth straight year and seventh season this decade with a new starting point guard. That is thanks to the unexpected departure of Travis Spivey, who started 32 of the Jackets' 33 games last year as a freshman. Spivey, who said he left Tech for academic reasons, transferred to Iowa State.

Spivey wasn't the only Yellow Jacket to skip town. Also leaving the program, rather unexpectedly, was 6-10 center Pablo Machado, who transferred to Loyola-Marymount.

The two transfers created a small firestorm in Atlanta. Cremins has now seen six players transfer elsewhere in the last three years, including his last two point guards, Spivey and Kevin Morris, who is now at Georgia State.

Spivey's high school coach even accused Cremins of forcing the guard to leave, an accusation Cremins vehemently denies.

"Travis was all for transferring," Cremins said. "He is the one who decided not to come back to summer school and I concurred with his decision. He's a good kid and I really hope he gets (to Iowa State) and goes forward."

Cremins certainly didn't want Machado, an athletic frontcourt presence, to leave either. The Jackets could have used the depth inside.

Tech could also have used Al Harrington, a 6-8 forward from Elizabeth, N.J., who was rated as the best high school player in the nation and the exact piece Cremins needed to have an awesome starting lineup. Tech was said to be one of the favorites to sign Harrington, but he opted to go pro. He was the No. 25 overall pick by the Indiana Pacers.

Freshman **Tony Akins** (28.6 ppg, 6.5 apg at Berkmar High School in Lilburn, Ga.) will inherit Spivey's spot at the point. The 6-0 guard was chosen the Georgia Player of the Year last year by the *Atlanta Journal-Constitution* and *USA Today*.

Spivey and Morris had similar credentials, and they had serious difficulties adjusting to play in the ACC. Cremins will throw Akins, a shooter in the mold of Travis Best, into the fire immediately and hope he can handle the challenge.

"He has a lot of skills," Cremins said. "But he has to go through the ACC and get some experience."

Pushing Akins at point guard will be 5-11 sophomore **T.J. Vines** (2.6 ppg, 44 assists), who spent last season as Spivey's backup. Vines played about 15 minutes per game. He had career highs of 12 points and six assists in the NIT victory over Georgetown. In that game, Vines keyed Tech's 16-point rally in the final 8:27 with three three-pointers, then made the winning free throw with 11 seconds left in overtime.

All but three of Vines' 25 field goals last season were from three-point range, but he could use some work from that distance. Vines shot .301 percent from behind the arc.

"At first, we were disappointed with his outside shot," Cremins said. "His shooting percentage was not what we hoped, but he can shoot it, and we want some scoring from him."

Joining Akins and Vines in the backcourt is 6-3 sophomore guard **Darryl LaBarrie**, who sat out last season after transferring from Florida A&M. LaBarrie averaged 12.1 ppg and 3.4 rpg in his only season at Florida A&M. He also passed for 63 assists and made 20 steals. LaBarrie led his team in scoring six times as a freshman, including a 25-point effort against Hampton. He scored 23 points against Boston University and 21 against Coppin State.

LaBarrie is considered a good shooter—his field goal percentage (.432) and three-point percentage (.316) were decent for a freshman. He was chosen to the Mid-Eastern Athletic Conference All-Freshman team in 1996-97.

Not landing Harrington leaves Cremins with an opening at small forward, the position Harpring owned for four consecutive years. Cremins will let 6-6 junior **Jason Floyd** and 6-8 sophomore **Jon Babul**, who returns this year after sitting out all of last year as a medical redshirt, battle it out for that slot.

Floyd (6.4 ppg, 2.4 rpg) has improved in each of his first two years at Tech, spending all of last season as Tech's sixth man. Though he is more of a slasher, Floyd is the best returning shooter on the team and could develop into an outside threat.

Babul (2.2 ppg, 2.8 rpg in 1996-97) is more fundamentally sound, but less gifted, especially as a shooter. Cremins will likely use him at power forward until Collier become available.

When the full squad is eligible, Cremins will have an unheard-of eight-man rotation. Cremins is one of the few coaches who has ever survived in the razor-sharp competition of the ACC with six, sometimes fewer, regulars.

He even has enough depth from walkons to run three squads in practice. **Ashley Kelley**, a 6-7 junior forward who averaged 1.3 points and nearly one rebound in his 11 games for the Yellow Jackets, is in his third year in that role. He is joined by four guards: 6-3 sophomore **Paul Trotti** (0.5 ppg, 0.3 rpg), 5-10 sophomore **Kyle Perry** (0.4 ppg, 0.4 rpg), 6-4 sophomore **Bert Culbreth** (1.0 ppg, 0.6 rpg) and 6-2 redshirt freshman **Steve Economos**.

adidas Blue Ribbon Analysis

BACKCOURT	**B**	**BENCH/DEPTH**	**C+**
FRONTCOURT	**A**	**INTANGIBLES**	**B**

Bobby's back and he has a few potential superstars coming with him. Glover proved last year that he will be a special player. If Jones can add some offense to go along with his defense, or effectively rely on Collier to score all the points, then the Yellow Jackets will have a great inside-outside combination.

Nevertheless, there are enough questions about Akins' ability to run a college team in the toughest league in the nation and the ability of Babul and Floyd to be productive that will keep the Jackets out of the upper half of the ACC.

This is still essentially a rebuilding year for Cremins. But at least he's not looking for the nearest ledge anymore.

(T.P.)

NORTH CAROLINA STATE

LOCATION	**Raleigh, NC**
CONFERENCE	**AtlanticCoast (ACC)**
LAST SEASON	**17-15 (.530)**
CONFERENCE RECORD	**5-11 (8th)**
STARTERS LOST/RETURNING	**2/3**
NICKNAME	**Wolfpack**
COLORS	**Red & White**
HOMECOURT	**Reynolds Coliseum (12,400)**
COACH	**Herb Sendek (Carnegie Mellon '85)**
RECORD AT SCHOOL	**34-30 (2 yrs.)**
CAREER RECORD	**97-56 (5 yrs.)**
ASSISTANTS	**Sean Miller (Pittsburgh '92)**
	Larry Harris (Pittsburgh '78)
	John Groce (Taylor '94)
TEAM WINS (last 5 yrs.)	**11-12-15-17-17**
RPI (last 5 yrs.)	**127-97-77-59-55**
1997-98 FINISH	**Lost in NIT first round.**

Herb Sendek had to laugh. It was the only thing that kept him from gushing tears.

Every time he seemed to be getting his North Carolina State program rolling, he'd get another call from the medical staff.

"Hey coach, your best player is out with a broken foot." "Hey coach, a not-so-good player is out with a broken foot." "Hey coach, one of your best freshman is out with a broken foot." "Hey coach, did you hear the one about the sophomore horsing around in the locker room and separating his shoulder? At least it's not a broken foot."

It got to be a broken record last year, as the Wolfpack saw its roster dwindle to only eight players, just in time to face top-ranked North Carolina. The results weren't pretty, in that game or during a season filled with constant setbacks on the medical front.

"We certainly endured a season full of disappointments," Sendek said in classic understatement. "Seven of our 12 players were hurt at some point in the season. That is almost incomprehensible. "

This year, the Wolfpack seems poised to enter the ACC's upper division for the first time under Sendek's tutelage. They will likely make a run at their first NCAA Tournament bid since 1991.

With the departure of seniors C.C. Harrison and Ishua Benjamin, the stalwarts of the offense last year, the Wolfpack has only three guards on its roster: Junior **Justin Gainey**, tiny sophomore shooter **Arch Miller** and incoming freshman **Adam Harrington**.

So Sendek will probably spend the preseason working on his team's zone offense, because opposing teams will surely be packed in, if you'll pardon the pun.

It will be completely opposite of last season, when injuries forced Sendek into a four-guard lineup with 6-8 forward **Kenny Inge** the team's only true post player. Was anyone surprised when, in back-to-back games, Virginia's Norman Nolan scored 35 and North Carolina's Antawn Jamison scored 36 against the Wolfpack?

But as players started to trickle back into the lineup, things improved dramatically for the Pack. In the second meeting with the Tar Heels, State went from having only one player taller than 6-4 to having a front line of Inge, 6-10 **Ron Kelley** and 6-11 **Cornelius Williams**, in a glimpse of what Wolfpack fans can expect this year.

That front line nearly cut Jamison's scoring in half and allowed him only 10 field goal attempts. Coupled with Harrison's remarkable 31-point performance, in which he hit eight of nine field goal attempts, the front line helped the Wolfpack knock off the top-ranked Tar Heels in the Smith Center, the biggest win for Sendek's team since it beat top-seeded Duke in the 1997 ACC Tournament.

Sendek, for the first time, should have a variety of options on the front line.

"We have been very small in our first two years here," said Sendek, entering his third season. "The first year, it was because of personnel and the second year, it was because of injuries.

"If this team turns out as it could, we'll finally be at the point where we have some options inside. It's been a long wait."

The primary reason for optimism is the return of 6-8, 238-pound sophomore power forward **Damon Thornton**, who could be a rising star in the conference if he stays healthy long enough to turn his potential in to productivity.

Thornton missed the final nine games of his promising freshman season with a prolonged hip injury that wasn't completely healed by the beginning of last season. That didn't matter after he broke his foot in the third game of last year and missed the rest of the season. Thornton got a medical redshirt and has three years of eligibility.

Thornton (6.7 ppg, 7.3 rpg in three games last year) made an immediate impact on the team in his first year, becoming the first freshman in school history to lead the team in rebounding. Sendek likes to remind people that Thornton was fourth in the ACC in rebounding that year, behind NBA first-round picks Tim Duncan, Antawn Jamison and Matt Harpring. A member of the ACC's All-Freshman team, Thornton led all ACC freshmen in rebounding, double-doubles and field goal percentage.

No wonder the coach is anxiously awaiting the return of a healthy Thornton, who spent the summer playing against stiff competition in a Raleigh summer league.

"I think he is 100 percent healthy," Sendek said. "He still has to scrape off a layer of rust, because he hasn't played a whole lot of basketball in the last 16 months. But I fully expect him to be healthy and raring to go."

Thornton excelled in the summer league, which is full of

1998-99 NORTH CAROLINA STATE SCHEDULE

Nov.	14	Maryland-Eastern Shore
	18	Campbell
	21	Coastal Carolina
	24	@Providence
	28	Charleston Southern
Dec.	1	Army
	5	@Duke
	12	Houston
	17	Winthrop
	21-23	#Puerto Rico Holiday Classic
Jan.	2	Georgia Tech
	5	@Clemson
	10	@Maryland
	14	Virginia
	16	North Carolina
	20	Wofford
	23	@Florida State
	28	Wake Forest
	30	Duke
Feb.	2	@Georgia Tech
	6	Clemson
	10	Maryland
	14	@Virginia
	17	@North Carolina
	21	Tulane
	24	Florida State
	28	@Wake Forest
Mar.	4-7	##ACC Tournament

@ Road Games
# San Juan, PR (vs. Middle Tennessee State, first round; also American University-PR, Mississippi, Oklahoma, St. Joseph's and UAB)
Charlotte Coliseum, Charlotte, NC

current and former ACC players and a handful of NBA players trying to keep the polish on their game. In his debut in the league, Thornton faced Duke center Elton Brand and gathered 17 points and eight rebounds to help his team win. Not bad for his first healthy trip on the court in more than 16 months. But can he play like the guy who made such an outstanding debut two years ago?

In his absence last year, Thronton's former high school teammate, 6-8, 211-pound forward Kenny Inge, stepped in and provided capable play on the inside. Playing against bigger opposition in almost every game, "Skinny Kenny" made the biggest impact of State's five freshmen last year, with his aggressive rebounding and his zeal for the game.

Or maybe it was just because he was one of the few who stayed healthy the entire year. Still, Inge was a durable and versatile inside player. Inge was selected to the ACC's All-Freshman team and played more minutes than anyone but Harrison and Benjamin. His 11 double-doubles were the most by any freshman in the league.

The front court will also get a solid boost from 6-10, 228-pound sophomore center **Ron Kelley** from Emory, Texas, and 6-11, 242-pound sophomore center **Cornelius Williams** from Fort McClellan, Ala. Both players had some limitations last year. Kelley (8.3 ppg, 4.7 rpg) suffered from a sprained right foot that kept him out of seven games last year.

When he returned, however, he played well. His 6-for-6, 13-point performance in the NIT against Georgia was a good starting point for his second season.

As for Williams (1.8 ppg, 1.8 rpg), his biggest limitation was his size. It's one thing to be a big man. It's another, he soon learned, to be a tubby guy, loaded with a layer of baby fat. He arrived on campus last August weighing more than 270 pounds.

The extra girth slowed him down and it was a while before Williams contributed. This fall, Williams reported to school at a more manageable 242 pounds, with the intent of losing a few more before fall drills began.

Added into the Wolfpack's frontcourt mix is 6-8 freshman forward **Keith Bean** of Fontana, Calif., by way of Maine Central Institute. He was one of 10 players from his prep school team to sign a college scholarship. Maine Central finished 35-0 last year and won the New England Prep Schools Championship.

Bean wasn't the highest-rated member on the team, but he is a versatile player who might step out on the perimeter every now and then. He should provide frontcourt depth. It's not exactly what Sendek needs the most, of course, but when you've suffered through as many injuries and setbacks as the coach had last year, there is no such thing as too much insurance.

It's the backcourt where Sendek has the most concerns. Last year's team relied heavily on senior guards Harrison and Benjamin for scoring, defense and leadership. For the last two years of his career, the 6-4 Harrison (16.6 ppg, 4.0 rpg) took almost every crucial shot the Wolfpack attempted. He was a fearless perimeter shooter, as he proved in the Pack's stunning upset of North Carolina.

He had one of the most remarkable shooting performances in the history of the league that afternoon, making seven consecutive three-point shots to break open the game and scoring a career-high 31 points in the 86-72 victory.

The 6-4 Benjamin (11.3 ppg, 3.4 rpg, 120 assists) was the Pack's most tenacious defensive player for two seasons. He struggled at times on offense, trying to play point guard when he is a natural off-guard.

He will be remembered by some for his frequent miscues at the worst possible times, but his legacy will remain as player who was instrumental in establishing the foundation of Sendek's program.

In the backcourt, 6-0 **Justin Gainey** and 5-9 **Archie Miller** will be counted on to handle the ball, while 6-6 redshirt freshman **Ron Anderson** and 6-4 freshman **Adam Harrington** will do the shooting.

Also adding some depth in the backcourt is a pair of walkon guards. Both 6-2 freshman **Brian Keeter** from Cary, N.C., and 6-2 freshman **Carl Lentz** from Norfolk, Va., will be counted on in practice to help the team prepare.

Gainey (5.3 ppg, 2.6 rpg) is finally recovered from a back injury that slowed him most of ACC schedule last season. Sendek says it's hard to gauge how much that injury, suffered late in January, hampered Gainey's game and slowed State's offense.

He only missed three games, but Gainey didn't practice with the team for nearly a month after suffering the lower-back strain against Florida State.

Gainey made an impression on many at the end of his freshman year, when he played all 160 minutes of State's run to the ACC Tournament title game. He hardly looked like the same guy whose poor shot selection and terrible turnover rate kept him out of the lineup earlier in the year. In the first 12 games of his college career, he had 23 turnovers and only 12 assists.

But he was forced into a starting role at the end of his freshman season because of Thornton's hip injury and he slowly began to develop confidence at the point. That allowed Benjamin to move to his more natural off-guard position.

In his first dozen games last year, Gainey had 47 assists and only 22 turnovers. Gainey isn't big, but when healthy he has a knack for getting big results by doing all the little things.

Miller (7.4 ppg, 1.1 rpg, .423 three-point percentage) is also a point guard, but he's also a bomber. If there is a place on the court too far out to shoot the basketball, Miller hasn't found it yet.

The ACC's second smallest player (behind Clemson's Terrell McIntyre) is fearless when it comes to pulling up for a three-pointer, even if he happens to be in the parking lot when he lets the ball loose.

And that's not such a bad thing, if he keeps hitting them like he did last year. Miller was second in the ACC with his .423 three-point shooting percentage.

He's awfully small and looks frail on the court, but looks are deceiving. Miller is a tough cookie; after all, he was one of the five players on the team that survived the season unscathed. (He did, however, have minor ankle surgery during the summer, but is expected to be at 100 percent for the season.)

What better exemplifies that than his 13-point performance in his first career start against No. 1 North Carolina? His size has hurt the Wolfpack defensively, of course, and that will be a major concern for Sendek.

Anderson (1.0 ppg, 1.2 rpg) never got the chance to show what he could do last year. He was one of the "Broken-Foot Boys," whose season ended last December after the Pack's sixth game. He, too, was granted a medical redshirt and has four years of eligibility remaining.

His absence didn't really affect last year's team because he was playing behind Harrison and Benjamin anyway. But it prevented Anderson from getting some actual game experience in the heat of the ACC, which would be nice to have going into this season.

Inge's former teammate at Hargrave Military Academy, Anderson entered State last fall with a limited reputation. He was not a particularly accomplished shooter at prep school. An athletic player, Anderson was more noted for his abilities to slash into the lane, which is why several recruiting analysts figured he will be more of a small forward than a shooting guard in college.

That's not where the Wolfpack needs him this year, so it will be interesting to see how well he works in the Pack's perimeter-poor offense.

Harrington, on the other hand, is known far and wide for his shooting prowess.

The shooting guard from Northfield, Mass., averaged an eye-popping 32.9 points as a senior, leading his team to the state Division III finals for the third consecutive year. Despite his 46 points in the state title game, his Pioneer Valley Regional High team lost its bid to win three straight state championships, 79-77.

Still, Harrington chosen the Massachusetts Player of the Year by *USA Today* and a third-team All-America honors by *Parade*.

He was also impressive this summer when he played on the USA Basketball junior team that won the gold medal in Junior World Championship Qualifying Tournament. Harrington scored 6.8 points in mostly reserve duty for that team.

Finally, 6-7 junior swing player **Tim Wells** probably will play more on the perimeter this season, if everyone in the frontcourt stays healthy. That's a more natural position for the athletically gifted, but still developing native of Winston-Salem, N.C.

Wells (4.9 ppg, 2.8 rpg) missed time in the preseason last year with a stress fracture in his leg, but used that time off to add nearly 20 pounds to his lanky frame. He also missed time in January, when he suffered a separated shoulder while rough-housing with a teammate in the locker room.

Still, he had the biggest moment of his career late in the season when he blocked a layup by Florida State's Kerry Thompson at the buzzer to seal the Wolfpack's victory over the Seminoles in an ACC first-round game.

Even though there are high hopes in Raleigh this year, the expectations might have been higher if Sendek hadn't suffered a couple of losses along the way. Two of those losses won't really hurt the Pack, but the others might keep Sendek's team out of the upper division of the league.

Luke Buffum, a 6-8, 211-pound forward who had one year of eligibility remaining, opted not to return for his fifth season. The former walkon, who averaged less than a point and a rebound per game last year, decided to enter graduate school at nearby University of North Carolina, preventing this year's team from having a single senior on its roster.

Rouldra Thomas, a 6-7, 194 pound forward, was a project who never really panned out. Even when the Pack was down to only eight healthy players, Thomas (0.5 ppg, 0.2 rpg) rarely got off the bench. He transferred to Temple in the offseason.

The bigger losses were of players who never actually stepped foot on N.C. State's campus. Sendek heavily wooed swing player Al Harrington, one of the nation's top-rated prep players right up until Harrington opted for a professional career instead of going to college.

Sendek also signed much-traveled Schea Cotton to a scholarship, in hopes the dynamic 6-5 swingman from California, who had signed letters of intent with Long Beach State and UCLA, would win his eligibility battle with the NCAA.

Cotton's case was fairly convoluted. He made his necessary qualifying score on the SAT under guidelines for someone with a learning disability. He was allowed a large-print test and unlimited time to take the exam.

The NCAA, however, did not recognize that score and Cotton refused to take the exam under normal circumstances for a non-learning disabled student. Cotton and his lawyer lost several appeals to the NCAA and in August Sendek announced that Cotton would not join the team.

The absence of Cotton in the recruiting class will leave the Wolfpack without some desperately needed outside shooting. But, in the grander sense, Cotton's failure to gain entry to the school might prevent some headaches later down the road.

Sendek, who rarely gets too excited, is anxious to get started with this season, mainly because he wants to erase some of the disappointments of last year. Still, there is reason for optimism.

In each of the last two years, the Wolfpack has knocked off one of the best teams in the nation, had some success in the ACC Tournament and advanced to postseason play. It wasn't the NCAA Tournament, but Wolfpack faithful believe that's where Sendek's third edition will end up.

adidas Blue Ribbon Analysis

BACKCOURT .... **C** **BENCH/DEPTH** .... **C**
FRONTCOURT .... **B+** **INTANGIBLES** .... **C+**

With the departure of Harrison and Benjamin, N.C. State is one of three teams in the ACC that doesn't have a senior on its roster. That's something to keep in mind for those Wolfpack fans who expect their team to challenge Duke, Maryland and North Carolina for the league crown.

On the other hand, no one really knows what to expect out of the Pack because it rarely had its entire team available last season. One of the reasons for such high expectations is that the Wolfpack entered preseason practice with everyone vertical.

"If we are healthy, we are going to put a hurtin' on some teams," Inge said just after last season ended.

One thing is for sure, even if the Pack is not healthy in the preseason, it should be able to beat the shorts off most of its non-conference schedule. Only one of its non-league games is against a team that finished higher than 215 in the RPI.

The rest is a collection of pushovers that may pad the victory total, but will not prepare Sendek's team for the stiff competition of the ACC.

In the end, the team's success will hinge on whether an inexperience and relatively thin backcourt will be able to get the ball to what could turn out to be one of the most formidable frontcourts in the league.

If that happens, then the Wolfpack should make its first return to the NCAA Tournament since 1991.

(T.P.)

adidas Blue Ribbon Analysis

GRADING SYSTEM

- A+ equal to very best in country—Final Four-caliber unit
- A among the best in the land—worthy of deep NCAA run
- B+ talented, versatile and experienced—NCAA-NIT ability
- B solid and productive winners—league and post-season contenders
- C+ average to above-average—may contend in a weaker league
- C average to mediocre—second division in a strong league
- D+ below average, inconsistent—second division in a weaker league
- D well below average—losing season virtually certain
- F non-Division I ability—an underdog every night

VIRGINIA

LOCATION .... **Charlottesville, VA**
CONFERENCE .... **Atlantic Coast**
LAST SEASON .... **11-19 (.367)**
CONFERENCE RECORD .... **3-13 (9th)**
STARTERS LOST/RETURNING **2/3**
NICKNAME .... **Cavaliers**
COLORS .... **Orange & Blue**
HOMECOURT .... **University Hall (8,457)**
COACH .... **Pete Gillen (Fairfield '68)**
RECORD AT SCHOOL .... **First Year**
CAREER RECORD .... **274-128 (13 yrs.)**
ASSISTANTS .... **Walt Fuller (Drexler '87)**
Bobby Gonzalez (Buffalo State '86)
Michael Malone (Loyola '94)
TEAM WINS (last 5 yrs.) **18-25-12-18-11**
RPI (last 5 yrs.) **19-11-57-29-91**
1997-98 FINISH .... **Lost in conference first round.**

At least Pete Gillen won't have to waste a lot of time learning the names of all his players.

With only five scholarship players returning and two incoming freshmen who were signed before Gillen took over the struggling Virginia program, there just aren't that many to commit to memory.

The biggest question for the new Cavaliers coach might be this: At what point in his attempt to take his sparse roster against the rest of the Atlantic Coast Conference will he be committed to a mental institution?

The Cavaliers are coming off their worst season in more than 30 years, the final straw in the school's downward-spiraling relationship with one of its own. At the end of the 11-19 season, Jeff Jones was asked to resign, which he did during last year's ACC Tournament.

It was an ugly, contentious breakup for the former point guard who had seen nothing but success in the first 17 years of his relationship with the school, as a player, assistant and the eventual successor to his mentor, Terry Holland.

He averaged 21 wins a season through his first five years, including an NIT title and four NCAA Tournament appearances.

But so many things went wrong, on and off the court. Jones, desperate to keep up with the UNCs, Dukes and even Clemsons of the ACC, brought in a handful of talented players with questionable backgrounds, and some of their activities brought shame and embarrassment to the school.

Those off-the-court problems, Jones' uncertain future as head coach and the mounting losses on the court, caused another problem for the Cavaliers: It made prep wonder Ronald Curry, a two-sport athlete who had committed to play football and basketball at Virginia last September, have second thoughts.

The Hampton, Va. native was listed as the best high school football and basketball player in the country and he wanted to play both in college. Virginia has a history of two-sport standouts over the years.

He never showed up. Whether he simply used Virginia to keep recruiters off his back, as some have suggested, or he didn't want to waste precious time on a rebuilding basketball team, Curry backed out of that non-binding commitment and headed south to North Carolina, a huge blow to Virginia's football and basketball programs and the collective egos of the state and university.

Meanwhile, Virginia finished the season with its worst record in three decades. It didn't help, of course, that the Cavs were also facing some of the toughest competition imaginable. They became the first team in NCAA history to play the country's top-ranked team five times in the same season, losing three times to Duke when the Blue Devils were No. 1 and twice to North Carolina when the Tar Heels were No. 1.

So, when the season mercifully ended, Jones was pressured out of his job. After a short search, Virginia athletics director Terry Holland hired Pete Gillen away from Providence, hoping the fast-talking funnyman could revive the moribund program.

Gillen's track record is impressive. The 50-year-old New Yorker has taken Xavier and Providence to the Final Eight. He's won more than two-thirds of his games, including a 72-53 record in four years at Providence.

Gillen couldn't be more different from the Virginia style that Holland began, oh, sometime during the Pleistocene Era. Holland's style, which he taught to Jones, relied heavily on intense defense. With Virginia's success over the years, there is no doubt that style was fundamentally sound. But that style created ugly basketball, alternating between boring and hard to stomach.

Gillen plans to change that, with an up-tempo style that will be fast-moving and fun to watch.

"Our style has always been to press and run and that is going to be our general theme this year," Gillen said.

"We are going to play fast. We're not going to hold the ball. We are not going to play a game in the 40s and 50s. We are going to try to play quicker. That's the way I have always coached and that's the way we are going to play."

Unfortunately for the coach, with last year's leading scorer Curtis Staples (18.1 ppg, 4.6 rpg, NCAA-leading 130 three-pointers) and leading rebounder Norman Nolan (21.2 ppg, 9.2 rpg) gone, it's going to be tough to get the program moving at that desired pace, mainly because of a lack of depth.

Three players—forward Monte Marcaccini and centers Craig McAndrew and Chase Metheny—decided to leave the program, eliminating some precious experience and depth.

"We certainly have a lot of work to do in building our program back up," Gillen said. "We have some good players in our program, we just don't have a lot of them. That's certainly a major concern. This style is one that needs lots of numbers."

Gillen plans to conduct a campus-wide open tryout to find a couple of players and scour the rest of the athletic department for a few bodies to help his team through this season.

The players who are still around have experienced little success during their college basketball careers. There are no seniors on the team and the three juniors on the roster arrived on campus right about the time things really started going down hill.

Gillen wasn't able to attract any recruits, and the team's only newcomers are a pair of marginal prospects signed by Jones last fall.

Gillen loves 6-9 junior center **Colin Ducharme**, a scrappy blue-collar player who has started in the middle for the last two seasons. Ducharme (7.8 ppg, 5.0 rpg, 34 blocked shots) is the team's top returning scorer and rebounder.

"He is a warrior," Gillen said. "He has no fear. He is going to be one of our cornerstones."

If, of course, he can stay on the floor. Ducharme led the team with 95 fouls last year and Gillen's mission is to make him less aggressive this year.

The only other returning post player is 6-10, 219-pound center **Kris Hunter** (1.8 ppg, 2.1 rpg, 29 blocked shots), a lanky, sometimes clumsy, presence inside. He saw more action as last season went along, but Gillen knows Hunter will have to get stronger and more productive this season.

There's a little more to work with in the backcourt. Junior swingman **Willie Dersch** (6.5 ppg, 3.6 rpg, .389 FG percentage, 99 assists) still has the most impressive resume of the remaining players. But the 6-5 former McDonald's All-American has been woefully unproductive as a college player, hidden in the shadows behind Harold Deane and Staples in his first two years.

"He doesn't have to be Atlas and carry the whole team on his shoulders, but Willie has to take on more of a role," Gillen said. "He is going to have to be more offensive-oriented. I don't expect him to be a superstar, but I do expect him to be a very solid player in this league."

Both **Donald Hand** and **Chezley Watson** were thrown into the fire as freshmen last year. The 5-11 Hand (4.7 ppg, 2.4 rpg, 99 assists, 80 turnovers, 37 steals) started in 21 of 30 games at point guard, but struggled from the field all season. He made only .329 percent of his field goals and .277 percent of his three-point shots.

The 6-1 Watson (2.2 ppg, 1.6 rpg, 55 assists) also started a few games at the point, but his freshman season was interrupted by surgery to remove his appendix.

The team's only other returning player is a walkon, 6-4 **Greg Lyons**, who appeared in only one game last year.

Gillen had little to do with the Cavalier recruiting class. Both **Adam Hall** and **Chris Williams**, a pair of 6-5 freshmen swingmen, signed with Virginia during the fall, before Jones' demise. Gillen tried desperately to lure some more freshmen to campus after he took over, but didn't want to take on the excess baggage that any available prospects at that time might have been carrying.

The coaches even looked to Europe for prospects, but the only player added to the roster was 6-3 shooting guard Keith Friel, a transfer from Notre Dame who won't be eligible this season.

Hall and Williams were marginal prospects when they were signed last fall, but they each improved their credentials during their senior seasons, even though neither ended up on recruiting analyst Bob Gibbons final Top 100 players in the country. *Prep Stars Recruiter's Handbook* ranked Williams No. 147 and Hall No. 158 on its list of the top 300 seniors

Williams who averaged 17.5 ppg and 10 rpg at Minor HS in Birmingham, Ala., led his team to the Alabama 6-A championship. However, he is a reluctant recruit for the Cavaliers.

After Jones departed, Williams asked for a release from his scholarship. His parents had wanted him to go to Alabama, where they both graduated, all along. But the school_desperate, no doubt, for bodies_didn't grant that release.

So, despite what seemed to be strong parental pressure, Williams showed up in Charlottesville.

Hall, who averaged 22.3 ppg as a senior and scored more than 2,500 points in his career at Katy (Texas) HS, had a busy summer. He played for the USA Basketball Men's Junior Championship Qualifying team, which won a gold medal in the Dominican Republic in July.

Gillen put his team on a rigorous summer program and is hoping everyone will come back stronger and better conditioned. They'll need to be, if they hope to keep up with Gillen's system.

As for Gillen, he's swimming in unfamiliar waters. He knows the ACC only by reputation and isn't exactly sure what will be waiting for him when his team takes the floor.

He's realistic enough to know that the prospects may be dim, at least until he gets some of his own players on campus.

"I know everybody is predicting gloom and doom," Gillen said. "I am sure they have some basis for what they are predicting. But we have some talent. The guys who are coming back have to play a bigger role and more important role.

"This is the hand we have, we have to do the best we can with it."

adidas Blue Ribbon Analysis

BACKCOURT .... **C** **BENCH/DEPTH** .... **F**
FRONTCOURT .... **D+** **INTANGIBLES** .... **D**

Pete Gilled isn't afraid to be stubborn. He knows that

1998-99 VIRGINIA SCHEDULE

Nov.	13	@Virginia Commonwealth
	20-22	#Top of the World Tournament
	25	Hampton
	28	Elon
Dec.	1	Florida State
	5	New Hampshire
	8	Liberty
	12	St. John's
	22	Virginia Military
	27	Delaware
	30	@Loyola College
Jan.	2	@Wake Forest
	7	Maryland
	10	@Duke
	14	@North Carolina State
	17	Clemson
	21	@North Carolina
	23	Georgia Tech
	27	*Virginia Tech
	30	@Florida State
Feb.	3	Wake Forest
	6	@Maryland
	11	Duke
	14	North Carolina State
	17	@Clemson
	20	North Carolina
	25	@Georgia Tech
Mar.	4-7	##ACC Tournament

@ Road Games
* Richmond Coliseum, Richmond, VA
# Fairbanks, AK (vs. Arkansas, first round; also Alaska-Fairbanks, Nebraska, New Mexico State, Villanova, Washington State and Wisconsin)
Charlotte Coliseum, Charlotte, NC

both Rick Barnes at Clemson and Herb Sendek at North Carolina State changed their basketball philosophy when they came into the league, switching from an up-tempo style to a more plodding, physical style in an attempt to bring more talented teams down to their levels.

Both had the same roster limitations Gilled now has, yet the Tigers managed to win five games in Barnes' first year and Sendek took the Wolfpack to the ACC championship game.

Oh, well. Gillen figures he will take his lumps with the philosophy that has been successful at Xavier and Providence.

"We are going to play our style," Gilled said. "We are going to press and run. At times, we will try and slow it down and be creative. But we are going to basically play an uptempo style and play the way we are going to play."

Will that play well in the country's best basketball league? To be honest, probably not. But with a seven-year contract in hand, Gilled figures he's in for the long haul, so why fiddle with what he thinks will eventually be successful?

That philosophy probably won't make this an easy season to watch for Virginia fans.

(T.P.)

ATLANTIC 10 CONFERENCE

adidas BLUE RIBBON FORECAST

EAST DIVISION

1. Temple
2. Massachusetts
3. Rhode Island
4. St. Bonaventure
5. St. Joseph's
6. Fordham

WEST DIVISION

1. Xavier
2. George Washington
3. Dayton
4. La Salle
5. Virginia Tech
6. Duquesne

TOP 40

George Washington, Massachusetts, Rhode Island, Temple and Xavier are ranked among the 1998-99 *adidas Blue Ribbon* Top 40. Extended profiles can be found in the Top 40 section of *Blue Ribbon.*

ALL-CONFERENCE TEAM

G—Shawnta Rogers, SR, George Washington
G—Lenny Brown, SR, Xavier
F—James Posey, SR, Xavier
F—Lamont Barnes, JR, Temple
C—Lari Ketner, SR, Massachusetts

PLAYER OF THE YEAR

James Posey, SR, Xavier

NEWCOMER OF THE YEAR

Lloyd Price, FR, Xavier

1998-99 CONFERENCE TOURNAMENT

Mar. 3-6, First Union Spectrum, Philadelphia, PA

1997-98 CHAMPIONS

Temple (East Division)
Xavier, George Washington and Dayton (West Division)
Xavier (conference tournament)

1997-98 POSTSEASON PARTICIPANTS

Postseason Record: 4-7 (.364)

NCAA

Rhode Island (Final Eight)
George Washington
Massachusetts
Temple
Xavier

NIT

Dayton (second round)
St. Bonaventure

TOP BACKCOURTS

1. Temple
2. Xavier
3. George Washington

TOP FRONTCOURTS

1. Temple
2. Massachusetts
3. Rhode Island

ON THE WAY UP

St. Bonaventure

ON THE WAY DOWN

Virginia Tech

INSIDE THE NUMBERS

- 1997-98 conference RPI: 7 (of 31)
- Conference RPI (last 5 yrs.): 6-9-8-8-7

DID YOU KNOW?

For the first time in its history, seven Atlantic 10 teams went to postseason play (including a second straight year of five in the NCAA Tournament). However, only Rhode Island and Dayton were able to win games in the NCAAs and NIT...Also for the first time in A-10 history, six teams won 21 or more games (Rhode Island, George Washington, Xavier, Dayton, Massachusetts and Temple)...Dayton's Ryan Perryman became the all-time leading rebounder in conference history. His 10.4 rpg in career league games eclipsed the record formerly held by George Washington's Mike Brown (9.8 rpg). Perryman's 1997-98 season average (12.5 rpg) was the second-best in league history, surpassed only by Sam Clancy of Pitt (12.8 ppg) in 1978-89...Temple's Pepe Sanchez set a league mark with 3.4 spg...Xavier's team total of 83.5 ppg was the highest in the conference since West Virginia averaged 87.3 ppg in 1990-91...Fordham's Bevon Robin (18.3 ppg) became the second freshman in as many years to lead the conference in scoring, following the record performance of La Salle's Donnie Carr in 1996-97...No decision has been made on where to hold the Atlantic 10 Tournament following this season, when a three-year contract expires with Philadelphia's First Union Spectrum...The best year-round source for Atlantic 10 information is the *A-10 Hoop Report* (a10hoops@pressroom.com).

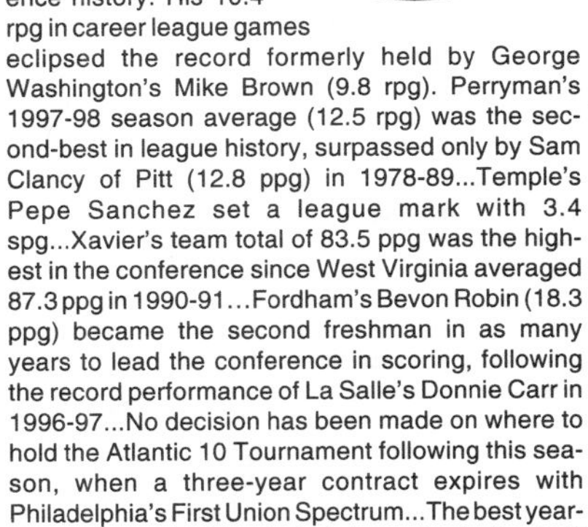

(J.L.)

DAYTON

LOCATION .... Dayton, OH
CONFERENCE .... Atlantic 10 (West Division)
LAST SEASON .... 21-12 (.733)
CONFERENCE RECORD 11-5 (t-1st)
STARTERS LOST/RETURNING 1/4
NICKNAME .... Flyers
COLORS .... Red & Blue
HOMECOURT .... U.D. Arena (13,455)
COACH .... Oliver Purnell (Dayton '75)
RECORD AT SCHOOL .... 56-60 (4 yrs.)
CAREER RECORD .... 157-135 (10 yrs.)
ASSISTANTS .... Frank Smith (Old Dominion '88)
Wade O'Connor (Bridgewater State '94)
Bill Comar (Kenyon College '93)
TEAM WINS (last 5 yrs.) 6-7-15-13-21
RPI (last 5 yrs.) 216-194-177-173-61
1997-98 FINISH .... Lost in NIT second round.

There is much to celebrate at the University of Dayton. The five-year climb from four victories in Conference USA (1992-93) to a share of the Atlantic 10 West Division title in 1997-98 must have seemed like forever to Dayton's large and loyal following.

You might even say the Flyers' progress has been a little like reading the Starr Report. Both are slow, painful and much more revealing than necessary.

Slow? The 4-23 nightmare back in '93 will not soon be forgotten, nor will the six- and seven-win seasons which immediately followed. Along the way came a new coach (Oliver Purnell), a new conference (A-10) and a rebuilding process the likes of which Dayton fans had never seen.

Painful? The whole process lost a year, maybe more, following the tragic death in February '96 of up-and-coming post prospect Chris Daniels. His loss had the Flyers reeling off the court, and left little star power on the court in support of recent U.D. stalwart Ryan Perryman.

Revealing? Now it's time for the really hard part. As far as the Flyers have come in the past half-decade, they are about to learn that the final few steps in program-building—the ones which put you in the NCAA Tournament—are indeed the toughest.

And, despite the 21 wins last year, despite the divisional co-championship, despite Dayton's second-round NIT showing, the Flyers are about to take a step backward before reaching anew for the brass ring. They don't want to hear that in Dayton, mind you, but facts are facts:

- There is no way to immediately replace the multiple contributions of Perryman (15.2 ppg, 12.5 rpg, .558 FG). The first-team All-A10 selection was the closest thing the Flyers had to a blue-chipper, and even he was a role player dressed up in star's clothing.
- The leading returnee, 6-7 senior **Coby Turner** (13.3 ppg, 4.8 rpg, .448 3PT) is another good—but not great—player. "This league is too good for that now," said one Atlantic 10 coach. "You've got to be able to say, 'Who are my all-league guys?'"
- The Flyers, much like fellow West Division import Xavier, still don't get the "schedule thing." Temple invented and Massachusetts later perfected the A-10 formula for stealing at-large bids from the more marquee conferences. Namely, play anybody...anywhere (preferably on television). It might cost you some wins, but the RPI will make it worth your while.

Instead, even though they already got their feet wet in the NIT a year ago, the Flyers are scheduling for little more than a return trip. The 1998-99 slate sounds tougher than it is. Among Dayton's non-conference opponents, only two—Cincinnati and Miami (Ohio)—are ranked in the *adidas Blue Ribbon* Top 40. That's not enough beef these days, when strength of schedule is king. It is an especially odd strategy for a team which plays six league games against the weak lower half of the Atlantic 10 West.

Dayton's final RPI from a year ago (No. 61) was just about right. Breakthrough conference victories over Xavier, Temple, George Washington and Rhode Island—all at home—were impressive. What the Flyers need next are non-league wins over better names than IUPUI and Kent, along with better road work along the A-10 trail.

Perryman was their lunch-pail star. "I've never had so much fun in my life," he told the *Dayton Daily News* after

1998-99 DAYTON SCHEDULE

Nov.	14	Kent
	18	IUPUI
	22	@Miami (Oh.)
	28	Marquette
Dec.	5	@Northwestern
	12	Toledo
	19	Eastern Michigan
	21	Louisville
	27	#Cincinnati
	30	DePaul
Jan.	2	Fordham
	6	St. Joseph's
	10	@Rhode Island
	14	@George Washington
	16	@La Salle
	21	Virginia Tech
	23	@Duquesne
	28	Massachusetts
	30	Xavier
Feb.	4	@Temple
	6	@St. Bonaventure
	14	George Washington
	17	Duquesne
	20	@Virginia Tech
	24	@Xavier
	27	La Salle
Mar.	3-6	##Atlantic 10 Tournament

@ Road Games
\# Gatorade Rock 'n Roll Shootout, Cleveland, OH
\#\# First Union Spectrum, Philadelphia, PA

the Flyers bowed out of the '98 NIT with a tight, homecourt loss to Penn State. "It's been a great run."

Four starters return from a club Purnell liked for its "balance and chemistry." They are led by small forward Turner, the league's most improved player and the nation's second-leading three-point shooter in 1997-98. He is joined in the frontcourt by 6-10 junior center **Mark Ashman** (11.7 ppg, 5.6 rpg), who was also a contender in the "most improved" category.

Yet sophomore sniper **Tony Stanley** (13.1 ppg, 3.5 rpg, .353 3PT, .851 FT) is clearly the Flyer with the greatest up side. The 6-5 Arlington, Va., native "had a great freshman year," said St. Joseph's coach Phil Martelli, setting a U.D. freshman scoring mark of 403 points (breaking the old record held by former NBA guard and coach Johnny Davis).

Alongside Stanley in the youngish backcourt is 6-2 junior point guard **Edwin Young** (8.2 ppg, 4.1 apg, .493 FG). Young is serviceable on offense, occasionally brilliant on defense, but, in a league of terrific point guards last year, was no more than average overall.

The unknown is how much Perryman made all the returning starters better. "His presence," suggested one Atlantic 10 scout, "was so important. They can replace a lot of his numbers, but how will they handle the 'bumps?'"

A stud sixth man or prominent recruit would be nice, but that will likely have to wait a year. Instead, the Flyers will again get by with top reserves **Andy Metzler**, a 6-3 junior (7.8 ppg, 2.3 rpg) and 5-11 senior **Josh Postorino** (2.6 ppg, .808 FT).

Neither is what Dayton needs most—namely, a power forward to make life easier for the still-developing Ashman and to draw defensive attention away from Turner and Stanley at the three-point line.

6-9 Nigerian import **Stephen Bamigbola**, the player formerly known as Stephen Bami, will get first crack at the position. Bamigbola (1.8 rpg, 1.2 rpg) is said to have a nice shooting touch. He connected on 55.6 percent in limited duty (5.4 minutes) a year ago.

Also in the mix at the power positions are 6-10 junior center **Matt Cooper** (1.4 ppg, 1.4 rpg) and 6-7 junior **Ted Fitz** (1.0 ppg, 1.2 rpg), a former walkon. Just as likely, if not more so, is that Dayton will go "small," utilizing Metzler and/or 6-7 sophomore **Cain Doliboa** (2.4 ppg, 0.9 rpg) on the wing. Turner could probably handle the rebounding chores in that alignment, but at least part of his long-distance prowess would be lost.

5-10 freshman **David Morris** (13.3 ppg, 3.9 apg, St. Vincent Pallotti HS/Laurel, Md.) is considered the best of the Dayton recruits. The excellent *A-10 Hoop Report* likens his game "to that of a young Tyson Wheeler." He will push Young at the point.

Morris shares a prep alma mater with 6-6 freshman Nate Green (11.1 ppg, 5.3 rpg), as the two combined to lead St. Vincent to a 26-9 record last year. Green was a first-team *Washington Post* All-Metro selection; Morris was named honorable mention to that group.

Also in uniform is 6-7 redshirt sophomore **Yuanta Holland** (17.3 ppg, 13.0 rpg, Dayton Christian HS/Dayton, Oh)., who did not qualify last season. Holland is a power player, but the level of his high school competition—along with the inevitable redshirt rust—make it likely he will not be a major contributor right away.

6-10 sophomore-to-be center Michael Harmon (0.5 ppg, 0.8 rpg, 12 appearances), nagged by injuries as a freshman, opted to transfer.

adidas Blue Ribbon Analysis

BACKCOURT	**B**	**BENCH/DEPTH**	**C+**
FRONTCOURT	**B**	**INTANGIBLES**	**B**

The math is pretty simple for the Flyers. With five Atlantic 10 teams reaching the NCAAs in each of the past two seasons, Dayton has to pass one of them to earn a coveted at-large bid.

Temple? Xavier? Massachusetts? Forget about it. The Flyers have neither the power nor the recent pedigree to bump the league's most well-positioned programs.

George Washington? Possible, but the presence of two (and possibly three) all-conference performers should be enough to keep the Colonials ahead of Dayton in the West.

Rhode Island? Also possible, but not too likely unless Lamar Odom is a complete bust and Jim Harrick has suddenly forgotten how to win.

Where does that leave the Flyers? In all probability, back in the NIT. It may sound distasteful to Dayton's suffering faithful, but the goal once again is to, well, keep the faith.

The school withstood an inquiry by the University of Virginia into the availability of native son Oliver Purnell. The Atlantic 10 Coach of the Year interviewed at U.Va., but already had an extension with the Flyers through 2002. Dayton also has a verbal commitment from in-state "super" Brooks Hall, a Top 50-caliber talent who is the kind of breakthrough recruit needed alongside the Stanley/Young/Ashman nucleus.

Fret not Flyer fans, your time is coming. Really.

(J.L.)

DUQUESNE

LOCATION	**Pittsburgh, PA**
CONFERENCE	**Atlantic 10 (West Division)**
LAST SEASON	**11-19 (.367)**
CONFERENCE RECORD	**5-11 (t-4th)**
STARTERS LOST/RETURNING	**3/2**
NICKNAME	**Dukes**
COLORS	**Red & Blue**
HOMECOURT	**A.J. Palumbo Center (6,200)**
COACH	**Darelle Porter (Pittsburgh '91)**
RECORD AT SCHOOL	**first year**
CAREER RECORD	**first year**
ASSISTANTS	**Josh Oppenheimer (No. Arizona '92)**
	Kenya Hunter (Duquesne '96)
	David Adelman (Pittsburgh '94)
TEAM WINS (last 5 yrs.)	**17-10-9-9-11**
RPI (last 5 yrs.)	**72-169-200-174-149**
1997-98 FINISH	**Lost in conference tourney first round.**

The sports fans of Pittsburgh have surely seen worse. The pre-Noll Steelers and post-Leyland Pirates come immediately to mind.

But the minority in the 'Burgh who actually care about college basketball—and the even smaller number who are loyal to Duquesne hoops—are in for the wrong kind of treat. We'll say it as gently as possible: The Dukes are going to be bad this year; in fact, they could be *really* bad.

How much worse could it get, you ask? Especially from a program which lost seven of its final eight games a year ago, which has exactly two winning seasons in the last 17 years and which is barely a rumor of the Norm Nixon salad days of the 1970s.

Oh, did we mention that Duquesne's response to this massive need to rebuild (again) was to hire an interim coach?

The Dukes got the first part of the decision right. Scott Edgar had to go.

Edgar—despite area roots, fine credentials and a Nolan Richardson pedigree—was woefully overmatched in the Atlantic 10. His teams were consistently at or near the

1998-99 DUQUESNE SCHEDULE

Nov.	14	SUNY-Albany
	18	West Virginia
	21	Buffalo
	23	@Maryland
	28	Akron
Dec.	2	South Florida
	5	@Radford
	7	@James Madison
	12	*Furman
	22	**Canisius
Jan.	2	George Washington
	6	@La Salle
	9	Xavier
	13	@Massachusetts
	19	Temple
	23	Dayton
	25	***Pittsburgh
	28	@George Washington
	30	Rhode Island
Feb.	3	Virginia Tech
	7	@Fordham
	9	@Xavier
	14	St. Bonaventure
	17	@Dayton
	20	La Salle
	25	@St. Joseph's
	27	@Virginia Tech
Mar.	3-6	#Atlantic 10 Tournament

@ Road Games
* Desmond Conference Challenge, Albany, NY
** Marine Midland Arena, Buffalo, NY
*** Civic Arena, Pittsburgh, PA
\# First Union Spectrum, Philadelphia, PA

bottom of the league's defensive statistics; a parade of junior college recruits was a near disaster; and the cupboard moving forward is darn near bare.

In his first three seasons, Edgar managed to underperform his two fired predecessors by winning even fewer games than Jim Satalin and John Carroll. The predictable player mutiny followed (not that mass defections would have made a difference), and athletic director Brian Colleary was forced to cut his losses.

"I like Scott," Colleary told the *Pittsburgh Post-Gazette*, "but the program wasn't moving forward. He worked really hard, we just didn't see the improvement."

For his part, Edgar wanted to serve the final year of his four-year deal. "I thought I had four years to build a program," he said. Instead, after refusing to resign, Edgar was fired.

That final year would not have mattered. After losing the threesome of point guard Mike James (17.5 ppg), power forward Kevin Price (13.5 ppg) and swingman Nick Bosnic (12.3 ppg), the Dukes were already taking on water. Keeping Edgar would have only postponed the inevitable.

The next decision was not quite so, well, decisive. Hometown hero Darelle Porter, the one-time Pitt star, was already on the staff (the only assistant retained, in fact). Duquesne could have hailed its future, sent a strong message to the local community and gained all sorts of goodwill by permanently promoting the first African-American to coach a major sport at either Duquesne or Pitt.

But Colleary was hamstrung by an administration unwilling to pay both Edgar and Porter head coach's money. So Porter got no more than a one-year contract, the satisfaction of being the nation's youngest head coach (at 29) and the difficult mission of surviving long enough to lose that distinction.

Now, no matter how much Porter is liked personally—and all indications are that the former point guard is beloved both on campus and around town—the 1998-99 won/loss record will be a factor in determining his long-term status. And it can't be all that easy to recruit while carrying around the dreaded "interim" label.

Is this any way to win games, now or later?

"We've had our share of talent," Porter told the *A-10 Hoop Report*. "We just have to keep them here. I don't think (recruiting in Pittsburgh) is a handicap. Last year, there were 10 Division I players from Western Pennsylvania."

Few are studs, however, and ever fewer choose Duquesne. Worse, Porter enters his one-and-maybe-done debut with virtually no proven Atlantic 10 players.

6-10 senior center **Kevin Shand** is the leading returnee (8.0 ppg, 5.4 rpg). 6-4 sophomore point guard **Courtney Wallace** (6.7 ppg, 3.6 rpg) has the most talent. The rest of the cast is young and unknown and, by all objective measurement, not good enough to make an impact at this level.

"We're definitely going to need Courtney to take control, because he's our point guard," Porter said. "Everyone else will have their part in pulling the team together."

Shand got 13 starts a year ago, Wallace a dozen. 6-9 junior forward **John Davis** (16 starts, 2.7 ppg, 3.1 rpg) and 6-5 sophomore guard **Aaron Lovelace** (13 starts, 3.8 ppg, 2.8 rpg) were also part-time starters, but even less productive. Those four, plus 6-7 freshman forward **Wayne Smith** (30.0 ppg, 15.0 rpg, Bathurst HS/North York, Ont.), are the team's likely top five.

Edgar called Smith "the best player he ever recruited." While that may be damning with faint praise, the truth is that no one knows if Smith is a real talent or simply the beneficiary of questionable competition.

Again, it won't matter this year. The Dukes are nowhere near challenging the top half of the conference.

They'll try to get by with a bunch of spare parts augmenting those above. Backcourt reserves include 6-4 sophomore **Shawn Tann** (3.7 ppg, 1.0 rpg), 6-4 sophomore **Charles Stanfield** (1.8 ppg, 0.9 rpg), 6-2 sophomore Matt Barker (two appearances) and 6-3 freshman **Austin Kegerreis** (15.0 ppg, 6.0 rpg, Chambersburg HS/ Chambersburg, Pa.).

Up front, the supporting cast consists of 6-7 junior **Devone Stephenson** (4.7 ppg, 2.3 rpg) and 6-7 sophomore **Jason Rackley-Mann** (one appearance). 6-11 junior Nyah Jones (2.8 ppg, 2.3 rpg) left school.

"We're going to work on their confidence," said Porter. "And, day-by-day, work to become better players and a better team."

adidas Blue Ribbon Analysis

BACKCOURT .... C BENCH/DEPTH C
FRONTCOURT .... D+ INTANGIBLES .... D

Porter may very well be the right guy for this job. He can't help but bring more structure, more respect and more pride to the program. The returning players applauded his selection, and he'll have at least a fighting chance to lure newcomers with a fresh personality and outlook.

The nagging question is whether or not Porter has already been set up to fail. The promise of a long-term contract is linked to this year's team, which is a certain loser. The new coach can only do much with the hand he's been dealt.

Porter's best chance is to control the damage, sign a local star or two, and have the current troops play hard enough to avoid embarrassment. His winning attitude may be all that stands between Duquesne and something like a 5-22 wipeout.

If Porter comes anywhere close to double-figure victories, the Dukes should sign-on for the long haul. If not, 1998-98 would have been yet another wasted year.

(J.L.)

FORDHAM

LOCATION .... **Bronx, NY**
CONFERENCE .... **Atlantic 10 (East Division)**
LAST SEASON .... **6-21 (.222)**
CONFERENCE RECORD .... **2-14 (6th)**
STARTERS LOST/RETURNING **1/4**
NICKNAME .... **Rams**
COLORS .... **Maroon & White**
HOMECOURT .... **Rose Hill Gym (3,470)**
COACH .... **Nick Macarchuk (Fairfield '63)**
RECORD AT SCHOOL .... **149-177 (11 yrs.)**
CAREER RECORD .... **298-305 (21 yrs.)**
ASSISTANTS .... **Nick Macarchuk III (Canisius '88)**
Edgar De La Rosa (St. Francis-NY '83)
Rob Senderoff (SUNY-Albany '95)
TEAM WINS (last 5 yrs.) **12-11-4-6-6**
RPI (last 5 yrs.) **243-244-260-243-223**
1997-98 FINISH .... **Lost in conference tourney first round.**

The baby steps were supposed to be in the past by now. If not running, Fordham should at least be walking after three full seasons in the Atlantic 10.

Instead, the Rams mostly stumble. Even the best squad (with the best player) of their Atlantic 10 era could manage just two conference victories. Overall, Fordham's three-year league record is an invisible 5-46.

1998-99 FORDHAM SCHEDULE

Nov.	24	*Boston College
	28	Holy Cross
Dec.	3-4	#Phoenix Classic
	12	Iona
	15	Florida International
	19	@St. John's
	27	@Manhattan
	30	Richmond
Jan.	2	@Dayton
	7	Massachusetts
	9	Temple
	13	@Rhode Island
	16	@St. Joseph's
	20	Xavier
	24	St. Bonaventure
	26	@Massachusetts
	31	@George Washington
Feb.	3	**Fairfield
	7	Duquesne
	10	@La Salle
	13	Virginia Tech
	16	St. Joseph's
	20	@St. Bonaventure
	24	@Temple
	28	Rhode Island
Mar.	3-6	##Atlantic 10 Tournament

@ Road Games
* Pepsi Arena, Albany, NY
** Madison Square Garden, NY
\# Hartford, CT (vs. Central Connecticut State, first round; also Hartford and Yale)
\## First Union Spectrum, Philadelphia, PA

So much for utilizing increased exposure from the A-10 to raid the New York City talent pool...

There is one major exception to this tale of woe. 6-2 sophomore **Bevon Robin** was not only an Atlantic 10 all-rookie selection, but he also led the league in scoring as a freshman (18.3 ppg, 3.4 rpg, 102 assists). Robin charged in from Rice High in the Bronx and single-handedly gave the Rams that one player who could win a game for you.

Witness a late February night against defending A-10 champion St. Joseph's. Robin took advantage of a hobbled Rashid Bey to post a conference freshman record of 35 points in a rare Fordham victory. Robin started all 27 games at point guard, ranking fourth in the league in free throw percentage (.812), seventh in three-point shooting (.384), 10th in assists (3.8 apg), 10th in steals (1.7 spg) and 12th in field goal percentage (.420).

He and senior Shawnta Rogers of George Washington were the only players to be listed among the leaders in that many A-10 statistical categories.

"Bevon had a tremendous year," said Fordham coach Nick Macarchuk. "He will take on even more responsibilities this year. One of his goals is to improve his defense and become the best defender in the Atlantic 10."

The Rams would settle for more of the same. And the return of former starter **Ray Carroll**, a 6-3 junior, might help. Carroll (12.4 ppg, 3.7 rpg as a sophomore) sat out last season, but was a solid performer at shooting guard during the 1996-97 campaign. He can also share some ballhandling duties, which could help Robin erase his freshman-like 3.8-to-4.0 assist-to-turnover ratio.

6-0 senior **Billy Lovett**, another guard who sat out the 1997-98 season, joins Carroll as a redshirt returnee with starting experience. Lovett is more of a point guard (4.4 ppg, 2.8 rpg, 94 assists as a junior), who could conceivably start and slide Robin toward a pure scoring role.

In fact, it would be no surprise to see all three guards—Lovett, Robin and Carroll—play together.

"We have a good feel for the guards," Macarchuk said. "We should get solid play from the backcourt." And that's not even counting a pair of part-time starters from a year ago.

6-4 junior **Scott Harmatuk** (7.6 ppg, 2.1 rpg, 22 starts) was third on the team in scoring despite playing the second half of the season with a stress fracture in his left leg. 5-9 sophomore **Jason Harris** (6.0 ppg, 2.9 rpg, 59 assists) got nine starts and was a good on-the-ball defender. Unfortunately, he played a lot of shooting guard alongside Robin and was not an especially good shooter (.322 FG, .302 3PT).

Up front, the big loss is 6-9 post man Maurice Curtis (16.3 ppg, 8.3 rpg), whose production really has no logical successor. Curtis himself tried to be the guy, appealing for an extra year of eligibility due to a prior injury, but that request was turned down by the NCAA.

Said Macarchuk: "And our returning frontcourt players haven't proven themselves."

You can say that again.

6-10 junior **Scott Pugh** (3.5 ppg, 3.0 rpg, 15 starts) will get the nod at center. Even if he doesn't learn to score consistently, Pugh will have to rebound aggressively in Curtis' absence. Same for 6-10 junior **Alexander Ziskunov** (1.6 ppg, 2.2 rpg), whose production actually dropped as a sophomore. Ziskunov was encouraged to play American college ball by George Washington star and fellow Belarus native Yegor Mescheriakov. Unfortunately, Ziskunov does not possess the same skill level as his mentor.

6-5 senior **Greg Griffin** (4.6 ppg, 3.9 rpg) is the best Fordham has to offer at small forward. Griffin, a one-time transfer from Bevill State (Ala.) CC, got 12 starts in his Ram debut, but is a more effective rebounder than scorer—and the Rams need points from the frontcourt.

6-8 sophomore **Alejandro Olivares** (3.1 ppg, 2.2 rpg), impressive at times after becoming eligible at mid-year, is also in the picture up front. 6-2 sophomore **Ken Aponte** (0.1 ppg, eight appearances) is the lone remaining guard.

"We've got six guys," said Macarchuk, "who played a lot last year." And two more, Carroll and Lovett, who were starters the year before that.

But what the Rams really need is for another newcomer to step up to Robin's level. If a true small forward was to emerge from the combination of 6-6 freshman **Steve Canal** (20.0 ppg, 13.0 rpg, 5.0 apg, 4.0 spg, 5.0 bpg, Nyack HS/Nyack, N.Y.) and 6-6 freshman **Teremun Johnson** (16.0 ppg, 8.0 rpg, 6.0 apg, St. Martin DePorres HS/ Detroit, Mich.), Fordham would have another position covered for the long run. Canal is more advanced at this stage, although Johnson's point guard experience from high school is intriguing.

6-9 freshman **Duke McKamey** (20.0 ppg, 13.0 rpg, Steelton-Highspire HS) and 6-7 **Arseni Kuchinsky** (17.0 ppg, 5.0 rpg, 5.0 apg, European Humanities University/ Minsk, Belarus) are the final signees. Obviously, there are plenty of frontcourt minutes available if either turns out to be ready for this level.

adidas Blue Ribbon Analysis

BACKCOURT .... B BENCH/DEPTH .... C+
FRONTCOURT .... C INTANGIBLES C

Fordham continues to take baby steps in its inexorable to struggle reach a competitive level in the Atlantic 10. Problem is, most of the league's true contenders are taking giant steps. The distance between the Rams and those from the conference who reach postseason play is still formidable.

"I don't know what the answer is," said one Atlantic 10 scout. "Robin is a start, but they don't have enough players at his level."

There is talk that time is running out on Nick Macarchuk, even though Fordham said going in that it would take five years to complete the transition from the non-scholarship Patriot League to contention in a major conference. For now, most Ram loyalists would settle for respectability.

As is often the case, Macarchuk is a victim of circumstance. John Wooden would have lost big as a coach in this situation, but he might have mined a few more New York stars by now. "And it's a shame," said a rival A-10 coach, "because what Fordham runs is as good as anything in the league."

Most of the players just aren't good enough to win with those sets at this level. The 1998-99 season will be better, but don't look for the Rams to leave the East Division basement anytime soon.

(J.L.)

adidas Blue Ribbon Analysis
GRADING SYSTEM

A+	equal to very best in country—Final Four-caliber unit
A	among the best in the land—worthy of deep NCAA run
B+	talented, versatile and experienced—NCAA-NIT ability
B	solid and productive winners—league and post-season contenders
C+	average to above-average—may contend in a weaker league
C	average to mediocre—second division in a strong league
D+	below average, inconsistent—second division in a weaker league
D	well below average—losing season virtually certain
F	non-Division I ability—an underdog every night

LA SALLE

LOCATION .... **Philadelphia, PA**
CONFERENCE .... **Atlantic 10 (West Division)**
LAST SEASON .... **9-18 (.333)**
CONFERENCE RECORD .... **5-11 (t-4th)**
STARTERS LOST/RETURNING **2/3**
NICKNAME .... **Explorers**
COLORS .... **Blue & Gold**
HOMECOURT .... **Hayman Center (4,000)**
COACH .... **William "Speedy" Morris**
RECORD AT SCHOOL .... **202-154 (12 yrs.)**
CAREER RECORD .... **202-154 (12 yrs.)**
ASSISTANTS .... **Tyrone Pitts (Pennsylvania '88)**
Bill Lange (Rowan '94)
Jim Phillips (La Salle '94)
TEAM WINS (last 5 yrs.) **11-13-6-10-9**
RPI (last 5 yrs.) **169-134-189-178-183**
1997-98 FINISH .... **Lost in conference tourney first round.**

Speedy Morris has been around this game a long time, winning big in Philadelphia both at the high school and college levels. Among other talents, he can add.

"To win in this league, and the Atlantic 10 is a very good league, you've got to have at least eight good players. Right now, we've got five."

Make it six if stud recruit Rasual Butler is eligible. The 6-7 Butler is one of those guys who can help you overcome a multitude of other shortcomings. He is a Top 25 signee would who give La Salle instant credibility, even at the high-est levels of the A-10.

For now, though, Butler sits. The Explorers hope he and his enormous high school credentials (26.7 ppg, 8.0 rpg, Roman Catholic HS/Philadelphia, Pa.) are eligible by the second semester. Simply put, his arrival could be the difference as La Salle seeks to avoid a sixth consecutive losing season.

The last three of those years have come since the Explorers finally landed in the Atlantic 10. Losing was not unexpected for La Salle as it sought to upgrade from prior stops in the MAAC and MCC. Losing indefinitely, however, is generally not an effective long-range plan.

Morris has been around long enough to understand that, too.

"We have to improve, and we are improved," he said. "We've made progress every year in the league. What killed us last year were two games."

Those would be the regular season finale and the conference tournament opener, both versus crosstown rival St. Joseph's. The Explorers were in position to win each. Instead, the more experienced Hawks pulled both contests out at the very end.

A win in the regular season closer would have given La Salle its most A-10 victories and sole possession of fourth place in the West Division. A win in the conference tourney would have been its first since joining the league.

"It left a sour taste for everyone at La Salle," Morris admitted. "We have to make it go away."

Butler would be a huge boost in that regard. His explosive offense from the wing, along with the ever-present sniping of 6-3 junior **Donnie Carr** (18.0 ppg, 2.2 rpg, 118 assists), would give the Explorers as good a 1-2 scoring punch as exists in the conference.

For his part, Carr was a much-improved player as a sophomore. "Less was more" for the gunner who led the nation's freshmen in scoring (sixth overall, 23.9 ppg) as a rookie.

Carr played more on the ball in 1997-98. In doing so, his upped his assist total from 55 to 118. Yet his three-point shooting dipped from .343 as a freshman to .309 as a soph.

This winter, Morris hopes to move Carr back to his natural off-guard position. He hopes his star remembers the more selective shooting and ball movement learned last season.

Of course, another point guard will have to emerge for Carr to slide over. There are two freshmen candidates, 6-2 **Julian Blanks** (18.2 ppg, 6.0 rpg, 3.4 apg, 2.2 spg, .516 FG, Cathedral Prep/Erie, Pa.) and 5-8 **Deon Jones** (23.0 ppg, 9.0 apg in 1996-97). Jones attended Christopher Robin (N.Y.) Academy last year, but did not play basketball. His stats are from Campus Magnet HS (Queens, N.Y.) one year earlier. The well-traveled Jones has also prepped at Bishop Loughlin HS (Brooklyn, N.Y.) and Oak Hill (Va.) Academy.

Blanks, a second-team All-State selection, is the leader in the preseason.

"I like his feel for the game," Morris said. "He passes when he's supposed to pass; shoots when he's supposed to shoot. This game isn't rocket science, you know. You just have to play it the right way."

The Explorers are counting on Butler as their eventual "three" man. In the meantime, 6-7 sophomore **Victor Thomas** (11.3 ppg, 4.7 rpg) will run at that spot. Thomas had a quiet but fine freshman year, starting 10 times and finishing strong. He also finished sixth in the conference in three-point shooting (.398).

Thomas and Butler can play together, particularly given the rebounding prowess of 6-7 senior post man **K'Zell Wesson** (13.2 ppg, 10.7 rpg). Wesson transferred in from South Carolina State and had an immediate impact. Guys who can average a double-double at this level typically don't fall off the transfer rack.

6-11 sophomore center **Garrett Bragg** (5.0 ppg, 3.3 rpg) was a 20-game starter last year, but has been slowed this fall by a stress fracture in his right foot. Bragg is in a cast for two months and could miss the start of the season.

"That's a setback," said Morris. "We don't have a lot of size."

Or much depth. The Explorers play their starters a ton of minutes—four at 29.6 per game or more, including Carr's 38.6—requiring a mostly zone defense approach to avoid fatigue and foul trouble.

The downside is that La Salle's zone is often too passive. Opponents shot a whopping .485 (.398 3PT) against the Explorers last year. That's why, despite four double-figure scorers, the team was outscored by nearly seven points per game last season.

Don't look for a different approach this time around. Instead, La Salle must hope for someone like 6-8 sophomore **James Jordan** (0.8 ppg, 2.6 rpg) or 6-10 junior **Bobby Collins** (two appearances) to emerge. The remaining recruits—6-7 redshirt freshman **Anwar Wilson** (13.7 ppg, 9.8 rpg in 1996-97 at John F. Kennedy HS/Bronx, N.Y.) and 6-8 freshman forward **Jermaine Peebles** (13.5 ppg, 9.1 rpg, Dudley HS/Greensboro, N.C.—are not yet ready to become major contributors.

"We can have a winning season and, next year, we can be a postseason team," Morris predicted. "We'll be there."

Speedy Morris fans everywhere are rooting for this Philly legend to be right.

adidas Blue Ribbon Analysis

BACKCOURT	**B**	**BENCH/DEPTH**	**D+**
FRONTCOURT	**B**	**INTANGIBLES**	**C+**

La Salle must get Rasual Butler, plain and simple. If not, it is hard to envision the Explorers scoring enough to offset their mediocre defense.

There is one other "X" factor: The Explorers actually have a homecourt to call their own. Hayman Center is complete on the La Salle campus and, while it ain't the Dean Dome, it beats piling players and students onto a bus to South Philadelphia.

"Every game was like a road game," Morris recalled. "We'd go to a hotel in the afternoon, even for home games. One time we got stuck in traffic and the other team (UMass) got to the Spectrum an hour before we did. It was crazy."

La Salle's entire program has been crazy for too long. Crazy league, crazy courts, crazy resourcing.

Speedy Morris deserves better. This year, if everything goes right, he has a chance to get it.

(J.L.)

1998-99 LA SALLE SCHEDULE

Nov.	14	@Mount St. Mary's
	21	Howard
	27-28	#Lobo Classic
Dec.	5	@Seton Hall
	11-12	##Boilermaker Classic
	19	Drexel
	23	Niagara
Jan.	3	@Temple
	6	Duquesne
	9	@George Washington
	12	Virginia Tech
	14	Pennsylvania
	16	Dayton
	21	@Rhode Island
	23	*St. Joseph's
	28	@St. Bonaventure
	31	@Virginia Tech
Feb.	3	George Washington
	6	Xavier
	10	Fordham
	16	@Xavier
	20	@Duquesne
	23	Massachusetts
	27	@Dayton
Mar.	3-6	###Atlantic 10 Tournament

@ Road Games
* First Union Spectrum, Philadelphia, PA
\# Albuquerque, NM (vs. Northeastern, first round; also Cornell and New Mexico)
\## West Lafayette, IN (vs. Eastern Washington, first round; also Purdue and Valparaiso)
\### First Union Spectrum, Philadelphia, PA

ST. BONAVENTURE

LOCATION .... **St. Bonaventure, NY**
CONFERENCE .... **Atlantic 10 (East Division)**
LAST SEASON .... **17-15 (.531)**
CONFERENCE RECORD .... **6-10 (4th)**
STARTERS LOST/RETURNING **2/3**
NICKNAME .... **Bonnies**
COLORS .... **Brown & White**
HOMECOURT .... **Reilly Center (6,000)**
COACH .... **Jim Baron (St. Bonaventure '77)**
RECORD AT SCHOOL .... **79-94 (6 yrs.)**
CAREER RECORD .... **153-165 (11 yrs.)**
ASSISTANTS . **Joe Lombardi (Youngstown State '81)**
Brian Nash (Keene State '92)
John Rhodes (Ohio '88)
TEAM WINS (last 5 yrs.) **10-18-10-14-17**
RPI (last 5 yrs.) **165-93-151-104-117**
1997-98 FINISH .... **Lost in conference quarterfinal.**

Just once, St. Bonaventure needs geography and reality to coincide.

Huh?

The Bonnies are among the western-most outposts in the Atlantic 10—and we do mean outposts—yet the school was slotted in the East Division when the conference expanded to 12 teams for the 1995-96 season. It must have seemed like a good idea at the time, as the East was by far the glamour division (with perennial heavyweights Temple and Massachusetts).

Well, so much for glamour. It can be argued that a shift in geography is all that is keeping the good people of St. Bonaventure from their first NCAA Tournament bid in two decades.

The Bonnies have been progressing ever so slowly under hard-working alum Jim Baron. They have also managed a pair of NIT bids in the past three seasons (including a first-round NIT victory in 1995). What the Bonnies have no control over is a double round-robin divisional schedule in which half of their conference games are against Temple, UMass, Rhode Island and St. Joseph's—all of whom are recent visitors to the Sweet 16.

You can't play Fordham enough to overcome that kind of meat-grinder. And now even the West Division is no bargain.

That's the bad news. The good is that even Baron thinks this is his best returning nucleus since coming home to Olean for the 1992-93 season. And, while the depth of the conference may consign the Bonnies to another NIT, it sure can't hurt to dream.

"This is the best core of returning players since I've been at St. Bonaventure," said Baron. "The nucleus of this team is good and versatile at what it can do. I'm comfortable with these players being able to play a number of different positions."

All of which is coach-speak, at least in part, for confidence. It's amazing what three victories over ranked opponents—Xavier, Rhode Island and Massachusetts (all at home)—will do for the collective ego. Said karma should more than compensate for the loss of leading scorer Rashaan Palmer (17.5 ppg, 5.1 rpg), who was a very high-maintenance guy away from the court.

Instead, Baron will hand over the leadership reins to juniors **Tim Winn** and **Caswell Cyrus**. They are two high-upside players who happen to man the most important positions.

The 5-10 Winn should move into the upper echelon of A-10 point guards this season. He was ready to do so a year ago, but he missed six starts with a very bad ankle sprain. Winn never returned to full strength, but still produced at a near all-league level (12.2 ppg, 3.3 apg, 107

1998-99 ST. BONAVENTURE SCHEDULE

Nov.	17	Liberty
	21	Canisius
	24	*Siena
	27	Rider
	30	@Southern California
Dec.	5	@Kent
	12	**Niagara
	18-19	#Hawaii Festival
	27	@Syracuse
	29	Delaware State
Jan.	3	@St. Joseph's
	6	@Temple
	9	Massachusetts
	13	@Xavier
	16	@Virginia Tech
	19	@Buffalo
	21	George Washington
	24	@Fordham
	28	La Salle
	30	Temple
Feb.	6	Dayton
	10	@Massachusetts
	14	@Duquesne
	16	Rhode Island
	20	Fordham
	24	@Rhode Island
	27	St. Joseph's
Mar.	3-6	##Atlantic 10 Tournament

@ Road Games
* Pepsi Arena, Albany, NY
** Marine Midland Arena, Buffalo, NY
# Honolulu, HI (vs. Northern Arizona, first round; also Eastern Illinois and Hawaii)
First Union Spectrum, Philadelphia, PA

assists, 70 steals).

It would help if this speedy dynamo was a better shooter (.353 FG, .267 3PT), but that should come given better offensive balance and a healthy set of wheels. And, even when not scoring consistently, Winn is a pesky defender for his size.

"I think he's an all-league guy," said one Atlantic 10 coach.

The same might be said for Cyrus (10.3 ppg, 6.3 rpg, .500 FG, 99 blocked shots). The emerging 6-9 center has made quantum leaps in each of his first two seasons. About 90 percent of the nation's Division I coaches would be thrilled to have him, and it is not at all a reach to suggest he might soon make a nice living playing basketball.

Cyrus has fabulous defensive instincts. That alone would be enough to keep him on the floor. Then Cyrus added some offense to his repertory, increasing his scoring average from 3.9 ppg as a freshman. He's come a long way in a short time, especially for someone who did not play high school basketball.

"He can alter a game," said St. Joseph's coach Phil Martelli, and he seems to do so when it matters most. Against ranked opponents, Cyrus averaged 13.8 ppg, 9.2 rpg, 2.6 bpg and shot 56.5 percent from the floor.

That, ladies and gentlemen, suggests a star in the making.

Baron will fill the middle of his rotation with a very Bonaventure-like combination of hard workers, rugged defenders and selective shooters. The lone exception might be 6-5 senior **Isaac King**, a one-time junior college transfer whose game is offense, offense and more offense.

King (5.6 ppg, 1.8 rpg) struggled through the usual transition from mid-level junior college ball to major Division I competition, but his touch is soft and his instincts for the basket are good. It would surprise no one if he doubled his scoring average from a wing position this year.

The antithesis of King is 6-3 redshirt junior **David Capers**, a defensive stopper who set or tied career-highs in steals, blocked shots and defensive rebounds. Capers (4.0 ppg, 3.5 rpg) also showed some offense late in the year, claiming career scoring highs seven times down the stretch. That run included a 16-point night at Vanderbilt in the NIT.

Figure on King and Capers to man the wing positions.

"A lot of our offense is predicated on defense," Baron said. "David will be a tremendous defender for us, and I feel good about what Isaac will be able to do for us this season."

The power forward spot remains in the hands of 6-7 senior Terrence Durham, who Baron liked enough to start 32 times despite an average of just 3.8 ppg. But Durham was the team leader (and 13th in the A-10) with 6.6 rpg. Not bad work for barely 25 minutes per game.

Durham is never going to be a scorer, but he keeps the play alive with decent ball movement and excellent timing on the offensive glass. He is the "dirty work" guy every good team needs.

The top frontcourt reserve is **Peter Van Paasen**, a 6-10 sophomore whose 1997-98 debut was better than expected (4.9 ppg, 4.3 rpg, 19.8 minutes). Van Paasen is comfortable at power forward despite his size, and he can team with Cyrus whenever the Bonnies go "big."

6-3 junior walkon **James Hayden** (0.9 ppg, nine appearances) is the final returnee.

"We've really developed the foundation for a successful program," Baron said. "Now is time for (the returnees) to lead us to the next level."

Bench help will have to come from the freshmen, led by 6-6 swingman **Vidal Massiah** (16.0 ppg, 9.0 rpg, 4.5 apg, 5.0 spg, 2.0 bpg, Eastern Commerce HS/Toronto, Ont.). Massiah continues the Bonnie trend of signees from north of the border, and he finished his prep career as runner-up for Player of the Year in Canada.

"Vidal is the complete package," said Team Toronto AAU coach Ro Russell, and the Bonnies could certainly use another creative player on the perimeter.

Another smaller forward, not as polished, is 6-6 late-bloomer Robert Cheeks (14.8 ppg, 6.7 rpg, St. Anthony's HS/Jersey City, N.J.). Said St. Anthony's coach Bob Hurley: "I think once (Robert) gets up there and puts on some weight, he will be a very good college player in the Atlantic 10." Cheeks had not qualified as of press time, but was enrolled at St. Bonaventure and paying his own way.

6-1 guard **Ernest "J.R." Bremer** (26.3 ppg, 5.8 rpg, 6.3 apg, .442 FG, Cleveland Heights HS/Cleveland, Oh.) will certainly see immediate time in the backcourt. At worst, he is good insurance against another injury to Winn. At best, he can occasionally team with Winn to create tempo and easier baskets for the mostly halfcourt Bonnies.

6-8 forward **Elton Ruddock**, a schoolmate of Massiah and Kentucky standout Jamal Magliore, did not suit up at Eastern Commerce HS. However, he once averaged a double-double (18.0 ppg, 12.5 rpg) in Toronto's AAU program.

adidas Blue Ribbon Analysis

BACKCOURT	B	BENCH/DEPTH	B
FRONTCOURT	B	INTANGIBLES	B+

Baron has his kind of team. There is a catalyst point guard (Winn), a defensive eraser (Cyrus) and just enough role players to keep the competition and defensive intensity keen.

Will there be enough points to help St. Bonaventure reach at least the NCAA bubble? That's up to King and rookie Massiah on the wing, although who's to say what Cyrus' upside might be as an offensive player?

Regardless, Bona fans should take heart. Unlike recent good teams which lost a Harry Moore or a David Vanterpool and then had to start over, these Bonnies are able to lose a Rashaan Palmer and probably improve. Plus, the heart of the squad—Winn, Cyrus and eventually Massiah—all return next season.

St. Bonaventure isn't going backward this time. The Bonnies are going back to the NIT, with the promised land getting closer every year.

(J.L.)

ST. JOSEPH'S

LOCATION .... **Philadelphia, PA**
CONFERENCE .... **Atlantic 10 (East Division)**
LAST SEASON .... **11-17 (.393)**
CONFERENCE RECORD .... **3-13 (5th)**
STARTERS LOST/RETURNING **3/2**
NICKNAME .... **Hawks**
COLORS .... **Crimson & Gray**
HOMECOURT ... **Alumni Memorial Fieldhouse (3,200)**
COACH .... **Phil Martelli (Widener '76)**
RECORD AT SCHOOL .... **56-37 (3 yrs.)**
CAREER RECORD .... **56-37 (3 yrs.)**
ASSISTANTS .... **Matt Brady (Siena '87)**
Monte Ross (Winston-Salem State '92)
Carlin Warley (St. Joseph's '95)
TEAM WINS (last 5 yrs.) **14-17-19-26-11**
RPI (last 5 yrs.) **85-48-63-12-138**
1997-98 FINISH .... **Lost in conference quarterfinal.**

The basketball gods finally got even with St. Joseph's last season. After two years of remarkable winning, close-game good fortune and magical chemistry, the Hawks fell off in 1997-98. And they fell hard.

It's a long way from the NCAA Sweet 16 to a 3-13 conference record. Last winter, Phil Martelli & Co. discov-

1998-99 ST. JOSEPH'S SCHEDULE

Nov.	28	@Tulsa
Dec.	1	*Villanova
	5	Tennessee-Chattanooga
	8	@Old Dominion
	10	Tennessee
	12	Akron
	21-23	#Puerto Rico Holiday Classic
	29-30	##Cable Car Classic
Jan.	3	St. Bonaventure
	6	@Dayton
	9	Virginia Tech
	14	@Temple
	16	Fordham
	18	*Pennsylvania
	20	Massachusetts
	23	**La Salle
	27	@Rhode Island
Feb.	4	Xavier
	7	@Massachusetts
	9	Temple
	12	@George Washington
	16	@Fordham
	18	*Drexel
	21	Rhode Island
	25	Duquesne
	27	@St. Bonaventure
Mar.	3-6	###Atlantic 10 Tournament

@ Road Games
* The Palestra, Philadelphia, PA
** First Union Spectrum, Philadelphia, PA
# San Juan, PR (vs. Mississippi, first round; also American University-P.R., Middle Tennessee State, North Carolina State, Ohio State, Oklahoma and UAB)
Santa Clara, CA (vs. San Francisco, first round; also Harvard and Santa Clara)
First Union Spectrum, Philadelphia, PA

ered just how far that was.

Hoping to milk a fourth-straight postseason appearance from the Rashid Bey-based nucleus, the Hawks instead lost one returning star to academics (Arthur Davis) and another potential star (**Damian Reid**) to an NCAA Clearinghouse rule which has since been changed. They also lost their way to the finish line, coughing up leads against good teams for the most basic of all reasons—not enough players.

"Just as winning begets winning, losing begets losing," said the affable Martelli, who was the same as a 26-game winner as he was a 17-game loser. "And, even though we were losing, the players never acted like losers."

Indeed, point guard Bey (16.9 ppg, 130 assists), forward Duval Simmonds (11.3 ppg, 5.1 rpg) and overachieving post man Harold Rasul (10.3 ppg, 8.8 rpg) gave it all they had for 28 games. Most nights, it just wasn't enough. Still, no one will forget their contributions to an Atlantic 10 champion or the prior NIT runner-up team.

Next up, the rebuilding begins. The 1998-99 Hawks will be, in a word, young. 6-8 senior **Rob Haskins** (11.5 ppg, 7.0 rpg, .392 3PT) is the only returnee with experience on a winner. The rest of the squad is a young and athletic nucleus the St. Joseph's coaching staff believes is the foundation of another run of postseason teams.

Haskins, for his part, can be explosive (career-high 33 points vs. Fordham) or invisible. He is a third-year senior who could regain a final season if, as expected, he graduates with his class. In the meantime, what the Hawks need is for him to accept a primary offensive role instead of hiding from the ball in key spots.

Haskins, who played mostly power forward a year ago, could be even better as a "three" man. His athleticism and face-up skills are fine, and he can defend the perimeter while not sacrificing good rebounding instincts.

Haskins will also be pushed at the position by emerging sophomore **Frank Wilkins**, a 6-9 swingman who got seven starts down the stretch a year ago. Wilkins (7.9 ppg, 3.6 rpg) could use more strength, but will take—and make—big shots if given the opportunity.

Wilkins has unusual skills for his body type. Wiry and quick, he has a pretty release and decent floor skills. However, he often gets lost while defending the perimeter and can be easily screened due to a lack of bulk. Yet he takes the ball to the basket and will get to the foul line.

6-6 junior transfer **Andre Howard**, a native Philadelphian (Overbrook HS) who sat out last year following a transfer from Pittsburgh, has emerged as the team leader without ever suiting up. Howard averaged just 2.7 ppg and 3.3 rpg as a Pitt sophomore, but has impressed everyone in the program with his work ethic and maturity.

Howard will start at power forward and become the team's primary rebounder. He'll have to get most of his points off the glass, as his shooting could use some work.

Reid makes a belated debut at center. The 6-9 Canadian (Bethune Collegiate Institute) is said to be the Hawks' best pivot signee since Rodney Blake in 1985. He averaged 26.0 ppg, 15.0 rpg and 5.0 bpg as a senior before playing one semester last year at Dawson College in Lennoxville, Quebec.

Reid has to shake off the rust and a few extra pounds, but has the requisite skills to compete at this level. He figures to learn on-the-job as a freshman, as will many of the rookie Hawks. Martelli will be employing up to three first-year starters.

"Damian thinks he's working hard right now," said Martelli. "Playing in this league will convince him to work even harder. He has the ability."

Reid also has the look. He was nicknamed the "Little Admiral" in Canada for his resemblance to NBA superstar David Robinson.

Backing up Reid will be another freshman center, 7-1 **Alexandre Sazanov** (Cardinal O'Hara HS, Pa./Moscow, Russia). Sazanov becomes the second Russian (following Dmitri Domani) and the first seven-footer to play at Saint Joseph's. He has good hands, decent footwork and a nice touch. Not surprisingly, he needs strength and may redshirt next year when the Hawks have more size to go around.

Even though 6-5 sophomore **Erick Woods** (4.1 ppg, 2.3 rpg) got 21 starts last season, he rarely performed like a starter at shooting guard. Woods wasn't recruited as a starter, but became one only after the wayward Davis missed the first semester and then a second before finally leaving school.

Woods will be pushed and probably surpassed by 6-5 redshirt sophomore **Naim Crenshaw** (Overbrook HS/Philadelphia, Pa.). Crenshaw led the Philadelphia Public League in scoring two years ago (25.5 ppg) before sitting out last season. The Hawks will need his offense, though it figures to come more as a slasher than as a stone shooter.

The point guard of the future, and perhaps the present, is 6-1 **Larry Jennings** (St. John's Prep/Astoria, N.Y.). Jennings put up gaudy numbers in the New York Catholic League (24.3 ppg, 6.0 rpg, 6.4 apg), but impressed Martelli most with his will to win and understanding of the game.

Jennings will likely share time this year with 6-2 junior **Tim Brown** (4.3 ppg, 2.0 rpg, 38 assists), a capable ballhandler and shooter who got 19.8 minutes per game a year ago. Brown can spot up nicely for open jumpers and is more athletic than he looks. Like Woods and Wilkins, however, he is not a perimeter defender of recent St. Joseph's vintage—Bey, Domani, and Mark Bass.

Crenshaw, on the other hand, has the body and toughness to defend, as does Howard. The latter may be undersized at times depending on how many minutes are gobbled by Reid and Sazanov.

6-7 sophomore **Chy Chy Ikenokwalu** (1.6 ppg, 1.3 rpg) and 6-8 sophomore **Lionel Ngounou** (seven appearances) are also in the frontcourt mix. 6-2 senior **Michael Mazzio** (0.3 ppg), 6-2 junior **Matt Zielenbach** (two appearances) and 6-2 junior **Ryan Leib** (two appearances) are the current walkons.

6-0 junior **John Gallagher** (six appearances) is the team's resident comic and vocal leader.

It is a likely nine-man rotation with more depth, speed and athleticism than anything St. Joseph's put on the floor last season. It is also greener than a bunch of new bananas.

"We know how young this group is," said Martelli. "We know what we're up against. We also know that everyone is back next year, so we're in this for the long haul."

Including Martelli, who was quietly the leading candidate at St. John's this past May before opting to remain close to his roots. Instead, the Johnnies overpaid for Mike Jarvis and St. Joseph's fans breathed a huge sigh of relief after keeping the coach who has won six postseason games in three short seasons.

adidas Blue Ribbon Analysis

BACKCOURT	**C**	**BENCH/DEPTH**	**C+**
FRONTCOURT	**B**	**INTANGIBLES**	**B**

Though a rugged schedule suggests a bumpy short-term, the Hawks will be back soon. In addition to the young talent ready to grow this winter, two Division I starters are sitting out as transfers—big man Bill Phillips (William & Mary) and wing guard Marvin O'Connor (Villanova). St. Joseph's should have all the required pieces a year from now.

Meanwhile, expect an unpredictable ride through 1998-99. The Hawks may not win any more games than last year's disappointment, but they're not expected to. It is a scenario which figures to allow an extremely young group to explore its upside with an upset or two.

"It's hard to win in this league when you're as young as we are," Martelli admitted.

Win consistently, that is. This year, St. Joseph's will look for a few shining moments on which to hang its hat for the Year 2000. It could be much like John's Griffin first team of 1990-91, when freshman guards Rap Curry and Bernard Blunt were the source of tremendous optimism. Two shredded knees later, there was little glory—only heartache.

If Martelli can keep the new Hawk youngsters healthy and together, the optimism may be hard to restrain this time next year.

(J.L.)

VIRGINIA TECH

LOCATION .... **Blacksburg, VA**
CONFERENCE .... **Atlantic 10 (West Division)**
LAST SEASON .... **10-17 (.370)**
CONFERENCE RECORD .... **5-11 (t-4th)**
STARTERS LOST/RETURNING **1/4**
NICKNAME .... **Hokies**
COLORS .... **Maroon & Burnt Orange**
HOMECOURT .... **Cassell Coliseum (10,052)**
COACH .... **Bobby Hussey (Appalachian State '62)**
RECORD AT SCHOOL .... **10-17 (1 yr.)**
CAREER RECORD .... **297-255 (19 yrs.)**
ASSISTANTS .... **Dean Keener (Davidson '88)**
Donnie Marsh (Franklin & Marshall '79)
Scott Davis (Virginia Tech '90)
TEAM WINS (last 5 yrs.) **18-25-23-15-10**
RPI (last 5 yrs.) **66-24-27-125-144**
1997-98 FINISH .... **Lost in conference tourney first round.**

The hospitality is great in Blacksburg, the press room food is the best we've ever seen and Cassell Coliseum is one of the underrated campus arenas anywhere. Problem is, it's all window dressing.

Virginia Tech's basketball program is going in the wrong direction.

Just look at the win totals above. The '95 NIT champions and '96 NCAA second-rounders are becoming a faded memory. Former coach Bill Foster, who built the program back to prominence through the early- and mid-'90s, has retired. And he left his successor, veteran mentor Bobby Hussey, a less than full cupboard.

That stock got even leaner following the 1997-98 season, when promising freshman guard Jenis Grindstaff (10.5 ppg, 2.8 rpg, 39 three-pointers) transferred to Tennessee. Grindstaff was no superstar, mind you, but he had outstanding range and was to be a career-long backcourt anchor.

The Hokies, who have been lacking in stars since the end of the Ace Custis era, can ill-afford to lose anyone with that kind of potential. Tech continues to play great team basketball, but it never hurts to have that one guy who can shine in dark moments.

The Hokies do have a potential star underneath. 6-6 sophomore **Rolan Roberts** (13.6 ppg, 6.4 rpg, .534 FG) is clearly the best player in the program, becoming the first Virginia Tech freshman in 20 years to lead the team in scoring.

Roberts is a beefy, yet athletic presence. He also led the squad in rebounding, shooting percentage and blocked shots (60). He was named to Atlantic 10 all-freshman team and was honorable mention all-freshman nationally according to *Basketball Times.*

"Roberts is legit," said one Atlantic 10 scout. "He could start for any team in the league."

Which begs the question, who else among the Hokies is worthy of a similar distinction? Grindstaff was their second-best player, even as a rookie, and now he is gone.

The top returning guard is 6-2 junior **Brendan Dunlop** (7.3 ppg, 2.9 rpg, 88 assists), who split time last season between the point and shooting guard. Dunlop started the final 11 games a year ago and will likely open the 1998-99 campaign at the point, where his sub-par shooting (.356 FG, .278 3PT) is less of a liability.

The Hokies have high hopes for 6-2 redshirt freshman **Kenny Harrell**, who was shelved after six games (2.2 ppg, 0.3 rpg) a year ago due to acute tendonitis in his left foot. Hussey likens him to Damon Watlington, a star from the NIT title team, and he'll have to be to help gobble up Grindstaff's minutes.

6-6 senior **Eddie Lucas** (9.1 ppg, 2.7 rpg, 10 starts) is Tech's swingman. While he is likely to start at small forward, the one-time transfer from Navy can also play big guard.

The same can be said for 6-4 junior **Andre Ray** (3.4 ppg, 4.3 rpg, 18 starts). Ray is an undersized forward, but he plays "three" most of the time because of his strong rebounding and defensive prowess. He is not the kind of explosive scorer one normally associates with the shooting guard position. However, it would not be surprising to see him in combination with Dunlop and Lucas if Harrell needs a longer adjustment period.

Also in the mix on the wing is 6-6 freshman **Rodrigo Viegas** (11.2 ppg, 5.1 rpg, Pitagoras HS/Belo Horizonte, Brazil), a former club team star who was also a member of the Brazilian 22-and-under national team. Viegas was a late signee and his role is likely to be minimal as a freshman.

In Roberts, Tech knows it has a full-time answer at power forward. Roberts was brought along nicely (27.0 minutes) as a rookie, meaning his production could easily jump along with his experience.

The center is 6-8 junior **Russ Wheeler** (9.6 ppg, 5.4 rpg, team-high 26 starts). Wheeler is a functional big man, but will never move into the upper echelon of pivots until he becomes a more consistent scorer (.475 FG).

Tech's top recruit, 6-9 freshman **Dennis Mims** (17.5 ppg, 9.5 rpg, 4.6 bpg, Freedom HS/Morgantown, N.C.), could become the first big man off the bench. Mims is quick and strong and an instinctive shot-blocker. The *A-10 Hoop Report* called him "a nationally underrated power player. Hokie coaches expect him to have a big impact, a la Rolan Roberts."

If that's the case, the Virginia Tech frontcourt will be well-manned for the next few years. It also leaves 6-9 senior **Alvaro Tor** (2.2 ppg, 2.5 rpg), 6-7 sophomore **David Whaley** (2.0 ppg, 0.4 rpg) and 6-9 redshirt freshman **Clinton McPherson** (Pace HS/Miami, Fla.) fighting for spare minutes.

The extra guards include 6-2 junior **Sean Floyd** (four

1998-99 VIRGINIA TECH SCHEDULE

Nov.	14	William & Mary
	19	East Tennessee State
	24	@Liberty
Dec.	1	North Carolina-Asheville
	5	@UNC Charlotte
	12	Wake Forest
	19	@West Virginia
	23	Coastal Carolina
	30	Winthrop
Jan.	2	@Massachusetts
	6	Xavier
	9	@St. Joseph's
	12	@La Salle
	16	St. Bonaventure
	21	@Dayton
	23	@Xavier
	27	*Virginia
	31	La Salle
Feb.	3	@Duquesne
	6	George Washington
	10	Rhode Island
	13	@Fordham
	16	Temple
	20	Dayton
	24	@George Washington
	27	Duquesne
Mar.	3-6	#Atlantic 10 Tournament

@ Road Games
* Richmond Coliseum, Richmond, VA
# First Union Spectrum, Philadelphia, PA

appearances), a walkon, and 6-0 junior **Jermaine Kimbrough** (St. Catherine JC, Ky./Shaker Heights, Oh.), a junior college transfer. Kimbrough averaged 12 points, five assists and three steals during an injury-marred 1997-98.

"We have a well-balanced squad," said Hussey, "and we have experience. We've got a good team here."

adidas Blue Ribbon Analysis

BACKCOURT .... **C+** **BENCH/DEPTH** .... **C+**
FRONTCOURT .... **B** **INTANGIBLES** .... **B**

Having just a "good team," as Hussey says, isn't good enough anymore in a league which sent seven of its 12 members to a postseason tournament. And the Virginia Tech recruiting class was rated 11th among those 12 by the *A-10 Hoop Report*.

That's the bad news. The good news is that Rolan Roberts is for real, Chris Mims might be and the Tech style—typically a possession game in an era full of road-racers—tends to keep the Hokies close. Cassell Coliseum is also a tremendous advantage when loud and rocking.

It will be the team's responsibility to make it so. The Hokies played before less than capacity crowds throughout 1997-98.

For 1998-99, the upside is no better than a .500 season overall. And Tech's conference record won't even be that good.

Virginia Tech is destined to fight La Salle for fourth place in the Atlantic 10 West Division.

(J.L.)

BIG EAST CONFERENCE

adidas BLUE RIBBON FORECAST

1. Connecticut
2. Syracuse
3. Miami
4. St. John's
5. Georgetown
6. Pittsburgh
7. Villanova
8. Rutgers
9. Providence
10. West Virginia
11. Seton Hall
12. Notre Dame
13. Boston College

TOP 40

Connecticut, Miami, St. John's, and Syracuse are ranked among the 1998-99 *adidas Blue Ribbon* Top 40. Extended profiles can be found in the Top 40 section of *Blue Ribbon*.

ALL-CONFERENCE TEAM

G—Khalid El-Amin, SO, Connecticut
G—Vonteego Cummings, SR, Pittsburgh
F—Richard Hamilton, JR, Connecticut
F—Tim James, SR, Miami
C—Etan Thomas, JR, Syracuse

PLAYER OF THE YEAR

Richard Hamilton, JR, Connecticut

NEWCOMER OF THE YEAR

Anthony Perry, SO, Georgetown

1998-99 CONFERENCE TOURNAMENT

March 3-6, Madison Square Garden, New York, NY

1997-98 CHAMPION

Connecticut (regular season - Big East 6)
Syracuse (regular season - Big East 7)
Connecticut (conference tournament)

1997-98 POSTSEASON PARTICIPANTS

Postseason Record: 8-7 (.533)

NCAA

Connecticut (Final Eight)
Syracuse (Sweet 16)
West Virginia (Sweet 16)
St. John's
Miami

NIT

Georgetown (2nd round)
Seton Hall

TOP BACKCOURTS

1. Connecticut
2. Pittsburgh
3. Villanova

TOP FRONTCOURTS

1. Syracuse
2. Connecticut
3. Miami

ON THE WAY UP

Pittsburgh

ON THE WAY DOWN

West Virginia

INSIDE THE NUMBERS

- 1997-98 conference RPI: 4th (of 30)
- Conference RPI (last 5 years): 4-5-5-4-4

DID YOU KNOW?

The big news in the conference is the return to a one-division format, after three years with the ridiculous, two-set configuration that had no geographic rhyme or reason. Worse yet, the previous model allowed for no scheduling symmetry. Not that a 1-through-13 design does. But it is an improvement. "I have thought from the very beginning that it should be 1-through-13," West Virginia coach Gale Catlett said. "Anybody who has any brains knows that the league should have done that, especially for the Big East tournament."...Conference coaches are thrilled with another change which will take place next year. The Big East will junk its current, 18-game league schedule in favor of a 16-game schedule. That gives each team two more chances to schedule easy wins that will help them come tournament selection time. Or, they could arrange two tough TV games that will help their power rating. Yeah, right...Once known for its sideline stability, the Big East has imported five new coaches in the last two years, with Providence's Tim Welsh and St. John's Mike Jarvis taking their bows this year...Seton Hall plays in the year's first regular-season game, when the Pirates meet Valparaiso Nov. 8 in the RCA Dome. Remember when basketball was a winter sport?...In other scheduling news of note, St. John's plays in the Preseason NIT, while Connecticut meets Washington in the Great Eight, Dec. 1 in Chicago...The Big East has four candidates for the John Wooden Player of the Year award, Connecticut's Richard Hamilton and Khalid El-Amin, Miami's Tim James and Pitt's Vonteego Cummings...It looks like it's time to make some new heroes in the league. Of the 10 players on last year's top two all-league teams, only four return.

(M.B.)

BOSTON COLLEGE

LOCATION .... **Boston, MA**
CONFERENCE .... **Big East**
LAST SEASON .... **15-16 (.484)**
CONFERENCE RECORD .... **6-12 (6th)**
STARTERS LOST/RETURNING **4/1**
NICKNAME .... **Eagles**
COLORS .... **Maroon & Gold**
HOMECOURT .... **Silvio O. Conte Forum (8,606**
COACH .... **Al Skinner (Massachusetts '74)**
RECORD AT SCHOOL .... **15-16 (1 yr.)**
CAREER RECORD .... **153-142 (10 yrs.)**
ASSISTANTS .... **Tim O'Shea (Boston College '84)**
Bill Coen (Hamilton '83)
Ed Cooley (Stonehill '94)
TEAM WINS (last 5 yrs.) **23-9-19-22-15**
RPI (last 5 yrs.) **24-159-44-28-121**
1997-98 FINISH .... **Lost in conference second round.**

Brian Barrio is now the oracle. Anybody who wants to remember the good times of Boston College basketball must visit the team's senior manager, who was there at Madison Square Garden in early March 1996, when the Eagles cut down the nets as Big East Tournament champions. It was the culmination of a long, hard drive for then-coach Jim O'Brien and made BC look for all the world like a future force in the conference, particularly with some of its biggest names on the wane.

Two years later, only Barrio remains to tell the tale. All 13 players who stood at midcourt in the Garden and celebrated the title are long gone, either graduated or transferred to other situations. O'Brien and his staff have moved west to Ohio State. And the team once thought to be so prepared for long-term success is now facing a huge rebuilding project that will no doubt land it in the basement of the 13-team Big East this year and could relegate it to second-division status for quite a while.

No matter how second-year coach Al Skinner wants to look at it, last year was a mirage. Even though BC went 15-16, the Eagles were one heckuva lot better than they will be this year. Only one starter, sophomore guard **Kenny Harley** returns. Boston College lost four double-figure scorers, one of whom, center Kostas Maglos, was supposed to play this year but was lured back to his native Greece by a professional contract. Two other role players transferred, leaving Skinner with only three scholarship holdovers from last year's team. It doesn't get much bleaker than that.

But Skinner is his customary optimistic self. Little seems to bother the guy, at least overtly, and he seems quite at ease with his situation. He freely admits that last year was better than he had hoped it would be and looks at this year's seven-man recruiting crop as a good start on the big job of turning things around.

"I got hired a little late last year and missed out on a recruiting class," said Skinner, who nonetheless brought in Harley and forward **Jonathan Beerbohm**. "This year, we made some inroads. I'm happy about the people we brought in. We need so much that it's tough to get it all at one time.

"Last year wasn't frustrating. In fact, it was a little more rewarding than I had anticipated. We were better than people thought and if forward **Mickey** (**Curley**) doesn't get hurt (he missed six games), we would have been even better. I'm happy with the way we played. For the most part, we held our own."

Now, it's time for the Eagles to be held—by the throat. Tightly. In a Big East where schools will be grouped in an all-inclusive pig pile for the first time, wins will be precious, because the difference between fifth and eighth place could be a win or two—and job security. Teams will love to see the Eagles on their schedule, preferably twice, and they won't hesitate to make the most of the opportunity. If this sounds particularly harsh, get used to it. The Eagles will need to scrape for every win they can manage. Should they reach four, there will be plenty of surprise around the league. Make it to six or seven, and Skinner deserves coach-of-the-year consideration. Really.

Here's how bad it is: BC returns a total of 9.5 ppg and 8.3 rpg. Its point guard is a former walkon who was given a scholarship midway through last year. Its starting small forward could be a transfer who averaged 1.1 ppg during his final year at his previous destination. Skinner was

1998-99 BOSTON COLLEGE SCHEDULE

Nov.	14	Marquette
	18	Harvard
	21	Monmouth
	24	*Fordham
	28	Fairfield
Dec.	5	St. John's
	8	Miami (Fla.)
	12	**Massachusetts
	19	Holy Cross
	23	@Northwestern
	30	@Seton Hall
Jan.	6	Connecticut
	10	@Pittsburgh
	13	@Villanova
	17	Providence
	21	@Syracuse
	24	Miami (Fla.)
	27	Notre Dame
Feb.	2	Seton Hall
	6	West Virginia
	10	@Connecticut
	13	@Rutgers
	17	@Georgetown
	20	Pittsburgh
	24	Syracuse
	28	@Notre Dame
Mar.	3-6	#Big East Tournament

@ Road Games
* Pepsi Arena, Albany, NY
** Centrum, Worcester, MA
\# Madison Square Garden, NY

hoping to have a Greek center, and he does. But instead of lining up a 6-10 senior capable of scoring 17-20 ppg, he gets a 6-9 rookie from Athens who is a giant unknown commodity. As usual, however, Skinner is undaunted.

"We've got young people who are excited about being here and competing," he said. "This team will have enthusiasm. The future is in front of them."

The present is there, too, glaring at Boston College like a hideous combination of Godzilla, King Kong and Rosie O'Donnell and ready to pounce.

So, where to start? The backcourt is actually this team's "strength", so that's a good candidate, even though it will be without two-man Damien Foster, who returned home to Buffalo, N.Y., after six games last year, and point Javier Rodriguez, who went back to Spain.

Dwayne Pina (1.4 ppg, 1.9 rpg, 1.6 apg), a 5-10 junior and the aforementioned walkon who was promoted last year, is the likely point man—he started the final eight games of last year. He'll take over for four-year starter Duane Woodward, who did a little bit of everything last year and most of it well. Skinner considers Pina "definitely part of the mix" but concedes that "everybody will have to handle the ball a little bit."

That means 6-5 freshman swingman **Kenny Walls** (Galileo HS/San Francisco, Calif.), the San Francisco Player-of-the-Year who averaged 23.2 ppg, 10.0 rpg and 4.1 apg last season, will get a chance to run the team, and Harley might even see some time there. This isn't all that unusual for the Eagles—Woodward wasn't a classic point guard last year, either.

"It's not a typical point-sguard situation," Skinner said. "We don't have one individual to dominate the ball."

adidas Blue Ribbon Analysis

GRADING SYSTEM

- A+ equal to very best in country—Final Four-caliber unit
- A among the best in the land—worthy of deep NCAA run
- B+ talented, versatile and experienced—NCAA-NIT ability
- B solid and productive winners—league and post-season contenders
- C+ average to above-average—may contend in a weaker league
- C average to mediocre—second division in a strong league
- D+ below average, inconsistent—second division in a weaker league
- D well below average—losing season virtually certain
- F non-Division I ability—an underdog every night

Harley returns as the leading candidate at the two spot. The 6-4 sophomore averaged 4.5 ppg and 3.5 rpg last year, but he'll need to improve his shooting considerably to be a real contributor. Harley shot just .391 percent from the field and was a dismal .275 percent from long range.

"He hit the wall last year but came back well at the end of the season," Skinner said. "I was pleased by that. He fought back. We can build on that. I'm happy with his progress.

"He can definitely shoot the ball better, and he showed that by making some big shots early in the year. He lost some confidence, and there weren't many easy nights for him to get it back. He played well late in the year against West Virginia, St. John's and Seton Hall and gave me some reason to be optimistic that he really does have what it takes."

Expect 6-3 freshman **Clinton Sims** (Maine Central Institute and Paris HS/Paris, Ky.), who scored 17.0 ppg, handed out 3.0 apg and had 4.0 spg last season, to fight it out with Harley for the two spot. Skinner considers Sims a solid shooter and good athlete who will provide necessary depth.

Another freshman, 6-1 **Willie Deane** (Schenectady HS/Schenectady, N.Y.), will figure in the rotation. Deane scored 1,500 career points and averaged 22.8 ppg in 1997-98, while leading his team to a 28-1 record and the state public school Class A title. Walk-on **Nicolas Dunn** (0.0 ppg, 0.3 rpg), a 6-3 soph who played in only four games last year, rounds out the backcourt.

Skinner was hoping Maglos would turn into a big-time Big East producer this season. Instead, he's playing for pay in Greece. That means the frontcourt situation is extremely unsettled, and BC will be vulnerable to pillaging by huskier foes. Beerbohm, a 6-7 sophomore who averaged 3.6 ppg and 2.3 rpg last year in 15.8 minutes per game, is the contingent's elder. He has to make significant progress in order to thrive.

"Jon is a tremendous leaper, but he thought he had to squat in order to take off," Skinner said. "He has to get quicker. He's good around the basket, but last year, he was a little surprised by the people he was going against. He'll be a little more comfortable this season."

Beerbohm will be challenged by the plum of the BC recruiting class, 6-7 freshman **Osei Millar** (Christ the King HS/Bronx, N.Y.), who averaged 13.2 ppg and 2.0 bpg on a team that went 23-4 and lost to Rice HS in the New York Catholic League title game.

"Osei is a fine athlete who can help us stretch the floor," Skinner said. "He has good quickness for his size and good foot speed. He came out of nowhere the last two years."

The BC interior will also include 6-8, 220-pound freshman **Brian Ross** (North Quincy HS/North Quincy, Mass.), a productive forward, who looks to be something of a project, despite ridiculous stats last year (36.7 ppg, 18.0 rpg, 4.0 apg), and 6-9, 235-pound freshman **Timos Papadimitriou**, who hails from Athens and will take over the pivot spot, provided the dramatic change to American college ball isn't too much for him.

The three spot shapes up as a fight between Walls, who could play any of the three perimeter positions, thanks to his athletic ability, and 6-4 junior **Michael Cotton**, a transfer from Oklahoma who averaged just 1.1 ppg and 1.1 rpg in 20 games (5.0 mpg) in 1996-97. A pair of walkons, 6-6 sophomore **Julian Bah** (0.0 ppg, 0.0 rpg) and 6-5 junior **Jim Boland** (0.0 ppg, 0.3 rpg) will again see limited action.

adidas Blue Ribbon Analysis

BACKCOURT	**C-**	**BENCH/DEPTH**	**C-**
FRONTCOURT	**D**	**INTANGIBLES**	**D**

How would you like to be selling season tickets for this group? About the only thing you'll be able to offer is a fine collection of opponents and good location. Here's a slogan: "Come out and see the Eagles; it beats a sharp stick in the eye." OK, we'll leave that stuff to the professionals, but you get the picture.

This freshman class does have some talent, most notably Millar and Walls, who should do well in the open court. But the point guard situation is a mess, and the frontcourt is even worse. Skinner thought it might take just one more recruiting class to make this program competitive, but he's looking at two more good ones to climb out of BC's present hole.

Things would have been better had Maglos stuck around, but in a way, it's almost better that he left. Now, Skinner can use all the youngsters in a sloppy baptism that could pay dividends down the road. Still, it won't be easy to take all the losses this year. Good thing Skinner is an upbeat guy. For now.

(M.B.)

GEORGETOWN

LOCATION	**Washington, DC**
CONFERENCE	**Big East**
LAST SEASON	**16-15 (.516)**
CONFERENCE RECORD	**6-12 (t-5th, Big East 7)**
STARTERS LOST/RETURNING	**1/4**
NICKNAME	**Hoyas**
COLORS	**Blue & Gray**
HOMECOURT	**MCI Arena (20,000)**
COACH	**John Thompson (Providence '64)**
RECORD AT SCHOOL	**589-233 (26 yrs.)**
CAREER RECORD	**589-233 (26 yrs.)**
ASSISTANTS	**Craig Esherick (Georgetown '78)**
	Mike Riley (Georgetown '78)
	Ronnie Thompson (Georgetown '92)
TEAM WINS (last 5 yrs.)	**19-21-29-20-16**
RPI (last 5 yrs.)	**33-26-8-57-115**
1997-98 FINISH	**Lost in NIT second round.**

What a great time it has been to hate the Hoyas. The last decade hasn't exactly been filled with Hoya Paranoia or Hoya Hysteria, rather a slow slide from the national scene, save a brief respite earlier this decade when Allen Iverson single-handedly led Georgetown to the Sweet 16. Other than that, coach John Thompson's team has been average, at best, and certainly not its old roughneck self.

The program is no longer synonymous with the Big East. Its games with quality non-conference opponents (when they play them) aren't big TV magnets. And even if the team is still known for playing great defense, it sure isn't attracting any attention for its offense. In fact, there are some who argue that Thompson doesn't even seem to devote any practice time to putting the ball in the basket. Ouch.

There's more. Hoya players have been involved in off-court problems. They have left the program. And top recruits aren't talking about coming to D.C. anymore. And, as if to add a slap in the face to the program, the Basketball Hall of Fame selection committee has once again decided against including Thompson among the Hall's august ranks. That's just wrong. Say what you want about the man's brusque personality or his various agendas, but don't let that stuff overshadow his accomplishments. Thompson has won 589 games. He has a national championship to his credit and a pair of runner-up finishes. His NCAA Tournament winning percentage is an impressive .642 percent. Thompson was the first black man ever to be elected president of the National Association of Basketball Coaches and the first to be an Olympic men's coach. Say what you want about him off the court, but don't belittle his achievements on it.

And don't get too comfortable knocking the Hoyas, either. If there is a sleeper in the Big East this year, it may well be Georgetown, which returns all but two key players from last year, will benefit greatly from the good health of center **Ruben Boumtje Boumtje** and welcomes three newcomers—particularly sophomore guard **Anthony Perry**—who should help out. We're not talking Patrick Ewing-style success here, but the Hoyas are certainly dangerous and extremely likely to improve, perhaps considerably, on last year's 6-12 league record.

Expect a different kind of Hoya team this year. Yes, Georgetown will have some size, with the 6-11 Boumtje Boumtje and 6-10, 244-pound senior **Jameel Watkins** providing the beef. But expect to see those two in tandem less and less as the Hoyas' younger, quicker players mature.

There is only one other player on the roster (**Rhese Gibson**) taller than 6-6 and a larger-than-usual assortment of mid-sized dervishes capable of tormenting rivals with aggressive defense. And, if Perry can do what most people expect of him, the Hoya offense might actually be pretty productive this year. Wouldn't that be a nice change?

That's not to say this team is without weaknesses. That's the furthest thing from the truth. It still doesn't shoot all that well as a group and definitely lacks a full-fledged point guard, now that Kenny Brunner has left town and is trying to extricate himself from various legal problems out in Jerry Tarkanian's playground at Fresno State. Believe it or not, Georgetown could also use a little help in the defensive department, after allowing Big East opponents to shoot .451 percent last year. But the team's smaller, quicker makeup should allow it to press more and be more aggressive in halfcourt sets.

1998-99 GEORGETOWN SCHEDULE

Nov.	10-11	#Coaches vs. Cancer Classic
	15	Hartford
	18	@Georgia State
	21	Grambling
	24	IUPUI
Dec.	2	Morgan State
	5	TBA
	8	Rutgers
	22	Maryland-Eastern Shore
	30	Miami (Fla.)
Jan.	2	@Connecticut
	4	@Seton Hall
	9	Providence
	11	@St. John's
	16	Syracuse
	19	West Virginia
	23	@Pittsburgh
	25	Connecticut
	30	@Villanova
Feb.	2	Pittsburgh
	6	@Miami (Fla.)
	10	@Notre Dame
	17	Boston College
	20	St. John's
	23	@Rutgers
	27	@Providence
Mar.	3-6	##Big East Tournament

@ Road Games
\# Madison Square Garden, NY (vs. Temple, first round; also Illinois and Wake Forest)
\#\# Madison Square Garden, NY

There is some promise here, especially in a Big East where Connecticut and Syracuse look like NCAA locks, and nothing else is certain. Sure, Miami and St. John's are defending tournament vets, but neither waltzed into March as an irresistible force, and each was unceremoniously bumped from the Madness in the first round. With so many teams jockeying for the first division in the conference—which now goes 1-through-13, instead of segmenting its members into ridiculously-named, uneven divisions—Georgetown has as good a shot as anybody of surviving.

Perry (St. Anthony HS/Jersey City, N.J.) will help fortify the backcourt, that's for sure. He sat out last year as a partial qualifier, a condition that hurt the Hoyas immensely. Without him, they were deprived of a true perimeter offensive force. The 6-3 Perry averaged 19.7 ppg 7.0 rpg, 3.0 apg and 3.0 spg while leading St. Anthony to a 29-1 record and the 1997 New Jersey state title. He can hit from the outside and get to the basket. He'll also set up his teammates. His arrival is extremely important for the Hoyas, although it remains to be seen whether the year off will hinder him for long.

The return of Boumtje Boumtje, a 6-11 sophomore who played in only six games last year before breaking his left wrist against Miami and shutting down for the year, is more good news.

Boumtje Boumtje averaged just 2.7 ppg, but grabbed 4.7 rpg and had 11 boards against Morgan State. Hoya fans are right to be excited about Boumtje Boumtje, because he has the ability to rebound and block shots. He's also quick enough to run the floor.

At 245 pounds, he's got the girth needed to hang tough in the Big East, and he does have an amazing up side. But he needs to produce, because the Hoyas don't' have much in the way of size. Just don't expect that production to take the form of big-time scoring, because Boumtje Boumtje's offensive game remains rudimentary.

Trez Kilpatrick's, however, does not—so long as his shooting eye improves. The 6-6 senior came to Georgetown last year from Neosho County CC and was expected to provide much-needed scoring pop. He did, to a point. Kilpatrick averaged 10.9 ppg and grabbed 4.8 boards a night, but he shot only .393 percent from the field, a figure that must increase. It should, particularly if he gets the chance to play the wing, which is his natural position, rather than inside, where he had to go last year when Boumtje Boumtje and Jahidi White suffered injuries.

Because of Georgetown's dearth of big men, it's imperative Watkins (4.5 ppg, 4.9 rpg) gives the Hoyas more than the 18.2 minutes per game he did last year. If not, then teams will be able to handle the Hoyas on the boards. The loss of Boubacar Aw may not hurt the offense that much, although he was the team's second-leading scorer, but his presence on the boards will be sorely missed. Thompson would like the 6-7, 230-pound Gibson (2.8 ppg, 3.3 rpg), a junior who is solid on the boards, to continue his development into an inside force.

Joining Perry in the backcourt could be 6-3 junior **Shenard Long**, who surprised many by scoring 13.1 ppg (3.6 rpg) last year, to lead the team. Long isn't the greatest three-point shooter around, though he did make .375 percent of his 80 shots. But he does slash to the basket well. The problem the Hoyas have with a Long-Perry combo is that neither is a point guard.

Brunner was supposed to be that man, but he left town midway through last year. Perhaps 6-2 senior **Joseph Touomou** (2.8 ppg, 1.8 rpg, 2.0 apg) could handle the job, because he started there toward the end of the season, but the job could go to 6-2 freshman **Kevin Braswell** (Maine Central Institute/Baltimore, Md.), who averaged 21.0 ppg, 9.0 apg and 4.3 rpg last year. Braswell can hit the open jumper, and he is an unselfish distributor who could make a big difference.

Another newcomer expected to make an immediate impact is **Willie Taylor** (La Vergne HS/La Vergne, Tenn.) a 6-5 swingman who scored 27.8 ppg and grabbed 10.7 rpg last year. He can shoot well (57 percent last season) and has the ability to play the two or three spots. Georgetown was fortunate enough to steal him from under the noses of Tennessee, Vanderbilt and Memphis.

Thompson has tremendous depth at his disposal along the perimeter, the better to inflict his aggressive defensive style on victims. **Daymond Jackson** (8.1 ppg, 3.6 rpg), a rock-solid 6-4 senior who gets to the basket with authority, can play either the two or three spots, as can 6-4 sophomore **Nat Burton** (5.3 ppg, 2.1 rpg). Burton, however, must improve on last year's .355 percent shooting. A pair of walkons, 5-10 senior **Dean Berry** (3.7 ppg, 0.6 rpg) and 6-3 junior **Damien Bolden** (2.3 ppg, 1.2 rpg), see enough time to be considered more than just the average practice players. Berry had three starts last year and has a pretty good shooting eye, while Bolden averaged 12.1 minutes in his 16 appearances.

adidas Blue Ribbon Analysis

BACKCOURT	B-	BENCH/DEPTH	B
FRONTCOURT	C+	INTANGIBLES	B+

Don't look for a return to the success of the mid-1980s, but these Hoyas could be tough.

Of course, a lot of things must happen first. Perry has to shake off the rust from a year off and be able to score. Boumtje Boumtje must be able to shake off the rust from a year off and rebound and defend. That would be a good start.

Those aren't the only problems. Watkins and Gibson must be consistent inside contributors. Kilpatrick has to shoot better. And somebody—Touomou? Braswell?—must be a reliable point man. If all that stuff happens, the Hoyas could have a great year. Shenard Long is an underrated backcourt performer. The bench is deep. Taylor could be a keeper.

It has been fun to bash the Hoyas these last few years, but that opportunity could be drying up. Georgetown looks like it might be pretty good this year —and beyond. Maybe even good enough to get Thompson into the Hall of Fame.

(M.B.)

adidas Blue Ribbon Analysis

GRADING SYSTEM

- A+ equal to very best in country—Final Four-caliber unit
- A among the best in the land—worthy of deep NCAA run
- B+ talented, versatile and experienced—NCAA-NIT ability
- B solid and productive winners—league and post-season contenders
- C+ average to above-average—may contend in a weaker league
- C average to mediocre—second division in a strong league
- D+ below average, inconsistent—second division in a weaker league
- D well below average—losing season virtually certain
- F non-Division I ability—an underdog every night

NOTRE DAME

LOCATION	**South Bend, IN**
CONFERENCE	**Big East**
LAST SEASON	**13-14 (.481)**
CONFERENCE RECORD	**7-11 (5th, Big East 6)**
STARTERS LOST/RETURNING	**2/3**
NICKNAME	**Fighting Irish**
COLORS	**Blue & Gold**
HOMECOURT	**Joyce Athletic Center (11,418)**
COACH	**John MacLeod (Bellarmine '59)**
RECORD AT SCHOOL	**92-108 (7 yrs.)**
CAREER RECORD	**182-177 (13 yrs.)**
ASSISTANTS	**Fran McCaffery (Pennsylvania '82)** **Parker Laketa (Kansas State '85)** **Terry Tyler (Detroit '78)**
TEAM WINS (last 5 yrs.)	**12-15-9-16-13**
RPI (last 5 yrs.)	**107-125-150-64-98**
1997-98 FINISH	**Lost in conference first round.**

It's a matter of timing in South Bend. Or, make that bad timing. Whenever the Fighting Irish have been strong in one area, there have been glaring weaknesses in the other. If the frontcourt looks good, the backcourt has been deficient. When coach John MacLeod has had guards, there have been holes up front. Take last year, for instance. Senior starters Pat Garrity and Derek Manner—particularly Garrity—gave Notre Dame solid, proven play up front. In fact, Garrity, a first-round NBA draft pick, provided the kind of star quality that had been missing at Notre Dame since the days when Digger Phelps was prowling the sidelines.

During McLeod's seven years at the school, he has never had the luxury of a roster without glaring holes. Not that he hasn't tried. But injuries, some bad recruiting luck and plain poor timing have hurt the Irish. Unfortunately, things don't look much better this year—at least in the won-loss column. Notre Dame will again be weak at the shooting guard spot. And although a solid crop of newcomers should fortify the frontcourt, none of the freshmen will approach the 23.2 ppg and 8.3 rpg Garrity posted last year.

So, expect another fight to approach .500. It will be unlikely if the Irish get back to the NIT, where they participated in 97. And with the Big East's new, 1-13 configuration, Notre Dame could find itself struggling to stay out of double figures in the standings. The future, it appears for the first time, may be a lot better. At least MacLeod thinks so.

"We had a good group of recruits last year, and this year's group is another good one," he says. "If we can pull together a year where we get three or four good players in '99, then we'll have a core of eight or ten players we can keep together, instead of having a dropoff."

This is a vital recruiting class for the Irish, because if the school doesn't import some more talent, then continued mediocrity will be forecast. Granted, Notre Dame has more stringent academic requirements than many of its Big East brethren, such as the inability to take partial qualifiers and an aversion to junior-college players. As a result, it has had to build block-by-block, rather than wholesale. It hasn't been easy.

"We don't go the junior college route, so that slows the process," MacLeod says. "We don't have the use of that band-aid."

But Notre Dame had better get well fast. It's not that the lynch mob is galloping toward MacLeod's office, but the rest of the Big East is improving. There is little doubt Notre Dame does not belong in this season's second group of Georgetown, Villanova, Pittsburgh, Rutgers, Providence and Seton Hall—at least at first glance. And if the school decides, as has been rumored of late, to join the Big Ten, things will be even tougher on the Irish—that conference has been stronger than the Big East in recent years. MacLeod needs to get players. He needs to keep them. He needs to develop them into winners.

With few exceptions, the Irish will be particularly young this year. Although a pair of anticipated starters, **Phil Hickey** and **Antoni Wyche**, are seniors, there is plenty of youth behind them. MacLeod should like that. It gives him a foundation for growth. There is not, however, any true standout on the roster, no one the Irish can count on for big production every night. And that's bound to be a problem.

Don't expect Wyche to become a big-time scorer. The 6-4 senior averaged 9.4 ppg and 3.2 rpg last year, but his

1998-99 NOTRE DAME SCHEDULE

Nov.	13	Miami (Oh.)
	15	Yale
	21	@Vanderbilt
	26-28	#Carr's Great Alaska Shootout
Dec.	1	Indiana
	5	Central Michigan
	8	@Providence
	19	Eastern Kentucky
	21	Stetson
	27	St. Francis-NY
	29	Syracuse
Jan.	2	Villanova
	5	Pittsburgh
	9	@Miami (Fla.)
	12	@Connecticut
	16	@Villanova
	19	Seton Hall
	23	Rutgers
	27	@Boston College
	30	Providence
Feb.	6	@Seton Hall
	10	Georgetown
	14	@West Virginia
	17	@Syracuse
	21	West Virginia
	24	@St. John's
	28	Boston College
Mar.	3-6	##Big East Tournament

@ Road Games
\# Anchorage, AK (vs. Duke, first round; also Alaska-Anchorage, Cincinnati, Fresno State, Iowa State, Southern Utah and Saint Mary's)
\## Madison Square Garden, NY

long-range shooting was poor (.299 percent), and he was especially inconsistent. If Notre Dame is to have any shot at .500 this year, Wyche must develop into a strong perimeter weapon. MacLeod is confident that will happen, but even he understands how some could be skeptical.

"He's going to get a ton of minutes," MacLeod says. "He'll be our captain, and his work ethic is superb. I think he's going to be good. Will he be the leading three-point shooter in the conference? I don't know. He improved his free throw percentage last year and reduced his turnovers. But he's always been a little spotty from the field, a little up and down.

"In some games, he doesn't do anything for 20 minutes, and then he scores 14 points in eight minutes."

While Wyche searches for his consistency, 5-11 sophomore **Martin Ingelsby** (6.6 ppg, 2.5 rpg, 5.6 apg, 1.5 spg) will continue to develop into a fine point guard. Ingelsby showed plenty during his debut, directing the Irish fast break well, making solid decisions in the halfcourt (his assist to turnover ratio was 2:1, strong for a freshman) and shooting well (.398 percent) from three-point range. Although he wore down a little toward the end of the season, there is little doubt he'll be an excellent college point man before he's through at Notre Dame. He needs work on the finer points of the game and must improve his free-throw shooting (.609 percent), but Ingelsby will be fine.

"The thing you have to like about Martin Ingelsby is that you only have to tell him things once," MacLeod says. "In high school, he could pass it over some people, but when you're going up against (Pittsburgh's) Vonteego Cummings, who's long and lean, that pass gets stolen. Martin went through an adjustment period where he had to learn to make the proper feed when covered by big people. He got a little tentative with his shooting, too, but we got that ironed out."

Depth in the backcourt will be a problem, particularly after 6-3 Keith Friel, who could play the point and two-guard spots, transferred to Virginia. That means the Irish will be forced to use fifth-year, 6-1 senior **Paul Rainey** (0.8 ppg, 0.3 rpg), a former walkon who was put on scholarship before this season, and 6-1 junior **Jimmy Dillon** (1.8 ppg, 0.9 rpg) as the main backups. That's not exactly a huge source of comfort for MacLeod, but it's all he has.

"Dillon played a lot better the last two or three months of last year," MacLeod says about the point guard. "He needs to be more consistent. He got stronger and moved his feet better on defense last year. He showed that he was quicker."

The rest of the backcourt includes little-used 6-3 sophomore **Tom Krizmanich** (0.8 ppg, 0.3 rpg), who appeared in only four games last year, and 6-3 junior **Matt MacLeod**, the coach's son, who saw action in five games last year and averaged 0.4 ppg and 0.0 rpg.

The 6-10 Hickey (10.7 ppg, 8.0 rpg, 1.1 bpg) is the sole returning frontcourt starter, and there will be plenty of pressure on him to increase his production. Some would argue that he could have scored more, had Garrity not been such a standout. Others say that to expect more than 10-12 ppg from him is unwise.

As in the case of Wyche, MacLeod is hopeful Hickey can continue to grow. He did shoot .496 percent from the field last year and took the second-most shots on the Irish team. But his putrid .539 percent free-throw shooting (.500 percent in league play) needs to improve considerably.

"I'm hoping he'll be more consistent, like Wyche," MacLeod says. "I think he'll have a big year. He went to Europe and played with the NIT All-Stars during the summer and attended Pete Newell's Big Man Camp.

"Phil's moving much better, and he's stronger than at any other point in his career here. He's playing with a lot of confidence and shooting the ball better. Last year, he would get tentative. I think that's over."

So, the center spot is set. The rest of the frontcourt, however, is not. The departures of Garrity and Manner mean that sophomores **Leviticus Williamson** and **Hans Rasmussen** are the only "experienced" players at the forward positions. And neither of them was exactly a revelation last year. Williamson, a 6-6, 200-pounder, averaged 2.0 ppg and 1.8 rpg in only 8.6 mpg last year, although he did battle injuries (back spasms) for part of the year. "He had some bright spots," MacLeod says. He's referring to a 10-point outburst against Northeastern last November.

The 6-9 Rasmussen (1.7 ppg, 2.1 rpg), who played 9.5 mpg last year and even earned four starts, shouldn't be expected to step into Garrity's shoes. That distinction will most likely go to 6-10, 230-pound freshman **Troy Murphy** (Delbarton HS/Morristown, N.J.), who averaged 33.0 ppg, 14.8 rpg and 3.2 bpg last year. He's a pretty big-time recruit for the Irish—*Prep Stars Recruiter's Handbook* ranked him No. 39 in last year's senior class—and MacLeod is clearly happy to have him.

"He scores the ball," MacLeod says. "He's not afraid to shoot it. He rebounds and blocks shots, too."

MacLeod says it's "not inconceivable" to think that Murphy and another freshman, 6-8 **Harold Swanagan** (University Heights Academy/Hopkinsville, Ky.) will play a lot together. Swanagan, who scored 20.0 ppg and grabbed 11.0 ppg while shooting an amazing .733 percent from the field against private school competition, should make Notre Dame tougher inside.

A third freshman, 6-6 **David Graves** (Lexington Catholic HS/Lexington, Ky.), was one of the three finalists for Kentucky's Mr. Basketball honor last year and averaged 19.3 ppg, 6.0 rpg and 3.2 spg as a senior. He can hit from the perimeter and brings some much-needed outside shooting to the equation.

The rest of the frontcourt includes 6-8 sophomore **Peter Okwalinga** (0.0 ppg, 0.0 rpg), 6-3 junior Skylard Owens (0.6 ppg, 1.2 rpg), 6-4 senior **Dennis Carroll**, a walk-on who elected not to play last year, and 6-7 junior **Todd Palmer** (1.6 ppg, 0.7 rpg). Only Palmer is expected to play any meaningful minutes.

adidas Blue Ribbon Analysis

BACKCOURT	C	BENCH/DEPTH	C
FRONTCOURT	C+	INTANGIBLES	C+

The Big East picked a bad year to go to the 1-through-13 format for keeping track of its teams, at least for Notre Dame. Had the two-division system remained intact, the Irish would have finished fifth—ahead of Boston College and might have even snuck into fourth, ahead of West Virginia. Now, it will fall into double figures, and that doesn't look good on anybody's resume.

But there is hope for the future. The three young forwards have some talent, particularly Murphy, and Ingelsby will be a first-rate point before it's all over. But the Irish need some more guards—badly. If they get them, then 1999-2000 and beyond could feature some post-season appearances.

As for this year, Wyche and Hickey will have to emerge as big-time producers if the Irish want to get above .500. Ingelsby will improve, and the newcomers will contribute, but those two seniors are the keys. If Wyche shoots and scores consistently, and Hickey can give 30-35 minutes of strong pivot play, Notre Dame might find itself creeping into the attack pack in the Big East. If not, there's always tomorrow. Again.

(M.B.)

PITTSBURGH

LOCATION	Pittsburgh, PA
CONFERENCE	Big East
LAST SEASON	11-16 (.407)
CONFERENCE RECORD	6-12 (t-6th, Big East 7)
STARTERS LOST/RETURNING	0/5
NICKNAME	Panthers
COLORS	Blue & Gold
HOMECOURT	Fitzgerald Field House (6,798) Pittsburgh Civic Arena (16,725)
COACH	Ralph Willard (Holy Cross '67)
RECORD AT SCHOOL	49-66 (4 yrs.)
CAREER RECORD	130-108 (8 yrs.)
ASSISTANTS	Jim Christian (Rhode Island '88) Troy Weaver (Prince George CC '91) Oliver Antigua (Pittsburgh '98)
TEAM WINS (last 5 yrs.)	13-10-10-18-11
RPI (last 5 yrs.)	82-112-134-62-129
1997-98 FINISH	Lost in conference first round.

Anybody trying to create a documentary on Ralph Willard's four years at Pittsburgh would be advised to consult the great disaster flicks of the 1970s for inspiration. Even though Willard's tenure has been far from cataclysmic, there is no denying that the Panther program has been hit with the kind of misfortune and bad luck that ran rampant in movies such as *Towering Inferno* and *Earthquake*. Injury and defection have taken tremendous tolls on Pittsburgh ever since Willard came to town from Western Kentucky and prevented the coach from transforming the team into a legitimate Big East contender.

Every time it seemed Willard was close to developing some momentum, graduation would sap his team's reserves. Or somebody would transfer or make a silly decision to leave for the NBA way too early. (Where have you gone, Mark Blount?) It's a wonder the affable Willard wasn't spending every available hour reading *When Bad Things Happen to Good People*. Somewhere, there had to be someone using a blue-and-gold voodoo doll for a pin cushion. Pitt couldn't catch a break.

Things may well change this year. For the first time in his tenure, Willard welcomes back a strong nucleus from the previous season. There is hope that defensive specialist **Kellii Taylor** may finally be clear of the injury problems that have ravaged him the last few seasons. And a solid cast of newcomers is on campus, ready to provide needed fortifications. You can bet Willard is still crossing the street to avoid black cats, treating mirrors with the utmost respect and picking up every penny he can find. But he is optimistic.

"Everything runs in cycles," he said. "If we're healthy this year, we could be a pretty darn good team."

The Panthers return all five starters from last year's team, including second-team all-league guard **Vonteego Cummings** and all-rookie squad choice **Ricardo Greer**, another guard. While it may be asking too much for the Panthers to vault from 11 wins (last year's total) to 20, there is no question this is a team ready to make a move—possibly to the postseason. Really. After wondering a little about how Willard could have been such a hot property, we may just get a chance to see what the guy can do, now that his team is healthy, deep and pretty talented.

It all starts with Cummings, who has put up some impressive numbers during his time at Pitt but perhaps lost some luster in the regional and national focus because his team wasn't winning. Cummings had a strong 1997-98 season, averaging 19.5 ppg, 4.1 rpg, 5.9 apg and 2.5 spg. The 6-5 senior has shown he can run a team, as well as score big, but this season, he must shoot the ball better (.426 field goal percentage, .315 percent three-point percentage, 69.4 percent free-throw percentage a year ago) and lead the team more successfully. If the Panthers are going to challenge for any kind of tournament invitation, Cummings must be the team's undisputed on-court chief.

"With the development of the younger players on our team, it's now a matter of his concentrating on making them better players," Willard said. "He needs to fulfill more of a role of the point guard.

"He's our leadership guy. There's no question the mantel is squarely on his shoulders."

It's not like Cummings will have to do it by himself. The 6-5 Greer (12.4 ppg, 6.7 rpg, 4.5 apg) showed last year that he could play well with Cummings and even supplant him

1998-99 PITTSBURGH SCHEDULE

Nov.	13	Maryland-Baltimore County
	17	St. Francis-PA
	20	@Wright State
	23	Texas-Pan American
	26-28	#Puerto Rico Shootout
Dec.	3	Prairie View A&M
	6	@Tennessee
	9	@St. John's
	12	Connecticut
	22	Howard
	30	Providence
Jan.	5	@Notre Dame
	10	Boston College
	16	@Connecticut
	19	@Villanova
	23	Georgetown
	25	*Duquesne
	30	Miami (Fla.)
Feb.	2	@Georgetown
	6	St. John's
	8	@Seton Hall
	11	@Rutgers
	13	Syracuse
	16	West Virginia
	20	@Boston College
	23	@Miami (Fla.)
	27	Seton Hall
Mar.	3-6	##Big East Tournament

@ Road Games
* Civic Arena, Pittsburgh, PA
# San Juan, PR (vs. Xavier, first round; also American University-P.R., Colorado, Kentucky, Maryland, San Francisco and UCLA)
Madison Square Garden, NY

at the point at times. Like Cummings, Greer must improve his marksmanship (.429 from the field, .256 from three-point range) and continue his development into a full-fledged off guard, but all that should come in time. Willard particularly likes the fact that at 220 pounds, Greer is strong enough to post up most guys guarding him, yet quick enough to go past forwards assigned to stop him.

Should Taylor rebound from a foot injury that limited him to just 10 games last year, the Panthers will be able to hit rivals with a versatile three-man backcourt alignment. Although Willard wondered about Taylor's availability in June, the 6-1 junior (7.2 ppg, 2.7 rpg) was running without pain by September and scheduled to be 100 percent for the start of practice.

Two seasons ago, Taylor registered a league-leading (third in the nation) 101 steals. But he's more than just a defensive force. He can also shoot and help the Panthers employ Willard's up-tempo style. "With Kellii and Vonteego in there, we can press and run," Willard said.

That's not all. The Panthers also return 6-3 junior **Jarrett Lockhart** (11.3 ppg, 4.3 rpg, .381 three-point percentage), last year's fourth-leading scorer who needs to become more consistent but could give Pitt some big help on the perimeter. And say hello to 6-3 freshman **Fred Primus** (Notre Dame Academy/Washington, D.C.), who will bolster the team's outside attack as well. Primus averaged 24.3 ppg and 5.5 rpg last year and had one game in which he tossed in 12 three-pointers.

Another newcomer, 6-3 junior college product **Jeremy Holmes** (Neosho County JC/Cleveland Heights HS/Cleveland Heights, Ohio), is a fine distributor (10.2 ppg, 7.5 apg) who will give Cummings a chance to play on the wing at times. Junior **Jason Boyd** is a 6-3 walkon who didn't appear in any games last year and might not get into any this season, either.

The Panther frontcourt, ravaged by graduation and Blount's early departure after the 1996-97 season, is in much better shape these days. Leading the way is 6-8 junior **Isaac Hawkins** (14.2 ppg, 9.2 rpg, 1.7 bpg, 54.1 percent FG), who made a tremendous transformation into a big-time Big East forward last year. He led the league in rebounding, finished second in field-goal percentage and was fourth in scoring. Hawkins is a great anchor on which to build the front line.

And he gives Willard hope that two more Panther big men, 6-9 sophomore **Attila Cosby** (11.6 ppg, 4.8 rpg, 2.0 bpg) and 6-8 sophomore **Stephen Flores** (5.9 ppg, 2.6 rpg), will make similar leaps. Cosby has added 20 pounds to his spindly frame and now goes about 225, while Flores has gotten stronger, too, something that should improve his defense.

"I think Attila will have a year like Isaac did last season," Willard predicts. "Attila only had 10 blocked shots going into January of last year, and he finished with 53. He's worked hard on his jump shot and now has a jump hook."

If Cosby and Flores falter, Willard can turn to 6-9, 230-pound freshman **Chris Seabrooks** (Winchendon [Mass.] School and Macon, Ga.), who missed all of last year with a torn ACL, but is expected to be at full strength this year. He'll give Pitt even more strength up front.

"He's a very, very good rebounder and a good shot blocker," Willard said. "He'll help us get out and run like we want to."

adidas Blue Ribbon Analysis

BACKCOURT .... B+ BENCH/DEPTH .... C+
FRONTCOURT .... B INTANGIBLES .... B

Because this team has struggled in recent years, it's tough to envision the Panthers making a big move. But Willard is right when he said the team could be strong—if healthy. Pitt has depth and talent in the backcourt, beginning with Cummings. If Taylor is healthy, the Panthers will be much more aggressive defensively, something they need—opponents made 47.8 percent of their field goal tries in league play last year.

Up front, Seabrooks bolsters an athletic group that could be one of the league's best. But Cosby must become more versatile offensively, and Flores has to play better defense. We already know about Hawkins, who will challenge for all-league honors.

Pitt looks free and clear of the injuries and defections that plagued it in recent years. Like Miami, which experienced a run of bad luck before blossoming into an NCAA Tournament team, the Panthers could be on the cusp of some success. Expect this year to bring an NIT bid, with the future pretty bright.

(M.B.)

PROVIDENCE

LOCATION .... Providence, RI
CONFERENCE .... Big East
LAST SEASON .... 13-16 (.448)
CONFERENCE RECORD .... 7-11 (4th-Big East 7)
STARTERS LOST/RETURNING 0/5
NICKNAME .... Friars
COLORS .... Black & White
HOMECOURT .... Providence Civic Center (13,410)
COACH .... Tim Welsh (Pottsdam State '84)
RECORD AT SCHOOL .... First Year
CAREER RECORD .... 70-22 (3 yrs.)
ASSISTANTS .... Steve DeMeo (SUNY-Buffalo '87)
King Rice (North Carolina '91)
Bob Walsh (Hamilton '94)
TEAM WINS (last 5 yrs.) 20-17-17-24-13
RPI (last 5 yrs.) 26-64-43-31-76
1997-98 FINISH .... Lost in conference second round.

You knew it was just a matter of time. The way Tim Welsh had it going up in New Rochelle, you just knew he was going to get back to the Big East. And this time, he wouldn't be an assistant. He would be boss. And he would be a good one.

Now, one year removed from a great season at Iona, in which he nearly scared the rest of the hair out of former boss Jim Boeheim's shiny pate, Welsh takes over for the suddenly intrepid Pete Gillen (didn't he say he wanted to stay at Xavier long enough to get a building named for him?) at Providence and tries to get the Friars back among the league's elite.

Friars fans will be cheered to know that Welsh sure knows his way around the league's environs. And he knows what to do once the ball is tossed in the air, too. There have been some changes since he left the conference three years ago, but Welsh won't need too much time to reacquaint himself with its personality.

"It is a different league all together," Welsh said. "The expansion has done that. You don't have the traditional way of everybody playing everyone twice. But it's still a unique conference. It's a difficult conference with great players."

Welsh may not have a whole lot of those "great players," but he doesn't walk into a hopeless situation by any means. Last year's 13-win season caused a little selective memory loss among some people who forgot that Providence was an overtime session away from going to the Final Four in 1997. Had the Friars not run out of gas against Arizona in the round of eight, Providence—not the Wildcats—would have been playing in Indianapolis, and we would have had a different champion.

But the loss of some key performers—Austin Croshere, Ruben Garces, God Shammgod and Derrick Brown—relegated the Friars to the league's slag heap with the rest of its mediocre horde (seven of the league's 13 teams had overall records below .500). And when Virginia came calling for Gillen, he bolted. He bolted for more money. He bolted for the prestige of coaching in the ACC. He bolted for a program that needs an awful lot of help.

And Welsh gets to step in to a situation that is better than one might expect. Everybody of consequence is back from last year's team, and three solid newcomers are eligible for immediate action. And after a year of watching Gillen's team walk the ball up, quite uncharacteristic for any of his squads, Friars fans will be happy to see Welsh turn his group loose. Providence isn't going to threaten Syracuse or Connecticut (or even Miami or St. John's), but it will make some trouble and has as good a chance as any of the other seven schools (Boston College and Notre Dame need not apply) to lead the league's second group.

"The core of players is solid," Welsh said. "We had some young players get valuable experience last year and play a lot of games. That can only be a positive. We have four seniors in the mix, so we have a good mix of youth and experience. We're starting off on the right foot."

Providence's biggest problem is a dearth of size up front. Nobody on the team is taller than 6-7, something that will concern Welsh at times. But in the grand scheme, that won't be all that troublesome. In fact, it will help when the Friars get out and run. There may be problems in the halfcourt, particularly on defense, but you can't have everything.

"I don't like to play slow," Welsh said. "My Iona teams always played up-tempo, trapping at halfcourt and opening the court up. We don't have a lot of set positions. I like to put my guards down on the baseline and my forwards up top sometimes and start the offense a lot of ways. We're going to change up a lot and try to keep teams off-balance."

The Friars will have some pretty good depth in the backcourt, beginning at the point positions, where jet-quick 5-9 sophomore **John Linehan** (5.6 ppg, 2.1 rpg, 2.7 spg) will probably get the start. Although not a particularly good shooter, Linehan impressed last year with his defense (50 steals), speed and no-nonsense approach to the game.

"What I saw from John Linehan was a guy who got better every week," said Welsh, who offers his assessments based on hours of tape watching. "He's a defensive guard, not a guy who looks to score. He showed he could guard a lot of people last year, even forwards. He's a tough kid who did a great job on (Syracuse forward Todd) Burgan

1998-99 PROVIDENCE SCHEDULE

Nov.	9	*Vanderbilt
	10	*Texas Christian
	14	Rhode Island
	21	Texas-Pan American
	24	North Carolina State
	28	@Cleveland State
	30	Maine
Dec.	5	Brown
	8	Notre Dame
	11	@Rutgers
	27	Purdue
	30	@Pittsburgh
Jan.	2	Seton Hall
	5	West Virginia
	9	@Georgetown
	12	@Syracuse
	17	@Boston College
	20	St. John's
	23	@Arkansas
	26	Villanova
	30	@Notre Dame
Feb.	3	@West Virginia
	7	Rutgers
	13	Miami (Fla.)
	15	@St. John's
	20	@Villanova
	22	Connecticut
	27	Georgetown
Mar.	3-6	##Big East Tournament

@ Road Games
* CoSIDA Classic, Providence, RI
Madison Square Garden, NY

last year. We're not going to be a great halfcourt team, so we'll need to get going by creating turnovers."

Linehan should team with 6-3 senior **Kendrick Moore** (9.2 ppg, 3.3 rpg, 3.1 apg), who finished second on the team in scoring but needs to improve on his 29.4 percent three-point shooting, or he'll risk losing time to a pair of talented incoming wing men, 6-4 sophomore **Jamaal Camah** (Notre Dame Academy/Salem, Mass.) and 6-4 freshman **Sean Connolly** (Bishop Fenwick HS/Peabody, Mass.). Camah was a non-qualifier who couldn't practice last year, but he'll bring an excellent all-around game to Providence. He averaged 13.4 ppg, 5.4 rpg and 3.5 as a prep senior and is a solid defender whom Welsh predicts will flourish in an up-tempo game. Connolly, meanwhile, was a top-50 recruit, according to several analysts and is an excellent long-range shooter. He scored 33 ppg and grabbed 11 rpg last year and totaled 2,473 points for his career, the fourth highest total in Massachusetts history.

"He's a great shooter, but he has a good head for the game," Welsh said of Connolly. "He moves well without the ball and can play on the wing or come off screens."

Expect 5-8 senior **Corey Wright** (2.4 ppg, 1.8 rpg, 2.7 apg) to be the primary point backup, although he'll need to improve his shooting (.273 percent from the field, .182 percent from three-point range) considerably. Walkon **Dennis Cleary** (0.3 ppg, 0.0 rpg), a 6-0 senior who played in just six games last year, will help out in practice situations.

Welsh understands that 6-6 senior **Jamel Thomas** (18.5 ppg, 6.9 rpg, 2.0 apg, 1.5 spg) needs some help. Even though Thomas scored so well last year, he shot just .358 percent from the field and was often the Friars' only legitimate offensive option. He shot more than twice as much as any other Friar and three or more times as often as most of his teammates. It would be a good sign for Providence if Thomas' point total falls a bit, because that would mean his teammates are contributing more.

"Opponents were too centered on him last year," Welsh said. "He's a terrific player, and we want him to be the focal point of our offense. But we have to have better balance. We need him to get better scoring opportunities."

The frontcourt is an interesting assortment of 6-6 and 6-7 players that could add up to be a pretty productive group. Welsh is high on 6-6, 230-pound freshman **Rahim Johnson** (Cedar Grove (Penn.) Academy/Maine Central Institute/ Queens, N.Y.), a lefty with good post moves who could give the Friars a much-needed interior scoring force. Johnson committed to USC after averaging 27 ppg during two seasons at MCI, but spent last year at a tiny prep school in the Philadelphia area. "He's an inside-outside guy," Welsh said. "He's a crafty lefthander with an unorthodox game who knows how to put the ball in the hole. He has a big body and can also shoot the three-pointer."

Welsh has another pair of swing players, **Justin Farley** and **Erron Maxey**, to fit into his up-tempo style. Farley (9.5 ppg, 2.8 rpg), a 6-6 senior, is a good shooter with a fair outside touch and pretty good passing skills. Maxey (7.3 ppg, 4.3 rpg) is a 6-6 sophomore and more of an inside player, despite weighing only 195 pounds. He's a strong finisher close to the basket and a good offensive rebounder.

A pair of part-time starters, **Llewellyn Cole** and **Ben Perkins**, will also figure prominently in Welsh's front line plans. Cole (6.9 ppg, 4.3 rpg), a 6-7 junior, is another player who works well close to the basket. He also blocked 25 shots last year. Perkins is a 6-7 sophomore who averaged 6.5 ppg and 3.2 rpg last year, but shot the ball inconsistently.

Two walkons, 6-5 sophomore **Peter Farrell-Marcellino** (0.0 ppg, 0.0 rpg) and 6-4 senior **Rick Cordella** (0.7 ppg, 0.3 rpg), combined to play just six minutes last year.

adidas Blue Ribbon Analysis

BACKCOURT .... C+ BENCH/DEPTH .... B-
FRONTCOURT .... C INTANGIBLES .... B

This isn't the perfect team for Welsh to coach, but it has some potential. In Thomas, the Friars have a proven scorer who will be an even better player this year should he get some support. And he should get some. Connolly will bring some much-needed scoring pop from the outside, while Linehan will be a more confident, experienced point man this year.

The style will help, too. By pressing and trapping, Providence will get some easy baskets and create a tempo that will allow it to get some layups and short jumpers, rather than have to live in halfcourt situations. That killed the Friars last year. Gillen never recruited any of these guys to walk it up, and they weren't very good at that last year.

The big question is up front, where Johnson needs to team with Cole and Perkins in a solid rotation that hits the boards and plays some good interior defense when the big guys come to call. If the front line produces, and Thomas gets some help on the offensive side of the ledger, Providence will be tough.

Of course, Welsh knows this team has flaws. And his first year will be as much about creating a culture and reviving the program as it will about winning 20 games. Providence is a definite postseason competitor (NIT, not NCAA), and Welsh has four scholarships to spend next year on his kind of players, plus some size. The Friars are definitely headed in the right direction with Welsh in control. It just might take a season to get rolling along.

(M.B.)

RUTGERS

LOCATION .... New Brunswick, NJ
CONFERENCE .... Big East
LAST SEASON .... 14-15 (.483)
CONFERENCE RECORD ....6-12 (t-5th, Big East 7)
STARTERS LOST/RETURNING 1/4
NICKNAME .... Scarlet Knights
COLORS .... Scarlet & White
HOMECOURT .... Louis Brown Athletic Center (8,500)
COACH .... Kevin Bannon (St. Peter's '79)
RECORD AT SCHOOL .... 14-15 (1 yr.)
CAREER RECORD .... 290-166 (16 yrs.)
ASSISTANTS Tod Kowalczyk (Minnesota-Duluth '88)
Rob Lanier (St. Bonaventure '90)
Dan Hurley (Seton Hall '96)
TEAM WINS (last 5 yrs.) 11-13-9-11-16
RPI (last 5 yrs.) 94-107-132-119-73
1997-98 FINISH .... Lost in conference semifinal.

Madison Square Garden was rocking. The TV cameras were focused in. Rutgers basketball was creating excitement again. Kevin Bannon had promised thrills, and he had delivered—for a couple days, at least. Rutgers may have won only 14 games last season, but its two Big East Tournament wins were extremely memorable and may just have been a glimpse into the program's potential.

First, RU dumped West Virginia, 72-65, in a No. 5 vs. No.12 opening-round game. No real big news there. Upsets happen all the time in the conference tournaments. And WVU hadn't had the best record in the Big East confab during its abbreviated time in the league.

It was the follow-up that made some news. When **Geoff Billet** hit a buzzer-beating runner to lift the Knights over Georgetown, 61-60, in the second round, people started to notice. How couldn't they? The shot was shown and reshown for the next few days, as sort of a precursor to the March Madness to follow. And Rutgers, which wasn't expected to accomplish anything, was playing Connecticut in the semis.

So what if the Huskies dealt RU a 14-point setback? A season that had featured more downs than ups had finished on an undeniable high point, and Rutgers was able to point to 1998-99 with hope and some deserved optimism. This isn't an NCAA Tournament team yet, but Bannon has certainly reversed the culture of losing in New Brunswick and appears ready to turn the team around.

"Our guys gave us everything they had last year," Bannon said. "What we did in the Big East tournament is pretty comparable to an NIT berth. The bang we got for that helped the program.

"We got three additional ESPN dates and some of the credibility we were looking for. We're moving in the right direction, and it's always good to see a team play well at the end of the season."

Okay, so maybe that stuff about the NIT berth is stretching things a little. But you can't blame Bannon for his optimism. Instead of cresting early, Rutgers ended the year on a roll, the perfect thing to do when building. How many recruits in the New York/New Jersey/Pennsylvania area got a chance to see Billet's shot again and again? Plenty, if the Scarlet Knights coaches were doing their jobs.

Not that they were asleep before the big moment. Rutgers welcomes one of the Big East's finest (if not the finest) recruiting classes to campus this season. But the biggest newcomer at the school hasn't even enrolled. New Rutgers athletic director Bob Mulcahy, who used to run the Meadowlands Sports Complex, brings much-needed savvy and respect to the Rutgers program.

Although Bannon said the commitment was there before Mulcahy arrived, you can bet things will be even better with him on board.

"I couldn't be happier with our situation," Bannon said. "All a coach asks for is a level playing field."

Joining the newcomers are four returning starters and a key frontcourt reserve. Among the recruits are two junior-college players, a strategy Bannon doesn't like to employ but a necessary evil in this case in order to provide a little more experience. If everybody pans out, Rutgers could have its deepest team in years. It certainly has talent.

Leading the way is Billet, a 6-0 senior who scored 13.9 ppg, grabbed 2.8 rpg and handed out 4.0 apg last year. Billet made .390 percent of his three-point shots, had a solid assist-to-turnover ratio (1.4:1) and was a strong leader. Although he won't ever be a dominant player from the point position, it's impossible not to be drawn to his charisma and not be impressed with his desire.

"He's an all-league player who's never been named all-league," Bannon said. "Night-in and night-out, he gives it to us at both ends of the floor."

Billet is part of an impressive perimeter lineup for the Knights. He's joined by a pair of returning wing players, 6-0 sophomore **Earl Johnson** (10.9 ppg, 3.4 rpg, 4.1 apg, .347 percent three-point percentage) and 6-5 sophomore **Jeff Greer** (10.0 ppg, 5.1 rpg, .347 percent three-point percentage). Both had impressive debuts last season and should continue to develop into strong parts of the program. Johnson can handle either the one or two spots, while Greer plays off-guard or small forward, but has the passing ability (2.8 apg) to trigger the offense.

And there's more. **Brian Samuels** (Allegany College/ Simon Gratz HS/Philadelphia, Penn.) is a 6-1 junior who averaged 9.6 ppg and 4.5 apg last year. He's a defensive-minded point guard who should help the Knights press more successfully and can swing to the two spot if necessary.

Freshman **Dahntay Jones** (Steinert HS/Hamilton, N.J.) goes 6-5 and gives Rutgers further flexibility along the perimeter. A first-team all-state choice who scored 24.2 ppg and grabbed 9.3 rpg last year, Jones is a slashing scorer who received high marks from several recruiting services. He won't have to be a big producer right away, but he will get the chance to score off the bench. Although Jones is just 17, Bannon thinks he's ready now.

"He's physically ready and a very versatile player," Bannon said. "He's ready to play against great competition."

Rounding out the backcourt is 6-2 senior **Ben Neville** (0.4 ppg, 0.3 rpg), who played in just eight games last year and confined his scoring to the free-throw line (three for four).

The big question at Rutgers is in the frontcourt, where several newcomers will be asked to help right away. At least one thing is certain. **Rob Hodgson** is back and ready to make more significant contributions. The 6-7 senior averaged 13.2 ppg and 5.4 rpg and shot .366 percent from three-point land. Another of Bannon's "all-league guys who weren't named all-league," Hodgson is a horse who

1998-99 RUTGERS SCHEDULE

Nov.	14	Wagner
	22	@James Madison
	27-29	#United Airlines Tip-Off Tournament
Dec.	3	Columbia
	5	Fairliegh Dickinson
	8	@Georgetown
	11	Providence
	19	Temple
	22	@Princeton
	27	Lehigh
	30	@West Virginia
Jan.	2	St. John's
	9	Villanova
	12	Miami (Fla.)
	16	@St. John's
	18	Syracuse
	23	@Notre Dame
	25	Lafayette
	31	West Virginia
Feb.	3	@Villanova
	7	@Providence
	11	Pittsburgh
	13	Boston College
	16	@Connecticut
	21	@Seton Hall
	23	Georgetown
	27	@Miami (Fla.)
Mar.	3-6	##Big East Tournament

@ Road Games
# Honolulu, HI (vs. Auburn, first round; also Hawaii and Wichita State)
Madison Square Garden, NY

averaged 35.2 minutes per game last year. He led the team in steals with 46 and free-throw shooting (.835 percent). Although Hodgson hasn't become the superstar many figured he would be out of high school, he is certainly a highly-productive Big East player who could be ready for a breakthrough season.

The biggest need at Rutgers this year is in the power plant, where starter Eric Clark is gone, and where the Knights were thin last year. It is almost imperative that 6-10 freshman **Eugene Dabney** (Fork Union Military Academy/Woodlawn HS/Birmingham, Ala.) steps in and contributes right away. Dabney averaged 13.0 ppg and 10.0 rpg last year at Fork Union and has the size, if not the girth (he goes 225), to contribute. He'll need to, because the only other player on the roster with any real height is 6-11 junior **Alvydas Tenys** (4.2 ppg, 4.4 rpg), who has promise, but remains raw.

"It's been an adjustment period for him," Bannon said. "Just the language barrier was tough. He didn't play against great competition before coming here. It's going to take some time."

Bannon likens 6-6, 265-pound freshman forward **Rashod Kent** (Fairmont Senior HS/Fairmont, W.Va.) to Miami strongman Mario Bland and would be thrilled if Kent could provide the same interior defensive presence and rebounding that the Hurricane force does. Kent averaged 15.9 ppg and 14.8 rpg last year and shot 69 percent from the field.

Expect 6-7 junior **Joel Salvi** (Allegany College/Springbrook HS/Silver Spring, Md.) to get an early opportunity to start. He scored 17.6 ppg last year and grabbed 10.6 boards a game at Allegany. "He's tough, physical and athletic," Bannon said.

The final newcomer is 6-7 freshman **Billy Collins** (Bishop Brady HS/Concord, N.H.), last year's Mr. Basketball in New Hampshire. Collins scored 30.0 points and grabbed nine boards each time out and brings multiple skills to the three spot. "He can make the three," Bannon said. "He can run and jump. I think he's a more athletic version of Hodgson."

Darko Matijasevic (0.0 ppg, 0.0 rpg), a 6-8 junior who played in just eight games last year, rounds out the frontcourt.

adidas Blue Ribbon Analysis

BACKCOURT	B-	BENCH/DEPTH	C+
FRONTCOURT	C+	INTANGIBLES	B

Bannon is right. Rutgers has created some excitement, generated interest and is pointed in the right direction. Mission one accomplished. Now comes the hard part. The Knights have to do more than threaten .500 with a late-season burst. They must become a competitive force in the Big East. This year's recruiting class takes a big step toward that goal. It's deep, versatile and talented. When combined with the solid perimeter holdovers and Hodgson, it gives Bannon some options.

Now, we'll see if Rutgers can find a way near the top of the second group in the Big East. Like Villanova, Pittsburgh, Providence, Seton Hall and Georgetown, the Knights return talent and fortified themselves with newcomers. Like those schools, however, Rutgers also has lots of questions.

The perimeter seems like it will be fine. Rutgers will be able to shoot it well and has good passers. It would help if the Knights cut down on their turnovers, but you can't have everything.

Up front, however, there are problems. Hodgson is solid, but Bannon needs his newcomers to be strong on the boards and defensively immediately. Rutgers was outrebounded last year and must show that it can hang with its bigger conference rivals, or it will struggle.

Bannon has proven that he was the right man for the job. But there is plenty of work to do. Rutgers must compete for a postseason bid—if not get there—this year, and the Knights must assemble another strong recruiting class, with an emphasis on size. Last year, particularly the Big East Tournament, was great, but that's not all Bannon had in mind when he came to New Brunswick.

(M.B.)

SETON HALL

LOCATION	South Orange, N.J.
CONFERENCE	Big East
LAST SEASON	15-15 (.500
CONFERENCE RECORD	9-9 (3rd, Big East 7)
STARTERS LOST/RETURNING	2/3
NICKNAME	Pirates
COLORS	Blue & White
HOMECOURT	Continental Airlines Arena (20,029)
COACH	Tommy Amaker (Duke '87)
RECORD AT SCHOOL	15-15 (1 yr.)
CAREER RECORD	15-15 (1 yr.)
ASSISTANTS	Rob Jackson (Northeastern '74)
	Tim O'Toole (Fairfield '88)
	Kerry Keating (Seaton Hall '93)
TEAM WINS (last 5 yrs.)	17-16-12-10-15
RPI (last 5 yrs.)	42-105-95-136-102
1997-98 FINISH	Lost in NIT first round.

Back when Tommy Amaker was looking for a way to make his smallish office look like a palace through some creative redesign and the proper use of color and furniture, there were many who thought the project was a metaphor for the Pirates' recent troubles. No longer a national force, Seton Hall was trying to convert its own diminutive persona into something capable of competing in the Big East and beyond. Without the resources of the larger schools against which it competed (including that state institution just to the south), the Hall needed something a little more. So, when Amaker was looking for a way to enhance his office, he was also searching for methods to boost the Pirates without millions of dollars.

Give him credit for a good start. Instead of taking the first-year nose-dive most expected, Amaker's Pirates finished .500 and qualified for the NIT. It wasn't quite 1989, when P.J. Carlesimo screamed and shouted the Hall to the Final Four, but it was a pretty good start.

"I'm very proud of what we were able to accomplish our first year," Amaker said. "We were picked to finish last in the Big East 7, and we still got a postseason berth. That's a heckuva start. If anybody told us coming in that we would have that kind of season, we would have taken it."

It almost ended too soon. When Michigan started trolling for a full-time coach after Brian Ellerbe's one-year apprenticeship, Amaker's name was mentioned—prominently. In one year, he had joined the ranks of the "hot young coaches" around the country.

Though he won't say whether it was his sweet shoe deal that kept him in South Orange, Amaker is back for a second season of rebuilding. But Pirate fans and administrators had better beware. There will be more suitors in the future, and the school will need to be creative themselves to keep Amaker around. Because no matter how much the school spews about its Big East membership and ticket to the big time basketball show, it is at a decided disadvantage when the Big Boys come calling, with their exceptional facilities, big budgets and secure futures in the NCAA spotlight.

"Last spring, because we had won some games, people recognized what's on the burner at Seton Hall," Amaker said. "Things are happening, and I received some inquiries. But I am happy to be at Seton Hall."

Whether Amaker will be happy come March is up for discussion. The Hall must replace its entire frontcourt from last year and find a way to rise above the six-team attack pack that is chasing the league's heavyweights. Should Seton Hall find some answers up front, it will be all right. If not, it could find itself sagging into the second division. Amaker understands that last year's 15-win effort is not necessarily a precursor to huge success this year. It was merely a good start in the building process. He must, however, continue the momentum or risk losing ground to several other programs.

"Last year was a huge positive step for the program," he said. "The kids worked hard and believed. They became a team. The next goal is to become a program. We have to continue to take steps to get better. We don't have a bunch of superstars. We do have one of the better point guards around (**Shaheen Holloway**) and some good kids who worked hard and improved.

"We just want to show progress."

Holloway will play a big role in any forward movement. The 5-10 junior improved last year, leading the team with 15.0 ppg, pulling down 3.8 rpg and handing out 6.5 apg, tops in the Big East. He cut down on his turnovers, averaged a solid 2.1 spg and logged a team-high 36.7 minutes per game. Although his shooting continued to be weak (.344 FG percent percentage, .242 three-point percentage), Holloway made significant strides under Amaker—himself an old point guard—and is in position to be even better this year.

"He improved his overall game," Amaker said. "His scoring was down (from 17.3 ppg in 1996-97), but his turnovers were down and his assists were up. He shot better from the free-throw line and just gave of himself for the team. We won five more games and went to the NIT, and he was able to see what he could do for the program.

"He's become a leader. He opened his eyes to the impact he can have and has taken responsibility for that."

Holloway will again be the focus of the Pirate attack. He penetrates with authority, creates well for his teammates and appears to be understanding how important it is to make sure everybody comes along for the ride. If he can improve his shooting over the next two years, Holloway could be one of the nation's best players.

Most coaches will tell you that the point guard spot is the most important on the team, so the Pirates are in good shape there. The rest of the roster, however, is not so settled. Amaker expects 6-5 junior **Gary Saunders**, who transferred from Georgia Tech after learning coach Bobby Cremins was recruiting over him, to play the two spot. Saunders averaged 11.6 ppg during the 1996-97 season and will be asked to improve on that production this year—the Pirates need an instant replacement for Levell Sanders, who scored 15.6 ppg last year.

"Gary has a chance," Amaker said. "He worked hard throughout the past year and established himself every day in practice. He has good size and is athletic. He has a scorer's mentality. He's not great at anything, but he can do everything pretty well. He shoots it, drives to the basket and is creative."

The Hall has plenty of depth along the perimeter, beginning with 6-4 junior **Rimas Kaukenas** (8.7 ppg, 3.8 rpg), who struggled some with his shot last year but nonetheless started 25 games. Amaker likes his toughness and defensive ability_"We put him on the best scorer on the other team last year," he said_and expects him to boost his offensive numbers this year to match his contributions on the other end.

Backing up Holloway will be 6-0 freshman **Ty Shine** (Milford (Conn.) Academy/Augusta, GA), who enrolled at Seton Hall last January and sat out the remainder of the season. Amaker expects Shine to play in place of and together with Holloway during the season, particularly if the Pirates are pressing. Shine is a pretty good shooter with solid quickness who might be able to give Holloway more rest. He averaged 16.0 ppg, 5.0 apg and 3.0 spg as a high school senior.

Another freshman, 6-4 **Darius Lane** (Totino Grace HS/Fridley, Minn.) will fight for time at the two and three spots.

1998-99 SETON HALL SCHEDULE

Nov.	8	*Valparaiso
	14	St. Peter's
	18	Drexel
	24	@Minnesota
	29	**Kean College (N.J.)
Dec.	5	La Salle
	9	Villanova
	12	@Syracuse
	19	Northwestern
	21	**Army
	30	Boston College
Jan.	2	@Providence
	4	Georgetown
	9	@St. John's
	13	West Virginia
	19	@Notre Dame
	23	@Connecticut
	27	@Miami (Fla.)
	30	Syracuse
Feb.	2	@Boston College
	6	Notre Dame
	8	Pittsburgh
	13	Connecticut
	21	Rutgers
	25	@West Virginia
	27	@Pittsburgh
Mar.	3-6	#Big East Tournament

@ Road Games
* NABC Classic, Indianapolis, IN
** Walsh Gymasium, South Orange, NJ
# Madison Square Garden, NY

Lane averaged 27.1 ppg and 12.0 rpg last year against some lesser competition, but Amaker likes his potential. "He's a strong kid and a scorer who will blossom into a very good player in the league," he said. "I like his maturity level, and he'll understand the physical play in the Big East."

Amaker thinks 6-2 sophomore **Chuck Moore** (4.4 ppg, 1.3 rpg), who was plagued with knee problems last year, has the potential to surprise at the off-guard position. Moore is a good shooter who needs to get stronger (he weighs just 175 pounds) and improve his ballhandling to get some serious minutes. **John Johnson** (0.2 ppg, 0.4 rpg), a 6-2 senior, rounds out the guard corps.

So, the backcourt looks pretty good. Up front, however, is a different story. The Pirates lost productive scorer Donnell Williams and rebounder Jacky Kaba from a crew that wasn't exactly all that deep. Now, Amaker must hope a pair of sophomores, 6-6 **Reggie Garrett** (2.2 ppg, 1.6 rpg) and **Ramon Cespedes** (1.6 ppg, 2.0 rpg) are capable of teaming with productive 6-6 senior **Duane Jordan** (6.5 ppg, 6.7 rpg) and a pair of newcomers in a group that can hang with the league's tough guys.

"We need inside help," Amaker said.

Jordan is a good start, even though he will never be a breakout scorer. But he works hard, has a strong body and doesn't back down. Amaker calls him last year's most improved player, and a similar jump would be appreciated this season. Over the final third of last year, he averaged 8.0 ppg and a whopping 10.1 rpg. Garrett is a solid athlete who can finish close to the hoop, while Cespedes is a capable defender and rebounder.

The big news is the arrival of 6-10 freshmen **Manga Charles** and **Damian Dawkins.** Charles (Adelphi Academy/Cameroon, Africa) weighs 225 pounds and averaged 15.7 ppg, 14.7 rpg and 4.8 bpg last year. He's wiry and agile and has the ability to play either the four or five spots.

Dawkins (Notre Dame Secondary HS/Brampton, Ontario), meanwhile, goes 260 pounds and averaged 18.0 ppg, 9.7 rpg and 6.0 bpg as a prep senior. As one might expect, he is more of a pivot but needs to convert his hulking frame into a solid piece of oak from its current jelly-filled state. Though neither Charles nor Dawkins needs to dominate, each must produce, or the Pirates will find themselves facing defenses stacked against their perimeter strength.

adidas Blue Ribbon Analysis

BACKCOURT	**B**	**BENCH/DEPTH**	**C**
FRONTCOURT	**C-**	**INTANGIBLES**	**B+**

The Pirates made a good start. The trick is to sustain. And if the big guys come around, there is no reason another flirtation with .500 and the postseason won't occur. Holloway is an excellent starting point, and the rest of the backcourt_particularly Kaukenas, Saunders and Shine_looks strong.

But there is little of the same confidence about the frontcourt. Although Jordan could threaten a double-double average, nobody else looks ready to make a significant contribution. Charles is raw. Dawkins needs to find the weight room. And though Garrett and Cespedes have potential, they'll probably make small steps.

Amaker has a pretty good situation at Seton Hall. As long as the Pirates keep moving ahead, he'll bolster his reputation. But don't think he's capable of miracles. The Hall has a long way to go_on and off the court. The team needs to improve its overall shooting (.398 percent last year) and play better defense. But another good recruiting class next year might put the Pirates into serious postseason contention. And make Amaker even hotter.

(M.B.)

adidas Blue Ribbon Analysis

GRADING SYSTEM

- A+ equal to very best in country—Final Four-caliber unit
- A among the best in the land—worthy of deep NCAA run
- B+ talented, versatile and experienced—NCAA-NIT ability
- B solid and productive winners—league and post-season contenders
- C+ average to above-average—may contend in a weaker league
- C average to mediocre—second division in a strong league
- D+ below average, inconsistent—second division in a weaker league
- D well below average—losing season virtually certain
- F non-Division I ability—an underdog every night

VILLANOVA

LOCATION	**Villanova, PA**
CONFERENCE	**Big East**
LAST SEASON	**12-17 (.633)**
CONFERENCE RECORD	**8-10 (4th)**
STARTERS LOST/RETURNING	**0/5**
NICKNAME	**Wildcats**
COLORS	**Blue & White**
HOMECOURT	**The Pavilion (6,500)** **First Union Center (19,010)** **First Union Spectrum (18,060)**
COACH	**Steve Lappas (CCNY '77)**
RECORD AT SCHOOL	**115-73 (6 yrs.)**
CAREER RECORD	**171-135 (10 yrs.)**
ASSISTANTS	**Steve Pinone (Villanova '87)** **Joe Jone (Oswego State '87)** **Peter Zaharis (New York University '87)**
TEAM WINS (last 5 yrs.)	**20-25-26-24-12**
RPI (last 5 yrs.)	**23-12-7-10-86**
1997-98 FINISH	**Lost in conference second round.**

And now an argument for the value of experience. After suffering through Villanova's worst season in five years, a distinct departure from the sizable success the Wildcats had experienced in the interim, the cast of characters returns, largely intact, to make things right again. At Villanova, 12 wins don't cut it, even if four starters leave town from the previous season. The alumni, who often lack patience and perspective, want more. A lot more.

These are the same people who weren't too happy when Steve Lappas won 95 games from 1993-97. The same people who started grumbling about his future after a 24-win season in 1996-97. The same people who sit on their hands during Wildcat games, preferring to cheer more loudly for increases in the Dow Jones average than for a 10-0 run against Syracuse.

It would be convenient to blame last year on Tim Thomas, because he was supposed to be hanging around for another year—at least in Lappas' grand scheme—scoring about 25 a game and generally being The Man. Instead, he took the one-year plan and bolted for the NBA, where he staggered through the second half of a rookie season, out of shape and out of gas, and his teammates struggled to pick up the slack.

"None of those guys played in the roles they had to last year," Lappas said, referring to the five returning starters. "We spent a lot of time last year trying to figure out who everybody is, trying to establish a pecking order."

It's true. In addition to losing Thomas from the 1996-97 team, the Wildcats also bade farewell to guard Alvin Williams, center Jason Lawson and forward Chuck Kornegay. Yes, Zeffy Penn returned from a redshirt year, but that was hardly a fair trade.

So, the Wildcats struggled. They shot the ball poorly (43.0 percent from the field). They got pounded on the boards (minus-3.8 rebounding deficit). They committed way too many turnovers. They fouled too much. And, truth be told, they were boring.

Lappas is convinced that's ready to change. Because the Wildcats spent last year acclimating themselves to their new roles, they'll be able to take off right away in 1998-99. There won't be any growing pains. In a Big East where the top group (Connecticut, Syracuse, Miami, St. John's) is defined and the next six or seven teams is anybody's guess, Villanova will be well-positioned to make a run for the top of that second pack.

"We were 8-10 in the league last year, and that's not like 3-15," Lappas said. "I don't think we're coming back from as far as a lot of people think. We were in the middle of things with a team that never really played that much together.

"Now, when I come into the locker room, I'll know what everybody can do. There's more of an upside. At least we have an idea. There are some questions that have been answered."

Lappas had better hope his assessment is right. Even though he still has a few years left on his contract, he remains a popular target for VU alumni and fans. This is clearly a big season for Lappas. If he generates some momentum in the early recruiting period and then turns the team into a postseason contender, he would turn the fire down a little.

It would be pretty tough to cut him loose, particularly if Villanova wins 17 or 18 games, plays beyond the Big East Tournament and gets some strong early commitments.

But the big question is whether the 'Cats can be that successful. Lappas thinks they can, but there are plenty more questions out there than were answered last year.

At least the backcourt seems pretty sturdy, thanks to the returns of starters **John Celestand**, **Howard Brown** and **Jermaine Medley**, top reserve **Brian Lynch's** continued development and the arrival of talented freshman **Bobby Smith**.

Celestand (13.2 ppg, 4.2 rpg, 5.1 apg, 1.7 spg) didn't exactly blister the nets last year, as evidenced by his .413 percent field-goal shooting (.326 percent form beyond the arc), but he did prove to be a pretty reliable point man, and he played well down the stretch. The 6-3 senior isn't going to blast past too many people off the dribble, but he does make some good decisions and plays strong defense. He rebounds well for his size and has scads of experience. But...

"I think he can shoot the ball better and cut down on his turnovers," Lappas said. "I think in the last six games last year, he was one of the three best guards in the Big East. The real John Celestand stood up then and came into his own."

Brown, a 6-5 senior, did the same thing, only his arrival came earlier than the final six games. He entered the year as an exciting open-court player who looked lost at times in the halfcourt and left it as the team's most productive outside shooter, a fact that astonished many. Brown (13.1 ppg, 5.3 rpg) shot .445 percent from the field, a huge improvement from his first two seasons in the program, and converted on 37 percent of his three-point shots, an enormous increase.

By the end of the year, he looked like the strong off-guard he had been promoted as when he came to Villanova. Although Brown will never be a 20 ppg guy who dominates games, he certainly has the capability to score in the 17-point range, something Lappas would welcome with open arms.

"He could have been the most improved player in the Big East last year," Lappas said of Brown. "He had an outstanding year. All the things people knocked him for during his freshman and sophomore years, he did last year. His three-point shooting was tremendous, and he handled the ball more."

Medley (6.2 ppg, 1.2 rpg) started 23 games last year and showed a few bursts of the talent that made him so coveted out of high school. But the 6-0 sophomore was out of control at times, and his shooting (.316 percent FG, .307 percent on three-pointers) was atrocious.

Medley did demonstrate the ability to run the team and showed quickness with the ball, but he needs to slow down a little and make more positive contributions this season or

1998-99 VILLANOVA SCHEDULE

Nov.	16	George Mason
	19-22	#Top of the World Classic
	27	Mount St. Mary's
Dec.	1	*St. Joseph's
	5	@Penn State
	9	@Seton Hall
	12	West Virginia
	15	Massachusetts
	22	Rider
	27	Howard
	30	@Connecticut
Jan.	2	@Notre Dame
	5	**Syracuse
	9	@Rutgers
	13	Boston College
	16	**Notre Dame
	19	Pittsburgh
	23	@West Virginia
	26	@Providence
	30	**Georgetown
Feb.	3	Rutgers
	6	@Syracuse
	13	@St. John's
	16	@Maimi (Fla.)
	20	Providence
	23	Pennsylvania
	27	St. John's
Mar.	3-6	##Big East Tournament

@ Road Games
* The Palestra, Philadelphia, PA
** First Union Center, Philadelphia, PA
# Fairbanks, AK (vs. Nebraska, first round; also Alaska-Fairbanks, Arkansas, New Mexico State, Virginia, Washington State and Wisconsin)
Madison Square Garden, NY

run the risk of losing some playing time to Smith (Maine Central Institute/East Chicago, Ind.), who may lack a little heft on his 6-2, 175-pound frame, but he is an unselfish player with a good handle and solid shot. Last year, he averaged 13.7 ppg, 3.5 rpg, 6.1 apg and 2.4 spg for an MCI team that went 35-0 and averaged 115 ppg.

It will be interesting to see what 6-6 junior **Brian Lynch** (8.1 ppg, 3.0 rpg) does this year. When he arrived on campus, his flair and lively play led Lappas to predict one night, "that kid's going to drive me crazy." But he meant it in a good way, because Lynch clearly had the ability to shine, even if he did drip some mustard. After spending much of the second half of the 1996-97 season on the bench, Lynch averaged 20 minutes per game last year and began to flash some of the offensive consistency he'll need to make serious contributions this season.

"He's gotten a lot stronger, and he just turned 20 years old," Lappas said. "He needed to mature some, and now he weighs about 200 pounds."

The picture up front isn't so clear. Villanova needs veterans **Malik Allen** and **Rafal Bigus** to produce, or it won't get near the first half of the new, 13-team Big East configuration.

Last year, Lappas thought the 6-10 Allen was ready for a big year. Instead, the junior averaged just 8.3 ppg and 5.8 rpg, hardly numbers befitting a real, live power forward. Lappas reports that part of the problem was that Allen wore down as the season went on. "He began the year at 248 pounds and ended it at 221," the coach said. "I could not believe he wore down like that."

Allen spent a good portion of the summer in the weight room, and that's good news for Villanova fans, because he must be much more productive at both ends this year. Allen must also stay clear of foul trouble (he was disqualified from five games last year) and hit the backboards with a fervor. Lappas believes Allen can do all of that. We'll see.

It's tough to tell what the coach thinks of Bigus, who was another disappointment last year. The 7-1 senior (8.2 ppg, 5.1 rpg) remains unsure of himself on the court and seemingly attracted to referees' whistles. Ten minutes into every game, it seemed as if "Biggy" had two fouls and was parking his sizable backside on the bench. Villanova doesn't need him to score all that much, although double figures would be nice. But the Cats do need him to rebound, defend and block more shots. And stay on the court.

"There's more to Biggy than we've seen," Lappas said about the player with whom he has had something of a love-hate relationship during the last three seasons. "I hope because it's the first time he'll really be playing without looking over his shoulder that he'll be better. He made a step last year, but it wasn't quite the step we needed him to make."

Lappas hopes he has some frontcourt depth this year, thanks to the maturation of 6-10 sophomore forward **Simon Ogunlesi** (1.2 ppg, 1.4 rpg), who played in only 10 games last year, because of injuries and lack of conditioning. Lappas believes Ogunlesi can be the guy who gives Villanova 10 minutes or so when Bigus gets his customary two quick fouls.

If not, Villanova will be relying heavily on 6-9, 210-pound freshman **Brooks Sales** (Northwest Catholic HS/Bloomfield, Conn.), the brother of former Connecticut women's standout Nykesha Sales. Although Sales (25.0 ppg and 16.0 rpg) does have some skills and was chosen the Gatorade Player of the Year in Connecticut, he needs to get stronger.

Because of Villanova's perimeter depth, there wasn't a whole lot of room at the three spot last year for 6-7 junior **T.J. Caouette** (4.3 ppg, 1.7 rpg), whom Lappas was forced to play at the four spot, not his best position. But that's where Caouette may end up again, if Ogunlesi and Sales can't step up, and the guards play well enough to keep a three-man backcourt rotation on the floor.

That wouldn't be the best news for 6-6 redshirt freshman **Johnny Holley** (McKinney HS/McKinney, Texas), who remains pretty skinny at 180 pounds and needs to get tougher before he can be a full-fledged Big East player. But he has four years ahead of him and is a fine athlete who could contribute more down the road.

Chris Lee (0.0 ppg, 0.5 rpg), a 6-5 walkon who played in just two games last year, rounds out the frontcourt.

adidas Blue Ribbon Analysis

BACKCOURT .... B+ BENCH/DEPTH .... B-
FRONTCOURT .... C+ INTANGIBLES .... C+

Throw Villanova in with Pittsburgh, Rutgers, Providence, Georgetown and Seton Hall in that second Big East group. The Wildcats could finish fourth or fifth in the league, or ninth or 10th. Their future depends on whether Allen and Bigus turn into a formidable frontcourt pairing, and if the guards can shoot the ball more accurately.

Lappas believes his team's increased experience will correct many of last year's sins. He may be right. It would also be nice to see Allen get tougher, Bigus stay on the floor for more than five minutes at a time, and Medley and Celestand take more reasonable shots. This is an important year for Lappas and the program, because another sub-.500 year won't be looked upon all that favorably by the administration. We already know what the fans would think. But it could also be a fine year, in which the returning starters play consistently, and people such as Lynch, Caouette and Smith provide quality depth.

The answer lies somewhere in the middle. Villanova should finish over .500, but not by much. The NIT is its most likely postseason destination. That's not bad, but not great, either. Remember, they want more on the Main Line. The Wildcats need to deliver it.

(M.B.)

WEST VIRGINIA

LOCATION .... Morgantown, WV
CONFERENCE .... Big East
LAST SEASON .... 24-9 (.727)
CONFERENCE RECORD .... 11-7 (3rd, Big East 6)
STARTERS LOST/RETURNING 5/0
NICKNAME .... Mountaineers
COLORS .... Blue & Gold
HOMECOURT .... WVU Coliseum (14,000)
COACH .... Gale Catlett (West Virginia '63)
RECORD AT SCHOOL .... 390-216 (20 yrs.)
CAREER RECORD .... 514-260 (26 yrs.)
ASSISTANTS .... Mike Brown (Vermont '73)
Mel Hankinson (Indiana, Pa. '65)
Drew Catlett (Randolph-Macon '85)
TEAM WINS (last 5 yrs.) 17-13-12-21-24
RPI (last 5 yrs.) 65-119-125-44-39
1997-98 FINISH .... Lost in NCAA third round.

1998-99 WEST VIRGINIA SCHEDULE

Nov.	14	Alabama A&M
	18	@Duquesne
	27-29	#Big Island Invitational
Dec.	2	Georgia
	9	Syracuse
	12	@Villanova
	17	@Ohio University
	19	Virginia Tech
	22	Robert Morris
	30	Rutgers
Jan.	2	@Syracuse
	5	@Providence
	9	Connecticut
	13	@Seton Hall
	16	Miami (Fla.)
	19	@Georgetown
	23	Villanova
	27	*Marshall
	31	@Rutgers
Feb.	3	Providence
	6	@Boston College
	9	St. John's
	14	Notre Dame
	17	@Pittsburgh
	21	@Notre Dame
	25	Seton Hall
Mar.	3-6	##Big East Tournament

@ Road Games
* Charleston, WV
# Hilo, HI (vs. Wisconsin-Green Bay, first round; also Evansville, Georgia Tech, Hawaii-Hilo, New Orleans, Saint Louis and Washington)
Madison Square Garden, NY

Last year, we tried a little sarcasm. Gale Catlett told us his team would be awful. He didn't have any faith in the Mountaineers. The backcourt was too small. The frontcourt was untested. If only Gordon Malone had stayed around for his senior year, then maybe West Virginia would have been able to accomplish something. But he didn't, so the 1997-98 season was destined to be a disaster of epic proportions. Poor Gale.

Well, we won't be doing that again. First of all, some people didn't quite get the joke. And those who did were only too happy to remind us come March about just how "badly" the Mounties did. How do a pair of wins in the NCAA Tournament grab you? How about a near-miss in the third round against the eventual national runner-up? If West Virginia stunk last year, like Catlett predicted, then maybe the Mountaineers should hope to be so aromatically challenged every season. As for Catlett, we won't be believing anything he said during the preseason any time soon.

Bet on that. So, even though WVU lost all five of its starters from last year's team and will be putting out a first five that has more question marks than the Riddler's costume, we refuse to put West Virginia in any sort of basement—especially with Boston College around. Of course, you know what Catlett's going to say about that.

"If somebody picks us higher than 13th (last) in the league, they ought to have their head examined," Catlett said.

OK, coach. You suggest the shrink, and we'll make an appointment. However, this year's team is certainly no match for last year's senior-laden unit, which included first-team all-league choice Damian Owens, the productive backcourt trio of Adrian Pledger, Greg Jones and Jarrod West—double-figure scorers all—and good soldier Brett Solheim.

The 1997-98 Mountaineers won 24 games and set a school record for turnovers forced. Blowing out Temple in the first round of the NCAA Tournament and then doing in Cincinnati on a buzzer-beater was borderline phantasmagoria. Had West Virginia beaten Utah (it lost, 65-62), it's possible Catlett may have been taken directly to the governor's mansion and installed as the state's executive by thousands of gleeful Mountaineer faithful.

"Last year's team was unique and will be one of the best-remembered in my coaching career," Catlett said. "I didn't think we'd get close to the Sweet 16. Our team the year before was better, but this team was tougher and had more chemistry. If you're going to write a book on chemistry, last year's team was the perfect subject.

"Plus, the (fullcourt) press was better. It was the same (stuff) we've done before, but the athletes were better, and they were seniors."

WVU will probably employ the same style as always, but now it's time to see what the understudies can do. Last year's starters dominated the team. They scored the points, grabbed the boards and made the steals. Now, they're gone. And it's time to look ahead.

This year's team begins with 6-8 junior forward **Marcus Goree**, who averaged 8.0 ppg, 5.2 rpg and shot .544 percent from the field in 23.6 minutes per game. He came to WVU heralded as a big-time frontcourt star, the kind of guy West Virginia needed to hang with the top clubs in the Big East. He has played pretty well to this point, but he certainly hasn't made good on his considerable promise yet.

"He's had a couple good years and is a talented young man," Catlett said. "This will be the first time he'll be a marquee player. He has the ability to be pretty darn good. It's a matter of how he accepts the responsibility."

Goree can shoot to 15 feet, but the Mountaineers will need him on the glass. He jumps well and quickly, gets out on the break and is the perfect forward for Catlett's system. If he becomes a star, WVU will be in good shape. If not, expect trouble, because the rest of the frontcourt rotation is shaky. It has to kill Catlett to see Marquise Gainous settling in at Texas Christian, in another up-tempo style. Had the 6-9 forward been eligible last year, he would be getting ready to team with Goree in a formidable pairing.

As it stands, Goree will look for help from newcomers and 6-6 senior **Elton Scott** (1.0 ppg, 1.5 rpg), who came to Morgantown last year at the end of the first term and never really got acclimated. A big-time scorer in junior college, Scott weighs only 190 pounds, so strength is a problem. But Catlett hopes Scott can be like Brian Lewin, another junior college import who struggled his first year but was very productive (7.6 ppg, 7.6 rpg) as a senior last season.

The rest of the frontcourt is anybody's guess. **Calvin Bowman** (San Jacincto JC/Brooklyn, N.Y.), a 6-10 JC import made the grades, but WVU will redshirt the junior and his quickness and athletic ability this year. But the

Mountaineers got good academic news about 6-7 freshman **Jackie Rogers** (Winchendon Prep/Syracuse, N.Y.), who weighs in at a stout 225 pounds. Rogers spent last year at Winchendon (Mass.) Prep after scoring more than 1,000 career points at Corcoran HS in Syracuse.

West Virginia must also rely on freshmen 6-8 **Chris Moss** (Lloyd C. Bird HS/Chesterfield, Va.) and 6-9 **John Oliver** (Maine Central Institute/Fayetteville HS/Manlius, N.Y.). Moss averaged 20.3 ppg, 12.3 rpg and 4.5 bpg as a senior, but will need some time to blossom into the versatile player Catlett hopes he can become. Oliver averaged 9.2 ppg, 5.9 rpg and 1.9 bpg at MCI last year and is a banger. WVU could use him.

The last frontcourt newcomer was supposed to be 6-8 Australian Paul Denman (Canberra School/Canberra, Australia), who played against West Virginia last year in an exhibition game and impressed Catlett. But he signed a pro contract and stayed on his home continent.

Rounding out the frontcourt are 6-6 sophomore **Brooks Berry** (1.6 ppg, 1.1 rpg), 6-0 senior **Tom Benyon** (0.3 ppg, 0.6 rpg) and 6-6 junior **Duane Lewis** (0.3 ppg, 0.3 rpg), none of whom will play that much—unless there is an emergency.

The backcourt could be in even tougher straits. Catlett will hand the ball to 6-5 sophomore **Jarett Kearse** (2.9 ppg, 1.4 rpg, 1.0 apg), who averaged 10.5 minutes per game last year, but was rarely the defensive stopper or future star that Catlett thought he would be. That could change this time around, because he'll have more opportunity to be on the court.

"Kearse didn't play nearly like I thought he was going to play," Catlett said. "Part of that wasn't his fault. There were three excellent guards ahead of him. He could have probably used some more minutes. Now, he'll step into the lead role, and we'll find out how good he is. He had some good moments last year, but not nearly as many as I thought."

Kearse has all the tools to be a highly-productive point, but his shooting (.398 percent from the field) must improve, and he has to play with more confidence. He had better, because Catlett doesn't have many options behind him.

Both backcourt newcomers, 6-0 freshman **Lionel Armstead** (Emanuel Baptist HS/Toledo, Ohio) and 6-1 junior **Brad McMillian** (Frank Phillips (Texas) JC/Huntington East HS/Huntington, W.Va.) are more two guards than points.

McMillian averaged 15.5 ppg and 4.1 apg last year and can fill it up from outside, while Armstead (32.7 ppg, 7.7 rpg, 5.5 apg) can fill it up. "He's a very good basketball player," Catlett said of Armstead. "I'm tickled to have him. He's definitely a Big East player."

Two 6-3 off-guards from McCook (Neb.) CC will also get a chance to impress. **Javis Johnson** (McCook CC/Natchez, Miss.) scored 10.9 ppg and grabbed 7.1 rpg last year, while **Kerry Murray** (McCook CC/Baton Rouge, La.) scored 11.7 ppg. Johnson is a junior, while Murray, who originally signed with UTEP but didn't play, will be a sophomore.

Catlett hopes 6-1 senior **Carl Williams** (1.6 ppg, 0.9 rpg), who came to WVU with a tremendous reputation for scoring, can produce consistently. "He had some moments last year," Catlett said. "He didn't have enough of them." Rounding out the backcourt is 6-1 junior **Jason D'Alesio** (0.5 ppg, 0.2 rpg), a deep reserve.

adidas Blue Ribbon Analysis

BACKCOURT	**C**	**BENCH/DEPTH**	**C-**
FRONTCOURT	**C+**	**INTANGIBLES**	**B-**

The Mountaineers were on a dream ride last season. They made it to the Sweet 16 and gave their fans plenty to cheer about. But all of that is over, and WVU must rely on another generation of players if it wants to keep its status as one of the top teams in the Big East.

That won't be easy. Goree and Kearse will be looked upon as the leaders of this team, and that won't necessarily be what the Mountaineers need. Both have plenty of potential, but neither is proven. As for the rest of the cast, it's dicey. The newcomers have some promise, but there are many of them, and none is proven.

Don't believe it when Catlett cries poor about his team's prospects this year. But don't expect all that many fireworks, either. West Virginia will be good for about 15 wins and could find itself in the NIT. That's not last year, but it's not bad, either. The real fun could come in 1999-2000, no matter what Catlett tells you.

(M.B.)

BIG SKY CONFERENCE

adidas BLUE RIBBON FORECAST

1. Northern Arizona
2. Montana State
3. Portland State
4. Weber State
5. Northridge State
6. Montana
7. Eastern Washington
8. Sacramento State
9. Idaho State

ALL-CONFERENCE TEAM

G—Brian Towne, SR, Portland State
G—Damien Baskerville, SR, Weber State
G—Danny Sprinkle, SR, Montana State
F—Nate Holmstadt, SR, Montana State
F—Jason Hartman, SR, Portland State

PLAYER OF THE YEAR

Nate Holmstadt, SR, Montana State

NEWCOMER OF THE YEAR

Harold Arceneaux, JR, Weber State

1998-99 CONFERENCE TOURNAMENT

March 4-6, at home court of regular-season champion

1997-98 CHAMPION

Northern Arizona (regular season)
Northern Arizona (conference tournament)

1997-98 POSTSEASON PARTICIPANTS

Postseason Record: 0-1 (.000)
NCAA
Northern Arizona

TOP BACKCOURTS

1. Eastern Washington
2. Northern Arizona
3. Weber State

TOP FRONTCOURTS

1. Montana State
2. Northern Arizona
3. Portland State

ON THE WAY UP

Portland State

ON THE WAY DOWN

Montana

INSIDE THE NUMBERS

- 1997-98 conference RPI: 21 (of 30)
- Conference RPI (last 5 years): 12-15-21-22-21

DID YOU KNOW?

Portland State has served its two-year NCAA-mandated compliance period and is eligible for the conference title and postseason play...Weber State coach Ron Abegglen has never had a losing season in 35 years as a head coach, including high school and junior college...The Big Sky has a combined record of 15-43 in NCAA Tournament play, with Idaho State recording eight of those wins. Weber State is next with five, including a 79-72 victory over Michigan State in 1995—the last victory by a league team...Last year's league tournament was a wild one, as three of the top four seeds lost their opening games. The lone favorite to win was Northern Arizona, which went on to win the tournament title and give Cincinnati a scare in the NCAA Tournament...Those tough winter flights through the mountains have proven to be a big obstacle. Three teams won all their league games at home last season: Northern Arizona, Weber State and Portland State. Eastern Washington and Montana only lost one league game at home...Five of the league's eight top scorers return, with Portland State's Jason Hartman (19.1 ppg) leading the way. Last year's leading scorer in the league—Tywan Meadows of Idaho State—transferred out of the conference.

(S.D.)

EASTERN WASHINGTON

LOCATION	**Cheney, WA**
CONFERENCE	**Big Sky**
LAST SEASON	**16-11 (.593)**
CONFERENCE RECORD	**10-6 (t-3rd)**
STARTERS LOST/RETURNING	**4/1**
NICKNAME	**Eagles**
COLORS	**Red & White**
HOMECOURT	**Reese Court (6,000)**
COACH	**Reese Court (Chandron State '71)**
RECORD AT SCHOOL	**26-53 (3 yrs.)**
CAREER RECORD	**214-193 (14 yrs.)**
ASSISTANTS	**Jerome Jenkins (Regis University '90)**
	Brian Priebe (Washington '95)
TEAM WINS (last 5 yrs.)	**5-6-3-7-16**
RPI (last 5 yrs.)	**263-280-300-276-164**
1997-98 FINISH	**Lost in conference quarterfinal.**

They finished with 11 losses and didn't win a game in the Big Sky Conference Tournament, but make no mistake: Last season was an historic one for the Eastern Washington Eagles. In fact the team has compiled a "Hoop-la" sheet which details exactly how big a year it was in Cheney, Wash.

Consider:

- The Eagles put together their best regular season and conference record in the '90s.
- They made their first postseason appearance in the decade, lasting until the quarterfinals of the Big Sky Tournament.
- They won seven of their last eight games in conference play.
- They had an 11-1 home record, a 10-1 record in games decided in the last three minutes, and beat Pac-10 foe Washington State in an overtime game in December.

The list of accomplishments goes on. Unfortunately so do the challenges ahead for Steve Aggers' Eagles.

EWU comes into what is expected to be a very competitive conference race with just one returning starter and only five players who have seen playing time. There is some talent and physical presence in the newcomers, but Aggers—the Big Sky's Coach of the Year last season—will have to perform his magic again for Eastern Washington to make a run.

"We certainly need the guys who were complementary players last year to step up and a fill a more meaningful role this year," Aggers said. "They have to step up and sustain what we are doing."

Much of that pressure will fall squarely on the shoulders of junior **Deon Williams** (12.3 ppg, 2.9 rpg, 164 assists, 36 steals), a 6-2 point guard who led the league in assists (6.1 per game) last year en route to first-team All Big Sky honors. Williams is just learning the nuances of the point-guard position, having made a name for himself mainly as a scorer during his high school days in Los Angeles. He did an admirable job of keeping his turnovers low (96), averaging one per every 9.3 minutes on the floor.

Williams didn't shoot all that well from the field last season (.399 percent), but was much better than average from three-point range, making 33 of 88 shots from behind the arc (.375 percent).

"He has a chance to be an absolutely wonderful player,

1998-99 EASTERN WASHINGTON SCHEDULE

Nov.	16	Concordia
	21	San Diego
	25	@California
	30	Gonzaga
Dec.	5	Washington State
	11-12	#Boilermaker Invitational
	17	@Cal Poly
	19	@San Jose State
	22	Evergreen State
Jan.	2	Idaho State
	7	@Northern Arizona
	9	@Northridge State
	14	Sacramento State
	16	Weber State
	21	Montana State
	23	Montana
	27	@Weber State
	30	@Portland State
Feb.	4	Portland State
	11	@Idaho State
	13	@Sacramento State
	18	Northridge State
	20	Northern Arizona
	25	@Montana State
	27	@Montana
Mar.	4-6	##Big Sky Tournament

@ Road Games
# West Lafayette, IN (vs. LaSalle, first round; also Purdue and Valparaiso)
At homecourt of regular-season champion.

we think, as he becomes more experienced," Aggers said. "He's really grown as a floor leader."

The other leader is expected to be **Shannon Taylor**, a 6-3 senior who vastly improved during conference play and will play shooting guard and small forward. He's the only senior on the roster. Taylor put up some big numbers in Big Sky play, especially in the last six games, when he averaged 24 points. That total included a 33-point effort in a road game at Idaho State.

Taylor (14.9 ppg, 3.8 rpg, 68 assists, 36 steals) is one of the better shooters in the conference, having shot .406 percent from three-point range last year. Taylor's 76 three-pointers were the second-highest single season total in school history. He's expected to start with Williams in what should be a potent backcourt.

"He plays very hard with great emotion and passion, but that has also gotten him into trouble with fouls," Aggers said. "We need to keep him on the floor, so playing under emotional control and reducing fouls are a key for him."

Aggers is counting on **Jason Humbert** (5.3 ppg, 3.9 rpg) and **Chris White** (2.9 ppg, 2.9 rpg) to become big contributors this season after filling smaller roles last year.

Humbert (5.3 ppg, 3.9 rpg), a 6-10, 245-pound senior, broke his hand in the conference opener last year and missed seven weeks. The injury limited his minutes, kept his statistics low and hurt the Eagles inside. The Eagles need much greater contributions from Humbert this season.

When Humbert when down last year, White stepped up. The thin, 6-9 sophomore didn't post great numbers (2.9 ppg, 2.9 rpg), but Aggers predicts a bright future and thinks the Phoenix, Ariz., product will break into the starting lineup this year. White can run, jump and play above the rim. Two years ago, he led the state of Arizona in shooting percentage. The problem is that he's only a sophomore, albeit one who finished his freshman year by nabbing 13 points and eight rebounds in the season finale against Northridge State.

The fifth starting job is open, but it might go to **Alex Carcamo**, a 6-7 junior transfer from Santa Monica (Calif.) JC. He averaged 19.0 ppg, 9.0 rpg and 3.0 spg a year ago. "Alex is a scorer who can put the ball on the floor and create off the dribble, but is also a good perimeter shooter and an even better offensive rebounder," Aggers said.

Rounding out the backcourt is 6-foot junior **Darrell Walker** (Everett CC, Wash.), 6-2 sophomore **Tony McGee**, 6-5 freshman **Marco Quinto** and 6-2 junior **Ryan Hansen** (Walla Walla CC, Wash.).

Of the four, Hansen and McGee should see the most playing time. Hansen is a spot-up shooter who can take advantage of Williams' creativity, having made 114 three-pointers last season while averaging 31.1 points per game.

McGee (2.8 ppg, 0.8 rpg) played about 10 minutes per game last year and became the team's defensive stopper.

Walker walked on in the fall of 1997 and was awarded a scholarship. Quinto, from Interlake HS in Bellevue, Wash., averaged 21.0 ppg and 8.0 rpg as a senior.

Competing for minutes in the thin frontcourt will be **Eddie Turner III**, **Dennis Fitzgerald**, **Chris Johnson** and **Will Levy**.

Turner, a 6-7, 260-pound sophomore, redshirted last year, but was impressive as a freshman the season before when he averaged 3.8 points and 2.2 rebounds in 9.2 minutes of work per game. EWU needs his size to bang around opponents inside.

Fitzgerald, 6-8, 230-pound junior from Chabot (Calif.) JC, will be counted on to back up both inside positions. Fitzgerald was a highly recruited football player who was overlooked as a basketball prospect but came into his own his final season at Chabot.

Levy, another JC transfer, is a little thin, but he's active and at 6-8 will be used as a shot blocker and rebounder. He averaged 18.0 ppg, 9.0 rpg and 2.5 bpg last season for Diablo Valley (Calif.) CC.

Johnson, a 6-11 freshman from Thomas Doherty HS in Colorado Springs, Colo., has bulked up to 225 pounds and is working hard in the weight room. He will likely redshirt.

adidas Blue Ribbon Analysis

BACKCOURT .... **C+** **BENCH/DEPTH** .... **C-**
FRONTCOURT .... **D+** **INTANGIBLES** .... **D+**

There's no question Aggers has the Eagles on the right track, but replacing four starters won't be easy.

The good news is that the Eagles are bigger, quicker and stronger than they were in years past. That alone gives Aggers something to work with. Having a point guard the quality of Deon Williams doesn't hurt, as he'll ease the transition for all the newcomers.

"I think we're cautiously optimistic," Aggers said. "We just need to have some people step up in a few places."

All that new talent has to mature through a non-conference schedule which includes California, Gonzaga, Washington State, the Purdue Boilermaker Invitational and a trip to underrated Cal Poly-SLO.

Considering that demanding non-conference schedule, will there be another 16-win season in Cheney this year? Probably not, but the program appears to have developed to the point where another three-win year (which is only three years in the past) isn't going to happen either.

(S.D.)

IDAHO STATE

LOCATION .... **Pocatello, ID**
CONFERENCE .... **Big Sky**
LAST SEASON .... **6-20 (.231)**
CONFERENCE RECORD .... **2-14 (8th)**
STARTERS LOST/RETURNING **2/3**
NICKNAME .... **Bengals**
COLORS .... **Red, White & Black**
HOMECOURT .... **Holt Arena (7,938)**
COACH .... **Doug Oliver (San Jose State '73)**
RECORD AT SCHOOL .... **First Year**
CAREER RECORD .... **First Year**
ASSISTANTS . **Jay McMillin (Nebraska Wesleyan '88)**
Louis Wilson (William Jewell '88)
TEAM WINS (last 5 yrs.) **18-18-11-14-6**
RPI (last 5 yrs.) **105-129-241-236-289**
1997-98 FINISH ... **Didn't qualify for postseason play.**

It's a long way from Palo Alto to Pocatello, but coach Doug Oliver is determined to make his new job a little more like his old hangout: Maples Pavilion.

The 12-year Stanford assistant has already sold a lot of the community on Idaho State men's basketball. He plans to canvass the campus and add strong support from the student body, turning Pocatello into a dreaded place to visit.

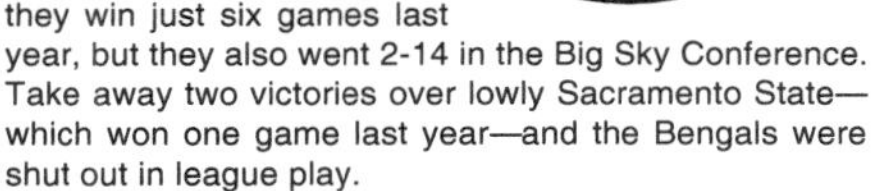

That is easier said than done.

The Bengals endured a miserable year in Herb Williams' lame-duck season. Not only did they win just six games last year, but they also went 2-14 in the Big Sky Conference. Take away two victories over lowly Sacramento State—which won one game last year—and the Bengals were shut out in league play.

The community noticed: Holt Arena's atmosphere rivaled the moon's. So Oliver's first task is to instill confidence in the players and the community.

"I think the personality of myself and the staff will be the

1998-99 IDAHO STATE SCHEDULE

Nov.	19	@Oregon State
	24	Western Montana
	28	@Boise State
Dec.	3	@Wyoming
	5	@Colorado
	7	Southern Utah
	12	Portland
	22	Boise State
	28	@Butler
	29	@Tennessee Tech
Jan.	2	@Eastern Washington
	4	@Northridge State
	7	Montana
	9	Montana State
	14	@Weber State
	16	@Portland State
	21	@Northern Arizona
	23	@Sacramento State
	28	Northridge State
	30	Northern Arizona
Feb.	6	@Montana State
	8	@Montana
	11	Eastern Washington
	13	Portland State
	17	Weber State
	20	Sacramento State
Mar.	4-6	#Big Sky Tournament

@ Road Games
# At homecourt of regular-season champion.

way we do that," he said. "We're going to be high energy and positive. There will, of course, be moments where we won't be happy with what we see, but our approach is such that the kids won't lack confidence from our viewpoint.

"We're going to demand the best of their abilities. At times that will be good enough to win, and at times it won't be good enough. We'll have to learn to deal with that."

Oliver has some talent to work with, but he has a long road ahead. The long-time assistant, who lists nearby Boise State on his resume, added five newcomers who will need to make an immediate impact.

One player who will need to make an immediate impact, especially with his shooting, is junior college transfer **Kevin Sweetwyne**. Sweetwyne, a 6-2 junior guard from Oakland, Calif., averaged 19.1 points and 4.2 assists last year while leading Chabot College to a 25-7 record. "Kevin will bring maturity to the program," Oliver said. "He has tremendous scoring ability, and we're excited about his perimeter shooting. Plus, he brings a physical presence to our perimeter."

The other junior college transfer is **Ammer Johnson**, a 6-4 junior from San Joaquin Delta College. He is expected to provide depth at shooting guard and small forward.

"I think they both have the ability to be impact players and play quality minutes," Oliver said. "They are two very capable winning-type of players."

Both will need to step up immediately because Idaho State loses its two top scorers in Tywan Meadows (20.9 ppg) and Johnny Mitchell (13.9 ppg). Meadows decided to transfer to Fort Hays State, and Mitchell, after being declared academically ineligible for the 1998-99 season, left school.

Sweetwyne is expected to shoulder a lot of the scoring burden, but Oliver also needs the three returning starters to each take their games to the next level.

Odell Stokes, a 6-7, 250-pound center, has some potential inside. The senior from Oklahoma averaged 6.7 points and 5.4 rebounds a year ago. The more telling statistics, however, come in his shooting percentage (.568) and minutes played per game (18.7). He would have averaged double figures if he'd played 30 minutes.

Playing beside him will be **Brandon Hearvey**, a 6-7 senior forward who played in 21 games and started 11 last year, averaging 4.4 points and 2.4 rebounds. He also shot the ball well (.532) but, like Stokes, it isn't because he's a good shooter. Both shot at about the 50 percent mark from the free-throw line.

The third returning starter is 6-5 junior **Cedric Robinson** (3.5 ppg, 3.4 rpg), who shot just 33 percent from the field and 51 percent from the free-throw line.

Other returnees include 6-1 sophomore guard **Brandon Vaughan** (4.3 ppg), who struggled to take his game from small-town Idaho basketball to the Division I level, and role players **Stephen Brown**, 6-0 junior, **Chadd Sukut**, a 6-0 junior, **Francis Junger**, a 6-8 senior and **Eric Skinner**, a 6-2 senior.

Of those last four, Brown had the highest scoring average (4.1), but it wasn't because of good shooting (just .338 percent). The others averaged around three points per game and also struggled to score.

It's a repeating theme with the Bengals, who shot just 42 percent from the field and scored less than the "Bitter Beer Face" guy. Those shooting woes also found their way to the free-throw line, where ISU shot 96 more freebies than its opponents, but made two less. "Our shooting is a big question mark," Oliver said. "Some of it will be solved with the recruiting, and I think maybe the style of play will assist the kids too."

One option to boost those shooting numbers will be to push the ball inside to Pocatello native **J.T. Nelson**, a 6-10 transfer from Loyola-Marymount. He's just a sophomore in eligibility, but that's a little misleading: He recently completed a two-year church mission.

Filling out the roster are two freshmen: **Brandon Anderson**, a 6-4 swingman from Salt Lake City, and **Andy Bybee**, a skinny, 6-foot guard from Pocatello.

"We have some pieces to the puzzle in place," Oliver said. "Now we're trying to fit in a new system and new players and try to come together as a unit by the time conference play comes around. I really think we're going to play nine or 10 or 11 players."

That takes care of what ISU will look like on the court. Oliver is also trying to building the surrounding atmosphere. He's worked hard at advertising his team and program, but admits that it is going to take time.

"I'm sure the fans are going to take a wait-and-see type of approach," he said. "If they come to the game and like the intensity and performance then they will come back. We've got to establish that here our first year.

"You've got to have a strong home-court advantage if you are going to win in college basketball."

adidas Blue Ribbon Analysis

BACKCOURT	**D+**	**BENCH/DEPTH**	**D**
FRONTCOURT	**D**	**INTANGIBLES**	**D+**

It's going to be an uphill road for Oliver, but the initial reviews for the new coach are strong. Getting that kind of positive initial success from his team will be harder, as the Bengals simply don't have enough skill players to compete in the Big Sky. In addition, the Bengals will have to learn Oliver's system through a brutal early-season schedule (road games to Oregon State, Boise State, Wyoming and Colorado).

Sweetwyne will help and make an immediate impact, but it just a band-aid. It will take several years—and all of Oliver's energy—to return Idaho State to contender status.

(S.D.)

MONTANA

LOCATION .... **Missoula, MT**
CONFERENCE .... **Big Sky**
LAST SEASON .... **16-14 (.533)**
CONFERENCE RECORD .... **9-7 (5th)**
STARTERS LOST/RETURNING **2/3**
NICKNAME .... **Grizzlies**
COLORS .... **Copper, Silver & Gold**
HOMECOURT .... **Sentinel High School (3,000)**
COACH .... **Don Holst (Northern Arizona '75)**
RECORD AT SCHOOL .... **First Year**
CAREER RECORD .... **First Year**
ASSISTANTS .... **Larry Krystkowiak (Montana '97)**
Jim Sampson (Wartburg College '81)
Todd Schmautz (Montana Tech '92)
TEAM WINS (last 5 yrs.) **19-21-20-21-16**
RPI (last 5 yrs.) **139-63-114-121-145**
1997-98 FINISH ...... **Lost in conference quarterfinals.**

Usually when a team discusses its need to be good in transition, the basketball parlance is clear. It's talking fast breaks and hustling defense, outlet passes and running the lanes. Not so in Missoula.

The University of Montana Grizzlies have transition concerns which transcend what happens on the court.

This season they'll be playing their games in a high school gym—and that's when they're lucky enough to be playing in Missoula. They have a midseason stretch where they play one home game in more than seven weeks.

The inconvenience comes as the team waits for its new $8 million arena, which will open next year.

1998-99 MONTANA SCHEDULE

Nov.	19	Southern Utah
	23	Carroll College
	28	@Idaho
Dec.	2	@Saint Mary's
	5	San Jose State
	11-12	#KGVO/Coca-Cola Classic
	15	Evergreen State
	19	@Youngstown State
	27	@Illinois-Chicago
Jan.	2	@Montana State
	7	@Idaho State
	9	@Weber State
	13	Northern Arizona
	17	Northridge State
	21	@Portland State
	23	@Eastern Washington
	27	@Sacramento State
	30	Montana State
Feb.	4	Weber State
	7	Idaho State
	11	@Northridge State
	13	@Northern Arizona
	18	Sacramento State
	25	Portland State
	27	Eastern Washington
Mar.	2-3	##Big Sky Tournament

@ Road Games
# Butte, MT (Idaho, Saint Mary's and Youngstown State)
At homecourt of regular-season champion.

The team will also be playing under a head coach with an interim tag hanging around his neck. Don Holst was selected as the acting head coach in April, replacing Blaine Taylor, who left to become an assistant at Stanford.

Holst, a long-time assistant at Montana, admits his interim status might be a distraction. "But I've got to control what I can control," he said. "I can't worry if I have a job when the new arena is built, or even if I'm going to have a job at all."

The bigger trick will be to get the players to have the same attitude. If they can tune out the distractions, Montana could be contending for a conference championship. If they can't, well, those cold nights in Missoula are going to feel even colder at Sentinel High School.

"It's going to be the toughest year Grizzly basketball has ever experienced," Holst said. "It's going to be interesting."

Holst does have some good news to report, however, and almost all of it comes on the basketball court. Montana returns nine lettermen and three starters. To that Holst can add four talented junior college players and two redshirt freshmen who should have an impact. In fact the Grizzlies have so many players that Holst's first task—besides finding the home locker room—will be dividing up the playing time.

The competition begins at the point guard spot, where senior **Cory Reiser** will battle **Kyle "KK" Keyes** and **Shane Christensen** for the starting role.

Reiser (5.8 ppg) is actually a shooting guard forced to play the point because he's only 6-foot, 167 pounds. The senior started 11 games last year.

Keyes is a more true point guard. The 6-2 junior can score, averaging 23.4 points at Bellevue Community College last year, but Holst said he has the skills to be the ball distributor the team needs. He should: Keyes is a former high school quarterback.

The best defender of the three is 6-1 redshirt freshman Christensen, a skinny player from Las Vegas who looks more like a cross-country runner than a Division I point guard. He plays really hard though, and Holst loves his attitude.

Joining the three-headed point guard in the backcourt will be **Mike Warhank** and **Eric Bowie**. Warhank (8.7 ppg), a 6-3 junior, came on at the end of last season, scoring in double figures seven of his last nine games. He's a great three-point shooter, making nine in one game (against Eastern Washington) and hitting .495 percent for the season. He needs to be shooting well to get time, however, as he's a liability defensively.

"He isn't the greatest athlete so he has to skew his defense so they can't penetrate on him," Holst said. "He has to give up a lot of ground."

Bowie (5.4 ppg), a 6-2 senior, started seven games last year. He's a better defensive option, and can score when he needs to, but he doesn't provide the instant offense like Warhank.

Starting at small forward will be 6-5 senior swingman **Mat Seidensticker** (7.0 ppg). Holst expects "Stick" to emerge as a scoring threat this season. He's the team's best perimeter defender and plays hard. In fact the biggest hurdle (an apt verb: he was a hurdler in high school) he must jump is his own confidence.

Backing "Stick" up is incoming junior-college transfers **Jason Collins**, who is known more for his penetrating skills than for his shooting, and **Ryan Slider**, a former high-school point guard who has a 7-foot wingspan on a 6-5 frame. Collins, a 6-5 junior, averaged 15.8 ppg at North Dakota State College.

The big key to the season—at least as far as the on-the-court stuff goes—comes inside with center **Bob Olson** (9.4 ppg, 5.8 rpg). The 6-10 senior has a nice touch and has added considerable weight, but he's never quite become a dominant player in the center-thin Big Sky. "It's a team game and we're going to share the scoring, but we really need him to play well," Holst said. "He's a big old kid you're going to have to guard because he'll score if you don't guard him. I'd like him to be a real force inside so that we have a lot of perimeter players to go inside-out too."

Jared Buckmaster (7.2 ppg), a 6-7 sophomore, is the team's power forward. He started 17 games last season as a freshman and has a nice shooting touch. He only weighs 215 pounds, however, so his toughness and durability is a question.

The darkhorse on the team is **Matt Williams**, a 6-7 junior forward who averaged 25 points and 12 rebounds for Columbia Junior College in California. "He's one of those guys where you ask, "How does he score?' Well, he hustles, he runs the floor and he's clever," the coach said. "Is he a great shooter? No. Is he a great hopper? No. He just has a nose for the ball.

"He's one of those guys that could be an all-league player this year or just a role player. It's hard to tell. He's very intriguing."

Rounding out the play on the inside is 6-7 freshman power forward **Travis Greenwalt**, who can bench 300 pounds but probably won't see too much time; backup center **Dominique Davis** (1.9 ppg, 2.1 rpg), a 6-10 junior; and 6-7, 265-pound junior power forward **Nate Sil**, a football player who came on to help out last year but won't see much time this season.

Incoming freshman Mike Card is expected to redshirt.

adidas Blue Ribbon Analysis

BACKCOURT	**C-**	**BENCH/DEPTH**	**C+**
FRONTCOURT	**D+**	**INTANGIBLES**	**D**

Holst's timing could've been better. First, there's the season-long road trip. Second, the usually weak league is looking strong from top to bottom.

Those distractions tend to dim Montana's on-the-court abilities. Even so, you get the feeling that the Grizzlies might be able to surprise teams this year. They have excellent senior leadership, a lot of depth, and an "us against the world" mentality. If they can survive December and January, the Grizzlies will have six of their final eight conference games in Missoula.

That stretch might decide Holst's future. "I think our leadership is really solid," Holst said. "We've got a lot of depth and I think that's a key. It'll be hard to find minutes for everyone, but that's a good problem to have because everyone should be playing hard."

That's a good thing, because the Grizzlies will need all the help they can get.

(S.D.)

adidas Blue Ribbon Analysis

GRADING SYSTEM

A+	equal to very best in country—Final Four-caliber unit
A	among the best in the land—worthy of deep NCAA run
B+	talented, versatile and experienced—NCAA-NIT ability
B	solid and productive winners—league and post-season contenders
C+	average to above-average—may contend in a weaker league
C	average to mediocre—second division in a strong league
D+	below average, inconsistent—second division in a weaker league
D	well below average—losing season virtually certain
F	non-Division I ability—an underdog every night

MONTANA STATE

LOCATION .... **Bozeman, MT**
CONFERENCE .... **Big Sky**
LAST SEASON .... **19-11 (.633)**
CONFERENCE RECORD .... **9-7 (4th)**
STARTERS LOST/RETURNING **2/3**
NICKNAME .... **Bobcats**
COLORS .... **Blue & Gold**
HOMECOURT .... **Worthington Arena (7,898)**
COACH .... **Mick Durham (Montana State '79)**
RECORD AT SCHOOL .... **113-116 (8 yrs.)**
CAREER RECORD .... **113-116 (8 yrs.)**
ASSISTANTS .... **Scott Carson (Mesa State '79)**
Jerry Olson (Minnesota-Morris '81)
TEAM WINS (last 5 yrs.) **16-21-21-16-19**
RPI (last 5 yrs.) **150-92-72-183-145**
1997-98 FINISH .... **Lost in conference semifinals.**

They were on top of their world—if not quite the Big Sky—when the collapse occurred.

First a horrible shooting slump caused the Bobcats to lose their last six games of the regular season, the longest losing streak at Montana State since 1988-89.

The ship was righted for one half, as the Bobcats rallied from a 10-point deficit to beat Montana in the quarterfinals of the league tournament. Then they collapsed again en route to a disappointing 77-50 loss to eventual champion Northern Arizona.

It was a disappointing way to end a season filled with so much promise, but don't shed too many tears for the Bobcats: They are poised for bigger and better things this year. And motivation won't be a problem, not with the taste of last year's failures still in their mouths. Coach Mick Durham sounds excited about this year's team—and he should be. The Bobcats return the league's best big man, one of its top all-around guards and several young players who are expected to make an immediate impact.

The team will revolve again around center **Nate Holmstadt**, a first-team all-Big Sky center last year after starting all 30 games and putting up a 16.9-point scoring average. He connected on 60 percent of his field goals, is already in the school's top 10 for rebounds and was the one player whose shooting didn't collapse last February.

Holmstadt scored 20 points 11 times last year, but Durham says he expects even more from the 6-8, 255-pound senior. "Nate has been one of the best players in the league in the last two years," Durham said, "but he needs to take that next step toward being a dominant player."

Luke Arthur is the team's frontcourt star of the future, but this season he will learn behind Holmstadt. He's a 6-11, 260-pound freshman who broke both thumbs last season as a redshirt. He's reported to be strong as a post player and a perimeter scorer.

The Bobcats return another all-league type player in **Danny Sprinkle** (13.5 ppg), whose numbers dropped off a bit last year but still has 1,000 points to his credit. The 6-2 senior guard's name is, uh, sprinkled throughout the school record book already. Unfortunately his normally reliable shooting stroke failed him at times last year, as he went from being a 48-percent three-point shooter to one who connects on just 35 percent.

That's by no means bad, but it's not what fans have expected out of Sprinkle. He also had a few games from the field which could only be described as awful, shooting 2 for 10 and 1 for 12 on back-to-back nights in February.

Backing up Sprinkle will be **Jamie Jordahl**. The sophomore didn't play in 9 of the last 10 games last year, but has good range on his jumpshot. He'll be pushed by **Justin Brown**, an athletic freshman who has good size at 6-4 and the potential to become the slasher the team needs.

Sprinkle's backcourt mate also returns in point guard **Jamie Hooper** (5.1 ppg). The 6-1 sophomore didn't score much last year, but he runs the offense well and had a great assist-to-turnover ratio (129-61). He should score more often this season as he becomes more comfortable with Division I basketball.

Jeff Riggs and **Shane Gamradt** will compete for time behind Hooper. Riggs, a 5-10 junior, redshirted last season after transferring from Oregon State.

Gamradt is an inch shorter than Riggs at 5-9. He's a freshman, however, so he has time to grow into the position.

Mike Henry (5.8 ppg) should assume the starting small-forward spot. The 6-5 senior is an athletic option who is probably the team's best defender. He's a liability at the end of the game, however, making just half of his free-throws.

"He is intriguing," Durham said. "He redshirted, then basically missed two years with a knee injury. He is a steady person that brings us some energy and athleticism."

Henry will be backed up by **Germaine Chase**, a 6-7 junior college transfer who has nice skills but needs to pick up some strength.

Sophomore **John Lazosky** (2.4 ppg in 1996-97) will play beside Henry as the starting power forward. He has the frame at 6-7, 230 pounds to be a solid asset and spent last year's redshirt season working on his jumpshot and defense. He needed help in those areas.

If Lazosky falters, 6-8 junior-college transfer **Rufus Nicholson** will get a good shot at replacing him. He was one of six players at Porterville (Calif.) Junior College who signed Division I scholarships, averaging 10 points and six rebounds.

Pete Conway, a 6-3 freshman guard, and **Aaron Rich**, a 6-6 freshman forward, are expected to redshirt. The team's third freshman signee, 6-10 center **Kyle Stirmlinger**, might play right away.

adidas Blue Ribbon Analysis

BACKCOURT	**B-**	**BENCH/DEPTH**	**C**
FRONTCOURT	**B**	**INTANGIBLES**	**C**

Give Durham his due: The Bobcat program is at the point where it is competitive year in and year out.

But the loyal fans in Bozeman are beginning to expect more: They want to win the darn thing. It could happen this year if Sprinkle regains his consistency (hard to believe he won't) and his teammates adjust to their new roles. That's a whopper of an "if", however, as up to 10 new faces could be on the floor this winter. Still, Durham does have the single-biggest weapon in the Big Sky Conference in Holmstadt. He should be able to carry the Bobcats through a good portion of their learning curve and any lingering shooting problems.

Then, once again, Montana State should be in business come February.

(S.D.)

1998-99 MONTANA STATE SCHEDULE

Nov.	20	Concordia
	27	*Wyoming
Dec.	1	@San Francisco
	5	Carroll College
	8	San Francisco
	10	@Fullerton State
	12	@San Diego
	22	@Minnesota
	28-29	#Bobcat Holiday Classic
Jan.	2	Montana
	7	@Weber State
	9	@Idaho State
	14	Northridge State
	16	Northern Arizona
	21	@Eastern Washington
	23	@Portland State
	25	@Sacramento State
	30	@Montana
Feb.	4	Sacramento State
	6	Idaho State
	11	@Northern Arizona
	13	@Northridge State
	20	Weber State
	25	Eastern Washington
	27	Portland State
Mar.	4-6	##Big Sky Tournament

@ Road Games
* First Interstate Bank Border War, Billings, MT
# Bozeman, MT (vs. Canisius, first round; also Boston University and Colorado)
At homecourt of regular-season champion.

NORTHERN ARIZONA

LOCATION .... **Flagstaff, AZ**
CONFERENCE .... **Big Sky**
LAST SEASON .... **21-8 (.724)**
CONFERENCE RECORD .... **13-3 (1st)**
STARTERS LOST/RETURNING **1/4**
NICKNAME .... **Lumberjacks**
COLORS .... **Blue & Gold**
HOMECOURT .... **J.L. Walkup Skydome (7,000)**
COACH .... **Ben Howland (Weber State '80)**
RECORD AT SCHOOL .... **58-51 (4 yrs.)**
CAREER RECORD .... **58-51 (4 yrs.)**
ASSISTANTS .... **Mike Adras (UC Santa Barbara '83)**
Jamie Dixon (Texas Christian '87)
Pat Sandie (San Francisco State '86)
TEAM WINS (last 5 yrs.) **13-8-6-21-21**
RPI (last 5 yrs.) **182-224-293-107-126**
1997-98 FINISH .... **Lost in NCAA first round.**

They captured the hearts of a town 800 miles away from their home. They made millions of basketball fans across the country sit up straight in excitement. They came in as a 15th-seed, took a six-point lead with 10 minutes to play against vaunted Cincinnati, sat on the verge of history. . . And then it all became history.

That's what is facing the Northern Arizona Lumberjacks after their dramatic run in the first round of the NCAA Tournament last March. They lost in a thriller when Cincinnati's D'Juan Baker hit a three-pointer with four seconds to play to silence a Boise, Idaho, crowd and send the Lumberjacks home as dejected—but proud—first-round losers. This time NAU's goal is clear. The Lumberjacks don't just want to win the Big Sky Conference, as they have the last two years. They don't want to just play in the postseason.

They want to dance for a while.

The prognosis is bright. NAU returns four starters, its renowned chemistry and much of its great shooting from last year's 21-win team. The Jacks have also won 22 of their last 23 games at home. Even so, head coach Ben Howland is trying to downplay expectations for what should be one of the best teams in school history.

"We won the Big Sky championship two years ago and it was a lot tougher the second time," he said. "Now we think it's going to be even tougher next year to three-peat."

The rest of the conference seems to think the race is

1998-99 NORTHERN ARIZONA SCHEDULE

Nov.	14	@Florida International
	17	@Arizona State
	21	Florida International
	24	Stephen F. Austin
	28	St. Martin's
Dec.	3	@San Diego
	5	@California-Irvine
	12	Colorado College
	18-19	#Nike Festival
	29	Elon
Jan.	2	Northridge State
	4	Sacramento State
	7	Eastern Washington
	9	Portland State
	13	@Montana
	16	@Montana State
	21	Idaho State
	23	Weber State
	30	@Idaho State
Feb.	6	@Northridge State
	11	Montana State
	13	Montana
	18	@Portland State
	20	@Eastern Washington
	25	@Sacramento State
	27	@Weber State
Mar.	4-6	##Big Sky Tournament

@ Road Games
# Honolulu, HI (vs. St. Bonaventure, first round; also Eastern Illinois and Hawaii)
At homecourt of regular-season champion.

NAU's to lose. "NAU is the class of the league by far," Eastern Washington coach Steve Aggers said. "I don't even think anyone can challenge them."

Northern Arizona was the nation's best three-point shooting team for the second-straight year last season, and it could easily make it three this year. **Kawika Akina**, **Billy Hix**, **Rod Hutchings**, **Ross Land**, **Patrick McGrath**, and **Michael McNair** have all shown that they can hit 40-percent of their three-point shots.

Akina (6.7 ppg, 46 percent three-point percentage) took over the starting point guard spot as soon as he became eligible. The 5-10 senior transferred from Hawaii. He had seven steals and five assists against Cincinnati—and also scored on a wild, one-handed, over-the-head shot which earned SportsCenter highlights.

"He plays big in big games," Howland said. "He's going to shoot more this year and he's already an outstanding defender. He's a big-time competitor."

Backing him up is Hutchings (6.3 ppg), a 5-7 junior who managed 89 assists last year while giving up just 38 turnovers.

Moving from shooting guard to small forward is the capable Land (10.7 ppg), a 6-5 junior who has been a starter ever since he first stepped into Flagstaff's dome as a freshman.

Land needs to work on his rebounding and post defense, but he's a great passer, solid defender and—of course—is in shooting range the moment he steps off the bench.

Rounding out the outside is freshman **Matthew Gebhardt** and **Michael McNair** (9.2 ppg), a 6-3 senior who has the skills but is still waiting for a breakout season. McNair needs to become more consistent, but that should happen now that a few distractions are behind him.

Gebhardt was a first-team all-state pick in football and basketball at Loveland (Colo.) HS, but what has Howland salivating is his 6-4 frame and beautiful shooting stroke.

The inside will be taken care of by 6-9 senior **Casey Frank** (10.7 ppg, 6.1 rpg), a first-team all-conference pick last year. His father Dennis played for the NFL's Philadelphia Eagles, so it's not surprising that Frank has the size to bang around in the Big Sky's soft insides. He'll be joined by Hix (6.6 ppg, 4.7 rpg), a 6-7 junior and the team's most physical player.

"He's our best screener, our best defender, our best guy at blocking out," Howland said of Hix. "He does all the little things you need to win. He's the glue that holds us together."

In case that isn't enough, NAU boosters can expect a bigger year from 7-foot junior **Dan McClintock** (9.6 ppg, 3.1 rpg), who has been dominating at times. The 255-pounder is athletic, but needs to work on his defense and rebounding.

Providing depth is 6-6 senior McGrath (3.3 ppg), who worked hard over the summer and increased his vertical leap from 29 to 34 inches. There is also **Andrew Wolthers** (1.6 ppg), a 6-8 junior who has been voted the team's most inspirational player the last two years. Howland said Wolthers had the best offseason of any player on the roster.

Also expected to eventually make an impact are freshmen **Casey Grundman** (6-10, 210 pounds) of Saint Mary's HS in Phoenix, Ariz. and **Joel Rieck** (6-6, 180 pounds) of Columbine HS in Littleton, Colo. Both need to add some weight, but they also fit in well with NAU's perimeter-based system.

adidas Blue Ribbon Analysis

BACKCOURT .... **B** **BENCH/DEPTH** .... **B+**
FRONTCOURT .... **B-** **INTANGIBLES** .... **B+**

The Lumberjacks have more chemistry than your average Fourth of July fireworks display, and that makes for a long night for most opponents. They rarely take bad shots or sell out on defense, can withstand an off night from anyone on the team and do better business from long distance than MCI and Ma Bell combined.

Howland won't let any of that change this year. True, the Lumberjacks are losing a good one in Big Sky MVP Andrew Mavis (14.3 ppg, 4.2 rpg), the 6-6 senior who shot .472 percent from three-point range a year ago, but they have enough coming back to compensate.

They also have a balanced schedule which features an opening four-game conference home stand. That's the good news. The bad: Six of NAU's last eight games—including the final four—are on the road. If the Lumberjacks improve their rebounding and defense just a little they should be shooting for another upset in March.

(S.D.)

NORTHRIDGE STATE

LOCATION .... **Northridge, CA**
CONFERENCE .... **Big Sky**
LAST SEASON .... **12-16 (.429)**
CONFERENCE RECORD .... **7-9 (6th)**
STARTERS LOST/RETURNING **3/2**
NICKNAME .... **Matadors**
COLORS .... **Red, White & Black**
HOMECOURT .... **The Matadome (1,600)**
COACH .... **Bobby Braswell (Northridge '84)**
RECORD AT SCHOOL .... **26-31 (2 yrs.)**
CAREER RECORD .... **26-31 (2 yrs.)**
ASSISTANTS .... **Michael Johnson (Purdue '91)**
Andre Chavalier (Northridge '91)
Eric Brown (Northridge '98)
TEAM WINS (last 5 yrs.) **8-8-7-14-12**
RPI (last 5 yrs.) **261-278-270-194-242**
1997-98 FINISH .... **Lost in conference semifinal.**

The Matadors know they have talent, quickness and skill. They always have.

And that's been the problem.

So this season, as the Matadors attempt to rebound from another wacky year, coach Bobby Braswell knows that rebuilding his team's attitude is just as important—if not more important—then finding three new starters to rebuild his roster.

"We're going to be a very athletic team in the Big Sky Conference," Braswell said. "We're young, but we'll hustle and we have talent. "We just need to find some chemistry." Chemistry appears to be all that separates Northridge from the conference favorites.

Last season Northridge had the reputation of being the most athletic team in the league, but late-season injuries and season-long attitude problems cost the Matadors dearly. The Matadors think they have those problems taken care of, however, and are aiming for a top-three finish in the conference.

They finally have a legitimate point guard, still might be the most athletic team in the conference, and boast a full-court defense which doesn't just press—it also sorts, folds and dry-cleans too.

And while it's true that the Matadors lose eight players with a combined 82 starts between them, they believe they have recruited enough talent to make up for the departing personnel.

Leading the way will be 6-1 redhirt freshman **Markus Carr**, a true point guard who will feel a lot of pressure this season because he'll probably have to start right away.

Carr is very flashy, thinks pass first, and was projected as the starter last year. Then he tore the ACL in his left knee, finishing his season before it had even begun.

Jason Crowe will battle Carr for the starting spot. The 6-4 junior transfer from American University is actually a better shooter (and three inches taller) than Carr, but may not have quite the same flash and instinct.

Between the two, Northridge should have a point guard it can trust. That's a big step up from last year.

Filling out the backcourt is 6-3 junior **Greg Minor**, 6-1 sophomore **Carl Holmes** and 6-3 senior **Derrick Higgins**. Minor was forced to play point guard last season—and he was never comfortable with it. He's a little slow on defense, but his strong outside shooting is a plus: He averaged 12.2 points while shooting 41 percent from three-point range.

Holmes (11.0 ppg) was the Big Sky Freshman of the Year last season. He can swing over to play small forward—where he gets pushed around a bit—but makes up for any lack of size with his intensity and smarts. He also lives with the coach, who just happens to be his uncle.

Higgins is the lone senior on the team. It's actually the second time he is beginning his senior season, but he hopes to finish this one: Last year he suffered a broken foot in his fifth game that required season-ending surgery. Luckily for Higgins he hadn't played in so many games he couldn't redshirt. He averaged 11.6 points per game in 1996-97, when he also set the school's single-season steal record with 74. He isn't much of a shooter, but reads the passing lanes well and has a 38-inch vertical leap.

The frontcourt received a big boost when **Andre Larry** transferred from the University of Oregon, where he was recruited by Braswell. He didn't exactly earn a reputation of being a coachable player at Oregon, but he and Braswell seem to get along well and he has Pac-10 credentials. Although he stands 6-9, Larry prefers to face the basket and create his own shot. He has nice range and should immediately take over a lot of the scoring duties.

The other forward will probably be 6-6 sophomore **Jermar Welch**, a Prop 48 player who redshirted last season. He is the best leaper on the team and rebounds like a pro. He is working hard to improve his outside game, but it's still not exactly a strength. He'll be depended on for eight to 10 points per game.

The rest of the frontcourt duties will rotate between **Larry Beard, Brian Heinle, Jeffrey Parris, Dan Read** and **Hewitt Rolle**.

Heinle and Read are essentially the same player: skinny guys who get pushed around inside but are deadly from the perimeter. Heinle, a 6-9 sophomore, averaged 6.9 points and 4.8 rebounds last year as a freshman. He closed the season by hitting six of his last 15 three-pointers. Read is a 6-10, 220-pound freshman from Eugene, Ore., who played with Holmes in high school.

The other three players will add the bulk and toughness inside. Beard a 6-9 junior, transferred from Angelina College. He needs to work on his defense, but is very coachable. He is also a shot-blocker, averaging seven blocks per game in junior college.

Parris, a 6-5 junior, averaged 7.6 points last year, but those numbers don't reflect his true worth. Short on skill, but long on hustle and desire, he does the dirty work inside and plays solid defense. And finally there is Rolle, another hard-working, tough-playing power forward who gives the team some muscle inside. The junior has good size at 6-7, 230 pounds, and has transferred into the system from Lon Morris College. He chose Northridge over Louisiana Tech, Oregon State and the University of San Francisco.

adidas Blue Ribbon Analysis

BACKCOURT .... **C-** **BENCH/DEPTH** .... **D+**
FRONTCOURT .... **D+** **INTANGIBLES** .... **C-**

The Matadors lost a lot from last year, but in some cases it's almost a case of addition by subtraction.

Maybe that's why Braswell sounds so enthused about this year. He has a number of players he describes as "hard-working" and "coachable." He also has a lot of local talent which decided that playing near home is suddenly a very attractive choice.

But the question—as always—is how well and how fast all those newcomers will come together as a team. There is only one senior on the team and, with six of the first eight games on the road, Northridge might be a year away from truly making some noise.

(S.D.)

1998-99 NORTHRIDGE STATE SCHEDULE

Nov.	14	@Long Beach State
	17	@Tennessee
	22	@San Jose State
	28	San Diego
	30	Southern California College
Dec.	3-4	#Power Bar Invitational
	11-12	##Cougar Classic
	19	@UCLA
	22	James Madison
	29	Lewis & Clark
Jan.	2	@Northern Arizona
	4	Idaho State
	7	Portland State
	9	Eastern Washington
	14	@Montana State
	17	@Montana
	20	Sacramento State
	21	Weber State
	28	@Idaho State
Feb.	6	Northern Arizona
	11	Montana
	13	Montana State
	18	@Eastern Washington
	20	@Portland State
	25	@Weber State
	27	@Sacramento State
Mar.	4-6	###Big Sky Tournament

@ Road Games
\# Honolulu, HI (vs. Hawaii, first round; also Coppin State and Georgia State)
\## Provo, UT (vs. Southern Utah, first round; also Brigham Young and Louisiana Tech)
\### At homecourt of regular-season champion.

PORTLAND STATE

LOCATION .... Portland, OR
CONFERENCE .... Big Sky
LAST SEASON .... 15-12 (.555)
CONFERENCE RECORD 10-6 (3rd)
STARTERS LOST/RETURNING 4/1
NICKNAME .... Vikings
COLORS .... Green & White
HOMECOURT .... The Rose Garden (21,538)
Memorial Coliseum (12,888)
Stott Center (1,775)
COACH .... Joel Sobotka (Arizona State '93)
RECORD AT SCHOOL .... First year
CAREER RECORD .... First year
ASSISTANTS .... Jason Tyrus (Washington '94)
Mark Folsom (Seattle-Pacific '95)
TEAM WINS (last 5 yrs.) N/A-N/A-N/A-9-15
RPI (last 5 yrs.) .... N/A
1997-98 FINISH .... Ineligible for postseason.

It's been an impressive run by Portland State, which restarted its basketball program just three years ago after a 15-year hiatus. In their first year the Vikings won nine games, including six in the Big Sky Conference. Last year those numbers improved to 15 and 10, good for third in the league.

Now Portland State expects to finish its climb. The Vikings return nine players, including two all-league first-team players, and expect to take advantage of the NCAA's decision to allow them to play in the postseason.

"We have a tremendous amount of pride to get to this point," new coach Joel Sobotka said. "Nobody thought we'd get this high this early in our rebuilding process. We have a whole lot of new expectations now, but I'd rather get picked near the top than near the bottom."

Sobotka was hired late—not until mid-September—and he can thank new Chicago Bulls coach Tim Floyd for his career break. When Floyd, the former Iowa State coach, bolted for the Chicago Bulls last spring, Utah State coach Larry Eustachy was hired to replace him. Utah State, in turn, hired Stew Morrill away from Colorado State. That meant Colorado State needed a coach, so the call went out to McKay.

After school officials talked briefly with other candidates—former Portland Trailblazers' coach Rick Adelman was one of them—they finally settled on Sobotka, McKay's former assistant.

The Vikings aren't going to sneak up on anyone this year: Not with returning all-league first-teamers like **Jason Hartman** and **Brian Towne**. Hartman is the conference's leading returning scorer, averaging 19.1 points in his first shots and 82 percent from the line, but can also post up or drive, too.

That versatility gives defenders a lot of match-up problems. "This year he's going to be asked to do more inside," Sobotka said. "What makes him a good scorer is that he can score in so many different ways."

Hartman, a 6-7 senior, has been working on his pull-up jumper. If he can get to the point where he can dribble once or twice and then knock down a jump shot, he'll have virtually every weapon in his arsenal.

If Hartman is getting double-covered—or having one of his few off-nights—then the Vikings can rotate the ball around to Towne, the best outside shooter in a league known for its perimeter game. The 6-3 senior made 43 percent of his three-point shots last year, the highlight coming when he hit a conference-record 12 in one game in a 40-point outburst against Sacramento State in February.

That game came just two days after Towne scored 38 points against Idaho State. He finished with a 15.6 ppg scoring average, but needs to work on being able to find a shot off the dribble.

The Vikings also return two other starters: Small forward **Derek Nesland** and point guard **Wayne Rhymes**.

Nesland, a 6-6 junior, is a former point guard who is expected to be the team's No. 3 scoring threat. Last year he averaged 6.6 points and 3.5 assists. "We need some increased scoring and we need him to be more of a factor defensively," Sobotka said.

Rhymes, a 6-3 sophomore, scored 16 points in the Vikings' landmark win over Oregon, but his game dropped off from that point. He has played some point guard, but has been moved to shooting guard. It's a better fit for him—Rhymes is more of a shooter than a passer.

The Vikings have five other players who return with playing experience. The one who should have the biggest impact is **Hasan Arthairee**, who at 6-5 is the team's best low-post scorer. At 235 pounds, he's built more like a tight end than a basketball player, but the Vikings are hoping the senior can play extended minutes this year. Last year he averaged 4.1 points and 3.0 rebounds.

"We're counting on him a lot this year," Sobotka said. "He says he's ready to accept his new role, and we're hoping that he is. This year he really has to take a huge leadership role in the post."

Another post player who should find more minutes is **Taplar Mvogo**, a 6-7 senior who almost transferred in the spring because of a lack of playing time. He only averaged 2.5 points last year, but Sobotka has described him as "a huge key for us this year."

Senior **Jamie Snook** will play behind Rhymes and Towne, but the 5-11 guard will get his minutes at shooting guard. He fills the Steve Kerr role on the team: He's a three-point specialist who will get five points in 10 minutes one night, then won't play the next. Known for being the toughest and most competitive member of the team, Snook hit 41 percent of his three-point shots last year en route to 4.4 points per game.

Ivan Garner will back up the point-guard spot. The 6-2 junior is the team's best perimeter defender. He averaged 2.4 points last year.

Sandy Bisaro, a 6-9 sophomore, averaged 1.8 points last year and needs to add some strength. He might play some mop-up duty in the post.

The one newcomer of note is junior-college transfer **Reggie Ball**, who should take over the point-guard role. The 6-1 guard averaged 8.2 assists last year at Highline (Wash.) Community College.

"He's a point guard in every sense of the word," Sobotka said. "Physically he can do everything you need him to do. Mentally he loves to be the guy who sets the table, so we expect him to be the guy to lead us offensively."

Freshmen **Ned James**, a 6-7 forward, and **Anthony Lackey**, a 6-5 swingman, are both expected to play this year. Lackey, in particular, has the potential to be a star: He already has an upperclassman's build.

adidas Blue Ribbon Analysis

BACKCOURT .... B- BENCH/DEPTH .... C-
FRONTCOURT .... C- INTANGIBLES .... B-

Last year the Vikings were one of the best teams in the Big Sky Conference—but it didn't matter because they were ineligible for postseason play. This year Portland State can play in the league tournament, and the Vikings have to be considered as one of the three teams with a legitimate shot of winning it (along with Northern Arizona and Montana State).

They key is two-fold: Rebounding and defense. Portland State can score with anyone in the conference, but even Sobotka admits that the Vikings defense "has to catch up with the offense." If that happens, everything might be turning up roses in Portland.

(S.D.)

adidas Blue Ribbon Analysis
GRADING SYSTEM

- A+ equal to very best in country—Final Four-caliber unit
- A among the best in the land—worthy of deep NCAA run
- B+ talented, versatile and experienced—NCAA-NIT ability
- B solid and productive winners—league and post-season contenders
- C+ average to above-average—may contend in a weaker league
- C average to mediocre—second division in a strong league
- D+ below average, inconsistent—second division in a weaker league
- D well below average—losing season virtually certain
- F non-Division I ability—an underdog every night

SACRAMENTO STATE

LOCATION .... Sacramento, CA
CONFERENCE .... Big Sky
LAST SEASON .... 1-25 (.038)
CONFERENCE RECORD 0-16 (9th)
STARTERS LOST/RETURNING 3/2
NICKNAME .... Hornets
COLORS .... Green & Gold
HOMECOURT .... Memorial Auditorium (2,803)
COACH .... Tom Abatemarco (Dowling College '73)
RECORD AT SCHOOL .... 1-25 (1 yr.)
CAREER RECORD .... 56-82 (5 yrs.)
ASSISTANTS .... Gregg Gotlieb (UCLA '95)
Preston Ivory (Texas-San Antonio '93)
TEAM WINS (last 5 yrs.) 1-6-7-3-1
RPI (last 5 yrs.) 294-294-281-283-305
1997-98 FINISH .... Did not qualify for conference tournament.

Tom Abatemarco refuses to call Sacramento State a rebuilding project. To rebuild, he said, you must have had something built at one time in the past. Sacramento State has yet to even lay a foundation of competitiveness.

"We're building from scratch," the second-year coach said. "I knew coming in that it was going to be this way. I'm looking forward to this season, but I looked forward to last season too. It's better to have a sorry team than no team."

Sorry is about the kindest description for the Hornets' play last year. They won one game, didn't win a Big Sky Conference game and were ranked 305th—out of 306 Division I teams—in the RPI. They lost in virtually every way imaginable. They lost one game in double overtime, two more with one overtime period, 10 games by 20 or more points and every game on the road.

"We were terrible last year," Abatemarco said. "We're starting over. And we're going to be a lot better."

The keys will be better guard play, full seasons by 6-8 senior **Sean Houston** and 6-6 junior **Eric Jorissen** and a quick learning curve by the tremendous influx of talent Abatemarco has brought in.

Houston (14.4 ppg, 10.7 rpg) is among the best rebounders in the league. He only played 14 games last season because of an injury, but came on and led the Hornets in scoring four times in February. He is a monster on the glass, leading Sacramento State in rebounds in 11 of his 14 games, including 18-board nights against Idaho State and Eastern Washington.

Houston's glaring weakness comes at the free-throw line, where he shot a Dennis Rodman-like 45 percent. That needs to come up, because Sac State needs Houston to be a reliable presence if it is going to climb out of the basement.

Jorissen (5.8 ppg) missed seven games because of an injury, but he's a good outside shooter whom Abatemarco plans to use more of this year. He isn't afraid to shoot the ball.

Beyond those two, nearly every other player on the roster is a mystery.

"When I took the job last year we had two players on scholarship," Abatemarco said. "I had like eight or nine players, and a lot of them couldn't play. We needed to make a complete overhaul of the roster."

The overhaul began this year with the signing of three junior college players and six high school recruits. There's some quality in there too, as Abatemarco's class was ranked among the top 50 in the country by some recruiting analysts.

Among those who will be quickly thrown to the fire are guards **Rene Jacques** and **Nate Murase**, two freshman who played together at St. Joseph Notre Dame High in Oakland, Calif., last year. Jacques is 6-1. Murase is 6-foot. They led their high school team deep into the state tournament last year, and Abatemarco believes they can lead his team out of the Big Sky basement this year.

"They are two of the better guards in the country," he said. "Any time you get two high school guards like that you are happy. Now, sure, they're going to struggle this year. They'll be up and down. But anytime you sign players like that, you are eventually going to be really good."

Providing depth for the freshmen will be 6-2 sophomore **Ryan Coleman** (4.1 ppg, 2.9 rpg, 140 assists, 17 steals), who led the team in steals and assists last year, but might be on the bench this time around. He needs to get stronger

1998-99 SACRAMENTO STATE SCHEDULE

Nov.	19	Lamar
	21	Saint Mary's
	23	@Cal Poly
	28	Pacific
Dec.	1	@Fresno State
	5	Houston
	9	San Jose State
	19	@New Mexico
	22	@Northern Illinois
	28	@Minnesota
Jan.	2	Weber State
	4	@Northern Arizona
	14	@Eastern Washington
	17	@Portland State
	20	@Northridge State
	23	Idaho State
	25	Montana State
	27	Montana
Feb.	4	@Montana State
	6	@Weber State
	11	Portland State
	13	Eastern Washington
	18	@Montana
	20	@Idaho State
	25	Northern Arizona
	27	Cal State Northridge
Mar.	4-6	#Big Sky Tournament

@ Road Games
# At homecourt of regular-season champion.

and improve his shooting.

Jimmy Landry (2.9 ppg) is also back after last year's disaster. The 6-3 sophomore swingman averaged 13 minutes as a freshman. Also expected to contribute in the backcourt are 6-0 freshman **Marcus Malone** (Freemont High in Oakland, Calif.) and 6-2 junior transfer **Antoine Bailey** (Siskiyous JC, in Weed, Calif.). Malone, in particular, can shoot the ball.

David Swift, a 6-2 senior, is also on the roster. He didn't score in four minutes of play last year.

"I need good guard play to my system, and we didn't have that last year," Abatemarco said. "But I think we've rectified that a bit."

The frontcourt has a little bit more experience with Houston and Jorissen. Also joining the rotation will be newcomers **Anthony Flood** at 6-8, 230-pound junior from Sierra College in Rocklin, Calif., **Tom Wiek**, a 6-7 junior from Solano Community College in Suisun, Calif. and 6-6 freshman **Arinze Anouro** of Burton High in San Francisco.

Abatemarco also signed 6-8, 225-pound **Troy Selvey** of Hanford, Calif. He might be the only incoming freshman who won't see much playing time. The others will jump right into a schedule which features Saint Marys, Pacific, Houston, New Mexico, Minnesota and an improved Big Sky.

It won't be easy, but Abatemarco remains optimistic. "We want to be the most improved team in the country," he said. "That's our goal. By the end of the year we want to become a factor in our conference."

adidas Blue Ribbon Analysis

BACKCOURT	**D**	**BENCH/DEPTH**	**D-**
FRONTCOURT	**D**	**INTANGIBLES**	**D+**

Like the perennial tornado survivor that it is, Sacramento State is trying to climb out of the cellar yet again this year. It might actually happen this time.

Abatemarco is a great recruiter who has brought in some nice talent, but the Hornets will be relying on freshmen and new junior-college transfers every night. That won't be easy against an imposing non-conference schedule and a Big Sky schedule which puts the Hornets on the road for four of their first five league games. The plus side to that? Sac State gets a lot of home games later in the year. That's good, because by then the team will have garnered some experience and might be able to make a run at clinching a spot for the postseason tournament.

Even if the Hornets fail, though, it's almost guaranteed that this season will seem a lot shorter than last year's.

(S.D.)

WEBER STATE

LOCATION .... **Ogden, UT**
CONFERENCE .... **Big Sky**
LAST SEASON .... **14-13 (.519)**
CONFERENCE RECORD .... **12-4 (2nd)**
STARTERS LOST/RETURNING **2/3**
NICKNAME .... **Wildcats**
COLORS .... **Purple & White**
HOMECOURT .... **Dee Events Center (12,000)**
COACH .... **Ron Abegglen (Brigham Young '62)**
RECORD AT SCHOOL .... **127-75 (7 yrs.)**
CAREER RECORD .... **236-120 (12 yrs.)**
ASSISTANTS .... **Guy Beach (Weber State '88)**
Joe Cravens (Texas-Arlington '77)
Kris Hill (DePaul '94)
TEAM WINS (last 5 yrs.) **20-21-20-15-14**
RPI (last 5 yrs.) **61-50-96-149-152**
1997-98 FINISH .... **Lost in conference semifinal.**

Ron Abegglen's final season as head coach promises to be one of his most intriguing. It has the potential to be one of his most successful, too. The seventh-year coach has brought in one of the most-heralded recruiting classes in Weber State history. He added seven new players—including two second-team junior-college All-Americans—to give the team some much-needed punch.

The big names are **Harold Arceneaux**, a 6-6 junior forward, and **Eddie Gill**, a 6-1 junior point guard. Both were among the best at their position in junior college last year. Both boast quickness and a take-charge mentality. And both will join with 6-3 senior **Damien Baskerville** to give Weber State what should be the best trio in the Big Sky.

"We've had some solid teams the last couple of seasons, but we've lacked some real speed and quickness, especially in the backcourt," Abegglen said. "Our main emphasis in recruiting was to improve in that area and I believe we have found those players."

Any talk of quick recruits usually centers around Gill, the MVP of the Scenic West Conference. He averaged 16.4 points and 6.4 assists last year and is reputed to have all the skills—shooting, passing, defending, leading—that a point guard needs. Gill was rated the 95th-best junior college sophomore in JC recruiting analyst Phil Henzel's Top 300 list.

Gill will combine with Big Sky first-teamer Baskerville (15.2 ppg) to give Weber State a strong backcourt. Baskerville is the team's top defender and led the team in scoring, assists (3.1) and steals (2.0) last year. He goes to the basket well, but has to learn to play more consistently.

"Damien is as good as he wants to be," Abegglen said. "With the new players we've signed to come in and play, there won't be as much pressure on him this season and I would expect him to play more at ease and take his game up a notch or two."

Arceneaux is expected to move into the starting small forward position. He averaged 17.6 points and 6.0 rebounds last year at Midland Junior College in Texas, which went 26-4. Arcenaux was ranked No. 37 in Henzel's list.

The starters in the post return from last year. Senior **Eric Ketcham** (6.2 ppg, 4.6 rpg) is more of a perimeter player, even with his height (6-9). He adds versatility to the lineup and is the only player to start all 27 games last year.

The cerebral **Andy Jensen** (10.2 ppg, 7.2 rpg), a 6-7 senior, is more suited to be a power forward instead of a center, but he can fill both positions. The left-hander is strong but not quick. He helped the Wildcats turn around their season after a disastrous 2-9 start. "He's very strong and physical underneath and intelligent with his moves," Abegglen said.

The player who might upset the mix—pushing Jensen to power forward and Ketcham into a sixth-man role—is 6-10 junior college transfer **Darius Beard.** The school spent the preseason worrying about his grades, but if he becomes eligible he'll add a nice high-post and center option. Beard averaged 13.0 ppg and 6.8 rpg at Utah Valley State.

Those are the probable starters.

The bench consists of **Luke Condill**, **Joey Haws**, **Noel Jackson**, **Marc Lawson**, **Shawn Moore** and four high school signees.

The one to watch is Moore, a 6-4 junior swingman, the fourth junior college transfer Weber State signed. He might

1998-99 WEBER STATE SCHEDULE

Nov.	13	@Southern Utah
	19	Brigham Young
	24	@UNLV
Dec.	1	Boise State
	4-5	#Northwestern Mutual Classic
	9	@Utah
	12	Mesa State
	15	Seattle
	19	*Utah State
	21-23	##Pearl Harbor Classic
Jan.	2	@Sacramento State
	4	@Portland State
	7	Montana State
	9	Montana
	14	Idaho State
	16	@Eastern Washington
	21	@Northridge State
	23	@Northern Arizona
	27	Eastern Washington
	28	Portland State
Feb.	4	@Montana
	6	Sacramento State
	17	@Idaho State
	20	@Montana State
	25	Northridge State
	27	Northern Arizona
Mar.	4-6	###Big Sky Tournament

@ Road Games
* Delta Center, Salt Lake City, UT
# San Francisco, CA (vs. Rice, first round; also Holy Cross and South Florida)
Laie, HI (vs. Alabama, first round; also BYU-Hawaii, Michigan State, Pepperdine, Texas Tech, Tulsa and Oregon State)
At homecourt of regular-season champion.

be the steal of the group, averaging 16.2 points for Ricks Junior College in Idaho. He has a 37-inch vertical leap. Moore turned up at No. 59 on Henzel's Top 300 list.

Lawson (5.0 ppg, 1.3 rpg), a 6-2 senior, came out of nowhere to earn a scholarship. The former walkon is a pressure player and can back up both guard positions. Condill (2.3 ppg), a 5-11 sophomore, proved himself in a 61-second span last year, hitting three three-pointers in that minute-plus against Northern Arizona. He can shoot and has a strong, stocky frame.

Jackson (5.1 ppg, 2.0 rpg 28 assists), a 6-0 senior, is the backup point guard. He's strong and a great defender, but couldn't make a basket in an empty gym. He made just one of 14 shots from beyond the three-point arc.

Haws (2.3 ppg), a 6-9 senior, will play six or seven minutes a game in the post.

Finally, there are the incoming freshmen. Guard **Jermaine Boyette**, 6-3, has nice quickness and averaged 23 points per game at Hammond High in Indiana last year. **Dan Del Vecchio**, a 6-7 forward from Guilford High School in Rockford, Ill., has a 40-inch vertical leap and is renowned for his ability to rebound. Swingman **Chris Woods**, 6-5, is known for his defensive ability, although he scored 15.8 points per game last year for East Central High in East Chicago, Indiana.

adidas Blue Ribbon Analysis

BACKCOURT	**B**	**BENCH/DEPTH**	**C**
FRONTCOURT	**C+**	**INTANGIBLES**	**C-**

The key to the season is obvious: Abegglen has to merge all the incoming talent with Baskerville and the rest of the squad. He's a good, experienced coach, so it's probably going to get done. The problem is that building all that chemistry might lead to another struggling start to the season. Last year Weber State opened at 2-9, then rallied down the stretch to make a big impact in conference play. This year the non-conference schedule includes Alabama, Utah, Brigham Young, UNLV, Utah State and Boise State. Possible tournament opponents include San Francisco, Michigan State, Texas Tech, Tulsa, Pepperdine and Oregon State.

That's a tough road for a team which will depend on players who were last playing the junior-college circuit, but Abegglen will make sure the Wildcats learn from any thumpings. By the time the conference season comes around, Weber State will be back.

(S.D.)

BIG SOUTH CONFERENCE

adidas BLUE RIBBON FORECAST
1. Radford
2. North Carolina-Asheville
3. Charleston Southern
4. Coastal Carolina
5. Liberty
6. Winthrop

ALL-CONFERENCE TEAM
G—Adam Larrick, SR, Charleston Southern
G—Leslie Ballard, SR, Radford
F—Marcus Stewart, SO, Coastal Carolina
F—Kevin Martin, SR, North Carolina-Asheville
C—Ryan Charles, JR, Radford

PLAYER OF THE YEAR
Kevin Martin, SR, North Carolina-Asheville

NEWCOMER OF THE YEAR
Peter Van Rij, FR, Charleston Southern

1998-99 CONFERENCE TOURNAMENT
Feb. 24-27, Asheville Civic Center, Asheville, N.C.

1997-98 CHAMPION
North Carolina-Asheville (regular season)
Radford (conference tournament)

1997-98 POSTSEASON PARTICIPANTS
Postseason Record: 0-1 (.000)
NCAA
Radford (1st round)

TOP BACKCOURTS
1. Radford
2. Charleston Southern
3. North Carolina-Asheville

TOP FRONTCOURTS
1. Radford
2. North Carolina-Asheville
3. Charleston Southern

ON THE WAY UP
Charleston Southern

ON THE WAY DOWN
Liberty

INSIDE THE NUMBERS
- 1997-98 conference RPI: 30 (of 30)
- Conference RPI (last 5 years): 26-22-28-23-30

DID YOU KNOW?
The Big South will add two members after this season when Elon (N.C.) College and High Point (N.C.) University officially join the conference in the fall of 1999...All six Big South teams will play Elon and High Point home and away this season, but the two newcomers aren't eligible for the conference championship...Maryland-Baltimore County left the Big South after last season...Radford has five players 6-10 or taller on its roster this season...Liberty has appeared in the Big South Tournament championship game three out of the last five years...All three new head coaches in the conference were assistants last season: Coastal Carolina's Pete Strickland at Dayton, Liberty's Mel Hankinson at West Virginia and Winthrop's Gregg Marshall at Marshall...Jeff Meyer, who will serve on Marshall's staff at Winthrop this season, was the head coach at Liberty for the last 16 years...No Big South team has ever made consecutive appearances in the NCAA Tournament...The top two teams in the final regular-season standings this season will receive byes into the semifinals of the Big South tournament.

(C.L.)

CHARLESTON SOUTHERN

LOCATION .... Charleston, S.C.
CONFERENCE .... Big South
LAST SEASON .... 5-22 (.185)
CONFERENCE RECORD 2-10 (7th)
STARTERS LOST/RETURNING 1/4
NICKNAME .... Buccaneers
COLORS .... Blue & Gold
HOMECOURT .... CSU Fieldhouse (1,000)
COACH .... Tom Conrad (Old Dominion '79)
RECORD AT SCHOOL .... 22-35 (2 yrs.)
CAREER RECORD .... 22-35 (2 yrs.)
ASSISTANTS .... Mark de Barros (St. Anselm '87)
Tony Bulford (Scranton '90)
TEAM WINS (last 5 yrs.) 9-19-15-17-5
RPI (last 5 yrs.) 242-130-187-143-301
1997-98 FINISH .... Lost in conference first round.

The cry last year surrounding the Charleston Southern basketball program was "Wait until next year."

Well, next year is here, and Buccaneers coach Tom Conrad couldn't be more excited.

It was only two years ago that Conrad, in his first season at Charleston Southern, guided his club to 17 wins and the school's first-ever trip to the NCAA Tournament.

But a year ago, the Bucs crash-landed and struggled through a forgettable 5-22 season. Their final RPI told a more dismal story than their record—301 out of 306 Division I teams.

"As a coach, I learned 10 times as much last year as I did the year before," Conrad said. "What this team has to do is overcome the disappointment of last year and forget about it. We have to get better every week. That's what happened two years ago. We started out 2-5, but put on a run at the end of the year.

"This team needs to accept what happened last year and move on."

And while improving on last season's seventh-place finish in the Big South is certainly a priority, you get the feeling the Bucs are thinking in much bigger terms.

As in the Big Dance.

"A lot of these kids felt like they let everybody down by not getting back to the NCAAs last year," Conrad said. "We'd love to go back. It was a thrill. The kids that were there will never forget it. I'll never forget it. I know it's not going to be my last time.

"If these kids work together, I think we have the potential to get back."

Four of the five starters from last season's team return, along with three newcomers Conrad will count on right away.

Three of the returning starters averaged in double figures—6-3 senior guard **Adam Larrick** (15.4 ppg, 3.6 rpg, 97 assists, 41 steals), 6-3 senior guard **Vincent Mitchell** (12.4 ppg, 3.6 rpg, 69 assists, 29 steals) and 6-5 junior forward **Marlin Parker** (12.6 ppg, 4.9 rpg, 28 steals).

Larrick was forced into playing point guard most of last season, and might have to do so again this season. Conrad was hoping talented 6-1 freshman Greg Lomax of Washington, D.C., could allow Larrick to move to his natural position of shooting guard. But that won't be possible, because Lomax didn't qualify.

The problem last season was that Larrick probably tried to do too much, and he wore down. Conrad hopes that won't happen again this year, though he might not have a choice but to play Larrick a lot.

"We want Adam to average the same amount of points, but take less shots," Conrad said. "We're going to cut his minutes because we want him to be fresh at the end of the season when it matters most."

If Conrad can find the right combination of minutes, he thinks the Bucs can be outstanding at shooting guard. Mitchell is a deadly perimeter shooter. He made 42 three-pointers last season, but struggled at times with his ball-handling.

"We need him to get some easier baskets," Conrad said. "He needs to take it by some people and get more free throws."

Also competing for time in the backcourt is 5-11 freshman walk-on **Brian McDermott**, who could play a reserve role at point guard after hurting his knee last season and redshirting.

Moving out on the wing, Parker remains the starter at small forward. But sophomore **Nick Mitchell** isn't too far behind. In fact, Conrad thinks the 6-5 Mitchell played as well as anybody down the stretch last season. Mitchell averaged 7.5 points, 4.0 rebounds and collected 24 steals. He wound up starting 10 games.

"I think those two guys could combine as the best (small forward) in the league," Conrad said. "Whoever's playing the best defense is probably going to be playing the most minutes because they both can score."

Parker, played some shooting guard last season, is more of a slasher. He's not a great outside shooter, but loves to go to the offensive glass.

Nick Mitchell, who weighs just 185 pounds, could use another 25 pounds on his frame. His long arms help him play even bigger, and he's capable of defending a shooting guard. Mitchell shot 55 percent from the field last season.

Returning at power forward is 6-7 junior **Andres Amaya**. He slumped a bit last season, but still managed to average 6.5 points and 4.2 rebounds. Foul trouble was a problem.

Senior **Dave Bradley** will vie for the starting center spot. The 6-10 Bradley (2.8 ppg, 2.2 rpg, 17 blocks) has battled leg injuries throughout his career at Charleston Southern.

Three of the newcomers should play early. **Peter Van Rij**, a 6-10 junior center, is a transfer from Fairfield. He redshirted last season. Originally from The Netherlands, Van Rij averaged 2.9 points and 1.7 rebounds at Fairfield two years ago.

"I think he can be one of the top newcomers in the league," Conrad said.

If Van Rij's not the top newcomer, Lomax might be. He's a true point guard who played on a Dunbar High School team that featured three point guards.

Yet another newcomer, 6-7 sophomore **Ibica Perica**, could push Amaya at power forward. The Croatian-born Perica comes to Charleston Southern from Yavatai Junior College in Prescott, Ariz. He's probably a better shooter than Amaya.

Charles White, a 6-6 freshman forward, could wind up redshirting if Parker and Nick Mitchell are doing the job at small forward. He averaged 14 points and 7 rebounds last year at Holly Hill Roberts High School.

adidas Blue Ribbon Analysis

BACKCOURT	**C+**	**BENCH/DEPTH**	**B**
FRONTCOURT	**B**	**INTANGIBLES**	**C**

One thing Conrad is counting on is being able to use

1998-99 CHARLESTON SOUTHERN SCHEDULE

Nov.	16	@Georgia Tech
	21	St. Peter's
	25	@Stetson
	28	@North Carolina State
Dec.	2	@Furman
	5	@Florida
	9	South Carolina State
	18	Erskine
	21-22	#College of Charleston Tournament
	30	Wingate
Jan.	9	High Point
	11	Elon
	16	@Radford
	18	@Liberty
	23	Winthrop
	25	North Carolina-Asheville
	30	@Coastal Carolina
Feb.	1	Hight Point
	6	Liberty
	8	Radford
	11	@North Carolina-Asheville
	13	@Winthrop
	17	@Elon
	20	Coastal Carolina
	24-27	##Big South Tournament

@ Road Games
# Charleston, SC (vs. Delaware, first round; also College of Charleston and Stony Brook)
Asheville Civic Center, Asheville, NC

different lineups depending on the situation in the game.

"I see us as a team that can go to a small, athletic lineup or be able to attack people in the middle with Van Rij," Conrad said. "I think we'll be able to create a lot of matchup problems for people."

This could have been a huge year for Larrick, who was hoping to have the added burden of playing point guard taken away by freshman Greg Lomax. But when Lomax didn't qualify, it meant more point-guard duties for Larrick.

Even without Lomax, newcomers will probably make the difference in whether the Bucs making a legitimate run at the title or finish somewhere in the middle of the pack. Our call is third place, but the real measure of Charleston Southern's season will come in the Big South Tournament.

"The Big South is all decided in the last three days," Conrad said. "You've got to get ready for the tournament, though, by playing consistently all year. We can't allow our work habits to be up and down like they were last year."

(C.L.)

COASTAL CAROLINA

LOCATION .... **Conway, SC**
CONFERENCE .... **Big South**
LAST SEASON .... **8-19 (.269)**
CONFERENCE RECORD .... **4-8 (5th)**
STARTERS LOST/RETURNING **2/3**
NICKNAME .... **Chanticleers**
COLORS .... **Coastal Green, Bronze & Black**
HOMECOURT .... **Kimbel-Brice Gymnasium (1,800)**
COACH .... **Pete Strickland (Pittsburgh '79)**
RECORD AT SCHOOL .... **First year**
CAREER RECORD .... **First year**
ASSISTANTS .... **Baker Neal (Glenville State'79)**
Ganon Baker (UNC-Wilmington '95)
Lewis Preston (VMI '93)
TEAM WINS (last 5 yrs.) **15-6-5-11-8**
RPI (last 5 yrs.) **179-270-299-225-300**
1997-98 FINISH .... **Lost in conference first round.**

Only once in the last four years has Coastal Carolina's win total reached double figures.

But don't tell that to first-year head coach Pete Strickland. He doesn't even plan on looking at tape of last year's team. For that matter, he couldn't care less about the past.

Strickland, a former assistant under Oliver Purnell at Dayton and Old Dominion, is ecstatic about his situation. He inherits seven returning seniors he says are hell-bent on going out in style.

First things first, though. And that's improving on last season's 8-19 finish.

"I think I've gotten their attention," said Strickland, who's making his collegiate head coaching debut. "They want to go out the right way, and I'd like to get off the right way. It's a perfect marriage."

It wasn't too long ago that Coastal Carolina was the Big South's most dominant team. The Chanticleers made trips to the NCAA Tournament in 1991 and '93.

Then came NCAA probation and crippling sanctions. Former head coach Michael Hopkins was never able to fully overcome the scholarship reductions, recruiting restrictions and postseason ban.

But he did leave Strickland a senior-laden nucleus that includes six players who started at least 11 games last season.

Even better, six of those seniors are junior college players—meaning they haven't necessarily been beaten down by losing for three straight years.

"These guys have invested so much this summer," Strickland said. "They don't want to leave here without reestablishing the tradition of Coastal Carolina basketball. And there's a genuine togetherness. That's something you don't always see with a losing team."

Strickland, a former guard at Pittsburgh, plans on stretching the defense every chance he gets this season. He played high school basketball for the legendary Morgan Wootten at DeMatha Catholic in Hyattsville, Md. Wootten was instrumental in Strickland's getting the Coastal job and even had John Wooden—yes, *the* John Wooden—make a call on Strickland's behalf.

"I don't know Pete Strickland," Wooden told Coastal Carolina officials. "But if Morgan Wootten is behind him, then I'm right behind Morgan."

1998-99 COASTAL CAROLINA SCHEDULE

Nov.	14	St. Andrews
	21	@North Carolina State
	24	@Campbell
	28	@Mercer
	30	@Florida
Dec.	3	Newberry
	5	South Carolina-Aiken
	16	@Wake Forest
	21	*The Citadel
	23	@Virgina Tech
Jan.	6	@North Carolina-Greensboro
	9	Elon
	13	High Point
	16	@Liberty
	18	@Radford
	23	@North Carolina-Asheville
	27	Winthrop
	30	Charleston Southern
Feb.	1	@Elon
	3	College of Charleston
	6	Radford
	8	Liberty
	11	@Winthrop
	13	@North Carolina-Asheville
	17	@High Point
	20	@Charleston Southern
	24-27	#Big South Tournament

@ Road Games
* Myrtle Beach Convention Center, Myrtle Beach, SC
# Asheville Civic Center, Asheville, NC

Wootten's style was to run and press, and Strickland won't veer too far away from what he learned under his mentor.

"I really believe this team will be able to defend because we have very good to excellent quickness," Strickland said. "Another thing is that they were 8-19 last year and created more turnovers than they committed. These guys are primed to catch fire."

Anchoring the collection of returning seniors is 6-6 sophomore forward **Marcus Stewart** (10.4 ppg, 6.6 rpg, 17 assists). Stewart was a member of the Big South's All-Rookie Team last year. Strickland likens Stewart to former NBA star Adrian Dantley.

"He moves people around," Strickland said. "He never jumps over you. He jumps around you and jumps through you. He's as good on the low block as anybody we had at Dayton."

Center **Andrew Hinton** is the lone four-year senior on the team. At 6-8, Hinton (6.4 ppg, 3.6 rpg) could provide a nice high-post complement to Stewart.

The player Strickland is most intrigued by is 6-6 senior **Michael Allen** (4.6 ppg, 3.2 rpg).

"I think (Allen) could defend the center or the two guard, and I think he could play either the center or the two guard positions," Strickland said. "He's like a utility infielder because he can do so many things. When you're extending the floor on defense, you can't have too many of those kind of guys."

Senior **Larry Roberts** (5.9 ppg, 3.3 rpg, 28 assists, 26 steals) started 14 games last season. The 6-5 Roberts is probably the best athlete on the team and figures in at the small forward spot this season.

The wildcard at small forward could be freshman **Torrey Butler**, who was the leading scorer in the Baltimore Catholic League last season while playing for Mount St. Joe. Butler, while undersized at 6-3, is an underrated three-point shooter.

"That's why a lot of the big schools stayed away," Strickland said. "He never had to shoot the three in high school, but he can really get to the rim."

Two other seniors, 6-8 **David Dannen** and 6-8 **Brent Johnson**, will also play key frontcourt roles. Dannen possesses a nice shooting touch from the high post. He averaged 3.8 ppg and 2.3 rpg last season. Johnson could play center, power forward or small forward. An extremely physical player, Johnson was hurt most of last season and averaged 1.7 ppg and 1.0 rpg.

In the backcourt, the point-guard job is up for grabs. Senior **John Moore**, junior **Todd Shannon** and freshman **Shane Wright** are the combatants. The 6-1 Moore (0.8 ppg, 0.5 rpg, 11 steals) had trouble shooting the ball last season, as did all the Coastal guards.

The 6-0 Shannon (3.2 ppg, 0.8 rpg, 32 assists) did manage to shoot .833 percent from the free-throw line. The 6-0 Wright averaged 24 ppg and 9.1 apg last season at St. Pius X High in Houston, Texas.

The favorite to win the shooting guard job is another senior, 6-5 **Nigel Berghan**. He averaged 6.2 ppg and 1.8 rpg last season and made 19 three-pointers. Strickland said Berghan lived in the weight room during the summer trying to get stronger.

Sophomore **Carl Moser** (4.5 ppg, 1.6 rpg) is more of a combo guard. At 6-3, Moser connected on 23 three-pointers last season, which leads the returnees. **Jerrod Paige**, a 6-1 junior walk-on, wound up starting in 11 games last season. He averaged 4.2 ppg and 2.3 rpg. None of the returning guards shot better than 40 percent from the field.

Steve Miles, the third of Strickland's three freshman signees, will also get an early look at shooting guard. He's 6-4, and, says Strickland, can defend, handle the ball and rebound. He played his prep ball at Hayfield HS in Woodbridge, Va.

adidas Blue Ribbon Analysis

BACKCOURT .... **C** **BENCH/DEPTH** .... **C+**
FRONTCOURT .... **C** **INTANGIBLES** .... **C+**

The Chanticleers didn't outshoot many teams last season, and they probably won't this season. That's why it's imperative they get some easy baskets from their pressure defense. Strickland plans on going deep into his bench, and that includes all three freshmen.

"It's an expensive style we're going to play," Strickland said. "Conditioning will be a key, as will willingness to be unselfish. Just looking at last year's stats, we've got to shoot it better."

The Chanticleers shot 39 percent from the field as a team.

The schedule is ambitious with road games at Wake Forest, Florida, North Carolina State and Virginia Tech. Adjusting to Strickland's up-tempo style could also take some time, although he likes this club's athletic ability.

Finishing in the upper half of the conference would be a nice accomplishment this season. Strickland is committed to building a solid base. He was able to sign all three of his freshmen this year despite taking the job just three days before the recruiting dead period.

That's some serious selling over the phone. "We have everything we need to get it done here," Strickland said.

But maybe not this year. Still, we look for a respectable fourth-place Big South finish.

(C.L.)

LIBERTY

LOCATION .... **Lynchburg, VA**
CONFERENCE .... **Big South**
LAST SEASON .... **11-17 (.393)**
CONFERENCE RECORD .... **5-7 (14th)**
STARTERS LOST/RETURNING **4/1**
NICKNAME .... **Flames**
COLORS .... **Red, White & Blue**
HOMECOURT .... **Vines Center (9,000)**
COACH .... **Mel Hankinson (Indiana-Pennsylvania '65)**
RECORD AT SCHOOL .... **First Year**
CAREER RECORD .... **325-276 (21 yrs.)**
ASSISTANTS .... **Otis Hughley (Livingston '87)**
Chad Hankinson (West Virginia '94)
Greg Tackett (Northeast State '92)
TEAM WINS (last 5 yrs.) **18-12-17-23-11**
RPI (last 5 yrs.) **155-188-180-115-282**
1997-98 FINISH .... **Lost in conference semifinal.**

Game programs and media guides will come in handy this season for anyone venturing into the Vines Center to catch a glimpse of the Liberty basketball team.

About the only thing that won't be new is the school's founder and chancellor, the Rev. Jerry Falwell. He remains the Flames' most ardent supporter.

Yet, even Falwell might have to do some homework on the cast of characters occupying the Liberty bench this season.

There's a new head coach, new coaching staff, nine new players and a new, fast-paced system.

Mel Hankinson, the top assistant under Gale Catlett at West Virginia the last five years, has taken over the Liberty program. Hankinson has 21 years of experience as a college head coach. This will be his sixth stop, one that will no doubt include a few growing pains along the way.

"It's going to be exciting for the fans," said Hankinson,

1998-99 LIBERTY SCHEDULE

Nov.	17	@St. Bonaventure
	21	Richmond
	24	Virginia Tech
	28	East Carolina
Dec.	2	@James Madison
	8	@Virginia
	12	@Virginia Commonwealth
	16	@Southern Methodist
	19	Augusta State
Jan.	2	@Norfolk State
	7	Tusculum
	9	North Carolina-Asheville
	12	Winthrop
	16	Coastal Carolina
	18	Charleston Southern
	23	@High Point
	27	Elon
	30	Radford
Feb.	1	Winthrop
	6	Charleston Southern
	8	Coastal Carolina
	11	Elon
	13	High Point
	17	@North Carolina-Asheville
	20	@Radford
	24-27	#Big South Tournament

@ Road Games
# Asheville Civic Center, Asheville,NC

a 28-year coaching veteran. "We predictably will be highly unpredictable. With a team like this making the adjustments, there are going to be nights where it looks like no one can beat them and nights where it looks like we might not win a game.

"That's what happens when you live and die with the three-pointer. That's what happens when you're inexperienced, and that's what happens when you're pressing and forcing the tempo."

If Hankinson sounds a bit negative, well, he really isn't. He eagerly awaits the challenge at Liberty.

"The uniqueness of basketball is displayed when you have a group of people that work hard and come together to overcome the obstacles in order to be successful," he said.

In no particular order, those obstacles this season are inexperience, injuries and a demanding schedule.

Only one starter returns from a team that went 11-17 last season, a year after the Flames compiled a school-best 23-9 record. The top three scorers and top two rebounders from last season are gone.

"We have signed six new players, and along with the returning players, I am excited about the program this season," Hankinson said. "However, I don't want our fans to have unrealistic expectations about this year's team.

"We'll have athleticism, quickness and shooting ability that should enable us to compete with anyone in the conference. Our inside offensive game and rebounding ability are major questions that could keep the team from winning the conference."

The non-conference schedule is probably not conducive to learning on the job. Liberty faces dates with Virginia, Virginia Tech, Virginia Commonwealth, Southern Methodist, East Carolina and Iona.

Center **Jeremy Day** is the lone holdover from the starting lineup, but his status is questionable. The 6-9 sophomore averaged 6.6 ppg and 2.9 rpg and blocked 13 shots last season, but herniated disks in his back may require surgery.

"His health is of major concern," Hankinson said. "We could very well lose him for a year."

If Day can't play, 6-10 senior **Adam Hopkins** (6.3 ppg, 3.9 rpg, 13 blocks) will likely be the answer in the middle. The 240-pound Hopkins is a huge presence in the middle.

Day isn't the only returnee trying to bounce back from an injury last season. Senior forward **Jay Boykin** (6.3 ppg, 3.1 rpg) has battled knee problems throughout his career and a series of rehabilitation stints. At 6-5, Boykin possesses a nice outside shooting touch and will contend for the starting small forward spot.

Boykin's competition will come from sophomore **Christyan Rios** and freshman **Keith Salscheider**. The 6-5 Rios sat out last season to complete his academic requirements. At Cornerstone Christian HS in San Antonio, Texas, Rios averaged 18 points and 9 rebounds.

The 6-5 Salscheider was a first-team all-state selection as a senior at Bemdji (Minn.) HS. He averaged 19 points and 8 rebounds. Hankinson likes Salscheider's explosiveness to the basket.

The power forward position also appears wide open. Freshman **Marvin Benjamin** sat out all of last season after undergoing knee surgery. The 6-7 Benjamin was selected as one of the country's 50 best prep players a year ago at Redemption Christian in Troy, N.Y. He's originally from Amsterdam, Holland.

Sophomore **Aaron Cullen** will also factor into the equation at power forward. He has good size at 6-8 and likes to operate with his back to the basket. Cullen transferred from Seminole Junior College in Seminole, Okla., where he averaged 14 points and 8 blocks.

Sophomore **Nathan Day** transferred to Liberty after playing a season at Tennessee Temple. The 6-7 Day averaged 10 points and 6 rebounds as a freshman.

The backcourt will also be made up of almost entirely newcomers. Nic Wright, who started 23 games last season as a freshman point guard, left the team during the summer.

Edward Marks is the only returnee. The 5-11 junior is one of the favorites to win the starting point guard job. He, too, had injury problems last season, missing nine games with a separated shoulder. Marks, a solid defender, averaged 2.6 ppg, 2.5 rpg and handed out 40 assists. He's one of the quickest players in the conference.

Two freshmen will battle Marks for playing time at the point guard. **Frankie Cabrera** averaged 25.1 ppg and 5.0 rpg last season at Cape Henry Collegiate HS in Virginia Beach, Va. The 6-1 Cabrera is a left-hander who finished as his school's all-time leading scorer with 2,306 career points.

Chris Caldwell averaged 24.1 ppg and 2.6 rpg at Willow Ridge HS in Houston, Texas last season. The 6-foot Caldwell is a deft penetrator, but also can spot up and shoot the three-pointer.

Junior college transfers **C.J. Cowgill** and **Delawn Grandison** will fight it out for the shooting guard job.

The 6-1 Cowgill, a junior, is a transfer from Eastern Wyoming JC in Torrington, Wyo. He averaged 18.8 points and 2.7 assists last season. The 6-5 Grandison, also a junior, transferred from Durham JC in Toronto, Ontario. An athletic guard, Grandison averaged 24 points, 5.0 rebounds and 2.0 assists last season and was chosen the Canadian junior college national tournament's MVP.

"Cowgill is one of the best shooters I've ever been around," Hankinson said. "He makes a 1,000 shots a day. This team is going to really be able to shoot the basketball. I think we have a chance to be as good as anybody at the 1, 2 and 3 positions."

Liberty also got a late addition in 6-1 **Jamal Bennett**, a freshman point guard from Berkeley, Calif. Bennett received the required score on a standardized test in July and signed in August.

adidas Blue Ribbon Analysis

BACKCOURT	C+	BENCH/DEPTH	C
FRONTCOURT	C	INTANGIBLES	B

Hankinson has proven that he can recruit. He brought in 10 of the 12 players that carried West Virginia to the Sweet 16 last season. He's especially had success in the junior college ranks.

His six latest signees will have a major impact on the Flames' success this season. There just simply isn't much coming back in the way of seasoned players.

And those who do return are iffy because of injuries. Whether Jeremy Day can recover from his back problems will be critical, and Marks needs to step up at point guard. Having a freshman shoulder the burden at point can be dangerous in any league.

But an even bigger question: Who's going to provide leadership? That problem could be ongoing.

And then there's the early non-conference schedule.

"I just hope the early season challenges will not demoralize the team before the conference begins," Hankinson said.

Given the multitude of inexperience, the Flames could be destined for a lower echelon finish. We see fifth place in Liberty's future.

(C.L.)

NORTH CAROLINA-ASHEVILLE

LOCATION	**Asheville, NC**
CONFERENCE	**Big South**
LAST SEASON	**19-9 (.678)**
CONFERENCE RECORD	**11-1 (1st)**
STARTERS LOST/RETURNING	**3/2**
NICKNAME	**Bulldogs**
COLORS	**Royal Blue & White**
HOMECOURT	**Justice Center (1,580)**
COACH	**Eddie Biedenbach (N.C. State '68)**
RECORD AT SCHOOL	**37-19 (2 yrs.)**
CAREER RECORD	**66-70 (5 yrs.)**
ASSISTANTS	**Monte Towe (N.C. State '75)**
	Pat Bryant (West Georgia '84)
	Jeff Crisp (UNC-Asheville '97)
TEAM WINS (last 5 yrs.)	**3-11-18-18-19**
RPI (last 5 yrs.)	**296-239-198-106-131**
1997-98 FINISH	**Lost in conference final**

No team in the Big South Conference has been more consistent or more productive the last two years than UNC-Asheville.

In Eddie Biedenbach's two years as head coach, the Bulldogs have compiled a 22-4 conference record, scored road victories over South Carolina and New Mexico State and just missed against Tennessee and Syracuse.

And yet, there have been no trips to the NCAA Tournament. Last season, Radford nipped UNC-Asheville at the buzzer in the conference championship game thanks to Kevin Robinson's rebound bucket. Two years ago, the Bulldogs fell, 67-57, in a semifinal to eventual tournament champion Charleston Southern.

"I think, for the most part, our kids have played to the best of their abilities the last two years," Biedenbach said. "We just haven't won the tournament."

Even with the gut-wrenching loss to Radford in last season's conference championship game, UNC-Asheville would have still been a candidate for an NIT bid had it held off Tennessee and Syracuse in November.

The Bulldogs squandered a 15-point lead against the Vols and held the lead inside the final two minutes. There were also losses to Arizona, Richmond, Maryland and Florida State—all NCAA Tournament teams.

"This team needs to put those things behind us," Biedenbach said. The Bulldogs, who've won the regular-season title each of the last two years, will have to manage as much without Josh Pittman—the two-time Big South Conference Player of the Year. The sweet-shooting guard bailed the Bulldogs out of countless jams the last two seasons.

"The whole thing comes down to this: We don't have someone like Pittman that we'll be able to go to in any situation," Biedenbach said. "He was a real player, I think the best that's been in our league in a long time.

"There are very few guys who are go-to guys. He was, and we'll miss that."

Senior forward **Kevin Martin** (13.4 ppg, 5.2 rpg, 73 assists, 38 steals) will help fill Pittman's void, but Biedenbach won't ask quite as much of Martin as he did Pittman. Even so, many consider the 6-5 Martin—a transfer from Ohio State—the best returning player in the conference.

His biggest adjustment? Getting his points when opposing defenses are geared to stop him, and not Pittman.

Other than Martin, the Bulldogs' frontcourt will be comprised of a bunch of fresh faces. Center **Dirk Lommerse** and power forward **Robert Stevenson** have moved on after dominating the middle last season.

Biedenbach said he will have six true frontcourt players this year, and all six will need to contribute. Height won't be a problem. The Bulldogs, who look better in airports than a lot of NBA teams, boast three 7-footers.

Sophomore **Adam Earnhardt** (2.1 ppg, 2.1 rpg, 17 blocks) will be a key at center. The 7-footer shot 55 percent from the field last season, but needs to get stronger physically. Senior **Remco Smits** (1.1 ppg, 0.9 rpg) has battled back problems his entire career. The 7-footer is the first cousin of Indiana Pacers center **Rik Smits**.

The tallest member of the team is redshirt freshman **Jason Horton**, who checks in at 7-2 and has beefed up to 235 pounds. Horton averaged 10.0 ppg, 11.0 rpg and 8.0

1998-99 NORTH CAROLINA-ASHEVILLE SCHEDULE

Nov.	13	@Purdue
	16	#St. John's
	28	Tennessee Tech
Dec.	1	@Virginia Tech
	3	@Auburn
	7	@East Tennessee State
	12	@Clemson
	19	@Mercer
	21	Marshall
	28	@Campbell
	30	@Michigan State
Jan.	2	@Texas Christian
	5	Montreat
	9	@Liberty
	13	Radford
	16	@Elon
	20	High Point
	23	Coastal Carolina
	25	@Charleston Southern
	30	Winthrop
Feb.	1	@Radford
	4	@High Point
	6	Elon
	11	Charleston Southern
	13	@Coastal Carolina
	17	Liberty
	20	@Winthrop
	25-27	##Big South Tournament

@ Road Games
\# Chase NIT (If the Bulldogs advance they will face either Massachusetts or Niagra on Nov. 18. Semifinals and finals are Nov. 25 and 27 in Madison Square Garden, NY)
\## Asheville Civic Center, Asheville, NC

bpg at Twin Springs High in Hiltons, Va., two years ago.

"I hope we can count on Horton," Biedenbach said. "If we can, we'll be a good team."

The Bulldogs will receive some help after the first semester when **John Risinger** becomes eligible. The 6-5 junior is a transfer from Evansville, where he averaged 5.0 ppg and 4.0 rpg two years ago. Biedenbach believes Risinger will be able to play either forward spot or either guard spot. He's that versatile.

Sophomore **Ben Ezell** (0.6 ppg, 0.7 rpg) will also be in the mix at power forward. At 6-7, Ezell must work on his offensive skills.

"A lot will depend on how Ezell, Earnhardt and Risinger come around," Biedenbach said. "Those three guys will make an impact whether they're starters or subs."

Also returning to the frontcourt is 6-7 junior forward **Matt Osikowicz**, who averaged 1.6 ppg and 1.1 rpg last season.

The backcourt is bolstered by the return of senior point guard **Mike Matthews** (5.5 ppg, 2.3 rpg, 52 assists). At 6-2, Matthews is an extension of Biedenbach on the floor. He makes good decisions, gets the ball to the right people in the right places and plays tenacious defense.

"Mike Matthews is the kind of guy you would like to have in your business or on your team," Biedenbach said. "He never has a bad day emotionally."

Juelian Flowers (5.5 ppg, 2.6 rpg, 20 assists, 21 steals) will play more of a swingman role for UNC-Asheville. The 6-3 senior was second on the team last season with 19 three-pointers and will need to be more of a consistent scorer this season.

After a tough sophomore season, junior guard **Brian Richerson** looks to rebound. The 6-0 junior averaged 1.9 ppg and 1.1 rpg last season and saw his playing time dwindle. He averaged 4.9 ppg as a freshman.

Richerson does have great three-point range, as does 6-3 senior guard **Jeff Coble** (1.7 ppg, 0.7 rpg). Coble pumped in 12 points against North Carolina his freshman season. If he can cut down his turnovers and improve his defense, his playing time will increase.

Providing depth in the backcourt will be 5-11 sophomore **Nick McDevitt** (0.4 ppg, 0.8 rpg).

A pair of freshmen could also play their way into the backcourt rotation. **Mike Smith**, at 6-2, averaged 11 ppg and 4 apg last year at St.

Johns Prospect Hall in Potomac, Md. **Nick Perkins**, at 6-3, poured in 25 ppg as a senior at Paulding County HS in Dallas, Ga.

adidas Blue Ribbon Analysis

BACKCOURT	**B**	**BENCH/DEPTH**	**C+**
FRONTCOURT	**B**	**INTANGIBLES**	**B+**

Outside of Martin and Matthews, there are a multitude of unknowns about this UNC-Asheville team.

One thing for sure, though, is that Biedenbach can coach. Rarely in his two years in the conference has UNC-Asheville floundered in a game it was supposed to win.

Depending on how players such as Earnhardt, Risinger and Horton develop, the Bulldogs could challenge Radford again for the conference title—or slip into the lower echelon of the league.

Replacing one player like Pittman is difficult enough. When you also have to replace the likes of Stevenson and Lommerse, the challenge is even more daunting.

But there's something to be said about the tradition the Bulldogs have established over the last two seasons.

"Our players realize how good those guys were that they're replacing," Biedenbach said. "They know to have that kind of success they're going to have to develop into that kind of player. We've made them aware of that. That's what a program is.

"Take Kentucky. They change head coaches, lose a few players to the pros and still win a national championship. Programs win, and I think we're developing a good program."

It's a program that shouldn't tumble out of the Big South Conference's top three this season. Look for a second-place regular-season showing and perhaps a rematch against Radford in the conference tournament championship game.

(C.L.)

RADFORD

LOCATION	**Radford, VA**
CONFERENCE	**Big South**
LAST SEASON	**20-10 (.666)**
CONFERENCE RECORD	**10-2 (2nd)**
STARTERS LOST/RETURNING	**3/2**
NICKNAME	**Highlanders**
COLORS	**Red, White & Blue**
HOMECOURT	**Dedmon Center (5,000)**
COACH	**Dr. Ron Bradley (Eastern Nazarene '74)**
RECORD AT SCHOOL	**121-80 (7 yrs.)**
CAREER RECORD	**217-131 (12 yrs.)**
ASSISTANTS	**Chris Hawkins (Radford '92)**
	Bill Lilly (Glenville State '82)
	Stephen Barber (Radford '92)
TEAM WINS (last 5 yrs.)	**20-16-14-15-20**
RPI (last 5 yrs.)	**162-195-236-182-170**
1997-98 FINISH	**Lost in NCAA first round.**

It was the shot heard around the Radford campus. For that matter, it was the shot heard around the college basketball world.

Kevin Robinson's loose ball rebound and frantic "jump-heave" at the buzzer to beat UNC-Asheville last season in the Big South Conference Tournament championship game established the Highlanders as a SportsCenter fixture.

Highlights and slow-motion replays of Robinson's thrilling game-winner were played and replayed a hundred times in the weeks leading to the NCAA Tournament.

March Madness had finally bounced Radford's way. "We had a marketing firm tell us that if we had to buy the air time that shot got us, it would have cost more than $20 million," marveled Dr. Ron Bradley, the Highlanders' coach.

Perhaps so, but what that shot afforded the Radford basketball program was priceless—a first ever trip to the Big Dance.

"I was at Maryland for 10 years," Bradley said. "I couldn't really conceive what (an NCAA Tournament berth) would mean for a small place like this, for the fans, for the students, for the university, as well as for the program."

Bradley has not made a habit of re-living Robinson's play. At least, not too often. He's watched the tape a few times with his family and during Radford's basketball camp this summer, but that's about it.

""It's still great when you see it and unbelievable for this place, but it's time to move on and try to do it again," Bradley said.

Radford, with eight straight winning seasons, will attempt to become the first team in Big South Conference history to make back-to-back trips to the NCAA Tournament. The Highlanders lost to Duke last season in the first round.

The Highlanders have the backcourt to pull off the repeat. Point guard **Rian Everett** (6.0 ppg, 1.7 rpg, 131 assists, 38 steals) is back for his third straight season as a starter after leading the conference in assists last season. The 6-foot junior will be counted upon to score more often this season. Look for him to be just as aggressive creating shots for himself as he is for others.

1998-99 RADFORD SCHEDULE

Nov.	17	Concord
	21	Davis & Elkins
	23	St. Peters
	28	@Richmond
	30	@Clemson
Dec.	2	Marshall
	5	Duquesne
	8	Virginia Commonwealth
	12	@James Madison
	29-30	#Capital City Classic
Jan.	6	@Norfolk State
	9	@Winthrop
	13	@North Carolina-Asheville
	16	Charleston Southern
	18	Coastal Carolina
	23	Elon
	27	@High Point
	30	@Liberty
Feb.	1	North Carolina-Asheville
	6	@Coastal Carolina
	8	@Charleston Southern
	11	High Point
	13	@Elon
	17	Winthrop
	20	Liberty
	24-27	##Big South Tournament

@ Road Games
\# Tallahassee, FL (vs. Niagara, first round; also, Florida A&M and Jacksonville)
\## Asheville Civic Center, Asheville, NC

Everett's backcourt mate, **Jon Belt** (5.4 ppg, 1.3 rpg, 36 assists, 30 steals), will also need to take on more of an offensive burden. But his defense has never been a problem. The 6-3 junior is extremely athletic and typically draws the assignment of defending the opposition's best offensive player. Belt also demonstrated last season that he can shoot the three-pointer, hitting 35 of 90.

"Jon developed more between his freshman and sophomore years than any other perimeter player we've had here," Bradley said.

Bradley has shown in the past that he's not afraid to play his best five players. During his first season at Radford, he started four guards and a 6-5 center.

With that said, don't be surprised if **Leslie Ballard** (11.5 ppg, 2.0 rpg, 52 assists) cracks the starting lineup this season. The 6-foot Ballard, the only senior on the team, was Radford's third leading scorer last season despite coming off the bench. He hit 68 of 194 three-point shots, and pound for pound, is probably the Highlanders' strongest player.

"Leslie sacrificed some minutes to come off the bench for us last year," Bradley said. "This is his time to shine."

Freshman **Mike Hornbuckle** has the quickness and athleticism to contribute at either guard spot. Bradley thinks the 6-1 Hornbuckle is as advanced as Anthony Walker was when he arrived at Radford a few years ago, and Walker wound up winning Big South Rookie of the Year honors.

Also returning in the backcourt are sophomores **Lamar King** and **Byron Hall**. King broke his foot playing basketball during the summer, but is expected to be ready to go for the start of practice. The 6-1 King (1.4 ppg, 0.7 rpg) is a slasher who will provide depth at point guard.

The 6-foot Hall (3.3 ppg, 0.8 rpg) broke his foot late last season. He should provide three-point firepower off the bench.

Walk-ons **Joey Rein** and **Ian Hanna** could see some playing time. At 6-4, Rein has a nice three-point stroke, while Hanna's specialty is defense.

All three frontcourt starters from last season are gone, including Academic All-American Corey Reed and Robinson, the Big South Tournament MVP.

Junior **Ryan Charles** will step in at center. At 6-11, Charles has beefed up to 235 pounds. He averaged 8.3 ppg, 4.2 rpg and blocked 17 shots last season, but played his best basketball down the stretch. During the Big South Tournament, Charles averaged 13.6 ppg while coming off the bench.

"He's probably the most skilled big man we've had here," Bradley said.

The most intriguing of the Radford newcomers is 6-11, 235-pound freshman **Andrey Savtchenko**. The St. Petersburg, Russia, native will need to adjust to the college game. Having faced so-so competition last year at the Blue Ridge School in Dyke, Va., Savtchenko is still awfully raw.

Who will play alongside Charles is still uncertain. The Highlanders will boast four players 6-10 or taller this season.

Junior **Lee Klag** played a year at Cleveland State before transferring to Gogebic Community College in Ironwood, Mich., where he battled an ankle sprain last season but still averaged 5.0 ppg, 6.0 rpg and 3.1 bpg. West and Klag rely more on finesse than they do power.

Nosa Obasuyi is a 6-10 freshman walk-on and a probable redshirt candidate.

One of the fiercest battles for playing time will come at the small forward position. Then again, Bradley may choose to go with three guards much of the time.

Nonetheless, sophomores **Jason Williams** and **Jamar Betz** are back after playing sparingly last season. The 6-5 Betz (1.9 ppg, 0.9 rpg) prefers to play inside. The 6-6 Williams (0.7 ppg, 0.4 rpg) played inside in high school. How well he develops on the perimeter will determine how much playing time he receives.

Freshman **Correy Watkins** played center in high school. At 6-7, he too will have to make the adjustment to the perimeter. Watkins averaged 18.4 ppg, 12.9 rpg and 5.3 apg last season en route to conference player of the year honors at North Stanly High in Badin, N.C.

adidas Blue Ribbon Analysis

BACKCOURT .... B+ BENCH/DEPTH .... B
FRONTCOURT .... B INTANGIBLES .... B+

In many ways, Bradley thinks his club unloaded a huge psychological weight last season by finally surviving the Big South semifinals. Before last season, Radford had lost in the semifinals seven of the last eight years.

"That's gone now," Bradley said. "Hopefully, that will make it easier to get back to the NCAAs."

The Highlanders enjoyed great chemistry last season. Eight players played all of the minutes. Four of those players are back. Four more return who played very little, and four others are completely new to the program.

"We'll be more athletic this year," Bradley said. "Last year was probably the least athletic team we've had."

What that means is that Radford is likely to turn up the heat on its pressure defense. And on offense, Bradley plans to overhaul the system the Highlanders have run the last three or four years.

Bradley is convinced the league will be stronger. Will it be strong enough to keep Radford from making a return trip to the NCAA Tournament?

Probably not.

(C.L.)

WINTHROP

LOCATION .... Rock Hill, S.C.
CONFERENCE .... Big South
LAST SEASON .... 7-20 (.259)
CONFERENCE RECORD 4-8 (6th)
STARTERS LOST/RETURNING 3/2
NICKNAME .... Eagles
COLORS .... Garnet & Gold
HOMECOURT .... Winthrop Coliseum (6,100)
COACH .... Gregg Marshall (Randolph-Macon '85)
RECORD AT SCHOOL .... First Year
CAREER RECORD .... First Year
ASSISTANTS .... Jeff Meyer (Taylor '76)
Shaun Golden (Georgia '93)
Damon Stephenson (Pikeville '92)
TEAM WINS (last 5 yrs.) 4-7-7-12-7
RPI (last 5 yrs.) 288-212-239-249-294
1997-98 FINISH .... Lost in conference first round.

Marshall Law is in effect this season for the Winthrop basketball program.

In this case, that would be Gregg Marshall_the man aiming to elevate the Eagles from the depths of the Big South Conference standings.

Marshall, a veteran assistant at the College of Charleston and Marshall the last few years, sprints enthusiastically into his first college head coaching gig. He starts from the back of the pack.

He takes over for Dan Kenney, who was fired after last season. Kenney failed to post a winning season in his six years at Winthrop. The Eagles have gone five straight years without winning a game in the Big South conference tournament.

Marshall's first goal is making his players believe they can win. "They've got to believe in what we're doing," Marshall said. "We worked them pretty hard this spring, and they responded. I think we can really get things going here, and I'm looking forward to it. I hope that in a couple of years they look back and say (Marshall's hiring) was a good decision, and we all benefited from it."

Marshall hopes to implement a blend of speed and quickness, aggressive in-your-face defense and suffocating pressure.

Whether the Eagles have the size and strength to pull it off remains to be seen. Two starters and seven more players who lettered return from last season's 7-20 team.

There was also a surprise of sorts over the summer. Junior guard **Tyson Waterman** returned to the team after leaving school for academic reasons two years ago. Marshall's wife tutored Waterman to help him regain his eligibility.

The 6-1 Waterman averaged 16.3 ppg and 4.1 rpg and handed out 126 assists in earning second-team All-Big South honors as a sophomore.

There are also six newcomers, including three junior college players. Previously, the Eagles didn't recruit the junior college ranks or take transfers.

The 35-year-old Marshall didn't make any promises of an instant winner when he took the job on April 2. His immediate goal: To have the Eagles playing their best basketball in late February.

"It's those three days in February during the conference tournament that count most," Marshall said. "The team that gets hot down the stretch can get to the Big Dance."

All eyes will be on Waterman, who will rotate between the point guard and shooting guard positions. He will have to adjust to not having the ball in his hands all the time.

"He ran the point previously when he was here, but with his scorer's mentality, I think he can also play the two-guard spot," Marshall said. "He will give us a lot of flexibility."

One of the other main cogs in the Winthrop attack this season will be 6-7 senior forward **Heson Groves** (10.9 ppg, 6.9 rpg, 30 blocked shots). Groves' natural position is power forward, where he can use his athleticism to beat slower defenders. But out of necessity, he may start out at center. Groves started in 25 games last season and led the team in minutes.

"He's a guy, athletically, who has a chance to play for pay," Marshall said of Groves. "He should be an all-conference performer if he does the things he needs to do. He needs to score in a variety of ways for us."

Another factor at the power forward position will be junior college transfer **Jacques Vandescure**. The 6-6, 210-pound junior averaged 16 points and 9 rebounds last season at Eastern Wyoming Junior College. Vandescure, originally from Brussels, Belgium, brings a certain toughness that Winthrop may have lacked last season. Vandescure was ranked the 98th best junior college sophomore in the nation by *Blue Ribbon*'s JC recruiting experts, Rick Ball and Phil Henzel.

"He's a good complement to Groves," Marshall said, adding that Groves and Vandescure could end up on the floor at the same time. "He's not an explosive athlete like Groves, but physical and not afraid to defend the other team's best low post player."

The development of 6-9 sophomore **Owen Barnes** could be pivotal to the Eagles' frontcourt. There simply isn't a proven center. Barnes, the tallest player on the team, signed with Winthrop in the fall of 1996, but sat out his freshman season after not qualifying academically.

Barnes averaged 12 points and 8 rebounds his senior season of high school at Malverne (N.Y.) High. If Barnes comes through, Groves will be able to remain at power forward.

Also vying for time at the center position will be junior walk-on **Juontonio Pinckney**, who played in 26 games last season and scored 11 points and grabbed 12 rebounds in a win over Charleston Southern. The 6-6, 245-pound Pinckney averaged 2.5 points and 2.7 rebounds.

The small forward position will be shared by a trio of undersized returnees_sophomore **Roger Toxey**, senior **Reggie Coles** and junior **Rob Wallace**.

The 6-3 Toxey (5.7 ppg, 3.1 rpg, 57 assists) alternated between point guard and shooting guard last season. He'll get a chance to play more of a swing position this season.

"We will be smaller at the three spot than what we would like in the future, but Roger can shoot the ball very well from that position," Marshall said.

The 6-4 Coles (3.6 ppg, 1.9 rpg) is more of a natural small forward, and the Eagles could desperately use his senior leadership.

"Reggie needs to give us solid minutes," Marshall said. "He's not a great shooter or a great ball-handler, but he needs to believe in himself, buy into what we're doing and step up as a senior."

1998-99 WINTHROP SCHEDULE

Nov.	14	Clinch Valley
	16	Mercer
	23	Furman
	28	@Minnesota
Dec.	2	@Central Florida
	5	Campbell
	8	@The Citadel
	17	@North Carolina State
	20	@Appalachain State
	30	@Virgina Tech
Jan.	2	North Carolina Wesleyan
	4	Belmont
	9	Radford
	12	@Liberty
	16	High Point
	20	@Elon
	23	@Charleston Southern
	27	@Coastal Carolina
	30	@North Carolina-Asheville
Feb.	1	Liberty
	4	Elon
	6	@High Point
	11	Coastal Carolina
	13	Charleston Southern
	17	@Radford
	20	@North Carolina-Asheville
	24-27	#Big South Tournament

@ Road Games
\# Asheville Civic Center, Asheville, NC

The 6-3 Wallace (3.2 ppg, 1.8 rpg, 36 assists) needs to rediscover his shooting touch from his freshman season. He played out of position some last season at point guard.

Dan Tollens, a 6-6 freshman, and **Corey Green**, a 6-7 redshirt sophomore, will play a support role off the bench after turning down Division II offers to walk on at Winthrop.

At the shooting guard spot, 6-4 sophomore **Robbie Waldrop** (9.2 ppg, 1.3 rpg, 25 assists) could be one of the surprises of the league. He tied for the team scoring lead in conference games last season (11.3 ppg) and also made a team-high 48 three-pointers. He erupted for 37 points in the win over Charleston Southern.

"Robbie's a big-time athlete and an exceptional shooter," Marshall said. "If he does the little things, he can be an all-conference player. He has tremendous upside potential."

Marshall has depth in his backcourt. **Jakub Juskowiak** will move to shooting guard after handling the Eagles' point guard duties down the stretch last season. The 6-1 junior averaged 3.7 points and1.7 rebounds and handed out 54 assists.

Adrian Stockman, a 6-0 junior, comes aboard from Cincinnati State Community College, where he averaged 16.3 points and 3.9 rebounds last season. Stockman turned up at No. 189 on Ball and Henzel's list of the top 300 JC players.

The point-guard job is likely **Pierre Wooten**'s to lose. The 6-3 freshman averaged 14 points, 5 rebounds and 6 assists last season at Winton Woods High in Cincinnati. He's exceptionally quick and a deft playmaker.

Stockman also played the point in junior college, while Juskowiak started the final nine games there last season for the Eagles. If Wooten hits some growing pains early, there are other options.

adidas Blue Ribbon Analysis

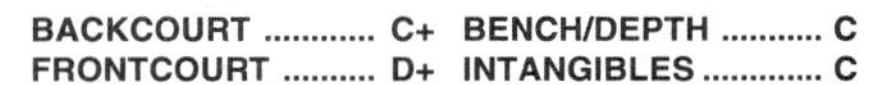

BACKCOURT .... C+ BENCH/DEPTH C
FRONTCOURT .... D+ INTANGIBLES C

Marshall's energy can't help but wear off on his players. Now he has to convince them that they can win in this league.

The Eagles have been slapped around for so long that a certain apathy seemed to rear its ugly head at certain points during the last few years. Kenney was well-liked in the community and respected for running a clean program. He was also one heck of a nice guy.

The problem?

Too many seasons of single-digit wins.

Marshall will need a few more recruiting classes before he can be fairly judged. He got a late start on his first one.

Getting Waterman back was huge. He has the ability to take over games down the stretch. But how rusty will he be?

Avoiding the cellar will be a chore this first season. But if a few of the JUCO players come through and Wooten grows up in a hurry, Winthrop could be the team nobody wants to face in the first round of the conference tournament.

(C.L.)

BIG TEN CONFERENCE

adidas BLUE RIBBON FORECAST

1. Michigan State
2. Purdue
3. Indiana
4. Minnesota
5. Illinois
6. Penn State
7. Ohio State
8. Wisconsin
9. Michigan
10. Iowa
11. Northwestern

TOP 40

Indiana, Michigan State, Minnesota and Purdueare ranked among the 1998-99 *adidas Blue Ribbon* Top 40. Extended profiles can be found in the Top 40 section of *Blue Ribbon.*

ALL-CONFERENCE TEAM

G—Mateen Cleaves, JR, Michigan State
G—A.J. Guyton, JR, Indiana
G—Michael Redd, SO, Ohio State
F—Antonio Smith, SR, Michigan State
C—Evan Eschmeyer, SR, Northwestern

PLAYER OF THE YEAR

Evan Eschmeyer, SR, Northwestern

NEWCOMER OF THE YEAR

Scoonie Penn, JR, Ohio State

1998-99 CONFERENCE TOURNAMENT

March 4-7, United Center, Chicago, IL

1997-98 CHAMPION

Michigan State and Illinois (co-champions)
Michigan (conference tournament)

1997-98 POSTSEASON PARTICIPANTS

Postseason Record: 16-7 (.696)

NCAA

Michigan State (Sweet 16)
Purdue (Sweet 16)
Illinois (2nd round)
Michigan (2nd round)
Indiana (2nd round)

NIT

Minnesota (champion)
Penn State (runner-up)
Iowa

TOP BACKCOURTS

1. Michigan State
2. Wisconsin
3. Ohio State

TOP FRONTCOURTS

1. Michigan State
2. Minnesota
3. Purdue

ON THE WAY UP

Ohio State

ON THE WAY DOWN

Michigan

INSIDE THE NUMBERS

- 1997-98 conference RPI: 3rd (of 30)
- Conference RPI (last 5 years): 1-8-6-3-3

DID YOU KNOW?

You'd have to go to the Big Ten archives to locate more tough backcourts in one season. Almost everybody has at least one skilled lead guard and a dependable three-point gunner. Many have more than one or combos who can interchange at the point and off guard...Ohio State unveils its $105 million, 19,500-seat Schottenstein Center, once dubbed "Value City Arena" after major contributors from the Columbus-based furniture chain. The original moniker quickly became a laughingstock—Michigan students held a banner at the '95 OSU-Michigan football game that read "Welcome Value City University"—and the Schottenstein family that owns Value City wised up...That makes three new league sports palaces in the last four seasons (Penn State's Jordan Center in '96; Wisconsin's Kohl Center '98). Hard to believe, but Illinois' mushroom-shaped Assembly Hall, once thought of as a futuristic marvel, is now the Big Ten's third-oldest arena (1963).

(D.J.)

ILLINOIS

LOCATION	**Champagne, IL**
CONFERENCE	**Big Ten**
LAST SEASON	**23-10 (.697)**
CONFERENCE RECORD	**13-3 (t-1st)**
STARTERS LOST/RETURNING	**5/0**
NICKNAME	**Fighting Illini**
COLORS	**Blue & Orange**
HOMECOURT	**Assembly Hall (16,450)**
COACH	**Lon Kruger (Kansas State '75)**
RECORD AT SCHOOL	**45-20 (2 yrs.)**
CAREER RECORD	**282-205 (16 YRS.)**
ASSISTANTS	**Robert McCullum (Birmingham Southern '76)**
	Rob Judson (Illinois'80)
	Mike Shepherd (Kansas State '90)
TEAM WINS (last 5 yrs.)	**17-19-18-22-23**
RPI (last 5 yrs.)	**32-42-62-25-24**
1997-98 FINISH	**Lost in NCAA second round.**

If we're to believe the business of major college basketball coaching has as much to do anymore with teaching as it does with recruiting, then Lon Kruger is about to prove once again he's at the top of his class.

The man who five years ago shocked the hoop world by taking a football school (Florida) to the Final Four last year took an Illinois team without a reliable post presence and ticketed for the middle of the Big Ten pack to a share of the league title.

Now he's facing a season without a single starter back. With exactly 9.4 points per game returning to the roster. And yet, you tend to believe Kruger when he says he's excited about building a team almost from scratch.

"Having seven seniors last year was special and I was so proud of that group," said Kruger of a team that lost in the NCAA second round. to Maryland "This year will be intriguing, equally enjoyable. That's the nature of the college game. Every year or two you have a new challenge."

There are more than a few Division I coaches who'd tremble at what Illinois faces this year: A point guard who hasn't played a minute of college ball. A center who's never played in an NCAA game. A pair of starting forwards who can't shoot. Almost no experience anywhere.

But Kruger is exactly the kind of man who not only keeps his cool in such a fix, but does it with a hint of a smile. Dale Carnegie could take classes from this guy. He sees not voids, but opportunities.

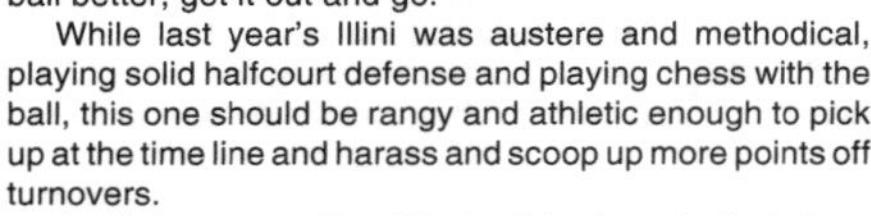

"This group actually may be able to do more things than last year's team," Kruger said. "I think we'll be able to extend more defensively. We'll rebound the ball better, get it out and go."

While last year's Illini was austere and methodical, playing solid halfcourt defense and playing chess with the ball, this one should be rangy and athletic enough to pick up at the time line and harass and scoop up more points off turnovers.

And it has something Illinois clubs have lacked since Lou Henson's "Flying Illini" made the Final Four in '89: Size. In fact, over the last decade, Illinois has fielded no one taller than 6-9 since the immortal Jens Kujawa in 1988. This team has six players 6-7 or taller.

And it has a genuine major appliance in 6-11, 285-pound sophomore **Festus Hawkins**. Felled by the NCAA Clearinghouse two years ago, Hawkins attended WestArk Community College last season to get his credits in order. There he averaged 19 points and eight rebounds and shot 62 percent from the field.

Those numbers would do nicely here and, frankly, they aren't out of reach in a league once again stripped of its best big men by the NBA.

Hawkins is not an oaf. He's skilled with his back to the hoop, possessing a nice baby hook. And Kruger says "he has a mind for the nuances of the game," something you don't see every day in a juco-transfer sophomore center. He takes pride in running the floor and also is capable of hitting the face-up jumper.

Speaking of which, Kruger sees a virus in Hawkins' game he intends to vaccinate at once—a tendency to drift away from the tin and work from the perimeter. Hawkins actually won a three-point shooting contest at an AAU all-star game. Kruger offers a last-thing-I-need chuckle and assures, "He won't be taking many threes this year."

If Hawkins gets up and down the floor like he says he can, the overall package sounds more like a family-size version of Lee Nailon than Robert Traylor. But, that remains to be seen.

Feeding Hawkins will be the other pivotal rookie, sophomore point guard **Cory Bradford** (Raleigh Egypt HS/ Memphis, Tenn.). Unable to qualify under Prop 42 standards, Bradford spent last season grinding through practices against now-departed Matt Heldman and Kevin Turner, giving them a reasonable scout-team facsimile of Mateen Cleaves on an everyday basis. He is big, strong and quick with the ball and should make an immediate impact on not only the Illini, but the league.

Lest anyone think starting a raw rookie at the point might wrinkle the meticulous Kruger's collar, consider that he's already done it twice with eye-opening results. Dan Cross at Florida and Steve Henson at Kansas State each started as teens and eventually led Kruger teams to the Final Four and Elite Eight, respectively. Bradford could be the third such success—maybe next season.

Anxious as Bradford is to mix it up, it might be a blessing that would-be starter Frankie Williams (Manual HS/ Peoria, Ill.) attained only partial qualification and must sit out. When the 6-4 McDonald's All-American arrives next season, he'll team with a seasoned leader who can swing between guard spots. That should make the Illini formidable.

If Bradford and Hawkins click and supply 30 points between them, life will be a lot easier for holdover forwards **Sergio McClain** (3.5 ppg, 3.1 rpg) and **Victor Chukwudebe** (2.0 ppg, 3.3 rpg). In Kruger's perfect world, both would start and develop some offensive finesse. Neither has shown evidence of doing so yet.

The 6-3, 230-pound McClain is built like a cinder block with a jumper to match (.339 FG percent). But the sophomore has proven indispensable because of an overall energy and knack for disrupting set-piece Big Ten offenses. He flat-out won the Illini's modest first-round NCAA decision by getting more involved in the South Alabama offense than the Jaguars themselves.

"Lots of times when freshmen don't shoot well, they don't do anything else well, either," said Kruger of McClain. "I think that speaks well to his air of being a winner."

Still, Kruger now wants McClain "to kind of take over" and flash the kind of skills he did when he was the state's Mr. Basketball while Williams' teammate at renowned Illinois high school power Manual.

Chukwudebe, a junior, most likely will never attain that sort of skill level and that'll be OK for Illinois as long as he boards and plays defense with authority. Often mechanical with the ball, he doesn't figure to be a high offensive option on this club no matter who Kruger puts on the floor. But at 6-7 and 230, the Nigerian-born former high school discus champ has shown hustle and heart that Kruger loves. He'll start on that alone.

The other starting spot, off guard, is the least certain and will depend a lot on the point production of the other four. If Kruger isn't getting enough potency, he'll probably keep plugging in streaky 6-2 senior **Arias Davis** (3.2 ppg, 0.8 rpg) and hope for the best. For Davis to play a lot, he needs to bomb in some threes. In seven minutes a game, he wasn't all that effective a year ago (.338 percent from three-point range). But when he was on—as in the Illini's climactic win at Indiana—Davis was a godsend.

Should Kruger not be desperate for points, he might opt for 6-4 junior transfer **Cleotis Brown** (Southern Union, Ala./Community College), a long-armed leaper perfect for trapping and assorted defensive nuisance. His juco averages of 21 points and nine rebounds at Southern Union suggest he might supply some points, too, if Davis sputters.

That core of players, even without much seasoning, looks to be plenty competitive in a weak Big Ten. But whether Illinois has enough depth to extend through February is a stickier wicket.

Certainly, Kruger can keep throwing long bodies out there. **Rich Beyers** (0.7 ppg, 0.9 rpg) won't win any slam dunk contests with his lift, but the sophomore is 6-8 and 230. Whether he can learn to play at the quickness level necessary is questionable. **Robert Archibald** is a 6-10, though only 215-pound freshman recruit from outside of St. Louis, originally way outside—Scotland. Though adept at finesse skills, how Archibald will handle Big Ten muscle is anyone's guess.

But the man most capable of filling the vital seventh spot in the rotation is 6-6, 207-pound sophomore **Carvell Ammons** (8.3 ppg, 6.5 rpg in '96-97), an evacuee from the last year of Ricky Byrdsong's funhouse at Northwestern. Before the NU situation completely unraveled late in the season, Ammons showed uncommon nerve for a freshman. The only question now is whether he's regained his spring and maintained confidence after ACL surgery a year ago. Ammons plays with the attitude of a power forward inside, but Kruger would like to see him develop his perimeter game more because of his size.

Freshmen **Damir Krupalija** (Boylan HS/Rockford, Ill.) and **Lucas Johnson** (Maine West H.S., Des Plaines, Ill.) are headed for lots of scout-team work and cheerleading. At 6-8 and 6-7, respectively, they'll further Illinois' revival in the All-Airport category.

adidas Blue Ribbon Analysis

BACKCOURT	B-	BENCH/DEPTH	D
FRONTCOURT	B	INTANGIBLES	B+

The paradox of this Kruger team is interesting. All the way back to his first job at tiny Pan American University on the dusty border of Texas and Mexico, Kruger has excelled at doing more with less, disguising his teams' weaknesses, emphasizing their strengths and building their confidence block by block. Although his teams have never been averse to accepting an open fast break, they've almost always maximized their talents with structure, patience and disciplined halfcourt play—at both ends.

Indeed, it was a concern of many Illini fans whether the corn-fed Kruger could recruit with such a style in the old Illini strongholds of the Chicago Public League, the vein that Henson and his longtime assistant Jimmy Collins used to mine. That concern remains to some degree, though his success at Peoria Manual makes it less relevant.

Now, here is Kruger looking at a group with as much raw teenage talent as he may have ever handled. And the best way to exploit it, at least this season, may be to loosen the leash and induce a degree of intentional chaos, a la Nolan Richardson and Arkansas' "40 Minutes of Hell." Risky, trapping defense and transition play whenever possible looks like the ticket for this squad.

It's a challenge in more ways than one for Kruger. The record shows he usually responds to such situations.

An NCAA berth might be asking a lot here, though the requisite RPI trophies lumber around on the non-conference schedule: Kansas, Clemson, Bradley, Valparaiso, Missouri, Saint Louis and the Coaches Versus Cancer Classic with Temple, Georgetown and Wake Forest.

We'll call it NIT this year. Then look out in '99-00.

(D.J.)

1998-99 ILLINOIS SCHEDULE

Nov.	10-11	#Coaches vs. Cancer Classic
	17	George Washington
	20	St. Louis
	23	Tennessee-Martin
	28	@Texas-Pan American
	30	Valparaiso
Dec.	5	*Bradley
	12	Eastern Illinois
	19	**Kansas
	22	***Missouri
	29	****Clemson
Jan.	3	@Indiana
	7	@Iowa
	9	Northwestern
	13	@Purdue
	16	Michigan State
	20	@Wisconsin
	23	Penn State
	28	@Michigan
	30	Ohio State
Feb.	3	@Minnesota
	6	Wisconsin
	11	@Michigan State
	13	Purdue
	17	@Northwestern
	21	Iowa
	23	Indiana
Mar.	4-7	##Big Ten Conference Tournament

@ Road Games
* United Center, Chicago, IL
** Sprint Shootout, Kemper Arena, Kansas City, MO
*** Kiel Center, St. Louis, MO
**** BI-LO Center, Greenville, SC
# New York, NY (vs. Wake Forest, first round; also Georgetown and Temple)
United Center, Chicago, IL

IOWA

LOCATION	Iowa City, IA
CONFERENCE	Big Ten
LAST SEASON	20-11 (.645)
CONFERENCE RECORD	9-7 (t-5th)
STARTERS LOST/RETURNING	3/2
NICKNAME	Hawkeyes
COLORS	Gold & Black
HOMECOURT	Carver-Hawkeye Arena (15,500)
COACH	Tom Davis (Wisconsin-Platteville '60)
RECORD AT SCHOOL	249-130 (12 yrs.)
CAREER RECORD	523-280 (27 yrs.)
ASSISTANTS	Gary Close (Arizona State '80)
	Rich Walker (Bowling Green '71)
	Frank DiLeo (Lafayette '75)
TEAM WINS (last 5 yrs.)	11-21-23-22-20
RPI (last 5 yrs.)	109-55-28-34-74
1997-98 FINISH	Lost in NIT first round.

Funny that Iowa is the only Big Ten state without a Great Lakes shore, because the Iowa Hawkeyes are looking a lot like the Edmund Fitzgerald these days: Tossed by storms and without a port in sight.

Their coach, 60-year-old Tom Davis, will step down after this season, his 27th as a Division I head coach. But there's no plan to hire one of his assistants, a la Tom Izzo following Jud Heathcote at Michigan State. That might have smoothed the transition, but Davis is not quite so beloved around these parts as Heathcote was in East Lansing.

That's particularly true in the athletic department, where director Bob Bowlsby has not been enamored with Davis. The edginess between the two began with, but has not been limited to, the 1996 suspension of Chris Kingsbury.

The undisciplined former Hawkeye guard tackled Danny Earl and threw a cheap-shot elbow at Pete Lisicky in a game against Penn State. Though referees didn't catch Kingsbury's handiwork, replays did and Bowlsby advocated a suspension that Davis reportedly disagreed with. Bowlsby, a former wrestler who held Dan Gable up as an example of the perfect coach, never thought Davis was enough of a disciplinarian.

Davis is now the definitive lame duck. He didn't make home visits during the fall recruiting period. And he might not have enough control over a team that eventually will add Wisconsin transfer Sam Okey.

Are the college hoop gods capricious? Hey, if he nabbed Raef LaFrentz, Davis was probably riding a new five-year extension to retirement at 65. But Kansas' Roy Williams outbattled him. Four years later, the Hawkeyes are coming off a first-round NIT loss and feeling gravity's effects.

Davis admitted last year he under-scheduled a team that could have sneaked into the NCAAs with some extra power-ranking juice. But a non-league schedule of bowling pins left the Hawkeyes with a lousy RPI and noses pressed against the Dance hall window. They were only the second Big Ten team to miss out with an above-.500 league record since the 64-team field was introduced in 1985 (Minnesota in 1996 was the other).

Davis? What, him worry? "It's been different," he said of his final preseason. "I've been putting in more time in the office, getting better organized, returning phone calls."

And figuring out how to plug a bunch of guys who aren't all that athletic into a system that demands as much. Davis always runs and presses. He's done it wherever he's been with whatever the material. This time, it will be a challenge.

The first unit isn't bad. That's even missing would-be sophomore Ricky Davis, who took his 15 points, five rebounds and rocket-thruster calves to the NBA after just one college season. Davis was chosen by the Charlotte Hornets and stands to make $2.5 million whenever the lockout settles.

Believe it or not, sore-backed Jess Settles, an All-Big Ten first-teamer three seasons ago, still had faint hopes of playing as of September. But even if a miracle cure for his chronic back malady is discovered, the NCAA still had to grant him a sixth year of eligibility. Dr. Tom isn't counting on any of it.

Okey? The Wisconsin problem child is a 6-7 senior forward (11.2 ppg, 8.5 rpg with the Badgers in '97) who quit the team in January after a pointless rebellion against UW coach Dick Bennett. He arrives with a chance to play the second semester (the conference schedule) if he completes required course work in the first. In September, Davis was calling it a 50-50 proposition.

On to the Hawkeyes, who definitely will be on hand. The backcourt is familiar and, like almost every backcourt in the league, very good.

Dean Oliver (8.8 ppg, 2.5 rpg, 4.2 apg), a 5-11 sophomore, had his ups and downs as a freshman starter on the point, but by and large played well. His assist-turnover ratio of 1.8 was fabulous for an 18-year-old.

What you look for in a kid Oliver's age starting at such a high-profile spot is resilience and progression. By March, Oliver was avoiding the plague of playground point men everywhere these days—aimless dribble penetration to a dead end in the paint. In the Hawks' final six games, Oliver committed just nine giveaways. He is smart and is clearly Iowa's best player.

As for 6-3 senior off-guard **Kent McCausland** (9.6 ppg, 2.2 rpg, 1.3 apg), nobody saw him coming except maybe his dad, the Hawkeye's radio announcer. Coming out of Waterloo West High, McCausland looked like the kind of barn hoop-trained homey that always gets the crowds whooping when the warm-ups come off with three minutes to go in 30-point games.

Nothing was farther from the truth. Once again, McCausland was Drano from the arc, hitting .460 (74 of 161), after a sophomore season in which he led the nation (.520).

McCausland isn't much of an athlete, but has a quick trigger and gets to his spots with dispatch, particularly when the Hawks are running. Without Davis darting around on the wing, he may need to get more of his points on the break this year.

And McCausland's defense doesn't scare anybody. He's pretty much a one-trick pony who continues to perform that trick extremely well.

J.R. Koch (6.9 ppg, 3.3 rpg), a 6-10 senior, is the latest in a long line of gawky forwards who play a lot better than they look. Koch is deceptively quick and gets off the floor well enough. With the loss of Davis, Ryan Bowen and Darryl Moore, Koch's scoring must rise considerably. And

1998-99 IOWA SCHEDULE

Nov.	15	*Western Illinois
	19	Northern Iowa
	25	Creighton
Dec.	1	@Drake
	4-5	#Hawkeye Invitational
	8	@Kansas
	12	Iowa State
	19	Missouri
	23	Coppin State
	31	Indiana
Jan.	3	@Northwestern
	7	Illinois
	12	@Ohio State
	16	@Minnesota
	21	@Michigan State
	23	Wisconsin
	27	Penn State
	30	@Michigan
Feb.	4	@Purdue
	6	Michigan State
	10	Minnesota
	13	Ohio State
	21	@Illinois
	23	Northwestern
	27 or 28	@Indiana
Mar.	4-7	##Big Ten Tournament

@ Road Games
* Mark of the Quad Cities, Moline, IL
# Iowa City, IA (vs. South Alabama, first round; also Detroit andGonzaga)
United Center, Chicago, IL

it should.

Like McCausland, his liabilities are more stark on defense. For his height, the senior is still skinny (220) and can be pushed around.

Junior **Guy Rucker** (6.6 ppg, 3.3 rpg) is an enigma Tom Davis needs an answer to. After a prodigious freshman season, his averages were virtually halved last year for no reason anyone can explain. At 6-10 and 270, he should, if nothing else, be throwing his weight around down low and grabbing eight boards a game.

"Maybe he thought it was going to be easier than it was," said Davis of Rucker's '98 season. "But I think the biggest thing was the loss of (All-America point) Andre Woolridge. He told Guy where to move, encouraged him, got him the ball where he needed it."

By midseason, Rucker's confidence grew so shaky that Davis removed him from the starting lineup.

"I thought he handled it real well," said Davis. "He knows what he's got to do. It's just a matter of doing it."

Davis needs Rucker to perform at center now. Iowa cannot afford another funk from him and contend for any sort of postseason tournament.

The fifth starter is at Davis' old spot, small forward. Pencil in 6-5 freshman **Joey Range** (Galesburg HS/ Galesburg, Ill.), a 6-5 slasher. Range is unselfish and a good passer, not something you often see out of heralded high school players these days. Unfortunately, this team may need instant points at the three.

The bench is awfully dependent on youngsters.

The most publicized is **Duez Henderson** (River Rouge HS/Detroit, Mich.), a 6-7 freshman small forward who played for Michigan's Class B state champs. He's said to be a good student and a hard worker as well as very athletic. Henderson looks to be the only quality bench player with any size. The backcourt is overpopulated.

Kyle Galloway (4.2 ppg, 1.8 rpg), a 6-5 sophomore shooting guard, and 5-11 junior point **Ryan Luehrsmann** (4.0 ppg, 1.9 rpg) are the only ones with any experience to speak of.

The spunky Galloway fared well as a spot-playing three-point shooter (.382) but he's not quick enough to do much more than that.

Luehersmann, on the other hand, gives Davis a real asset as a very astute back-up point and a good shooter (.390 from three-point range) when asked. Luehrsmann would be a starter on a lot of mid- and high-major teams, but Oliver must play in front of him here.

With those two 100-assist men in front of him, 6-0 junior transfer **Jason Price** (Marshalltown CC/Carver HS/Chicago, Ill.) won't get many chances to prove himself. He'd better make the most of his athletic ability by pushing it strong on the break.

The others are borderline players at best. **Jason Bauer** (0.8 ppg, 0.7 rpg) is a 6-3 senior, homestate kid and a brilliant math student who got in a lot of mop-up duty because he can play some defense and rebounds well for a guard.

He'll only play if the kids in front of him flop.

The reserve size on this team is not impressive.

Jacob Jaacks (Marshalltown CC/Washington HS/Cedar Rapids, Iowa) is a 6-8, 235-pound four man who played with Luehrsmann in high school before attending junior college with Price. He'll play a few quality sub minutes by default.

Antonio Ramos (DeLaSalle HS/Minneapolis) is an absolute project. At a hard-to-believe 7-2 and 215 pounds, the freshman will almost certainly redshirt. One year may not be long enough.

Marcello Gomes (0.6 ppg, 2.0 rpg) is a 6-6 sophomore forward and another foreign product who's strictly a practice player. So is 6-6, 230-pound freshman forward **Rod Thompson** (Galesburg HS/Galesburg Ill.), a tag-along from Range's high school.

adidas Blue Ribbon Analysis

BACKCOURT	**B**	**BENCH/DEPTH**	**D**
FRONTCOURT	**C-**	**INTANGIBLES**	**D-**

A lot could go wrong for Iowa. The Hawkeyes lost a ton of talent and scoring in Bowen, Davis and Moore and don't seem to have replaced it adequately.

Worse, Tom Davis has a tendency to rely too much on the press and transition even when he doesn't have the horses.

"I hate the slow down game," Davis said. "When we were outmatched, I tried holding the ball early in my career. But I hated doing it, even though it was successful at times."

With nothing to prove and nothing to hold him back, Davis will run kamikaze missions with this group that will hold up only as long as Oliver is out there. This is not a team equipped to press, and it will get burned.

The Hawkeyes are going to have enough trouble defending their end in a halfcourt situation without giving up easy hoops, too. It doesn't look promising.

In the halfcourt offense, McCausland and Oliver will find it hard getting space if Koch or Rucker don't develop some weaponry they so far haven't displayed.

Looks like whomever replaces Davis will be working from the bottom when he arrives in April, 1999.

(D.J.)

MICHIGAN

LOCATION	**Ann Arbor, MI**
CONFERENCE	**Big Ten**
LAST SEASON	**25-9 (.735)**
CONFERENCE RECORD	**11-5 (4th)**
STARTERS LOST/RETURNING	**3/2**
NICKNAME	**Wolverines**
COLORS	**Maize & Blue**
HOMECOURT	**Crisler Arena (13,562)**
COACH	**Brian Ellerbe (Rutgers '85)**
RECORD AT SCHOOL	**25-9 (1 yr.)**
CAREER RECORD	**59-56 (4 yrs.)**
ASSISTANTS	**Scott Trost (Minnesota-Morris '85)**
	Kurtis Townsend (Western Kentucky '85)
	Lorenzo Neely (Eastern Michigan '92)
TEAM WINS (last 5 yrs.)	**24-17-20-24-25**
RPI (last 5 yrs.)	**5-47-37-22-10**
1997-98 FINISH	**Lost in NCAA second round.**

It's true Michigan athletic director Tom Goss contacted 37 candidates before choosing assistant Brian Ellerbe to be Steve Fisher's successor as U-M basketball coach. That doesn't necessarily mean Ellerbe was at the bottom of the list, right?

Well, that's pretty much what everyone thought when Ellerbe was hired last fall at the end of a chaotic hiring process at the worst possible time of year for a basketball program.

You don't start looking for a college basketball coach in October. Waiting until then pretty much assures what happened to Michigan.

Rather than give serious consideration to a job with a school in hot NCAA water—right in the middle of the autumn recruiting window, no less—most candidates tried to use overtures from Goss to pad new deals with their own schools. The administration wound up appearing very foolish. Even after all its recent success in basketball, U-M still looked like a football school that hasn't a clue about hoops.

The irony was that former athletic director Bo Schembechler had hired then-assistant Fisher to replace Bill Freider in 1989 with the huffy proclamation: "A Michigan man will coach Michigan."

And here, eight years later, Ellerbe was getting the job six months after coming to U-M off a firing as the head coach at Loyola College. A Michigan man? He hadn't even stepped on the Crisler Arena floor for a game yet.

Well, you have to give Ellerbe credit. He got a veteran unit that had never concentrated longer than the average teenage PlayStation freak to focus for at least seven games. That's how long it took for the Wolverines to brutalize Indiana, 112-64, put on a finishing regular-season kick, climb to fourth in the league and plow through Iowa, Minnesota and Purdue for the inaugural Big Ten Tournament title.

Two games into the NCAAs they were done, felled by UCLA, and center Robert Traylor was free to start counting money. As a first-round NBA Draft choice, that is.

Maceo Baston and Jerod Ward, two of the Fab Five successors who were supposed to carry on the Wolverines' tradition of elite eight and Final Four appearances, are also gone, leaving a legacy of under-achievement and listless, middle-of-the-pack finishes.

It's fair to say no one thought Ellerbe could get these guys to carry a pulse last season. So, who's to say he can't take a limited group like this year's and whip it into a surprise contender?

We'll take that calculated gamble. He can't. This team has a good, experienced backcourt in seniors **Robbie Reid** and **Louis Bullock**. But everyone in the Big Ten has a strong backcourt. The Wolverines haven't had such an apparently weak frontcourt in decades. There appear to be zero scoring options down low, and there is no depth at any position. If one injury strikes this team, it could very easily finish last.

What a way for Bullock (17.1 ppg, 3.3 rpg), the 6-3 senior, to end a sparkling Michigan career. He's among the best perimeter shooters the Big Ten has ever produced (93 of 207 from three-point range—.449 percent—last season) but he's so much more. Bullock takes care of the ball, has a sense for time and situation and is a rock on the free-throw line late in games.

The problem for him this year will be getting free for shots. Ellerbe ran lots of stuff for him last season, but it won't be nearly as easy to get loose with defenders ignoring the interior. Bullock improved at creating his own shot last season. He'll need to improve further to merely keep his scoring average where it was.

Compounding the problem, Bullock wants to play in the NBA, but knows he must get work at the point this year to have a shot. The big league is not overpopulated with 6-3 shooting guards. Can Bullock play lead and score as much as this team needs him to?

Reid (8.2 ppg, 2.4 rpg, 3.4 apg), a 6-1 senior, is almost as good a three-point shooter (74-175, .423) but was timid much of last season trying to blend into an offense with many other options.

In March, he blossomed and played his best basketball since transferring from Brigham Young. In the Wolves' five-game postseason, Reid averaged 13.4 ppg and was 21 for 31 on three-pointers.

Reid didn't realize how tough it would be to get back in hoop shape after a two-year Mormon mission to Greece in which he never picked up a basketball. He was rounding into condition most of last season. He'll need every ounce of energy he can muster this year.

Reid is a deft ballhandler and can make plays at the point as well as Bullock. If Ellerbe does what he did last year, whoever gets the outlet pass after a defensive board will assume the lead guard role.

Now, the headaches start for Ellerbe.

He would prefer that 6-7 sophomore **Brandon Smith** (3.2 ppg, 1.3 rpg) start at small forward. In 10 minutes a game last year, Smith showed remarkable leaping and spectacular dunks when he got a lane to the hole. A late-blooming phenom in the '96 summer camps, he got looks from North Carolina and Duke before picking the Wolverines.

But whether Smith is ready to start stroking the corner jumper and help loosen up the middle for the Wolverines' questionable big men is another matter. He simply didn't get enough quality playing time last year to prove his .613 FG percentage (38 of 62) isn't a mirage. And if he doesn't hit the J, highlight forays to the hoop will be a lot harder to come by this season.

What happens down low is anybody's guess. The plan is for 6-11 junior **Peter Vignier** (0.3 ppg, 0.7 rpg) and 6-11 sophomore **Josh Asselin** (2.7 ppg, 2.7 rpg) to do the twin-towers thing—Vignier at the pivot, Asselin at the four. That's the plan.

But Vignier has never shown a smidgen of offensive confidence in two years of almost exclusive mop-up time

1998-99 MICHIGAN SCHEDULE

Nov.	13	@Florida International
	16	Ball State
	19	Detroit
	23-25	#Maui Classic
	30	Towson
Dec.	2	Bradley
	6	*Western Michigan
	9	@Eastern Michigan
	12	@Duke
	21	Hampton
	27	@Florida
	30	Wisconsin
Jan.	2	@Penn State
	5	Indiana
	9	@Michigan State
	16	Ohio State
	20	@Minnesota
	23	@Purdue
	28	Illinois
	30	Iowa
Feb.	4	@Northwestern
	7	Minnesota
	9	@Ohio State
	16	Michigan State
	21	@Indiana
	23	Penn State
	27 or 28	@Wisconsin
Mar.	4-7	##Big Ten Tournament

@ Road Games
* Grand Rapids, MI
# Maui, HI (vs. Clemson, first round; also Chaminade and Syracuse)
United Center, Chicago, IL

(4.1 minutes per game in '97-98). Every time he gets the ball on the blocks, he looks like he's holding a bomb. Not only is he unrefined on the post, he's been a fish on the boards.

Vignier spent the summer at home in Teaneck, N.J., and is said to have worked on his game in the competitive North Jersey court scene. Reid said he looked surprisingly confident when the team convened for informal workouts in September.

If that's for real, it would mean a ton to the Wolverines. Vignier can run well enough, and he's not bad on defense. If he can score 10 points a game and pull down the boards he should get, Ellerbe can live with him.

If not, Ellerbe will be forced to go with a three-guard lineup he'd rather not use. Not that the third guard, 6-5 freshman **Leon Jones** (12.4 ppg, 3.7 rpg at Winchendon, (Mass.) Prep Academy/Battle Creek HS, Battle Creek, Mich.), isn't athletically equipped. He is. But he's inexperienced and can't be counted on to produce what Michigan needs most—points.

The best of two newcomers, Jones originally committed to Iowa, but changed his mind. He was forced to attend prep school as a non-qualifier. Ellerbe and his staff are happy with him and he'll play plenty regardless, as either the third guard or the first—and only—guard off the bench.

Asselin is ideally the power forward. In 12 minutes a game last year, he showed more of an offensive repertoire than Vignier and surprised people with his hustle. Eight rebounds in a December win over Duke opened eyes. So did nine points in the first half against Purdue.

When Asselin is active, he has a knack for keeping offensive rebounds alive. But there's no Baston or Traylor or Ward to clamp it now. He has to rebound.

Bottom line, Asselin should be a sixth-man role player. But on this team, he has to start.

The only viable frontcourt reserve is 6-9 freshman **Chris Young** (Central Catholic HS/Plymouth, Mich.). In a perfect world, from all indications Young should be redshirting this year instead of playing. He's been cramming in the weight room all summer just to get from 210 to 220. Young got by on his height in high school. Even though the Big Ten is in for one of its worst years in the frontcourt, this still ain't high school.

That's it. Ellerbe almost surely must live with those seven because the others just aren't ready for Big Ten-caliber ball or never will be. They are practice players.

Six-foot senior point **Ron Oliver** (0.7 ppg, 0.3 rpg) is the closest thing to game-ready. He's been awarded a scholarship the last three years because of his pinball hustle. He's one for one in his career from the arc, so he can claim a better three-point percentage than Bullock.

Darius Taylor (0.8 ppg, 0.2 rpg) is a 6-4 senior who walked on two years ago. He plays small forward. Very small forward.

Donte Scott (0.6 ppg, 0.4 rpg) is a 6-2 sophomore and second-year walkon who plays off guard on the scout team.

And 6-6 senior forward **Erik Szyndlar**'s (1.4 ppg, 0.8 rpg) claim to fame is that he survived going head-to-head against Traylor in practice for two years. Some might rather be Mike Tyson's sparring partner.

adidas Blue Ribbon Analysis

BACKCOURT	**B+**	**BENCH/DEPTH**	**D**
FRONTCOURT	**D**	**INTANGIBLES**	**C**

It's important to remember amid all this that Ellerbe has dealt with less material than this. He's a bright guy who will recruit this program back into the thick of the Big Ten—eventually.

But for now, it's grim. God forbid Bullock goes down or Ellerbe can close his eyes and pretend he's back leading a 9-18 Loyola (Md.) College team.

The experience of dealing with low-major talent at Loyola (excepting the wonderful Mike Powell) should serve Ellerbe well here. And he doesn't have any whining holdovers to make his job harder. Bullock and Reid are mature and they can be counted on to shepherd the raw kids along until they can stand on their own.

That said, this is not a pretty picture. Michigan's glory days are clearly behind it and a new program must be rebuilt in Ellerbe's image. It might take a while.

(D.J.)

NORTHWESTERN

LOCATION .... **Evanston, IL**
CONFERENCE .... **Big Ten**
LAST SEASON .... **10-17 (.370)**
CONFERENCE RECORD .... **3-13 (10th)**
STARTERS LOST/RETURNING **1/4**
NICKNAME .... **Wildcats**
COLORS .... **Purple & Black**
HOMECOURT .... **Welsh-Ryan Arena (8,117)**
COACH .... **Kevin O'Neill (McGill '79)**
RECORD AT SCHOOL .... **10-17 (1 yr.)**
CAREER RECORD .... **150-137 (9 yrs.)**
ASSISTANTS .... **Bob Beyer (Alfred State '84)**
Brian Gregory (Oakland '90)
Billy Schmidt (Wake Forest '92)
TEAM WINS (last 5 yrs.) **15-5-7-7-10**
RPI (last 5 yrs.) **81-234-230-204-188**
1997-98 FINISH .... **Lost in conference first round.**

It's usually a telltale sign of a team in total despair when the highlight of its season is a loss.

Northwestern seems to fit the bill. The Wildcats' major accomplishment of 1997-98 was an overtime loss to eventual Big Ten co-champion Michigan State.

But couched in the ultimate failure of that game were a pair of bright spots that give the 'Cats reason for hope this season, Kevin O'Neill's second at the suburban Chicago private school.

First, Northwestern's All-Big Ten center **Evan Eschmeyer** was unstoppable. Time and again, NU went to the well inside and the Spartans could do nothing to alter the outcome. Eschmeyer piled up 30 points.

Second, rookie shooting guard **Sean Wink** didn't look like any rookie Northwestern has had in a long time. Unafraid and unintimidated, he bombed away with disdain for the Spartans and even tied the game in the final seconds of regulation with a looping three.

Indeed, the 6,053 fans who wandered into NU's rehabbed old arena saw a treat, even if MSU did eventually win. After all, don't the Wildcats *always* lose any game of importance?

And what's O'Neill doing at this outpost, anyway? Isn't there an easier place for a recruiting madman to make a living? Someplace where it's easier to get marginal academic qualifiers admitted? Someplace with a little hoop tradition or at least a big facility to help you out?

Someplace like, uh, Tennessee?

Well, that's kind of why O'Neill is here. After recruiting the Volunteers into the '90s, he came to loggerheads with athletic director Doug Dickey. So last year, O'Neill landed at NU which, if it isn't exactly college basketball's dream job, is at least close to established O'Neill recruiting turf (he took Marquette, of nearby Milwaukee, to the Sweet 16 in '93).

You get the feeling this probably isn't O'Neill's last stop, either. But while he's here, Northwestern should be ecstatic to have him. There couldn't be a better-equipped man to raise this program out of the slop left by the bizarre Ricky Birdsong regime.

What NU has always had less of than every school in the league is talent. That's exactly what O'Neill produces. He's been a successful recruiter every place he's been and he's already nabbing better players for NU than its had in a while. He claims the steep academic standards of the Big Ten's most prestigious school are not an impediment.

"I've honestly found it's not that hard (to recruit)," O'Neill said. "You're dealing with a smaller pool of kids who're available to you. The other thing is, you immediately have the interest of kids who want a great education. One year into the job, I'm really glad I took it."

Don't let him kid you. Yes, it can be done. Gary Barnett has managed to recruit here and won back-to-back Big Ten football titles because of it. But it's tough. Very tough.

It won't get an easier, either, because of a point-shaving scandal that hit the school, full details of which only were revealed in March by a federal indictment of former players Kenneth Dion Lee and Dewey Williams. O'Neill can rightly claim that the scandal is residue left over from the Birdsong era. But what effect it has on recruiting won't be fully apparent until the November signing period.

Talent is the only way to turn around a program that hasn't won more than 10 games since the 1994 NIT team in Birdsong's first year. Certainly, O'Neill didn't have much to work with last season.

"Aside from Eschmeyer, we had a group of guys a little over their heads," said O'Neill. But we played pretty well the last eight or 10 games."

They'll be better this year, too, because Eschmeyer and Wink return and the first concentrated wave of O'Neill recruits arrive.

Eschmeyer (21.7 ppg, 10.7 rpg), like Danny Earl at Penn State, has been granted a rare sixth year of eligibility by the NCAA. Unlike Earl, Eschmeyer's medical problems are well behind him. Foot fractures that kept him out his first two seasons are no longer a factor.

And with the departure of Robert Traylor, Brad Miller, Ryan Bowen and Jason Collier, he becomes the unquestioned top returning post player in the conference. He should destroy this league inside. Other than Penn State's Calvin Booth and perhaps Illinois' Fess Hawkins, no one is even in his class.

Eschmeyer has shot .613 and .610 from the field the last two years with teams doubling his post moves almost without fail. He's become slick enough inside to wriggle between defenders or spin around them, routinely getting either a good look or a foul.

In fact, if Eschmeyer was a better free-throw shooter (just .613 last season), he might score 30 a game. Because he *lives* at the line. His 171 free-throw attempts last season in league games threatened Terry Dischinger's 36-year-old Big Ten record (179). He might beat it this year.

Wink (12.1 ppg, 2.4 rpg) was a wonderful surprise as a viable second option. The Californian made more threes than anyone in the league (86, an NU record) and placed third in percentage (.457). O'Neill will be delighted if Wink does nothing but equal his 1998 numbers for the next three years.

Like all great jump shooters, Wink never shied from a big shot. O'Neill loved that. So he ran all sorts of picks and double picks to get the kid shots.

And Wink's shooter's attitude made up for O'Neill's initial trepidation about a driveway-shooter body tone.

"I told him after last summer, 'Just don't come to school'," said O'Neill. "He wasn't working out. I thought he was a soft pansy. But he's put on 15 pounds of muscle since then. He's not a great player. But he's a great shooter."

So, that's two players. Anybody else?

Maybe. O'Neill is enthused about his freshman point guard, 6-3 **David Newman** (Hoover HS/Des Moines, Iowa), whom he stole right from under Iowa's nose.

If he's as good as O'Neill thinks he is, Newman will bring a Scott Skiles demeanor and a scoring attitude to the Wildcats. Exactly what this program needs—points and toughness.

Newman is already penned in as the starter and plans are for him to play as long as he can last—as many as 35 minutes per. In a league that's as tough as it's ever been at point guard, that'll be a cruel baptism. And even O'Neill admits Newman so far "can't guard his lunch in a kindergarten classroom." In other words, hang in there, kid.

How the forward spots shake out is a wide-open ques-

1998-99 NORTHWESTERN SCHEDULE

Nov.	17	Maine
	21	Oakland
	25	St. Francis (NY)
	28	Furman
Dec.	5	Dayton
	14	Wisconsin-Milwaukee
	19	@Seton Hall
	23	Boston College
	27	Long Beach State
Jan.	3	Iowa
	6	@Minnesota
	9	@Illinois
	13	@Indiana
	16	Wisconsin
	20	Penn State
	23	Texas-Pan American
	27	Purdue
	30	@Michigan State
Feb.	4	Michigan
	6	@Penn State
	10	@Wisconsin
	13	Indiana
	17	Illinois
	20	@Ohio State
	23	@Iowa
	27	Minnesota
Mar.	4-7	#Big Ten Tournament

@ Road Games
# United Center, Chicago, IL

tion. A cushy November and December in which the Wildcats see the road just once (at Seton Hall) in nine games and play no one more challenging than Dayton may not immediately provide the answers.

Certainly the holdovers are lacking job security. O'Neill is happier with the effort of 6-9 senior power forward **Joe Harmsen** (3.9 ppg, 3.1 rpg) than he is with his performance. He'll probably start just because of his work ethic.

But long-armed 6-7 freshman **Tavaras Hardy** (Providence HS/Joliet, Ill.) will push him and may eventually take his job. Hardy will have to score to do it; at 215, he's awfully light for the rough stuff.

The three spot is completely up for grabs. Based on experience, the safe choice is 6-3 sophomore swingman **Napoleon Harris** (4.9 ppg, 5.1 rpg), whose aggressive rebounding belies his size. But, knowing O'Neill, freshman **Collier Drayton** (Lyons HS/Lyons, N.Y.), a 6-3 freshman mutt whose on-ball defense is said to be outstanding, may get a look, too.

The other candidate is another rookie, freshman **Steve Lepore** (St. Edward HS/North Olmstead, Ohio), a strong 6-5 shooter from suburban Cleveland. Lepore filled it up for the U.S. World Junior team but he could be overmatched on defense against the quicker Big Ten three-men.

First man off the bench is 6-1 senior **Julian Bonner** (9.0 ppg, 4.1 apg), a kid you have to feel badly for. Stuck on some awful teams, he has always come ready to compete. Last year, because O'Neill had no one else, Bonner was forced to play the point. He didn't do too badly either (1.2-1 assists-turnovers), especially considering he averaged an obscene 39.4 minutes in 16 Big Ten games and 38.8 over NU's 27-game season. Bonner should be happy to play 25-28 and rediscover fresh legs. Because he's neither a true point nor a shooter (.273 three-point percentage), that will be his lot.

The fourth guard is either 23-year-old Israeli **Danny Allouche**, a 6-5 senior transfer from Missouri whose good sense outshines his physical gifts, or holdover **Nate Pomeday** (3.5 ppg, 1.9 apg), a 6-3 senior who can hit the stand-still three (.400 three-point percentage) but has chronic knee pain.

The poster boy of this program's Poppin' Fresh past is junior **Aron Molnar** (4.5 ppg, 2.7 rpg), a doughy Clydesdale whose specs (6-11, 242) have always looked better on a roster sheet than on a court.

Matt Kammrath (0.0 ppg, 0.3 apg), a 6-1 junior guard from Boca Raton, Fla., has the team's best second serve.

adidas Blue Ribbon Analysis

BACKCOURT	**C**	**BENCH/DEPTH**	**D**
FRONTCOURT	**B-**	**INTANGIBLES**	**C**

Throughout his career, O'Neill has always stressed defense. Lacking great talent, he's always willing to play guys who bust a gut on D at the expense of points. Witness a five-game Big Ten stretch last year in which NU scored an *average* of 45 points. Or a taffy-pull two years ago at Penn State when the Lions and his young Tennessee team finished regulation tied at 33.

But he gets results. This program is going nowhere until it toughens up. O'Neill, a biting, often profane city guy with a propensity for straight-on, unvarnished criticism, will accomplish that. His players will know where they stand.

"I'm telling them we should be able to play in the postseason right now." said O'Neill. "And I mean other than the Big Ten tournament.

"Then, we'll go through a year where we're really young ('99-00). And by the fourth year, we should be pretty damn good."

This group has a shot at the NIT simply because 8-2 against the potted plants on its non-league schedule is entirely possible. Then 6-10 in the league would lock it up.

Regardless, the Wildcats figure to be progressively more annoying for Big Ten visitors to Welsh-Ryan. When the February dog days roll around and all the contenders are looking for their customary breather against the Purple People, don't be surprised to see O'Neill's boys pick off one or two. This league simply isn't good enough to avoid it.

(D.J.)

adidas Blue Ribbon Analysis

GRADING SYSTEM

- A+ equal to very best in country—Final Four-caliber unit
- A among the best in the land—worthy of deep NCAA run
- B+ talented, versatile and experienced—NCAA-NIT ability
- B solid and productive winners—league and post-season contenders
- C+ average to above-average—may contend in a weaker league
- C average to mediocre—second division in a strong league
- D+ below average, inconsistent—second division in a weaker league
- D well below average—losing season virtually certain
- F non-Division I ability—an underdog every night

OHIO STATE

LOCATION	**Columbus, OH**
CONFERENCE	**Big Ten**
LAST SEASON	**8-22 (.266)**
CONFERENCE RECORD	**1-15 (11th)**
STARTERS LOST/RETURNING	**1/4**
NICKNAME	**Buckeyes**
COLORS	**Scarlet & Gray**
HOMECOURT	**Jerome Schottenstein Center (19,500)**
COACH	**Jim O'Brien (Boston College '72)**
RECORD AT SCHOOL	**8-22 (1 yr.)**
CAREER RECORD	**243-239 (16 yrs.)**
ASSISTANTS	**Rick Boyages (Bowdoin '85)**
	Paul Biancardi (Salem State '85)
	Dave Spiller (Canisius'78)
TEAM WINS (last 5 yrs.)	**13-6-10-10-8**
RPI (last 5 yrs.)	**69-199-157-132-176**
1997-98 FINISH	**Lost in conference first round.**

Jim O'Brien had an idea of what lay ahead for the 1997-98 season after his very first Big Ten game. With 1:09 left against bottom-feeder-to-be Wisconsin, the Buckeyes held a 59-58 lead. With the ball. At home.

Four straight turnovers later, OSU had absorbed its first league loss. O'Brien sensed a trend.

"When you look up and down this conference, it seems to me there's not going to be many opportunities like this to win games at the end," said the former Boston College coach. "You tell me. Do you think we're going to have better chances to win games? I think not."

Perceptive, the new guy.

He knew the odds against him. With a kid who'd never played the point (**Carlos Davis**) being asked to do so. With three potential starters removed from his roster by injury and disciplinary moves. With the spiritual bacteria of Randy Ayers' squalid final years as coach still infecting the program. No way the Buckeyes were going to compete.

They didn't. Seventeen Big Ten losses and several school records for futility later, a hoop version of the Bataan death march was finally over.

After a 7-3 start, the young Bucks had lost 19 of their last 20. They had absorbed two of the three worst home losses in school history—within 72 hours (84-58 to Michigan State; 107-75 to Purdue).

They had lost 17 straight, 14 straight in the league, 20 straight in the league over two seasons. All were school records.

And yet, somehow, Buckeye backers sensed tangible reasons for optimism. In fact, they rallied around a team that, though completely ill-equipped, refused to quit. OSU's last eight games all were decided by seven points or fewer.

When the Buckeyes finally won at Wisconsin in the next-to-last regular-season game, overcoming a season's worth of brick-laying at the free-throw line with eight made in a row, the celebration ensued. True, avoiding the distinction of becoming the second Big Ten team in 51 years to lose 'em all seemed scant reward. But more, it was vindication of a very good coach and players who believed in his teachings against all concrete evidence.

Ohio State fans gave O'Brien a loud ovation in the last game at 41-year-old St. John Arena and he returned the favor, thanking the loyal fans for their unflagging support.

Truth is, they liked the style of this Easterner who'd shown no hesitance in running undisciplined players out of the program where his predecessor had been a lenient Pollyanna. They liked the way his team fought. They liked him.

Now, the question is, can that enthusiasm, O'Brien's old point guard from Boston College and the excitement of a new arena be translated into wins?

The guess here is yes. Ohio State still has significant liabilities, in particular, the lack of either a proven rebounder or scorer around the tin. Still, the vibes are so positive in Columbus and the Big Ten so down across the board that the Buckeyes actually could challenge for an NCAA Tournament berth on the heels of a 22-loss season.

Crazy? Consider:

Where O'Brien was happy simply to see Davis get the ball across midcourt, make that first pass and disappear, he now has a guy who could become the best point guard in the league.

Scoonie Penn, a 5-10 junior, knows exactly what he's doing out there. The former Big East Freshman of the Year ('96) and Big East Tournament MVP ('97) is a classic dribble penetrator with eyes in his temples and a waterbug's moves. The ball is a yo-yo in his hands. He will make every man on the team better. Penn averaged 13.1 points and handed out 81 assists in his final season at BC

Michael Redd (21.9 ppg, 6.5 rpg, 91 assists, 61 steals), a 6-5 sophomore, was the Big Ten Freshman of the Year after a season in which he led the league in scoring (the first rookie ever to do so) and led the nation's freshmen in scoring. He should immediately become more effective because of Penn. Forced to create his own shots constantly a year ago, Redd developed a lethal crossover and first-step to move through heavy traffic. Now, given space created by defenders' respect for Penn, Redd's perimeter jumper should improve. He shot well early in the season before a 37.9 average in minutes sapped his legs a year ago. Redd will probably switch permanently to the three spot, a more natural fit that can exploit his one-on-one skill.

Penn's presence should also help, though to a lesser extent, center **Ken Johnson**, a 6-11, 220-pound junior. Young and raw, Johnson (6.8 ppg, 4.2 rpg, 58 blocked shots) can look mechanical in the pivot and doesn't have a natural head for the game. But he shows flashes of physical talent that make O'Brien's mouth water. Once in a while, a flawless sky hook, a rebound snared way above the rim or an emphatic rejection show what Johnson could become. A 15-point, 10-rebound effort in OSU's narrow Big Ten Tournament loss to Indiana was encouraging. O'Brien would take that every night this season.

What the Buckeyes need most out of Johnson is smart hip movement for board position, a minimum of mental errors with the ball and sweat. If he can develop into a top-five rebounder in the league, the Buckeyes will have a triangle of strength in place to challenge for a top-division finish.

The rest of the team consists of role players. **Neshaun Coleman**, a 6-3 senior, is ticketed for a starting spot at shooting guard. An ankle injury before the first exhibition game last season cost Coleman (6.5 ppg, 2.5 rpg) his starting job. Redd took it as a blessing in disguise. Inconsistent from three-point range a year ago and a disaster in a few dabbles at the point, Coleman should get better looks with Penn nearby. Whether he knocks them down is another matter, though his .344 percentage from behind

1998-99 OHIO STATE SCHEDULE

Nov.	13	Oakland
	15	Alabama
	18	Robert Morris
	20	Penn State
	22	Army
	24	Tennessee Tech
	28	@Vanderbilt
Dec.	5	@Toledo
	14	Tennessee-Martin
	17	Florida Atlantic
	21-23	#Puerto Rico Holiday Classic
	27	@Miami
Jan.	2	@Wisconsin
	9	Indiana
	12	Iowa
	16	@Michigan
	19	Purdue
	23	Minnesota
	27	@Michigan State
	30	@Illinois
Feb.	6	@Purdue
	9	Michigan
	13	@Iowa
	17	@Indiana
	20	Northwestern
	24	Wisconsin
	27	@Penn State
Mar.	4-7	##Big Ten Tournament

@ Road Games
\# San Juan, PR (vs. UAB, first round; also American University-PR, Middle Tennessee State, Mississippi, North Carolina State, Oklahoma and St. Joseph's)
\## United Center, Chicago, IL

the arc led Ohio State last season.

O'Brien might end up starting 6-7, 225-pound sophomore **Jon Sanderson** (9.1 ppg, 5.5 rpg, 60 assists) at power forward simply by default. Sanderson's awkward screwball jumper is streaky and he's not really big enough. But he's unafraid to stick his nose in traffic and is a deceptively tough rebounder.

First off the bench looks like 6-6 senior **Jason Singleton** (10.7 ppg, 4.8 rpg, 43 assists, 33 steals) who, along with Coleman, represent the only remaining links to the Ayers regime. He can't shoot a lick. In fact his countless misses from five feet and in became a pitiful symbol of the Buckeyes' futility. But the kid's a fighter. Somehow, Singleton came up with a big offensive night in a narrow loss to Kansas in the Rainbow Classic, throwing in all manner of runners and stickbacks in an improbable Buckeye surge to a late lead. O'Brien likes him because he has a warrior's attitude and plays defense with fangs.

The only other returners are bit-part players. **Shamar Herron** (1.6 ppg, 1.5 rpg), a 6-9, 247-pound sophomore, actually started three games when O'Brien attempted to light a fire under Johnson late in the year. He played in 27, the best being a six-point, four-rebound effort. An intelligent kid with good grades, he's a plow horse who won't play except to fill in for those in dire need of rest.

Kwadjo Steele (0.4 ppg, 0.4 rpg), a 6-7 junior, is a walk-on practice player. He saw a smidgen of legit action last year. Competitive and smart, he tries hard.

Among four freshmen, the most important are a power forward and a driveway shooter.

George Reese, a 6-7, 220-pound junior, will play because he's a JC transfer from John A. Logan College in Carterville, Ill., where he averaged 21 points and 11 rebounds. He's a local kid who played at Independence High in Columbus three years ago. Signed by South Florida out of high school, he didn't get along with the coaching staff there and transferred out with academic problems.

Reese returned home, attended Columbus State University to get his grades in order and did not play basketball in 1996-97. He played on Johnson's team in the well-regarded Worthington summer AAU league last summer and has added weight, but he looks to need tone and conditioning. Whether O'Brien can get 15 dependable minutes of boards and D out of Reese is a pivotal question if OSU is to make the quantum leap to tournament contender.

The other newcomer of note is **Slobodan "Boban" Savovic**, a 6-5 220-pound freshman from the Serbian republic of Montanegro by way of East Side High in Newark, N.J. There, he averaged 24 points, 8.0 rebounds and 6.0 assists. Savovic allegedly can fill it up as a spot-up man from the arc. He was chosen championship-game MVP in the Boston Shootout AAU tournament in June with 29 points and 10 rebounds.

Savovic has become something of a cult legend already among Columbus' Serbian community. One Serb greeted him at the airport during his recruitment last spring after waiting three hours for his flight. Then, to the astonishment of a stunned OSU assistant, Savovic was whisked off to a Serbian church on the city's East Side where 30 people welcomed him. He is now living with a Serbian family in the suburb of Bexley.

O'Brien has hopes Savovic could eventually start at shooting guard. He has quick feet, but plays flat-footed defense in the European tradition.

The other freshmen are high school teammates who probably won't play much. **Brian Brown** is a 6-3 combo guard from Bishop Loughlin High in New York City. He supposedly has a decent three-point shot. It remains to be seen how consistent it is with people actually slapping some stiff defense on him.

Loughlin teammate **Will Dudley** a 6-8 forward, is for two years down the road. Lean up top, he had a good AAU season but isn't ready for Big Ten muscle.

adidas Blue Ribbon Analysis

BACKCOURT	**B**	**BENCH/DEPTH**	**C**
FRONTCOURT	**C-**	**INTANGIBLES**	**A-**

If this were chess, O'Brien would be playing with two queens and 10 pawns. In Penn and Redd, the Buckeyes have two superior pieces who can whoosh about the board in sweeping strokes, flashing one-on-one skills the others can't dream of. The key is whether one other player (Johnson? Savovic? Sanderson?) can become a bishop or knight at the offensive end.

If so, O'Brien is in business. Give this guy something to work with and he won't disappoint. And his teams will always play defense.

Enthusiasm is bound to build as fans settle into the shiny new 19,500-seat, $105 million Schottenstein Center, scheduled to be ready by the Buckeyes' first exhibition game on Nov. 3. Seat licenses are 90-percent sold already at $4,000, $7,500 and $15,000 a pop—all that simply for the right to buy tickets for the next 40 years.

A good start and there's no telling where this season could lead. Fourth place in the league is not out of the question. Sixth would be satisfying enough.

(D.J.)

PENN STATE

LOCATION	**State College, PA**
CONFERENCE	**Big Ten**
LAST SEASON	**19-13 (.593)**
CONFERENCE RECORD	**8-8 (6th)**
STARTERS LOST/RETURNING	**1/4**
NICKNAME	**Nittany Lions**
COLORS	**Blue & White**
HOMECOURT	**Jordan Center (15,261)**
COACH	**Jerry Dunn (George Mason '80)**
RECORD AT SCHOOL	**50-38 (3 yrs.)**
CAREER RECORD	**50-38 (3 yrs.)**
ASSISTANTS	**Mike Boyd (Northern Michigan '70)**
	Chuck Swenson (Indiana '76)
	Christian Appleman (Penn State '90)
TEAM WINS (last 5 yrs.)	**13-21-21-10-19**
RPI (last 5 yrs.)	**91-65-20-133-83**
1997-98 FINISH	**Lost in NIT final.**

It happened on the basketball floor at Madison Square Garden, but it might just as well have been out in the alley off 33rd Street.

Penn State power forward **Jarrett Stephens** was rising for a breakaway dunk in the first half of a National Invitation Tournament semifinal when Georgia's Larry Brown, clearly too far behind to affect the shot, opted for a two-handed takedown instead.

In the next second, a promising 1998-99 season, for Penn State and Stephens, was thrown into doubt.

Brown, who also played tight end for Georgia's football team, drove Stephens into the wood; the Big Ten's top shooter landed with a sickening thud.

Stephens' left knee bounced off the court with the sound of badly-thrown bowling ball. His anterior cruciate ligament in that knee was ripped and cartilage was torn.

Penn State won the game, but it hardly mattered. A subsequent 79-72 loss to Minnesota in the NIT title game was a lot less important to a program struggling for respect than Stephens' health this year.

And, as of late September, it was still unclear whether PSU's most important cog would play this season. And to what effect if he did.

It's this simple: If Stephens plays and is even 90 percent of his old self, the Lions are a logical choice for as high as second place in the Big Ten and are a clear contender for an NCAA at-large bid. If the senior doesn't play or struggles to recapture the spring and Barkley-esque mobility that so marked his pre-injury game, the Nittany Lions are in for a fight just to finish in the first division and are darkhorses for the Dance.

That's how much the Ferndale, Mich., native means to this team. That Stephens (14.1 ppg, 5.9 rpg) was overlooked as an All-Big Ten pick in 1998 is a farce, part a result of coach Jerry Dunn's odd insistence on bringing him off the bench and part because of Stephens' substance-over-style manner.

Stephens led the Big Ten in field goal percentage. In 51 years the Big Ten has been keeping that stat, Stephens' .643 ranks in a tie for No. 7 among seasonal leaders. The six players above him on the list all played in the NBA or will—Evan Eschmeyer ('97), Steve Scheffler ('90), Loy Vaught ('89), Ken Norman ('86), Ron Charles ('80) and Jerry Lucas ('60, '62).

Stephens' sense for the game and quick hands allowed him to also lead the team in steals (48). Find another player who pulls off that double (steals, FG percentage) and you've found a player.

Listed at 6-7 but really barely over 6-5, Stephens is stocky of build yet possesses a remarkable bounce in his muscular calves and upper thighs. He lost 15 pounds during strenuous summer therapy sessions and looks to be in the best shape of his life. But all that matters is a knee that was initially diagnosed as a 6-to-9-month rehab project.

If Dunn has the old Stephens available, every weak-side rebound is his, every shot from within six feet he takes is as good as made, every fast break he runs has one of the league's best finishers filling a lane. And every entry pass to senior center **Calvin Booth** on the low blocks may draw a double-team only at great risk.

If Stephens isn't out there, Booth becomes a lot less effective with his growing arsenal of shots. A team that already ranked dead last in rebounding takes a huge hit on the glass. And a top returning scorer versatile enough to post up bigger defenders or win a game with his only three-pointer of the season is lost.

Penn State never seems to get a break from this sort of thing. This could be the fifth consecutive Penn State season (and sixth in the last seven) in which a starter from the previous year will be forced to redshirt the season. It happened to Danny Earl in '98 (knee) and '97 (back); Rahsaan Carlton in '96 (knee); and Matt Gaudio in '95 and '93 (back). Two others were valuable enough that they started the year after a redshirt season—Michael Jennings in '92 (hamstring) and Titus Ivory in '97 (foot).

So, if Stephens is held out, that will make eight potential starters lost in eight seasons.

Without Stephens, PSU still has a shot at its third NCAA berth in nine seasons, but it will be a struggle.

Booth (11.8 ppg, 6.5 rpg, 4.5 bpg) is getting looks from NBA scouts, mainly because of his uncanny timing and reach as a shot-blocker. He was chosen the Big Ten defensive player of the year in '98.

Already owning 333 blocks, including 140 last season, Booth should finish this season among the top five on the all-time NCAA Division I list. That's a group that includes current NBA stars Shaquille O'Neal, David Robinson, Theo Ratliff and Alonzo Mourning.

Booth stepped up his productivity with the ball last season, too. He moved better, learned a drop-step, smoothed his baseline turnaround into a dependable option and added 20 pounds (now 6-11 and 230) to what was a rail-thin frame. By the time he returned from a summer stint with the gold-medal-winning U.S. Goodwill Games team in July, he was looking like a real post player instead of the lower-case Manute Bol that was pushed around by league centers his sophomore year.

But Booth's value has always grown exponentially with a tough, scoring power forward at his side. All-Big Ten first-teamer Matt Gaudio ('96) and Stephens ('98) took the heat off him.

If Stephens can't go, it's unclear whether his likely replacement, 6-7 sophomore **Gyasi Cline-Heard** (3.0 ppg, 2.2 rpg), is ready to supply the same sort of pop.

Certainly, Cline-Heard has potential. The son of former NBA veteran and current Detroit Pistons assistant coach Garfield Heard was the most intriguing development of the late season.

Though still a little edgy with the ball, his sheer athleticism and willingness to stick his nose in traffic gets him points. His 14 points and five boards in place of Stephens in the NIT final suggest he can quickly become a scoring force if he continues to develop a steady baseline jumper. Cline-Heard's .682 field goal percentage (15-22) in nine minutes per Big Ten game bodes well.

1998-99 PENN STATE SCHEDULE

Nov.	16	Virginia Military Institute
	20	@Ohio State
	23	Lehigh
	28	@George Mason
Dec.	1	Temple
	5	Villanova
	9	@Bradley
	12	Pennsylvania
	21	Bucknell
	28-30	#Fiesta Bowl Tournament
Jan.	2	Michigan
	6	Purdue
	9	@Minnesota
	13	Wisconsin
	20	@Northwestern
	23	@Illinois
	27	@Iowa
	31	Indiana
Feb.	2	Michigan State
	6	Northwestern
	13	@Wisconsin
	17	Minnesota
	20	@Purdue
	23	@Michigan
	27	Ohio State
Mar.	4-7	##Big Ten Tournament

@ Road Games
# Tucson, AZ (vs. Florida International, first round; also Arizona and Holy Cross)
United Center, Chicago, IL

But he can't hope to replace his mentor as a rebounder and that's what the Lions would need most in Stephens' absence.

Junior power forward **Carl Jackson** (1.8 ppg, 1.9 rpg) is a plow horse Dunn started most of the season because of his hard work on defense. The 6-9, 247-pound Jackson isn't a Big Ten-level talent, but he's a veteran in a league without many on the baseline.

Dunn also can get a few legit minutes from sophomore center **Scott Witkowsky** (0.6 ppg, 1.2 rpg). Not any sort of all star while a high schooler in Colorado, Witkowsky is nonetheless huge (7-0, 270) and ingrained with work ethic. His foot work inside isn't bad for a guy his size, but he hasn't logged the minutes yet to develop any game outside of bump-and-grind.

The perimeter should be a strength. Three freshmen who saved the season a year ago are back for their sophomore years. They give Penn State promise of backcourt depth for years to come.

The man most responsible for Penn State's late-season run of nine wins in 13 tries (including NIT wins in tough homecourts at Dayton and Georgia Tech) was sophomore point guard **Joe Crispin** (9.6 ppg, 1.9 rpg, 107 assists, 25 steals).

Dunn and the 5-11 Crispin are inseparably intertwined. Nobody of any magnitude wanted Crispin out of tiny Pitman (N.J.) High School. Other than Penn State, only low-major Fairfield offered him a scholarship.

While Dunn was the only one to see the fire in Crispin's eyes, the freshman's nerve and guile no less than saved the season—and ultimately maybe even Dunn's job down the road.

Fifth-year senior **Danny Earl**, counted on to run the offense, went down with a torn ACL in the season's fifth game against Lehigh and was lost for the season for the second straight year. Penn State had already been through this before with disastrous results. In '96-97, Earl couldn't go because of a chronic back ailment and was replaced by true freshman **Ryan Bailey.** The Lions pinballed through a horrific 3-15 Big Ten season and quit on Dunn down the stretch.

Barely 18, Crispin vowed after his second game, a 1-for-7, five-turnover outing in a loss at VMI, that the same thing wouldn't happen again.

It didn't.

Crispin's stats weren't overwhelming. His 107-99 assist-turnover ratio was made mediocre by a bad habit of crossing over his dribble in front of more experienced guards. And he takes risks with passes.

But Crispin has a propensity for the big play and a sense for time and situation that a player either has or doesn't. He has an ingrained confidence that's just a notch short of cocky and tends to raise the level of those around him. In short, he's a winner, he loves the game and he'll only get better.

Sophomore swingman **Titus Ivory** (5.4 ppg, 2.9 rpg, 63 assists, 35 steals), also started as a 6-4 third guard. Ivory—a big-boned, quick-handed clone of former PSU standout Monroe Brown—overcame a foot injury that sidelined him all of 1996-97 and immediately became State's best on-ball defender.

When PSU was 3-6 in the league and sliding to 10-9 overall, seemingly headed for another rendezvous with oblivion, Ivory's defense was a constant, a stabilizer. But when he began hitting big three-pointers (his .368 three-point percentage against the Big Ten was a team-high), the Lions got an offensive jolt, too. Already 21, Ivory has a year of prep school behind him and is a mature, upbeat personality who's great for team chemistry.

The third sophomore is **Greg Grays** (6.0 ppg, 1.8 apg), a quick, 6-foot off guard whose guts in tight situations stood out. He banged in a pair of big threes and had 18 points and four steals in the win at Georgia Tech. Grays is a terrific asset on the break. But he needs to tweak his three-point shot (.347) to help fill the void of departed gunner Pete Lisicky (15.6 ppg, 2.8 rpg, 113 assists, 35 steals, .368 three-point percentage). Trey accuracy will determine whether he gets 20 minutes a game or 10.

Rounding out the backcourt is Earl (8.4 ppg, 3.2 rpg 3.8 apg in five games last season) whose stay at Penn State only seems like it stretches back to the Eisenhower administration. Granted a rare sixth year of eligibility by the NCAA, Earl has seen the entire Big Ten history of this program. He was recruited even before Penn State's painful inaugural season and his rise as the team's unquestioned playmaker and floor boss paralleled the program's ascent to respectability. From his very first minute wearing No.10, Earl has started at the point.

Now Dunn has a dilemma: Does he pull his young fighter pilot Crispin off the point and give the job back to Earl (the most likely scenario)? Or does he allow Crispin, a superior penetrator, to keep starting at the point and play Earl as a combo—starting off-guard and sub point-man?

While Crispin made several important threes last year with games in the balance, he's short (5-11) and wasn't a good triple shooter for the entire span of games (.324). In no way is he a prototype two-guard. Earl, on the other hand is tall enough (6-3) to get clear looks and is a .401 career three-point shooter (137-342).

One thing's for sure: With PSU depleted at small forward because of the April transfer of junior Greg Stevenson, the Lions need points from the guards. However Dunn can get them will dictate his decisions.

Others in the mix are bit-players, rookies and walk-ons. The only one who figures to get any minutes outside of mop-up is freshman power forward **Stephan Bekale** (Notre Dame Academy/Middleburg, Va., and T.C. Williams HS/ Washington, D.C.). A 6-8, 225-pounder with a cut-up physique, Bekale is a native of Libraville, Gabon on the Ivory Coast of Africa. He is a raw offensive player. If Dunn can get three or four rebounds out of him in 6-8 minutes, he'll be happy.

The other recruit is a project—6-7 forward **Tyler Smith** (Lake Forest HS/Lake Forest, Ill.) who won't play much but is very intelligent and may eventually fill a Glenn Sekunda role as a wing shooter.

Not eligible is the most notable recruit in the '98 class, 6-5 forward Rob Walls of St. Joseph's HS in West Chester, Ill. From the same alma mater as Isiah Thomas, Walls would have given the Lions a slasher on the wing. But his transcripts were red-flagged by the NCAA Clearinghouse and he'll spend at least one year in prep school.

Titcus Pettigrew (1.3 ppg, 0.6 rpg in 1997) could also take another stab at hoops. A cornerback/wideout on the football team, Pettigrew is 6-4, was a high school hoop star in North Carolina and might see time as a defensive specialist for a handful of minutes.

Tim McGovern (0.0 ppg, 0.3 rpg), a 6-0 junior; **Pete Rogowski** (0.0 ppg, 0.5 rpg) and **Jon Branam** (1.5 ppg, 0.0 rpg), a 6-0 junior, are walkons who won't play except for blow-outs. Branam is a valuable practice player who actually hit four treys last season.

adidas Blue Ribbon Analysis

BACKCOURT .... **B+** **BENCH/DEPTH** .... **B-**
FRONTCOURT .... **C** **INTANGIBLES** .... **C**

This team could finish anywhere from second to seventh depending on the health of Stephens and, to a lesser degree, Earl. Their knee rehabs make Penn State a tough pick.

Based on the known quantities, the Lions need a dependable scorer and big-play guy to replace the departed Lisicky. Though he sometimes shot the Nittany Lions out of games, Lisicky also won a bunch with his clutch three-point shooting. Somebody has to acquire that knack to give PSU a good shot at the NCAAs because this group simply isn't athletic enough to win big by other means. If it's not Earl and not Grays, who is it?

The other potential debacle is rebounding. State managed .500 in the league last year even though it consistently was outjumped and outflanked for rebounds. If Stephens can't go or isn't his old springy self, Cline-Heard and Bekale will have to make quantum leaps to keep the Lions from getting destroyed on the glass.

For once, a presentable non-conference schedule should answer these questions before the New Year. Villanova and Temple visit State College for the first time in years. Arizona is a likely opponent on its home floor in the Fiesta Bowl Classic final at Tucson. That's if the Lions can get by revenge-seeking former PSU guard Damien McKnight of Florida International. McKnight feuded with Dunn two years ago and transferred to FIU.

Penn State continues to recruit outside of Pennsylvania to remain competitive. Cursed with no urban turf it can call its own and constantly in the shadow of Joe Paterno's football behemoth, the Lions will suit up without a single scholarship player from the home state this season. Only a small handful of Division I teams can say the same. And none is a consistent Top 25 inhabitant.

Dunn is close to nabbing the recruit that could give this program visibility in Philadelphia or Pittsburgh or Washington, D.C. But he hasn't sealed such a deal yet. Until he does, this will continue to be a hand-to-mouth program that, while competitive, must always live in fear of the big injury.

(D.J.)

WISCONSIN

LOCATION .... **Madison, WI**
CONFERENCE .... **Big Ten**
LAST SEASON .... **12-19 (.387)**
CONFERENCE RECORD .... **3-13 (t-9th)**
STARTERS LOST/RETURNING **1/4**
NICKNAME .... **Badgers**
COLORS .... **Cardinal & White**
HOMECOURT .... **Kohl Center (17,142)**
COACH .... **Dick Bennett (Ripon '65)**
RECORD AT SCHOOL .... **47-44 (3 yrs.)**
CAREER RECORD .... **407-233 (22 yrs.)**
ASSISTANTS .... **Brad Soderberg (Wisconsin-Stevens Point '85)**
Shawn Hood (Cleveland State '88)
Brian Hecker (Indiana '90)
TEAM WINS (last 5 yrs.) **18-13-17-18-12**
RPI (last 5 yrs.) **28-102-67-36-101**
1997-98 FINISH .... **Lost in conference second round.**

Program propaganda at Wisconsin has mentioned that this is the first year that coach Dick Bennett has a UW roster made up entirely of players he recruited. This is, at once, a good and bad thing.

On one hand, there are no Sam Okeys. On the other, there are no Sam Okeys. Wisconsin fans know what we mean.

While the old-school Bennett has no star scorer/ rebounder to hang his hat on this season, he also probably doesn't have to worry about the petulant nonsense that infected and ultimately destroyed last year's Badgers.

Okey's suspension for missing a team training session, then defection the next day—on the eve of Wisconsin's opening of its beautiful new Kohl Center—was a body blow from which the Badgers never recovered. They already were missing tough point guard **Ty Calderwood**, redshirted because of a knee injury, and were playing without a true pivot man because NBA draftee Paul Grant had not been adequately replaced.

When Okey left and later decided to transfer to Iowa for his senior year, any chance the Badgers had of participating in the postseason went out the door with him.

Okey's departure also may have been symptomatic of pervasive selfishness in today's college game, one Bennett can't and won't tolerate as some other coaches do. Okey wanted to play at a quicker pace, something Wisconsin couldn't hope to win at considering its lack of depth. Frantic pace is also not a trend the crew-cut Bennett is likely to adopt soon. So, Okey left.

It's hard to watch a man like Bennett fail. Demanding of technique and precision, he is a persnickety teacher of the game who will never recruit himself a Big Ten title. But, entering the fourth season of a five-year contract, he'd take a team competitive enough to challenge for an NCAA berth.

These Badgers should make bubble conversation come March. But Bennett knows if somebody doesn't fill Okey's void inside, the bubble will probably burst.

"I'll be surprised if we aren't a much more cohesive team," Bennett said. "I think we're moving toward the nucleus we want. We're strong in the guard area. I like this team."

Indeed, in a year when the Big Ten has an obvious pack leader (Michigan State) and everybody else is puttering along on training wheels, Wisconsin is an intriguing squad because of a backcourt full of experience and skill. And the hot conduit between Bennett and his five seasoned guards, four of them seniors, will give UW a fighting chance.

Calderwood (8.8 ppg, 3.2 rpg in '96-97), apparently at 100 percent again after suffering chronic tendinitis in his patella after surgery last year, brings an overall game of hustle, nerve and energy. The guts of the 1996-97 team who made game-winning plays in the Badgers' NCAA-clinching upset of Minnesota will be warmly welcomed back to the point.

How valuable is Calderwood? He led the team two years ago in steals, assists, free-throw percentage (.792) and minutes. And when Calderwood didn't start the NCAA first-rounder against Texas because Bennett was infuriated that he'd been 12 minutes late for a team meal, the Badgers fell behind and were held at arm's length throughout the game.

At Calderwood's side is perhaps the most underrated

1998-99 WISCONSIN SCHEDULE

Nov.	14	Loyola
	16	Wisconsin-Milwaukee
	20-22	#Top of the World Tournament
	28	@Rhode Island
Dec.	2	Northern Illinois
	5	@Illinois State
	9	@Temple
	12	Pepperdine
	15	@Texas
	23	@Marquette
	27	Fresno State
	30	@Michigan
Jan.	2	Ohio State
	6	Michigan State
	10	Purdue
	13	@Penn State
	16	@Northwestern
	20	Illinois
	23	@Iowa
	30	Minnesota
Feb.	3	@Indiana
	6	@Illinois
	10	Northwestern
	13	Penn State
	21	@Michigan State
	24	@Ohio State
	27 or 28	Michigan
Mar.	4-7	##Big Ten Tournament

@ Road Games
# Fairbanks, AK (vs. New Mexico State, first round; also Air Force, Arkansas, Nebraska, Villanova, Virginia and Washington State)
United Center, Chicago, IL

player in the Big Ten, 6-2 off-guard **Sean Mason** (15.5 ppg, 2.9 rpg, .815 FT percentage). Calling Mason the Badgers' leading returning scorer doesn't do him justice. Not only was he remarkably consistent (26 of 31 games in double figures) after coming off surgeries on each knee in consecutive years, he was the only Badger capable and willing to accept an offensive challenge during a string of impotent Wisconsin performances late in the season. Yet, Mason is one of the few players in the league—indeed, in the nation—with a sense of time and situation. Even with the ship sinking around him, Mason rarely forced his game until desperation dictated he must. If his sore knees hold up, he's capable of a first-team All-Big Ten season.

The third guard in what will often be a three-guard set is probably 6-3 sophomore **Mike Kelley** (4.2 ppg, 2.0 rpg, 1.9 spg). Kelley was thrust into the starting point guard spot when Calderwood went down and that made him wiser than his years. He's the kind of physical, defense-minded mutt Bennett loves, able to body up on driveway shooters and get in their heads. Though not a waterbug, he's quick and savvy enough to have collected 58 steals a year ago without having seen his competition before.

First guard off the bench is 6-1 senior **Hennssy Auriantal** (7.2 ppg, 2.1 apg), another defensive specialist who has slowly improved as a playmaker during three seasons of grinding in Bennett's set-piece system. Auriantal's offensive repertoire won't scare anybody. But he's quick and, by now, knows the moves of every point in the league.

His playmakers and defenders established, what Bennett could really use is a hired gun who can play 15-20 minutes and bomb in a few threes. Such was lacking in '98; Wisconsin had no one in the league top 10 in either three-pointers made or three-point percentage.

The two main candidates for that role are 6-5 junior **Duany "Doc" Duany** (4.5 ppg, 1.7 rpg), who got his nickname in high school because he once "operated" on defenses, and Division II transfer **Jon Bryant**, a 6-2 junior.

Duany operated more like Frank Burns last season. His jumper was flat and his contribution was a flat line—a disastrous .198 from the arc (16 of 81). Bryant, we know, can stroke it against Division II competition. He was .468 on treys (87 of 186) for St. Cloud (Minn.) State. If the Badgers can get him looks, he might be a valuable man to have around.

Had enough guards? Wait. There's more. The forgotten man might be 6-1 senior **David Burkemper** (0.7 ppg, 0.8 rpg), who actually started on the NCAA team in '96 and could be headed for a coaching position someday. "I thought he was smarter than that," says Bennett. Burkemper doesn't do anything exceedingly well, but he's another mature senior who takes care of the ball, can play either backcourt spot in a pinch and won't whine for PT.

Travon Davis (Nazareth Academy, Summitt, Ill.), 5-10, and **John Moriarity** (Oostburg H.S., Oostburg, Wisc.), 6-5, are freshmen guards and likely practice fodder.

Now, the caveat. If Bennett can't find someone to score, board and defend on the baseline, the backcourt depth won't matter.

Nobody exactly jumps out at you. Among sophomores **Andy Kowske** (5.1 ppg, 3.9 rpg), **Mark Vershaw** (5.3 ppg, 2.7 rpg) and **Maurice Linton**, the three kids forced to tote big minutes a year ago, none appears ready to carry a primary offensive load.

Kowske, 6-8, looks like the toughest, which is a start. He grabbed 10 rebounds against athletic Fresno State and started nine of UW's last 10 games because Bennett liked his guts. Vershaw, 6-9, has some attitude, too, and is an alert passer. The 6-9 Linton, who played the least, made the biggest shot—a 16-foot turnaround with three seconds to go in the Badgers' one-point Big Ten Tournament upset of Penn State.

The wildcards are two freshmen. **Maurice Sessoms** (Berkshire School, Teaneck, NJ) is 6-8 and 220 but probably not ready for Big Ten pounding. More intriguing is **Charlie Wills** (Angola H.S., Angola IN), a 6-8, 235-pound banger who redshirted a year ago and has a more mature body. "He's a good passer from the high post, he's smart and he'll do whatever you ask him to do," said Bennett.

In other words, he's no Okey.

adidas Blue Ribbon Analysis

BACKCOURT .... A- **BENCH/DEPTH .... C+**
FRONTCOURT .... C- **INTANGIBLES .... B**

Give Dick Bennett a bunch of tough, experienced guards and he's proven to be a very tough out against anyone. He has exactly that this season which makes this Wisconsin team impossible to dismiss for the field of 64.

Points will be hard to come by, but they always are for a coach who plays a wool-socks-and-hightops style. It was no aberration that UW finished first in the league in points allowed (62.6) and last in points scored (60.5) a year ago.

But Bennett doesn't need to roll up points to make his system work. What he needs is to make possessions count. One or two guys who can knock down some threes at the end of trips against opponents sick of playing defense would do wonders for this club.

And if Bennett can mine someone to do the dirty work inside and gets a levy-en-masse attitude from his big men across the board, the Badgers might then be able to get by without a big-scoring forward.

"This is the first team that will play the game like I want to play since I've been here," assured Bennett. "I think this group is tough and tough-minded."

Whether a guy like Bennett can survive in the age of brainless AAU ball when so many recruits only want to run and score is a point open for debate. This season will go a long way toward providing the answer.

(D.J.)

adidas Blue Ribbon Analysis
GRADING SYSTEM

- A+ equal to very best in country—Final Four-caliber unit
- A among the best in the land—worthy of deep NCAA run
- B+ talented, versatile and experienced—NCAA-NIT ability
- B solid and productive winners—league and post-season contenders
- C+ average to above-average—may contend in a weaker league
- C average to mediocre—second division in a strong league
- D+ below average, inconsistent—second division in a weaker league
- D well below average—losing season virtually certain
- F non-Division I ability—an underdog every night

BIG 12 CONFERENCE

adidas BLUE RIBBON FORECAST

1. Oklahoma State
2. Kansas
3. Oklahoma
4. Texas
5. Nebraska
6. Missouri
7. Kansas State
8. Texas Tech
9. Iowa State
10. Colorado
11. Texas A&M
12. Baylor

TOP 40

Kansas, Oklahoma, Oklahoma State and Texas are ranked among the 1998-99 *adidas Blue Ribbon* Top 40. Extended profiles can be found in the Top 40 section of *Blue Ribbon*.

ALL-CONFERENCE TEAM

C—Venson Hamilton, SR, Nebraska
F—Marcus Fizer, SO, Iowa State
G—Kris Clack, SR, Texas
G—Adrian Peterson, SR, Oklahoma State
G—Rayford Young, SR, Texas Tech

PLAYER OF THE YEAR

Adrian Peterson, SR, Oklahoma State

NEWCOMER OF THE YEAR

Keyon Dooling, FR, Missouri

1998-99 CONFERENCE TOURNAMENT

March 5-8, Kemper Arena, Kansas City, MO

1997-98 CHAMPION

Kansas (regular season)
Kansas (conference tournament)

1997-98 POSTSEASON PARTICIPANTS

Postseason Record: 2-6 (.250)

NCAA

Kansas (2nd round)
Oklahoma State (2nd round)
Nebraska
Oklahoma

NIT

Kansas State
Missouri

TOP BACKCOURTS

1. Oklahoma State
2. Texas Tech
3. Kansas

TOP FRONTCOURTS

1. Nebraska
2. Kansas
3. Kansas State

ON THE WAY UP

Oklahoma State

ON THE WAY DOWN

Kansas

INSIDE THE NUMBERS

- 1997-98 conference RPI: 6th (of 30)
- Conference RPI (last 5 years): 3-1-2-2-6

DID YOU KNOW?

Texas A&M opens its new building, 12,500-seat Reed Arena, a year behind schedule because of construction problems...Texas Tech gets into its new building next season...New coaches in the league this season are Rick Barnes (Clemson) at Texas, Melvin Watkins (UNC Charlotte) at Texas A&M and Larry Eustachy (Utah State) at Iowa State. None of those Big 12 programs were in the postseason last year, but all of the new coaches took their former teams to the NCAA Tournament...The NCAA will leave Overland Park, Kansas for Indianapolis next summer, but the NABC is staying in town. Actually the coaches' group will move its office from Overland Park to venerable Municipal Auditorium in downtown Kansas City and plans to conduct an annual marquee game and open a coaches hall of fame...The conference held its own against other major leagues last season, finishing 3-3 against the ACC, 4-3 against the Big Ten and 5-4 against the Pac-10. But the Southeastern Conference (4-8) and Western Athletic Conference (5-11) owned the Big 12..Kansas won only one Big Eight Tournament in eight years under Roy Williams, but the Jayhawks are two for two in Big 12 Tournaments. If Kansas makes it three straight, it will do so without the player chosen MVP of the previous two, Paul Pierce, who left for the NBA with a year of eligibility remaining...Other streaks on the line for Kansas this season: The Jayhawks have won four straight conference championships and 60 straight games in Allen Field House. They've also posted consecutive 15-1 league records...A Big 12 all-star team won four of six games on a summer tour of Germany and Holland. The team was coached by Texas Tech's James Dickey and included at least one player from each team...The NBA strike nixed what would have been an interesting exhibition game. The Chicago Bulls and coach Tim Floyd were scheduled to come through Ames, Iowa. Wonder what kind of reception Floyd would have received?

(B.K.)

BAYLOR

LOCATION .... **Waco, TX**
CONFERENCE .... **Big 12**
LAST SEASON .... **14-14 (.500)**
CONFERENCE RECORD .... **8-8 (t-5th)**
STARTERS LOST/RETURNING **3/2**
NICKNAME .... **Bears**
COLORS .... **Green & Gold**
HOMECOURT .... **Ferrel Center (10,084)**
COACH .... **Harry Miller (Texas Lutheran '74)**
RECORD AT SCHOOL .... **50-63 (4 yrs.)**
CAREER RECORD .... **50-63 (4 yrs.)**
ASSISTANTS .... **Mike Wilson (Southwestern)**
Rodney Terry (St. Edwards '90)
Brad Autry (Northwester Oklahoma '91)
TEAM WINS (last 5 yrs.) **16-9-9-18-16**
RPI (last 5 yrs.) **135-238-214-93-99**
1997-98 FINISH .... **Lost in conference quarterfinal.**

Last year was the strangest of seasons for Baylor. Injuries decimated the team early, and losses to Lamar and Northwestern State in the first three games took the wind from the team's sails. Even coach Harry Miller admitted before the calendar turned to December that it would be tough for the Bears to overcome those losses if Baylor became NCAA Tournament-worthy later in the season.

Then Big 12 play started and the Bears looked like world beaters. They started 5-0, with victories at Texas and Texas Tech. The streak was capped by a thrilling, 97-95 double-overtime triumph over nationally ranked Oklahoma State. For a few days, Baylor sat on top of the league standings. Miller knew the streak couldn't last.

"Man, if we finished in second place there'd be a ticker tape parade in downtown Waco," Miller said. "Confetti and everything."

The slide was just as abrupt. The Bears returned to earth by losing five straight and seven of eight. Baylor limped home and became Texas A&M's lone victim in Big 12 play. In all, it was a crushing season for the Bears, who had high hopes entering the season because of the return of center Brian Skinner.

Skinner (18.1 ppg, 9.5 rpg, 98 blocked shots, 38 steals), the Bears' leading scorer and rebounder, is gone and so are other double digit scorers Patrick Hunter (12.8 ppg, 3.4 rpg, 106 assists, 33 steals) and Roddrick Miller (11.9 ppg, 97 assists, 28 steals). The rebuilding project begins now.

Sadly for the Bears, they couldn't come up with a postseason tournament appearance in the Skinner era. He leaves as one of the program's best players, a real find for Baylor. Skinner blossomed while in college and finished his career as the program's third-leading career scorer and leader in rebounds and blocked shots. He was drafted in the first round (22nd overall) by the Los Angeles Clippers.

Life without the top three scorers doesn't look promising. The returning starters were largely role players who will be asked to step up. Forward **Jamie Kendrick** (6.0 ppg, 3.9 rpg, .393 FG percentage, .318 three-point percentage), a 6-8 junior, started the first 10 league games before returning to the bench. Kendrick doesn't have much of a touch and needs to cut down on his attempts behind the arc.

Kendrick is capable of decent scoring games. He had career-high scoring performances in consecutive games, with 14 against Texas A&M and 16 against Kansas State. Kendrick played on a Big 12 all-star team that toured Europe in August, so perhaps he put in some work on his shooting.

Shooting was also a problem for the other returning starter, 6-6 junior shooting guard **Leon Morris** (6.3 ppg, 4.9 rpg, .364 FG percentage, .279 three-point percentage, .490 FT percentage). As poorly as Morris shot free-throws, he rallied for that figure by hitting .764 percent in the final six games.

Perhaps the most effective player with experience is 6-7 senior forward **Gabe Ramirez** (5.1 ppg, 3.3 rpg, .415 FG percentage, .368 three-point percentage). Ramirez suffered knee problems throughout most of the conference schedule. He and Skinner were the only Baylor players to shoot higher than 50 percent in league games. Ramirez hit .537 percent from the floor and .464 percent on three-pointers against Big 12 opponents. The Bears could have used much more than that.

Forward **Kish Lewis** (5.8 ppg, 4.7 rpg, .427 FG percentage, .460 FT percentage), a 6-7 junior, is the only other player returning who showed any signs of competing on a major college level.

The others, 6-6 junior **David Jones** (3.0 ppg, 1.1 rpg), 6-3 junior **B.J. Sellers** (2.2 ppg, 0.5 rpg), 5-9 senior **Grant**

1998-99 BAYLOR SCHEDULE

Nov.	16	@Arkansas State
	21	Texas-Arlington
	24	Southwest Texas State
	27-29	#Honolulu Thanksgiving Shootout
Dec.	2	@Creighton
	5	Nevada
	8	Texas Christian
	12	McNeese State
	19	@Marquette
	22	Jacksonville
	30	Texas-Pan American
Jan.	2	@Texas Tech
	6	Kansas
	9	Oklahoma State
	13	@Texas
	16	Nebraska
	20	@Oklahoma State
	23	Texas A&M
	30	@Missouri
Feb.	3	Oklahoma
	6	@Texas A&M
	10	Texas Tech
	13	@Kansas State
	16	@Iowa State
	20	Colorado
	24	Texas
	27	@Oklahoma
Mar.	4-7	##Big 12 Tournament

@ Road Games
\# Honolulu, HI (vs. Virginia Commonwealth, first round; also Hawaii-Pacific, Hofstra, Illinois State, Iona, Missouri-Kansas City and Southern Mississippi)
\## Kemper Arena, Kansas City, MO

McCasland (0.4 ppg, 0.6 rpg) and 6-8 senior **Jeff Gipson** (1.5 ppg, 1.3 rpg) saw action, but contributed little. It was a measure of Baylor's problems last year that Jones, Sellers and Gipson started three games each.

What this means, of course, is newcomers will have a chance to make a splash. But there are only three new faces. Two, actually. One is **Marcus Golson**, a redshirt freshman forward who played in only one game last season.

The top recruit and likely starting point guard is **Tevis Stukes**, a 5-11 junior who transferred from Independence (Kan.) Community College. Stukes averaged 25 points and seven assists as a sophomore. The Bears would settle for half of those numbers.

The same goes for freshman guard **Robert Thornton**, who averaged 25.3 points and 6.9 rebounds for Harrah HS in Oklahoma.

adidas Blue Ribbon Analysis

BACKCOURT .... **D** **BENCH/DEPTH** .... **D**
FRONTCOURT .... **D** **INTANGIBLES** .... **D**

Miller is one of the funniest guys in the Big 12. To wit: Describing a blowout loss to Kansas, "I know how the Ethiopians must have felt facing the German army during World War II, armed only with spears and loin cloths." And comparing his defense with Arkansas' "40 minutes of hell." Remember, Baylor is a Baptist school: "We like to call it 40 minutes of hostility."

Miller's going to need his sense of humor this year. This one may remind him of the bad old days. The Bears won only nine games in each of his first two years. Even with a weak non-conference schedule, that many wins may not be possible this season.

(B.K.)

COLORADO

LOCATION .... **Boulder, CO**
CONFERENCE .... **Big 12**
LAST SEASON .... **13-14 (.481)**
CONFERENCE RECORD .... **7-9 (t-7th)**
STARTERS LOST/RETURNING **3/2**
NICKNAME .... **Buffaloes**
COLORS .... **Black & Gold**
HOMECOURT .... **Coors Events Center (11,198)**
COACH .... **Ricardo Patton (Belmont '80)**
RECORD AT SCHOOL .... **39-32 (3 yrs.)**
CAREER RECORD .... **39-32 (3 yrs.)**
ASSISTANTS .... **David Moe (Texas Lutheran '86)**
Terry Dunn (Northern Colorado '77)
Shane Wagner (Ohio '93)
TEAM WINS (last 5 yrs.) **13-22-14-10-10**
RPI (last 5 yrs.) **163-76-131-39-120**
1997-98 FINISH .... **Lost in conference first round.**

Colorado basketball over the last few seasons has been like the stock market of last summer: Record gains followed by stunning drops. Just take a peek at the Buffaloes' RPI the last five years.

Colorado peaked in 1997 with 22 victories and a triumph over Indiana in the first round of the NCAA Tournament. The team was led by sophomore Chauncy Billups, who left after that season, and coach Ricardo Patton was a hot commodity. But it was back to reality for the Buffaloes in 1997-98, a season school officials, like Wall Street analysts, call an "adjustment."

At Colorado, adjusting meant rebuilding. The Buffs lost nearly all their scoring threats and had to reinvent themselves last season. The results weren't bad. Colorado clawed its way to some unexpected outcomes, like a victory at Texas and an overtime loss at Oklahoma State. A 7-9 league record speaks to Patton's coaching. In the program's leaner times of the '70s and '80s, Colorado would have shown no signs of life. A year ago, the Buffs were at least competitive.

Now comes the difficult part for Patton. A year ago, a losing record could be excused because of the personnel losses. Now, he has to convince the Big 12's most fickle fans that he has the program on solid ground and that he has been able to recruit top talent to Boulder.

The good news is the return of top scorer **Kenny Price** (14.5 ppg, 4.4 rpg, .407 FG percentage, .421 three-point percentage, .800 FT percentage, 54 assists, 21 steals, 31.2 minutes), a 6-4 senior shooting guard with excellent range. Price transferred in from junior college and made an immediate splash. He was selected the league's top newcomer in one poll.

The Buffs have had their share of three-point threats over the last few seasons, but Price's 90 bombs were a school record for a season. He personally kept Colorado close in several games. He saved his best for last, scoring a career-high 28 in the regular-season finale victory over Texas. Price made a school-record eight three-pointers in that game. He led the Big 12 in three-pointers made and three-point percentage.

The starting backcourt returns intact with 5-11 senior **Dwight Jones** (4.0 ppg, 43 assists, .409 three-point percentage) at the point. Actually, Jones was a part-time starter, but his 2.52-1 assist-turnover ratio was one of the best in the Big 12. Jones committed just 17 turnovers in 26 games. He averaged nearly 17 minutes on the floor.

Will Smith, a 6-6 junior forward, showed signs of becoming a force as a freshman, when he averaged 4.5 points and 2.0 rebounds in the shadow of Billups and made the Big 12 All-Freshman team. But Smith didn't step up last season when his numbers jumped only slightly to 5.5 points and 2.6 rebounds. His field-goal percentage actually dipped from .341 to .336.

Power forward **Jamahl Mosley** (4.4 ppg, 4.0 rpg, .429 FG percentage), a 6-8 sophomore, turned in a nice freshman season until a fractured left hand slowed him in January. Mosley eventually returned to form, setting career highs in minutes (32), field-goals made (seven), field-goals attempted (12), rebounds (11), steals (two) and points (15) in the last two games of the season.

Mosley was more productive than fellow rookies **Ernest Renfroe** (2.2 ppg, 1.4 rpg, .438 FG percentage), a 6-7 sophomore, and **Aki Thomas** (4.4 ppg, 2.3 rpg, .388 FG percentage, .205 three-point percentage), a 6-8 sophomore. Any or all could have benefited by a redshirt year, but the Buffs couldn't afford to spare a body. Thomas had occasional flashes of potential. He had a career-high 14 points against Nebraska and a personal-best 10 boards against Northwestern State.

There's plenty of opportunity for newcomers, and of the seven additions to the roster, 6-4 sophomore swingman **Tyron Manlove** appears to be the best. He was twice chosen Oregon's top high school player three years ago and enrolled at Oregon. He redshirted in 1997, then transferred to Colorado. Manlove is a scorer, something the Buffs sorely lacked last season.

There is also room for a big man, which could put a pair of 6-10 players in the mix right away. Freshman **Carlton Carter** played power forward at Solebury Academy/Trenton, N.J., where he averaged 14.5 points and 4.5 blocks last season.

Junior **Steve Ryan** played center and forward at North Idaho Junior College, where he averaged 11.1 points and 5.3 rebounds but only shot .455 percent from the floor. Ryan grew up in Sydney, Australia, and played high school ball in Baton Rouge, La. He was Patton's first signee as Colorado's head coach, but wound up going to junior college.

Four others will vie for backcourt time. **Jose Winston**, a 6-0 freshman point guard, from Vincent HS/Milwaukee, Wisc., could be the best of the bunch. One recruiting service chose him the nation's 42nd best prospect.

Nick Mohr, a 6-4 freshman from Columbine HS/Littleton, Col. will be a local favorite; 6-3 junior **Jaquay Walls** led Compton, (Cal.) Junior College to the California JC championship by averaging 14.3 points and 5.2 assists; **Kyle Williams** is a 6-6 freshman shooting guard from Burlington HS/Burlington, N.J., who averaged 21.2 points last season.

adidas Blue Ribbon Analysis

BACKCOURT .... **C** **BENCH/DEPTH** .... **C**
FRONTCOURT .... **D** **INTANGIBLES** .... **D**

The low grade for intangibles is given for potential chemistry problems with seven newcomers. This could be a rough year for Patton and the Buffaloes, who can only dream of what might have been had Chauncey Billups stayed for his junior and senior seasons.

The NCAA Tournament is out of the question for the Buffs. An NIT berth might be another year away. The skid continues.

(B.K.)

1998-99 COLORADO SCHEDULE

Nov.	14	Denver
	17	Colorado State
	20	Elon
	22	Stephen F. Austin
	26-28	#Puerto Rico Shootout
Dec.	2	Virginia Commonwealth
	5	Idaho State
	9	@Wyoming
	21	Texas-Arlington
	28-29	##Montana State Invitational
Jan.	2	Texas
	9	@Oklahoma
	13	@Iowa State
	16	Missouri
	20	@Kansas State
	23	@Nebraska
	27	Iowa State
	30	@Kansas
Feb.	3	Nebraska
	7	Kansas
	10	Oklahoma State
	13	@Missouri
	17	Texas A&M
	20	@Baylor
	24	@Texas Tech
	27	Kansas State
Mar.	4-7	###Big 12 Tournament

@ Road Games
\# San Juan, Puerto Rico (vs. Kentucky, first round; also American University-PR, Maryland, Pittsburgh, San Francisco, UCLA and Xavier)
\## Bozeman, MT (vs. Boston, first round; also Canisius and Montana State)
\### Kemper Arena, Kansas City, MO

IOWA STATE

LOCATION .... **Ames, IA**
CONFERENCE .... **Big 12**
LAST SEASON .... **12-18 (.400)**
CONFERENCE RECORD .... **5-11 (11th)**
STARTERS LOST/RETURNING **1/4**
NICKNAME .... **Cyclones**
COLORS .... **Red & Gold**
HOMECOURT .... **Hilton Coliseum (14,020)**
COACH .... **Larry Eustachy (Long Beach State '79)**
RECORD AT SCHOOL .... **First year**
CAREER RECORD .... **159-86 (8 yrs.)**
ASSISTANTS .... **Steve Barnes (Azusa Pacific '80)**
Leonard Perry (Idaho '91)
Terry Caroll (Northern Iowa '78)
TEAM WINS (last 5 yrs.) **21-14-23-2-12**
RPI (last 5 yrs.) **97-19-15-24-133**
1997-98 FINISH .... **Lost in conference first round.**

Iowa State fans knew for two years Tim Floyd would leave for the Chicago Bulls. They knew it, could prepare emotionally for it, deal with it. But when it finally happened, there was a deeper sense of despair than anybody thought possible.

Was Floyd so terribly ambitious that he'd punt away the program he nurtured into one of the nation's best? Didn't he turn down overtures and offers from other schools such as North Carolina State and Tennessee because he had a case of the warm fuzzies for the Iowa State community?

And last year, the 12-18 record, that was a blip on the screen. It was Floyd's first losing record in 12 years as a Division I coach and it wasn't going to happen again.

But the talk wouldn't disappear. Floyd wouldn't—and we know now, couldn't—reassure the community that he was in Ames for the long haul. Phil Jackson quit and the talk heated up. Other NBA assistants interviewed, but it was all a ruse. Floyd, the fishing buddy, was always Chicago general manager Jerry Krause's man.

Now Larry Eustachy is Iowa State's man. He served on Floyd's first staff, at Idaho in 1986-87, and had been Utah State's head coach for the last five seasons, compiling an impressive 98-53 record. Twice he was chosen Big West Coach of the Year, including last season when he guided the Aggies to a 25-8 record and their first NCAA Tournament appearance since 1988.

Eustachy got the call from Cyclones athletic director Gene Smith a day after Floyd announced his resignation. Nobody else interviewed.

"He's an excellent recruiter," Smith said. "We needed someone who would go out and sell the university with the same passion we have for Iowa State."

Eustachy assured Smith and university president Mar-

1998-99 IOWA STATE SCHEDULE

Nov.	23	Chicago State
	25-28	#Great Alaska Shootout
Dec.	2	@Northern Iowa
	4-5	##Cyclone Challenge
	8	Drake
	12	@Iowa
	19	*Arizona
	22-23	###ISU Holiday Classic
	29	Southern
Jan.	3	Oklahoma
	6	@Texas
	9	@Kansas
	13	Colorado
	16	@Texas A&M
	23	Texas Tech
	27	@Colorado
	30	Nebraska
Feb.	2	@Oklahoma State
	6	Kansas State
	8	Missouri
	13	@Nebraska
	16	Baylor
	20	@Kansas State
	24	@Missouri
	28	Kansas
Mar.	4-7	####Big 12 Tournament

@ Road Games
* Las Vegas Shootout, Las Vegas, NV
# Anchorage, AK (vs. Saint Mary's, first round; also Alaska-Anchorage, Cincinnati, Duke, Fresno State, Iowa State and Southern Utah)
Ames, IA (vs. North Texas, first round; also Princeton and Western Illinois)
Ames, IA (vs. New Orleans, first round; also Rice and Saint Mary's (CA))
Kemper Arena, Kansas City, MO

tin Jischke that it could be done. Eustachy said all the right things when he was fed to the media on July 31.

"A week earlier I thought I was going to be in Logan, Utah for a long time," Eustachy said. "It took something special to get me to leave what we had. If Iowa State was in New York City we wouldn't be here. We're here because of Ames, because of the state and the people."

And what is the state of Iowa State basketball these days? It's going to better than last season, when the Cyclones—as they usually did under Floyd—fooled everybody. After he lost four starters and cried proverty in 1996, Floyd recruited the class that included Dedric Willoughby and Kelvin Cato and started the best two-year run in the program's history.

When he lost his starting lineup after the 1997 season, nobody bought Floyd's cries. Fool me once, shame on you. Fool me twice...

So Iowa State, which finished second in the inaugural Big 12 season, didn't figure to fall off the face of the earth last year. But that's what happened. Hints of trouble came early. The Cyclones lost the opener at home to Northern Iowa. When December ended, Iowa State stood 7-6 and had played only two ranked teams, losing to Iowa and getting throttled by Texas Christian.

The Big 12 portion of the schedule was even uglier. Iowa State had so many inexperienced players, Floyd didn't know what to do with the starting lineup. Eleven players started at least three games.

Some gems emerged. None better than 6-8, 240-pound sophomore forward **Marcus Fizer** (14.9 ppg, 6.7 rpg, 20 assists, 32 steals, 27 blocked shots). His terrific play wasn't unexpected. He was the Cyclones' first McDonald's All-American. He assured Iowa State fans he wasn't overrated when he dropped in 20 against Texas-Arlington in his second game. He went on to lead Big 12 freshmen in scoring and was second in rebounding.

"He was our go-to guy," Floyd said before departing to the Bulls. "That was terrible to put that much pressure on a freshman, but that's where we were."

The Big 12 was filled with solid freshman a year ago, but nobody had a bigger impact for his team than Fizer. His big frame allows him to be a rugged finisher, yet he has a soft touch around the hoop (.474 field goal percentage). "He was by far the most impressive freshman we encountered last year," said St. Louis coach Charlie Spoonhour.

Not surprisingly, Fizer cleaned up when it came time to handing out postseason honors. He was the Big 12 Freshman of the Year, made the league's all-freshman team and was a third-team All-Big 12 pick. He was also chosen Iowa State's MVP.

Fizer was the Cyclones' lone double-digit scorer, a condition you might expect from what was, by far, the Big 12's lowest-scoring team. Iowa State averaged 63.7 points, about eight fewer than the 11th-place team. Mostly, that was Floyd's style: Playing every possession like the game depended on it. But it also was a matter of few offensive weapons. Iowa State also finished last in the conference in team three-point percentage (.294).

With .771 percent of the scoring returning, this won't be a case of teaching old dogs new tricks. Eustachy preaches rebounding and defense. The player who may most benefit by the new hire is 6-9 senior forward/center **Klay Edwards** (9.3 ppg, 7.7 rpg, 24 blocked shots). Edwards is a favorite son from Morning Sun, Iowa. He doesn't shoot much (6.6 attempts per game). That has to increase, because at .527 percent he's one of the team's most accurate shooters.

Edwards is a better-than-average rebounder. He led the Cyclones and was sixth in the Big 12 in that department last year. Edwards grabbed a career-high 15 boards in that disastrous Northern Iowa game.

Stevie Johnson (7.2 ppg, 3.7 rpg), a 6-4 junior forward, hung on to his starting role with a fast finish. He averaged 10.3 points in the final six games. Johnson came to Iowa State through family connections. Tim Floyd used to baby-sit Johnson's high school coach, Matt O'Keefe, as a youngster. Johnson is the son of Cleophus Johnson, who played for three NFL teams.

The other returning starter is 6-1 sophomore guard **Lee Love** (3.9 ppg, 1.9 rpg, 84 assists), who was typical of the Tim Floyd non-scoring point guard. He took just 88 shots in 23 games, 19 of them starts.

The top players off the bench were 6-10 junior forward **Paul Shirley** (8.1 ppg, 6.0 rpg) and 6-9 sophomore **Martin Rancik** (5.7 ppg, 2.8 rpg). Shirley started 14 of the final 23 games and led the Cyclones in shooting at .566 percent.

Rancik, a native of Slovakia, followed former Cyclone forward Julius Michalik to Iowa State. He showed some of the same kind of skills, making eight of hist last 23 three-pointers (.348 percent). He scored a career-high 15 points against Missouri and had a personal-best seven rebounds against Kansas State. Rancik got some excellent experience over the summer when he played for a Big 12 all-star team that toured Europe.

The Cyclones' frontcourt will get a boost by the return of 7-foot junior **Tony Rampton**, who saw action in only two games last season with an injured back. Rampton, a New Zealand native, showed signs of progress two years ago when he averaged 3.3 points and 2.2 rebounds and was voted the team's most improved player.

Dewayne Johns, a 7-1, 280-pound junior transfer from College of Eastern Utah, gives the Cyclones another frontcourt banger. When he logs his first minute, Johns will be the tallest player in Iowa State history. John, who wears a size 19 shoe, isn't a scorer. But he averaged 1.9 blocks last season.

The other frontcourt newcomer is 6-6 junior forward **Deionta Hagwood**, who averaged 9.5 points and 5.5 rebounds for Bakersfield (Calif.) College a year ago.

Floyd targeted the backcourt for recruiting help and he signed four guards. The best is 5-11 junior point guard **Michael Nurse**, who went largely unrecruited out of tiny Monroe (N.Y.) College, which doesn't offer athletic scholarships. Once Floyd got on him, other big-time schools followed, but Nurse stuck with the Cyclones.

Nurse was a second-team Division III junior college All-American, averaging 23.4 points, 4.7 assists and 3.3 steals. He's quick, can shoot off the dribble and reminds Floyd of a player he coached as an assistant at Texas-El Paso—Tim Hardaway.

Anthony Lloyd, a 6-3 freshman who averaged 13.4 assists at Perris High in Perris, Calif., will get a look at the point.

Competing at shooting guard are 6-3 junior **Lamar Gregg**, who averaged 21 points at Hiwassee (Tenn.) College, and **Rodney Hampton**, a second-team Division II junior college All-American at Lakeland (Ohio) CC. The 6-2 junior averaged 28.1 points and shot .404 percent on three-pointers at Lakeland.

Of the new faces, Nurse should make the greatest impact.

adidas Blue Ribbon Analysis

BACKCOURT	**C-**	**BENCH/DEPTH**	**C**
FRONTCOURT	**B**	**INTANGIBLES**	**C**

Eustachy is a good hire. He's won big at Idaho and Utah State. The stakes are much higher in the Big 12, but good coaching is good coaching. And it's not as if Floyd left the program in a shambles. If he had left a year earlier, that may have been the case. But Fizer may be as good a player to build around as there is in the Big 12. And Iowa State is excited about Nurse.

The rest of the team is dominated by role players who must step out of roles and take on more responsibility, namely Edwards, Johnson and Shirley.

One of Eustachy's better moves was to sign up Terry Carroll on the staff. Carroll moves over from Indian Hills Community College in Iowa and is a hometown hero. He was a standout player on Ames High's 1973 state championship team and was introduced into the state's hall of fame two years ago. With Carroll's ties to junior college basketball, the Cyclones should stay stocked with talent.

Eustachy has never had a losing season, and with some luck, he'll get Iowa State back over .500 and into the NIT this year.

(B.K.)

KANSAS STATE

LOCATION	**Manhattan, KS**
CONFERENCE	**Big 12**
LAST SEASON	**17-12 (.586)**
CONFERENCE RECORD	**7-7 (t-4th)**
STARTERS LOST/RETURNING	**2/3**
NICKNAME	**Wildcats**
COLORS	**Purple & White**
HOMECOURT	**Bramlage Coliseum (13,500)**
COACH	**Tom Asbury (Wyoming '68)**
RECORD AT SCHOOL	**56-56 (4 yrs.)**
CAREER RECORD	**181-115 (10 yrs.)**
ASSISTANTS	**David Campbell (Saint Mary's '80)**
	Mark Fox (Eastern New Mexico '91)
	Butch Hawking (Air Force '92)
TEAM WINS (last 5 yrs.)	**17-10-17-12-20**
RPI (last 5 yrs.)	**40-86-41-112-81**
1997-98 FINISH	**Lost in NIT first round.**

If the memory of the previous game can be erased, there are reasons to believe this will be a breakthrough year for the Wildcats.

Kansas State ended last season with one of the ugliest losses in Tom Asbury's tenure—a 59-39 defeat at North Carolina State in the first round of the NIT. The Wolfpack defense made many teams look bad last season, but this was ridiculous. It was only the second time since the shot clock was instituted in 1985 that the Wildcats were held under 40 points. Kansas State scored just eight points in the final 12 minutes. Asbury seethed after the game, then he turned his thoughts to this season, which alleviated the anger.

"We have a great opportunity," Asbury said. "This team definitely has a chance to get to the NCAA Tournament. There may be some predictions that this is the deepest and best team we've had in a while."

It's true. The Wildcats return 10 lettermen and four who started at least 13 games. The schedule is tougher than usual, which should only help in March when the selection committee pours over at-large contenders.

Asbury can use a winner to break the trend. Four years at Kansas State have produced a loser, winner, loser and winner. The 1996 team was his only one to make the NCAA Tournament. The Wildcats figured that would be an annual destination when Asbury was hired from Pepperdine in '94. After all, he had taken the Waves to the tournament in three of his final four years there.

But it's been difficult to find consistency at a program that for years has relied heavily on junior college players. It's no coincidence this year that the reason for Kansas State optimism is a starting lineup that will include four players who have been in the program for at least three years.

Three of them, forwards **Manny Dies, Shawn Rhodes** and **Ayome "Paco" May**, are fourth-year seniors. Dies' career has been marked by controversy. He spent four days in jail over the summer on a disorderly conduct charge. Dies has said and done all the right things since then.

Knee surgery in April kept the 6-9, 230-pound Dies (15.7 ppg, 7.6 rpg, .547 FG percentage, 49 blocked shots) on the shelf over the summer, but Asbury expects him to return to the form that made him the Wildcats' top scorer and rebounder and maybe the Big 12's most improved player last season. In face, he was chosen to the Big 12 All-Improved team, and was a second-team All- Big 12 pick by the Associated Press and third-team by the league's coaches.

At 6-11, Rhodes (11.2 ppg, 5.5 rpg, 45.7 FG percentage, 36.0 three-point percentage, 38 blocked shots) is two inches taller than Dies, but Rhodes is more of an outside threat. He attempted a three-pointer in every game. But Rhodes does have some muscle. With 12 more blocked shots, he'll own the school's career record (104). Rhodes traveled Europe in August with a team of Big 12 all-stars.

1998-99 KANSAS STATE SCHEDULE

Nov.	13	Saint Mary's
	16	Fullerton State
	18	Washburn
	23-25	#Maui Classic
	29	Georgia State
Dec.	1	Loyola
	8	Wichita State
	12	@Long Beach State
	19	Missouri-Kansas City
	21	Coppin State
	28	*St. Louis
Jan.	2	@Oklahoma State
	6	Missouri
	9	Texas Tech
	13	@Nebraska
	16	@Texas
	20	Colorado
	23	Oklahoma
	27	@Missouri
Feb.	1	Kansas
	6	@Iowa State
	10	@Texas A&M
	13	Baylor
	17	@Kansas
	20	Iowa State
	24	Nebraska
	27	@Colorado
Mar.	4-7	##Big 12 Tournament

@ Road Games
* Earth Grains Basketball Classic, TWA Dome, St. Louis, MO
# Maui, HI (vs. Indiana, first round; also Arizona State and Utah)
Kemper Arena, Kansas City, MO

The 6-6 May (7.6 ppg, 3.5 rpg, .408 FG percentage, .300 three-point percentage) slipped as a junior. He lost his starting role and saw his numbers fall in nearly all significant categories. But May remains one of the team's better one-on-one players. In a narrow defeat at Kansas, it was May who got the call out of a time-out late in the game.

The point guards are Pac-10 transfers. **Duane Davis** (7.3 ppg, 1.5 rpg, 76 assists, 30 steals), a 5-11 junior, started his career at Arizona State. He isn't much of a scorer, but every now and again he could burn people. His six-for-six three-point shooting night against Coastal Carolina was the year's best long-range performance in the Big 12.

Davis is handy to have around for other reasons. His 2.11-1 assist-turnover ratio ranked third in the Big 12. He committed just 36 turnovers in 23 games. Davis was chosen to the league's All-Newcomer team.

Chris Griffin (3.2 ppg, 1.9 rpg, 62 assists), a 6-2 senior, was shoved into the starting lineup for an injured Davis in February and made nine starts. His best game came against Kansas in the Big 12 tournament with a career-high 14 points. Griffin's career started at Washington State.

Shooting guard **Josh Reid** (6.9 ppg, 2.5 rpg, .432 FG percentage) and small forward **Ty Sims** (6.3 ppg, 3.3 rpg, .535 FG percentage) each produced a showcase game. Reid, a 6-6 junior, had 28 against Missouri. Sims, a 6-5 senior, scored 26 against Texas A&M. Both were part-time starters and give Kansas State depth many Big 12 teams don't have.

The roster's only true center is 7-0, 245-pound sophomore **Joe Leonard** (1.7 ppg, 1.7 rpg, 6.1 minutes, 20 games). He's a project who has a difficult time keeping pace. Leonard had ankle surgery after last season, slowing his summer play, which didn't help his development.

Jay Heidrick (0.3 ppg, 12 games), a 6-6 senior, turned down scholarship offers at small Division I schools to walk on. **David Ries** (0.2 ppg, 12 games), a 6-6 junior, moved over from the football team. Both players help fill in the cracks.

Both junior college transfers should help immediately. Shooting guard **Cortez Groves** (11.7 ppg, 4.0 apg), a 6-5 junior, comes from Moberly (Mo.) Community College, which also produced former K-State stars Mitch Richmond and Anthony Beane. Forward **Tony Kitt** (20.8 ppg, 10.2 rpg, 2.3 blocks), a 6-8 junior, started his career at Elon College in North Carolina before transferring to Colby (Kan.) Junior College, where he was a unanimous all-Jayhawk Conference pick.

The three high school signees will have time to develop. Two are point guards. **Kenyatta Dix**, 6-1, averaged 22.9 points for Buchholz High in Gainesville, Fla. **Josh Kimm**, 6-1 and the son of Florida Marlins bullpen coach Josh Kimm, averaged 21.5 points and 4.5 assists for Prairie HS in Cedar Rapids, Iowa.

Travis Reynolds, a 6-7 power forward, makes the short trip over from Junction City, Kan., where he averaged 19.7 points and 9.7 rebounds.

adidas Blue Ribbon Analysis

BACKCOURT .... **C** **BENCH/DEPTH** .... **B**
FRONTCOURT .... **B** **INTANGIBLES** .... **C**

Kansas State is on the rise. Last season, the Wildcats improved in areas that had doomed them in recent seasons, namely field-goal percentage. K-State was the league's second-best shooting team last year at .456 percent, up considerably from the bottom-half finishes of previous years. Last year was Asbury's most disciplined team. It showed not only in shot selection, but in the reduction of turnovers and personal fouls.

Now comes the hard part, building on a little success. This is not an all-or-nothing season, but an important one. The Wildcats have the experience and enough talent to be better than last year and make a run at the NCAA Tournament. Dies and Rhodes give Kansas State solid players to feature in the offense. Both are potential all-conference picks.

(B.K.)

MISSOURI

LOCATION .... **Columbia, MO**
CONFERENCE .... **Big 12**
LAST SEASON .... **17-15 (.531)**
CONFERENCE RECORD .... **8-8 (t-5th)**
STARTERS LOST/RETURNING **2/3**
NICKNAME .... **Tigers**
COLORS .... **Black & Gold**
HOMECOURT .... **Hearnes Center (13,300)**
COACH .... **Norm Stewart (Missouri '56)**
RECORD AT SCHOOL .... **614-324 (31 yrs.)**
CAREER RECORD .... **711-366 (37 yrs.)**
ASSISTANTS .... **Rich Daly (NE Missouri '62)**
Kim Anderson (Missouri '77)
Lynn Hardy (Missouri '93)
TEAM WINS (last 5 yrs.) **17-16-18-20-28**
RPI (last 5 yrs.) **3-17-80-80-59**
1997-98 FINISH .... **Lost in NIT first round.**

Wait 'till next millennium.

Not to suggest Missouri won't be good this season. The Tigers may very well be good enough to get back to the NCAA Tournament for the first time since 1995, if they can find a way to win on an opponents' home floor (the losing streak is 23).

But with a terrific recruiting class and only two seniors on the roster, Missouri is setting up rather nicely for the next millennium. Maybe the Tigers will have more postseason luck in that century. They ended last season with a first-round home loss to UAB in the NIT.

Missouri has to get through 1998-99 first, and coach Norm Stewart has issued a warning for the Tigers faithful who are depending on this touted freshmen class to carry the day.

"I don't think it's ever in the hands of the group that's coming in," Stewart said. "It has to come from the guys who are here. They have to know what's expected of them, and they've got to take responsibility to do the things that are necessary."

Besides, in mid-September, Missouri lost one of those promising newcomers, Travis Robinson, who decided to attend Fresno State instead.

So it's up to guys like 6-5, 238-pound junior forward **Albert White** (10.9 ppg, 4.9 rpg, 42 assists) and 6-3 senior shooting guard **John Woods** (11.4 ppg, 2.4 rpg, .386 three-point percentage) to show the way.

White is potentially a big-time player. He transferred from Michigan and after sitting out two semesters, made an immediate impact. In his second game, White scored 16 points and had 11 rebounds to spark a victory over Illinois. He has the ability to carry Missouri in stretches. In a victory over Oklahoma State, White scored nine straight that turned a deficit into the lead.

And he did all this on a bum ankle. White missed three games with the injury. It showed. The Tigers' only triumph in that stretch was at home over a Texas A&M team that finished 1-15 in the Big 12. Even though he played only half the season, White emerged as the Tigers' leader.

"Early in the season we were hurting for confidence and he gave us a tremendous charge," Stewart said. "Everybody seemed to improve their play."

Woods, who wears his shorts low and socks high—just below the kneecap—made the league's all-newcomer team and could end up being the Tigers' scoring leader this year. He blended in well in his first season after transferring from Connors State JC in Texas and was one of the team's more dependable perimeter shooters.

Never was that more evident than at Kansas. The Jayhawks owned a 19-point lead before Woods went to work. He made five of six three-pointers, the last one a rainbow from the right side that cut the KU lead to 66-63 with 3:53 left. Kansas won by 10, but Woods, who had 16 of his 18 in the second half, was a hero.

Now the Tigers need more heroes from their returning class. Point guard is in the capable hands of 6-0 sophomore **Brian Grawer** (5.9 ppg, 2.4 rpg, 79 assists, 45 steals, .789 FT percentage). His assist-turnover ratio in Big 12 games was 2.1-1 and he knocked down 30 of 36 free-throws (.833 percent) in the final four minutes of games.

Swingmen **Jeff Hafer** (5.8 ppg, 3.4 rpg, 2.1 apg, .462 FG percentage) and **Johnnie Parker** (3.7 ppg, 2.2 rpg, .358 FG percentage) are two of the team's better athletes. Hafer, a 6-5 junior, is a leaper; Parker, a 6-6 sophomore, is a slasher.

Hafer had a fairly productive sophomore season. He scored in double figures seven times, including a career-high 18 against Coppin State. Hafer led the Tigers in field-goal percentage, was second in steals (42) and third in assists (67). In August, Hafer hooked up with a team of Big 12 all-stars that toured Europe.

What to make of senior **Monte Hardge** (7.0 ppg, 5.9 rpg)? He's the biggest player in the Big 12 at 6-11, 330-plus pounds and can bother the heck out of opposing centers. But as you might guess from somebody that size, stamina is a problem. Hardge's 19.8 minutes were the fewest of the top seven players.

Still, Hardge had his moments, especially in Big 12 games. He reached double figures in scoring nine times last season, all against league opponents. His best game of the season was a double-double—a career-high 20 points and 13 boards against Colorado. Hardge made the Big 12's All-Improved team.

Where do the newcomers fit in? Perhaps prominently. Freshman point guard **Keyon Dooling**, a third-team *Parade* All-American, is one of the highest-profile recruits Stewart has signed. The Fort Lauderdale, Fla., native was the state's large class player of the year. He averaged 23 points and five assists. Dooling was ranked as the country's 18th-best senior by *Prep Stars Recruiter's Handbook*.

The 6-3 Dooling had transferred to Dillard High as a senior to be with his longtime friend, **Clarence Gilbert**, who also signed with the Tigers. Gilbert, a 6-2 freshman

1998-99 MISSOURI SCHEDULE

Nov.	13	Jackson State
	18	#Southwest Missouri State
	23	Austin Peay
	29	Southwest Texas State
Dec.	1	Nicholls State
	5	Idaho
	9	Arkansas-Pine Bluff
	12	@Southern Methodist
	19	@Iowa
	22	*Illinois
	30	Centenary College
Jan.	2	Nebraska
	6	@Kansas State
	9	@Texas A&M
	11	Kansas
	16	@Colorado
	24	@Kansas
	27	Kansas State
	30	Baylor
Feb.	3	Texas Tech
	6	@Nebraska
	8	@Iowa State
	13	Colorado
	15	Oklahoma
	20	@Oklahoma State
	24	Iowa State
	27	@Texas
Mar	4-7	##Big 12 Tournament

@ Road Games
* Kiel Center, St. Louis, MO
# Chase NIT (If the Tigers advance, they will face either Southern Methodist or Stanford on Nov. 20. Semifinals and finals are Nov. 25 & 27 at Madison Square Garden, NY)
Kemper Arena, Kansas City, MO

shooting guard, was the state's top player as junior. He averaged 25 points last season. The dynamic duo backcourt led Dillard to a 27-7 mark and a spot in the 6A final four. Gilbert was also a top-100 player, turning up at No. 72 on *Prep Stars*' list.

Two other freshmen may have less of an impact. Seven-footer **Pat Schumaker** from Hazelwood Central HS/St. Louis was a third-team all-metro pick who averaged 11.7 points and 8.1 rebounds.

Power forward **Matt Rowan**, 6-7 and 230 pounds, led Liberty HS/Liberty, Mo., to a 31-0 record and the state 5A championship with averages of 11.6 points and 8.5 rebounds.

adidas Blue Ribbon Analysis

BACKCOURT .... B BENCH/DEPTH C
FRONTCOURT .... C INTANGIBLES C

Missouri has been a notoriously slow-starting team, and this year should be no different as the Tigers attempt to blend talented youth with experienced players.

"We'll probably have to keep things simple at first to get everyone on the same page," Stewart said.

Getting them on the same page could be another challenge. When a newcomer group as talented as this one arrives, responsibilities sometimes get blurred. Remember the 1994 North Carolina team? This is a smaller scale, but it's a potential issue for Stewart, who has a team capable of the NCAA Tournament this year and is sitting in a potential powerhouse in two years.

(B.K.)

NEBRASKA

LOCATION .... Lincoln, NE
CONFERENCE .... Big 12
LAST SEASON .... 20-12 (.625)
CONFERENCE RECORD 10-6 (4th)
STARTERS LOST/RETURNING 1/4
NICKNAME .... Cornhuskers
COLORS .... Scarlet & Cream
HOMECOURT .... Bob Devaney Center (14,200)
COACH .... Danny Nee (St. Mary of the Plains '71)
RECORD AT SCHOOL .... 223-225 (12 yrs.)
CAREER RECORD .... 330-225 (19 yrs.)
ASSISTANTS .... Jimmy Williams (Ashland '69)
Cleo Hill Jr. (North Carolina Central '88)
Randy Roth (Ohio '83)
TEAM WINS (last 5 yrs.) 20-20-20-18-21
RPI (last 5 yrs.) 22-53-48-53-41
1997-98 FINISH .... Lost in conference first round.

Nebraska's 1998 season went largely unappreciated.

The Cornhuskers received votes in only four polls all season. Early losses to Tulsa, Creighton and two in the Rainbow Classic doused expectations. Even the fans turned their backs. It's rare when Nebraska draws better on the road, but that was the case last season when an average of only 9,431 showed up in the 14,200-seat Devaney Center.

But ever-so-quietly, Nebraska got its act together after starting 4-6 in conference play. The Huskers took advantage of a weak Big 12 and slipped into fourth place by winning their final six league games, including three on the road. Toss in the first-round victory in the conference tournament and Nebraska won seven straight against league foes for the first time since 1978.

Point guard Tyronn Lue played to his all-conference capability, leading Nebraska in scoring in each of the final nine games. He wound up with 1,577 points, seventh on the school's all-time scoring list, before leaving with one year of eligibility remaining. Lue was drafted by the Denver Nuggets as the 23rd pick in the first round.

Defense was the real key to Nebraska's late surge. It held those last six opponents to a collective 36 percent from the field and 29 percent from behind the arc. In that span, the Cornhuskers led opponents in blocked shots 37-20 and steals 73-58. In their final 175 minutes of the regular season, Nebraska only trailed for 3:06. In a victory over Baylor the 'Huskers held the Bears to three second-half field-goals. It was a focused team coming down the stretch.

The rally got the Cornhuskers back in the NCAA Tournament for the first time since 1994, and history wasn't on Nebraska's side. The program hadn't won a first-round game in its previous five appearances, and last season made it six, although the 11th-seeded Cornhuskers threw a major scare into Arkansas.

1998-99 NEBRASKA SCHEDULE

Nov.	14	North Carolina-Greensboro
	19-22	#Top of the World Classic
	28	North Carolina A&T
Dec.	1	Tulsa
	4-5	##Ameritas Classic
	9	Creighton
	12	@Colorado State
	19	Minnesota
	27	@San Francisco
	30	@Missouri-Kansas City
Jan.	2	@Missouri
	10	Texas
	13	Kansas State
	16	@Baylor
	20	@Oklahoma
	23	Colorado
	27	Kansas
	30	@Iowa State
Feb.	3	@Colorado
	6	Missouri
	10	@Kansas
	13	Iowa State
	17	Oklahoma State
	20	@Texas Tech
	24	@Kansas State
	27	Texas A&M
Mar.	4-7	###Big 12 Tournament

@ Road Games
\# Fairbanks, AK (vs. Villanova, first round; also Alaska-Fairbanks, Arkansas, New Mexico State, Virginia, Washington State and Wisconsin)
\## Lincoln, NE (vs. Southwest Texas State, first round; also Colgate and Davidson)
\### Kemper Arena, Kansas City, MO

The season was enough of a success that fans should eagerly be looking forward to this year, despite the loss of Lue. Every other significant player returns. Six have started at least 10 games.

The best of the bunch is center **Venson Hamilton** (11.2 ppg, 9.8 rpg, 58 assists, 53 steals, 66 blocked shots), a 6-10, 245 pound senior, who is poised for a breakout season. Hamilton will become the school's career rebound leader in December and is likely to wind up second on the career blocked shot list.

Athleticism runs in the family. Hamilton is the youngest of four brothers: Alex Mayse played at Robert Morris, Jabbar Mayse played football at South Carolina and Victor Hamilton played hoops at East Carolina.

A year ago, Nebraska coach Danny Nee touted his senior center Mikki Moore as a NBA prospect. The evaluation was inflated. Nee sounds a little more reserved when talking about Hamilton, who actually is a better player.

"He's on the verge of becoming a dominant big man," Nee said. "We need a little more on the offense end."

Hamilton is sometimes indecisive on offense, though he did shoot 51 percent from the field. Once he gets that worked out, Hamilton could be the Big 12's best big man.

Rebounding and shot blocking are clearly Hamilton's strengths. A year ago he was second in the league, behind Raef LaFrentz of Kansas, in rebounding. He paced the Big 12 with his average of 4.4 offensive boards a game, and was fifth in defensive rebounds (5.4). Hamilton was third in the conference with his average of 2.1 blocks per game.

Hamilton also led the Big 12 with his 17 double-doubles last season. He was chosen to play on the league's all-star team that toured Europe in August.

With players such as Kelvin Cato and Tony Battie out of the league, Hamilton rises to the upper-echelon of Big 12 centers. With continued improvement—reducing turnovers is the key—he'll bid for all-league honors.

"He is our go-to big guy," Nee said. "There's so much with him we haven't seen, great passing ability, good basketball instincts. The mistakes are the only thing keeping him from becoming a great player."

Also bidding to be the conference's best at his position is 6-4 junior shooting guard **Cookie Belcher** (11.1 ppg, 3.9 rpg, 124 assists, 75 steals, .443 FG percentage), who, like Hamilton, has the defensive part down. It's the shooting that must improve. Especially distressing was Belcher's three-point shooting, which dipped from .395 percent as a freshman to .284 percent (29 of 102) last season.

Belcher finished third in the Big 12 with 2.3 steals per game, and could become the school's career leader in that category this year. Perhaps more than anybody, Belcher will miss Lue. They're third cousins and were soulmates on the floor. But Nee believes the loss of Lue could help Belcher.

"He's kind of been in Tyronn's shadow the past two years, so this could be the year he makes a name for himself," Nee said. "He got better as the season went on, and he adjusted to the college game very well. He has a chance to be one of the better players to come out of our program."

Small forward **Larry Florence** (9.0 ppg, 3.7 rpg, 32 assists, 32 steals), a 6-5 senior, started 18 of the final 20 games. He's battled injuries (surgery on each knee) and poor shooting throughout his Nebraska career. He gets by as a good defensive player who is usually matched up with the opposing team's best swing player.

When the Cornhuskers needed to get a little quicker, 6-8 senior forward **Andy Markowski** (6.6 ppg, 6.6 rpg, 46.4 FG percentage) usually went to the bench. He started the first 23 games last season, then came off the bench during the team's six-game winning streak to end the regular season. Filling the spot was 6-6 sophomore **Chad Johnson** (3.8 ppg, 2.9 rpg), who started the final nine games.

Johnson's big moment came at Colorado, when he scored seven in a row late in the game to seal a victory. Johnson averaged 6.2 points and 3.2 rebounds in the final nine games.

Besides Lue, 6-5 senior **Troy Piatkowski** (6.4 ppg, 2.5 rpg, .362 three-point percentage), was the team's top offensive threat. When Piatkowski, the younger brother of former Nebraska great Eric Piatkowski, was in the game, his orders were clear. Shoot. He nearly beat Kansas by himself, knocking in five treys for 18 points in an 11-point home loss.

Piatkowski will get more playing time if can get his three-point numbers higher.

It was slow going early for 6-10, 250-pound sophomore center **Brant Harriman** (2.0 ppg, 2.6 rpg). But when Nee started pushing buttons late, Harriman got more time. He averaged 15.7 minutes in the final nine games and had at least five rebounds in five of the final seven games. He'll battle Hamilton in practice and for playing time.

So who replaces Lue, who was rarely off the floor in averaging 36 minutes last season? Nee dipped into the junior college ranks and plucked 5-11 junior **Joe Holmes** from Tyler Junior College in Texas. Holmes played high school ball at Seat Pleasant, Md. At Tyler, he averaged 10.4 points and 8.1 assists.

Holmes won't come close to being the offensive threat Lue was. Leadership will have to come from the returning players, not the point guard.

Nee could slide one of his shooting guards into the point, and that's what will happen with 6-4 **Todd Smith**, who gets a second shot at a freshman season. Smith had steel rods placed in both lower legs to repair stress fractures and was cleared to play in November. But after six games, the pain was so great, he gave up the season and was granted a medical redshirt. Smith will get time at the point. He played some there at Baldwin HS/Milledgeville, Ga., and shot 45 percent on three-pointers.

Another guard, **Cary Cochran** (pronounced CO-horn), is getting a second freshman season. He sat out last year after having surgery in September to reattach a ligament in his right ankle. The 6-2 Cochran will be a designated shooter and should be one of the team's top three-point threats.

The gem of the recruiting class is **Louis Truscott**, a 6-7 freshman forward from Milby HS/Houston, Texas. Truscott averaged 17.2 points and 11.1 rebounds. One recruiting service had him ranked No. 63 among the nation's prospects. He'll battle for time at power forward.

Shooting guard **Rodney Fields** a 6-4 junior, was a teammate of Holmes' at Tyler Junior College. Field originally signed with Nebraska out of Tampa Bay Tech HS/Tampa. Fla.) but didn't meet academic requirements. He averaged 15 points and six boards last season.

adidas Blue Ribbon Analysis

BACKCOURT .... C BENCH/DEPTH C
FRONTCOURT .... B+ INTANGIBLES C

Nebraska becomes a different team without Lue. Everything revolved around the point guard, who became a first-round NBA draft pick. Now, the focus is on the four other positions where starters return.

Hamilton and Belcher are keys. Both rank among the league's defensive best, but better shooting is needed. Those guys are going to lead the team in minutes, so both need to kick up their scoring average. About three or four points more a game from each will do.

After missing the NCAA Tournament in the previous three seasons, fans were getting restless with Nee. But he responded to his critics with a fantastic finish and tournament berth. Nee owns six of the program's 10 season of 20 or more victories.

But Nebraska demands more. A great football program and overall athletic success at the school has forced Nee to keep up. The next step is a victory in the tournament.

It could happen. Point-guard production will be a big factor. The defense is solid and Nebraska is the most experienced team in the Big 12. Those factors should get the Cornhuskers back to the tournament.

(B.K.)

TEXAS A&M

LOCATION .... **College Station, TX**
CONFERENCE .... **Big 12**
LAST SEASON .... **7-20 (.259)**
CONFERENCE RECORD .... **1-15 (1st)**
STARTERS LOST/RETURNING **2/3**
NICKNAME .... **Aggies**
COLORS .... **Maroon & White**
HOMECOURT .... **Reed Arena (12,500)**
COACH .... **Melvin Watkins (UNC Charlotte '77)**
RECORD AT SCHOOL .... **First year**
CAREER RECORD .... **42-20 (2 yrs.)**
ASSISTANTS .... **Tom Billeter (Illinois '83)**
Porter Moser (Lew Hill '87)
Bobby Kummer (UNC Charlotte '96)
TEAM WINS (last 5 yrs.) **10-19-14-11-7**
RPI (last 5 yrs.) **99-167-176-137-237**
1997-98 FINISH .... **Lost in conference first round.**

Tony Barone's A&M tenure came to a sad conclusion. The Aggies had to show some improvement, and early on there appeared to be some hope. A&M defeated the teams it was supposed to beat, lost to some tougher non-conference opponents at the buzzer, and headed into Big 12 play with no reason to believe it couldn't have some success.

Ugh. The conference season couldn't have been uglier. Injuries played havoc with the lineup. But even in a down year for the Big 12, the Aggies could find a victory nowhere. Perhaps the toughest loss came at home against Texas by one point when A&M couldn't get a final shot to fall. It was one of five games A&M led in the final 15 minutes, only to lose.

The conference-game losing streak reached 15 games. A&M finally broke through in the regular-season finale, and the final game played in G. Rollie White Coliseum, against Baylor. At that point, nothing short of a national championship was going to save Barone's job, and the Aggies ended the suspense a week later, falling to the Bears in the first round of the Big 12 Tournament.

The coaching search came up with several possibilities, but none more intriguing than the one A&M hired. Melvin Watkins seemed to have a good thing going at UNC Charlotte and wasn't looking to move. After all, he played for the 1977 Final Four team and served as a 49ers assistant for 18 years. He was the only person in the program who had been associated with all eight of the school's postseason appearances.

"I pretty much have never looked for another opportunity," Watkins said. "But when an opportunity knocked you on the head, it wakes you up a little."

The opportunity is this: The Big 12 conference is on a slightly higher level than Conference USA. A&M, although it has no basketball tradition, desperately wants a winner and will do everything it can (including throwing tons of cash at Watkins) to help Watkins turn things around.

The new facility is already in place. Reed Arena is open for business. It's a beautiful place. The Aggies had trouble filling 7,000-seat White Coliseum, but let's not spoil things yet. And White isn't dead. The Aggies will play an exhibition game there before moving into Reed permanently on Nov. 13.

Watkins has work to do in College Station, beginning with repairing the team's wounded psyche. The Aggies have underachieved in their two Big 12 years, and Watkins needs to get his guys to live up to their potential, starting with 6-8 junior forward **Jerald Brown**.

No player better reflected A&M sagging fortunes than Brown, who was the league's freshman of the year in 1997. Look at what happened to Brown's numbers: Scoring—10.1 to 7.4. Field-goal percentage—.361 to .290. Three-point percentage—.351 to .248.

Brown is too good a talent to give up on, but Watkins may have to downgrade Brown to a role player if his shooting doesn't improve.

The nucleus of the team are two other returning starters and a starter from the 1997 season who missed all of last year.

Small forward **Shanne Jones** (18.0 ppg, 6.7 rpg, .504 FG percentage), a 6-5 senior, came on strong in his second season with the Aggies after transferring from Stetson, where he was chosen the Trans-America Athletic Conference Freshman of the Year in 1994-95. Jones led A&M in scoring, was second in rebounding and was chosen to the league's all-underrated team. He's the Big 12's top returning scorer.

Last season, Jones was seventh in the league in scoring, 12th in rebounding and sixth in field-goal percentage. He was a consistent scoring threat, reaching double figures in all 27 games. Nine times, he scored 20 or more points.

Jones also had six double-doubles last season, all in conference play. His best game of the season came against Texas, which he scorched for 32 points and 11 boards. Jones had a career-high 12 rebounds against Baylor and Iowa State.

Also in the mix is 6-1 junior guard **Steve Houston** (9.5 ppg, 3.7 rpg, 119 assists, 67 steals). Houston is one of the Big 12's top defenders and led the league in steals at 2.5 per game. That earned Houston a spot on the Big 12's All-Defensive team.

He's also a fair shooter, making 35 percent of his three-pointers. He had a career-high 22 points, to go with seven assists, against Texas Tech in his best game of the season. Houston had a career-best 10 assists against Stephen F. Austin and also grabbed 10 boards against Southern. For good measure, he tossed in his personal-best steals game (seven) against Washington State.

The Aggies got bad news in early September when they learned power forward Calvin Davis (13.8 ppg, 7.1 rpg, .515 FG percentage, .807 FT percentage), a 6-8 senior, would be unavailable for the season. Davis, who could become the fourth player in A&M history to score 1,000 points with 500 rebounds and 100 blocked shots, is out after having back surgery to repair two herniated disks in his back. He missed the final 14 games last season with the ailment.

The Aggies get a frontcourt boost with the return of 6-9, 230-pound senior **Dario Quesada**, a former member of the Spanish national team. Quesada suffered a bulging disk in September, 1997 and sat out last year as a medical redshirt. He slipped to 6.2 points in 1996-97, but averaged 11.0 in 1995-96.

A&M has no shortage of athletes up front. **Chris Richards** (4.0 ppg, 1.9 rpg), a 6-10, 245-pound senior, was the team's best shooter at .623 percent in 20 games after transferring from Texas Christian.

Newcomers **Jason Boeker**, a 6-10 junior who started 15 games at Division II Alabama-Huntsville in 1997 when he averaged 7.1 points and 5.6 boards; 6-10, 255-pound freshman **Larry Jackson**, who averaged 14.2 points and 9.5 rebounds at St. Josephs HS/Trumbull, Conn.; and 6-10 freshman **Joe White**, who averaged 14.2 points and 8.3 rebounds at Taft HS/San Antonio, Texas) should make the Aggies one of most impressive airport teams this season.

Forward **Aaron Jack** (8.3 ppg, 6.8 rpg) was everything the Aggies hoped he would be after transferring from Penn State. Jack, a 6-8, 235-pound sophomore, never played there after suffering a concussion on the first day of practice. Jack's father, Bobby, was a standout at Oklahoma in the early 1970s. Jack, in his fourth year of college after sitting out a regular- then medical-redshirt season at Penn State, could blossom into one of the team's top players.

The Aggies need to develop some backcourt depth. Gone is point guard Brian Barone (3.2 ppg, 2.2 rpg, 125 assists, 61 steals), the coach's son who brought stability to the lineup. Barone transferred to Marquette after flirting with Texas.

As a freshman, 6-5 shooting guard **Michael Schmidt** (8.9 ppg, 3.0 ppg, 73 assists) had some big games, including a 26-point performance against Baylor. He was chosen to the Big 12 All-Bench team. Schmidt came on strong, and his .426 three-point percentage was the best in the conference in Big 12 games.

Chris Clayton (6.8 ppg, 1.1 rpg, .333 three-point percentage), a 6-3 senior, started twice last year and tied a White Coliseum record with seven three-pointers against Maryland-Eastern Shore. He missed the final eight games with a broken foot.

T.J. Brown (1.1 ppg, 0.6 rpg), a 6-1 sophomore, had a similar problem, suffering a knee injury after 10 games and missing the rest of the season.

New to the backcourt is 6-1 junior point guard **Clifton Cook**, who averaged 17.1 points and 8.2 assists for Howard College in Tyler, Texas, last year.

adidas Blue Ribbon Analysis

BACKCOURT	**D**	**BENCH/DEPTH**	**C**
FRONTCOURT	**C**	**INTANGIBLES**	**C**

Watkins got an early look at his team during an August tour of Germany and Holland. The Aggies went 1-4 against professional teams. The highlight was a victory in the finale over German team Brandt-Hagan, a game in which Clayton knocked in 34 points and made 10 three-pointers.

There's enough talent here for A&M to be vastly improved over last season. It's a matter of finding the right chemistry and responding to a new coach. Watkins got the most out of UNC Charlotte over the last two season—who can forget the 49ers' overtime loss to Final Four-bound North Carolina in the second round of the NCAA Tournament last year? But he has no horses at A&M like he had in DeMarco Johnson at Charlotte.

Six or seven conference victories isn't out of the question, and such a record would put the Aggies in the right direction. From there, it's a matter of Watkins learning Texas.

(B.K.)

1998-99 TEXAS A&M SCHEDULE

Nov.	13	North Texas State
	19	@Stephen F. Austin
	21	Centenary
	28	@Oral Roberts
Dec.	1	Alabama
	3	@Sam Houston State
	6	Lamar
	9	Tulane
	19	Arizona State
	28	@Southern
Jan.	2	@Kansas
	6	Oklahoma State
	9	Missouri
	13	@Texas Tech
	16	Iowa State
	23	@Baylor
	27	Texas Tech
	30	@Oklahoma State
Feb.	3	@Texas
	6	Baylor
	10	Kansas State
	13	@Oklahoma
	17	@Colorado
	20	Texas
	24	Oklahoma
	27	@Nebraska
Mar.	4-7	#Big 12 Tournament

@ Road Games
Kemper Arena, Kansas City, MO

TEXAS TECH

LOCATION .... **Lubbock, TX**
CONFERENCE .... **Big 12**
LAST SEASON .... **13-14 (.481)**
CONFERENCE RECORD .... **7-9 (t-7th)**
STARTERS LOST/RETURNING **4/1**
NICKNAME .... **Red Raiders**
COLORS .... **Scarlet & Black**
HOMECOURT .... **Lubbok Municipal Coliseum (8,174)**
COACH .... **James Dickey (Central Arkansas '76)**
RECORD AT SCHOOL .... **132-72 (7 yrs.)**
CAREER RECORD .... **132-72 (7 yrs.)**
ASSISTANTS .... **James Pinkey (Wayland Baptist '86)**
Robert Brasher (Texas Tech '90)
James Rike (Texas Tech '96)
TEAM WINS (last 5 yrs.) **13-18-30-20-17**
RPI (last 5 yrs.) **113-88-12-33-105**
1997-98 FINISH .... **Lost in conference first round.**

Rarely has James Dickey gone into a season with this little knowledge about a team, and rarely has he been this excited about coaching.

To understand, you have to go back to the end of last season. The Red Raiders, who once talked about a possible NIT appearance, finished the regular season with a 17-point loss at Nebraska and a 33-point home loss to Oklahoma. The margin was a

1998-99 TEXAS TECH SCHEDULE

Nov.	19	Texas-San Antonio
	21	@North Texas State
	25	New Mexico State
	28	@Southwestern Louisiana
Dec.	2	Southern Methodist
	5	Stephen F. Austin
	8	@Texas Christian
	12	Texas-Arlington
	17	Texas-Pan American
	21-23	#Pearl Harbor Shootout
	30	Nevada
Jan.	2	Baylor
	6	@Oklahoma
	9	@Kansas State
	13	Texas A&M
	17	Oklahoma State
	23	@Iowa State
	27	@Texas A&M
	30	Oklahoma
Feb.	3	@Missouri
	6	Texas
	10	@Baylor
	13	Kansas
	17	@Texas
	20	Nebraska
	24	Colorado
	27	@Oklahoma State
Mar.	4-7	##Big 12 Tournament

@ Road Games
# Laie, HI (vs. Tulsa, first round; also Alabama, BYU-Hawaii, Michigan State, Oregon State, Pepperdine and Weber State)
Kemper Arena, Kansas City, MO

record for a defeat at home, topping the 31-point beating the Red Raiders absorbed from Texas Christian in the season opener.

The home finale loss was especially sad for Cory Carr, who passed up a chance at the NBA draft to return for his senior season. But Carr, who had been part of only winners in his previous three seasons, including the tremendous 30-2 team of 1996, went out on a losing note. In the locker room after the game, Dickey made it a point to thank the classy Carr for his efforts that season.

Tech could muster no enthusiasm for the conference tournament and bowed out quietly to a Texas team that had even less to play for. For the Red Raiders, it was one of those seasons that couldn't end soon enough.

A highlight? Maybe one. Tech tied an NCAA record by scoring 25 points in overtime in a 99-94 victory over Nevada. But that was it. The season marked Dickey's first losing season in seven at Texas Tech.

Which is why Dickey is looking forward to 1998-99, even though he has no player the caliber of Carr, or Tony Battie or Jason Sasser, his all-conference players of the last four seasons.

"One of the things we'll be looking forward to is more balance," Dickey said.

Nobody with a 22-point average, although 5-11 junior point guard **Rayford Young** (15.4 ppg, 3.2 rpg, 116 assists, 46 steals, 11 blocked shots, .843 FT percentage) can light it up. He's extremely quick, but his shooting (.415 percent from the field, .393 percent from three-point range) runs like a faucet. When he's on, the league doesn't have a hotter shooter. When he's off, like the six for 34 stretch at midseason, he can kill you. Rayford ended that skid by hitting a career-best six three-pointers and scoring 27 points against Missouri.

But Young's defense and free-throw shooting are always there. He made 27 straight from the line last year. Against Baylor, he held Patrick Hunter to a season-low three points.

The strength of shooting guard 6-3 senior **Stan Bonewitz** (12.9 ppg, 4.9 rpg, 113 assists, 31 steals, .422 three-point percentage, 3.1 three-pointers per game, .813 FT percentage) is three-point accuracy but he'll need to develop into a more all-around player without Carr. But the guy can shoot. He tied the school record with seven treys against Texas A&M and made at least two three-pointers in 25 of 27 games.

"Rayford and Stan have to have their best years," Dickey said. "They're the strength of this team. Stan will continue to have the green light. But we want to see more of a medium-range jumper and see him get to the free-throw line more often."

The backcourt depth will come from Midland (Texas) Junior College transfers **Jevon Banks** and **James Ware**. The 5-11 Banks, a sophomore, will have three years in the office. He handed out a team-high 88 assists, a nice total for junior college competition. Ware, a 6-5 junior shooting guard, can also play small forward. He started his career at Colorado State. Banks averaged 5.6 points and Ware 6.6 last season.

Tech certainly missed Battie last year. The Red Raiders outrebounded only seven opponents, which is why the recruiting emphasis was placed on front liners.

Forward **Cliff Owens** (10.2 ppg, 7.7 rpg, .592 FG percentage) is the best of the returning players. He tied for second in the Big 12 with his 8.4 rebound average in conference games and, in his first year as a starter, was about all Tech had up front. With a few more attempts, Owens would have led the Big 12 in field-goal percentage.

Center **Johnny Phillips** (5.2 ppg, 3.0 rpg, 17 blocked shots.592 FG percentage), a 6-10 sophomore, was thrust into the starting lineup before he was ready. But Dickey had no choice. Phillips was backed up by 6-10 junior **Ross Carmichael** (3.5 ppg, 4.4 rpg, 26 blocked shots, .532 FG percentage), who led Tech in blocked shots coming off the bench.

So the recruiting call went out to big men. The Red Raiders signed four, with **Andy Ellis** leading the way. Ellis, a 6-10 freshman, led Lamesa HS/Lamesa, Texas, to a 32-4 record with averages of 21.6 points and 11.2 rebounds. Ellis needs a year of strength training (he came to Tech at 200 pounds), but there will be no redshirt season. Tech can't afford that.

Brodney Kennard started his career at Wisconsin-Milwaukee and transferred to Tech from Tyler (Texas) Junior College, where he averaged 10.0 points and 8.0 rebounds. Kennard is a 6-8 junior power forward and may be the best rebounder of the newcomers.

The other new forwards are of the swing variety, and both come from the Texas junior college ranks. **Mario Layne**, a 6-6 junior, averaged 15.2 points and 4.7 boards while shooting .495 percent from the floor at South Plains College. And 6-5 junior **Jayson Mitchell** averaged 11.2 points and 6.5 rebounds at McLennan Community College. Like Ware, Mitchell started his career at Colorado State.

adidas Blue Ribbon Analysis

BACKCOURT	**B**	**BENCH/DEPTH**	**C**
FRONTCOURT	**D**	**INTANGIBLES**	**C**

We may have seen the passing of a golden era for Tech hoops. Dickey had constructed a power that peaked with the 1996 NCAA Tournament run to the Sweet 16. NCAA troubles cost the Red Raiders a follow trip in 1997 and now the significant players of the decade are all on NBA rosters.

There is hope for the future. Tech will move into a new home the following season. There's only senior on the roster—Bonewitz—and the Big 12 appears to have no major powers.

But a postseason appearance this year is asking too much.

(B.K.)

BIG WEST CONFERENCE

adidas BLUE RIBBON FORECAST

EASTERN DIVISION

1. Idaho
2. Boise State
3. Utah State
4. New Mexico State
5. North Texas
6. Nevada

EASTERN DIVISION

1. Cal Poly
2. Long Beach State
3. Pacific
4. Fullerton State
5. California-Irvine
6. California-Santa Barbara

ALL-CONFERENCE TEAM

G—Avery Curry, SR, Idaho
G—Mike Wozniak, JR, Cal Poly
F—Roberto Bergersen, SR, Boise State
F—Ike Harmon, JR, Fullerton State
C—Donnie Johnson, SR, Utah State

PLAYER OF THE YEAR

Avery Curry, SR, Idaho

NEWCOMER OF THE YEAR

Ramel Lloyd, SO, Long Beach State

1998-99 CONFERENCE TOURNAMENT

March 5-7, Lawlor Events Center, Reno, NV

1997-98 CHAMPION

Utah State (East Division)
Pacific (West Division)
Utah State (conference tournament)

1997-98 POSTSEASON PARTICIPANTS

Postseason Record: 0-2 (.000)

NCAA
Utah State
NIT
Pacific

TOP BACKCOURTS

1. Idaho
2. Cal Poly
3. Long Beach State

TOP FRONTCOURTS

1. Utah State
2. Long Beach State
3. New Mexico State

ON THE WAY UP

Idaho State

ON THE WAY DOWN

Pacific

INSIDE THE NUMBERS

• 1997-98 conference RPI: 18 (of 30)
• Conference RPI (last 5 years): 21-14-18-14-18

DID YOU KNOW?

Cal Poly finally was given its due by the NCAA and was cleared to participate in the Big West tournament and compete for the league's automatic berth to the NCAA Tournament. The Mustangs have waited four of the previously required eight years of the Division I waiver period. Cal Poly coach Jeff Schneider was getting hurt in recruiting without the guarantee his players could compete for an NCAA berth...Stew Morrill (Utah State) and Bob Williams (California-Santa Barbara) are the two new coaches in the league...Pacific coach Bob Thomason needs five wins to reach 100. He would be the fourth coach in conference history to win 100 or more games in the league, joining Jerry Tarkanian (UNLV, Long Beach State), Neil McCarthy (New Mexico State) and Jerry Pimm (California-Santa Barbara)...Pacific center Michael Olowokandi was selected as the No. 1 pick in the draft by the Los Angeles Clippers. He was the second No. 1 pick in Big West history. UNLV's Larry Johnson was selected No. 1 in 1991 by the Charlotte Hornets...Boise State has two players who received a sixth-year of eligibility in Roberto Bergersen and Steve Shephard, both because of knee injuries...The Big West had two postseason teams for the second straight season in 1997-98.

(A.K.)

BIG WEST

BOISE STATE

LOCATION .... Boise, Idaho
CONFERENCE .... Big West (Eastern Division)
LAST SEASON .... 17-13 (.557)
CONFERENCE RECORD 9-7 (3rd)
STARTERS LOST/RETURNING 2/3
NICKNAME .... Broncos
COLORS .... Blue & Orange
HOMECOURT .... BSU Pavillion (12,380)
COACH .... Rod Jensen (Redlands '75)
RECORD AT SCHOOL .... 46-39 (3 yrs.)
CAREER RECORD .... 46-39 (3 yrs.)
ASSISTANTS .... Ed Boyce (Pacific Lutheran University '84)
Shambic Williams (Boise State '95)
Don Kenney (Fresno State '92)
TEAM WINS (last 5 yrs.) 17-17-15-14-17
RPI (last 5 yrs.) 94-88-124-153-148
1997-98 FINISH .... Lost in conference quarterfinal.

Boise State had its fate this season resting in the hands of the Big West and the NCAA. The Broncos would have been looking at having to qualify for the Big West Tournament if **Roberto Bergersen** (19.4 ppg, 3.1 rpg, 2.4 apg, 1.5 spg, .514 FG, .417 three-PT, .779 FT) wasn't granted a sixth year of eligibility for his hardship of dealing with a knee injury. He was given the year, and as a result, Boise State is suddenly a contender for the title instead of scrambling just to make the tournament.

Bergersen isn't Michael Jordan. He's not Michael Olowokandi. He may not even be Mike Wozniak, the league's leading scorer and Cal Poly's shooting guard. However, Bergersen is the Broncos' leader, on the court and off, and can provide the Broncos with the necessary scoring punch to take over games.

The Big West Eastern Division, and for that matter the Western Division, too, is fragile. One player can make a difference between finishing first and last, or contending and qualifying for the tournament. When one NCAA bid and, at times one NIT berth, are at stake, one player can save jobs, let alone programs.

Rod Jensen wasn't in trouble but he could be secure (read: extension) if he's able to turn Bergersen's extra season into a postseason berth. The Broncos have been stable through Jensen's first three years but unable to push into the postseason the way Bobby Dye's teams did in the Big Sky. Jensen has been the defensive mind at Boise State since he arrived as an assistant in 1983. When he took over for Dye, he instituted a matchup zone, but didn't have the same personnel New Mexico State had to deploy the defense that demands quickness.

The Aggies were the only team using the defense in the Big West before Boise State arrived, but the Broncos did little to unseat the Aggies as the most frustrating team to face. While last season's 69.1 points per game allowed average was a tad higher than the past few years, it was the 15th straight season at 69 points or less. The Broncos did lead the league in turnovers caused and ranked second in turnover margin and steals.

The forced turnovers, nearly 21 a game, actually led to a more improvised fast break. Bergersen was able to get out on the wing with 6-1 senior point guard **Gerry Washington** (11.4 ppg, 3.1 rpg, 3.3 apg, 1.7 spg, 38.4 FG, 77.7 FT) usually running the break. The Broncos averaged just under 73 points a game, the fifth time since 1982 that a Boise State team has scored more than 70 points a game.

"There's no question that having Berto back is a big thing for this team," said Jensen. "He's a first team all-conference performer who plays with a lot of emotion and who's been through the battles. Those are two big pluses, especially on a team with so many young players."

Having Bergersen, Washington and two other seniors who join 10 freshmen and sophomores gives the Broncos one of the most experienced rosters in the league. It shouldn't be that way, but the turnover in the Big West has allowed a handful of veterans to suddenly give a program favored status.

"You look at our roster and see all of the freshmen and sophomores and instantly the idea of a young, inexperienced team pops in your mind," said Jensen. "We do have youth, there's no question, but two of those sophomores started for us last year and you combine that with the four returning seniors and all of a sudden it's not as inexperienced a group as you first think."

The 6-6 Bergersen scored in double figures in 27 of 30 games last season and was the go-to player with an average of 19.7 points a game. He's a tweener and can play shooting guard and small forward. He's able to create his own shot on the perimeter as well as cut to the basket. He's a player-of the-year-candidate and was the only Big West player to rank among the league's top 10 in scoring, field-goal, free-throw and three-point percentage as well as three-point baskets.

He'll likely stay at shooting guard with Washington remaining at the point. He's not the quickest player around, but he's dependable. He'll average close to 12 points a game but needs to raise his assist numbers to closer to five to six a game instead of a sub-par three. Washington has made 121 threes in his career and will be counted on to knock down that shot as the Broncos continue to rely more on the perimeter.

Jensen has options of pushing Bergersen to small forward with the return of 6-3 senior **Steve Shephard** (2.8 ppg, 1.6 apg), who, like Bergersen, is back for a sixth year. Shephard had two consecutive knee injuries which prevented him from playing from 1994-96. He was a backup at shooting guard in 26 games last season and is finally strong enough to be more than a token contributor.

The Broncos were second in the Big West in three-point percentage (.394), making 221 threes. **Delvin Armstrong** (Diablo Valley College/Vallejo HS, Calif.), a 6-4 redshirt sophomore, could pad that number this season. Jensen thinks he'll be the spot shooter the Broncos need behind Bergersen and Shephard.

Clint Hordemann (Clackamas College, Idaho/Eagle HS/Idaho), a 6-3 redshirt sophomore, is more of a defensive worker who will try to make things happen on the offensive end through his defense.

Don't be surprised if 6-foot freshman **C.J. Williams** (Westchester HS/Inglewood, Calif.), who will likely back up Washington at the point, and 6-5 freshman **Dustin Van Weerdhuizen** (LaCenter HS/Wash.), earn time off the bench. Williams could be the quickest player on the team and Van Weerdhuizen is another shooter—he made110 threes last season.

While the Broncos are loaded by their standards along the perimeter, they've still got to develop a post game to overtake Utah State, New Mexico State and, favorite Idaho. **Kejuan Woods** (7.0 ppg, 3.0 rpg, 1.5 spg), 6-6, will either start at small forward (if Bergersen's at shooting guard) or slide over to power forward. He was on the Big West all-freshman team but still averaged only three rebounds a game. He's active but can't seem to find the basketball at the defensive end. His offensive rebounding was a factor as 58 percent of his boards were on the offensive end. He scored in double figures 10 times and the Broncos were 8-2 in those games.

Jensen may go with Woods and 6-7 senior **Justin Lyons** (4.6 ppg, 1.6 rpg) for experience and leadership, but that might not last if 6-8 redshirt freshman **Richard Morgan** (Terry Fox Secondary/Port Coquitlam, B.C.), 6-11 sophomore **Trever Tillman** (2.7 ppg, 2.3 rpg, 1.3 bpg) or 7-foot freshman **Michael Gely** (Blaise Pascal Secondary/Toulouse, France) can steal the spot.

Lyons missed most of last season with a knee injury, playing in only five games. Lyons is more suited for small forward with his ability to put the ball on the floor and cut to the basket. Morgan can play either the finesse forward—he made 39 percent of his threes as a high school senior—or bang bodies underneath. He bulked up over the course of his redshirt season while going against Tillman in practice. He averaged 1.3 blocks. but wasn't able to use his 85-inch wingspan to his advantage. He was hoping that a stint at Pete Newell's big man camp in Honolulu this summer would raise his game this season.

Gely still needs to adapt to American basketball, but has the size to cause problems in the league. The Broncos may not have the luxury of redshirting 6-6 freshman swing forward **Jamal O'Quinn** (Artesia HS/Gardena, Calif.) or 6-7 freshman **Abe Jackson** (Bishop Kelly HS/Boise, Idaho), Idaho's A-2 player of the year as a junior and senior.

"With the guys we've got coming back and the new guys we're going to have make some changes in our matchup," says Jensen. "We don't have the personnel to run as much. We're stronger and deeper but we're not as athletic as we have been in the past. There are several ways we go each night. We could go big, we could go small."

1998-99 BOISE STATE SCHEDULE

Nov.	17	Northwest Nazarene
	21	@Loyola Marymount
	25	@Eastern Michigan
	28	Idaho State
	1	@Weber State
	5	Washington
	11-12	#Indiana Classic
	22	@Idaho State
Jan.	2	Gonzaga
	7	@Cal Poly
	9	@California-Santa Barbara
	14	California Irvine
	16	Cal-State Fullerton
	21	Utah State
	23	Nevada
	28	@Long Beach State
	30	Idaho
Feb.	4	@North Texas
	6	@New Mexico State
	11	North Texas
	13	New Mexico State
	18	@Nevada
	20	@Utah State
	25	Pacific
	27	@Idaho
Mar.	5-7	##Big West Tournament

@ Road Games
\# Bloomington, IN (vs. Indiana, first round; also Bowling Green and Grambling)
\## Reno, NV

adidas Blue Ribbon Analysis

BACKCOURT	B+	BENCH/DEPTH	B-
FRONTCOURT	C	INTANGIBLES	C-

Bergersen has been given a new lease on his college career and wants nothing more than to finish with a postseason berth. His hunger should carry over to the rest of the team. However, Jensen needs to get a set lineup and figure out which way he wants to play. He'll have to switch his defense and go to a more halfcourt set than a pestering matchup zone with some fullcourt pressure. He doesn't have the personnel to stretch the defense and the inexperience inside doesn't help.

Bergersen can carry the team to a top two finish, but the Broncos' ability to win the East Division will depend on Washington's aggressive play at the point and, at least two of the frontcourt players anchoring the inside and rebounding well enough to jump-start fast breaks.

The schedule isn't laced with NIT possibilities. The Broncos have eight road games. They've got to win four to have a chance at an NIT bid. Finishing with five of their last eight Big West games on the road doesn't help their postseason chances, either. Bergersen will have an all-Big West season but the Broncos look like a team headed for 18 wins, which means they would fall short of the NIT and the NCAA.

(A.K.)

CAL POLY

LOCATION .... San Luis Obispo, CA
CONFERENCE .... Big West (Western Division)
LAST SEASON .... 14-14 (.500)
CONFERENCE RECORD 7-9 (2nd)
STARTERS LOST/RETURNING 0/5
NICKNAME .... Mustangs
COLORS .... Green & Gold
HOMECOURT .... Robert A. Mott Gym (3,500)
COACH .... Jeff Schneider (Virginia Tech '82)
RECORD AT SCHOOL .... 44-43 (3 yrs.)
CAREER RECORD .... 44-43 (3 yrs.)
ASSISTANTS .... Kevin Bromley (Colorado State '83)
Brian Loyd (Tulsa '91)
Bob Schneider (Salem College '66)
TEAM WINS (last 5 yrs.) 9-1-16-14-14
RPI (last 5 yrs.) N/A-302-253-218-228
1997-98 FINISH .... Not eligible for conference tournament.

Mitch Ohnstad left a year too soon.

Ohnstad left behind a starting job and returned to his native Minnesota last summer, for what seemed like a good reason at the time: He wanted to play for a program that had a chance to be in the NCAA Tournament.

Little did he know what was about to happen.

In August, Jeff Schneider got the news he has been waiting for the last four years. The Mustangs had been given a reprieve from the rule that forced new Division I teams to wait eight years before becoming

1998-99 CAL POLY SCHEDULE

Nov.	16	@Fresno State
	21	Simon Fraser
	23	Sacramento State
	28	@Portland State
Dec.	12	Cal Baptist
	15	Southern
	17	Eastern Washington
	22	@Missouri-Kansas City
	29-30	#All College Tournament
Jan.	7	Boise State
	9	Idaho
	14	@Utah State
	16	@Nevada
	20	California-Santa Barbara
	23	@North Texas
	28	California-Irvine
	30	Fullerton State
Feb.	4	@Pacific
	6	@Long Beach State
	11	Pacific
	13	Long Beach State
	18	New Mexico State
	20	@California-Santa Barbara
	25	@Fullerton State
	27	@California-Irvine
Mar.	5-7	##Big West Tournament

@ Road Games
# Oklahoma City, OK (vs. Oral Roberts, first round; also Oklahoma and Western Kentucky)
Lawlor Events Center, Reno, NV

eligible to compete for their league's automatic bid to the NCAA Tournament. With four years of waiting already behind them, the Mustangs were relieved of their last four when the NCAA reduced the mandatory rule from eight years to two.

The story, no doubt relegated to a sentence or two in most newspapers, may not have meant much to the rest of the nation. But to Cal Poly, it means the Mustangs can finally play for something. Getting into the NCAA Tournament as an at-large team was almost impossible. Earning an NIT bid seemed just as remote without a chance to pad their record in the Big West Tournament.

Now, they have no excuse. The Mustangs, favored to win the Big West West Division, can not only compete for the conference tournament title, they can actually go to the NCAA Tournament.

And now, perhaps, they can keep all of their players for four years. If anyone does leave, it won't be because the Mustangs don't have a shot at the Big Dance.

"Eight years was too long," Schneider said. "When you're in a situation like we were, where we were 1-26 and then jumped to the Big West and can't compete for the title, it's hard to overcome that. Had this not happened, I might not have been able to keep my freshmen and sophomores for four years."

Schools like the College of Charleston and Tennessee-Martin had to wait the full term. Charleston was able to earn an NCAA bid with a near-perfect record. Cal Poly was never able to come close to that, barely hovering around .500.

That should change this season. The Mustangs have a chance to be one of the sleeper teams on the West Coast, with five starters back, a substantial bench and a style that could drive teams wild in a crazed, renovated Mott Gym. There, the Mustangs' loyal fans will now have a seat, rather than a bench.

"All of our good young players just wanted to have an opportunity to try and win the tournament," Schneider said. "We weren't good enough the past two years to compete for the tournament berth, not good enough to win the Big West. But last year, we still would have been the second seed and instead Fullerton was and got into the semis. We return our top eight players and now we're closer to that level."

Mott Gym's transformation from a glorified high school venue to a cozy arena should pose a potential threat to any visiting team, including UNLV—the highest profile non-conference opponent.

Schneider's optimism hasn't been lost on any other coach in the Big West. All of them are quick to point out that Schneider is confident the Mustangs can win the West. It's OK to boast. He can.

This may be the same team that lost to Sacramento State (the Hornets' only win last season) but the Mustangs are a year older, have more depth and the Big West has slipped with the departures at Pacific in the West and Utah State in the East.

"This is the first year where we've had any type of experience back," Schneider said. "We've been very, very young, but not as athletic in the past. Instead of playing a bunch of freshmen, we have a few guys who have been in the program for four years. We can be as athletic as any team in the league."

Cal Poly had one of the hardest Big West schedules last season, opening at Boise State and Idaho before hosting Utah State and Nevada. The Mustangs lost all four games. The winless start could have devastated them, but they rallied and won seven of their final 12 games, including six of the final nine.

"I was pleased we were still able to get to 14-14," Schneider said.

The Mustangs begin with 6-0 senior point guard **Ben Larson** (7.2 ppg, 2.7 rpg, 126 assists, 53 turnovers). Larson isn't going to get style points like Idaho's Avery Curry or Long Beach State's Charles O'Neal, but he can run Cal Poly's offense and that's all he has to do. He doesn't turn the ball over much, can defend adequately and won't hurt the Mustangs by being on the floor. Last year, Larson became the school's all-time leader in steals with 224.

Schneider will use 5-9 freshman **Jason King** (Lake Washington HS/Redmond, Wash.) behind Larson and expects him to be a scoring point at some stage, banking on him being a three-point shooter off the bench. King averaged 18.0 points as a senior.

Eventually, Schneider may move 6-3 sophomore **Jabbar Washington** (8.5 ppg, 5.4 rpg, 45 assists, 58 turnovers, 488 FG percentage, .472 three-point percentage, .688 FT percentage, 19.0 minutes) to the point because of his quickness. However, Washington will probably stay at one of the wings, where he can slash to the basket. He still needs to be more of a three-point threat like **Mike Wozniak**.

The 6-2 junior was the second-leading scorer in the Big West last season behind Pacific's Michael Olowokandi. Wozniak (20.4 ppg, 2.6 rpg, 63 assists, 74 turnovers, 32.9 minutes, .422 FG percentage, .417 three-point percentage, .890 FT percentage) thrives in Schneider's Rick Pitino-like system. Wozniak has a quick release and can hit the stop-and-pop jumper and pull-up three-pointer on the break. He was the 1996-97 Big West Freshman of the Year and reached the 1,000-point mark in just his second season—a first for a Cal Poly player. His 3.1 threes a game put him at 162 in two seasons.

Schneider rotates Larson, Washington, Wozniak and 6-2 sophomore **Watende Favors** (10.0 ppg, 3.4 rpg) around the perimeter, sometimes using all four in a smaller lineup but at least three all the time. Favors, a gift from former Georgia coach and Schneider mentor Tubby Smith after he decided not to sign with the Bulldogs two years ago, has given the Mustangs the athleticism at guard they lacked in Schneider's first year.

He has shown flashes of being a go-to player with 33 points against Sacramento State and 29 against Southern University. "He's gotten stronger and should continue to average in double figures," Schneider said.

Anchoring the middle is last year's Big West Freshman of the Year—6-9 sophomore **Chris Bjorklund** (17.3 ppg, 5.5 rpg, 36 assists, 19 blocked shots, .345 three-point percentage). Bjorklund was a find for Schneider last season, reaching double figures in all but three games, including season highs of 31 against Eastern Washington and 32 against Long Beach State. He put up 28 in one of the two games against Olowokandi.

"With Wozniak and Bjorklund, it gives us two of the better players returning in the league," Schneider said. "Both understand how to score and take advantage of our system."

Bjorklund created the shift inside with some help from 6-8 sophomore **Jeremiah Mayes** (4.3 ppg, 3.9 rpg), 6-8 senior **Ross Ketcham** (8.5 ppg, 5.4 rpg, .369 three-point percentage) and 6-7 sophomore **Brandon Beeson** (3.4 ppg, 3.1 rpg).

The bench got deeper with the addition of 6-7 freshman **David Henry** (Cardinal Newman HS/Santa Rosa, Calif.) and 6-5 **James Grace III** (MacArthur HS/San Antonio, Texas), who will both probably push out 6-5 senior **Steve Fleming** (2.0 ppg, 1.8 rpg, 9.3 minutes, 53.8 FG, 47.6 FT). Henry averagbed 17.5 points and 9.2 rebounds a year ago, Grace 14.9 points and 7.0 rebounds.

Ketcham is a skilled forward in line with the type at Pacific. Schneider gives him the freedom to step out and take the three-pointer. Beeson will stay home more often, needed to simply finish inside.

"I really do feel comfortable with our inside game," said Schneider, who believes Bjorklund can be as physical as anyone in the Big West, including Fullerton's Ike Harmon.

adidas Blue Ribbon Analysis

BACKCOURT	B	BENCH/DEPTH	B
FRONTCOURT	B	INTANGIBLES	B

The sore spot for the Mustangs has been on the boards, where they were outrebounded 41-35 on average last season. Bjorklund cannot neglect rebounds, and neither can the newcomers. Without them, the Mustangs can't get out on the break to generate their high-octane offense, which at 84.5 points a game was good for ninth in the nation.

The incentive—a chance to play in the Big West Tournament for the first time—is in place for the Mustangs. The perimeter is loaded by Big West standards and the inside game should be able to hold its own. Cal Poly should be able to sweep Irvine, Fullerton, Santa Barbara and Pacific. A split with Long Beach State should give the Mustangs the West title.

They catch a break by getting East frontrunners Boise State and Idaho at home, two must-wins that open the Big West season. If they can sweep that homestand, the Mustangs can win the conference. Without a sweep or a win against Long Beach State at home, then the Mustangs may not have the necessary wins to get an NIT bid if they don't win the Big West Tournament.

(A.K.)

CALIFORNIA-IRVINE

LOCATION ...... **Irvine, CA**
CONFERENCE ...... **Big West (Western Division)**
LAST SEASON ...... **9-18 (.333)**
CONFERENCE RECORD ...... **6-10 (t-3rd)**
STARTERS LOST/RETURNING **2/3**
NICKNAME ...... **Anteaters**
COLORS ...... **Blue & Gold**
HOMECOURT ...... **Brent Evans Center (5,000)**
COACH ...... **Pat Douglass (Pacific '72)**
RECORD AT SCHOOL ...... **9-18 (1 yr.)**
CAREER RECORD ...... **9-18 (1 yr.)**
ASSISTANTS ...... **Len Stevens (Sacramento State '71)**
Todd Lee (South Dakota '86)
Calvin Byrd (Villanova '93)
TEAM WINS (last 5 yrs.) **10-13-15-1-9**
RPI (last 5 yrs.) **238-156-192-302-241**
1997-98 FINISH ...... **Lost in conference quarterfinal.**

Thank heaven for the Big West. There's no other conference in the West that could have provided a similar safe haven for a first-year Division I coach. Pat Douglass could be branded a savior after turning a one-win team into a nine-win, conference tournament qualifying team. It took one season for the Anteaters' credibility to be regained and Douglass did it with a bunch of no-names.

The Big West has slipped since UNLV and New Mexico State left their perches as regular postseason teams. Any coach at any program can come into the league and turn a dismal team into a contender, or at least a pretender, by qualifying for the tournament. Douglass came to Irvine with a plan.

"The thing we tried to do was establish our hard working principles," said Douglass, who built a perennial Division II power at Cal State-Bakersfield before arriving at Irvine last year. "We tried to teach kids who hadn't been successful before. They had to realize that they could be successful. Everyone predicted us for last and we surpassed those expectations. We've got a better awareness with the kids who are back. We're still in the developmental stages but the kids have the right attitude. I couldn't ask for anything more."

Earning a berth in the tournament can build that kind of confidence. Four teams from each side get to go. It might not seem like much, but it does instill confidence and create a sense of accomplishment. Douglass has been able to build off of that during the offseason.

He can harp on his principles because he's got all of his own players. In just one season he has gutted his entire program, leaving it free of former coach Rod Baker's players.

Junior forward **Adam Stetson** (12.1 ppg, 4.0 rpg, 1.2 apg) gives the Anteaters a go-to player after scoring 20 points or more four times and leading the Anteaters in scoring nine times. He's an inside-outside player who will have to continue to improve his rebounding numbers if the Anteaters are to reach the tournament for two consecutive seasons.

While the 6-7 Stetson was the only player to average in double figures, he wasn't the only one ending the season on a streak. Sophomore guard **Jason Flowers** (8.2 ppg, 2.5 rpg, 1.7 apg) scored 78 points in the last five games (15.6 a game). He was a walkon, but should be given a scholarship after helping the Anteaters to late-season

1998-99 CALIFORNIA-IRVINE SCHEDULE

Nov.	17	@Pepperdine
	24	Cal State-Stanislaus
	28	@Oregon State
	30	@Portland
Dec.	5	Northern Arizona
	14	@Arizona
	20	James Madison
	22	Brigham Young
	28	Southern Oregon
Jan.	2	@San Diego
	7	North Texas
	9	New Mexico State
	14	@Boise State
	16	@Idaho
	21	Pacific
	23	Long Beach State
	28	@Cal Poly
	30	@California-Santa Barbara
Feb.	4	Nevada
	6	Fullerton State
	11	@Utah State
	13	@Fullerton State
	18	@Long Beach State
	20	@Pacific
	25	California-Santa Barbara
	27	Cal Poly
Mar.	5-7	#Big West Tournament

@ Road Games
# Reno, NV

upset wins over Long Beach State and UC Santa Barbara, the two wins that were the difference between finishing fourth and earning a place in the tournament or sixth and taking an early spring vacation.

The 6-1 Flowers was tied for third on the team in three-point baskets and was the team's second best free-throw shooter, making 36 of his final 38.

Douglass' youth movement was led by 6-7 sophomore guard **Ben Jones** (8.8 ppg, 3.9 rpg, 1.2 apg), a member of the All-Big West freshman team. Jones was the team's second leading scorer behind Stetson, was second in three-pointers and third at the line. The problem with Stetson and Jones is that they're more finesse players than physical specimens. Neither stays inside too often. Yet, Douglass has to force the pair to play more underneath because of the void in size.

Matt Willard (5.7 ppg, 3.8 rpg, 0.7 apg), a 6-9 senior forward, will have to help some, but impact has to come from 6-8 sophomore forward **Stan Divranos** (Butte College, Calif.), 6-10 freshman **Matt Gottschalk** (Trout Lake HS/Wash.) and 6-6 junior **Marek Onders** (Mira Costa College/Calif.).

Willard averaged 15 points and eight rebounds and shot 80 percent from the field as an All-Golden Valley Conference player in California. Gottschalk averaged 17 points,10 rebounds and 4.5 blocked shots and was an all-star in the state high school game. Onders averaged 19.7 points, 7.2 rebounds and shot 65 percent from the field as the Pacific Coast Conference MVP.

"We need to get that inside presence," said Douglass. "We've got the kids who can shoot and score some points. But we need an inside attack so that they don't extend out on us so far."

Gottschalk is still a project in waiting but will be forced to produce earlier than expected. Divranos is mostly a dunker and his power game will be welcome simply because it was nonexistent last season. Onders has the ability to score from different spots on the floor. The latter two could replace either Jones or Stetson. However, a more likely scenario has the six rotating in the frontcourt and playing center and power forward by committee.

Douglass' hope on the perimeter doesn't rest with Flowers nor three seldom used reserves: 6-2 senior **Brian Scoggin** (3.2 ppg, 1.3 rpg, 1.3 apg), 6-foot sophomore **Malachi Edmond** (2.8 ppg, 1.5 rpg, 0.8 apg) or 6-4 junior Anthony DelaCruz (0.0 ppg, 0.5 rpg, 0.0 apg).

Douglass is banking on 6-3 freshman **Zamiro Bennem** (Magnolia HS/Anaheim, Calif.), who was the Orange County Player of the Year after averaging 23.6 points, 5.8 rebounds and 6.0 assists a game; 5-10 freshman **Gabe Cagwin** (North Mason HS/Belfair, Wash.), an all-state player who averaged 24.0 points, 6.0 assists and 5.0 rebounds a game; and 6-3 freshman **Jerry Green** (Pomona HS/Calif.), who was all-state and All-Southern California after averaging 31 points, 8.0 rebounds and 5.0 assists.

All three can score, handle the ball and play some pressure defense.

adidas Blue Ribbon Analysis

BACKCOURT	D	BENCH/DEPTH	D
FRONTCOURT	D	INTANGIBLES	C+

More experience will come in a year when the Anteaters add 6-5 swing guard Sean Jackson, who transferred from Cal. The game experience of this group won't come until the Big West season, when the Anteaters have a chance to finish fourth and qualify for the tournament again.

However, they'll have to prove they can rebound, score and defend inside. Their perimeter shooting has to improve with the newcomers, too.

Douglass and the Anteaters have a chance to match last year's record with six wins in the Big West and nine overall.

That would still be a sign of improvement.

(A.K.)

CALIFORNIA-SANTA BARBARA

LOCATION	**Santa Barbara, CA**
CONFERENCE	**Big West**
LAST SEASON	**7-19 (.269)**
CONFERENCE RECORD	**4-12 (6th, West)**
STARTERS LOST/RETURNING	**3/2**
NICKNAME	**Gauchos**
COLORS	**Blue & Gold**
HOMECOURT	**The Thunderdome (6,000)**
COACH	**Bob Williams (San Jose State '76)**
RECORD AT SCHOOL	**First Year**
CAREER RECORD	**First Year**
ASSISTANTS	**Marty Wilson (Pepperdine '89)** **Jon Wheeler (Cal '87)** **Greg Clink (Chico State '94)**
TEAM WINS (last 5 yrs.)	**13-13-11-12-7**
RPI (last 5 yrs.)	**188-164-224-212-272**
1997-98 FINISH	**Didn't qualify for conference tournament.**

The UC Santa Barbara had hit a rut, unable to make a play for the postseason for the last four years. The program had grown stale. The players had grown disinterested, nearly reverting to a mutiny when they went to the athletic director to attempt a possible revolt during the season. Coach Jerry Pimm's fate was cast and he couldn't save his job.

Athletic director Gary Cunningham had to start fresh, go young and take a chance. You may not have heard of his choice, but the rest of California has, for the last eight years.

Bob Williams, the former UC Davis coach with a Division II national championship to his credit, was familiar with the UC system. He knew the academic restrictions. He understood the politics. He wasn't going in with any false pretenses about how to rebuild a program under adverse conditions at a university where athletics aren't a priority.

And he has won.

Williams, 44, won the Division II national title last season with a 31-2 record, finishing his eight years with a 158-76 record. In his final four seasons, Davis took the Aggies to four Division II NCAA Tournaments, four 20-win seasons and an overall record of 95-28.

"Davis prepared me for this opportunity," Williams said. "I can do the same type of thing in terms of the people we recruit. I understand what it takes to be successful in the UC system on the floor and in the classroom. I understand this type of public school that a private-school person may not. I understand that you have to have students who can handle sitting in a classroom where the average SAT is closer to 1200. Most of the students are serious academic people. You have to bring in the right kids."

Williams had done what he could at Davis in arguably the toughest Division II league in the country. The national champion has come from this league four of the last six years, between Davis and Cal State-Bakersfield. One of the two years the two teams didn't play for the title, conference member UC Riverside did.

Last year, Bakersfield's Pat Douglass joined the Big West, taking over UC Irvine and—stunningly—leading the Anteaters to a third-place finish with six wins in the West. Williams could do the same.

He's familiar with central and southern California after serving as recruiting coordinator at Pepperdine for two seasons under Tom Asbury.

Williams will build around **B.J. Bunton**. The 6-7 senior forward is the team's best returning player and maybe its most talented after losing its most electric in shooting guard Raymond Tutt. Bunton (10.8 ppg, 6.2 rpg, 28.7 minutes, .545 FG percentage) gives the Gauchos hope that they can contend in a weak interior league.

"B.J. has the ability to score inside and out," Williams said. "He's very quick off his feet and he can be our consistent go-to guy. We'll play similar to Kansas and North Carolina with quick hitters for guys in various different positions. We can post him up, bring him off double-teams and staggers. He can pass the ball well and he helps make players better."

And he has help.

The Gauchos were a respectable sixth in rebounds, but Bunton and Tutt had more to do with it than 6-9 senior **Josh Merrill** (6.7 ppg, 3.7 rpg, 17.8 minutes .738 FT percentage) and 6-9 sophomore **Mike Vukovich** (2.8 ppg, 2.5 rpg, .74.1 FT percentage).

That has to change. Merrill, Vukovich and 6-5 sophomore **Chris Lynch** (4.1 ppg, 2 rpg, .473 FG percentage, .375 three-point percentage, .800 FT percentage) have to be more assertive on the boards and on defense if the Gauchos are to be this season's UC Irvine.

"It's our best position and Merrill is our most versatile player," Williams said. "Lynch is a versatile three-man and one of our most athletic players."

However, Merrill has to find his niche. It isn't shooting, where he shot under 40 percent (poor for a supposedly inside player) and was under 30 percent when he stepped past the three-point line. Williams promises to make him more of an option this season—closer to the basket. He's also hoping Vukovich uses his strength more often and becomes more of a wide-body inside than simply another space eater in the post.

If he can't handle the heat, Williams is convinced a late signee, 6-8 sophomore **Adama Ndiaye** (Barton County JC/Kansas/Senagal, Africa) will help immediately.

"He'll factor in there," Williams said. "He's very athletic, gives us shot blocking and is a pretty good back-to-the-basket player. He's young and doesn't have as much basketball experience, but he'll improve every month."

Williams plans on using 6-5 sophomore **Matt Blakely**, a transfer from the University of New Hampshire, as a scrappy, physical player off the bench. Blakely, originally from San Diego's University High School, will compete with 6-7 freshman **Mark Hull** (Hoover HS/Glendale, Calif.) and 6-5 freshman forward **Eric Hare** (McKinney HS/Texas) for minutes.

1998-99 CALIFORNIA-SANTA BARBARA SCHEDULE

Nov.	14	@Pepperdine
	18	San Francisco
	21	Westmont
	24	@Portland
	28	Loyola Marymount
Dec.	5	Southern California
	17	@Santa Clara
	19	@Saint Mary's
	23	Western Colorado State
	30	San Jose State
Jan.	7	Idaho
	9	Boise State
	14	@Nevada
	16	@Utah State
	20	@Cal Poly
	23	@New Mexico State
	28	Fullerton State
	30	California-Irvine
Feb.	4	@Long Beach State
	6	@Pacific
	11	Long Beach State
	13	Pacific
	18	North Texas
	20	Cal Poly
	25	@California-Irvine
	27	@Fullerton State
Mar.	5-7	#Big West Tournament

@ Road Games
# Lawlor Events Center, Reno, NV

Hull, who averaged 27.9 points and 13.9 rebounds a game last season, is a scorer who will be given a chance to shoot early in the season to prove he can make the transition. Hare is an undersized post player who will give the Gauchos truer front-line play when he's at small forward.

"He could be our best back-to-the-basket post-up guy," Williams said. "He's strong and quick but if he doesn't figure into the mix early and in the top eight, we could redshirt him."

While Williams is enthused about his frontcourt, the perimeter is wide open. **Brandon Payton**, a 6-foot sophomore, is the likely starter at the point after a decent year as a freshman.

Payton (7.9 ppg, 2.0 rpg, 2.3 apg, .368 three-point percentage, .760 FT percentage) was the team's third-leading scorer, but couldn't hang with the top point guards in a point-guard-loaded league. He has to assert himself as one to watch if the Gauchos move out of the cellar.

"He can shoot the ball better, but he has great instincts," Williams said. "We could use him at off-guard, too. He also needs to defend better."

Williams may interchange all of the guards, including 6-1 sophomore **Tory Woodward** (2.5 ppg, 1.0 rpg). He has become the team's best defender, but wasn't an offensive option. Williams is contemplating trying him at the point, taking advantage more of his playmaking and Payton's scoring.

Larry Bell, a 6-1 junior point guard out of Compton College (Calif.), could be the quickest player and top defender on the team. Bell (11.5 ppg, 5.8 apg at Compton, which won the California state championship) still isn't a good enough shooter, but if he switches Payton and Woodward, he may not need Bell to do anything but run the team and play defense.

Derrick Allen, a 6-foot junior guard out of Porterville Junior College (Calif.), could be the team's "warrior," but not much else without an offensive game. **Erick Ashe**, a 6-2 junior guard from Fullerton (Calif.) CC, is more of a shooting guard and could beat out Payton or Woodward for significant time if he can shoot. Losing Tutt puts three-point shooting (he led the team with 34) as a high priority. If Ashe can make threes, he'll be on the court.

adidas Blue Ribbon Analysis

BACKCOURT	D	BENCH/DEPTH	D
FRONTCOURT	C-	INTANGIBLES	C+

Williams makes the Gauchos sound better than the propaganda the school puts out on the team, and it may be true. No one thought Irvine was going to finish as high as third last season. But few thought the West was as poor—with the exception of Pacific—as it was last season.

Williams' knowledge of the game, his energy to revive the program and his Midas touch after winning the Division II championship give the Gauchos more hope than any of the players.

"There's a small difference between the top and bottom of this league," Williams said. "There's not a lot of difference physically. Realistically, everybody has a chance to win the West."

Realistically? Yes. Possibly? No. Expect the Gauchos to finish anywhere from fourth to sixth.

(A.K.)

adidas Blue Ribbon Analysis

GRADING SYSTEM

- A+ equal to very best in country—Final Four-caliber unit
- A among the best in the land—worthy of deep NCAA run
- B+ talented, versatile and experienced—NCAA-NIT ability
- B solid and productive winners—league and post-season contenders
- C+ average to above-average—may contend in a weaker league
- C average to mediocre—second division in a strong league
- D+ below average, inconsistent—second division in a weaker league
- D well below average—losing season virtually certain
- F non-Division I ability—an underdog every night

FULLERTON STATE

LOCATION	Fullerton, CA
CONFERENCE	Big West (West Division)
LAST SEASON	12-16 (.429)
CONFERENCE RECORD	6-10 (t-3rd)
STARTERS LOST/RETURNING	3/2
NICKNAME	Titans
COLORS	Blue, Orange & White
HOMECOURT	Titan Gym (4,000)
COACH	Bob Hawking (Northridge State '71)
RECORD AT SCHOOL	38-70 (4 yrs.)
CAREER RECORD	38-70 (4 yrs.)
ASSISTANTS	Todd Johnson (Oklahoma '91) Bob Thornton (UC Irvine '98)
TEAM WINS (last 5 yrs.)	8-7-6-13-12
RPI (last 5 yrs.)	257-220-251-202
1997-98 FINISH	Lost in conference semifinal.

When it's time to rebuild at Fullerton State, the foundation is usually as unstable as the ground beneath the school.

The Titans were supposed to have their best team under Bob Hawking a year ago and still won only six games in the Big West. They did win 12 overall and fell just four games shy of a .500 record. Also, they won a game in the Big West tournament, which is as rare as an above-.500 record.

However, it's not enough to feel satisfied. The Titans had a chance to make more noise in the league, but lost their first two at home, both within three points to Idaho and Boise State. That set up a string of five losses in six games that took them out of contention early. No one thought they would ever catch Pacific, but the Titans had enough talent to make it a more interesting race.

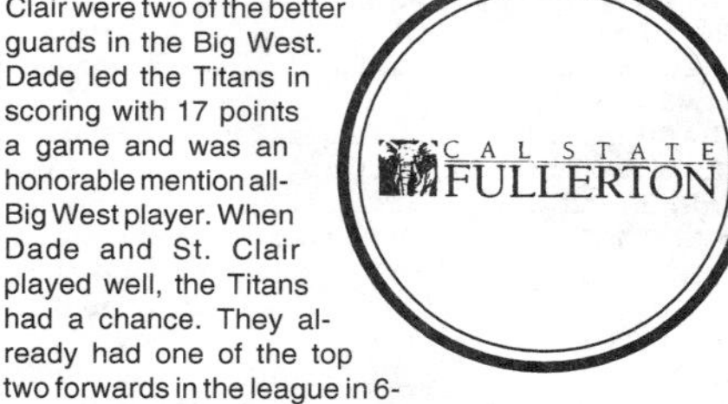

Chris Dade and Chris St. Clair were two of the better guards in the Big West. Dade led the Titans in scoring with 17 points a game and was an honorable mention all-Big West player. When Dade and St. Clair played well, the Titans had a chance. They already had one of the top two forwards in the league in 6-7 junior **Ike Harmon**. However, he needed their help to avoid teams doubling down on him. He got it during the wins, didn't as much in the losses, and now he's desperate for someone to replace Dade and St. Clair.

Harmon (15.3 ppg, 6.4 rpg) is a running forward who can get out ahead of defenders on the break. He's one of the best-conditioned athletes in the Big West and is akin to former Washington forward Mark Sanford. He could be the player who gets the Titans 20 points a game and delivers nearly eight rebounds. Someone will have to pick up the scoring load lost by Dade and it will likely fall on Harmon.

The Titans lost wing Craig Whitehead and his 6.5 points and 3.0 rebounds a game. He provided some help, but Harmon will need more from returnees 6-7 senior **Mark Richardson** (5.4 ppg, 4.8 rpg) and 6-5 senior forward **Jason Cunningham** (5.0 ppg, 3.9 rpg). Richardson and Cunningham are both bangers and not much else. They'll need to develop more offensive skills to keep some of the defensive pressure off of Harmon.

Josh Fischer, a 6-9 freshman, could be the answer. Fischer (La Habra HS/Calif.) averaged 18 points and 10 rebounds and is similar to Pacific's Rayne Mahaffey. The Tigers' former forward was the typical skilled three-to-four man who can step out and hit the three-pointer but also do some banging inside. Harmon has the paint taken care of, but needs a forward who can step out and shoot from 15 feet and beyond to stretch the defense.

Matt Caldwell, a 6-8 sophomore, will be more of a backup for Harmon in the post. Caldwell (4.3 ppg, 3.6 rpg) was limited offensively and needs to be more of a defensive presence.

Mitch Deve, a 7-2 freshman from La Cueva High School in Albuquerque, N.M., is a project and can't start practicing until he gets a cast off his right foot. He has been battling a stress fracture and could be a redshirt candidate, even though the Titans desperately needs his size.

Harmon would love to play small forward, but that won't happen with this group, especially with 6-4 freshman **Brandon Campbell** (Cardinal Ritter HS/St. Louis, Mo.) and 6-6 freshman **Josh Helbig** (East Belleville HS/Belleville, Ill.) expected to compete for Whitehead's minutes. Hawking is expected to keep more of a traditional rotation with Harmon at power forward and Richardson or Cunningham next to him. One of these freshman, more likely Campbell (13.5 ppg last year), could find himself at small forward.

None of it will matter if the Titans can't find someone to shoot from the perimeter and drive from the point. **Kenroy Jarrett**, a 5-11 junior, will be the starting point guard. He's not exceptionally quick, but in his defense, he didn't get a chance to prove he could play with Dade and St. Clair taking the majority of minutes. Jarrett (4.8 ppg, 1.0 rpg, 1.5 apg .42.1 three-point percentage, .818 FT percentage) is one of the better three-point shooters on the team. He'll have to be to replace Dade's 54 threes and St. Clair's 58. Jarrett made 24 and will easily get twice as many looks. The Titans lost their other shooter when Dane Plock took his 21 threes and decided to skip his senior season.

Mark Murphy, a 6-foot junior from Mesa Community College in Arizona, is the only other true ball handler. Murphy, who averaged nine points as a freshman at Grand Canyon College in Arizona, averaged 23 points and shot 51 percent on threes and made 90 percent of his free-throws. If he's good enough to get to the line, knock down threes and run a team, he could replace Jarrett. He could start next to him if he can score. The unknown is 6-5 freshman guard **Danny Italiano**, a former member of the Israeli army. Italiano is supposed to be a scorer, but he hasn't seen competition at this level the last two years. **Matt Donahue**, a 6-1 freshman guard from Etiwanda High School in Rancho Cucamonga, Calif., will probably be the last option.

adidas Blue Ribbon Analysis

BACKCOURT	D	BENCH/DEPTH	D
FRONTCOURT	C-	INTANGIBLES	D

Harmon's presence gives the Titans one grade above a D. He could and should be an all-Big West player and is the only one on the roster who could play professionally when he's done. However, this isn't the same team as a year ago. The Titans were better and finished with six Big West wins.

The schedule is similar and littered with a few wins in the nonconference, but the Titans are looking at last place unless Harmon gets help from shooting guards Jarrett and Murphy, finesse play from Fischer at forward and grunt, body-banging work from Richardson and Cunningham. Harmon could push them ahead of California-Santa Barbara and California-Irvine, but he can't get them any higher alone.

(A.K.)

1998-99 FULLERTON STATE SCHEDULE

Nov.	16	@Kansas State
	21	San Diego State
	28	Pepperdine
Dec.	2	@Loyola Marymount
	5	Saint Mary's
	10	Montana State
	12	@Saint Louis
	19	@Portland
	22	Quincy
	27	@San Jose State
Jan.	7	New Mexico State
	9	North Texas
	14	@Idaho
	16	@Boise State
	21	Long Beach State
	23	Pacific
	28	@California-Santa Barbara
	30	@Cal Poly
Feb.	4	Utah State
	6	@California-Irvine
	11	@Nevada
	13	California-Irvine
	18	@Pacific
	20	@Long Beach State
	25	Cal Poly
	27	California-Santa Barbara
Mar.	5-7	#Big West Tournament

@ Road Games
# Reno, NV

IDAHO

LOCATION .... **Moscow, ID**
CONFERENCE .... **Big West (Eastern Division)**
LAST SEASON .... **15-12 (.556)**
CONFERENCE RECORD .... **9-7 (4th East)**
STARTERS LOST/RETURNING **1/4**
NICKNAME .... **Vandals**
COLORS .... **Silver & Gold**
HOMECOURT .... **ASUI Dome (10,000)**
COACH .... **Dave Farrar (Andersen College '69)**
RECORD AT SCHOOL .... **15-12 (2 yrs.)**
CAREER RECORD .... **78-85 (6 yrs.)**
ASSISTANTS . **Steve Forbes (Southern Arkansas '88)**
Derek Zeck (Kansas '93)
TEAM WINS (last 5 yrs.) **18-12-12-13-15**
RPI (last 5 yrs.) **112-166-206-196-142**
1997-98 FINISH .... **Lost in conference quarterfinal.**

Dave Farrar has taken his second chance at coaching and made sure he wouldn't have to seek a third.

Idaho should be the team to beat in the Big West Eastern Division, and the favorite to win the outright title in the conference tournament.

It was just three years ago Farrar was forced out at Middle Tennessee State. Though lacking the high-profile name it usually takes to get back into the job rotation, Farrar settled at Idaho, expecting to work under Kermit Davis Jr. indefinitely. But Davis unexpectedly left Moscow after one season to return to the South and become an assistant for his friend John Brady at LSU.

The Vandals were in disarray after looking toward their third coach in three seasons. At least, that's what it seemed from the outside.

What most people didn't know was that Farrar had helped recruit **Avery Curry** from Florida State. Curry wasn't content being a backup point guard to Lamar Greer and wanted to find a place where he could shine.

He has in Idaho.

Curry, a 6-2 senior, is the preseason favorite to be the player of the year in the Big West after averaging 19.7 points as a junior, leading the Vandals to a stunning 15-12 record, 9-7 in the Big West. Qualifying for the conference tournament was not even a consideration for the Vandals last season, especially with New Mexico State in the division. However, Idaho slid by the Aggies into fourth and earned the final spot in the tournament.

The offseason has been just as kind to Idaho, with Farrar signing a five-year contract to ensure security. It continued with the commitments from 6-5 Barton County Junior College junior guard **Gordon Scott** and 6-6 junior forward **Michael Jackson**, a Barton County teammate of Scott's. The revelation to the rest of the league that Curry will be back despite being listed as a senior all season, something the Idaho athletic department said was merely a typo, confirmed Idaho's status.

This year, Idaho is a team wearing the tag of favorite. "We are definitely not going to sneak up on people from this point on," Farrar said. "There is talk we'll be the preseason pick in the league. We don't lose very many key players and we had a stable recruiting year. Where do I expect us to be? I expect our team to be a contender for the league and a contender for postseason play."

Curry is the basis for Farrar's optimism. He's been given free reign to score in Farrar's offense and he hasn't disappointed. Curry was the third-leading scorer in the Big West behind Pacific's Michael Olowokandi and Cal Poly's Mike Wozniak.

"I've coached a long time and he's the type of player who can score at the end of the games when the coaching is over," Farrar said. "You always have a chance to be competitive. He can just raise up and score over the defense. You need that quality in today's game."

Curry alone couldn't lead the Vandals to a Big West title. So, Farrar tried to go out and mirror Utah State's backcourt from last season. He already had the Marcus Saxon-type point guard in Curry (19.7 ppg, 3.9 rpg) and the Justin Jones-type shooting guard in 6-5 senior **Cameron Banks**. What he lacked was the shooting/slashing scorer like a Kevin Rice.

Farrar found one in Scott, ranked the No. 7 junior college player in the country by analysts Rick Ball and Phil Henzel. How did Idaho get Scott? He decided to follow his junior college coach, Steve Forbes, now on Farrar's staff. Forbes was kind enough to bring along Jackson, too. The package deal immediately gave the Vandals the type of scoring at swing guard and small forward that had been lacking last season.

"Traditionally the better players in this league are in that in-between size," Farrar said. "You need perimeter players who have the star-like ability. Olowokandi was a plus for this league and he improves the visibility but Avery's the stereotypical player in the league."

The three-guard lineup of Curry, Banks and Scott should be the most productive in the conference. All three can defend as well, making it the toughest threesome to face at either end.

While Curry is the scoring point, Banks (11 ppg, 3.0 rpg, .485 FG percentage) is the hustle player who can ignite a scoring run with a mid-range jumper, a dive for a loose ball or a drive to the basket for a layup. He was considered the most improved player on the team. However, he has to make himself more of an option as a three-point threat. Banks made only .208 percent of his three-pointers last season, but he didn't have to shoot from behind the arc as much with Curry making 40 percent of his shots from that range.

Scott takes even more pressure off Banks. He holds the Barton County Junior College single-game record with nine three-pointers in one game. He averaged 22 points and made 48 percent of his shots, including 100 threes last season.

"One thing about Gordon is that he loves to play," Farrar said. "We'll definitely play all three at the same time and our style of play is for two wings and a point," Farrar said. "The four and five players are interchangeable."

Farrar has depth behind Curry, Scott and Banks with 6-3 junior **Devon Ford** (Northeastern JC/Denver, Colo.) getting the first look off the bench. Ford sat out last season at Idaho. He was a scorer in junior college, averaging 24 points and eight rebounds while making 58 percent of his shots. He's more suited for the big guard or small forward. When he's in the game, Ford will be asked to go to the boards rather than bust out for the fast break.

The fifth guard in the rotation could be late signee **Terrence Chapman**, a 6-2 guard out of Garden City (Kan.) Junior College. Farrar has other bodies in 6-4 freshmen **Anthony Lewis** (Franklin HS/Seattle, Wash.) and **Nathaniel Watson** (Eastglen HS/Edmonton, Alberta), 6-5 sophomore **Jon Harris** (3.0 ppg, 2.0 rpg), 6-2 senior guard **Josh Toal** (4.6 ppg, 2.4 rpg) and 5-10 sophomore **Adam Miller** (0.5 ppg, 0.6 rpg). However, the minutes won't be there behind the four regulars.

Ford would have had to battle Clifford Gray for time but the 6-5 senior forward will redshirt so nagging leg and ankle injuries can heal. He became a starter out of Dodge City (Kan.) JC, averaging 11 points and grabbing 6.3 rebounds a game. His specialty was scoring close to the basket, finishing the season with a .535 field-goal percentage.

Jackson can step in and become just as productive.

The 6-6 junior forward is a leaper with limited offensive skills, but has an ability to be around the basketball. His activity will force points as he gets his hands on rebounds for putbacks. He should be the best runner on the floor, finishing with jams. He has a 40-inch vertical leap, enabling him to play taller.

There will have to be a place for 6-4 junior forward **Trywone Still**, who sat out last season after fracturing his shin bone.

"He can be a double-figure scorer and he's another one of those in between size guys," Farrar said.

The middle will probably belong to 6-9 senior center **Kevin Byrne** (4.5 ppg, 2.9 rpg). Byrne's a lanky center who still needs to hold his own on the low block but could step out and hit the jumper. He's a near-80 percent free-throw shooter and can help the Vandals by getting to the line more often. He'll have less pressure on him once 6-6 senior forward **Mao Tosi** (4.1 ppg, 5.5 rpg) gets back from football. Tosi is 270 pounds and can literally clear out space inside.

Tosi was a force last season, putting up double-digit rebound games three times, with his season-high of 12 coming against New Mexico State.

While Tosi's at football practice, 6-8 sophomore forward **Kaniel Dickens** from Tyler (Texas) JC, will get more of a look. Dickens is the complete opposite of Tosi and is much more of a leaper. Farrar won't play Dickens and Jackson at the same time, but he could rotate the two next to Byrne and then Tosi when he returns.

adidas Blue Ribbon Analysis

BACKCOURT .... **B+** **BENCH/DEPTH** .... **C+**
FRONTCOURT .... **C** **INTANGIBLES** .... **B**

The three-guard lineup worked for Utah State, because the Aggies didn't have a dominant low-post game. What they did have was rebounders, passers, screeners and interior defenders. So it is with Idaho.

Junior college players sometimes take a year to adjust to Division I. Picking Idaho to win the Big West is putting pressure on that theory to fail. However, the Big West is filled with teams faced with this dilemma. Idaho has the most talent of any of them, and the best returning guard. Idaho should win the East and the Big West tournament.

Unfortunately, if the Vandals get beat in the tournament, they won't have enough quality power-rating wins to earn an at-large NCAA Tournament berth. But an NIT spot just might be waiting.

(A.K.)

1998-99 IDAHO SCHEDULE

Nov.	19	*Western Oregon
	24	@Florida State
	28	Montana
Dec.	5	@Missouri
	11-12	#KGVO/Coca-Cola Classic
	20	Washington State
	22	@Gonzaga
Jan.	2	Long Beach State
	7	@California-Santa Barbara
	9	@Cal Poly
	14	Fullerton State
	16	California-Irvine
	21	Nevada
	23	Utah State
	28	@Pacific
	30	@Boise State
Feb.	4	@New Mexico State
	6	@North Texas
	11	New Mexico State
	13	North Texas
	18	@Utah State
	20	@Nevada
	28	Boise State
Mar.	5-7	##Big West Tournament

@ Road Games
* Nampa, ID
# Butte, MT (Montana, Saint Mary's and Youngstown State)
Lawler Events Center, Reno, NV

LONG BEACH STATE

LOCATION .... **Long Beach, CA**
CONFERENCE .... **Big West (Western Division)**
LAST SEASON .... **10-19 (.345)**
CONFERENCE RECORD .... **5-11 (5th)**
STARTERS LOST/RETURNING **3/2**
NICKNAME **49ers**
COLORS .... **Black & Gold**
HOMECOURT .... **The Pyramid (5,000)**
COACH .... **Wayne Morgan (St. Lawrence '73)**
RECORD AT SCHOOL .... **23-33 (2 yrs.)**
CAREER RECORD .... **23-33 (2 yrs.)**
ASSISTANTS .... **Clyde Vaughan (Pittsburgh '84)**
Tom Lewis (Pepperdine '90)
Reggie Warford (Kentucky '76
TEAM WINS (last 5 yrs.) **17-20-17-13-10**
RPI (last 5 yrs.) **146-56-126-115-251**
1997-98 FINISH .... **Lost in conference quarterfinal.**

Wayne Morgan didn't have a chance. He came out of nowhere during the hiring process two years ago, shocking a number of observers in the West Coast. He was replacing a vocal coach in Seth Greenberg, who had drawn attention to himself and to the program.

So far, Morgan hasn't able to do either, at least not for reasons he would prefer.

Long Beach State didn't qualify for the Big West Tournament in Morgan's first season, despite having two of the more talented players in the league in James Cotton, an eventual second-round NBA draft pick (Denver Nuggets) and **Brandon Titus**.

Morgan was supposed to have Cotton back with his brother Schea, a highly recruited freshman, last season. But James left early for the NBA and Schea wasn't eligible. The latter eventually signed at UCLA, but didn't land there, either.

Last season, Morgan should have had both Cottons next to 7-foot transfer Andrew Betts, an eventual second

1998-99 LONG BEACH STATE SCHEDULE

Nov.	14	Cal State Northridge
	17	@Loyola Marymount
	21	Pepperdine
	24	@Southern California
	28	@San Diego State
Dec.	1	Cal State Dominguez Hills
	5	Utah
	9	@Southwest Missouri State
	12	Kansas State
	27	@Northwestern
Jan.	2	@Idaho
	7	Nevada
	9	Utah State
	14	@New Mexico State
	16	@North Texas
	21	@Fullerton State
	23	@California-Irvine
	28	Boise State
	30	@Pacific
Feb.	4	California-Santa Barbara
	6	Cal Poly
	11	@California-Santa Barbara
	13	@Cal Poly
	18	California-Irvine
	20	Fullerton State
	27	Pacific
Mar.	5-7	#Big West Tournament

@ Road Games
# Reno, NV

round pick of the Charlotte Hornets. It would have been enough to unseat Pacific in the Western Division and beat Utah State in the conference tournament. It would have meant an NCAA Tournament berth. Instead, the 49ers barely made the Big West Tournament, lost to Utah State in the quarterfinals (the first round in an eight-team tournament) and were left to ponder a 10-19 record.

After two years, Morgan has gone from the can't-miss coach to the coach who has missed too much.

Things could be different this season, as Morgan seems to have some players, enough to seriously challenge for a division title and a postseason berth. But misfortune struck again when junior college transfer Charles O'Neal couldn't gain eligibility. There's a chance O'Neal could return for the second semester. If he does, the 49ers' outlook could change.

"We've got a chance to be competitive," says Morgan. "We've never felt like we were under the gun. We had high expectations but a number of things happened. There were higher expectations the next year. Then, James goes hardship and it was a devastating blow. And then his brother decides he can't come. If you put Betts with both Cotton brothers and a point guard, we're as good as any team last year."

Ramel Lloyd, a 6-4 sophomore from the Bronx, N.Y., will immediately step in at shooting guard after sitting out last season. Morgan had signed him at Syracuse when he was an assistant. Lloyd obviously was more loyal to Morgan than upstate New York. Put Lloyd next to the 6-3 junior O'Neal (Florida CC/Jacksonville, Fla.) and the 49ers have the most athletic guard tandem in the league. Cal Poly has the deepest and most productive perimeter, but no two guards will be as difficult to defend as Lloyd and O'Neal. The tandem should be just as dangerous defensively, pressuring opposing guards at halfcourt.

"O'Neal and Lloyd give us an explosive offense and I believe they will be recognized as one of the best backcourts in America," Morgan said. "Our backcourt will be our strength. Lloyd can score and people can't stop him from scoring. He's got a body like Herschel Walker and Arnold Schwarzenegger. He looks so strong."

Lloyd, nicknamed "Rock," was a *Parade* All-American out of Cardinal Hayes High School in the Bronx. O'Neal, who sat out last season with Lloyd, led Florida CC to the state finals of the Florida JC tournament in 1997.

Morgan had to do a bit of scrambling to shore up the point guard spot in O'Neal's absence. First, he reinstated 5-9 senior point guard **Tommie Davis**, who wasn't on the team a year ago. The 49ers also picked up 6-1 freshman **Ron Johnson** out of Helix Walton High School in San Diego.

If someone can play the point in O'Neal's absence, that would allow **Antrone Lee** (11.7 ppg, 4.1 rpg) to return to his natural position at small forward or swing guard. The 6-7 Lee had to play the point, but couldn't adjust to the position and the 49ers suffered. He may have led the 49ers with 89 assists, but only because he had no other choice. Lee can play shooting guard or small forward and allows Morgan to go with a quick lineup with Lee next to O'Neal and Lloyd.

Lee has to become a better three-point shooter if he's going to be more of a scorer at a wing. He made only .241 percent of his three-point shots. He did lead the team in steals (64) and blocked shots (51) and can become even more effective with his reach at the wing, especially coming off some helpside defense for Lloyd.

Morgan will probably rotate 6-6 senior **D'Cean Bryant** (12.7 ppg, 6.9 rpg) with Lee. Bryant, the lone senior on the team, played small forward last season, but will play some power forward with Lee's return to his natural position. Bryant comes out of the same mold as Lee, and continues the athletic, versatility of the new-look 49ers. He's a better shooter, hitting .416 percent of his threes. If Bryant comes off the bench, it gives the 49ers the shooting punch they'll need to beat teams like Cal Poly.

Bryant isn't the rebounder needed for the other forward. Morgan is banking on 6-8 junior **Richie Smalls** (St. Catherines CC/KY., Bronx, NY) to be the banger at power forward. Smalls brings his East Coast brashness to the West Coast and would give the 49ers the toughness they lacked last season.

If Smalls stumbles in his transition, 6-8 sophomore **Grant Stone** (5.2 ppg, 5.0 rpg) will have to provide the necessary rebounding. Stone started every game as a freshman, taking over at center after 6-10 sophomore **Ian Milley** (Mercersburg Prep, Pa./Oak Hills, Calif.) was hurt in the season opener, fracturing a finger. He came back eight games later but his rust showed—he averaged 0.7 points and 1.1 rebounds in limited action.

Morgan may slow down the middle, but give it some size if Milley is healthy and 6-11 junior **Mate Milisa** (Pensacola JC/Fla./Zagreb, Croatia) produces as expected. Dubbed the M&M boys, Milley is the physical side while Milisa is the more finesse, skilled center. Betts was a reliable player in the low post for the 49ers last season. The M&M boys should be able to equal his production of 18.7 points and 10.1 rebounds.

Milisa, ranked No. 74 on on a list of the country's top 300 JC sophomores, averaged 17.1 points and 8.2 rebounds a year ago.

"We shouldn't have to hesitate to go inside," Morgan says.

The rest of the depth comes from 6-5 junior **Allan Gomez** (East Los Angeles CC/Calif.), who can be a slashing wing and 6-5 senior **Jared Frey** (2.5 ppg, 2.9 rpg), who played 12.9 minutes a game last season and built a following with his leaping abilities. **Ugonna Onyekwe**, a 6-8 freshman from Mercersburg Prep (Pa.) and originally from Crydon, England, could be a candidate for a redshirt season.

adidas Blue Ribbon Analysis

BACKCOURT	**B**	**BENCH/DEPTH**	**C+**
FRONTCOURT	**C**	**INTANGIBLES**	**C+**

There would have been no excuse, had guard Charles O'Neal gained eligibility for the first semester, but his absence will hurt. If he returns in time for conference play, Long Beach State should be a contender for the West title.

Lloyd and O'Neal have to be as good as advertised. Lee, Bryant, Smalls, Milley and Milisa give the 49ers the most athletic team in the league, but that has to translate into wins. A year ago, the 49ers couldn't shoot well enough to move ahead of Cal Poly and they may not have enough punch this season, depending on O'Neal's situation. But they should be able to shut down the Mustangs with their quickness.

If Lloyd and O'Neal produce, the 49ers can overcome any inexperience in the frontcourt. Any chance of an NIT bid could hinge on a nonconference schedule that includes five road games and a home game against Utah. The 49ers have to go 4-2 in that stretch to give them a cushion before they get into the Big West. Finishing with three straight wins at home against Irvine, Fullerton and Pacific could be the edge they need to claim the West title.

(A.K.)

NEVADA

LOCATION	**Reno, NV**
CONFERENCE	**Big West (Eastern Division)**
LAST SEASON	**16-12 (.571)**
CONFERENCE RECORD	**11-5 (2nd)**
STARTERS LOST/RETURNING	**5/0**
NICKNAME	**Wolf Pack**
COLORS	**Silver & Black**
HOMECOURT	**Lawlor Events Center (11,200)**
COACH	**Pat Foster (Arkansas '61)**
RECORD AT SCHOOL	**82-63 (6 yrs.)**
CAREER RECORD	**358-185 (19 yrs.)**
ASSISTANTS	**Jason Glover (Grand Canyon '85)** **David Spencer (Delaware '72)**
TEAM WINS (last 5 yrs.)	**11-18-16-21-16**
RPI (last 5 yrs.)	**211-87-143-74-132**
1997-98 FINISH	**Lost in conference semifinal.**

Recruiting doesn't have to be an exact science. The goal is to go out and find the best players you can. What you don't want to do is get caught without a returning starter, or even a proven player.

Nevada did and the Wolf Pack will pay for it by going into the season with little clue about how they'll come out in March.

The Wolf Pack lost nine players off last season's team, including their starting backcourt in Robin Kennedy, Paul Culbertson and Jimmy Carroll. The inside tandem of Marvin Wilson and David Morgan checked out, too.

Nevada has been able to find the balance of finishers inside with pesky defenders and shooters on the perimeter. It has worked to stay in the top tier of the Big West during Foster's six years. He has averaged 17.8 wins the past four seasons, dwarfing the 13.9-win-per-season average from the last 24 years.

Having the tournament on the Wolf Pack's homecourt for the fourth straight season has provided added incentive. It'll have to this season with the Wolf Pack a reach to finish as high as fourth in the Big West Eastern Division, above North Texas and New Mexico State.

"We lost everything," Foster said. "We're starting with all new players and one that I had last year. But I still think we can have an upper-level player at each position."

Foster is obviously believing all of the publicity on his newcomers. And even that might be a reach because most of them were unheralded.

Derrick Anderson, a 6-5 junior point guard from Los Angeles City College, will have to be as talented as Foster predicts if the Wolf Pack can reclaim their status in the Big West. Foster has handed him the starting job in the summer and expects him to be a "Magic-type" of point guard.

"He's not your typical point guard because he can back the ball in like Magic," Foster said. "He can be a good passer and post his man up and score outside, too. He's got a chance to be really, really good."

There's no reason to doubt that contention. Anderson played with Rico Harris last season at Los Angeles City College, forming one of the better inside-out combinations in the California junior college league.

Anderson will have to be a hawk on the ball to make up for Kennedy or even off the ball the way Culbertson was able to shut down wings. Foster is banking on him being like Avery Curry for Idaho or Marcus Saxon for Utah State. Curry and Saxon were able to take over their teams, dictating tempo, leading the defense and forcing defenses to neutralize them.

Point guard won't be the only position gone big. Foster is looking at 6-5 junior **Calvin Criddle** (Santa Monica College/Calif.) at one wing, 6-6 sophomore **Lamont Bonner** (2.0 ppg, 2.0 rpg, .531 FG percentage) at the other. Bonner never got a chance to show he could shoot from long range, playing behind Culbertson and Morgan. He'll look to stay close to the basket, slash and rebound. However, he'll have to make open shots.

"Bonner's best asset is rebounding for his size, and he was one of the best rebounders on our team last year," said Foster, even though Bonner had only 27 rebounds in 165 minutes on the court. "He could have the best rebound numbers this year. He won't take too many shots, but he could be like Bo Outlaw and be a real good athlete. He's not tall, but he could be a better shooter. He gets the ball

1998-99 NEVADA SCHEDULE

Nov.	14	@San Diego State
	23	Wyoming
Dec.	2	UNLV
	5	@Baylor
	9	San Diego State
	15	Saint Mary's
	17	Stanford
	21	Seattle
	30	@Texas Tech
Jan.	2	@Colorado State
	7	@Long Beach State
	9	@Pacific
	14	California-Santa Barbara
	16	Cal Poly
	21	@Idaho
	23	@Boise State
	28	New Mexico State
	30	North Texas
Feb.	4	@California-Irvine
	6	Utah State
	11	Fullerton State
	13	@Utah State
	18	Boise State
	20	Idaho
	25	@North Texas
	27	@New Mexico State
Mar.	5-7	#Big West Tournament

@ Road Games
# Reno, NV

in the basket and at 6-6 can be an all-purpose type of player."

Foster's high on Bonner's passing, too. He'll need to look for Criddle, who can create his own shot. Carroll made 74 three-pointers last season. Someone will have to knock down threes and Criddle is supposedly a shooter.

"He can score and he plays hard," Foster said of the Oakland native whose father played at Bradley. "He's the other guy (aside from Bonner) who can be a power player for us."

If Criddle can't consistently shoot, 6-3 junior guard **John Burrell** (Antelope Valley College/Calif.) could be the sleeper off the bench to ultimately replace Carroll.

"That's what our guys recruited him for and he comes with that reputation and we're sure he can do that," Foster said. "He's always been a scorer."

Bonner is way ahead of another big guard/forward, junior 6-8 **Chris Bacon** (Porterville College/Calif.). In fact, Bacon may have trouble cracking the top seven or eight. So, too, may 6-3 junior guard **Tommy Zapata** (2.4 ppg, 1.2 rpg), who will have trouble getting time behind Anderson.

Zapata will likely be passed over by freshmen guards, 6-2 **Damon Caldwell** (Basic HS/Henderson, Nev.) and 6-2 **Dan Galvanoni** (Capo Valley HS/Mission Viejo, Calif.).

The uncertainties continue up front where Foster is hoping for a healthy return to the court from 6-7 senior **Andre McLeod**, who received a medical redshirt last season but averaged only a point and less than a rebound two years ago.

McLeod is a physical player but his offense is obviously limited. It won't be plentiful from either center 6-9 freshman forward **Joao Santos** (Club Portugal Telecom/Lisbon, Portugal) and 6-9 sophomore center **Demetrios Marmarinos** (Athens, Greece). Marmarinos was a late summer addition and put Foster at ease by providing him another body up front. Both are strong and can board, but neither has the offensive skills to intimidate anyone in the Big West.

"We had to get those up-front kids," Foster said. "We're still encouraged. The key is getting the point. We had the big point guard when I was at Houston and that can be a great asset. He gives us a lot at that position."

adidas Blue Ribbon Analysis

BACKCOURT .... **C** **BENCH/DEPTH** .... **D**
FRONTCOURT .... **D** **INTANGIBLES** .... **C**

Nevada lost 97.9 percent of its scoring, 91.7 percent of its rebounding, 95.3 percent of its assists and 90.1 percent of its steals from a year ago. Replacing that kind of production will be left up to newcomers whom no one seems to know.

Foster has been able to take the Wolf Pack deep into the Big West Tournament, but has fallen short of an NCAA bid a few times. He won't get that close this season. In fact, he may not even get to the tournament. The Wolf Pack will go as far as Anderson can take it, but comparing him to Saxon or Curry isn't fair at this juncture of his career.

The schedule may hurt Nevada in its bid to claim the fourth and final spot tournament spot in the East. The Wolf Pack finish at North Texas and New Mexico State, two teams that should be vying for the final berth in the tournament.

(A.K.)

NEW MEXICO STATE

LOCATION .... **Las Cruces, NM**
CONFERENCE .... **Big West (Eastern Division)**
LAST SEASON .... **18-12 (.600)**
CONFERENCE RECORD .... **8-8 (5th)**
STARTERS LOST/RETURNING **3/2**
NICKNAME .... **Aggies**
COLORS .... **Crimson & White**
HOMECOURT .... **Pan American Center (13,071)**
COACH .... **Lou Henson (New Mexico State '55)**
RECORD AT SCHOOL .... **191-83 (10 yrs.)**
CAREER RECORD .... **681-343 (35 yrs.)**
ASSISTANTS .... **Russ Bradburd (North Park '80)**
Thomas Trotter (Wisconsin-Parkside '84)
TEAM WINS (last 5 yrs.) **23-25-11-19-18**
RPI (last 5 yrs.) **75-43-207-78-150**
1997-98 FINISH .... **Didn't qualify for conference tournament.**

Lou Henson was entrusted to resurrect his alma mater after a turbulent end to Neil McCarthy's reign.

He didn't seem to have much chance of doing that right away, with seven scholarships to fill and an NCAA penalty forbidding New Mexico State from recruiting junior college players. But his luck changed after pulling off a unique recruiting coup. Henson signed the entire starting five from a disbanding Division I program.

Raiding Northeastern Illinois may have been the only way to avoid a complete overhaul. Last October the school announced it was dropping basketball, which meant every player was free to transfer to another school and not have to sit out a year. Henson snapped up five NIU players, four of whom could help immediately.

In a league where all it takes is one or two impact players to rise from the cellar, the Aggies may have found a way to beat the NCAA sanctions.

"It was the last year of our probation and we couldn't recruit JC kids when I got here," says Henson, who signed a four-year contract extension last year. "It has worked out."

The first move was to hire Northeastern Illinois assistant Thomas Trotter. Signing the players was the natural progression in the process. Henson knew Trotter from his tenure at Illinois when Henson was recruiting the state. "We first started with a few of the guys and then it went on from there," Henson says.

The additions allow the Aggies to play with the full complement of 13 scholarship players for the first time in three years. The NCAA penalties, which ended on Aug. 1, were put in place because of the Aggies' role in an academic fraud case involving the Southeastern Bible College in Florida, where students were registered for correspondence classes but failed to do the work. The Aggies weren't allowed to play in the postseason for one season and prevented from recruiting junior college athletes.

McCarthy had gotten around it by signing two junior college transfers, of which one was last year's leading scorer Louis Richardson, before the penalty began. He also picked up a transfer in Washington State point guard Donminic Ellison. However, McCarthy only coached Richardson for one season and didn't see Ellison play after being forced out before the season began by new athletic director Jim Paul.

Henson was a natural replacement, considering he was retired but still had a home in Las Cruces. This is his second tour of duty at the school—he took the Aggies to their lone Final Four appearance in 1970.

Henson took over a team accustomed to a matchup zone and put in his disciplined man-to-man defense, leading the Aggies to an 18-12 record, which included wins over Virginia, Ohio State and Big West champion Utah State. It wasn't enough to earn an NIT bid, mainly because the Aggies slumped later in the year and couldn't get into the Big West tournament.

They should be able to earn a bid this season as the fourth team in the East Division and have the potential to climb as high as second. But the Northeastern Illinois transfers must be impact players, able to make the leap from the Mid-Continent to the Big West.

William Keys, a 6-2 junior from Northeastern Illinois, will be the starting point. Keys (12.7 ppg, 3.5 rpg, 5.6 apg in 1996-97) is a scoring point guard who should grab the leadership role on the first day of practice.

"We needed someone to rely on," Henson says.

The Aggies should be able to rely on Keys. He set a school record with 158 assists two years ago. He didn't play last season once the school announced it was dropping basketball, because he wanted to protect his eligibility.

Keys will have to play 30-plus minutes—the only other true ball handler is 5-10 freshman **Ben Karam** (Eastwood HS/El Paso, Texas/17.0 ppg, 7.0 apg), who is basically a defensive replacement more than a scorer.

Brad Bestor, a 6-2 junior transfer from Northeastern Illinois, and 6-4 freshman **Eric Channing** (Warrenville South HS/Wheaton, Ill.) will replace Denmark Reid at shooting guard, alternating time. Bestor (12.4 ppg, 3.5 rpg, 66 three-pointers) is a pure shooter who impressed the coaching staff with his touch during their preseason individual drills in the fall. Bestor, who is left-handed, was the 14th-leading scorer in the Mid-Continent and shot 46 percent from three-point range. His best game was a 27-point effort against Mid-Continent champion Valparaiso.

Henson is high on Channing, whom he considers the find of this recruiting class. He was the winnner of Illinois' state three-point shooting contest and finished averaging 19.5 points and 6.5 rebounds as a senior.

"The Big Ten missed out on him," says Henson, who spent 21 years at a Big Ten institution at Illinois. "He could end up starting for us."

Henson has options at small forward. One candidate is 6-6 sophomore and Northeastern Illinois transfer **Daveeno Hines** (12.1 ppg, 8.5 rpg in 1996-97), who like Keys didn't play last season once he knew the program was shutting down. Another NIU transfer, 6-6 junior **Gerard Moore** (12.0 ppg, 4.0 rpg, 1 bpg in 1996-97), will compete with Hines. Moore didn't play last season because of a knee injury.

Another freshman, 6-4 **Damond Williams** (Hyde Park HS/Chicago, Ill./19 ppg, 7.0 rpg), is also in the small-forward mix..

Hines is a rebounder with quick reflexes, an active mindset on the boards and some three-point range. He's a typical, wiry three-man for the Aggies who would have fit in perfectly in McCarthy's system. Moore is a scorer around the basket and will be called upon more when the Aggies look to go stronger in the post. Williams is a scorer who can create shots off the dribble and penetrate.

The only returning experience is up front, where 6-8 senior **Charles Gosa** (12.5 ppg, 8.1 rpg, 1.7 apg, .548 FG percentage) could be an all-Big West first-team member. Gosa was forced to start during the Aggies' first year on probation when they struggled to win only 11 games. He has developed his offensive skills where he can score in the post and hit the mid-range jumper.

1998-99 NEW MEXICO STATE SCHEDULE

Nov.	13	@UTEP
	20-22	#Top of the World Tournament
	25	@Texas Tech
	28	UTEP
Dec.	1	Western New Mexico
	15	Texas Southern
	19	@Washington
	22	@San Diego State
	29	Alaska
Jan.	2	@New Mexico
	7	@Fullerton State
	9	@California-Irvine
	14	Long Beach State
	16	Pacific
	19	New Mexico
	21	North Texas
	23	California-Santa Barbara
	28	@Nevada
	30	@Utah State
Feb.	4	Idaho
	6	Boise State
	11	@Idaho
	13	@Boise State
	18	@Cal Poly
	20	@North Texas
	25	Utah State
	27	Nevada
Mar.	5-7	##Big West Tournament

@ Road Games
# Fairbanks, AK (vs. Wisconsin, first round; also Alaska-Fairbanks, Arkansas, Nebraska, Villanova, Virginia and Washington State)
Lawlor Events Center, Reno, NV

Gosa became the Aggies' top rebounder and their third option. He'll move up to No. 1, but will need Keys' help. His best game was a 29-point effort against North Texas.

Aaron Brodt, a 6-9, 240-pound junior, will be the Aggies' version of a space eater, hoping to give them some strength in the post. He has developed into a decent defender but is still limited offensively (5.1 ppg, 5.5 rpg, .504 FG percentage).

The three unknowns in terms of production are: 6-7 senior **Rhonte' Davis** (3.3 ppg, 2.9 rpg, .518 FG percenntage), who is an athletic power forward and defender but still struggles with his role on the court; 6-7 sophomore **Mikko Noopila** (3.5 ppg, 1.9 rpg, .422 three-point percentage), a native of Finland who is a typical foreign forward with more three-point shooting skills than rebounding abilities; and 6-10 freshman **Simon Bredenberg** (Capital HS/Santa Fe, N.M.), who is still a year or two away from having any kind of impact.

The fifth NIU transfer, 6-3 sophomore **Zachary Norvell** (11.4 ppg, 3.5 rpg, 1.7 apg last year) isn't eligible yet and Henson will make a decision in mid-December whether to redshirt him or have him play the final 22 games.

adidas Blue Ribbon Analysis

BACKCOURT .... **C** **BENCH/DEPTH** .... **C-**
FRONTCOURT .... **C** **INTANGIBLES** .... **C**

=

The Aggies have reason to be excited about picking up the NIU transfers. It helped solve a recruiting nightmare. But how good are they? No one quite knows if Keys, Hines, Bestor and Moore can be impact players in the Big West. The Mid-Continent must be a competitive league, though—Valparaiso proved that in the NCAA Tournament. But it's still too early to tell how productive this foursome will be when mixing in with Brodt, Gosa and Noopila.

The newcomers may not change the Aggies' woeful road record. They won only two games out of Las Cruces and the schedule got tougher with the Aggies' picking up the Top of the World Tournament in Fairbanks, Alaska, Texas Tech, San Diego State, Washington and New Mexico, once Kenny Thomas is reinstated.

"The day of New Mexico State winning 20 games all the time is over," said Henson, taking a shot at McCarthy's previously soft scheduling. "This is a very tough schedule. I don't know how many teams, even those in the top 10, that can go on the road and win some of these games."

The Big West schedule won't ease the pain, either. The Aggies have to sweep Idaho, Boise State and Utah State at home to have a chance to finish higher in the league race. Pulling off an upset on the road against one of the top three is a must, too. It doesn't help that the Aggies drew West favorite Cal Poly on the road. Henson has found a way to salvage the program, but it won't be enough to earn a postseason berth.

(A.K.)

NORTH TEXAS

LOCATION .... **Denton, TX**
CONFERENCE .... **Big West (East Division)**
LAST SEASON .... **5-21 (.192)**
CONFERENCE RECORD .... **4-12 (6th)**
STARTERS LOST/RETURNING **4/1**
NICKNAME .... **Eagles**
COLORS .... **Green & White**
HOMECOURT .... **The Super Pit (10,032)**
COACH .... **Vic Trilli (Midwestern State '76)**
RECORD AT SCHOOL .... **5-21 (1 yr.)**
CAREER RECORD .... **5-21 (1 yr.)**
ASSISTANTS .... **Melvin Haralson (Auburn '89)**
Nate Sheahan (Westmont College '92)
Chris Beard (Texas '94)
TEAM WINS (last 5 yrs.) **14-14-15-10-5**
RPI (last 5 yrs.) **197-216-190-226-233**
1997-98 FINISH .... **Failed to qualify for conference tournament.**

North Texas is the mystery team in the Big West and to itself. No one knows what to expect from this group.

The Eagles return only one player, three if you include a redshirt and a walkon. The schedule is once again loaded with high-major teams. But on paper, the Eagles have recruited well, added the necessary quickness and shooting to make their high-octane offense run. But once again, they lack size and in the end will likely find themselves at the bottom of the Big West wondering what can they do next to try and overhaul the program.

Vic Trilli arrived a year ago with the intent of making North Texas basketball a happening. He promised a lot of points and scheduled matchups the alumni could be proud of, even if they were road games. What he couldn't deliver was wins.

North Texas averaged 79.4 points a game, good for third in the Big West, but gave up 87.8 points a game. The Eagles were near or at the bottom in almost every other defensive statistic.

"We made tremendous progress last year," Trilli said. "Our recruiting class tells you about what we were able to accomplish. Do we have great players? No. Do we have better players than we did before? Yes. I think people are looking and watching and waiting for something to happen. They know that there's something going on up there, but I don't know if they believe it yet."

Trilli believes he can make inroads in Texas recruiting, the way he did for eight seasons as an assistant for Tom Penders at the University of Texas. Nine of his newcomers come from Texas.

"Nobody recruited Texas in the late '70s and early '80s and now it's one of the best places to recruit," Trilli said. "We want to keep as many of those kids in the state. I was very pleased with what we were able to do this year. For us to go into Dallas Kimball (High School) and get a couple of kids is huge. You've got TCU, SMU and us in the area and we should be competitive in our own backyard."

Charles Washington is the one exception, but he was already at North Texas. Washington, a 6-4 senior, played junior college basketball in Texas at Navarro College, but is from Jackson, Miss. It wouldn't matter where he played, Washington has been adopted as a native son.

Washington (10.5 ppg, 8.7 rpg, .40.7 three-point percentage, .744 FT percentage, 56 steals) is an undersized small forward who can flourish in a league filled with tweeners trying to control the backboards. He finished second in the Big West in rebounding and ended the year with four straight double-doubles. His best game came in a loss to Texas when he scored13 points and grabbed 17 rebounds.

Washington needs help inside and he'll get it from 6-8 junior forward **Sam Funches** (Connecticut/Murrah HS/Jackson, Miss.) but not until mid-December when he's eligible. Funches never fit in at Connecticut. He should fit in fine at North Texas, where he'll feel more wanted.

Until Funches is eligible, 7-foot sophomore center **Graeme Anstey** will probably start at center. Anstey (San Jose State/Melbourne, Australia) sat out last year and worked out with the Eagles. However, Anstey is still a project and doesn't seem to fit the Eagles' uptempo style. He doesn't stand straight enough to truly utilize his size. He may be the brother of Dallas Mavericks first-round pick Chris Anstey but he's got a way to go before he can be a Division I contributor.

The likely starter in place of Funches at power forward is 6-8 junior **Brandon Gilbert** (Kilgore JC/Texas). Gilbert, who averaged 10.3 points and 8.0 rebounds last season, signed at TCU last spring, but got out of his national letter of intent. He ended up at North Texas and will see more time than he would have in Fort Worth.

The rest of the frontcourt depth is young, athletic but obviously untested. **Chris Davis**, a 6-6 freshman, has the best credentials. He averaged 23.8 points and 15 rebounds at Dallas' Kimball High School and was a third-team Class 5A all-state pick and first-team all-area by the *Dallas Morning News*. He averaged 22.8 points at Nimitz High School in Irving before transferring to Kimball.

Deginald Erskin, a 6-6 freshman from Gonzales High School in Texas, was a second-team Class 4A all-state pick after averaging 23.4 points and 16 rebounds as a senior. Like Davis, he's undersized but can rebound, and could play more power forward in the Big West. The feeling at North Texas is that Erskin may be more polished than Davis and better-suited to start earlier in his career.

Chris Kepley, a 6-8 redshirt freshman, got a medical redshirt at Tulsa and sat out a year before transferring to North Texas. He could factor in there, as well. So, too, should 6-6 freshman **Dexter Tennell** (Nimitz HS/Irving, Texas), who could play either big guard or small forward. Tennell was a first-team Class 5A all-state pick after averaging 30.5 points, 10.3 rebounds, 2.3 assists and 2.3 steals. He's a scorer and should fit into the rotation off the bench, but more as a shooting guard than a forward. Tennell could find himself at shooting guard if he can knock down threes.

The point is probably going to be shared by 6-4 junior **Dominic Hardie** (Frank Phillips College/Texas/Lincoln HS/Port Arthur, Texas) and 6-foot sophomore **Calvin Williams** (Midland College/Texas/Kimball HS/Dallas, Texas). Hardie was plagued by injuries last season and averaged only 6.3 points and 2.3 rebounds and 2.4 assists. He did shoot 47 percent overall, 67 percent from the line and 50 percent on threes.

Williams played one year of junior college ball and averaged a mere 3.6 points, 2.6 assists and 2.2 steals. He played in 30 games and had just 36 turnovers, getting more assists than turnovers in 26 of the team's 30 games.

Trilli has depth with 6-4 freshman **Kenneth Mangrum** (University HS/Waco, Texas), a Class 4A third-team all-state pick after averaging 21.2 points and 4.8 rebounds; 6-4 freshman **Wes Allen** (Amarillo HS/Texas), who averaged 14.1 points and 3.4 rebounds last year; and 6-1 senior walkon **Joe Ervin** (McLennan CC/Texas/University HS/Waco, Texas).

"It takes a highly conditioned athlete to play this style of basketball and it gives a lot of people a chance to play," Trilli said. "I don't think teams can play at that level for 40 minutes. All of these kids have been successful and are more athletic. The only negative is youth and it doesn't frighten me, it excites me. Young people have a lot of energy and all of these kids have a scorer's mentality."

1998-99 NORTH TEXAS SCHEDULE

Nov.	13	@Texas A&M
	21	Texas Tech
Dec.	1	@Texas Christian
	4-5	#Cyclone Challenge
	8	@Tulsa
	12	Wyoming
	19	@Louisiana Tech
	23	@Maryland
	30	@Arkansas
Jan.	7	@California-Irvine
	9	@Fullerton State
	14	Pacific
	16	Long Beach State
	21	@New Mexico State
	23	Cal Poly
	28	@Utah State
	30	@Nevada
Feb.	4	Boise State
	6	Idaho
	11	@Boise State
	13	@Idaho
	18	@California-Santa Barbara
	20	New Mexico State
	25	Nevada
	27	Utah State
Mar.	5-7	##Big West Tournament

@ Road Games
\# Ames, IA (first round vs. Iowa State; also Princeton and Western Illinois)
\## Reno, NV

adidas Blue Ribbon Analysis

BACKCOURT .... **D** **BENCH/DEPTH** .... **D**
FRONTCOURT .... **D** **INTANGIBLES** .... **D**

North Texas is in for another rebuilding year and will struggle to make the Big West Tournament. The Eagles will score in bunches again, but will have a hard time stopping anyone. They've got players who can play at this level, but can they play together? And the size will catch up to them when they play Utah State, Idaho, Boise State and New Mexico State.

Trilli is still convinced that the Eagles played defense well enough to win games, but the offense stalled last season. However, the statistics support the opposite, at least in the Big West. The Eagles will have plenty of players to hawk the ball on the perimeter, but no one's quite sure who can be a consistent three-point threat or even a reliable penetrator into the paint.

"Talent-wise and size-wise we will be a lot better than last year," Trilli said. "The exciting thing is that most of the kids will be around for four years. How fast will they mature? How game-ready will they be? There's a group out there called Boyz 2 Men. How fast can we go from boys to men?"

Not fast enough to win more than five games.

(A.K.)

PACIFIC

LOCATION .... **Stockton, CA**
CONFERENCE .... **Big West (Western Division)**
LAST SEASON .... **23-10 (.697)**
CONFERENCE RECORD .... **14-2 (1st)**
STARTERS LOST/RETURNING **4/1**
NICKNAME .... **Tigers**
COLORS .... **Orange & Black**
HOMECOURT .... **Alex J. Spanos Center (6,150)**
COACH .... **Bob Thomason (Pacific '71**
RECORD AT SCHOOL .... **160-131 (11 yrs.)**
CAREER RECORD .... **287-207 (18 yrs.)**
ASSISTANTS Tony Marcopulos (Stanislaus State '87)
Ron Verlin (Sacramento State '90)
Alan Major (Purdue '92)
TEAM WINS (last 5 yrs.) **17-14-15-24-23**
RPI (last 5 yrs.) **178-145-167-79-82**
1997-98 FINISH .... **Lost in NIT first round.**

Few would have noticed Bob Thomason's face coming into the picture. TNT's cameras were focused on Michael Olowokandi as the No. 1 pick in the NBA draft. After the big center hugged a few family members, Thomason was next. And why not? Olowokandi was about to become a multi-millionaire because of Thomason. And the coach could forever claim that he had coached a No. 1 pick. Olowokandi helped put Pacific on the map and Thomason was the prime beneficiary.

But here comes the real test of Olowokandi's worth. He led the Tigers to the NCAA Tournament two years ago, the Big West's Western Division title and an NIT berth a year ago. He's gone and Thomason has to prove that he was able to use his name in recruiting after having to completely rebuild the roster.

"Once you have a good program, you have to readjust," said Thomason. "We're looking forward to this year. We're fired up. We'll make the adjustments and move on. We're still the champs until someone beats us."

Olowokandi—the most dominant low-post player in the league—wasn't the only player to leave the program.

Adam Jacobsen was the spirit of the team, leading the Tigers from the perimeter and giving the team a pulse on the court. While Olowokandi was the scorer, Jacobsen was the type of player who would dive on the floor, rally the team from behind with a few screams and knock down a critical three-pointer to spark a rally.

Aaron Woliczko and Rayne Mahaffey were two of the most underrated forwards in the league. Both had three-point range despite playing in the lane. Their ability to hit the mid-range and long-range jumpers extended the defense off of Olowokandi.

Thomason is banking on a new cast of characters to create a similar level of success. **Jason Williams** (8.7 ppg, 5.1 rpg, 1.3 apg), a 6-7 senior forward, will have to become the new Olowokandi. He's not even close. Still, Williams can be a low-post scorer that can at least get Thomason points in the teens. Williams had his moments last season but they were usually as a result of teams doubling down on Olowokandi. His production sagged once he missed four games during the Big West season after he was injured. Williams lost his starting spot to Mahaffey and never recovered. He'll have to be the focus from the outset of the season in November.

"He has to keep working on his shot and his ballhandling," said Thomason, who uses his forwards from 15-feet out in his flex system. "He needs to gain some maturity. He could become the best forward I've ever coached. He has the capability to score 20 points and grab 10 rebounds every game."

If Williams is to produce those kind of numbers, the Tigers will need an impact year from either 6-10 redshirt freshman **Ross Mills** (North Salem HS/Salem, Ore.) or 6-9 freshman **Mike Preston** (Omaha Westside HS/Omaha, Neb.). One of the two will likely start next to Williams, but both have to be factors to save the Tigers from slipping too far in the standings.

Mills is the better offensive player, but Preston is the better defender and rebounder. Mills had the benefit of going against Olowokandi every day in practice last season and has been yearning to get his own shot at leading the team in the middle. Preston is more versatile and can play either center or power forward. Preston was a second-team all-state player in Nebraska and was able to score 21.3 points and snare 10.2 rebounds in Class A basketball.

Tim Johnson, a 6-10 freshman from Glencoe HS in Hillsboro, was a second-team all state selection in Oregon. Thomason has no clue which one of the three centers will establish himself as the main man, but all three will have to contribute for the Tigers to have a chance.

Barry Marvel (2.9 ppg, 3.0 rpg, 1.7 apg), a 6-7 junior forward, doesn't have the same kind of perimeter prowess that Woliczko and Mahaffey possessed.

Thomason's early line on the frontcourt has Williams alongside or being backed up by Marvel with Mills probably at center. He's convinced that Mills can be the best shooting big man the program has had since he arrived. If he's better than Woliczko and Mahaffey, then Thomason's already ahead with this team. What Thomason loses inside with this group is toughness and aggressive rebounding. Olowokandi intimidated teams going into the lane. That won't be the case with Mills, Williams or any of the other newcomers.

The sleepers in this frontcourt could be 6-7 freshmen twins **Andy** and **Matt Abernethy** (Carmel HS/Ind.), 6-7 freshman **Mike Hahn** (Lincoln Northeast HS/Lincoln, Neb.) and 6-7 freshman **Dan Masters** (Plattsmouth HS/Neb.).

The Abernethys were both all-state players in Indiana, Andy averaging 17.9 points and seven rebounds and Matt 16.5 points and 9.0 rebounds. Hahn was the player of the year in Nebraska and averaged 20.3 points and 11.3 rebounds. His scoring total included a 54-point game. Masters was a fellow all-state selection in Nebraska. Don't be fooled by the height—all of these players are adept on the perimeter.

Earl Clark (3.1 ppg, 1.6 rpg, 2.6 apg), a 6-1 junior point guard, 6-1 junior **Clay McKnight** (3.6 ppg, 1.0 rpg, 1.1 apg) and 5-8 senior guard **Scott Thomason** (2.6 ppg, 0.8 rpg, 1.3 apg) all return to the backcourt, but none will strike fear in the hearts of most of their Big West counterparts, especially with the likes of Long Beach State's Ramel Lloyd and Charles O'Neal entering the conference.

Thomason will need immediate help from 6-2 redshirt freshman **Nathan Davis** (San Ramon Valley HS/Danville, Calif.), who will share shooting guard with McKnight. Clark and Thomason will likely split time at the point. With the four taking control of two spots, that doesn't leave much for 6-6 redshirt freshman **Eli Kiedrowski** (Lodi HS/Calif.) or 6-6 sophomore **Bill Walton** (0.7 ppg, 0.5 rpg).

"We've got to establish somebody," Thomason said. "Jason can shoot the three and score inside and hopefully he can drive the ball to the basket better. He's the guy who will be most active and do things for us. Michael [Olowokandi] was a stud inside but Jason can score in some different ways. He can be our big four-man and we can be quicker and run some things off of him. I think Mike Hahn will help us. We've got to make some adjustments, but I think this team will be tougher and more interesting."

adidas Blue Ribbon Analysis

BACKCOURT .... **D** **BENCH/DEPTH** .... **C-**
FRONTCOURT .... **C+** **INTANGIBLES** .... **C+**

Thomason sounds like everything will be fine. It won't. Williams looks like the type of player who could develop into an all-Big West first team member, but he's not talented enough to carry this team to the postseason, let alone the Western Division title. The backcourt lacks leadership, a proven scorer and doesn't look like it will be able to handle pressure. The rest of the frontcourt, outside of Williams, is all new and untested.

Pacific has had success maximizing the talent of the unknowns, and that's why it's so difficult to predict this Tiger team. But one thing is certain, they will fall from their perch of the past two seasons. The title no longer goes through Stockton.

Let the post-Olowokandi era begin, but don't expect it be anything like his reign. The Tigers will return to relying on their disciplined offense and position defense to carry them rather than the talent of certain individuals.

(A.K.)

1998-99 PACIFIC SCHEDULE

Nov.	14	Santa Clara
	20	Chico State
	24	San Jose State
	28	@Sacramento State
Dec.	7	@Fresno State
	12	@Loyola Maramount
	19	Stanford
	21	@Portland State
	30	Lewis & Clark
Jan.	7	Utah State
	9	Nevada
	14	@North Texas
	16	@New Mexico State
	21	@California-Irvine
	23	@Fullerton State
	28	Idaho
	30	Long Beach State
Feb.	4	Cal Poly
	6	California-Santa Barbara
	11	@Cal Poly
	13	@California-Santa Barbara
	18	Fullerton State
	20	California-Irvine
	25	@Boise State
	27	@Long Beach State
Mar.	5-7	#Big West Tournament

@ Road Games
\# Reno, NV

UTAH STATE

LOCATION .... **Logan, UT**
CONFERENCE .... **Big West (Eastern Division)**
LAST SEASON .... **25-8 (.758)**
CONFERENCE RECORD .... **13-3 (1st)**
STARTERS LOST/RETURNING **3/2**
NICKNAME .... **Aggies**
COLORS .... **Navy Blue & White**
HOMECOURT .... **Smith Spectrum (10,270)**
COACH .... **Stew Morrill (Gonzaga '74)**
RECORD AT SCHOOL .... **First Year**
CAREER RECORD .... **218-138 (11 yrs.)**
ASSISTANTS .... **Tony Fuller (Pepperdine '83)**
Randy Rahe (Buena Vista '82)
Don Verlin (Stanislaus State '89)
TEAM WINS (last 5 yrs.) **14-21-18-20-25**
RPI (last 5 yrs.) **174-72-164-96-51**
1997-98 FINISH .... **Lost in NCAA first round.**

Larry Eustachy had done all he could at Utah State. Stew Morrill had done the same at Colorado State.

It was time to move.

Eustachy took a step up to Iowa State. Morrill took a side step to Utah State. It couldn't have worked out any better for all parties.

Iowa State gets another Tim Floyd clone. Utah State gets a coach who wants to be in Logan.

"It just made sense," Morrill says. "In the coaching business, sometimes you need to recharge yourself at a new place. Don't get me wrong, CSU was great to me and my family for seven years."

However, Morrill reached a stagnant point. The Rams had never been to the NCAA Tournament under his watch and he was constantly being reminded of the two years Boyd Grant took his team to the NCAAs. Winning 20 games wasn't enough in Fort Collins, especially when it didn't get them an NIT berth. They went twice in Morrill's seven years. It didn't help him that the athletic director (Tom Jurich) who had hired him at Colorado State and given him two extensions left for Louisville in the spring. Morrill got along with the new athletic director (Tim Weiser) but it was clear he wasn't banking on getting another extension.

Utah State had just hired a new athletic director and the slate was clean for Morrill. Signing a five-year contract would give him a new lease on his career and if he got an extension, he could coach well into his 50s. The money was similar and maybe even more because of a richer camp deal.

The final reason for making the move rested with his family. Morrill didn't take the Brigham Young job a year ago because his son was a senior in high school. The timing wasn't right. It was for Utah State, where he can challenge BYU and Utah for in-state talent, especially members of the Mormon Church, considering that he's a member himself.

"The facilities are the top in the Big West and the budget is too," Morrill says. "It's a very attractive job. I'm very comfortable here. I'm really starting over."

He'll have to with this team.

Eustachy took the Aggies to the NCAA Tournament on the strength of a backcourt of Marcus Saxon, Justin Jones and Kevin Rice.

"It was 90 percent of the scoring and 70 percent of the minutes," Eustachy said before he left Utah State. "I knew we would be good last year. (Utah State) will have no

1998-99 UTAH STATE SCHEDULE

Nov.	9	Simon Fraser
	20	Colorado-Colorado Springs
	24	@San Diego State
	28	Whitworth
Dec.	5	Colorado State
	10	@Fresno State
	19	*Weber State
	23	Utah
	29-30	#Gossner Classic
Jan.	2	@Brigham Young
	7	@Pacific
	9	@Long Beach State
	14	Cal Poly
	16	California-Santa Barbara
	21	@Boise State
	23	@Idaho
	28	North Texas
	30	New Mexico State
Feb.	4	@Fullerton State
	6	@Nevada
	11	California-Irvine
	13	Nevada
	18	Idaho
	20	Boise State
	25	@New Mexico State
	27	@North Texas
Mar.	5-7	##Big West Tournament

@ Road Games
* Salt Lake City, UT
# Logan, UT (vs. Norfolk State, first round; also Troy State and Lafayette)
Reno, NV

experience in the backcourt and that makes for a challenging year. (The Aggies) will struggle early but could play the best at the end."

Eustachy was a master at stashing junior college and transfers away at Utah State, only to sneak them up on the rest of the league. Saxon and Rice were both all-stowaway. Morrill will likely take a different approach, looking for the more traditional way of recruiting through the high schools. However, he still has a few transfers who will make an impact on this year's roster.

Troy Rolle, a 6-3 junior guard from Chipola (Fla.) JC and Phillips HS/Orlando, Fla., could be one of those typical Utah State players. Eustachy said he was as athletic as Rice and could be a slashing, scoring player from the wing.

That would mesh quite well with the returning frontcourt of 6-6 senior **Donnie Johnson** (9.5 ppg, 7.5 rpg) and 6-5 senior **Pharoah Davis** (8.8 ppg, 6.4 rpg). Johnson was the hardest working rebounder in the Big West last season and was constantly overmatched inside. It was clear during the Maryland game in the first round of the NCAA Tournament that Johnson couldn't handle the taller, power players. It wasn't as much of an issue during the Big West.

Eustachy said he expected Johnson to be the team's leading scorer. He said he has better perimeter skills than have been shown. Morrill has a knack for getting more out of low-post players who have some finesse skills. He'll love Johnson's work ethic. Davis is in the same mold with his knack for being around the basketball. His activity will keep him on the court and his leadership is a blessing for Morrill, who will look for players to assert themselves during this transition.

Morrill would like to have a more true frontcourt and he could leave Davis and Johnson with 7-foot sophomore **Dmitri Jorssen** (Lassen JC/Calif./Belgium).

"If Dmitri were 6-foot tall, he would still play basketball," Eustachy said of him earlier this year. "There are a lot of seven footers who play basketball because they are seven feet. He likes to play regardless of size. His potential is unlimited. He has the right mental makeup and work ethic. We will have him for three years, but I don't want the expectations on him to be too high because everyone is excited when someone that big signs with you and they have big expectations, but he could be a force before he leaves."

Morrill will enjoy coaching someone like Jorssen for the same reasons he'll dive into dissecting Johnson's game.

The other factor in the frontcourt will be 6-7 sophomore **Brandon Birch** (4.1 ppg, 2.6 rpg), who was one of two substitutes for Johnson and Davis last year. Birch is a better defender than offensive talent and handled Pacific's Michael Olowokandi during a stint on the floor in the Big West Tournament. The other three forwards are 6-5 sophomore forward **Brad Wilden** (Utah Valley State/Alta HS/Sandy, Utah), 6-5 sophomore **Brennan Ray** (Mesa JC/Ariz./ Chandler, Ariz.), who just returned from a two-year Mormon Church mission and was looking for a school as late as mid-August, and 6-8 freshman **Spencer Nelson** (Pocatello HS/Idaho).

Nelson was the Idaho Player of the Year, averaging 22 points and 11 rebounds for Pocatello High. He's one of the better high school players the Aggies have signed recently, but will probably only play one season before going on a Mormon Church mission. Wilden is back from a mission and hasn't played in two years. His rust could slow his contribution.

Rolle will get a chance to start in the backcourt, as will 6-4 freshman **Tony Brown** (Mountain Crest HS/Hyrum, Utah). He was the 1998 Utah High School Player of the Year after averaging 26.3 points and 6.2 rebounds a game. He's a .438 percent three-point shooter and brings a toughness to either the wing or the point. However, with a few point guards back, Brown will likely play shooting guard.

Morrill has the choice of 5-9 redshirt junior **Rashad Elliott** (George Wallace JC/Ala./Davis HS/Montgomery, Ala.), who sat out last season while Saxon dominated the position; 6-3 senior **Rick Randall** (1.9 ppg, 0.7 rpg, five assists); or 6-1 senior **Tyrone Allick** (1.4 ppg, 0.6 rpg, 10 assists). The latter two didn't get many reps, either, with Saxon at the point.

"Tyrone and Rashad are still really good," Eustachy said of his former players. "They're waterbug-type guards. Rolle, Brown and Wilden make them strong at the one, two and three. Tyrone and Rashad will be out there but it will be tough to keep Tony Brown and Troy Rolle off the court."

The depth continues with 6-5 sophomore **Mark Thurston** (1.1 ppg, 0.6 rpg) and 5-9 redshirt freshman Dax Anderson. Eustachy also signed 6-foot junior **Melvin Farmer** (Rio Hondo JC/Calif./Lynwood HS/Los Angeles, Calif.). He averaged 22.1 points a game and 26.9 points a game as a sophomore while shooting 63 percent.

"He is obviously very talented," Rio Hondo coach Ernie Carr said. "He is small but he is still growing physically and mentally. He really stepped up for us this year."

adidas Blue Ribbon Analysis

BACKCOURT .... C **BENCH/DEPTH** C
FRONTCOURT .... B **INTANGIBLES** .... B

Utah State has hope because of Johnson, Davis, Jorssen and Morrill. He loves to coach big men and will have a field day with this trio. The guard play should be decent enough to hang with Idaho, Boise State and New Mexico State.

The Aggies have the talent to contend for the title, but that says just as much about the division. Morrill will bring more ball control to the offense, but the team won't be as aggressive defensively as it was under Eustachy.

Look for the Aggies to fall a game or two short of the title, but finish well enough to cause some fits in the Big West Tournament. A semifinal loss and no postseason is the likely scenario.

(A.K.)

COLONIAL ATHLETIC ASSOCIATION

adidas BLUE RIBBON FORECAST
1. Old Dominion
2. James Madison
3. North Carolina-Wilmington
4. George Mason
5. Richmond
6. William & Mary
7. Virginia Commonwealth
8. American
9. East Carolina

ALL-CONFERENCE TEAM
G—Randy Bracy, SR, William & Mary
G—Stan Simmons, SR, North Carolina-Wilmington
F—Mark Poag, SR, Old Dominion
F—Chatney Howard, SR, James Madison
C—George Evans, SO, George Mason

PLAYER OF THE YEAR
Randy Bracy, SR, William & Mary

NEWCOMER OF THE YEAR
Evaldas Jocys, JR, East Carolina

1998-99 CONFERENCE TOURNAMENT
Feb. 25-27, Richmond Coliseum, Richmond, VA

1997-98 CHAMPION
North Carolina-Wilmington, William & Mary (regular season)
Richmond (conference tournament)

1997-98 POSTSEASON PARTICIPANTS
Postseason Record: 1-2 (.333)
NCAA
Richmond (second round)
NIT
North Carolina-Wilmington (second round)

TOP BACKCOURTS
1. Old Dominion
2. William & Mary
3. North Carolina-Wilmington

TOP FRONTCOURTS
1. Old Dominion
2. George Mason
3. James Madison

ON THE WAY UP
George Mason

ON THE WAY DOWN
East Carolina

INSIDE THE NUMBERS
• 1997-98 conference RPI: 15 (of 30)
• Conference RPI (last 5 years): 20-21-17-12-15

DID YOU KNOW?
For the fourth time in 13 years, the Richmond Spiders advanced past the first round of the NCAA Tournament after handing Southeastern Conference power South Carolina its second straight first-round loss...With its 13-3 conference record and first-place tie with William & Mary last season, North Carolina-Wilmington extended its streak to five seasons of finishing no worse than third in the league, recording at least 10 league wins each year...William & Mary recorded just its fifth 20-win season in school history, the first since 1983, and its second winning season in 15 years...Old Dominion was 18th in the country in field-goal percentage defense (.396 percent)...Richmond coach John Beilein is the only coach in the country to record 20-win seasons at four different levels of coaching—junior college, NAIA, NCAA Division I and Division II...ODU senior swingman Mark Poag set an NCAA single-game record by hitting nine of nine shots from beyond the three-point line in an 84-69 victory over VMI.

(D.B.)

AMERICAN

LOCATION .... Washington, D.C.
CONFERENCE .. Colonial Athletic Association (CAA)
LAST SEASON .... 9-19 (.321)
CONFERENCE RECORD 5-11 (7th)
STARTERS LOST/RETURNING 1/4
NICKNAME .... Eagles
COLORS .... Red & Blue
HOMECOURT .... Bender Arena (5,000)
COACH .... Art Perry (Rutgers '75)
RECORD AT SCHOOL .... 9-19 (1 yr.)
CAREER RECORD .... 15-39 (2 yrs.)
ASSISTANTS ... Scott Spinelli (Boston University '89)
Kevin Broadus (Bowie State '90)
Tom Devitt (Boston College '93)
TEAM WINS (last 5 yrs.) 8-9-12-11-9
RPI (last 5 yrs.) 221-231-194-192
1997-98 FINISH .... Lost in conference semifinal.

Although it certainly didn't seem like it at the time, a great thing happened to the American Eagles on Feb. 28 of last season. They lost.

The significance isn't because they lost, but how they lost. The scenario: A young team with a first-year coach plays through a tumultuous regular season with more valleys than peaks, only to find itself a tip-in away from the league tournament championship game. Unfortunately for the Eagles, seeded No. 7 in the tournament, the aforementioned tip-in fell in the favor of Richmond, seeded third. The Spiders ultimately won the tournament championship and advanced to the second round of the NCAA Tournament after defeating third-seeded South Carolina in the first round.

For the Eagles, the loss was an exclamation point on a disappointing season. Lack of depth and inexperience were factors throughout the season as American finished just 1-8 in games decided by six points or less. The final shot decided seven of those games, including the loss to Richmond in the tournament semifinal.

"Last year, we were really searching for our identity," second-year coach Art Perry said. "We had our ups and downs and we played that way most of the season. During the CAA Tournament, we made significant strides understanding who we are and what it took to be successful. That made us believe in ourselves and allowed us to understand what it takes to be champions."

Perry is confident he has the recipe for success at American—he just needs time to gather the ingredients. Fortunately, his specialty is recruiting and he has six freshmen on this year's roster as proof. "Last year, I inherited the team and basically molded the players to my style and this year we recruited players to our style," Perry said. "It's certainly a more comfortable transition when you know you've recruited players for your particular style."

The return of four starters and eight lettermen gives Perry a mix of experienced veterans to go with his crop of new talent, but he isn't fearful of the Eagles ability to gel.

With veteran **Jarion Childs** (8.8 ppg, 4.9 rpg, 73 steals) returning at the point, Perry has the quarterback he needs to run the up-tempo style he wants to implement. Childs, a 6-0 junior, had a breakout sophomore season in which he led the league in steals and led the Eagles with 3.3 assists a game. Childs has the ability to score, but his quickness and athleticism earned him a CAA All-Defensive selection. His 73 steals were the fourth-highest total in school history and Perry's quick, full-court press style is a perfect fit.

He grabbed three or more steals in 15 games last season, including an eight-steal effort against James Madison on Feb 21. Missing from the backcourt is All-CAA selection Nathan Smith, the league's third-leading scorer (16.3) who averaged 3.25 three-pointers a game. For his career, Smith finished in AU's top 10 in six categories.

Taking over for Smith will likely be 6-5 junior **Ossie Jones** (6.3 ppg, 2.5 rpg), a starter in 12 games last season who turned in some brilliant performances in the CAA tournament. Against Richmond in the tournament semifinal, Jones broke out with 21 points and four threes. He also had a 16-point, seven-rebound performance against William & Mary and 17 points against VCU. He shot 39 percent from three-point range.

Adding backcourt experience off the bench will be 6-0 senior point guard **Jim Spadafore** (1.0 ppg, 0.1 rpg) and 5-9 junior shooting guard **David Olson** (1.8 ppg, 0.4 rpg). Spadafore is a true point guard who averaged 5.9 minutes a game and handed out 11 assists. Olson struggled from the field last season, shooting just .273 percent, but made 10 of 11 free throws after transferring from The Citadel.

The senior leadership Perry seeks will probably come from 6-6 swingmen **Dave Small** (10.1 ppg, 7.1 rpg) and **Matt Brown** (8.9 ppg, 5.2 rpg), a couple of versatile veterans who can make things happen. Small, a senior, stepped in at power forward much of last season and performed admirably, finishing seventh in the league in rebounding and fifth in free-throw percentage (77.1). Brown is a fifth-year senior at AU who sparked the Eagles to an upset of second-seeded William & Mary in a CAA Tournament quarterfinal with a 20-point performance that included four threes. Perry is counting on his versatile senior duo to shoulder the leadership load this year.

"They've played a lot together and experienced a lot of ups and downs and they have the knowledge and experience to lead us, particularly to lead a young group like we are going to have," Perry said.

Perry is excited by the evolution of the Eagles' post play in just one season. A big reason for that was the emergence of 6-8 sophomore center **Saliou-Binet Telly** (7.7 ppg, 5.2 rpg), a starter in 23 games as a freshman and a CAA All-Rookie selection. Telly showed the ability to excel in all facets of the game around the basket. He finished third in the league with 44 blocks, the second-best season total in school history. Seven of those blocks came in one game against James Madison. Now at 220 pounds, Telly has added size and strength in the offseason while playing in D.C.'s competitive Kenner League, where he displayed his shot-blocking ability. Telly had at least one blocked shot in the final 15 games last season.

He led the Eagles in field goal percentage (.478) and had four double-doubles.

Spelling Telly in the post is 6-9 junior **Henry Marquiss** (2.0 ppg, 2.4 rpg), who struggled from the field, shooting just .270 percent. Marquiss started three games and scored a career-high nine points in the season-opener against George Washington and grabbed eight rebounds against Old Dominion.

Evidence that Perry is on board for the long haul can be found in his first recruiting class of six freshmen. Focusing on the long term instead of the short, Perry did what he does best in the offseason, recruit versatile, athletic players around whom he can mold his teams of the future.

The gem of the bunch is 6-4 guard **Bobby Thompson**, one of the highest-rated recruits ever at AU. Rated the No. 34 high school prospect by recruiting analyst Bob Gibbons last fall, Thompson is an all-around offensive player from Victory Christian (N.C.) Prep. There, he led the state in scoring (27.2), the highest single-season average in Mecklenburg County history. He also averaged 8.4 rebounds in leading Victory Christian to its fourth straight Class A Independent Schools state championship.

Joining the backcourt mix along with Thompson are 6-3 **Hasheem Alexander** and 6-1 **Omar Vanderhorst**.

Alexander spent last year at Mercersburg (Pa.) Academy, where he averaged 18.0 points and 10.0 assists. As a senior at Thomas Johnson (Md.) HS, Alexander averaged 18.4 points, 8.0 assists and 6.0 rebounds.

Vanderhorst is a talented point guard who could see considerable playing time spelling Childs. A four-time all-region, three-time all-state and the 1997 Lowcountry Player of the Year at Middleton (S.C.) HS, Vanderhorst spent last year at Notre Dame (Mass.) Academy and averaged 18 points and eight assists.

Keith Gray is another highly rated recruit for Perry. A 6-8, 220-pound forward, Gray was rated in the top 100 recruits by Gibbons, was a McDonald's All-America honorable mention, was selected among *USA Today*'s top seniors in the South and two-time district MVP at Pine Tree (Texas) HS, where he averaged 15.1 points, 11.3 rebounds, five blocks and two steals as a senior. A gifted athlete, Gray was a second team all-district receiver in football and a regional qualifier in track with a high jump of 6-9.

Patrick Doctor is somewhat of a mystery because he didn't attract much attention until his senior season at Gwynn Park (Md.) HS. A 6-9, 230-pound bruiser, Doctor averaged 19.8 points, 13.4 rebounds and 2.0 blocks in leading his team to the Class AAA title. Along the way, he collected 19 double-doubles and shot 51 percent from the field.

Bryan Wynn is a 6-8, 220-pound forward who comes to the nation's capital by way of Fork Union (Va.) Academy, where he averaged 14.3 points last season. As a senior at Monroe (N.C.) HS, Wynn was a *Street & Smith's* All-America honorable mention and was nominated for the McDonald's All-America game after averaging 23.4 points, 13.0 rebounds, 4.0 assists and 3.5 blocks.

adidas Blue Ribbon Analysis

BACKCOURT .... C+ BENCH/DEPTH C
FRONTCOURT .... C INTANGIBLES .... C+

Art Perry has been involved with some big-time programs like Maryland, Rutgers, Old Dominion and Connecticut and he also spent a year at Delaware State. Now in his second year at American, Perry can best be described as a builder. A recruiting specialist, Perry faced a tough situation when he arrived in the nation's capital before last season. The Eagles averaged just 11 wins a season under previous coach Chris Knoche. Despite just nine wins in his initial season, Perry is determined to build for the long run. Standing by his word, Perry welcomes a talented six-pack of freshmen to campus this year, three of whom have a year of prep school under their belts.

However, the immediate concern this year is turning around the offensive woes that haunted the Eagles last season when they shot a miserable .401 percent from the field and scored just 61.6 points a game. With four starters and eight lettermen returning to go with the crop of new talent, Perry will have an opportunity to go nine- or ten-deep on his bench this season, compared with just six- or seven-deep last year. The Eagles will also be more athletic and continue to pressure the ball defensively.

"It may be a little more up-tempo than it was last year," Perry said. "Certainly, we will play a little more pressure defense than we did. If we do those two things, it will give us the opportunity to play more people and it will also give us a chance to exploit our athleticism. We have some experience in the starting lineup to give us a solid base. When you add the newcomers who have a lot of skill and athleticism to that, those veterans can relay some of their experience to the young players. Then we'll be the athletic and up-tempo team we want to be."

Perry is lining up the ingredients for success at American and he's building a foundation for the future. Unfortunately, the Eagles haven't experienced much success lately and that won't change immediately. Until those freshmen can get experience on the Division I level, the Eagles will be mistake-prone. They will, however, be athletic enough to surprise a team or two during the season, but an eighth-place finish seems about right.

(D.B.)

1998-99 AMERICAN SCHEDULE

Nov.	14	Delaware
	18	@Howard
	21	Catholic
	24	Western Maryland
	30	@Boston University
Dec.	2	George Washington
	5	@East Carolina
	7	@UNC-Wilmington
	9	Marist
	21	@USC
	23	@UCLA
	30	@Towson
Jan.	2	@Virginia Commonwealth
	9	Geoge Mason
	13	William & Mary
	16	@Old Dominion
	20	Richmond
	23	James Madison
	27	@William & Mary
Feb.	3	Virginia Commonwealth
	6	@Richmond
	8	@James Madison
	10	Old Dominion
	13	East Carolina
	15	UNC-Wilmington
	20	@George Mason
	25-28	#CAA Tournament

@ Road Games
# Ricmond Coliseum, Richmond, VA

EAST CAROLINA

LOCATION .... **Greenville, NC**
CONFERENCE .. **Colonial Athletic Association (CAA)**
LAST SEASON .... **10-17 (.370)**
CONFERENCE RECORD .... **5-11 (t-7th)**
STARTERS LOST/RETURNING **4/1**
NICKNAME .... **Pirates**
COLORS .... **Purple & Gold**
HOMECOURT .... **Minges Coliseum (7,500)**
COACH .... **Joe Dooley (George Washington '88)**
RECORD AT SCHOOL .... **44-38 (3 yrs.)**
CAREER RECORD .... **44-38 (3 yrs.)**
ASSISTANTS .... **Barry Sanderson (Alabama '90)**
Richard Morgan (Virgina '89)
Darren Savino (Jersey City State '93)
TEAM WINS (last 5 yrs.) **15-18-17-17-10**
RPI (last 5 yrs.) **149-171-171-97-217**
1997-98 FINISH .... **Lost in conference third round.**

Joe Dooley must be wondering what hit him. Expectations were high last season as Dooley entered his third year. Coming off consecutive 17-win seasons, the Pirates had a solid nucleus of veterans returning from the league's third-place team in 1996-97, the school's best conference finish.

Those expectations were never met. Losing streaks of five, four and three games during the season sank the Pirates' ship to its worst finish in six years and a frustrating seventh-place tie in the CAA. Injuries nagged the Pirates throughout the season and they played 13 of 26 regular season games with just eight players.

"It was a season that wasn't a lot of fun," Dooley said. "But I think we learned some things and now it's time to move on."

Fundamentally, the Pirates struggled throughout last season. That played no small part in the fact that they were unable to turn the corner in close games—they lost 12 times by 10 points or less. While he was certainly disappointed with last season's results, Dooley remains undeterred.

"We're going to get back to where we were two years ago," Dooley said. "We just have to get back to doing all the little things that enable us to compete and have a chance to win."

Four starters and eight lettermen are gone from last year, but Dooley is determined to build the program from scratch.

"Two years ago we made a conscientious effort to bring guys in here for four years and we've got our program now to the point where we can build the continuity that we want to be successful," Dooley said.

The lone senior and starter returning is 6-0 **Alico Dunk** (4.8 ppg, 2.2 rpg), a starter in 26 games who isn't exactly an offensive standout, shooting just .402 percent from the field, .302 percent from long range, and .596 percent from the free-throw line. Defense, however, is where Dunk excels. He led the team in steals (29) and assists (78).

The former Tennessee transfer also provides leadership, and Dooley is counting on Dunk to take charge this season. Ten of the 13 players on the roster are in their first or second year in the program.

"He has to just set the tone with getting guys to understand what it takes to win at this level," Dooley said.

Joining Dunk in the backcourt is 6-2 junior **Garrett Blackwelder** (7.6 ppg, 1.6 rpg), who turned it on as a sophomore. He shot .416 percent in making 37 three-pointers and averaged 10.8 points in the Pirates' final eight games. He also shot .804 percent from the free-throw line.

"Garrett had a great second half of last season and he had a great off-season," Dooley said. "He's in great shape and has worked very hard. We'll see how he'll evolve."

Larry Morrisey (0.5 ppg, 0.5 rpg) is a 6-2 sophomore who appeared in 11 games as a freshman.

Looking to step into the starting lineup is 6-5 swingman **Vinston Sharpe** (1.5 ppg, 1.6 rpg). As a freshman, Sharpe started three games and struggled from the floor, shooting just .300 percent from the field and .217 percent from three-point range.

Dooley can only hope the Pirates' frontcourt fortunes improve in 1998-99.

Last season, he lost a trio of key inside players to injury. **Neil Punt** (2.5 ppg, 1.4 rpg) and **Alphons van Ierland** (2.7 ppg, 2.4 rpg) missed much of the season with injuries, severely hampering Dooley's options. Punt is a 6-8 junior who appeared in nine games before breaking his right foot on Dec. 20 against UNC-Asheville. He didn't return until late February.

For his brief season, the 225-pound Punt shot 50 percent from the field and the free-throw line and managed four blocks. van Ierland, 7-0 and 230 pounds, suffered a fracture in his left hand in early December and sat out seven games. Despite appearing in 20 games, he never found his rhythm and will look for redemption this season.

Quincy Hall is a highly touted 7-footer from Northland Pioneer (Ariz.) JC, who was forced to redshirt last season because of lingering knee problems. With a full year of rehabilitation and workouts behind him, Hall could have an impact season in 1998-99. At Northland, Hall averaged 10 points and five rebounds despite suffering through knee problems. Northland Pioneer was 9-0 with Hall in the lineup before the injury to his left knee limited his playing time the rest of the way.

Also back in the frontcourt mix are 6-7 sophomore **Steven Branch** (1.8 ppg, 3.0 rpg, 15 blocked shots) and 6-5 junior **J.J. McQueen** (0.6 ppg, 0.5 rpg). Branch started five games as a freshman and shot a team-best .528 percent. McQueen appeared in 13 games and could compete for time at small forward.

Dooley has raised the expectations for his returning players up front. "Our frontcourt guys have to step up," Dooley said. "Punt is healthy again, van Ierland is healthy again, Branch is a year older, Quincy Hall is eligible and those guys are going to have to step up for us."

Also expected to step in and produce right away is the talented quartet of recruits Dooley landed.

The jewel of the class is certainly 6-9 junior **Evaldas Jocys**, a consensus first-team NCJAA All-American last season at Western Nebraska CC, where he averaged 16 points and seven rebounds. Jocys, ranked the No. 5 JC player in the country by recruiting analyst Phil Henzel, is expected to compete for starting time at small forward immediately and could well carry the Pirates on both ends of the court. Having lured Jocys to Greenville despite competing with some high-profile programs for his services, Dooley knows the native Lithuanian has the potential of being an impact player in the CAA. "He's the guy who makes other people better," Dooley said. "He's an excellent passer and he really knows how to play and those are the kinds of things he has and the other guys on the floor will enjoy playing with him."

David Taylor comes to Greenville via Athens, Ga., where he played in 23 games in 1996-97 for the Georgia Bulldogs as they tied a school record with 24 victories. Taylor, a 6-4 native of Gastonia, N.C., sat out last season after transferring, but practiced with the Pirates and should contribute right away. As a freshman for Georgia, Taylor averaged 0.8 points and 0.7 rebounds in a limited role. That role will change with the Pirates.

The most highly-touted freshman for Dooley is 6-4 **Kenyatta Brown**, considered a top 100 prep prospect by some recruiting analysts. Brown is from Paul Roberson (N.Y.) HS in Brooklyn, where he averaged 18.0 points and 5.0 rebounds as a senior. "Kenyatta is long and athletic," Dooley said. "He needs more size and strength, but he's hungry and wants to be successful at this level."

Rounding out the new class for the Pirates is versatile 6-2 freshman guard **Brandon Hawkins** of East Burke (N.C.) HS. Considered one of the top guards in the state last season, Hawkins can play either backcourt position and averaged 17 points and five rebounds as a senior.

adidas Blue Ribbon Analysis

BACKCOURT	**C**	**BENCH/DEPTH**	**C**
FRONTCOURT	**C**	**INTANGIBLES**	**C**

With a promising season gone awry in 1997-98, Joe Dooley and the Pirates find themselves on their heels as they try to regain the form that led them to consecutive 17-win seasons and a school-best third-place finish in the CAA just two years ago. Missing from last year's club are four starters and eight lettermen. That can be bad or good, depending on how you look at it. Dooley sees it as an opportunity. Just one senior remains, and Dooley is determined to stick to his guns and build the program with young players for stability and continuity. Despite a veteran team last season, the Pirates struggled fundamentally. With such a young team—10 of 13 players are in either their first or second year in the program—Dooley must start from scratch in many facets of the game.

"We have to be very fundamental," Dooley said. "Maybe do fewer things but be very fundamental in what we do and be very good at a few things as opposed to try and do a whole bunch. And as we get good at some things, then add a wrinkle here and there."

With the addition of four talented players, including junior college All-American Evaldas Jocys and prep standout Kenyatta Brown, Dooley is building the foundation for the future in Greenville. Though less experienced, the Pirates will certainly be more athletic than a year ago. If the Pirates can turn that atheticism into better fundamental play, they'll win their fair share of close games, something they were unable to do last season. If their youth and inexperience drags them down, then it could be another long season in Greenville. With so many teams in the CAA returning veteran players in 1998-99, it will most likely be the latter for the Pirates, who will fall to the league cellar before returning to their impressive form of a couple of years ago.

(D.B.)

1998-99 EAST CAROLINA SCHEDULE

Nov.	14	@Jacksonville State
	21	@Campbell
	24	Southwestern Louisiana
	28	@Liberty
	30	Appalachian State
Dec.	5	American
	8	@Wisconsin-Green Bay
	12	Evansville
	19	@South Carolina
	22	@Georgia
	28	Francis Marion
Jan.	2	@Richmond
	6	Virginia Commonwealth
	9	@James Madison
	13	Old Dominion
	16	@William & Mary
	18	George Mason
	23	@North Carolina-Wilmington
	30	William & Mary
Feb.	1	@Old Dominion
	3	James Madison
	10	@Virginia Commonwealth
	13	@American
	15	@George Mason
	17	Richmond
	20	North Carolina-Wilmington
	25-28	#CAA Tournament

@ Road Games
\# Richmond Coliseum, Richmond, VA

GEORGE MASON

LOCATION .... **Fairfax, VA**
CONFERENCE .... **Colonial Athletic**
LAST SEASON .... **9-18 (.333)**
CONFERENCE RECORD .... **6-10 (5th)**
STARTERS LOST/RETURNING **0/5**
NICKNAME .... **Patriots**
COLORS .... **Green & Gold**
HOMECOURT .... **Patriot Center (10,000)**
COACH .... **Jim Larranaga (Providence '71)**
RECORD AT SCHOOL .... **9-18 (2 yrs.)**
CAREER RECORD .... **207-187 (14 yrs.)**
ASSISTANTS .... **Bill Courtney (Bucknell '92)**
Mike Gillian (N. Adams St. '86)
Derek Kelloff (Massachusetts '95)
TEAM WINS (last 5 yrs.) **10-7-11-10-9**
RPI (last 5 yrs.) **226-258-255-219-202**
1997-98 FINISH .... **Lost in conference first round.**

Most coaches would have a hard time finding solace in a season in which his team lost twice as many games as it won. Considering the situation Jim Larranaga found himself in entering his first season at George Mason, it isn't difficult to comprehend the Patriots taking a string of moral victories from their nine-win season.

After all, Larranaga inherited a program without two key ingredients for success: Experience and depth. To make matters worse, two returning starters were lost with season-ending injuries and Larranaga was left with just four lettermen returning.

Expectations were not high and the Patriots were picked last in the preseason coaches' poll. But a three-game winning steak late in the season lifted George Mason to a respectable fifth-place finish in the CAA. Larranaga's aggressive defensive philosophy kept the Patriots within striking distance most games. Despite some early-season blowout losses, the Patriots allowed

1998-99 GEORGE MASON SCHEDULE

Nov.	13	@George Washington
	16	@Villanova
	20-21	#AT&T Shootout
	24	Toledo
	28	Penn State
Dec.	1	Howard
	5	@James Madison
	12	@College of Charleston
	28	Sacred Heart
Jan.	2	William & Mary
	4	Old Dominion
	9	@American
	13	Richmond
	16	@North Carolina-Wilmington
	18	@East Carolina
	20	Virginia Commonwealth
	23	@Bucknell
	27	@Richmond
	30	James Madison
Feb.	6	@Old Dominion
	10	@William & Mary
	13	North Carolina-Wilmington
	15	East Carolina
	17	@Virginia Commonwealth
	20	American
	25-28	##CAA Tournament

@ Road Games
# Fairfield, CT (vs. Portland, first round; also Fairfield and Long Island)
Richmond Coliseum, Richmond, VA

just 68.5 points a game, down from a whopping 83.4 points a game in 1996-97, Paul Westhead's final season. George Mason also led the CAA with more than eight steals a game.

What a difference a year makes. Five starters return this season and, with a solid recruiting class in the fold, Larranaga isn't faced with the experience and depth problems that plagued the Patriots a year ago. "We have some experience, everybody's back and they are more familiar with the system," Larranaga said. "We have depth at each position, experience at each spot and we'll have additional athletic ability with our newcomers."

Leading the resurgence in Fairfax is 6-2 senior point guard **Jason Miskiri** (15.9 ppg, 4.4 rpg, 92 assists), a second-team All-CAA selection as a junior. Along with William & Mary point guard Randy Bracy, Miskiri was one of only two players in the league to be in the top five in scoring, assists and steals.

Although he finished third in the league in assists, Miskiri isn't afraid to pull the trigger himself. A proven scorer, Miskiri must improve his field-goal percentage (.386), long-range accuracy (.270 percent from three-point range) and his turnovers (83) while continuing to use his athleticism to create shots for himself and his teammates.

Flanking Miskiri on the perimeter is 6-2 junior **Ahmad Dorsett** (9.8 ppg, 2.7 rpg), a sharpshooter who finished seventh in the league in three-point accuracy (.405) and led the team with 49 threes. Also a tenacious defender, Dorsett looks to have a breakout year on both ends of the court.

Giving Miskiri a breather at the point will be the talented tandem of 6-1 senior **Lee Brown** (6.2 ppg, 1.9 rpg) and 5-8 sophomore **Tremaine Price** (3.7 ppg, 1.9 rpg). Brown is a defensive specialist and was voted the team's most improved offensive player as a junior. Price is a true point guard who started 17 games as a freshman while Miskiri was awaiting his eligibility. He shot just .320 percent, but passed for 38 assists and had 16 steals. Price could also score when needed— he had a career-high 14 points against Penn State.

Tom Carroll (0.5 ppg, 0.8 rpg) is a 6-2 senior who provides some insurance minutes off the bench.

Swingman **Erik Herring** (10.1 ppg, 3.8 rpg) made an immediate impact when he became eligible midway through his freshman season, scoring 19 points in his debut against Northern Illinois, a 73-66 victory that snapped a five-game losing streak for the Patriots. More impressively, Herring, a 6-5 sophomore, had practiced but one day before that performance.

Overall, Herring shot .425 percent from the field, including .329 percent from beyond the arc, was fifth in the league in steals per game (1.62) and was third on the team with 34 steals.

Returning to the lineup after a medical redshirt season is 6-5 senior **Avery Carey** (11.1 ppg, 4.9 rpg), who started 20 games as a junior in 1996-97 and led the Patriots in field goal percentage (.449). Carey is a true inside-out player who can work the baseline, around the basket or drift out to the perimeter.

A point guard in high school, Carey causes match-up problems because of his size and athleticism. Twice as a junior, Carey displayed his offensive ability with 26-point efforts. Carey scored in double figures 15 times, including 14 of the final 22 games two seasons ago.

Perhaps the brightest aspect of last season for the Patriots was the surprising emergence of 6-7 sophomore post player **George Evans** (13.4 ppg, 8.2 rpg), the CAA Rookie of the Year. Evans was somewhat of a mystery as freshman because he played for the non-traditional Aberdeen (Md.) Army Base team, which plays against other military bases, prep schools and collegiate junior varsity teams. There, he averaged 40.0 points and 18.0 rebounds for a team that averaged better than 100 points per game.

Last season, Evans shot .527 percent from the field, blocked 41 shots and came up with 40 steals. He was third in the CAA in rebounding, fifth in field-goal percentage and blocked shots and sixth in steals. He scored in double figures 19 times and came up with seven double-doubles.

The final starter returning is 6-6 junior power forward **Nsilo Abraham** (4.5 ppg, 2,8 rpg), who shot .511 percent from the field and .500 percent from the line. Abraham showed flashes of brilliance as a sophomore. He scored a career-high 12 points at East Carolina, and grabbed nine rebounds at Old Dominion. In league play, Abraham shot .563 percent from the floor over the final 14 games.

Backing up Evans underneath will be 6-9 senior **Nik Mirich** (3.8 ppg, 3.7 rpg), the tallest player on the roster. As a junior, Mirich was upstaged by Evans, but started 19 games and managed to shoot .435 percent from the field and .651 percent from the free-throw line.

Despite the amount of experience returning from last season, the Patriots still needed help. Larranaga hopes to have addressed that with the addition of four players, all versatile forwards. Expected to contribute right away is 6-6 swingman **Keith Holdan**, a transfer from Campbell College who sat out last season.

As a sophomore, Holdan averaged 7.9 points, 4.3 rebounds, and 3.0 assists while shooting .426 percent from the field. He finished 10th in the Trans America Athletic Conference in three-point percentage (392) and led his team with 80 steals.

Rob Anderson is a 6-5 freshman swingman who was a local prep standout at Wakefield (Va.) HS in Arlington. There, Anderson averaged 17.5 points, 9.2 rebounds, 3.7 assists and 3.0 blocked shots as a senior.

"Rob is a very versatile performer," Larranaga said. "His size, speed and athletic ability allow him to play effectively in and around the basket and his ball-handling skills allow him to play on the perimeter as well."

Anderson shot 52 percent from the field, including 47 percent from three-point range, and 69 percent from the line while leading Wakefield to a 22-4 record and the semifinals of the Northern Virginia playoffs.

Terrance Nixon is a 6-6 sophomore who practiced with the Patriots last season, but was ineligible for games. As a senior at Oxon Hill (Md.) HS, Nixon averaged 20 points, 15 rebounds and five blocks while leading the Clippers to a 15-5 record. A tenacious rebounder, Nixon was a first-team All-Metropolitan selection by the *Washington Post.*

Rounding out the fresh faces is freshman **Quilninious "Q" Randall**, a 6-7, 205-pound forward from Thayer Academy in Boston, where he became the first three-year player in school history to grab more than 700 rebounds.

A two-time, first-team Independent League and all-state selection, Randall averaged 16 points and nine rebounds while shooting 52 percent from the floor and 70 percent from the line. He helped lead Thayer to its second straight New England Prep Class B title.

adidas Blue Ribbon Analysis

BACKCOURT	**C+**	**BENCH/DEPTH**	**C+**
FRONTCOURT	**C**	**INTANGIBLES**	**C**

Jim Larranaga doesn't have the George Mason basketball program where he wants it. However, after just one season on the job, Larranaga and the Patriots certainly have caught the attention of the CAA. Just how far does Larranaga expect George Mason to progress? Perhaps it's best described in the motto he has adopted for the Patriots: E Pluribus Unum : "Out of Many, One."

The Latin phrase certainly has a plethora of interpretations, but it best applies to the Patriots in terms of steps. After all, George Mason was a far cry from the top of the CAA when Larranaga arrived, and he was quick to warn his players, fans and administration about expecting too much too soon. Thus, in order to ascend to the top of the league once again, the Patriots must make one positive step at a time. Last season was the first step in that process. However, it was still a weak season in Fairfax and exposed a number of areas that became depleted in the run-and-gun era of former coach Paul Westhead. Larranaga acknowledges the time it takes to build a contender in the ever-improving CAA.

"We were the weakest rebounding team in the conference and we must improve in this area," Larranaga emphasizes. "We have to recognize good shots and make those shots. Yes, we have made progress and it would be easy for us to be optimistic.

"But, only wins will give us confidence."

Because of a depleted lineup last season, Larranaga was unable to run his vaunted 'scramble' defense with any regularity. That should slowly change this season. Also, with the addition of four athletic and versatile forwards, George Mason is certain to improve its rebounding woes. Other keys include shutting opponents down in close games and improved free-throw shooting. The Patriots shot just 61 percent last season.

The Patriots raised some eyebrows with a respectable fifth-place finish in the league a year ago. Look for another step forward and a fourth-place finish in 1998-99.

(D.B.)

JAMES MADISON

LOCATION .... **Harrisonburg, VA**
CONFERENCE .. **Colonial Athletic Association (CAA)**
LAST SEASON .... **11-16 (.407)**
CONFERENCE RECORD .... **6-10 (t-5th)**
STARTERS LOST/RETURNING **1/4**
NICKNAME .... **Dukes**
COLORS .... **Purple & Gold**
HOMECOURT .... **JMU Convention Center (7,612)**
COACH .... **Sherman Dillard (James Madison '78)**
RECORD AT SCHOOL .... **11-16 (1 yr.)**
CAREER RECORD .... **40-68 (4 yrs.)**
ASSISTANTS .... **Herb Krusen (East Carolina '80)**
Chris Theobald (Southwest Minnesota '86)
Bill Old (Randolph-Macon '94)
TEAM WINS (last 5 yrs.) **20-16-10-16-11**
RPI (last 5 yrs.) **84-168-204-129-197**
1997-98 FINISH .... **Lost in conference first round.**

Sherman Dillard applies a simple motto to life experiences: "That which doesn't kill you makes you stronger."

Sherman can only hope that motto aptly applied to his first year coaching his alma mater. It is certainly his intention.

When Dillard returned to Harrisonburg before last season, he stepped into the legendary coaching shoes of Lefty Driesell, whom he assisted for seven years at Maryland. Three consecutive mediocre seasons under Driesell led the James Madison administration to seek a new direction.

Dillard seemed the perfect replacement—he was an All-American and Academic All-American at JMU, where he graduated magna cum laude in 1978.

Dillard's first year back on campus was tumultuous. After starting the season with three wins in four games, Dillard lost his leading scorer to injury. As a result, the Dukes struggled and won just three of their next 16 games, falling to last place in the league. But JMU closed out the regular season with five wins in six games, three on the road, and rallied for a fifth-place tie in the CAA.

"We were encouraged by the way we finished up last year," Dillard said. "I thought we got off to a decent start before some injuries hit us, but what I was most proud of was the way we rebounded at the end of the season. It was a year of growth for us and, obviously, the one thing we gained was experience."

Four starters and nine lettermen return and Dillard can only hope the Dukes can pick up where they left off last season. The potential is there, but consistency remains a concern.

"We took some steps last year, albeit maybe some baby steps and now we have to try and get into some strides," Dillard said. "We have to understand that it's a process and I feel confident that with the success we had at the end of last season, we've already had the attitude adjustment that we can compete with anybody."

For all practical purposes, Dillard has five starters returning. The backcourt duo of **Ned Felton** (7.5 ppg, 2.3 rpg) and **Jamar Perry** (14.0 ppg, 2.7 rpg) are expected to provide solid perimeter play for the Dukes.

Felton, a 5-11 senior point guard, has started 33 consecutive games at JMU. As a junior, Felton shot just .364 percent from the field and .320 percent from beyond the arc, but he handed out 66 assists and came up with 23 steals.

Perry, a 6-4 junior, picked up the scoring slack with a team-high 47 three-pointers. He shot .382 percent from three-point range. He also finished third in the league in free-throw percentage (.800), passed for a team-high 69 assists and had 29 steals, but also averaged 2.74 turnovers a game.

Perry, who played sparingly as a freshman, immediately caught the eye of Dillard last season.

"Jamar Perry's improvement was remarkable last year," Dillard said. "A lot was thrown at him and he gained some valuable experience and should be a much better player again this year."

Dwayne Braxton (4.3 ppg, 1.7 rpg) is a 6-3 sophomore who started two games as a freshman, shooting just .315 percent from the field and .255 percent from three-point range.

Rounding out the backcourt experience is 5-10 sophomore point guard **Mark DiCicco** (0.2 ppg, 0.2 rpg), who appeared in nine games as a freshman.

Providing the biggest impact in Harrisonburg is the return of 6-4 senior **Chatney Howard** (15.4 ppg, 7.6 rpg), who played just five games before being sidelined for the season with a back injury. The 1997-98 CAA Preseason Player of the Year, Howard was certainly missed last season.

As a junior in 1996-97, Howard led the Dukes and finished fourth in the league in scoring and was a first-team All-CAA selection. He led the Dukes or tied for the team lead in scoring 16 times and in assists 12 times. He led JMU with 51 three-point goals and averaged a team-high 34 minutes.

Now that he's back at full strength, Howard will be the catalyst for the Dukes again this season.

"Chatney gives us someone who can be creative off the dribble and can score in bunches," Dillard said. "I think we lacked that at times last year when our offense got stale and we didn't really have anybody to create and find a way to manufacture points. Chatney has that capability."

With the loss of Howard early in the season, the Dukes' focus turned to **Eugene Atkinson** (14.2 ppg, 7.0 rpg), a 6-5 senior. Atkinson finished eighth in the league in scoring and rebounding and sixth in free-throw percentage (.769). He shot .425 percent from the field and .370 percent from beyond the arc and led the Dukes with 71 offensive rebounds.

Atkinson proved his versatility by playing four positions as a junior. "Eugene Atkinson is deceptive in what he accomplishes on the court in that he is not exceptionally quick and he doesn't jump that well, but he is a guy that has a knack for finding the ball and putting it in the hole," Dillard said.

The biggest surprise for Dillard could well have been the performance of 6-10, 285-pound junior center **Rob Strickland** (5.4 ppg, 5.7 rpg), who started 18 games and shot .547 percent from the field and blocked 42 shots, fourth-best in the league.

"One guy who stepped up last year and made a difference in what we were doing was Rob Strickland," Dillard said. "We want to make sure he becomes a meaningful part of our offense. I don't want to shortchange his ability and contributions."

Dillard has made it a priority to work the ball into Strickland's hands even more this season.

"We'll push the ball when we have the opportunities to push and we should also be able to run a good, set, half-court offense and be go inside and power it in with Strickland," Dillard said.

Kevan Johnson (2.8 ppg, 3.1 rpg) is a versatile 6-6 junior who started three games last season and displayed strong rebounding ability and also blocked 15 shots.

Marvin Zaandam (0.3 ppg, 0.3 rpg) is a 6-7 junior who appeared in 12 games.

Eligible after sitting out last season is 6-0 junior guard **Jabari Outtz**, a transfer from Howard who will press Felton right away at the point. At Howard, Outtz was the Mid-Eastern Athletic Conference Freshman of the Year in 1995-96 when he averaged 17.7 points, 3.6 rebounds and 3.7 assists. He started every game as a freshman and led Howard in scoring, assists, steals (32), minutes per game (33.8) and threes (67). In eight games as a sophomore, Outtz averaged 14.3 points, 3.6 rebounds and 3.1 assists.

"Jabari is going to give us the depth we needed at the point guard," Dillard said. "He is a very powerful point guard that is quick, explosive, can get into the paint and also has the ability to shoot the ball from the perimeter. Having that depth on the perimeter will give us an opportunity to be a little bit more aggressive defensively."

A trio of freshmen will compete for minutes.

Charlie Hatter is a 6-4 sharpshooter who was a standout at Stuarts Draft (Va.) HS before missing his senior season because of a lacerated forearm suffered in a preseason scrimmage. As a junior, he averaged 27.4 points and 6.0 rebounds in earning all-region honors. A gifted athlete, Hatter quarterbacked Stuarts Draft into the regional football playoffs as a junior.

Clayton Brown and **Tim Lyle** are a couple of 220-pound bruisers who will provide much-needed frontcourt depth for the Dukes. Brown, 6-7, scored 2,446 career points at Palmyra (N.J.) HS, completing his prep career as the 17th-leading scorer in New Jersey history. In leading his team to the South Jersey finals as a senior, Brown averaged 27.5 points and scored in double figures in 95 of 97 games, including the final 63.

Lyle was a three-sport standout at Poca (W.Va.) HS and had 1,598 points and 727 rebounds as a three-year letterman in basketball. Lyle was recruited by several Division I football programs, excelled in track and field and graduated as his class valedictorian. In 72 games, Lyle averaged 22.2 points and 10.1 rebounds while shooting 66 percent from the field.

adidas Blue Ribbon Analysis

BACKCOURT	B	BENCH/DEPTH	B
FRONTCOURT	B	INTANGIBLES	B

Two months into his first season at his alma mater had Sherman Dillard dazed and confused. After a quick start with three wins in five games, Dillard and the Dukes found themselves just 6-14 overall with a single league victory entering February. Injuries certainly played a major part as Chatney Howard, the league's preseason player of the year, was sidelined after just five games with a back injury. The Dukes didn't find their rhythm again until the second week of February, when they started a string of five wins in six games that lifted JMU into a fifth-place tie in the CAA.

The Dukes struggled offensively and shot just .405 percent from the field. With Howard back at full strength and the addition of Jabari Outtz at the point, the Dukes should be better offensively. If Rob Strickland continues to improve underneath the basket, Dillard will have scorers at every position.

While the Dukes were able defenders last season, they need to extend their defense and improve their full-court pressure. A solid and deep perimeter should make that possible.

Perhaps the most important key for JMU, however, is confidence. "Getting the kids we have in the program to believe in themselves and putting forth that championship-type effort is important for us right now," Dillard said.

Unlike last season, Dillard will have the ability to put five proven players on the court at the same time. With more proven players coming off the bench and a trio of talented freshmen added in, the Dukes are poised to return to the rightful spot in the upper-echelon of the CAA with a runner-up finish.

(D.B.)

1998-99 JAMES MADISON SCHEDULE

Nov.	13	Morgan State
	18	@North Carolina A&T
	22	Rutgers
	28	Maryland-Eastern Shore
Dec.	2	Liberty
	5	George Mason
	7	Duquesne
	12	Radford
	20	@California-Irvine
	22	@Northridge State
	31	@St. Peter's
Jan.	2	@North Carolina-Wilmington
	6	@Old Dominion
	9	East Carolina
	11	@Richmond
	16	Virginia Commonwealth
	20	William & Mary
	23	@American
	27	Old Dominion
	30	@George Mason
Feb.	3	@East Carolina
	6	North Carolina-Wilmington
	8	American
	10	Richmond
	17	@William & Mary
	20	@Virginia Commonwealth
	25-28	#CAA Tournament

@ Road Games
# Richmond Coliseum, Richmond, VA

NORTH CAROLINA-WILMINGTON

LOCATION	**Wilmington, NC**
CONFERENCE	**Colonial Athletic**
LAST SEASON	**20-11 (.640)**
CONFERENCE RECORD	**13-3 (1st)**
STARTERS LOST/RETURNING	**1/4**
NICKNAME	**Seahawks**
COLORS	**Green, Gold & Navy Blue**
HOMECOURT	**Trask Coliseum (6.100)**
COACH	**Jerry Wainwright (Colorado College '66)**
RECORD AT SCHOOL	**65-52 (4 yrs.)**
CAREER RECORD	**65-42 (4 yrs.)**
ASSISTANTS	**Brad Brownell (DePauw '91)** **Mike Winiecki (Richmond '89)**
TEAM WINS (last 5 yrs.)	**18-16-13-16-20**
RPI (last 5 yrs.)	**134-151-136-113-79**
1997-98 FINISH	**Lost in first round of NIT.**

Jerry Wainwright has a pretty simple approach as he enters his fifth season at the helm of UNC-Wilmington: Set lofty goals and reach them.

That might seem a bit elementary, but the Seahawks have responded under Wainwright and have suddenly become the model of consistency in the improving CAA, finishing no worse than third for five straight seasons.

Since Wainwright's arrival in 1994-95, the Seahawks have averaged 16.3 wins a season and reached the 20-win level for the first time last season with a 20-11 record. As a result, UNCW found itself in the postseason for the first time with an appearance opposite Wake Forest in the first round of the NIT.

In four seasons, Wainwright is already the second winningest active coach in the league with a .662 winning percentage. He also ranks fifth on the all-time list for CAA victories.

With shares of the last two regular season championships, the Seahawks went undefeated at home and sport a 16-game home winning streak. Now, Wainwright is setting his sights even higher as the Seahawks welcome back a veteran cast for the 1998-99 campaign at UNC Wilmington.

"We always approach each year with three goals," said Wainwright "One is to win the regular season CAA title. Two is to win the CAA tournament championship. And three is to advance more than one round in the NCAAs. I think the kids whet their appetite for postseason play last year. The NIT was a great experience, but it's not like going to the NCAAs. That's our ultimate goal."

Reaching their ultimate goal won't be easy for the Seahawks. In fact, building on last season's success is a formidable challenge in itself. The 1997-98 squad set 24 team records and 10 individual marks in the most memorable season the Seahawks have had in 20 years at the Division I level.

Wainwright was even surprised at the Seahawks' resiliency last season, when 7 of 11 losses came at the hands of nationally-ranked opponents such as Clemson, Rhode Island, Princeton, Connecticut and Maryland. "Overall, we were very proud of what that team accomplished," he said. "It was a great trip. It was truly a team that believed it could win every game."

Although the Seahawks won't win every game this year, they should be able to play with anyone on their schedule. That's because four starters and 11 lettermen return to defend their back-to-back CAA championships. The Wilmington fans will expect success, but Wainwright remains cautiously optimistic.

With a track record that is paving the way to a bright future in Wilmington, the Seahawks enter the 1998-99 season dead set on not taking a step back. The key will be whether or not they can maintain their dominance on defense. UNCW led the league in scoring defense (61.5) and turnover margin (+3.55) and held five opponents under 50 points last season. The result was a lot of close games, most of which the Seahawks were able to win. In fact, UNCW finished 9-1 in games decided by three or fewer points.

The heart and soul of the 1998-99 Seahawks will be found on the perimeter. Leading the way is crafty point guard **Billy Donlon** (6.9 ppg, 2.6 rpg, 173 assists), a 6-1 senior who started all 31 games and set school records for

1998-99 NORTH CAROLINA-WILMINGTON SCHEDULE

Nov.	13	@Memphis
	16	@Washington
	21	Princeton
	25	@DePaul
	27-28	#Coca-Cola Spartan Classic
Dec.	2	Campbell
	7	American
	19	@Illinois-Chicago
	30	@Cincinnati
Jan.	2	James Madison
	7	@William & Mary
	9	@Richmond
	13	Virginia Commonwealth
	16	George Mason
	20	@Old Dominion
	23	East Carolina
	27	@Virginia Commonwealth
	30	Richmond
Feb.	3	William & Mary
	6	@James Madison
	11	Wisconsin-Green Bay
	13	@George Mason
	15	@American
	17	Old Dominion
	20	@East Carolina
	25-28	##CAA Tournament

@ Road Games
# East Lansing, MI (vs. Central Florida, first round; also Michigan State and Western Michigan)
Richmond Coliseum, Richmond, VA

minutes played (1,112) and assists in a game (12). He led the league in total assists and finished second in assists per game (5.58) and committed just 72 turnovers.

Flanking Donlon on the perimeter is diminutive-but-dangerous **Stan Simmons** (15.7 ppg, 4.9 rpg, .399 three-PT percentage), a 5-11 senior shooter who led the team and finished sixth in the league in scoring as a junior. An All-CAA selection, Simmons is a candidate for the Frances Pomeroy-Naismith Award and needs just 104 points to reach 1,000 for his career.

Wainwright has high expectations for his senior backcourt duo. "Our perimeter players will be the key to what we do," said Wainwright. "They should bring a high level of play to the floor this year because they have played a lot of games."

The Seahawks will miss the long range accuracy of Mark Byington (11.6 ppg, 3.0 rpg), who graduates with nearly every three-point field goal record in Wilmington. However, Donlon and Simmons have proven to be capable from beyond the arc, combining for 205 of 540 long-range shots over the last three seasons.

Wainwright is counting on Donlon to call on his own number more frequently than he did a year ago, when he had Byington on the wing. "Part of Mark's scoring will be taken up by Billy Donlon," Wainwright said. "He will have to score more this year. He will look to score more. His outside shooting will be a factor."

Ready to fill the void left by Byington and 6-6 swingman Keith Spencer (7.4 ppg, 3.2 rpg) is 6-5 senior **Tadearl Pratt** (6.8 ppg, 3.2 rpg, 20 steals), a part-time starter as a junior. Pratt shot .474 percent from the field and .400 percent from three-point range and should help take the offensive pressure off Donlon and Simmons with his ability to create shots both inside and out.

adidas Blue Ribbon Analysis

GRADING SYSTEM

- A+ equal to very best in country—Final Four-caliber unit
- A among the best in the land—worthy of deep NCAA run
- B+ talented, versatile and experienced—NCAA-NIT ability
- B solid and productive winners—league and post-season contenders
- C+ average to above-average—may contend in a weaker league
- C average to mediocre—second division in a strong league
- D+ below average, inconsistent—second division in a weaker league
- D well below average—losing season virtually certain
- F non-Division I ability—an underdog every night

"Experience off the bench will come from 6-4 junior **Danny Dahl** (2.5 ppg, 2.0 rpg, 16 steals), 6-3 sophomore **Dominick Scott** (2.2 ppg, 1.4 rpg, 14 steals), and 6-4 junior **Paul Tharp**, who appeared in 11 games as a sophomore.

While the Seahawks will be driven by their perimeter play, quality depth and experience returns up front. Leading the way is 6-10 senior **Oleg Kojenets** (6.1 ppg, 2.7 rpg, .821 FT percentage), a solid performer who started 23 games and averaged 17.9 minutes.

Also returning to the front line is 6-9 sophomore **Marcus Green** (2.5 ppg, 3.3 rpg, 8 blocks), who struggled with his shot (.386 percent) in 22 starts as a freshman.

Wainwright also has the luxury of bringing two experienced post players off the bench in 6-8 senior **Michael Gibbs** (0.8 ppg, 0.5 rpg) and 6-8 junior **Victor Ebong** (1.1 ppg, 1.4 rpg).

As far as new faces, the coaching staff is high on newcomer **Ramond Perine**, a junior college transfer who could make an immediate impact with his defensive tenacity and rebounding prowess. The 6-4, 200-pound guard averaged 10.0 points, 5.0 rebounds and 5.0 assists last season at Three Rivers Community College in Poplar Bluffs, Mo. "He is a multiposition player," Wainwright said. "Ray is big enough to play small forward. At the same, time, he gives us our first big point guard. He defends well, so his immediate impact will be defense and rebounding. Billy played way too many minutes last year, so this should give us a better rotation and the kids won't tire as much."

A late signee for the Seahawks was Russian import **Dmitri Khorokhorine** (pronounced Di-Meet-tree Hora-horin), a 6-10, 215-pound forward from Moscow who is immediately eligible and has three years of eligibility remaining.

"We're very excited about what Dmitri brings to our program, both to the court and to the personality of our team," said Wainwright. "His size and mobility hopefully will give us an added dimension to our offense that we have not had since I've been here. Without question, he also brings much-needed depth to our frontcourt."

Also joining the team this season is 6-7, 210-pound redshirt freshman **Stewart Hare**, a former standout at East Gaston (N.C.) HS in nearby Mt. Holly.

adidas Blue Ribbon Analysis

BACKCOURT	**B**	**BENCH/DEPTH**	**B**
FRONTCOURT	**C+**	**INTANGIBLES**	**B**

Life at the top is anything but easy. Just ask Jerry Wainwright, the fifth-year coach of UNC Wilmington, coach of arguably the top program in the CAA. The Seahawks have finished in the top three in the league for five straight seasons. No other program can say that.

How has Wainwright been able to maintain such a high level of consistency in a league with higher profile programs like Old Dominion, Virginia Commonwealth, Richmond and James Madison, to name a few? Defense.

The Seahawks led the league in scoring defense, steals and turnover margin last year and won 9 of 10 games decided by three points or less. That translates into success, particularly late in the season. On its way to the first 20-win season in school history, UNCW had a nine-game winning streak, went undefeated at home and currently has the ninth-longest home court winning streak in the nation at 16 games.

Despite the success, one thing has eluded Wainwright and the Seahawks: A league tournament championship and the automatic bid to the NCAA Tournament that goes with it. They came one step closer last year with a regular-season championship and a trip to the NIT, where they lost to Wake Forest, 56-52, in the first round.

Solid defense has kept the Seahawks in more than a few games during the Wainwright era. However, when it comes time for trading baskets with a high-octane, powerful offense, the Seahawks struggle mightily. In their 11 losses, the average margin of defeat was 16.4 points. In 20 wins, the average margin was 9.8 points.

The offense will suffer further with the loss of playmakers Mark Byington and Keith Spencer, who combined for 19 points.

If the Seahawks can elevate their inside game to the level of their perimeter play, they could find themselves in the Big Dance come March. However, offensive production remains the Achilles heel in Wilmington. A sixth-straight top-three finish in the CAA is likely, but just barely.

(D.B.)

OLD DOMINION

LOCATION	**Norfolk, VA**
CONFERENCE	**Colonial Athletic**
LAST SEASON	**12-16 (.420)**
CONFERENCE RECORD	**8-8 (4th)**
STARTERS LOST/RETURNING	**1/4**
NICKNAME	**Monarchs**
COLORS	**Slate Blue & Silver**
HOMECOURT	**Norfolk Scope (10,239)**
COACH	**Jeff Capel (Fayetteville State '77)**
RECORD AT SCHOOL	**73-52 (4 yrs.)**
CAREER RECORD	**152-117 (9 yrs.)**
ASSISTANTS	**Mark Cline (Wake Forrest '88)** **Jim Corrigan (Duke '80)** **James Johnson (Ferrum '93)**
TEAM WINS (last 5 yrs.)	**21-21-18-22-12**
RPI (last 5 yrs.)	**102-83-145-91-174**
1997-98 FINISH	**Lost in conference second round.**

A 10-game turnaround for the worse in just one season would be the death knell for many college basketball programs, particularly those lurking in the shadows at a mid-level Division I conference. That's precisely the situation facing Old Dominion and its fifth-year coach Jeff Capel. After two conference tournament championships in three years and a 22-win season, the Monarch slipped to 12-16 overall last season and finished fourth in the CAA at 8-8, their worst season in 11 years.

OLD DOMINION UNIVERSITY

In the process, Capel had to say goodbye to Brion Dunlap (3.1 ppg, 2.5 rpg, 5.6 apg), the point guard who had been with him for all 73 of his coaching victories at ODU. Most coaches in Capel's shoes would probably hit the pink stuff pretty hard.

Capel isn't sulking, though. In fact, he's energized and banking on his players following suit.

Why? Because Capel likes life at the top of the league and has every intention of returning there. He doesn't plan on waiting, either. Helping ease the pain is the return of four starters and three more veterans. With two transfers now eligible and a couple of touted freshmen in the fold, Capel believes he has the solution to his problems.

The Monarchs return 91 percent of their scoring and 86 percent of their rebounding. Last season they ranked 18th in the country in field-goal percentage defense, limiting opponents to just .396 percent from the floor. It was the second straight year ODU finished in the top 20 nationally in that category.

Despite the sub-par season, Capel isn't mincing words when describing his expectations this season.

"We've got a good team," Capel said. "I'm not going to downplay this team because we should be pretty good. We're really excited about this team because we have five seniors and we've added some depth. That should mean a lot."

While Dunlap handled the ball almost exclusively during his tenure in Norfolk, it will be a point guard by committee approach this season. Just as opponents and game situations change throughout the season, so will the point-guard duties at ODU. The result should be less half-court sets on offense and more running and creativity with the ball.

Capel has the luxury of the point guard rotation because he has two skilled veterans in 6-2 senior **Mike Byers** (12.7 ppg, 3.9 rpg) and 6-3 sophomore **Michael Williams** (5.0 ppg, 1.7 rpg). Byers started 27 games at shooting guard last season and came on strong late, averaging 19.3 points in ODU's final eight games. He led the Monarchs in steals with 36 and finished eighth in the league with 84 assists. He shot .426 percent from the field, .379 percent from long range, and .735 percent from the free-throw line.

Williams made four starts as a freshman and could benefit the most from Capel's quicker offensive game plan. An athletic and versatile guard, Williams can create off the dribble and slash his way to the basket. However, he must pick his spots, be more patient and improve on his field-goal percentage (.343) and decision making (62 turnovers).

Capel is counting on the combination of Byers and Williams in the backcourt to take the heat off 6-6 senior swingman **Mark Poag** (15.3 ppg, 3.8 rpg).

"I think one of the areas of concern is getting more consistency with our outside shooting from someone other than Poag," Capel said. "Mike Byers and Michael Williams are going to have to become more consistent with their outside shots."

Regardless of who runs the point, the main objective will be finding Poag, a three-year starter for Capel who can pull the trigger from almost anywhere on the court. Poag finished seventh in the league in scoring, 11th in field-goal percentage (.481), first in three-point field goal percentage (.474) and third in free-throw percentage (.828). One of the top three-point shooters in the country, Poag set an NCAA single-game record by hitting nine of nine shots from beyond the arc in an 84-69 win over VMI. He ranked 16th nationally with 3.2 threes a game and was 13th in three-point field-goal percentage.

Experienced depth on the perimeter will come in the form of 6-3 junior **Freddie Bryant** (1.0 ppg, 0.6 rpg), who averaged 5.0 minutes in 21 games as a sophomore.

Anchoring the frontcourt is 6-10, 255-pound senior power forward **Cal Bowdler** (10.2 ppg, 8.8 rpg), who led the CAA in rebounding and blocked a league-high 68 shots, 23rd in the nation. He swatted seven shots in four games and had 10 double-doubles. In ODU's 62-57 victory over eventual league-tournament champion Richmond, Bowdler scored 20 points and grabbed 17 boards.

If he has a weakness, it's shot selection. Bowdler shot just .421 percent from the field as a junior.

Flanking Bowdler down low is 6-9, 245-pound senior center **Reggie Bassette** (7.6 ppg, 7.5 rpg), who finished tied for fourth in the league in rebounding and second in blocks (40). He shot .459 percent from the field and grabbed a team-best 76 offensive rebounds.

Another potential starter is 6-8, 245-pound senior **Skipper Youngblood** (6.3 ppg, 5.0 rpg), another shot blocker who finished seventh in the league with 30 blocks in a reserve role. Youngblood started 10 games as a junior and shot .493 percent from the field.

The Monarchs could well have the deepest frontcourt in the league with only the players returning from last season's active roster. With two highly-touted sophomore transfers now eligible, it's a no-brainer. **Clifton Jones** and **Andre McCullum** practiced with the Monarchs last season but were forced to sit out after transferring from Duquesne and North Carolina State, respectively. Both will factor into the Monarchs' equation right away.

Jones, 6-7, averaged 5.9 points and 2.3 rebounds as a freshman at Duquesne. He was the Dukes' leading free-throw shooter at 80 percent and scored 17 points against Illinois State and 15 at Western Kentucky.

McCullum, 6-6, is capable of playing anywhere from shooting guard to the post. He averaged 1.9 points and 1.3 rebounds in a limited role with the Wolfpack, but averaged 20 points, 12 rebounds, three assists and three steals for Whiteville (N.C.) HS. McCullum scored 24 points and grabbed 10 rebounds in being selected MVP of the North Carolina East-West high school all-star game two years ago. Jones and McCullum will provide Capel with depth in the frontcourt and could work their way into the starting lineup before the end of the season.

1998-99 OLD DOMINION SCHEDULE

Nov.	14	Wright State
	16	Elon College
	18	Hampton
	21	UNC Charlotte
	24	Virginia Military
	28	@Tennessee-Chattanooga
Dec.	4	*North Carolina
	5	*South Carolina
	8	St. Joseph's
	12	@George Washington
	28-30	#Hilo Holiday Shootout
Jan.	4	@George Mason
	6	James Madison
	9	@Virginia Commonwealth
	13	@East Carolina
	16	American
	18	Richmond
	20	North Carolina-Wilmington
	23	@William & Mary
	27	@James Madison
	30	Virginia Commonwealth
Feb.	1	East Carolina
	6	George Mason
	8	@Richmond
	10	@American
	13	William & Mary
	17	@North Carolina-Wilmington
	25-28	##CAA Tournament

@ Road Games
* Food Lion MVP Classic, Charlotte, NC
# Honolulu, HI (vs. Hawaii-Hilo, first round; also Buffalo and Central Connecticut)
Richmond Coliseum, Richmond, VA

"I expect for both of them (transfers) to push for starting positions right away," Capel said. "At times last year they were the most dominating guys in our practices. I think the fact that they were able to practice gives them a leg up on a freshman coming in here for the first time. Both of them will add some key depth and give us more flexibility because now we can be really, really big with some of our lineups."

With McCullum and Jones at his disposal, Capel has toyed with the idea of having the two of them joined on the court by Bowdler, Bassette and Poag for a huge lineup.

"That's not something we would play a lot, but it certainly would be intriguing in certain situations," Capel said.

Shoring up the backcourt are a couple of highly-touted freshmen. **Lavar Hemphill** is a 6-3 guard from Hargrave (Va.) Military Academy where he averaged 12.5 points and 3.2 assists last season. **Pierre Greene**, 6-2, averaged 15.4 points and five assists for Simeon (Ill.) HS in Chicago and is skilled at either backcourt position. With an abundance of experience at his disposal, Capel plans on nurturing his freshmen this season.

adidas Blue Ribbon Analysis

BACKCOURT .... B+ BENCH/DEPTH .... B+
FRONTCOURT .... A INTANGIBLES .... B+

For the first time in Jeff Capel's coaching tenure at Old Dominion, the Monarchs realized what it felt like to be an average team in the Colonial Athletic Association. Neither Capel nor his players liked the feeling and they're determined to do something about it this season. Experience, talent and depth abounds in Norfolk and the terms "transition" or "rebuilding" certainly won't apply to the Monarchs, despite their lackluster 12-16 overall record in 1997-98.

With 91 percent of its scoring and 86 percent of its rebounding back from last year, ODU is poised to return to the top of the CAA in 1998-99. The Monarchs have the deepest and most talented frontcourt in the league, arguably the best long-range shooter in three-year starter Mark Poag and a number of capable veterans to handle the ball. Add two sophomore transfers and two standout freshmen into the mix and it's no wonder Capel is giddy about ODU's chances.

"We like our team a lot," Capel said. "It's really hard to predict the future, but I think long before I got here it was a really solid program and we're just trying to build on that and we have it headed in the right direction."

The Monarchs will have an abundance of senior leadership this season, something they sorely lacked a year ago. That will translate into more consistency on offense, especially because Capel has implemented a more wide open, transition-type style. Match that with one of the best defenses in the country and you get a winning combination. ODU will make last season's fourth-place finish in the CAA a distant memory as it returns to the top of the league in 1998-99.

(D.B.)

RICHMOND

LOCATION .... Richmond, VA
CONFERENCE .. Colonial Athletic Association (CAA)
LAST SEASON .... 23-8 (.742)
CONFERENCE RECORD 12-4 (3rd)
STARTERS LOST/RETURNING 2/3
NICKNAME .... Hawks
COLORS .... Red & Blue
HOMECOURT .... Robbins Center (9,171)
COACH .... John Beilein (Wheeling Jesuit '75)
RECORD AT SCHOOL .... 23-8 (1 yr.)
CAREER RECORD .... 370-213 (20 yrs.)
ASSISTANTS .... Phil Seymour (Canisius '89)
Jeff Neubauer (La Salle '93)
Matt Brown (Shippensburg '94)
TEAM WINS (last 5 yrs.) 14-8-8-13-23
RPI (last 5 yrs.) 138-233-229-167-66
1997-98 FINISH .... Lost in NCAA second round.

What's John Beilein going to do for an encore?

No stranger to success, Beilein was lured to Richmond away from Canisius after the 1996-97 season. That wasn't an easy task for Richmond athletic director Chuck Boone. Beilein had amassed a five-year record of 89-62 at Canisius and led the Golden Griffins to three straight postseason appearances, including a berth in the 1996 NCAA Tournament and an NIT semifinal appearance in '95. More importantly, Beilein was content at Canisius and felt embraced by the people in Buffalo, where his family started forming roots. Ultimately, Boone's sales pitch proved successful and Beilein was announced as Bill Dooley's successor on April 2, 1997.

Looking back, the timing was perfect for everyone involved. The Spiders assembled two winning streaks of seven games and rode a wave of excitement all the way to the second round of the NCAA Tournament. Their 23-8 record was the best season at Richmond in 10 years. Victims along the way included Virginia and, most importantly, South Carolina in the first round of the Big Dance. The big break came when the Spiders advanced to the CAA Tournament championship by virtue of a buzzer-beating tip-in that gave them a two-point victory over American.

1998-99 RICHMOND SCHEDULE

Nov.	14	Campbell
	19	@Connecticut
	21	@Liberty
	28	Radford
Dec.	1	@Drexel
	5	@William & Mary
	18-19	#Arkansas-Little Rock Tournament
	28	Florida Atlantic
	30	@Fordham
Jan.	2	East Carolina
	4	Southern Methodist
	9	North Carolina-Wilmington
	11	James Madison
	13	@George Mason
	18	@Old Dominion
	20	@American
	23	Virginia Commonwealth
	27	George Mason
	30	@North Carolina-Wilmington
Feb.	6	American
	8	Old Dominion
	10	@James Madison
	13	@Virginia Commonwealth
	17	@East Carolina
	20	William & Mary
	25-28	##CAA Tournament

@ Road Games
# Little Rock, AR (vs. High Point, first round; also Centenary and Richmond)
Richmond Coliseum, Richmond, VA

A 15-point victory over UNC-Wilmington in the championship allowed the Spiders to maintain their trend of giant killing when they shocked the Gamecocks in the first round of the Southest Regional of the NCAA Tournament. "It was amazing how things fell into place," Beilein said. "We were extremely fortunate to win our semifinal game against American. Everything started to break our way at the end of February and early March."

Beilein had a sneaking suspicion that he stumbled upon something special when he accepted the position. "I saw a rare situation where I thought, with the four seniors we had, it wasn't a time to start building for the future," Beilein said. "It was a great time to try and win that first year. Those were four seniors coach Dooley spent a lot of time nurturing. I was fortunate enough to dot the Is and cross the Ts in order to make it work."

Beilein certainly had the Spiders clicking on all cylinders throughout much of last season. They led the league in scoring (69.6), three-point field goals made (7.77), field-goal percentage (.456), three-point field-goal percentage (.398) and free-throw percentage (.698) while finishing second in the league in turnover margin (+3.39) and scoring margin (+8.0) and third in scoring defense (61.9).

Trying to maintain that type of consistency, particularly with the fundamentals, is a top priority for Beilein and the Spiders, who lost four seniors and two starters from last season. "The intangibles that made us so good last year can't go unnoticed," Beilein said. "Staying together early and learning when we're young is going to be very important and we have to keep our players eager to learn."

Just as the frontcourt production of the now departed Jarod Stevenson and Eric Poole carried Richmond last season, the leadership load will fall in the backcourt in 1998-99. Stevenson and Poole combined for more than 30 points and 13 rebounds last year, leaving most of the question marks up front for Beilein.

"We're going to have to find ways to create baskets," Beilein said. "Hopefully, we'll be as fundamentally sound as we were last year. Things like that we still have to dwell on, but we'll be so young up front and I always felt, backcourts are good and centers are good, but forwards are always key to winning."

The backcourt is good because running the show in Richmond this season is 5-9 junior point guard **Marseilles Brown** (9.6 ppg, 1.7 rpg), who started 26 games as a sophomore and finished fifth in the league in assists (107) and 10th in threes per game (1.83). Brown is an exciting player who can score outside or off the drive and has an assists-to-turnover ratio of 2.06-to-1.

On the receiving end of many of Brown's assists is 6-1 senior sharpshooter **Jonathan Baker** (9.6 ppg, 3.1 rpg), who made 71 shots from beyond the arc while shooting 44.7 percent from long range, third-best in the league. A member of the CAA All-Tournament team, Baker finished seventh in the league with a team-high 45 steals and shot 45.9 percent from the field overall.

Adding backcourt experience off the bench is 6-4 sophomore **Rick Houston** (3.0 ppg, 1.2 rpg), who played in 30 games as a freshman. Anchoring the frontcourt will be 6-7 senior **Nick Patrick** (7.4 ppg, 5.5 rpg), a model of consistency throughout his junior season. He averaged 25.6 minutes a game and shot .476 percent from the field while handing out 42 assists, coming up with 23 steals and blocking 23 shots.

Tyler Phillips (0.8 ppg, 0.2 rpg) is a versatile 6-4 sophomore who has the ability to provide depth on the front line. A former walkon, Phillips appeared in 10 games as a freshman. Competing for time in the post will be 6-9 senior **David Hensel** (1.1 ppg, 1.2 rpg) and 6-9 sophomore **Scott Kauffman** (0.7 ppg, 0.6 rpg). At 210 pounds, Hensel is a long and athletic big man who appeared in 23 games last season, shooting .455 percent from the field and blocking 13 shots. Kauffman is the biggest of the Spiders at 230 pounds and should make his presence felt this season after appearing in just 17 games as a freshman.

If the Spiders carry their momentum from last season, it will largely depend on the ability of seven newcomers adjusting to Beilein's system. A talented group of six freshmen and a sophomore transfer gives Beilein a solid foundation for the future.

Bringing championship experience to the table is the duo of **Marques Cunningham** and **Charles Stephens**, high school teammates who led George Washington (Va.) HS to the state title last season. Cunningham is a 6-1 point guard who averaged 15.5 points and 4.3 assists for George Washington, the former high school of former Spider and current Denver Nugget Johnny Newman.

"Marques is a deceptively quick point guard who understands the pace of a game," Beilein said. "He can shoot the three off the catch or off the dribble. He shows the personality of a great leader, which is essential for the position."

Stephens, a 6-5 swingman, was selected player of the year in Virginia and averaged 20.1 points and 8.3 rebounds.

"Charles is an excellent athlete who is a strong shooter and scorer," Beilein said. "He is physically ready to play the college game."

If Beilein needs another point guard, he can turn to 5-10 freshman **Cordell Roane**, who signed with the Spiders to play football and basketball. He played quarterback, defensive back and return specialist at Varina (Va.) HS and was selected the *Richmond Times-Dispatch* Player of the Year in football after rushing for 764 yards and passing for another 654. He ran for16 touchdowns and threw eight more. On defense, he made 35 tackles and had three interceptions.

Roane's offensive production continued on the basketball court, where he led the Richmond area in scoring with a 28.0 average as a senior.

Another versatile addition for Beilein is 6-5 sophomore **Kinte Smith**, who sat out last season after transferring from Atlantic 10 power George Washington, where he averaged 2.3 points and 8.4 minutes in 14 games as a freshman.

Scott Ungerer is a 6-7 freshman forward from Westhill (N.Y.) HS, where he averaged 13 points and seven rebounds in leading his team to the New York State Public High School Class B title.

Johnathan Collins, a 6-10 freshman, comes to Richmond from Ryan (Va.) Academy, where he averaged 16.8 points and 12.4 rebounds in being selected the Virginia Independent Schools Division II Player of the Year. "Along with his size, Johnathan has great jumping ability and great feel away from the basket," Beilein said. "He has strong perimeter skills and can block some shots. He must continue his overall physical development, but he has tremendous skills."

Rounding out the new class is 6-11, 200-pound freshman **Tim Faulconer**, who attended Williston Northhamption (Mass.) Prep School last year and averaged 18 points, 10 rebounds and seven blocked shots. Beilein has Faulconer on a plan that will add a pound a week to his lean frame in an effort to beef him up enough to handle the physical play underneath the basket.

adidas Blue Ribbon Analysis

BACKCOURT	**B+**	**BENCH/DEPTH**	**C**
FRONTCOURT	**C**	**INTANGIBLES**	**B**

Now that John Beilein has had an opportunity to catch his breath, he might be able to settle in to his role as coach of the Richmond Spiders. No doubt the players, fans and administration are willing to do whatever it takes to keep him comfortable in his new surroundings.

Beilein certainly knows how to make a first impression. In joining a program that won a total of 43 games in the four-year tenure of its previous coach, Beilein took full advantage of the situation handed him and it led all the way to the second round of the NCAA Tournament. A first-round victory over South Carolina returned the Richmond program to national prominence and lifted Beilein's name to the top of the wish lists at some higher profile programs seeking to fill coaching vacancies. Beilein stayed put.

With two starters and seven lettermen gone from last year's magical team, uncertainty abounds in Richmond. As a result, Beilein's coaching ability will be tested even more this year. One thing is certain. Beilein coaches fundamentals and gives his team a chance to win. Can the Spiders come close to last year's success?

"I don't have many expectations for the long run," Beilein said. "All of mine are short-term. Last year, we were one of the few senior-laden teams, but I see this season as having a lot of talent at the top of the classes in this league. It will be a topsy-turvy type of league and we will have to grow up quickly, very quickly."

Without any proven leaders in the frontcourt, the Spiders won't be able to grow up fast enough this season and will find the road much tougher come tournament time. Let's call it a fifth-place finish and, who knows, maybe another magical run for the giant killers?

(D.B.)

VIRGINIA COMMONWEALTH

LOCATION	**Richmond, VA**
CONFERENCE	**Colonial Athletic Association**
LAST SEASON	**9-19 (.321)**
CONFERENCE RECORD	**4-12 (9th)**
STARTERS LOST/RETURNING	**2/3**
NICKNAME	**Rams**
COLORS	**Black & Gold**
HOMECOURT	**Siegel Center (7,500)**
COACH	**Mack McCarthy (Virginia Tech '74)**
RECORD AT SCHOOL	**First Year**
CAREER RECORD	**243-122 (12 yrs.)**
ASSISTANTS	**Mike Ellis (North Carolina '88)**
	Chris Cheeks (Virginia Commonwealth '90)
	E.J. Sherod (Old Dominion '97)
TEAM WINS (last 5 yrs.)	**14-16-24-14-9**
RPI (last 5 yrs.)	**63-98-65-131-245**
1997-98 FINISH	**Lost in conference quarterfinal.**

Sonny days might be over at Virginia Commonwealth, but the horizon isn't dim.

With the departure of popular coach Sonny Smith to retirement after last season, plus a new, state-of-the-art facility set to welcome new head coach Mack McCarthy, a Smith protégé, the buzz around campus is filled with comments such as "fresh start" and "opportunity."

Despite a less-than-memorable season in which the Rams struggled to a nine-win, last place finish in the CAA, Smith set the table for McCarthy, his coaching pupil and, more importantly, close friend.

Smith and McCarthy have had stops together at Virginia Tech, East Tennessee State and Auburn, where they teamed to land recruits such as Charles Barkley in the early 1980s. After helping turn the Tigers into an SEC powerhouse, McCarthy was lured away to Tennessee-Chattanooga in 1985. There, he became the winningest coach in Southern Conference history and took the Mocs to five NCAA Tournaments and three NIT appearances.

Under McCarthy, Chattanooga won eight regular-season conference championships and, in 1997, the 14th-seeded Mocs became the darlings of the Big Dance with victories over 3rd-seeded Georgia and 6th-seeded Illinois

1998-99 VIRGINIA COMMONWEALTH SCHEDULE

Nov.	13	Virginia
	18	Western Kentucky
	21	@Southern Illinois
	23	Maryland-Eastern Shore
	27-29	#Honolulu Thanksgiving Shootout
Dec.	2	@Colorado
	8	@Radford
	12	Liberty
	19	Norfolk State
	22	@Georgia State
	30	Southern Mississippi
Jan.	2	American
	6	@East Carolina
	9	Old Dominion
	13	@North Carolina-Wilmington
	16	@James Madison
	20	@George Mason
	23	@Richmond
	25	William & Mary
	27	North Carolina-Wilmington
	30	@Old Dominion
Feb.	3	@American
	6	@William & Mary
	10	East Carolina
	13	Richmond
	17	George Mason
	20	James Madison
	25-28	##CAA Tournament

@ Road Games
# Honolulu, HI (vs. Baylor, first round; also Hawaii-Pacific, Hofstra, Illinois State, Iona, Missouri-Kansas City and Southern Mississippi)
Richmond Coliseum, Richmond, VA

before falling to 10th-seeded Providence in the Sweet 16. Despite that resume, McCarthy was unable to land a higher profile gig when coaching vacancies became available at some of the larger programs in the southeast, including Auburn, Tennessee and Georgia.

Smith, knowing his retirement was imminent, lured McCarthy to VCU before last season and made him associate head coach. McCarthy left behind a solid program in Chattanooga, but felt right at home alongside Smith. McCarthy is a native Virginian and a Virginia Tech graduate.

"It was great to work with Sonny again," McCarthy said. "We are such great friends that despite the less-than-optimal year, we really enjoyed each other's company and enjoyed the battle. He and I both changed a lot since the last time we worked together, but the friendship had not changed. We probably clashed basketball-wise more than we used to, but we still enjoyed it very much."

The welcome mat in front of McCarthy's head-coaching office can be found at the Stuart C. Siegel Center, a just-completed, 7,500-seat, on-campus facility that gives the Rams a true home court for the first time.

McCarthy can only hope his second season in Richmond is smoother than his first, when he had a lifetime's worth of point guard problems. After signing arguably the top junior college point guard in the country in Bootsy Thornton, VCU lost him when he failed to qualify academically just days before practice began. Somehow, he landed at St. Johns. Then, freshmen point guards **Scott Lilly** and **LaMar Taylor** suffered severe knee injuries early on, forcing Smith and McCarthy to change their game plan.

The combination of a healthy Lilly (8.2 ppg, 2.8 rpg, 69 assists) and Taylor (8.6 ppg, 2.8 rpg, 89 assists) will certainly set the tempo for the Rams.

Lilly is a 6-2 sophomore who suffered a partially torn ligament in his right knee during preseason workouts last year, but returned and appeared in all 28 games as a freshman. Along the way, he led the Rams in minutes (898), three-point field goals (51) and threes attempted (148). Against Old Dominion, Lilly hit seven of 12 from the field, including six of nine from beyond the arc, and scored a career-high 23.

Likewise, Taylor, a 5-10 sophomore, suffered cartilage damage in the preseason and missed eight games. He returned after a strenuous, post-surgery rehabilitation and was impressive. A CAA All-Rookie selection, Taylor scored a career high 22 points against William & Mary on February 22 and managed 31 steals in 20 games.

Another freshman guard thrown into the fire last season was **Hunter Hoggatt** (4.2 ppg, 1.4 rpg), who averaged 15.8 minutes. McCarthy will be counting on the 6-3 Hoggatt to improve on his field goal percentage (.278) and three-point field goal percentage (.266).

Just two players return to the VCU frontcourt, but both were starters last season. **Patrick Kodjoe** (5.2 ppg, 5.0 rpg) is a 6-7 junior and former walkon who started 22 games and is the Rams' leading returning rebounder. Also an excellent student, Kodjoe is a first-team CAA All-Academic selection with a 3.28 cumulative grade-point average in marketing.

Fellow 6-7 junior **Simon Moore** (4.2 ppg, 3.8 rpg, 19 blocks) was a spot starter as a sophomore and struggled after dislocating a shoulder in December. He scored a season-high 14 points against James Madison and grabbed a career-high 10 rebounds against William & Mary.

Frontcourt depth will come in the form of 6-6 junior walk-on **Chris Whitlow**, who appeared in six games as a sophomore.

Although the Rams have a nucleus of experienced players returning, much of their success or failure will fall squarely on the shoulders of seven first-year players. McCarthy spent his first offseason in Richmond addressing the weaknesses that plagued the Rams all last season.

Boosting the perimeter game will be 6-5 junior **Garland Raglar**, who is capable of playing all three perimeter positions and gives McCarthy a versatile player on both ends of the court. As a sophomore at Catonsville (Md.) CC, Raglar averaged 20 points, nine rebounds and seven assists while leading his team to a 24-7 record.

Scott Moore is a 6-5 freshman from Oviedo (Fla.) HS, where he averaged 18 points and eight rebounds as a senior. A third-team all-state selection, Moore was chosen Oviedo's MVP while leading his team to a 21-7 record and No. 5 state ranking.

The sparkplug in the Rams backcourt could well be sophomore **Leroy "Bo" Jones**, who transferred to VCU from Atlanta Metropolitan JC during the second semester last year. As a result, he was able to practice with the Rams. A former Virginia prep standout, Jones led the state in scoring as a senior (29 ppg.) He established school records in career points, assists and steals at Richmond's Huguenot HS.

The gem of McCarthy's recruiting class is 6-8 freshman **Shawn Hampton**, a 230-pound force from St. Francis Academy in Baltimore. There, he averaged 21 points, 10 rebounds and five blocked shots. Hampton received the Catholic Player-of-the-Year award, was a first-team all-state and all-metro selection and led his team to four consecutive regular-season championships. Hampton is a talented and versatile big-man who will play extensively right away.

Also expected to play right away in the frontcourt is 6-11 freshman **Reggie Okosa**, whom McCarthy describes as an "interesting player." He uses that description because Okosa, who starred at Brandywine (Del.) HS, has grown three inches and gained 30 pounds in the last 18 months. Okosa excelled in all facets of the game as a senior and was selected Gatorade State Player of the Year after averaging 18 points, 12 rebounds and four blocks while leading Brandywine to a 25-2 record and a state championship. *Hoop Scoop* rated Okosa the 14th-best center prospect in the country.

Like Okosa, freshman **Matt Treadwell** is a 6-11 post who has to add bulk to his 200-pound frame. As a senior at Saint Mary's (Md.) Academy, Treadwell was an all-state, all-conference and all-county selection after averaging 13 points, 10 rebounds and three blocks. Rounding out the recruiting class is 6-6, 220-pound junior swingman **Shannon Martin**, who could wind up logging the most playing time among the incoming class.

Martin averaged 16 points, seven rebounds and two steals for Otero (Colo.) JC, where he shot a league-best 51 percent from three-point range.

adidas Blue Ribbon Analysis

BACKCOURT	**C+**	**BENCH/DEPTH**	**C**
FRONTCOURT	**C**	**INTANGIBLES**	**C+**

Mack McCarthy has certainly had a wild ride over the last year and a half. After becoming the most successful coach in the history of the Southern Conference with a postseason run that saw his 1997 Chattanooga Mocs reach the Sweet 16 of the NCAA Tournament, McCarthy, in the prime of his coaching career, took a year off as head coach. Instead of running his own program, he returned to his home state of Virginia, reunited with old friend and colleague Sonny Smith and assumed the role of coach-in-waiting at Virginia Commonwealth.

Now, with a new on-campus facility and a plethora of incoming talent ready to greet VCU fans this year, McCarthy is ready to make his mark in Richmond. With nary a senior on the roster of a team that managed just nine wins and finished last in the league last season, the task ahead of McCarthy is daunting. However, in 12 years in Chattanooga, he never suffered a losing season and averaged 20 wins a year. That's the kind of consistency VCU fans have come to expect. Also, McCarthy has a knack for playing to his roster's strengths and finding ways to the postseason, as evidenced by his five trips to the NCAA Tournament and three NITs.

The key for the Rams this season will be confidence. Of four juniors on the squad, just two have Division I experience. No one on the roster has experienced any level of success in Division I. If McCarthy can mold his returning players with his recruits and get his system in place, the Siegel Center could be a terror for opponents by the end of February.

However, if the Rams reveal their youth and show any reluctance to learn McCarthy's system, it could be another long season in Richmond.

The Rams won't rebound from last season's misery overnight. The future looks bright at VCU, but the 1998-99 season looks like a seventh-place finish in the CAA.

(D.B.)

WILLIAM & MARY

LOCATION .... **Williamsburg, VA**
CONFERENCE .. **Colonial Athletic Association (CAA)**
LAST SEASON .... **20-7 (.741)**
CONFERENCE RECORD .... **13-3 (t-1st)**
STARTERS LOST/RETURNING **2/3**
NICKNAME .... **Tribe**
COLORS .... **Green, Gold & Silver**
HOMECOURT .... **William & Mary Hall (10,000)**
COACH .... **Charlie Woollum (William & Mary '62)**
RECORD AT SCHOOL .... **50-58 (4 yrs.)**
CAREER RECORD .... **368-279 (23 yrs.)**
ASSISTANTS .... **Mark Lezanic (Bucknell '86)**
Bobby Woollum (Bucknell '89)
Kihlon Golden (Bucknell '96)
TEAM WINS (last 5 yrs.) **4-8-10-12-20**
RPI (last 5 yrs.) **272-247-238-186-106**
1997-98 FINISH .... **Lost in conference first round.**

Redemption.

That just about sums up last season for Charlie Woollum and William & Mary.

In his fourth season at his alma mater, Woollum has brought the Tribe back to life. Just 4-23 the season before he arrived, William & Mary has steadily improved each season under Woollum.

The Tribe's ascension reached its pinnacle last season when it did the unexpected. Picked seventh in the preseason coaches poll, the Tribe managed to assemble two seven-game winning streaks and suffered just a single home loss in a remarkable season that lifted it to an overall record of 20-7 and a tie for first in the league with North Carolina-Wilmington at 13-3.

Woollum's leadership didn't go unnoticed, either, as he was selected CAA Coach of the Year by the league media and District 4 Coach of the Year by the National Association of Basketball Coaches. A loss in the first round of the league tournament ended just the fifth 20-win season in the 94-year history of the school and first since 1983. It was just the second winning season for William & Mary in 15 years.

"We had a great year," Woollum said. "All of the kids came to play every night and, barring a couple of injuries, we might have even gone farther. I was extremely pleased that we were pretty much injury-free most of the year, so it works on both ends."

Woollum wasn't exactly surprised by his team's accomplishments. The Tribe swept regular-season champion Old Dominion two years ago, a feat it matched again last season. Among the losses was a two-point loss to Big East member Virginia Tech and a two-point, overtime loss at Wichita State.

"We've been getting better every year," Woollum said. "Some of the top teams haven't beaten us in two years. I felt like we gained respect a long time ago. I don't think anybody takes us lightly."

1998-99 WILLIAM & MARY SCHEDULE

Nov.	14	@Virginia Tech
	17	Furman
	21	Albright College
	24	@Wake Forest
	28	@Hampton
	30	@North Carolina-Greensboro
Dec.	2	@Citadel
	5	Richmond
	21-22	#Stanford Invitational
	28	North Carolina-Greensboro
Jan.	2	@George Mason
	7	North Carolina-Wilmington
	13	@American
	16	East Carolina
	20	@James Madison
	23	Old Dominion
	25	@Virginia Commonwealth
	27	American
	30	@East Carolina
Feb.	3	@North Carolina-Wilmington
	6	Virginia Commonwealth
	10	George Mason
	13	@Old Dominion
	17	James Madison
	20	@Richmond
	25-28	##CAA Tournament

@ Road Games
\# Stanford, CA (vs. Santa Clara, first round; also Elon and Stanford)
\## Richmond Coliseum, Richmond, VA

While the Tribe won't be overlooked, the team certainly will have a new look. That's because four of the top seven players graduated, including almost the entire frontcourt. However, Woollum is licking his chops with the return of arguably the best Tribesman in recent memory, 6-1 senior point guard **Randy Bracy** (17.2 ppg, 5.6 rpg), the league's leading returning scorer. The first player in school history selected first-team All-CAA, Bracy finished fourth in the league in assists (107), second in steals (57) and fifth in threes per game (2.5). He did, however, commit a league-high 101 turnovers, almost four a game.

"No question he's a good player," Woollum said. "He's an extremely talented player. If he stays healthy and plays as well as I think he can, he will be a major for us and our league. He has worked hard to get to this point."

Bracy shot .410 percent from the field, .378 percent from long range, .697 percent from the free-throw line and displayed his athletic ability by blocking 23 shots.

"We're not going to out-talent a lot of people in the sense that we're not going to just physically dominate anybody," Woollum said. "But Bracy will certainly hold his own with any guard he plays in the nation. He's a very good talent and has a shot at the next level if he continues to improve."

The rest of the players returning in the backcourt combined for just 5.8 points and 3.1 boards a game last season. Most likely to step into the shooting-guard spot is 6-5 junior **Brian Brown** (0.7 ppg, 0.3 rpg), who played sparingly in 23 games as a sophomore and shot just .292 percent from the field.

Mit Winter (3.7 ppg, 1.8 rpg) is a 6-6 sophomore pure shooter who gained confidence on the court as a freshman and is poised to have a breakthrough season. Winter shot .471 percent from the field, .500 percent from beyond the arc and .759 percent from the free throw line.

Alex Klein (1.0 ppg, 0.5 rpg) is a 6-4 sophomore and former walkon who has the capability to play any position on the perimeter.

Spelling Bracy at the point will be 5-11 junior **Scotty Scott** (0.4 ppg, 0.5 rpg), who appeared in 13 games last season.

Gone from last year's frontcourt are 6-9 Bill Phillips and 6-7 David Grabuloff, who combined for 16.4 points and 11.9 rebounds for the Tribe. Phillips, the Tribe's sixth man, transferred to St. Joseph's and Grabuloff graduated. Returning to the front line is 6-7, 240-pound senior power forward **Jermaine Harmon** (7.0 ppg, 5.3 rpg) and 6-7 sophomore **Jim Moran** (8.2 ppg, 4.3 rpg).

Harmon, co-captain with Bracy, is a powerful force under the basket. He shot 50 percent from the floor, blocked a team-high 29 shots and grabbed a team-high 54 offensive boards.

Moran was a CAA All-Rookie selection and is an intense player. After adding more than 20 pounds in the offseason, Moran will be able to hold his own down low and bang around the basket. A starter in 24 games last season, Moran shot 46 percent from the floor, blocked 15 shots and came up with 41 steals, second best on the team.

Moran went down with an injury just before the league tournament last year and didn't return. Without him providing frontcourt depth, the Tribe lost in the first round.

A possibility at center is 7-1, 230-pound sophomore **Jarad Houston** (0.7 ppg, 1.3 rpg), the tallest player in school history. In just 22 minutes last season, Houston grabbed 12 rebounds and blocked three shots.

Versatility up front will come in the form of 6-6 junior **James Haunty** (0.1 ppg, 0.9 rpg), who appeared in seven games as a sophomore. In the offseason, Haunty participated in the Marine Corps boot camp and bulked up his already impressive physique.

Nary a player remains from before Woollum arrival in Williamsburg. The new faces on campus this fall will include two guards and two forwards, all freshmen.

Justin Jackette is a 6-2 shooter from Iona (N.Y.) Prep, where he averaged 22 points last season. He was the Gannet Suburban Newspaper Player of the Year and also played for Riverside AAU, which posted an impressive record of 100-4 last year, including the European National Championship in France.

Cody Carbaugh joins the backcourt mix after a stellar prep career at Chambersburg (Penn.) HS, where he averaged 17 points as a senior and scored 1,300 career points. A two-time first-team Mid-Penn selection, Carbaugh was selected to Pennsylvania's Associated Press Big School All-State team the last two years.

Much-need frontcourt help will come in the form of **Bill Davis** and **Tom Strohbehn**. Davis, 6-8, led Windsor, Ontario's Catholic Central HS to the Southwestern Ontario championship the last two years and a fourth-place finish in the provincial championships. The two-time all-city selection averaged 24.5 points, 12 rebounds and 1.8 blocks while being selected the city's Mr. Basketball.

Strohbehn, 6-9, played at Blue Valley North (Kan.) HS, where he set 10 school records, including career points (1,193), rebounds (559) and blocked shots (130). His .701 field goal percentage was a single-season record at the school and he was a two-time all-state selection.

adidas Blue Ribbon Analysis

BACKCOURT	**B**	**BENCH/DEPTH**	**C**
FRONTCOURT	**C**	**INTANGIBLES**	**C+**

In just four years on the job, Charlie Woollum has restored the level of respect at William & Mary, a once-proud basketball program that had been beaten down over the last several years.

The four-win season before Woollum arrived is now a distant memory. With an improved record every season since, the Tribe took the league by storm last season and finished in a first-place tie with North Carolina-Wilmington at 13-3.

Old Dominion, widely regarded as the measuring stick in the ever-improving CAA, can certainly attest to Woollum's impact, having been swept by the Tribe the last two seasons. A big reason for the impressive turnaround is Woollum's ability to teach solid, fundamental skills. He also gets consistency from his players, often less talented than their opponents.

"We're going to have some awful good teams in this league this season," Woollum said. "We're going to be real young other than a couple of guys.

"We had a great chemistry last year and we have to replace that, but my goal is that we always perform to the best of our ability. If that's good enough, then we're happy. Last year it was good enough most of the time. Right now, we have a lot of young players and with Bracy and Harmon as our leaders, they have to do the same kind of job that our seniors did last year."

Matching last year's accomplishments certainly won't be easy. Without a proven big man, post play remains the biggest question mark, but Woollum has toyed with the idea of going small. Playing three forwards and two guards should give Woollum the best opportunity of getting his most talented lineup on the court.

Senior Randy Bracy is arguably the best point guard in the league and should help the young players adjust to Woollum's system. Versatile players Jim Moran and Jermaine Harmon will provide consistency. However, the Tribe is young. A great portion of their depth has little or no game experience. As a result, it might take some time to jell. With senior-laden teams throughout the CAA this season, the Tribe will be pushed early and often. Without much experience or depth, the Tribe will slide to sixth in the league in 1998-99.

(D.B.)

CONFERENCE USA

adidas BLUE RIBBON FORECAST

AMERICAN CONFERENCE

1. Cincinnati
2. Saint Louis
3. DePaul
4. Marquette
5. Louisville
6. UNC Charlotte

NATIONAL CONFERENCE

1. Memphis
2. UAB
3. South Florida
4. Southern Mississippi
5. Houston
6. Tulane

TOP 40

Cincinnati, Memphis and UAB are ranked among the 1998-99 *adidas Blue Ribbon* Top 40. Extended profiles can be found in the Top 40 section of *Blue Ribbon.*

ALL-CONFERENCE TEAM

G—Quentin Richardson, FR, DePaul
G—Neil Reed, SR, Southern Mississippi
C—Kenyon Martin, JR, Cincinnati
F—Omar Sneed, SR, Memphis
F—Matt Baniak, SO, Saint Louis

PLAYER OF THE YEAR

Omar Sneed, SR, Memphis

NEWCOMER OF THE YEAR

Quentin Richardson, FR, DePaul

1998-99 CONFERENCE TOURNAMENT

March 3-6, Birmingham-Jefferson Civic Center, Birmingham, AL

1997-98 CHAMPION

Cincinnati (regular season)
Cincinnati (conference tournament)

1997-98 POSTSEASON PARTICIPANTS

Postseason Record: 7-7 (.500)

NCAA

Cincinnati (2nd round)
UNC Charlotte (2nd round)
Saint Louis (2nd round)

NIT

Marquette (3rd round)
Memphis (2nd round)
UAB (2nd round)
Southern Mississippi

TOP BACKCOURTS

1. Memphis
2. DePaul
3. Cincinnati

TOP FRONTCOURTS

1. Cincinnati
2. Memphis
3. St. Louis

ON THE WAY UP

South Florida

ON THE WAY DOWN

UNC Charlotte

INSIDE THE NUMBERS

- 1997-98 conference RPI: 8th (of 30)
- Conference RPI (last 5 years): N/A-N/A-4-9-8

DID YOU KNOW?

New Houston coach Clyde Drexler scored 22,195 points in his NBA career, making him one of a handful of NBA players to reach the coveted 20,000-point plateau. It also gives him more than a third of all the NBA points scored by current Division I coaches. There are 20 other Division I coaches who played in the NBA, and their scoring totals ranged from Clem Haskins' 8,743 points to three by Mount St. Mary's coach Jim Phelan...Louisville will not be eligible to compete in the Conference USA Tournament because of league bylaw 4.05; being ineligible for NCAA competition means being ineligible in the league. Ironically, when the Cardinals belonged to the Metro Conference, they were cost an NCAA bid in 1987 when that league allowed Memphis to compete in its tournament while banned from the NCAA. Memphis defeated the Cardinals in the league title game, and they weren't chosen as an at-large team...Louisville's absence from the tournament means this will be the second time in C-USA's four years of existence it will have an 11-team tournament. Five teams will be awarded first-round byes; the top two in each division and the team with the next-best record...With new hires at Houston and UNC Charlotte, 20 different men have been head coaches in the league and only five schools (Cincinnati with Bob Huggins, Louisville with Denny Crum, Marquette with Mike Deane, Saint Louis with Charlie Spoonhour and Tulane with Perry Clark) have had the same coach for the league's four seasons...The capacity for Houston's Hofheinz Pavilion has dropped from 10,000 to 8,479 because of a construction project to add luxury suites to the arena...Cincinnati has an 18-game homecourt winning streak in place...Tulane is entering its final season in tiny Fogelman Arena, where the only thing more scarce than bleacher seats is parking. The trouble is, Fogelman holds 3,500 and the Green Wave isn't filling it. The New Orleans Sports Arena has room for 20,000...Pfeiffer University in North Carolina, where Bobby Lutz turned the program into an NAIA power while serving as head coach, has named its in-season tournament the Bobby Lutz Tournament in his honor...South Florida was the only Division I school to offer Cedric Smith a scholarship when he was at Fork Union Military Academy in Virginia. He averaged 9.8 points and 4.9 rebounds as a freshman...Houston is the only team in the league whose three top salesman—the three coaches permitted to recruit off-campus—all attended the university where they work...As a freshman, Memphis guard Marcus Moody scored 18.4 percent of his season's points in one game, getting 41 against Oklahoma. He didn't top that in any four consecutive games the rest of the season...Conference USA as a whole does not have even half as many former McDonald's All-Americans on its rosters (three) as Duke does on its own (eight)...UAB has had 12 seasons of 20 or more wins in two decades of operating a program and is averaging 20 wins a year...Cincinnati has held opponents under 40 percent shooting for three consecutive seasons, something it had not done since 1960-63...Last season, Louisville's schedule was ranked No. 2 in the nation according to the RPI report...Conference USA insiders who believe competing in a 12-team league has hurt their chances to receive NCAA Tournament bids might want to consider the real reason they've gotten a combined seven bids the past two years: Not enough good players. Consider that members of the first two C-USA all-freshman teams have now had time to play a combined 25 seasons of college basketball—three each for the five-man '96 team, two each for the '97 team—and that those seasons have produced three double-figure scoring totals. Four of those 10 players aren't even in the league any more: former Southern Miss center Anthony Richards, former South Florida forward Dan Luczywko, former Saint Louis guard Jeramy Biles and former DePaul guard Doc Taylor.

(M.D.)

DEPAUL

LOCATION .... **Chicago, IL**
CONFERENCE .... **Conference USA (American)**
LAST SEASON .... **7-23 (.233)**
CONFERENCE RECORD .... **3-13 (6th)**
STARTERS LOST/RETURNING **1/4**
NICKNAME .... **Blue Demons**
COLORS .... **Royal Blue & Scarlet**
HOMECOURT .... **Rosemont Horizon (17,500)**
COACH .... **Pat Kennedy (Kings College '78)**
RECORD AT SCHOOL .... **7-23 (1 yr.)**
CAREER RECORD .... **333-213 (18 yrs.)**
ASSISTANTS .... **Larry Harrison (Pittsburgh '78**
Tracy Dildy (Illinois-Chicago '91)
Brian Kennedy (Monmouth '92)
TEAM WINS (last 5 yrs.) **16-17-11-3-7**
RPI (last 5 yrs.) **64-60-108-231-193**
1997-98 FINISH .... **Lost in conference first round.**

Words on paper. This is what they are to most DePaul fans at the moment. The words about **Quentin Richardson**, **Bobby Simmons** and **Lance Williams** have been mostly flattering, and probably accurate, but until Blue Demons followers actually see what these three players look like on a college basketball floor, they can't really know how good these next few years will be.

In a way, because they are entering a program that has been so lacking in hope, Richardson, Simmons and Williams are the most eagerly anticipated freshman class to enter any Division I school since the Fab Five took over Michigan in 1991. There may be more talent in UCLA's incoming class; there may not be. But there can be no doubt DePaul needs more help.

The last few years have been grim: Only 10 victories in two years. A lot of the problems were quite likely self-inflicted by the DePaul administration, but there is hope, now, in the form of three local products who decided they would pursue their college careers at the school that once brought you Mark Aguirre, Dallas Comegys and Terry Cummings.

"This is excited as I've ever been," said DePaul coach Pat Kennedy. "My last few years at Florida State were difficult for me, realizing we'd kind of hit the ceiling. Here—it's already been done here. That's what we sold to these kids. We're not creating something out of fantasy land."

Richardson would seem to be a sort of fantasy player: Fine student, great talent, champion. His team at Chicago's Whitney Young High won the Chicago Public League title, the state Class AA championship and 30 of 31 games.

A 6-6, 215-pound shooting guard, Richardson set a record with 20 rebounds in the state title game and averaged 25 points, 12.3 rebounds and .440 three-point shooting in his senior season at Young.

He was a player many analysts looked upon favorably as he entered the summer before his senior season, but the more he played the higher he climbed.

Richardson was a lock top 25 pick after his week at the Nike All-American Camp. By the end of the July 1997 evaluation period, he was one of the top dozen players in the nation. After he tore through the high school season and was dominant in both the McDonalds All American Game (19 points, 10 rebounds) and Derby Festival (40 points, 18 boards), it became clear no one could be as good a pick to finish as national freshman of the year in 1998-99.

He is a very springy, upright player who moves quickly, with bursts of forward motion that defenders find difficult to contain because of his strength. He has no wasted motion in his shot, which is one reason it has become so reliable for him. He also is not bound to either the three-point line or the post. Richardson understands how to create shots for himself at a variety of distances in between.

"Quentin is a kid that's so admired in this community," Kennedy said. "The real basketball fans of Chicago—they admire his tenacity as a winner. People will go watch him, and he won't shoot the ball for the first 12 minutes of the game, and some of them will be wondering what the fuss is about. Then the game gets on the line, and he'll score the last 15. He's a youngster that will create what it is he wants to create, and it's usually winning basketball games."

Because Simmons is a more natural forward, the only difficulty in combining him with Richardson is in deciding who shoots and how often. Having two such extraordinary threats is hardly a burden, though, as the U.S. junior team discovered in the World Championship Qualifying tournament last summer.

A 6-7 , 210-point small forward from Chicago's Simeon High, Simmons averaged 12.2 points as a sixth man while Richardson started and averaged 13.7 points. Syracuse coach Jim Boeheim, who worked with the U.S. team, sent Kennedy a note at one point during the team's workouts that included a fairly succinct message: Simmons equals Pippen.

"He can play four positions," Kennedy said. There were recruiting analysts who called Simmons the best player in Illinois last year, even over Richardson, Williams, Arizona recruit Michael Wright and guard Frankie Williams, who will belong to Lon Kruger's Illini.

"He's got wide shoulders, is an excellent passer and a good shooter," Kennedy said. "There's a whole lot to him. He may be better than good."

Although he may be the least talented of the three, Williams is as important as any of DePaul's recruits because of the Blue Demons' lack of inside play the past few years.

At 6-9, 230, Williams is a powerful low-post presence. He was the first of the program's heralded recruits to commit and went on to average 25 points and 15 rebounds for Julian High. In the postseason, he scored 19 points and got five rebounds in the Magic Johnson Roundball Classic.

"Lance Williams will always be very special to me personally because he was the first guy to step forward and say, 'I believe that this can get done. I want to be a part of this,' " Kennedy said.

"Lance is a very skilled interior player. The thing I like about Lance_watching him in Magic's game—he was one of the few kids on the court who understood his position. He ran block-to-block. He's got a very simple game, but very effective ... almost a Danny Fortson. He's not as strong, but has a very soft touch. His consistency around the basketball could be a key."

Because these three players are so talented, and because each is a hometown product, all the recruits with them appear to be afterthoughts.

In fact, point guard **Kerry Hartfield** is probably as important as any of them to DePaul's potential for success the next two seasons. Hartfield is a 6-1 junior from Southeastern (Iowa) Community College who averaged 16.4 points and 3.4 assists in his sophomore season, which was affected by a broken thumb that kept him out for five games and limited him in seven others.

Hartfield, from Benton Harbor High in Michigan, was far more productive his first season, averaging 20.2 points and eight assists. His natural tendency is to be a scoring point guard, but depending on how quickly the freshmen adjust to the college game, he may need to resist that impulse and concern himself with serving as a playmaker.

Had not Jermaine Watts lapsed into academic ineligibility, ending his career at DePaul, the Blue Demons would have returned a proven point guard who averaged 15.9 points and proved many times he could create shots for teammates, even though they couldn't make the shots.

Without him, DePaul will be dependent on Hartfield making a rapid adjustment to major college as a playmaker and leader. "We needed a lead guy, a guy we can really give the basketball to," Kennedy said. "At the point, he's great with the ball, and at the two, he can score. I just love guards like Kerry. Those are the kind of guards I have traditionally had on my teams, so he fits the mold perfectly. As soon as I saw him, I feel in love with him."

The incoming freshman will certainly permit DePaul to quit relying on walkons, guys like 5-11 senior **Jerry Fitzgerald** (1.0 ppg) and 6-2 junior David Bruno (2.5ppg.), and scholarship players like 6-2 senior **Devon Phillips** (3.4 ppg.) and 6-1 sophomore **Brian Cashin** (0.8 ppg).

The two great freshman wings will most likely displace 6-5 junior **DeMarcus Gaines** (6.8 points, 7.9 rebounds) and 6-5 senior **Thomas Cooper** (7.4 points. 4.5 rebounds), but these are players destined to be career reserves at the Conference USA level who instead wound up starting a fair number of games.

Although their starting jobs will be gone, Gaines and Cooper could actually help the Demons to win more games if they do not view playing off the bench as a demotion.

Gaines has decent leaping ability and has grown into a strong, hustling player, but even though he averaged 31 minutes as a junior he never scored more than 13 points. He does not handle the ball well (18 assists, 47 turnovers). Cooper has always been solid as a defender and ballhandler, but he has no shooting touch and still has been forced to fire throughout his career because there was no one else to do it.

In three seasons, Cooper has attempted 220 three-point shots despite making only .245 percent of them.

Cooper can handle either wing position as a defensive specialist and to provide stability. Gaines will be a rebounder filling in at both forward spots when the points are coming freely from other sources but DePaul needs someone to chase the ball on the boards.

DePaul's plans are to use 6-1 senior **Willie Coleman** as a high-quality third guard, subbing for Hartfield at the point and Richardson at shooting guard. Coleman (15.8 ppg, 84 assists) can play both positions and handled the point during the dozen games Watts missed because of injury.

Coleman is not an overwhelming talent, but would be ideal in the reserve role because of his extraordinary competitiveness. It is not easy for a player to maintain intensity when the defeats start numbering in the high teens, but there was Coleman pumping out 19 in a two-point loss to Marquette at the Conference USA tournament and 27 in an overtime defeat at home to Louisville in the final regular season game.

In 30 games, Coleman led the Blue Demons in scoring 20 times and assists 15, and he also was No. 3 in the nation in steals with 100. He is a powerful guard whose three-point shooting will likely go from last season's .351 (71-202) to a more acceptable number in the .400 range once he is surrounded by more threatening offensive players. He certainly is good enough, as well, to handle the starting point guard job if Hartfield fails.

The other option at the point is 5-9 freshman **Rashon Burno**, a product of successful programs at St. Anthony's in Jersey City and the Winchendon School in Massachusetts. He averaged 15 points and 11 assists at Winchendon last season, but increased his scoring to 22 points a game in the second half of the year and alienated some teammates—seven signed at Division I schools—with his shoot-first style.

Kennedy called Burno "the consummate point guard," and Burno did run three consecutive state title teams at St. Anthony's, the latter two winning 61 of 62 games. Although he's just coming into college, Burno already is 20 years old and thus should carry along some degree of maturity, but he doesn't figure to play a great deal unless Plan A gets fouled up.

A year of operating with only 6-8 **Ayinde Avery** (8.2 points, 6.1 rebounds) standing taller than 6-6 convinced Kennedy he needed more than just Williams to address the size issue. Recruiting in that regard did not go exactly as planned.

Power forward Antonio Latimer failed to qualify for freshman eligibility, and the best the Demons could do in their spring search for a center was 6-11 junior Lamar Butler of Polk (Fla.) Junior College. In the 1995-96 season as a part-time player at Loyola (Md.), where Butler played before blowing out his knee and missing a year and then choosing to attend junior college, he averaged 2.3 points and 2.1 rebounds. Kennedy believes recovering from the knee injury has allowed Butler to make progress, but this is still a short-term project.

The Demons were a bit more fortunate to take advantage of the misfortunes of Northeastern Illinois athletes.

1998-99 DEPAUL SCHEDULE

Nov.	13	*New Mexico
	22	@Alabama State
	24	North Carolina-Wilmington
	28	California
Dec.	1	Chicago State
	6-7	#BB&T Classic
	12	Texas-Pan American
	17	@Kansas
	19	@Louisville
	30	@Dayton
Jan.	2	Houston
	6	@Cincinnati
	9	Marquette
	14	UAB
	17	Louisville
	24	@Marquette
	28	@South Florida
	30	@Tulane
Feb.	3	UNC Charlotte
	6	Cincinnati
	11	Saint Louis
	13	Memphis
	18	@Southern Mississippi
	20	@Saint Louis
	24	Duke
	27	@UNC Charlotte
Mar.	3-6	##Conference USA Tournament

@ Road Games
* BCA Classic, Albuquerque, NM
\# Washington, DC (vs. George Washington, first round; also Maryland and Stanford)
\#\# Birmingham-Jefferson Civic Center, Birmingham, AL

Their program was disbanded after last season, which means 6-10, 210-pound senior center **Roman Peoples** is eligible immediately to play his senior year at DePaul. He averaged 6.6 points and 2.8 rebounds while making 10 starts. He had career highs of 17 points and seven rebounds, but it's clear there are limitations to a player whose highest minutes total was 30 despite the fact he is so tall. At least he has Division I experience.

It's unlikely either player will make a huge contribution on his own, but the two combined might be able to help to spell Williams and Avery, who is a junior playing his second season after sitting out as a freshman. There never was a time last season when Avery was not under pressure to avoid foul trouble and to ward off opposing interior defenders. With bigger bodies around him, Avery's quickness and agility should permit him to develop into a player who averages in the 12-point, seven-rebound neighborhood.

"With those two guys and Ayinde, now all of a sudden we've got some bulk, we've got some speed, got some quickness and got some skill people," Kennedy said. "If they gel and get better, we have a shot to be a tournament team. At the same time, we could be talented and youthful and a .500-type team."

adidas Blue Ribbon Analysis

BACKCOURT .... B+ BENCH/DEPTH .... C+
FRONTCOURT .... B INTANGIBLES C

It's only reasonable to assume this will not be an easy process, hence the average rating on the intangibles meter. Kennedy has not yet coached the most important players on this team, and they have not yet played major-college ball. These guys do not have a talented group of veterans to lead them, the way Duke's freshmen did last season, and thus will be counted on to provide so much more.

That said, there aren't many teams that will be putting two better wings on the floor than Richardson and Simmons, and Kentucky showed us in 1996 and Arizona confirmed a year later—not to mention what the Chicago Bulls have accomplished throughout this decade—that great wing players who commit to excellence at both ends of the floor can dominate a game.

Knowing that 1997-98 was a transitional season for DePaul, Kennedy experimented with different schemes on offense and defense to see how they would play in Conference USA. He now says it was "just a great learning process. You learn a lot about yourself as a coach, and that was exciting."

It will be more exciting for Kennedy to know he's not going into a season unarmed. DePaul's biggest adjustment will be on defense, where top talents generally need more time to develop. Kennedy says he prefers to play 94 feet with "a lot of pressure man-to-man and trapping." He also intends to push the ball on offense, using all his ballhanders to run the break.

There also is a problem with a schedule that is far too ambitious: At New Mexico, California, at George Washington, at Kansas. If DePaul can get to its first league game, at Louisville, with a 5-4 record, it will be time to think seriously about whether this is a tournament club. Anything better, and college basketball is in for a revolution.

(M.D.)

HOUSTON

LOCATION .... Houston, TX
CONFERENCE .... Conference USA (National)
LAST SEASON .... 9-20 (.310)
CONFERENCE RECORD 2-14 (5th)
STARTERS LOST/RETURNING 1/4
NICKNAME .... Cougars
COLORS .... Scarlet & White
HOMECOURT .... Hofheinz Pavilion (8,479)
COACH .... Clyde Drexler (Houston '83)
RECORD AT SCHOOL .... First Year
CAREER RECORD .... First Year
ASSISTANTS .... George Walker (Houston '83)
Reid Gettys (Houston '83)
Reid Martinka (Washington '83)
TEAM WINS (last 5 yrs.) 8-9-17-11-9
RPI (last 5 yrs.) 224-219-86-152-224
1997-98 FINISH .... Lost in conference first round.

Clyde Drexler is, without a doubt, the greatest player to grace Conference USA with his presence. But he's not here at Houston to play. He's here to coach.

Many of Drexler's new peers are fond of saying they can't take a shot for their players or go chase rebounds, and he is now similarly constricted.

So what can Drexler do for Houston, aside from convince success-starved Houston fans to buy a few thousand tickets? Can he recruit the sort of players to become Cougars that Bob Huggins is getting to Cincinnati and Tic Price is landing at Memphis and Pat Kennedy is drawing at DePaul? Can he strategize at the same level as Marquette's Mike Deane, Denny Crum of Louisville, Charlie Spoonhour of Saint Louis and Seth Greenberg of South Florida?

This is a fairly exclusive party Drexler has crashed. You could say the same about the NBA, but he prepped to play in the league with a lifetime of practice and three years of high-level competition as a member of the Phi Slamma Jamma squad at Houston. What has he done to prove he can coach?

The truth is, nothing.

It's also true, though, that every assistant who gets a head job also has not proven he can do those things that are exclusively done by head coaches. The assistant may have done them all along, but no one knows to what degree.

"Being in basketball my whole life, I do know a lot of people involved and they are all familiar with you," Drexler told *Basketball Times*. "It's not every day that people get a call from an NBA player. It doesn't take much to get to know people."

Drexler, who retired from the Houston Rockets to accept this job, has brought name-recognition to the Houston coaching position, which surely was missing during the five years Alvin Brooks spent on the bench. Brooks was a nice man and nearly got this thing turned, but a bit of bad luck, the slow death of the Southwest Conference and his own recruiting and coaching mistakes did not help matters.

He left behind some fine athletes and a couple of nice recruits when he was fired last March, but there aren't a whole lot of really good basketball players, which was the Cougars' problem throughout last season.

The turnover numbers are almost staggering. With no true point guard for the final 27 games of a 29-game season, the Cougars averaged 21.8 turnovers and committed nearly two turnovers for every one assist they recorded. They committed 32 against Arkansas-Pine Bluff, for goodness sake.

Clyde Drexler will not solve that problem alone, but **Roy Spears** (4.0 ppg, 6.5 rpg) might be a start. A 6-1 junior recruited to play the point from Shorter College in Arkansas, Spears blew out an ACL after two games, both of which Houston won. He committed six turnovers in his first game, that wild win over Pine Bluff, but in his second time out had six assists and only two turnovers in leading a win against Sam Houston State.

Spears is a strong player who grew up in Memphis and averaged 10.8 points and 7.4 assists in his last full season, as a sophomore at Shorter. He was the only true major-college point guard in the program at the start of last season. Without him, Houston was lost, with no offensive flow, no chance to beat a press. Shamahn McBride, who had been promised a full-time move to shooting guard and averaged 24.5 points when playing alongside Spears, had to accept more ballhandling responsibility and slipped to an 11.4 scoring average by the end of his final season with the Cougars.

With Spears back in the lineup, presuming he's 100 percent healthy, Houston need not embarrass itself once again. Because the skill and direction a solid point guard could bring to this team were the Cougars' most significant deficiencies.

The picture is not entirely golden elsewhere, but it's not entirely grim, especially if you're looking at 6-5 sophomore shooting guard **Chad Hendrick** (8.1 ppg, 4.7 rpg) and 6-9 junior forward **Kenny Younger** (10.0 ppg, 6.6 rpg). They were two of the better first-year players in the league last season, Younger having scarified his freshman season to academic ineligibility.

Younger is an efficient player who ranked eighth in C-USA in field-goal percentage (.488) and is not limited to put-backs and dunks. He has a decent mid-range shot and had the freedom to use it under Brooks. His range does not extend to three-point land, but it could in time.

Like all Houston players, Younger needs some work on his ballhandling skills, but his turnover numbers (91) should decrease simply by not being forced into as many difficult situations. He closed the season with double-figure efforts in six of his final eight games and shot 41 of 74 from the field in that stretch. Younger also showed greater aggression on the boards, with two double-digit games in his last five, indicating he was making significant progress amid all the distress.

Younger has help inside size-wise, but not in terms of production. The other three returning frontcourt players did not average 10 points combined, and none was a particularly effective rebounder or defender. Junior **Early Smith** (3.2 ppg, 2.5 rpg, .543 FG) is a 6-8, 265-pound power forward who never once hit double figures in points or rebounds but only occasionally hit double-figures in minutes, even with Galen Robinson dogging it through his senior year.

Smith transferred from Mississippi State and left little doubt why the Bulldogs had no use for him. But Drexler has some hope. He calls Smith "very capable."

William Stringfellow (3.1 ppg, 3.9 rpg, 12 blocks), a 6-8, 215-pound junior, transferred from Wake Forest and joined the Cougars after the first semester. He also never reached double-figures in points or rebounds and also struggled to get major minutes, averaging less than 15 a game.

Stringfellow is athletic, but not terribly skilled. "William Stringfellow has some incredible abilities that he needs to recognize," Drexler said. "He's a hard worker and a good shot-blocker. I think he can thrive in our system."

The other veteran forward is **Charles Fordjour** (2.5 ppg, 1.8 rpg), a 6-6, 200-pound sophomore who is a fine athlete but has much to learn about how to play. He scored12 points against Cincinnati as the Cougars came back from a 26-point deficit. He also was turnover-prone and shot poorly from the field and can use whatever coaching Drexler and his staff may offer.

Hendrick is less gifted as a player than Younger, but could be the program's most imposing athlete. He started 22 games and hit double-figures nine times, including three of the final four games. He became more confident at the offensive end, attempting double-figure shots in six of the last eight games and making 7 of 15 from three-point range to close out the season after breaking an 0-of-11 slump.

At his size (210 pounds), Hendrick could play small forward in a three-out, two-in look. His passing ability, which resulted in 62 assists as a freshman, might be better utilized in that role than at the shooting-guard spot. "I expect Chad to take a more assertive role," Drexler said. "He has the talent to do more things, and we're going to try to get him to the point where he is very consistent and more effective."

There are two other returning starters, but this is like one of those good news/bad news jokes yearbook preview writers are tempted to drag out each year.

Forward **Willie Moore** (4.5 ppg, 3.2 rpg), a 6-5 junior, is a former walkon who is certainly several steps above walkon level but would not play more than a few minutes a game for any of the league's first-division teams. He is a decent athlete who scored 15 in a game against Cincinnati and 13 against UAB, but his shooting touch (10 of 41 on threes, .313 FG) does not merit the sort of time the Cougars were forced to give him.

Point guard **Treva Cosby** would struggle to play full-time at Texas' abundance of mid-major schools. It must have been his long-range shooting (37 of 108 on threes) that convinced Brooks to offer him a scholarship, because he is abysmal as a ballhandler. He committed 79 turnovers

1998-99 HOUSTON SCHEDULE

Nov.	17	Texas
	21	@Rice
	23	Sam Houston State
	28	Indiana/Purdue-Indianapolis
	30	LSU
Dec.	3	@California
	5	@Sacramento State
	12	@North Carolina State
	22	@Cincinnati
	28-29	#Lobo Invitational
Jan.	2	@DePaul
	7	Southern Mississippi
	9	@UAB
	13	Saint Louis
	17	Memphis
	21	@Southern Mississippi
	23	@Tulane
	30	South Florida
Feb .	4	UAB
	6	@Memphis
	11	@South Florida
	13	Tulane
	16	@Louisville
	23	UNC Charlotte
Mar.	3-6	##Conference USA Tournament

@ Road Games
\# Albuquerque, NM (vs. Portland State, first round; also New Hampshire and New Mexico)
\## Birmingham-Jefferson Civic Center, Birmingham, AL

and passed for only 35 assists despite starting 13 games at the point. His inability to control the ball gave the Houston coaches fits once Spears went down.

If Spears is healthy, Cosby can settle into a spot-shooting role. If there is any reliance on Cosby to run the show for extended periods, the Cougars could be again struggling to hit double-digits in wins.

Most of Houston's better recruits (and better basketball names) will show up in the backcourt, after all. **Gee Gervin**, a 6-2 junior guard who can play either guard spot, was signed from San Jacinto College. He is the son of former San Antonio Spurs great George Gervin. Gee Gervin began his college career at Arizona State, got into trouble there and moved on to San Jac, where he averaged 16.7 points and 3.7 assists last season.

"Gee Gervin plays just like his dad," Drexler said. "He is silky smooth and has a great shooting touch."

That may be a bit of an exaggeration. Gervin was not even one of the top junior college players in the nation, having been selected only second-team all-region, but he is the sort of athlete Houston needs to build depth in the program.

More promising is 6-5 freshman **Moses Malone Jr.**, whose father, you might have guessed, is Moses Malone Sr. He does not play just like his dad, but one aspect of the difference is that he can shoot from the outside. Really shoot.

He made 79 threes as a junior. Malone averaged 25.1 points and 8.5 rebounds at Friendswood (Tex.) High and was generally considered a top 50 recruit.

It's unlikely Malone will come in and begin busting threes like he's Chris Mullin, but it's almost a given that he'll start. The perimeter lineup could be Spears, Malone and Hendrick or Gervin, Malone and Hendrick, but it's hard to imagine there not being a place for Malone in the middle of that mix.

Houston's other recruits were too much like Houston's recruits have been in the last few years. **Justin Wiggins** is a 6-6 sophomore small forward who attended Tulsa, but did not play. As a senior at Episcopal High in Houston, he averaged 18.0 points and 6.7 rebounds and was second-team all-city. **Torrence Botts** is a 6-1 freshman point guard from Clear Brook High in Friendswood, Tex., where he twice was first-team all-district and averaged 15.2 points and 5.6 assists.

Jake Ballis is a 6-8, 230-pound freshman power forward from Stratford High in Houston who averaged 15 points and nine rebounds and chose to walk on with the Cougars. He reportedly was offered scholarships by Hawaii and Pepperdine.

Brooks Bassler, a 6-4, 180-pound sophomore, is walking on after skipping his freshman season at Houston. He averaged 20.2 points and 8.4 rebounds at Rockdale (Tex.) High. Forward **Tega Moceanu**, a 6-7, 235-pound junior, attended College of the Canyons, but left no statistical trail because he did not play. It's not an imposing collection of talent. Drexler has much work to do in retirement.

adidas Blue Ribbon Analysis

BACKCOURT	C-	BENCH/DEPTH	D+
FRONTCOURT	D+	INTANGIBLES	C-

The similarly dreadful current state of Tulane basketball gives Houston some hope it can avoid last place in the National Division in particular and Conference USA in general. But DePaul has lifted itself from the company of these two, which means there'll be one less game that looks winnable on the schedule.

Drexler is promising to play an uptempo game, which his athletes seem suited to do at the defensive end, but moving fast requires guards who can handle the ball at top speeds and think quickly. That seems to be a weakness here.

The offense will mostly have to come from the perimeter, because Younger is the only legitimate inside threat. Drexler will have to figure out how to best utilize his talents. It's problematic to have a big man with mid-range skills when there are so few guys who can be counted upon to chase down his misses. Malone and Gervin at least offer the suggestion of improved perimeter offense, and Hendrick has the ability to improve.

"I guarantee you we will be one of the hardest-working teams in the nation," Drexler said.

That may be the only good thing to say about this program, for now.

(M.D.)

LOUISVILLE

LOCATION .... **Louisville, KY**
CONFERENCE .... **Conference USA (American)**
LAST SEASON .... **12-20 (.375)**
CONFERENCE RECORD .... **5-11 (5th, American)**
STARTERS LOST/RETURNING **1/4**
NICKNAME .... **Cardinals**
COLORS .... **Red, Black & White**
HOMECOURT .... **Freedom Hall (18,865)**
COACH .... **Denny Crum (UCLA '58)**
RECORD AT SCHOOL .... **625-253 (27 yrs.)**
CAREER RECORD .... **625-253 (27 yrs.)**
ASSISTANTS .... **Jerry Eaves (Louisville '86)**
Vince Taylor (Duke '82)
Scott Davenport (Louisville '78)
TEAM WINS (last 5 yrs.) **28-17-19-26-12**
RPI (last 5 yrs.) **9-32-17-17-90**
1997-98 FINISH .... **Lost in conference first round.**

On the list of all-time NCAA Tournament appearances, Louisville trails only Kentucky, UCLA and North Carolina. On the list of Final Fours reached, it's UCLA, North Carolina, Kentucky, Duke, Kansas and Ohio State. Now, the Cardinals are keeping historic company with Kansas, Kentucky and UCLA in another category: Being banned from the NCAA Tournament. Indeed, it's happened to the best of 'em.

Whatever hope Louisville had of immediately bouncing back from last year's first-ever 20-loss season with a 22nd NCAA Tournament appearance for coach Denny Crum was destroyed at 2 p.m. on the afternoon of Sept. 22, when Bonnie Slatton of the NCAA's committee on infractions announced the Cardinals would not be permitted to enter postseason play and would forfeit one scholarship each of the next two seasons because of its second incidence of major rules violations in the last three years.

Crum said he was "saddened by the decision ... I am ultimately responsible for our basketball program, and I feel bad that it has had such a negative effect on our program and this university."

Slatton said Louisville got the tournament ban, a punishment rarely applied in the last half-decade, because of its status as a "repeat violator." The infractions committee essentially said to the Cardinals they'd been let off with a warning the first time, and now there was no choice but to throw the book at them.

So what is there to play for? The Cards cannot compete in the Conference USA Tournament, either. They have had removed the greatest incentive players have to expend extra energy in the pursuit of improvement. It's just a regular season, and that's it. They're coming off a year in which progress always seemed elusive into one in which progress seems almost pointless.

Louisville will again plunge itself into a meat-grinder of a schedule, having apparently learned nothing from the experience of overtaxing last year's overmatched team. The Cardinals played reasonably well in early games against Georgia Tech, North Carolina, Arkansas and Mississippi, and even beat St. John's and Kentucky, but there was never an opportunity to develop confidence or continuity or some idea of how to consistently achieve success.

The Cards learned how to lose, not how to win. Next time you hear a major-college fan complain about that game against Southeastern Louisiana, remember what happened to Louisville in 1998.

How much more difficult will it be to get through those games knowing that whatever RPI points the Cardinals might score by playing those games and winning some will not amount to anything on Selection Sunday?

Louisville remains a reasonably talented basketball team with a few significant weaknesses. Chief among them is point guard, where 6-0 senior **Cameron Murray** (8.8 ppg, 2.0 rpg, 134 assists) is an extremely skilled player who looks like he's been a victim of middle-aged spread. Murray was fit when he was a prep player, but after sitting out a year from competition upon transferring from Southern California to Louisville, he returned puffy and pudgy and unable to keep even mediocre players from beating him into the lane.

Murray was Louisville's most obvious defensive liability, allowing such players as Cincinnati's Michael Horton (17), DePaul's Willie Coleman (27) and Southern Miss' Mel Cauthen (17) to enjoy huge scoring nights—and that was just in the last four games. Murray also was sloppy with the ball, allowing Horton to set a school record with seven steals in a January game at Cincinnati.

Murray can shoot the ball. Surely it runs in the family. His brother Tracy was one of the best shooters in college basketball in the last decade. Cameron hit 38 of 96 from three-point range, but he wasn't nearly tough enough when finishing shots closer to the goal (.412, 96 of 233).

Frustration with Murray even led Crum to start 6-5 sophomore **Jeff McKinley** (1.5 ppg, 0.9 rpg, 28 assists) in four games, and he is no more a point guard than he is a high-major player. McKinley was about even in the assist/turnover department and represented a golden opportunity for exploitation whenever he entered the game.

Crum has turned borderline talents into contributors in the past, but depth of talent allowed them to be hidden in practice until they were ready. You didn't see much of B.J. Flynn or Brian Kiser until they were ready to help. Crum has got three years still to work with this one, but if McKinley is ever to contribute, it will be as a shooting guard. If he's back at the point this year, it can't be good news.

Louisville thus was determined to find someone in spring recruiting to push Murray to compete or push him out of the way, but 6-1 guard Caleb Gervin did not establish freshman eligibility. That leaves only 6-1 sophomore **Travis Best** (0.9 ppg, 1.0 rpg, 13 assists), another player who was a reach in recruiting and is not ready to become a significant performer in Conference USA.

The situation is not so desperate or disappointing at shooting guard, where 6-4 sophomore **Marques Maybin** (10.0 ppg, 1.7 rpg) figures to continue his progress toward becoming an outstanding player. Again, the only problem with Maybin is that he was asked to do too much, too soon. He started his opening game at Louisville, becoming only the 11th player to do that under Crum, but probably the least prepared of all.

Maybin had sat out a full year after failing to become eligible his freshman year, when he had signed at Tennessee. He was thrown into a situation where he had to be a primary offensive option and where even a shoulder problem that bothered him early in the year had to be quickly dismissed.

He did an effective job as a shooter (45 of 118, .381 on threes) but did not appear to know how to use his athletic ability. Maybin can be a high-flying player but needs to perform with greater aggression.

Maybin started because Crum was determined to keep 6-3 senior **Eric Johnson** (7.9 ppg, 2.8 rpg) in reserve. Johnson started just one game last year and has 24 starts in his career. He is an outstanding athlete capable of remarkable shooting streaks, including his eight-of-10 performance (3 of 3 from three-point range) in the Kentucky win at Rupp Arena. He is a big-game player, but an emotional one who tends not to do as well when he perceives there to be an absence of incentive. He scored a combined 16 points the five games that followed Louisville's home loss to UNC Charlotte, which was viewed

1998-99 LOUISVILLE SCHEDULE

Nov.	22	Western Kentucky
Dec.	5	@Mississippi
	7	Towson State
	17	@North Carolina
	19	DePaul
	21	@Dayton
	26	Kentucky
	30	Morgan State
Jan.	2	@Michigan State
	6	Saint Louis
	10	@South Florida
	13	@Marquette
	17	@DePaul
	21	Cincinnati
	23	UCLA
	28	@Saint Louis
	30	UNC Charlotte
Feb.	4	Memphis
	6	Marquette
	11	@UNC Charlotte
	14	Georgia Tech
	16	Houston
	18	@Tulane
	21	@Cincinnati
	25	UAB
	27	@Southern Mississippi
March	3-6	#Conference USA Tournament

@ Road Games
* NABC Classic, RCA Dome, Indianapolis, IN
# Birmingham-Jefferson Civic Center, Birmingham, AL

as the final toll of the bell for the Cardinals, then gunned in 12 in 18 minutes at Cincinnati against the Bearcats in the conference tournament quarterfinals—a game played in his hometown.

Johnson will probably serve in the same role once again this season, backing up Maybin and 6-6 junior small forward **Nate Johnson** (12.3 ppg, 5.9 rpg). He is one of three players eligible to transfer because the sanction period covers the remainder of his eligibility and might have been the most likely to go. But because the penalty was not delivered until late September, and because there's so much administrational nonsense for players in this circumstance to navigate, the NCAA believes it would be unlikely for any such transfer to occur before the semester break. Thus, he plans to stay put.

Kevin Smiley, a junior from Allegany College in Maryland who is originally from Louisville, is a 6-6 junior who is expected to play primarily shooting guard but also may wind up getting some time at the small-forward spot. He averaged 10.1 points, 5.2 rebounds and 3.7 assists for an outstanding JC team that was upset at the NJCAA national tournament. He played strong down the stretch, averaging 16.9 points over the final 13 games, but some scouts who've seen him do not believe Smiley will make a major impact. Louisville also added a walkon who has long-term possibilities: 6-3 **Quintin Bailey**, who averaged 18.1 points, 9.2 rebounds and 2.5 assists at Iroquois High in Louisville and was selected third-team all-state.

If Smiley does not emerge, that should not hurt a great deal, although Louisville needs all the quality players it can get. The Cardinals are reasonably set with Nate Johnson, who regressed as a sophomore but still has the potential to be one of the best players in this league. His work habits slipped terribly as a sophomore, and it was learned he was having some off-court disciplinary problems. He seemed to be distracted by the investigation of his father's hotel stay in Louisville during his freshman year, the incident that led Louisville to be kicked from the tournament this year.

Johnson was rarely the stirring, breakdown offensive player he'd been as a freshman. He averaged 18 point and 6.4 rebounds over the final nine games, but it was almost like he didn't start to try until it didn't matter any longer. Johnson needs to play assertively to matter. He is as effective as any player in the college game at driving the baseline, but his lack of emphasis in that area can be noticed from the fact he attempted the same number of free-throws as in his freshman season even though his shot attempts increased by 60. He was counted upon to be a breakthrough star as a sophomore and instead regressed.

The more one thinks about Johnson's ability, the more one realizes how dangerous it can be not to consider him an all-star candidate. But another year like the last is not going to embarrass any prognosticators. With enthusiasm, Johnson is one of the three or four best players in the league. Without it, he's just good.

And if he's just good, there'll be that much more reason to play 6-7 junior **Tony Williams** (9.1 ppg, 5.0 rpg), who would be a dynamite player on a better team but whose contributions get lost when rolled into another defeat. Limited role players, of which Williams is one, tend to look more limited when employed by losing teams. Williams is not laterally quick and not good with the ball (72 turnovers in 24 minutes a game), but he hustles, blocks out his man on the boards (110 at the defensive end, even though he played a lot at two-guard) and is a terrific three-point shooter (51 of 138) who is difficult to guard because of his height.

There aren't many guys as long as he is who'll stick you as ably from beyond the arc. He is harder to hide on a team that does not guard particularly well, but he may become more dangerous as Louisville presumably upgrades its inside game.

Senior **Alex Sanders** (10.5 ppg, 6.0 rpg), 6-7 and 260 pounds, has played center each of his two seasons with the Cardinals. He has done what he can, but occasionally has shown frustration because of the difficulty of playing against taller players so often inside. Sanders never has become the star he might have if allowed to perform his entire career at power forward.

Sanders passes and shoots the ball well, which does fit the requirements for a center in Louisville's scheme, but opponents who've had reasonably mobile centers have not had a hard time guarding him. He fired too often from three-point range for a player with his bulk and poor accuracy (32 of 104) but part of that probably came from the knowledge that he was too short to get a lot done inside.

There are two juco recruits who may be able to move Sanders to forward: 6-9 junior **Dion Edward** of Westark Community College and 6-9 junior **Tobiah Hopper** of St. Catherine Junior College. Edward is the more likely of the two, a powerful presence who drew serious interest from Cincinnati and Xavier before his academic struggles led them to surrender. Louisville hung in because of its thirst for post players and will be rewarded with a guy who averaged 23.4 points and 8.2 rebounds as a sophomore at Westark and was rated by some analysts as a top-10 prospect.

Edward is mobile and strong and is extremely dangerous when he plays aggressively.

Hopper averaged 20 points and 9.2 rebounds for St. Catherine and also was a top-25 JC player. He considered Tennessee, St. John's and Minnesota, but chose to remain closer to home and become a Cardinal. He is willing to take the three-point shot, like Sanders, but also hit .555 percent from the field and .732 from the free throw line.

The question for either or both will be whether they can adapt to Crum's offense. It is not common and requires players to invest a great deal of concentration in practice. If Edward grasps the system, he could become a capable center for the Cardinals and permit the team to grow out of the size problem that affected the last two teams.

Hajj Turner, a 6-8 redshirt freshman from Charlottesville, Va., was one of the players Crum hoped would do that a year ago, but he tore knee ligaments before the start of the season and spent his freshman year rehabilitating. He averaged 21.5 points and 14.9 rebounds for a bad high school team and is not the caliber athlete that Edward is, but at least he gives Louisville one more big body than filled the practice gym last season.

adidas Blue Ribbon Analysis

BACKCOURT	**C+**	**BENCH/DEPTH**	**C+**
FRONTCOURT	**B-**	**INTANGIBLES**	**B-**

This will be a season to forget for the Cardinals, no matter how many memorable wins they might achieve. There could be a few. This is not a team devoid of talent, no matter how much its detractors screech.

But where is the program headed? Sanders and Eric Johnson are gone after this year, leaving a small stable of decent wing athletes and no apparent future at point guard. Recruiting has not been promising of late.

It seems a shame that Crum's final seasons do not appear to be moving in a positive direction. He is one of three active coaches in the Hall of Fame and the guy who made Final Four appearances the standard by which Louisville basketball is judged—as absurd as that may be.

If Crum can squeeze 16 wins out of this team, it will be one of his supreme achievements in coaching. You are free to bet against him, but it's at your own risk.

(M.D.)

MARQUETTE

LOCATION	**Milwaukee, WI**
CONFERENCE	**Conference USA**
LAST SEASON	**20-11 (.645)**
CONFERENCE RECORD	**8-8 (4th, American)**
STARTERS LOST/RETURNING	**3/2**
NICKNAME	**Golden Eagles**
COLORS	**Blue & Gold**
HOMECOURT	**Bradley Center (19,150)**
COACH	**Mike Deane (Potsdam State '74)**
RECORD AT SCHOOL	**86-40 (4 yrs.)**
CAREER RECORD	**345-187 (18 yrs.)**
ASSISTANTS	**Dan Thiess (Plattsburg State '81)**
	Rob Jeter (UW-Platteville '91)
	Brian Bidlingmyer (Siena '95)
TEAM WINS (last 5 yrs.)	**24-21-23-22-20**
RPI (last 5 yrs.)	**17-58-22-56-62**
1997-98 FINISH	**Lost in NIT third round.**

It is four years into Mike Deane's residence at Marquette, and at last the program is his. It couldn't belong to him until he had his own man at point guard, and he couldn't have his own man until Tony Miller and Aaron Hutchins had passed through.

It is hard to complain about having two such gifted players as Miller and Hutchins in charge of your offense and, indeed, Deane is not. He sometimes itched at Miller's lack of shooting ability and privately bristled at Hutchins lack of cooperation, but always Deane understood his team was in capable hands when those guys were on the floor.

Cordell Henry, though, is a Mike Deane point guard.

1998-99 MARQUETTE SCHEDULE

Nov.	14	@Boston College
	16	Morgan State
	19-20	#Zippy's Invitational
	28	@Dayton
Dec.	1	Northeastern
	4-5	##Blue and Gold Coca Cola Classic
	8	Wisconsin-Milwaukee
	13	South Florida
	19	Baylor
	23	Wisconsin
	31	Illinois-Chicago
Jan.	3	@Cincinnati
	6	@UAB
	9	@DePaul
	13	Louisville
	16	Saint Louis
	21	@UNC Charlotte
	24	DePaul
	28	Tulane
	30	@Saint Louis
Feb.	6	@Louisville
	10	Cincinnati
	13	UNC Charlotte
	21	@Memphis
	24	Southern Mississippi
	27	@Houston
Mar.	3-6	###Conference USA Tournament

@	Road Games
#	Honolulu, HI (vs. Oklahoma State first round; also Hawaii and Nicholls State)
##	Milwaukee, WI (vs. Cornell, first round; also Tulsa and Vermont)
###	Birmingham-Jefferson Civic Center, Birmingham, AL

He wants speed, he wants shooting ability, he wants intelligence and maybe a bit more speed. He wants Marc Brown. He wants Doremus Bennerman. Those are the guards who helped make Deane a success at Siena, who helped bring him to high-major basketball with the Golden Eagles.

Hutchins most certainly could play that style of ball, which is why Marquette was so outstanding when he did through most of the 1995-96 season, through the Conference USA Tournament in '97 and the first 10 games of '97-98. But there always was something holding Hutchins back, whether it was injuries or attitude or some combination of the two.

Henry, a freshman, arrives with no such baggage. He isn't big enough to carry it, for one thing. He is 5-9, 160 pounds, but was big enough to direct Whitney Young High in Chicago to a 31-1 record and the Illinois AA championship. Although he averaged 13.7 points and 4.0 assists, he was chosen second-team all-state in one of the richest years for talent in Illinois' recent history.

"Cordell's not strong by any means, but he's a very good athlete," Deane said. "Cordell is a guy that can get people excited because of his explosiveness and his speed. He's a guy that can run the break. He's unselfish, and yet he can score."

He also is an astonishing athlete, graced not only with the quickness you might expect, but also explosive leaping ability. "He has the highest vertical jump of any player I've been around," Deane said. "He can dunk it anyway you want it. It's amazing how high he can jump. He's a guy you can't press because he can dribble through the thing."

Deane is not yet conceding that Henry will be his starting point guard from day one, but consider that his other option is 6-5 junior **Bart Miller** (1.1 ppg), who passed for precisely one assist as a sophomore and averaged 3.1 minutes in 15 games. Miller may be sufficient to give Henry an adequate backup, but even that is in question. If Henry does not open the year in charge of the Golden Eagles, the early part of the season will tell little about their future.

"Any time you come into the season without a proven point guard, you're concerned," Deane said. But going in with a promising point guard is preferable to going in with one who has no opportunity to excel.

Having Henry on the floor will make it more difficult for Marquette to play its patented man-to-man defense this season, because teams that wish to exploit his size can attempt to post up their point guards, as Cincinnati could do with Michael Horton or UAB could with LeAndrew Bass. That's OK, because it wasn't Deane who owned the patent.

He came to Marquette with a reputation as an exceptional offensive coach, but the nature of the players left behind dictated an emphasis on defense. The Golden Eagles led the nation in field goal defense in 1996-97, playing the physical man-to-man that former coach Kevin

O'Neill preferred. Deane has always liked to use matchup zone, but needs more quickness and athletic ability to make it proficient. His current roster will be better able to do use that scheme, although it's still got a ways to go before that is a full-time tactic.

Marquette still has more big, burly centers than most leagues, but they serve the Golden Eagles well. **Jarrod Lovette** (10.8 ppg, 6.9 rpg), a 6-10 senior, has been among C-USA's most underrated players from the moment he arrived. He has an exceptional shooting touch (he made11 three-pointers last year)) and understands the game and his role in it.

Lovette knows how to use his feet to defend the post and establish position on offense and is especially good at using his body for rebounding position, although he's not quick to the ball. He will not have nimble Richard Shaw beside him this season, which will probably mean less shot-blocking help but more assistance in the rebounding department.

"I think the only thing that happens with Jarrod is what experience adds to it," Deane said. "He'll be there every night. He comes to play. You talk about centers in the league, I don't think there's anybody better. In terms of size, shooting the ball, low-post scoring—he can do some things."

What Deane wants from Lovette is better conditioning, which always has been a problem. Lovette tends to need a blow every three or four minutes, which didn't work badly when Shaw was around. Lovette sat out 13 minutes on the average night one year ago, but even with two decent backups, that's not what Marquette needs. He needs to be able to go seven minutes at a time, and toward that end is working to begin the season at 245 pounds, down about 10 pounds from his typical playing weight.

The reserves behind him both have size: 6-11, 255-pound sophomore **Greg Clausen** (2.1 ppg, 2.3 rpg) and 6-10, 225-pound sophomore **John Mueller** (0.9 ppg, 1.4 rpg).

Mueller was a walkon whom Deane planned to redshirt last season, but he wound up playing in 17 games. Mueller is a long way from being a top-line C-USA player, or even a second-rank C-USA player, but he is there to provide what Deane wants: Another big body in case of emergency and someone with enough physical promise to perhaps become a significant contributor.

Mueller is reasonably athletic for a player his size. He grabbed a rebound for every 2.6 minutes on the floor, which was by far the best figure for any Marquette big man. His rebounds were split almost evenly between the offensive and defensive ends, indicating an eagerness to chase the ball wherever it was available.

Clausen does not have Mueller's feet, but has a body that looks like it was made to be worn by a 10-year NBA backup center. He is rugged-looking, powerful and needs only to use that body to its full effect to be an important player for the Golden Eagles this season. He is the more logical choice to use for the purpose of spelling Lovette. Clausen averaged 8.1 minutes per game as a freshman and shot well from the floor (.523 percent).

He is not as agile as Shaw was, or Mueller is now, so it'll be tougher for Deane to play two big men at once, as he often did the last three seasons. But that fits more toward the idea of using a quicker team and playing the matchup zone.

Marquette has options at the power forward spot it has not had in recent years. Faisal Abraham was a very capable player in years past, but always limited offensively. Deane hopes 6-7, 215-pound freshman **Jon Harris** of Edwardsville, Ill., and 6-7, 210-pound freshman **Oluoma Nnamaka** of Uppsala, Sweden, will provide similar athleticism to Abraham, but more offensive skill.

Harris averaged 21.8 points and 14.0 rebounds and was the *St. Louis Post-Dispatch* Player of the Year. The most promising aspect of his resume, perhaps, was his success in tryouts for the U.S. team in the Junior World Championship qualifying tournament, the team top DePaul recruits Quentin Richardson and Bobby Simmons dominated. Harris made it out of the tryouts and was one of the final players cut.

Nnamaka made the Swedish national team—the only player under 19 to do so. He may be the best athlete and best defender on the roster, and his experience in high-level international competition could make him extremely well-prepared to begin a Division I career. He appears to be most likely to start at the big forward spot, but Harris will push him for the job.

"They're men, physically, and that's usually the biggest drawback for freshmen," Deane said. "We're asking questions of athletes now, instead of big, strong guys. Maybe we're not as good defensively, because we're not as big, but now, you can be a little bit better offensive club."

If it's not a freshman starting a power forward, it will be 6-8, 235-pound junior **John Polonowski** (1.8 ppg, 0.9 rpg) who gets the job. But Marquette has waited through three years—one of them spent as an injury redshirt—waiting for him to play to his potential.

Deane spoke before Polonowski's freshman season about how underrated he was because of his deceptive athletic ability and pure basketball skills. Now the "under" word for Polonowski is "underachiever."

"This is a year we're hoping he can give us more," Deane said. "Certainly, the opportunity is there at the four spot, and he has some athletic abilities and skills. He's a big question mark in all of our minds. He's certainly a guy we'd love to get something out of."

The small forward spot remains problematic for Deane, as it has since Roney Eford concluded his career. **Mike Bargen** (6.7 ppg, 4.4 rpg), a 6-7 senior, started there last season, but does not play with the confidence necessary to produce to the level of his talent. His .398 shooting and particularly his .323 three-point accuracy are far below what he ought to manage.

Bargen has a sweet stroke and does not fire a lot of improvised threes, so the percentage ought to be closer to .400. But no one makes shots if he's wondering whether they might go in, and this has been Bargen's problem throughout his time at Marquette. On an all-star tour of Europe he took with Deane as coach last summer, he was the team's second-leading scorer, playing a much freer, more versatile game in which he scored from many spots on the floor and even dunked a few.

"I don't know how good he's supposed to be, but he's been a solid player for us," Deane said. "Mike's done exactly what he is asked to do. He's probably an ideal sixth man, but he's had to start. He could go from six a game to a solid 10. That would be tremendous."

In the time Bargen is not at the small-forward spot, it could be manned by either one of the freshman power forwards (an unlikely scenario) or 6-5 sophomore **Brian Wardle** sliding up from his spot at shooting guard. Wardle figures to start in the backcourt alongside his former AAU teammate, Henry, after a rookie year in which he was named to the C-USA All-Freshman team and was the league's sixth-man of the year. There are other options at this spot, though, which could lead to more of a three-out, two-in type of alignment.

Deane loves Wardle, although there are some who follow the league who wonder what he sees. His detractors can point to Wardle's .356 field goal percentage and .293 three-point shooting, and often do. They also look at him and see someone who does not appear to be laterally quick or slick enough to get to the basket or to defend athletic shooting guards.

In fact, it was Wardle who defended UNC Charlotte point guard Sean Colson in the league tournament and held him to 2-of-12 shooting and five points, although Marquette eventually lost the game by eight. "Brian Wardle was the best defender on our team," Deane said.

The only player who would keep Wardle from starting in the backcourt is 6-2 junior **John Cliff** (5.3 ppg, 1.6 rpg), who spent last year living off the memory of his three-point outburst against Cincinnati in the 1997 league tournament. Cliff is strong and has terrific range, but he was only 33 of 110 (.300) as a sophomore. He is not a great ballhandler on offense, but can lock up an opponent when he concentrates at the defensive end.

Through the summer and preseason, Cliff was playing exceptionally well, causing Deane to consider using him as a starter. **David Diggs**, a 6-4 freshman from Dayton, Ohio, is another option at that position. He averaged 25.3 points and 10.3 rebounds and is a brilliant student, which should make his mental transition to the college game go smoothly. Diggs is not an exceptional athlete, but in time should be an effective addition to the Golden Eagles.

"That's our most solid position," Deane said. "We're solid there, and we're solid there for a couple years. I'm excited about these kids. I love the attitude. I recognize we've got some work to do. I'm looking at this as more a two-year mission than a one-year mission. We're looking at the big picture, but we'll take it a day at a time."

adidas Blue Ribbon Analysis

BACKCOURT .... **B-** **BENCH/DEPTH** .... **B-**
FRONTCOURT .... **C+** **INTANGIBLES** .... **B+**

Marquette has 16 games on the schedule before Jan. 9, a scheduling trick that would have worked better last year—when Hutchins was healthy before the Christmas break—than it will now that so much of the team is inexperienced.

At this point, Deane is not certain which of his young players will fit where and who is ready to make a quick transition to the college game. And some of the freshmen will have to play.

"We will be better athletically, but still the biggest team in the league," Deane said. "I think this team will look different than the other teams we've had. We will be able to play four skilled guys at once, rather than three."

Marquette could easily ride strong rookie seasons from Henry and one or both of the power forwards and Deane's coaching acumen to a first-division finish in Conference USA. That would not be a shock. But the offensive inconsistency from Bargen and occasionally Wardle leaves some questions about whether this team is ready for that.

Wardle is likely to have a fine sophomore season, lifting his percentages to more respectable levels, but will that be enough for the Golden Eagles to make a run at the NCAA Tournament? Probably not this year. They have won 20 games for six consecutive seasons, something only seven other programs have matched or exceeded currently. That will be tough to extend another year, although there is a strong possibility this will be an NIT team once again.

(M.D.)

SAINT LOUIS

LOCATION .... **St. Louis, MO**
CONFERENCE .... **Conference USA (American)**
LAST SEASON .... **22-11 (.666)**
CONFERENCE RECORD .... **11-5 (3rd)**
STARTERS LOST/RETURNING **1/4**
NICKNAME .... **Billikens**
COLORS .... **Blue & White**
HOMECOURT .... **Kiel Center (20,000)**
COACH .... **Charlie Spoonhour (Ozarks '61)**
RECORD AT SCHOOL .... **106-74 (5 yrs.)**
CAREER RECORD .... **304-155 (15 yrs.)**
ASSISTANTS **Greg Lackey (Southern Mississippi '80)**
Derek Thomas (Missouri-St. Louis '89)
Jay Spoonhour (Pittsburgh State '94)
TEAM WINS (last 5 yrs.) **23-23-16-11-21**
RPI (last 5 yrs.) **43-36-89-172-42**
1997-98 FINISH .... **Lost in NCAA second round.**

Why are the Billikens here? This is what so many want to know. And they're not wondering why the Billikens are here rather than in the front of the book among the nation's elite teams. No, they want to know why the Bills are in the book at all. They want to know why Saint Louis is bothering to field a team now that Larry Hughes has done his 100-meter dash through the program.

There are so many who knee-jerk figure this team is history because Hughes entered the NBA draft after one of the best freshman seasons any college player enjoyed this decade. Indeed, between his points and assists, Hughes accounted for better than 37 percent of SLU's offense last season, and he also averaged 5.1 rebounds. Everything he did offensively enabled his teammates to operate with greater freedom and confidence. He was as important to Saint Louis as any single player was to any team that reached the NCAA Tournament one year ago. So Saint Louis will not be able to replace him. But it may survive him.

"I don't think you do it with any one person or one thing," said coach Charlie Spoonhour. "You have to get everybody to pull a little bit more of the load. Hopefully, some of the people here will have some of the characteristics he had."

Hughes, a 6-5 guard, averaged 20.9 points, more than double what any other Saint Louis player managed. He scored 40 against Marquette, 30 against UAB, 32 against Louisville and 37 against UAB. He was kept out of double-figures only once in 32 games. He was not an ideal long-range shooter, hitting only .290 on three-pointers, but had his percentages depressed because he was forced to generate offense at all times.

Without him, Saint Louis is an entirely different operation, but that doesn't guarantee it will collapse. It's important to remember Hughes was not the only reason the Billikens' freshman class last season was so highly regarded and that Spoonhour has made a career of doing more with less.

If there is a single reason to be optimistic about this team beyond Spoonhour—and it's only fair there should be, because Mike Deane and Denny Crum are certainly proven coaches, as well—it is 6-9, 235-pound sophomore forward **Matt Baniak**.

With a freshman year in which he averaged 8.7 points and 5.0 rebounds, Baniak only hinted at what he is capable of doing with more playing time and more responsibility. He was chosen to the Conference USA All-Freshman team along with Hughes, shooting .537 from the floor and

1998-99 SAINT LOUIS SCHEDULE

Nov.	13	Arkansas State
	20	@Illinois
	23	@San Francisco
	27-29	#Big Island Invitational
Dec.	5	Grambling
	12	Fullerton State
	15	@Southern Illinois
	20	UNC Charlotte
	23	Kansas
	28	Kansas State
Jan.	2	Southwest Missouri State
	6	@Louisville
	9	Tulane
	13	@Houston
	16	@Marquette
	20	South Florida
	23	@Cincinnati
	28	Louisville
	30	Marquette
Feb.	3	Southern Mississippi
	6	@UNC Charlotte
	8	Murray State
	11	@DePaul
	14	Cincinnati
	18	@Memphis
	20	DePaul
	27	@UAB
Mar.	3-6	##Conference USA Tournament

@ Road Games
# Hilo, HI (vs. Evansville, first round; also Hawaii-Hilo and Washington)
Birmingham-Jefferson Civic Center, Birmingham, AL

blocking a shot a game. Baniak has excellent feet and large hands and plays a rugged game. He faces the basket well, but needs to refine his moves after he catches the ball in the post. He still moves a little mechanically in that circumstance, and the slow development of his move allows the defense to react appropriately.

"If we hadn't had Larry Hughes, people would have thought Matt had a great freshman year," Spoonhour said. Without Hughes, Baniak will unquestionably have to be an offensive target, a player who can catch the ball inside and break down a defense or flash away from the lane to receive a pass and launch a shot.

Baniak played less than 24 minutes a game last season, but he should be a 30-plus player this season. The question is whether he'll operate at power forward or center.

If Banika lines up at forward, Saint Louis can field a big team with 6-11 sophomore **Chris Heinrich** (4.3 ppg, 3.0 rpg) at center. The two only occasionally played together last season, but Heinrich made decent progress at the close of his rookie year, playing his finest game of the season in the NCAA Tournament loss to Kentucky: 16 points, 10 rebounds, both tops among the Billikens.

"The idea has got some merit," Spoonhour said about playing a big lineup. "I think Baniak has the ability to go out away from the basket. The whole thing has to be, can they handle the basketball away from the goal?"

Spoonhour likes Heinrich's shooting touch. Heinrich has an ideal frame and simply needs to smooth away his rough edges. He is not in the best condition at all times. He tends to bump into opponents underneath the basket, causing foul problems. He is not polished with the ball and passed for only 10 assists in 501 minutes. But like Baniak, he will use his body to accomplish what is necessary. He is not a Kaspars Kambala inside, but Heinrich does not back away from contact.

The two of them and 6-8 fifth-year senior **Ryan Luechtefeld** (9.8 ppg, 5.7) form a reasonable post rotation. A former walkon, Luechtefeld started all 33 games as a junior and showed himself to be as versatile and competitive as Spoonhour could hope for him to be. Luechtefeld shoots well from three-point range (25-of-72, .347), passes nicely (78 assists) and picked up 34 steals despite not having the game's quickest hands or feet. He understands how to play. He is not the most physical player, and thus there are times he can be taken advantage of on defense, but he rarely allows his man to be a difference-maker.

To complement these three, Saint Louis signed 6-10, 225-pound freshman **Chris Braun** of Waterloo, Ill. (15.0 ppg, 8.0 rpg). He is an excellent free-throw shooter (84 percent). Spoonhour believes Braun "has the potential to be a fine player." But that moment has not arrived, and Saint Louis does not need it now. He will have time to learn.

Saint Louis has another option if Spoonhour is uncomfortable playing big, although it will not become available until the second semester: 6-6 sophomore forward **Justin Tatum**, who sat out last season after battling the NCAA to achieve freshman eligibility. He is a former prep teammate of Hughes at Christian Brothers College H.S., averaging 20 points, 10 rebounds and four assists as a senior. He is probably the most athletic forward Spoonhour has coached with the Billikens.

Tatum is not a great shooter, which is why he could end up playing inside. He's got the feet to guard small forwards, though, and conceivably could team with Heinrich and Baniak on the most physically powerful front line in Spoonhour's half-dozen years with the Billikens.

If you don't believe in the interior guys, you probably aren't falling for the idea that Saint Louis will be good. The nature of the team almost certainly has to change. Not dramatically, but at least slightly.

Spoonhour still believes in the guys he'll have on the wings: 6-5 freshman **Charles Cranford**; 6-2 junior **Justin Love**; and 6-4 senior **Virgel Cobbin** (8.0 ppg, 2.2 rpg). He'll cut them loose on Conference USA opponents with orders to attack the goal with the same abandon as Hughes, although they'll come one at a time, whereas Hughes looked like he was three guys at once.

Cranford, who played last season at St. Thomas More prep school in Connecticut, averaged 22 points, seven rebounds and four assists before missing part of February and all of March to recover from an ankle injury. Cranford, considered one of the top 10 players in prep school by analyst Clark Francis, "has had an outstanding offensive career to this point," Spoonhour said.

Cranford, who averaged 33 points as a high school junior at Cardozo in New York City, will be getting the ball with some opportunities to create offense for himself and occasionally for teammates. In that way, he'll be similar to Hughes. But "to put undue pressure on him and to think he's going to take Larry Hughes' role would be unfair to him. He will still need to adjust to the way we do things and to major-college basketball," Spoonhour said. "He can take the ball, go to the goal, dribble, go places. It'll take him a little while to understand, but his skills complement the way we do things."

Cobbin (8.0 ppg, 2.2 rpg) has never averaged more than 9.2 points, and that was in his freshman season, but he recovered his long-range touch after a dismal sophomore season and hit .423 from three-point range as a junior. He also improved his efficiency inside the line, although he rarely tried anything that wasn't a three—only 59 shots in 33 games.

"He doesn't make many mistakes, because he's a conservative player," Spoonhour said. It is likely Cobbin will move into the shooting guard spot, where he can work to position himself behind the arc while the wing forward and point guard initiate the offense. Spot-shooting is extremely important in Spoonhour's scheme and is something Cobbin does as well as most anyone in C-USA.

Love was the co-player of the year among California junior colleges, averaging 22 points, six rebounds and five assists. He is a fine shooter, having hit 83 percent from the line as a freshman and 53 percent from the field that year. "He's always been the guy that hits the big shot," Spoonhour said. "He's always done things at a high level of success.

Love will be able to spell 5-11 senior **Jamall Walker** at the point, but Walker has been with the Bills four seasons and is unlikely to be handing off his job after 60 career starts. If Love is as ready for Division I as Spoonhour believes he is, he'll be able to get minutes at both guard spots with an emphasis on scoring points for the Bills.

This is the problem Saint Louis faced before Hughes, and thus it has to solve once again now that he's gone.

Walker (6.1 ppg, 2.2 rpg, 128 assists) has been nothing if not steady during his career at Saint Louis. Never great. Never awful. He does not create a lot, but does not undo a lot. He was just short of two assists for every one turnover committed, but averaged only 3.9 assists—even with Hughes at his side.

Walker has been the very definition of OK. He can be better than that—at the least, pretty good—but he must be more aggressive about feeding the post and more selective about when to attempt three-pointers. Saint Louis has a fairly large collection of OK players. There's not much bad to say about 6-4 junior **Troy Robertson**, but not a lot of good, either. He hit .478 on three-pointers, but played only 13 minutes a game because he played the same position as Hughes. If he accepts the challenge, he could make it difficult for Cranford and Love to get playing time early.

Robertson is not exceptionally quick, though, and turns over the ball far too often (one a game while not even playing half the game). He has a thick frame and plays aggressively around the basket but appears most likely to keep a role similar to last year's.

Spoonhour also found extensive use last season for 6-7 junior forward **Larry Simmons** (2.7 ppg, 1.4 rpg in 11.6 minutes) and 6-1 junior guard **John Redden** (3.5 ppg, 2.4 rpg in 16.6 minutes).

Simmons has offensive potential and scored 15 points against Southern Illinois, but he's not been able to stay on the court long enough to make extensive use of a decent shooting touch. Redden is outstanding as a ball-pressure defender. His strength and quickness facilitated 35 steals, and he easily would have ranked among the best in C-USA had he not missed 10 games with a broken foot.

The odd thing about Redden is that it's offensive ability that keeps him off the floor, and yet he made 6 of 15 from three-point range for a .400 percentage.

If he can improve his comfort with the ball, Redden could easily be a 25-minute player. It's more likely he'll again be used as a defensive stopper; in fact, that role will be more important with so many inexperienced players in the backcourt and Hughes not around to outscore the other guys.

There will not be enough playing time for all of SLU's perimeter recruits, and the ones who figure to be fighting hardest to be noticed are 6-4 junior **Dave Fergerson** of San Jose City College and 6-5 freshman **Drew Diener** of Goodrich High in Fond du lac, Wisc.

Fergerson averaged 13.6 points and 5.2 assists for a junior college team that won 63 consecutive games. If Love is uncomfortable at the point, Fergerson will become the backup there. "We've lacked the quickness to slash to the basket, other than Hughes. He can take the ball and go by people," Spoonhour said.

Diener averaged 20 points and 7.4 rebounds and was twice chosen all-state. He is considered to be an outstanding shooter—he made 170 three-pointers and hit .427 from three-point range for his career.

"I like the mix of guys we've got," Spoonhour said. "I think Hughes' presence helped us recruit a couple kids with size, and the guys who came in, who we thought would fit around Larry, are going to have to assume a little more of the load more quickly."

adidas Blue Ribbon Analysis

BACKCOURT .... **B-** **BENCH/DEPTH** .... **B**
FRONTCOURT .... **B+** **INTANGIBLES** .... **B+**

After a couple years of regression, Hughes allowed Saint Louis basketball to start moving forward again. Certainly if he still were with the team, it would be racing ahead this season, but that does not mean the progress must be aborted because of his departure. How many times have we seen teams with a star player continue to function well after he left for the NBA?

"I think we have some people coming in with the ability to score," Spoonhour said. "The thing I don't want to do is put too much pressure on a Justin Love or Ricky Cranford. I think those kids can put some points up. I think they'll be pretty significant additions."

With Diener's shooting ability and decent work from Love and Cranford, Saint Louis figures to be an improved three-point team. Last year's team hit .354, which was third in C-USA, but its 183 three-pointers ranked fourth in a poor-shooting league.

Most important is that Saint Louis finds a way to improve defensively and to get as much as possible out of its big players. Its .429 defensive field-goal percentage last season was better than in some recent years when the Bills were smaller, but now that they're deeper they should play more aggressively. They've been among the worst rebounding teams in the league forever, and using Heinrich and Baniak in tandem would easily solve that concern.

"I've seen us picked anywhere from dead to dying," Spoonhour said. OK, so call it a miracle if you see the Billikens in the NCAA Tournament next spring. But it could happen.

(M.D.)

adidas Blue Ribbon Analysis

GRADING SYSTEM

A+	equal to very best in country—Final Four-caliber unit
A	among the best in the land—worthy of deep NCAA run
B+	talented, versatile and experienced—NCAA-NIT ability
B	solid and productive winners—league and post-season contenders
C+	average to above-average—may contend in a weaker league
C	average to mediocre—second division in a strong league
D+	below average, inconsistent—second division in a weaker league
D	well below average—losing season virtually certain
F	non-Division I ability—an underdog every night

SOUTH FLORIDA

LOCATION .... **Tampa, FL**
CONFERENCE .... **Conference USA (National)**
LAST SEASON .... **17-13 (.567)**
CONFERENCE RECORD .... **7-9 (3rd)**
STARTERS LOST/RETURNING **1/4**
NICKNAME .... **Bulls**
COLORS .... **Green & Gold**
HOMECOURT .... **Sun Dome (10,044)**
COACH ...... **Seth Greenberg (Fairleigh Dickinson '78)**
RECORD AT SCHOOL .... **25-31 (2 yrs.)**
CAREER RECORD .... **130-101 (8 yrs.)**
ASSISTANTS .... **David Zimroth (Florida State '78)**
Jimmy Dixon (District of Columbia '83)
Mike Madagan (Northern Illinois '88)
TEAM WINS (last 5 yrs.) **10-18-12-8-17**
RPI (last 5 yrs.) **125-81-152-213-119**
1997-98 FINISH .... **Lost in conference first round.**

There are those in the college basketball world who figure they know two things about the game as it will exist this season in the Tampa Bay area: South Florida will host the Final Four there this season, and the Bulls will not be crashing their own party. Ah, but they're getting closer.

Not since 1992 has USF made an appearance in the NCAA Tournament, but that could change this year, if everything goes just right. If not, the Bulls are almost certainly bound for postseason play in the NIT and would be expected to make the big show in 2000.

It is fairly remarkable to see that these things are possible so soon after coach Seth Greenberg took over a program that resembled a building burned to the ground. In 1996-97, he had one legitimate Division I player returning from the previous season_and the situation was so dire Greenberg had to turn Brian Lamb from a promising shooting guard into a passable point guard.

Last season, with three freshmen playing major roles and another making periodic appearances, South Florida executed a 15-game turnaround_nine more wins, six fewer defeats_and fell just short of an NIT bid. There are only two seniors on this squad, and the starting lineup is likely to average less than two years of experience.

There is, however, for the first time in many years, serious depth of talent on this club. USF has somewhere between seven and nine players who could contribute to any team in the league. (Which is to say, they could crack the rotations at Memphis or Cincinnati).

"We'll be better," Greenberg said. "I'm cautiously optimistic. I think we'll have good athletes, more depth. You're talking about some hard-playing, athletic kids that can make some things happen.

"You look at where we were two years ago, and look where we are today, as a school that people don't wake up at night and say, 'I want to go to South Florida.' My goal is to get to where people do say that."

B.B. Waldon already did.

Waldon is a 6-7 freshman wing from Kathleen High in Lakeland, Fla., rated among the nation's top 35 prep seniors last season by HoopScoop, ESPN and Bob Gibbons' All-Star Sports. The third-team *Parade* All-American is probably the most highly regarded player ever recruited by South Florida, which is important, but he also could bring to this team the injection of offensive dynamism necessary to lift it toward the 20-win plateau.

The Bulls played hard and physically and held opponents to .417 shooting despite blocking only 90 shots, which ranked eighth in Conference USA and was the lowest number among the top five field goal defense teams in the league. But one team you could always count on shooting worse than USF's opponents was USF.

Its .393 shooting percentage was third from the bottom in the league. No regular recorded an acceptable figure from the floor. No one. The best was Chonsey Asbury's .433. No kidding.

So what Waldon might be able to do for the Bulls could approximate what Larry Hughes did for Saint Louis in his freshman season. The presence of Hughes as a scoring threat made the Billikens as a group far more productive, and though Waldon is not Hughes, he is coming into a situation where the players are bigger, stronger and more experienced.

"He does so many things well. There's not a facet of the game that he doesn't excel at, at some level," Greenberg said. "He'll post you up, step you out. He rebounds. For a young player, he has a very complete game.

"I think he's got to come to the gym every day with a lunch bucket and carve out some space for himself. I'm not giving anyone anything. You're not walking in here and claiming a position."

This is more a matter of fact than a matter of concern. Greenberg expects Waldon to fight for a job. "The kid is about winning. There are a lot of guys who play the game and aesthetically they look good, but at the end of the game they have one less point than the other team. That's not him."

Teaming with fellow recruit **Altron Jackson**, Waldon led his Tampa Stars team to a victory at the AAU 22-and-under national tournament this summer, even though both of them are well under 22. He averaged 26.9 points and 12.2 rebounds for a 22-8 Kathleen team this year. The year before, he led Kathleen to a 4-A state title.

Waldon is almost certain to start, but whether it's at the shooting guard or small forward spot depends upon his adjustment to the college game and how he best works into the lineup.

Jackson, a 6-6 forward, also figures in among USF's top eight players. He is a slasher who averaged 29 points and 10 rebounds at Sarasota's Riverview High and was a top 100 prospect in a number of recruiting lists. "To me, he's a young Lucious Harris," Greenberg said. He likes that comparison a lot and has made it on many occasions. Harris started for Greenberg's Long Beach State teams in the early 1990s and has been in the NBA several season as a rugged, intense shooting guard.

"I think both kids ... people had no clue of how good they were going to be," Greenberg said. "They're both very skilled and can really excel on the defensive end."

The playing time will be more difficult for Jackson to gain because he faces competition from such veterans as 6-6 sophomore **Chonsey Asbury** (9.0 ppg, 4.0 rpg), 6-7 sophomore **Artha Reeves** (4.0 ppg, 3.7 rpg) and 6-4 sophomore **Cedric Smith** (9.8 ppg, 4.9 rpg).

Smith will continue to play both wing positions, and Asbury and Reeves will play both forward spots. Each of them is more experienced and probably more physical than Jackson, though not as purely talented.

Asbury had an excellent freshman year, improving with each game and leading the Bulls in scoring in C-USA games (11.2). He scored 20 points in two of his final five games, including the season-ender against Louisville. He is the sort of player who helps a team win, more than the kind who'll make one win on his own. Asbury is not a great perimeter shooter, but uses his strength well and is a ferocious offensive rebounder. He got nearly twice as many boards at that end of the court as on defense. He is likely to be a primary beneficiary of whatever lift Waldon can give to the USF offense.

Reeves began the season as a starter, but eventually was beaten out by Asbury and will have to work hard to get back playing time. Greenberg likes his athleticism and his mid-range shooting, but strength and injuries were problems his first year. Reeves broke his thumb in late February and missed the close of the season, save one minute against Louisville in the league tournament.

There was a point during the season when Reeves was rebounding very well. He got 12 against Michigan State and Rice, 11 against St. Francis (N.Y.) and eight against Ohio State and Rutgers. But that slipped as competition began to become consistently more stern. Greenberg believes Reeves might have hit the wall and has little doubt he'll be a significant contributor this season.

Waldon fits most comfortably into Smith's position, but taking Smith out of the mix does not appear to be an option. "We'll find a place for Cedric Smith," Greenberg said. Rightfully so. Smith made 40 threes as a freshman and shot .323 from long distance. This does not make him a proficient shooter, but it makes him better than most at USF, and you have to figure maturity, strength and a more fluid offense will lift that toward a more respectable number, say something between 36-38 percent.

His long arms are suited to Greenberg's preference for physical defense and he chases the ball on the boards as well as most any shooting guard in America. "He was the silent but effective member of our freshman class," Greenberg said. "He came in with no expectation and left with no adulation.

But how many freshmen averaged 10 points, five rebounds and two steals?"

Greenberg also has available 6-4 junior transfer **Sam Sanders**, who comes to USF from Rutgers, where he played two seasons. Sanders scored 12 points in a visit to the Sun Dome in 1996-97 and averaged 5.1 points and 5.3 rebounds that season.

With those six players to man the perimeter, USF stacks up as well as just about any team in the league, rivaling top picks Memphis and Cincinnati. The problem is that the Bulls have not made as much progress as yet in recruiting the point and post.

1998-99 SOUTH FLORIDA SCHEDULE

Nov.	21	@Texas
	24	Central Michigan
Dec.	2	@Duquesne
	5	Florida Atlantic
	13	@Marquette
	17	*Central Florida
	19	**Tennessee
	22	Long Island
	29	Austin Peay
Jan.	2	@Cleveland State
	7	Memphis
	10	Louisville
	13	@Southern Mississippi
	16	UAB
	20	@Saint Louis
	23	@Memphis
	28	DePaul
	30	@Houston
Feb.	2	@Florida State
	6	@Tulane
	11	Houston
	13	Southern Mississippi
	18	@UAB
	20	@UNC Charlotte
	25	Cincinnati
	27	Tulane
Mar.	3-6	#Conference USA Tournament

@ Road Games
* Tropicana Field, St. Petersburg, FL
** Tampa Bay Shootout, Tampa, FL
\# Birmingham-Jefferson Civic Center, Birmingham, AL

Power forward **Raheim Brown** could help in that regard. A 6-9, 200-pound redshirt freshman from Orlando, he broke his leg and missed last season and then in June tore the meniscus in the same leg. He had arthroscopic surgery and missed three weeks of workouts. Brown runs well and is a capable shooter. He averaged 26.3 points, 10.4 rebounds and once made five consecutive three-pointers in a high school game.

He may be the best shot-blocker on the roster, which isn't saying much, but it could add a bit more defensive bite inside.

He also could free center **Scott Johnson** (12.0 ppg, 5.2 rpg) for even more work on the perimeter. Johnson, a 6-11 junior, played his first season with USF last year after transferring from Virginia. He is the league's best-shooting big man and, with 47 three-pointers, was USF's most prolific long distance shooter.

But there isn't much backup for Johnson, aside from Brown. "We can't afford Scott Johnson to get hurt," Greenberg said. And Johnson is an effective big player, but does not necessarily play big. He was terribly weak as a sophomore but may be improved in that regard; he is listed at 260 pounds and a year ago was no better than 240.

"He's done a great job with his body this summer," Greenberg said. "He's got to play to his body, believe in his body. He's got to establish himself inside-out. We'll move him around the floor a lot."

Johnson will do well enough for this team to win, but it could win big if there were greater certainty at the point. The most prominent candidate is 6-2 sophomore **Haven Jackson** (4.9 ppg, 32 assists), who started four games as a freshman and is beginning to look more like a shooting guard whose team needs him to run the offense.

He is a powerful player and shows signs of being able to shoot the ball, despite only hitting 18-of-63 on threes (.286) last season. But his assist to turnover ratio was slightly below break even and he did not appear to be comfortable in command of the ball or the offense. He has a ways to go as a distributor and creator and needs to understand that sacrificing his own game could make the team better and bring greater glory his way.

But a player with a year in that position might be better suited to succeed. "Haven's got to have a solid year," said Greenberg, who most likely will know after a few weeks of practice if this is coming along as he wants. If not, he may be forced to convert still another shooting guard to the point: 6-3 senior **Shaddrick Jenkins** (10.6 ppg, 6.3 rpg).

Jenkins, who started last year, is really more of a rebounding guard. He is not proficient from long range, but can take his man into the lane and score from there. He was the first guard in school history to lead the team in rebounding. He is a big-game player, as well, averaging 13.3 points and 8.5 rebounds against the 11 teams the Bulls played that reached the postseason.

Because he's not a great shooter, it would be no extreme sacrifice to put Jenkins at the point. There's no doubt Jackson has the ability to become the better point guard, but if he doesn't make that happen, USF could be the better team with Jenkins holding the ball and Waldon at his side.

The more conventional point guards on USF's roster are 5-10 freshman **William Copeland**, a native of Sweden who played high school ball in the Miami area last season, and 5-10 senior **Andrikk Frazier** (4.0 ppg, 61 assists). Copeland has a great shooting touch and averaged 22.7 points last season but may take time to adjust to Division I. Frazier handles the ball well and plays with a great deal of energy but is not a threat to score himself or to create for others. He is an adequate point guard backup but is likely to play primarily when others threaten to press.

adidas Blue Ribbon Analysis

BACKCOURT .... **C+** **BENCH/DEPTH** .... **B+**
FRONTCOURT .... **B** **INTANGIBLES** .... **B**

If there is a darkhorse team in Conference USA, this is it. The Bulls were fortunate to win seven games last season by a basket or less, but this also was a testament to their mental and physical toughness.

"We have three criteria that we look for: play hard, be athletic, shoot the basketball. If they don't hit two of the three, we won't recruit them. And I won't recruit a soft player," Greenberg said. "Playing hard isn't an option here. Practicing hard isn't an option. Soft kids will not survive this program."

Greenberg has a lot of options available to him_"We have enough players now that people can second guess me"_which will allow him to switch out the players who aren't performing well, but there is not a lot of variety among those players. They basically have the same strengths (strength) and the same weaknesses (shooting).

That means Greenberg will have to be as creative on offense as he is insistent on defense. He will try to use his guards to post-up defenders and bring Brown and Johnson away from the basket often to keep opposing centers from growing comfortable in the lane.

The homecourt advantage at the Sun Dome can be phenomenal because of the proximity of the fans to the court, and can only improve as more fans than last season (4,652) see reason to attend.

If they are looking for perfection, they won't find it this season unless they can squeeze in the doors of Tropicana Field for the Final Four. But that won't be the only place to find quality basketball in the Tampa Bay area this season.

(M.D.)

SOUTHERN MISSISSIPPI

LOCATION .... **Hattiesburg, MS**
CONFERENCE .... **Conference USA (National)**
LAST SEASON .... **22-11 (.667)**
CONFERENCE RECORD .... **9-7 (3rd)**
STARTERS LOST/RETURNING **3/2**
NICKNAME .... **Golden Eagles**
COLORS .... **Crimson & Gray**
HOMECOURT .... **Reed Green Coliseum (8,095)**
COACH .... **James Green (Mississippi '83)**
RECORD AT SCHOOL .... **34-62 (2 yrs.)**
CAREER RECORD .... **34-62 (2 yrs.)**
ASSISTANTS .... **Terry Reed (Henderson State '73)**
Jeff Norwood (Mississippi State '86)
Kyle Roane (Southern Miss '97)
TEAM WINS (last 5 yrs.) **15-17-12-12-22**
RPI (last 5 yrs.) **73-61-101-142-71**
1997-98 FINISH .... **Lost in NIT first round.**

Far removed from Digger Phelps, even farther removed from Bob Knight, **Neil Reed** has a new home at Southern Mississippi. This is a good thing for Reed. This is a very good thing for Southern Mississippi.

If you remember the player who dazzled at the 1993 McDonald's All-America Game—a game that produced more flameouts than a waterlogged fireworks display—you probably are convinced there is a potential in Reed that never was realized while playing his first three seasons for Knight at Indiana. If you remember the player who so impressed in his first month with the Hoosiers that *Sports Illustrated* could not help but do a story about him, you know that talent translates to the Division I level.

And if you remember that he finished that season playing basically with one arm because of a paralyzing shoulder injury, you know he's got the competitive toughness to make whatever team employs him better.

Reed transferred to Southern Miss after a tempestuous conclusion to his Indiana career. He said he was told by Knight he was no longer wanted at IU and thus would transfer to another school. Reed then was harangued by Phelps, butting in on the Fabulous Sports Babe's radio program, in an almost embarrassingly bad interview. Reed then decided USM, where his father is an assistant coach, would be just the right place to try to rescue one pleasurable season from his college experience.

It could be just that. Reed is precisely what the Golden Eagles need to improve as a basketball team. Well, truth be told, they need more than he alone can offer, but Reed is an excellent addition to a promising team. Southern Miss concluded last season with nine wins in its last 13 games and looked very much like a team the NCAA selection committee might consider, regardless of a weak nonconference schedule. The Golden Eagles were snubbed, probably rightly so, then got drilled in an NIT opener against Auburn.

The two most important players on that team concluded their careers in that Auburn loss: shooting guard Jimmie Floyd (13.9 ppg, 4.2 rpg, 64 assists) and power forward Kelly McCarty (14.6 ppg, 8.1 rpg). Each played brilliantly in the season's final month, with McCarty averaging just under 10 rebounds in the last five games and Floyd drilling 40 percent of his three-point shots.

Reed cannot replace the rebounding and frontcourt defense McCarty delivered, but he is a more versatile scoring threat than Floyd, who was no more accurate shooting regular shots than he was on threes and whose assist/turnover ratio was well into negative numbers. Reed, a 6-3 shooting guard, averaged 12.6 points and shot .404 from three-point range in his junior season with the Hoosiers and passed for 135 assists and shot .455 on threes when playing the point as a sophomore. This is a fundamentally sound player who has spent the last 18 months working intensely at improving his game.

"I don't think there's any question he'll be a go-to guy," said USM coach James Green. "He's very capable, understands the game, loves to compete. He's the kind of guy who'll take the last shot, who'll want the ball in crucial situations.

"Offensively, we will play off him quite a bit, just because he knows how to play. We'll probably use him more in a scoring role, because we want to get our best players on the floor, and to do that, **Mel Cauthen** and **Arthur Stapleton** will have to play on the perimeter."

Cauthen and Stapleton shared the point guard job last year, Cauthen eventually claiming it for his own during the stretch run. Green is most likely to use those two and Reed in a three-guard offense, this because USM lacks a small forward who can handle the ball and facilitate offensive flow.

A 6-0 sophomore, Cauthen (6.5 ppg, 125 assists) is a solid quarterback, especially for a guy who has been in college only a year. He shot .487 from the field and was strong defensively. He might be even better if he allows himself to be more confident with his shooting touch.

The problem with this alignment is that Stapleton (4.8 ppg, 60 assists), a 6-3 senior, is not much of a scorer or creator. He would be likely to handle the defensive assignment should the opposition come packing a stud small forward, but his lack of shooting ability could make this lineup ineffectual offensively. Of course, Green's style is to worry about the defensive end first and then figure out how to get the ball in the basket. It was a philosophy he polished while at Iowa State under Tim Floyd, and it has served him well in two seasons as a head coach.

The Golden Eagles play strong pressure defense along the perimeter, using their athletic ability and proper positioning to unravel opponents. The three-guard setup would work well in this regard, and it also would allow the Golden Eagles to push the ball more often in transition. They would have three players ostensibly capable of accepting an outlet pass and running the break.

There is improved depth at the guard spot, with 6-1 junior **Earl Flowers** of Meridian (Miss.) C.C. (17.0 ppg, 10.0 apg) to help at the point. He started as a freshman at Nicholls State before transferring out and is considered by Green to be "a creator, with more ability to score than Mel." The wing guard reserves are 6-3 senior defensive specialist **Kevin Winn** (1.7 ppg) and 6-4 freshman **Tobias Brinkley**, who averaged 20 points and 6.0 rebounds for Lovejoy High in Jonesboro, Ga. There is one walkon reserve at guard, 6-3 senior **Robert Lewis** (0.8 ppg)

Southern Miss would not be in the position of contemplating the revamped lineup if not for the fact 6-5 senior **Pedro Phillips** (7.6 ppg, 2.8 rpg) struggles to handle the ball and 6-6 sophomore **Kilavorus Thompson** was not eligible as a freshman. **George Giuria**, a 6-5 junior from Meridian CC, is unlikely to surpass either of them on the depth chart.

1998-99 SOUTHERN MISSISSIPPI SCHEDULE

Nov.	19	Southwestern Louisiana
	24	South Alabama
	27-29	#Honolulu Thanksgiving Shootout
Dec.	3	Jackson State
	5	@Southwestern Louisiana
	8	Nicholls State
	10	Mississippi Valley State
	19	Northeast Louisiana
	21	@Northern Iowa
	28	@Memphis
	30	@Virginia Commonwealth
Jan.	2	@Tulane
	7	@Houston
	9	Cincinnati
	13	South Florida
	16	@UNC Charlotte
	21	Houston
	27	@Oklahoma State
	30	Memphis
Feb.	3	@Saint Louis
	7	@UAB
	11	Tulane
	13	@South Florida
	18	DePaul
	20	UAB
	24	@Marquette
	27	Louisville
Mar.	3-6	##Conference USA Tournament

@ Road Games
\# Honolulu, HI (vs. Hofstra, first round; also Baylor, Hawaii-Pacific, Illinois State, Iona, Missouri-Kansas City and Virginia Commonwealth)
\## Birmingham-Jefferson Civic Center, Birmingham, AL

Thompson was all-state in Louisiana and was a player many expected to help USM as a freshman, but being forced to sit a full season quite possibly will hold him back, and he's got the added problem of recovering from a knee injury. If Thompson is ready to go, he could force a change in Green's plans.

"He's got a chance to be a really good player," Green said. "He's very athletic. We wish he could have been out there practicing with us. Right now, in this particular state of Southern Miss basketball, a guy who's a great athlete with some ability can get to the floor quickly if he just does the work."

None of USM's non-point guard regulars turned over the ball as often as Phillips (64 in 769 minutes), and that caused Green eventually to remove him from the starting lineup and use him as a spot reserve. As a result, his turnovers were cut down once the Conference USA season began.

"We want Pedro to be able to do whatever we want him to do," Green said. "He's crafty around the basket and got into what we were doing defensively. There's not a guy that likes to play more." If defense becomes a problem with a three-guard set, Phillips will become USM's answer.

Another key to moving toward the different lineup is being able to move 6-9 junior **Vandarel Jones** (8.3 ppg, 4.6 rpg) from center to power forward and rely on 6-10 junior recruit **Carlos Booker** of Okaloosa-Walton (Fla.) CC to hold down the middle. The Golden Eagles also have another big body in 6-10 freshman **Mark Schwab** of St. Paul High in Covington, La., who averaged 22.5 points and 10.5 rebounds as a senior.

Jones shot .713 percent from the floor last year, which leads to the natural question of why he didn't shoot more often_the answer being that if he did, he wouldn't have shot .713 from the floor. Jones still is developing as an offensive player. He was more a putback man as a first-year sophomore and rarely was used as an offensive target.

"I'm hoping he's got it to where he can step away from the basket and be a threat from 10-12 feet," Green said. "I think with the three guys on the perimeter, we've got to establish ourselves back to going inside-out. I think we have a legitimate guy down there, that if we can get it in his hands at the right spot, we've got a legitimate chance to score. He needs touches."

Booker, originally from Clarksdale, Miss., was USM's key recruit, even though his averages (10 ppg, 10 rpg) in the two major categories were not overwhelming. Where he was dominant was in blocking shots; he led the nation as a freshman and was close with last season's four rejections per game. Although the Golden Eagles held opponents to .396 shooting, Jones had only 40 blocks and the team just 123. Booker turned up at No. 46 on the list of the nation's top 300 JC sophomores put together by analysts Rick Ball and Phil Henzel.

"They both have pretty good feet, some ability around the basket," Green said. "Booker is a pretty good passer in the post. We wanted a big guy to intimidate shots around the basket, because of the way we like to pressure the perimeter. Booker played into that real big."

adidas Blue Ribbon Analysis

BACKCOURT .... B- BENCH/DEPTH .... C+
FRONTCOURT .... C+ INTANGIBLES .... A-

"We've got to find a new identity," Green said. Southern Miss is a team that will defend its territory as well as anyone in the conference, but personnel is dictating a likely change in the structure of its lineup. Whether that will affect how well the Golden Eagles can guard shall decide whether they can employ a three-guard set.

Reed's offensive ability will liberate this team to some degree, as will an increased reliance on Jones inside, although he has to prove he can catch, turn and score and also demonstrate that he can defeat double-teaming defenses by passing out of the post.

But what if Stapleton just can't guard a good three-man? Do the Eagles change the nature of their team and insert Phillips each time they match up against a Pete Mickeal, Omar Sneed or Nate Johnson? This is Green's predicament, and the only way to resolve it is to have Thompson make a sudden adjustment to major-college ball and prove to be a fine Division I player or for Stapleton to hold up at both ends of the court.

Neither is a given, which is why the Golden Eagles are leaning toward the lower half of the National Division. But that is not a given, and this portion of Conference USA is strong enough that another NIT bid could result from a fourth-place finish. The schedule is more imposing, which is good in the sense it might help the league's and the program's power rating, but this team may not be as ready to make visits to Southwestern Louisiana, Virginia Commonwealth and Oklahoma State.

"I think we've got a more talented team than we've had since I've been here," Green said. "'Potentially, we've got a chance to maybe be a better basketball team from a skill standpoint. Can we create the toughness that we did last year?

"I think we'll be taken seriously in every game we play. I don't know if that means we'll win the same number of games."

(M.D.)

TULANE

LOCATION .... New Orleans, LA
CONFERENCE .... Conference USA (National)
LAST SEASON .... 7-22 (.241)
CONFERENCE RECORD 2-14 (6th)
STARTERS LOST/RETURNING 2/3
NICKNAME .... Green Wave
COLORS .... Olive Green & Sky Blue
HOMECOURT .... Fogelman Arena (3,600)
COACH .... Perry Clark (Gettysburg '74)
RECORD AT SCHOOL .... 153-119 (9 yrs.)
CAREER RECORD .... 153-119 (9 yrs.)
ASSISTANTS .... Greg Gary (Tulane '92)
Julius Smith (Morehouse '78)
Kim Lewis (Tulane '95)
TEAM WINS (last 5 yrs.) 18-23-22-20-7
RPI (last 5 yrs.) 67-35-38-66-220
1997-98 FINISH .... Lost in conference first round.

There was hope a year ago. There were three outstanding freshmen, a class Tulane fans were optimistically comparing to the Honeycutt-Allen class, and there was the promise of a new homecourt just two seasons away.

Precisely 22 losses later, hope is a casualty. Football, once given up for dead, has been thriving on the Tulane campus, while the once-cruising basketball program has produced almost no excitement. The Green Wave could not even fill Fogelman Arena last season, even when a top 25 team such as Cincinnati was in town. Recruiting yielded four players, but none with the reputation or accomplishments that had been common in previous classes.

1998-99 TULANE SCHEDULE

Nov.	19	Prairie View A&M
	24	Nicholls State
	28	Stetson
Dec.	1	Samford
	5	Alabama
	9	@Texas A&M
	12	Lamar
	28	Hartford
	30	UAB
Jan.	2	Southern Mississippi
	7	UNC Charlotte
	9	@Saint Louis
	14	@Memphis
	16	New Orleans
	21	@UAB
	23	Houston
	28	@Marquette
	30	DePaul
Feb.	3	@Cincinnati
	6	South Florida
	11	@Southern Mississippi
	13	@Houston
	18	Louisville
	21	@North Carolina State
	24	Memphis
	27	@South Florida
Mar.	3-6	#Conference USA Tournament

@ Road Games
\# Birmingham-Jefferson Civic Center, Birmingham, AL

It almost as seems as though Louisville and Tulane are in a race to see which program can deteriorate more quickly.

Coach Perry Clark kept as much of his spirit and good humor as possible through what he endured last winter. He insists last season was an aberration and that Tulane basketball will return to what it once was, but the news only got worse once the season ended.

Chris Owens, a 6-8, 225-pound power forward considered a jewel of the freshman class, decided he wanted out after he averaged only 6.1 points and 5.0 rebounds. Owens seemed almost not to care as the defeats mounted upon him and his teammates. There were those entering the year who thought Owens had been overrated—he was a consensus top 15 player according to *The Sporting News*' poll of recruiting analysts—but almost nothing about his play for the Green Wave indicated he was that sort of talent.

In early-season games against weak competition, Owens averaged 12.6 points and 7.8 rebounds, but as the competition stiffened and the losses piled up, he immediately began to regress. The nadir was in Tulane's late-December Conference USA opener against Memphis, when Owens went through 23 minutes without a point. He had only two more double-figure games the rest of the way, played just 21 minutes combined in the final two games and then announced his decision to transfer. He wound up at UCLA.

That leaves Tulane with only two members of that prized class, and this is not a program that can afford to be sacrificing talented players at the moment. The good news is that 6-6 sophomore wing **Byron Mouton** (15.3 ppg, 3.9 rpg) really is a fine offensive player, and that 6-7 sophomore power forward **LeDaryl Billingsley** (5.0 ppg, 3.6 rpg) is every bit as energetic and competitive as he suggested during his high school career in the Chicago area. They are what's left from that class, and they are something to build around.

Mouton did not shoot well last season (.360 FG percentage, .324 three-PT percentage), but part of the reason was he had so little help on offense that he forced shots. Another reason was that he played too passively, taking nearly half his shots from three-point range even though he wasn't that accurate. He showed as a prep player that he can attack the basket because of his quickness and ballhandling skill, but he did not make use of that talent as often as he should have while playing as a freshman.

He made it tougher for 6-4 junior **Dylan Osean** (6.2 ppg, 1.7 rpg) to find time. Osean is not athletic enough to compete in Conference USA and did not shoot well (16 of 49 on threes) as a sophomore. He started 10 games early, but disappeared from the rotation as the season progressed. He could still have some value as a spot-up shooter, but has to regain his touch.

Billingsley had some injury problems in his rookie year and early in the season had trouble finding a position. With Owens gone, it's likely that spot will be power forward, next to 6-10 junior center **Morris Jordan** (7.0 ppg, 4.6 rpg). Billingsley, gets off the floor well, plays a rugged game, is not afraid to bang inside and is productive on the offensive boards. He has a decent mid-range jumpshot.

One thing Billingsley does poorly is shoot free-throws, which is a handicap given that he's a decent threat in the post. It doesn't do much good to earn free-throws if you can't make a decent percentage.

Jordan won the center job away from Lawrence Nelson as the latter performed dispassionately throughout his senior season. Nelson is another Tulane player who made few improvements over the course of his career, much like Honeycutt before him. Jordan has plenty of room to get better. He more than doubled his production from his freshman season, but remains an agile player who appears not to understand the game's finer points.

He is not a great shot-blocker, getting 21 last season, which will be a difference from when shot-blocking was all Nelson could or would do. His 49 blocks last year was part of the reason Tulane held opponents as low as .440 percent from the field—not great, but not as bad as you might expect for a team that won seven games.

Competition was one reason for that low number. In conference games, where there are no patsies, Tulane was last in C-USA in field-goal defense at .464. That's a reflection on how sloppy the Green Wave players were, because their athleticism on the wings enabled them to hold opposing shooters to .280 on threes, which tied for the league lead.

Jordan became a more significant offensive threat in the late stages of his sophomore season and could return as an important part of the Tulane attack. He hit double figures in eight of his final 10 games and was 11 of 14 from the field in a game against South Florida, one of the better defensive teams in Conference USA. His progress will be a major factor as the Wave battles to stay out of the National Division basement.

Two players who've been major disappointments at Tulane remain the most likely starters at small forward. Junior **Sterling Davis** (4.0 ppg, 3.0 rpg) and senior **Keith Harris** (3.9 ppg, 3.0 rpg) have never fulfilled the promise they brought into the program, each of them standing 6-7, each one considered to be a top-100 prospect.

Davis is not athletic and has not shot the ball well enough to be as stationary as he is. He scored 11 points against Tulsa and UNC Charlotte and 13 against Houston, but otherwise was nondescript. Although he's got a strong frame that should permit him to do damage in closer to the basket, he does not have the ball skills to work his way into position. His three-point shooting (14 of 40) adds little to the offense.

Harris was predicted by league coaches to be the top freshman in C-USA four years back. That wasn't fulfilled, and neither was anything else about his career. He plays as if bewildered or unconcerned. After opening last season with 13 points against Texas-Arlington, he was shut out by Tulsa and wound up posting eight goose eggs over the course of the year.

If those two remain laggards, Clark could turn to 6-7 senior **Ted Kritza** (6.7 ppg, 3.4 rpg), but he is effective as a reserve and likely to remain in that role. Kritza, a transfer from Colorado, gave Tulane a productive 18 minutes a game off the bench last season, but was not in top condition and saw his production fade as the season progressed. Of his eight double-figure scoring efforts, six occurred in the first 12 games. And three came against Tulsa, Memphis and UNLV, so it was not just a matter of the competition improving.

Kritza is a scrapper, so once again the dwindling incentive likely played a part in his decline.

Tulane added some depth to the frontcourt by reaching into Chicago, where most of this year's recruiting success was transacted, for 6-8 power forward **Linton Johnson**, who averaged 18 points and 14 rebounds at Providence St. Mel High, a perennial Chicago power.

Tulane's most obvious problem as a basketball team has persisted for the last five seasons. The Green Wave has gone years without a decent point guard, with the exception of the time LeVeldro Simmons spent running the club when he should have been enjoying his time at shooting guard.

It's true Tulane was unlucky that injuries ruined the career of Derrick Moore, who was counted on to turn the Honeycutt teams into NCAA clubs. But one would think the guy who landed Honeycutt, Mouton and Owens could find himself someone else to run the show at least marginally well. That hasn't happened.

The players who shared the position last year were consistently ineffective. **P.J. Franklin** (5.6 ppg, 1.8 rpg, 2.1 apg), a 5-10 junior who plays for the football team, closed the year as a starter, but never displayed the sort of grip on the game a point guard must. The Green Wave turned over the ball 18.8 times per game, which was mitigated only by their own ability to force the ball from the opposition.

He is quick and strong, as one would expect from a punt

returner, but committed 67 turnovers against 53 assists and shot .307 percent (31 of 101) from three-point range. It wasn't bad, really, for a guy getting his first real shot at playing major-college ball, but the question is whether he could improve while devoting so much of the autumn to football. It seems unlikely. He noticeably tired at the end of last season, scoring only 11 points in his final four games and committing nine turnovers.

It's more likely the point-guard job will be firmly in the hands of 6-1 junior **Marlo Miles**, a Chicago native who averaged 13.0 points and 9.0 assists at hometown Kennedy King JC, by the time Franklin is free to play basketball. Miles was a third-team NJCAA All-American. Tulane's other recruits also were backcourt players: 6-2 freshman **Waitari Marsh** of Chicago's Julian High, who averaged 22 points and 8 rebounds and also could play the point; and 6-2 junior **Wade Mason**, who scored 11.9 points and grabbed 4.1 rebounds at Tyler (Tex.) Junior College.

Although there is no difference-maker in the class, save possibly for Miles, it is a group that expands the Wave's talent base beyond what was in place last year with the likes of Billy Wells and Jon Citrin.

adidas Blue Ribbon Analysis

BACKCOURT .... C- **BENCH/DEPTH** .... C-
FRONTCOURT .... C **INTANGIBLES** .... C-

The pressure defense Clark likes to employ worked surprisingly well for a team that accomplished so little otherwise last season. Whether that's because teams came to take the Green Wave lightly or Tulane just was good at it, it's a matter of conjecture, but this remains the cornerstone of the plans to return to prominence.

Forcing turnovers from the opposition and actually making something out of them could help Tulane lift itself from the depths of Conference USA. There has to be more spirit and leadership among the players, though. A soft schedule at the start of the year could help build confidence. But once again, whether this team will become a success depends largely on whether it finds someone who can run an offense at the Conference USA level.

Last season, Tulane had the advantage of playing in the less competitive of the league's two divisions and still faltered. This year, the top four teams in the National Division may be better as a group, which makes climbing out of the basement all the more difficult. It may be possible for Tulane to keep Houston's recovery delayed another year, but there are as many good players on the Cougars' roster as on the Wave's.

If there is to be a difference between the teams, Mouton must become a more efficient player, Jordan needs to defend effectively in the post and all those turnovers the opposition commits have to be converted into points by a lead guard who knows how to distribute the ball. There just is so much uncertainty.

(M.D.)

UNC CHARLOTTE

LOCATION .... **Charlotte, NC**
CONFERENCE .... **Conference USA (American)**
LAST SEASON .... **20-11 (.645)**
CONFERENCE RECORD .... **13-3 (2nd)**
STARTERS LOST/RETURNING **3/2**
NICKNAME **49ers**
COLORS .... **Green & White**
HOMECOURT .... **Dale F. Halton Arena (9,105)**
COACH .... **Bobby Lutz (UNC-Charlotte '80)**
RECORD AT SCHOOL .... **First Year**
CAREER RECORD .... **181-91 (9 yrs.)**
ASSISTANTS .... **Orlando Early (Gardner-Webb '90)**
Land Odom (High Point '89)
Rob Moxley (Pfeiffer '94)
TEAM WINS (last 5 yrs.) **16-19-14-22-20**
RPI (last 5 yrs.) **54-39-66-26-25**
1997-98 FINISH .... **Lost in NCAA second round.**

Of all the many teams included within this book's many, many pages, it is hard to imagine one that will be asked to survive more significant player losses than UNC Charlotte. DeMarco Johnson and Sean Colson. Inside and outside. Heart and soul. How does a team recover from this?

It helps to have a lot of highly regarded players around, as North Carolina does as it moves on to a future without Vince Carter and Antawn Jamison. UNC Charlotte happens to have mostly good players and could struggle to make this adjustment. The prediction that places UNCC at the bottom of the American Division is made with not great confidence, though. It's just a reflection of how many more variables the 49ers must deal with and how deeply they depended on Johnson and Colson the past two seasons.

Consider that Johnson led UNCC in scoring and rebounding and Colson led in assists, three-pointers and free-throw percentage. Johnson played in all 31 games and led the scoring in 22. Colson missed most of preseason practice and the opener at Miami for disciplinary reasons and the 49ers wound up with a nearly disastrous 3-5 start—a start that led to a No. 8 NCAA Tournament seed and likely cost them the opportunity to play in the Sweet 16.

By the way, did we mention UNCC has a new coach? "Obviously, we'll miss them tremendously," said Bobby Lutz, previously the top assistant for Melvin Watkins and hired as his replacement once Watkins chose to head for the big money offered by Texas A&M.

It might help in some ways that the transition came now. Watkins had been successful in his two seasons playing a pound-it-inside style that perfectly suited Johnson and Colson. There's no reason to believe he couldn't have changed the 49ers to something else, but there's no way to be sure he'd have been comfortable in another system. Now, that won't be a concern. Lutz will shift UNCC into a higher gear and play a more open-court game, the way he did when he was head coach at Pfeiffer College in North Carolina and turned that school into an NAIA power.

"I would just as soon have those guys in uniform, but it's kind of exciting, too," Lutz said. "We feel like we have some good young players. We'll be a lot different team this year.

"Coach Watkins and I saw eye-to-eye on a lot of things, but I think it's going to be exciting to allow some guys to have a little more offensive opportunity than we did. I think some of these guys are ready for that."

The principal beneficiary of the fast-paced style Lutz wants to incorporate could be 6-7 senior wing **Galen Young** (8.5 ppg, 5.2 rpg), who started nearly all of his junior season but was primarily used as a defensive stopper. Young is from Memphis and played his first two years in junior college, so you know he understands how to play basketball at full speed. He will start at small forward for the 49ers.

Young is extremely athletic and stronger than a lot of Memphis products, but he's not a great shooter from the perimeter (.290 on three-pointers) and did not exercise great shot selection, firing more than a quarter of his attempts from long distance. Without Johnson in the paint, though, there may be more room for Young to operate inside and lift that shooting percentage.

If he does not improve a great deal in that regard, he still will be valuable for his ability to shut down opposing wings. "I felt Galen was really good defensively," Lutz said. "He was a little foul-prone, and he can't do that this year. I honestly don't know where our scoring is going to come from, but I think guys like Galen Young and **Kelvin Price** can step up their contributions."

Price, a 6-8 senior, is the other returning starter. He was the center beside Johnson in his first season and could easily handle that job once again. But the nature of the 49ers roster may squeeze him over to power forward, a position for which he is better suited, anyway. Price (9.5 ppg, 8.0 rpg) is not a low-post scorer and is smaller than a lot of centers.

He shot .552 from the field in his first season after transferring from Southwestern Louisiana, primarily by only attempting stick-backs and layups. He does not have shooting range and desperately needs to improve his free-throw shooting (.481). By hitting .700 from the line, he would have lifted his scoring average by a full point.

The only other player who might be a natural power forward is 6-8 freshman **Charles Hayward**, whose return to the court will be one of this season's most heartwarming stories. Hayward was a top 75 recruit for the 49ers last year who spent the season fighting—leukemia—rather than playing. He went through chemotherapy and was pronounced by doctors to be free of the disease last spring. He has been lifting and working on his game since and reports that he'll again be the player who entered school with such promise.

Whether Hayward will be ready to help the 49ers this year is hard to say. His teammates are extremely pleased he is recovered and are hoping for the best. The other option is athletic but undersized **Tremaine Gardiner**, a 6-5, 210-pound junior who sat out last season with a knee injury. He scored a career-high 14 points against Utah in the 1997 NCAA Tournament, Gardiner's last game before the injury, and averaged 3.3 points and 3.1 rebounds as a spot reserve that season. He is tough and will be a valuable reserve, but a frontcourt that features Gardiner and Price would likely to be too small to avoid that sixth-place finish.

That leaves Lutz to consider the possibility of employing one or all of several untested players in the middle: 6-9 redshirt freshman **Osseynou Kane**, the highest-rated of the bunch; 6-10 sophomore **Jonathan Neely**, who sat out last year as an ineligible freshman; and 6-10 freshman **Kenny Whitehead**.

"We'll probably do this by committee," said Lutz. "We have a lot of young guys we're excited about, but don't know which one will play the most. It's a matter of who comes along the quickest, and who plays in November may not be the guy that finishes the year."

Neely is from Richmond High in Rockingham, N.C., and was a top 100 player as rated by *All-Star Sports* analyst Bob Gibbons and No. 129 by *Prep Stars* analyst Brick Oettinger. Neely has a bench-press of more than 300 pounds—rare for a basketball player—and is UNCC's strongest player.

"He doesn't jump well, but he's just so big," Lutz said. "He's going to establish a post presence both offensively and defensively, and he can really step out and shoot the basketball."

A native of Senegal who attended Washington's Dunbar High and averaged 16.1 points and 7.4 rebounds, Kane is a defensive specialist, which is nice for a lot of the teams in this league but may be a luxury UNCC struggles to afford. He blew out his knee before last season began, tried to go in six games but played a combined 24 minutes and was 0-for-5 from the field. Lutz admits Kane will have to make progress in order to score at the Division I level.

As school started, Kane had a slight problem. He returned home to Senegal for the summer, but had trouble getting a visa in order to return to the United States. Lutz is hopeful the problem can be worked out by the second semester.

Whitehead's injury problems might have preceded his arrival at UNCC. He had knee surgery in each of the last two years and averaged just 6.9 points and 4.9 rebounds as a senior at St. Vincent Pallotti in Maryland. A native of Arlington, Va., he is clearly a long-term project and is expected to fall behind the other two big men on the depth chart.

"We have a lot of choices," Lutz said. "I'm confident we have enough depth there, whereas last year we didn't have a lot of options."

The 49ers also are deep in the backcourt, but aren't fast at all, which might limit their ability to excel in an uptempo system. Point guard **Diego Guevara** is an outstanding shooter, possibly the best in Conference USA and almost certainly the league's best clutch shooter. He nailed an off-balance three-pointer that put the 49ers into overtime with top-ranked North Carolina in last March's NCAA Tournament second-round game. He also struck from behind a screen with a three-pointer that gave UNCC a one-point lead at Cincinnati in the game that decided Conference USA's regular-season title. Guevara had a combined 30 points in those games. UNCC lost both times, but he'd done what he could and proved he was getting substantially better as the season advanced.

1998-99 UNC CHARLOTTE SCHEDULE

Nov.	17	@Boston University
	21	@Old Dominion
	23	Miami
	29	George Washington
Dec.	2	Kent
	5	Virginia Tech
	8	@Davidson
	10	VMI
	12	@North Carolina
	20	@Saint Louis
	27-30	#Rainbow Classic
Jan.	7	@Tulane
	10	Memphis
	14	Cincinnati
	16	Southern Mississippi
	21	Marquette
	24	@UAB
	30	@Louisville
Feb.	3	@DePaul
	6	Saint Louis
	11	Louisville
	13	@Marquette
	17	@Cincinnati
	20	South Florida
	23	@Houston
	27	DePaul
Mar.	3-6	##Conference USA Tournament

@ Road Games
\# Honolulu, HI (vs. Murray State, first round; also Florida State, Hawaii, Mississippi State, Princeton, Southwestern Louisiana and Texas)
\## Birmingham-Jefferson Civic Center, Birmingham, AL

Guevara (5.7 ppg, 45 assists, 22 steals) is a 6-1 sophomore from Venezuela and played in high school at Washington Academy in Tennessee. He is strong and shot .422 from three-point range, but is not a cat-quick point and not expert at setting up teammates. What he brings to the UNCC offense is the ability to stretch a defense but not the quickness to get into the seams.

This should not be construed as a weak position for the 49ers. They are better set in terms of talent at the point than most teams in the league—even though 6-1 senior **Chris Dwiggins** (0.4 ppg), and 5-11 junior **Kedric Smith** (2.1 ppg) are not overwhelming backups—but the question is whether Guevara can facilitate the attack Lutz wants to employ.

The same is true at shooting guard, where 6-5 sophomore Dalonte Hill figured to start before he underwent knee surgery in late September. Hill will sit out the season as a redshirt.

Arthroscopic surgery revealed significant damage to the anterior cruciate ligament in Hill's knee. "Obviously, we're very disappointed for the team and for Dalonte," Lutz said.

Hill's injury could mean 6-6 senior **Marlon Thomas** will step into the starting shooting guard job.

Thomas was something of a disappointment as a first-year transfer. Watkins had promised big things from Thomas, but his numbers (3.6 points, 1.4 rebounds) did not measure up. The one thing he did reasonably well was shoot three-pointers (.417, 10-of-24), which UNCC will need with a lineup so short on scorers.

Thomas is every bit the marginally athletic, upright, stationary shooter he looked to be in high school, that Watkins insisted he no longer was. Thomas may have a decent vertical leap, but he's not able to translate that to basketball productivity. He doesn't have the ballhandling skill to shoot off the dribble or beat a man to the basket.

"Sometimes the transition from junior college doesn't go as smoothly as everybody wants," Lutz said. "There was a stretch there where he struggled offensively, but to his credit, he continued to work hard. In limited minutes down the stretch, he made shots and contributed, which is really hard to do.

"We need him to do more this year. I know he wasn't personally happy with what he was able to do. He came in, said he's going to play more, contribute more. We need him to step up."

Although 6-4 sophomore **Dee Toliver** (2.4 points, 0.7 rebounds) has a year in the system, freshman **Jobey Thomas** is the likely fourth guard, but he'll have to prove he's good enough to make this a four-guard rotation. A 6-4 product of Charlotte's Independence High, he averaged 22.6 points and 6.1 rebounds as a senior and was ranked No. 82 by Gibbons and No. 102 by Oettinger.

"He can handle the ball as a second guard and can bring the ball up, which in my scheme is very important," Lutz said. "He's a good outside shooter ... the three-point line is not the extent of his range. He isn't going to back down from anybody. I think he will find a way to get some time. He is that kind of player."

adidas Blue Ribbon Analysis

BACKCOURT	**C+**	**BENCH/DEPTH**	**C**
FRONTCOURT	**C**	**INTANGIBLES**	**B**

Watkins clearly knew that if he was ever going to leave UNC Charlotte—which was not a sure thing, given that he'd spent two decades there—this was going to be the time.

Losing two such gifted players meant it was unlikely he'd be this hot again for a while, and who knew if there'd be another A&M out there throwing around the cash?

His departure opens the opportunity for Lutz, an excellent coach who will have to work extremely hard to keep this club out of the basement. It's not impossible. There's not a whole lot of difference between No. 2 and No. 6 in the American Division. The team that gets the breaks, works hardest and does the best taking advantage of its strength will likely wind up as runner-up to Cincinnati.

Charlotte has decent players, but it needs strength at a few positions to approach the level of the last two years. There aren't enough good scorers and not enough good athletes to successfully do what Lutz wants to do.

"Last year, we didn't get anybody open except DeMarco, and Sean got himself open. We're going to have to do more in our offensive system ... set more screens. Last year, we basically got Sean the ball, and he could create and make things happen.

"We'll do things differently. We really want to play uptempo. We still probably aren't quite there. We need a jet at the point to do what I want to do. That's a recruiting priority. We'll press more, but certainly not as much as we will two years from now." Lutz could probably say the same about victories. The 49ers will win, but not as much as in the future.

(M.D.)

IVY LEAGUE

adidas BLUE RIBBON FORECAST

1. Pennsylvania
2. (tie) Princeton
   (tie) Harvard
4. Columbia
5. Cornell
6. Dartmouth
7. Brown
8. Yale

ALL-CONFERENCE TEAM

G—Brian Earl, SR, Princeton
G—Tim Hill, SR, Harvard
G—Michael Jordan, JR, Pennsylvania
F—Gabe Lewullis, SR, Princeton
F—Geoff Owens, JR. Pennsylvania

PLAYER OF THE YEAR

Michael Jordan, JR, Pennsylvania

NEWCOMER OF THE YEAR

Wallace Prather, FR, Cornell

1997-98 CHAMPIONS

Princeton

1997-98 POSTSEASON PARTICIPANTS

Postseason Record: 1-1 (.500)

NCAA

Princeton (second round)

TOP BACKCOURTS

1. Pennsylvania
2. Princeton
3. Harvard

TOP FRONTCOURTS

1. Princeton
2. Columbia
3. Pennsylvania

ON THE WAY UP

Harvard

ON THE WAY DOWN

Brown

INSIDE THE NUMBERS

- 1996-97 conference RPI: 20th (of 30)
- Conference RPI (last 5 yrs.): 27-30-20-15-20

DID YOU KNOW?

The law of averages would suggest that it is impossible, but Princeton coach Bill Carmody still has not lost a game in the Ivy League. In his first two seasons, Carmody is 28-0...Since the 1962-63 season, just five teams have won the Ivy title: Columbia in '67-68, Brown in '85-86, Cornell in '87-88 and Princeton and Pennsylvania taking the rest. Since 1988, Penn and Princeton have shut out the rest of the league, with the Tigers winning seven and the Quakers gaining four (the two shared the 1995-96 title)...Relatively speaking: Princeton's Chris Krug is the brother of Penn's Todd, Columbia's Tony Mboya is the brother of Penn's George. And Cornell's A.J. McGuire is the grandson of legendary Marquette coach Al...Even though there is no postseason conference tournament for the Ivy League, there are always two dates to circle on the schedule. When will Penn and Princeton square off? This year, Princeton goes to the Palestra on Feb. 16 and the Quakers return the favor on March 2, the final game for both squads. Many years, the league's automatic NCAA Tournament berth is on the line in that final game.

(B.A.)

BROWN

LOCATION	**Providence, RI**
CONFERENCE	**Ivy League**
LAST SEASON	**6-20 (.231)**
CONFERENCE RECORD	**3-11 (8th)**
STARTERS LOST/RETURNING	**2/3**
NICKNAME	**Bears**
COLORS	**Seal Brown, Cardinal Red and White**
HOMECOURT	**Pizzitola Sports Center (2,800)**
COACH	**Frank "Happy" Dobbs (Villanova '84)**
RECORD AT SCHOOL	**63-119 (7 yrs.)**
CAREER RECORD	**63-119 (7 yrs.)**
ASSISTANTS	**Jeff Estis (Miami '94)**
	Eric Blackiston (Brown '96)
	David Martinelli (Brown '98)
TEAM WINS (last 5 yrs.)	**12-13-10-4-6**
RPI (last 5 yrs.)	**187-205-227-266-277**
1997-98 FINISH	**No conference tournament.**

They may call Brown coach Frank Dobbs "Happy," but he definitely wasn't pleased with his team's performance last season.

Everyone associated with the Bears had high expectations going into last season. After a grueling schedule in 1996-97, Brown thought it had a chance to break through in '97-98. Didn't happen. For the second consecutive year, Brown managed just one win on the road and for the second straight year, it was at Columbia (not exactly Cameron Indoor Stadium).

Now Dobbs and his staff have to once again attempt to resurrect a program. And this year, the Bears will be better described as Cubs. Seven freshmen and four sophomores are on the preseason roster, making this team too young to be full-fledged Bears.

"We going to be young, but very talented," Dobbs said. "With the influx of an outstanding freshman class, you'll definitely see a more exciting Brown team this year."

One of the returnees is 6-8 senior forward **Kamal Rountree** (8.3 ppg, 4.3 rpg), whose inside game made him one of the Ivy League's top performers last season. Against Pennsylvania, he had a huge game, scoring 18 and grabbing 13 rebounds. With the graduation of Paul Krasinski, Rountree is the team's leading scorer and rebounder and he will be called on to do both frequently in order for Brown to improve. Dobbs knows this and has chosen the Montclair, N.J. native as team captain.

The rest of the frontcourt will be a mystery, with no one more experienced than a sophomore fighting for court time. The other four forwards on the roster are all freshman. **Shaun Etheridge** (Xavier HS/Portland, Conn.), 6-7, averaged a double-double last season (23 ppg, 14 rpg) and has emerged as the favorite to join Rountree in the starting rotation. He will be pushed by 6-4 **Travis Brown** (Northfield-Mount Herman Prep/Upper St. Clair, Pa.), who was a scorer in high school (16.5 ppg).

Also in the hunt at forward will be 6-7 power forward **Quinn Tamm** (Cherry Hill HS/Cherry Hill, N.J.) and 6-6 **Josh Meyer** (Roncalli Catholic HS/Omaha, Neb.), with both seeing time backing up Rountree. Tamm averaged 19 points and eight rebounds per game as a senior, while Meyer did him one better in each category (20.0 ppg, 9.0 rpg).

Sophomore **Tyrone Driggers** (1.5 ppg, 1.1 rpg), a 6-8 center, should see most of the time in the middle. He appeared in 17 games last season off the bench and is aggressive on offense. Look for him to assist Rountree a bit on the offensive end.

Also set in the middle will be 6-8 sophomore **Graham Amon** (1.0 ppg, 0.8 rpg) and 6-9 freshman **John Verdeaux** (King Phillip Regional HS/Norfolk, Mass.).

Up front, the Bears are returning just under 11 points per game. That would seem to say the Brown offense will come from the little guys.

The main little guy for Brown is 6-0 junior **Corey**

1998-99 BROWN SCHEDULE

Nov.	14	@New Hampshire
	17	Northeastern
	20-21	#Mohegan Sun Classic
	24	@Rhode Island
	28	Maine
Dec.	1	Cleveland State
	3	@Providence
	9	Holy Cross
	21	Quinnipiac
	28	@Robert Morris
	30	@New Orleans
Jan.	8	@Princeton
	10	@Pennsylvania
	16	Yale
	23	@Yale
	30	@Dartmouth
	31	@Harvard
Feb.	5	Columbia
	6	Cornell
	12	Pennsylvania
	13	Princeton
	19	@Cornell
	20	@Columbia
	26	Harvard
	27	Dartmouth

@ Road Games
\# New Britain, CT (vs. Central Connecticut, first round; also Delaware State and New Hampshire)

Vandiver (5.9 ppg, 2.4 apg). Vandiver took over the point-guard position late in the season and responded beautifully. Against Ivy powerhouse Princeton last year, he scored 13 points and showed flashes of brilliance.

When Vandiver has to come out of a game, the Bears will suffer little as he will be spelled by 6-1 freshman **Omari Ware** (St. John's Prep/Washington, D.C.), an explosive point man. In his senior season, Ware averaged 15 points and 10 assists.

The two-guard position may be the deepest spot on the floor for the Bears, as six players will vie for floor time. First on the list is 6-3 sophomore **Patrick Nee** (5.3 ppg, 1.8 rpg, .821 FT%). Nee was forced to play at the small-forward position for much of last year, but will be more comfortable in his regular off-guard spot. His laser-eye will be perfectly suited for the role, as Nee led the team in three-pointers with 24 last year.

Another player moving to the off-guard spot this year will be 6-0 junior **Joe Bucci** (5.0 ppg, 1.5 rpg). For the first three-quarters of 1997-98, Bucci was forced into the point guard role. He moved to shooting guard late in the season and played well.

One more intriguing name in the backcourt is 6-2 junior **Matt D'Antoni** (5.0 ppg, 1.2 rpg). He started 16 games last season and dropped in a season-high 14 against Holy Cross. D'Antoni came to Providence from Loyola and seemed a bit rusty after missing a year. Dobbs is hoping his skills will return and give Brown another outside scoring threat.

Another question mark is 6-3 sophomore **Peter Johnson** (3.5 ppg, 0.7 rpg), who was limited to 14 games because of a shoulder injury, but showed enough talent to earn a selection to the all-tournament team at the Fairfield Tournament last year. If Johnson is healthy, Brown hopes he will add even more depth to this spot in the lineup.

Rounding out the backcourt are 6-2 senior **Scott Sienkiewicz** (1.2 ppg, 0.4 rpg), 6-1 junior **James Perry** (1.9 ppg, 0.9 rpg) and 6-3 freshman **Jesse Wood** (Northfield Mount Herman Prep/Buena Vista, CO).

Sienkiewicz saw action in 11 games last season, all off the bench. Perry, a first-team all-Ivy League selection as a quarterback in 1997, played in seven games last season. Wood could be the wildcard in this scenario. A first-team, all-state selection in high school, Wood averaged 19.0 points and seven assists in high school and 12.0 points and four assists at prep school last year.

adidas Blue Ribbon Analysis

BACKCOURT	C+	BENCH/DEPTH	C
FRONTCOURT	C	INTANGIBLES	C

"Happy" Dobbs has his work cut out for him, but at least he's going to have something to work with this season. The talent is there, but it is awfully young. Probably too young.

Rountree is a definite player, and will certainly make anyone's definition of an all-Ivy team. Vandiver was a solid point guard last year and Ware seems to possess all of the tools. All of this plus a more realistic schedule than the previous two years seem to make Brown's chances better this year.

The question is: Is this enough?

Unfortunately, it doesn't seem so. With so many young players, the Bears' play will be erratic. It's a shame Rountree has only one year left, because with him, this could be a solid squad in 1999-2000.

Dobbs and his team should be satisfied with 10 wins this season, a four-game improvement. That may be enough to move up a level in the Ivy—not enough to catch Princeton or Penn, but maybe closer to the second tier than the last few editions have been. Not much in the grand scheme of things, but small steps forward are better than the steps back the program has taken during the last few years.

(B.A.)

COLUMBIA

LOCATION	New York, NY
CONFERENCE	Ivy League
LAST SEASON	11-15 (.423)
CONFERENCE RECORD	6-8 (t-4th)
STARTERS LOST/RETURNING	1/4
NICKNAME	Lions
COLORS	Columbia Blue and White
HOMECOURT	Levien Gymnasium (3,400)
COACH	Armond Hill (Princeton '85)
RECORD AT SCHOOL	24-54 (3 yrs.)
CAREER RECORD	24-54 (3 yrs.)
ASSISTANTS	Paul Lee (Columbia '86)
	Bill Johnson (Nebraska '88)
	Lyman Casey (Santa Clara '93)
TEAM WINS (last 5 yrs.)	6-4-7-6-11
RPI (last 5 yrs.)	288-299-279-284-239
1997-98 FINISH	No conference tournament.

Columbia coach Armond Hill is in his fourth year of a rebuilding project, so you should excuse his optimism. While last year's fourth-place finish and 11 wins may not seem like much to many teams, at Columbia those numbers are huge. Both were the program's best in five years and the team showed some heart by winning four league games in a row on the road despite the tough Ivy travel schedule.

The Lions' success this season should hinge again on 6-2 senior guard **Gary Raimondo** (14.7 ppg, 7.1 rpg, 2.4 apg, 2.4 spg), who is an outstanding all-around player. A second-team, all-Ivy League selection last year, Raimondo was among the top in the Ivy in steals (1st), scoring (6th), and rebounding (4th). He is also just 126 points shy of becoming the program's 20th 1,000 point scorer. For all of these reasons and more, Hill has chosen Raimondo team captain, the first time in 10 years that a Columbia player has earned that title two years in a row.

Joining Raimondo in the backcourt will be 6-2 senior **Abe Yasser** (2.0 ppg, 2.6 rpg, 2.5 apg), a steady point guard who started all 26 games for the Lions last season. In addition to running the offense, Yasser is an excellent defender who was second on the team in steals a year ago.

Coming off the bench will be 6-2 sophomore **Tony Mboya** (5.0 ppg, 2.9 rpg, 1.0 apg), who had a solid rookie year. The Columbia coaching staff is hoping that Mboya, an athletic talent, can attain the promise that he showed offensively last year.

Two freshmen, 6-0 **Victor Munoz** (Harvard-Westlake Prep/South Gate, Calif.) and 6-5 **Craig Austin** (St. Francis HS/Marilla, N.Y.), will vie for time as backups in the backcourt. Munoz, who will spell Yasser at the point, passed for 17 assists in a game last year at the Las Vegas Holiday Tournament and is an excellent passer. Austin, the most valuable player in the Buffalo City All-Star Game, was a fine scholastic scorer (averaging 22 ppg).

The forward positions are anchored by two returning starters—one of them, 6-7 senior **Erik Crep** (10.3 ppg, 3.5 rpg), is a shooter who is not afraid of mixing it up in the post. A year ago, he was the team's best three-point shooter (.380) and free-throw shooter (.821).

Crep is joined by 6-8 senior forward **Justin Namolik** (11.3 ppg, 4.4 rpg). Namolik has started all but one of Columbia's games since joining the program, and is right behind Raimondo in the hunt for 1,000 points, needing 248 to reach the goal.

The rest of the forward mix looks a little more murky. Injuries crippled the Lions here last year and how the players return could make the difference. **Steve Brown**, a 6-5 junior forward (1.7 ppg, 1.1 rpg), is working to come back from knee problems (patella tendonitis). He spent much of last season trying to rehabilitate and is hoping to gain the power forward post.

Also returning from injuries last year are 6-4 sophomore **Ty Ugolyn** (2.0 ppg, 0.5 rpg), who played just two games last year because of a stress fracture, and 6-5 sophomore **Brad Gloger** (Santa Margarita Catholic HS/Mission Viejo, Calif.), who missed the year with bilateral tarsal tunnel syndrome.

Also, look for 6-3 sophomore **Sheldon Jackson** (0.9 ppg, 0.9 rpg) to see time in the swing position. Jackson played in 10 games last year, but attempted just eight shots.

In addition, three freshmen will provide depth up front. At 6-8 **Joe Case** (East HS/Morningside, Iowa) will play at forward while also seeing time in the middle. He averaged a double-double in high school (20.2 ppg, 11.2 rpg) and was the conference most valuable player in addition to being chosen first-team all-state.

Marc Simon (Shipley School/Rydal, Pa.), 6-6, also averaged a double-double in high school, and is thought to be a standout passer and rebounder. Finally, there's 6-7 **Chris Van Ens** (Pomona HS/Arvada, Co.), who impresses the Columbia coaching staff with his size, weighing in at 225 pounds.

Although the Lions seem to have a lot of candidates in the middle, there is not a sure-fire starter. Sophomore **Mike Merley** 6-7 (1.9 ppg, 2.0 rpg) did start nine games in his first year and saw action in every game, but did not have much of an impact.

Two freshmen will push him for time. At 6-9 **Chris Fidyk** (Thousand Oaks HS/Thousand Oaks, Calif.), was hampered by injuries during his final year of high school basketball, but the staff likes his upside. However, he will need to add strength throughout the year.

The other freshman is 6-8 **Mike McBrien** (Jesuit HS/Carmichael, Calif.), who was a Northern California all-star his senior season. Rounding out the center position is 6-7 sophomore **Zach Schiller** (2.0 ppg, 0.0 rpg), who saw scant action in two contests last season.

adidas Blue Ribbon Analysis

BACKCOURT	C	BENCH/DEPTH	D+
FRONTCOURT	C	INTANGIBLES	C

While last year may have given Columbia hopes for the future, there is too little for Hill and his coaches to work with this season. The four main guys (Raimondo, Namolik, Crep and Yasser) are solid, but with the exception of Mboya, there is not much behind them.

The Lions may be able to equal last season's talent on the will of that solid nucleus alone, but on those deadly Ivy back-to-back weekends, there is just not enough ammunition.

Even in his fifth year of rebuilding, Hill needs to locate some more bricks. But, Columbia fans may want to enjoy this brief renaissance—four of the starters are seniors. Doesn't bode well for the 1999-2000 season, does it?

One thing working to Columbia's advantage is a blitz on the early schedule. As was the case last year, the Lions play early and often, with nine games on the docket before Dec. 8. With a senior team that is woefully thin in numbers,

1998-99 COLUMBIA SCHEDULE

Nov.	15	@Holy Cross
	18	@Lafayette
	21	Quinnipiac
	23	@St. John's
	27-28	#Pepsi-Marist Classic
Dec.	3	@Rutgers
	5	Army
	7	Stony Brook
	27	@Nevada-Las Vegas
Jan.	2	@Lehigh
	8	Darthmouth
	9	Harvard
	18	@Cornell
	24	Cornell
	29	Princeton
	30	Pennsylvania
Feb.	5	@Brown
	6	@Yale
	12	@Harvard
	13	@Dartmouth
	19	Yale
	20	Brown
	26	@Pennsylvania
	27	@Princeton

@ Road Games
\# Poughkeepsie, NY (vs. Vermont, first round; also, Colgate and Marist)

these games may be helpful as the troops will be fresh. They then take almost three weeks off before getting back at it with a difficult post-Christmas journey to UNLV (December 27). This team should probably linger over their holiday celebrations.

(B.A.)

CORNELL

LOCATION .... **Ithaca, NY**
CONFERENCE .... **Ivy League**
LAST SEASON .... **9-17 (.346)**
CONFERENCE RECORD .... **6-8 (t-4th)**
STARTERS LOST/RETURNING **2/3**
NICKNAME .... **Big Red**
COLORS .... **Carnelian Red and White**
HOMECOURT .... **Newman Arena (4,473)**
COACH .... **Scott Thompson (Iowa '76)**
RECORD AT SCHOOL .... **24-28 (2 yrs.)**
CAREER RECORD .... **129-177 (11 yrs.)**
ASSISTANTS .... **Ray Jones (La Salle '69)**
Desmond Oliver (Dominican '92)
Jonathan Tsipis (North Carolina '96)
TEAM WINS (last 5 yrs.) **8-9-10-15-9**
RPI (last 5 yrs.) **250-279-240-168-257**
1997-98 FINISH .... **No conference tournament.**

Now, there's not too many times when a team coming off of a nine-win season can feel good about the upcoming season. But Cornell may have one of those teams.

The Big Red's tie for fourth place last year in the Ivy League marked the program's best league finish in five years. That, plus nine returning players—including three starters—has led to some excitement in Ithaca.

The offensive onus will probably fall upon 6-5 sophomore forward **Ray Mercedes** (12.6 ppg, 4.2 rpg), who was the squad's leading scorer last season. He started 17 games in a solid freshman season, during which he netted double figures 17 times, including 10 in a row.

Two juniors, 6-8 **Derek Kruse** (5.3 ppg, 2.6 rpg, .558 FG) and 6-6 **Keirlan Brown** (3.8 ppg, 3.1 rpg), will compete for time at the power-forward spot. Kruse, who missed some time last season with a deep thigh bruise, is athletic and ran cross country in high school. Despite his injury last year, he did have three games in double-digit scoring and will add some offense up front.

Brown, also the squad's backup center, is small in height but able to throw his 230 pounds around effectively. He is also an excellent offensive rebounder, grabbing 66 of his 130 career rebounds on the offensive end.

Two freshmen will also vie for time at forward. The tallest of the two is 6-10, 220-pound **Trevor Tarpley** (Cherry Creek HS/Englewood, Co.), who averaged 9.6 ppg, 10.4 rpg and 4.1 bpg in high school. He was athletic enough to letter in soccer in high school, following in the footsteps of his father, Tim, who was a first-team, All-American in soccer at Cal-Berkeley in the early '60s.

His high school teammate, 6-5 **Luke Vernon** (Cherry Creek HS/Englewood, Co.) will also work for some time up front. Vernon, who averaged 10.1 ppg and 5.7 rpg, was first-team all conference as a senior.

Rounding out the inside game is 6-11 senior center **Jeffrion Aubry** (8.9 ppg, 7.0 rpg, 53 blocks). The team's captain, Aubry needs to match his blocks total from last year to become the program's all-time-leading shot blocker. He makes it difficult for opponents to do anything in the lane. Besides Brown, another center backup will be 6-8 sophomore **Cody Bradshaw** (0.4 ppg, 0.8 rpg), who saw very limited action last season.

The Big Red backcourt will see some changes this year. **Kevin Cuttica** (8.1 ppg, 3.4 rpg, 79 assists), a 6-3 sophomore, will move to shooting guard despite starting every game as a point guard last season. He is moving to allow 5-9 freshman **Wallace Prather** (Cedar Grove HS/Decatur, Ga.) to step into the point-guard position. Prather is a scorer, averaging 25.5 ppg and 4.1 assists in his senior year and was a two-time all-Georgia selection by *USA Today*.

Also in the backcourt will be 6-2 sophomore **Quran Pender** (2.7 ppg, 0.8 rpg), saw action last season in a backup role and should challenge for time as a two-guard. Other returning members of the backcourt are 6-3 senior **RaShan Hilton** (1.9 ppg, 2.5 rpg) and 6-2 junior **Jim Pieri** (1.9 ppg, 0.7 rpg).

Two freshmen join Prather at guard: 6-0 **Pete Carroll** (Glenbrook North HS/Northbrook, Ill.) and 6-5 **A.J. McGuire** (Phillips Exeter Academy/Winchester, Mass.). Carroll averaged 17.2 ppg, 5.8 rpg and 8.2 assists as a senior while McGuire, the grandson of legendary Marquette coach Al McGuire, suffered a season-ending injury during his post-graduate year at Exeter.

1998-99 CORNELL SCHEDULE

Nov.	17	Buffalo
	21	Bucknell
	24	Penn State-Behrend
	27-28	#Lobo Classic
Dec.	4-5	##First Bank Classic
	12	Marist
	20	@Colgate
	30	@Lehigh
Jan.	2	@Army
	8	Harvard
	9	Dartmouth
	16	Columbia
	18	Lafayette
	23	@Columbia
	29	Pennsylvania
	30	Princeton
Feb.	5	@Yale
	6	@Brown
	12	@Dartmouth
	13	@Harvard
	19	Brown
	20	Yale
	26	@Princeton
	27	@Pennsylvania

@ Road Games
\# Albuquerque, NM (vs. New Mexico, first round; also LaSalle and Northeastern)
\## Milwaukee, WI (vs. Marquette, first round; also Tulsa and Vermont)

adidas Blue Ribbon Analysis

BACKCOURT	**C**	**BENCH/DEPTH**	**C**
FRONTCOURT	**C**	**INTANGIBLES**	**C**

Despite some promise, this turns out to be an average team—with one caveat. They are young, with just two seniors. Look for the Big Red to be a force in the 1999-2000 season.

To put the ball into the hands of a freshman, even a talented one like Prather, is risky. Thompson has some confidence in the youngster, but will suffer some growing pains.

So, be patients Cornell fans. This year will not be the best, but better things await.

(B.A.)

DARTMOUTH

LOCATION .... **Hanover, NH**
CONFERENCE .... **Ivy League**
LAST SEASON .... **7-19 (.269)**
CONFERENCE RECORD .... **4-10 (7th)**
STARTERS LOST/RETURNING **2/3**
NICKNAME .... **Big Green**
COLORS .... **Dartmouth Green and White**
HOMECOURT .... **Leede Arena (2,100)**
COACH .... **Dave Faucher (New Hampshire '72)**
RECORD AT SCHOOL .... **85-97 (8 yrs.)**
CAREER RECORD .... **85-97 (8 yrs.)**
ASSISTANTS .... **Mike Maker (California Baptist '88)**
Rob Summers (Dartmouth '90)
Jay Tilton (Hobart '92)
TEAM WINS (last 5 yrs.) **10-13-16-18-7**
RPI (last 5 yrs.) **233-202-149-117-271**
1997-98 FINISH .... **No conference tournament.**

Many around the country were starting to take notice of the Big Green in recent years. This is a team that won 18 games and was 117 in the RPI after the 1996-97 season. Maybe this was a program to mention in the same breath as Penn and Princeton in the Ivy League.

Not so fast. Last year's dropoff wasn't a shock to most Dartmouth observers, as the program lost a ton from its previous successful years. But a drop to seventh in a weak Ivy last year was out of the question.

Well, maybe it wasn't. Dave Faucher learned what countless other coaches have learned before him—without a point guard the offense doesn't go. Last year, the offense was a mess, as the Big Green scored nine less points per game than its opponents.

Well, the sign of a good coach is to see a need and fill it. Faucher hopes he has done that by adding 6-0 freshman **Flinder Boyd** (Fairfax HS/Los Angeles, Calif.), who turned down several scholarship offers to make his way to Hanover. He is billed as a textbook study of a point guard—meaning he plays defense and thinks of the pass before scoring. With credentials like that, he should be a fan favorite in the tradition-rich Ivy League, once he matures.

Unfortunately, his backup also has little experience. **Justin Whisenant** (2.2 ppg, 0.9 rpg), a 6-2 sophomore, missed much of last season with ankle problems, playing in just five games.

The other backcourt position will be filled after a battle among four other players. **Greg Buth** (5.6 ppg, 1.9 rpg), a 6-3 sophomore, is the leading contender, having turned in a solid, if unspectacular, rookie year. He was banged up early last season, suffering from a knee injury.

A pair of juniors, 6-4 **Brian Laibow** (2.8 ppg, 1.4 rpg) and 6-2 **Jason Kemp** (0.7 ppg, 1.0 rpg), will also see some time in the backcourt. Laibow has a 20-point performance (vs. Colgate last season) in his resume, while Kemp started six games last year after missing two years because of a Mormon mission. Also, look for 6-4 freshman **Charles Harris** (White Station HS/Memphis, Tenn.), who led his team to the state tournament final in his senior season.

Three other players round out the backcourt corps. **Brad Stooks**, (0.0 ppg, 0.0 rpg), a 5-9 sophomore, shooting guard, played sparingly in 13 games last season and failed to make a shot in six attempts. **Aaron Wilkinson** (0.3 ppg, 0.3 rpg), a 6-3 sophomore, was also little-used, seeing action in eight games and making one of his two shot attempts. **Nick Murphy**, a 6-0 freshman (Hilton Head Prep/Blufton, S.C.), can play either guard position.

Up front is where the experience is, especially with 6-7 junior **Shaun Gee** (18.3 ppg, 6.0 rpg) and 6-8 sophomore **Ian McGinnis** (8.5 ppg, 8.0 rpg). Gee was the Ivy's leading scorer last year and earned a berth on the all-conference team. A powerful forward, he causes defensive trouble throughout the league and will again be the Big Green's best weapon.

McGinnis' strength lies under the boards. He grabbed eight rebounds a game last year and led the Ivy. His 207 boards were the most by a first-year player in Hanover since 1973-74—all of this despite being hampered with a back injury throughout the year.

Backing up these two are a junior, a sophomore and two freshmen. The junior is 6-6 **Chris Ellis** (1.9 ppg, 1.0 rpg), who has a nice scoring touch from the outside, but his lack of weight hurts him in the paint. **Chris Swanson** (0.4 ppg, 0.9 rpg), a 6-6 sophomore, appeared in just seven games last year and was hampered by nagging injuries all

1998-99 DARTMOUTH SCHEDULE

Nov.	14	Lafayette
	18	@Vermont
	21	Colgate
	28	Keene State
Dec.	1	@Holy Cross
	13	New Hampshire
	16	@Harvard
	19	North Carolina
	21	@Navy
	28	@Denver
	31	@Wyoming
Jan.	2	@Air Force
	8	@Columbia
	9	@Cornell
	13	Harvard
	23	Denver
	30	Brown
	31	Yale
Feb.	5	@Pennsylvania
	6	@Princeton
	12	Cornell
	13	Columbia
	19	Princeton
	20	Pennsylvania
	26	@Yale
	27	@Brown

@ Road Games

season.

The freshmen are 6-9 **Mark Kissling** (Okemos HS/ Okemos, MI), who was an all-state selection in his senior year, and 6-5 **Vedad Osmanovic** (Dwight School/New York, NY), who may see time in the swing position. Like Boyd, Osmanovic turned down scholarship offers to play for the Big Green.

The middle has the potential of causing many problems for Dartmouth, with no real player available to step up. The starter after two years as a backup will be 6-9 junior **Ryan Smerek** (3.4 ppg, 3.2 rpg). Also in the mix is 6-11 **Jay Jenckes** (Lawrenceville (N.J.) School/Houston, Tex.), who has a major-league body but will certainly experience growing pains getting adjusted to the college game. Also, McGinnis will slide over from the power forward spot when needed.

adidas Blue Ribbon Analysis

BACKCOURT .... C BENCH/DEPTH .... D+
FRONTCOURT .... C+ INTANGIBLES C

If there is ever a mandatory senior class trip throughout the Ivy League that would last the entire basketball season, then Dartmouth would certainly be among the favorites to repeat. The Green Wave does not have one senior on the roster, and all of that inexperience could be harmful.

That having been said, it also means there is a tremendous potential upside to this team. Gee and McGinnis are known commodities. But what if Boyd is the real deal as his credentials seem to suggest? That could put Dartmouth into a position to contend in the Ivy.

But, that may be a bit presumptuous. In reality, next year would seem to be a better year in Hanover. But, in 1998-99, Big Green fans should look for improvement and be satisfied . That, along with the uptempo offense that Faucher plans to install, should keep the Leede Arena jumping this season.

(B.A.)

HARVARD

LOCATION .... **Cambridge, MA**
CONFERENCE .... **Ivy League**
LAST SEASON .... **13-13 (.500)**
CONFERENCE RECORD .... **6-8 (t-4th)**
STARTERS LOST/RETURNING **1/4**
NICKNAME .... **Crimson**
COLORS .... **Crimson, Black and White**
HOMECOURT .... **Lavietes Pavilion (2,195)**
COACH .... **Frank Sullivan (Westfield State '73)**
RECORD AT SCHOOL .... **72-110 (7 yrs.)**
CAREER RECORD .... **186-196 (14 yrs.)**
ASSISTANTS .... **Kevin O'Brien (Tufts '80)**
Bill Holden (Bentley '90)
James White (Harvard '95)
TEAM WINS (last 5 yrs.) **9-6-15-17-13**
RPI (last 5 yrs.) **269-288-184-130-207**
1997-98 FINISH .... **No conference tournament.**

When you are a student on Harvard's famous Yard, basketball may not seem as important as producing a Nobel Prize winner or seeing an alum elected to the U.S. Senate. What the Crimson has accomplished the last three seasons, though, has made people take notice.

For the first time in 34 years, Harvard's squad has posted three straight winning seasons outside the Ivy. In that time, the Crimson has posted the league's second-best record—even better than perennial powerhouse Pennsylvania. In fact, the last three years has been the winningest stretch in school history (45). If they can manage 12 victories this season, the Harvard seniors will have set the mark for wins in a four-year stretch (57).

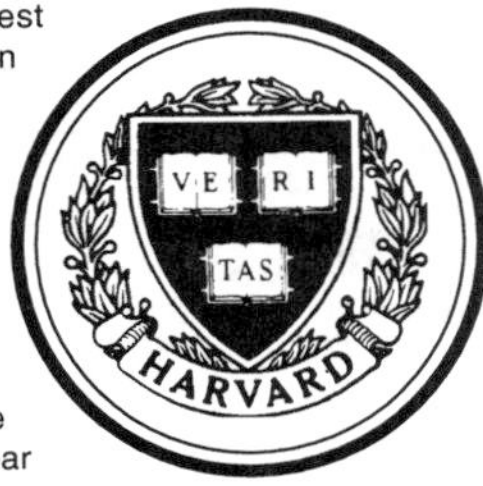

That means the pressure is on for Frank Sullivan's squad. Luckily for Harvard fans, it doesn't seem as if 1998-99 will be any different in Cambridge than the previous three. Four starters and five reserves are back, making the Crimson one of the early favorites to challenge for the upper tier of the Ivy.

The one big change will be the loss of Mike Scott to graduation. With him leaves 15.1 points, 5.9 rebounds and 3.0 assists per game. That will be a huge gap to fill.

Just under 58 points of offense is returning, including second-team, all-Ivy League point guard **Tim Hill** (14.9 ppg, 2.5 rpg, 5.3 apg). The 5-11 senior is just 30 points away from becoming Harvard's 19th player to go above the 1,000-point plateau and has a chance to become the program's all-time assist leader.

1998-99 HARVARD SCHEDULE

Nov.	18	@Boston College
	24	Holy Cross
	28	Lehigh
Dec.	1	@Marist
	5	Sacred Heart
	8	Boston University
	11	@Colgate
	16	Dartmouth
	19	@Northeastern
	21	@Hartford
	29-30	#Cable Car Classic
Jan.	4	@Navy
	8	@Cornell
	9	@Columbia
	13	@Dartmouth
	30	Yale
	31	Brown
Feb.	5	@Princeton
	6	@Pennsylvania
	12	Columbia
	13	Cornell
	19	Pennsylvania
	20	Princeton
	26	@Brown
	27	@Yale

@ Road Games
# San Jose, CA (vs. Santa Clara, first round; also San Francisco and St. Joseph's)

An extremely solid point guard, Hill is stingy with the ball, dishing 2.3 assists to every turnover and going 16.9 minutes between miscues. Also working in his favor is his durability. In the last two years, Hill has led the Ivy League in minutes played (1,005 in 1996-97 and 998 in 1997-98).

Joining him in the starting backcourt will be 6-2 senior **Mike Beam** (8.7 ppg, 2.6 rpg, 28 assists). Beam is a steady and amazingly accurate from the perimeter. His .513 shooting percentage from beyond the three-point arc was good for fourth-best in the country and set a Harvard record.

Occasionally, the Crimson like to employ a three-guard offense. When they do, expect that third guard to be 6-2 junior **Damian Long** (4.0 ppg, 2.0 rpg). Long, who can play either guard position, thinks offense. Like Beam, he is an effective outside shooter, making 46 percent of his treys. Last season, Long notched three double-digit efforts, including a career-high 17 against intra-state rival Holy Cross.

Behind them will be three freshmen fighting for time. **Andrew Gellert** (Newtown HS/Newtown, CT), a 6-2 point guard and all-state selection as a senior, will vie for minutes as Hill's backup. Also seeing action will be 6-1 guard **Patrick Harvey** (Brother Rice HS/Chicago, IL) and 6-1 guard **Alex Lowder** (Bishop Arnat HS/West Covina, CA). Harvey is an outside scoring threat, while Lowder will be able to play both guard positions.

One of last season's biggest surprises was 6-7 sophomore forward **Dan Clemente** (13.8 ppg, 5.3 rpg). The Ivy League Rookie of the Year in 1996-97, Clemente tied two of the program's three-pointer records—most in a game (6) and most consecutive games with a trey (18). He was the team's most prolific outside scorer, hitting a Harvard-best 48 three-pointers last year. This year, he will fill Scott's small forward spot, moving over from the power forward position he occupied a year ago.

Finding someone to fill Clemente's old role will be a challenge. Four players will be vying for the spot, with two sophomores leading the way. **Tim Coleman** (1.6 ppg, 1.8 rpg), 6-8, was solid a year ago, showing promise especially on the offensive boards where he gathered half his 30 rebounds. **Chris Lewis** (0.6 ppg, 0.8 rpg), 6-7, is a good defender but undersized for the position.

Also inside will be senior captain, 6-8 center **Paul Fisher** (10.7 ppg, 7.7 rpg, 19 blocked shots). He has shored up the middle, grabbing 7.7 boards a game, second-best in the Ivy, and blocking 19 shots, best by a Crimson player since 1993 when Arturo Llopis had 37.

Fisher will be backed up by 6-9 senior **Bill Ewing** (1.6 ppg, 2.2 rpg), a solid defender and shot blocker. Ewing blocked 16 shots a year ago. Coupled with Fisher, Ewing gives Harvard a defense that will force opponents to stay outside.

Rounding out the frontcourt will be 6-8 forward **Ethan Altaratz**, a transfer from Samford who sat out last year, and 6-6 senior forward **Chris Dexter** (2.0 ppg, 1.2 rpg), who suffered through an injury-plagued season in 1996-97. Dexter is a good outside shooter who could see some time at small forward if healthy.

adidas Blue Ribbon Analysis

BACKCOURT .... B BENCH/DEPTH .... C+
FRONTCOURT .... B INTANGIBLES .... C+

This should be a telling year in Cambridge. The team is experienced and good, two words that should spell success in the Ivy League.

Are the Crimson good enough to crash the Princeton/ Penn party that has ruled the league for a decade? Possibly. If Hill and Clemente are as good as they were last year and the rest of the offense continues to click, then this team could contend. Sullivan has been around long enough to know which buttons to push.

If there's a weakness, it's defense. Last year, the Crimson's opponents shot 46 percent from the floor and they surrendered 69 points per game. Both numbers need to be lower if Harvard is to be successful.

Look for good things coming out of Cambridge this year. With so many returnees, this has to be the year, as the program will spend next season rebuilding. With Princeton rebuilding this season (or having as close to a rebuilding year as the Tigers can have), look for the Crimson to be playing a major role in the Ivy race come late February.

(B.A.)

PENNSYLVANIA

LOCATION .... **Philadelphia, PA**
CONFERENCE .... **Ivy League**
LAST SEASON .... **17-12 (.586)**
CONFERENCE RECORD .... **10-4 (2nd)**
STARTERS LOST/RETURNING **1/4**
NICKNAME .... **Quakers**
COLORS .... **Red and Blue**
HOMECOURT .... **The Palestra (8,700)**
COACH .... **Fran Dunphy (La Salle '70)**
RECORD AT SCHOOL .... **152-91 (9 yrs.)**
CAREER RECORD .... **152-91 (9 yrs.)**
ASSISTANTS .... **Gil Jackson (Elizabethtown '69)**
Steve Donahue (Ursinus '84
TEAM WINS (last 5 yrs.) **22-25-17-12-17**
RPI (last 5 yrs.) **50-79-113-153-125**
1997-98 FINISH .... **No conference tournament.**

In this league, can it be any surprise that a team with a name starting with "P" is a favorite to take the title? Penn and Princeton have dominated Ivy League basketball since the early '60s and this year looks to be no different. But this year, the league title should return to Philadelphia.

The Quakers return four of their five starters from a year ago and also get back 6-11 junior center **Geoff Owens**, who missed all of last year because of a heart condition. He returns to shore up a frontcourt that should be one of the best in the league.

Still, when you talk about Penn, you must start in the backcourt. There, it is led by 6-0 junior guard **Michael Jordan** (15.3 ppg, 4.4 rpg, 131 assists, 45 steals), who has lived up to the pressure associated with the name of his boyhood idol. Jordan is one of the premier players in the Ivy League, leading his team in almost every scoring category.

He will be joined in the backcourt by 6-5 junior **Matt Langel** (13.5 ppg, 3.8 rpg), a good shooting guard who can light it up from anywhere. Together, they form one of the best backcourts around.

Backing up at the point position is 6-0 sophomore **Lamar Plummer** (4.3 ppg, 0.7 rpg), who had a decent rookie season last year and is expected to step right in off the bench.

Up front will be an area of strength that did not always exist for Penn last year. Owens was sorely missed in the middle—his absence forced other Quakers to play out of position. **Jed Ryan** (10.1 ppg, 4.0 rpg), a 6-7 senior, will be able to become a better offensive player and can move outside where he is more comfortable.

He will be paired with fellow 6-7 senior **Paul Romanczuk** (14.0 ppg, 6.3 rpg, 22 blocks), the team's leading rebounder and interior defender last season. He and Owens should provide a formidable force inside for the Quakers.

Owens, the only true center on the Penn roster, blocked 40 shots as a freshman (a program rookie record) and

1998-99 PENNSYLVANIA SCHEDULE

Nov.	18	Kansas
	23	Temple
Dec.	3	Lehigh
	5	@Villanova
	12	@Penn State
	26-27	#ECAC Holiday Festival
Jan.	5	@Lafayette
	8	Yale
	9	Brown
	14	La Salle
	16	Colgate
	18	St. Joseph's
	21	Drexel
	29	@Cornell
	30	@Columbia
Feb.	5	Dartmouth
	6	Harvard
	12	@Brown
	13	@Yale
	16	Princeton
	19	@Harvard
	20	@Dartmouth
	26	Columbia
	27	Cornell
Mar.	2	@Princeton

@ Road Games
# New York, NY (vs. Iona, first round; also Georgia Tech and Hofstra)

should be a more balanced player in 1998-99.

Coming off the bench up front is 6-6 senior forward **George Mboya** (2.4 ppg, 3.0 rpg), who was called on for defensive purposes often last season. Also up front is 6-8 sophomore **Josh Sanger** (1.6 ppg, 2.4 rpg), who was forced to start half of the Quakers' games at center because of Owens' injury.

Also seeing time as a reserve will be 6-6 senior **Frank Brown** (5.9 ppg, 4.4 rpg). Brown has been injured both of the last two years. If his knee holds up, he is an athletic addition to the Penn roster as he can play small forward or shooting guard.

Mike Sullivan (1.1 ppg, 0.8 rpg), a 6-6 senior forward, saw spotty time last season. Rounding out the roster are 6-5 junior forward **Matt Koller** (Greybull HS/Greybull, Wyo.), 6-7 sophomore forward **Jon Tross** (Madison, Conn./Hamden Hall) and 6-6 freshman forward **Dan Solomito** (St. Andrews School (Fla.)/Montclair, N.J.).

adidas Blue Ribbon Analysis

BACKCOURT .... **B** **BENCH/DEPTH** .... **C+**
FRONTCOURT .... **B** **INTANGIBLES** .... **B+**

This should be the year the Penn Quakers take back the Ivy crown from Princeton, which has been among the nation's best in the last two seasons.

The return of Owens automatically makes the Quakers better and puts them above the rest of the Ivy League. He should be among the candidates for the all-Ivy team.

Jordan is a stud—certainly a favorite for the Ivy League Player of the Year. He has so many weapons that it is nearly impossible to guard him.

Those two players plus the experience among the starting lineup give the Quakers all they will need to make a return trip to the NCAA Tournament. Factor in Fran Dunphy, one of the best unsung coaches in the nation, and you have to believe that there is a Wharton School alum already creating the league championship t-shirts just to have ready. It would be hard to argue with that business strategy.

(B.A.)

PRINCETON

LOCATION .... **Princeton, NJ**
CONFERENCE .... **Ivy League**
LAST SEASON .... **27-2 (.931)**
CONFERENCE RECORD .... **14-0 (1st)**
STARTERS LOST/RETURNING **3/2**
NICKNAME .... **Tigers**
COLORS .... **Orange and Black**
HOMECOURT .... **Jadwin Gym (6,854)**
COACH .... **Bill Carmody (Union '75)**
RECORD AT SCHOOL .... **51-6 (2 yrs.)**
CAREER RECORD .... **51-6 (2 yrs.)**
ASSISTANTS .... **Joe Scott (Princeton '87)**
John Thompson (Princeton '88)
Howard Levy (Princeton '85)
TEAM WINS (last 5 yrs.) **18-16-22-24-27**
RPI (last 5 yrs.) **141-153-55-40-22**
1997-98 FINISH .... **Lost in NCAA second round.**

Last season was finally the year. After years of being David against Goliath, the Princeton Tigers were actually a college basketball giant. Ranked eighth in the country at the end of the season, Princeton got to wear the home uniforms in the NCAA Tournament and didn't have to worry about pulling off the upset. All it had to guard against was preventing one.

It was a wonderful year: Another perfect Ivy League sweep (two straight years) and a third-straight league title. Does it get any better than this?

Fortunately for the rest of the Ivy, the answer is no. Princeton is not going to dominate the league this year. In fact, the Harvard Crimson may give it a run for its money for that second spot behind Pennsylvania. How can the Tigers go from the lofty end of 1998 to a battle for second in '99? Easy, take away three experienced starters of the ilk of center Steve Goodrich, point guard Mitch Henderson and James Mastaglio.

Bill Carmody, yet to lose an Ivy League game in his tenure at Princeton, will have to figure out a way to make this work. But, you would be hard-pressed to bet against him. One of the best young coaches in the nation, Carmody has the second-best record of any coach after two years. They're heavy numbers, but numbers that he seems to wear easily.

Not that the cupboard is completely depleted, but it sure is close. Thankfully for Tigers fans, first-team All-Ivy Leaguer **Gabe Lewullis** (14.2 ppg, 5.3 rpg, 35 steals, 74 assists), a 6-6 senior forward, and second team, All-Ivy **Brian Earl** (13.1 ppg, 2.7 rpg, 50 steals, 62 assists), a 6-2 senior guard, top the returnees for the Tigers.

Lewullis is just 167 points shy of the 1,000-point plateau and is fifth all-time from behind the three-point arc. One of the guys he trails in both categories is Earl, who has 986 career points and 212 career treys, just 23 away from the program's record. Earl is also a multi-dimensional talent, with ballhandling skills that will aid the point guard and defensive skills to guard against the opponents' best guard.

After that, the team is thin. **C.J. Chapman** (2.3 ppg, 0.5 rpg), a 6-1 sophomore, played in 23 games last year and has a difficult job to take over for Henderson. A sure-handed guard who rarely turns the ball over, Chapman will have to work to get his teammates scoring opportunities.

Another returning member of the backcourt will be 6-3 sophomore **Lance Walters** (0.7 ppg, 0.1 rpg), who appeared in just nine games last season. (As a point of trivia, Walters does possess the best vertical leap among the Tigers. Maybe the Princeton track coach should take a look.)

Also in the backcourt is 6-5 sophomore **Anthony Taylor** (0.0 ppg, 0.6 rpg), who saw spotty action in 12 games. **Eugene Baah** (Northfield-Mount Hermon/New York, N.Y.), a 6-5 freshman, will also add some depth to the guard spot.

A gaggle of forwards will join Lewullis up front. **Mason Rocca** (2.7 ppg, 2.2 rpg), a 6-7 junior, spent much of last season at center, but the coaches hope he will be able to team with Gabe at power forward. That would give Princeton a size advantage over most of the teams on its schedule.

Nathan Walton (1.7 ppg, 2.2 rpg), a 6-7 junior forward will also spend time at power forward. Like Rocca, he spent some time in the middle last season, but should see the majority of his time down low in '98-99.

Phil Belin (2.3 ppg, 0.8 rpg), a 6-4 junior, is a quality three-point shooter who should swing between the two-guard and small-forward positions.

Two other returners, 6-7 sophomore **Terence Rozier-Byrd** (0.8 ppg, 0.7 rpg) and 6-6 senior **Chris Kilburn-Peterson** (0.0 ppg, 0.4 rpg), will share hyphens on the Tigers' bench.

Four freshmen will round out the Tigers' forward crew: 6-6 **Mike Bechtold** (Lebanon HS/Lebanon, Penn.), a solid three-point shooter; 6-4 **Ahmed El-Nokali** (Chartiers Valley HS/Pittsburgh, Penn.), a swing player; and 6-5 **Phil Jackman** (San Ramo HS/Danville, Calif.) and 6-7 **Ray Robbins** (Pasorobeles HS/Pasorobeles, Calif.), a pair of prolific scorers from the Golden State.

The center spot should be an interesting battle. The Tigers have brought in three freshmen named Chris who will vie for time in the middle: **Chris Krug** (Germantown Academy/Philadelphia, Penn.), 6-9, joins his brother Todd in the Ivy League (Pennsylvania) and looks to be the front-runner of the group. **Chris Young** (Highland Park HS/Dallas, Texas) is the tallest at 6-10, and the most athletic. He also stands on the pitchers' mound in the spring for the Tigers, packing a 90 mph fastball. The last Chris is 6-8 **Chris Martin** (Episcopal HS/Olney, Md.). If none of the Chrises are ready, look for Rocca or Walton to take over the spot.

1998-99 PRINCETON SCHEDULE

Nov.	18	@Lafayette
	21	@North Carolina-Wilmington
	28	@Monmouth
Dec.	4-5	#Cyclone Challenge
	9	Bucknell
	15	@UAB
	19	*Maryland
	22	Rutgers
	27-30	##Rainbow Classic
Jan.	8	Brown
	9	Yale
	25	Union
	29	@Columbia
	30	@Cornell
Feb.	5	Harvard
	6	Dartmouth
	12	@Yale
	13	@Brown
	16	@Pennsylvania
	19	@Dartmouth
	20	@Harvard
	26	Cornell
	27	Columbia
Mar.	2	Pennsylvania

@ Road Games
* Baltimore Arena, Baltimore, MD
# Ames, IA (vs. North Texas State, first round; also Iowa State and Western Illinois)
Honolulu, HI (vs. Florida State, first round; also Hawaii, Murray State, Mississippi State, Southwestern Louisiana, Texas and UNC Charlotte)

adidas Blue Ribbon Analysis

BACKCOURT .... **C+** **BENCH/DEPTH** .... **C**
FRONTCOURT .... **C+** **INTANGIBLES** .... **B**

It's hard to believe, but Princeton will struggle. Well, maybe not as much as some the other Ivy teams struggle, but the Tigers will struggle compared with what they have become used to.

There is just too much talent gone and and not enough talent to replace it. Beyond Earl and Lewullis, Carmody will be shaking his head searching for answers. And the Tigers will play a schedule that befits a team that was in the top 10 during the previous year. Dates at the Iowa State Cyclone Challenge, at Maryland on ESPN, at the Rainbow Classic in Honolulu and against Florida State loom. Unfortunately, that could spell disaster for the Tigers, who barely resemble that team from a year ago.

In the Ivy, Princeton will be hard-pressed to stay undefeated again. The Tigers could escape January without losing in the league, but two games against Harvard and Pennsylvania follow. There is potential that the mighty Tigers could fall to third in the Ivy League, a momentous occasion in the league this decade.

The intangibles are Carmody and that "Princeton Mystique." Maybe Carmody is that genius everybody says he is and he can pull a rabbit out of the hat. Basketball fans can only hope so, because it is awfully fun to watch the Tigers battle the big boys in March.

(B.A.)

YALE

LOCATION	**New Haven, CT**
CONFERENCE	**Ivy League**
LAST SEASON	**12-14 (.462)**
CONFERENCE RECORD	**7-7 (3rd)**
STARTERS LOST/RETURNING	**2/3**
NICKNAME	**Elis, Bulldogs**
COLORS	**Blue and White**
HOMECOURT	**John J. Lee Amphitheater (3,100)**
COACH	**Dick Kuchen (Rider '66)**
RECORD AT SCHOOL	**147-167 (12 years)**
CAREER RECORD	**230-281 (19 years)**
ASSISTANTS	**Greg Herenda (Merrimack '83) Stephen Graham (North Carolina Central '92)**
TEAM WINS (last 5 yrs.)	**10-9-8-10-12**
RPI (last 5 yrs.)	**245-284-282-241-218**
1997-98 FINISH	**No conference tournament.**

There was some joy in New Haven last year as the Elis won 12 games, the most since the 1991-92 season. Well fans, don't expect a repeat.

The Bulldogs are young and two key components, Emerson Whitley (16.1 ppg, 6.8 rpg, 48 steals) and Matt Ricketts (10.9 ppg, 2.3 rpg, .880 FT), have graduated and moved away from the Pound. That leaves a void in the lineup that will be hard to fill.

Stepping into that vacuum is 6-6 senior **David Tompkins** (9.9 ppg, 7.3 rpg, .724 FG in Ivy contests). He will move to the power-forward spot that is more natural than center, where he played most of last season. After spending much of his first two seasons on the bench, Tompkins made the most of his extended playing time last season, starting all but one game and leading the team in rebounding.

Joining him in the frontcourt is 6-1 senior **Charlie Petit** (7.0 ppg, 1.9 rpg), who will serve as the team's captain. Petit, who will float between small forward and shooting guard, is a good shooter from beyond the three-point arc. He's made 110 in his career, fifth on Yale's all-time list.

Two juniors will also see action in the frontcourt. 6-6 **Ted Smith** (1.8 ppg, 1.7 rpg) is coming off of a knee injury, but did have 10 steals in the 10 games he played.

John Kirkowski (0.8 ppg, 1.6 rpg), 6-6, came off the bench behind Whitley and played in 13 games last year. Smith and Kirkowski bring little offense to the table, combining to shoot nine for 32 from the field last year.

A senior and four freshmen make up the rest of the forward corps. **Ken Marschner** (1.2 ppg, 1.6 rpg), a 6-6 senior, saw action in 18 games last season, with some at forward and some at center. A receiver on the Eli football team, Marschner should add some power inside.

The four freshmen are: 6-7 **James Ahern** (St. Rose Belmar HS/Sea Girt, N.J.), who averaged a double-double as a high school senior (15 ppg and 10 rpg); 6-7 **David Huhs** (Mercer Island HS/Mercer Island, Wash.), a strong inside presence who grabbed nine rebounds a game in high school; another double-double performer in 6-7 **Tyrone Powell** (Redwood HS/Visalia, Calif.), who averaged 10 points, 10 rebounds and three blocks in his senior season; and 6-5 **Brad Reusch** (Highland HS/Medina, Ohio), a prolific scholastic scorer who averaged 26 points and nine rebounds to make him Highland's second-leading all-time scorer.

Rounding out the frontcourt are two 6-10 sophomore centers. **Neil Yanke** (3.6 ppg, 2.2 rpg) has the Bulldogs' staff buzzing. Yanke is an athletic 6-10 who can run and has a good scoring touch—two rare qualities for big men.

Giving Yanke a run for playing time is **Tom Kritzer** (2.6 ppg, 1.1 rpg), who suffered with a back injury through most of last year but seems healthy now. To get both players on the floor as much as possible, look for one to slide over to power forward at times.

In the backcourt is 5-11 senior **Marlon Simpkins** (5.0 ppg, 2.2 rpg, 37 steals), the team's best defensive player. Simpkins, a quick two-guard, did have a number of good outings last year and is the best the Elis have at guard.

He will be joined by 5-10 sophomore point guard **Isaiah Cavaco** (2.0 ppg, 0.9 rpg), who was hampered by an injury midway through last season. He was Yale's best freshman last year and needs to step in and have a solid season for the Elis to entertain any thoughts of competing this season.

Athletic forward **Jason Williams** (3.8 ppg, 1.5 rpg), a 6-4 junior, will play the shooting-guard and small-forward spots. He appeared in all but one of the Bulldogs' games last year and brings some stability to the backcourt.

Mark Bratton (0.7 ppg, 0.0 rpg), a 6-2 sophomore, was limited to just 25 games last year because of a knee injury. How he rehabilitates will tell how much depth Kuchen has in the backcourt.

Onaje Woodbine (Lawrenceville Prep [N.J.]/Boston, Mass.), a 6-2 freshman, is going to be given a look after averaging 14.5 ppg and 6.0 apg as a high school senior.

adidas Blue Ribbon Analysis

BACKCOURT	**D+**	**BENCH/DEPTH**	**C**
FRONTCOURT	**C+**	**INTANGIBLES**	**C**

Yale is going to struggle. Too much has been lost for the Elis to really compete in an Ivy League that is looking stronger from top to bottom than it has in recent years. A lot of inexperience should spell doom for Yale.

Things could get better if Cavaco has a big sophomore season and the two centers perform beyond what is expected. But they will be tested with games at Notre Dame and at the Wyoming Cowboy Classic.

Although this year looks like a wash in New Haven, Bulldogs fans should take heart. At some of the most skilled positions, Yale will be young. No consolation for 1998-99, but hope for the future.

(B.A.)

1998-99 YALE SCHEDULE

Nov.	13	@Holy Cross
	15	@Notre Dame
	19	Lehigh
	28	New Hampshire
Dec.	3-4	#Phoenix Classic
	7	@Army
	9	@Vermont
	26-27	##Cowboy Shootout
Jan.	8	@Pennsylvania
	9	@Princeton
	16	@Brown
	18	Swarthmore
	23	Brown
	25	Denver
	30	@Harvard
	31	@Dartmouth
Feb.	5	Cornell
	6	Columbia
	12	Princeton
	13	Pennsylvania
	19	@Columbia
	20	@Cornell
	26	Dartmouth
	27	Harvard

@ Road Games
# Hartford, CT (vs. Hartford, first round; also Central Connecticut and Fordham)
Laramie, WY (vs. Wagner, first round; also Louisiana Tech and Wyoming)

METRO ATLANTIC ATHLETIC CONFERENCE

adidas BLUE RIBBON FORECAST

1. Iona
2. Rider
3. Siena
4. Canisius
5. Niagara
6. Fairfield
7. Loyola College
8. Marist
9. Manhattan
10. St. Peter's

ALL-CONFERENCE TEAM

G—Greg Burston, SR, Rider
G—Marcus Faison, JR, Siena
F—Kashif Hameed, SR, Iona
F—Tariq Kirksay, JR, Iona
C—Roderick Platt, SR, Loyola (Md.)

PLAYER OF THE YEAR

Kashif Hameed, SR, Iona

NEWCOMER OF THE YEAR

Steve Grant, JR, Marist

1998-99 CONFERENCE TOURNAMENT

Feb. 26-March 1, Marine Midland Arena, Buffalo, NY

1997-98 CHAMPION

Iona (regular season)
Iona (conference tournament)

1997-98 POSTSEASON PARTICIPANTS

Postseason Record: 0-2 (.000)
NCAA
Iona
NIT
Rider

TOP BACKCOURTS

1. Siena
2. Rider
3. Loyola (Md.)

TOP FRONTCOURTS

1. Iona
2. Canisius
3. Rider

ON THE WAY UP

Siena

ON THE WAY DOWN

Manhattan

INSIDE THE NUMBERS

- 1997-98 conference RPI: 13th (of 30)
- Conference RPI (last 5 years): 18-20-13-21-13

DID YOU KNOW?

The MAAC has been an incubator of coaches of late—producing Tim Welsh (Iona to Providence), Fran Fraschilla (Manhattan to St. John's), Mike Deane (Siena to Marquette), Brian Ellerbe (Loyola College to Michigan), Skip Prosser (Loyola College to Xavier), Steve Lappas (Manhattan to Villanova) and up-and-comer John Beilein (Canisius to Richmond) in the 1990s alone. FYI: The next hot commodity out of this league appears to be Siena's John Leonard...Speaking of coaches, there are three new ones in the MAAC this season—former Iona alum/NBA All-Star Jeff Ruland at Iona, long-time La Salle assistant Joe Mihalich at Niagara and former Seton Hall assistant Tim O'Toole at his alma mater Fairfield. O'Toole's previous stops as an assistant include stints under Jim Boeheim at Syracuse ('92-95) and Mike Kryzewski at Duke ('95-97)...Loyola College point guard Jason Rowe was in the top 10 in the MAAC in six categories last year...Canisius' 13-14 record represented the Golden Griffs' first losing record since '92-93...St. Peter's enters the '98-99 season in the midst of a 10-game losing streak. It could be 11 with Seton Hall as the season opener...Of the 21 new head coaches who had never been a Division I head coach before, only three of them—North Carolina's Bill Guthridge (34-4), Georgia's Ron Jirsa (20-5) and Wyoming's Larry Shyatt—finished with more victories last season than Rider's Don Harnum...Iona's trip to the '98 NCAA Tournament was the school's first in 13 years.

(B.D.)

CANISIUS

LOCATION .... **Buffalo, NY**
CONFERENCE .... **Metro Atlantic Athletic (MAAC)**
LAST SEASON .... **13-14 (.481)**
CONFERENCE RECORD .... **9-9 (t-5th)**
STARTERS LOST/RETURNING **1/4**
NICKNAME .... **Golden Griffins**
COLORS .... **Blue & Gold**
HOMECOURT .... **Koessler Athletic Center (1,800)**
Marine Midland Arena (19.500)
COACH .... **Mke McDonald (St. Bonaventure '88)**
RECORD AT SCHOOL .... **13-14 (1 yrs.)**
CAREER RECORD .... **13-14 (1 yrs.)**
ASSISTANTS .... **Terry Zeh (St. Bonaventure '90)**
Damone James (Canisius '95)
Brian Miller (St. Bonaventure '88)
TEAM WINS (last 5 yrs.) **22-21-19-17-13**
RPI (last 5 yrs.) **74-82-73-124-135**
1997-98 FINISH .... **Lost in conference first round.**

To say that Canisius coach Mike McDonald is anxious to get the 1998-99 season started is an understatement. That's because, after a 9-4 start in his first season as the Golden Griffins' head man, his team stumbled to the finish line with a 13-14 record. That included an overtime loss to Siena in the first round of the MAAC Tournament.

"That loss was a tough pill to swallow," said McDonald, thinking about the 13-point lead that his team blew down the stretch. "When you lose a game like that, you want to get right back on the court and play again. We have to wait nine months to make amends."

The late-season tailspin was a result of a lot of factors—the two biggest being the fact that every starter but one (the departed Kevin Thompson) was playing his first season as an impact player and also the fact that starting center **Matt Tribul**, a 6-9 junior, suffered a stress fracture in his foot, leaving the Griffs vulnerable in the middle.

His loss left 6-10 sophomore **Darren Fenn** as the only center on the roster. Fenn (6.0 ppg, 4.7 rpg, 35 blocked shots, 12 steals) made the most of his opportunity as a freshman, earning a place on the all-MAAC rookie team and getting invited to try out for the USA Basketball men's junior team last June in Colorado Springs.

"I thought Matt was doing a great job for us and was getting better each time out, but Darren had a great year and the extra minutes will benefit him this season," said McDonald.

Fenn is just one of four returning starters for Canisius. Double-figure scoring forwards **Jamie Cammaert** and **Keith Lambkin** are also back, as is point guard **Kevin Worley**, who was arguably the most-improved player in the MAAC last season. Cammaert (13.9 ppg, 6.7 rpg, 74 assists, 21 steals), a 6-5 senior, started all 27 games at power forward in 1997-98 and was a force inside. He led the Golden Griffins in scoring 12 times and in rebounding 13 times, notching five double-doubles in the process.

Lambkin (12 ppg, 5.7 rpg, 49 assists, 29 steals), a 6-4 senior, has steadily improved throughout his career—averaging 3.4 ppg as a freshman, 6.4 as a sophomore and 12 ppg last year. He scored a career-high 25 points in a home win over Siena last season.

"Jamie and Keith were our stabilizers," said McDonald. "I thought they both matured over the course of the year and are ready this season to take over the leadership responsibilities of the club."

Few would have guessed that Worley, a 6-2 senior, would have made such an impact last season. In his first two years, Worley was little more than a footnote for the Golden Griffs—shooting only .235 percent from the field and averaging a scant 2.2 ppg as Bam Moore's backup. As a junior, though, the Maryland native averaged 8.7 points and 3.2 assists, shot 42 percent from the field and led the team in three-pointers made (39).

"During his first two years, our boosters would yell "Oh no, Kevin's on the floor!' " said McDonald. "Last year, when I took him out, all I heard was "Oh no, Kevin's not on the floor'."

Worley's understudy is 6-0 sophomore **Clive Bentick** (0.6 ppg, 0.2 rpg). The New York City native saw limited action last season, but the coaching staff thinks that he has all the tools to be a successful point guard in the MAAC.

"Clive will see more court time this year," said McDonald. "He's outstanding on defense and, like Worley, needs playing time in order to have the confidence in his game at the offensive end."

Thompson (12.7 ppg), Worley's backcourt running mate last season, has graduated, but McDonald hopes that junior college import **Dorian McClure** of Macomb (Mich.) Community College can fill Thompson's hightops. McClure, a 6-2 junior, averaged 23.7 points (sixth-best in school history) and 4.9 rebounds per game for Macomb 1996-97. He signed in November of 1996, but did not enroll in classes at Canisius until last January.

If McClure doesn't pan out, then Lambkin might have to move to shooting guard. That's because sophomore Damon Young, who was being counted on to take on some minutes at the shooting guard slot, injured his ACL this summer and is probably lost for the season.

Even though Cammaert and Lambkin are the incumbents at the forward spots, they will have to contend with athletic junior **Dale Sawyers** and incoming freshmen **Alex Barnhill** and **Andre Jackson**. Cammaert is versatile enough to fill in for Lambkin at small forward should the senior need to move to the off-guard.

The 6-8 Sawyers (3.6 ppg, 2.2 rpg) closed the 1997-98 season with a flourish, making 23 of his last 29 shots (.793 percent) from the field. The 6-4 Barnhill averaged 19 points and seven rebounds last season for Bridgeton (Maine) Academy, which finished 20-11. Jackson, 6-5, averaged 14.5 points and 7.8 boards at Gwynn Park (Md.) High last season and was the MVP of the Maryland-Pennsylvania all-star game after scoring a career-high 27 points.

"We really upgraded our talent from a year ago at the three and four spots," said McDonald. "Jamie and Keith are much better, Dale is on the verge of breaking out and having a great year and the two freshman are very talented."

Fenn will be part of a center-by-committee approach by McDonald. Tribul, who missed 14 early-season starts in 1997-98, has rehabilitated his foot injury and is ready to return, while 6-8 redshirt freshman **Andrew Bush** is ready to fight for playing time in the pivot, too.

"There were times in practice that Andrew dominated Darren and Matt," said McDonald. "Andrew is capable of playing both the four and five spots. He's strong and aggressive near the basket and will give us another dimension in the middle."

adidas Blue Ribbon Analysis

BACKCOURT	**C+**	**BENCH/DEPTH**	**C**
FRONTCOURT	**B**	**INTANGIBLES**	**B**

Mike McDonald's squad is anxious to get started this season after the wheels fell off down the stretch in 1997-98. Canisius has lots of versatility at the three and four spots, with double-digit scorers Keith Lambkin and Jamie Cammaert back in the fold. Plus, McDonald has a solid leader at the point in Kevin Worley, arguably the MAAC's most-improved player last season.

However, despite the return of four starters, there are minor questions in the middle and major ones at the vacant two-guard spot. Those are more question marks than MAAC frontrunners Iona, Rider and Siena have.

Call it a fourth-place regular season finish—behind the three aforementioned teams. But the Golden Griffins could be dangerous in the MAAC Tournament, which is played on their homecourt.

(B.D.)

1998-99 CANISIUS SCHEDULE

Nov.	21	@St. Bonaventure
	24	@Buffalo
Dec.	4	Iona
	6	St. Peter's
	12	Buffalo
	19	@Xavier
	22	Duquesne
	28-29	#Bobcat Holiday Classic
Jan.	3	Colgate
	8	@Marist
	10	@Siena
	14	@Fairfield
	16	Marist
	18	Loyola College
	21	Rider
	23	Manhattan
	30	@Iona
Feb.	1	@St. Peter's
	4	Siena
	6	Niagra
	8	@Manhattan
	11	Fairfield
	15	@Niagara
	18	@Loyola
	20	@Rider
26-Mar.	1	##MAAC Tournament

@ Road Games
\# Bozeman, MT (vs. Montana State, first round; also Boston University and Colorado)
\## Marine Midland Arena, Buffalo, NY

FAIRFIELD

LOCATION .... **Fairfield, CT**
CONFERENCE .... **Metro Atlantic Athletic (MAAC)**
LAST SEASON .... **12-15 (.444)**
CONFERENCE RECORD .... **7-11 (t-7th)**
STARTERS LOST/RETURNING **1/4**
NICKNAME .... **Stags**
COLORS .... **Red, Black & White**
HOMECOURT .... **Alumni Hall (2,479)**
COACH .... **Tim O'Toole (Fairfield '87)**
RECORD AT SCHOOL .... **First Year**
CAREER RECORD .... **First Year**
ASSISTANTS .... **Jerry Hobbie (Fordham '85)**
Fred Quartlebaum (Fordham '89)
Matt Roe (Maryland '91)
TEAM WINS (last 5 yrs.) **8-13-20-11-12**
RPI (last 5 yrs.) **204-181-75-227-175**
1997-98 FINISH .... **Lost in conference first round.**

For the first time in school history, Fairfield will play basketball at Alumni Hall with one of its alums in charge. That's because last April 2, Tim O'Toole (class of 1987) was hired as the school's new head coach.

If nothing else, O'Toole has been well-schooled as an assistant coach, working under the likes of Duke's Mike Krzyzewski and Syracuse's Jim Boeheim. Most recently, O'Toole had been for Tommy Amaker, who is trying to rebuild the hoops fortunes at Seton Hall. But when his alma mater called, O'Toole couldn't help but listen. One of his former bosses, for one, thinks that Fairfield has gotten a real up-and-comer who has the right stuff to run his own program.

"Tim is as good a young assistant as I've ever been involved with and I've been involved with Rick Pitino and a whole bunch of other guys," said Boeheim, for whom O'Toole worked from 1992-95. "I can't recommend anyone as highly as Tim. He's an outstanding young coach. He'll coach just like he played—100 percent, full-blast, year-round."

Fortunately, O'Toole inherits a team which returns four starters: senior forward **Didier Boucard**, senior guard **Kyle Commodore**, junior forward **Darren Phillip** and junior center **Sunday Eniojukan**. All four were part of Fairfield's magical run to the 1997 NCAA Tournament and would love nothing better than to get backin '99.

Eniojukan has been a starter pretty much since he first arrived on campus two years ago. The 6-7 sophomore averaged 6.3 ppg and 4.9 rpg last season and has played in 57 consecutive games. He always shows up for work (which is good) but he must post bigger scoring numbers in the post, if Fairfield has any hope of competing with the MAAC's elite teams.

His backup in the middle will be 6-9 senior **Mike Horan** (3.8 ppg, 3.2 rpg). Horan wasn't at full effectiveness (thanks to a severe ankle injury), but still managed to play in 19 games last season. Horan and Eniojukan averaged just more than eight rebounds per game between them, a number O'Toole will need to significantly increase for the Stags to get anywhere near an NCAA bid.

The forward position seems solid with Boucard and Phillip both back in uniform. The 6-4 Boucard puts the "small" in small forward, but he posted big numbers last season-averaging 10.3 ppg and a team-best 6.6 rpg. He also gained a reputation as one of the MAAC's top shot blockers, rejecting 56 (2.1 per game) to rank among both the league and national leaders .

The 6-9 Phillip has been injury-plagued throughout his first two seasons at Fairfield. When he was out there, Phillip was effective, finishing as one of the team's most accurate marksman (.557 FG percentage) and top scorers (10.7 ppg). Phillip, who played well last summer as part of the MAAC's all-star team which toured Japan, might be ready to blossom into one of the league's top forwards, if he can just stay healthy. He has the quickness necessary to be successful around the basket, both offensively and defensively.

1998-99 FAIRFIELD SCHEDULE

Nov.	14	@Duke
	17	@Fordham
	20-21	#AT&T Shootout
	26	@Boston College
Dec.	2	@Central Michigan
	5	@Loyola
	7	Rider
	12	San Francisco
	23	@Connecticut
Jan.	3	@Marist
	6	Niagara
	8	@St. Peter's
	12	Siena
	14	Canisius
	17	Manhattan
	21	@Iona
	23	Loyola
	26	@Manhattan
	28	St. Peter's
Feb.	1	@Siena
	6	@Rider
	11	@Canisius
	13	@Niagara
	16	Iona
	20	Marist
26-Mar.	1	##MAAC Tournament

@ Road Games
# Fairfield, CT (vs. Long Island, first round; also George Mason and Portland)
Marine Midland Arena, Buffalo, NY

Junior **Andy Buzbee** and sophomore **Chris Rivers** will also figure prominently in the frontcourt picture. The 6-6 Buzbee has been a starter and a valued reserve during his career. He handled both roles pretty well last season, as he averaged 4.5 points and 3.9 rebounds in 27 games (including nine starts). Buzbee is adept at stepping out and hitting the 12-to 15-footer, which can draw the defense out and open things up inside for others, such as Boucard or Phillip.

The slender Rivers (6-7, 185) ranked as one of the team's all-around best shooters (49 percent from the field and 70 percent from the free-throw line). Rivers appears to have a bright future after averaging 3.9 points and 2.1 boards as a freshman.

The leader of this pack of Stags will be 5-11 senior point guard Commodore. The homegrown product is the team's top three-point shooter, connecting on 32 percent (33 of 88) of his shots from behid the arc. He also led the team in assists, handing out a meager 2.9 per game. While Commodore will once again run the show, the second-guard position is still up for grabs.

The list of suspects to land that spot include 6-3 sophomore **Leroy Robertson**, 6-0 sophomore **Charles "Boo" Farrow** and 6-5 freshman **Jermaine Clark**.

After playing secondary roles last season, look for Robertson and Farrow to take on more of the load in 1998-99. Robertson appeared in 24 of the team's 27 games, averaging 5.7 points and 1.4 rebounds. The bad news for O'Toole is that Roberston isn't the world's best long-distance shooter (isn't that part of the job description?). He shot 50 percent (35 of 70) inside the arc, but only 18 percent outside the three-point line.

Farrow's progress, on the other hand, was slowed by a broken hand which forced him to miss six games. He still appeared in 21 games and averaged 4.7 points and 2.2 assists.

If neither pans out, O'Toole can always turn to Clark—who played for perennial power St. Patrick's (N.J.), the 1998 New Jersey state champs and the same school that produced Shaheen Holloway and 1998 NBA early entrant Al Harrington. Clark mixes dependable ball-handling skills with the ability to stroke the perimeter jumper. How did the proven winner land at Fairfield? O'Toole hired Jerry Hobbie, an assistant coach at St. Patrick's for the last four years, as one of his assistants at Fairfield. That could turn out to be a smart hire, because St. Patrick's turns out Division I players as regularly as Detroit churns out mini-vans.

The unproven lot of shooting guards will be tested early and often against a rough-as-sandpaper schedule. The Red and White open against Duke at Cameron Indoor Stadium on November. Can you say blowout? The Stags also play two Big East teams on the road, Connecticut (yet another top-three team) and Boston College, before Christmas.

Is that any way to treat an alum?

adidas Blue Ribbon Analysis

BACKCOURT	C-	BENCH/DEPTH	C
FRONTCOURT	C+	INTANGIBLES	C+

Tim O'Toole returns to his alma mater with tons of outstanding behind-the-scenes experience as an assistant under the likes of Jim Boeheim and coach K. Now, it's O'Toole's turn to run the show. Expect him to be intense and prepared. The problem is that he appears to have middle-of-the-pack MAAC talent.

His squad is undersized, but solid at the forward slots. That's the good news? On the downside, O'Toole doesn't have a proven shooting guard and his depth isn't great. Still, he has some upperclassmen who have been to the Big Dance before. Add it all up and it looks like a fifth- or sixth-place finish in the 10-team MAAC in Year One of the O'Toole regime.

Our guess? Make it sixth place.

(B.D.)

IONA

LOCATION	**New Rochelle, NY**
CONFERENCE	**Metro Atlantic Athletic (MAAC)**
LAST SEASON	**27-6 (.818)**
CONFERENCE RECORD	**15-3 (1st)**
STARTERS LOST/RETURNING	**2/3**
NICKNAME	**Gaels**
COLORS	**Maroon & Gold**
HOMECOURT	**Mulcahy Center (3,200)**
COACH	**Jeff Ruland (Iona '91)**
RECORD AT SCHOOL	**First Year**
CAREER RECORD	**First Year**
ASSISTANTS	**Craig Holcomb (Brockport State '86)** **Tony Chiles (Columbia '89)** **Rob O'Driscoll (Villanova '94)**
TEAM WINS (last 5 yrs.)	**7-10-21-22-27**
RPI (last 5 yrs.)	**271-254-69-103-43**
1997-98 FINISH	**Lost in conference first round.**

After Iona's boy wonder coach Tim Welsh headed for literally greener pastures at Providence this offseason, it was a no-brainer as to who would replace him.

The man who was at Welsh's side as the Gaels won three straight MAAC regular season titles. Welsh's right-hand man as Iona went to the Big Dance for the first time in 13 years. That's right, former NBA All-Star and Iona alum Jeff Ruland. Since his hiring on April 6, Ruland has aggressively pursued his goal of returning Iona to the level it attained in the late 1970s and early 1980s, when he and then-head coach Jim Valvano put the Gaels on the college basketball map.

During the press conference to announce his hiring, Ruland vowed that he was going to strengthen the Gaels' schedule, as he proclaimed: "We will play anybody, anywhere, anytime."

Ruland has been a man of his word thus far. He has accepted invitations to play perennial Atlantic 10 power Massachusetts on Jan. 5 and to play in two high-profile tournaments—the Hawaiian Hoops Classic (the field includes TCU, Southern Mississippi and Illinois State) and the ECAC Holiday Festival (which includes Georgia Tech).

Why shouldn't Ruland take on all comers? His frontcourt is loaded, thanks to the return of reigning MAAC Player of the Year **Kashif Hameed**. After playing last season at center, Ruland vows to move the 6-8 Hameed to his natural position of power forward for his senior year. Wherever he plays, Hameed figures to be a force on both ends of the court. Last season, he led the Gaels in scoring (15.3 ppg) and blocked shots (2.5 bpg), while also grabbing 6.2 rebounds per game. In addition to being a candidate to repeat as MAAC Player of the Year, Hameed will also attract some NBA scouts to Iona's Mulcahy Center.

While they're there, the NBA scouts might want to start taking notes on 6-6 junior forward **Tariq Kirksay**, a high-major Division I talent toiling in the MAAC just as current Kentucky star Heshimu Evans did at Manhattan a couple of years back. Kirksay is easy to spot because of his entertaining style of play and his odd fashion statement of wearing a blue and white-striped tube sock at full mast (think stripes like those in a Dr. Seuss hat) on his left foot and just tape on his right foot. Kirksay, like Hameed, is a quick leaper who fills up lots of columns on the stat sheet night in, night out. Kirksay played in all 33 games for the Gaels last season, averaging 14.2 ppg and leading the team in rebounding (7.2 rpg), steals (2.3 spg) and three-point field goal percentage (.385).

Ivo Kresta, a 6-9 junior from the Czech Republic, was the Gaels' most improved player last season. He gives Ruland another talented option along the front line. His athletic ability and emotional style of play earned him a starting spot just four games into last season. Like many international forwards, Kresta (6.3 ppg, 3.2 rpg) has a smooth stroke from three-point range—which prevents opposing defenses from just surrounding Hameed on the low blocks.

Kresta might be the first big man off the bench rather than a starter for Iona in 1998-99—if Ruland sticks to his plan of moving Hameed to power forward. That move would open up the starting center spot for burly 6-9 sophomore **Nakiea Miller**, who impressed the coaches with his late-season play. In just 18 games last season, the powerfully built lefty averaged 4.2 points and 4.1 rebounds and shot a remarkable 68 percent from the field. In addition to his wide array of moves on the low block, Miller can step out and hit the 15-foot jumper from the high post. Miller looks like he has the makeup to be a major force on the boards and at the rear of the press, where his wing span of a 7-footer will wreak havoc.

Miller's backups at the five-spot will be Hameed (when Ruland opts to play him with Kirksay and Kresta) and 6-11, 250-pound sophomore **Ned Rolsma**, who has a clean bill of health after being an injury redshirt last year. Rolsma, Iona's tallest recruit in the 1990s, saw action in only three games last season. But Rolsma—who seems to be a pet project of Ruland's— possesses a soft shooting touch and has worked hard in the offseason to improve his strength and footwork.

There's still even more talented athletes in Iona's frontcourt—which is one of the best on the East Coast. Senior forward **Jamal Dunmore**, a 6-7 junior college import, returns for his second season with the Gaels. He's one of the best pure athletes on the team, along with Kirksay. Dunmore (3.8 ppg, 2.4 rpg) possesses outstanding quickness and leaping ability. As a result, he's a force at the point of Iona's fullcourt pressure.

Like Dunmore, heralded freshman **Dyree Wilson** from Rice High School in the Bronx seems suited to thrive in the open court. The 6-5 Wilson is still raw, but he figures to develop quickly into a player just by going against Kirksay every day in practice.

While the Gaels are loaded in the frontcourt, they will be somewhat inexperienced in the backcourt with tough-as-nails floor general John McDonald and starting two-guard Donell Mitchell both lost to graduation. Both were double-figure scorers last season. McDonald's lethal first step and fearlessness heading into the tall trees had ESPN analyst Bill Raftery running on empty in the adjective department in last season's MAAC title game. McDonald figures to play pro ball overseas, while Mitchell already is—in Korea.

First in line to replace McDonald at lead guard is hard-nosed 6-2 junior **Jason Young**, who was the first guard off the bench for the Gaels last season. Young appeared in all

1998-99 IONA SCHEDULE

Nov.	27-29	#Honolulu Shootout
Dec.	4	@Canisius
	6	@Niagara
	8	Hofstra
	12	@Fordham
	15	St. Francis (NY)
	20	Morgan State
	26-27	##ECAC Holiday Festival
Jan.	2	Loyola
	5	@Massachusetts
	8	Rider
	10	@St. Peter's
	13	@Loyola
	15	Manhattan
	21	Fairfield
	24	@Siena
	28	@Rider
	30	Canisius
Feb.	1	Niagara
	4	@Idaho
	7	Marist
	10	St. Peter's
	13	@Manhattan
	15	@Marist
	18	@Fairfield
	21	Siena
26-Mar.	1	###MAAC Tournament

@ Road Games
# Honolulu, HI (vs. Hawaii-Pacific, first round; also Baylor, Hofstra, Illinois State, Missouri-Kansas City, Southern Mississippi and Virginia Commonwealth)
New York, NY (vs. Pennsylvania, first round; also Georgia Tech and Hofstra)
Marine Midland Arena, Buffalo, NY

33 games, taking over the point from McDonald and allowing him to move to the two-guard spot at times. Young (5.2 ppg, 1.8 rpg, 2.8 apg) only played 18 minutes per night, but appears to ready for the job—which is to pump the ball into the frontcourt stalwarts as often as possible.

Like most freshman, point guard **Javar Cheatham** (0.7 ppg, 0.3 apg) struggled last season in adjusting to the college game. But the 6-0 Cheatham has the foot speed and talent—remember, he was a first-team All-New York City selection as a high school senior—to thrive in Iona's helter-skelter style. He'll split the point-guard duties with Young.

The Gaels have two sharpshooters who will step in and see minutes at the two-guard spot. Sophomore **Phil Grant** (5.3 ppg, 2.4 rpg), a lanky 6-foot-7 player, had an impressive rookie season and will see time at two guard and small forward. His long arms and quick feet make him a dogged defender. Plus, he's equally adept at shooting the three-pointer or putting the ball on the floor and going to the basket.

Also expected to see time at the shooting guard is fellow sophomore **Steve Armistead**, a 6-3 shooter. Armistead (2.0 ppg) saw limited time, but did appear in 26 games last season. He has unlimited range on his near-textbook jumper. If neither one steps up, then Ruland might opt to put Kirksay, a Stacey Augmon-esque talent, at the two-guard spot.

Rounding out the roster is exciting newcomer **Leland Norris**, a 6-2 freshman combo guard from Newark, N.J. He's a hard worker who can shoot the ball from distance and also possesses fine ballhandling skills and court vision. He'll see some time as a freshman.

adidas Blue Ribbon Analysis

BACKCOURT .... **B-** **BENCH/DEPTH** .... **B+**
FRONTCOURT .... **A-** **INTANGIBLES** .... **B+**

Iona has won three consecutive regular-season MAAC titles. A fourth straight title is not a given, because Rider and Siena return most of their teams from last season and will provide stiff competition once again.

Iona has two of the five best players in the league in 1998 MAAC Player of the Year Kashif Hameed and 6-6 Tariq Kirksay, but appears to be vulnerable in the backcourt, where backups must step up to replace the fine backcourt of John McDonald and Donell Mitchell. Junior Jason Young seems to seasoned enough to take over at lead guard, but the major question mark is at the two-guard spot.

Our guess? New coach Jeff Ruland will use the tough preseason games to figure out if he has enough talent at the guard spots. If he doesn't, then he'll move Kirksay from small forward to two-guard to plug that hole. That move alone should be enough to secure a fourth straight MAAC crown for Iona in a photo-finish over Rider and Siena.

(B.D.)

LOYOLA COLLEGE

LOCATION .... **Baltimore, MD**
CONFERENCE .... **Metro Atlantic Athletic (MAAC)**
LAST SEASON .... **12-16 (.429)**
CONFERENCE RECORD .... **9-9 (t-5th)**
STARTERS LOST/RETURNING **1/4**
NICKNAME .... **Greyhounds**
COLORS .... **Green & Gray**
HOMECOURT .... **Reitz Arena (3,000)**
COACH .... **Dino Gaudio (Ohio '81)**
RECORD AT SCHOOL .... **12-16 (1 yr.)**
CAREER RECORD .... **48-88 (5 yrs.)**
ASSISTANTS .... **Dae Wojcik (Loyola '91)**
Darrell Brooks (Bowie State '79)
TEAM WINS (last 5 yrs.) **17-9-12-13-12**
RPI (last 5 yrs.) **121-212-160-191-171**
1997-98 FINISH .... **Lost in conference third round.**

Everyone—the coaching staff, players, even Loyola basketball fans—knew it would take some time for the 1997-98 Greyhounds to hit their stride. With seven newcomers and a first-year coach who promised a radically different style of play, a period of adjustment was a foregone conclusion.

And as expected, Loyola was a much better team at the end of the season than it was at the beginning, playing one game over .500 in its last 23 games, including a stunning win over eventual Metro Atlantic Athletic Conference champ Iona.

"It takes time for players to understand the system and what the coaches are looking for," said second-year coach Dino Gaudio, who came to Loyola after four years at Army. "This year, the coaches have a very good understanding of every player's capabilities."

For one thing, they know that they can count on highlight-film plays galore and great senior leadership from thrill-a-minute point guard **Jason Rowe** and powerful center **Roderick Platt**. The 5-10 Rowe ranked among the MAAC's top 10 in six categories on his way to earning second-team all-conference honors.

Meanwhile Platt, a 6-10, 262-pound bruiser, led the conference in rebounding and earned third-team all-MAAC honors. Obviously, both are legitimate candidates for first-team all-MAAC accolades in 1998-99.

Rowe was second in the conference in scoring (18.5 ppg) and assists (5.4 apg), while finishing first in the MAAC and fourth in the nation in steals (3.1 spg). Rowe also ranked among the MAAC's top 10 in field-goal percentage, three-point shooting and free-throw shooting and established school single-season records for steals (86), three-pointers made (57) and attempted (168). He combined with the now-departed, first-team all-MAAC two-guard Mike Powell to form the nation's second-highest scoring backcourt (41.2 ppg).

Replacing Powell (22.7 ppg) won't be an easy proposition, but 6-5 sophomore **Jamal Hunter** will give it a whirl. Hunter bounced in and out of the starting lineup as a freshman. For the season, the swingman appeared in 28 games, starting nine, and averaged 9.8 ppg on .429 percent marksmanship, including .354 shooting from three-point range. He really blossomed down the stretch, scoring in double figures in nine of the final 11 games, including a breakthrough 27-point effort against Iona in a MAAC Tournament semifinal.

A pair of newcomers—freshman **Damien Jenifer** and junior **Jerome Adams**—will battle for the backup point guard spot. Jenifer's versatility might give him a slight edge at this point, but both are tenacious defenders. That's imperative, because Loyola likes to apply full-court pressure most of the time. The 6-foot Jenifer averaged 22 points, 10 rebounds and 7.9 steals while leading Mervo Prep (Md.) to its first-ever regional championship.

Adams, 5-11, comes to Loyola with two years of junior college experience at Garrett (Md.) Community College, where he scored a remarkable 990 points.

Also competing for backup guard minutes will be sophomores **Brant Mack** and **James Tallarico** as well as junior **Mike Langley** and freshman **Anthony Walker**.

The best bet to get significant playing time from among this group is the youngest of the bunch. The 6-3 Walker brings one thing to the table that Loyola has been lacking in recent years—a consistent threat from the outside. Walker, an outstanding pure shooter, led Charleston High School in Massachusetts to a three-year record of 58-8, earning all-Boston honors of some sort after each of those seasons. He averaged 22.6 ppg, 14 rpg and 6.0 apg as senior at Charleston.

If the other guards are on the court, it's probably a signal of a blowout one way or the other. The 6-1 Mack was a backup point guard as a freshman, but saw limited duty, appearing in 17 games and averaging just 0.5 ppg in 3.8 minutes of action per night. Tallarico (1.0 ppg) is a 5-11 walkon who saw action in only two games. The 6-1 Langley, too, is a seldom-used walkon who appeared in just 12 games last season, averaging 0.3 ppg.

Loyola used a three-guard lineup much of last season, with 6-4 sophomore **Ryan Blosser** filling in as the third guard. This year, Gaudio hopes to use a more traditional lineup. That leaves Blosser to compete with 6-4 freshman **Melvin Robinson** for the starting small-forward slot. Another freshman, **Clifford Strong**, a high school power forward who needs to add some serious beef to his skinny bones (6-7, 190), might start his career as a small forward.

Blosser rebounded from an early-season shoulder injury to start 18 games., averaging 4.7 ppg and 2.5 rpg in 21.1 minutes of action. He's a fundamentally sound player who started 18 straight games before giving way to Hunter in the MAAC Tournament. He'll face stiff competition from a pair of prized New York City imports.

Robinson was one of the finest scorers in the New York City Public League last season. He averaged 23 ppg, 12 rpg and three apg as a senior at Cardozo High, where he notched 1,001 career points.

Strong is one the most heralded recruits in recent Loyola history. A versatile performer, Strong was recruited by many East Coast programs out Bishop Loughlin High, one of New York's perennial powers. Strong earned first-team All-Catholic honors as well as all-city and all-borough accolades as a senior.

One of the most spirited battles of the season figures to take place at the power-forward spot , where Strong will battle 6-7 junior **Blanchard Hurd** and 6-8 sophomore **Brian Carroll** for the starting job.

1998-99 LOYOLA COLLEGE SCHEDULE

Nov.	14	Howard
	19-21	#Battle for Baltimore
	28	Kent State
Dec.	2	@Siena
	5	Fairfield
	7	Denver
	19	Mount St. Mary's
	30	Virginia
Jan.	2	@Iona
	6	Manhattan
	10	@Rider
	13	Iona
	16	@Niagara
	18	@Canisius
	21	Siena
	23	@Fairfield
	27	@Marist
	29	@Manhattan
Feb.	2	@Denver
	5	Marist
	7	St. Peter's
	12	Rider
	14	@St. Peter's
	18	Canisius
	20	Niagara
26-Mar.	1	##MAAC Tournament

@ Road Games
# Towson, MD (vs. Maryland-Baltimore County, first round; also Morgan State and Towson)
Marine Midland Arena, Buffalo, NY

Carroll is the incumbent starter, having moved into that role after missing eight games last year with a stress fracture in his foot. Carroll is a strong, wiry player with excellent shot blocking skills. He started in 16 of his 20 appearances last year, averaging 4.2 ppg and 5.5 rpg in 26.1 minutes per outing. Carroll paced the team in blocked shots with 26 (1.3 per game), despite missing eight games with the foot problem. A lefty, Carroll has solid post moves and can step out to 15 feet and bury an open jumper.

Hurd, a Baltimore native, came to Loyola with a gaudy resume from Milford Hill High School. However, he has seen his first two season cut short by knee injuries. Hurd didn't play at all last season. His return would provide a huge boost, because at 235 pounds, Hurd provides a much-needed physical presence at both ends of the floor.

One position where there is no debate as to who will start is center, where preseason MAAC Player of the Year candidate Platt returns. Platt is a tireless worker on and off the court who has added 20 pounds of muscle since arriving at Loyola. He enjoyed a breakthrough season in 1997-98, grabbing a MAAC-leading 9.1 rebounds to go along with his 12.2 ppg in 32.4 minutes. He scored in double figures 21 times, including in 15 of the final 18 contests. He's still a work in progress at the offensive end, but is capable of averaging a double-double for the Greyhounds this season.

While Platt is clearly the top dog in the pivot for the Greyhounds, 6-7 sophomore **Apostolis Nasiou** from Trikala, Greece, is available should Platt need an occasional break. Actually, Nasiou will be backup at center and power forward—just as he was last season. He actually started eight games last year among his 28 appearances, averaging 3.0 ppg and 2.6 rpg on .474 shooting in 17.5 minutes. He's a very physical player who is foul-prone.

"I think the additions of Blanchard Hurd and Clifford Strong, along with the solid inside play of Rod Platt, will make us a formidable offensive team in the paint," said Gaudio. "But the key to that is our backcourt, which can be sensational. With Jason (Rowe) and Jamal (Hunter), we are far from one-dimensional and that could help make things much easier for our frontcourt players."

adidas Blue Ribbon Analysis

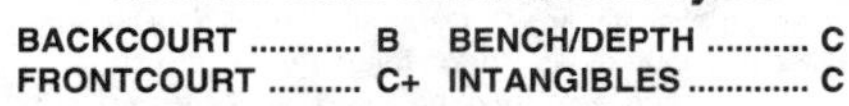

BACKCOURT .... **B** **BENCH/DEPTH** .... **C**
FRONTCOURT .... **C+** **INTANGIBLES** .... **C**

Loyola is the mystery guest in the MAAC. The Greyhounds have proven firepower in Jason Rowe and Roderick Platt and a possible budding star in Jamal Hunter. The problem areas remain the same: Defense and rebounding.

The Greyhounds' aggressive, pressing style often allows the opposing team to get easy buckets, if they have solid guard play and can break the press. As a result, while Loyola can score (76.5 ppg), it often can't stop the opposition (79.2 ppg). This must improve, or Loyola isn't going anywhere in the standings.

Plus, despite the fact that their roster includes the MAAC daddy of rebounders in Platt (a league-best 9.1 per game in 1997-98), the Greyhounds were still out-rebounded last season. They'll need to shore that area to be a title contender. Their only hope in that regard is that their front-line players stay healthy. Injuries have been a problem the last two years.

As a result, Loyola—arguably the MAAC's most exciting team to watch (as well as one of its most talented)—won't be its most successful in 1998-99. It looks like another second-division finish for Greyhounds, unless they do a much better job than expected on the boards and on defense.

(B.D.)

MANHATTAN

LOCATION .... **Riverdale, NY**
CONFERENCE .... **Metro Atlantic Athletic (MAAC)**
LAST SEASON .... **12-17 (.413**
CONFERENCE RECORD .... **7-11 (t-7th)**
STARTERS LOST/RETURNING **3/2**
NICKNAME .... **Jaspers**
COLORS .... **Kelly Green & White**
HOMECOURT .... **Draddy Gymnasium (3,000)**
COACH .... **John Leonard (Manhattan '82)**
RECORD AT SCHOOL .... **21-25 2 yrs.)**
CAREER RECORD .... **21-25 2 yrs.)**
ASSISTANTS .. **Sean Cleary (Franklin & Marshall '91)**
Marc Turner (Millersville '87)
John Dunne (Ithaca '92)
TEAM WINS (last 5 yrs.) **19-26-16-9-12**
RPI (last 5 yrs.) **86-45-98-235-168**
1997-98 FINISH .... **Lost in conference third round.**

In his attempt to return Manhattan to its high level of hoops in the mid-1990s, coach John Leonard is filling his roster with more new faces than even a clock manufacturer sees. The result? A team that was already young last season gets even younger this year as five new players join the program.

"We were young last year, but somehow we're getting even younger this year," said Leonard. "Well, maybe not younger. Maybe just newer."

But in this case, will "new" mean improved? We'll have to wait and see as there are lots of job openings on this team, which returns only two starters and lost its three top scorers to graduation.

Not surprisingly, those two returning starters are young: sophomore guards **Alvin Anderson** and **Mars Mellish** (an all-name team fixture the next couple years, to be sure). The 6-2 Anderson is back after earning MAAC All-Rookie honors as the Jaspers' point guard last year. Anderson (9.6 ppg, 4.0 rpg, 111 assists, 24 steals) was fourth in the MAAC in assists and is the top returning scorer for the Jaspers. Simply put, he's a star in the making.

"Alvin had an outstanding freshman year and has become one of the better younger players in our league. I'm expecting big things from him," said Leonard. "This season, I want to see him play like a veteran by developing more consistency in his shooting and decision-making. He certainly has the ability."

The 6-1 Mellish (6.3 ppg, 3.3 rpg, 37 assists, 29 steals) burst on to the scene as the starting two-guard and posted a career-high 14 points in the opener against Fairleigh Dickinson. Then, at season's end, he calmly sank eight of 10 free throws as Manhattan upset Rider in the MAAC Tournament.

Serving as the two primary backups to the all-sophomore starting tandem will be the threesome of 6-4 senior **Kyle Dye**, 6-5 freshman **Noah Coughlin** and 5-11 junior **Phil "Boo" Lane**. Dye (1.6 ppg, 0.5 rpg) has yet to start a game for Manhattan, but has appeared in 60 in his career.

Coughlin is one three freshmen recruits. He joins the Jaspers from Tabor (Mass.) Academy, where he posted team-best averages of 18 ppg and seven rebounds for a 19-6 team. His strengths include his perimeter shooting skills as well as his maturity for a freshman—the result of living away from home the last two years at Tabor.

Lane (3.2 ppg, 1.9 rpg, 67 assists, 27 steals) is a solid understudy to Anderson at the point. Lane has started 25 times in his career (only twice last season), so he knows the system. Plus, he is quick, which makes him pesky at the defensive end of the court.

Rounding out the backcourt rotation are a pair of 6-foot walkons in senior **Kevin Noone** and sophomore **Daryl Palmieri**. Noone (0.7 ppg, 0.3 rpg) appeared in a career-high 10 games last year, but his appearances were brief in nature (his longest being three minutes). Like Noone, Palmieri was primarily a practice player. He appeared in just nine games as a freshman and made one of his two three-point attempts for his only three points of the 1997-98 season.

The center spot is loaded with candidates, none a standout. **Kyle Crandall** (6-10, 240) is the only senior with any starting experience on the Jaspers' roster. Crandall (1.8 ppg, 2.0 rpg, 14 blocked shots) played in all 29 games last season, starting the first 12. The junior-college import was supposed to be the answer last season. But he seemed to be rushed into the starting lineup and never looked comfortable.

If he doesn't work out, perhaps junior **Badou Kane**, a 6-7, 225-pounder from Senegal, could be the man at the five spot. That is, if he could ever stay healthy. A wrist fracture as a freshman and recurring back problems last season limited his availability.

Besides Kane and Crandall, Leonard has two newcomers to turn to at the power positions in freshman **Justin Boeker** and sophomore **Phil Murray**. Boeker, a 6-9, 230-pounder from Strake Jesuit High in Houston, is another guy who will try to plug the hole in the middle. He averaged a double-double last season (13.7 ppg, 12.2 rpg), Leonard likes the fact that Boeker can step away from the basket and either pass out of the high post or score from there.

Murray (6-8, 235) is another new face for Leonard to consider. A New York City product, Murray decided to come home after seeing little time at Bowling Green. He'll be eligible after the fall semester.

One of the starting forward spots should go to 6-7 sophomore **Durelle Brown**, who saw a great deal of playing time as a freshman, including 11 starts. Brown is the team's leading rebounder and saved his best for last a year ago. He shot .761 percent over the last six games and .833 percent in the MAAC Tournament. He has lots of savvy around the hoop and just needs to get a little stronger to blossom.

Brown won't be handed a starting job, though. That because Leonard landed two recruits that he likes a lot in 6-6 freshman **Tydrayll Coleman** and 6-9 San Jose State transfer **Ken Kavanaugh**. Coleman averaged 20.5 ppg and 12.4 rpg last season for Valhalla (N.Y.) High and he could be the best all-around athlete on the Jaspers' roster. Kavanaugh, a junior, is more of a blue-collar worker who scraps and claws underneath. He'll be a solid board man and will draw fouls from opponents with his aggressive nature inside.

And they're not the only viable option. After sitting behind two seniors, 6-6 sophomore **Frank Drejaj** (1.2 ppg, 0.6 rpg) should see more opportunity to play meaningful minutes at small forward. He had his moments last year, including a nine-point performance (on four of six shooting) against Niagara.

adidas Blue Ribbon Analysis

BACKCOURT .... **C** **BENCH/DEPTH** .... **C**
FRONTCOURT .... **C** **INTANGIBLES** .... **C+**

This team has more unanswered questions than a season-ending episode of *Melrose Place*. The all-sophomore backcourt of Alvin Anderson and Mars Mellish will continue to go through growing pains. As will the rest of the Jaspers—thanks to the presence of six sophomores and three freshmen on coach John Leonard's roster.

Color this another season of growing—and losing—at Manhattan. But, on the bright side, the Jaspers should be better at the end of the season than they are at the beginning, as all the youngsters get more accustomed to the college game.

(B.D.)

1998-99 MANHATTAN SCHEDULE

Nov.	28	@Fairleigh Dickinson
Dec.	1	Buffalo
	4	@Rider
	6	Marist
	10	Army
	22	@Boston University
	27	Fordham
	30	@Colgate
Jan.	2	@Denver
	6	@Loyola College
	9	@Lehigh
	12	Niagara
	15	@Iona
	17	@Fairfield
	21	@Niagara
	23	@Canisius
	26	Fairfield
	29	Loyola College
	31	Rider
Feb.	3	@St. Peter's
	6	Siena
	8	Canisius
	11	@Siena
	13	Iona
	18	@Marist
	21	St. Peter's
26-Mar.	1	#MAAC Tournament

@ Road Games
\# Marine Midland Arena, Buffalo, NY

MARIST

LOCATION .... **Poughkeepsie, NY**
CONFERENCE .... **Metro Atlantic Athletic (MAAC)**
LAST SEASON .... **11-17 (.393)**
CONFERENCE RECORD .... **7-11 (t-7th)**
STARTERS LOST/RETURNING **3/2**
NICKNAME .... **Red Foxes**
COLORS .... **Red & White**
HOMECOURT .... **McCann Center (3,944)**
COACH .... **Dave Magarity (St. Francis-Pa. '74)**
RECORD AT SCHOOL .... **168-173 (12 yrs.)**
CAREER RECORD .... **228-249 (17 yrs.)**
ASSISTANTS ...... **Stephen Sauers (SUNY-Albany '90)**
Van Macon (Southampton '94)
George Siegrist (Marist '95)
TEAM WINS (last 5 yrs.) **14-17-22-6-11**
RPI (last 5 yrs.) **183-148-99-289-203**
1997-98 FINISH .... **Lost in conference second round.**

In his case, Marist coach Dave Magarity is hoping that 13 turns out to be lucky. His last two seasons have been tough ones as the Red Foxes have won six and 11 games, respectively. He's hoping that Year Two as a MAAC member, not to mention his 13th season at Marist, will be much better than Marist's inaugural MAAC season.

To ensure that it is, Magarity and his assistants had a mission: Find two big men who could step in immediately and a backcourt of the future that could serve as understudies in 1998-99. Mission accomplished—maybe. Magarity and his staff landed one of the MAAC's finest recruiting classes.

Magarity knew his team was set this season at the guard positions with senior point guard **Borja Larragan** from Madrid and senior two-guard **Bobby Joe Hatton** from Puerto Rico both back in the fold. The 6-2 Larragan (14.1 ppg, 101 assists), a third-team all-MAAC performer, is a heady leader with a wealth of international experience. He scored in double figures 23 times last season and also led the squad in assists. Larragan is a lethal weapon in the closing minutes when Marist is ahead and playing keep-away. He's adept at dribbling, so it's hard to strip him. And fouling Larragan, a Providence transfer, is not an option because he was 11th in the nation in free throw percentage (.882).

The 6-2 Hatton, like his backcourt mate Larragan, is another top-notch foreign import. He started 27 games for the Red Foxes and led the team in scoring for a second straight season (14.9 ppg). He took a 21-game double-figure scoring streak into the season. Hatton didn't rest on his laurels, helping Puerto Rico's 22-and-under team win the bronze medal at the World Games in Australia this summer. He got immeasurably better this summer just by going head-to-head with former Massachusetts stars Edgar Padilla and Carmelo Travieso every day in practice.

Magarity hopes his two prize freshman backcourt recruits—6-2 **Sean Kennedy** and 6-3 **Richard Smith**—will learn the ropes the same way by battling Hatton and Larragan every day in practice. Magarity went to Billy Joel country (Oyster Bay, Long Island) to snag Kennedy, one of

1998-99 MARIST SCHEDULE

Nov.	24	Middle Tennessee State
	27-28	#Pepsi Marist Classic
Dec.	1	Harvard
	4	Siena
	6	@Manhattan
	9	@American
	12	@Cornell
	22	@Arizona State
	30	Army
Jan.	3	Fairfield
	5	@St. Peter's
	8	Canisius
	10	Niagara
	16	@Canisius
	18	@Niagara
	23	St. Peter's
	27	Loyola
	30	@Siena
Feb.	2	Rider
	5	@Loyola
	7	@Iona
	10	@Rider
	15	Iona
	18	Manhattan
	20	@Fairfield
26-Mar.	1	##MAAC Tournament

@ Road Games
# Poughkeepsie, NY (vs. Colgate, first round; also Columbia and Vermont)
Marine Midland Arena, Buffalo, NY

the top players in New York. Kennedy averaged 23 points, 10 assists and six steals for St. Dominic's (N.Y.) High last season. He was a *USA Today* all-state selection and he enters the season as the heir apparent to Larragan at lead guard.

Smith was a key member of one of the nation's most powerful high school teams (Maryland's St. Vincent Pallotti) last year. Five players from that squad signed with Division I schools, including Smith, who finished his career there with 1,183 points. He tallied 13.3 ppg, 4.7 rpg, 2.2 spg and 1.9 apg in his senior year and should be Marist's shooting guard of the future.

The frontcourt needed some immediate retooling for the Red Foxes to be able to compete in the MAAC. Sure, 6-5 junior swingman **Joe McCurdy** can slash to the basket and score (8.2 ppg). And 6-9 sophomore **Tomasz Cielebak** from Poland can hit the glass some (team-best 5.1 rpg).

But, Magarity's not stupid. His best board man averaged just five per game, so he knew he needed help. Lots of help. And Magarity needed it yesterday. So, he headed for the mountains of Utah and brought home what he thinks are two junior college aces in 6-9 **Steve Grant** and 6-8 **Jason Hastings**.

Grant, a junior and true center, looks like a good get for Magarity and Co. He was rated by Rick Ball's Junior College Scouting Service to be one of the top 15 centers in JUCO ball last season. Magarity sure hopes so. Grant averaged 13.5 points and 7.5 boards while leading Snow (Utah) Junior College to a 21-11 overall record and a semifinal berth in the regional junior college tournament.

Hastings, a junior, isn't bad either. In fact, he helped Salt Lake (Utah) Community College to a 24-7 record and a berth in the regional tournament last season. Hastings averaged 15 points for the Bruins and led the Scenic West Athletic Conference in rebounding, averaging 9.2. A polished operator in the low post, Hastings was also second in the league in scoring and first in field goal percentage (.630).

Expect Grant to win the starting center spot and for 6-10 junior **Thomas Kenney** (4.3 ppg 3.9 rpg) to serve as his backup. Cielebak will battle Hastings for the starting four spot.

Rounding out the frontcourt rotation are a pair of small forwards—6-6 sophomore **Drew Samuels** and 6-5 freshman **Mark Prosser**—who will fight McCurdy for minutes. Samuels, an intense competitor, appeared in 22 games last season as a freshman, averaging 2.4 points in 8.9 minutes per night. Prosser scored 18 points and hauled down seven rebounds per game last season at Lawrenceville (N.Y.) High School.

adidas Blue Ribbon Analysis

BACKCOURT	B-	BENCH/DEPTH	C-
FRONTCOURT	C	INTANGIBLES	D

Marist could be a long-shot sleeper team, if the JUCO imports both work out. Now, we all know that junior college players are a crapshoot. But if 6-9 center Steve Grant and 6-8 power forward Jason Hastings can score in double figures and hit the glass with verve, then the Red Foxes (picked by some to finish last) could be dangerous. Their all-senior backcourt of Borja Larragan and Bobby Joe Hatton is proven, and the wings are OK.

But let's face it, landing two quality JUCO big men—unless you're Cincinnati or Fresno State—is unlikely. So let's project a second-division finish for the Red Foxes, unless coach Dave Magarity hits the jackpot with these big guys.

(B.D.)

NIAGARA

LOCATION	Niagara University, NY
CONFERENCE	Metro Atlantic Athletic (MAAC)
LAST SEASON	14-13 (.519)
CONFERENCE RECORD	10-8 (t-3rd)
STARTERS LOST/RETURNING	2/3
NICKNAME	Purple Eagles
COLORS	Purple & White
HOMECOURT	Gallagher Arena (3,200) Marine Midland Arena (19,500)
COACH	Joe Mihalich (La Salle '78)
RECORD AT SCHOOL	First Year
CAREER RECORD	First Year
ASSISTANTS	Tom Parrott (Fordham '88) Kandia Milton (Niagara '94)
TEAM WINS (last 5 yrs.)	6-5-13-11-14
RPI (last 5 yrs.)	262-273-193-217-128
1997-98 FINISH	Lost in conference second round.

We've all heard of the seven-year itch. Well, Joe Mihalich suffered from the 17-year itch. After 17 seasons as an assistant at La Salle, Joe Mihalich decided to scratch that itch by taking the head-coaching job at Niagara.

He inherits a team that was 9-4 in its final 13 games and was proud owner of 20-point victories over St. John's and Mihalich's old employer, La Salle, last season. The Purple Eagles had a winning record for the first time in five seasons and hope to challenge for the school's first MAAC title.

While Niagara isn't likely to do that, it does appear to have enough talent to finish in the top half of the MAAC standings. Three starters return from last year's team, as well as several others who saw extensive playing time. Mihalich believes that the combination of senior leadership and the addition of some talented new faces is vital to any success that Niagara has.

The starting backcourt of seniors **Jeremiah Johnson** and **Alvin Young** is back for the 1998-99 season. After leading Niagara in assists each of the last two seasons, the 5-9 Johnson ranks ninth all-time at NU with 330 career assists. Erratic at the point early in his career, Johnson has improved his decision-making skills a great deal over the years, as evidenced by the fact that he committed 32 less turnovers last season than he did the year before. Johnson (10 ppg, 3.3 rpg, 127 assists, 50 steals) is more than just a passmaster, though. He scored in double figures 17 different times last season and Niagara was 12-5 in those games.

The 6-3 Young, last season's leading scorer, will handle the two-guard spot. Young averaged 15.7 points and 2.4 assists. Young's forte is to drive into the teeth of the defense and fire up an array of shots in the lane. As a result of going strong to the bucket so often, Young led the Purple Eagles in free- throws made and attempted last year. He's also an excellent rebounder for his size, as his 5.1 per game average in 1997-98 attests.

"We're hoping that Alvin picks up where he left off last year," said Mihalich. "Hopefully, he will improve his outside shooting to add to his game inside the lane."

Junior **Luke Dobrich** and freshman **Daryl Greene** will split the backup point guard duties. The 6-2 Dobrich (3.7 ppg, 1.0 rpg, 50 assists, 8 steals) is a steady player who can knock down the three-pointer if opponents don't guard him closely enough. In fact, he is Niagara's top returning three-point threat (24-62, .387) and also notched 50 assists, despite logging just 14 minutes per night as a sophomore.

Greene, 6-0, is a classic combo guard who comes from DeMatha Catholic, one of the top prep programs in America.

"We feel good about our point guards," says Mihalich. "We have an experienced, athletic point guard in Jeremiah Jackson, a well-schooled point guard in Daryl Greene and a heady, Steve Kerr-like player in Luke Dobrich. Hopefully, we have the right guy for every situation."

Akbar Waheed (2.0 ppg, 0.7 rpg, 19 assists, 2 steals), a 6-3 senior, will be the backup at the two-guard spot. Though he isn't much of a scorer, Waheed gets valuable minutes because he's one of Niagara's top defenders. He scored a career-high seven points on three occasions last season and is an 86 percent career free-throw shooter. Dobrich and Greene will also see time at shooting guard.

Junior-college import **Terry Edwards** looks to be the favorite to man the small-forward spot. The 6-7 Edwards, a junior, signed with Wichita State out of high school, but was a non-qualifier and ended up at Paris (Tex.) Junior College. He's equally adept driving to the hoop and spotting up behind the three-point line.

Junior **Nate Bernosky** and sophomore **Danny Amponsah**—both 100 percent healthy after injury-shortened 1997-98 seasons—will push for time at the three-spot as well. The 6-4 Bernosky (1.7 ppg, 2.6 rpg, 22 assists) missed 13 games last season because of a broken jaw suffered while diving for a loose ball against Youngstown State. He started the first six games of last season before becoming a bench player the rest of the year. With the loss of three-point bomber Jeff O'Connor, look for Bernosky's minutes to increase.

The 6-4 Amponsah also saw his 1997-98 season derailed by injury. He appeared in 10 games before suffering a season-ending foot injury. Amponsah (0.5 ppg, 0.7 rpg, 2 assists) is a dogged defender when healthy, capable of giving the team a lift by his intense effort alone.

Seniors **Mike Piwerka** and **Kevin Jobity** will join Edwards to form the starting front line. Jobity, a 6-10 center, averaged 11.6 points and 5.9 rebounds as a junior. He finished second on the team in field-goal percentage (.605) and led Niagara in blocks (53) for a third-straight season. Jobity had 17 double-figure scoring games as a junior.

Piwerka, a 6-9 power forward, started 16 games last season and averaged 5.6 points and 5.2 rebounds.

Newcomer **Christos DeFoudis** and **Peter Strobl** will provide frontcourt depth. DeFoudis, a 6-9 import from Athens, Greece, is a powerfully-built player who should give Mihalich another much-needed banger. Strobl, a 6-8 junior, appeared in 16 games last season. Strobl (0.9 ppg, 0.6 rpg) can play either forward spot-if called upon.

adidas Blue Ribbon Analysis

BACKCOURT	C+	BENCH/DEPTH	C+
FRONTCOURT	C+	INTANGIBLES	B

First-year head coach Joe Mihalich left La Salle after 17 years as an assistant to take over at Niagara. He appears to have a much better chance to succeed than his old boss Speedy Morris, who is very much on the hot seat at La Salle.

While Mihalich doesn't appear to have the horses to win

1998-99 NIAGARA SCHEDULE

Nov.	13	Buffalo
	16	#Massachusetts
	21	@Maryland-Eastern Shore
	30	@Long Island
Dec.	4	St. Peter's
	6	Iona
	12	St. Bonaventure
	23	@La Salle
	29-30	##Capital City Classic
Jan.	2	Siena
	6	@Fairfield
	10	@Marist
	12	@Manhattan
	16	Loyola College
	18	Marist
	21	Manhattan
	23	Rider
	30	@St. Peter's
Feb.	1	@Iona
	6	@Canisius
	8	@Siena
	13	Fairfield
	15	Canisius
	18	@Rider
	20	@Loyola College
26-Mar.	1	###MAAC Tournament

@ Road Games
# Chase NIT (If the Purple Eagles advance, the will face either North Carolina-Asheville or St. John's on Nov. 18. Semifinals and finals are Nov. 25 & 27 at Madison Square Garden, NY)
Tallahassee, FL (vs. Radford, first round; also Florida A&M and Jacksonville)
Marine Midland Arena, Buffalo, NY

the MAAC, his team does have a proven backcourt and one of the league's most productive centers. That should be enough to help him finish in the upper-half of this 10-team conference. Barely. Let's call it fifth place in the MAAC for Niagara's rookie coach—behind Iona, Rider, Siena and Canisius.

(B.D.)

RIDER

LOCATION .... **Lawrenceville, NJ**
CONFERENCE .... **Metro Atlantic Athletic (MAAC)**
LAST SEASON .... **18-10 (.634)**
CONFERENCE RECORD .... **12-6 (2nd)**
STARTERS LOST/RETURNING **1/4**
NICKNAME .... **Broncs**
COLORS .... **Cranberry & White**
HOMECOURT .... **Alumni Gymnasium (1,650)**
COACH .... **Don Harnum (Susquehanna '86)**
RECORD AT SCHOOL .... **18-10 (1 yr.)**
CAREER RECORD .... **18-10 (1 yr.)**
ASSISTANTS .... **Jim Engles (Dickinson '90)**
Tony Newsome (Niagara '93)
TEAM WINS (last 5 yrs.) **19-21-18-10-18**
RPI (last 5 yrs.) **87-115-97-188-113**
1997-98 FINISH .... **Lost in NIT first round.**

In 1997-98, there were 61 new head coaches in NCAA Division I. Of those 61, Rider University head coach Don Harnum compiled the 12th best record (18-10).

Not bad for a rookie head coach.

In fact, of the 21 new head coaches who had never been a Division I head coach before, only three—North Carolina's Bill Guthridge (34-4), Georgia's Ron Jirsa (20-5) and Wyoming's Larry Shyatt (19-9)—finished with more victories than Harnum. Harnum also took Rider to the NIT for the first time in school history and finished second to Iona in Metro Atlantic last season, the Broncs' first in the MAAC.

So what does he do for an encore? With the return of his top three scorers and three of his top four rebounders, Harnum is thinking MAAC title and automatic NCAA Tournament berth—despite the fact that everyone in the media seems to conceding the crown to Iona, even though the Gaels lost their starting backcourt.

"That is our goal every year: To win the regular season, win the conference tournament and advance to the NCAA Tournament," said Harnum. "Even though we did not reach all of our goals, last season has to be considered a success by the fact that we did so many good things that had not been done here in a long time, if ever."

While his team didn't make it into the NCAA Tournament, Harnum was excited to go the NIT "Being invited to the NIT was real big for our program," Harnum said. "At that time of year, there were only 96 still playing and it was nice to be one of them."

This season, Harnum's club should be in the postseason again, thanks to the return of four starters. The best of the lot is 1998 first-team All-MAAC guard **Greg Burston** and second-team All-MAAC center **Kevin McPeek**. Burston (14.1 ppg, 3.8 rpg, 72 assists, 33 steals), a 6-3 senior, has led the Broncs in scoring the last two years.

"We challenged Greg to step up and be a leader," said Harnum. "He was the heart and soul of this team last year, the emotional leader as well as the leading scorer. With the talent we have this year, he shouldn't have to log as many minutes as he did last season."

McPeek returned to peak form after missing the previous season with a knee injury. A fifth-year senior, the 6-8, 225-pound McPeek (11.6 ppg, 5.3 rpg, 25 assists, 21 blocks, 15 steals) is strong and savvy enough to overpower lots of the MAAC's four and five men.

"He's not flashy, but he is so much stronger than he was," said Harnum. "He is one of the best finishers in MAAC, and he's the anchor of our defense. Being in his fifth year, he's more mature, both physically and mentally, than most players he'll face this season."

Starting power forward **Ken Lacey**, a 6-7 junior, also returns. Lacey (8.4 ppg, 5.5 rpg, 28 assists, 19 blocked shots) logged a lot of air miles this summer, traveling to Ireland with the Irish National team and to Japan with the MAAC all-star team. Lacey struggled with leg and back injuries—as well as the move from center to power forward. However, he played well down the stretch (averaging 11.7 points and 8.7 boards over the final seven games of the season) and performed well this summer.

"I think Kenny is really going to explode and come into his own this year," Harnum said.

Senior point guard **Kevin Finefrock** is the fourth returning starter for Rider. The 5-9 Finefrock was the Broncs' third-leading scorer last season (9.7 ppg) and handed out 71 assists. He made 39 three-pointers and is an outstanding free-throw shooter (.842 percent, 80 for 95, last season).

"Finny gives us a certain toughness in the backcourt and never seems to turn the ball over," said Harnum. "He's a tough defender, he makes his open shots and has a great understanding of the game."

Other key returnees include 6-7 junior **Jonathan McClark**, 6-0 sophomore guard **Michael Crawford** and 6-5 sophomore forward **Brian Bigos**. McClark (4.8 ppg, 4.5 rpg, 47 assists, 13 steals) shot a team-high .573 percent from the field, despite sitting out the1996-97 season.

"Jonathan had a typical first year for a big guy," said Harnum. "He was a bit rusty and inconsistent at times after missing a season, but his adjustment period is over now. He should be one of the best rebounders in the MAAC this season."

As a Rider rookie, Crawford played more as the season wore on. Crawford (4.8 ppg, 1.3 rpg, 49 assists, 14 steals) logged 18 minutes in a game just once in the first 12 games of the season. Then he played 18 minutes 13 times in the final 15 games. The young point guard continued his maturation process by playing well for the MAAC all-stars this summer in Japan.

Bigos was in a tough situation, playing behind a pair of proven seniors in TaTa Touomou (5.4 ppg) and Derrick Perry (8.6 ppg) last season. As a result, Bigos (0.2 ppg, 0.2 rpg) rarely got any court time, appearing in only nine games. His minutes should increase greatly in 1998-99.

The six-pack of newcomers are **Winston Grey, Dave Hutchinson, Mario Porter, Mike Scott , R.J. Wicks** and redshirt freshman **Mark VanSickle**.

Grey is a 6-6 freshman forward who averaged 11 points and 10 rebounds at Norwalk (Conn.) High School last season. Grey is quick and has some tools, including an innate shooting blocking ability (6.0 blocks per game as a high school senior).

Hutchinson is a 6-4 freshman guard who finished third on nearby Steinert (N.J.) High School's career scoring list with 1,190 points—just 229 points behind Bigos, now a Rider teammate. He's a gym rat who averaged 17.8 ppg for his 26-2 team last year.

Porter, a 6-6 freshman, earned Essex County Player-of-the-Year honors as well as a spot on the second-team all-New Jersey squad last year. The swingman posted averages of 22.1 points, 13 rebounds, 3.5 steals and 2.7. Scott and Wicks are a pair of 6-4 freshmen guards. Scott, from Hyattsville, Md., scored 20.4 points and grabbed 7.8 boards per game in 1997 at Northwestern High before taking off last season to work. Wicks joins the program after earning all-state honors at Bridgeport (Mich.) High School, where he led his team to the Class B state quarterfinals and finished with a school-best 1,149 career points.

VanSickle is the largest Bronc (6-10, 240), He redshirted last year after earning *Street & Smith's* honorable mention All-America honors as a senior at East Liverpool (Ohio) High. "The redshirt year was great for Mark," said Harnum. "He was able to adjust without the pressure of having to perform right away. He's done a terrific job getting in better basketball shape, now it's a matter of competing for playing time."

1998-99 RIDER SCHEDULE

Nov.	18	@Bucknell
	23	@Delaware
	27	@St. Bonaventure
Dec.	4	Manhattan
	7	@Fairfield
	12	Monmouth
	22	@Villanova
	29-30	#Dr Pepper Classic
Jan.	2	St. Peter's
	8	@Iona
	10	Loyola College
	13	Maryland-Eastern Shore
	16	@St. Peter's
	18	@Siena
	21	@Canisius
	23	@Niagara
	28	Iona
	31	@Manhattan
Feb.	2	@Marist
	6	Fairfield
	10	Marist
	12	@Loyola College
	14	Siena
	18	Niagara
	20	Canisius
26-Mar.	1	##MAAC Tournament

@ Road Games
\# Chattanooga, TN (vs. Tennessee-Chattanooga, first round; also Hampton and Samford)
\## Marine Midland Arena, Buffalo, NY

adidas Blue Ribbon Analysis

BACKCOURT	**B**	**BENCH/DEPTH**	**B+**
FRONTCOURT	**B**	**INTANGIBLES**	**B+**

Rider is the MAAC's forgotten powerhouse. Everybody's preseason title talk seems to center around either defending champ Iona with alum Jeff Ruland now coaching, or Siena, where "hot" young coach Paul Hewitt, a one-time Villanova assistant, is being talked about as the next MAAC coach to get a big-time offer.

Don't overlook the Broncs, though. They return four starters from last season's second-place MAAC regular-season finisher, including all-league types in guard Greg Burston and center Kevin McPeek. They'll be in the MAAC title chase all year—along with Iona and Siena.

(B.D.)

ST. PETER'S

LOCATION .... **Jersey City, NJ**
CONFERENCE .... **Metro Atlantic Athletic (MAAC)**
LAST SEASON .... **8-19 (.296)**
CONFERENCE RECORD .... **4-14 (10th)**
STARTERS LOST/RETURNING **5/0**
NICKNAME .... **Peacocks**
COLORS .... **Blue & White**
HOMECOURT .... **Yanitelli Center (3,200)**
COACH .... **Rodger Blind (Ursinus '72)**
RECORD AT SCHOOL .... **36-46 (3 yrs.)**
CAREER RECORD .... **36-46 (3 yrs.)**
ASSISTANTS Chris Casey (Western Connecticut '86)
Bill Maranz (Winston-Salem '89)
Nick Marinello (Trenton State '92)
TEAM WINS (last 5 yrs.) **14-19-15-13-8**
RPI (last 5 yrs.) **186-95-133-205-243**
1997-98 FINISH .... **Lost in conference first round.**

The Super Bowl jinx is alive and well. It's just residing in Jersey City, not some AFC metropolitan area.

Last Super Bowl Sunday (Jan. 25), it appeared Saint Peter's College had turned the corner. The Peacocks had won their third straight game, 77-57 over Niagara, to improve their record to 8-9 overall and 4-5 in the Metro Atlantic Athletic Conference. Then, the Broncos upset the Packers and the jinx needed a new zip code to reside in and, for some reason, chose "07306." The once-proud Peacocks didn't win a game the rest of the season—dropping 10 straight games and finishing 8-19.

That's the bad news. On the bright side, all five starters are back for coach Rodger Blind, including 6-2 junior **Rick Bellinger** and 6-foot senior **Jamar Hunter**. Both were third-team All-MAAC performers as St. Peter's employed a three-guard set much of last season.

Hunter, playing his natural two-guard role after a stint at the point as a sophomore, raised his scoring average from 13.9 ppg to 16.2 ppg last year. He reached double figures in 23 of 27 games and made a team-best 40 three-pointers. Hunter is almost certain to become St. Peter's next 1,000-point scorer. He's currently perched at 928 points. Still, even though he's one of the best long-distance shooters on the team, his overall shooting percentage was seriously lacking (.408)—a seemingly contagious disease on this team that can't shoot straight. Because of that, opposing teams often opted to play off him, willing to gamble against his jump shot rather than be beaten off the dribble.

Bellinger suffered a similar fate. No player in the MAAC is better at getting to the rim or getting his shot off the dribble than Bellinger. He followed his strong freshman season (16.3 ppg) with almost a carbon copy in his sophomore season (team-best 16.5 ppg). And he's done all this scoring with an erratic—at best—jumper. St. Peter's sup-

1998-99 ST. PETER'S SCHEDULE

Nov.	14	*Seton Hall
	21	@Charleston Southern
	23	@Radford
	29	Lafayette
Dec.	4	@Niagara
	6	@Canisius
	9	Northeastern
	19	@Wagner
	23	@Monmouth
	31	James Madison
Jan.	2	@Rider
	5	Marist
	8	Fairfield
	10	Iona
	14	@Siena
	16	Rider
	23	@Marist
	28	@Fairfield
	30	Niagara
Feb.	1	Canisius
	3	Manhattan
	7	@Loyola College
	10	@Iona
	14	Loyola College
	19	Siena
	21	@Manhattan
26-Mar.	1	#MAAC Tournament

@ Road Games
* Continental Airlines Arena, East Rutherford, NJ
# Marine Midland Arena, Buffalo, NY

porters—try saying that five times fast—are encouraged that the junior-to-be seemed to find his jumper this summer. Turns out, it was living in Japan. Bellinger picked it back up as a member of the MAAC All-Star team that toured Japan this summer. He shot 27 of 48 (.563) during the tour.

There are some whispers that Bellinger might be moved to the point-guard spot this season to take advantage of his penetration skills. However, the x-factor in the guard picture remains 6-2 **Kalief Allen**, a pure point guard who will be a junior. Hunter and Bellinger, both natural two-guards, are the Peacocks' best players. Ineligible as a freshman, Allen was handed the keys to the offense last year as coach Blind was willing to gamble on a small lineup.

However, given the late-season collapse and the addition of two newcomers with true small-forward size, the best lineup might be a more conventional frontline and two highly-skilled all-conference guards, even though neither is a true point guard.

Regardless of whether he starts, Allen has the talent to make an impact. He was one of the top high school guards in New Jersey as a high school senior, but he sat out his freshman year at St. Peter's because of academic problems. In his first collegiate start, Allen scored 16 points and handed out 15 assists and folks in Jersey City were excited. Unfortunately, things were never that easy the rest of the way. In 25 games (including 15 starts), Allen averaged just 5.5 ppg. He showed potential, but his 1997-98 season was filled with peaks and valleys. He'll need to minimize the number of valleys, as players often do with experience, to live up to his promise.

Antoine Moore, a 5-9 sophomore, is another pure point guard who is quick and fearless. Orr flashed some ability on both ends of the court as a freshman in 1997-98, averaging 2.5 ppg and, like Allen, playing solid on-the-ball defense. He'll need to improve his outside shot (five of 22 from three-point range) and his assists-to-turnover ratio (32-to-33 as a freshman) to earn more minutes.

Depending on how the frontline shakes out, junior-college import **Damian Spencer** could easily swing from small forward to either guard spot, which is where he played a lot at Brown Mackie (Kan.) College (28-8 last season). Spencer (10.9 ppg), a 6-4 junio, was chosen to the all-tournament team of the NJCAA Division II Tournament, where he averaged 16 ppg as Brown Mackie finished fourth.

In the frontcourt, Blind appears tempted to go with a more conventional look after playing three guards and two post players last season. That means that either Spencer or fellow newcomer **Rodney Rodgers**, a sophomore and Drexel transfer, will get a chance to nab the small-forward spot. Rodgers (6-7, 210) averaged just 2.5 ppg and 2.8 rpg for a 22-9 Drexel team before deciding to transfer back home. Rodgers starred, along with current NBA player Tim Thomas and current St. Peter's teammate Jermaine Johnson, at Paterson (N.J) Catholic a few seasons back. Rodgers possesses an inside-outside game, although his numbers at Drexel didn't match the hype surrounding Rodgers when he came out of high school.

The starting power forward figures to be 6-5, 275-pound sophomore **Kamaal McQueen** (8.5 ppg, 5.5 rpg). This "Big Mac" is built like a defensive lineman, but is surprisingly nimble inside. His freshman season ended on a sour note, though. A respiratory illness made him virtually unavailable from mid-February on. His absence seemed to fuel the Peacocks' skid down the stretch.

If a positive came from McQueen's late-season absence, it was the reemergence of JUCO import **Rich Brown**, who had slumped after a solid start. Brown, a 6-7 senior, had six double-figure scoring games in the first 14 games, but then opened February with a four-game stretch of a combined three points and three rebounds. Overall, Brown averaged 7.1 ppg and 4.3 rpg and finished second on the team in field-goal percentage at .497, trailing only McQueen (.576).

Jermaine Johnson (6-7, 230), a powerfully-built junior, also got an opportunity to play a bit more late in the season. Johnson has been slowed by missing two different seasons within the past four years (a redshirt freshman year at Austin Peay and a year sitting out as a transfer) as well as knee surgery last fall. Perhaps spurred on by playing in the final four games of the season, Johnson worked hard in the weight room this offseason and looks ready to play a more significant role.

The last forward on the roster is 6-5 sophomore **Keith Sellers** (3.8 ppg). The quiet, slender Sellers has the ability to stroke the long-range jumper, a absolute rarity at St. Peter's (which shot a MAAC-worst .294 as a team from behind the arc in 1997-98).

While the forward mix is a jumble at this point, the center spot belongs to 6-11, 270-pound **Jake Holmes**—the only true pivot on Blind's roster. Holmes (7.4 ppg, 9.1 rpg, 15 assists, 26 blocks) became eligible after the fall semester last season and made an immediate impact. Appearing in 21 games (13 starts), Holmes had a team-best six double-doubles and was second in the MAAC in rebounding (9.1 per game).

adidas Blue Ribbon Analysis

BACKCOURT	**C**	**BENCH/DEPTH**	**C**
FRONTCOURT	**C**	**INTANGIBLES**	**D**

Rodger Blind's squad fell apart down the stretch last season, losing its final 10 games. As a result, Blind is toying with the idea of going with a more conventional lineup rather than the three-guard attack he favored last year.

Good move. Three-guard lineups usually are utilized when teams have three unbelievable shooters on the perimeter that must get into the game at the same time. While 6-2 junior Rick Bellinger and 6-foot senior Jamar Hunter are both scorers, neither are shooters. What's more, last year's point man Kalief Allen endured more ups and downs than the Dow Jones. With those three guards in the starting lineup, St. Peter's still managed to shoot a MAAC-worst .294 as a team from behind the arc in 1997-98—which led to the 10-game losing skid, not mention countless jokes that Blind was leading the blind at St. Peter's.

They'll have to shoot better from distance and figure out their jumbled frontcourt in order to get back on the winning track. Don't bet on it as the Peacocks look closer to the MAAC outhouse than the penthouse in 1998-99.

(B.D.)

SIENA

LOCATION	**Loudonville, NY**
CONFERENCE	**Metro Atlantic Athletic (MAAC)**
LAST SEASON	**17-12 (.643)**
CONFERENCE RECORD	**10-8 (t-3rd)**
STARTERS LOST/RETURNING	**0/5**
NICKNAME	**Saints**
COLORS	**Green & Gold**
HOMECOURT	**Pepsi Arena (6,900)**
COACH	**Phil Hewitt (St. John Fisher '85)**
RECORD AT SCHOOL	**17-12 (1 yr.)**
CAREER RECORD	**17-12 (1 yr.)**
ASSISTANTS	**Robert Burke (Haverford '88)**
	Cliff Warren (Mount St. Mary's '90)
	Steve Evans (Union '94)
TEAM WINS (last 5 yrs.)	**14-17-19-9-17**
RPI (last 5 yrs.)	**44-263-247-245-123**
1997-98 FINISH	**Lost in conference title game.**

Siena coach Paul Hewitt knows all about inflated expectations. A few seasons ago, he was an assistant at Villanova under Steve Lappas. And at that time, Hewitt had played an integral role in the Wildcats landing everybody's prep All-American forward Tim Thomas. The signing of the 6-9 Thomas—to go along with 6-10 center Jason Lawson

1998-99 SIENA SCHEDULE

Nov.	14	@Bethune-Cookman
	21	@Hartford
	24	St. Bonaventure
Dec.	2	Loyola College
	4	@Marist
	8	@Colgate
	12	*Fairleigh Dickinson
	23	George Washington
	29-30	#Sparkletts Invitational
Jan.	2	@Niagara
	5	Quinnipiac
	10	Canisius
	12	@Fairfield
	14	St. Peter's
	18	Rider
	21	@Loyola College
	24	Iona
	30	Marist
Feb.	1	Fairfield
	4	@Canisius
	6	@Manhattan
	8	Niagara
	11	Manhattan
	14	@Rider
	19	@St. Peter's
	21	@Iona
26-Mar.	1	##MAAC Tournament

@ Road Games
* Desmond Conference Challenge, Albany, NY
# Malibu, CA (vs. Eastern Michigan, first round; also Pepperdine and Rhode Island)
Marine Midland Arena, Buffalo, NY

and 6-3 point guard Alvin Williams—had folks on Philadelphia's Main Line thinking big. How big? There was talk of a Big East title and perhaps, a serious Big Dance advance.

Of course, it never panned out as the Mildcats flamed out in round two of NCAAs. Shortly after the NCAA Tournament loss, Thomas was one-and-done—declaring for the NBA draft after his freshman year. Of course, Lawson and Williams, both seniors, were NBA-bound, too. And Hewitt headed off to Siena to run his own program.

Last year was his first season at Siena and a rousing success. The Saints, picked to be a bottom-feeder, turned into a MAAC machine, almost doubling their win total in one season (from nine in 1997-97 to 17 last season). And they came within spitting distance of the Big Dance by going all the way to the MAAC Tournament title game before losing to regular-season champ Iona, 90-75.

Hence, the greater expectations for Hewitt's bunch, with many factors in their favor. For the first time in three years, Iona looks slightly vulnerable, as the Gaels must break in a new coach and a new backcourt. Plus, the Saints return all five starters from last year's 17-12 squad-led by a guard combination which is arguably the best in the MAAC.

However, after his experience with great expectations at Villanova, Hewitt is cautiously optimistic. "These guys are pretty young," says Hewitt. "And what if they decide they're not going to work as hard as they did a year ago?"

That doesn't seem likely with this bunch, though. The floor leader in the backcourt is 5-11 senior **Melvin Freeny** (7.8 ppg, 4.0 rpg, 5.6 apg). Freeny has come a long way in the last two years, especially in terms of his decision-making and ability to run a team. The only wart on his game right now is his not-always-reliable jumper (.399 FG percentage). Teams lay off Freeny and dare him to shoot the deep shot, and he often obliges. Freeny reportedly worked hard in the offseason to correct this flaw, so it will be interesting to see if he can get his shot to drop more consistently.

Freeny's running mate will again be 6-5 junior **Marcus Faison** (16.1 ppg, 6.8 rpg, 2.7 apg), the Saints' best player and a first-team all-MAAC performer last season. He might end up being the MAAC Player of the Year by season's end, as nobody does more things to help his team win. He has the ability to break his man down in one-on-one situations with the shot clock winding down. He's a relentless defender (team-best 65 steals) who never shies away from a difficult assignment and is an excellent rebounder for a two-guard (6.5 per game).

Providing instant offense off the bench for Hewitt will

once again be 6-3 sophomore guard **Scott Knapp** (12.3 ppg, 1.9 rpg, 3.2 apg). Knapp was the MAAC Rookie of the Year last season. Further backcourt depth will be provided by 6-3 sophomore **Isaiah Stewart** (2.9 ppg, 1.0 rpg, 0.7 apg), who also struggled with his shooting (.333 percent as a freshman) and 6-6 freshman swingman **Dwayne Archbold** from Paul Robeson High in Brooklyn.

The final two guard possibilities are 6-4 junior **Micah Ogburn** and seldom-used 5-9 sophomore **Brian Scalzo**. Ogburn was a medical redshirt last season, but he's OK now and should get some meaningful playing time. The same can't be said of Scalzo (.3 ppg, 0.2 apg) a walkon who rarely gets to walk on the court—other than in practice.

Siena's frontcourt features one leading man and two best-supporting-actor-types. The frontcourt star is 6-8 junior **Jim Cantamessa**, who led the nation in three-point percentage (.564) last season, But Cantamessa (14 ppg, 5 rpg, 1.6 apg) is more than just a long-range jacker; he's a complete player. He can hurt opposing defenses just as easily with his outside game as with his post-up moves.

His two frontcourt mates, 6-7 junior **Corey Osinski** (8.1 ppg, 2.6 rpg) and 6-10 junior **Dave Deters** (5.5 ppg, 2.8 rpg) are unselfish, hard-working guys near the bucket. They won't lead the league in headlines, but they'll set screens, rebound and hustle from the opening tap to the final buzzer.

Quality depth up front should be provided by 6-6 senior **Brandon Fields** (7.4 ppg, 3.7 rpg) and a pair of freshman in 6-8 **James Clinton**, who averaged 16 points and 11 boards at St. Augustine (N.J.) High, and **Dale Taylor**, a 6-9 forward-center from Thayer (Mass.) Academy. Clinton looks like a future star, as soon as he can add some meat to his 200-pound frame.

adidas Blue Ribbon Analysis

BACKCOURT .... **B+** **BENCH/DEPTH** .... **C+**
FRONTCOURT .... **B-** **INTANGIBLES** .... **B**

Most preseason prognosticators are conceding the MAAC regular-season crown to Iona, winners of three straight. But this will be a legitimate three-horse race among Iona, Rider and Siena.

Siena possesses the MAAC's best backcourt, led by legit league Player of the Year candidate Marcus Faison. The Saints have the MAAC's hottest young coach (now that Iona's Tim Welsh headed to greener pastures at Providence). The frontline contains two working-class heroes in Corey Osinski and Dave Deters and a budding star in 6-8 junior Jim Cantamessa.

Is that combination enough to win the MAAC and go to the Big Dance? We won't know for sure until the Ides of March.

(B.D.)

MID-AMERICAN CONFERENCE

adidas BLUE RIBBON FORECAST

EAST DIVISION

1. Miami (Ohio)
2. Akron
3. Ohio
4. Marshall
5. Bowling Green
6. Kent
7. Buffalo

WEST DIVISION

1. Toledo
2. Ball State
3. Western Michigan
4. Northern Illinois
5. Eastern Michigan
6. Central Michigan

TOP 40

Miami (Ohio) is ranked among the 1998-99 *adidas Blue Ribbon* Top 40. An extended profile can be found in the Top 40 section of *Blue Ribbon*.

ALL-CONFERENCE TEAM

G—Jami Bosley, JR, Akron
G—Damon Frierson, SR, Miami (Ohio)
F—Wally Szczerbiak, SR, Miami (Ohio)
F—Anthony Stacey, JR, Bowling Green
C—T.J. Lux, SR, Northern Illinois

PLAYER OF THE YEAR

Wally Szcerbiak, SR, Miami (Ohio)

NEWCOMER OF THE YEAR

LaDrell Whitehead, SR, Ohio

1998-99 CONFERENCE TOURNAMENT

Feb. 27, March 2-3, SeaGate Centre, Toledo, Ohio
(Quarterfinal games at campus sites)

1997-98 CHAMPION

Akron (East Division)
Ball State, Western Michigan (co-champions-West)
Eastern Michigan (conference tournament)

1997-98 POSTSEASON PARTICIPANTS

Postseason Record: 1-3 (.250)

NCAA
Western Michigan (2nd round)
Eastern Michigan

NIT
Ball State

TOP BACKCOURTS

1. Akron
2. Miami (Ohio)
3. Ohio

TOP FRONTCOURTS

1. Miami (Ohio)
2. Ohio
3. Northern Illinois

ON THE WAY UP

Ohio

ON THE WAY DOWN

Eastern Michigan

INSIDE THE NUMBERS

- 1997-98 conference RPI: 14 (of 30)
- Conference RPI (last 5 years): 14-12-14-11-14

DID YOU KNOW?

Buffalo joins the Mid-American Conference this season, boosting the league roster to 13 schools. The Bulls left the Mid-Continent Conference after posting a 15-13 record and going 9-7 (fifth) in the league. Marshall and Northern Illinois joined the MAC last year...The MAC once again has a two-division format. The East Division includes Akron, Bowling Green, Buffalo, Kent, Marshall, Miami (Ohio) and Ohio, while the West Division includes Ball State, Central Michigan, Eastern Michigan, Northern Illinois, Toledo and Western Michigan. The team with the best overall regular-season conference winning percentage will be considered the MAC champion...Five teams return all five starters (Akron, Bowling Green, Kent, Marshall and Miami) while two schools (Buffalo and Eastern Michigan) will field completely new starting units...Returning first-team All-MAC players are Northern Illinois center T.J. Lux and Miami (Ohio) forward Wally Szczerbiak. Second team all-conference returnees are Akron guard Jami Bosley and Miami (Ohio) guard Damon Frierson...MAC players taken in the NBA draft were Ball State's Bonzi Wells, the 11th pick in the first round by the Detroit Pistons; Toledo's Casey Shaw (second round by the Philadelphia 76ers) and Eastern Michigan's Derrick Dial (second round by the San Antonio Spurs). Eastern Michigan's Earl Boykins had a three-day tryout with the Washington Wizards just before the NBA imposed a lockout...Eastern Michigan vacated 41-year-old Bowen Field House after last season and is moving into the new, $29.6 million Convocation Center next to Rynearson Stadium. The Convocation Center seats 8,824...Marshall's Cam Henderson Center underwent a $4.6 million renovation. The "new" Henderson Center seats 9,043...MAC head coaches working at their alma mater are Charlie Coles (Miami '65), Larry Hunter (Ohio '71), Stan Joplin (Toledo '79), Ray McCallum (Ball State '83) and Greg White (Marshall '82)...Veteran Division I referee Eric Harmon is the league's new supervisor of officials. Harmon, 32, has worked games in the Big 10, Big East, Western Athletic, Missouri Valley, Conference USA, Big 12 and Mid-Continent conferences...Ball State and Western Michigan shared the Reese Cup as MAC schools with the best overall men's athletic programs in 1998. Their respective basketball teams also tied for first place in the West Division.

"A New Era" Mid-American Conference MAC

(R.M.)

AKRON

LOCATION .... Akron, OH
CONFERENCE .... Mid-American (East)
LAST SEASON .... 17-10 (.630)
CONFERENCE RECORD 13-5 (1st)
STARTERS LOST/RETURNING 0/5
NICKNAME .... Zips
COLORS .... Blue & Gold
HOMECOURT .... James A. Rhodes Arena (5,942)
COACH .... Dan Hipsher (Bowling Green '77)
RECORD AT SCHOOL .... 28-51 (3 yrs.)
CAREER RECORD .... 154-96 (9 yrs.)
ASSISTANTS .... John Pigatti (Dayton '85)
John Burns (Wittenburg '95)
Saint Crawford (Bowling Green '97)
TEAM WINS (last 5 yrs.) 8-8-3-8-17
RPI (last 5 yrs.) 256-209-289-229-134
1997-98 FINISH .... Lost in conference first round.

Akron coach Dan Hipsher is building his program one step at a time:

Three victories in 1995-96, followed by eight victories in 1996-97, then 17 wins and a Mid-American Conference East Division title last season.

The Zips actually cut down the nets at JAR Arena after clinching first place. Akron went to the eight-team MAC Tournament for the first time in six seasons as a league member, played host to a quarterfinal game and lost to neighboring rival Kent, 95-88. Akron had whipped Kent by 17 points only nine days earlier.

The turnaround didn't go unnoticed, as Hipsher was selected MAC Coach of the Year in voting by the media, and he was chosen Ohio College Coach of the Year in voting by his peers, receiving more votes for the state award than Cincinnati's Bob Huggins, who coached the Zips from 1985-89.

More importantly, Hipsher also received a three-year contract extension.

Despite last year's success—and the loss of only one reserve guard, Scott Gooden (8.5 ppg, 1.8 rpg)—Hipsher knows the Zips haven't arrived yet.

"We showed the ability to compete and win last season," Hipsher said. "Now the slate is clean. We've gotten better, but a lot of other teams have gotten better, too."

All five starters are back, led by 6-0 junior guard **Jami Bosley** (16.3 ppg, 4.5 rpg). Much of Akron's success was linked to the arrival of Bosley, a transfer from Ohio State. Bosley's injury-plagued season included 18 starts in 21 games. He was sidelined early by a back injury, then by a hip problem late in the year.

With a healthy Bosley playing alongside 5-10 junior point guard **Jimmal Ball** (14.7 ppg, 3.8 rpg, 93 assists), the Zips have one of the MAC's best backcourts. Bosley earned second-team All-MAC honors and Ball was chosen honorable mention all-conference.

Bosley is an intense competitor who makes players around him better with his hustle and relentless style of play.

"He brings the lunch bucket every day," Hipsher said. "Jami is very good in our motion offense. He makes good decisions, plays well without the ball. He just competes well and has the skills to play the game."

Ball followed his 1997 MAC Freshman-of-the-Year season with another solid performance last season. With the addition of Bosley to pick up some of the scoring load, Ball was free to concentrate more on his point-guard duties. He was eighth in the league in assists, third in steals (2.3 per game) and third in assist-to-turnover ratio (1.79).

Also returning in the backcourt are 6-2 senior guard **Adam Benton** (3.9 ppg, 1.9 rpg) and 6-3 senior **Ali Kart** (1.2 ppg, 0.6 rpg). Benton's season was limited to only eight games because of an ankle injury. Sophomore guard **Todd Casey** (0.6 ppg, 0.5 rpg) appeared in eight games.

Hipsher expects 6-5 sophomore **Nate Schindewolf** to have an impact. Schindewolf, a transfer from Miami (Ohio), sat out last season. He played in six games for Miami as a freshman and averaged 2.3 points.

Schindewolf, an outstanding athlete, played at Akron's Manchester HS, where he was a teammate of Zips' forward **Ryan Andrick**. Schindewolf averaged 26 points as a high school senior and won Ohio's Division III Player-of-the-Year honors for the second time. He also was the quarterback on his high school football team.

Freshman **Cornell Felton**, a 6-0 point guard, was the Northern Virginia Player of the Year at Hayfield HS in Alexandria, Va. He averaged 19 points, four rebounds and six assists while making 122 steals.

"Cornell is the kind of point guard that accounts for about 30-35 points each game," Hipsher said. "He either scores 20 points with five assists or scores 10 points and has 10 assists. He knows what needs to be done on a given night in order to win."

Bosley shared the team MVP award with 6-6, 215-pound senior forward **George Phillips** (12.4 ppg, 6.4 rpg) Phillips led the conference in blocked shots with 42. He shot 48 percent from the field and is a primary option in the offense.

The one-two punch at forward includes the 6-7, 240-pound Andrick (10.1 ppg, 5.2 rpg), a junior who led the MAC in field-goal percentage (.565). Andrick made a successful return from a knee injury that wiped out his 1996-97 season.

Forward **Jawanza Moore** (6.1 ppg, 3.5 rpg) is a 6-5 senior who makes steady contributions off the bench.

Adding depth and quality to the frontcourt is 6-6 junior **Kirene Johnson** from Penn Valley (Mo.) CC, where he averaged 18 points and six rebounds.

"Kirene is a great competitor who goes to battle every night," Hipsher said. "He can run the floor, score around the basket and rebound the ball. He'll really help us inside."

Akron's shaky three-point shooting (31 percent) might get a boost from 6-7 freshman **David Falknor**, an Ohio Division II all-state player who averaged 22.4 points at Bellevue H.S.

Two returning sophomore centers are 6-11, 220-pound **Bruce Weinkein** (5.3 ppg, 3.6 rpg) and 6-9, 240-pound **Klaas Zollner** (0.5 ppg, 0.7 rpg). Weinkein is an athletic pivot who needs to put on some weight and muscle. Zollner, a native of Hannover, Germany, has the needed bulk, but his offensive game is still developing.

adidas Blue Ribbon Analysis

BACKCOURT .... B+ BENCH/DEPTH .... C+
FRONTCOURT .... B INTANGIBLES .... B

Between 1992 and 1997, Akron averaged seven victories per season. Last year's 17 victories was the school's most since 1989.

Zips coach Dan Hipsher is obviously moving the program in the right direction.

Akron was ranked among the MAC leaders in four key categories—scoring (75.3), scoring defense (67.6), field-goal percentage (.472) and field-goal percentage defense (.429).

And everybody is back from last year's team.

Repeating as the MAC East champion won't be easy, but the Zips have all the ingredients to do it. A collapse in the MAC Tournament might have cost Akron an NIT bid, something the Zips are capable of earning this season, if they don't grab an NCAA bid.

(R.M.)

1998-99 AKRON SCHEDULE

Nov.	20	@Illinois State
	23	Florida International
	25	@Western Kentucky
	28	@Duquesne
Dec.	2	Eastern Michigan
	5	@Buffalo
	8	College of Wooster
	12	@St. Joseph's
	19	@Loyola
	21	Cleveland State
	30	Toledo
Jan.	6	Kent
	9	Marshall
	13	@Bowling Green
	16	@Miami
	20	Ohio
	23	Northern Illinois
	27	@Ball State
	30	@Central Michigan
Feb.	3	Western Michigan
	10	@Eastern Michigan
	13	@Kent
	15	@Northern Illinois
	17	Bowling Green
	20	Ball State
	24	@Ohio
27, Mar.	2-3	#MAC Tournament

@ Road Games
# First round Feb. 27 at campus sites. Remainder of tournament March 2-3 at SeaGate Centre, Toledo, OH

BALL STATE

LOCATION .... Muncie, IN
CONFERENCE .... Mid-American (West)
LAST SEASON .... 21-8 (.724)
CONFERENCE RECORD 14-4 (t-1st)
STARTERS LOST/RETURNING 2/3
NICKNAME .... Cardinals
COLORS .... Cardinal & White
HOMECOURT .... University Arena (11,500)
COACH .... Ray McCallum (Ball State '83)
RECORD AT SCHOOL .... 88-56 (5 yrs.)
CAREER RECORD .... 88-56 (5 yrs.)
ASSISTANTS .... Tim Buckley (Bemidji State '86)
Jerry Francis (Ohio State '91)
John Fitzpatrick (Bowling Green '80)
TEAM WINS (last 5 yrs.) 16-19-16-16-21
RPI (last 5 yrs.) 129-73-105-108-77
1997-98 FINISH .... Lost in NIT first round.

Life without Bonzi will be difficult.

Ball State basketball was the Bonzi Wells show last year when the talented All-American forward led the Cardinals to a 21-8 record.

Even Wells couldn't get Ball State a coveted NCAA Tournament berth, though. When the bids came out, Ball State, which lost in overtime to eventual MAC Tournament champion Eastern Michigan in the semifinals, was relegated to the NIT, where it lost a first-round game at Memphis, 90-67.

Not that the NIT was bad, but the Cardinals wanted more.

For the fourth time in history, the MAC received multiple NCAA bids.

Eastern Michigan went as the tournament champion. So did surprising at-large pick Western Michigan, which lost in the MAC Tournament's quarterfinals to Miami (Ohio), 67-63.

Ball State beat Western Michigan twice during the year and posted a big victory over 13th-ranked Mississippi.

Ball State coach Ray McCallum expected his team—the MAC West Division co-champion_to receive an at-large bid to the NCAA Tournament.

"I had no reason not to think so, having defeated (Western Michigan) twice, earning the No. 1 seed for the MAC Tournament and winning a quarterfinal game," McCallum said. "I thought we had separated ourselves from Western (Michigan)."

At least three things hurt Ball State's chances. One was a lower RPI (77) than Western Michigan (53). Also, Western Michigan's 21-win season included two wins over Eastern Michigan. Finally, schedule strength also worked against Ball State, which had wins over NAIA Montana Tech and Division II Quinnipiac.

"That had to be it," McCallum said.

Whatever the reason, Ball State didn't go to the Big Dance, and with Wells gone, things don't look quite as good as last year.

Wells was chosen the MAC's Player of the Year for the second time after winning it as a sophomore. Last season, Wells led the team in scoring (22.8), rebounds (6.3), steals (103) and tied for the lead in assists (95). The Detroit Pistons made Wells the 11th pick in the NBA draft.

Records set by Wells include the all-time MAC scoring record of 2,476 previously held by Ron Harper of the Chicago Bulls, who scored 2,377 points for Miami (Ohio) from 1982-86. Wells also set the league career record for steals with 346, which ranks second in NCAA history behind Eric Murdock of Providence (1987-91).

Wells shattered the Ball State career scoring record previously held by his coach, who didn't mind a bit.

"We were very proud of Bonzi Wells' accomplishments while at Ball State," McCallum said. "He brought a lot of national attention to our program because of his outstanding career. He will be greatly missed and there will be a major void to fill in our program, but we are looking forward to that challenge."

The Cardinals will also miss 6-4 sophomore guard Lamont Roland (12.1 ppg, 3.5 rpg), who became eligible at midseason, played in 19 games and is now at Barton County (Kan.) CC, and departed seniors Mitch Hankins (9.0 ppg, 3.0 rpg), Ryan Reed (6.3 ppg, 5.3 rpg), Doug Clark (1.1 ppg, 0.6 rpg) and Charles Smith (3.0 ppg, 2.4 rpg).

Left to continue the tradition at Ball State, which has seven postseason appearances in the last 10 seasons,

1998-99 BALL STATE SCHEDULE

Nov.	16	@Michigan
	28	Indiana State
Dec.	4-5	#Cardinal Varsity Club Classic
	8	Wright State
	12	@Butler
	22	@Ohio
	27-28	##Hoosier Classic
Jan.	2	Northern Illinois
	7	@Central Michigan
	9	@Eastern Michigan
	13	Western Michigan
	16	Toledo
	21	@Buffalo
	23	@Kent
	27	Akron
	30	Bowling Green
Feb.	3	@Marshall
	6	@Northern Illinois
	10	Miami
	13	Central Michigan
	17	@Western Michigan
	20	@Akron
	24	Buffalo
27, Mar.	2-3	###MAC Tournament

@ Road Games
\# Muncie, IN (vs. St. Joseph's-Indiana, first round; also Jacksonville and South Carolina State)
\## Indianapolis, IN (vs. Bucknell, first round; also Drake and Indiana)
\## First round Feb. 27 at campus sites. Remainder of tournament March 2-3 at SeaGate Centre, Toledo, OH

are six returning lettermen and five recruits.

Three returning starters are 6-0 junior guard **Duane Clemens** (10.6 ppg, 2.1 rpg, 95 assists), 5-11 junior guard **Mickey Hosier** (3.7 ppg, 1.9 rpg, 64 assists, 46 steals) and 6-7, 250-pound senior forward **Wayne Johnson** (4.5 ppg, 2.3 rpg).

Other returning lettermen are 6-5 sophomore forward **Jerome Davis** (5.9 ppg, 4.0 rpg), 6-5 senior forward **Marcus Mason** (3.7 ppg, 2.3 rpg) and 5-8 sophomore guard **Billy Lynch** (1.0 ppg, 0.2 rpg).

Clemens ranked third in the MAC in assist-to-turnover ratio (1.7 to1.0), fifth in steals (62), 10th in assists (3.3) and is the Cardinals' leading returning scorer. He reached double figures in 20 games, including a career-high 19 points against Northern Illinois.

Hosier played in 26 games with 22 starts and received the Ray McCallum Award for making outstanding contributions in the areas of academics, attitude and achievement. Johnson is a veteran who has played in all 86 games in his three seasons. He shot .545 against MAC opponents last season.

"We are going to count a lot on our experienced players, Wayne Johnson, Marcus Mason, Duane Clemens and Mickey Hosier," McCallum said. "They have all been starters at some point in their careers, and we will rely on them for their leadership.

"We are going to have a team this year that should have good speed and quickness. It is a young team with very good talent."

Ball State's freshman recruiting class, ranked as the nation's best among mid-majors by the High Potential Scouting Service, has some high-scoring potential. The biggest scorer in the group is 6-5 swingman **Floyd Campbell**, who averaged 26.1 points and 8.1 rebounds at Toledo (Ohio) Whitmer HS.

Other freshmen are 6-7 forward **Josh Murray**, who averaged 17.4 points and 9.1 rebounds at Indianapolis North Central HS; 6-8, 230-pound center **Corey Harris**, who averaged 10.5 points and 7.3 rebounds at Chicago's Whitney Young HS; 6-11, 215-pound center **Lonnie Jones**, who averaged 13 points and 11 rebounds at Gary (Ind.) Wallace HS; and local favorite **Patrick Jackson**, a 5-10 guard who averaged 19 points and 3.4 rebounds at Muncie (Ind.) Delta HS.

As with most top programs, McCallum has been stockpiling players.

Brian Burns, a 6-9 center, and 6-2 guard **Cedric Moodie** sat out last season as redshirt freshmen. **Nick Wise**, a 6-4 sophomore forward, was on the team but didn't play in any games.

Shane Franks, a 5-11 junior guard, also sat out as a transfer from Mercer, where he averaged 4.7 points as a freshman. Franks, who played at Monticello (Ind.) Twin Lakes HS, made 27 of 97 three-point shots at Mercer.

adidas Blue Ribbon Analysis

BACKCOURT .... **B** **BENCH/DEPTH** .... **C**
FRONTCOURT .... **C** **INTANGIBLES** .... **B**

One of Ball State's biggest assets this year is a tremendous homecourt advantage at 11,500-seat University Arena, where the Cardinals led the MAC in average attendance (7,407).

Ball State has won 29 of its last 30 home games and is 84-12 overall at University Arena since 1992, an .875 winning percentage.

The Cardinals will need all the support they can muster because the adjustment to playing without Bonzi Wells will take some time. You just don't lose a first-round NBA draft pick and carry on without some dropoff.

Cardinals coach Ray McCallum is well-stocked in the frontcourt, but looking for help on the inside.

How quickly the newcomers make an impact will be the key to Ball State's season.

(R.M.)

BOWLING GREEN

LOCATION .... **Bowling Green, OH**
CONFERENCE .... **Mid-American (East)**
LAST SEASON .... **10-16 (.385)**
CONFERENCE RECORD .... **7-11 (t-4th)**
STARTERS LOST/RETURNING **0/5**
NICKNAME .... **Falcons**
COLORS .... **Orange & Brown**
HOMECOURT .... **Anderson Arena (5,000)**
COACH .... **Dan Dakich (Indiana '85)**
RECORD AT SCHOOL .... **10-16 (1 yr.)**
CAREER RECORD .... **10-16 (1 yr.)**
ASSISTANTS .... **Keith Noftz (Heidelberg '78)**
Jamal Meeks (Indiana '92)
Artie Pepelea (Wisconsin-Parkside '94)
TEAM WINS (last 5 yrs.) **18-16-14-22-10**
RPI (last 5 yrs.) **92-121-135-73-206**
1997-98 FINISH .... **Did not qualify for conference tournament.**

Seven Bowling Green players were members of a Mid-American Conference championship team two years ago, including five who played significant roles. They haven't forgotten how to win, despite last year's disappointing season.

Those five players—**Anthony Stacey**, **Tony Reid**, **Dave Esterkamp**, **DeMar Moore** and **Kirk Cowan**—form the nucleus for this year's team and could be the starting five.

"Our strength is going to have to be having veteran players who are mentally tough," second-year coach Dan Dakich said. "They have been through the whole gamut, up and down. They've won a championship and experienced a less-than-successful season a year ago."

Along with its championship experience, Bowling Green also returns every player from last season and has added some talented newcomers. Maybe the depth is good enough that assistant coach Jamal Meeks, a former Indiana player, won't be forced to practice as he did at times last year.

The Falcons went through most of the 1997-98 season with only nine players.

"Our depth was non-existent last season," Dakich said.

Many questions exist, but none bigger than the status of junior forward **Anthony Stacey** (12.4 ppg, 4.6 rpg). The 6-4 Stacey earned MAC Freshman-of-the-Year honors in 1996, but his sophomore season was a bust. Stacey played in only five games last season. He missed the season opener while recovering from mononucleosis, then suffered a torn plantar facia on the bottom of his right foot on Nov. 29 and again on Jan. 5 in his third game back after the first incident.

1998-99 BOWLING GREEN SCHEDULE

Nov.	24	Detroit
	28	Illinois-Chicago
Dec.	2	@Ohio
	5	@Eastern Michigan
	8	Oakland University
	11-12	#Indiana Classic
	19	@Wisconsin-Green Bay
Jan.	2	Toledo
	6	@Buffalo
	9	@Kent
	14	Akron
	19	Marshall
	23	Ohio
	27	@Miami
	30	@Ball State
Feb.	3	Nothern Illinois
	6	@Toledo
	10	Central Michigan
	13	Buffalo
	17	@Akron
	20	Miami
	24	@Marshall
27, Mar.	23	##MAC Tournament

@ Road Games
\# Bloomington, IN (vs. Grambling, first round; also Boise State and Indiana)
\## First round Feb. 27 at campus sites. Remainder of tournament March 2-3 at SeaGate Centre, Toledo, OH

Stacey received a medical hardship season. He returned to the court in the summer and is expected to be ready for the start of practice in October.

If healthy, Stacey is one of the league's top players. A two-time honorable mention All-MAC selection, Stacey posted 13 double-doubles in his first two years, while averaging 15.1 points and seven rebounds. He has scored in double figures in 54 of 64 career games.

"We expect Anthony to be back at 100 percent," Dakich said. "But you never know until practice starts and he gets that constant pounding. That kind of injury can be one which bothers him the rest of his career at times or he might not have any more problems.

"But at this point we're hoping he can stay healthy and be a big part of the team this season."

Last year's leading scorer was Reid (16.7 ppg, 3.5 rpg), a 6-3 senior who played shooting guard and small forward. Reid was the eighth-leading scorer in the league, despite being targeted by opposing defenses. He also ranked second in free-throw percentage (101-121, .835) and made 49 of 120 three-point shots (.408), ranking ninth in the MAC.

Reid had a six-game stretch in the middle of the season when he averaged 23.3 points.

Moore (12.3 ppg, 3.4 rpg), a 6-1 senior, returns at point guard, where he handed out 92 assists and committed 62 turnovers.

Reid and Moore form a potent three-point shooting combination. Moore was 43 for 112 on three-point shots last year and earned the MAC's Defensive Player-of-the-Year award as a sophomore.

Cowan (11.2 ppg, 8.7 rpg), a lean 6-7, 190-pound senior, manned the center's job for the Falcons, and he played it well. He improved his sophomore numbers (4.4 ppg, 3.6 rpg) and was third in the MAC last year in rebounding.

And like Cowan, the role of Esterkamp (12.7 ppg, 5.0 rpg), a 6-7 junior forward, dramatically increased from his freshman season. Esterkamp averaged only 4.1 points and 2.3 rebounds as a freshman in 1996-97.

Dakich has numerous other options in the backcourt, where 6-2 sophomore **Jay Keys** (5.8 ppg, 1.7 rpg) and 6-3 sophomore **Dubrey Black** (5.2 ppg, 1.8 rpg) combined to start 10 games. Keys started six games and Black four.

Howard Chambers (0.8 ppg, 0.4 rpg), a 5-6 senior, and 6-4 junior **Dave Furlin** (0.5 ppg, 0.7 rpg) will provide depth in the backcourt.

Javier Crespo (1.7 ppg, 2.5 rpg), a 6-8 senior forward, also returns.

The key addition arrives at the end of the first semester on Dec. 18 when 6-4 sophomore guard **Trent Jackson** becomes eligible after transferring from Ohio State. Jackson might be the best all-around player on the team with the ability to score, rebound and defend. He averaged 2.9 points in 14 games for Ohio State in 1996-97 with a high of 12 points against Illinois.

The combination of Jackson and Moore gives the Falcons a terrific defensive backcourt.

Dakich expects two freshmen frontcourt players to have an impact: 6-9 **Len Matela** from Dakich's hometown of Merrillville, Ind., where he averaged16.4 points, 8.2

rebounds and 3.4 blocked shots at Andrean HS; and 6-8 **Brent Klassen** from Kimball, Neb. Klassen played last season at New Hampton (N.H.) Prep School and averaged 15 points and nine rebounds.

adidas Blue Ribbon Analysis

BACKCOURT .... B+ BENCH/DEPTH C
FRONTCOURT .... B+ INTANGIBLES C

The adjustment period to Dan Dakich's demanding coaching style isn't over yet, but the Falcons are getting there.

Anthony Stacey's return makes the Falcons better, and additional depth is another plus.

In only his second year as a Division I head coach, Dakich, the former player and assistant to Bobby Knight at Indiana, is putting the pieces together for a good team.

"The ideal team is one in which the players have to battle every day to keep their spot," Dakich said. "Hopefully, with the kids coming in and the ones returning, we'll have a battle every day."

Bowling Green should field a team that can score. Defense was a problem last year and must improve.

This team will get better throughout the year and could make a run in the MAC Tournament.

(R.M.)

BUFFALO

LOCATION .... **Buffalo, NY**
CONFERENCE .... **Mid-American (East)**
LAST SEASON .... **15-13 (.536)**
CONFERENCE RECORD .... **9-7 (5th-Mid-Continent)**
STARTERS LOST/RETURNING **4/1**
NICKNAME .... **Bulls**
COLORS .... **Royal Blue & White**
HOMECOURT .... **Alumni Arena (8,464)**
COACH .... **Tom Cohane (Navy '67)**
RECORD AT SCHOOL .... **73-68 (5 yrs.)**
CAREER RECORD .... **217-211 (16 yrs.)**
ASSISTANTS .... **Frank Valenti (Rollins '70)**
Fred Batchelor (Valley Forge Christian '88)
Ron Torgalski (Hamilton '89)
TEAM WINS (last 5 yrs.) **10-18-13-17-15**
RPI (last 5 yrs.) **282-157-211-134-191**
1997-98 FINISH .... **Lost in conference second round.**

Buffalo becomes the 13th member of the Mid-American Conference this season. The Bulls hope that's not an unlucky number.

They left the Mid-Continent Conference after last season and joined the MAC this year in all sports but football, which is being elevated from NCAA Division I-AA status to I-A, with some restrictions.

To become a full-fledged league member, possibly in 1999, Buffalo must meet certain requirements in football, including upgrading its stadium to 30,000 seats from 17,200. Its football team must average 17,000 paid tickets this fall or else.

Or else what?

"Then probably the rest of our teams would be coming out," of the MAC, said Bob Arkeilpane, the school's associate athletic director.

The basketball Bulls were placed in the much-improved MAC East along with Akron, Bowling Green, Kent, Marshall, Miami (Ohio) and Ohio.

Not only are they joining a new and stronger league, but the Bulls are virtually starting over again with a team that lost four starters, including two of the top scorers in school history.

"We welcome the challenge and recognize that the MAC had as many players chosen in the NBA draft this year as the Big East and the Big 10," said coach Tim Cohane. "The challenge is greater, the risk is greater, but the reward is also greater as well."

The departed seniors will be hard to replace, especially the high-scoring guard tandem of Rasaun Young (19.8 ppg, 4.1 rpg) and Mike Martinho (17.3 ppg, 3.3 rpg). Young is Buffalo's all-time scoring leader (1,908) while Martinho finished third on the list (1,708). Buffalo also lost swingman Matt Clemens (9.8 ppg, 4.4 rpg) and forward Scott McMillin (8.9 ppg, 3.3 rpg).

Young tied with Valparaiso's Bryce Drew for the Mid-Continent scoring title.

Ryan Peterson (2.3 ppg, 2.0 rpg, 152 assists, 53 turnovers), a 5-11 sophomore point guard, is the only returning starter. Peterson was impressive from the start as a freshman and logged more minutes (704) than anyone but the four seniors. Peterson led all freshmen in the nation in assists (5.85 per game).

"He was all we hoped he would be," Cohane said. "He managed to break into a very experienced team on the perimeter and play a lot of minutes. I expect he'll be a team leader at point guard."

Cohane said 6-3 redshirt freshman **Louis Campbell** "is the best athlete we've ever had at guard."

Freshman **Koran Godwin**, a 6-4 guard, has the opportunity to play right away because he is one of the Bulls' best shooters. Godwin comes to Buffalo from Abraham Clark HS in Roselle, N.J.

Two walkon guards, 5-11 freshman **Davis Lawrence** and 5-9 freshman **Malik Winn**, will provide depth while Buffalo waits for 6-5 Damien Foster, a Boston College transfer, to become eligible next year.

The Bulls have only two forwards with game experience. Junior **Jon Kleidon** (2.6 ppg, 2.0 rpg) is a 6-6, athletic player with great leaping ability who was slowed last season by a knee injury he suffered in high school. He averaged only 9.6 minutes in 26 games last season Kleidon still showed flashes of the ability the coaching staff recognized when he transferred from Wichita State two years ago.

"Jon had a decent season despite his knee flaring up," Cohane said. "The big question with him is if this knee problem is recurring."

Senior forward **Robert Harris** (5.2 ppg, 5.4 rpg) is Buffalo's top returning scorer. Harris is 6-4, 230, and loves to bang inside. He is one of only six Buffalo players with more than 500 career points and rebounds.

Redshirt freshman **Will Campbell**, is a physical force at 6-7, 230. Another freshman is 6-7 Lithuanian **Bogdan Karebin**, who will get an opportunity to play quickly.

Post player **Nikolai Alexeev**, a former Belarus National Team player, adjusted to the American game quickly as a freshman. The 6-11, 240-pound Alexeev (4.2 ppg, 3.0 rpg, 27 blocks) shot 81 percent at the foul line and made seven of 17 three-point shots.

"Nick really had a good freshman season," Cohane said. "He's great at the high-post area because he has a soft touch and passed the ball well. He also proved he could make big plays by saving the game against Niagara with a blocked shot and his three-point shooting against Youngstown State won that game for us."

Nate Johnson (2.8 ppg, 3.8 rpg in '96-97) returns as a senior after missing last season because of a shoulder injury. Johnson, a 6-9, 225 center, is a good defender and rebounder who worked to improve his offensive skills during the layoff.

Another player in the low-post mix is 6-8, 230-pound sophomore **Maliso Libomi** (1.8 ppg, 1.4 rpg). Libomi, native of Zaire, Africa, averaged 4.9 minutes in 20 games with two starts

"Maliso played very well when he got in games last season," Cohane said. "This year he'll have a chance to play serious minutes. He's the most athletic big man we have."

Freshman walkon **Jay Jackson**, 6-6, 225 forward, adds more size off the bench.

adidas Blue Ribbon Analysis

BACKCOURT .... C BENCH/DEPTH C
FRONTCOURT .... C+ INTANGIBLES C

With only one returning starter, two seniors, and 10 freshmen and sophomores on the roster, Buffalo will have a difficult time contending against the game-tested teams in the MAC's East Division.

The Bulls have the size inside to compete in the MAC, but too many questions exist at other positions.

"The good news is we're excited because it's a new challenge for us, a new mountain to climb," second-year coach Tim Cohane said. "The success of this year's team will depend on how quickly the inexperienced kids can get seasoned and how hard they work this fall."

That mountain is probably too tall this year. The Bulls look to be a year or two away from being a strong team in the MAC.

(R.M.)

1998-99 BUFFALO SCHEDULE

Nov.	13	@Niagra
	17	@Cornell
	21	@Duquesne
	24	Canisius
Dec.	1	@Mahattan
	5	Akron
	8	@North Carolina
	12	@Canisius
	21	@Central Michigan
	28-30	#Hilo Holiday Shootout
Jan.	2	@Kent
	6	Bowling Green
	8	Miami
	14	@Marshall
	16	@Ohio
	19	St. Bonaventure
	21	Ball State
	23	Central Michigan
	28	@Northern Illinois
	30	@Western Michigan
Feb.	3	Eastern Michigan
	6	Kent
	11	@Toledo
	13	@Bowling Green
	17	Marshall
	20	Northern Illinois
	24	@Ball State
27-Mar.	1	##MAC Tournament

@ Road Games
# Honolulu, HI (vs. Central Connecticut State, first round; also Hawaii-Hilo and Old Dominion)
First round Feb. 27 at campus sites. Remainder of tournament March 2-3 at SeaGate Centre, Toldeo, OH.

CENTRAL MICHIGAN

LOCATION .... **Mount Pleasant, MI**
CONFERENCE .... **Mid-American (West)**
LAST SEASON .... **5-21 (.192)**
CONFERENCE RECORD .... **3-15 (6th)**
STARTERS LOST/RETURNING **2/3**
NICKNAME .... **Chippewas**
COLORS .... **Maroon & Gold**
HOMECOURT .... **Dan Rose Arena (5,200)**
COACH .... **Jay Smith (Saginaw Valley '84)**
RECORD AT SCHOOL .... **5-21 (1 yr.)**
CAREER RECORD .... **28-27 (2 yrs.)**
ASSISTANTS .... **Dave Grube (Kent '66)**
Mark Montgomery (Michigan State '92)
TEAM WINS (last 5 yrs.) **5-3-6-7-5**
RPI (last 5 yrs.) **254-287-261-272-256**
1997-98 FINISH .... **Did not qualify for conference tournament.**

Do you like new? If so, you'd love Central Michigan's basketball team.

A dozen new faces dot an expansive roster of 19 players, and second-year coach Jay Smith likes what he sees.

Central Michigan lost six lettermen, but returns seven players who earned letters, three of them starters. The Chippewas have 14 underclassmen—nine freshmen and five sophomores—and no seniors.

"With such an influx of new players, the team attitude and chemistry will be critical to our success," Smith said.

Although only 5-21 overall and 3-15 in the MAC last year, the Chippewas fired a season-ending warning shot that was heard around the league. Their 73-71 victory at home over NIT-bound Ball State could some day prove to be the turning point for Smith's program.

Smith knows success isn't always measured by wins and losses.

"We knew that we did not have as much talent as other teams," he said. "The biggest thing we had to do was establish a tremendous work ethic, not only in games but every day in practice. We also wanted to instill a team attitude. We wanted them to sacrifice for the team. Everyone has a role and that is to do whatever it takes to help the team win.

"I feel we accomplished both goals. We turned the corner in both those areas without question."

Central Michigan missed qualifying for the MAC Tournament for the sixth consecutive season and averaged only three league victories per year during that period.

The most significant losses from last year's team were guard Jerry Glover, the leading scorer (11.8 ppg, 4.2 rpg) and forward Aaron Brown (11.3 ppg, 4.3 rpg).

Returning starters are 6-5 junior forward **Dan Schell**, 6-

1998-99 CENTRAL MICHIGAN SCHEDULE

Nov.	14	Rochester College
	17	@Wright State
	21	@Wisconsin-Milwaukee
	24	@South Florida
	30	Robert Morris
Dec.	2	Fairfield
	5	@Notre Dame
	9	@Detroit
	12	Miami
	21	Buffalo
	30	@Marshall
Jan.	2	@Ohio
	7	Ball State
	13	@Northern Illinois
	16	Western Michigan
	20	@Eastern Michigan
	23	@Buffalo
	27	Toledo
	30	Akron
Feb.	3	@Kent
	6	Ohio
	10	@Bowling Green
	13	@Ball State
	18	Northern Illinois
	20	@Toledo
	24	Eastern Michigan
27, Mar.	2-3	#MAC Tournament

@ Road Games
\# First round Feb. 27 at campus sites. Remainder of tournament March 2-3 at SeaGate Centre, Toledo, OH

2 sophomore guard **Tim Kisner** and 6-1 sophomore guard **Jon Borovich**.

Schell (10.5 ppg, 4.8 rpg) is a hometown product of Mount Pleasant HS who shot 45 percent from the field and 70 percent at the free-throw line. He made 14 of 51 three-point shots (.275) and his 1.27 blocks per game ranked fourth in the league.

In Central Michigan's 122-121 double-overtime loss at Ohio, Schell scored 32 points and grabbed eight rebounds. Schell also recorded a double-double (15 points, 10 rebounds) in a loss to Bowling Green and scored 20 points in the victory over Ball State.

Kisner (12.1 ppg, 3.4 rpg) wasn't expected to contribute much as a freshman, then went out and contributed a lot. Kisner made two clutch free-throws with eight seconds left and scored 15 points in Central Michigan's upset victory over East Division champion Akron. Kisner went 11 for 11 at the free-throw line in a loss to Eastern Michigan when he also scored a season-high 25 points. He scored 18 in another loss to Eastern Michigan, 18 against Toledo and 17 against Northern Illinois.

Kisner played in 21 games, started 16 and averaged 30.9 minutes. He was second on the team in assists with 66.

Borovich (6.8 ppg, 3.5 rpg) came on strong as the starting point guard, making significant contributions as a freshman. He led the team with 79 assists, but also led in turnovers with 99.

The other four returning players, all walkons, are 5-8 sophomore guard **Brent Larson** (3.5 ppg, 0.5 rpg); 6-1 sophomore guard **Luke Johnson** (2.9 ppg, 1.3 rpg); 5-7 sophomore guard **Ted Baggett** (0.0 ppg, 0.0 rpg); and 6-4 junior forward **Todd Simmons** (0.7 ppg, 0.7 rpg).

Smith's recruiting contacts from seven years as an assistant on Michigan's staff under Steve Fisher helped land 6-6 junior **Jason Webber**, a Michigan State transfer, and his brother, 6-2 freshman **David Webber**. The Webbers' older brother, Chris, played at Michigan and is with the NBA's Sacramento Kings.

Jason Webber was redshirted last year. David Webber was a standout at Country Day HS in Farmington Hills, Mich.

Jamar Hill, a 6-3 junior guard/forward transfer from Cuesta (Calif.) CC, was also redshirted last year. Hill averaged 17 points, six rebounds and four assists at Cuesta CC.

Junior forward **Rudy Gaytan** transferred from Lansing (Mich.) CC. The 6-8, 200-pound Gaytan is a strong interior defender and rebounder.

Freshman recruits include 6-6 forward **Omar Zeigler**, an all-state player at Redford HS in Detroit, where he averaged 21 points and 11 rebounds.

"Omar increases our athletic ability and quickness on the perimeter," Smith said. "He is a proven scorer who'll give us an offensive touch. He is a good fit for our program. I look for him to contribute immediately."

Other freshmen scholarship players are 6-4 guard/forward **Derrick Bird**, 6-4 guard/forward **Robert Brown**, 6-5 forward **Mike Manciel** and 6-2 guard **Joe Shepherd**.

Freshman walkons are 6-6 **Chad Pleiness**, 6-7 **Ben Feeney** and 6-7 **Andrew Neidlinger**. Each can play power forward or center.

Pleiness is on a football scholarship. As a senior at Mason County Central HS in Scottville, Mich., he caught 28 passes for 383 yards and had a 43.3 punting average. He earned all-state honors in football and basketball.

adidas Blue Ribbon Analysis

BACKCOURT	**C**	**BENCH/DEPTH**	**C**
FRONTCOURT	**C**	**INTANGIBLES**	**C**

Most schools would be disappointed with winning only three conference games, but at Central Michigan, it was enough to build some hope.

Second-year coach Jay Smith pulled every ounce of available energy from his players. A team that could have quit never did, and that's a credit to Smith and the players.

"Those wins showed our players that if you work hard and play together as a group, a lot can be accomplished," Smith said. "I think we surprised some people. A lot of people had written us off, but we were competitive in almost every game.

"Everything was not peaches and cream, but I think everyone finished the season with respect for one another. We have built some momentum."

Will the Chippewas be better this season? Certainly. They have nowhere to go but up.

(R.M.)

EASTERN MICHIGAN

LOCATION	**Ypsilanti, MI**
CONFERENCE	**Mid-American (West)**
LAST SEASON	**20-10 (.667)**
CONFERENCE RECORD	**13-5 (3rd)**
STARTERS LOST/RETURNING	**5/0**
NICKNAME	**Eagles**
COLORS	**Dark Green & White**
HOMECOURT	**Convocation Center (8,824)**
COACH	**Milton Barnes (Albion '79)**
RECORD AT SCHOOL	**42-20 (2 yrs)**
CAREER RECORD	**42-20 (2 yrs.)**
ASSISTANTS	**Todd Lickliter (Butler '79)**
	Tony Harvey (Cameron '90)
	Chad Walthall (Concordia '91)
TEAM WINS (last 5 yrs.)	**15-20-25-22-20**
RPI (last 5 yrs.)	**159-75-31-77-67**
1997-98 FINISH	**Lost in NCAA first round.**

Eastern Michigan coach Milton Barnes laughed when asked who is going to carry the scoring load for Eastern Michigan this season.

"That question will be answered Nov. 25 when we play our first game," Barnes said. "Hopefully we have somebody who can score. Maybe we don't."

It's not a laughing matter, but the third-year coach has some serious holes to plug after losing five senior starters who accounted for 91 percent of the scoring and 84 percent of the rebounding for last year's Mid-American Conference Tournament champions.

Those seniors went 87-36 the last four seasons, winning 20 or more games all four years. They led the Eagles to the NCAA Tournament twice (1998, 1996) and to the NIT in 1995.

Eastern Michigan finished third in the MAC West, then roared through the conference tournament with wins over Toledo, Ball State and Miami (Ohio) and advanced to the NCAA Tournament for the second time in four years and the fourth time in school history. The Eagles put up a good fight against Michigan State in the NCAA first round before losing to the Big Ten Conference co-champions, 83-71.

The Eagles' departed starters are first team All-MAC point guard Earl Boykins (25.7 ppg, 2.3 rpg), second-team All-MAC guard Derrick Dial (20.9 ppg, 6.7 rpg), forwards Jon Zajac (6.6 ppg, 5.9 rpg) and James Head (10.8 ppg, 6.7 rpg) and center Nkechi Ezugwu (7.7 ppg, 6.7 rpg).

You just don't replace that kind of production overnight.

"It's an era that just comes to an end," Barnes said. "Everything at some point must end. We hope the winning tradition doesn't change, but when you're talking about back-to-back 20-win seasons, that's hard to duplicate."

1998-99 EASTERN MICHIGAN SCHEDULE

Nov.	25	Boise State
	28	@Colorado State
Dec.	2	@Akron
	5	Bowling Green
	9	Michigan
	12	@Minnesota
	19	@Dayton
	21	@Kent
	29-30	#Sparkletts Invitational
Jan.	2	@Marshall
	6	Miami
	9	Ball State
	13	@Ohio
	16	@Northern Illinois
	20	Central Michigan
	27	@Western Michigan
	30	Toledo
Feb.	3	@Buffalo
	6	Marshall
	13	@Miami
	17	Ohio
	20	Western Michigan
	24	@Central Michigan
27-Mar.	2-3	##MAC Tournament

@ Road Games
\# Malibu, CA (vs. Siena, first round; also Pepperdine and Rhode Island)
\#\# First round Feb. 27 at campus sites. Remainder of tournament March 2-3 at SeaGate Center, Toledo, Ohio.

Nobody can take the place of the incomparable Boykins, the 5-5 mighty mite who led the MAC in scoring and won the Naismith Award as the nation's top player under 6-0. Boykins, who had 160 assists and 93 turnovers last season, finished his career second in school history with 2,211 points. He set the career assists record with 624.

Boykins was chosen to *Basketball Weekly*'s All-Small Team and was featured in *Sports Illustrated* as "The Best Little Player in America."

NBA teams apparently didn't like the size of Boykins and passed him over in the draft. He was contacted by several teams and could end up in someone's training camp, whenever the NBA lockout ends.

Boykins picked up many of his assists on feeds to the 6-5 Dial, who was fourth in the league in scoring and finished third in school history (1,891). Dial was drafted by the San Antonio Spurs in the second round.

Zajac, Head and Ezugwu combined to give the Eagles a strong front line.

"Put that talent together with experience and it's very difficult to replace," Barnes said. "It's a very, very difficult situation, but I am excited about the season. It's a challenge."

The Eagles also lost forwards Sharif Fordham (2.7 ppg, 1.6 rpg) and Corey Tarrant (3.2 ppg, 2.3 rpg) because of academic deficiencies.

Barnes turns to his most experienced returnee, 6-1 sophomore **Avin Howard** (2.3 ppg, 1.5 rpg), to replace Boykins at point guard. Howard spent his freshman year backing up Boykins. He played in all 30 games and made 12 starts while averaging about 17 minutes per game.

The center position could go to 6-10, 220-pound senior **Ajani Williams** (2.3 ppg, 2.0 rpg), who played in 26 games with one start. Williams, a native of Kingston, Jamaica, joined the Eagles last season after a year at McClennan JC in Waco, Texas, where he averaged 11 points and seven rebounds. He was selected to play on Jamaica's national team in 1995.

Two returnees who played sparingly in the frontcourt are 6-8, 280-pound senior **DeWayne Geeter-Burns** (0.8 ppg, 1.0 rpg) and 6-5 junior **Jermaine Sheffield** (0.3 ppg, 0.6 rpg). Junior guard **Charlie Eibeler**, 6-5, returns after missing last season with back problems. Eibeler averaged 2.3 points in 1996-97.

Barnes is leaning heavily on eight newcomers to provide immediate help.

Two Detroit high school products, 6-7 sophomore forward **Tyson Radney** and 6-6 sophomore forward **Ken Richardson**, sat out the 1997-98 season as Prop 48 players and are eligible this season. Radney averaged 19 points and seven rebounds at Detroit's Northern HS, while Richardson averaged 19.2 points and five rebounds at Martin Luther King Jr. HS.

Solomon McGee, a 6-7, 230-pound junior forward, is a transfer from Coastal Carolina, where he averaged 4.9 points and 4.2 rebounds as a sophomore.

The *Future Stars* recruiting report said the Eagles made a "major steal" by signing 6-10 junior center **K.C. Tanner** from Olney (Ill.) CC. Tanner averaged 12 points and nine rebounds at Olney CC last season.

"He will be a defensive force in the MAC," the report said.

Wing player **Larry Fisher** is a 6-4 junior transfer from Three Rivers (Mo.) CC. Fisher, a guard, averaged 18.7 points and 3.2 rebounds last season.

Also expecting to contribute is 6-3 junior guard **DeSean Hadley**, who averaged 17.8 points and 8.9 rebounds at Sinclair (Ohio) CC. **Craig Erquhart**, a 6-6 junior forward, joins the Eagles after averaging 14.6 points and 6.3 rebounds at Owens Tech (Ohio) CC last season.

"We signed four junior-college players and I'm hoping that gives us a chance to keep it at a certain level," Barnes said. "I'm hoping this year we can be competitive. When you have so many new faces it's difficult to still compete at the same level you've been competing at."

The only freshman recruit is 6-6 forward **Calvin Warner** from Sandalwood HS in Jacksonville, Fla. He averaged 18 points and 8.1 rebounds last season.

adidas Blue Ribbon Analysis

BACKCOURT .... C **BENCH/DEPTH .... C**
FRONTCOURT .... C **INTANGIBLES .... C**

Eastern Michigan has a new basketball arena and basically an entirely new team to put on the court.

The Eagles moved out of antiquated Bowen Field House, its basketball home since 1955, and into the $29.6 million Convocation Center at the south end of Rynearson Stadium.

Eastern Michigan coach Milton Barnes wishes the Convocation Center was the only thing new this season.

It is definitely a rebuilding year at Eastern Michigan, and that has nothing to do with the basketball arena. With five talented senior starters lost to graduation, the Eagles reloaded with four junior-college transfers and a freshman recruit.

"There are going to be some long nights," Barnes said. "The key thing for me and my staff is patience."

Playing in the MAC, a league that Barnes said is "enormously tough," doesn't make it any easier.

Barnes probably wishes he had brought home some of the players he worked with this summer as an assistant coach with the gold medal-winning U.S. team in the Goodwill Games.

(R.M.)

KENT

LOCATION .... Kent, OH
CONFERENCE .... Mid-American (East)
LAST SEASON .... 13-17 (.433)
CONFERENCE RECORD 9-9 (t-2nd)
STARTERS LOST/RETURNING 0/5
NICKNAME .... Golden Flashes
COLORS .... Navy Blue & Gold
HOMECOURT .... M.A.C. Center (6,327)
COACH .... Gary Waters (Ferris State '75)
RECORD AT SCHOOL .... 22-35 (2 yrs.)
CAREER RECORD .... 22-35 (2 yrs.)
ASSISTANTS .... Kevin Heck Wayne State '92)
Garland Mance (St. Bonaventure '94)
Larry DeSimpelare (Spring Arbor '91)
TEAM WINS (last 5 yrs.) 13-8-14-9-13
RPI (last 5 yrs.) 167-211-175-206-204
1997-98 FINISH .... Lost in conference semifinal.

Kent's Golden Flashes are no longer loosers.

Coach Gary Waters and his team fooled last year's pollsters who picked them to finish sixth (last) in the Mid-American Conference East Division by rising up to a second-place tie with Miami (Ohio). Kent's league record of 9-9 was its best in eight years.

Then, the Golden Flashes fooled everybody by whipping Akron, the East Division champion, 95-88 in the conference tournament quarterfinals. It was Kent's first tournament victory in nine years.

The breakthrough season for Waters ended with a 64-59 loss to Miami in the semifinals.

"Now we're ready to take another step," Waters said. "As a team one of our goals is to be above .500 in everything we do. We want to have a chance to win our division."

Waters enters his third season with a team that has adjusted to his fast-paced, full-court style. He thinks that style will pay dividends in the MAC.

"We play different than everyone else," Waters said. "The way we press, nobody else does that. It gives us something unique."

Senior guard Scott Effertz (6.0 ppg, 1.9 rpg) is the only key figure missing from the 1997-98 team.

Effertz, who lead the MAC in three-point shooting (30 of 69, .435), is a pre-medicine student with a 3.9 grade-point average and is devoting all his time to academics.

Sophomore forward Tim Martin (0.8 ppg, 1.7 rpg) left school after averaging 6.1 minutes in 19 games last season.

Everyone else is back, including the five who started against Miami in the tournament. They are 6-2 senior guard **Ed Norvell** (9.0 ppg, 3.3 rpg, 161 assists), 6-1 junior guard **Jose Davis** (6.9 ppg, 1.9 rpg), 6-2 senior guard **John Callaway** (6.1 ppg, 3.4 rpg), 6-8, 235-pound junior forward **John Whorton** (11.4 ppg, 6.5 rpg) and 6-10, 210-pound sophomore center **Mike Perry** (5.9 ppg, 3.5 rpg).

Sophomore **Kyrem Massey** (12 ppg, 3.8 rpg) was suspended for the semifinal game after the 6-6 guard decked Akron's Jami Bosley with a flagrant elbow in the quarterfinals.

"Massey would have helped us immensely in the Miami game," Waters said. "He's young. He's got to learn how to carry and conduct himself. He came back and worked hard this summer. He made a commitment to do whatever is necessary to help us."

The 6-6 Massey missed a total of seven games because of the suspension and a stress fracture in his foot, but was still chosen to the MAC All-Freshman team. He led the team in scoring in nine games, reached double figures in 14 games and had a season-high 26 points against Marshall.

Norvell earned honorable-mention All-MAC honors for the second straight year and has missed only one game in three seasons. With 419 career assists, he is well within reach of Anthony Grier's school record (503) set from 1981-85.

"If Ed Norvell gets going, we go," Waters said. "He's our leader out there on the floor."

The big man on campus is Whorton. His career started with a 20-point game against Ferris State the first time he stepped on the court, and he's been on a roll ever since.

Whorton is coming off a strong season and has All-MAC potential. He was second on the team in scoring behind Massey and led the Golden Flashes in rebounding while swatting away a school-record 37 shots. Big John also has a nice shooting touch, ranking third in the league in field-goal accuracy (.563).

The coaches received a glowing report on Whorton's performance at a big-man camp this summer in Tennessee.

"He was voted one of the better ones there, and a lot of the good players were there," Waters said.

Kent has to wait on the services of Davis, the starting quarterback on the football team. He joined the basketball team last season on Nov. 24 and provided immediate help.

1998-99 KENT SCHEDULE

Month	Date	Opponent
Nov.	14	@Dayton
	18	Youngstown State
	22	@Ball State
	28	@Loyola College
Dec.	2	@UNC Charlotte
	5	St. Bonaventure
	9	St. Joseph
	12	@Cleveland State
	19	@Toledo
	21	Eastern Michigan
	30	@Western Michigan
Jan.	2	Buffalo
	6	@Akron
	9	Bowling Green
	16	@Marshall
	20	Miami
	23	Ball State
	27	Ohio
	30	@Northern Illinois
Feb.	3	Central Michigan
	6	@Buffalo
	10	Western Michigan
	13	Akron
	20	@Ohio
	24	@Miami
27-Mar.	3	#MAC Tornament

@ Road Games
\# First round Feb. 27 at campus sites. Remainder of tournament March 2-3 at SeaGate Centre, Toledo, OH.

Callaway came to the Golden Flashes last year after two seasons at McCook (Neb.) CC. He was a starter in 16 of 30 games and finished the season strong. His six double-figure scoring games included 17 against both Marshall and Ohio late in the year and 19 against Akron in the tournament.

Perry displayed his potential as a freshman with 18 points and 10 rebounds against Loyola College in the fourth game of the season. He shot .461 percent from the field, second-highest on the team among players with at least 100 shots.

One of the reasons Kent set a school record with 190 three-point goals was the shooting of 6-4 junior **Nate Meers** (8.8 ppg, 1.5 rpg), who made 54 of 133 (.406 percent) from three-point range. Meers showed little rust after taking a year off to work on academics, and his playing time increased as the season went along. He averaged 15.1 minutes in 25 games.

Meers ranked sixth in the MAC in three-pointers per game (2.16) and was eighth in three-point percentage. He had six three-pointers in two games, against Central Michigan and Marshall.

Forward **Al Moore** (4.6 ppg, 2.6 rpg) was one of five players who played in every game. The 6-7 junior played 13 minutes a game, all in a reserve role.

Kent's other returnees are 6-5 junior guard **Ryan Lehrke** (0.6 ppg, 0.2 rpg), 6-6 junior forward **Geoffrey Vaughn** (4.0 ppg, 3.3 rpg) and 6-7, 245-pound sophomore forward **Rashaun Warren** (3.3 ppg, 2.1 rpg).

Waters also welcomes 6-0 sophomore guard **Andrew Mitchell** and 6-5 sophomore forward **Eric Thomas**, who were academically ineligible last season as freshmen. Mitchell averaged 21 points and was an all-city point guard at Detroit's East Catholic HS, leading the team to the Class D state championship. Thomas averaged 18 points and nine rebounds at Springfield (Ohio) North HS.

As partial qualifiers, Mitchell and Thomas practiced with Kent last season, but were ineligible for games.

"They're going to contribute immediately," Waters said.

adidas Blue Ribbon Analysis

BACKCOURT .... B **BENCH/DEPTH .... C+**
FRONTCOURT .... B **INTANGIBLES .... C+**

Kent is coming off its best season of the '90s.

Advancing to the MAC semifinals was a good experience for a group of young players. Kent returns nine lettermen, all five starters and statistical leaders in almost every category.

It's no wonder the Golden Flashes have their sights set on winning a MAC East title.

"We're going to have one here one day," Kent coach Gary Waters said. "We hope it's sooner rather than later."

Maybe the time is now.

(R.M.)

MARSHALL

LOCATION .... Huntington, WV
CONFERENCE .... Mid-American (East)
LAST SEASON .... 11-16 (.407)
CONFERENCE RECORD 7-11 (t-4th)
STARTERS LOST/RETURNING 0/5
NICKNAME .... Thundering Herd
COLORS .... Kelly Green & White
HOMECOURT .... Cam Henderson Center (9,043)
COACH .... Greg White (Marshall '82)
RECORD AT SCHOOL .... 31-25 (2 yrs.)
CAREER RECORD .... 150-179 (12 yrs.)
ASSISTANTS .... Steve Snell (Radford '88)
Bryan Poore (West Virginia State '88)
TEAM WINS (last 5 yrs.) 9-18-17-20-11
RPI (last 5 yrs.) 251-177-148-98-213
1997-98 FINISH .... Lost in conference first round.

Marshall left the Southern Conference two years ago feeling good about itself. And why not? Greg White's team won 20 games and dropped a one-point overtime loss to Tennessee-Chattanooga in the Southern Conference Tournament finals.

Then reality set in. Marshall returned to the Mid-American Conference after a 28-year absence. Marshall was a MAC member from 1953 until 1969, when it was booted out after

1998-99 MARSHALL SCHEDULE

Nov.	14	Bluefield State
	17	Northern Illinois
	23	@Georgia
	28	Morehead State
Dec.	2	@Radford
	5	Massachusetts
	8	@Miami
	17	Rio Grande
	19	@Western Michigan
	21	@North Carolina-Asheville
	30	Central Michigan
Jan.	2	Eastern Michigan
	6	@Toledo
	9	@Akron
	14	Buffalo
	16	Kent
	20	@Bowling Green
	23	Miami
	27	@West Virginia
	30	@Ohio
Feb.	3	Ball State
	6	@Eastern Michigan
	10	@Northern Illinois
	13	Toledo
	17	@Buffalo
	24	Bowling Green
27-Mar.	3	#MAC Tournament

@ Road Games
# First round Feb. 27 at campus sites. Remainder of tournament March 2-3 at SeaGate Centre, Toledo, OH

a major football recruiting scandal and because of its poor athletic facilities.

Moving from the Southern Conference to the MAC provided a wake-up call. Marshall qualified for the eight-team MAC Tournament last season, but just barely. As the eighth-seeded team, the Herd was dispatched to Muncie, Ind., to face Ball State, and lost to the Cardinals for the third time.

Marshall's basketball team was the proverbial 98-pound weakling with the MAC kicking sand in its face. That's why, after being eliminated from the tournament in late February, players went straight to the weight room.

"Our weakness, no question, is strength," said White, a former Marshall point guard. "It really shows defensively."

Marshall enters its second MAC season with Paul Helsel as a full-time strength coach. Helsel came from the University of Alabama, where he worked with the basketball and football teams.

The poster child for the strength program is 6-6 sophomore guard **Joda Burgess** (10.3 ppg, 2.1 rpg) who made 63 of 153 three-point shots (.412) and was chosen to the MAC All-Freshman Team. At times Burgess was sensational. At other times he was overpowered by stronger players.

Burgess reported as a freshman weighing 168 pounds and now tips the scales at about 190.

"We were looking for someone to put some bulk on our guys," White said. "Paul Helsel came highly recommended. He's a taskmaster. Strength and conditioning are his specialties."

Marshall had some moments last season. Its upset of Wake Forest and a two-point loss to Massachusetts were highlights, along with a regular-season victory over Western Michigan.

On the down side, Marshall lost to Morehead State, which went 3-23 last season.

"I knew it would be a bumpy ride," White said. "It was."

Leading scorer **Carlton King** (13.7 ppg, 4.7 rpg), a 6-5 senior forward, returns from an honorable mention All-MAC season. Forward **Derrick Wright** (8.2 ppg, 6.9 rpg), a 6-6 junior, and 6-8 senior center **Terrell McKelvy** (8.6 ppg, 6.9 rpg) also return, along with 6-1 sophomore point guard **Travis Young** (11.3 ppg, 3.1 rpg, 117 assists). Young was chosen the MAC Freshman of the Year.

King, Wright, McKelvy and Young each started last season. Wright led the team's field-goal percentage (.520) and McKelvy wsan't far behind (.511).

Others returning are 6-5 junior guard **Deon Dobbs** (9.1 ppg, 2.2 rpg), 6-6 senior forward **VonDale Morton** (5.2 ppg, 3.4 rpg), 6-9 senior center **Vince Carafelli** (3.4 ppg, 2.6 rpg) and 6-3 junior guard **Brian Faulknier** (1.5 ppg, 0.8 rpg). Dobbs started four games, Carafelli had three starts and Morton two. Faulknier played in only four games.

White also welcomes a newcomer who should have an impact, 6-3 sophomore guard **Cornelius Jackson**, a transfer from Tennessee. Jackson was a starter in 21 games two season ago as a freshman at Tennessee, where he averaged 3.6 points and was second on the team with 2.3 assists per game.

When coach Kevin O'Neill left Tennessee for Northwestern after the 1997-97 season, Jackson started looking elsewhere. He came home to West Virginia, where he was the 1996 state player of the year at Oak Hill HS.

"Corny Jackson helps us instantly," White said.

Another transfer who's eligible is 6-7 junior forward **Josh Perkey**, a hometown product of Huntington's Vinson HS. Perkey is a hard-working inside player who averaged 13.7 points and 6.6 rebounds as a sophomore at Division II University of Charleston (W.Va.)

White recruited Perkey for Charleston, but did not coach him there. Shortly after Perkey signed, White left to take an assistant's position at UCLA, where he spent a year on Jim Harrick's staff before taking the Marshall job.

Perkey paid his way to school last year, but was put on scholarship this summer when one of the Herd's recruits didn't qualify academically.

"With Corny (Jackson) and Josh Perkey sitting out last year they practiced with us and they know our system," White said.

For the second straight year, Marshall's recruiting class was rated as the MAC's best. The group includes two high school players of the year in their respective states: 6-9 post player **J.R. VanHoose** from Paintsville, Ky., and 6-7 wing **Tamar Slay** from Beckley, W.Va. The other signee is 6-8 freshman forward **Edwin Johnson** of St. Petersburg, Fla., who played last year at Hargrave (Va.) Military Academy.

Signing VanHoose was a major coup. He was recruited by many top Division I schools, but not the Kentucky Wildcats, which opened the door for the Herd. White was relentless in his efforts to land VanHoose, who was ranked No. 33 in the senior class by *Regional Basketball Report* and No. 50 by *Prep Stars Recruiter's Handbook.*

White's 2-year-old son, Hunter, even got into the act. Hunter White, with his father's help, wrote a letter in crayon to VanHoose's 2-year-old brother, Alex, asking if it was OK for J.R. to come to Marshall.

The strategy must have worked. VanHoose received more than 1,000 telephone calls and 5,000 letters from recruiters before he narrowed a lengthy list down to two schools and picked Marshall over Vanderbilt.

"Needless to say J.R. had his pick of the litter," White said. "I think J.R. VanHoose is one of the top post players in America and will make an outstanding player in the Mid-American Conference."

VanHoose, averaging 25.8 points and 14.6 rebounds as a senior, led the voting for Kentucky's all-state team for the second straight year after leading Paintsville to a state runner-up finish. He scored 3,095 career points—18th-best in state history—and established career Kentucky records with 2,069 rebounds and 541 blocks.

Slay, who averaged 21 points and seven rebounds, led Beckley to a 22-3 record and its second consecutive Class AAA state title.

"Tamar is an oversized shooting guard at 6-7 that reminds me a lot of George Gervin and Scottie Pippen," White said.

adidas Blue Ribbon Analysis

BACKCOURT	**B**	**BENCH/DEPTH**	**B**
FRONTCOURT	**B**	**INTANGIBLES**	**B**

Much has changed since the summer of '97, when Marshall was concerned about replacing three seniors, John Brannen, Keith Veney, and Sidney Coles, who accounted for 65 percent of the offense in the 1996-97 season.

This year's team has 97 percent of its scoring intact, a banner crop of recruits and, its fans hope, a lot more muscle.

No wonder Marshall coach Greg White is excited.

"We've got these kids sold on being the top team in the MAC," White said. "Talent-wise we're going to be better, but you still have to play the games."

The Herd will play its games a lot better this season and will continue coming on strong.

(R.M.)

adidas Blue Ribbon Analysis

GRADING SYSTEM

- A+ equal to very best in country—Final Four-caliber unit
- A among the best in the land—worthy of deep NCAA run
- B+ talented, versatile and experienced—NCAA-NIT ability
- B solid and productive winners—league and post-season contenders
- C+ average to above-average—may contend in a weaker league
- C average to mediocre—second division in a strong league
- D+ below average, inconsistent—second division in a weaker league
- D well below average—losing season virtually certain
- F non-Division I ability—an underdog every night

NORTHERN ILLINOIS

LOCATION	**DeKalb, IL**
CONFERENCE	**Mid-American (West)**
LAST SEASON	**10-16 (.385)**
CONFERENCE RECORD	**6-12 (5th)**
STARTERS LOST/RETURNING	**1/4**
NICKNAME	**Huskies**
COLORS	**Cardinal & Black**
HOMECOURT	**Chick Evans Field House (6,044)**
COACH	**Brian Hammel (Bentley '75)**
RECORD AT SCHOOL	**97-97 (7 yrs.)**
CAREER RECORD	**188-167 (13 yrs.)**
ASSISTANTS	**Benjy Taylor (Richmond '89)**
	Andy Greer (SUNY-Brockport '84)
	Ryan Marks (USC '93)
TEAM WINS (last 5 yrs.)	**10-19-20-12-10**
RPI (last 5 yrs.)	**239-150-110-211-234**
1997-98 FINISH	**Did not qualify for conference tournament.**

Last season, the number of first-year players at Northern Illinois outnumbered the veterans, 8-5, so sacrificing short-term goals for long-term gains became a necessity.

Not surprisingly, the Huskies struggled in their first season out of the Midwestern Collegiate Conference. Coach Brian Hammel anticipates better days as a second-year member of the Mid-American Conference, having lost only three players and one starter, guard Donte Parker (9.7 ppg, 2.3 rpg, 88 assists).

"In contrast to last year we have a lot more experience under our belts," Hammel said. "A lot of guys, especially first-year players in our system, played a lot of minutes. Having signed four good ones who are capable of playing, court time will be a lot more competitive. Those guys who played a lot of minutes may not have to this year. There's no question we have a lot more depth."

The one player Hammel can definitely count on is 6-9, 220-pound center **T.J. Lux** (18.6 ppg, 11.1 rpg), dubbed the "King of the Double-Doubles" by the school's sports information staff. The senior from Merrillville, Ind., was one of 19 players in the nation with double-figure averages in points and rebounds. He doubled up in a conference-best 17 games last year and has done it 45 times in 83 career games. Lux shot 46 percent from the field last year and 73 percent from the free-throw line. He also led the team in blocked shots (36) and steals (29).

His most impressive double-double, however, is his success on the court and in the classroom. He earned first team All-MAC honors in basketball while also being chosen a first team GTE/CoSIDA Academic All-American with a 3.5 GPA as a math education major.

Lux was seventh in the league in scoring and first in rebounding. He was sixth nationally in rebounding and could become Northern Illinois' career leading scorer and rebounder.

"T.J. defends, he passes, he understands the value of the ball, he has good blockout technique, he plays big in the post, he can shoot it, he can put the ball on the floor and he has good vision," Hammel said. "If I had to get 40 words down to one word—complete."

Chicago native **Burton Anderson**, a 6-4 senior forward, came on strong for the Huskies as a transfer from Porterville (Calif.) JC. Anderson (9.2 ppg, 4.7 rpg) averaged 10.2 points in league games. Another returning starter is 6-0 junior guard **Rey Jones** (4.6 ppg, 3.3 rpg), who is the team's defensive stopper. Jones generally handled defensive assignments against taller opponents. MAC Player of the Year Bonzi Wells from Ball State worked hard to score 17 points on Jones, hitting only 6 of 18 shots. Jones made six steals against the Cardinals.

The fourth returning starter is 6-9, 204-pound sophomore **Steve Determan** (6.2 ppg, 4.4 rpg). Determan started

1998-99 NORTHERN ILLINOIS SCHEDULE

Nov.	14	Chicago State
	17	@Marshall
	21	New Orleans
	24	@Illinois-Chicago
	28-29	#Florida International Thanksgiving Tournament
Dec.	2	@Wisconsin
	15	Ohio
	19	@Lamar
	22	California State-Sacramento
	30	@Miami
Jan.	2	@Ball State
	9	@Western Michigan
	13	Central Michigan
	16	Eastern Michigan
	21	@Toledo
	23	@Akron
	28	Buffalo
	30	Kent
Feb.	3	@Bowling Green
	6	Ball State
	10	Marshall
	15	Akron
	18	@Central Michigan
	20	@Buffalo
	24	Toledo
27, Mar.	2-3	##MAC Tournament

@ Road Games
# Miami, FL (vs. Georgia Southern, first round; also Bucknell and Florida International)
First round Feb. 27 at campus sites. Remainder of tournament March 2-3 at SeaGate Center, Toledo, OH

16 games at power forward and has added some muscle to his frame.

Hammel expects increased production from 6-8, 228-pound sophomore forward **Charlie Ries** (1.6 ppg, 1.5 rpg), 6-4 senior forward/guard **Benjamin Ross** (1.9 ppg, 1.3 rpg), and 6-9 junior forward/center **Jeremy Roach** (0.0 ppg, 0.6 rpg). Roach was limited to only five games by a foot injury.

"We have a great anchor underneath in T.J. and Burton certainly came on like gangbusters late in the year," Hammel said. "Determan needs more strength to go with his offensive skills and Ries has the potential to turn into a real power player. Roach and Ross need to develop their confidence."

Others returning players include 6-0 senior **Phiffney Dukes** (2.0 ppg, 1.7 rpg, 47 assists), who started late in the season at point guard; 6-2 senior guard **Andre Williams** (6.2 ppg, 2.4 rpg); and 6-0 sophomore guard **Mike Brown** (5.9 ppg, 1.5 rpg, 46 assists).

Dukes started 15 games and averaged 18.6 minutes in 24 games. Williams started five games and Brown started three.

The guards will be pushed by swift 5-10 junior guard **Ephraim Eaddy**, a transfer from Moraine Valley (Ill.) CC, and 6-1 freshman guard **Garrett Thomas** from Riverton (Ill.) HS.

Eaddy was a two-time team MVP at Moraine Valley, where he led the Marauders to a 26-7 record and averaged 20.6 points. Thomas averaged 22.1 points and was a first-team all-state player. He finished his high school career with 354 three-pointers.

Northern Illinois also added some size by signing 6-7 freshman forward **Leon Rodgers** from Columbus (Ohio) Eastmoor HS and 6-9, 220-pound freshman forward/center **Matt Nelson** of Albion (Neb.) HS.

Rodgers averaged 22.8 points, 10.5 rebounds and shot .588 from the field, earning All-Columbus City League honors.

Nelson is his school's career leader in points (1,093), rebounds (695) and blocked shots (202). He averaged 14.3 points and 8.5 rebounds and shot 61 percent from the field as a senior.

Recruiting analyst Bob Gibbons placed Rodgers and Thomas within the third-highest rating group, giving them "marginal high-major player" status. Jerry Mullens of *Roundball Review* said Northern Illinois got a steal in Nelson.

Hammel likes his recruits.

"Leon Rodgers oozes potential," he said. "He has great ability and offensive skills, which prove he can be a real talent. Matt Nelson's combination of size and strength is exciting. Eaddy brings quickness to our backcourt, and Thomas certainly has outstanding shooting range. The entire class can give us immediate help."

adidas Blue Ribbon Analysis

BACKCOURT .... **C+** **BENCH/DEPTH** .... **B**
FRONTCOURT .... **B** **INTANGIBLES** .... **C+**

The Huskies finished fifth in the six-team MAC West race and didn't qualify for the league tournament, but they were close—really close—to having a pretty good year.

They averaged 67.8 points and gave up 68.1 per game, numbers that usually equate to a better record. They outrebounded opponents by plus-2.2 per game, another statistic that usually leads to more victories.

Of their 16 defeats, 11 were by 10 points or less. That's how close the Huskies were.

Along with Toledo, the Huskies return the best nucleus of players in the MAC's West Division.

"It's time to lace 'em up tighter and hang on for the ride," Hammel said.

The Huskies look to be in for a pretty good ride.

(R.M.)

OHIO

LOCATION .... **Athens, OH**
CONFERENCE .... **Mid-American (East)**
LAST SEASON .... **5-21 (.192)**
CONFERENCE RECORD .... **3-15 (6th)**
STARTERS LOST/RETURNING **2/3**
NICKNAME .... **Bobcats**
COLORS .... **Ohio Green & White**
HOMECOURT .... **Convocation Center (13,000)**
COACH .... **Larry Hunter (Ohio '71)**
RECORD AT SCHOOL .... **147-114 (9 yrs.)**
CAREER RECORD .... **452-190 (22 yrs.)**
ASSISTANTS .... **Mike Elfers (Wittenburg '85)**
James Jones (Albany '86)
Geno Ford (Ohio '96)
TEAM WINS (last 5 yrs.) **25-24-16-17-5**
RPI (last 5 yrs.) **35-44-112-94-250**
1997-98 FINISH .... **Did not qualify for conference tournament.**

Larry Hunter is ready to follow up his worst season at Ohio with one that might be one of his best.

Nobody had much fun around the Convocation Center last season. As time expired in a late-season home game, a 32-point whipping by Miami (Ohio), forward **Diante Flenorl** slammed the basketball to the floor, letting his frustrations out. The sound reverberated through the nearly-empty arena. The ball bounced about 20 feet into the air.

Two more defeats, sandwiched around a pride-saving Mid-American Conference win over Kent in the season finale, and the season finally ended.

The worst record in school history was in the books and would soon be forgotten, Hunter hoped.

The Bobcats are out to prove their last-place finish in the MAC East was a fluke.

"Last season, we were just boys, but this season we will be men," Hunter said.

Missing from last year's team are forward Basra Fakhir (8.4 ppg, 7.9 rpg) and guard Jim Peterson (10.9 ppg, 2.2 rpg, 71 of 210 three-point shots). Also missing is forward Seth Martin (4.5 ppg, 2.8 rpg), who transferred to California (Pa.), a Division II team. Forward Matt Jager called it quits after two ankle surgeries. Jager didn't play last season.

The good news is that last year's team MVP and leading scorer, 6-6, 230-pound junior guard **Sanjay Adell** (16.1 ppg, 6.0 rpg, .432 FG percentage) returns with a stronger supporting cast. Adell is joined by second-leading scorer Flenorl (11.2ppg, 7.9 rpg), a 6-8 senior forward, and 5-10 junior guard **Corey Reed** (5.4 ppg, 3.4 rpg, 22 assists in five games). Reed suffered a season-ending knee injury in the fifth game of the season and received a medical redshirt.

Those three form Ohio's "Milwaukee Connection." Adell played at Messmer HS while Flenorl and Reed were teammates at Rufus King HS.

More good news comes with the addition of transfers **LaDrell Whitehead** from Wyoming and **Shaun Stonerook** from Ohio State.

Stonerook, a 6-8 junior forward, transferred to Ohio last year and sat out. He averaged 11.6 points, 7.7 rebounds and 3.7 assists two years ago at Ohio State.

Whitehead, a 5-9 senior guard, was Wyoming's starting point guard two years ago and averaged 21.7 points, 2.9 rebounds, 3.4 assists and 34.6 minutes. Whitehead suffered a dislocated elbow during that the season, but managed to return for the last two regular-season games. He then decided to transfer.

Ohio welcomes back five lettermen, including three starters, to join eight newcomers.

"One of our strengths will be our versatility," Hunter said. "We have many multi-position players."

Adell was one of the most highly-recruited players ever signed by the Bobcats. He sat out his freshman year to concentrate on academics and came on strong last year. He was chosen to the league's all-freshman team and was an honorable mention All-MAC selection. He is a talented scorer, good rebounder and outstanding passer who had 54 assists last season.

Adell shot 166 free throws last year, the fourth-highest total in school history. He shot .651 from the line (108 for 166).

The Bobcats can go with a big lineup with Adell in the backcourt, or they can play him at a forward position.

"Sanjay will be one of our primary offensive options, but may end up as our second- or third-leading scorer," Hunter said. "He can post people up and also take the ball to the basket. He should have a great season because he will have less pressure."

Whitehead, from New Albany, Ind., is a starting candidate at both guard positions. In three seasons at Wyoming, he averaged 17.7 ppg. He was chosen to the Western Athletic Conference All-Defensive team as a sophomore. He is a candidate for the Naismith Award given to the nation's top player under 6-0.

Whitehead is Wyoming's career leader in three-point goals (168) and he is also first in three-point shots (459), third in steals (150), fourth in assists (274) and 13th in scoring (1,321).

"We have great anticipation to see LaDrell play," Hunter said. "He is a leader who is smart and unselfish. He can score and play defense and is the complete package."

Another key backcourt player is 5-10 sophomore guard **Dustin Ford** (8.3 ppg, 3.0 rpg), the team leader in assists (85) and steals (31). Ford is a gritty competitor who was forced to play 32.4 minutes a game because of Reed's injury. Ford's brother, Geno, was an All-MAC guard for Ohio in 1996-97, and is now on the coaching staff.

Ohio's newcomers include 6-5 freshman **Jason Crawford**, a late signee from Withrow HS in Cincinnati. Crawford missed the first half of his senior season because of an ankle injury, but returned in time to lead Withrow to the Division I state semifinals. In 12 games, he averaged 12 points, seven rebounds and five assists. The team went 10-2 with him in the lineup.

Crawford is nicknamed "The Sheriff" because of his ability to shut down the opponents' top scorer.

"He is one of those players who loves to play defense

1998-99 OHIO SCHEDULE

Nov.	28	Wilmington College (Ohio)
Dec.	2	Bowling Green
	4-5	#Carrier Classic
	8	@Cleveland State
	12	Rhode Island
	15	@Northern Illinois
	17	West Virginia
	22	Ball State
	28	@Central Florida
	30	@George Washington
Jan.	2	Central Michigan
	6	@Western Michigan
	9	@Toledo
	13	Eastern Michigan
	16	Buffalo
	20	@Akron
	23	@Bowling Green
	27	@Kent
	30	Marshall
Feb.	3	@Miami
	6	@Central Michigan
	13	Western Michigan
	17	@Eastern Michigan
	20	Kent
	24	Akron
27-Mar.	2-3	##MAC Tournament

@ Road Games
# Syracuse, NY (vs. Syracuse, first round; also Illinois-Chicago and Santa Clara)
First round Feb. 27 at campus sites. Remainder of tournament March 2-3 at Seagate Centre, Toledo, OH.

and takes pride in it," Hunter said.

Jeremy Thrapp, a 6-4 sophomore forward, didn't play last season, but is a promising shooter. Freshman twins **Jason** and **Justin LaFerla**, both 5-11 guards, might be redshirted. The twins committed to Hunter as sophomores at St. John the Baptist HS on Long Island, N.Y.

Flenorl plays small forward at 6-8, 215 pounds and is a tough matchup for most players at the position. At times Flenorl was one of the better players in the MAC, but at other times he was average. "Hopefully he can put it all together," Hunter said.

Stonerook was one of Ohio's best practice players last season. The 230-pound Stonerook, who's from Westerville, Ohio, is expected to have an all-conference type season. He was sixth in the Big Ten in rebounding two years ago and was the Buckeyes' third-leading scorer. He had eight double-doubles while earning honorable mention All-Big Ten honors.

The Bobcats will probably use Stonerook at center to anchor a formidable front line that also includes Adell and Flenorl.

"He's a force on the floor," Hunter said of Stonerook.

Backing up Stoneook is 6-11, 250-pound sophomore **Nick Terry** (2.8 ppg, 1.7 rpg). The new center is 6-10, 220-pound freshman **Asa Jewett** of Blue Creek, Ohio and Portsmouth West HS.

Another frontcourt player with promise is 6-8 freshman **Patrick Flomo** of Columbus (Ohio) and Groveport Madison HS. Flomo reminds Hunter of Bill Russell because of his defensive skills.

adidas Blue Ribbon Analysis

BACKCOURT .... B BENCH/DEPTH .... C+
FRONTCOURT .... B+ INTANGIBLES .... B

This is not anything close to the same team Ohio put on the court last season.

The immediate impact of transfers LaDrell Whitehead and Shaun Stonerook should be tremendous. Both could be all-conference players and should provide the leadership the Bobcats were lacking.

"We are expecting great things," Hunter said.

A worst-to-first scenario is altogether possible, although Ohio is in the rugged MAC East, and that's where the league's strength is this season.

It looks like they'll be having more fun in the Convo, anyway.

(R.M.)

TOLEDO

LOCATION .... **Toledo, OH**
CONFERENCE .... **Mid-American (West)**
LAST SEASON .... **15-12 (.556)**
CONFERENCE RECORD .... **10-8 (4th)**
STARTERS LOST/RETURNING **1/4**
NICKNAME .... **Rockets**
COLORS .... **Midnight Blue & Gold**
HOMECOURT .... **John F. Savage Hall (9,000)**
COACH .... **Stan Joplin (Toledo '79)**
RECORD AT SCHOOL .... **28-26 (2 yrs.)**
CAREER RECORD .... **28-26 (2 yrs.)**
ASSISTANTS .... **Tony Jones (Concordia '93)**
Monte Mathis (Toledo '91)
Tim Saliers (Aquinas '92)
TEAM WINS (last 5 yrs.) **15-16-18-13-15**
RPI (last 5 yrs.) **148-123-111-170-147**
1997-98 FINISH .... **Lost in conference first round.**

Toledo coach Stan Joplin isn't staying awake nights plotting ways to replace one valuable player. He's too busy figuring ways to find enough playing time to distribute to a team that returns six of its top seven scorers and has an impressive recruiting class.

But Joplin hasn't completely dismissed Casey Shaw from his thoughts.

Shaw, a rugged 6-11 center drafted by the Philadelphia 76ers in the second round, was Toledo's leading scorer (14.2 ppg), rebounder (10.0), shot blocker (41) and shooter (.529 percent) while earning second-team all-conference honors.

For his career, Shaw finished as Toledo's fourth-leading scorer (1,562 points), fifth-leading rebounder (871) and second-leading shot blocker (112).

1998-99 TOLEDO SCHEDULE

Nov.	16	Grand Valley State
	21	Albany State
	24	@George Mason
	28	Oakland
	30	Mississippi Valley State
Dec.	5	Ohio State
	9	Xavier
	12	@Dayton
	19	Kent
	28	@Western Michigan
	30	@Akron
Jan.	2	@Bowling Green
	6	Marshall
	9	Ohio
	13	@Miami
	16	@Ball State
	21	Northern Illinois
	23	Western Michigan
	27	@Central Michigan
	30	@Eastern Michigan
Feb.	6	Bowling Green
	11	Buffalo
	13	@Marshall
	17	Miami
	20	Central Michigan
	24	@Northern Illinois
27, Mar.	3	#MAC Tournament

@ Road Games
# First round Feb. 27 at campus sites. Remainder of tournament March 2-3 at SeaGate Centre, Toledo, OH

"No one person can ever replace Casey Shaw," Joplin said. "Hopefully we can do it by committee."

Joplin, a former Toledo star guard whose buzzer-beating shot beat Iowa in the 1979 NCAA Tournament and propelled the Rockets into the Sweet 16, enters his third season as coach with a much more athletic team than he had the two previous seasons.

Maybe that burst of speed and quickness will provide the missing intangibles that Toledo lacked in a season of close calls. Folks in Toledo were starting to get the postseason fever until the Rockets faltered down the stretch, losing six of their last eight games.

"We were very close last year," Joplin said.

Other than the loss of Shaw, the team returns almost intact. The only other departing senior was forward Joel Howard (2.7 ppg, 1.8 rpg).

The backcourt appears to be strong with a three-guard rotation featuring 6-0 junior **Clayton Burch** (8.3 ppg, 2.0 rpg, 85 assists), 6-3 senior **Art Norman** (10.6 ppg, 4.0 rpg, 62 assists) and 6-1 junior **Chad Kamstra** (10.2 ppg, 2.5 rpg, 59 assists).

Burch shot only 40 percent from the field, but Joplin believes his shooting will improve if he gets some help handling the basketball. Norman is the Rockets' leading returning scorer after reaching double figures in 15 games.

Kamstra displayed moments of brilliance, like when he scored 30 points on seven-of-eight shooting from the three-point line at Central Michigan and when he scored 25 points, including 21 in the first half, at Miami (Ohio). He is one of the MAC's best three-point shooters (53 of 147, or .361 percent) and its best free-throw shooter (60 of 70, .857).

"Chad is like our Steve Kerr," Joplin said. "If he gets his feet squared away, we just feel like he's going to make it every time. We need to set more screens for Chad."

Kamstra is also an outstanding student who made the GTE-CoSIDA Academic All-District team with a 3.77 grade-point average as a pre-business major.

Both freshmen backcourt recruits—6-2 **Sammy Bacino** and 6-3 **Justin Hall**—can play either guard position. Walkon sophomore guard Bernard Scott (0.1 ppg, 0.3 rpg) played in eight games last season.

The most experienced players are 6-4 senior guard-forward **Robert Kizer** (8.7 ppg, 5.9 rpg) and 6-7, 230-pound senior forward **Brett Fedak** (4.8 ppg, 3.2 rpg). Each can play shooting guard.

Kizer and Fedak are Toledo's co-captains.

Kizer is Toledo's master of steals and best defender. He had 59 steals, second-best in Rockets' history to Craig Thames' 82 in 1996. In addition to his defensive skills, Kizer was also usually assigned to guard the opponent's top scoring threat on the perimeter.

"Robert is our defensive stopper," Joplin said.

Fedak is another sound defensive player, but in the low post.

Sophomore **Greg Stempin** (9.2 ppg, 5.0 rpg) was chosen to the MAC's All-Freshman team a year ago. Stempin, who started the last season games of the season, is a versatile big man at 6-8, 202 pounds. He can post up or play on the wing, as evidenced by his team-leading three-point shooting percentage (29 of 73, .397).

"Greg is our most athletic big guy," Joplin said. "He showed flashes of being a big-time player last year. If he can get stronger physically and mentally, I would expect him to have a big year for us. I could see Greg averaging six or seven rebounds and maybe 15 points a game."

Also back is 6-6 junior **Calvin Meikle** (0.7 ppg, 0.9 rpg), who played in 15 games.

Robierre Cullars, a 6-4 sophomore guard/forward, returns after sitting out his freshman year while academically ineligible.

Joplin expects 6-7, 225-pound freshman **Albert Wilson** to be an impact player. Wilson, averaging 15 points and 13 rebounds as a senior in high school, played on back-to-back Ohio Division II state championship teams at Cleveland's Benedictine HS.

"He's what we need," Joplin said. "He has good speed, size and quickness."

With Shaw gone, the Rockets will play without a true center much of the time. That doesn't mean they won't have a force in the middle, however, because 6-8, 245-pound **Rickey Strong** is waiting for his chance. Strong is a transfer from Independence (Kan.) CC, where he averaged 12.5 points and 7.2 rebounds.

Independence (24-7) was ranked among the nation's Top 25 junior-college teams. Strong was one of four Division I signees on the team.

"We went the junior-college route because we had to fill a need right now," Joplin said. "Rickey will help fill the void left by Casey Shaw and Joel Howard. He's strong, big, a good passer and he runs the floor well."

Providing depth at center is 6-11 sophomore **Craig Rodgers** (1.2 ppg, 0.9 rpg).

adidas Blue Ribbon Analysis

BACKCOURT .... B+ BENCH/DEPTH C
FRONTCOURT .... B- INTANGIBLES C

Toledo coach Stan Joplin likes his returnees, but he also speaks highly of the newcomers on the team.

He's reloading in the post-Casey Shaw season, and has plenty of quality players to work with.

"We recruited Rickey Strong because he's a junior-college player, someone who can come in and hold down the fort," Joplin said. "Casey was a big presence inside. Now we've got guys who can get to the basket and make plays. We've got guards who can dunk the ball now. I like that. That's the direction we wanted to go in."

Expect the Rockets to become more of a transition team, pushing the basketball up the court and doing more things defensively.

Toledo has a great chance in the wide-open MAC West.

(R.M.)

WESTERN MICHIGAN

LOCATION .... **Kalamazoo, MI**
CONFERENCE .... **Mid-American (West)**
LAST SEASON .... **21-8 (.724)**
CONFERENCE RECORD .... **14-4 (t-1st)**
STARTERS LOST/RETURNING **4/1**
NICKNAME .... **Broncos**
COLORS .... **Brown & Gold**
HOMECOURT .... **University Arena (5,800)**
COACH .... **Bob Donewald (Hanover '64)**
RECORD AT SCHOOL .... **130-122 (9 yrs.)**
CAREER RECORD .... **338-243 (20 yrs.)**
ASSISTANTS .... **Kirk Manns (Michigan State '91)**
Chris Davis (Michigan '83)
Christian Wilson (Northern Michigan '92)
TEAM WINS (last 5 yrs.) **14-14-15-14-21**
RPI (last 5 yrs.) **130-128-104-145-53**
1997-98 FINISH .... **Lost in NCAA second round.**

So, what does Western Michigan do for an encore after a terrific season?

First of all, it keeps the coach. Bob Donewald was awarded a five-year contract extension after leading the Broncos to only their second NCAA appearance. Donewald's record at Western Michigan (130-122) includes seven consecutive non-losing seasons.

"We are pleased to have

1998-99 WESTERN MICHIGAN SCHEDULE

Nov.	16	@Indiana State
	24	Wisconsin-Milwaukee
	27-28	#Coca-Cola Spartan Classic
Dec.	1	Detroit
	6	*Michigan
	12	Oakland
	19	Marshall
	21	@Bowling Green
	23	@Loyola
	27	Toledo
Jan.	2	@Miami (Ohio)
	6	Ohio
	9	Northern Illinois
	13	@Ball State
	16	@Central Michigan
	23	@Toledo
	27	Eastern Michigan
	30	Buffalo
Feb.	3	@Akron
	6	Miami
	9	@Kent
	17	Ball State
	20	@Eastern Michigan
27-Mar.	2-3	##MAC Tournament

@ Road Games
* Grand Rapids, MI
# East Lansing, MI (vs. Michigan State, first round; also Central Florida and North Carolina-Wilmington)
First round Feb. 27 at campus sites. Remainder of tournament March 2-3 at SeaGate Centre, Toledo, OH

Bob for another five years," director of athletics Kathy Beauregard said. "His commitment and loyalty to the Broncos, along with the coaching staff he has in place, ensures Western Michigan a competitive program for many seasons to come."

It's too bad they couldn't retain some of the key players as well.

The "Triple Threats"—shooting guard Saddi Washington (21.6 ppg, 4.2 rpg), penetrating guard Rashod Johnson (19.1 ppg, 2.3 rpg) and playmaker Jason Kimbrough (19.7 ppg, 1.9 rpg, 166 assists)—are all gone. Forward Aaron Toothman (4.1 ppg, 4.9 rpg) also departed as his eligibility ended, leaving 6-7 senior forward **Shaun Jackson**, the leading rebounder, as the only returning starter.

Donewald has his work cut out.

"There are three keys in looking ahead toward this season," Donewald said. "First is determining who will be our leaders. Second is finding out who will be our scorers. Finally, (third) is seeing if we can establish the same type of defensive pressure we had a year ago (70.4 ppg allowed) which I think was the best we had in my nine years here."

The Broncos were co-champions of the MAC West Division last season, sharing the top spot with Ball State. They lost to Miami in an emotion-charged first-round league tournament game. Miami coach Charlie Coles suffered a heart attack and collapsed on the bench in the first half with the teams tied, 14-14. After a lengthy delay, Miami gutted out a 67-63 victory.

Resigned to the fact that the NIT was probably in their future, Western Michigan's players didn't even get together to watch the NCAA Tournament pairings show on television. The Broncos gathered quickly enough when it was revealed they had indeed received an at-large bid and would be joining MAC Tournament champion Eastern Michigan in the NCAA Tournament.

The bid rewarded a tough non-conference schedule and a solid regular season.

"I told my players that I doubted we'd get a bid to the NCAA, but that they deserved it," Donewald said. "I'm gratified that the NCAA recognized the strength of our schedule and our performance against strong teams.

"We beat Michigan and UNC Charlotte, gave Indiana a very good game and beat Eastern Michigan twice."

The 11th-seeded Broncos stunned Clemson, a sixth seed, 75-72, in their Midwest Regional opener—a win that many considered the greatest in school history. Western Michigan's dreams ended, though, with a loss to Final Four-bound Stanford, 83-65, in the second round.

Now, what about that encore?

Washington, Johnson, Kimbrough and Toothman accounted for 69 percent of the scoring in 1997-98. Washington was chosen first-team All-MAC, Johnson was chosen to the second team and Kimbrough was chosen honorable mention.

Some frontcourt depth returns with Jackson and 6-7 junior **Brad Van Timmerman**. Jackson (9.6 ppg, 7.5 rpg) shot almost 55 percent from the field in his transition to Division I from Labette (Kan.) JC. He is capable of taking on some of the scoring burden.

Van Timmerman (2.2 ppg, 3.2 rpg) was a tri-captain a year ago and started five games, averaging 12.6 minutes in 29 games.

Another former junior-college transfer, 6-4 senior swingman **Isaac Bullock** (7.1 ppg, 2.9 rpg) started nine games and shot .507 percent from the field. Bullock has played in two NCAA Tournament. He signed with Murray State out of high school and was a member of that school's 1996 Ohio Valley Conference championship squad. His other stop was at Olney Central (Ill.) JC.

Ready to play shooting guard is 6-0 sophomore **Kylo Jones** (4.4 ppg, 1.0 rpg). He made 21 of 50 three-point shots last season.

The other returnees are 6-5 senior forward **Ryan Black** (0.4 ppg, 0.6 rpg) and 6-3 sophomore guard-forward **Tony Collins** (0.2 ppg, 0.2 rpg).

Sensing the need for immediate help, Donewald hit the recruiting trail and landed the school's biggest class ever. Eight newcomers join the program this season.

"Our recruiting tried to touch all of the bases, replacing the perimeter people we lost and also trying to establish an inside game built around natural inside players that we haven't really had in the last two years," Donewald said. "How quickly they adapt to new roles and our style will be very important."

Incoming players include 6-4 transfer guard **Thadus Williams** from Indianapolis and Lincoln Trail (Ill.) CC. Williams averaged 17 points, 4.9 rebounds and 2.5 assists in his second year of junior college. He was a two-time All-Region 24 and All-Great Rivers Athletic Conference player.

"Thadus is a wing player who adds athleticism and the ability to get the ball in the basket from the perimeter," Donewald said.

Other junior-college signees are 6-1 junior point guard **Rod Brown** from Dallas and Pratt (Kan.) CC; 6-2 junior guard **Tony Barksdale** from Topeka, Kan. and Coffeyville (Kan.) CC; and 6-9, 240-pound junior **Emil Mulic**, a Bosnian who played high school ball in Toronto and transferred to Westerm Michigan from Garden City (Kan.) CC.

Brown, Barksdale and Mulic each earned All-Region VI and All-Jayhawk East Conference honors.

The freshman class includes 6-10, 280-pound center **Thomas Haskell** from Albany Alexander (Ohio) HS; 6-6, 200-pound **Darren Kahl** from Crown Point (Ind.) HS; 6-8, 210-pound **Jesse Slauter** from Cincinnati Northwest HS; and 5-9 point guard **Tim O'Neill** from Chicago's Brother Rice HS.

adidas Blue Ribbon Analysis

BACKCOURT	**C+**	**BENCH/DEPTH**	**C+**
FRONTCOURT	**C+**	**INTANGIBLES**	**C+**

The guard trio of Saddi Washington, Rashod Johnson and Jason Kimbrough provided much excitement and most of the scoring last season, and replacing their production won't be easy.

Shaun Jackson, a 6-7 senior center/forward, will be asked to lead the team in their absence.

Western Michigan's roster is loaded with new faces and talented prospects, but they are also unproven players.

Broncos coach Bob Donewald has a solid bench, and that's a plus. He has had just three losing seasons during a 20-year career at Western Michigan and Illinois State. He won't have one this year, either.

A shift in power from the MAC West to the East this year helps Donewald as he reloads. The West title is up for grabs. Expect the Broncos to be somewhere in the mix.

(R.M.)

MID-CONTINENT CONFERENCE

adidas BLUE RIBBON FORECAST

1. Oral Roberts
2. Youngstown State
3. Southern Utah
4. Valparaiso
5. Western Illinois
6. Missouri-Kansas City
7. Chicago State
8. Indiana/Purdue-Indianapolis

ALL-CONFERENCE TEAM

C—Zoran Viskovic, SR, Valparaiso
C—Kenyatta Clyde, SR, Southern Utah
F—Derrick Taylor, JR, Oral Roberts
G—Jermaine Hicks, JR, Chicago State
C—Jimmy Keller, SR, UMKC

PLAYER OF THE YEAR

Kenyatta Clyde, SR, Southern Utah

NEWCOMER OF THE YEAR

Justin Kaliszewski, FR, Southern Utah

1998-99 CONFERENCE TOURNAMENT

Feb. 28-March 2, Mark of the Quad Cities, Moline, Ill.

1997-98 CHAMPION

Valparaiso (regular season)
Valparaiso (conference tournament)

1997-98 POSTSEASON PARTICIPANTS

Postseason Record: 2-1 (.667)
NCAA
Valparaiso (Sweet 16)

TOP BACKCOURTS

1. Youngstown State
2. Western Illinois
3. Chicago State

TOP FRONTCOURTS

1. Oral Roberts
2. Southern Utah
3. Valparaiso

ON THE WAY UP

Southern Utah

ON THE WAY DOWN

Valparaiso

INSIDE THE NUMBERS

- 1997-98 conference RPI: 23rd (of 30)
- Conference RPI (last 5 years): 23-27-26-18-23

DID YOU KNOW?

For the second season in a row, the conference has two new members. This year, Indiana/Purdue-Indianapolis and Oakland replace Buffalo and Northeastern Illinois. Oakland isn't eligible for full-blown Division I status this season...Valparaiso is the only Division I school in the country to capture both the conference regular season title and the tournament championship in each of the last four years...Southern Utah has three state Mr. Basketball winners on its squad: Justin Kaliszewski of Colorado, Kenyatta Clyde of Nevada and Jeff Monaco of Arizona.

MID CONTINENT CONFERENCE

(T.D.)

CHICAGO STATE

LOCATION	Chicago, IL
CONFERENCE	Mid-Continent
LAST SEASON	2-25 (.074)
CONFERENCE RECORD	2-14 (9th)
NICKNAME	Cougars
COLORS	Green & White
HOMECOURT	Dickens Center (2,500)
COACH	Maurice "Bo" Ellis (Marquette '77)
RECORD AT SCHOOL	First Year
CAREER RECORD	First Year
ASSISTANTS	James Farr (Creighton '89) Donnie Kirksey (Roosevelt '85) Mike Rice (Fordham '91)
TEAM WINS (last 5 yrs.)	4-6-2-4-2
RPI (last 5 yrs.)	291-253-298-279-303
1997-98 FINISH	Failed to qualify for conference tournament.

The Indians have become perennial winners. The Rock & Roll Hall of Fame is a reality. The highly rated *Drew Carey Show* beams positive feedback into America's living rooms every week. There is a resurgent downtown scene. Even the Browns are about to return.

Cleveland is no longer "The Mistake by the Lake." The title is up for grabs.

Fortunately, there are five Great Lakes, and hugging Lake Michigan is a city that looks ready to take a shot. May we suggest Chicago, Ill., home of perhaps the most inept college basketball program in the country?

The Chicago State Cougars are in the midst of one of the longest-running stretches of hapless play in Division I history. Since stepping up to Division I play in 1984, the school has never achieved a winning season, and has posted double-digit victories just once. The last three years have been especially bru- tal—just eight wins sprinkled around a revolving door of head coaches.

Former NBA sharpshooter Craig Hodges couldn't get the job done. Two years ago, he was fired six games into the season, and Phil Gary took over. Gary finished Hodges' incomplete season by going 4-17, then followed up last year with a 2-25 record. The Cougars drew an average of 257 fans to their 11 home games.

Have a nice summer, coach Gary. And don't bother coming back for fall practice, OK?

That left Chicago State with yet another coaching vacancy last spring. The city's most famous basketball coach was soon to be out of a job, but chances are Phil Jackson experienced some sort of Zen vibe telling him to run as fast as he could in the opposite direction. Athletic director Al Avant instead handed the whistle and clipboard to Maurice "Bo" Ellis, who spent the last 10 years as an assistant with the very successful Marquette program.

Ellis is a winner, a guy who played under Al McGuire on Marquette's 1977 national champion team and a former NBA first-round pick. A good recruiter and a smart hoops guy, he knows what it's like to be around a winning program. Ellis told his players at his first team meeting, "Our preparations are geared toward winning the Mid-Continent Conference championship. It is a waste of time to prepare for any other goals. If you believe that it can be accomplished, then I expect you to do everything it takes, academically and athletically, to make that goal a reality."

Ellis' brave public face aside, few expect the Cougars to challenge right away. Chicago State lost two starters from last year's two-win squad. No, this season will be about putting Humpty Dumpty together again, not expecting him to run the floor, stop on a dime and hit the open three.

As if the situation weren't bleak enough for Ellis, he has to face this reality: His best returning player is 5-6. But while junior point guard **Jermaine "Squirt" Hicks** (17.7 ppg, 3.5 rpg, 134 assists, 53 steals) may be small in size, he sure plays like a big boy. The Mid-Continent's Co-Newcomer of the Year and a media selection for the all-conference second team, he was the team's leader in scoring, assists, steals, three pointers and minutes played. *Basketball Times* put him on its All-Midwest honorable-mention list.

In fact, Hicks comes back as the conference leader in scoring, assists and steals. In short—so to speak—this is no novelty act. He's a legitimate contender for player-of-the-year honors, a guy fulfilling the potential he showed three years ago at Weber State, from which he transferred after his freshman season.

Hicks' problem—and Chicago State's, too—last season was that he was essentially a one-man band. The need to do it all himself may explain his mediocre .363 shooting percentage. "He accomplished a great deal individually last season," Ellis said. "Now we want to teach him how to bring his teammates to the next level with him."

Ellis may opt to play 6-3 junior **Marques Buford** alongside Hicks in the starting backcourt. A knee injury wiped out Buford's entire season a year ago; it would have been his first in Division I after transferring from Northwest JC, where he helped his team win the Wyoming Junior College Conference championship as a sophomore. The coach is confident that Buford has healed and looks for him again to show his ability to get himself open and hit the outside shot. "With Marques, last year's team would have been more successful," Ellis said. "The injury was an unfortunate blow for Marques. But he is an outstanding young man and a solid ballplayer. He will be a key player for us this season."

Hicks and Buford are this year's co-captains.

Hicks' primary backup at the point is 6-0 senior **Jason Daniel** (8.4 ppg, 2.3 rpg), a nine-game starter as a junior. Daniel was the Cougars' third-leading scorer and second-best assist man, with 43. And with 32 steals, he showed himself to be a hard-nosed defender with a toughness Ellis admires. Daniel will often find himself matched against the opponent's two guard.

Backing up Buford at shooting guard and seeing a fair amount of time at small forward will be 6-3 junior swingman **Jason Strojinc**, a transfer from Illinois-Chicago. Strojinc completed his scholastic career as Buffalo Grove High School's second-leading career scorer and third-leading career rebounder, earning *Street & Smith's* and McDonald's All-America honors as a senior.

At UIC, he averaged just 4.0 ppg. Ellis made Strojinc his first recruit despite the lackluster numbers. "Jason is a legitimate outside shooter (who) gives us some flexibility in the lineup," he said.

Also providing backcourt depth is 6-3 senior **Matt Normand** (2.3 ppg, 1.6 rpg), who played in all 27 CSU games, starting five.

The team's only freshman guard is 6-0 **Terrence West** (Leo HS/Chicago, Ill.), who had committed to Utah State, then opted for his hometown school when Aggies head coach Larry Eustachy announced his departure for Iowa State. That has to be considered a big break for Ellis. Starting for Leo, which finished fourth in its class in the state, West averaged 13.0 ppg, six assists a game and three steals a game. He is a standout student.

A pair of starters return up front, led by 6-6 forward **Pierre Shuttlesworth** (8.0 ppg, 7.0 rpg), Chicago State's leading rebounder. His 36 steals were second best on the team. While Ellis considers Shuttlesworth a talented player near the hoop, the coach still wants to "teach a few more things that will make him an asset in the paint." Take that to mean that while he hits the boards hard, Shuttlesworth needs to work on his interior shooting. He shot just .386 from the field last season.

The other returning starter is 6-6 senior forward **Demont Payton** (5.0 ppg, 2.6 rpg), who appeared in all 27 games, starting 15. Payton needs to take the ball to the hoop more often, having attempted just 12 free throws his entire junior season. At least he made nine of them.

The team's only true center, and its tallest player, is 6-8 sophomore **Federico Carlotta** (1.1 ppg, 1.6 rpg), a native of Argentina who made the most of his limited playing time by swatting away 13 shots in just 148 minutes. A .286 shooter from the floor, Carlotta, too, must work on his offensive game.

Payton's twin, 6-7 junior forward **Demetrius Payton** (1.9 ppg, 1.4 rpg), rounds out the returning frontcourt rotation. He saw action in 21 games and started three times.

One of the Cougars' most pressing needs is a player who can take charge around the offensive basket, and Ellis thinks he's found the guy in 6-7 junior **Derrick Bolton** (Lewis & Clark CC/Chicago, Ill.). A brawny 235 pounds, Bolton led Lewis & Clark his sophomore year with 14.0 ppg and 9.5 rpg. The performance led to team MVP honors and to selections to the Midwest Community College Athletic Conference first team and the Region 24 All-Region team.

Ellis has visions of a maniacal presence on both ends. "Derrick is an explosive athlete and is very strong," he said. "He will provide us with inside scoring punch and give us a shot blocker on the defensive end."

In addition to Bolton, athletic 6-7 junior forward **Lizet Wilks** (Eastern Oklahoma State CC/Jackson, Miss.) joins Chicago State as a transfer. Wilks, who averaged 10.0 ppg and 8.5 rpg as a sophomore, can take the ball to the hole with authority. He played his scholastic ball at Murrah HS, the same Jackson, Miss., school that produced NBA players Lindsey Hunter and Othella Harrington. Ellis hopes some of that magic rubbed off. "Lizet comes from a good basketball background," he said. "He is a tough, strong player that will provide us with maturity and quality depth in the frontcourt."

The freshman forwards include 6-7 **Andre Wiggins** (Westinghouse HS/Chicago, Ill.) and 6-6 **Devin Friday** (American HS/Miami, Fla.). Wiggins, who averaged 15.0 ppg and 8.0 rpg as a senior, is a versatile offensive player. He played at the same high school as Kory Billups, Chicago State's all-time leading scorer and the Mid-Continent Conference's all-time leading rebounder. Friday averaged 15.0 ppg, 8.0 rpg and 3.0 bpg as a senior for his Dade County champion team.

1998-99 CHICAGO STATE SCHEDULE

Nov.	14	@Northern Illinois
	17	Loyola-Chicago
	21	@Xavier
	23	@Iowa State
	28	Western Illinois
Dec.	1	@DePaul
	17	@Oregon State
	19	@Gonzaga
	22-23	#Coors Lite Classic
	28	@Wright State
Jan.	2	@Missouri-Kansas City
	4	@Oral Roberts
	7	Indiana/Purdue-Indianapolis
	9	Oakland
	14	@Indiana/Purdue-Indianapolis
	16	Southern Utah
	21	Valparaiso
	23	@Western Illinois
	28	Oral Roberts
	30	Missouri-Kansas City
Feb.	4	@Youngstown State
	11	Youngstown State
	13	@Oakland
	18	@Valparaiso
	20	@Southern Utah
27-Mar.	2	##MCC Tournament

@ Road Games
\# Fresno, CA (vs. Fresno State, first round; also Miami-Ohio and San Diego)
\## The Mark of the Quad Cities, Moline, IL

adidas Blue Ribbon Analysis

BACKCOURT	C+	BENCH/DEPTH	D
FRONTCOURT	D	INTANGIBLES	C

Stop us if you've heard this before—let the rebuilding begin. Again.

First-year head coach Bo Ellis is the latest to take a crack at Chicago State's ever-elusive target: A winning season. He is optimistic about his chances, saying, "The response has truly been amazing. The people are excited. There are a lot of coaches and teachers in Chicago who are alums, and they want a winner here. I think the school understands that once we turn the program around, that will bring students. I feel good about the challenge."

At the very least, Ellis has a legitimate talent playing the most important position in college basketball. Point guard Jermaine "Squirt" Hicks, despite his stature, could wind up as the Mid-Continent Conference's Player of the Year. Led by the incomparable Hicks, Chicago State is a swift team, and Ellis pledges to adapt his game plan to that quickness. Look for the Cougars to gamble on defense and try to run, but even Ellis admits he needs his frontcourt to get the job done for the team to succeed. After all, Hicks was sensational last year, yet CSU won only twice.

Improvements in shooting and defense are paramount. The Cougars shot an anemic .370 from the floor, while opponents schooled them for .507.

Ellis figures, correctly, that Valparaiso is highly vulnerable and that the Mid-Con will be much more balanced this season. He also figures, incorrectly, that Chicago State has as much of a shot as any other conference team to "dethrone the king."

We disagree. The Cougars will play hard for Ellis, who knows winning basketball when he sees it—he's been around winners nearly all his life. And if Chicago State can manage to be something more this season than The Bo & Squirt Show, then the program is on the right track. Even if that happens, don't expect a winning record—not this year, anyway.

(T.D.)

INDIANA/PURDUE-INDIANAPOLIS

LOCATION	Indianapolis, IN
CONFERENCE	Mid-Continent
LAST SEASON	18-9 (.667)
CONFERENCE RECORD	N/A
STARTERS LOST/RETURNING	3/2
NICKNAME	Jaguars
COLORS	Red, Gold & Black
HOMECOURT	IUPUI Gymnasium (2,000)
COACH	Ron Hunter (Miami, Ohio '86)
RECORD AT SCHOOL	72-40 (4 yrs.)
CAREER RECORD	72-40 (4 yrs.)
ASSISTANTS	Kevin Jones (Eastern Illinois '87)
	Todd Howard (Louisville '93)
	Sean Richardson (IUPUI '97)
TEAM WINS (last 5 yrs.)	N/A
RPI (last 5 yrs.)	N/A
1997-98 FINISH	N/A

Pop quiz, kids. IUPUI is:

A chain of islands in the South Pacific.

The top-secret international terrorist organization Pierce Brosnan will battle in the next James Bond film.

A brand-new Division I basketball school.

Gold stars to all who answered (c.) IUPUI is Indiana University Purdue University-Indianapolis, one of two new Division I teams to begin play in the Mid-Continent Conference this season.

As such, information on the Jaguars—formerly the Metros—is a little tough to come by. They did win 18 games at the Division II level last year, and fifth-year head coach Ron Hunter has yet to have a losing season at the school.

The challenge inherent in the program's advance to Division I is enhanced by the loss of three starters, including scoring machine Carlos Knox (30.0 ppg, 5.4 rpg) and rebounder extraordinaire Marcus Overstreet (10.9 ppg, 7.1 rpg), and the need to work 11 newcomers into the lineup.

Oh, and did we mention that the roster contains one player with Division I experience?

Welcome to the bigs, fellas.

On the positive side, Hunter must be doing something right, because last year's team excelled in every important area. They shot and defended well, hitting .486 percent from the floor and holding opponents to .419 percent shooting. They hit the long ball and were tough on the perimeter, netting a startling .416 percent of their three-point shots while keeping foes at .338 percent. They made their free throws, shooting .700 percent from the line. And they cleaned the glass, outrebounding the opposition 40.9 rpg to 34.9 rpg.

"Playing in a conference and a competitive Division I schedule are challenges we have been looking forward to for a long time," Hunter said. Hope he means it, because he's going to get those challenges, in spades.

Multi-talented guard **Derek Williams** (4.5 ppg, 3.3 rpg), a 6-3 junior, will begin the season as the starter at shooting guard after starting 17 games last season as a swingman. In addition to shooting .485 percent from the field,

Williams ranked second on the team in steals, with 50, and in assists, with 61. These skills were on full display in a Dec. 27 game against Virgin Islands, when he set a school record with 11 steals and also compiled seven assists.

Junior **Rodney Thomas** (6.0 ppg, 1.3 rpg), a 6-2 sniper, will provide backup at shooting guard. Thomas played in 26 games, starting once and connecting for 35 three-pointers, third best on the team. He is capable of the occasional big night, as seen in his 21-point performance against Drury.

Hunter will have to sift through five newcomers to find someone to play the point for the Jags. The only player to have seen Division I action is 6-5 sophomore transfer **Matt Hermes** (Maine South HS/Park Ridge, Ill.), who scored a single basket and grabbed one board in seven games as a freshman at Drake in 1996-97.

The other newcomers at guard are 6-2 junior transfer **Brian Ponder** (Cooley HS/Detroit, Mich.), who played at Owens Community College; 6-4 freshman **Patrick Cunningham** (Providence St. Mel HS/Oak Park, Ill.); 6-3 freshman swingman **Shaun Clarke** (Vaughn Secondary School/Thornhill, Ont.); and 6-1 freshman **Taj Hawkins** (Oak Hill HS/Washington, D.C.).

Similarly, only two letterwinners return in the frontcourt. One is 6-6 sophomore **Don Carlisle**, the starting small forward, who averaged 6.3 ppg and 4.8 rpg. A 20-game starter, Carlisle was a .456 percent field-goal shooter who displayed a decent all-around game, with 34 assists, 25 steals and 14 rejections. He totaled 11 rebounds twice. Carlisle is IUPUI's top returning scorer and rebounder, and is probably the team's best player.

The other returning frontcourt player is 6-6 forward **Mohammed Witherspoon** (3.4 ppg, 2.3 rpg), the Jaguars' only senior. Witherspoon appeared in 20 games and made one start. His .610 shooting from the floor was best on the team. Still, while the percentage is gaudy, Witherspoon took just 41 shots for the year.

One JC transfer joins three freshmen at forward. The transfer is 6-6 **Vito Knighton** (Detroit Cody HS/Detroit, Mich.), who was at Owens CC last season. The freshmen are 6-8 forward/center **Josh Fitzwater** (Crawfordsville HS/Crawfordsville, Ind.), 6-5 **Rocky Clouse** (Center Grove HS/Greenwood, Ind.) and 6-6 **Jovan Fisher** (Althoff Catholic HS/Belleville, Ill.).

A pair of sizable rookies will compete for the starting job at center. Sophomore transfer **Katoni Waller** (Manasquan HS/Manasquan, N.J.) comes from Keystone JC and provides bulk at 6-8, 254 pounds. Slightly taller and substantially lighter is the 6-10, 210-pound freshman **Herbert Lambert** (Providence St. Mel HS/Chicago, Ill.).

adidas Blue Ribbon Analysis

BACKCOURT	D	BENCH/DEPTH	D
FRONTCOURT	D+	INTANGIBLES	C+

Ron Hunter has enjoyed success with IUPUI over the last several seasons. That may help the Jags steal a few games this year—they're led by a guy who knows how to win.

But IUPUI will find quickly that the opponents they face have better players, and ultimately, that's what it always comes down to. None of the returnees averaged in double figures last year, and 11 new faces will make the adjustment that much harder. Don't look for this team to win a whole lot of games. A double-figure victory total is out of the question.

The good news is that this team is very young. It loses only one player after this season, which will permit Hunter a couple of seasons of teaching his guys how to play the more advanced game before he has to start filling holes.

If nothing else, IUPUI will probably have company at the bottom of the Mid-Continent Conference—Oakland, which doesn't yet have full-blown Division I status. The real test will be whether the Jaguars can learn from this season's inevitable obstacles and apply the lessons to future challenges.

(T.D.)

1998-99 INDIANA/PURDUE-INDIANAPOLIS SCHEDULE

Nov.	14	West Virginia State
	18	@Dayton
	21	Alcorn State
	24	@Georgetown
	28	@Houston
Dec.	5	Oral Roberts
	7	Missouri-Kansas City
	12	Eastern Kentucky
	19	Florida Atlantic
	28	Alcorn State
Jan.	2	@Youngstown State
	4	Southern Utah
	7	@Chicago State
	9	Western Illinois
	14	Chicago State
	18	Belmont
	21	@Oakland
	23	@Valparaiso
	28	@Southern Utah
	30	Youngstown State
Feb.	1	@Butler
	4	@Oral Roberts
	6	@Missouri-Kansas City
	11	Oakland
	13	@Western Illinois
	16	@Belmont
	20	Valparaiso
	27	@Texas-Pan American
28-Mar.	2	#MCC Tournament

@ Road Games

\# The Mark of the Quad Cities, Moline, IL

MISSOURI-KANSAS CITY

LOCATION	Kansas City, MO
CONFERENCE	Mid-Continent
LAST SEASON	9-18 (.333)
CONFERENCE RECORD	7-9 (16th)
STARTERS LOST/RETURNING	1/4
NICKNAME	Kangaroos
COLORS	Blue & Gold
HOMECOURT	Municipal Auditorium (9,827)
COACH	Bob Sundvold (South Dakota State '77)
RECORD AT SCHOOL	19-35 (2 yrs.)
CAREER RECORD	101-73 (5 yrs.)
ASSISTANTS	Bernie Pearson (Friends '87)
	Brian Ostermann (Wisconsin-Lacrosse '88)
	Mike Sharpe (Kansas State '90)
TEAM WINS (last 5 yrs.)	15-12-12-10-9
RPI (last 5 yrs.)	185-184-272-216-228
1997-98 FINISH	Lost in conference quarterfinal.

The record doesn't indicate it, but last season really did mark something of a turnaround for Missouri-Kansas City.

On the surface, the situation seemed static. The 9-18 record was a game worse than that of two years ago. The 7-9 Mid-Continent record and sixth-place conference finish was exactly the same.

But dig a little deeper. Realize that head coach Bob Sundvold had gone for the industrial-size recruiting class, importing eight new faces a season after injuries and suspensions had left his Kangaroos wondering whether the team mascot was permitted to suit up. Consider trying to rebuild not by adding a piece here, a piece there, but by tearing down the whole thing and reconstructing practically from the ground up.

Do these things, and the long, hard season endured by the 'Roos starts to make sense. The 3-13 start. The 41-point mauling at Texas A&M. The season-ending five losses in six games. And the successes, too: The two-point loss to talented Oral Roberts, followed by five straight victories. Wins in the final five home games. Holding opponents to .290 three-point shooting, the second-lowest percentage in conference history.

UMKC's successes should seem considerably more impressive this year. Now in his third season with the Kangaroos, Sundvold finally finds himself working with a team that has slowed down the revolving door of new players. Four starters and six seniors return. The top four scorers are back, as are the top five rebounders. Team introductions, mercifully, will be shorter as well, with three freshmen being the only newcomers to stroll through the locker room.

The entire starting frontcourt returns intact and is anchored by a pair of players who shone in their initial seasons with UMKC. Each was chosen to an all-newcomer team_6-2 junior forward **Sherod Dent** (9.8 ppg, 4.1 rpg) by the conference's coaches and 6-5 senior center **Jimmy Keller** (11.2 ppg, 5.7 rpg) by media members.

Team MVP Keller, more a power forward than a true center, was the squad's leading scorer and rebounder, and he paced the 'Roos with a .568 field goal percentage. Dent, an 11-game starter, poured it on in the season's second half and finished as UMKC's second-leading scorer. He, too, shot well from the floor (.515 percent).

Look for 6-4 sophomore **Jack Savage** (6.2 ppg, 4.3 rpg) to complete the starting rotation up front. Savage started 20 games as a freshman, shooting a sparkling .542 percent from the field and leading the Kangaroos in steals, with 35. In addition, his 50 assists were third on the team.

Coming off the bench to spell Dent will be 6-6 junior **Brad Mann** (4.2 ppg, 2.7 ppg), who averaged nearly 11 minutes in 26 games as a sophomore, with one start. Mann has a decent shooting touch, hitting .443 percent from the floor and .356 percent from beyond the arc, but his 18 free-throw attempts are far too few for a forward his size.

Further experience comes from a pair of big men, 6-9 senior center **Seth Breitkreutz** (2.9 ppg, 2.1 rpg), a six-game starter, and 6-7 senior forward **Hal Lewis**, who sat out last season after transferring from Alabama-Birmingham. Breitkreutz appeared in 23 games, averaging just over 10 minutes a night, while the 225-pound Lewis was permitted to practice with the team. Together, they give Sundvold some reliable beef up front.

1998-99 MISSOURI-KANSAS CITY SCHEDULE

Nov.	14	@South Alabama
	18	Creighton
	21	William Penn
	23	@Southwest Missouri State
	27-29	#Hawaii-Pacific Shootout
Dec.	6	@Valparaiso
	7	@Indiana/Purdue-Indianapolis
	12	@Wisconsin-Milwaukee
	16	Texas-San Antonio
	19	@Kansas State
	22	Cal Poly
	30	Nebraska
Jan.	2	Chicago State
	4	Western Illinois
	7	Oral Roberts
	9	@Southern Utah
	14	@Youngstown State
	18	@Oakland
	21	Southern Utah
	28	@Western Illinois
	30	@Chicago State
Feb.	4	Valparaiso
	6	Indiana/Purdue-Indianapolis
	10	@Denver
	13	@Oral Roberts
	18	Oakland
	20	Youngstown State
28-Mar.	2	##MCC Tournament

@ Road Games
# Honolulu, HI (vs. Illinois State, first round; also Baylor, Hawaii-Pacific, Hofstra, Iona, Southern Mississippi and Virginia Commonwealth)
The Mark of the Quad Cities, Moline, IL

The frontcourt's only freshman is promising 6-7 forward **Will Palmer** (Truman HS/Independence, Mo.), a two-time all-state pick who averaged 23.9 ppg and 11.3 rpg while shooting 60 percent from the floor. Palmer will be Keller's primary backup.

The backcourt is a bit thin, though what is there isn't bad. Point guard looked to be a major trouble spot when starter Mooch Williams blew out a knee 16 games into the season. However, **Eddie Smith**, a 6-0 senior, stepped in nicely despite redshirting the previous year at the junior-college level. Smith started 19 games and appeared in all 27 of UMKC's games, and finished the season with 9.4 ppg—third best on the squad—and 3.2 rpg. His 56 assists were a team high, and his solid play helped the 'Roos play .500 ball in the season's second half.

Shooting guard Anthony Perry was the team's only lost starter. The leading candidate to replace him is 6-2 senior **Nick Richmond** (8.6 ppg, 1.9 rpg), whose 44 treys were tops on the squad. While he played well from downtown, Richmond could stand to improve his shooting from more moderate ranges: He hit only .395 percent from inside the arc. He started nine times last season, so changing to a more leading role shouldn't pose too much of a problem.

Anton Hall, a 6-2 senior, also will get some consideration at shooting guard. Hall (6.3 ppg, 4.2 rpg) was a 14-game starter as a junior, and his 52 assists were good for second on the team. Like Richmond, he should be spending some time in the gym working on his jumper in an effort to improve his pedestrian .359 field goal percentage.

Anthony Love, a 5-9 sophomore, returns to the Kangaroos after sitting out last season as an injury redshirt. Love averaged 4.9 ppg and knocked down 31 three-pointers in his freshman year of 1996-97.

The freshmen guards are 6-2 **Robby Graves** (Lee's Summit HS/Lee's Summit, Mo.) and 6-3 **Marc Stricker** (Christian Brothers College/St. Louis, Mo.). The dynamic Graves averaged 18.6 ppg and 6.4 rpg, and his 4.3 assists a night should lead Sundvold to give him a look at the point. In addition, the first-team all-state selection won the slam-dunk contest at a Missouri-Kansas all-star game. Stricker (18.4 ppg, 3.7 rpg) is a long-range bomber whose 80 treys set a school record and helped him earn all-state second-team honors. Like Graves, he can spread the ball around as well.

Sundvold isn't giving his 'Roos many breaks in scheduling. The nonconference slate includes games against South Alabama, Nebraska, Creighton and Kansas State. Those contests should help UMKC prepare for contests within the Mid-Con, where it played respectably last season.

adidas Blue Ribbon Analysis

BACKCOURT	C	BENCH/DEPTH	D
FRONTCOURT	C+	INTANGIBLES	D+

This is a critical year for the Missouri-Kansas City program. Now that he has a set roster, Bob Sundvold needs to start producing some wins.

A key for this year's squad is to create more scoring opportunities. Thanks to a smothering perimeter defense, last year's team was outscored by an average of only 4.5 points a game. Just a couple of buckets a night—or a few extra trips to the foul line. The Kangaroos went to the line nearly 100 times fewer than their opponents, and hit only 321 shots, the second-lowest in the conference. In addition, though UMKC shot fairly well from the floor, its 68.2 ppg were the worst in the conference, and its 129 treys last. Pushing the ball to the hoop and spreading it around in the half-court set should help in all of these areas.

Sherod Dent and Jimmy Keller offer hope in the frontcourt, and Eddie Smith and Nick Richmond have the ability to produce from the backcourt. Sundvold needs to find reliability at the point, however, and the 'Roos' relative lack of height—only one guy reaches 6-9—will be a concern again; UMKC blocked just 50 shots a season ago.

Sundvold's plan a season ago to work many different players into the starting lineup may not have produced many wins, but it did give his roster a generous dollop of quality-time experience that should come in useful this year. This year's freshman class looks good, too. If the 'Roos' potential-laden squad can show some real improvement in its level of play, a .500 season is in reach, and would be a major step on the road back.

(T.D.)

ORAL ROBERTS

LOCATION ..... **Tulsa, OK**
CONFERENCE ..... **Mid-Continent**
LAST SEASON ..... **19-12 (.613)**
CONFERENCE RECORD ..... **12-4 (2nd)**
STARTERS LOST/RETURNING **2/3**
NICKNAME ..... **Golden Eagles**
COLORS ..... **Vegas Gold, Navy & White**
HOMECOURT ..... **Mabee Center (10,575)**
COACH ..... **Barry Hinson (Oklahoma State '83)**
RECORD AT SCHOOL ..... **19-12 (1 yr.)**
CAREER RECORD ..... **19-12 (1 yr.)**
ASSISTANTS ..... **Tommy Deffebaugh (Drury'85)**
Tom Hankins (Northestern '90)
Scott Sutton (Oklahoma State '94)
TEAM WINS (last 5 yrs.) **6-10-18-21-19**
RPI (last 5 yrs.) **279-260-142-63-146**
1997-98 FINISH ..... **Lost in conference final.**

Year One of the Barry Hinson Era at Oral Roberts coincided with Year One of the Mid-Continent Conference Era for the Golden Eagles. And, as a recently departed legend once crooned, it was a very good year.

Just not quite good enough.

Hinson had inherited from Bill Self a swiftly rebuilt team that soared from six wins to 21 in only four seasons. Last year's squad was fresh off an NIT appearance and had landed on its feet in the Mid-Con after drifting through the nebulous world of independent programs for a while. Finally, ORU could set its sights—legitimately—on an NCAA Tournament appearance, no longer needing to worry about an at-large bid and all of the headaches that entails.

And Hinson had the horses—three returning starters, a deep bench, and some quality performers. Expectations were high on the Oral Roberts campus, and not unreasonably. The puzzle was nearly put together.

In almost every respect, the Golden Eagles enjoyed a very successful season. Nineteen wins are nothing to scoff at, and the team's 12-4 conference record left them in second place, just a game out of the top spot. Seniors Tim Gill and Rocky Walls copped all-conference first-team honors, leading an offensive attack of uncommon potency. Oral Roberts was the first team in Mid-Con history to lead the league in scoring (80.2 ppg), field-goal accuracy (.482) and three-point shooting (.402), and it scored at least 100 points five times.

The Golden Eagles were 6-4 after 10 games, then lost their next four. A 12-3 streak left the team confident heading into the conference tournament—too confident, perhaps. Lowly Southern Utah, which had managed just seven wins the entire season, scared the pants off ORU, extending it to double overtime before falling, 94-84.

That set up a championship match against Valparaiso, with which Oral Roberts had split the regular-season series. It was a matchup featuring the class of the conference, and Valpo was a bit better, notching a 14-point win, advancing to the NCAA Tournament, and leaving the Golden Eagles tasting the sourness of unmet expectations.

1998-99 ORAL ROBERTS SCHEDULE

Nov.	14	@Texas Christian
	18	@Arkansas State
	21	@Denver
	28	Texas A&M
Dec.	2	Texas
	5	@Indiana/Purdue-Indianapolis
	7	@Valparaiso
	13	@Tulsa
	22	Arkansas State
	29-30	#All College Tournament
Jan.	2	Western Illinois
	4	Chicago State
	7	@Missouri-Kansas City
	14	@Oakland
	16	@Youngstown State
	19	Denver
	23	Southern Utah
	30	@Western Illinois
Feb.	4	Indiana/Purdue-Indianapolis
	6	Valparaiso
	11	@Southern Utah
	13	Missouri-Kansas City
	18	Youngstown State
	20	Oakland
28-Mar.	2	##MCC Tournament

@ Road Games
# Oklahoma City, OK (vs. Cal Poly, first round; also Oklahoma and Western Kentucky)
The Mark of the Quad Cities, Moline, IL

Gill (18.1 ppg, 3.2 rpg) and Walls (13.6 ppg, 10.5 ppg) are significant losses. Each started every game, and each was a significant component of ORU's success last year. However, the Golden Eagles return three starters and eight lettermen, so the outlook isn't exactly bleak, despite a frightening car accident involving three players in late September.

Senior guard Nathan Binam had the index finger of his shooting hand amputated after he injured it in a car accident. He will sit out the season as a medical redshirt, work as a student coach and, he hopes, return to play in 1999-2000.

Binam, guard Eric Perry, and center Blake Moses were injured when the pickup truck Binam was driving missed a curve and rolled over.

Perry sustained severe cuts and scrapes on his back and arms. The junior was able to rejoin the team within a week. Moses had to have stitches in his face and lost three front teeth. He underwent oral surgery and returned to practice inside of a month.

The tendons in the index finger of Binam's left hand were destroyed in the

accident, which took place three miles west of his hometown of Claremore, Okla.

This season's anchor will be 6-5 junior forward **Derrick Taylor** (13.6 ppg, 5.7 rpg), a .563 percent field goal shooter who nearly tripled his scoring average from the season before and was rewarded by being chosen to the all-conference second team. Though undersized for a power forward, Taylor is able to play—and play well—above his height. He has a knack for finding his way to the free-throw line, and could help his team even more if he improved on his .532 percent shooting from there.

Joining Taylor up front is 6-6 senior swingman **Chad Wilkerson** (6.7 ppg, 3.3 rpg), a fine shooter from all parts of the court (.511 from the field, .418 beyond the arc, .763 from the line). Wilkerson played a little off-guard last season, but saw most of his time at small forward, where he started 16 games. With Gill gone, look for him to play less in the frontcourt and more in the backcourt. Hinson gave Wilkerson a great deal more responsibility and playing time last year, and he responded with his best season. ORU needs him to step up his game even more this year.

Oral Roberts' biggest question mark a year ago was at the point. Hinson handed the ball to level-headed 6-0 guard Perry (9.1 ppg, 2.8 rpg), who responded with a respectable 131 assists to 70 turnovers, as well as 41 steals, .358 percent three-point shooting, and an .821 free throw average. Taking over from three-year point man Earl McClellan, Perry proved himself a capable ballhandler and shooter unafraid to assert himself. A junior, he is ORU's unquestioned floor leader.

That's not a bad threesome. If Hinson can dig out a couple of able forwards from among the returning reserves and newcomers, he may find himself with a starting contingent that can do some damage.

The pair likely to get first crack at the starting lineup were 6-8 senior center Moses and Binam. Moses (6.4 ppg, 3.9 rpg) started 12 times last year, but failed to progress as Hinson had hoped. The coach had been counting on him for 12 to 14 points a night, but despite shooting .488 from the field, Moses ended up with even worse numbers than those he posted as a sophomore.

As for Binam (6.1 ppg, 2.9 rpg), a 15-game starter, he was, as advertised, every bit the long-range sniper. An excellent all-around athlete, Binam made 46 treys on .377 shooting. Who knows how his finger injury will affect his shooting?

Lightning-quick **Phillip Owens** (4.8 ppg, 0.9 rpg), a 5-9 sophomore, served as Perry's backup last season. He saw action in all 31 games, averaging 14 minutes a night, and hit 39 percent of his three-pointers. His 29 steals are impressive, though the 37 assists against 49 turnovers leave something to be desired.

The remaining returning players didn't see much action and didn't contribute a whole lot when they played. **Jay Henderson** (1.3 ppg, 1.2 rpg), a 6-8 senior center, appeared in 22 games, at five minutes a night, while 6-2 junior guard **David Sumrall** (1.1 ppg, 0.4 rpg) played only 14 times.

That should leave plenty of opportunity for the Golden Eagles' large contingent of newcomers. Eight Oral Roberts rookies will attempt to help plug the holes and carry the team over the hump.

The most intriguing is 6-6 freshman forward **Rodney Bond** (Gateway Christian HS/St. Louis, Mo.), who put up impressive numbers as a senior (17.4 ppg, 15.6 rpg). Walls' departure leaves a big opening for anyone who can rebound, and if Bond shows himself able, he'll get the chance to contribute.

Another possibility is 6-9 freshman center **Brandon Rabel** (Wyandotte HS/Wyandotte, Okla.), who also posted some nice scholastic stats (18.0 ppg, 9.5 rpg).

Elsewhere up front, junior college import **Leon Irving** (Carl Albert JC/Oklahoma City, Okla.), a 6-6 junior forward, will try to make the jump to Division I after a good sophomore season (15.3 ppg, 5.8 rpg). **Paul Brandt** (Thousand Oaks HS/Thousand Oaks, Calif.), a 6-11 junior center, was on the preseason roster last year but never played. He averaged 10 points, eight rebounds and three blocked shots two years ago at Rhema Bible College.

Brandt and 6-8 freshman forward **Kyle Stewart** (Bartlesville HS/Bartlesville, Okla.) seem destined for lots of bench time. Stewart averaged 15 points, eight rebounds and two blocks.

A trio of rookies will vie for time in the backcourt. The most-traveled among them is 6-3 junior **Reggie Tate** (Connors State College/Oklahoma City, Okla.), who averaged 12.0 points, 5.0 rebounds and 5.0 assists as a sophomore. Tate originally signed with Oklahoma State, then attended St. Gregory's College in Shawnee, Okla., for a season. He played one season at Connors State.

The Golden Eagles may have found a sniper in 6-5 freshman shooting guard **Micah Ratzlaff** (Hillsboro HS/Hillsboro, Kan.), a 60 percent field goal shooter last season. In his junior year, Ratzlaff averaged15.2 points, 5.6 rebounds and 5.6 assists. **Stacy Barrett**, a 6-3 freshman, rounds out the rotation. He averaged 22 points, eight rebounds and six assists as a senior.

adidas Blue Ribbon Analysis

BACKCOURT	**C+**	**BENCH/DEPTH**	**D+**
FRONTCOURT	**B**	**INTANGIBLES**	**B**

The transition year behind them, the Golden Eagles enter the season knowing what to expect out of the teams of the Mid-Continent Conference. They weren't quite good enough to knock off a very strong Valparaiso squad last year, but graduation drained the Crusaders much more severely than it did Oral Roberts.

There are definite bright spots to this team. Derrick Taylor will be a star this year, Chad Wilkerson looks ready to hit double figures and Eric Perry proved himself an able point man last season. But the rest of the starting lineup is iffy, and the bench is by and large a collection of guys with no significant Division I experience.

Figure the three returning starters to play at least as well, if not better, than they did last season. If Blake Moses, Nathan Binam and Phillip Owens can step up their games—and they appear fully capable of doing so—and if two or three of the newcomers play solid ball, ORU should have another winning season. A critical area to watch is turnover margin, where Oral Roberts, despite 19 wins, ranked last in the conference a year ago at minus1.3 per game.

For the first time in a long while, the league title truly is wide open, and it is not out of the question to suggest that the Golden Eagles will contend for it again this season.

(T.D.)

SOUTHERN UTAH

LOCATION	**Cedar City, UT**
CONFERENCE	**Mid-Continent**
LAST SEASON	**7-20 (.259)**
CONFERENCE RECORD	**4-12 (7th)**
STARTERS LOST/RETURNING	**1/4**
NICKNAME	**Thunderbirds**
COLORS	**Scarlett & White**
HOMECOURT	**Centrum (5,300)**
COACH	**Bill Evans (Southern Utah '72)**
RECORD AT SCHOOL	**84-87 (6 yrs.)**
CAREER RECORD	**84-87 (6 yrs.)**
ASSISTANTS	**Bob Lowe (George Fox '85)**
	Barrett Peery (Southern Utah '95)
TEAM WINS (last 5 yrs.)	**16-17-15-9-7**
RPI (last 5 yrs.)	**194-248-215-214-284**
1997-98 FINISH	**Lost in conference quarterfinal.**

Picture yourself as the new kid in school. It's your first day, and you're not sure yet who hangs out with whom, which kids are the nerdy ones, who's going to try to steal your lunch money, and so on.

Now picture yourself as this new kid, but with only one of the five books you're supposed to be carrying to make it through a full day of classes.

This was life last season for Southern Utah, the new kid in the Mid-Continent Conference.

In addition to being conference newcomers, the Thunderbirds of 1997-98 returned—for the third year in a row—just one starter. Is it any wonder the team won just seven games?

Remember, this is not a program plagued by chronic losing. It posted consecutive seasons of 16, 17 and 15 wins as recently as three- to five years ago. And until last season, Southern Utah hadn't had a losing home record in 18 years. But last season's squad boasted just two seniors, and the inexperience was telling. The Thunderbirds took their lumps.

Ain't that tough enough?

"I don't think there is any question that our young kids got a lot of battle experience (last) year," said seventh-year head coach Bill Evans, who will move into second place on SUU's all-time victories list with his team's next win.

Evans' point is well taken. Southern Utah's early-season troubles did not cause its players to give up. The Thunderbirds managed January wins against Youngstown State and Northeastern Illinois, posted two straight victories over Missouri-Kansas City and Chicago State in February, then stretched a very good Oral Roberts team to double-overtime before falling in a Mid-Con Tournament quarterfinal by 10.

"We had four or five guys play a lot of minutes and some backup guys that also got some good time," Evans said. "That should be good for the future."

Indeed, the Thunderbirds welcome back four starters as well as a player who started for most of two seasons before embarking on a two-year church mission. Three of the returning bench players saw lots of quality time last year, and Evans likes what he sees in his newcomers.

Finally, the addition of Oakland and Indiana/Purdue-Indianapolis to the conference means Southern Utah quickly sheds its status as the new kid in school.

SUU looks solid up front, where 6-8 senior **Kenyatta Clyde** (14.4 ppg, 6.0 rpg, 39 blocks) patrols at both center and forward. Clyde's first season with Southern Utah was a wonderful one, earning him co-newcomer of the year honors and a selection to the all-conference second team. He returns as the Mid-Con's top returning shot blocker and its second-leading scorer. Clyde is *Blue Ribbon*'s preseason choice as Mid-Con Player of the Year.

Evans would love to get his star some interior help. "Kenny's a guy that can dominate a game, and he did that several times last year, even though he played a lot of minutes at center," Evans said. "We need our big guys to step up and take some pressure off Kenny in the post. If that happens, he could have a great, great year."

It's hard to imagine getting much more production out of 6-5 senior forward **Tarvish Felton** (12.0 ppg, 7.6 rpg, 48 steals), the team's leader in rebounding, steals and minutes played last year. The conference's top returning rebounder, Felton also shot .465 from the floor and notched 56 assists and 39 blocked shots. In short, he is probably the Thunderbirds' most complete player, a guy who can get the job done at both ends of the floor and every point in between.

Because his shooting skills have improved, Felton may even shift to the off-guard slot if Evans wants to go with a big backcourt. "One of the best things about Tarvish is that he's been very consistent both seasons he's been here," the coach said. "I look for that to continue."

An intriguing question for Southern Utah is whether 6-6 junior forward **Jim Faulkner** has blown away enough cobwebs to contribute. The aggressive Faulkner started 21 of 28 games as a sophomore in 1994-95, when he averaged 6.9 ppg and 3.8 rpg and helped SUU win the American West Conference championship. He spent the next two years on a mission to Pennsylvania and redshirted last season.

The broken ankle he sustained in May surely won't help Faulkner scrape off the rust, though team officials insist he's ready to go. "Jimmy was a big part of our two most successful seasons, and he brings a lot to the table," said Evans. "He does all the non-glamour things, like rebounding, defending (and) passing, and plays with a lot of passion."

A pair of veterans will provide experience and depth off the bench. A three-game starter who appeared in 23 games, 6-7 senior **Brian McKee** (2.7 ppg, 2.0 rpg) helped out Clyde in the paint. Despite his size, McKee managed 12 blocks in only 215 minutes, and shot .455 percent from the floor.

Former walkon **Mark Bailey** (3.9 ppg, 1.7 rpg) was one of just three SUU players to see action in all 27 games. Bailey, who started twice, shot .867 percent from the free-throw line and 34 percent from three-point land, and reached double figures three times.

Evans would be ecstatic if 6-11 freshman center **Chris Wallin** (Mountain View HS/Mesa, Ariz.) is able to step in and play the pivot right away. True talent from a true big man would let Clyde slide over to forward, where he could do even greater damage. Wallin's high school team won the Arizona state championship last year.

Looking to add grit on his front line, Evans signed junior college players **Tyson Hancock** (Snow JC/Roosevelt, Utah) and **Nate Pugmire** (Utah Valley State College/Laketown, Utah), both 6-7 junior forwards. Hancock has a nice perimeter touch, while Pugmire is a solid interior defender who rebounds well. He averaged 4.2 ppg and 2.7

1998-99 SOUTHERN UTAH SCHEDULE

Nov.	13	Weber State
	17	Montana Tech
	19	@Montana
	25-28	#Great Alaska Shootout
Dec.	3	Youngstown State
	7	@Idaho State
	11-12	##Cougar Classic
	19	California Baptist
	28	@UNLV
Jan.	2	@Valparaiso
	4	@Indiana/Purdue-Indianapolis
	9	Missouri-Kansas City
	11	Denver
	14	@Western Illinois
	16	@Chicago State
	21	@Missouri-Kansas City
	23	@Oral Roberts
	28	Indiana/Purdue-Indianapolis
	30	Valparaiso
Feb.	4	@Oakland
	6	@Youngstown State
	11	Oral Roberts
	13	@Denver
	18	Western Illinois
	20	Chicago State
	23	Oakland
28-Mar.	2	###MCC Tournament

@ Road Games

\# Anchorage, AK (vs. Cincinnati, first round; also Alaska-Anchorage, Duke, Fresno State, Iowa state, Notre Dame and Saint Mary's)

\## Provo, UT (vs. Northridge State, first round; also Brigham Young and Louisiana Tech)

\### The Mark of the Quad Cities, Moline, IL

rpg last season. "Tyson and Nate will both be factors this season," Evans said. "Both of them fill needs we felt had to be addressed, and both will bring a toughness that we sometimes lacked last year."

The final newcomer up front, 6-9 freshman forward **Nic Fitzgerald** (Hillcrest HS/Sandy, Utah), needs to bulk up if he wants to get more than a passing glance.

Both starters return at guard. Handling the point is 6-1 senior **Tyrone Ellis** (5.3 ppg, 2.4 rpg), who handed out a team-high 94 assists against only 55 turnovers. Ellis, a 20-game starter with appearances in every SUU contest, also had 37 steals and shot .788 percent from the line. And he blocked 10 shots to boot.

His backcourt mate is 6-0 sophomore **Jeff Monaco** (9.9 ppg, 2.1 rpg), who also appeared in all 27 games. Monaco started 16 times as a freshman and finished the season as the Thunderbirds' third-leading scorer and second-best assist man (87). Like Ellis, he shot well from the free-throw line, (.853 percent). Monaco also hit 43 treys at a .344 clip.

Ellis will need to be replaced next year, so look for Evans to give plenty of minutes to 6-0 freshman **Justin Kaliszewski** (Chatfield HS/Littleton, Colo.), who was Colorado's Mr. Basketball last year. Kaliszewski was ranked among the state's top five high school prospects by *Student Sports* magazine.

SUU should also get quality minutes from 5-10 senior shooting guard **Greg Harton** (3.9 ppg, 1.7 rpg), a former walkon who played in 24 games, averaging 14.3 minutes, and started seven times early in the year. Harton's 21 three-pointers ranked behind only Monaco; he sank two clutch free-throws and buried a deep three-pointer to seal the Thunderbirds' overtime win against Idaho State.

A pair of newcomers round out the guard rotation. Local product **David Almadova** (Cedar City HS/Cedar City, Utah), 5-10, redshirted last season. That redshirt year followed two years of a church mission to Ohio. He averaged 20.1 ppg, 5.3 apt and 2.0 rpg in 1993-94, his last season of high school. **Stan Johnson** (Taylorsville HS/Salt Lake City, Utah), a 6-2 freshman, was a second-team all-state pick.

adidas Blue Ribbon Analysis

BACKCOURT .... **C+** **BENCH/DEPTH** .... **C**
FRONTCOURT .... **B** **INTANGIBLES** .... **C+**

Cedar City, Utah, can hardly be said to sit in the middle of the continent. In fact, its distance from the cities that house the rest of the teams of the Mid-Continent Conference probably contributed to last season's tough times for the Thunderbirds.

That won't change this year. What is different is the substantial experience of the returning players, a factor head coach Bill Evans believes "should make them much better this time around."

Look for Southern Utah to rely heavily on its veteran nucleus. Kenyatta Clyde and Tarvish Felton are legit frontline players, and Tyrone Ellis and Jeff Monaco comprise a reliable backcourt that won't make many mistakes.

"No doubt about it, we return a good nucleus and one that is more experienced than any group we've had in a while," Evans said. "They all know what it takes to play at this level, and that should really help us."

Solid play from freshman center Chris Wallin, highly touted rookie guard Justin Kaliszewski and returning missionary Jim Faulkner, combined with continued contributions from its role players, would give SUU depth and potential at every position. In the suddenly balanced Mid-Con, that could be enough for the T'birds to emerge as a dark horse in the league race.

(T.D.)

adidas Blue Ribbon Analysis

GRADING SYSTEM

- A+ equal to very best in country—Final Four-caliber unit
- A among the best in the land—worthy of deep NCAA run
- B+ talented, versatile and experienced—NCAA-NIT ability
- B solid and productive winners—league and post-season contenders
- C+ average to above-average—may contend in a weaker league
- C average to mediocre—second division in a strong league
- D+ below average, inconsistent—second division in a weaker league
- D well below average—losing season virtually certain
- F non-Division I ability—an underdog every night

VALPARAISO

LOCATION .... **Valparaiso, IN**
CONFERENCE .... **Mid-Continent**
LAST SEASON .... **23-10 (.697)**
CONFERENCE RECORD .... **13-3 (1st)**
STARTERS LOST/RETURNING **4/1**
NICKNAME .... **Crusaders**
COLORS .... **Brown & Gold**
HOMECOURT ..... **Athletics-Recreation Center (4,500)**
COACH .... **Homer Drew (William Jewell '66)**
RECORD AT SCHOOL .... **144-147 (10 yrs.)**
CAREER RECORD .... **413-269 (22 yrs.)**
ASSISTANTS .... **Scott Drew (Butler '93)**
Steve Flint (UC-San Diego '84)
Mark Morefield (Valparaiso '98
TEAM WINS (last 5 yrs.) **20-20-21-24-23**
RPI (last 5 yrs.) **116-111-123-67-70**
1997-98 FINISH .... **Lost in NCAA Sweet 16.**

It was the kind of shot that every kid who has ever laced up sneakers and lobbed balls at the hoop over the garage dreams of making.

Last March 13, down by two to 4th-seeded Mississippi in the first round of the NCAA Tournament, Valparaiso's players and coaches watched helplessly as the Rebels' Ansu Sesay stood at the free-throw line for a pair of shots that could ice the game and finish their season.

The Valpo players hope for a miracle and get it—Sesay misses twice. The Crusaders, a No. 13 seed, grab the rebound and call timeout. Two and a half seconds are left. Jamie Sykes, inbounding from the baseline, heaves a baseball pass downcourt and hits Bill Jenkins, who barely touched the ball before passing to star guard Bryce Drew. Off-kilter, Drew launches a prayer from the right wing and beyond the arc as time runs out.

Swish.

Bedlam.

Valpo's wildly improbable, 70-69 upset over the Rebels was its first NCAA Tournament win ever. The game appeared to cap another fine season, one that resulted in a fourth straight trip to the Big Dance. Except the Crusaders weren't done. They sent thousands more crumpled office pools spiraling into trash cans with an 83-77 overtime win against Florida State to advance to the Sweet 16.

The clock turned midnight against Rhode Island, which ended the magic and dropped Valparaiso by six points.

When the dust settled, Valpo had finished the season ranked 23rd in the country in the *USA Today*/ESPN poll. It was the only Division I school to win its conference's regular season and tournament championships for each of the last four years, and only the fourth team ever to accomplish this feat. And the one or two people who didn't know about the Crusaders a year ago had been educated.

Drew, the Mid-Continent Conference's Player of the Year for the second straight season and a third-team All-America pick by *Basketball Times*, was taken by the Houston Rockets in the first round of the NBA draft as the 16th selection overall. He finished his career as just the second player in Mid-Con history to amass 2,000 points and 600 assists, and spent his entire career among the Division I leaders in scoring, field goal and free-throw percentage, assists, steals and three-point shooting. To top it off, he was chosen the conference's male Scholar-Athlete of the Year by the league's faculty athletic representatives.

And now, Valpo fans, take a deep breath.

Leading scorer and assist man Drew (19.8 ppg, 155 assists) and leading rebounder Jenkins (7.5 rpg) have graduated, along with Sykes (8.7 ppg, 2.7 rpg, 107 assists), 7-0 center Antanas Vilcinskas (8.3 ppg, 5.2 rpg) and Jenkins' twin, reserve forward Bob Jenkins (5.2 ppg, 4.8 rpg). All told, the Crusaders have lost four starters and five members of the eight-man rotation that saw the bulk of the action last season.

That leaves Bryce's father, 11th-year head coach Homer Drew, with quite a lot of work to do. The core of players who produced Valparaiso's astoundingly successful four-year run has moved on, and in their place is a big-time youth movement. There are eight newcomers, including five freshmen.

The notable exception among all these kids is 6-11 center **Zoran Viskovic** (13.6 ppg, 6.1 rpg), the team's only returning starter and its sole senior. The Croatian native was second on the team in rebounding, and his 49 rejections paced the squad. Along with Vilcinskas, he formed the "V Towers," a pair of very large European players patrolling the paint for the Crusaders. Viskovic, a second-team all-conference pick, shot .629 percent from the floor—good for sixth in the country—including an 11-for-11 performance against Chicago State. He also hit for 71 percent from the line, so look for him to take a lot of shots this season.

Viskovic's role on this year's Valpo squad can't be overstated. Against Mississippi, he scored 19 points, and in the season-ending loss to Rhode Island, he totaled 13 points and seven boards. Viskovic has shown himself to be a money player. Now, with Bryce Drew and most of his supporting cast gone, it will be up to him to raise his game even higher, to the level of "go-to" guy.

The unenviable job of replacing Drew at the point falls to 5-11 sophomore **Jared Nuness** (5.8 ppg, 1.7 rpg, 51 assists, 25 steals). Nuness played a major role in his freshman season—no doubt coach Drew had more than a casual eye on the potential difficulties of replacing so many seniors. He sank 34 treys for a success ratio of .358, draining six of six from beyond the arc against Belmont. No one expects Nuness to be the second coming of his predecessor, but his quickness and big-game experience should help him progress nicely.

Look for 6-6 sophomore **Marko Punda** (1.8 ppg, 0.6 rpg) to have the inside track on the starting shooting guard slot. Punda, a Croatian, played in 20 games last year, showing a nice outside touch that could keep opposing defenses from sagging on Viskovic. His significant international playing time will help as well.

Drew also may give a shot to 6-4 freshman **Milo Stovall** (Notre Dame Academy/Kalamazoo, Mich.), who posted nice numbers as a senior: 26.4 ppg, 8.0 rpg, and 4.2 apg and 3.0 spg. Throw in 51 percent shooting from the field and 42 percent from three-point range and you have a guy who may contribute right away.

The other guards include 6-3 sophomore **Aric Graham** (0.6 ppg, 0.5 rpg), who played for just 22 minutes over 11 games; 6-0 junior **Chris Sparks**, a redshirt attempting to return from an injury; and 6-3 junior **Tarrance Price** (Barton County College/Junction City, Kan.), a junior college transfer. The remaining freshmen in the backcourt are 6-3 **Ryan Sexson** (Jefferson HS/Lafayette, Ind.) and 6-3 **Greg Tonagel** (LaPorte HS/LaPorte, Ind.). Tonagel averaged 18.0 ppg and 6.0 apg in helping his team reach the state Final Four as a junior, while Sexson tallied 16.5 ppg, 2.8 rpg and 4.0 assists per game in his junior season.

Junior walkon **Dwayne Toatley** (Eden Prairie HS/Eden Prairie, Minn.), a 6-2 transfer from Minnesota-Duluth, doesn't figure to play much.

The starting small forward is likely to be 6-8 sophomore **Jason Jenkins** (2.5 ppg, 1.3 rpg), a part of Valpo's eight-man rotation a season ago. Jenkins came off the bench in all but one of his 30 appearances, and proved adept at providing a lift from the outside. Chances are that he'll be joined in the starting frontcourt by 6-10 junior forward-center **Ivan Vujic**, a transfer from Vincennes University, where he averaged 7.3 ppg and 4.1 rpg as a freshman. Mobile despite his height and 240-pound bulk, Vujic hails

1998-99 VALPARAISO SCHEDULE

Nov.	15	Northland College
	23	Kendall College
	28	@Norfolk State
	30	@Illinois
Dec.	2	Norfolk State
	5	Missouri-Kansas City
	7	Oral Roberts
	11-12	#Boilermaker Invitational
	22	@Wisconsin-Green Bay
Jan.	2	Southern Utah
	7	@Oakland
	9	Youngstown State
	11	Belmont
	16	@Western Illinois
	21	@Chicago State
	23	Indiana/Purdue-Indianapolis
	28	Oakland
	30	@Southern Utah
Feb.	4	@Missouri-Kansas City
	6	@Oral Roberts
	11	Western Illinois
	13	@Youngstown State
	18	Chicago State
	20	@Indiana/Purdue-Indianapolis
	22	@Belmont
28-Mar.	2	##MCC Tournament

@ Road Games
# West Lafayette, IN (vs. Purdue, first round; also Eastern Washington and La Salle)
The Mark of the Quad Cities, Moline, IL

from the same Croatian town as Punda, and Crusader backers are already speculating on his joining Viskovic in a new version of the "V Towers."

The only other frontcourt veteran is 6-7 junior role player **Aaron Thomason** (1.1 ppg, 0.5 rpg), a hard worker and enthusiastic performer who played in only 11 games. Drew will have no choice but to hope that some of his many newcomers can adapt to the Division I game quickly. In addition to Vujic, these include 6-9 freshman center **Phil Wille** (Hilliard-Davidson HS/Hilliard, Ohio) and 6-10 forward **Marty Perry** (Jacksonville HS/Jacksonville, Ind.). Despite his size, Wille's numbers weren't grand—only 8.0 ppg and 5.0 rpg as a high school junior. Perry performed better, hitting for 18.0 ppg and 7.0 rpg while shooting 53 percent from the floor.

With the loss of experience and depth, Drew has eased up a bit on the schedule, perhaps in an effort to spare his players any unnecessary early-season whippings. Illinois, Purdue and Wisconsin-Green Bay are the highlights for the young Crusaders.

adidas Blue Ribbon Analysis

BACKCOURT .... C BENCH/DEPTH .... D+
FRONTCOURT .... C+ INTANGIBLES .... B+

Below the rarefied air where the elite of the college hoops world lives and plays—the Kentuckys and Dukes, the North Carolinas and Connecticuts—the majority of Division I teams exist in a world of perpetual ascendance and rebuilding. To sustain a four-year run of excellence in this realm, as Valparaiso has done, is a truly amazing feat.

So shed no tears for the Crusaders, whose dynasty will come to an end this year.

Homer Drew must replace more than 50 ppg and 24 rpg. He must account for a wealth of leadership and experience. He must do without Bryce Drew, his son and one of the country's most outstanding players.

And it ain't gonna be easy. Only big man Zoran Viskovic has proven himself. The rest of the team is young and green. While a few of the returnees saw quality time last season, most rode the pine. Sophomore Jared Nuness and freshman Milo Stovall look like nice players, but in large part this is a team that will need a lot of time for its players to find their roles and settle into them.

Drew can coach, though, and he'll need to do a fair amount of it this year. The Crusaders are young, and will play like it this season. Viskovic, the team's only senior, can put the ball in the basket with regularity, but the issue of who will get him the ball is just one of many question marks for Valparaiso.

No one is calling for a repeat of the recently ended halcyon days any time soon, which is a good thing—only time will tell whether this bunch can gel. For now, it's someone else's turn in the Mid-Con.

(T.D.)

WESTERN ILLINOIS

LOCATION .... Macomb, IL
CONFERENCE .... Mid-Continent
LAST SEASON .... 16-11 (.593)
CONFERENCE RECORD 11-5 (t-3rd)
STARTERS LOST/RETURNING 3/2
NICKNAME .... Leathernecks
COLORS .... Purple & Gold
HOMECOURT .... Western Hall (5,128)
COACH .... Jim Kerwin (Tulane '64)
RECORD AT SCHOOL .... 87-80 (6 yrs.)
CAREER RECORD .... 87-80 (6 yrs.)
ASSISTANTS ..... Brad Underwood (Kansas State '86)
Marc Lowe (Missouri Valley College '89)
TEAM WINS (last 5 yrs.) 7-20-17-19-16
RPI (last 5 yrs.) 265-138-178-123-179
1997-98 FINISH .... Lost in conference quarterfinal.

For a team that wasn't supposed to make much noise last year, Western Illinois had a season that wasn't half-bad. The Leathernecks posted 16 wins and defeated every team in the Mid-Continent Conference, including Sweet 16 entry Valparaiso, at least once. Their turnover margin was best in the conference, and their three-point percentage second best.

On the individual side, three players hit for double-digit scoring averages, Tony Ackerman was chosen to the all-conference second team and **Shawn Doles** was selected to the all-newcomer team.

1998-99 WESTERN ILLINOIS SCHEDULE

Nov.	15	*Iowa
	18	St. Ambrose
	24	Augustana College
	28	@Chicago State
Dec.	4-5	#Cyclone Challenge
	10	@Eastern Illinois
	19	@Bradley
	21	Oakland
	29-30	##Cessna Classic
Jan.	2	@Oral Roberts
	4	@Missouri-Kansas City
	7	Youngstown State
	9	@IUPUI
	14	Southern Utah
	16	Valparaiso
	21	@Youngstown State
	23	Chicago State
	28	Missouri-Kansas City
	30	Oral Roberts
Feb.	3	Wisconsin-Milwaukee
	5	@Oakland
	11	@Valparaiso
	13	IUPUI
	18	@Southern Utah
28-Mar.	2	###MCC Tournament

@ Road Games
* The Mark of the Quad Cities, Moline, IL
# Ames, IA (vs. Princeton, first round; also Iowa State and North Texas)
Wichita, KS (vs. Mississippi Valley State, first round; also Mercer and Wichita State)
The Mark of the Quad Cities, Moline, IL

All in all, it was a worthy year for a team that had to play with a totally rebuilt frontcourt. Alas for seventh-year head coach Jim Kerwin, a large influx of newcomers will nudge expectations even lower than last season's. Can this year's Western Illinois squad overachieve as last year's did, if only ever so slightly?

Look for the Leathernecks to go about nine- or 10-players deep most nights, and as Kerwin gazes at his preseason roster, he sees eight or nine guys as potential starters.

Penciled into the starting lineup are the top two scorers last season, 5-10 senior guard **Brandon Creason** (11.7 ppg, 1.9 rpg, 64 treys, 29 steals) and 6-4 senior swingman Doles (10.4 ppg, 4.0 rpg, .448 field-goal percentage). Creason did a nice job at the point last year, notching 89 assists against only 47 turnovers, but this year will play both guard spots. He shot .403 from beyond the arc and .831 from the free-throw line, giving WIU a reliable all-around presence on the perimeter. Creason's 22nd three-pointer will give him the school record.

Doles proved a solid offensive threat for Kerwin, scoring in double digits 15 times (including 10 of the last 11 games). The Division I rookie hit the boards well for a 6-4 player and even managed to garner 26 steals. A 13-game starter a season ago, Doles will play both shooting guard and small forward, offering the Leathernecks some versatility.

If 5-7 junior junior-college import **Curtis Haggins** (LaCanada JC/Redwood City, Calif.) is the point guard Kerwin hopes he is, Creason can relinquish floor general duties and concentrate on sniping from long range. Haggins is described as strong and quick, with good defensive skills. He averaged nearly 10 points and 7.5 assists last season.

The most experienced backcourt reserve is 6-2 sophomore **Bill Heisler** (6.3 ppg, 1.3 rpg), who played well in his freshman season. Heisler appeared in all 27 games, starting six of them, and he made .436 percent of his three-pointers, tops on the squad. He also passed for 46 assists and grabbed 34 steals, making him a valuable role player.

Joining Heisler on the bench are a pair of freshmen, 6-2 **Cory Fosdyck** (Macomb HS/Macomb, Ill.) and 6-5 **Jake Wessel** (Prairie HS/Cedar Rapids, Iowa). Hometown boy Fosdyck redshirted last season, which should give him a leg up. He is an athletic leaper who can shoot, and will likely get a longer look than Wessel, a good ballhandler who may not get much game time with Haggins and Heisler ahead of him at the point.

It appears, at least early on, that Kerwin intends to go with a couple of his newcomers to join Doles in the starting frontcourt. The early favorite at power forward is 6-7 junior **Chris Canaday** (Mineral Area CC/Ste. Genevieve, Mo.), a beefy 235-pounder who can hold down either the three or four position. Canaday has a good outside touch, though with his frame he may want to mix it up inside more often than pulling up for the perimeter shot. He averaged 10.5 points and 6.5 rebounds as a sophomore.

Look for 6-5 senior **Geoff Alexander** (2.9 ppg, 4.3 rpg) to make a strong push at Canaday, however. Alexander did start 16 games last season and appeared in 26 games. He was the Leathernecks' third-leading rebounder and hauled in 14 boards in Western Illinois' upset victory over Bradley.

Another experienced player is 6-10 junior **Fernando Coloneze** (7.3 ppg, 4.2 rpg, .508 field-goal shooting), who played in 25 games and showed marked improvement during the course of the season. Coloneze alternated between forward and center as a sophomore and is expected to do so again this year.

Probably slated for bench roles are 6-8 senior **Chad Breedlove** (3.3 ppg, 1.7 rpg) and 6-8 junior **Nathan Anderson** (Brown Mackie JC/Brooklyn, N.Y.). Breedlove played in 18 games as a junior, while Anderson, a fine defender, needs to work on his offensive skills quite a bit. He averaged 10.0 points and 6.0 rebounds a year ago and blocked 32 shots.

Doles' likely backup at small forward is 6-4 junior **Marlon Sears** (Seward County CC/Wichita, Kan.), an athletic junior college import who can contribute at both ends of the floor. Like Doles, Sears may see some time in the backcourt.

As noted, Coloneze should see some time in the paint, although Kerwin plans to give 6-9 junior **Juan Martinez** (Indian Hills JC/Quincy, Ill.) first crack at the starting job. Martinez's pedigree is a good one, as he played for a two-time national junior college champion. He can run, score down low, hit the boards and defend inside, and Kerwin considers him the most athletic big man he has coached at Western Illinois. Martinez averaged 8.6 points and 5.8 rebounds for a deep and talented team that won 72 straight and was 76-1 in his two seasons.

Another solid defender in the middle is 6-11 sophomore **Brian Nagle** (Barton County CC/Topeka, Kan.), Kerwin's tallest-ever player. At 250 pounds, Nagle takes up a lot of floor space, which he uses to clear room on defense and to crash the boards.

adidas Blue Ribbon Analysis

BACKCOURT .... C+ BENCH/DEPTH C
FRONTCOURT .... C INTANGIBLES .... C+

Western Illinois enters the season with an awful lot of questions to answer, largely because there are so many new players with no Division I experience.

The most pressing issue is determining who's going to put the ball in the basket. The Leathernecks appear to have no one ready to be a significant scorer, although Brandon Creason and Shawn Doles could find themselves in that role if circumstances are right. Again, though, that depends on other questions being answered.

Such as: Is Curtis Haggins the real deal at the point? Can Juan Martinez be the true center WIU needs so badly? Who on earth is going to play power forward?

To his credit, Bill Kerwin recognized last season's problem areas—defense and rebounding—and recruited large, athletic newcomers who can address them. But where's the excitement going to come from? Who's going to threaten to light it up for 30 points and 12 boards on any given night?

Like we said, too many questions. Kerwin is too good a coach not to answer at least some of them, so look for a middle-of-the-pack finish for the Leathernecks.

(T.D.)

adidas Blue Ribbon Analysis
GRADING SYSTEM

A+	equal to very best in country—Final Four-caliber unit
A	among the best in the land—worthy of deep NCAA run
B+	talented, versatile and experienced—NCAA-NIT ability
B	solid and productive winners—league and post-season contenders
C+	average to above-average—may contend in a weaker league
C	average to mediocre—second division in a strong league
D+	below average, inconsistent—second division in a weaker league
D	well below average—losing season virtually certain
F	non-Division I ability—an underdog every night

YOUNGSTOWN STATE

LOCATION .... **Youngstown, OH**
CONFERENCE .... **Mid-Continent**
LAST SEASON .... **20-9 (.690)**
CONFERENCE RECORD .... **11-5 (3rd)**
STARTERS LOST/RETURNING **2/3**
NICKNAME .... **Penguins**
COLORS .... **Red & White**
HOMECOURT .... **Beeghly Center (8,000)**
COACH .... **Dan Peters (Kent State '76)**
RECORD AT SCHOOL .... **64-73 (5 yrs.)**
CAREER RECORD .... **224-126 (12 yrs.)**
ASSISTANTS Gary Grzesk (Wiconsin-Green Bay '94)
Mark Coffman (Western New Mexico '80)
Andre Smith (Youngstown State '95)
TEAM WINS (last 5 yrs.) **5-18-12-9-20**
RPI (last 5 yrs.) **293-174-262-277-137**
1997-98 FINISH .... **Lost in conference final.**

Ask the casual basketball fan what he knows about the Mid-Continent Conference, and you'll likely hear lots of breathless praise for the collegiate cagers from Valparaiso, Ind. The name Bryce Drew will sneak into the conversation quite a bit, as will that of the former Valpo star's pop, coach Homer Drew.

That's a shame. Because in Youngstown, Ohio, a town famous for its gridiron warriors and their fans, there is quite an interesting basketball story happening.

Four seasons ago, Dan Peters took a team that had won just five times the year before and drove it to 18 victories. Things tailed off after that, and Youngstown State entered last season sentenced by most pundits to do hard time at the bottom of the Mid-Continent Conference standings. With the Penguins welcoming back just two returning starters from a last-place team and trying to work a host of freshmen into the mix, the prediction was hardly unfounded.

After a 2-2 start, YSU tore off six wins in a row. A 2-3 stretch followed. The Penguins then took seven straight, including games against league titans Valparaiso and Oral Roberts. Youngstown State dropped three of its last four to close the regular season, then rediscovered the magic in the Mid-Continent Tournament. The team sent Missouri-Kansas City and Oral Roberts home to study for finals before its season came to an end with a 19-point loss to Valpo in the title game.

When the dust had settled, the Penguins were 20-game winners for the first time since the program graduated to Division I in 1981. They ended with a league record of 11-5, their best since joining the Mid-Con five years ago and good for a third-place tie. Peters became the first YSU head man to earn conference Coach-of-the-Year honors, and was rewarded with a three-year contract extension in June.

More significantly, perhaps, the Youngstown State student body and alumni now have something to do after football season ends. Two of the Penguins' February games—a heartbreaking, last-second loss to Valparaiso and a 21-point schooling of Oral Roberts—drew home crowds of 5,000-plus, for the first time in 13 years.

"One of our main goals when I came here five years ago was to fill Beeghly Center," Peters said. "The excitement that was generated for that (ORU) game was one that I know I will never forget."

Peters's teams always play hard, defend ferociously and hit the boards, and last season's squad was no exception. The Penguins led the league in rebounding, shooting defense and, for the fourth straight year, opponents' points per game, and were second in rejections. Most observers figured YSU would come up lacking in shooting the ball, but the club did well enough to climb into the middle of the Mid-Con pack in that area. In addition, it was second in three-point goals.

Guard Anthony Hunt (14.4 ppg, 3.9 rpg, 139 assists) earned All-Conference first-team honors, and forward Willie Spellman (13.9 ppg, 5.4 rpg, .370 beyond the arc) was chosen to the second team.

"Last year was an exciting one for me," Peters said. "Our guys put it out on the line night in and night out. It was great to see Beeghly Center packed on a few occasions. I think our players enjoyed that the most."

Hunt and Spellman, alas, are gone, leaving Peters to take on yet another challenge as he enters his sixth year. His returnees are solid and the newcomers show promise, however, and there is a well-rounded aspect to this team that should serve it well.

"We need someone to step into (Hunt's and Spellman's) positions immediately," the coach said. "It will be interesting to see which players will fill those roles."

The only player to have locked up a starting slot is 6-1 senior off-guard **DeVon Lewis** (11.3 ppg, 3.5 rpg), who started all 29 games a season ago. A multi-talented performer, Lewis handed out 91 assists last year, good for second on the squad, and shot 46.1 percent from the floor while raising his scoring average by more than eight points a night. He dropped 22 points on Oral Roberts durin what was his finest offensive season ever. In addition, Lewis is the Penguins' defensive whiz, a guy who managed 27 steals despite guarding many of the opposition's top scorers.

"DeVon will be a key component to our success this season," Peters said. "Offensively, we need him to guide from the outside, and defensively, he is one of the top defenders in the league."

Because of Lewis' versatility—he can play either guard slot—the coach anticipates heated competition to determine who will start alongside him. A pair of bench players, 6-2 sophomore **Craig Haese** (5.4 ppg, 1.8 rpg) and 6-3 sophomore **Andrew Hannan** (5.5 ppg, 3.4 rpg), saw quality time and responded well as freshmen, and should get the chance to crack the starting lineup when Lewis plays the point.

Haese made .345 percent of his three-point attempts, and Hannan 40.4 percent . In addition, Hannan turned out to be a real sparkplug who jump-started the Penguins whenever he entered the game. When Spellman had to cut back his time after an injury, Hannan filled in; against Northeastern Illinois. He scored 24 points in his first collegiate start.

If Peters opts to play Lewis at shooting guard, look for 6-2 junior **Albert Crockett** (New Mexico JC/Philadelphia, Pa.), a junior-college import who averaged 16.0 ppg and an impressive 7.0 assists per game, to serve as YSU's floor general. The other newcomer in the backcourt, 5-10 sophomore **Ryan Patton** (Valley Forge HS/Parma, Ohio), is projected to see time as a backup.

Up front, the Penguins feature three returning starters and a fair amount of that quality you can't coach—height.

Four frontcourt men reach 6-8 or more, including 6-8 sophomore center **David Brown** (5.4 ppg, 7.4 rpg), whose splendid freshman season landed him on the conference's all-newcomer team.

Brown led YSU in rebounding and blocked shots (39) and showed a surprising touch for a big man, sinking .566 percent of his field-goal tries, also a team high. He started 28 games in his first season, so despite Peters' talk about competition, it would raise more than a few eyebrows if Brown saw most of his minutes as a backup this year.

Youngstown State's third returning starter is 6-8 senior forward **Maurice Anderson** (7.2 ppg, 3.9 rpg), who played decently in his first season with the Penguins after transferring from San Jacinto Junior College. He was one of three YSU players to start every game, but his poor shooting skills may relegate him to the bench if Peters can find a better alternative.

The best bet to step up his game in the frontcourt is 6-5 sophomore **Desmond Harrison** (7.1 ppg, 4.9 rpg), who was fifth on the team in scoring and third in rebounding, despite seeing all of his action as a backup. As a freshman he averaged more than 20 minutes a game and shot 46.1 percent from the field, giving the Penguins reason to hope for even greater success over the next three seasons.

The frontcourt newcomers have size and athleticism. In particular, 6-9 junior center **Ricky McClanahan** (Allan Hancock JC/Columbus, Ohio) elicits raves from Peters. The bulky McClanahan averaged 23.0 ppg and 6.0 rpg at the junior-college level last season, numbers that excite Peters. "If McClanahan can live up to his potential, he will be on the floor," the coach said. "He may be our first legitimate post player who can score with his back to the basket."

The other rookies are 6-4 junior swingman **Elmer Brown** (Howard JC/Akron, Ohio) and 6-9 junior center **Robbie Robinson** (Barton CC/Philadelphia, Pa.). Brown (19.0 ppg, 6.0 rpg) displayed nice inside and outside skills in junior college, while Robinson (10.0 ppg, 6.0 rpg) can shift from the paint to power forward if Peters wants to go big.

Little-used forward **Christopher McGill** (1.4 ppg, 1.0 rpg, 12 games), a 6-7 senior, and **Greg Robinson** (0.3 ppg, 1.5 rpg, four games), a 6-11 senior, round out the frontcourt rotation.

1998-99 YOUNGSTOWN STATE SCHEDULE

Nov.	18	@Kent State
	20	Slippery Rock
	24	@Hofstra
	28	@Loyola (IL)
Dec.	3	@Southern Utah
	11-12	#KGVO Coca-Cola Classic
	16	@Fairleigh Dickinson
	19	Montana
	23	Hofstra
Jan.	2	Indiana/Purdue-Indianapolis
	4	Oakland
	7	@Western Illinois
	9	@Valparaiso
	14	Missouri-Kansas City
	16	Oral Roberts
	21	Western Illinois
	23	@Oakland
	27	Central State
	30	@Indiana/Purdue-Indianapolis
Feb.	4	Chicago State
	6	Southern Utah
	11	@Chicago State
	13	Valparaiso
	18	Oral Roberts
	20	Missouri-Kansas City
28-Mar.	2	##MCC Tournament

@ Road Games
# Butte, MT (Idaho, Montana and Youngstown State)
The Mark of the Quad Cities, Moline, IL

adidas Blue Ribbon Analysis

BACKCOURT .... **C+** **BENCH/DEPTH** .... **C**
FRONTCOURT .... **C+** **INTANGIBLES** .... **B**

Last year's ride was fun while it lasted, but Dan Peters is under no illusions about what his team did and did not accomplish.

"Advancing to the NCAA Tournament is definitely one of our main objectives," he says. "We were close last season, but lost to a great Valparaiso team. We knew how close we were, and now we have to work harder to achieve our goal."

Indeed, the Penguin overachievers of last season have lost their two best players in Anthony Hunt and Willie Spellman, so Peters doesn't want to take anything for granted.

"Starting in October, practice is going to be extremely competitive. We have many new faces, and our players are going to be competing for playing time," Peters said.

Youngstown State has a potential All-Conference guard in DeVon Lewis, and center David Brown and forwards Maurice Anderson and Desmond Harris provide a solid nucleus in the frontcourt. However, there is some legitimate concern about who will spell Hunt at the point, and while there is some depth, most of the bench is unproven at the Division I level.

Peters has YSU fans buzzing about hoops for the first time in a long while, and for good reason. His Penguins work like demons, and the guy can flat-out coach. Peters has assembled some promising players to join this year's seniors, and because his history suggests a fair amount of successful on-the-job training for his players, the learning curve shouldn't be too painful.

The Penguins don't look to have the tools to make a serious run at the league title, but appear ready to hang around the upper division, gaining valuable seasoning in the process. Lewis will be this year's only significant graduation loss. The future looks bright.

(T.D.)

MID-EASTERN ATHLETIC CONFERENCE

adidas BLUE RIBBON FORECAST

1. South Carolina State
2. Coppin State
3. Morgan State
4. Hampton
5. Florida A&M
6. Maryland-Eastern Shore
7. Delaware State
8. North Carolina A&T
9. Howard
10. Bethune-Cookman
11. Norfolk State

ALL-CONFERENCE TEAM

G—Rasheed Sparks, SR, Morgan State
G—Fred Warrick, SR, Coppin State
C—Raheem Waller, SR, South Carolina State
F—Tarvis Williams, JR, Hampton
F—Damian Woolfolk, JR, Norfolk State

PLAYER OF THE YEAR

Rasheed Sparks, SR, Morgan State

NEWCOMER OF THE YEAR

Tajai Young, JR, Hampton

1998-99 CONFERENCE TOURNAMENT

March 3-6, Richmond Coliseum, Richmond, VA

1997-98 CHAMPION

Coppin State (regular season)
South Carolina State (conference tournament)

1997-98 POST-SEASON PARTICIPANTS

Post-Season Record: 0-1 (.000)
NCAA
South Carolina State

TOP BACKCOURTS

1. Hampton
2. South Carolina State
3. Morgan State

TOP FRONTCOURTS

1. South Carolina State
2. Hampton
3. Morgan State

ON THE WAY UP

Hampton

ON THE WAY DOWN

Howard

INSIDE THE NUMBERS

- 1997-98 conference RPI: 28th (of 30)
- Conference RPI (last 5 years): 32-32-32-29-28

DID YOU KNOW?

Rasheed Sparks of Morgan State is the lone first-team all-conference performer from last season returning...Hampton is eligible for the MEAC Tournament and a bid to the NCAA Tournament this season after the NCAA ruled this summer that new Division I schools did not have to wait eight years, just two, to achieve full D-I status...Howard's Xaiver Singletary, who earned rookie-of-the-year and first-team all-conference honors as a freshman last season, has transferred to Boston College...Hampton coach Steve Merfeld is now officially the head coach of the Pirates after serving in an interim capacity last season...Center Jerome James of Florida A&M gave the MEAC some publicity last summer when he was selected in the second round of the NBA draft by the Sacramento Kings. James was a first-team all-conference performer and all-tournament selection last year...The Richmond Coliseum will be the site for the MEAC Tournament for the second straight year...Coppin State has won six straight regular-season titles and seven of the last eight...In the las six years, South Carolina State has never finished lower than second and has won two of the last three MEAC Championships, beating Coppin State each time...Mel Coleman is the interim coach at Norfolk State this year, taking over for Michael Bernard, who was let go last summer. Norfolk will conduct a search after the season and Coleman is rumored to want the permanent job. Bernard landed on his feet as he got the head-coaching job at Division II power Fayetteville State...For the second straight year, a MEAC team will host national power North Carolina. Last year it was Bethune-Cookman, and this year it's Hampton...Kirk Saulny, a former assistant at North Carolina-Wilmington, is the new head coach at Howard.

(M.G.)

BETHUNE-COOKMAN

LOCATION .... **Daytona Beach, FL**
CONFERENCE .... **Mid-Eastern Athletic (MEAC)**
LAST SEASON .... **1-26 (.037))**
CONFERENCE RECORD .... **1-17 (11th)**
STARTERS LOST/RETURNING **1/4**
NICKNAME .... **Wildcats**
COLORS .... **Maroon & Gold**
HOMECOURT .... **Moore Gymnasium (3,000)**
Ocean Center (9,000)
COACH .... **Horace Broadnax (Georgetown '86)**
RECORD AT SCHOOL .... **1-26 (1 yr.)**
CAREER RECORD .... **1-26 (1 yr.)**
ASSISTANTS .... **Cliff Reed (Bethune-Cookman '91)**
Rick Waldron (Methodist '75)
TEAM WINS (last 5 yrs.) **9-12-15-12-1**
RPI (last 5 yrs.) **276-250-290-263-306**
1997-98 FINISH .... **Lost in conference first round.**

Thankfully, there's nowhere to go but up for the Bethune-Cookman basketball program.

The Wildcats hit bottom last year as they staggered to a 1-26 season, easily the worst in school history. Bethune-Cookman was in danger of a winless season until a late-season victory over North Carolina A&T salvaged a little pride for the program.

First-year coach Horace Broadnax, a former star at Georgetown, has now been on both ends of the Division I spectrum. When he played for the Hoyas in the 1980s, he played for a program that was traditionally one of the best in the country and always competed for Big East championships and national titles.

At Bethune-Cookman last year, Broadnax coached the team with the nation's lowest RPI (306). If Broadnax gets double-digit victories out of this year's team, it would be a surprise.

Still, it was a team that never quit last year. The Wildcats even took conference power Coppin State to double-overtime before losing, 92-89. In the MEAC Tournament play-in game, they went overtime with Howard before losing, 79-68.

Bethune-Cookman must improve its offense. Last season, it shot .370 from the field, .560 from the free-throw line, .240 from three-point range and averaged 60 points.

"Last year we played good defense, we just couldn't put the ball in the hole," Broadnax said. "We hope to be stronger this year and improve our outside shooting."

Broadnax is cautiously optimistic. "The second year is always a lot better," he said. "You have a better fit. You feel a little more confident. You know the nucleus of your team better, you know when to push and when not to push. The returning players know what to expect from me. It's not an adjustment for them anymore. We obviously played hard and aggressively, but we just lacked experience and leadership. This year should be an improvement because of seven guys returning with more experience and the leadership of **Freddie Cole**."

The Wildcats were facing a tough year last season with four starters gone from the '96-97 team that went 12-16. Then Cole, the only returning starter, got hurt. The 6-4 junior shooting guard missed last season with a fractured foot and Bethune-Cookman's season crumbled. Cole averaged 11.1 points, 2.2 rebounds and shot better than 40 percent from three-point range in '96-97.

The return of Cole will be a welcome break for 6-6 senior small forward **Johnny McClenton** (13.1 ppg, 4.3 rpg). McLenton was the only Wildcat to average in double figures last year and he was consistently Bethune-Cookman's only scoring threat. He led the team in scoring in 15 games. He missed the previous two seasons for personal reasons.

Also returning is 6-6 sophomore forward **Derricus Lockwood** (6.8 ppg, 4.0 rpg). Lockwood hopes for a better sophomore season after a rough rookie year. He was second on the team in three-point goals, but made just 29 percent from the field and 51 percent from the free-throw line.

A bright spot for the Wildcats last season was the improved play of 6-6 junior forward **Valder Ned** (8.2 ppg, 5.7 rpg). Ned can play both forward positions and shooting guard, but last year he was mainly an inside player. He led the Wildcats in rebounding and shot 48 percent from the field. He averaged about one point and one rebound the previous season.

The center job could be taken this season by 6-8 junior **Delvin Thomas** (5.2 ppg, 4.5 rpg). Thomas missed the '96-97 season because of injuries, but shot 54 percent from the field last season. He was worse from the free-throw line, shooting 51 percent. He had 40 blocked shots.

The Wildcats' inside game will also be helped by the return of 6-6 senior forward **J.R. Allen** (3.2 ppg, 1.6 rpg). Broadnax is looking for a lot more production and defense from him this season.

A newcomer who should help Bethune-Cookman's frontcourt and perimeter game is 6-5 freshman forward **Brent King**, who comes to Bethund-Cookman from Lawrence Central HS in Indianapolis.

"Brent King brings us a little versatility," Broadnax said. "At 6-5, he can play the perimeter, he can play inside if neccessary and he's a strong rebounder and defender."

The Wildcats will start over at point guard as 5-7 junior **Javon Duke** (2.7 ppg, 1.4 rpg) and a newcomer, 6-1 freshman **Tyhron Crawford**, joins the program from Auburndale (Fla.) HS.

Bethune-Cookman struggled at the point last year and Duke, who only averaged 17 minutes per game, led the team in assists with just 39. He made 73 turnovers. If Duke wants to start in front of Crawford, he will need to improve.

"Tyhron is a freshman point guard who can break the defense down off the dribble and we believe he should be a solid player down the line for us," said Broadnax.

When Broadnax was hired last year from Valencia (Fla.) CC, he wanted to establish a pressing, aggressive

1998-99 BETHUNE-COOKMAN SCHEDULE

Nov.	14	Siena
	17	@Detroit
	21	*Florida A&M
	23	@Florida
	30	Georgetown
Dec.	9	Stetson
	12	@Florida Atlantic
	15	@North Carolina A&T
	17	@South Carolina State
	29	@Auburn
Jan.	2	@Delaware State
	4	Maryland-Eastern Shore
	9	@Coppin State
	11	@Morgan State
	16	Hampton
	18	Norfolk State
	25	Howard
	30	North Carolina A&T
Feb.	1	South Carolina State
	6	Delaware State
	8	Maryland-Eastern Shore
	13	Coppin State
	15	Morgan State
	20	@Hampton
	22	@Norfolk State
	26	Florida A&M
Mar.	3-6	#MEAC Tournament

@ Road Games
* Orlando Arena, Orlando, FL
# Richmond Coliseum, Richmond, VA

offensive and defensive team. That was the way his teams played at Georgetown. The only problem: Broadnax needs a few more bodies to do that at Bethune-Cookman. The Wildcats have just nine players on their roster. All the Wildcats should get plenty of playing time.

adidas Blue Ribbon Analysis

BACKCOURT .... **D** **BENCH/DEPTH** .... **D-**
FRONTCOURT .... **D-** **INTANGIBLES** .... **D**

It will be another long winter for Bethune-Cookman. There just isn't a lot of talent in this program right now, and what makes things really tough for Wildcats coach Horace Broadnax this year is the lack of depth. He has just nine players.

Broadnax wants to play an aggressive style this year, but that won't be easy with so few bodies.

While Broadnax was at Valencia CC, the team went from 9-21 to 20-10 in his two years. There is a little chance of that kind of turnaround at Bethune-Cookman this year.

Turning this program around is going to take time and several recruiting classes. Look for the Wildcats to finish 10th in the MEAC, but also look for a few more victories than last year. Not many more, though.

(M.G.)

COPPIN STATE

LOCATION .... **Baltimore, MD**
CONFERENCE .... **Mid-Eastern Athletic (MEAC)**
LAST SEASON .... **21-8 (.724)**
CONFERENCE RECORD .... **17-1 (1st)**
STARTERS LOST/RETURNING **4/1**
NICKNAME .... **Eagles**
COLORS .... **Royal Blue & Gold**
HOMECOURT .... **Coppin Center (3,000)**
COACH .... **Ron "Fang" Mitchell (Edison State '84)**
RECORD AT SCHOOL .... **226-128 (12 yrs.)**
CAREER RECORD .... **453-173 (20 yrs.)**
ASSISTANTS .... **Derek Brown (Coppin State)**
Eric Skeeters (Coppin State '86)
TEAM WINS (last 5 yrs.) **22-21-19-22-21**
RPI (last 5 yrs.) **110-132-159-127-107**
1997-98 FINISH .... **Lost in conference final.**

A year ago, Coppin State was the toast of the little guys of college basketball.

In the 1997 NCAA tournament, the Eagles, a No. 15 seed, shocked No. 2 seed and SEC champion South Carolina in the first round. Two days later, Coppin State lost to Texas, 82-81, and just missed a trip to the Sweet 16.

Coach Ron "Fang" Mitchell's unheralded group had become a Cinderella team, and the nation cheered.

That NCAA success didn't do a thing for the Eagles last year, when they were snubbed in the postseason, despite an outstanding season. After going 17-1 in the MEAC, the Eagles lost to South Carolina State, 66-61, in the championship of the league tournament.

The Eagles, who upset Missouri, 78-70, and gave top-ranked Arizona a scare before losing, 99-82, did not receive an at-large bid into the NCAA Tournament, or even a berth in the NIT.

Some thought Coppin State had been shortchanged. Mike Lupica of the *New York Daily News* criticized the NIT on ESPN's Sports Reporters for snubbing Coppin State.

It has been a good run for the Eagles, who are 93-7 in the MEAC over the last six year, but they might struggle to continue that success this year.

The Eagles graduated four starters from last year's team, including the talented backcourt of MEAC Player of the Year Antoine Brockington (20.3 ppg, 3.3 rpg) and Danny Singletary (14.7 ppg, 3.3 rpg, 79 assists). Other starters gone are 6-7 forward Kareem Lewis (10.8 ppg, 6.8 rpg) and guard Troy Lewis (4.1 ppg, 1.6 rpg).

With new personnel this year, Mitchell could change his game plan drastically.

Instead of relying on his backcourt and perimeter scoring, Coppin State might become an inside-oriented team this year.

"We should be better inside with the depth we have," Mitchell said. "The play of our big men will be key to our success. It's going to be tougher to score because we lost players like Antoine, Danny, Kareem and Troy, but I believe we will be a better scoring team inside and have more balance than we did last season. We have guys who can get the job done. I'm cautiously optimistic."

1998-99 COPPIN STATE SCHEDULE

Nov.	13	@Fresno State
	15	@Oregon
	19	@Syracuse
	21	@Oklahoma
Dec.	3-4	#PowerBar Invitational
	7	@California
	12	Morgan State
	14	Howard
	21	@Kansas State
	23	@Iowa
	31	@New Mexico
Jan.	2	@North Carolina A&T
	4	@South Carolina State
	9	Bethune-Cookman
	11	Florida A&M
	16	@Delaware State
	18	@Maryland-Eastern Shore
	23	@Hampton
	25	Norfolk State
Feb.	1	@Howard
	6	South Carolina State
	8	North Carolina A&T
	13	@Bethune-Cookman
	15	@Florida A&M
	20	Delaware State
	22	Maryland-Eastern Shore
	27	@Morgan State
Mar.	2-6	##MEAC Tournament

@ Road Games
\# Honolulu, HI (vs. Georgia State, first round; also Hawaii and Northridge State)
\## Richmond Coliseum, Richmond, VA

The four starters who are gone accounted for 50 points per game. One player who should assume some of the scoring load this year is 6-5 senior guard/forward **Fred Warrick** (12.9 ppg, 4.4 rpg), the Eagles' third-leading scorer last year. Warrick has averaged more than 12 ppg while coming off the bench the last two seasons. He is a solid long-range threat after making 60 of 162 three-point shots (.370 percent) last year.

"Fred is a big-time player," Mitchell said. "He was a team player his first two years and let the upperclassmen take most of the shots. He'll get the opportunity to show what he can do this season."

Also back at shooting guard is 6-3 senior **Jerel Seamon** (3.9 ppg, 2.1 rpg), who struggled at times last year after he missed the first seven games with a broken foot. He's heathy now and should be more of a factor. Seamon and Warrick will be co-captains and Mitchell is counting on their leadership.

"One of the most important things Fred and Jerel will need to provide is leadership, especially with as many new players as we have," Mitchell said.

Expected to provide depth in the backcourt are two freshmen: 6-3 **Jason Downing** and 6-4 **Terrance Lee**.

Downing, a shooting guard from Largo (Md.) High School, averaged 11 ppg last year. Lee, who can play shooting guard or small forward, averaged 14 ppg last year at Hazelwood High School in St. Louis.

The big question for the Eagles this year is at point guard.

Alfonso Jones, a 5-10 junior guard, was expected to play a big role in the backcourt this year, but he was dismissed from the team in August. Jones (3.1 ppg, 0.9 rpg) could have played either guard position.

That could leave the point guard job in the hands of 6-2 freshman **Rasheem Sims** , a graduate of basketball power Simon Gratz High School in Philadelphia. Mitchell believes Coppin State may have a sleeper in Sims, who averaged 12.7 points and 7.2 assists during an injury-riddled senior season.

Warrick could also play point guard.

"Point guard is a key area for us because of our inexperience there," Mitchell said. "What we're looking for from that position is a steady job, (someone to) get the ball to the right people and work hard on the defensive end."

In the frontcourt, Mitchell has several options, starting with 6-7 senior **Dorian Pena** (4.3 ppg, 5.5 rpg) and 6-9 senior **Rafi Reavis** (4.1 ppg, 4.2 rpg). They split time at power forward last season with Pena starting the first 14 games of the year and Reavis starting the last 15.

Pena is one of Coppin State's strongest players and is a very good rebounder. Despite not starting in the last half of the season, Pena averaged 7.4 points and 6.8 rebounds in the the Eagles last 10 games.

Reavis moved from small forward to the paint in the second half of the year and immediately helped Coppin's inside game.

"They do the little things well," Mitchell said. "Rafi gives us size and quickness. It's hard for big men to get by him or shoot over him. Dorian gives us everything he has. He played with so much confidence at the end of the year, we'll need that when the season starts."

Pena and Reavis will be pushed by two newcomers and a returnee in the frontcourt. **Tyran Watkins** (1.0 ppg, 2.0 rpg), a 6-8 junior forward, played in 25 games last season and averaged 9.6 minutes per game. He was third on the team in blocked shots with 13. Since last year, he has worked to improve offensively.

Shatee Cooks, a 6-7, 250-pound sophomore forward, didn't play last season as a partial qualifer, but he practiced with the team. Cooks was a teammate of Sims at Simon Gratz. Mitchell likes Cooks' aggressive defense and his strength.

Kofi Pointer, a 6-9 junior, transferred to Coppin State last winter from Providence. Pointer, who averaged 0.6 ppg and 0.4 rpg at Providence last year, will be eligible after the first semester.

Another returnee, 6-7 forward **Greg Hammond**, should be a factor in the frontcourt. Hammond (2.1 ppg, 1.0 rpg) played at Boston University as a freshman before transfering to Coppin State two years ago.

The tallest player in school history, 7-1 sophomore **Jason Iacona** (0.5 ppg, 0.2 rpg), will probably be redshirted this season.

adidas Blue Ribbon Analysis

BACKCOURT .... **C** **BENCH/DEPTH** .... **C**
FRONTCOURT .... **C** **INTANGIBLES** .... **B**

Coppin State has been the premier team in the MEAC, so don't bet against Ron "Fang" Mitchell and Co.

However, several questions surround this year's team, primarily in the backcourt. The Eagles seem to have a solid frontcourt, but they must fill some holes on the perimeter.

Coppin State has won six straight regular-season MEAC titles, and Mitchell is a coach who loves a challenge. He's got one this year.

The Eagles will be hungry. Look for them to finish second in the MEAC behind South Carolina State, and the two teams could meet again for the tournament championship.

(M.G.)

DELAWARE STATE

LOCATION .... **Dover, DE**
CONFERENCE .... **Mid-Eastern Athletic (MEAC)**
LAST SEASON .... **9-18 (.333))**
CONFERENCE RECORD .... **7-11 (6th)**
STARTERS LOST/RETURNING **2/3**
NICKNAME .... **Hornets**
COLORS .... **Columbus Blue & Red**
HOMECOURT .... **Memorial Hall (3,000)**
COACH .... **Jimmy DuBose (New York Tech '82)**
RECORD AT SCHOOL .... **9-18 (1 yr.)**
CAREER RECORD .... **9-18 (1 yr.)**
ASSISTANTS .... **Mike Bramucci (Ramapo '92)**
TEAM WINS (last 5 yrs.) **8-7-11-7-9**
RPI (last 5 yrs.) **289-298-280-293-281**
1997-98 FINISH .... **Lost in conference quarterfinal.**

Finally there appears to be some continuity at Delaware State.

Last season, Jimmy DuBose was the Hornets' third head coach in three years and the fourth in five years. Not too many programs endure that kind of coaching turnover.

But DuBose seems to have brought some calm to the program. He is also a veteran of the program's coaching shuffles. This is his fifth year with the Hornets. In his first three years, DuBose was an assistant under two coaches. He got his chance to be the top man last season.

DuBose started from scratch, working on fundamentals, and it paid off with a 9-18 season—two more victories than the previous season—and a 7-11 league record.

And the Hornets did it without a dependable point guard. They committed 581 turnovers, averaging an astounding 22 per game.

"We learned a lot last year," DuBose said."We learned what you have to do to play hard and how a program is suppossed to be organized. We made some strides and became a lot more competitive. We were 9-18, but that easily could have been 18-9 if we had made some better decisions at crucial times. Hopefully, we'll make better decisions this year."

Last year, DuBose brought in eight new players. This year, he welcomes seven newcomers, players he hopes can bolster the frontcourt and fill the need at point guard.

Delaware State shouldn't have to worry about a shooting guard with 6-4 senior **Terence Hood** (14.8 ppg, 3.2 rpg, 45 three-pointers) returning and ready for an even better year. Hood can look forward to a few more shots.

"We want Terence to shoot the ball more," DuBose said. "He had to be one of the most economical players in America last year considering how many times he shot the ball (11 shots per game) and what he averaged. Sometimes he's too unselfish and this year we want him to shoot more and have a coming-out party for him. I really think he can be a player-of-the-year candidate this year and that's what we're going to try and do for him."

Hood will quickly become the 13th player in school history to reach 1,000 career points. He enters the season with 994. Hood also needs just 25 three-pointers to become the school's all-time leader.

Delaware State returns a versatile player in 6-3 junior guard **Demond Wilkerson** (5.1 ppg, 2.3 rpg). He can play shooting guard, small forward, point guard or even power forward if the Hornets employ a four-guard attack.

"Demond is a jack of all trades for us," DuBose said. "He can do a lot of different things on the floor that can help us. We plan to use him primarily at the two or three this year, and we think he'll be best at either spot."

Another candidate at small forward is 6-7 junior **Barrington Clarke** (9.7 ppg, 4.1 rpg). Clarke was the Hornets' third-leading scorer and rebounder last season and led the team in field-goal percentage (.500).

"Barrington has grown up a little bit and is a lot more wiser this year," DuBose said. "Just the fact he's matured and grown up should make him a better player. He'll push for playing time at (small forward) and hopefully he'll be able to give us even more this season than he did last year."

Also battling for playing time at several positions will be 6-3 senior guard/forward **Brian Butler** (6.9 ppg, 1.7 rpg). Butler has gained 15 pounts, to 215, and that extra strength should help this year.

"Brian gives us some size out on the perimeter this year," DuBose said. "His 215 pounds is all muscle and he should be able to post up people this year and cause match-up problems for a lot of opponents."

This season could be a redemption year for 6-6 senior forward **Darien Robinson** (3.5 ppg, 3.9 rpg). A transfer last season from Kilgore (Texas) JC, Robinson was expected to be a key frontcourt player, but didn't quite meet those expectations. DuBose hopes for better from Robinson this year.

"Darien didn't live up to his billing last year and hopefully things will be different," DuBose said. "He was a great rebounder at (Kilgore JC) and he needs to play like he did there for us. He's got a different attitude this year and hopefully that will produce a better performance on the floor this year."

At center, two players from last year should battle for playing time along with some talented newcomers. The returnees are 6-9 sophomore center **Brandon Calvert** (3.2 ppg, 3.1 rpg) and 6-6 senior forward/center **Ousmane Traore** (3.1 ppg, 3.0 rpg). Each should be improved after a year of Division I ball.

Traore was born in France and played for the its national team.

"Ousmane is a special kid who's still learning the game," DuBose said. "He plays great defense in the post and he should be better this year with some experience under his belt."

Five junior-college transfers join the program this year, and if they live up to their billing, the Hornets could be in the MEAC race.

Along with the five junior-college signees, two freshmen with outstanding credentials join the program. Many believe this is one of Delaware State's best recruiting classes.

"We think we've really answered some needs with our recruiting class," DuBose said. "We've brought in experienced players who should be able to help us right away."

The Hornets' biggest need last season was a dependable point guard. That shouldn't be a problem this season with the arrival of 6-1 junior **Stephan Malliet** from State University of New York at Farmingdale. Malliet was a junior-college All-American last year after averaging 25 points, seven rebounds and six assists. DuBose can't wait to get the Long Island native on the court.

"Stephan brings us a new dimension this year at the point-guard spot," DuBose said. "He's a real floor general who knows how to get the ball into the right people's hands at the right time. He can also score and is an outstanding shooter. We're really excited about having him in our program and we think he can make a real difference this year."

Freshman guard **Marty Bailey** will help Malliet at the point this year. Bailey, 6-2, enjoyed an outstanding career at Easton (Md.) HS, where he averaged 19 points and four rebounds last season. He was Maryland's runner-up for state player of the year and could find some valuable playing time this year, despite being a freshman.

"Marty is a real smart kid who can also distribute the ball quite well," DuBose said. "He's played against great competition during his career and should be able to fit in with us."

Two brothers from United Tribes Tech College in Bismark, N.D., could also help this year: 6-3 junior guard **Tanner Alkbers** (25.0 ppg) and 6-6 junior forward **Travis Alkbers** (10.0 ppg, 9.9 rpg). Tanner could be a steal and is an outstanding perimeter shooter. He was headed to Arkansas-Little Rock, but decided to join his brother at Delaware State.

"Tanner could make an impact with us right away because he is an outstanding three-point shooter," DuBose said. "He shot better than 60 percent in his career out there from the three-point line and that is really going to make us a better basketball team this year."

DuBose also likes the other freshman, 6-7 forward **Amin Norris** (14.8 ppg, 8.0 rpg), who played at national prep power St. Anthony's HS in Jersey City, N.J.

"Amin is a diamond in the rough," DuBose said. "He's a very skilled big man who is just going to get better and better with experience. I really believe he could be Deleware State's all-time leading scorer before his career is over if he develops the way we hope he does. We feel really good about getting him."

Also joining the team are two players frm College of the Desert in Palm Desert, Calif: 6-7 junior forward **Leon Piper** and 6-10 center **Darnel Cromer**. They could be the key to the Hornets' inside game, but they won't be eligible until Dec. 12.

"Leon is an excellent shooter and Darnel has some excellent big-man skills," DuBose said. "They both should give us an inside presence that we haven't had in the past. We're going to just try and hang on until Dec. 12 when they're eligible to play."

adidas Blue Ribbon Analysis

BACKCOURT	C	BENCH/DEPTH	B-
FRONTCOURT	C	INTANGIBLES	C

Delaware coach Jimmy DuBose has the kind of enthusiasm you can't help but like. It may be what this long-suffering progam needs.

Still, there will be a transition period with seven new players, and DuBose can't turn the program around over night.

The point-guard job will be in better hands this season with Stephan Malliat, who averaged 25 points in junior college. Can he make the transition from a scoring point guard to a passing point guard? He'd better. Malliat will need to get the basketball to Terence Hood.

The Hornets have the talent for a winning season and that will be an accomplishment. It hasn't happened in eight years at Delaware State. Look for a seventh-place finish this year, but keep your eye on this program. DuBose seems to be building it the right way.

(M.G.)

1998-99 DELAWARE STATE SCHEDULE

Nov.	18	@Delaware
	20-21	#Mohegan Sun Classic
	24	@Drake
Dec.	1	@UCLA
	7	@Hampton
	10	@Maryland-Eastern Shore
	14	@Norfolk State
Jan.	2	Bethune-Cookman
	4	Florida A&M
	9	@Stonybrook
	11	@Howard
	16	Coppin State
	18	Morgan State
	23	@North Carolina A&T
	25	@South Carolina State
	30	Hampton
Feb.	1	Norfolk State
	3	Lehigh
	6	@Bethune-Cookman
	8	@Florida A&M
	15	Howard
	20	@Coppin State
	22	@Morgan State
	27	Maryland-Eastern Shore
Mar.	2-6	##MEAC Tournament

@ Road Games
\# New Britain, CT (vs. New Hampshire, first round; also Brown and Central Connecticut)
\## Richmond Coliseum, Richmond, VA

FLORIDA A&M

LOCATION .... **Tallahassee, FL**
CONFERENCE .... **Mid-Eastern Athletic (MEAC)**
LAST SEASON .... **11-17 (.393)**
CONFERENCE RECORD .... **8-10 (5th)**
STARTERS LOST/RETURNING **2/3**
NICKNAME .... **Rattlers**
COLORS .... **Orange & Green**
HOMECOURT .... **Gaither Center (3,365)**
COACH .... **Mickey Clayton (Florida A&M '75)**
RECORD AT SCHOOL .... **21-42 (2+ yrs.)**
CAREER RECORD .... **21-42 (2+ yrs.)**
ASSISTANTS .... **Melvin Smith**
Jim Baxter
TEAM WINS (last 5 yrs.) **4-5-8-8-11**
RPI (last 5 yrs.) **298-300-301-285-261**
1997-98 FINISH .... **Lost in conference semifinal.**

Florida A&M made some more strides toward respectability last season, reaching the semifinals of the MEAC Tournament for the first time in several years.

The Rattlers' 11 victories were the most for the program since the 1992-93 season. After the season, 7-1 center Jerome James (19.9 ppg, 10.4 rpg, 4.6 blocks per game) was drafted in the second round by the Sacramento Kings.

This year, Florida A&M could take some more strides in the right direction.

Losing James will hurt, but coach Mickey Clayton has the program moving forward. They might not be ready to win the MEAC, but they should still have a solid season.

"We feel like the MEAC is broken up into three tiers," Clayton said. "We're not in the top half with Coppin and South Carolina State, but we believe we're in the middle tier and moving up. We're making progress, but we're not where we want to be just yet. Obviously we're going to miss Jerome We were ranked in the top 10 nationally in defense the past two years and he was a big reason why. But we're going to be OK.

"We're going to have a different look this year. We've got some more speed to play more of an up-tempo game and play more pressure defense, and I'm excited about that."

The Rattlers' top player this year should be 6-3 senior shooting guard **Monroe Pippins** (10.3 ppg, 3.4 rpg, 63 steals, 43 three-pointers). Pippins was a transfer last year from Fulton-Montgomery (N.Y.) CC who helped the Rattlers down the stretch.

"Monroe will be the key to our defensive pressure this year," Clayton said. "We need him to get our defense going, but I'm confident he can do that. Monroe is an explosive scorer who can score in bunches. He took awhile to get started last year, but once he got going, he really played great for us. Monroe should be even better this year."

Another transfer who played for the Rattlers last year, 6-4 senior guard/forward **Roderick Seay** (10.0 ppg, 3.8 rpg, 39 assists) also got off to a slow start before coming on at the end of the season. The Furman transfer had reason for a slow start after having surgery on both shoulders before the season. Despite that, he was the team's third-leading scorer.

"Roderick had some problems early because of the injuries to his shoulders, but he had pretty good numbers despite all he went through," Clayton said. "Like Monroe, he really played well for us at the end of the season. Roderick will play either the (shooting guard or small forward) this season. He's a great penetrator who can score in traffic. He's very athletic and that makes him a good defender, and with us playing more pressure defense this year that should come in handy."

Also looking for playing time at shooting guard will be 6-4 junior **Travis Grant** (4.3 ppg, 1.4 rpg, .490 three-point percentage). Grant has played sparingly, but this could be a breakout year for him.

"Travis is a real zone buster," Clayton said. "He's one of our better shooters and we're going to try and get him the ball some this year so he can help us with three-point

1998-99 FLORIDA A&M SCHEDULE

Nov.	16	@Auburn
	21	*Bethune-Cookman
	24	Jacksonville State
Dec.	5	@Troy State
	12	@North Carolina A&T
	15	@South Carolina State
	19	@Wichita State
	28-29	#Capital City Classic
Jan.	2	@Maryland-Eastern Shore
	4	@Delaware State
	9	@Morgan State
	11	@Coppin State
	16	Norfolk State
	18	Hampton
	23	@Howard
	30	South Carolina State
Feb.	1	North Carolina A&T
	6	Maryland-Eastern Shore
	8	Delaware State
	13	Morgan State
	15	Coppin State
	20	@Norfolk State
	22	@Hampton
	26	@Bethune-Cookman
Mar.	3-6	##MEAC Tournament

@ Road Games
* Orlando Arena, Orlando Florida
# Tallahassee, FL (vs. Jacksonville, first round; also Niagara and Radford)
Richmond Coliseum, Richmond, VA

shooting."

Florida A&M's small forward spot could be the deepest in the league with the addition of 6-5 sophomore forward **Brian Johnson**. Johnson enjoyed a solid freshman season two years ago at California-Irvine, earning all-rookie honors in the Big West after averaging 12.3 points. He sat out last season.

"Brian is very athletic and knows how to finish a play off," Clayton said. "We think he could play either the three or the four for us this year."

Another small forward who could have a big season is 6-6 sophomore **Kendric Green** (3.5 ppg, 1.4 rpg). Green was the leading scorer in Miami and Dade County coming out of high school, but wasn't eligible until December and didn't play his best ball until the end of the season.

"Kendric could be a real force for us," Clayton said. "Last year was tough because he couldn't play until December, but he got better and better as the year went on. He's a good three-point shooter and another very athletic player on the perimeter for us."

The point-guard job was suppossed to be held by senior Willie Bullock, but he decided to transfer to Pfeiffer College. Bullock shot just .330 from the field and averaged two assists a game.

Bullock's replacement could be 6-0 sophomore **Morris Scott** (3.9 ppg, 2.8 rpg, 38 assists), who played well for the Rattlers in the second half of the season. Clayton believes Scott can do the job. Scott didn't play in the early part of the season because of a broken hand sustained when James stepped on it during a practice.

"Morris bounced back well from getting hurt by Jerome and played really well for us in the second half of the year," Clayton said. "We even managed to start him a few games in the last half of the year and he really responded. Morris can do the job for us this year."

Scott will battle for the starting job at point guard with **John Cuyler**, a 6-0 freshman from Dunbar HS in Glenndale, Md. Cuyler averaged 19.5 points and 10.5 assists last season.

"John's a true point guard who is very quick and very athletic," Clayton said. "He just needs a more consistent jumper, but he'll definitely battle for playing time at the point this year."

Frank Oliver Jr. (2.5 ppg, 1.5 rpg), a 5-11 junior guard, played sparingly last season, but made 15 three-point shots. He will vie for more time this season.

The biggest challenge will be replacing James, but Clayton believes he has some options, starting with 6-10 senior center **Kevin George** (4.6 ppg, 3.1 rpg). George wasn't eligible until the second semester and played in 11 games. He started nine games and was brought along slowly by Clayton. He could be a sleeper after an offseason of hard work.

Also joining the team will be 6-9 forward/center **Jamal Rhodes** from San Jacinto JC in Houston. Rhodes could give A&M a shot blocker who can rebound and score.

Also in the mix is 6-9 senior center **Herb Woodard** (1.2 ppg, 1.8 rpg). He will provide depth behind George and Rhodes.

"You can't replace Jerome but we have some players that we think can do a good job inside and give us what we want in the pivot," Clayton said.

Also expected to play power forward is 6-7 junior **Jamie Johnson**, a transfer from Jacksonville. The Tallahassee native could play either frontcourt position.

"Jamie could give us some inside scoring that we lost with Jerome," Clayton said. "He's an athletic player who knows how to score inside and that's an area we will need help with this year."

Also looking for playing time in the post will be 6-5 senior forward **Derrick Magee** (2.2 ppg, 1.8 rpg) and 6-5 senior forward **Norris Fletcher** (3.4 ppg, 3.5 rpg). Both have experience and should provide depth in the frontcourt.

adidas Blue Ribbon Analysis

BACKCOURT .... **C-** **BENCH/DEPTH** .... **C**
FRONTCOURT .... **C-** **INTANGIBLES** .... **C**

Florida A&M should be even better than last year, despite the loss of 7-1 center Jerome James.

Rattlers coach Mickey Clayton likes to play a pressing style and with this year's team he should be able to do that. There's some good talent with players such as Monroe Pippins and Roderick Seay returning along with newcomers Brian Johnson and Jamie Johnson.

If Morris Scott can do the job at point guard, Florida A&M could earn its first winning season in a number of years.

However, the Rattlers probably won't make a move into the top of the MEAC standings. This program is still another good recruiting class from making a push into the top three in the conference.

The Rattlers are definitly moving in the right direction, though. Look for a fifth-place finish and perhaps a berth in the MEAC semifinals again.

(M.G.).

HAMPTON

LOCATION .... **Hampton, VA**
CONFERENCE .... **Mid-Eastern Athletic (MEAC)**
LAST SEASON .... **14-12 (.538)**
CONFERENCE RECORD .... **11-7 (t-3rd)**
STARTERS LOST/RETURNING **1/4**
NICKNAME .... **Pirates**
COLORS .... **Royal Blue & White**
HOMECOURT .... **Convocation Center (7,200)**
COACH .... **Steve Merfield (Wisconsin-Lacrosse '84)**
RECORD AT SCHOOL .... **14-12 (1 yr.)**
CAREER RECORD .... **14-12 (1 yr.)**
ASSISTANTS .. **Bobby Collins (Eastern Kentucky '90)**
Richard Morgan (Virginia '89)
Walter Mebane (North Carolina '87)
TEAM WINS (last 5 yrs.) **19-19-9-8-14**
RPI (last 5 yrs.) **N/A-N/A-234-291-210**
1997-98 FINISH .... **Not eligible for conference tournament.**

Christmas came early for Hampton last summer.

That's because the NCAA changed its eight-year mandatory waiting period for new Division I schools to be eligible for the NCAA Tournament.

Now schools just have to wait two years before becoming eligible to make an appearance in the Big Dance. And Hampton, which had been a Division I member for four years, is now eligible. The Pirates can now take part in the MEAC Tournament, which they couldn't play in before for fear they might have won, thus handing a team ineligible for the NCAA Tournament the league's only automatic bid.

This is all very good news for several obvious reasons, perhaps most importantly for recruiting.

The Pirates were the surprise of the MEAC last season, but they won't surprise people this year. Most of the coaches in the league believe Hampton could contend for the conference title.

"You've got Coppin and South Carolina State but Hampton's going to be right up there," said Deleware State coach James DuBose.

"I look for Hampton to make a real impact in the MEAC race this year and be one of the teams to beat," said South Carolina State coach Cy Alexander, coach of the defending MEAC champions and the preseason pick to win it again this year.

Second-year coach Steve Merfeld won't make such bold predictions.

Last year, he was the interim coach, replacing Byron Samuels, who left in the summer of '97 to join Jerry Green's staff at Tennessee. Merfeld had served as an assistant under Samuels for two years.

Merfeld did an outstanding job after branching out on his own, molding a young team into a winner. The Pirates' last six games were on the road, and with no postseason berth at stake, they played for a winning season and won four of their last six. That mission was accomplished, and there was even an added bonus—third place in the MEAC.

"We had a nice year last season," Merfeld said. "We were able to stay injury free and got some breaks in a couple of games down the stretch to pull out some wins. Being in an interim situation isn't easy for anyone, but to our players' credit and out staff's credit, we made the most of it and things worked out."

While Merfeld has reason to be cautiously optimistic, the Pirates do appear to be talented. They return four starters and 11 lettermen and have added three newcomers, including former Norfolk State star **Tajai Young**.

"We have depth this year and that's always a positive when you have that," Merfeld said.

Last year Merfeld had a newcomer who produced in a big way: 6-8 junior center **Tarvis Williams** (12.2 ppg, 6.4 rpg, 83 blocked shots), who earned MEAC Rookie-of-the-Year honors.

"Tarvis was a pleasant surprise because he developed so early," Merfeld said. "We knew he had the potential to be good, but we wanted to take it slowly. But he kept developing and we had to put him in the starting lineup because he kept producing for us. He's so athletic and very explosive with the ball. He also helps our defense because he's a great shot blocker."

Also back is 5-10 senior shooting guard **Torrey Farrington** (**12.5** ppg, 3.4 rpg, 70 three-point goals). Farrington has improved each season, along with the Pirates.

"Torrey has grown with our program and has done a great job for us at the shooting-guard position," Merfeld said. "He's a leader and accepts that role quite well. Torrey shoots the three very well and should be ready to have a great senior season."

Hampton has a good situation at point guard with the return of two game-tested players from last season. They are 5-10 senior **Ramont Hawkins** (4.6 ppg, 2.5 rpg, 79 assists) and 5-10 junior **Damany Smith** (3.5 ppg, 3.1 rpg, 95 assists). They split playing time and should do the same this year.

"Ramont and Damany did a great job for us at the point and we're real fortunate to have two high-quality point guards who we can play and understand their role," Merfeld said. "We're concerned about Damany's health because he's had some foot problems in the offseason and we're going to bring him back slowly. We think he'll be ready by the time practice comes but we're going to be cautious with

1998-99 HAMPTON SCHEDULE

Nov.	14	@Maine
	18	@Old Dominion
	23	North Carolina
	25	@Virginia
	28	William & Mary
Dec.	4	Maryland-Eastern Shore
	7	Delaware State
	12	Norfolk State
	21	@Michigan
	29-30	#Dr Pepper Classic
Jan.	4	@Howard
	9	North Carolina A&T
	11	South Carolina State
	16	@Bethune-Cookman
	18	@Florida A&M
	23	Coppin State
	25	@Morgan State
	30	@Delaware State
Feb.	1	@Maryland Eastern Shore
	8	Howard
	13	@North Carolina A&T
	15	@South Carolina State
	20	Bethune-Cookman
	22	Florida A&M
	27	@Norfolk State
Mar.	4-6	##MEAC Tournament

@ Road Games
# Chattanooga, TN (vs. Samford, first round; also Rider and Tennessee-Chattanooga)
Richmond Coliseum, Richmond, VA

him."

The newcomer who should make an impact is Young, a 6-5 junior transfer. Young played at Norfolk State two seasons ago in the Spartans' last year of Division II and earned Central Intercollegiate Athletic Association Rookie-of-the-Year honors. He left Norfolk after one year and transferred to Seminole (Okla.) JC, where he averaged 11 points, five rebounds and six assists. He is a versatile player who can play in the frontcourt or perimeter.

"Tajai can play the point-guard position and either forward spot," Merfeld said. "We feel good about getting him and believe he can help us. Because of his versatility, he can do a lot of different things and we plan to take advantage of that this season."

Senior guard/forward **Greg Brown** (12.4 ppg, 5.1 rpg) could be ready to have a big season at small forward. He can also play shooting guard.

Brown, 6-3, is a solid long-range shooter who was second on the team last year with 62 three-pointers.

"Greg is a very mature player who we really like," Merfeld said. "We plan to use him at the two or the three this year because he shoots the ball very well from the three-point line. He's difficult to guard on the perimeter and we expect him to have another good season for us."

Merfeld has high hopes for 6-6 junior forward **Doug Belton** (10.8 ppg, 4.4 rpg), who should help the Pirates' frontcourt again. Belton was Hampton's sixth man last season and was second on the team in field-goal percentage (.510).

"You'd like to have 13 Doug Belton's on your team," Merfeld said.

Senior center **Kenyo Hunter** (2.7 ppg, 2.6 rpg) struggled last year after transferring to Hampton from Otero (Colo.) JC. Merfeld expects better play from the 6-8 Hunter after a year of adjustment to Division I.

"Kenyo struggled some last year but he's had a year to figure things out and should be better for it," Merfeld said. "We graduated a pretty good center in Brent Johnson (4.3 ppg, 4.6 rpg) and that's what we'd like Kenyo to do this season is try and replace Brent."

Providing depth in the backcourt this year will be 6-2 sophomore **Treston Dowell** (2.6 ppg, 1.4 rpg), 6-3 freshmen guard **Tommy Adams** and 6-4 freshman guard **Ricky Moore**. Adams played at Hylton HS in Woodbridge, Va. and averaged 19 points and five rebounds. He is an excellent shooter who could provide some scoring.

Moore averaged 31 points and 11 rebounds at tiny Word of God Academy in Raleigh, N.C. Moore was an explosive scorer in a very small league.

The frontcourt will have depth with 6-5 senior forward **Jason Jackson** (0.5 ppg, 0.5 rpg) and 6-6 sophomore forward **Dain Ervin** (2.7 ppg, 1.0 rpg). Neither played much a year ago.

adidas Blue Ribbon Analysis

BACKCOURT	**B-**	**BENCH/DEPTH**	**C+**
FRONTCOURT	**C+**	**INTANGIBLES**	**B-**

There's a lot to like about this Hampton team.

The Pirates aren't waiting for players to become eligible, and they're not counting on freshmen. There are two talented point guards, Ramont Hawkins and Damany Smith, and a proven newcomer, Tajai Young.

However, Hampton won't sneak up on anybody. Coaches around the league see the Pirates as a tough bunch, possibly even contenders for the league title.

That doesn't seem likely, though, so look for a fourth-place finish and a very bright future. After this season, the Pirates might be picked near the top for the next several years.

(M.G.)

adidas Blue Ribbon Analysis

GRADING SYSTEM

- A+ equal to very best in country—Final Four-caliber unit
- A among the best in the land—worthy of deep NCAA run
- B+ talented, versatile and experienced—NCAA-NIT ability
- B solid and productive winners—league and post-season contenders
- C+ average to above-average—may contend in a weaker league
- C average to mediocre—second division in a strong league
- D+ below average, inconsistent—second division in a weaker league
- D well below average—losing season virtually certain
- F non-Division I ability—an underdog every night

HOWARD

LOCATION .... **Washington, DC**
CONFERENCE .... **Mid-Eastern Athletic (MEAC)**
LAST SEASON .... **8-20 (.286)**
CONFERENCE RECORD .... **6-12 (8th)**
STARTERS LOST/RETURNING **2/3**
NICKNAME .... **Bison**
COLORS .... **Blue, Red & White**
HOMECOURT .... **Burr Gymnasium (2,700)**
COACH .... **Kirk Saulny (Southeast Louisiana '79)**
RECORD AT SCHOOL .... **First year**
CAREER RECORD .... **First year**
ASSISTANTS Lamont Franklin (UNC-Wilmington '97)
Darrell Bruce (Towson '90)
TEAM WINS (last 5 yrs.) **10-9-7-7-8**
RPI (last 5 yrs.) **268-282-292-292-292**
1997-98 FINISH .... **Lost in conference quarterfinal.**

Howard is starting over under first-year coach Kirk Saulny, who inherits a tough job. Saulny, an assistant at North Carolina-Wilmington for four years under Jerry Wainwright, also worked for Benny Dees at New Orleans, so he's been associated with some good head coaches. He'll need all the wisdom he absorbed from his former bosses, and then some.

At the end of a sub-par season, Howard coach Mike McLese was fired. Saulny took over in June, way too late to do any serious recruiting.

As if that wasn't a difficult enough start to his career, Saulny suffered a serious setback in August when first-team all-conference guard Xavier Singletary decided to transfer to Boston College. Singletary led the MEAC in scoring last year, averaging 22.2 points and 6.1 rebounds.

"On paper, it doesn't look good," Saulny said. "We have our work cut out for us in a tough conference and I'm sure we'll be picked pretty low when predictions come out, but we can't worry about that because thankfully games aren't played on paper."

Saulny hated to lose Singletary, but tries to put a positive spin on it.

"I'm looking forward to coaching the guys here," Saulny said. "Xavier had a tough decision and I tried to advise him and to look at both sides. He did and I know he tossed and turned with it, but he decided to move on and we wish him well."

The problem for Saulny right now is numbers. Howard has just 10 players. That means lots of playing time for everbody—possibly too much. And with a few exceptions, there's not a whole lot of scoring returning.

"We have some guys on the roster that we want to play good defense, rebound and help us do a lot of little things," Saulny said. "However, with such a small roster, that's not a good sign when you have so many players who you're asking to do that."

One player who can score is 5-8 sophomore point guard **Ali Abdullah** (9.5 ppg, 2.8 rpg, 235 assists). Abdullah had a solid freshman season and earned first-team all-rookie honors. Saulny hopes for an even better season from the New Jersey native.

"Ali is a talented player who has the potential to be even better," Saulny said. "The big thing for him is he has to learn to make decisions quicker when he has the ball. We also need him to be a leader, a boss on the floor but not in a bossy way."

Also looking to score more this season is 6-4 senior swingman **Melvin Watson** (12.1 ppg, 4.4 rpg). Watson will get his points, but Saulny is looking for more than just scoring from him.

"We need Melvin to be a leader both on and off the court this year," Saulny said. "He's a quiet kid, but certainly a proven scorer and we'll need him for that this season. But what I'd really like is for him to be a leader for this team."

Junior **Jermaine Holloway** (6.8 ppg, 3.7 rpg) will probably play power forward this year. Saulny likes the potential of the 6-5 Holloway.

Competing for playing time will be 6-10 senior center **Ogoumi Real** (0.7 ppg. 1.4 rpg,), but the Cameroon native isn't a big scorer. "Ogoumi is in unbelievable shape and what we want from him this year is to clog up the middle, rebound and block some shots," Saulny said. "He hasn't played the game long and lacks certain knowledge of the game, but we're going to put him out on the high post every now and then and let him shoot from there and see what happens."

Also expected to play center is 6-7 sophomore **Dave Libbett** (3.8 ppg, 3.8 rpg). Libbett missed the Bisons' first 10 games last season, but proved to be an effective rebounder later in the year. He had 13 rebounds in a home victory over Bethune-Cookman and also had seven rebounds in three other games.

"I compare Dave to Dennis Rodman in the way he gets rebounds and his intensity for the game," Saulny said. "We want Dave to rebound and defend this year and score if he can."

Also returning is 6-3 junior shooting guard **Antonio Mitchell** (0.9 ppg, 0.5 rpg), who didn't play much last year but is a good defensive player. He needs to work on his shooting and limit his turnovers to get more playing time.

One player Saulny is anxious to work with is 6-8 junior forward **Garrett McCormick** (1.4 ppg, 1.2 rpg). Several Big East, Atlantic 10 and Colonial Conference schools looked at McCormick before he decided to attend Howard. McCormick can play either power forward or center.

"I remember Garrett out of high school and a lot of schools were interested in him," Saulny said. "Things haven't worked out for him here so far, so I think with the coaching change he'll have a fresh start with me and we'll go from there. He's definitely got some talent and I'm looking forward to working with him. I think Garrett has a chance to help us inside."

While some of Howard's players will specialize in defense and rebounding, 5-9 senior guard **Byron Bailey** (2.3 ppg, 0.5 rpg) could need to score more points.

"Byron has a reputation as a great stand-still shooter who hasn't been used much in the past," Saulny said. "We're going to see if we can get him some shots this year and help our offense. Being a senior, we're also looking for leadership from him. He's one of our few older kids and we'll need him to be positive and work with us."

Another Bison who could have more of an impact this year will be 6-6 redshirt freshman forward **Byron Alvin**. Alvin could be an inside scorer.

"Byron appears to be a real good scorer with an unorthodox way of doing it," Saulny said. "He could be pretty effective for us this year if we play a lot of half-court basketball which we might very well have to do. Byron is an Adrian Dantley type-scorer that seems to know how to get the ball in the hoop."

The only freshman is 5-10 guard **Marquis Strange** from Cathedral City (Cal.) HS. He seemed destined for Howard. If Strange succeeds, it would be one of the better stories in college basketball.

"I had just gotten the job when Marquis wrote me a very interesting letter about how it was his dream to play at Howard," Saulny said. "He was getting offers from other places, but the place he wanted to be was Howard. I liked the magnetism of the letter and I had him send a tape. I got the tape and I was impressed with his athleticism and decided this is the kind of person we want in our program."

adidas Blue Ribbon Analysis

BACKCOURT	**C**	**BENCH/DEPTH**	**D**
FRONTCOURT	**D**	**INTANGIBLES**	**C**

Howard coach Kirk Saulny's luck has gotten a little

1998-99 HOWARD SCHEDULE

Nov.	14	@Loyola
	18	American
	21	@LaSalle
	25	Delaware
Dec.	1	@George Mason
	5	Lafayette
	7	@Morgan State
	14	@Coppin State
	22	@Pittsburgh
	28	@Villanova
Jan.	2	Norfolk State
	4	Hampton
	9	Maryland-Eastern Shore
	11	Delaware State
	16	@North Carolina A&T
	18	@South Carolina State
	23	Florida A&M
	25	Bethune-Cookman
	30	Morgan State
Feb.	1	Coppin State
	6	@Norfolk State
	8	@Hampton
	13	@Maryland-Eastern Shore
	15	@Delaware State
	20	North Carolina A&T
	22	South Carolina State
Mar.	2-6	#MEAC Tournament

@ Road Games
\# Richmond Coliseum, Richmond, VA

better. He sold his house and had his family move from Wilmington, N.C. just before Hurricane Bonnie hit North Carolina's coast in late August.

Saulny can only hope his good luck continues this season.

The Bison will play a half-court game this year. They'll play tough defense and try to stay in games.

Howard has only two proven scorers in Melvin Watson and Ali Abdullah and its inside game consists of players Saulny simply wants to rebound and play defense.

There won't be a lot of victories, but this program will turn around soon. Not this year, though. Look for a ninth-place finish in the MEAC.

(M.G.)

MARYLAND-EASTERN SHORE

LOCATION .... **Princess Anne, MD**
CONFERENCE .... **Mid-Eastern Athletic (MEAC)**
LAST SEASON .... **9-18 (.333)**
CONFERENCE RECORD .... **7-11 (7th)**
STARTERS LOST/RETURNING **3/2**
NICKNAME .... **Fighting Hawks**
COLORS .... **Maroon & Gray**
HOMECOURT .... **Physical Ed. & Athletic Complex (5,000)**
COACH .... **Lonnie Williams (Eastern Washington '80)**
RECORD AT SCHOOL .... **20-35 (2 yrs.)**
CAREER RECORD .... **171-158 (11 yrs.)**
ASSISTANTS .... **Arturo Ormond (Texas-Pan American ('93)**
TEAM WINS (last 5 yrs.) **16-13-11-11-9**
RPI (last 5 yrs.) **237-265-287-280-276**
1997-98 FINISH .... **Lost in conference quarterfinal.**

Shhhh. Third-year Maryland Eastern Shore coach Lonnie Williams believes he has a pretty good basketball team, but he doesn't want people to know.

He wants to sneak up and suprise people.

Williams is trying to build a winner at a school that doesn't have a lot of tradition. In more than 20 years of Division I basketball, the Fighting Hawks have had just one winning season. This year could be the year they get their second.

Why? For the first time since Williams has taken over, his program has depth. Nine new players, including some impact players, should make the Fighting Hawks a MEAC contender this season.

Also, the Fighting Hawks will play in a new arena this season. The Health and Physical Education facility will seat 5,000 and will be one of the finest in the MEAC.

"We're very optimistic about the upcoming year," Williams said. "We feel like we've got a good team back, plus some good players coming into the program who can help us right away, and we're really excited about the new arena. That's going to help us in recruiting and should give us a real homecourt advantage."

At the midpoint of the 1997-98 season, Maryland-Eastern Shore had a 7-8 record and was 5-2 in the MEAC before injuries crept up and stopped its momentum. It went 2-10 mark in the last month of the season and lost to Morgan State in the first round of the league tournament.

"Injuries just killed us down the stretch and that's where our lack of depth came in," Williams said. "We didn't have enough depth to make up for some of the injuries."

Coaches seldom count on newcomers, but Williams is confident some of his can contribute early this season.

"We like the players we have coming back but we feel some of the new guys we have coming in can make us a better basketball program right away," he said. "The new guys we have coming in will help prevent us from struggling down the stretch like we did last year if we have any injuries."

Several returnees will help too, including 6-0 senior point guard **Joel Hoover** (10.8 ppg, 3.4 rpg, 100 assists, 74 steals). Hoover has been the Hawks' starter at point guard the last two seasons and he led the nation in steals two seasons ago. However, his starting job isn't guaranteed and Williams wants to see some improvement from Hoover.

"Joel's worked hard this summer to get better and we need him to be more consistent this year," Williams said.

1998-99 MARYLAND-EASTERN SHORE SCHEDULE

Nov.	14	@North Carolina State
	21	Niagara
	23	@Virginia Commonwealth
	28	@James Madison
Dec.	4	@Hampton
	6	@Norfolk State
	10	Delaware State
	22	@Georgtown
	29	@St. Francis (PA)
Jan.	2	Florida A&M
	4	Bethune-Cookman
	9	@Howard
	13	@Rider
	16	Morgan State
	18	Coppin State
	23	@South Carolina State
	30	Norfolk State
Feb.	1	Hampton
	6	@Florida A&M
	8	@Bethune-Cookman
	13	Howard
	20	@Morgan State
	22	@Coppin State
	25	@Delaware State
Mar.	3-6	#MEAC Tournament

@ Road Games
\# Richmond Coliseum, Richmond, VA

"But he's going to get some competition this year and that should help make him better."

Hoover will get competition for the point-guard job from 6-3 junior-college transfer **Edwin Colbert** and 5-9 freshman **Joshua Hickman**. Colbert comes from Carl Albert State (Okla.) CC, while Hickman is an in-state player from Pocomoke (Md.) HS, where he played for a state championship team.

"We feel really lucky about getting Edwin, because he's a big-time player who will be pushing for a starting job in the backcourt," Williams said. "Joshua is a very smart and steady player who will give us some depth here."

The Hawks' biggest question this year is at shooting guard, where leading scorer Cryhten Langhorne (16.2 ppg, 5.4 rpg, 32 three-pointers) must be replaced. Langhorne was injured late last year and missed the last five games, during which the Hawks went 0-5.

Williams has tried to replace Langhorne with 6-5 junior-college transfer **Demetric Reese** of Columbia State (Tenn.) JC.

"We feel like Demetric is a mid-major player who will be able to step right in and help us," Williams said. "He's very strong and a great athlete who can shoot the ball quite well."

Adding depth at shooting guard will be 6-5 junior **Jason Conway** (3.4 ppg, 1.8 rpg) and 6-6 junior newomer **Kevin Wallace** from Casper CC in Casper, Wyo.

In the frontcourt, the Fighting Hawks could be solid if everything falls into place, starting with 6-8 senior forward **Jeremy Jones** (8.9 ppg, 4.5 rpg), who was a second-team all-conference player last season. Jones shot 50 percent rom the field, and Williams believes he can be even more effective this year.

"Jeremy is a solid player for us on the block who is going to be even better with some players around him," Williams said. "He's one of the best big men in the MEAC and we think he's ready to have a great year."

Newcomers who are going to help Jones this year include 6-8 junior-college transfer **Sheridan James**, who comes from Fulton-Montgomery (N.Y.) CC. He averaged 18 points and 13 rebounds last season. Also, 6-7 junior forward **Cederick Rashaw** of Southwestern Christian College in Terrell, Texas should help the Hawks' rebounding.

"Sheridan is an inside player who can score, while Cederick reminds me off a Dennis Rodman type who can rebound everything in site," Williams said.

Hoping for more playing time will be 6-5 senior forward **Ron Christian** (2.9 ppg, 2.5 rpg).

Senior forward **Bram Reynolds** (3.7 ppg, 1.0 rpg), a 6-5 returnee, has some offensive ability. He had 21 three-point goals last season, third-best on the team.

Also vying for more playing time will be 6-6 junior forward **Jamie White** (1.7 ppg, 1.2 rpg), but the minutes will be hard to come by.

The center spot will be taken by two newomers, and Williams likes both of them: 7-0 sophomore center **Brett Hughes** and 6-8 freshman center **Cecil Watson**. Hughes joins the program from Marion (Ala.) Military Academy, while Watson is from Gwynn Park HS in Brandywine, Md.

"Brett Hughes is a sleeping giant who we think is going to be a great player for us," Williams said. "He's a player who's a great shot blocker and is just going to get better and better for us. We didn't bring him to look good in the airport. We got him to play and he will. Cecil is very strong and a good athlete who will grow with our program"

adidas Blue Ribbon Analysis

BACKCOURT .... **C-** **BENCH/DEPTH** .... **C-**
FRONTCOURT .... **C-** **INTANGIBLES** .... **C**

With all the newcomers, Maryland-Eastern Shore coach Lonnie Williams expects to be picked near the bottom of the MEAC standings. That's OK with him.

"We know we'll be picked toward the bottom based on the past years we've had here and all the new guys we have," Williams said. "But one of our goals this year is to play higher than where we're picked."

Williams wants his team to be challenged, and that, in part, should help the Fighting Hawks escape the MEAC cellar.

Williams has a team that could finish with a winning record, but look for a sixth-place finish in the MEAC and a better record than last season.

(M.G.)

MORGAN STATE

LOCATION .... **Baltimore, MD**
CONFERENCE .... **Mid-Eastern Athletic (MEAC)**
LAST SEASON .... **12-16 (.429)**
CONFERENCE RECORD .... **11-7 (3rd)**
STARTERS LOST/RETURNING **2/3**
NICKNAME .... **Bears**
COLORS .... **Orange & Royal Blue**
HOMECOURT .... **Hill Field House (6,000)**
COACH .... **Chris Fuller (SUNY-Buffalo '73)**
RECORD AT SCHOOL .... **28-54 (3 yrs.)**
CAREER RECORD .... **28-54 (3 yrs.)**
ASSISTANTS .... **Chris Watson (Morgan State '97)**
TEAM WINS (last 5 yrs.) **8-5-7-9-12**
RPI (last 5 yrs.) **284-293-278-268-216**
1997-98 FINISH .... **Lost in conference semifinal.**

Baltimore will have two teams battling for the Mid-Eastern Athletic Conference championship this year.

Coppin State will again make a run at the title, but this year look for its crosstown rival, Morgan State, to make a move.

Chris Fuller begins his fourth year as the Bears coach, and he hopes to continue steady improvement in the program.

Morgan State is 28-54 during Fuller's tenure, but last year the Bears jumped to a third-place league finish with an 11-7 record. The Bears, who advanced to the semifinals of the conference tournament, won more league games than any Morgan State team since the 1977-78 season.

This could be the year Morgan State becomes a contender.

The Bears return three starters, 11 lettermen and have brought in some talented newcomers. That has Morgan State fans excited about the upcoming season, now that the stench of NCAA probation has worn off. Fuller seems to have the once-proud program moving upward.

"We wish we had won some more games the past few years but we're making progress," Fuller said. "We're moving in the right direction. We've managed to increase our win total each season and hopefully we can continue to do that this year."

Fuller is optimistic his team can continue to move in the right direction this season.

"We're still a young team," Fuller said. "But a lot of our young guys got some great experience last season. If we can grow up a little bit, then we have a chance to be a good team."

One big reason for optimism is the return of 6-3 senior guard/forward **Rasheed Sparks** (14.8 ppg, 6.0 rpg). Sparks enjoyed a stellar junior year and is the only 1997-98 first-team All-MEAC player returning this season. He led Morgan State in scoring and rebounding last year and shot 48 percent from the field. He scored 36 in a game against Coppin State last season.

Fuller expects the Newark, N.J. native to be even better this season.

"Rasheed has worked very hard in the offseason to get ready for this year," Fuller said. "I expect him to be a player-of-the-year candidate in the conference this year. To do that, he has to improve his shooting and his defense.

1998-99 MORGAN STATE SCHEDULE

Nov.	13	@James Madison
	16	@Marquette
	19-21	# Battle for Baltimore
	23	@ Xavier
Dec.	2	@Georgetown
	7	Howard
	12	Coppin State
	20	@Iona
	30	@Louisville
Jan.	2	@South Carolina State
	4	@North Carolina A&T
	9	Florida A&M
	11	Bethune-Cookman
	16	@Maryland Eastern Shore
	18	@Delaware State
	23	@Norfolk State
	25	Hampton
	30	Howard
Feb.	6	North Carolina A&T
	8	South Carolina State
	13	@Florida A&M
	15	@Bethune Cookman
	20	Maryland-Eastern Shore
	22	Delaware State
	27	Coppin State
Mar.	4-6	##MEAC Tournament

@ Road Games
\# Towson, MD (vs. Towson, first round; also Loyola College and Maryland-Baltimore County)
\## Richmond Coliseum, Richmond, VA

Rasheed has great ability and he showed that last year. He can just take a game over and we wouldn't mind him doing that about 27 times this season."

Sparks will be backed up by 6-2 junior forward **Ronnie Van Hook** (6.7 ppg, 1.5 rpg). The walkon will probably be the Bears' first player off the bench this year and Fuller likes what he gives the team.

"Ronnie is a tempo changer," Fuller said. "He has the quickest first step I've ever seen. He's so explosive and makes things happen. Ronnie is like our sixth starter."

One of the Bears' biggest questions this year is at point guard. Departed Lorenzo Hutchinson led the MEAC with 146 assists last season, setting a school record his senior year.

Fuller hopes he has a replacement in 5-10 junior guard **Jimmy Fields** (7.6 ppg, 2.6 rpg, 77 assists). Last year, Fields came to Morgan State as a highly touted transfer from UNC Charlotte.

In last year's season opener, Fields, a Baltimore native, scored 28 points in an overtime loss to NCAA Tournament participant Iona, but that was his season's highlight. He struggled from the field, shooting just 36 percent. His 91 turnovers overshadowed 77 assists.

"I don't care who you are but when you transfer, sit out a year and then come back and play, it takes time to adjust, and Jimmy's no different," Fuller said. "He's worked hard in the offseason and he's excited about this season. Jimmy will be ready this year and ready to do the job."

Another contender for the point guard job will be 5-10 junior **Angelo Herron** (2.3 ppg, 1.4 rpg in 1996-97). Herron didn't play last season but started some two years ago. He could play some this year.

"Angelo is a steady guard who knows how to play," Fuller said. Sparks is a versatile player, having played four positions during his career.

Other backcourt players are 6-2 junior guard **Hedrick McBride** (3.5 ppg, 1.1 rpg), 6-2 junior guard **Jason Demory** and 6-1 redshirt freshman guard **Corey McNeill.**

McBride is a walkon who played in 24 games and gave the Bears some quality minutes. He shot 50 percent from the field and 69 percent from the free-throw line.

Demory, who has good range on his jump shot, missed last year after averaging 1.7 points and 0.4 rebounds in 1996-97. McNeill injured his ankle in the preseason and played in just one game.

The frontcourt could be the Bears' strength. Two Philadelphia natives from Roman Catholic High School should handle the the bulk of the workload: 6-7 sophomore forward **Curtis King** (7.2 ppg, 3.4 rpg) and 6-11 sophomore center **Michael Canady** (6.5 ppg, 4.5 rpg). They return and are battle tested from their freshmen seasons.

"Curtis and Michael should be ready to have good years," Fuller said. "They played a lot last year and hit the wall late in the year, which I knew would happen. They struggled at times down the stretch, but they know what to expect this year and should be even tougher this season."

King earned first team all-rookie honors in the MEAC last year. He and Canady were two of the MEAC's best at blocking shots. King blocked 39 shots to finish fifth in the conference, while Canady blocked 43 to place fourth.

Canady earned second-team all-rookie honors last year, but Fuller fully expects improvement on his modest statistics from a year ago. "At 6-11, he's a very athletic player who wants to be great," Fuller said. "He works hard and longs to be out on the floor. We also need his defense to get better, but I expect it to this season."

Doug Qualls (2.7 ppg, 1.3 rpg), a 6-7 junior forward, should also help the Bears this year.

Also battling for playing time in the frontcourt will be 6-5 senior forward **Jerle Lewis** (5.2 ppg, 1.3 rpg). Last year, Lewis started and played in Morgan's first 10 games, scoring a career-high 20 points against Texas Christian. He missed the second half of the season after being declared academically ineligible. He needs work on his shooting (37 percent from the field, 46 percent from the line in '97-98).

Also returning are 6-7 sophomore forward **Brandon Dalton** (2.3 ppg, 0.6 rpg) and 6-8 sophomore center **John Doreinvil** (0.7 ppg, 0.8 rpg).

One of the keys to Fuller bringing the Morgan program back has been the ability to recruit in the Baltimore and Philadelphia area. Eight players on this year's roster hail from either Baltimore or Philadelphia.

Fuller signed two freshmen who could make an impact this season and—you guessed it—one is from Philly and the other from Baltimore.

Freshman forward **Reggie Bullock**, 6-7, of Philadelphia and 6-7 freshman forward **Brandon Reece** of Baltimore could be two key players for Morgan this year.

Bullock is a swingman who played at Franklin Learning Center and led his team to the Philadelphia's Public League Championship.

"I'm confident Reggie will find a place this year," Fuller said. "He's a great leaper who has a lot of defensive ability and has a good attitude. He could play a lot for us this year."

Reece went to St. Francis High School and was a starter on a team that won two straight Catholic League titles in Baltimore.

"Brandon is a banger who will play inside for us but he's also a good shooter who can hit the three," Fuller said. "He's a tough kid who we're glad to have in the program."

adidas Blue Ribbon Analysis

BACKCOURT	C+	BENCH/DEPTH	C+
FRONTCOURT	B-	INTANGIBLES	C+

A year ago, Morgan State was a surprise team that was perhaps a year from contending for the MEAC title.

The Bears were indeed a surprise, finishing third after being picked to finish anywhere from fourth to seventh.

Now, Morgan State's time to contend has arrived. The Bears should do it.

Rasheed Sparks may be best player in the MEAC this year, and Jimmy Fields should get the job done at the point guard spot. The Bears are loaded with talented inside players and if everybody understands their roles and playing time, good things should happen to this team.

Will they win the MEAC? Maybe. The big question is how will they handle the pressure of being a contender and not being able to sneak up on other people?

Look for a third-place finish behind South Carolina State and Coppin State.

(M.G.)

adidas Blue Ribbon Analysis

GRADING SYSTEM

- A+ equal to very best in country—Final Four-caliber unit
- A among the best in the land—worthy of deep NCAA run
- B+ talented, versatile and experienced—NCAA-NIT ability
- B solid and productive winners—league and post-season contenders
- C+ average to above-average—may contend in a weaker league
- C average to mediocre—second division in a strong league
- D+ below average, inconsistent—second division in a weaker league
- D well below average—losing season virtually certain
- F non-Division I ability—an underdog every night

NORFOLK STATE

LOCATION ... **Norfolk, VA**
CONFERENCE ... **Mid-Eastern Athletic (MEAC)**
LAST SEASON ... **6-22 (.222)**
CONFERENCE RECORD ... **N/A**
STARTERS LOST/RETURNING ... **1/4**
NICKNAME ... **Spartans**
COLORS ... **Green & Gold**
HOMECOURT ... **Echols Arena (7,600)**
COACH ... **Mel Coleman (Edward Walters '67)**
RECORD AT SCHOOL ... **First year**
CAREER RECORD ... **First year**
ASSISTANTS ... **Erik Rashad (Guilford '85)**
TEAM WINS (last 5 yrs.) ... **25-25-24-17-6**
RPI (last 5 yrs.) ... **NA-NA-NA-NA-268**
1997-98 FINISH ... **Not eligible for postseason tournament.**

Last year was Norfolk State's first season in Division I. It was a young team that played 19 games on the road and finished with a predictable record.

Progress was slow and steady for coach Michael Bernard, but despite that, his contract wasn't renewed in the summer.

Enter assistant coach Mel Coleman, who was announced as interim coach for the 1998-99 season. Suddenly, the program seems in chaos.

"I was in shock when it happened and I'm still in shock," Coleman said. "We're just going to try and keep going. Life isn't easy and obviously this isn't easy, but we'll just keep going and make the best of it."

Coleman will coach the team this year and Norfolk State will take applications for the position next year. Where does that leave Coleman?

"We'll worry about that when the time comes and let the chips fall where they may. Right now we can't be concerned about that," Coleman said.

The Spartans have brought in six new players to try and meet some needs. Getting a dependable point guard and some inside players were top priorities, and Coleman believes that has been accomplished.

"We feel good about our recruiting class," Coleman said. "We think we've got some people that can help us right away and make a difference."

One returning player who should help is 6-5 junior shooting guard/small forward **Damian Woolfolk** (18.3 ppg, 3.1 rpg). Woolfolk was the MEAC's fourth-leading scorer last year, but Coleman says he needs help this season.

"Damian scored most of his points in the first half of games last year and then because we didn't have much behind him, he didn't score much in the second half," Coleman said. "We need to get him some help because we don't need him playing close to 40 minutes per game like he did a year ago. We need to be a little more diverse on offense and have other people step up and score."

Coleman seems to have filled a need for a solid point guard, bringing in two: 6-2 sophomore **Dion Dove** from Allen (Kan.) CC and 6-0 freshman **Terrence Wilson** from nearby Wilson HS in Portsmouth, Va. Dove averaged 11 points last season, while Wilson averaged 18 points.

"Dion and Terrence should both help us this year," Coleman said. "They'll both have a crack at starting at the point this season, but both will play. We think both have the capability of getting the job done here this season and making us better."

Senior **Kevin Perry** (14.7 ppg, 2.0 rpg) started the season as the point guard, without good results. Perry, 6-3, made 134 turnovers and had 83 assists. He led the Spartans with 46 three-pointers and will probably play shooting guard this year.

"It just didn't work out with Kevin at the point, so we're going to move him back to the two-guard where he's most comfortable," Coleman said. "We think he'll fit better there."

Expected to play small forward will be 6-5 senior **Will Brooks** (9.4 ppg, 3.2 rpg). Coleman is looking for more consistency from Brooks this season and for him to improve his .360 field-goal percentage.

Returning to the frontcourt is 6-8 sophomore forward **Darrell Neal** (5.4 ppg, 3.7 rpg) and 6-6 senior **Maurice Howell**, back after taking a year off. Howell played a significant role in the '96-97 season, when the Spartans

1998-99 NORFOLK STATE SCHEDULE

Nov.	18	@McNeese State
	25	Georgia State
	28	Valparasio
Dec.	2	@Valparasio
	6	Maryland-Eastern Shore
	12	@Hampton
	14	Delaware State
	19	@Virginia Commonwealth
	28-29	#Utah State Christmas Tournament
Jan.	2	@Howard
	4	Liberty
	6	Radford
	9	South Carolina State
	11	North Carolina A&T
	16	@Florida A&M
	18	@Bethune-Cookman
	23	Morgan State
	25	@Coppin State
	30	@Maryland-Eastern Shore
Feb.	1	@Delaware State
	6	Howard
	13	@South Carolina State
	15	@North Carolina A&T
	20	Florida A&M
	22	Bethune-Cookman
	27	Hampton

@ Road Games
# Logan, UT (vs. Utah State, first round; also Lafayette and Troy State)
Richmond Coliseum, Richmond, VA

won their last CIAA championship.

Coleman signed four players destined for the frontcourt: 6-7 junior **Jeff Richardson** from Carl Sandburg (Ill.) CC, 6-6 junior **Neal Roberts** from Alleghany CC in Pittsburgh, 6-8 junior **Kala Dawson** from Salem CC in Carneys Point, N.J. and 6-8 freshman center **George Bailey** from St. John Newman HS in Philadelphia.

Richardson (18.0 ppg, 11.0 rpg) should be the Spartans' starting center. Coleman likes the Illinois native's toughness.

"Jeff Richardson is a warrior and we're going to need his leadership this season," Coleman said. "He's very strong and has a solid low-post game and we think he'll be our starting center this season.

Roberts, who averaged 13 points and 7.0 rebounds last year, could play either forward spot and is known as a great shooter.

Dawson averaged 10 points and eight rebounds last season and will battle for the starting strong-forward spot with Roberts.

Bailey, who averaged 17 points and 10 rebounds last season, appears to be a player of the future for the Spartans.

Sophomore **Clyde Abney** (5.4 ppg, 3.7 rpg) is a 6-9 center who will provide depth in the frontcourt.

adidas Blue Ribbon Analysis

BACKCOURT .... **C-** **BENCH/DEPTH** .... **D**
FRONTCOURT .... **D+** **INTANGIBLES** .... **D**

It looks like a tough year for Norfolk State.

With Mel Coleman serving as an interim coach and uncertainty in the program, it does not bode well for the Spartans. If they get off to a tough start and with nothing to play for—not even the conference tournament—things could go sour in a hurry. The Spartans have benefitted from an NCAA decision last summer to lower the waiting period from eight years to two before new Division I schools can become eligible for the NCAA Tournament. But there's another year to go, and Norfolk State, as a result, can't even play in its conference tournament.

Norfolk is another MEAC team that is counting on new players to help immediately. Look for a last-place finish in the MEAC from the Spartans, who could struggle to match last year's record.

(M.G.)

NORTH CAROLINA A&T

LOCATION .... **Greensboro, NC**
CONFERENCE .... **Mid-Eastern Athletic (MEAC)**
LAST SEASON .... **8-19 (.296)**
CONFERENCE RECORD .... **7-11 (8th)**
STARTERS LOST/RETURNING **2/3**
NICKNAME .... **Aggies**
COLORS .... **Navy Blue & Old Gold**
HOMECOURT .... **Corbett Sports Center (6,700)**
COACH .... **Roy Thomas (Baylor '74)**
RECORD AT SCHOOL .... **48-64 (4 yrs.)**
CAREER RECORD .... **290-202 (14 yrs.)**
ASSISTANTS .... **Curtis Hunter (North Carolina '87)**
Bill Sutton (North Carolina A&T '57)
TEAM WINS (last 5 yrs.) **16-15-10-15-8**
RPI (last 5 yrs.) **195-201-265-230-279**
1997-98 FINISH .... **Lost in conference quarterfinal.**

Aggie pride took a bit of a beating last season.

North Carolina A&T, traditionally one of the best teams in the MEAC, stumbled last year, and there were some good reasons for the fall.

Coach Roy Thomas had 10 new players and most of them were freshmen. There was also a challenging non-conference schedule with games against Duke, Tulane and Colorado.

It was tough for a program with great tradition. The Aggies won seven straight MEAC titles in the 1980s and won two more league titles in the '90s.

"No one here was satisfied with what happenned here last year," Thomas said. "But out of 14 players, we had 10 who had never worn an A&T uniform, so we knew things would be kind of tough. We hung in there most of the way, but our inexperience just killed us at crucial times. We plan to be better this year and know we have to be better this season, and I think we can be better."

After the disappointing season, Thomas said his team seems focused.

"I like what I see so far," Thomas said. "Before we even started preseason conditioning, our guys were running at 6:30 in the morning without any of the coaches' knowledge. I had people around school telling me that they saw our guys running at 6:30 and I didn't believe them at first."

Leading the list of returnees is sophomore **J.J. Miller** (4.6 ppg, 1.1 rpg), a 5-11 point guard who earned second-team all-rookie honors in the MEAC last season. Miller was one of the Aggies' freshman pushed into an early role, and Thomas believes that experience will help this year.

"J.J. has really matured from last season and he'll be better this year simply because he's learned to play within the system," Thomas said. "He's really quick on the perimeter and that makes his defense really good. That's so important in our league because of the outstanding guards you have. We need somebody to guard those guards and we think J.J. is one of the guys who can do it."

Working with Miller at the point is 5-11 senior **Jonathan Richmond** (11.9 ppg, 1.9 rpg). Thomas expects a lot from Richmond, the Aggies' second-leading scorer last season.

"Jonathan Richmond will be a key player for us because we're going to need his senior leadership for a still-young team," Thomas said. "We're looking for a lot more consistency from him this year and better shot selection."

The shooting-guard job could belong to 6-2 sophomore **Marque Carrington** (6.3 ppg, 3.4 rpg) and 6-4 junior-college transfer **Vashon Murphy**. Murphy was signed out of Saint Catharine (Ky.) JC, where he averaged 16 points and eight rebounds.

"We expect big things from Marque this season," Thomas said. "He's versatile enough to play the point and the two, but we'll probably keep him at the two this season. His best trait is his defense, because he's a stopper. Vashon is very athletic and he can play either the shooting guard spot or the small forward slot. He's also an excellent shooter who can come off a pick and hit a jumper, and that's something we'll need this season."

Providing depth in the backcourt will be 6-1 sophomore **Jemaine Price** (2.0 rpg, 1.1 rpg).

The small-forward job could be a battle between 6-5 sophomore **Anthony Debro** (2.5 ppg, 1.3 rpg) and 6-6 freshman **Bruce Jenkins.** Debro earned valuable playing time as a freshman and should be another Aggie who's wiser for it. Jenkins is a highly touted newcomer from Blair HS in Silver Spring, Md, where he averaged 18 points and 12 rebounds.

"We think Anthony will give us a lot of help this year," Thomas said. "He's a good shooter who's gotten stronger in the offseason and that should make him more effective this year. We're expecting a lot of help from Bruce Jenkins. He can play either the three or the four. He's got a lot of tools that make him a good player at either forward spot. One big way he'll help us is rebounding, and we needed help in that area last season."

The inside game should be led this year by 6-7 senior forward **Maurice Chambers** (2.3 ppg, 2.4 rpg). Thomas wants to see improvement in his rebounding this season.

"We need a lot more consistency from Maurice this year," Thomas said. "We want him to really work on rebounding and get us between 7 to 10 rebounds per game. If he can do that, that will be a big help to our inside game."

Junior forward **Tony Mitchell** (2.9 ppg, 1.7 rpg) is one of the Aggies' most versatile players. He can play either forward spot and shooting guard. Mitchell, 6-6, has great potential, but hasn't lived up to it.

"We keep waiting for Tony to make that jump and be the player we expected when we recruited him," Thomas said "He's athletic and a good shooter, but we need for him to come through for us this season."

Thomas is more upbeat about 6-6 sophomore forward **Tarrell Robinson** (5.4 ppg, 2.7 rpg). He played a great deal as a freshman and should be another young Aggie who will benefit from it.

"We're really pleased with Tarrell because he's really worked hard and improved," Thomas said. "He can play either the three or the four because he's a good ballhandler but he can also play inside because he's so athletic. We really expect Tarrell to have a good year for us."

The Aggies struggled at the defensive end last season, and that had to trouble Thomas. He takes pride in defense and couldn't be happy with the 75 points allowed on the average game last season. Opponents shot .480 from the field against the Aggies, who ranked last in the league in field-goal percentage defense. Two years ago, the Aggies tied for first in that category.

The Aggies hope to improve on that with better frontcourt play.

A possible help inside will be 6-8 freshman center **Jafar Taalib** from Powers HS in Decatur, Ga. Taalib averaged 19 points and 11 rebounds as a senior.

"Jafir is a real good athlete who is a super shot blocker and that's what we need and hope he can give us," Thomas said. "He's still got a lot to learn, but he's got a lot of potential and he's showing a willingness to work to get better."

Kelvin Clyburn (5.2 ppg, 4.5 rpg) is a 6-5 junior forward who could help the Aggies at either of the forward positions or at center. However, his playing time will depend on how he recovers from a foot injury he suffered last year.

"K.C. is about 80 percent right now and we're trying to bring him along slowly," Thomas said. "He's an excellent post defender and if he can get 100 percent healthy this

1998-99 NORTH CAROLINA A&T SCHEDULE

Nov.	18	James Madison
	23	Elon
	25	@LSU
	28	@Nebraska
Dec.	2	@South Carolina State
	5	@North Carolina-Greensboro
	12	Florida A&M
	15	Bethune Cookman
	20	@Duke
	28	@Georgia State
Jan.	2	Coppin State
	4	Morgan State
	9	@Hampton
	11	@Norfolk State
	16	Howard
	20	*North Carolina Central
	23	Delaware State
	25	@Maryland-Eastern Shore
	30	@Bethune-Cookman
Feb.	1	@Florida A&M
	6	@Morgan State
	8	@Coppin State
	13	Hampton
	15	Norfolk State
	20	@Howard
	27	South Carolina State
Mar.	3-6	#MEAC Tournament

@ Road Games
* Greensboro Coliseum, Greensboro, NC
# Richmond Coliseum, Richomind, VA

year he could be a player to really help us."

Junior **Ves Tetterton,** a 6-5 forward, was brought in last season to help the Aggies' frontcourt, but injured his knee early and only played one game before being redshirted. Thomas believes a healthy Tetterton could be a starter at power forwrd.

Albert Perkins (9.2 ppg, 2.9 rpg), a 6-7 senior forward, started most of last season at power forward and led the Aggies in shooting percentage (.540).

"I was pleased with the job Albert did last season as he improved and got mentally tougher as the year went on," Thomas said. "He's also got a nice outside shot that we'll try to take advantage of this year."

Freshman **Travis Totten**, a 6-8 center from nearby Western Alamance HS in Burlington, N.C., is raw, but has good potential. Totten averaged 18 points and 12 rebounds last year but has only been playing organized basketball for three years.

adidas Blue Ribbon Analysis

BACKCOURT .... D BENCH/DEPTH .... C-
FRONTCOURT .... C- INTANGIBLES C

It wasn't a season to remember for North Carolina A&T. Along with its losing record, the Aggies also lost to Bethune-Cookman, which won just one game in 1997-98.

Not much offense returns as Jonathan Richmond is the only double-figure scorer coming back. If the Aggies have trouble scoring, their defense must improve.

Roy Thomas is known as one of the better coaches in the MEAC and he will have to try and move his team back to the upper half of the league's standings.

That probably won't happen this year. Look for the Aggies to finish eighth in the MEAC, but by season's end, they will be a team not many MEAC foes will be eager to play.

(M.G.)

SOUTH CAROLINA STATE

LOCATION .... Orangeburg, SC
CONFERENCE .... Mid-Eastern Athletic (MEAC)
LAST SEASON .... 22-8 (.733)
CONFERENCE RECORD 16-2 (2nd)
STARTERS LOST/RETURNING 2/3
NICKNAME .... Bulldogs
COLORS .... Garnet & Blue
HOMECOURT .... Memorial Center (3,200)
COACH .... Cyrus Alexander (Catwaba '75)
RECORD AT SCHOOL .... 186-134 (11 yrs.)
CAREER RECORD .... 186-134 (11 yrs.)
ASSISTANTS .... Francis Simmons (Voorhees '71)
Jamal Brown (South Carolina State '97)
TEAM WINS (last 5 yrs.) 16-15-22-14-22
RPI (last 5 yrs.) 208-249-156-209-103
1997-98 FINISH .... Lost in NCAA first round.

South Carolina State coach Cy Alexander continues to build one of the Mid-Eastern Athletic Conference's top programs in Orangeburg, S.C.

Last year, for the second time in three years, the Bulldogs claimed the MEAC championship by rallying past Coppin State in the league championship game, 66-61. It made Alexander's team 2-0 against the Eagles in MEAC title games and 5-3 against the MEAC's glamour team over the last four years.

Coppin State may have been the team to beat in the MEAC the last few years, but South Carolina State has established itself as one of the top teams in the conference under Alexander's watch.

And the Bulldogs may very well be the team to beat this year. The Bulldogs must replace a very talented backcourt, including MEAC Player of the Year Roderick Blakney.

Still, Alexander's team has a talentened frontcourt, some impressive newcomers and a strong desire to get back to the NCAA Tournament after last year's 82-67 loss to national champion Kentucky in the first round. The Wildcats blew past St. Louis and UCLA in the NCAAs after getting a tough game from the Bulldogs.

Being respectable, though, wasn't what Alexander was looking for in that game with Kentucky.

"We were down 10 with eight minutes to go and had two free throws," Alexander said. "We missed them both and they hit a three and that was it. If we could have gotten it below 10, we could have made a real run.

"And that game has motivated us. We did a good job in the backcourt against them but they killed us in the frontcourt. We know to take our program even higher we need to get stronger up front. Our work ethic last spring was just terrific. We started working out as soon as we got back from the regionals, determined to get there again."

The Bulldogs should be strong in the frontcourt again this year. There is some question about the backcourt, where South Carolina State must replace Blakney and Tyler Brown, who combined for 36 points per game last year.

"It's tough to replace a backcourt as talented as the one we had," Alexander said. "You don't just replace people like Roderick Blakney but we have everyone else back and some good players coming in and I'm cautiously optimistic."

The Bulldogs strong front line, starts with 6-8, 250-pound senior center **Raheem Waller** (7.0 ppg, 7.9 rpg). Waller was a second-team All-MEAC selection last year and was the team's top rebounder. He shot 51 percent from the field and was a defensive standout.

Alexander wants to see even more from him this year.

"Raheem did a great job for us last year, but he can get even better," Alexander said. "First and foremost, he's got to become a better free-throw shooter. He only shot 51 percent from the line last season and that must get better. Secondly, we're challenging him to be a better rebounder. With his strength, his future is to rebound. We think if he puts his mind to it and keeps working hard, he can be one of the nation's top rebounders. We want him to set a goal to be in the top five or top 10 in rebounding this year."

Joining Waller in the frontcourt will be 6-10 junior center **Duane Johnson** (5.8 ppg, 5.4 rpg). Johnson led the Bulldogs in blocked shots with 45.

"Duane has improved his offensive game and that should help him this season," Alexander said. "He's got some great game experience from last season and that should help him, as well. We're looking for Duane to block some shots, get some rebounds and average 10 to 11 points per game. He's a tough kid from Philadelphia who should be ready to have a great year for us this season."

Expected to provide depth in the frontcourt will be 6-8 junior center **Edmund Alston** (1.4 ppg, 0.2 rpg). And 6-8 sophomore forward **Dexter Hall**, who sat out last season under NCAA Prop 48 guidelines, should also bolster the frontcourt.

"Edmund continues to improve and he'll help us some this year," Alexander said. "What we look from Dexter when he plays is to give us some energy. We want him to come into the game, block some shots and get us going. He's a player of the future for us and we just want him to keep working and developing."

Another returnee to the frontcourt is 6-8 junior forward **Bryan Neis** (4.0 ppg, 2.9 rpg). Neis started six games last year and gave the Bulldogs some quality minutes. He should help again this year, but could see his playing time drop with all of the newcomers.

Blakney will be hard to replace, but 6-4 junior **James Jones** (9.5 ppg, 3.3 rpg) should be able to add some offensive punch in the backcourt. Jones was also sidelined because of Prop 48 two years ago, but immediately made an impact for the Bulldogs last season. He was the team's third-leading scorer, and Alexander expects him to be more of a factor this year.

"James will be one of our co-captains this season and we expect big things from him," Alexander said. "He'll be expected to take over some of the scoring load and he should be able to do that. James averaged close to 10 points per game in about 16 minutes last season. This year he'll play close to 30 minutes and should be able to average even more than he did last year."

The big task for the Bulldogs this year will be replacing Blakney at point guard.

Not only did Blakney average 20.7 points per game but he handed out 4.7 assists per game. One of the newcomers, 6-0 junior **Mike Wiatre**, could replace Blakney. Wiatre played last season at Fashion Institute of Techonology in his hometown of New York City.

"We feel very, very lucky to get a player like Mike and I think he'll do a great job as our point guard," Alexander said "He's got a great work ethic. He's a hard-nosed player from Brooklyn who should give us some real toughness this year. He's also a great shooter and has tremendous knowledge of the game. I think he's just what the doctor ordered for our club this year."

Pushing Wiatre for time in the backcourt will be 6-1 sophomore guard **John Shivers** (0.8 ppg, 0.5 rpg) and 5-10 junior guard **Evans Gilliard** (0.9 ppg, 0.2 rpg).

Also looking for playing time in the backcourt will be 5-10 junior **Charles Jackson** (1.0 ppg, 0.1 rpg) and 5-11

1998-99 SOUTH CAROLINA STATE SCHEDULE

Nov.	21	@Duke
	28	@Alabama A&M
Dec.	2	North Carolina A&T
	4-5	#Cardinal Varsity Club Classic
	9	@Charleston Southern
	15	Florida A&M
	17	Bethune-Cookman
	21	@Clemson
	27	@Maryland
	29	@South Carolina
Jan.	2	Morgan State
	4	Coppin State
	9	@Norfolk State
	11	@Hampton
	18	Howard
	23	Maryland-Eastern Shore
	25	@Delaware State
	30	@Florida A&M
Feb.	1	@Bethune-Cookman
	6	@Coppin State
	8	@Morgan State
	13	Norfolk State
	15	Hampton
	22	@Howard
	27	@North Carolina A&T
Mar.	2-6	##MEAC Tournament

@ Road Games
# Muncie, IN (vs. Jacksonville, first round; also Ball State and St. Joseph's-Indiana)
Richmond Coliseum, Richmond, VA

sophomore **Rayner Moore**.

One transfer could be an impact player, 6-5 junior guard/forward **Terry Smith-Harris**, who joins South Carolina State from Chicago State. Smith-Harris sat out last year after transfering and Alexander looks forward to getting the Los Angeles native on the court.

"Terry is a tremendous shooter who is very versatile," Alexander said. "He can play the (point, shooting guard and small forward) and may do all of that this year. He's another tough kid who knows what tough competition is all about. He's played against major college competition in the Los Angeles area and he played against some tough teams when he was at Chicago State.

"He's probably going to be our first guy off the bench and the only thing Terry needs to learn is what a good shot is. He's an outstanding shooter who thinks he can hit from anywhere and it's my job to show him what a good shot is."

The small forward spot should be a position of strength with 6-5 junior forward **Coray Davis** (5.8 ppg, 2.7 rpg) returning and 6-6 junior forward **Arthur Carlisle** transferring from the University of South Carolina. Carlisle averaged 3.5 ppg, 2.2 rpg, and 12.8 minutes per game in 1996-97.

Carlisle won't be eligible until after the first semester, but Alexander is excited to have the former Gamecock..

"What Arthur also gives us is the total package," Alexander said. "He can score, rebound and defend. We think he'll really help us this year and have a great season."

Unlike last year, when Blakney was the show, Alexander wants to have a balanced team this year.

"What I want is seven to eight guys scoring betweeen eight to 13 points per game," Alexander said. "This will make it awful tough for teams to key on one player and should make us a lot tougher to defend. If we can do that, I think we could have a really good season and be a factor for the MEAC championship again."

adidas Blue Ribbon Analysis

BACKCOURT .... C BENCH/DEPTH .... B-
FRONTCOURT .... B- INTANGIBLES .... C+

There's a lot to like about this South Carolina State team, and it's easy to like Bulldogs coach Cyrus "Cy" Alexander, a personable guy.

Alexander is proud of the program he's built in 11 years at South Carolina State, which has carved its niche in a state that has nine Division I basketball programs and is in the heart of Southeastern Conference and Atlantic Coast Conference country.

Yes, star guard Roderick Blakney is gone, but an impressive frontcourt with some experienced returning players and some game-proven newcomers should make South Carolina State the best team in the MEAC.

If Mike Wiatre can handle the tall task of replacing Blakney, the Bulldogs will be tough to beat. Look for South Carolina State and Coppin State to battle for the MEAC title, once again.

(M.G.)

MIDWESTERN COLLEGIATE CONFERENCE

adidas BLUE RIBBON FORECAST

1. Detroit
2. Wisconsin-Green Bay
3. Cleveland State
4. Illinois-Chicago
5. Loyola (Ill.)
6. Butler
7. Wright State
8. Wisconsin-Milwaukee

ALL-CONFERENCE TEAM

G—Jermaine Jackson, SR, Detroit
G—Keion Brooks, SR, Wright State
G—James Madison, JR, Cleveland State
F—Javan Goodman, SR, Loyola
F—Jerry Carstensen, JR, Wisconsin-Green Bay

PLAYER OF THE YEAR

Jermaine Jackson, SR, Detroit

NEWCOMER OF THE YEAR

Bryant Notree, SR, Illinois-Chicago

1998-99 CONFERENCE TOURNAMENT

Feb. 27-March 2, UIC Pavilion, Chicago, Ill.

1997-98 CHAMPION

Detroit and Illinois-Chicago (regular season)
Butler (conference tournament)

1997-98 POSTSEASON PARTICIPANTS

Postseason Record: 1-3 (.250)
NCAA
Detroit (second round)
Butler
Illinois-Chicago

TOP BACKCOURTS

1. Detroit
2. Illinois-Chicago
3. Wright State

TOP FRONTCOURTS

1. Detroit
2. Cleveland State
3. Butler

ON THE WAY UP

Cleveland State

ON THE WAY DOWN

Butler

INSIDE THE NUMBERS

- 1997-98 conference RPI: 10th (out of 30)
- Conference RPI (last 5 years): 11-19-15-24-10

DID YOU KNOW?

The MCC will be hard-pressed to come up with an encore for last year's breakthrough season. The MCC sent three teams (Butler, Illinois-Chicago, and Butler) to the NCAA Tournament for the first time...Loyola hired former Rhode Island assistant coach Larry Farmer as its new head coach. Farmer, who played for John Wooden during the glory years at UCLA, holds the distinction of playing for a team with the best three-year record in NCAA Division I men's basketball history (89-1)...Detroit guard Jermaine Jackson was the lone MCC representative invited to this summer's Team USA trials. The 6-4 Jackson, a legitimate NBA prospect, averaged 12.1 ppg and owned a stellar 2.48-to-1 assist-to-turnover ratio as a junior for the Titans...Detroit's trip to the NCAAs was the school's first in 19 years, while Illinois-Chicago's NCAA berth was the school's first...Butler coach Barry Collier must replace the most successful class in the history of Bulldogs hoops. Jon Neuhouser, Matthew Graves, Rolf van Rijin, Jeff Rogers and Dan Dudukovich combined to win a four-year, school-record 79 games and made trips to the NCAA Tournament the last two seasons...Two imports from major Division I programs, 6-5 swingman Bryant Notree (Illinois) and 6-9 senior center Ins Norville (UMass), should be one-year wonders at Illinois-Chicago and Wright State, respectively. DePaul transfer Ricardo Crumble will be a tough customer inside the next two years at Cleveland State...Players from big-time programs will keep trickling in next season as Louisville transfer Jerry Johnson becomes eligible at Butler and Ohio State defector Damon Stringer joins Rollie Massimino at Cleveland State.

(B.D.)

BUTLER

LOCATION	Indianapolis, IN
CONFERENCE	Midwestern Collegiate
LAST SEASON	22-11 (.666)
CONFERENCE RECORD	8-6 (3rd)
STARTERS LOST/RETURNING	5/0
NICKNAME	Bulldogs
COLORS	Blue & White
HOMECOURT	Hinkle Fieldhouse (11,043)
COACH	Barry Collier (Butler '76)
RECORD AT SCHOOL	151-114 (9 yrs.)
CAREER RECORD	151-114 (9 yrs.)
ASSISTANTS	Thad Matta (Butler '90)
	Jim Price (Louisville '72)
	Mark Bailey (Wisconsin-Parkside '95)
TEAM WINS (last 5 yrs.)	16-15-19-23-22
RPI (last 5 yrs.)	136-136-83-88-52
1997-98 FINISH	Lost in NCAA first round.

When first asked about the prospects for his 1998-99 squad, Butler University coach Barry Collier tried to make a grim assessment sound funny: "Well everyone has graduated from Butler—but me."

He's not kidding, because last year's NCAA Tournament-qualifying Butler team contained more seniors than a church bingo night. And of course, last May's graduation day saw the most successful class in Butler hoops history walk across the stage and grab diplomas. Before picking up their sheepskins, Jon Neuhouser, Matthew Graves, Rolf van Rijn, Jeff Rogers and Dan Dudukovich led the Bulldogs to a four-year school-record 79 victories, two Midwestern Collegiate Conference tournament titles, one MCC regular season crown and NCAA Tournament trips the last two years.

Neuhouser, the team's working-class dog, finished his fine career as one of only three Butler players to score more than 1,400 points and haul down 700 boards. Graves sits second on Butler's all-time list for three-point field goals, while the 7-2 van Rijn finished as Butler's all-time leader in blocked shots and Rogers stands No. 2 on the school's all-time assist list. Dudukovich, a dogged defender, started 63 times over the last two seasons.

If that weren't enough turnover for one guy to endure, Collier suffered an unexpected loss when the team's only returning starter, 6-3 senior-to-be Otis Frazier (9.4 ppg, 4.9 rpg, 43 steals) withdrew from school. Frazier, who notched 17 double-figure scoring games last season for Butler, eventually transferred to Purdue-Calumet over the summer.

"Those guys had a great run, but we'll have an all-new starting five this season," said Collier. "But I resent the fact that just because you have some new faces in the starting lineup that people assume you're not going to be very good. I'm not ready to resign myself to that fact and neither are these players. We've done a lot of winning here lately and guys have gotten used to that. The older guys know what it takes to win and they'll make sure that the young guys work hard enough to succeed."

It appears that the Bulldogs might have more than just new pups in the starting lineup in 1998-99—they might be playing a whole different brand of basketball. The last couple years, the Bulldogs have opted for a half-court style of offense featuring more screens than a multiplex theater. This season, it appears that Collier will play at a slightly quicker pace—which seems to suit his 1998-99 personnel just fine. "Frankly, my plan is for this team to play a lot faster than my last couple teams have," said Collier. "But we'll see what happens. Sure, playing at a break-neck speed is fun. But we're not in this for fun; we're in this to succeed. So we'll just have to wait and see how we're best suited to play."

The keys to this more souped-up offense will be handed over to 6-foot freshman **Thomas Jackson**, who finished third in the balloting for "Mr. Basketball" in Michigan last year. The 160-pound Jackson averaged 20.0 points, 7.5 rebounds, 6.0 assists and 6.5 steals as a senior at East Lansing (Mich.) High School.

"Thomas isn't experienced yet, but he has more of the tools that we want in our point guard than anybody else on our roster," said Collier. "He can get up under someone on defense and really guard them tightly. His quickness will also allow him to help his teammates out and still be able to recover. Plus, he can really shoot the basketball. He'll be an impact newcomer for us."

The arrival of the highly-touted Jackson means that last year's matching set of 6-3 sophomore backup point guards, **LaVall Jordan** and **Michael Hicks**, will see time at both guard spots.

The 185-pound Jordan could well be the team's starter at shooting guard, giving the Bulldogs one of the league's more athletic, albeit inexperienced, starting backcourt combos. Jordan (0.9 ppg, 0.9 rpg, 16 assists) appeared in 30 games last season, getting increased minutes during the second half of the year. He scored three points in the Bulldogs' 79-62 first round NCAA Tournament loss to New Mexico last March.

Hicks (1.4 ppg, 1.0 rpg) played in 26 games as a deep reserve for last year's senior-laden squad. Even though their 1997-98 numbers are puny, their arduous work in the weight room could result in both cracking the starting lineup as Collier toys with the notion of using a three-guard set.

"Jordan and Hicks will be completely different players this winter, if their offseason work translates into success," Collier said. "They both added 10-15 pounds of muscle to their frames and should be better-equipped to excel at the D-I level. I can see us playing all three of those guards together, at times, which will allow us to play a much faster brand of basketball."

Of course, Jordan and Hicks will have to battle with 6-2 junior **Andrew Graves** (1.3 ppg, 0.6 rpg, 18 assists), Matthew's younger brother, for playing time if he's healthy. Graves was much more effective as a freshman (2.2 ppg, 65 assists) than he was last season when he struggled with injuries (sprained ankle). As a result, Graves—whose job description reads "zone buster"—couldn't hit the broad side of a barn from the field last year (8-27, .286 FG percent).

"Andrew really struggled last season," Collier said. "But he also worked hard this offseason and time will tell if that hard work will pay off."

Whoever earns the starting two-guard spot figures to be keeping it warm until 6-3 Louisville transfer Jerry Johnson becomes eligible next winter. Johnson, a two-time all-state high school player from Atlanta, possesses a 40-inch vertical leap. He just never really got much of a chance to play for Denny Crum and Co.

"We're excited that Jerry will be a part of our program," said Collier. "He's our best athlete. Of course, he'll sit out this year and will have two years of eligibility left. He'll really help us down the road." But that's next season. Rounding out the guard rotation this year will be some things old—6-foot senior **Andy Hirschy** and 6-1 sophomore **Jason Myers**—as well as something new—6-2 freshman **Ryan Murray**.

Hirschy (1.3 ppg, 0.7 rpg) appeared in 27 games last year, including an impressive season-high 11-point performance against eventual Final Four team Stanford. Myers (0.6 ppg, 0.2 rpg) is a walkon guard who served as a practice player and Butler's victory cigar last season. When he appears in the game (which he did in 13 different times in 1997-98), then Collier's bunch usually has things well in hand.

Murray, on the other hand, could battle for meaningful minutes this season, if he's not redshirted. An honorable mention all-state selection last year, Murray was a starting guard for Noblesville High School, one of the top Class 4A schools in Indiana. He averaged 16.7 points per game and 3.8 assists as a high school senior.

The frontcourt will be retooled around returnees **Mike Marshall** and **Bjorn Gieseck,** plus well-decorated freshman **Ryland Hainje**. The 6-4, 235-pound Marshall (4.3 ppg, 5.0 rpg, 23 assists, 14 steals) is one tough hombre

1998-99 BUTLER SCHEDULE

Nov.	14	Southwest Missouri State
	19	Xavier
	21	@Indiana State
	23	@Belmont
Dec.	5	@Evansville
	8	Western Kentucky
	12	Ball State
	19	*Purdue
	23	Florida State
	28	Idaho State
Jan.	2	@Illinois-Chicago
	4	@Loyola
	9	@Wright State
	14	Cleveland State
	16	Detroit
	18	Florida International
	23	@Wisconsin-Milwaukee
	25	@Wisconsin-Green Bay
	28	Illinois-Chicago
	30	Loyola
Feb.	1	Indiana/Purdue-Indianapolis
	6	Wright State
	11	@Detroit
	13	@Cleveland State
	18	Wisconsin-Milwaukee
	20	Wisconsin-Green Bay
27-Mar.	2	#MCC Tournament

@ Road Games
* Market Square Arena, Indianapolis, IN
# UIC Pavilion, Chicago, IL

whose muscles-on-top-of-muscles frame would be the envy of a quite a few NFL linebackers.

Marshall was a one-time all-state linebacker from Ohio who had Big 10 football factories Michigan, Penn State and Ohio State mighty interested. The burly junior brings a football mentality to the hardwood.

"Mike's enthusiasm and intensity are phenomenal," said Collier. "He's the most obvious leader that I've ever been around in my 10 years of coaching. Guys like playing with and seem to gravitate toward him when they're looking for someone to follow.

"Plus, he's just a superior athlete. He weighs 235 pounds, but he's a great leaper who can get that weight nearly 40 inches off the ground. He will step up and fill the leadership void on this team, by playing hard and saying the things that need to be said."

The man in the middle for Collier's club will once again be a foreign import as the 6-10 senior Gieseck (2.9 ppg, 1.4 rpg), from Hagen, Germany, replaces the 7-2 Dutchman van Rijn. Gieseck appeared in all 33 games last year.

"Bjorn has made significant gains athletically during his first three years here and I think he's poised to have a little bit of a breakout year as a senior," Collier said.

The other frontcourt regular will be the 6-6, 225-pound Hainje—whom Collier jokingly calls "my other starting linebacker." Like Marshall, Hainje was a two-sport star in high school, playing football as well as averaging 16.8 points and nine rebounds as a high school senior at nearby Cathedral High School in Indianapolis. Like any self-respecting Hoosier state product, Hainje opted for roundball over football, despite the fact that Big Ten schools Michigan, Purdue and Indiana were all ready to give him football scholarships.

"He's a big-time athlete who will make an impact right away," said Collier. "He just loves the game and has a terrific work ethic."

If Collier needs further frontcourt help, he can either turn to 6-5, 210-pound senior **Mike Pflunger** or a pair of newcomers in 6-7 freshman forward **Lewis Curry** or 6-9 freshman **Mike Moore**. Pflunger appeared in 22 games last year and averaged a meager 1.3 points and 0.7 boards. "But I've had a lot of guys really step up their level of play as seniors as they see the sand of their playing careers start to disappear through the hourglass," said Collier. "And Pflunger could be one of those types of guys."

Curry figures to garner more minutes than Pflunger, though. The 6-7, 210-pounder just looks like a basketball player. He's long, lean and can leap. Curry averaged 18 points and nine rebounds as a senior at Concordia High School in Fort Wayne, Indiana.

"Lewis Curry is one of those guys that passes the eye test when you're recruiting," said Collier. "By that, I mean that he has everything you're looking for in terms of athleticism. He just needs to improve his intensity and he'll develop into a fine player."

The 6-9 Moore (10 ppg, 7 rpg as a senior at Alter HS/Kettering, Ohio) figures to see less time than Curry. He can play either the four or five spots, but must add serious weight to his frame (which is currently as skinny as a Q-tip at only 210 pounds). He's a probable redshirt candidate.

adidas Blue Ribbon Analysis

BACKCOURT .... **C+** **BENCH/DEPTH** .... **C+**
FRONTCOURT .... **B-** **INTANGIBLES** .... **C+**

After making two straight NCAA Tournament trips, the Bulldogs don't figure to have a three-peat performance. Butler looks like a middle-of-the-pack type of team that can finish anywhere from third to sixth in the balanced eight-team MCC. The key to the season will be how quickly freshman Thomas Jackson and Rylan Hainje adjust to the rigors of D-I ball. Both have impressive prep resumes, but they'll be literally thrown to the wolves early this season against a tough-as-nails non-league schedule—which includes pre-Christmas dates with 1998 NCAA Tournament teams Xavier, Purdue and Florida State. Ouch!

With all the new faces, figure on the Bulldogs slipping to fifth or sixth place in the MCC. But with all of the talented underclassmen getting much-needed seasoning this year, plus the addition of Louisville transfer Jerry Johnson, these Dogs figure to have much more bite in 1999-2000.

(B.D.)

CLEVELAND STATE

LOCATION .... **Cleveland, OH**
CONFERENCE .... **Midwestern Collegiate**
LAST SEASON .... **12-15 (.444)**
CONFERENCE RECORD .... **6-8 (5th)**
STARTERS LOST/RETURNING **4/1**
NICKNAME .... **Vikings**
COLORS .... **Forest Green & White**
HOMECOURT .... **Henry J. Goodman Arena (13,610)**
COACH .... **Rollie Massimino (Vermont '56)**
RECORD AT SCHOOL .... **21-34 (2 yrs.)**
CAREER RECORD .... **448-312 (25 yrs.)**
ASSISTANTS .... **Mitch Buounaguro (Boston College '77)**
Harold Presley (Villanova '86)
Paul Molinari (Villanova '90)
TEAM WINS (last 5 yrs.) **14-10-5-9-12**
RPI (last 5 yrs.) **176-259-273-233-127**
1997-98 FINISH .... **Lost in conference first round.**

It's hard to believe, but thirteen (that's right, 13) years have passed since coach Rollie Massimino engineered one of the greatest upsets in NCAA hoops history, the almost-flawlessly played 66-64 win by Villanova over Patrick Ewing and Georgetown.

So what's "Grand-Daddy Mass" up to now, you ask? He's in year three of what he originally estimated would be a five-year rebuilding plan at Cleveland State. His battle plan has been to schedule games against the roughest customers he can find, in order to toughen his troops and get the attention of local Cleveland high school players.

This season will be no different. Schools from eight conferences, in addition to the Midwestern Collegiate Conference, are scattered on the 26-game schedule. Including the three MCC teams—Butler, Detroit and Illinois-Chicago—that participated in the 1998 NCAA Tournament, CSU will face off against six teams that advanced to postseason play last season. Atlantic 10 power Rhode Island and Prairie View A&M went to the '98 Big Dance, while UAB went to last spring's NIT. In addition, Massimino's squad will tangle with Providence in late November and South Florida from Conference USA on Jan. 2 in an ESPN2 game.

"Once again we are bringing into Cleveland outstanding national powers so that the fans of Cleveland can enjoy big-time college basketball," said Massimino.

The $64,000 question: Is Daddy Mass' plan working? It appears to be, albeit slowly. The win totals have increased modestly from nine in Year One to 12 victories last season. And each year, Massimino keeps more and more home-grown talent from driving over the state lines. His 1998-99 roster includes six Ohio-born players, and that doesn't include a pair of transfers (including former Ohio State passmaster Damon Stringer, eligible in 1999-2000) who are homegrown.

"Cleveland State is a team to watch in the MCC," said Butler coach Barry Collier. "Rollie is doing a good job of keeping the local kids at home and seems to be adding quality size to the program."

1998-99 CLEVELAND STATE SCHEDULE

Nov.	14	SUNY-Stonybrook
	24	@UAB
	28	Providence
Dec.	1	@Brown
	8	Ohio
	12	Kent
	19	Prairie View A&M
	21	@Akron
	23	Sacred Heart
	27	*Rhode Island
	29	@Tulsa
Jan.	2	South Florida
	4	@Wisconsin-Milwaukee
	7	Illinois-Chicago
	9	Loyola
	14	@Butler
	16	@Wright State
	23	Detroit
	28	Wisconsin-Green Bay
	30	Wisconsin-Milwaukee
Feb.	4	@Illinois-Chicago
	6	@Loyola
	11	Wright State
	13	Butler
	20	@Detroit
27-Mar.	2	#MCC Tournament

@ Road Games
* Rock-N-Roll Shootout, Gund Arena, Cleveland, OH
# UIC Pavilion, Chicago, IL

Gobbling up local products has helped fellow MCC teams Detroit and Illinois-Chicago put themselves on the NCAA radar screen, so why not Cleveland State? In fact, expect the 1998-99 Vikings to add to their win column and end up in the first-division of the MCC—thanks to the return of three full-time starters along with some talented new faces and a trio of players that rotated into a fourth starting spot.

If nothing else, Massimino's squad looks wing-loaded. That's because the best of the returnees are a pair of underclassmen: 6-2 junior shooting guard **James Madison** and 6-6 sophomore small forward **Theo Dixon**. Madison (15.3 ppg, 2.8 rpg, 61 assists, 23 steals) can stroke the ball from behind both lines (.356 three-point percentage, .844 FT percentage) and is a legit candidate for MCC Player-of-the-Year honors. He's the Lord of the Wings for the Vikes, but Dixon (10.0 ppg, 4.0 rpg, 41 assists, 27 steals) is also a top-notch young talent.

A homegrown product from Cleveland Heights, Dixon made the quantum leap to Division I basketball without a hitch in 1997-98, except for his assist-to-turnover ratio (41 assists, 71 turnovers). If he can learn to take better care of the basketball, he'll blossom into a star in this league.

"Since we arrived here, we have been committed to recruiting local players and taking CSU to another level," Massimino said. "Theo Dixon will help us make that happen."

Joining Dixon as a familiar frontcourt face is **Carter Arnett**, a 6-9 senior center who started 20 games last season. Arnett (6.2 ppg, 5.7 rpg, 26 assists, 13 blocked shots) transferred to Cleveland State from Wichita State and won the starting pivot job from now-departed 6-8 Brian Hovecar. Arnett's biggest weakness is literally his weakness (he's only 215 pounds) for a five-man. As a result, he'll be pushed for the starting center spot by burly 6-8 junior **Ricardo Crumble**, a DePaul transfer.

Rejoining Arnett and Dixon up front are three frontcourt guys who drew starting assignments in 6-7 sophomore **Anthony Jackson** (two starts in 1997-98), 6-6 senior **JoVonn Jefferson** (13 starts), 6-7 senior **Leonidas Skoutaris** (one start), and 6-8 senior **Steve Bowie** (nine starts).

Jackson (2.9 ppg, 1.9 rpg, 9 blocked shots) is a work in progress. He sprouted nine inches between his freshman year in high school and his senior year and is still getting accustomed to the rough-and-tumble life near the bucket (.458 FG percentage last season). Jefferson is another late bloomer who didn't play organized basketball until his senior year in high school. After spending two years at Johnson County (Kan.) Community College, Jefferson made a decent impact at Cleveland State last season, averaging 4.9 points and 2.8 boards.

"JeVon Jefferson makes us a more athletic basketball team because of his jumping ability, defense and his great quickness around the basket," said Massimino.

Skoutaris (3.3 ppg, 1.0 rpg, 14 assists, 12 steals), a former standout in Greece's 19-under league, has struggled with his shot in the states. He hit only one of every three shots (21 of 63) last season after shooting just .364 as a sophomore in 1996-97. He'll struggle to get much playing time this season, thanks to the long list of returnees and three promising frontcourt newcomers.

The final frontcourt player who got starting assignments last year was Bowie, a Cleveland native who arrived at CSU via Moberly (Mo.) Community College. Bowie was fourth on the team in scoring at 6.4 ppg and also finished third on the team in rebounding average at 5.3 rpg. Jackson, Jefferson, Skoutaris and even Bowie all figure to lose significant minutes in 1998-99, thanks to the arrival of two ballyhooed transfers in Crumble and 6-8 junior **David Barrett**, plus a well-decorated freshman in **Sonny Johnson**.

The well-traveled 235-pound Crumble is a Cleveland prep product who played at Oak Hill Academy and DePaul before landing at CSU. Crumble, not the nation's most skilled post player but still a hard worker, didn't fit into Pat Kennedy's rebuilding project at DePaul. He figures to post numbers at Cleveland State after averaging five points and five rebounds as a freshman at DePaul.

Barrett has played the last two seasons at Snead State (Ala.) Community College. He averaged 12 points and 10 rebounds as a sophomore at Snead State, while shooting 64 percent from the floor.

The other new frontcourt face is the 6-5, 225-pound freshman Johnson from Garfield Heights, Ohio. Selected Mr. Basketball in Ohio last year, Johnson doesn't need a compass to fine his way to the hoop. He averaged 34 points and 17.6 rebounds last season and is expected to see quality time at both the three and four spots.

Rounding out the frontcourt types for the Vikings will be seldom-used 6-6 senior forward **Shawn Kenney** (0.2 ppg, 1.0 rpg). Joining Madison in the backcourt will be 5-10 senior **Melvin McKey** and 6-1 sophomore **Jamaal Harris**. McKey (4.3 ppg, 2.0 rpg, 45 assists, 14 steals) arrived along with Arnett as a Wichita State transfer after Randy Smithson was hired as the Shockers' coach. McKey, a New Yorker, will start at the point for Massimino this winter. Harris, a 6-1 sophomore, was sidelined by academic woes last season, but he should split time at the point with McKey.

adidas Blue Ribbon Analysis

BACKCOURT .... **C+** **BENCH/DEPTH** .... **B-**
FRONTCOURT .... **B** **INTANGIBLES** .... **B+**

This is a program on the rise in the MCC. Cleveland State has adopted the same formula that fellow MCC schools Detroit and Illinois-Chicago used to land NCAA berths last year. Namely, they acquire local high school talent in bulk. In year three of his building project, Rollie Massimino has landed three top-notch frontcourt recruits in DePaul transfer Ricardo Crumble, JUCO import David Barrett and 6-5 freshman Sonny Jackson, the 1998 Mr. Basketball in Ohio. The addition of this threesome to a nucleus that already includes a pair of double-digit wing scorers in 6-2 junior James Madison (15.3 ppg) and 6-6 sophomore Theo Dixon (10.0 ppg) makes this bunch dangerous.

If Massimino can blend this talent into a cohesive unit, the Vikings could push prohibitive favorite Detroit for league supremacy this year. Our guess? Cleveland State will finish third in the conference, behind only Detroit and Wisconsin-Green Bay, in 1998-99. But watch out for the Vikes in 1999-2000, when Ohio State castoff Damon Stringer—a true point guard (the only obvious missing piece to the puzzle)—joins the mix.

(B.D.)

adidas Blue Ribbon Analysis

GRADING SYSTEM

- A+ equal to very best in country—Final Four-caliber unit
- A among the best in the land—worthy of deep NCAA run
- B+ talented, versatile and experienced—NCAA-NIT ability
- B solid and productive winners—league and post-season contenders
- C+ average to above-average—may contend in a weaker league
- C average to mediocre—second division in a strong league
- D+ below average, inconsistent—second division in a weaker league
- D well below average—losing season virtually certain
- F non-Division I ability—an underdog every night

DETROIT

LOCATION .... **Detroit, MI**
CONFERENCE .... **Midwestern Collegiate**
LAST SEASON .... **25-6 (.806)**
CONFERENCE RECORD .... **12-2 (t-1st)**
STARTERS LOST/RETURNING **3/2**
NICKNAME .... **Titans**
COLORS .... **White & Blue**
HOMECOURT .... **Calihan Hall (8,837)**
COACH .... **Perry Watson (E. Michigan '72)**
RECORD AT SCHOOL .... **88-68 (5 yrs.)**
CAREER RECORD .... **88-68 (5 yrs.)**
ASSISTANTS .... **David Greer (Bowling Green '83)**
Mickey Barrett (Xavier '90)
Michael Jackson (Detroit '95)
TEAM WINS (last 5 yrs.) **16-13-18-16-25**
RPI (last 5 yrs.) **119-165-88-151-36**
1997-98 FINISH .... **Lost in NCAA second round.**

Even though Detroit "officially" lost four starters from the team that played in the NCAA Tournament last March, coach Perry Watson firmly believes he has four starters back. Perhaps last year's success—the school's finest season since some fast-talking guy named Dick Vitale roamed the Titans' sidelines—has made Watson delusional.

Whatever the reason, that's Watson's story and there's no telling him otherwise. "We had eight players who were capable of starting for us last year," Watson said, trying to explain his "Starting Eight" theory. "As the newcomers among them got better, so did we as a team. All eight of them got starter's minutes and all of them were important to what we did. The fact that we bring back four experienced players can't be discounted. They all played 20-plus minutes a game and they were instrumental in us winning 25 games, getting to the NCAA Tournament and beating St. John's once we got there."

The Titans did indeed take their coach on a magic carpet ride—their 25 wins matched the most recorded in a single season in school history and their NCAA berth was the school's first in 19 years. And the Titans, a 10th seed, weren't just happy to be there. They decided to wreck some office pools for good measure, taking out St. John's in the first round of the Midwest regional before bowing out against Purdue in round two.

When the dust settled, Watson had been chosen MCC Coach of the Year. Now, the Titans enter the 1998-99 season without four seniors from that team: All-MCC center Brian Alexander, two-time All-MCC guard Derrick Hayes, guard EJ Haralson and reserve forward Perry Robinson. Between them, they averaged 37.6 points and 18.9 rebounds per game and were major reasons Watson registered his fourth winning season in five years.

Despite the huge lose of personnel, expect the winning to continue at Detroit. The reason? Watson's roster still has more tough guards than a state penitentiary.

That stellar group of perimeter players includes 6-4 senior point man **Jermaine Jackson**, a bonafide NBA prospect as well as the early-line favorite to win 1999 MCC Player of the Year honors. Jackson, the Titans' starting point guard for the last three seasons, was the only Midwestern Collegiate Conference player to be invited to the Team USA Basketball tryouts last summer. His invitation was well-deserved after a junior season during which Jackson finished second on the Titans in scoring (12.1 ppg) and fashioned a sparkling 2.48-to-1 assist-to-turnover ratio (career-best 149 assists vs. only 60 miscues).

"Our team starts with Jermaine," Watson said of his senior passmaster. "He's really entrusted with running the show and getting all of our players on the same page. I think he's poised to have a great senior season."

The Titans' potent perimeter also boasts the 1998 MCC Newcomer of the Year, 5-9 junior **Rashad Phillips**, as well as 6-6 junior swingman **Desmond Ferguson** and a pair of new faces in 6-3 sophomore **Brandon Gray** and 6-4 freshman **Darius Belin.**

After sitting out his freshman year for academic reasons, Phillips burst on to the scene last year. Despite coming off the bench, Phillips was fourth on the team in scoring (10.0 ppg). He was also third in the MCC in assists (3.3 per game), third in assist-to-turnover ratio (1.82 to 1) and fourth in steals (1.7 per game). Phillips will move from the "starting eight" into the starting five this season and will combine with Jackson to form one of the best backcourts in the Midwest.

"Rashad is a tremendously talented young man," Watson said. "He had some outstanding games and some average ones last year, which is indicative of what a first-year player usually does. I look for Rashad to be a lot more consistent this year."

Like Phillips, Ferguson was a newcomer last season, having come in as a transfer from Missouri. He averaged 8.9 points per game and proved that there's no zone he can't shoot over. Ferguson made 70 threes last season while connecting at a .407 clip from behind the arc. He should blossom into a more complete double-figure scorer this season.

"Desmond gave us a deep threat last year and I look for him to really improve this season," said Watson. "I think he'll add to his long-range shooting by putting the basketball on the floor and by getting to the offensive glass and becoming more well-rounded in his play."

A former Michigan all-stater, Gray practiced with, but did not compete with the Titans last season. He was redshirted because of the log jam at guard in 1997-98. Belin, one of six Detroit high school products on the Titans' roster, is capable of playing both guard spots. Watson really likes Belin, saying that he reminds him of a young Jackson.

Up front, the Titans return starting forward **Bacari Alexander**, a bruising 6-5 senior who never backs down from a tough assignment. He averaged 4.2 points and 3.5 boards in his first season with Detroit—after spending his first two years at Robert Morris—and always thinks defense first.

"Bacari gives us a tremendous presence inside and on the boards," said Watson. "Bacari will contribute to us in more ways this year based on the fact that he's played in the MCC for a year."

Detroit also returns two sophomores inside—6-6 forward **Michael Jordan** (no relation to CEO Jordan) and 6-10 center **Walter Craft**. Jordan (0.0 ppg, 0.6 rpg) appeared in only seven games last year before a shoulder injury sidelined him for the remainder of the season. He'll have to really improve if he's to get any significant playing time, because Watson recruited three highly-touted frontcourt types.

Craft (1.2 ppg, 0.8 rpg) will be asked to fill the large hightops of Brian Alexander at center. Alexander was a three-time MCC All-Defensive team selection. The 250-pound Craft figures to benefit from the fact that he joined Jackson this summer as a regular at St. Cecelia's, a Detroit-area basketball haven where Motor City products Chris Webber, Jalen Rose and Voshon Lenard regularly play.

Three newcomers—junior college imports **Daniel Whye** and **Julian Van Dyke** along with 6-7 freshman **Terrell Riggs**—should all make an immediate impact in the frontcourt. The 6-8 Whye comes to Detroit from Allegany (Md.) College, the nation's top-ranked junior college team most of last season, where he averaged 14.0 ppg.

The other JUCO transfer is Van Dyke, a former high school teammate of Desmond Ferguson who averaged 11.6 ppg last year at Fort Scott (Kan.) Community College.

1998-99 DETROIT SCHEDULE

Nov.	17	Bethune-Cookman
	19	@Michigan
	24	@Bowling Green
	28	Texas Southern
Dec.	1	@Western Michigan
	4-5	#Iowa/Super Chevy Shootout
	9	Central Michigan
	28-29	##Sun Bowl Classic
Jan.	2	@Wisconsin-Milwaukee
	4	Wisconsin-Green Bay
	7	Loyola
	9	Illinois-Chicago
	14	@Wright State
	16	@Butler
	23	@Cleveland State
	28	Wisconsin-Milwaukee
	30	Wisconsin-Green Bay
Feb.	4	@Loyola
	6	@Illinois-Chicago
	11	Butler
	13	Wright State
	20	Cleveland State
27-Mar.	2	###MCC Tournament

@ Road Games
# Iowa City, IA (vs. Gonzaga, first round; also Iowa and South Alabama)
El Paso, TX (vs. Grambling, first round; also Texas-El Paso and Washington State)
UIC Pavilion, Chicago

Whye is the more accomplished offensive player of the JUCO imports, while the 235-pound Van Dyke will be asked to play defense and rebound at the four and five spots. Riggs is another new face to watch. He was rated among the top 65 high school seniors in the nation by *Basketball Times* and led Detroit Finney High School to the state Class A semifinals.

adidas Blue Ribbon Analysis

BACKCOURT .... **A-** **BENCH/DEPTH** .... **B**
FRONTCOURT .... **B** **INTANGIBLES** .... **B+**

The Titans are the team to beat in the Midwestern Collegiate. Sure, they have a question mark in the middle, but everywhere else this team is strong. Point guard Jermaine Jackson and shooter Rashad Phillips form the conference's most lethal backcourt combo.

How good is Jackson? NBA teams came to Detroit games last season to see senior Derrick Hayes and left talking about Jackson, who possesses excellent size (6-4), good decision-making skills and a reliable jumper. Phillips was a double-digit scorer off the bench last season and should really blossom this season, as should small forward Desmond Ferguson (8.9 ppg in 1997-98). Starting power forward Bacari Alexander is back and coach Perry Watson has plenty of options to fill the final starting spot.

Sophomore Walter Craft and newcomers Daniel Whye, Julian Van Dyke and Terrell Riggs are all possibilities there. That gives Watson a talented 8-to-10 man rotation, just like last year. So, expect another 20-plus win season and another NCAA Tournament berth for the Titans. Just like last year.

(B.D.)

ILLINOIS-CHICAGO

LOCATION .... **Chicago, IL**
CONFERENCE .... **Midwestern Collegiate**
LAST SEASON .... **22-6 (.786)**
CONFERENCE RECORD .... **12-2 (t-1st)**
STARTERS LOST/RETURNING **4/1**
NICKNAME .... **Flames**
COLORS .... **Navy Blue & Fire Engine Red**
HOMECOURT .... **UIC Pavilion (8,000)**
COACH .... **Jimmy Collins (New Mexico State '70)**
RECORD AT SCHOOL .... **37-20 (2 yrs.)**
CAREER RECORD .... **37-20 (2 yrs.)**
ASSISTANTS .... **Dick Nagy (Hardin-Simmons '67)**
Mark Coomes (Western Illinois '74)
Gene Cross (Illinois '94)
TEAM WINS (last 5 yrs.) **20-18-10-15-22**
RPI (last 5 yrs.) **95-114-183-157-34**
1997-98 FINISH .... **Lost in NCAA first round.**

After the most successful season in school history, Illinois-Chicago coach Jimmy Collins faces a rebuilding project so large in scale it might even make Bob Vila throw up his hands.

Gone are 1998 MCC Player-of-the-Year Mark Miller (19.7 ppg), his backcourt running mate Anthony Coomes (13.5 ppg) as well as forwards Bryant Lowe (15.1 ppg) and Konstantine Stavropoulos (9.2 ppg). That foursome represented 76 percent of UIC's scoring a year ago, and took the Flames to the NCAA Tournament.

The losses of Coomes (now playing in Holland) and Lowe (finishing up his course work) were expected. Both were seniors. However, the early defections of Miller, who declared for the NBA draft and then went undrafted, and Stavropoulos, who decided to play pro ball in Greece, were quite a surprise.

If that weren't enough, the team's next top returning scorer and one of the Flames' quicker returnees, Theandre Kimbrough (6.5 ppg), was ruled academically ineligible.

But before you throw a pity party for Collins, remember that no one was predicting an at-large berth to the NCAA Tournament for the Flames this time last year.

"Anybody who predicted that before last season would have been taken to the hospital," said Collins after the Flames fell to UNC-Charlotte in the first round of the Big Dance last March. "This program has come a long way."

Whether it has staying power will be determined by a group of eight newcomers—led by 6-5 senior swingman sub in 1998-99, averaged 18 points and 4.6 rebounds as a senior at Ladue (Mo.) High School.

1998-99 ILLINOIS-CHICAGO SCHEDULE

Nov.	16-18	#Purdue
	24	Northern Illinois
	28	@Bowling Green
	30	@Alabama State
Dec.	4-5	##Carrier Classic
	13	@Michigan State
	17	Florida International
	19	North Carolina-Wilmington
	21	@Southern Illinois
	23	@Illinois State
	27	Montana
	31	@Marquette
Jan.	2	Butler
	4	Wright State
	7	@Cleveland State
	9	@Detroit
	14	Wisconsin-Milwaukee
	16	Wisconsin-Green Bay
	23	Loyola
	28	@Butler
	30	@Wright State
Feb.	4	Cleveland State
	6	Detroit
	13	@Wisconsin-Milwaukee
	15	@Wisconsin-Green Bay
	20	@Loyola
27-Mar.	2	###MCC Tournament

@ Road Games
# Chase NIT (If the Flames advance, they wil face either Gonzaga or Memphis on Nov. 18. Semifinals and final are Nov. 25 and 27 at Madison Square Garden, NY)
Syracuse, NY (vs. Santa Clara, first round; also Syracuse and Ohio)
UIC Pavilion, Chicago, IL

Bryant Notree, a University of Illinois transfer. Notree played three seasons for the Fighting Illini, including two when Collins was an assistant to Lou Henson. He averaged 7.9 points and 3.7 boards as a junior before opting to transfer to be reunited with Collins.

Notree's best season was in 1995-96, when he was a sophomore and earned honorable mention All-Big Ten honors. That season, he averaged 10.5 ppg and shared the team's rebounding lead with Jerry Gee at 6.1 boards per game. He should be a force in the Midwestern Collegiate Conference, especially with four starters gone and plenty of shots to be taken.

Joining Notree in what Collins hopes is a "quick-fix" approach are a pair of highly regarded JUCO imports: 6-2 guard **Joel Bullock** and 6-7 forward **Tarrie Monroe**.

Bullock, who will be a sophomore, averaged 20.1 points, 4.2 rebounds and 3.1 assists en route to all-region honors at Malcolm X Junior College. Bullock shot an amazing .561 percent from three-point range and .849 percent from the free-throw line. He looks like the starting two-guard.

Monroe should start at the power-forward spot, alongside Notree (the likely starting three-man). Monroe (16.7 ppg, 6.7 rpg, 70 assists, 27 steals) was a key figure in Vincennes University's 31-5 season and fifth-place finish at NJCAA Tournament in Hutchinson, Kansas last year. Monroe shot a sizzling .558 percent from the floor and should be able to score in the paint for Collins and Co.

Three rookies have yet to take to the court, but who spent last season getting adjusted to college life are 6-5 sophomore swingman **Cory Little**, who sat out under Prop 48, and 1997-98 redshirts **Jordan Kardos** and **T.J. Mixson**. Little is the best of that trio. He was an all-state selection by the *Chicago Sun-Times* after averaging 23 points, 10.1 rebounds and 6.2 assists two years ago at Addison Trail High School. He'll start at guard, along with Bullock.

The two redshirts, 6-2 guards Kardos and Mixson, will be counted on to provide quality depth-along with two freshman, 6-6 forward **Ian Hanavan** and 6-2 guard **Jon Pierre Mitchom**.

The two best players in that foursome of off-the-bench types appear to be Kardos and Hanavan. As a senior at Glenbrook (Ill.) North High, Kardos averaged 22.6 points, 4.0 rebounds and 2.2 assists. His specialty is long-range shooting. Kardos hit 93 threes as a high school senior and shot 47 percent from behind the three-point arc.

Hanavan contributed 15.8 points and 11.8 rebounds per game last season at Moline (Ill.) High School on his way to Associated Press honorable mention all-state honors

Mixson joined the Flames last season as a walkon after lettering for four years at Thornwood (Ill.) High School. As the Thunderbirds' point guard, Mixson averaged 16.1 points, 5.3 steals and 6.2 assists as a high school senior. Mitchom, who like Mixson figures to be a deep backcourt sub in 1998-99, averaged 18 points and 4.6 rebounds as a senior at Ladue (Mo.) High School.

While the long list of newcomers will ultimately decide whether the Flames flicker out early this season, there are some returnees for Collins. The two familiar faces who figure to see the most playing time are 6-8 senior **Anton Collins** and 6-11 sophomore **Thor Solverson**. They'll split the center duties.

Collins played in 27 of UIC's 28 games last year, including 12 starts at center. Collins (1.6 ppg, 3.1 rpg) will be counted on to hit the glass with verve. The wafer-thin Solverson (1.3 ppg, 1.5 rpg) finally started to live up to his first name by hitting the weight room with a vengeance this offseason. Despite his countless hours of work, Solverson still weighs just 205 pounds. He's obviously a work in progress.

The other returnees from last year's NCAA Tournament team are swingman **Frank Walker** as well as walkons **Jason Ayers**, **Frank Wade** and **J.T. Wilson**. Walker (3.8 ppg, 2.2 rpg, 5 assists, 5 steals) will see time, while the walkons will only see action in blowouts.

adidas Blue Ribbon Analysis

BACKCOURT .... **B** **BENCH/DEPTH** .... **C**
FRONTCOURT .... **C** **INTANGIBLES** .... **B**

Coach Jimmy Collins has his work cut out for him in 1998-99. The bar was raised last year when the Flames made their first NCAA Tournament trip on the strength of a Phoenix Suns-like three- and sometimes four-guard attack and a high RPI. The latter was thanks to a rough-as-sandpaper schedule.

Collins will try the same approach in 1998-99. However, this time he'll take a group of largely unproven, but talented new faces into battle. The rough schedule starts with a trip to Purdue in the preseason NIT and also includes trips to Syracuse for the Carrier Classic and games at Michigan State, Illinois State and Marquette.

The leader of this year's bunch will be Bryant Notree, an Illinois transfer who won't wilt against the top-notch competition. He was an honorable mention All-Big 10 player as a sophomore. The question is how well the rest of the projected starting five (guards Joel Bullock and Cory Little, forward Tarrie Monroe and center Anton Collins) will respond.

Our guess is that they'll struggle in 1998 and then get better after the ball drops in Times Square and league play begins. Still, with four new starters, look for the Flames to drop a few spots in the MCC standings to fourth place.

But be forewarned: These guys could be dangerous in the MCC Tournament, which will be played on their homecourt.

(B.D.)

LOYOLA

LOCATION .... **Chicago, IL**
CONFERENCE .... **Midwestern Collegiate**
LAST SEASON .... **15-15 (.500)**
CONFERENCE RECORD .... **6-9 (t-5th)**
STARTERS LOST/RETURNING **1/4**
NICKNAME .... **Ramblers**
COLORS .... **Maroon & Gold**
HOMECOURT .... **Joseph J. Gentile Center (5,200)**
COACH .... **Larry Farmer (UCLA '73)**
RECORD AT SCHOOL .... **First year**
CAREER RECORD .... **95-77 (6 yrs.)**
ASSISTANTS .... **Pete Trgovich (UCLA '75)**
Lance Irvin (Idaho '92)
Jeff Dunlap (UCLA '86)
TEAM WINS (last 5 yrs.) **8-5-8-12-15**
RPI (last 5 yrs.) **225-283-243-259-171**
1997-98 FINISH .... **Lost in conference first round.**

In hopes of bringing its college hoops program back into national prominence, the powers-that-be at Loyola-Chicago have chosen the most successful college basketball player in history as their head coach.

Loyola's new sideline boss is 47-year-old Larry Farmer, who played from 1970-73 on John Wooden-coached UCLA teams that went 89-1 and won three national championships. Farmer comes to Loyola from the University of Rhode Island, where he served as the top assistant coach under Jim Harrick last year. The Rams were 25-9 and

1998-99 LOYOLA SCHEDULE

Nov.	14	@Wisconsin
	17	@Chicago State
	21	Eastern Illinois
	23	@Bradley
	28	Youngstown State
Dec.	1	@Kansas State
	5	@Drake
	8	@Portland
	12	Indiana State
	19	Akron
	23	Western Michigan
	29	@Oakland
Jan.	2	Wright State
	4	Butler
	7	@Detroit
	9	@Cleveland State
	12	Wisconsin-Milwaukee
	18	Wisconsin-Green Bay
	23	@Illinois-Chicago
	28	@Wright State
	30	@Butler
Feb.	4	Detroit
	6	Cleveland State
	8	@Wisconsin-Green Bay
	11	@Wisconsin-Milwaukee
	20	Illinois-Chicago
27-Mar	2	#MCC Tournament

@ Road Games
# UIC Pavilion, Chicago, IL

made a run to the Elite Eight last season.

"For me, it's an opportunity of a lifetime," said Farmer of his new position. "I look at the places I've been and the jobs I've had, and I love and appreciate every one of them. This is certainly a blessing. I've coached all over the world, and my family and I couldn't be more excited about coming to Loyola."

The folks at Loyola are pretty excited to have landed Farmer, too. "Larry Farmer embodies the qualities we value at a Jesuit university," said Loyola President John J. Piderit. "He values academic excellence and growth of the individual student-athlete and expects each player not only to excel on the court, but also, more importantly, in the classroom. He's been a champion since his playing days at UCLA, so it is fitting that he now joins the only school in Illinois with an NCAA men's basketball championship."

Farmer comes to Loyola with literally a world's worth of experience. After his playing days were over, Farmer returned to Westwood as an assistant coach from 1975-81 and then as the head coach from '81-84, helping the Bruins to two Final Four appearances in '76 and '80. During that time, he served as an assistant under Gene Bartow, Gary Cunningham and Larry Brown. He was 61-23 as UCLA's head man.

After UCLA, Farmer was the head coach at Weber State from 1985-88, finishing with a disappointing three-year mark of 34-54. His best club was the '85-86 squad which finished 18-11. Farmer was fired from that job and accepted an offer to coach national and club basketball teams in Kuwait. While he was in the midst of preparing to leave for the Middle East, Kuwait was invaded by Iraq and the apartment building that Farmer was going to live in was shelled by an Iraqi tank.

Farmer did eventually coach in Kuwait—after the Gulf War ended. He'd return to the United States for four months during college basketball season to work as a television commentator.

"I was around Division I basketball—doing the television, watching the practices, talking to the players and coaches—for five years," Farmer said. "By about the third year, I started to feel like I really wanted to get back and be involved."

That happened last season when Harrick, himself a former UCLA head coach, hired Farmer as his top assistant at Rhode Island. His credentials and history of being around winning programs from UCLA to Rhode Island made him an attractive candidate to replace Ken Burmeister, who was fired after four seasons at Loyola because his "Fastbreak on the Lake" attack produced lots of excitement, but not enough wins.

"I've paid a lot of dues, been a lot of places," said Farmer. "I think I'm a much better person and coach now. I think I'm far more qualified at age 47 than I was at age 30, when I first became a head coach."

Unlike most new coaches, Farmer inherits a pretty good situation at Loyola. The Ramblers were 15-15 last season, their best mark in a decade, and four starters return from that squad.

The best of that lot is 6-8, 230-pound senior forward **Javan Goodman**, a first-team All-MCC selection last year. League opponents had a difficult time keeping this particular Goodman down in 1997-98, as he was the only player in the conference to finish in the top three in both scoring (16.8 ppg) and rebounding (8.4 rpg) a year ago. Goodman also led the MCC with 29 double-digit scoring games and notched nine double-doubles last year. This Nassau, Bahamas, product is the best power player in the MCC.

Also returning is point guard **Earl Brown**, who led the conference in steals and assists and was a member of the MCC All-Defensive team. Brown, a 6-0 junior, averaged 10.3 points, 5.6 assists and 2.23 steals in 1997-98. He'll be joined in the backcourt by 6-4 junior **Damien McSwine** (12.1 ppg, 3.4 rpg, 44 assists, 27 steals) and 6-4 sophomore **Mike Hare** (7.9 ppg, 2.4 rpg, 42 assists, 17 steals).

Hare started 25 games, the most starts by a Rambler freshman since Javan Goodman's rookie year, and was among the MCC leaders in three-point field goal percentage (.420) and in threes made (38).

The rest of the backcourt rotation includes some things old (6-5 senior **Carlos Gallo**, 6-2 sophomore **Marc McDonald** and 6-foot sophomore **Ndueso Udolwood**) and something new (6-3 freshman **Chris Williams**). Gallo (2.7 ppg, 1.2 rpg, 34 assists, 21 steals) , a native of Buenos Aires, Argentina, appeared in 29 games for the Ramblers last season. McDonald (1.5 ppg, 0.1 rpg, 11 assists) made appearances in 13 games, but struggled mightily with his touch from the floor (7 of 21, .333) and the free-throw line (2 of 5, .400). Udolwood (1.1 ppg, 0.3 rpg, 7 assists) saw precious little time as a freshman (62 total minutes in 22 games).

Williams, a combo guard, was a member of the powerhouse Fenwick (Ill.) High School team. Fenwick was a top-10 fixture in the *USA Today* national polls last year. In addition to Williams, Fenwick's roster also included everybody's high school All-American, forward Corey Maggette, a Duke signee.

Aside from Goodman, the list of frontcourt returnees isn't sending shivers down the spines of MCC coaches. **Brad Tice** (1.7 ppg, 2.1 rpg, 11 assists, 13 blocks), a 6-9 junior, is probably the opening day starter at center. But he'll probably relinquish that spot before too long. That's because Goodman figures to have a legit tag-team partner on the backboards when University of Iowa transfer **Alvin Robinson** becomes eligible at the start of the second semester.

The 6-8, 250-pound Robinson is a former Windy City prep product who decided to return home after being unable to crack the crowded frontcourt at Iowa. Robinson averaged 0.9 ppg and 2.2 rpg as a sophomore reserve for Dr. Tom Davis. He's as raw as sushi at the offensive end, but this wide body should be a force on the backboards in the MCC.

The other three frontcourt returnees are role players, at best. **Drew Petersen** (0.7 ppg, 0.4 rpg), a 6-8 senior, showed promise when he first arrived at Loyola, but any progress he hoped to make was thwarted by a series of stress fractures. **Wayne Plowman** (0.6 ppg, 0.8 rpg, 4 blocks), a 6-7 sophomore, showed glimpses of potential in his brief appearances in 1997-98 (129 minutes played in 23 appearances).

The final returnee is 6-4 senior forward **Kevin Gill**, who didn't see any action last season. After Robinson becomes eligible, Tice and Plowman figure to provide minutes off the bench—along with freshmen 6-8 **Jonathan Freeman** and 6-7 **Jarod Fry**.

adidas Blue Ribbon Analysis

BACKCOURT	**B**	**BENCH/DEPTH**	**C**
FRONTCOURT	**C+**	**INTANGIBLES**	**C**

With one-time UCLA Bruin player and coach Larry Farmer at the controls, the Ramblers will adopt many of John Wooden's philosophies—and they hope with it some of the Wizard of Westwood's winning ways.

Farmer hasn't been a college head coach since 1987-88, his final year at Weber State. But he's convinced that he's much better equipped to be a Division I head coach now than he was then.

A better-than-.500 record is quite possible this season, because for the most part the Ramblers' non-league schedule is softer than a 10-year-old mattress. Plus, the Ramblers seem well-stocked at the guard spots and at power forward, where 1999 MCC Player-of-the-Year candidate Javan Goodman patrols the paint.

The problem area will be the rest of the frontcourt, where burly University of Iowa transfer Alvin Robinson (6-8, 250) must step up after two undistinguished years with the Hawkeyes. If he does, the Ramblers could be the MCC's success story in 1999.

More than likely, though, it will take the Loyola players some time to adjust to the much more structured system of Farmer. So call it a fifth-place finish in the MCC in 1997-98, but watch for these guys to be a possible sleeper in the MCC Tournament in Chicago come March.

(B.D.)

WISCONSIN-GREEN BAY

LOCATION	**Green Bay, WI**
CONFERENCE	**Midwestern Collegiate**
LAST SEASON	**17-12 (.586)**
CONFERENCE RECORD	**7-7 (4th)**
STARTERS LOST/RETURNING	**2/3**
NICKNAME	**Phoenix**
COLORS	**Green & White**
HOMECOURT	**Brown County Arena (5,600)**
COACH	**Mike Heidman (UW-LaCrosse '71)**
RECORD AT SCHOOL	**56-30 (3 yrs.)**
CAREER RECORD	**122-55 (7 yrs.)**
ASSISTANTS	**Bob Semling (UW-Eau Claire '81)**
	Ben Johnson (UW-Green Bay '92)
	Woody Wilson (UW-Oshkosh '65)
TEAM WINS (last 5 yrs.)	**27-22-25-13-17**
RPI (last 5 yrs.)	**49-68-21-166-100**
1997-98 FINISH	**Lost in conference title game.**

Some folks have forgotten this, but Wisconsin-Green Bay actually wrote the script for Midwestern Collegiate Conference success in the 1990s: Schedule RPI-enhancing nonconference games, play in-your-face defense, recruit like crazy out of your home state and suddenly you're a team nobody wants to face come March.

An office-pool wrecker, if you will.

But the other MCC coaches aren't dumb. They've stolen the not-so-secret formula. And guess what? It's worked, particularly at Detroit and Illinois-Chicago, where deep reservoirs of inner-city talent exist. As a result, the Phoenix has slipped a bit the last two seasons under Mike Heideman, the successor to wildly successful Dick Bennett (now at Wisconsin). But the Phoenix does seem to be rising again.

After a .500 season in 1996-97, Wisconsin-Green Bay nearly made it back to the Big Dance last season. In the MCC Tournament, Wisconsin-Green Bay knocked off regular-season co-champ Detroit in the semis before losing—on its homecourt—to a Butler team that featured more seniors than a church bingo night.

This year, the title game has been moved to Chicago, but no one would be surprised if Wisconsin-Green Bay makes another appearance. Oh sure, Heideman has some holes to fill. Second-team all-conference selection Wayne Walker (13.0 ppg), a slashing southpaw swingman with a knack for slicing through the heart of the defense and then drawing fouls, must be replaced. Ditto Kevin Olm, the heady point guard who started for the last three years and was selected to the MCC All-Defensive team two straight years.

But all is not lost—far from it, in fact. Three starters return, led by 6-4 junior **B.J. LaRue** (10.8 ppg, 3.5 rpg, 34 assists, 26 steals). LaRue's two free throws with two seconds remaining iced the Phoenix's MCC semifinal win over Detroit. He appears more than ready to accept the mantle of go-to guy after posting games of 21 points and 26 points in MCC Tournament wins over Cleveland State and Detroit.

Also back for Heideman and Co. is two-thirds of last season's starting frontcourt in 6-7 junior **Jerry Carstensen** and 6-10 forward/center **Matt Hill**. Carstensen (9.5 ppg, 3.4 rpg, 14 blocked shots, 20 steals) returns as the team's designated banger with two years experience, a no-nonsense attitude and like LaRue, all-conference potential. His lunch-pail approach earned him league-wide respect as well as a spot on the MCC's All-Defensive squad by season's end. Hill is another tough customer inside, having averaged 9.9 points, 2.9 boards and 1.5 blocks last year. Hill displayed more and more confidence as last season wore on and can stick the occasional perimeter jumper, in addition to scoring inside.

Who will fill the two vacancies in the starting lineup? Actually, a pair of 6-1 seniors in **Luke Kiss** and **Ryan Bonowicz** are two likely candidates—if Heideman elects to go with a three-guard look.

Kiss figures to assume the starting point guard slot from his mentor Olm. Groomed for the job, Kiss (1.0 ppg, 1.7 rpg, 67 assists, 20 steals) isn't much of a scorer, but he did fashion a 2:31-to-1 assists-to-turnover ratio a year ago. Kiss averaged 17 minutes per game in 1997-98, a statistic which increased to 20.3 in MCC play. An old-fashioned pass-first point guard, Kiss is a gutty and tough-minded

1998-99 WISCONSIN-GREEN BAY SCHEDULE

Nov.	13	@Southwest Texas State
	18	@Illinois State
	21	Northern Michigan
	27-29	#Big Island Invitational
Dec.	6	Miami of Ohio
	8	East Carolina
	12	Northern Iowa
	19	Bowling Green
	22	Valparaiso
	29-30	##Pepsi-Oneida Classic
Jan.	4	Detroit
	7	Wisconsin-Milwaukee
	16	@Illinois-Chicago
	18	@Loyola
	20	Cleveland State
	23	Wright State
	26	Butler
	28	@Cleveland State
	30	@Detroit
Feb.	3	@Appalachian State
	5	@Wisconsin-Milwaukee
	8	Loyola
	11	@North Carolina-Wilmington
	15	Illinois-Chicago
	18	@Wright State
	20	@Butler
27-Mar.	2	###MCC Tournament

@ Road Games
# Hilo, HI (vs. West Virginia, first round; also Georgia Tech, New Orleans, Saint Louis, Evansville, Washington and Hawaii-Hilo)
Milwaukee, WI (vs. Air Force, first round; also Drexel and Texas Southern)
UIC Pavilion, Chicago, IL

leader who played in every game last season. He made 11 starts.

The other starter could be the hometown hero Bonowicz, if he's 100 percent healthy. He has battled injuries throughout his career, but he can be one of the deadliest perimeter shooters in the MCC when he's well.

Bonowicz (6.1 ppg, 0.9 rpg, 27 assists, 13 steals) made 44 of his 112 three-point shots and led the Phoenix in scoring three times last season. His most impressive night was a seven of nine performance, including five of seven work on three-pointers against Michigan Tech.

If Heideman elects to go with a bigger lineup, then Kiss and LaRue will start in the backcourt with Carstensen, Hill and perhaps 6-8 senior **Mike Nabena** (2.0 ppg, 1.2 rpg) up front. At 240 pounds, Nabena gives Heideman another banger. His career-best 10-rebound performance against Northeastern Illinois last season showed what Nabena is capable of, if he gets some playing time.

But Nabena isn't the only frontcourt option for Heideman, who bought big men in bulk as four of his six-pack of recruits can play either forward or center.

Ryan Mueller, a 6-6 redshirt freshman, was a former all-state prep player at Waupan (Wisc.) High School who originally signed with Northeastern Illinois. Realizing that NE Illinois was disbanding its program at the end of last season, Mueller sat out the entire year. At the very least, Mueller will see some reserve minutes. At best, Mueller will fill the opening at the small forward spot left by Walker's graduation.

But Mueller isn't the only suspect. Swingman **Chancellor Collins** (13.2 ppg, 7.5 rpg as a senior at Thornridge [Ill.] HS), a 6-4 freshman, might also be the answer to the loss of Walker. He's a Walker clone in that he's strong and adept at slashing to the bucket.

Another possibility is 6-5, 215-pound junior **Jeremy Pfister**, who played in 10 games last season for the Phoenix before being sidelined by a knee injury. He averaged 3.2 minutes in his 10 appearances last season, but did play in 23 games the year before when he was healthy.

The other two frontcourt freshmen look like probable redshirt material. Forward **Greg Babcock** (18 ppg, 9.3 rpg), a 6-9 freshman from Mishawakan, Indiana, is growing like ragweed—he sprouted 10 inches during his four years of high school—and needs some time to adjust.

Scott Sowinski, a freshman swingman from Xavier (Wisc.) High School, was chosen the *Appleton Post-Crescent* Player of the Year last season. He's a walkon who needs to add some serious meat to his skinny frame (6-4, 175 pounds).

Quality backcourt depth will be provided by a pair of youngsters in 6-3 sophomore **Paul Kraft** as well as by 5-10 freshman **DeVante Banks**. Kraft, a Green Bay native, showed uncanny poise for a freshman—that is, until he was slowed during the second half of the season by a back injury. Kraft (2.8 ppg, 0.9 rpg) flashed his potential when he played a major role in guarding eventual 1998 first-round draft pick Bryce Drew of last year's feel-good story Valparaiso.

Kraft guarded Drew for much of the game, a 60-52 Phoenix win, and helped hound Valpo's shooting star into a 5-for-15 shooting night. He also held his own on offense that night, making three of his four three-pointers in only his fifth game. He'll see tons of playing time, if he's healthy.

Banks will be Kiss' understudy at the point-guard slot in 1998-99. He averaged 13.1 points and nearly seven assists, leading his Gordon Tech team to a 21-8 mark last season.

Rounding out the roster, and the backcourt rotation, will be seldom-used 6-1 junior **Ben Royten** (0.4 ppg, 0.3 rpg) and 6-1 freshman walkon **Gene Evans** (another serious redshirt candidate).

Royten, a walkon, was three for three from behind the arc in one exhibition game last season, but is little more than a practice player.

adidas Blue Ribbon Analysis

BACKCOURT .... **B** **BENCH/DEPTH** .... **B+**
FRONTCOURT .... **C+** **INTANGIBLES** .... **B**

While Detroit is everybody and their uncle's choice—and ours too—to win the Midwestern Collegiate, the battle for second place looks like a tight three-horse race among Wisconsin-Green Bay, Illinois-Chicago and Rollie Massimino's up-and-coming Cleveland State team. The educated guess here is that Wisconsin-Green Bay will finish as the regular-season MCC runner-up to Detroit.

Looking for reasons? First, the Phoenix play one of the nation's most tenacious brands of defense. Second, there are three returning starters, some experienced hands off the bench and some promising new recruits who should help right away. And third, there is a legitimate go-to guy in 6-4 junior guard B.J. LaRue.

The reason they won't topple Detroit for league honors, though, is the lack of proven scoring punch at the point-guard spot—where Detroit possesses the MCC's best player in Jermaine Jackson and the Phoenix counter with steady, but unspectacular senior Luke Kiss and unproven freshman DeVante Blanks.

(B.D.)

WISCONSIN-MILWAUKEE

LOCATION .... **Milwaukee, WI**
CONFERENCE .... **Midwestern Collegiate**
LAST SEASON .... **3-24 (.125)**
CONFERENCE RECORD .... **2-12 (8th)**
STARTERS LOST/RETURNING **1/4**
NICKNAME .... **Hawks**
COLORS .... **Black & Gold**
HOMECOURT .... **Klotsche Center (5,000)**
COACH .... **Ric Cobb (Marquette '70)**
RECORD AT SCHOOL .... **20-62 (3 yrs.)**
CAREER RECORD .... **20-62 (3 yrs.)**
ASSISTANTS .... **Kirk Earlywine (Campbell '87)**
Bob Piercy (Marquette '96)
Shawn Chism (Chicago State '96)
TEAM WINS (last 5 yrs.) **10-3-9-8-3**
RPI (last 5 yrs.) **232-292-205-253-244**
1997-98 FINISH . Lost in conference tournament first round.

For the first time in his tenure at Wisconsin-Milwaukee, Ric Cobb (affectionately known as "The Elevator Man" because of his vertical leap during his playing days for Al McGuire at Marquette) thinks he can get the Panthers' moribund program off the ground floor. Color us skeptical, though. In each of his three seasons at Wisconsin-Milwaukee, Cobb's win totals have plummeted from nine to eight to just three last season.

So why is Cobb feeling so upbeat? "For the first time, I finally have all of the players I've wanted in the program," said Cobb. "And I think our strength this season will be the experience this team has and its ability to play cohesively as a unit."

While Cobb's club looks more like a cellar-dweller than a team that's ready for the MCC penthouse in 1998-99,

1998-99 WISCONSIN-MILWAUKEE SCHEDULE

Nov.	16	@Wisconsin
	21	Central Michigan
	24	@Western Michigan
	28	@SUNY-Stonybrook
Dec.	1	@Indiana State
	5	Sam Houston State
	8	@Marquette
	12	Missouri-Kansas City
	14	@Northwestern
	20	Tri-State
	29	Trinity
Jan.	2	Detroit
	4	Cleveland State
	7	@Wisconsin-Green Bay
	12	@Loyola
	14	@Illinois-Chicago
	21	Wright State
	23	Butler
	28	@Detroit
	30	@Cleveland State
Feb.	3	@Western Illinois
	6	Wisconsin-Green Bay
	11	Loyola
	13	Illinois-Chicago
	18	@Butler
	20	@Wright State
27-Marl	2	#MCC Tournament

@ Road Games
# UIC Pavilion, Chicago, IL

there is one reason to be excited about the future of Panthers' basketball: The sophomore class, which accounted for 47 percent of the Panthers' scoring last season.

The leader of Cobb's quintet of sophomores is 6-8, 255-pound center **Damon Ninkovic**, an MCC All-Newcomer selection last season. Ninkovic (9.0 ppg, team-best 6.1 rpg) led the Panthers in scoring eight times last season and had a career-high 24 points against eventual MCC regular-season champ Detroit. He was also UW-Milwaukee's top rebounder 12 times.

Just behind Ninkovic in terms of top returning scorers is 6-9, 230-pound center/power forward **Chad Angell**, who was the only Panther to start all 27 games last season. Angeli averaged 8.8 ppg and 3.9 rpg last season.

Also back is 6-5 sophomore swingman **Jared Hardwick** (8.6 ppg, 5.1 rpg, 1.1 apg). Rounding out the sophomore class is 6-5 guard **Reggie Wheeler** (2.9 ppg), who played in more than half of the Panthers' games, and 6-1 guard **Donte Jackson** (1.1 ppg, 1.1 apg), who appeared in 13 games and even started one.

"This outstanding sophomore class already has played a lot of quality minutes," said Cobb. "Their experience will make us very competitive in the MCC. With this class on board, the future of UWM men's basketball looks bright."

Yes, it does—thanks to the aforementioned sophomores and three solid guard recruits Cobb has added to the mix. However, the $64,000 question is whether Cobb will be a part of that future. A grand total of 20 wins in three seasons doesn't exactly ensure job security.

With his frontcourt in decent, albeit young hands, Cobb set out this offseason to bolster his backcourt. He appears to have done that by bringing in junior college transfers **Shawn Fountain** (5-10, 175) and **Roy King** (6-0, 180) as well as freshman **Ronnie Jones Jr.** (5-9, 165).

Fountain averaged 12 points, 6.1 assists and 4.2 steals last year at Owens Junior College in Toledo, Ohio. He shot 58 percent from the field and 47 percent from three-point range, helping his squad to a 27-6 record and a final ranking of No. 2 in the last NJCAA Division II poll. Pencil him in as the starting point guard.

"Shawn brings the leadership that we need on the floor," Cobb said. "He makes sound decisions as a point guard, which is necessary to run a successful basketball team. He is a very good all-around athlete."

King averaged 20.4 ppg as a freshman at Kaskaskia Junior College in Centralia, Ill and 18.6 ppg and 4.6 apg as a sophomore. He'll push senior **Cyrus Caldwell** and Jones, for the starting two-guard spot.

"Roy is a very tough competitor who will help us on both ends of the floor," Cobb said. "He is a good shooter from the perimeter and he can take it to the basket with authority."

Jones, the only freshman in the group, averaged 19.5 points, 4.7 assists and 3.6 rebounds as a senior point guard at Las Vegas (Nev.) High School. He also canned three three-pointers per game and shot 40 percent from behind the arc.

"Ronnie has a great feel for the game," Cobb said. "He has outstanding court awareness and knowledge of the total game. He will definitely be one of our three-point threats."

While the younger guys and newcomers figure to make most of the headlines, Cobb desperately needs his seniors Caldwell, **Larry Treadwell** and **Keith Seigel** to step up and be leaders.

Caldwell, a 6-1 point guard, is the most talented of the lot, averaging 8.0 ppg, a team-best 4.7 apg and 2.7 rpg. He started all but one game in 1997-98 and will back up Fountain.

Seigel, a 6-7 forward, scored 3.7 ppg and hauled down 3.0 rebounds per game, fourth-best on the team. Treadwell, a 6-4 guard, averaged 5.1 ppg and should battle for the starting two-guard slot.

"One of the biggest challenges this team faces in 1998-99 will be how fast everyone blends in together," said Cobb. "It is this group of seniors that will need to bring the new guys along faster."

One additional new face will be 6-7, 245-pound redshirt freshman **Kyle Kickert**. He'll be hard-pressed to get playing time this season, though. That's because, in addition to Kickert, Cobb can call on a trio of juniors off the bench in guard **Danny Johnson** (6-2, 160) and forwards **Bryan LaFave** (6-7, 200) and **Tim Gullette** (6-5, 185).

Johnson (2.8 ppg) played in all 27 games last season, including five starts. LaFave and Gullette worked hard in weight room over the summer, but still need to add some weight to their frames to be consistent contributors.

Add it all up and the Panthers are certainly more talented than last year. But is it enough for the Elevator Man, if he pushes the right buttons, to get his team out of the MCC basement? Probably not.

adidas Blue Ribbon Analysis

BACKCOURT .... C BENCH/DEPTH .... D
FRONTCOURT .... C INTANGIBLES .... D

Another year, another season in the MCC basement. But for the first time in Ric Cobb's tenure, it appears that this team has a future with a solid all-sophomore frontcourt to build around.

If the team's JUCO imports Shawn Fountain and Roy King can fill the two starting guard spots, then maybe the Panthers can win a few more games and get out of the league's cellar. However, one of the sophomores—none of whom were double-figure scorers last year—or a new face must develop into a go-to guy.

If they don't, then the UMW powers-that-be might have no choice but to give Cobb his walking papers. He's produced single-digit win totals in each of his first three seasons. A fourth straight would be too much for anyone to take.

(B.D.)

WRIGHT STATE

LOCATION .... Dayton, OH
CONFERENCE .... Midwestern Collegiate
LAST SEASON .... 10-18 (.357)
CONFERENCE RECORD 3-11 (7th)
STARTERS LOST/RETURNING 2/3
NICKNAME .... Raiders
COLORS .... Green & Gold
HOMECOURT .... Ervin J. Nutter Center (10,632)
COACH .... Ed Schilling (Miami-Ohio '88)
RECORD AT SCHOOL .... 10-18 (1 yr.)
CAREER RECORD .... 10-18 (1 yr.)
ASSISTANTS .... Will Rey (NE Illinois '76)
Ken Barer (George Washington '88)
Red Foster (UCLA '88)
TEAM WINS (last 5 yrs.) 12-13-14-7-10
RPI (last 5 yrs.) 227-154-118-265-185
1997-98 FINISH ... Lost in conference second round.

Ed Schilling has been on a whirlwind ride up the coaching ranks.

As recently as 1995, Schilling was coaching at Logansport (Ind.) High School. He spent his summers wisely, working as a station master at Howard Garfinkel's Five-Star Basketball Camp in Coraopolis, Pa., just a chest pass away from Moon, Pa. (the birthplace of John Calipari). So, of course, coach Cal got to know Schilling during his recruiting trips back to his old stomping grounds (Calipari, too, was a station master at Five-Star) and he eventually hired Schilling as an assistant at UMass before the 1995-96 season.

Things fell quickly into place for Schilling after that. The Minutemen went 35-2 and reached the 1996 Final Four before losing to eventual national champ Kentucky.

Calipari liked Schilling's work so much that he took him to the swamps of Jersey as an assistant coach with the New Jersey Nets for the 1996-97 season. From there, he was chosen the head coach at Wright State on March 18, 1997.

Pretty heady stuff, to be sure. But Schilling's carpet ride hit some turbulence last season—in the form of a 10-18 record. There were bright spots though, specifically a first-round MCC tournament upset over heavily-favored Illinois-Chicago and the all-around brilliance of 6-3 junior guard **Keion Brooks**.

If the memorable moments are to continue in 1998-99, chances are that Brooks will be in the middle of them. Brooks (14.7 ppg, 4.2 rpg, 76 assists) was the model of consistency for Schilling last season, scoring in double figures in all but one of the Raiders' games. The tough-to-defend slasher enters his senior season as the school's 12th all-time leading scorer with 1,207 points. How good is Brooks? If he can significantly improve his perimeter touch (just 17 of 52 from behind the arc last year), then he'll get some NBA looks.

Rejoining Brooks in the Raiders' starting backcourt will be 6-1 sophomore **Brandon Pardon**, Schilling's first-ever recruit at Wright State. If Pardon (6.1 ppg, 1.8 rpg, 105 assists) can improve his perimeter jumper too (.388 FG percentage), then he'll join Brooks to form one of the MCC's finest backcourts. The third returning starter is 6-5 senior small forward **Sherman Curry** (8.2 ppg, 3.7 rpg, 15 blocked shots). Curry missed games early in the season with a balky knee, but this JUCO import made his presence felt as the season wore on. His high point last year was a 20-point, 10-rebound game against Prairie View A&M two days after Christmas.

Additional help on the wings will come from 5-11 freshman point guard **Marcus May** (12.6 ppg, 4.0 spg, 2.5 apg for perennial prep powerhouse Indianapolis North High School). He's the heir apparent to Pardon at the point.

Pushing Curry for the starting small forward slot will be 6-6 sophomore **Kevin Melson**, an honorable mention JUCO All-American last season at Schoolcraft (Mich.) Community College. Melson was second in the junior college ranks in scoring (28.6 ppg) and also averaged 9.8 boards per game. Melson led the Ocelots to their best season in a decade (a 24-7 record). He will have three years of eligibility left after missing his entire freshman season because of an injury.

Giving Brooks an occasional break will be 6-4 freshman swingman **Louis Holmes** (31.3 ppg, 13 rpg, 5.0 apg, 2 spg for Orange Christian Academy in suburban Cleveland last year). Holmes is a zone-busting jump-shooter extraordinaire who collected more than 100 three-pointers last season and had three games of 40 points or better. In addition to his on-court skills, Holmes is a true student-athlete as his selection as his senior class valedictorian and membership in his high school's National Honor Society indicate. "Louis is a great addition to our program," said Schilling. "He is an outstanding long-range shooter who will keep the defense honest."

The new faces on the perimeter won't just be handed playing time. They'll have to earn it. Melson and Holmes, for instance, figure to do battle with Curry and 6-4 junior swingman **Steve Yeagle** (2.2 ppg, 1.2 rpg), who appeared in 27 games last year, for quality minutes.

While there are options at the three perimeter spots, there are some questions at the four and five spots—where double-figure scorers Thad Burton (12.8), a 6-8 power forward, and Marvin Rodgers (12.3 ppg), a 6-9 pivot, have both departed.

The five spot will be manned by 6-9, 271-pound transfer **Inus Norville**, who was highly recruited out of high school but spent lots of time on the pine—first behind 1996 lottery pick Marcus Camby and then Lari Ketner at UMass. Norville, a 23-year-old fifth-year senior, figures to be an impact player in the MCC, where 270-plus pound centers aren't in great supply. At UMass, he had much more of an impact on defense (69 career blocks) than he ever had on offense, though.

Backing up Norville, Wright State's new Big Man on Campus, will be 7-foot sophomore **Bruno Petersons**. While Norville will be 24 by the time he picks up his college diploma this spring, Petersons is a young 'un (he didn't turn 19 until July 22). Since arriving at Wright State, Petersons (0.8 ppg, 0.8 rpg, 14 blocks) has added nearly 25 pounds to his frame and he could start to blossom this season.

Another guy who is devouring second and third helpings at the school cafeteria is 6-7 sophomore **Onome Scott-Emuakpor** (1.7 ppg, 1.6 rpg). Scott-Emuakpor arrived at Wright State as skinny as Kate Moss (6-7, 180 pounds). But thanks to a diligent eating and weight-training regimen, he's now 206 pounds and is much better equipped to deal with the hand-to-hand combat of Division I ball.

1998-99 WRIGHT STATE SCHEDULE

Nov.	14	@Old Dominion
	17	Central Michigan
	20	Pittsburgh
	23	*Kentucky
	28	Sacred Heart
Dec.	5	Denver
	8	@Ball State
	12	@Denver
	14	@Northern Iowa
	19	Morehead State
	21	Prairie View A&M
	28	Chicago State
Jan.	2	@Loyola
	4	@Illinois-Chicago
	9	Butler
	14	Detroit
	16	Cleveland State
	21	@Wisconsin-Milwaukee
	23	@Wisconsin-Green Bay
	28	Loyola
	30	Illinois-Chicago
Feb.	6	@Butler
	11	@Cleveland State
	13	@Detroit
	18	Wisconsin-Green Bay
	20	Wisconsin-Milwaukee
27-Mar.	2	#MCC Tournament

@ Road Games
* The Crown, Cincinnati, OH
\# UIC Pavillion, Chicago, IL

Fellow sophomore **Ryan Grose** (2.9 ppg, 1.8 rpg), 6-7, figures to also battle for the vacant power forward slot—along with Israeli import **Israel Sheinfeld**, a 6-10 freshman. The 22-year-old Sheinfeld has spent the last three years in the Israeli army.

"Although Israel was not highly recruited, we saw tremendous potential as we watched him play and got to know him as a person," says Schilling. "He has the potential to improve his skills as he becomes more acquainted with the game in the United States. Israel is not an immediate answer to all of our NCAA Tournament dreams, but he can certainly be a piece to help us improve."

adidas Blue Ribbon Analysis

BACKCOURT .... B BENCH/DEPTH C
FRONTCOURT .... C+ INTANGIBLES C

Everyone is confident that Ed Schilling is Mr. Right at Wright State. But rebuilding tasks take time, even for boy wonders like Schilling. It's only Schilling's second season and most Division I rebuilding projects are five-year propositions, so expect some peaks (such as the all-around play of NBA prospect Keion Brooks) and lots of valleys (with a sophomore point guard and lots of frontcourt questions).

Add it all up and it looks like a 12-14 win season and a seventh-place finish in MCC—unless frontcourt transfers Inus Norville and Kevin Melson take the league by storm.

(B.D.)

adidas Blue Ribbon Analysis

GRADING SYSTEM

- A+ equal to very best in country—Final Four-caliber unit
- A among the best in the land—worthy of deep NCAA run
- B+ talented, versatile and experienced—NCAA-NIT ability
- B solid and productive winners—league and post-season contenders
- C+ average to above-average—may contend in a weaker league
- C average to mediocre—second division in a strong league
- D+ below average, inconsistent—second division in a weaker league
- D well below average—losing season virtually certain
- F non-Division I ability—an underdog every night

MISSOURI VALLEY CONFERENCE

adidas BLUE RIBBON FORECAST

1. Creighton
2. Southwest Missouri State
3. Illinois State
4. Wichita State
5. Bradley
6. Evansville
7. Indiana State
8. Southern Illinois
9. Northern Iowa
10. Drake

ALL-CONFERENCE TEAM

G—Marcus Wilson, SR, Evansville
G—Maurice Evans, SO, Wichita State
F—Rodney Buford, SR, Creighton
F—Chris Thunell, JR, Southern Illinois
C—Danny Moore, SR, Southwest Missouri State

PLAYER OF THE YEAR

Rodney Buford, SR, Creighton

NEWCOMER OF THE YEAR

Tarise Bryson, SO, Illinois State

1998-99 CONFERENCE TOURNAMENT

Feb. 26-March 1, Keil Center, St. Louis, MO

1997-98 CHAMPION

Illinois State (regular season)
Illinois State (conference tournament)

1997-98 POSTSEASON PARTICIPANTS

Postseason Record: 1-2 (.333)

NCAA

Illinois State (second round)

NIT

Creighton

TOP BACKCOURTS

1. Creighton
2. Southwest Missouri State
3. Bradley

TOP FRONTCOURTS

1. Southwest Missouri State
2. Illinois State
3. Southern Illinois

ON THE WAY UP

Southwest Missouri State

ON THE WAY DOWN

Northern Iowa

INSIDE THE NUMBERS

- 1997-98 conference RPI: 12 (of 30)
- Conference RPI (last 5 years): 17-10-12-10-12

DID YOU KNOW?

Jason Perez, Wichita State's honorable-mention All-MVC junior, broke a bone in his foot on Sept. 3 during a pickup game. Surgery was performed and Perez was expected to miss the Shockers' first two weeks of practice...Creighton is making a big deal of trying to become the first MVC school to improve its overall and conference record for five straight seasons—for good reason. The only other team to do it was Henry Iba's Oklahoma A&M squad. Iba was one of seven inductees in the Valley's first Hall of Fame class (1997)...Junior big man Cory Jenkins won't be eligible for the first semester at Northern Iowa. Jenkins' academic difficulties will keep him out of games in November and some in December...Illinois State will try to continue a remarkable streak this season. For seven consecutive years, the Redbirds have won at least 12 conference games. Most years, that's meant at least a .667 winning percentage...For the second straight season, Bradley led the Valley in attendance with 9,769 fans per game in 1997-98. The Braves have been in the NCAA's top 50 in attendance the last five seasons...The Missouri Valley's career three-point goals leader, Shane Hawkins of Southern Illinois, will trade in his sneakers for a clipboard this season. Hawkins will be an undergraduate assistant to Salukis first-year coach Bruce Weber...Indiana State is going for its first back-to-back winning seasons since 1980. The Sycamores would need to win a highly improbable 33 games to tie the two-year win mark that the '78-79 and '79-80 teams achieved...Southwest Missouri State didn't play any other Division I teams from inside the state last season, but the Bears have all four (Missouri, Saint Louis, Missouri-Kansas City and Southeast Missouri State) on this year's schedule...Evansville's sixth-best free-throw percentage nationally last season was no fluke. The Aces shot 75.7 percent, with four players shooting 85 percent or better...Not only has Drake lost all 36 of its conference games over the last two seasons, but last year the Bulldogs got within six points of a league opponent just twice—in home games against Southern Illinois and Wichita State.

(K.S.)

BRADLEY

LOCATION ..... **Peoria, IL**
CONFERENCE ..... **Missouri Valley**
LAST SEASON ..... **15-14 (.517)**
CONFERENCE RECORD ..... **9-9 (t-6th)**
STARTERS LOST/RETURNING **1/4**
NICKNAME ..... **Braves**
COLORS ..... **Red & White**
HOMECOURT ..... **Carver Arena (10,825)**
COACH ..... **Jim Molinari (Illinois Wesleyan '77)**
RECORD AT SCHOOL ..... **115-92 (7 yrs.)**
CAREER RECORD ..... **157-109 (9 yrs.)**
ASSISTANTS ..... **Pat Donahue (Elmhurst '88)**
Duane Broussard (Bradley '93)
George Barber (Asbury '86)
TEAM WINS (last 5 yrs.) **23-20-22-17-15**
RPI (last 5 yrs.) **71-54-30-102-139**
1997-98 FINISH ..... **Lost in conference semifinal.**

When you play the kind of defense that Jim Molinari teaches at Bradley, the upsides are numerous.

Bradley was the nation's second-best defensive team last season, allowing opponents to shoot only .382 percent from the field. The Braves were also ninth-best in scoring defense, allowing 61.1 points a night. The downside? Take a look at Bradley's offensive numbers. Semi-offensive, really.

Despite respectable field-goal, three-point and free-throw percentages, the Braves averaged a meager 64.6 points—eighth in the 10-team Missouri Valley Conference.

The problem is simple: When Bradley makes opponents use up 30 to 34 seconds of the shot clock, it doesn't give the Braves as many offensive possessions of their own. Bradley was last in MVC field goals last season. "That is an issue for us," Molinari said. "But a lot of it is caused by our defense. Our defense is very position-oriented. It takes teams a lot of time to get shots off.

"I think we did see the last 12 games we really did start pushing the ball more last season."

Which brings us to the Braves' magical statistic: Since Molinari took over in 1991, Bradley is 66-10 (.868) when it scores 70 or more points. Last season, Bradley was 7-2 when scoring at least 70 (8-12 when under 70). So expect the Braves to get into more of a running game this season—or at least attempt to get more transition baskets, which in Bradley vernacular is fast-break basketball.

Bradley scored more than 70 points in just three of its first 17 games last season, but did it five times over the last dozen to finish 8-4 down the stretch.

Fortunately for the Braves, the guys who will get the ball moving are experienced and talented. Big guard **Rob Dye** and point man **Eric Roberson** were two of Bradley's three full-time starters last season. Dye (12.5 ppg, 4.8 rpg, 94 assists, 37 steals), a 6-1 junior, averaged more than 35 minutes a game and took over as the Braves' three-point threat. Dye attempted 147 three-pointers, but just as importantly, he's quick enough to blow by defenders and get to the basket.

Roberson (8.2 ppg, 6.0 rpg, 105 assists, 71 steals), a 6-4 junior, was among Division I's top 30 in steals per game (2.4). Maybe the Braves' most all- around player—he was the team's No. 2 rebounder with 6.0 a game—Roberson has good size and quick hands, but needs to improve his 57-percent free-throw shooting from a year ago.

It will be up to these two to quicken Bradley's tempo, which won't be easy with the Braves playing 30-35 seconds of harassing defense during every opponent's possession.

"On the perimeter, those guys have gotten a lot of experience early," Molinari said. "They made some mistakes when they were young, but they're athletic and competitive. They're going to be a very good pair of guards."

Backup guard minutes will go to **Jerome Robinson**, **Fred Atkins** and **Reggie Hall**. Robinson (3.1 ppg, 2.0 rpg), a 6-3 sophomore, is an athletic player who earned valuable experience last season. Atkins (5.9 ppg, 2.3 rpg, 33 assists) can play either big guard or small forward and has a year of inconsistency behind him. Hall, a sophomore from Chicago who didn't qualify academically last year but went to school at BU, could be a pleasant surprise at one of the wing spots. He has a good jump shot and is also able to penetrate to the basket.

Jim Vershaw (0.5 ppg, 0.3 rpg), a 6-4 senior, is a walkon who didn't play much last season.

Also on the perimeter will be **Gavin Schairer** (5.1 ppg. 1.8 rpg), a 6-7 small forward who is Bradley's only senior with any experience. Schairer has been a role player his entire career, but the Braves could use more out of him in his final season.

"Gavin came on during the stretch last year and he's going to have to add some leadership," Molinari said. "He's also going to have to be the guy to make some three-point shots." Schairer shot .432 percent from three-point range last season and is sure to take more than the 74 he hoisted last season.

No matter who's running the show on the perimeter, what will make Bradley either a Valley contender or pretender is a front line that enters the season woefully short on scoring, rebounding and big-game experience. The front line is also short one dominating center—Adebayo Akinkunle, a first-team All-Valley player and defensive player of the year who graduated. "We'll miss Bayo because those are the hardest-type players to recruit," Molinari said. "You don't replace a long, athletic 6-9 player who's

1998-99 BRADLEY SCHEDULE

Nov.	17	Southeast Missouri State
	21	Tennessee-Martin
Dec.	2	@Michigan
	5	*Illinois
	9	Penn State
	19	Western Illinois
	22	Indiana State
	26	@George Washington
	30	@Creighton
Jan.	3	Northern Iowa
	6	@Southern Illinois
	9	@Drake
	13	@Southwest Missouri State
	16	Wichita State
	20	@Illinois State
	23	Evansville
	27	Creighton
	30	@Indiana State
Feb.	3	@Northern Iowa
	6	Drake
	10	Illinois State
	13	Southwest Missouri State
	17	@Evansville
	20	@Wichita State
	22	Southern Illinois
26-Mar.	1	#MVC Tournament

@ Road Games
* United Center, Chicago, IL
\# Kiel Center, St. Louis, MO

versatile, so we'll try to do it by committee."

Problem is, the committee doesn't have an obvious chairman. **Ed Cage, Matt Moran, Aba Koita, Matthew Lee** and **Milo Kirsch** are all members looking for a promotion.

Cage (7.6 ppg, 3.5 rpg, 32 assists), a 6-7 junior, has faced the basket more often than not in his first two seasons. A starter in 17 games last season, Cage will need to boost his rebounding numbers. Koita (2.3 ppg, 1.7 rpg), a 6-9 junior center, gives the Braves their biggest body. Koita played almost 10 minutes a game last season but has an accurate shooting touch. Lee (2.3 ppg, 1.7 rpg), a 6-8 junior, should see more than the 9.5 minutes he averaged last season.

Kirsch, a 6-7 freshman from Indianapolis Lawrence Central High, joins the program as a strong leaper who should help defensively.

Moran (4.1 ppg, 2.6 rpg), a 6-8 junior, may have the best shot of doing the most damage. He transferred to Bradley from Northwestern and sat out the 1996-97 season, then a broken foot and broken hand wiped out almost half of his '97-98 games. When he's healthy and applies himself, he's a sharp inside player. But his injured foot acted up again in September, making Moran's status questionable as the season began.

"They really don't bring anything yet," Molinari said of his front-line candidates. "Lee's a pretty good athlete. Aba has a lot of size and a lot of fight. Moran was coming on at the end of last year and he has a good touch around the basket.

"We don't have a proven inside player, but that doesn't mean they can't become good players."

adidas Blue Ribbon Analysis

BACKCOURT .... B+ BENCH/DEPTH C
FRONTCOURT .... D+ INTANGIBLES C

Bradley would love to average 70 points this season, but it'll be tough. When the Braves' stifling defense continues to limit possessions, and an inside game lacks the rebounding and scoring strength to make much of an impact, another scoring average in the low- to mid-60s wouldn't be a surprise.

Scoring averages aside, another strong defensive team will keep Bradley in almost every game and win some that the Braves probably don't deserve. But this is a defense unlike the last few, in that Akinkunle isn't the last line of protection in the middle. Opposing penetrators can take it to the middle with less fear of having a shot swatted across Carver Arena.

If the front-line committee can pass a resolution of acceptable scoring and rebounding numbers, and keep opposing big men from having huge nights, Bradley will challenge for an upper-division Missouri Valley finish. If not, the opposition will target Roberson and Dye and a middle-of-the-pack finish will be a best-case scenario.

Either way, don't look for the Braves to return to the NCAA Tournament or NIT, which they missed out on last season for the first time in five years.

(K.S.)

CREIGHTON

LOCATION .... Omaha, NE
CONFERENCE .... Missouri Valley
LAST SEASON .... 18-10 (.643)
CONFERENCE RECORD 12-6 (2nd)
STARTERS LOST/RETURNING 2/3
NICKNAME .... Bluejays
COLORS .... Blue & White
HOMECOURT .... Omaha Civic Auditorium (9,493)
COACH .... Dana Altman (Eastern New Mexico '80)
RECORD AT SCHOOL .... 54-59 (4 yrs.)
CAREER RECORD .... 137-126 (9 yrs.)
ASSISTANTS .... Greg Grensing (Southwest Texas State '79)
Len Gordy (Arizona '77)
Kevin McKenna (Creighton '93)
TEAM WINS (last 5 yrs.) 7-7-14-15-18
RPI (last 5 yrs.) 260-214-161-138-89
1997-98 FINISH .... Lost in NIT first round.

Very quietly, Dana Altman has rebuilt the Creighton basketball program into a Missouri Valley Conference contender.

The four years of building came almost in baby steps. There was the "get-your-feet-wet" 7-19 season in 1994-95, still an improvement from the year before Altman arrived. Then the near-.500 second season, a 15-15 mark in 1996-97, and then last year's explosion into an 18-10 squad that finished second in the Valley and earned an NIT bid. Only last season's record was unexpected.

1998-99 CREIGHTON SCHEDULE

Nov.	14	Towson
	18	@Missouri-Kansas City
	25	@Iowa
	29	Centenary
Dec.	2	Baylor
	5	Southern Illinois
	9	@Nebraska
	12	@Drake
	20	Oklahoma State
	22	Mississippi Valley State
	30	Bradley
Jan.	2	@Indiana State
	4	Evansville
	10	@Southwest Missouri
	17	Indiana State
	20	@Evansville
	23	Illinois State
	27	@Bradley
	30	@Northern Iowa
Feb.	1	@Southern Illinois
	6	@Wichita State
	10	Northern Iowa
	14	@Illinois State
	17	Southwest Missouri
	20	Drake
	22	Wichita State
26-Mar.	1	#Missouri Valley Conference Tournament

@ Road Games
\# Kiel Center, St. Louis, MO

The Bluejays had NBA prospect **Rodney Buford** to carry the load, but plenty of no-names and newcomers around him. Thing is, the newcomers filled in tremendously around Buford and Creighton finished with its best record since 1990-91. This time, with all important cogs remaining in place, more improvement seems natural. Creighton has 13 lettermen back and is eyeing its first conference crown in eight years.

"I guess it's the next step," Altman said. "We've made good progress and I'm pleased with the efforts of our young men."

The Bluejays start, but don't end, with Buford (18.9 ppg, 7.3 rpg, 58 assists, 43 steals), a 6-5 senior small forward who is the favorite for league player-of-the-year honors. Already with 1,540 points, Buford could become Creighton's career scoring leader by late in the season. Buford has a wonderful inside-outside game, able to drive to the basket or stop on a dime and hit a 17-footer. But where he could help Creighton most this season is in other areas.

"The place I'd like to see Rodney carry us more is rebounding and on the defensive end," Altman said. "We don't have to get 20-something from him every night. As the team matures, some guys are going to step forward for us."

Rebounding started to become one of Buford's assets last season. He had at least eight boards in 13 games, leading the Bluejays in rebounding in 16 of 28 games. That should dispel the notion that Buford is a one-dimensional player.

"I think the two things I've always talked to Rodney about are improvements defensively and becoming more physical," Altman said. "He has lifted weights with a little better regimen this summer and I hope that helps him. If his game is going to improve, he needs to be more consistent in those areas."

With Buford in the backcourt will be a foursome of guards: 6-0 sophomore **Ryan Sears**; 6-2 sophomore **Ben Walker**; 6-0 senior **Corie Brandon**; and 6-4 junior swingman **Matt West**.

Sears (10.5 ppg, 3.0 rpg, 134 assists, 62 steals) was the Valley's Freshman of the Year after taking over playmaking duties. Third in the league in assists and steals, Sears provided Creighton a reliable point man to run the show.

"Ryan is a worker and he'll work even harder this year," Altman said. "He'll find ways offensively to find us some more easy baskets. He won't have to look over at the bench nearly as much. He'll have an idea what he wants to run for himself."

Walker (5.6 ppg) and Brandon (7.2 ppg, 70 assists) split time at shooting guard last season. Both shot 41 percent from three-point range, though neither tried nearly as many as Buford and Sears. Altman wants Walker to make more strides in his sophomore season, especially on defense. He is an animal on the offensive boards, gathering a team-high 52 last season.

Brandon was picked to the Valley's All-Bench team and is the more-legitimate three-point threat. Both will spell Sears at point guard.

West (4.6 ppg) was Creighton's top three-point percentage man (.423) and made key threes in early season wins over Nebraska, Towson State and Northern Iowa. West should continue to see considerable minutes as a backup to Buford.

Other guards vying for playing time are 6-2 junior **Dan Kolder** (0.5 ppg) and 6-1 junior **Jason Ourada** (0.1 ppg). Kolder and Ourada each averaged less than two minutes a game last season.

Second-year players such as Sears and Walker got more experience last May, when the Bluejays took a two-week trip to Europe and compiled a 5-1 record against club teams.

"It gave us an opportunity to go out for two weeks and spend a lot of time together," Altman said. "We played a very physical brand of basketball and that's something we need to improve upon."

Playing physically was the biggest problem for Creighton's front-liners last season, including 6-10 senior center **Doug Swenson** (11.3 ppg, 4.4 rpg, 57 blocked shots), a junior-college transfer who blossomed as the Valley shot-blocking leader. Swenson was used exclusively off the bench, yet blocked more than two shots a game.

With big man Kevin Mungin (5.5 ppg, 3.5 rpg) no longer on the team (failure to meet team standards), Swenson will see much more than the 20 minutes he averaged last season. Swenson will be the starting center and have to watch foul trouble, which got him disqualified six times last season.

Offensively, Swenson has nice shooting range (.530 FG, .740 FT) and complements Sears' outside shooting and Buford's all-around game.

Swenson, who along with Sears was a Valley All-Newcomer pick, should be helped inside by the addition of 6-8, 235-pound junior forward **Nerijus Karlikanovas**, a Lithuanian who averaged 19.5 points and six rebounds as an all-conference player at Mid-Plains Community College in North Platte, Neb.

Karlikanovas is Creighton's first foreign player and has the size to be the physical player Altman is looking for. He's also the only addition to the Jays' roster.

"It's definitely going to be a transition for him, but I hope not for long," Altman said of Karlikanovas' ascension to Division I. "He's got good size and a good body, and he can post up and give us some things inside."

More inside depth will come from 6-4 sophomore forward **Justin Haynes** and 6-7 junior forward **Donnie Johnson**. Haynes (5.0 ppg) was one of four Bluejays on the bench rotation last season, while Johnson sat out after transferring from State Fair Community College in Sedalia, Mo. He averaged 13.0 points, 8.3 rebounds and 3.6 blocks in 1996-97.

Other front-line players are 26-year-old **Cliff Bates**, a 6-4 senior forward; 6-9 sophomore center **Alan Huss** (1.0 ppg); and 6-5 redshirt freshman **John Klein.**

Bates (1.9 ppg) came to Creighton from Iowa Western Community College with the reputation of a scorer, but needs to improve his defense to earn more playing time. Huss is coming back from knee surgery last season and will be Swenson's backup.

adidas Blue Ribbon Analysis

BACKCOURT .... B+ BENCH/DEPTH C
FRONTCOURT .... B INTANGIBLES .... B

No Missouri Valley Conference team has ever improved its overall and conference records in five consecutive seasons. Creighton should be the first. Altman's concerns are few. His team will score, and although the Jays' press can give opponents fits, he'd like to see his half-court defense shut some foes down.

Buford will once again be the leader, but as the Bluejays proved last season, it's the guys around Buford that makes this team complete. Another year of seasoning for Sears and Walker, plus a solid senior season from Swenson, should put Creighton in the driver's seat for the Missouri Valley crown.

(K.S.)

DRAKE

LOCATION .... **Des Moines, IA**
CONFERENCE .... **Missouri Valley**
LAST SEASON .... **3-24 (.111)**
CONFERENCE RECORD .... **0-18 (10th)**
STARTERS LOST/RETURNING **1/4**
NICKNAME .... **Bulldogs**
COLORS .... **Blue & White**
HOMECOURT .... **Knapp Center (7,000)**
COACH .... **Kurt Kanaskie (LaSalle'80)**
RECORD AT SCHOOL .... **5-50 (2 yrs.)**
CAREER RECORD .... **212-157 (13 yrs.)**
ASSISTANTS .... **Marty Bell (South Carolina '87)**
Lennie Parham (Gonzaga '87)
Kevin Reynolds (Bloomsburg '91)
TEAM WINS (last 5 yrs.) **11-12-12-2-3**
RPI (last 5 yrs.) **202-140-139-255-293**
1997-98 FINISH ..... **Lost in conference play-in round.**

Drake is a resounding 0-36 in the Missouri Valley Conference over the last two seasons. It has gotten to the point where the standing coach's line, "On any given night ..." doesn't apply anymore. The Bulldogs have been so overmatched the last two seasons, their games have become gimmes for opponents. The challenge for Bulldogs coach Kurt Kanaskie, who begins his third season with a 5-50 overall record, is to begin to make some strides.

Drake was just plain bad in Kanaskie's first year and overwhelmed in his second.

"I don't think we've been as bad as our record," Kanaskie said, "but we have not had the talent to compete in the Valley." If things are going to change any in Des Moines this season, it has to come from six newcomers Kanaskie believes have more athletic ability than his lettermen. The returning players, while adequate, won't be able to get the Bulldogs out of the conference cellar by themselves.

"We inherited a program that, quite frankly, was in a tough situation," Kanaskie said. "We didn't have many upperclassmen at all, and because of Drake's academic situation, we couldn't go to junior-college kids unless they were good students."

This season, though, Drake will lean heavily on three junior-college players: 6-8 junior **Aaron Deeter**, 6-8 junior **Dontay Harris** and 6-5 sophomore **Abdul Collier**.

Deeter, a 225-pound frontliner, averaged 12.2 points and 6.5 rebounds at Collin County (Texas) Junior College last season. He's an inside banger who should give the Bulldogs some physical play, which has been missing. Harris, who earned all-conference honors at San Jose (Calif.) City Junior College, averaged 7.2 points and 6.0 rebounds and helped San Jose to 63 victories in his two seasons.

Last season, the Bulldogs had two inside players average almost 10 points each. But neither were reliable scoring threats. Kanaskie hopes Deeter and Harris will cure that problem.

"The two junior-college post players are very mature and skilled and skilled outside," Kanaskie said. "They can both step out and shoot. We haven't had much of that."

Collier, from Marshalltown (Iowa) Junior College, averaged 4.6 points and 1.8 rebounds as a freshman last season. He's a big guard at 210 pounds and will provide some outside shooting depth. But it's the two freshmen the Bulldogs hope will provide some continuity for four years. Talented **Kareem Lee**, a 6-2 point guard, and **Jonathan Anderson**, a 6-4 shooting guard, will push Drake veterans for playing time in the backcourt.

Lee, who averaged 22.5 points and 4.1 assists at Trinity Catholic High in Stamford, Conn., is a highly sought-after point man who was an all-state pick in Connecticut. Lee shot 48 percent from three-point range as a prep senior, but it's his ballhandling and speed that will make Drake's offense more diverse than in the past.

"We have had no one who could break down the defense on the dribble," Kanaskie said. "I think now we have several guys who can do that." Including Anderson, a freshman who averaged 20.5 points at Mount Tahoma High in Tacoma, Wash. Anderson can score outside and inside, especially with a 39-inch vertical leap. Anderson recently had his high school jersey number retired—the first Mount Tahoma athlete to be so honored since Ahmad Rashad.

On a three-win team, you'd think that Lee and Anderson would be in the starting lineup on opening night. But if there's any depth to the Bulldogs, it's on the perimeter, where 6-2 junior guard **Armand LeVasseur** and 5-11 junior point guard **Matt Woodley** return. They are the closest things Kanaskie has to seniors this season.

LeVasseur (10.9 ppg, 1.8 rpg, 47 assists) strengthened his big-guard game over the last half of last season, scoring more than 20 points in three of Drake's final six games. As an outside shooter, his three-point percentage (.400) was better than the entire team's field-goal percentage (.396). "LeVasseur really came on at the end of the year last year," Kanaskie said. "He's always been a pretty decent shooter, now he's quicker off the dribble."

Woodley (10.1 ppg, 3.1 rpg, 111 assists, 61 steals) owned two of the Bulldogs' three top-10 conference statistical finishes. He finished second in steals, sixth in assists. But he also shot a mediocre .329 percent from three-point range, attempting a team-high 6.3 treys per game.

Backup guard minutes will come from **Aaron Thomas** (2.1 ppg, 1.7 rpg), a 6-4 sophomore, and **Jason VandeBrake**, a 6-4 junior swingman. VandeBrake averaged 9.9 points and 9.0 rebounds last season at Iowa Lakes Junior College.

Drake will be without part-time starter Kory Petzenhauser (4.0 ppg, 2.3 rpg), a senior who transferred to South Dakota.

Inside, Drake was outrebounded badly last season. Opponents grabbed seven more boards per night, and only departed senior Rashad Thomas averaged more than 3.7 rebounds. For Drake to make strides, the front line needs to get better.

Last season, 6-8 sophomore **Joey Gaw** had to be the Bulldogs' rock as a freshman, even though he wasn't ready for the role. Gaw (9.8 ppg, 3.7 rpg, 37 assists) seemed to wear down as the rigors of a long Missouri Valley schedule caught up with him. But Gaw, like many of the Bulldogs, have put more emphasis into weight training during the offseason.

"I think Gaw had to do too much as a freshman," Kanaskie said. "All the other good freshman kids in the Valley had time to work themselves into things. But we had to rely on him and I thought he wore down." A terrific free-throw shooter (.767 percent), Gaw's lack of stamina showed in a .384-percent shooting year. He hit a third of his three-point shots, but needs to become more of a threat with his back to the basket.

Harris and Deeter should help take some of the pressure off. Forward help will also come from **Myron Richardson** (7.5 ppg, 3.5 rpg, 34 steals), a 6-7 junior. Richardson started 13 games last season and showed spurts where he was Drake's best athlete. Kanaskie hopes with more quality athletes around him, Richardson can blossom in his second season in Des Moines. **Justin Ohl** (2.6 ppg, 2.2 rpg), a 6-6 sophomore, will see backup minutes at small forward.

Brandon Donaldson (2.7 ppg, 1.6 rpg) is a 6-10 sophomore center who could back up Gaw or possibly redshirt.

1998-99 DRAKE SCHEDULE

Nov.	18	New York-Stony Brook
	24	Delaware State
	28	Lamar
Dec.	1	Iowa
	5	Loyola-Chicago
	8	@Iowa State
	12	Creighton
	19	Illinois State
	27-28	#Hoosier Classic
Jan.	2	Evansville
	4	@Wichita State
	9	Bradley
	13	@Illinois State
	16	@Southwest Missouri State
	18	@Southern Illinois
	24	Northern Iowa
	27	Southwest Missouri State
	30	@Evansville
Feb.	4	Indiana State
	6	@Bradley
	11	Wichita State
	13	@Indiana State
	17	Southern Illinois
	20	@Creighton
	22	@Northern Iowa
26-Mar.	1	##MVC Tournament

@ Road Games
\# Indianapolis, IN (vs. Indiana, first round; also Ball State and Bucknell)
\#\# Kiel Center, St. Louis, MO

adidas Blue Ribbon Analysis

BACKCOURT .... **C** BENCH/DEPTH .... **D+**
FRONTCOURT .... **D** INTANGIBLES .... **D**

Winning five games in two seasons isn't the only thing that has made Kurt Kanaskie pull his hair out as Drake's head coach. Also contributing was the methodical offense, the lack of a fast break, being outrebounded badly most nights and giving up easy baskets on defense.

There was a common denominator for all those woes: A lack of athleticism. Take away Lynnrick Rogers two years ago and Kanaskie hasn't had a player who can light it up offensively or compete athletically with the rest of the conference. This season, Kanaskie hopes that starts to turn around. Don't misunderstand improvement with contention—the Bulldogs are still miles away from the Missouri Valley's upper division, most less the penthouse. Even a simple escape from the conference cellar would be considered a good season. But unless the newcomers mesh and contribute quickly, it will be hard for Drake not to be looking up at all nine Valley foes again.

(K.S.)

EVANSVILLE

LOCATION .... **Evansville, IN**
CONFERENCE .... **Missouri Valley**
LAST SEASON .... **15-15 (.500)**
CONFERENCE RECORD .... **9-9 (6th)**
STARTERS LOST/RETURNING **4/1**
NICKNAME .... **Purple Aces**
COLORS .... **Purple & White**
HOMECOURT .... **Roberts Stadium (12,300)**
COACH .... **Jim Crews (Indiana '76)**
RECORD AT SCHOOL .... **232-150 (13 yrs.)**
CAREER RECORD .... **232-150 (13 yrs.)**
ASSISTANTS .... **Lennox Forrister (Evansville '92)**
Kirk Sarff (Millikin '84)
Marty Simmons (Evansville '88)
TEAM WINS (last 5 yrs.) **21-18-13-17-15**
RPI (last 5 yrs.) **114-85-120-89-190**
1997-98 FINISH .... **Lost in conference quarterfinal.**

To find an Evansville losing stretch as bad as the one experienced late last season, you have to go back to Jim Crews' first season, 1984-85. The Aces lost 9 of 10 that year. That dismal streak was matched by Evansville at the end of last season.

Yet Crews, who begins his 14th season in Evansville, can't remember a team he liked coaching more than last year's 15-15 squad. "We just weren't quite good enough," Crews said. "They worked hard and had good attitudes. We didn't get better results, but I was pleased with them. They didn't get off-track with anything."

Nine players return from the Aces team that finished 9-9 and in a sixth-place tie in the Missouri Valley. Evansville brings back a good chunk of its talent, but the question is whether the Aces can make enough significant improvement to become a conference contender.

Marcus Wilson is a good start. Wilson (18.3 ppg, 3.7 rpg, 61 assists), a 6-3 senior, was the Missouri Valley's top shooting guard (.466 field-goal percentage and was second among Valley three-point shooters (.441). A first-team All-MVC pick last season, Wilson needs to repeat his 1997-98 scoring average to finish as the Aces' No. 2 career scorer. "Marcus has been a good scorer and late in the year he became a better rebounder," Crews said. "But I think he is capable of doing better in terms of going after loose balls and causing some havoc from that standpoint."

Joining Wilson on the perimeter are two sophomores who were big contributors as freshmen—6-1 **Jeremy Stanton** and 6-5 **Kyle Runyan**. Stanton (4.0 ppg, 2.4 rpg, 119 assists) started every game he played in, taking over quickly as the Aces' point guard. Stanton was one of three MVC freshman point guards of impact and finished fourth in the league in assists with 4.6 a game.

"He'll be more offensive-minded this year," Crews said. "He was thinking pass first last year, but he needs to be more aggressive." Crews wants Stanton to drive to the basket more in his second season.

Runyan (10.8 ppg, 2.1 rpg, 47 assists) came to Evansville with the reputation of a scorer, and didn't disappoint. Starting a third of the games, he settled into the small-

1998-99 EVANSVILLE SCHEDULE

Nov.	14	Western Kentucky
	18	@Tennessee-Martin
	22	Sacred Heart
	27-29	#Big Island Invitational
Dec.	5	Butler
	8	@Eastern Illinois
	12	@East Carolina
	16	Tennessee Tech
	19	Indiana State
	29	@Morehead State
Jan.	2	@Drake
	4	@Creighton
	7	Northern Iowa
	9	Wichita State
	13	@Northern Iowa
	16	Illinois State
	20	Creighton
	23	@Bradley
	27	Southern Illinois
	30	Drake
Feb.	4	@Wichita State
	6	@Southwest Missouri State
	10	@Indiana State
	13	@Southern Illinois
	17	Bradley
	20	@Illinois State
	22	Southwest Missouri State
26-Mar.	1	##Missouri Valley Conference Tournament

@ Road Games
# Honolulu, HI (vs. Saint Louis, first round; also Georgia Tech, Hawaii-Hilo, New Orleans, Washington, West Virginia and Wisconsin-Green Bay)
Kiel Center, St. Louis, MO

forward spot and attempted 135 three-pointers, hitting 43 percent (sixth-best in the conference).

With the graduation of Wilson's partner in scoring, 6-6 Chris Hollender (16.5 ppg, 7.4 rpg), Stanton and Runyan will need to take on some of the scoring burden. But both players were hampered by injuries last season. Stanton missed four games with a stress fracture in his foot, while Runyan missed three games with an infection to his elbow. The infection made it necessary for three surgeries to be performed.

"I think hopefully that we'll have some guys who were young but scored a little bit last year," Crews said. "I really think we'll have a better offensive team."

That's hard to imagine—the Aces shot a solid .476 percent from the field last season. Evansville was also the nation's sixth-best free throw-shooting team, making .757 percent.

"I think we can score in different ways, other than just being good shooters," Crews said. "I'd like to see us get more off the offensive boards or in post play."

Four guards should provide backup minutes—6-2 freshman **Clint Keown**, 6-3 freshman Adam Seitz, 6-2 sophomore **Josh Robinson** and 6-0 sophomore **Drew Church**.

Keown and Seitz were second and third, respectively, among Indiana high school scoring leaders last season. Keown finished hundreths of a point ahead, averaging 26.8 points at Evansville Memorial High. Seitz finished with 26.8 a game for Petersburg Pike Central. Neither Robinson (1.5 ppg, 0.7 rpg) nor Church (0.3 ppg, 0.8 rpg) played more than four minutes a night last season.

Hollender is the only significant loss from last season's roster. Hollender was a 55-percent shooter from the field, .853 percent from the free-throw line. He was Evansville's gritty, do-anything-needed player and will be missed. But the Aces have replacements for Hollender in the power forward spot. **Craig Snow** (6.5 ppg, 3.8 rpg, 35 assists), a 6-7 sophomore, started 19 games last season but often didn't play at his natural position. Snow tried 83 three-pointers last season, but will probably see more time inside this year.

"Chris had a lot of flexibility and he was the kind of guy you liked to have on your team," Crews said. "But we had a kid last year, Craig Snow, who kind of played out of position because of Chris. He'll be playing in Chris' position this year."

Competition for forward minutes will come from **Curt Begle**, a 6-9 senior, and **Charles Hedde**, a 6-8 freshman. Begle (3.3 ppg, 2.4 rpg) was an inside backup last season, while Hedde averaged 17.5 points and 8.3 rebounds for Vincennes (Ind.) Lincoln High.

Kwame James returns as the Aces' center, hoping to provide more consistency than his first two seasons. James (7.1 ppg, 4.9 rpg), a 6-8 junior, made strides last season and needs that to continue to help Evansville's inside game compete in the conference. Crews hopes James, a native of Trinidad, can avoid over-analyzing situations which tended to paralyze him in games last season.

Zack Anderson and **Matt Vidoni** should provide backup bulk. Anderson (0.6 ppg, 0.8 rpg), a 6-10 sophomore, played less than three minutes a game last season. Vidoni, a 6-9 junior from Black Hawk College in Illinois, is an Australian who should see some reserve minutes. He averaged 14 points and 11 rebounds last season at Black Hawk.

adidas Blue Ribbon Analysis

BACKCOURT	**B+**	**BENCH/DEPTH**	**C**
FRONTCOURT	**C**	**INTANGIBLES**	**C+**

When Evansville joined the Missouri Valley Conference in 1994, it was thought the Aces would provide another strong, traditional basketball program to help strengthen the league.

In many ways, that's exactly what has happened. Evansville has provided a consistently tough team, never finishing below .500 in the conference. But the Aces also haven't showed the same kind of success that they enjoyed in the Mid-Continent Conference. Three of Jim Crews' MCC teams earned berths in the NCAA Tournament, while two more got into the NIT. In the Valley, though, the Aces have come up empty in the postseason.

Evansville has never finished higher than fifth in the Valley standings and has yet to win a Valley tournament game in four tries. Things may not change much this season.

Behind Wilson, Runyan and Stanton, the Aces will have enough talent to keep their heads above water in the Valley. But there's not enough depth and not enough of an inside game to help Evansville challenge for the conference championship. It's a team that will certainly be good enough to win half its conference games. But a finish above fifth or sixth place depends on the Aces taking their games up another level.

(K.S.)

ILLINOIS STATE

LOCATION	**Normal, IL**
CONFERENCE	**Missouri Valley**
LAST SEASON	**25-6 (.806)**
CONFERENCE RECORD	**16-2 (1st)**
STARTERS LOST/RETURNING	**4/1**
NICKNAME	**Redbirds**
COLORS	**Red & White**
HOMECOURT	**Redbird Arena (10,200)**
COACH	**Kevin Stallings (Purdue '82)**
RECORD AT SCHOOL	**107-48 (5 yrs.)**
CAREER RECORD	**107-48 (5 yrs.)**
ASSISTANTS	**Chad Altadonna (Illinois State '96)**
	Tom Richardson (St. Xavier '77)
	Alvin Williamson (Tulsa '95)
TEAM WINS (last 5 yrs.)	**26-20-22-24-25**
RPI (last 5 yrs.)	**122-84-64-41-27**
1997-98 FINISH	**Lost in NCAA second round.**

It has become such an easy thing to do around the Missouri Valley Conference: Put Illinois State at the top of the conference and let everybody slug it out for second place.

Opting to stay put instead of leaving for a higher-profile job, Kevin Stallings has built himself a mini-dynasty in the Valley. The last two years, he had such a deep, talented and together ballclub that it was sometimes poetry in motion. Two NCAA appearances were the result.

But poetry time ended last March. Three seniors graduated, and Valley MVP Rico Hill opted to turn professional after the June NBA Draft. His 18.4 points and 7.5 rebounds went with him. So is it time to feel sorry for Stallings? Not just yet.

You see, Illinois State will have a freshman point guard whom Stallings thinks is going to be a good one. A first-year sophomore may start at shooting guard and some former Redbirds are already calling him the best player during Stallings' tenure. Two transfers will occupy spots inside (by the way, did we mention that both have two years of Division I experience and are big, bulky and talented? And burly center **Leroy Watkins** returns as the only starter back, getting another season of eligibility because he graduated school in four years.

1998-99 ILLINOIS STATE SCHEDULE

Nov.	15	Oakland
	18	Wisconsin-Green Bay
	20	Akron
	25-27	#Hawaii-Pacific Shootout
Dec.	2	Alcorn State
	5	Wisconsin
	8	@Purdue
	12	Wichita State
	19	@Drake
	23	Illinois-Chicago
	29	Eastern Illinois
Jan.	2	@Wichita State
	9	Northern Iowa
	13	Drake
	16	@Evansville
	20	Bradley
	23	@Creighton
	27	Indiana State
	30	@Southern Illinois
Feb.	3	Southwest Missouri State
	7	Southern Illinois
	10	@Bradley
	14	Creighton
	17	@Northern Iowa
	20	Evansville
	22	@Indiana State
26-Mar.	1	##MVC Tournament

@ Road Games
# Honolulu, HI (vs. Missouri-Kansas City, first round; also Baylor, Hawaii-Pacific, Hofstra, Iona, Southern Mississippi and Virginia Commonwealth)
Kiel Center, St. Louis, MO

There are a lot of questions in Normal this fall. There may be some pretty good answers by conference time.

"I think there's far too many unknowns to expect us to be the favorite," Stallings said. "I'm not saying that we're not going to have a capable team, because I think we will have a capable team. But the last two years, I didn't think there was any way we wouldn't win the league championship, and this year I certainly can't say that."

ISU was in danger of not having a single starter returning until Watkins, a 6-7 senior, passed summer school courses in August. Originally a non-qualifier, Watkins (10.1 ppg, 4.3 rpg, 24 blocked shots) graduated during the summer and was one of the first student-athletes to take advantage of new NCAA bylaws allowing a fourth year of eligibility for student-athletes who graduate before their fifth year of school begins.

Watkins' return was great news for Stallings, who earlier had lost Hill to the pros. Watkins may be only 6-7, but he's the Valley's strongest player and a load for any center to handle.

"Whether or not it produces a tremendous difference in our victory total, I couldn't tell you that," Stallings said of Watkins' return. "But from a leadership and experience standpoint, it certainly helps us."

Watkins will be joined inside by two transfers, **Sean Riley** and **L. Dee Murdock**, who sat out last season but practiced with the Redbirds. Riley, a 7-0 junior, averaged 9.8 points and 4.7 rebounds for North Texas in 1996-97. Stallings appreciates Riley's feel for the game and his shooting touch, both of which you don't often find in 7-footers.

Murdock, a 6-9 junior, averaged 5.4 points and 2.3 rebounds in 12.2 minutes a game for Missouri in 1996-97. Not great numbers, but he's a good shooter (.543 percent) and should make more waves in the Valley than he did in the Big 12.

Trouble is, that's it for Illinois State's front-line depth. **Ronald van Velzen** (1.3 ppg, 1.0 rpg), a 6-10 senior, was lost for the season when he tore two ligaments in his right knee in an August pickup game. "Losing Ronald hurts us because we thought we had a very sturdy group of guys who were all big and strong and either fairly athletic, fairly skilled, or both," Stallings said. "It will limit our depth and cause us to have to do some other things."

Namely, **Kenneth Pierson** will probably move from small forward to power forward. Pierson (1.4 ppg, 1.2 rpg), a 6-8 senior, had knee problems of his own last season and wasn't 100 percent most of the time. At 185 pounds, he's not a true frontliner, but ISU's depth problems will make him one.

Depth isn't nearly the concern on the perimeter, though experience is. Only **Kyle Cartmill** returns with much experience, but **Tarise Bryson** and **Vic Williams** will both be thrown into the rigors of Division I basketball quickly.

Cartmill (7.0 ppg, 1.9 rpg, 60 assists, 30 steals), a 6-0 senior, is more comfortable at the shooting guard spot and is vying for his first full-time starting job. A terrific leaper, Cartmill has been a valuable backup guard in the past and could see the same duty again if Bryson and Williams live up to their potential. Cartmill, subbing for an injured Jamar Smiley, etched his name into Illinois State basketball history last March. With 1.9 seconds left in the Redbirds' first-round NCAA Tournament game against Tennessee, he whipped a pass to a wide-open Dan Muller that led to the winning layup.

Bryson, a 6-2 sophomore, sat out last season after failing to meet NCAA academic standards. But he was chosen to the ISU athletic director's honor roll in both semesters and is ready to play. He averaged 27.6 points and 3.9 rebounds as a senior at Stephen Decatur (Ill.) High, but more importantly gained 20 pounds last year to get up to 175.

A leading candidate for Missouri Valley Newcomer of the Year, Bryson is a complete player. He can take it to the basket, hit the three-pointer, and also comes with the reputation of being a good defender. "According to guys who have been in the program before, he has a chance to be one of the best players, if not the best player, we've ever had here," Stallings said. "After having sat out a year, I don't think we're going to see that this year, but maybe some day."

Williams, a 5-10 freshman, led his Kansas City (Kan.) Wyandotte High team to a state championship last season, averaging 27.3 points in the three-game tournament. A better shooter than the departed Smiley, Williams is also quicker and will have the starting job from day one.

Both Bryson and Cartmill could see backup minutes as the playmaker. **Shawn Jeppson**, a 6-2 freshman, averaged 23 points last season at Spring Valley (Ill.) Hall High and was Illinois' small-class player of the year. Jeppson's biggest asset is an accurate three-point shot, but he'll have a hard time penetrating the three-guard rotation of Williams, Bryson and Cartmill.

Nic Stotler (0.3 ppg, 0.1 rpg), a 6-0 junior, is a walkon who saw late-game action 15 times last season.

Among all the unknowns and unprovens, the small forward spot is the biggest question mark. The likely man for the job is **Tyrone Brown**, a 6-5 junior who averaged 15.1 points and 3.6 rebounds at Butler County (Kan.) Community College last season. Brown is a fluid open-court player who knows his strengths. "I think Tyrone is going to make open jump shots and he's going to make baskets in transition because he's a great finisher," Stallings said. "He's also going to get offensive-rebound points. He scores in the ways you need him to."

Ryan Crowley (1.1 ppg, 0.5 rpg), a 6-5 junior, and **Joe Hein** (0.6 ppg, 0.3 rpg), a 6-7 junior, will compete for backup minutes at small forward. Neither has had much of an opportunity to play and may be nudged out again.

adidas Blue Ribbon Analysis

BACKCOURT	C+	BENCH/DEPTH	C
FRONTCOURT	B	INTANGIBLES	B+

Stallings has won at least 20 games in each of his four years at Illinois State, and he'll probably get there again. But this could be his toughest job as Redbirds coach, trying to mesh freshmen, transfers and untested players into a cohesive bunch by conference time.

Much will be asked of first-year players Williams and Bryson, and there probably will be more heat on them than front-liners Watkins, Riley and Murdock. Small forward is a key spot, too, with Brown needing to make the adjustment from junior college to Division I.

Maybe the biggest factor is injuries, which could deplete an ISU roster that's already lacking depth. Let's not pencil Illinois State in as Valley favorites this time—but don't forget the Redbirds, either. The potential is there for a third straight conference championship. It's just a matter of everyone adjusting to new roles. Even if that doesn't happen, Stallings has the personnel to keep his team among the Valley's top three and in some kind of postseason tournament.

(K.S.)

INDIANA STATE

LOCATION .... **Terre Haute, IN**
CONFERENCE .... **Missouri Valley (MVC)**
LAST SEASON .... **16-11 (.593)**
CONFERENCE RECORD .... **10-8 (t-5th)**
STARTERS LOST/RETURNING **2/3**
NICKNAME .... **Sycamores**
COLORS .... **Blue & White**
HOMECOURT .... **Hulman Center (10,206)**
COACH .... **Royce Waltman (Slippery Rock '64)**
RECORD AT SCHOOL .... **16-11 (1 yr.)**
CAREER RECORD .... **205-97 (11 yrs.)**
ASSISTANTS .... **Dick Bender (Western Maryland '86)**
Greg Lansing (South Dakota '90)
Rick Ray (Grand View '94)
TEAM WINS (last 5 yrs.) **4-7-10-12-16**
RPI (last 5 yrs.) **264-240-217-163-111**
1997-98 FINISH .... **Lost in conference quarterfinal.**

Royce Waltman and Indiana State's basketball program enjoyed a natural honeymoon last season. With fans around Terre Haute having little to be excited about since Larry Bird and the Sycamores' 1979 NCAA final, Waltman continued his pattern of turning around programs and led Indiana State to a 16-11 record in his first season. Considering that ISU hadn't enjoyed a winning record since 1979-80, even a 3-8 finish didn't damper hopes that a complete turnaround is in progress.

But in year two, the honeymoon ends. The Sycamores will again try for an upper-division finish in the Missouri Valley Conference, but this time it will be without its top two scorers from Waltman's first season.

"The main feeling among the whole program is a need for improvement," Waltman said. "We all enjoyed the interest that people showed last year and the credit they gave us for making some headway.

"But at the same time, we are very realistic in that we have a long ways to go, and with that in mind, we are taking a more serious approach towards trying to improve."

Improvement in Waltman's first season came with help from 6-7 forward Jayson Wells (16.7 ppg, 8.4 rpg), a first-team all-Valley selection who made tremendous strides in his senior season. Steve Hart (12.9 ppg, 3.1 rpg), an athletic swingman, also benefited from Waltman's tutelage in his final season.

"I don't think we will have one guy that will be able to step in and replace what Jayson gave us last year," Waltman said. "However, we do think that with our recruiting class, we have a couple of guys who can step in and hopefully replace those numbers. One guy may have to score a little more and the other will have to rebound a little more, but I don't see one person filling that position."

With Wells and Hart gone, Indiana State's biggest strength becomes the backcourt. Junior **Nate Green** and sophomore **Michael Menser** are two reliable players to build around.

"Almost every coach would agree it's like trying to play baseball without a pitcher. You can't even start the game," Waltman said of his backcourt. "We feel good about the fact that we do have Nate and Michael back, because without sound guard play you really don't have a chance to win."

Green (8.1 ppg, 5.2 rpg, 131 assists, 54 steals, 35 blocked shots), a 6-5 point guard, is a versatile player who this year could develop into one of the Valley's best. A taller point man, Green has good passing skills and also is a threat in posting up against smaller guards. But offensively, Green is strongest as a slashing penetrator to the basket.

Menser (10.5 ppg, 3.2 rpg, 78 assists, 40 steals), a 5-11 sophomore, was one of three promising freshmen point men in the MVC last season. A former runner-up for Mr. Basketball in Indiana, he has been a starter since his opening game and shares ballhandling duties with Green. Menser was a 36-percent three-point shooter last season, but also excels at driving to the basket.

There are plenty of players to back up Green and Menser, but only one has collegiate experience. **Chad Adkins** (6.8 ppg. 1.7 rpg), a 6-2 senior, is the Sycamores' best three-point threat. A reserve his first three seasons, Adkins is a career 36-percent three-point shooter who will help take some pressure off Green and Menser.

The other reserve guards—**Abasi Thompson**, **Andy Williamson** and **Kelyn Block**—all come to Indiana State with good credentials but no Division I experience. Thompson, a 6-5 junior, figures to be the newcomer ready to make the biggest impact. He averaged 22.8 points and 9.7 rebounds at Chicago's Kennedy-King Junior College. He'll be a big guard-small forward, as will Williamson, a 6-5 freshman who averaged 18.3 points and 5.1 rebounds at Hamilton Heights High in Arcadia, Ind.

Block, a 6-2 freshman, averaged 22 points and 5.1 rebounds for Kansas City (Kan.) Sumner Academy. Block, also a standout football player, led Sumner to the Kansas Class 4A championship.

There's little doubt that Green and Menser will be the strength of the ISU lineup. Problem is, the rest of the Valley knows it. But ISU hopes the most promising first-year player, small forward **Chad Hunter**, can help out. Hunter, a 6-6 sophomore who averaged 19.7 points and 8.5 rebounds as a high school senior in New Albany, Ind., wasn't an academic qualifier as a freshman and sat out last season.

"He (Hunter) helps us athletically and he will rebound and score for us," Waltman said. "His shortcoming is that he has missed that year of development and experience, but he gives us a very athletic guy at the three and four spot."

Inside, the Sycamores will try to develop players who haven't had to play important roles in the past. **Matt Renn**, **Ben Anderson**, **Brian Giesen** and **Jon Luchetti** are key cogs in an Indiana State team needing some front-line help to take pressure off the perimeter.

Renn (6.6 ppg, 4.6 rpg), a 6-6 sophomore, started a third of Indiana State's games as a freshman. A power forward with good scoring skills inside, Renn takes over as the team's best bet to come up with scoring punch in the paint. He shot 54 percent from the field last season.

Anderson (4.0 ppg, 2.4 rpg), a burly 6-6, 240-pound center, has been primarily a bench player in his two seasons. He comes in and gives ISU a physical, won't-be-pushed-around presence inside. But Anderson isn't much of a scoring threat and will have to improve his rebounding prowess.

Giesen (1.5 ppg, 0.7 rpg), a 6-9 big forward, has good low-post moves but didn't get many opportunities last season. He averaged less than six minutes a game, but should get more this season with Wells' departure. Luchetti (0.6 ppg, 0.3 ppg), has seen his playing time go down in each of his first three seasons.

Djibril Kante, a 6-7 freshman, is the only newcomer up front. He averaged 10.2 points and 7.4 rebounds at Bloomington (Ind.) North High last season, and at 235 pounds, is already big enough to show his muscle in the Valley.

adidas Blue Ribbon Analysis

BACKCOURT	C+	BENCH/DEPTH	C
FRONTCOURT	D+	INTANGIBLES	C

Interest in Indiana State basketball is back, but Waltman enters his second season with many new challenges. Green and Menser are already established guards in the

1998-99 INDIANA STATE SCHEDULE

Nov.	14	@Indiana
	16	Western Michigan
	18	@Eastern Illinois
	21	Butler
	24	Eastern Kentucky
	28	@Ball State
Dec.	1	Wisconsin-Milwaukee
	5	Northern Iowa
	12	@Loyola-Chicago
	19	@Evansville
	22	@Bradley
Jan.	2	Creighton
	7	Wichita State
	9	@Southern Illinois
	17	@Creighton
	20	Southern Illinois
	23	Southwest Missouri State
	27	@Illinois State
	30	Bradley
Feb.	4	@Drake
	6	@Northern Iowa
	10	Evansville
	13	Drake
	18	@Wichita State
	20	@Southwest Missouri State
	22	Illinois State
26-Mar.	1	#MVC Tournament

@ Road Games
\# Kiel Center, St. Louis, MO

Missouri Valley, but both will have to step up their scoring production while an inexperienced front line encounters on-the-job training. It's certainly not a make-or-break year for the Sycamores, but it could be a good indicator of how quickly Waltman can turn around a program waiting for sustained success.

With Green and Menser, Indiana State's backcourt can compete with any in the Missouri Valley. Problem is, there are too few inside threats to make the Sycamores a serious contender in a rough-and-tumble conference. An upper-division finish would be a great second year for Waltman, but seventh place is more realistic.

(K.S.)

NORTHERN IOWA

LOCATION .... **Cedar Falls, IA**
CONFERENCE .... **Missouri Valley**
LAST SEASON .... **10-17 (.370)**
CONFERENCE RECORD .... **4-14 (9th)**
STARTERS LOST/RETURNING **2/3**
NICKNAME .... **Panthers**
COLORS .... **Purple & Old Gold**
HOMECOURT .... **UNI-Dome (10,000)**
COACH .... **Sam Weaver (Henderson State '84)**
RECORD AT SCHOOL .... **First Year**
CAREER RECORD .... **20-60 (3 yrs.)**
ASSISTANTS .... **Grady Bean (Henderson State '80)**
Ron Smith (Illinois State '76)
TEAM WINS (last 5 yrs.) **16-8-14-16-10**
RPI (last 5 yrs.) **161-237-122-85-226**
1997-98 FINISH ..... **Lost in conference play-in round.**

Sam Weaver is one of two new coaches in the Missouri Valley this season, but he's no newcomer to the league. Weaver was an assistant to Rich Herrin at Southern Illinois from 1989-93, and also served under Gary Garner at Drake in 1987-88.

But Weaver, who most recently was Tim Floyd's assistant at Iowa State, doesn't think his MVC knowledge will be of any help to him as he takes over the Panthers program.

"It scares the hell out of me, to tell you the truth," Weaver said. "I know how good the conference is."

To be sure, Weaver knows the job ahead of him. He's taking over a Northern Iowa program that has a marginal following, plays in a football stadium (the cavernous UNI-Dome) and is trying to recover from last season's crumbling 10-17 finish in which there were injuries and a breakdown in team cohesiveness. Eldon Miller, Weaver's predecessor who was at the helm for 12 years, probably did as much as he could with the program, resigning after last season with a 164-178 record.

"I don't know if I'll be changing a whole lot," said the 40-year-old Weaver, who was head coach at Alcorn State from 1993-96. "I thought Eldon's teams were great defensively, and we're going to build from that end and continue building until we get to the other end."

The Panthers won't have to do a lot of building in the backcourt, even though No. 2 scorer Darian DeVries (12.6 ppg, .440 three-point percentage) was lost to graduation.

Leading scorer **Tony Brus**, point guard Terry Cress and swingman **TyJuan Finley** all give Weaver some experience.

Brus (15.4 ppg, 2.7 rpg, 71 assists, 35 steals), a 6-0 senior, was only a part-time starter last year and was usually more effective as the first player off the bench. Brus shot 34 percent from three-point range, but is at his best when he's driving to the basket.

"I think he's a young man with a tremendous work ethic," Weaver said. "He put himself with our strength coach this summer and did a great job getting stronger. Tony's going to work himself into a starting position."

Brus will join Cress (4.5 ppg, 2.6 rpg, 74 assists, 30 steals), a 6-2 junior who led the MVC in assists early in the conference schedule. Cress is a reliable ballhandler who will get more playing time. As a result, he needs to work on his free throws (.561) if he's going to have the ball late in games.

Three point guards have been brought in to strengthen the position. Before his resignation, Miller signed 6-1 junior **Murphy Carter**, who averaged 11 points, 8.2 assists and five rebounds last season at Blackhawk (Ill.) Community

1998-99 NORTHERN IOWA SCHEDULE

Nov.	16	@Bowling Green
	19	@Iowa
	23	@Tennessee State
	27	@Miami
Dec.	2	Iowa State
	5	@Indiana State
	12	@Wisconsin-Green Bay
	14	Wright State
	21	Southern Mississippi
	30	Southwest Missouri State
Jan.	3	@Bradley
	7	@Evansville
	9	@Illinois State
	13	Evansville
	16	Southern Illinois
	21	@Southwest Missouri State
	24	@Drake
	27	@Wichita State
	30	Creighton
Feb.	3	Bradley
	6	Indiana State
	10	@Creighton
	13	Wichita State
	17	Illinois State
	20	@Southern Illinois
	22	Drake
26-Mar.	1	#MVC Tournament

@ Road Games
\# Kiel Center, St. Louis, MO

College. In late August, Weaver signed 6-0 sophomore **Robbie Sieverding** from Marshalltown (Iowa) Junior College. Sieverding averaged 19 points at Marshalltown and once scored 62 points at Bellevue (Iowa) Marquette High.

Both should push Cress for playing time. **Terry Rouse** (13.0 ppg, 7.0 rpg at Shorter, Ark., Junior College), a 6-6 junior, could also see time at the point.

Sean Stackhouse, who averaged 21.5 ppg at Kaskaskia (Ill.) Junior College, is a 6-3 sophomore who should push Brus for off-guard minutes. Stackhouse was a late signee by Weaver, who was impressed with Stackhouse's performance in the national junior-college tournament. Stackhouse is a good shooter (120 of 240 from three-point range) with a quick release, and more importantly, he represents Weaver's first Chicago-area recruit. Weaver terms Windy City recruiting a priority.

Finley (9.1 ppg, 4.3 rpg), a 6-5 senior, is the team's returning rebound leader, though that's not saying much. Playing small forward, Finley made 13 starts last season before breaking his ankle in an early February game. He missed the last four regular-season games, reappearing for a few minutes in the Panthers' only MVC tournament game.

Three other Panthers will compete for guard minutes: 6-1 freshman **Marius Boyd**; 6-6 freshman **Aaron Middendorf** and 6-2 sophomore **Tim Scheib.** Boyd, who averaged 16.0 ppg at Whitefish Bay (Wisc.) High, was a Miller signee, while Middendorf redshirted last season.

Scheib (0.7 ppg) is a walk-on who played in nine games. The inside game is clearly the Panthers' biggest concern. Northern Iowa wasn't a good rebounding team last season, and its 39.2-percent shooting meant there weren't many easy baskets coming from post players.

Part-time starter **Cory Jenkins** (4.5 ppg, 3.5 rpg) may be Northern Iowa's key inside player. When Weaver first looked at a stat sheet from last season, Jenkins, a 6-8 junior small forward, was one of the players whom Weaver thought was cheated out of some baskets and boards.

"We're going to need more production out of him this season," Weaver said. Same with **Burt Lappe** (5.8 ppg, 3.3 rpg), a 6-9 junior forward-center, and **Tyler Peterson** (3.0 ppg, 1.8 rpg). Lappe started 11 of 24 games last season, averaging 14 minutes behind departed seniors Chris Burdine, Sean Hawkins and Brian Heying.

Peterson, who played at Iowa State before transferring after the 1995-96 season, averaged 10.2 minutes of playing time last year. The 7-foot, 235-pound junior has been slowed by tendonitis in his knees. Past those three front-line returners, it gets thin quickly.

Joe Breakenridge (1.4 ppg, 1.8 rpg), a 6-5 sophomore, got off to a quick start last season before a broken wrist was discovered in January. He started the Iowa State game and had 10 points against Chicago State. **Brian Lubeck**, a 6-6 freshman, is a walkon redshirt.

Weaver has emphasized weight training, trying to get his players bigger and stronger in an attempt to play more physically inside. That could help the rebounding and inside scoring, but defense is another priority. Last season, the Panthers allowed opponents to shoot 44 percent—bad enough for eighth in the Valley.

adidas Blue Ribbon Analysis

BACKCOURT .... **C+** **BENCH/DEPTH** .... **C**
FRONTCOURT .... **D** **INTANGIBLES** .... **C**

In his first season, Weaver could certainly use the same kind of start that Miller's last team enjoyed. The Panthers won at Iowa State to open the season (Weaver was an assistant on the other bench) and reeled off six wins in seven tries. The other big win was a six-point home decision over Iowa which, coupled with two wins over Drake, gave Northern Iowa a 4-0 record against in-state rivals.

But what's ahead for the Panthers more likely is a tough first season under Weaver. He doesn't inherit much talent, but he hopes some new faces can breath some life into the squad.

"We're going to have to peddle harder than anyone else," Weaver admits. It's hard to imagine Northern Iowa finishing any better than seventh in the Valley. More likely, the Panthers are destined for eighth or ninth in a 10-team race and left with building for the future.

(K.S.)

SOUTHERN ILLINOIS

LOCATION .... **Carbondale, IL**
CONFERENCE ..... **Missouri Valley Conference (MVC)**
LAST SEASON .... **14-16 (.467)**
CONFERENCE RECORD .... **8-10 (8th)**
STARTERS LOST/RETURNING **2/3**
NICKNAME .... **Salukis**
COLORS .... **Maroon & White**
HOMECOURT .... **SIU Arena (10,000)**
COACH .... **Bruce Weber (Wisconsin-Milwaukee'78)**
RECORD AT SCHOOL .... **First Year**
CAREER RECORD .... **First Year**
ASSISTANTS .... **Alan Major (Purdue '92)**
Matt Painter (Purdue '94)
Rodney Watson (Eastern Illinois '82)
TEAM WINS (last 5 yrs.) **23-23-11-13-14**
RPI (last 5 yrs.) **41-34-197-140-157**
1997-98 FINISH .... **Lost in conference quarterfinal.**

When you spend 18 years as an assistant coach for the same basketball program, you're either darn happy where you are or you're biding your time for the right head-coaching opportunity to come along. In Bruce Weber's case, both are true.

"It's been a dream being at Purdue and being named head basketball coach at SIU is like a second dream coming true for me," Weber said. "It's one of the most exciting happenings in my life."

Weber, 41, was Gene Keady's assistant coach at Purdue for plenty of good times. The Boilermakers had only one losing season in those years, but more importantly won six Big Ten Conference championships and were in postseason play 17 times.

So, Weber knows how to win. But he takes over a Southern Illinois program that is at an interesting crossroads in its history. In the early 1990s, the Salukis were the Missouri Valley's top dogs. They didn't win every regular-season title, but they snared three straight postseason tournament crowns and were NCAA Tournament regulars under Rich Herrin.

But the last three seasons have been rough in Carbondale. SIU won just 11 games in 1995-96, 13 the next year and then 14 last season, the third straight losing mark. The program was on the decline under Herrin, and it was easy to tell. Many different players would take all kinds of shots, many of them of the highly questionable variety.

With Herrin's forced resignation last spring, it gave SIU a chance to reverse field. The school hopes Weber has ability to do it. At first glance, it looks as if Weber inherited a bare cupboard. Forward Rashad Tucker (15.8 ppg, 7.8 rpg) and guard Shane Hawkins (14.2) are two big players to lose. Hawkins finished his career as the Valley's career leader in three-point goals.

But there is plenty to work with up front, especially with Valley rebounding champ Chris Thunell back for his second season. He led a charge last season that finished SIU as the sixth-best Division I team in rebounding margin (+8.6).

"I feel good about our inside players, our front line with

1998-99 SOUTHERN ILLINOIS SCHEDULE

Nov.	14	@Murray State
	21	Virginia Commonwealth
	28	Oregon
Dec.	5	@Creighton
	12	Southwest Missouri State
	15	St. Louis
	21	Illinois-Chicago
	23	@Western Kentucky
	28	*Southeast Missouri State
Jan.	2	Tulsa
	6	Bradley
	9	Indiana State
	13	Wichita State
	16	@Northern Iowa
	18	Drake
	20	@Indiana State
	23	@Wichita State
	27	@Evansville
	30	Illinois State
Feb.	1	Creighton
	7	@Illinois State
	10	@Southwest Missouri State
	13	Evansville
	17	@Drake
	20	Northern Iowa
	22	@Bradley
26-Mar.	1	#Missouri Valley Conference Tournament

@ Road Games
* Trans World Dome, St. Louis, MO
# Kiel Center, St. Louis, MO

guys like **Chris Thunell, Monte Jenkins, Derrick Tilmon, James Jackson** and **James Watts** returning," Weber said. "They no doubt know how to rebound." Thunell (12.6 ppg, 8.6 rpg, 69 assists), a 6-9 junior, was chosen Missouri Valley Newcomer of the Year after becoming a dominant inside player after his transfer from Florida International. Thunell has a nose for the ball and should be even more of a scorer this season. And bad news for the rest of the Valley: Thunell has added 15 pounds to his frame, getting up to 227 pounds. Many other Salukis return at the forward and center spots, giving Weber plenty of options.

Jenkins (13.5 ppg, 4.6 rpg, 77 assists, 40 steals), a 6-4 senior, is SIU's best returning scoring threat from the outside. He averaged almost 12 shots a game last season, with more than four out of 10 coming from three-point range. With a combined 743 shots gone with the departures of Tucker and Hawkins, Jenkins will be called upon for more.

Tilmon (6.3 ppg, 4.5 rpg), a 6-7 junior, and Jackson (4.5 ppg, 4.8 rpg), a 6-6 senior, will man the center spot. Tilmon made 13 starts last season to Jackson's 12, and both should improve their rebounding numbers from last season.

Watts (3.6 ppg, 3.8 rpg), a 6-8 senior, can be another off-the-bench spark. He averaged almost four boards in 14 minutes per game last season.

Where Southern Illinois fans will have to buy programs is for the perimeter, where five newcomers are expected to battle for starting spots and playing time. Weber signed four guards, looking especially to shore up the point-guard spot.

Two first-year Salukis—**Ricky Collum** and **Brandon Mells**—figure to share the playmaking duties. Collum, a 5-11 junior, averaged 12.0 points and 4.9 assists last season for Kankakee (Ill.) Community College. He's the more seasoned player of the two and is known as a good ballhandler and assist man.

Mells, a 6-1 freshman, was signed in July out of Memphis (Tenn.) Central High. He averaged 17.1 points, 7.3 assists and 5.4 rebounds last season. Another above-average ballhandler, Mells should complement Collum and give SIU some much-needed stability at the point.

Ryan Hammer (0.5 ppg, 0.2 rpg), a 6-1 guard, will continue to see backup time at point guard.

Everybody and his brother will compete for second-guard time. **Abel Schrader** (1.3 ppg, 0.4 rpg), a 6-4 sophomore, averaged 7.5 minutes as a freshman, but should get more in his second year. Schrader is a good outside shooter, canning 8 of 15 three-point tries in a six-game tour of the Dominican Republic in August. He was the Southern Illinois Player of the Year as a high school senior.

A pair of California junior college transfers will also help. **Ashanti Miller**, a 6-4 junior, averaged 12.2 points and 6.6 rebounds for College of the Desert (Palm Desert, Calif.) last season. He signed with the Salukis in August. **Gianandrea Marcaccini**, a 6-4 junior, averaged 12.2 points and 5.2 rebounds for Los Angeles City College and was another summer signee.

Lance Brown (1.3 ppg, 0.4 rpg), a 6-3 junior guard, and **Josh Cross** (3.2 ppg, 2.1 rpg), a 6-4 sophomore guard, are expected to be perimeter backups. Cross can cross over and play some point guard.

adidas Blue Ribbon Analysis

BACKCOURT .... D+ BENCH/DEPTH C
FRONTCOURT .... B INTANGIBLES C

What may help the new-look Salukis more than anything else was an opportunity to play six games—and more importantly, practice 10 times—in an August tournament in the Dominican Republic. The Saluki returnees were under Weber's tutelage for the first time and won five of six games. Some things won't change under Weber. Southern Illinois should have another hellacious rebounding bunch and Thunell will lead the way, most likely in rebounding and scoring.

But Saluki fans are hoping other facets change. Newcomers have to contribute quickly at point guard, and SIU could use progression from inside players such as Jackson and Tilmon.

If that happens, SIU could make a run at the Missouri Valley's first division. More likely, the Salukis will try to work out the kinks in Weber's first year and finish around seventh or eighth. But that wouldn't necessarily mean Weber and SIU aren't on the right track.

(K.S.)

SOUTHWEST MISSOURI STATE

LOCATION .... Springfield, MO
CONFERENCE .... Missouri Valley
LAST SEASON .... 16-16 (.500)
CONFERENCE RECORD 11-7 (t-3rd)
STARTERS LOST/RETURNING 1/4
NICKNAME .... Bears
COLORS .... Maroon & White
HOMECOURT .... Hammons Student Center (8,846)
COACH .... Steve Alford (Indiana '87)
RECORD AT SCHOOL .... 56-37 (3 yrs.)
CAREER RECORD .... 134-66 (7 yrs.)
ASSISTANTS .... Sam Alford (Franklin '64)
Hosea Lee (East Texas State '93)
Steve Lynch (Manchester '93)
TEAM WINS (last 5 yrs.) 12-16-16-24-16
RPI (last 5 yrs.) 173-120-91-51-118
1997-98 FINISH .... Lost in conference final.

Last season was one in which Southwest Missouri State was supposed to break through all the obstacles and find a spot in the NCAA Tournament. Steve Alford's team appeared solid, with a good mix of everything. There seemed to be no reason the Bears shouldn't earn one of those coveted 64 bids.

Then the Bears fell apart. Not all season, just long enough to force a mushy record (16-16) and no berths to anything but an early spring break. That was enough to make Alford hit the recruiting trail for leaner, meaner, quicker bodies.

"We've kind of gone full-circle," Alford said. "We tried the big thing and we didn't care for that. Now we're going back to the way we've done it in the past."

No longer will the Bears trudge down the floor. The plan is to get back to the up-tempo game that netted the Bears a 40-21 record in Alford's first two seasons.

"I really enjoyed (Coleco) Buie's senior group (1996-97)," Alford said. "That was a team that might have overachieved a little bit (24-9) because of their attitudes. Last year's team did not have the attitude I like in my teams, and I think that showed."

Alford heads into his fourth season looking forward to his team as much as any he's coached. Ten of his 14 players are upperclassmen, yet the six newcomers are what excites Alford. "I thought a priority was toughness and the ability to make plays," Alford said. "These six individuals, when you add them to the guys we have coming back, I think we now have an abundance of guys that can make plays and know how to win and want to win."

With its only significant loss coming from the graduation of 6-5 forward Ben Kandlbinder (12.9 ppg, 5.5 rpg), the

1998-99 SOUTHWEST MISSOURI STATE SCHEDULE

Nov.	14	@Butler
	18	@Missouri
	20-27	#Missouri
	23	Missouri-Kansas City
Dec.	4-5	##Pizza Hut Classic
	9	Long Beach State
	12	@Southern Illinois
	19	Texas Christian
	22	Southeast Missouri State
	30	@Northern Iowa
Jan.	2	@St. Louis
	5	Illinois State
	10	Creighton
	13	Bradley
	16	Drake
	18	@Wichita State
	21	Northern Iowa
	23	@Indiana State
	27	@Drake
	31	Wichita State
Feb.	3	@Illinois State
	6	Evansville
	10	Southern Illinois
	13	@Bradley
	17	@Creighton
	20	Indiana State
	22	@Evansville
26-Mar.	1	###Missouri Valley Conference Tournament

@ Road Games
# Chase NIT (If the Indians advance, they will face either Southern Methodist or Stanford on Nov. 20. Semifinals and finals are Nov. 25 and 27 at Madison Square Garden, NY)
Springfield, MO (vs. Texas Southern, first round; also Louisiana Tech and Texas-Pan American)
Kiel Center, St. Louis, MO

Bears will be built around two seniors—6-10 center **Danny Moore**, 6-1 guard **Ryan Bettenhausen**—and two juniors—6-3 shooting guard **Kevin Ault** and 6-3 guard **William Fontleroy**.

Moore (15.7 ppg, 6.0 rpg, 33 blocked shots) is without a doubt the Missouri Valley's top inside scorer. He has a sweet shooting touch to 17 feet and uses his body and long arms to hit tough shots in traffic. Foul Moore and he'll make you pay—he's an 84-percent free-throw shooter.

But although he led the Bears in scoring and rebounding the last two seasons, his numbers dropped last season after averaging 19.5 points and 7.3 boards as a sophomore. He also dropped from first-team All-Valley in 1997 to second team last season. Alford blames that on the Bears' emphasis to make Moore a tougher inside player.

"I think we made the mistake of listening to everybody about how he's got to bulk up and get stronger," Alford said. "He wasn't in good shape last year, and I think the added weight really affected him. I don't think Danny's strength is ever going to be a strength for him. But we've got to get him the ball more."

The battle for Kandlbinder's power forward spot should be the most interesting. Candidates are all newcomers: 6-6 junior **Ron Bruton**, 6-8 freshman **Scott Brakebill** and 6-5 junior **Allen Phillips**. Bruton may be the most athletic of the three, averaging 10 points and 10 rebounds for Hutchinson (Kan.) Community College. He's a better defensive player, capable of guarding anyone from a big guard to center.

Phillips averaged 18.4 points at SMSU-West Plains last season, leaving school as the program's career scoring leader. Phillips, who shot 60 percent, is a three-point threat. He was ranked No. 52 in the list of the nation's top 300 junior college sophomores compiled by *Blue Ribbon* contributors Rick Ball and Phil Henzel.

Brakebill is the youngest of the power forward candidates, but he may be Southwest Missouri's star of the future. Averaging 19.9 points and 11.7 rebounds at Bolivar (Mo.) High, Brakebill owns a 38-inch vertical leap and the versatility to play outside and inside. "He potentially could be an outstanding scorer in our league down the road," Alford said. "We're excited to see how he's going to develop. He's probably the most intriguing of all of them (the newcomers)."

A mixture of newcomers and bench returners will fill in inside. **Matt Reuter** (0.8 ppg, 1.0 rpg), a 6-8 sophomore, played sparingly behind upperclassmen last season. Senior **Paul Murans** (1.3 ppg, 0.5 rpg), a 6-8 big forward, averaged 4.2 minutes last season. **Brian George**, a 6-10 freshman, averaged 15 points and 8.2 rebounds at Springfield (Mo.) Kickapoo High. One of his first tasks as a Bear has been to add to his 210-pound frame.

Even without new recruits, Southwest's guard combos

would be in good shape. Ault (14.8 ppg, 3.7 rpg, 65 assists, 52 steals) is a prototype shooter, while Fontleroy (7.5 ppg, 2.7 rpg, 135 assists, 45 steals) is an explosive point guard. Throw in versatile backup Bettenhausen (6.7 ppg, 2.8 rpg, 111 assists, 31 steals) and it's already one of the Missouri Valley's best backcourts.

Ault had a standout sophomore season, hitting 43 percent of his three-pointers and shooting 90 percent from the line, good for fourth nationally. He's a reliable outside threat when defenses are packing it in on Moore. Or when they're not.

"I think last year was a pretty good breakout year for Kevin," Alford said. "Now, we're just hoping he'll ride a lot of confidence. Now he should come out with a personality that's aggressive and confident. That's a key when you're a shooting guard."

Brandon Miller, a 6-0 freshman, is from Alford's hometown of New Castle, Ind. Alford's dad and assistant coach, Sam, was Miller's coach during his freshman season. Miller averaged 18.1 points and 3.9 assists last season and should push for point-guard minutes.

Eric Judd, a 6-1 junior and teammate of Phillips at SMSU-West Plains, averaged 17.8 points and made 42 percent of his three-point shots. He'll be used at both guard spots. He turned up at No. 80 on the top 300 list compiled by junior college experts Ball and Henzel.

Two returners will compete for time at small forward. Senior **Ken Stringer** (7.4 ppg, 4.8 rpg, 69 assists), 6-4, started 25 games last year and improved throughout his first season as a Bear. An athletic player with an ability to take the ball to the basket, Stringer may have the inside track over 6-6 senior **Butch Tshomba** (2.6 ppg, 1.3 rpg), another junior-college transfer in his second SMS season.

It's the wing forward and big guard who will make the difference in SMS' rebounding this season. Moore's forte isn't on the boards, and none of the other inside players have played much.

"I think it's going to be situation where it's going to be rebounding by committee, much like two years ago," Alford said. "We weren't a good rebounding team last year. I thought we were slow reacting to the ball and we didn't have a lot of guys who got after it. I think this is a team that's more athletic and more live on its feet and gets after things harder on both ends. When that happens, I think rebounding takes care of itself."

adidas Blue Ribbon Analysis

BACKCOURT	**B+**	**BENCH/DEPTH**	**B**
FRONTCOURT	**B**	**INTANGIBLES**	**B**

Steve Alford has quality perimeter players coming out of his ears and he has the Missouri Valley's best inside scorer. Things are set up for Southwest Missouri State to make a run for the school's first Valley title in its seven years as a league member.

The only thing that can keep the Bears out of contention is the kind of funk they fell into at times last season. An early season slump against a good schedule—all but one of the quality games were away from the Hammons Student Center—put the Bears at 4-10 and fading fast. But SMS won 12 of its final 18 games and played the basketball that the entire conference expected it to play. If the Bears are back in that frame of mind this season, watch out.

Alford recognized last season's flaws and addressed them in recruiting. He got rid of dead weight (and heavyweights) and brought in quicker, more athletic players. They should fit in nicely and help Southwest Missouri go nose-to-nose with Creighton for the MVC title.

(K.S.)

adidas Blue Ribbon Analysis

GRADING SYSTEM

- A+ equal to very best in country—Final Four-caliber unit
- A among the best in the land—worthy of deep NCAA run
- B+ talented, versatile and experienced—NCAA-NIT ability
- B solid and productive winners—league and post-season contenders
- C+ average to above-average—may contend in a weaker league
- C average to mediocre—second division in a strong league
- D+ below average, inconsistent—second division in a weaker league
- D well below average—losing season virtually certain
- F non-Division I ability—an underdog every night

WICHITA STATE

LOCATION .... **Wichita, KS**
CONFERENCE .... **Missouri Valley**
LAST SEASON .... **16-15 (.516)**
CONFERENCE RECORD .... **11-7 (t-3rd)**
STARTERS LOST/RETURNING **2/3**
NICKNAME .... **Shockers**
COLORS .... **Yellow & Black**
HOMECOURT .... **Levitt Arena (10,545)**
COACH .... **Randy Smithson (Wichita State '81)**
RECORD AT SCHOOL .... **30-28 (2 yrs.)**
CAREER RECORD .... **330-107 (13 yrs.)**
ASSISTANTS .... **Carlos Diggins (Kansas State '93)**
Don Parr (Washburn '85)
Fred Andrews (Purdue'95)
TEAM WINS (last 5 yrs.) **9-13-8-14-16**
RPI (last 5 yrs.) **205-152-225-135-122**
1997-98 FINISH .... **Lost in conference quarterfinals.**

Randy Smithson's first two years as Wichita State coach both ended with records one game above .500. Certainly much better than the seven-year drought before his arrival, but the Shockers the last two seasons have endured many ups and downs.

There was a hot start the first year with an end-of-season falter. Last year, the Shockers stumbled early, only to win six of seven in February and finish with the school's first winning Missouri Valley record since 1989. It's Year 3 now and Smithson wouldn't mind getting off the roller-coaster rides.

"Hopefully we can bring the best of both those seasons together," Smithson said. "There were definitely some good things that happened in both."

It's an intriguing collection of players Smithson has to challenge for another upper-division finish in the conference. He has two established standouts in guards **Jason Perez** and **Maurice Evans**, yet no other player who has proven he's a Division I regular. Ten—count 'em, 10—Shockers will play their first season of Division I ball.

"To win a lot of games, we've got to get some inside help," Smithson said. "To be a great team, our point guards are going to have to be awfully good."

At least Perez and Evans are two good ones to start with. Perez (13.5 ppg, 5.5 rpg, 62 steals, 51 assists), a 6-4 junior, earned team MVP honors with a sophomore season that was solid but not as flashy as when he was a freshman. All he did was come close to setting the Shocker record for single-season steals, lead the team in scoring, finish second in assists and darned-near led the team in rebounding.

"Jason does a lot of tough things on the court," Smithson said. "A lot of timing things, savvy things that not a lot of players can do."

Perez will continue to be the Shockers' top outside threat and should get more three-point opportunities with the departure of guards Terry Hankton and Chris Grill, and forward Ty Rhodes. They combined for 301 three-point tries last season.

Evans (12.1 ppg, 4.1 rpg, 30 steals), a 6-5 sophomore, will man the other wing and is a much different player than Perez. Evans had a better three-point percentage last season (.329 to Perez's .308), but Evans would rather break down a defender and head to the basket. He has also bulked up to 225 pounds, which helps him post up a guard or small forward. Smithson knows Evans is the franchise, and often put him in big-game, need-a-basket situations last season.

This is even after Evans missed playing with the team in the summer of 1997 because of back problems, then missed weeks of early practice with a stress fracture in his foot.

"You can learn from your successes, but the great ones learn from not making it," Smithson said. "We have had to put Mo in tough situations and accelerate his growth."

Perez and Evans form a terrific offensive duo. Trouble is, there's little experience on the perimeter to help them. Wichita State will need contributions from a bunch of guards, including **Carl Lemons**, **Jay Lewis, Terrell Benton**, **Juston White** and walkons **Craig Steven** and **Reggie Smithson** (the coach's son).

Lemons (4.0 ppg, 1.8 rpg), a 6-3 junior, is the only point-guard candidate who's not a freshman. He started 12 games at shooting guard as a freshman, then was planning to redshirt last season when two guards left the Shocker program in December.

Lemons got into uniform and learned the point-guard spot on the fly, giving Smithson some strong minutes late in the season. Still, he had only 18 assists in 295 minutes of playing time.

"Carl's learning to take charge," Smithson said. "I think his decision-making is going to be the key. He's going to score and be able to handle the ball."

Lemons gets first shot as the starter, but plenty of potential replacements wait in the wings. Benton, a 6-5 freshman, averaged 20.8 points and 5.6 rebounds at Derby (KS) High last season. He played point and shooting guard, displaying a good shooting touch. Probably more of a two-guard, he'll still challenge for the starting job at the point while learning the ropes behind Perez and Evans on the wing.

Lewis, a 6-0 freshman from Anchorage (AK) Bartlett High, averaged 16 points and seven assists and signed with the Shockers during the spring period. Smithson is encouraged by Lewis' ability to get the ball inside to big men.

Lewis' jumper isn't a big asset yet, though he can hit it when open. White, a 6-6 freshman from Wichita's East High, averaged 16.2 points and 6.2 rebounds and gives Smithson a long-armed swingman who isn't much of a scorer, but he'll earn time by becoming a defensive stopper.

Steven, a 6-3 freshman and all-state football player from Wichita's Bishop Carroll High, chose to walk on at Wichita State and could provide a valuable backup at point guard. A crisp passer and good floor leader who averaged 14.3 points and eight assists at Carroll, Steven needs to work on his jump shot but could compete for a starting job in a wide-open point guard race.

Smithson, a 6-0 freshman who averaged 14.8 points last season at Augusta (KS) High, becomes a third-generation Shocker player or coach. Randy Smithson, of course, was a Shocker player from 1979-81 for his father, Gene, who coached eight seasons.

Inside, the Shockers have one part-time starter back and a bunch of new faces. **Darrin Williams** (6.7 ppg, 4.6 rpg, 21 blocks), a 6-8 junior power forward, has had two mediocre seasons. On occasion, he shows signs of becoming a dominating big man. But most times, he's passive and not much of a contributor.

"Darrin's going to have to decide if he's going to be more special than he has been," Smithson said. "He can't fear demands and expectations." Expectations could be higher on Williams this year—the other two big men returning aren't expected to help much.

Seniors **James Bunch** (1.1 ppg, 1.5 rpg), a 6-10 center, and **Luke Utting** (0.2 ppg), a 6-8 forward, are best at setting picks and being physical inside. Wichita State's needed success inside will have to come from new faces, such as 6-9 freshman **Troy Mack**, 6-10 freshman **Mahrnord**

1998-99 WICHITA STATE SCHEDULE

Nov.	18	Florida Atlantic
	24	@Pepperdine
	27-29	#United Airlines Tipoff Classic
Dec.	5	Texas-San Antonio
	8	@Kansas State
	12	@Illinois State
	19	Florida A&M
	21	Chaminade
	29-30	##Cessna Classic
Jan.	2	Illinois State
	4	Drake
	7	@Indiana State
	9	@Evansville
	13	@Southern Illinois
	16	@Bradley
	18	Southwest Missouri State
	23	Southern Illinois
	27	Northern Iowa
	31	@Southwest Missouri State
Feb.	4	Evansville
	6	Creighton
	11	@Drake
	13	@Northern Iowa
	18	Indiana State
	20	Bradley
	22	@Creighton
26-Mar.	1	###Missouri Valley Conference Tournament

@	Road Games
#	Honolulu, HI (vs. Auburn, first round; also Hawaii and Rutgers)
##	Wichita, KS (vs. Mercer, first round; also Mississippi Valley State and Western Illinois)
###	Kiel Center, St. Louis, MO

Martina, 6-9 freshman **Bart Westgeest**, 6-9 freshman **Kurt Flowers** and 6-8 freshman **Mike Watkins**.

Mack and Flowers both sat out their first seasons at Wichita State—Mack as an academic non-qualifier, Flowers as a medical redshirt (back surgery). Mack can play facing the basket, and Smithson hopes he can contribute immediately. Mack averaged 17.2 points and 10 rebounds as a prep senior in Detroit.

Flowers, who averaged 18.5 points and 14 boards at tiny Alexis (Ill.) High as a senior, was the Shockers' most impressive rebounder in preseason practice before back trouble sidelined him. He's not a scorer, but could join Bunch and Utting as players who can provide backup minutes here and there.

Martina and Westgeest, both from the Netherlands, are the Shockers' most intriguing newcomers. Both are more seasoned than average freshmen because they played on junior club teams in Europe. Westgeest, who averaged 20 points and 18 rebounds for his club team, is the more polished player of the two.

Smithson compares him to the Bulls' Toni Kukoc—a tall left-hander who is comfortable playing outside. But with the Shockers' depth at small forward, Westgeest may see more time at big forward. Martina (25 ppg, 12 rpg, 3 bpg for his club team) is more raw as a 6-10 forward-center, but he has long arms and could become a shot-blocking presence. He'll live in the Shocker weight room in an attempt to become stronger inside.

Watkins (9.5 ppg for Derby High) is a big, raw player who won't have to contribute much in his first season. With a 16-man roster, Smithson said Watkins is the most likely redshirt candidate.

adidas Blue Ribbon Analysis

BACKCOURT	B	BENCH/DEPTH	C
FRONTCOURT	C	INTANGIBLES	B

By the end of last season, Wichita State's grittiness and determination were winning it some games it probably shouldn't have won, considering the team's woeful shooting (.381). Forty-percent shooting might have gotten the Shockers three or four more wins, and that's a big key this season.

A lot will be asked of some young kids, primarily Lewis and Benton at point guard and Mack, Martina and Westgeest inside. They don't need to become stars, just consistent contributors to put around Perez and Evans, two of the Missouri Valley's top offensive players on the perimeter.

A much easier non-conference schedule than last season will help a young team develop. Wichita State may be a year away from challenging for the Valley's top spot, instead challenging for third place again. But don't be surprised to see 17 or 18 wins and an outside shot at the NIT.

(K.S.)

NORTHEAST CONFERENCE

adidas BLUE RIBBON FORECAST

1. St. Francis (NY)
2. Mount St. Mary's
3. Fairleigh Dickinson
4. Wagner
5. Maryland-Baltimore County
6. Long Island
7. St. Francis (PA)
8. Central Connecticut State
9. Monmouth
10. Robert Morris
11. Quinnipiac

ALL-CONFERENCE TEAM

G—Rick Mickens, JR, Central Connecticut State
G—Gregory Harris, JR, Mount St. Mary's
G—Richie Parker, JR, Long Island
F—Richy Dominguez, SO, St. Francis (NY)
C—Frantz Pierre-Louis, SR, Wagner

PLAYER OF THE YEAR

Gergory Harris, JR, Mount St. Mary's

NEWCOMER OF THE YEAR

Melvin Whitaker, FR, Mount St. Mary's

1998-99 CONFERENCE TOURNAMENT

Feb. 25-March 1, Spiro Sports Center, Staten Island, NY

1997-98 CHAMPION

Long Island University (regular season)
Fairleigh Dickinson (conference tournament)

1997-98 POSTSEASON PARTICIPANTS

Postseason Record: 0-2 (.000)

NCAA

Fairleigh Dickinson (1st round)

NIT

Long Island University (1st round)

TOP BACKCOURTS

1. Maryland-Baltimore County
2. St. Francis (NY)
3. Mount St. Mary's

TOP FRONTCOURTS

1. Mount St. Mary's
2. Wagner
3. St. Francis (NY)

ON THE WAY UP

Mount St. Mary's

ON THE WAY DOWN

Long Island University

INSIDE THE NUMBERS

- 1997-98 conference RPI: 22nd (of 30)
- Conference RPI (last 5 years): 24-23-19-20-22

DID YOU KNOW?

The Northeast Conference will be hard-pressed to come up with an encore for last year's fine season. The NEC had the nation's top scorer (Long Island's Charles Jones) and the nation's second-best rebounder (St. Francis [PA] strongman Eric Taylor). Plus, the conference sent two teams (Fairleigh Dickinson to the NCAAs, Long Island to the NIT) to the postseason for just the second time in the 1990s...The NEC welcomes two new members for the 1998-99 season: Maryland-Baltimore County (UMBC) and Quinnipiac. UMBC competed in the Big South last season, while Quinnipiac moves up from the Division II ranks...Wagner's brand new Spiro Center will play host to the 1999 NEC men's and women's basketball tournaments. The top eight teams in the NEC will advance to the tournament, but Quinnipiac is ineligible because it's just in its first season as a Division I program...Graduation took away many of the NEC's brightest stars, as nine of the 11 first- and second-team all-NEC performers are gone from last year, including seven of the NEC's top 10 scorers and five of the 10 top rebounders...Long Island has a new coach in Ray Martin, a former Notre Dame player who most recently served as an assistant coach at Miami (Ohio)...Central Connecticut State had the youngest Division I team in the nation last season with just one junior, five sophomores and six freshmen...At 29, Monmouth's Dave Calloway is the second-youngest coach in Division I. Mount St. Mary's coach Jim Phelan is at the other end of the spectrum. At age 69, Phelan is the "most mature" coach in Division I. As a point of reference, Phelan had already compiled a 281-97 record at the Mount before Calloway was born.

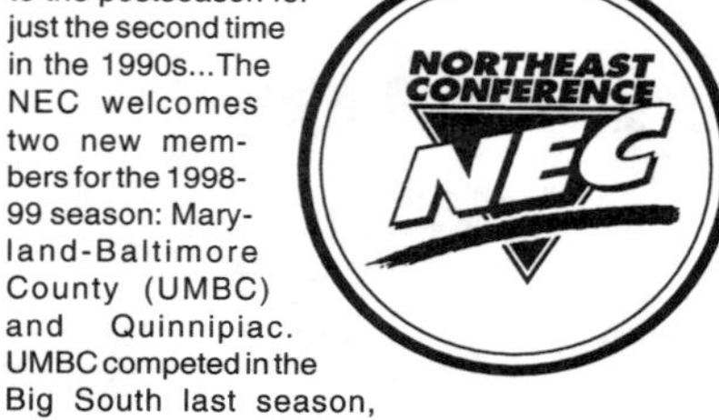

(B.D.)

CENTRAL CONNECTICUT STATE

LOCATION .... New Britain, CT
CONFERENCE .... Northeast (NEC)
LAST SEASON .... 4-22 (.154)
CONFERENCE RECORD 3-13 (9th)
STARTERS LOST/RETURNING 1/4
NICKNAME .... Blue Devils
COLORS .... Blue & White
HOMECOURT William H. Detrick Gymnasium (4,500)
COACH. Howie Dickenman (Central Connecticut '69)
RECORD AT SCHOOL .... 12-41 (2 yrs.)
CAREER RECORD .... 12-41 (2 yrs.)
ASSISTANTS .... Steve Pickiell (Connecticut '90)
Steve Hayn (SUNY-Stony Brook '91)
TEAM WINS (last 5 yrs.) 4-8-13-8-4
RPI (last 5 yrs.) 301-264-218-264-295
1997-98 FINISH .... Lost regular-season finale.

Howie Dickenman knows all about building and doing it with plenty of patience. Dickenman began his collegiate coaching career as an assistant at Connecticut in 1982. Back then the Huskies were just a middle-of-the-road team in a still new and largely unproven conference called the Big East.

By the time the early 90's arrived, the Big East was an elite conference and UConn, thanks significantly to Dickenman's recruiting efforts, was a national power.

So with the resume secure after 10 years as Jim Calhoun's top assistant, Dickenman moved into the head-coaching job at his alma mater in the spring of 1996. Reclamation project number two was just beginning.

Another change for the better came a year later, when Central Connecticut State ended its stint as the geographically-challenged member of the Mid-Continent conference and joined the Northeast Conference.

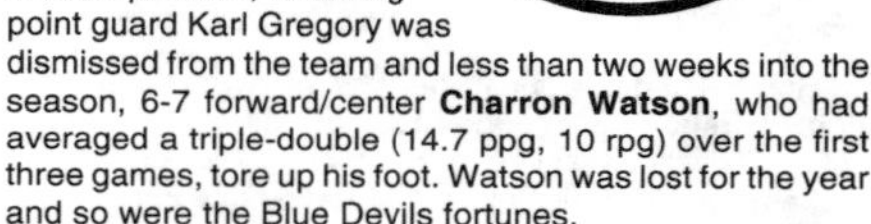

The good news ended there, however. A few weeks into preseason practice, returning point guard Karl Gregory was dismissed from the team and less than two weeks into the season, 6-7 forward/center **Charron Watson**, who had averaged a triple-double (14.7 ppg, 10 rpg) over the first three games, tore up his foot. Watson was lost for the year and so were the Blue Devils fortunes.

Central Connecticut State, which was believed to be the youngest team in Division I, lost its first seven games and won just four all season.

The biggest problem was at the point. Without Gregory, Dickenman used a pair of freshmen—6-4 **Dean Walker** (7.7 ppg, 5.0 rpg, 76 assists, 98 turnovers, .385 FG percentage) and 6-0 **Richard Ijeh** (4.5 ppg, 1.9 rpg, 46 assists, 65 turnovers, .398 FG percentage)—and it didn't work. Both proved to be too young and simply gave up the ball too much.

Their sloppiness was apparently contagious. Not one Blue Devil had more assists than turnovers. The poor shooting wasn't mutually exclusive of Walker and Ijeh either. No player on CCSU who played more than 11 games shot above 45 percent. The Blue Devils were outscored by an average of more than 11 points per game.

Dickenman hopes he has the solution at the point in 6-2 junior transfer **Tomas Brookins** (Genesee CC/Brooklyn, N.Y.) and hopes that will in turn have a mushroom effect on the rest of the team.

Walker should move to a more comfortable home at small forward. He should be more effective closer to the basket. The sophomore made just five of 32 three-pointers a year ago.

Ijeh will remain a reserve, where he was after the first nine games last season. He will back up Brookins at the point and 6-4 junior **Rick Mickens** (19.8 ppg, 3.8 rpg, 60 assists, 76 three-pointers)—CCSU's best player. Mickens was a second-team all-NEC choice last season after leading the conference in free-throw percentage (85.1 percent) and finishing second in scoring and fifth in steals (60). With little help, Mickens put it up 456 times, led CCSU in scoring in all but seven games, and played more than 35 minutes per game.

Dickenman hopes Brookins will get Mickens the ball with more ease than Walker and Ijeh did, but Mickens will still be asked to carry most of the load.

Bryan Finley (College of Canyons C.C./Saugus, Ca.), a 6-2 junior, is another junior college transfer who could help, but will be in a battle for minutes.

Brenden Floyd (1.4 ppg, 0.7 rpg), a 6-2 senior, played

1998-99 CENTRAL CONNECTICUT STATE SCHEDULE

Nov.	20-21	#Mohegan Sun Classic
	25	Army
Dec.	3-4	##Phoenix Classic
	7	@Fairleigh Dickinson
	10	Mount St. Mary's
	12	Maryland-Baltimore County
	22	@Northeastern
	28-30	###Hilo Holiday Shootout
Jan.	2	@Quinnipiac
	4	@Wagner
	7	St. Francis (PA)
	9	St. Francis (NY)
	16	@Long Island
	18	@St. Francis (NY)
	21	Robert Morris
	23	Long Island
	28	@St. Francis (PA)
Feb.	2	@Monmouth
	4	Wagner
	6	Monmouth
	11	@Maryland-Baltimore County
	13	@Mount St. Mary's
	15	Fairleigh Dickinson
	18	@Robert Morris
	20	Quinnipiac
25-Mar.	1	####NEC Tournament

@ Road Games
# New Britain, CT (vs. Brown, first round; also Delaware State and New Hampshire)
Hartford, CT (vs. Fordham, first round; also Harford and Yale)
Honolulu, HI (vs. Buffalo, first round; also Hawaii-Hilo and Old Dominion)
Spiro Sports Center, Staten Island, NY

in just 11 games and is likely to suffer the same fate this season.

Getting Watson back for his senior year will be a big plus for the Blue Devils. He is thin (listed anywhere from 185 to 200 pounds), but was talented enough to have scored 15 points and grabbed 10 rebounds against Boston College. If his foot stays healthy, he becomes the centerpiece of the front line and another offensive option after Mickens.

The long-awaited arrival of 6-8 freshman **Corsley Edwards** (Lake Clifton Eastern HS/Baltimore, Md.) will also be a big boost in more ways than one. Edwards checks in at 280 pounds. The Baltimore native originally committed to Bowling Green and sat out last year as a partial qualifier.

Victor Payne (6.7 ppg, 6.7 rpg, 40 steals), a 6-4 senior forward, started 19 games a year ago, but may find himself playing behind Walker this season. Payne doesn't have much offensive range, but is a worker around the basket, as evidenced by his status as the Blue Devils top rebounder in 1997-98.

Shawn Dreyer (6.2 ppg, 3.4 rpg), a 6-5 junior, offers just the opposite at the small-forward spot. Dreyer is more of a shooter with range. He was second behind Mickens in three-pointers made (26) and percentage (.371). Neither are numbers to retire on, but Dreyer can be a quick-hitter off the bench on any given night. When Payne went out with a hand injury for three games, Dreyer stepped in to average 14.3 points and 9.3 rebounds. He just needs to round himself into a more consistent player.

Behind Watson and Edwards up front, Dickenman will look to 6-9 sophomore **Jason Smith** (1.5 ppg, 2.4 rpg) and 6-10 sophomore **Jeremy Bergh** (3.4 ppg, 3.4 rpg). They each were rushed into duty last season, but now have 48 games of experience between them. That's time they wouldn't have gotten if Watson stayed in the lineup. Neither was very productive, although Bergh did block 27 shots, fifth in the conference. Smith and Bergh are much better suited to the reserve roles they will have this year.

Harvey Van Stein (Nova/Haarlem, Holland) is a 6-6 sophomore who failed to qualify last year. He was looked at by some Big East schools, so the talent is there. However, it's likely Van Stein will need time to adapt to American basketball.

adidas Blue Ribbon Analysis

BACKCOURT .... C **BENCH/DEPTH** .... D+
FRONTCOURT .... D+ **INTANGIBLES** C

Central Connecticut State won just four games last season as the youngest team in Division I, starting three freshmen and two sophomores most of the year, but strides were made individually, if not collectively.

Mickens proved to himself and the rest of the league that he was a bona fide scorer. Payne's scrappy play earned him co-NEC Player-of-the-Week honors in early February. He was the first Blue Devil to be so honored. And now Dickenman has Watson and Edwards in the fold to provide a legitimate mix of size and talent up front. CCSU did suffer a blow when Marijus Kovaliukas (12.2 ppg) decided not to return for his sophomore year. The Lithuanian native earned a spot on the NEC All-Newcomer team.

The addition of Brookins and the subsequent position change for Walker should help make up for any lost offense. This Blue Devil team should be much more versatile and diverse.

The program is still a long way from making any huge inroads in the standings, but if health does not play a factor, Dickenman has himself a much more talented—and experienced—club.

CCSU needs to take baby steps to respectability and the first foot forward should be getting out of the NEC basement and qualifying for the conference tournament. A little success should breed more success with a coach like Dickenman. And a little success is just what the Blue Devils need.

(C.C.)

FAIRLEIGH DICKINSON

LOCATION .... **Teaneck, N.J.**
CONFERENCE .... **Northeast**
LAST SEASON .... **23-7 (.767)**
CONFERENCE RECORD .... **13-3 (2nd)**
STARTERS LOST/RETURNING **4/1**
NICKNAME .... **Knights**
COLORS .... **Blue, White and Black**
HOMECOURT .... **Rothman Center (5,000)**
COACH .... **Tom Green (Syracuse '71)**
RECORD AT SCHOOL .... **260-174 (15 yrs.)**
CAREER RECORD .... **260-174 (15 yrs.)**
ASSISTANTS .... **Elloyna "Tiny" Green (Upsala '80)**
Neal Biscaldi (Rowan '95)
TEAM WINS (last 5 yrs.) **14-16-7-18-23**
RPI (last 5 yrs.) **177-149-257-105-92**
1997-98 FINISH .... **Lost in NCAA first round.**

One of the biggest commodities at the Rothman Center this season will be game programs. As in "you can't tell the players without a scorecard."

The Knights have lost four starters from last year's Northeast Conference champions and bring in eight new players. Change will be the only constant on the floor this year.

One of the toughest spot to fill will be at the point-guard position, where Elijah Allen (17.8 ppg, 159 assists) has vacated for a roster spot in France. **Lamont Perry** (Southwestern JC/Brooklyn, N.Y., 14.2 ppg, 7.3 apg, 6.3 rpg), a 6-3 junior from New York City with strong ball-handling skills, will take over running the show. His only drawback is perimeter shooting.

He will be backed up by 5-10 junior **Antoine Ross** (San Joaquin Delta JC/Stockton, Calif.), a speedy guard with a nice defensive presence.

The newcomers will be aided in the backcourt by the only returning starter from the NCAA team, 6-4 senior **Daryl Todd** (9.9 ppg, 5.3 rpg). He is going to be asked to pick up a lot of the scoring for the players lost.

The rest of the shooting guards looks like a United Nations contingent: 6-2 senior **Jesper Rasmussen** (7.2 ppg, 1.7 rpg) hails from Denmark; freshmen twins 6-6 **Tom Vanderkeere** and 6-7 **Wim Vanderkeere** come to Teaneck from Blankenberge, Belgium; and 6-3 junior transfer **Danny Sampson** (Riverside JC) comes all the way from Queens, N.Y. (okay, so that's not that too far from Teaneck).

Rasmussen is a solid outside scorer who will be needed to score off the bench. Wim Vanderkeere is a perimeter player who needs to add strength. Sampson averaged 20.9 ppg and 7.4 rpg last year and is able to score from outside on the drive.

Sampson, along with Tom Vanderkeere, will also play some at the small-forward position. Vanderkeere (17 ppg, 7.0 rpg, 5.0 apg), who is the slated starter at small forward, is a good scorer and passer who can also drive to the basket. He and Sampson should help the Knights on offense.

The front line is inexperienced. The only senior down low will be 6-7 **Jemo King** (3.4 ppg, 3.2 rpg), who is a decent rebounder. However, the starting nod will probably go to 6-8 junior college transfer **Donald Williams** (Irvine, Calif./Irvine Valley College), who is a power player inside. His addition could help make up for the loss of Rahshon Turner, who averaged 17.8 ppg and 10.8 rpg last season.

The Knights do have some intriguing possibilities at center. Three foreign players, all 6-10 and taller, will vie for time. The leading candidate is 6-10 import from Iceland **Baldur Olafsson**, who has a sweet shooting touch from outside.

Also pushing for the starting nod is 6-10 sophomore **Jonas Sinding** (1.9 ppg, 2.9 rpg), a native of Denmark who is a bruising defensive presence in the middle. Also in the middle will be 7-0 freshman **Jorn Grundman** (Hamburg, Germany/Adelphia Academy), a good-hands guy and a decent shooter. He will take some time to get accustomed to the American style of play.

Rounding out the roster are two little-used guards 5-9 senior **Damian Ware** (0.7 ppg, 0.5 rpg) and 5-11 junior **Jomaree Pinkard** (0.3 ppg, 0.7 rpg). Ware played in just six games last season, while Pinkard made it to the floor just three times.

1998-99 FAIRLEIGH DICKINSON SCHEDULE

Nov.	21	Maine
	28	Manhattan
Dec.	5	@Rutgers
	7	Central Connecticut State
	12	*Siena
	16	Youngstown State
	22	@St. John's
	30	Quinnipiac
Jan.	2	@St. Francis (PA)
	4	@Robert Morris
	7	Long Island
	11	@Monmouth
	13	@St. Francis ((NY)
	16	Wagner
	18	Maryland-Baltimore County
	21	St. Francis (PA)
	25	Mount St. Mary's
	28	@Maryland-Baltimore County
	30	@Mount St. Mary's
Feb.	1	Robert Morris
	3	@Long Island
	6	St. Francis (NY)
	11	Monmouth
	13	@Quinnipiac
	15	@Central Connecticut State
	20	@Wagner
25-Mar.	1	#NEC Tournament

@ Road Games
* Desmond Conference Challenge, Albany, NY
# Spiro Sports Center, Staten Island, NY

adidas Blue Ribbon Analysis

BACKCOURT .... **C+** **BENCH/DEPTH** .... **C**
FRONTCOURT .... **C+** **INTANGIBLES** .... **C**

The Knights have so much to make up for in 1998-99, it will take a miracle for them to repeat as NEC champs. This team is so young and the NEC is still strong at the top.

How this team makes up for the 67 points lost from last year's squad is a mystery. This will be one of the toughest coaching jobs in recent years, but Tom Green has the experience.

FDU is still good enough to finish in the top half of the Northeast Conference, but the youth will be hard-pressed to do much better. On the bright side, the recruiting class makes this one of the best "future" teams around.

(B.A.)

adidas Blue Ribbon Analysis

GRADING SYSTEM

- A+ equal to very best in country—Final Four-caliber unit
- A among the best in the land—worthy of deep NCAA run
- B+ talented, versatile and experienced—NCAA-NIT ability
- B solid and productive winners—league and post-season contenders
- C+ average to above-average—may contend in a weaker league
- C average to mediocre—second division in a strong league
- D+ below average, inconsistent—second division in a weaker league
- D well below average—losing season virtually certain
- F non-Division I ability—an underdog every night

LONG ISLAND

LOCATION .... Brooklyn, NY
CONFERENCE .... Northeast (NEC)
LAST SEASON .... 21-11 (.656)
CONFERENCE RECORD 14-2 (1st)
STARTERS LOST/RETURNING 3/2
NICKNAME .... Blackbirds
COLORS .... Blue & White
HOMECOURT .... Schwartz Athletic Center (1,300)
COACH .... Ray Martin (Notre Dame '77)
RECORD AT SCHOOL .... First Year
CAREER RECORD .... First Year
ASSISTANTS ... Julius Allen (Southern Nazarene '81)
Monte Ross (CUNY '76)
TEAM WINS (last 5 yrs.) 3-11-9-21-21
RPI (last 5 yrs.) 290-255-264-81-97
1997-98 FINISH .... Lost in conference final.

Ray Martin was going to play it cool if Long Island University called back and offered him the head coaching job. Cool as a cucumber. Cool as Puff Daddy. Do you hear me, cool?

Of course, when LIU athletic director John Suarez did call and offered Martin the chance to be the school's 10th head men's basketball coach, calm and cool went right out the window. After all, Martin—an 18-year assistant coach—had waited his entire adult life for this phone call.

"I told him to hold on for a second, and I put down the phone and started screaming," Martin recalled as he stood at the podium last June 20 as LIU's newest basketball coach. "I think my kids thought I was freaking out or something. I was extremely happy. It's a dream come true for me. I paid my dues."

Martin, 43, is coming home. He grew up in Long Island and became an All-Catholic guard at Mater Christi High (now St. John's Prep). From there, he signed with Digger Phelps and Notre Dame, where he was a four-year letterman and one of the Fighting Irish captains as a senior. One of the highlights of his fine career at Notre Dame was knocking off UCLA to snap the Bruins' 88-game winning streak.

With a degree in economics from one of America's most prominent institutions in his pocket, Martin probably made his econ professors cringe when he chose one of the lowest-paying, unstable professions in the world, becoming an assistant varsity coach and head freshman coach at Harvard back in 1977-78. But hoops was in his blood. He bounced all over as an assistant coach, including stops at Florida Atlantic, SMU, North Carolina State, Tennessee and Miami (Ohio). One of the highlights of his assistant coaching career was his eight-year stint on Tobacco Road with the late Jim Valvano at North Carolina State, especially the 1983 national championship season.

"Things that I remember most is his love for his players, his love for his family and his passion for the game," said Martin. "His players would always come into his office and they'd feel that they could talk about anything. And Jimmy didn't take himself too seriously. Those are the traits that I'm going to try and bring with me in putting this program together."

It's a program that has been successful the last two seasons with invites to the NCAAs in 1997 and the NIT last year. However, previous coach Ray Haskins ran into some problems with the school's administration, who thought the LIU coach was running a program with the emphasis too much on the athlete and not enough on the student-athlete.

The criticisms might have been valid considering that the Blackbirds logged almost 26,000 miles of air travel by the end of December last season. Flying so frequently is great if you're an up-and-coming rock band, not so great if you're trying to earn passing grades toward a diploma.

Martin will bring a different approach—not only cutting down significantly on the school's frequent flier miles (he's already talking about renewing age-old backyard rivalry with St. John's), but also slowing down the team's offense a bit from its NASCAR-like speeds the last two seasons.

It will be interesting to see how the slower style is accepted by students and players alike. Because despite what his critics say, Haskins did put the LIU program on the map with its run-and-stun style. His teams won 21 games in each of the last two seasons in addition to earning postseason tournament bids.

However, this will be a down year at LIU, which must replace 6-3 scoring machine Charles Jones and all-around whiz Mike Campbell. Jones averaged a Division I-best 29.0 points last year to become just the seventh player in NCAA history to win back-to-back scoring titles. He is hoping to latch on with some NBA team after the lockout is over. Jones, the 1998 NEC Player of the Year, did more than just score for the Blackbirds, averaging 7.4 apg, 5.2 rpg and 2.9 spg in LIU's wide-open attack.

The other star who must be replaced is the underrated 6-6 Campbell, a first-team All-NEC performer who averaged 19.7 points, 8.3 rebounds and 2.8 assists per game. Campbell has offers to play overseas, but also wants to give the NBA a whirl as a free agent after the lockout ends.

"I think next year is going to be a struggle," Suarez said to the *New York Post* at the time of Martin's hiring, citing the departures of Jones and Campbell.

All told, Martin must find replacements for six players, all lost to graduation, who accounted for 62 percent of the Blackbirds' offense. What the Blackbirds will have going for them is veteran leadership at the guard position as well as one of the top talents in the league in junior swingman **Richie Parker**. The 6-5 Parker will be asked to step into more of a leadership role with Jones and Campbell both gone. Parker, probably more well-known nationally for his infamous past rather than his stellar first two seasons at LIU, certainly has talent. He averaged 15.9 ppg and 7.3 rpg while shooting 51 percent from the floor last year.

The starting backcourt will be solid too, with 6-1 senior **Karee Anderson** and 6-3 senior **Issiah Francis** both returning. Anderson averaged 5.1 points and 2.4 assists in the team's first 19 games before being forced to miss the rest of the season with a knee injury. His weakness is his perimeter shot—or lack thereof. Last season, Anderson was a woeful 8 of 32 from behind the arc.

His running mate in the backcourt will be Francis, who has long arms and may be the best on-the-ball, man-to-man defender in the NEC. As a junior, Francis was one of the conference's premier sixth men, averaging 10.1 points, 3.7 rebounds and 2.6 steals.

A pair of juniors, 6-5 **Jonathan Frank** (2.4 ppg, 1.9 rpg, 16 steals) and 6-4 **Ray Rivera** (5.2 ppg, 2.8 rpg, 21 assists, 24 steals), will back up Francis and Anderson at the guard spots. Frank struggles mightily from the free-throw line (11 of 33, .333 percent, last season), while Rivera is shaky from the three-point line (28 of 290, .311). Further backcourt depth was expected from JUCO imports Hassan Ringer and Paul Ruddock, but both were lost because of academic deficiencies.

In addition to Parker, the frontcourt returns 6-9 senior and starting center **John Morganstern** (2.7 ppg, 2.2 rpg), whose numbers were underwhelming in the Blackbirds' guard-oriented, pedal-to-the-floor attack. He's no lock to start though, as 6-10 junior **Cheikh Fall** and 7-0 sophomore **Mike Ansley** both figure to push him. Fall averaged a modest 1.2 points and 2.1 rebounds in 1997-98, while Ansley redshirted last season. Ansley, a 300-pounder, is strong, but he's a work in progress. Another pivot possibility will be 6-10 sophomore **Jason Schnelle** (0.9 ppg, 0.6 rpg), but he appears to be a longshot at best.

The other starting frontcourt spot could belong to 6-6 senior **Robin Dickerson**, who started six times last season. He averaged 2.4 points and 2.7 rebounds, but had his troubles shooting straight last season (.319 FG percentage, .609 FT percentage). Another possibility to fill Campbell's vacant forward spot is 6-7 junior **Virgil Smiley**, who starred at Monroe Community College last year.

1998-99 LONG ISLAND SCHEDULE

Nov.	20-21	#AT&T Shootout
	30	Niagara
Dec.	5	Wagner
	7	Robert Morris
	10	@St. Francis (PA)
	12	@Robert Morris
	20	@Florida
	22	@South Florida
	28	@Georgia
Jan.	2	Mount St. Mary's
	4	Maryland-Baltimore County
	7	@Fairleigh Dickinson
	9	@Monmouth
	11	@St. Francis (NY)
	16	Central Connecticut State
	21	@Quinnipiac
	23	@Central Connecticut State
	28	Monmouth
Feb.	3	Fairleigh Dickinson
	6	Quinnipiac
	8	@Wagner
	11	St. Francis (PA)
	14	St. Francis (NY)
	18	@Maryland-Baltimore County
	20	@Mount St. Mary's
25-Mar.	1	##NEC Tournament

@ Road Games
# Fairfield, CT (vs. Fairfield, first round; also George Mason and Portland)
Spiro Sports Center, Staten Island, NY

adidas Blue Ribbon Analysis

BACKCOURT	C+	**BENCH/DEPTH**	C
FRONTCOURT	C+	**INTANGIBLES**	C+

First-time head coach Ray Martin has taken on a tough task here. LIU has been the NEC's most exciting team (96.9 ppg in 1997-98), as well as one of its most successful (42 wins, postseason berths in '97 and '98) the last two seasons.

This year, he takes over a team that has lost 62 percent of its scoring to graduation, including the remarkable Charles Jones—the NCAA scoring champ the last two seasons.

Just how far will LIU tumble? Richie Parker, one of the NEC's best all-around players, is back along with the makings of a solid backcourt. But while the Blackbirds will be strong on the outside, they look vulnerable down low. As a result, they appear to be a middle-of-the-pack team in 1998-99. Let's call it sixth place in the 11-team NEC—perhaps higher if the frontcourt (particularly the power forward and center spots) gets straightened out.

(B.D.)

MARYLAND-BALTIMORE COUNTY

LOCATION .... Baltimore, MD
CONFERENCE .... Northeast (NEC)
LAST SEASON .... 14-14 (.500)
CONFERENCE RECORD .... 6-6 (3rd-Big South)
STARTERS LOST/RETURNING 1/4
NICKNAME .... Retrievers
COLORS .... Black & Gold with Red
HOMECOURT .... UMBC Fieldhouse (4,024)
COACH .... Tom Sullivan (Fordham '72)
RECORD AT SCHOOL .... 179-189 (13 yrs.)
CAREER RECORD .... 24-58 (3 yrs.)
ASSISTANTS .... Randy Monroe (Cheyney '85)
Doug Nicholas (Gettsburg '89)
Bill Zotti (Seton Hall '95)
TEAM WINS (last 5 yrs.) 6-13-5-5-14
RPI (last 5 yrs.) 255-196-292-297-254
1997-98 FINISH .... Lost in conference semifinals.

Nothing against the Big South Conference, from which UMBC escaped after last season, but veteran coach Tom Sullivan found himself spending more time on buses than a country western singer when the Retreivers were in that league.

""Some trips down to Winthrop and Coastal Carolina were a good eight-hour bus ride," Sullivan said. ""It was kind of like minor-league baseball. The Northeast Conference is a better fit for the university in terms of travel, and we're also more compatible with the other teams in the league. We're the southern-most school in the league now, but everybody's within three hours of us. That's a lot better situation."

To be sure, Sullivan brings a road-tested team to the NEC. But the Retreivers have some talent, too. Young talent.

Last year, UMBC finished third in the Big South with three freshman playing a lot of minutes. Forward **Kennedy Okafor**, swingman **Rich Giddens** and point guard **Terence Ward** all made the Big South's All-Rookie team in 1997-98. The three youngsters led the Retreivers to a .500 record and helped Sullivan earn the league's coach-of-the-year honors.

Okafor (12.1 ppg, 9.3 rpg, 39 assists, 19 steals, 19 blocked shots), a 6-7, 252-pound sophomore who was redshirted the year before, became the Retreivers' second-straight Big South Rookie of the Year after leading the league in rebounding. Okafor, who also earned second-team All-Big South honors, displayed a good shooting touch as a freshman, shooting 51 percent from the field and 74 percent from the free-throw line. Considering he had a year's worth of rust to dust off after injuring his knee and redshirting in 1996-97, Okafor's debut was impressive.

""Even though he was getting his timing back after a year off, you could see Kennedy is a player who can contribute a lot at this level," Sullivan said. "Kennedy is a very physical player. His presence enables him to get a lot of interior points and rebounds. He's an excellent rebounder on both ends, and he can get some points off the offensive

1998-99 MARYLAND-BALTIMORE COUNTY SCHEDULE

Nov.	13	@Pittsburgh
	17	@Maryland
	20-21	#Beltway Classic
Dec.	3	Mount St. Mary's
	5	St. Francis (PA)
	10	@Quinnipiac
	12	@Central Connecticut State
	19	Towson
	23	Navy
Jan.	2	@Wagner
	4	@Long Island
	7	Wagner
	9	Robert Morris
	11	@Mount St. Mary's
	16	@Monmouth
	18	@Fairleigh Dickinson
	23	Monmouth
	28	Fairleigh Dickison
	30	Quinnipiac
Feb.	4	St. Francis (PA)
	6	@Robert Morris
	11	Central Connecticut State
	16	@St. Francis (NY)
	18	Long Island
	20	St. Francis (NY)
25-Mar.	1	##NEC Tournament

@ Road Games
# Baltimore, MD (vs. Loyola, first round; also Morgan State and Towson)
Spiro Sports Center, State Island, NY

glass."

UMBC's answer to Okafor, who does most of his damage in the post, is Giddens, a 6-5 sophomore who has a great stroke from three-point range. Last season Giddens (15.5 ppg, 3.9 rpg, 83 assists, 41 steals, 11 blocked shots) a second-team All-Big South pick, scored the most points ever by a Retriever freshman (434) and tied a school record for three-pointers in a season (80).

Giddens shot a team-high .394 percent from behind the arc, but isn't one dimensional. With his size, Giddens can post up smaller defenders. He led UMBC in scoring last season.

""Last year, we spotted Rich up for three-pointers a lot," Sulivan said. ""He can really shoot it. And as he understands our system, he'll get open more and more. He's a great athlete who can play two postitions. And with his size, he's capable of helping us out on the boards."

The third sensational sophomore is the 6-1 Ward (12.9 ppg, 2.6 rpg, 106 assists, 43 steals), who was second on the team in scoring and paced the Retrievers in assists and steals.

"Terence is still learning to play the point at the college level," Sullivan said. "He's adjust to the physical nature of the game. But he really makes us go on offense. And he's an excellent shooter."

Last season Ward shot .387 percent from three-point range and 81 percent from the free-throw line.

Still a fourth sophomore, 6-5 **Brad Martin** (4.0 ppg, 3.0 rpg), saw his share of action last year, starting 11 times in 22 games. He averaged 14.4 minutes on the floor. "He's come back bigger and stronger," Sullivan said. ""He's a kid that can play the three or four spot for us."

Before we move on from the sophomore class, we'd be remiss if we didn't mention 6-0 guard **Tim Hyland**, who was having a good year in his own right until he factured his wrist in the ninth game of the season. Hyland (6.3 ppg, 1.8 rpg, 32 assists, .929 FT percentage), isn't afraid to hoist three-pointers, and his range is deep. He scored 13 points in consecutive games against Bucknell and North Carolina-Asheville last season.

Other players competing for backcourt minutes include 5-11 senior **Rod Harrison** (3.1 ppg, 1.1 rpg, 40 assists) and 6-2 junior **Jason Womble** (3.7 ppg, 1.9 rpg, 22 assists).

Isaac Green (7.6 ppg, 5.0 rpg, 35 assists, 24 steals), a 6-6, 225-pound junior, will team with Okafor in UMBC's frontcourt. Green, the 1996-97 Big South Rookie of the Year, is a physical presence who shot 48 percent from the field last year, including 59 percent in his final six games. Green was the Retrievers' second-leading rebounder.

Kerry Martin (3.6 ppg, 2.1 rpg, .580 FG percentage), a 6-7 junior, had a solid season on offense and defense. He shot 58 percent from the field and 77 percent from the free-throw line, and also blocked a team-high 23 shots.

Michael van Heen (2.3 ppg, 1.9 rpg), a 6-4 senior, and **Nick Grella**, a 6-8, 250-pound sophomore, will provide backup help in the frontcourt. Grella's minutes decreased in the final third of last season, but he started 11 games. Van Heen (2.3 ppg, 1.9 rpg) is reported to be a good outside shooter, but last year, he made just five of 26 three-point shots (.192 percent).

Sullivan brought in three newcomers, including junior college transfer **Ricardo Dalmau**, a 6-3 combo guard from South Florida Community College. Dalmau averaged 16.3 points last season.

Two freshman join the program. **Brett Kindelmann**, a 6-10 center, will be worked into the lineup slowly. He averaged a double-double Huntington (N.Y.) High School (14.8 ppg, 11.7 rpg).

Neil Streeter, a 6-3 guard, averaged 16.9 ppg and 9.0 rpg at the Bullis School in Washington, D.C.

adidas Blue Ribbon Analysis

BACKCOURT	**B**	**BENCH/DEPTH**	**C**
FRONTCOURT	**C+**	**INTANGIBLES**	**C**

The Retrievers logged more miles than the girls in Lilith Fair last season, traveling to such remote Big South outposts as Coastal Carolina and Charleston Southern. They will welcome a switch to the NEC, where the farthest school is no more than a three-hour bus ride. That beats an eight-hour ride any day of the week, and should make UMBC fresher and ready to compete in its new league.

Sullivan has one of the best young lineups in the conference. Kennedy Okafor is a quality front-line player who could be a league player-of-the-year type. Rich Giddens is already one of the NEC's best shooters, and Terence Ward is developing into a solid point guard.

With so many sophomores and freshmen on the roster, UMBC might not be ready, experience wise, to challenge for the NEC title, but a middle-of-the-pack finish wouldn't be out of the question for its rookie year in the league. And watch out when all those sophomores get to be juniors and seniors.

(C.D.)

MONMOUTH

LOCATION	**West Long Branch, NJ**
CONFERENCE	**Northeast (NEC)**
LAST SEASON	**4-23 (.148)**
CONFERENCE RECORD	**3-13 (8th)**
STARTERS LOST/RETURNING	**2/3**
NICKNAME	**Hawks**
COLORS	**Blue & White**
HOMECOURT	**Boylan Gymnasium (2,500)**
COACH	**Dave Calloway (Monmouth '91)**
RECORD AT SCHOOL	**3-10 (1 yr.)**
CAREER RECORD	**3-10 (1 yr.)**
ASSISTANTS	**Mark Calzonetti (Bently '85)**
	Kevin Nickleberry (Virginia Wesleyan '86)
	Ron Krayl (Sioux Falls '68)
TEAM WINS (last 5 yrs.)	**18-13-20-18-4**
RPI (last 5 yrs.)	**133-180-84-118-288**
1997-98 FINISH	**Lost in conference quarterfinal.**

Monmouth College looked into its not-too-distant past to hire the man that will shape its future. Dave Calloway has bled Monmouth blue and white since his days as a player from 1987-91. Calloway earned the reputation as one of the deadliest shooters in the Northeast Conference and Monmouth history. He is fourth on the school's all-time Division I scoring list with 1,404 points and is the school's all-time leader in three-pointers (260).

With 13 games left in the 1997-98 season, the school needed a replacement for long-time coach Wayne Szoke, who had coached and shaped the lives of Calloway and countless others during his decade as the Hawks head man. Calloway took over, and the team struggled to win just three of its final 13 games.

But all of that is now forgotten. "We had our first meeting and we said that last season was an aberration," said Calloway. "I want to restore Monmouth to its old level of winning basketball. And I think we've started to do that by recruiting talented players who come from some of the East Coast's finest high school programs. The freshmen that were brought in here are winners."

While the seven newcomers will shape the future of Monmouth hoops, the leader of this year's edition of Hawks is 6-3 guard **Maurice Williams**, the only senior on the roster. Williams (9.7 ppg, 2.5 rpg, 59 assists, 27 steals) is the team's top returning scorer, but struggled with his long-distance shooting (.293 percent from three-point range). He's not a rah-rah guy by nature, but is blossoming into a leader or sorts—Williams leads by example.

"Maurice has become a little more vocal," said Calloway. "And he's working extremely hard on his own game. He's the first one in the weight room or the gym and the last to leave. That's what you look for out of your seniors, a guy who shows your young guys the ropes."

His running mate in the backcourt will be one of those fresh-scrubbed youngsters—**Raheem Carter**, a 6-3 freshman from Long Branch (N.J.) High School who averaged 12.2 ppg, 5.3 rpg and 5.0 assists in his senior season. Carter, who finished his career with 1,103 points, was a second-team all-state selection by the *Newark Star-Ledger* and The Associated Press.

"Raheem Carter is a leader. He's strong with the ball and he just flat-out wins," said Calloway. "He's the epitome of a point guard. He has games when he scores 16, 18 or 20 points. And he has games where he scores four points and you leave the gym thinking he played even better than he did in those high-scoring games. Simply put, he does whatever it takes to help the team win."

Carter is just one of three freshman guards Calloway likes. The other two are 6-2 **Cameron Milton** and 6-3 **Aaron Faulkner**. Milton transferred from Philadelphia's Bodine High—where he did everything but sell programs—to traditional Philly power Franklin Learning Center for his senior season. His scoring average dropped from 22.0 ppg to 8.9 ppg, but his team went 23-4 and reached the Philadelphia Public League title game.

Faulkner also started for one of the nation's most powerful high school teams—St. Vincent Pallotti in Greenbelt, Md., a squad which included five Division I signees and was ranked as high No.15 in the country by *USA Today*. Faulkner averaged 6.5 ppg, 2.7 rpg and 3.5 apg last season.

"Milton and Faulkner are going to be pretty good players for us," said Calloway. "They both played in highly successful high school programs and both sacrificed a lot of their own personal success to be team players. They're the type of kids we want in our program."

The slew of new faces will battle with returnee **Sean Collins** for time in the backcourt, opposite Williams. Collins (4.5 ppg, 2.7 rpg, 52 assists, 20 steals), a 6-2 junior, appeared in 27 games last season, including 13 starts. He excels at long-range shooting, making 24 of 57 three-pointers (.421 percent) last year).

Calloway and his assistant coaches, including Mark Calzonetti (with seven years of experience at Fairfield) and Kevin Nickelberry (with his Maryland-Washington, D.C.-area ties from his days at Howard) also worked hard to increase the talent level in the frontcourt. And it looks like they've succeeded.

The best of new frontcourt faces is 6-5 freshman small forward **Alpha Bangura**, who originally committed to George Washington but changed his mind after Mike Jarvis left the school to take the St. John's head coaching job. Nickelberry's connections in the nation's capitol no doubt aided the Hawks in their efforts to land Bangura. He should be a four-year starter for Calloway after averaging 22.3 ppg and 5.0 rpg for a 14-10 Roosevelt (Lanham, Md.) High School team which reached the Maryland 4A semifinals.

"Any time we can get a player who committed to an Atlantic 10 school, we're thrilled," said Calloway. "Alpha will be a player for us."

Two other newcomers show lots of promise in the frontcourt, if they can live up to their press clippings.

1998-99 MONMOUTH SCHEDULE

Nov.	18	Sacred Heart
	21	@Boston College
	24	@Drexel
	28	Princeton
Dec.	7	Quinnipiac
	10	St. Francis (NY)
	12	@Rider
	22	St. Peter's
Jan.	2	@Robert Morris
	4	@St. Francis (PA)
	7	@St. Francis (NY)
	9	Long Island
	11	Fairleigh Dickinson
	16	Maryland-Baltimore County
	18	@Wagner
	21	@Mount St. Mary's
	23	@Maryland-Baltimore County
	28	@Long Island
Feb.	1	Wagner
	2	Central Connecticut State
	4	Mount St. Mary's
	6	@Central Connecticut State
	8	@Quinnipiac
	11	@Fairleigh Dickinson
	13	Robert Morris
	17	St. Francis (PA)
25-Mar.	1	#NEC Tournament

@ Road Games
# Spiro Sports Center, Staten Island, NY

Calloway believes that he has landed Monmouth's center of the future in 6-10 freshman **Kevin Owens**, the younger brother of University of Pennsylvania center Geoff Owens. The only problem is that the 200-pound Owens needs to put some serious meat on his bones. Still, Owens is highly skilled—as his 16.0 ppg and 8.0 rpg averages and 64 percent field-goal percentage as a senior at Camden (N.J.) Catholic High suggest.

"Kevin obviously needs to get stronger," said Calloway. "But 6-10 guys don't grow on trees. He needs a year or two of serious strength and conditioning to become a force, but he has skills and talent in a 6-10 body."

The final frontcourt imports are 6-8, 220-pound freshman forward **Steve Bridgemahon** and 6-5, 210-pound freshman **Andre Williams**. Bridgemahon, a second-team Group II all-state selection last season for North Brunswick (N.J.) High, scored 16.3 points and grabbed 9.5 boards per game. He also possesses a knack for blocking shots (2.5 per game in 1997-98).

Williams is gifted enough to be a starter from the time he steps on the court. A second-team all-state selection by the *Newark Star Ledger*, Williams was one of the top players in South Jersey last season. Williams (16.5 ppg, 9.3 rpg) is the only player in Bishop Eustace High School history to top the 1,000-point and rebound plateaus. He finished with 1,272 points and 1,105 rebounds and led his team to the No. 4 ranking in the state last year.

"These guys are more than just skilled players," said Calloway. "They're winners."

In order to start, Williams must beat out the Hawks' best frontline returnee, 6-6 junior **Quin Hayes**. Hayes appeared in all 27 games last season for the Hawks, including 10 starts. He was fourth on the team in scoring (8.9 ppg) and can stroke the three-ball (63-151, .417 percent).

Rounding out the frontcourt possibilities are 6-6, 220-pound junior **Joe Potkay** (3.6 ppg, 3.7 rpg, 10 assists, 23 steals), who gave the Hawks some valuable minutes off the bench last year, and 6-5, 210-pound **Darren Kennedy**, who redshirted last season.

adidas Blue Ribbon Analysis

BACKCOURT .... **C+** **BENCH/DEPTH** .... **C+**
FRONTCOURT .... **C** **INTANGIBLES** .... **C**

Monmouth could be on the road to recovery after a four-win season in 1997-98. Oh sure, this Hawks' team is about as young as the cast of *Dawson's Creek*, but at least Monmouth's boy wonder coach Dave Calloway and his hard-working assistants have brought a much-needed ingredient into the program: Talent.

Still, teams with seven newcomers generally take a year or so to gel. That will be the case with the Hawks, who figure to play a lot of different combinations this season. But after another second-division finish this season, watch out for these guys in 1999-2000.

(B.D.)

MOUNT ST. MARY'S

LOCATION .... **Emmitsburgh, MD**
CONFERENCE .... **Northeast (NEC)**
OVERALL RECORD .... **13-15 (.464)**
CONFERENCE RECORD .... **8-8 (5th)**
STARTERS LOST/RETURNING **3/2**
NICKNAME .... **Mountaineers**
COLORS .... **Blue & White**
HOMECOURT .... **Knott Arena (3,196)**
COACH .... **Jim Phelan (LaSalle '51)**
RECORD AT SCHOOL .... **785-428 (44 yrs.)**
CAREER RECORD .... **785-428 (44 yrs.)**
ASSISTANTS .... **Milan Brown (Howard '93)**
Don Anderson (Franklin & Marshall '82)
TEAM WINS (last 5 yrs.) **14-17-21-14-13**
RPI (last 5 yrs.) **213-143-71-171-200**
1997-98 FINISH .... **Lost in conference semifinal.**

One of the most famous graduates in the history of Mount St. Mary's is Father Flanagan, the founder of Boy's Town. The joke going around the Mount's campus these days is that the school's bow-tie wearing, future Hall of Fame coach Jim Phelan has turned into Father Flanagan.

The reason? Phelan, the winningest active coach in college basketball with 785 victories and counting, has the most talked-about newcomer in the Northeast Conference. However, for the second time in three years, the NEC's most-discussed new face comes to the school with a rap sheet.

1998-99 MOUNT ST. MARY'S SCHEDULE

Nov.	14	LaSalle
	22	@Santa Clara
	28	@Villanova
Dec.	3	@Maryland-Baltimore County
	6	*Bucknell
	7	St. Francis (PA)
	10	@Central Connecticut State
	12	@Quinnipiac
	19	@Loyola
	30	@Georgia Tech
Jan.	2	@Long Island
	4	@St. Francis (NY)
	7	Robert Morris
	9	Wagner
	11	Maryland-Baltimore County
	16	@St. Francis (PA)
	18	@Robert Morris
	21	Monmouth
	25	@Fairleigh Dickinson
	28	Quinnipiac
	30	Fairleigh Dickinson
Feb.	4	@Monmouth
	6	@Wagner
	13	Central Connecticut State
	18	St. Francis (NY)
	20	Long Island
25-Mar.	1	#NEC Tournament

@ Road Games
* Hoops For Jake Benefit, Harrisburg, PA
# Spiro Sports Center, Staten Island, NY

Three years ago, the newcomer was Richie Parker, Long Island's small forward with his well-chronicled problems. This season, it's 6-10 Mount St. Mary's center **Melvin Whitaker**.

You might remember that Whitaker, a high school All-American, signed with the University of Virginia out of Oak Hill Academy. But Whitaker was charged with assault after slashing the face of a Virginia football player with a box cutter after a dispute that began during a pickup game. The football player needed 73 stitches to close the wound and Whitaker was found guilty of malicious wounding and was sent to prison.

He's not scheduled to get out of jail until some time in October, but he's committed to start playing for Mount St. Mary's on Dec. 19th—even though he hasn't played organized hoops in more than three years. And even though some folks at this quiet, small school on the Maryland-Pennsylvania border aren't too thrilled about Whitaker getting a scholarship.

Hence, the Father Flanagan references. Despite the wisecracks, Whitaker is coming to the Mount. And if the one-time ACC signee is anywhere near playing shape, he could make the Mountaineers the team to beat in the Northeast Conference.

That's because Phelan's squad already possesses one of the league's most feared perimeter talents in 6-3 junior combo guard **Gregory Harris** (15.5 ppg, 4.9 rpg, 156 assists, 51 steals), the ninth-leading scorer in the NEC despite the fact he was forced to play out of position at point guard last year. Harris, a DeMatha High product, is a more natural shooting guard, but a lack of a true answer at the point made Harris the best option to play there.

Harris, a bonafide NEC Player-of-the-Year candidate, is still liable to spend most of his time at the point-guard slot this season. That's because 6-8 junior swingman **Rob Balgac**, a Yugoslavian import, has made tremendous strides this offseason—thanks to some intense work in the weight room.

Balgac (4.0 ppg, 2.2 rpg, 28 assists, 16 steals), the designated gunner off the bench last year, has added 20 pounds to his once-frail frame and has increased his vertical leap significantly in the process.

Balgac has undergone such a transformation that he figures to battle 6-foot senior **Eric Bethel** (8.8 ppg, 2.0 rpg, 43 assists, 19 steals) for the starting two-guard spot. Whoever loses the heated battle figures to be the first guard off the bench.

Of course, Harris figures to see some action at the shooting-guard spot, if skinny sophomore point guard **A.J. Herbert** is 100 percent after ankle problems dogged him last year, or if 5-11 freshman **Jerry Lloyd** is ready to run the show. The 5-10 Herbert (0.8 ppg, 0.7 rpg) is just 155 pounds, but he's very quick. However, recurring ankle injuries limited him to just 12 games last season. Phelan would like to see him gain some bulk in order to be able to be a stronger on-the-ball defender. Aside from getting to know the weight room a little better, Herbert also needs to improve his perimeter jumper after making just three of his 15 shots last year.

When Lloyd—a preseason honorable-mention All-America selection by *Blue Ribbon* before last season—was first recruited, it was believed he could handle the point-guard slot. But that transition could take some time, because Lloyd looks more like a smallish two-guard at this point of his career. Still, Lloyd arrives in Emmitsburg with a gaudy resume from Whitehall (Pa.) High, where he was an all-area performer as a junior and senior. Lloyd figures to come off the bench as a freshman.

The other backcourt possibilities are a pair of seldom-used sophomores in 6-3 **Jason Grace** (2.0 ppg, 0.0 rpg in nine games) and 5-11 **Stephen Moore** (0.3 ppg, 0.3 rpg in seven games).

The frontcourt has a chance to be the NEC's finest, if Whitaker is as good as advertised (despite the three years of inactivity) and if 6-8 Newton Gayle, a starter at power forward last season, is granted an extra year of eligibility by the NCAA.

Whitaker, an honorable mention McDonald's All-American, was supposed to be the answer to former Virginia coach Jeff Jones' prayers. But things didn't work out—either for Jones (who was fired last spring) or Whitaker. So how did Whitaker end up at the Mount? While he was a player at Oak Hill Academy, one of his teammates was from Gettysburg, Pa. As a result, Whitaker became close friends with the entire family and during visits to their home, he wandered over to the Mount (just a hop, skip and a jump from Gettysburg) to play in some pickup games. He liked the campus, the facilities and some of the players and committed there last year.

Whitaker won't have as much pressure on him, if Gayle is granted an extra year of eligibility. As of mid-September, Phelan and his coaching staff were hopeful it would happen because the 6-8, 235-pound Gayle lost a year of eligibility when he was forced to transfer when Niagara rescinded his scholarship. Because the decision to transfer to the Mount—and as a result, the lost year—wasn't his but Niagara's, Gayle figures to be granted an extra season. Gayle (7.8 ppg, 5.5 rpg, 24 assists, 17 steals) would give Phelan a rugged rebounder who already knows the system. His presence would allow Whitaker to ease into the frontcourt picture.

Even if Gayle doesn't return, Phelan can turn to hard-working 6-5 senior **Tony Hayden**, one of the team's co-captains, to play small forward and power forward. Hayden (9.1 ppg, 5.8 rpg, 43 assists, 23 steals) isn't the fastest player in world or can't jump out the gymnasium; he just out-works his opponents and gets every ounce he can out of his ability. He'll start again this season.

Phelan is excited about Hayden's understudy at small forward, 6-7 rail-thin freshman **Terrence Wilson**. At just 175 pounds, Wilson is as skinny as a super model, but he does have skills. As a senior at Nansemond River (Va.) High School, Wilson was an all-county selection. Thanks to his athleticism, Wilson has a substantial upside, however he must become a fixture in the weight room first.

Two other members of the Mount's deep reservoir of frontcourt talent who figure to log significant minutes are 6-9, 250-pound junior **Michael Cook** and 6-9 junior **Konata Springer**, a transfer from Manhattan. Neither Cook (1.4 ppg, 0.9 rpg) nor Springer is the second coming of Patrick Ewing on the low blocks, but both are much-needed bangers who won't hurt Phelan's club if they're on the court in limited minutes.

The last man off the bench figures to 6-11 senior **Todd Kessler** (1.2 ppg, 0.2 rpg in just five appearances in 1997-98). Kessler is Phelan's victory cigar, appearing when the Mountaineers are on their way to yet another win in Phelan's illustrious career.

adidas Blue Ribbon Analysis

BACKCOURT .... **B-** **BENCH/DEPTH** .... **B**
FRONTCOURT .... **B+** **INTANGIBLES** .... **B**

St. Francis (N.Y.), with nearly everybody back from last season, is the popular pick to win the Northeast Conference. While St. Francis looks like the best team right now, our hunch is that Mount St. Mary's could be the NEC's finest come March.

By then, highly-touted 6-10 center Melvin Whitaker will have peeled some of the rust off his game after a three-year prison sentence. If 1997-98 starter Newton Gayle is granted an extra year of eligibility by the NCAA and Whitaker can regain his past form—or something near it—then the Mount will win the Northeast Conference Tournament and the automatic bid to the Big Dance.

Looking for reasons we like St. Francis to win the regular-season crown, but the Mount to ultimately get the NCAA bid? The Mountaineers possess a future Hall of Fame coach in Jim Phelan, who should pass the 800-win mark this season. And they possess one of the top perimeter talents in Gregory Harris (15.5 ppg in 1997-98) and one of the NEC's hardest workers in senior co-captain Tony Hayden (9.1 ppg, 5.8 rpg). That combination should do the job in the postseason.

(B.D.)

QUINNIPIAC

LOCATION .... **Hamden, CT**
CONFERENCE .... **Northeast (NEC)**
LAST SEASON .... **4-23 (.148)**
CONFERENCE RECORD .... **N/A**
STARTERS LOST/RETURNING **4/1**
NICKNAME .... **Braves**
COLORS .... **Blue & Gold**
HOMECOURT .... **Burt Kahn Court-Athletic Center (1,500)**
COACH .... **Joe De Santis (Fairfield '79)**
RECORD AT SCHOOL .... **9-43 (2 yrs.)**
CAREER RECORD .... **9-43 (2 yrs.)**
ASSISTANTS .... **Tom Blake (Connecticut '78)**
TEAM WINS (last 5 yrs.) **13-12-5-5-4**
RPI (last 5 yrs.) .... **N/A**
1997-98 FINISH .... **Lost in final Division II game.**

Say a prayer or 12 for poor Joe DeSantis, if you get a chance. The third-year Quinnipiac College coach takes the Braves into the Division I ranks after the school competed for 47 seasons at the NAIA and Division II level. The scary part? The Braves were having a tough enough time holding their own as a Division II school the last two years, so Lord knows how gruesome things could get in year one at the D-I level.

Last season, the Braves were 4-23—which marked the least wins and the most losses in program history. Not exactly awe-inspiring stuff for a team about to move up to college basketball's highest level. In addition, the team has notched just 14 wins in the last three years, and hasn't had a winning season since 1992-93.

So what team does DeSantis schedule for his team's opponent in its first-ever game as an "official" Division I team? That's right, Connecticut—a legit national title contender. Sure, Quinnipac would have a chance to win a mensa contest against the Huskies. After all, Quinnipiac is rated among the top 10 Northern regional universities in *U.S. News and World Report*'s 1999 edition of *America's Best Colleges*. But this is basketball.

Things don't figure to get much easier for the Braves after the Huskies bludgeon them in the opener. That's because it will take DeSantis a couple years just to flush all of the Division II players out of the program. Plus, the Braves also play at Syracuse on Dec. 1. What is this guy, a masochist? DeSantis' feeling is that the two early-season games against the Big East heavyweights will give his school some much-needed name recognition, because UConn and Syracuse figure to be preseason top-25 types. That means the name "Quinnipiac" will be on the bottom of the ESPN screen every 20 minutes or so and that the box scores will appear in newspapers all up and down the East Coast—which is invaluable publicity for a first-year Division I program.

This season, DeSantis might need more leadership out of his senior co-captains than any other coach in the country. He'll need the two individuals, senior guards **Andrew Mackenzie** and **Sean Tabb**, to keep the team's spirits from getting crushed as the losses pile up. And trust us, they will pile up.

The 6-3 Mackenzie (11.5 ppg, 2.1 rpg, 28 assists, 7 steals) played in all 27 games for Quinnipiac as a junior. After becoming a fixture in the starting lineup in January, Mackenzie averaged 17 points per game. A dean's list student, Mackenzie was the 26th most accurate free-throw shooter in Division II ball last season (.847 percent).

"Andrew is a terrific role model for any student-athlete," said DeSantis. "He has excelled in the classroom. and he's continued to improve on the court. We look for him to have a great season."

On the surface, Tabb appears to be an odd choice to be a co-captain. After all, he transferred from Hartford to Quinnipiac last December and won't become eligible until the conclusion of the first semester. The 6-3 guard played three seasons for Hartford and will complete his eligibility this spring. Tabb, who joins his younger brother, **Colin**, on the Quinnipiac roster, amassed 2,095 career points and netted all-state honors three times at Somers High School.

"Although Sean has only been here for one semester, he has a nice combination of leadership qualities and three years of Division I experience," DeSantis said. "Sean comes to Quinnipiac after playing valuable minutes in a tough conference (America East). I feel he will be one of the better three-point shooters in the league."

Two other key contributors are back in 6-6 junior forward **Ivoree Stanley** (if he's healthy) and 6-7 junior **Chris Stone**. Despite having not played in nearly two seasons after transferring from Bridgeport, Stanley displayed some potential by averaging 9.2 points and 7.0 rebounds in five games against Division I competition before suffering a season-ending foot injury. If he's 100 percent—or near it—he'll probably start.

Stone (2.8 ppg, 2.0 rpg) appeared in 22 games last season, including one start. He should fight for some minutes off the bench as DeSantis' lineup card figures to go through more new combinations than a lock manufacturer. Three sophomore returnees—5-9 **Rashad McCormick**, 6-9 **Jason Rosato** and 6-7 **Bon McNeish**—will battle with a six-pack of newcomers to earn quality minutes.

McCormick (1.4 ppg, 0.7 rpg, 33 assists) figures to be a deep reserve at the point-guard slot. Rosato (250 pounds) and McNeish (230 pounds), on the other hand, are two of the biggest bodies in the program, so they'll see action this season. Rosato (1.7 ppg, 2.1 rpg, 10 blocks) appeared in 20 games (for an average of 8.5 minutes per game) last season. After shooting a woeful 14 of 46 from the floor last year, Rosato will need to improve his shooting touch to warrant more playing time.

McNeish (3.0 ppg, 3.2 rpg, .556 FG percentage) was a decent contributor when he was on the floor, but injury problems limited him to just 10 games last season.

McNeish figures to battle 6-8, 250-pound freshman **Bill Romano** for the starting power-forward slot. Romano, who picked Quinnipiac despite drawing interest from Manhattan, Niagara and Northeastern, earned all-state honors as a junior and senior at Wethersfield (Conn.) High School. A four-year starter in high school, Romano compiled 1,679 career points and 977 career boards while averaging 23.2 ppg and 13.8 rpg in his senior season.

"Bill is a big man with excellent touch. We will look for him to score inside and out to the three-point line," said DeSantis.

In addition to Romano, JUCO import **Alphah East** should be an immediate impact performer. The 6-6, 225-pound East, a junior, has decided to move back to the New England states after spending the last two seasons at Cowley County (Kan.) College. During his scholastic career, East led Greenfield High to the Massachusetts state finals as a senior. The biggest question mark about East is his health. He averaged 12 points and seven rebounds last season at Cowley, but his season was cut short after just seven games because of a broken wrist.

"With his strength and athletic ability, Alphah will establish himself as a strong inside presence, especially on the defensive end," said DeSantis.

DeSantis also signed three more guards. One of the newcomers, JUCO transfer **Nate Poindexter**, could be the answer at point guard. The 6-4 junior joins the Braves after averaging 15 points, 7.6 rebounds, 9.2 assists and 4.3 steals for Hesser (N.H.) College. Poindexter led Hesser to the junior-college national tournament and was chosen to the all-tournament team after handing out a school single-game record 15 assists against Sinclair.

"Nate is a very versatile guard who is an outstanding passer," said DeSantis. "We are looking for Nate to contribute immediately."

Ditto 6-3 sophomore guard **Jamar Fields**, a former starter for perennial New York City prep power St. Raymond's. Fields was receiving interest from Providence and St. Louis before enrolling in Dixie (Utah) Junior College last fall. He stayed there one semester before transferring to Quinnipiac. He'll get playing time as soon as he becomes eligible at the end of the fall semester. Fields is a typical New York City guard—meaning that he can drive to the hole against all comers.

"Jamar is a strong guard who can slash to the basket very well," said DeSantis. "He is an unselfish player who can play any guard position."

The final guard signee is 6-3 freshman **Jared Grasso**, who averaged 23 points, eight assists and seven rebounds as a senior at St. Anthony's (N.Y.). He was the school's first four-year starter and finished with 1,275 career points.

"Jared is a combination guard who will be looked upon to run the team and score points," said DeSantis. "He's a gym rat who will only improve."

DeSantis only hopes the same is true for the rest of his young Braves.

1998-99 QUINNIPIAC SCHEDULE

Nov.	15	@Connecticut
	18	Army
	21	@Columbia
Dec.	1	@Syracuse
	7	@Monmouth
	10	Maryland-Baltimore County
	12	Mount St. Mary's
	21	@Brown
	30	@Fairleigh Dickinson
Jan.	2	Central Connecticut State
	5	@Sienna
	9	St. Francis (PA)
	11	@Wagner
	16	@Robert Morris
	18	@St. Francis (PA)
	21	Long Island
	23	Robert Morris
	28	Mount St. Mary's
	30	@Maryland-Baltimore County
Feb.	4	@St. Francis (NY)
	6	@Long Island
	8	Monmouth
	11	St. Francis (NY)
	13	Fairleigh Dickinson
	18	Wagner
	20	@Central Connecticut State
25-Mar.	1	#NEC Tournament

@ Road Games
\# Spiro Sports Center, Staten Island, NY

adidas Blue Ribbon Analysis

BACKCOURT	**C**	**BENCH/DEPTH**	**F**
FRONTCOURT	**C-**	**INTANGIBLES**	**F**

Quinnipiac is everybody and their third cousin's choice to finish in the NEC basement (yes, that includes *Blue Ribbon*). This might be the lowest-rated Division I team in the RPI ratings, in fact. The Braves struggled mightily last year at the Division II level, so how in the world do they expect to compete as a Division I team? They'll build around their six newcomers and a couple decent returnees, play an occasional big-name foe like UConn and Syracuse to build name recognition, and be patient as the losses pile up in the first year or two.

Coach Joe DeSantis hopes that after about three seasons, he will have a roster full of legitimate D-I players and be able to compete in the NEC. Until then, times will be tough.

(B.D.)

ROBERT MORRIS

LOCATION .... **Moon Township, PA**
CONFERENCE .... **Northeast**
LAST SEASON .... **8-19 (.296)**
CONFERENCE RECORD .... **4-12 (7th)**
STARTERS LOST/RETURNING **2/3**
NICKNAME .... **Colonials**
COLORS .... **Blue & White**
HOMECOURT .... **Charles L. Sewell Center (3,056)**
COACH .... **Jim Boone (West Virginia State '81)**
RECORD AT SCHOOL .... **12-42 (2 yrs.)**
CAREER RECORD .... **240-113 (12 yrs.)**
ASSISTANTS **Glenn Gutierrez (West Liberty State'85)**
Dave Pilipovich (Thiel '86)
John Mahoney (Robert Morris '98)
TEAM WINS (last 5 yrs.) **14-4-5-4-8**
RPI (last 5 yrs.) **172-291-297-287-283**
1997-98 FINISH .... **Lost in conference first round.**

Jim Boone is smack in the middle of a rebuilding project. He knows it. After all, it's been his life's calling of late. First, he transported California (Pa.) from an afterthought into the Division II limelight. Now he's in year three of his overhaul of the once-proud Robert Morris program that won an NEC-record five league titles between 1982 and '92.

Lately, though, the Colonials have been NEC bottom feeders with three straight last-place finishes between 1995 and '97 and RPIs near 300 each season during that stretch. Last year, Boone's squad made baby steps forward as the Colonials finished seventh in what was a nine-team league. So what's Boone looking for in 1998-99? Continued progress.

"I feel strongly that we can use this year to pave the way toward being a conference contender," says Boone. "We now have a foundation in place, from which, by virtue of the last two years, we can take off and be the best we can be."

If Boone's squad is to continue its slow forward crawl, then Robert Morris' three returning starters (**Chris Hopkins, Keith Jones** and **Niall Phelan**) must blend with eight newcomers to form a cohesive unit.

Jones and Hopkins return to be the building blocks up front. Jones, a 6-6 senior, led the Colonials by averaging 12 points and 6.6 rebounds (the latter was eighth-best in the NEC last season).

1998-99 ROBERT MORRIS SCHEDULE

Nov.	14	Bucknell
	18	@Ohio State
	24	LaRoche
	30	@Central Michigan
Dec.	5	@St. Francis (NY)
	7	@Long Island
	10	Wagner
	12	Long Island
	22	@West Virginia
	28	Brown
Jan.	2	Monmouth
	4	Fairleigh Dickinson
	7	@Mount St. Mary's
	8	@Maryland-Baltimore County
	16	Quinnipiac
	18	Mount St. Mary's
	21	@Central Connecticut
	23	@Quinnipiac
	28	St. Francis (NY)
Feb.	1	@Fairleigh Dickinson
	6	Maryland-Baltimore County
	8	St. Francis (PA)
	11	@Wagner
	13	@Monmouth
	18	Central Connecticut
	20	@St. Francis (PA)
25-Mar.	1	#NEC Tournament

@ Road Games
# Spiro Sports Center, Staten Island, NY

Meanwhile, Hopkins (8.4 ppg, 5.5 rpg, 31 assists, 7 steals), a 6-10 senior, was much like the hare in the old hare and tortoise story. Hopkins started last season fast and then cooled off as the season progressed. But the 245-pound Hopkins does perform those valuable chores—such as leaning on the opponent's pivot man for about 30 minutes every night. Still, Jones and Hopkins need to be more consistent as seniors, if the Colonials are to climb up from the depths.

"Keith has teased us with his ability," says Boone. "He's dabbled in success, but he has to be successful on a more regular basis for the team to benefit. He's had a good summer and he's developed the confidence to know he can step up and produce without forcing the action."

While all three frontcourt newcomers—**Robert Shirley**, **Steve Pettyjohn** and **Matt Smith**—hope to contribute early, Shirley is the favorite to do the most damage. Although he did not play organized basketball in his native Brooklyn, N.Y., Shirley, a 6-7 junior, was a standout at Erie Community College in Buffalo, averaging 25 points and 10 rebounds over his two seasons there. Pettyjohn and Smith are a matching set of 6-foot-8 freshmen from Ohio.

Naron Jackson, a 6-5 sophomore who was academically ineligible last season, and 6-4 senior **Jamir Washington** (1.1 ppg, 1.2 rpg) round out the frontcourt rotation.

While the frontcourt features more questions than a week's worth of episodes of Jeopardy, the backcourt appears to be in good hands. **Gene Nabors**, a 6-2 junior, takes over for four-year starter Javier Smith at the point-guard spot. A transfer from LSU, where he averaged 5.1 points, 2.5 rebounds and 5.8 assists as the Tigers' starting point guard for two years, Nabors could blossom into a star in the NEC.

"Offensively, we want to be more up-tempo and Gene can make that happen," says Boone. "He's the kind of player who makes everyone else better."

His running mate in the backcourt will be either 6-3 sophomore **Kevin Covert** or Phelan. Bet on Phelan because Covert, who scored more than 2,600 points in high school, remains a medical question mark. After his 1995-96 season at the University of Akron, Covert tore the ACL in his right knee and then transferred to Robert Morris. His luck wasn't better at his new locale, as he tore the ACL in his left knee just 14 minutes into the Colonials' season-opening exhibition game last year.

His ongoing Battle of Wounded Knees opened the door for Phelan, a native of Dublin, Ireland, to start at the two-guard slot. And Phelan, a 6-3 junior, excelled. He was second on the Colonials in scoring (11.4 ppg) while logging almost 33 minutes per night. He and Smith were pressed into extra duty last year because of a lack of backcourt depth, but that doesn't seem to be the case this season.

Help is on the way in the person of JUCO import **Brandon Welsch**, a 6-6 junior guard who started his career at the University of Iowa two seasons ago. He spent last season at Kirkwood (Iowa) Community College and is expected to make an impact at shooting guard and small forward.

Further depth will be provided by 6-2 senior **Dan Alcorn** and 6-5 sophomore **Wesley Fluellen**. Alcorn (4.3 ppg, 1.3 rpg, 43 assists, 15 steals) has logged quality minutes off the bench the last three seasons, though he has struggled mightily to find his shooting touch (34- of 106, .321 percent). Fluellen (4.2 ppg, 2.3 rpg, 6 assists, 4 steals) is still adjusting to life away from the basket. He looked more comfortable playing with his back to the basket as a freshman.

adidas Blue Ribbon Analysis

BACKCOURT	C	BENCH/DEPTH	C-
FRONTCOURT	C	INTANGIBLES	C

Continued progress. That's all that Robert Morris coach Jim Boone is looking for this season.

His team won four games in his first season and eight last season. The Northeast Conference has expanded to 11 teams with the addition of Maryland-Baltimore County and Quinnipiac, yet only eight schools will make the postseason tournament in Staten Island, N.Y.

Robert Morris' 1998-99 team aims to make the NEC Tournament with room to spare. Will it happen? Well, Robert Morris appears to be on the bubble, a team which figures to finish anywhere from eighth to 10th.

If the Colonials are to be tournament worthy, then the eight newcomers will have to make a sudden impact—particularly at the offensive end, where Robert Morris was either last or second-to-last in scoring offense (63.0 ppg), field goal percentage (.417), three-point field goal percentage (.309) and three-pointers made (3.96 per game).

Expect another second-division finish for the Colonials and a short stay in the NEC Tournament—that is, if they're lucky enough to make it.

(B.D.)

ST. FRANCIS (N.Y.)

LOCATION .... **Brooklyn Heights, N.Y.**
CONFERENCE .... **Northeast**
LAST SEASON .... **15-12 (.555)**
CONFERENCE RECORD .... **10-6 (t-3rd)**
STARTERS LOST/RETURNING **2/3**
NICKNAME .... **Terriers**
COLORS .... **Red & Blue**
HOMECOURT .... **Pope Physical Education Center (1,250)**
COACH .... **Ron Ganulin (LUI-Brooklyn '68)**
RECORD AT SCHOOL .... **71-121 (7 yrs.)**
CAREER RECORD .... **98-144 (9 yrs.)**
ASSISTANTS .... **Glenn Braica (Queens '88)**
TEAM WINS (last 5 yrs.) **1-9-9-13-15**
RPI (last 5 yrs.) **300-281-286-242-189**
1997-98 FINISH .... **Lost in conference first round.**

St. Francis coach Ron Ganulin isn't stupid. Five years ago, you could count his team's win total on one finger. So recruiting stateside—where each July is treated like the Paris fashion season with prospects put on display in camps and AAU tourneys before talent-hungry coaches who can look, but can't touch or even talk to—was fruitless.

Few, if any, New York City hoop talents were going to sign on the dotted line with a guy with one stinking win. So Ganulin started looking into the foreign import business. He wasn't the first to mine overseas talent, but he's gotten good at it: Ganulin's current 10-man roster includes five players born outside the United States. One of his reserve forwards, **Marcel Dimberg** of Cameroon, has lived in five countries and speaks four languages fluently. Three of his top four returning scorers are from Columbia, the Canary Islands and Cameroon, respectively.

And you know what? Ganulin's foreign invasion has paid dividends. Serious dividends, as the wins are starting to pile up nearly as fast as the frequent flier miles. In fact, folks are talking about the Terriers as a legit NEC title contender for the next two years. And it's not far-fetched talk thanks to the world of talent that Ganulin has been able to scarf up.

The best of the foreign imports is 6-6 sophomore swingman **Richy Dominguez** (11.4 ppg, 4.1 rpg, 55 assists, 27 steals), a native of Choco, Columbia, and winner of the Northeast Conference Newcomer of the Year last season. Dominguez, a former two-time Junior National Player of the Year in Columbia, is clearly the Terriers' top dog. Dominguez, a born slasher, must only learn to improve his defense and his woeful free-throw shooting (.561) to blossom into one of the NEC's brightest stars.

Rejoining Dominguez in the starting lineup are 6-7 junior forward **Angel Santana** from the Canary Islands and 6-11 sophomore center **Heberth Reyes**. Santana (10.7 ppg, 3.7 rpg, 33 assists, 30 steals) has scored in double figures in both of his seasons at St. Francis. The only wart on his game is that his long-range jumper is often about as accurate as the editorial content of a supermarket tabloid. Santana shot just .350 from the field last season. But he's a lock to start. He moved into the lineup at Long Beach State last Dec. 20, scored a season-high 24 points, and never left the starting five after that.

The other starting forward spot will be manned by 6-7 sophomore **Henry LaLane** (9.2 ppg, 3.4 rpg, 25 assists, 11 steals). Like Santana, LaLane is a fine athlete who is more effective in transition then he is standing still and firing up long-range bombs (52 of 170 from three-point range, .306 percent).

Santana and LaLane will have to do better than that with their perimeter jumpers, in order to open things up inside for Reyes. The new pivot will be asked to pick up more of the scoring load, now that second-team All-NEC power forward Roque Osorio (team-best 11.7 ppg) is gone. The somewhat mechanical Reyes (3.5 ppg, 3.7 rpg, 25 assists, 21 blocks) will never be confused with Hakeem Olajuwon on the low blocks, but he's certainly capable of doubling his scoring average this season.

Aside from replacing the lost points of Osorio, the other gaping hole that Ganulin must plug is at point guard, where John Thomas (11.3 ppg) must be replaced. Thomas did more than just lead the Terriers in assists (109) last season. He also would take (and often make) the big shot and had a knack of rallying the troops when times were tough.

His replacement at the point will be 5-10 sophomore **Greg Nunn** (1.3 ppg, 1.8 rpg, 42 assists, 17 steals). Nunn isn't much of a shooter (.297 FG percentage) and is more steady than spectacular, but he'll try to get everyone involved like Thomas did.

Nunn will have an able (or rather an Abel) backup. That's because 5-11 senior **Solomon Abel** (1.7 ppg, 0.9 rpg, 9 assists, 10 steals) returns to give Nunn an occasional breather. Abel's minutes were limited last season because Thomas was so valuable and because Abel was still rounding back into shape after undergoing reconstructive knee surgery in 1996-97. Before the surgery, Abel was a double-figure scorer for Ganulin, scoring 10.4 ppg as a sophomore.

Further perimeter depth will be provided by a proven hand in 6-4 senior **Ray Mineland** (also from Cameroon). A transfer from Davidson, Mineland (8.8 ppg, 3.4 rpg, 46 assists, 33 steals), who started last season's first 13 games and appeared in 23 games overall, is the younger brother of former St. John's standout Charles Mineland. Mineland's instant offense is critical to the Terriers. He scored in double figures 11 times last season and the Terriers were 7-4 in those games.

Rounding out the backcourt rotation will be 6-3 senior **Tim Rail**, who appeared in just seven games as a reserve last season, playing just 28 minutes. Rail averaged 1.9 ppg and 0.1 rpg as a junior—quite a dropoff from his sophomore season with the Terriers (7.0 ppg, 2.2 rpg).

Frontcourt depth will come from two old faces and a new one. The returnees include the 6-7 Dimberg, who appeared in 19 games last season. Dimberg (2.4 ppg, 2.5 rpg, 9 blocks) actually started nine games in 1997-98. Another valuable bench jockey is 6-7 senior **Anthony**

1998-99 ST. FRANCIS (NY) SCHEDULE

Nov.	16	@Lehigh
	25	@Northwestern
	30	@St. John's
Dec.	5	Robert Morris
	7	Wagner
	10	@Monmouth
	16	@Iona
	18	Caldwell College
	27	@Notre Dame
Jan.	4	Mount St. Mary's
	7	Monmouth
	9	@Central Connecticut State
	11	Long Island
	13	Fairleigh Dickinson
	18	Central Connecticut State
	21	@Wagner
	23	St. Francis (PA)
	28	@Robert Morris
	30	@St. Francis (PA)
Feb.	4	Quinnipiac
	6	@Fairleigh Dickinson
	11	@Quinnipiac
	14	@Long Island
	16	Maryland-Baltimore County
	18	@Mount St. Mary's
	20	@Maryland-Baltimore County
25-Mar.	1	#NEC Tournament

@ Road Games
# Spiro Sports Center, Staten Island, NY

Rogers, whose numbers (2.5 ppg, 2.3 rpg, 5 blocks) are similar to Dimberg's.

The new kid on the low blocks will be 6-7 junior-college import **Gerald Walker** from McCook (Neb.) Junior College. Walker (10 ppg, 6 rpg) was part of a powerhouse McCook squad which finished 29-3. How good was McCook? Two of Walker's teammates from last season will attend West Virginia, one will attend St. John's and another will play for Oregon this winter.

adidas Blue Ribbon Analysis

BACKCOURT .... **B-** **BENCH/DEPTH** .... **B-**
FRONTCOURT .... **B** **INTANGIBLES** .... **B**

Thanks to all of the foreign imports, head coach Ron Ganulin has directed quite a turnaround at St. Francis. The $64,000 question is: Can a coach who is 50 games under .500 during his first seven years in Brooklyn Heights finish the job and take his team to the Big Dance? We think so, although the Terriers will be pushed hard by defending champ Fairleigh Dickinson and perhaps Mount St. Mary's (if 6-10 prize recruit Melvin Whitaker can shake off the rust after spending the last three years in prison).

The Terriers are the NEC's best on the wings, but they must find replacement parts for their starting point guard John Thomas (no small task) and their most reliable inside scorer in Roque Osorio, a second-team All-NEC performer.

Several guys have the talent to develop into the squad's brand new go-to guys, particularly Richy Dominguez and Angel Santana. Whether they do could make the difference in whether Ganulin's squad can actually win the NEC tournament and with it, the golden ticket to the NCAAs.

(B.D.)

ST. FRANCIS (Pa.)

LOCATION .... **Loretto, PA**
CONFERENCE .... **Northeast**
LAST SEASON .... **17-10 (t-3rd)**
CONFERENCE RECORD .... **13-3 (1st)**
STARTERS LOST/RETURNING **3/2**
NICKNAME .... **Red Flash**
COLORS .... **Red & White**
HOMECOURT .... **DeGol Arena/Maurice Stoke Center (3,500)**
COACH .... **Tom O'Connell (Point Park '84)**
RECORD AT SCHOOL .... **76-88 (6 yrs.)**
CAREER RECORD .... **76-88 (6 yrs.)**
ASSISTANTS .... **Andy Helton (Miami-Ohio '92)**
John Sanow (Indiana-Pa. '87)
TEAM WINS (last 5 yrs.) **13-12-13-12-17**
RPI (last 5 yrs.) **193-208-162-216-172**
1997-98 FINISH .... **Lost in conference first round.**

During his six-year tenure at St. Francis, Tom O'Connell hasn't been looking for anything flashy—just solid defense and strong board work.

He got plenty of both ingredients last season as the Red Flash posted a 17-10 record, including a 10-6 league mark which was good enough for a third-place tie in the Northeast Conference. By limiting opponents to just .410 percent shooting from the field and by holding the rebounding edge in 23 of 27 games, St. Francis went on to register its first winning season since 1991 and just its fourth since '81.

So, if it ain't broke, don't fix it, right? O'Connell would love to incorporate the same formula again in 1998-99. There's one small problem: His big people are unproven commodities, so the Red Flash might have to play a more run-and-gun style this winter. That's because the Red Flash bid farewell to six lettermen, including two-time All-Northeast Conference center Eric Taylor.

How good was the glass-eating Taylor? So good that some opposing NEC head coaches probably dispatched one of their trusted assistants to St. Francis' graduation ceremony last spring to make sure the big fella left.

Taylor was among the nation's top rebounders the last two seasons and led the team in scoring (17.5 ppg), rebounding (11.9 rpg second in the nation), field-goal percentage (.567) and minutes played (940) last season.

Also gone is Taylor's tag-team partner underneath, 6-6 power forward Emmanuel Adekunle (9.6 ppg, 5.5 rpg, 105 career blocked shots) and 6-9 Jeff Churchill, Taylor's backup last season. The backcourt also has some holes to

1998-99 ST. FRANCIS (PA) SCHEDULE

Nov.	17	@Pittsburgh
	21	@North Carolina-Greensboro
	28	North Carolina-Greensboro
Dec.	3	@Bucknell
	5	@Maryland-Baltimore County
	7	@Mount St. Mary's
	10	Long Island
	12	Wagner
	22	@Utah
	29	Maryland-Eastern Shore
Jan.	2	Fairleigh Dickinson
	4	Monmouth
	7	@Central Connecticut State
	9	@Quinnipiac
	16	Mount St. Mary's
	18	Quinnipiac
	21	@Fairleigh Dickinson
	23	@St. Francis (NY)
	28	Central Connecticut State
	30	St. Francis (NY)
Feb.	4	Maryland-Baltimore County
	8	@Robert Morris
	11	@Long Island
	13	@Wagner
	17	@Monmouth
	20	Robert Morris
25-Mar.	1	#NEC Tournament

@ Road Games
\# Spiro Sports Center, Staten Island, NY

patch, now that bench scorers Walt DeVan (8.4 ppg, 2.6 rpg, 3.3 apg) and Sotiris Aggelou (7.7 ppg) are long gone too.

Still, the strength of the Red Flash figures to be its backcourt, thanks to the return of sophomore starters **Sam Sutton** and **Jamal Ragland**. The 6-3 Sutton, a solid defender who can play either the shooting guard or small forward slot, started 18 of 25 games last season. He finished third on the team in scoring (9.3 ppg) and rebounding (3.9), earning a spot on the NEC's All-Newcomer team in the process.

Ragland (5.6 ppg), a 5-10 point guard, started 26 of 27 games and led the Red Flash in assists (110) and tied for the team lead in steals with 32. Yet another Division I player for Bob Hurley Sr.'s fertile St. Anthony's (N.J.) program, Ragland was also second on the team in minutes played, behind Taylor.

Ragland won't have to log the same iron-man type of minutes this season. That's because 5-8 sophomore **Earl Foreman** is now eligible after sitting out his freshman year under Proposition 48. As a senior at Frankford High School in Philadelphia, the cat-quick Foreman averaged 22.8 points, 5.7 rebounds and 8.1 assists and earned all-public league honors. He'll split time with Ragland at the point.

Another key contributor on the perimeter will be 6-2 junior **John McLean**, who came on strong as the season wore on. He could start at the two-guard slot and push Sutton to small forward. McLean started the last 10 games of the season and averaged 10.1 points during that span, pushing his season average up to 5.7. McLean also produced one of the most memorable individual performances of last season when he knocked down 10 of 17 shots from the field, including five of six from three-point range, en route to a career-high 31 points against Wagner last February.

Expected to challenge McLean for playing time is fellow junior **Rob Krimmel** (3.3 ppg, 1.0 rpg, 17 assists, 3 steals), a 6-2 two-year letterman who started three games last season, and 6-4 **Arthur Wills**, a 6-4 freshman from the Newport School (Md.). Wills averaged 17 points and eight boards a game for Newport and he'll see time at both guard spots.

Additional backcourt depth will be provided by **John Silva**, the lone senior on the roster, and sophomore **Clinton Crouch**. Both played sparingly last season and should expect to again this year. The 6-2 Silva (0.3 ppg, 0.5 apg) saw action in 12 games as a backup two-guard in 1997-98, while Crouch (0.6 ppg, 0.6 rpg, 0.2 apg) appeared in just nine games as a freshman.

For McConnell, the biggest problem area is his depleted frontcourt. Not only will the Red Flash sorely miss Taylor and Adekunle's inside presence, St. Francis will enter the year without a true center on its roster. Junior **Tom Fox** (3.9 ppg, 1.6 rpg, 10 assists, 3 steals) is the tallest player on the roster at 6-7. But Fox is as thin as the plot line of a WB comedy series, at only 190 pounds.

Melvin Scott (2.0 ppg, 1.8 rpg, 9 assists, 22 blocked shots), a 6-6 leaper, will be asked to increase his scoring and rebounding totals this season. Fellow junior **Matt Walter**, a 6-5 two-year lettermen, doesn't figure to see increased time after tallying just 1.2 ppg and 0.4 rpg in limited duty last season.

So who will fill the voids up front? The freshmen will try, particularly **Shawn Crosbie**, **Pete Fox** (Tom's younger brother) and **Bryan Martin**. The 6-5, 200-pound Crosbie was chosen team MVP at Paterson Catholic (N.J.) last season after averaging 13 points and 10 boards for a 19-5 squad.

The 6-5 Pete Fox is expected to swipe some of Sam Sutton's minutes at the small forward slot after averaging 17 points, nine rebounds and five assists at St. Ignatius (Ohio) High School. Martin, 6-6, will swing between the two- and three-man spots after averaging 18 points and seven boards for Hatboro-Horsham (Pa.) High.

adidas Blue Ribbon Analysis

BACKCOURT .... **C+** **BENCH/DEPTH** .... **C+**
FRONTCOURT .... **D** **INTANGIBLES** .... **C**

Lacking the muscle and inside strength of his previous teams (St. Francis' tallest player is 6-7), look for head coach Tom O'Connell to favor a much more up-tempo style this season in an attempt to keep the Red Flash among the NEC's elite.

It won't work. Preseason league favorites St. Francis (N.Y.), Mount St. Mary's and defending champ Fairleigh Dickinson all either have veterans who can score underneath or highly-touted newcomers who can score an easy bucket inside every once in while.

Making matters tougher for the Red Flash is the fact that O'Connell has put together a challenging non-conference schedule that includes dates with NCAA runner-up Utah and Pittsburgh. This will be a rebuilding year for the Red Flash.

(B.D.)

WAGNER

LOCATION .... **Staten Island, NY**
CONFERENCE .... **Northeast**
LAST SEASON .... **13-16 (.448)**
CONFERENCE RECORD .... **7-9 (6th)**
STARTERS LOST/RETURNING **2/3**
NICKNAME .... **Seahawks**
COLORS .... **Green & White**
HOMECOURT .... **Spiro Sports Center (2,100)**
COACH .... **Tim Capstraw (Wagner '82)**
RECORD AT SCHOOL .... **95-130 (8 yrs.)**
CAREER RECORD .... **95-130 (8 yrs.)**
ASSISTANTS .... **Scott Fielder (Washington-Mo. '91)**
Stephen Norberg (St. John's '93)
Chris Kelly (Staten Island '97)
TEAM WINS (last 5 yrs.) **16-10-10-10-13**
RPI (last 5 yrs.) **157-228-233-238-236**
1997-98 FINISH .... **Lost in conference semifinal.**

Tim Capstraw hopes that a recent trend—teams just a short outlet pass from the Big Apple going to the Big Dance—continues in the Northeast Conference.

Two years ago, it was the run-and-stun style of Long Island University that resulted in an NCAA Tournament bid. Last year, Fairleigh Dickinson, fueled by a 43-point performance by point man Elijah Allen, scared Connecticut in round one of March Madness, before falling short.

This year, it could be Wagner—the Staten Island-based school with the breathtaking views of the New York Harbor, the Atlantic Ocean and the Verrazano Narrows Bridge from its residence halls—that enjoys a view from the top of the NEC standings.

But reaching the summit of the NEC might have more to do with Frantz than New York City. As in 6-8, 255-pound post player **Frantz Pierre-Louis**, one of the most talented frontcourt performers in the conference, when he's on the court. As a sophomore, a shoulder injury forced him to miss much of the season. And last year, he was only able to appear in 18 games, averaging 13.6 ppg (second on the team) and a team-best 9.4 rpg.

If he's able to play an entire season, the Seahawks could have the NEC's most imposing frontline. That's because 6-7 senior **Ryan Reed** and 6-6 senior **Bobby Bok** also return.

Reed is equally adept at scoring (8.6 ppg) and hitting the glass (7.0 rpg). Bok, who replaced Pierre-Louis in the starting lineup late in the 1997-98 season, averaged 8.4 points and 4.4 boards. Reed and Bok will both have to blossom into double-figure scorers in order for the Seahawks to overcome the loss of their leading scorer Dan Seigle (19.3 ppg), a tough customer from Western Pennsylvania who could beat you in so many ways (5.7 rpg, 53

1998-99 WAGNER SCHEDULE		
Nov.	14	@Rutgers
	28	@College of State Island
Dec.	5	@Long Island
	7	@St. Francis (NY)
	10	@Robert Morris
	12	@St. Francis (PA)
	19	St. Peter's
	21	@Lehigh
	27-28	#Cowboy Shootout
Jan.	2	Maryland-Baltimore County
	4	@Central Connecticut State
	7	@Maryland-Baltimore County
	9	@Mount St. Mary's
	11	Quinnipiac
	16	@Fairleigh Dickinson
	18	Monmouth
	21	St. Francis (NY)
	30	Central Connecticut State
Feb.	1	@Monmouth
	6	Mount St. Mary's
	8	Long Island
	11	Robert Morris
	13	St. Francis (PA)
	18	@Quinnipiac
	20	Fairleigh Dickinson
25-Mar.	1	##NEC Tournament

@ Road Games
# Casper, WY (vs. Yale, first round; also Louisiana Tech and Wyoming)
Spiro Sports Center, Staten Island, NY

three-pointers in 1997-98).

Taking over Bok's role as first frontcourt player off the bench will be 6-6 sophomore **Steve Moore** (2.8 ppg, 3.0 rpg, 10 assists, 13 steals), who appeared in 24 games last season. But he'll be pushed for the sixth-man spot by highly-touted newcomer **Lesli Myrthil**, a 6-7, 220-pound freshman from Sweden who has played for several years for the Solna Vikings Club team. He averaged 10.0 ppg and 4.5 rpg for Solna last season and has played for the Swedish National team and the Swedish Junior National team. He's regarded as one of the top three players in his age group in Sweden.

Another new face in the frontcourt is 6-6, 200-pound freshman **Chris Jackson** of Redwood (Calif.) High School. Jackson was tabbed a first-team Marin County Athletic League selection after he averaged 14.9 points, 8.3 rebounds, 4.0 steals and 2.7 assists last season.

While there seem to be plenty of answers in the frontcourt, there are questions abound in the backcourt, as Capstraw must replace a double-figure scorer at two-guard in Jason Roberts (10.5 ppg), as well as a true floor general in passmaster Mick Wheeler (197 assists in 1997-98).

The man expected to replace Roberts is designated long-distance bomber **Frank DeBlasi** (5.4 ppg, 1.3 rpg, 36 assists, 18 steals). There was nothing blasé about DeBlasi's work outside the arc—he hit 34 of his 76 three-point shots for a tough-to-match .447 success rate.

The point should be manned by 1997-98 part-time starter **Damian McClimont**, who started 15 games last season. McClimont, a hometown boy from Staten Island, averaged 3.1 points and nearly an assist per game last season.

Capstraw makes no bones about the fact that he'll be replacing his lost starting backcourt tandem by committee this season. In addition to DeBlasi and McClimont, Capstraw has two other returnees as well as two backcourt newcomers he likes a lot. The two returning guards are 5-9 sophomore **Bilal Rodgers** and 6-foot senior **Vinson Smalls**.

Rodgers will vie with McClimont for the starting lead guard spot. The smallish (just 155 pounds), but lightning-quick Rodgers is a North Jersey product who appeared in all 29 games, but struggled to adjust to Division I ball like many freshman do. However, the coaching staff expects Rodgers (1.7 ppg, 0.9 rpg, 49 assists, 10 steals) to begin to blossom this season. Meanwhile, Smalls made big strides last season—more than doubling up his scoring average from 1.9 points per game to 4.1 points last season.

The two new faces in the backcourt are 6-4 freshman shooting guard **Jeff Klauder** and 5-9 freshman point guard **Yves Kabore**. Klauder saw his senior season at Washington Township (N.J.) cut short by a broken leg. The injury caused Klauder to miss 11 games, but he still earned all-South Jersey honors by averaging 23 ppg, 8.0 rpg and 4.0 apg when he was in the lineup. To succeed at the D-I level, Klauder will have to go up for seconds of the school cafeteria's entree offerings, because he's a stringbean at just 180 pounds.

The final newcomer is Kabore, one of the top point guards in the always-tough New York City Catholic League last year. Kabore averaged 14 points. But perhaps more important to the Wagner coaching staff, he fashioned a 3:1 assist-to-turnover ratio. He'll get a crack at the starting lead-guard spot, along with McClimont and Rodgers.

adidas Blue Ribbon Analysis

BACKCOURT	C	BENCH/DEPTH	C+
FRONTCOURT	B	INTANGIBLES	B

The Seahawks have fallen on hard times in recent years. But coach Tim Capstraw appears to have the makings of one of the NEC's most feared frontcourts, that is if oft-injured pivot Frantz Pierre-Louis can stay on the court this season. Sure, leading scorer Dan Seigle will be tough to replace at the small forward slot, but Capstraw appears to have another proven commodities to make up for Seigle's lost points.

The major area of concern is the backcourt, where Capstraw has plenty of suspects to replace Jason Roberts (10.5 ppg) and Mick Wheeler (197 assists), but no sure things.

If the backcourt situation is solidified and Pierre-Louis can make it through an entire season, then Wagner could push for the top spot. More likely though is a fourth-place finish during the regular season-behind preseason favorites St. Francis (N.Y.), Mount St. Mary's and Fairleigh Dickinson.

(B.D.)

OHIO VALLEY CONFERENCE

adidas BLUE RIBBON FORECAST

1. Murray State
2. Tennessee State
3. Austin Peay
4. Southeast Missouri State
5. Middle Tennessee State
6. Eastern Kentucky
7. Eastern Illinois
8. Tennessee-Martin
9. Tennessee Tech
10. Morehead State

ALL-CONFERENCE TEAM

G—Jamie Roberts, SO, Tennessee State
G—Trenton Hassell, SO, Austin Peay
F—Ryan DeMichael, SR, Tennessee-Martin
F—Isaac Spencer, JR, Murray State
C—Bud Eley, SR, Southeast Missouri State

PLAYER OF THE YEAR

Isaac Spencer, JR, Murray State

NEWCOMER OF THE YEAR

Trenton Hassell, SO, Austin Peay

1998-99 CONFERENCE TOURNAMENT

Feb. 23, top four seeds host first round at campus sites.
Feb. 27-28, Nashville Arena, Nashville, TN.

1997-98 CHAMPIONS

Murray State (regular season)
Murray State (conference tournament)

1997-98 POSTSEASON PARTICIPANTS

Postseason Record: 0-1 (.000)
NCAA
Murray State

TOP BACKCOURTS

1. Austin Peay
2. Tennessee State
3. Southeast Missouri State

TOP FRONTCOURTS

1. Murray State
2. Southeast Missouri State
3. Tennessee State

ON THE WAY UP

Tennessee State

ON THE WAY DOWN

Eastern Illinois

INSIDE THE NUMBERS

- 1997-98 conference RPI: 19th (of 30)
- Conference RPI (last 5 years): 29-26-22-27-19

DID YOU KNOW?

Murray State has won or shared the OVC regular-season title 10 times in the last 11 years. During that span, the Racers are 131-33 (.799) against league opponents...Tennessee State has had the OVC Freshman of the Year for the last three seasons: Jamie Roberts, Kevin Samuel and Jason Johnson...Bill Hodges, who coached Larry Bird at Indiana State in the late 1970s, is an assistant on Tevester Anderson's staff at Murray State...Tennessee-Martin will be eligible for the OVC Tournament for the first time since joining the league in 1992-93...North Carolina will play at Middle Tennessee State University's Murphy Center on Nov. 30...Almost half the players on Eastern Kentucky's roster this season are from Michigan. Second-year coach Scott Perry was an assistant coach for Michigan's Wolverines before taking over the Colonels...Tennessee State returns five of its top six scorers from last season...Jeff Lebo's father, Dave Lebo, will serve on his son's staff this season at Tennessee Tech. Dave Lebo coached Jeff at Carlisle (Pa.) High School.

(C.L.)

OVC
OHIO VALLEY CONFERENCE

AUSTIN PEAY

LOCATION	**Clarksville, TN**
CONFERENCE	**Ohio Valley (OVC)**
LAST SEASON	**17-11 (.607)**
CONFERENCE RECORD	**11-7 (4th)**
STARTERS LOST/RETURNING	**3/2**
NICKNAME	**Governors**
COLORS	**Red & White**
HOMECOURT	**Dunn Center (9,000)**
COACH	**Dave Loos (Memphis '70)**
RECORD AT SCHOOL	**110-119 (8 yrs.)**
CAREER RECORD	**192-172 (12 yrs.)**
ASSISTANTS	**Bret Campbell (Valdosta State '83)**
	Tony Collins (Virginia State '79)
	Andy Blackston (David Lipscomb '98)
TEAM WINS (last 5 yrs.)	**13-13-19-17-17**
RPI (last 5 yrs.)	**236-172-124-199-159**
1997-98 FINISH	**Lost in conference semifinal.**

For years, Austin Peay coach Dave Loos has heard that the Ohio Valley Conference is a guard's league.

If that's the case, the Governors should be in dandy shape this season.

They feature a brand new backcourt that has everyone in the conference talking. Sophomores **Nick Stapleton** and **Trenton Hassell**, both of whom sat out last season as NCAA non-qualifiers, are that good.

AP

"You look back when we had Bubba Wells come in here, but we've never had a combination like Stapleton and Hassell in the same year," said Loos, entering his ninth season at Austin Peay.

The 6-1 Stapleton will handle the Governors' point-guard duties. A native of Flint, Mich., Stapleton averaged

1998-99 AUSTIN PEAY SCHEDULE

Nov.	16	@Vanderbilt
	19	Tennessee-Chattanooga
	23	@Missouri
	28	@Mississippi
Dec.	3	Southeast Missouri State
	5	Eastern Illinois
	12	@Georgia Southern
	15	@Tennessee-Chattanooga
	29	@South Florida
Jan.	2	Tennessee State
	7	@Morehead State
	9	@Eastern Kentucky
	12	@Southeast Missouri State
	14	Tennessee Tech
	16	Middle Tennessee State
	21	@Tennessee-Martin
	23	@Murray State
	26	Belmont
	30	@Tennessee State
Feb.	4	Morehead State
	6	Eastern Kentucky
	11	@Tennessee Tech
	13	@Middle Tennessee State
	18	Tennessee-Martin
	20	Murray State
	23-28	#OVC Tournament

@ Road Games
\# First round Feb. 23 at campus sites. Semifinals and final Feb. 27-28 at Nashville Arena, Nashville, TN.

22.4 ppg as a senior at Carman Ainsworth High School. He served further notice of his ability with 51 points, including 12 three-pointers, in the 1997 Michigan All-Star game.

"The key for us and him is Nick adopting the right philosophy at the point-guard position," Loos said. "If he does, look out. He can punish you in so many ways."

Stapleton's partner in the backcourt, Hassell, is a scoring machine. He tore up the Nashville summer league this year, and some are calling him Austin Peay's most talented recruit since James "Fly" Williams burst on the scene back in the early 1970s.

The 6-5 Hassell averaged 23.3 ppg, 12.7 rpg and 4.5 apg as a senior at Clarksville (Tenn.) High School. He was rated the 65th-best prospect in the nation by ESPN.

"Trenton can really be a special player," Loos said. "He can take it to the basket, can post you up, has great moves inside and is a great competitor. He's got a chance to really be good."

With so much attention being focused on Stapleton and Hassell, almost lost in the shuffle is the return of 6-5 senior forward **Jerome Jackson**. Last season, Jackson (13.4 ppg, 5.7 rpg, 35 steals) led Austin Peay in scoring and shot 57 percent from the floor. He was a second-team All-OVC selection.

"Outside of (Murray State's) Isaac Spencer, I think Jerome is as good a low-post scorer as there is in this league," Loos said.

The Governors are also set at small forward, where 6-5 sophomore **James Stewart** will move over from shooting guard. Stewart (9.5 ppg, 2.7 rpg) made 34 three-pointers last season, but also has the ability to score inside.

Stewart was chosen to the OVC's All-Freshman team last season.

"He showed flashes last year of being a really good player," Loos said. "He's athletic and can score on the perimeter or inside. He got 25 points against Murray State."

The only starting job up for grabs is at center, where junior **Mike Head** will get a long look. The 6-8 Head (2.8 ppg,1.5 rpg) has been plagued by illness and injury during his career. He's a good shooter and could present matchup problems with his ability to make the perimeter jump shot.

"There is no beating around the bush," Loos said. "We have a great deal of talent. Going into the season, at least on paper, the only question we have is the five spot."

Loos says the center's job is Head's to lose, at least early in the season. "We know he can score," Loos said. "Now he has to develop a stronger, tougher presence inside."

The key for Austin Peay could very well be its depth off the bench. One of the more valuable players will be 6-7 senior **Scott Combs**, who can play shooting guard, small forward or power forward.

Combs (3.3 ppg, 2.7 rpg, 34 assists) is one of two seniors on the team. The transfer from Missouri will be counted on for leadership.

"Scott is such a mature person the other players really respect as a player and person," Loos said. "I think he may be that guy we are going to need to be that calming influence out there."

There is also depth behind Stapleton at point guard. Junior **J.J. Halliburton** started 11 games last season. At 5-8, Halliburton (4.0 ppg, 1.4 rpg, 55 assists) is ultra-quick, but Loos would like to see him make better decisions and finish better once he gets around the basket.

The best pure three-point shooter on the team is probably 6-2 junior guard **Joey Tuck** (2.6 ppg, 0.5 rpg). Tuck hit 17 three-pointers last season, but will likely get a few more opportunities this season.

Also returning in the backcourt is 6-2 junior **Jeremy Qualls** (0.2 ppg, 0.3 rpg).

Freshman **Kevin Easley**, a third player who sat out last year, can play either guard position. At 6-1, Easley is an outstanding long-range shooter. He was a part-time student last year and retained four years of eligibility. Easley played for Peabody High School in Trenton, Tenn. two years ago.

Loos' son, 6-2 freshman **Brad Loos**, rounds out the backcourt. Loos was redshirted last season after averaging 10 points as a senior at Clarksville (Tenn.) Northeast High School.

Playing a swing position this season will be 6-4 junior **Willie Ivory**, who was sixth on the team in minutes played last season. Ivory (4.7 ppg, 2.8 rpg, 36 assists, 30 steals) is a versatile player. He was a bit streaky last season, but is one of the Governors' better defenders.

"Willie has got to become more consistent," Loos said. "If he does that and keeps his focus, he can be a real asset to us."

Loos signed two junior college post players. **Richard Whitfield**, a 6-9 junior, averaged 10.3 points and 6.1 rebounds last season at Bacone (Okla). Community College and could challenge Head for playing time at center.

Andrew Dagner, a 6-7, 230-pound junior, could wind up serving as Jackson's backup at power forward. Dagner averaged 10.7 points and six rebounds at Rend Lake (Ill.) Community College last season.

"Hopefully, at least one of them can give us something because we're going to need depth at the inside positions," Loos said.

adidas Blue Ribbon Analysis

BACKCOURT	**B+**	**BENCH/DEPTH**	**C**
FRONTCOURT	**B**	**INTANGIBLES**	**B**

Glancing over the Austin Peay roster, it's no secret where teams will attack the Governors this season.

Four of the five starters will stand 6-5 or under, although 6-5 Jerome Jackson plays much bigger than his size. Most of the team's height rests with unproven newcomers.

This is the first year in Austin Peay history that it will play a schedule that includes all Division I opponents. The Governors open on the road at Vanderbilt. Loos, with good reason, is excited about the possibilities, but he warns that there will be a certain adjustment period for Nick Stapleton and Trenton Hassell. Still, it shouldn't take long.

If the Governors are going to make a run at unseating Murray State, Loos said three things will have to happen.

For starters, Stapleton will have to adopt the proper mindset at point guard. The second will be the right chemistry developing and the third will be someone becoming a threat in the frontcourt.

"It's going to be a matter of these guys all pulling in the same direction," Loos said. "I'd be surprised if they don't. They're pretty proud and want to win."

(C.L.)

EASTERN ILLINOIS

LOCATION	**Charleston, IL**
CONFERENCE	**Ohio Valley (OVC)**
LAST SEASON	**16-11 (.593)**
CONFERENCE RECORD	**13-5 (2nd)**
STARTERS LOST/RETURNING	**2/3**
NICKNAME	**Panthers**
COLORS	**Blue & Gray**
HOMECOURT	**Lantz Gym (5,600)**
COACH	**Rick Samuels (Chadron State '71)**
RECORD AT SCHOOL	**262-254 (18 yrs.)**
CAREER RECORD	**262-254 (18 yrs.)**
ASSISTANTS	**David Cason (Illinois State '95)**
	Mike Church (Northeast Missouri '73)
	Mike Painter (Purdue '93)
TEAM WINS (last 5 yrs.)	**12-16-13-12-16**
RPI (last 5 yrs.)	**214-198-212-251-151**
1997-98 FINISH	**Lost in conference first round.**

In just its second year as a member of the Ohio Valley Conference, Eastern Illinois proved that it belonged last season.

The Panthers roared to a 13-5 conference record and second-place finish, only to be upset in the first round of the tournament by Tennessee State.

Rick Samuels, the winningest coach in school history, said his club simply had a knack for finding a way to win.

An encore could prove tricky, particularly without Rick Kaye. The do-it-all guard averaged 21.1 ppg and 4.6 rpg last season, and more importantly, was the team's leader.

1998-99 EASTERN ILLINOIS SCHEDULE

Nov.	16	Missouri Baptist
	18	Indiana State
	21	@Loyola
	29	@Purdue
Dec.	3	@Tennessee State
	5	@Austin Peay
	8	Evansville
	10	Western Illinois
	12	@Illinois
	18-19	#Nike Festival
	29	@Illinois State
Jan.	2	Morehead State
	4	Eastern Kentucky
	7	@Tennessee Tech
	9	@Middle Tennessee State
	12	Tennessee State
	14	Tennessee-Martin
	16	Murray State
	23	Southeast Missouri State
	28	@Morehead State
	30	@Eastern Kentucky
Feb.	2	Austin Peay
	4	Tennessee Tech
	6	Middle Tennessee State
	11	@Tennessee-Martin
	13	@Murray State
	20	@Southeast Missouri State
	23-28	##OVC Tournament

@ Road Games
\# Honolulu, HI (vs. Hawaii, first round; also Northern Arizona and St. Bonaventure)
\## First round Feb. 23 at campus sites. Semifinals and finals Feb. 27-28 at Nashville Arena, Nashville, TN.

"We're not going to have an individual like Rick Kaye, who at times could carry us last year," Samuels said. "But we're going to miss all of our seniors. It was a good group that provided guidance when we really needed it. Hopefully, our (three) returning starters can carry over that leadership."

Jack Owens (11.2 ppg, 3.8 rpg, 124 assists, 55 steals) is one of the better point guards in the league. A 6-0 senior, Owens ranked second in the conference in assists and third in steals last season and was also voted Eastern Illinois' top defender.

"He's a real gritty kid," Samuels said. "I like that trait, especially with this year's team. Jack's going to have to provide a lot of leadership."

Owens worked extensively on his perimeter shot over the summer. Samuels is counting on Owens hitting the open jump shots in the Panthers' motion offense.

Junior **Marc Polite** (10.3 ppg, 3.3 rpg, 28 assists) returns as the starting small forward. Perhaps more than any other Panther, Polite needs to have a big year for Eastern Illinois to be successful. The 6-5 Polite is the top returning field-goal shooter on the team (.447 percent).

"Marc's a great spot-up shooter," Samuels said. "If he's open, he can get on some great runs. He's worked hard this summer, though, coming off the dribble and scoring."

A third starter, 6-7 junior center **John Smith**, won't be eligible until after the fall semester because of academic reasons, meaning he will miss the Panthers' first two OVC games in December. Smith (5.7 ppg, 4.5 rpg) started 13 games last season.

Samuels would prefer to move Smith to the power forward position this season. For that to happen, someone else needs to take over at center.

One of the top candidates is 6-10 senior **Michael Shaver**, who has battled injuries the last two seasons. He finally appears healthy after averaging 1.3 ppg and 1.7 rpg in 15 games a year ago.

Another returning veteran, 6-7 senior forward **Keith Hibbler**, will get an extended look in the post with Smith out of action. Hibbler (1.8 ppg, 2.6 rpg) is one of the better rebounders on the team and is also a good jump shooter.

One of the big surprises this season could be **Merv Joseph**, a 6-3 power forward from St. John's, Antigua. Joseph, a sophomore, sat out last season after coming to Eastern Illinois from John Wood CC in Quincy, Ill. without graduating.

"He plays like he's 6-7," Samuels said of Joseph. "You'd probably like to play him at the three spot, but he's so powerful and a great leaper. He can post you up and rebound."

Samuels signed three frontcourt freshmen, and two of them could be forced into action early. **Luke Sharp** of Irvington, Ill., was a 6-8 center at Centralia (Ill.) HS. He will move to power forward at Eastern Illinois. **Todd Bergmann** of Elk Grove, Ill., is more of a center prospect. Samuels had hoped to bring the 6-7 Bergmann along slowly, but he may not have that luxury. Bergmann played for Conant HS in Hoffman Estates, Ill.

The third freshman post signee, 6-11 **Jan Thompson** of Waterloo, Ind., is a redshirt candidate who played for DeKalb HS.

In the backcourt, there should be some pretty fierce competition. The point guard's job clearly belongs to Owens, but his running mate at shooting guard, as well as his backup, have yet to be determined.

Samuels would like to see one of the two backcourt returnees emerge at point guard, either 5-10 sophomore **Greg Ktistou** (3.8 ppg, 1.3 rpg, 36 assists) or 6-2 sophomore **Kyle Hill** (5.4 ppg, 2.1 rpg).

Ktistou played in 24 games last season and served as Owens' backup. Hill spent most of the season getting adjusted to college. Both players are good shooters.

"At least one of those guys, maybe both, are going to have to play a lot of minutes for us this year," Samuels said.

A couple of newcomers will battle for the shooting guard job. Freshman **Henry Domercant** of Lisle, Ill., was a *Chicago Sun-Times* All-Area selection last season at Naperville North HS. The 6-2 Domercant didn't turn 17 until late in his senior year and could develop into a small forward.

Junior **Michael Forest** played point guard for John Logan CC last season. At 6-3, Forest, a native of Hopkinsville, Ky., is probably more of a shooting guard, which is where he will play at Eastern Illinois.

"He's more of a scorer than he is a shooter," Samuels said. "He can take it to the basket. But right now, I'm not real confident in his three-point range."

Also expected to battle for playing time in the backcourt is 6-1 junior guard **Matt Britton**, a transfer from the University of Indianapolis, an NCAA Division II school.

Freshman **Luke Mueller** is a 5-11 walkon from Crystal Lake, Ill., who will play a reserve role.

adidas Blue Ribbon Analysis

BACKCOURT .... **C+** **BENCH/DEPTH** .... **C**
FRONTCOURT .... **C** **INTANGIBLES** .... **C+**

Eastern Kentucky could be in for a rough ride early, especially with center John Smith sidelined through December.

Of course, Smith's absence could also be a blessing. One of the younger inside players will have no choice but to mature, which could provide valuable depth for the stretch run in the conference.

Jack Owens and Marc Polite will have to carry the Colonels early. If they get help as the season continues, Eastern Illinois has a chance to remain in the league's upper echelon.

If not, it could be a long year.

"We're going to have to be a team this year and mature in a hurry," Samuels said. "We may take our lumps early. But hopefully by conference time, we will have found the right chemistry."

With so many young players, the Colonels will probably battle inconsistency. Last year's team won a bundle of close games on the road, and that may be asking too much of this club, which features just two seniors.

(C.L.)

adidas Blue Ribbon Analysis

GRADING SYSTEM

- A+ equal to very best in country—Final Four-caliber unit
- A among the best in the land—worthy of deep NCAA run
- B+ talented, versatile and experienced—NCAA-NIT ability
- B solid and productive winners—league and post-season contenders
- C+ average to above-average—may contend in a weaker league
- C average to mediocre—second division in a strong league
- D+ below average, inconsistent—second division in a weaker league
- D well below average—losing season virtually certain
- F non-Division I ability—an underdog every night

EASTERN KENTUCKY

LOCATION .... **Richmond, KY**
CONFERENCE .... **Ohio Valley (OVC)**
LAST SEASON .... **10-17 (.370)**
CONFERENCE RECORD .... **8-10 (t-6th)**
STARTERS LOST/RETURNING **2/3**
NICKNAME .... **Colonels**
COLORS .... **Maroon & White**
HOMECOURT .... **McBrayer Arena (6,500)**
COACH .... **Scott Perry (Wayne State '86)**
RECORD AT SCHOOL .... **10-17 (1 yr.)**
CAREER RECORD .... **10-17 (1 yr.)**
ASSISTANTS .... **Tom Souder (Bluffton '78)**
Tom Sandler (Michigan '96)
TEAM WINS (last 5 yrs.) **13-9-13-8-10**
RPI (last 5 yrs.) **215-242-220-275-211**
1997-98 FINISH .... **Lost in conference first round.**

The infusion of new blood at Eastern Kentucky this season is staggering. The Colonels have 10 new players, with no full-time starters and only three returnees from last season.

Quite a transition, right?

Well, maybe not as extreme as it sounds. Second-year coach Scott Perry has little doubt that this will be a more talented team than his first one at Eastern Kentucky.

"We're better off now than we were at this same point a year ago," Perry said.

When Perry surveys his recruiting class, he has reason to be confident. Some are calling it the best class in Eastern Kentucky history. Perry signed seven new players, and three others are now eligible after sitting out last season.

"Several of those guys will play prominent roles," said Perry, who was Michigan's ace recruiter before taking the Eastern Kentucky job. "I don't think there's any doubt that we've taken a step in the right direction."

How quickly it all comes together remains to be seen. "You never know quite how long it's going to take," Perry said. "You'd like to see it happen as quickly as possible. But whether it takes the preseason or midway through the conference season or the full year, I'm encouraged by our level of talent."

Three of the newcomers are not new to the program. Junior **Charles Thomas**, who transferred from Minnesota, practiced with the Colonels last season.

At 6-4, Thomas will step in at shooting guard. He was the first player off the bench for the Golden Gophers in 1996-97 when they went to the Final Four, averaging 7.2 ppg and 1.5 rpg. A native of Harlan, Ky., Thomas was the Kentucky High School Player of the Year in 1995.

"He can shoot, is strong and can beat people off the dribble," Perry said. "He also has the experience and maturity. We expect big things from Charles."

Sophomore forward **Ronnie Griffin** also sat out last season as a non-qualifier. The 6-9 sophomore originally signed with Louisville, and at one time was ranked among the top 20 high school juniors in the country. Two years ago, Griffin averaged 19.1 ppg and 11.2 rpg at Maine Central Institute.

Perry said Griffin has a nice touch on his jump shot and will play either the power forward or center position.

The third Colonel who didn't play last season is 6-2 sophomore **Darius Acuff**, the frontrunner to win the point guard job. As a senior at Pershing High School in Detroit, Acuff averaged 14.2 ppg, 8.1 rpg and 6.2 apg.

"He's a classic point guard that comes from probably the top high school program in Detroit," Perry said. "He can penetrate and find people in transition."

Three seniors also return after starting seven games each last year.

Chris Fitzgerald (5.7 ppg, 1.1 rpg, 24 three-pointers), a 6-0 guard, is an excellent shooter. **Warren Stukes** (1.9 ppg, 3.8 rpg), a 6-6 power forward, led the team in field-goal percentage (.579). Stukes was plagued by injuries, but provided a spark off the bench.

"Both of those kids are extremely unselfish and are team guys," Perry said. "I think they've found their niche in our program, and I expect both to have even better years now that they know what I expect."

Ibrahim Myles, a 6-7 senior forward, returns after averaging 4.8 ppg and 4.6 rpg last year.

Guard Mark Williams, who averaged 13.3 points and made 57 three-pointers last season, won't be back. He left the team for personal reasons.

The top catch in this signing class, 6-6 junior forward Mario Duncan, won't be academically eligible this year. Duncan averaged 22.3 ppg and 12.4 rpg last season at Walker (Ala.) Junior College.

Duncan's teammate at Walker Junior College, **Darick Mattox,** will be eligible this season. The 6-8 junior forward averaged 20.2 ppg and 10.3 rpg last season and is athletic enough to play both forward positions.

The bulk of Perry's signing class consisted of freshmen, headed by 5-11 point guard **Whitney Robinson** of Detroit. Robinson averaged 27.2 ppg and 5.3 apg last season at Notre Dame High School.

Perry, who knows a thing or two about recruiting in Michigan, said Robinson was one of the top six or seven seniors in that state last year.

"He plays with tremendous energy," Perry said. "I don't think you will find many players who will play with more energy than he will. He has a great passion for the game."

Robinson will combine with Acuff to give Eastern Kentucky a talented one-two punch at point guard, with Thomas at shooting guard. It's a brand new backcourt, but much more athletic than last year.

"It was important that we add some quickness and athleticism back there, and we did," Perry said.

Will Morris, 6-4 freshman guard/forward from Maine Central Institute, will also get a shot at one of the wing positions. He averaged 10.1 ppg and 4.2 rpg last season on an undefeated prep school team that sent just about its entire roster into college basketball.

"He didn't have gaudy numbers, but I think he's somebody that will get better every year he's here," Perry said.

Rounding out the freshman class are a trio of Detroit, Mich., products: 6-6 forward **Keanan Weir**, 6-8 forward **Sam Hoskin** and 6-2 guard **Damon Allison**.

Weir averaged 16.3 ppg, 9.6 rpg and 4.1 apg last season at Martin Luther King High School.

Hoskin averaged 20.6 ppg and 11.4 rpg at Detroit's Bishop Borgess High last year. He has the body to be a power forward (240 pounds), and could also get a look at center.

Allison was a late addition to the class. He averaged 12.2 ppg, 6.1 rpg and 4.3 apg at Southfield Lathrop High last season.

"I think we'll be able to broaden our attack, both offensively and defensively," Perry said. "Our new recruits will take a while to jell, but we're excited with the overall addition of size to our team, which should give us more of a presence in the middle."

adidas Blue Ribbon Analysis

BACKCOURT .... **C+** **BENCH/DEPTH** .... **C**
FRONTCOURT .... **C** **INTANGIBLES** .... **C+**

Scott Perry is a proven recruiter who knows how and where to mine a little gold. Notice how many players in his latest class are from the Detroit area.

There's no question that this team will be more talented and athletic than Perry's first at Eastern Kentucky, but with so many new faces, how long will it take for the right chemistry to develop?

The bulk of the production should come from Charles

1998-99 EASTERN KENTUCKY SCHEDULE

Nov.	17	@Kentucky
	19	Belmont
	24	@Indiana State
Dec.	3	Tennessee-Martin
	5	Murray State
	10	@Southeast Missouri State
	12	@Indiana/Purdue-Indianapolis
	19	@Notre Dame
	22-23	#Golden Bear Classic
	30	Georgia State
Jan.	4	@Eastern Illinois
	7	Tennessee State
	9	Austin Peay
	12	@Tennessee-Martin
	16	Morehead State
	21	@Tennessee Tech
	23	@Middle Tennessee State
	30	Eastern Illinois
Feb.	2	@Murray State
	4	@Tennessee State
	6	@Austin Peay
	13	@Morehead State
	16	Southeast Missouri State
	18	Tennessee Tech
	20	Middle Tennessee State
	23-28	##OVC Tournament

@ Road Games
# Oakland, CA (vs.California, first round. also Mississippi State and Southwestern Louisiana).
First round Feb. 23 at campus sites. Semifinals and finals Feb. 27 & 28 at Nasvhille Arena, Nashville, TN.

Thomas, Ronnie Griffin and Darius Acuff_three guys who've been around the program, but didn't play last season. Not having Mario Duncan right away will hurt.

Perry said the Colonels need to take care of the ball better, rebound better, cut down on their fouls and shoot free throws better if they're going to make a significant move upward this season.

"We've taken a step with our new players," he said. "It remains to be seen how many steps we've taken."

Eastern Kentucky will probably need another stellar recruiting class before it's ready to make a move into the upper echelon of the conference.

(C.L.)

MIDDLE TENNESSEE STATE

LOCATION .... **Murfreesboro, TN**
CONFERENCE .... **Ohio Valley (OVC)**
LAST SEASON .... **19-9 (.679)**
CONFERENCE RECORD .... **12-6 (3rd)**
STARTERS LOST/RETURNING **3/2**
NICKNAME .... **Blue Raiders**
COLORS .... **Blue & White**
HOMECOURT .... **Murphy Center (11,520)**
COACH .... **Randy Wiel (North Carolina '79)**
RECORD AT SCHOOL .... **38-21 (2 yrs.)**
CAREER RECORD .... **70-71 (5 yrs.)**
ASSISTANTS .... **Andy Herzer (UNC-Asheville '84)**
Victor Newman (UNC-Asheville '96)
Jim Ryan (Montclair State '90)
TEAM WINS (last 5 yrs.) **8-12-15-19-19**
RPI (last 5 yrs.) **281-246-85-156-136**
1997-98 FINISH .... **Lost in conference semifinal.**

Randy Wiel, the multi-talented Middle Tennessee State coach, has an interesting spin on this season.

"We won't be young, but we will be inexperienced," Wiel said.

If the Blue Raiders can demonstrate the same versatility as their coach, they should be in good shape. Wiel, beginning his third season at MTSU, represented The Netherlands as a sprinter in the 1968 Olympics and as a swimmer in the 1967 Pan-American games.

He's fluent in six languages and plays jazz and classical guitar.

His record as a basketball coach is equally impressive. He guided MTSU to 19 wins in each of his first two seasons after helping resurrect the program at UNC-Asheville.

If that's not enough, Wiel has managed to get his alma mater, perennial power North Carolina, to come to Murphy Center this season on Nov. 30.

Wiel anticipates another good year for the Blue Raiders.

"I'd like to think that we will be able to challenge for the league again," Wiel said. "We'll need to find some scorers and rebounders among some of our new players."

The Blue Raiders will boast four seniors and five juniors this season, but five of those players are newcomers to the program. A mixture of junior-college transfers, players who transferred from other programs and players who sat out last season have joined the team.

The two returning starters are 6-5 junior forward **Freddie Martinez** (12.3 ppg, 2.8 rpg, 66 of 162 three-point shots) and 6-2 senior point guard **Richard Duncan** (9.8 ppg, 2.1 rpg, 117 assists, 54 steals).

Martinez is an outstanding shooter, but he's coming off offseason knee surgery to repair a partially torn ligament in his knee. It could be a while before Martinez is back to full speed.

"Freddie's really more of a two guard," Wiel said. "With K.J. Harden (6.3 ppg, 2.5 rpg) leaving, we could move him there. I don't know yet. The positions will be wide open."

That also goes for the point-guard job. Duncan was the starter there for 27 games last season. He improved his statistics in every category and also had to undergo the transformation from a scoring point guard to a playmaker.

His competition will come from 5-10 junior guard **Allen Hatchett**, a transfer from Southeast Missouri State. Hatchett started every game for the Indians two years ago and averaged 10.2 points and 2.9 rebounds with 89 assists and 29 steals.

"The good thing is that Allen can play both guard positions," Wiel said. "He's more of a combo guard."

The little bit of experience the Blue Raiders possess is in the backcourt.

Kent Ayer, a 6-1 senior, made four starts last season, averaging 4.8 points and 1.3 rebounds and handing out 54 assists. He's the second-best outside shooter on the team behind Martinez and will probably play both guard positions.

Reggie Marshall, a 6-0 sophomore, will provide additional depth in time. He underwent surgery on his ankle in the summer and is still rehabilitating. Marshall (1.3 ppg, 0.3 rpg) was bothered by the ankle all of last season and played in just 12 games.

Kevin White, a 6-2 sophomore, played on the wing last season. White (3.0 ppg, 0.8 rpg) is more of a defensive specialist than a scorer, but can make the perimeter jump shot.

Wiel hopes the Blue Raiders will have more depth this season. A year ago, they jumped out to a 17-4 start, but Aylton Tesch and **Ali McGhee** both suffered ankle injuries and were hobbled the rest of the way. The result was five losses in the last seven games.

"If we missed one guy last year, we really suffered," Wiel said. "I think we might have a little more balance this year."

In the frontcourt—not counting Martinez—Wiel has two players coming back with a combined five starts. The rest are newcomers.

McGee, a 6-6 senior forward, played well toward the end of last season, averaging 7.0 points and 2.3 rebounds. He didn't become eligible until the second half of the season, so he should be more settled into the system. McGhee could also play shooting guard if needed.

Lee Nosse, a 6-11 sophomore center, was the backup last season behind Mantia Callender (5.7 ppg, 6.1 rpg). Nosse (2.9 ppg, 2.4 rpg, 19 blocks) could be one of the Blue Raiders' most improved players this season.

"He's physically stronger and worked very hard this offseason," Wiel said. "We will need him to play a big role this season. He's not a great athlete, but a good basketball player."

The long list of newcomers in the frontcourt is made up primarily of transfers.

Cedrick Wallace, a 6-5 junior from Northeast Mississippi CC, comes to MTSU with a reputation as an accomplished scorer. He signed last year, but had to retake a class before he graduated from junior college. Wallace averaged 26.0 points and 7.8 rebounds in eight games in 1996-97 before a knee injury ended his season. In two years at Northeast Mississippi CC, Wallace scored 40 or more points six times.

Ellious Swanigan, a 6-8 junior forward from Shorter (Ark.) College, is more of a rebounder and scorer. He played his freshman season at UNC Charlotte. **Johnny Cobb**, a 6-8 junior from Hutchinson (Kan.) CC, is another big, strong player Wiel hopes will add some scoring punch in the frontcourt.

At a wing position, **Dale Thomas**, a 6-6 sophomore, joins the team after sitting out last season under Proposition 48. Thomas, who's from Cleveland, Ohio, should be able to play both forward positions.

"We wanted some experience with our inside guys," Wiel said. "When you have a freshman big man who has to play, that's usually like throwing him to the wolves."

Sam Hylton, a 6-7 senior forward, is a walk-on who will provide depth. He won't become eligible until after the first semester.

Gerald King, a 6-3 sophomore guard/forward, is a walkon who was an all-state player at Murfreesboro (Tenn.) Oakland High School. King did not play or practice last season after transferring from Coastal Carolina.

1998-99 MIDDLE TENNESSEE STATE SCHEDULE

Month	Date	Opponent
Nov.	16	East Tennessee State
	21	Erskine
	24	@Marist
	28	@East Tennessee State
	30	North Carolina
Dec.	3	@Western Kentucky
	5	Tennessee Tech
	12	Belmont
	21-23	#Puerto Rico Christmas Shootout
Jan.	2	@Tenessee-Martin
	4	@Murray State
	7	Southeast Missouri State
	9	Eastern Illinois
	12	@Tennessee Tech
	14	@Tennessee State
	16	@Austin Peay
	21	Morehead State
	23	Eastern Kentucky
	28	Tennessee-Martin
	30	Murray State
Feb.	1	@Belmont
	4	@Southeast Missouri State
	6	@Eastern Illinois
	11	Tennessee State
	13	Austin Peay
	18	@Morehead State
	20	@Eastern Kentucky
	23-28	##OVC Tournament

@ Road Games
\# San Juan, PR (vs. North Carolina State, first round; also American University-PR, Mississippi, Ohio State, Oklahoma, St. Joseph's and UAB)
\## First round Feb. 23 at campus sites. Semifiinals and final Feb. 27 & 28 at Nashville Arena, Nashville, TN.

adidas Blue Ribbon Analysis

BACKCOURT .... **B** **BENCH/DEPTH** .... **C+**
FRONTCOURT .... **C+** **INTANGIBLES** .... **B**

As coach Randy Wiel says, Middle Tennessee State's season depends on how the new guys work out. The Blue Raiders' entire frontcourt will be new.

"Hopefully, we'll develop the kind of chemistry you'd like," Wiel said.

During Wiel's tenure, MTSU has been one of the better defensive teams in the OVC. The Blue Raiders led the league in defensive field-goal percentage last season (.424) and will need to be near the top again this season.

Another key will be rebounding, which was anything but a strength a year ago.

Somewhat unsettling to Wiel is that he can't predict where most of the points will come from this year.

"That's a little frustrating, but we'll play a team-oriented game," Wiel said. "It is nice, though, that if you struggle, you have somebody to go to."

Toward the end of last season, teams began to key on Freddie Martinez. Finding someone to share the scoring burden with Martinez this season will be critical.

If one or more of the big men have a good year, the Blue Raiders should be among the top four or five teams in the OVC again.

(C.L.)

MOREHEAD STATE

LOCATION .... **Morehead, KY**
CONFERENCE .... **Ohio Valley (OVC)**
LAST SEASON .... **3-23 (.115)**
CONFERENCE RECORD .... **2-16 (10th)**
STARTERS LOST/RETURNING **2/3**
NICKNAME .... **Eagles**
COLORS .... **Blue & Gold**
HOMECOURT .... **Johnson Arena (6,500)**
COACH .... **Kyle Macy (Kentucky '80)**
RECORD AT SCHOOL .... **3-23 (1 yr.)**
CAREER RECORD .... **3-23 (1 yr.)**
ASSISTANTS .... **Wayne Breeden (Kentucky '83)**
Darrin Horn (Western Kentucky '95)
Diego McCoy (Lincoln Memorial '95)
TEAM WINS (last 5 yrs.) **14-15-7-8-3**
RPI (last 5 yrs.) **222-179-285-288-296**
1997-98 FINISH .... **Did not qualify for postseason.**

Kyle Macy isn't accustomed to losing games, and certainly not in the state of Kentucky.

But Macy, attempting to resurrect the Morehead State program, lost 23 times last season in his first year of what continues to be a major rebuilding job. The Eagles won only three games, and at one point were down to just eight players. Only six of them were on scholarship.

The disappointment associated with losing so many games wore on Macy, a former two-time All-America guard at Kentucky, but not to the point where he gave up hope.

Last season was just the start of Macy's rebuilding project, albeit a rough one.

"We didn't win last year, but I thought we got a lot of things accomplished off the court," said Macy, who played seven seasons in the NBA. "We built a new weight room, made improvements to our gymnasium, made it more fun to come to our arena, created a new image with our new uniforms and built new offices."

And most importantly, Macy hopes he created a new mindset among his players.

"This program had deteriorated to the point where it had almost hit rock bottom," Macy said. "But now, from a coach's standpoint, I'm starting to get excited.

"I've seen that these guys want to play and want to get

1998-99 MOREHEAD STATE SCHEDULE

Nov.	16	Huntington
	18	Asbury
	24	@Vanderbilt
	28	@Marshall
Dec.	3	Murray State
	5	Tennessee-Martin
	17	Jacksonville State
	19	@Wright State
	21	@Florida
	29	Evansville
Jan.	2	@Eastern Illinois
	4	@Southeast Missouri
	7	Austin Peay
	9	Tennessee State
	12	@Murray State
	16	@Eastern Kentucky
	21	@Middle Tennessee State
	23	@Tennessee Tech
	28	Eastern Illinois
	30	Southeast Missouri
Feb.	2	@Tennessee-Martin
	4	@Austin Peay
	6	@Tennessee State
	13	Eastern Kentucky
	18	Middle Tennessee State
	20	Tennessee Tech
	23-28	#OVC Tournament

@ Road Games
# First round Feb. 23 at campus sites. Semifinals and final Feb. 27 & 28 at Nashville Arena, Nashville, TN.

better. We inherited some players last year where that just wasn't the case. They really weren't Division I players. Now, we're getting better talent and guys with the attitude that they want to become better players. We're headed in the right direction. We'll be better this year, not great, but better."

Only four returnees are back from last season. Three of those returnees, senior point guard **Ted Docks**, junior forward **Jeremy Webb** and sophomore center **Dewayne Krom**, finished the year as starters.

Their jobs are anything but secure this year. Macy isn't guaranteeing any starting spots—not even to Docks, who started 22 games last year.

"Everybody on the team is aware of that," Macy said. "That will be good for our team in the long run. We had guys who started for us most of last year, but hey, we only won three games. It wasn't like we were undefeated."

The 5-8 Docks averaged 5.3 ppg, and 4.6 rpg, handed out 114 assists and collected 49 steals last season. The team's only senior, Docks isn't known as a great shooter (.320 from the field last year).

"He brings that experience to the table that we'll need to have," Macy said.

Webb, at 6-5, can play inside or outside, but will probably fit in more as a small forward. Webb (10.3 ppg, 5.2 rpg, 36 three-pointers, 33 steals) was the second-leading scorer on the team last season.

Krom, 6-8, averaged 9.6 ppg and 4.6 rpg and started 22 games as a freshman.

"We look for him to build from a good freshman season," Macy said.

The only other returnee from last season is 6-4 sophomore guard **Thomas Jenkins** (3.3 ppg, 2.1 rpg, 21 assists). Jenkins battled injuries for much of last season.

Macy hit the recruiting trail during the offseason and signed seven new players. By design, five of those were junior-college players.

"I felt like they would help give us a jump start with a higher maturity level than freshmen," Macy said. "We needed to sign players that could come in and play right away. We couldn't afford to wait a year for them to develop."

Two of the junior college transfers will add some muscle to the Eagles' inside game. **Dwane Samuels**, a 6-8 junior forward, transferred from Hiwassee (Tenn.) College, where he averaged 16 ppg and 8.5 rpg last season. A former standout at Richmond (Va.) Hermitage High, Samuels has the type of athleticism Morehead State was lacking last season.

Scott Charity, a 6-7 junior forward/center, is from Santa Rosa (Calif.) Community College. At 225 pounds, Charity, who averaged 10 ppg and 6.0 rpg last season, has more bulk than Samuels, who is listed at 210 pounds.

Three junior college guards were also signed. **Bobby Washington Jr.** is a 6-0 junior point guard who played last season at Belleville Area (Ill.) Community College, averaging 10 ppg and 4.5 apg. He is the son of Bobby Washington, head coach at Bryan Station High in Lexington, Ky.

"We think Bobby has outstanding leadership qualities," Macy said.

Brad Cleaver, a 6-3 junior transfer from Kansas City Community College, and **Brett Bohanan**, a 6-4 junior transfer from Spoon River (Ill.) Junior College, are both shooting guards.

Cleaver averaged 17 ppg and 5 apg last season. Macy said Cleaver could also play point guard. Bohanan, a pure shooter, averaged 17.4 ppg last season and made 115 three-pointers.

There are two freshman signees: 6-5 forward **Eric Brown**, who averaged 23.5 ppg and 8.4 rpg last season at Bryan Station (Ky.) High school, is versatile enough to play either forward position. He's a good perimeter shooter.

"We're very high on him and think he can turn into an outstanding player for us," Macy said. "He's still growing and just got better every year in high school."

Kyle Umberger, a 6-6 forward from Paul Blazer High School in Ashland, Ky., was rated as one of the top players in Kentucky heading into his senior year. He had a bit of a transition year as a senior after a new head coach took over, but still averaged 19 ppg and 10 rpg. Umberger's former high school coach, Wayne Breeden, is now on Macy's staff at Morehead State.

Bernard Evans, a 6-5 junior forward, is a walkon from Covington, Ky. He averaged 9.8 ppg and 7.0 rpg at St. Petersburg (Fla.) Community College last year.

adidas Blue Ribbon Analysis

BACKCOURT	**D+**	**BENCH/DEPTH**	**C**
FRONTCOURT	**C**	**INTANGIBLES**	**C+**

This was Kyle Macy's first real shot at recruiting after being hired by Morehead State in late April of '97. It's safe to say he made some headway. Next year will be an even better indication of where the program is headed.

Macy is nothing short of a legend in Kentucky. He's still revered from his playing days on the 1978 national championship team. His stature should certainly help him in stockpiling talent.

"The name recognition helped open a few doors, but you still have to produce a product," Macy said. "I feel good about the direction we're headed, but it's going to take a while. We knew that when we came here."

If the Eagles are going to avoid the cellar for a second straight year, they will need several of the newcomers to contribute right away. Sophomore center Dewayne Krom could use some immediate help from Dwane Samuels and Scott Charity inside, and it shouldn't be long before freshman forward Erik Brown cracks the starting lineup.

The big question: Who's going to score in the backcourt? That's where newcomers Brett Bohanan and Brad Cleaver come in.

Still, it could be another long year in Morehead.

(C.L.)

MURRAY STATE

LOCATION	**Murray, KY**
CONFERENCE	**Ohio Valley (OVC)**
LAST SEASON	**29-4 (.879)**
CONFERENCE RECORD	**16-2 (1st)**
STARTERS LOST/RETURNING	**2/3**
NICKNAME	**Racers**
COLORS	**Blue & Gold**
HOMECOURT	**Regional Special Events Center (8,200)**
COACH	**Tevester Anderson (Arkansas AM&N '62)**
RECORD AT SCHOOL	**First year**
CAREER RECORD	**First year**
ASSISTANTS	**Bill Hodges (Marian College '70)** **Bob Eskew (Tennessee State '69)** **Chris Woolard (UCLA '96)**
TEAM WINS (last 5 yrs.)	**23-21-19-20-29**
RPI (last 5 yrs.)	**90-139-106-161-48**
1997-98 FINISH	**Lost in NCAA first round.**

Better later than never. At least, that's Tevester Anderson's philosophy as he settles into his first collegiate head coaching job after serving for more than 35 years as a high school coach and college assistant.

Anderson, 61, takes over for Mark Gottfried at Murray State, a program that has dominated the Ohio Valley Conference. The Racers, coming off a 29-4 season, have won or shared the regular-season championship 10 of the last 11 years.

Last season, Murray State won its seventh OVC Tournament title in the last 11 years and earned a No. 9 seed in the NCAA Tournament—the highest seed for an OVC team since the NCAA bracket was expanded. The Racers lost to Rhode Island, 97-74, in the first round.

1998-99 MURRAY STATE SCHEDULE

Nov.	14	Southern Illinois
	21	@Belmont
	27-28	#Sooner Classic
Dec.	3	@Morehead State
	5	@Eastern Kentucky
	8	Hanover College
	12	@Alabama State
	19	Western Kentucky
	27-30	##Rainbow Classic
Jan.	2	Tennessee Tech
	4	Middle Tennessee State
	9	Tennessee-Martin
	12	Morehead State
	14	@Southeast Missouri State
	16	@Eastern Illinois
	21	Tennessee State
	23	Austin Peay
	28	@Tennessee Tech
	30	@Middle Tennessee State
Feb.	2	Eastern Kentucky
	6	@Tennessee-Martin
	11	Southeast Missouri State
	13	Eastern Illinois
	18	@Tennessee State
	20	@Austin Peay
	23-28	###OVC Tournament

@ Road Games
# Norman, OK (vs. Arkansas-Little Rock, first round; also Oklahoma and Western Carolina)
Honolulu, HI (vs. UNC Charlotte, first round; also Florida State, Hawaii, Mississippi State, Princeton, Southwestern Louisiana and Texas)
First round Feb. 23 at campus sites. Semifinals and final Feb. 27-28 at Nashville Arena, Nashville, TN.

If there's pressure to keep the Racer machine rolling, Anderson says he doesn't feel it. He's simply honored to have the opportunity.

"It wasn't one of those deals where I had gone out every year looking for a head coaching job," said Anderson, who coached under Sonny Smith at Auburn and Hugh Durham at Georgia.

"I really haven't applied for many head jobs at all. In this business, if you're applying for them all the time, you're probably not going to get it because they're going to come looking for you. I guess I was like, 'If it happens, it happens.' I never really thought that much about being passed over and didn't dwell on it. I was always happy to be an assistant. I liked teaching and the recruiting part of it."

Anderson couldn't have picked a better situation to get his first shot at the head coaching rigors. He's coached at Murray State for three years under Gottfried and knows his personnel and the rest of the league.

And it's not like he faces a rebuilding job, either.

"The people here love basketball," Anderson said. "Murray State is a basketball school, and it's been a good basketball program for a long, long time."

The Racers' frontcourt should be among the best in the league, headed by 6-6 junior forward **Isaac Spencer**. He burst onto the scene last season as an immediate starter after sitting out as a freshman. Spencer averaged 13.8 ppg, 8.3 rpg and shot .633 percent from the field. Showing his versatility, he handed out 69 assists, blocked 50 shots and collected 27 steals.

Many around the league consider Spencer the best returning player. He's a relentless rebounder on the offensive boards.

"I don't know if he's the best player, but he comes to compete and come out on top when he competes," Anderson said. "He comes to win every day."

Middle Tennessee State coach Randy Wiel said Spencer's unflappable will is what makes him so good.

"There may be players in the league who have better basketball skills, but no one plays with his heart and intensity," Wiel said. "He's a warrior out there."

Spencer's running mate at forward is 6-7 junior **Rod Murray**, who played through injuries last season but started 28 of 33 games. Murray (9.5 ppg, 4.7 rpg, 53 assists) shot .542 percent from the field. He, too, was playing his first season after sitting out as a freshman. Spencer and Murray were high school teammates at Jefferson Davis HS in Montgomery, Ala.

The center position will once again be secured by 6-9 senior **Duane Virgil**, who started every game last season. Virgil (8.2 ppg, 5.9 rpg, 20 blocks) is probably more of a power forward than a center, but the Racers need him in the middle.

While the three frontcourt starters are set, questions loom in the backcourt. De'Teri Mayes and Chad Townsend are gone after combining for more than 35 points per game last season.

"We're truly going to miss their leadership and their talent," Anderson said.

At the shooting guard, junior **Marlon Towns** is braced to step in for the high-scoring Mayes. The 6-5 Towns began his career at Arkansas, where he started as a freshman. He then transferred to Northern Oklahoma Junior College, where he averaged 14.5 ppg last season.

Anderson thinks Towns has a chance to be one of the better newcomers in the league.

"He can shoot the three-pointer pretty well, all the way out to the NBA line," Anderson said. "But he's also a big, strong two guard who can post you up. And he loves to pass the ball."

The favorite to win the point guard job is 6-0 junior **Aubrey Reese**, who was Townsend's backup last season. Reese averaged 4.6 ppg, 1.8 rpg and handed out 68 assists. With Townsend playing so many minutes last year, Reese didn't get to play as much as Anderson would have liked.

As the season progresses, don't be surprised if 5-10 freshman **Jay Ragan** makes a strong bid for playing time at the point. Ragan, from Biloxi (Miss.) HS, is super-quick and loves to force the tempo. He averaged 7.4 ppg and 4.7 apg as a senior last season and earned all-state honors.

Depth shouldn't be a problem for the Racers, who welcome back several players who saw extensive action off the bench a year ago. Anderson thinks he will be able to go 10 or 11 players deep.

The frontcourt depth is especially good. **Michael Floyd**, a 6-7 senior, backed up Spencer at power forward last season. Floyd (3.8 ppg, 3.6 rpg) played his best basketball down the stretch.

Marvin Gay, a 6-8 senior, will likely back up Virgil at center. Gay (3.2 ppg, 2.6 rpg) is an athletic player who should perform better in Anderson's pressing style.

Also inside, 6-7 junior forward **Mike Turner** (1.9 ppg, 1.5 rpg) is back and will provide depth at the power forward and center positions. Turner is one of the team's best passing big men.

A pair of 6-5 returnees will provide firepower on the wings. Sophomore **Ray Cunningham** (2.0 ppg, 1.5 rpg) injured his thumb last season and was awarded a medical redshirt. He might be the most athletic player on the team and is an outstanding defensive player.

Aaron Page (6.6 ppg, 2.6 rpg) is more of a long-range shooter. A 6-5 junior guard, Page hit 48 of 122 three-point shots last season and also had 42 assists. Page may be a little slow getting started. He broke his hand during the summer and was just getting back to full strength as school started in the fall.

Justin Burdine, a 6-1 freshman guard from Savannah, Tenn., will add depth to the backcourt. Burdine averaged 21.0 ppg as a junior and 24.0 ppg last year at Hardin County HS. **Blair Hogg**, a 6-2 freshman point guard from British Columbia, is more of a long-range project.

David Greene, a 6-5 redshirt freshman forward from Murray, Ky., and Calloway County HS, is a walkon who could be a factor in a couple of years. He averaged 18.1 ppg and 6.8 rpg as a high school senior and practiced with the Racers last season.

adidas Blue Ribbon Analysis

BACKCOURT	B+	BENCH/DEPTH	B
FRONTCOURT	C+	INTANGIBLES	B

Knocking Murray State off its perch atop the Ohio Valley Conference will prove difficult, even though the Racers are without De'Teri Mayes and Chad Townsend, the excellent starting guard tandem of the last two years.

First-year coach Tevester Anderson thinks the Racers' backcourt could be suspect. That concerns him most.

"In this league, if you have a really good backcourt, you have a chance to win," he said. "We've won it the last three years because we had a good backcourt, and usually the teams that played us the closest had a good backcourt. That could be our Achilles heel this year."

The addition of Marlon Towns will help. Towns is athletic enough to do a little bit of everything on the perimeter, but either Aubrey Reese or Jay Ragan needs to have an impact at point guard.

The Isaac Spencer-led frontcourt should give Murray State a chance in every game. This is a team that knows how to win, which shouldn't change this season.

(C.L.)

SOUTHEAST MISSOURI STATE

LOCATION .... **Cape Girardeau, MO**
CONFERENCE .... **Ohio Valley (OVC)**
LAST SEASON .... **14-13 (.519)**
CONFERENCE RECORD .... **10-8 (5th)**
STARTERS LOST/RETURNING **1/4**
NICKNAME .... **Indians**
COLORS .... **Red, Black & White**
HOMECOURT .... **Show Me Center (7,000)**
COACH .... **Gary Garner (Missouri '65)**
RECORD AT SCHOOL .... **14-13 (1 yr.)**
CAREER RECORD .... **262-176 (15 yrs.)**
ASSISTANTS .... **Anthony Beane (Kansas State '94)**
Keno Davis (Iowa '95)
Tom Schuberth (Mississippi State '80)
TEAM WINS (last 5 yrs.) **10-13-8-12-14**
RPI (last 5 yrs.) **274-215-258-223-198**
1997-98 FINISH .... **Lost in conference first round.**

If Southeast Missouri State is going to make a move in the Ohio Valley Conference, this would seem to be the year.

Four starters return from a team that went 14-13 last season and finished fifth in the conference. One of those starters is 6-10 center **Bud Eley,** who withdrew his name just before the NBA draft and is back for his senior season.

Another starter, senior guard **Cory Johnson**, is back after leading the Indians in scoring last season.

"We have the majority of our team returning," Southeast Missouri State coach Gary Garner said. "I'm not sure that's all good because we only won 14 games last season, but I can tell you that we're excited about this year."

Eley, projected as a certain second-round NBA draft pick, should be the most dominant big man in the OVC this season. He has averaged 17.1 ppg and 9.5 rpg during his career at Southeast, and he's already the school's career leader in blocked shots with 104.

The only question: Can he stay healthy?

Eley (15.0 ppg, 6.8 rpg, 16 blocked shots) played in only 11 games last season because of broken bones in both feet. He was a first-team All-OVC choice as a sophomore. Eley is a 250-pounder who runs the floor well, blocks shots and has soft hands on the interior.

"Bud never really got going last year," Garner said. "He appears to be very healthy now. Having him back will definitely be a big plus for us. Where we hope he has a great year is on the defensive end."

When Eley exited the lineup for good last season, 6-8 senior **David Montgomery** stepped in at center. Montgomery (12.0 ppg, 5.3 rpg, 38 assists, 24 blocks) averaged 17 ppg during Eley's absence.

With Eley back in the middle, Montgomery could move to the power forward position, although he's more comfortable catching the ball with his back to the basket. Montgomery ranked eighth nationally last season in field-goal percentage (.621).

Firepower in the frontcourt shouldn't be a problem. **Roderick Johnson**, a 6-6 junior forward, transferred from Wisconsin-Milwaukee, where he was a second-team All-Mid-Continent selection as a freshman during the 1995-96 season.

Johnson averaged 14.5 ppg and 7.1 rpg in his first season at Wisconsin-Milwaukee and then left the team midway through the 1996-97 season. He spent last year at Southeast Missouri and practiced with the team.

Brian Bunche, a 6-8 junior center, will add bulk as a backup at both post positions. He averaged 10.0 ppg and 7.0 rpg last season at Southwest Missouri-West Plains Community College.

One of Garner's freshman signees, 6-7 forward Drew DeMond of Rockton, Ill., is questionable for this season. He tore his Achilles tendon last spring in track and probably will have to redshirt. DeMond averaged 16.0 ppg and 8.0 rpg last season in high school.

"We'll have to be a better rebounding team than we were last year," said Garner, in his second year at Southeast Missouri State. "That's the area that sticks out the most to me. Hopefully, with Bud coming back and Roderick coming in, we'll have the size and athleticism alone to make us a better rebounding team."

At the small-forward spot, returnees **Nathan Owen** and **Demetrius Watson** will battle junior-college transfer **Mike Branson** for the starting job. There is also the possibility that the Indians will utilize a three-guard offense at times.

Owen, a 6-2 sophomore, played some at small forward and shooting guard last season. He started nine games, averaging 5.3 ppg and 1.6 rpg, but was hampered by injuries.

Watson, a 6-4 senior, is more of a true small forward. He started in 11 games last season, averaging 8.8 ppg and 5.2 rpg.

Branson, a 6-6 junior, was a second-team Division II All-American last season at Merrimack (Mass.) College, where he averaged 18.4 ppg and 8.9 rpg.

"We as coaches, always at this time of year, like to compare last year's team to this year's team," Garner said. "And you ask yourself: Are we going to be better? The one thing that keeps popping up is our depth. We have a lot more depth and quality depth than we had all of last year."

The backcourt is anchored by the 6-0 Johnson, an outstanding shooter. Johnson (14.5 ppg, 2.8 rpg, 62 assists) ranked fifth nationally last season in three-pointers made (95 for 219). He earned second-team All-OVC honors and was runner-up for OVC Newcomer of the Year honors last season.

Kahn Cotton, a 5-10 senior, returns at the point guard. Cotton (12.3 ppg, 4.0 rpg) led the team with 104 assists last season. He is probably more comfortable at shooting guard and could split time there this season.

One of the Indians' top newcomers is sophomore point guard **Jeramy Biles**, who sat out last season but practiced with the team after transferring from St. Louis University.

The 5-11 Biles was a member of the All-Freshman team in Conference USA after averaging 7.6 ppg and playing in all 29 games during the 1996-97 season.

Freshman **Fred Abraham** of Catholic High School in Paterson, N.J., will add depth at the point-guard position. The 6-0 Abraham averaged 16.0 ppg and 8.0 apg as a senior.

Returnee **Matt Morris,** a 6-2 sophomore, will also play a reserve role in the backcourt after averaging 2.5 ppg and 1.1 rpg last season.

adidas Blue Ribbon Analysis

BACKCOURT	B	BENCH/DEPTH	C+
FRONTCOURT	B	INTANGIBLES	C+

Inconsistency and a lack of depth were big problems for Southeast Missouri State last season, but second-year coach Gary Garner thinks he's corrected the depth problem.

If senior center Bud Eley stays healthy, he has the kind of physical tools to dominate games. His defensive presence will be a huge boost.

Watch Roderick Johnson, too. He should provide a perfect complement inside to Eley and could emerge as the Indians' top inside scorer.

Cory Johnson, with his sweet shooting from the perimeter, should make things easier for the two big men inside.

If this team comes together as Garner hopes, a run at the OVC championship is certainly possible. Jeramy Biles, though, needs to establish himself as a steady point guard.

"This is the year that I hope we can really get into the race," Garner said.

(C.L.)

1998-99 SOUTHEAST MISSOURI STATE SCHEDULE

Nov.	14	Southern Illinois-Edwardsville
	17	@Bradley
	20	Central Methodist
	23	Louisiana Tech
	28	@Oklahoma State
Dec.	3	@Austin Peay
	5	@Tennessee State
	8	@Arkansas State
	10	Eastern Kentucky
	22	@Southeast Missouri
	28	@Southern Illinois
Jan.	4	Morehead State
	7	@Middle Tennesse State
	9	@Tennessee Tech
	12	Austin Peay
	14	Murray State
	16	Tennessee-Martin
	23	@Eastern Illinois
	30	@Morehead State
Feb.	2	Tennessee State
	4	Middle Tennessee State
	6	Tennessee Tech
	11	@Murray State
	13	@Tennessee-Martin
	16	@Eastern Kentucky
	20	Eastern Illinois
	23-28	#OVC Tournament

@ Road Games
\# First round Feb. 23 at campus sites. Semifinals and final Feb. 27 & 28 at Nashville Arena, Nashville, TN.

TENNESSEE-MARTIN

LOCATION .... **Martin, TN**
CONFERENCE .... **Ohio Valley (OVC)**
LAST SEASON .... **7-20 (.259)**
CONFERENCE RECORD .... **5-13 (t-8th)**
STARTERS LOST/RETURNING **2/3**
NICKNAME .... **Skyhawks**
COLORS .... **Royal Blue, Orange & White**
HOMECOURT .... **Skyhawk Arena (6,700)**
COACH .... **Cal Luther (Valparaiso '51)**
RECORD AT SCHOOL .... **59-131 (8 yrs.)**
CAREER RECORD .... **486-444 (37 yrs.)**
ASSISTANTS .... **Sean McDonough (Marquette '91)**
Ernest Neal (Maryland-Eastern Shore '74)
Bob Ward (Murray State '74)
TEAM WINS (last 5 yrs.) **5-7-13-11-7**
RPI (last 5 yrs.) **297-276-226-252-278**
1997-98 FINISH .... **Not eligible for postseason.**

The shackles have been lifted off Tennessee-Martin's basketball program.

For the first time since joining the Ohio Valley Conference in 1992-93, the Skyhawks are eligible to play in the conference tournament and earn the league's automatic bid to the NCAA Tournament.

At long last, the transition period from Division II to Division I is over.

"It's been a tough haul," said veteran Tennessee-Martin coach Cal Luther, who will be in his 38th season as a collegiate head coach. "The recruiting part of it has been devastating, when a kid knows he can't play in his own conference tournament, much less the NCAA.

"This is the biggest thing that's happened to us, obviously, in the last eight years."

There is reason for optimism this year. The top three scorers from last season's 7-20 team return, including first-team All-OVC selection **Ryan DeMichael**. The 6-9 senior forward was third in the league in scoring last season (14.9 ppg) and led the league in rebounding (9.8 rpg) and blocked shots (52). He shot 51 percent from the field.

DeMichael became just the second Tennessee-Martin player in history to earn first-team All-OVC honors.

"Ryan's a tremendous athlete for his size," Luther said. "He's a good shooter, but not a great shooter. He can take you inside or outside and is an excellent leaper."

In many ways, DeMichael reminds Luther of former Portland Trail Blazers star Jerome Kersey, whom Luther coached at Longwood College. "They just find ways to score," Luther said.

DeMichael will be joined in the frontcourt by returning starter **Joe Crumby**, a starter since his freshman season. The 6-8 senior averaged 13.1 ppg and 5.3 rpg last season and led the team with 37 steals.

Crumby entered the Tennessee-Martin program weighing around 185 pounds, but is now pushing 220.

"Joe isn't quite the athlete Ryan is, but he plays with such great enthusiasm," Luther said. "He's an excellent jump shooter and has a great work ethic. He plays all out every minute."

In the past, the Skyhawks have played a double low-post set with DeMichael and Crumby. But this season, Luther plans to play one on the wing and the other in the post.

"We'll change it up a little bit and rotate them inside and outside," Luther said.

The third returning starter is senior guard **Jason Ohlsen**, who started 22 games last season at shooting guard. The 6-2 Ohlsen (10.5 ppg, 1.9 rpg, 53 assists, 34 steals) is not a great ball handler and struggled at times last season when asked to to do so. His forte is shooting—he made 58 for173 three-pointers a year ago.

Another returning post player figures to play a reserve role. **Adam Hassett**, a 6-9 senior center, returns to give Tennessee-Martin some depth inside. He averaged 2.8 ppg and 2.3 rpg last season.

On the perimeter, sophomore guards **Sean Griffin** and **Nick DeVilder** should be improved with a year of experience. The 6-1 Griffin (1.1 ppg, 0.4 rpg) has beefed up to 185 pounds. The 6-5 DeVilder (0.9 ppg, 0.5 rpg) has excellent size for a shooting guard. Both are good shooters.

Newcomers will play a significant role for the Skyhawks, and several will get a chance to play right away.

Freshman **Andrae Betts** gives Tennessee-Martin the kind of quickness at the point-guard position it was lacking last season. The 5-9 Betts averaged 16.5 ppg and 5.8 assists last season for Marion (Ind.) HS, which reached the state championship game in its division. He is extremely quick and can shoot.

Eric Johnson, another 5-9 freshman, will push Betts at the point-guard spot. Like Betts, Johnson, who's from Atlantic Shores HS in Chesapeake, Va., is a blur up and down the court. Johnson averaged 12.5 ppg and 4.3 assists last year. Luther isn't ruling out playing Johnson and Betts at the same time.

Junior college transfer **Steve Jordan** will also factor in to the backcourt mix. The 6-3 junior played last season at Okaloosa-Walton (Fla.) Junior College, averaging 14.5 ppg and 4.0 rpg. He's a good enough ball handler to play the point, where he played some last season, but he's big enough and a good enough shooter to play on the wing.

Luther signed two other freshmen and will try to bring them along gradually. **Morris Robinson**, a 6-7 forward from Jackson (Tenn.) Northside HS and **Ben Corley**, a 6-5 forward from Wayne HS in Fort Wayne, Ind., round out the recruiting class. Robinson averaged 10.0 ppg and 7.0 rpg last season, while Corley averaged 21.0 ppg.

Corley, who played in the Kentucky-Indiana all-star series, may have a better shot at playing earlier.

The Skyhawks received a double dose of bad news during the offseason. Junior college transfer **Daniel Grubbs** and sophomore Brian Lyon both suffered serious knee injuries. Grubbs, a 6-7 junior from Scottsdale (Ariz.) Community College, has a chance to get back by the middle of the year, but Lyon is out for the season.

Lyon, a 6-6 forward, was starting for the Skyhawks last season during the opening exhibition game, but tore the anterior cruciate ligament in his knee. He came back from that injury and was shooting the ball well, but tore the ACL in his other knee and had reconstructive surgery.

"Those were two guys we were really counting on being factors," Luther said.

adidas Blue Ribbon Analysis

BACKCOURT	**C**	**BENCH/DEPTH**	**D+**
FRONTCOURT	**B**	**INTANGIBLES**	**C+**

Seniors Ryan DeMichael and Joe Crumby are both proven players on the inside for the Skyhawks, and senior guard Jason Ohlsen figures to be improved now that he has a better feel for the league.

But when it comes to game experience, those three have all of it at Tennessee-Martin.

Skyhawks coach Cal Luther is anxious to see how well his freshmen adjust and what kind of player 6-3 guard/forward Steve Jordan will become. Chances are Jordan will be in the lineup from the start.

"We're going to have to get some help from the new guys handling the ball and scoring," Luther said. "If we get that, I think we'll have a chance to be competitive."

For the two freshman point guards, Andrae Betts and Eric Johnson, it will be an opportunity for early playing time in their college careers.

"I'm optimistic about our potential," Luther said. "Crumby and DeMichael and the other seniors are determined to do something this year as seniors, and I think a couple of our young people are good enough to step in and help.

"It's just nice knowing that we're at least going to have a chance to play in the tournament. Down the road, that's really going to help the level of talent we get in here."

(C.L.)

1998-99 TENNESSEE-MARTIN SCHEDULE

Nov.	16	Lyon College
	18	Evansville
	21	@Bradley
	23	@Illinois
	28	@Mississippi State
	30	Bethel
Dec.	3	@Eastern Kentucky
	5	@Morehead State
	14	@Ohio State
Jan.	2	Middle Tennessee State
	4	Tennessee Tech
	9	@Murray State
	12	Eastern Kentucky
	14	@Eastern Illinois
	16	@Southeast Missouri
	21	Austin Peay
	23	Tennessee State
	28	@Middle Tennessee State
	30	@Tennessee Tech
Feb.	2	Morehead State
	6	Murray State
	8	Brescia
	11	Eastern Illinois
	13	Southeast Missouri
	18	@Austin Peay
	20	@Tennessee State
	23-28	#OVC Tournament

@ Road Games
\# First round Feb. 23 at campus sites. Semifinals and final Feb. 27-28 at Nashville Arena, Nashville, TN.

TENNESSEE STATE

LOCATION .... **Nashville, TN**
CONFERENCE .... **Ohio Valley (OVC)**
LAST SEASON .... **13-16 (.448)**
CONFERENCE RECORD .... **8-10 (t-6th)**
STARTERS LOST/RETURNING **0/5**
NICKNAME .... **Tigers**
COLORS .... **Royal Blue & White**
HOMECOURT .... **Gentry Complex (10,500)**
COACH .... **Frankie Allen (Roanoke College '71)**
RECORD AT SCHOOL .... **96-103 (7 yrs.)**
CAREER RECORD .... **152-164 (11 yrs.)**
ASSISTANTS .... **Thomas Hunter (Illinois State '94)**
Marc Joffe (UCLA '80)
Shayne Carey (Stephen F. Austin '94)
TEAM WINS (last 5 yrs.) **19-17-15-9-13**
RPI (last 5 yrs.) **145-155-166-239-196**
1997-98 FINISH .... **Lost in conference final.**

Frankie Allen has heard the lofty predictions before.

Not that Allen is down on his Tennessee State team. He's just naturally hesitant about bestowing too much praise before the Tigers play a game.

But his Ohio Valley Conference cohorts? That's a much different story.

Almost everybody in the conference is gushing over the returning talent at Tennessee State, plus a handful of newcomers who made their mark in summer-league ball.

"I've heard that same thing from the time I got here eight years ago," Allen said with a chuckle. "We have a chance to be pretty good this year, or just middle of the pack. It's one of those things you never know until you get into it."

The Tigers struggled much of last season, finishing13-16, but they played their best basketball at the end and sprinted all the way to the OVC Tournament championship game. Murray State ended Tennessee State's run with a 92-69 victory, but the seed had been planted for this season.

"We want to try and build on that positive experience," Allen said. "We took Murray right down to the championship game. You take those four or five minutes away when they pulled away, and we might be talking about a team that was on the chopping block most of the year righting itself at the right time. We were about three minutes away from going to the NCAA Tournament."

The Tigers return their entire starting lineup from last season, including a pair of marquee players who deserve mention on preseason all-conference checklists.

Sophomore guard **Jamie Roberts** (14.9 ppg, 4.4 rpg, 55 assists, 44 steals) was the 1997-98 OVC Newcomer of the Year. He has great range, as evidenced by his 86-for-228 three-point shooting. Roberts is a big-time scorer.

"When he loads up that three, he's dangerous from NBA range," Allen said.

The 6-3 Roberts has also improved his ability to go to the basket. Allen believes Roberts will be a more effective defensive player this season.

Senior **Jason Johnson** (13.4 ppg, 7.4 rpg, 30 blocks) has earned second-team All-OVC honors each of the last two seasons. He's a three-year starter at power forward. Johnson, 6-8, is one of only two players in school history to surpass 1,000 points and 500 rebounds in a career.

"He can play with his back to the basket or face it," Allen said. "His leadership will be invaluable to us."

The Samuel brothers from Albany, Ga., will give the Tigers some nice inside-outside flexibility.

Allen says **Kevin Samuel**, a 6-3 junior, is Tennessee State's best defensive player and rebounder, pound for pound. He averaged 12.8 points and 5.0 rebounds, passed for a team-high 91 assists and had a team-high 48 steals. He also made 65 of 192 three-point shots.

Keith Samuel, a 6-6 junior, fits somewhere between a power forward and small forward. Allen said he has the body of a power forward but plays more like a small forward. Last season, Keith Samuel (7.6 ppg, 4.2 rpg) was an effective shooter from the 17- to 18-foot range.

The center position will once again be held by 6-10 junior **Julian Bankston**, who started 20 games last season. Bankston (5.2 ppg, 4.6 rpg, 26 blocks) improved as much as any player on the team. His continued develop-

1998-99 TENNESSEE STATE SCHEDULE

Nov.	15	@Tennessee
	20	Trevecca Nazarene
	23	Northern Iowa
	28	Spalding
Dec.	3	Eastern Illinois
	5	Southeast Missouri State
	19-20	#UNO Christmas Classic
	29	@Kentucky
Jan.	2	@Austin Peay
	7	@Eastern Kentucky
	9	@Morehead State
	12	@Eastern Illinois
	14	Middle Tennessee State
	16	Tennessee Tech
	21	@Murray State
	23	@Tennessee-Martin
	28	Belmont
	30	Austin Peay
Feb.	2	@Southeast Missouri
	4	Eastern Kentucky
	6	Morehead State
	11	@Middle Tennessee
	13	@Tennessee Tech
	18	Murray State
	20	Tennessee-Martin
	23-28	##OVC Tournament

@ Road Games
# New Orleans, LA (vs. Troy State first round; also Maine and New Orleans)
First round Feb. 23 at campus sites. Semifinals and final Feb. 27-28 at Nashville Arena, Nashville, TN.

ment this season could be one of the keys to the Tigers' success.

There will be times when Tennessee State goes with a three-guard set this season. Senior **Brian Williams** is the likely starter at point guard after providing some stability there down the stretch last season. The 6-0 Williams (4.9 ppg, 2.4 rpg) started the last six games. He had 62 assists and 32 turnovers last season.

"Brian was a godsend down the stretch last year," Allen said. "The team was struggling, and he came in and gave them a lift. The team rallied behind him. He's a true point guard who makes the team better."

The Tigers will welcome three newcomers who were around the program last season but sat out as NCAA non-qualifiers.

Ralph Martin is a 6-8 sophomore forward/center from Decatur, Ga. He will serve as Bankston's backup. **DeMario Jones** is a 6-7 sophomore forward, also from Decatur, Ga. Jones is more of a swingman who could spell Keith Samuel at the small-forward position.

John Strong, a 6-3 sophomore point guard, will be Williams' backup. Strong, who's from Albany, Ga., isn't a big scorer, but he's a solid playmaker.

The Tigers have just one signee who will be eligible immediately, and he's a good one. Junior **Corey Williams**, a 6-7 junior forward from Imperial Valley (Calif.) CC, should make an immediate impact. He averaged 20 points and 12 rebounds last season and was just as impressive this summer in the Nashville Summer League. He's very active around the basket.

"I think we're going to have more depth," Allen said. "Last year, we were more or less confined to our starting five, and that was it. But with the kids coming back and Corey Williams, we're going to have the ability to play nine or 10 people. We'll be able to go to the bench and not have a big dropoff."

Three walkons will play support roles this season. **George Parker** (2.2 ppg, 0.8 rpg) is a 6-5 senior forward. **Harold Spencer** (0.5 ppg, 0.5 rpg) is a 6-0 senior guard. **Bryant Herbert** (1.5 ppg, 1.3 rpg) is a 6-4 forward.

There could be more help on the way after the first semester. **Ryan Beane**, a 6-9 junior power forward from Jacksonville State (Texas) CC, won't be eligible until the second semester. The same goes for **Darwin Carter**, a 6-1 junior point guard from Santa Monica (Calif.) JC. Leon Murray, the quarterback on the TSU football team, has also expressed an interest in joining the team after football season.

adidas Blue Ribbon Analysis

BACKCOURT .... **B** **BENCH/DEPTH** .... **B**
FRONTCOURT .... **B+** **INTANGIBLES** .... **B+**

This is as many quality players as Tennessee State has had since the Carlos Rogers days. Jamie Roberts and Jason Johnson could play just about anywhere, and if the reviews from the Nashville Summer League are accurate, Corey Williams will be a candidate for newcomer-of-the-year honors in the OVC.

The versatile Samuel brothers, Keith and Kevin, figure to be improved this year, and Tigers coach Frankie Allen is especially excited about the improvement of center Julian Bankston in the summer. Brian Williams has proven he's a capable point guard.

So where are the weaknesses?

There aren't many, except that this TSU team has yet to prove on the court that its talent is as good as advertised.

"If we're going to have success, it's going to have to be our returning guys who set the tone," Allen said. "The new guys will need to fit in where needed, but it's up to Jamie, Kevin, Jason and those guys who've been in our program for a while to show the way."

Tennessee State hasn't won the tournament title since 1994, although it shared the regular-season title with Murray State in 1995.

If anyone can knock the Racers off their throne, Tennessee State has the team to do it.

(C.L.)

TENNESSEE TECH

LOCATION .... **Cookeville, TN**
CONFERENCE .... **Ohio Valley (OVC)**
LAST SEASON .... **9-21 (.300)**
CONFERENCE RECORD .... **5-13 (t-8th)**
STARTERS LOST/RETURNING **2/3**
NICKNAME .... **Golden Eagles**
COLORS .... **Purple & Gold**
HOMECOURT .... **Eblen Center (10,152)**
COACH .... **Jeff Lebo (North Carolina '89)**
RECORD AT SCHOOL .... **First year**
CAREER RECORD .... **First year**
ASSISTANTS .... **John Shulman (ETSU '89)**
Tracy Garrick (Furman '91)
Dave Lebo (Elizabethtown College '66)
TEAM WINS (last 5 yrs.) **10-13-13-15-9**
RPI (last 5 yrs.) **270-222-223-221-270**
1997-98 FINISH .... **Lost in conference first round.**

Everywhere Jeff Lebo has traveled during his basketball career, winning has seemed to follow.

As a highly coveted high school player in Carlisle, Pa., he led his team to three straight Class AAAA state championships. From there, Lebo headed south to play for the legendary Dean Smith at North Carolina. The sweet-shooting guard started for three-and-a-half seasons and still holds several Tar Heel records.

His college coaching career was born just eight years ago when he served on the staff at East Tennessee State. The Bucs won the Southern Conference Tournament and advanced to the NCAA Tournament in each of Lebo's two years there, defeating No. 3 seed Arizona in 1992.

Lebo joined Eddie Fogler at Vanderbilt in 1992-93, and the Commodores also reached the NCAA Tournament. He spent the last six years at South Carolina, helping Fogler resurrect the program there.

Given his credentials, it's no surprise that the people at Tennessee Tech are upbeat about Lebo's arrival as the Golden Eagles' new coach.

Lebo, 31, is just as excited about getting a chance at such a young age.

"It boiled down to having a good gut feeling about Tennessee Tech and the people here, the administration and their commitment to wanting to have a good basketball program," said Lebo, regarded as one of the top young assistants in the country the last few years.

"I feel good that this will be a great start for me and a great start to my coaching career. Like many places, there's a lot of work to do, and not a lot of time to do it."

Lebo takes over for Frank Harrell, who resigned as the Golden Eagles struggled through the 1997-98 season. Three of the top four scorers from that team are gone.

Despite not getting started on the job until well into March, Lebo was able to sign three new players. Harrell had already signed one in the early period.

Lebo's first order of business will be changing a few attitudes.

"They lost a lot last year, and it was a bad experience," Lebo said. "They had 10 new guys last year, a whole new group of people. We've got to erase that bad experience, get it out of their minds and focus on what we can achieve here."

Three frontcourt players who ended last season as starters return, but one of those, 6-8 sophomore center **Adonis Hart** (4.5 ppg, 3.0 rpg, 14 blocked shots), is trying to recover from offseason reconstructive knee surgery.

"He's at home plate and just headed for first," Lebo said. Hart came to Tennessee Tech on a football scholarship as a tight end and just started to develop as a basketball player during the latter part of last season.

Senior forward **Wesley Whitehorn** (10.0 ppg, 6.0 rpg, 22 steals) is the Golden Eagles' leading returning scorer after starting in 26 games last season. The 6-6, 225-pound Whitehorn is more of a power player inside, but has the ability shoot the three-pointer. His problem last season was 102 turnovers to go with 28 assists.

The third returning starter is 6-7 senior **Reggie Nelson**, who can play both forward positions. Nelson (6.8 ppg, 4.3 rpg) was slowed by a stress fracture in his shin early last season, but had a strong finish. He suffered a stress fracture in his other leg during the offseason and is coming off surgery. Lebo expects him to be ready for the start of practice.

Forward Alex Franco, who led Tennessee Tech in scoring and rebounding last season, has quit the team. He returned to his native Canary Islands before last season ended.

A player Lebo is especially high on is 6-10 junior **Eric Akins,** who started 15 games last season. Akins (6.8 ppg, 5.6 rpg, 33 blocked shots) will contend for the starting power forward or center position.

The reports are equally glowing on 6-8 freshman forward **Arnaldo Febres**, who sat out last season as a partial qualifier. Febres, a native of Canovanas, Puerto Rico, may wind up being one of the Golden Eagles' better inside scorers.

Charles Haney, a 6-4 junior, is also capable of playing the power forward position. His size, though, makes him more of a small forward. Haney averaged 1.8 ppg and 0.9 rpg last season in only 12 games.

"It's going to be very competitive for those inside positions," Lebo said.

Lebo has tried to bolster the Eagles' three-point shooting by signing two outstanding perimeter shooters.

Joey Westmoreland, a 6-6 freshman guard/small forward from Dalton, Ga., has NBA range. Westmoreland is accurate two or three steps behind the three-point line and is a good enough athlete to dunk in traffic. Last season, he averaged 18.2 points, 8.4 rebounds, 3.8 steals and 3.3 assists and was chosen to *The Chattanooga Times* All-Tri-State first team and the *Atlanta Journal-Constitution*'s All-State second team.

Josh Heard, a 6-2 shooting guard from Roane State (Tenn.) Community College, is another solid perimeter shooter. He averaged 21.3 points last season and set a school record with eight three-point baskets in a game. His nine three-pointers is a single-game record at Hart County (Ga.) High School.

Two returnees factor prominently in Lebo's plans as swing players. **DeAntoine Beasley**, a 6-6 sophomore guard, can do a little bit of everything. Beasley (2.9 ppg, 1.3 rpg, 38 assists, 12 blocked shots) saw extensive time at point guard last season, but Lebo thinks his best position is small forward.

"He needs a little more confidence shooting the ball, but he can do a lot of things," Lebo said. "He has great skills with the ball, can put it down, pass, rebound and knows how to play. We're hoping for good things from him."

Ricardo Woodfine, a 6-2 senior, is an outstanding leaper who would rather take it to the basket than shoot the

1998-99 TENNESSEE TECH SCHEDULE

Nov.	14	Belmont
	19	@Alabama
	24	@Ohio State
	30	Appalachian State
Dec.	5	@Middle Tennessee State
	16	@Evansville
	19	Montreat College
	21	Bryan College
	29	Idaho State
Jan.	2	@Murray State
	4	@Tennessee-Martin
	7	Eastern Illinois
	9	Southeast Missouri
	12	Middle Tennessee State
	14	@Austin Peay
	16	@Tennessee State
	21	Eastern Kentucky
	23	Morehead State
	28	Murray State
	30	Tennessee-Martin
Feb.	4	@Eastern Illinois
	6	@Southeast Missouri
	11	Austin Peay
	13	Tennessee State
	18	@Eastern Kentucky
	20	@Morehead State
	23-28	#OVC Tournament

@ Road Games
# First round Feb. 23 at campus sites. Semifinals and final Feb. 27-28 at Nashville Arena, Nashville, TN.

jumper. Woodfine (5.8 ppg, 1.9 rpg, 36 assists) played little after the midway point of last season. Lebo hopes Woodfine can be a defensive stopper on opposing shooting guards.

The only pure point guard on the roster is 6-1 junior **Corey Hemphill,** who played last season at Dodge City (Kan.) Community College. Hemphill, who averaged 11.3 points and had 95 assists last year, is exceptionally quick and can handle the ball.

"He can go all day," Lebo said. "He's one of those kids who never fatigues."

Junior **Ronnie Braxton** will also get a look at the point, although he might play some at shooting guard. The 6-2 Braxton (2.5 ppg, 0.7 rpg) played in six games last season. He started his career at LaSalle and wasn't eligible until midway through last season.

Freshman **Martin Fears** of Lithonia, Ga., was signed before Lebo took the job. Even though he's only 5-8, Fears is probably more of a shooting guard. Freshman **Collins Rouse** of Greenville, S.C., is a walkon and will play a support role in the backcourt.

adidas Blue Ribbon Analysis

BACKCOURT	C	BENCH/DEPTH	D
FRONTCOURT	C	INTANGIBLES	B

There will be a certain adjustment period for Tennessee Tech's basketball program, but first-year coach Jeff Lebo doesn't plan on wasting any time in getting his message across.

"Our goal this year is to get the kids to understand the importance of playing hard, playing unselfishly, playing for the front of the jersey and not the name on the back," Lebo said.

Improving on last season's eighth-place finish in the OVC will be difficult. A new system and a new starting backcourt usually makes for problems. How well Corey Hemphill develops at point guard will be critical.

The Golden Eagles need a big year from Wesley Whitehorn, and the two new perimeter shooters in the program will need to take pressure off Whitehorn in the post.

There aren't many proven scorers on this team. Somebody needs to emerge. Eric Akins is one to watch.

Growing pains are a fact of life in any rebuilding job. But then, Lebo isn't looking for a quick fix.

(C.L.)

PACIFIC-10 CONFERENCE

adidas BLUE RIBBON FORECAST

1. Stanford
2. Washington
3. Arizona
4. UCLA
5. California
6. USC
7. Oregon
8. Arizona State
9. Oregon State
10. Washington State

TOP 40

Arizona, California, Stanford, UCLA and Washington are ranked among the 1998-99 *adidas Blue Ribbon* Top 40. An extended profile may be found in the Top 40 section of *Blue Ribbon*.

ALL-CONFERENCE TEAM

G—Arthur Lee, SR, Stanford
G—Baron Davis, SO, UCLA
F—A.J. Bramlett, SR, Arizona
F—Tim Young, SR, Stanford
C—Todd MacCulloch, SR, Washington

PLAYER OF THE YEAR

Todd MacCulloch, SR, Washington

NEWCOMER OF THE YEAR

Dan Gadzuric, FR, UCLA

1997-98 CHAMPION

Arizona

1997-98 POSTSEASON PARTICIPANTS

Postseason Record: 11-5 (.688)

NCAA

Stanford (Final Four)
Arizona (Final Eight)
UCLA (Sweet 16)
Georgetown (Sweet 16)

NIT

Arizona State

TOP BACKCOURTS

1. Stanford
2. California
3. UCLA

TOP FRONTCOURTS

1. Stanford
2. California
3. Arizona

ON THE WAY UP

California

ON THE WAY DOWN

Washington State

INSIDE THE NUMBERS

- 1997-98 conference RPI: 5th (of 30)
- Conference RPI (last 5 years): 9-6-7-5-5

DID YOU KNOW?

The Pac-10 comes off its second straight season of advancing four teams to the Sweet 16 round of the NCAA Tournament. With an 11-4 record in NCAA play last season, the conference is 24-8 in the tournament over the last two seasons and 36-16 during the last four...The Pac-10 has advanced a team into the Final Four in four of the last five years with UCLA ('95) and Arizona ('97) claiming titles...Compared to a year ago when most of the league's top talent was returning, only two of the Pac-10's top scorers from 1997-98 are back: Washington's Todd MacCulloch (fourth at 18.6 ppg) and Cal's Geno Carlisle (eighth at 17.9 ppg)...By contrast, five of the league's top nine rebounders, the top five shot blockers, the top four field-goal percentage leaders and the top three free-throw shooters all return...Rob Evans' arrival as coach at Arizona State marks the seventh consecutive year the league has experienced at least one head coaching change...With eight players selected in the NBA Draft, three of them in the first round, the Pac-10 had more players drafted than any other conference in the nation...A Pac-10 fathers-sons game might wind up embarrassing for the kids. Dads of current conference players include these former NBA standouts: Center Bill Walton (son Luke at Arizona); power forward Lonnie Shelton (Marlon at Washington); small forward Glenn McDonald (Mike at Stanford); and guards Slick Watts (Donald at Washington), Paul Westphal (Michael at Washington), and Fred Brown (Terik at Oregon, Bryan at Washington)...Pac-10 rosters feature players from 22 states (plus Washington, D.C.) and 10 foreign countries.

(J.F.)

ARIZONA STATE

LOCATION	Tempe, AZ
CONFERENCE	Pacific-10
LAST SEASON	18-14 (.263)
CONFERENCE RECORD	8-10 (t-5th)
STARTERS LOST/RETURNING	2/3
NICKNAME	Sun Devils
COLORS	Maroon & Gold
HOMECOURT	Wells Fargo Arena (14,198)
COACH	Rob Evans (New Mexico State '68)
RECORD AT SCHOOL	First Year
CAREER RECORD	86-81 (6 yrs.)
ASSISTANTS	Tony Benford (Texas Tech '86)
	Russ Pennell (Pittsburgh State '89)
	Dan O'Dowd (Bethany College '86)
TEAM WINS (last 5 yrs.)	18-24-11-10-18
RPI (last 5 yrs.)	78-22-154-187-63
1997-98 FINISH	Lost in NIT first round.

Things rarely are as good or as bad as they first appear, and so it is with the Arizona State program new coach Rob Evans inherited. Evans, hired April 7 to replace one-year interim coach Don Newman, figured to immediately reap the benefits of three starters returning from an 18-win team, while battling to overcome a recent legacy of scandal in the ASU program.

Turns out, the Sun Devils won't enjoy the full bloom of their experience from the outset of Evans' debut season. Senior forward **Mike Batiste** (15.3 ppg, 7.8 rpg, .566 FG) must sit out the first eight games because of academic shortcomings. Then there were brief rumblings last summer from junior shooting guard **Eddie House** (11.3 ppg, 3.0 rpg, 2.5 apg, .401 three-point percentage) about a possible transfer.

Evans, who led Mississippi to unprecedented back-to-back NCAA Tournament appearances in 1997 and '98, didn't have time to sweat much about the doings of his returning players. He arrived in Tempe in full sprint, quickly signing five recruits before beginning an enthusiastic public-relations tour of the community and the state.

That was followed by a return to the recruiting front, which seemed to reap positive results last summer. After stating that he intended to make in-state recruiting a priority, Evans got a July commitment from 6-foot-8 forward Donnell Knight, regarded as a top-25 national prospect from Corona Del Sol HS in Tempe.

Residue from the point-shaving scandal that received hands-on attention from the FBI and ultimately drove out coach Bill Frieder a year ago hardly impacted Evans' early efforts.

"It's a clean slate as far as I'm concerned—new people, new ideas," Evans said. "We know what we've got to do to get this thing going. In recruiting, I have not had a lot of problems with negativity because the point-shaving issue is a national issue, not just an institutional issue. It could happen anywhere."

In addition to the point-shaving episode, in which ex-Sun Devils Stevin "Hedake" Smith and Isaac Burton were implicated in a scheme that involved four games during the 1993-94 season, 13 other ASU players were linked to the transgressions ranging from rape, assault and credit card theft during Frieder's tenure.

To make sure the program took a new direction, athletic director Kevin White hired Evans, 51, who arrived with a record of 42-16 at Mississippi the previous two years and a reputation as a disciplinarian.

"Rob Evans has worked night and day to put his program in place and headed in the direction wherein we could realize our objectives, to consistently be in the top three in the Pac-10 and the top 10 in the NCAA," White told the *Arizona Republic.*

Evans understands the concept of first things first. He knows the Sun Devils aren't likely to crack the top three of a ferocious Pac-10 this season.

"Obviously, the Pac-10 is a league that in the last few years has really burst upon the national scene," said Evans, who directed Ole Miss to back-to-back Southeastern Conference West Division titles and NCAA Tournament appearances. "I'm leaving one difficult conference and going to another."

Evans' immediate priorities, in addition to recruiting, are to establish the foundation of his program and to build a stronger fan base.

"I've been through this before. I understand the nature of this, with a new coach coming in," he said. "There's a certain way we're going to do things, and we're not going

1998-99 ARIZONA STATE SCHEDULE

Nov.	13	San Jose State
	17	Northern Arizona
	23-25	#Maui Classic
Dec.	1	New Orleans
	5	*UNLV
	8	Stephen F. Austin
	19	@Texas A&M
	22	Marist
	28-29	##Arizona State Christmas Classic
Jan.	2	@Southern California
	4	@UCLA
	7	Washington
	9	Washington State
	13	Arizona
	21	@Oregon State
	23	@Oregon
	28	California
	30	Stanford
Feb.	4	@Washington State
	6	@Washington
	10	@Arizona
	18	Oregon
	20	Oregon State
	25	@Stanford
Mar.	4	UCLA
	6	Southern California

@ Road Games
* America West Arena, Phoenix, AZ
# Maui, HI (vs. Utah, first round; also Chaminade, Clemson, Indiana, Michigan, Syracuse, Utah and Western Kentucky)
Tempe, AZ (vs. Navy, first round; also Alaska-Anchorage and Southern Methodist)

to waffle on it. We're not going to bend.

"There's not a whole lot of rules, but the ones we have, we're going to enforce. You've got to have discipline."

Likewise, he knows first-hand the value of support at home. In posting consecutive 20-victory seasons for the first time in 60 years, Mississippi went 13-0 at home and sold out every SEC home game last season. Already, Evans has helped arrange a $5 million title sponsorship for the arena formerly known as the University Activity Center.

"It's really been tremendous, the reception that we've gotten," Evans said. "People are really excited about us being here and the things we are going to try to do. We have a great city, a great facility, a great league."

And a great in-state rival just down the road in Tucson. Evans said he respects the job Lute Olson has done at Arizona, but won't get hung up on comparing his program to any other in the conference.

"There's a lot of programs that are model programs," he said. "People talk about wanting to beat Arizona. We want to beat everybody. I hope the model program will be at Arizona State."

Those who know Evans have little doubt he will succeed at ASU. "What he did at Ole Miss was nothing short of a miracle," Kentucky coach Tubby Smith said. "His team exemplified great energy and effort. They were the best defensive teams I've played against in my career."

Anchoring Evans' first ASU team will be 6-9 senior forward **Bobby Lazor**, the one-time Syracuse defector, who is the club's top returning scorer (16.8 ppg) and rebounder (7.8 rpg). Lazor added strength through an off-season weight program, and should assume a leadership role on the team with the graduation of school scoring king Jeremy Veal.

"I'm really excited about Bobby," Evans said. "He's very athletic, he can play a number of positions, and he's a leader. He will be a very big key for us."

When the 6-8 Batiste returns for the Dec. 19 game at Texas A&M, he's likely to team up front with Lazor in what may once more be a three-guard alignment. "Mike has size, physical ability and intelligence on the basketball court," Evans said.

The Sun Devils anxiously await a progress report on the comeback of 6-8 junior forward **Okeme Oziwo**, who missed all of last season after a preseason car accident. "How effective he will be remains to be seen," Evans said.

Early, 6-7 junior forward **Lohnnie Tape** (23.4 ppg, 8.1 rpg at Santa Ana CC in Esperanza, Calif.) figures to be given a good shot at Batiste's spot. Tape (pronounced ta-PAY), a one-time California state track entry in the high hurdles, will battle 6-9 freshman **Chad Prewitt** (18 ppg, 10 rpg at Greeway HS in Phoenix) for time up front.

Rounding out the candidates up front is 6-6 freshman **Willie Hendricks** (Franklin HS in Seattle, Wash.).

"Somebody needs to step to the forefront to help us on the front line," Evans said. "But I'm not adverse to playing three guards."

That's been pretty much a staple with recent Sun Devils teams. ASU made it work last year with a depth-deprived squad that featured the backcourt of Veal (20.8 ppg), House and departed senior point guard Ahlon Lewis, whose 9.19 apg led the nation.

If House is in order, the 6-1 shooting guard provides Evans with a player who can score in various ways and last year had more steals (64) than turnovers (43). House has played 24 turnover-free games in his two-year career, with nearly a 2.5-to-1 assist-to turnover ratio.

"The thing he brings to the table is his athletic ability," Evans said. "He really gets his shot off quick, and I think he can play the point or the off guard."

More likely, the point will be handled by newcomer **Alton Mason**, a 6-2 sophomore who originally signed with Marquette, but transferred to Barton County CC (Great Bend, Kansas), where last season he averaged 10.0 ppg, 8.3 apg and 3.3 spg for a 29-4 team.

"Alton brings a tremendous of physical ability," Evans said. "He's very, very intelligent—he can run a basketball team."

Mason will be challenged by 6-4 freshman **Kenny Crandall** (14.1 ppg and 6.1 apg for a 28-1 state finalist Mountain View HS in Mesa, Ariz.).

Also vying for backcourt time will be 6-4 junior **Jason Patton** (6.1 ppg, 2.6 rpg), 6-3 freshman **Chris Bryant** (25 ppg, 8 rpg, 3 apg at Washington HS in Peoria, Ariz.), and 6-4 junior **Derrick Davis** (17.6 ppg, 5.3 rpg at Cowley County CC in Abbeville, Ala.)

Walkons **Ron DuBois** (1.3 ppg, 0.4 rpg), a 5-10 senior, and **D'Angelo Jones** (0.3 ppg, 0.4 rpg), a 5-10 sophomore, round out the roster.

adidas Blue Ribbon Analysis

BACKCOURT	C+	BENCH/DEPTH	B
FRONTCOURT	C	INTANGIBLES	C

Even before Frieder arrived in Tempe nearly a decade ago, ASU has been considered a sleeping hoops giant, a program waiting to take its place among the Pac-10's elite. Getting the Sun Devils to that point is Evans' goal and his mandate. But it won't happen this year.

ASU burst out of the gate quickly a year ago, with Newman guiding the club to a berth in the Preseason NIT semifinals. By March, the momentum was gone, and a 46-point loss at USC in the Pac-10 finale sealed a return trip to the NIT.

These Sun Devils will have to overachieve, too, if they hope to still have NCAA hopes entering the final weekend of the season. ASU has no depth up front and no established floor leader.

"I'm always optimistic," Evans said. "We do have three starters returning, once we get Mike back. But we lost the leading scorer in the league and the leading assist man in the country.

"We won 18 games last year, but lost 14. I'm more worried about the losses than the wins."

Evans may well prove to be the right man for the job. He talks about bringing in good people who want to be part of something special. Right now he's playing with a hand largely dealt to him by someone else. Maybe it will work, maybe it will take some time.

In the meantime, he will attack the big picture by focusing on the detail work. "If you take care of your immediate needs," Evans said, "I think your long-range goals will come in time."

(J.F.)

OREGON

LOCATION	Eugene, OR
CONFERENCE	Pacific-10
LAST SEASON	13-14 (.481)
CONFERENCE RECORD	9-10 (5th)
STARTERS LOST/RETURNING	3/2
NICKNAME	Ducks
COLORS	Green & Gold
HOMECOURT	McArthur Court (9,087)
COACH	Ernie Kent (Oregon '77)
RECORD AT SCHOOL	13-14 (1 yrs.)
CAREER RECORD	103-94 (7 yrs.)
ASSISTANTS	Greg Graham (Oregon '77)
	Don Newman (Idaho '87)
	Mark Hudson (Northwestern '92)
TEAM WINS (last 5 yrs.)	10-19-16-17-13
RPI (last 5 yrs.)	181-23-87-61-108
1997-98 FINISH	No conference tournament.

It feels like old times again at Oregon for coach Ernie Kent. This is what he expected last season when he returned to his alma mater after 20 years. But he didn't anticipate things might start falling into place so quickly.

Kent, who has always seen the glass as half full, hopes the Ducks can take a big sip of success this season after being gradually more competitive in his debut campaign.

"When we took over the program, you knew that you were going to struggle, that there would be some lean years," he said. "There wasn't much talent left and things were out of sync. But considering the way our kids really bought into our program and locked in and performed, particularly the second half of the season, I was really pleased."

1998-99 OREGON SCHEDULE

Nov.	15	Coppin State
	28	@Southern Illinois
	30	@Minnesota
Dec.	5	Brigham Young
	12	Portland State
	14	@Santa Clara
	19	Alcorn State
	22	*Vanderbilt
	28	St. Martin's
Jan.	2	@California
	4	@Stanford
	7	Southern California
	9	UCLA
	14	@Washington State
	16	@Washington
	21	Arizona
	23	Arizona State
	30	@Oregon State
Feb.	4	@UCLA
	6	@Southern California
	11	Washington State
	13	Washington
	18	@Arizona State
	20	@Arizona
	27	Oregon State
Mar.	4	Stanford
	6	California

@ Road Games
* Rose Garden, Portland OR

Oregon, expected to finish near the bottom of the Pac-10 standings, instead wound up in a three-way tie for fifth. The Ducks needed perhaps just one more victory to have earned an NIT bid, and Kent likes to point out they had the third-best record in the conference over the second half of the Pac-10 schedule.

Oregon hired Kent—a member of the Ron Lee-led "Kamikaze Kids" teams of the mid-1970s—to help revive tradition and past success. Kent's the perfect man for that assignment and his voice rises with excitement as he talks about the potential of playing in cozy but hostile McArthur Court, built in 1926.

"The biggest thing for us is team play, and understanding we have such a powerful home-court advantage here at Mac Court," he said. "If we can come together on and off the floor, it can really work well. The community started feeding off our team and Mac Court came alive again and then the team started feeding off the fans."

The feeding frenzy reached a crescendo Feb. 5 when the Ducks routed sixth-ranked UCLA, 97-81, behind 22 points from guard **Terik Brown**.

Eight players, including Brown, return from that team, and the Ducks refueled well, adding five newcomers. The best of those are guards **Frederick Jones**, the top prep prospect to emerge from the state of Oregon in several years, and **Alex Scales**, who arrives from powerhouse JC San Jacinto (Texas) College.

While Arizona and UCLA drew raves for their recruiting classes, Kent is thrilled with the batch of new talent headed to Eugene after just one year selling his program.

"We feel we had, for us, an unbelievable recruiting class, too," he said. "In my opinion, it throws us into the thick of things with everybody else, Stanford being maybe the lone exception."

Kent believes the Ducks will compete with the likes of Cal and USC for a spot just above the league's equator, giving them a shot at a postseason bid.

No doubt, the Ducks are well-equipped at the wing spots. Brown (12.8 ppg, 3.0 rpg, .387 three-point shooting) was the club's top scorer a year ago. The 6-1 senior scored in double figures 17 times, including nine of the final 10 games, and five times topped the 20-point plateau.

Kent expects Brown to become a better defender, and he wants to see a more consistent scorer than the player who averaged 14.3 ppg at home but just 8.8 away from Mac Court. "He's got to have the courage to display that on the road," Kent said.

The arrival of Jones and Scales gives the Ducks a chance to play big in the backcourt when they feel the need.

Jones is a two-time Oregon player of the year who averaged 29.9 ppg last season at Gresham HS. At 6-3, he also contributed 8.1 rpg, 4.0 apg, 3.4 bpg and 2.5 spg. He was a first-team *Long Beach Press-Telegram* Best in the West selection.

Kent doesn't hedge on how good Jones can become for the Ducks. "Freddie Jones, in my opinion, has the potential to be the best player, or one of the best players, to play at Oregon," Kent said. "He's an explosive player who has the complete package. He can score inside, shoot the ball, pass the ball. He's going to have an instant impact on our team."

Scales gives the Ducks a third weapon on the wing. A native of Racine, Wis., the 6-4 junior averaged 15 ppg for a 29-4 San Jacinto JC team after helping it to a 36-1 mark as a freshman.

"He can score going to the basket, he's an excellent defender and he's such a physical specimen," Kent said.

The point-guard spot has even more depth, albeit not the same quality. The returnees are 6-4 junior **Mike McShane** (4.7 ppg, 3.3 apg, .359 FG), a starter 23 times, and 6-1 junior **Yasir Rosemond** (5.2 ppg), who had more turnovers (66) than assists (38). Added to the mix and a potential starter is 6-0 junior **Darius Wright** (17.0 ppg, 9.8 apg for West Valley College in Saratoga, Calif.), who led his team to a 30-4 record and the California JC quarterfinals last year.

"McShane and Rosemond came a long way last year. When they were on, that's when we were at our best," Kent said. "At the same time, I felt we needed more consistency this year. What Wright brings to the table is a prototype throwback to the old days as a heady point guard. He's totally team-oriented in his play."

Rounding out the backcourt is 6-1 sophomore walkon **Kristian Christensen** (0.4 ppg, 0.1 rpg in 8 games).

The Ducks have high hopes for their interior players, but less tangible evidence to support that outlook. Gone is 6-6 forward Henry Madden (12.6 ppg, a team-best 5.4 rpg), but there is plenty of beef.

Center **Mike Carson** (7.5 ppg, 4.5 rpg in 6 games) is back for a fifth season after being granted a medical redshirt last season. The 7-foot senior injured his ankle Dec. 16, then encountered knee problems that forced him to miss the remainder of the season. He had a 15-point performance against Santa Clara before being sidelined.

"If we could get him back to the point he was when he was injured we would be happy," Kent said. "He's certainly healthy enough now, but he lost all the confidence he had developed."

Backing up Carson will be 7-2, 275-pound freshman **Chris Cristoffersen**, a former teammate of Christensen at Nordoff HS in Ojai, Calif. Christoffersen, a native of Roenne, Denmark, averaged 15.0 ppg, 9.0 rpg and 5.0 bpg a year ago.

Christofferson played water polo, soccer and volleyball before taking up basketball, so Kent believes he will develop quickly. "He's a project, but he's not your typical project because he is athletic and has great hands," Kent said.

The Ducks hope 6-9, 260-pound sophomore power forward **Flo Hartenstein** (3.9 ppg, 4.2 rpg) will be one of the league's most improved players. The native of Germany is Oregon's strongest player and is an intense rebounder and defender.

Hartenstein will be pushed by 6-8, 230-pound junior **Skouson Harker** (14.0 ppg, 8.0 rpg at McCook CC in McCook, Neb.), a native of Alberta, Canada.

The team's most versatile frontline player is 6-8 junior forward **A.D. Smith** (10.4 ppg, 4.4 rpg, .448 FG), who had seven double-figure scoring performances in the Ducks' final eight games.

Junior **Donte Quinine** (2.4 ppg, 1.0 rpg) is a 6-6 small forward Kent rates as perhaps the team's best all-around athlete and top defender.

Kent believes he and his staff_which now includes former Arizona State interim head coach Don Newman—have fortified the Ducks in all areas.

"We feel we're two and three deep at every position," he said. "At the same time, we felt like we were one of the (physically) weaker teams in the league last year. Now we feel we're one of the stronger ones.

"We now have the ability to play small or play big, play fast or play in the halfcourt. It's just a matter of bringing it all together."

adidas Blue Ribbon Analysis

BACKCOURT	**B**	**BENCH/DEPTH**	**C+**
FRONTCOURT	**C**	**INTANGIBLES**	**B**

There is little doubt Oregon will be better than a year ago. The problem is, everyone else in the middle of the pack is also improved, and those at the top aren't likely to slide enough to make a difference.

Kent envisions a scenario where several of the league's clubs—including Arizona and UCLA—have been so drastically rebuilt that their fortunes aren't easily predicted. "Some people are coming back to the pack a little bit," he said. "There's a lot of unknowns out there."

Surely that's the case with Oregon, too. The Ducks seem well-stocked at the wing spots, but their point guard logjam must be resolved and there is muscle, but little proven scoring punch in the frontline.

"We're definitely going to have the scoring in the backcourt and wings. We need to find someone who can score consistently on the low block," Kent said. "One of those five guys has to emerge as an offensive threat. That would be our biggest concern."

Kent has recruited well, sparked renewed fervor from fans and sold his players on his philosophies. In the old days—his playing days—of the conference, that would have been enough to vault a team into the upper echelon.

This isn't your father's Pac-10, though—it's deeper and tougher. Oregon will be better, but cracking the upper division may take another year or two.

(J.F.)

OREGON STATE

LOCATION .... **Corvallis, Ore.**
CONFERENCE **Pacific-10**
LAST SEASON .... **13-20 (.394)**
CONFERENCE RECORD .... **3-15 (t-9th)**
STARTERS LOST/RETURNING **3/2**
NICKNAME .... **Beavers**
COLORS .... **Orange & Black**
HOMECOURT .... **Gill Coliseum (10,400)**
COACH .... **Eddie Payne (Wake Forest '73)**
RECORD AT SCHOOL .... **26-61 (3 yrs.)**
CAREER RECORD .... **185-170 (12 yrs.)**
ASSISTANTS .... **Leroy Washington (Montana '88)**
Rich Wold (Oregon State '90)
Chad Forcier (Seattle Pacific '95)
TEAM WINS (last 5 yrs.) **6-9-4-7-13**
RPI (last 5 yrs.) **196-122-203-190-180**
1997-98 FINISH .... **No conference tournament.**

Nowhere in the Pac-10 will you find a bigger proponent of addition by subtraction than Oregon State coach Eddie Payne.

Perhaps it's merely a self-defense mechanism, but Payne is confident the Beavers can be improved this season, despite losing eight players from a year ago—four to graduation, three as transfers to other schools and sophomore star Corey Benjamin to the NBA.

"I actually feel pretty good about our team," Payne said. "It'll be different. There'll be some things we'll be much better at. We'll be a better shooting team, and consequently, a better free-throw shooting team. We should get more productivity out of the post.

"We've got a club with a much better distribution offensively. We have many more people who can score."

Without question, the Beavers will miss Benjamin's offensive explosiveness and star quality. The 6-6 wing averaged 19.8 ppg and 5.0 rpg, leading the team in scoring 13 times. He had five games of 30 points or more, including 36 against Oregon and Arizona State, before the Chicago Bulls plucked him from the first round of the NBA draft.

"Corey's situation for us, at this point in time, is unique," Payne said. "Those are things that happen."

The reality is, even with Benjamin, the Beavers were a sub-.500 team last year, and finished tied for last in the conference. After four straight single-digit victory totals—the previous two under Payne—last season was expected to be the year OSU made a significant breakthrough.

There were hints it might happen, including potential upsets against Arizona and Oregon late in the season. Free-throw failures sabotaged those efforts, but Payne believes a new recipe this season can continue the building process.

Despite some speculation, the Beavers' new look doesn't include the coaching spot. New athletic director Mitch Barnhart extended Payne's contract, giving him four more years on the payroll. Ultimately, the school and its fans may not be willing to wait that long for some real progress, but Barnhart seems fully behind Payne and his program.

"The biggest thing about Mitch Barnhart is he understands what we're up against," Payne said. "There are some different issues here that relate to facilities and student seating, and he's attentive to that. That attitude in general extends to every issue that comes up with the program."

Payne's immediate concern relates to assembling a team from a roster that includes five newcomers.

Besides Benjamin, the Beavers lost four seniors, including center Terrill Woods (5.1 ppg, 4.1 rpg) and guard Jerome Vaden (10.8 ppg), and departing transfers John-Blair Bickerstaff (8.6 ppg, 4.7 rpg), Nick Greene and Ronnie Walton.

The losses total 50.8 ppg and 22.2 rpg, leaving just two players who contributed more than 3.7 ppg a year ago. "A couple of the guys could tell their opportunities weren't great to play the minutes they wanted," Payne said.

The two key returnees are junior guard **Ron Grady** and sophomore point guard **Deaundra Tanner**. Grady averaged 10.4 ppg and 4.1 rpg last season before suffering a lacerated kidney in an on-court collision against Washington in mid-January. That forced him to miss the final 13 games.

Payne said the Beavers could not replace Grady's perimeter defense or his leadership qualities last season. The 6-3, 200-pounder is physically OK now, but Payne won't know how well he's recovered emotionally until the team is back on the floor.

"His biggest challenge after such a prolonged period of inactivity is to get him back in the mental frame of mind he had," Payne said. "I don't know if he's really regained his mental edge. It was basically a question of lying flat on your back for eight weeks, then walking around on eggshells for another month."

Payne said Grady won't have to step right back in and contribute huge numbers. "I think we'll rely more on the whole than the parts," he said. "Ron can play within the system. He can contribute mightily with his competitive nature."

The 6-1 Tanner (9.0 ppg, 2.5 rpg, 90 assists, 50 steals) is being touted in Corvallis as perhaps the school's best point-guard prospect since Gary Payton. He averaged 10.9 ppg in Pac-10 play as a freshman, and led the team in scoring in five of the season's final seven games, including a career-high 25 points at Stanford.

Now Payne believes Tanner can assume a leadership role. "It takes that long sometimes for a freshman to get into that position," he said. "He's got a lot of valuable experience. He works hard, his teammates like him, and he's very much an optimistic type of guy. Players gravitate toward him because of that."

Newcomers will play a key role on the squad, because there is no alternative. The three mostly likely contributors are 6-5 sophomore **Josh Steinthal**, 6-5 junior **Ramunas Petraitis** and 6-8 junior **Clifton Jones.**

Steinthal averaged 32.0 ppg as a senior at Sumner HS in Washington, signed with Memphis, left after one year and did not play basketball last season while attending a junior college.

"Steinthal's a shooter," said Payne, who expects to use a three-guard alignment much of the time. "Josh is a gym rat. He's fanatical in his approach to the game."

Petraitis, a native of Lithuania, came to OSU from Weatherford JC in Texas, along with his girlfriend, Reda Kakeranaite, a newcomer to the women's basketball team. A member of the Lithuanian national junior team, Petraitis averaged 13.7 ppg and 6.0 rpg at Weatherford last year.

"He's a kid who can do a lot of things," Payne said. "He's a really good passer, he can motor the ball upcourt, he can

1998-99 OREGON STATE SCHEDULE

Nov.	19	Idaho State
	28	California-Irvine
Dec.	1	*Colorado State
	4	Arkansas-Pine Bluff
	17	Chicago State
	21-23	#Pearl Harbor Classic
	30	College of Notre Dame (CA)
Jan.	2	@Stanford
	4	@California
	7	UCLA
	9	Southern California
	14	@Washington
	16	@Washington State
	21	Arizona State
	23	Arizona
	30	Oregon
Feb.	4	@Southern California
	7	@UCLA
	11	Washington
	13	Washington State
	18	@Arizona
	20	@Arizona State
	27	@Oregon
Mar	4	California
	6	Stanford

@ Road Games
* Rose Garden, Portland OR
\# Laie, HI (vs. BYU-Hawaii, first round; also Alabama, Michigan State, Pepperdine, Texas Tech, Tulsa and Weber State)

make shots, get to the basket."

Jones, a candidate for the power forward slot, averaged 13.6 ppg and 9.7 rpg and blocked 113 shots last year at Skyline JC in the San Francisco Bay Area. "He's not a great scorer and he's a little lean," Payne said, "but he's athletic and a good rebounder."

The three newcomers also give the Beavers some valuable experience Payne said he hasn't enjoyed in all his time at OSU. "Ever since I've been here, it seems like we've been infants," he said. "That maturity is going to help us."

Returnees include 6-11 sophomore **Jason Heidi** (3.6 ppg, 2.7 rpg), who will be given a chance to win the starting center spot. Heidi scored 12 points in 16 minutes against Stanford last year, but needs to improve his conditioning to become a consistent factor.

Junior **Iyan Walker** (3.7 ppg, 2.1 rpg), a 6-8 junior forward, and **Sasa Petrovic** (1.3 ppg, 1.3 rpg), a 6-8 senior forward, also should see playing time.

The Beavers will try to find minutes for 7-1, 232-pound junior center **George von Backstrom**, a native of Pretoria, South Africa, who red-shirted last year after arriving as a JC transfer.

Payne recruited two high school players, neither of whom figure to see significant action this season. **Adam Masten** is a 6-5 point guard and the son of his coach at Sprague HS in Salem, Ore. **Moses Olson** is a 6-3 shooting guard from Churchill HS in Eugene, Ore.

"I feel better about this team and program than I ever have," Payne said. "We're molding ourselves into a group of people who are committed to what we're doing.

"We're unfortunate in the fact that we happened to find ourselves in this predicament when the league was at its unprecedented best. I think the question remains: What does improvement mean to your relative position in the league?"

adidas Blue Ribbon Analysis

BACKCOURT .... C BENCH/DEPTH C
FRONTCOURT .... D INTANGIBLES .... D+

The likely answer to Payne's final question is that improvement by the Beavers may not be evident in their place in the conference standings. Optimism and new blood notwithstanding, this is no time to be playing in the Pac-10 Conference without big-time talent, and the Beavers still don't have enough.

Oregon State appears in good hands with Tanner at the point, and there should be ample scoring from the wings. But nearly every team in the conference can make those claims, and what separates the better clubs is a complementary frontcourt game. The Beavers are lacking in that department.

"The league is a bear right now," Payne said.

And the Beavers are still prey.

(J.F.)

SOUTHERN CALIFORNIA

LOCATION .... Los Angeles, CA
CONFERENCE Pacific-10
LAST SEASON .... 9-19 (.321)
CONFERENCE RECORD 5-13 (8th)
STARTERS LOST/RETURNING 3/2
NICKNAME .... Trojans
COLORS .... Cardinal & Gold
HOMECOURT ..... Los Angeles Sports Arena (15,509)
COACH .... Henry Bibby (UCLA '72)
RECORD AT SCHOOL .... 26-39 (3 yrs.)
CAREER RECORD .... 26-39 (3 yrs.)
ASSISTANTS .... David Miller (Springfield '85)
Silvey Dominguez (New Mexico '75)
Joe Callero (Central Washington '86)
TEAM WINS (last 5 yrs.) 16-7-11-17-9
RPI (last 5 yrs.) 118-193-116-54-177
1997-98 FINISH .... No conference tournament.

This whole business of losing basketball games in the Pac-10 Conference has been fairly awkward for Henry Bibby. He's not comfortable with it, certainly not resigned to it, but mostly not familiar with it.

Bibby, beginning his fourth season as coach of the Trojans, knew the conference in a different era, when it was the Pac-8, or more accurately UCLA and the Seven Dwarfs.

The point guard for the Bruins during his playing days, Bibby was the point guard on teams that were 87-3 and won three NCAA titles from 1969-72. UCLA didn't lose a conference game his junior and senior seasons.

"It's completely different now," Bibby said of the conference. "During those times, we would beat the Stanfords and the Cals and the Washingtons, people like that.

"When I first came back, because I hadn't been part of the league for a while, I thought those teams (still) couldn't play any basketball. But there's a major difference in the conference from when I played.

"Stanford wasn't even a team you'd think about when I played," he said. "It was an automatic win. Now you can't win at Maples (Pavilion). You just don't walk into the Pac-10 and win a game."

Having seen life on the other side, Bibby is determined to guide his Trojans into the upper half of an increasingly challenging Pac-10. "It gets better every year," he said.

The Trojans, by all accounts, should also be improved this season. The most compelling bit of evidence was their strong finish a year a year ago. On the heels of a seven-game skid that left their record at 7-19, the Trojans scored a 91-90 overtime conquest of defending national champ Arizona and a 46-point thrashing of win-starved Arizona State.

Bibby hopes the rewards of those season-ending victories—marking the first time since 1983 USC won its final two games of the year—serve as motivation this year.

"You don't know how things like that happen," he said. "One day the light turns on and the kids decide they believe what you're saying. Beating a powerhouse like Arizona can change everything around you, give you a lot of confidence.

"I think we were growing at the end of last year. We were in a lot of ballgames—we just weren't good enough to win some of the games we should have won. I think this year we'll be better overall."

USC features a deep and balanced roster, but Bibby said he will rely on three upperclassmen—6-8 junior forward **Jarvis Turner**, 6-2 senior guard **Larry Ayuso** and 6-7 senior forward **Adam Spanich**.

Turner (10.6 ppg, 5.3 rpg) broke his hand just before the Pac-10 season, forcing him to sit out six games, all of which the Trojans lost. He had 19 points and 11 rebounds in the upset of Stanford, and led the team in rebounding seven times in 18 conference games.

"Turner can be a leader for us," Bibby said. "He's one of the oldest guys on the team. He's been here. He's going to be a stable factor for us. He's a guy we have to depend on. He can go inside, he can go outside, he can rebound with people. He can be as good as he wants to be."

Bibby expects Ayuso (8.8 ppg, 1.6 rpg, 36 assists, 24 steals .359 three-point percentage) to be a more consistent shooter this season. "Ayuso has to come through," Bibby said. "He didn't have a great year shooting the ball. People who saw the Arizona and Arizona State games, they saw the old Larry Ayuso."

Ayuso, who converted just under 40 percent of his three-pointers as a sophomore, averaged 19.0 ppg and shot 50 percent from beyond the arc in his final three games last year. "Who knows why he shot the ball in those games and couldn't shoot the basketball in those other games," Bibby said.

Spanich (12.0 ppg, 2.8 rpg, .420 three-point percentage) is the team's top returning scorer and led the Pac-10 with 73 three-pointers, despite starting just seven games. "He does so many things for us," Bibby said. "He has a nose to rebound and gives you instant offense."

A key newcomer will be 6-3 junior guard **Quincy Wilder** (23.1 ppg, 6.5 rpg, 3.7 apg, 3.2 spg at Highline CC in Des Moines, Wash.), who is versatile enough he could play any of three backcourt positions.

"He's very physical, very athletic," Bibby said of Wilder, who scored 20 points or more in 23 games last season. "He's a mentally tough player and an excellent defensive player. The kid's going to meet the challenge. But we're giving him time to make the adjustments. He had a very good junior college career, but it's a different ball game once you get to Division I."

Kevin Augustine (6.3 ppg, 2.3 rpg, 96 assists 22 steals), a 6-0 sophomore, figures to wind up as the starting point guard after drawing 10 starting assignments a year ago. "Kevin can do a lot of things," Bibby said. "He gives us a lot of leadership and brings a winning attitude."

Bibby is reluctant to identify a firm starting lineup, or anything close to it.

"Sure, you'd like to have five (players set)," he said. "We weren't good enough last year to have five."

Other returnees include three sophomores_6-4 shooting guard **Jeff Trepagnier** (5.3 ppg, 3.5 rpg in 16.4 minutes), 6-6 forward **Shannon Swillis** (3.7 ppg, 5.9 rpg), and 6-8 forward **Greg Lakey** (5.3 ppg, 3.7 rpg). All three should have escalated roles this season.

The Trojans' incoming recruiting class, headlined by Wilder, was rated No. 15 in the nation by ESPN, and Bibby expects many of the newcomers to lend a hand.

Brian Scalabrine (16.1 ppg, 9.6 rpg in 1996-97 at Highline CC in Des Moines, Wash.), is a 6-9, 240-pound sophomore who sat out last season after teaming with Wilder to build a 31-1 record two years ago.

Likewise, the four freshmen have winning backgrounds in common. **Sam Clancy** (17.5 ppg, 10.5 rpg, 2.0 bpg at St. Edwards HS/Cleveland, Ohio) is a 6-8, 240-pound forward who earned fourth-team *Parade* All-America honors after leading his team to Ohio's large-school state title.

Teammates at Westchester HS in Los Angeles, 6-7, 215-pound forward **David Bluthenthal** (21 ppg, 11 rpg) and 5-10 point guard **Brandon Granville** (12 ppg, 10 apg, 3 spg) guided the Comets to a 30-3 record and the California Division I state title. Bluthenthal was chosen L.A. City Section 4-A Player of the Year, and Granville was a *USA Today* honorable mention All-America selection.

Another freshman possibly headed the team's way is 6-4, 220-pound small forward **Jason Thomas** (23 ppg as a junior at Dominguez HS/Compton, Calif.)., who is a quarterback on the Trojans' football team.

"I'm looking for winners," Bibby said. "There are a lot of (talented) individuals out there, guys who don't win. We want to play winning basketball. We're looking for guys who know what it feels like to win."

The Trojans are young, but that doesn't scare Bibby. "That's what I'm excited about," he said. "It takes time to build a program. How long did it take Stanford to get where they are? It took them a long time. That's what we're doing here. It's hard to be patient, but I'm not concerned with what people think. My concern is, are we working to get there? Are we getting some of the kids we need?"

Gradually, Bibby sees it happening.

1998-99 SOUTHERN CALIFORNIA SCHEDULE

Nov.	17	San Diego State
	20	@Nevada-Las Vegas
	24	Long Beach State
	30	St. Bonaventure
Dec.	4	@California-Santa Barbara
	9	Loyola Marymount
	12	@Kansas
	21	American
	29	Arkansas State
Jan.	2	Arizona State
	4	Arizona
	7	@Oregon
	9	@Oregon State
	14	Stanford
	16	California
	20	UCLA
	28	@Washington
	30	@Washington State
Feb.	4	Oregon State
	6	Oregon
	11	@California
	13	@Stanford
	17	@UCLA
	25	Washington
	27	Washington State
Mar.	4	@Arizona
	6	@Arizona State

@ Road Games

adidas Blue Ribbon Analysis

BACKCOURT .... C+ BENCH/DEPTH .... B
FRONTCOURT .... C+ INTANGIBLES C

Once more, the Trojans are perhaps the toughest team in the Pac-10 to pigeonhole. They seem to have talent, depth and balance, but they are very young, have no winning track record at the Division I level and probably lack the muscle up front to contend with the league's best teams.

Frankly, no one is really sure what to make of the Trojans, least of all Bibby.

One thing's for sure, USC will have to play better defense than a year ago if it hopes to make a serious bid at cracking the league's upper division. The Trojans ranked last in the Pac-10 in field-goal percentage defense (46.5 percent) and eighth in scoring defense (80.4 ppg).

That will come, Bibby believes, if the Trojans embrace a team approach. "I think we're solid at every position. I don't think we're great at every position," he said. "The team concept is going to be very important for us. If we can play team ball, we can be in a lot of games."

And what will that net the Trojans in the final ledger?

"I don't really expect anything," Bibby said, declining to put limits on his team's potential. "We have to motivate them and get them to a point where they are going to be competitive. I think we can be in there with anybody."

Maybe they can be. But Bibby, like almost everyone else, will have to wait and see.

(J.F.)

WASHINGTON STATE

LOCATION .... **Pullman, WA**
CONFERENCE **Pacific-10**
LAST SEASON .... **10-19 (.345)**
CONFERENCE RECORD .... **3-15 (t-9th)**
STARTERS LOST/RETURNING **1/4**
NICKNAME .... **Cougars**
COLORS .... **Crimson & Gray**
HOMECOURT .... **Friel Court (12,058)**
COACH .... **Kevin Eastman (Richmond '77)**
RECORD AT SCHOOL .... **59-59 (4 yrs.)**
CAREER RECORD .... **183-134 (11 yrs.)**
ASSISTANTS .... **Warren Riley (Indiana '87)**
Jeff Maher (Penn State '85)
Lorenzo Hall (Cal State Hayward '95)
TEAM WINS (last 5 yrs.) **20-18-17-13-10**
RPI (last 5 yrs.) **50-70-68-144-184**
1997-98 FINISH .... **No conference tournament.**

A cynic might wonder if coach Kevin Eastman has spent too much time in Pullman, Wash. How else can you explain this statement?

"I found last year to be one of the most enjoyable years we've had," Eastman said of a season that produced just 10 wins overall and left the Cougars in a share of the Pac-10 basement.

Hey coach, you thought last season was big fun, wait 'til you get a load of the competition in the Pac-10 this year.

But Eastman thinks of himself as a realist, and he knows the road still is rough for WSU. He knew it heading into last year, too, and that's at the heart of why he came away with at least some sense of satisfaction.

"The team played so hard and we were in games we shouldn't have been in," he said. "The attitude was fantastic all year. That team really overachieved."

The Cougars, in fact, lost six games by three points or fewer, plus another game in overtime. With any luck in those games, WSU might have been a .500 team, or close to it.

And considering who the Cougars had on their roster—and who they didn't—that's probably not too bad.

Aside from perhaps the Florida Marlins, no team in sports seemingly has lost more personnel in recent years than the Cougars. Starting in the spring of 1996, when he dismissed point guard Donminic Ellison for a series of off-the-court problems, Eastman has seen the exit of six key players for reasons other than graduation.

The defectors last year were would-be starting guard Beau Archibald, who transferred after his father died of prostate cancer, and projected starting shooting guard Ron Selleaze, who never qualified academically after signing a letter-of-intent out of junior college. Selleaze wound up at BYU, where he was the Cougars' top scorer.

On the eve of the Pac-10 season, the Cougars lost starting small forward Rodrigo de la Fuente, who signed a professional contract in his native Spain.

The result was a team that relied on workhorse power forward Carlos Daniel, but had little depth or experience. Daniel averaged 16.1 ppg and 10.1 rpg, but now has also exited, via graduation.

Eastman says he has no regrets about the way he's run his program. The two dismissals were necessary, he says, and he will not compromise his standards for the bottom line.

Eventually, though, that bottom line is how his program will be judged, and he has no illusions about that. "College basketball is a results business, regardless of how anybody may try to sugarcoat it," he said. "Our players understood that. Because we were very open and honest and realistic with them, it helped us in terms of reacting to the year.

"The team definitely knew that had we kept the guys, it would have been a whole different story last year."

Now the Cougars face the prospect of a third-straight losing season, after six years of winning. Some of that comes with the territory, Eastman believes.

"You look at Washington State's history, and it's been a little cyclical," he said, alluding to seven straight losing seasons before the run of success that began in 1991. "It's not what you see in an Arizona or a UCLA."

There will be no mistaking the Cougars for either of those teams this year, although Eastman remains optimistic that his squad will outdistance expectations. "We'll be improved," he said.

How much the Cougars progress is likely to be a direct result of how much three newcomers are able to contribute.

Eastman expects instant offense from 6-2 junior guard **Jan-Michael Thomas** (20.5 ppg at San Joaquin Delta JC/Stockton, Calif.), who hit 138 three-pointers a year ago as an honorable mention JC All-America pick.

"I really liked his game when I saw him the previous summer," Eastman said. "He's able to drive it to the basket, he's got good quickness and he can shoot the ball. He's the kind of guard I really like."

Freshman **Mike Bush**, a 6-6 wing, could also have significant early impact. Bush averaged 20 ppg and 11 rpg at Mercersburg Academy in Pennsylvania two years ago, then transferred to Kent HS in Washington, where he lived with an older brother last year.

After starting five games at tight end for the football team, however, Bush's eligibility was called into question, and school officials discovered he already had played four years of high school sports. That kept him off the basketball court last season.

Eastman said Bush reminds him of ex-Lakers guard Michael Cooper. "He's a real slasher, very good at stealing passes," Eastman said. "He has that kind of game where if someone asked, 'Was Michael Cooper a great shooter?' You'd say no. But he gets into passing lanes, runs the floor real well and is a slithery type of guy."

Mostly, Eastman is banking on the possibility that Bush will blossom as a basketball player given the chance to concentrate on a single sport. "He's a very good athlete," Eastman said.

Another mystery arrival is **Eddie Miller**, a 6-8, 225-pound sophomore forward, who sat out last basketball season for a different set of reasons. Miller played his freshman year at Ventura (Calif.) CC, which shut down its program after the 1997 season.

"Eddie has a scorer's mentality and had a full year to work on his individual playing skills," Eastman said. "He can score inside, but he also can shoot the 15-16 footer. Carlos (Daniel) was so locked inside. Eddie probably isn't as good as Carlos inside, but he's better outside."

Anchoring WSU's returning group are forward **Chris Crosby** and point guards **Blake Pengelly** and **Kab Kazadi**.

Crosby (11.8 ppg, 3.2 rpg, .414 FG percentage) is a 6-7 junior forward who made 19 starts a year ago. He scored 21 points at BYU, hitting five of six three-pointers, and had a stretch of four games where he averaged three three-pointers per game.

But Crosby wasn't a consistent shooter, hitting just .315 from beyond the arc in conference play. "Chris has skill. He can shoot the ball," Eastman said. "He'll get more comfortable on the floor as he lets the game come to him."

Crosby, who grew up in Littleton, Colo., spent several weeks during the summer training at the Colorado School of Mines, where he worked out with Bill Romanowski and Ed McCaffrey of the Super Bowl champion Denver Broncos. "He learned what a real workout is," said Eastman, who hopes Crosby can be a better rebounder this year. "He said Romanowski was at times super-human. It was an eye-opener for him."

Pengelly (8.0 ppg, 4.1 apg, .398 three-point percentage) is a 5-10, 163-pound junior whom Eastman called the team's strongest player, pound for pound. The problem is, Pengelly doesn't have any extra pounds, and that by going nearly 37 minutes per game in conference play, he wore himself down.

He should get more help at the point this year from Kazadi (7.3 ppg, 3.1 rpg), who was forced to slide over to the shooting-guard slot at midseason when de la Fuente turned pro.

"Both guys had to play major minutes last year and we took some lumps because of it," Eastman said.

Eastman wants Pengelly to shoot more and Kazadi to foul less (he fouled out of nine games a year ago). He hopes both can help WSU improve on its last-place conference ranking in turnover margin (minus-3.3 per game).

The Cougars hope 6-10, 272-pound senior **Leif Nelson** (5.5 ppg, 4.4 rpg, .496 FG percentage) can hold down the center spot. Nelson started 24 games last year, but averaged fewer than 17 minutes per game. "He's just got to go in spurts," conceded Eastman, who will use 6-10 sophomore **Brian Stewart** 1.0 ppg, 0.9 rpg) as Nelson's backup.

The Cougars have high hopes for 6-5 senior forward **Kojo Mensah-Bonsu** (9.2 ppg, 4.5 rpg), who scored 21 points in a non-conference game vs. Boise State, but fouled out of six games. "Kojo's a pretty difficult player to match up with," Eastman said. "He's really an inside player, but he has the ability to take you off the dribble and is a good enough shooter you can't leave him wide open."

Senior forward **Steve Slotemaker** (5.8 ppg, 3.0 rpg), a 6-9 former walkon, could also see his role elevated. "Slotemaker has good skills," Eastman said. "The biggest thing with him is he's got to have confidence in himself. I have confidence in him."

Rounding out the squad will be 6-3 senior guard **Will Hutchens** (2.1 ppg, 0.9 rpg) and wiry 6-8 freshman forward **Milton Riley** (Compton HS/Compton, Calif.), who could end up being redshirted.

1998-99 WASHINGTON STATE SCHEDULE

Nov.	16	Central Washington
	19-22	#Top of The World Classic
	28	@Gonzaga
Dec.	2	Portland State
	5	@Eastern Washington
	8	Brigham Young
	20	@Idaho
	28-29	##Sun Classic
Jan.	3	*Washington
	7	@Arizona
	9	@Arizona State
	14	Oregon
	16	Oregon State
	21	@Stanford
	23	@California
	28	Southern California
	30	UCLA
Feb.	4	Arizona State
	6	Arizona
	11	@Oregon
	13	@Oregon State
	18	California
	20	Stanford
	25	@UCLA
	27	@Southern California
Mar.	6	@Washington

@ Road Games
* Spokane Arena, Spokane, WA
\# Fairbanks, AK (vs. Alaska-Fairbanks, first round; also Arkansas, Nebraska, New Mexico State, Villanova and Wisconsin)
\## El Paso, TX (vs. UTEP, first round; also Detroit and Grambling)

adidas Blue Ribbon Analysis

BACKCOURT .... **C+** **BENCH/DEPTH** .... **C**
FRONTCOURT .... **D** **INTANGIBLES** .... **C**

Things won't get dramatically easier for the Cougars, but at least they should be more stable. If WSU can simply get through a season without losing a player to misbehavior, academics, European pro ball or alien abduction, Kevin Eastman may feel a sense of calm he hasn't enjoyed in a while.

WSU should be a deeper and more athletic team than a year ago, but in this league that's all relative. Virtually everyone else in the conference also is improved, and a couple of those that slipped a notch did so from very high vantage points.

The Cougars still are not as physical up front as most teams in the Pac-10, and will rely heavily on newcomers. In a nutshell, there are still more questions than answers.

Washington State is not an easy place to win, given its remote geography and modest basketball history. Eastman excelled his first two seasons, but there is a growing sense he did that with ex-coach Kelvin Sampson's players.

Sure, there have been real and defensible reasons for the Cougars' difficulties over the last two years, but Eastman understands the program must eventually produce success again.

With two years remaining on his contract, Eastman will want to show some progress this season in order to get a tangible vote of confidence from athletic director Rick Dickson.

It's hard to imagine that progress will be significant in terms of wins and losses.

(J.F.)

adidas Blue Ribbon Analysis
GRADING SYSTEM

- A+ equal to very best in country—Final Four-caliber unit
- A among the best in the land—worthy of deep NCAA run
- B+ talented, versatile and experienced—NCAA-NIT ability
- B solid and productive winners—league and post-season contenders
- C+ average to above-average—may contend in a weaker league
- C average to mediocre—second division in a strong league
- D+ below average, inconsistent—second division in a weaker league
- D well below average—losing season virtually certain
- F non-Division I ability—an underdog every night

PATRIOT LEAGUE

adidas BLUE RIBBON FORECAST
1. Navy
2. Bucknell
3. Lehigh
4. Lafayette
5. Colgate
6. Army
7. Holy Cross

ALL-CONFERENCE TEAM
G—Brett Eppenhimer, SR, Lehigh
G—Brian Ehlers, JR, Lafayette
G—Skip Victor, SR, Navy
F—Martin Gilliard, SR, Bucknell
F—Ben Wandtke, SR, Colgate

PLAYER OF THE YEAR
Ben Eppenhimer, SR, Lehigh

NEWCOMER OF THE YEAR
Ryan Serravalle, FR, Holy Cross

1998-99 CONFERENCE TOURNAMENT
Feb. 27-28, March 4, Christl Arena, West Point, NY

1997-98 CHAMPION
Lafayette, Navy (regular season)
Navy (conference tournament)

1997-98 POSTSEASON PARTICIPANTS
Postseason Record: 0-1 (.000)
NCAA
Navy (1st round)

TOP BACKCOURTS
1. Army
2. Lafayette
3. Lehigh

TOP FRONTCOURTS
1. Bucknell
2. Navy
3. Lafayette

ON THE WAY UP
Lehigh

ON THE WAY DOWN
Holy Cross

INSIDE THE NUMBERS
• 1997-98 conference RPI: 27 (of 30)
• Conference RPI (last 5 years): 30-28-33-28-27

DID YOU KNOW?
Lehigh senior guard Brett Eppenhimer's 24.7 ppg last season ranked fourth in the country, and makes him the second-leading returning scorer in Division I this year...Look for Lafayette junior guard Brian Ehlers to become the league's 31st 1,000-point scorer. He needs 241 points to reach the milestone...The conference tournament's quarterfinal and semifinal rounds will be played at Army, with the championship game to be played at the home of the highest remaining seed...CBS will televise the Army-Navy matchup at Annapolis on Feb. 13...Bucknell and Army were among the top 20 schools drawing the highest number of people tuning in to their games via the Teamline call-in service...Navy's Hassan Booker, who graduated last spring after two selections to the all-league team, won the second annual Chip Hilton Award, given to a player who has demonstrated personal character on and off the court. Booker's uniform and shoes are in a display at the Basketball Hall of Fame in Springfield, Mass.

(T.D.)

ARMY

LOCATION .... **West Point, NY**
CONFERENCE .... **Patriot League**
LAST SEASON .... **8-19 (.296)**
CONFERENCE RECORD .... **2-10 (7th)**
STARTERS LOST/RETURNING **1/4**
NICKNAME .... **Cadets, Black Knights**
COLORS .... **Black, Gold & Gray**
HOMECOURT .... **Christl Arena (5,043)**
COACH .... **Pat Harris (Army '79)**
RECORD AT SCHOOL .... **8-19 (1 yr.)**
CAREER RECORD .... **8-19 (1 yr.)**
ASSISTANTS .... **Denny Carroll (Dayton '71)**
Walt Corbean (Xavier '91)
Marty Coyne (Army '81)
TEAM WINS (last 5 yrs.) **7-12-7-10-8**
RPI (last 5 yrs.) **277-266-307-290-285**
1997-98 FINISH .... **Lost in conference quarterfinal.**

Well, well, well, what's this? Signs of life in West Point?

Could be. On the surface, the Patriot League's whipping boy didn't have much of a season last year. Pat Harris began his Army coaching career by watching his team experience a 33-point schooling at the hands of Duke on opening day. That's bad enough, but when one considers that Harris played for the Blue Devils' Mike Krzyzewski at the Point 20 years ago, it's even tougher to take.

The Cadets' first two victories came against non-Division I schools. Still, midway through its schedule, Army stood at a fairly respectable (well, for Army) 6-7. That's when the wheels came off. Eight straight losses consigned the team to its usual resting place at the bottom of the league.

After a couple of February wins, the Cadets were pounded by Navy in the opening round of the conference tournament. Their eight wins were two fewer than the team managed the season before. Fourteen of the team's 19 losses came by at least 14 points; eight games ended in losses of 20 points or more.

Talk about a wake up call. Harris did a fine job playing the point for the last Army teams to enjoy substantial success: 20 wins in 1976-77 and a National Invitation Tournament appearance a year later. Those were the days, eh?

"We felt like we were caught between a rock and a hard place last season," he said. "We had only one senior on our roster, and because of the timing of my hiring, we were way behind in recruiting."

Hmmm, you're thinking at this point. I thought you said something about "signs of life."

Coach?

"I felt as though last season was a successful season," Harris said. "As a coaching staff, we learned a lot about ourselves and our players. The kids were indoctrinated into our type of system, so now they know what to expect. We accomplished everything we wanted. We faced a lot of adversity throughout the season, and I thought we handled it well."

Harris is overstating the case a bit. Had the Cadets accomplished everything they wanted, surely the win total would have been higher. That aside, there are many reasons to believe that this program has—finally—turned a corner. And while Army isn't ready to compete for the league championship just yet, this season should prove far less painful than the last several.

Four starters return, including arguably the Patriot's best backcourt. A pair of players were chosen to the league's all-rookie team last year. And the team's recruiting efforts—helped enormously by Harris' irrepressible boosting of the entire West Point experience—seem to be paying dividends.

Mindful of the pressure any Army freshman faces, Harris is taking care not to put undue pressure on his newcomers. The Cadets finally have a chance to work young players into the lineup, rather than throw them to the wolves and watch the resulting carnage. The coach also plans to intensify practices in hopes of proving his point that "competition makes people better." Throw in a little depth and some lucky breaks, and the result may be a light at the end of the tunnel.

"We were really thin at some positions last season," Harris said. "In many cases, we were just one-deep at certain spots, and that forced our hand a little bit. That shouldn't be the case this season. Our team will be young this year. If we are patient with these kids, we are going to see some great things from them in the future."

For the present, Army will rely on its veteran backcourt to set the pace. The starters are 6-0 senior point guard **Babe Kwasniak** (9.1 ppg, 2.9 rpg) and 6-2 senior swingman **George Tatum** (13.1 ppg, 4.4 rpg).

Team captain Kwasniak posted team highs in assists (107) and steals (39) while playing a whopping 34.3 minutes a game. He also hit .338 percent of his three-pointers and .813 percent of his free-throws. On the minus side, he turned over the basketball 91 times and shot a mediocre .353 percent from the floor. Kwasniak showed signs of wear by season's end, a reflection of his status as the team's only true point man. However, he provided a sterling example of hustle to Army's younger players.

Tatum was a preseason all-league pick last year, but an abdominal muscle injury limited his effectiveness for the entire season. He led the Cadets in scoring and was second in steals, but did not shoot the ball well and saw his production drop from his sophomore season. If healthy, Tatum is a multi-pronged threat, capable of dropping 20 points on an opponent and grabbing 10 boards on any given night.

Army's backcourt rotation should receive a tremendous boost with the return of 5-10 senior **Jamie Uptgraft**, who spent last season away from West Point. Uptgraft began his Black Knight career as the starting point man, and in addition to handling the basketball with care, he is a dangerous outside shooter who averaged 10.1 ppg and 2.8 rpg two years ago. That gives Harris options: He can rest Kwasniak when necessary, for example, as well as go with a three-guard setup capable of putting points on the board in a hurry.

He may not play a whole lot, but 6-1 senior guard **Chris Crawford** (2.8 ppg, 0.9 rpg) is nonetheless a valuable player. He provides 10 to 15 minutes a night, is a decent shooter and can spot-start as necessary. Crawford also has shown some leadership skills, which will prove valuable on this young team.

All in all, Army's guards will be the team's bedrock.

"Collectively, our senior class offers so much to the program," Harris said. "Babe Kwasniak provides a lot of energy, George Tatum carries force, Chris Crawford is just a great person on and off the court, and Jamie Uptgraft is much more mature and confident in the direction he wants to pursue. That's going to provide some very positive leadership at the top for our underclassmen."

A trio of players who saw little time a season ago will vie for more minutes in the backcourt this year. The most promising is 6-2 sophomore **Aaron Horn** (4.0 ppg, 1.0 rpg), who earned a late-season call up from the JV squad and impressed the coaching staff with a 31-minute performance in his only varsity game.

Horn can play both guard slots, which is a plus. He'll be joined by 6-0 sophomore **Clifton Kyle** (0.4 ppg, 0.4 ppg)

1998-99 ARMY SCHEDULE

Nov.	14	@Vanderbilt
	18	@Quinnipiac
	22	@Ohio State
	25	@Central Connecticut
	28	Bethany
Dec.	1	@North Carolina State
	2	@Wofford
	5	@Columbia
	7	Yale
	10	@Manhattan
	21	@Seton Hall
	30	@Marist
Jan.	2	Cornell
	5	Lehigh
	9	@Colgate
	13	@Bucknell
	16	@Lafayette
	19	Navy
	24	Holy Cross
	26	SUNY-New Paltz
	30	@Lehigh
Feb.	3	Colgate
	6	Bucknell
	9	Lafayette
	13	@Navy
	17	@Holy Cross
27-Mar.	5	#Patriot League Tournament

@ Road Games
\# First and second rounds Feb. 27-28 at West Point, NY. Championship game March 5 at homecourt of highest remaining seed.

and 6-0 junior **Chris Dempsey** (2.0 ppg, 0.4 rpg), each of whom played in 16 games last year.

Several freshmen will try to work their way into the lineup at both the point- and two-guard positions. At the former are 5-11 **Chris Spatola** (Lawrence Academy/Pepperell, Mass.), 5-11 **Frank Schafer** (Roswell HS/Roswell, Ga.) and 6-1 **Joe Quinn** (Xaverian HS/Brooklyn, N.Y.).

The newcomers at off-guard are 6-4 **Parker Allie** (Crowley HS/Fort Worth, Texas) and 6-5 **Neil Forbes** (North Kingstown HS/North Kingstown, R.I.), a couple of good shooters with size.

Army is hurt up front by the two-year loss of starting forward Dax Pearson (9.1 ppg, 2.9 rpg), who is in Chile on a Mormon mission. He'll be back in the fall of 2000 with two years of eligibility remaining.

However, Harris welcomes back two returning starters who enjoyed all-rookie seasons as freshmen a year ago. **Joe Clark** (8.4 ppg, 4.6 rpg), a 6-5 sophomore swingman, proved to be a presence from the floor and on the boards. Particularly impressive is his .391 shooting from beyond the arc. Clark spent much of the offseason trying to round out his offensive game. His only worry may be the ankle he broke in the spring, although he was expected to be at full strength when practice started.

The Cadets' other freshman find last season was 6-5 **Seth Barrett** (7.7 ppg, 4.9 rpg), the team's leading rebounder and its top returning shot blocker (13 blocked shots last year). The muscular Barrett got better as the season went on. He played in the pivot a great deal as a freshman and should benefit tremendously if Harris can find a center and allow him to move to power forward.

Depth could prove to be a problem at forward, as the reserves are either newcomers or little-used career bench warmers. Count 6-4 junior **Jeff McFarland** (1.5 ppg, 0.8 rpg), who saw action in 23 games, among the latter. A preseason knee injury limited 6-5 sophomore **Mohamed Desoky** (0 points, 0 rebounds) to two games, while 6-6 sophomore **Josh Richardson** (0.8 ppg, 0.8 rpg) played in only five games after his promotion to the varsity squad at midseason.

Harris is very high on 6-7 freshman **Jont Harrell** (Charlotte Latin HS/Charlotte, N.C.), an athletic youngster who shined on several fronts as a scholastic player. He could contribute right away, as could 6-5 freshman **Charles Woodruff** (Lubbock HS/Lubbock, Texas), who played well at USMA Prep last year.

Because of the weak bench, 6-6 freshmen **Jonathan Freeman** (Marquette HS/Clarkson Valley, Mo.) and **Cory Scott** (Homestead HS/Mequon, Wis.) could get their shots as well.

As usual, the Cadets must rely on unproven players in the paint. In fact, 6-10 freshman **Matt Rutledge** (Cy-Fair HS/Cypress, Texas) and 6-9 freshman **Willie Bass** (Indian Springs HS/Birmingham, Ala.) will get the chance to step in immediately. Rutledge is the more polished player, with a nice offensive touch perhaps giving him the advantage. Bass spent last season at USMA Prep. Importantly, each offers size, a valuable commodity on a team that blocked only 56 shots a year ago.

Veterans **Jonathan Westfield** (1.6 ppg, 1.5 rpg), a 6-7 junior, and **Tom Dunaway** (1.4 ppg, 0.8 rpg), a 6-7 sophomore, will probably continue to see little time if either Rutledge or Bass plays decently.

adidas Blue Ribbon Analysis

BACKCOURT	B+	**BENCH/DEPTH**	D
FRONTCOURT	C+	**INTANGIBLES**	C

Second-year head coach Pat Harris hopes that this is the season that breaks Army's rut of 7-to 12-win seasons, and he could be right. A veteran, talented backcourt, anchored by Babe Kwasniak and George Tatum, should provide both performance and leadership, while developing stars Joe Clark and Seth Barrett appear set to contribute at forward for several years.

In addition, Harris put together a nice recruiting class, and if his starters remain healthy, the coach can ease his newcomers into the lineup, offering them gradual seasoning. And if Jamie Uptgraft has found himself, Army will have yet another weapon at its disposal.

That said, Cadet fans shouldn't expect miracles. Center remains a problem area, with Harris hoping for immediate help from freshmen. And beyond the starting lineup is a frightening paucity of reliable, experienced bench help, especially in the frontcourt. Beyond that, non-stop losing is a cycle not typically broken in one or two seasons. Army is a unanimous pick by the Patriot League's coaches and SIDs to finish in last place, and with good reason.

But surprises are not out of the question. If that which can go right does, the Cadets may—may—find themselves within striking distance of .500, which would be a major achievement for this program.

(T.D.)

BUCKNELL

LOCATION	**Lewisburg, PA**
CONFERENCE	**Patriot**
LAST SEASON	**35-15 (.464)**
CONFERENCE RECORD	**8-4 (3rd)**
STARTERS LOST/RETURNING	**1/4**
NICKNAME	**Bison**
COLORS	**Orange & blue**
HOMECOURT	**Davis Gym (2,300)**
COACH	**Pat Flannery (Bucknell '80)**
RECORD AT SCHOOL	**61-51 (4 yrs.)**
CAREER RECORD	**61-51 (4 yrs.)**
ASSISTANTS	**Terry Conrad (Bloomsburg '80)**
	Carl Danzig (Baker '87)
	Don Friday (Lebanon Valley '90)
TEAM WINS (last 5 yrs.)	**10-13-17-18-13**
RPI (last 5 yrs.)	**253-206-202-193-219**
1997-98 FINISH	**Lost in conference semifinal.**

Paging Pat Flannery. Your reality check is here.

Up until last season, Bucknell's head man seemed to have the Midas touch. Two of his first three seasons in Division I ended with Flannery winning Patriot League Coach-of-the-Year honors, and the 1996-97 Bison came within a hair of earning an invitation to the NCAA Tournament.

Expectations were high last year, among not only pundits but also Flannery himself. But he came to realize that what the basketball gods give, they also may take away.

They gave Bucknell an all-league first-team pick, J.R. Holden, who averaged 18.2 ppg. They gave players with gifted shooting touches; the Bison led the loop with a .452 field-goal percentage and a .362 three-point percentage. They gave the team an All-League second team pick, **Martin Gilliard**, and a former rookie of the year, **Dan Bowen**.

Ah, but the gods took away as well. They removed defense, as opponents shot .425 from the floor and .377 from behind the arc, and tallied 39 more steals than the Bison. And they certainly must have taken all of Bucknell's lucky socks from their suitcases; the team went just 5-12 on the road.

The Bison's up-and-down season resulted in a 12-14 overall record and an 8-4 league record, good for third place, as play in the Patriot tournament began. With Holden and Gilliard scoring 15 points each and Bowen snaring seven boards, Bucknell squeaked by Holy Cross by four points in the first round. But the team's spotty play caught up with it in a semifinal, when Navy handed the Bison a 19-point trashing, ending their season.

Under Flannery for the last four seasons, the Bison have been rather charming underachievers considered by most observers to be nearly ready, though not totally prepared, to reach the next level. It will be interesting to see how the coach and his players react to lower expectations and the realization that last year, for the first time, all of them disappointed.

Flannery, for one, expects the happy days to return quickly.

"I think the common thread in this group of players is that they have all been involved with winning programs throughout their high school careers, and that success has continued here at Bucknell," he said. "So these players know how to win and know the hard work and effort that it takes to be successful. I think that says a lot about our program."

The most significant challenge is to replace Holden, the work horse point guard who assisted on 116 baskets, totaled 43 steals and poured in 69 treys—all team highs—to go along with his team-high scoring average. The presence of four returning starters and last year's top five rebounders should provide a lift. More importantly, perhaps, is that Flannery has seen a host of his young players emerge quietly into capable, solid performers prepared to make their own marks.

Take 6-4 senior small forward Gilliard, for example. He has steadily improved his game, plays lots of minutes, and is able to contribute from both the frontcourt and the backcourt. In addition to averaging a very respectable 12.0 ppg and 4.6 rpg, he is the guy assigned to guard the opposition's top scorer. And Gilliard, a tenacious defender, is up to the task, making 34 steals a season ago. His intensity is an asset to the Bison; now he must develop some leadership skills. Gilliard is a preseason all-league selection.

The likely starter at power forward is 6-7 junior **Valter Karavanic** (9.2 ppg, 4.8 rpg), a Croatian native. He started all 28 games a year ago and was Bucknell's leading free-throw shooter, at .816 percent. Flannery is counting on Karavanic to provide more offensive punch this year, as the team looks to account for Holden's points, and to hit the boards harder.

Karavanic, like Gilliard, is a versatile player who should see action in other slots. In fact, the two give the Bison a wonderful outside touch in the frontcourt. Each notched 27 treys, with Karavanic taking 76 three-point shots and Gilliard 67.

Bowen (8.8 ppg, 5.7 rpg), a 6-8 junior, was Bucknell's top rebounder and shot blocker, with 37 rejections. He has started 57 consecutive games at center since arriving in Lewisburg, and shot an amazing .566 percent from the floor as a sophomore.

Flannery is optimistic that his starting frontcourt will pick up the slack.

"Last year, there were times when Dan Bowen, Martin Gilliard and Valter Karavanic would end up with big numbers," he said. "Now, for us to be successful, those players will have to do that night in and night out. They know what they need to do, they know what we've lost, and it's their time."

The supporting players up front include 6-8 senior forward **Max Wetzel** (3.9 ppg, 1.8 rpg), a nine-game starter as a junior. Wetzel didn't shoot much, but made the most of his chances, making .543 percent of his shots from the field and dropping in half of his 42 three-point shots. His rebounding and shot blocking (just a pair of snuffs) weren't too impressive for a player of his size, though.

Providing beef down low is 6-6 junior forward **Dyrika Cameron** (3.5 ppg, 3.6 rpg), who put up decent numbers in a shade over 14 minutes a game. A dependable presence on defense, he could crack the starting lineup if his scoring and rebounding continue to improve.

Barring injury, Bowen will play as many minutes in the paint as Flannery can squeeze out of him. That won't leave many opportunities for 6-10 senior **Tom Hauser** (0.9 ppg, 0.6 rpg) and 6-9 sophomore **John McBride** (0.8 ppg, 0.3 rpg). McBride played in only 12 games last season, though he averaged 7.0 ppg and 5.2 rpg in 11 junior varsity games. Hauser shot 4 of 4 from the field in only nine varsity games.

The team's only freshman is 6-5 forward **Peter Santos** of Notre Dame HS in New Haven, Conn., an all-state pick who averaged 16.3 ppg and 9.8 rpg his senior year, when his school made it to the state championship game. Santos has the skills to see quality time as a Bison rookie.

Holden was a dominating point guard, and while the two men who will compete to start in his place have potential, neither will be confused for his predecessor. The more experienced of the pair is 6-2 senior **Willie Callahan** (5.6 ppg, 2.1 rpg), who can fill it up from downtown and slash to the hole. However, the majority of Callahan's playing time over his first three seasons came at the off-guard.

The other candidate is 6-1 sophomore **Nyambi Nyambi** (0.7 ppg, 0.1 rpg), who saw most of his action with the JV squad, for which he averaged 15.1 ppg and nearly three

1998-99 BUCKNELL SCHEDULE

Nov.	14	@Robert Morris
	18	Rider
	21	@Cornell
	23	Scranton
	28-29	#FIU/Money Store Tournament
Dec.	3	St. Francis
	6	*Saint Mary's
	9	@Princeton
	21	@Penn State
	27-28	##Hoosier Classic
Jan.	2	Carnegie Mellon
	6	@Navy
	9	@Holy Cross
	13	Army
	16	Lehigh
	20	@Colgate
	23	George Mason
	27	Lafayette
	31	Navy
Feb.	3	Holy Cross
	6	@Army
	10	@Lehigh
	13	Colgate
	21	@Lafayette
27-Mar.	5	###Patriot League Tournament

@ Road Games
# Miami, FL (vs.Florida International, first round; also Georgia Southern and Northern Illinois)
Indianapolis, IN (vs. Ball State, first round; also Drake and Indiana
First and second rounds Feb. 27 and 28 at West Point, NY. Championship game March 5 at homecourt of highest remaining seed.

assists. He played for just 51 minutes over 17 games as a freshman, giving Holden the occasional breather, but his athleticism and superior ball-handling skills could give him the edge.

If Flannery opts to go with Callahan at the point, he'll probably tap 6-6 junior **Brian Muckle** (4.6 ppg, 3.6 rpg) or 6-4 sophomore **Jake Ramage** (3.9 ppg, 1.6 rpg) to complete the starting backcourt.

Muckle started Bucknell's final 10 games last season, averaging 6.2 ppg and 4.8 rpg in that stretch. A multi-talented player who can shoot, dribble, pass and leap, he has the versatility to play either backcourt slot as well as some small forward.

Ramage was expected to contribute much more than he did, but a foot injury early in the season cost him a dozen games. He did make it back for the last 12 games, scoring 4.7 ppg, and showed himself to be a hard-nosed guy who likes to shoot.

The JV team's best player was 6-4 junior **Shaun Asbury** (1.1 ppg, 0.6 rpg), who saw little action with the varsity squad. He averaged 18.5 ppg and 7.2 rpg as a junior varsity player, and can play guard and forward.

Having watched last year's team flame out on the road, Flannery will send his Bison packing for 10 of their first 12 games this season in an effort to overcome the problem. The schedule includes Rider, Princeton, Penn State and George Mason, and tournaments with Florida International, Georgia Southern and Northern Illinois, and Indiana, Drake and Ball State.

adidas Blue Ribbon Analysis

BACKCOURT .... **C+** **BENCH/DEPTH** .... **C+**
FRONTCOURT .... **B** **INTANGIBLES** .... **B**

The smart money says not to expect a whole lot out of Bucknell this year. The team's best player is gone, and there is no superstar waiting in the wings. After coaxing significant over-achievement out of his team during his first three years, Pat Flannery returned to earth in 1997-98, when a squad with postseason aspirations skidded through a mostly mediocre season. Has the magic gone?

Not necessarily. One doesn't win two coach-of-the-year awards in three seasons without having some ability, and Flannery is smart enough to know that J.R. Holdens are special. They don't come along every year, so when such a player leaves, a smart coach can't anoint one guy to serve as his successor. Rather, the coach will try a scoring-by-committee approach, spreading the ball around to four or five guys with the ability to reach double figures on a nightly basis.

Flannery can do this because he has good shooters on the floor. More significantly, he has improving players who have consistently taken steps to shore up their games. "With J.R. gone, the opportunity to score and be on the line at crunch time is now there," he said. "It's their team now, and the players coming back have demonstrated that they are ready to rise to that challenge."

He had better hope so. Bucknell's frontcourt is solid, though not spectacular, and the guard rotation looks shaky, especially at the critical point position. In addition, the Bison need someone become a leader. Off nights will be fatal; there is no one to whom they can hitch their wagon while they enjoy the ride. However, the pressure is off, and with lower expectations, the team may be able to relax a bit and play its game.

The call here is for a .500 record, an upper-division finish and more than a passing chance to make some noise in the league tournament. Such a performance proved disappointing last season; this year, it wouldn't be half bad.

(T.D)

COLGATE

LOCATION .... **Hamilton, NY**
CONFERENCE .... **Patriot**
LAST SEASON .... **10-18 (.357)**
CONFERENCE RECORD .... **5-7 (4th)**
STARTERS LOST/RETURNING **1/4**
NICKNAME .... **Red Raiders**
COLORS .... **Maroon, Gray & White**
HOMECOURT .... **Cotterell Court (3,100)**
COACH .... **Emmett Davis (St. Lawrence '81)**
RECORD AT SCHOOL .... **First Year**
CAREER RECORD .... **First Year**
ASSISTANTS .... **Rod Balanis (Georgia Tech '94)**
Dennis Csensits (Allentown '90)
TEAM WINS (last 5 yrs.) **17-17-15-12-10**
RPI (last 5 yrs.) **189-118-158-210-246**
1997-98 FINISH .... **Lost in conference semifinal.**

Forgive Colgate basketball fans for declining to dwell on last season's dismal 10-18 record. Forgive them for refusing to focus on the graduation loss of the team's best player. Forgive them for remembering what the Bobby Knights of the world tend to forget: That basketball is just a game.

Forgive the Colgate faithful these and other transgressions. Last Dec. 19, the Red Raiders learned the hard way that there are things more important than hoops. On that sad day, just six games into the season, popular head coach Jack Bruen lost his battle with pancreatic cancer.

The Red Raiders already had significant obstacles to overcome. With superlative center Adonal Foyle leaving school a year early for the first round of the NBA draft, Colgate faced some serious rebuilding for the first time in a long while. Still, Bruen was optimistic. He had told his players of his illness last October, and though his health deteriorated through the beginning of the season, the team was playing .500 ball at the time of his passing. After the tragedy Colgate, led by assistant Paul Aiello, won just seven of its remaining 22 games. The squad posted a one-point win over Lehigh in the opening round of the Patriot League Tournament, then lost by six to Lafayette in the semifinals.

Bruen had just begun his ninth season. His tenure coincided with the Red Raiders' recent glory days, and the legacy he left is impressive: Two league titles, two NCAA Tournament appearances, two Patriot League Coach of the Year awards, dozens of players made better by his tutelage and good humor. Jack Bruen was a large man in ways besides his stature; his shoes are considerable ones to fill.

Colgate will attempt to turn around its floundering program with a longtime Patriot League assistant. Emmett Davis, a 12-year assistant at Navy, was hired as the Red Raiders' new head coach in late April. The Midshipmen played in the NCAA Tournament in five of Davis' 12 seasons in Annapolis. The Colgate job is his first head coaching job, and he has quite a task in front of him.

"I've been working toward this goal for 16 years," Davis said when he was hired. "I've always wanted to work for an institution with a strong academic reputation, and a school like Colgate that is known throughout the country. I also come from upstate New York, which makes it exciting for me. I'm ready for the challenge that lies ahead."

In selecting Davis, the Colgate administration had both pedigree and geography in mind.

"He's worked under one of the finest head coaches in the country in Don DeVoe, and is ready to become a head coach," said Red Raider athletic director Mark Murphy. "His work as Navy's recruiting coordinator has been impressive. Emmett's familiarity with the Patriot League as well as his experience at St. Lawrence, (Davis' alma mater and the place where he began coaching) and his upstate New York roots will allow him to make a smooth transition to the position."

The good news for Davis is that his team welcomes back four starters, including a second-team All-Patriot League selection and three double-figure scorers. The bad news is that the Red Raiders have lost all-league guard Seth Schaeffer, along with his 17.6 ppg, to graduation, and appear to have no one able to step up and be a similar go-to guy on offense.

Colgate's best returning player is 6-6 senior forward **Ben Wandtke** (11.9 ppg, 6.9 rpg), who led the squad in rebounding and was second in scoring. A second-team all-league pick, he shot fairly well from the floor (.437 percent), from behind the three-point line (.344 percent) and from the free-throw line (.790 percent). Wandtke also showed a knack for hard inside play, so look for Davis to slide him into the pivot on occasion.

The returning starter at small forward is 6-5 senior **Chad Wiswall** (11.8 ppg, 4.3 rpg), who has decent defensive skills (41 steals, team-high 27 blocked shots) to go along with double-figure scoring. Wiswall's junior season produced evidence of some nice improvements over the season before, and he has the tools to be a star.

In the Red Raiders' season-ending loss to Lafayette, he led the team in scoring and rebounding. Still, Wiswall's entire collegiate career has been marked by motivation problems. Davis believes that with greater mental fortitude, he could blossom into a potential all-league player. Will this be the year?

The versatile Wandtke's stature is more reflective of a small forward, so he may spell Wiswall there at times. With the Red Raiders having little depth at this slot, a pair of freshmen will get shots at quality time: 6-5 **Jordan Harris** (Brophy Jesuit Prep/Peoria, Ariz.), who averaged 15 ppg and 8 rpg, and 6-5 swingman **LaMarr Datcher** (Episcopal HS/Washington, D.C.), who posted 16.4 ppg and 7.0 rpg.

Colgate shows more promise at power forward, where Wandtke's primary backup, at least initially, will be 6-8 sophomore **Robert Akers** (2.0 ppg, 1.8 rpg).

Akers' freshman numbers were nothing to write home about, but his performance in the league tournament left the Raiders high on him. In just 18 minutes over two games, he made three of three from the field and five of six free throws, snared eight boards, and rejected three shots. And keep an eye on 6-6 freshman **Pat Campolieta** (Bishop Ludden HS/Syracuse, N.Y.), whose 21.9 ppg and 10.5 rpg landed him on the All-State Class "C" second team. Wandtke will play all over the frontcourt, and Akers is hardly a proven commodity, so Campolieta should get a chance to contribute right away.

As an assistant at Navy, Davis coached the Midshipmen centers, an experience he should be prepared to repeat. Colgate is weak in the paint, where 6-6 junior **Pat Diamond** is the returning starter. The undersized Diamond put up modest numbers (5.5 ppg, 5.4 rpg), starting only 18 games, and is the Red Raiders' only true center.

Davis will try to make do with a squadron of power forwards backing up Diamond in the pivot: Wandtke and Akers will shift there from time to time, as will 6-8 sophomore **Terry Zinn** (0.8 ppg, 0.7 rpg) and 6-7 sophomore **Dave Brown** (0.7 ppg, 0.4 rpg), neither of whom played much as freshmen.

At the critical point-guard slot, the Red Raiders are looking to answer the same questions they asked a year ago. The situation looks more promising this season, however. **Chester Felts**, a 6-3 senior, started all 28 games as a junior, though some were at the two guard. Felts (10.5 ppg, 3.8 rpg) was hardly sparkling as a ballhandler, with his team-best 92 assists being offset by 82 turnovers, but he made 44 steals and is the leading returning player in minutes played.

Last season was Felts' best as a scorer, and ideally Davis would like to start him at off guard and let 6-0 senior **Mike Tilley** get the bulk of the time at the point. Tilley (3.8 ppg, 1.6 rpg) battled injury problems as a junior, though he played in every game, starting nine. His 79 assists against just 27 turnovers would suggest he knows what to do. If his durability and shooting (.374 percent from the floor) improve, Davis can turn his attention to other areas.

With two seniors poised to see substantial time at the point, 6-0 freshman **Devin Tuohey** (10.0 ppg, 2.0 rpg at Gonzaza HS/Washington, D.C.) and 5-11 freshman **Bill Kern** (14.0 ppg, 3.0 rpg at Brecksville-Broadview HS/Brecksville, Ohio) may struggle to find minutes.

Colgate's largest hole is at shooting guard, where Schaeffer held down the fort for the entire team last season. Felts will see some action here, as will 6-3 junior **Mike Chemotti** (2.7 ppg, 1.2 rpg), a 40 percent field goal shooter in 27 games, and 6-2 senior **Mike O'Donnell** (1.8 ppg, 1.4 rpg), who appeared in 26 games. The freshman possibilities are 6-5 **Rico Cabrera** (Worcester Academy/Los Angeles, Calif.) and 6-3 Jim **Detmer** (Scarsdale HS/Scarsdale, N.Y.). Cabrera averaged 17.1 ppg and 4.1 rpg, and Detmer 20.3 ppg and 7.0 rpg; both showed fine shooting touches as high schoolers. And if there's one thing these Red Raiders need, it's someone who can put the ball in the basket consistently.

1998-99 COLGATE SCHEDULE

Nov.	17	@Syracuse
	21	@Dartmouth
	27-28	#Marist Tournament
Dec.	1	Delaware
	4-5	##Ameritas Classic
	8	Siena
	11	Harvard
	18	Keuka
	20	Cornell
	30	Manhattan
Jan.	3	@Canisius
	6	@Holy Cross
	9	Army
	13	@Lehigh
	16	@Pennsylvania
	20	Bucknell
	23	@Lafayette
	27	@Navy
	30	Holy Cross
Feb.	3	@Army
	7	Lehigh
	13	@Bucknell
	17	Lafayette
	20	Navy
27-Mar.	5	###Patriot League Tournament

@ Road Games
\# Poughkeepsie, NY (vs. Marist, first round; also Columbia and Vermont)
\## Lincoln, NE (vs. Davidson, first round; also Nebraska and Southwest Texas State)
\### First and second rounds Feb. 27 and 28 at West Point, NY. Championship game March 5 at homecourt of highest remaining seed.

"Chemotti has been working hard over the summer developing his skills, and Felts has experience at this position," Davis says. "We also have a couple of other options with our freshman class."

adidas Blue Ribbon Analysis

BACKCOURT .... C BENCH/DEPTH .... D
FRONTCOURT .... C+ INTANGIBLES C

With the untimely passing of Jack Bruen, last season's expected rebuilding project turned instead into a lengthy state of suspended animation for the entire Colgate squad. The project begins in earnest *again* this year, led by new head man Emmett Davis.

In Ben Wandtke, Chad Wiswall and Chester Felts, Davis has some players with the potential to be pretty good contributors, though none of them looks headed for stardom. Pat Campolieta, Rico Cabrera and Jim Detmer are a trio of freshmen who provide hope for the future.

Colgate's present is not bright, however. The Red Raiders are short and they shoot poorly, connecting on just .414 percent from the field last season. Center is a wasteland, and the backcourt is a collection of ifs and hopefullys. The appearance of a new head coach, combined with the need for his team to get accustomed to a new style, will put unanticipated stress on a program that was already struggling to find a new direction.

This year's team will lose five seniors, including its best players, to graduation. Until then, Davis plans to use their experience. "I'm going to put a lot of emphasis on those players in terms of getting after other teams defensively and improving some of the rebounding statistics from last year," he says. "This basketball team has the potential to be very competitive in the league and have a successful season with the players in the program."

The coach's optimism aside, a more realistic view is that shedding the seniors sooner rather than later may help the program to adjust to Davis more swiftly than it would otherwise. For now, things could get worse before they get better.

(T.D)

HOLY CROSS

LOCATION .... Worcester, MA
CONFERENCE .... Patriot League
LAST SEASON .... 7-20 (.259)
CONFERENCE RECORD 3-9 (6th)
STARTERS LOST/RETURNING 2/3
NICKNAME .... Crusaders
COLORS .... Royal Purple
HOMECOURT .... Hart Center (3,600)
COACH .... Bill Raynor (Dartmouth '74)
RECORD AT SCHOOL .... 47-63 (4 yrs.)
CAREER RECORD .... 47-62 (4 yrs.)
ASSISTANTS .... Roger Breslin (Holy Cross '93)
Chad O'Donnell (Springfield '94)
TEAM WINS (last 5 yrs.) 14-15-16-8-7
RPI (last 5 yrs.) 198-200-242-296-291
1997-98 FINISH .... Lost in conference quarterfinal.

This season, for the first time ever, Patriot League schools are permitted to offer merit-based scholarships to their athletes. For Holy Cross, the move comes not a moment too soon.

Anything that will result in an influx of better players will be welcomed by the hoops faithful in Worcester, Mass. The former league stalwarts are in danger of falling below even perpetually bottom-dwelling Army in the Patriot.

Under fifth-year head coach Bill Raynor, Holy Cross has steadily regressed. His first two seasons were winning ones, though the team required outstanding second halves to scratch its way above .500. Two years ago there was a mere eight wins. But the nadir was last season. The seven-win train wreck was no illusion: Holy Cross was outperformed in nearly every statistical category, and thoroughly earned its 20 losses. The team's season-ending defeat to Bucknell in the opening round of the conference tournament was like a mercy killing.

Having more than taken their lumps recently, the Crusaders will attempt to regroup this year. The departures are limited to just two starters and a reserve, leaving an experienced team joined by a handful of the new scholarship players.

The initial go-to guy will be 6-0 senior point guard **John Hightower** (11.1 ppg, 3.5 rpg), who led Holy Cross in assists, with 99, and in steals, with 32. Hightower is no more than an adequate floor leader though. Eighty-seven turnovers are too many, considering his assist total. Then again, when one takes in the enormous number of minutes he played—a team-high 35.6 a game last year—that turnover tally can seem a bit low.

1998-99 HOLY CROSS SCHEDULE

Nov.	13	Yale
	15	Columbia
	18	Hartford
	21	@Vermont
	24	@Harvard
	28	@Fordham
Dec.	1	Dartmouth
	4-5	#Northwestern Mutual Classic
	9	@Brown
	23	@Boston College
	28-30	##Fiesta Bowl Classic
Jan.	3	Sacred Heart
	6	Colgate
	9	Bucknell
	13	@Lafayette
	16	@Navy
	23	@Army
	27	Lehigh
	30	@Colgate
Feb.	3	@Bucknell
	6	Lafayette
	10	Navy
	17	Army
	20	@Lehigh
27-Mar.	5	##Patriot League Tournament

@ Road Games
\# San Francisco, CA (vs. San Francisco, first round; also Rice and Weber State)
\## Phoenix, AZ (vs. Arizona, first round; also Florida International and Penn State)
\### First and second rounds Feb. 27 and 28 at West Point, NY. Championship game March 5 at homecourt of highest remaining seed.

Hightower is the top returning scorer, and while he is capable of the occasional 20-point outburst, it is not accurate to call him an offensive force. He shot a so-so .441 percent from the floor, and attempted just 32 treys, hitting eight of them.

That leaves Raynor looking to his two-guard for some serious points. The starter at the beginning of last season was 6-5 junior **James Stowers** (8.2 ppg, 1.5 rpg), but he couldn't capitalize on the role and was sent to the bench. As a reserve, however, he found his game, especially toward the end of the season, when he hit for double figures in five of the last eight games. The Crusaders' top free throw shooter at .884 percent, Stowers also made an impressive .456 of his three-pointers in Patriot League play. He should see time at shooting guard and at small forward.

Also expected to challenge for a starting job are 6-1 junior **Chris Spitler** (3.7 ppg, 1.6 rpg) and 6-3 junior **Malik Waters** (6.2 ppg, 2.5 rpg). Spitler is a former walkon who began last year as Holy Cross' 12th man, only to find himself starting eight of the last nine games. Displaying a nice outside touch, he scored 11 points in his first start, against Bucknell, and finished the season with a 5.9-ppg average as a starter.

Spitler's progress meant diminished time for Waters, who fought back from a debilitating knee injury two seasons ago and earned 12 starts in the middle of the year, hitting double figures in six of them. Waters can shoot, knocking down 25 of 72 treys, and should earn an extra look because of it.

If highly touted Canadian rookie **Ryan Serravalle** (Northfield-Mt. Hermon/Thorold, Ont.), a 6-0 freshman, plays well enough, he may get the nod at the point and shift Hightower to shooting guard. Serravalle was a 30.1-ppg scholastic player who earned All-Canada honors in leading his team to the national championship in 1996

After high school, he played for a season at Northfield-Mt. Hermon, averaging 18 ppg and seven assists and shooting 44 percent beyond the arc. The Crusader faithful already have seen the damage Serravalle can do; he dropped 27 points—including six for eight from three-point land—on the Holy Cross JV squad last December.

Reliable 5-10 senior **Thomas Nelson** (1.1 ppg, 0.9 rpg) again will provide depth at the point. He's no scorer, and he doesn't play much, but when Nelson is in the game, the basketball is in good hands. He handed out 16 assists against just five turnovers in 127 minutes last year. Raynor hoped to fit Army transfer **Tony Gutierrez** (4.1 ppg, 1.0 rpg), a 6-4 junior, into the starting lineup a season ago, but he proved to be a better bench player. After starting the first six games, he settled into his reserve role, playing gutty basketball in 14 more games off the bench.

The forward rotation is young, led by three sophomores who all saw significant time as freshmen. The man who appears to have broken Raynor's recruiting drought is 6-5 **Jared Curry** (7.7 ppg, 5.4 rpg), who started the final 19 games of the season at small forward on his way to all-rookie honors. Curry brought an all-around spark to the Crusaders, displaying scoring, rebounding and passing skills. Holy Cross will count on him a great deal in 1998-99.

Pencil in 6-6 sophomore **Juan Pegues** (7.0 ppg, 4.9 rpg) to start at power forward. He was the first Holy Cross freshman to earn a starting role in 12 seasons, and was the first player in Patriot history to earn three straight rookie-of-the-week nods. Pegues faded a bit down the stretch, though, and after starting the Crusaders' first 20 games, he gave way to senior Brian Hopkins and came off the bench for six of the last seven. He is athletic and strong on the boards, and may regain his spot in the starting lineup this year.

The third sophomore to earn a good look is 6-8 **Colin Boddicker** (2.9 ppg, 2.0 rpg), a two-game starter who played in all 27 games. One of Raynor's first subs, he'll earn more time this season if he can hone the quickness to the hoop he showed last year.

Appearing only 11 times last year was 6-6 sophomore **Dylan Kalbacher** (1.8 ppg, 1.1 rpg), who provides some bulk inside. Because the Crusaders aren't terribly deep at forward, 6-8 freshman **Dekker McKeever** (Santa Margarita HS/LaGuna Niguel, Calif.) could see some significant action. Raynor doesn't appear ready to rush his tallest forward into the lineup, but he may have no choice. McKeever averaged 14 ppg and 9.0 rpg as a senior.

The Crusaders' biggest problem area looks to be center. Jon Kerr held down the position last season, and did a fine job, earning all-league second-team honors. He played so much, though—more than 31 minutes a night and in every game—that backup **Scott Hall** saw painfully little action.

Now a 6-7 sophomore, Hall (1.5 ppg, 1.6 rpg) appeared in only eight games, for a total of 40 minutes, as a freshman. He did manage to hit six of his 14 shots and posted a four-point, six-rebound performance against New Mexico.

A more likely scenario has Raynor giving 6-9 freshman **Pat Whearty** (Our Lady of Lourdes HS/Poughkeepsie, N.Y.) a chance to start in the paint. Whearty averaged 17 ppg, 11 rpg and three blocked shots a night as a senior, and his size would be a real asset in the height-starved Patriot League. If Whearty is a bust, the Crusaders will use their abundance of forwards and swingmen to go small.

Help will arrive next season in the form of 7-1 transfer Josh Sankes, who is sitting out this season after leaving Rutgers. Sankes, who played high school ball with Spitler, is permitted to practice with Holy Cross, and he'll be the guy Whearty faces there. Raynor would like nothing more than to have Whearty hang in this year, then shift to power forward and let Sankes man the pivot.

adidas Blue Ribbon Analysis

BACKCOURT .... C BENCH/DEPTH .... D+
FRONTCOURT .... C INTANGIBLES .... D

This is a critical season for Bill Raynor. The turnaround he has brought about at Holy Cross is not the kind anyone likes—seasons of 15 and 16 wins his first two years, and seasons of eight and seven wins the last two years.

It appears, however, that Raynor finally may have stopped the bleeding. He unearthed a couple of recruits who can play in Jared Curry and Juan Pegues, and this year's rookies, especially Ryan Serravalle, show promise.

The Crusaders also feature John Hightower, who is a good player but lacks star quality. He'll be Holy Cross's leader, but Raynor really needs someone to step up and help. Hightower can't do it alone. There are several players who scored in the six-to-nine ppg range a year ago, and if any can reach inside and hit for double figures on a nightly basis—are you listening, James Stowers? Malik Waters?—HC would at least be competitive again.

The backcourt has plenty of players and almost as many question marks. The frontcourt looks more settled, but its performers are young and, despite displaying some potential, unproven. Until the Crusaders see what kind of player Josh Sankes will be next season, center is an indefinite question mark. And can Raynor wring more than seven or eight wins out of a team that is entirely his, with no traces of his predecessor's players?

As noted, it will be a critical season. Look for Holy Cross to turn a tiny corner, but there's still a long road back.

(T.D.)

LAFAYETTE

LOCATION ...... **Easton, PA**
CONFERENCE ...... **Patriot League**
LAST SEASON ...... **19-9 (.697)**
CONFERENCE RECORD ...... **10-2 (t-1st)**
STARTERS LOST/RETURNING **0/5**
NICKNAME ...... **Leopards**
COLORS ...... **Maroon & White**
HOMECOURT ...... **A.P. Kirby Field House (3,500)**
COACH ...... **Fred O'Hanlon (Villanova '70)**
RECORD AT SCHOOL ...... **37-46 (3 yrs.)**
CAREER RECORD ...... **37-46 (3 yrs.)**
ASSISTANTS ...... **Pat Brogan (Dickinson '90)**
Mike McKee (Lehigh '94)
Mike Burden (Rowan'95)
TEAM WINS (last 5 yrs.) **9-2-7-11-19**
RPI (last 5 yrs.) **266-297-275-267-143**
1997-98 FINISH ...... **Lost in conference final.**

This was going to be the Leopards' year.

It was going to be the season when Lafayette truly came into its own, shucking off Navy and Bucknell and claiming its well-deserved spot—alone—at the top of the Patriot League.

It all ended in one heartbreaking moment in North Jersey this summer.

When 1997-98 Patriot Player of the Year Stefan Ciosici hit the deck at a Seton Hall summer camp, an anterior cruciate ligament shredded inside his knee, the thump also described the Leopards' plummeting chances of defending their crown.

Which is a shame. Lafayette has come a long way in a little time. It won all of two games four years ago, and had welcomed the 1990s with seven straight losing seasons. Truly Lafayette was one of the perennial laughingstocks of Division I basketball.

But these Leopards were quite different, especially after unexpectedly clinching a share of the league crown last year. While its maturity happened about a season earlier than most had anticipated, few observers were surprised at the complete turnaround engineered by fourth-year head coach Fran O'Hanlon. In the beginning, the first season after the two-win disaster, O'Hanlon had to teach his squad how to play. Now, he teaches his players how to play well. The difference is monumental.

Last year's squad contained no seniors and was expected just to hang around the upper division of the league and maybe make life difficult for the top teams. Instead, the Leopards posted a respectable 9-7 nonconference record while cruising through the Patriot League for 10 wins in 12 games, earning the school a tie with Navy for its first-ever conference championship.

The turning point came after a midseason funk that produced three straight losses. Lafayette then regrouped and closed the regular season with nine consecutive wins. A six-point victory over Colgate in the Patriot tournament semifinal earned the Leopards a matchup with Navy in the championship game.

Perhaps unnerved by their success and unaccustomed to the spotlight of national television, the Leopards fell behind the Midshipmen by 21 points late in the first half. But Lafayette rallied, clawing its way back to a 77-all tie with 3:37 left in the game. With 37 seconds remaining, it was Navy by three, and the Mids converted their free throws to send the Leopards back to Easton with an eight-point loss.

Last season should have been a mere warm-up. Before Ciosici's injury, Lafayette was to have returned all five starters as well as the league's rookie of the year. In O'Hanlon the team has the defending Patriot League Coach of the Year, making last year's Lafayette team the first in league history to sweep the major post-season awards.

Winning breeds winning. With the Leopards now accustomed to victory, the task now is to sustain the edge that has allowed them to progress to the very doorstep of the NCAA Tournament.

Lafayette fans may need to wait a little longer, though. The devastating effect of Ciosici's loss cannot be overstated. The 6-11 senior center, who averaged 17.0 ppg, 7.9 rpg on his way to the player of the year award, was the preseason pick to repeat this year.

O'Hanlon, who played and coached in Sweden after his collegiate career ended, was serving as an assistant at Penn a few years ago when he was clued into the Romanian native by a European friend. Ciosici already had a deft shooting touch, and learning the nuances of the American game allowed him to come into his own last season.

Ciosici shot .584 percent from the floor, highlighted by a 15-for-17 performance against Lehigh on Jan. 7. He led the Leopards in scoring 16 times and in rebounding 16 times, and became just the fifth Patriot League player to amass 1,000 career points and 600 career rebounds. Defense may be the one chink in his armor, as Ciosici blocked only 14 shots, a relatively low number for a pivot man nearly seven feet tall.

He is petitioning the NCAA for a medical redshirt and hopes to return next season as a fifth-year senior.

Meanwhile, O'Hanlon must scramble to replace his fallen star. The returning starters at forward are 6-6 senior **Ross Harms** (3.8 ppg, 3.3 rpg) and 6-7 senior **Ted Cole** (5.8 ppg, 3.9 rpg), a versatile pair whose skills complement Ciosici's nicely. Harms, for example, led the team in rejections, with 28, and was second in assists, with 63. In addition, he connected on 11 of 28 three-point shots, opening up the inside game ever so slightly. Cole, who provided scoring and rebounding punch, was a .458 percent shooter from the floor while starting 26 games.

Joining these talented role players is be 6-7 senior **Dave Klaus** (6.2 ppg, 4.1 rpg), a solid outside shooter who knocked down .462 percent from the field and 40.4 percent from behind the three-point arc. Typically the first forward off the bench, he'll be penciled into the starting lineup as the season begins. Like Cole and Harms, Klaus is experienced; he appeared in all 28 of Lafayette's games, and started seven of them.

Playing in 23 games was 6-6 sophomore forward **General Butler** (1.9 ppg, 1.5 rpg), while **Nathan Klinkhammer** (0.4 ppg, 1.2 rpg), a 6-8 junior forward, was limited by injuries to just 10 games.

Ciosici was to have seen the lion's share of minutes at center, of course. His loss opens up opportunities for **Frank Barr**, a 6-11 sophomore center who sat out last season after transferring from Hofstra. Barr (Pennwood HS/Upper Darby, Pa.) tallied 15.1 ppg and 10.2 rpg as a scholastic player.

The only freshman up front is 6-6 forward **Rob Worthington** (St. Thomas Academy/St. Paul, Minn.), an all-state selection who averaged 15.2 ppg and 7.5 rpg.

In the backcourt, the Leopards welcome back all-league second teamer **Brian Ehlers** (16.3 ppg, 5.4 rpg, 76 assists), a 6-4 junior who led the squad in assists and minutes played and was second in rebounding. A former all-rookie pick, Ehlers also amassed 30 steals, and was tops on the team with an .838 free throw percentage. In Lafayette's losing effort against Navy in the Patriot League championship game, his 31 points and 10 boards were team highs. He is a preseason pick to the all-league team.

The starter at point guard is 5-11 sophomore **Tim Bieg** (5.2 ppg, 2.0 rpg, 42 steals). He received a good amount of seasoning last year, starting 21 games as a freshman. With Ciosici and Ehlers taking most of the shots, Bieg didn't need to score to contribute last season. He may want to pick up his scoring more this year, and he can also stand to handle the ball better; O'Hanlon probably doesn't want his starting point man to dish out just 54 assists against 48 turnovers.

In addition to these two solid players, Lafayette's backcourt includes the returning Patriot League Rookie of the Year. Sophomore **Tyson Whitfield** (9.6 ppg, 3.8 rpg), a 6-4 swingman, was a 15-game starter who knocked down 50 three-pointers, good for second in the league.

Providing solid minutes off the bench is 6-4 junior **Mike Homer** (5.1 ppg, 1.5 rpg), who contributed 32 treys. The gritty **Peter Van Siclen** (6.0 ppg, 0.9 rpg), a 6-1 sophomore, made the most of his 12.6 minutes per game. Despite his limited playing time, only four Leopards scored more than he did, and he burned opponents from beyond the arc, shooting .455 percent on three pointers.

The guard rotation looks full, but freshmen **Brian Burke** (Germantown Academy/Lafayette Hills, Pa.) and **Reggie Guy** (Suffield Academy/Harrisburg, Pa.) can take solace in the fact that O'Hanlon does not hesitate in the least to play his rookies. The 6-5 Burke ended his high school career with 1,429 points, and his 23.1 ppg average as a senior landed him on the all-state second team. Guy, a 6-3 guard, scored 10.3 ppg while helping his team to the semifinal round of the New England Prep School Tournament.

adidas Blue Ribbon Analysis

BACKCOURT	B	BENCH/DEPTH	B
FRONTCOURT	C+	INTANGIBLES	B+

Fran O'Hanlon had been building toward this season for quite a while. Surely he had pleasant off-season dreams, imagining his Leopards as a complete team entering the season with a great deal of tools, plenty of confidence, and valuable experience gained from last year's league tournament. O'Hanlon is one of the country's best young coaches, and he has managed to resurrect a moribund program very, very quickly.

Stefan Ciosici's loss changes all of that. Sure, the Leopards still have an All-League performer in Brian Ehlers, a star-in-waiting in Tyson Whitfield, and a splendid supporting cast of players who know their roles.

Lafayette knows how to play the game. Its players have on-court smarts: They're not just good, but intelligent as well.

Not to mention tough. The Leopards spread around the rebounding duties, and the guards are not afraid to stick their noses into the paint to grab some boards. That toughness will be tested this season.

You don't replace a player of the year. You can't, unless you have another player of the year waiting in the wings—which O'Hanlon doesn't. The Leopards are now a team with a very good backcourt and a bunch of nice, reliable role players up front, not unlike about a zillion other teams in college basketball. Ciosici was a rare breed, and the dominant Patriot League big man. He is what would have made this team special.

Still, Lafayette is a veteran, talented, deep team that can score, rebound and play defense. Throw in O'Hanlon's intensity and savvy, and the Leopards are still likely to win more than they lose. Any more than that doesn't appear likely.

(T.D)

1998-99 LAFAYETTE SCHEDULE

Nov.	14	@Dartmouth
	18	Princeton
	22	@Purdue
	29	@St. Peter's
Dec.	2	Swarthmore
	5	@Howard
	10	Columbia
	12	*Delaware
	22	@Towson
	29-30	#Gossner Classic Tournament
Jan.	5	Pennsylvania
	9	@Navy
	13	Holy Cross
	16	Army
	18	@Cornell
	20	@Lehigh
	23	Colgate
	25	@Rutgers
	27	@Bucknell
Feb.	1	Haverford
	3	Navy
	6	@Holy Cross
	9	@Army
	14	Lehigh
	17	@Colgate
	21	Bucknell
	26-28	##Patriot League Tournament

@ Road Games
* Desmond Conference Challenge, Albany, NY
# Logan, UT (vs. Troy State, first round; also Norfolk State and Troy State)
First and second rounds Feb. 27 and 28 at West Point, NY. Championship game March 5 at homecourt of highest remaining seed.

adidas Blue Ribbon Analysis

GRADING SYSTEM

A+ equal to very best in country—Final Four-caliber unit
A among the best in the land—worthy of deep NCAA run
B+ talented, versatile and experienced—NCAA-NIT ability
B solid and productive winners—league and post-season contenders
C+ average to above-average—may contend in a weaker league
C average to mediocre—second division in a strong league
D+ below average, inconsistent—second division in a weaker league
D well below average—losing season virtually certain
F non-Division I ability—an underdog every night

LEHIGH

LOCATION .... Bethleham, PA
CONFERENCE .... Patriot
LAST SEASON .... 10-17 (.370)
CONFERENCE RECORD 4-8 (5th)
STARTERS LOST/RETURNING 0/5
NICKNAME .... Mountain Hawks
COLORS .... Brown & White
HOMECOURT .... Stabler Arena (5,600)
COACH .... Sal Mentesana (Providence '69)
RECORD AT SCHOOL .... 11-43 (2 yrs.)
CAREER RECORD .... 11-43 (2 yrs.)
ASSISTANTS .... Jeff Wilson (East Stroudsburg '86)
Joe Mantegna (Ithica '91)
Todd Painton (East Stroudsburg '93)
TEAM WINS (last 5 yrs.) 10-11-4-1-10
RPI (last 5 yrs.) 258-251-302-304-264
1997-98 FINISH .... Lost in conference quarterfinal.

If the journey of a thousand miles begins with the first step, then it can be said fairly that Lehigh took quite a few steps last season.

In seeking to make the thousand-mile journey back from the one-win gulag of two years ago, the Mountain Hawks effected the greatest one-season turnaround in Division I last year, improving their win total by nine games. It was something of an up-and-down season, as Lehigh won its first three, dropped four in a row, took the next two, lost six straight, won a pair, lost the next five, then won three of the final four games entering the Patriot League Tournament.

Along the way were heartbreaking losses—by one to Harvard, by two to Penn, by three to Lafayette—and outright pastings, such as a 52-point loss to Stanford.

The first round of the league tournament pitted the Mountain Hawks against Colgate. The Red Raiders led by a point at halftime, and despite a 30-point effort from **Brett Eppehimer** and 19 points and eight boards by **Fido Willybiro**, Lehigh fell by one, 84-83.

"The program is definitely on the rise," said third-year head coach Sal Mentesana. "I like that we are building the program in increments, because I want to build the foundation for a solid program for the next 20- to 25 years. It is a slow process, and I think that eventually the program will be one that the university, students, faculty, administration and the community will be proud of."

Barring injuries, Lehigh should take even greater strides on that thousand-mile journey this season. All five starters return, including Eppehimer, an all-league pick and the country's second-leading returning scorer. And with just two seniors on the roster, the Mountain Hawks look poised to make some noise for a few years to come, as Mentesana hopes.

For now, however, the coach is still teaching. Lehigh continues to adapt to the running style Mentesana has implemented, and he aims for all of the pieces to be in place by the time the Mountain Hawks begin the Patriot League portion of the schedule.

"It's a mental process as well as a physical process," Mentesana said. "I think our team is physically ready—we are strong enough and fast enough—but I don't think we are mentally ready yet. I think that will come at some point this season."

The amazing Eppehimer (24.6 ppg, 2.2 rpg, 46 steals), a 5-11 senior shooting guard, again will be called on to carry the scoring load. Any way you slice it, Eppehimer's junior season was nothing short of sensational. The league leader in scoring, three-point shooting and steals, he started all 27 games, Eppehimer hit .398 percent of his shots from beyond the arc and .877 percent of his free throws, 15th best in the country.

To top it off, Eppehimer and his father form a four-time South Jersey Beach Horseshoe Champion team. He is such a lover of the Jersey Shore that he and teammate **Dan Handerhan** used 700 pounds of sand, a live palm tree, beach chairs and an umbrella to turn their frat house room into an indoor replica of the beach.

Eppehimer's on-court accomplishments are equally impressive. Not bad for a guy too many observers said was too short to make it.

"Everyone has talent. It is a matter of how you develop your talent that makes the difference," Mentesana said. "He has put forth an uncommon amount of work to develop his talent. ... He is a better person than he is a basketball player, and that is what makes him such a good player."

A major reason for both Eppehimer's blossoming last season and Lehigh's resurgence was 6-1 sophomore **Tiwaun Hawkins** (2.8 ppg, 2.5 rpg), the guy Mentesana unearthed to play the point. Hawkins didn't score much—he attempted only 65 shots all season—but he started 26 games, and his 121 assists were the best in the Patriot League. His 1.61:1 assists:turnover ratio was second best in the league and provided vivid evidence of poise that is uncommon for a freshman.

Most important, Hawkins gave the Mountain Hawks a reliable floor leader and enabled Eppehimer to play shooting guard full-time. Hawkins will play a key role in any continued improvement for Lehigh this season.

Hawkins' backup was 5-10 guard **Steve Aylsworth** (3.3 ppg, 1.7 rpg), whose relentless defensive pressure is an important component of the Mountain Hawks' running game. Aylsworth played in every game, starting one, and he compiled 56 assists against only 37 turnovers. He and Hawkins have Lehigh covered at the point.

Eppehimer will continue to see nearly all of the minutes at shooting guard. A variety of swingmen will spell him at that slot as well as look to contribute at small forward. Second-leading scorer **Jared Hess** (10.8 ppg, 3.9 rpg), a 6-5 junior, nearly doubled his scoring and rebounding output over his freshman year. A former all-rookie selection, Hess started every game as a sophomore, hitting 38 three-pointers. A midseason slump that mirrored his team's shows that he still has work to do, but if he keeps improving, it will force teams to play Eppehimer more honestly.

Sophomore guard **Bobby Willis** (2.5 ppg, 1.0 rpg), 6-4, made an immediate splash, scoring 10 points in his first college game, a win over Wagner. He played in 22 games, but needs to round out his game if he hopes to take over for Eppehimer next season.

Another swingman who provided valuable minutes was unflappable 6-3 junior **Michael Fry** (4.0 ppg, 2.0 rpg), who played for hallowed St. Anthony's as a high schooler. Fry lost his eligibility six games into his freshman year, but showed lots of grit by hitting the books hard and spending considerable time in the gym and weight room. He now can run the floor, drive to the hoop and hit the outside shot.

Looking for more minutes is 6-0 backup point guard **Bobby George** (0.8 ppg, 0.6 rpg), an unselfish role player who can contribute when Hawkins and Aylsworth are in foul trouble.

Joining Hess in the starting frontcourt is 6-6 junior power forward Willybiro (8.4 ppg, 6.7 rpg), an athletic player who led the team in rebounding. Willybiro has had to learn on the job in his first two seasons, but has shown sufficient development to warrant extended court time. He started 26 games last year, hitting in double figures 11 times, making 29 steals and blocking 19 shots, second best in the league. A former all-rookie pick, Willybiro should see his numbers rise this season if the Mountain Hawks can find some guys to help him inside; in years past he was typically guarded by the opponent's centers.

Mentesana hopes for big things from 6-5 sophomore forward **Edil Lacayo** (2.9 ppg, 2.5 rpg), who played in just one of Lehigh's first five games, but in 19 of its last 22. Lacayo shifted from small forward to power forward and, despite being undersized, responded well and proved to be a physical presence in the paint. He hits the glass very hard, grabbing 50 boards in just 192 minutes of play.

A pair of 6-5 freshmen could step in immediately at forward. **Bobby Mbom** (Bishop Ford HS/Brooklyn, N.Y.) averaged 17.0 ppg and snared 12.0 rpg as a senior, when he earned McDonald's All-America honors and was chosen to the All-CHSAA first team, the *New York Daily News* second team and the New York City Empire State Team. **Scott Taylor** (Newton North HS/Newton, Mass.) tallied 17.0 ppg and 7.0 rpg on his way to the Bay State League MVP award and the *Boston Herald* All-Scholastic Team.

Perhaps more than anyone else, Handerhan (1.1 ppg, 0.5 rpg), Eppehimer's roommate, struggled with the new system Mentesana put in place. A 6-6 senior, he saw his court time decrease because he is less athletic and more of a halfcourt player.

Another forward who will look to increase his minutes is 6-3 sophomore **Anson Ferguson** (1.2 ppg, 0.6 rpg), who appeared in 14 games as a freshman. Ferguson hustles and is physical, which may earn him more action this year.

The returning starter at center is 6-6 junior **Peter DeLea** (7.7 ppg, 5.7 rpg), who put up some nice numbers in spite of his size. DeLea, like Fry, foundered academically as a freshman and was kicked off the team after six games. Also like Fry, he pulled himself together to have a solid sophomore year, closing the season by averaging 15.0 ppg and 8.7 rpg over the last six games. While he may start the year at center, if one of the youngsters steps up he'll shift to his more natural power forward slot. DeLea shot .491 percent from the floor, and if he can continue to improve his outside shot, it should ease the pressure on the interior players.

Injuries and dismissals led to a kind of jury-rigged rotation in the paint, which helped 6-10 sophomore **Sah-U-Ra Brown** and 6-9 sophomore **Kyle Gloff** earn extra time. Brown (1.1 ppg, 1.5 rpg) rejected 12 shots in only 123 minutes of playing time, and has put on two inches and 20 pounds since signing with Lehigh. He still needs some seasoning, but could prove to be a force to be reckoned with. Gloff (1.5 ppg, 1.9 rpg) played inconsistently over 22 games.

Lehigh was outrebounded by four boards a game last year, so Mentesana made sure to recruit a big man to play the pivot. **Marshall Rumney** (E.C. Glass HS/Lynchburg, Va.), a 6-8 freshman, averaged 11.1 ppg and 9.8 rpg and was picked to the All-Western Virginia District first team.

1998-99 LEHIGH SCHEDULE

Nov.	13	Vermont
	16	St. Francis
	19	@Yale
	23	@Penn State
	28	@Harvard
Dec.	3	@Pennsylvania
	7	Drew
	19	Hobart
	21	Wagner
	27	@Rutgers
	30	Cornell
Jan.	2	Columbia
	5	@Army
	9	Manhattan
	13	Colgate
	16	@Bucknell
	20	Lafayette
	23	Navy
	27	@Holy Cross
	30	Army
Feb.	3	@Delaware State
	7	@Colgate
	10	Bucknell
	14	@Lafayette
	17	@Navy
	20	Holy Cross
27-Mar.	5	#Patriot League Tournament

@ Road Games
\# First and second rounds Feb. 27 and 28 at West Point, NY. Championship game March 5 at homecourt of highest remaining seed)

adidas Blue Ribbon Analysis

BACKCOURT	B	BENCH/DEPTH	C
FRONTCOURT	C	INTANGIBLES	C

In a sense, Sal Mentesana has done the easy part—there was nowhere to go but up. He has finally made Lehigh a competitive squad, one that should be able to play with the rest of the teams in the Patriot League night in and night out. The hard part begins now, as he tries to drive his team into the league's upper ranks.

The Mountain Hawks have flaws, as Mentesana freely acknowledges: "We need to get better defensively. Our field-goal percentage needs to be better. We need to be a better rebounding team. Our defense is based on deflections and how much we can disrupt the other team's offense. I think we did a good job at that, but we didn't finish it."

However, Lehigh also has Patriot League Player-of-the-Year candidate Brett Eppehimer. It has a highly stable rotation at point guard. And it has some hard workers up front who could crack double-figure scoring. Those aren't bad things to have.

What the Mountain Hawks really need is a legitimate big guy who can eat up minutes and suck down rebounds in the paint, forcing opponents to ease off Eppehimer. Otherwise, it will be like last year all over again, with undersized forwards doing their best while playing out of position and Lehigh struggling to mount a decent perimeter attack.

Mentesana offers a *realistic* prediction of 14 to 15 wins this year, and that sounds about right. The real key, of course, is whether Lehigh—which went 4-8 in the Patriot last season—can pick up its game when playing against league opponents. If so, and if some breaks go their way, the Mountain Hawks could be a darkhorse in the conference race.

(T.D.)

NAVY

LOCATION .... **Annapolis, MD**
CONFERENCE .... **Patriot League**
LAST SEASON .... **19-11 (.633)**
CONFERENCE RECORD .... **10-2 (t-1st)**
STARTERS LOST/RETURNING **3/2**
NICKNAME .... **Midshipmen**
COLORS .... **Blue & Gold**
HOMECOURT .... **Alumni Hall (5,710)**
COACH .... **Don DeVoe (Ohio State '64)**
RECORD AT SCHOOL .... **99-73 (6 yrs.)**
CAREER RECORD .... **427-301 (25 yrs.)**
ASSISTANTS .... **Jimmy Allen (Emory & Henry '93)**
Nathan Davis (Randolph-Macon '97)
Doug Wojcik (Navy '87)
TEAM WINS (last 5 yrs.) **17-20-15-20-19**
RPI (last 5 yrs.) **207-158-248-147-165**
1997-98 FINISH .... **Lost in NCAA first round.**

Read carefully:

"When I first started coaching, I thought defense was everything," said Don DeVoe. "But now, I am putting more stress on offense."

This is not a misprint.

DeVoe, the seventh-year head coach at Navy and a man famous for preaching the virtues of a ravenous man-to-man defense, actually is thinking about opening things up a bit. This on top of the occasional lapses into a zone.

But, hey, don't be too surprised. After all, you don't wind up 126 games over .500 in your career, one of only 11 coaches to take three Division I schools to the Big Dance, with appearances in three of the last five NCAA Tournaments, by being unwilling to alter your theories and try new approaches from time to time.

Besides, Navy can't kick on the cruise control and glide its way through the Patriot League. The competition is too good, and the Midshipmen were hit hard by graduation.

They have lost three starters and seven lettermen, among them top scorer Michael Heary (13.6 ppg, 3.8 rpg), an all-league first-teamer, and leading rebounder Hassan Booker (12.0 ppg, 7.8 rpg), who was selected to the second team. Players who represented sixty-four percent of last year's points and 52 percent of its boards are sailing the high seas now, fulfilling their obligation to Uncle Sam.

So what's a coach to do? Adapt_but not too much.

"I feel like this Navy basketball team can be effective pushing the ball when the opportunity presents itself," DeVoe said, "yet our main offense will be halfcourt-set."

Last year's squad ho-hummed its way to a 6-8 non-league record, but played very well against Patriot opponents. A pair of consecutive February defeats by Lafayette and Bucknell were the Mids' only league losses, and they rolled into the conference championship game after dispatching Army and Bucknell with little difficulty. A hard-fought win over Lafayette landed Navy in the East Region of the NCAA tourney, where top-seeded North Carolina handed it the expected pasting.

That successful season doesn't obscure the hard road ahead, though. What may help the Midshipmen is that DeVoe played with a long bench last year. He went 10 to 12 deep on a lot of nights, which means that the guys charged with replacing all the departed bodies saw a great deal of action that mattered. That seasoning should prove tremendously valuable this year.

Among DeVoe's many accomplishments at Navy is a consistent rebuilding effort that has kept his team competitive no matter how many performers he has to replace. And so, despite this year's turnover, he is optimistic.

"We lost seven quality players off of last year's squad, seven players who did a lot for this program," he said. "That said, I feel like we have an outstanding nucleus coming back. This will probably be the most athletic team we have put on the floor since I have been here."

If anyone personifies the hard-nosed Navy defense of old and its emerging offensive mindset, it is 6-2 senior shooting guard **Skip Victor** (8.9 ppg, 4.2 rpg). Victor is the man loosed upon the opponent's top scorer, and for good reason_witness his 50 steals last season. In addition, he is a solid ballhandler who began the season manning the point and tallied 86 assists for the year.

Just before last Christmas, with his lackluster squad standing at 4-5, DeVoe decided a backcourt shakeup was the answer. He shifted Heary to the point and installed Victor as his starting off-guard before Navy's game against Harvard, and Victor and the Midshipmen responded quite nicely. The team won 15 of its final 21 games, while Victor averaged 11 ppg in his new role, finished with a .474 shooting percentage and was chosen most valuable player of the Patriot League Tournament.

The all-league second-team pick, little-used the season before, exploded into stardom last year with a game that improved in nearly every area. Now he needs to take up the leadership reins. "I am confident he will get the job done," DeVoe says.

Heary's graduation leaves a significant hole at the point. His likely replacement is 6-2 sophomore **Reggie Skipworth** (1.9 ppg, 0.3 rpg). A late-season call-up from the junior-varsity squad, Skipworth impressed with his ballhandling skills and speed. He managed nine assists and two steals in his 57 minutes of varsity time.

While Victor will see some time at the point, Skipworth's primary understudy is 6-0 sophomore **Chris Worthing** (Inman HS/Inman, Kan.), who played no varsity ball last season. DeVoe likes his athleticism but would like to see Worthing improve at the defensive end of the floor.

A pair of underclassmen will provide depth at shooting guard. The more experienced is 6-5 sophomore **John Williams** (1.3 ppg, 0.6 rpg), who will also see time at forward. Williams, one of Navy's many gritty hustlers, played in 21 games last year. Appearing 16 times was 6-6 junior **Jeremy Toton** (1.7 ppg, 1.0 rpg), a hard-working sharpshooter who provides size in the backcourt.

As damaging as Heary's loss is to the guard rotation, Booker's graduation hurts the frontcourt equally hard. Senegal native **Sitapha Savane** (5.4 ppg, 4.4 rpg), a 6-7 junior dubbed the "Senegal Sensation," gets first crack at succeeding him. An all-rookie pick last year, the surprising Savane led the Midshipmen with 37 blocked shots and delivered a clutch performance in the Patriot League title game, scoring 15 points and snaring six boards.

"I am expecting him to continue to improve this year," DeVoe said. "He has that rare ability to block a shot without fouling. Offensively, he really improved as the year went along and should be a force for us inside."

The athletic **Chris Williams** (6.0 ppg, 2.8 rpg, 31 steals), a 6-5 sophomore, showed a nice resiliency by returning from preseason knee surgery to play in 25 games. In the league tournament, he scored 30 points, hauled down 14 rebounds and pocketed a tournament-record 13 steals in three games. Williams could have a breakout season; expect him to start.

Also in the mix are 6-3 sophomore **Shawn Murray**, 6-7 sophomore **Robert Reeder** and 6-6 senior **Seth Schuknecht**. Murray (Benson HS/Portland, Ore.) posted good number at the JV level, averaging nearly 20 ppg, but DeVoe would like him to step up his defense. The bulky Reeder (2.3 ppg, 2.0 rpg) played decently in 21 games as a freshman. The Mids like his sound fundamental approach and hope he can put some more points on the board.

Perhaps the team's most perplexing mystery this season is Schuknecht (2.5 ppg, 2.3 rpg). After being chosen to the league's all-rookie team as a freshman, he faltered a bit as a sophomore, then hit a wall last season, when his scoring and rebounding decreased. Still, he plays well with his back to the hoop, and DeVoe pledges not to let last year's downturn prevent him from getting his minutes.

Also at forward is 6-7 sophomore **Josh Hill** (Camarillo HS/Camarillo, Calif.).

Navy has a returning starter in the paint, 6-11 senior **Josh Williams** (6.0 ppg, 4.0 rpg, 30 blocks), who stepped back into his starting role after Mike Palumbo's knee injury a year ago. Throughout his career, the Mids have tended to play as well, or as poorly, as he does. Williams played markedly better as a junior than as a sophomore, but has yet to put together a consistent season. He is astoundingly mobile for a big man and defends quite well, but needs to shoot and score more to help his team this season.

It is very important that Williams limit his foul trouble, because the depth at center is unproven. Give the post reserves this, though: They are big. **Michael Cunningham** (Antosian Col. Prep/San Antonio, Texas), a 6-11 sophomore, had a good year with the JV team, while 6-9 junior **Lance Day** (Servite HS/Fullerton, Calif.), who weighs 260 pounds, provides bulk.

1998-99 NAVY SCHEDULE

Nov.	16	Rice
	20	Northeastern
	23	Davidson
	28	@Air Force
Dec.	3	@Belmont
	5	@Wofford
	7	Coast Guard
	19	Auburn
	21	Dartmouth
	23	@Maryland-Baltimore County
	28-29	#Tribune Classic
Jan.	2	Gettysburg
	4	Harvard
	6	Bucknell
	9	Lafayette
	17	Holy Cross
	19	@Army
	23	@Lehigh
	27	Colgate
	31	@Bucknell
Feb.	3	@Lafayette
	10	@Holy Cross
	13	Army
	17	Lehigh
	20	@Colgate
27-Mar.	5	##Patriot League Tournament

@ Road Games
\# #Tempe, AZ (vs. Arizona State, first round; also Alaska-Anchorage and Southern Methodist)
\## First and second rounds Feb. 27 and 28 at West Point, NY. Championship game March 5 at homecourt of highest remaining seed.

adidas Blue Ribbon Analysis

BACKCOURT .... **B** **BENCH/DEPTH** .... **C**
FRONTCOURT .... **C+** **INTANGIBLES** .... **B+**

Don DeVoe begins his seventh year at Navy with plenty of questions to answer, not least of which is how to replace all of the contributions of his seven departed lettermen. One answer, he thinks, is a more aggressive offensive approach.

But don't think DeVoe is going to abandon the tactics that have gotten him where he is. A common refrain from the coach regarding this year's team is that all a player needs to do is "work on his defense" to "be a force in the league," or words to that effect.

So defense and fundamentals survive and live on as major ingredients in the Midshipmen's recipe for success. In addition, Skip Victor, a preseason all-league pick, is the real deal. But there are other questions whose answers won't be known until play starts: Can Josh Williams put it together night in and night out? Can Reggie Skipworth handle a full season at the point? Can Seth Schuknecht recover the form that made him so valuable as a freshman? Can Navy's youngsters make the jump from JV?

DeVoe's determination to play so many guys last year should help Navy weather some of its departures. And many of the young players who were exposed to important action show tremendous upsides and plenty of potential.

In addition to the above questions, however, the bench looks rather thin, not to mention unproven. But while DeVoe probably would like more tools, the season-ending injury sustained by Lafayette's Stefan Ciosici will have a ripple effect. Among its primary results is to make Navy the league favorite. It may not be the most honorable way to win a conference title, but will anyone remember come March?

(T.D.)

SOUTHEASTERN CONFERENCE

adidas BLUE RIBBON FORECAST

EAST DIVISION

1. Kentucky
2. Tennessee
3. Georgia
4. South Carolina
5. Florida
6. Vanderbilt

WEST DIVISION

1. Arkansas
2. Auburn
3. Mississippi
4. Mississippi State
5. Alabama
6. LSU

TOP 40

Arkansas, Georgia, Kentucky, South Carolina and Tennessee are ranked among the 1998-99 *adidas Blue Ribbon* Top 40. Extended profiles can be found in the Top 40 section of *Blue Ribbon.*

ALL-CONFERENCE TEAM

G—B.J. McKie, SR, South Carolina
G—Tony Harris, SO, Tennessee
F—Jumaine Jones, SO, Georgia
F—Scott Padgett, SR, Kentucky
C—Tyrone Washington, SR, Mississippi State

PLAYER OF THE YEAR

B.J. McKie, SR, South Carolina

NEWCOMER OF THE YEAR

Chris Porter, JR, Auburn

1998-99 CONFERENCE TOURNAMENT

Mar. 4-7, Georgia Dome, Atlanta, GA

1997-98 CHAMPIONS

Kentucky (regular season)
Kentucky (conference tournament)

1997-98 POSTSEASON PARTICIPANTS

Postseason Record: 14-8 (.636)

NCAA

Kentucky (national champion)
Arkansas (2nd round)
Mississippi
South Carolina
Tennessee

NIT

Georgia (semifinals)
Vanderbilt (3rd round)
Auburn (2nd round)
Florida

TOP BACKCOURTS

1. Tennessee
2. Arkansas
3. Georgia

TOP FRONTCOURTS

1. Kentucky
2. Tennesssee
3. Auburn

ON THE WAY UP

Florida

ON THE WAY DOWN

Vanderbilt

INSIDE THE NUMBERS

• 1997-98 conference RPI: 2nd (of 30)
• Conference RPI (last 5 years): 7-4-3-6-2

DID YOU KNOW?

Of the league's three new head coaches, all are from the Western Division. And two of those, Rod Barnes of Mississippi and Rick Stansbury of Mississippi State, have never been a head coach before on any level. Mark Gottfried comes to Alabama having been a successful head coach at Murray State...In the last six years, SEC teams have made eight appearances in the Final Four, more than any other conference. The ACC is a distant second with five. Arkansas, Kentucky, Florida and Mississippi State are the four SEC teams to play in the Final Four in that span...The SEC leads the nation in NCAA Tournament winning percentage over the last five years (.710, 49-20). The Pac 10 is second at .656...That success is impressive considering how poorly SEC teams have fared in the tournament's first round the last two years. In 1997, four league teams lost in the first round, and last year, Tennessee, South Carolina and Mississippi all bit the dust after one game. Adding to the league's frustration was that each of those losses were by one point...Since 1980-81, each of the 12 SEC schools has won either a league division, overall or tournament title.

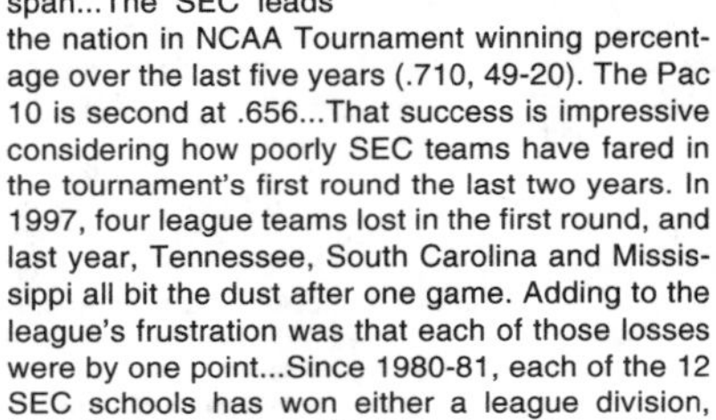

(C.D.)

ALABAMA

LOCATION .... Tuscaloosa, AL
CONFERENCE ...... Southeastern (Westerm Division)
LAST SEASON .... 15-16 (.483)
CONFERENCE RECORD 6-10 (t-4th)
STARTERS LOST/RETURNING 2/3
NICKNAME .... Crimson Tide
COLORS .... Crimson & White
HOMECOURT .... Coleman Coliseum (15,043)
COACH .... Mark Gottfried (Alabama '87)
RECORD AT SCHOOL .... First year
CAREER RECORD .... 68-24 (3 yrs.)
ASSISTANTS .... Tom Kelsey (David Lipscomb '86)
Philip Pearson (Alabama '93)
Robert Scott (Alabama '80)
TEAM WINS (last 5 yrs.) 20-23-19-17-15
RPI (last 5 yrs.) 46-33-54-87-84
1997-98 FINISH .... Lost in conference second round.

It had to be the least suspenseful coaching search in the history of Division I basketball.

Even before last season began, Alabama fans and—especially—the media, speculated that former Crimson Tide coach David Hobbs, who couldn't quite maintain the level of success established by predecessor Wimp Sanderson, was a goner. The people's choice to replace him was Mark Gottfried, a star guard on some of Sanderson's best teams and a successful young head coach at Murray State.

Several Alabama newspapers made the trek to Murray, Ky. to write extended profiles on Gottfried, weeks before Hobbs' fate was known. Callers to radio talk shows around the state insisted all season that Hobbs' firing and Gottfried's hiring were done deals, and that there would be a statewide insurrection of Tide fans if they weren't.

When Hobbs' long-anticipated depature was announced, no one was shocked. And it was even less surprising that Gottfried, the native son, was hired to replace him. Suffice to say Alabama fans everywhere were pleased.

"The reception we've been given has been great," Gottfried said. "People are excited about the future. There's a lot of enthusiasm around the state and around our program. It's been terrific."

Alabama's 1998-99 season will be slightly less than terrific, but Gottfried is prepared for whatever happens. Not many people in college basketball can pick up the phone and call John Wooden for advice, but Gottfried, who coached at UCLA under Jim Harrick and called on the Wizard of Westwood often, can. Wooden always offers good advice.

"Coach Wooden and I talked about this job before I took it," Gottfried said. "He thinks it was a great move. He did tell me that at your alma mater, expectations are a little higher. But he told me that's something you should never be afraid of."

The Tide probably won't live up to anyone's expectations this season, but who knows? Under Gottfried's uptempo system, perhaps his new team will develop quickly. There are plenty of bodies for Gottfried to run in and out.

"We have a large number of players, and they all do something different well," Gottfried said. "But not many of them have made an impact on the SEC level."

Three players who have made an impact return, all of them starters a year ago: 6-1 senior guard **Brian Williams** (161. ppg, 4.2 rpg, 78 assists, 33 steals), 6-1 senior guard **Chauncey Jones** (9.9 ppg, 2.7 rpg, 109 assists, 40 steals) and 6-10 junior center **Jeremy Hayes** (9.3 ppg, 7.3 rpg, 56 blocked shots, 33 steals).

Williams is Alabama's most talented player, but can sometimes be his own worst enemy. He's a great scorer—last season Williams tossed in 28 points against Kentucky, 27 against Mississippi and 26 against Mississippi State—who can get to the basket in a hurry and has three-point range. On the minus side, he also had more turnovers (89) than assists.

"Brian is one of those guys who can do a lot of things," Gottfried said. "He's really good with the ball in transition and can create shots for himself. We're going to put the ball in his hands a little bit more than he had it last year. It's going to be like pruning a fruit tree with Brian. Cut off some branches here and there, and what you have is a real polished player."

Hayes made a lot of progress last season and is one of the league's top centers. He started 28 of 31 games, and became a feared shot blocker and consistently good rebounder. He got better as the season went along, averaging 14 points and 12 rebounds in his last six games. That rebound total included an 18-board effort against Vanderbilt in the SEC Tournament.

Hayes had four double-doubles last season, including a 26-point, 10-rebound night against Florida. He led the Tide and was seventh in the SEC in blocked shots.

"With his size, Jeremy's got a nice presence inside," Gottfried said. "He's proven he can score and rebound. He's going to have to shoulder even more of the scoring responsibility this season and emotionally take his game to another level."

Williams' running mate at guard last season was Jones, who lived up to his junior college reputation by fitting in quickly at the Division I level. Jones led the Tide in assists—he had a career-high nine against Alabama State—and steals. His shooting could use some work—Jones shot just 38 percent from the field and 25 percent from three-point range a year ago.

Three other veteran guards return. **Tarik London** (2.1 ppg, 1.2 rpg, 40 assists), a 6-1 sophomore, backed up

1998-99 ALABAMA SCHEDULE

Nov.	15	@Ohio State
	19	Tennessee Tech
	22	Boston University
	25	McNeese State
	28	Jacksonville State
Dec.	1	@Texas A&M
	5	@Tulane
	8	Alabama State
	12	*South Alabama
	17	Northeast Louisiana
	21-23	#Pearl Harbor Classic
Jan.	2	Georgia
	6	@Mississippi
	9	Mississippi State
	13	@LSU
	16	South Carolina
	20	@Arkansas
	23	Auburn
	27	@Florida
	30	@Tennessee
Feb.	3	@Mississippi State
	6	Kentucky
	10	LSU
	13	@Auburn
	21	@Vanderbilt
	24	Mississippi
	27	Arkansas
Mar.	4-7	##SEC Tournament

@ Road Games
* Birmingham-Jefferson Civic Center, Birmingham, AL
# Honolulu, HI (vs. Weber State, first round; also BYU-Hawaii; Michigan State, Pepperdine, Texas Tech, Tulsa and Oregon State)
Georgia Dome, Atlanta, GA

Jones at the point last season and earned two starts. **Chris Rollins** (2.4 ppg, 2.9 rpg), a 6-5 senior, started four early-season games after transferring from junior college, but a broken wrist ended his season prematurely. **Terrance "Doc" Martin** (2.8 ppg, 1.5 rpg), a 6-3 sophomore, played nine minutes a game and showed some promise. He had 10 points against Arkansas, making four of six shots. Martin is recovering from offseason knee surgery.

Besides Hayes, three other frontcourt players with varying degrees of experience return. **M.C. Mazique** (2.3 ppg, 3.3 rpg), a 6-10, 240-pound senior, played in 21 games and started four times. **Neil Ashby**, a 6-8 sophomore, played in 25 games his freshman season. His best effort came against Jacksonville State, when he scored 10 points and grabbed six rebounds. **Alfred Moss** (2.7 ppg, 1.2 rpg) played in just six games as a redshirt sophomore before suffering an elbow injury that required surgery.

Five freshman and a junior college transfer will bid for playing time. The freshman who's the most advanced and has the best chance of helping the Tide this year is 6-8, 235-pound **Sam Haginas**. Haginas was chosen Alabama's Mr. Basketball in 1998 after averaging 16.4 ppg and 7.6 rpg as a senior at UMS-Wright in Mobile, Ala.

"Sam can step in and physically be ready to play," Gottfried said. "He's not your typical freshman who needs to spend time in the weight room."

Haginas, who can play inside or on the perimeter, was ranked the 99th-best senior in the country by *Prep Stars Recruiter's Handbook*.

Gottfried was able to take one of his Murray State recruits with him to Alabama. **Travis Stinnett**, a 5-11 guard from Alcoa (Tenn.) HS, orginally signed with the Racers because of Gottfried, and when the coach left, Stinnett wanted to leave also. After much discussion, Murray State released Stinnett, who will be eligible to play this season. He's a good three-point shooter and also has leadership qualities.

Cedric Patton is painfully thin at 6-7, 169 pounds, but was second-team all-state at Huntsville's Grissom HS last season. He's a good perimeter shooter Hobbs likened to former Alabama star Keith Askins.

Two freshmen who redshirted last season return. **Ray Johnston** is a 6-1 guard who was a first-team all-state pick at Montgomery (Ala.) Academy two years ago. **Sam Williams** is a 6-8, 230-pound forward who averaged 16.8 ppg, 8.2 rpg and 2.4 bpg two years ago at Demopolis (Ala.) HS.

adidas Blue Ribbon Analysis

BACKCOURT	B	BENCH/DEPTH	B
FRONTCOURT	C	INTANGIBLES	C

There's no question Alabama athletic director Bob Bockrath made the right decision when he replaced ousted coach David Hobbs with Mark Gottfried. Gottfried is one of the brightest young coaches in the business, and he's smart and humble enough to realize there is much he can learn from his mentors, including the legendary John Wooden and Rhode Island coach Jim Harrick. Gottfried has applied much of what he's learned from the two former UCLA coaches and come up with a system that is fun for his players to execute and exciting for fans to watch. When Gottfried was at Murray State, the Racers kept the scoreboard clock operators busy.

"I'm not sure, personnel-wise, which style our players are best in," Gottfried said. "But we're going to try and open it up some, try to get in the 80s and 90s. Last year, Alabama only averaged about 69 points a game. We want to push it up the other way."

Gottfried will get the job done at Alabama, but it might take a while. Hobbs and his staff struggled with their recruiting efforts, and as a result, the talent level is down in Tuscaloosa. Gottfried was hired too late to get much done in recruiting, though he did manage to bring one of his Murray State recruits, Travis Stinnett, along. Stinnett, though, will be more of a complementary player than an impact player.

Several teams in the SEC West look better than Alabama. Look for the Tide to finish fifth in the division this season, but better days are ahead.

(C.D.)

AUBURN

LOCATION .... **Auburn, AL**
CONFERENCE .... **Southeastern (Western Division)**
LAST SEASON .... **16-14 (.533)**
CONFERENCE RECORD .... **7-9 (3rd)**
STARTERS LOST/RETURNING **1/4**
NICKNAME .... **Tigers**
COLORS .... **Burnt Orange & Navy Blue**
HOMECOURT .... **Beard-Eaves Memorial Coliseum (12,500)**
COACH .... **Cliff Ellis (Florida State '68)**
RECORD AT SCHOOL .... **67-55 (4 yrs.)**
CAREER RECORD .... **415-267 (23 yrs.)**
ASSISTANTS .... **Eugene Harris (Florida State '68)**
Mike LaPlante (Maine '89)
Shannon Weaver (Middle Tennessee '93)
TEAM WINS (last 5 yrs.) **11-16-19-16-16**
RPI (last 5 yrs.) **120-101-93-100-58**
1997-98 FINISH .... **Lost in second round of NIT.**

A season that includes 16 wins and a trip to the NIT would no doubt be considered a bitter disappointment for some of college basketball's elite programs. Not at Auburn. For the Tigers, those 16 wins and NIT trip represent real progress.

The NIT appearance netted the Tigers' first postseason victory in 10 years. Auburn fans are excited, and hopeful that this year, the Tigers can take one more step forward and play in the NCAA Tournament, something the program hasn't done since 1988.

Fifth-year coach Cliff Ellis isn't side-stepping those expectations.

"When you look at where things were in 1994, we have taken this program to another level," Ellis said. "Now our goal is to take it to another level. We've had four straight winning seasons and the first postseason win in 10 years. Now, in the next four to five years, we want to have this group go on to another level. Now, the expectations move up a little bit."

Ellis isn't afraid to meet those expectations head-on because he knows that, for the first time in his four seasons at Auburn, he has a deep roster. Ellis and his staff have added seven newcomers to a nucleus of six veterans. Included in that recruiting class, which was ranked as high as sixth in the country by three recruiting analysts, is a true impact player, 6-7 junior **Chris Porter**, who transferred from Chipola Junior College in Marianna, Fla.

Porter comes with excellent credentials. He was ranked the No. 2 junior college player in the country by Blue Ribbon experts Rick Ball and Phil Henzel. That opinion was shared by recruiting analyst Bob Gibbons.

"(Porter is) Auburn's best signee since Charles Barkley," Gibbons said. "He's great. He's one of the top two junior college players in the nation, which makes him like a top five high school player. He's a major impact player."

Porter is mobile, athletic and plays with relentless effort. That makes him a great rebounder—he averaged 11.8 boards, to go along with 24.4 points per game, as a JC ll-America honors.

"Chris Porter has a lot of skills," Ellis said. "We signed him out of high school, but he eventually went to junior college. He certainly performed at the junior college level in the way that we thought he would when we signed him out of high school. He had a great two years as a junior college player, coming out as one of the top power forwards in America."

Porter scored 1,332 points in 58 career games at Chipola, averaging 22.9 ppg in his two seasons there. He's expected to step right into the starting power forward job and probably become the Tigers' leading scorer and rebounder. For that reason, *Blue Ribbon* chose Porter as its preseason newcomer of the year in the SEC.

Porter will be joined on Auburn's front line by **Bryant Smith** (13.3 ppg, 6.6 rpg, 64 assists, 67 steals), a 6-5 junior who was chosen second-team All-SEC by the league's coaches. Smith led the Tigers in scoring and was second in rebounding. He also paced the Tigers with 92 offensive rebounds, which helps account for his team-leading field-goal percentage (.506). That figure was third best in the SEC.

Smith isn't much of a perimeter threat—he shot just .211 percent from three-point range last year—but he's capable of putting big numbers on the board. A year ago he had five double-doubles, including a 26-point, 13-rebound, six-steal effort against Wofford. He also had 25 points and nine rebounds against UAB, 21 points and six boards against Alabama and 20 points and five rebounds against South Carolina.

Smith provides an added bonus—he's also the Tigers' best defender, often given the task of guarding the opposition's best scorer.

"We are looking for maturity and a leadership role from Bryant Smith," Ellis said. "He is primed for his senior year in giving us the necessary things to lead us."

At center, **Mamadou N'diaye** will continue as a work-in-progress. A year ago, N'diaye (8.0 ppg, 6.9 rpg, 73 blocked shots), a 7-0 junior, started all 30 games and became a feared shot blocker. N'diaye was second in the league to Tennessee's C.J. Black with his average of 2.4 blocks per game.

N'diaye also made some advances offensively, finishing as the team's fouth-leading scorer and shooting .503 percent from the field.

"He continually gets better," Ellis said of the native of Dakar, Senegal. "He always has had tremendous shot-blocking ability. In each season, he has also improved his game from the offensive end. Given the fact that he has two years experience, hopefully he'll continue to grow as an inside presence. It's very difficult to score over him, and I see his offensive game progressing."

The only other returning frontcourt player is 6-5, 235-pound senior **Adrian Chilliest** (2.4 ppg, 3.5 rpg), who started eight times a year ago.

The backcourt is in the capable hands of 6-2 junior **Doc Robinson** (12.4 ppg, 3.7 rpg, 131 assists, 35 steals) and **Scott Pohlman** (10.6 ppg, 2.6 rpg, 44 assists, 35 steals), Auburn's second- and third-leading scorers of a year ago.

Robinson shared the job with Wes Flanigan two years ago, but last year stepped into the starter's role and responded with a solid season. Robinson was sixth in the league in assists and second on the team in steals. He also shot a respectable .339 percent from three-point range.

"With his experience, Doc should be primed and ready to be one of the top point guards in the conference," Ellis said. "He showed his character and leadership in a lot of key conference games."

Pohlman surprised a lot of people with his aggressive offensive game. He started 29 games at shooting guard and wound up on the SEC's All-Freshman team. Pohlman is a threat from the outside (team-high 53 three-pointers) and can also get to the basket. And when he got fouled last season, Pohlman could cash in. He led the team in free-throw percentage (.831).

Another backcourt veteran is 6-5 junior **Daymeon Fishback** (6.9 ppg, 3.2 rpg), a potential game-breaking shooter. He was third on the team in three-pointers made (39) and shot 35 percent from behind the arc. When his stroke is on, Fishback can score points in a hurry. He dropped a career-high 24 points on Arkansas, making five of nine three-pointers. He made four of seven threes in 28 minutes against Ole Miss, scoring 14 points.

Several members of Auburn's huge recruiting class will have to help out. One player who could have a big impact, though not to the extent of Porter's, is 6-9, 225-pound freshman **David Hamilton**. The Tigers went all the way to California to land Hamilton, who was ranked the 111th-

1998-99 AUBURN SCHEDULE

Nov.	13	Southeastern Louisiana
	16	Florida A&M
	19	Central Florida
	23	BYU
	27-29	#United Airlines Tip-Off Classic
Dec.	3	UNC-Asheville
	6	@Florida State
	12	*UAB
	15	Wofford
	19	@Navy
	29	Bethune-Cookman
Jan.	2	Tennessee
	6	Arkansas
	9	@LSU
	13	@Mississippi
	16	Florida
	20	@Kentucky
	23	@Alabama
	27	Mississippi State
	30	@Georgia
Feb.	3	@South Carolina
	6	LSU
	9	Mississippi
	13	Alabama
	17	Vanderbilt
	24	@Arkansas
	27	@Mississippi State
Mar.	4-7	##SEC Tournament

@ Road Games
* Hardwood Classic, Birmingham, AL
# Honolulu, HI (vs. Rutgers, first round; also Hawaii and Wichita State)
Georgia Dome, Atlanta, GA

best player in nation by the *Recruiter's Handbook*. Hamilton averaged 17.8 ppg, 11.3 rpg and 2.5 bpg as a senior at Compton HS.

"David brings a hard-nosed game to us from a different part of the country, which I think is good," Ellis said. "He is an excellent rebounder, can score down low and play defense. David is one of those freshmen who can make an impact early-on."

Another frontcourt player who will be asked to contribute right away is 6-7 **Mack McGadney** from LeFlore HS in Mobile, Ala. He averaged 15.3 ppg and 8.5 rpg a year ago and played in the Alabama-Mississippi All-Star game last summer along with fellow Auburn freshman **Jay Heard**, a 6-3 shooting guard.

Heard, from Oxford (Ala.) HS, was a first-team all-state pick last year when he averaged 29.0 ppg and 9.0 rpg. "Jay Heard, in my opinion, was the best two-guard in the state," Ellis said. "He's big and strong, and I like the fact he can not only shoot the ball, but take you to the hole."

Corey Watkins is another freshman guard who can help. He comes with good credentials from Winchendon (Mass) Prep, where he was the only player among 10 future Division I signees to start every game. The 6-2 Watkins led Winchendon in steals and averaged 12.8 ppg. Before Winchendon, Watkins went to Mountain Brook HS in Birmingham, Ala, where he was a second-team all-state pick as a junior.

Abe Smith, a 6-7 freshman, averaged 18.9 ppg and 8.7 rpg last season at Roswell (Ga.) HS, the same school that produced Pohlman. A good athlete, Smith is also a pitcher in baseball. He has a fastball in the 90 mph range.

The final newcomer is 6-1 sophomore **Reggie Sharp**, who redshirted a year ago after transferring from West Georgia. As a freshman, he helped lead West Georgia to a Gulf South Conference title and 24-6 record, averaging 6.0 ppg and 3.2 apg.

adidas Blue Ribbon Analysis

BACKCOURT .... B   BENCH/DEPTH .... C+
FRONTCOURT .... B   INTANGIBLES .... B

After a trip to the NIT last season, Auburn coach Cliff Ellis is hungry for more. Ellis talks about taking the Tigers to the next level, which can mean only one thing—the NCAA Tournament.

Auburn has the makings of a tournament team, starting in the backcourt, where Doc Robinson and Scott Pohlman form a potent pair. The frontcourt is solid with senior stalwart Bryant Smith and emerging center Mamadou N'diaye returning. The addition of 6-7 junior college transfer Chris Porter gives the Tigers a true impact player, and other newcomers should be able to contribute right away.

Is this blend of talent enough to get Auburn to its first NCAA Tournament appearance since 1988?

"I think for the first time I feel comfortable that we can compete no matter who we play," Ellis said. "Does that mean we are going to win? That still remains to be seen. (But) this is the most talented team because of one thing—for the first time, I have depth."

Arkansas, as is almost always the case, will be the team to beat in the Western Division, but we see Auburn as a solid second. If the SEC is as good as Ellis thinks, that could be enough for that long-coveted NCAA Tournament bid.

"It's just time that the SEC gets six to seven teams in the NCAA Tournament," Ellis said.

If the the SEC place that many teams in the Big Dance, Auburn should be one of them.

(C.D.)

FLORIDA

LOCATION .... Gainesville, FL
CONFERENCE .... SEC (Eastern Division)
LAST SEASON .... 14-15 (.483)
CONFERENCE RECORD 6-10 (6th)
STARTERS LOST/RETURNING 2/3
NICKNAME .... Gators
COLORS .... Orange & Blue
HOMECOURT .... O'Connell Center (12,000)
COACH .... Billy Donovan (Providence '86)
RECORD AT SCHOOL .... 27-32 (2 yrs.)
CAREER RECORD .... 62-52 (4 yrs.)
ASSISTANTS .... John Pelphrey (Kentucky '92)
Anthony Grant (Dayton '87)
Donnie Jones (Pikeville '88)
TEAM WINS (last 5 yrs.) 16-29-17-13-14
RPI (last 5 yrs.) 12-38-60-160-75
1997-98 FINISH .... Lost in first round of NIT.

Further evidence of Florida's recovery under the leadership of coach Billy Donovan was provided last year, as the scrappy Gators played their way into the NIT. Donovan was pleased with that accomplishment in just his second season, but acknowledges his program has a long way to go before it reaches the level to which he's accustomed.

It's only fitting that the former assistant to Rick Pitino at Kentucky uses the SEC's best program as a barometer.

"Kentucky's been to something like 37 NCAA Tournaments," Donovan said. "In a given year, they're going to get hot and maybe win it all, just like they did last year. Our ultimate goal here at Florida is to win the national championship. But a lot of people don't realize the school has only been to the NCAA Tournament five times in its history.

"Our goal right now should be getting to the NCAA Tournament every year. We want to establish that tradition."

The Gators might not get to the Big Dance this season, but Donovan will trot out the best Florida team Gator fans have seen since Lon Kruger took a band of upstarts to the Final Four in 1994.

Florida has been fortified with a great recruiting class that most analysts ranked among the top five in the country. Included in that haul are four freshmen who should be able to provide immediate contributions: 6-8 forward **Mike Miller**, 5-10 guard **Ted Dupay**, 6-4 guard **LaDarius Halton** and 6-8 post **Udonis Haslem.**

Those four will join a solid nucleus led by 6-8 senior **Greg Stolt**, 5-11 senior **Eddie Shannon** and 6-4 junior **Kenyan Weaks**.

Because of a mid-summer incident involving a Florida coed, Weaks won't be around for the first nine games of the season, having been suspended for breaching the university's conduct code. Weaks will miss games against Florida State and Duke, but returns in time for a late-December game against Michigan.

"Kenyan's situation is really disappointing to me because he didn't use better judgement," Donovan said. "He had an unbelievable offseason and would have been one of the most improved players in the conference."

Weaks (12.7 ppg, 4.8 rpg, 33 assists, 39 steals, 10 blocked shots) blossomed under Donovan's guidance last season, becoming one of the feared shooters around. He shot .513 percent from the floor, but an even more impressive .508 percent (fifth in the nation) from three-point range.

Weaks' woes might hamper the Gators early, but they might also have a positive effect. His absence could allow Dupay or Halton to play more minutes, thus indoctrinating them into the college game that much faster.

Both are scorers. Dupay, ranked the No. 22 prospect in the nation by *Prep Stars Recruiter's Handbook* and a McDonald's All-American, was the most prolific scorer in Florida high school history. Dupay is a great shooter who averaged 41.5 points as a senior for Mariner High School in Cape Coral, Fla. He finished his career with 3,744 points (you read that correctly) and last season was chosen the state's Mr. Basketball.

Some have compared Dupay to none other than his coach, himself an undersized but scrappy guard who could shoot a little bit.

"I hope he's a lot better than I was," Donovan said. "The first two years, I cheated Providence College. I'd compare Ted more to (former Kentucky player) Travis Ford, but with maybe a little more quickness and speed."

Halton was runnerup to Dupay in Mr. Basketball voting last season, and he too scored a few points during his career at New Smyrna (Fla.) HS. Halton averaged 32.9 points as a senior and finished with 2,860 in his career. He was ranked No. 57 on *Prep Stars*' list.

One freshman who might already have earned a starting job is Miller, ranked No. 7 by analyst Bob Gibbons and No. 21 by *Prep Stars*. Like Dupay, Miller was also a McDonald's All-American. Miller doesn't exactly come from a high school hoops hotbed—he played for Mitchell (S.D.) High School—but he was heavily recruited and narrowed his choices to Florida, Kansas and Kentucky. Miller, who can play either small forward or big guard, averaged 26.6 points and 10.5 rebounds as a senior.

"Mike no doubt will have an opportunity to play right away," Donovan said. "He's very gifted and loves to play. He's a good shooter, but he can really put it on the floor and passes it well."

Miller could join veterans Stolt and Shannon in the starting lineup.

Stolt is another Donovan success story. Most thought he would be too plodding to fit into the coach's uptempo system, but Stolt has flourished. A great shooter, Stolt (12.0 ppg, 4.6 rpg, 32 blocked shots) connected on .458 percent of his three-pointers last season, 19th in the country. Not bad for a power forward.

"I think our style has really helped Greg," Donovan said. "He's a good runner north and south and a phenonmenal three-point shooter. When you've got a four-man who can shoot like that, it really poses difficult matchups."

Shannon (11.6 ppg, 3.4 rpg, 123 assists, 53 steals), a four-year starter, should handle the point this year, but he can also move over to shooting guard if the need arises. Shannon isn't quite the three-point shooter Weaks and Stolt are, but a year ago he shot a respectable .323 percent from behind the arc. He was second on the team in assists and tied for the lead in steals.

"Eddie's a hard worker and a great kid," Donovan said. "He's not overly talented, but he's a super competitor. We really need him to step up and provide leadership."

The only other returning guard on Florida's roster is 5-7 junior walkon **Mark Timinski** (0.0 ppg, 0.0 rpg). The Gators have a lot more returning depth in the frontcourt.

Obiora Nnaji (3.6 ppg, 2.5 rpg) is a 6-11, 240-pound center entering just his third year of organized basketball. He gained valuable experience playing for an Athletes in Action team that toured Croatia and Switzerland last summer.

Donovan is looking for an inside scorer to complement his perimeter shooters and hopes Nnaji can become the man. Last year, Nnaji played just 12.5 minutes per game, but he shot .494 percent from the field and blocked 23 shots. Donovan sees promise.

Sophomores **Brent Wright** and **Major Parker** were members of Donovan's first recruiting class. Wright (7.4 ppg, 4.3 rpg, 30 steals), 6-7, earned 10 starts and was the Gators' fifth-leading scorer. Parker (5.3 ppg, 2.1 rpg), 6-3, is a bit undersized, but he's a rugged competitor. He played 15.0 minutes per game as a freshman.

Donovan is hoping to get some contributions from **Greg Cristell**, whose career has been plagued by injuries. Cristell (2.3 ppg, 1.7 rpg), a 6-9, 236-pound junior, played in just 15 games last year. So far, he's come back from a dislocated knee cap, a stress fracture in a toe and a herniated disk. The latter injury kept him out of early-season action a year ago, but he returned and eventually worked his way into the rotation, playing 19.5 minutes per game in two SEC Tournament appearances.

Patrick O'Connor (0.0 ppg, 0.4 rpg) is a 6-5 sophomore walkon. He played in just five games as a freshman.

The final newcomer is the monstrous (275 pounds) Haslem, who keeps Florida's pipeline into Miami Senior High School flowing. Haslem averaged 14.2 points and 8.0 rebounds as a senior. *Prep Stars* ranked him No. 131 in the senior class.

"Haslem is going to play because he's a 6-8 low-post scorer with good footwork, a wide body and good touch around the basket," Donovan said.

adidas Blue Ribbon Analysis

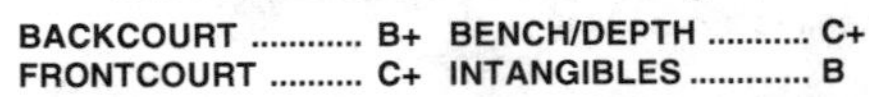

BACKCOURT .... B+   BENCH/DEPTH .... C+
FRONTCOURT .... C+   INTANGIBLES .... B

Gator fans have to be pleased at how the program is progressing under Donovan, one of the youngest head coaches in the nation (33), but one of the best.

So far, Donovan and his staff have been able to attract several high-caliber players to Gainesville. Donovan's first recruiting class was solid, and his second was sensational. He signed several players who will fit right in to his high-octane offense, including Ted Dupay, the most prolific

1998-99 FLORIDA SCHEDULE

Nov.	16	Georgia Southern
	20	@Florida State
	23	Bethune-Cookman
	30	Coastal Carolina
Dec.	5	Southern
	9	@Duke
	12	Jacksonville
	20	Long Island
	22	Morehead State
	27	*Michigan
Jan.	2	@Kentucky
	6	Vanderbilt
	10	Georgia
	13	@South Carolina
	16	@Auburn
	20	@LSU
	23	Tennessee
	27	Alabama
	30	@Mississippi State
Feb.	4	Kentucky
	6	Mississippi
	10	@Tennessee
	13	@Georgia
	16	Arkansas
	24	South Carolina
	27	@Vanderbilt
Mar.	4-7	

@ Road Games
* Orange Bowl Basketball Classic, Miami, FL
\# Georgia Dome, Atlanta, GA

scorer in Florida high school history and Mike Miller, the best player in South Dakota history.

The new players will join holdovers such as Greg Stolt and Kenyan Weaks and give the Gators a potent offense. If Obiora Nnaji or freshman Udonis Haslem can become the low-post scorer Donovan needs, Florida can become one tough out.

In most other conferences in the country, the Gators could be expected to make a rapid rise this season. But in the SEC's tough Eastern Division, where five teams won 20 or more games last season and all six played in a postseason tournament, a dramatic vault up the standings might be impossible. Kentucky, Tennessee, South Carolina and Georgia are all more experienced than the young Gators.

Call it fifth place for Florida, but that will include another NIT trip. Next season, with gifted West Virginia high school point guard Brett Nelson having already committed to join the young talent pool at Florida, look for the Gators to finally get that NCAA Tournament bid Donovan covets.

(C.D.)

LOUISIANA STATE

LOCATION .... **Baton Rouge, LA**
CONFERENCE .... **SEC (Western Division)**
LAST SEASON .... **9-18 (.333)**
CONFERENCE RECORD .... **2-14 (6th)**
STARTERS LOST/RETURNING **2/3**
NICKNAME .... **Tigers**
COLORS .... **Purple & Gold**
HOMECOURT .... **Pete Maravich Assembly Center (14,164)**
COACH .... **John Brady (Belhaven '76)**
RECORD AT SCHOOL .... **9-18 (1 yr.)**
CAREER RECORD .... **98-95 (7 yrs.)**
ASSISTANTS Kermit Davis Jr. (Mississippi State '82)
Butch Pierre (Mississippi State '84)
Donnie Tyndall (Morehead State '94)
TEAM WINS (last 5 yrs.) **11-12-12-10-9**
RPI (last 5 yrs.) **104-106-117-114-161**
1997-98 FINISH .... **Lost in conference first round.**

This should be the year LSU's downward spiral halts, for a lot of reasons: Better players, another year of the John Brady system; and an easier schedule.

Start with the schedule.

"I want to play 15-to 17 home games every year, plus the SEC," Brady said. Consider it done. LSU will play just two non-conference road games and one is at lowly Houston on Nov. 30. Then the Tigers go to Arizona on the unlikely date of Feb. 13, right in the midst of the SEC schedule. Otherwise, LSU plays host to the likes of Texas-Pan American, McNeese State, Prairie View, Troy State and Belmont. Yeah, there are visits from pesky North Carolina A&T and Texas, but clearly the burden on LSU this season will be to improve from its woeful 2-14 SEC finish as it tries to get back to postseason play for the first time since 1993.

That year capped a stretch of 10 consecutive NCAA Tournament appearances but also marked the beginning of the end for former coach Dale Brown. He finished his storied 25-year career with four losing seasons, so Brady was dealt a tough hand when he took over last year.

There was progress, for sure, as LSU finished 9-18 with occasional flashes of brilliance. But the progress is better measured in what LSU accomplished in practice in installing a new system and in the signing of a whopping 11 players. Ten of them made it to LSU and combined with just three returning players, a transfer who sat out last season and a few walkons, the Tigers will have a totally different look in 1998-99.

But, wait, there's more. There always seems to be with LSU basketball. In this case, it was an NCAA investigation that was concluding as *Blue Ribbon* was going to press. In a nutshell, LSU was charged with a number of violations, mostly revolving around Lester Earl, a Baton Rouge product who started at LSU in 1996-97 but then transferred to Kansas, and his brother, Louis, who was a senior for LSU last year.

LSU was accused of giving improper medical treatment to both, and former assistant coach Johnny Jones, now at Memphis, was accused of giving Lester Earl up to $12,000 in cash. A Baton Rouge doctor already admitted giving Earl cash. Louis Earl and LSU admitted to the medical treatment, and his mother admitted that LSU helped her and her daughter find jobs.

A subsequent investigation by LSU led to the school's self-imposing the penalties of relinquishing five scholarships over three years, limiting recruiting visits and forfeiting the games in which Lester Earl played early in the 1996-97 season before he quit the team. LSU appeared before the NCAA in August, and Brady believes that will be the end of it. He is confident the NCAA will accept the self-imposed sanctions and that LSU will be neither kept off TV nor out of postseason play.

"The taking of scholarships will hurt us a little bit in normal growth development and normal progress, but if we keep what we have and are able to add one or two players in the next couple of years, I think we'll be fine," Brady said.

Keeping what it has should be no problem for nine of those 10 recruits, but the status of one of them, the most coveted, is still uncertain. Stromile Swift, the 6-9 forward/center from Fair Park HS in Shreveport, La. (21.5 ppg, 10.2 rpg, 3.3 bpg) moved to Baton Rouge in the early summer. But going into October, Swift, one of the most highly rated players in the nation last year, had yet to qualify academically under NCAA standards.

He had two more opportunities to take the ACT to become eligible and enroll at LSU after one semester. That meant he would miss five games. In the meantime, Swift was auditing six hours at LSU and keeping in constant touch with the coaches. But there's a catch. Swift did not sign a national letter of intent. So while the other freshmen enrolled at LSU, he didn't and had the option of leaving and going somewhere else if the NCAA sanctions were not to his liking. In all probability, Swift will be a Tiger, but there was always that chance because he left himself an out.

Swift was living with a relative in Baton Rouge and taking an ACT prep course.

Brady couldn't comment about Swift, because he isn't yet on scholarship. But suffice to say a player of Swift's considerable skills can elevate the Tigers' talent level in a hurry.

In the meantime, LSU will be led by three returning seniors. **Maurice Carter**, a 6-4 guard (14.4 ppg, 3.7 rpg, 44 assists, 21 steals) established himself as a solid SEC performer, especially with a marked improvement in his three-point shooting (44 of 131, .336 percent). "And I don't see any reason why he won't improve more this season," Brady said. "He's worked hard and he's also become a more committed defender."

Willie Anderson (12.0 ppg, 3.2 rpg, 64 assists, 31 steals). also 6-4, survived an up-and-down season after arriving as a junior-college transfer and had some big games.

"He was our best perimeter defender, developed that and got better at that," Brady said. "He played well offensively the first half of the year, and then he hit a stretch where he lost his confidence in his making of shots. He started pressing on offense and never found the groove he had the first half of the season. But he continued to work. He got down on himself, but that, too, was a learning experience for him. He had a tremendous offseason of work. There's not a player on our team who has put the time into developing his game as well as Willie has in the spring and throughout the summer."

Cedric Carter (8.1 ppg, 6.1 rpg), at just 6-7, was forced to play the post last season for the undermanned and undersized Tigers. Carter, however, will probably move to a reserve role as 6-11 junior **Jabari Smith** takes over at center. Carter is obviously flexible: Because LSU signed so many players, Brady took his scholarship, so Carter offered to pay his own way to remain part of the team.

"Cedric Carter will play, especially early on because of his experience," Brady said. "He's special because he chose to stay at LSU. He was willing to give up his scholarship and play as a walkon, because he wants to finish his degree from LSU. He played well at times last year against some SEC teams."

Just three others return, all walkons. **Jack Warner**, a 6-5 junior, played in just five games before breaking his hand and missing the rest of the season. **Jeremy Comeaux**, a 6-3 sophomore, played just four minutes, and **Brandon Landry**, a 6-1 guard, never got off the bench. But all are adept in running Brady's motion offense, which makes them invaluable in practices that can be most demanding.

One who survived them last season was **Brian Beshara**, a 6-7 sophomore forward who couldn't play last season after transferring from Rice. The product of Dallas averaged 3.4 ppg, 2.0 rpg for the Owls in 1996-97, but figures to start for LSU this season along with the three seniors. He's a tough kid who's not afraid to bang and should fit well into Brady's offense.

The other starter at first should be 6-1 junior point guard **Jamaal Wolfe**, a product of Baton Rouge who returns home after transferring from Lon Morris (Texas) JC (10.6 ppg, 2.3 rpg, 7.0 apg). "It will be interesting to see who emerges to play behind Jamal, and I say Jamal simply because he is a junior college player and I have recruited him to secure the majority of minutes at point guard at this writing," Brady said.

1998-99 LOUISIANA STATE SCHEDULE

Nov.	16	Texas-Pan American
	21	McNeese State
	25	North Carolina A&T
	30	@Houston
Dec.	12	Jackson State
	16	Prairie View A&M
	19	Texas
	22	Troy State
	29	Belmont
Jan.	2	Arkansas
	6	@Tennessee
	9	Auburn
	13	Alabama
	16	@Mississippi State
	20	Florida
	23	Vanderbilt
	27	@Arkansas
	30	@Kentucky
Feb.	3	Mississippi
	6	@Auburn
	10	@Alabama
	13	@Arizona
	17	South Carolina
	20	@Georgia
	24	Mississippi State
	27	@Mississippi
March	4-7	#SEC Tournament

@ Road Games
# Georgia Dome, Atlanta, GA

The competition includes 6-3 freshman **Omar Mance** from Lithonia (Ga.) HS (21 ppg, 6 rpg, 5 apg); 6-2 freshman **Darryl Cooper** from Redan Central HS in Stone Mountain, Ga. (21.2 ppg, 6.0 rpg, 3.5 apg); and 6-4 freshman **Collis Temple III**, a product of LSU's University High (26.9 ppg).

Anderson will also fill in some at the point as he did last year. The reason the point-guard spot is available is DeJuan Collins was not invited back by Brady. Collins, a junior college transfer who played one season for LSU (8.8 ppg, 3.7 rpg, 3.4 apg), was involved in an early-season altercation with Beshara in the weight room and broke his hand when he hit his bigger teammate. It went downhill from there for Collins, who is one of seven players who didn't return.

Forward Louis Earl (3.4 ppg, 3.0 rpg) and guard Reggie Tucker (1.8 ppg, 2.6 rpg) were the team's only seniors. Forward Rogers Washington would have been (9.2 ppg, 4.1 apg) but flunked out and transferred to nearby Southwestern Louisiana, where he'll sit out this year. Two others were not invited back, forwards Rhodaria Caston (4.1 ppg, 4.3 rpg) and Chico Potts (2.9 ppg, 2.2 rpg), while forward Leroy Womack (2.2 ppg, 1.6 rpg) left the team after five games last season.

LSU never really had a center last season, but that role should be filled by Smith. Smith, who was a standout at Atlanta Metropolitan JC (18.0 ppg, 12.0 rpg) didn't play basketball last season so he could earn his associate degree and get himself academically prepared to enter LSU. By all accounts, he's an excellent big man.

"He needs to get in shape," Brady said, admitting the year off didn't help Smith. "It's been an adjustment for him, but his concern is getting in tip-top condition. But Jabari Smith will make a significant contribution to our team."

LSU will still run a five-man motion, but will score more out of the post. However Smith and Swift are more than capable of moving out for a 15-footer. That's where two freshmen from Baton Rouge fit in.

Jermaine Williams and **Marqus Ledoux** were teammates on three state championship teams at Parkview Baptist High School. Williams, a 6-6 forward (11.6 ppg) was a complement to the 6-8 Ledoux (14 ppg, 6 rpg, 2 bpg) on a talented team. Both figure to play key reserve roles for LSU this season after being strongly recruited by other schools.

"They're both in the mold of the LSU player we want to recruit. Not restricted to the post but can play in the post and also have the skill level it takes to play out on the floor, which makes the motion offense most effective," Brady said. "Both of them will play some quality minutes and as the season goes on, they'll play more and more."

Two other big freshmen, 6-8 **Brad Bridgewater** from Pointe Coupee HS in New Roads, La. (19.0 ppg, 7.0 rpg) and 6-9 **Brian Helquist** of University Christian in Jacksonville, Fla. (17.0 ppg, 14.0 rpg), will likely be redshirted, although don't be surprised if Bridgewater makes his way into the rotation. One signee, Darryl Robbins of Istrouma HS in Baton Rouge, failed to make the grade and went to a junior college.

adidas Blue Ribbon Analysis

BACKCOURT	**C+**	**BENCH/DEPTH**	**B-**
FRONTCOURT	**B+**	**INTANGIBLES**	**B**

Regardless of the NCAA outcome, LSU is on the way back.

LSU ranked first in the SEC in points allowed (65.4), first in opponents' rebounds (32.8), third in opponents' three-point field-goal percentage (.334) and fourth in rebound margin (3.2). Obviously Brady recognized that LSU's deliberate style of offense affected those numbers. "But we tried to get a quality shot and rebound the ball well. We outrebounded 20 of our 27 opponents last season," he said.

Perhaps, but LSU finished last in the league in scoring (62.2), 10th in rebounding (36.0), ninth in field-goal percentage (.424), ninth in opponents' field-goal percentage (.424), ninth in three-point percentage (.328), 11th in three-pointers per game (5.2), 10th in free-throw percentage (64.5) and last in blocks (1.7), turnover margin (-4.1) and scoring margin (-3.1). LSU was also 11th in steals (6.1).

And now Brady has to start over, in a sense. Teaching his motion offense is no small task. Assistant coach Kermit Davis Jr., who left as head coach at Idaho to join Brady at LSU, shares in the teaching of the relentless scheme, which they installed from day one and worked on every practice thereafter. "The problem we have now is just three players are returning who were part of that operation a year ago," he said. "We have better players, more talented players and more character on our team because of recruiting, but what we don't have is the experience to become a better motion team.

"But the players we do have are intelligent enough to be able to pick it up, and with the help of the leadership of Maurice Carter, Willie Anderson, Cedric Carter and Brian Beshara, hopefully we'll come along and grasp the offense and be a good offensive team sometime in January."

At the very least, the losing streak should end. How much progress LSU makes in the always-tough SEC remains to be seen.

(L.F.)

MISSISSIPPI

LOCATION .... **Oxford, MS**
CONFERENCE .... **Southeastern (Western Division)**
LAST SEASON .... **22-7 (.758)**
CONFERENCE RECORD .... **12-4 (1st)**
STARTERS LOST/RETURNING **2/3**
NICKNAME .... **Rebels**
COLORS .... **Cardinal Red & Navy Blue**
HOMECOURT .... **Tad Smith Coliseum (8,135)**
COACH .... **Rod Barnes (Mississippi '88)**
RECORD AT SCHOOL .... **First year**
CAREER RECORD .... **First year**
ASSISTANTS ... Marc Dukes (Mississippi College '77)
Eric Bozeman (Arkansas Tech '81)
Wayne Brent (Northeast Louisiana '89)
TEAM WINS (last 5 yrs.) **14-8-12-20-22**
RPI (last 5 yrs.) **106-184-141-48-16**
1997-98 FINISH .... **Lost in first round of NCAA Tournament.**

Rob Evans finally got an offer he couldn't refuse.

His work in reviving Mississippi's basketball program had turned Evans into a commodity, a man whose name was bandied about in connection with seemingly dozens of job openings. Evans eventually began receiving offers, and to his credit, he resisted them for as long as he could. But when Arizona State came calling last spring, Evans couldn't say no. The challenge of building a program in a great league and in a part of the country where he had once lived was appealing. The money wasn't too bad either.

After Evans' departure, Ole Miss administrators said they wanted an experienced head coach to replace him. Southern Mississippi's James Green's name was mentioned prominently—he's an Ole Miss graduate who has plenty of name recognition in the talent-rich state.

The two sides never could come to an agreement, though. The man chosen to replace Evans didn't exactly fit the job description. Rod Barnes, Evans' 32-year-old former assistant, had never run his own program on any level. But he too is a former Ole Miss player, and was the overwhelming choice of the players Evans left behind.

That he doesn't have any prior experience as a head coach doesn't worry Barnes a bit.

"Well, let me ask you this," Barnes told the *Jackson Clarion-Ledger*. "How much experience did the previous head coach have before he got the job?"

The answer: None. After 25 years as an assistant, Evans' time to be the boss had come when he took the Ole Miss job in 1992. Barnes doesn't have 25 years in the business, but he does have certain intangible qualities that make those who know him say he's right for the job.

"Rod always wanted to coach," said former Ole Miss coach Ed Murphy, who coached Barnes. "You have players occasionally who you know this is the profession they belong in. He's one of them."

"Rod's been a leader all his life," Mississippi chancellor Robert Khayat said. "And this is a leadership role. I have all the confidence in him. He's mature far beyond his years. I'm sure he'll learn some on the job, but I'm 60 years old and I'm still learning."

All his life, Barnes has faced down challenges and come out on top. Many wondered whether the gawky, skinny kid from Satartia, Miss. could even play SEC-level basketball when he showed up in Oxford in 1984, but he eventually made the all-conference team.

"I have always been the underdog," Barnes said. "I just try to prove (naysayers) wrong. It's like a journey."

The journey that Barnes begins at Ole Miss includes a couple of experienced tour guides. In guards **Keith Carter**, a 6-4 senior, and **Michael White**, a 6-1 senior, the Rebels have one of the most experienced backcourts in the league. Carter and White have 159 career starts between them as they helped Evans orchestrate the return of Ole Miss basketball.

With the departure of All-SEC forward Ansu Sesay (18.6 ppg, 7.6 rpg, 80 assists, 36 steals, 26 blocked shots), a second-round draft pick of the Dallas Mavericks, Carter will become the Rebels' go-to scorer this season. Not that Carter, a game-breaking shooter, didn't occasionally carry the Rebels offensively even while Sesay was around.

A year ago, Carter (14.8 ppg, 6.2 rpg, 53 assists, 40 steals), was Ole Miss' second leading scorer and its third-best three-point shooter (.372). He was second on the team with 58 three-pointers, and added another dimension to his game by becoming the team's third-leading rebounder.

Carter had some big-time performances last season, like the night he dropped 33 points on Temple. He also had 15 rebounds in that game and made a school-record seven three-pointers. Carter had a career-high 16 rebounds against Long Island.

After finishing ranked among the SEC's leaders in scoring (seventh), three-point percentage (eighth), rebounding (13th) and free-throw percentage (seventh), Carter was a second-team All-SEC pick.

"Keith will handle the new role well because he is a very intelligent player," Barnes said. "He understands the game, and he knows that the opposition will come after him and put pressure on him this year. He's been waiting his turn to step up and lead this team. I feel Keith is ready for this role mentally and physically, and he is ready to be the leader of this team."

Carter gained invaluable experience over the summer while playing for the gold medal-winning United States Goodwill Games team. Carter was the U.S. team's sixth-leading scorer, averaging 7.8 points. He also shot .481 perecent from the field, .400 percent from three-point range and 78 percent from the free-throw line.

White is a smart point guard who knows his limits and never tries to exceed them. Last season he led an unselfish Ole Miss team with 87 assists. He was also the Rebels' top three-point threat, percentage-wise, though he was economical with his attempts. White made 28 of 59 three-pointers (.475 percent) and also shot .485 percent from the floor. Barnes will probably need White to shoot more often this season.

"Michael has been a very solid player for us the past three years," Barnes said. "He is our floor leader, and we expect him to have an outstanding seasn for us. He has continued to work hard and is improved in every phase of the game."

Jason Flanigan, a 6-1 sophomore, will see plenty of action behind White. Flanigan (4.1 ppg, 1.6 rpg, 51 assists) played shooting guard in high school, but made the transition to point guard in his freshman year and wound up fourth on the team in assists. Flanigan didn't forget how to shoot—he made nine of 10 three-pointers in the Rebels' last 12 games.

The only returning guard behind Carter is 6-0 senior **Hunter Carpenter** (2.0 ppg, 0.4 rpg) who played in just 10 games a year ago.

The Rebels will miss Sesay and center Anthony Boone (5.3 ppg, 4.1 rpg), their inspirational leader, but they do have a solid veteran returning in the frontcourt. **Jason Smith** (9.8 ppg, 6.5 rpg, 39 assists, 48 steals) is a 6-6 senior who's a great defender and rebounder. He does pretty well offensively, too, for a guy who doesn't have much of a jumper. He had 20-point nights against Florida and South Carolina last year.

The opposition's high scorer hates to see Smith coming—he's a relentless defender who excelled in Evans' defensive-minded system. Smith led the Rebels in steals the last three years and was seventh in the SEC in steals (1.7 spg) a year ago.

1998-99 MISSISSIPPI SCHEDULE

Nov.	13	Alabama State
	16	Belmont
	18	@Temple
	23	Alabama A&M
	28	Austin Peay
Dec.	2	Northeast Louisiana
	5	Louisville
	7	West Alabama
	12	@Memphis
	21-23	#Puerto Rico Holiday Classic
	29	Prairie View A&M
Jan.	2	@Vanderbilt
	6	Alabama
	9	@Arkansas
	13	Auburn
	16	Kentucky
	20	Mississippi State
	23	Georgia
	27	@South Carolina
	30	Arkansas
Feb.	3	@LSU
	6	@Florida
	9	@Auburn
	17	Tennessee
	29	@Mississippi State
	24	@Alabama
	27	LSU
Mar.	4-7	##SEC Tournament

@ Road Games
# San Juan, PR (vs. St. Joseph's, first round; also American University-PR, Middle Tennessee State, North Carolina State, Ohio State, Oklahoma and UAB)
Georgia Dome, Atlanta, GA

Another defensive stalwart on the front line is 6-9 senior **Johnnie Rogers** (3.2 ppg, 2.8 rpg, 48 blocked shots), who made the most of his 10 minutes of playing time a game. He led the team and was 10th in the SEC in blocked shots. Rogers' playing time should increase substantially this season.

Two other frontcourt players return: 6-8 sophomore **Rahim Lockhart** (3.5 ppg, 3.1 rpg) and 6-8 senior **Jon Cantrell** (3.9 ppg, 1.7 rpg). At 245 pounds, Lockhart is a load to move out of the post. He shot .481 percent from the field as a freshman. Cantrell is a good perimeter shooter—he made 24 of his 57 three-point shots (.421 percent) last season. Cantrell spent a lot of time in the weight room over the summer so he can see some duty in the low post.

Marcus Hicks, a 6-6 junior from Northwest Mississippi CC, will give the Rebels a big lift in the frontcourt. Had the school hired anyone but Barnes as coach, Hicks might have signed elsewhere. He averaged 18.9 ppg and 9.0 rpg as a sophomore and was chosen a junior college All-American. Hicks was ranked as the eighth-best junior college player in the country by analyst Phil Henzel.

Two freshmen will also bid for playing time in the frontcourt. **John Engstrom** is a 7-footer who redshirted last year after suffering a torn ACL in the preseason. He averaged 12 points, eight rebounds and four blocked shots two years ago at Ridgecrest HS in Paragould, Ark.

Ole Miss also tapped Arkansas for 6-6 freshman **Darrian Brown**, who averaged 22 points and 12 rebounds while leading West Memphis HS to the Class 4A state championship.

Yet another freshman from Arkansas is 6-3 guard **Matt Pruitt**, who averaged 21.2 ppg, 6.2 rpg and 5.1 apg at Jonesboro HS.

Other players who will bid for backcourt minutes are **Lataryl Williams**, a 6-6 junior from Northwest Mississippi CC and 6-2 freshman **Syniker Taylor**.

Williams was a two-time junior college all-state pick as he averaged 12.0 ppg and 4.6 rpg in 67 career games at Northwest. Taylor, of Gulfport (Miss) HS, was chosen to the *Jackson Clarion-Ledger*'s All-State first team after averaging 27.8 ppg, 4.8 rpg, 4.2 apg and 3.1 spg. He missed the final 19 games of the year after breaking his right leg while driving for a dunk. Barnes will have to wait for the Ole Miss football team to get finished with Taylor, who was also a first-team all-state pick as a running back/linebacker.

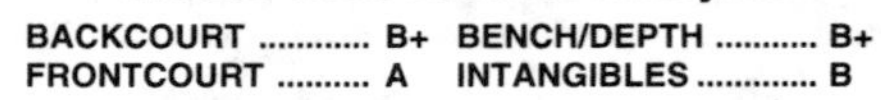

BACKCOURT	**B+**	**BENCH/DEPTH**	**B+**
FRONTCOURT	**A**	**INTANGIBLES**	**B**

After former head coach Rob Evans departed for Arizona State, Ole Miss wanted to hire an experienced head coach to replace him. Some would say the school took a risk by hiring Rod Barnes, who has never been a head coach at any level. Other think Barnes is a natural leader who was born to be a coach.

Barnes inherits a program that was revived under Evans' leadership, but the Rebels might not be quite as good as they were with first-team All-SEC and NBA draft pick Ansu Sesay. Several players will try and fill the void left by Sesay.

The logical candidate to become the Rebels' go-to scorer is senior Keith Carter, who has great range on his jump shot and is a strong jumper and rebounder. Michael White, Carter's running mate in the backcourt, is a steady point guard who needs to shoot more often this season.

In the frontcourt, returning veteran Jason Smith will be joined by heralded newcomer Marcus Hicks, a 6-6 junior college transfer, and a group of players who will try to fill the low-post void left by the departure of Anthony Boone.

Barnes will have to learn on the job this season, but *Blue Ribbon* thinks he won't fare badly. We look for the Rebels to finish third in the SEC's Western Division. They might not have quite as much fun as they did their two previous seasons, when they won the division championship, but it should be enough for another postseason tournament berth.

(C.D.)

MISSISSIPPI STATE

LOCATION .... **Starkville, MS**
CONFERENCE .... **Southeastern (Western Division)**
LAST SEASON .... **15-15 (.500)**
CONFERENCE RECORD .... **4-12 (5th)**
STARTERS LOST/RETURNING **2/3**
NICKNAME .... **Bulldogs**
COLORS .... **Maroon & White**
HOMECOURT .... **Humphrey Coliseum (10,000)**
COACH .... **Rick Stansbury (Campbellsville '82)**
RECORD AT SCHOOL .... **First year**
CAREER RECORD .... **First year**
ASSISTANTS .... **Greg Carter (Mississippi State '91)**
Robert Kirby (Pan American '83)
RPI (last 5 yrs.) **57-14-10-120-112**
TEAM WINS (last 5 yrs.) **18-22-26-12-15**
1997-98 FINISH .... **Lost in conference first round.**

Before the end of last season, after it had become apparent former Mississippi State coach Richard Williams' tenure was all but over, Bulldog fans wondered about his potential successor. Would a nationwide search be needed to hire a coach who could bring the program back to the level it had reached during a Final Four appearance in 1996?

As it turned out, the search began and ended in Starkville. Suffice to say Rick Stansbury had paid his dues to become a head coach. Sixteen years as an assistant, the last eight at Mississippi State, had helped him stake a claim to Williams' job. Stansbury had laid the groundwork by recruiting most of the players who took the Bulldogs to the Final Four. And he has long been popular with fans, alumni and the media—let's just say he mingles better than his old boss.

"He can put people at ease," Williams said. "He has that way about him that's much different than my way. Where maybe I put people on the edge, he puts people at ease."

Stansbury also has the requisite work ethic and passion for the game. "It's his passion," said Stansbury's wife, Meo. "But it's more than that. It's his life. He and basketball are intertwined as one."

OK, so we've established that Stansbury is a swell guy who loves basketball. Now the question is, can he coach? Though Stansbury has toiled on the sidelines of basketball courts most of his adult life, it has never been as the head man.

That question can't be answered fairly for a few years. But Stansbury does talk like a man who has carefully considered the job he's taken over and is prepared to handle it. He will add his own wrinkles to Williams' system, which had been successful for most of the '90s.

"We'll continue to do most of the things we've done," Stansbury said. "But there will be differences. We'll do more things from the fullcourt than we've done in the past. My attitude is to play from an aggressive standpoint. I'd like to be very aggressive defensively, and offensively to attack the basket."

Stansbury will have a few players who can do just that, though the talent level is clearly down a few notches from two years ago. Everything Mississippi State does this year will start with 6-10, 260-pound senior **Tyrone Washington** (12.9 ppg, 9.3 rpg, 61 blocked shots), who might be the best center in the SEC.

Last season, Washington was a third-team All-SEC pick after finishing in the top five in three statistics—field-goal percentage (.531, first), rebounding (second) and blocked shots (fourth). Washington is on *Blue Ribbon*'s preseason All-SEC team.

"There are a lot of expectations for Tyrone this season," Stansbury said. "For this team to be as good as we all want it to be, Tyrone's got to be big for us. But he's capable of doing that. He's our best player and go-to guy."

Washington had some big games last season, despite having to share the frontcourt scoring load with the departed Horatio Webster (17.0 ppg, 5.2 rpg) a two-time All-SEC pick. Washington had nine double-doubles, including a 22-point, 15-rebound effort against Mississippi. He had 13 double-figure rebound games, with a high of 17 against Auburn. Washington was a defensive presence last year as well—he blocked three or more shots in 13 games.

Stansbury's frontcourt is painfully thin, but he's hoping to get some help by the second semester in the form of Tyrus Boswell, a 6-7, 235-pound freshman who was still trying to gain eligibility during the fall. Originally from Mountain Brook (Ala.) HS, where he was an all-state selection, Boswell attended Winchendon (Mass). Prep last year in hopes of scoring well enough on the ACT to qualify for a Division I scholarship.

Boswell didn't get the score, but decided to keep trying to take the test in the fall. If he's successful, Boswell could play in January.

"Tyrus would give us a different kind of player on the back line," Stansbury said. "He gives you great athletic ability—he can really rebound and has the ability to run and jump and score some points. And being in prep school, he brings more maturity."

Without Boswell, the Bulldogs wouldn't have much to surround Washington. Quentin Smith, a 6-9 junior, has to sit out this season after a bizarre series of events a year ago when he transferred to Southern Mississippi, changed his mind after Stansbury was hired and then came back to Starkville.

That leaves 6-7, 245-pound **Oral Roberts** (3.5 ppg, 3.3 rpg) and 6-7 sophomore **Tang Hamilton** (4.4 ppg, 3.1 rpg) as Stansbury's only experienced frontcourt reserves. And Roberts and Hamilton barely qualify as experienced. A year ago, Hamilton played 14.6 minutes a game as a freshman, and Roberts just 12.2 minutes as a junior college transfer.

Hamilton seems to have SEC-level talent, and Stansbury is hoping he can claim the small forward job. Hamilton showed signs as a freshman. He scored 16 points against Centenary in his debut, and also had a double-double (16 points, 12 boards) against LSU.

Roberts, says Stansbury, "has all the ability in the world," but was slow to make the adjustment to Division I basketball.

Whatever happens to Boswell, another freshman could steal several minutes a game in the frontcourt. Stansbury reached all the way to Milwaukee to find 6-8, 250-pound **Robert Jackson**, a freshman who can play power forward or center. Jackson was a first-team all-state selection after averaging 17.4 points and 8.7 rebounds for Washington High School. "I think even though he'll be a freshman, Robert has a lot of ability to score points," Stansbury said.

Mississippi State has a solid, if not spectacular, backcourt. **Detrick White** (12.2 ppg, 4.9 rpg, 166 assists, 49 steals) had a great first season in '97-'98 after transferring from junior college. The 6-1 senior led the SEC in assists and was ninth in steals. He was also the Bulldogs' third-leading scorer.

White had his own version of a double-double on two occasions. He scored 10 points and passed for 10 assists against American and had 13 and 11 against Vanderbilt. He came within a whisker of getting the first triple-double in school history with a 17-point, nine-rebound, eight-assist effort against Alabama. White is a fair shooter (.468 percent from the field, .327 percent from three-point range) and sure-handed—his assists to turnover ratio was better than two to one.

"You know what you're getting with Detrick," Stansbury said. "Whether it's a shoot-around, walk-through or practice, he gives you the same effort, every day. He's a very solid player for us."

Bart Hyche, a 5-11 senior, will get the first look at shooting guard. A career 35 percent three-point shooter, Hyche (6.8 ppg, 1.2 rpg), slumped to 32 percent from behind the arc last season. He started the last five games a year ago, after coming off the bench most of the season.

Backcourt reserves include **Todd Myles** (2.9 ppg, 1.7 rpg, 67 assists), a 6-4 junior, and **T.J. Billups**, a 6-4 sophomore coming off a redshirt year. He averaged 2.1 points and 1.4 rebounds two seasons ago.

Another newcomer who could fit in right away is 6-2 sophomore **Joe Marshall**, who averaged 13.8 points, 2.1 rebounds and 2.1 assists last season at the College of Southern Idaho. He shot 43 percent from three-point range in his only junior college season.

Marckell Patterson, a 6-5 freshman, will also try to find time in the backcourt. A shooting guard, Patterson was a first-team all-state pick for Eupora (Miss.) High School after averaging 29.4 points, 9.5 rebounds, 6.7 assists and 2.6 steals a year ago.

1998-99 MISSISSIPPI STATE SCHEDULE

Nov.	17	*Arkansas-Pine Bluff
	21	**Northwestern State
	25	Belmont
	28	Tennessee-Martin
	30	Sam Houston State
Dec.	2	Jacksonville State
	8	Centenary
	12	Southeastern Louisiana
	21-22	#Golden Bear Classic
	27-30	##Rainbow Classic
Jan.	2	South Carolina
	6	@Georgia
	9	@Alabama
	13	Arkansas
	16	LSU
	20	@Mississippi
	23	@Kentucky
	27	@Auburn
	30	Florida
Feb.	3	Alabama
	6	@Tennessee
	10	Vanderbilt
	13	@Arkansas
	20	Mississippi
	24	@LSU
	27	Auburn
Mar.	4-7	###SEC Tournament

@ Road Games
* Mississippi Coliseum, Jackson, MS
** Tupelo Coliseum, Tupelo, MS
# Oakland, CA (vs. Southwestern Louisiana, first round; also California and Eastern Kentucky)
Honolulu, HI (vs. Texas, first round; also Florida State, Hawaii, Mississippi State, Murray State, UNC Charlotte, Princeton, and Southwestern Louisiana)
Georgia Dome, Atlanta, GA

adidas Blue Ribbon Analysis

BACKCOURT	**C**	**BENCH/DEPTH**	**C**
FRONTCOURT	**C**	**INTANGIBLES**	**C**

Nearly everyone who keeps up with Mississippi State basketball agrees. Rick Stansbury deserved his chance to become the Bulldogs' head coach after former coach Richard Williams resigned after last season. Stansbury is a long-time assistant who was responsible for recruiting most of the players who took Mississippi State to the Final Four in 1996. Clearly, Stansbury knows how to recruit.

But does he know how to coach? That question should be partially answered this season. Stansbury won't have the best talent in the SEC, but he's got enough to be competitive if he pulls the right strings. And if recruit Tyrus Boswell becomes eligible by the second semester, the Bulldogs just might be pretty good.

If Boswell doesn't make it, the Bulldogs could be fairly average, despite the presence of preseason All-SEC pick Tyrone Washington and Detric White, a better-than-average point guard.

We'll call it fourth place in the SEC Western Division. If the Bulldogs manage 15 victories, as they did a year ago, they just might find their way into the NIT.

(C.D.)

adidas Blue Ribbon Analysis

GRADING SYSTEM

- A+ equal to very best in country—Final Four-caliber unit
- A among the best in the land—worthy of deep NCAA run
- B+ talented, versatile and experienced—NCAA-NIT ability
- B solid and productive winners—league and post-season contenders
- C+ average to above-average—may contend in a weaker league
- C average to mediocre—second division in a strong league
- D+ below average, inconsistent—second division in a weaker league
- D well below average—losing season virtually certain
- F non-Division I ability—an underdog every night

VANDERBILT

LOCATION .... **Nashville, TN**
CONFERENCE .... **SEC (Eastern Division)**
LAST SEASON .... **20-13 (.606)**
CONFERENCE RECORD .... **7-9 (5th)**
STARTERS LOST/RETURNING **3/2**
NICKNAME .... **Commodores**
COLORS .... **Black & Gold**
HOMECOURT .... **Memorial Gymnasium (15,311)**
COACH .... **Jan van Breda Kolff (Vanderbilt '74)**
RECORD AT SCHOOL .... **90-66 (5 yrs.)**
CAREER RECORD .... **113-95 (7 yrs.)**
ASSISTANTS .... **Chris Walker (Villanova '92)**
Jerry Meyer (David Lipscomb '96)
Gib Arnold (Brigham Young '95)
TEAM WINS (last 5 yrs.) **20-13-18-19-20**
RPI (last 5 yrs.) **51-94-61-43-46**
1997-98 FINISH .... **Lost in third round of NIT.**

Vanderbilt coach Jan van Breda Kolff has been around the SEC's Eastern Division long enough to know what he's up against. A case could be made that the East is among the college game's tougher affiliations. Consider that last year, five of its six teams won at least 20 games, and all six played in a postseason tournament. Four East Division teams earned NCAA Tournament bids.

That's pretty fast company, literally. Which brings us to a change in philosophy that van Breda Kolff will spring on the rest of the division this winter. Though you wouldn't exactly call the Vanderbilt teams of recent vintage plodding, the Commodores haven't been as quick or athletic as their division mates. Having emphasized those commodities in his recruiting efforts the last two years, van Breda Kolff now feels confident to tweak Vanderbilt's style a bit.

"We're improved every year in terms of adding more athletic players," van Breda Kolff said. "For the first time, we feel that, athletically speaking, we're competitive with the rest of the league.

"We have the depth now to play an uptempo style with pressing and pushing the ball upcourt. We can do it for 40 minutes. Last year, we weren't able to sustain it due to some injuries and having three redshirts."

This season, the Commodores won't be as experienced as in years past, but as van Breda Kolff said, quickness and athleticism will be in abundant supply. Considering that no single player could offset the loss of guard Drew Maddux (16.8 ppg, 4.1 rpg, 134 assists, 68 steals), center Austin Bates (13.8 ppg, 5.5 rpg, 30 blocked shots) and forward Billy DiSpaltro (11.8 ppg, 5.7 rpg), Vanderbilt's top three scorers a year ago, van Breda Kolff will do it by committee.

Heading the committee will be a newcomer, a player talented enough to become a double-figure scorer in his first season. **Michael LeBlanc** is a 6-6 sophomore who had the luxury of practicing with the Commodores last season while redshirting after transferring from Connecticut. Though LeBlanc, from Sugar Land, Texas, was a top 50-ranked high school player, he didn't get much of an opportunity to play at UConn behind All-America Richard Hamilton. As a freshman, LeBlanc averaged four minutes on the floor and 1.8 ppg.

Though that was hardly enough action to judge LeBlanc against big-time competition, van Breda Kolff has seen enough of the player in practice to know what he can do.

"He's a true scorer," van Breda Kolff said.

Some longtime Vanderbilt observers compare LeBlanc to former All-SEC guard Ronnie McMahan, who is the school's No. 2 all-time scorer. LeBlanc has the skills to create his own shot, but like McMahan, he also has deadly range from the perimeter.

LeBlanc should battle incumbent small forward **Vince Ford**, a 6-4 senior, for the starting job. Ford (7.4 ppg, 3.1 rpg, 57 assists, 42 steals), was last year's breakthrough player for the Commodores. Ford played sparingly his first two years, but last season he started all but three games and averaged 24 minutes.

"Vince is solid," van Breda Kolff said. "He does good things game in and game out. He gives a great effort. He shoots the ball extremely well from three-point range. From 15 feet away, he's as consistent a perimeter shooter as we have. He's a consummate team player and leader."

Ford had impressive shooting numbers last season, making .525 percent of his shots, including .453 percent from three-point range. He didn't have any huge offensive games, but reached double figures 11 times. Not bad for a player who had averaged 0.9 ppg the season before.

LeBlanc and Ford will wage a battle for the small forward job, but the other frontcourt positions appear set. **Dan Langhi** (6.3 ppg, 2.9 rpg), a 6-11 junior, will start at power forward. Undersized at 205 pounds, Langhi does most of his damage from the outside—he shot 35 percent from three-point range a year ago. Langhi finished the season strong, averaging 12.0 ppg and 6.1 rpg in the Commodores' last seven games. He dropped a career-high 19 points on Wake Forest in a second-round NIT game.

"He has a slight build, but he's much stronger than he looks," van Breda Kolff said. "He has the ability to be a go-to type player and one of our top scorers. This team needs Dan more than last year's team."

Greg LaPointe, a 6-9, 235-pound sophomore, will start at center after a season in which he made the SEC's All-Freshman team. LaPointe (5.3 ppg, 3.3 rpg) is only the fourth Vandy player to be so honored.

LaPointe started the last 10 games after DiSpaltro broke a foot. During that time he displayed good skills, but more importantly a real feel for the game.

"He's as fundamentally sound as any player I've coached," van Breda Kolff said. "He knows what to do in every situation."

LaPointe will get the ball more in the low post this year, where he can do damage with some good moves and the ability to shoot with either hand. LaPointe should also get to the free-throw line more often, where he has the ability (.696 percent a year ago) to cash in.

Anthony Williams (2.8 ppg, 3.3 rpg) is the only returning frontcourt reserve. The 6-7 Williams is a rebounding machine—he was the leading rebounder in Alabama high school history. He showed flashes of those skills in limited duty last season.

A pair of juniors will handle the guard positions. **Atiba Prater**, 6-1, made great strides last year despite a nagging groin injury that hampered his play in February and March. Prater (8.9 ppg, 2.2 rpg, 152 assists, 64 steals) was second in the league in steals (2.2 spg) and fourth in assists (5.1 apg).

In addition to running the show, Prater also improved his shooting. He was second on the team in three-pointers (47) and was markedly better from the free-throw line (.698 percent to .514 percent) than he was as a freshman. Prater tossed in a career-high five three-pointers against Tennessee and had a career-high 19 points against Arkansas. Prater had two 10-assist games a year ago, against Saint Louis and Florida. He picked Tennessee-Martin's pockets for eight steals, also a career-high.

"Attiba was one of the leading steals guys in the country until his injury," van Breda Kolff said. "He's a very good passer and a very unselfish player. He has the ability to improvise in the open court. Defensively, he's very, very good."

James Strong (5.4 ppg, 2.5 rpg, 46 assists, 51 steals), 6-3, will join Prater in the backcourt. Strong might be Vanderbilt's most athletic player and has the ability to change the tempo of a game any time van Breda Kolff puts him in. Strong can take the ball to the basket, and he excels in transition. Because he's such a good leaper, Strong can play small forward.

Walkon **Brian Williams**, a 6-1 junior, is Vanderbilt's only other returning guard. Williams (0.4 ppg, 0.0 rpg) saw action in just eight games last year, and none after Feb. 28.

Besides LeBlanc, several other newcomers will have to contribute if Vanderbilt is to come close to its success of previous seasons. Like LeBlanc, 6-4 freshman **Sam Howard** and 7-1 freshman **Darius Coulibaly** were redshirted last season and should have a grasp on van Breda Kolff's system.

Howard, like Maddux and former Kentucky star Ron Mercer, played for Nashville's Goodpasture Christian school. A great outside shooter, Howard is the all-time leading scorer in Nashville high school history with 3,063 points. Howard averaged 24.0 ppg, 4.0 rpg and 3.5 apg two years ago. He's got excellent shooting touch and will be groomed to take over Maddux's old spot at shooting guard.

Coulibaly, from the Ivory Coast in West Africa, grew up playing soccer and has limited basketball experience. But because of his long frame and athletic ability, Vanderbilt coaches are excited about him and see him emerging as a shot-blocking force in the middle.

Coulibaly should be a willing and capable student. He excels in the classroom and can obviously retain a lot—he speaks English, French, German and two African dialects. If Vanderbilt can get the same sort of contributions from Coulibaly as Auburn has from Mamadou N'diaye, another foreign-born 7-footer with little prior basketball experience, van Breda Kolff would be happy.

A more polished newcomer is 6-9, 240-pound freshman **Iiro Tenngren**, a native of Finland who played high school basketball in the United States for one season at Episcopal in Lynchburg, Va. He averaged 25.8 ppg and 11.0 rpg at Episcopal.

"He's a guy that can play three frontcourt positions," van Breda Kolff told *The Commodore Report*. "He is a physical player that can play inside and outside. He can be a significant player for us as a freshman, similar to Greg LaPointe."

Another talented signee won't have as much of an early impact as Tenngren. He's 6-6 **Sam Lekwauwa**, who didn't turn 17 years old until September. The native of Nigeria lived in Winston-Salem, N.C. for 10 years and averaged 14.3 ppg, 10.0 rpg, 3.6 apg and 1.7 bpg last year at Mt. Tabor High School. At least two ACC schools encouraged Lekwauwa to attend a prep school this season, but Lekwauwa thought he was physically ready for Division I competition. Still, Lekwauwa is a likely candidate for a redshirt year.

If Prater needs relief, 5-10 freshman **Deandre Moore** can provide it. He's a natural point guard with good quickness and decision-making skills. Moore averaged 18.0 ppg and 8.0 apg as a senior. If van Breda Kolff wants to go with an ultra-quick backcourt, he can slide Prater over to the two-guard spot and play Moore at the point.

1998-99 VANDERBILT SCHEDULE

Nov.	9	*Providence
	10	*Rhode Island
	14	Army
	16	Austin Peay
	21	Notre Dame
	24	Morehead State
	28	Ohio State
	30	Florida A&M
Dec.	5	@Memphis
	19	Campbell
	22	@Oregon
	30	Alabama A&M
Jan.	2	Mississippi
	6	@Florida
	9	Kentucky
	13	@Georgia
	20	South Carolina
	23	@LSU
	27	Tennessee
	30	@South Carolina
Feb.	3	Georgia
	6	Arkansas
	10	@Mississippi State
	13	@Tennessee
	17	@Auburn
	21	Alabama
	24	@Kentucky
	27	Florida
Mar.	4-7	#SEC Tournament

@ Road Games
* CoSIDA Classic, Providence, RI
# Georgia Dome, Atlanta, GA

adidas Blue Ribbon Analysis

BACKCOURT	**C+**	**BENCH/DEPTH**	**B**
FRONTCOURT	**B**	**INTANGIBLES**	**B**

Looking around the SEC, it wasn't hard for Vanderbilt coach Jan van Breda Kolff to spot a trend. Most of the teams in the league are quick and athletic and play an uptempo style. In order to keep pace, van Breda Kolff reasoned, the Commodores would have to make a few changes.

This year, Vanderbilt will have a different look. Reliant on slower-footed post players in recent years, the Commodores will now utilize speed and athleticism to get the job done. They will press at every turn, try to force turnovers and score in transition.

There seems to be enough depth and talent on hand to play that style. Point guard Atiba Prater elevated his game last year, and if he makes the same kind of improvement this season, should be one of the best at his position in the SEC. James Strong is an exciting guard who should excel in an uptempo game. Newcomer Michael LeBlanc, the Connecticut transfer, will remind Vanderbilt fans of former Commodores star Ronnie McMahan. That's no bad thing—McMahan is the No. 2 scorer in school history.

When Vandy does have to slow down, there are some players who should be able to get the ball in the post and score. Dan Langhi is now resigned to the fact his position in college is power forward, even though he has great touch from the perimeter. Greg LaPointe was impressive as a freshman, showing an ability to score in the paint and great court awareness.

The Commodores also have depth, though many newcomers will have to provide it.

All this adds up to another nice Vanderbilt team, but five other schools in the league have a head start playing the uptempo game. Call it a sixth-place finish in the SEC's Eastern Division, but that isn't as bad as it sounds. As Florida showed last year, even the last-place team in such a rugged division can get into postseason play.

(C.D.)

SOUTHERN CONFERENCE

adidas BLUE RIBBON FORECAST

NORTH DIVISION

1. Davidson
2. Appalachian State
3. East Tennessee State
4. Virginia Military Institute
5. North Carolina-Greensboro
6. Western Carolina

SOUTH DIVISION

1. College of Charleston
2. Tennessee-Chattanooga
3. Furman
4. Wofford
5. The Citadel
6. Georgia Southern

ALL-CONFERENCE TEAM

G—Jason Bell, SR, Virginia Military Institute
G—Greg Stephens, SR, East Tennessee State
F—David Phillips, JR, Tennessee-Chattanooga
F—Marshall Phillips, SR, AppalachianState
C—Sedric Webber, SR, College of Charleston

PLAYER OF THE YEAR

Greg Stephens, SR, East Tennessee State

NEWCOMER OF THE YEAR

Jody Lumpkin, SO, College of Charleston

1998-99 CONFERENCE TOURNAMENT

Feb. 25-28, Greensboro Coliseum, Greensboro, NC

1997-98 CHAMPIONS

Davidson, Appalachian State (North Division)
Tennessee-Chattanooga (South Division)
Davidson (conference tournament)

1997-98 POST-SEASON PARTICIPANTS

Post-Season Record: 0-1 (.000)
NCAA
Davidson

TOP BACKCOURTS

1. College of Charleston
2. Appalachian State
3. Davidson

TOP FRONTCOURTS

1. Davidson
2. College of Charleston
3. Tennessee-Chattanooga

ON THE WAY UP

Furman

ON THE WAY DOWN

The Citadel

INSIDE THE NUMBERS

- 1997-98 conference RPI: 24 (of 30)
- Conference RPI (last 5 years): 22-29-27-19-24

DID YOU KNOW?

The College of Charleston joins the Southern Conference after five years of dominating the Trans-Atlantic Athletic Conference (TAAC). The Cougars, seeking their sixth straight postseason berth, return all five starters from last year's 24-6 team and welcome transfer Jody Lumpkin, a bruising post player from Rice, to this year's lineup...Tennessee-Chattanooga has nine newcomers and has bolstered its frontcourt in a big way. Oliver Morton, a transfer from Mississippi who practiced with the Mocs last year, should be one of the league's top post players, and junior-college transfers Cory Hart and Clark Costa give the Mocs even more frontcourt power, which was a weakness last season...East Tennessee State's Greg Stephens returns after leading the conference in scoring last year (17.2 ppg), and the Bucs will also benefit inside from Leo Murray, a transfer from Xavier who practiced last season while sitting out as a redshirt...Wofford got two breaks from the NCAA over the summer months when senior forward Alfred Forbest was granted another year of eligibility and the Terriers were cleared to play in the postseason, thanks to the NCAA's reducing the probation period for teams moving from Division II to I from eight years to two...Furman has its first junior-college transfer in almost 20 years, 6-8 power forward Stanislav Makshantsev, who will replace last season's conference player of the year, Chuck Vincent...Davidson has added more international flavor to its roster with the signing of guard Michael Bree of Ireland and forward Chris Pearson of England...Georgia Southern lost a potential starter when sophomore guard Arkee Thompson decided to play football in 1998...Appalachian State will replace all-conference forward Kareem Livingston with junior-college transfer Cedrick Holmes, who comes to Boone, N.C. with great expectations.

(D.L.)

APPALACHIAN STATE

LOCATION .... **Boone, NC**
CONFERENCE .... **Southern (North Division)**
LAST SEASON .... **21-8 (.724)**
CONFERENCE RECORD .... **13-2 (t-1st)**
STARTERS LOST/RETURNING **2/3**
NICKNAME .... **Mountaineers**
COLORS .... **Black & Gold**
HOMECOURT .... **Varsity Gymnasium (8,000)**
COACH .... **Buzz Peterson (North Carolina '86)**
RECORD AT SCHOOL .... **35-32 (2 yrs.)**
CAREER RECORD .... **35-32 (2 yrs.)**
ASSISTANTS .... **Lavell Hall (Western Carolina '79)**
Houston Fancher (Middle Tennessee State '88)
George Singleton (Furman '94)
TEAM WINS (last 5 yrs.) **16-9-8-14-21**
RPI (last 5 yrs.) **153-274-259-152-109**
1997-98 FINISH .... **Lost in conference championship.**

In his first two seasons as basketball coach at Appalachian State, Buzz Peterson spent much of his time stressing the importance of a good work ethic.

Maybe the Mountaineers got the message. They better have. Peterson doesn't want to preach the same thing this year.

"I'm tired of saying the words, 'Lets's work hard,'" Peterson said. "It should be automatic. I had to harp on that so much the last two years."

Peterson's harping must have done some good. After going 14-14 two years ago, the Mountaineers came within a victory of reaching the 1998 NCAA Tournament before losing to Davidson, 66-62, in the championship of the 1998 Southern Conference Tournament.

It was the Mountaineers' third loss of the season to Davidson. The two teams tied for the North Division title, but Davidson earned the division's top seeding in the league tournament by sweeping two regular-season games from the Mountaineers.

"Davidson had our number last year," Peterson said. "We had some battles. Coach (Bob) McKillop does a good job and they have a good program."

Peterson wants to build that kind of program in Boone, and he laid down a foundation for it during his first two years.

Three starters return from last year's team, but the Mountaineers must replace two key players: 6-5 guard Tige Darner (11.8 ppg, 4.7 rpg) and 6-7 forward Kareem Livingston (12.4 ppg, 4.7 rpg). Livingston was chosen all-conference by the league's coaches and media.

Still, Peterson believes he has the personnel to make another push for the North Division title. "I like the chemistry and the makeup of the guys coming in," Peterson said. "Hopefully we can continue to build on it."

Three returning starters will make the building a little easier.

Leading the way will be 6-5 senior forward **Marshall Phillips** (11.3 ppg, 7.4 rpg) and 5-9 junior point guard **Tyson Patterson** (10.0 ppg, 3.0 rpg, 159 assists, 56 steals).

Phillips was chosen to the coaches' 10-player all-conference team and was also voted to the all-tournament team. He was fifth in the league in rebounding, spending much of his time in the post.

This year, Peterson plans to move Phillips to his more natural position on the wing. Phillips may not have reached his potential. His first taste of organized basketball came as a college freshman at Campbellsville (Ky.), an NAIA school, and he played two years ago at Hiwassee (Tenn.) Junior College.

"He's just been unelievable for us," Peterson said. "His work ethic is unbelievable. We played him all over the floor. He's played point, and he's been a post guy."

Phillips won't have to play much more point, not with Patterson returning. Patterson was third in the league in assists last season and fifth in steals. He started 18 games as a freshman two years ago and set a school record for assists by a freshman (107). He set the school's assist record for a sophomore last year.

"He's a true point guard who's not looking to shoot the ball, but to pass," Peterson said. "He's always looking to give it up. He's a very good defensive player, but he needs to improve his free throws and three-point shooting. (.597 FT, 11 for 54 three-point shooting in '97-98)"

Also returning after starting last season is 6-5, 220-pound guard **Blair Adderley** (7.3 ppg, 4.0 rpg), a versatile player best suited to play the wing. At times last season, Adderley found himself playing in the post, but Peterson will try to avoid that this year.

"He's played all over in the past," Peterson said. "We hope he steps up and has a big senior year. When he's on his game, we're a good team."

Two returning guards, 6-0 junior **Matt McMahan** (5.3 ppg, 1.2 rpg) and 5-11 senior **Ian Adams** (5.0 ppg, 1.6 rpg) will give the Mountaineers some perimeter scoring punch off the bench. Last season, Adams was second on the team in three-point goals (30 for 78) and McMahon was third (19 for 67).

Also returning to the backcourt are 6-6 junior guard/forward **Kent Phillips** (1.5 ppg, 1.3 rpg) and 5-10 junior guard **Seneca Fritts** (0.3 ppg, 0.3 rpg).

One newcomer, 6-6 junior forward **Cedric Holmes**, figures into Peteson's frontcourt plans as the replacement for Livingston. Holmes, who weighs 230, will play one of the two post spots. "Our four and five (post positions) are pretty much the same," Peterson said.

Peterson hopes Holmes can give him pretty much the same production that Livingston did. Last year at Okaloosa-Walton (Fla.) Junior College, Holmes averaged 18.3 points and 10.7 rebounds. He played on a Class 2A state championship team at Harriman (Tenn.) High School.

1998-99 APPALACHIAN STATE SCHEDULE

Nov.	13	@North Carolina
	17	King College
	21	@Minnesota
	23	Greensboro College
	30	@East Carolina
Dec.	2	South Carolina-Spartanburg
	5	@Georgia Tech
	8	Georgia
	20	Winthrop
	29	The Citadel
Jan.	2	@Davidson
	4	College of Charleston
	9	Virginia Military Institute
	11	@Wofford
	14	@Tennessee-Chattanooga
	16	East Tennessee State
	18	Western Carolina
	23	@East Tennessee State
	25	North Carolina-Greensboro
	30	@Georgia Southern
Feb.	1	@North Carolina-Greensboro
	3	Wisconsin-Green Bay
	8	Furman
	13	@Virginia Military Institute
	15	@Western Carolina
	20	Davidson
	25-28	#Southern Conference Tournament

@ Road Games
# Greensboro Coliseum, Greensboro, NC

There will be much expected of Holmes. "We're hoping he can fill Kareem's shoes," Peterson said. "He's 6-6 with long arms and a nice touch inside. He's going to need to score with his back to the basket."

Senior center **Josh Grover,** a 7-footer, will be expected to start with Holmes in the frontcourt. Grover (3.2 ppg, 2.9 rpg, 13 blocks) played in 29 games last season, averaging 15 minutes, and is coming off a productive offseason. He shot 56 percent from the field last season.

Mike Coffey, a 6-7 redshirt freshman center, played in five games last season before a stress fracture in his left leg put him out for the rest of the year. Coffey averaged 1.8 points and 1.8 rebounds before the injury.

Perhaps the marquee player in Peterson's '98 class of signees is 6-2 guard **Shawn Alexander** of T.C. Roberson High School in Asheville, N.C. Alexander, who will play shooting guard, averaged 21.5 points and 8.2 rebounds last year and earned co-player of the year honors in North Carolina.

Another signee who could have an impact this year is 6-3 sophomore guard/forward **Roderick Stevenson**, a Detroit native who transferred from Oxnard (Calif.) Junior College. Stevenson, who played at Kettering High in Detroit, averaged 19 points and 8.6 rebounds last season at Oxnard.

Jonathan Butler, a 6-0 freshman point guard, will back up Patterson. Butler averaged 12.1 points, 6.6 rebounds and 10.1 assists last season at North Forsyth High School in Winston-Salem, N.C.

Andrew Davis, a 6-7 freshman, will play power forward. Davis averaged 18 points and 11 rebounds last year at Troup County (Ga.) High School.

Mikah Hill, a 6-5 sophomore forward, is a walkon who averaged 19.3 points and 9.1 rebounds as a senior at South Wayne High in Dudley, N.C.

Blue Ribbon Analysis

BACKCOURT .... B+ BENCH/DEPTH .... B
FRONTCOURT .... B- INTANGIBLES .... B+

Once a promising assistant coach, Buzz Peterson has quickly established himself as one of the nation's top young head coaches. It took him only two years at Appalachian State to show his stuff.

"We're excited about the way things have gone," Peterson said. "We've made strides the first two years."

There is no reason to think the program won't keep making strides under Peterson, who was voted Southern Conference Coach of the Year in 1997-98 by the league's coaches and media.

With the arrival of junior-college forward Cedrick Holmes, Peterson believes he has a replacement for all-conference forward Kareem Livingston.

Senior forward Marshall Phillips will move from the post to the wing this season. With Phillips and Blair Adderley on the wings and Tyson Patterson at the point, the Mountaineers have a formidable backcourt.

That will make Appalachian State a tough team to beat, especially with Peterson calling the shots. Peterson hasn't solved the Davidson problem yet, but give him time. For now, put the Mountaineers second in the North Division behind the Wildcats.

(D.L)

COLLEGE OF CHARLESTON

LOCATION .... Charleston, SC
CONFERENCE .... Southern (South Division)
LAST SEASON .... 24-6 (.800)
CONFERENCE RECORD .... 14-2 (1st, TAAC East)
STARTERS LOST/RETURNING 0/5
NICKNAME .... Cougars
COLORS .... Maroon & White
HOMECOURT .... John Kresse Arena (3,500)
COACH .... John Kresse (St. John's '64)
RECORD AT SCHOOL .... 465-118 (19 yrs.)
CAREER RECORD .... 465-118 (19 yrs.)
ASSISTANTS .... Jim Yarbrough (Florida State '87)
Ben Butts (Roanoke College '90)
Chris Evans (Genesco State '87)
TEAM WINS (last 5 yrs.) 24-23-25-29-24
RPI (last 5 yrs.) 59-62-70-49-78
1997-98 FINISH .... Lost in NCAA first round.

It's time for veteran coach John Kresse and the College of Charleston to take on bigger and better challenges.

After dominating the Trans-Atlantic Athletic Conference (TAAC) for five years, the Cougars join the Southern Conference this season. They do so with plenty of momentum.

Returning are five starters from the 1997-98 team that continued its rule of the TAAC. Charleston was 80-6 in five TAAC seasons. It won the regular season champion every year. In their only two TAAC Tournaments, the Cougars left as champions. They weren't eligible for the tournament the three previous seasons after making a move from NAIA status to Division I in 1990-91, but still managed one at-large bid to the NCAA Tournament and an NIT berth. These guys are that good.

Kresse, in his 20th season at College of Charleston, says the move into the Southern Conference will be be a good test.

"From top to bottom, it will be a much tougher league than the Trans-Atlantic Athletic Conference," Kresse said. "There is more tradition, larger facilities and much better ball clubs that will challenge us each and every night."

It is a challenge that will help College of Charleston and the Southern Conference. The Cougars will join the South Division, which was the weaker of the league's two divisions last year. However, with Tennessee-Chattanooga reloading with talent and Furman and Wofford making a push, the division looks to be much stronger this year.

Look for some new and much-needed rivalries to develop with the Cougars' arrival in the conference. Their game at Davidson on Jan. 30 will be a feature matchup between division favorites and possibly a preview of the tournament championship game. The Cougars and Tennessee-Chattanooga could become bitter division rivals. College of Charleston will have instate rivals in The Citadel (also located in Charleston), Wofford and Furman.

It looks like College of Charleston and the Southern Conference are a perfect match.

"For our fans, players and coaches, it will certainly be more exciting to play with these natural rivalries like The Citadel, Furman and teams in our geographical area," Kresse said.

Kresse and the Cougars will be seeking their fifth straight postseason appearance. Two years ago, they stunned No. 22-ranked Maryland in the first round of the NCAA Tournament before losing to eventual national champion Arizona, 73-69, in the second round.

In the '98 NCAA Tournament, the Cougars lost to No. 11 Stanford, 67-57.

It looks like the Cougars have enough talent to continue their impressive run.

Leading the returnees is 6-6 senior forward/center **Sedric Webber** (15.1 ppg, 7.9 rpg), who should quickly prove one of the top players in the Southern Conference. Last season, Webber was chosen the co-player of the year in the TAAC along with Central Florida's Mark Jones.

Webber, who was also the TAAC Tournament's MVP, shot .510 from the field and .697 from the free-throw line, led the Cougars with 67 steals and had 29 blocked shots. He was also their leading scorer and rebounder.

An outstanding athlete, Webber has played mostly in the post at College of Charleston, but is learning to move to the perimeter a bit more. Kresse and his staff want Webber to play under control at all times, and if Webber does that, he could be an even better player.

Kresse, ever the team coach, will not focus his attention on one player. Webber might be the marquee player, but Kresse wants the team to come first.

"We do have talented kids," assistant coach Chris Evans said. "From Day One we preach team, team, team, and it really carries over."

One newcomer, 6-8, 240-pound sophomore center **Jody Lumpkin**, should make the Cougars even more formidable. A transfer from Rice, Lumpkin sat out last season after transferring but practiced with the Cougars. He averaged 4.7 points and 3.3 rebounds as a freshman at Rice.

Late last summer, Webber went to visit Evans just after finishing a workout with Lumpkin.

"How's Jody playing?" Evans asked Webber.

"I think he'll be one of the best assets ever for College of Charleston," Webber said.

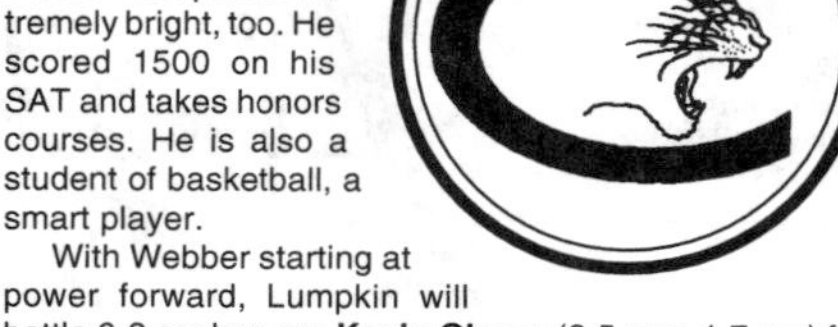

Lumpkin is a big, physical player. His teammates call him "The Beast." Lumpkin is extremely bright, too. He scored 1500 on his SAT and takes honors courses. He is also a student of basketball, a smart player.

With Webber starting at power forward, Lumpkin will battle 6-8 sophomore **Kevin Glover** (2.5 ppg, 1.7 rpg) for the center's job.

Glover is a wiry player who is still adapting to the college game. He is a good defensive player and shot blocker.

The Cougars are loaded at power forward with Webber and 6-5 senior **Carlos Brown** (9.4 ppg, 6.3 rpg), who started all 30 games last year and was the team's fourth-leading scorer. Brown shot .486 from the field last year. If he's not in the starting lineup this year, Brown won't stay on the bench for long.

1998-99 COLLEGE OF CHARLESTON SCHEDULE

Nov.	13	@Charleston Southern
	16	#Georgia
	23	Pfeiffer
Dec.	1	Massachusetts
	4	*South Carolina
	5	*North Carolina
	12	George Mason
	17	Francis Marion
	21-22	##College of Charleston Classic
	28	Western Carolina
Jan.	2	@Georgia Southern
	4	@Appalachian State
	9	The Citadel
	11	@Furman
	16	Wofford
	18	Tennessee-Chattanooga
	23	North Carolina-Greensboro
	25	@Wofford
	30	@Davidson
Feb.	1	Georgia Southern
	3	@Coastal Carolina
	6	@The Citadel
	8	Virginia Military Institute
	13	@Tennessee-Chattanooga
	15	@East Tennessee State
	20	Furman
	25-28	###Southern Conference Tournament

@	Road Games
*	Food Lion MVP Classic, Charlotte, NC
#	Chase NIT (If the Cougars advance, they will face either Florida International or North Carolina on Nov. 18. Semifinals and finals are Nov. 25 and 27 at Madison Square Gardeny, NY).
##	Charleston, SC (vs. Stony Brook, first round; also Charleston Southern and Delaware).
###	Greensboro Coliseum, Greensboro, NC

Carl Thomas, a 6-7 senior, is the likely starter at small forward. Thomas (10.8 ppg, 4.3 rpg) started 15 games last year and was the team's second-leading scorer. He shot .488 from the field and made 24 of 61 three-point shots.

In his third year at College of Charleston, Thomas began his college career at Western Kentucky. He has worked to become a solid shooter and defensive player. Last season, Thomas was third on the team in three-point goals (24 of 61).

Danny Johnson, a 6-3 senior, can play either small forward or shooting guard. Johnson (7.7 ppg, 3.6 rpg) started 16 games last season and was second on the team in three-point goals (25 for 73).

Micheal Feenane, a 6-6 junior forward, will battle for more playing time this year, but that won't be easy with the senior-laden team. Feenane (0.9 ppg, 0.8 rpg) played in 14 games last year.

Kresse is fortunate to have two talented guards, 5-11 senior **Jermel President** (10.3 ppg, 2.0 rpg, 49 assists) and 5-11 senior **Shane McCravy** (7.3 ppg, 2.3 rpg, 136 assists).

McCravy started 27 games last year at point guard and should hold down that job again. An outstanding defender, McCravy was second on the team in steals (63) and shot .470 from the field.

President, who started 13 games, can play point guard or shooting guard. He missed the first three games last season with a knee injury after having arthroscopic surgery Nov. 11. It didn't slow him too much.

President, chosen third-team All-TAAC, led the Cougars in three-point goals, making 26 of 79. He is extremely quick and a natural shooting guard and scorer, but has learned to play point guard over the years.

Two returning guards will provide depth in the backcourt: 6-1 sophomore **Kyle Lourie** (0.8 ppg, 0.3 rpg) and 5-11 sophomore **Tyrone Nelson** (1.1 ppg, 0.6 rpg).

Jeff Bolton, a 6-3 freshman guard, was redshirted last season. As a senior at Butler HS in Augusta, Ga., Bolton averaged 20.3 points, 7.7 rebounds and 4.1 assists.

Kresse also signed three freshmen, and they should benefit greatly from practicing against the Cougars' strong lineup of returnees.

"The two redshirts, Jody Lumpkin and Jeff Bolton, we are hoping those two players will certainly make great contributions to our season, and we do have three freshmen who will hopefully help us a great deal in the future," Kresse said.

Leighton Bowie, a 6-6 freshman forward, averaged 21 points, 11 rebounds and 3.0 assists last season at Port Charlotte (Fla.) HS.

Rodgie Leggett, a 6-7 freshman forward, averaged 17 points, 10 rebounds and three blocks as a senior at Spring Valley HS in Columbia, S.C. One of Leggett's teammates at Spring Valley, 6-6 forward **Marco Sanders**, also signed with the Cougars. Sanders averaged 12 points and 9.0

rebounds for Spring Valley last year.

adidas Blue Ribbon Analysis

BACKCOURT .... **A** **BENCH/DEPTH** .... **B+**
FRONTCOURT .... **A-** **INTANGIBLES** .... **B+**

The College of Charleston isn't just loaded with players. Its coach, John Kresse, has the third-highest winning percentage (.798) for an active coach behind Fresno State's Jerry Tarkanian and Roy Williams of Kansas.

Kresse, chosen the TAAC's coach of the year last season, is 125-23 in the last five years. The 23 losses ties Kentucky for the fewest in the last five years.

If any coach can make a team play to its billing, Kresse can. With 6-6 senior forward/center Sedric Webber leading the way, Kresse has enough talent to continue its winning ways in his first season in the Southern Conference.

"We're banking on our senior leadership," Kresse said.

Kresse will get a chance to test his team during a rugged non-conference schedule that includes games against Georgia, Massachusetts, South Carolina and North Carolina.

"It is the toughest non-conference schedule in my 20 years as head coach at the College of Charleston," Kresse said.

It should have the Cougars ready for their new foes in the Southern Conference. Is the Southern Conference ready for the Cougars? Good question. They'll be awfully hard to beat.

(D.L.)

THE CITADEL

LOCATION .... **Charleston, S.C**
CONFERENCE .... **Southern (South Division)**
LAST SEASON .... **15-13 (.536)**
CONFERENCE RECORD .... **6-8 (t-2nd)**
STARTERS LOST/RETURNING **2/3**
NICKNAME .... **Bulldogs**
COLORS .... **Citadel Blue & White**
HOMECOURT .... **McAlister Field House (6,000)**
COACH .... **Pat Dennis (Washington &Lee '78)**
RECORD AT SCHOOL .... **70-92 (6 yrs.)**
CAREER RECORD .... **70-92 (6 yrs.)**
ASSISTANTS .. **Marty McGillan (UNC-Wilmington '90)**
Brian Frazier (Lenoir-Rhyne '95)
TEAM WINS (last 5 yrs.) **11-11-10-13-15**
RPI (last 5 yrs.) **231-268-276-203-222**
1997-98 FINISH .... **Lost in conference semifinal.**

Slowly but surely, The Citadel's basketball program has prospered under seventh-year coach Pat Dennis. Last season, the Bulldogs posted their first winning season (15-13) since the 1988-89 team also went 15-13.

Dennis compares his project at The Citadel to the old tortoise and the hare fable.

"We keep creeping along and getting better," Dennis said. "It's like the tortoise and the hare. We're moving along slower than some people want, but we feel real good about what we've accomplished. I think the program has gotten better every year."

Two years ago, the Bulldogs won 13 games—the most since the '88-89 team—and they didn't slow down last year, going 6-8 and tying Wofford for second place in a balanced South Division. The Citadel also snapped a 13-game losing streak in the conference tournament and posted victories over Davidson and College of Charleston, each an NCAA Tournament team.

Two starters are gone from last year, including 6-1 guard Jamie Jenkins (14.1 ppg, 3.6 rpg, 44 assists), an all-conference choice by the league's coaches. Still, Dennis believes he has reloaded his roster with one of his best recruiting classes, which consists of six freshmen.

Not only will The Citadel have some new faces, it will also have a new style of play.

"We'll go from a big, slow team to a smaller, more athletic team," Dennis said. "That's something we're excited about. We'll be a different type of team. I think we'll play a little more pressure defense. In the past we've played more of a contain defense and we've done it well because of our size. We'll play a little more pressure defense and I think we'll have the ability to get out and run the floor more than we've done in the past. I also think we'll be a much better shooting team."

If that's the case, the Bulldogs will have some new people supplying the scoring punch. The Citadel lost each of its top four scorers and rebounders, including 6-8 starting center Matt Newman (10.4 ppg, 4.2 rpg) and 7-0 backup center Kirill Misyuchenko (6.5 ppg, 7.4 rpg) and 6-5 forward Virgil Stevens (13.3 ppg, 5.0 rpg), one of the league's top non-starters last season.

Dennis is confident the Bulldogs can ride a strong perimeter game.

"I feel if you've got good guards you've got a chance to win, but we're young in other areas," Dennis said. "Our forwards are young and we'll have to play some guys early to get them experience, but I'm optimistic because we've got good guards."

Dennis will rely on his perimeter players, in particular 5-10 junior guard **Bryan Patton** (4.7 ppg, 3.1 rpg, 105 assists) and 5-10 sophomore guard **Mike Roy** (4.2 ppg, 2.0 rpg, 41 assists) They will share the point guard and shooting guard jobs.

Last year, Patton was seventh in the league in assists and shot .786 percent from the free-throw line. He started 26 games, averaging 27.4 minutes, despite suffering from a couple of foot injuries.

Patton is a gritty player. After his stint at The Citadel, Patton wants to become a Navy Seal.

"He's got the toughness to do it," Dennis said. "He was having a very good year early before he got two stress fractures in his feet. His time really fell off. They operated on him in the summer and he's ready to go again. We need his leadership and his toughness."

With Patton's feet hurting, Roy's minutes increased drastically. Averaging 16.8 minutes in 27 games, Roy came on strong late in the year and scored 17 against Virginia Military Institute in a 77-66 quarterfinal victory in the league tournament.

"We knew how good Roy was all along," Dennis said. "It was a matter of how we'd get him the minutes with Patton (and Jenkins). When Patton got hurt, Roy really came on. I really think he will be a very good player here."

Jerald Freeman, 6-3 senior swingman, should also start again this year. Freeman (3.6 ppg, 3.1 rpg, 76 assists) was second on the team in assists last season and started 23 games.

"He's a 6-3 athlete," Dennis said. "He's just real solid. He's an exceptional defensive player, he handles the ball well and he makes good decisions. He just needs to score more."

Dennis will also look for scoring from three freshman guards: 6-2 **Travis Cantrell** of Floyd County (Va.) High School, 6-1 **Trevor Crafton** of Hanover (Ind.) Southwestern High School, and 6-5 swingman **Alan Puckett** of Hot Springs (Ark.) Lake Hamilton High School.

Cantrell averaged 24 points and six assists last season and earned first-team all-state honors. He set a school record with 1,871 career points.

Crafton averaged 18 points last season and also earned first-team all-state honors. Puckett averaged 21 points, six rebounds and four assists and was chosen Garland County Player of the Year and first-team all-state.

"We brought in three players who are swing guards or forwards who can really shoot the ball," Dennis said. "Cantrell was the most valuable player of the Virginia all-star game after he knocked down six threes from NBA range. He really knows how to play. Crafton has the ability to break you down one-on-one and he can also shoot it, and Puckett can light it up. I think we've helped ourselves shooting the ball."

Also returning is 6-2 junior guard **Johan Rat** (1.4 ppg, 1.0 rpg), who played in five games last year. Rat should get some playing time at shooting guard.

Leading the returnees in the frontcourt will be 6-8 senior forward **Ryan Sears** (6.4 ppg, 3.4 rpg), who shot 50 percent from the field while playing alongside the massive Misyuchenko and Newman last year. Sears isn't taking his senior season lightly.

"He's worked harder than ever," Dennis said. "He has a good feel for the game. He's a good athlete for his size and he has a good degree of toughness. Offensively, he got a lot better last year. He knows we're counting on him and he's worked very hard."

Several players will compete for time at the forward positions, including three freshmen: 6-7 **Kevin Longley**, 6-6 **Rod Shiver** and 6-6 **Cliff Washburn**.

Longley averaged 15 points and 11 rebounds last season at Vandalia-Butler (Ohio) High School. "He's very athletic and a very skilled player," Dennis said. "He'll play some (small forward) for us."

Shiver averaged 15.7 points, 8.0 rebounds and 2.5 blocks as a senior at Lower Richland High School in Columbia (S.C.) last season and played in the South Carolina high school all-star game. "Athletically, he's probably as good as anybody in the Southern Conference," Dennis said of Shiver. "He'll probably play four (power forward) for us this year but eventually he'll be a three man (small forward)."

Washburn averaged 15.5 points and 10 rebounds last season at Shelby (N.C.) High School. He will play power forward.

1998-99 THE CITADEL SCHEDULE

Nov.	17	Anderson College
	20	@Georgia Tech
	23	Toccoa Falls
	28	@South Carolina
Dec.	2	William & Mary
	5	@Stetson
	8	Winthrop
	12	Lynchburg
	19	University of the South
	21	@Coastal Carolina
	29	@Appalachian State
Jan.	4	@Furman
	9	@College of Charleston
	11	Georgia Southern
	13	North Carolina-Greensboro
	16	Tennessee-Chattanooga
	18	@Davidson
	23	Furman
	25	@East Tennessee State
	30	@Wofford
Feb.	1	Virginia Military Institute
	6	College of Charleston
	9	@Tennessee-Chattanooga
	13	Western Carolina
	15	@Georgia Southern
	20	Wofford
	25-28	#Southern Conference Tournament

@ Road Games
# Greensboro Coliseum, Greensboro, NC

Jonathan Kunz, 6-5 senior forward, will look for the playing time that has eluded him since his freshman year. Kunz (3.6 ppg, 1.3 rpg) played in 16 games last season.

"Kunz started as a freshman and hasn't played much the last two years," Dennis said. "We look for him to get more minutes this year."

Returning for his sophomore season will be 6-8 forward **Tim Wilson** (1.0 ppg, 1.2 rpg), who played in six games last season.

adidas Blue Ribbon Analysis

BACKCOURT .... **B** **BENCH/DEPTH** .... **C**
FRONTCOURT .... **C** **INTANGIBLES** .... **C**

It's not an easy job winning at a military school, but Pat Dennis has found out how to do it in his six years at The Citadel.

Dennis likes his chances of winning again this season, thanks to the return of talented backcourt players Bryan Patton, Jerald Freeman and Mike Roy. Still, there are questions to be answered in the frontcourt, in particular this one: Can Ryan Sears, 6-8 senior forward, have a big senior year?

The Bulldogs will be more athletic and have better shooters this year, but they won't have near they size they've had in recent years. Can they make the adjustment from being a big team to a small team? Another good question.

With six newcomers, several of whom are expected to contribute, Dennis will need to mesh this team quickly. Can he do it?

"We're sort of an unknown," Dennis said. "People ask me what I think and I say I won't really know till they all get here and see what kind of chemistry we have."

Dennis is a promising young coach and he says this could be his best freshman class at The Citadel, but the Bulldogs lost a bunch of points and rebounds from last season's team. Fifth place in the South Division looks like their spot.

(D.L.)

DAVIDSON

LOCATION .... **Davidson, NC**
CONFERENCE .... **Southern (North Division)**
LAST SEASON .... **20-10 (.666)**
CONFERENCE RECORD .... **13-3 (1st)**
STARTERS LOST/RETURNING **1/4**
NICKNAME .... **Wildcats**
COLORS .... **Red & Black**
HOMECOURT .... **Belk Arena (5,700)**
COACH .... **Bob McKillop (Hofstra '72)**
RECORD AT SCHOOL .... **138-120 (9 yrs.)**
CAREER RECORD .... **138-120 (9 yrs.)**
ASSISTANTS .... **Steve Shurina (St. John's '88)**
Matt Matheny (Davidson '93)
Jason Zimmerman (Davidson '94)
TEAM WINS (last 5 yrs.) **22-14-25-18-20**
RPI (last 5 yrs.) **100-204-79-110-93**
1997-98 FINISH .... **Lost in NCAA first round.**

In his 10 years as Davidson's coach, Bob McKillop has found a system that works. It might sound simple. It isn't.

McKillop travels the globe to find players, then for four years weaves them into his system. Davidson always seems to put a veteran team on the floor. It is that kind of team that will make defending North Division co-champion Davidson the team to beat again this year.

The Wildcats are an experienced bunch that is hungry for another NCAA Tournament bid.

"That's the trademark of our program: Building the program class by class and always being able to find veteran players to pave the way for younger kids coming in," McKillop said.

McKillop has plenty of those veterans this year. He has experienced players in the frontcourt and backcourt.

Leading the way will be 6-0 senior point guard **Ali Ton** (4.9 ppg, 2.9 rpg, 193 assists), who led the Southern Conference in assists last year and was 16th in the nation. He was ninth in the nation in assists as a sophomore.

"Ali Ton is a winner," McKillop said. "He makes the team better. He has clearly demonstrated that in his two years as a starter and his initial year coming off the bench. He has learned to make defenders respect him and has worked hard to be more of an offensive threat. I think that will be the change in him this year."

Joining Ton in the backcourt will be 6-3 junior guard **Davor Halbauer** (6.4 ppg, 2.3 rpg, 41 assists), who started 25 games last season. A native of Croatia, Halbauer has good range on his jump shot and made 34 of 95 three-pointers (.358) last season.

"Davor came on strong at the end of the season and he had a very productive and impressive spring," McKillop said. "I see him stepping up to the plate this year."

Adding depth to the backcourt will be 6-3 junior guard **Jeff Bergmann** (0.8 ppg, 0.5 rpg) and 5-10 sophomore guard **James Hampton** (0.8 ppg)

McKillop has built his program by signing versatile players who fit his motion offense. Several players could play small forward, but McKillop doesn't like to restrict his players to one spot on the floor.

Three players have the ability to play small forward, power forward or low post: 6-7 junior forward **Landy Kosmalski**, 6-7 senior forward **Ben Ebong** and 6-9 senior center **Chadd Holmes**.

A starter in all 30 games last year, Kosmalski (9.3 ppg, 6.2 rpg) shot .468 from the field and was 12 of 34 (.343) from three-point range. The son of former Tennessee star Len Kosmalski, Landry ranked 11th in the conference in rebounding last season.

McKillop said Kosmalski is the type of player who makes his system work.

"We have tremendous versatility at the swing spots in the post," McKillop said. "I believe that will be one strength of this team."

Ebong (9.4 ppg, 6.2 rpg) would also fit that mold. Last season, Ebong, the team's third-leading scorer, was the Wildcats' super sub. He started just two games, but averaged 22.7 minutes in 30 games. Ebong shot .516 from the field, but didn't make enough shots to meet the minimum of five per game to be ranked in NCAA or league statistics.

At last year's conference tournament, Ebong was chosen most outstanding player after scoring 36 points and grabbing 25 rebounds in three games. He had nine points and eight rebounds in the Wildcats' 80-61 loss to Michigan in the first round of the NCAA Tournament. He led the Wildcats with 23 blocked shots last year.

"He performed well enough to be chosen player of the game against Michigan," McKillop said. "Clearly he has made a statement as a guy who plays well coming off the bench. Whether he's best coming off the bench or as a starter isn't clear right now, but he will be a major contributor to our team. He's very athletic and he plays with great passion. There are a lot of great athletes out there, but to bring passion like Ben plays with is an important part of his makeup."

Holmes (5.2 ppg, 3.1 rpg) played in all 30 games last year and started five. His 14 blocks were second on the team.

Stephen Marshall, 6-8 junor center, is also back after starting 25 games last year. Marshall (9.6 ppg, 4.5 rpg) was second on the team in scoring, just ahead of Ebong and Kosmalski.

His spot is the low post, but McKillop likes the way Marshall can surprise people with his outside shot.

"He has very talented back-to-the-basket skills but he can also step out and shoot the three-pointer," McKillop said. Marshall was 13 of 30 (.400 percent) from three-point range last year.

Making a push for more playing time this year will be 6-7 senior forward **David Burns** (5.3 ppg, 1.4 rpg) and 6-4 sophomore forward **Emeka Erege** (2.8 ppg, 1.8 rpg). Erege was slowed by a leg injury last year, but was impressive as a small forward.

McKillop signed three freshmen, and one of them continues his trend of signing players from overseas.

Chris Pearson, a 6-7, 210-pound freshman forward, played for Deallam Secondary School in Cottingham, England. Pearson averaged 24.0 ppg, 9.0 rpg, and shot 53 percent from the field last year.

Michael Bree, a 6-0 redshirt freshman guard, signed with Davidson last year out of Summerhill College High School in Sligo, Ireland. Bree, who averaged 24.0 ppg, 9.0 assists, and 4.5 steals as a high school senior, practiced with the Wildcats last year. McKillop plans to continue his long-range recruiting.

"If you look at my roster (over the years) you can see my overseas connections are extensive and strong," McKillop said. "That's historical even when I was a high school coach. With 17 or 18 years of experience overseas, obviously it will produce dividends."

McKillop's other two signees are 7-2, 280-pound freshman center **Martin Ides** of East Burke High School in Icard, N.C., and 6-4 freshman guard/forward **Brian Turner** of Moorestown Friends High in Cinnaminson, N.J.

Ides averaged 13.0 ppg and 9.0 rpg last year, while Turner averaged 25.5 ppg and 13.5 rpg.

The freshmen won't be pushed into early duty, but will work their way into the system. It is a process that has worked well for McKillop, and he doesn't plan to change it.

"All four are very capable and very talented, but they'll be going against people who have two or three years of college experience," McKillop said.

adidas Blue Ribbon Analysis

BACKCOURT .... **B+** **BENCH/DEPTH** .... **B+**
FRONTCOURT .... **B+** **INTANGIBLES** .... **B+**

Davidson is favored to win the North Division title and should challenge the College of Charleston in the league tournament, but don't tell the Wildcats. Their coach, Bob McKillop, doesn't want them taking anything for granted.

"Any time you have 12 teams in a league, it's a chaotic situation," McKillop said. "For one team to emerge a winner is a challenge and a formidable task. Add Charleston, and the task becomes even more formidable."

That's just what Davidson will be again this year—a formidable team.

Davidson must replace one starter, all-conference guard Mark Donnelly (14.6 ppg, 4.5 rpg). For some teams, filling the spot of a player like Donnelly would be a tall order. Not for Davidson. McKillop has plenty of players who have waited for their chance.

Led by senior point guard Ali Ton and junior guard Davor Halbauer, the Wildcats have a strong backcourt. The frontcourt may be even better, led by senior Ben Ebong and juniors Stephen Marshall and Landry Kosmalski, who can also play small forward.

It looks like another winning team for McKillop, but that shouldn't surprise anyone.

(D.L.)

1998-99 DAVIDSON SCHEDULE

Nov.	17	*Duke
	23	@Navy
	28	@Wake Forest
	30	Elon
Dec.	4-5	#Ameritas Classic
	8	North Carolina-Charlotte
	19	Washington College
	29	@Massachusetts
Jan.	2	Appalachian State
	4	@Virginia Military Institute
	9	@East Tennessee State
	11	@North Carolina-Greensboro
	16	Western Carolina
	18	The Citadel
	23	@Tennessee-Chattanooga
	25	Virginia Military Institute
	30	College of Charleston
Feb.	1	@Western Carolina
	3	Furman
	6	North Carolina-Greensboro
	8	@Georgia Southern
	13	East Tennessee State
	16	@Wofford
	20	@Appalachian State
	25-28	##Southern Conference Tournament

@ Road Games
* Charlotte Coliseum, Charlotte, NC
\# Lincoln, NE (vs. Colgate, first round; also Nebraska and Southwest Texas)
\## Greensboro Coliseum, Greensboro, NC

EAST TENNESSEE STATE

LOCATION .... **Johnson City, TN**
CONFERENCE .... **Southern (North Division)**
LAST SEASON .... **11-16 (.407)**
CONFERENCE RECORD .... **6-9 (5th)**
STARTERS LOST/RETURNING **1/4**
NICKNAME .... **Buccaneers**
COLORS .... **Navy Blue & Old Gold**
HOMECOURT .... **Memorial Center (12,000)**
COACH .... **Ed DeChellis (Penn State '82)**
RECORD AT SCHOOL .... **18-36 (2 yrs.)**
CAREER RECORD .... **18-36 (2 yrs.)**
ASSISTANTS .... **Jerry Pelphrey (ETSU '94)**
Dave Siepert (Muhlenberg '86)
TEAM WINS (last 5 yrs.) **16-14-7-7-11**
RPI (last 5 yrs.) **173-192-271-273-267**
1997-98 FINISH ...... **Lost in first round of conference tournament**

For the first time in his three years at East Tennessee State, Ed DeChellis can realistically look forward to a winning season and possibly making a run at the Southern Conference title. Many Buccaneer faithful share the coach's optimism.

DeChellis was a realist when he was hired at ETSU for the '96-97 season. With nine scholarship players, the Bucs went 7-20, 2-11 in the league. At times, the last thing on DeChellis' mind was winning.

"It wasn't like, "Wow, I'm going to walk into this situation and win games'," he said. "My first year I wasn't sure we could score 18 points in a game."

Those woes eased a bit for the Bucs last season on their way to an 11-16 record. It was the type of improvement DeChellis expected when he was hired to revive a program that was the league's most dominant from the late '80s to the early '90s.

With four starters returning—three of them seniors—DeChellis says his rebuilding project is right on schedule this season.

"On paper, this looks like a better basketball team," DeChellis said. "This is my third year and the first time we have a chance to win more than we lose. It's another step in the right direction. We went from seven wins my first year to 11 wins last year. Hopefully we'll be around the .500 mark this year."

That wouldn't satisfy DeChellis, though. He enters the season looking for better.

"We can compete with any team in the Southern Conference now," he said. "We have the ability to win any game we play, whether it's at home or on the road."

One reason for such confidence is 6-3 senior point guard **Greg Stephens** (17.2 ppg, 4.6 rpg, 133 assists), who led the conference in scoring and was fourth in assists. Stephens, dubbed a "point forward" by the league's media, will be one of the league's top players.

Amazingly, Stephens was snubbed in the media's all-conference voting at the end of the season, but he did make the coaches' all-conference team. He shot 45.9 percent from the field, 76.3 percent from the line and made 32 of 87 three-point shots.

It might be the intangibles that make Stephens one of

1998-99 EAST TENNESSEE STATE SCHEDULE

Nov.	14	Anderson College
	16	@Middle Tennessee State
	19	@Virginia Tech
	28	Middle Tennessee State
Dec.	3	@Clemson
	7	North Carolina-Asheville
	10	Michigan State
	19	@Wake Forest
	22	Ferrum
Jan.	2	Virginia Military Institute
	5	Western Carolina
	9	Davidson
	11	@Tennessee-Chattanooga
	16	@Appalachian State
	18	@North Carolina-Greensboro
	20	Belmont
	23	Appalachian State
	25	The Citadel
	30	@Western Carolina
Feb.	1	Furman
	4	@Wofford
	6	@Virginia Military Institute
	8	North Carolina-Greensboro
	13	@Davidson
	15	College of Charleston
	20	@Georgia Southern
	25-28	#Southern Conference Tournament

@ Road Games
\# Greensboro Coliseum, Greensboro, NC

the league's best. After transferring from Navy and sitting out the '96-97 season, Stephens was everything DeChellis expected last year.

"Greg is the glue to the team," DeChellis said. "If you asked if he does anything exceptional, probably not, but he does do a lot of things extremely well. The thing he has that makes him stand out is his competitiveness. When you need someone to step up and make a play, he's going to do it. You can't coach that instinct."

Kyle Keeton, a 6-0 senior, gives the Bucs experience at shooting guard. Keeton (10.2 ppg, 2.6 rpg, 61 assists) has played in 80 games during his career and ranks among the top 10 career assist leaders at ETSU.

Last year, Keeton moved from point to shooting guard, so the Bucs have an adequate sub for Stephens, if needed. Like Stephens, Keeton has strengths that don't show in boxscores.

"Kyle may be the hardest working player I've ever coached," DeChellis said. "You always know that he's going to give you 100 percent in every game and every single day in practice. He made the transformation to the two-guard spot last year, so he'll be more comfortable there this year. He is a tough player."

DeChellis should benefit from more depth in the backcourt than in his pervious two seasons at ETSU. One of the Bucs' top reserves will be 6-0 junior **Gabe Lisicky** (4.6 ppg, 0.8 rpg). Lisicky is the brother of Penn State guard Pete Lisicky, whom DeChellis coached while an assistant with the Nittany Lions.

Two years ago, Gabe Lisicky started 13 games, but he couldn't break into the starting lineup last season. Lisicky has the ability to hit a hot streak, as evidenced by his five-for-seven shooting from three-point range against Charleston Southern last season.

"Gabe has played very well at times and his goal is to become more consistent with his shooting," DeChellis said.

Two other guards are veterans of the ETSU program and will provide depth: 6-2 sophomore **D.J. McDuffie** (4.6 ppg, 2.1 rpg) and 6-0 junior **Erskin Anavitarte** (0.9 ppg, 0.4 rpg).

"D.J. had a great spring and he is going to be able to step up offensively and defensively this season," DeChellis said. "Erskin is a good shooter and I think that if he could grasp our system better, he could really make an impact."

Andy Huckabay, a 6-2 sophomore swing player, will push for more playing time this season. Last season, Huckabay (0.6 ppg, 0.6 rpg) saw action in 13 games.

It isn't just the Stephens-led backcourt that has DeChellis excited about this year's team. He expects to see a vastly improved frontcourt with two starters back: 6-7 senior **Reggie Todd** at power forward and 6-6 sophomore **Adrian Meeks** at center.

Todd (12.8 ppg, 8.6 rpg) tied for the league's rebounding championship with North Carolina-Greensboro's Demetrius Cherry. Todd was also third in the league in field-goal percentage (52.7 percent).

A Seventh Day Adventist, Todd missed three games last season while practicing his religious beliefs, which prohibit him from playing games from sundown on Fridays to sundown on Saturdays. He missed two games against Appalachian State and one against VMI. Not surprisingly, ETSU lost all three.

"Reggie has the ability to be one of top players in the Southern Conference," DeChellis said. "He's a great rebounder because he has long arms and can jump. We're hoping he can become a more consistent scorer."

DeChellis believes Meeks (6.3 ppg, 6.4 rpg) will be the Bucs' most improved player this season. Meeks was forced into the college game quickly—he started 24 games at center—and responded by making the coaches' all-conference freshman team.

Meeks was thrown into early action when 6-9 **Ryan Wilson** hurt his ankle in the preseason, missed nine games, and never could go full speed. Wilson, a junior who was on the league's all-freshman team two years ago, hurt his ankle again last spring and had major surgery. Meeks again enters the race for the center's job with a big lead because of Wilson's injury.

"We really had to throw Meeks into the fire last year because Wilson couldn't play," DeChellis said. "I think his offensive skills will be much more developed next season and he will be an overall better player."

Wilson (3.5 ppg, 2.9 rpg) would give the frontcourt a big boost if he fully recovers. Last season, Wilson hobbled through 18 games, averaging 14 minutes per game, and wasn't close to full speed. Listed at 222 pounds, Wilson is closer to 240 after some work in the weight room.

"Ryan is a big, strong player who can shoot the ball well," DeChellis said. "If he can get healthy, he can really help us. His return will be a big key for us."

Gareth Davis, 6-9 junior, gives the Bucs added depth in the post. Davis (2.3 ppg, 2.1 rpg) played in 26 games and started five, but saw his playing time decrease as the season progressed. "Gareth has had some bright moments," DeChellis said. "We just want more of them."

One newcomer is expected to give the Bucs plenty of bright moments—6-5, 250-pound junior forward **Leo Murray**.

Murray sat out last season after transferring to ETSU from Xavier, where his playing time was limited in two seasons. He averaged 2.3 minutes in 1996-97 when the Musketeers finished the season ranked No. 13 nationally. As a freshman, Murray averaged 6.3 minutes, scoring a career-high 12 points against St. Francis (Pa.)

"He looks like a defensive end or a tackle," DeChellis said. "He's an athlete, strong and tough. He's got low post skills, but he also can step out on the perimeter and shoot. He can run, he can pass and he's a very good shooter."

Two freshmen join the program this year: 6-3 shooting guard **Dimeco Childress** from Columbia (Tenn.) Central High School and 6-0 point guard **Cliff Decoster** from Miramar (Fla.) High School.

Childress averaged 20 points, 4.1 rebounds and 2.7 assists as a senior, leading his team to a 31-3 record and state tournament berth. He played in the prestigious Tennessee-Georgia All-Star game in early August. Decoster averaged 15 points and five assists as a senior, 10 points and four assists as a junior.

"We're very pleased with our two incoming freshmen," DeChellis said. "Cliff Decoster is a point guard that we can build around for the future. He can push the ball, he's strong, he's got a great work ethic and he's a great competitor. (Demeco) also has a chance to be very good and I think he will give us an offensive punch when we need it. He's very athletic."

adidas Blue Ribbon Analysis

BACKCOURT	B	BENCH/DEPTH	C
FRONTCOURT	B	INTANGIBLES	C

Fans of ETSU basketball yearn for the glory days of not so long ago, when the Buccaneers went to the NCAA Tournament four straight years (1989-92). Perhaps third-year coach Ed DeChellis has them on the path back.

Only one player is gone from last year's 11-16 team, and DeChellis should be able to replace senior guard Troy Seymour, who averaged 7.1 points. Senior swingman Greg Stephens will be among the league's top players and he could help carry the Buccaneers back toward the top of the North Division.

ETSU will tune up for the league with a rugged non-conference schedule, including three games against teams that reached the 1998 postseason: Clemson and Michigan State, which played in the NCAA Tournament, and Wake Forest (NIT). ETSU also has two games against North Division rival Davidson, which played in the NCAA Tournament a year ago.

Once ETSU gets into league play, it could be a dangerous team, but the Bucs won't be alone. "The conference is more balanced and I don't think anybody is going to run away with the title," DeChellis said. "Teams like us are creeping back into it so it should be an exciting conference race."

ETSU will creep a little closer to the top this year, but look for a third-place finish in the tougher of the league's two divisions.

(D.L.)

FURMAN

LOCATION .... **Greenville, SC**
CONFERENCE .... **Southern (South Division)**
LAST SEASON .... **9-20 (.310)**
CONFERENCE RECORD .... **5-9 (4th)**
STARTERS LOST/RETURNING **1/4**
NICKNAME .... **Paladins**
COLORS .... **Purple & White**
HOMECOURT .... **Timmons Arena (5,000)**
COACH .... **Larry Davis (Asbury '78)**
RECORD AT SCHOOL .... **9-20 (1 yr.)**
CAREER RECORD .... **9-20 (1 yr.)**
ASSISTANTS ... **Ken Potosnak (Randolph-Macon '90)**
Mike Jones (Howard '90)
Ryan Odom (Hampden-Sydney '96)
TEAM WINS (last 5 yrs.) **10-10-10-10-11**
RPI (last 5 yrs.) **217-277-254-258-290**
1997-98 FINISH . **Lost in conference tournament first round.**

It was too bad Furman fans couldn't enjoy a banner season in 1997-98 while watching the Southern Conference player of the year, departed power forward Chuck Vincent.

Instead, Furman and second-year coach Larry Davis endured a 9-20 season that was marred by turnover after turnover and some horrid perimeter shooting. As a result, the Paladins clanked their way to a fourth-place finish in the South Division.

With opponents focusing on Vincent inside, the Paladins certainly had their share of open three-point shots, but could seldom connect. Their 28 percent shooting from three-point range was worst in the league, and their 93 three-pointers made were the fewest in the league, 25 behind the next closest team (The Citadel made 118).

This year, Davis says goodbye to the 6-7 Vincent—he's now playing in Spain—and he hopes goodbye to that woeful shooting of last year.

"We knew going into the season that would be our biggest problem," Davis said. "Our guards handled the ball fine, but our big guys didn't. They led the team in turnovers, but that wasn't our biggest problem. The big thing was our perimeter shooting."

Davis has done his best to correct that problem. He signed two sharpshooting high school guards, **Anthony Thomas** and **Kyle Julius**, and also sent his returnees a memo: Work on your shooting.

"We signed two outstanding shooters in Julius and Thomas," Davis said. "They both can really shoot the basketball and both will definitely play. We've also worked on our shooting. **Bubba Smith**, **Marcus Dilligard** and **P.J. Brown** each shot 300 balls a day this summer."

That can't hurt. Neither will the experience of Smith, Dilligard and Brown. Furman may have lost Vincent (17.2 ppg, 7.9 rpg), but it returns most of the '97-98 team. Junior guard **Que Gaither** (2.2 ppg, 1.3 rpg), who transferred to Francis Marion in Florence, S.C., is the only other Paladin not returning.

Furman's four returning starters aren't guaranteed their old jobs, though. Davis expects a fight for playing time, thanks to the solid class of newcomers.

Dilligard (5.8 ppg, 2.7 rpg, 44 assists), a 6-4 sophomore swing player, started at point guard last year, but that might not be his spot this year. Not if 6-0 freshman point **Paul Foster** can forge his way into the lineup.

Foster, who signed during the early signing period in November, was a true point guard at Wallace-Rose Hill High in Teachey, N.C., and averaged 10.5 ppg and 8.5 apg, leading the team to a 31-0 record and state championship.

"(Foster) is a point guard who can run the whole show, and there are few who can do it better," said recruiting analyst Bob Gibbons. "He'll develop into a fine floor leader and keep turnovers to a minimum."

Furman could use that kind of help. Last season, the Paladins had the worst turnover ratio in the league (minus 4.3).

"It will be Dilligard or Foster at point guard," Davis said. "Dilligard has the experience at point guard, but we'd like to move him around. He has the funniest positions on the team, point guard and small forward. He's potentially a better scorer, but because we played him at point it kept his scoring down."

Smith, a 6-4 senior, returns at shooting guard after starting 29 games last year. Smith (10.8 ppg, 3.3 rpg), who can also play point, led Furman in assists (75) last season

1998-99 FURMAN SCHEDULE

Nov.	14	Stetson
	17	@William & Mary
	23	@Winthrop
	28	@Northwestern
Dec.	2	Charleston Southern
	4	@Georgia
	9	Mercer
	12	*Duquesne
	19	Greensboro College
	26	Clemson
Jan.	2	Wofford
	4	The Citadel
	9	@Georgia Southern
	11	College of Charleston
	16	North Carolina-Greensboro
	18	Georgia Southern
	23	@The Citadel
	25	@Tennessee-Chattanooga
	30	Virginia Military Institute
Feb.	1	@East Tennessee State
	3	@Davidson
	6	Western Carolina
	8	@Appalachian State
	13	@Wofford
	15	Tennessee-Chattanooga
	20	@College of Charleston
	25-28	#Southern Conference Tournament

@ Road Games
* Desmond Conference Challenge, Albany, NY
\# Greensboro Coliseum, Greensboro, NC

and minutes (33.9 per game).

"I think Bubba is the best perimeter defender in the Southern Conference," Davis said. "He's a good athlete, very strong, and he has experience. Mark Donnelly (of Davidson) only had six points against him. Every time he had a defensive assignment, Bubba would shut him down.

"I look for Bubba to score more this year. One reason he didn't score more last year was because he was playing so many minutes and he always got the toughest defensive assignments."

Thomas, a 6-4 guard from Atlanta Woodward Academy, and Julius, a 6-3 guard from Cathedral High in Thunder Bay, Ontario, should help Smith get some rest when he needs it.

Thomas, who will also play small forward, was rated among the nation's top 150 players by Gibbons and No. 200 by *Prep Star Magazine.* Last year, Thomas averaged 21.5 ppg, 7.3 rpg and earned all-state honors. He shot 54 percent from the field and 73 percent from the line for his career.

Julius was the Paladins' last signee in the spring. He averaged 14 points last season for Cathedral High, one of Ontario's basketball powers, and shot 50 percent from the field and 48 percent from three-point range. Cathedral went 33-0 and was ranked No. 1 in Ontario.

"Julius and Thomas will both play significant minutes," Davis said. "I think that will help Bubba."

Brown (2.0 ppg, 1.3 rpg), a 6-1 sophomore, can play all three backcourt positions. "He's a versatile guy, strong and athletic," Davis says.

Terry McGann (0.9 ppg, 0.9 rpg), a 6-0 senior, returns as a backup point guard after playing in 28 games last season. **Michael Campbell** (0.0 ppg, 0.3 rpg), a 6-2 junior guard, is also back.

Returning at small forward is 6-6 junior **Andre Kerr** (11.1 ppg, 5.2 rpg), who started all 29 games. Davis would like to see Kerr's shooting improve this season. Kerr shot .414 percent from the field but was erratic from outside.

"He's a big, strong, athletic kid, but he was an inconsistent shooter from the perimeter," Davis said. "In fairness to him, he was coming off a redshirt year for an injury (to his back). He will have his hands full keeping that spot."

As a freshman in '95-96, Kerr averaged 12.1 ppg and 5.5 rpg and was voted to the league's all-freshman team, despite having knee problems that required offseason surgery.

Replacing Vincent at power forward became one of Davis' biggest recruiting tasks. Davis found his man in 6-8 junior **Stanislav Makshantsev**, a transfer from Northeast Nebraska Community College.

Makshantsev, native of Alama-Alta, Kazakhstan, is the Paladins' first junior-college transfer in 20 years (what true Furman fan can forget Tobe Jackson?). Makshantsev is coming off an outstanding season after averaging 23.5 ppg and 10.4 rpg at Northeast Nebraska and earning third-team All-America honors. Blue Ribbon junior college recruiting analysts Rick Ball and Phil Henzel ranked Makshantsev No. 87 in their list of the country's top 300 JC sophomores.

"I'd be surprised if he doesn't start," Davis said. "He's a very good scorer, a very good rebounder. He can shoot the three, drive it and post up inside. He has more of a total game than Chuck. Will he do what Chuck did remains to be seen, but he's a very good player."

Davis likes the Paladins' depth in the post. Four players, including 6-11, 240-pound freshman **Stevan Petrovic**, could be used at center.

Petrovic, a native of Yugoslavia, averaged 14.6 ppg and 7.5 rpg last season at Norfolk (Neb.) HS.

Daniel Quigley (7.3 ppg, 7.4 rpg), 6-7 senior center, started 21 games last season and tied for seventh in the league in rebounding. **Will Coles** (4.8 ppg, 4.5 rpg), a 6-8, 230-pound senior center, was the team's top shot blocker with 24 and can be a scoring threat, as evidenced by consecutive 14-point games last season against Tennessee-Chattanooga and The Citadel.

"Quigley will certainly play a lot inside and so will Coles," Davis said. "They're both solid players inside."

Patrick Garner (2.6 ppg, 2.1 rpg), a 6-9 power junior forward/center, gives the Paladins more depth in the post.

"All four guys will play significant minutes (at center)," Davis said. "Who starts doesn't matter. All four are good enough to play and we plan to play all four of them."

Steven Hamrick (0.0 ppg, 0.0 rpg), a 6-5 forward, returns after playing three games last season.

The Paladins' non-conference schedule includes games at Northwestern and Georgia, and they play host to Clemson in the brand-new Bi-Lo Center in downtown Greenville, S.C.

It might take a few games for Davis to settle into a rotation of players. "We'll have much more competitive practices," Davis said. "Everybody's job will be on the line. That wasn't the case last year."

adidas Blue Ribbon Analysis

BACKCOURT	C	BENCH/DEPTH	B
FRONTCOURT	B	INTANGIBLES	C

So much for a one-man show. Second-year Furman coach Larry Davis saw enough of that last year when Chuck Vincent, the Southern Conference player of the year, was often the Paladins' only offensive threat.

Davis says junior-college transfer Stanislav Makshantsev, a 6-8 power forward/center, has a better all-around game than Vincent and four other newcomers could steal the jobs, or at least some playing time, from the four returning starters.

Before being hired, Davis was recruiting coordinator at Minnesota, and he has put together a good class of Paladins this year. Time restraints hampered his first effort, and given the time, Davis got the five players he needed this time.

He looks forward to the post-Vincent days. "There was so much focus on Chuck last year, but we played very well a couple of times when he wasn't in the game," Davis said. "This year we should have much more firepower. How quickly we mature will determine how good we are. We will certainly be more talented, but we're young."

Furman needs to find a playmaker, and freshman point guard Paul Foster was signed as the man of the future. Whether he's ready this year is still a question. If he isn't, swingman Marcus Dilligard will be back at the point again.

Two other newcomers, Anthony Thomas and Kyle Julius, will shore up the backcourt. If the new players can contribute and the Paladins can improve their perimeter play, they could be dangerous.

Still, third place in the South Division looks like a safe bet, and that—like the division—is better than last year.

(D.L.)

GEORGIA SOUTHERN

LOCATION	Statesboro, GA
CONFERENCE	Southern (South Division)
LAST SEASON	10-18 (.357)
CONFERENCE RECORD	4-10 (5th)
STARTERS LOST/RETURNING	1/4
NICKNAME	Eagles
COLORS	Blue & White
HOMECOURT	W.S. Hanner Fieldhouse
COACH	Gregg Polinsky (Northern Arizona '82)
RECORD AT SCHOOL	23-59 (3 yrs.)
CAREER RECORD	23-59 (3 yrs.)
ASSISTANTS	Sammy Jackson (Montevallo ('86)
	Stu Brown (Wake Forest '89)
	Dave Coradini (Georgia Southern '96)
TEAM WINS (last 5 yrs.)	14-8-3-10-10
RPI (last 5 yrs.)	199-289-305-271-273
1997-98 FINISH	Lost in conference quarterfinal.

Sometimes, a return to normalcy isn't all bad. Just ask fourth-year Georgia Southern coach Gregg Polinsky.

For his first two years, Polinsky battled scholarship restrictions mandated by the NCAA that he inherited from his predecessor, Frank Kerns.

Now Polinsky has the program almost back to normal.

1998-99 GEORGIA SOUTHERN SCHEDULE

Nov.	14	Piedmont
	16	@Florida
	19	Jacksonville State
	21	High Point
	28-29	#Florida International Tournament
Dec.	3	Tennessee-Chattanooga
	7	@Belmont
	12	Austin Peay
	20	@Florida State
	29	North Georgia
Jan.	2	College of Charleston
	4	@Tennessee-Chattanooga
	9	Furman
	11	@The Citadel
	16	@Virginia Military Institute
	18	@Furman
	23	Wofford
	25	@Western Carolina
	30	Appalachian State
Feb.	1	@College of Charleston
	6	@Wofford
	8	Davidson
	13	@North Carolina-Greensboro
	15	The Citadel
	20	East Tennessee State
	25-28	##Southern Conference Tournament

@ Road Games
\# Miami, FL (vs. Northern Illinois, first round; also Bucknell and Florida International)
\#\# Greensboro Coliseum, Greensboro, NC

And that can feel pretty good.

"Last year was like our first normal year," Polinsky says. "We're still in the process of building. We think we have a solid freshman class (of six players). I'm not sure if we'll set the world on fire, but we're headed in the right direction."

His '98 class of signees could keep the Eagles moving that way. It includes two freshman guards, three freshman forwards and a freshman center, plus a junior-college transfer at guard.

Donta Humphries, 6-0 freshman, should make a push for a starting job at point guard. Humphries is a local favorite. He played at Statesboro (Ga.) High School and last season averaged 18 points, seven assists and four steals, earning second-team all-state honors.

Also competing for the job at point guard will be 6-2 sophomore guard **Toby Frazier**, who sat out last season as a Proposition 48 signee out of Jacksonville (Fla.) Paxon High School.

"Both guys (Frazier and Humphries) have a good feel for the game," Polinsky said. "They're young and they'll make their share of mistakes. I'm not sure how they'll do under fire. They might not be as quick as some guys at that position, but they add another dimension because of their feel for the game."

With Humphries or Frazier at the point, Polinsky could move 6-1 senior **Fernando Daniel** to shooting guard. Last season, Daniel (7.5 ppg, 2.0 rpg, 107 assists, 81 turnovers) played point guard and led the Eagles in assists. He shot 78 percent from the free-throw line and made 38 of 107 three-point shots.

If needed, Daniel could return to point guard.

"Fernando has been there and he can shoot the basketball," Polinsky said. "He's played point guard and he'll be able to take some pressure off the younger guys."

Polinsky will again employ a three-guard offense, and several players will compete for the third perimeter spot with 6-4 junior **Quentin Martin**, a top candidate if he's healthy.

Last season, Martin (10.5 ppg, 3.6 rpg, 69 assists) started all 28 games, but he's coming off knee surgery in May.

"He's a guy who can score," Polinsky said. "We want him to improve his outside shot but he's good at taking the ball to the basket. If he can come back and he's healthy, he can play either two (guard) or three (small forward). The biggest thing is how he comes back."

Demarlo Slocum, a 6-2 guard who transferred from Dixie (Utah) Junior College, will also play shooting guard or small forward. Slocum averaged 10 points, three rebounds and three assists last season and led Dixie JC to a 28-5 record and a No. 4 national ranking.

Duane Goebel, 6-4 senior, will also be in the guard/small forward mix. Goebel (3.9 ppg, 3.4 rpg) played in 16 games last season, started four and averaged 20 minutes, but was hampered by a knee injury. He also played hurt during his sophomore season.

"He's only been healthy his freshman year," Polinsky said. "We think if he's healthy, he'll have a solid senior season. He's not an explosive scorer, but he knows how to play and he's been in the program. From the leadership standpoint, he could be great for us."

Also returning to the backcourt are 6-4 senior guard **Andre Wilkes** (2.0 ppg, 1.3 rpg) and 6-0 junior guard **Omar Gunn** (1.1 ppg, 0.4 rpg). Wilkes played in 22 games last season and started eight, while Gunn played in 13 games without a start.

Polinsky must replace several spot starters from last year's lineup.

Elvardo Rolle, (10.5 ppg, 1.3 rpg), a 6-0 guard, started eight games last season as a senior after coming back from a wrist injury. Also gone is 6-1 sophomore guard Arkee Thompson (6.3 ppg, 3.5 rpg) and 6-8 forward Quincy Wright (10.5 ppg, 3.5 rpg, .456 fg). Thompson, now a safety with the Georgia Southern football team, played in 27 games last year and started five.

Wright, who would have been a senior, played in 24 games, averaging 23 minutes, before being dismissed from the team before the conference tournament.

Polinsky will be counting heavily on two returning starters in the frontcourt, 6-8 senior forward **Cedric McGinnis** and 6-7 junior forward **Hamp Jones.** McGinnis has the potential to be one of the better inside players in the league.

Last season, McGinnis (12.8 ppg, 6.1 rpg) learned the Eagles' system after transferring from Butler County (Kan.) Community College, where he averaged 13.3 points and was an honorable mention JC All-American. McGinnis led the Eagles in blocked shots (18) and was second in steals (42) in '97-98. He shot 47 percent from the field and 72 percent from the free-throw line.

"McGinnis is our biggest threat in the interior, no question," Polinsky said. "We need him to have a big senior season. With a year under his belt, he'll be more comfortable. He's real agile and real skilled. He can put the ball down and do a lot of different things."

McGinnis will start at one spot in the frontcourt with Jones (7.8 ppg, 6.2 rpg) also a likely starter. Jones came to Georgia Southern as a walkon out of Jenkins County (Ga.) High School and has become one of Polinsky's favorite players.

Jones started all 28 games last year and shot 58 percent from the field, but he didn't take enough shots (he was 91 for 156) to meet the minimum number of five shots per game to be ranked in conference statistics. He would have ranked second in field-goal percentage.

And Jones works at defense. Last season, he was second on the team in blocks (17) and led in steals (55).

"He's been a great role player," Polinsky said. "He does all the intangibles. He came in as a walkon and he's been a joy to coach. He's quick, he takes high-percentage shots and he's our best interior defender."

Polinsky has added some depth to the frontcourt with four freshmen: 6-9 forward **Kashien Latham**, 6-7 forward **Edward Keith**, 6-6 forward **Wayne Wooley**, and 6-9 forward/center **Tywon Thomas.**

Latham averaged 18.5 points and 9.6 rebounds last season at Bradwell Institute in Hinesville, Ga.

Keith averaged 6.0 points and 8.5 rebounds last season and helped Dougherty High School in Albany, Ga., to a 25-7 record and the Class 3A state championship.

Wooley was a three-year starter at Southwest Dekalb High School near Atlanta. He averaged 11 points, eight rebounds and two blocks last season.

Thomas averaged 10 points, nine rebounds and four blocks last season at Treutlen High School in Soperton, Ga.

"We think our new inside guys can run the floor," Polinsky said. "Of course, they all have to learn. Keith and Wooley are guys who run well and their skill level will have to improve. The new guys will have to rebound and run the floor and leave the scoring to the more experienced players."

adidas Blue Ribbon Analysis

BACKCOURT .... **C-** **BENCH/DEPTH** .... **C**
FRONTCOURT .... **B** **INTANGIBLES** .... **C**

In the heart of football country, Georgia Southern coach Gregg Polinsky is trying to build a basketball program. Polinsky's '98 recruiting class, six freshmen and one junior-college transfer, is probably his best in four years at the school.

Several of the newcomers will be expected to contribute this season, but they won't likely push the Eagles into the South Division race this year. It might take them time to develop.

"The key will be how well we defend and rebound and how well our new players and old players mesh," Polinsky said. "Our new players will have to play a big part. If we can get a healthy blend of young and old, we can be a good basketball team."

It's tough to win when you're counting on that many new players. The Eagles look like they're headed for sixth place in the South.

(D.L.)

NORTH CAROLINA-GREENSBORO

LOCATION .... **Greensboro, NC**
CONFERENCE .... **Southern (North Division)**
LAST SEASON .... **9-19 (.321)**
CONFERENCE RECORD .... **6-9 (t-4th)**
STARTERS LOST/RETURNING **3/2**
NICKNAME .... **Spartans**
COLORS .... **Gold, White & Navy Blue**
HOMECOURT .... **Fleming Gymnasium (2,320)**
COACH .... **Randy Peele (Virginia Wesleyan '80)**
RECORD AT SCHOOL .... **39-49 (3 yrs.)**
CAREER RECORD .... **39-49 (3 yrs.)**
ASSISTANTS .... **Robert Williams (American International '87)**
Joe Gallagher (Pembroke State '68))
Darryl Kosciak (North Carolina-Greensboro '95)
TEAM WINS (last 5 yrs.) **15-23-20-10-9**
RPI (last 5 yrs.) **192-99-121-232-229**
1997-98 FINISH .... **Lost in conference quarterfinal.**

In mid-January last season, North Carolina-Greensboro was 4-2 in the Southern Conference and its coach, Randy Peele, was feeling like a contender for a league title.

Peele couldn't hide his optimism. "I think we've got a chance to be a pretty good team," Peele told his assistants. He spoke too soon.

Soon after that proclamation, freshman guard **Nathan Jameson** suffered an MCL tear in his knee, and the Spartans' hopes for a North Division title slowly crumbled. They won four more league games, but entered the conference tournament without 6-8 forward **Demetrius Cherry**, who broke a toe with three games left in the regular season.

Even without Cherry and Jameson, the Spartans beat Western Carolina, 60-59, in a play-in game in the conference tournament when since-departed Derrick Nix made a three-point shot from half court at the buzzer. The Spartans then flirted with an upset before losing to Tennessee-Chattanooga, 56-55, in a quarterfinal game.

Inspired by his team's resiliency last season, Peele enters the '98-99 season with high hopes. Peele might not have the most talented team in the league, but he believes the Spartans can match any other team in guts.

"I'd like to think we'll be in the mix at tournament time," Peele said. "It's all about winning close games. Maybe we can sneak up on some people. I think once the end of February hits, we can be a factor."

That will likely depend on the return of Cherry and Jameson.

A senior, Cherry has struggled with his once-broken little toe, which he reinjured in June. "Cherry will be a major key to what we're trying to do," Peele said. "He's shown the ability to make the tough shots at crucial parts of the game."

Last season, Cherry (12.9 ppg, 8.6 rpg, 30 steals) tied for the league's rebounding title. Shooting .541 percent from the field, Cherry, a power forward, was voted to the media's all-conference second team and to the coaches' 10-player all-conference team.

Peele thinks Cherry's movement away from the ball and his strength inside gives him a chance to be one of the league's premier post players.

"When other kids wear down, Cherry has the physical strength that really helps him," Peele said. "Offensively, he's unorthodox enough that he is very effective. He's left-handed and he is very efficient with his jump hook, plus he has the ability to rebound offensively. He also shoots free throws well (.694 percent). Last year he was more of an offensive threat than I anticipated. Can he average 15 points this year? I think he has a chance."

Jameson, a 6-2 sophomore, will also play a key role in the Spartans' season. Last year, Jameson (8.1 ppg, 2.6 rpg, 44 assists) played 15 games before suffering the knee injury. He can play point guard or shooting guard.

"I think he could very easily have been rookie of the year if he hadn't been injured," Peele said. "He's a combination guard. He can legitimately play both guard positions."

Jameson, chosen to the league's all-freshman team, will likely play the point this year. During the summer, Jameson, hoping to strengthen his knee and get in shape for the preseason, played in Europe with a touring team.

Two freshmen, **Courtney Eldridge** and **Ray Henry,** will give Jameson some help in the backcourt.

Eldridge, a 5-9 guard from Thayer Academy in Boston, averaged 17 points and nine assists last season. An outstanding defender, Eldridge earned honorable mention All-America honors in *Street & Smith's College Basketball Yearbook*. He could figure into the Spartans' plans this year.

"He's a tough kid," Peele said. "We think he can play. We recruited him to create competition. It's anybody's job. Everything on the perimeter is open."

Henry, a 6-3 shooting guard, averaged 20 points, 12 rebounds and five assists last year at Rush Henrietta (N.Y.) High School, where he was a teammate of Cherry for one season. Henry, the player of the year in Rochester, N.Y., chose to attend UNCG over closer-to-home Niagara.

"Henry is really a slasher," Peele said. "He can get it to the basket and score off the dribble. We think he'll help us."

Warren Cunningham, a 6-2 junior, is a true point guard who can also play shooting guard. Cunningham (1.2 ppg, 0.8 rpg, 42 assists) played in 27 games, starting 10, and averaged 16.6 minutes. His role last year increased dramatically when Jameson was hurt.

That will only help Cunningham this year, but Peele wants to see him become more of an offensive threat.

"We want him to be more of a scorer," Peele said. "We want to see him try to create more opportunities off the dribble and knock down open shots. He's a leader and a tough kid. He was a great backup, but can he be a starter? That's the key."

Several players could contend for the job at small forward with 6-5 senior **Justin Stewart** (6.5 ppg, 3.3 rpg, 30 three-pointers) leading the race. Stewart is one of the team's top three-point shooters—he made 30 of 66 (.454 percent) last year—and shot 71 percent from the line.

"He can really shoot the ball," Peele said. "He can shoot with anybody in the country. Now there's a challenge: His ability to defend and play the open court."

Geoff Williams (1.9 ppg, 0.8 rpg), 6-4 sophomore, also plays small forward. Last year, Williams played in 28 games, started two, and averaged 8.3 minutes.

The Spartans must replace two of their frontcourt players last season, 6-9 Larry Gilbert (8.9 ppg, 4.3 rpg) and 6-5, 210-pound bruiser Matt Javit (8.9 ppg, 4.7 rpg). Also gone is Nix (11.9 ppg, 3.0 rpg), whose running three-pointer that stunned Western Carolina in the conference tournament won't soon be forgotten by Spartan fans.

Aaron Chavis, a 6-7, 245-pound power forward, will be expected to carry much of the frontcourt load on his broad shoulders. Chavis (4.6 ppg, 3.4 rpg), like Javit, is a bruiser. Peele says Chavis is all muscle.

"I don't think there's any question that we can win with Chavis in the post," Peele said, "but he must continue to improve and become a better scorer."

Peele expects to get some quick frontcourt help from **Sam Brinson,** a 6-7 junior power forward from Northeastern (Colo.) Junior College. Brinson, a native of Miami who played one year at the University of Wyoming, averaged 12 points and nine rebounds last season.

1998-99 UNC-GREENSBORO SCHEDULE

Nov.	14	@Nebraska
	18	@Wake Forest
	21	St. Francis (PA)
	28	@St. Francis (PA)
	30	William & Mary
Dec.	5	North Carolina A&T
	7	Virginia Military Institute
	22	@Tennessee
	28	@William & Mary
	30	@Duke
Jan.	4	Wofford
	6	Coastal Carolina
	9	Western Carolina
	11	Davidson
	13	@The Citadel
	16	@Furman
	18	East Tennessee State
	23	@College of Charleston
	25	@Appalachian State
	30	Tennessee-Chattanooga
Feb.	1	Appalachian State
	6	@Davidson
	8	@East Tennessee State
	13	Georgia Southern
	15	@Virginia Military Institute
	20	@Western Carolina
	25-28	#Southern Conference Tournament

@ Road Games
# Greensboro Coliseum, Greensboro, NC

"He's a lot like Cherry, almost a clone, but he may be better offensively," Peele said.

Also returning to the frontcourt will be 6-7 senior forward **Randy Woodard** (2.7 ppg, 1.8 rpg), who played in 20 games last season.

UNCG's tallest player, 6-10 junior center **Ricardo Trevisan,** has only been playing since his sophomore season at Maury (Va.) High School. If Trevisan (2.1 ppg, 1.7 rpg) continues to mature, he should be a factor at low post. Last year, he played in 24 games and averaged 8.4 minutes.

Two freshman forwards, 6-6 **James Maye** and 6-8 **Luke Boythe,** round out the frontcourt. Maye averaged 13.1 points and five rebounds last year, shot 47 percent from the field and an impressive 51 percent from three-point range.

Boythe, who played at Charlotte (N.C.) Christian School, averaged 13 points and seven rebounds as a junior and was rated among the state's top 25 prospects by recruiting analyst Bob Gibbons.

"I feel very good about our interior," Peele said. "We have six quality players inside. We're deep and talented there. If you asked me if we're good enough to challenge in the Southern Conference in the post, I'd say yes."

Can the Spartans challenge for the league's North Division title? That may depend on Cherry's toe and Jameson's knee and how quickly the Spartans' newcomers can fit into Peele's system.

adidas Blue Ribbon Analysis

BACKCOURT .... **C** **BENCH/DEPTH** .... **C**
FRONTCOURT .... **C** **INTANGIBLES** .... **B**

When North Carolina-Greensboro finished tied for fourth in its first season in the Southern Conference's North Division, Spartans coach Randy Peele wasn't too pleased. Peele thought with a couple of breaks—or minus two injuries—the Spartans could have been much better.

Well, that's the breaks, and Peele hopes to get a few good ones this time around. Much of the Spartans' success will depend on the healthy return of 6-8 senior forward Demetrius Cherry and 6-2 guard Nathan Jameson. They need some help, though. In particular, the perimeter players must improve for the Spartans to be successful.

"We may be a team that's a year away with our underclassmen (eight are freshmen or sophomores)," Peele said. "On the perimeter, I like our talent but we're not real experienced. We've improved our athleticism, which should help us defensively."

Like Peele says, the Spartans might be a year away. They appear to be the fifth-best team in the North Division this year.

(D.L.)

TENNESSEE-CHATTANOOGA

LOCATION .... **Chattanooga, TN**
CONFERENCE .... **Southern (South Division)**
LAST SEASON .... **13-15 (.464)**
CONFERENCE RECORD .... **7-7 (1st)**
STARTERS LOST/RETURNING **0/5**
NICKNAME .... **Mocs**
COLORS .... **Blue, Gold & Silver**
HOMECOURT .... **UTC Arena (11,218)**
COACH .... **Henry Dickerson (Morris Harvey '73)**
RECORD AT SCHOOL .... **13-15 (1 yr.)**
CAREER RECORD .... **13-15 (1 yr.)**
ASSISTANTS .... **John Gibson (Tennessee-Chattanooga '88)**
Jon Goddard (Tennessee-Chattanooga '90)
L.J. Kilby (Lincoln Memorial '75)
TEAM WINS (last 5 yrs.) **23-19-1524-13**
RPI (last 5 yrs.) **58-147-210-111-205**
1997-98 FINISH .... **Lost in conference semifinal.**

It wasn't just a job when Henry Dickerson took over for Mack McCarthy as Tennessee-Chattanooga's basketball coach in the summer of '97. It was an adventure. Dickerson saw it all last season.

On his first road trip of the year, to Charlotte, N.C., for the Harris-Teeter Pepsi Challenge, Dickerson had to wait several hours with his players before they could check into their hotel. It was on fire.

Once the Mocs checked in, Dickerson was bumped to another room. Throughout the first night, someone kept pounding on Dickerson's door. Nothing like a good night's sleep to get yourself ready for North Carolina.

The adventure continued the next two nights in the Charlotte Coliseum, where the Mocs lost to the then-No.3-ranked Tar Heels, 68-38, and to then-No.5-ranked South Carolina, 67-55.

That tournament set the tone for a frustrating season that saw several of the Mocs' former patsies in the Southern Conference gain a measure of revenge. The Mocs were pitiful on the road (2-8 and 1-3 in neutral sites) and even lost four times in their own Roundhouse, a place where they had been nearly unbeatable in league play.

Despite it all, the Mocs managed to win the Southern Conference South Division, but they suffered their first non-winning season (13-15) since McCarthy's 1989-90 team went 14-14 and their first losing season since Murray Arnold's 1979-80 team went 13-14.

Through it all, Dickerson, who had been McCarthy's top assistant for eight years, never lost his enthusiasm for the job.

"I was very excited last year because it was my first head coaching job," Dickerson said. "I'm even more excited this year, not because I'm a head coach, but because we'll be better. I learned a lot last year. There are a lot of things I did last year that I won't do this year."

Dickerson will have a lot more options this year, thanks to a restocked roster. He has nine newcomers, several of whom will battle returning starters for jobs.

"Nobody will be given a spot," Dickerson said. "I hate to admit it, but last year we gave some spots to people. We played the best people we had. I've been sending notes to the returning players and the incoming players each week explaining the situation. They understand it."

Sure, there will be competition for all jobs, but it will be difficult for a newcomer to replace two returning starters, 5-10 senior point guard **Wes Moore** and 6-5 junior forward **David Phillips**.

Moore, who played high school ball at Chattanooga Christian School, walked on with the Mocs in '95 and started 24 games. He has started ever since. Moore is anything but a flashy player, but Dickerson wouldn't trade him for any point guard in the league.

Last season, Moore (9.4 ppg, 3.9 rpg, 93 assists) led the conference in three-point shooting percentage (.423) and was fourth in three-pointers (58 of 137). He was eighth in the league in assists. He shot .417 from the field and .791 from the free-throw line, and his 55 steals were one shy of tying his own school record.

Perhaps most impressive was Moore's assist-to-turnover ratio (3.10), which led the league. Moore committed just 30 turnovers while leading the team in minutes (34.1 per game).

"I admire Wes as a person first," Dickerson said. "I know he will be just as successful in life as in basketball. He's one guy I'll never forget. He came here as a walkon and has started since day one. Wes runs the show. He plays hard, hits the open shots and never turns the ball over. He does just what we need him to do."

In the Mocs' season opening victory over Wofford last year, Moore scored 33 points, making nine of 11 three-point shots. It sent a quick message to the Mocs' future opponents: Keep an eye on Moore.

That was easy to do last year with the Mocs' lack of a solid inside game. For the rest of the season, opponents blanketed Moore and his backcourt mates and let the frontcourt run free.

"Wes will be a better player this year because he's as good as the players he has around him," Dickerson said. "He's a steady kid you can count on. He can't create his own shots, but he will hit the open shots."

Phillips (12.5 ppg, 5.4 rpg, .439 fg) will be another player on whom Dickerson is counting. Last season, Phillips was often forced to play with his back to the basket, and that's not his style.

A tough, hard-nosed player, Phillips was chosen to the coaches' all-conference team and to the media's second team. Phillips loves to lift weights and has muscled up to 195 pounds this year.

"David is a one-position player, a three man," Dickerson said. "He grew up a lot in the second half of the year when we were able to get him to play from 15 feet in. We had to move him out to three and then to four (power forward), where he had to try to guard those guys. If we get David at the three and keep him there, he will be a much better player."

With Moore at point and Phillips at small forward, the Mocs' other job on the perimeter, at shooting guard, is open. One candidate will certainly be 6-6 senior **Isaac Conner** (10.9 ppg, 3.9 rpg, 75 assists), who can play all three backcourt positions.

Conner joined Moore and Phillips as the only three players to start and play in all 28 games last year. Like many of his teammates, Conner often found himself playing out of position.

"We played him at every position," Dickerson said. "It was a big burden on Ike. He wanted to be a leader for us last season. Without an inside game, it really hurt Ike."

1998-99 TENNESSEE-CHATTANOOGA SCHEDULE

Nov.	17	Tennessee Wesleyan
	19	@Austin Peay
	24	@Tennessee
	28	Old Dominion
Dec.	3	@Georgia Southern
	5	@St. Joseph's
	15	Austin Peay
	17	West Virginia State
	19	@Southern Methodist
	29-30	#Dr Pepper Classic
Jan.	2	@Western Carolina
	4	Georgia Southern
	9	@Wofford
	11	East TennesseeState
	14	Appalachian State
	16	@The Citadel
	18	@College of Charleston
	23	Davidson
	25	Furman
	30	@North Carolina-Greensboro
Feb.	1	Wofford
	9	The Citadel
	13	College of Charleston
	15	@Furman
	20	@Virginia Military Institute
	25-28	##Southern Conference Tournament

@ Road Games
\# Chattanooga, TN (vs. Rider, first round; also Hampton and Samford).
\## Greensboro Coliseum, Greensboro, NC

Other returnees contending for the job at shooting guard are 5-11 senior **Chuck Barker** and 6-3 sophomore **Idris Harper.**

Barker (6.8 ppg, 1.5 rpg) enjoyed a five-game starting stint early in the season. A transfer from Miami (Fla.), Barker sat out the '96-97 season but practiced with the Mocs.

"Chuck will be a factor because he's a senior and he can score," Dickerson said. "The only thing that hurts Chuck is his defense. He's not real quick on his feet."

Harper (4.3 ppg, 2.6 rpg) earned a starting job for 11 games late in the season. He scored the winning basket, on a putback, in the Mocs' 56-55 victory over UNC-Greensboro in the quarterfinals of the conference tournament.

Many thought Harper, who played at Chattanooga City High School, should have been chosen to the league's all-freshman team.

"Idris is probably our best athlete as far as quickness and speed," Dickerson said. "We had to throw him into the frying pan and he made some freshman mistakes, but you could see in spurts he had the talent. He just needs to be more aggressive and not as passive."

Dickerson also returns one of his best pure shooters, 6-9 senior forward **Juraj Grabaric,** a native of Croatia who transferred to UTC from Saint Gregory's (Okla.) Community College last year. Grabaric (4.5 ppg, 1.7 rpg) started six games last year and made 20 of 50 three-points shots, but needs work on his defense.

Two junior-college transfers, 6-5 guard **Rashun Coleman** from Columbia State (Tenn.) Junior College and 6-4 guard **Marc Smith** from Wallace State (Tenn.) Junior College, are also expected to vie for playing time in the backcourt. Each may be rusty after sitting out last year while concentrating on academics.

Coleman, a native of Pulaski, Tenn., averaged 17.4 points, 8.0 rebounds and 2.9 assists two years ago at Columbia State. Smith, who played for in-state power Chattanooga Brainerd High School, averaged 20.8 points and 10 rebounds in two years at Wallace State.

"Coleman is a great athlete and he can shoot the ball," Dickerson said. "He's a strong player who reminds me of (former UTC player) Gary Robb, except that he shoots the ball better than Gary did.

"Marc Smith is also a great athlete. Depending on how much time he gets, Marc could lead the conference in offensive rebounding. He's a great athlete who runs the floor. He can score, but he's not a great shooter. He runs the break and loves to dunk."

Renaldo Atkins, 6-2 freshman guard from Pasadena, Tex., will add depth at shooting guard. Atkins averaged 18.1 points, 7.3 rebounds, 2.3 assists and shot 49 percent from the floor and 79 percent from the line last season at South Houston High School. He averaged 15.4 points and 6.4 rebounds for his career.

While Dickerson reloaded with some perimeter power, he didn't overlook the need for frontcourt help. Not in the least. Three newcomers are expected to make those post-play woes of 1997-98 a distant memory.

Leading the way will be 6-10 sophomore center **Oliver Morton**, who practiced with the Mocs last season after transferring from the University of Mississippi. A native of Gatlinburg, Tenn., Morton played in 18 games for Ole Miss in '96-97 and averaged 2.0 points and 1.5 rebounds. He is expected to be the sturdy low post player the Mocs so desperately needed last year.

"He's a big factor," Dickerson said. "He has soft hands, he can run and he can score around the block. He's a strong, physical player who can bang you for 40 minutes and take a toll on you."

Two junior-college transfers, 6-8 **Clark Costa** from Navarro (Texas) Junior College and 6-9 **Cory Hart** from Indian Hills (Iowa) Junior College, will bolster the frontcourt.

Costa, who weighs 260, averaged 6.0 points and 4.0 rebounds in 14 games, missing much of the season with an ankle sprain. He averaged an astounding 20.3 rebounds and 21.4 points as a senior at Coosa Valley (Ala.) High School, which won the private schools state championship.

"Hands-wise, once he grabs the ball, you can't take it away," Dickerson said. "Out of our four big men, Costa is probably close to being the best athlete. He can run, jump and block shots."

Hart, coming off a broken leg that sidelined him for the '96-97 season, averaged 5.8 points and 3.9 rebounds in a backup role last season when Indian Hills went 38-0 and won the junior college national championship. Hart, no lightweight himself at 240, was a three-time all-state selection at Rocky Mount (N.C.) High School, where he averaged 18.6 points and 11.8 rebounds as a senior.

"He's another big kid who can score on the block," Dickerson said. "He was one of the top 50 or 70 kids in the nation coming out as a senior in high school. We know he can play. His thing is scoring on the block."

Dickerson won't forget about two key players on last year's team, 6-8 sophomore forward **Otis Donald** and 6-8 senior forward **Francisco Colon.**

Donald (2.3 ppg, 3.2 rpg) started 18 games last season, which was much sooner than Dickerson wanted him in the starting lineup. Offensively, Donald needs some work. He had trouble scoring around the basket, shooting .306 from the floor, and his free throws were an adventure; he made 13 of 43, shooting several air balls.

Regardless, Donald was a defensive intimidator at times and led the team with 18 blocks. He was chosen to the league's all-freshman team.

Colon (11.1 ppg, 5.8 rpg) was UTC's most consistent player in the low post, but that wasn't his natural position. Despite starting 17 games, Colon seemed more comfortable coming off the bench. He has good range on his jump shot and made 18 of 45 three-point shots last year.

During the offseason, Colon had arthroscopic surgery to clean up some tendinitis in his knee.

The Mocs' other freshmen are 6-8 forward **John Cape**, 5-11 point guard **J.B. Watkins** and 6-4 swingman **Tim Parker.**

Cape averaged 18 points and 10 rebounds last season at Greater Atlanta Christian School. Watkins averaged 21.4 points, 3.1 rebounds, 4.0 assists and 3.6 steals last season at Ooltewah High School in Chattanooga.

Parker, native of Tuscaloosa, Ala., averaged 20.9 points and 10.3 rebounds last year at Baylor School in Chattanooga.

adidas Blue Ribbon Analysis

BACKCOURT	B+	BENCH/DEPTH	A
FRONTCOURT	B	INTANGIBLES	B

After adding plenty of muscle to his frontcourt, Tennessee-Chattanooga coach Henry Dickerson can't wait for the new season to get started. Led by 6-10, 260-pound transfer Oliver Morton, the Mocs should get back to playing their kind of basketball.

"We'll be able to do what I've always loved to do, attack people from the inside out," Dickerson said. "That's what we were always able to do with Mack (McCarthy as coach)."

Tennessee-Chattanooga also did a lot of winning with McCarthy as its coach, and that should happen again this year, thanks to the influx of newcomers.

With the College of Charleston joining the South Division this year, the Mocs will have some stiff competition for the title. There should be some good battles between those two teams in the future, but for now, give the new guys an edge.

It looks like the Mocs will finish second to College of Charleston this year in the South.

(D.L.)

VIRGINIA MILITARY INSTITUTE

LOCATION	Lexington, VA
CONFERENCE	Southern (North Division)
LAST SEASON	14-13 (.519)
CONFERENCE RECORD	8-7 (3rd)
STARTERS LOST/RETURNING	2/3
NICKNAME	Keydets
COLORS	Red, White & Yellow
HOMECOURT	Cameron Hall (5,029)
COACH	Bart Bellairs (Warren Wilson '79)
RECORD AT SCHOOL	54-56 (4 yrs.)
CAREER RECORD	54-56 (4 yrs.)
ASSISTANTS	KennyBrooks (James Madison '92) Kirby Dean (Eastern Mennonite '92) Ramon Williams (VMI '90)
TEAM WINS (last 5 yrs.)	5-10-18-12-14
RPI (last 5 yrs.)	292-267-169-208-221
1997-98 FINISH	Lost in conference quarterfinal.

In the small town of Lexington, Va., fans have learned to love the fast-paced basketball played by their Virginia Military Institute Keydets. The fans aren't the only ones caught up in a scoring frenzy.

"We play a fast-paced game," VMI coach Bart Bellairs said. "Our goal is to score 80 points a game. Our fans like it. I like it. Our players love it."

Who wouldn't? Fast-paced basketball is fun to watch, and it's Bellairs' style. Last season, Bellairs' fourth as VMI's coach, the Keydets averaged 75.4 points per game and led the Southern Conference in scoring for the third straight year.

It was a style that worked for the Keydets, whose third-place finish in the tough North Division was impressive enough. The Keydets also posted their first victory at Virginia Tech since 1954 and beat Penn State for their first victory over a Big Ten Conference team.

Half of the Keydets' outstanding backcourt tandem is gone with the departure of 6-1 senior guard Darryl Faulkner (15.4 ppg, 2.9 rpg, 134 assists), who was fifth in the league in scoring and assists. That's the bad news.

The good news: **Jason Bell**, a 6-1 senior guard, is back for his senior year. Bell (16.3 ppg, 3.8 rpg, 79 steals) was the league's fourth-leading scorer last year, ranked eighth in field-goal shooting (.406) and ninth in free-throw shooting (.738). Bell's 79 steals led the league and ranked ninth nationally.

Faulkner was chosen to the media's all-conference first team, while Bell made the second team.

"Bell anticipates as well as anybody and he's a tough player," Bellairs said. "He has the ability to score a lot of points. He needs to find consistency in his shooting and if he does that, he's capable of scoring 20 points a game."

Bell will be the shooting guard, with 5-11 junior **Andre Quarles** the likely starter at point guard.

Quarles was redshirted last season, but was a starter in 1996-97 before being suspended at Christmas for a semester because of excessive demerits. He averaged 6.9 points, 1.9 rebounds, and had 42 assists and 20 steals before his suspension two years ago.

"Quarles was one of the best players we had in practice last year," Bellairs said. "If he can transfer that over to games, we'll be in good shape."

Two freshmen, 5-7 **Renard Phillips** and 6-2 **Mark Grigsby**, will back up Quarles at the point.

Phillips averaged nine points and five assists last season at national power DeMatha High School in Hyattsville, Md.

Grigsby, who can also play shooting guard, led James Monroe High School in Lindside, W.Va., to the Class 3A state championship two years ago, averaging 17.5 points, four rebounds and five assists, but he has been on a Mormon mission in Argentina the last two years.

Also returning to the backcourt is 6-3 sophomore **Richard Bruce** (6.1 ppg, 2.1 rpg, 46 assists), who played in 27 games last season and averaged 20.9 minutes. Bruce made 26 of 78 three-point shots.

"We threw Bruce into the fire last year because we asked him to play backup point guard," Bellairs said. "He'd never played point guard in his life, even in high school. He's a competitor."

Aaron Demory, a 6-3 junior guard/forward, returns after starting 26 games last season. Demory (10.7 ppg, 5.7 rpg) can play either forward position. He spent the summer in China with a Sports Outreach program.

Bellairs says Demory has all-conference potential. "What a great kid, too," Bellairs says. "He's a fantastic leaper, he's strong as an ox and he can shoot the three (13 for 31 last year). He's a versatile player."

Another Keydet who could develop that kind of versatility is 6-8 sophomore forward **Richard Trombley** (2.5 ppg, 1.4 rpg). Trombley, who's from Anchorage, Alaska, played in 22 games last year after coming to VMI from Fork Union (Va.) Military. He can play either forward position.

"I believe he's got the potential to play at the next level," Bellairs said. "At 6-8 he's so versatile. He's a slasher and can play anything from two (shooting guard) to four (power forward)."

Nick Richardson, a 6-7 sophomore, is another one of those versatile players who fits into Bellairs' up-tempo style. Richardson (6.4 ppg, 2.6 rpg) played in 26 games last year, averaging 14.3 minutes.

Last year Richardson lived up to his billing as the Keydets' most decorated recruit. "He can shoot the three or take it to the hole," Bellairs said. "The key to our system is getting versatile players like him. He's strong and quick."

Matt Matheny (4.5 ppg, 2.5 rpg), 6-4 senior foward, returns after playing in 27 games last season and starting five.

Anchoring the frontcourt is 6-9 junior forward **Eric Mann** (6.6 ppg, 7.3 rpg), who was second in the league in blocks (47) and seventh in rebounds. Mann, a good athlete for his size, has worked on his shooting and gained some weight, up to about 205 pounds, since last year.

The Keydets were dealt a blow in July when Brent Conley, a 6-7, 230-pound forward, decided to transfer to Lindsey Wilson College, an NAIA school in Columbia, Ky. Conley was redshirted last year after serving a similar suspension as Quarles' at the halfway point of the '96-97 season. He was averaging 17.3 points and 9.2 rebounds at the time of his suspension.

Conley, the Southern Conference Freshman of the Year in 1995-96, would have given the Keydets a formidable front line alongside Mann. Bellairs won't dwell on what could have been. That's life at a military school.

"I think we still have a lot of potential," Bellairs said.

Two freshmen will provide depth in the frontcourt. **Zach Batte,** a 6-9 forward, averaged 16 points and 11 rebounds last year at Skyline High School in Idaho Falls, Id., where he earned all-state honors.

Tim Cole, a 6-9 forward/center, averaged 9.8 points and 7.0 rebounds at Fork Union (Va.) Military a year ago.

adidas Blue Ribbon Analysis

BACKCOURT	B	BENCH/DEPTH	B
FRONTCOURT	C	INTANGIBLES	B

Even with the departure of All-Southern Conference candidate Brent Conley in July, Virginia Military Institute has the personnel to battle its counterparts in the league.

Bellairs must also replace one of the league's best players in '97-98, guard Darryl Faulkner, and he may have just the guy in Andre Quarles.

With Conley, VMI could have made a run at the North Division title. Without Conley, the Keydets will still be competitive, thanks to several athletic swing players and senior guard Jason Bell, who should be one of the league's best.

VMI should give the league's title contenders plenty of

1998-99 VIRGINIA MILITARY INSTITUTE SCHEDULE

Nov.	14	Elon
	16	@Penn State
	24	@Old Dominion
	30	Wake Forest
Dec.	2	@Elon
	5	Randolph Macon
	7	@North Carolina-Greensboro
	10	@North Carolina-Charlotte
	18	Shenandoah
	22	@Virginia
Jan.	2	@East Tennessee State
	4	Davidson
	9	@Appalachian State
	11	@Western Carolina
	16	Georgia Southern
	18	Wofford
	23	Western Carolina
	25	@Davidson
	27	Southern Virginia
	30	@Furman
Feb.	1	@The Citadel
	6	East Tennessee State
	8	@College of Charleston
	13	Appalachian State
	15	North Carolina-Greensboro
	20	Tennessee-Chattanooga
	25-28	#Southern Conference Tournament

@ Road Games
\# Greensboro Coliseum, Greensboro, NC

trouble, but don't look for the Keydets to finish among the North's top three teams. Give them fourth in the North.

(D.L.)

WESTERN CAROLINA

LOCATION .... **Cullowhee, NC**
CONFERENCE .... **Southern (North Division)**
LAST SEASON .... **12-15 (.444)**
CONFERENCE RECORD .... **6-9 (t-4th)**
STARTERS LOST/RETURNING **4/1**
NICKNAME .... **Catamounts**
COLORS .... **Purple & Gold**
HOMECOURT .... **Ramsey Center (7,826)**
COACH .... **Phil Hopkins (Gardner-Webb '72)**
RECORD AT SCHOOL .... **43-41 (3 yrs.)**
CAREER RECORD .... **43-41 (3 yrs.)**
ASSISTANTS .... **Chad Dollar (Milligan '95)**
Dave Feuer (Massachusetts '93)
Terry Rogers (Gardner-Webb '70)
TEAM WINS (last 5 yrs.) **12-14-17-14-12**
RPI (last 5 yrs.) **210-229-186-201-247**
1997-98 FINISH .... **Lost in conference first round.**

There's a whole new ball game in Cullowhee, N.C., where Western Carolina's basketball program has undergone a facelift under fourth-year coach Phil Hopkins.

Four starters are gone from last year's 12-15 team that finished in a three-way tie for fourth in the Southern Conference's North Division. Hopkins has tried to replace those four starters with nine newcomers, and many are expected to contribute.

Also gone is the Catamounts' style of recent years. It will no longer be one of the more athletic teams in the league, no longer the fast-breaking, high-scoring team of recent years. Hopkins, however, has his biggest team at Western Carolina, and he wants it to be his most physical.

Hopkins, in fact, will be a man surrounded by new faces. Even his coaching staff has changed.

"It will be a totally different game," Hopkins said. "We have (nine) new players, a whole new coaching staff. I didn't want to totally get away from our athleticism of the past, but we really needed size. We will be a different style of team. We'll be more controlled and a lot more physical. We won't score as many points, but I think we'll be a better team."

It won't be easy for Hopkins to replace three departed starters. Bobby Phillips, a 6-6 forward, was the coaches' choice for Southern Conference Player of the Year. He was the league's third-leading scorer (16.9 ppg) and free-throw shooter (78.9 percent) and ninth-leading rebounder (6.9). Joel Fleming (11.0 ppg, 2.9 rpg) was a three-year starter at point guard and was second in the league in assists (161). Jarvis Graham (9.6 ppg, 5.1 rpg), a 6-7 forward, was a veteran of 108 games.

Also gone is 6-3 junior shooting guard Derrick Drummond (4.3 ppg, 1.3 rpg), who failed to qualify academically. He started 19 games last season after transferring from Hutchinson (Kan.) Community College.

"We may start four new players," Hopkins said. "With this many new players, chemistry will be so imporant for us."

Hopkins said he may start two players who are point guards, 6-0 freshman **Casey Rogers** and 6-0 junior **Michael Plavich**. Rogers, from Morganton (N.C.) Freedon High School, averaged 16 points and 10 assists last season. He was a three-time all-state point guard and led Freedon High to the Class 4A state championship.

Plavich averaged 16 points and 5.1 assists last season at Aquinas Junior College in Nashville (Tenn)., where he played point guard and shooting guard. He could play the same role this year.

"I hope we can play them together," Hopkins said of Plavich and Rogers. "They're both real good shooters and both are very good passers.If somebody else doesn't step in, one of them could be the two-guard."

Two players expected to provide depth in the backcourt are 5-10 sophomore guard **Chad Wall** and 5-11 sophomore guard **Robert Anderson**. Wall (1.8 ppg, 0.0 rpg) played in six games last season, while Anderson failed to see action.

One of the top returnees will be 6-3 sophomore **Stacy Ervin** (6.7 ppg, 1.3 rpg), and he will contend for the starting job at shooting guard. Ervin started seven games last season and had 54 three-pointers, fifth in the league. He was chosen to the league's all-freshman team. As a senior at Twin Springs High School in Nickelsville (Va.), Ervin was the state's all-time leading scorer (2,687 points) and led the state in scoring that year with a 33-point average.

"Ervin played a lot for us last year as a freshman (18.8 minutes per game)," Hopkins said. "He's a very good shooter. We look for him to contribute again."

Hopkins' only returning starter is 6-6, 200-pound senior forward **Dondrell Whitmore** (10.6 ppg, 7.7 rpg), the league's fourth-leading rebounder last year. He shot 55 percent, but didn't make enough shots (he was 114 for 207) to meet the five per game average needed to be ranked in the NCAA and league statistics. Whitmore spent most of last season playing in the post, but that should change this year.

"Whitmore played inside for us because we didn't have any post players," Hopkins said. "We'll be able to play him at the three (small forward), which is his natural position. He will benefit from that. He's very athletic, the slasher type. He has a decent jump shot and I think he can be a good defender on the perimeter."

Hopkins also expects 6-5 junior forward **Joey Bryson** (5.4 ppg, 2.6 rpg) to be a factor on the perimeter. Bryson was the team's leading scorer off the bench last season. After missing most of his first two seasons for illness and injuries, Bryson was honored as the team's comeback player of the year in 1997-98.

"Joey is really a hard-nosed kid," Hopkins said. "He plays extremely hard. It's going to be a dog fight at his position. We have a lot of depth at wing."

As for the Catamounts' revamped post game, Hopkins went the junior-college route for some quick help. Only one returnee, 6-6 senior Leon Davis, had a chance to push for playing time, but he was suspended from the team in August. Davis (3.6 ppg, 3.1 rpg) could return for the second semester.

Michael Green and **Todd Seibert**, each a 6-9 junior-college transfer, are expected to compete for starting jobs in the post.

Green averaged 18 points and 14 rebounds last season at Aquinas Junior College, where he played alongside Plavich. Green and Plavich are longtime teammates dating back to their days at Dalton (Ga.) High School, and they came to Western Carolina as a package deal. Green will play power forward.

"Green is just a good player inside," Hopkins said. "He can step out on the floor and shoot the 12- to 15-foot jump shot. He's a good rebounder and very active around the basket."

Seibert averaged eight points and six rebounds last season for Northern Oklahoma Junior College, which advanced to the NJCAA Tournament.

"With Todd's junior-college experience, I would suspect he has a chance to come in and start (at low post)," Hopkins said. "He's rugged, real aggressive. He's a good rebounder and a pretty good defender. Todd will set screens and he likes to set screens. He's athletic, very strong and aggressive."

Other newcomers are 6-6 freshman forward **Cory Largent** of Morganton (N.C.) Freedom High School; 6-4 freshman guard **John Lewis** of Fork Union (Va.) Military; 6-4 junior guard **Thomas Mosely** of Ellsworth (Iowa) Junior College; 6-9 freshman center **Colin Kearns** of Rockledge (Fla.) High School; and 6-6 freshman forward **Dewayne Hood** of Texarkana (Ark.) High School.

Largent was a teammate of Rogers' last season at Freedom High and averaged 11 points and six rebounds.

Lewis averaged 15 points and eight rebounds at Fork Union and is somewhat of a hometown hero. He played at Smoky Mountain High in Cullowhee, about three miles from the Western Carolina campus, and averaged 25.6 points and 12 rebounds as a senior.

Hood averaged 10 points and nine rebounds as a senior at Texarkana. Mosely, of Gary, Ind., averaged 15 points and seven rebounds.

"We lost some outstanding players and leaders that helped bring a lot of great moments to this basketball program, but I'm really excited about the new players we have signed and our chances of putting a competitive team on the floor in the coming season," Hopkins said. "We will be a much bigger team that should be able to rebound, score and play tougher inside on both ends of the floor with a lot of flexibility in the backcourt."

adidas Blue Ribbon Analysis

BACKCOURT	**D+**	**BENCH/DEPTH**	**C**
FRONTCOURT	**C**	**INTANGIBLES**	**C**

With nine new players on the roster, Phil Hopkins will be looking for the right combination this season.

It could take some time to find it. The Catamounts might start four newcomers along with 6-6 senior Dondrell Whitmore (10.6 ppg, 7.7 rpg), who played inside last season and will move to his more natural small forward position this year.

Hopkins has some size to work with, and that's a first for him at Western Carolina. But junior-college transfers Todd Seibert and Michael Green must prove themselves in the Southern Conference.

"Our balance and depth will be significantly better," Hopkins said. "My only concern about this team at this time is chemistry. It is going to take time for nine new players to mesh into our system."

Can Western Carolina be transformed from the athletic teams of recent years into a physical, controlled team? Wait and see.

There are plenty of question marks to be answered with this team. The project may take some time. Western Carolina looks to be headed for sixth in the North.

(D.L.)

1998-99 WESTERN CAROLINA SCHEDULE

Nov.	14	@Maryland
	19	@Clemson
	21	Anderson
	27-28	#IGA Sooner Holiday Tournament
	30	@Tennessee
Dec.	7	@Arkansas
	10	Newberry
	12	Tennessee Wesleyan
	28	@College of Charleston
Jan.	2	Tennessee-Chattanooga
	5	@East Tennessee State
	9	@North Carolina-Greensboro
	11	Virginia Military Institute
	13	Tusculum
	16	@Davidson
	18	@Appalachian State
	23	@Virginia Military Institute
	25	Georgia Southern
	30	East Tennessee State
Feb.	1	Davidson
	6	@Furman
	8	Wofford
	13	@The Citadel
	15	Appalachian State
	20	North Carolina-Greensboro
	25-28	##Southern Conference Tournament

@ Road Games
\# Norman, OK (vs. Oklahoma, first round; also Murray State and Arkansas-Little Rock)
\## Greensboro Coliseum, Greensboro, N.C.

WOFFORD

LOCATION .... **Spartanburg, S.C.**
CONFERENCE .... **Southern (South Division)**
LAST SEASON .... **9-18 (.333)**
CONFERENCE RECORD .... **6-8 (.429)**
STARTERS LOST/RETURNING **4/1**
NICKNAME .... **Terriers**
COLORS .... **Old Gold & Black**
HOMECOURT .... **Benjamin Johnson Arena**
COACH .... **Richard Johnson (The Citadel '76)**
RECORD AT SCHOOL .... **188-164 (13 yrs.)**
CAREER RECORD .... **188-164 (13 yrs**
ASSISTANTS .... **Mike Young (Emory & Henry '86)**
Simon Cote (Tennessee '95)
TEAM WINS (last 5 yrs.) **21-17-4-7-9**
RPI (last 5 yrs.) **N/A-N/A-294-300-274**
1997-98 FINISH **Ineligible for conference tournament**

Richard Johnson has endured a liftime of growing pains in his 14 seasons as Wofford College basketball coach. His approach: No pain, no gain.

Wofford was a longtime NAIA member when Johnson was hired, and he watched the Terriers grow into the Division II ranks for the 1988-89 season.

Four years ago, the Terriers made the move to Division I. It was tough on Johnson and his team, which went 4-22 and 7-20 in its first two years as a Division-I independent.

Facing another challenge last season, Wofford jumped into the Southern Conference and made the most of its chance. Picked to finish fifth in the South Division in the preseason, Wofford—with an 9-18 overall record—finished tied for second in the division at 6-8.

Maybe the Terriers surprised some people. Not Johnson, and he has realistic hopes for even more success. This will be the first time Johnson enters a season with a roster of

1998-99 WOFFORD SCHEDULE

Nov.	13	@Brigham Young
	16	@Air Force
	19	Montreat
	23	@South Carolina
	30	Toccoa Falls
Dec.	2	Army
	5	Navy
	15	@Auburn
	16	@Georgia Tech
Jan.	2	@Furman
	4	@North Carolina-Greensboro
	9	Tennessee-Chattanooga
	11	Appalachian State
	16	@College of Charleston
	18	@Virginia Military Institute
	20	@North Carolina State
	23	@Georgia Southern
	25	College of Charleston
	30	The Citadel
Feb.	1	@Tennessee-Chattanooga
	4	East Tennessee State
	6	Georgia Southern
	8	@Western Carolina
	13	Furman
	16	Davidson
	20	@The Citadel
	25-28	#Southern Conference Tournament

@ Road Games
\# Greensboro Coliseum, Greensboro, NC

players recruited for the Division I level.

"We had a small measure of success last year," Johnson said. "It's tempered by the fact that we don't have many inside players. If anything, we'll be even smaller than last year. We were able to turn it into an advantage last year."

Johnson will do the same this season, relying on a solid group of perimeter players, led by 6-3 sophomore shooting guard **Ian Chadwick**, last year's conference freshman of the year.

"Our perimeter game is very solid with Ian Chadwick and **Alfred Forbes** coming back," Johnson said. "They will provide experience and leadership out there. The question again will be the four and five (positions), and can we hang with people on the boards and defend people inside."

Forbes and Chadwick—along with experienced point guards **Donald Davis** and **Jon Pryor**—must carry the load as the Terriers try to overcome their shortcomings in the frontcourt.

When last season ended, Forbes' collegiate future was very much in doubt, but in June he was granted a fifth year of eligibility by the NCAA. Forbes played just five games for Army during the 1995-96 season, then transferred to Wofford for the second semester. He watched from the sidelines the rest of the '96-97 season.

His return last season was a rousing success, and it was a chance for Forbes (11.8 ppg, 4.6 rpg) to show his versatility—he played all five positions. The Jonesboro, Ga., native was the team's second-leading scorer and leading rebounder. He also led the Terriers in steals (37) and was third in assists (50).

This fall, Forbes is taking chemistry classes in preparation for graduate school. He will likely be pushed into duty at the power forward spot.

"He's a very good athlete in a couple of ways," Johnson said. "He's big, strong and lanky. We're obviously glad to have him back for another season. His presence on the court and in the locker room has such a positive influence on our younger players. He really came into his own the last month of the season and was very instrumental in some of our bigger victories."

Chadwick (12 ppg, 2.7 rpg, 47 assists) should benefit from Forbes' return. He is the younger brother of Seth Chadwick—Wofford's leading scorer as a senior in '96-97 and the school's all-time leading three-point shooter—and while not being the pure shooter his older brother was, Ian is more of a scorer.

"Ian Chadwick is just an exceptional athlete," Johnson said. "He has a 10.8 second 100-meter time and can triple jump 47 feet. With the speed and quickness he possesses, he's a threat from anywhere on the floor to beat someone off the dribble. What compounds that is the fact he's an exceptional shooter. He has a great stroke and a great first step."

Last season, Chadwick led the Terriers in scoring while shooting .385 percent from the field and .694 percent from the line. He led the team in three-point goals (61 of 165, 37 percent), ranking fifth in the conference.

Johnson feels comfortable with his two point guards. Davis (6.7 ppg, 2.5 rpg, 70 assists) started 23 games and shot .756 percent from the line and made 20 of 76 (.350 percent) from three-point range.

Pryor (2.7 ppg, 1.6 rpg) was second on the team in assists (59) while starting just four games and averaging 16 minutes per game. He gives Johnson two point guards with different strengths.

"You have to respect Donald because of the way he's able to get to the hole," Johnson said. "Pryor is very important to us because of his ability to spark the team. He's more of a steady player than Donald and a good defensive player, but he can't do some of the things Donald can do."

Johnson welcomes back several other part-time starters who will push for full-time jobs this fall. Leading those players is 6-4 sophomore forward **Terenthial White** (3.5 ppg, 2.6 rpg), who started 12 games at low post. Although more of a power forward, White will probably again be pushed into duty under the basket.

Another player competing for that job will be 7-foot sophomore **Brandon Boyce** (1.9 ppg, 1.3 rpg), the first 7-footer to play at Wofford. Boyce was considered a project out of Dacula (Ga.) High and has made some strides, but just how effective he can be at the college level is still in question.

Rashane DeLoach (3.1 ppg, 2.6 rpg), a 6-7 junior, could also play either the power forward or center position. Averaging 11 minutes last season, DeLoach appears ready to push for a starting job—or even a breakout season.

"Rashane DeLoach has come along and made a lot of strides," Johnson said. "He has a great body and he's very athletic, but he's raw. We're still pleased with his progress. I'd have to guess it will be DeLoach or White (at low post)."

Reggie DeGray could have emerged as a starter in the post, but decided to leave the team for personal reasons. His decision wasn't a timely one for Johnson. DeGray informed the Terriers' coach he was leaving in April.

Also gone is 6-8, 220-pound center McCarthy Crenshaw (3.3 ppg, 3.7 rpg), who started 19 games last season in the post.

Starzee Walker (5.7 ppg, 2.5 rpg), a 6-3 junior, started six games last season at small forward, and sophomore **Bishop Ravenel** (2.2 ppg, 1.8 rpg) started five games at both forward positions.

Walker will be expected to start this season after seeming to find his niche with the team toward the end of last season. Averaging 19 minutes per game, Walker was the team's leading free-throw shooter at .826 percent (38 of 46).

"Walker comes in with some experience," Johnson said. "He's turned into a good shooter and a good rebounder. We're solid right there (at small forward)."

Johnson has two newcomers: 6-3 freshman guard **Colon Largent**, who averaged 14.5 points and 5.0 rebounds last season at Fork Union (Va.) Military; and 6-7 freshman forward **Matt Tucker**, who averaged 11.7 points and 7.0 rebounds at Hazelton (Pa.) High School.

"Largent is a two or a three, but he played point last year," Johnson said. "He's very quick, an exceptionally quick defender. He gives us somebody with more size who can play point, or he can play two or three. He shoots it real well.

"Tucker probably isn't projected to step in and play big minutes, but he developed late and he's starting to play real well. He's a four who could be pressed into duty at five."

Johnson knows he must bolster his inside game in the future and win on the road to become a contender in the Southern Conference. The Terriers, 1-15 on the road last season, beat Georgia Southern for their only road win in the league. With 13 freshmen and sophomores, Johnson expects a few more growing pains.

"It's an important year, not only in terms of doing well, but getting contributions from our younger players," Johnson said.

Once again, the non-conference schedule is rugged. The Terriers play road games against Brigham Young, Air Force, South Carolina, Auburn, Georgia Tech and North Carolina State. They play host to Army and Navy.

Wofford could not compete in the Southern Conference tournament last season because of an NCAA regulation requiring eight years of Division I eligiblity before a team can earn an automatic NCAA Tournament bid. That changed during the summer after legislation to decrease the eight-year wait to two years was enacted by the NCAA.

adidas Blue Ribbon Analysis

BACKCOURT	**B**	**BENCH/DEPTH**	**C**
FRONTCOURT	**D**	**INTANGIBLES**	**B**

When senior forward Alfred Forbes was granted a fifth year of eligibility by the NCAA last summer, Wofford coach Richard Johnson must have been dancing in the streets of Spartanburg, S.C. Perhaps it was a sign of good things to come for the Terriers, who last year finished in a surprising second-place tie in their first year in the Southern Conference's South Division. Johnson hopes so, anyway. Forbes played a key role last year and Johnson expects him to do the same this year.

Forbes will have some help, largely from sophomore guard Ian Chadwick, the conference's freshman of the year in '97-98. The Terriers are talented around the perimeter, but lack size and depth in the post. Johnson likes to think his team can turn that weakness into a strength by utilizing its quickness and shooting skills.

This will be Johnson's most talented team in his 14 years at Wofford, his first team of Division I recruits. Johnson doesn't just want to play in the Southern Conference. He wants to contend for titles, like he did when Wofford was a Division II power.

Don't look for Wofford to push for a title this year, not without a better frontcourt. Johnson won't be happy with a fourth-place finish in the improved South, but that looks to be a likely finish for the Terriers.

(D.L.)

SOUTHLAND CONFERENCE

adidas BLUE RIBBON FORECAST

1. Texas-San Antonio
2. Southwest Texas State
3. Lamar
4. Northeast Louisiana
5. Nicholls State
6. McNeese State
7. Texas-Arlington
8. Stephen F. Austin
9. Sam Houston State
10. Southeastern Louisiana
11. Northwestern State

ALL-CONFERENCE TEAM

G—Demond Mallet, JR, McNeese State
G—Donte Mathis, SR, Southwest Texas State
F—Jason McCutcheon, SR, Nicholls State
F—Leon Watson, SR, Texas-San Antonio
C—Jeff Foster, SR, Southwest Texas State

PLAYER OF THE YEAR

Donte Mathis, SR, Southwest Texas State

NEWCOMER OF THE YEAR

Mike Smith, JR, Northeast Louisiana

1998-99 CONFERENCE TOURNAMENT

TBA

1997-98 CHAMPIONS

Nicholls State (regular season)
Nicholls State (conference tournament)

1997-98 POSTSEASON PARTICIPANTS

Postseason Record: 0-1 (.000)
NCAA
Nicholls State

TOP BACKCOURTS

1. McNeese State
2. Southwest Texas State
3. Lamar

TOP FRONTCOURTS

1. Texas-San Antonio
2. Nicholls State
3. Southwest Texas State

ON THE WAY UP

Lamar

ON THE WAY DOWN

Northwestern State

INSIDE THE NUMBERS

- 1997-98 conference RPI: 26th (of 30)
- Conference RPI (last 5 years): 28-25-25-26-26

DID YOU KNOW?

Lamar is a returning member of the Southland Conference. It won league titles in 1978, '79, '80, '81, '83, and '84. Then the school became a charter member of the the American South Conference in 1987-88. The ASC merged with the Sun Belt and Lamar played in the SBC from 1991-92 through last season. Just once, in 1988, has Lamar won more than 15 games since leaving the SLC...How balanced could the league be this year? "I think this is one of those years when the parity is going to show," McNeese State coach Ron Everhart said. Said Southwest Texas coach Mike Miller, "It's the most balanced league I've ever seen. This is my eighth year here and I spent a year at Sam Houston (as an assistant). I've seen nine league races and looking at who's returning and where people finished last year, it's going to be the most balanced ever."...If only Texas-San Antonio didn't have to play Texas-Arlington. UTA, the sixth seed in the Century Cellunet Southland Classic, ousted the third-seeded Roadrunners in the semifinals last season. It was UTA's seventh victory over UTSA in eight tries...Few teams have ever lost more in one season. Northwestern State lost five senior starters and five other players...UTA's media guide last season featured a quote from *Sports Illustrated* about its arena that said Texas Hall was "The Best Place to Watch College Basketball." UTA went 7-5 at home last season, 4-4 in the league...The only category in which Southeastern Louisiana had better numbers than opponents was in three-point shots taken and made. SLU hit 227 of 633. The Lions led the SLC and ranked eighth nationally at 8.7 per game. Eight times the Lions hit 10 or more threes, but in the last four games, they made just nine...Lamar will play at Drake Nov. 28, because that's the home of senior guard Matt Sundblad. "I try to take our seniors home," Lamar coach Grey Giovanine said. "Rock Winston's a New Orleans kid (so Lamar plays at Tulane, Dec. 12), but I couldn't get a game in Nairobi, Kenya, for (senior center) Frank Obudo."...One player who has the league buzzing is Northeast Louisiana forward Mike Smith, a transfer from Bossier Parish (La.) CC. "That guy's going to be an NBA player," said McNeese's Everhart.

(L.F.)

LAMAR

LOCATION .... **Beaumont, TX**
CONFERENCE .... **Southland**
LAST SEASON .... **15-14 (.517)**
CONFERENCE RECORD .... **7-11 (7th in Sun Belt)**
STARTERS LOST/RETURNING **2/3**
NICKNAME .... **Cardinals**
COLORS .... **Red & White**
HOMECOURT .... **Montagne Center (10,080)**
COACH .... **Grey Giovanine (Central Missouri '81)**
RECORD AT SCHOOL .... **63-74 (5 yrs.)**
CAREER RECORD .... **63-74 (5 yrs.)**
ASSISTANTS .. **Leonard Drake (Central Michigan '78)**
Ric Wesley (Central Michigan '80)
Terrell Wilson (Lamar '94)
TEAM WINS (last 5 yrs.) **10-11-12-15-15**
RPI (last 5 yrs.) **218-241-208-169-178**
1997-98 FINISH .... **Lost in conference semifinal.**

Lamar coach Grey Giovanine couldn't be happier about leaving the Sun Belt Conference for the Southland.

"I think it's a great thing for us," said Giovanine, whose team finished in seventh place in the SBC last year. "It's a natural. We're in the middle of the league (geographically). When Lamar had its success (in the late 1970s and through the late '80s), that's the league they were in. It was absolutely a no-brainer for us to get into the Southland."

It will look even better if the Cardinals can stay healthy this season. Last year, Lamar won its first five games and stood at 6-1, including victories against Baylor, LSU and Nicholls State, before being decimated by injuries. **Landon Rowe** hurt his knee and **Matt Sundblad** broke his jaw. **Marvin Hill**, became eligible long enough to injure his knee. Things ended up well, however, because Sundblad never seemed to miss a beat, Rowe made it back for the SBC Tournament and Lamar won its first two games, winning in the conference tournament for the first time in 10 years and guaranteeing back-to-back winning seasons for the first time since 1984-85 (20-12) and '85-86 (18-12).

"We were 15-12, but it was really a big step of progress for us, because of the wins in the tournament and that, hey, we have a winning program now," Giovanine said.

Sundblad, a 6-2 senior guard (11.3 ppg, 2.9 rpg, 54-159 three-pointers, 36 assists, 27 steals), is not only good on the floor, he's an academic All-American off it with a 4.0 GPA in pre-med/psychology. "He's the consummate student-athlete," Giovanine said of his leading returning scorer. The leader last year, guard Ronald Nunnery (14.4 ppg, 5.0 rpg) was a senior. Nunnery, guard Rod Jones (6.2 ppg, 2.2 rpg) and forward Donny Coryell (8.6 ppg, 4.9 rpg) were Lamar's only significant losses.

Three other experienced players return in Rowe, a 6-8 junior forward (2.8 ppg, 2.0 rpg), 6-10 senior **Frank Obudo** (2.5 ppg, 3.8 rpg, 18 blocked shots) and 6-8 junior **Marlone Jackson** (8.7 ppg, 6.7 rpg). But the stats are misleading on Rowe, who marked his late-season return with 19 points, and 10 rebounds in Lamar's upset of Arkansas State in the SBC Tournament.

Obudo, a product of Kenya, hadn't played much basketball. "But he's had a tremendous summer. The learning curve on those foreign kids is awful steep," Giovanine said. "But he's really going to help us."

Those two and Jackson give Lamar a potentially powerful front line and certainly one that will be fairly strong in the SBC. And **Rock Winston**, a 6-4 senior (5.5 ppg, 4.0 rpg) actually posts up despite his size. Hill, a 6-2 junior (4.6 ppg, 1.9 rpg), played in just 22 games, starting 11. Giovanine has high hopes for him this season.

There are five newcomers, led by 5-8 junior **Malcolm McCreight**, a transfer from Jackson (Tenn.) CC, where he averaged 18.0 ppg and 11.0 apg. "He's a key guy, because he's the new starting point guard and we recruited him with that in mind," Giovanine said of the speedy McCreight.

Two junior college transfers with similarly unusual names could figure into the mix. **Brom Knop**, a 6-4 junior, played at Independence (Kan.) CC, and averaged 10 ppg and 7.0 rpg a year ago, while 6-5 junior **Tyler Ropp** of Fort Scott, Kan., came from Florida College (17 ppg, 8 rpg). Ropp is a walkon. **Kenyon Spears** (1.3 ppg), a 6-3 sophomore, served as a backup point guard last year and could get more playing time this year.

Brennen White, a 6-6 forward from Kennedy HS in New Orleans (17.3 ppg, 8.4 rpg), and **Lewis Arline**, a 6-6 freshman from Silsbee (Texas) HS (15.8 ppg, 12.1 rpg), probably won't see too much playing time.

One of Arline's high school teammates, 6-0 freshman Thaydeus Holden, is trying to get eligible for the second semester. Also on the roster is 6-0 junior walkon **Von Shelton.**

adidas Blue Ribbon Analysis

BACKCOURT .... **C+** **BENCH/DEPTH** .... **B-**
FRONTCOURT .... **B** **INTANGIBLES** .... **B**

Last season, Southeastern Louisiana made the switch from the Trans America Athletic Conference to the Southland and got crushed night in and night out. Lamar doesn't expect the transition to be quite as tough. "We think we should immediately be a contender," Giovanine said matter of factly.

He's probably right, because had Lamar escaped all those injuries, the Cardinals might have challenged for the Sun Belt lead. This year in the SLC, things should be different, not only because there is no clear-cut favorite but also because Giovanine has the makings of an outstanding club.

1998-99 LAMAR SCHEDULE

Nov.	19	@Sacramento State
	24	Texas A&M-Kingsville
	28	@Drake
Dec.	2	Loyola (LA)
	6	@Texas A&M
	12	@Tulane
	16	Southwestern Louisiana
	19	Northern Illinois
	28	@Nicholls State
	30	@Southeastern Louisiana
Jan.	2	Texas-San Antonio
	4	Southwest Texas State
	7	@Northeast Louisiana
	9	@Northwestern State
	16	Sam Houston State
	21	Stephen F. Austin
	23	@McNeese State
	28	Souteastern Louisiana
Feb.	4	@Stephen F. Austin
	6	@Texas-Arlington
	11	@Sam Houston State
	13	Texas-Arlington
	18	Nicholls State
	20	@Texas-San Antonio
	25	McNeese State
	27	Northwestern State
Mar	3-6	#Southland Tournament

@ Road Games
# TBA

Sundblad and Rowe make for a strong inside-outside threat, Obudo is improving and could become a force on defense, and Winston, Hill and Jackson give Lamar enough experience and depth to contend for the SLC crown, a title it last won in 1984 under coach Pat Foster.

(L.F.)

MCNEESE STATE

LOCATION .... **Lake Charles, LA**
CONFERENCE .... **Southland**
LAST SEASON .... **7-19 (.269)**
CONFERENCE RECORD .... **4-12 (t-9th)**
STARTERS LOST/RETURNING **2/3**
NICKNAME .... **Cowboys**
COLORS .... **Blue & Gold**
HOMECOURT .... **Burton Coliseum (8,000)**
COACH .... **Ron Everhart (Virginia Tech '85)**
RECORD AT SCHOOL .... **51-59 (4 yrs.)**
CAREER RECORD .... **51-59 (4 yrs.)**
ASSISTANTS .... **Carl Klein (McNeese '95)**
Jason Hamm (South Alabama '98)
Julius Allen (South Nazarene '81)
TEAM WINS (last 5 yrs.) **11-11-15-18-7**
RPI (last 5 yrs.) **247-236-188-180-286**
1997-98 FINISH .... **Didn't qualify for conference tournament.**

McNeese State struggled last season as coach Ron Everhart patiently dealt with a team that had no seniors, choosing to field a team with only nine scholarship players. Now he'll find out if it paid off. If the performance last year of a young and promising backcourt is any indication, the Cowboys have good reason to think they'll be back in the SLC hunt this season.

"Obviously we did not perform at the level that we have been in terms of wins and losses, but it was probably the most rewarding year I've had here at McNeese, because I saw a group of young guys that stayed dedicated, remained excited and continued to improve all year long," Everhart said.

He'll be counting on 6-1 junior **Demond Mallet** (18.9 ppg, 2.3 rpg, 68 assists, 44 steals), who led the league in scoring and made the All-SLC first team. Mallet averaged 24 points over the last six games of the season, putting the finishing touches on a year in which he hit 94 of 258 three-pointers (.364), the most in a single season in the SLC. Mallet is McNeese's third all-time three-point shooter with 146 in 368 attempts. Michael Cutright is the all-time school leader with 461, followed by Damon Woodlaw.

Mallet was by no means alone in the McNeese backcourt, as 6-2 sophomore **Tierre Brown** (13.3 ppg, 3.5 rpg, 75 assists, 34 steals) couldn't have been too far behind Sam Houston's Jeremy Burkhalter for SLC freshman-of-the-year honors.

Everhart gets a tremendous effort from **Franklin Paul**, a 6-3 senior (11.3 ppg, 7.6 rpg, 43 steals), who is just as capable of playing on the perimeter as he is outside. Paul not only ranked fourth in the league in rebounding, he averaged 8.1 boards in SLC play.

One other experienced reserve returns, 6-1 senior **Todd Briley**, (6.7 ppg, 1.2 rpg), who has filled a role as an occasional starter or, as Everhart calls him, "super sub." Another returning player is 6-3 sophomore walkon **Jeff LeJeune** (0.7 ppg, 0.3 rpg).

But it could be the newcomers who take McNeese from the bottom half of the SLC to the top, giving the Cowboys the height and strength they lacked last season.

Quaysean Nicholson, for example, is a 6-5 forward from Southwood HS in Shreveport. Last summer he played on a team that included two of the nation's top recruits, Brandon Dean (Ark.) and Stromile Swift (LSU), and was chosen the MVP of the Louisiana under-19 state tournament. Nicholson averaged 21.0 ppg and 7.0 rpg as a senior.

Fred Gentry had to sit out last season as an academically ineligible freshman. But the 6-8 sophomore from DeQuincy (La.) HS is expected to start this year. "I think before it's all said and done he'll be one of the best big guys to come through here," said Everhart, who normally plays things a little closer to the vest.

So impressive is Gentry that one time last spring, while he was working out in the McNeese weight room (the 235-pounder can bench press 360), that scouts from the New York Giants called Everhart to inquire about him. "He's a physical specimen," Everhart said. Gentry averaged 18.0 ppg and 8.5 rpg two years ago.

Adrian Floyd, a 6-7 junior from Indianapolis who transferred from Gulf Coast (Fla.) JC, "will add a lot for us up front." He averaged 17.5 ppg and 7.8 rpg as a sophomore at Gulf Coast. Another Adrian, 6-7 Adrian Johnson of Bossier City HS in Shreveport, La., is "one of the freshmen I'm really excited about," Everhart said. Johnson averaged 15.0 ppg and 8.0 rpg in his final season at Bossier City.

Another freshman, 6-7 **Nathan Smith** of Crowley (Texas) HS, will see some playing time. What's more, he makes McNeese the only team in America with two players from two different Crowleys—Briley is from tiny Crowley, La. Smith averaged 14.4 ppg and 6.0 rpg as a senior.

Two other newcomers should redshirt because of injuries, 6-6 forward **Paul Beik** of Lake Mary HS in Orlando, Fla., and 6-5 junior **Leroy Mayo**, a transfer from San Jose (Calif.) CC. Beik averaged 24.0 ppg and 7.5 rpg as a senior. Mayo averaged 10.6 ppg and 6.5 rpg in his final season at San Jose.

The backcourt also gets a boost.

"We're really excited about our backcourt because we've got so much depth there," Everhart said.

Last season, 6-2 sophomore **Terrance Scott** from Istrouma HS in Baton Rouge, La., was an academically ineligible freshman, but he should see plenty of playing time this year. Scott averaged 12.0 ppg and 5.6 apg in his senior season at Istrouma two years ago. And **Quentin Gilmore**, a 6-0 freshman from Fenwick HS in Chicago, is a highly touted player who will also compete for playing time. Gilmore averaged 15.0 ppg as a senior.

And there's one more, yet another tie to Everhart's Tulane connection. He was an assistant there before he took the job at McNeese. Last year, two of his assistants were former Tulane players, Greg Gary and Carlin Hartman. Gary left to go to Tulane's staff, while Carlin took a job as a high school coach in Houston. But it was because of them last year that **Khalid Morris** transferred from Tulane to McNeese and the 6-5 junior swingman from Los Angeles "is going to help us a lot," Everhart said.

Morris played sparingly at Tulane, but Everhart said he could make quite an impact for the Cowboys.

"I'm really looking forward to him taking the court for us. There's no harder worker in our program or anywhere," Everhart said. "I've never been around a kid who works harder. He's really made himself a very good basketball player."

adidas Blue Ribbon Analysis

BACKCOURT	**B**	**BENCH/DEPTH**	**C+**
FRONTCOURT	**C+**	**INTANGIBLES**	**C**

McNeese State has reloaded with huge group of newcomers, several of whom can compete for quality minutes in their first seasons.

Can the recruits get the Cowboys competitive right away? There is the typically tough non-conference schedule that includes games at Colorado State, LSU, Alabama and Baylor to help indoctrinate them to college basketball. Two years ago, the Cowboys put together McNeese's best season in a decade. This season may decide if last year was just a stumbling block or if more rebuilding is in order.

"I'm very excited about this team," said Everhart, who needs five victories to become the fifth-winningest coach in school history. "I don't know how good we'll be this year, simply because of chemistry. But this is a group that if they stay together athletically and talent-wise, we can be very good down the road."

(L.F.)

1998-99 MCNEESE STATE SCHEDULE

Nov.	14	@Colorado State
	18	Norfolk State
	21	@Louisiana State
	25	@Alabama
	30	@Southwestern Louisiana
Dec.	12	@Baylor
	15	Central Florida
	21	@New Mexico
	28	@Southeastern Lousiana
Jan.	2	Southwest Texas State
	4	Texas-San Antonio
	7	Northwestern State
	9	@Northeast Louisiana
	14	Sam Houston State
	18	Nicholls State
	21	Texas-Arlington
	23	Lamar
	28	@Texas-San Antonio
	30	@Southwest Texas State
Feb.	4	@Texas-Arlington
	6	@Stephen F. Austin
	11	Northeast Louisiana
	13	@Sam Houston State
	17	Southeastern Louisiana
	25	@Lamar
	27	Stephen F. Austin
Mar.	3-6	#Southland Tournament

@ Road Games
# TBA

NICHOLLS STATE

LOCATION .... **Thibdaux, LA**
CONFERENCE .... **Southland**
LAST SEASON .... **19-10 (.655)**
CONFERENCE RECORD .... **15-1 (1st)**
STARTERS LOST/RETURNING **2/3**
NICKNAME .... **Colonels**
COLORS .... **Red & White**
HOMECOURT .... **Stopher Gymnasium (3,800)**
COACH .... **Rickey Broussard (Southwestern Louisiana '70)**
RECORD AT SCHOOL .... **109-112 (8 yrs.)**
CAREER RECORD .... **109-112 (8 yrs.)**
ASSISTANTS .... **Quinn Strander (Nicholls State '96)**
Blaine Russell (Centenary '91)
Daryl Thrower (Nicholls State student)
TEAM WINS (last 5 yrs.) **19-24-5-10-19**
RPI (last 5 yrs.) **171-59-274-244-141**
1997-98 FINISH .... **Lost in NCAA first round.**

Nicholls State coach Rickey Broussard had to regroup last summer in more ways than one. Sure, he lost a couple of outstanding seniors, but that's nothing unusual for a basketball coach. Broussard, however, had to deal with the loss of the ring finger on his right hand. It was literally pulled off when his championship ring got caught on a nail as he lowered himself after addressing a group of his camp coaches.

The bizarre incident occurred in late July at Bubba's II, a restaurant in Thibodaux, La., that is the gathering place of choice for Nicholls fans and coaches. Broussard stood up above the group to talk to them and when he went to get down, he reached up to a beam that he grabbed for support. However, his 1995 Southland Conference championship ring got caught and as he jumped down, his finger was yanked off.

Oddly enough, it was just a week earlier that he compared last season to 1995, a year that also saw the Colonels win the SLC's NCAA Tournament berth. Just as in '95, when Nicholls lost Gerard King and Reggie Jackson, last year's team lost Russell McCutcheon (16.8 ppg, 3.4 rpg, 70 assists, 49 steals), and Kenderick Franklin (16.7 ppg, 5.1 rpg, 49 assists, 29 steals).

"But here's the difference," Broussard said. "In '95, when we lost those two guys, I also lost a starting point guard who played every game in four years. I mean, we lost our top six guys. This year, we have three starters back and not only that, my No. 6, 7, 8 and 9. My first four guys off the bench are all returning. So even those we lost two quality players like that, we're not going to be in the same boat that we were in '96."

No, that 1996 team won five games. This year's team should be much better than that, especially because Broussard signed players who will contribute and has a transfer who could make an impact. Nicholls is coming off an almost dream season. A team picked to finish in the middle of the pack was one game from going through the SLC season undefeated. The addition of McCutcheon and his younger brother, 6-7 senior forward **Jason McCutcheon** (14.2 ppg, team-high 5.9 rpg, .512 FG percentage, 37 blocked shots), was big as they became eligible after sitting out the previous year after transferring.

Now there's another, **Terrence McCutcheon**, a 6-3 sophomore guard who transferred after one year at the College of Southern Idaho (6.3 ppg, 2.1 spg, 2.0 apg). Jason McCutcheon will start at one forward, while Terrance will compete for time in the backcourt.

The point guard should be 6-3 junior **James Banks** (7.0 ppg, 4.6 rpg, 134 assists, 69 steals), who established himself as one of the better guards in the league last season. The two McCutcheons and Franklin earned All-SLC honors.

The other guard could be 6-1 senior **Taurus Howard** (2.4 ppg, 0.9 rpg, 45 assists, 23 steals), who is back for a fifth year. The backcourt will also include **Zach Ray**, a 6-4 freshman from Baton Rouge who sat out last season after transferring from North Texas.

Linzie Green, a 6-3 senior (10.9 ppg, 2.5 rpg, 37

1998-99 NICHOLLS STATE SCHEDULE

Nov.	13	@Centenary
	15	Loyola (LA)
	19-20	#Zippy's Invitational
	24	@Tulane
	30	@Southwestern Louisiana
Dec.	8	@Southern Mississippi
	12	@Oklahoma
	14	@Cincinnati
	19	Missouri Valley
	28	Lamar
Jan.	2	@Texas-Arlington
	4	@Stephen F. Austin
	7	@Sam Houston State
	14	Texas-San Antonio
	16	Southwest Texas State
	18	McNeese State
	21	@Northwestern State
	23	Southeastern Louisiana
	28	Stephen F. Austin
	30	Texas-Arlington
Feb.	1	@Northeast Louisiana
	4	Sam Houston State
	11	@Southwest Texas State
	13	@Texas-San Antonio
	18	@Lamar
	20	@Southeastern Louisiana
	25	Northeast Louisiana
Mar.	3-6	##Southland Tournament

@ Road Games
\# Honolulu, HI (vs. Hawaii, first round; also Marquette and Oklahoma State)
\## TBA

assists, 28 steals) is the ideal swingman in Broussard's uptempo offense, along with 6-5 senior **Tracy Blake** (3.5 ppg, 2.3 rpg), who also should start.

The center will be 6-7 junior **Lorenzo Wright** (4.0 ppg, 3.7 rpg). **Cedric Marie**, a 7-footer from France who sat out last season while mending a broken collarbone, returns a better player. He averaged 4.0 points and 3.5 rebounds in 1996-97. Marie "is looking much better," Broussard said.

Chicagoan **Chris Worrell**, a 6-4 junior transfer from Mashalltown CC (10.0 ppg, 8.0 rpg, 2.5 spg), will also be in the mix. "I think he's going to be a really good addition to our team," Broussard said.

Nicholls also has two first-year freshmen, 6-3 **John Fontenot** of Washington-Marion HS in Lake Charles, La., and 6-8 **Clifton Jones** from Oakdale (La.) HS.

adidas Blue Ribbon Analysis

BACKCOURT	**B**	**BENCH/DEPTH**	**B-**
FRONTCOURT	**C+**	**INTANGIBLES**	**B+**

Just like last year, no one is expecting too much from the Colonels.

"I think we're going to be all right," Broussard said. "We're not going to be the odds-on favorite to win, either." No, but other coaches know not to count Nicholls out. Not with Jason McCutcheon and a group of experienced players who have exceptional quickness and athletic ability.

"The beauty of this year is we signed two junior college players and three high school kids and I think the three high school kids are all going to be very good players," Broussard said. "But we're not in the position we have to depend on them. We're going to need them to play and play well, but not in starting roles. Supporting roles, mostly."

Don't be surprised if this collection of supporting-role players has the Colonels challenging for the SLC lead.

(L.F.)

adidas Blue Ribbon Analysis
GRADING SYSTEM

- A+ equal to very best in country—Final Four-caliber unit
- A among the best in the land—worthy of deep NCAA run
- B+ talented, versatile and experienced—NCAA-NIT ability
- B solid and productive winners—league and post-season contenders
- C+ average to above-average—may contend in a weaker league
- C average to mediocre—second division in a strong league
- D+ below average, inconsistent—second division in a weaker league
- D well below average—losing season virtually certain
- F non-Division I ability—an underdog every night

NORTHEAST LOUISIANA

LOCATION .... **Monroe, LA**
CONFERENCE .... **Southland**
LAST SEASON .... **13-16 (.448)**
CONFERENCE RECORD .... **8-8 (t-5th)**
STARTERS LOST/RETURNING **3/2**
NICKNAME .... **Indians**
COLORS .... **Maroon & Gold**
HOMECOURT .... **Ewing Coliseum (8,000)**
COACH .... **Mike Vining (Northeast Louisiana '67)**
RECORD AT SCHOOL .... **307-196 (17 yrs.)**
CAREER RECORD .... **307-196 (17 yrs.)**
ASSISTANTS .... **John Gullatt (LSU '88)**
Brad Hodge (Athens State College '96)
Keith Brown (Belhaven '81)
TEAM WINS (last 5 yrs.) **19-14-16-14-13**
RPI (last 5 yrs.) **143-163-147-181-188**
1997-98 FINISH .... **Lost in conference first round.**

You could make some great jokes if the situation were not so serious.

For whom does Maurice Bell toil? Not for NLU, not after getting arrested the night before the SLC Tournament last March. You could say that Bell had one steal too many.

The problem was it was the middle of the night and he was caught stealing a stereo out of a car that wasn't his. What made things worse was that coach Mike Vining purposely took the team home from Shreveport back to Monroe after practice that day so no one would get in trouble. Instead, he lost the team's best player in Bell, a 6-4 forward who led NLU in scoring (15.3 ppg), and rebounding (6.2 rpg) and was fourth in assists (36) and steals (32). Bell's absence was no small part of NLU's season-ending defeat, but it's not impossible he could play this season.

While not listed on the preseason roster, Bell, who is from Monroe, stayed on scholarship and in school. He was working out with the team in preseason weight training and drills, but the best that could be said as school started was his NLU future was very much in doubt. His return could make quite a difference, because he was arguably one of the top few players in the league last season, his first after transferring from nearby Louisiana Tech.

Off-the-court problems plagued Vining since the middle of last season.

Guard Brandun Hughes, who transferred from Michigan and figured into this season's plans a year ago, went through the first semester as a member of the team and then simply left the squad last January. So did sophomore swingman Terrell Jeter, the team's third-leading scorer (12.1 ppg) and second-leading rebounder (6.1). Jeter, who played in 17 games, starting 14, went home to tiny Princeton, La., last January and never rejoined the team.

"He just went home and didn't come back," a beleaguered Vining said. "He'd go home before and miss a practice, but you'd call him and get on him and his mother or grandmother would bring him back. After the fourth or fifth time, I wasn't going through two more years of that, so I just let him stay. Now he called and said he wants to come back, but he's not eligible."

Raymond Gill, a 6-6 forward who would have been a senior, was suspended from school because of academics and won't play this season. He played 28 of NLU' s 29 games, averaging 9.7 ppg, 2.3 rpg.

So what does it all mean?

"We've got a whole new team," Vining said. "We lost everybody. Everybody. Well, not everybody. But close."

Marcus Anthony, a 6-2 junior guard, is the most experienced returnee. He was second to Bell in scoring (15.0 ppg), averaged 2.7 rpg and added 47 steals and 46 assists. Two others return, backup point guard **Joe Childress**, a 5-10 senior (3.3 ppg, 0.8 rpg), 34 assists), and 6-5 sophomore **Jayde Hixon** (1.4 ppg, 0.4 rpg), a walkon who got a leftover scholarship. Accordingly, newcomers will have to move right in. One who should quite easily is 6-7 junior swingman **Michael Smith**, a product of West Monroe who transferred from Bossier Parish (La.) CC, where he averaged 28.0 ppg.

"Michael Smith is a tremendous athlete, a great shooter, jumps well, has good size," Vining said. "He can just do everything."

Smith was ranked No. 21 on junior college recruiting expert Phil Henzel's list of the top 300 JC sophomores.

Todd Daniels is a 5-9 point guard from Foxworth, Miss., by way of Pearl River (Miss.) JC, where he averaged 16 ppg, 9.0 apg and 5.0 rpg. "We think he will be a very good player for us," Vining said. Daniels was ranked 78th on Henzel's list.

One conversation and connection led to another and Vining signed a player from Lancashire, England, in 6-5 junior **Matt Hogarth**. "He's a very good player. Offensively he'll be very good," Vining said.

David Walker, a 6-5 forward from Washington, D.C., by way of Copiah-Lincoln (Miss.) JC (7.0 ppg, 8.0 rpg) should help defensively and give some depth to the frontcourt.

A sleeper could be **Marlon McCoy**, a 6-2 guard from Southern Lab in Baton Rouge, La., where he averaged 18.0 ppg. And NLU now has its first 7-footer, freshman **Wojciech Myrda**, a Pole who finished high school in Monroe at Ouachita Parish, where he averaged 12.4 ppg, 11 rpg, 7.2 bpg).

Two others will miss the first five games of the season, which includes contests at Michigan State, Memphis, Arkansas and Ole Miss, because they won't be academically eligible until the end of the first semester. But Vining figures that 6-2 guard **Chris Weakley** and 6-7 forward **Jermaine Stokes** will help the Indians quite a bit. Weakley is a transfer from Southern Union (Ala.) JC, where he averaged 19.8 ppg, while Stokes will be a sophomore after averaging 10 ppg for Dekalb (Ga.) JC.

Weakley was ranked No. 42 on Henzel's list of the top 300 JC sophomores, giving NLU three among the top 78. That influx of talent and experience should go a long way.

adidas Blue Ribbon Analysis

BACKCOURT	**C+**	**BENCH/DEPTH**	**C-**
FRONTCOURT	**C**	**INTANGIBLES**	**C**

NLU perennially makes itself a team to beat in the Southland and last year was no exception. The Indians struggled all season before winning three of four down the stretch to gain a spot in the SLC Tournament. But despite cutting a 12-point lead to two late and 30 points from Anthony, they lost to Southwest Texas 90-87 without Bell.

"Last year we had all these problems," Vining said. "We needed shooters, so we got shooters and then lost them. One gets homesick, one loses confidence, one decides he wants to play football, one decides he needs a stereo. I thought we were going to have a good team last year and we were ready to make a run at the conference tournament."

In most cases, you would call this a total rebuilding effort, but Vining has been through reconstruction before and has always fared well. After all, NLU has been to the NCAA Tournament five times in the 1990s and somehow, some way is in the hunt every year.

1998-99 NORTHEAST LOUISIANA SCHEDULE

Nov.	13	@Michigan State
	21	@Memphis
	24	Samford
	28	@Arkansas
Dec.	2	@Mississippi
	17	@Alabama
	19	@Southern Mississippi
	21	Arkansas-Monticello
	28	@Southwest Texas State
	30	@Texas-San Antonio
Jan.	2	Sam Houston State
	7	Lamar
	9	McNeese State
	14	@Stephen F. Austin
	16	@Texas-Arlington
	21	Southeastern Louisiana
	23	@Northwestern State
	30	@Sam Houston State
Feb.	1	Nicholls State
	4	Texas-San Antonio
	6	Southwest Texas State
	11	@McNeese State
	13	Northwestern State
	20	Texas-Arlington
	25	@Nicholls State
	27	Southeastern Louisiana
Mar.	3-6	#Southland Tournament

@ Road Games
\# TBA

"We've got good talent," Vining said, "if we can get them on the floor all at one time."

Winning the off-the-court battles will be the key to NLU's success on it.

(L.F.)

NORTHWESTERN STATE

LOCATION .... **Nachitoches, LA**
CONFERENCE .... **Southland**
LAST SEASON .... **13-14 (.481)**
CONFERENCE RECORD .... **10-6 (t-2nd)**
STARTERS LOST/RETURNING **5/0**
NICKNAME .... **Demons**
COLORS .... **Purple, White & Orange**
HOMECOURT .... **Prather Coliseum (5,000)**
COACH .... **J.D. Barnett (Winona State '66)**
RECORD AT SCHOOL .... **44-64 (4 yrs.)**
CAREER RECORD .... **335-237 (20 yrs.)**
ASSISTANTS . Clinton Sampson (Louisiana Tech '80)
Jason Tinsley (Northwestern State)
TEAM WINS (last 5 yrs.) **11-13-5-13-13**
RPI (last 5 yrs.) **246-210-296-224-232**
1997-98 FINISH .... **Lost in conference semifinal.**

It's been a long time since J.D. Barnett, who enters his 21st year as a head coach, has had to rebuild an entire team. But such is the case at Northwestern State, which lost five senior starters and five other players.

But Barnett, a tireless recruiter, has been down this road before. So he went out and got players, which couldn't have been that hard a sell. After all, any newcomer with a decent game is going to get his share of playing time.

"The first year I came here I had two players in the program. So the first year was a major rebuilding," Barnett said. "And we recruited every kid after signing day and we still had a good year. The good thing about this group is they're much more athletic. The bad thing is they just haven't been through the wars in Division I basketball."

The departed seniors: 6-9 center Seth LeGrand (13.8 ppg, 7.1 rpg), 6-3 guard Charles Duncan (13.7 ppg, 5.4 rpg), 6-7 forward Dameon McQuarters (11.2 ppg, 4.6 rpg), 6-5 senior Sam Alexander (10.2 ppg, 3.4 rpg) and 6-0 Ryan Bundy (7.6 ppg, 2.2 rpg). They also accounted for nearly all the team's assists and steals.

Just three Demons who played last season return, sophomore guards **Alann Polk** and **Josh Hancock** and sophomore center **Charles Thompson**. They'll be the foundation for a team that won't have a senior, but has four junior-college transfers and a few freshmen who figure heavily into the mix.

Polk, a 6-3 off-guard (6.3 pgg, 1.8 ppg), played in all 27 games, starting three. "He's strong and has excellent shooting range," Barnett said.

Hancock, 5-11, was a backup point guard last season (2.9 ppg, 1.3 rpg, 50 assists, 25 steals). "He has a lot of heart and doesn't make a lot of mistakes," Barnett said.

Thompson is 6-8 (2.4 ppg, 2.1 rpg) and played 13 minutes a game last year. Barnett said he's improved his strength and toughness, but remains thin. "But he can catch, he can shoot and he can pass," Barnett said. "He wants to be a player."

One of the junior college products is **Richard Taylor**, a 6-3 swingman from Tallahassee, Ala., who transferred from Faulkner (Ala.) State (18.0 ppg, 9.0 rpg). "He's a very good player and can do a little bit of everything," Barnett said. "And he can defend. Last year we did not have one guy who could really defend. As a team we were OK, but we didn't have that one guy." **Brent Shropshire** is a 5-11 junior guard from Dallas by way of Lon Morris (Texas) CC (11.0 ppg, 3.0 rpg, 4.0 apg). He'll play the point for Barnett, who said Shropshire—the son of a high school coach—has good shooting and leadership skills.

Kenton Fisher is listed as a 6-5 junior from Minneapolis and played at Minneapolis JC (16.0 ppg, 8.0 rpg). "He's about 6-4 and plays 6-6," Barnett said. "He's an excellent rebounder. He's getting better and has worked very hard."

The other two junior college players are **Amidd Sardinea**, a 6-6 forward from Houston and Weatherford (Texas) CC, and **Will Burks**, a product of Decatur, Ala., who is a sophomore from Motlow State JC in Tullahoma, Tenn.

Northwestern has four freshmen, two with strong football roots. **Jerrold McRae Jr.** is the son of the former Tennessee State and Kansas City Chiefs tight end of the same name. The younger McRae is 6-4 and a product of Glencliff HS in Nashville, Tenn.

Ryan Foppe is a 6-2 guard from Kimball HS in Dallas. His father was a very good receiver at Louisiana Tech in the 1970s.

Jamal Coles is a 6-3 guard from Keller HS in Keller, Texas, and **Ryan Duplessis** is a 6-1 guard from St. Augustine HS in New Orleans. Walkon **Martin Reisons**, a 6-2 junior guard who played 19 minutes last season, will be on the team again this year. So might **Chris Oney**, a transfer from Mississippi now enrolled at Northwestern State.

Oney, a 6-3 guard from Talullah, La., who earlier transferred from Texas A&M, played the 1995-96 season (2.8 ppg, 1.4 rpg) at Ole Miss and then played in the first five games of last season, hitting five of seven free-throws. But he developed migraine headaches and never played again as Ole Miss waited for medical clearance that never came. Oney finished the spring semester at Ole Miss and hopes to get eligible for the Demons.

adidas Blue Ribbon Analysis

BACKCOURT .... **C** **BENCH/DEPTH** .... **C-**
FRONTCOURT .... **C** **INTANGIBLES** .... **C**

Even though Northwestern lost seven of its final 10 games, last season was a good one. Expectations were higher, but Northwestern's 10-6 SLC record was its best since joining the league in the 1987-88 season. What's more, the second-place finish was its best ever in the SLC. Matching that is highly unlikely, although these Demons survived Barnett's annual rigorous preseason training program that includes many miles of running and meeting time requirements.

"We go for 21 straight days and we just tear their bodies completely down to a wreck," Barnett said. "But a part of it is to make them tough. That's how we succeeded last year to a certain degree. We didn't have the consistency we should have had, but down the stretch in some close games we had some toughness."

But with so much turnover, even on the coaching staff, you have to wonder if a totally new group will blend together. As *Blue Ribbon* went to press, Barnett was looking for a third assistant, because coach Kurt Young left the staff late in the summer to take a job as coach at Thomas College. "We recruited four JC players. Hopefully they'll come in and do the kind of job we need them to for us to be competitive," Barnett said. "I'm pleased with them. I think they all have a chance to be pretty good players."

(L.F.)

1998-99 NORTHWESTERN STATE SCHEDULE

Nov.	14	@Oklahoma
	16	@Oklahoma State
	21	@Mississippi State
	24	@Grambling
	30	Louisiana Tech
Dec.	5	@Centenary
	17	Belhaven
	31	Louisiana College
Jan.	4	Sam Houston
	7	@McNeese State
	9	Lamar
	14	@Texas-Arlington
	16	@Stephen F. Austin
	21	Nicholls State
	23	Northeast Louisiana
	28	@Southwest Texas State
	30	@Texas-San Antonio
Feb.	1	Southeastern Louisiana
	4	Southwest Texas State
	6	Texas-San Antonio
	9	@Sam Houston State
	13	@Northeast Louisiana
	18	Texas-Arlington
	20	Stephen F. Austin
	25	@Southeastern Louisiana
	27	@Lamar
Mar.	3-6	#Southland Tournament

@ Road Games
TBA

SAM HOUSTON STATE

LOCATION .... **Huntsville, TX**
CONFERENCE .... **Southland**
LAST SEASON .... **9-17 (.346)**
CONFERENCE RECORD .... **7-9 (7th)**
STARTERS LOST/RETURNING **2/3**
NICKNAME .... **Bearkats**
COLORS .... **Orange & White**
HOMECOURT .... **Bob Marlin (Mississippi State '81)**
RECORD AT SCHOOL .... **First Year**
CAREER RECORD .... **123-35 (5 years)**
ASSISTANTS .... **Darby Rich (Alabama '93)**
Neil Hardin (West Florida '95)
Abar Rouse (Baylor '97)
TEAM WINS (last 5 yrs.) **7-7-11-8-9**
RPI (last 5 yrs.) **275-285-231-260-265**
1997-98 FINISH .... **Didn't qualify for conference tournament.**

Defeating Southwest Texas in its last regular-season game, Sam Houston won exactly one game more a year ago than it did the previous season. Then coach Jerry Hopkins went out and signed eight players, a class about which he was excited. But then he got fired, reassigned within the university.

Then nothing happened. No coach. No one attending to the details of the upcoming season. You could just imagine Yosemite Sam uttering his famous line from those Bugs Bunny cartoons: "What in the name of Sam Houston is a goin' on here?"

Finally, on Aug. 4, Sam Houston announced the hiring of Bob Marlin as its new coach. The bad news was it was Aug. 4, putting Marlin well behind schedule for an incoming coach. The good news was it was Marlin, an accomplished, well-respected coach who was an assistant the last three years at Alabama. He lost his job when Alabama forced out head coach David Hobbs.

Once at Sam Houston, Marlin had to order equipment, handle paperwork, re-recruit the recruits and totally regroup. "There's definitely a learning curve," he said with a laugh.

Last Dec. 27, Alabama defeated Sam Houston, 77-58, in a tournament in Oklahoma City. Sam Houston actually led by a few at halftime. Little did Marlin know he was looking at his next team. "But I knew a little bit about them when the job came open," Marlin said.

Marlin has an impressive resume. As a head coach, he went 123-35 in five seasons at Pensacola (Fla.) Junior College, where that team won the 1993 junior college championship. He has also been an assistant at Northeast Louisiana, Marshall and Houston Baptist. This is his first go-round into the Southland Conference.

"We've got a lot of new faces," Marlin said in the biggest understatement of his head-coaching career so far.

A few holdovers will be all too familiar to SLC foes, including last year's league freshman of the year, **Jeremy Burkhalter**. "Burkhalter's a good athlete. He's long, he can get to the basket and he's a good outside shooter," Marlin said.

The 6-4 sophomore (14.9 ppg, 3.3 rpg, 43 assists, 20 steals, 58 three-pointers) scored in double figures in all but one SLC game. However, the product of Channelview, Texas, was in a car accident in May and cracked a vertabrae in his neck. He underwent surgery, but got clearance to play in August.

"We're closely monitoring the situation," Marlin said. "He's lifting weights, doing conditioning and individual workouts, but we don't want to get him hurt."

Boney Watson, a 5-11 junior (7.3 ppg, 3.0 rpg, 142 assists, 45 steals), became a pretty good point guard last season. "He's very steady. He's small, but he's a great competitor and a very good student," Marlin said.

Watson will get plenty of competition from **Bobby Willis**, a 6-1 product of Tulsa who transferred from Seward County (Kan.) CC (7.1 ppg, 2.3 rpg).

David Amaya, a 6-7 junior (11.2 ppg, 4.7 rpg) was one of Sam Houston's nicest surprises last season. He came on very strong late in the year and established himself as a solid player. "We're counting him to help us inside," Marlin said.

One other player returns, 6-7 junior **Ricky Fernandez** (5.1 ppg, 3.6 rpg).

Of the eight signees, seven showed up for the first day of classes. Jason Russell, a 6-8 product of Garland, Texas who averaged 19 ppg in high school, qualified academi-

1998-99 SAM HOUSTON STATE SCHEDULE

Nov.	15	@Tulsa
	19	St. Edward's
	23	@Houston
Dec.	3	Texas A&M
	5	@Wisconsin-Milwaukee
	17	@Oklahoma
	20	@Florida State
	28	Texas-Arlington
	30	Stephen F. Austin
Jan.	2	@Northeast Louisiana
	4	@Northwestern State
	7	Nicholls State
	14	@McNeese State
	16	@Lamar
	21	Southwest Texas State
	30	Northeast Louisiana
Feb.	4	@Nicholls State
	6	@Southeastern Louisiana
	11	Lamar
	13	McNeese State
	18	Texas-San Antonio
	20	@Southwest Texas State
	25	@Stephen F. Austin
	27	@Texas-Arlington
Mar.	3-6	#Southland Tournament

@ Road Games
\# TBA

cally, but went to a junior college instead.

Obviously the newcomers will have to contribute. **Charles Dixon**, a 6-7 transfer from Moorpark (Calif.) CC in his hometown (14.1 ppg, 6.2 rpg), should start at one forward spot. The other newcomer who will probably start is 6-3 guard **Demetrius Smith** (16.1 ppg, 5.2 rpg), a product of Amarillo who transferred from Frank Phillips (Texas) JC.

Brian Jordy, a 6-7 freshman from Huntsville HS (8.6 ppg, 6.2 rpg), chose to stay at home.

Harold McKinley, "an excellent freshman guard prospect" is a 6-1 product of Nimitz HS in Houston (15.1 ppg, 6.0 rpg).

Nick Christopher, a left-handed 6-8 forward from Tomball (Texas) HS (9.8 ppg, 7.6 rpg) "has to gain some strength and weight, but has a chance to be a good player while he's here," Marlin said. "But I don't know how soon."

Collin Degge, a 6-9, 235-pound teammate of Christopher's from Tomball (12.1 ppg, 6.2 rpg), "can shoot it, has a nice touch and a big body, and we may be forced to play him this year, which can only help us and him," Marlin said.

adidas Blue Ribbon Analysis

BACKCOURT	B+	BENCH/DEPTH	B
FRONTCOURT	C-	INTANGIBLES	C

Sam Houston opens its season on a Friday the 13th at Florida State. Marlin doesn't inherit a basketball power. Far from it—Sam Houston has never had a winning season in its 12-year Division I history. But Marlin could have done worse.

"Player-wise, no question," he admitted. But he is behind for now.

"Getting here late, in August, it was a situation where I was basically locked in. I wasn't able to recruit and didn't have any scholarships," Marlin said. "I'm inheriting the team we've got and the schedule we've got. But I think we've got a chance to be OK." And the future is bright: Sam Houston has no seniors. "I'm excited," Marlin said. "But it's going to be my biggest challenge."

(L.F.)

SOUTHEASTERN LOUISIANA

LOCATION .... **Hammond, LA**
CONFERENCE .... **Southland**
LAST SEASON .... **6-20 (.231)**
CONFERENCE RECORD .... **2-14 (10th)**
STARTERS LOST/RETURNING **2/3**
NICKNAME .... **Lions**
COLORS .... **Green & Gold**
HOMECOURT .... **University Center (7,500)**
COACH .... **John Lyles (Louisiana College '77)**
RECORD AT SCHOOL .... **43-66 (4 yrs.)**
CAREER RECORD .... **43-66 (4 yrs.)**
ASSISTANTS .... **Ron Cox (McNeese State '88)**
Terry Waldrop (Northeast Louisiana '86)
TEAM WINS (last 5 yrs.) **10-12-15-10-6**
RPI (last 5 yrs.) **244-227-195-298-302**
1997-98 FINISH Ineligible for conference tournament.

The defining moment for Southeastern Louisiana came at midseason, a dagger in the heart of a long year that would seemingly never end. Earlier that evening at the University Center, the visiting Texas-Arlington women trounced SLU. Then, in the men's game, the UTA men basically did the same thing. And as they walked off the court, the SLU men were serenaded by the UTA women, who loudly told them, "Welcome to the SLC, baby!" Welcome, indeed.

"We came in the league, we were picked last—where we should have been picked—and we came into a better league than we were in and we came in at the bottom," SLU coach John Lyles said. "We're just hoping through our recruiting—and we recruited pretty good—that we'll work our way up the ladder and move up in the league."

There is just one way to go, of course, for the Lions, who had a stranglehold on last place in the SLC after moving over from the Trans America Athletic Conference.

"In the TAAC, in which we were very competitive every year, you had College of Charleston, which was a dominant program, and then everyone else was at a whole, complete different level," Lyles said. "The Southland Conference, when we moved in there, there was maybe no one quite as good as College of Charleston, but everyone else was better than everyone else in the TAAC.

"So the teams were more athletic, much more athletic, and we were caught in a situation where we were not quite there. Night in and night out we were playing most people quite close but just weren't good enough to get over the hump at the end of the games."

At one point SLU lost 16 games in a row, tying the school record for such a skid, before finally winning at Sam Houston State. The Lions lost their next two games, however, before winning at Northeast Louisiana to close the season.

SLU led the league in scoring (79.4 ppg), but also ranked last in scoring defense (85.8 ppg).

SLU had four seniors, but only one, swingman Glenn Charles (10.5 ppg, 4.0 rpg), played significant minutes. Also gone is forward Andre Lewis (6.5 ppg, 6.0 rpg) who gave help on defense and the boards. Center Brennen Shingleton (1.1 ppg, 0.5 rpg) and guard Eric Myles (4.8 ppg, 1.4 rpg) were seniors; forward Mark Gulina (4.7 ppg, 2.2 rpg) and center Stuart Drury (3.2 ppg, 2.6 rpg) transferred.

However, Lyles gets back a reasonably talented group that not only includes last season's top four scorers, but one who should provide senior leadership.

Cory Combs, a 6-6 senior forward, overcame an early-season slump and emerged as the team's leading scorer (12.0 ppg) and third-leading rebounder (5.5 rpg) while adding 28 assists, 22 steals and 10 blocks.

Maurice Clark, a 6-4 senior guard (11.9 ppg, 2.8 rpg, 22 assists, 21 steals) hit 56 of 112 three-pointers (.412). **Noble Evans**, another 6-6 senior (11.6 ppg, 6.6 rpg, 38 assists), led with 34 steals, while 5-10 senior **Troy Green** (11.3 ppg, 1.3 rpg) led with 128 assists (4.9 apg) and hit 50 of 136 three-pointers (.368).

Two others return: 5-11 sophomore guard **Lee Carney** (3.1 ppg, 1.1 rpg, 65 assists, 23 steals) and 6-8 junior **James Randolph** (1.6 ppg, 1.2 rpg in 1996-97), who redshirted last season.

Lyles is excited about a group of newcomers that includes 7-foot transfer **Kelland Payton**, a junior from Biloxi, Miss. who sat out last season after transferring from Seton Hall. Another player who sat out last season is redshirt freshman **Jason Elloie**, a 6-7 forward who averaged 14.0 ppg, 7.0 rpg at St. Augustine HS in New Orleans.

SLU signed three junior college players: 6-1 guard **Tawaski Lawton**, from Hill (Texas) JC; **Marcus Mackey**, a 6-6 forward from Lumberton, Miss., by way of Pearl River (Miss.) JC; and **Jeremy Hall**, a 6-0 guard from Garrett, Ky., and St. Catherine (Ken.) JC, who played as a freshman at Wisconsin. "We definitely improved our talent, but we were behind," Lyles said. "It's a league where if you get a couple of players you have a chance to move up and I'm hoping we do that."

The Lions will have just one freshman, 6-6 forward **Shawn Ashworth** from tiny Plainview, La., a Class C school.

"Our needs were so immediate because of the talent gap we had to fill from changing leagues that we had to go more the junior-college route than normal," Lyles said.

adidas Blue Ribbon Analysis

BACKCOURT	B-	BENCH/DEPTH	C
FRONTCOURT	D+	INTANGIBLES	C-

SLU plays three Southeastern Conference road games, at Auburn, Mississippi State and Arkansas. It might be a good time to point out that the Lions were 2-12 on the road last season. But by the time SLC play begins, the Lions should be a much-improved team. And the style won't change. "We're committed to pressing and we're committed to uptempo basketball because we feel in the long run we're going to be able to recruit better players that way," Lyles said. "Players want to play that way, fans want to watch players play that way. It helps recruiting, because it's hard to recruit players when you play slow.

"We play fast and that's the way we're always going to play. We were able to win in the TAAC playing that way and we'll be able to play and win that way in this league when our recruiting catches up."

It probably won't catch up this season, but the addition of Payton, combined with the four returning top scorers, should give the Lions a chance to get out of the cellar.

(L.F.)

1998-99 SOUTHEASTERN LOUISIANA SCHEDULE

Nov.	13	@Auburn
	17	Grambling University
	21	Louisiana College
Dec.	2	Centenary
	5	@Southern
	12	@Mississippi State
	16	@Arkansas
	23	Texas College
	28	McNeese State
	30	Lamar
Jan.	2	@Stephen F. Austin
	4	Texas-Arlington
	14	Southwest Texas State
	16	Texas-San Antonio
	21	@Northeast Louisiana
	23	@Nicholls State
	28	@Lamar
	30	Stephen F. Austin
Feb.	1	@Northwestern State
	6	Sam Houston State
	11	@Texas-San Antonio
	13	@Southwest Texas
	17	@McNeese State
	20	Nicholls State
	25	Northwestern State
	27	Northeast Louisiana
Mar.	3-6	#Southland Tournament

@ Road Games
\# TBA

SOUTHWEST TEXAS STATE

LOCATION .... **San Marco, TX**
CONFERENCE .... **Southland**
LAST SEASON .... **17-11 (.607)**
CONFERENCE RECORD .... **10-6 (t-2nd)**
STARTERS LOST/RETURNING **2/3**
NICKNAME .... **Bobcats**
COLORS .... **Maroon & Gold**
HOMECOURT .... **Strahan Coliseum (7,200)**
COACH .... **Mike Miller (East Texas '87)**
RECORD AT SCHOOL .... **56-53 (4 yrs.)**
CAREER RECORD .... **56-53 (4 yrs.)**
ASSISTANTS .... **Doug Novsek (Southern Illinois '87)**
Jim Elgas (Illinois State '93)
Mike VandeGarde (Illinois State '95)
TEAM WINS (last 5 yrs.) **25-12-11-16-17**
RPI (last 5 yrs.) **103-221-250-175-154**
1997-98 FINISH .... **Lost in conference semifinal.**

Southwest Texas enters this season with what appears to be an excellent blend of inside strength, outstanding guard play, experience and youth. After all, no other team in the league can boast the second-leading scorer (**Donte Mathis**), leading rebounder (**Jeff Foster**) and leading free-throw shooter (**Clifton Ellis**).

"I think we've got a chance," coach Mike Miller said. "We feel real good that we've got Donte and Jeff back and that they've started for us basically since they've been freshmen.

"They've been through the wars. They've seen the

good and the bad and the ups and the downs. Hopefully they're going to see this thing through. We've got some question marks on our team. We're fortunate we have our guard play."

That starts with Mathis, a 6-4 senior who established himself as one of the better guards in the league. The first-team All-SLC player averaged 18.6 ppg (second in the league) and 5.5 rpg, hitting 22 of 52 (.423) of his three-pointers. He also was a 77 percent free-throw shooter and added 79 assists and 43 steals. Mathis scored in double figures in every game, became the ninth player in school history to surpass 1,000 points for his career and finished the season fifth on the all-time SWT list.

Ellis, a 6-0 senior (5.7 ppg, 2.3 rpg, 91 assists, 28 steals), returns at point guard after leading the team in assists and free-throw percentage (72 of 80, .900 percent).

And inside is 6-11 senior Foster (12.8 ppg, 10.2 rpg, 44 assists, 37 steals, 29 blocked shots). He made the All-SLC second team.

The other starters should be 6-3 junior guard **Wesley Williams** (5.5 ppg, 1.7 rpg) and either 6-9 senior **DaVvon Bethea** (3.6 ppg, 3.2 rpg), who started two games last year and certainly brings one of the more unusual names to the game, or 6-7 sophomore **Theo Stephens** (0.5 ppg, 0.6 rpg), who played sparingly last season.

Justin Hardin, a 6-3 sophomore (1.0 ppg, 23 assists, 26 steals) served well as the backup point guard and should fill that role again this season. The Bobcats lost Carlos Morris (10.4 ppg, 5.5 rpg), who was a senior guard last year and perhaps the team's best defender, Ross Johnson (5.0 ppg, 3.6 rpg), who was SWT's best post defender, and Max Schleder (5.9 ppg, 2.3 rpg). But plenty of newcomers and young players should fill in.

"We have an experienced team in that we have eight returning players, but of our 13 scholarshipped players, seven are freshmen or sophomores," Miller said.

One of the newcomers, junior Jasper Smith, should be a big factor. The 6-0 guard from Spearsville, La., is a transfer from Jacksonville Baptist College in Texas (20 ppg).

Miller signed 6-7 **Byron Hobbs** of West Columbia (Texas) HS (21.0 ppg, 12.0 rpg), 6-3 guard **Clay Click** from San Alamo Heights (Texas) HS (30.0 ppg) and 6-9 **Daryl Hamilton** from LaMarque (Texas) HS (13.4 ppg, 10.2 rpg, 3.5 bpg). Later, he got 6-6 forward **Jason Blair** from Shadow Mountain HS in Phoenix, who was a prep teammate of Mike Bibby's on a state-championship team. Click is a spot-up shooter who should see plenty of playing time.

adidas Blue Ribbon Analysis

BACKCOURT .... B BENCH/DEPTH .... B-

FRONTCOURT .... B- INTANGIBLES .... B

After losing four in a row and five of six last season, SWT made a tremendous late-season charge, winning six of its last seven regular-season games. Then the Bobcats held off Northeast Louisiana in a Southland Conference Tournament quarterfinal, 90-87, before losing to eventual champion Nicholls State in a semifinal game. It was typical of the season, as SWT played 10 games decided by four points or less, winning five and losing five.

This year's team figures to win more than its share of the close ones, although a schedule that includes a season-opener at home against Wisconsin-Green Bay and trips to Baylor, Missouri and Nebraska will be challenging.

"We're going to get tested," Miller said. "It is the most challenging schedule we've ever had. Some of that is by design, but we have some returning players and we need to find out where we're at and what we have to do to be a good team. With that schedule, we're going to find that out."

The rest of the league's coaches think he'll like the answers, but you know how coaches are.

"I know people are picking us high and that's fine," Miller said. "It's a compliment that people think we've got some guys are some pretty solid players. But for us to make that jump (to the next level), we have to prove some things."

(L.F.)

1998-99 SOUTHWEST TEXAS STATE SCHEDULE

Nov.	13	Wisconsin-Green Bay
	24	@Baylor
	29	@Missouri
Dec.	4-5	#Ameritas Classic
	8	Howard Payne
	15	New Mexico Highlands
	21	@Samford
	28	Northeast Louisiana
Jan.	2	@McNeese State
	4	@Lamar
	7	Stephen F. Austin
	9	Texas-Arlington
	14	@Southeastern Louisiana
	16	@Nicholls State
	21	@Sam Houston State
	23	Texas-San Antonio
	28	Northwestern State
	30	McNeese State
Feb.	4	@Northwestern State
	6	@Northeast Louisiana
	11	Nicholls State
	13	Southeastern Louisiana
	18	@Stephen F. Austin
	20	Sam Houston
	27	@Texas-San Antonio
Mar.	3-6	##Southland Tournament

@ Road Games
# Lincoln, NE (vs. Nebraska, first round; also Colgate and Davidson)
TBA

STEPHEN F. AUSTIN

LOCATION .... Nacogdoches, TX
CONFERENCE .... Southland
LAST SEASON .... 10-16 (.385)
CONFERENCE RECORD 6-10 (8th)
STARTERS LOST/RETURNING 3/2
NICKNAME .... Lumberjacks
COLORS .... Purple, White & Red
HOMECOURT .. William R. Johnson Coliseum (7,203)
COACH .... Derek Allister (Chico State '76)
RECORD AT SCHOOL .... 22-31 (2 yrs.)
CAREER RECORD .... 22-31 (2 yrs.)
ASSISTANTS . Andrew Prince (Abilene Christian '75)
Dennis Cutts (Albany '90)
Sean McDonough (Marquette '91)
TEAM WINS (last 5 yrs.) 9-14-17-12-10
RPI (last 5 yrs.) 221-241-197-181-249
1997-98 FINISH .... Did not qualify for conference tournament.

Last year, freshman point guard **Aaron Radl** (6.7 ppg, 2.3 rpg, 102 assists, 60 steals) was force-fed into the college game. An injury to starter Jermaine Lyons, a 5-9 sophomore, forced Radl's rapid indoctrination to the Southland Conference, but Stephen F. Austin could be better this season as a result of Radl's early playing time.

"He was an untested freshman who was thrown to the wolves. Now he's a very veteran sophomore because at the end of the year he was playing 40 minutes a game. And I think he's superb," coach Derek Allister said.

With the return of a healthy Lyons, point guard has become a position of strength for the Lumberjacks.

"I think that gives us two of the better point guards in the conference," Allister said.

SFA also has one of the better forwards in the conference in 6-9 senior **Keith Tate** (14.0 ppg, 5.0 rpg), who has bulked up from 200 to 230 pounds. "Keith has responded with hard work and some good performances despite all the defensive attention he was getting," Allister said.

Those three players, Allister said, "are a good place to start in the rebuilding."

SFA lost four key players, swingman Davanzio Carter (13.9 ppg, 4.8 rpg), the team's best shooter; forward David Henry (10.0 ppg, 5. 7 rpg), who did everything well; forward Tysmon Jolivetter (7.4 ppg, 2.5 rpg); and Wayne Allen (9.8 ppg, 6.1 rpg) who was lost to an injury midway through last season while leading the team in rebounding. And before the season began, Lyons was lost to an injury.

That's a lot of talent to replace, and Allister is trying to sort from several newcomers and holdovers.

The small forward will be 6-5 sophomore **Patrick Gusters** (10.8 ppg, 4.0 rpg, 32 assists, 21 steals), who also benefited from all the injuries. "He had flashes of brilliance," Allister said. "As a sophomore he gives us a very good small forward."

The off-guard should be 6-3 **Kevin Daniels**, a junior transfer from Vacaville, Calif., by way of Contra Costa JC (18 ppg, 6 rpg), but 6-2 junior **Will Porter**, the all-time three-point shooting leader from Northland Pioneer JC (14.2 ppg, 2.0 rpg), should see plenty of playing time. Daniels originally went to Loyola Marymount and is a strong leader.

The other forward spot? "That's going to be a tossup," Allister said, admitting it could be the key to the Lumberjacks' success.

Phillip Clayton, a 6-8 sophomore who started six games last season (2.4 ppg, 1.7 rpg) is probably in the lead, but he's more of a perimeter player who might serve SFA better on the wing and coming off the bench. So **Stephen Cobb**, a 6-11 freshman who redshirted last season, might be the answer.

So might **Matt Brown**, 6-10 leaper from Roseburg, Ore., who has a personal best of 6-10 in the high jump, or **Travis Beavers**, a 6-8 product of Plano (Texas) HS (10.0 ppg, 5.0 rpg).

"If there's one position I'm a little concerned about, it's how we're going to fill that spot," Allister said.

Also on the team are newcomers **Colt Clark**, a 6-7 freshman forward from Kansas (Okla.) HS; 6-2 junior **Will Porter** of Tucson, Ariz., who transferred from Northland Pioneer (Ariz.) JC (14.2 ppg, 2.0 rpg); and **Terrance Lofton**, a 6-4 junior swingman from Grandview, Mo., who transferred from Carl Sandberg JC. **Kirk White** is a 6-4 freshman guard from Tascosa HS in Amarillo, Texas.

adidas Blue Ribbon Analysis

BACKCOURT .... B- BENCH/DEPTH .... B-

FRONTCOURT .... B- INTANGIBLES .... B

The Lumberjacks were last in the league in three-point field-goal percentage (.314) and ninth in rebounding margin (-4.6). But it's not likely that injuries will decimate SFA as they did last season when Allister struggled through his longest season because of such high expectations.

Now he has a team with an experienced point guard in Radl and a potential star with Tate.

"I think our guards are really good, I feel really comfortable with all our perimeter players, I think we're deep at the point and Radl will really step up," Allister said. "That forward spot really concerns me." But at least he has a handful of taller players to stick in there and plenty of them. "How that one spot comes out may really determine how we do," Allister said.

The odds are they'll do better.

(L.F.)

1998-99 STEPHEN F. AUSTIN SCHEDULE

Nov.	19	Texas A&M
	22	@Colorado
	24	@Northern Arizona
Dec.	1	@Rice
	2	Texas College
	5	@Texas Tech
	8	@Arizona State
	21	Southern Methodist
	30	@Sam Houston State
Jan.	2	Southeastern Louisiana
	4	Nicholls State
	7	@Southwest Texas State
	9	@Texas San-Antonio
	14	Northeast Louisiana
	16	Northwestern State
	21	@Lamar
	23	Texas-Arlington
	28	@Nicholls State
	31	@Southeastern Louisiana
Feb.	4	Lamar
	6	McNeese State
	11	@Texas-Arlington
	18	Southwest Texas State
	20	@Northwestern State
	25	Sam Houston
	27	@McNeese State
Mar.	3-6	#Southland Tournament

@ Road Games
# TBA

TEXAS-ARLINGTON

LOCATION .... **Arlington, TX**
CONFERENCE .... **Southland**
LAST SEASON .... **13-16 (.448)**
CONFERENCE RECORD .... **8-8 (t-6th)**
STARTERS LOST/RETURNING **2/3**
NICKNAME .... **Mavericks**
COLORS .... **Royal Blue & White**
HOMECOURT .... **Texas Hall (4,200)**
COACH .... **Eddie McCarter (UAB '75)**
RECORD AT SCHOOL .... **69-97 (6 yrs.)**
CAREER RECORD .... **69-97 (6 yrs.)**
ASSISTANTS .... **Mark Stone (Texas Christian '74)**
Tony Stubblefield (Nebraska-Omaha '95)
Scott Cross (UTA '98)
TEAM WINS (last 5 yrs.) **7-10-11-12-14**
RPI (last 5 yrs.) **278-256-244-240-240**
1997-98 FINISH .... **Lost in conference final.**

Texas-Arlington was so close last year.

Coach Eddie McCarter made a late-season lineup switch that paid off big for the Mavericks as they nearly knocked off Nicholls State in the Southland Tournament championship game. But Nicholls rallied from a 78-69 deficit with just more than five minutes left for an 84-81 victory that propelled the Colonels into the NCAA Tournament.

UTA's **Bill Washington** squared up from the left side and swished a three-pointer that would have won the game, but the officials waved it off because he took it after the buzzer.

But there were two bright spots in the disappointment. **Donald Harris**, a 6-5 senior (13.8 ppg, 4.0 rpg, 37 assists, 26 steals) who was moved to forward from guard down the stretch, averaged 20.8 ppg the final five games, including 30 in the title match against Nicholls. Accordingly, he was chosen MVP of the Southland Tournament.

Washington, a 6-5 junior, (12.9 ppg, 8.7 rpg) averaged 16.4 ppg in that stretch as he also made the all-tournament team. Washington, who finished third in the league in rebounding, also added 57 assists and 56 steals.

A third starter also returns, 6-8 senior **Jared Hiple** (7.7 ppg, 4.5 rpg). "We need to Hiple to get tougher for us," McCarter said. "But in all fairness to him, he had a good sophomore year and then last year he had a bad knee and didn't want to have it operated on until after the season. He'll come back and be a lot better player for us."

Chad Jones, a 6-5 junior (5.4 ppg, 1.1 rpg) also had knee surgery and he wasn't expected to be back until mid-October for the start of practice. "We plan on him playing, but we just don't know," McCarter said.

Gabe Isaac might have been the point guard, but he was lost to grades. So the job falls to 5-10 junior **Jermaine Johnson** (1.9 ppg, 1.7 rpg, 93 assists, 17 steals), who played in 27 games last year. Point guard is a big concern for McCarter, who figures to get help there from **Jason Arbuckle**, a 6-0 sophomore from Houston who sat out last season after transferring from Portland.

Three junior-college products should contribute right away, especially **Dewayne Marable**, a 6-8 forward from Lawson State (Ala.). "We feel he'll be a real big plus. He can shoot the ball and can post up. He has to get a lot stronger," McCarter said.

Tony Jones is a 6-6 junior from Bevill State (Ala.) CC. He's described by McCarter as "a fine offensive player."

And **Keith Green** is a 6-3 junior from Bossier Parish (La.) CC, where he averaged 15 points and hit .417 percent of his three-pointers. "He shoots it real well. He handles it well," McCarter said. "All three of those guys will play. If they're not starting, they'll be close."

A player who redshirted last year, 6-3 freshman guard **Walter Louis**, could contend for playing time, while 6-0 freshman guard **Dakendrick Smith** will redshirt this season.

adidas Blue Ribbon Analysis

BACKCOURT	**B-**	**BENCH/DEPTH**	**B-**
FRONTCOURT	**C**	**INTANGIBLES**	**C**

UTA has had an annual problem of starting off slow and finishing strong. "We've got to stay healthy and get off to a good start," McCarter said. "We need to have some luck, too."

The Mavericks ought to be able to come out of the preseason with a strong record, considering they play home games against McMurry College, Texas Wesleyan and Samford. They have tough road trips, though, to Baylor, UAB, Texas Tech and Colorado.

Cross was a big loss, because he was a settling factor for the sometimes helter-skelter Mavs. How well Johnson and Arbuckle come through will probably determine how well UTA does this season.

(L.F.)

1998-99 TEXAS-ARLINGTON SCHEDULE

Nov.	21	@Baylor
	24	McMurry College
Dec.	1	@UAB
	5	Texas Wesleyan
	12	@Texas Tech
	16	Samford
	19	@Air Force
	21	@Colorado
	28	@Sam Houston State
Jan.	2	Nicholls State
	4	Southeastern Louisiana
	7	@Texas-San Antonio
	9	@Southwest Texas State
	14	Northwestern State
	16	Northeast Louisiana
	21	@McNeese State
	23	@Stephen F. Austin
	30	@Nicholls State
Feb.	4	McNeese State
	6	Lamar
	11	Stephen F. Austin
	13	@Lamar
	18	@Northwestern State
	20	@Northeast Louisiana
	25	Texas-San Antonio
	27	Sam Houston State
Mar.	3-6	#Southland Tournament

@ Road Games

TEXAS-SAN ANTONIO

LOCATION .... **San Antonio, TX**
CONFERENCE .... **Southland**
LAST SEASON .... **16-11 (.593)**
CONFERENCE RECORD .... **10-6 (t-2nd)**
STARTERS LOST/RETURNING **1/4**
NICKNAME .... **Roadrunners**
COLORS .... **Navy Blue & White**
HOMECOURT .... **Convocation Center (5,100)**
COACH .... **Tim Carter (Kansas '79)**
RECORD AT SCHOOL .... **39-42 (3 yrs.)**
CAREER RECORD .... **50-48 (4 yrs.)**
ASSISTANTS .... **Al Grushnik (Oglethorpe '75)**
Roland Ware (Oklahoma '92)
Owen Miller (Mississippi College '94)
TEAM WINS (last 5 yrs.) **12-15-14-9-16**
RPI (last 5 yrs.) **234-182-191-294-215**
1997-98 FINISH .... **Lost in conference quarterfinal.**

Texas-San Antonio might have lost the Southland Conference Player of the Year in guard Roderic Hall, but coach Tim Carter doesn't appear worried.

"I feel a whole lot better about who we're going to war with now than I did a year ago because I really didn't know where we'd stack up with all the injuries we'd had two years ago," Carter said. Hall led his team in scoring (17.4 ppg), added 4.3 rebounds, averaged 2.3 apg, and hit 62 of 199 three-pointers (.312). But he scored just 11 points in his team's season-ending loss to Texas-Arlington in a Southland Tournament quarterfinal.

"Rod was a phenomenal shooter. Hopefully we can have somebody pick up the load offensively, but defensively, we're going to really, really pick up, because Rod did not play the best defense," Carter said.

Hall, was the only senior who played any significant minutes. Center **Leon Watson** leads a group of solid young players that should keep UTSA in the hunt all season. Watson, a 6-8 junior, did it all: 14.1 ppg, second in the SLC at 9.7 rpg, SLC-best 65 blocks, SLC-best .616 shooting percentage. But he only made the All-SLC second team. "Leon did a heck of a lot more than I thought he could do," Carter admitted. Actually he didn't plan for Watson to play such a big role, but injuries gave him the opportunity.

"The thing I like about Leon is he loves the game," Carter said.

While Watson takes care of things inside, 6-3 senior guard **Steve Meyer** (15.9 ppg, 4.9 rpg) takes care of things outside. "Steve Meyer was our best player and our most consistent player and that he didn't make second team (All-SLC) is a joke," Carter said. He hit 30 three-pointers last season and twice hit game-winning shots. "He's a complete player. He can shoot it, rebound and defend," Carter said. "It's his team."

Lloyd Williams, a 5-9 junior guard (7.0 ppg, 4.0 rpg, 4.3 apg), should again start at point guard. Last seasn, he was fifth in the league in steals and assists. But the job is not a lock, because 6-0 senior **Jerome Riley** (5.6 ppg, 2.8 rpg, 77 assists, 34 steals) "had a great summer" Carter said, and could challenge for the starting spot.

Others back include 6-6 sophomore **Juston Pendleton** (6.2 ppg, 4.4 rpg) and 6-5 senior **Ricky Reed** (3.8 ppg, 2.2 rpg).

Three reserves from a year ago didn't return: 6-2 junior Terrence Jones (0.6 ppg, 0.6 rpg), Willie Robinson (4.1 ppg, 3.0 rpg) and Mike Clemons (5.3 ppg, 2.7 rpg). But a handful of newcomers will make an immediate impact, especially 6-4 freshman guard **Devin Brown**, the *San Antonio Express-News* All-Greater San Antonio Basketball Player of the Year (32.3 ppg, 10.2 rpg), who will start at one of the wing spots.

"We were very fortunate because he could have gone a lot of places bigger than us," Carter said.

Another Texan who could start at wing is 6-4 **Reggie Minnieweather** of Dallas Skyline HS (18 ppg).

Other newcomers include **Machoe "Punchy" Parker**, a 6-8 forward from Northeastern Oklahoma JC (17.0 ppg, 11.1 rpg); **Terrance Herbert**, a 6-7 forward from East Central CC (18.0 ppg, 11.0 rpg); and **McEverett Powers**, a 6-7 freshman from Memphis Ridgeway HS (18.0 ppg, 11.0 rpg).

adidas Blue Ribbon Analysis

BACKCOURT	**B**	**BENCH/DEPTH**	**C**
FRONTCOURT	**C+**	**INTANGIBLES**	**C**

UTSA struggled early last season, but then put together a string of six victories that extended into eight of nine as the Roadrunners challenged for second place in the league. It marked the school's best season since going 21-8 in 1992. Winning three one-point conference games was an important part of the late-season success.

Although Carter was thrilled to win 16 games, considering how bleak things looked a year ago, UTSA nonetheless ended the season with three defeats, including its second of the year to Texas-Arlington. The non-conference schedule is typically difficult, as the Roadrunners play at Texas Tech, Tulsa, UTEP and Wichita State early. They also play five of seven SLC games on the road in January.

If they get the help Carter expects from the newcomers and continue to win the close ones, the Roadrunners could be atop the league by season's end.

(L.F.)

1998-99 TEXAS-SAN ANTONIO SCHEDULE

Nov.	19	@Texas Tech
	22	Texas College
	24	@Tulsa
	28	Troy State
Dec.	1	@Texas-El Paso
	5	@Wichita State
	16	@Missouri-Kansas City
	30	Northeast Louisiana
Jan.	2	@Lamar
	4	@McNeese State
	7	Texas-Arlington
	9	Stephen F. Austin
	14	@Nicholls State
	16	@Southeastern Louisiana
	23	@Southwest Texas State
	28	McNeese State
	30	Northwestern State
Feb.	4	@Northeast Louisiana
	6	@Northwestern State
	11	Southwestern Louisiana
	13	Nicholls State
	18	@Sam Houston State
	20	Lamar
	25	@Texas-Arlington
	27	Southwest Texas State
Mar.	3-6	#Southland Tournament

@ Road Games
# TBA

SOUTHWESTERN ATHLETIC CONFERENCE

adidas BLUE RIBBON FORECAST

1. Texas Southern
2. Southern
3. Grambling State
4. Jackson State
5. Alabama State
6. Alcorn State
7. Mississippi Valley State
8. Prairie View
9. Arkansas-Pine Bluff

ALL-CONFERENCE TEAM

G—Dionte Harvey, SR, Southern
G—Leland Redmond, SR, Texas Southern
G—Reuben Stiff, SR, Alcorn State
F—Chris Thomas, JR, Grambling State
C—Adarrial Smylie, JR, Southern

PLAYER OF THE YEAR

Dionte Harvey, SR, Southern

NEWCOMER OF THE YEAR

Willie Gross, JR, Jackson State

1998-99 CONFERENCE TOURNAMENT

March 3-6, Dallas Convention Center, Dallas, TX

1997-98 CHAMPION

Texas Southern (regular season)
Prairie View (conference tournament)

1997-98 POSTSEASON PARTICIPANTS

Postseason Record: 0-1 (.000)
NCAA
Prairie View

TOP BACKCOURTS

1. Southern
2. Alabama State
3. Texas Southern

TOP FRONTCOURTS

1. Grambling State
2. Texas Southern
3. Alabama State

ON THE WAY UP

Alabama State

ON THE WAY DOWN

Jackson State

INSIDE THE NUMBERS

- 1997-98 conference RPI: 29th (of 30)
- Conference RPI (last 5 years): 31-31-29-31-30

DID YOU KNOW?

Prairie View won its first-ever SWAC Tournament championship with a 59-57 comeback victory last season over Texas Southern. The Panthers became the 14th team to ever reach the NCAA Tournament with a losing record and their RPI ranking of 263 was the lowest of any team ever participating in the "Big Dance"...Alcorn State plays its home games in the Davey Whitney Complex, named in honor of the Braves' coach from 1969-89 and 1996-present. Whitney, entering his 22nd season, is one of only three current coaches whose team plays in the arena named for him. (The College of Charleston's John Kresse and UTEP's Don Haskins are the others)...Whitney needs 36 victories to reach 500 for his career...Texas Southern has established itself as the SWAC team of the 1990s with four regular-season championships and three tournament titles during this decade...Southern center Adarrial Smylie had left junior college and was working at a Baton Rouge supermarket when he decided to enroll with the Jaguars...SWAC teams are 4-18 in NCAA Tournament play. Alcorn State won first-round games over South Alabama in 1980, Xavier in 1983 and Houston Baptist in 1984. Southern won a first-round game over Georgia Tech in 1993...The SWAC Tournament returns to Dallas for the third straight year, its longest stay in one city since the event was staged in Baton Rouge from 1992-95.

(S.G.)

ALABAMA STATE

LOCATION .... **Montgomery, AL**
CONFERENCE .... **Southwestern Athletic (SWAC)**
LAST SEASON .... **11-17 (.393)**
CONFERENCE RECORD .... **6-10 (t-6th)**
STARTERS LOST/RETURNING **0/5**
NICKNAME .... **Hornets**
COLORS .... **Old Gold & Black**
HOMECOURT .... **Joe L. Reed Acadome (8,000)**
COACH .... **Rob Spivery (Ashland '72)**
RECORD AT SCHOOL .... **19-38 (2 yrs.)**
CAREER RECORD .... **193-183 (13 yrs.)**
ASSISTANTS .... **Calvin Cochran**
Davis Oness
Joe Proctor
TEAM WINS (last 5 yrs.) **19-11-9-8-11**
RPI (last 5 yrs.) **191-262-295-281-287**
1997-98 FINISH .... **Lost in conference semifinal.**

Looking for a darkhorse in the Southwestern Athletic Conference? Then look no further than Alabama State, which is the only current SWAC member that has not won either a regular-season or tournament championship.

The Hornets return all five starters and could contend for their first upper-division finish since the 1993-94 team ended in third place, two games behind regular-season champion Texas Southern and one game behind runner-up Jackson State.

"We only lost two players from last year's team, so we will have experience on our side," coach Rob Spivery said. "**Jasaun Moncrief** led us through the SWAC Tournament, so he will already be battle-tested. We return all five starters plus most of our bench. I'm expecting good things from this team."

The Hornets showed tremendous improvement in Spivery's second season, splitting their first eight games and losing to eventual champion Prairie View in the second round of the SWAC Tournament. They ranked first among the nine conference teams in three-point percentage (.359) and rebounding margin (plus-1.7), third in scoring defense (73.7) and field-goal percentage (.445), fifth in free-throw percentage (.627), sixth in scoring margin (minus-5.4) and eighth in scoring offense (68.4).

Alabama State's returning starters are Moncrief, the 5-9 senior guard (7.9 ppg, 2.1 rpg, 64 assists, 36 steals), 6-1 sophomore guard **Tobarie Burton** (5.4 ppg, 2.7 rpg, 48 assists, 47 steals), 6-4 senior forward **Corey Williams** (14.4 ppg, 5.5 rpg, 50 steals, 45 assists), 6-6 senior forward **Courtney Stephens** (7.3 ppg, 4.3 rpg, 28 steals, 25 assists) and 6-7 junior center **Terrence Simmons** (13.0 ppg, 7.3 rpg, 17 steals).

Simmons ranked fifth in the SWAC in rebounds and sixth in field-goal percentage and Williams ranked seventh in scoring and ninth in steals. Moncrief, a Kent transfer who ranked fourth in free-throw percentage, directed the Hornets after starter Richard Mason left the team 18 games into the season.

Alabama State's other returning players are 6-8 senior center **Muhammad Sisay** (2.5 ppg, 4.2 rpg), 6-9 sophomore center **Jeffrey Thomas** (2.7 ppg, 2.0 rpg), 6-7 junior forward **Milton Brownlee** (2.3 ppg, 1.9 rpg) and 6-3 sophomore forward **Dupree McKenzie** (2.2 ppg, 1.0 rpg).

The Hornets added four players, including three forwards. Their newcomers are 6-2 freshman guard **Joey Ball**, 6-5 freshman forward **Tyrone Levett**, 6-6 freshman forward **Richard Milsaps** and 6-9 freshman forward **Alvin Pettway**.

"I believe that we've brought in some top quality student-athletes," Spivery said. "In Joey Ball and Alvin Pettway, you have two players that represented Alabama in the Alabama-Mississippi All-Star game. Pettway and Tyrone Levett are two of the top players in the country, not just in the state. In Richard Millsaps, we get a player who can play two or three positions."

Once again, Alabama State will be challenged by a schedule that features five opponents who participated in the NCAA Tournament last season. The Hornets' non-conference schedule includes home games against DePaul, Illinois-Chicago and Murray State and road games against Southeastern Conference members Mississippi, Arkansas and Alabama.

1998-99 ALABAMA STATE SCHEDULE

Nov.	13	@Mississippi
	17	@Arkansas
	22	DePaul
	30	Illinois-Chicago
Dec	5	Montevallo
	8	@Alabama
	12	Murray State
	19	Jackson State
	21	Grambling
Jan.	2	@Arkansas-Pine Bluff
	4	@Mississippi Valley State
	9	@Alabama A&M
	12	Auburn-Montgomery
	16	Southern
	18	Alcorn State
	23	@Prarie View A&M
	25	@Texas Southern
	30	Arkansas-Pine Bluff
Feb.	1	Mississippi Valley State
	6	Alabama A&M
	13	@Southern
	15	@Alcorn State
	20	Prarie View A&M
	22	Texas Southern
	25	@Jackson State
	27	@Grambling
Mar.	3-6	#SWAC Tournament

@ Road Games
\# Dallas Convention Center, Dallas, TX

adidas Blue Ribbon Analysis

BACKCOURT	**B**	**BENCH/DEPTH**	**C**
FRONTCOURT	**B**	**INTANGIBLES**	**C**

Without a doubt, this could be Spivery's best team.

Alabama State needed name tags last season for a roster that featured nine new players, including five junior-college transfers. If the final month, when Moncrief took over for Mason, was any indication, the Hornets could be one of the teams to watch this season. The adage a year older, a year wiser definitely applies to this team.

It would come as little surprise if Alabama State challenged such teams as Alcorn State, Grambling State, Southern and Texas Southern for the championship.

(S.G.)

ALCORN STATE

LOCATION .... **Lorman, MS**
CONFERENCE .... **Southwestern Athletic (SWAC)**
LAST SEASON .... **12-15 (.444)**
CONFERENCE RECORD .... **8-8 (5th)**
STARTERS LOST/RETURNING **2/3**
NICKNAME .... **Braves**
COLORS .... **Purple & Old Gold**
HOMECOURT .... **Davey Whitney Complex (7,000)**
COACH .... **Davey Whitney (Kentucky State '53)**
RECORD AT SCHOOL .... **418-232 (22 yrs.)**
CAREER RECORD .... **472-295 (27 yrs.)**
ASSISTANTS .... **Sam West (Texas Southern '77)**
TEAM WINS (last 5 yrs.) **3-7-10-11-12**
RPI (last 5 yrs.) **295-295-267-247-269**
1997-98 FINISH .... **Lost in conference quarterfinal.**

Time is running out for Davey Whitney, who led Alcorn State to eight Southwestern Athletic Conference regular-season championships from 1969-89.

He returned to the Braves in 1996-97, promising to turn around the once-proud program in short order before leaving it with a hand-picked successor.

This could be Whitney's do-or-die season. Alcorn State returns seven players from last year's team, which was picked to challenge for the school's first championship since '85-86, but never recovered after losing three of its first four SWAC games.

"We will be in the thick of the race for the conference championship," he said. "We have a little more depth and the quality of players on the roster will make up a better squad."

The Braves have increased their victory total in the last five seasons, from three in 1993-94 to 12 in '97-98. They ranked second in the SWAC in field-goal percentage (.454) and rebounding margin (plus-0.4), third in scoring offense (73.9) and three-point percentage (.334), fourth in scoring defense (75.6), fifth in scoring margin (minus-1.6) and sixth in free-throw percentage (.617).

"If they can acquire another level of maturity and can continue to want to work hard," Whitney said, "we can be very successful. We will not really know until the opening tip."

Alcorn State's returning starters are 5-foot-11 senior guard **Reuben Stiff** (11.9 ppg, 3.5 rpg, 151 assists, 55 steals), 6-6 junior forward **Brian Adams** (11.1 ppg, 5.4 rpg, 35 assists, 24 steals, 13 blocks) and 6-10 senior center **Orko Guyton** (7.8 ppg, 5.7 rpg, 29 steals, 29 blocks, 25 assists).

Stiff, arguably the conference's best player under 6-feet, ranked second in assists and third in steals. Guyton ranked fourth in field-goal percentage and ninth in blocked shots and Adams ranked eighth in field-goal percentage.

"Guard play is one of our chief areas of concern," Whitney said. "We must have good guard play for this team to reach its potential."

Other returning players are 6-5 junior forward **Terrance Cameron** (8.0 ppg, 4.1 rpg, 20 steals, 14 assists), 6-0 sophomore guard **Devon Pack** (1.2 ppg, 0.4 rpg), 6-5 sophomore forward **Howard Newkirk** (0.9 ppg, 1.2 rpg) and 6-4 sophomore guard **John Jobe** (0.8 ppg, 0.0 rpg).

Alcorn State landed four guards, four forwards and one center in one of the SWAC's largest recruiting hauls. The newcomers are 5-11 junior guard **Tremaine Chambers**, 6-3 junior guard **Wallace Harris**, 6-4 junior guard **Donald Flemming**, 6-5 freshman guard **Toir Harris**, 6-4 freshman forward **Jason Cable**, 6-4 freshman forward **Jason Griggs**, 6-6 senior forward **Keldrick Brown**, 6-8 junior forward **Marcus Flemming** and 6-8 freshman center Walter Harper.

The Braves will be tested early in a preconference schedule that includes road games against Alabama-Birmingham, Illinois State, SMU, Oregon and Wyoming and a home game against South Alabama in the Davey Whitney Complex.

Interestingly, the Braves are one of three schools currently playing in an arena named for the current head coach (UTEP and the College of Charleston are the others).

1998-99 ALCORN STATE SCHEDULE

Nov.	14	@UAB
	18	South Alabama
	23	Texas Southern
	25	Prairie View A&M
Dec.	2	@Illinois State
	5	@Southern Methodist
	12	Tougaloo
	19	@Oregon
	22	@Wyoming
	28	@Indiana/Purdue-Indianapolis
Jan	2	@Jackson State
	4	@Grambling
	9	Mississippi Valley State
	11	Arkansas-Pine Bluff
	16	@Alabama A&M
	18	@Alabama State
	23	Southern
	30	Jackson State
Feb.	1	Grambling
	6	@Mississippi Valley State
	8	@Arkansas-Pine Bluff
	13	Alabama A&M
	15	Alabama State
	20	@Southern
	25	@Texas Southern
	27	@Prairie View A&M
Mar.	3-6	#SWAC Tournament

@ Road Games
# Dallas Convention Center, Dallas, TX

"Some people feel that the crowd acts as the sixth man on the court at all times," Whitney said. "When they are alive, they provide much-needed support and poise for us."

adidas Blue Ribbon Analysis

BACKCOURT	B	BENCH/DEPTH	B
FRONTCOURT	C	INTANGIBLES	B

Whitney smiled when asked if he was excited about the possibilities of this year's team.

"Yes I am," he said.

And with good reason. The Braves have three key ingredients already in place. Stiff is one of the best point guards in a guard-oriented league, Adams is a versatile forward who has yet to experience a breakthrough season and Guyton is one of the league's tallest players.

Whitney is the wild card. Known as "The Wiz" because of his teams' incredible feats against tough competition, he has taken Alcorn State to 11 postseason appearances and his 1979-80 team became the first from a historically black school to compete in the NCAA Tournament. If anyone can get his team to reach its potential, it is Whitney. And this team is loaded with potential.

(S.G.)

ARKANSAS-PINE BLUFF

LOCATION	**Pine Bluff, AR**
CONFERENCE	**Southwestern Athletic (SWAC)**
LAST SEASON	**4-23 (.148)**
CONFERENCE RECORD	**3-13 (9th)**
STARTERS LOST/RETURNING	**1/4**
NICKNAME	**Golden Lions**
COLORS	**Black & Gold**
HOMECOURT	**Health & Phys Ed Recreation Complex (4,500)**
COACH	**Harold Blevins (Arkansas-Pine Bluff '65)**
RECORD AT SCHOOL	**23-51 (3 yrs.)**
CAREER RECORD	**23-51 (3 yrs.)**
ASSISTANTS	**Van Holt**
TEAM WINS (last 5 yrs.)	**N/A-N/A-9-10-4**
RPI (last 5 yrs.)	**N/A**
1997-98 FINISH	**Ineligible for postseason.**

No doubt Arkansas-Pine Bluff's second season in NCAA Division I was one that coach Harold Blevins would rather forget. The Golden Lions were one of the nation's worst teams last season, winning just four games, with losing streaks of 10 games from late November to early January and eight games from late January to late February.

Arkansas-Pine Bluff competed as an affiliate member of the SWAC, meaning its games counted in the standings even though the Golden Lions were ineligible for the regular-season championship and postseason tournament.

"One of our biggest problems last year was playing hard throughout the duration of a game," Blevins said. "We played well for a half on several occasions, only to give the game away in the second half. We have to get better at playing 40 minutes of solid basketball. Hopefully the lessons learned last season will do that."

There is good news and bad news on Arkansas-Pine Bluff's roster. The good news is that the Golden Lions return four starters. The bad news is that they must replace forward Fred Luckett, who led the team in scoring (14.1) and rebounding (8.0).

They ranked sixth among nine SWAC teams in scoring defense (78.0), eighth in field-goal percentage (.392) and three-point percentage (.280) and ninth in scoring offense (64.7), scoring margin (minus-13.3), free-throw percentage (minus-6.2) and rebounding margin (minus-6.2).

Arkansas-Pine Bluff's returning starters are 5-foot-7 junior guard **Antonio Moore** (1.8 ppg, 2.1 rpg, 68 assists, 52 steals), 6-3 sophomore guard **Derion Gipson** (2.4 ppg, 1.0 rpg, 31 assists, 14 steals), 6-6 senior forward **Patrick Chambers** (13.7 ppg, 7.5 rpg, 45 steals, 29 assists, 28 blocks) and 6-7 senior forward **Terrance Duncan** (9.3 ppg, 3.9 rpg, 27 assists, 22 steals, 13 blocks).

Chambers was one of the rare bright spots, ranking first in field-goal percentage and fourth in rebounds, eighth in blocks and ninth in scoring. Moore ranked fifth in steals.

The Golden Lions' other returning players are 5-11 junior guard **Damon Horton** (6.4 ppg, 1.3 rpg, 39 assists, 16 steals); 6-0 sophomore guard **Marcus Swygart** (2.5 ppg, 0.9 rpg); 6-1 junior guard **Dwayne Stephens** (0.9 ppg, 0.7 rpg); 6-4 junior guard **Vincent Callaway** (1.9 ppg, 0.8 rpg); 6-4 junior forward **Calvis Craig** (0.8 ppg, 0.4 rpg); 6-5 junior forward **Shawn Eldridge** (4.1 ppg, 3.9 rpg); 6-5 sophomore forward **Troy Brown** (2.7 ppg, 1.1 rpg); and 6-5 sophomore forward **Effrence Smith** (1.3 ppg, 0.6 rpg).

"This will be an important season for our program," Blevins said. "We have to forget about last season and concentrate on what we need to do in order to be successful in the SWAC. I think we'll be competitive in the conference. We're playing a tough nonconference schedule and that should help us prepare for the always-tough schedule against our conference opponents."

Arkansas-Pine Bluff added just two guards and one center from its recruiting class. The Golden Lions' newcomers are 6-2 freshman guard **Jermaine Rollins**, 6-3 freshman guard **Melvin O'Neil** and 6-8 junior center **Kristopher Landers**.

Arkansas-Pine Bluff will be sorely tested by a preconference schedule that includes road games against Clemson, Mississippi State, Memphis, New Mexico, Oregon State and Missouri.

adidas Blue Ribbon Analysis

BACKCOURT	D	BENCH/DEPTH	D
FRONTCOURT	D	INTANGIBLES	D

This is a team full of question marks.

Can Arkansas-Pine Bluff improve on last year? Are the returning players talented enough to compete on a nightly basis in the SWAC? Will they have any confidence left after the treacherous nonconference schedule? All things con-

1998-99 ARKANSAS-PINE BLUFF SCHEDULE

Nov.	13	@Clemson
	17	@Mississippi State
	21	*Arkansas-Little Rock
	30	@Memphis
Dec.	2	@New Mexico
	4	@Oregon State
	7	Mississippi Valley State
	9	@University of Missouri
Jan.	2	Alabama State
	4	Alabama A&M
	9	@Southern
	11	@Alcorn State
	16	Texas Southern
	18	Prairie View A&M
	23	@Grambling
	25	@Jackson State
	30	@Alabama State
Feb.	1	@Alabama A&M
	3	@Philander Smith
	6	Southern
	8	Alcorn State
	13	@Texas Southern
	15	@Prairie View A&M
	20	Grambling
	22	Jackson State
	24	Philander Smith
	27	@Mississippi Valley State
Mar.	3-6	#SWAC Tournament

@ Road Games
* Pine Bluff Convention Center, Pine Bluff, AR
# Dallas Convention Center, Dallas, TX

adidas Blue Ribbon Analysis
GRADING SYSTEM

A+	equal to very best in country—Final Four-caliber unit
A	among the best in the land—worthy of deep NCAA run
B+	talented, versatile and experienced—NCAA-NIT ability
B	solid and productive winners—league and post-season contenders
C+	average to above-average—may contend in a weaker league
C	average to mediocre—second division in a strong league
D+	below average, inconsistent—second division in a weaker league
D	well below average—losing season virtually certain
F	non-Division I ability—an underdog every night

sidered, the Golden Lions are several years away from making noise in the SWAC. Until they do, single digits in the victory column will be the rule rather than the exception.

(S.G.)

GRAMBLING

LOCATION .... **Grambling, LA**
CONFERENCE .... **Southwestern Athletic (SWAC)**
LAST SEASON .... **16-12 (.571)**
CONFERENCE RECORD .... **10-6 (t-3rd)**
STARTERS LOST/RETURNING **2/3**
NICKNAME .... **Tigers**
COLORS .... **Black, Red & Gold**
HOMECOURT .... **Memorial Gymnasium (2,648)**
COACH.. Lacey Reynolds (Mississippi Industrial '74)
RECORD AT SCHOOL .... **38-45 (3 yrs.)**
CAREER RECORD .... **38-45 (3 yrs.)**
ASSISTANTS .... **Brian Brooks**
Scott Monarch
TEAM WINS (last 5 yrs.) **9-11-12-10-16**
RPI (last 5 yrs.) **293-290-269-282-230**
1997-98 FINISH .... **Lost in conference quarterfinal.**

Grambling State coach Lacey Reynolds vowed that his team would not finish last in the Southwestern Athletic Conference last season. Sure enough, not only did the Tigers defy the oddsmakers who had relegated them to the basement, they shared third place with Southern for their first upper-division finish since 1988-89.

Grambling lost three of its first four conference games before climbing into contention with a five-game winning streak in January and a four-game winning streak in February.

"I think it should be an interesting conference race this season," Reynolds said. "I'm certain that a lot of schools are coming back with a lot of zeal and enthusiasm. I don't know if we can make a dent in the SWAC race or not. We just want to line up and go play—we're still dreamers at this point.

"I like the direction in which this program is headed. We're capable of competing with anyone if we can stay away from injuries. This is a 10-team league this season, so hopefully we'll finish higher than 10th."

The Tigers return three starters from last season's team, which finished 16-12 overall and 10-6 in the conference. They ranked first in free-throw percentage (.686), second in scoring defense (73.5), fourth in scoring margin (minus-1.0), field-goal percentage (.445) and rebounding margin (minus-0.6) and fifth in scoring offense (72.5) and three-point percentage (.305).

"We had a mixture of young and old players," Reynolds said. "We thought we had a chance. Watching the kids work early and seeing their work ethic, you get a sense of how good the team could be. Being picked last gave us something to fight for. We had to prove ourselves every game, but we would haved liked to have reached the championship circle."

Grambling's returning starters are 6-foot-1 senior guard **Kenneth Haynes** (13.1 ppg, 4.5 rpg, 130 assists, 75 steals), 6-7 junior forward **Chris Thomas** (13.4 ppg, 6.5 rpg) and 6-10 senior center **Thomas Dodd** (11.8 ppg, 6.3 rpg, 48 assists, 38 blocked shots, 16 steals).

All three of the Tigers' returning starters boast legitimate all-conference credentials. Haynes led the SWAC in steals and ranked third in assists and free throw percentage. He was 18th in the nation in steals.

Thomas ranked 16th in the nation in field-goal percentage (.598) and was ninth in the SWAC in rebounding. Dodd was right behind at10th in rebounding.

Grambling's other returning players are 6-3 sophomore guard **Quadree Drakeford** (3.1 ppg, 1.3 rpg); 6-5 senior forward **Kala Bragg** (1.6 ppg, 1.7 rpg); 6-6 junior forward **Brandon Thomas** (1.7 ppg, 1.2 rpg); 6-7 sophomore forward **Devin Ewing** (1.4 ppg, 0.7 rpg); 6-8 sophomore forward **Royal Maxwell** (1.2 ppg, 0.8 rpg); and 6-8 senior center **Mario Hinds** (2.0 ppg, 1.8 rpg).

"I feel good about this group," Reynolds said. "They tasted success. The guys are working really hard. They have to represent themselves. They have to prove last year isn't a fluke. We have all the guys focused. They're on the right page. We're trying to move up. I think we're competitive. We're growing. I like the direction of the program.

"It all depends on how much they learned from last season from always being the underdog and fighting hard to prove themselves. They have to bring back some of the tenacity. I'm excited."

The Tigers signed three forwards and two guards. Their newcomers are 6-2 freshman guard **Jimmy Lawson**, 6-4 freshman guard **Sean Jackson**, 6-5 junior forward **Geramie Wilson**, 6-5 freshman forward **Dion Smith** and 6-7 junior forward **Charley Bass**.

Grambling plays a highly competitive preconference schedule that includes road games against Georgetown and St. Louis as well as tournaments at Indiana and Texas-El Paso.

"We're playing an all-Division I nonconference schedule with some tough games," Reynolds said. "It's hard to say how we'll do. If we survive that and learn from the experience, it may help us during our conference season. We're trying to put a good product on the floor. Playing good teams makes us better. The guys are on a mission. Something good could happen for us."

adidas Blue Ribbon Analysis

BACKCOURT	**B**	**BENCH/DEPTH**	**C**
FRONTCOURT	**B**	**INTANGIBLES**	**B**

Grambling has not won the SWAC championship since 1988-89, when it shared the title with Southern and Texas Southern. These Tigers are loaded. Haynes, Chris Thomas and Dodd are three of the best players at their positions in the conference. This team has made steady improvement under Reynolds, reaching new heights last season with a third-place tie.

The only surprise this season would be if Grambling doesn't challenge for the regular-season and tournament championships.

(S.G)

1998-99 GRAMBLING SCHEDULE

Nov.	17	@Southeastern Louisiana
	21	@Georgetown
	24	Northwestern Louisiana
Dec.	5	@St. Louis
	11-12	#Indiana Classic
	19	@Alabama A&M
	21	@Alabama State
	28-29	##Sun Classic
Jan.	2	Southern
	4	Alcorn State
	9	@Prarie View A&M
	11	@Texas Southern
	16	Jackson State
	23	Arkansas-Pine Bluff
	25	Mississippi Valley State
	30	@Southern
Feb.	1	@Alcorn State
	6	@Prarie View A&M
	8	@Texas Southern
	13	@Jackson State
	20	@Arkansas-Pine Bluff
	22	@Mississippi Valley State
	25	Alabama A&M
	27	Alabama State
Mar.	4-7	###SWAC Tournament

@ Road Games
# Bloomington, IN (vs. Bowling Green, first round; also Boise State and Indiana)
El Paso, TX (vs. Detroit, first round; also UTEP and Washington State)
Dallas Convention Center, Dallas, TX

JACKSON STATE

LOCATION .... **Jackson, MS**
CONFERENCE .... **Southwestern Athletic (SWAC)**
LAST SEASON .... **14-13 (.519)**
CONFERENCE RECORD .... **11-5 (2nd)**
STARTERS LOST/RETURNING **5/0**
NICKNAME .... **Tigers**
COLORS .... **Royal Blue & White**
HOMECOURT Williams Athletics & Assembly Center (8,000)
COACH .... **Andy Stoglin (UTEP '65)**
RECORD AT SCHOOL .... **138-128 (9 yrs.)**
CAREER RECORD .... **171-152 (11 yrs.)**
ASSISTANTS .... **Chris Giles (UAB '82)**
Travis Gordon (Jackson State '96)
Eric Strothers (Jackson State '92)
TEAM WINS (last 5 yrs.) **25-19-12-16-14**
RPI (last 5 yrs.) **160-226-168-200-227**
1997-98 FINISH .... **Lost in conference quarterfinal.**

1998-99 JACKSON STATE SCHEDULE

Nov.	13	@Missouri
	15	@Arkansas
	18	@Tulsa
	21	Tougaloo
	24	@UTEP
	30	@McNeese State
Dec.	3	@Southern Mississippi
	8	@Memphis
	12	@LSU
	19	@Alabama State
	21	@Alabama A&M
Jan.	2	Alcorn State
	4	Southern
	9	@Texas Southern
	11	@Prairie View A&M
	16	@Grambling State
	23	Mississippi Valley State
	25	Arkansas-Pine Bluff
	30	@Alcorn State
Feb.	1	@Southern
	6	Texas Southern
	8	Prairie View A&M
	13	Grambling
	20	@Mississippi Valley State
	22	@Arkansas-Pine Bluff
	25	Alabama State
	27	Alabama A&M
Mar.	3-6	#SWAC Tournament

@ Road Games
# Dallas Convention Center, Dallas, TX

Give Jackson State coach Andy Stoglin credit. What does he do to prepare one of the most inexperienced teams during his career? Why, he goes to Mexico of course.

Stoglin took his Tigers south of the border during the summer for an international tour that was designed to develop the chemistry of a team that features no returning starters, nine returning players and nine newcomers.

"Our trip to Mexico helped us out tremendously," he said. "We played against a Mexican national team, which is equal to our NBA. The team competed well against the other teams. Out of the six games we played, I believe my guys had a chance to win three of those games. I was really pleased with the player's spirits because they didn't give up."

Jackson State started slowly last season, winning three of 10 nonconference games in a brutal schedule that included road games at Oklahoma, Arkansas, Southern Miss, Memphis, LSU, Oklahoma State and UAB.

The Tigers finished strong with four straight victories to end the regular season, but lost in the first round of the SWAC Tournament to eventual champion Prairie View and ended the season 14-13 overall and 11-5 in conference play.

They ranked first in scoring defense (67.9), second in scoring margin (plus-2.0), third in free-throw percentage (.653) and rebounding margin (minus-0.4), fifth in field-goal percentage (.416), sixth in three-point percentage (.291) and seventh in scoring offense (69.9).

Jackson State's starting lineup of senior guards Michael Hall and DeCarto Draper, senior forwards Trent Pulliam and Doug Williams and senior center Robert Fairley combined for 47.9 points and 22.4 rebounds. That's a lot of production to be replaced.

"This year's team is different from last year's team," Stoglin said. "Last year our team had a lot more experience. Six of our seniors were starters. Out of those six players, four were starters for four years. "This year we have some talented players. They are very coachable.

"Their talent will make up for their inexperience. What makes this team unique is the abundance of talent. If one player fails to pull his weight, there is another player ready to take his place."

The Tigers' returning players are 6-foot-1 sophomore guard **Eric Large** (0.5 ppg, 0.7 rpg); 6-2 senior guard **Terry Bradley** (0.7 ppg, 0.4 rpg); 6-2 junior guard **Timmy Marks** (3.5 ppg, 1.2 rpg); 6-3 junior guard **Marino Walker** (1.7 ppg, 0.9 rpg); 6-4 junior guard **Roy Dixon** (4.0 ppg, 1.4 rpg); 6-4 sophomore forward **Richard Bradley** (5.1 ppg, 3.2 rpg); 6-7 senior forward **Fidel Woods** (1.6 ppg, 2.0 rpg); 6-8 senior center **Brad Collier** (1.3 ppg, 1.8 rpg); and

6-11 junior center **Vincent Jones** (3.5 ppg, 2.9 rpg).

Of that group, only three players started at least one game. Walker started in four of 27 games, Richard Bradley one of 26 games and Terry Bradley one of 20 games.

"Although we lost five starters, this year's team will be an exciting group to watch," Stoglin said. "We may be young, but there is so much talent on this team. This is the first team I have been truly excited about since Lindsey Hunter's senior year (1992-93). Once this year's team learns how to use their talents, we should have a very successful season."

Jackson State's newcomers features five guards, three forwards and one center. The new Tigers are 5-10 junior guard **Willie Gross**, 5-11 freshman guard **Lawrence Myers**, 6-0 junior guard **Jamari Francis**, 6-3 senior guard **Antwan McAfee**, 6-5 freshman guard **Perry Fletcher**, 6-6 junior forward **Deon Burns**, 6-7 senior forward **Joseph McKinney** 6-9 freshman forward **Brian Nicholls** and 7-0 junior center **Darren Robinson**.

This young team will be sorely tested by another one of Stoglin's difficult preseason schedules. Jackson State's nonconference schedule includes road games against Missouri, Arkansas, Tulsa, UTEP, Memphis and LSU.

"The players to watch this year will be Richard Bradley, Deon Burns, Darren Robinson and Marino Walker," Stoglin said. "However, these are not the only players to watch. We have an abundance of talent. I believe this year's players are equally talented. All of the players will stand out this year because they are young and talented.

"I think we have a legitimate chance to finish in the top four this year. I believe we will fare well against the other teams in this league. By being a young team, we will be a team to watch."

adidas Blue Ribbon Analysis

BACKCOURT .... **C** **BENCH/DEPTH** .... **B**
FRONTCOURT .... **C** **INTANGIBLES** .... **B**

As Stoglin said, this could be a team to watch simply because no one knows quite what to expect.

Taking his team on an international trip during the summer was a good move. At least the team has some idea of what it can do, even if opposing teams do not.

SWAC teams may have to wait until home games against Alcorn State and Southern in early January before knowing if these are just paper Tigers.

(S.G.)

MISSISSIPPI VALLEY STATE

LOCATION .... **Itta Bena, MS**
CONFERENCE .... **Southwestern Athletic (SWAC)**
LAST SEASON .... **6-21 (.222)**
CONFERENCE RECORD .... **6-10 (t-6th)**
STARTERS LOST/RETURNING **5/0**
NICKNAME .... **Delta Devils**
COLORS .... **Green & White**
HOMECOURT .... **Harrison Health Complex (6,000)**
COACH .... **Lafayette Stribling (Mississippi Industrial '57)**
RECORD AT SCHOOL .... **216-222 (14 yrs.)**
CAREER RECORD .... **216-222 (14 yrs.)**
ASSISTANTS .... **Ira Peterson (Mississippi State)**
Harvey Wardell (Alcorn State '69)
TEAM WINS (last 5 yrs.) **10-17-22-19-6**
RPI (last 5 yrs.) **273-23-144-189-298**
1997-98 FINISH .... **Lost in conference quarterfinal.**

Mississippi Valley State was one of the most disappointing teams in the Southwestern Athletic Conference last season. Picked to challenge for their fifth regular-season or tournament championship of the 1990s, the Delta Devils never recovered after losing their first 10 games.

They won back-to-back games just twice and finished 6-21 overall and 6-10 in the SWAC, their worst records in 14 seasons under coach Lafayette Stribling. Things don't look much brighter this season for Mississippi Valley, which must replace six lettermen and all five starters from last year. One of those starters is 6-6 Kenyon Ross, who was 10th in the country in rebounding (10.8 per game)

"We'll be a young team," Stribling said. "We definitely will be in the rebuilding stage. As the season goes, we'll get better, but not a threat to win the championship."

1998-99 MISSISSIPPI VALLEY STATE SCHEDULE

Nov.	16	Jacksonville State
	19	Talledega College
	30	@Toledo
Dec.	2	@Kansas State
	7	@Arkansas-Pine Bluff
	10	@Southern Mississippi
	22	@Creighton
	29-30	#Cessna Classic
Jan	2	Alabama A&M
	4	Alabama State
	9	@Alcorn State
	11	@Southern
	16	Prarie View A&M
	18	Texas Southern
	23	@Jackson State
	25	@Grambling State
	30	Alabama A&M
Feb.	1	@Alabama State
	6	Alcorn State
	8	Southern
	13	@Prarie View A&M
	15	@Texas Southern
	20	Jackson State
	22	Grambling State
	27	Arkansas-Pine Bluff
Mar.	3-6	##SWAC Tournament

@ Road Games
\# Wichita, KS (vs. Western Illinois, first round; also Mercer and Wichita State)
\## Dallas Convention Center, Dallas, TX

The Delta Devils ranked fourth among the nine conference teams in scoring offense (73.7), fifth in rebounding margin (minus-0.9), seventh in three-point percentage (.284), eighth in scoring margin (minus-8.5) and free-throw percentage (.580) and ninth in field-goal percentage (.370). To make matters worse, their four returning players from last season combined for just 17 starts, 14.1 points and 8.0 rebounds as freshmen.

"Last year's team was quicker and more experienced," Stribling said. "This team will be talented but does not have enough experience to win big. We'll have more depth and more size. We are excited about this young team. We'll have to play hard every night in order to be competitive."

Mississippi Valley's returning players are 6-foot-2 sophomore guard **Tyson Rivels** (6.2 ppg, 2.4 rpg, 17 assists, 14 steals); 5-11 sophomore guard **Eltra Leigh** (3.9 ppg, 1.1 rpg, 36 assists, 22 steals); sophomore forward **LaDarryl Campbell** (2.5 ppg, 1.1 rpg); and 6-10 sophomore center **Derrick McInnis** (1.5 ppg, 3.4 rpg, 27 blocks).

Rivels, who played in 24 games and started three, made 49 of 173 field goals overall, 31 of 109 from three-point range. Leigh, who played in 22 games and started none, made 39 of 126 field goals overall and 24 of 71 from three-point range. Campbell played in all 27 games and started three and McInnis played in 24 games and started seven.

In addition, the Delta Devils welcome back 6-3 junior **Faragi Phillips**, who missed all of last season. Phillips averaged 12.2 points and 2.9 steals with 43 assists and 31 steals in 1996-97 and is being touted for all-conference honors.

"Hopefully this team will showcase talent at the guard position," Stribling said. "We should have a good outside game because our guards should be our strength. We should be able to handle any test the opponents put before us.

"In the past, we've led the league in rebounding, but a lack of experience inside will slow us from regaining our rebounding title. Our inside game will suffer from the lack of experience. Defensively and offensively, our speed will be in question from our big people."

Mississippi Valley's newcomers are 5-9 freshman guard **Ashley Robinson**, 6-0 junior guard **Marcus Metcalf**, 6-1 junior guard **Johnny Dotson**, 6-2 junior forward **Michael Blivens**, 6-3 freshman forward **James Nelson** and 6-10 sophomore center **Henry Jordan**.

The Delta Devils have another difficult preconference game with road games against Toledo, Kansas State, Southern Mississippi and Creighton. "We will have to be patient and let the new players learn the system and blend with the old players," Stribling said. "With the players we have recruited, we shouldn't have any problem being able to score. If one of our recruits can step in and help us, we will be a better team."

adidas Blue Ribbon Analysis

BACKCOURT .... **C** **BENCH/DEPTH** .... **D**
FRONTCOURT .... **D** **INTANGIBLES** .... **C**

This could be another long season for Mississippi Valley. Simply put, the Delta Devils don't have enough talent or experience to compete on a nightly basis with such teams as Alabama State, Alcorn State, Grambling State, Southern and Texas Southern. In fact, they are so inexperienced that a last-place finish is not out of the question. Phillips has been through the SWAC wars before, but he alone can't lift this team to greater heights. None of the other returning players know how to win.

Mississippi Valley will have to learn that lesson before it expects to challenge for the upper division.

(S.G.)

PRAIRIE VIEW A&M

LOCATION .... **Prairie View, TX**
CONFERENCE .... **Southwestern Athletic (SWAC)**
LAST SEASON .... **13-17 (.433)**
CONFERENCE RECORD .... **6-10 (t-6th)**
STARTERS LOST/RETURNING **1/4**
NICKNAME .... **Panthers**
COLORS .... **Purple & Gold**
HOMECOURT .... **Billy Nicks Building/Baby Dome (5,000)**
COACH .... **Elwood Plummer (Wiley College '72)**
RECORD AT SCHOOL .... **134-173 (14 yrs.)**
CAREER RECORD .... **310-379 (24 yrs.)**
ASSISTANTS .... **Ed Phillips (Alabama A&M '73)**
Robert Vanderbilt (Wiley College '72)
TEAM WINS (last 5 yrs.) **5-6-4-10-13**
RPI (last 5 yrs.) **299-301-202-278-252**
1997-98 FINISH .... **Lost in NCAA first round.**

The Panthers' postseason appearance was the crowning moment for a program that lost all 28 games in 1991-92 and 27 of 28 games in '92-93. Only one starter returns for Prairie View, which rallied from a 20-point deficit in the Southwestern Athletic Conference Tournament final to become only the 14th team to reach the NCAA field with a losing record.

"Our biggest concern will be that we have nine freshmen on our roster," Panthers coach Elwood Plummer said. "So I'd have to say that a lack of experience may be our greatest enemy. I think our young guys will have to grow quickly. If they can mature and we can gel together, we will be in pretty good shape."

Prairie View finished 13-16 overall and 6-10 in the SWAC with a team that featured seven seniors who combined for 55.5 points and 24.2 rebounds.

The Panthers ranked fifth among the nine conference teams in scoring offense (72.5), seventh in scoring defense (80.1), scoring margin (minus-7.6), field-goal percentage (.397) and free-throw percentage (.602), eighth in rebounding margin (minus-5.4) and ninth in three-point percentage (.267).

Prairie View's lone returning starter is 6-foot-8 junior center **Aron Thompson** (5.1 ppg, 4.5 rpg, 26 blocks, 22 steals).

The Panthers' other returning players are 5-8 senior guard **Sylvester Lilly** (1.6 ppg, 1.6 rpg); 6-2 senior guard **Decedric Giron** (1.6 ppg, 0.8 rpg); 6-4 senior guard **Jocquinn Arch** (7.0 ppg, 2.6 rpg); and 6-6 junior forward **Omari Taylor** (1.9 ppg, 2.4 rpg).

"Last year's team was more experienced because we had seven seniors and this year we'll have nine freshmen," Plummer said. "We'll be a much bigger team than last year, but I think last year's team was a little more experienced because of our senior leadership.

"If I had to put a difference between the two, the positive part was that our team last year was led by our seniors. We had four starters that were seniors, but this year we might have three freshmen who could start and possibly four."

Prairie View signed two-junior college transfers in 6-7 junior forward **Randall Williams** and 6-8 junior forward **Jermaine Johnson**. The Panthers also signed eight high school players in 6-3 guard **Jesse Bibbs**, 6-4 guard Jason Anderson, 6-4 guard **Patrick Willybiro**, 6-5 guard **Jason Ivey**, 6-5 forward **Keith Toney**, 6-7 forward **Terry Smith**, 6-9 center **Ivan Coulter** and 6-11 center **Landry Barnes**.

They will be challenged immediately by a schedule that includes road games against Tulane, Pittsburgh, LSU, Cleveland State, Wright State and Ole Miss. Two of its first four games are SWAC road contests against contenders Southern and Alcorn State.

"Our schedule is probably the same that it has been for the last two or three years even though we have a couple

1998-99 PRAIRIE VIEW A&M SCHEDULE

Nov.	17	Texas College
	19	@Tulane
	23	@Southern University
	25	@Alcorn State
Dec.	3	@Pittsburgh
	6	@Southwestern Adventist
	16	@Louisiana State
	19	@Cleveland State
	21	@Wright State
	29	@ Mississippi
Jan.	9	Grambling
	11	Jackson State
	16	@Mississippi Valley State
	18	@Arkansas-Pine Bluff
	23	Alabama State
	25	Alabama A&M
	30	@Texas Southern
Feb.	6	@Grambling
	8	@Jackson State
	13	Mississippi Valley State
	15	Arkansas-Pine Bluff
	20	@Alabama State
	22	@Alabama A&M
	25	Southern
	27	Alcorn State
Mar.	3-6	#SWAC Tournament

@ Road Games
# Dallas Convention Center, Dallas, TX

of new opponents," Plummer said. "The tough competition we have at the beginning of the season should help us tremendously when we get to conference play.

"Of course, we would like to win the SWAC just like everybody else, but if we could finish in the middle of the pack, then I would be very happy."

adidas Blue Ribbon Analysis

BACKCOURT .... D BENCH/DEPTH .... D
FRONTCOURT .... D INTANGIBLES C

There's little hope on the prairie one year after the Panthers made their first NCAA appearance.

Simply put, Prairie View has too many inexperienced players to challenge such veteran teams as Alabama State, Alcorn State, Grambling State, Southern and Texas Southern. If last season was considered a miracle by the Panthers' standards, it will take another one for them to finish higher than eighth place.

(S.G)

SOUTHERN

LOCATION .... Southern, LA
CONFERENCE .... Southwestern Athletic (SWAC)
LAST SEASON .... 14-13 (.519)
CONFERENCE RECORD 10-6 (t-3rd)
STARTERS LOST/RETURNING 2/3
NICKNAME .... Jaguars
COLORS .... Columbia Blue & Gold
HOMECOURT .... F.G. Clark Activity Center (7,500)
COACH .... Tommy Green (Southern '78)
RECORD AT SCHOOL .... 24-30 (2 yrs.)
CAREER RECORD .... 24-30 (2 yrs.)
ASSISTANTS .... Roman Banks (Northwestern'92)
TEAM WINS (last 5 yrs.) 16-13-18-10-14
RPI (last 5 yrs.) 220-286-201-299-280
1997-98 FINISH .... Lost in conference quarterfinal.

Will the real Southern Jaguars please stand up? Was it the team that won seven straight games from late January to mid-February by a whopping 26.0-point margin? Or was it the team that finished the season with six straight losses, including an embarrassing 23-point loss to underdog Alabama State in the first round of the Southwestern Athletic Conference Tournament?

Even Southern coach Tommy Green would like to know. "We just have to do a better job of finishing strong," he said. "If you can get out quick and maintain, you should be able to finish strong. We had nine new guys and they didn't really know what to expect. You have to be a mature bunch to know how to handle the situation. We're banking that we've learned from it."

Still, the Jaguars were one of the surprise teams in the SWAC last season, challenging for the regular-season championship despite being picked to finish in the lower division in Green's second year.

Southern ranked first among the nine conference teams—and sixth in the nation—in scoring offense (86.4), first in scoring margin (plus-6.1) and field-goal percentage (.457), second in three-point percentage (.343), seventh in rebounding margin (minus-2.9) and eighth in scoring defense (80.3).

The Jaguars could have one of the most balanced teams in the SWAC even though 10 of the 14 players on their roster can play either point guard or shooting guard.

"I think we have a great chance," Green said. "We have a great nucleus coming back. Any time you have 11 lettermen coming back, you have to like your chance. It's up to them to want to finish the season stronger."

Southern's returning starters are 6-2 senior guard **Kendrick Davis** (7.1 ppg, 2.0 rpg, 79 assists, 38 steals); 6-4 senior guard **Dionte Harvey** (18.7 ppg, 3.0 rpg, 55 steals, 41 assists); and 6-7 senior center-forward **Adarrial Smylie** (15.0 ppg, 8.6 rpg, 32 blocks, 29 steals, 20 assists).

Harvey and Smylie were first-team all-conference performers last season. Harvey ranked second in scoring, third in three-point percentage and fifth in free-throw percentage and Smylie ranked second in rebounds, sixth in blocked shots and free-throw percentage and 10th in field-goal percentage.

Harvey, Blue Ribbon's SWAC Preseason Player of the Year, also turned up in national statistics. He was 61st in the country in scoring and 31st in three-pointers per game (3.0).

The Jaguars also return 6-5 senior guard-forward **Aaron Bates** (11.2 ppg, 2.6 rpg, 25 steals, 19 assists); 6-0 sophomore guard **Devan Clark** (4.3 ppg, 1.4 rpg, 91 assists, 38 steals); 6-7 sophomore center-forward **Greg Martin** (8.0 ppg, 5.8 rpg, 20 steals, 11 blocks, 5 assists),;6-9 senior center-forward **Wesley Lamb** (2.1 ppg, 1.1 rpg); and 6-8 senior center **Chris Grant** (0.5 ppg, 0.8 rpg).

"They've worked real hard during the summer," Green said. "Adarrial should be a better player. He'll have a whole season under his belt rather than starting after the first semester. Dionte really has a taste for it. Last season was an experience for him. He may have worked the hardest of all during the offseason."

Southern's newcomers are 6-1 sophomore guard **Emmerine Womack**, 6-2 sophomore guard **Coy Landry**, 6-6 senior guard-forward **Keith Williams** and 6-7 freshman guard **Irving Richardson**.

The Jaguars' schedule features season-opening home games against SWAC rivals Texas Southern and Prairie View, road games against Georgia State, Cal Poly-San Luis Obispo and Rice and a home game against Texas A&M.

"Obviously we'd like to put ourselves in position to compete for the championship," Green said. "That's our main goal. Not only do we want to compete for the championship, but we want to be able to finish strong and win it as well.

1998-99 SOUTHERN SCHEDULE

Nov.	21	Texas Southern
	23	Prarie View A&M
Dec.	1	West Alabama
	5	Southeastern Louisiana
	10	@Georgia State
	15	@Cal Poly
	20	Rice University
	28	Texas A&M
Jan.	2	@Grambling
	4	@Jackson State
	9	Arkansas-Pine Bluff
	11	Mississippi Valley State
	16	@Alabama State
	18	@Alabama A&M
	23	@Alcorn State
	25	Texas College
	30	Grambling
Feb.	1	Jackson State
	6	@Arkansas-Pine Bluff
	8	@Mississippi Valley State
	13	Alabama State
	15	Alabama A&M
	20	Alcorn State
	25	@Prarie View A&M
	27	@Texas Southern
Mar.	3-6	#SWAC Tournament

@ Road Games
# Dallas Convention Center, Dallas,TX

"This team wants to have its own identity. It's already created an identity. It's just a matter of coming together and achieving it."

adidas Blue Ribbon Analysis

BACKCOURT .... B BENCH/DEPTH .... B
FRONTCOURT .... B INTANGIBLES .... B

Southern's late-season collapse remains a total mystery. How else to describe the finish of a talented team that sparked interest from one of the national tournaments?

It remains to be seen if this team learned from that experience. If so, the Jaguars could have their best team since 1992-93, when they last won the SWAC Tournament and advanced to the NCAA second round for the first time in school history.

Southern does have one big factor in its favor. The Jaguars boast a roster with experience and depth at every position. If Harvey and Smylie play to their potential, this could be a dangerous team from the first game to the last.

(S.G.)

TEXAS SOUTHERN

LOCATION .... Houston, TX
CONFERENCE .... Southwestern Athletic (SWAC)
LAST SEASON .... 15-16 (.484)
CONFERENCE RECORD 12-4 (1st)
STARTERS LOST/RETURNING 2/3
NICKNAME .... Tigers
COLORS .... Maroon & Gray
HOMECOURT .... Health & Physical Education Arena (7,500)
COACH .... Robert Moreland (Tougaloo '62)
RECORD AT SCHOOL .... 372-297 (23 yrs.)
CAREER RECORD .... 372-297 (23 yrs.)
ASSISTANTS .... Kevin Adams (Texas Southern '98)
Chris Parker (Abilene Christian)
Carlin Warley (St. Joseph's '91)
TEAM WINS (last 5 yrs.) 19-22-11-12-15
RPI (last 5 yrs.) 131-110-256-256-214
1997-98 FINISH .... Lost in conference final.

Texas Southern surprised some people last season after being picked to finish in fourth place. Instead, the Tigers rebounded from a horrendous start in which they lost their first eight games and ended with records of 15-16 overall and 12-4 in the SWAC.

"We won 15 out of our last 20 games," Texas Southern coach Robert Moreland said. "I was very pleased with the way we came back and did what we needed to do, especially in terms of our conference and our conference championship."

The Tigers ranked second in scoring offense (75.1) and free-throw percentage (.684), in winning their seventh regular-season or tournament championship. They finished third in scoring margin (minus-0.9), fourth in three-point percentage (.305), fifth in scoring defense (76.0) and sixth in field-goal percentage (.412) and rebounding margin (minus-2.0).

The Tigers do have some big holes to fill in the backcourt with the departure of All-SWAC guards Randy Bolden (19.9 ppg, 3.1 rpg, 68 assists, 34 steals) and Russell Evans (12.1 ppg, 6.2 rpg, 42 assists, 35 steals), who combined for 43 percent of the offense last season. Bolden was the two-time conference player of the year, and ranked 36th in the country in scoring and 24th in three-pointers per game (3.0).

"Nobody should underestimate Texas Southern basketball," Moreland said. "In the 1990s, we have won seven conference championships. I would think by now that people know that Texas Southern is going to be a very competitive ballclub and one of those teams that you are going to have to beat out for a championship."

Texas Southern returns three starters in 6-foot senior guard **Leland Redmond** (8.1 ppg, 5.9 rpg, 167 assists, 34 steals); 6-7 junior forward **Ifey Anyanwu** (8.7 ppg, 7.2 rpg, 28 assists, 24 steals); and 6-8 junior forward **John Rhodes** (7.3 ppg, 5.3 rpg, 31 assists, 26 blocks, 17 steals).

Redmond led the SWAC in assists and the improved Anyanwu ranked sixth in rebounds and ninth in field-goal percentage. The Tigers' other returning players are 5-10 sophomore guard **Roderick Beechem** (2.9 ppg, 0.7 rpg); 6-3 junior guard **Patrick Dyse** (5.2 ppg, 1.7 rpg, 38 steals, 22 assists); 6-4 junior guard **Lindsey Adams** (4.3 ppg, 1.5 rpg); 6-6 junior forward **Derick Malone** (4.0 ppg, 3.5 rpg) and 6-8 sophomore forward **Rahmeen Underwood** (3.9

1998-99 TEXAS SOUTHERN SCHEDULE

Nov.	21	@Southern
	23	@Alcorn State
	28	@Detroit
	30	Tougaloo
Dec.	4-5	#Pizza Hut Classic
	15	@New Mexico State
	17	@Texas-El Paso
	29-30	##Pepsi Oneida Classic
Jan.	9	Jackson State
	11	Grambling
	16	@Arkansas-Pine Bluff
	18	@Mississippi Valley State
	23	Alabama A&M
	25	Alabama State
	30	Prairie View A&M
Feb.	2	@Prarie View A&M
	6	@Jackson State
	8	@Grambling
	13	Arkansas-Pine Bluff
	15	Mississippi Valley State
	20	@Alabama A&M
	22	@Alabama State
	25	Alcorn State
	27	Southern
Mar.	4-6	###SWAC Tournament

@ Road Games
# Springfield, MO (vs. Southwest Missouri State, first round; also Louisiana Tech and Texas-Pan American)
Green Bay, Wisconsin (v s. Wisconsin-Green Bay, first round; also Air Force and Drexel)
Dallas, TX

ppg, 2.3 rpg).

"We have eight returning lettermen who had good playing time from last year," Moreland said, "but offensively we need lots of maturing."

Texas Southern added three newcomers in 6-1 freshman guard **Demonse Williams**, 6-6 freshman guard **Harold Boston** of Piney Woods (Miss.) HS and 6-11 freshman center **Eddie Stewart**. Boston was one of Mississippi's Dandy Dozen and Stewart was one of the top recruits in the Houston area.

The Tigers have little margin for error. Their schedule opens with road games against SWAC contenders Southern and Alcorn State and includes nonconference road games against Detroit, Louisiana Tech, New Mexico State and UTEP.

"As always, we'll be competitive," Moreland said. "With a bit of luck, we could be in the hunt for another championship."

adidas Blue Ribbon Analysis

BACKCOURT .... **B** **BENCH/DEPTH** .... **C**
FRONTCOURT .... **B** **INTANGIBLES** .... **B**

Texas Southern keeps producing top guards such as Kevin Granger and Randy Bolden and just keeps winning.

Any thoughts that the Tigers might struggle without Bolden and Russell Evans might have been erased when Moreland returned to his Mississippi roots to sign Harold Boston, and kept local product Eddie Stewart from leaving the city. Texas Southern has enough returning talent to go along with its signees to mount a serious bid to win back-to-back regular-season championships for the third time in this decade.

(S.G.)

adidas Blue Ribbon Analysis

GRADING SYSTEM

- A+ equal to very best in country—Final Four-caliber unit
- A among the best in the land—worthy of deep NCAA run
- B+ talented, versatile and experienced—NCAA-NIT ability
- B solid and productive winners—league and post-season contenders
- C+ average to above-average—may contend in a weaker league
- C average to mediocre—second division in a strong league
- D+ below average, inconsistent—second division in a weaker league
- D well below average—losing season virtually certain
- F non-Division I ability—an underdog every night

SUN BELT CONFERENCE

adidas BLUE RIBBON FORECAST

1. Florida International
2. Arkansas State
3. Southwestern Louisiana
4. Louisiana Tech
5. Western Kentucky
6. Arkansas-Little Rock
7. South Alabama
8. New Orleans

ALL-CONFERENCE TEAM

G—Lonnie Cooper, SR, Louisiana Tech
G—Chico Fletcher, JR, Arkansas State
F—Raja Bell, SR, Florida International
F—Ryan Moss, SR, Arkansas-Little Rock
F—Reginald Poole, SR, Southwestern Louisiana

PLAYER OF THE YEAR

Chico Fletcher, JR, Arkansas State

NEWCOMER OF THE YEAR

Gerrod Henderson, JR, Louisiana Tech

1998-99 CONFERENCE TOURNAMENT

Feb. 27-28, March 2, Cajundome, Lafayette, LA

1997-98 CHAMPIONS

Arkansas and South Alabama (regular season)
South Alabama (conference tournament)

1997-98 POSTSEASON PARTICIPANTS

Postseason Record: 0-1 (.000)
NCAA
South Alabama

TOP BACKCOURTS

1. Arkansas State
2. Florida International
3. Louisiana Tech

TOP FRONTCOURTS

1. Southwestern Louisiana
2. Florida International
3. Arkansas-Little Rock

ON THE WAY UP

Louisiana Tech

ON THE WAY DOWN

South Alabama

INSIDE THE NUMBERS

- 1997-98 conference RPI: 16th (of 30)
- Conference RPI (last 5 years): 13-18-16-16-16

DID YOU KNOW?

The Sun Belt Conference continues this season an affiliation with ESPN that dates to when the all-sports network was a fledgling venture back in 1979. The Sun Belt was the first conference to sign a long-term agreement with ESPN...Dennis Felton becomes just the 11th head coach in the tradition-rich 79 years of basketball at Western Kentucky...Predictions are just that, predictions. For the last two seasons, a team picked to finish in the lower half of the Sun Belt Conference has at least claimed a share of the league's regular-season title...South Alabama has won 17 straight conference home games, third-best in league history behind New Orleans (23) and former member UAB (20)...Southwestern Louisiana registered the third-best attendance surge among Division I schools last season, going from 2,925 fans per game in 1996-97 to 5,427 last season...Among Division I conferences, the Sun Belt ranked 15th in average attendance at 3,208 per game, led by Arkansas State at 6,625 per game...With Florida International's invitation to play North Carolina in the Chase NIT, the Sun Belt has a team playing in the prestigious tournament for a third straight season and fifth time in the last six.

(G.P.)

ARKANSAS-LITTLE ROCK

LOCATION .... Little Rock, AR
CONFERENCE .... Sun Belt
LAST SEASON .... 15-13 (.536)
CONFERENCE RECORD 10-8 (4th)
STARTERS LOST/RETURNING 2/3
NICKNAME .... Trojans
COLORS .... Maroon & Silver
HOMECOURT .... Barton Coliseum (8,303)
COACH .... Wimp Sanderson (North Alabama '59)
RECORD AT SCHOOL .... 73-43 (4 yrs.)
CAREER RECORD .... 338-161 (16 yrs.)
ASSISTANTS .... Clarence Finley (Arkansas-Pine Bluff '79)
Porter Moser (Creighton '90)
Kevin Fricke (Nebraska '84)
TEAM WINS (last 5 yrs.) 13-17-23-18-15
RPI (last 5 yrs.) 203-135-56-141-160
1997-98 FINISH .... Lost in conference quarterfinal.

When his Arkansas-Little Rock team starts the season Nov. 21 against Arkansas-Pine Bluff, head coach Wimp Sanderson will coach his 500th game in his 17th season, the last four in Little Rock, Ark.

With a nice balance of returning veterans and promising newcomers, the Trojans plan to return to the Sun Belt prominence they achieved in Sanderson's first three years as coach.

"This group of returning players should be able to tell the new guys what to expect from me, from the conference and what it is going to take to win," said Sanderson, the former Alabama coach.

Under Sanderson, the Trojans have never posted a non-winning season, although last year's 15 victories were the fewest during his tenure.

However, that came during a rebuilding year that could pay dividends this season—especially if power forward **Ryan Moss** (14.5, 9.7 rpg), a 6-7 senior, continues to emerge as a force in the league. The native of Nassau, Bahamas, who played at national power Hutchinson (Kan.) JC, was chosen the Sun Belt's Newcomer of the Year last season.

Moss was second in the country last season in shooting percentage (.657), making 167 of 257 shots, and his rebounding total (272) ranked 26th in the country. He also had a team-high 55 blocked shots, third-best in school history.

Despite Moss' production last season, Sanderson is expecting more.

"Ryan had a very good season last year," Sanderson said. "He is going to have to continue to work very hard and get the job done defensively and on the boards for us to be successful."

The small forward job will again be held by 6-7 forward **Maurice Bowie** (7.1 ppg, 5.4 rpg), who started 19 games last season. The former transfer from East Central (Mo.) CC has scoring ability, as evidenced by his career-high 24 points against Gonzaga in the season's second game.

Bowie didn't continue the early hot streak and had just one other 20-point game the rest of the season.

"Maurice started the season very well last year," Sanderson said. "He needs to be aggressive looking for the rebound. With his size, we need him to help with our rebounding total. He needs to take good shots as well."

The other returning starter is 5-10 senior **Chris Green** (15.2 ppg, 2.5 rpg), a versatile point guard who can score (team-high 63 three-pointers last season) and find the

1998-99 ARKANSAS-LITTLE ROCK SCHEDULE

Nov.	21	@Arkansas-Pine Bluff
	23	Albany
	27-28	#IGA/Super Thrift Holiday Classic
Dec.	2	@Florida International
	12	@Oklahoma State
	18-19	##TCBY Holiday Classic
	22	@UTEP
Jan.	2	Florida International
	4	@Texas-Pan American
	7	Southwestern Louisiana
	13	@Louisiana Tech
	16	@Arkansas State
	19	Texas-Pan American
	23	New Orleans
	25	@Southwestern Louisiana
	28	Western Kentucky
	31	South Alabama
Feb.	4	@New Orleans
	6	@South Alabama
	8	Denver
	10	@Western Kentucky
	13	Arkansas State
	16	Louisiana Tech
	20	@Denver
27-Mar.	2	###Sun Belt Tournament

@ Road Games
# Norman, OK (vs. Murray State, first round; also Oklahoma and Western Carolina)
Little Rock, AR (vs. High Point, first round; also Centenary and Richmond)
Cajundome, Lafayette, LA

open man (team-high 104 assists). Despite his height, Green can move to shooting guard and not hurt the team defensively.

"We need Chris to be more consistent this year," Sanderson said. Green scored 33 in a conference tournament victory over Louisiana Tech. "He shows flashes, but he needs to be very consistent."

The Trojans also return four players who gained significant playing time last season, especially 6-1 senior guard **Steve Rector** (5.1 ppg, 2.5 rpg), a strong defender who can play either backcourt position. He started 11 games, including nine straight during one stretch, and the team's two conference tournament games.

Battling for playing time at center or power forward is 6-8, 225-pound sophomore **Michael Neal** (2.1 ppg, 1.9 rpg), who played in every game a year ago. The only freshman to play for the Trojans last season, Neal showed immediate promise by scoring 11 points and grabbing five rebounds in his first college game.

Although averaging just 7.2 minutes in 17 games last season, 6-6 swingman **Tavares Davis** (1.4 ppg, 0.9 rpg) has the athletic ability to be an impact player, especially offensively. One reason the third-year sophomore has been slow to reach his potential is a daily struggle with Sickle Cell disease, which limits his strength and stamina.

Rounding out the returning reserves is 6-2 senior guard **Maurice Jones** (0.0 ppg, 1.0 rpg), who played in 12 games, but didn't make a shot in 12 attempts.

There are seven newcomers on the team, including 6-5 junior forward **Ryan Gore**, a hometown product who guided Little Rock Parkview HS to a Class 4A state championship.

Gore sat out last season after transferring from Henderson State (Ark.), a Division II program. A leaper and great dunker, Gore could have the most impact of any newcomer.

"Ryan is a kid that could really help us, if he keeps his head together," Sanderson said. "The year that he spent with us last year as a redshirt should really help him. He will really help us on the inside."

Another player redshirted last year, 6-1 freshman guard **Adrian Brown**, gained valuable experience practicing with the team. He is a gritty, defensive-minded point guard who was a two-time all-state player at Jacksonville (Ark.) North Pulaski HS.

Adding depth at forward will be 6-5 senior Tommy Cradup (0.0 ppg, 1.0 rpg), who played in two games last year.

Also joining the team are three junior-college transfers: 6-4 junior guard **Alan Barksdale**, who averaged 18.6 points per game at Meridian (Miss.) JC after transferring there from Colorado.; 6-2 junior guard **Michael Lovitt**, an athletic player from Florida CC in Jacksonville; and 6-7 sophomore forward **James Joseph**, who enrolled on the first day of the school year.

Joseph averaged 13 points and eight rebounds at Temple (Texas) JC last season. He missed his senior year of high school with two stress fractures in the middle of his back. Joseph's spot on the roster came open when 6-8 junior forward Tyren Johnson was declared medically unfit to play after breaking his foot and eventually redshirting last season.

The only freshman on the team is 6-1 guard **Jesse Peeples,** who averaged 16.9 points and 6.3 rebounds last season at Stone Mountain (Ga.) HS.

"The new guys are going to have to work very hard to reach the level they need to play at in the Sun Belt," Sanderson said. "These guys should really add depth and the ability to score to our team."

adidas Blue Ribbon Analysis

BACKCOURT	**C**	**BENCH/DEPTH**	**C**
FRONTCOURT	**B**	**INTANGIBLES**	**B**

Arkansas-Little Rock had become known for producing outstanding backcourt talent such as former Sun Belt Player-of-the-Year Derek Fisher, now playing for the Los Angeles Lakers, and the league's leading scorer two seasons ago, Malik Dixon.

As it often does in the transient Sun Belt Conference, the talent level for the Trojans has shifted to the frontcourt, where Ryan Moss is as talented as any player in the league.

The style of play Wimp Sanderson's teams have featured through the years begins and often ends with athletic play on the perimeter, which opens up a solid game in the post. That trend is now reversed at Arkansas-Little Rock.

If the Trojans are to post another winning season under Sanderson, there is little doubt what has to come through—the backcourt. To help in that area, the Trojans signed five guards.

In Sanderson, Arkansas-Little Rock has a coach who can adapt to his personnel, and with the departure of Western Kentucky's Matt Kilcullen, Sanderson becomes the dean of Sun Belt coaches in just his fifth season in the conference.

That's good for a few victories in itself.

(G.P.)

ARKANSAS STATE

LOCATION	**Jonesboro, AR**
CONFERENCE	**Sun Belt**
LAST SEASON	**20-9 (.690)**
CONFERENCE RECORD	**14-4 (t-1st)**
STARTERS LOST/RETURNING	**2/3**
NICKNAME	**Indians**
COLORS	**Scarlet & Black**
HOMECOURT	**Convocation Center (10,563)**
COACH	**Dickey Nutt (Oklahoma State '82)**
RECORD AT SCHOOL	**44-39 (3 yrs.)**
CAREER RECORD	**44-39 (3 yrs.)**
ASSISTANTS	**Dennis Nutt (Texas Christian '86)** **Charlie Fenske (Wisconsin-Stout '74)** **Tony Madlock (Memphis State '91)**
TEAM WINS (last 5 yrs.)	**15-8-9-15-20**
RPI (last 5 yrs.)	**115-269-235-164-85**
1997-98 FINISH	**Lost in conference first round.**

Arkansas State has been playing basketball 71 seasons, and last year's 20-9 record was just one of five 20-win seasons in the program's history.

Thus, Arkansas State rewarded fourth-year coach Dickey Nutt—last season's Sun Belt Coach of the Year—with a contract extension through the 1999-2000 season. With that came a $30,000 per year raise. Even his assistants got their pay bumped upward.

With all that—and three returning starters and a key reserve—the expectations have risen for the Indians, who were upset by seventh-seeded Lamar in their league tournament opener and denied a postseason berth.

"We had a good year," Nutt said. "Winning the Sun Belt (regular season) co-championship was great, but we didn't finish like we wanted. Our No. 1 goal is to reach the NCAA Tournament."

That is uncharted territory for Arkansas State, which has never been to the Big Dance. It's a fact that is on the mind of Nutt, whose brother Houston is the new head football coach at Arkansas.

Nutt's coach-of-the-year honor wasn't the only accolade garnered by the Indians last season. They lose two 1,000-point career scorers in backcourt leader Micah Marsh and forward Jabari Myles.

However, the good news outweighs the bad, considering Arkansas State returns the reigning Sun Belt Player in the Year, 5-6 sophomore point guard **Chico Fletcher** (13.2 ppg, 3.7 rpg, 240 assists), and last year's league defensive player of the year, key reserve **Freddy Hicks** (7.6 ppg, 5.6 rpg). Hicks is a 6-7 senior power forward who is expected to leave his sixth-man role for a starting job in the post.

Add two other returning starters, 6-4 senior guard **Antonio Harvey** (14.4 ppg, 4.3 rpg), the team's top returning scorer, and 6-8 senior forward/center **Eric Beatty** (7.3 ppg, 4.0 rpg), and it's easy to see why the Indians are again considered a team to beat in the Sun Belt.

"We're excited about the talent we have coming back," Nutt said. "We feel like we had a good year last year and that we only lose two players from that team. We are excited about the future.

"One of the best things about our team and the returning players is that they all got significantly better last year."

Especially Fletcher, the nation's top returning assists leader after his 8.3 per game was second-best in the country a year ago. That included a school-record 15 assists against Jacksonville. The Indians let Fletcher run the show.

While the in-state product is in the midst of a great basketball career, the former three-time Arkansas all-state football player nearly didn't play basketball.

"It really made a big difference that Chico has had a year and a half of being a full-time basketball player," Nutt said. "It was very tough to make the transition from football. We know that every player and team will be gunning for Chico. This will be a tremendous challenge for him. Chico has a heart of a lion, a warrior. He will be fine."

Fletcher played a team-high 36.7 minutes per game last year, but Nutt plans to spell him more this year at point guard with either **DeShawn Denson**, a 6-2 junior transfer from Northern Oklahoma CC, or 6-0 sophomore **Wes Wagner** (0.7 ppg, 0.5 rpg), who played in 19 games last season.

Joining Fletcher in the backcourt will be Harvey, who made a school-record 88 three-point shots last season, including a school-record eight in one game. The former walkon and former high school track star out of Jacksonville, Fla., shot almost 44 percent from three-point range (88 for 202)

Despite starting just one game, Hicks emerged as the league's premier defender, breaking his own school record with 65 blocked shots. Four times he was chosen the league's defensive player of the week.

This season, though, Hicks is expected to provide more scoring and rebounding after shooting .560 from the field a year ago. He needs 153 rebounds to reach 500 for his career. As for Indians fans, they most surely want Hicks to resume his flair for the dramatic with his amazing leaping ability.

The other returning starter is Beatty, a rugged inside player who can score when he has to, as evidenced by a career-high 23 points against Pan American last year.

Depth at either backcourt position and small forward again will come from 6-3 senior **Jeremaine Ezell** (1.3 ppg, 0.8 rpg), who played in the last 11 regular-season games.

Also pushing for playing time in the backcourt will be 6-

1998-99 ARKANSAS STATE SCHEDULE

Nov.	13	@Saint Louis
	16	Baylor
	18	Oral Roberts
	23	@Texas Christian
	28	@Denver
Dec.	5	Alabama A&M
	8	Southeast Missouri State
	17	Denver
	22	@Oral Roberts
	27	@San Diego State
	29	@Southern California
Jan.	4	Florida International
	9	@Southwestern Louisiana
	14	New Orleans
	16	Arkansas-Little Rock
	21	@Western Kentucky
	23	@Florida International
	25	@Memphis
	28	@Louisiana Tech
	30	Western Kentucky
Feb.	2	@South Alabama
	6	@New Orleans
	11	Southwestern Louisiana
	13	@Arkansas-Little Rock
	18	South Alabama
	20	Louisiana Tech
27-Mar.	2	#Sun Belt Tournament

@ Road Games
# Cajundome, Lafayette, LA

3 senior **Jeff Holloway** (2.4 ppg, 1.3 rpg), an explosive jumper who has been hobbled by a foot stress fracture, and 6-0 senior **Daniel Sexton** (0.6 ppg, 0.6 rpg).

Available again is 6-9 junior forward/center **Geoff Williams** (1.0 ppg, 1.5 rpg), who played in four games before being redshirted because of knee injuries. Nutt plans on Williams playing significant minutes.

"We feel like that year of sitting out has definitely helped him," Nutt said of Williams, a former transfer from Coahoma (Miss.) JC. "We think that he's going to be a nice addition to our team for the next two years."

Another redshirted player, 6-3 freshman guard **Cody Mears**, becomes eligible and provides even more depth in the backcourt.

Perhaps the best player of the incoming recruiting class is 6-4 junior swingman **C.J. Pepper**. He was a junior-college regional most valuable player last season at Moberly (Mo.) JC, where he was chosen third-team junior college All-American after averaging 20.7 points and nine rebounds as a sophomore and 21.4 points and nine rebounds as a freshman. Pepper was No. 16 on JC recruiting expert Phil Henzel's list of the top 300 sophomores.

"C.J. has a chance to be a very good player," Nutt said of Pepper, who chose Arkansas State over Iowa State, South Alabama, Western Kentucky, Minnesota and Saint Louis. "He has a chance to step in and be a good player for us immediately."

The Indians have two incoming freshmen, 6-7 forward/center **Luis Rivas,** who played at high school power Quincy (Ill.) HS, and 6-2 guard Norman Stewart, who was rated the No. 34 senior in Texas last season out of Garland HS.

Sitting out the season is 6-9 forward/center Kolin Weaver, a transfer from Siena College who will not be eligible until next season.

"This season will be more of the same, an uptempo style like last season and (we will) try to add a more full-court game defensively," Nutt said. "We will try to create more scoring off our defense, and we're really trying to develop a bench for this year."

adidas Blue Ribbon Analysis

BACKCOURT .... B+ BENCH/DEPTH .... C+
FRONTCOURT .... C+ INTANGIBLES .... B

While Florida International swaggers into the Sun Belt in its debut season heralded as a contender, Arkansas State should again be the team to beat.

In Dickey Nutt, the Indians have one of the bright young coaches in the country, and Arkansas State wasted no time in rewarding him with a contract extension and raise after last year's 20-win season.

There is talent and athleticism at Arkansas State, especially in Chico Fletcher, a waterbug-like guard who can break down defenses off the dribble as well as any point guard in the country.

If the Indians are to advance to the NCAA Tournament for the first time, however, they must get solid inside play, even though their pace will again be fast and furious.

Arkansas State was left hungry after losing in the conference tournament last season. Nutt used that as offseason motivation. Now, the Indians must prove it on the court before they can be called postseason contenders.

(G.P.)

FLORIDA INTERNATIONAL

LOCATION .... Miami, FL
CONFERENCE .... Sun Belt
LAST SEASON .... 21-8 (.724)
CONFERENCE RECORD 13-3 (2nd)
STARTERS LOST/RETURNING 0/5
NICKNAME .... Golden Panthers
COLORS .... Blue & Yellow
HOMECOURT .... Golden Panther Arena (5,000)
COACH .... Marcos "Shakey" Rodriguez (Florida International '75)
RECORD AT SCHOOL .... 50-36 (3 yrs.)
CAREER RECORD .... 50-36 (3 yrs.)
ASSISTANTS .... Jose Ramos (Regents '96)
Tyrone Hart (Howard '76)
Bernard Wright (Grambling '80)
TEAM WINS (last 5 yrs.) 11-11-13-16-21
RPI (last 5 yrs.) 206-217-237-177-87
1997-98 FINISH .... Lost in conference final.

Florida International isn't afraid to break new ground.

First, the Golden Panthers turned a few heads in 1995 by hiring Miami (Fla.) Senior High School basketball coach Shakey Rodriguez to turn his alma mater's basketball fortunes around.

Three seasons later, all FIU did was post a school-record 21-8 record in its 17th and final year in the Trans America Athletic Conference. And the Golden Panthers darn near beat perennial TAAC strongboy College of Charleston on its homecourt in the league tournament's championship game.

That's all in the rearview mirror now. Florida International has moved its entire athletics program into the Sun Belt Conference, where it is not only picked as a player with five starters and 10 lettermen returning, but predicted to win it outright.

"More than anything else, the Sun Belt is just a better league from top to bottom," Rodriguez said. "The nucleus of the Trans America is near the bottom of the conference ratings, while the Sun Belt is in the middle of the pack with prospects to improve.

"Game in and game out, we will have a struggle in the Sun Belt."

Not that the TAAC was a breeze. Florida International always played second fiddle to College of Charleston, which Rodriguez claimed could have been beaten if the tournament had been played at a neutral site.

"That was a tough place to go and come out with a win, especially with the NCAA Tournament berth on the line," Rodriguez said. "I honestly believe if we would have played them the last two years on a neutral site, we would have won both times."

Instead, the reality of being second best in a lowly-rated conference hit home when the NIT selection committee said thanks, but no thanks to the Golden Panthers, who thought 21 wins—including solid victories at Alabama and at home against Long Beach State—might have made a difference.

Florida International doesn't want to leave the postseason—where it has been just once, a 92-56 loss to UCLA in the 1995 NCAAs—to chance this year.

"Like any team, we're going to have to stay healthy," Rodriguez said of his team's prospects. "We're going to have to get continual improvement from our post game, most of all."

That was evident last season when the Golden Panthers, in the opinion of their coach, were the worst rebounding team in the TAAC the first half of the season, only to turn that around and become the league's best in the second half.

But if the team has a strength, it has to be the backcourt, which fuels Florida International's high-throttled offense that averaged 87.3 points per game last season. Expect more of the same from the Golden Panthers, whose fast-break offense will fit in nicely with the Sun Belt's penchant for scoring early and often.

"We run a lot," Rodriguez said. "We're very much uptempo. We want to be among the top teams in the nation in scoring. And we have eight guys back who I consider excellent three-point shooters."

Directing the offense again is 6-2 sophomore point guard **Carlos Arroyo** (12.0 ppg, 4.7 apg, 2.3 spg), the lightning-quick quarterback of the team whose 135 assists set a school record. He also had 66 steals, second-best in the TAAC. The all-league newcomer peaked in the conference semifinal win over Georgia Southern with a career-high 28 points.

"We have one of the better point guards in the country," Rodriguez said. "He is tremendous handling the ball, but he can score, too. He's a one-man with two-man skills He's very strong and explosive and really knows how to play the position. He was one of the better freshmen in the country last year."

His running mate again will be 6-2 senior guard **Damien McKnight** (8.5 ppg, 1.4 rpg), a transfer from Penn State. McKnight is FIU's chief outside threat, shooting .395 percent (49-124) from behind the arc. He started out last season at point guard, but was quickly moved to the shooting slot with Arroyo's emergence.

Leading scorer **Raja Bell** (16.6 ppg, 4.1 rpg), a 6-5 senior forward, scored 20 or more points 14 times last season on his way to 481 points, fifth-best in program history. A transfer from Boston University, where he was chosen North Atlantic Conference Rookie of the Year, Bell was voted all-league and all-newcomer in the TAAC after sitting out the previous season.

"Raja's a tremendous athlete," Rodriguez said. "He scores in so many different ways, and he's capable of playing above the basket. And he especially shoots well when changing ends of the floor."

Bruising **Darius Cook** (10.9 ppg, 6.1 rpg), a 6-9, 242-pound junior, is back at center. The hometown product attended Miami Northwestern and Miami-Dade Community College. He sometimes disappeared during the season, but tended to come up big in big games, notching 14 points and 15 rebounds against Alabama, scoring 20 points to outduel Villanova's 7-1 center **Rafael Bigus**, and scoring 17 points against College of Charleston in a nationally televised ESPN game.

"Darius is going to be a much-improved player," Rodriguez said. "The reason he wasn't a double-double kind of player last year was that he had never been pushed to get in the best physical condition.

"He's much bigger now than last year, but there's much less body fat. He should be much quicker. He needs to be the go-to guy in our halfcourt set, a first option. And if he can get up to 30 to 32 minutes a game (compared to 22.9 last season), he can produce those kind of numbers."

Back at power forward is 6-9 senior **Anthony Harris** (6.7 ppg, 2.9 rpg), who blocked five shots in one game, but finished with just nine for the season. He's solid with a good touch, making .744 percent of his free throws.

Improving **Karel Rosario** (4.8 ppg, 3.5 rpg), a 6-9 sophomore, has gained more than 20 pounds since the start of last season. His three straight double-doubles during a late stretch notched an average of 14.3 points and 11 rebounds during the run.

"Between Cook, Harris and Rosario, we will have the best post game we've had since I've been here," Rodriguez said.

The bench accounted for 38 percent of FIU's scoring last year, much of which came from 6-6 senior forward **Gene Derkack** (9.1 ppg, 4.5 rpg). He scored a season-high 24 points against Jacksonville that included going 8 for 8 from the field and 7 for 7 from the free-throw line.

Another high-octane reliever is 5-11 senior guard **Marcus Carreno** (5.0 ppg, 1.9 rpg), a former walkon who two years ago ranked fourth nationally in three-point shooting. A streak shooter, he missed his first nine three-pointers two years ago, but then made 52 of the next 95 (.547 percent). A former player for Rodriguez at Miami Senior, Carreno cooled off a bit last season to a still-impressive .404 percent (38 of 94).

Other returnees include 6-2 junior guard **Joe Cross** (3.6 ppg, 1.3 rpg), the brother of former Florida star Dan Cross; 6-9 junior **Raymon Aybar** (1.1 ppg, 1.4 rpg); and 6-0 junior guard **Leinad Cross** (0.8 ppg, 0.8 rpg).

Rodriguez signed only one newcomer, reaching all the way to Givataim, Israel to get **Eran Klein**, a 6-5 sophomore guard. After high school, Klein served three years in the Israeli army, so he comes with some maturity. He averaged 21.0 points, 3.0 rebounds and 4.5 assists in his senior year at Kalay High School in 1994-95.

The Golden Panthers will find out how ready they are for a step up when they become the third straight Sun Belt team—and fifth in the last six years—to play in the Chase NIT to open the season. On the agenda for Nov. 16 is a road trip to North Carolina.

1998-99 FLORIDA INTERNATIONAL SCHEDULE

Month	Date	Opponent
Nov.	13	Michigan
	14	Northern Arizona
	16	#North Carolina
	21	@Northern Arizona
	23	@Akron
	28-29	##FIU/Money Store Tournament
Dec.	2	Arkansas-Little Rock
	15	@Fordham
	17	@Illinois-Chicago
	20	@UTEP
	22	South Alabama
	28	###Bank One Fiesta Bowl Classic
Jan.	2	@Arkansas-Little Rock
	4	@Arkansas State
	12	Western Kentucky
	14	@South Alabama
	18	@Butler
	23	Arkansas State
	28	@New Orleans
	30	@Louisiana Tech
Feb.	2	@Western Kentucky
	6	Louisiana Tech
	13	Southwestern Louisiana
	15	New Orleans
	17	@Southwestern Louisiana
27-Mar.	2	####Sun Belt Tournament

@ Road Games

Chase NIT (If the Panthers advance, they will face either the College of Charleston or Georgia on Nov. 18. Semifinals and finals are Nov. 26 & 28 at Madison Square Garden, NY)

Miami, FL (vs. Bucknell, first round; also Georgia Southern and Northern Illinois)

Tucson, AZ (vs. Penn State, first round; also Arizona and Holy Cross)

Cajundome, Lafayette, LA

adidas Blue Ribbon Analysis

BACKCOURT .... B BENCH/DEPTH .... B
FRONTCOURT .... B INTANGIBLES .... B

While Florida International will be tested more on a nightly basis in the new Sun Belt Conference, it is a program that is seemingly on the rise. And the fact that FIU is the largest school (30,094 students) in the largest market in the Sun Belt Conference is not lost on Rodriguez.

"It's a new school that has unlimited potential," he said. "There is a tremendous upside to our program. Like the school, we're still in a building stage."

It doesn't hurt that Rodriguez has vast connections among former fellow high school coaches throughout Florida, which annually produces among the best and most Division I-A talent in the country.

"This is a great city and a great state for basketball," Rodriguez said. "We need to take advantage of that."

Which makes the team's Sun Belt debut a pivotal season. Earning the school's second postseason berth in its short Division I history would only cement the team as a viable player in a large market that is often driven by professional sports.

(G.P.)

LOUISIANA TECH

LOCATION .... Ruston, LA
CONFERENCE .... Sun Belt
LAST SEASON .... 12-15 (.444
CONFERENCE RECORD 9-9 (t-5th)
STARTERS LOST/RETURNING 2/3
NICKNAME .... Bulldogs
COLORS .... Red & Blue
HOMECOURT .... Thomas Assembly Center (8,000)
COACH .... Jim Wooldridge (Louisiana Tech '77)
RECORD AT SCHOOL .... 52-59 (4 yrs.)
CAREER RECORD .... 229-147 (13 yrs.)
ASSISTANTS .. Charles Baker (Eastern Kentucky '90)
Marcus Stribling (Georgia State '95)
TEAM WINS (last 5 yrs.) 2-14-11-15-12
RPI (last 5 yrs.) 286-173-232-150-181
1997-98 FINISH .... Lost in conference first round.

Jim Wooldridge isn't ready to declare his Louisiana Tech program at a crossroads. But he does admit having done some soul-searching during the offseason as he enters his fifth year at the helm of his alma mater.

After all, Wooldridge inherited a Bulldogs team that won just two games before producing double-figure wins in each of Wooldridge's first four seasons.

But are the Bulldogs ready to take that next step and become annual contenders in the conference?

"This is what I have come up with," Wooldridge said of his contemplations. "Over a four-year period, we have basically made our teams and the program competitive. We have played in a 10-team league, and right now we are currently tied for fifth place in this league over a four-year period in terms of wins and losses."

The 8.5 league wins per year is respectable, sure, but it's still four league wins a season behind New Orleans, the conference leader in wins during the same stretch.

"Obviously, we have room to go if we are ever going to call ourselves champions," Wooldridge said. "But we're not at the bottom and having to start over. We've been happy with certain aspects of our four-year period and disappointed in others.

"To summarize, I do believe we have put ourselves in the position to make a run to the top."

Maybe that means three returning starters, including two-time all-league pick in 6-4 senior guard **Lonnie Cooper** (17.0 ppg, 4.4 rpg, 5.1 apg, team-high 41 steals), who ranked in the top three in the league last season in scoring, assists and free throw percentage (.803).

Or it could mean that there is a wealth of untapped talented in the eight newcomers that will surely be called upon this season if the Bulldogs are to surge to the top.

Then again, no one knows the expectations that surround a Louisiana Tech program that produced Karl Malone better than Wooldridge, who played for the Bulldogs in the mid-1970s.

"We've had a roller-coaster ride with that," Wooldridge said of the program's talent level, which he is convinced

1998-99 LOUISIANA TECH SCHEDULE

Nov.	18	@Baylor
	23	@Southeast Missouri State
	30	@Northwestern State
Dec.	4-5	#Southwest Missouri State Tournament
	11-12	##BYU Tournament
	19	North Texas
	22	@Texas-Pan American
	27-28	###Cowboy Shootout
Jan.	4	@Southwestern Louisiana
	9	South Alabama
	13	Arkansas-Little Rock
	16	@South Alabama
	21	@New Orleans
	23	Southwestern Louisiana
	28	Arkansas State
	30	Florida International
Feb.	1	Texas-Pan American
	4	@Western Kentucky
	6	@Florida International
	11	New Orleans
	13	Western Kentucky
	16	@Arkansas-Little Rock
	20	@Arkansas State
27-Mar.	2	####Sun Belt Tournament

@ Road Games
\# Springfield, MO (vs. Texas-Pan America, first round; also Southwest Missouri State and Texas Southern)
\## Provo, UT (vs. BYU, first round; also Northridge State and Southern Utah)
\### Laramie, WY (vs. Wyoming, first round; also Wagner and Yale)
\#### Cajundome, Lafayette, LA

has improved. "On a piece of paper, we are more talented than we have ever been."

That's because the Bulldogs have created—for the first time under Wooldridge, anyway—a balance between the perimeter and interior.

"What we have is a more balanced talent pool to work with," Wooldridge said. "I hope that turns into more wins."

Again, the place opponents first must focus is Cooper, who ranked sixth in the league in three-point field goal percentage (63 of 164 for .384). He scored a career-high 33 points last season against Arkansas State. The four-year starter is a workhorse, too, averaging a team-high 35.8 minutes per game last season.

"Lonnie really has developed into a terrific overall player," Wooldridge said. "Some players are good offensively and not so good on defense. He can do a lot of things on the basketball floor. He doesn't have to go out and score 20 points a game to be a good player."

Not that Cooper will have to, either. And look for his minutes to remain about the same, considering the Bulldogs will have four other players—two returnees and three newcomers—to rotate among point guard, shooting guard and small forward.

Also back is 6-2 junior **Derek Smith** (14.9 ppg, 3.9 rpg), the Sun Belt Freshman of the Year two seasons ago. He's also dependable, having started all 27 games and ranking behind just Cooper in minutes played (31.1).

"Derek is an explosive athlete who has learned over the last two years to better use his explosives," Wooldridge said of the former Atlanta prep star, who finished his high school career as the state's No. 8 all-time scorer with 4,098 points. "He has made great strides. We're expecting more out of him this year."

The Bulldogs will also depend again on 6-4 junior guard **Omar Cooper** (11.9 ppg, 4.1 rpg), whose point guard mentality wouldn't allow him to attempt a three-pointer last season.

"Omar is the best athlete on our team," Wooldridge said. "He was our most-improved player last season. He became a better decision-maker. His improvement was attributable to his playing time."

Three new faces will round out the rotation, including prize recruit **Gerrod Henderson**, a 6-4 sophomore guard who was a two-time Class AA Louisiana Mr. Basketball out oft Haynesville High School.

Henderson originally enrolled at Iowa State, but transferred to Louisiana Tech and has three years of remaining eligibility. Wooldridge admits the Bulldogs will depend heavily on Henderson, who averaged 32.5 points as a senior and 34.3 points as a junior in high school.

Coming out of high school, Henderson was listed by one recruiting service as one of the top 50 prep players in the country.

"(Henderson) is truly a gifted player," Wooldridge said. "We would be disappointed if he didn't make a huge impact on this team."

Providing depth will be 6-1 junior guard **Craig Jackson**, an Arkansas product who averaged 21.3 points per game last season at Shorter College in North Little Rock, Ark.

"He's a proven scorer who can shoot it deep," Wooldridge said of Jackson. "He's a strong athlete who can play both guards. He, too, must make an immediate impact."

Versatile **Ira Miller**, a 6-5 junior who also played at Shorter College by way of Christ the King High School in New York City, can play point and shooting guards as well as small forward.

Just like the backcourt will be built around Cooper and company, the frontcourt will be manned by committee as well with three returning lettermen and five newcomers.

Among the suspects down low will be newcomers **Curtis Williams**, a 6-9, 215-pound junior also out of Shorter College; **Mike Pawelczak**, a 6-8, 235-pound junior out of Jacksonville (Texas) College; and returnee **Jon Fowler** (1.1 ppg, 1.6 rpg), a 6-10 sophomore who played in seven games last season.

The Bulldogs expect Florida transfer and Baton Rouge native **Kendrick Spruel**, a 6-9 junior, to provide good minutes in the paint, but Wooldridge won't be averse to letting Spruel let fly with outside jumpers, including treys.

"We believe that Kendrick is going to give us some real ammunition at this position," Wooldridge said of Spruel, whose arm span makes him look 7-2. "We'll run at the four (power forward), but he will be on the perimeter a lot."

Providing depth along the front line will be two returnees: 6-6 junior **Fred Smith** (2.9 ppg, 3.8 rpg) and 6-6 junior **Walker McDonald** (1.1 ppg, 0.7 rpg). **John Gist**, a 6-8 redshirt sophomore, is also available.

The lone freshman in the bunch is 6-7 forward **Karelius Paul**, who earned district co-MVP at Richardson (Texas) High School.

adidas Blue Ribbon Analysis

BACKCOURT .... B+ BENCH/DEPTH .... C+
FRONTCOURT .... C+ INTANGIBLES .... C+

If the Bulldogs can mesh the new faces with the returnees that include Cooper, they might make a run at the league title. But that's a big if.

It's especially so up front, where Louisiana Tech will mix and match until something works.

"We'll just see how that goes," Wooldridge said of the frontcourt situation. "It will be done by committee, unless somebody rises up and shows he deserves the time and the role. Then, we will give it to him."

No doubt, the overall talent at Louisiana Tech—on paper, anyway—appears to be at its best since Wooldridge took over five seasons ago. And most programs are judged on their fourth and fifth seasons.

Most notable improvement should come in point production, where the Bulldogs averaged a meager 68.5 points per game last season.

Louisiana Tech has steadily made progress under Wooldridge, a talented coach whose star has been on the rise for years. Still, there comes a time to produce. This might have to be Louisiana Tech's year in that regard.

(G.P.)

adidas Blue Ribbon Analysis
GRADING SYSTEM

- A+ equal to very best in country—Final Four-caliber unit
- A among the best in the land—worthy of deep NCAA run
- B+ talented, versatile and experienced—NCAA-NIT ability
- B solid and productive winners—league and post-season contenders
- C+ average to above-average—may contend in a weaker league
- C average to mediocre—second division in a strong league
- D+ below average, inconsistent—second division in a weaker league
- D well below average—losing season virtually certain
- F non-Division I ability—an underdog every night

NEW ORLEANS

LOCATION .... **New Orleans, LA**
CONFERENCE .... **Sun Belt**
LAST SEASON .... **15-12 (.555)**
CONFERENCE RECORD .... **9-9 (t-5th)**
STARTERS LOST/RETURNING **4/1**
NICKNAME .... **Privateers**
COLORS .... **Royal Blue & Silver**
HOMECOURT .... **Lakefront Arena (10,000)**
COACH .... **Joey Stiebing (Louisiana State '85)**
RECORD AT SCHOOL .... **15-12 (1 yr.)**
CAREER RECORD .... **15-12 (1 yr.)**
ASSISTANTS Anthony Anderson (McNeese State '95)
Mike Giorlando (Spring Hill '80)
Nikita Johnson (West Georgia '89)
TEAM WINS (last 5 yrs.) **20-20-21-22-15**
RPI (last 5 yrs.) **62-109-52-75-155**
1997-98 FINISH .... **Lost in conference quarterfinal.**

With a school-record 13 straight winning seasons, New Orleans has become a perennial postseason contender out of the Sun Belt Conference.

During the last 12 years, the Privateers have reached the postseason nine times, and they have won seven regular-season conference championships in the last 11 seasons.

Those are the flashy records. Now, New Orleans must try to continue playing up to those lofty standards under second-year coach Joey Stiebing.

The Privateers return only two lettermen, a school-record low. Also, New Orleans' 16 road opponents is a record high. New Orleans plays only 12 home games at Lakefront Arena, also a program low.

With just one returning starter and nine newcomers, it's easy to see why this could be called a rebuilding year for the Privateers, who had won at least 20 games five straight seasons before posting 15 victories last season.

"The program is in a transition period right now," said Stiebing, who was an assistant under former New Orleans and Iowa State coach Tim Floyd. "Chemistry is going to play a big part on our team this season. There are a lot of question marks on this team. We have a lot of inexperience."

There are no questions surrounding the team's only returning starter, sophomore **Tory Walker** (9.0 ppg, 3.1 rpg), a 6-7 small forward who was chosen the Sun Belt's Freshman of the Year last season.

The former New Orleans high school star and all-state player from Archbishop Shaw High School led the league's freshmen in scoring, rebounding, three-point field goals (44 for 101) and three-point field-goal percentage (.436). His continued production is crucial to New Orleans' chances for a successful season.

The only other returning letterman is another small forward, 6-6 junior **Carlos Hines** (5.2 ppg, 2.9 rpg). He played in all 27 games and ranked fifth on the team in rebounding and scoring. He scored in double figures five times.

"We're very comfortable at small forward because Tory and Carlos are back," Stiebing said. "They complement each other very well. We may even play them together early in the season until others step up and develop."

From there, the Privateers will piece together a team with the newcomers, six of whom come from junior colleges, two more from Division I schools and one from high school.

The best of the bunch may be 6-8 junior forward **Curtis Wilson**, a bruising 215-pounder who will probably get the starting job at power forward. While earning all-conference honors and helping Porterville (Calif.) JC to a 29-6 record, the Wisconsin native averaged 10.1 points and 6.8 rebounds.

"Curtis is a very good rebounder and very strong," Stiebing said. "He's athletic, and he can score around the basket. He plays hard, and he's a guy who will come in and compete for a starting position."

Also contending for time at power forward is the team's only freshman, 6-8 **Rhett Reed**, the all-time scoring and rebounding leader at Greenfield (Ind.) HS. He averaged 13.2 points, 8.0 rebounds, 3.0 assists and 2.1 blocked shots while shooting .511 from the field last season.

Outside scoring is expected from 6-2 junior guard **Frank Clardy**, who helped Mount San Jacinto (Calif.) JC to a 30-7 record, averaging 17 points and four rebounds.

"Frank is a scorer. He'll break you off the dribble, get to the basket and finish plays," Stiebing said. "If he makes his perimeter shots, he's going to be a really good player in the Sun Belt."

Pushing Clardy for the start at shooting guard will be a two more junior-college transfers, 6-3 junior **Desmond Baxter** of Chipola (Fla.) JC and 6-3 sophomore **Tim Brinker** of East Central (Mo.) JC.

Baxter has a deft outside shooting touch, evidenced by his two-year shooting average on three-point shots (.408, making 116 of 284) in junior college. Of the eight junior-college transfers, Brinker is the only one with three years eligibility remaining. Brinker averaged 11.6 points, 3.2 rebounds and 2.8 assists last year.

The Privateers lost sophomore point guard Edderick Womack (3.9 ppg, 2.6 rpg, team-high 103 assists) when he decided to transfer late in the spring semester. That leaves the point-guard job open.

Two transfers will battle for playing time there: 6-0 junior **Andre Blackmon** and 6-2 senior **Markell Sneed**.

Blackmon, a former all-state high school player in Mobile, Ala., transferred from Tennessee-Martin after starting his college career at Howard (Texas) JC. Three seasons ago, Blackmon had two 30-point games.

Sneed will not be eligible until at least mid-December while fulfilling academic requirements. The Duquesne transfer practiced with the Privateers last season. He averaged 2.0 points and 2.1 assists at Duquesne after starting his college career at Shorter (Ark.) JC.

Also joining the Privateers are two 6-0 junior guards, **Dexter Young** from Porterville (Calif.) JC and **Robert Griffin** from Irvine Valley (Calif.) JC. Young, a Chicago native, averaged 15.2 points and 5.6 assists last season, while Griffin, from Tustin, Calif., averaged 11.4 points, 2.8 rebounds and 3.7 assists.

The center job will be shared by two 6-9 juniors from junior colleges: **Byron Wilson** (no relation to teammate Curtis Wilson) and **Kevin Pickings**, a bruiser at 230 pounds.

A former standout from Chicago's Manley HS, Wilson was chosen all-conference last season after helping Mineral Area (Mo.) JC to a 25-7 record, including a school-record 15-0 record at home.

Pickings averaged 7.4 points, 3.5 rebounds and a team-high 1.8 blocked shots at Western Nebraska JC, which went 22-14 and won its region tournament for a second straight year with Pickings in the middle.

Even with so many new players on the roster, Stiebing believes his team should show cohesion by the time conference play begins.

"I think we'll all be on the same page," he said. "We'll spend a lot of time together on the road early in the season (with 11 of the first 17 games away). We've got to come together and do things unselfishly. We'll have to do the little things to win games."

1998-99 NEW ORLEANS SCHEDULE

Nov.	18	@Texas Christian
	21	@Northern Illinois
	27-29	#Big Island Invitational
Dec.	1	@Arizona State
	12	Centenary
	15	Denver
	19-20	##UNO Christmas Classic
	22-23	###ISU Holiday Classic
	30	Brown
Jan.	4	@Denver
	6	South Alabama
	9	@Western Kentucky
	14	@Arkansas State
	16	*Tulane
	18	@South Alabama
	21	Louisiana Tech
	23	@Arkansas-Little Rock
	28	Florida International
	30	@Southwestern Louisiana
Feb.	4	Arkansas-Little Rock
	6	Arkansas State
	11	@Louisiana Tech
	15	@Florida International
	18	Western Kentucky
	20	Southwestern Louisiana
27-Mar.	3	####Sun Belt Tournament

@ Road Games
* Nokia Sugar Bowl Classic, New Orleans, LA
\# Hilo, HI (vs. Georgia Tech, first round; also West Virginia and Wisconsin-Green Bay)
\## New Orleans, LA (vs. Maine, first round; also Tennessee State and Troy State)
\### Ames, IA (vs. Iowa State, first round; also Saint Mary's and Rice)
\#### Cajundome, Lafayette, LA

adidas Blue Ribbon Analysis

BACKCOURT .... **C** **BENCH/DEPTH** .... **D+**
FRONTCOURT .... **C+** **INTANGIBLES** .... **C+**

Although starting just his second season as coach at New Orleans, Joey Stiebing has a familiarity and understanding of the Privateers' program.

Stiebing is one of just three current Sun Belt coaches who have been in the league continuously since 1991-92. The others are Arkansas State head coach Dickey Nutt and Arkansas-Little Rock assistant Clarence Finley.

Even more important is Stiebing's relationship with his players.

"Every player on this year's team was recruited while I was head coach," Stiebing said, "and I believe that's a positive thing."

But the Privateers are definitely in a rebuilding mode, considering the influx of players and the lack of returnees. How they mesh is critical and it makes predicting New Orleans' season difficult.

Still, New Orleans is one of the league's premier programs, and anything less than an upper-division finish would be a surprise.

(G.P.)

SOUTH ALABAMA

LOCATION .... **Mobile, AL**
CONFERENCE .... **Sun Belt**
LAST SEASON .... **21-7 (.750)**
CONFERENCE RECORD .... **14-4 (t-1st)**
STARTERS LOST/RETURNING **4/1**
NICKNAME .... **Jaguars**
COLORS .... **Red, White & Blue**
HOMECOURT .... **Mitchell Center (10,000)**
COACH .... **Bob Weltlich (Ohio State '67)**
RECORD AT SCHOOL .... **21-7 (1 yr.)**
CAREER RECORD .... **240-277 (18 yrs.)**
ASSISTANTS .... **Tommy Wade (Southeast Missouri State '92)**
Dale Osbourne (South Alabama '87)
Chris Jones (Indiana State '93)
TEAM WINS (last 5 yrs.) **13-9-12-23-21**
RPI (last 5 yrs.) **156-235-221-82-60**
1997-98 FINISH .... **Lost in conference quarterfinal.**

South Alabama is hoping that new faces can take the Jaguars to familiar places during coach Bob Weltlich's second season.

The Jaguars are coming off their first season under Weltlich. It was somewhat of a disjointed season that found the former Mississippi head coach taking over for departing Bill Musselman, who resigned on Oct. 7, just a week before the start of preseason practice.

At the time, Musselman was quoted as saying about South Alabama athletics director Joe Gottfried: "I can't stand working one more day for that guy."

Well, apparently Weltlich can, and the fit worked for the Jaguars, who posted a 21-7 record en route to defending their Sun Belt Conference regular season co-championship.

As drastic and sudden a coaching change that occurred last season, the same can be said this time around with South Alabama's personnel. Gone are six seniors, including four starters who accounted for 90 percent of the team's offense and nearly 70 percent of its rebounding.

That's a lot of production considering the Jaguars finished the season ranked nationally in several categories, including second in scoring defense (54.5), ninth in rebound margin (7.6), 13th in field-goal percentage (.485), 16th in three-point field-goal percentage (.398), and 23rd in two categories, scoring margin (10.5) and won-lost percentage (.750).

"Every team has its own personality," said Weltlich, who dropped the interim label to his South Alabama job on Feb. 10 when he signed a four-year contact through the 2001-02 season. He previously had head coaching stints at Ole Miss (1977-82), Texas (1983-88) and Florida International (1991-95).

"When we lost the seniors," he said, "we lost the one tangible thing, leadership. There's no way of evaluating how we'll replace that. Last year, the seniors had been through a conference season and knew more than I did. They knew what they had to do."

The Jaguars signed seven players during the spring recruiting period to go with two transfers who become

1998-99 SOUTH ALABAMA SCHEDULE

Nov.	14	Missouri-Kansas City
	18	@Alcorn State
	24	@Southern Mississippi
	29	UAB
Dec.	4-5	#Hawkeye Invitational
	9	Colorado State
	12	*Alabama
	16	Alabama A&M
	22	@Florida International
	30	@Colorado State
Jan.	4	Western Kentucky
	6	@New Orleans
	9	@Louisiana Tech
	14	Florida International
	16	Louisiana Tech
	18	New Orleans
	21	@Southwestern Louisiana
	25	Texas-Pan American
	28	Southwestern Louisiana
	31	@Arkansas Little-Rock
Feb.	2	Arkansas State
	6	Arkansas-Little Rock
	11	@Texas-Pan American
	18	@Arkansas State
	20	@Western Kentucky
27-Mar.	2	##Sun Belt Tournament

@ Road Games
* Arby's Hardwood Classic, Birmingham, AL
# Iowa City, IA (vs. Iowa, first round; also Detroit and Gonzaga)
Cajundome, Lafayette, LA

eligible and four returning players, two of whom have never played collegiately.

The only returning starter is 6-5 senior forward **Darrian Evans** (11.6 ppg, 7.6 rpg), the team's third-leading scorer and top rebounder last season. He is best known for his defense, however, having finished the season ranked second in the Sun Belt at 2.2 steals per game (61 total).

Having started all 28 games last season, Evans will be called upon from the start for leadership. His solid and consistent play was best exhibited through his team-record field-goal percentage (.623). He was chosen the league's player of the week during one stretch when he made 15 of 17 shots in two games.

Also back from a key reserve role and expected to challenge for a starting job at small forward and shooting guard is 6-4 junior **Dusty Dubbs** (3.4 ppg, 1.8 rpg, 28 assists). Averaging 17 minutes a game, he led the team in free-throw percentage (.815). He played in 26 games, starting three.

Challenging for a starting job in the backcourt will be 6-4 senior **Clayton Dye** (2.7 ppg, 0.9 rpg), who played in 18 games and started two. When he did play, the former transfer from Pratt (Kan.) CC was solid, shooting almost 49 percent from the field.

The only other returnee with playing experience at South Alabama is 6-2 senior guard **Garrett Theriot** (1.2 ppg, 1.4 rpg, 23 assists), a second-year walkon who played in 18 games and started two. He filled in two games last season for injured point guard Jerome Coaxum, but is not expected to challenge for a starting job this season.

The Jaguars gain the eligibility of three players who were with the team last season, including two transfers: 6-5 junior guard **Josh Hotz**, a transfer from Southwest Missouri State, and 6-0 freshman guard **Tom Titus**, who transferred from Youngstown State. Also ready this season will be 6-10, 270-pound junior center **Jason Maronge**, who was redshirted last season while recovering from knee surgery.

Hotz started 10 games, including the last seven, two seasons ago at Southwest Missouri. He averaged 5.2 points, 1.9 rebounds and 1.5 assists while shooting .407 percent from the field, including 38.2 percent from three-point range.

Before walking on at Youngstown State in 1996-97, Titus underwent surgery on his right bicep. He has fully recovered from that injury, however. Titus is a scrappy defender who will contend for a starting job at point guard.

Maronge is a bulky center who will provide depth in the post. He is a former signee at Rutgers, where he played 24 games as a freshman during the 1995-96 season. Maronge, who came to South Alabama from Lee JC in Texas, is still questionable because of the knee injury.

With the signing of seven recruits in the spring, the South Alabama incoming class was ranked 47th in the nation by one national recruiting service.

In August, Weltlich signed 6-10, 240-pound sophomore **Virgil Stanescu** of Bucharest, Romania. Stanescu averaged 19.6 points and 10.8 rebounds per game last season for SOCED—a Division I club team in Romania. He is expected to battle Maronge for playing time at center.

Of the eight new players, only one is a freshman, 6-4 swingman **Alvin Payton**, a three-year starter at tradition-rich Valdosta (Ga.) High School. He earned second-team all-state and first-team all-region honors last season in helping his team to a 26-1 record. He averaged 12 points and six rebounds while shooting 53 percent from the field.

The continuing sojourn of 6-8, 210-pound sophomore **Brian Bland** has landed the Houston native at South Alabama. After starring at Temple CC in Texas, Bland signed with Cincinnati. But after suffering two broken noses and having to deal with a death in the family, Bland enrolled at Temple. Bland is the leading candidate to start at power forward.

Also contending for playing time down low is 6-6 junior **Bruce Williams**, a burly 218-pounder out of Okaloosa-Walton CC in Florida. He followed former Hiwassee (Tenn.) JC coach Bruce Stewart to the Florida junior college, where Williams averaged eight points and six rebounds last season.

Depth along the front line will also come from 6-6 forward **Michael Stewart**, who averaged 7.0 points, 4.2 rebounds, 2.4 assists and 1.5 steals last season for Marshalltown (Iowa) CC.

The leading candidate to start at point guard is 6-0 junior **James Broussard**. He was a do-it-all player for Lee (Texas) JC last season, averaging 10 points, three rebounds, five assists and 1.5 steals en route to being chosen honorable mention All-Texas among its junior-college players.

Perhaps the most athletic player for the Jaguars will be 6-3 junior guard **Melvin Cochran**, who toured Australia before last season on the U.S. National Junior College All-Star team. He didn't quite live up to preseason third-team All-America billing last year, but still averaged 12 points, four rebounds and 2.5 assists at Belleville (Ill.) Area College.

The most heralded recruit is 6-5 junior forward **Jerrick Kellum**, ranked No. 69 on JC recruiting analyst Phil Henzel's list of the top 300 sophomores. He helped Three Rivers (Mo.) CC to a 48-16 record the last two seasons, including a No. 17 national ranking last season when he averaged 13 points and six rebounds and shot 63 percent from the field.

"I think we'll be more athletic and deeper," Weltlich said. "We'll have more players to choose from. ... We should be more competitive in our drills, and that should give us more options. We recruited players who were versatile for that reason."

Even so, there is very little Division I experience on the roster—a fact not lost on Weltlich.

"We'll have a lack of playing experience at this level," he said, "and we have to develop some team continuity. Besides being new guys, (the new players) have to learn our system. And they have absolutely no idea what to expect in the Sun Belt Conference race."

Weltlich plans to install a more uptempo style of play that will be reliant on a motion offense and man-to-man defense.

adidas Blue Ribbon Analysis

BACKCOURT	C	BENCH/DEPTH	C
FRONTCOURT	D+	INTANGIBLES	C

Through the years, Bob Weltlich has proven to be a top-flight coach. He took over the Jaguars' program last season on short notice and guided them to a regular season co-championship. Weltlich joined Kentucky's Tubby Smith, Rhode Island's Jim Harrick and Texas Christian's Billy Tubbs as just one of four coaches to take three different teams to the NCAA Tournament.

The talent that garnered South Alabama back-to-back 20-win seasons is gone, however, and Weltlich has had to reload with eight new players, not counting three more players who were with the team but weren't available until this season.

The Jaguars catch no break from a tough schedule that certainly has caught Weltlich's attention:

"The one disservice for these players is that we have a very difficult schedule," Weltlich said. "We should be playing this year's schedule with last year's team."

It's certainly a season of uncertainty for the Jaguars, and it seems realistic to envision the program taking a step or two backward as it reloads for the future.

(G.P.)

SOUTHWESTERN LOUISIANA

LOCATION .... **Lafayette, LA**
CONFERENCE .... **Sun Belt**
LAST SEASON .... **18-13 (.581)**
CONFERENCE RECORD .... **12-6 (3rd)**
STARTERS LOST/RETURNING **4/1**
NICKNAME .... **Ragin' Cajuns**
COLORS .... **Vermillion & White**
HOMECOURT .... **Cajundome (12,800)**
COACH .... **Jessie Evans (Eastern Michigan '72)**
RECORD AT SCHOOL .... **18-13 (1 yr.)**
CAREER RECORD .... **18-13 (1 yr.)**
ASSISTANTS .... **Robert Lee (Nichols State '91)**
Bobby Champagne (South Alabama '90)
Paul Johnson (Harding '97)
TEAM WINS (last 5 yrs.) **22-7-16-12-18**
RPI (last 5 yrs.) **56-252-127-185-130**
1997-98 FINISH .... **Lost in conference final.**

Second-year Southwestern Louisiana coach Jessie Evans will not approach any season differently, regardless of circumstances.

Last season, Evans inherited a senior-laden team that won 18 games and came within three points of winning the Sun Belt Tournament and an NCAA Tournament berth.

Evans expects to challenge for the postseason every year. After all, the former Arizona assistant under Lute Olson is used to playing winning basketball.

"I want to emulate the Arizona program," said Evans, who helped coach the Wildcats to the 1997 national championship. "We want to build on last year. That means getting better as a team and becoming more consistent."

Evans said there will be several constants in his USL program, including high expectations.

"I want this team to progressively get better each game and each season," Evans said. "And it is our goal every year to make the NCAA Tournament. That will not change."

The Ragin' Cajuns came within a whisker of making the NCAA Tournament last season, losing to South Alabama in the nationally -televised championship game.

Duplicating last season's success will be difficult, considering Evans said goodbye to the team's top four scorers, who accounted for 52.2 points per game.

The most glaring absences will come in the backcourt, where All-Sun Belt players Casey Green (16.9 ppg, 2.7 rpg) and Tryone Foster (16.0 ppg, 2.5 repg) have departed.

That's the bad news. The good news is that USL returns nine lettermen, including former all-conference player **Reginald Poole**, a 6-10 power forward. Poole is back for his senior season after sitting out last year.

Poole was picked by several publications as the league's preseason player of the year in 1997-98, and for good reason. The Ragin' Cajuns' leading scorer (16.0) and rebounder (10.3) in 1996-97 was considered the league's premier post player. He was sixth in the nation in rebounding and had 15 double doubles.

But Poole was diagnosed just before the season with a benign bone tumor. Subsequent surgery to remove the tumor cost Poole the season.

"From what I have seen in individuals workouts, Reggie is back 100 percent," Evans said of Poole, USL's career leader in blocked shots (144). "He's a very exciting player who will give us what we want inside and outside."

Poole has added some weight and is up to 218 pounds, but Evans said he is "cut and looking good."

Joining Poole inside to give USL one of the league's premier frontcourts is 6-9, 250-pound sophomore center **Brett Smith** (6.5 ppg, 6.1 rpg), the team's leading rebounder last season and only returning starter.

Smith was the only Ragin' Cajun who started all 31 games last season and emerged as a dependable player in the low post. He ranked 10th in rebounding in the Sun Belt. Although he is a graduate of Baton Rouge (La.) Walker HS, Smith is a product of Australia, where he was a member of the All-Australian team as a junior in high school.

Inside depth will come from 6-9, 240-pound junior **Kendall Regis** (5.6 ppg, 4.7 rpg). He played in all 31 games, starting eight, and shot .545 from the field (72 of 132). In the 1996-97 season, Regis started 18 games as a freshman.

Two newcomers, **Lester Bruno** of Hutchinson (Kan.) JC and **Lonnie Thomas** of Phillips (Okla.) JC, are 6-8 juniors who will provide more depth in the frontcourt.

"We've got some beef inside," Evans said. "But we will still be a 94-foot team"

The vacated backcourt jobs are up for grabs, but the best candidate is 6-3 sophomore guard **Blaine Harmon**, who was academically ineligible last season. He was a proven scorer at Rayne (La.) HS, where he averaged 19.4 points as a senior, and he looked good practicing with the team last season.

"Blaine will give us both quickness and size," Evans said. "He's similar to (former Arizona guard) Khalid Reeves. He's a big guard that can really move in traffic and be creative and score."

The point guard job will be taken by either 5-10 junior **David Patrick** (3.5 ppg, 0.9 rpg, 40 assists), who played in 28 games and started 10, or 6-2 sophomore **Orlando Butler**, who sat out last season as a Prop 48 player.

Depth in the backcourt will come from 6-4 sophomore **William Howell** (3.1 ppg, 1.6 rpg), who started nine games last season; 6-2 sophomore **Chris Funderburk** (1.5 ppg, 1.3 rpg), who played in 28 games; and 6-6 sophomore **Shea Whiting** (5.0 ppg, 2.3 rpg), who played in all 31 games.

Also playing this season is combo guard **Jarret Evans**, a 6-3 sophomore who knows the coach quite well. Jarret is Jessie Evans' son.

The small forward job is also wide open, although Pepperdine transfer **Billy Jones**, a 6-5 sophomore and former high school star from New Orleans, looks like a strong candidate.

Southwestern Louisiana has two freshmen signees, 6-6 forward **Anthony Johnson** of Chicago Martin Luther King HS and 6-4 guard **Robert Jupiter** of Baton Rouge (La.) Parkview Baptist HS.

There is one wild card in the equation. Former LSU signee Darryl Robbins, a 6-7 swingman out of Baton Rouge, has decided to attend USL, but his status is in question as he waits to meet entrance requirements.

Also, other academic troubles could slow the team's progress, especially early. Howell and Whiting—as well as newcomers Jones, Butler and Robbins—will not be eligible until the end of the first semester in early December.

adidas Blue Ribbon Analysis

BACKCOURT	**C**	**BENCH/DEPTH**	**C+**
FRONTCOURT	**B+**	**INTANGIBLES**	**B**

Two seasons ago, Southwestern Louisiana coach Jessie Evans was helping Lute Olson prepare Arizona for a season that would eventually land the Wildcats a national championship.

Evans is a proven recruiter and a coach with a bright future. The Ragin' Cajuns didn't miss a beat last season, even without star power forward Reginald Poole.

Southwestern Louisiana is a program that could be poised for a run of league dominance, as long as Evans sticks around. He can recruit and coach, and that's a winning combination.

As for this year's team, Poole can't carry it and he won't have to. Although USL is traditionally a high-scoring team, this year's team will play defense and play well in the halfcourt, especially defensively.

If the program can overcome academic mishaps like this season, when at least five players are ineligible at the start, then look for Southwestern Louisiana to not only remain among the league's elite, but climb to the top of the pack.

(G.P.)

1998-99 SOUTHWESTERN LOUISIANA SCHEDULE

Nov.	19	@Southern Mississippi
	24	@East Carolina
	28	Texas Tech
	30	McNeese State
Dec.	5	Southern Mississippi
	12	@Cincinnati
	16	@Lamar
	21-22	#Golden Bear Classic
	27-30	##Rainbow Classic
Jan.	4	Louisiana Tech
	7	@Arkansas-Little Rock
	9	Arkansas State
	14	@Texas-Pan American
	16	@Western Kentucky
	21	South Alabama
	23	@Louisiana Tech
	25	Arkansas-Little Rock
	28	@South Alabama
	30	New Orleans
Feb.	6	Western Kentucky
	11	@Arkansas State
	13	@Florida International
	17	Florida International
	20	@New Orleans
	22	Texas-Pan American
27-Mar.	2	###Sun Belt Tournament

@ Road Games
# Oakland, CA (vs. Mississippi State, first round; also California and Eastern Kentucky)
Honolulu, HI (vs. Hawaii, first round; also Florida State, Mississippi State, Murray State, Princeton, Texas and UNC Charlotte)
Cajundome, Lafayette, LA

WESTERN KENTUCKY

LOCATION ..... **Bowling Green, KY**
CONFERENCE ..... **Sun Belt**
LAST SEASON ..... **10-19 (.345)**
CONFERENCE RECORD ..... **6-12 (t-8th)**
STARTERS LOST/RETURNING **2/3**
NICKNAME ..... **Hilltoppers**
COLORS ..... **Red & White**
HOMECOURT ..... **Diddle Arena (11,300)**
COACH ..... **Dennis Felton (Howard '85)**
RECORD AT SCHOOL ..... **First Year**
CAREER RECORD ..... **First Year**
ASSISTANTS ..... **Pete Hermann (SUNY-Genesco '70)**
Ken McDonald (Providence '92)
Kevin Baggett (St. Joseph's '83)
TEAM WINS (last 5 yrs.) **20-27-13-12-10**
RPI (last 5 yrs.) **52-25-129-176-209**
1997-98 FINISH ..... **Lost in conference quarterfinal.**

How quickly the mighty mid-major has fallen. It hasn't been that long_four seasons, to be exact—since Western Kentucky was a perennial entry into the NCAA Tournament and a solid top 30 team in both ranking and RPI.

And even the changing of the guard, when former coach Ralph Williard left for Pittsburgh and was replaced by former Jacksonville head man Matt Kilcullen, seemed to be the correct answer. Kilcullen became the first Division I coach to be chosen coach of the year in the same conference after consecutive seasons.

But because Kilcullen's 27-win debut season (in 1994-95) was followed by a steady decline to 10 wins last year and three straight losing seasons, it didn't take long for him to be unceremoniously shown the door before last season was even complete.

There are various theories for the decline, which just so happened to coincide with an overall rating decline for the league, which many relate in part to the Hilltoppers' disappearance from the postseason. But the talent level at Western withered the past four seasons, as did the support of fans and administration alike.

Enter Dennis Felton, 34, a phenom of a coach who becomes the youngest of the Hilltoppers' coaches who have tried in vain to rekindle the glory days of legendary E.A. Diddle (who began his 42-year run at the age of 27).

Felton has the coaching pedigree, albeit of the assistant variety. He is most noted for being a top assistant of Rick Barnes the last six years at Clemson (1994-98) and Providence (1992-94). During that stretch, Barnes-coached teams had six winning seasons and visited the postseason every year (four NCAAs and two NITs). Last season, Felton had climbed to the status of associate head coach.

"I learned how to build and operate a program from square one in a very comprehensive way," Felton said of his days under Barnes, which were preceded by assistant coaching stops at St. Joseph's, Tulane and Delaware.

"We sweated every detail and left nothing for doubt. We always controlled everything we could control. We didn't allow things to slip through the cracks and develop as they may. Rick was excellent at running an entire program."

A top athlete out of Surrattsville (Md.) High School, Felton starred at Prince George's Community College before becoming an All-Mid-Eastern Athletic Conference selection at Howard University, where he graduated cum laude in 1985 with a degree in radio and television and film production.

It was during his senior year of college that Felton began his coaching career as an assistant at Oxon (Md.) High School. He then moved on to Charles County Community College in LaPlate, Md., before joining the staff at Delaware in 1986.

"I feel like I am well-prepared for this moment because of my past experiences with different head coaches I've worked with," Felton said of his first head coaching job.

Felton considers his philosophy to rebuilding WKU's hoops fortunes a hybrid of lessons learned. But there is one adjective he repeats when asked for an approach—intensity.

"I would say I'll be intense in terms of how I accept challenges and how we attack things in a comprehensive manner to this program," Felton said. "We're going to take into account every single aspect of building a successful program."

And after a trio of losing seasons for the Hilltoppers, Felton knows where to begin.

"Clearly, we need to learn as a team what goes into greatness and learn to embrace those characteristics," said Felton, who rattles off such qualities as commitment, discipline, work ethic, intelligence, togetherness, etc. Competitiveness is the major thing we need to develop. And mental toughness comes with competitiveness."

That's all fine and good, but will it win games? Hard to say, especially this season, when the cupboard is not well-stocked. It will surely take two to three recruiting classes for Felton to get the kind of athlete he wants to coach.

But for now, he's saddled with the good news and the bad news of three returning starters and six other returning lettermen that stumbled to a less-than-Western type of season.

If Western is to return to league-title contention, it will have to ride the sturdy shoulders of 6-8, 215-pound senior center **Ravon Farris** (10.9 ppg, 6.9 rpg), who battled back from an injury in the season opener to play in 20 games.

Farris shot 50.9 percent from the field and scored in double figures in half his games, including 20 points against Lamar in the regular-season finale in which he made all seven of his shots. He also notched 10 or more rebounds five times, including a career-high 13.

"Ravon is the single post player in our program," Felton said. "I hope he can really do the work of three or four post players. He needs to have a tremendous presence inside on both offense and defense. As a senior, he must show the kind of leadership and desire to make something special of his last year."

Just who will accompany Farris down low is anybody's guess. It was supposed to be former Memphis Central High star and Southern California transfer Maurice Strong, but it didn't take long for Felton and Strong to butt heads. Guess who departed?

From there, there are very few prospects and just a few suspects.

The Hilltoppers keep waiting for former Georgia high school star **Melvin Adams** (5.0 ppg, 2.9 rpg), a 6-6, 225-pound senior forward, to show up in the paint. He played in all 29 games last season, starting five, but only scored in double figures five times.

Felton also hopes that **Lee Lampley** (3.6 ppg, 2.4 rpg), a 6-6 junior, can do battle inside, but his 195 pounds tend to push him more to the small forward slot. On the horizon is 6-8 freshman forward **Ben Mauck**, who averaged 20

1998-99 WESTERN KENTUCKY SCHEDULE

Nov.	14	@Evansville
	18	@Virginia Commonwealth
	22	@Louisville
	25	Akron
	30	Belmont
Dec.	3	*Middle Tennessee State
	5	UAB
	8	@Butler
	19	@Murray State
	23	Southern Illinois
	29-30	#All College Tournament
Jan.	4	@South Alabama
	9	New Orleans
	12	@Florida International
	16	Southwestern Louisiana
	21	Arkansas State
	28	@Arkansas-Little Rock
	30	@Arkansas State
Feb.	2	Florida International
	4	Louisiana Tech
	6	@Southwestern Louisiana
	10	Arkansas-Little Rock
	13	@Louisiana Tech
	18	@New Orleans
	20	South Alabama
27-Mar.	2	##Sun Belt Tournament

@ Road Games
* Nashville Arena, Nashville, TN
# Oklahoma City, OK (vs. Oklahoma, first round; also Cal Poly and Oral Roberts)
Cajundome, Lafayette, LA

points and 10 rebounds per game at Savannah (Tenn.) Harding County High School. But Felton has yet to see Mauck, a November signee under Kilcullen, play a game. Mauck was selected to play in the Tennessee-Georgia All-Star game in August, an indicator that he has some talent. Tennessee put a strong team on the floor.

Also available will be 6-5 senior forward **Kareem Abdul-Jabbar** (1.8 ppg, 1.4 rpg), who missed most of last season with a broken bone in his left hand. But by tournament time, Abdul-Jabbar showed promise against South Alabama, scoring eight points in just five minutes. And, yeah, he's the son of you know who.

That's about it for the frontcourt, but the backcourt features two returning starters, three returning lettermen and three two newcomers vying for playing time.

Let's start with the starters. If Felton is seeking hard-nosed, then 6-4 senior guard **Joe Harney** (9.1 rpg, 2.9 rpg, 32 steals) fits the bill. Harney also was sidelined with a hand injury, but not before notching a career-high 23 points against Arkansas-Little Rock, two points better than his season-opening effort against Kansas.

Before the injury, though, Harney had stepped up, connecting on 16 of 30 field goals, including 8 of 14 on three-point shots. He made 37 of 102 (.363) treys last season.

Returning to point guard, where he started the last 10 games, should be 6-1 senior **Vince Edwards** (2.3 ppg, 1.4 apg). His had eight points and six assists in his best game of the season, against Southwestern Louisiana.

The wildcard for the Hilltoppers this season is ever-promising **Nashon McPherson** (6.5 ppg, 1.6 rpg), a 6-4 sophomore swingman who left Queens (N.Y.) Springfield Gardens High School as the most heralded recruit under Kilcullen's regime.

But he sat out his freshman year with a broken wrist and was slowed last season by a knee injury. He finally broke into the starting lineup late in the season and averaged 9.6 points during the last 11 games, including a career-high 21 against Pan American. The southpaw sharpshooter/slasher must come up big for the Hilltoppers to compete.

"I haven't seen him play either," Felton said of McPherson, "but I know that he is a very strong, gifted athlete."

Two other guards gained experience last season—6-5 senior **Kyle Chapman** (3.0 ppg, 0.7 apg) and 6-0 sophomore **Roshon Brown** (5.2 ppg, 3.3 apg). Chapman played in 19 games, starting three, and during one late stretch made 8 of 12 treys. Brown played in just one of the first nine games, but every one after that with nine starts.

The only incoming freshman signed by Felton was 6-4 guard **Tremaine Rowles**, who averaged 30 points and 8.5 rebounds for Baltimore Gwynn Lake School last season.

"He plays the game and approaches it in a very mature way," Felton said of Rowles. "He has a lot of poise, and he can really shoot the ball."

The other incoming freshman is 6-3 guard **Casey Simpson**, who played for his father, Ernie Simpson, at in-town Bowling Green High School. A scrappy player, he set school records for career points (1,508) and three-point shots made (162).

Felton admits not knowing much about his charges. But that will soon change.

"It's normal because I just haven't been exposed to the team a lot," he said. "We'll get to know them better, sure. Until you get in the trenches with somebody, you don't know what they're made of."

adidas Blue Ribbon Analysis

BACKCOURT .... **C+** **BENCH/DEPTH** .... **C**
FRONTCOURT .... **C+** **INTANGIBLES** .... **C+**

Talk about tradition, Western Kentucky fans will remind you in a heartbeat that the Hilltoppers are among the winningest programs in all of college basketball. But 1971 seems like a long time ago. That was the year of the program's only Final Four visit.

Sure, there have been blips on the radar screen, like the late '80s teams of Clem Haskins, the early-'90s surge under Ralph Willard, and even the 27-win season under Matt Kilcullen. Thing is, when coaches leave Western, they do it in one of two ways—to a better job (like Gene Keady to Purdue, Haskins to Minnesota, and Willard to Pittsburgh) or the coaching unemployment line (like Willard predecessor Murray Arnold, now at Stetson; and Kilcullen).

Felton has a long battle in a league in flux. Western officials and fans always talk about talking to other conferences, but the Hilltoppers need to worry about returning to the top of the Sun Belt Conference before considering a move elsewhere, whether it be up or down.

In the meantime, Felton appears to be a savvy recruiter and excellent judge of talent. He's also personable enough to help thwart the long shadows of in-state powers Kentucky and Louisville.

And Felton was also smart enough to surround himself with college coaching veteran Pete Herrmann, the former Navy head coach and Virginia assistant.

Time will only tell if Felton wins at Western and becomes attractive to other schools; or, worse yet, doesn't get the job done and leaves Western in languor.

In the meantime, the Hilltoppers will struggle to be average in a very average league.

(G.P.)

TRANS-AMERICA ATHLETIC CONFERENCE

adidas BLUE RIBBON FORECAST

1. Georgia State
2. Central Florida
3. Samford
4. Jacksonville
5. Centenary
6. Florida Atlantic
7. Stetson
8. Jacksonville State
9. Mercer
10. Campbell
11. Troy State

ALL-CONFERENCE TEAM

G—Ronnie McCollum, SO, Centenary
G—Damon Arnette, SR, Florida Atlantic
F—Brad Traina, SR, Central Florida
F—Will Daniel, JR, Samford
F—Quincy Gause, SR, Georgia State

PLAYER OF THE YEAR

Ronnie McCollum, SO, Centenary

NEWCOMER OF THE YEAR

Anton Reese, JR, Georgia State

1998-99 CONFERENCE TOURNAMENT

Feb. 25-27, Jacksonville Coliseum, Jacksonville, FL

1997-98 CHAMPION

College of Charleston (regular season, East Division)
Georgia State (regular season, West Division)
College of Charleston (conference tournament)

1997-98 POSTSEASON PARTICIPANTS

Postseason Record: 0-1 (.000)
NCAA
College of Charleston

TOP BACKCOURTS

1. Georgia State
2. Samford
3. Central Florida

TOP FRONTCOURTS

1. Georgia State
2. Jacksonville
3. Central Florida

ON THE WAY UP

Florida Atlantic

ON THE WAY DOWN

Campbell

INSIDE THE NUMBERS

- 1997-98 conference RPI: 25 (of 30)
- Conference RPI (last 5 years): 25-24-24-30-25

DID YOU KNOW?

The offseason was a tumultuous one for the conference. In addition to the already announced departure of College of Charleston to the Southern Conference, and the addition of Jacksonville from the Sun Belt, the league was stunned by the sudden pullout of Florida International. TAAC bylaws require a two-year notice for members desiring to leave the league, and there's a financial penalty for non-compliance. FIU decided to make the move anyway, eventually replacing Jacksonville in the Sun Belt. The loss of FIU reduced the conference to 11 members. The odd number of schools eventually led league administrators to do away with the conference's old East-West division alignment...Perhaps no conference in the country was more thrilled with the NCAA Management Council's decision to revise its old "Eight-Year Rule". Schools moving from Division II to Division I that were normally required to wait eight years before becoming eligible for an NCAA automatic bid, now must wait only two years for that privilege. That means that TAAC members Florida Atlantic, Jacksonville State and Troy State will now be eligible to compete in the NCAA and TAAC tournaments. Like most mid-major conferences normally receiving one bid, the TAAC would not allow its members that fell under the "Eight-Year Rule" to compete in the conference tournament. The league's fear was the potential loss of NCAA Tournament revenue that would have resulted if an ineligible team had won the conference tournament and left the league without an NCAA representative...In addition to Hugh Durham arriving with new league member Jacksonville, there is only one new head coach in the TAAC after the conference underwent wholesale changes a year ago. Mark Turgeon, who spent last season as an assistant coach with the Philadelphia 76ers, takes over for Bill Jones at Jacksonville State...With Georgia State's first win this season, Lefty Driesell will join a select group of coaches to have won 700 career games. That group includes such notables as Dean Smith, Adolph Rupp, Henry Iba, Phog Allen, Ray Meyer and Bobby Knight.

(G.C.)

CAMPBELL

LOCATION .... **Buies Creek, NC**
CONFERENCE .... **Trans-America Athletic (TAAC)**
LAST SEASON .... **10-17 (.370)**
CONFERENCE RECORD .... **4-12 (6th-East Division)**
STARTERS LOST/RETURNING **3/2**
NICKNAME .... **Camels**
COLORS .... **Orange & Black**
HOMECOURT .... **Carter Gymnasium (945)**
COACH .... **Billy Lee (Atlantic Christian '71)**
RECORD AT SCHOOL .... **175-190 (13 yrs.)**
CAREER RECORD .... **296-278 (20 yrs.)**
ASSISTANTS .... **Cliff Dillard (Campbell '89)**
Rob Dooley (Western New England '93)
Steve Roberts (Lander '84)
TEAM WINS (last 5 yrs.) **20-8-17-11-10**
RPI (last 5 yrs.) **154-217-172-248-266**
1997-98 FINISH .... **Lost in conference first round.**

In a place as backwoods sounding as Buies Creek, it's easy to imagine finding yourself stuck in the mud, or perhaps quicksand. That has to be the feeling Campbell coach Billy Lee is having these days.

Just a few years removed from an unlikely appearance in the NCAA Tournament, Lee's Camels have been struggling as of late. Campbell has won just 21 games the last two seasons and things don't appear to be getting any easier this time around.

Lee has no double-figure scorers returning, but is facing the season with the same kind of zeal and sense of humor that has made him something of a folk hero around these parts of the basketball world.

"We do have a lot of unanswered questions about what our strengths and weaknesses will be," said Lee, who is just four victories shy of his 300th career coaching win. "That leaves us with a lot of holes to fill both defensively and offensively. But overall, I like our team personality and enthusiasm. We're going to work on performance. Just as night follows day, winning will follow performance. We're always con-

1998-99 CAMPBELL SCHEDULE

Nov.	14	@Richmond
	18	@North Carolina State
	21	East Carolina
	24	Coastal Carolina
	28	Mars Hill
Dec.	2	@North Carolina-Wilmington
	5	@Winthrop
	17	@Belmont
	19	@Vanderbilt
	28	North Carolina-Asheville
Jan.	2	@Central Florida
	4	@Florida Atlantic
	7	Central Florida
	9	Florida Atlantic
	14	@Georgia State
	16	@Mercer
	21	Samford
	23	Jacksonville State
	28	Stetson
	30	Jacksonville
Feb.	4	@Troy State
	6	@Centenary
	11	@Samford
	13	@Jacksonville State
	18	Georgia State
	20	Troy State
	25-27	#TAAC Tournament

@ Road Games
# Jacksonville Coliseum, Jacksonville, FL

cerned with doing things right."

With little or no "star quality" on this year's team, Lee is counting on eight returning players and five newcomers to make Campbell competitive.

"If we had to start tomorrow, I couldn't tell you what the starting lineup would be," he said. "Out of quantity comes quality. We have no preconceived notions of who is ahead of the other, especially with five new players. The keys for this team are to see how well we play defensively, how we rebound, and if easy baskets are going to come for us. I hope that every basket will not be as laborious as last year. We've got to find guys who can step up and knock down shots so that we don't have to work so hard for every bucket."

While Lee may not know where to start looking for contributions, we'll begin with 6-2 junior guard **Matt Mardis** (8.5 ppg, 1.7 rpg, 40 assists, 23 steals), who ranked second on the team in scoring last year and is one of two returning starters. Mardis is a left-hander with an excellent mid-range game. He scored in double figures in three of Campbell's last four games, including a career-high 23 points against Stetson in the regular-season finale. Lee hopes his scoring average will soar if he can place him a couple of steps closer to the basket.

"We have tried for two years to play Matt outside the three-point line, but his strength is around the basket where he can use his moves and fakes to get off shots," said Lee. "He's a wiggler with a middle game and is a Campbell version of a Damon Bailey, a 6-2 or 6-3 player who can score down low. He will be playing against people who are bigger, stronger and quicker each night. So Matt's got to be tougher, smarter and more mentally prepared than his opponent."

The Camels' other returning starter is 6-5 junior forward **Jamie Simmons** (5.4 ppg, 4.9 rpg, 21 blocks, 20 steals), who was hampered most of last season with a foot injury. Simmons is an excellent rebounder, having led the squad in that category as a freshman. He is a good defender and passer, and a career .525 shooter from the field.

Sophomore **Eddie Walker** (5.1 ppg, 2.0 rpg, 38 assists) could join Mardis in what could potentially become a three-man starting backcourt. Walker, a natural two-guard at 6-3, played at the point for much of last season due to an injury to departed senior Corey Best. A slender player with a nice jumper, Walker will probably start out the season at the point, but could eventually move to off-guard if 5-11 freshman **Wes Layton** is the answer to Campbell's point-guard prayers.

Campbell has played without a true point guard for much of the last two seasons, something akin to death in Lee's intricate motion offense. Layton averaged 10.9 points and 5.2 assists last season at Olathe (Kan.) East HS. Layton is being billed as a heady ballhandler and distributor who can also step up and hit the open jumper.

"Wes was the quarterback on the football team, played in the state tournament in tennis, and has won everywhere he has been," said Lee. "He has a chance to be a very good guard here, but it's hard for any freshman to come in and take over in terms of leadership. Eddie did a very admirable job at the point last season. He also has the versatility to move to the two if Wes proves he can handle the point as a freshman."

There are a host of newcomers set to join Simmons as pieces to Lee's frontcourt puzzle.

Junior forward **Darrin Hucks** (5.7 ppg, 1.9 rpg) played in 27 games last season and made seven starts. A good three-point shooter, the 6-5 Hucks shot .352 (38 of 108) from beyond the arc. His is mostly a stand-still shooter, however, and is limited defensively.

Tyreck Knox (3.1 ppg, 1.7 rpg), a 6-6 junior forward, is an excellent offensive rebounder and a good athlete. His minutes were limited last season because of an ankle injury and the presence of leading scorer George Miller (13.1 ppg) up front.

Senior forward **Brian Paine** (1.6 ppg, 0.9 rpg) appeared in 21 games a year ago, but will be ineligible to start the season after he switched his major, causing him to miss NCAA satisfactory progress requirements. Paine is a good outside shooter.

The center slot could become a two-headed version consisting of 6-8 senior **Jason Smith** (3.9 ppg, 2.8 rpg) and 6-9 sophomore **Andy Miller** (0.7 ppg, 1.0 rpg). Smith is an excellent athlete and is strong (240 pounds). He finished fourth in last year's TAAC outdoor track and field championships in the 110-meter high hurdles. His achievements on the hardwood have been much more sporadic, mainly because of a propensity for committing fouls. He was whistled for 61 fouls in just 331 minutes. Miller is a work in progress who is still learning to compete at the Division I level. He has soft hands and a nice jump shot, making his up side worth the investment.

In addition to Layton, four other newcomers will be competing for playing time.

Guard **Adam Fellers**, a 6-3 freshman, averaged 18.5 points and 4.8 assists last season for Pine Forest HS in Fayetteville, N.C. He hit 112 three-pointers during his senior season, but will have to learn how to use picks to get his shot off within Lee's offense.

Forwards **Quincy Hinton** and **Joey Smith** will vie for minutes at small forward. Smith is a 6-4 junior transfer from Kansas City (Kan.) CC, where he averaged 13.3 points and 6.5 rebounds last season. Hinton, a 6-4 freshman, averaged 14.0 points and 10.0 rebounds as a senior at Ramsey HS in Birmingham. Both players can put the ball on the floor and score and are good defenders.

Bobby Jones, a 6-6 freshman from White Oak HS in Jacksonville, N.C., has size and strength, but needs to work on his ball handling. He averaged 13.1 points and 10.0 rebounds last season. Jones might just be willing to put the time in to become a player at this level. His dad is a retired drill instructor.

adidas Blue Ribbon Analysis

BACKCOURT	C	BENCH/DEPTH	D+
FRONTCOURT	D+	INTANGIBLES	C

Campbell appears to have just two problems heading into this season—offense and defense.

With no double-figure scorers returning on a team that shot just .405 from the field last season, and without a pure go-to guy in sight, the Camels are going to have run their motion offense to perfection and hope to limit the number of possessions in each game in order to win. Win that is, if they have a reasonable chance of stopping the opposing team at the other end of the floor.

"Inexperience usually shows up quicker on defense than on offense," said Lee. "An inexperienced player might be out of position by three or four steps on defense, so we've got to spend a lot of time on that aspect in the preseason. But, if we can't pass and shoot well, then that translates into us playing more defense."

Sounds like an ominous statement from a man who has been around the scene for quite a while. With that said, we'll pick the Camels to finish 10th.

(G.C.)

CENTENARY

LOCATION .... **Shreveport, LA**
CONFERENCE .... **Trans-America Athletic (TAAC)**
LAST SEASON .... **10-20 (.333)**
CONFERENCE RECORD .... **8-8 (3rd-West Division)**
STARTERS LOST/RETURNING **2/3**
NICKNAME .... **Gentlemen (Gents)**
COLORS .... **Maroon & White**
HOMECOURT .... **Gold Dome (4,000)**
COACH. Billy Kennedy (Southeastern Louisiana '86)
RECORD AT SCHOOL .... **10-20 (1 yr.)**
CAREER RECORD .... **10-20 (1 yr.)**
ASSISTANTS .... **Kevin Johnson (Texas-Pan American '88)**
Steve Prohm (Alabama '97)
Scott Stapler (Auburn '96)
TEAM WINS (last 5 yrs.) **16-10-11-9-10**
RPI (last 5 yrs.) **200-230-246-269-263**
1997-98 FINISH .... **Lost in conference first round.**

1998-99 CENTENARY SCHEDULE

Nov.	14	Nicholls State
	21	@Texas A&M
	29	@Creighton
Dec.	2	@Southeastern Louisiana
	5	Northwestern State
	8	@Mississippi State
	12	@New Orleans
	18-19	#TCBY Tournament
	30	@Missouri
Jan.	2	@Jacksonville
	4	@Stetson
	9	Jacksonville
	11	Stetson
	16	Samford
	18	@Jacksonville State
	23	Central Florida
	25	Florida Atlantic
	28	@Troy State
	30	@Mercer
Feb.	6	Campbell
	8	Georgia State
	13	@Florida Atlantic
	15	@Central Florida
	18	Jacksonville State
	20	@Samford
	25-27	##TAAC Tournament

@ Road Games
# Richmond, VA (vs. Richmond, first round; also, Arkansas-Little Rock and High Point)
Jacksonville Coliseum, Jacksonville, FL

The snapshots of **Ronnie McCollum** on opposition blackboards around the TAAC might be getting larger this season.

McCollum (17.5 ppg, 2.9 rpg, 32 assists), a 6-3 sophomore, did what few players at the Division I level are able to in their first season—compete for a conference scoring title. Though outdistanced by Central Florida's Mark Jones (20.8 ppg), McCollum did finish second, setting him up for the possibility of some extra defensive attention in year two.

"Defensively, this year is going to be more of a challenge for him," said coach Billy Kennedy. "People are going to gear their defenses to take him out. We are going to have to find new ways to get him open, and we're also going to need somebody else to step up and score."

McCollum came to Centenary with the reputation as a big-time shooter. His 101 three-pointers last season solidified that status and also established school and conference single-season records. His three-point total was the fourth highest for a freshman in NCAA history.

McCollum shot .419 from downtown and .455 from the field. He hit seven three-pointers in a game on two occasions. To his credit, McCollum has refused to rest on his laurels during the offseason. He has hit the gym hard, working on improving defensively and in being able to create shots for himself off the dribble. "He is in better shape and is a better player today than he was when he got here," said Kennedy.

McCollum's first season has Centenary fans begging for more and is one reason the future looks brighter for a program that has been the epitome of mediocrity over the last four years.

Two other reasons for optimism that come quickly to mind are the return of 5-10 senior point guard **Tim Law** (11.5 ppg, 3.2 rpg, 138 assists, 64 steals) and the arrival of some size on a front line that did not have a starter taller than 6-6 in 1997-98.

Law is the perfect running mate for McCollum. Extremely quick and a good leaper, his success is predicated on how effectively he can penetrate into the lane and create opportunities for himself and others. Law ranked fifth in the TAAC in assists. Many of his forays into the lane last season resulted in kick-outs to McCollum for uncontested threes.

"One of the things that makes him (McCollum) so good is we have a point guard that complements him," said Kennedy.

Law was a bit inconsistent offensively last season (especially at home), something that he will need to straighten out in a hurry if opposing teams begin to key more on McCollum. He also committed 121 turnovers.

Up front, two newcomers—6-7 freshman forward **Ed Dotson** and 6-8 junior forward/center **Srdjan Lalic**—

could be in the starting five.

Dotson played at Cooley HS in Detroit and was the Gents' most sought-after recruit. He is an excellent player around the basket with his ability to score, rebound and block shots.

Lalic comes to Centenary from Pratt (Kan.) CC, where he averaged 12.0 points and 8.0 rebounds as a sophomore. Lalic, from Serbia, has an excellent overall game.

Dotson and Lalic will try to compensate for almost 25.0 points and 14.0 rebounds per game lost because of the departure of starters Herbert Lang (16.3 ppg, 6.6 rpg) and Reggie Love (8.2 ppg, 7.4 rpg).

Cornell Hardman (7.5 ppg, 5.6 rpg, 20 steals, 18 blocked shots), a 6-6 senior, started 28 of 30 games last season. He can play all three frontcourt positions, providing an interesting blend of tenacity around the basket and touch on the perimeter. Hardman shot .419 (18 of 43) from three-point range and also tied for the team lead in blocked shots.

Lloyd Cook (3.3 ppg, 2.9 rpg, 16 blocks), a 6-6 sophomore, was the Gents' sixth man for most of last season. Cook was a starter for the first part of the season, but his lack of proficiency at the free-throw line (.431) cost him minutes and opportunities as the year wore on. He is effective going to the basket, runs well and can also knock down an occasional 15-foot jumper.

Darian Burton (1.2 ppg, 1.3 rpg), a 6-7 sophomore, saw action in 22 games last season. The tallest member on last year's squad, Burton was chained to the bench early before ending the season as the seventh player in Kennedy's rotation. A hard worker on defense, Burton also showed some promise as a scorer and rebounder. He shot .522 in limited attempts from the floor.

The new big man on campus is 6-11 junior **Ben Horn**, who played last season at Meridian (Miss.) CC. Although he's very unpolished, expect Horn to see meaningful minutes this season fulfilling such roles as rebounding and setting picks.

Two other newcomers in the frontcourt are 6-9 freshman **Brein Rabenhorst**, who averaged 13.0 points and 10.0 rebounds at Catholic HS in Baton Rouge, and 6-5 freshman **Delrick Brown** from Pearland (Tex.) HS. Brown averaged 16.0 points and 9.0 rebounds last season The Gents coaching staff is high on his shooting ability and all-around game. Brown played on a state championship team last season.

The backcourt reserve corps is headed by 6-0 junior **Thomas Foster** (1.5 ppg, 1.0 rpg), who played in 29 games last season. Foster, who spelled McCollum and Law, is a heady player who isn't afraid to step up and take big shots.

Competing with Foster for playing time will be 6-0 freshman **Warren Harris** from Clear Brook HS in Priestwood, Tex.

adidas Blue Ribbon Analysis

BACKCOURT	**B**	**BENCH/DEPTH**	**D+**
FRONTCOURT	**C**	**INTANGIBLES**	**C**

Centenary's 8-8 conference record last season was a good "pick-me-up" for a team that got brutalized playing its early-season non-conference schedule. The Gents dropped 10 of their first 11 games and looked to be doormat material heading into league competition.

After that respectable league showing, there are plenty of positives to ponder heading into 1998-99. First off, the backcourt of McCollum and Law should be competitive with, or outperform, any in the TAAC. Second, Kennedy seems to have recruited to fill a need, specifically the Gents' lack of size on the front line. That should bode well for a coach who likes to stress defense and rebounding, and prefers to keep the scores of games in the 60- to 70 range.

How good the Gents ultimately are will depend a lot on how good the likes of Brown and Lalic are, and how much the holdovers in the frontcourt have improved during the offseason.

"We went after some size with our recruiting class," said Kennedy. "We're bigger and stronger than we were last year. Whether or not we're better, only time will tell. Our goal is to win more games than last year and we think we have the opportunity to do that. We've got some guys returning who know how we want to play, and we have a recruiting class that we think can help us."

For now, Centenary appears to be a slightly better-than-average unit in the TAAC. Pencil the Gents in for a fifth-place finish.

(G.C.)

CENTRAL FLORIDA

LOCATION .... **Orlando, FL**
CONFERENCE .... **Trans-American Athletic (TAAC)**
LAST SEASON .... **17-11 (.607)**
CONFERENCE RECORD .... **11-5 (3rd-East Division)**
STARTERS LOST/RETURNING **4/1**
NICKNAME .... **Golden Knights**
COLORS .... **Black & Gold**
HOMECOURT .... **UCF Arena (5,100)**
COACH .... **Kirk Speraw (Iowa '80)**
RECORD AT SCHOOL .... **67-74 (5 yrs.)**
CAREER RECORD .... **67-74 (5 yrs.)**
ASSISTANTS .... **Don Burgess (Radford '94)**
Jorge Fernandez (Stetson '85)
Chris Mowry (St. Ambrose '84)
TEAM WINS (last 5 yrs.) **21-11-11-7-17**
RPI (last 5 yrs.) **144-243-219-301-169**
1997-98 FINISH .... **Lost in conference semifinal.**

Click! Click!

That sound you just heard was Central Florida locking the back door now that TAAC rivals College of Charleston and Florida International have taken their considerable "game" to other conferences.

No team in the league figures to benefit more this season from the departure of the two TAAC powerhouses. The Golden Knights finished behind the Cougars and the Golden Panthers in the East Division last year, despite the presence of TAAC Player of the Year Mark Jones (20.8 ppg, 7.2 rpg, 62 assists, 49 steals).

UCF should be able to see the top of the mountain clearly now. Most TAAC observers figure that the Golden Knights should be wrestling for the top spot this year with Lefty Driesell's Georgia State squad. UCF will get to gauge its top competitor early. The Golden Knights and Panthers will hook up twice in early January, long before the meat of the conference schedule.

"We should be a part of that (the TAAC championship race)," said coach Kirk Speraw. "We think we would have been even with the changes in the league."

UCF's success will probably be predicated on how effectively it makes up for the loss of Jones, and how it adjusts to life as a league frontrunner. The Golden Knights went from seven wins to 17 last season, snapping College of Charleston's 33-game TAAC home winning streak in the process with a 70-68 overtime victory on Feb. 21. Those kind of achievements won't allow them the opportunity to sneak up on any opponents this year.

"We won't replace Mark and all the different things he did," said Speraw.

"At the same time, we've got a more experienced team now. We've played the last two years with a lot of underclassmen. That game experience should evolve into some added production this year."

UCF will be led this season by solid senior **Brad Traina** (15.4 ppg, 4.8 rpg, 62 assists, 45 steals, 14 blocks), a 6-5 swingman. Traina finished ninth in the conference in scoring last season. A versatile offensive performer, Traina can penetrate from the wing, shoot three-pointers and pass. He shot .482 percent from the field and .398 (53 of 133) from three-point range. In addition, he made .759 (85 of 112) of his free-throw attempts.

"Brad can do a lot of things," said Speraw. "He has continued to improve every year he has been here. He's a hard worker and he sets the tone for us."

Traina has the ability to take over a game offensively. He scored 37 points at Stetson last season, the second-most scored in a game in UCF's Division I history. The beauty of all of this is that Traina may not be asked to do any more on offense than he has in the past, even with the departure of Jones.

The Golden Knights are a versatile and deep team. Last year's sixth man—6-2 junior **D'Quarius Stewart** (10.3 ppg, 2.5 rpg, 60 assists, 41 steals)—will bring his considerable offensive talents to the front as he takes over for Jones at off-guard.

It is also expected that the center tandem of 6-6 junior **Davin Granberry** (7.1 ppg, 4.1 rpg, 15 blocks) and 6-9 senior **Bucky Hodge** (6.8 ppg, 4.5 rpg, 33 blocks) will become more of a focal point offensively.

Stewart finished third on the team last season in scoring. He is an athletic player who can create his own shot. His numbers have been hampered by the fact he has played behind the Golden Knights' top scorer for the last two years (Harry Kennedy in 1996-97 and Jones last season). Stewart has worked hard on developing his perimeter game since arriving at UCF. He shot .347 percent (33 of 85) from three-point range last season.

"Stewart has had his best offseason as far as working on his game," said Speraw. "Hopefully, that will result in better production. He's capable of having some big offensive games."

Granberry set a school record for field-goal percentage (.672) last season. He is extremely strong, but also has good quickness in the post. Granberry will need to improve his free-throw shooting considerably if he wants to be on the floor during crunch time. He shot just .358 (24 of 67) from the line last season.

Hodge, a transfer from Georgia Tech, ranked fifth in the conference in blocked shots. He is the team's best defensive frontcourt player and a good face-up shooter from 15 feet. Hodge needs only to be more aggressive in order to step up his production.

"They (Granberry and Hodge) give us two people that can shore things up inside," said Speraw. "They do different things. One is a lanky shot-blocker type and one is a rough, physical type., They contrast each other, but as we got into the year last season, they complimented each other as well."

Mario Lovett (5.7 ppg, 4.8 rpg, 33 assists, 12 blocks), a 6-7 junior, is the incumbent starter at power forward. He is one of the team's better ball-handlers and passers, and can play the role of the Charlotte Hornets' Anthony Mason when it comes to breaking pressure defenses. Lovett is reported to be in the best shape of his career.

Lovett should be pushed at the power-forward slot by Seton Hall transfer **Roy Leath**, a 6-7 junior. Leath was a high school teammate of Hodge's who only played two minutes of an exhibition game during his last season with the Pirates before deciding to transfer. He will be eligible to play after the fall semester.

Cory Perry (5.5 ppg, 3.4 rpg, 142 assists, 59 steals), a 5-11 junior, is the Golden Knights' only true point guard. He will be counted on to play heavy minutes. Perry pushes the ball up the floor hard and can get inside opposing defenses. He ranked second in the conference in assists per game (5.1) and is also UCF's best perimeter defender. Perry does not shoot the ball well from any angle. He hit just .380 from the field, .258 from three-point range, and .558 from the free-throw line.

Taking over Stewart's sixth man role this season could be 6-4 redshirt sophomore guard **Inyo Cue**. A left-hander, Cue is the team's most athletic player and a great leaper. He shoots the ball well from long range and is extremely good at going to the basket from his left. Cue averaged 2.7 points and 1.8 rebounds as a freshman. As a high school player at Buckholz HS in Gainesville, Fla., he scored 51 points in a game to break Vernon Maxwell's single-game school record.

Forward **Beronti Simms** (1.7 ppg, 1.8 rpg), a 6-7 sophomore, should also get the chance to spread his wings a little more in 1998-99. Simms played in just 15 games last season, but could be the team's most-improved player. Simms, originally from Seoul, South Korea, is an improved outside shooter after adopting a higher

1998-99 CENTRAL FLORIDA SCHEDULE

Nov.	13	Rollins College
	19	@Auburn
	27-28	#Spartan Coca-Cola Classic
Dec.	2	Winthrop
	11	@Miami
	15	@McNeese State
	17	@South Florida
	20	Barry
	28	Ohio
Jan.	2	Campbell
	4	Georgia State
	7	@Campbell
	9	@Georgia State
	14	Jacksonville
	16	Stetson
	20	@Florida Atlantic
	23	@Centenary
	28	@Samford
	30	@Jacksonville
Feb.	4	Mercer
	6	Troy State
	9	@Stetson
	15	Centenary
	18	@Jacksonville
	20	Florida Atlantic
	25-27	##TAAC Tournament

@ Road Games
# East Lansing, MI (vs. North Carolina-Wilmington, first round; also Michigan State and Western Michigan)
Jacksonville Coliseum, Jacksonville, FL

release point on his shot. He is also a very quick leaper underneath the basket.

Redshirt freshman **Jason Thornton** will be fighting for playing time behind Traina, Stewart and Cue at the off-guard and small forward slots. A heady player with a good shot and average quickness, the 6-5 Thornton averaged 22.0 points and 8.0 rebounds per game as a senior at Central Florida Christian HS in Orlando.

The only freshman newcomer to the Golden Knight program this season is 6-5 forward **Ikechi Nnakwe**, who played at Community HS in Normal, Ill. Nnakwe will play at the small-forward and power-forward positions after competing in high school as a center. A good physical specimen at 220 pounds, Nnakwe wears a size 17 shoe. He could be redshirted this season.

adidas Blue Ribbon Analysis

BACKCOURT	**C**	**BENCH/DEPTH**	**C+**
FRONTCOURT	**B**	**INTANGIBLES**	**C+**

UCF seems to have all of the pieces in place to be a solid contender in the TAAC.

For starters, the Golden Knights have a go-to player in Traina, who should be in the running for conference player of the year honors. Traina, Stewart and Cue are all threats on the perimeter as well as slashing to the basket, giving UCF good offensive balance on the perimeter. The return of Perry also ensures that the motion offense will be directed properly. He is the leading returning assists man in the league. Down low, the presence of Granberry, Hodge and Lovett gives the Golden Knights a nice combination of size, defensive intimidation, quickness and ballhandling.

Statistically, UCF was the top rebounding team in the TAAC last season, as well as the second best offensive unit.

Perhaps the Golden Knights could use a little more depth. That can be said of most teams in the TAAC, however. For now, UCF looks like a solid second place team behind Georgia State.

(G.C.)

FLORIDA ATLANTIC

LOCATION .... **Boca Raton, FL**
CONFERENCE .... **Trans-America Athletic (TAAC)**
LAST SEASON .... **5-22 (.185)**
CONFERENCE RECORD .... **5-11 (5th-East Division)**
STARTERS LOST/RETURNING **1/4**
NICKNAME .... **Owls**
COLORS .... **Blue & Gray**
HOMECOURT .... **FAU Gymnasium (5,000)**
COACH .... **Kevin Billerman (Duke '75)**
RECORD AT SCHOOL .... **30-51 (3 yrs.)**
CAREER RECORD .... **30-51 (3 yrs.)**
ASSISTANTS .... **Alfonzo Duncan (Winston-Salem State '90)**
Brian Lane (Transylvania '90)
Scott Williams (Florida Atlantic '90)
TEAM WINS (last 5 yrs.) **3-9-9-16-5**
RPI (last 5 yrs.) **280-257-263-215-260**
1997-98 FINISH .... **Not eligible for postseason.**

The 1997-98 season was a one-way roller coaster for Florida Atlantic. And it started lurching downhill before the season even began with the tragic death of 6-8 freshman Walter Turner.

Picked to finish near the bottom of the conference in the preseason, the Owls went 0-10 in non-conference play to start the year and didn't grab their first win until defeating Samford on Jan. 3. FAU then won four of its first five league games before winning just once in its final 12 games.

Brighter days could be ahead, however. For starters, the Owls are one of three teams in the TAAC now eligible to compete in the conference tournament because of changes in NCAA rules governing new Division I members.

The old rule made schools ineligible to receive an automatic bid to the NCAA Tournament for eight years, which would have meant that FAU would not have been allowed to compete until 2001. That rule has now been adjusted to two years. The TAAC could have allowed its affected schools to compete in the conference tournament, but would have forfeited its automatic bid and substantial NCAA Tournament revenue if one of them had won the event.

1998-99 FLORIDA ATLANTIC SCHEDULE

Nov.	13	Miami
	16	St. Thomas
	18	@Wichita State
	29	@Southern Methodist
Dec.	1	@Oklahoma State
	5	@South Florida
	12	Bethune-Cookman
	17	@Ohio State
	19	@Indiana/Purdue-Indianapolis
	28	@Richmond
Jan.	2	Georgia State
	4	Campbell
	7	@Georgia State
	9	@Campbell
	14	Stetson
	16	Jacksonville
	20	Central Florida
	25	@Centenary
	30	@Samford
Feb.	1	@Jacksonville State
	6	Mercer
	8	Troy State
	10	@Jacksonville
	13	Centenary
	18	@Stetson
	20	@Central Florida
	25-27	#TAAC Tournament

@ Road Games
# Jacksonville Coliseum, Jacksonville, FL

"Our players will have a realistic goal to accomplish at the end of the season," said coach Kevin Billerman. "With our conference rating, it was not reasonable to expect an at-large bid to the NCAA Tournament unless you win 25 or 26 games in a 27-game schedule. I know our players are extremely excited about this opportunity."

Billerman also has to be excited to finally have a true point guard on his roster in 6-2 sophomore **Jevon Glenn**, a transfer from Jacksonville. Last season's team was dealt a setback when the NCAA failed to grant senior Phillip Huyler (14.7 ppg, 5.7 rpg, 94 assists in 1996-97) an extra season of eligibility. That thrust the ballhandling chores onto the shoulders of off-guards **James Turner** (10.4 ppg, 2.6 rpg, 65 assists), **Damon Arnette** (16.1 ppg, 6.6 rpg, 57 assists, 56 steals) and **Ryan Hercek** (5.6 ppg, 1.0 rpg, 38 assists).

"At the point guard position, we have a returning starter in James Turner," said Billerman. "But, the ball's being placed in the hands of Jevon Glenn."

Glenn is a physical point guard with a hard-nosed attitude. He is not considered a scorer, but rather a player who can get the ball up the court and get the Owls into their offense, a quality the team has been lacking for the last two seasons.

Arnette, a 6-4 senior, is FAU's go-to player and figures to benefit immensely from Glenn's presence. Always good at putting the ball on the floor and finding the basket, Arnette has become a proficient three-point shooter as well. He shot .343 (35 of 102) from three-point range after attempting just 14 treys two years ago. Arnette is also considered the Owls' top defender.

"Damon, who came to us as a post player, has evolved through hard work into a polished wing player," said Billerman. "Last year he was not only our best scorer, but our best defender and rebounder. Each year he has come back with his skills increased by 20 percent. If he does that this year, he'll have a legitimate shots at playing professionally after college."

Turner, a 6-3 sophomore, will return to his more natural wing position this year. He has explosive offensive ability, as evidenced by his 30-point outburst in a game against Florida International last January. A good penetrator and leaper, Turner also led the Owls in three-pointers made with 40.

"James' development will be keyed by better shot selection, which will increase his shooting percentage (.360)," said Billerman. "In addition, a decrease in his turnovers will hopefully take place because he will no longer be playing the point."

Hercek, a 6-5 junior, will play in the backcourt and frontcourt this season. A left-hander, he is considered the team's best pure shooter. He was inconsistent from the floor last season, shooting .323 from the field and .284 from three-point range, but was probably hampered by a lack of playing time.

Senior swingman **Gary Durrant** (10.9 ppg, 4.1 rpg, 30 assists, 16 steals) is another perimeter-oriented Owl. He ranked second on the team in scoring last season and first in three-point percentage at .371 (39 of 105). Durrant is a bit too streaky with his shot at times and needs to improve defensively.

With a perimeter corps five players deep in front of him, the impact of highly regarded 6-3 freshman guard **Rino Bevis** remains to be seen. Bevis averaged 14.2 points, 4.3 rebounds and 4.3 assists last season Tampa Prep HS in Tampa. He was an honorable mention high school All-America selection and one of only 110 players nationally to be invited to the prestigious Nike camp in 1997.

Billerman will need a consistent presence down low if the Owls are going to make the jump to contender status in the TAAC. FAU returns three players—6-6 junior forward **Otis Kitchen** (4.8 ppg, 3.1 rpg, 30 assists), 6-8 sophomore forward/center **Eric Lawson** (1.9 ppg, 2.4 rpg) and 6-6 senior forward/center **Chris Clemons** (1.6 ppg, 2.7 rpg)—who saw action last season at the power slots.

"They (Kitchen, Lawson and Clemons) need to show signs of increased strength in order to improve their scoring and rebounding," said Billerman.

Kitchen, who started 19 games last season, is a good outside shooter and can also handle the ball. Kitchen was the only player among the three to score in double figures in a game last season. He did so just twice with 12-point outings against Miami (Fla.) and Minnesota.

Lawson is not afraid to bang underneath and is the bulkiest player on the team at 235 pounds. Clemons played behind starter Akbar Cook (7.3 ppg, 3.5 rpg) last season. A good rebounder with lots of potential, he could be the Owls' starting center.

Junior **Rob Rollins** (1.7 ppg, 1.6 rpg), a 6-5 forward, played in 21 games last season and started the final two contests. He is a versatile performer who will bang inside and also step outside and connect from the perimeter.

Two players whocould have an impact on the frontcourt after gaining their eligibility in January are 6-8 junior forward **Ashley Baumgardner**, a transfer from Houston, and 6-7 redshirt freshman forward/center **Robert Peterkin**.

Baumgardner hasn't played since the 1995-96 season, when he appeared in 22 games for the Cougars and averaged 1.5 points and 1.9 rebounds. Peterkin, a raw big man, came to FAU from Miami Senior HS.

Two other newcomers who figure to be caught in a numbers games in the backcourt are 6-1 freshman **Cedric Powell** from T.R. Robinson HS in Tampa, and 6-4 redshirt freshman **Jason Stelmacki** from Estero HS in Fort Myers. Stelmacki is a good outside shooter, while Powell is quick and an excellent scorer.

adidas Blue Ribbon Analysis

BACKCOURT	**B**	**BENCH/DEPTH**	**C+**
FRONTCOURT	**D+**	**INTANGIBLES**	**C+**

The Owls were hit hard last season by graduation and the unfortunate denial of Huyler's fifth season.

Despite winning just five games a year ago, FAU coach Kevin Billerman has to be walking with a little more spring in his step this season. The NCAA ruling, combined with a good returning nucleus, is cause for optimism.

"I think Georgia State on paper has the best talent in the TAAC," said Billerman. "Central Florida and Samford are next, and everything is a tossup after that. I feel we have the opportunity to make new strides if we can make these young men more mature."

FAU should indeed be able to compete with any team in the league on the perimeter. The Owls have good shooters and, Billerman believes, a competent floor leader now in Glenn.

The frontcourt picture is still sketchy, however. Until a player steps up with a breakthrough season and becomes a force inside, the Owls still seem destined for a middle-of-the-pack finish at best. Put FAU down for sixth place in the TAAC.

(G.C.)

adidas Blue Ribbon Analysis
GRADING SYSTEM

A+	equal to very best in country—Final Four-caliber unit
A	among the best in the land—worthy of deep NCAA run
B+	talented, versatile and experienced—NCAA-NIT ability
B	solid and productive winners—league and post-season contenders
C+	average to above-average—may contend in a weaker league
C	average to mediocre—second division in a strong league
D+	below average, inconsistent—second division in a weaker league
D	well below average—losing season virtually certain
F	non-Division I ability—an underdog every night

GEORGIA STATE

LOCATION .... **Atlanta, GA**
CONFERENCE .... **Trans-America Athletic (TAAC)**
LAST SEASON .... **16-12 (.571)**
CONFERENCE RECORD ...... **11-5 (1st-West Division)**
STARTERS LOST/RETURNING **2/3**
NICKNAME .... **Panthers**
COLORS .... **Royal Blue, White & Crimson**
HOMECOURT .... **GSU Arena (4,200)**
COACH .... **Lefty Driesell (Duke '54)**
RECORD AT SCHOOL .... **16-12 (1 yrs.)**
CAREER RECORD .... **699-347 (36 yrs.)**
ASSISTANTS .... **Scott Adubato (Upsala '87)**
Phil Cunningham (Campbellville '90)
Michael Perry (Richmond '81)
TEAM WINS (last 5 yrs.) **13-11-10-10-16**
RPI (last 5 yrs.) **228-245-245-186-195**
1997-98 FINISH .... **Lost in conference semifinal.**

Now that Panther fans have had their appetizer, it's time for the main course.

Lefty Driesell's first season at GSU was a success by traditional Panther standards. Driesell guided the school to only its fourth winning season (and first since 1991-92) and a program-best 11-5 conference record.

The upswing should continue. Despite the loss of point guard Rodney Hamilton (16.0 ppg, 3.4 rpg, 171 assists, 61 steals) and off-guard Shellord Pinkett (14.8 ppg, 2.9 rpg, 67 assists, 21 steals), the Panthers enter this season as the favorite in the TAAC.

The reason for such optimism is twofold—the loss of conference kingpins College of Charleston and Florida International and the eligibility of sophomore **Kevin Morris** and juniors **Anton Reese** and **Brad Stricker**. The trio sat out last season after transferring from Georgia Tech, Alabama and Texas A&M, respectively.

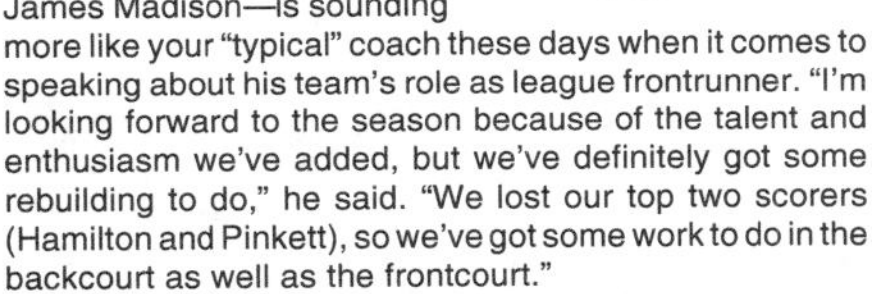

The venerable Driesell—who at age 66 is just one win shy of 700 for his career after successful tours at Davidson, Maryland and James Madison—is sounding more like your "typical" coach these days when it comes to speaking about his team's role as league frontrunner. "I'm looking forward to the season because of the talent and enthusiasm we've added, but we've definitely got some rebuilding to do," he said. "We lost our top two scorers (Hamilton and Pinkett), so we've got some work to do in the backcourt as well as the frontcourt."

The backcourt Driesell speaks of rebuilding probably looks like a finished product to the rest of the TAAC. With the arrival of the 6-0 Morris at point and the 6-3 Reese at off-guard, the Panthers have the conference's best guard tandem on paper. "Our guards both have a lot of natural ability," said Driesell. "But, the thing that worries me is that they haven't played in an actual game for over a year. They've got the physical ability, but they've got to adjust to our system."

The 6-0 Morris is coming off a foot injury that forced him to miss the second half of practice last season. As a freshman in 1996-97 at Georgia Tech, he started 23 of 27 games and averaged 5.9 points and 3.3 assists. Included in his efforts that season were a 17-point, five three-pointer outing in his first game against Wofford, a 10-assist performance in a win against Temple, and a five-steal game versus Maryland.

Overall, he scored in double figures five times. As a senior at Martin Luther King Jr. HS, Morris was chosen the New York City Public School Athletic League Player of the Year.

Reese is *Blue Ribbon*'s selection as the TAAC's Newcomer of the Year. He is without a doubt one of the best talents to grace the Panther program and could have pro potential. Reese played two seasons for the Crimson Tide before running into trouble off the court. He started 17 games as a sophomore, averaging 10.1 points and 3.1 rebounds.

Reese should be one of the top point-producers in the conference this season. He has excellent range on his jumper and possesses the natural ability and strength to put the ball on the floor and get to the basket. Reese had several big scoring nights during his second season at Alabama. He had 25 points against Alabama, 21 against North Texas State, 20 against LSU and 17 in an early-season upset of nationally ranked Minnesota.

Stricker is a well-traveled 6-11 center who could give the Panthers the kind of physical presence (265 pounds) in the middle few teams in the TAAC ever possess. He averaged only 3.5 points and 2.0 rebounds two seasons ago at Texas A&M, but showed excellent touch, shooting .580 from the field and .740 from the line. He scored in double figures three times.

Stricker will not be eligible until the second semester after originally transferring to Arizona State. The Sun Devils' coaching shakeup prompted his quick change of direction to Georgia State.

While Stricker sits, GSU will make do with 6-7 junior **Torquin Gresham** (7.3 ppg, 5.4 rpg, 43 blocked shots) in the middle. Gresham started 17 of 28 games last season and led the conference in rejections. He is a strong leaper around the basket and a good shooter. He shot .594 from the field, but still needs to improve his ballhandling and passing skills. When conference season rolls around, Gresham should split time at the center and power forward positions.

Quincy Gause (12.9 ppg, 7.6 rpg, 35 assists, 36 steals, 15 blocks), a 6-6 senior, is GSU's top returning scorer. He started all 28 games last season and scored in double figures 21 times. His efforts included eight double-doubles, which helped him rank fifth in the conference in rebounding. Gause played most of last season with his back to the basket, but should be free to face up more this season. He is a good mid-range shooter and an excellent defender. He was normally assigned to guard the opposition's top frontline scorer.

Senior **Maurice Robertson** (11.0 ppg, 5.7 rpg, 39 assists, 13 blocks), 6-5, was a solid performer last season after becoming eligible during the fall. He started 17 games and scored in double figures 11 times. Robertson was a heralded recruit for Tennessee in 1995 and ended up in a starting role for the first five games of his freshman year. Robertson passes and shoots well, and has enough heft to muscle opponents at the small forward slot. He is a former high school teammate of the New Jersey Nets' Kerry Kittles.

The Panthers' other returning letterman is 6-5 junior swingman **Chad Searcy** (5.7 ppg, 2.9 rpg), who started the first five games of last season at small forward before Robertson became eligible. Searcy is a good outside shooter and the Panthers' top returning three-point marksman at .390 (16 of 41). Searcy, who is mobile and has good leaping ability, can also slash to the basket.

Besides Morris and Reese, there are three other newcomers of note on this year's roster. GSU could have a star in the making in 6-7 freshman swingman **Donnie Davis** from Collins Hill HS in Lawrenceville, Ga. Davis averaged just 10.4 points and 7.0 rebounds last season, but was listed as a top-25 recruit in the state after moving to an outside position and recovering from an early-season wrist injury. He averaged 15.0 points and 8.0 rebounds as a junior.

The Panthers' other two recruits of note both come from the junior college ranks.

Jarrod Hill, a 6-8 junior forward, averaged 11.0 points, 9.0 rebounds and 2.0 blocks last season at Pasco-Hernandez CC in New Port Richey, Fla. He is an extremely athletic player who uses a combination of quickness and intensity around the basket.

Markeal King, a 6-9 junior forward/center, played last season at Coffeyville (Kan.) College. A good rebounder and interior defender, King averaged 5.0 points, 6.0 rebounds and 1.5 blocks last season. He is considered a banger inside. He has limited shooting range, but probably won't be counted on to score.

1998-99 GEORGIA STATE SCHEDULE

Nov.	18	*Georgetown
	21	North Florida
	25	@Norfolk State
	29	@Kansas State
Dec.	4-5	#Hawaii Powerbar Invitational
	10	Southern
	18	Miami
	22	Virginia Commonwealth
	28	North Carolina A&T
	30	@Eastern Kentucky
Jan.	2	@Florida Atlantic
	4	@Central Florida
	7	Florda Atlantic
	9	Central Florida
	14	Campbell
	16	@Troy State
	19	@Mercer
	23	Samford
	25	@Jacksonville State
	28	Jacksonville
	30	Stetson
Feb.	6	@Fresno State
	8	@Centenary
	11	Jacksonville State
	13	@Samford
	18	@Campbell
	20	Mercer
	25-27	##TAAC Tournament

@ Road Games
* Georgia Dome, Atlanta, GA
# Honolulu, HI (vs. Coppin State, first round; also Hawaii and Northridge State)
Jacksonville Coliseum, Jacksonville, FL

adidas Blue Ribbon Analysis

BACKCOURT	**B**	**BENCH/DEPTH**	**C**
FRONTCOURT	**C+**	**INTANGIBLES**	**B**

The Panthers should have the inside track on the TAAC's automatic bid now that College of Charleston (Southern Conference) and Florida International (Sun Belt Conference) have vacated the league landscape.

While Driesell obviously doesn't have the same kind of talent that he had back in his heyday at Maryland, he has more than enough to compete at the highest level in the TAAC. The returning frontcourt of Gause, Robertson and Gresham was one of the league's best before the arrival of Stricker. It should now be the conference's best and deepest.

Morris and Reese have the potential and the bloodlines to be an even more effective guard combination than last year's stellar tandem of Hamilton and Pinkett. The one glaring weakness is the absence of any reliable backups to handle the ball and give the pair a rest.

If that bump in the road can be smoothed and if Stricker can help the team improve on its -2.2 rebounding margin of a year ago, GSU should be set and Driesell ready to claim his 13th conference regular-season championship.

(G.C.)

JACKSONVILLE

LOCATION .... **Jacksonville, FL**
CONFERENCE .... **Trans-American Athletic (TAAC)**
LAST SEASON .... **8-19 (.296)**
CONFERENCE RECORD .... **6-12 (t-8th, Sun Belt)**
STARTERS LOST/RETURNING **3/2**
NICKNAME .... **Dolphins**
COLORS .... **Green & Gold**
HOMECOURT .... **Jacksonville Coliseum (10,000)**
COACH .... **Hugh Durham (Florida State '95)**
RECORD AT SCHOOL .... **8-19 (1 yr.)**
CAREER RECORD .... **536-330 (30 yrs.)**
ASSISTANTS .... **Clayton Bates (Florida '95)**
Doug Durham (Georgia Southern '92)
Charlton Young (Georgia Southern '94)
TEAM WINS (last 5 yrs.) **17-18-15-5-8**
RPI (last 5 yrs.) **117-103-155-274-248**
1997-98 FINISH .... **Lost in conference first round.**

These Dolphins are now swimming in shallow waters. After a long and sometimes successful stint in the Sun Belt Conference, Jacksonville is now the newest member of the TAAC.

While the Sun Belt probably has a reputation for being a more competitive league, the TAAC may be a better fit for the Dolphins in the long run. Jacksonville was the smallest and only private school in the Sun Belt and had won just 13 games over the last two seasons.

"We are excited about the Trans America because it gives us the opportunity to develop some rivalries right here in Florida with three other conference schools nearby," said coach Hugh Durham.

Durham took over a program in disarray before last season and squeezed out three more wins from a diminished talent base. He sent seven players packing before the season and his leading scorers—6-3 forward Micah Ross (12.6 ppg, 7.5 rpg, 33 steals, 25 blocks) and 6-1 guard John Knox (12.1 ppg, 2.5 rpg, 26 steals)—were holdovers from the previous regime.

There will be no mistaking Durham's stamp on this year's team, however. With seven newcomers and improved athleticism, the Dolphins should be set to scrap their more deliberate style of play for the kind of pressing and running scheme that Durham has long favored.

All in all, it's a formula that could land Jacksonville in the thick of the TAAC championship hunt. Many observers are picking the Dolphins near the top of the conference and most consider Durham's recruiting class to be the league's best.

1998-99 JACKSONVILLE SCHEDULE

Nov.	18	Florida Tech
	25	Palm Beach Atlantic
	30	@South Carolina
Dec.	4-5	#Cardinal Varsity Club Classic
	12	@Florida
	17	Florida State
	22	@Baylor
	29-30	##Capital City Classic
Jan.	2	Centenary
	7	Stetson
	9	@Centenary
	14	@Central Florida
	16	@Florida Atlantic
	23	Troy State
	25	Mercer
	28	@Georgia State
	30	@Campbell
Feb.	4	Samford
	6	Jacksonville State
	10	Florida Atlantic
	13	@Mercer
	15	@Troy State
	18	Central Florida
	20	@Stetson
	25-27	###TAAC Tournament

@ Road Games
# Muncie, IN (vs. South Carolina State, first round; also Ball State and St. Joseph's-Indiana)
Tallahassee, FL (vs. Florida A&M, first round; also Niagara and Radford)
Jacksonville Coliseum, Jacksonville, FL

"The team is ahead of where we were last year because our staff was totally new to the returning players and the players entirely new to staff so there was no carryover experience," said Durham. "This year, we have five players that have been with us for a year. Now, that certainly does not make us an experienced team, because having said we have five means we have seven people who are totally new.

"This is their first association with Jacksonville University, first time to participate, first opportunity for our coaches and players to work together. So, while we may be ahead of last year, we are a long way from being ahead."

Two players who should have an immediate impact on the program are 6-3 sophomore guard **Shawn Platts** from Florida CC in Jacksonville, and 6-5 junior guard **Calvin Slaughter** from Neosho County (Kan.) CC.

Slaughter played in the highly regarded Jayhawk Conference and was that league's player of the year last season after averaging 24.6 points and 9.3 rebounds. A warrior underneath the basket, Slaughter earned second-team juco All-America honors. The Dolphins beat out Arizona State, Oregon State and Georgia for his services. Slaughter should start at the power-forward slot.

Platts was another player who drew some attention from high-profile schools. He is extremely strong for a guard and, in addition to playing both backcourt positions, can also compete at small forward. Platts could begin the season as the Dolphins' starting point guard, taking over for 5-11 senior **Ty Jackson** (7.4 ppg, 2.5 rpg, 70 assists, 30 steals).

Jackson was a walkon who ended up starting 19 games last season. He can stick an open three-pointer and is a hard worker. Jackson shot .362 from the field, .346 (28 of 81) from three-point range, and .771 from the free-throw line, but could be more valuable as a backup than he was as a starter.

Stepping into Knox's shoes at off-guard could be either 6-0 junior **Jameel Anderson** or 6-2 junior **Ivan Gunder**.

Anderson played last season at Coffeyville (Kan.) CC and competed against Slaughter in the Jayhawk Conference. He can play either the point- or off-guard position and is an excellent outside shooter.

Gunder averaged 12.0 points and 3.0 assists last season at Chipola (Fla.) JC. He originally signed at Western Illinois and is a local product from Ribault HS in Jacksonville. Gunder is a good outside shooter, as evidenced by his nine three-pointers in a game last season against Gulf Coast (Fla.) CC.

Besides Slaughter, others who figure to see significant action in the frontcourt are 6-7 senior **Jamar Bailey** (10.7 ppg, 6.0 rpg, 24 steals, 23 blocks), 6-5 junior **Jamal Childs**, 6-5 junior **Amos Conyors**, 6-10 freshman **Jeremy Davis** and 6-8 senior **Nate Stewart** (6.0 ppg, 4.3 rpg, 25 steals, 7 blocks).

Bailey is the Dolphins' leading returning scorer. He does most of his damage in the post and spent time last season at power forward and center. Bailey came on strong toward the end of last season, scoring 25 points in a win against Texas-Pan American and 23 points in a victory over Western Kentucky. Bailey shot just .419 (96 of 228) from the field, but managed to get to the free-throw line 140 times.

Childs was a former teammate of Bailey's at Mt. San Antonio (Calif.) College. Childs averaged 15.0 points last season and is a strong finisher around the basket. He is also the team's best defender on the perimeter, something that should earn him additional playing time in the backcourt.

Conyors played last season at Gulf Coast CC, where he averaged 21.0 points and 8.0 rebounds. Although not as physically talented as other members of the Dolphin team, Conyors is a fundamentally sound player with good all-around skills.

Davis was redshirted last season while battling health problems related to an esophagus condition. The tallest Dolphin, Davis played for current Jacksonville assistant Doug Durham (Hugh's son) at Walton Academy in Loganville, Ga. He was an all-state performer his senior year after averaging 16.0 points and 7.0 rebounds. Davis came to Jacksonville listed at just 195 pounds, but has since added 15 pounds.

Stewart played in 23 games last season and made 11 starts. He incurred knee problems late in the year that led to surgery during the summer.

Swingman **Jason Dangerfield** (4.8 ppg, 3.1 rpg, 26 steals), a 6-4 sophomore, showed flashes of potential last season. He averaged 18 minutes per game in 25 appearances. Dangerfield shot just .376 (38 of 101) from the field and .261 (six of 23) from three-point range and will need improved consistency in order to maintain his playing time.

One other newcomer on the Dolphin roster is 6-0 freshman guard **Kevin Sheppard** from Tigan HS in the Virgin Islands. Sheppard is an exceptionally quick player, but is recovering from a broken foot that required the insertion of a pin. Sheppard was signed after the Dolphin coaches watched him make 13 three-pointers in an AAU tournament game in Chicago.

adidas Blue Ribbon Analysis

BACKCOURT .... C **BENCH/DEPTH** C
FRONTCOURT .... C+ **INTANGIBLES** .... C+

Talk about starting over. New conference. New system. Almost an entirely new team. The times sure are changing at Jacksonville.

Hugh Durham brings his revamped Dolphins into the TAAC after winning just a handful of games a season ago. Don't bet on that kind of finish this time.

Durham has hit the junior college ranks with all the subtlety of a hurricane lashing the Florida coast. Of the eight newcomers on this year's team, six played at the juco level last season. Of the four holdovers from last year, three also came to Jacksonville from junior colleges after being recruited by Durham.

There is no denying that Durham's efforts have resulted in huge gains for the Dolphins in the talent category. However, blending all of the new faces into a cohesive unit may take some time. Durham, with 30 years of Division I coaching experience, knows more than most about that kind of thing. It also stands to reason that the man knows exactly what it takes to assemble a winning team.

We will predict a slow start for the Dolphins this season, but a strong finish. Put them down for fourth in the TAAC but keep on eye on them come conference tournament time.

(G.C.)

JACKSONVILLE STATE

LOCATION .... **Jacksonville, AL**
CONFERENCE .... **Trans-America Athletic (TAAC)**
LAST SEASON .... **12-14 (.461)**
CONFERENCE RECORD .... **13-3 (1st)**
STARTERS LOST/RETURNING **2/3**
NICKNAME .... **Gamecocks**
COLORS .... **Red & White**
HOMECOURT .... **Pete Mathews Coliseum (5,500)**
COACH .... **Mark Turgeon (Kansas '87)**
RECORD AT SCHOOL .... **First Year**
CAREER RECORD .... **First Year**
ASSISTANTS .... **Ted Boyle (Kansas '85)**
Brandon Johnson (Georgia State '97)
TEAM WINS (last 5 yrs.) **17-24-10-10-12**
RPI (last 5 yrs.) **N/A-N/A-252-270-275**
1997-98 FINISH ...... **Not eligible for postseason play.**

Mark Turgeon could very well be the right man, at the right place, at the right time.

After 24 years as head coach of the Gamecocks, Bill Jones, who won 449 games and led the school to the 1985 NCAA Division II national championship, called it quits after last season.

The 33-year old Turgeon, who was hired to replace Jones in April, comes to Jacksonville State with impeccable credentials. He spent last season as an assistant under Larry Brown with the Philadelphia 76ers. Before that, he was an assistant at Oregon under present Tennessee coach Jerry Green, and an assistant at Kansas under Brown and Roy Williams. As a player at Kansas, Turgeon performed for both Brown and Roy Williams and was the first player in Jayhawk history to compete in four consecutive NCAA Tournaments.

"Most of my philosophy, both in coaching and in life, in general, can be attributed to coach Brown, coach Williams and my high school coach, Ben Meseke," said Turgeon. "They have had a tremendously positive influence on my life, both on and off the floor. Many of the things we'll be doing here at Jacksonville State will be as a direct result from what I've learned from these three outstanding men."

What makes Turgeon's arrival at JSU perhaps more exciting than coaching philosophy or pedigree is timing. The program is stocked with a fair amount of returning talent and should be headed for its first-ever appearance in the TAAC Tournament. That's because the NCAA has recently reduced the amount of time new Division I schools must wait to be eligible for an automatic bid to the NCAA Tournament from eight years to two. That will allow the TAAC to include the Gamecocks in the conference tournament as the league will no longer be concerned with a team not eligible for an automatic bid entering its tournament and winning. JSU is entering its fourth season as a Division I member.

"This a positive for our program," said Turgeon. "There is not an asterisk by our program any more. The players on the team now have something to look forward to."

Turgeon got a late recruiting start because of his April hiring, but did manage to secure five newcomers, including two players from the junior-college ranks. Turgeon is hopeful that those newcomers can help the Gamecocks overcome their three most pressing problems—finding a starting point guard, a reliable power player, and replacing high-scoring swingman Jay Knowlton (16.2 ppg, 5.7 rpg, 29 steals, 14 blocked shots).

The Gamecocks lost starter Jamael Hickman (5.7 ppg, 3.5 rpg, 123 assists, 26 steals) at the point and will rely heavily on 5-10 freshman **Rashard Willie** from Lee HS in Huntsville, Ala., and 6-3 freshman **Jason Lewis** from Churchill HS in Eugene, Ore., to fill the void. "Even though we're going to be young, we're going to throw them in there and let them grow," said Turgeon.

Willie, who averaged 18.0 points, 5.0 assists and 4.0 steals last season, is extremely quick and a good defender. "We were lucky to get him," said Turgeon. "I was shocked he was still around. He's one of those guys when you sign him, you know you will be tough to press for the next four years."

Lewis is not in Willie's class as far as being able to handle pressure, but he's a heady point guard with a knack for getting the ball to the right people at the right time. He averaged 11.2 points and 4.8 assists last season. "I spent five years at Oregon, so I knew Jason, and I knew his coach," said Turgeon. "We felt like he was one of the better point guards in the state."

Also competing for playing time at the point will be 6-1 junior **Bryan Taylor** (1.1 ppg, 0.5 rpg, 26 assists, 10 steals), who appeared in 25 games last season. Taylor is a competent outside shooter who averaged just 8.0 minutes per game in 1997-98.

While the point guard slot is in need of a fix, the same can't be said of the off-guard slot. **Derrell Johnson** (16.8 ppg, 3.8 rpg, 27 assists, 20 steals), a 6-1 junior, was the Gamecocks' leading scorer last season. He ranked third in the conference in scoring and shot .446 from the field and .382 (63 of 165) from three-point range. In addition to his perimeter game, Johnson also has excellent quickness and is a good penetrator. He averaged just 3.4 points per game two seasons ago. Johnson scored 20 or more points nine times last season, including a 28-point effort in a win against Troy State.

"Derrell fits in to our system because he likes to play defense and likes to play up-tempo," said Turgeon. "From everything I've seen, he should be a big factor this season."

Backing up Johnson this season should be 6-1 junior **Marlon Gurley**, a transfer from Snead State (Ala.) CC. Gurley averaged 28.7 points last season and was a Division II Junior College All-American. "Marlon is a complete offensive player," said Turgeon. "He can shoot outside and can create. He's a solid passer and an adequate ballhandler. He loves the game of basketball. When I took the job, one of the first calls I made was to him."

Also at the off-guard slot is 6-3 sophomore **Jeremy Wilson** (2.3 ppg, 1.3 rpg), who played in just 15 games last

1998-99 JACKSONVILLE STATE SCHEDULE

Nov.	14	East Carolina
	16	@Mississippi Valley State
	19	@Georgia Southern
	24	@Florida A&M
	28	@Alabama
Dec.	2	@Mississippi State
	4-5	#Tom Roberson Coca-Cola Classic
	8	@UAB
	17	@Morehead State
Jan.	2	Mercer
	4	@Troy State
	7	@Mercer
	9	Troy State
	14	@Samford
	18	Centenary
	23	@Campbell
	25	Georgia State
	30	Central Florida
Feb.	1	Florida Atlantic
	4	@Stetson
	6	@Jacksonville
	11	@Georgia State
	13	Campbell
	15	Samford
	18	@Centenary
	25-27	##TAAC Tournament

@ Road Games
\# Jacksonville, AL (vs. West Georgia, first round; also Brewton-Parker and North Georgia)
\#\# Jacksonville Coliseum, Jacksonville, FL

season.

The frontcourt will be anchored by 6-5 sophomore small forward **Alex Beason** (11.6 ppg, 4.2 rpg, 38 assists, 18 steals), who should see additional offensive opportunities with the loss of Knowlton. Beason is an excellent outside shooter, hitting .411 (51 of 124) from beyond the arc last season, but can also score in other ways.

"Alex is a real talent," said Turgeon. "The only thing is, things may have always come easily for him. We're going to try and push him to another level. He has natural ability to score. He was one of the best freshman in the conference last season. Now, we want him to become one of the best players in the conference."

The power positions are largely unsettled. **Wes Fowler** (4.2 ppg, 4.0 rpg, 17 blocks), a 6-8 junior center, started 12 games last season. Fowler is a good face-up shooter from 15 feet, has quick feet, and can also handle the ball. He scored in double figures just once, but in that contest recorded a double-double of 15 points and 10 rebounds against Thomas College.

David Ash (2.7 ppg, 2.8 rpg), a 6-8 senior forward/center, played in 26 games last season and made five starts. Ash, also a good jump shooter, has put on additional weight, which should help him compete more effectively under the boards.

Other returnees up front are 6-7 junior center **Jeff Bellamy** (1.9 ppg, 1.9 rpg) and 6-7 junior forward/center **Niki Okalovitch** (2.8 ppg, 2.0 rpg). Bellamy can shoot, pass and catch, but needs to become more physical. Okalovitch joined the team as a walkon last season. He played in just 14 games, but managed to score 14 points in an early-season victory over Alabama State.

The frontcourt should be bolstered by the additions of 6-7 junior forward **Shawn Philpotts**, a transfer from Dodge City (Kan.) CC, and 6-9 freshman center **Ben Moates** from G.W. Long HS in Skipperville, Ala.

Philpotts averaged 16.0 points, 8.0 rebounds and 4.0 blocks last season. "Shawn has frontcourt potential," said Turgeon. "He is big, strong, athletic, can block shots, and his offensive skills can get better. He has a chance to play a lot of minutes."

Moates averaged 18.0 points, 10.0 rebounds and 4.0 blocks as a senior.

adidas Blue Ribbon Analysis

BACKCOURT	C+	BENCH/DEPTH	C
FRONTCOURT	D+	INTANGIBLES	C+

Not only did Turgeon hit the ground running at JSU, it appears he will be asking the Gamecocks to do the same thing.

"At Kansas, we always tried to average around 90 possessions a game," he said. "I don't know if that is going to be possible with our personnel this season, but we would like to get around 80 possession per game, and then in future years, improve that to about 90. We are going to run the Kansas-style break, and play a passing game. We won't necessarily be a pressing team, although we'll put one on now and then. But, we will try and take teams out of their offense."

JSU will have to overcome some hurdles to achieve the kind of success Turgeon is accustomed to.

For starters, the Gamecocks must get production from the point-guard spot. Johnson will also need to continue to score at last season's pace, and Beason will need to make the jump to the next level.

Without some additional help, however, even that might not be enough to elevate the Gamecocks very far in the TAAC standings. JSU was the second-worst defensive and rebounding team in the conference last season. Although some renewed enthusiasm on the defensive end could help, the Gamecocks are still without a dominant shot blocker or rebounder inside.

And that spells trouble, or more specifically, eighth place in the TAAC.

(G.C.)

MERCER

LOCATION	Macon, GA
CONFERENCE	Trans-America Athletic (TAAC)
LAST SEASON	5-21 (.192)
CONFERENCE RECORD	2-4 (6th-West Division)
STARTERS LOST/RETURNING	1/4
NICKNAME	Bears
COLORS	Black & Orange
HOMECOURT	Macon Centreplex (2,500)
COACH	Mark Slonaker (Georgia '80)
RECORD AT SCHOOL	5-21 (1 yr.)
CAREER RECORD	46-42 (3 yrs.)
ASSISTANTS	Mike Gillespie (Morehead State '95) Dewey Haley (Chadron State '91) John Lykins (Georgetown, Ky. '89)
TEAM WINS (last 5 yrs.)	5-15-15-3-5
RPI (last 5 yrs.)	267-191-290-305-304
1997-98 FINISH	Did not qualify for conference tournament.

The Bears spent most of last season in hibernation. Some observers might have mistaken it for a more serious type of sleep disorder.

After starting its season 3-3, Mercer won just twice in its next 20 games to finish out of contention for the TAAC Tournament for the second straight year.

Mark Slonaker's honeymoon season as a Division I head coach was interrupted early when the Bears' best player—senior point guard Bruce Simms (14.9 ppg, 3.5 rpg)—was declared academically ineligible after eight games. Simms was off to a phenomenal offensive start, shooting .597 from the field and .565 from three-point range

After Simms' departure, the Bears simply did not have enough punch to win on most nights. Mercer lost eight games by six points or less.

Sometimes that sort of adversity can be a blessing in disguise. With four starters and nine lettermen returning, and with two highly regarded transfers set to become its go-to players, Mercer just might be on the road back to respectability.

"We only won five games last year, but we felt like we were in there in a lot of games," Slonaker said. "Our kids never gave up. We went out and recruited this year to try and balance our classes. Hopefully, that will get us to a situation were we can be competitive every year. We're trying to build this program the right way."

The transfers are 6-2 junior guard **Earnest Brown**, who averaged 2.0 points and 2.0 rebounds in limited playing time two years ago at Auburn, and 6-8 sophomore forward/center **Terry Lawyer**, who averaged 1.1 points and 1.1 rebounds as a freshman at Mississippi State.

Brown should start at off-guard in place of departed starter Mark Johnson (13.2 ppg, 2.8 rpg, 52 assists, 37 steals). Brown is an excellent outside shooter and is being counted on to open up the Bear offense. Johnson scored plenty last year but did not shoot well enough—.372 from the field and .310 from three-point range—to prevent opposing defenses from sagging inside.

"Earnest is a very good three-point shooter," Slonaker said. "He really enhanced his whole game in practices last season. He should be one of the better guards in the TAAC. It may take him 20 games to get there because he hasn't played in two years, but by the end of this year or the beginning of next year, he should be there."

Lawyer is thin at just 205 pounds, but is a quick leaper and has mid-range offensive skills. Although lacking in bulk, he should be able to hold his own at center in the traditionally undersized TAAC.

"Terry brings SEC tougness and experience," Slonaker said. "He is a finesse player with a good mid-range jump shot. We felt like he was just a cut off of being a productive player in the SEC. He should be a good player in our league and he will complement **Mark Adamson** very well."

Brown and Lawyer could be just the ticket that Adamson, a 6-6 junior forward needs to further his development. Adamson (13.0 ppg, 9.5 rpg, 42 assists, 23 steals, 21 blocked shots) led the conference in rebounding last season and shot a lofty .547 from the floor. Adamson, a left-hander who posted 10 double-doubles, was the subject of more than one defender's attention on many occasions last season and wound up taking less than 10 shots per game. He should get easier scoring opportunities this year as his chances to work against solo coverage on the blocks ought to increase.

"Mark really stepped up last year, but when your best player is one that scores most of his points within five feet of the basket, it's tough," Slonaker said.

Evans Davis (11.0 ppg, 5.9 rpg, 41 assists, 27 steals), a 6-4 senior, started 25 games last season. His production slowed as the season wore on, a reflection probably of the fact that he was forced to move from small forward to power forward late in the year due to injuries.

Davis, who should reclaim his starting slot at small forward, can do a little bit of everything offensively and is a tenacious competitor. He was leading the conference in three-point percentage before making just three of his final 23 attempts in the last nine games of the season. He wound up shooting .359 percent (33 of 92) from three-point range and .389 (103 of 265) from the field. Davis had some of his best games against big-time competition, scoring 23 points against Georgia and 21 against Duke.

Korey McCray (8.0 ppg, 3.8 rpg, 75 assists, 23 steals), a 6-1 sophomore, was thrust into a starting role at the point last season after the loss of Simms. McCray's style of play at the point is a little like that of the Indiana Pacers' Mark Jackson. He uses his strength to back opponents into the post, can stick a three-pointer if left alone, and takes good care of the basketball. McCray started slowly after moving into the starting lineup. He did not register a point in his first three games as a starter, but became a reliable double-figure scorer thereafter.

Last year's starter at center was 6-5 walkon **Isaac Stallworth** (9.2 ppg, 4.2 rpg). Stallworth, a senior, earned a scholarship with his play last season. He became the Bears' starter when **Chris Ott** (4.2 ppg, 2.6 rpg 11 blocks) suffered a torn anterior cruciate ligament. Stallworth gives up plenty of size in the post, but is an extremely physical player. He also has the ability to take bigger opponents off the dribble.

Ott, a 6-11 senior, made 12 starts last season before being shelved. He is an agile big man and a smart player, but simply did not rebound enough for his size. His status for the start of the year is still uncertain after last season's injury. He most likely would not have regained his starting berth even if he was at 100 percent.

Another big man who should see limited action is 6-9 junior **Jesse McMillan** (1.1 ppg, 1.5 rpg). McMillan has long arms and can block shots, but spends too much of his

1998-99 MERCER SCHEDULE

Nov.	13	@Georgia
	16	@Winthrop
	19	@Kentucky
	21	@Wake Forest
	28	Coastal Carolina
Dec.	5	Covenant
	9	@Furman
	19	North Carolina-Asheville
	29-30	#Cessna Classic
Jan.	2	@Jacksonville State
	4	Samford
	7	Jacksonville State
	9	@Samford
	14	@Troy State
	16	Campbell
	19	Georgia State
	23	@Stetson
	25	@Jacksonville
	30	Centenary
Feb.	4	@Central Florida
	6	@Florida Atlantic
	13	Jacksonville
	15	Stetson
	18	Troy State
	20	@Georgia State
	25-27	#TAAC Tournament

@ Road Games
\# Wichita, KS (vs. Wichita State, first round; also Mississippi Valley State and Western Illinois)
\#\# Jacksonville Coliseum, Jacksonville, FL

time on offense away from the basket.

The backcourt reserve corps is full of interesting stories and possibilities.

Steve Davis (3.2 ppg, 1.4 rpg, 21 steals), a 6-0 fifth-year senior, will back up McCray at the point. Davis was a highly touted player coming out of high school but missed almost two full years of action after anterior cruciate ligament injuries to both knees. He is still one of the fastest players on the team and is the only player remaining from the Bear squad that advanced to the TAAC Tournament championship game in 1995-96.

Sophomore off-guard **Rodney Kirtz** (4.2 ppg, 2.6 rpg) came to Mercer with the reputation of being a big-time shooter. The 6-3 Kirtz struggled with his shot last season, however, connecting on just .264 of his shots from the field and .185 of his three-point shots. If he finds his touch and confidence, Kirtz could see plenty of action.

The Bear coaching staff is particularly excited about freshman **Noel West**, a 6-2 off-guard. West was a teammate of Florida signee Ted Dupay at Cape Coral Mariner HS in Ft. Myers, Fla. and might have been just a bit overshadowed by Dupay, who was Florida's all-time high school scoring leader. West, a good scorer in his own right, averaged 26.0 points last season. West is an athletic player who can shoot and defend. He is being looked at the Bears' designated stopper off the bench.

"We got a steal in him," Slonaker said. "He should give us a dimension that we didn't have last year. He is very quick on the perimeter, can get to the basket, and can shoot three-pointers. We expect him to score for us."

Another freshman with intriguing potential is 6-4 swingman **Aleam Muhammed** from W.D. Mohammed HS in Ellenwood, Ga. He averaged 25.0 points last season, but did not compete against top-flight competition. Muhammed has long arms, is a great leaper, and can shoot. The possibility exists that he could be redshirted as he adjusts to competing at the Division I level.

Rounding out the roster this season will be 6-4 senior forward **Russell Golden** (0.2 ppg, 0.3 rpg), a walkon who appeared in 11 games last season, and 6-0 sophomore redshirt guard **John Pat Pickles**.

adidas Blue Ribbon Analysis

BACKCOURT .... **C** **BENCH/DEPTH** .... **D+**
FRONTCOURT .... **C** **INTANGIBLES** .... **C**

Slonaker appears to have done a credible job of assembling a cast that should allow the Bears to be more competitive.

Everything hinges on the additions of Brown and Lawyer. If that pair is as good as advertised, it will make opposing defenses have to pay attention to more than one player at a time.

The returnees, with the exception of possibly Adamson, are role players who were asked to contribute more than they could have been expected to last season. That could change this season, but don't expect things to change dramatically enough to make the Bears a contender.

After finishing with the worst record in the TAAC last season, Mercer should escape the basement this year. Put the Bears down for ninth place.

(G.C.)

SAMFORD

LOCATION	**Birmingham, AL**
CONFERENCE	**Trans-America Athletic (TAAC)**
LAST SEASON	**14-13 (.518)**
CONFERENCE RECORD	**9-7 (2nd-West Division)**
STARTERS LOST/RETURNING	**1/4**
NICKNAME	**Bulldogs**
COLORS	**Red & Blue**
HOMECOURT	**Siebert Hall (4,000)**
COACH	**Jimmy Tillette (Our Lady of Holly Cross '75)**
RECORD AT SCHOOL	**14-13 (1 yr.)**
CAREER RECORD	**14-13 (1 yr.)**
ASSISTANTS	**Paul Kelly (Tulane '87)**
	Mike Morris (Alabama-Huntsville '91)
	Lance Richardson (Samford '96)
TEAM WINS (last 5 yrs.)	**10-16-17-19-14**
RPI (last 5 yrs.)	**248-187-173-222-225**
1997-98 FINISH	**Lost in conference first round.**

1998-99 SAMFORD SCHEDULE

Nov.	23	@Northeast Louisiana
	28	Belmont
Dec.	1	@Tulane
	12	North Georgia
	14	@UTEP
	16	@Texas-Arlington
	21	Southwest Texas
	29-30	#Dr Pepper Classic
Jan.	2	@Troy State
	4	@Mercer
	7	Troy State
	9	Mercer
	14	Jacksonville State
	16	@Centenary
	21	@Campbell
	23	@Georgia State
	28	Central Florida
	30	Florida Atlantic
Feb.	4	@Jacksonville
	8	@Stetson
	11	Campbell
	13	Georgia State
	15	@Jacksonville State
	20	Centenary
	25-27	#TAAC Tournament

@ Road Games
\# Chattanooga, TN (vs. Hampton, first round; also Rider and Tennesssee-Chattanooga)
\# Jacksonville Coliseum, Jacksonville, FL

Samford coach Jimmy Tillette forgot one important item when he took his Bulldogs on the road last season. "The most important implement I could have had was a night light, because these kids were scared to death on the road," he said.

Indeed it seemed that way. Samford went 11-1 at home last season, but was just 3-12 away from the friendly confines of Siebert Hall. Given the fact that the Bulldogs were the youngest team in Division I last season, starting four sophomores and playing five freshmen off the bench, it was perhaps a forgivable offense. With an added year of experience, Bulldog opponents shouldn't have such an easy time defending their home turf in 1998-99.

"There are two factors that will help this year's team over last year," said Tillette. "Number one is experience and number two is competition. We've got a year in our system on offense. What that means is, we can spend more time addressing defense. We've got talented players with our returnees and newcomers, all of whom will be trying to get more playing time."

Samford lost just one key performer from last season's team in center Freddie Williams (12.0 ppg, 6.6 rpg, 52 assists). Every other key performer is back, including double-figure scorers in third team all-conference performer **Will Daniel** (13.0 ppg, 4.3 rpg, 63 assists, 27 steals, 24 blocked shots), **Reed Rawlings** (12.1 ppg, 4.9 rpg, 56 assists, 32 steals, 12 blocks), and **Mario Lopez** (10.2 ppg, 2.8 rpg, 92 assists).

"We've got a nice blend of skill and athleticism with this team," said Tillette. "Also, the leaders are more comfortable with their roles. They were kind of thrown into leadership roles right before practice last year after we lost a couple of seniors."

Daniel, a 6-4 junior swingman, was the Bulldogs' top scorer and shot blocker last season, and also ranked second on the club in assists and steals. Daniel is strong around the basket and can also step out on the perimeter and knock down jumpers. He shot .301 (44 of 146) from three-point range and .730 (54 of 74) from the foul line. Daniel had 25 points last season against Stetson and 24 against Northwestern State.

Rawlings, a 6-7 junior, is an outstanding perimeter player despite his size. He was the Bulldogs' leading three-point shooter with 46 treys. He hit .368 from behind the arc, and has unlimited range. Rawlings also has a knack for putting the ball on the floor and either scoring or getting fouled. He was Samford's top free-throw shooter in terms of attempts (118), makes (97) and percentage (.822). His best game last season was a 25-point effort in the Bulldogs' conference tournament game against Central Florida.

"Reed is a very explosive player," said Tillette. "He is a nice mix. He can go to the rim but is also a great three-point shooter. He is athletic and just coming into his own. He graduated from high school at age 16, so he's a 19-year old junior. We think he has tremendous ability."

Lopez, a 6-1 junior, stepped into a starting role at the point when senior Tyler Davis went down for the season with a knee injury. "It worked out well for Mario because he got tremendous minutes at the point," said Tillette. "He's our best on-the-ball defender and a leader on the floor. He's also a good three-point shooter and can go to the hole. He's probably our most solid all-around player."

Lopez shot a respectable .462 from the field and .361 (39 of 108) from long range.

While Daniel, Rawlings and Lopez will probably be the main guns in Samford's arsenal, there are more than a few solid complementary players on hand.

Junior **Boyd Kaiser** (7.3 ppg, 3.7 rpg, 40 assists), a 6-5 forward, started 26 games last season. A former walkon, Kaiser is a solid offensive player with an uncanny knack for getting open. He had an 18-point outing in a win against Monmouth and shot a lofty .571 overall from the field.

"Boyd's a good all-around player," said Tillette. "He doesn't do anything great, but does everything well. He's very bright and understands how to play."

Marc Salyers (6.1 ppg, 3.2 rpg), a 6-9 sophomore, played mostly at power forward last season, but is being groomed this season to replace Williams at center. Salyers has a nice blend of inside-outside offensive skills and has improved his strength. He was benching over 300 pounds in preseason workouts. Salyers showed flashes of his vast potential last season, scoring 20 points against New Orleans and leading the team in rebounding on four occasions.

Salyers should be spelled in the middle by 6-9 sophomore **Gabe Skypala** (1.6 ppg, 0.8 rpg), who appeared in 16 games last season. Tillette had hoped to redshirt the athletic Skypala in 1997-98, but was forced to keep him on the roster because of injuries.

Sophomore **Corey Green** (4.1 ppg, 2.1 rpg), a 6-3 swingman, should serve as a backup to Daniel. Thin and wiry, he is the prototypical slasher with a limited outside shot. Green scored 24 points last season against Florida International, but struggled at times to fit into Tillette's system. "He's a kid we got from a different type of system. He was an up-tempo player in high school," said Tillette. "That is the antithesis of what we do, but he is certainly a capable player and should be better this year because of his experience."

Two additional returnees in the backcourt are 6-0 sophomore guard **Chris Sparks** (1.9 ppg, 0.6 rpg) and 6-1 junior guard **Lee Burgess** (1.5 ppg, 0.1 rpg). Sparks is an excellent outside shooter who began to play meaningful minutes toward the end of last season. Burgess is a walkon who appeared in just eight games.

Tillette has three newcomers in 6-2 freshman guard **David Hall**, 6-6 freshman center **Joey Howard** and 6-2 freshman guard **Chris Weaver**.

Hall, who played on an Alabama 6A state championship team at Minor HS in Birmingham, can play both guard positions but isn't expected to see much action in his first season.

Howard, who has good offensive skills but needs additional strength, played last season at Central Private HS in Baton Rouge, La. He is originally from Wagga Wagga, Australia.

Of the three newcomers, Weaver has the best chance to see significant action. He was the top offensive player in Alabama last season, averaging 27.8 points. Weaver, who played at Arab (Ala.) HS, is an excellent shooter with tremendous range.

adidas Blue Ribbon Analysis

BACKCOURT .... **C+** **BENCH/DEPTH** .... **C**
FRONTCOURT .... **C+** **INTANGIBLES** .... **C**

Tillette likes a deliberate style of play and emphasizes halfcourt motion offense and halfcourt man-to-man defense. Last year's winning record was made more remarkable by the fact that Tillette was in his first year on the job and had to adjust his returning players and newcomers to his particular style, even though the system was the same run by former coach John Brady. That won't be much of a problem this time.

Samford ended up doing exactly what it wanted to on offense last season as it kept most games in the 60-70 point range. The Bulldogs averaged 68.9 points per game and were also one of the better rebounding teams in the TAAC.

Therefore, it is easy to see where the improvement must come from if Samford is to make that jump to the next level. Samford gave up just 67.0 points per outing, but let too many games within the conference slip into higher ranges.

"Tangibly, we have to be able to defend better," said Tillette. "We spent a lot of time teaching offense last year because we were so young. Defense was one of our weak points last year, and we have to improve there."

The rest of this team's improvement should come more as a result of nature rather than Tillette's readjustments. "You can't expedite experience," said Tillette. "If this team is more mature with a season under its belt, hopefully we will be a better team on the road."

Everything seems to be coming together. With a solid season to build on, the Bulldogs should finish third in the TAAC, behind Georgia State and Central Florida.

(G.C.)

STETSON

LOCATION .... **DeLand, FL**
CONFERENCE .... **Trans-America Athletic (TAAC)**
LAST SEASON .... **11-15 (.423)**
CONFERENCE RECORD .... **8-8 (4th-East Division)**
STARTERS LOST/RETURNING **2/3**
NICKNAME .... **Hatters**
COLORS .... **Green & White**
HOMECOURT .... **Edmunds Center (5,000)**
COACH .... **Murray Arnold (American University '60)**
RECORD AT SCHOOL .... **11-15 (1 yr.)**
CAREER RECORD .... **376-189 (19 yrs.)**
ASSISTANTS .. **Andy McClouskey (Oregon State '82)**
Wylie Tucker (Montevallo '78)
Derek Waugh (Furman '93)
TEAM WINS (last 5 yrs.) **14-15-10-9-11**
RPI (last 5 yrs.) **212-162-249-295-235**
1997-98 FINISH .... **Lost in conference first round.**

Murray Arnold didn't exactly play the part of the savior on his return home to DeLand, Fla., last year. But he did turn a few heads.

The well-traveled Arnold, who once coached at DeLand HS and won the school's only state championship in 1963, returned to his old stomping grounds to direct the Stetson program after college head coaching stints at Birmingham Southern, UT-Chattanooga, Western Kentucky and Okaloosa-Walton (Fla.) CC and a brief layover as a Chicago Bulls assistant..

In his first year, he put a little fun back into the Edmunds Center, increasing Stetson's scoring output by more than seven points per game.

"We're definitely a more up-tempo team now and hopefully we're more aggressive defensively," said Arnold. "The kids enjoy playing that style and the fans like it. That translated into two more wins overall for us last season and eight TAAC wins. Hopefully, that's going in the right direction."

The Hatters' roster this season is comprised of five returning lettermen, including three starters, and six newcomers.

Stetson has at least one proven scorer in 6-3 senior swingman **Garrett Davis** (13.2 ppg, 3.7 rpg, 54 assists). He was the team's second-leading scorer last season. Davis shot .384 (33 of 86) from three-point range and ranked first in the conference in free-throw percentage at .888 (87 of 98). He led the Hatters in scoring on six occasions, including a 26-point effort in an early-season loss at Florida.

"Davis is a good offensive player and should have a fine senior year," said Arnold. "He is an excellent shooter who began to expand his ability to score late last season. He's going from being a shooter to more of a composite scorer. That's important because the more he does that, the more he will get to the free-throw line."

Davis played a wing position last year alongside the smallish starting backcourt of 6-1 **Kennith Johnson** (6.7 ppg, 1.8 rpg, 41 assists, 30 steals) and 5-10 **Mario Haynes** (3.7 ppg, 2.0 rpg, 83 assists, 23 steals).

Johnson, a senior, is a defensive stopper, while Haynes, a junior, was the Hatters' only pure point guard last season. He ranked ninth in the TAAC in assists per game (3.2) and is the son of a high school coach. Neither player is much of a threat from the perimeter. Johnson hit just .295 percent (28 of 95) of his three-point shots, while Haynes made just one of 19 from behind the arc.

Still, Arnold likes having his three perimeter players on the floor at the same time. "We think that kind of variety can create perimeter mismatches to our advantage," he said. "It makes people defend us all over the floor."

Sophomore **Will Robertson** (8.1 ppg, 4.3 rpg), a 6-6 forward, should see increased playing time with the departure of frontcourt starters Jeff Warbritton (14.3 ppg, 8.9 rpg) and Chad Lambert (10.2 ppg, 6.2 rpg, 26 blocks). Robertson missed the final three games of last season because of a knee injury. When healthy, he is a good inside-outside scorer.

"Will is an explosive player," said Arnold. "He can run, jump and shoot.

If we can use that explosiveness and control it with mental maturity, he should have a fine season. Of course, we hope his knees hold up."

Stetson's other returning player is 6-8 sophomore forward/center **Steve Hoffert** (2.7 ppg, 2.6 rpg). He appeared in 26 games last season and showed flashes of offensive potential. "Hoffert backed up Warbritton and Lambert last year, so his minutes were limited," said Arnold. "He's a good, solid contributor—somewhere between a factor and a force. He is a good post-up player, but can also knock down the three. His versatility is what we like so much about him."

The Hatters' six newcomers should provide some of the punch that some of the returnees seem to be lacking.

Shamar Johnson, a 6-2 junior, should see heavy minutes in the backcourt after averaging 15.8 points and 3.9 rebounds last season at Monroe (N.Y.) CC. "Johnson is strong and athletic, and can give us some scoring punch on the perimeter that we need," said Arnold. "He can also defend. He could be a double-figure performer at one end of the floor and a defensive force on the other."

Maryland transfer **Kelly Hite**, a 6-3 sophomore, should back up Davis on the wing once he becomes eligible after the first semester. Hite is a good shooter who saw little action with the Terrapins. He averaged just 1.2 points per game as a freshman. "We think he will be a good player in the TAAC," said Arnold. "Our concern is with his being on the Maryland bench for that year, it is now going to be two and a half seasons since he has played competitively."

Another transfer who could figure into the frontcourt picture is 6-5 sophomore forward **Sebastian Singletary**, who averaged 16.2 points and 10.3 rebounds last season at Central Florida CC. Singletary is a strong player with a soft touch. "We thought he was one of the top five juco players in the state of Florida last season," said Arnold.

The incoming freshman class has size in the form of 6-8 **Ricky McConnell** from Leto HS in Tampa, and 6-7, 270-pound **Santos Hampton** from Monroe HS in Albany, Ga. McConnell averaged 26.3 points and 7.8 rebounds last season, while Hampton averaged 11.5 points and 5.8 rebounds. McConnell is listed at 215 pounds and needs to mature physically to be effective, while Hampton needs work in the conditioning department.

Arnold's other freshman signee is 6-1 guard **Van Morris** from Pickering HS in Leesville, La. Morris averaged 18.4 points and 5.1 rebounds last season. "Morris has a lot of physical tools," said Arnold. "He was a great high school quarterback, so this is the first time he has touched a basketball in September and October. That's why we think he's going to be a good one. We look at him maybe the way the Knicks looked at Charlie Ward."

The roster is filled out by walkon freshmen **Jason Weiss**, a 6-3 guard from Osceola HS in Kissimmee, Fla., and **Mark Thompson**, a 6-3 guard from Battle Ground Academy in Nashville, Tenn.

1998-99 STETSON SCHEDULE

Nov.	14	@Furman
	16	@Clemson
	21	Flagler
	25	Charleston Southern
	28	@Tulane
Dec.	5	The Citadel
	9	*Bethune-Cookman
	19	Belmont
	21	@Notre Dame
	29	Anderson
Jan.	4	Centenary
	7	@Jacksonville
	11	@Centenary
	14	@Florida Atlantic
	16	@Central Florida
	21	Troy State
	23	Mercer
	28	@Campbell
	30	@Georgia State
Feb.	4	Jacksonville State
	6	Samford
	9	Central Florida
	13	@Troy State
	15	@Mercer
	18	Florida Atlantic
	20	Jacksonville
	26-27	#TAAC Tournament

@ Road Games
* Ocean Center, Daytona Beach, FL
# Jacksonville Coliseum, Jacksonville, FL

adidas Blue Ribbon Analysis

BACKCOURT .... **C** **BENCH/DEPTH** .... **C**
FRONTCOURT .... **D+** **INTANGIBLES** .... **C+**

Arnold doesn't seem to be putting the cart before the horse when he talks about this season's Hatter team.

"We're trying to do things here at Stetson in a way that will help us build a solid, stable program," said Arnold. "One of the most elusive things these days in college basketball is stability. There are lots of things out there that can create chaos in a program—players transferring, coaches leaving or teams changing conferences. We felt good about last year. We thought we had a solid year of progress to give us a foundation. We feel like we had a good, solid recruiting year. Hopefully, that's going to move us into competitor status this year, then perhaps contender status down the road from there."

Last year was indeed a good start to what seems to be a promising future. But based on this year's group of returning players, and the uncertainty that always centers around newcomers, the Hatters don't appear poised to make a big push toward the top this season. If history holds true, however, it won't be long before the Hatters savor some additional success.

Arnold has been successful at his other stops—his teams have appeared in four NCAA tournaments and two NITs. Stetson's losing season in 1997-98 was just the fourth experienced by Arnold in his college coaching career. This season will be his fifth. Put the Hatters down for a seventh-place finish in the TAAC.

(G.C.)

TROY STATE

LOCATION .... **Troy, AL**
CONFERENCE .... **Trans-America Athletic TAAC**
LAST SEASON .... **7-20 (.259)**
CONFERENCE RECORD ...... **5-11 (5th-West Division)**
STARTERS LOST/RETURNING **3/2**
NICKNAME .... **Trojans**
COLORS .... **Cardinal, Gray & Black**
HOMECOURT .... **Trojan Arena (4,000)**
COACH .... **Don Maestri (Southern Mississippi '69)**
RECORD AT SCHOOL .... **270-182 (16 yrs.)**
CAREER RECORD .... **270-182 (16 yrs.)**
ASSISTANTS .... **David Felix (Troy State '77)**
Billy Jeffcoat (Troy State '94)
TEAM WINS (last 5 yrs.)
27-15-9-16-7
RPI (last 5 yrs.)
252-232-268-155-297
1997-98 FINISH
Not eligible for conference tournament.

For a coach coming off his worst season, Don Maestri sure is smiling a lot these days.

"Really, this is one of the best teams in terms of outlook that we've had here in years," said Maestri. "There are a lot of new, positive things surrounding this program."

New is the operative word here. Starting with the roster—which contains three junior-college transfers, one Division I transfer, and three freshmen—and ending with a refurbished arena. The Trojans' old home (Sartain Hall) is now called Trojan Arena after an offseason overhaul that increased its seating capacity by almost 1,000.

Also contributing to Maestri's giddy demeanor is the fact that TSU is now eligible to compete in the TAAC Tournament. During the summer, the NCAA changed from eight to two the number of seasons new Division I members are required to wait to be eligible for NCAA Tournament participation.

"This is the first year we actually feel like a Division I program," said Maestri. "It's the first year that we can be a part of things that are afforded to Division I teams."

Of course, with the TAAC Tournament consisting of just the top eight teams in the league, the Trojans will have to improve plenty if they want to taste the finer things in life this season.

A good start would be finding a way to put the ball in the basket on occasion. Last season, TSU was anemic offensively, shooting just .376 from the field, .262 from three-point range, and .663 at the free-throw line. One of the new assets of the Trojans' renovated arena is air-conditioning. Maestri may not feel like turning it on if his team doesn't find a way to begin warming up on its own.

"We weren't a good shooting team last year, and to top that off, we weren't a very good defensive team," said Maestri, who had to scrap his normally frenetic pressing and up-tempo scheme early last year when it was apparent

		1998-99 TROY STATE SCHEDULE
Nov.	16	@UNLV
	28	@Texas-San Antonio
Dec.	1	Belhaven
	5	Florida A&M
	14	Huntingdon
	19-20	#UNO Christmas Classic
	22	@Louisiana State
	28-29	##Gossner Classic
Jan.	2	Samford
	4	Jacksonville State
	7	@Samford
	9	@Jacksonville State
	14	Mercer
	16	Georgia State
	21	@Stetson
	23	@Jacksonville
	28	Centenary
Feb.	4	Campbell
	6	@Central Florida
	8	@Florida Atlantic
	13	Stetson
	15	Jacksonville
	18	@Mercer
	20	@Campbell
	25-27	###TAAC Tournament

@ Road Games
# New Orleans, LA (vs. Tennessee State, first round; also Maine and New Orleans)
Logan, UT (vs. Lafayette, first round; also Norfolk State and Utah State)
Jacksonville Coliseum, Jacksonville, FL

the Trojans wouldn't be able to find the basket. "When you can't shoot, you can't press because if you don't make shots you're never going to be able to get in it. Then, you have to play halfcourt defense, which is something this team wasn't very accustomed to doing."

Only three players who played significant minutes—6-3 junior guard **Joey Raines** (10.8 ppg, 2.8 rpg), 6-1 senior guard **Aldo Hudson** (10.2 ppg, 2.6 rpg, 84 assists, 31 steals) and 6-8 sophomore **Rammy Morrison** (1.7 ppg, 1.2 rpg)—return from last season. A fourth returnee—6-7 sophomore forward **Brad Grant** (3.2 ppg, 2.8 rpg)—appeared in five games a year ago before being redshirted.

"We're really a very young team in terms of experience," said Maestri. "We have a mix of redshirts, jucos and high school kids that, credential-wise, can shoot the ball fairly well and are athletic. We hope that gives us a chance to be a better team."

Hudson, who came to TSU from junior college, is the team's only senior.

He is extremely quick, but shot just .384 from the field and .197 from three-point range last season. "Hudson is one of the quickest and fastest players in the conference," said Maestri. "He struggled some with his ability to score. As quick as he is, he also struggled with the pressing system. Hopefully, he will be better with one year's experience."

Raines, a walkon last season, is an excellent three-point shooter, which made him something of a rarity at Troy. Rains shot .403 percent (50 of 124) from behind the arc in 1997-98. "We're expecting him to be on of the better three-point shooters in the league," said Maestri. "He can stand still and shoot and is also good at using pump fakes to free himself. He is the type of player that can get on a roll and make five or six three-pointers in a row. He can definitely do some damage when hot."

Morrison averaged almost seven minutes per game a year ago. He is an athletic big man but still needs to get stronger and become more physical to compete consistently. "He got taken to school in games against big-time post players," said Maestri.

Grant is an intriguing player who can rebound and also is the best jump shooter in the Trojan frontcourt. He played in 22 games as a freshman two years ago before falling victim to injury early last season.

The TSU front line should get a boost this season with the arrival of 6-7 junior **Johna Seay**, a transfer from Georgia Southern. Seay saw extensive playing time in his two seasons at Georgia Southern, averaging 8.5 points and 6.0 rebounds as a sophomore, and 11.1 points and 6.2 rebounds as a freshman.

"Johna is a legitimate post player," said Maestri. "He can play defense in the post. He's not a great jumper, but is a good position player. He has one or two solid post moves on offense and will be counted on to make some big contributions for us."

Maestri's junior college recruits include teammates **Eugene Christopher** and **Nek Daniels**, guards from Pensacola (Fla.) JC. Christopher, a 6-3 junior, averaged 6.3 points and 5.0 rebounds last season, while Daniels, a 6-1 junior, averaged 8.0 points. Both players participated in the Florida Junior College All-Star Game.

"Christopher is a competitor, he competes on every play," said Maestri. "He is a very balanced player and an excellent athlete. Daniels is an excellent defender. He is a point guard who is quick and a good passer. He didn't shoot the ball a lot last season, but when he did his decisions on when to shoot were excellent."

The team's other transfer is 6-6 forward **Nick Cherry** from Jones County (Miss.) JC. Cherry averaged 14.7 points and 6.8 rebounds last season. His game is a combination of athleticism and intensity. "He may be the best athlete on this campus," said Maestri. "He runs like a deer. He's not as skilled as our other two junior-college recruits, but because of his intensity, he will be a factor. He is the kind of player that goes to the water fountain hard."

Maestri describes his freshman class of 6-1 guard **Robert Rushing**, 6-6 forward **Donnie Pemberton**, and 6-5 forward **Ryan Blankson** as "one of the best freshman classes since I've been at this university."

Rushing, who averaged 17.6 points, 4.1 rebounds and 5.2 assists at Randolph-Clay HS in Ft. Gaines, Ga., last season, is an excellent shooter with a good all-around game.

Pemberton, who averaged 18.6 points, 8.2 rebounds and 3.0 assists at Bainbridge (Ga.) HS, is already the strongest Trojan, as he has benched more than 300 pounds in preseason workouts.

Blankson, a late addition out of Chicago, is also a strong inside player with good court instincts.

"All three of these freshmen will play this year, but in the long haul, this will be the group the puts us in a real successful situation here at Troy State," said Maestri. "This group will be the continuity we haven't had in this program."

adidas Blue Ribbon Analysis

BACKCOURT .... **D+** **BENCH/DEPTH** .... **C**
FRONTCOURT .... **D+** **INTANGIBLES** .... **C**

TSU is a program on the mend. The Trojans did not have a double-figure scorer returning last season and the results were predictable, especially given Maestri's preference for up-tempo, full-court basketball.

Although not standouts be any means, TSU does have two double-figure scorers returning this year in Raines and Hudson. Seay should also have a positive influence in the middle. That improvement may be just a band-aid solution for a program that is in need of major surgery.

The rest of the cast is too unproven to allow us to move the Trojans up very far in the TAAC standings. The Trojans will once again be on the outside looking in when postseason play rolls around, and will probably also be looking up from the bottom of the TAAC standings.

(G.C.)

WEST COAST CONFERENCE

adidas BLUE RIBBON FORECAST

1. Pepperdine
2. Gonzaga
3. Saint Mary's
4. San Francisco
5. Santa Clara
6. Portland
7. San Diego
8. Loyola Marymount

ALL-CONFERENCE TEAM

G—Jelani Gardner, SR, Pepperdine
G—Matt Santangelo, JR, Gonzaga
F—Eric Schraeder, SR, Saint Mary's
F—Gerald Zimmerman, SR, San Francisco
C—Brad Millard, JR, Saint Mary's

PLAYER OF THE YEAR

Matt Santangelo, JR, Gonzaga

NEWCOMER OF THE YEAR

Nick Sheppard, JR, Pepperdine

1998-99 CONFERENCE TOURNAMENT

Feb. 27-March 1, Toso Pavilion, Santa Clara, Calif.

1997-98 CHAMPION

Gonzaga (regular season)
San Francisco (conference tournament)

1997-98 POSTSEASON PARTICIPANTS

Postseason Record: 1-2 (.333)
NCAA
San Francisco
NIT
Gonzaga (second round)

TOP BACKCOURTS

1. Gonzaga
2. San Francisco
3. Saint Mary's

TOP FRONTCOURTS

1. Saint Mary's
2. Gonzaga
3. Pepperdine

ON THE WAY UP

Pepperdine

ON THE WAY DOWN

Santa Clara

INSIDE THE NUMBERS

- 1997-98 conference RPI: 11th (of 30)
- Conference RPI (last 5 years): 16-13-11-17-11

DID YOU KNOW?

Gonzaga was the preseason pick in the annual coaches' poll, but it was close. Four teams received first-place votes: The Zags, Pepperdine, Saint Mary's and Santa Clara. Gonzaga returns four starters from a team that reached the second round of the NIT under first-year coach Dan Monson. Monson did a terrific job and earned well-deserved coach-of-the-year honors...Pepperdine, on the upswing after enduring three poor seasons, is trying to win its first conference crown since 1993. The Waves are easily the most athletic team in the league...Saint Mary's center Brad Millard's injury (a broken foot two games in to the season) dramatically changed the league race a year ago. Millard, at 7-foot-3 and 345 pounds the largest player in Division I, is healthy now and ready for a monster year...Santa Clara's finish last year was forgettable—the Broncos dropped their last three regular-season games and did a free-fall from first to third. It got worse in the offseason. All-WCC guard Brian Jones (15.6 ppg) dislocated his right kneecap playing summer ball. He might return in December. Meanwhile, the Broncos will be treading water...The 1997-98 season saw WCC teams post a .581 winning percentage against Division I opponents (54-39), the second-best in league history. That mark included wins over the ACC, SEC, Big Ten, WAC and Pac-10....WCC schools were 37-4 at home in non-league play, a conference record. Gonzaga was 11-1, Pepperdine 10-2 and USF 10-3. It was dog-eat-dog in the league season, as usual: Home teams went 34-22 in WCC play...Millard, shoe size 24, dwarfs the league's other big men. Loyola-Marymount's Haywood Eaddy, 5-4 and 140 pounds, is one of the smallest players in Division I.

(P.B.)

GONZAGA

LOCATION .... Spokane, WA
CONFERENCE .... West Coast
LAST SEASON .... 24-10 (.742)
CONFERENCE RECORD 10-4 (1st)
STARTERS LOST/RETURNING 1/4
NICKNAME .... Bulldogs
COLORS .... Blue, Red & White
HOMECOURT .... Martin Centre (4,000)
COACH .... Dan Monson (Idaho '85)
RECORD AT SCHOOL .... 24-10 (1 yr.)
CAREER RECORD .... 24-10 (1 yr.)
ASSISTANTS .... Mark Few (Oregon '87)
Bill Grier (Oregon '90)
Scott Didrickson (Washington '95)
TEAM WINS (last 5 yrs.) 22-21-21-15-24
RPI (last 5 yrs.) 79-90-82-184-65
1997-98 FINISH .... Lost in NIT second round.

Everyone knew it would be a silky-smooth transition when veteran assistant Dan Monson slid 16 inches to his left and replaced Dan Fitzgerald as Gonzaga's head coach. Monson couldn't rant and rave in Fitz's league, but he knew his Xs and Os.

At 36, Monson was the youngest active head man in the WCC, but he had all the tools, not to mention the genes, to be successful. He had Bakari Hendrix, too. So nobody was totally surprised when the Zags won the 1998 WCC regular-season championship—their third title in five years—and advanced to the second round of the NIT with a school-record 24 victories.

Dan Monson, the son of ex-Idaho and ex-Oregon coach Don Monson (Jud Heathcote's fishing buddy), carved a reputation as a terrific recruiter during a five-year run that saw Gonzaga go 103-45 and make three postseason appearances.

During Monson's first year as head coach, Hendrix was player of the year and point guard **Matt Santangelo** was first-team all-WCC. Did we mention Monson was WCC Coach of the Year and national rookie coach of the year as judged by *Basketball Times*?

Noisy Martin Centre, capacity 4,000, remained one of the least hospitable venues in the country. The Zags, meanwhile, had a different look under the aggressive Monson. There was less "flex" on offense and more pushing the ball up the floor. Gonzaga pressured more, shot a ton of three-pointers (679 attempts) and averaged a league-high 80 points per game. It wasn't exactly UNLV, but it was sizzling stuff compared to some previous GU teams.

Hendrix is gone, no doubt bound for the NBA, but four starters return and the Zags have been given the honor (kiss of death?) of being No. 1 in the preseason, just ahead of Pepperdine, Saint Mary's and Santa Clara.

Gonzaga can't complain about a lack of national exposure this season: The Zags are in the preseason NIT. They play at Kansas on Nov. 13 and ESPN will televise the game regionally. It is an excellent chance for Santangelo to make an impression as one of the top guards on the West Coast.

There is no getting around it. This little 5,000-student school in Spokane, Wash., has become a basketball dynasty (albeit on a low-profile scale). The Zags are 156-80 (.661) since the 1990-'91 season, the best overall record in the WCC in that span. It translates into an average of 19.5 victories per year in the '90s, with a league-high five 20-win seasons.

Hendrix, a versatile 6-8 forward, averaged 19.9 points and basically carried the Zags over the rough spots last year. "When you lose a player of that caliber, the MVP of the league, it's tough to know how your team will respond," Monson said. "It will have to be a team effort to pick up the slack, not one man."

Santangelo is now the big man on campus. The 6-1 junior from Portland, Ore., was co-freshman of the year in '97, all-WCC in '98 and now he's a potential league MVP. Santangelo is the top returning scorer in the league (16.2 ppg). He ranked in the league's top five in assists (4.1), three-point percentage (.430) and three-pointers made (74). He also led the league in minutes played (1,129).

With Santangelo and 6-5 junior **Richie Frahm** (12.1 ppg, 3.8 rpg, 60 assists, 23 steals) the Zags have perhaps the top backcourt in the league in terms of firepower. The two players combined for 151 made three-pointers and shot 45 percent combined from long range. Frahm has a chance to make all-WCC.

Quentin Hall, the 5-8 senior sparkplug from the Bahamas (8.6 ppg, 2.5 apg) appeared in 33 games and served as a catalyst off the bench. Hall earned his spurs for Monson with 18 points in the Zags' upset of No. 5 Clemson in the Top of the World Classic at Fairbanks, Alaska.

The other guards on the roster include 6-1 junior **Ryan Floyd** (2.4 ppg, 1.3 apg) and 6-5 junior **Mike Nilson** (2.8 ppg, 1.7 rpg).

The Zags return two experienced front-line players in 6-11 junior **Axel Dench** (5.3 ppg, 4.1 rpg) and 6-7 senior **Mike Leasure** (5.0 ppg, 3.3 rpg). The other front-line spot could be a tussle among 6-8 sophomore **Casey Cavalry** (3.7 ppg, 2.7 rpg), 6-9 redshirt senior **Jeremy Eaton** (5.4 ppg, 3.8 rpg in '96-'97) and 6-8 sophomore **Mark Spink** (1.5 ppg, 1.9 rpg).

Calvary, considered one of the best freshmen big men in GU history, became the first freshman to lead the conference in blocked shots (46). Calvary did his damage while averaging just 14 minutes per game. He had 0.1 blocks per minute played. By comparison, 7-3 Brad Millard of Saint Mary's averaged 0.105 blocks per minute in '97 en route to 97 rejections—the second-highest total in WCC history.

There is a Hendrix on the roster. The Zags recruited 6-5 **Damany Hendrix** from Vallejo, Calif. He is one of three freshmen on the team. The others are 6-8 forward **Zach Gourde** and 7-1 center **Eric Chilton**.

adidas Blue Ribbon Analysis

BACKCOURT	B+	BENCH/DEPTH	C
FRONTCOURT	C+	INTANGIBLES	B

Pepperine has more athleticism and Saint Mary's has man-mountain Brad Millard in the middle, but Gonzaga has it rolling and there is no reason to believe the Zags won't at least contend for another WCC title. There is enough experience and firepower to win it outright. If Santangelo and Frahm have a great year, the loss of Hendrix won't be insurmountable, but somebody has to step forward on the front line.

With each of the contenders facing serious questions, this is not an easy race to handicap. Monson believes it will be a dogfight all year. "The league is as competitive as ever in the ten years I've been around it," he said. "Four teams have a legitimate shot to win it and all eight can beat anybody on a given night."

Monson's personal pick is Santa Clara, but that was before the Broncos lost Brian Jones to injury.

(P.B.)

1998-99 GONZAGA SCHEDULE

Nov.	13	@Kansas
	16-18	#Memphis
	22	St. Martin's College
	28	Washington State
	30	@Eastern Washington
Dec.	4-5	##Hawkeye Invitational
	8	Washington
	19	Chicago State
	22	Idaho
	28	@Texas-Pan American
	30	@Texas Christian
Jan.	2	@Boise State
	7	Loyola Marymount
	9	Pepperdine
	13	Portland
	16	@Portland
	22	@San Francisco
	23	@Santa Clara
	28	Santa Clara
	30	San Francisco
Feb.	4	@San Diego
	6	@Saint Mary's
	11	Saint Mary's
	13	San Diego
	19	Pepperdine
	20	Loyola Marymount
27-Mar.	1	###WCC Tournament

@ Road Games
# Chase NIT (If the Bulldogs advance, they will play either Purdue or Illinois-Chicago on Nov. 18. Semifinals and finals are Nov. 25 & 27 at Madison Square Garden, NY)
Iowa City, IA (vs. Detroit, first round; also Iowa and South Alabama)
Toso Pavilion, Santa Clara, CA

LOYOLA MARYMOUNT

LOCATION .... Los Angeles, CA
CONFERENCE .... West Coast
LAST SEASON .... 7-20 (.259)
CONFERENCE RECORD 3-11 (8th)
STARTERS LOST/RETURNING 3/2
NICKNAME .... Lions
COLORS .... Crimson & Columbia Blue
HOMECOURT .... Gersten Pavilion (4,156)
COACH .... Charles Bradley (Wyoming '81)
RECORD AT SCHOOL .... 7-20 (1 yr.)
CAREER RECORD .... 44-63 (4 yrs.)
ASSISTANTS .... Ronnie Stubbs (Southern Utah '80)
Bill Garnett (Metro State '95)
John Schweitz (Richmond '88)
TEAM WINS (last 5 yrs.) 6-13-18-7-7
RPI (last 5 yrs.) 121-212-160-254-255
1997-98 FINISH .... Lost in conference quarterfinal.

In the tradition of Spud Webb and Mugsy Bogues, a little point guard is trying to lead Loyola Marymount out of the basketball wilderness: 5-4 senior **Haywood "Beatstreet" Eaddy**, a non-stop dynamo from Baltimore, Md., who averaged 15.2 ppg and 4.9 apg last season.

Eaddy, a transfer from Casper (Wyo.) Community College, single-handedly kept the 7-20 Lions in many games. He won two of them with last-second shots. But this was a high-scoring team that couldn't stop anybody even though it led the league in rebounding and blocked shots.

Loyola Marymount was last (3-11) in the WCC for the second year in a row despite a coaching change that swept John Olive out the door and brought in former Wyoming All-American Charles Bradley.

Bradley rolled up his sleeves and found out there is much work to be done at LMU. "You've got to take it piece by piece," he said. "We haven't proven anything yet. We've got to go out and do it on the floor.

"This is almost like my first year. We've got some players now who are more conducive to the style of play I can coach. Sometimes my biggest problem is losing my patience ... but I know I have to be patient."

No one can say the Lions don't have an interesting roster. They have the smallest player in the history of the conference (Eaddy), a 6-11 center from Kenya (**Silvester Kainga**) and two eagerly-anticipated JC transfers (**Ed Wolfe** and **Rupert McClendon**) as Bradley enters Year Two of his rebuilding job.

As usual, the rest of the league's coaches had little respect for the Lions. They were picked last, and Bradley can't argue too loudly. Loyola Marymount must win some games to earn respect. "A season like we had last year, we can do nothing but improve," Bradley said. "We were in almost every game, but we just didn't have quite enough."

Eighth-seeded in the WCC tournament, the Lions nearly shook up the form chart. A few days after a 23-point loss at 1997-98 league champ Gonzaga, Loyola Marymount played the No. 1-seeded Zags at Toso Pavilion and lost 79-78. It left Bradley wondering what might have happened if the Lions had squeezed into the semifinals.

Five new players join a team top-heavy with guards. Eaddy ranked ninth in league scoring and was high in several other categories. LMU officials were stunned when he was left off the all-conference team.

"You look at Haywood, and you do think about players like Mugsy and Spud Webb," Bradley said. "But he's a much better shooter (than those guys). He can't jump like a Spud Webb, but he has his own identity, which is good.

"I was involved in the World Games (assistant coach) and I got a chance to see some of the better players. I think Haywood Eaddy is not only one of the premier players in this conference, but in the country. I really believe that."

LMU averaged nearly 74 points per game last year, and Eaddy scored or passed off for 24.9 points per game. By comparison, the second-best mark among returning players is owned by Gonzaga's Matt Santangelo (24.4).

Willie Allen, a 5-11 senior, returns at shooting guard for LMU. A former walkon who spent a year at Cypress (Calif.) JC, Allen (9.2 ppg, 1.7 rpg, 59 assists, 21 steals) shot just 37 percent from the floor.

The rest of the backcourt includes 6-4 senior **Leo Saucedo** (6.6 ppg, 3.0 rpg, 26 assists, 21 steals) and 6-5 sophomore **Elton Mashack** (6.5 ppg, 3.1 rpg, 27 assists). Mashack was a highly regarded local recruit a year ago who has yet to make a big impact in Division I. There is also little-used 6-1 senior **Chris Evelyn** (1.0 ppg, 0.8 rpg) and spot player **Mihail Papadopulo** (0.5 ppg, 0.4 rpg), a 5-10

1998-99 LOYOLA MARYMOUNT SCHEDULE

Nov.	17	Long Beach State
	21	Boise State
	25	Southern California College
	28	@California-Santa Barbara
Dec.	2	Fullerton State
	5	San Diego State
	9	@Southern California
	12	University Of Pacific
	19	@Utah
	21	@Xavier
	29	@UCLA
Jan.	2	California Baptist
	7	@Gonzaga
	9	@Portland
	15	San Francisco
	16	Santa Clara
	21	@San Diego
	23	@Saint Mary's
	29	Saint Mary's
	30	San Diego
Feb.	3	Pepperdine
	6	@Pepperdine
	12	@Santa Clara
	13	@San Francisco
	19	Portland
	20	Gonzaga
26-Mar.	1	#WCC Tournament

@ Road Games
# Toso Pavilion, Santa Clara, CA

senior who started two games in midseason when Eaddy injured his hand.

The new recruits are 6-3 freshman **Robert Davis**, a *USA Today* honorable mention All-American (22 ppg) from Tempe, Ariz., and 6-6 **Curtis Slaughter** (17.0 ppg, 5.0 rpg, 4.0 apg) from Los Angeles.

The front line? Bradley is starting fresh, having lost starters Ben Ammerman (10.9 ppg), Kenny Hotopp (8.0 ppg) and Peter Cornell (8.0 ppg).

One lock for a spot somewhere is 6-5 senior **Tim Kennedy** (7.7 ppg, 3.3 rpg, 41 assists), a versatile player who can shoot from outside and post up. "A strong body that can defend," Bradley said.

There is one center listed on the roster. Kainga, who came to LMU from Nairobi, Kenya via Midland (Texas) JC, broke into the starting lineup for six games late in the year. His numbers aren't impressive (2.0 ppg, 2.7 rpg, 19 blocked shots) but he did come within one blocked shot of tying the school record after swatting away five against San Jose State.

"He worked hard in the spring and summer and made some very good strides," Bradley said. "I can see the improvement in his game. I can see him playing a lot of center for us."

Pablo Machado, 6-10 and 235, is being groomed for the future. Machado, a junior, transferred from Georgia Tech in August and will redshirt. He played in 22 games for the Yellow Jackets as a sophomore, averaging 1.5 points and 1.6 rebounds. He is a native of Venezuela who moved to the U.S. in 1991.

Wolfe is a 6-7, 225-pound junior from Cochise (Ariz.) JC who should start at power forward. He plays inside, can shoot from outside, and he has experience at center. "He's got the power inside that we need," Bradley said.

Wolfe led his junior college to its first 20-win season and a trip to the playoffs. He averaged 14 points and 5.1 rebounds as a sophomore.

McLendon, 6-5 junior, is slated to start at small forward. Bradley said McLendon (15.0 ppg, 4.0 rpg) is quick and explosive with the ability to create. McClendon's athleticism will stand out.

adidas Blue Ribbon Analysis

BACKCOURT .... **C** **BENCH/DEPTH** .... **D**
FRONTCOURT .... **C** **INTANGIBLES** .... **D**

If Wolfe and McClendon make an impact, the Lions will be much more dangerous than league coaches have predicted. Eaddy is one of the most exciting players to watch in the country. Kainga is a shot-blocking specialist who needs a shooting touch. Mashack was a high school superstar, but is still adjusting to college basketball.

If this group comes together, then Bradley has himself a WCC tournament darkhorse. If not, LMU will settle into its accustomed position at the bottom of the standings.

(P.B.)

PEPPERDINE

LOCATION .... **Los Angeles, CA**
CONFERENCE .... **West Coast**
LAST SEASON .... **17-10 (.630)**
CONFERENCE RECORD .... **9-5 (2nd)**
STARTERS LOST/RETURNING **2/3**
NICKNAME .... **Waves**
COLORS .... **Blue, Orange & White**
HOMECOURT .... **Firestone Fieldhouse (3,104)**
COACH .... **Lorenzo Romar (Washington '80)**
RECORD AT SCHOOL .... **23-31 (2 yrs.)**
CAREER RECORD .... **23-31 (2 yrs.)**
ASSISTANTS .... **Randy Bennett (San Diego '86)**
Darwin Cook (Portland '80)
Ken Ammann (Stanford '91)
TEAM WINS (last 5 yrs.) **19-8-10-6-17**
RPI (last 5 yrs.) **93-213-196-262-114**
1997-98 FINISH .... **Lost in conference quarterfinal.**

After three seasons of humbling seventh-place finishes, Pepperdine returned to respectability in WCC basketball. The Waves were 6-21 during coach Lorenzo Romar's forgettable rookie season in 1996-97. They rebounded sharply, finishing 17-10 last year and claiming second in the league race. It was the second-best one-year improvement in Division I basketball and the third-best improvement in the history of the league. Now, the program is poised to win its first WCC crown since 1993 with a little help from Notre Dame and LSU.

The Waves lost all-WCC performers Gerald Brown (16.9 ppg) and Bryan Hill (12.2 ppg) but they return all-WCC point guard **Jelani Gardner** (14.1 ppg, 4.1 rpg, 145 assists, 50 steals) and transfers **David Lalazarian** and **Nick Sheppard** are expected to make an immediate impact—tempering the news that troubled senior center omm'A Givens won't return to the school that overlooks the Malibu coastline.

Around the WCC, it is conceded Pepperdine may have the best athletes. But team cohesion can be difficult when transfers dominate the roster. Romar may actually have an easier job in that regard with the distraction of Givens gone. "I'm excited about the makeup of this year's team," he said. "Our focus will be on developing a stronger bond of team chemistry."

Romar wants a fast start. "It took awhile for us to mesh last year," he said. "We didn't play that badly, but we really didn't play our best basketball until the second half of the league season when we won seven of our last nine."

Pepperdine's returning starters include 6-6 sophomore forward **Kelvin Gibbs** (4.7 ppg, 4.3 rpg) and 6-5 senior guard **Tommie Prince** (7.8 ppg, 3.8 rpg). Price broke his foot in the offseason and didn't have the cast removed until mid-September.

Gibbs was the Waves' starting power forward. Sixth man **Marc McDowell** (4.4 ppg, 2.8 rpg) also returns. McDowell, 6-7, is one of just three seniors on the roster. He was the Waves' starting power forward in 1996-'97. "They're both back, so I just don't know (who will get the job)," Romar said. "Kelvin and Marc are blue-collar types. They work hard and are willing to contribute in any way to help the team succeed."

Brown and Hill accounted for more than 44 percent of the Waves' scoring, so Romar will be scratching for point production. The key is Gardner, a 6-6 senior who began his career at Cal.

"No doubt, a lot is riding on his shoulders," Romar said.

When WCC play started, Gardner turned his game up a notch (14.1 ppg, 6.1 apg). "Talent-wise, he's definitely one of the top guards on the West Coast," Romar said. "He did a lot of work this summer on his conditioning. He worked hard on his shooting."

Same with Prince, a two-year starter who figures to shift from small forward to off-guard this season assuming he comes back 100 percent from his summer injury. Prince was the top defensive player on a team that led the league by allowing just 65.9 points per game.

Behind the starting guards there are 6-1 junior **Tezale Archie** (1.4 ppg, 1.2 rpg), 6-1 junior **Robert Fomby** (2.8 ppg, 1.0 rpg) and 6-3 sophomore walkon **Al Minahan** (1.5 ppg, 0.3 rpg). Freshman recruits **Brandon Armstrong** (6-5) and **Craig Lewis** (6-3) may represent Pepperdine's backcourt of the future.

With Prince moving to join Gardner in the backcourt, 6-7 Notre Dame transfer Lalazarian (5.3 ppg, 2.0 rpg) is the likely starting small forward. Lalazarian established a reputation as a dead-eye three-point shooter when he played for the Fighting Irish. He has three years of eligibility remaining.

"Not the quickest player around, but a relentless worker who can shoot the basketball," Romar said.

The announcement in mid-June that Givens wouldn't return will push 6-11, 240-pound LSU transfer Sheppard into a starting role. Sheppard, a junior, averaged 7.1 ppg and 5.5 rpg as a sophomore at LSU during the 1996-'97 season. He'll send bodies flying in the post, but he may not be at full strength when practice begins because of a sore foot.

Romar tries to downplay the impact of his two transfers. "It's important they do well, but it's a lot to ask of two young men who haven't been in a competitive environment in nearly 18 months," Romar said.

"David can really shoot the ball from the perimeter and isn't afraid to drive to the basket. Nick gives a real presence in the middle and you have to guard him because he can score. If Nick's in condition, he can really help us with his size."

Frontline backups include 6-11 redshirt freshman **Cedric Suitt** (14.0 ppg, 11.0 rpg at Mays HS in Atlanta, Ga.); 6-10 freshman **Jeremy Vague** (who broke his wrist during summer league play); and 6-7 freshman **Ross Varner**. "Varner will challenge our four men (power forwards) for playing time," Romar said.

Pepperdine's schedule has an interesting footnote. Besides playing Kansas at the Arrowhead Pond in Anaheim in the John Wooden Classic, the Waves host a late-December tournament at Firestone Fieldhouse that includes Jim Harrick's Rhode Island team.

Harrick, a legend at Pepperdine, compiled a nine-year record of 167-97 when he was head coach. His Rhode Island team came within one game of advancing to the Final Four last season.

Romar would be happy just to make the NCAAs. If he did, it would be quite a story considering how far the Waves fell after the glory years under Harrick and Tom Asbury (who left for Kansas State).

adidas Blue Ribbon Analysis

BACKCOURT .... **C+** **BENCH/DEPTH** .... **C**
FRONTCOURT .... **B** **INTANGIBLES** .... **B**

Romar's contagious enthusiasm has the Pepperdine program moving in the right direction. If Lalazarian and Sheppard are good as advertised, this is a dangerous team that, barring injuries, could contend for a league championship.

Gardner, who took some time getting comfortable after his transfer from Cal, is a terrific player who could make the jump to great player with little difficulty. He has that kind of talent. Just ask anyone at Cal, his previous school.

1998-99 PEPPERDINE SCHEDULE

Nov.	14	California-Santa Barbara
	17	California-Irvine
	19	Fresno State
	21	@Long Beach State
	24	Wichita State
	28	@Fullerton State
Dec.	5	*Kansas
	12	@Wisconsin
	17	Southern California College
	21-23	#Pearl Harbor Basketball Classic
	29-30	##Sparkletts Invitational
Jan.	2	@San Jose State
	7	@Portland
	9	@Gonzaga
	15	Santa Clara
	16	San Francisco
	21	@Saint Mary's
	23	@San Diego
	29	San Diego
	30	Saint Mary's
Feb.	3	@Loyola Marymount
	6	Loyola Marymount
	12	@San Francisco
	14	@Santa Clara
	19	Gonzaga
	20	Portland
27-Mar.	1	###WCC Tournament

@ Road Games
* Arrowhead Pond of Anaheim, Anaheim, CA
# Laie, HI (vs. Michigan State, first round; also Alabama, BYU-Hawaii, Oregon State, Pepperdine, Texas Tech, Tulsa and Weber State)
Malibu, CA (vs. Rhode Island, first round; also Eastern Michigan and Siena)
Toso Pavilion, Santa Clara, CA

Even if the Waves don't beat out Gonzaga or Saint Mary's for the regular-season title, they will be a team no one wants to face in the WCC tournament.

(P.B.)

PORTLAND

LOCATION .... **Portland, OR**
CONFERENCE .... **West Coast**
LAST SEASON .... **14-13 (.519)**
CONFERENCE RECORD .... **7-7 (t-4th)**
STARTERS LOST/RETURNING **1/4**
NICKNAME .... **Pilots**
COLORS .... **Purple & White**
HOMECOURT .... **Chiles Center (5,000)**
COACH .... **Rob Chavez (Mesa College '80)**
RECORD AT SCHOOL .... **63-50 (4 yrs.)**
CAREER RECORD .... **91-77 (6 yrs.)**
ASSISTANTS .... **Jim Shaw (Western Oregon '85)**
Richard Lucas (Northridge State '93)
Carlin Warley (Oregon '91)
TEAM WINS (last 5 yrs.) **13-21-19-9-14**
RPI (last 5 yrs.) **180-100-85-246-187**
1997-98 FINISH .... **Lost in conference quarterfinal.**

With a month to go in the WCC regular season, the Portland Pilots were tied for first place. They had no reason to believe they would not contend for a championship. But all of a sudden, trainer Tom Fregoso was getting all the minutes. By the end of the year, the Pilots had lost most of their inside strength to injuries. They limped into the WCC tournament as the No. 6 seed and were mercifully taken out by Santa Clara.

Coach Rob Chavez doesn't have to worry about lofty preseason expectations. The Pilots are picked seventh, and Chavez figures that's fair: This is a team with one senior on the roster in 6-6 forward **Jimmie Rainwater**. The Pilots lost a pair of excellent guards in Dionn Holton (WCC assists leader with 151) and team MVP Chivo Anderson (UP-leading 13.3 ppg). Point guard figured to be a problem all year until 6-3 sophomore **Travis Andrews** emerged on the team's tour of Germany and Paris.

Staying healthy is a major goal. Last year, Chavez was shaking his head when Luke Palumbis (torn ACL), Brian Jackson (torn ankle ligament) and **Philip Dejworek** (broken foot) went down within 10 days. "All front-line players," Chavez said. "It pretty much decimated us inside. It made it very difficult for us to defend and rebound in the post."

If Portland's young players feed off the adversity of a year ago, the Pilots could play the role of spoiler. They are especially tough (10-4 last season) in their own Chiles Center, which gives hope for at least another break-even league season.

"Everyone wants to point to the injuries as the reason we stumbled at the end of last season," Chavez said. "That's the obvious (cause), but it indirectly affected the whole team. I think our younger guys got worn down. Mentally, they were tired. And maybe they were physically tired, too."

Chavez has no trouble nominating probable starters at four positions:

Rainwater (8.6 ppg, 3.1 rpg) ranks sixth on UP's career three-point list (102). He'll be a key player in whatever the Pilots do. "He's got to have a banner season," Chavez said. "He's more or less our designated perimeter shooter. He's also become a solid defensive player."

Troy Collins is a 6-6 junior forward (7.6 ppg, 5.8 rpg) who led the team in rebounding and ranked No. 9 in the WCC in that department. All this after missing his first season with a heart problem. "He's the workhorse type," Chavez said.

Jason Franklin is the team's top returning scorer (10.1 ppg, 2.1 rpg, 32 assists, 42 steals). The 6-4 junior guard has explosive ability, judging from his 22-points-in-28-minutes burst at Oregon State his freshman season.

"His strongest position is off-guard, although he played some point on our tour," Chavez said. "Jason's a slasher and a good penetrator. He's a streaky offensive player who can get it going when he's on."

German junior national center Dejworek, 6-9, played in 25 games as a freshman despite his injuries (foot and ankle). Dejworek (6.6 ppg, 3.1 rpg) shot nearly 50 percent from the field when he was healthy. "He'll be a go-to guy," said Chavez, who will need all the size he can throw together against some of the league's beefier teams.

Sophomore **Eric Sandrin**, 6-9, started 11 games at forward. Sandrin (2.8 ppg, 1.9 rpg) led the Pilots with 16 blocked shots. **Brian Jackson**, a 6-5 junior forward, averaged five points and three rebounds in 24 games but he fought ankle problems the last third of the year. **Travis Andrews** is a 6-3 sophomore who played in 26 games (4.8 ppg, 1.8 rpg), showing flashes of outside brilliance with 16 three-pointers.

Jackson's sore ankle complicated Chavez' juggling act with the roster. "Before he got hurt, he was rounding into form as our best low-post scorer," Chavez said.

Daniel Sandrin, a 6-7 true freshman, joins his brother on the team. The slender forward averaged 18 points and 10 rebounds as a prep at Bothell (Wash.) High.

The most intriguing Pilot signee is 6-11 transfer center **Chukwuma Neboh**, who escaped Nigeria's political unrest three years ago and fled to Salt Lake (Utah) CC where a relative was working as a professor.

Neboh, literally recruited out of the hallways, played two years, averaging 5.3 points and 4.7 rebounds as a sophomore to go with 35 blocked shots. Neboh is a project, but loaded with potential. The junior is a shot-blocker who can only get better offensively.

Redshirt freshman **Jason Robbins**, 6-6, played in just two games before injuring a shoulder. Chavez said he could contend for time at small forward. Robbins scored more than 2,000 career points at Seattle's Franklin High.

Chavez said 6-3 true freshman **Ryan Jones** is a multitalented guard who should get minutes. Jones is one of four freshmen coming to the Bluff. He sat out last season, but averaged 31 points and eight rebounds at Olympia (Wash.) High.

Who will play the point? Chavez isn't hurting for candidates. Andrews positioned himself to take the job during the 11-day European trip that gave the Pilots a nice jump-start on their season.

"We knew Travis had good skills, but with Dionn Holton (getting the PG minutes) we really didn't get a chance to see them," Chavez said.

"Travis has good skills. He's much more of an offensive player than Dionn, a good three-point shooter and a good passer. But defensively, Dionn was as good as anybody in the country. You don't replace that."

Ross Jorgusen, a 6-1 redshirt freshman, is in the point guard hunt. Trouble is, Jorgusen is more scorer than distributor. He led the state of Washington in scoring last year at 34.6 ppg. Meanwhile, 5-10 freshman **Davon Johnson** from Inglewood, CA (24.0 ppg, 7.0 apg) brings in glossy stats. And 6-7 freshman **Bryan Mills** (15.0 ppg, 7.0 rpg, 5.0 apg) will make a bid. If Mills wins the job, he would be the tallest point guard in the WCC. Chavez said he's a threat to start at all three perimeter positions.

adidas Blue Ribbon Analysis

BACKCOURT .... **C** **BENCH/DEPTH** .... **D**
FRONTCOURT .... **C** **INTANGIBLES** .... **D**

Although the long arm of UP recruiting stretched to Enugu, Nigeria, the Pilots didn't merit much respect in the preseason coaches' poll. Those nay votes could change if Portland's freshmen come through and the team stays injury-free.

Chavez got the Pilots into the NCAA tournament in 1995-96 and seemed on track for another banner year in '97-'98 until it all fell apart. If Rainwater, Collins, Franklin and Dejworek stay out of the trainer's room, this team is better than seventh place. Andrews' ability to replace Holton at point guard is crucial.

If nothing else, Portland will be fun to watch with a 6-7 point guard on the floor at times and 6-11 Nigerian center Chukwuma Neboh, who didn't pick up a basketball until coaches spied him roaming the halls two years ago at Salt Lake CC.

(P.B.)

1998-99 PORTLAND SCHEDULE

Nov.	17	Patten College
	20-21	#AT&T Shootout
	24	California-Santa Barbara
	30	California-Irvine
	5	Eastern Oregon
	8	Loyola
	12	@Idaho State
	19	Fullerton State
	22	@San Jose State
	30	@Washington
Jan.	2	@Rice
	7	Pepperdine
	9	Loyola Marymount
	13	@Gonzaga
	16	Gonzaga
	22	@Santa Clara
	23	@San Francisco
	28	San Francisco
	30	Santa Clara
Feb.	4	@Saint Mary's
	6	@San Diego
	11	San Diego
	13	Saint Mary's
	19	@Loyola Marymount
	20	@Pepperdine
27-Mar.	1	##WCC Tournament

@ Road Games
\# Fairfield, CT (vs. George Mason, first round; also Fairfield and Long Island)
\## Toso Pavilion, Santa Clara, CA

SAINT MARY'S

LOCATION .... **Moraga, CA**
CONFERENCE .... **West Coast**
LAST SEASON .... **12-15 (.444)**
CONFERENCE RECORD .... **7-7 (t-4th)**
STARTERS LOST/RETURNING **1/4**
NICKNAME .... **Gaels**
COLORS .... **Blue & Red**
HOMECOURT .... **McKeon Pavilion (3,500)**
COACH .... **Dave Bolwinkel (California '72)**
RECORD AT SCHOOL .... **12-15 (1 yr.)**
CAREER RECORD .... **70-98 (6 yrs.)**
ASSISTANTS .... **Tim Murphy (Colorado State '84)**
Kyle Manary (Stephen F. Austin '95)
David Carter (Saint Mary's '89)
TEAM WINS (last 5 yrs.) **13-18-12-23-12**
RPI (last 5 yrs.) **190-96-146-92-187**
1997-98 FINISH .... **Lost in conference quarterfinal.**

Flash back 12 months, and Saint Mary's was a legitimate contender. First-year coach Dave Bollwinkel was convinced of it, and 7-3, 345-pound center **Brad Millard** had his back. Bollwinkel could talk tough because he just *knew* Millard could take care of San Francisco, Pepperdine or Santa Clara.

"He was the most dominant force in the league," said Bollwinkel.

But Millard couldn't get through warmups in the Gaels' third game of the season. It was at Cal in late November. A simple layup drill. "He felt something go 'pop' and that was it," said Bollwinkel. The result was freakish, and final: Millard broke a bone in his size 24 left foot, shattering any hope the Gaels had of being in the title hunt.

It said something that Saint Mary's won the game. "We knew the foot was a problem," Bollwinkel said, reliving a nightmare. "He hadn't practiced all week. We tried to treat it to see what would happen.

"I told the guys, 'we can either mail this sucker in, or find another way to win'. The whole season was like that. I can't say I'm happy with fourth place, but ... we kind of sucked it up."

Surgery, and a subsequent bone graft, dispelled the myth that all the king's horses and all the king's men couldn't put Millard back together again. All-WCC as a sophomore after averaging 12.4 ppg and 7.6 rpg, Millard bumped heads with Tim Duncan in the NCAAs. He spent more time with doctors and nurses than he did in the key in a washout junior season. He's been granted an extra year of eligibility, and this WCC version of *My Left Foot* will have a direct impact on the league race.

Millard did have a second surgery to make sure the foot would heal properly, but Bollwinkel said the prognosis is excellent. The Gaels are being extremely cautious with Millard, but they expected him to be able to go full speed when fall practice started.

"Our biggest key, literally and figuratively, is Brad's return to good health," Bollwinkel said. "No one else in the league will add a player of equal impact."

No Millard meant no prayer in 1997-'98, but Saint Mary's played the rest of the season anyway. The Gaels worked hard under Bollwinkel without their starting center. They finished 12-15 overall and 7-7 in WCC play. Not bad, considering.

Four starters return, assuming Millard gets a clean bill of health, and Saint Mary's was picked third in the preseason coaches' poll. Such is the respect for Millard, the biggest player in Division I, and Bollwinkel's ability to coax maximum effort out of his players.

Saint Mary's will be tested early. The Gaels play just two home games in the first five weeks of the season. Iowa State and possibly Cincinnati await in the Great Alaska

1998-99 SAINT MARY'S SCHEDULE

Nov.	13	@Kansas State
	18	San Jose State
	21	@Sacramento State
	25-28	#Great Alaska Shootout
Dec.	2	Montana
	5	@Fullerton State
	11-12	##KVGO Coca-Cola Classic
	15	@Nevada
	19	California-Santa Barbara
	22-23	###Cyclone Classic
	28	Xavier
Jan.	8	@Santa Clara
	9	@San Francisco
	13	San Diego
	16	@San Diego
	21	Pepperdine
	23	Loyola Marymount
	29	@Loyola Marymount
	30	@Pepperdine
Feb.	4	Portland
	6	Gonzaga
	11	@Gozaga
	13	@Portland
	18	San Francisco
	20	Santa Clara
	26-29	####WCC Tournament

@ Road Games
# Anchorage, AK (vs. Iowa State, first round; also Alaska-Anchorage, Cincinnati, Duke, Fresno State, Notre Dame and Southern Utah)
Butte, MT (Idaho, Montana and Youngstown State)
Ames, IA (vs. Rice, first round; also Iowa State and New Orleans)
Toso Pavilion, Santa Clara, CA

Shootout.

Two-time All-WCC guard David Sivulich (19.4 ppg, 238 career treys) is gone, but tough 5-10 junior point guard **Frank Allocco** (9.6 ppg, 2.8 rpg, 105 assists, 20 steals) returns and he'll pair with 6-2 junior **Frank Knight** (9.5 ppg, 3.1 rpg, 29 assists).

"I'll take the Millard for Sivulich swap any time," Bollwinkel said.

Allocco had a 1:72.1 assists-to-turnovers ratio, the best among starting point guards back this season in the WCC. "He surprised everybody the way he upped his level of play," Bollwinkel said.

Senior **Eric Knapp** (3.5 ppg, 3.0 rpg) gives the Gaels a big guard (6-5) off the bench. Depth at the position includes 6-1 sophomore **Frankie King** (1.5 ppg, 1.0 rpg); 6-4 sophomore **Dorian Williams**;(1.4 ppg, 0.5 rpg) and 6-2 junior **Rekato Cole** (0.4 ppg, 0.4 rpg).

Eric Schraeder is a 6-9 senior forward who should be all-league at the end of the year. Schraeder (15.7 ppg, 6.9 rpg, 35 assists) led the WCC in free throw shooting (.868). A little research revealed he is the tallest player to ever pace the league in that category.

"He's a 6-9 guy who can run and can shoot with range," Bollwinke said. "He's more of a runner-shooter than a low-post type, but with Brad gone last year we used Eric down low, too."

The power forward spot probably goes to 6-7 junior **Josh Greer** (8.4 ppg, 5.9 rpg). Bollwinkel said Ricks College transfer **Seth Dahle**, a 6-6 junior, adds defensive toughness and rebounding to the front line and he'll push Greer. "Because of his toughness," said the coach.

The Gaels' other newcomer is 6-3 freshman guard **Dan Pangrazio** from Fairfield, Conn.

Reliable **Jesse Bond** is the 6-9, 230-pound center who will be Millard's latest insurance policy. Bond (1.5 rpg, 2.0 rpg) started seven games last year. He has also battled injuries in his career, having broken a foot early in the 1996-97 season.

O'Neil Kamaka, a 6-5 senior, started three games last year and figures to be one of the first players off the bench. Kamaka (4.9 ppg, 2.6 rpg) had some productive games. Adding more size is 6-8 senior forward/center **Brett Varga** (1.8 ppg, 1.5 rpg).

Bollwinkel isn't concerned about depth. Eleven of his top 12 scorers returned, making Saint Mary's the most experienced team in the conference. "We have the scoring tools," Bollwinkel said. "What was need to improve in is how we defend and rebound."

Millard should help. A lot.

adidas Blue Ribbon Analysis

BACKCOURT	C	BENCH/DEPTH	C
FRONTCOURT	B	INTANGIBLES	C

Millard, also known as "Big Continent," must remain healthy all season for the Gaels to make noise in the championship race. If he does, Saint Mary's has one of the top frontcourt scoring combinations in the league in Millard and Schraeder. The Gaels also have a nice backcourt combination in Frank Allocco and Frank Knight.

It is more likely the Gaels will have their moments in the regular season and finish in the first division. When it comes time for the WCC tournament, few teams will want a piece of Saint Mary's if Millard is back fighting for another shot in the NCAAs.

(P.B.)

SAN DIEGO

LOCATION .... **San Diego, CA**
CONFERENCE .... **West Coast**
LAST SEASON .... **14-14 (.500)**
CONFERENCE RECORD .... **5-9 (7th)**
STARTERS LOST/RETURNING **3/2**
NICKNAME .... **Toreros**
COLORS .... **Columbia Blue, Navy & White**
HOMECOURT .... **USD Sports Center (2,500)**
COACH .... **Brad Holland (UCLA '79)**
RECORD AT SCHOOL .... **56-55 (4 yrs.)**
CAREER RECORD .... **79-86 (6 yrs.)**
ASSISTANTS .... **Kyle Smith (Hamilton College '92)**
Terry Bosel (Oregon State '86)
David Frizdale (USD '96)
TEAM WINS (last 5 yrs.) **18-11-14-17-14**
RPI (last 5 yrs.) **128-185-140-146-163**
1997-98 FINISH .... **Lost in conference semifinal.**

Few tears will be shed when the decrepit USD Sports Center gives way to the new Jenny Craig Pavilion that opens in 2000.

Coaches here have privately complained about the league's worst facility for years. A $10 million gift by school Board of Trustee member Jenny Craig (yes, that Jenny Craig) should give USD a much bigger profile in the years to come.

"We're anxiously anticipating what it might bring in terms of opening doors for recruiting," said coach Brad Holland.

In the spirit of Jenny Craig, the Toreros lost 610 pounds over the offseason when Brian Miles (16.8 ppg), Nosa Obasohan (9.1 ppg) and Alex Parker (10.1 ppg) ran out of eligibility. Parker, the starting point guard at 5-11, somehow led the team in blocked shots (11).

USD was 14-14 last season (7th in league play), and somewhat unlucky because its first four WCC losses were by a total of just 10 points.

The Toreros were picked sixth in the preseason. "I don't care about any of that stuff," Holland said. "I wouldn't care if we were ranked second. Any coach who knows exactly what he has in September has been holding illegal workouts.

"Can we crack the top four or five? I don't know."

This is a young team (10 players sophomores or younger), but it could finish in the upper half of the conference race if everything breaks right.

"Our young people have to play well," Holland said. "We didn't have good senior leadership a year ago. I think we'll have it this year."

Holland is counting on 6-6 senior forward **Ryan Williams**, 6-5 senior guard **Brock Jacobsen** and hustling 6-2 senior swingman **Lamont Smith** to lead the way.

Williams (15.1 ppg, 6.3 rpg) is the Toreros' top returning scorer. He is a career 55 percent shooter who also led the team in minutes played. He has also beaten the odds, having missed the entire 1996-'97 season after knee surgery.

"Ryan's one of those players you love to coach because you always know what you're getting," Holland said. "He's Mr. Steady, game in and game out. He's left-handed, and a somewhat unorthodox offensive player, but he's very efficient. He knows his way around the basket."

Jacobsen (7.3 ppg, 2.5 rpg, 88 assists, 28 steals) didn't have the huge junior year that was expected, but he shot 50 percent from three-point range in WCC play (and .397 percent in all games). He was the WCC Freshman of the Year in 1996. His junior swoon was somewhat of a mystery.

"It's important for our ballclub that he have a big senior year," Holland said. "Last year was a disappointment for him and for us as well. Last year was far below what we expected ... but I see a fire in his gut. He and I have had many conversations and I'm happy to say Brock's back to his old self."

1998-99 SAN DIEGO SCHEDULE

Nov.	17	Concordia
	21	@Eastern Washington
	23	@Portland State
	28	@Cal State Northridge
Dec.	3	Northern Arizona
	5	*Texas
	12	Montana State
	19	@San Diego State
	22-23	#Coors Lite Classic
	30	Occidental
Jan.	2	Irvine
	8	@San Francisco
	9	@Santa Clara
	13	@Saint Mary's
	16	Saint Mary's
	21	Loyola Marymount
	23	Pepperdine
	29	@Pepperdine
	30	@Loyola Marymount
Feb.	4	Gonzaga
	6	Portland
	11	Portland
	13	Gonzaga
	18	Santa Clara
	20	San Francisco
	27-1	##WCC Tournament

@ Road Games
* Sports Arena, San Diego, CA
# Fresno, CA (vs. Miami-Ohio, first round; also Chicago State and Fresno State)
Toso Pavilion, Santa Clara, CA

Smith (2.5 ppg, 1.7 rpg) started 10 games last season and was respected enough to be chosen co-captain. "His hustle and team attitude are contagious," Holland said of his best defensive player.

Holland will go with 6-foot sophomore **Dana White** (4.6 ppg, 2.2 rpg) at point guard. White started four games last year and was second on the team with 69 assists. He was a stellar two-sport athlete (also a football player) in high school. "We wanted to redshirt him last year because he didn't turn 18 until January," Holland said. "But he ended up winning some games for us. He's quick, he's fast, and he's learning to make better decisions."

Andre Laws, a 6-1 freshman from Anchorage, Alaska, averaged 20 points in high school. Jim Brewer Jr., a 6-3 sophomore, decided to leave the program with Holland's blessing. Brewer is the son of ex-Minnesota Golden Gopher great Jim Brewer, a teammate of Holland's on the Lakers.

Freshman **Scott Boardman**, 6-4, won't be in the rotation unless Holland runs into injury problems but 6-6 redshirt freshman **Tim Lippold** could end up being the starting small forward. Lippold played in just one game last year.

Junior **Jeff Knoll** is the center at 7-foot, 275 pounds. Knoll (4.0 ppg, 3.2 rpg, .575 shooter) would be the biggest player in the league if it wasn't for Saint Mary's Brad "Big Continent" Millard. Knoll is one of the WCC's most improved players over the last two seasons and a graduate of Pete Newell's prestigious Big Man's Camp in Hawaii.

"If Jeff's able to hold the post, he can be dangerous (offensively) because he's so big," Holland said. "He's a quality passer with a great understanding of the game, but his best strengths are rebounding and defense."

The Toreros got immediate help inside with 6-7 sophomore transfer **Cameron Rigby** from Bradley. Rigby is a 235-pound Aussie who averaged six points per game at his old school. Holland calls him a "complete ballplayer. He does a little bit of everything. If he's what we think he is, he'll be a quality four man'."

The Toreros recruited Rigby out of high school, but ran out of scholarships. "We couldn't pull the trigger on him," Holland said.

But the story had a happy ending for USD.

Steve Ross, 6-6 freshman swingman, averaged an eye-popping 33 points in Canada. USD's depth includes 6-9 redshirt freshman **Jason Powell**; 6-10 freshman **Kevin Hanson**; and 6-9, 235-pound UC-Santa Barbara transfer Tyler Field, who will sit out this season.

Michael Blackmon, a 6-6 sophomore forward with potential, tore his ACL and will miss the entire year.

adidas Blue Ribbon Analysis

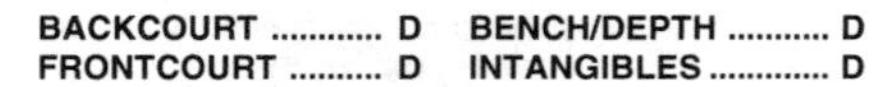

BACKCOURT	D	BENCH/DEPTH	D
FRONTCOURT	D	INTANGIBLES	D

When the $15 million Jenny Craig Pavilion opens, USD basketball enters a new era. "It's one of the missing pieces to our puzzle," Holland said. The Toreros have been consistently average in the WCC. They are the only team in the league to have posted 10 or more wins in each of the last nine years but they have clearly fallen behind in terms of putting together contending teams.

The Toreros' youth suggests this team may start slowly, then build toward tournament time. Holland said his three seniors will have a lot to say about where USD finishes. Looks like fifth or sixth.

(P.B.)

SAN FRANCISO

LOCATION .... **San Francisco, CA**
CONFERENCE .... **West Coast**
LAST SEASON .... **19-11 (.651)**
CONFERENCE RECORD .... **7-7 (t-4th)**
STARTERS LOST/RETURNING **3/2**
NICKNAME .... **Dons**
COLORS .... **Green & Gold**
HOMECOURT .... **Memorial Gym (5,300)**
COACH .... **Philip Mathews (Cal-Irvine '72)**
RECORD AT SCHOOL .... **51-35 (3 yrs.)**
CAREER RECORD .... **348-92 (13 yrs.)**
ASSISTANTS .... **Bill Carr (USF '88)**
John Wade (Eastern Washington '83)
Phil Galvin (Mount St. Mary's '94)
TEAM WINS (last 5 yrs.) **18-10-15-16-19**
RPI (last 5 yrs.) **124-160-102-158-94**
1997-98 FINISH .... **Lost in NCAA first round.**

Philip Mathews took just three seasons to get San Francisco back into the NCAA Tournament. He did it last year despite a rash of injuries. He did it with two freshmen guards, **Ali Thomas** and **Dony Wilcher**. USF's first NCAA appearance since 1982 was hard-earned, too, with WCC tournament victories over '97 co-champs Saint Mary's and Santa Clara and '98 regular-season champion Gonzaga.

But two-time all-WCC forward Hakeem Ward (15.4 ppg), M.J. Nodilo, Jamal Cobbs, Damian Cantrell and Ra'oof Sadat are gone. The 1998-'99 Dons are young, inexperienced, potentially hurting inside and picked no better than fifth in the preseason coaches' poll. A word of warning, however: USF is likely to be dangerous at tournament time given Mathews' history since he entered the league after winning 10 championships at Ventura College.

"We're young. It's a big switch from the experience we've had the last few years," Mathews said. "But our kids are talented, so we don't have to rebuild. I don't like to rebuild."

UCLA, Indiana, and Nebraska loom on the schedule. The Dons don't have to worry about being tested early with a roster that includes four freshmen, a junior college transfer and a redshirt. The Dons must replace six of their top seven scorers, nine players who accounted for 54.7 points per game last year.

With 6-6 senior **Gerald Zimmerman** (10.1 ppg, 4.3 rpg in '96-'97) back from knee surgery, USF's strength is definitely on the perimeter: The 6-2 Thomas (11.1 ppg, 2.2 rpg) knocked down a school-record 75 three-point shots and was the league's freshman of the year. He made 80 percent from the free-throw line and tied for the team lead with 34 steals.

Thomas' leadership ability is a plus. "He'll be a great force for us," Mathews said. "He spent the summer working out and getting stronger. His attitude toward the game is very much needed on this team. It's a 'we play hard, never quit, we're going to try and beat you any way we can' mindset."

The kind of attitude Thomas showed in the NCAAs when he drilled three straight three-pointers to try and rally the Dons against Utah.

The 5-10 Wilcher (4.4 ppg, 1.7 apg) shared the point guard minutes with talented freshman **LyRyan Russell**, a 6-foot local prep star (3.9 ppg, 1.7 apg) who impacted many games. It was Wilcher's ability to push the ball that helped transform a Dons' team potentially crushed by Zimmerman's season-ending injury. Russell, even quicker, turned up the tempo yet another notch.

Over the last six games leading into the WCC tournament, Wilcher averaged 5.8 points, 4.7 assists and 1.3 steals. "When he's on the floor he makes things happen," Mathews said. "His speed and strength are big plusses for him."

When Mathews decided to start Thomas and Wilcher, USF won its final six regular-season games. In a blistering stretch before the NCAA Tournament, the Dons outscored opponents 87.3-68.3 and forced 18.2 turnovers per game.

Mathews' teams are known for their ability to defend and rebound. Even if the Dons are reloading, they won't lose those qualities. Zimmerman, for instance, is an excellent defender. Wilcher is a terror on defense. And Mathews said 6-6 Ventura College transfer **James Lee** (15.4 ppg, 9.6 rpg) fits the same mold. Lee has three years of eligibility. "A great athlete who can slash, dunk, and rebound," Mathews said.

Russell was a preseason pick for newcomer of the year in the league. Mathews won't forget how he shut down Santa Clara's Brian Jones in a rare victory at Toso Pavilion. "LyRyan might be the quickest player in the league from point A to point B," Mathews said.

Freshman guard **Glen Summerall**, 6-4, fits perfectly into the USF system. Summerall (18.8 ppg, 11.0 rpg, 3.1 blocked shots) was a league MVP at Fontana (Calif.) High. Walkon **Booker T. Harris**, a 6-1 junior, adds depth but figures to have a difficult time getting minutes.

What about the paint? Good question. Mathews said a pair of junior college transfers will fill key roles. Lee is one of them. "He can make the medium-range shot, but his strength is driving to the basket," Mathews said. "He will go way up for rebounds and finish plays."

Terrence Moore, a 6-7, 270-pound junior from Chaffey (Calif.) College, is the guy who'll be asked to bump heads with the likes of 7-3 Brad Millard from Saint Mary's. Moore (17.0 ppg, 9.0 rpg) has size, strength and a phenomenal 73 percent shooting touch. "He plays similar to Hakeem Ward, but he's much bigger," said Mathews. "He gives us a big body (inside) and he can shoot from 17-18 feet."

The Dons can throw more big bodies on the floor. **Eugene Brown** (12.0 ppg, 6.0 rpg) is a mobile 6-10 freshman from Avondale, Ariz., who shot 71 percent from the floor and reportedly chose USF over Arizona State.

Hondre Brewer, 6-11 and 225 pounds, is a freshman from prestigious St. Joseph's-Alameda HS (Jason Kidd's alma mater). He is the Dons' big man of the future. Brewer saw limited action as a high school senior because of a knee injury, but USF liked the risk-reward potential. Brewer grew seven inches between his sophomore and senior seasons and now has a 7-3 arm span. He's a blocked shot waiting to happen.

Derek Christensen is a 6-5 redshirt freshman from Honolulu who should add outside shooting. Christensen (19.0 ppg) led his league in scoring and three-pointers made.

adidas Blue Ribbon Analysis

BACKCOURT	**B**	**BENCH/DEPTH**	**C+**
FRONTCOURT	**C**	**INTANGIBLES**	**B**

Given the athletes on this team, fifth place may be harsh. Mathews' squad has quickness, athletic ability, and a tenaciousness on defense that may overcome youth and inexperience. There isn't a quicker backcourt combination in the league than the Thomas-Wilcher-Russell group. If Zimmerman is back to his old form, the Dons will terrorize opponents on the perimeter.

The guess here is that Lee and Moore will fit in nicely underneath. USF looks better than fifth in the regular season, and the Dons should be fighting for another NCAA berth when it comes time for the WCC tournament. If they don't, they will at least leave some black and blue marks. Mathews' teams, above all else, play hard for 40 minutes.

(P.B.)

1998-99 SAN FRANCISCO SCHEDULE

Nov.	18	@California-Santa Barbara
	23	Montana State
	26-28	#Puerto Rico Shootout
Dec.	4-5	##Northwestern Mutual Classic
	8	@Montana State
	10	@Fairfield
	17	St. Louis
	20	@Indiana
	23	@Rhode Island
	27	Nebraska
	29-30	###Cable Car Classic
Jan.	8	San Diego
	9	Saint Mary's
	15	@Loyola Marymount
	16	@Pepperdine
	22	Gonzaga
	23	Portland
	28	@Portland
	30	@Gonzaga
Feb.	3	@Santa Clara
	6	Santa Clara
	12	Pepperdine
	13	Loyola Marymount
	18	@Saint Mary's
	20	@San Diego
27-Mar.	1	####WCC Tournament

@ Road Games
# San Juan, RP (vs. UCLA, first round; also American University-PR, Colorado, Kentucky, Maryland, Pittsburgh and Xavier)
San Francisco, CA (vs. Holy Cross, first round; also Rice and Weber State)
San Jose, CA (vs. St. Joseph's, first round; also Harvard and Santa Clara)
Toso Pavilion, Santa Clara, CA

SANTA CLARA

LOCATION .... **Santa Clara, CA**
CONFERENCE .... **West Coast**
LAST SEASON .... **18-10 (.643)**
CONFERENCE RECORD .... **8-6 (3rd)**
STARTERS LOST/RETURNING **2/3**
NICKNAME .... **Broncos**
COLORS .... **Bronco Red & White**
HOMECOURT .... **Taso Pavilion (5,000)**
COACH .... **Dick Davey (Pacific '64)**
RECORD AT SCHOOL .... **107-63 (6 yrs.)**
CAREER RECORD .... **107-63 (6 yrs.)**
ASSISTANTS .... **Steve Seandel (San Jose State '81)**
Vic Couch (Santa Clara '85)
Jason Sedlock (Santa Clara '97)
TEAM WINS (last 5 yrs.) **13-21-20-16-18**
RPI (last 5 yrs.) **170-51-32-109-80**
1997-98 FINISH .... **Lost in conference semifinal.**

Coach Dick Davey may have his hands full. Junior point guard **Brian Jones**, a first team all-WCC pick, dislocated his right knee cap in June while playing summer ball. The bone and tissue damage was extensive, and the Broncos' leading scorer (15.6 ppg, 4.8 rpg, 115 assists) is out until at least December. There is the possibility Jones may redshirt. It would be akin to the Broncos' NCAA team of a few years past losing Steve Nash.

Santa Clara surprised some people in 1997-98 by going 18-10 overall and finishing third in the league race. With Jones showing the way, the Broncos were in first place with three games to go in the regular season. They would ultimately slip to third, or Davey might have had another Cinderella story to tell his grandchildren.

Entering his seventh season as head coach after replacing Carroll Williams, Davey's record is 107-63 (55-29 WCC). The three-time WCC Coach of the Year has steered Santa Clara to three regular-season championships, one tournament title, three NCAA appearances and four wins over top 25 teams. He almost got the worst-shooting team in the WCC (.416) into the NCAAs last year.

Jones scored more points in his first two seasons (812) than any player in school history, including Nash, Kurt Rambis and Harold Keeling. He had surgery July 2 and began his rehab in August.

"We're hopeful, but at the same time not overly optimistic," Davey said. "It looks like the kind of injury that will take a long time to heal. We don't want to bring him back if he's not where he needs to be ... we're going to have to live through it, but it's unfortunate for him. He has a chance to play at the next level."

With no Jones, and no go-to guy, it may take smoke and mirrors to keep the Broncos afloat in the title chase. They were picked third in the preseason coaches' poll. "The big question is how we'll be able to defend," Davey said. "We're not as quick or athletic as we've been in the past, but we're bigger, stronger, and more physical." With one little problem: "We don't shoot the ball real well," Davey said.

Santa Clara lost guards Craig Johnson (12.6 ppg) and

Lloyd Pierce (11.2 ppg), so Davey can only guess about what kind of firepower this team will have. With Jones down, 6-4 junior **Nathan Fast** (10.1 ppg, 4.3 rpg, 1.2 apg) is now the point guard and 6-foot sophomore **Delano D'Oyen** (2.4 ppg 0.6 rpg) the backup with 6-2 true freshman **Brian Vaka** filling spot duty.

Fast, who would have started at off-guard, came off the bench to shoot a team-high 46 percent from the floor last year. He had the highest scoring average by a Broncos' reserve in 10 years.

Transfer **Darrell Teat**, a 6-3 junior from West Valley (Calif.) JC, is penciled in at shooting guard. Teat (15.4 ppg, 5.1 apg, 4.2 rpg) could automatically become the team's most accurate marksman. "A good shooter who will fit right in," Davey said.

The Broncos have more experience in the frontcourt where 6-10, 250-pound senior **Alex Lopez** (5.2 ppg, 3.3 rpg) returns at center. Lopez started slowly after transferring from the University of Washington, but the schedule might have been a factor. His first two games were against a pair of NBA lottery picks in Kansas' Raef LaFrentz and Pacific's Michael Olowokandi.

Lopez could have run from the gym screaming, but he grew more comfortable in the final nine games when he averaged 9.1 points, 4.2 rebounds and shot 61 percent from the floor.

The small forward slot goes to 6-7 junior **Todd Wuschnig** (8.4 ppg, 5.8 rpg), the team's leading rebounder in his freshman and sophomore seasons. Wuschnig can score over bigger players and he can maneuver off the dribble. The power forward is 6-8 junior **Jamie Holmes** (6.5 ppg, 4.1 rpg), an important contributor off the bench last season who must now adjust to being a starter.

The depth inside is impressive, with 6-8 junior **Chris Gomes** (1.6 ppg, 3.7 rpg), 6-11 redshirt freshman **David Emslie**, 6-11 sophomore **Stephen Dely** (0.9 ppg, 0.5 rpg) and 6-7 redshirt freshman **Justin Holbrook**. Freshman **Andre Bobbitt**, 6-7, is also on the squad.

adidas Blue Ribbon Analysis

BACKCOURT	**C-**	**BENCH/DEPTH**	**C**
FRONTCOURT	**C**	**INTANGIBLES**	**B**

No Jones, no prayer? Afraid so. If the Broncos get their star player back before the end of the season, all bets are off. Santa Clara probably won't recover in time to get back in the league chase, but the Broncos will be dangerous in the WCC tournament. Trouble is, Jones' injury was devastating. It would be a miracle if he played before Christmas.

Poor shooting was a problem last year, when Santa Clara ranked last in the WCC. If the Broncos can't shoot straight, they better be able to defend and rebound. Davey has a lot of big, experienced players to pound opponents inside. That might be Santa Clara's best hope for finishing in the top three. If Jones returns, and looks like last year's version, watch out.

(P.B.)

1998-99 SANTA CLARA SCHEDULE

Nov.	14	@Pacific
	19	@UCLA
	22	Saint Mary's
Dec.	1	*San Jose State
	4-5	#Carrier Classic
	14	Oregon
	17	California-Santa Barbara
	21-22	##Apple Invitational
	29-30	###Cable Car Classic
Jan.	8	Saint Mary's
	9	San Diego
	15	@Pepperdine
	16	@Loyola Marymount
	22	Portland
	23	Gonzaga
	28	@Gonzaga
	30	@Portland
Feb.	3	San Francisco
	6	@San Francisco
	12	Loyola Marymount
	13	Pepperdine
	18	@San Diego
	20	@Saint Mary's
27, Mar.	1	####WCC Tournament

@ Road Games
* San Jose Arena, San Jose, CA
# Syracuse, NY (vs. Illinois-Chicago, first round; also Ohio and Syracuse)
Stanford, CA (vs. William & Mary, first round; also Elon and Stanford)
San Jose, CA (vs. Harvard, first round; also San Fracisco and St. Joseph's)
Toso Pavilion, Santa Clara, CA

WESTERN ATHLETIC CONFERENCE

adidas BLUE RIBBON FORECAST

PACIFIC DIVISION

1. New Mexico
2. Utah
3. Fresno State
4. Hawaii
5. San Diego State
6. Brigham Young
7. UTEP
8. San Jose State

MOUNTAIN DIVISION

1. UNLV
2. Texas Christian
3. Tulsa
4. Southern Methodist
5. Wyoming
6. Colorado State
7. Rice
8. Air Force

TOP 40

New Mexico, Texas Christian, UNLV and Utah are ranked among the 1998-99 *adidas Blue Ribbon* Top 40. Extended profiles can be found in the Top 40 section of *Blue Ribbon*.

ALL-CONFERENCE TEAM

G—Andre Miller, SR, Utah
G—Chris Herren, SR, Fresno State
F—Kenny Thomas, SR, New Mexico
F—Lee Nailon, SR, TCU
F—Hanno Mottola, JR, Utah

PLAYER OF THE YEAR

Lee Nailon, SR, TCU

NEWCOMER OF THE YEAR

Shawn Marion, JR, UNLV

1998-99 CONFERENCE TOURNAMENT

March 2-6, Thomas & Mack Center, Las Vegas, NV

1997-98 CHAMPION

Texas Christian (Pacific Division)
Utah (Mountain Division)
UNLV (conference tournament)

1997-98 POSTSEASON PARTICIPANTS

Postseason Record: 12-9 (.571)

NCAA

Utah (national runnerup)
New Mexico (2nd round)
Texas Christian (2nd round)
UNLV

NIT

Fresno State (consolation game)
Hawaii (3rd round)
Wyoming
Colorado State

TOP BACKCOURTS

1. Fresno State
2. New Mexico
3. Utah

TOP FRONTCOURTS

1. New Mexico
2. Texas Christian
3. UNLV

ON THE WAY UP

Tulsa

ON THE WAY DOWN

Colorado State

INSIDE THE NUMBERS

- 1997-98 conference RPI: 9 (of 30)
- Conference RPI (last 5 years): 10-11-10-7-9

DID YOU KNOW?

The WAC is breaking up. It was the story of the summer in college athletics. Five presidents—Colorado State, Air Force, Wyoming, Utah and Brigham Young—met on May 22 at Denver's International Airport and plotted a departure from the WAC. The reasons: A proposed alignment splitting Air Force, Colorado State and Wyoming apart and the declining revenue. The five invited three other schools—New Mexico, UNLV and San Diego State—and announced their intentions to leave at the WAC president's meeting June 1. The official split will occur next July, leaving a geographically fractured eight to survive on their own: Fresno State, San Jose State, Hawaii, UTEP, Texas Christian, Southern Methodist, Tulsa and Rice. The two sides squabbled all summer over a number of issues, including the $2.6 million in NCAA Tournament basketball revenue earned by the league. The NCAA determined that the money has to stay with the remaining WAC members. NCAA President Cedric Dempsey said the basketball units earned from the NCAA Tournament aren't transferred to another league. Tulsa had to leave its units with the Missouri Valley Conference when it left to join the WAC in 1996. However, 28 of the 33 units in question were earned by the departing eight. The units from this season will have to stay with the WAC, too. Units (at $80,000 a share) are accumulated over a rolling six-year period. There was a chance the WAC would split into the same divisions for this season but that was voted down. Instead, the western teams will join with Utah, Brigham Young, New Mexico and UTEP, putting a division together that has seven of its eight members as old WAC teams. The only new member is San Jose State...The WAC had four players taken in the NBA draft—two by Orlando (Utah's Michael Doleac and UNLV's Keon Clark) and two in the second round (Fresno State's Rafer Alston to Milwaukee and the Bulldogs' Tremaine Fowlkes by Denver)...The only two new faces coaching in the WAC are former Portland State coach Ritchie McKay at Colorado State and former Texas Christian assistant coach Steve McClain at Wyoming...Wyoming won a legal battle, forcing former coach Larry Shyatt (now at Clemson) to pay the school $286,000 for the final four years of his contract...All three of the WAC's basketball tournaments as a 16-team league will have been played in Las Vegas...WAC Commissioner Karl Benson was retained by the remaining eight and wasn't offered a contract, nor asked for one, by the departing eight...The next fight between the two sides will be the ESPN contract, with Big Monday as the goal for each league...Neither league has decided if it will have a postseason tournament in 2000...The NCAA hasn't decided if it will give either side an automatic berth to the 2000 NCAA Tournament.

(A.K.)

AIR FORCE

LOCATION .... Colorado Springs, CO
CONFERENCE .... WAC (Mountain Division)
LAST SEASON .... 10-16 (.385)
CONFERENCE RECORD 2-12 (8th)
STARTERS LOST/RETURNING 2/3
NICKNAME .... Falcons
COLORS .... Blue & Silver
HOMECOURT .... Clune Arena (6,002)
COACH .... Reggie Minton (Wooster '63)
RECORD AT SCHOOL .... 132-260 (14 yrs.)
CAREER RECORD .... 143-275 (15 yrs.)
ASSISTANTS .... Paul Drake (Springfield '78)
Maj. Dean Christian (Air Force '82)
David Taylor (Cal Poly '91)
TEAM WINS (last 5 yrs.) 8-8-5-7-10
RPI (last 5 yrs.) 229-225-272-250-208
1997-98 FINISH .... Did not qualify for conference tournament.

Perhaps the WAC should have adopted a Reggie Minton clause, allowing Air Force a better chance to earn a berth to the WAC tournament. Air Force had several of its best teams over the last five seasons for a coach who is one of the league's best citizens, but still couldn't qualify for the conference tournament.

Did the Falcons earn it? No. They finished eighth, but it would have been nice to at least see Minton's team get a shot at pulling off an upset.

The WAC will split into two eight-team divisions after this season, but the rules about qualifying to the league tournament still apply. Only the top six teams in each division earn a bid. Air Force will probably have to score an upset or two to sneak ahead of Rice and Colorado State for the sixth spot in the Mountain Division. Without Jarmica Reese (18.8 ppg, 4.1 rpg, 43 assists, 40 steals), last year's leading scorer, it doesn't seem likely.

"I've always been an advocate of all of the teams making the tournament," Minton said. "It makes sense. I don't get any satisfaction seeing the end of the league, but there has to be more sensitivity. It's the last year in the WAC and we can't worry about it any more. We'll just move on now."

The Falcons may have more balance, but they'll struggle to score from the perimeter and they won't be strong in the frontcourt. They'll battle defensively, bodying up teams and contending with them on the defensive boards. Look for them to struggle on the road.

Minton will be counting on 6-6 senior forward **Louis Stewart** (7.4 ppg, 3.4 rpg, 37 assists, 12 steals). Stewart, who can play either forward position, was the third-leading scorer last year, but will have to take on a bigger portion of the scoring load for the Falcons to have a chance. A year ago, he shot 47 percent from the field and 34 percent from three-point range (16 of 47).

Glen Gonzales, a 5-10 senior, may need to replace Reese at point guard. Minton could pull some players off the junior varsity in a worst-case scenario. Gonzales (1.2 ppg, 0.4 rpg) appeared in only 12 games, averaging 4.8 minutes, in relief of Reese.

If Gonzales doesn't secure the point-guard job, the Falcons could move one of the four wing players to the position.

Those candidates will be 6-3 junior **Dylan Pope** (6.0 ppg, 1.8 rpg), who started seven times and averaged 20.7 minutes; 5-10 junior **Lawrence Yazzi** (3.0 ppg, 0.7 rpg), who played in 24 games; 6-4 sophomore **Jarvis Croff**, who played for Air Force's junior varsity after a high school career at Beaumont (Texas) West Brook HS.; and 6-4 junior **Tyron Wright**, who also played for the junior varsity after a high school career at Lexington HS in West Columbia, S.C.

Pope slumped after a freshman year when he averaged 7.6 points and was one of the team's catalysts. Pope needs to become more aggressive and work on his shooting and defense.

Yazzi should battle Gonzales for time at the point, but isn't a true playmaker. He'll have to become one to earn more time.

Croff led the junior varsity in scoring (21.4 ppg), and that's almost like leading a junior-college team. He also averaged 6.5 rpg, shot .428 from the field, .701 from the line and .359 from three-point range.

"I think he's got a chance to be very, very good on the perimeter," Minton says. "He's got long arms and a good shot."

Wright, who averaged 9.5 rpg and was second behind Croff in JV scoring (18.7 ppg) last year, could play either guard position and small forward. Wright is a slasher who knows how to get to the free-throw line, where he shot .733.

One player who could find his way into the lineup is 6-6 junior **Miguel Garcia**, who started 20 of 26 games last season but didn't put enough points on the board. Garcia (4.0 ppg, 3.0 rpg) did a solid job running the offense, despite his lack of scoring.

Also adding depth in the backcourt is 6-3 senior **Jovan Hollins** (1.7 ppg, 0.8 rpg). He played in 21 games and averaged 7.1 minutes.

The Falcons are hoping several players develop this season, including 6-7 sophomore forward **David Schuck** (4.9 ppg, 5.0 rpg); 6-6 junior forward **Billy Humphrey** (4.3 ppg, 3.3 rpg); and 6-9 sophomore **Steve Kincannon** (1.8 ppg, 1.3 rpg).

Schuck is a tough, scrappy player who is a strong rebounder. He has become a better defender, but still needs work there.

The two newcomers in the frontcourt are 6-6 sophomore **Byron Nicholson**, who played for the junior varsity last season, and 6-5 freshman **John Nodilo** of Saguaro HS in Phoenix.

Nicholson averaged 7.0 ppg and 6.0 rpg for the junior varsity last year, shooting 56 percent from the field. He could spell Pope, Wright or Humphrey at small forward. Nodilo is still probably a year away from contributing.

"We hope we can steal a few wins," Minton says of the WAC. "We'll have a bunch of young guys who will allow us to spread the ball around more. (But the key) could be Louis Stewart. He's a senior and he should be an outstanding player. He should be able to step up and surprise people in a different role."

adidas Blue Ribbon Analysis

BACKCOURT	D	BENCH/DEPTH	D
FRONTCOURT	D	INTANGIBLES	D

Louis Stewart's new role will be to replace Jarmica Reese as the Falcons' premier player, and that won't be easy.

Air Force may be getting out of the WAC just in time. The Falcons will have a tough time winning in the league this year and making the tournament seems to be a reach. The 16-team WAC hasn't been good to Air Force and Minton. He'll probably leave it without ever playing in the tournament.

(A.K.)

1998-99 AIR FORCE SCHEDULE

Nov.	13	Doane
	16	Wofford
	18	Regis
	21	Colorado-Colorado Springs
	28	Navy
Dec.	5	@Portland State
	19	Texas-Arlington
	29-30	#Pepsi-Oneida Classic
Jan.	2	Dartmouth
	6	Denver
	9	@UNLV
	14	Tulsa
	16	Rice
	21	@Texas Christian
	23	@Southern Methodist
	28	Colorado State
	30	Wyoming
Feb	6	UNLV
	11	@Rice
	13	@Tulsa
	16	@Denver
	18	Southern Methodist
	20	Texas Christian
	25	@Wyoming
	27	@Colorado State
Mar	2-6	##WAC Tournament

@ Road Games
# Milwaukee, WI (vs. Wisconsin-Green Bay, first round; also Drexel and Texas Southern)
Thomas & Mack Center, Las Vegas, NV

adidas Blue Ribbon Analysis
GRADING SYSTEM

- A+ equal to very best in country—Final Four-caliber unit
- A among the best in the land—worthy of deep NCAA run
- B+ talented, versatile and experienced—NCAA-NIT ability
- B solid and productive winners—league and post-season contenders
- C+ average to above-average—may contend in a weaker league
- C average to mediocre—second division in a strong league
- D+ below average, inconsistent—second division in a weaker league
- D well below average—losing season virtually certain
- F non-Division I ability—an underdog every night

BRIGHAM YOUNG

LOCATION .... Provo, UT
CONFERENCE .... WAC (Pacific Division)
LAST SEASON .... 9-21 (.300)
CONFERENCE RECORD .... 4-10 (6th Mountain)
STARTERS LOST/RETURNING 2/3
NICKNAME .... Cougars
COLORS .... Blue & White
HOMECOURT .... Marriott Center (23,000)
COACH .... Steve Cleveland (UC-Irvine '76)
RECORD AT SCHOOL .... 9-21 (2 yrs.)
CAREER RECORD .... 9-21 (2 yrs.)
ASSISTANTS .... David Rose (Houston '83)
Nate Call (BYU '93)
Heath Schroyer (Armstrong State '94)
TEAM WINS (last 5 yrs.) 22-22-15-1-9
RPI (last 5 yrs.) 48-46-100-261-167
1997-98 FINISH .... Lost in conference first round.

Steve Cleveland had everything planned. He signed Ron Selleaze last year at midseason and had Mike Garrett sitting out. His two former Fresno City College players would have given him two-thirds of his perimeter lineup this season. He would have been a contender for an NIT berth and a top-five finish in the WAC's Pacific Division.

The Cougars will be fortunate to finish fifth. Selleaze was an all-WAC newcomer, leading the Cougars to sixth place in the Mountain Division. However, the euphoria of BYU's late-season run to the WAC tournament, which included a shocking upset at New Mexico that ended the Lobos' 40-game homecourt winning streak and a triple-overtime win at UTEP, was tempered a few weeks later.

Selleaze was caught with possession of marijuana in Garrett's apartment. It was deemed a misdemeanor but the BYU code-of-conduct committee ruled that it was a violation of the school's honor code. Selleaze was banned for one year and despite appeals to the contrary, so too, was Garrett. Selleaze didn't have a year to sit after redshirting during junior college. Garrett decided to go back to Fresno City and can return to BYU as a junior next fall. Selleaze is done and is headed to a Division II school in California.

So much for Cleveland's plans.

"We'll still have a competitive group," Cleveland said. "We may have more overall talent than last year and depth but we don't have a player as good as Ron and Mike. There's no question that this team will be better in its second year together. Once we get this program into its fourth and fifth years, we'll be able to compete with anybody."

With a number of returning missionaries, the Cougars will be banking on their quick adjustment back to the Division I level in order for them to edge out UTEP and San Diego State for one of the final two spots in the league tournament.

"We can play together and I hope somehow we can win 13-14 games and make the WAC tournament," Cleveland said. "Making it last year gave us tremendous credibility. I was a non-Division I coach and getting the wins at New Mexico and UTEP got our confidence and got people

1998-99 BRIGHAM YOUNG SCHEDULE

Nov.	13	Wofford
	19	@Weber State
	23	@Auburn
	28	Arizona
Dec.	1	Denver
	5	@Oregon
	8	@Washington State
	11-12	#Cougar Classic
	19	California
	22	@California-Irvine
Jan.	2	Utah State
	9	@Utah
	14	@San Diego State
	16	@Hawaii
	21	San Jose State
	23	Fresno State
	28	@UTEP
	30	@New Mexico
Feb.	6	Utah
	11	Hawaii
	13	San Diego State
	18	@Fresno State
	20	@San Jose State
	25	New Mexico
	27	UTEP
Mar.	2-6	##WAC Tournament

@ Road Games
# Provo, UT (vs. Louisiana Tech, first round; also Cafornia-Northridge and Southern Utah)
Thomas & Mack Center, Las Vegas, NV

excited. I don't think people are wondering if we can coach. We can't let the Ron and Mike thing be a distraction. We've got to go forward. Our biggest problem we're facing in the program is our scholarship imbalance by having so many players on missions."

If the travails of Garrett and Selleaze weren't bad enough, the Cougars got more bad news in August when 6-9 sophomore **Mekeli Wesley** (13.5 ppg, 5.0 rpg) was suspended for the first semester (eight games) for breaking the school's honor code. Wesley will sit out the semester at Salt Lake Community College.

Wesley was a throw-in recruit last year, signed under the former staff. He was a local player from Provo and the Cougars weren't sure if he could make the adjustment to Division I quick enough to help. He became the Cougars' lone inside scorer. Wesley bullied his way around the basket, turning offensive rebounds into layups. It sounds simple, but no one else was doing it.

"He's not the most athletic player, but he's efficient," Cleveland said. "He can score."

The Cougars can survive portions of the nonconference season without Wesley, but not much more if they want to contend for the sixth and final spot out of the Pacific Division for the WAC Tournament.

Cleveland needs 6-11 junior **Bret Jepsen** (2.9 ppg, 3.3 rpg) to return to his form of three years ago. Jepsen ended his freshman season as one of the bright young stars in the WAC. He went on a mission and floundered on his return last season. Jepsen went off to Pete Newell's Big Man camp in Honolulu to shore up his inside game. He needed to work on his footwork and his aggressive behavior in the post. He has the size but not the demeanor to play strong. The Cougars can't compete with Utah, New Mexico, Hawaii or Fresno State if Jepsen doesn't get tougher inside.

"He will be better next year," Cleveland said. "He's been home for a year and he's playing with more confidence. He has to be more of defensive force for us. He's got the ability to be a scorer and now he has to do it."

The third frontcourt player should be 6-7 junior **Silester Rivers** of Utah Valley State College. Rivers was the Cougars' No. 1 recruit in the spring. He gives them a slashing scorer and a defender at small forward. The Cougars have always struggled to defend small forwards such as former New Mexico player Clayton Shields. Rivers gives them a chance to hang with the Lobos' Lamont Long or Fresno State's Terrance Roberson.

"He's got a chance to be a really good player," Cleveland said. "He's undersized but he can play on the perimeter, so he can help us out in different spots."

Cleveland is looking for Wesley and Rivers to each put up 15-20 points a game, but that might be pushing their production capabilities. Wesley can do that, but Rivers may be more of a 10-12 scorer, at least the first few months of the season. He has to help out on the boards, because Jepsen hasn't proven he can rebound in double figures.

The depth up front will come from two of Rivers' junior college teammates: 6-8 junior walkon **Jacob Hawkins** and 6-10 junior center **Mark Michaelis**.

"It'll take Mark until the WAC season to really feel comfortable, but he'll help us," Cleveland said. "Hawkins could play either forward and could be a factor off the bench."

Cleveland should have enough shooters on the perimeter.

He'll probably start 6-3 freshman **Michael Vranes** (Taylorsville HS/Utah) at the point and 6-1 sophomore **Todd Christensen** (returning missionary) at shooting guard. Christensen played the point three years ago, but was erratic and may be better suited to be an off-guard.

Cleveland will have trouble keeping 6-5 sophomore **Nathan Cooper** (returning missionary) off the court. Cooper started alongside Christensen before he went on a mission. He was a fiery competitor who helped energize a struggling team. He has the ability to board and could play some small forward behind Rivers. He might have to if Cleveland wants to work 6-4 freshman **David Nielsen** (Brighton HS/Salt Lake City, Utah) and 6-6 freshman guard **Mark Bigelow** (Olympia HS/Wash.) into the perimeter rotation. Both will be needed to knock down shots.

Danny Bower, a 6-4 senior guard, was forced to start on last season's thin team. Bower (11.3 ppg, 2.6 rpg) could hold onto his starting position if Cleveland wants to reward him for his good service last season. However, he'll probably get beaten out by either Christensen or Cooper. He was an erratic shooter but he finished making .364 percent of his threes and, regardless of when he plays, he'll be needed to at least match that number this year.

Brian Hamilton (6.7 ppg, 3.1 rpg, 2.3 apg), a 6-0 senior guard, falls into the same category. Cleveland may start the season with him at one shooting guard and let Christensen try and beat him out for the starting position.

Hamilton was a decent three-point shooter at 32 percent. He was nearly 1-1 in his assist-to-turnover ratio.

Brian Dignan (3.8 ppg, 2.2 rpg, 4.0 apg) started at point because no one else could be trusted at the position. The 6-3 senior will likely suffer the same fate as Hamilton and lose his starting position to someone more talented (Vranes).

"Michael still has to learn how to play that position," Cleveland said of his future point guard. "We'll be competitive at guard with Todd, Danny and Nathan. They're not the prettiest things to watch but they're efficient and good defenders. Mark Bigelow will play substantial minutes, but if Ron had been here, we would have redshirted him."

adidas Blue Ribbon Analysis

BACKCOURT	**D+**	**BENCH/DEPTH**	**C-**
FRONTCOURT	**C**	**INTANGIBLES**	**C**

The Cougars have a decent frontcourt with Wesley, Rivers and Jepsen, but the loss of Wesley for the first eight games of the season will hurt. And the backcourt is painfully short on experience. Cleveland's program won't take a step back—it just may not go too far up this season. BYU may reach double figures in wins, but could have pushed 18-20 with Selleaze and Garrett and a full season from Wesley.

The Cougars will battle with UTEP and San Diego State for fifth and sixth. One team won't get to the tournament. Cleveland's teams have played hard for him and he was able to maximize almost nothing last year. Look for the Cougars to be more of a homecourt threat and steal one or two more road wins behind a productive frontcourt, provided, of course, that Wesley returns.

(A.K.)

COLORADO STATE

LOCATION	**Fort Collins, CO**
CONFERENCE	**WAC (Mountain Division)**
LAST SEASON	**20-9 (.590)**
CONFERENCE RECORD	**8-6 (4th)**
STARTERS LOST/RETURNING	**4/1**
NICKNAME	**Rams**
COLORS	**Green & Gold**
HOMECOURT	**Moby Arena (9,001)**
COACH	**Ritchie McKay (Seattle-Pacific '87)**
RECORD AT SCHOOL	**First Year**
CAREER RECORD	**24-29 (2 yrs.)**
ASSISTANTS	**Brad Soucie (Christian Heritage '90)**
	Scott Didrickson (Washington'95)
	Dale Layer (Eckerd College '70)
TEAM WINS (last 5 yrs.)	**15-17-18-20-20**
RPI (last 5 yrs.)	**137-144-81-69-72**
1997-98 FINISH	**Lost in NIT first round.**

Ritchie McKay was the right choice for Colorado State at the right time. He had gone through a rebuilding process, dealing with endless obstacles in resurrecting a dormant program at Portland State.

Colorado State has never been dead, but it wasn't bubbling, either. The Rams needed new life after hitting a wall of 17-20 wins with only two postseason appearances to show for the usually unimpressive schedule. With only one returning starter, the Rams were ripe for an overhaul. Stew Morrill found a gig that fit his lifestyle better at Utah State.

Enter McKay.

In two years at Portland State, McKay took a program that had sat without basketball for 15 years and brought it to the top tier of the Big Sky. His record may have been only 24-29, but he had the Vikings on the verge of challenging for the Big Sky title this season.

At Portland State, he led an 11-man roster with six freshmen, two sophomores and three juniors to a 9-17 record in his first season against a Big Sky Conference schedule. Two of the wins came over Big Sky champion Northern Arizona and the previous league champ Montana State. He was eventually selected as a finalist for the Clair Bee Coach of the Year Award after bringing the program back to respectability in just one season.

McKay prepped for the Portland State job with assistant stints at Washington and Bradley. He knew the West and the Midwest. He'll have to know both at Colorado State, where the Rams have lacked a real recruiting base this decade.

"It'll be an interesting year because we don't have a lot of expectations," McKay said. "The players will have to get a feel for our style and it may not be determined with this group. Any time you've got a first-year program, you've got to lay the foundation. We'll be characterized by a great work ethic and will play an exciting brand of basketball. That suits me and my style."

McKay's energy rekindled the Portland State basketball fans. His youthful enthusiasm got him the job at CSU. He was competing with Kansas assistant Neil Dougherty for the job, but won over the CSU administration with his passion for the position.

"This program has great potential," said McKay, worried that he had just uttered a typical coach cliché. "But it does in this league and the new league [with the breakaway eight members of the WAC in 1999-2000]."

McKay inherited at least a core of talent to be competitive and challenge for the last WAC Tournament spot in the Mountain Division. Wyoming should finish at least fifth, leaving CSU to beat out Rice and Air Force for the tournament berth.

Ceedric Goodwyn, **John Sivesind** and **Milt Palacio** should be the nucleus of this team. They all immediately took to McKay when he arrived in late August, and they're all hungry. Goodwyn and Sivesind sat out last year and Palacio needs to show he can be a leader at the point.

McKay will try and play uptempo on offense and a tight man-to-man defense. The style will be a bit more open than CSU fans are used to at Moby Arena, but it should get the joint jumping.

A lot of that will have to do with Goodwyn. The 6-8 junior

1998-99 COLORADO STATE SCHEDULE

Nov.	14	McNeese State
	17	@ Colorado
	21	Montana Tech
	25	@Texas-Pan American
	28	Eastern Michigan
Dec.	1	@Oregon State
	5	@Utah State
	9	@South Alabama
	12	Nebraska
	20	Denver
	30	South Alabama
Jan.	2	Nevada
	7	@Tulsa
	9	@Rice
	14	SMU
	16	TCU
	23	Wyoming
	28	@Air Force
	30	@UNLV
Feb.	4	Rice
	6	Tulsa
	11	@SMU
	13	@TCU
	20	@Wyoming
	25	UNLV
	27	Air Force
Mar.	2-6	#WAC Tournament

@ Road Games
# Thomas & Mack Center, Las Vegas, NV

sat out last season after averaging 19.1 points and 4.7 rebounds at Midland CC in Texas the year before. Goodwyn, who prepped at Lubbock Coronado High School, signed with the Rams out of Midland, but didn't qualify. He chose to stay at CSU rather than go play for a school in a lower division. He's one of nine players who has never suited up for the Rams, but he's clearly the most talented.

Morrill said he was looking forward to coaching Goodwyn all season and was impressed by how much he "took care of his business." That's off the court. On the court, Goodwyn is an impact player and could have been the difference between an NIT and NCAA berth last season. He can score in the low block and has some slashing moves to the basket. He should thrive in McKay's more uptempo system.

He'll feed off of Palacio, the 6-3 senior, who spent the summer playing for Belize. He's from Los Angeles, but his parents are from the Central American country. Palacio (9.8 ppg, 3.6 rpg, 148 assists, 33 minutes, .478 FG percentage, .377 three-point percentage) emerged as the team's best on-ball defender and a reliable playmaker, but still didn't shoot the ball as well as he needed to. He has to do a better job at the free-throw line, especially with his ability to get deep into the lane and draw fouls.

He won't have to shoot as well if Sivesind, a 6-3 sophomore from Sioux Falls, S.D., can be the impact player at shooting guard. Sivesind spent one year at Wright State before transferring to Colorado State. He started every game for Wright State, averaging 19.5 points and shooting 58 percent, 45 on threes. He lit up Cleveland State with 23 points in one game and had a high of seven boards against Illinois-Chicago. Morrill considered Sivesind one of the top two or three shooters he had ever coached.

The sleeper newcomer could be 6-6 **Shawn Harris** (San Jose City College/Gunderson HS/San Jose, Calif.), who could slip in at small forward. Harris averaged 14 points and had six rebounds for San Jose City and has a decent mid-range game. He won't be expected to do more than board, body up the small forwards on defense and hit the shots in the high post. He could be like former Rams James Smith or Delmonte Madison, the type of players who helped them guard the more athletic wings in the WAC.

The other choices could be 6-5 sophomore **Tony Trimble** (San Bernardino CC/Calif./Cal State-San Bernardino/Miller HS/Fontana, Calif.), a slasher who is more of a defender and screener than scorer after averaging just four points and two rebounds; 6-9 sophomore **Paul Martin** (Colorado School of the Mines/Heritage HS/Littleton, Colo.); or 6-7 sophomore **Garrett Patik**. Martin transferred last year and sat out after averaging 14 points and nine rebounds at Colorado School of the Mines. Morrill considered him to be extremely active inside. Patik (1.2 ppg, 1.1 rpg) got into 12 games and was a non-factor last season. He has the size to contribute on the boards.

With Goodwyn at power forward, Morrill left McKay with some options at center with 7-2 junior **Philip Von Backstrom** (Western Nebraska JC/Pretoria, South Africa), 6-9 junior **John Ford** (2.4 ppg, 1.9 rpg, 10 minutes, 62.8 FG, 30.0 FT) or 6-10 sophomore **David Fisher** (SW Missouri State JC/Fordland, Mo.). The three will probably share the position by committee. Von Backstrom, whose identical twin brother plays at Oregon State, is the strongest of the lot. He averaged five points and four rebounds last season and will have to do more to help the Rams.

Ford was a blip on the frontcourt screen last season and will have to do even more than Von Backstrom to get McKay's attention. Fisher averaged 10.1 points and shot 48 percent for SW Missouri CC, not State. This is not the same school that Steve Alford coaches. Fisher's another unheralded player, but does have a big body.

The guards have more legitimate help with 6-1 senior **Andre McKanstry** (3.8 ppg, 1.0 rpg, 1.2 apg, 13.1 minutes, .750 percentage); 6-3 freshman **Sam Adamo** (Strake Jesuit HS/Houston, Texas); and 6-3 freshman **Erik Smith** (Dulles HS/Sugar Land, Texas). Smith can play the point and back up Palacio. McKanstry can be a combo, but his shooting has to improve. And Adamo, a 17.5 point, seven-rebound and seven-assist performer in high school, has a chance to be a scorer. He'll likely rotate in behind Sivesind or slide behind Harris at small forward.

adidas Blue Ribbon Analysis

BACKCOURT	**C**	**BENCH/DEPTH**	**C**
FRONTCOURT	**C**	**INTANGIBLES**	**B**

The intangible with this team is McKay. He instantly brings more enthusiasm because of his thirst for the job. He galvanized a dormant Portland State program and should be able to pump up the Rams.

Goodwyn gives the new coach a marquee talent to build with the next two seasons. McKay has a point in Palacio and a shooter in Sivesind. He can't bank on much else.

Colorado State should be able to defend, but rebounding is still uncertain. So, too, are the number of wins. CSU is in a tough side of the WAC and can't expect to get ahead of UNLV, TCU, Tulsa or SMU. The Rams' only hope is to beat out Wyoming for fifth. They'll likely fight Rice for sixth.

Morrill thought this group could overachieve. Under McKay, it still will.

(A.K.)

FRESNO STATE

LOCATION .... **Fresno, CA**
CONFERENCE .... **WAC (Pacific Division)**
LAST SEASON .... **21-13 (.618)**
CONFERENCE RECORD .... **10-4 (2nd, Pacific)**
STARTERS LOST/RETURNING **2/3**
NICKNAME .... **Bulldogs**
COLORS .... **Cardinal & Blue**
HOMECOURT .... **Selland Arena (10,159)**
COACH .... **Jerry Tarkanian (Fresno State '55)**
RECORD AT SCHOOL .... **63-36 (3 yrs.)**
CAREER RECORD .... **688-158 (27 yrs.)**
ASSISTANTS .... **Wil Hooker (Fresno State '96)**
Danny Tarkanian (UNLV '84)
John Welch (UNLV '86)
TEAM WINS (last 5 yrs.) **21-13-22-20-21**
RPI (last 5 yrs.) **70-178-51-68-69**
1997-98 FINISH .... **Lost in NIT consolation game.**

Fresno State can't have any more excuses for failing to reach the NCAA Tournament or dealing with off-court problems. There have been too many NITs and far too many distractions the last three seasons.

Last year was the worst.

The Bulldogs had 12 suspensions, all but three of them for drug offenses. Fresno State may have had the strictest policy for testing, but it had too many offenders. The distractions were endless.

The year began with an assault charge against point guard Rafer Alston. It continued with Terrance Roberson sitting for a few weeks in practice because of the drug policy. The next offender was Daymond Forney. **Chris Herren** followed and missed three weeks of the season and five games for heading off to a drug rehabilitation center in Salt Lake City. Forney would slip again. Avondre Jones and Tremaine Fowlkes would also fall prey to the policy. Forney did again and sat one other time for failing to produce community service documents from an assault charge the previous summer.

Jones and Forney came back for a final time, but then left soon after and were gone for the season—Forney because he didn't want to deal with the rules of his reinstatement; Jones because of his involvement in a nationally-publicized assault with a samurai sword.

That incident involved Georgetown transfer Kenny Brunner and both were still waiting to have their cases heard on the matter. Brunner left because of that incident and spent the summer in a Los Angeles County jail because of an attempted robbery.

On the court, the Bulldogs somehow managed to piece together practices and games with sometimes only six players. The chemistry worked well enough to put them on the verge of claiming an NCAA Tournament berth with a trip to the WAC Tournament final. That didn't happen. Fresno State couldn't get past hometown UNLV in a semifinal game.

But the Bulldogs got by Pacific in the first round on the road, Memphis in the second at home and Hawaii in the third in Honolulu and reached the NIT Final Four in New York. An overtime loss to eventual champion Minnesota was the final "good" thing about the season. The consolation-game loss to Georgia was a dismal effort and left everyone thinking about the lost season.

Gone is Alston a year early, taken by Milwaukee in the second round. Gone is Fowlkes a year early, who ended up finishing in the top five in rebounding and was taken in the second round by Denver.

Gone is Winfred Walton two years early, who was the most disappointing newcomer in the nation. He wasn't drafted, but signed with an agent and is expected to surface in a pro league overseas.

Gone is Jones, who threw away a chance to play professionally with his actions last March.

Gone is Forney, who did the same with his failure to stay on the court.

Could all the bad luck have left with those players? That's what Fresno State hopes, especially with its booster group's slogan of it being a "New Dog Day."

Here's why: A calmer, more mature Herren. A hungry **Courtney Alexander**. A driven **Terrance Roberson**. A stable **Larry Abney**. A developing **Melvin Ely**. A bench that won't settle for limited playing time.

Herren (15.4 ppg, 2.3 rpg, 138 assists, 54 steals), a 6-3 senior, was a first-team all-WAC Pacific Division choice by the coaches and media and is a player-of-the-year candidate. He was expected to declare for the draft, but pulled his name out a few days after the deadline. The two reasons: He realized he could get academically eligible for his fifth year and he saw a chance to play the point with Alston declaring for the draft.

Herren had withdrawn from school the second semester and had three incompletes from the first semester because of his rehab stint. He faced a brutal summer to get eligible, and it was still pending as *Blue Ribbon* went to press. But he was expected to make it. He wanted to play the point because he knew that's where he would land in the NBA.

Herren will have to take a reduced scoring role if he's to achieve his goal of becoming a true playmaker. He says he has already proven he can score. Herren's best move is driving to the basket, finding his way into the lane, especially from his right. However, he shied away from it last season, looking for the deep three-pointer instead of the drive. He'll have to do that more with Alexander.

That's not to say Herren won't put up similar numbers on occasion, like the 33 points he scored against SMU or the six of nine three-pointers he made against TCU. Herren will have to get inside, drive and dish out to Alexander and Roberson for threes. He still has trouble brushing back a player and launching the three-pointer. He's great coming off a screen for a three-pointer or pulling up on the break, or even off of a reverse pass for a three-pointer.

"I really believe Chris can play the point and accept the role as a playmaker," coach Jerry Tarkanian said. "He's already proven he can shoot the ball. He has to let everyone in the country know he can guard the quickest point guards in the country and I think he can do that. We'll be pressuring and he can go out and guard quicker people."

Alexander, a 6-5 junior transfer from Virginia, is the best scorer on the team and might be the most prolific scorer in the West. He can get his shot off against any defender, taking it at the top of his jump. He can push a defender back without having to use a cross-over dribble. He can also drive and post up. He still needs to prove he can be as good on defense. However, he has the leaping ability to flush dunks inside the lane, coming from a wing to help with rebounding. He'll also benefit from alley-oops on the break.

Alexander, who sat out last season at Fresno State, averaged 14.3 points, 3.6 rebounds and shot .452 percent

1998-99 FRESNO STATE SCHEDULE

Nov.	13	Coppin State
	16	Cal Poly
	19	@Pepperdine
	25-28	#Great Alaska Shootout
Dec.	1	Cal State Sacramento
	4	Minnesota
	7	Pacific
	10	Utah State
	19	*Georgia
	22-23	##Coors Lite Classic
	27	@Wisconsin
	31	Temple
Jan.	4	New Mexico
	7	@San Jose State
	14	UTEP
	23	@Brigham Young
	25	@Utah
	28	San Diego State
	30	Hawaii
Feb.	4	San Jose State
	6	Georgia State
	11	@UTEP
	13	@New Mexico
	18	Brigham Young
	20	Utah
	25	@San Diego State
	27	@Hawaii
Mar.	2-6	###WAC Tournament

@ Road Games
* Georgia Dome, Atlanta, GA
\# Anchorage, AK (vs. Alaska-Anchorage, first round; also Cincinnati, Duke, Iowa State, Notre Dame, Southern Utah and Saint Mary's)
\## Fresno, CA (vs.Chicago State, first round; also Miami-Ohio and San Diego)
\### Thomas & Mack Center, Las Vegas, NV

from the field and 464 percent on threes as a sophomore at Virginia. He was an honorable-mention all-ACC member as a sophomore and was on the all-ACC freshman team the previous year. The key to this team will be how Herren and Alexander get along on the perimeter.

"What makes Courtney stand out is that he's one of the few players who can get his own shot," Tarkanian said. "He has that ability. He can get one any time he wants. You can't guard him one-on-one. You've got to hope he's not hitting. We haven't had anybody since I've been here who can do that."

Roberson (14.6 ppg, 4.9 rpg, 77 assists, 54 steals) will be content to get his share. His best move is still getting to the corners and taking the three-pointer. He doesn't have the foot speed to dribble past someone and tends to turn the ball over when he tries to use his power dribble to get past a defender on a drive from the free-throw extended or the corner. Roberson can post up and has improved his spin move around the baseline. He has to continue to improve his rebounding and may be forced to play some power forward, which could be a problem defensively.

Roberson still has to watch disappearing at times. He can go on a streak of hitting six threes (against Wisconsin) and then go out and miss all his shots. He tends to lose focus and when he does that, his defense goes with him. When he's attentive, his long reach makes him one of the most dangerous players on the Bulldogs' amoeba zone or man-to-man defense. Roberson can pick off steals, get the break going and finish with either a three-pointer or a jam. Roberson can put up 20-plus easily and joins Herren and Alexander as the most productive trio of guards in the West and possibly the nation.

"Terrance has had great games for us and turned into a tremendous shooter," Tarkanian said. "He has to do it every time and get consistent."

The Bulldogs plan on using four players out and one center at times, which could mean the 6-8 Abney's time could be cut. However, the junior has become a fan favorite and is one of those players who makes things happen on the court. He's always around the ball, and was instrumental in keeping the Bulldogs' season alive during Jones' and Fowlkes' absences last season.

Without Abney, the NIT may not have even been a reality. Abney started 13 games and scored 15 points and had 11 rebounds against Hawaii in a critical win on the Island for the Bulldogs. He was seven for seven from the field in that game and ended up leading the Bulldogs in field-goal percentage.

Abney (5.5 ppg, 4.1 rpg, .607 FG percentage) spent the summer working on his game and gained considerable confidence playing on a team touring in Greece. He was the recipient of a number of fast-break passes from Seton Hall guard Shaheen Holloway on that trip.

Abney's spirited play, ability to flush the ball on the break and his improved 15-foot jumper will make the Bulldogs even tougher to defend. Abney has to improve on his defensive rebounding. He wasn't able to get to the ball with Fowlkes always flying around the backboard. He has to help the 6-10 Ely (Thornton Township HS/Harvey, Ill.).

No player has as much expectations as this sophomore. Alexander has already done damage in college, but Ely was supposed to last season. He was a McDonald's All-American after posting 15.5 points and 9.3 rebounds as a senior in Illinois. However, he didn't qualify academically and had to sit out the season.

Ely's game is defensive post play and shot blocking first, offense second. He has a soft hook but tends to shoot the ball too often from his palm and doesn't get the full release. He still needs to add to his moves before he can be counted on to score. He doesn't have the quick leaping ability the way Abney does around the basket. However, he's strong and has a presence.

"Melvin has to give us an inside presence both offensively and defensively," Tarkanian said. "He'll have to play a lot of minutes. He can't commit silly fouls and offensive fouls. He has to do a lot of things and play intelligently."

He's also alone.

Abney is the only other player who could play the post. The others will have to play by committee. **Randy Holcomb**, a 6-8 sophomore from Lincoln Park High School in Chicago, sat out the year with Ely. He averaged 20 points and 10 rebounds, but was considered a sleeper. He'll awaken teams this season. He's the strongest player in the program and can rip rebounds and jam with anyone on the team. Holcomb has to hone his temperament and has to funnel toward controlled, but aggressive play. He's still developing his offensive moves but can really help on defense, where he'll body up anyone who comes in the post.

Andrea Bona, a 6-7 freshman from Redemption Christian Academy in Troy, N.Y., could find some minutes at power forward. Bona, who is originally from Rome, Italy, is a tough, hard-nosed player who plays well above his size. He can bang with any player and could be used to add muscle in the post, rebound and play defense.

The depth behind Herren, Roberson and Alexander gives Tarkanian hope that this team will be his quickest, most athletic and best on defense.

Travis Robinson (Mt. Zion Academy/Durham, N.C.), a 6-7 freshman, could be the first off the bench if he can gain a waiver to be eligible this season. Robinson signed at Missouri in November 1997, but got out of his national letter of intent because he had to attend a trial in his hometown.

He was a witness when his cousin was murdered, and Robinson thought it would take the fall semester. It didn't, and his mother wanted him out of the area. He went west to Fresno, where he'll wait to see if he can help immediately. Robinson has the potential to help inside with his ability to spin and score. He can on the perimeter because of his three-point range. And he can on defense because of his reach.

Willie Farley, a 6-5 senior, is the sleeper on the team. He started five of six games last season before abruptly quitting. Farley (8.3 ppg, 5.0 rpg in six games) left because he thought his playing time would be gone when Herren returned. He went to North Florida, but never enrolled. He returned in the summer and immediately was welcomed back onto the team. He's still one of the best defenders, hardest workers and most versatile players on Fresno State's roster. He can slash to the basket for points, hit threes and defend away from and on the ball.

Herren has company at the point with 6-foot junior **Shomario Richard** (Chaffey College/Rancho Cucamonga, Calif. and Nogales HS/La Puente, Calif.) and 6-foot sophomore **Demetrius Porter** (3.1 ppg, 0.9 rpg, 68 assists, 26 steals).

As fall practice began, Richard was waiting to become eligible and probably wouldn't know his fate until November. He still needed clearance on his associate of arts degree. If he's cleared, Richard gives the Bulldogs a true point who can slice into the lane and distribute. He's not a shooter, but a true playmaker. He can be an above average ball defender.

Porter is a combo guard in a point-guard's body. He had his moments (scoring 15 points against San Diego State) and his assists to turnovers ratio (36 turnovers) was good. He won't hurt the Bulldogs on the court and is a point guard who does what's he supposed to on the floor.

Damon Jackson, a 6-3 freshman from Perris High School in San Diego, and 6-foot junior Nick Irvin (College of Southern Idaho/Carver HS/Chicago, Ill.) are both academically ineligible and will sit out the season.

"Our depth is fine everywhere except at center," Tarkanian said. "We've got depth at every other spot. We had it at center but we lost Steve Eldridge (a junior-college recruit who didn't make it academically). We've got speed, shooting ability and quickness and everything except a good backup big man."

adidas Blue Ribbon Analysis

BACKCOURT	A	BENCH/DEPTH	B
FRONTCOURT	B	INTANGIBLES	B

The backcourt could be the best in the nation, certainly the most productive. Teams will have a tough time defending Herren, Roberson and Alexander. Tarkanian will try and use a swarm team off the bench as a gimmick to force the defensive tempo.

This should be the first team that finally plays the way Tarkanian wants to at Fresno State. The inside game will be thin, but the quickness and scoring on the perimeter will make up for any depth deficiencies.

The keys for this team will be the same as it's been the last three years: Off-court problems and team chemistry. If the Bulldogs can avoid the first one and accomplish the second, then they finally can get Tarkanian back to the NCAA Tournament. The schedule gives them a chance to pick up power-rating points early. They can't blow it and try to climb during the WAC. Their fate may be determined in December, when Minnesota, Wisconsin, Georgia and Temple are on the schedule. Expect the Bulldogs to be right on the bubble in March again. If they can get in, they'll be dangerous in the first round.

(A.K.)

HAWAII

LOCATION	Honolulu, HI
CONFERENCE	WAC (Pacific Division)
LAST SEASON	21-9 (.700)
CONFERENCE RECORD	8-6 (4th, Pacific)
STARTERS LOST/RETURNING	4/1
NICKNAME	Rainbows
COLORS	Green & White
HOMECOURT	Specia Events Arena (10,000)
COACH	Riley Wallace (Centenary '84)
RECORD AT SCHOOL	176-152 (11 yrs.)
CAREER RECORD	191-179 (13 yrs.)
ASSISTANTS	Bob Nash (Hawaii '84) Jackson Wheeler (Marymount '82) Jaime Dixon (Texas Christian '87)
TEAM WINS (last 5 yrs.)	18-16-11-21-21
RPI (last 5 yrs.)	83-91-165-52-44
1997-98 FINISH	Lost iin NIT third round.

Hawaii coach Riley Wallace is used to worrying about finding talent, but he always seems to be put at ease late in the summer.

It never fails. Just when it looks like the Rainbows are ready for a complete overhaul, primary recruiting assistant Jackson Wheeler finds a few junior college players to replace departing players.

Wheeler did it again last summer and the Rainbows should again contend for a postseason berth.

The backcourt of Anthony Carter and Alika Smith is gone, along with forwards Micah Kroeger and Eric Ambrozich. However, Wheeler found the usual replacements: A combo guard, a power forward and a few role players.

"We had a lot to fill but we'll be more athletic than we were a year ago," Wallace said. "We can end up being pretty good."

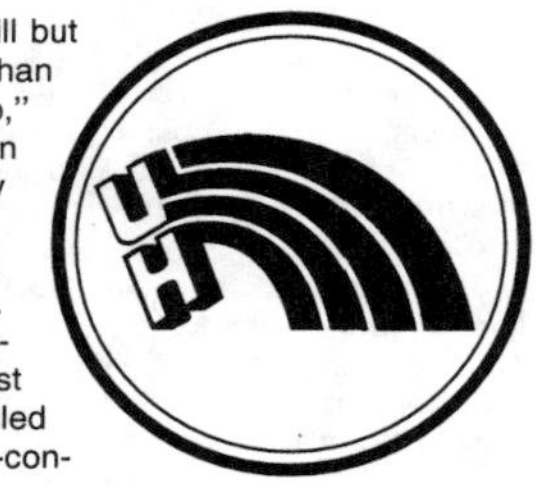

The Rainbows will again be a sleeper. Hawaii became the darling of the nation last December when it pulled off an improbable non-conference run.

Hawaii swept through its first tournament, the United Airlines Tipoff Tournament, upsetting Indiana and Illinois State. The upset streak continued with victories over Tulane, Southern Illinois and Long Island before an injury to Smith hurt the Rainbows' chances in a home-court loss to Arkansas State.

The Rainbows rebounded with six straight wins, including the most significant in Hawaii's recent history—a 76-65 win over second-ranked Kansas in the championship of the Rainbow Classic. The win, fueled by a 17-point second half from Carter, was televised by ESPN and sent the Rainbows into the top 25 and into the hearts of writers and fans across the country. ESPN analyst Dick Vitale hailed the Rainbows' backcourt as the most underrated in the nation.

However, reality hit the Rainbows hard when they struggled in the WAC. Contributing to the struggles were Smith's sore toe, Carter's nagging shoulder injury and a heart procedure to Wallace that kept him benched for a few games.

Hawaii regrouped and ended the regular season with a five-game winning streak, creeping back onto the NCAA Tournament bubble. But the Rainbows lost to UNLV in the first round of the WAC Tournament and had to settle for an NIT berth. The too advantage of the invitationak, advancing to the third round before losing at home to Fresno State.

Thanks to this year's signees, the Rainbows anticipate another run toward a postseason berth. That might not have been possible if Wheeler hadn't signed 6-9 junior forward **Marquette Alexander** of San Francisco City College and Balboa (Calif.) HS and 6-2 junior guard **Johnny White** of Brevard (Fla.) Community College and Orlando Jones (Fla.) HS. They give the Rainbows a solid inside-outside combination.

Returning are two experienced forwards: 6-8 seniors **Erin Galloway** (7.6 ppg, 6.4 rpg, .583 FG percentage) and **Mike Robinson** (8.6 ppg, 6.0 rpg, .498 FG percentage).

They give Wallace four solid players who should help the Rainbows push for at least a fourth-place finish in the Pacific Division.

"Our recruiting is a lot different than it used to be because of national television," Wallace said. "It has drawn us closer to the mainland. We've had our share of TV (appearances) and the Rainbows have benefited. I trust Jackson (to recruit quality players). He gets a feel for players and can tell if they can be big-time for us."

Robinson wasn't supposed to be back, but the Rain-

1998-99 HAWAII SCHEDULE

Nov.	15	California
	19-20	#Zippy's Invitational
	27-29	##United Airlines Tip-Off Tournament
Dec.	4-5	###Powerbar Invitational
	18-19	####Nike Festival
	27-30	#####Rainbow Classic
Jan	7	@UTEP
	9	@New Mexico
	16	Brigham Young
	18	Utah
	23	San Diego State
	28	@San Jose State
	30	@Fresno State
Feb.	4	UTEP
	6	New Mexico
	11	@Brigham Young
	13	@Utah
	20	@San Diego State
	25	San Jose State
	27	Fresno State
Mar.	2-6	######WAC Tournament

@ Road Games
# Honolulu, HI (vs. Nichols State, first round; also Marquette and Oklahoma State)
Honolulu, HI (vs. Wichita State, first round; also Auburn and Rutgers)
Honolulu, HI (vs. Northridge State, first round; also Coppin State and Georgia State)
Honolulu, HI (vs. Eastern Illinois, first round; also Northern Arizona and St. Bonaventure)
Honolulu, HI (vs. Southwestern Louisiana, first round; also Florida State, Mississippi State, Murray State, Princeton, Texas and UNC Charlotte)
Thomas & Mack Center, Las Vegas, NV

bows won an appeal with the NCAA, which granted him an extra year of eligibility. The appeal was based on a year of junior college when he played just a couple of games. Robinson has matured as a post player and looks for his best season ever. He has developed more of a low-post game, displaying soft touch on his hook shot and a good mid-range jump shot.

Galloway, nicknamed Helicopter, has a vertical leap that can cause problems defensively, but he must learn to do more than dunk. He is a sound defender and rebounder, in part because of his leaping ability.

"One of the things that made me feel good about this season was getting Robinson back and having Galloway there, too," Wallace said. "Getting two experienced guys back there will really help us."

Alexander gives the Rainbows more of a true power post player. He's a wide body at 250 pounds and can add muscle while Robinson and Galloway leap over everyone for jams. If Wallace puts them on the court at the same time, he'll probably play Galloway at small forward, Robinson at center and Alexander at power forward.

"(Alexander) gives us that different look and he can score better than anyone we've had inside," Wallace said. "We should get more points inside than last year."

If that's the case, White, who averaged 17.0 ppg, 4.0 rpg, 6.0 apg and 2.3 spg at Brevard CC last year, need only be a playmaker. He's not going to score like Carter in the lane or shoot like Smith from the three-point line, but if White can simply get the ball to the forwards, then the Rainbows should click.

"We beat out Nebraska, LSU and Florida State for him," Wallace said. "White might be a better shooter than we think."

Casey Cartwright (5.4 ppg, 1.9 rpg), a 6-5 senior guard, could be ready for a greater role after playing behind Kroeger and Smith. Wallace might not have a great three-point threat, but he will have his most athletic team since he's been at Hawaii with White, Cartwright, Galloway, Alexander and Robinson.

Smith and Carter clearly tired at the end of last season, especially in the NIT game against Fresno State. Carter was pressing and trying to do too too much, taking shots out of his range and not in his repertoire. Smith's shooting became erratic.

That won't happen if Wallace gets the lift from several other players, including 6-4 sophomore **Gary Gillman**, who sat out last season after averaging 14.2 points his freshman year at Cuesta (Calif). Junior College. He played at Morrow Bay (Calif.) HS.

Also expected to contribute more will be 6-4 junior **Geremy Robinson**, who averaged 17.8 points, 13 rebounds and nine assists last season at Pearl River (Miss.) Junior College; 6-4 junior **Damon Lee** from Monterey Peninsula (Calif) College and El Cerrito HS in Oakland; and 6-2 freshman **Mike Macintyre** of Long Beach (Calif) Poly SH.

Robinson and Lee are shooting guards who can defend and run the lanes on the fast break. Macintyre can back up White at the point and Gillman could play either guard or small forward.

"Geremy has a 41-inch vertical (leap) and he'll be able to help us rebound," Wallace said. "We've got good perimeter athletes and good players who can shoot the basketball. Hopefully we can blend them all together. We've got Jaime (Dixon) back to coach them. The last time Jaime was here we went to the NCAA Tournament (in 1994). We've just got to get them in the gym and get them going."

The other returnees are 6-5 redshirt freshman **Philipp Czermin** of Pacific Palisades (Calif.) HS and 7-foot senior center **Bryan Moeller** (1.3 ppg, 8.0 rpg). Wallace likes Czermin's toughness and Moeller's big body in practice. Moeller is another strong post player who can bang in practice with 6-4 sophomore forward Predrag Savovic, a transfer from UAB who will be eligible in 1999-2000.

"It looks like we've got the depth at the (perimeter) positions we needed," Wallace said. "We'll be better inside and it may take a while for us to replace (Carter) and Alika offensively but we're capable once we click on all cylinders."

adidas Blue Ribbon Analysis

BACKCOURT	**C+**	**BENCH/DEPTH**	**B**
FRONTCOURT	**B**	**INTANGIBLES**	**B**

Hawaii coach Riley Wallace may be high on his backcourt this year, but Johnny White and Casey Cartwright need to prove themselves in the heat of competition.

The Rainbows' frontcourt is strong with Erin Galloway, Mike Robinson and Marquette Alexander. Of the three, Alexander is more the scorer, while Galloway and Robinson are the active defenders, shot-blockers and finishers who will make the Rainbows difficult to match up with inside.

Look for the Rainbows to battle through a lighter non-conference schedule than last year's. The Pacific Division won't be so easy. Hawaii will have a tough time moving ahead of Utah or New Mexico in the division race, but the Rainbows could catch Fresno State.

Hawaii will be fortunate to earn an NCAA Tournament bid, but the NIT seems quite possible.

(A.K.)

RICE

LOCATION	**Houston, TX**
CONFERENCE	**WAC (Pacific Division)**
LAST SEASON	**6-22 (.214)**
CONFERENCE RECORD	**3-11 (7th)**
STARTERS LOST/RETURNING	**2/3**
NICKNAME	**Owls**
COLORS	**Blue & Gray**
HOMECOURT	**Autry Court (5,000)**
COACH	**Willis Wilson (Rice '82)**
RECORD AT SCHOOL	**80-88 (6 yrs.)**
CAREER RECORD	**80-88 (6 yrs.)**
ASSISTANTS	**Marty Gross (Jacksonville '77)**
	Todd Smith (Valparaiso '89)
	John Herndon (Washington & Lee '85)
TEAM WINS (last 5 yrs.)	**15-15-14-12-6**
RPI (last 5 yrs.)	**151-137-109-126-199**
1997-98 FINISH	**Failed to qualify for conference tournament.**

Everyone shares in the blame for overestimating the talent at Rice last season. No one is exempt—not the coaching staff, the players or the media.

Everyone is doing it again this season—to a lesser extent. Rice should be decent, a WAC Tournament team and a spoiler to cause fits for teams such as TCU, Tulsa, SMU and, maybe, even UNLV in its attempts to reach the postseason.

That statement is not as lofty as proclaiming the Owls an NIT team. But it's still a positive forecast for a six-win program that couldn't make the WAC Tournament in a Pacific Division that was weak toward the bottom.

"It looks like things are moving in the right direction," said coach Willis Wilson, who despite his sub .500 record could win any game against any coach if a pleasant personality were a prerequisite.

"Our guys understand that they are the reason we win and they're the reason we lose," Wilson said. "Our veteran guys are embarrassed by what happened last season. They understand that six wins wasn't enough. We lost six games by three points or less, four by nine points or less. We're talking about possessions. Our confidence and attitude has been incredible this offseason and that's the difference between winning and losing."

So, too, is scheduling and health.

Wilson overscheduled last season with games to open the season against Florida State and Kansas. Playing West Virginia, South Florida and Iowa didn't help, either. Drawing NCAA Tournament runnerup Utah as the cross-over game from the Mountain Division wasn't Wilson's fault, but it crushed any chance the Owls had of catching a break in the WAC.

Small forward Jesse Cravens was lost for the season—even before it began—with a back injury and guard Bobby Crawford never shook a preseason ankle injury. Crawford's erratic shooting became the pulse of the team. When he was off, the Owls were bad. When he was on, they were OK, but never complete.

Forward Jarvis Kelley Sanni was exciting to watch, but showed why he wasn't able to crack Arizona's lineup. He lacked the skills beyond the first few feet from the basket. Neither became the leader Wilson had envisioned when he took them as transfers three years ago.

"Cravens would have given us experience, minutes that never saw the floor," Wilson said. "Bobby saw the floor but he was hurt and when he broke down, he wasn't able to give us a lot. The team that was supposed to play that schedule never saw the floor. This year's schedule is conducive to a young, hungry team."

The team that will play Navy on the road, in average tournaments at San Francisco and Iowa State, Houston, Missouri-Rolla, Stephen F. Austin, Louisiana College, Southern and Portland at home will be led by two transfers who share Wilson's hunger.

Jason Skaer, a 6-7 senior, never felt comfortable at Oklahoma State and wasn't able to find the freedom under Eddie Sutton's watch. Skaer (6.7 ppg, 4.1 rpg in 1996-97) will be given free reign under Wilson. He's healthy after a leg injury sidelined him for a bit during his redshirt season.

Skaer has no other choice but to produce with only one season left in college.

"He's got the toughness and the strength to play power forward," Wilson said. "The thing I like about him is his versatility. He can do a lot of things for us. He can rebound, score and defend."

Joining Skaer inside will be 6-6 sophomore **Erik Cooper**, a transfer from Loyola (Md.) College. Cooper (8.0 ppg, 4.0 rpg at Loyola) tore his anterior cruciate ligament during his redshirt season, but has been cleared to play this fall. He should be the shooter the Owls needed in Cravens' absence the last two seasons.

Wilson thinks he has his most experienced frontline with 6-11 junior center **Alex Bougaieff** (5.0 ppg, 5.9 rpg) given the nod to replace Kelley Sanni. Bougaieff played for a Canadian team this summer and added some bulk. He'll have to be stronger in the post to defend Tulsa's Brandon

1998-99 RICE SCHEDULE

Nov.	13	Texas-Pan American
	16	@Navy
	21	Houston
	23	Missouri-Rolla
Dec.	1	Stephen F. Austin
	4-5	#Northwestern Mutual Classic
	9	Louisiana College
	20	Southern
	22-23	##ISU Holiday Classic
	29	Houston Flight
Jan.	2	Portland
	7	Wyoming
	9	Colorado State
	14	UNLV
	16	@Air Force
	23	Tulsa
	28	Southern Methodist
	30	Texas Christian
Feb.	4	@Colorado State
	6	@Wyoming
	11	Air Force
	13	UNLV
	20	@Tulsa
	25	@Texas Christian
	27	@Southern Methodist
Mar.	2-6	###WAC Tournament

@ Road Games
# San Francisco, CA (vs. Weber State, first round; also, Holy Cross and San Francisco)
Ames, IA (vs. Saint Mary's, first round; also, Iowa State and New Orleans)
Thomas & Mack Center, Las Vegas, NV

Kurtz, TCU's Lee Nailon or UNLV's Kaspars Kambala.

There is decent depth and size up front. **Ferron Morgan**, a 6-10 freshman center from East High School in Aurora, Colo., joins a bench of 6-10 sophomore **Hugh Thomson** (0.8 ppg, 1.2 rpg) and 6-8 sophomore and part-time starter **Derek Michaelis** (6.9 ppg, 4.2 rpg).

Wilson believes Thomson will finally shine after struggling during his first year in America. The Australian has gotten stronger and simply needs to bang, rebound and finish around the basket. Morgan has the size and strength to push Thomson in practice and earn some minutes. Michaelis, who will rotate with Skaer at small forward, gives the Owls another offensive threat from 19 feet and in, but he has to continue to put the ball on the floor and drive.

"Jason and Derek give us two quality power forwards while Hugh and Morgan give us versatility in the post," Wilson said. "We can even move Skaer out to the perimeter at a three spot if we want at times."

Shawn Tyndell, a 6-5 sophomore, will probably spell Cooper as the seventh player in the frontcourt rotation. Tyndell (1.5 ppg, 1.3 rpg) was a bit of a disappointment as a freshman. Cooper allows Wilson a breather from pushing Tyndell in too soon. He may not be ready to be more than a spot player again, but he'll have to shoot better than 22 percent.

Crawford made the Owls rely too much on perimeter shooting last season. The deeper frontcourt pushes the offense further inside. Still, point and shooting guard could be a surprise. **Mike Wilks**, a 5-10 sophomore, will return as the point. Wilks (4.8 ppg, 2.6 rpg, 72 assists, 58 turnovers) played a reserve role last season. If he had any fears, they should be shelved this year with the ball in his hands from day one.

"He has the jets to create for us at both ends of the court," Wilson said. "I think our guys are comfortable with him in that role."

Keenan Holmes, a 6-3 freshman guard from Heritage High School in Richmond, Va., will be the backup, but could play alongside Wilks, too. He has the quickness to push the ball, but his offensive skills are too untested to be trusted right away.

No other spot seems to get Wilson as excited as shooting guard, where he's adamant that 6-4 senior **Robert Johnson** (11.6 ppg, 3.3 rpg, 50 assists, 54 turnovers) will be the most improved player in the WAC.

"His attitude this summer was unmatched by any other player," Wilson said. "He has put in the time in the gym. He will help us win games."

T.J. Armstrong (2.6 ppg, 1.1 rpg, 13.1 minutes, 13 assists, 28 turnovers) will be his backup and rotate some at small forward. The 6-5 senior hasn't produced the numbers in his previous three seasons, but could be a leader off the bench.

Don't expect as much time for the backup point, 6-2 junior **Josh Stringer** (3.6 ppg, 1.7 rpg) and 6-6 redshirt sophomore **Christian Lockwood**. They'll probably join 6-11 sophomore T.J. McKenzie, a transfer from Providence College sitting out this season, on the scout team.

adidas Blue Ribbon Analysis

BACKCOURT	C-	BENCH/DEPTH	C
FRONTCOURT	C+	INTANGIBLES	C

Wilson should be optimistic with a team that has hunger and heart. But the unknown will hurt the Owls from being anything more than a contender to make the WAC Tournament, competing with Air Force, Colorado State and Wyoming for the final two spots. The Owls will probably have to beat out CSU and Air Force, which will only happen if Skaer can be a double figure scorer, Cooper is a nine- to 10-point scorer, Bougaieff can grab eight to 10 rebounds a game, Wilks is the jet Wilson thinks he is and Johnson's summer was really that good.

Expect Rice to be in the thick of the race for the final Mountain Division tournament spot, a potential 10-win team and a better competitor with a more realistic schedule.

(AK.)

adidas Blue Ribbon Analysis

GRADING SYSTEM

- A+ equal to very best in country—Final Four-caliber unit
- A among the best in the land—worthy of deep NCAA run
- B+ talented, versatile and experienced—NCAA-NIT ability
- B solid and productive winners—league and post-season contenders
- C+ average to above-average—may contend in a weaker league
- C average to mediocre—second division in a strong league
- D+ below average, inconsistent—second division in a weaker league
- D well below average—losing season virtually certain
- F non-Division I ability—an underdog every night

SAN DIEGO STATE

LOCATION .... **San Diego, CA**
CONFERENCE .... **WAC (Pacific Division)**
LAST SEASON .... **13-15 (.464)**
CONFERENCE RECORD .... **5-9 (6th)**
STARTERS LOST/RETURNING **3/2**
NICKNAME .... **Aztecs**
COLORS .... **Scarlett & Black**
HOMECOURT .... **Cox Arena (12,414)**
COACH .... **Fred Trenkle (Idaho State '70)**
RECORD AT SCHOOL .... **51-61 (4 yrs.)**
CAREER RECORD .... **51-61 (4 yrs.)**
ASSISTANTS . **James Holland (S.C.-Spartanburg '84)**
Steve Green (Oklahoma Christian '74)
Craig Koch (Tarleton State '91)
TEAM WINS (last 5 yrs.) **12-11-15-12-13**
RPI (last 5 yrs.) **185-218-170-198-158**
1997-98 FINISH .... **Lost in conference quarterfinal.**

Fred Trenkle would like to begin again, wipe away his previous four years and start his San Diego State coaching career today.

If only life were that easy.

Trenkle has to live with an Aztec past that has been blessed by hard work and overachieving, but blemished by constant attrition and bad luck. The results have been four years of subpar performances by a program constantly struggling to achieve respect.

After four years, some of that respect has finally arrived, but it isn't clear if it has arrived too late. Trenkle has put together his best recruiting class in his time at San Diego State. He nabbed most of the top players in the San Diego area, minus one who escaped to Arizona. Cox Arena received rave reviews as a basketball venue in its first year and Trenkle finally has some recruiting advantages that he has never enjoyed.

However, the patience has worn thin at San Diego State, where Trenkle has to offset a hunger by some administrators to lure Utah's Rick Majerus if he will be had. Trenkle has time left on his contract and if he can make a run for fourth place in the Pacific Division, get near .500 and pull off a few upsets to galvanize the local fickle fan base, then he should be here to stay.

Pressure? Certainly.

"If I were walking in this year, I'd be tickled because of the players, the facility and the schedule," Trenkle says. "If we keep them solid and keep them in school, with two or three more signings then a year from now, we can be really good. We've got choices now. I had no need for neck muscles on my right side the past few years because there was no sense looking to the right on the bench. We didn't have anyone."

The Aztecs haven't had any players under Trenkle whom he would consider even worthy of playing in the NBA. He's not ready to anoint 6-7 freshman **Vincent Okotie** (Grossmont HS/El Cajon, Calif.) or 6-foot freshman **David Abramowitz** (University of San Diego HS/San Diego, Calif. and Tijuana, Mexico) as future pros, but at least he believes they can come close through hard work.

"We've never had guys who even had pro reputations, but those two guys will play somewhere when they're done," Trenkle says. "Talent-wise, this is the best we've had. We've had more experience but we've got size, quickness and physical ability with this group. They're young, but there's nothing that says freshmen can't win. We'll convince them they can beat anybody."

Abramowitz will start at the point. He has the toughness and aggressiveness with the basketball and on the defensive end to make the Aztecs' offense and defense jump when he's on the floor. He has had a history of injuries, mainly with his ankle, but his ballhandling and quickness, especially laterally, will allow him to match up with any point in the WAC.

Trekle has an option behind Abramowitz and won't hesitate to use 6-3 junior college transfer **Donte Wilson** (South Plains JC/Midland, Texas). He can play either point or shooting guard, thus giving the Aztecs another athlete at the position. He was erratic last season and needs to do a better job of moving without the ball.

Trenkle will work those two with 6-3 freshman **Jeffrey Berokoff** (Sonora HS/Whittier, Calif.) and 6-3 senior **Matt Watts** (12.9 ppg, 4.1 rpg, 3.8 apg, 35.6 minutes), who is the only true returning starter. Berokoff is a strong player who looks older than a freshman. He has the potential to bust out with a few high-scoring games and should be one of the better three-point threats off the bench.

Watts was all over the place last season, slashing to the basket in the halfcourt, running the break fullcourt, popping the occasional three-pointer and mid-range jumper. He finished up well, leading the Aztecs in scoring in three of the final six games. When point guard Jason Richey went down with a foot injury in the final few weeks, Watts was able to take over control of the team, handling the ball and showing poise and leadership under adverse situations. His best game may have been his last, when he scored 24 points in a blowout 92-57 loss to Fresno State in the WAC tournament quarterfinals.

Trenkle's son, Brady, a 5-11 senior, probably won't be allowed to play after sitting out last season with a heart ailment. **David Kaplansky** (1.1 ppg, 0.3 apg), a 5-9 senior walkon, should return to provide a few breathers.

Trenkle will likely start with Abramowitz at the point and Watts at shooting guard with either Wilson or 6-5 freshman **Julien Sormonte** (Milford Academy/Conn./Montpelier, France) at small forward. Sormonte played alongside of UCLA recruit Jerome Moiso in high school and has better perimeter skills. Trenkle sees him as a tireless worker who can shoot the three-pointer, post-up and pass out of the post and from the free-throw extended, proving that he can get the ball inside, too. He has the ability to take the ball off one dribble and slam it.

If Sormonte isn't ready, though, Trenkle believes 6-6 freshman forward **Myron Epps** (Tulare Union HS/Tulare, Calif.) will be eager to take his place. Epps is still raw offensively, but he can get to the boards and should be able to rebound effectively at the Division I level. Epps was passed over in the Central Valley, and Trenkle believes he's one of the steals of this freshmen class.

The unknown of the bunch is 6-7 freshman **Jackson Jones** (Jefferson HS/Cedar Rapids, Iowa). He has three-point skills but can also be a banger similar to former San Diego State forward Paul Jarrett. He has the ability to lumber out to the three-point line and hit the three-pointer, while also working inside well enough to be a factor on the boards.

Ideally, Trenkle would like to have Okotie play small forward and have one of the bruisers develop as a power forward. However, he doesn't feel comfortable enough with his other potential power forwards, or for that matter his centers, to leave Okotie too far out of the lane.

He's the most talented player on the roster and was the first legitimate talent to stay home in San Diego. He can play facing the basket or with his back to it. His touch around the rim is soft ,but he can also jam with anybody in the league. He'll run the floor well and should be able to receive plenty of slams from Abramowitz passes on the break.

If 6-10 freshman center **Joe Mann** (Poway HS/San Diego, Calif.) or 6-10 sophomore **Marcelo Correa** (4.1

1998-99 SAN DIEGO STATE SCHEDULE

Nov.	14	Nevada
	18	@Southern California
	21	@Fullerton State
	24	Utah State
	28	Long Beach State
Dec.	2	Southern California College
	5	@Loyola Marymount
	9	@Nevada
	19	San Diego
	22	New Mexico State
	27	Arkansas State
Jan.	2	Pacific
	7	@New Mexico
	9	@UTEP
	14	Brigham Young
	16	Utah
	23	@Hawaii
	28	@Fresno State
	30	@San Jose State
Feb.	8	New Mexico
	6	UTEP
	11	@Utah
	13	@Brigham Young
	20	Hawaii
	25	Fresno State
	27	San Jose State
Mar.	2-6	#WAC Tournament

@ Road Games
\# Thomas & Mack Center, Las Vegas, NV

ppg, 4.0 rpg, 19.9 minutes, 45.2 FG, 57.4 FT) can't play strong enough in the post, then Okotie may play center with Epps at power forward and either Jackson or Sormonte at small forward.

Trenkle has options, but he'd rather have Correa, who started 15 of 28 games last season, produce. He had games where he was a no-show and he others where he found his touch and suddenly looked like he knew how to score in the low post. Mann has better hands and is a worker. He has more potential to play above the rim than Correa, who gives the Aztecs more finesse than strength.

adidas Blue Ribbon Analysis

BACKCOURT .... C BENCH/DEPTH C
FRONTCOURT .... C INTANGIBLES C

This team has the potential of being worthy of watching throughout the season. The freshmen class is as good as this school has recruited in the last 10 years. The question is, will Trenkle be around to see them to their sophomore season? That's up to them.

The pressure on this group won't be as intense as it was on Michigan's famed Fab Five recruiting class of the early '90s, but the newcomers do have the weight of the program and Trenkle's job security on their shoulders. Abramowitz can't afford to have a high assist-to-turnover ratio and he has to be a pest on defense. Okotie will have to produce points in double figures, possibly on the boards, too.

The sleeper players such as Sormonte, Epps, Jackson and Mann have to develop quicker than they would in most other programs. And Watts has to tone down his erratic shooting. If he can become the one senior leader and coexist with Abramowitz in the backcourt, then the Aztecs have a chance to cause Hawaii fits for fourth. If they struggle early and get frustrated, then fending off BYU and UTEP for fifth will be their fate.

Trenkle has had success getting more out of less. He finally has more talent, but has to produce even more than before. This may be his toughest challenge.

(A.K.)

SAN JOSE STATE

LOCATION .... San Jose, CA
CONFERENCE .... WAC (Pacific Division)
LAST SEASON .... 3-23 (.115)
CONFERENCE RECORD .... 1-13 (8th in Pacific)
STARTERS LOST/RETURNING 1/4
NICKNAME .... Spartans
COLORS .... Gold, White & Blue
HOMECOURT .... The Event Center (5,000)
COACH .... Phil Johnson (East Central Oklahoma '81)
RECORD AT SCHOOL .... First Year
CAREER RECORD .... First Year
ASSISTANTS .... Mike Kruszynski (Mary '86)
Eddie Hill (Washington State '84)
Gary Patterson (Utah State '93)
TEAM WINS (last 5 yrs.) 15-4-13-13-3
RPI (last 5 yrs.) 140-261-179-122-253
1997-98 FINISH .... Failed to qualify for conference tournament.

Chuck Bell wanted to get into the WAC for years, constantly pushing his superiors at Utah State. But for all his efforts, Utah State never got in the league, so Bell did the next best thing_he left the Big West school to become athletic director at San Jose State.

Phil Johnson wasn't necessarily looking for the same thing, but wanted a head coaching job, regardless of league affiliation. He jumped at the chance when San Jose State made him an offer.

Both men have to wonder what happened.

Less than a month after the coach and the athletic director signed on, San Jose State was left behind as eight WAC schools left to form their own conference, effective June 30, 1999. Suddenly, coaching San Jose State doesn't seem to be as good a job in a remaining WAC that includes Fresno State, Hawaii, UTEP, TCU, SMU, Tulsa and Rice. But don't tell that to Johnson.

"I don't have a problem with the breakup," says Johnson, who spent the last five years as an assistant at Arizona. "If anything, it will give us flexibility in the schedule. I think it will be a good solid league."

The question is, where will San Jose State fit into it? The Spartans have dropped off considerably the last two years since the player formerly known as Olivier Saint-Jean left for the NBA. The Spartans won only three games last season and could have been shut out. The prospects for this season are just as grim.

1998-99 SAN JOSE STATE SCHEDULE

Nov.	13	@Arizona State
	18	@Saint Mary's
	22	Northridge State
	24	@Pacific
	27	Menlo College
Dec.	1	Santa Clara
	5	@Montana
	9	@Cal State Sacramento
	19	Eastern Washington
	22	Portland
	27	Fullerton State
	30	@California Santa Barbara
Jan.	2	Pepperdine
	7	Fresno State
	13	New Mexico
	16	UTEP
	21	@Brigham Young
	23	@Utah
	28	Hawaii
	30	San Diego State
Feb.	4	@Fresno State
	11	@New Mexico
	13	@UTEP
	18	Utah
	20	Brigham Young
	25	@Hawaii
	27	@San Diego State
Mar.	2-6	#WAC Tournament

@ Road Games
# Thomas & Mack Center, Las Vegas, NV

"We have a lot of kids interested in us because we have positions open," Johnson says. "They've seen our style at Arizona. We've reached the bottom here and now it's time to make a move. We're at the rock bottom and playing time will be one of our best sells."

Johnson has little else. Eight of nine players and a redshirt may have returned from last season's team, but that's not anything to tout.

"In our case, we're recruiting to every position because we have to start completely over at every spot," Johnson says. "If you look at some of the scores from last year, they got annihilated. They were last in the WAC in steals, rebounding and scoring. We've got to improve the talent, the way we play and the way we coach them. We've got a long way to go."

Michael Quinney (15.8 ppg, 3.2 rpg, 2.8 apg), a 5-10 senior point guard, is the only returning Spartan who averaged in double figures. Quinney, who was an intramural player two years ago, was the Spartans' only legitimate perimeter threat. He set a single-season school record for three-pointers with 174 and connected on .362 percent, but shot only 38 percent overall. Quinney's backcourt mate was 6-3 senior **Shawn McCullough** (4.0 ppg, 2.2 rpg, .739 FT percentage), who struggled the first two-thirds of the season. McCullough never could find his shooting touch and wasn't a threat to score.

The help is going to have to come from 5-10 junior **Jeff Jacoway** (Mesa JC/Ariz.), 6-5 junior **Ben Sanders** (Fullerton College/Calif./UNLV) and 6-1 **Reggie Wilcox** (Atlanta Metro College/Ga.). Jacoway and Wilcox are playmaking guards, while Sanders is a scorer at the wing. **Ulysses Preston**, a 6-3 freshman from Lee HS in Huntsville, Ala., will get a chance, too.

"Ben Sanders will have to help us, but anybody we bring in will have to help us," Johnson says. "Ben's at least got some experience at UNLV. He's been at this level and knows what it's about. Everybody on the team needs to be good defensively.

"If you are a perimeter player, you need to be able to defend against quick players and put pressure on them. We need players who can make baskets and score. We are not a very powerful team inside or out, but we want to take advantage of our quickness."

The only significant loss last season was versatile forward Marmet Williams, who averaged 12 points and 6.9 rebounds. His dozen points were part of the woeful 59.7 points a game average.

The only two players on the team who are 6-9 or taller are 6-9 senior **Shaun Murray** (8.2 ppg, 5.0 rpg, 23.8 minutes) and 7-foot sophomore **Maik Mertens** (2.7 ppg, 2.0 rpg, 11.7 minutes). Murray was an effective mid-range shooter and the team's top field-goal percentage shooter. Mertens, a transfer from Germany at the end of December, wasn't ready for the college game. He has to contribute more this season for the Spartans to have a chance.

Brent Boe (3.2 ppg, 1.6 rpg), a 6-6 senior, was a disappointment. He went through stretches when he couldn't hit a three-pointer, which was supposed to be his forte. He'll have to find ways to contribute to stay on the floor.

Brad Kennett (4.3 ppg, 2.6 rpg), a 6-6 sophomore and 6-5 sophomore **Reggie Cooks** (0.5 ppg, 0.6 rpg) were both ineffective, too. All three of them will probably start the season behind the aforementioned perimeter players.

Will Trawick (7.4 ppg, 6.4 rpg), a 6-7 senior, and returning redshirt **Eric Griffin**, a 6-7 sophomore transfer from Pepperdine, will rotate with Mertens and Murray inside. Trawick, the team's top shot blocker with a 0.9 average, was the Spartans' most productive player in the second half of the season, averaging 9.6 points and 7.9 rebounds in the WAC.

"Eric gives us a big body and he'll shore up the rebounding weaknesses," Johnson says. "Hopefully the JC transfers will be more effective during their second years. We need Griffin, Murray and Trawick to be relentless on the glass."

adidas Blue Ribbon Analysis

BACKCOURT .... D BENCH/DEPTH .... D
FRONTCOURT .... D INTANGIBLES C

San Jose State might be the worst major Division I program. However, Johnson's experience at Arizona brings hope. Johnson will have to take some risks with junior college players and sprinkle in a few transfers and high school recruits in order to build back the talent level.

The object this season is to save face. Ten of the 27 regular season games are against '98 postseason teams. San Jose State won't earn the sixth and final WAC Tournament spot out of the Pacific Division and can expect to be shut out for the second straight year. The Spartans' goal should be to beat three wins.

(A.K.)

SOUTHERN METHODIST

LOCATION .... Dallas, TX
CONFERENCE .... WAC (Mountain Division)
LAST SEASON .... 18-10 (.643)
CONFERENCE RECORD .... 6-8 (5th Pacific)
STARTERS LOST/RETURNING 2/3
NICKNAME .... Mustangs
COLORS .... Red & Blue
HOMECOURT .... Moody Coliseum (8,998)
COACH .... Mike Dement (East Carolina '76)
RECORD AT SCHOOL .... 42-42 (3 yrs.)
CAREER RECORD ....(164-165 12 yrs.)
ASSISTANTS .... Jimmy Tubbs (Bishop College '72)
Robert Lineburg (Roanoke College '91)
TEAM WINS (last 5 yrs.) 6-7-8-16-18
RPI (last 5 yrs.) 201-207-199-116-104
1997-98 FINISH .... Lost in conference quarterfinal.

Mike Dement wanted to bring some instant respect to Southern Methodist University's basketball program. It took him only about three years.

SMU is poised to make a run at a '99 postseason berth, which many Mustang fans wanted as the 1997-98 season came to an end.

It could happen this season. The Mustangs have a solid backcourt, and if the newcomers in the frontcourt can have an impact, they should push for a fourth-place finish in the Mountain Division.

"We still haven't beaten the top guys like Tulsa and (Texas Christian) at our place or Hawaii and Fresno State last year," Dement said. "We've got to play extremely well at home and put up a good record at home. Once we get over that hump, then we can be thought of like that. Our big guys have to do something and change our ways. We've had good ones in Jay Poerner and Bobby Dimson, but we need guys who can provide shot blocking and help around the basket."

Dement's rebuilding job has been anchored by consecutive top-50 recruiting classes. The result has been a stretch in which SMU has won 36 of its last 59 games.

Last season, Dement won his 40th game sooner than any previous SMU coach. In the WAC Tournament, Dement led the Mustangs to their third consecutive first-round upset of a higher-seeded team, despite starting two freshmen and a sophomore.

"For the third year in a row, we will rely on our freshman

1998-99 SOUTHERN METHODIST SCHEDULE

Nov.	18	@Stanford
	29	Florida Atlantic
Dec.	2	@Texas Tech
	5	Alcorn State
	14	Hardin-Simmons
	16	Liberty
	19	Tennessee-Chattanooga
	28-29	#Arizona State Christmas Classic
Jan.	2	Texas-Pan American
	4	@Richmond
	11	TCU
	14	@Colorado State
	16	@Wyoming
	21	UNLV
	23	Air Force
	28	@Rice
	30	@Tulsa
Feb.	6	@TCU
	11	Colorado State
	13	Wyoming
	18	@Air Force
	20	@UNLV
	25	Tulsa
	27	Rice
Mar.	2-6	##WAC Tournament

@ Road Games
# Tempe, AZ (vs. Alaska-Anchorage, first round; also Arizona State and Navy)
Thomas & Mack Center, Las Vegas, NV

class to step forward and be forced to compete on a high level for this team to be successful," Dement said. "It's a very young team. Hopefully, they'll mature quickly and be ready for another tough WAC division. We can be a deeper team and hopefully become a better defensive team."

Dement is focusing heavily on his four freshmen in the frontcourt: 6-11 **Jon Forinash** of Newman Smith High School in Carrollton, Texas; 6-8 **Michael Niemi** of Katy High in Katy, Texas; 6-10 **Nigel Smith** of Kennedale High in Arlington, Texas; and 6-8 **DeWayne Ford** of West Orange-Stark High in Orange, Texas.

"We haven't had a shot blocker the last three years," Dement said. "Jay (Poerner) gave us a player at the line at the end of the game, but not a shot blocker. We're hoping the freshmen will give us a presence defensively. We could play three of the four together, get some points and press."

Smith, who was selected Texas' 3A player of the year after averaging 16.6 points, 13.3 rebounds and 4.9 blocks last season, is the shot blocker Dement wanted. Forinash, a second-team all-Dallas area player after averaging 11.5 points and 7.9 rebounds last year, gives the Mustangs a big body inside.

Ford, who averaged 17.5 points, 14.8 rebounds and three blocks last season, is the runner in the lane the Mustangs needed on the fast break. Niemi, an all-state selection after averaging 12 points, 7.0 rebounds and 2.5 blocks last year, may be the strongest of the bunch.

"We need two or three of them to step up," Dement said.

Returning forward **Josh Ihde** (1.7 ppg, 0.2 rpg), a 6-8 senior, will battle the incoming freshmen for playing time.

Jeryl Sasser, the WAC Pacific Freshman of the Year, played all three perimeter positions last season, perhaps displaying more versatility than his older brother Jason, who played for Texas Tech. The 6-6 Sasser (15.0 ppg, 8.3 rpg, 104 assists, 42 steals, 15 blocked shots) followed backcourt teammate **Stephen Woods** as the second consecutive freshman of the year in the WAC.

Sasser, an all-WAC second-team player, became the first SMU player to lead the team in rebounding, assists and steals. He was the second freshman to score more than 400 points (he scored 420) and was among the WAC leaders in scoring (17th), rebounding (8th), assists (16th) and steals (17th). He finished with 10 double-doubles.

"Sasser has a great nose for the ball," Dement said. "He can be like a Clayton Shields (formerly of New Mexico) for us. He's got such a tremendous work ethic. I just hope he doesn't have a sophomore jinx."

The 6-foot Woods (13.3 ppg, 3.0 rpg, 79 assists, 38 steals) followed up his freshman-of-the-year honor with a steady sophomore season. He led the team in minutes played (935), three-pointers (74), three-pointers attempted (177), three-point percentage and free-throw percentage (.808). He was the fifth most accurate three-point shooter in school history (.391 percent).

"There's no question about the positive impact Stephen Woods has had on this team," Dement said. "He's an all-conference candidate. He's a leader and we're never at our best unless he's on the floor."

Dement would prefer Sasser bring the ball up the court to force matchup problems and to free Woods to shoot. He will also have 6-6 sophomore **Willie Davis** (7.0 ppg, 1.0 rpg, 38.4 FG) as the third option.

Davis, who missed the first seven games last year with a knee injury, took over as a starter midway through the season. Davis became one of the most active players in the second half of the season, averaging 10.7 points and 5.9 rebounds in the last 12 games.

Chad Elsey, a 6-7 guard who looks like a forward, could steal the starting spot from Davis. Elsey (8.2 ppg, 3.3 rpg, 48 assists, 24 steals) is a solid shooter, but needs to be a more aggressive rebounder.

"He needs to drive more so he's not so one-dimensional," Dement said. "I've never had a team in 12 years as a head coach that had three freshmen (Sasser, Davis and Elsey) have any better years than this threesome. Each is versatile in their game. If they can stay healthy, they will impact the upcoming season greatly as they did as freshmen."

The Mustangs could have more perimeter depth than any team in the Mountain Division. Sophomore **Renaldo Bratton**, 6-foot transfer from LSU who never actually played for the Tigers, 6-3 freshman **Damon Hancock** of Lancaster (TX) High School and 6-3 junior **Anthony Anderson** (3 ppg, 0.8 rpg), the Mustang's sixth-man award winner last season, will work in the rotation.

Bratton, who was a two-time Louisiana All-State player at Arcadia High School, gives the Mustangs more quickness at wing and a leaper. He was signed by former LSU coach Dale Brown, but left when Brown retired and was replaced by John Brady. Bratton averaged 23.o points and 5.0 assists as a senior.

Hancock averaged 21 points, nine assists and eight rebounds last season and gives the Mustangs another penetrating playmaker.

"Stephen Woods was our only point two years ago and now we can move him off of that position with Jeryl, Bratton and Hancock," Dement said. "We cause some problems defensively."

adidas Blue Ribbon Analysis

BACKCOURT	**B**	**BENCH/DEPTH**	**B**
FRONTCOURT	**C**	**INTANGIBLES**	**C+**

The Mustangs have a solid backcourt that can shoot, play defense and beat opponents with its quickness, but the frontcourt is too green to make a run at an NCAA Tournament bid.

Not yet, anyway.

"We have the depth and defensive strengths we haven't had lately and we've been in foul trouble and had fatigue," Dement said. "We shouldn't have that (problem) this year. We should be able to provide good pressure and extend our defense up court without fearing that we'll run out of guards."

The Mustangs will be a pest for opponents with their renewed faith in pressure defense and the quick shot. If the freshmen forwards can provide shot-blocking, defense and the occasional putback, then SMU could surprise and finish ahead of Tulsa. Beating out UNLV and Texas Christian probably won't happen.

Winning 20 games and securing a bid to the NIT would be another step forward for a program on the rise. Maybe a year from now, the Mustangs will finish the season in the NCAA Tournament.

(A.K.)

TULSA

LOCATION	**Tulsa, OK**
CONFERENCE	**WAC (Mountain Division)**
LAST SEASON	**19-12 (.613)**
CONFERENCE RECORD	**9-5 (3rd, Pacific)**
STARTERS LOST/RETURNING	**1/4**
NICKNAME	**Golden Hurricane**
COLORS	**Old Gold, Royal Blue & Crimson**
HOMECOURT	**Donald W. Reynolds Center (8,300)**
COACH	**Bill Self (Oklahoma State '85)**
RECORD AT SCHOOL	**19-12 (1 yr.)**
CAREER RECORD	**74-66 (4 yrs.)**
ASSISTANTS	**Norm Roberts (Queens College '87)** **Billy Gillispie (Southwest Texas State '83)** **John Phillips (Oklahoma State '73)**
TEAM WINS (last 5 yrs.)	**23-24-22-24-19**
RPI (last 5 yrs.)	**34-16-42-18-96**
1997-98 FINISH	**Lost in conference quarterfinal.**

Tulsa expects to be in the NCAA Tournament every season. It doesn't matter if there's a new coach, a few new players or a new league. The Golden Hurricane has come to expect success.

And that's why last season's postseason shutout was so hard to swallow. Tulsa lost three games to start the WAC season, losses that ultimately cost them a postseason bid. **Eric Coley** wasn't with the team during that stretch, returning home to grieve with his family over his mother's death.

1998-99 TULSA SCHEDULE

Nov.	15	Sam Houston State
	18	Jackson State
	22	@Alabama-Birmingham
	24	Texas-San Antonio
	28	St. Joseph's
Dec.	1	@Nebraska
	4-5	#Blue and Gold Coca-Cola Classic
	8	North Texas
	12	Oral Roberts
	21-23	##Pearl Harbor Classic
	29	Cleveland State
Jan.	2	@Southern Illinois
	7	Colorado State
	10	Wyoming
	14	@Air Force
	16	@UNLV
	23	@Rice
	28	TCU
	30	SMU
Feb.l	4	@Wyoming
	6	@Colorado State
	13	Air Force
	15	UNLV
	20	Rice
	25	@SMU
	27	@TCU
Mar.	2-6	###WAC Tournament

@ Road Games
# Milwaukee, WI (vs. Vermont, first round; also Cornell and Marquette)
Laie, HI (vs. Texas Tech, first round; also Alabama, BYU-Hawaii, Michigan State, Oregon State, Pepperdine and Weber State)
Thomas & Mack Center, Las Vegas, NV

The Golden Hurricane wasn't the same without Coley. Tulsa struggled in a four-point home loss to a then-brutal Brigham Young, went to Rice and lost by 13 and then nearly upset Fresno State before losing by four points. The three straight losses could have sent the Golden Hurricane into a terrible spin. Instead, Tulsa ripped off a streak of eight wins in nine games, the only loss coming by two points in overtime to TCU.

It was nearly enough to earn a bid, but three losses in the final five games, even though they were at Hawaii, to TCU and to New Mexico in the WAC Tournament, were enough to keep Tulsa home in mid-March. It wasn't enough to dampen the drive of this program.

"We lost three games at home that were costly to us and we had a great chance to win all three as poorly as we played," second-year coach Bill Self said. "At 22-9 we would have had a great year. Last year's team isn't that far off from a solid season. So much of the game is luck and keeping guys healthy. It seemed like we didn't get any in the first semester. We were one of the better teams in the league in the second."

Tulsa shouldn't have two identities this season. Self made sure of that by recruiting one of the top classes in the WAC. This team should be good from the start.

"If guys stay healthy, with our good attitude, I'd be disappointed if we didn't surpass our expectations," Self said. "Why? Recruiting. The return of Coley. **Michael Ruffin**. A new arena. We're deeper, stronger and more committed."

First: Recruiting.

Self needed help for Ruffin inside, who has been asked to do more than he's capable in the post. He went out and grabbed 6-10 junior **Brandon Kurtz** (Bakersfield College/Bakersfield, Calif.) and 6-10 freshman **DeAngelo McDaniel** (John Marshall HS/Oklahoma City, Okla.) to form one of the toughest frontcourts in the league. Tulsa has been above average defensively. Now, the Hurricane will be even tougher to defend.

Kurtz (19.6 ppg, 11.3 rpg, third-team All-American and California JUCO Player of the Year) brings with him immediate respect in the post. Why? He can score on the low block.

McDaniel (15.7 ppg, 13.7 rpg and third-team McDonald's All-American) gives the Golden Hurricane a more athletic forward/center, who brings with him more of a shot-blocking mentality. Kurtz will likely start next to Ruffin with McDaniel the first off the bench.

Here's what Kurtz and McDaniel do for Ruffin: they give him freedom. Ruffin (10.5 ppg, 9.5 rpg, 78 blocked shots), a 6-8, 230-pound senior, was never supposed to be a big-time low-post scorer. He was thrust into the role after Rafael Maldonado and Shea Seals moved on last season. Ruffin is a rebounder who can finish and get to the free-throw line. He's not a low-post threat who can be depended on to dictate the outcome of the game. Kurtz can help offset any added coverage on him and McDaniel will demand attention with his activity and quickness to the ball.

Ruffin is a two-time WAC all-defensive team member and as a junior was chosen to the first team All-WAC Pacific Division. He was among the nation's leaders in rebounding (27th) and block shots (14th). He has had 47 double-figure rebounding games and 39 double-digit scoring games in 95 career games.

While Kurtz will step in next to Ruffin, he'll likely push 6-8 junior **Zac Bennett** (6.8 ppg, 5.9 rpg) to the bench. He's a banger and a decent defender, but needs to be more of a role player, not a counted-on contributor.

"Michael had to do some things that weren't what he does best last year," Self said. "Having someone next to him who can score will help him become a better defender, shot blocker and rebounder. He can score but it's not in his mindset. Kurtz can cover up for his deficiencies."

The third factor in the frontcourt recruiting puzzle is 6-7 **Kevin Johnson** (HCYA home school/Missouri City, Texas). Johnson, who scored 24.3 points and 11 rebounds for a team comprised of home schooled students, could play some power forward and rotate in with Bennett, McDaniel, Ruffin and Kurtz.

"Michael and Brandon will play the majority of minutes and either DeAngelo and Kevin have a chance to play quite a bit of minutes," Self said. "We've got depth at those positions."

That's because there are two other returnees: 6-9 junior **John Cornwell** (4 ppg, 1.8 rpg) and 6-10 sophomore **Jay Spurlock** (2.4 ppg, 1.6 rpg). Cornwell is strictly role-player material with limited skills, but Spurlock could become more of a scorer and could aid in Kurtz' development in the post. He spent two weeks with a People to People touring team in Greece and reportedly improved markedly, especially with his post move.

Self was just as self-assured in filling his needs at the point, where he expects 6-foot junior **Tony Heard** (Seward County CC/KS and John Marshall HS/Oklahoma City, Okla.) and 6-2 freshman **Greg Harrington** (Newman Smith HS/Carrollton, Texas) to compete for time at the point and off-guard. Heard, who averaged 14 points, seven assists and four steals last season, is a true point and should share the time with 5-10 senior **Shawn Williams** (5.2 ppg, 1.2 rpg, 47 assists, .406 three-point percentage, .862 FT percentage). Harrington, who averaged 23.5 points, 6.7 assists and 5.5 rebounds, could be the shooter the Golden Hurricane lacked last season.

"Heard is a little guy who knows how to win," Self said. "He's ready to run a team right now. We will miss Rod (Thompson's) leadership and he made big shots, but we've got guys who can help us recover that."

Thompson took with him a 15-point scoring average, but Heard could replace that in a hurry. So, too, could Williams, who is expected to take on more of the three-point shooting load. The former walkon was the team's most reliable threat. He moved into the starting lineup after the first 18 games and never lost the job.

He has help from 6-3 senior **Jonnie Gendron** (7.3 ppg, 1.9 rpg, 48 assists) and 6-5 sophomore **Marcus Hill** (5.2 ppg, 2.2 rpg, 35 assists,.371 three-point percentage). Gendron, whose ankle injury allowed Williams to step into the lineup, had started 51 career games for the Hurricane. He struggled from the perimeter, but should be the spot-shooter off the bench this season. Hill is more of a slasher and needs to put a sub-par freshman year behind him that was limited mostly by playing time.

And then there's the 6-5 Coley.

Coley, a junior, made the Hurricane move. He was the team's spirit at both ends of the court and his personal duress weighed on the team. Coley tied Ruffin for scoring and led the team in steals, was second in assists and blocks and third in rebounding. His tenacious defense earned him a spot next to Ruffin on the all-defensive team.

When Coley (10.4 ppg, 5.5 rpg, 31.0 minutes, .487 FG, .340 three-point percetange, 74 assists) was out of the lineup for four games, Tulsa was 1-3. When he returned, his team won nine of the final 13. He scored in double digits eight times, including a career-best 19 against Rice.

His primary backup at small forward was 6-6 sophomore **Robert Bell** (2.5 ppg, 1.4 rpg). He'll be the main reserve for him again. Both can become two of the better three-point shooters on the team and Bell will give the Hurricane a lift when he replaces Coley on the floor.

adidas Blue Ribbon Analysis

BACKCOURT .... C+ BENCH/DEPTH .... B
FRONTCOURT .... B INTANGIBLES .... B

The backcourt can't get the full blessing until it proves itself at the high- major Division I level. However, it's easy to share Self's enthusiasm. He already had more than enough talent to get a postseason bid this season, and he's added even more muscle, scoring and shooting through a good recruiting class.

"We're going to be very deep and big," Self said. "We didn't have the depth inside last year. This year we've got seven guys 6-8 or bigger. I'm excited because they are more athletic and can bring something different to the table."

Self's best team on the court has Heard at the point, Coley at shooting guard and the frontcourt of Kurtz, Ruffin and McDaniel. He'll likely start Williams next to Heard and shift Coley to a wing. He could also put Hill at shooting guard in place of Williams and be even more athletic.

If it can knock down the necessary open shots to keep defenses from collapsing on the frontcourt, Tulsa will be one of the toughest teams to defend. Look for the Golden Hurricane to push TCU and UNLV for the Mountain Division title and be on the bubble come NCAA Tournament time.

(A.K.)

UTEP

LOCATION .... El Paso, TX
CONFERENCE .... WAC (Mountain Division)
LAST SEASON .... 12-14 (.462)
CONFERENCE RECORD 3-11 (7th)
STARTERS LOST/RETURNING 1/4
NICKNAME .... Miners
COLORS .... Orange, White & Blue
HOMECOURT .... Don Haskins Center (12,222)
COACH .... Don Haskins (Oklahoma A&M '52)
RECORD AT SCHOOL .... 703-342 (37 yrs.)
CAREER RECORD .... 703-342 (37 yrs.)
ASSISTANTS .... G. Ray Johnson (Western New Mexico '85)
Luster Goodwin (Texas-El Paso '86)
TEAM WINS (last 5 yrs.) 18-20-12-13-12
RPI (last 5 yrs.) 101-69-174-99-148
1997-98 FINISH .... Did not qualify for conference tournament.

UTEP seems to have hit a rut. It has lasted three years, but it probably can't last forever.

It looks like a change is needed in recruiting. Don Haskins is still getting the most of his players, but his talent appears to be lacking.

The Miners haven't won more than 13 games in any of the last four years. They haven't been to the NCAA Tournament since 1992, and it doesn't look like they'll return soon.

The Miners' recruiting pipeline to Chicago has dried up and they're not getting the type of NBA players like Tim Hardaway or Greg Foster—or even the all-WAC players like Prince Stewart, Eddie Rivera or George Banks.

The 16-team WAC has been in existence for two years and UTEP missed both tournaments. The Miners could easily miss a third.

"We're not as talented a team on the offensive end and that has to be better," Haskins said "We spent more days doing two-a-days last year and we still couldn't get the ball in the basket."

That won't change unless 6-8 senior **Sharif Fajardo** becomes a dominant player in the post. Fajardo (15.4 ppg, 7.4 rpg, 43 assists, 30 steals, 18 blocked shots) emerged as a low-post threat but still wasn't able to carry the team. He needs to this season, especially without the scoring guards Haskins usually possesses.

Fajardo, the fourth-leading returning scorer and sixth returning rebounder among WAC players, has a soft hook and can finish a play inside.

"Early in the year he made tremendous improvement," Haskins says of Fajardo. "He wasn't good at all the last seven games and that's when you've got to be good."

Where will the help come from? Probably not inside.

Brandon Wolfram, a 6-8 sophomore, and 6-8 sophomore **Louis Radford** have shown positive signs. Wolfram (6.8 ppg, 5.0 rpg, 13 blocked shots, .576 FG percentage) started 10 games. He scored 13 points in a 71-49 loss to Utah. Radford (2.8 ppg, 2.0 rpg) put in a lot of work on his game over the summer.

"Wolfram was our best shooter," Haskins says. "He didn't take bad shots. He's got a chance to be good in time, but he only played one year in high school. Louis will be a pleasant surprise because he's a heck of a defensive player. He doesn't take many shots."

Jon Bomba, a 6-11 senior center, has been bothered by nagging back injuries throughout his career. Bomba (1.3 ppg, 2.6 rpg) has to concentrate on rebounding and defense and work on his scoring in the post.

An unknown is 6-8 junior forward **Jose Escobedo** (2.4 ppg, 3.5 rpg), a former walkon who averaged 12 minutes as a sophomore. Escobedo hopes to get more playing time this year.

"Jose could shoot a better percentage," Haskins said. "We're hoping they all do. We can't win with the way we shot, no matter who we play. We couldn't score enough to get away from teams."

The backcourt offers more promise than the frontcourt, even with a three-point shooting percentage of .308 from last year. UTEP's overall shooting percentage was .411.

Alton Sanders, a 5-10 senior point guard, is back after gaining academic eligibility in the summer. Sanders (7.0 ppg, 2.5 rpg, 87 assists, 35 steals) needs to work on his shooting and needs to work on driving the lane.

William Smith, a 6-3 junior guard/forward, has a chance to be the slashing scorer the Miners had hoped for when they signed him. Smith (12.7 ppg, 4.2 rpg, 54 assists, 19 steals, 14 blocked shots) was the team's most versatile player last year and the only other double-figure scorer beside Fajardo.

"He's a 6-foot inside player but we're trying to play him at guard," Haskins said. "He's very poor defensively."

Rico Nelson (5 ppg, 1.2 rpg, 19 assists), a 6-1 junior guard, needs to be a more reliable playmaker when he subs for Sanders.

Haskins hopes the two newcomers can be impact players on the perimeter and give the Miners an offensive lift.

Winfred McRae is a 6-1 junior guard from Tallahassee (Fla.) Community College. McRae, who played at Redempton Christian Academy in Troy, N.Y., is a combination guard. He averaged 13 ppg and 9.0 apg in junior college and is the slasher the Miners needed.

Jarvis Mullahon, a 6-4 junior shooting guard from the College of Southern Idaho, has good range on his jump shot. Mullahon, from Navajo Pines HS in Crystal, N.M., could be one of the team's best shooters. He averaged 12.0 ppg at at College of Southern Idaho and 35.0 ppg at Navaho Pines.

adidas Blue Ribbon Analysis

BACKCOURT .... D BENCH/DEPTH C
FRONTCOURT .... C INTANGIBLES .... B

The Miners allowed almost 66 points per game last year. Their defense was the team's strength. They outrebounded teams by three rebounds per game.

1998-99 UTEP SCHEDULE

Nov.	13	New Mexico State
	21	TCU
	24	Jackson State
	28	@New Mexico State
Dec.	1	Texas-San Antonio
	5	@TCU
	12	Lubbock Christian
	14	Samford
	17	Texas Southern
	20	Florida International
	22	Arkansas-Little Rock
	28-29	#Sun Classic
Jan.	7	Hawaii
	9	San Diego State
	14	@Fresno State
	16	@San Jose State
	23	New Mexico
	28	Brigham Young
	30	Utah
Feb	4	@Hawaii
	6	@San Diego State
	11	Fresno State
	13	San Jose State
	20	@New Mexico
	25	@Utah
	27	@Brigham Young
Mar.	2-6	##WAC Tournament

@ Road Games
# El Paso, TX (vs. Washington State, first round; also Detroit and Grambling-)
Thomas & Mack Center, Las Vegas, NV

Their trouble was scoring. They averaged 64.2 ppg.

Don Haskins has always been a defensive-minded coach. Playing the Miners won't get any easier, but if they can't change their scoring habits—specifically improving on Jarvis Mullahon's shooting, Winfred McRae's slashing, William Smith's all-around game, and Sharif Fajardo's play in the post—then the Miners will be in for another long year.

"I didn't think we were that bad last year," Haskins says. "The problem was we couldn't score and the opposition was tremendous."

That won't change.

(A.K.)

WYOMING

LOCATION .... **Laramie, WY**
CONFERENCE .... **WAC (Mountain Division)**
LAST SEASON .... **19-9 (.679)**
CONFERENCE RECORD .... **9-5 (3rd)**
STARTERS LOST/RETURNING **3/2**
NICKNAME .... **Cowboys**
COLORS .... **Brown & Yellow**
HOMECOURT .... **Arena Auditorium (15,028)**
COACH .... **Steve McClain (Chadron State '84)**
RECORD AT SCHOOL .... **First Year**
CAREER RECORD .... **First Year**
ASSISTANTS .... **Steve Roccaforte (Lamar '89)**
Tony Barbee (Massachusetts '93)
John Adams (Iowa State '95)
TEAM WINS (last 5 yrs.) **14-13-14-12-19**
RPI (last 5 yrs.) .... **147-133-128-158—56**
1997-98 FINISH .... **Lost in first round of NIT.**

Walkons do count. They can get you a job if you treat them as equals. Just ask Wyoming athletic director Lee Moon. Or Steve McClain.

It wasn't the primary reason for McClain to be hired at Wyoming, but it didn't hurt that McClain had started a relationship with Moon's son, Lee, when the latter walked on at Texas Christian. McClain, an assistant to Billy Tubbs at the time, made sure he talked to Moon at the WAC Tournament in Las Vegas in March 1997.

Joby Wright was expected to be out as coach and Moon was in search of a replacement, albeit not publicly. McClain wanted to touch base with the Wyoming athletic director. He didn't get the job—at least right away.

It took a year before the two would talk again, but this time the subject was about McClain, not Moon's son.

When Larry Shyatt abruptly left Wyoming after one year to return to Clemson, Moon turned to one person—McClain—to repair the shambles from Shyatt's bitter departure.

"I was looking for someone with quality experience," Moon said. "I wanted someone who had been involved in building a Division I program from the ground up, and Steve certainly was involved in that at TCU. He has been a head coach, and won a national championship (at Hutchinson JC in Kansas). To win a national championship at the intercollegiate level is a tremendous accomplishment."

McClain's hiring culminated a wild week of events for McClain and Wyoming that didn't calm down until late August, when Moon and the school settled with Shyatt for $286,000. The school filed a suit against Shyatt for his breach of contract and was on the verge of filing an injunction from allowing him to coach at Clemson without paying part of his contract back to Wyoming. Shyatt had four years remaining on the deal.

Meanwhile, McClain had left TCU after last season and was hired as the top assistant to new coach Melvin Watkins at Texas A&M. That lasted a few weeks before Moon was on the phone.

"When Melvin got the A&M job, he approached me about coming there and after four years with Billy, I felt we had accomplished what we wanted to by putting TCU basketball on the national map," McClain said. "I wanted another challenge. But when the opportunity came to be a head coach, there was no doubt what I had to do. I had gotten to know Lee the year before at the WAC Tournament and we just kept up. The good thing for me is that I know this league."

And he knows how to coach uptempo basketball. Shyatt's departure left a bitter taste with Wyoming administration and McClain is unintentionally wiping away any reference to the Shyatt era with a dramatic switch in the style of play.

Wyoming was one of the most physical teams in the West last season, bruising its way to 19 wins, including victories over Utah and New Mexico at home. The defense was stingy but the offense often stunk.

McClain obviously doesn't want the defense to change, but he's looking at a completely different look offensively.

The Cowboys will run, hoping to make the 7,000-plus altitude a factor in Laramie. Whether they can sustain it to the level of TCU depends on the talent. The newcomers Shyatt's staff had recruited were better suited for an uptempo style than the previous lineup. But it will still take some time before Wyoming can be known for a high-octane offense. Benny Dees was able to pull it off for a few years in the early 1990s, but it didn't last. Wright and Shyatt never made pushing the basketball their objective.

"These kids were excited about playing that style when I got the job," McClain said. "They want to press and run. That's the way kids want to play today. We've improved ourselves athletically with the newcomers and they can play this style."

The one player who was caught in the middle of the coaching move was 6-7 junior forward **LeDarion Jones**, a Clemson transfer from Bartow (Fla). High School. Jones left Clemson to join Shyatt in Laramie, sat out the year and was burned when Shyatt returned to Clemson this spring.

Jones isn't bitter anymore and has welcomed the new staff. He knows he'll be the go-to player underneath. That's a role he coveted at Clemson as he envisioned himself an eventual replacement for Greg Buckner. He performed admirably, shooting .556 percent from the field in reserve duty in 41 games over two years with the Tigers.

"He'll be our guy in the post at either the three or four," McClain said.

Pasha Bains, a 6-4 freshman from Richmond Secondary School in Richmond, B.C., is probably suited more for McClain's style than Shyatt's. He averaged 38.4 points, 8.0 rebounds and 6.0 assists as a senior in leading his school to the British Columbia championship. He scored more than 40 points 10 times and more than 50 points three times. Wyoming beat out New Mexico and interest from Washington State and Stanford for him.

"He can stroke it and has big-time scoring ability," McClain said. Bains has been compared to Steve Nash, but only because they're both from the same area. Bains doesn't have the ballhandling skills Nash had, but may be a better shooter. He'll play either wing, which should be interchangeable in McClain's system.

If McClain wants to add another newcomer to the starting lineup, he could go with 6-9 freshman **Josh Davis** (Salem Academy/Salem, Ore.). Davis was a considered a top 100 player last year after averaging 20 points and 12 rebounds.

"He reminds me of a young Keith Van Horn," said McClain. "He can play on the perimeter at 6-9 but can go in the post and handle the ball well. He's got real good passing skills."

But he's not as deft with the ball as 5-10 freshman point guard **Chris McMillian** (Brea Olinda HS/Brea, Calif.). McClain has already compared McMillian to TCU point guard Prince Fowler. His quickness, penetration and scoring mentality make him a perfect fit to lead the change in the offense.

The all-newcomer starting five could be complete if McClain opts to go with 6-9 freshman **John Pettersson** (Lulea, Sweden) or 6-5 freshman swing guard **Jimmy White** (Western HS/Las Vegas, Nev.).

Pettersson averaged eight points and six rebounds, last season, but gives the Cowboys a finesse post player who can step out and hit the three-pointer while Jones handles the bruising inside. If McClain wants to go quicker, he can move White into the lineup and hope he comes close to matching his 20 points and nine rebounds in high school. It's not likely, but White does have a scorer's mentality, plays tenacious defense and can rebound well for his size, which will fit in better with this system.

McClain isn't forgetting about the returnees, but they all could be replaced. The Cowboys shot .418 percent overall last season and that was with Jeron Roberts and Gregg Sawyer, the starting backcourt that finished its eligibility after accounting for 33 of the team's 63 points per game.

Andy Young (4.9 ppg, 2.3 rpg, 2.1 apg, 26.0 minutes, .361 FG percentage, .321 three-PT percentage, .821 FT percentage), a 6-foot junior point guard, started all 28 games as a sophomore. He wasn't an offensive threat, but did get to the free-throw line often and was able to convert. He was the first line of defense in the Cowboys' stingy approach and he will be used in some form.

So, too, will 6-foot sophomore **Brett McFall** (3.4 ppg, 1.7 rpg, 1.1 apg, 12.9 minutes, .322 FG percentage, .276 three-PT percentage, .714 FT percentage), who played in 27 of 28 games as a reliable reserve. He didn't hurt the team, but didn't wow any opponent, either. The intriguing guard in the mix is 6-2 junior **Anthony Blakes**, who redshirted with a broken foot after playing in four games last season. He has the quickness over Young and could be in the lineup more with this system.

Justin French (6.1 ppg, 3.7 rpg, 1.5 apg, 27.1 minutes, .382 FG percentage, .280 three-PT percentage, .768 FT percentage), a 6-6 junior forward, started 27 of 28 games last season and was the perfect position player for Shyatt's system. He did what he was told, moved the basketball and got into the right spots for rebounds and screens. He'll still have a role, but his offensive limitations could keep out of the starting lineup.

Brad Mann (4.8 ppg, 1.4 rpg), a 6-6 senior forward, was the Cowboys' best three-point shooter by percentage (.442), but wasn't counted on to be more than a spot shooter off the bench. Don't expect that role to change. **Antone Lostetter** (2.7 ppg, 1.5 rpg), a 6-8 junior forward, got into 26 of 28 games but never was able to pick up his pace on the court. His slow game could get lost in this system.

The one returning player who could crack the lineup more under McClain is 6-8 sophomore **Ugo Udezue** (3.5 ppg, 4.2 rpg). He was a physical player in every game for the Cowboys and his offense is progressing. If he becomes a better rebounder, he could mimic the role by former TCU forward Dennis Davis, who was a rebounder by trade for the Horned Frogs last season.

"Ugo can give us production in the post," McClain said. "He can get us 10-12 rebounds a game. In our style he can score 14-16 because he'll get easy baskets."

1998-99 WYOMING SCHEDULE

Nov.	17	Denver
	23	@Nevada
	27	@Montana State
Dec.	3	Idaho State
	5	*Arizona
	9	Colorado
	12	@North Texas
	21	Alcorn State
	27-28	#Cowboy Shootout
	31	Dartmouth
Jan.	7	@Rice
	10	@Tulsa
	14	TCU
	16	SMU
	23	@Colorado State
	28	@UNLV
	30	@Air Force
Feb.	4	Tulsa
	6	Rice
	11	@TCU
	13	@SMU
	16	Texas-Pan American
	20	Colorado State
	25	Air Force
	27	UNLV
Mar.	2-6	##WAC Tournament

@ Road Games
* Phoenix, AZ
# Casper, WY (vs. Louisiana Tech, first round; also Wagner and Yale)
Thomas & Mack Center, Las Vegas, NV

adidas Blue Ribbon Analysis

BACKCOURT	**C+**	**BENCH/DEPTH**	**C+**
FRONTCOURT	**C**	**INTANGIBLES**	**C+**

Shyatt's legacy won't be the lawsuit, it will be his recruiting class. The Cowboys would have been on the verge of building a potential postseason team every year. It will still happen, but with a different look.

However, it won't be this season. The Cowboys won't be able to move past UNLV, Tulsa, TCU and SMU, but could be a strong fifth and pull off an upset or two during the season and in the WAC tournament.

Wyoming will be one of the most interesting teams to watch as it tries to play uptempo at the highest altitude in the nation. The newcomers are the key with Jones and Bains candidates for all-league honors. If McClain can mesh this group early enough through a nonconference schedule that has only one certain loss (at Arizona), then look out for the Cowboys to be a spoiler during the WAC race. They'll struggle on the road, but expect them to pull off a few upsets, just as they did last year.

(A.K.)

DENVER

LOCATION .... **Denver, CO**
CONFERENCE .... **Independent**
LAST SEASON .... **7-20 (.259)**
CONFERENCE RECORD .... **N/A**
STARTERS LOST/RETURNING **2/3**
NICKNAME .... **Pioneers**
COLORS .... **Crimson & Gold**
HOMECOURT .... **Denver Fieldhouse (1,800)**
COACH .... **Marty Fletcher (Maryland '73)**
RECORD AT SCHOOL .... **7-20 (1 yr.)**
CAREER RECORD .... **220-251 (16 yrs.)**
ASSISTANTS .... **Todd Rinehart (Bowling Green '90)**
Byron Jones (Central Oklahoma '93)
Anthony Barone (Texas A&M '94)
TEAM WINS (last 5 yrs.) **17-18-22-14-7**
RPI (last 5 yrs.) .... **N/A**
1997-98 FINISH .... **Lost in final regular season game.**

You need not have passed geography back in grammar school to know that Denver—or any part of the Rocky Mountains, for that matter—is not a part of the Sun Belt.

Not so fast, proclaims University of Denver coach Marty Fletcher. Denver has 300 days of sunshine a year. Then it's fair to make the not-so-logical leap that Denver is a natural to become the newest member of the Sun Belt Conference. Not bad for a program that jumps from NCAA Division II status for a return run with the Division I big boys after more than a 20-year hiatus.

The connection and eventual alignment between Denver and the Sun Belt Conference was fostered by Fletcher, who took over the Pioneers' program after spending 11 seasons as head coach of Sun Belt Conference member Southwestern Louisiana. It was Fletcher's relationship with Sun Belt Commissioner Craig Thompson that not only began discussions of the unlikely partnership, but helped influence Denver administrators and fans that joining the mid-major conference was a great place to start building a program.

"My relationship with Craig had an impact, sure," Fletcher said. "But make no mistake: This was a decision ultimately made by our chancellor (Daniel Ritchie) and the university.

"And we're delighted. Next year, in our second season of Division I, we'll have a chance to compete in the conference tournament and earn a berth in the NCAA Tournament."

Also part of the deal is Denver's petitioning the NCAA to waive its standard eight-year probation period for new members. "The purpose of the rule is so people just won't throw a conference together to get the NCAA berth and money," Fletcher said. "The fact that we were joining the Sun Belt was a factor in the NCAA waiving the rule."

Another factor, Fletcher contends, was Denver's prior status in NCAA in basketball, as well as current Division I status in such other sports as gymnastics and hockey.

The overriding factor, however, might have been the construction of Denver's new arena—the Daniel L. Ritchie Center, which will open next season and seat 7,200. And Fletcher's reputation as a successful coach didn't hurt, either. While at Southwestern Louisiana, the Ragin' Cajuns averaged 18 wins per season and had four 20-win seasons, including a 21-11 record in 1991-92 that earned the team an NCAA Tournament berth and Fletcher the league coach-of-the-year honor.

Before USL, Fletcher took a Virginia Military Institute program that went 2-25 in his first season in 1992-83 to 16-14 in just his third season. He was chosen coach of the year in the Southern Conference for that effort.

"I've always felt I was a program-builder," said Fletcher, 47. "Denver afforded me an opportunity to certainly build a program from the ground level up. We have accomplished a lot in a short period of time, especially joining a conference with a great basketball tradition like the Sun Belt."

Another marker Fletcher thinks is significant is Denver's schedule, which produced a 7-20 record last season but the program's first win over a Division I opponent—Loyola-Chicago—in more than 20 years. On the agenda this year are road trips to Colorado, Colorado State, Brigham Young and Wyoming, as well as home-and-home duels with future Sun Belt opponents New Orleans, Arkansas State and Arkansas-Little Rock.

"I build for the long term," Fletcher said. "If I was concerned originally with the wins and losses, I would have not put together the kind of schedule we're going to play the next two years. I think this is the best way to do it."

Scheduling is one thing; competitiveness is another. And just how far and how fast the Pioneers can come is anybody's guess—including Fletcher. "It's difficult to say how long it will take," Fletcher said of the building process. "I do know that I wanted to get the best schedule I could to open our building. We've done that.

"Now, I want to recruit the best student-athletes available who can handle Denver's strong academics and compete on the Division I level."

In as much, the Pioneers will feature six new recruits, but just two junior college signees—teammates **Ty Church**, a 5-10 junior guard, and **Brandt Wilcox**, a 6-8 junior center, from Ricks College in Rexburg, Idaho. Both have completed Mormon missions and are older than their teammates. Both will play immediately.

After playing at Utah as a freshman out of Salt Lake City, Church transferred to Ricks College, where he led his team to a 28-10 record and an eighth-place finish in the national tournament. Church averaged 11 points and seven assists last season. He shot 47 percent from behind the three-point line.

Last season, Wilcox averaged 10 points and 9.4 rebounds—tops in the Scenic West Athletic Conference. His 20 points and eight rebounds lifted Ricks College past Dixie College and into the national junior college tournament.

"In Ty and Brandt, we have added two players who have competed at the highest level of competition," Fletcher said. "These are two guys we think can play."

Although Church is in the fold, 5-7 senior **Norman Daniels** (106 assists and 36 steals, both team highs), also a former junior college player, is the incumbent at point guard. He is the only returning Pioneer to start every game last season.

Whoever the point guard is, he will be flanked in the backcourt by the team's top scorer last season—6-1 senior guard **Russell Martin** (16.3 ppg), who played a team-high 999 minutes and only missed an average of three minutes a game.

"He's a good athlete who jumps well. He is a solid Division I player," Fletcher said of Martin. "Russell has done a good job for us."

Also back at power forward is 6-8 senior **Eric Dow** (10.6 ppg), who led the team in rebounding (7.3) and field-goal percentage (.526). Competing for the post position will be 6-11 senior **Michael Nachreiner**, who started three games last season.

Backing up at shooting guard again will be 6-2 senior **Mike Deatly** (2.1 ppg, 0.4 rpg). Also providing depth again in the backcourt will be a pair of sophomores—6-3 **Matt Paul** (6.2 ppg, 23 steals), who played 15.8 minutes per game; and 6-3 **Arthur Ireland** (4.4 ppg), who played 12.6 minutes.

Fletcher signed four freshmen during the early signing period. Of the quartet, 6-6 forward **Wahhab Carter** will probably see the most action the soonest. Carter was considered Oklahoma's top prospect by many publications. But because he was also a top football prospect at El Reno High School, a lot of the top hoops programs in the area backed off. Carter wanted to play basketball, though, and proved he could by being chosen the Class 5-A state tournament most valuable player after guiding El Reno to the championship game and a 24-4 record. He was twice chosen all-state, all-region and all-district and was picked as the state's player of the year by *USA Today*, *Hoop Scoop* and *Midwest Basketball Services*.

Carter was also included in the Oklahoma "Super 5" team. As a senior, Carter averaged 19 points, eight rebounds and three blocked shots.

"He's my kind of player," Fletcher said. "He can run the floor and shoot the basketball. But we'll probably used him at power forward."

Also in the incoming freshman class is 6-8, 240-pound forward/center **Aaron Gottschalk**, 5-10 guard **Phillip Heath** and 5-10 guard **Tyrone Turner**. Gottschalk averaged 15 points and nine rebounds for Hays (Kan.) High School, where he was all-county and all-conference twice and second-team all-state as a senior.

Heath helped guide Ranier Beach (Wash.) High to a 27-2 record and the Class AAA state championship. His team was later voted the sixth-best team on the West Coast by *USA Today*. A floor leader and defensive specialist, Heath averaged 13 points, six rebounds and four assists as a senior.

Turner is a local product from Denver's George Washington High School, where he was chosen all-city and second-team all-state after averaging 18 points, seven assists and three steals per game last season. He was second in the state in assists.

"What we like about all of the freshmen is that they are great students and wonderful young people," Fletcher said of his freshman class. "It's a great group to start building a program with."

1998-99 DENVER SCHEDULE

Nov.	14	@Colorado
	17	@Wyoming
	21	Oral Roberts
	28	Arkansas State
Dec.	1	@Brigham Young
	5	@Wright State
	7	@Loyola College
	12	Wright State
	15	@New Orleans
	17	@Arkansas State
	20	@Colorado State
	28	Dartmouth
Jan.	2	Manhattan
	4	New Orleans
	6	@Air Force
	11	@Southern Utah
	19	@Oral Roberts
	23	@Dartmouth
	25	@Yale
	30	@Texas-Pan American
Feb.	2	Loyola College
	8	@Arkansas-Little Rock
	10	Missouri-Kansas City
	13	Southern Utah
	16	Air Force
	18	Texas-Pan American
	20	Arkansas-Little Rock

@ Road Games

adidas Blue Ribbon Analysis

BACKCOURT .... **C** **BENCH/DEPTH** .... **D+**
FRONTCOURT .... **D+** **INTANGIBLES** .... **D+**

The long uphill fight to build a competitive Division I program has begun at Denver under Marty Fletcher, who was used to playing solid basketball at Southwestern Louisiana.

"That seems like a long time ago," he now reflects upon his days at USL, which ended dubiously two years ago. Obviously, it will be different going back there to play (in Sun Belt) games."

But that's the least of Fletcher's concerns these days. Denver is a long way from competing in a solid mid-major conference, where the emphasis on athleticism is paramount. Still, Fletcher is establishing a solid foundation—from recruiting to scheduling to facilities—that could put Denver on the fast track in the league.

Just how long it will take for the Pioneers to become competitive is another story. If Fletcher has a strength, it's identifying and luring talent that slips through the cracks from the major programs. He's not afraid to take chances, but he won't have the luxury of taking marginal students as in the past while building a program at Denver.

(G.P.)

adidas Blue Ribbon Analysis
GRADING SYSTEM

- A+ equal to very best in country—Final Four-caliber unit
- A among the best in the land—worthy of deep NCAA run
- B+ talented, versatile and experienced—NCAA-NIT ability
- B solid and productive winners—league and post-season contenders
- C+ average to above-average—may contend in a weaker league
- C average to mediocre—second division in a strong league
- D+ below average, inconsistent—second division in a weaker league
- D well below average—losing season virtually certain
- F non-Division I ability—an underdog every night

TEXAS-PAN AMERICAN

LOCATION .... **Edinburg, TX**
CONFERENCE .... **Independent**
LAST SEASON .... **3-24 (.111)**
CONFERENCE RECORD .... **3-15 (10th-Sun Belt)**
STARTERS LOST/RETURNING **2/3**
NICKNAME .... **Broncs**
COLORS .... **Green & White**
HOMECOURT .... **UTPA Fieldhouse (5,000)**
COACH .... **Delray Brooks (Providence '88)**
RECORD AT SCHOOL .... **3-24 (1 yr.)**
CAREER RECORD .... **3-24 (1 yr.)**
ASSISTANTS .... **George Morgan (Valparaiso '79)**
Patrick Harrington (Rollins '86)
Jason Patterson (Brigham Young '95)
TEAM WINS (last 5 yrs.) **20-8-9-3-3**
RPI (last 5 yrs.) **142-126-239-303-258**
1997-98 FINISH .... **Lost in conference first round.**

Don't look for Delray Brooks to head for the quick fix to resurrect Texas-Pan American basketball—which makes the second-year Broncs coach unique to the program.

After all, the ailing team, which departs the Sun Belt Conference to compete independently this season, has not been anywhere near the upper echelon of the college game.

Sure, there has been success in the past for the Broncs. Their No. 126 RPI that followed a 20-win season four years ago might be considered the program's high point.

But that was followed by several unsettling dealings with the NCAA and a subsequent coaching change. Enter Brooks, the former Providence star who worked under former Kentucky and current Boston Celtics coach Rick Pitino.

Success on the court was always understood by Brooks. And now he understands that turning the program around won't happen overnight. The progress will be measured in small steps.

The first marker, however, could well be the first full recruiting class lured by Brooks to Texas-Pan American. You won't find a junior-college transfer in the bunch. All seven are freshmen in a recruiting class that was tabbed by some publications of being top-50 caliber.

"I have never been a big proponent of going the junior-college route, although I am not completely against junior college players," said Brooks, who was disappointed but undeterred with his coaching debut last season "It's just that the good juco players are going to the big-time schools, and the ones that we would get, by the time they learn our system and get acclimated to Division I, they're leaving."

Instead, Brooks will build the Texas-Pan American program with freshmen.

The four returning lettermen won't be forgotten, but those departing will not be missed a great deal, either.

"The kids that I brought in will absolutely destroy the kids that we lost," Brooks said. "We will be a lot better this year than last year, although we'll be depending upon a lot of unproven and young talent."

The biggest recruiting coup in the incoming class was the signing of 6-7 power forward **Larry Gibbs**, a bruiser who has added bulk over the summer. The New York native was a highly-touted recruit from Cheshire Academy in Connecticut. Gibbs, one of five Division I players at Cheshire Academy, averaged 14.5 points and 8.5 rebounds.

"That was a great get for us," Brooks said. "Larry is as talented for a guy his size that you will find. He's going to be around 6-8 and 235 pounds, but he can put it on the floor. He has great moves and is an extremely good passer. He has unlimited potential."

The other marquee recruit was 6-7 forward **Kirby Lemons** of Midland (Texas) HS, the state's Class 5A state champion. Lemons, however, will be academically ineligible for the first semester, but could become eligible for the second semester.

Lemons was recruited by New Mexico and Arizona State, among other high-profile programs. He averaged 26 points and 12 rebounds as a senior, earning all-state honors for the second straight year, and led Midland to a 34-2 record.

"I'm very excited about having Kirby in our program," Brooks said. "He's extremely talented and comes from a program with a great winning tradition."

A native of Gary, Ind., Brooks is no stranger to basketball in the Chicago area, and he returned to his roots on the recruiting trail and landed two standouts: 6-4 combo guard **Watra Banks** of Chicago Julian HS, and 6-6 swingman **Brucal Green** of Hillside (Ill.) Proviso West HS.

Banks is used to playing at the top level, considering Chicago Julian was ranked among the top high school teams in the country last season. He was chosen all-city after averaging 16 points, five rebounds and four assists and shooting 40 percent from three-point range.

Banks was invited to the prestigious adidas ABCD camp, where he ranked among the top seniors. The lightning-quick athlete is expected to be among the team's leading scorers.

"Watra is an athletic player who will really excel in our pressing, up-tempo style," Brooks said. "He's got real good court savvy. I like his ability to create."

Green was the most valuable player of Chicago's West Suburban Conference after averaging 15.2 points and 7.6 rebounds for Proviso HS.

"Brucal is an athletic player who will create matchup problems for folks," Brooks said. "He will benefit from our style of play. I like the way he rebounds and scores inside, but also his ability to handle the ball on the perimeter."

Another recruit who will see early action is 6-1 point guard **Charles Baker**, a three-year starter at Houston's Westbury Christian HS, which won four straight Texas private school state championships.

Baker averaged 14 points and 6.8 rebounds, and he isn't afraid to go inside and mix it up in the post. The hard-nosed Baker will fit in nicely with the defensive demands of a point guard under Brooks.

"Charles is a winner," Brooks said. "I like the fact that he comes from a winning program and that he has worked so hard on his game. He's got a great basketball body and is very athletic."

Brooks also signed Baker's teammate, 6-7 forward **George Simpkins**. He led Westbury in scoring (20.6), rebounding (7.6) and blocked shots (78) while shooting 64 percent from the field.

"George has a knack for being around the basketball," Brooks said. "He can score inside as well as from the perimeter. He rebounds and passes the ball well. He knows how to play the game."

Another key member of the incoming class will be 6-9 center **Dewayne Watson**, who helped East St. Louis (Ill.) HS to a 19-5 record by averaging 10 points and 11 rebounds. He will provide immediate help in the post.

"Dwayne is a very strong rebounder," Brooks said. "He will be asked to make his presence felt inside. I like his basketball frame and his upside potential."

While all seven freshmen will push for playing time and probably end up starting much of the time, the Broncs return four lettermen to go with two transfers.

The team's leading returning scorer and rebounder is 6-5 small forward **Larry Jackson** (17.3 ppg, 5.7 rpg), also a product of the Chicago area out of Farragut Academy.

Texas-Pan American's only senior is 5-10 point guard **Lalo Rios** (9.2 ppg, 3.5 rpg), who led the Sun Belt last season with 3.2 steals per game. He also ranked third in the league with 4.7 assists per game.

Two 6-9 inside players, junior **Matt Palmquist** (6.7 ppg, 3.5 rpg) and **Micah McAdams** (2.3 ppg, 2.3 rpg), return to provide muscle in the frontcourt.

1998-99 TEXAS-PAN AMERICAN SCHEDULE

Nov.	13	@Rice
	16	@LSU
	21	@Providence
	23	Pittsburgh
	25	Colorado State
	28	Illinois
Dec.	4-5	#Pizza Hut Classic
	8	@New Mexico
	12	@DePaul
	17	@Texas Tech
	22	Louisiana Tech
	28	Gonzaga
	30	Baylor
Jan.	2	@Southern Methodist
	4	Arkansas-Little Rock
	14	Southwestern Louisiana
	19	@Arkansas-Little Rock
	23	@Northwestern
	25	@South Alabama
	30	Denver
Feb.	1	@Louisiana Tech
	11	South Alabama
	16	@Wyoming
	18	@Denver
	22	@Southwestern Louisiana
	27	Indiana/Purdue-Indianapolis

@ Road Games
# Springfield, MO (vs. Louisiana Tech, first round; also Southwest Missouri State and Texas Southern)

Palmquist started 25 games last season and shot .563 from the field (71-126). He led the team with 13 blocked shots. McAdams played in 23 games, starting two.

Two sophomore transfers, 6-4 swingman **John Braxton** from Houston and shooting guard **Brian Merriweather** of Cumberland College, will vye for starting jobs after sitting out last season and practicing with the Broncs.

adidas Blue Ribbon Analysis

BACKCOURT .... **D** **BENCH/DEPTH** .... **D**
FRONTCOURT .... **D** **INTANGIBLES** .... **D**

It was a tough coaching debut for Delray Brooks, who endured the season knowing better times were ahead.

In the cellar of the Sun Belt Conference, the program must show considerable improvement if talks with potential league membership in the Southland or Trans-America conferences could come to fruition.

"It depends on how you look at the situation," Brooks said of competing as an independent. "If you're in a conference, you have a chance to go to the NCAA Tournament, but let's be realistic, only one (team) is going to go most years anyway. But what a conference does is allow you to have some slip-ups during the season and still put it together at the end of the season."

For now, Brooks is more concerned with getting the program headed in the right direction, and that not only means bringing in better talent—which he has done—but also working on his players from the neck up.

"The thing that disappointed me the most last year wasn't the success of wins and losses," he said. "It was the caliber of players that I was coaching from an effort standpoint. Effort is part of talent and our players just didn't work hard at times last year."

Brooks won't stand for it, especially now that at least seven of the players on the team are his recruits. They should know what to expect.

"Sometimes it is going to sound like a broken record," Brooks said. "But I am going to continue to point to things that emphasize our philosophy of hard work. We're not going to out-talent teams. Not yet, anyway. But there is no excuse for not outworking them."

(G.P.)

THE HIGH SCHOOLS

BEN WILSON HIGH SCHOOL TOP 44

by Brick Oettinger, PREP STARS RECRUITER'S HANDBOOK

BEN WILSON

Ben Wilson was *Blue Ribbon*'s 1984-85 Co-High School Player of the Year. As a junior he led Chicago Simeon High School to the Illinois state title. In the summer of '84 he was chosen the top player at the Nike/ABCD Camp of Princeton, N.J. and entered his senior year generally regarded as the top high school senior in the country. Just a few days before the first game of his senior year, Wilson was shot within a block of Simeon's campus. He died in a Chicago hospital less than a day later.

Anyone who saw Wilson play knows he would have gone on to become one of the all-time greats to ever come out of Chicago. His memory is yet another reminder of the toll random, senseless violence has taken on us all. It is in the memory of Ben Wilson that the *adidas Blue Ribbon College Basketball Yearbook* again dedicates its High School Top 44.

Name	Height	Class	High School	Hometown & State
FIRST TEAM				
Casey Sanders	6-11	Senior	Tampa Prep	Tampa, FL
Donnell Harvey	6-8	Senior	Randolph-Clay	Cuthbert, GA
Jason Kapono	6-8	Senior	Artesia	Lakewood, CA
Keith Bogans	6-5	Senior	DeMatha	Hyattsville, MD
Dajuan Wagner	6-1	Sophomore	Camden	Camden, NJ
SECOND TEAM				
Marvin Stone	6-11	Senior	Grissom	Huntsville, AL
Jason Parker	6-8	Senior	West Charlotte	Charlotte, NC
Brian Cook	6-10	Senior	Lincoln Community	Lincoln, IL
DeShawn Stevenson	6-5	Junior	Washington Union	Fresno, CA
Brett Nelson	6-3	Senior	St. Albans	St. Albans, WV
THIRD TEAM				
Samuel Dalembert	6-11	Senior	St. Patrick's	Elizabeth, NJ
Alton Ford	6-9	Junior	Milby	Houston, TX
DerMarr Johnson	6-9	Prep	Maine Central Institute	Pittsfield, ME
Kareem Rush	6-6	Senior	Pembroke Hill	Kansas City, MO
Jason Williams	6-2	Senior	St. Joseph's	Metuchen, NJ
OTHER TOP 44 MEMBERS				
Jonathan Bender	6-11	Senior	Picayune	Picayune, MS
Ronald Blackshear	6-4	Prep	Hargrave Military Academy	Chatham, VA
Steven Blake	6-3	Senior	Miami Senior	Miami, FL
LaVell Blanchard	6-7	Senior	Pioneer	Ann Arbor, MI
Matt Bonner	6-9	Senior	Concord	Concord, NH
Carlos Boozer	6-9	Senior	Juneau Douglas	Juneau, AK
Nick Collison	6-9	Senior	Iowa Falls	Iowa Falls, IA
Mike Dunleavy	6-7	Senior	Jesuit	Portland, OR
Chuck Eidson	6-8	Senior	Pinewood Prep	Summerville, SC
Joe Forte	6-4	Senior	DeMatha	Hyattsville, MD
Kevin Gaines	6-3	Senior	Clark	Las Vegas, NV
Jason Gardner	5-11	Senior	North Central	Indianapolis, IN
Andrew Gooden	6-9	Senior	El Cerrito	El Cerrito, CA
Rod Grizzard	6-7	Senior	Central Park Christian	Birmingham, AL
Casey Jacobsen	6-6	Senior	Glendora	Glendora, CA
Majestic Mapp	6-1	Senior	St. Raymond's	Bronx, NY
Josh Moore	7-0	Senior	St. Anthony's	Jersey City, NJ ??
Derrick Payne	6-6	Senior	Mt. Zion Christian	Durham, NC
Jason Richardson	6-6	Senior	Arthur Hill	Saginaw, MI
Tony Robertson	6-3	Senior	St. Andrew's	Barrington, RI
Kenny Satterfield	6-2	Senior	Rice	Manhattan, NY
Imari Sawyer	6-1	Junior	Martin Luther King	Chicago, IL
Leon Smith	6-10	Senior	Martin Luther King	Chicago, IL
Marcus Taylor	6-3	Junior	Waverly	Lansing, MI
Brian Wethers	6-5	Senior	Murrieta Valley	Murrieta, CA
Damien Wilkins	6-6	Senior	Newport School	Kensington, MD ??
Marshall Williams	6-5	Senior	Vincent	Milwaukee, WI
Wesley Wilson	6-11	Prep	Maine Central Institute *or* Winchendon School	Pittsfield, ME Winchendon, MA
Doug Wrenn	6-7	Prep	Milford Academy	Milford, CT

1998-99 adidas Blue Ribbon
100 MORE STARS OF THE FUTURE

Name	Ht	Cl	City & State/High School
Carlton Aaron	6-9	Sr	Chesapeake, VA/Atlantic Shores Christian
Leland Anderson	6-8	Sr	Attleboro, MA
Nick Anderson	6-7	Jr	Baton Rouge, LA/Southern Lab
Gilbert Arenas	6-4	Sr	Van Nuys, CA/Grant
Carl Baker	6-8	Sr	Wheatley, AR/Palestine-Wheatley
George Baker	6-3	Sr	Lexington, KY/Dunbar
Julius Barnes	6-1	Sr	Rowland Heights, CA/Rowland
Lubos Barton	6-7	Sr	Mouth of Wilson, VA/Oak Hill
Mike Bauer	6-8	Sr	Hastings, MN
Todd Billet	6-0	Sr	Lincroft, NJ/Christian Brothers
Tony Bobbitt	6-4	Sr	Daytona Beach, FL/Mainland
Curtis Borchardt	6-10	Sr	Redmond, WA/Eastlake
Jamie Brewer	6-3	Sr	East Point, GA/Tri-Cities
Greg Brittian	6-5	Sr	Mt. Dora, FL
Andre Brown	6-9	Jr	Chicago, IL/Leo
Taliek Brown	5-11	Jr	Astoria, NY/St. John's Prep
Cardell Butler	6-4	Sr	San Mateo, CA
Caron Butler	6-6	Sr	Racine, WI/Washington Park
Cameron Carr	6-7	Sr	West Linn, OR
Matt Carroll	6-6	Sr	Horsham, PA/Hatboro-Horsham
Rashaad Carruth	6-3	So	Decatur, GA/Cathedral Academy
Tyson Chandler	7-0	So	Compton, CA/Dominguez
Scott Clark	6-4	Pr	Winchendon, MA/Winchendon School
Omar Cook	6-1	Jr	Middle Village, NY/Christ the King
Clifford Crawford	6-3	Sr	Winston-Salem, NC/Parkland
T.J. Cummings	6-8	Jr	Homewood, IL/Homewood-Flossmoor
Eddy Curry	6-10	So	South Holland, IL/Thornwood
Marquis Daniels	6-7	Sr	Durham, NC/Mt. Zion Christian
Brent Darby	6-0	Sr	River Rouge, MI
Jemel Davila	6-4	Jr	Miami, FL/Miami Senior
Erwin Dudley	6-8	Sr	Uniontown, AL/R.C. Hatch
Chris Duhon	6-1	Jr	Slidell, LA/Salmen
Ebi Ere	6-5	Sr	Tulsa, OK/McLain
Antonio Falu	6-4	Sr	Houston, TX/Waltrip
Desmond Farmer	6-4	Jr	Flint, MI/Northwestern
Amoury Fernandez	6-9	So	Lakewood, CA/Artesia
Courtland Freeman	6-9	Sr	Socastee, SC
Reese Gaines	6-4	Sr	Madison, WI/West
Eddie Griffin	6-8	Jr	Philadelphia, PA/Roman Catholic
Gavin Groninger	6-5	Sr	Plainfield, IN
Justin Hamilton	6-4	Sr	Sarasota, FL/Booker
Jerome Harper	6-5	Jr	Columbia, SC/Keenan
Vincent Hart	6-7	Sr	Gary, IN/Roosevelt
Scott Hazelton	6-7	Jr	Lawrence, MA/Central Catholic
Ray Henderson	6-9	Sr	Charlotte, NC/East Mecklenburg
Jon Higgins	6-3	Sr	Shaker Heights, OH
Myron Hodge	6-7	Jr	Evansville, IN/Bosse
Tahj Holden	6-9	Sr	Little Silver, NJ/Red Bank
Nick Horvath	6-10	Sr	Arden Hills, MN/Mounds View
Jerrance Howard	6-1	Sr	Peoria, IL/Central
Josh Howard	6-7	Pr	Chatham, VA/Hargrave Military
Steve Hunter	6-11	Sr	Durham, NC/Mt. Zion Christian
Jared Jeffries	6-9	Jr	Bloomington, IN/North
Ben Johnson	6-3	Sr	Minneapolis, MN/DeLaSalle
Joe Johnson	6-7	Sr	Little Rock, AR/Central
Shawnson Johnson	6-9	Sr	Shreveport, LA/Green Oaks
Zachery Johnson	6-9	Sr	Shreveport, LA/Woodlawn
Donnell Knight	6-7	Sr	Phoenix, AZ/St. Mary's
Antonio Latimer	6-9	Pr	Winchendon, MA/Winchendon School ??
Kenneth Lawrence	6-1	Sr	North Little Rock, AR/West
George Leach	6-11	Sr	Charlotte, NC/Olympic
Reo Logan	6-10	Jr	Country Club Hills, IL/Hillcrest
Tim Lyles	6-0	Sr	Durham, NC/Mt. Zion Christian
Tito Maddox	6-4	Sr	Compton, CA
Kei Madison	6-8	Pr	New Hampton, NH/New Hampton School
Roger Mason	6-4	Sr	Wheaton, MD/Good Counsel
Darius Miles	6-8	Jr	East St. Louis, IL/Lincoln
Cornelius Mitchell	6-0	So	Augusta, GA/Josey
Jamario Moon	6-7	Sr	Coosa, AL/Central ??
Gregory Morton	6-7	Sr	Bronx, NY/St. Raymond's
Jeffrey Newton	6-9	Sr	Atlanta, GA/Benjamin E. Mays
Johnathan Oden	6-8	Sr	Scottsdale, AZ/Carl Hayden *or* St. Louis, MO/Cardinal Ritter
Jerrell Parker	6-4	Sr	Chicago, IL/St. Francis DeSales
Hollis Price	6-1	Sr	New Orleans, LA/St. Augustine
Zach Randolph	6-9	Jr	Marion, IN
Justin Reed	6-7	Jr	Jackson, MS/Provine
Chip Richmond	6-10	Sr	Memphis, TN/Booker T. Washington
Larry Satchell	6-8	Sr	Waco, TX
Shane Schilling	6-6	Sr	Excelsior, MN/Minnetonka
Andre Scott	6-10	Jr	Hyattsville, MD/DeMatha
Scooter Sherrill	6-3	Jr	Mt. Ulla, NC/West Rowan
Demetrius Smith	6-4	Jr	LaGrange, GA/Calloway
John Stewart	7-0	Sr	Indianapolis, IN/Lawrence North
Andrew Sullivan	6-7	Sr	Richland, NJ/St. Augustine
Julian Swartz	6-6	Sr	Waukesha, WI/South
Kelvin Torbert	6-4	So	Flint, MI/Northwestern
Harris Walker	6-1	Pr	Chatham, VA/Hargrave Military
Kenny Walker	6-9	Sr	Jacksonville, FL/Wolfson
Donnie Wallace	6-9	Sr	Wichita, KS/Goddard
Travis Watson	6-7	Sr	Mouth of Wilson, VA/Oak Hill
Robert Whaley	6-9	So	Benton Harbor, MI
Luke Whitehead	6-6	Jr	San Francisco, CA/St. Ignatius
Chris Wilcox	6-8	Jr	Whiteville, NC
DeShaun Williams	6-3	Sr	Paterson, NJ/Paterson Catholic
Ezra Williams	6-4	Sr	Marietta, GA
George Williams	6-8	Sr	Missouri City, TX/Elkins
Brian Woodward	6-3	Sr	Bayside, NY/Cardozo
Glen Worley	6-7	Jr	Iowa City, IA/West
Ricky Wright	6-7	Sr	East Chicago, IN/Central
Andrew Zahn	6-10	Jr	Redondo Beach, CA/Redondo Union

adidas Blue Ribbon high school material provided by PREP STARS RECRUITER'S HANDBOOK
and the ACC AREA SPORTS JOURNAL • P.O. Box 4323 • Chapel Hill, NC • 27515-4323
For subscription information, call (800) 447-7667 or (919) 967-7789. Also access the *Recruiter's Handbook* online at "www.prepstars.com".
Read Brick Oettinger online at www.prepstars.com and also at The Sporting News website. Many thanks to my astute young colleague at the *Prep Stars Recruiter's Handbook* and the *ACC Area Sports Journal*, Dave Telep, for his invaluable insights and suggestions.

1998-99 adidas Blue Ribbon

HONORABLE MENTION HIGH SCHOOL ALL-AMERICA TEAM

Compiled by David Benezra and Mark Mayemura, *Recruiting USA*

Name	Ht	Cl	City/High School
ALABAMA			
Mario Alston	6-7	Jr	York, AL/Sumpter County
Chris Brock	6-7	Jr	Thomasville, AL
Michael Christian	6-2	Sr	Birmingham, AL/West End
Rodney Clark	6-3	Sr	Mobile, AL/LeFlore
Adrian Davidson	6-5	Jr	Huntsville, AL/Butler
Jonathan Deveridge	6-3	Sr	Troy, AL/Charles Henderson
Michael Draper	5-11	Sr	Huntsville, AL/Butler
Trey Ferguson	6-5	Sr	Hoover, AL
Keith Gamble	6-4	Sr	Mobile, AL/LeFlore
Chris Jones	6-3	Sr	Bessemer, AL/Academy
Danny L. Jones	6-6	Sr	Birmingham, AL/Carver
Greg Jones	6-5	Sr	Phenix City, AL/Central
Carl Landry	6-1	Jr	Huntsville, AL/Johnson
Jamario Moon	6-7	Sr	Rockford, AL/Coosa Central
Wesley Rimes	6-3	Sr	Hoover, AL
Muhammad Sanders	6-7	Sr	Florence, AL/Bradshaw
Lloyd Savage	6-0	Sr	Birmingham, AL/Shades Valley
Marcus Snow	6-7	Sr	Selma, AL/Southside
Emmitt Thomas	6-5	Jr	Birmingham, AL/John Carroll
Gerald Wallace	6-7	Jr	Childersburg, AL
Chris White	6-5	So	Huntsville, AL/Grissom
Henry Williams	6-6	Sr	Mobile, AL/LeFlore
Derrick Underwood	6-6	Sr	Boaz, AL
ALASKA			
Howard Bellamy	6-2	Sr	Anchorage, AK/East
Clarence Cole	6-5	Sr	Anchorage, AK/Bartlett
John Coon	6-0	Sr	Colony, AK
Doug Lamb	6-1	Sr	Anchorage, AK/East
Garland Perry	6-4	Sr	Anchorage, AK/Bartlett
ARIZONA			
Justin Adams	6-5	Sr	Phoenix, AZ/Brophy Prep
Adrian Aguayo	6-7	Sr	Phoenix, AZ/Mountain Point
Jason Blair	6-7	Sr	Phoenix, AZ/Shadow Mountain
Nathan Bloom	7-0	Sr	Mesa, AZ/Westwood
Brett Cox	6-0	Sr	Mesa, AZ/Mountain View
Prileu Davis	6-2	Jr	Phoenix, AZ/Moon Valley
Jason Dickens	6-6	Sr	Tucson, AZ/Salpointe Catholic
Pat Donaher	6-9	Sr	Phoenix, AZ/Camelback
Jason Fontenet	5'8	So	Phoenix, AZ/St. Mary
Robbie Green	5'11	So	Scottsdale, AZ/Horizon
Ryan Haggerty	6-10	Jr	Scottsdale, AZ/Saguaro
Anthony Hill	6-5	Jr	Peoria, AZ
Jon Howard	6-5	Jr	Phoenix, AZ/Brophy Prep
Darryl Isaac	7-0	Jr	Peoria, AZ
Byron Jackson	6-6	Sr	Phoenix, AZ /Trevor Browne
Donnie Jackson	6-6	Sr	Phoenix, AZ/Shadow Mountain
Jeff Kirkaby	6-6	Sr	Phoenix, AZ/Thunderbird
Ricky Luenberg	6-10	Sr	Gilbert, AZ
Chris Mardis	6-9	Sr	Phoenix, AZ/Moon Valley
Jamar Murphy	6-4	Jr	Tucson, AZ/Amphitheatre
Andrew Pawling	6-5	Jr	Scottsdale, AZ/Chaparral
Hakim Rasul	6-6	Sr	Tucson, AZ/Tucson Magnet
Brady Richeson	5-10	Sr	Mesa, AZ/Mountain View
Mike Schwertley	6-5	Sr	Phoenix, AZ/Brophy Prep
Jamal Scott	6-5	Jr	Phoenix, AZ/Shadow Mountain
Tanner Shell	6-6	Sr	Mesa, AZ/Mountain View
Tommy Smith	6-8	Sr	Phoenix, AZ/North
Wyatt Spencer	6-9	Jr	Sierra Vista, AZ/Buena
Jimmy Tricco	6-4	Sr	Phoenix, AZ/Brophy Prep
G.T. Turley	6-9	Jr	Chino Valley, AZ
Ryan Walcott	6-2	Jr	Phoenix, AZ /Shadow Mountain
Josh Wallace	6-10	Sr	Casa Grande, AZ/Casa Grande Union
Chris Walls	7-0	Sr	Phoenix, AZ/Thunderbird
Scott Watson	5-11	Jr	Gilbert, AZ
Marcus West	6-5	Sr	Tempe, AZ/McClintock
Ronnie West	6-3	Jr	Phoenix, AZ/Brophy Prep
Kevin Woodberry	6-0	Sr	Phoenix, AZ/Trevor Browne
ARKANSAS			
LeManuel Allen	6-4	Jr	Fayetteville, AR
Andre Amos	6-2	Sr	Little Rock, AR (Central)
Steve Ausler	6-7	Sr	Morrilton, AR
Michael Bollman	6-7	Sr	Clarksville, AR
Jay Brogden	6-6	Sr	Highland, AR
Will Bryant	6-5	Jr	Lockesburg, AR
Bobby Chaten	6-1	Sr	Little Rock, AR (Parkview)
Fred Dandridge	5-10	Sr	Little Rock, AR (Parkview)
Josh Daniel	5-11	Sr	Jonesboro, AR
Jason Diggs	6-8	Sr	North Little Rock, AR
Jackson Dunn	6-0	Sr	Hartford, AR
Spencer Flowers	5-11	Jr	Fayetteville, AR
Tyaun Forte	5-11	Sr	Little Rock, AR (J.A. Fair)
Micah Gibson	head	6-8	Sr
			Mount Vernon, WA
Ryan Wildenborg	6-10	Sr	Kirkland, WA/Juanita
Josh Williams	6-7	So	Yakima, WA/Davis
Gene Woodward	6-5	Sr	Seattle, WA/O'Dea
CALIFORNIA			
Aaron Abrams	6-3	Sr	Vista, CA/Rancho Buena Vista
Michael Ahmad	6-7	Sr	Glendora, CA
Steve Albitre	6-2	Sr	La Puente, CA/Bassett
Lamarr Alexander	6-5	Sr	Los Angeles, CA/Dorsey
Tony Alexander	6-2	Sr	Seaside, CA
Corey Anderson	6-8	Sr	Richmond, CA
Jason Anderson	6-2	Sr	Richmond, CA/Salesian
Jason Anderson	6-8	Sr	Van Nuys, CA/Montclair Prep
Shea Anderson	6-6	Sr	Long Beach, CA/Poly
Justin Saad-Anthony	6-5	Jr	Woodland Hills, CA/El Camino Real
Koko Archibong	6-7	Sr	Pasadena, CA/Poly
Jacoby Atako	5-10	Jr	Santa Monica, CA
Bryson Atkins	5-7	Sr	San Fernando, CA
Chaun Ballard	6-4	Sr	San Bernardino, CA/Pacific
Mike Bayer	6-6	Sr	Santa Ana, CA/Mater Dei
Jerome Beasley	6-10	Sr	Moreno Valley, CA
Chad Bell	6-11	So	Los Angeles, CA/Westchester
David Bell	5-10	Sr	Hayward, CA
Chris Bennett	6-8	Sr	Pasadena, CA/Marshall Fundamental
Geormel Benson	6-5	So	San Francisco, CA/Lincoln
Rafael Berumen	6-9	Sr	Simi Valley, CA
Richard Bluette	5-9	Jr	Los Angeles, CA/Verbum Dei
Nick Booker	6-6	Jr	La Jolla, CA (Bishop-s)
Tony Booker	6-5	Sr	Torrance, CA/Bishop Montgomery
Scott Borchart	6-7	So	West Hills, CA/Chaminade
Jason Bow	6-3	Sr	Clovis, CA/Clovis West
Jesse Boyd	6-8	Sr	Manhattan Beach, CA/Mira Costa
Cedric Bozeman	6-2	So	Santa Ana, CA/Mater Dei
Josh Bridges	5-9	Sr	Roseville, CA
Keith Brooks	6-5	Jr	Compton, CA (Dominguez)
Kevin Brown	6-2	Jr	Playa Del Rey, CA (St. Bernard's)
Solomon Brown	6-2	Jr	Anaheim, CA/Savannah
Travon Bryant	6-8	Jr	Long Beach, CA (Jordan)
Josh Burnett	6-1	Sr	Rialto, CA
Craig Calloway	6-1	Sr	Long Beach, CA/Jordan
Nehemiah Campbell	6-4	Sr	Los Angeles, CA/Washington
Jacquay Carlisle	6-6	Sr	Riverside, CA/J.W. North
Tony Champion	6-7	Sr	Oakland, CA/Bishop O'Dowd
Chris Chatman	6-4	Jr	Tustin, CA
Josh Childress	6-6	So	Lakewood, CA/Mayfair
Chad Clark	6-6	Sr	Glendora, CA
Chris Clark	6-6	Sr	Glendora, CA
Doyle Cole	6-4	Jr	Gardena, CA/Serra
Sean Cole	6-6	So	Santa Monica, CA/St. Monica
Clayton Coleman	6-5	Sr	Pasadena, CA
Casey Cook	6-7	Jr	Sacramento, CA/El Camino
Cayce Cook	5-10	Sr	West Hills, CA/Chaminade
Jeremy Cooley	6-7	Sr	Aliso Viejo, CA/Aliso Niguel
Keyon Cooley	6-6	Sr	Long Beach, CA/Poly
Derrick Craven	6-1	So	Torrance, CA/Bishop Montgomery
Errick Craven	6-1	So	Torrance, CA/Bishop Montgomery
Marcel Cummings	6-3	Jr	Elk Grove, CA/Laguna Creek
Kenny D'Oyen	5-7	So	Torrance, CA/Bishop Montgomery
Deryon Dale	6-3	Sr	Long Beach, CA/Jordan
Omosalewa Daramola	6-5	Sr	Los Angeles, CA/Crenshaw
Anthony Davis	6-4	So	Los Angeles, CA/Locke
Justin Davis	6-8	Sr	Pasadena, CA
Justin Davis	6-9	Sr	Alameda, CA/St. Joseph
Leroy Dawson	5-11	Sr	Los Angeles, CA
Jamaal Dean	6-2	Jr	Los Angeles, CA/Verbum Dei
Jake Dederer	6-9	Sr	Rolling Hills Estates, CA/Peninsula
George DeJohnette	6-2	Sr	Pasadena, CA

Name	Ht	Cl	City/High School
Kent Dennis	6-3	Sr	Reseda, CA/Cleveland
McKenzie Dent	6-6	Sr	Los Angeles, CA/Westchester
Nick Dodson	6-8	Sr	Los Angeles, CA/Verbum Dei
Eddie Droughan	6-5	So	Lakewood, CA/Mayfair
Josh Dunaj	5-11	So	Riverside, CA/Poly
Jerry Dupree	6-6	Sr	Moreno Valley, CA/Valley View
Trenell Eddings	5-10	Sr	Rialto, CA/Eisenhower
Nick Enzweiler	6-6	Jr	Walnut Creek, CA/Campo Lindo
Osa ìSkipî Esene	6-6	Sr	Inglewood, CA
Edward Esteban	6-1	Sr	Pacific Palisades, CA/Palisades
Noel Felix	6-8	Sr	Inglewood, CA
Blandon Ferguson	6-4	Sr	Alameda, CA/St. Joseph
Chris Ferguson	6-1	Sr	Irvine, CA
Evan Fields	6-3	Jr	Mission Viejo, CA/Trabuco Hills
Sandy Fletcher	6-2	Sr	Inglewood, CA
Chris Ford	5-10	Sr	Sacramento, CA/Kennedy
Keilon Fortune	5-11	So	Compton, CA/Dominguez
Jesse Foster	6-7	Jr	North Hollywood, CA/Campbell Hall
Isaiah Fox	6-9	So	Santa Monica, CA/Crossroads
Branduinn Fullove	6-3	Jr	Simi Valley, CA
Roy Gilad	6-5	Sr	Danville, CA/San Ramon Valley
Joe Gilliam	6-2	Sr	Fresno, CA/Edison
Michael Goldman	6-1	Sr	Calabasas, CA
DeShaun Good	6-2	So	Los Angeles, CA/Dorsey
Chad Gordon	6-1	Sr	Santa Monica, CA/Crossroads
Alex Graham	6-10	So	Redlands, CA
Ramesh Graham	6-3	Sr	Los Angeles, CA/Mid-City Magnet
Matt Grundy	6-4	Jr	San Dimas, CA
Larry Guess	6-4	Sr	Oakland, CA/Fremont
Brandon Guyton	6-1	Sr	Lodi, CA/Tokay
Nathan Hair	6-4	Sr	Mission Viejo, CA/Capistrano Valley
Aaron Hamilton	6-5	Sr	Lakewood, CA/Artesia
Johnny Hardwick	6-9	Sr	Los Angeles, CA/Manual Arts
Reggie Harmon	5-7	Jr	Pasadena, CA
Jermaine Harper	6-3	Sr	Gardena, CA
Dawayne Harris	6-7	Jr	Gardena, CA
E.J. Harris	6-2	Jr	Los Angeles, CA/Crenshaw
Jamie Harris	6-6	Jr	Canoga Park, CA
Jovan Harris	6-3	Sr	El Cerrito, CA
B.J. Hart	6-3	Jr	Rolling Hills Estates, CA/Rolling Hills Prep
Rasheed Hayes	6-2	Jr	Woodside, CA
Shaun Hemsley	6-9	Sr	Los Angeles, CA/Crenshaw
Aaric Hickerson	6-4	Sr	San Jose, CA/Piedmont Hills
John Hoffert	6-10	Sr	Davis, CA
Alex Holloway	6-4	So	San Francisco, CA/Lincoln
Gary Holmes	6-6	Sr	Fontana, CA
Keith Holmes	6-3	Sr	Duarte, CA
Rashad Hooks	6-2	Sr	San Jose, CA/Piedmont Hills
Terry Hosendove	6-4	Sr	Compton, CA
Gabriel Hughes	6-10	Sr	Torrance, CA/Bishop Montgomery
Jerry Inzunza	5-6	Sr	Fullerton, CA/Troy
Marvin Isaacs	6-2	Sr	Inglewood, CA
Chris Jackson	6-4	Sr	Bakersfield, CA/West
Alex Jenkins	6-6	Sr	Goleta, CA/Dos Pueblos
Gerrold Jenkins	6-6	Sr	Inglewood, CA
Dalron Johnson	6-8	Sr	Los Angeles, CA/Verbum Dei
Earvin Johnson	6-3	So	South Gate, CA
Larry Johnson	6-4	Jr	Irvine, CA/University
Phillip Johnson	6-11	So	Arroyo Grande, CA
Roderick Johnson	6-7	Sr	Moreno Valley, CA/Canyon Springs
Ronald Johnson	6-4	Sr	South Gate, CA
Tommie Johnson	6-4	Jr	Los Angeles, CA/Fairfax
Willie Johnson	6-4	Sr	Fresno, CA/Edison
David Joiner	6-4	Jr	Rialto, CA
Nick Jones	6-4	Sr	Oxnard, CA/Santa Clara
Lamar Kerr	6-8	Sr	Pomona, CA
Keith Kincade	6-5	Sr	Compton, CA/Dominguez
Jeremiah "Carnival" King	5-6	Sr	El Cerrito, CA
Joe Kirchofer	6-9	Sr	Laguna Creek, CA/Elk Grove
Eric Knight	6-1	Sr	Los Angeles, CA/Westchester
Larry Knox	6-3	Jr	Reseda, CA/Cleveland
Charlie Kundrat	6-3	Sr	Rolling Hills Estates, CA/Peninsula
Russell Lakey	5-11	Jr	Studio City, CA/Harvard-Westlake
Derrick Lambeth	6-4	Sr	Oakland, CA/Bishop O'Dowd
Kharie Lands	6-5	Sr	Newark, CA/Newark Memorial
Garrett Lee	6-4	Sr	Torrance, CA/Bishop Montgomery
Donny Legans	6-1	Sr	Compton, CA
Shantay Legans	5-10	Sr	Goleta, CA/Dos Pueblos
Kamron Leonard	6-9	Sr	Riverside, CA/J.W. North
Gary Lenoir	6-0	Sr	Lynwood, CA
Earl Lewis	6-5	Sr	Gardena, CA/Serra
Chris Lopez	6-7	Sr	Clovis, CA/Clovis West
Danny Lubinsky	6-2	Sr	Manhattan Beach, CA/Mira Costa
Reid Luszeck	6-9	Sr	Redlands, CA/East Valley
Michael Malloy	6-4	Sr	San Diego, CA/University of San Diego
James Marshall	5-10	Sr	Elk Grove, CA
Brandon Martin	6-4	Sr	Trabuco Canyon, CA/Trabuco Hills
Brennen Martin	6-6	Jr	Trabuco Canyon, CA/Trabuco Hills
Derek Martinez	6-4	Sr	San Jose, CA/Bellarmine Prep
Jack Martinez	6-7	So	Lakewood, CA/Artesia
Jack May	6-7	Sr	Chino Hills, CA/Ayala
Donyare Mayfield	5-6	Jr	San Diego, CA/Vista
Brian McCollom	6-6	Jr	Ridgecrest, CA/Burroughs
Eskias McDaniels	6-4	Sr	Valencia, CA
Jason McGlaston	5-11	Sr	Alameda, CA/St. Joseph
Glen McGowan	6-5	Sr	Los Angeles, CA/Venice
Jeremee McGuire	6-8	Jr	San Diego, CA/Lincoln
Micah McKinney	6-3	Jr	Compton, CA/Dominguez
Steve McMaryion	6-3	Jr	Pacific Palisades, CA/Palisades
Devin Montgomery	5-11	Sr	Mission Hills, CA/Alemany

Name	Ht	Cl	City/High School
Bret Michel	6-6	Jr	Simi Valley, CA
Shaun Michel	6-0	So	Simi Valley, CA
Ryan Mollins	6-4	Jr	Los Angeles, CA/Loyola
Eugene Moore	6-8	Jr	Los Angeles, CA/Washington
Marcus Moore	6-4	Sr	Compton, CA/Dominguez
Steve Moore	6-2	Jr	Compton, CA/Dominguez
Brandon Moorer	6-7	Sr	Los Angeles, CA/Manual Arts
Roy Morris	6-2	Sr	Chula Vista, CA/Bonita Vista
Jason Morrisette	6-3	Jr	Los Angeles, CA/Fairfax
Jeremy Murphy	6-2	So	Agoura, CA/Oak Park
Ellis Myles	6-6	Jr	Compton, CA
James Neal	5-10	Jr	Los Angeles, CA/Dorsey
Joe Nichols	6-5	Sr	Whittier, CA/California
Preston Norman	6-4	Sr	Moreno Valley, CA/Rancho Verde
Floyd North	6-3	So	San Diego, CA/Helix
Marquez Ologbosele	6-9	Sr	Oakland, CA/Castlemont
Marcus Outland	6-4	Jr	Norwalk, CA/Glenn
Chris Osborne	6-8	Sr	Los Angeles, CA/Westchester
Brandon Owens	5-8	Sr	Los Angeles, CA/Pacific Hills
Adam Parada	6-10	Sr	Alta Loma, CA
Antoine Parker	5-11	So	Los Angeles, CA /Washington
DeWayne Parker	6-3	Sr	Los Angeles, CA/Crenshaw
Jon Parker	6-4	Sr	Pasadena, CA/Muir
Marlon Parmer	6-0	Sr	Los Angeles, CA/Verbum Dei
DeVaughn Peace	6-0	So	Torrance, CA/Bishop Montgomery
Cody Pearson	6-0	So	Sherman Oaks, CA/Notre Dame
Lonnel Penman	6-3	Jr	Long Beach, CA/Poly
Marvin Perez	6-4	Sr	Torrance, CA/Bishop Montgomery
Darren Peterson	6-4	Sr	Long Beach, CA/Jordan
Marquis Poole	6-2	Sr	Compton, CA/Centennial
David Popoola	6-2	Jr	Los Angeles, CA/Westchester
Andre Porter	5-10	Sr	San Diego, CA/St. Augustine
James Profit	6-6	Jr	San Diego, CA/Serra
Brian Pruitt	6-5	Jr	Torrance, CA/Bishop Montgomery
Perry Pugh	5-11	Sr	Berkeley, CA
Marquis Revels	6-4	Sr	Rialto, CA
Tyrone Riley	6-6	Jr	Los Angeles, CA/Jordan
Ryan Romberg	6-8	Sr	Anaheim, CA/Canyon
Eric Rowher	6-9	Sr	Burbank, CA
Janou Rubin	6-2	Jr	Union City, CA/Logan
Jamaal Sampson	6-9	So	Santa Ana, CA/Mater Dei
Aerick Sanders	6-8	Jr	Gardena, CA/Serra
Darius Sanders	6-4	Fr	Compton, CA
Marques Sargent	6-2	Sr	Long Beach, CA/Poly
Shomari Sarpy	6-9	Sr	Pomona, CA
Chris Schlatter	6-5	Jr	Concord, CA/De La Salle
Dustin Schultz	6-8	Sr	Exeter, CA/Exeter Union
Steve Scoggin	6-1	Jr	Santa Ana, CA/Mater Dei
Joe See	5-9	So	Concord, CA/De La Salle
Bo Segeburg	6-8	Sr	Phelan, CA/Serrano
Josh Shavies	6-6	Sr	Oakland, CA/Fremont
Marcus Shelby	6-5	So	Santa Monica, CA/St. Monica
Daniel Sherman	6-6	Sr	Chino Hills,CA/Ayala
Will Sheslow	5-11	Fr	Agoura, CA
Joe Shipp	6-4	Sr	Los Angeles, CA/Fairfax
Eric Siess	6-3	Sr	Redlands, CA
Joe Skiffer	6-1	Sr	San Francisco, CA/St. Ignatius
Brandon Smith	6-0	Sr	Rancho Cordova, CA
Gary Smith	6-0	So	Hayward, CA/Tennyson
Ryan Stacey	6-5	Jr	Rancho Santa Margarita, CA/Santa Margarita
Shamell Stallworth	6-4	Sr	Fresno, CA/Washington Union
Jon Steffanson	6-3	Fr	Lakewood, CA/Artesia
Scottie Stern	6-4	Jr	Los Angeles, CA
Jonathon Stevens	6-4	Jr	Anaheim, CA/Esperanza
Riccardo Stewart	5-9	Jr	La Verne, CA/Bonita
Wesley Stokes	5-9	Jr	Long Beach, CA/Poly
Mike Stowell	6-3	Sr	Mission Viejo, CA/Capistrano Valley
Mikey Strawberry	6-3	Fr	Santa Ana, CA/Mater Dei
Ricardo Suazo	6-5	Sr	Los Angeles, CA/Verbum Dei
Aaron Thomas	6-5	Sr	Pomona, CA
Armand Thomas	6-8	Sr	Los Angeles, CA/Verbum Dei
Cedric Thompkins	6-6	Sr	Compton, CA/Dominguez
Stanley Thorne	5-8	Sr	Los Angeles, CA/Fairfax
J.J. Todd	6-10	Sr	West Hills, CA/Chaminade
Ismael Torres	6-2	Jr	Los Angeles, CA/Fairfax
Joe Travis	6-7	Jr	Long Beach, CA/Poly
Jeremiah Turner	6-6	Sr	Sylmar, CA
Jamaal Walls	6-6	Fr	Anaheim, CA/Canyon
Chris Walton	6-6	Jr	San Diego, CA/University of San Diego
Kam Walton	6-8	Jr	San Diego, CA/University of San Diego
Jeffrey Washington	6-1	Sr	Pasadena, CA/Muir
Christian Wiedemann	6-9	Sr	Danville, CA/San Ramon Valley
Alfred Williams	6-4	Jr	Bakersfield, CA
Bryan Williams	6-2	So	Corona, CA/Centennial
DeMarcus Williams	6-7	Jr	Upland, CA
Felipe Williams	6-3	Jr	Santa Monica, CA/Crossroads
Jamaal Williams	6-5	So	Corona, CA/Centennial
Marques Williams	5-9	Sr	Oakland, CA/Fremont
Marqui Worthy	6-3	Sr	La Habra, CA/Sonora
George Wrighster	6-4	Sr	Sylmar, CA
James Wright	5-11	Sr	Los Angeles, CA/Manual Arts
Lou Wright	6-5	Jr	Los Angeles, CA/Westchester
Joey Youman	6-7	Sr	Sylmar, CA
Mike Zepeda	6-9	Sr	Santa Ana, CA/Century

COLORADO

Name	Ht	Cl	City/High School
Bob Austin	6-4	Sr	Littleton, CO/Heritage Ranch
Greg Barnes	6-2	So	Littleton, CO/Colombine
Rodney Billups	5-10	So	Denver, CO/Washington

Name	Ht	Cl	City/High School
Jim Blair	6-7	Sr	Gypsum, CO/Eagle Valley
Matt Carroll	6-7	So	Aurora, CO/Smoky Hill
Jimmy Dadiotis	6-2	Jr	Denver, CO/East
Anthony Draper	6-6	Sr	Denver, CO/Thomas Jefferson
Mark Elasier	6-5	Sr	Denver, CO/Montbello
Mike Folda	5-9	Sr	Pueblo, CO/East
Richard Fox	6-10	Sr	Denver, CO/Regis Jesuit
Joel Gerlach	6-6	Jr	Lakewood, CO/Bear Creek
Ryan Goral	5-11	Jr	Thornton, CO/Horizon
Brian Green	6-7	Sr	Thornton, CO/Horizon
John Hawk	6-6	Sr	Denver, CO/Mullen
Martin Iti	6-11	Fr	Denver, CO/East
Stan King	6-3	Jr	Denver, CO/East
Matt Krause	5-10	Jr	Denver, CO/East
Keith Landers	6-2	Jr	Denver, CO/Manual
Arzelle Lewis	6-2	Jr	Denver. CO/East
Keith Lewis	6-7	Sr	Kim, CO
Rondrill Lipsey	6-8	Sr	Westminster, CO
Derek McCoy	6-4	Sr	Thornton, CO/Skyview
Russ Mendelson	6-5	Sr	Grand Junction, CO/Central
Cleophus Morris	5-10	Jr	Denver, CO/East
Derek Noyes	6-4	Jr	Denver, CO/East
Eric Olsen	6-4	Jr	Englewood, CO/Cherry Creek
Heath Orvis	6-0	Sr	Longmont, CO
Andy Osborne	6-8	So	Longmont, CO
Demond Parrish	6-6	Jr	Denver, CO/Manual
Evan Pope	6-2	Sr	Aurora, CO/Smoky Hill
Daniel Rose	6-4	Jr	Lakewood, CO/Bear Creek
Jonathan Sanders	6-7	Jr	Westminster, CO/Belleview Christian
Ross Schraeder	6-3	So	Denver, CO/Regis
Patrick Simpson	6-8	So	Denver, CO/Manual
Steve Smiley	6-1	Sr	Arvada, CO/Pomona
D.J. Stelley	6-3	Sr	Aurora, CO/Overland
Ryan Strain	5-9	Sr	Englewood, CO/Cherry Creek
Alex Smith	6-6	Jr	Denver, CO/Mullen
Walt Stauffer	6-4	Sr	Arvada, CO/Faith Christian
Jaison Williams	6-1	So	Aurora, CO/Smoky Hill
Blair Wilson	6-6	Jr	Westminster, CO

CONNECTICUT

Name	Ht	Cl	City/High School
Andoni Alberdi	6-3	Jr	Windsor, CT
Reggie Alston	6-7	So	New Haven, CT/Hillhouse
Austin Andrews	6-7	Jr	West Hartford, CT/Northwest Catholic
Harold Bailey	6-3	Sr	Wallingford, CT/Choate School
Olani Beckels	6-7	Sr	Cheshire, CT/Cheshire Academy
Rob Benedetto	6-5	Sr	Trumbull, CT/St. Joseph
Jason Benton	6-6	Jr	New Haven, CT/Wilbur Cross
Micah Brand	6-10	Sr	Milford, CT/Milford Academy
Randy Brooks	6-4	Sr	Waterbury, CT/Sacred Heart
Sequan Canady	6-5	Sr	New Britian, CT
Nick Cavallo	6-4	Jr	Plainville, CT
Marcus Cox	6-4	Sr	Bridgeport, CT/Kolbe Cathedral
Kelsey Cross	6-2	Sr	Waterbury, CT/Crosby
Tony Feliciano	6-1	Sr	Manchester, CT
Joe Gaetano	6-1	Sr	Wallingford, CT/Sheehan
Derek Glasper	6-3	Sr	Plainville, CT
Reynaldo Gosby	6-0	Sr	New London, CT
Brandon Hawkins	6-2	Pr	Oakdale, CT/St. Thomas More
Mike Hayes	6-7	Sr	Manchester, CT
Kevin Jeffreys	6-2	Jr	Bridgeport, CT/Kolbe Cathedral
Kevin Johnson	6-7	Pr	Milford, CT/Milford Academy
Mark Jones	6-1	So	East Lyme, CT
Dave Kashetta	6-3	Jr	Westport, CT/Staples
Abraham Keita	6-9	Sr	Oakdale, CT/St. Thomas More
B.J. Laffitte	6-4	Jr	Kent, CT/Kent School
Harry Lum	6-3	Sr	Kent, CT/Kent School
Nolan McBride	6-4	Jr	Hartford, CT/Weaver
Rahsheen McClain	6-1	Fr	Waterbury, CT/Sacred Heart
Abdul Mills	6-3	Pr	Milford, CT/Milford, CT
Winston Moncrief	6-7	Sr	Bridgeport, CT/Central
Danny Oglesby	6-1	So	Hamden, CT/Hall
Andrew Parker	6-5	So	Waterbury, CT/Sacred Heart
Jamel Riddle	5-9	Sr	Meriden, CT/Platt
Marvin Roundtree	6-4	Sr	Waterbury, CT/Crosby
Sharonne Sinvilcin	6-0	Sr	Stamford, CT/Trinity Catholic
Mike Stallings	6-0	So	Waterbury, CT/Sacred Heart
Nick Vander Laan	6-10	Sr	Oakdale, CT/St. Thomas More
Kendall Williams	6-1	Jr	Hartford, CT/Weaver
Mike Wilson	6-2	Sr	Naugatuck, CT
Jeff Wolfinger	6-8	Sr	Reading, CT/Barlow

DELAWARE

Name	Ht	Cl	City/High School
Troy Childress	6-6	Sr	Wilmington, DE/Concord
Carlos Hawkins	6-2	Jr	Tatnall
Josh Hill	6-6	Jr	Sanford
Arron Holden	6-8	Sr	Hockessin, DE/Sanford
Andre Matthews	6-4	Sr	Seaford, DE
Brian Polk	6-3	Jr	Georgetown, DE/Sussex Central
Mike Stevenson	6-4	Sr	Lake Forest
Janavor Weatherspoon	6-1	Sr	Camden Wyoming, DE/Caesar Rodney
Troy Wiley	6-8	Sr	Hodgson

DISTRICT OF COLUMBIA

Name	Ht	Cl	City/High School
Howard Blue	6-6	Jr	Washington, DC/Gonzaga
Brian Chase	5-10	Sr	Washington, DC/Dunbar
O'Neil Cover	6-3	Jr	Washington, DC/Roosevelt
Tony Dobbins	6-3	Sr	Washington, DC/Maret
Charles Dunnington	6-8	Sr	Washington, DC/Anacostia
Quinton Fairman	6-2	So	Washington, DC/Maret
Mike Harris	6-0	Jr	Washington, DC/Woodson
David Hawkins	6-4	Jr	Washington, DC/Archbishop Carroll
Chakowby Hicks	6-2	Jr	Washington, DC/Spingarn
David Holmes	6-6	Jr	Washington, DC/Dunbar
Andrew Jackson	6-6	Sr	Washington, DC/Ballou
James Johnson	5-10	So	Washington, DC/Woodson
Ramon Johnson	6-6	Jr	Washington, DC/Woodson
Jay Karimah	6-6	Jr	Washington, DC/Spingarn
Herbert Kennedy	6-4	Jr	Washington, DC/St. John's
Tom McCloskey	6-7	Sr	Washington, DC/Gonzaga
Anton Miller	6-6	So	Washington, DC/Woodson
Pat Mitchell	6-7	Sr	Washington, DC/Gonzaga
Xavier Moore	6-8	Jr	Washington, DC/Spingarn
Laydon Reed	5-11	Sr	Washington, DC/Cardozo
Robert Reed	6-8	Sr	Washington, DC/Archbishop Carroll
Deon Saunders	6-6	Jr	Washington, DC/Spingarn
Duane Shackleford	5-11	Jr	Washington, DC/Anacostia
Michael Stewart	6-4	Jr	Washington, DC/Coolidge
Cortez Sutton	6-7	Jr	Washington, DC/Eastern
Omar Weaver	6-6	Sr	Washington, DC/Coolidge
David Wilkerson	6-6	Sr	Washington, DC/Cardozo

FLORIDA

Name	Ht	Cl	City/High School
Rich Alexis	6-3	So	Boca Raton, FL/Pope John Paul II
Mike Arnold	6-0	Fr	Coral Springs, FL/Douglas
Eddie Baker	6-5	Jr	Jacksonville, FL /Ribault
Antwan Barbary	6-7	Sr	Miami, FL/Pace
Brandon Barber	6-6	Jr	Lake City, FL/Columbia
Jimmy Baxter	6-6	Jr	St. Petersburg, FL/Boca Ciega
Malerick Bedden	6-4	Sr	Pensacola, FL/Escambia
Frank Bennett	6-7	Jr	Pompano Beach, FL/Ely
Brock Benton	6-3	Jr	Gainesville, FL/Buchholz
Cedric Booth	5-9	Sr	Gainesville, FL/P.K. Yonge
John Braswell	6-3	So	Wellington, FL
Jabahri Brown	6-10	Sr	Hialeah, FL/Champagnat Catholic
Tony Brown	6-5	Jr	Fort Lauderdale, FL/St. Thomas Aquinas
Jermaine Bryant	6-4	Jr	Orlando, FL/Dr. Phillips
Harrell Butler	6-5	Sr	Jacksonville, FL/Ribault
Garth Campbell	6-5	Jr	Fort Lauderdale, FL/St. Thomas Aquinas
Manny Clifton	6-5	Sr	Cocoa, FL
Bonell Colas	6-8	Jr	Miami, FL /North Miami
Steve Cowherd	5-11	Fr	Coral Springs, FL/Douglas
Elbert Crumbley, Jr.	5-11	Jr	St. Petersburg, FL/Lakewood
Chris Cummings	5-11	Jr	Lake Butler, FL/Union County
James Daniels	6-3	Sr	Port St. Joe, FL
Jerry Daniels	6-8	Sr	Hallandale, FL
Joel Davila	6-1	Fr	Miami, FL/Miami Senior
Cecil Davis	6-1	Jr	Pompano Beach, FL/Ely
Delvis Diaz	6-7	Jr	Cape Coral, FL/Mariner
Andy Dietrich	6-4	Sr	Lakeland, FL/Santa Fe Catholic
Nigel Dixon	6-11	Sr	Orlando, FL/Edgewater
Larry Dortly	5-10	Jr	Lake City, FL/Columbia
Bryon Durias	5-9	Sr	Mt. Dora, FL
Jerald Fields	6-3	Jr	Gainesville, FL
Gene Francois	6-6	Jr	Lake Worth, FL
Damion Fray	6-8	Jr	Miami, FL/Miami Senior
Charles Frederick	6-0	So	Boca Raton, FL/Pope John Paul II
Chris Gay	6-4	Jr	Cape Coral, FL
Marcus Ghent	6-2	Sr	Lakeland, FL/Jenkins
Darrance Gillion	6-3	Jr	Fort Lauderdale, FL/Northeast
O.J. Gilmore	6-8	So	Jacksonville, FL/Arlington Country Day
Gary Godsey	6-8	Sr	Tampa, FL/Tampa Jesuit
Scott Goodwin	6-7	Jr	Orlando, FL/Edgewater
Leroy Gore	6-4	Jr	Miami, FL/Pace
Orien Green	6-3	Jr	Gainesville, FL
Tremaine Hall	5-10	So	Boca Raton, FL
Robert Hanson	6-8	Jr	Bellview, FL
Mark Henderson	5-11	Jr	Jacksonville, FL/Bishop Kenny
Anwar Hunt	6-3	Jr	Pompano Beach, FL/Ely
Adrian Jackson	5-10	Jr	Pompano Beach, FL/Ely
Dominic "Pee Wee" Jackson	6-2	So	Immolakee, FL
Pascal Jean-Charles	6-5	Sr	Miramar, FL
Julius Jenkins	6-2	Sr	Deerfield Beach, FL
Antoine Johnson	5-10	Sr	Pompano Beach, FL/Ely
Alexander Jones	6-6	Sr	Ocala, FL/Vanguard
James Jones	6-8	Sr	Miami, FL/American
Demetrius King	6-2	Sr	Malone, FL
Reggie Kohn	5-9	Sr	Winter Springs, FL/Lake Howell
Shavis Linder	6-7	Sr	Fort Lauderdale, FL /Dillard
Jackie Manuel	6-4	So	West Palm Beach, FL/Cardinal Neuman
Jerry McGill	6-4	Sr	Miramar, FL
Melvin McCray	6-4	Jr	Gainesville, FL
Joseph McNeal	6-5	Jr	Alachua, FL/Santa Fe
Gerrick Morris	6-8	Sr	West Palm Beach, FL/Wellington
Zack Moss	6-5	Sr	Pompano Beach, FL/Ely
Michael Nattiel	6-1	Sr	Newberry, FL
Garrick Nicholson	6-7	Sr	Jacksonville, FL/Wolfson
Purvis Pasco	6-9	Sr	Clearwater, FL
Ricky Phillips	5-8	So	Fort Lauderdale, FL/Dillard
David Pierce	6-0	Jr	St. Petersburg, FL/Dixie Hollins
Sylvester Pittman	6-4	Jr	Orlando, FL/Dr. Phillips
Derek Ponder	6-1	Sr	Ocala, FL/Vanguard
Sredrick Powe	6-6	Jr	Brandon, FL
Torin Ragin	6-5	Sr	Miami, FL/Norland
Napolean Rhodes	6-6	Sr	Ocala, FL/Vanguard
Willie Roberts	6-7	Jr	Miami, FL/Southridge
Djahue Rodrique	6-7	Sr	Miami, FL/Northwest Christian

Name	Ht	Cl	City/High School
Larry Scroggins	6-2	Sr	Clearwater, FL
Mike Senna	6-7	Jr	Boca Raton, FL/Pope John Paul II
Sewell Setzer	6-5	Sr	Jacksonville, FL/Ribault
Marquis Shead	6-3	Sr	Pompano Beach, FL/Ely
Lavar Sheppard	5-10	Sr	Cape Coral, FL
Sylvester Smalls	6-5	Sr	Lakeland, FL/Kathleen
D.J. Smith	6-2	Jr	Alachua, FL/Santa Fe
Johnell Smith	6-2	Sr	Interlachen, FL
Nick Smith	7-0	Jr	Valrico, FL/Bloomingdale
Theron Smith	6-7	Sr	Tampa, FL/Auburndale
Josh Snyder	6-1	Sr	Ocala, FL/Vanguard
Tavares Spillman	6-0	Sr	Hollywood, FL/Hollywood Hills
John Spivey	6-6	Jr	Miami, FL/South Miami
Jerome Stamper	6-5	Jr	Jacksonville, FL/Ribault
Duval Taylor	6-6	Jr	Lake Worth, FL
LaKendrick Taylor	6-5	Sr	Alachua, FL/Santa Fe
Donovan Thomas	6-7	Sr	Fort Lauderdale, FL/St. Thomas Aquinas
Tyrone Tiggs	6-1	Sr	Malone, FL
Enzenwa Ukeagu	6-7	Sr	Coral Springs, FL
T.J. Walden	6-5	So	Lakeland, FL/Kathleen
Greg Walker	6-1	Jr	Fort Lauderdale, FL/Cardinal Gibbons
Kenny Walker	6-9	Sr	Jacksonville, FL/Wolfson
Reggie Warren	6-4	Sr	Pensacola, FL/Tate
Marques Washington	6-0	Sr	Neptune Beach, FL/Fletcher
David Watford	6-1	Sr	Graceville, FL/Poplar Springs
Darryl Williams	6-2	Sr	Alachua, FL/Santa Fe
Javorie Wilson	6-6	Sr	Miami, FL/Miami Senior
Cornelius Wright	6-6	Sr	Miami, FL/Miami Senior
Darrell Wright	6-5	Sr	Port St. Lucie, FL
Tim Yarn	5-9	Sr	Citra, FL/North Marion
Chris Young	6-0	Sr	Port St. Lucie, FL

GEORGIA

Name	Ht	Cl	City/High School
Alexi Adediran	6-6	So	Covington, GA/Newton County
Richard Bailey	6-7	Jr	Marietta, GA/Pope
Jeff Braswell	6-0	Sr	Cuthbert, GA/Randolph-Clay
Michael Benton	6-9	Sr	Covington, GA/Newton County
Mike Brelan	6-3	Sr	Atlanta, GA/Marist
Jeremy Brooks	5-11	Sr	Valdosta, GA
Kendrick Brown	6-10	So	Brunswick, GA/Glynn Academy
Armond Burnett	6-7	Sr	Macon, GA/Southwest
Alvin Carter	6-2	So	Tyrone, GA /Sandy Creek
Mark Causey	6-2	So	Gainesville, GA/East Hall
Josh Clark	6-6	Sr	South Atlanta, GA
Jason Crouse	6-5	So	Evans, GA
Chris Daniels	6-5	Jr	Albany, GA/Monroe
Travis Davenport	6-6	Sr	Fairburn, GA/Creekside
Ndu Egekeze	6-7	Sr	Augusta, GA/Westside
Ricky Fisher	6-5	Sr	Decatur, GA/Catheral
Willie Francis	6-4	Jr	Dunwoody, GA
Eric Freeman	6-7	Sr	Columbus, GA/Carver
Jon Gardner	6-5	Jr	Roswell, GA
Leigh Gayden	5-9	Sr	Fairburn, GA/Landmark
Tavares Green	6-3	So	Augusta, GA/Josey
Quraishy Harris	6-3	So	Atlanta, GA/W.D. Mohammed
Oscar Harvey	6-4	Jr	Camilla, GA/Mitchell-Baker
Jarvis Hayes	6-5	Sr	Atlanta, GA/Douglass
Jonas Hayes	6-5	Sr	Atlanta, GA/Douglass
Tyrone Hayes	6-5	Sr	Augusta, GA/Josey
Marcus Henderson	6-7	Sr	Adairsville, GA
Chris Hewitt	6-8	Sr	Rome, GA
Karl Hollingsworth	6-4	So	Jonesboro, GA/Mt. Zion
Nehemiah Ingram	6-8	So	Milledgeville, GA/Baldwin
Brian Kekeisen	6-9	Jr	Suwanee, GA/Collins Hill
Allan Kyburz	6-3	So	Marietta, GA
Rocky Lane	6-8	Sr	Tifton, GA/Tift County
Gabriel Lee	6-7	Sr	Camilla, GA/Mitchell-Baker
Chris Lowe	6-5	Jr	Roswell, GA
A.J. Meredith	6-1	Jr	East Point, GA/Tri-Cities
Cornelius Mitchell	6-0	So	Augusta, GA/Josey
Ismail Muhammed	6-4	So	Atlanta, GA/W.D. Muhammed
Ajene Moye	6-4	Jr	Atlanta, GA/Westlake
Cornelius Mitchell	6-0	So	Augusta, GA/Josey
Ismail Muhammed	6-4	So	Atlanta, GA/W.D. Muhammed
Jeffrey Newton	6-9	Sr	Atlanta, GA/Mays
Sohylar Pace	6-1	Jr	Cedartown, GA
Byron Parker	6-0	Sr	Stone Mountain, GA
James Pattman	6-0	So	Roswell, GA
Brendan Plabich	6-1	Jr	Dalton, GA
Donte Porter	6-2	Sr	Chamblee, GA
David Prophitt	6-6	Sr	Snellville, GA/South Gwinett
Amir Abdul-Rahim	6-3	Sr	Marietta, GA/Wheeler
J.R. Reid	5-9	So	Greensboro, GA/Greene-Taliaferro
Jamey Richardson	6-6	Jr	Moultrie, GA/Colquitt County
Gerald Riley	6-6	Jr	Milledgeville, GA/Baldwin
Robert Rushing	6-2	Sr	Fort Games, GA/Randolph Clay
Reggie Shell	5-10	Sr	Carrollton, GA
Demetrius Smith	6-3	Jr	Hogansville, GA/Callaway
Jarvis Smith	6-7	Sr	Milledgeville, GA/Baldwin
Jimil Smith	5-7	Jr	Ellenwood, GA/Towers
Marcus Smith	5-10	Jr	East Point, GA/Tri-Cities
Mike Smith	6-7	Sr	Decatur, GA/Towers
Shawn Smith	6-5	So	Covington, GA/Newton County
Tarvis Smith	6-7	Sr	Milledgeville, GA/Baldwin
Keenan Stephens	6-4	Sr	Greensboro, GA/Greene-Taliaferro
Michael Stringer	5-9	Jr	Smyrna, GA/Campbell
Quentin Strong	6-1	Jr	Greensboro, GA/Greene-Taliaferro
Darius Swain	6-4	So	Tucker, GA
Greg Tinch	6-4	So	Albany, GA /Westover
John Toombs	6-9	Sr	Columbus, GA/Carver
Mike Thurmond	6-1	Jr	Gainesville, GA
Rodney Tucker	6-8	Sr	Stone Mountain, GA
Larry Turner	6-8	Jr	Milledgeville, GA/Baldwin
Mike Walton	6-0	Sr	Macon, GA/Southwest
Antoine Welchel	6-4	Sr	Gainesville, GA/East Hall
Batavia Weldon	5-7	Sr	Atlanta, GA/Crim
Antione Whelchel	6-5	Sr	Gainesville, GA/East Hall
Ezra Williams	6-4	Sr	Marietta, GA
Kerry Willis	5-10	Sr	Atlanta, GA/Westlake
Richard Wilson	6-3	Sr	Augusta, GA/Butler
Robert Wilson	6-4	Sr	Augusta, GA/Josey
Dennis Young	6-7	Jr	Warrenton, GA
Kalley Young	6-1	Jr	Atlanta, GA/Mays
Kenny Zeigler	6-5	Sr	Lithonia, GA

HAWAII

Name	Ht	Cl	City/High School
Brad Anderson	6-6	Sr	Honolulu, HI/Iolani
Cord Anderson	6-5	Sr	Honolulu, HI/Iolani
Brandon Brooks	6-6	Sr	Honolulu, HI/Punahou
Levon Freeman	6-2	Sr	Kailua, HI/Kalaheo
Ryan Rogue	6-7	Sr	Kailua, HI/Kalaheo
Julian Sensley	6-8	Jr	Kailua, HI/Kalaheo
Matt Vivas	6-5	Sr	Honolulu, HI/St. Louis
Joe Udell	6-3	Fr	Honolulu, HI/Iolani

IDAHO

Name	Ht	Cl	City/High School
Josh Bradshaw	6-6	Sr	Boise, ID/Capital
Kevin Fellos	6-9	So	Meridien, ID
Spencer Lynn	6-0	Sr	Caldwell, ID/Wilder

ILLINOIS

Name	Ht	Cl	City/High School
Imonichie Akhibi	6-5	Jr	Chicago, IL/Morgan Park
Chris Alexander	6-10	Jr	Harvey, IL/Thornton
Greg Alexander	6-1	So	Lincoln, IL/Community
Desmond Altman	6-4	Sr	Oak Lawn, IL/Richards
Jamar Avant	6-7	Jr	Cairo, IL
David Bailey	5-3	Sr	Chicago, IL/Westinghouse
Cedric Banks	6-1	Jr	Chicago, IL/Westinghouse
Jeremy Bell	6-6	Jr	Jacksonville, IL
Marlon Brooks	6-0	Sr	Peoria, IL/Manual
Demarcus Brown	6-6	Sr	Cahokia, IL
Anthony Bumgartner	6-4	Jr	Chicago, IL/St. Patrick
Shawn Bunch	6-0	So	Lincoln, IL/Community
Jason Burk	6-9	Sr	Centralia, IL
Will Bynum	5-7	So	Chicago, IL/Crane
Steve Callahan	6-4	Jr	Hinsdale, IL/Central
Aaron Carr	6-3	Jr	Chicago, IL/Lincoln Park
Marcus Catchings	6-2	Sr	Chicago, IL/King
Ross Cherepkai	6-0	Jr	Roxana, IL
Chris Clemons	6-6	Sr	Chicago, IL/Whitney Young
Jamie Cotton	6-8	Sr	Virginia, IL
Eric Crockrell	6-5	Sr	Chicago, IL/Robeson
Laban Cross	6-0	Sr	McLeansboro, IL
Brian Cuttica	6-2	Jr	Hinsdale, IL/Central
Vernon Dandridge	5-9	Sr	Chicago, IL/Morgan Park
Emmanuel Dildy	5-10	Sr	Chicago, IL/Mount Carmel
Jermimah Dobine	6-5	Sr	Chicago, IL/South Shore
Aaron Doss	6-5	Jr	Streamwood, IL
Brian Duncan	5-10	So	Palatine, IL/Fremd
Najeeb Echols	6-6	So	Chicago, IL/Whitney Young
Cameron Echolls	6-5	Jr	Chicago, IL/Simeon
Matt Engstrom	6-8	Sr	Payson, IL/Seymour
Darnell Fields	6-6	Sr	Zion, IL/Zion-Benton
Stanley Gaines	6-5	Fr	Chicago, IL/Providence-St. Mel
Max Galt	6-0	Sr	Junction, IL/Gallatin County
Armon Gates	5-10	So	Chicago, IL/Whitney-Young
Albert Gatheright	6-6	Sr	Chicago, IL/Morgan Park
Phillip Gilbert	6-1	Jr	East St. Louis, IL
Bill Goehrke	6-4	Jr	Hoffman Estates, IL
Brian Grasle	5-9	Sr	Dupo, IL
Nate Gurnsey	5-11	So	Springfield, IL/Southeast
Jeremy Harrington	6-4	Jr	Chicago, IL/Prosser
Billy Harris	6-4	Sr	Carbondale, IL
Jabari Harris	6-7	Sr	Oak Park, IL/Fenwick
Chris Hill	5-8	So	Chicago, IL/Whitney-Young
Corey Hodges	6-3	So	Champaign, IL/Centennial
Glen Hopson	6-7	Sr	Blue Island, IL/Eisenhower
Ron Howard	6-4	So	Chicago, IL/Whitney Young
Anthony Johnson	6-5	Sr	Chicago, IL/Farragut
Brandon Johnson	6-5	Sr	Chicago, IL/Providence-St. Mel
Sam Johnson	6-1	Jr	Springfield, IL
Darris Jones	5-10	Sr	East St. Louis, IL
Che Jordan	6-3	So	Champaign, IL/Centennial
Jon Knoche	5-8	Sr	Mt. Vernon, IL
Karl Krass	6-7	Sr	Zion, IL/Zion-Benton
Corley Lee	6-5	Sr	Decatur, IL/MacArthur
Anthony Lenoir	6-4	So	Evanston, IL
Sonny Lewis	6-6	Sr	Champaign, IL/Centennial
Dave Liker	6-7	Jr	Plainfield, IL
D.P. Lipke	5-9	Jr	Lisle, IL/Benet Academy
Matt Lottich	6-3	Jr	Winnetka, IL/New Trier
Jabari Maddox	6-1	Jr	Westchester, IL/St. Joseph
Cameron "CC" Malone	6-5	Sr	Chicago Heights, IL/Bloom Township
Jevon Mamon	6-2	Jr	Flossmoor, IL/Homewood-Flossmoor
Brandon Mason	6-3	Sr	Chicago, IL/Morgan Park
Albert McBeth	6-5	Jr	Chicago, IL/Morgan Park

Name	Ht	Cl	City/High School
Scotty McBride	6-4	Sr	Chicago, IL/Lindblom
Anthony McClellan	6-3	Jr	O-Fallon, IL
Anthony McClellan	6-3	Sr	O-Fallon, IL
Brett Melton	6-4	Jr	Mahomet, IL/Seymore
Kevin Menard	6-6	So	New Lenox, IL/Lincoln-Way
Adam Miller	5-10	So	Peoria, IL/Central
Carlton Mims	6-0	Sr	Evanston, IL/Evanston Township
Shawn Moore	6-4	Sr	Collinsville, IL
Mike Morrison	6-6	Sr	Deerfield, IL
Justin Naughton	6-8	Sr	Chicago, IL/St. Ignatius
Kyle Nelson	6-0	Sr	Rockton, IL/Hononegah
Les Norman	6-1	Sr	Lebanon, IL
Tim O'Brien	6-4	So	Springfield, IL/Southeast
Brett Olson	6-1	Sr	Park Ridge, IL/Maine South
Alvin Palmer	6-8	Sr	Quincy, IL
Anton Palmer	6-5	So	Chicago, IL/Julian
Jordon Pals	6-6	Sr	Effingham, IL/Effin
Brandon Parker	6-3	Sr	Rockford, IL/Boylan Catholic
Marque Perry	6-1	Sr	Chicago, IL/Prosser
Rueben Perry	6-7	Sr	Chicago, IL/Robeson
Pierre Pierce	6-1	So	Westmont, IL
Maurice Pitts	6-7	Sr	Chicago, IL/Hales Franciscan
Roger Powell	6-5	So	Joliet, IL/Township
Darrell Price	6-4	Sr	Chicago, IL/Calumet
Shaun Riley	6-3	Jr	O-Fallon, IL
Nate Rogers	6-9	Sr	Harvey, IL/Thornton
Jerry Sanders	6-6	Sr	Chicago, IL/Gordon Tech
Steve Schmitt	6-3	Sr	Carlinville, IL
Joe Scott	6-7	Sr	Palos Hills, IL/Stagg
Levar Seals	6-3	So	Chicago, IL/Providence St. Mel
Andre Senegal	6-5	So	Chicago, IL/St. Rita
T.J. Silas	6-3	So	Carbondale, IL
Tyrone Silas	6-3	Jr	East St. Louis, IL
Luke Siller	5-9	Jr	Plainfield, IL
Kelvin Smallwood	6-5	Sr	Chicago, IL/Dunbar
Marcus Smallwood	6-5	Jr	Elgin, IL
Dwayne Smith	6-2	Sr	Rantoul, IL
Hodges Smith	5-11	Sr	Chicago, IL/Gordon Tech
Jason Smith	6-3	Jr	O-Fallon, IL
Mike Smith	5-8	So	Normal West, IL
Perry Smith	6-4	Sr	Maywood, IL/Proviso East
Jason Straight	5-10	So	Chicago, IL/Dunbar
Marcellus Summerville	6-5	So	Peoria, IL/Central
Tim Szatko	6-7	Sr	Naperville, IL/Naperville Central
Stanley Thomas	6-5	Jr	Chicago, IL/King
Byron Thompson	6-5	Sr	Aurora, IL/Aurora West
Reggie Tillitt	6-2	Sr	Murphysboro, IL
Eric Tolar	6-4	Sr	Maywood, IL/Proviso East
Todd Townsend	6-5	Jr	Chicago, IL/Morgan Park
Kevin Troc	6-4	So	Lockport, IL
Thomas Trotter	5-10	Jr	Flossmoor, IL/Homewood-Flossmoor
Joe Tulley	6-2	Sr	Rockford, IL/Boylan Catholic
Perry Vaughn	6-5	Jr	Cairo, IL
Adam White	5-9	So	Lincoln-Way, IL
Damian Williams	6-7	Jr	Chicago, IL/Whitney Young
DeAndre Williams	5-9	Jr	Chicago, IL/St. Francis De Sales
Demetrius Williams	6-8	Sr	Chicago, IL/King
Dwayne Williams	5-10	Jr	Chicago, IL/Simeon
Kent Williams	6-4	Sr	Mount Vernon, IL
Marquis Williams	6-7	So	Chicago, IL/Julian
Shohn Williams	6-5	Sr	Chicago, IL/Lindblom
Fenelle Woodson	5-8	Sr	Tamms, IL/Tamms Egyptian
Kin Yanders	6-2	Sr	Decatur, IL/MacArthur
Jitim Young	6-1	Jr	Chicago, IL/Gordon Tech
Brian Zirkle	5-6	Jr	Kankakee, IL/Bishop McNamara
Matt Zachary	6-1	So	Rockford, IL/Christian Life

INDIANA

Name	Ht	Cl	City/High School
Levi Adams	6-8	Jr	Terre Haute, IN /North Vigo
Jerod Adler	6-7	So	Monroe, IN /Adams Central
Matt Backs	6-6	Jr	Marion, IN
Carlton Baker	6-6	Sr	East Chicago, IN/Central
Derek Bechtel	6-4	Jr	Edinburgh, IN
Edwin Belardo	6-1	Jr	Columbus, IN /East
Mike Bennett	6-2	Jr	Indianapolis, IN /Brebeuf
David Betch	6-5	Jr	West Lafayette, IN /Harrison
Adam Bontreger	6-0	Jr	Westfield, IN /Westfield-Washington
Brody Boyd	5-11	Jr	Dugger, IN /Union
Adam Broderick	6-8	Sr	Indianapolis, IN/Brebeuf
Aaron Brothers	5-11	Jr	Evansville, IN /Memorial
Martin Brothers	6-7	Sr	Indianapolis, IN/Arlington
Eddie Brown	5-9	Sr	Indianapolis, IN/Pike
Justin Brown	6-5	So	Floyds Knobs, IN /Floyd Central
Phil Brown	6-1	Sr	Indianapolis, IN/Cathedral
Marcus Burham	6-6	So	Bloomington, IN /South
Brett Buscher	6-7	Jr	Chesterton, IN
Braden Bushman	6-3	Jr	Gas City, IN /Mississinewa
Reed Carmichael	6-3	So	Bloomington, IN /South
Jake Childress	6-5	So	Indianapolis, IN /Decatur Central
Brennon Clemmons	6-1	Sr	Indianapolis, IN/Northwest
Bryan Claybourne	6-0	Jr	Evansville, IN /Reitz
Bryan Clossman	6-4	Jr	Elwood, IN
Terry Collins	6-0	Jr	Fort Wayne, IN /South Side
Ryan Cook	6-6	So	Martinsville, IN
Dennis Cootee	6-4	So	Jeffersonville, IN
Patrick Danley	6-8	Sr	Gary, IN/Westside
Jay Dawson	6-4	So	Oxford, IN /Benton Central
Aaron Drake	6-5	Jr	Cambridge City, IN /Lincoln
Mark Drake	6-0	Jr	Shelbyville, IN
Doug Dzybinski	6-6	Jr	Valparaiso, IN /Boone Grove
Adam Fedak	6-4	Jr	Merrillville, IN
Mark Ferris	6-6	Sr	Indianapolis, IN/Pike
Demetrius Files	6-1	Sr	Ft. Wayne, IN/Concordia Lutheran
Jamarr Gaines	5-10	Sr	Indianapolis, IN/Ben Davis
Sean Gillespie	6-2	Jr	Indianapolis, IN /Arlington
Ajagbe Gillis	6-3	Sr	East Chicago, IN/Central
Alan Goff	6-3	Sr	Terre Haute, IN/North
Traver Griffin	6-5	Jr	Pendleton, IN /Pendleton Heights
John Hamilton	6-3	Jr	Greenfield, IN /Central
Kyle Hankins	6-2	So	Bloomington, IN /South
Willie Harmon	6-1	Sr	North Vernon, IN/Jennings County
Bandon Haughey	5-10	Jr	Westville, IN
Krunti Hester	6-6	Sr	Indianapolis, IN/Brebeuf
C.J. Hill	6-2	Jr	Indianapolis, IN /Ben Davis
Zac Hill	5-7	Jr	Mishawaka, IN /Penn
Ryan Hixson	6-3	Jr	Milan, IN
Aaron Hogg	6-5	Sr	Indianapolis, IN/Warren Central
Jon Holmes	6-0	Sr	Bloomington, IN/South
Jake Howe	6-5	So	Evansville, IN /Harrison
Harold Jackson	6-5	Sr	Gary, IN/Wirt
Nick Johnson	5-10	So	Thorntown, IN /Western Boone
Brandon Jones	5-10	So	Peru, IN
Jay Jones	6-0	So	Indianapolis, IN /Ben Davis
Brian Kane	6-7	Jr	Mishawaka, IN /Penn
Darmetreis Kilgore	6-3	Sr	South Bend, IN/Washington
Demar King	6-2	So	New Albany, IN
Adam Kizer	6-7	Jr	Anderson, IN
Matt Kleymeyer	6-2	Jr	Indianapolis, IN /Park Tudor
Sean Kline	6-6	So	Huntington, IN
Paul Kopanski	6-6	So	Michigan City, IN
Kenneth Lampley	6-2	So	Gary, IN/Roosevelt
Fred Long	6-6	Jr	Indianapolis, IN /Lawrence North
Chris Loveless	5-10	Jr	Mooresville, IN
Kenny Lowe	6-3	Sr	Gary, IN/Westside
Adam Mark	6-6	Jr	Bremen, IN
Mickey McGill	6-2	Jr	Rossville, IN
Jeff McGowan	6-2	Jr	Newburgh, IN /Castle
Ross McGregor	6-8	Jr	Fort Wayne, IN /North Side
Brandon McLemore	6-4	Jr	Fort Wayne, IN /South Side
Nathan Meshberger	6-6	Jr	Berne, IN /South Adams
Johnnie Miller	6-1	So	Muncie, IN /Central
Faruk Mujezinovic	6-8	Sr	Jasper, IN
Andre Owens	6-0	Jr	Indianapolis, IN /Perry Meridian
Austin Parkinson	5-10	Jr	Kokomo, IN /Northwestern
Aaron Patterson	6-5	So	Indianapolis, IN /Ben Davis
Brian Prevost	6-7	Jr	Monrovia, IN
Jon Patterson	6-1	So	Decatur, IN /Bellmont
Jamie Petrowski	6-4	So	Terre Haute, IN /North
Shane Power	6-6	Jr	Merrillville, IN /Andrean
Matthew Poynter	6-6	Sr	Lawrence, IN/Jefferson
Lonnie Randolph	6-1	So	Merrillville, IN
Joey Ray	5-10	Sr	Bedford, IN/North Lawrence
Bryan Reed	6-5	Sr	Terre Haute, IN/North
Zach Rueter	6-5	So	Martinsville, IN
Nathan Richwine	6-5	So	Elwood, IN
Cory Ryan	6-5	Sr	Richmond, IN/Northeastern
Adam Schaper	6-6	So	Wheatfield, IN /Kankakee Valley
Zack Scott	6-10	So	Muncie, IN /Central
Otis Shannon	5-8	So	Indianapolis, IN /Cathedral
Quinn Shepherd	5-11	Jr	Carmel, IN
Eric Sills	5-10	Sr	Bluffton, IN
Spank Simmons	6-4	Jr	Linton, IN /Linton-Stockton
Jeremy Smith	6-3	Jr	Fort Wayne, IN /North Side
Jamaal Southern	6-3	Jr	Gary, IN / Lew Wallace
John Standeford	6-3	Jr	Monrovia, IN
Chris Thomas	6-1	So	Indianapolis, IN /Pike
Jeremy Thompson	6-5	Jr	Avon, IN
Clarence Washington	6-5	So	Gary, IN /West Side
Nick Washington	5-8	So	Indianapolis, IN /Ben Davis
Brandon Webb	6-5	Jr	Knox, IN
Chaz Winston	6-2	Sr	East Chicago, IN/Central
Richard Wright	6-6	Sr	East Chicago, IN/Central
Derek Yoder	6-3	Jr	Topeka, IN /Westview

IOWA

Name	Ht	Cl	City/High School
Ryan Borman	6-9	Sr	Preston, IA
Craig Callahan	6-7	Sr	Cascade, IA
Josh Cerveny	6-9	Sr	Indianola, IA
Justin Cooper	6-1	Sr	Sioux City, IA/East
Greg Danielson	6-8	Sr	Des Moines, IA/Hoover
Brad Davis	6-1	Sr	Knoxville, IA
Brody Frame	6-2	Sr	Van Horne, IA/Benton Community
Kirk Hinrich	6-3	Sr	Sioux City, IA/West
Sean Hughley	5-10	Sr	Clear Lake, IA
Aaron Jennings	6-11	Sr	Van Horne, IA/Benton Community

Name	Ht	Cl	City/High School
Joshua Kirkpatrick	6-7	Jr	Grundy Center, IA
Craig Lewis	6-1	Sr	Keokuk, IA
Kyle Kerver	6-6	Sr	Pella, IA
Tony Miller	6-7	Jr	Pomeroy, IA/Pomeroy/Palmer
Claudell Mims	6-4	Jr	Cedar Rapids, IA/Jefferson
John Reuter	6-1	Sr	Kuemper, IA
Adam Robinson	6-9	Sr	Cedar Falls, IA
Jason Sarchet	6-8	Sr	Newell, IA/Newell-Fonda
Derrick Schantz	6-5	Sr	Center Point, IA/Center Point-Urbana
Kurt Spurgeon	6-6	Sr	DeWitt, IA/DeWitt Central

KANSAS

Name	Ht	Cl	City/High School
Quentin Buchanan	6-7	Sr	Junction City, KS
Elisha Fields	6-5	Jr	Junction City, KS
Daniel Gilchrist	7-2	So	Topeka, KS/East
Mario Gunter	5-9	Sr	Wichita, KS/Southeast
Karwin Johnson	6-2	Jr	Topeka, KS/Highland Park
Clinton Jones	6-5	Sr	Wichita, KS/Southeast
Dennis Latimore	6-9	So	Halstead, KS
Brandon Lucas	6-6	Sr	Overland Park, KS/Blue Valley North
Kelvin Manning	6-9	Sr	Tecumseh, KS/Shawnee Heights
C.J. Martin	6-4	Sr	Wichita, KS/Wichita Heights
Scott Miller	6-2	Sr	Lawrence, KS
Casey Mulligan	6-7	Sr	Overland Park, KS/Blue Valley North
Ryan Murphy	6-6	Sr	Circle, KS
Melvin Sanders	6-4	Sr	Liberal, KS
Javin Tindall	5-7	Jr	Wichita, KS/South
Travis Walk	6-6	Sr	Wichita, KS/Wichita Heights
Donnie Wallace	6-9	Sr	Wichita, KS/Goddard
Rashad Washington	6-4	Sr	Wichita, KS/Southeast
Bret Wise	6-6	Jr	Emporia, KS
Ryan Woodman	6-11	Sr	Andover, KS

KENTUCKY

Name	Ht	Cl	City/High School
Ryan Barnett	6-9	Jr	Hopkinsville, KY/University Heights
Brandon Bender	6-9	So	Louisville, KY/Ballard
Johnny Brooks	6-6	Jr	Louisville, KY/Pleasure Ridge Park
Joshua Carrier	6-4	So	Bowling Green, KY
Blake Downing	6-3	Jr	Louisville, KY/Pleasure Ridge Park
Norton Edmonds	5-10	Sr	Louisville, KY/Moore
Marquis Estill	6-10	Sr	Richmond, KY/Madison Central
Alonzo Evans	6-2	Sr	Louisville, KY/Western
Don Fielder	6-4	So	Lexington, KY/Bryan Station
Nathan Forterner	6-7	Jr	Hartford, KY/Ohio County
Brent Gibson	6-5	Sr	Henderson, KY/County
Tony Green	6-6	Jr	Shelbyville, KY/Shelby County
Matt Heissenbuttel	6-4	Jr	Lexington, KY/Catholic
Freddie Holifield	6-3	Sr	Hopkinsville, KY
Billy Howell	6-9	Sr	Vanceburg, KY/Lewis County
Scott Hundley	6-5	Jr	Lexington, KY/Dunbar
Charlie Jackson	6-5	Sr	Hopkinsville, KY
Maurice Johnson	6-3	Jr	Frankfort, KY
Rick Jones	6-1	Sr	Georgetown, KY/Scott County
Tony Key	6-10	So	Hendersonville, KY
Duane King	6-4	Sr	Louisville, KY/Pleasure Ridge Park
Cedric Knight	6-5	Jr	Louisville, KY/Ballard
T.J. McKee	5-11	Jr	Flemingsburg, KY/Fleming County
Ervin Miller	6-3	Jr	Henderson, KY/Henderson County
Brandon Moore	6-6	So	Louisville, KY/St. Xavier
Larry O'Bannon	6-3	So	Louisville, KY/Male
Dan Offut	6-3	Jr	Lexington, KY/Catholic
Nathan Popp	7-1	Sr	Lexington, KY/Catholic
Beau Powers	6-7	So	Brandenburg, KY/Meade County
Marlous Scott	5-10	Jr	Lebanon, KY/Marion County
Chris Shumate	6-5	Sr	Louisville, KY/Male
Derek Smith	6-7	Sr	Ft. Thomas, KY/Highlands
Patrick Sparks	6-1	So	Greenville, KY/Muhlenberg North
Matt Spencer	6-7	Jr	Louisville, KY/Ballard
Derek Springate	5-11	Sr	Boyle County
Joe Sykes	6-9	Sr	Radcliff, KY/North Hardin
Tanner Turley	6-0	Sr	Bowling Green, KY/Greenwood
Neil Warren	5-8	Jr	London, KY/South Laurel
Mac Wilkinson	6-8	Jr	Louisville, KY/Ballard
Jonathon Williams	6-5	So	Brownsville, KY/Edmonson County
Tyler Zornes	6-1	Jr	Ashland, KY/Boyd County

LOUISIANA

Name	Ht	Cl	City/High School
Jerminey Bennett	5-9	So	Baton Rouge, LA/Glen Oaks
Brad Boyd	6-4	Jr	Lafayette, LA/St. Thomas More
Aaron Branch	6-1	So	Pine, LA
Torris Bright	6-3	Sr	Slidell, LA
Chevis Brimmer	5-10	Jr	Mereaux, LA/Archbishop Hannan
Brandon Brown	6-8	Sr	Houma, LA/Terrebonne
Kedrick Brown	6-6	Sr	Zachery, LA
Dwight Campbell	6-3	Sr	Marrero, LA/Ehret
Barry Carter	6-5	Sr	White Castle, LA
Michael Clayton	6-3	So	Baton Rouge, LA/Christian Life
Eugene Costello	5-8	Sr	New Orleans, LA/St. Augustine
Kendell Dartez	6-9	Jr	Cecelia, LA
Robert Davis	6-6	Sr	Baton Rouge, LA/Glen Oaks
Brandon Dickerson	6-3	Sr	Woodlawn
Chris Farrell	6-8	Sr	Slidell, LA
Anthony Greenup	6-7	Sr	Baton Rouge, LA/Istrouma
Draper Housley	6-4	Sr	Coushatta, LA
Bernard King	6-3	Sr	Gibsland, LA/Gibsland Coleman
Charski McDonald	6-3	Jr	Baton Rouge, LA/Glen Oaks
Antonio Meeking	6-7	Sr	Farmerville, LA
Jeremy Monceaux	5-11	Fr	Reeves, LA
Clarence Moore	6-5	Sr	Galliano, LA/South LaFourche
Brandon Mouton	6-4	Jr	Lafayette, LA/St. Thomas More
Ernest Nixon	6-4	Sr	Ellender
Jai Pradi	6-6	Sr	Rayne, LA
Hollis Price	6-1	Sr	New Orleans, LA/St. Augustine
Ryan Prillman	6-7	Sr	New Orleans, LA/McDonogh #35
Reggie Rambo	6-8	So	Alexandria, LA/Peabody
Trayvean Scott	6-2	Sr	Baton Rouge, LA/Southern Lab
Andy Slocum	6-11	Sr	West Monroe, LA
Troy Smith	6-3	Jr	Slidell, LA/Salmen
Wendall Spurlock	6-6	Sr	Baton Rouge, LA/Southern Lab
Branden Vincent	6-6	Jr	Marrero, LA/Ehret
Victor Tarver	5-8	Sr	Baton Rouge, LA/Southern Lab
Courtney Trask	6-4	Sr	Baton Rouge, LA/Parkview Baptist
Charlie Thompson	6-0	Jr	Lake Charles, LA/St. Louis
Will Watson	5-10	Jr	Baton Rouge, LA/Belaire
Juemichael Young	6-3	Jr	Hammond, LA
Derrick Zimmerman	6-2	Sr	Monroe, LA/Wossman

MAINE

Name	Ht	Cl	City/High School
Braden Clement	6-0	Sr	Skowhegan, ME
Bradley Jackson	5-10	Pr	North Bridgeton, ME/Bridgeton Academy
Roger Levesque	6-2	Sr	Falmouth, ME
Al Miller	6-0	Sr	Pittsfield, ME/Maine Central Institute
Ryan Moore	5-11	Sr	Cony, ME
Avery Queen	5-6	Jr	Pittsfield, ME/Maine Central Institute
Tory Reed	6-7	Sr	Pittsfield, ME/Maine Central Institute
DeLonnie Southall	6-8	Sr	Pittsfield, ME/Maine Central Institute
Darrell Tucker	6-8	Pr	Pittsfield, ME/Maine Central Institute

MARYLAND

Name	Ht	Cl	City/High School
Derrek Ahren	6-9	Sr	Hyattsville, MD/DeMatha
Sam Armstead	6-3	Jr	Hyattsville, MD/DeMatha
Keith Barnes	6-7	Sr	Largo, MD
Nick Barnes	6-8	Sr	Kensington, MD/Newport
Antonje Becks	6-10	Jr	Hagerstown, MD/South Hagerstown
Derrick Brelane	5-9	Jr	Laurel, MD/St. Vincent Palotti
Reggie Bryant	6-3	Sr	Towson, MD/Calvert Hall
Jordan Collins	6-10	So	Hyattsville, MD/DeMatha
Dontaz Dean	6-6	Sr	Baltimore, MD/Dunbar
Mohamed Diakiti	6-11	Jr	Frederick, MD/St. John's at Prospect Hall
Charlie Forbes	6-1	So	Baltimore, MD/Gibbons
Sherrod Ford	6-6	Jr	Brandywine, MD/Gwynn Park
Cairo Frank	6-7	Sr	Randallstown, MD
Mohammad Fufana	6-9	Jr	Potomac, MD/Bullis
Travis Garrison	6-7	So	Hyattsville, MD/DeMatha
James Golden	6-3	Jr	Seat Pleasant, MD /Central
Derrick Goode	6-10	Sr	Severn, MD/Archbishop Spaulding
Gil Goodrich	5-8	Jr	Baltimore, MD/Cardinal Gibbons
Lee Green	6-2	Sr	Hagerstown, MD/St. Maria Goretti
Arthur/AJ Harris	5-11	Sr	Wheaton, MD/Good Counsel
Marcus Hatten	6-2	Sr	Baltimore, MD/Mervo
Delonte Holland	6-5	Jr	Greenbelt, MD/Eleanor Roosevelt
Earl Hunt	6-4	Sr	Wheaton, MD/Good Counsel
Joseph Ison	6-5	Sr	Baltimore, MD/Douglas
Hekima Jackson	6-1	Jr	Oxon Hill, MD
Damien Jenifer	5-11	Sr	Baltimore, MD/Mervo
Keith Jenifer	6-2	Jr	Towson, MD/Catholic
Isaiah ìZekeî Johnson	6-7	Jr	Baltimore, MD/Southern
LaFonte Johnson	5-9	Sr	Towson, MD/Towson Catholic
Margues Johnson	6-3	Jr	Annapolis, MD
Pierre Johnson	6-5	Sr	Kensington, MD/Newport Prep
Sean Johnson	6-7	Sr	Baltimore, MD/Mt. St. Joseph
Steve Johnson	6-6	Sr	Towson, MD/Towson Catholic
Craig Jones	6-8	Jr	Potomac, MD/Bullis
Jocaru Knight	5-11	Jr	Laurel, MD
Antonio Leppegard	6-7	Sr	Largo, MD
B.J. Maigler	6-0	Jr	Seat Pleasant, MD/Central
Roger Mason	6-5	Sr	Wheaton, MD/Good Counsel
Patrick Massey	6-6	Jr	Largo, MD
Joe Karim McCoy	6-5	So	Wheaton, MD/Good Counsel
Kevin Mickens	6-8	So	Baltimore, MD/Mt. St. Joseph
Ronald Miller	6-7	Jr	Oxon Hill, MD
Chris Monroe	6-3	Sr	Wheaton, MD/Good Counsel
Joseph Morris	5-9	Jr	Clinton, MD/Surrattsville
Andre Mouzon	5-10	So	Baltimore, MD/Lake Clifton
John Day Owens	6-6	Sr	Hyattsville, MD/DeMatha
Tim Payne	6-5	Jr	Baltimore, MD/St. Francis
Pat Pope	5-10	Sr	Clinton, MD/Surrattsville
Delbert Randall	6-3	Jr	Baltimore, MD/Calvert Hall
Brandon Reese	6-6	Sr	Baltimore, MD/St. Francis
Tremaine Robinson	6-2	Jr	Severn, MD/Archbishop Spalding
John Sadusky	6-0	Sr	Hyattsville, MD/DeMatha
Victor Sammick	6-8	Jr	Kensington, MD/Newport
Andre Scott	6-9	Jr	Hyattsville, MD /DeMatha
Larry Scott	6-6	Sr	St. James, MD
Melvin Scott	6-2	So	Baltimore, MD/Southern
William Shanklin	6-7	So	Largo, MD
Ricky Shields	6-2	Jr	Riverdale, MD/Parkdale
Matt Slaninka	7-4	Jr	Hyattsville, MD/DeMatha
Kevin Smith	6-5	Sr	Baltimore, MD/Lake Clifton
Derrick Snowden	6-0	Jr	Severn, MD/Archbishop Spalding
Mike Sweetney	6-6	Jr	Oxon Hill, MD
Sherrod Teasley	6-4	Sr	Frederick, MD/St. John's at Prospect Hall
Mack Thornton	6-3	Sr	Riverdale, MD/Parkdale
Tank Walhmann	6-7	Sr	Kensington, MD/Newport
Levi Watkins	6-6	Jr	Laurel, MD/St. Vincent Palotti

Name	Ht	Cl	City/High School
Robert Went	6-6	Jr	Hyattsville, MD/DeMatha
James White	6-4	So	Kensington, MD/Newport
Erik Wills	5-11	Sr	Kensington, MD/Newport
Maurice Young	6-5	Jr	Forestville, MD/Bishop McNamara

MASSACHUSETTS

Name	Ht	Cl	City/High School
Anthony Anderson	5-10	Jr	Lynn, MA
Dustin Arnold	6-7	Sr	Peabody, MA/Bishop Fenwick
Jeff Babul	6-2	Jr	North Attleboro, MA
Toby Brittian	6-4	Sr	Marion, MA/Tabor Academy
Dennis Desmont	5-9	Sr	Marion, MA/Tabor Academy
John Devlin	6-2	Sr	Wayland, MA
Neil Fingleton	7-5	Jr	Worcester, MA/Holy Name
Adam Lapham	6-4	Sr	Mansfield, MA
Chris McCarthy	6-5	Sr	Melrose, MA
Cullen McCarthy	6-8	Sr	Mansfield, MA
Keith McCloud	6-3	Sr	Winchendon, MA/The Winchendon School
Tommy McLoughlin	6-3	So	Andover, MA
Diarra Modibo	6-10	Jr	Fitchburg, MA/Notre Dame
Steve Patrick	6-5	Sr	Marion, MA/Tabor Academy
Keith Quimby	6-4	Sr	Bridgewater, MA/Bridgewater Raynam
Kyle Quimby	6-4	Sr	Bridgewater, MA/Bridgewater Raynam
Marshall Strickland	6-1	So	Winchendon, MA/The Winchendon School
Matthew Symes	6-6	Sr	Shrewsbury, MA/St. John's
Jermaine Watson	6-1	So	Sudbury, MA/Lincoln-Sudbury

MICHIGAN

Name	Ht	Cl	City/High School
Chris Aguwa	6-5	So	Birmingham, MI/Brother Rice
Ashton Aikens	6-3	So	Birmingham, MI/Detroit Country Day
Curtis Allen	5-10	Sr	Southfield, MI
Aloysius Anangonya	6-7	Sr	Detroit, MI/St. Martin DePorres
Laddie Andahazy	6-2	So	Beverly Hills, MI/Roeper
Javon Anderson	6-0	So	Detroit City, MI
Marcus Anthony	6-3	So	Willow Run, MI
Raphael Ball	5-9	Sr	Harper Woods, MI/Bishop Gallagher
Glenn Batemon	6-8	Jr	Detroit, MI/Cass Tech
Jeremy Battier	6-4	Jr	Birmingham, MI/Detroit Country Day
Joseph Bauer	6-8	Sr	Williamston, MI
Jason Bird	5-10	So	Ypsilanti, MI
Andre Booze	5-11	So	Ferndale, MI
James Bridgewater	6-2	So	Ann Arbor, MI/Pioneer
Taylor Bro	6-7	Sr	Rockford, MI
Robert Brooks	6-8	Jr	Saginaw, MI/Arthur Hill
Eric Brown	6-7	So	Birmingham, MI/Detroit Country Day
Mario Brown	5-10	So	Flint, MI/Powers
Kelly Butler	6-7	Jr	Grand Rapids, MI/Union
Jevon Caldwell	6-1	So	Redford, MI/Bishop Borgess
Brian Carter	6-10	Jr	Southgate, MI/Aquinas
DeShaun Chapman	6-1	Sr	Detroit, MI/Cooley
Derrick Clark	5-11	Jr	Detroit, MI/Cody
Javon Clark	6-0	Sr	Detroit, MI/Cass Tech
Lloyd Cowan	6-0	So	Detroit, MI/Renaissance
Charles Crawford	5-11	Sr	Grand Rapids, MI/Union
Omari Daniels	5-8	Sr	Detroit, MI/Murray-Wright
James Davis	6-3	Jr	Detroit, MI/Murray-Wright
John Davis	6-10	Jr	Detroit, MI/Douglass
Donald DeFoe	6-4	Sr	Detroit, MI/King
Joel DeFormer	6-6	Sr	Allendale, MI
Donald Didlake	6-1	Jr	Detroit, MI/Redford
Colin Dill	6-7	Sr	Beverly Hills, MI/Detroit Country Day
Thomas Dillard	6-4	Jr	Kalamazoo, MI/Central
Mike Eatmon	6-6	So	Detroit, MI/Murray-Wright
Lamont Ely	6-0	Sr	Grand Rapids, MI/Union
Glen Fenderson	6-2	Jr	Hamtramck, MI
Joe Finland	6-7	Jr	Bloomfield Hills, MI/Lahser
Justin Fiori	6-9	Jr	Sterling Heights, MI/Ford
Bryan Foltice	6-0	Sr	Wyoming, MI/Tri-Unity Christian
Kevin Ford	5-8	So	Lansing, MI/Sexton
Tim Fralick	6-1	Sr	Troy, MI
Chris Garwood	6-6	Jr	Romulus, MI
Garrett Gibbons	6-2	So	Cadillac, MI
Herb Golliday	6-3	So	Ferndale, MI
Jermaine Gonzalez	6-3	Jr	Orchard Lake, MI/St. Mary's
C.J. Grantham	5-10	Sr	Belleville, MI
Steve Green	6-8	So	Detroit, MI/Lutheran West
Ray Guthrie	5-9	Jr	Birmingham, MI/Detroit Country Day
Nick Hall	6-3	Jr	Walled Lake Central, MI
Leonard Harden	6-6	So	Ferndale, MI
Darius Harris	6-2	Jr	Flint, MI/Beecher
Jaquin Hart	5-10	So	Flint, MI/Northern
Eric Haut	6-1	Sr	Lansing, MI/Walter French Academy
Paul Haynes	6-3	So	Pontiac, MI/Northern
Clark Headen	6-9	Jr	Detroit, MI/Mumford
Adam Hess	6-4	Sr	Grosse Pointe, MI/South
R.J. Hollywell	6-6	Sr	Clinton Township, MI/Chippewa Valley
Josh Holmes	6-4	Sr	Ludington, MI
Ryan Hoover	6-3	Jr	Mt. Clemens, MI/L'Anse Creuse
Sam Hopes	6-2	Sr	Detroit, MI/King
Marcus Hughes	5-10	Sr	Detroit, MI/St. Martin DePorres
Rodney Hughes	6-6	Sr	Southgate, MI/Aquinas
Princeton Jiles	5-11	So	Bay City, MI/Central
Arthur Johnson	6-8	Jr	Detroit, MI/Pershing
Deargel Johnson	6-2	So	Muskegon Heights, MI
Eric Jones	5-9	Jr	Westland, MI/John Glenn
Ryan Kaul	5-7	So	Clarkston, MI
Mike Kordoba	6-5	Sr	Canton, MI/Plymouth-Salem
Adam Kulesaza	6-6	Sr	Lansing, MI/Catholic Central
Kevin Lee	5-11	Sr	Lansing, MI/Everett
Martise Lee	6-0	Sr	Detroit, MI/Pershing
Hillary Marks	6-6	Sr	Detroit, MI/Murray-Wright
Mark Maxwell	6-8	Sr	Detroit, MI/Murray-Wright
Jason McGowan	6-0	Sr	Detroit, MI/Cooley
Chris McLavish	5-10	So	Flint, MI/Kearsley
Jimmy Mehlbert	5-9	So	Oakland, MI/Christian
Mike Mikel	5-10	So	Farmington, MI
Nick Moore	6-0	Sr	Redford, MI/Central Catholic
Ricky Morgan	6-0	So	Pontiac, MI/Central
Curtis Morrow	5-9	Sr	Detroit, MI/MacKenzie
Yaku Moten	6-7	Jr	Westland John Glenn, MI
Justin Ockerman	6-9	So	Redford, MI/Central Catholic
Alex Ofili	6-3	So	Ypsilanti, MI
Reggie Parker	6-3	So	Detroit, MI/Pershing
Williams Pyant	6-2	So	Beverly Hills, MI/Roeper
Jeremy Rau	6-7	Jr	Saginaw Swan Valley, MI
Phillip Reed	6-4	So	Detroit, MI/Rogers
Robert Richardson	6-4	So	Detroit, MI/MacKenzie
Dennis Ridley	6-4	So	Detroit, MI/Redford
Pete Ritzma	7-0	Jr	Clarkston, MI
Chuck Rogers	6-5	Jr	Saginaw, MI
Randy Royal	6-2	Sr	Ferndale, MI
Biley Russell	5-10	So	Southfield, MI
Walker D. Russell	5-8	So	Rochester, MI
Cory Santee	5-10	So	Flint, MI/Northern
Chris Schell	6-4	Jr	Mt. Pleasant, MI
Courtney Scott	6-6	Jr	Lansing, MI/Waverly
Eugene Seals	6-5	Jr	Saginaw, MI
Maurice Searight	6-3	Jr	Orchard Lake, MI/St. Mary's
Kevin Shorter	6-5	Jr	Clinton Township, MI/Chippewa Valley
Odell Simmons	6-0	Jr	Detroit, MI/Pershing
Jamie Smith	6-5	Sr	Kalamazoo, MI/Loy-Norrix
Nucleus Smith	6-3	Sr	Pontiac, MI/Northern
Travis Spaman	6-3	So	Kalamazoo, MI/Christian
Andrew Squirewell	5-7	So	Detroit, MI/DePorres
Bret Stephenson	6-4	Jr	Galesburg-Augusta
Earold Stephens	6-3	So	Ferndale, MI
James Theus	6-0	Jr	Detroit, MI/King
Ricardo Thomas	6-7	Sr	Detroit, MI/Comm. Media Arts
Kelvin Torbert	6-4	So	Flint, MI/Northwestern
Jimmy Twyman	6-1	Sr	Detroit, MI/Central
Jarend Vant' hof	5-9	Jr	Grand Rapids, MI/Christian
Jeremy Veenstra	6-4	Sr	Kalamazoo, MI/Kalamazoo Christian
Willie Wallace	6-6	Sr	Flint, MI/Southwestern
Zach Warlock	6-7	So	Kalamazoo, MI/Kalamazoo Christian
Robert Whaley	6-8	So	Benton Harbor, MI
Rodney Whaley	5-8	So	Detroit, MI/Mumford
Deverson White	6-4	Jr	Detroit City, MI
Nathon White	6-4	So	Detroit, MI/Douglass
Colin Wilkerson	6-2	Sr	Dearborn, MI
Curtis Williams	6-3	So	Detroit, MI/Murray Wright
James Williams	5-9	Jr	Detroit, MI/Cooley
Marlon Williamson	6-0	Sr	Detroit, MI/Cass Tech
Marcus Willis	5-7	Jr	Flint, MI/Northwestern
Tyree Wright	6-0	So	Detroit, MI/Central
Marcus Young	6-4	So	Redford, MI/Bishop Borgess

MINNESOTA

Name	Ht	Cl	City/High School
Grant Anderson	6-7	Sr	Minnetonka, MN
Troy Bell	6-0	Sr	Minneapolis, MN /Holy Angels
Adam Boone	6'1	Jr	Minneapolis, MN/Washburn
John Breneman	6-7	Sr	Minneapolis, MN/Minnehaha Academy
Kevin Buth	6-0	Sr	Edina, MN
Drew Carlson	6-1	Sr	Belle Plaine, MN
Steve Esselink	6-5	Sr	Hills, MN
John Gilbert	6'8	Jr	Minneapolis, MN/Patrick Henry
Pete Hegseth	6-1	Sr	Forest Lake, MN
Erick Holmstadt	6-8	Sr	Monticello, MN
Jibraun Ike	6-1	Sr	St. Anthony
Ben Johnson	6-2	Sr	Minneapolis, MN /De La Salle
Levi Jones	6-9	Sr	Minneapolis, MN/North
Gerald Kingbird	6-0	Sr	Red Lake, MN
Jason Krone	6-5	Sr	Roccora, MN/Cold Springs
Reid Kuschel	6-8	Sr	Crosby, MN/Crosby-Ironton
Rory Larson	6-2	Sr	St. Francis, MN
Drew Lemme	6-6	Sr	Minneapolis, MN/North
Steve Neigamasabo	6-7	Sr	Mound, MN
Rick Rickert	6-9	So	Duluth, MN/East
Steve Ruda	6-7	Sr	Long Prairie, MN
Shane Schilling	6-6	Sr	Minnetonka, MN
Andy Skoglund	7-0	Jr	Minnetonka, MN
Jake Sullivan	6'0	Jr	Oakdale, MN/Tartan
Alfonso Triguero	6-10	Sr	Monticello, MN

MISSISSIPPI

Name	Ht	Cl	City/High School
Earl Barron	6-10	Sr	Clarksdale, MS
Ricky Bennett	6-1	Sr	Picayune, MS
Jimmy Boykin	6-6	Sr	Jackson, MS /Murrah
Kelvin Butler	6-2	Sr	Shelby, MS/Broad Street
Jason Campbell	6-5	Jr	Taylorsville, MS
Tony Carter	6-6	Jr	Gulfport, MS
Quentin Christian	6-7	Jr	Mendenhall, MS
Devin Davis	6-8	Jr	Gulfport, MS/Harrison Central
David Drain	6-4	Sr	Calhoun City, MS
Ronald Dupree	6-6	Sr	Biloxi, MS
Antwain Ellis	6-7	Sr	Jackson, MS/Lanier
Kendrick Fox	6-5	So	Oxford, MS/Lafayette County
Billy Funchess	6-4	Sr	Utica, MS/Hinds

Name	Ht	Cl	City/High School
Sims Gilliam	6-7	Sr	Greenville, MS
John Gunn	6-10	Sr	Oxford, MS
Aaron Harper	6-5	Sr	Jackson, MS/Provine
Germaine Harris	5-9	Sr	Gulfport, MS
Quintarrius Hodges	5-11	Sr	Indianola, MS/Gentry
Leroy Hurd	6-6	Sr	Moss Point, MS
Dennis Isom	6-5	Sr	Byhalia, MS
Tommy Kelly	6-7	Sr	Jackson, MS/Provine
Timothy Latiker	6-4	Jr	Durant, MS
Alonzo Lane	6-6	Sr	Canton, MS
Lee Miles	6-4	Sr	Biloxi, MS
Korey Moore	6-0	So	Jackson, MS/Jim Hill
Mario Myles	6-4	Sr	Jackson, MS/Callaway
Willie Neal	6-5	Sr	Raymond, MS
Milas Randle	6-2	Sr	Indianola, MS/Gentry
Steven Redd	5-10	Sr	Florence, MS
Justin Reed	6-6	Jr	Jackson, MS/Provine
Darius Rice	6-8	Jr	Jackson, MS/Lanier
Matthew Roebuck	6-8	Sr	Decatur, MS/Newton County Academy
Trey Sanders	6-3	Sr	Jackson, MS/Jim Hill
Lincoln Smith	6-9	Sr	Hollandale, MS/Simmons
Leonard Taylor	6-6	Sr	Clinton, MS
Reggie Taylor	6-0	Jr	Brandon, MS
Marcus Terrell	6-1	Sr	Jackson, MS/Provine
James Thomas	5-8	Jr	Jackson, MS/Lanier
Cornelius Torrence	5-7	Sr	Jackson, MS/Lanier
Sedric Travis	6-3	Sr	Magnolia, MS/South Pike
Dewey Turner	6-3	Jr	Gulfport, MS/Harrison Central
Rodney Turner	6-4	Sr	Jackson, MS/Forest Hill
Joseph Ward	6-6	Sr	Clinton, MS
James West	5-8	Sr	Natchez, MS
Derrick White	6-3	Sr	Laurel, MS/Northwest Jones
Maurice Williams	6-0	So	Jackson, MS/Murrah

MISSOURI

Name	Ht	Cl	City/High School
Nick Benson	6-5	Sr	Jennings, MO
Kenneth Brown	6-9	Sr	Hazelwood, MO /Hazelwood West
Jabari Buchanon	6-5	Sr	St. Louis, MO /Cardinal Ritter
James Collins	6-2	Sr	Warrensburg, MO
Shawn Dunson	5-8	Sr	Kansas City, MO /Pembroke Hill
Justin Gage	6-4	Sr	Jefferson City, MO
Patrick Harmon	6-3	Jr	St. Louis, MO/Cardinal Ritter
Ben Hart	6-7	Jr	Columbia, MO/Rock Bridge
Nathan Johnson	6-3	Sr	Kansas City, MO /Ruskin
Ryan Johnson	6-0	Sr	St. Louis, MO /Christian Brothers
Jibran Kelley	6-7	Sr	Lees Summit, MO /North
Brian Kreider	6-9	Jr	Webster Groves, MO
Dominique Leake	6-6	So	Jefferson City, MO
Robin Lucas	6-1	Sr	Blue Springs, MO /Blue Springs South
Paul Miller	6-8	So	Jefferson City, MO/Blair Oaks
Mike Nelke	5-11	Jr	Florissant, MO/McCluer
John Oden	6-8	Sr	St. Louis, MO /Cardinal Ritter
Kenny Oliver	5-11	So	Raytown, MO/Raytown South
John Pace	6-2	Sr	Troy, MO /Buchanan
Joseph Principe	6-10	Sr	Kansas City, MO /Rockhurst
Joe Ries	6-6	Jr	St. Louis, MO/DeSmet
Jarriot Rook	6-5	Sr	Troy, MO /Buchanan
Phillip Rootz	6-7	Jr	Warrenton, MO
Tim Scheer	6-5	Sr	New Haven, MO
Ryan Stock	6-3	Sr	Springfield, MO/Kickapoo
Mike Sutherland	6-6	Sr	St. Louis, MO/Lutheran North
Jeff Taylor	6-2	Sr	St. Louis, MO /Cardinal Ritter
Jayce Tingler	5-7	Sr	Smithville, MO
Brian Turner	6-0	Jr	St. Louis, MO/Beaumont
Thomas White	7-2	Jr	Moberly, MO
Blake Will	6-6	Sr	Springfield, MO /Glendale
Kyle Wolfe	6-1	Sr	New Haven, MO

MONTANA

Name	Ht	Cl	City/High School
Danny Faaborg	6-4	Sr	Bozeman, MT
Spencer Hay	6-7	Sr	Bridger, MT

NEBRASKA

Name	Ht	Cl	City/High School
Jason Boyd	6-5	Sr	Omaha, NE/Benson
Omar Bynum	6-7	Sr	Omaha, NE/Northeast
Eric Dunnigan	6-0	Jr	Grand Island, NE
Tyler Engel	6-6	Sr	Kearney, NE
Ty Gifford	6-0	Sr	Lincoln, NE/Southeast
Tryon Graham	5-11	Jr	Lincoln, NE
Ty Graham	5-7	Sr	Lincoln, NE
Derek Hack	6-6	Sr	Fremont, NE
Shane Ideus	6-2	Sr	Filley, NE
Derek Lacey	6-5	Sr	Grant, NE
Adam Lamprecht	6-3	Jr	Fremont, NE
Cody Levinson	6-2	Jr	Bellevue, NE/West
Andy Lund	6-9	Sr	Omaha, NE/Burke
Tee Mason	6-1	Sr	Lincoln, NE/Northwest
Ryan McLaughton	6-6	So	Bellevue, NE/West
Dan Morrow	6-5	Sr	Louisville, NE
Luke Olsen	6-2	Sr	Norfolk, NE
Derek Paben	6-5	Sr	Beatrice, NE
Shawn Redhage	6-7	Sr	Lincoln, NE/East
Nick Svehla	6-4	Sr	Omaha, NE/Creighton Prep
Eric Tesmer	6-0	Sr	Grand Island, NE
Derric Werner	6-8	Fr	Elkhorn Valley, NE
Chris Whittgren	6-6	Sr	Lincoln, NE/Southeast
Greg Wood	6-0	Sr	Omaha, NE/North

NEVADA

Name	Ht	Cl	City/High School
Lance Buoncristiani	5-8	Sr	Reno, NV/Galena
Demetrius Hunter	6-3	Sr	North Las Vegas, NV/Rancho
Jason Johnson	6-5	Sr	Las Vegas, NV/Cimarron-Memorial
Brian Lang	6-2	Sr	Las Vegas, NV/Cimarron-Memorial
Jamie Manor	6-1	Sr	Las Vegas, NV/Clark

NEW HAMPSHIRE

Name	Ht	Cl	City/High School
Mark Durham	6-1	Sr	Derry, NH/Pinkerton
Ryan Faulkner	5-9	Sr	Lebanon, NH
Josh Kroenke	6-4	Pr	New Hampton, NH/New Hampton School
Steve Lavolpicelo	5-11	Sr	North Sutton, NH/Kearsarge
Jeff Morse	6-3	Jr	Lebanon, NH
Kyle Purinton	6-6	Sr	Northwood, NH/Coe-Brown-Northwood

NEW JERSEY

Name	Ht	Cl	City/High School
John Allen	6-3	So	Camden, NJ
Rick Apodaca	6-2	Sr	North Bergen, NJ
Chris Arnold	6-3	Sr	Pennsauken, NJ/Bishop Eustace
Marcus Austin	6-8	So	Elizabeth, NJ /St. Patrick's
Sean Axani	6-7	Sr	Little Silver, NJ/Red Bank
Arthur Barclay	6-5	Jr	Camden, NJ
Kevin Bower	6-7	Sr	Westville, NJ/West Deptford
Tory Cavalerio	5-6	Jr	Atlantic City, NJ
Mike Cleaves	5-11	Jr	Paterson, NJ /Catholic
Jon Crispin	6-2	Sr	Pitman, NJ
Kalif Dieye	6-4	Sr	Newark, NJ/East Side
Colin Donahue	6-2	Sr	Pennsauken, NJ/Bishop Eustace
Ernie D'Orazio	6-0	Jr	Cherry Hill, NJ /Camden Catholic
Rashid Dunbar	6-3	Jr	Bayonne, NJ/Marist
Keith Duncan	6-7	Sr	Rahway, NJ
Tim Ferguson	6-4	Sr	Mt. Holly, NJ /Rancocas Valley
Kevin Garrity	6-11	Jr	Edison, NJ/Wardlaw Hartridge
Bennie Glasper	6-3	Sr	Medford, NJ /Lenape
Marcus Grant	6-6	So	Pennsauken, NJ /Bishop Eustace
Harvey Harrington	6-3	So	Elizabeth, NJ /St. Patrick
Jerome Holman	5-9	Sr	Elizabeth, NJ /St. Patrick
Tywan Holmes	6-5	Sr	Richland, NJ /St. Augustine Prep
Justice Howell	5-9	Jr	Elizabeth, NJ /St. Patrick
Matt Hudgins	6-1	Jr	Absecon Highlands, NJ/Absegami
Junior Ighodaro	6-7	Jr	Richland, NJ /St. Augustine
Jamal Jackson	5-8	Sr	Elizabeth, NJ /St. Patrick
Maurice Jackson	6-9	Sr	Jersey City, NJ /St. Anthony
Mark Jerz	6-0	Sr	Oradell, NJ /Bergen Catholic
Abraham Johnson	5-9	Jr	Newark, NJ /East Side
Brian Keenan	5-10	Sr	Newark, NJ /St. Benedict
Jeremia King	5-11	So	Passaic, NJ
Andre Kirkland	6-4	Jr	Atlantic City, NJ
Brandin Knight	6-0	Sr	West Orange, NJ /Seton Hall Prep
John Paul Kobryn	6-6	So	Jersey City, NJ /St. Anthony
Herve Lamizana	6-8	Jr	Elizabeth, NJ /St. Patrick-s
Justin Leith	6-6	Sr	Princeton, NJ /Princeton Day School
Shawn Marx	6-0	Sr	Bayonne, NJ /Marist
Wayne McClinton	6-2	Sr	Elizabeth, NJ /St. Patrick
Amil Mitchell	5-9	Sr	West Orange, NJ /Seton Hall Prep
Jeff Mitchell	6-10	Sr	Cherry Hill, NJ /West
Johnnie Moore	6-1	Jr	Morristown, NJ
Sean Mullholland	5-10	Jr	Medford, NJ /Shawnee
Walter Price	6-0	Jr	Elizabeth, NJ /St. Patrick's
Bill Raferty	6-4	Sr	Morristown, NJ /Delbarton
Juan Rozier	6-3	Jr	Pennsauken, NJ /Bishop Eustace
Jamar Smith	6-7	Jr	Pine Hill, NJ
Andrew Sullivan	6-7	Sr	Richland, NJ /St. Augustine
Tony Tate	5-11	So	Jersey City, NJ/St. Anthony
Ernest Turner	6-2	So	Somerdale, NJ/Sterling
Sal Thompson	5-9	Sr	Newark, NJ /East Side
Jerome Tradwick	6-8	Sr	East Orange, NJ/Clifford Scott
Ryan Wigmore	6-2	Sr	Delran, NJ
DeShawn Williams	6-2	Sr	Paterson, NJ/Catholic
Marcelo Williams	5-11	Sr	Teaneck, NJ
Walik Wilson	6-4	Sr	Jersey City, NJ /St. Anthony
Mark Jarrell-Wright	6-4	Sr	Newark, NJ /St. Benedict

NEW MEXICO

Name	Ht	Cl	City/High School
Ed Abreu	6-3	So	Albuquerque, NM/Valley
Isaac Acosta	5-11	Sr	Hagerman, NM
Ryan Ashcraft	6-2	Sr	Albuquerque, NM/La Cueva
Michael Cooper	6-1	Sr	Albuquerque, NM/La Cueva
Dathan Culpepper	6-0	Jr	Portales, NM
Toby Foote	6-1	Sr	San Jon, NM
Victor Garcia	6-0	Sr	Albuquerque, NM
R.T. Guinn	6-9	Sr	Albuquerque, NM/Valley
Kevin Henry	6-2	Sr	Hobbs, NM
Matt King	6-5	Jr	Albuquerque, NM/La Cueva
Damon Martin	6-9	Sr	House, NM
Shawn Mason	6-5	Sr	Albuquerque, NM/West Mesa
Jesus Moreno	6-3	Sr	Wagon Mound, NM
Bill Parkhurst	6-6	Sr	Albuquerque, NM/Sandia
Jared Quintana	6-0	Sr	Santa Fe, NM/Santa Fe Indian

NEW YORK

Name	Ht	Cl	City/High School
Uka Agbai	6-7	Sr	Briarwood, NY/Archbishop Molloy
Sagari Allegne	7-0	Fr	New York, NY/Frederick Douglass
Pierre Anthony	6-3	So	Flushing, NY/Holy Cross
Deon Ayala	6-5	Sr	Bronx, NY/Cardinal Hayes

Name	Ht	Cl	City/High School
Juma Allen	6-5	Jr	Flushing, NY/Christ the King
Andre Barrett	5-7	Jr	New York, NY/Rice
Simeon Belk	5-9	Jr	Brooklyn, NY/Bishop Loughlin
Kevin Bell	6-2	Sr	New York, NY/Rice
Kevin Bishop	6-1	So	East Elmhurst, NY/Monsignor McClancy
Carl Bolton	5-8	Jr	East Elmhurst, NY/Monsignor McClancy
Darryl Boykins	6-1	Jr	East Elmhurst, NY/Monsignor McClancy
Mike Boynton	6-1	Jr	Brooklyn, NY/Bishop Loughlin
Famous Brown	6-0	So	New York, NY/La Salle
Jessie Brown	6-4	Sr	Bronx, NY/Taft
Reggie Brown	6-3	Sr	Jamaica, NY/Archbishop Molloy
Tom Byrnes	5-10	So	Staten Island, NY/Moore Catholic
Miguel Caballero	6-6	Sr	New York, NY/La Salle
Lionel Chalmers	5-11	Sr	Schenectady, NY/Bishop Gibbons
Korie Clarke	6-1	Jr	Bronx, NY/St. Raymond
Michael Clarke	6-4	So	Brooklyn, NY/Grady
Leslie Cole	6-0	Sr	Bronx, NY/Cardinal Hayes
Jason Coleman	6-3	Sr	Brooklyn, NY/Lincoln
John Connor	5-11	Jr	New York, NY/La Salle
Khari Council	6-2	Jr	East Elmhurst, NY/Monsignor McClancy
Stephen Cox	6-2	Jr	Brooklyn, NY/Boys & Girls
Kyle Cuffe	6-6	Jr	New York, NY/Rice
Alwan Curtis	6-1	Sr	Brooklyn, NY/Bishop Loughlin
Ernest Dancy	6-0	Sr	Brooklyn, NY/Brooklyn Tech
Shawn Danzler	6-3	So	Bronx, NY/Christopher Columbus
Aaron Davis	6-4	Sr	Brooklyn, NY/Boys and Girls
Nick Delfico	6-4	Sr	New Rochelle, NY/Iona Prep
Mamadu Diene	6-7	Jr	Troy, NY/Redemption Christian
Arthur Drumgo	6-6	Sr	Troy, NY/Redemption
Tommie Eddie	6-4	So	Brooklyn, NY/Boys & Girls
Obinna Efobi	6-6	Sr	New York, NY/Stuyvesant
Rodney Eperson	6-7	Jr	New York, NY/La Salle
Anthony Epps	6-0	So	Bronx, NY/St. Raymond
Bryan Evans	6-0	Sr	Brewster, NY
Courtney Fields	6-8	Sr	New York, NY/Rice
Fab Fisher	5-6	Sr	Brookville, NY/Long Island Lutheran
Justus Flavors	6-0	Jr	Brooklyn, NY/Bishop Loughlin
Davonne Folks	6-3	Fr	Bronx, NY/St. Raymond
Craig Forth	6-11	So	East Greenbush, NY/Columbia
Jason Gibson	6-4	Sr	Briarwood, NY/Archbishop Molloy
Wendell Gibson	6-7	So	Briarwood, NY/Archbishop Molloy
James Hamlet	6-3	Sr	New York, NY/Frederick Douglass
Johnny Helton	6-6	Sr	Buffalo, NY/Turner-Carroll
Charles Henson	6-6	Jr	Bronx, NY/All Hallows
Darryl Hill	5-5	So	Bayside, NY/Cardozo
Julius Hodges	6-0	So	Bronx, NY/St. Raymond's
Shad James	6-2	So	Brooklyn, NY/Bishop Loughlin
Reginald Jenkins	6-2	Sr	Bronx, NY/Taft
O'Neil Johnson	6-0	Sr	Bronx, NY/Cardinal Spellman
Lee Jones	6-6	Sr	Albany, NY
Andrew Joseph	6-5	Sr	Bronx, NY/Walton
Jamell Kelly	6-1	Jr	Flushing, NY/Christ the King
Todd Klimkowski	5-10	Sr	Briarwood, NY/Archbishop Molloy
Chase Licata	6-4	So	Brooklyn, NY/Packer Institute
Andre Logan	6-4	Jr	Brooklyn, NY/Poly Prep
J.C. Mathis	6-7	Jr	Bronx, NY/Kennedy
Mark McCarroll	6-8	Sr	Flushing, NY/Christ the King
Matthew McCloskey	6-3	Jr	Albany, NY
Marvin McCullough	5-10	Fr	Bronx, NY/All Hallows
Chris McRae	6-4	So	Bronx, NY/St. Raymond
Jave Meade	6-1	Sr	Flushing, NY/Christ the King
Darnell Miller	6-2	Jr	Bronx, NY/St. Raymond
Justin Miller	6-7	Jr	Jamestown, NY/Southwestern
Kaishon Mims	6-4	Sr	Flushing, NY/Christ the King
Steve Mitchell	6-3	Sr	Staten Island, NY/St. Peter
Aswan Morris	5-5	Sr	Brooklyn, NY/Canarsie
Gregory Morton	6-8	Sr	Bronx, NY/St. Raymond
Ted Mumford	5-8	So	Brooklyn, NY/Bishop Loughlin
Drew Nicholas	6-3	Sr	Brookville, NY/Long Island Lutheran
Karl Nickerson	6-5	Sr	Bronx, NY/Kennedy
Quan Pickeny	5-10	so	Bronx, NY/St. Raymond
William Poole	5-10	Sr	Middle Village, NY/Christ the King
Andreas Pope	6-3	So	Brooklyn, NY/St. Edmund
Courtney Prichard	5-9	Jr	Center Moriches, NY
Richard Pyle	6-5	Sr	Brooklyn, NY/Robeson
John Quantara	6-0	So	Brooklyn, NY/Lincoln
Omari Roberts	6-4	Sr	Brooklyn, NY/Berkeley Carroll
Akwasi Rose	6-7	Sr	Brooklyn, NY/Bishop Loughlin
Mike Sherrod	5-9	Jr	Brooklyn, NY/Paul Robeson
Eric Siegrist	6-3	Sr	Poughkeepsie, NY/Spackenkill
John Sikiric	6-3	So	Briarwood, NY/Archbishop Molloy
Tremayne Singletary	6-5	Jr	Bronx, NY/St. Raymond
Calvin Smith	6-5	So	Brooklyn, NY/Xaverian
Jamaal Smith	6-2	Sr	New York, NY/M.L. King
Eric Sterling	6-3	So	New York, NY/La Salle
Leonard Stokes	6-5	Sr	Buffalo, NY/Turner-Carroll
Andre Sweet	6-5	Jr	New York, NY/Rice
Atiba-Rekeim Taylor	6-1	Jr	Spring Valley, NY/Ramapo
Terrell Taylor	6-1	Sr	Peekskill, NY/Ossining
James Thomas	6-7	Sr	Schenectady, NY
Obinna Uzuchukwa	6-7	Sr	Brooklyn, NY/Lincoln
Daniel Walker	6-6	Sr	Brooklyn, NY/Robeson
Darius Waters	6-4	Sr	Brooklyn, NY/New Utrecht
Terrance Watkins	6-2	Jr	Brooklyn, NY/Bishop Loughlin
Kevin White	6-3	So	Fresh Meadows, NY/St. Francis Prep
Sherman Whittenberg	5-11	Sr	Queens, NY/Hillcrest
Durron Williams	6-7	Sr	Rochester, NY/Edison Tech
Zach Williams	6-7	Jr	Flushing, NY/Christ the King
Phillip Wilson	6-2	Jr	Brooklyn, NY/Canarsie
Jason Wingate	5-11	Fr	New York, NY/Rice
Brian Woodward	6-1	Sr	Bayside, NY/Cardozo
Maurice Yearwood	5-10	Sr	Brooklyn, NY/Tech

NORTH CAROLINA

Name	Ht	Cl	City/High School
Dan Anderson	6-0	Jr	Lenoir, NC/West Caldwell
Imo Archibong	6-0	Sr	Winston-Salem, NC/Bishop Guinness
Turner Battle	5-7	So	Kernersville, NC/East Forsyth
Derrick Beckham	6-3	Sr	Kinston, NC
Von Bittle	6-0	So	Winston-Salem, NC/North Forsyth
Kenny Booker	6-8	Sr	Durham, NC/Mount Zion
Cory Broadnax	6-4	Sr	Raleigh, NC/Leesville Road
Ben Brooks	6-3	Jr	Charlotte, NC/Latin
Brandon Burke	5-9	Sr	Trinity, NC
Jason Burns	6-4	Sr	Durham, NC/Mt. Zion
Marcus Campbell	6-11	So	Durham, NC/Mt. Zion
Ryan Carson	6-2	Jr	Charlotte, NC/Providence Day
Calvin Clemmons	6-9	Sr	Charlotte, NC/Olympic
Brandon Clifford	6-8	Jr	Greensboro, NC/Page
Dwon Clifton	6'3	Jr	Raleigh, NC/Millbrook
Chris Clyburn	6-4	Jr	Charlotte, NC/Providence Day
Preston Davis	6-7	Sr	Charlotte, NC/Independece
Deon Dixon	6'8	Jr	Fayetteville, NC/71st
Del Douglas	6-5	Sr	Charlotte, NC/West Charlotte
Ronald Dowdy	6'5	Jr	Fayetteville, NC/Pine Forest
Adam Duggins	6-9	Sr	Greensboro, NC/Page
Redmond Dunlap	6-1	Sr	Winston-Salem, NC/R.J. Reynolds
Lester Dunn	6-4	So	High Point, NC/Andrews
Dovonte Edwards	6-0	So	Chapel Hill, NC
Justin Ellerbe	6-5	Jr	Greensboro, NC/Dudley
Dwayne Ellis	6-6	Sr	Morganton, NC/Freedom
Chris Garnett	6-9	Sr	Durham, NC/Mount Zion
Jeremy Grier	6-0	Jr	Huntersville, NC/Vance
David Hairston	6-3	Sr	Winston-Salem, NC/Carver
Kenneth Hammond	6'4	Jr	Monroe, NC/Sun Valley
Kenneth Harrell	6-4	Sr	Durham, NC/Mount Zion
Mike Harris	6-9	Sr	Charlotte, NC/East Mecklenberg
Chris Hobbs	6'7	Jr	Chapel Hill, NC/East
Elijah Holland	6'0	Jr	Camp LeJeune, NC/LeJeune
Shannon Huffstetler	6-6	Sr	Mt. Holly, NC/East Gaston
Nick Huge	6-3	Sr	Charlotte, NC/Charlotte Christian
Will Johnson	6-8	Sr	Hickory, NC
Michael Joiner	6'5	Jr	Fayetteville, NC/71st
Zach Jordan	6-4	Sr	Charlotte, NC/Providence Day
Tom Lange	6-9	Sr	Concord, NC/Central Cabarrus
Reginald Love	6'3	Jr	Charlotte, NC/Providence Day
Cory Lundeen	6-7	Sr	Charlotte, NC/Charlotte Christian
Tim Lyles	5-10	Sr	Durham, NC/Mt. Zion
Scooter McBride	5-9	Sr	High Point, NC/Central
Rod McCollum	6-6	So	High Point, NC/Andrews
Idris Mayo	6-3	Jr	Hillsborough, NC/Orange
Nicholas Means	5-10	Sr	Thomasville, NC
Brian Mobley	5-10	Sr	Greensboro, NC/Western Guilford
Thomas Mobley	6-5	Sr	Charlotte, NC/Providence
Marcus Oliver	6-2	Sr	Charlotte, NC/West Charlotte
Lechez Patterson	6-4	So	High Point, NC/Andrews
Scott Pettis	6-7	Sr	Charlotte, NC/Garinger
Cornelius Pigford	6-6	Jr	Elizabethtown, NC/East Bladen
Darmarcus Powell	6-6	Sr	Newton, NC/Conover
Demetrius Powell	6-2	Jr	Cerro Gordo, NC/West Columbus
James Powell	6-6	Sr	Newton, NC/Newton-Conover
Travis Pritchard	5-10	Jr	Morganton, NC/Freedom
Mark Saunders	6-2	Sr	Ramseur, NC/Eastern Randolph
Tommy Saunders	5-7	Sr	Greensboro, NC/Western Guilford
Lance Searcy	6-2	So	Winston-Salem, NC/North Forsyth
Cory Seels	6'9	Jr	Asheville, NC/Christ School
Scooter Sherrill	6'1	Jr	Mt. Ulla, NC/West Rowan
Tony Simmons	6-8	Jr	Fayetteville, NC/71st
Roach Stevenson	6-2	Sr	High Point, NC/Central
Charles Taylor	6-2	Jr	Siler City, NC/Jordan Matthews
Tony Taylor	6-5	Sr	Durham, NC/Mount Zion
Weston Taylor	6-6	Jr	Raleigh, NC/Southeast Raleigh
Dominque Townes	6-1	Sr	Charlotte, NC/West Charlotte
Alton Washington	6-6	Sr	Kinston, NC
Damion White	6-3	Jr	Charlotte, NC/West Charlotte
Rodney White	6-7	Sr	Durham, NC/Mount Zion
Tracy White	5-7	Jr	Charlotte, NC/West Charlotte
Chris Wilcox	6'8	Jr	Whiteville, NC
Marques Williams	6-7	Sr	Durham, NC/Mt. Zion
Nate Williams	6-8	Sr	Raleigh, NC/Ravenscroft
Wes Wilmoth	6-4	Jr	Dobson, NC/North Surry
Kelly Winstead	6-9	Sr	Wilson, NC Beddingfield

NORTH DAKOTA

Name	Ht	Cl	City/High School
Chuck Archambault	5-11	Sr	Bismarck, ND
Jeff Brandt	6-5	Sr	Minot, ND
John Godfread	6-11	Jr	Grand Forks, ND/Red River
Jared Keaveny	6-2	Sr	Wahpeton, ND
Travis Kraft	6-6	Sr	Mayville, ND/Mayville-Portland-Cliffors-Galesburt
Brian Verdouw	6-7	Jr	Bismarck, ND/St. Mary's

OHIO

Name	Ht	Cl	City/High School
Steve Albany	6-8	Sr	Canton, OH/Glen Oaks
Benjamin Alexander	6-9	Sr	Stow, OH
Josh Almonson	6-7	Jr	Bowling Green, OH
Jason Andreas	6-9	Sr	Sugarcreek, OH/Garaway
Malcom Andrews	5-8	So	Cincinnati, OH/Western Hills
Romeo Augustine	6-6	Sr	Youngstown, OH/Rayen

Name	Ht	Cl	City/High School
Ray Austin	6-7	Sr	Youngstown, OH/Liberty
B.J. Barre	6-1	Jr	Toledo, OH/Whitmer
Marvin Black	6-6	Sr	Cleveland, OH/John Hay
Mike Black	6-3	So	Newark, OH
Donovan Brown	6-7	So	Dayton, OH/Dunbar
Larry Brown	6-5	Jr	Cincinnati, OH/Princeton
Rashod Brown	5-8	Fr	Cleveland, OH/Benedictine
Brandon Bryant	6-5	Jr	Cincinnati, OH/Purcell-Marion
Jared Calhoun	6-2	Jr	Cleveland, OH/St. Joseph
Leonard Campbell	5-9	So	Canton, OH/McKinley
Frank Cardwell	5-10	Sr	Columbus, OH/Brookhaven
Maverick Carter	6-4	Jr	Akron, OH/St. Vincent-St. Mary
Brandon Childress	5-9	Jr	Bedford, OH/Chanel
Kameron Chones	6-4	Fr	Orange, OH
Kendall Chones	6-4	Fr	Orange, OH
Kyle Chones	6-3	Fr	Orange, OH
Henry Coffee	5-11	Jr	Dayton, OH/Dunbar
Jermaine Crosby	6-7	Sr	Cleveland, OH/Benedictine
Preston Dean	6-6	Sr	Columbus, OH/Mifflin
Terrance Dials	6-8	So	Youngstown, OH/Boardman
Larry Drake	6-5	Sr	Groveport, OH/Groveport-Madison
Jeremy Duncan	5-10	Sr	Cincinnati, OH/Moeller
Phillip Dupree	6-6	Sr	Columbus, OH/Brookhaven
Adam Ellis	6-4	Jr	Springfield, OH/North
Jamison Evans	6-4	So	Shaker Heights, OH
Jimmy Fisher	6-5	Jr	Huron, OH
Damon Francis	6-1	So	Springboro, OH
Mike Gansey	6-4	So	Olmstead Falls, OH
Brandon Green	6-1	Jr	Akron, OH/Central Hower
Greg Guiler	6-1	Jr	Chanel, OH/Winchester
Brooks Hall	6-6	Sr	Troy, OH
Bernard Harris	6-5	Sr	Riverside, OH/Stebbins
Josh Helm	6-5	Jr	Grove City, OH
Jason Hicks	5-9	So	Cleveland, OH/St. Joseph
Jawad Hillman	6-7	So	Lakewood, OH/St. Edward
Tyree Hinkston	6-6	Sr	Mt. Healthy, OH
Andy Hipsher	6-8	Sr	Akron, OH/Hoban
Brian Hipsher	6-3	So	Akron, OH/Hoban
Andre Hodge	5-11	Jr	Zanesville, OH
Lance Hood	6-7	So	Mansfield, OH
Dorian Hoover	6-9	Jr	Dayton, OH/Belmont
Danny Horace	6-6	So	Cincinnati, OH/Western Hills
Chase Howard	6-3	So	Columbus, OH/Brookhaven
Adam Howell	6-3	Sr	Lexington, OH
Keith Jackson	6-4	So	Cincinnati, OH/Purcel Marian
Jan Jagla	6-11	Jr	Medina, OH/Highland
Isaac Jefferson	6-3	Sr	Columbus, OH/West
Jermeny Johnson	6-7	Fr	Akron, OH/Hoban
Julius Johnson	6-5	Jr	Garfield Heights, OH
David Junius	6-5	Jr	Akron, OH/Buchtel
John King	6-4	Sr	Cleveland, OH/Benedictine
Forest Kirby	6-6	Sr	East Liverpool, OH
Scott Klingbiel	6-10	Jr	North Royalton, OH
Brian Lakes	5-11	Sr	Cincinnati, OH/Roger Bacon
Chris Lee	6-2	Fr	Xenia, OH/Beavercreek
Lenny Love	5-7	So	Cincinnati, OH/Withrow
T.J. Madison	6-3	So	Columbus, OH/Brookhaven
Matt Marinchick	6-11	Jr	Hudson, OH
Chester Mason	6-4	Jr	Cleveland, OH/John Hay
Ed McCants	6-4	Jr	Marion, OH/Marion Catholic
Rich McFadden	6-6	Jr	Struthers, OH
Antwan McGinnis	6-6	Jr	Columbus, OH/East
Clay McGowen	6-9	Jr	Westerville, OH/North
Scott Melle	6-6	Sr	Cleveland, OH/St. Joseph
Brady Merchant	6-3	Sr	Lebanon, OH
Sasha Mijalovic	6-10	Sr	Massillon, OH/Washington
Mike Monserez	6-5	Sr	Cincinnati, OH/Moeller
Eddie Mosley	6-5	Jr	East Cleveland, OH/Shaw
Mike Newman	6-3	Jr	Lakewood, OH/St. Edward
Slobodan Ocukiljic	6-8	Sr	Massillon, OH/Washington
Robbie Owens	6-5	Jr	Columbus, OH/Hartley
Eyuless Palmer	6-3	Jr	Toledo, OH/Libbey
Darryl Peterson	6-4	So	Cincinnati, OH/Western Hills
Rian Powell	6-4	Fr	Lakewood, OH/St. Edward
Jabari Ray	6-4	Jr	Columbus, OH/Ready
Tory Reed	6-8	Sr	Cleveland, OH/Cleveland Heights
Darrin Robinson	6-7	So	Cleveland, OH/East Tech
Robert Siwo	6-1	Fr	Xenia, OH
Rollie Smith	5-10	Sr	Cleveland, OH/St. Joseph
Sammy Smith	6-4	Jr	Worthington, OH/Christian
Adam Sommer	6-5	So	Columbus, OH/St. Charles
Ladetres Stallworth	6-7	Jr	Cincinnati, OH/Hughes
Thomas Stephens	6-0	Sr	Springfield, OH/South
Brew Story	6-2	So	Cleveland, OH/Benedictine
Brian Swift	5-10	So	Bedford, OH/Chanel
Matt Sylvester	6-6	So	Cincinnati, OH/Moeller
Derrick Tarver	6-3	Sr	Akron, OH/St. Vincent-St. Mary
Brian Thompson	6-5	Jr	Norton, OH
Keith Triplett	6-2	Jr	Toledo, OH/Bowsher
Michael Tucker	6-6	Sr	Cleveland, OH/Shaker Heights
Adam Waleskowski	6-8	So	Kettering, OH/Alter
Benjamin Walters	6-8	Sr	Youngstown, OH/Austintown
Omari Westley	6-7	Jr	Cleveland, OH/JFK
Danny Williams	6-4	So	Toledo, OH/Scott
Doug Williams	6-5	Sr	Beaver, OH/Eastern Pike
Kamil Wilson	6-3	Jr	Bedford, OH
Adam Wolfe	6-9	Sr	Westerville, OH/South
Mike Yelley	6-7	Jr	Wheelersburg, OH
Billy Younger	5-11	Jr	Reynoldsburg, OH

OKLAHOMA

Name	Ht	Cl	City/High School
Stephen Alexander	6-5	Jr	Midwest City, OK
Junior Amous	6-6	Sr	Oklahoma City, OK/Bishop McGuiness
Jamie Armstead	6-3	Sr	Tulsa, OK/Central
Jonathan Barnett	5-11	Sr	Tulsa, OK/Victory Christian
Alan Blount	5-11	Sr	Tulsa, OK/Booker T. Washington
Jonathan Bluitt	5-8	So	Oklahoma City, OK/McGuiness
Micah Boylan	6-4	Sr	Edmond, OK/Deer Creek
Nate Boylan	6-3	Sr	Norman, OK
Ty Bridwell	6-4	Sr	Blanchard, OK
March Brown	5-11	Sr	Sand Springs, OK/Charles Page
Michael Byrd	6-0	Sr	Oklahoma CIty, OK/John Marshall
Brian Cardwell	6-9	Sr	Sapulpa, OK
Eric Castro	6-7	So	Oklahoma City, OK/Mt. St. Mary
Terrence Crawford	6-6	Jr	Oklahoma City, OK/McGuiness
Joe Cummings	6-4	Sr	Pocola, OK
Greg Davis	6-8	Jr	Tulsa, OK/Washington
Luke Dobbins	6-1	Jr	Tahlequah, OK
Hank Dooley	6-7	Jr	Yale, OK
Cue Doyle	6-7	Jr	Tulsa, OK/McClain
Randy Gabler	6-9	Sr	Altus, OK
Mathew Gastel	6-9	Jr	Jenks, OK
Percy Green	6-6	Sr	Oklahoma City, OK/Western Heights
Asher Hall	6-3	Jr	Coweta, OK
Sean Kelly	6-1	Sr	Tulsa, OK/Bishop Kelley
Jack Marlow	6-10	Jr	Tulsa, OK/Tulsa Union
Pat Moore	6-7	So	Pawnee, OK
JoJo Noles	6-1	Jr	Tulsa, OK/Central
Antonio Reed	6-1	Sr	Tulsa, OK/Booker T. Washington
Dave Schaefer	7-3	So	Tulsa, OK/Victory Christian
Shelden Williams	6-7	Fr	Midwest City, OK
Jaime Waltonbaugh	5-9	Sr	Tulsa, OK/Hale

OREGON

Name	Ht	Cl	City/High School
Elliott Alexander	6-3	Sr	Salem, OR/North
Jim Anderson	6-9	Sr	Junction City, OR
Heath Bailey	6-10	Jr	Beaverton, OR
Boomer Brazzle	6-6	Sr	Portland, OR/Benson Tech
Brandon Brooks	5-10	Jr	Portland, OR/Jefferson
Devon Carr	6-3	So	West Linn, OR
Ben Coffee	6-6	Sr	Portland, OR/Benson Tech
Tim Frost	6-10	Sr	Klamath Falls, OR /Henley
Nick Gibbs	6-7	Sr	Gresham, OR/Centennial
Terrance Green	6-3	Sr	Portland, OR/Benson Tech
Brian Jackson	6-9	Sr	Astoria, OR/Knappa
Elijah Jackson	6-3	Sr	Portland, OR/Wilson
Luke Jackson	6-5	Jr	Creswell, OR
Michael Lee	6-1	So	Portland, OR/Jefferson
Quintae McKinney	6-7	Jr	Portland, OR/Cleveland
Brian Michaelson	6-4	Jr	Portland, OR/Jesuit
Aaron Miles	5-11	So	Portland, OR/Jefferson
Jamar Mitchell	6-9	Jr	Portland, OR/Madison
Matt Nelson	6-6	Sr	West Linn, OR
Colin Orirard	6-6	Sr	Corvallis, OR/Crescent Valley
Greg Smith	6-11	Sr	Cottage Grove, OR
Blake Stepp	6-3	Jr	Eugene, OR/South
Salim Stoudamire	6-0	So	Portland, OR/Lincoln
Tionte Tims	5-10	Sr	Portland, OR/Benson Tech
John Tinnon	6-7	Jr	Portland, OR/Benson Tech
Tom Watson	6-11	Sr	Tualatin, OR
Renaldo Williams	6-6	Sr	Portland, OR/Westview

PENNSYLVANIA

Name	Ht	Cl	City/High School
Carnell Adams	6-8	Sr	Philadelphia, PA/Cedar Grove
John Allen	6-3	So	Coatesville, PA
Phillip Alston	6-1	Jr	Philadelphia, PA/Frankfort
Chas Bailey	6-4	Jr	Philadelphia, PA/Neumann
Hassan Benton	6-5	Jr	Philadelphia, PA/Cedar Grove
Kenyette Bey	5-7	Sr	Philadelphia, PA/Roman Catholic
Danny Bosnic	6-5	Jr	Fairchance, PA/Gallentin
Brandon Bridgeman	6-8	So	Philadelphia, PA /Neumann
Maurice Bryant	5-5	So	Coatesville, PA
Pat Carroll	6-5	So	Horsham, PA /Hatboro-Horsham
Sharod Carroll	6-4	Sr	Philadelphia, PA/Simon Gratz
Purcell Coles	6-2	Jr	Philadelphia, PA/Simon Gratz
Chris Copp	6-0	Jr	Bernville, PA/Tulpehocken
Greg Corum	6-3	Jr	Pottstown, PA
David Crawford	5-9	Jr	Philadelphia, PA/Roman Catholic
Jason Curry	5-10	Sr	Slippery Rock, PA
Melvin Eason	6-3	Sr	Philadelphia, PA/Edison
Doug Fairfax	6-3	Sr	Havertown, PA/Haverford Township
Donnel Feaster	5-8	Sr	Philadelphia, PA/West
Contrell Fletcher	5-8	So	Philadelphia, PA /Neumann
Tahric Gosley	6-9	Sr	Philadelphia, PA/Simon Gratz
Marques Green	5-6	Jr	Norristown, PA
John Grove	6-10	Sr	Grove City, PA/George Republic
Jarrod Gruber	6-6	Jr	Hamburg, PA
Billy Guess	6-4	Sr	Plymouth Meeting, PA/Plymouth Whitemarsh
Andre Henry	5-6	So	Harrisburg, PA
Dave Hindenlang	6-7	Sr	Johnstown, PA
Robert Hostetter	6-3	Sr	Lancaster, PA/Lancaster Memnonite
Ashley Howard	5-9	Sr	Philadelphia, PA/St. Joseph Prep
Abdul Johnson	6-5	Jr	Philadelphia, PA/West Catholic
Justin Luber	5-8	Jr	Jenkintown, PA/Abington Friends
Breagan Moore	6-1	Jr	Harrisburg, PA
Andre Morton	6-6	Sr	Philadelphia, PA/Chester
Brian Novitsky	6-3	So	Ft. Washington, PA /Upper Dublin

Name	Ht	Cl	City/High School
Ugonna Onyekwe	6-9	Pr	Mercersburg, PA/Mercersburg Academy
Stephon Pelle	6-8	Sr	Mercersburg, PA/Mercersburg Academy
Scott Pennwell	6-5	Jr	Camp Hill, PA/Cedar Cliff
Charles Pringle	6-8	Sr	Philadelphia, PA/Christian Academy
Eric Pugh	6-5	Sr	Philadelphia, PA/Dobbins Tech
Jermaine Robinson	6-2	Sr	Philadelphia, PA/Simon Gratz
Jason Roseto	6-11	Sr	Harborcreek, PA
Benjamin Slater	6-6	Sr	Jenkintown, PA/Abington Friends
Ben Slater	6-6	Jr	Jenkintown, PA/Abington Friends
Zakee Smith	5-11	Sr	Philadelphia, PA/Christian Academy
Terrence Stokes	5-10	Jr	Philadelphia, PA/Simon Gratz
Brent Storm	6-0	Jr	Philadelphia, PA/Penn Charter
Alex Thompson	5-10	Jr	Philadelphia, PA/Olney
Anthony Thompson	6-5	So	Harrisburg, PA
Jamal Weeks	6-5	Sr	Philadelphia, PA/Franklin Learning Center
Tim Whitworth	6-3	Sr	Philadelphia, PA/Chestnut Hill
Michael Wild	6-2	Jr	Philadelphia, PA/Roman Catholic
Karem Wright	6-9	Sr	Mercersburg, PA/Mercersburg Academy
David Young	6-3	Sr	New Castle, PA

RHODE ISLAND

Name	Ht	Cl	City/High School
Robert Griffin	6-0	Sr	Providence, RI/St. Raphael
Tim Murphy	6-3	Sr	Providence, RI/La Salle
Jason Nickerson	6-4	Sr	Warwick, RI/Bishop Hendricksen
Joshua Odugbela	6-8	Sr	Barrington, RI/St. Andrew's

SOUTH CAROLINA

Name	Ht	Cl	City/High School
C.W. Bankhead	6-5	Jr	Mauldin, SC
Jerrod Coefield	5-6	So	Columbia, SC/Keenan
Pat Cooper	6-5	So	Newberry, SC
Zebulon Cope	6-7	Jr	Columbia, SC/Hammond School
Charles Copeland	5-11	Sr	Spartanburg, SC
Ben Daniels	6-1	Sr	North Charleston, SC
Marcus Gerald	6-2	So	Mullins, SC
Jamal Grey	6-7	Jr	Chester, SC
Derrick Hamilton	6-4	Jr	Dillon, SC
Alexander Harper	6-2	So	Columbia, SC/Keenan
Michael Hayes	6-7	Sr	St. Matthews, SC/Calhoun County
Brandon Howard	6-7	Sr	Greer, SC /Riverside
Ivan Howell	6-7	Sr	Hopkins, SC/Lower Richland
Rolando Howell	6-8	Jr	Hopkins, SC/Lower Richland
Robert Jackson	6-1	Sr	Greenville, SC
Van Jamison	6-5	Sr	Holly Hill, SC/Roberts
Antwon Jones	6-8	Sr	Anderson, SC/Westside
Clary Judge	5-11	Sr	North Charleston, SC
Brian Latimer	6-0	Jr	Columbia, SC/Richland Northeast
Cedric McHaney	6-7	Jr	Iva, SC/Crescent
Kenny Ruby	6-3	Sr	Taylors, SC/Eastside
Benjamin Ryan	6-0	Jr	Lexington, SC
Edward Scott	5-11	Sr	Hopkins, SC/Lower Richland
Marques Strong	6-2	Jr	Great Falls, SC
Charles Sullivan	5-11	Sr	Greenville, SC/J.L. Mann
Chavis Thompson	6-9	Jr	Florence, SC/Wilson
Troy Washington	6-7	So	Denmark, SC
Derek Watson	6-3	Sr	Williamston, SC/Palmetto
Jarred Weeks	6-6	So	Columbia, SC/Keenan
Cooper Wilson	6-3	Jr	Sumpter, SC/Wilson Hall
Robert Wylie	6-4	So	Columbia, SC/Keenan

SOUTH DAKOTA

Name	Ht	Cl	City/High School
Steve Anderson	6-8	Jr	Rapid City, SD/Central
Shad Carney	6-6	So	Sioux Falls, SD/Roosevelt
J.R. Johnson	6-3	Sr	Groton, SD
Chris Knight	6-2	Jr	Aberdeen, SD/Central
Jason LaFave	6-1	So	Selby, SD
Vance Newman	6-6	Jr	Watertown, SD
Derek Paulsen	6-4	Jr	Custer, SD
Jared Reiner	6-10	Jr	Tripp, SD/Tripp Delmont
Chris Stoebner	6-3	Sr	Harrisburg, SD
Denver Ten Broek	6-4	Sr	McIntosh, SD
Tony Young	6-2	Sr	Mitchell, SD

TENNESSEE

Name	Ht	Cl	City/High School
Jared Austin	6-7	Sr	Sparta, TN/White County
Gary Bledsoe	6-4	Sr	Memphis, TN/Hamilton
Dujuan Bogan	6-4	Sr	Memphis, TN/Northside
Danny Brown	5-8	Sr	Memphis, TN/Oakhaven
Jace Bryant	6-4	Jr	Collinwood, TN
Antonio Burkes	6-1	Sr	Memphis, TN/Booker T. Washington
Kevin Cal	6-4	Sr	Chattanooga, TN/Tyner
Corey Carr	6-2	Jr	Memphis, TN/East
Renaldo Curry	6-2	Jr	Memphis, TN/East
Ashley Champion	6-5	Sr	Bolivar, TN/Central
Shawn Davis	6-5	Jr	Memphis, TN/Hamilton
Jason Etherton	6-2	Sr	Dandridge, TN/Jefferson County
Brian Felts	6-6	Sr	Knoxville, TN/Austin-East
Josh Harr	6-6	Jr	Cleveland, TN/Bradley
Jason Harrell	6-6	Sr	Troy, TN/Obion Central
Tim Harris	6-6	Sr	Clarksville, TN/Northeast
Dave Harrison	6-9	So	Brentwood, TN/Brentwood Academy
Demarcus Hence	6-5	Sr	Memphis, TN/Fairley
Marcus Hill	5-7	So	Memphis, TN/Central
Jason Holwerda	6-4	So	Chattanooga, TN/Chattanooga Christian
Thomas Jackson	6-7	Sr	Memphis, TN/Whitehaven
Terrance Johnson	6-9	So	Memphis, TN/Hillcrest
Brent Jolley	6-5	Sr	Sparta, TN/White County
James Kimber	6-2	Sr	Knoxville, TN/Austin East
George Laney	6-3	Sr	Memphis, TN/White Station
Ryan Lawson	6-2	Sr	Rogersville, TN/Cherokee
Nathaniel McCoy	6-2	Jr	Pigeon Forge, TN
Scooter McFadgon	6-3	Jr	Memphis, TN/Raleigh-Egypt
Fred McGhee	6-3	Jr	Memphis, TN/East
Travis Mull	6-1	Sr	Memphis, TN/Kingsbury
Mike Palmer	6-8	Sr	Dyer, TN/Gibson County
Bronson Parker	6-5	Sr	Dandridge, TN/Jefferson County
Craig Price	6-4	Sr	Oliver Springs, TN
Antonio Rambo	5-10	Jr	Memphis, TN/Hamilton
Billy Richmond	6-3	Jr	Memphis, TN/Hamilton
Charles Richmond	6-10	Sr	Memphis, TN/Booker T. Washington
Craig Sexton	6-7	Sr	Sevierville, TN/Sevier County
Ron Slay	6-6	Sr	Nashville, TN/Pearl-Cohn
Justin Smith	6-1	Jr	Memphis, TN/Hamilton
Witt Smith	6-6	Sr	Dandridge, TN/Jefferson County
Andy Starrett	6-5	Sr	Collierville, TN
Antonio Whitehead	6-2	Sr	Nashville, TN/Pearl-Cohn
Odei Williams	6-3	Sr	Memphis, TN/Trezvant
Travis Williams	6-1	Sr	Oliver Springs, TN
Qyntel Woods	6-7	Sr	Memphis, TN/Carver

TEXAS

Name	Ht	Cl	City/High School
Danny Allen	5-10	Jr	Dallas, TX/Lincoln
Jovanni Allen	6-3	Sr	Ft. Worth, TX/Southwest
Vincent Anderson	6-8	Sr	Houston, TX/Waltrip
Ronald Banks	6-0	Jr	Gainesville, TX
Ryan Belcher	5-10	So	Houston, TX/Mt. Carmel
Winston Blake	6-4	Sr	Plano, TX
Brian Boddicker	6-9	Jr	Duncanville, TX
Chris Booker	6-7	Jr	Ft. Worth, TX/Diamond Hill
Willie Broughton	6-5	Jr	Plano, TX/East
Devin Brown	6-3	Sr	San Antonio, TX/West Campus
Roosevelt Brown	6-4	Sr	Duncanville, TX
Andrew Bryant	6-7	Jr	Denison, TX
Jason Burke	6-5	Sr	Plano, TX/Plano East
Nolan Butterfras	6-9	Jr	Houston, TX/Cypress Creek
Jermaine Byrd	5-7	Jr	Houston, TX/Reagan
Cameron Campbell	6-5	Jr	Katy, TX/Cypress Springs
Golden Corner	6-0	So	Beaumont, TX/Westbrook
DoJuan Covington	6-0	Sr	Kileen, TX
Donald Crabtree	6-5	Jr	Dallas, TX/Madison
Andre Craddock	6-2	Sr	Farmersville, TX
Carl Crawford	6-2	Sr	Houston, TX/Jefferson Davis
Regis Davonish	6-4	Jr	Alief, TX/Alief-Elsik
Edmond Eddings	6-6	Jr	Houston, TX/Kempner
Michael Edwards	6-3	Jr	Garland, TX
Nick Egland	6-4	So	Houston, TX/Westfield
Brandon Evans	6-9	Sr	Houston, TX/Kempner
Daniel Ewing	6-3	So	Sugarland, TX/Willowridge
James Felder	6-6	Sr	Dallas, TX/Skyline
Aaron Flick	6-8	Sr	Garland, TX/North Garland
Terrance Ford	5-10	So	Sugarland, TX/Willowridge
Xavier Gaines	6-2	So	Dallas, TX/Carter
Maurice Gardner	6-3	Jr	Lancaster, TX
Jason Gibson	6-9	Sr	Plano, TX/Plano East
Daniel Glaser	6-9	Jr	Austin, TX/Bowie
Wendell Greenleaf	6-2	Sr	Houston, TX/North Shore
Barry Hairston	6-4	Sr	Harlingen, TX/Marine Military Academy
Matt Hall	6-0	Jr	Katy, TX
Meador Hall	6-7	Sr	Lubbock, TX/Coronado
Mario Hamilton	6-7	Pr	Harlingen, TX/Marine Military Academy
Jason Hammick	6-7	Jr	The Colony, TX
Chris Harris	6-4	So	Houston, TX/Boys Prep
Richard Hashaway	6-4	Jr	Dallas, TX/Kimball
Jon Havens	6-2	Sr	Lewisville, TX
Ronald Hobbs	6-5	Sr	Everman, TX
Leonard Hopkins	6-3	Jr	Dallas, TX/Lincoln
Justin Hurbert	6-1	Jr	San Antonio, TX/Taft
Anthony Ikeakor	6-8	Jr	Houston, TX/Westbury Christian
Antoine Jackson	6-8	Jr	San Antonio, TX/Jay
Carl Jones	6-9	Sr	Humble, TX
Dandric Jones	6-1	So	Dallas, TX/Kimball
Philip Jones	6-4	Sr	Kileen, TX
Roger Jordan	6-4	Jr	League City, TX/Clear Creek
James Kidd	6-2	Sr	Sulphur Springs, TX
Shane King	6-10	Jr	Allen, TX
Jason Klotz	6-10	Jr	Houston, TX/Klein Forest
Logan Kosmalski	6-8	Jr	Trinity, TX
Rodney Lee	6-5	Sr	Ft. Worth, TX/Southwest
Keith Lemons	6-1	Sr	Houston, TX/Sharpstown
Craig Lewis	6-5	Jr	Garland, TX/North Garland
Kendrick Lincoln	6-5	Sr	Dallas, TX/Lincoln
Dylan Loal	6-5	Jr	Houston, TX/Stratford
Trammell Martin	6-5	Jr	Bellaire, TX/Episcopal
Melroy McElvey	6-7	Sr	Houston, TX/Kashmere
Ivan McFarlin	6-7	Jr	Missouri City, TX
J.B. McGee	6-2	Sr	Bryan, TX
Roy McKinney	6-6	Jr	Denton, TX/Ryan
Bingo Merriex	6-7	Sr	Wichita Falls, TX
Jermichael Miller	6-7	Jr	Houston, TX/Wheatley
Eddie Moten	5-11	Jr	Lancaster, TX
Curtis Nash	6-4	Sr	Hurst, TX/L.D. Bell
Nate Nelson	6-2	Sr	Burkburnett, TX
Chris Ogden	6-7	Sr	Seminole, TX
Quinn Parker	5-9	Jr	Justin, TX/Northwest
Dominque Perkins	6-8	So	Amarillo, TX

Name	Ht	Cl	City/High School
Ed Persia	6-0	Jr	Beaumont, TX/Monsignor Kelly
Jason Pritchard	6-8	Sr	Livingston, TX
Ruben Randall	6-5	Jr	Wortham, TX
Chris Rhodes	6-7	So	Houston, TX/Westbury
Isaac Rollins	6-5	So	Sugarland, TX/Willowridge
Hamilton Rucker	6-6	Sr	League City, TX
Larry Satchell	6-6	Sr	Waco, TX
Marcus Shropshire	6-2	Jr	Grand Prairie, TX/South Grand Prairie
Marcus Simmons	5-11	Sr	Houston, TX/Milby
Marcus Sloan	6-5	So	Houston, TX/Eisenhower
Roy Smallwood	6-5	Sr	Sugarland, TX/Dulles
Howard Smith	6-1	Sr	Killeen, TX
Mike Smith	6-8	Sr	Richardson, TX
Clayton Southerland	6-8	Sr	Richardson, TX/Berkner
Shawn Spikes	6-0	Sr	Dallas, TX/Bryan Adams
David Stephens	6-10	Sr	Fort Worth, TX/Crowley
Darren Stephens	6-2	Jr	Lewisville, TX
David Sykes	6-4	Sr	Duncanville, TX
Damien Tasby	6-6	Sr	Houston, TX/Yates
Charles Tatum	5-11	Sr	Midland, TX
Brandon Thompson	6-6	Sr	La Marque, TX
Juan Valdez	6-5	Sr	San Antonio, TX/Holmes
Hunter Wall	6-3	Jr	Coppell, TX
Bryan Williams	6-7	Jr	Gainesville, TX
Field Williams	6-3	Jr	Dallas, TX/Kimball
George Williams	6-8	Sr	Missouri City, TX/Elkins
Columbus Willis	6-3	Jr	Carrollton, TX/Newman-Smith
Rashard Wright	6-3	Sr	Sugarland, TX/Austin
William Wyatt	6-6	Sr	Grand Prairie, TX/South Grand Prairie

UTAH

Name	Ht	Cl	City/High School
Lance Allred	6-10	Sr	Salt Lake City, UT /East
Jackson Brown	6-4	Sr	Sandy, UT/Jordan
Jake Chrisman	6-8	Jr	Provo, UT
Lawrence Cowan	6-4	Jr	Salt Lake City, UT/Brighton
Derrick Dawes	6-10	Jr	Salt Lake City, UT/Cottonwood
Kevin Dorenbusch	6-7	Sr	Magna, UT/Cyprus
Lance Ellett	6-9	So	Magna, UT/Cyprus
Noah Eyre	6-6	Sr	Salt Lake City, UT/East
Darrin Hammer	5-11	Jr	Salt Lake City, UT/East
Blake Hanson	6-6	Sr	Salt Lake City, UT/Hillcrest
Luke Hendrix	6-1	Jr	Salt Lake City, UT/Brighton
Tim Henry	6-4	Sr	Orem, UT/Mountain View
Mike Higgins	6-8	Jr	South Jordan, UT/Bingham
Aaron Hill	6-3	Sr	Gunnison, UT
Tyler Holt	6-3	Jr	South Jordan, UT/Bingham
Chris Huber	6-2	Sr	Tremonton, UT/Bear River
Schaeffer Jackson	6-2	Jr	Provo, UT
Jared Jensen	6-8	So	Plain City, UT/Fremont
Judd Lyon	6-4	Sr	Salt Lake City, UT/Hillcrest
Garners Meads	6-8	Jr	Salt Lake City, UT/Brighton
Josh Neeley	6-2	Sr	Salt Lake City, UT/Cottonwood
Shawn Opunui	5-11	Sr	Orem, UT
Jesse Pinegar	6-9	Jr	Salt Lake City, UT/Brighton
Kenyon Rodgers	5-9	Sr	Salt Lake City, UT/Granite
Cliff Scholer	6-7	Sr	Clearfield, UT
Jake Schroeder	6-2	Sr	South Jordan, UT/Bingham
Morgan Sharp	6-1	Jr	Sandy, UT/Jordan
Trevor Stokes	6-0	Sr	Smithfield, UT/Sky View
Travis Viscentin	6-7	Sr	Heber City, UT/Wasatch

VERMONT

Name	Ht	Cl	City/High School
Jeff Dixon	6-7	Sr	Brattleboro, VT
David Hannah	6-2	Sr	Randolph, VT
Matt Scheftic	6-7	Sr	Essex, VT
Jeff Weld	5-11	Sr	Windsor, VT

VIRGINIA

Name	Ht	Cl	City/High School
John Alexander	5-11	Sr	Fairfax, VA/St. Paul VI
Ben Bates	6-10	Sr	Middleburg, VA/Notre Dame Academy
Val Brown	6-1	Sr	Springfield, VA/Robert Lee
Jason Buston	6-3	Sr	Reston, VA/South Lakes
Aaron Chambliss	5-11	Sr	Hampton, VA
Almondo Curry	5-6	Sr	Hampton, VA
David Fanning	6-2	Sr	Chesapeake, VA/Western Branch
Jamal Gilcrist	5-11	Sr	Middleburg, VA/Notre Dame Academy
Ron Ginyard	6-4	Sr	Fairfax, VA/Paul VI
Derrick Goode	6-10	Sr	Severn, MD/Archbishop Spaulding
Marcus Green	6-2	Sr	Alexandria, VA/Episcopal
Terry Green	6-4	Sr	Middleburg, VA/Notre Dame Academy
Jonathon Harget	6-1	So	Highland Springs, VA
Cliff Hawkins	6-2	Jr	Mouth of Wilson, VA/Oak Hill
Matt Hillary	6-8	Sr	Manassas, VA/Seton
Phillip Janney	6-1	Sr	Richmond, VA/Collegiate
Shamar Johnson	6-6	Sr	Arlington, VA/Washington-Lee
Dominic Jones	6-0	Jr	Chesterfield, VA/Bailey Bridge
Demetrius Lee	6-1	Sr	Norfolk, VA/B.T. Washington
Allen Lovette	6-4	Jr	Mouth of Wilson, VA/Oak Hill
Nate McEachin	7-0	Sr	Norfolk, VA/Ryan Academy
Paul Michael	6-6	Sr	Newport News, VA/Menchville
Alex Miloserdov	6-5	Jr	Lynchburg, VA/Virginia Episcopal
Luke Minor	7-3	Sr	Dyke, VA/Blue Ridge School
Camara Mintz	6-0	Sr	Lynchburg, VA/Heritage
Daniel Mogels	6-11	Sr	Fairfax, VA/Paul VI
Greg Pettis	6-8	Sr	Lynchburg, VA/Virginia Episcopal
Tevon Raikes	6-0	Jr	Newport News, VA/Heritage
Robert Reed	7-0	Sr	Lynchburg, VA/Virginia Episcopal
Sylbrin Robinson	6-9	Pr	Hargrave Military/Chatham, VA
Jason Rogers	6-10	Sr	Staunton, VA/Robert E. Lee
Michael Rowson	6-7	Sr	Fairfax, VA/Robinson
Tyrone Sally	6-6	Jr	Richmond, VA/Benedictine
Ronald Slay	6-6	Sr	Mouth of Wilson, VA/Oak Hill
James Smith	6-6	Jr	Norfolk, VA/Booker T. Washington
Bryson Spinner	6-3	Sr	Alexandria, VA/Episcopal
Tyree Spinner	6-4	Jr	Fairfax, VA/Paul IV
Johnnie Story	6-4	Jr	Hampton, VA
Morten Szmiedowicz	6-10	Jr	Lynchburg, VA/Virginia Episcopal
Anthony Tyler	6-8	Sr	Norfolk, VA/Ryan Academy
Tim Washington	6-8	Sr	Chatham, VA/Hargrave Military
Rico Waters	5-8	Jr	Hampton, VA/Phoebus
Travis Watson	6-7	Sr	Mouth of Wilson, VA/Oak Hill
Bobby Weismiller	6-3	Sr	Middleburg, VA/Notre Dame Academy
Maurece Wilkins	6-3	Jr	Alexandria, VA/West Potomac
Keith Willis	6-7	Sr	Norfolk, VA/Norview
Jerrian Younger	6-8	Sr	Danville, VA/George Washington

WASHINGTON

Name	Ht	Cl	City/High School
Yuself Azez	6-3	Sr	Seattle, WA/Foster
Ross Benson	6-8	Sr	Everett, WA/Cascade
Tyler Besecker	6-5	Sr	Mercer Island, WA
Dante Branham	6-8	So	Everett, WA/Mariner
Nate Burleson	6-2	Sr	Seattle, WA/O'Dea
Mark Campbell	6-2	Sr	Mount Vernon, WA
Jamal Crawford	6-4	Sr	Seattle, WA/Rainier Beach
Troy DeVries	6-0	So	Mt. Vernon, WA
Tim Ellis	6-4	Jr	Seattle, WA/Rainier Beach
Ricky Frazier	5-8	Jr	Seattle, WA/Rainier Beach
Amon Gordan	6-3	Jr	Everett, WA/Mariner
Jimmy Haywood	6-3	Sr	Seattle, WA/Franklin
Teyo Johnson	6-6	Jr	Everett, WA/Mariner
Eddie Lincoln	6-4	Jr	Seattle, WA/O'Dea
Matt Logie	6-3	Sr	Mercer Island, WA
Elliott Prasse-Freeman	6-0	Sr	Mercer Island, WA
Luke Ridnour	6-1	Jr	Blaine, WA
Jesse Rossmeier	6-6	Sr	Auburn, WA
Paul Roth	6-10	Sr	Seattle, WA/O'Dea
Jay Sherell	6-8	Sr	Spanaway, WA/Bethel
Bryan Whitehead	6-8	Sr	Mount Vernon, WA

WEST VIRGINIA

Name	Ht	Cl	City/High School
Drew Smith	6-4	Sr	Beckley, WV/Woodrow Wilson
John Smith	6-10	Sr	Dunbar, WV

WISCONSIN

Name	Ht	Cl	City/High School
Taron Barker	5-10	Sr	Racine, WI/J.J. Case
Donald "Lou" Chapman	5-11	Sr	Milwaukee, WI/Bay View
Kamarr Davis	6-5	So	Milwaukee, WI/Washington
Dave Edwards	6-2	Jr	Milwaukee, WI/Washington
Latrell Fleming	6-2	So	Whitefish Bay, WI/Dominican
Gabriel Green	5-10	So	Milwaukee, WI/Vincent
Quemont Greer	6-6	So	Milwaukee, WI/Vincent
Marcus Ivey	6-4	Sr	Milwaukee, WI/Riverside
Brian Jordan	6-0	So	Whitefish Bay, WI/Dominican
Marques Lewis	6-6	So	Milwaukee, WI/Tech
Dave Mader	6-10	Sr	Appleton, WI/East
Scott Merritt	6-9	Jr	Wauwatosa, WI/East
Lewis Monroe	6-4	Sr	Madison, WI/East
Pat Rodgers	6-7	So	Milwaukee, WI/Vincent
Terry Sanders	6-7	Sr	Milwaukee, WI/Vincent
Angelo Smith	6-2	Fr	Glendale, WI/Nicolet
Julian Swartz	6-4	Sr	Waukesha, WI/South
Dejuan Turner	6-1	Jr	Milwaukee, WI/Washington
Cory Turrintine	6-0	Fr	Milwaukee, WI/Hamilton
Brian Weber	6-10	Sr	Oak Creek, WI
Eugene Webster	5-10	Sr	Racine, WI /Horlick
Dan Weisse	5-11	Sr	Oshkosh, WI/North
James Wright	6-6	Sr	Milwaukee, WI/Vincent

WYOMING

Name	Ht	Cl	City/High School
Jacque Finn	6-2	Sr	Natrona County
Sundance Wicks	6-4	Sr	Campbell County

BEN WILSON HIGH SCHOOL TOP 44 PROFILES

by Brick Oettinger, PREP STARS RECRUITER'S HANDBOOK

FIRST TEAM

KEITH BOGANS, *6-5, 203 lbs., senior, wing guard/small forward, DeMatha Catholic HS/Hyattsville, MD*

Entering the 1998-99 season, we rank Keith Bogans the number one senior prospect (by a narrow margin over Donnell Harvey) because we believe he's closer to becoming a superstar than anyone else in the class. Interestingly, Bogans has been quoted as saying, "It doesn't really matter about the ranking. I could be ranked like 100 and it wouldn't matter to me."

But that's a lot of baloney. It's obvious from the way he plays that he takes great pride in being, at the minimum, a serious contender for No. 1 nationally in the senior class.

MAJOR ACCOMPLISHMENTS: Bogans is a true rarity, in that he became a key player for the always-powerful DeMatha Stags during his freshman season in 1995-96. Coming off the bench, he averaged 12.7 points, 3.8 rebounds and 2.0 assists. Versus heralded Paterson (NJ) Paterson Catholic in the Holiday Invitational Tournament at Raleigh (NC), he racked up 29 points in 22 minutes.

Bogan's statistics as a sophomoreomore and junior were nearly identical, but that fact masks his clear improvement as a player during the course of those two seasons. As a sophomore, he averaged 19.0 points, 6.5 rebounds and 4.5 assists. In 1997-98, the figures were 19.2 points, 6.1 rebounds and 3.4 assists, along with a field-goal percentage of 55, for a 34-1 team that wound up No. 3 in USA Today's final national rankings and amassed the second-highest victory total is DeMatha's storied history.

In the city title game in March, Bogan scored 20 points and was chosen MVP as the Stags defeated Anacostia. His season high of 30 points came in DeMatha's only loss, a stunning 68-63 decision to quick Anderson (IN) High in the DeMatha Invitational at the MCI Center in D.C. Actually, his career game high of 38 points came as a sophomore.

The last two seasons, he was first-team All-Metro D.C. and *USA Today* All-USA Honorable Mention. As a junior, he made *Parade*'s All-America second-team, with first-team choice DerMarr Johnson the only non-senior listed ahead of him. This spring, *USA Today* chose Bogans as one of the Top 15 Juniors (rising seniors) to Watch nationally.

In summer play, a year ago he attended the adidas ABCD Camp in Teaneck (NJ) for two days, which was long enough for him to showcase his array of talents. A couple of weeks later, he combined with Johnson and others to pace D.C. Team Assault to the championship of the 186-team adidas Big Time tournament in Las Vegas. For his efforts in Vegas, he was an obvious choice for the All-tournament team.

The 1998 summer provided a different, less auspicious story for Bogans, who attended summer school (although his grade-point averaged reportedly is 2.8) and adhered to famed DeMatha coach Morgan Wootten's wishes by not attending the adidas ABCD Camp despite constant reports that he would arrive a couple of days late. He did excel locally in the Kenner Pro-Am Summer League, but the sole national event he participated in (flying in the day that pool play ended) was, again, the adidas Big Time, which contained an incredible 224 teams.

This time, despite the presence of Johnson (whose play was sub-par), big-time forward Derrick Payne, and a host of guards who are high Division 1 prospects, D.C. Assault struggled to reach the quarterfinals, fell apart down the stretch and lost shockingly by an 81-66 count to the Madison Broncos, a New York City area team with no big national names on its roster. But don't blame Bogans (or Payne), who played reasonably well by his stratospheric standards but got betrayed by mediocre play from Johnson and the touted guards.

Because of his team's stunning defeat and the fact that he missed a couple of games, Bogans was not selected to the 35-man All-tournament team. Don't, however, view that as a referendum on his ability.

STRENGTHS AND AREAS NEEDING WORK: A top athlete with outstanding skills and savvy, Keith has lots of heart and confidence, which nearly always rubs off on his teammates. He understands the game, is fundamentally sound, and possesses loads of poise.

On offense, he plays within the team concept, yet he scores so well off the dribble that (as with Michael Jordan) defenders must try to make him pull up and shoot a contested jump shot. They simply seek to contain him, because they know they can't really stop him.

Besides his talent at driving, elevating and completing the play, Bogans is a good but not great three-point shooter. His three-point field-goal percentage of 28 last season belies the current accuracy of his shot, although we wouldn't call him the same kind of "pure" perimeter marksman that DeMatha teammate Joe Forte is. This is the area that Bogans needs to work on more than any other.

Additionally, he is a good passer and solid (though unspectacular) handler who sees the court well. With his leaping ability, he's certainly capable of grabbing more than six rebounds per game (although DeMatha has four players at least 6-10), and he can be a true stopper at the defensive end, thanks to his quickness, strength, intensity and floor I.Q.

COLLEGIATE PREFERENCES: His final four college choices are Kentucky, Georgia Tech, Michigan and Connecticut. Early co-favorite (along with Kentucky) North Carolina strangely stopped calling Bogans, then started again, but apparently thinks Kentucky has the inside track and thus was tepid in its pursuit until eliminated from consideration.

Our gut feeling is that it will be difficult for anyone to come in now and get him away from the Wildcats.

BOTTOM LINE: Barring injury, he will get more attention than any other prep senior because he's the marquee player on probably the No. 1-ranked high school team in the nation.

CASEY SANDERS, *6-11, 205 lbs., senior, center, Tampa Preparatory HS/Tampa, FL*

Our choice as the No. 1 senior center *prospect* (the key word) in the nation is Casey Sanders, who at times during the last two years has flashed absolute shades of brilliance. At other times, however, it is abundantly clear that he is not yet a fully polished product by any means. But because he only began playing in the ninth grade, that should be expected.

MAJOR ACCOMPLISHMENTS: Based on his play last season for Tampa Prep, *USA Today* chose him All-USA Honorable Mention and, even more prestigiously, one of the Top 15 Juniors to Watch nationally. A first-team All-state selection, he was Florida Class 2-A Player of the year and runner-up to Florida-bound backcourt scorer Ted Dupay for overall Player of the year in the state.

What earned him these honors were junior statistics of 21.4 ppg, 11.2 rpg and 7.5 bpg, plus shooting percentages of 68 on FGs and 74 on FTs, for a 30-5 team that reached the state semifinals in its classification.

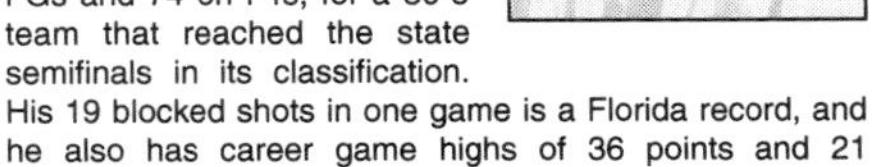

His 19 blocked shots in one game is a Florida record, and he also has career game highs of 36 points and 21 rebounds.

Sanders also has made his mark in summer play the last two years. He has attended the Nike All-America Camp in Indianapolis, and he's also starred in AAU competition for the Florida Stars. After the 1997 Nike Camp, he was widely identified as one of the top 10 rising junior prospects nationally. The big question at that time was whether Casey or Alabaman Marvin Stone was the best big man in the prep class of 1999.

This spring, Sanders played relatively subpar (for him) at the Boo Williams Spring Invitational tournament in Newport News (VA). The Stars were upset in the quarterfinals by the host Boo Williams team, and despite high expectations based on his huge reputation, Casey simply wasn't spectacular.

Nevertheless, *Prep Stars Recruiter's Handbook* colleague Dave Telep reports that Sanders made one of the best plays of the year in this tournament when he sprinted downcourt to foil a breakaway layup by smashing it so hard against the backboard that the shooter visibly trembled.

While he didn't scintillate overall in Newport News, Sanders did stand out two months later at the Nike Camp, where a lot more college coaches were in the stands. We ranked him among the top five performers in the camp, which showcased a total of 14 of our top 44 high school players (regardless of class) in the nation.

STRENGTHS AND AREAS NEEDING WORK: A truly outstanding athlete for his size, Sanders has long arms, exceptional quickness and mobility, and solid fundamentals. When it comes to speed up and down the court, he rates in the very top echelon of players taller than 6-9. He keeps the ball high, is a good outlet passer, and has a smooth and reliable jump shot to 15 feet. On defense, he possesses quick lateral movement and anticipation; hence he's a prime time rejector, potentially of the highest order.

While Sanders is starting to fill out a bit and plays stronger than he looks, he's still thin. He has been listed as heavy as 215 but weighed in barefoot at 200 at the Nike Camp. Before going to war at the collegiate level, he needs to gain weight and strength so that he won't be outmuscled in the paint.

He also must continue to polish his low post moves (he already brandishes some spins and quick maneuvers) and perhaps develop a jump hook to complement his jumpshot.

The other area that he needs to beef up is his academic credentials. At the end of his junior year, his core curriculum grade-point average reportedly was 2.3, and he had not yet taken the SAT or ACT. Although he hasn't qualified yet for collegiate freshman eligibility, Duke is still recruiting him. Obviously, the Blue Devils and many others expect him to ultimately qualify by the end of next spring.

COLLEGIATE PREFERENCES: Casey has pared his list to seven schools—Duke (the staff feels good but not great about its chances to land him), Florida (he's the missing link for a potential run at the NCAA title), Florida State (where Steve Robinson badly needs to sign a national blue-chipper), Miami (don't count Leonard Hamilton out), Syracuse, South Florida and Kansas. We expect the first four on the list have the best shots.

BOTTOM LINE: He's been a little up and down, but with his size, agility and hard work in the weight room, it's scary what he could accomplish on the hardwood.

DONNELL HARVEY, *6-8, 220 lbs., senior, power forward, Randolph-Clay HS/Cuthbert, GA*

At this point, Keith Bogans' strongest competition for best senior prospect in the nation is Donnell Harvey, who only needs a better jump shot to quickly ascend to the top rung. Harvey *is* the most consistently dominating prepster. In the apt words of Dave Telep of the *Prep Stars Recruiter's Handbook*, he "lives out in the country, cleans the backboards with virtually unmatched aggressiveness and tenacity, and says grace at dinner."

MAJOR ACCOMPLISHMENTS: Widely touted since his sophomore season, Donnell has been a major figure on the national prep scene for two years. This spring, he made *Parade*'s fourth-team All-America (just eight juniors were in the top 40), and he also was listed by *USA Today* as an All-

adidas Blue Ribbon high school material provided by PREP STARS RECRUITER'S HANDBOOK
and the ACC AREA SPORTS JOURNAL • P.O. Box 4323 • Chapel Hill, NC • 27515-4323
For subscription information, call (800) 447-7667 or (919) 967-7789. Also access the *Recruiter's Handbook* online at "www.prepstars.com".
Read Brick Oettinger online at www.prepstars.com and also at The Sporting News website.

USA Honorable Mention and in the Top 15 Juniors to Watch nationally.

Within his home state, Harvey was selected to the Georgia Terrific 10 after averaging 17.4 ppg, 14.8 rpg, 3.0 bpg, 3.6 apg and 2.0 spg for a 26-2 team. He shot 56 percent from the field and 60 percent from the free-throw line. Entering his senior season, he has career game highs of 34 points and 25 rebounds.

In May, he led the state champion Atlanta Celtics to the title of the loaded, 17-under division at the Reebok/Bob Gibbons Tournament of Champions in the Triangle area of North Carolina. An obvious choice for the All-tournament team, he was edged out for MVP by Joe Forte, whose prolific scoring carried the D.C. Stars to the title game. While Forte averaged over 20 ppg more than Harvey (32.8 vs. 12.4) in the 28-team tournament, many observers thought the Georgia southpaw was even more valuable to his team.

In July, he played and excelled at the adidas ABCD Camp in Teaneck (NJ), the adidas Big Time tournament in Las Vegas and the AAU Junior Boys (17-under) National Championship in Orlando (FL). At the adidas ABCD Camp, he averaged 12.3 ppg, 8.6 rpg (third among 250 participants), and connected on 56 percent of his field goals. Selected (of course) to the camp Senior All-Star Game, he had 14 points and nine rebounds in 16 minutes of action for the losing side.

At the gargantuan adidas Big Time tournament, Harvey was the inside force at both end of the court for the Celtics. An extremely difficult draw had them face the talented and deep Michigan Mustangs in the semifinals a few hours after the Atlantans had nipped the very strong Illinois Fire, 77-73, in the quarterfinals. The Celtics ultimately fell in a 69-64 decision to the eventual tournament champions, but Harvey was his usual sensational self and a cinch for the All-tournament team.

Then came a long flight to Orlando for the AAU Junior Boys National Championship. There, the weary Celtics reached the quarterfinals, where they lost to the ultimate runner-up Central Jersey Hawks in a 62-49 stunner. Harvey injured a wrist in the first half when knocked to the floor while leaping for a rebound. He left the game and later returned briefly, but was obviously handicapped. Nevertheless, he made the AAU Junior Boys All-America first team.

STRENGTHS AND AREAS NEEDING WORK: Astute basketball observers don't look first at the point sheet for Harvey. They look at the havoc he causes for opponents. To say he "plays big" doesn't really do him justice, because his priorities, which he pursues with a passion, are to challenge virtually every shot that approaches the basket, and to collar every single rebound.

He says he wants to be like Dennis Rodman, minus the tattoos and the attitude. Consequently, he's one of our favorite players to watch, as he *always* plays extremely hard, he'a a monster on the boards and he affects numerous plays at both ends of the court, even without necessarily scoring a great deal.

He changes games with his defensive presence by rejecting or (more often) altering shots of would-be intruders into the paint. On offense, he gets down the court like a track dash man, has earned a reputation as a vicious dunker and if we were creating a video on how to finish strong, he would be the star. The result is that he's a master of the old-fashioned three-point play, as his leap, strength and body control enable him to get clobbered and still put the ball in the basket from nearby.

Harvey also has quick and effective inside moves to the hoop, but his shooting is another story, as his jump shot and free throw stroke both require considerable honing. The problem is that he shoots the ball off the palm of his hand rather than his fingertips, and his shot has a little sidespin on it. At most, his current legitimate shot range is 15-16 feet, and that may be stretching it, although we have seen him hit one three-pointer.

In Las Vegas, however, Harvey assured us that he was going to work very hard every day to improve his shot. We believe him.

COLLEGIATE PREFERENCES: Many colleges are presently involved with Harvey, who reportedly has a 2.7 grade-point average. The eight schools mentioned most often are Kentucky (which envisions him as part of a blockbuster recruiting class), Clemson (he likes new coach Larry Shyatt's staff), Georgia (Ron Jirsa badly needs to snare him), Georgia Tech, Texas, Alabama, Georgetown and Connecticut.

It remains conceivable that others could still enter the picture.

BOTTOM LINE: Harvey takes care of business and leaves with a smile on his face. Any college coach would love to have this consummate roundball warrior.

JASON KAPONO, *6-8, 218 lbs., senior, small forward, Artesia HS/Lakewood, CA*

If you were looking for a current NBA player to compare Jason Kapono to, it would be Tom Gugliotta, although on the court Kapono is far ahead of where Gugliotta was at the same age. If someone, through outstanding defense, is able to take a part of his game away, or if (for example) he's not shooting well, he'll find another way to contribute. Most players lack the versatility and mental toughness to do this.

MAJOR ACCOMPLISHMENTS: Close followers of prep basketball first saw Kapono's name during his freshman year at perennial power Artesia, when he was recognized as one of the premier young prospects in the nation. That reputation has continued to grow, though we (until this summer) were a dissenter, viewing him as an overrated role player rather than a true main man. After watching him very closely in July, we're willing to admit that we were wrong—far wrong.

His play last season at Artesia earned him All-USA Honorable Mention in *USA Today*, and the same publication chose him one of the Top 15 Juniors to Watch nationally. Still, we were apprehensive until we observed him at the adidas ABCD Camp in Teaneck (NJ), where 24 of our national top 44 high school players were present.

There, we rated him among the top six or seven performers. He averaged 12.1 points and 6.0 rebounds in eight games, while shooting 55 percent from the field and an astounding camp-best 57 percent (12-21) on three-pointers. He was chosen to play in the Senior All-Star Game at the camp, and while he didn't post big numbers (four points and six rebounds in 16 minutes), he unsurprisingly was on the winning team.

From Jersey, Kapono went to the Double Pump West Coast All-Star Camp at California State-Dominguez Hills, where was one of a handful of elite players, and then to Las Vegas for the 224-team adidas Big Time tournament. At the Big Time, Kapono was definitely a "main man" in carrying QBL Lakewood to the Open Division (championship bracket) round of 32, where it lost, 80-68, to defending tournament champion D.C. Assault. Even in defeat, Jason was superb, and his play landed him a berth on the All-tournament team.

STRENGTHS AND AREAS NEEDING WORK: Kapono's playing style reminds us of some other current players, besides Tom Gugliotta. Another Jason, North Carolina freshman forward and 1998 McDonald's All-American Jason Capel, is also a good but not great athlete who knows how to play and has a lot of the same attributes, except Artesia's Jason has a smoother jump shot stroke. And Kapono's good friend Casey Jacobsen, who's also among our top 44 prep players nationally, is similar in that each is a widely talented, *extremely* intelligent wing forward who almost always plays under control.

Skill-wise, Kapono is a fine ballhandler and shooter, a pretty good rebounder, and a heady defender with a nose for the ball. His hands are extremely sure, he can score on the move, and he's an excellent free-throw shooter, especially in the clutch. Particularly impressive is how he skillfully distributes the ball in transition, sometimes with a crisp, solid pass and at other times with a spectacular pinpoint, behind-the-back bounce pass.

We also admire his mental and physical toughness. At the July events, he played wearing goggles and a mask in order to protect a broken nose, yet he literally stuck his nose in and played just as aggressively as anyone except perhaps Donnell Harvey.

Some players are quicker than Jason, and some jump higher, though his quickness and leap aren't at all bad. Regardless, we would take him before any other high school small forward in the nation.

COLLEGIATE PREFERENCES: Kapono is looking for a strong college program where he can come in as a freshman, see immediate playing time, and make an important contribution. In the summer, he specified 13 schools as possibilities, although we believe those with the best chance to corral him include Southern California (the staff of which is trying to convince him he could be "The Man" for the Trojans), Stanford, California, UNLV, Utah, Kentucky, Syracuse and North Carolina State. Others on his list are UCLA (already loaded in the frontcourt), Duke, Missouri, Oregon State and Rhode Island, where former UCLA head coach Jim Harrick has built a very good program.

BOTTOM LINE: Kapono doesn't just make great decisions; he makes fantastic *plays.*

DAJUAN WAGNER, *6-2, 176 lbs., sophomore, point guard/wing guard, Camden HS/Camden, NJ*

Now we've seen a young point guard who is unquestionably better at the same age than previous phenoms such as Stephon Marbury, Allen Iverson, Kenny Anderson and Isiah Thomas. No kidding.

MAJOR ACCOMPLISHMENTS: As a 15-year old freshman, Wagner served notice upon the national scene by averaging 27.3 points and nine assists against good competition for Camden (NJ) High. The Associated Press chose him second-team All-state, while *USA Today* made him an All-USA Honorable Mention selection.

Wagner is the son of Milt Wagner, a former Camden star in his own right who made All-America and played on a national championship team at Louisville and played two seasons in the NBA. The younger Wagner has earned invitations to the USA Youth Development Festival in Colorado Springs and the Nike All-American Camp in Indianapolis. He took full advantage of these opportunities by more than living up to the advance billing and stratospheric expectations.

At the Youth Development Festival in June, he helped lead the East team to a gold medal by scoring 20 points in the championship game and averaging 14.3 ppg in five games. The sophomore class nationally is absolutely loaded with talent and might just be the best high school crop since the class of 1979 (Ralph Sampson, James Worthy, Isiah Thomas, Dominique Wilkins, Sam Bowie, Clark Kellogg, Steve Stipanovich, Antoine Carr et al.), and Wagner was clearly the best sophomore performer in Colorado Springs.

The same thing was true at the Nike Camp, where the only other point guards we thought played comparably to DaJuan were senior Jason Williams and junior Marcus Taylor. We believe Wagner's *potential* is even greater than either of those two, hence we've placed him as the point guard on the first five nationally.

STRENGTHS AND AREAS NEEDING WORK: Despite his youth, Wagner looks like he belongs, with a maturity well beyond his years. We hear so much about "precocious" players, and we wonder how much is true. In this case, it all is, and more.

Wagner simply is a stupendous talent who is already an all-around player, not just a scorer. Yes, he has his father's sweet jump shot from three-point territory, but he also is poised, takes command of the offense and runs it, and is a slick passer, especially on the fast break. As noted by Camden teammate Arthur Barclay, "You never can take your eyes off of him because you never know when he's gonna pass it to you."

But he's certainly a scoring machine, too. He can score all over the court, from the perimeter or near the basket. He can get his shot off the dribble, and he also moves smartly without the ball to shake free. Wagner is virtually automatic when open beyond the three-point stripe, but perhaps even more dazzling is his ability to score on the move in traffic.

An amazing finisher among the trees, he is able to succeed because he has exceptional body control and athleticism, concentration, touch and an eye for the hoop. Simply put, he gets to the basket and creates a way to put it in.

Wagner actually can play either guard, and he will probably grow at least a couple of more inches, given that his father is 6-5. If this happens, and he continues to work hard on his game and avoids serious injury, he might be the closest we've seen to the "next Jordan."

COLLEGIATE PREFERENCES: Let's start with the caveat that he's so young, any mention of colleges is speculation of the purest kind. Still, might Louisville, his dad's alma mater with a strong track record of recruiting Camden players (e.g., current forward Nate Johnson), be the team to beat?

Although his mother and father have never married, and Wagner has lived his entire life with his mother, Lisa Moore, his parents have reportedly maintained a good relationship, and there appears to be a bond between father and son. Remember that DaJuan has taken the last name of his unabashably proud papa (who's still playing professionally in Germany), rather than that of his mom.

We should also note that Wagner resides in the heart of Big East territory; that Atlantic Coast Conference members traditionally recruit quite successfully from the Northeast; and that DaJuan, if he desires, will likely have a realistic opportunity to go directly from high school to the NBA as a high first-round draft choice in 2001.

BOTTOM LINE: "DaJuan and only" (pardon the pun, but it's accurate) has a swagger, in the words of Dave Telep of the *Prep Stars Recruiter's Handbook*, that says, "Hey, it doesn't matter how old I am. I belong out here with you." Of that, there is no doubt.

SECOND TEAM

MARVIN STONE, *6-11, 240 lbs., senior, center/power forward, Grissom HS/Huntsville, AL*

When you are ranked by most scouts as the No. 1 player in your class nationally, as Marvin Stone was entering the summer of 1998, it's only natural to feel some pressure, because you're Wyatt Earp and everyone is gunning for you. Stone disclosed to us that he felt some pressure, but he embraced the challenge. That attitude is just as impressive as his basketball talents.

MAJOR ACCOMPLISHMENTS: Since the ninth grade, Stone has been widely heralded and the subject of an off-and-on recruiting war among Huntsville high schools. An outstanding sophomore year was followed by a superb showing at the 1997 Nike Camp, where he led his team to the camp finals.

Last season, Stone averaged 19.2 ppg, 14 rpg, 5.5 bpg and 5.4 apg while connecting on 65 percent of his field goals and 68 percent of his free-throws, as Grissom High finished with a 26-5 record. Consequently, he was honored by *Parade* as an All-America third-team, and by *USA Today* as All-USA Honorable Mention and one of the Top 15 Juniors to Watch nationally. He was Alabama Class 6-A (large-school) Player of the year and first-team All-state.

In AAU-type competition after the season, Stone was most impressive in the Boo Williams Invitational Tournament at Newport News (VA) in April. This event was loaded with talent from around the nation, and he was the trump card for the Alabama Lasers, who reached the semifinals. His surprising ability to step outside and drill three-pointers buffaloed his opponents when combined with his obvious prowess around the basket.

Before the prestigious July events, however, Marvin severely sprained an ankle. Although he didn't advertise his injury, it forced him to play hurt (and subpar) at the Nike All-American Camp in Indianapolis and kept him from playing for the Lasers in the Nike Super Showcase at Orlando (FL).

Part of his problem at the Nike Camp was that he wasn't fed the ball in scoring position by his teammates. In addition, he was physically hammered by some of his match-ups (such as 6-9, 255-pound Indiana junior Zach Randolph), no doubt because of his reputation as No. 1. Nevertheless, we thought Stone performed well at the camp—just not exceptionally, which is what everyone expected from him.

STRENGTHS AND AREAS NEEDING WORK: Along with his smooth jump shot to 20 feet, which is extremely rare for players his size, his ability to convert inside stands out. A broad-shouldered horse who is very hard to budge in the paint, Stone isn't really explosive but utilizes a picture-perfect spin move to draw fouls near the hoop. Besides his turnaround jumper, he has a creditable jump hook in the lane, and he uses the glass well on angle shots.

The rest of Stone's game is equally solid, even though he has steadily gained weight (from 205 pounds two years ago to at least 240 now) and subsequently has lost some of his former exceptional athleticism. In fact, we believe he's improved very little in the last year, but he's still plenty good.

As for those other attributes, he plays extremely hard and smart, is very strong, remains a good (but not great) leaper, and has lots of polish. He hustles downcourt, pounds the backboards, keeps the ball high, catches everything he can touch and passes skillfully. He's also a fine defender who understands positioning and blocks some shots via good timing.

COLLEGIATE PREFERENCES: We believe that Kentucky is the strong leader for Stone's services and likely will sign him in November. Others still in the chase are Alabama, Auburn and Florida State. Should he wait until spring to sign a national letter-of-intent, it's conceivable (but unlikely) that North Carolina, which was high on his early summer list, might enter the picture.

BOTTOM LINE: His toughness, aggressiveness and skills will spell NBA in a few years.

JASON PARKER, *6-8, 260 lbs., senior, power forward/center, West Charlotte HS/Charlotte, NC*

Just looking at him, you'd think this burly, imposing-looking young man with huge hands he utilizes better than any other prepster might be nicknamed "Papa Bear." He certainly merits that kind of respect among coaches and scouts.

MAJOR ACCOMPLISHMENTS: A starter and prime player since his sophomore season at West Charlotte, his progress was steady until this summer, which was a "breakout" period for him on the national scene. It was obvious during the spring and summer of 1997 that he was going to be a good prospect, but the key question then was "how good?"

Even as a junior, when he averaged 18.5 ppg, 12.0 rpg, 4.0 bpg and 4.0 spg for a team that reached the Western Regional finals (state semifinals), some questions remained. He was Associated Press Co-Player of the year in North Carolina and *USA Today* All-USA Honorable Mention, yet we had watched him struggle in a pair of holiday games at the Beach Ball Classic in Myrtle Beach (SC) versus strong national competition.

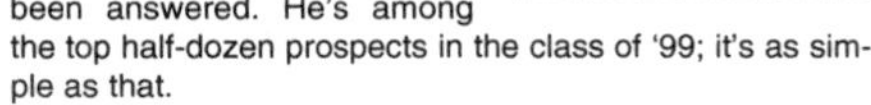

Starting with the Reebok/Bob Gibbons Tournament of Champions during late May in the Triangle area of North Carolina and building to a crescendo at the adidas Big Time tournament in Las Vegas, all questions about Parker have been answered. He's among the top half-dozen prospects in the class of '99; it's as simple as that.

Three and a half weeks after the Tournament of Champions, where he averaged 14.3 ppg in four games for the state AAU champion Charlotte Royals and made the All-tournament team, he attended the NBA Players Association Camp at Princeton (NJ). Present at the camp were 88 players, all highly touted, and he was clearly among the most impressive three or four.

Almost two weeks later, Parker was among 250 carefully selected participants at the adidas ABCD Camp in Teaneck (NJ). Playing on a camp team with several other especially big names (Brett Nelson, Brian Wethers and 6-8 Texan George Williams), he averaged 7.4 points, 4.1 rebounds and 1.1 blocked shots in eight games while shooting .527 percent from the field. Despite his stats, he was selected to the camp's Senior All-Star Game, in which he scored four points and grabbed six rebounds in 16 minutes for the winning side.

It was at the 224-team adidas Big Time, however, where Parker broke loose and fully demonstrated what he's capable of doing. Despite being double-teamed virtually all of the time, he was a dominant force for the Team Carolina Sonics, who reached the championship game of the Open Division (winners bracket) before inadequate backcourt play keyed a 98-76 loss to the deep and talented Michigan Mustangs.

In that game, his 19 points included two monster slams off stunningly quick baseline spin moves from the low post. During that game, an upper-level Division I assistant coach called Parker "the best player here," which isn't bad considering that 27 of our top 44 high school players were at the Big Time. Naturally, he was named to the All-tournament team.

Later in July, an obviously exhausted Jason played for the Charlotte Royals in the AAU Junior Boys (17-under) National Championship in Orlando (FL), where he was an AAU second-team All-American, and briefly at the one-day Pepsi Mid-Summer Chalenj (sic) in Greensboro (NC).

STRENGTHS AND AREAS NEEDING WORK: By far the best interior passer in high school ball today, he instinctively and unselfishly looks for (and finds) the open man when he's doubled up. He also takes full advantage of his huge body and great strength near the basket, where his weapons include quick and polished post moves (his footwork is good), an arching turnaround jump shot to 15 feet, and a reliable baby hook. Whether a bear or merely a horse, his overall exploits around the basket are quite impressive.

Parker doesn't run nearly as fast as Duke's Elton Brand (whom he otherwise plays a lot like), but he works very hard at both ends of the court. He uses his body effectively to block out on the boards and rebound strongly. Although not a straight-up leaper, he actually gets in the air pretty well with a running start.

On defense, his strength is a major asset, although at times he needs to move his feet better. He anticipates well and blocks shots via good timing.

COLLEGIATE PREFERENCES: Parker thought he'd be committed to the North Carolina Tar Heels by August, but the Tar Heels asked him to wait until spring so that they could monitor his hoped-for academic progress. Parker reportedly enters his senior year lacking both the core curriculum grade-point average and the standardized test score required by the NCAA for collegiate freshman eligibility.

He says he will wait until spring before reaching a college decision, although he plans to take official visits to Michigan and perhaps Kentucky in the fall. North Carolina still probably will land Parker if it offers a scholarship. Meanwhile, hometown UNC Charlotte is definitely involved, and South Carolina plus most of the ACC could more strongly enter the picture later on, should his academics improve significantly and the Tar Heels (strangely) not offer him.

BOTTOM LINE: Parker will be a success because, along with all his physical assets and basketball skills, he has fire in him.

BRIAN COOK, *6-10 1/2, 220 lbs., senior, power forward/small forward, Lincoln Community HS/Lincoln, IL*

When we reached this summer Nike All-America Camp in Indianapolis, everyone was talking about 7-5 Chinese sensation Yao Ming, who had been dominating the first two days. But then he had to match up with Brian Cook, a fluid, versatile inside/outside package who proceeded to give Ming a taste of how it is to play against a truly elite American frontcourt man. In fact, no one at the camp did a better job versus Yao at either end of the court than Cook.

MAJOR ACCOMPLISHMENTS: Cook is the son of former Kansas star forward Norman Cook, a prep All-American at Lincoln who played two years in the NBA. Hence, a great deal has been expected of Brian since he entered high school. Unfortunately, a broken ankle forced him to miss eight games during his sophomore season, but he still was able to show considerable promise.

When we saw him in action in the summer of 1997, we were impressed by his skills and savvy, but he was very thin and played too "soft" near the basket. His junior season at Lincoln was when he really began to assert himself. The team finished with a 25-3 record and won the King Cotton Holiday Classic in Pine Bluff (AK) against a strong national field. Cook was MVP.

Cook wound up averaging 16.7 ppg, 9.3 rpg and 2.3 bpg while shooting .535 percent from the floor, 45 percent on three-point field goals, and 75 percent from the free-throw line. His high games were 29 points and 14 rebounds, and he was selected first-team All-state. This spring *USA Today* selected him All-USA Honorable Mention and one of the Top 15 Juniors to Watch in the nation.

He attended the NBA Players Association Camp in Princeton (NJ) in June. Most observers thought he played as well or better than anyone else there, although Rhode Island guard Tony Robertson was chosen MVP.

We saw him two and a half weeks later at the Nike All-America Camp in Indianapolis, where we judged him to be among the top five or six performers. Besides showing his mettle versus Ming, he played just as hard against less-publicized foes and had even greater success.

STRENGTHS AND AREAS NEEDING WORK: A very good run/jump athlete whose skills are polished and fundamentals are impeccable, Cook already knows how to play the game and no doubt has the tools to be a combination forward. In fact, he reportedly has said that he believes he is a perimeter player, but we beg to differ. The truth is his future success almost certainly lies at big forward, not on the wing.

Yes, he has a consistent and accurate mid-range jump shot and is a fine three-point marksman when stationary. He runs extremely well, is very quick for his size and dribbles proficiently and passes alertly, like a wing forward should; and he finishes high-post drives and in transition with either hand.

But, in reality, Cook reminds us more of Samaki Walker (thank you, Dr. Grerald Moore) than of Danny Manning, because he's *also* a good leaper who enjoys mixing it up on the boards and, consequently, rebounds quite well. Additionally, his prowess on defense is more reminiscent of Walker than of even the young, pre-injured knee Manning.

What Cook needs to add at this point is a back-to-the-basket game in the post, and we have no doubt that he will soon. This, along with more weight and strength that should come naturally with physical maturity, will make him even more multi-talented than he already is.

COLLEGIATE PREFERENCE: Despite his father's background as a Jayhawk, Cook made a very early commitment to home-state Illinois. In fact, in the fall of 1999, Cook will join a superb crop of Illini newcomers that will feature two other McDonald's All-Americans (current juco insider Marcus Griffin and academic partial qualifier Frank Williams, a point guard), besides almost certainly himself.

BOTTOM LINE: At age 17, Cook already is almost 6-11 and approaching 225 pounds. How many perimeter players in the NBA fit that description?

DESHAWN STEVENSON, *6-5 1/2, 210 lbs., junior, wing guard/small forward, Washington Union HS/Fresno, CA*

You'd be hard-pressed to find a better run/jump athlete than DeShawn Stevenson. Just a junior, he's without question one of the top three players (along with senior forwards Jason Kapono and Casey Jacobsen) in the talent-full state of California, despite the notoriety of others such as insider Andrew Gooden and wing Brian Wethers, who are in our national top 44 list.

MAJOR ACCOMPLISHMENTS: Stevenson began to edge into the national limelight as just a freshman, when as a 6-

4 wing guard he averaged 18.0 ppg, 7.0 apg, 5.0 rpg, 3.0 spg and 1.0 bpg for a good Washington Union team. We first saw him after that season at the 1997 adidas ABCD Camp, where he showed considerable promise yet didn't look quite like a national top five player in his class.

Stevenson's 1997-98 sophomore statistics (18.0 ppg, 12.0 rpg, 6.0 apg, 3.0 spg and 1.0 bpg) weren't a whole lot different from the previous year, but this was accomplished while sharing top billing with 6-8 teammate Chris Jeffries, a talented senior forward who signed with Arkansas and was ranked number 113 nationally in the prep class of '98 by us.

USA Today obviously was impressed with Stevenson, choosing him All-USA Honorable Mention and one of the Top 10 Sophomores to Watch in the nation. During the summer of 1998, Stevenson moved up another notch by demonstrating at several major events that he really is among the best four junior prospects in the USA.

In May he was a standout at the well-attended Spiece Run 'N Slam Tournament at Purdue University in West Lafayette (IN), and he began the month of July by sizzling at the prestigious adidas ABCD Camp at Teaneck (NJ). In Jersey, he averaged 12.3 ppg, 2.1 rpg and 1.8 apg while drilling 40 percent of his three-point shots and 89 percent of his free-throws in eight camp games. Selected (of course) to play in the camp's Underclassman All-Star Game, he rammed home a game-high 18 points for the losing team.

A couple of days later, the next stop for Stevenson was the Double Pump West Coast All-Star Camp at California State-Dominguez Hills. There he played on the same team as blue-chip senior power forward Carlos Boozer, and both were among the few truly elite players present. In fact, each of them outclassed virtually all of their competition at this camp.

But we were most dazzled by Stevenson later that same month at the 224-team adidas Big Time tournament in Las Vegas, where he played for a power-packed EBO-Fresno team that also showcased two other top 44 players, Boozer and PG Brett Nelson, plus 6-8 Floridian Napoleon Rhodes, a deluxe rebounder. Stevenson was, in our opinion, clearly the most effective player on the team, which was upset 67-64 in the round of 16 by the unheralded Capital Players from Burke (VA).

Others obviously agreed with our conclusion, as Stevenson was the only member of EBO-Fresno to make the 35-man All-tournament team, which included just five other underclassmen. In six games at Vegas, he averaged a team-high 20.2 ppg.

STRENGTHS AND AREAS NEEDING WORK: What most people notice first about the well-built swingman Stevenson is that he's a cloud-piercing leaper with remarkable hang time. Sensational in transition and extremely quick and explosive with or without the ball, he's a fine scorer on the move who seems to be able to drive to the basket almost whenever he wants to. Once he gets there, this spectacular finisher routinely elevates over taller players to score, while making it look easy.

While he's not a great three-point shooter, he's improved his stroke in the past year and become a pretty dangerous perimeter marksman who will burn you if you don't respect his jump shot. He's especially effective at backing in on smaller or less-athletic defenders and drilling short to mid-range turnarounds.

Stevenson also is an alert passer (though he forces a few that aren't there), at least an adequate rebounder for a wing player (yet given his hops, he could be better), and a capable defender. He uses his quickness to get steals and his leap to spectacularly reject shots by much taller players, but he also on occasion is caught out of position and called for holding on defense.

If Stevenson continues to hone his three-point jump shot, further polishes his ballhandling, and avoids serious injury, he will be a contender to become the closest thing to "the next Jordan" that we've seen.

COLLEGIATE PREFERENCES: Because he's just a junior, it may be at least slightly premature to speculate about Stevenson's favorite colleges, assuming he doesn't go directly into the 2000 NBA draft (certainly a possibility) after high school. Nevertheless, we believe that the collegiate decision this season of his EBO-Fresno buddy, Carlos Boozer, may well provide a hint of Stevenson's likely college destination.

Although Boozer claims to still have nine schools on list, there have been widespread reports for months that UCLA is the team to beat. Even though the Bruins already have plenty of young frontcourt talent, their staff loves Carlos, and three UCLA assistant coaches trailed him from event to event in July.

Should Boozer head to Westwood, we wouldn't be at all surprised if Stevenson followed suit a year later, although that might change if UCLA signs swingman Kareem Rush this year to go with current freshmen wing guard Ray Young and small forward JaRon Rush. Anyway, as outstanding as Stevenson is, he almost certainly will be courted by many of the nation's premier hoop powers.

BOTTOM LINE: He takes athleticism to a level seen extremely rarely, as he's not just a good or even great athlete, but an absolutely *fantastic* one who must be seen in action to be fully appreciated.

BRETT NELSON, *6-3, 170 lbs., senior, point guard/wing guard, St. Albans HS/St. Albans, WV*

With Brett Nelson, there are at least two things you don't have to worry about: (1) Can he get his own shot off the dribble? Answer: Is MJ a clutch player? And (2) Where is he going to college? Answer: Florida.

MAJOR ACCOMPLISHMENTS: Nelson is a prep phenom who originally established a reputation as a high school freshman and then significantly enhanced it by sparkling at the Five-Star Camp's famed Development League for rising sophomores in the summer of 1996. The following season, he led the state of West Virginia in scoring with over 29 ppg as a sophomore, while adding 9.0 apg, 6.0 rpg and 2.0 spg. At the Beach Ball Classic in Myrtle Beach (SC) during late December of 1996, he mesmerized fans with his outstanding shooting on the move and clever ballhandling.

Nelson's notoriety continued to escalate during the summer of 1997, when he performed quite well for the Dakota Schoolers (with future Florida teammate Mike Miller) at both the Reebok/Bob Gibbons Tournament of Champions in Triangle area of North Carolina and the adidas Big Time tournament in Las Vegas, where he made the All-tournament team.

In between these two events, Nelson attended the prestigious adidas ABCD Camp in Teaneck (NJ) and acquitted himself quite well overall against many of the nation's best prep point guards. Consequently, entering his junior season he was generally regarded as one of the nation's top 10 players in the prep class of 1999.

His play last season certainly didn't adversely affect his reputation. Nelson once again led the state in scoring, amassing 31.1 ppg, plus 8.0 apg, 6.0 rpg, 2.0 spg and 1.0 bpg for an 18-7 St. Albans team that reached the state Class 3-A quarterfinals. He knocked in 57 percent of his shots, 78 percent of his free-throws. He had high games of 52 points and 16 assists, and made a triumphant return to the Beach Ball Classic, where he once again wowed onlookers as well as opponents.

At the conclusion of his junior season, *Parade Magazine* selected Nelson to its All-America fourth team, while *USA Today* recognized him as All-USA Honorable Mention and among the Top 15 Juniors to Watch nationally. He was first-team All-state for the second straight year, and the West Virginia University Touchdown Club declared him Player of the year in the state.

In the late spring and summer of 1998, Nelson played well at a variety of different events, yet none of the teams he played for reached even the semifinals of a major tournament. At the Spiece Run 'N Slam Tournament in West Lafayette (IN), his performance actually was very good, and the same is true for his play at the outstanding adidas ABCD Camp in Teaneck (NJ). At the latter, he averaged 10.0 ppg, 3.0 apg, 2.1 rpg and 0.9 spg in eight camp games while connecting on .385 percent of his three-pointers. In the camp's Senior All-Star Game, Nelson totaled seven points and eight assists in 16 minutes of action for the losing side.

The mammoth 224-team adidas Big Time tournament was a bummer this year compared with 1997. The impressive-on-paper EBO-Fresno team that Nelson played for (along with power forward Carlos Boozer and junior sensation DeShawn Stevenson from our national top 44) was eliminated in the round of 32 by the untouted Capital Players of Burke (VA). Subsequently, Nelson was not chosen for the All-tournament team.

STRENGTHS AND AREAS NEEDING WORK: Much like the incomparable Pete Maravich, Nelson is a flashy player with absolutely great basketball skills and fundamentals. He's capable of getting plenty of points and assists versus nearly any foe.

A creative ballhandler who throws behind-the-back, over-the-shoulder, alley-oop and lookaway passes with touch and pinpoint accuracy very rarely seen, he is quick and fast, and he has a knack for scoring off the dribble.

In an open-court, fast-break offense, you know he'll see the entire floor and either pass the ball to the open man or score himself, yet he also can intelligently set the offense up in a half-court game. His advanced penetration maneuvers are delightful to watch and feature a superb crossover dribble known to wrong-foot opponents.

When his top-of-the-line ballhandling and floor leadership are coupled with his smooth and accurate jumpshot to 22 feet, the result is so many weapons that even the most talented and hard-working defender is likely in deep trouble trying to contain Nelson without help. His ability to drain long-range three-pointers off the dribble is at least comparable to any current high school player in the nation. While he has the tools to play wing guard if needed, it's clear that point guard is his natural and best position.

On defense, Nelson makes good use of his quickness, anticipation and long arms to get lots of steals, but his relative lack of strength can be a handicap when he's matched up with an athletic "power guard." Still, he's able to compensate most of the time by utilizing his brain (his grade-point average is 3.75) to play cerebrally.

COLLEGIATE PREFERENCE: As noted above, Nelson has given Florida a very early commitment and plans to sign a national letter-of-intent with the Gators in November of 1998. The other finalists were Duke (which then landed point guard Jason Williams) and Kentucky, although West Virginia received an unofficial campus visit.

Florida had the inside track all along because Nelson attended coach Billy Donovan's summer camp while in junior high, when Donovan was at Marshall. Nelson likes and trusts Billy a great deal. Nelson also calls Donovan "the best coach to prepare me for the NBA." Interestingly, after playing in college and, he hopes, the NBA, Nelson's goal is to become a big-time college coach.

BOTTOM LINE: IF Florida is to succeed in making the transition from pretender to Southeastern Conference and NCAA title contender during the next few years, Nelson will have to be a big part of it, because his talent is unique.

THIRD TEAM

SAMUEL DALEMBERT, *6-11 1/2, 230 lbs., senior, center, St. Patrick's HS/Elizabeth, NJ*

Question: How many prepsters who didn't start as a junior, sat out half of that season because of a knee injury, and averaged 8.1 ppg, 6.9 rpg and 3.0 bpg have been considered preseason national top 15 prospects and viewed as premier run/jump athletes the very next year? Answer: (to our recollection) One, Samuel Dalembert.

MAJOR ACCOMPLISHMENTS: Early last season we heard from a reliable source that St. Patrick's had a big junior who had recently transferred in from the Ivory Coast and was battling a knee problem (that ultimately prevented his playing the first half of the season), yet who was an incredible athlete who might possess even more *potential* than senior teammate Al Harrington. Our interest was definitely piqued, because we then had (and continued to have) Harrington ranked as the number one prospect nationally in the prep class of 1998.

The truly remarkable thing about Dalembert is that he entered the summer of 1998 having only played in a total of approximately 50 games of organized basketball. His improvement has been extremely rapid, which bodes well for the future.

Actually, when we heard our colleague Dave Telep of the *Prep Stars Recruiter's Handbook* report on Dalembert after watching him play in January, 1998, we were a bit disappointed. Even though Telep emphasized Dalembert's stupendous athletic ability, he also noted his raw offensive skills. Dalembert was eloquently described as shooting knuckleball jump shots so flat and hard that they resembled laser beams fired at the basket.

However, at the end of the season, he had managed to hit 57 percent of his field goals and 68 percent of his free-throws as St. Patrick's compiled a 27-3 record, won the New Jersey Tournament of Champions, and earned a final national team ranking of No. 8 from *USA Today*. Dalembert's high games were 16 points, 14 rebounds and nine blocked shots. Don't look for at least the first two of those career highs to last very long in the 1998-99 season.

Three and a half months after the season ended, a "new" Samuel Dalembert erupted upon the national scene at the prestigious Nike All-America Camp in Indianapolis. This version was arguably at least as dominant as any of the 200 touted players who were present.

He played better than Marvin Stone (who was hampered by a sprained ankle) and as well as Casey Sanders, whom he may have slightly outplayed in their head-to-head matchup. We ranked Dalembert among the top half-dozen performers at the camp and immediately raised him into the 12-15 senior prospects nationally.

STRENGTHS AND AREAS NEEDING WORK: Dalembert truly is an outstanding athlete with an NBA frame and good strength already. This nice young man has worked very hard this year to gain weight and become physically stronger, and he has certainly succeeded. On the court, he runs very well (in spite of his recent knee problems), gets up quickly and high on the boards to rebound aggressively at both ends, and is an elite, long-armed defender with lateral mobility who makes his mark in every game rejecting and altering shots and intimidating opponents.

Dalembert wasn't super all of the time this summer—who was?—but much of the time he was very close to that level. Though still far from fully polished at the offensive end, he drilled soft jump shots (with arch and some backspin!) from as far away as the high post at the Nike Camp, showed that he had developed a usable jump hook, converted stickbacks, exhibited a couple of quick and effective low post moves to the basket and even passed the ball pretty well.

His game has advanced every bit as far during the last eight months as he had to travel to get to New Jersey. Now he needs repetitions in practice and experience in games, more than anything else, in order to more fully tap into his vast wealth of potential.

We believe that Dalembert has a definite chance to become not only the best center in the high school class of 1999, but also the No. 1 prospect (and player?), regardless of position.

COLLEGIATE PREFERENCES: Because Dalembert is at a disadvantage now on at least the verbal part of the SAT or ACT, some coaches and scouts question whether he'll be able to fully qualify academically for 1999 collegiate freshman eligibility.

Dalembert has indicated that he's "wide open" on colleges. Among the many colleges who are in the chase (just in case he qualifies) and closely monitoring his progress both on the court and in the classroom are Seton Hall, Rutgers, Massachusetts, Georgia Tech, Syracuse, Kentucky (in the unlikely possibility that they sign neither Marvin Stone nor Casey Sanders), Villanova, Connecticut, Kansas, Florida and Georgia.

BOTTOM LINE: Will Dalembert work as hard and tirelessly on his post moves, shot and ballhandling as former teammate Al Harrington did (a year ago) in order to not only polish his game but also to become the number one player in his class nationally? Stay tuned.

ALTON FORD, *6-9, 260 lbs., junior, power forward/center, Milby HS/Houston, TX*

Alton Ford has been considered one of the premier prospects nationally in the class of 2000 since the ninth grade, so you might think he has little to prove. Not so. To the contrary, he really went after it this summer, playing every bit as hard as he is physically big until he almost ran out of gas in Orlando (FL), at the AAU Junior Boys (17-under) National Championship.

MAJOR ACCOMPLISHMENTS: During his freshman season in 1996-97, Ford averaged 15.7 ppg, 9.7 rpg, 3.5 apg, 3.1 bpg and 2.7 spg for Milby versus strong Houston area competition. The following summer, he showed considerable promise while playing for the Houston Select 17 AAU team at the Reebok/Bob Gibbons Tournament of Champions in North Carolina, and he stood out as one of the very best rising sophomores present at the 1997 adidas ABCD Camp in Teaneck (NJ).

Last season, his performance as a sophomore was a full step beyond his play the previous year. He averaged 22.4 ppg, 14.6 rpg, 3.7 bpg. 2.0 spg and 1.4 apg. *USA Today* listed Ford as one of the Top 10 Sophomores to Watch nationally, and we rated him the number two rising junior in our 1998 pre-summer national rankings.

In late May he returned to the Reebok/Bob Gibbons Tournament of Champions, but somewhat strangely played for the Houston Select 16 team in the 16-under division, even though there were two different Houston teams (that could have used him) in the larger, more competitive 17-under division. Regardless, he naturally made the All-tournament team in his division after averaging 25.4 ppg in five tournament games.

At the adidas ABCD Camp in early July, Ford stepped up a notch and was our choice as the best junior there. His averages of 9.0 ppg and 4.1 rpg in eight camp games are deceptive and don't do justice to his true value for his team. In the Underclassman All-Star Game at the camp, he contributed 11 points and seven rebounds to the winning team and was chosen game MVP.

Less than twp weeks later came the above-mentioned AAU Junior Boys (17-under) National Championship, where his exhaustion was readily apparent, and he didn't shoot nearly as accurately as he usually does. Nevertheless, he did enough other things well for the Houston Select 17 squad to be selected AAU second-team All-American. By the end of the major summer events, Ford had edged past Michigan combo guard Marcus Taylor and ascended into the number one slot in our latest national rankings of the junior class.

STRENGTHS AND AREAS NEEDING WORK: Ford can beat you a lot of different ways. Not fat but quite muscular, he has a wide base that, combined with his advanced skills, helps make him very difficult to defend in the paint. As a consequence, he gets fouled a great deal near the basket, where he adeptly utilizes strong and quick post moves to the hoop.

He runs fairly well, and if you see him coming at you with a full head of steam, better get out of his way. Taking a charge from Ford is definitely not a good idea, if you value your health.

His hands are sure, and jump shot reliable, whether a short turnaround or a soft, arching shot facing the basket to 19-20 feet. He passes skillfully from the high- or low-post and can rebound with forceful authority in traffic, although he doesn't always do it when he's particularly tired.

As his game has continued to steadily improve, very few foes are able to butt heads down low with this "beast with a touch." Surprisingly quick for 260 pounds, he also outmuscles virtually all opponents. A steady diet of double-teams is required to even slow (but not halt) this physical specimen.

At the defensive end, Ford is a pretty good shot-blocker whose leap is not bad but unexceptional, by elite standards. Wisely, he uses his bulk quite effectively for positioning purposes.

COLLEGIATE PREFERENCES: Because he's just a junior, it may be a bit premature to speculate about Ford's future college decision, especially because entering the 2000 NBA draft would appear to be a possibility, though not a probability. If he opts to attend a university for at least a couple of years, then we would expect hometown Houston, with a high-profile new head coach in local hero Clyde "The Glide" Drexler, to be a strong contender.

Also don't forget Texas, with a big-name new coach of its own in Rick Barnes, and a burning desire to become a national power. Then there's Nebraska, which has had recent recruiting success in Houston. And given Ford's talent and prominence, won't many traditional national powers try to get involved?

BOTTOM LINE: The "next Karl Malone" is ... (drum roll, please) Alton Ford!

DERMARR JOHNSON, *6-9 1/2, 200 lbs., senior, small forward, Maine Central Institute/Pittsfield, ME*

The pressure on DerMarr Johnson to be the best high school player in the class of 1999, and to become the next prepster to go directly to the NBA, has taken a definite toll. He didn't have a great junior year, nor did he perform up to his press clippings during the summer of '98. It would be refreshing to see this extremely talented young man at least once in a while wear a smile on his face, looking like he's enjoying what he's doing when he's on the court.

MAJOR ACCOMPLISHMENTS: A senior at Maine Central Institute now, but actually a fifth-year prep, Johnson became a national name with his spectacular play in the 16-under division of the Bob Gibbons Tournament of Champions in North Carolina during the late spring of 1996. At that point, he already played a lot like Scottie Pippen, in that he was a wiry, superb athlete and a skilled ballhandler (especially for his size) who could take over a game in sensational fashion.

Johnson had really begun high school in 1994-95 as a freshman at Bladensburg (MD) High, but poor grades prevented him from playing that season. He then transferred to Parkdale HS in Riverdale (MD), where he played one year and averaged more than 16 ppg, but still lacked sophomore credits when we first saw him play Mamorial Day weekend of '96 at the Dean Smith Center in Chapel Hill (NC). His play at times was breathtaking, and we were awed at how precocious he was.

The next stop for Johnson was the Newport School in Kensington (MD), where he repeated his sophomore year in 1996-97 and was an academic junior in 1997-98. His first year there he averaged 16.2 ppg, 8.6 rpg, 5.1 apg, 3.1 bpg and 2.2 spg. By the summer of 1997, we had Johnson ranked as the No. 1 prospect nationally in his class.

Unfortunately, he played significantly more consistently at major events during that summer than he has since then. A year ago, he performed quite well at the adidas ABCD Camp in Teaneck (NJ) and was even better at the 186-team adidas Big Time tournament in Las Vegas, where he (and Keith Bogans) led D.C. Team Assault to the championship, and he was selected MVP.

The pressure of rising expectations had really escalated by the 1997-98 season, which was his second, and as it turned out, last at the Newport School. As a highly publicized junior on a team that lacked a true big man (hence he was used part of the time out of position, as a post player), Johnson didn't really shine relative to his enormous talents, even though he averaged 20.5 ppg, 8.2 rpg, 4.5 apg, 3.2 bpg and 2.0 spg. With an improved jumpshot, he knocked in 41 percent of his three-point shots as Newport finished with a 30-6 mark after losing in the Maryland private school title game.

By the spring of 1998, his reputation had begun to exceed his actual calibre of play. Thus he was the sole junior chosen first-team All-America by *Parade Magazine*. More deservedly, USA Today selected Johnson as All-USA Honorable Mention and among the Top 15 Juniors to Watch nationally.

During the late spring and summer of 1998, Johnson again played in the Reebok/Bob Gibbons Tournament of Champions, the adidas ABCD Camp and the adidas Big Time Tournament. At the TOC, he played for the first time with the Tim Thomas Playaz out of Philadelphia. The team lacked organization, Johnson again was played part of the time out of position in the post, and although he averaged 16 ppg and was somewhat generously put on the All-tournament team, his stock with many scouts was beginning to edge downward.

The same trend continued at the adidas ABCD Camp, even though he demonstrated at times that he was among the very best *prospects* present. In eight camp games, Johnson averaged 9.3 ppg, 5.0 rpg, 2.3 apg and 0.8 bpg; his field-goal percentage was a mediocre .377, yet he proved he could hit arching, knuckleball three-pointers when he drilled five of them for all 15 of his points for the losing side in the camp's Senior All-Star Game.

The lowest point for Johnson during the summer of '98 occurred at the massive 224-team adidas Big Time in Las Vegas, the scene of his biggest triumph exactly a year earlier. He at times was bothered by nagging injuries, at other times sat at the end of the bench and seemed to pout, and too often when on the court played uninspired and seemingly with little thought.

With relatively little contribution from Johnson, defending champion D.C. Assault was shocked in the quarterfinals of the Open Division (winners bracket) 81-66 by the unheralded New York-based Madison Broncos. Incredibly, Johnson was "rewarded" with a berth on the 35-man All-tournament team. Hey fellas, watch the games.

STRENGTHS AND AREAS NEEDING WORK: Johnson is a superior run/jump athlete who handles the ball quite well and is at his best facing the basket, going one-on-one, and utilizing his passing skills. As noted previously, he was played out of position (at power forward) often this summer, and he is just adequate inside, where his lack of weight and strength is a handicap.

His game really is best suited to creating opportunities for himself primarily outside the paint and for his teammates near the basket. His style and size are similar to Magic Johnson, but Johnson (although a highly capable passer) doesn't make as consistently good decisions with the ball as Magic did. On the other hand, D. Johnson can play superb defense, which is something M. Johnson was never accused of.

At 200 pounds, Johnson remains very thin and not ready, physically or mentally, for the NBA, regardless of past rumors that he would skip college. Although some scouts believe that his biggest current problem is that he doesn't play consistently hard, we think his erratic decision-making is a bigger culprit, although there's no doubt that Johnson turns his aggressiveness on and off.

On the positive side, his hands are excellent, he's a quick leaper, his passing *can* be (but isn't always) extremely alert and creative, and he has at his disposal a passel of big-time dribble moves to the hoop. On those occasions when his sometimes erratic outside shot is falling, and he's making primarily wise decisions, he's virtually impossible to stop.

But then there's the issue of his academic credentials. Maine Central is his fourth high school in the last five years, and it's no secret that Johnson has transferred into veteran coach Max Good's outstanding program in order to (1) better prepare for the next level of basketball, (2) get more direction in his life, and (3) reach 820 on the SAT or an average of 17 on the ACT and thus qualify for collegiate freshman eligibility, assuming he ends up with a core grade-point average of at least 2.5.

COLLEGIATE PREFERENCES: Of course, "will he qualify?" is a vital question in this regard. Coaches at many reputable universities appear to be assuming that he'll ultimately meet NCAA standards by the end of next spring and thus be able to play as a freshman in 1999-2000. Right now, Pittsburgh, UNC Charlotte (ex-Newport teammate Dalonte Hill is a sophomore guard for the 49ers), and Michigan are strongly involved, but others still could enter the picture.

BOTTOM LINE: Despite the negatives, we believe that Johnson has a lot in reserve that no one has seen yet. He possesses the sheer ability to be the best prep player in the nation this season, and he can also fill the seats.

KAREEM RUSH, *6-6, 200 lbs., senior, wing guard/small forward, The Pembroke Hill School/Kansas City, MO*

The Rush brothers from Kansas City are quite an anomaly in the prep basketball world, in that it's virtually unheard of for a pair of brothers to be ranked so high nationally in consecutive years. Jaron, a 6-7 right-handed small forward who's now a freshman at UCLA, was our number seven high school senior in the country last spring, while "little" brother Kareem enters this season as a national top-15 calibre prospect in the strong prep class of 1999.

MAJOR ACCOMPLISHMENTS: Although the Rushes had led Pembrook Hill to a state Class 2-A title in 1996-97, Rush's status as a big-time talent really was cemented by his play at the Nike All-American Camp in Indianapolis (IN) early in July of 1997, after his sophomore year of high school. There, he was a key player for one of the camp's top two teams, and he was just about as impressive as the older and more touted Jaron.

Last season, Pembroke Hill captured its second consecutive state 2-A championship behind Jaron's 27.1 ppg and 10.3 rpg, and Rush's 20.5 ppg, 9.5 rpg, 4.3 apg and 2.0 bpg. Rush also shot .572 percent from the field but a surprisingly poor .592 percent from the free-throw line. He made first-team All-state and first-team All-Metro Kansas City, and *USA Today* selected him to its All-USA Honorable Mention.

In May of 1998, the younger Rush played well at the Spiece Run 'N Slam Tournament in West Lafayette (IN) and then two weeks afterward earned MVP honors at the St. Louis Eagles Invitational tournament, where he paced the Kansas City Rebels to the championship while averaging 24.0 ppg (second-high in the event) in five games.

His next major stop was a return to the Nike All-American Camp. There, despite hampered by a toe injury, he was outstanding each time we watched him. The fine athlete repeatedly swished left-handed NBA-range three-pointers in an awesome display of marksmanship. We ranked his overall performance among the top half-dozen at the camp.

STRENGTHS AND AREAS NEEDING WORK: Rush is such a sweet downtown shooter (especially standing rather than on the move) because his stroke is picture-perfect in form, and his shot release is very quick, which permits him to get it off even when guarded closely. The vast majority of the time his shot is "on," so look out.

Besides his superb jump shot, the next best asset Rush has is good body control, which enables him to often finish plays when contested by bigger players. He has learned to jump in to draw contact and get to the free-throw line, because the call nearly always goes against the defender in that case. Still, he has begun to gain even more effectiveness by sometimes pulling up and finishing with short jump shots instead of taking it all the way and risking rejection by the skyscrapers.

As for the rest of his game, Rush is a good transition player who runs the floor swiftly, and he's a fine leaper who scraps on the boards. His passing is skillful, as his ballhandling is plenty solid for wing guard. A bit more of a finesse player than Jaron, Rush knows the game and plays aggressive defense, where he gets steals through anticipation and good (not great) quickness.

COLLEGIATE PREFERENCES: Missouri and UCLA are the frontrunners for his services at this writing, though it's conceivable that might change. Rush also lists Arizona and Duke as possibilities, but neither is really recruiting him hard right now.

If he stays near home and plays for the Tigers, his friends and family can come to watch him play. Should he opt to join Jaron at UCLA, he knows that the Bruins are already loaded with excellent players, so playing time likely would come more slowly then at Missouri. Of course, UCLA also has a better shot than Missouri at winning the NCAA championship, which is a dream of nearly all outstanding prep prospects.

BOTTOM LINE: You can blink and he's hung 25 points on you.

JASON WILLIAMS, *6-2 1/2, 195 lbs., senior, point guard/wing guard, St. Joseph's HS/Metuchen, NJ*

No current high school player affects others on the court more than Jason Williams. An outstanding student/athlete with a 3.6 grade-point average and a 1,080 SAT entering his senior year, William sets up the offense, directs traffic and communicates with teammates (and sometimes officials) in an effective and efficient manner that any coach would love.

MAJOR ACCOMPLISHMENTS: Williams was MVP of his high school team and third-team All-state as a sophomore, but he didn't attend the major national camps and tournaments during the 1997 summer and thus entered last season lacking the big reputation that some of his classmates already had. This quickly changed, as he had a blockbuster junior season, with averages of 22.0 ppg, nearly 7.0 rpg, and 5.0 apg while shooting 48 percent on field goals and 82 percent on free-throws for 24-4 St. Joseph's.

His game highs were 41 points and 12 assists, and the awards streamed in. The Associated Press chose him first-team All-state, he was Central Jersey Player of the year, and *USA Today* placed him on its All-USA Honorable Mention.

It was at the Reebok/Bob Gibbons Tournament of Champions in North Carolina during late May, however, that William became universally recognized as one of the very best point guards in the class of '99. At this talent-stocked event, while playing with two bad ankles, Williams still managed to rack up 24.8 ppg (including a high of 35 vs. the touted New Orleans Jazz) in four games for the New Jersey All-Stars en route to All-Tournament honors.

Next for William was the Nike All-America Camp in Indianapolis, where he established a strong claim as the best senior point guard present. We also ranked him among the top six performers (regardless of position) among 200 participants at this prestigious camp.

STRENGTHS AND AREAS NEEDING WORK: Williams is very athletic, strong and quick, a natural playmaker, and a fine shooter with a beautiful stroke and three-point range. He has a dynamic first step with the ball, pushes it relentlessly downcourt ala Mike Bibby, and makes consistently good decisions leading the break, where he is an acrobatic finisher and a clever, highly skilled passer. We especially like William's adept use of nifty bounce passes to set up his teammates.

His dribbling is quite slick, featuring a crossover that frequently wrong-foots foes. It seems as if he creates his opportunities at will. As a physical, highly competitive player who works very hard, his muscular body is an asset a both ends of the court. Defensively, he's smart as well as tough and quick, and his lightning-fast hands persistently hawk the ball.

Williams' scoring tools are such that he could certainly play wing guard if needed. But he lacks ideal height for that position, and he truly is a deluxe "pure" point guard.

COLLEGIATE PREFERENCE: On August 28 William committed to Duke during an unofficial visit to its campus. In the process, he canceled a planned trip that same weekend to Georgetown, and he personally telephoned John Thompson and Rutgers head coach Kevin Bannon to disclose his decision. He termed the calls "one of the hardest things I've had to do."

Interestingly, just a few days before his journey to Durham, N.C., Williams had said that he was leaning toward Rutgers, located very close to home. In contrast, while at the Tournament of Champions in May, he had been quoted as saying, "I've always wanted to play in the Carolinas."

Besides Rutgers (for whom he was a "must sign" recruit) and Georgetown, he also considered Connecticut, Notre Dame, Seton Hall and Clemson. Colleague Dave Telep of the *Prep Stars Recruiter's Handbook* jokes that Duke's high powered offense "would have been a Porsche without William and will be a Ferrari with him."

BOTTOM LINE: Personable, articulate and confident without being cocky, Williams lets his teammates know if they don't do the right thing on the court. Most importantly, he does it in a nice, classy way that they respond to positively. He'll be an excellent representative of Duke or, for that matter, any university.

OTHER TOP 44 CAPSULES

JONATHAN BENDER, *6-11, 195 lbs., senior, center/power forward, Picayune HS/Picayune, MS*

Widely heralded since he exhibited superior shotblocking and rebounding ability at the 1997 adidas ABCD Camp, Jonathan Bender apparently decided he was a perimeter player and, consequently, has since played himself out of the national top 12 in the class of '99. What a shame. Why would a young, extremely agile (albeit very thin) 6-11 leaper prefer to roam the perimeter 20 feet from the basket jacking up jump shots (hitting a few) rather than play in the paint, where he can elevate over foes to score easily via a soft, arching jumper or jump hook?

In high school play, Bender averaged 18.0 ppg, 8.0 rpg, 3.0 bpg and 2.0 apg as a sophomore. Last season he upgraded those stats to 20.9 ppg, 11.0 rpg, 4.2 bpg, 2.0 apg ad 1.0 spg, while shooting an impressive 62 percent from the field and 81 percent on free-throws, as Picayune finished with a 27-7 mark. He made first-team All-state, *Parade Magazine* All-America fourth team, and *USA Today's* All-USA Honorable Mention and Top 15 Juniors to Watch nationally.

In 1998 summer events, he averaged 14.5 ppg for the New Orleans Jazz in two games at the Reebok/Bob Gibbons Tournament of Champions and didn't make All-Tournament, scored 16 points in the Senior All-Star Game at the adidas ABCD Camp after shooting just .351 percent from the floor in camp games, and was an All-Tournament selection at the adidas Big Time.

The talent of this gifted, long-armed athlete is indisputable. He can run, jump, shoot, rebound, dribble, pass and dominate on defense with his lateral quickness. But he still must gain weight and strength, better utilize post moves, and use his height as an advantage.

He has a fluctuating list of college possibilities that includes Mississippi State, Memphis, Oklahoma, Florida, Kansas, Kentucky, Tennessee, longshot Tulane and perhaps others.

RONALD BLACKSHEAR, *6-4, 195 lbs., fifth-year senior, wing guard, Hargrave Military Academy/Chatham, Va.*

A gunner with reckless disregard for the three-point line, Ronald Blackshear is a 1998 all-state choice and *USA Today* All-USA Honorable Mention at Camilla (GA) Mitchell-Baker who didn't qualify last spring for collegiate freshman eligibility and thus is prepping for a year at Hargrave.

We liked his potential when we watched him at the 1997 Reebok/Bob Gibbons Tournament of Champions and the adidas ABCD Camp, but he was much more exciting a year later. When the ball is inbounded, he thinks it's within his range (he's usually right!) and thus has the trigger cocked.

This summer, Blackshear was a key performer for the Atlanta Celtics I team that reached the semifinals of the adidas Big Time tournament before falling by five points to the Michigan Mustangs, the ultimate champion. Demonstrating impressive athleticism in finishing drives as well as his smooth jump shot with a high release and 26-feet range (yes!), he earned a berth on the All-tournament team. Although he usually looks to shoot the ball himself, he made some slick dishes on the break, plus he hustled on defense and helped on the boards, utilizing his fine leaping ability.

In the spring of 1998 Blackshear made official campus visits to Georgia, Auburn and North Carolina State. Those three schools plus perhaps Kentucky (where he really wants to go?) appear to be the frontrunners for his services, though this may be subject to change.

STEVEN BLAKE, *6-3, 170 lbs., senior, point guard, Oak Hill Academy/Mouth of Wilson, VA*

While not a great athlete, Steven Blake is a winner who was the floor leader last season for Miami (FL) Miami Senior High's 36-1 powerhouse that won its third consecutive Class 6-A (large school) state title and finished the season ranked No. 4 nationally by *USA Today.* That same publication named Blake All-USA Honorable Mention, even though his statistics (9.1 ppg, nearly 7.0 apg and 3.2 spg) were not auspicious. He also played a vital role the previous year for Miami Senior's championship team.

Blake will play at perennial power Oak Hill this season because the Florida High School Athletic Association has declared him (and four former teammates) ineligible to play in Florida for allegedly violating association rules by receiving housing assistance from Miami Senior High employees and fans.

Blake edged out athletically gifted Arizona small forward Donnell Knight for the last top 44 spot. This summer Steven was impressive enough at trials in Colorado Springs to be selected to the 1998 USA Junior World Championship Qualifying Team (18-under) that won the Americas Region tournament held in the Dominican Republic. Only three other members of that team have remaining high school eligibility.

He made the USA team because he is mentally tough and smart, handles the ball quite capably, knows how to settle things down and run a team, shoots well from the perimeter when open and works hard on defense, where he can sometimes be physically overmatched. He needs to be more physical and to improve his ability to get his shot off the dribble.

Blake has committed to Maryland after giving serious consideration to Miami-Florida and Syracuse. While we doubt that he'll be a big star for the Terps, he should do a good job of running the show, directing traffic, and getting the ball to the right people.

LAVELL BLANCHARD, 6-7, *195 lbs., senior, small forward/power forward, Pioneer HS/Ann Arbor, MI*

LaVell Blanchard had an outstanding summer, with no weak performances and plenty of excellent ones. He was among the four most impressive players at the NBA Players Association Camp, led all scorers at the adidas ABCD Camp with 16.8 ppg while adding 5.9 rpg and a 54.0 percent field-goal average, and capped off July by being chosen Camp Most Outstanding Player at the best Pittsburgh week of the famous Five-Star Camp, even though he played on a possible broken leg after the second day.

The new item he showcased this summer was a much improved jump shot, with legitimate three-point range. Even without much of an outside shot, he had enough other weapons to average 25 ppg, 14.0 rpg and 4.0 bpg as a soph in 1996-97, and 28 ppg, 10 rpg and 5 bpg the following season, when he was selected All-USA Honorable Mention by *USA Today.*

The best thing that Blanchard does is make plays. A terrific run/jump athlete, he reacts to the ball very quickly, plays taller than his actual size (especially in rebounding), isn't at all afraid to stick his nose in versus bigger players, and brandishes a polished set of inside moves to the hoop. Whether in transition or in a set offense, he's going to get his points, particularly now that his jump shot is regularly finding the net.

When it comes to college possibilities, LaVell keeps a poker face and won't tip his hand, even though hometown Michigan (where he almost certainly would be an immediate starter) is located almost within sight of his home. He also mentions Georgetown, Wisconsin, "the ACC and Big Ten." Does all this mean he wants to leave Ann Arbor? We doubt it, but stay tuned!

MATT BONNER, *6-9, 235 lbs., senior, power forward, Concord HS/Concord, NH*

Probably the best player to ever come from New Hampshire is Matt Bonner, who is somewhat mechanical but usually efficient and very skillful. When all is said and done, he compiles big statistics, even versus top-calibre competition.

As a junior he averaged nearly 30 ppg, 13.3 rpg, 3.8 bpg, 3 apg and 3 spg. USA Today tabbed him as both All-USA Honorable Mention and one of the Top 15 Juniors to Watch nationally. Additionally, he was New Hampshire Gatorade Player of the year for the second consecutive year and first-team All-state for the third straight season.

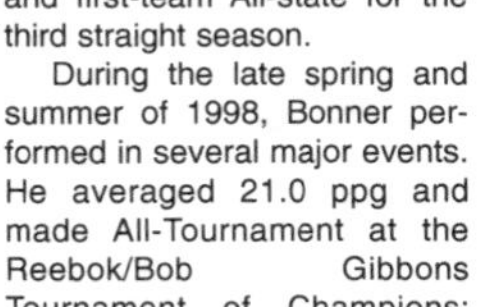

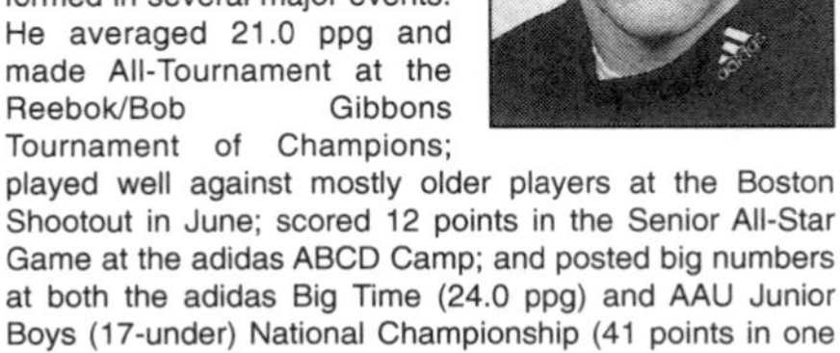

During the late spring and summer of 1998, Bonner performed in several major events. He averaged 21.0 ppg and made All-Tournament at the Reebok/Bob Gibbons Tournament of Champions; played well against mostly older players at the Boston Shootout in June; scored 12 points in the Senior All-Star Game at the adidas ABCD Camp; and posted big numbers at both the adidas Big Time (24.0 ppg) and AAU Junior Boys (17-under) National Championship (41 points in one game), although he made the All-tournament team at neither.

When he makes a concerted effort to play primarily inside and take advantage of his size and soft touch, he's a better player, but he has said that he sees himself as a wing forward, hence he spends a lot of time on the perimeter, which is cause for concern. He does possess a fine jump shot with three-point range, some strong and polished moves (e.g., up and under) with the ball, a nice jump hook in the lane, and the abilities to dribble and pass skillfully, and to score on the move.

Still, he needs to get inside and rebound more. When he's near the basket, he actually rebounds quite proficiently. While he appears to be just a slightly above average athlete, he's good enough to have won the slam dunk contest last season at a 16-team tournament in Florida. When the other team has the ball, Matt has pretty good reject timing and is an alert post defender, but he can be driven by, especially if he's trying to guard a quick forward.

An excellent student with a grade average of 97 and a reported SAT score of 1,330, he has committed to Florida, where he'll join good friends Mike Miller (a current Gator freshman) and Brett Nelson in the fall of 1999. Virginia was his second choice, while Syracuse finished third in the Bonner sweepstakes.

CARLOS BOOZER, *6-9, 230 lbs., senior, power forward, Douglas HS/Juneau, AK*

If there has ever been a better *prospect* from Alaska than Carlos Boozer, we've never seen him (move over, Trajan Langdon)! Boozer, who seriously contemplated a transfer to Fresno (CA) Washington Union but decided he preferred to live in Juneau, emerged on the national scene with an outstanding showing at the 1997 adidas ABCD Camp.

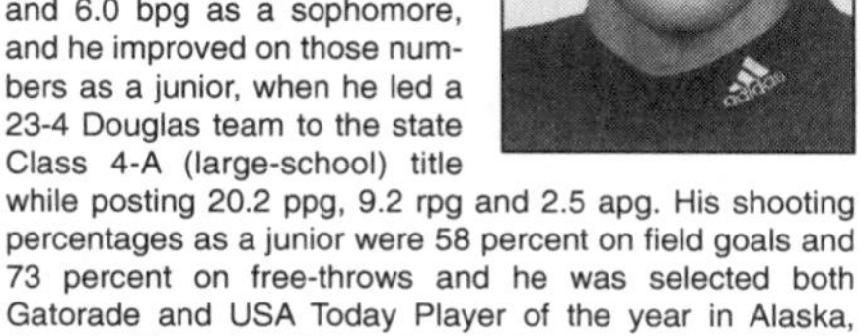

The previous season he had averaged 19.0 ppg, 12.0 rpg and 6.0 bpg as a sophomore, and he improved on those numbers as a junior, when he led a 23-4 Douglas team to the state Class 4-A (large-school) title while posting 20.2 ppg, 9.2 rpg and 2.5 apg. His shooting percentages as a junior were 58 percent on field goals and 73 percent on free-throws and he was selected both Gatorade and USA Today Player of the year in Alaska, *Parade Magazine* All-America third team, and one of the Top 15 Juniors to Watch nationally by *USA Today.*

In the four and a half months after the 1997-98 season, Carlos was outstanding at the Spiece Run 'N Slam Tournament, one of the premier performers (again) at the adidas ABCD camp (where he averaged 13.9 ppg in camp games and scored 12 points in the Senior All-Star Game), and dominant at the Double Pump West Coast All-Star Camp. He didn't make the All-tournament team at the adidas Big Time, as the touted EBO-Fresno team he played for was a disappointment.

One of the best prep talents in the USA, Boozer has a complete offensive package very few can match. But he sometimes coasts through at least parts of games, which is a bad habit that needs correction. When he's playing hard, he's very skilled as well as extremely athletic, has an explosive first step, and makes everything look easy, whether a reverse layup, mid-range jumper, or hanging power jam in traffic.

Boozer is an acrobatic, ambidextrous finisher, and he can be (but isn't always) a strong and reliable rebounder. While his dribble moves to the hoop are clever as well as strong, his selection on his jump shot is something that could be improved.

Boozer has indicated that he's considering nine schools, with UCLA (whose entire coaching staff followed him around all summer), Duke, Kansas, Maryland and Kentucky generally considered prime contenders. Others on his list are Syracuse, St. John's, Connecticut and Southern California.

NICK COLLISON, *6-9, 220 lbs., senior, power forward/center, Iowa Falls HS/Iowa Falls, IA*

Nick Collison's national stock rose markedly this summer, when he played for the USA Junior World Championship Qualifying Team (18-under) that won the Americas Region tournament, made the All-tournament team at the adidas Big Time (where he averaged 21.2 ppg), and was chosen AAU first-team All-America at the AAU Junior Boys (17-under) and the Senior Boys (19-under) National Championships. In the latter, the Martin Brothers Select team he starred for reached the title game before falling 89-68 to the older Boo Williams All-Stars.

Before the Junior World Championship Qualifying Team trials in Colorado Springs, he excelled at the Spiece Run 'N Slam Tournament and was chosen to the All-tournament team at the Reebok/Bob Gibbons Tournament of Champions, where he averaged 18.3 ppg. In high school play, Collison made *USA Today's* All-USA Honorable Mention for his performance as a junior.

The apple of many big-time recruiters' eyes, Collison is the son of a high school coach, and it shows. He's polished, confident, fundamentally sound, intelligent, skilled and surprisingly athletic. He scores proficiently in the paint via quick spin moves and a soft jump shot, which he can also drill when he steps out to 19 feet.

He constantly puts out the effort, and the numbers take care of themselves. Scrappy on the boards, Collison has good hands and runs the court well. On defense, he has impressive shot-block timing and stands in to draw charges.

Collison has narrowed his collegiate choices to two schools, Kansas (he wears Raef LaFrentz's number) and Duke. Interestingly, the Blue Devils are avidly recruiting him even though they already have a commitment from 6-10 Minnesota power forward/center Nick Horvath, who was a member of the USA World Youth Games (17-under) Team. Coaching changes at Iowa and Iowa State apparently cost both major home-state universities a good chance to land him.

MIKE DUNLEAVY, *6-7, 200 lbs., senior, small forward/wing guard, Jesuit HS/Portland, OR*

As good a player as Portland Trail Blazers head coach Mike Dunleavy, Sr., was at South Carolina and in the NBA, his son Mike Jr., may well turn out to be better. The younger Dunleavy played as a sophomore at Mequon (WI) Homestead, while his father coached the Milwaukee Bucks, and when we observed Mike Jr. in action at the 1997 adidas ABCD Camp, we weren't particularly excited.

A year later, after a strong junior season (21 ppg, 8 rpg, 4 apg and 2 spg) at Jesuit High in Portland (OR) that gained him All-USA Honorable Mention from *USA Today*, he looked like a completely different, and much better, player. At the adidas ABCD Camp, he averaged 10.1 ppg for his camp team, drilled 48.1 percent of his three-pointers, and contributed 12 points and four assists to the winning side in the Senior All-Star Game.

Next came the Double Pump West Coast All-Star Camp, where he was one of the best three or four players present. But the clincher was his stellar all-around play at the adidas Big Time for the Pump & Run I team out of Chatsworth (CA). Dunleavy played a critical role as his team reached the Open Division quarterfinals, and he deservedly made the All-tournament team.

When Mike Sr. says that his son "really knows how to play the game," he's not kidding. Mike Jr. is very aggressive, a super open shooter who buries three-pointers, smart, highly motivated and fundamentally sound in every way, from his shooting form to the way he throws a two-hand chest pass. He's solid, consistent, alert, and a better athlete (e.g., grabbing rebounds in traffic) than he initially appears.

His hands are excellent, he moves well without the ball and he's a tricky passer who sees the entire court but sometimes forces things too much. Because he already knows what to do, coaches won't have to spend time teaching and re-teaching him things.

On the negative side, his quickness isn't exceptional, he's not the most sure ballhandler in a crowd (despite his skill in the open court), he doesn't often play above the rim, he's not physically strong and he has trouble guarding either a quick perimeter player or a strong insider, even though he does anticipate wisely on defense.

Dunleavy, who has a 3.57 grade-point average and a reported 1,130 SAT as a junior, has narrowed his field of potential colleges to four: Duke, North Carolina, Stanford and Kentucky. All four have already offered him a scholarship, the coaching staffs of all four are to make September in-home visits with Dunleavy and his family and he plans to take official visits during the fall to each campus.

CHUCK EIDSON, *6-7, 185 lbs., senior, small forward/wing guard, Pinewood Prep/Summerville, SC*

Another coach's son, southpaw swingman Chuck Eidson, played pretty well this summer at the Nike All-America Camp but was absolutely sensational in the adidas Big Time tournament at Las Vegas and is better than generally advertised. Eidson played on private schools state championship teams as a freshman and junior at Pinewood Prep, and he was Region Player of the year the last two seasons.

As a junior, he averaged 26.9 ppg, 11.2 rpg and 5.7 apg while shooting 52 percennt from the floor and 73 percent from the free-throw line. *USA Today* selected him All-USA Honorable Mention, and after the season he played on the USA team in the Albert Schweitzer Games in Mannheim, Germany. It's worth providing a few details about Eidson's splendid play for the Team Carolina Sonics in Vegas. The team lost in the championship game of the Open Division despite Eidson's game-high 28 points. He averaged 20.6 ppg in eight games and was an obvious choice for the all-tournament team.

As a player, Eidson is intelligent, virtually always in the right place, athletic and a skilled, unselfish ballhandler who gets the ball to the people around him but gets his points, too. He makes good decisions, runs the court and finishes the break, drives quickly and effectively, and throws up a high-arching long-range (to 23 feet) shot that lacks back-

spin yet often goes in.

Additionally, Eidson is a good leaper and solid rebounder for small forward (though more strength would be an asset), and a heady defender who get some steals but is no one-on-one stopper. In fact, on defense he's better suited by far for small forward than for wing guard. Put it all together, assume normal improvement, and you have a player with the potential to be an All-Southeastern Conference performer down the road.

Eidson made a junior year commitment to South Carolina, and the Gamecocks have to feel fortunate that they were able to corral him so early, before he really emerged as a national factor.

JOE FORTE, *6-4, 190 lbs., senior, wing guard, DeMatha Catholic HC/Hyattsville, MD*

Although Joe Forte emerged during his sophomore season as a key player for powerful DeMatha and averaged as many points and rebounds last season as more heralded teammate Keith Bogans, it wasn't until the Reebok/Bob Gibbons Tournament of Champions in May of 1998 that he established himself as a truly elite prospect and moved into the national spotlight. Because Bogans didn't come to this event, Forte moved from the No. 2 option to the main man for the D.C. Stars, and he capitalized remarkably well at first fiddle by making nearly every jump shot, averaging 32.8 ppg to lead the Stars into the tournament finals and earning the MVP award.

At DeMatha last season he contributed 19.0 ppg, 5.8 rpg, 4.1 apg, and shot 50 percent from the field, 34 percent on three-pointers and 79 percent from the foul line as the Stags won the Washington (DC) Metro title with a 34-1 record and were ranked No. 3 in the nation by *USA Today*. Joe, who was MVP of two tournaments (over Bogans!), was chosen first-team All-Metro D.C., and *USA Today* named him to its All-USA Honorable Mention.

After the season and before the Tournament of Champions, Forte was on the USA Junior team that played in the Albert Schweitzer Games at Mannheim, Germany. During the summer of '98, he attended summer school, played for DeMatha in the Reebok Summer League in D.C. and briefly attended the Nike All-America Camp against the wishes (reportedly) of venerable Stags' coach Morgan Wootten.

A smart team player with fine shot selection, solid ballhandling skills and good but not great quickness, he can create his own shot via a sneaky first step and crafty stop-and-go dribble moves. He scores not only on smooth three-point pushes (low release) but also on mid-range pull-ups and fadeaways, hanging finishes near the hoop and power slams on the break.

Forte is a good leaper who helps on the boards, and he can dish skillfully on the move. He has quick hands on defense, and he's proven to be an excellent clutch performer.

Forte has reduced the field to four colleges—North Carolina, Georgia Tech (his family moved to D.C. from the Atlanta area), Villanova and North Carolina State. We understand that the Tar Heels have a very good shot at landing Forte, but must first offer him a scholarship.

KEVIN GAINES, *6-3 1/2, 186 lbs., senior, point guard/wing guard, Edward Clark HS/Las Vegas, NV*

Kevin Gaines is among the best five senior point guards nationally and might be the most athletic of the lot. As a high school junior, he averaged 23.0 ppg, 8.0 apg and 8.0 rpg with shooting percentages of 46 from the field and 64 on free-throws en route to recognition by *USA Today* as All-USA Honorable Mention.

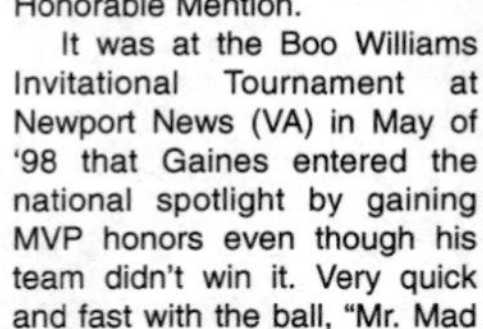

It was at the Boo Williams Invitational Tournament at Newport News (VA) in May of '98 that Gaines entered the national spotlight by gaining MVP honors even though his team didn't win it. Very quick and fast with the ball, "Mr. Mad Moves" blows by defenders and usually completes the play, though he struggled some with this aspect of his game at the Nike All-America Camp this summer.

His play at the adidas Big Time in his hometown was as scintillating as it was in Virginia three months earlier. On a relatively poor team, Gaines led everyone in this 224-team extravaganza with 29.8 ppg, including a high game of 46 points, while playing with a thigh bruise. He was a clearcut choice for the All-tournament team.

Besides his outstanding ability to break down his defender, penetrate to the basket and either score or dish, Gaines also hits three-pointers with a stroke that looks OK yet is sometimes inconsistent. An excellent transition player who pushes the ball downcourt at every opportunity and thrives in an up-tempo forum, he's also plays aggressive defense and presents matchup problems at both ends for guards not as big and athletic as he is.

Gaines is occasionally careless with the ball, and his feet are sometimes quicker than his brain, but the latter is not necessarily always a detriment on the court.

He committed to Michigan in late August, and we anticipate that he'll be an immediate starter for the Wolverines. Apparently Michigan was his clear-cut choice, with no other school really challenging Brian Ellerbe' program, even though Saint Louis wanted Gaines badly. His list also contained Stanford and Duke, but neither seemed to be recruiting him that hard.

JASON GARDNER, *5-11, 170 lbs., senior, point guard, North Central HS/Indianapolis, IN*

Jason Gardner was one of four players with remaining high school eligibility to be picked for the 1998 USA Junior World Championship Qualifying Team (18-under) that won the Americas Region tournament. That provides an excellent indicator of his level of talent.

As a prep sophomore in 1996-97, he made first-team all-state and was chosen Indianapolis Player of the year after averaging 15.3 ppg, 5.0 apg, and 4.0 rpg, and shooting 53 percent on field goals and 73 percent on free-throws. At the Nike All-America Camp in July of 1997, he impressed us a great deal with his super quickness, ballhandling skill and ability to penetrate virtualy at will.

Last season Gardner moved his game up another notch. He averaged 21.4 ppg, 4.0 rpg, 3.4 apg and 2.5 spg for 14-7 North Central, and his shooting percentages were 50 percent from the floor and 73 percent (again) from the foul line. *USA Today* selected him Indiana Player of the year and All-USA Honorable Mention, while *Parade Magazine* placed him on its All-America fourth team.

In late spring of 1998, he excelled at the Spiece Run 'N Slam Tournament, and when we saw him in action in July for the No Excuses team from Indianapolis at the adidas Big Time tournament, he was absolutely superb despite a bruised knee. Jason gets by opponents with his clever low dribbling and quicks.

His crossover dribble and hesitation (stop-and-go) move are both top-caliber, and he sees the court and passes creatively and skillfully. Unlike many athletic prep point guards, he's not only explosive but also under control. He draws lots of fouls on drives where he gets his shoulder past his defender and then jumps in to assure comtact.

Gardner isn't a bad three-point shooter (he hit 40 percent as a junior), though he doesn't try a whole lot. We love the way he hounds opponents on defense and uses his quick feet to draw charges.

In July of '98 he committed to Arizona (where the climate benefits his asthma) over power programs Kansas, Purdue and Duke shortly after returning from the Americas Region tournament in the Dominican Republic. Maybe he won't make Wildcat fans totally forget Mike Bibby, but he will get a chance to direct one of the best teams in the nation.

ANDREW GOODEN, *6-9, 211 lbs., senior, power forward/center, El Cerrito HS/El Cerrito, CA*

After a good but not great junior season in which he averaged 16.5 ppg, 13.5 rpg, 3.2 bpg, 2.1 apg and 2.1 spg, Andrew Gooden performed so consistently well at the adidas ABCD Camp this summer that he improved his national reputation arguably (or is it?) more than any other prepster. At this event, he paced his unbeaten (8-0) camp team in both scoring (14.6 ppg, third-high for the entire camp) and rebounding (a camp-high 9.8 per game), while hitting a high percentage of his shots (59.8% FGA) and rejecting or altering shots impressively.

In the camp's Senior All-Star Game, he scored eight points in 16 minutes of play for the winning side. Later that same month, Gooden didn't hurt his new-found status a bit at the huge adidas Big Time tournament. Playing for the Oakland Slam N Jam, he made the All-tournament team even though his team wasn't especially strong. By then, his stock had soared "from Duquesne to Duke!"

Gooden's game seems to get started at the defensive end, and then good things happen for him on offense. With excellent mobility, long arms and a fine leap, he's one of the best defenders and shot blockers in the senior class, and also a good and persistent rebounder despite less than ideal physical strength.

A very good student as well as athlete, he has developed both a smooth jump shot with 18-feet range and an effective jump hook. He's also an adept passer and not a bad dribbler, especially for his size. He uses spin moves inside, but still needs to work on his post moves, besides gaining more strength.

Gooden is listing seven colleges, with no leanings indicated. The contenders for his services are California, Kansas, Duke (whose first choice is Nick Collison), UCLA, Michigan, Arkansas and Southern California. Don't count the Razorbacks out; his mother resides in Fayetteville (AR).

ROD GRIZZARD, *6-7, 180 lbs., senior, wing guard/point guard/wing forward, Central Park Christian School/ Birmingham, AL*

Until bursting on the scene with a spectacular showing this spring at the Boo Williams Invitational Tournament, Rod Grizzard was a genuine national "sleeper," and there aren't many of those. A private school player in Alabama, last season he led Central Park Christian to a 31-0 record and state title in its classification by averaging 25.3 ppg, 8.1 rpg and 7.3 apg.

He shot 49 percent from the field, 81 percent from the free-throw line, and had game highs of 41 points, 18 rebounds and 12 assists. He was chosen first-team all-state, and *USA Today* recognized him on its All-USA Honorable Mention. Following his scintillating play at the Boo Williams Invitational, Grizzard combined participation in the Nike All-America Camp and the Nike Super Showcase (in Orlando) with summer school attendance.

Unfortunately, at the Nike Camp he was played out of position (as a combo forward) for his camp team and thus didn't perform nearly as well as he's capable. Less than two weeks later, this rangy southpaw flashed his awesome potential potential at times, but didn't consistently step up in Orlando for the Alabama Lasers, who were beaten easily by ultimate finalist Potomac Blue Devils.

When used at wing guard (his best position), he brings to the table an array of weapons and the kind of athletic ability few possess. A great athlete who reminds us of Scottie Pippen in his ability to finish plays, he has a superior handle (although he sometimes over dribbles), is able to skywalk over defenders for easy shots and sometimes looks unstoppable. Grizzard sees the floor well, is a very good passer, has lightning-quick hands and can drill NBA-range three-point jumpshots with a smooth stroke.

Though not really out of control, he's so physically talented that he sometimes plays at too high a speed for his teammates to keep up. At those times, he needs to limit the flash and dash a little bit, yet on other occasions he seems too laid back and doesn't play with enough intensity.

The two big questions related to his collegiate future are (1) will he qualify academically for freshman eligibility in 1999?; and (2) if so, will he leave the state of Alabama for college? Right now, hometown UAB wants him to be the centerpiece of its program (ala Larry Hughes at St. Louis last season), while Alabama and Auburn are also strongly in contention. Others involved include Florida State, Connecticut and South Carolina.

CASEY JACOBSEN, *6-6, 195 lbs., senior, small forward/wing guard, Glendora HS/Glendora, CA*

The captain and star of the USA World Youth Games Team (17-under) that won the title by beating Russia this summer in Moscow was Casey Jacobsen. He scored 23 points in the championship game and averaged 25.4 ppg for the tournament. In the trials at Colorado Springs that resulted in his selection to this team, he led all scorers with 19.3 ppg.

Obviously, then, Jacobsen is a deluxe scorer, as he has also proven in high school play, where he averaged 26 ppg (plus 6.0 rpg and 3.5 apg) as a sophomore and 32 ppg last season. His other junior statistics were 9.0 rpg, 5.0 apg and 2.0 spg. He shot 57 percent from the field and 77 percent on free-throws as 31-2 Glendora captured the California Southern Section Division I championship. He was chosen first-team all-state, Southern Section Division I Player of the year, and *USA Today* All-USA Honorable Mention.

Before the Colorado Springs trials, he was a member of the Belmont Shore (CA) team in the Reebok/Bob Gibbons Tournament of Champions. There he averaged 25 ppg in five games and made the All-tournament team.

Although not the fastest, strongest, nor best leaper, Jacobsen is a consummate basketball player because he plays plays skillfully, with toughness, and very intelligently, like his good friend Jason Kapono. In fact, along with Kapono and junior DeShawn Stevenson, Jacobsen is one of the top three prep players in the loaded Golden State.

He comes off screens and squares up to the basket with precision, gets off and knocks down jump shots to 21 feet with a high release, has a deceptively quick first step to the hole, always finds his man and works hard on defense, and leads the team in floor burns. A consistent player, he understands how to get open, dribbles and passes the ball well (his hands are ultra-quick), and leaps well enough to slam alley oops and snare his share of rebounds.

Jacobsen is a real competitor who hates to lose. What he lacks in speed at both ends of the court, he more than makes up with intensity, desire and fundamentals. Vitale will love him.

An excellent student with a 3.94 grade-point average and more than 1,000 on the PSAT, Jacobsen appears likely to wind up at either Duke (his first choice, but the Blue Devils are waiting on Mike Dunleavy's decision before offering Casey a scholarship) or Stanford. His third finalist is Utah, but we hear that the Utes know they're unlikely to get him.

MAJESTIC MAPP, *6-2, 180 lbs., senior, point guard, St. Raymond's HS/Bronx, NY*

Perhaps the most aptly named prep player is Majestic Mapp (Scientific's brother—no kidding), because his game is truly majestic, in some important ways. He entered the lineup at always-strong St. Anthony's as a sophomore and averaged 10.0 ppg, 7.0 apg and 3.0 spg. A year later, his stats had beefed up to 19.0 ppg, 5.0 apg, 5.0 rpg and 2.0 spg.

During the 1998 spring and summer, Mapp played for the New York Ravens in the Reebok/Bob Gibbons Tournament of Champions, where he averaged 16.4 ppg and should have, but didn't make the all-tournament team. Mapp could not compete at the NBA Players Association Camp because of injury, but scored 14 points in the Senior All-Star Game at the adidas ABCD Camp after leading the camp in assists (5.5 per game), averaging 10.6 ppg, and drilling .538 percent of his three-point shots. He was selected to the all-tournament team at the adidas Big Time, where he again played for the New York Ravens.

One of the nation's top-five senior point guards, he is a deft handler who is extremely clever with the ball, a sweet assist man who sees the floor and finds the open man and a pretty good, improving jump shooter. While he hits some three-pointers, he still sometimes shoves his jump shot. This excellent student-athlete often puts on a clinic, exploding past defenders on offense and shutting down opposing point guards with his quick, highly physical defense.

In fact, we consider him the best prep point guard defender in the nation. Just as important is the way he runs his team. A pure point guard in St. Raymond's well-structured program, Mapp is an outstanding leader who plays cerebrally, and who relates well to his teammates (and virtually everyone else) with his dynamic personality. He had a summer job working on Wall Street, and this is the kind of person any coach would love to have in his program.

The program Mapp plans to play for has already been determined, as he became Pete Gillen's first recruit at Virginia by committing to the Wahoo head coach on August 28, during an unofficial campus visit. Gillen, who outdueled finalist Conecticut, must be delighted and is no doubt hoping that Majestic will help draw other prime prospects to Charlottesville.

JOSH MOORE, *7-0 1/2, 280 lbs., senior, center, St. Thomas More Academy/Oakdale, CT*

One part of Josh Moore's game already compares favorably with Shaquille O'Neal—his feet. Moore's size 22 shoes resemble ski boots, but he still is able to run OK, although certainly not great. We also admire Moore's spunk for telephoning our colleague Dave Telep at the *Prep Stars Recruiter's Handbook* to say that he's better than those big men ahead of him on our senior list. We're pleased that he reads us and cares so much about where he's ranked.

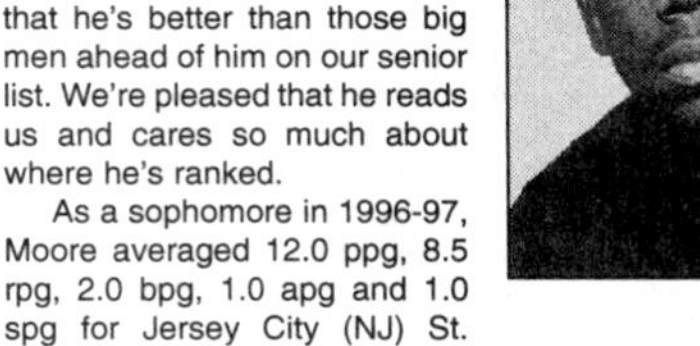

As a sophomore in 1996-97, Moore averaged 12.0 ppg, 8.5 rpg, 2.0 bpg, 1.0 apg and 1.0 spg for Jersey City (NJ) St. Anthony's, which won the New Jersey state Tournament of Champions. We thought he was highly promising at the 1997 adidas ABCD Camp, and he began his junior season in fine form, averaging 15.0 ppg, 7.5 rpg, 1.5 bpg and 1.0 spg in the first 14 games for powerful St. Anthony's. At that point, however, coach Bob Hurley, Sr. booted Moore from the team for violating unspecified team rules, and St. Anthony's (minus Moore from then on) finished with a 22-5 record after losing in the state semifinals.

Last summer he again was a participant at the adidas ABCD Camp. There he averaged 8.9 ppg, 6.3 rpg (sixth-best at the camp), 1.0 bpg and connected on .630 percent of his shots. In the camp's Senior All-Star Game, he scored four points in 16 minutes of action for the losing side. We were amused and impressed that he was smart enough to quickly introduce himself to many fellow campers who looked like point guards, assumedly to make sure they knew who the seven-footer was and got him the ball.

The young Goliath now is bound for another prep power, St. Thomas More, after also considering Cheshire Academy in Connecticut. On the court, when Moore doesn't envision himself as a face-the-basket mid-range jumpshooter, he can be very effective. He has a good offensive package down low, with sound power moves, a jump hook and a soft turnaround jump shot.

He catches the ball well, passes it skillfully (e.g., give-and-go), and rebounds strongly. While not a plodder, he's not a top run/jump athlete either, and sometimes he looks a bit awkward. Moore, who could be more of a defensive factor with added commitment and lateral agility, certainly doesn't need any more weight beyond the 280 pounds that he already is.

Although his academic credentials are reportedly questionable when it comes to qualifying in 1999 for collegiate freshman eligibility, at this point he likes Rutgers, Seton Hall, St. John's, Syracuse, Kansas, Villanova and maybe Connecticut.

DERRICK PAYNE, *6-6, 220 lbs., senior, small forward/power forward, Mount Zion Christian Academy/Durham, NC*

After a subpar showing this May for the disorganized Carolina Sonics in the Reebok/Bob Gibbons Tournament of Champions cost Derrick Payne his spot in our pre-summer national top 25, he told *Prep Stars Recruiter's Handbook* colleague Dave Telep that he wanted and intended to get back into the top 25. Then Payne went out this summer and did it.

We've been very high on Payne since his sophomore year, when he averaged 22.0 ppg, 11.3 rpg, 3.0 apg, 2.0 bpg and 2.0 spg for Washington (DC) Coolidge versus strong urban competition. He was impressive at the 1997 adidas ABCD Camp, and then had an excellent junior season for a very good Coolidge team, with his scoring increasing to 24.0 ppg, and other stats of 9.0 rpg, 4.0 spg and 2.0 apg. *USA Today* selected him for its 1997-98 All-USA Honrable Mention list.

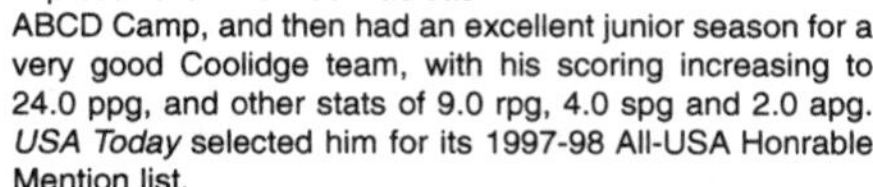

After the Tournament of Champions debacle, Payne redeemed himself at the adidas ABCD Camp by averaging 15.3 ppg (second-high for the entire camp), 3.8 rpg and 1.1 spg while hitting one-third of his three-point field goal attempts. In the camp's Senior All-Star Game, he led the winners with 17 points in 16 minutes.

Payne's next appearance was at the adidas Big Time tournament for touted the D.C. Assault team that also contained Keith Bogans and DerMarr Johnson. Although the team was upset in the Open Division quarterfinals by the upstart Madison Broncos from the New York City area, it wasn't because of Payne's play. He was terrific, repeatedly drilling off-the-dribble jump shots and driving powerfully, elevating and converting. He somehow missed making the All-tournament team, but everyone knew that the real Derrick was back, and that meant serious Payne for opposing defenders.

Very strong, he can get up in the air with just about anyone, and he also can step outside and drain three-pointers, though his perimeter shot occasionally flattens out too much, and he'll force a few. His best position definitely is wing forward, but he can play the high post, turn, and explode past his defender to the hoop. This high-flyer also is tough on the boards, passes alertly off the drive and plays aggressive defense, blocking more shots than his previous high school statistics indicate.

In early September, his top four collegiate preferences appear to be Cincinnati, Maryland, Virginia and Kentucky, although this could be subject to modification.

JASON RICHARDSON, *6-6, 210 lbs., senior, small forward/wing guard, Arthur Hill HS/Saginaw, MD*

Before this summer, Jason Richardson was on no one's national top 25 list of senior prospects; now he's on everyone's. A truly gifted athlete with a rapidly expanding offensive arsenal, he helped himself as much by his play in July as anyone in the nation. He had made *USA Today*'s All-USA Honorable Mention as a junior, when he averaged 18.0 ppg, 12.0 rpg, 4.0 apg, 3.2 spg and 3.0 bpg on the same team with big-time forward DeAndre Hulett, but he certainly wasn't a household name.

His summer rise started at the adidas ABCD Camp, where he played very well, averaging 14.5 ppg (fifth-high in the camp), 5.3 rpg and 1.6 apg, and connecting on .314 percent of his three-point shots. Richardson was chosen for the camp's Senior All-Star Game, but Michigan high school rules prevented him (plus LaVell Blanchard and combo guard Brent Darby) from playing in it.

At the adidas Big Time, Richardson took his game to a different, even higher level. He led the Michigan Mustangs to the Open Division (winners bracket) championship of this 224-team event, scoring 20 points in the title game (a 98-76 romp over the Team Carolina Sonics) and earning the tournament's MVP award.

Richardson is not only a sensational athlete with superb quickness and leaping ability, but also a versatile player who (even though he's just a pretty proficient dribbler) gets to the basket in the blink of an eye, thanks to an incredible first step. Very quick off his feet, he plays tall and tough inside, where he out-jumps taller players to corral rebounds and reject shots spectacularly, yet he can also go out on the floor, pass the ball crisply and hit three-pointers.

Richardson's reactions to the ball compare favorably with anyone his size, and he's especially dangerous in transition, where he slam dunks alley oops and stickbacks with breathtaking body control and coordination. All in all, it will be a battle royal for Player of the year in Michigan, and Richardson will be in the thick of it.

On the recruiting front, don't be surprised if he opts for the same college as friend and Mustangs teammate Brent Darby. Jason is a particularly high-priority target for homestate Michigan, and the Wolverines might be the team to beat, although Michigan State and Connecticut apparently round out his top three, and Georgetown and Cincinnati are also under consideration.

TONY ROBERTSON, *6-3, 195 lbs., senior, wing guard/point guard, St. Andrew's School/Barrington, RI*

Combo guard Tony Robertson has posted some big high school numbers already, and his play this summer clearly established him as a national top-30 calibre senior prospect. A two-time all-state choice, he averaged approximately 30.0 ppg as both a sophomore and junior, while also contributing 8.0 rpg, 6.0 apg, 5.0 spg and 2.0 bpg this past season, when he made the All-New England Prep first team and *USA Today*'s All-USA Honorable Mention. St. Andrew's finished with a 28-1 record and won the New England Class E prep school championship.

When we watched Robertson in May of 1998 at the Reebok/Bob Gibbons Tournament of Champions, we were disappointed, especially compared with his play a year earlier in the same event. However, the team (Tim Thomas Playaz from Philadelphia) that he played for this year lacked structure, and this worked to Robertson's detriment. He didn't make the All-tournament team and shouldn't have made it, but we knew he was better than he showed.

Things turned around for him at the NBA Players Association Camp, where he was (controversially) chosen MVP and was certainly among the best four performers. At the adidas ABCD Camp, Robertson played fairly well, averaging 8.8 ppg, 3.5 rpg and 1.4 apg while shooting .412 percent from the field. In the camp's Senior All-Star Game he stepped up big, scoring a game-high 18 points while playing for the losing side.

We also observed him at the adidas Big Time, and we thought he played quite well for the Long Island Panthers, even though he wasn't picked for the somewhat arbitrary All-tournament team. He amply demonstrated that he is one of the best players in the senior class with the ball in his hands.

An extremely athletic driver with an excellent first step and super crossover dribble that can break a defender's legs, he gets to the basket swiftly and with relative ease, sees the court and generally is a good finisher who uses his strong frame to covert in the paint among the trees. Probably more effective at wing guard than point guard, Robertson also moves well without the ball and possesses a scorer's mentality.

He's a good but not great jump shooter with arch and backspin; an occasional three-pointer goes in, but he's much more reliable on short- to mid-range jumpshots off the bounce. When he's aggressive with the ball (as he wasn't in the Tournament of Champions), he plays a lot better. With his strong and sturdy frame and outstanding hops, he could post up other guards more often than he does.

In late August, Robertson announced that he would sign in November with the Connecticut Huskies. Florida finished second in the widespread war to land him.

KENNY SATTERFIELD, *6-2 1/2, 180 lbs., senior, wing guard/point guard, Rice HS/Manhattan, NY*

One of the most consistently impressive players we saw this spring and summer was Kenny Satterfield, a brilliant scorer who shoots accurately from beyond the three-point line with a quick shot release, but is best as a cat-quick, crafty driver who can take his defender off the dribble, slash to the basket easily and finish the play himself or via a slick pass. He first established a reputation in AAU-type competition for 15 and 16 year olds, and as a sophomore he cracked the lineup for strong Rice High.

It was last season when Satterfield really stepped forward and began to show more of what he is capable of doing. Rice won the New York Federation Class A (large-school) state title, compiled a 24-4 record versus a very strong schedule, and was nationally ranked No. 11 by *USA Today* in its final rankings. The balanced team's primary go-to player was forward Anthony Glover, a St. John's signee, but Satterfield played a major role by averaging 14 ppg (second only to Glover's 17.5), 5.0 apg, 4.0 rpg and 2.5 spg. He was chosen all-conference, first-team All-Bronx/Manhattan, and second-team all-county.

Playing for the New York Ravens in the Reebok/Bob Gibbons Tournament of Champions, Satterfield averaged a sizzling 27.3 ppg in six games and made the All-tournament team. A few weeks later, he was chosen to the USA World Youth Games Team (17-under) after tallying 15.8 ppg and shooting 53.5 percent from the field and 92 percent from the free-throw line at the trials in Colorado Springs; however, he turned down the spot because he was scheduled to attend summer school classes.

Satterfield did play in July at the adidas ABCD Camp and the adidas Big Time tournament, and he was a standout at both events. At ABCD, he annihilated Notre Dame recruit Mike Monserez in a head-to head matchup and averaged 11.8 ppg and 4.0 apg (tied for fourth at the camp) while shooting .522 percent from the field in eight camp games. This earned him a place in the Senior All-Star Game, in which he had 12 points and eight assists in 16 minutes for the losing team.

Surprisingly, he failed to be chosen for the All-tournament team at the adidas Big Time even though he averaged 23.5 ppg in four games for the New York Ravens. Regardless, everyone knows now that this "quiet assassin" is an elite senior prospect.

Actually, Satterfield does everything well on the court, and he can double as a point guard in a pinch, which is a major asset. He has a fairly slender build, but that doesn't adversely affect his ability to take the ball to the hoop successfully. A particularly outstanding finisher on the fast break, he has excellent body control and no one scares him away from the basket.

On defense, he is quick, smart and hard-working, which combine to reap him many steals. Most importantly, his versatility and clutch play make it difficult to keep him off the court.

Expected to qualify academically, Satterfield lists nine colleges that he is contemplating. They are Cincinnati, North Carolina State, Clemson, Connecticut, Seton Hall, Pittsburgh, Villanova, St. John's and Xavier. Will he reach a decision by November or wait until spring? Stay tuned.

IMARI SAWYER, *6-1, 170 lbs., junior, point guard, Martin Luther King HS/Chicago, IL*

One of the nation's best four junior prospects, Imari Sawyer is a very quick athlete who is both an outstanding scorer and a deluxe playmaker off the dribble. He stepped straight into the MLK lineup as a freshman and averaged an extremely impressive 17.0 ppg, 9.0 apg, 5.0 rpg and 3.5 spg versus tough Chicago competition. That following summer (1997), he was was of the few rising sophomores to be invited to adidas ABCD camp, where he understandably struggled at times against top players who were two years older.

Last season, Sawyer's game continued to mature, and he averaged 24.0 ppg, 10.0 apg and 3.0 spg for King High's fine team, which also featured current senior insider Leon Smith, among others. *USA Today* chose Sawyer to its All-USA Honorable Mention but not to its Top 10 Sophomores to Watch, which seems like a mistake, using hindsight.

In May of 1998, Sawyer played very impressively in the Spiece Run 'N Slam Tournament, and he built on that performance by shining in a return trip to the adidas ABCD Camp. There, his statistics (6.6 ppg, 4.4 apg which was second-high for the camp, 1.0 spg, 3.3 turnovers per game and .333 from the field) didn't do justice to the general high quality of his play. He was chosen to play in the Underclassman All-Star Game and contributed nine points and six assists for the winning side. We judged him to be the best junior point guard at the camp.

But it was at the adidas Big Time that Imari really stepped up and performed superbly for the Illinois Fire. He was the floor leader and sparkplug as the Fire reached the quarterfinals of the Open Division (winners bracket) before losing by four points to the Atlanta Celtics I (Donnell Harvey, Ronald Blackshear et al.) in a great game. In six games at Vegas Sawyer averaged 23.8 ppg, and he was an obvious choice for the All-tournament team.

He plays with a maturity beyond his years, drilling three-pointers and mid-range pull-up jumpshots with a fine stroke, getting to the basket on quick drives, throwing clever passes with fine court vision and scrapping on defense. A slick dribbler with terrific spin moves to shake free, he's an acrobatic finisher who gets fouled a lot. Though his free-throw stroke isn't real pretty, he hits most of them.

Because Sawyer is only a junior, it's too early to have a full bead on his likely collegiate choices. Our guess is that the college decision during the current school year by his outstanding MLK and Illinois Fire teammate Leon Smith (assuming Leon qualifies academically) may well shed light on what Sawyer will do in another year. Smith, by the way, has indicated interest in DePaul, Syracuse, Georgetown and others.

LEON SMITH, *6-10 1/2, 235 lbs., senior, power forward/center, Martin Luther King HS/Chicago, IL*

Very wide at the shoulders but relatively sleek otherwise, Leon Smith is an outstanding athlete and physical specimen whose physique reminds us of Shawn Kemp. Yet many college scouts have been more concerned about what exists above Smith's shoulders, ever since the top senior prospect in talent-laden Chicago was ejected from the 1998 NBA Players Association Camp at Princeton for sitting on the floor and refusing to leave the court so a substitute could enter. Shades of Joe Don Looney.

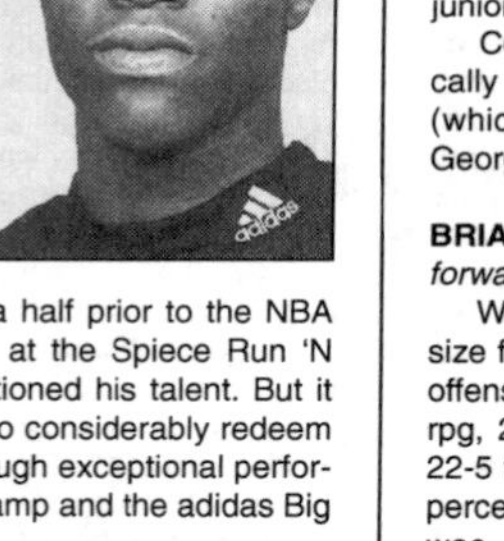

Smith averaged 20.0 ppg, 15.0 rpg, 8.0 bpg, 2.0 spg and 1.0 apg last season for a very strong King team that also features elite underclass point guard Imari Sawyer. A month and a half prior to the NBA Camp travesty, he was a standout at the Spiece Run 'N Slam Tournament, so no one questioned his talent. But it was in July that he was really able to considerably redeem himself in the eyes of recruiters through exceptional performances at both the adidas ABCD Camp and the adidas Big Time tournament.

At the former, his stats in camp games were good but not great great—7.9 ppg, 6.8 rpg (fifth-best), 1.95 spg (tied for fourth-best), 0.9 bpg, 54 percent from the field and a poor 45 percent from the free-throw line. However, in the camp's Senior All-Star Game, Smith was MVP, with 14 points and a game-high 11 rebounds in 16 minutes for the winning team.

Then, at the adidas Big Time he averaged 19.7 ppg in six games and played a key role as the Illinois Fire reached the Open Division (winners bracket) quarterfinals before falling 77-73 to the powerful Atlanta Celtics I team. Smith, who played consistently hard at both adidas events, was chosen to the Big Time's 35-man All-tournament team.

Smith is very mobile and not a pure center. He plays just as well facing the basket as he does with his back to it, hence he plays the high post as often (and as effectively) as the low post. He runs the court well, leaps impressively, and is very active on the boards, as his statistics indicate. A powerful dunker in traffic, he is also a budding defensive rejector, and his quick reactions are a major asset at both ends of the court.

No one knows how good Smith could become, because his physical attributes primarily have carried him to this point. Still, some of his fundamentals are OK. He meets passes smartly, and he has also developed some quick and strong inside moves to the basket, though he doesn't always finish them successfully.

We lack reliable information on Smith's academic credentials, and they obviously are a factor in his recruitment by Division I universities. The reported favorites to sign him are DePaul, Syracuse and perhaps Georgetown, although others might also be in the picture.

MARCUS TAYLOR, *6-3, 180 lbs., junior, point guard/wing guard, Waverly HS/Lansing, MI*

Ever since Marcus Taylor averaged 39.0 ppg versus eighth-grade competition in 24-minute games, he's been marked as one of the very best prospects in the prep class of 2000. Thus far, he's let no one down. As a freshman, he averaged 25.0 ppg, 6.0 rpg, and 6.0 apg while connecting on 48 percent of his field goals and 85 percent of his free-throws. This gained him recognition as first-team Michigan All-state and City MVP, and a spot on *USA Today*'s Top 5 Freshmen to Watch nationally.

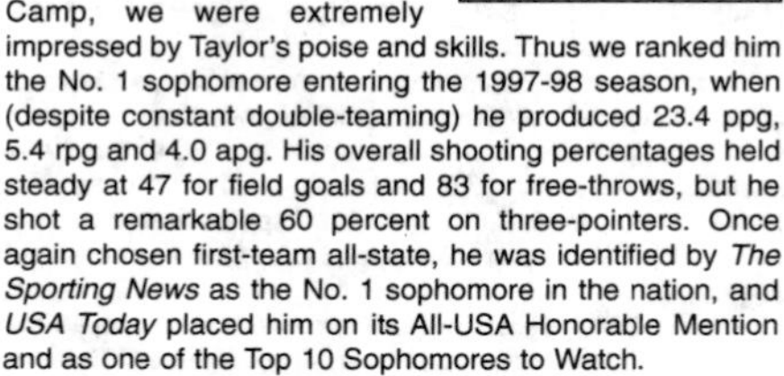

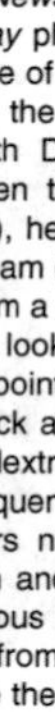

At the 1997 Nike All-America Camp, we were extremely impressed by Taylor's poise and skills. Thus we ranked him the No. 1 sophomore entering the 1997-98 season, when (despite constant double-teaming) he produced 23.4 ppg, 5.4 rpg and 4.0 apg. His overall shooting percentages held steady at 47 for field goals and 83 for free-throws, but he shot a remarkable 60 percent on three-pointers. Once again chosen first-team all-state, he was identified by *The Sporting News* as the No. 1 sophomore in the nation, and *USA Today* placed him on its All-USA Honorable Mention and as one of the Top 10 Sophomores to Watch.

During the summer of 1998, Taylor was invited to the USA Youth Development Festival in Colorado Springs, where even though he was among the leading scorers (17.4 ppg), he was not selected for the USA World Youth Games Team (17-under), in something of a surprise. When we saw him a couple of weeks later at the Nike All-America Camp, he looked the same not-so-old Taylor, drilling arching three-pointers off the dribble, slashing past defenders with a quick and strong first step and finishing athletically and ambidextrously.

Consequently, we currently rate him among the best four juniors nationally, along with Alton Ford, DeShawn Stevenson and Imari Sawyer. Taylor admittedly idolizes a more famous Lansing product, Earvin Johnson, and has borrowed from Magic's game in the hope that one day he too can be the greatest player in the world.

Taylor, who can play either guard, sees the court well and is very focused. A heady performer who excels in the clutch, he plays older than he is. He's also cerebral in the classroom, with a 3.0 grade-point average entering his junior year.

College still is nearly two years off, but Taylor has publically expressed interest in hometown Michigan State (which hardly can afford to miss him), Michigan, Georgetown, Arizona, North Carolina and UCLA.

BRIAN WETHERS, *6-5, 210 lbs., senior, wing guard/small forward, Murrieta Valley HS/Murrieta, CA*

Wethers Wethers is a prototypical wing scorer with ideal size for a wing guard and a wide variety of weapons in his offensive arsenal. As a junior, he averaged 22.6 ppg, 10.2 rpg, 2.7 spg and 2.5 apg for a 22-5 team while knocking in 54 percent of his field goals. He was chosen MVP of the Mountain View League, All-Valley, and All-California Interscholastic Federation.

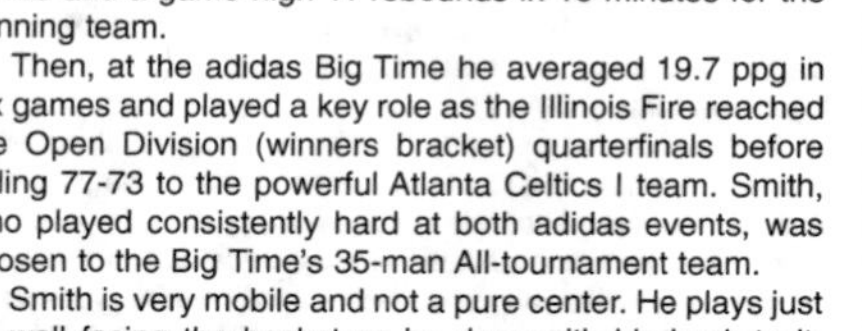

Wethers got a considerable taste of national competition during the spring and summer of 1998, and he fared well overall. Playing for the Los Angeles Rockfish, he performed solidly at the Spiece Run 'N Slam Tournament and better than that at the Reebok/Bob Gibbons Tournament of Champions, where he averaged 18.3 ppg in three games and was selected to the all-tournament team.

At the adidas ABCD Camp, his statistics were just average (4.7 ppg, 2.1 rpg, .425 percent from the field). Although we thought he actually played better than the numbers might indicate, he was not chosen for the senior all-star game. The adidas Big Time Tournament 10 days later was provided a different story, as Wethers averaged 18.3 ppg for the Rockfish and made the all-tournament team.

He has a very versatile game, in that he can score from the perimeter via line-drive jumpshots to 21 feet, pull up smoothly off the dribble to stick short to mid-range jumpers, drive and finish athletically, see the court well and pass very effectively for a wing guard. On the fast break, he relishes filling a lane and elevating to slam alley oops.

An intelligent young man on and off the court, he's a good defender (at least most of the time), and he consistently rises to the occasion when the game is on the line. He will be a good addition in the fall of 1999 for the California Golden Bears, to whom he committed on September 1, 1998.

Wethers picked Cal over finalists Southern California, Connecticut, Notre Dame and Kansas. At Berkeley he'll be joined by (at least) two of his Rockfish teammates, 5-10 point guard ShanTay Legans and 6-10 center Nick Van Der Laan, who have also declared for the Bears.

DAMIEN WILKINS, *6-5 1/2, 217 lbs., senior, small forward/power forward/wing guard, Dr. Phillips HS/Orlando, FL*

Wilkins Wilkins' bloodlines stack up with any other prep player in the nation. His father Gerald plays for the Orlando Magic, and uncle Dominique is a virtually certain Hall of Famer who still competes in Europe after exiting the NBA. Interestingly, Wilkins is a good leaper capable of acrobatic finishes on the break, yet when it comes to elevating, both his uncle and dad jumped higher in their primes.

The youngest Wilkins, who attended powerful Frederick (MD) St. John's at Prospect Hall as a sophomore and junior, has reputedly been among the best talents in his class for the last two or three years. Until this fall, his primary residence has been with his mother in suburban Atlanta. In 1996-97, he contributed nearly 18.0 ppg and 10.0 rpg for 24-1 Prospect Hall, and last season he averaged 21.4 ppg, 9.6 rpg and 2.2 apg in 19 games for a 25-0 team that finished ranked No. 1 nationally by *USA Today*.

As a junior, he was MVP of both the Iolani Classic in Honolulu and the Charm City Classic in Baltimore, and Most Outstanding Player in the Glaxo Wellcome Holiday Invitational in Raleigh (NC). He was suspended by Prospect Hall for six games for a violation of the school's conduct code, reinstated by court order and thus played in the crucial finale versus Mouth of Wilson (VA) Oak Hill Academy. But, he was later expelled. *USA Today* recognized him as All-USA Honorable Mention and among the Top 15 Juniors to Watch nationally.

At the end of the 1997-98 school year he appeared bound for the Newport School in Kensington (MD), where he would join friend DerMarr Johnson. But Johnson decided this summer to transfer to Maine Central Institute, and Wilkins finally opted to live with Gerald in Orlando and enroll at perennial power Dr. Phillips.

The spring and summer of '98 were also busy for Wilkins on the court. He played for the Georgia Stars in several events, including the St. Louis Eagles Invitational, in which he averaged 25.0 ppg and made All-Tournament, and the Reebok/Bob Gibbons Tournament of Champions, where he was poked in the eye in the first game and never got on track after that. At the Nike All-America Camp, he was one of the two most impressive senior wing forwards, even though he didn't really play great.

Then at the Nike Super Showcase in Orlando, Wilkins stepped up and was outstanding as the Georgia Stars reached the semifinals before falling 59-54 to the The Challege, an Alabama aggregation that won the title. During that event, he twice hit game-winning three-pointers with the clock running down to keep his team alive.

Wilkins' goal is to become the best player in the nation, and that might not be impossible. He is a versatile player who knows how to play the game, although he forces some shots. Not only a fine jump shooter, he likes to drive, yet had some trouble this summer when he tried to beat really quick small forwards off the dribble. We believe he's most effective when playing in an organized system.

His body is strong, and he uses it well to post up and score inside via power moves. Also a good interior passer, he plays solid, physical defense that is especially effective near the basket.

His most likely collegiate destination looks to be Georgia Tech (near his mother), Kentucky, Syracuse, North Carolina State or Michigan, although others are also involved. He has indicated interest in both North Carolina and Duke, but neither was recruiting him hard at this writing.

MARSHALL WILLIAMS, *6-5, 205 lbs., senior, wing guard/small forward, Vincent HS/Milwaukee, WI*

During the last year, Williams Williams has improved his perimeter jump shot and ball handling considerably. Consequently, he has become, at the minimum, a national top 35 senior prospect. He began to get attention as a sophomore, when he posted 17.0 ppg, 8.0 rpg, 3.0 apg, 3.0 spg and 1.2 bpg for Vincent's Division I state championship team.

During the summer of 1997, he attended the adidas ABCD camp but wasn't among the premier performers, because his game still had some holes in it. Last season Vincent finished with a 26-1 record, again won the state title (its third in a row), and was ranked No. 9 nationally by *USA Today*. Williams earned first-team all-state and *USA Today* All-USA Honorable Mention by averaging nearly 18 ppg, plus 7.3 rpg, 3 apg, 3 spg and 2 bpg.

During May of 1998, he helped lead Milwaukee DTA to the finals of the Spiece Run 'N Slam Tournament, where he scored 16 points in a 59-58 overtime loss to Bray Center Nike of Racine (WI). Then he played for the same DTA team in the Reebok/Bob Gibbons Tournament of Champions. There, he averaged 14.8 ppg in five games and did not make the all-tournament team, although he had to have gotten serious consideration.

At the adidas ABCD Camp, Williams performed extremely well, averaging 14.3 ppg (sixth-high at the camp) and adding 4.1 rpg and 1.0 spg. His three-point field goal percentage was just .289, but that was the sole negative. In the camp's Senior All-Star Game, he scored 11 points in 16 minutes for the losing side.

Williams followed that up with another strong showing, this time at the adidas Big Time Tournament. At this 224-team event, he averaged 19.0 ppg in six games as DTA Team Wisconsin reached the round of 32 before losing 72-67 to a Jason Gardner-led No Excuses team from Indiana. This gained him a spot on the all-tournament team.

Williams is an extremely active player who has emerged as a real weapon on the court. A good (not great) athlete with a strong body that he hurls recklessly around the court, he has developed some slick dribble moves which he uses to quickly take the ball to the basket and often get fouled. He's very effective in transition and now is dangerous to 21 feet with his arching jump shot and quick shot release.

Williams' shot selection sometimes could be better, but he follows his own shot unusually well, and he's a fine leaper who gets more than his share of rebounds. To top it off, he plays hustling, aggressive defense.

The six colleges that appear to have the best shot at corraling Williams are Cincinnati, Missouri, Wisconsin, Michigan, Memphis and Marquette. The opportunity for other schools to jump into the picture may still be there.

WESLEY WILSON, *6-11, 230 lbs., fifth-year senior, Maine Central Institute/Winchendon, ME*

Wilson Wilson has been well-regarded as a prospect for quite awile, as he was invited to attend the 1996 Nike All-America Camp after his sophomore year at Vallejo (CA) High. Last season he averaged 17 ppg and 12 rpg for Vallejo, and we ranked him in the *Prep Stars Recruiter's Handbook* as the No. 82 senior nationally. Since then, however, this fifth-year prepster, who will attend powerful Maine Central Institute after considering the Winchendon School in Massachusetts, has proven that he's better than that.

In fact, he could be a beast in college, as he already possesses the type of strong body that many NBA players wish they had. Wilson is a very active rebounder who looks to throw the outlet pass to start the break, and he blocks lots of shots with his long arms, even though he's not real quick laterally.

On offense, this specimen has a bit of a game, including a decent short jump shot and jump hook. But overall, he lacks polish and especially needs to hone his low-post power moves. He needs to assert himself every time down the court, and if he does, he could become a dominant player down the road.

Wilson has committed to Georgetown over finalists California and Michigan. He must yet qualify academically for collegiate freshman eligibility in 1999.

DOUG WRENN, *6-7, 210 lbs., fifth-year senior, small forward, Milford Academy/Milford, CT*

It can be frustrating to watch Wrenn Wrenn, because he looks capable of more than he sometimes accomplishes on the court. After a junior season in which he led Seattle (WA) O'Dea to the state Class 2-A championship by averaging 18.5 ppg, 8.6 rpg, 5.3 apg, 3.1 spg and 2.2 bpg, we first saw him at the 1997 adidas ABCD Camp. He was (and is) clearly among the best run/jump athletes in high school basketball, yet he managed to miss far too many easy shots near the basket.

As a senior at O'Dea, he increased his production to 22.0 ppg and 11.0 rpg, and *USA Today* (which picked him Washington Player of the year as a junior) chose him All-USA Honorable Mention for the second consecutive year. *Parade* put him on its All-America fourth team, and we ranked him as the No. 44 senior in the Prep Stars Recruiter's Handbook.

Wrenn attended the 1998 adidas ABCD Camp, but as a camp counselor rather than camper, hence he worked out with collegians such as Duke's Chris Burgess, Seton Hall's Shaheen Holloway, UConn's Kevin Freeman, and Clemson's Terrell McIntyre. Ten days later, we liked what we saw of him at the adidas Big Time tournament, where he played quite well (missing fewer easy shots) for the Long Island Panthers, even though he was not chosen for the All-tournament team.

Wrenn is a sensationally explosive leaper who consistently plays high above the basket and loves to dunk. This acrobatic skywalker soars for highlight-reel layup-finishes and short jump shots that are virtually impossible to stop. He's very quick off the dribble, but sometimes drives into traffic and trouble. His smooth jump shot looks good, with nice backspin, arch and 20 feet range, yet it remains a bit inconsistent.

The rest of his game is solid. He uses his leap to rebound well, and he's also an alert passer. Particularly impressive is his ability on defense, where he plays with intensity and is a true stopper.

He actually signed with home-state Washington this spring after considering overtures from Kansas, Georgia Tech and (until they got tired of waiting for his decision and backed off) Minnesota. Now, however, he is a fifth-year prep at Milford Academy and says, "the only time I will be back in Washington is to visit my mother."

He should get a lot of exposure and opportunity to shine as the centerpiece of a very good Milford team, yet some high-profile college coaches refuse to recruit him because of unspecified "character" issues. While it's not clear who is seriously courting him this fall, Wrenn says he particularly likes Michigan, Georgia Tech, Connecticut and Syracuse.

NCAA MEN'S TOURNAMENT INFORMATION

EAST REGION

First and Second Rounds
March 12 & 14—Fleet Center, Boston MA
March 12 & 14—Charlotte Coliseum, Charlotte, NC

Semifinals and Finals
March 19 & 21—Carrier Dome, Syracuse, NY

SOUTH REGION

First and Second Rounds
March 11 & 13—Orlando Arena, Orlando, FL
March 11 & 13—RCA Dome, Indianapolis, IN

Semifinals and Finals
March 18 & 20—Thompson-Boling Arena, Knoxville, TN

MIDWEST REGION

First and Second Rounds
March 12 & 14—Bradley Center, Milwaukee, WI
March 12 & 14—Louisiana Superdome, New Orleans, LA

Semifinals and Finals
March 19 & 21—TWA Dome, St. Louis, MO

WEST REGION

First and Second Rounds
March 11 & 13—Key Arena, Seattle, WA
March 11 & 13—McNichols Arena, Denver, CO

Semifinals and Finals
March 18 & 20—America West Arena, Phoenix, AZ

FINAL FOUR

March 27 & 29—Tropicana Field, St. Petersburg, FL
(Semifinals: East vs. West; Midwest vs. South)

FUTURE FINAL FOUR SITES

2000 (April 1 & 3)—RCA Dome, Indianapolis, IN
2001 (March 31 & April 2)—Hubert H. Humphrey Metrodome, Minneapolis, MN
2002 (March 30 & 31)—Georgia Dome, Atlanta, GA
2003—Louisiana Super Dome, New Orleans, LA
2004—Alamodome, San Antonio, TX
2005—TWA Dome, St. Louis, MO
2006—RCA Dome, Indianapolis, IN
2007—Georgia Dome, Atlanta, GA

NCAA WOMEN'S TOURNAMENT INFORMATION

EAST REGION

First and Second Rounds
March 12 & 14 or 13 & 15—campus sites

Semifinals and Finals
March 20 & 22—Greensboro Coliseum, Greensboro, NC

MIDEAST REGION

First and Second Rounds
March 12 & 14 or 13 & 15—campus sites

Semifinals and Finals
March 20 & 22—Shoemaker Center, Cincinnati, OH

MIDWEST REGION

First and Second Rounds
March 12 & 14 or 13 & 15—campus sites

Semifinals and Finals
March 20 & 22—Redbird Arena, Normal, IL

WEST REGION

First and Second Rounds
March 12 & 14 or 13 & 15—campus sites

Semifinals and Finals
March 20 & 22—Los Angeles Sports Arena, Los Angeles, CA

FINAL FOUR

March 26 & 28—San Jose Arena, San Jose, CA

FUTURE FINAL FOUR SITES

2000 (March 31 & April 2)—CoreStates Center, Philadelphia, PA
2001 (March 30 & April 1)—Kiel Center, St. Louis, MO
2002 (March 29 & 31)—Alamodome, San Antonio, TX